MIRRORS & WINDOWS

Connecting with Literature

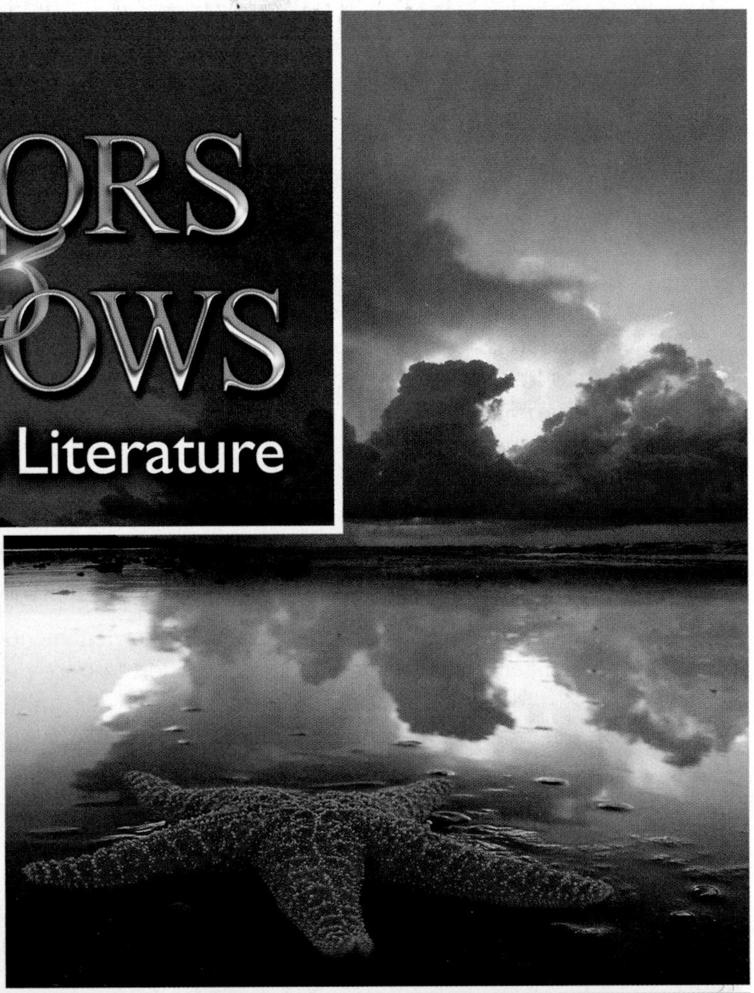

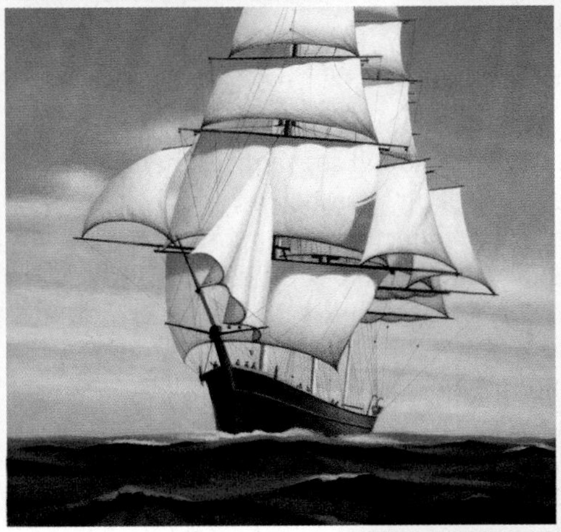

Annotated Teacher's Edition

Level III

EMC Publishing

ST. PAUL • INDIANAPOLIS

Staff Credits

Senior Editor: Brenda Owens
Editor: Nancy Papsin
Associate Editor: Carley Bomstad
Editorial Assistants: Erin Saladin,
Lindsay Ryan
Permissions Coordinator: Valerie Murphy
Photo Researcher: Brendan Curran
Marketing Managers: Bruce Ayscue,
Laurie Skiba
Cover Designer: Leslie Anderson

Text Designer: Ronan Design
Page Layout Designers: Jack Ross,
Matthias Frasch
Production Editor: Courtney Kost
Production Specialist: Petrina Nyhan
Project Manager: Sara Dovre Wudali,
Buuji, Inc.
Editorial Development and Production:
Nieman Inc.
ATE Composition: Parkwood Composition

Literary Acknowledgments: Literary Acknowledgments appear following the Glossary of Vocabulary Words. We have made every effort to trace the ownership of all copyrighted material and to secure permission from copyright holders. In the event of any question arising as to the use of any material, we will be pleased to make the necessary corrections in future printings. Thanks are due to the authors, publishers, and agents for permission to use the materials indicated.

Art and Photo Credits: Art and Photo Credits appear following the Literary Acknowledgments.

ISBN 978-0-82196-034-9

© 2012 by EMC Publishing, LLC
875 Montreal Way
St. Paul, MN 55102
E-mail: educate@emcp.com
Web site: www.emcp.com

EMC's *Mirrors & Windows*
Is 100% Aligned with the
Common Core State Standards

for English Language Arts

Your *Best* Resource for Meeting College and
Career Readiness Standards in English Language Arts

Grades 6–12

EMC's *Mirrors & Windows* presents a rigorous and balanced program in reading, writing,
speaking and listening, and language. This innovative 6–12 literature program provides extensive
and varied preparation opportunities and materials for the Common Core State Standards
assessments as well as College and Career Readiness Standards in English Language Arts.
The *Mirrors & Windows* program is designed to encourage students to be excellent
communicators and lifelong learners.

Help Your Students Meet Common Core State Standards with Correlated Support Materials

Meeting the Standards Unit Resources

Practice and Apply Strategies and Skills for College and Career Readiness Standards Mastery

- Unit Study Guide with Practice Test correlated to Common Core State Standards in English Language Arts
- Active Reading Model Lessons
- Guided Reading Lessons
- Directed Reading Lessons
- Comparing Literature Lessons
- Independent Reading Lessons
- Writing Workshops

Program Planning Guide and E-Lesson Planner

- Lesson Plans for all the selections in the unit correlated to the Common Core State Standards
- Alternative Teaching Options
- Evaluation Guidelines
- All Common Core State Standards reading text types covered in every grade level

Mirrors & Windows Prepares Your Students for Success on Common Core State Standards Assessment Tests

The *Mirrors & Windows* program contains extensive opportunities and support materials to help prepare your students for taking Common Core State Standards assessments.

- Each unit in the textbook offers a fully developed Test Practice Workshop correlated to the English Language Arts Common Core State Standards in reading, writing, and revising and editing. Writing practice includes narrative, expository, and argumentative writing prompts.
- The Language Arts Handbook in the back of each textbook provides an in-depth section on Test-Taking Skills.

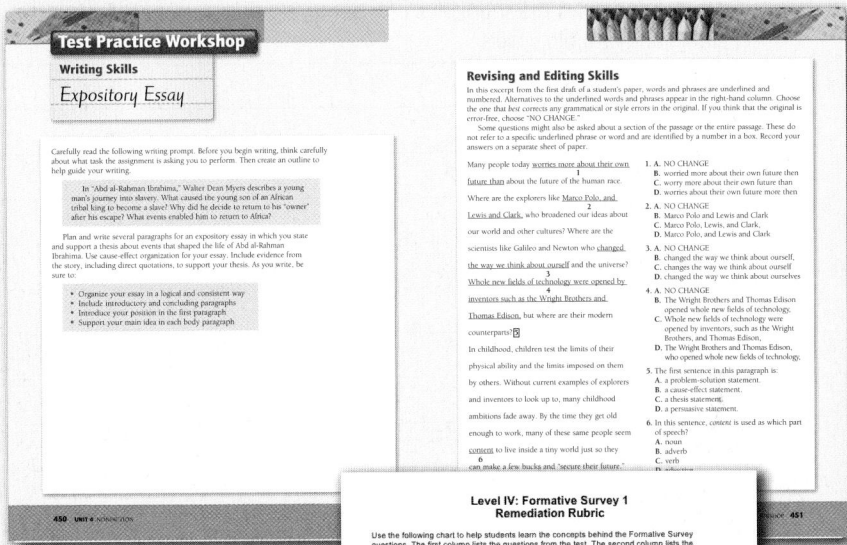

Assessment Guide and ExamView® Assessment Suite

- Selection Test questions in ExamView® are correlated to the English Language Arts Common Core State Standards and labeled by level of difficulty as Easy, Medium, or Difficult.
- Assessment tools include lesson tests and unit exams, oral reading fluency tests, and formative reading surveys correlated to the Common Core State Standards and accompanied by rubrics that prescribe remediation activities provided in the program.

- *Meeting the Standards* unit resource books include a practice test for each unit correlated to the Common Core State Standards.

EMC's *Mirrors & Windows* Common Core State Standards Edition includes the full Range of Text Types for Grades 6–12 in every grade level!

Common Core State Standards Range of Text Types	Grade 6	Grade 7	Grade 8	Grade 9	Grade 10	Grade 11	Grade 12
Literature							
Stories: Includes the subgenres of adventure stories, historical fiction, mysteries, myths, science fiction, realistic fiction, allegories, parodies, satire, and graphic novels							
adventure stories	•	•	•	•	•	•	•
historical fiction	•	•	•	•	•	•	•
mysteries	•	•	•	•	•	•	•
myths	•	•	•	•	•	•	•
science fiction	•	•	•	•	•	•	•
realistic fiction	•	•	•	•	•	•	•
allegories	•	•	•	•	•	•	•
parodies	•	•	•	•	•	•	•
satire	•	•	•	•	•	•	•
graphic novels	•	•	•	•	•	•	•
Drama: Includes one-act and multi-act plays, both in written form and on film							
one-act plays	•	•	•	•	•	•	•
multi-act plays	•	•	•	•	•	•	•
Poetry: Includes the subgenres of narrative poems, lyrical poems, free verse poems, sonnets, odes, ballads, and epics							
narrative poems	•	•	•	•	•	•	•
lyrical poems	•	•	•	•	•	•	•
free verse poems	•	•	•	•	•	•	•
sonnets	•	•	•	•	•	•	•
epics	•	•	•	•	•	•	•
Nonfiction: Includes the subgenres of exposition, argument, and functional text in the form of personal essays, speeches, opinion pieces, essays about art or literature, biographies, memoirs, journalism, and historical, scientific, technical, or economic accounts (including digital sources) written for a broad audience							
personal essays	•	•	•	•	•	•	•
speeches	•	•	•	•	•	•	•
opinion pieces	•	•	•	•	•	•	•
essays about art or literature	•	•	•	•	•	•	•
biographies	•	•	•	•	•	•	•
memoirs	•	•	•	•	•	•	•
journalism	•	•	•	•	•	•	•
historical, scientific, technical, or economic accounts (including digital sources) written for a broad audience	•	•	•	•	•	•	•

EMC *Mirrors & Windows,* Correlation to Common Core State Standards, Grade 8

English Language Arts Standards, Grade 8	EMC Pages That Cover the Standards
Reading Standards for Literature	
Key Ideas and Details	
RL.1. Cite the textual evidence that most strongly supports an analysis of what the text says explicitly as well as inferences drawn from the text.	17, 30, 44, 53, 62, 73, 76, 85, 94, 152, 166, 178, 187, 198, 207, 221, 237, 289, 298, 311, 333, 339, 353, 480, 483, 491, 496, 500, 508, 511, 515, 521, 546, 550, 553, 559, 564, 570, 584, 589, 593, 638, 677, 759, 771, 777, 784, 790, 796, 803, 807, 813, 817, 828, 835
RL.2. Determine a theme or central idea of a text and analyze its development over the course of the text, including its relationship to the characters, setting, and plot; provide an objective summary of the text.	5, 153, 154, 156, 165, 166, 211, 221, 335, 512
RL.3. Analyze how particular lines of dialogue or incidents in a story or drama propel the action, reveal aspects of a character, or provoke a decision.	11, 13, 21, 22, 24, 29, 30, 35, 40, 178, 210, 311, 621, 796
Craft and Structure	
RL.4. Determine the meaning of words and phrases as they are used in a text, including figurative and connotative meanings; analyze the impact of specific word choices on meaning and tone, including analogies or allusions to other texts.	76, 94, 198, 345, 479, 483, 497, 521, 544, 559, 755, 835
RL.5. Compare and contrast the structure of two or more texts and analyze how the differing structure of each text contributes to its meaning and style.	221, 491, 504, 521, 593, 777
RL.6. Analyze how differences in the points of view of the characters and the audience or reader (e.g., created through the use of dramatic irony) create such effects as suspense or humor.	148, 559, 566, 570, 625
Integration of Knowledge and Ideas	
RL.7. Analyze the extent to which a filmed or live production of a story or drama stays faithful to or departs from the text or script, evaluating the choices made by the director or actors.	447, 682
RL.8. Delineate and evaluate the argument and specific claims in a text, including the validity of the reasoning as well as the relevance and sufficiency of the evidence.	Not Applicable to Literature per CCSS guidelines
RL.9. Analyze how a modern work of fiction draws on themes, patterns of events, or character types from myths, traditional stories, or religious works such as the Bible, including describing how the material is rendered new.	796, 803, 813, 821
Range of Reading and Level of Text Complexity	
RL.10. By the end of the year, read and comprehend literature, including stories, dramas, and poems, at the high end of grades 6–8 text complexity band independently and proficiently.	96, 104, 129, 244, 254, 261, 372, 376, 379, 523, 525, 527, 594, 598, 601, 714, 729, 836, 850, 855

EMC *Mirrors & Windows,* Correlation to

Reading Standards for Informational Text	
Key Ideas and Details	
RI.1. Cite the textual evidence that most strongly supports an analysis of what the text says explicitly as well as inferences drawn from the text.	210, 321, 345, 358, 369, 405, 409, 413, 418, 425, 436, 444
RI.2. Determine a central idea of a text and analyze its development over the course of the text, including its relationship to supporting ideas; provide an objective summary of the text.	312, 314, 316, 321, 396, 398, 401, 403, 414
RI.3. Analyze how a text makes connections among and distinctions between individuals, ideas, or events (e.g., through comparisons, analogies, or categories).	321, 369, 409, 413, 444
Craft and Structure	
RI.4. Determine the meaning of words and phrases as they are used in a text, including figurative, connotative, and technical meanings; analyze the impact of specific word choices on meaning and tone, including analogies or allusions to other texts.	179, 281, 301, 308, 341, 345
RI.5. Analyze in detail the structure of a specific paragraph in a text, including the role of particular sentences in developing and refining a key concept.	314, 315, 317, 319, 398, 401, 403
RI.6. Determine an author's point of view or purpose in a text and analyze how the author acknowledges and responds to conflicting evidence or viewpoints.	290, 292, 341, 347, 358, 414, 421, 433, 439
Integration of Knowledge and Ideas	
RI.7. Evaluate the advantages and disadvantages of using different mediums (e.g., print or digital text, video, multimedia) to present a particular topic or idea.	467
RI.8. Delineate and evaluate the argument and specific claims in a text, assessing whether the reasoning is sound and the evidence is relevant and sufficient; recognize when irrelevant evidence is introduced.	312, 315, 317, 318, 319, 345
RI.9. Analyze a case in which two or more texts provide conflicting information on the same topic and identify where the texts disagree on matters of fact or interpretation.	208, 209, 299, 412, 420
Range of Reading and Level of Text Complexity	
RI.10. By the end of the year, read and comprehend literary nonfiction at the high end of the grades 6–8 text complexity band independently and proficiently.	372, 376, 379, 448, 459, 729

Writing Standards	
Text Types and Purposes	

W.1. Write arguments to support claims with clear reasons and relevant evidence.
    a. Introduce claim(s), acknowledge and distinguish the claim(s) from alternate or opposing claims, and organize the reasons and evidence logically.
    b. Support claim(s) with logical reasoning and relevant evidence, using accurate, credible sources and demonstrating an understanding of the topic or text.
    c. Use words, phrases, and clauses to create cohesion and clarify the relationships among claim(s), counterclaims, reasons, and evidence.
    d. Establish and maintain a formal style.
    e. Provide a concluding statement or section that follows from and supports the argument presented.
	485, 730–732, 735, 939–940

W.2. Write informative/explanatory texts to examine a topic and convey ideas, concepts, and information through the selection, organization, and analysis of relevant content. a. Introduce a topic clearly, previewing what is to follow; organize ideas, concepts, and information into broader categories; include formatting (e.g., headings), graphics (e.g., charts, tables), and multimedia when useful to aiding comprehension. b. Develop the topic with relevant, well-chosen facts, definitions, concrete details, quotations, or other information and examples. c. Use appropriate and varied transitions to create cohesion and clarify the relationships among ideas and concepts. d. Use precise language and domain-specific vocabulary to inform about or explain the topic. e. Establish and maintain a formal style. f. Provide a concluding statement or section that follows from and supports the information or explanation presented.	130–133, 135, 380, 381–382, 384, 385, 421, 460–462, 465, 528–530, 533, 856–858, 863, 939–940
W.3. Write narratives to develop real or imagined experiences or events using effective technique, relevant descriptive details, and well-structured event sequences. a. Engage and orient the reader by establishing a context and point of view and introducing a narrator and/or characters; organize an event sequence that unfolds naturally and logically. b. Use narrative techniques, such as dialogue, pacing, description, and reflection, to develop experiences, events, and/or characters. c. Use a variety of transition words, phrases, and clauses to convey sequence, signal shifts from one time frame or setting to another, and show the relationships among experiences and events. d. Use precise words and phrases, relevant descriptive details, and sensory language to capture the action and convey experiences and events. e. Provide a conclusion that follows from and reflects on the narrated experiences or events.	62, 262–264, 266, 269, 384, 530, 602–604, 605, 607

Production and Distribution of Writing

W.4. Produce clear and coherent writing in which the development, organization, and style are appropriate to task, purpose, and audience. (Grade-specific expectations for writing types are defined in standards 1–3 above.)	134, 266, 384, 464, 532, 606, 734, 860
W.5. With some guidance and support from peers and adults, develop and strengthen writing as needed by planning, revising, editing, rewriting, or trying a new approach, focusing on how well purpose and audience have been addressed. (Editing for conventions should demonstrate command of Language standards 1–3 up to and including grade 8 on page 52.)	131–134, 263–266, 381–384, 461–464, 529–532, 603–606, 731–734, 857–860
W.6. Use technology, including the Internet, to produce and publish writing and present the relationships between information and ideas efficiently as well as to interact and collaborate with others.	134, 266, 345, 384, 439, 464, 504, 532, 589, 606, 734, 835, 860, 946

Research to Build and Present Knowledge

W.7. Conduct short research projects to answer a question (including a self-generated question), drawing on several sources and generating additional related, focused questions that allow for multiple avenues of exploration.	62, 92, 94, 208, 238, 242, 333, 344, 358, 378, 419, 421, 458, 485, 490, 553, 568, 678, 759, 782, 796, 813, 856–860
W.8. Gather relevant information from multiple print and digital sources, using search terms effectively; assess the credibility and accuracy of each source; and quote or paraphrase the data and conclusions of others while avoiding plagiarism and following a standard format for citation.	62, 92, 94, 208, 238, 242, 333, 344, 358, 378, 419, 421, 458, 485, 490, 553, 568, 678, 759, 782, 796, 813, 857, 951–952

W.9. Draw evidence from literary or informational texts to support analysis, reflection, and research.
    a. Apply *grade 8 Reading standards* to literature (e.g., "Analyze how a modern work of fiction draws on themes, patterns of events, or character types from myths, traditional stories, or religious works such as the Bible, including describing how the material is rendered new").
    b. Apply *grade 8 Reading standards* to literary nonfiction (e.g., "Delineate and evaluate the argument and specific claims in a text, assessing whether the reasoning is sound and the evidence is relevant and sufficient; recognize when irrelevant evidence is introduced").
	17, 30, 44, 53, 62, 73, 76, 85, 94, 152, 166, 178, 187, 198, 207, 210, 221, 237, 289, 298, 311, 321, 333, 339, 345, 353, 358, 369, 405, 409, 413, 418, 425, 436, 444, 480, 483, 491, 496, 500, 508, 511, 515, 521, 546, 550, 553, 559, 564, 570, 584, 589, 593, 638, 677, 759, 771, 777, 784, 790, 796, 803, 807, 813, 817, 828, 835, 953–954

Range of Writing	
W.10. Write routinely over extended time frames (time for research, reflection, and revision) and shorter time frames (a single sitting or a day or two) for a range of discipline-specific tasks, purposes, and audiences.	30, 44, 85, 103, 130–135, 210, 262–267, 289, 333, 345, 358, 375, 380–385, 460–465, 504, 511, 521, 526, 528–533, 546, 580, 602–607, 610, 683, 712, 728, 730–735, 759, 784, 803, 856–861

Speaking and Listening

Comprehension and Collaboration	

SL.1. Engage effectively in a range of collaborative discussions (one-on-one, in groups, and teacher led) with diverse partners on *grade 8 topics, texts, and issues,* building on others' ideas and expressing their own clearly.
    a. Come to discussions prepared, having read or researched material under study; explicitly draw on that preparation by referring to evidence on the topic, text, or issue to probe and reflect on ideas under discussion.
    b. Follow rules for collegial discussions and decision-making, track progress toward specific goals and deadlines, and define individual roles as needed.
    c. Pose questions that connect the ideas of several speakers and respond to others' questions and comments with relevant evidence, observations, and ideas.
    d. Acknowledge new information expressed by others, and, when warranted, qualify or justify their own views in light of the evidence presented.
	137, 271, 333, 387, 405, 447, 535, 609, 737, 865, 964–965, 969

SL.2. Analyze the purpose of information presented in diverse media and formats (e.g., visually, quantitatively, orally) and evaluate the motives (e.g., social, commercial, political) behind its presentation.	737, 865, 963
SL.3. Delineate a speaker's argument and specific claims, evaluating the soundness of the reasoning and relevance and sufficiency of the evidence and identifying when irrelevant evidence is introduced.	137, 387, 737, 865, 963
Presentation of Knowledge and Ideas	
SL.4. Present claims and findings, emphasizing salient points in a focused, coherent manner with relevant evidence, sound valid reasoning, and well-chosen details; use appropriate eye contact, adequate volume, and clear pronunciation.	386–387, 534–535, 736-737, 864–865

SL.5. Integrate multimedia and visual displays into presentations to clarify information, strengthen claims and evidence, and add interest.	387, 784, 865, 970
SL.6. Adapt speech to a variety of contexts and tasks, demonstrating command of formal English when indicated or appropriate. (See grade 8 Language standards 1 and 3 on page 52 for specific expectations.)	136–137, 270–271, 386–387, 534–535, 608–609, 736–737, 864–865

Language Standards

Conventions of Standard English	
L.1. Demonstrate command of the conventions of standard English grammar and usage when writing or speaking. a. Explain the function of verbals (gerunds, participles, infinitives) in general and their function in particular sentences. b. Form and use verbs in the active and passive voice. c. Form and use verbs in the indicative, imperative, interrogative, conditional, and subjunctive mood. d. Recognize and correct inappropriate shifts in verb voice and mood.*	334, 684, 902, 917, 937
L.2. Demonstrate command of the conventions of standard English capitalization, punctuation, and spelling when writing. a. Use punctuation (comma, ellipsis, dash) to indicate a pause or break. b. Use an ellipsis to indicate an omission. c. Spell correctly.	95, 167, 324, 893, 900, 927, 929, 931
Knowledge of Language	
L.3. Use knowledge of language and its conventions when writing, speaking, reading, or listening. a. Use verbs in the active and passive voice and in the conditional and subjunctive mood to achieve particular effects (e.g., emphasizing the actor or the action; expressing uncertainty or describing a state contrary to fact).	Exceeding the Standards: Grammar & Style 67–69, 937
Vocabulary Acquisition and Use	
L.4. Determine or clarify the meaning of unknown and multiple-meaning words or phrases based on *grade 8 reading and content*, choosing flexibly from a range of strategies. a. Use context (e.g., the overall meaning of a sentence or paragraph; a word's position or function in a sentence) as a clue to the meaning of a word or phrase. b. Use common, grade-appropriate Greek or Latin affixes and roots as clues to the meaning of a word (e.g., *precede, recede, secede*). c. Consult general and specialized reference materials (e.g., dictionaries, glossaries, thesauruses), both print and digital, to find the pronunciation of a word or determine or clarify its precise meaning or its part of speech. d. Verify the preliminary determination of the meaning of a word or phrase (e.g., by checking the inferred meaning in context or in a dictionary).	346, 432, 581, 639, 886, 887, 889–890, 891

L.5. Demonstrate understanding of figurative language, word relationships, and nuances in word meanings.
  a. Interpret figures of speech (e.g. verbal irony, puns) in context.
  b. Use the relationship between particular words to better understand each of the words.
  c. Distinguish among the connotations (associations) of words with similar denotations (definitions) (e.g., *bullheaded, willful, firm, persistent, resolute*).
	179, 497, 755, 891, 892, 893

L.6. Acquire and use accurately grade-appropriate general academic and domain-specific words and phrases; gather vocabulary knowledge when considering a word or phrase important to comprehension or expression.	19, 33, 46, 54, 61, 63, 74, 78, 84, 86, 154, 168, 180, 188, 200, 208, 211, 220, 222, 238, 281, 290, 299, 302, 312, 322, 325, 335, 341, 347, 354, 359, 370, 372, 376, 396, 407, 410, 414, 419, 423, 426, 433, 437, 440, 445, 478, 481, 484, 488, 493, 498, 501, 505, 509, 512, 514, 516, 519, 523, 525, 543, 548, 551, 554, 557, 560, 566, 571, 578, 582, 585, 587, 590, 592, 594, 619, 640, 678, 685, 708, 747, 760, 773, 778, 786, 791, 793, 798, 804, 808, 814, 818, 822, 829

Language Progressive Skills

Conventions of Standard English

L.3.1f. Ensure subject-verb and pronoun-antecedent agreement.	31, 77, 912, 918–919
L.3.3a. Choose words and phrases for effect.	730, 731, 733, 734, 735
L.4.1f. Produce complete sentences, recognizing and correcting inappropriate fragments and run-ons.	713, 902, 934
L.4.1g. Correctly use frequently confused words (e.g., to/too/two; there/their).	134, 384, 797, 892, 900
L.4.3b. Choose punctuation for effect.	324, 926–931
L.5.1d. Recognize and correct inappropriate shifts in verb tense.	266, 340, 605, 909–910
L.5.2a. Use punctuation to separate items in a series.	167, 927–928
L.6.1c. Recognize and correct inappropriate shifts in pronoun number and person.	77, 547, 907
L.6.1d. Recognize and correct vague pronouns (i.e., ones with unclear or ambiguous antecedents).	907
L.6.1e. Recognize variations from standard English in their own and others' writing and speaking, and identify and use strategies to improve expression in conventional language.	939–940
L.6.2a. Use punctuation (commas, parentheses, dashes) to set off nonrestrictive/parenthetical elements.	324, 927, 931
L.6.3a. Vary sentence patterns for meaning, reader/listener interest, and style.	134, 406, 556, 903–904, 935–936
L.6.3b. Maintain consistency in style and tone.	132, 938, 940
L.7.1c. Place phrases and clauses within a sentence, recognizing and correcting misplaced and dangling modifiers.	772, 785, 920

Common Core State Standards, Grade 8

L.7.3a. Choose language that expresses ideas precisely and concisely, recognizing and eliminating wordiness and redundancy.	266
L.8.1d. Recognize and correct inappropriate shifts in verb voice and mood.	340

Range of Text Types

Literature	
Stories: Includes the subgenres of adventure stories, historical fiction, mysteries, myths, science fiction, realistic fiction, allegories, parodies, satire, and graphic novels	
adventure stories "Pecos Bill" "Blackbeard's Last Fight" "Paul Bunyan of the North Woods"	760 793 814
historical fiction "A Mother in Mannville" "The Drummer Boy of Shiloh"	32–44 54–60
mysteries *The Dying Detective*	620
myths "Legend of the Feathered Serpent" "Coyote Steals the Sun and Moon" "Where the Girl Rescued Her Brother"	747 773 778
science fiction "Flowers for Algernon"	104
realistic fiction "The Treasure of Lemon Brown" "A Mother in Mannville" "The Journey" "The Drummer Boy of Shiloh" "Gary Keillor" "Checkouts" "Last Night" "Raymond's Run" "The Tell-Tale Heart" "Born Worker" "Sweet Potato Pie" "Miss Butterfly" "The Ransom of Red Chief" "Men on the Moon" "The Medicine Bag" "Moon" "Luke Baldwin's Vow" "Lose Now, Pay Later"	19 33 46 54 63 78 86 96 145 154 168 180 188 200 211 222 244 254
allegories "The Old Grandfather and His Little Grandson" "The People Could Fly"	220 786

parodies "Frog"	861–864
satire "The Ant and the Grasshopper"	865–868
graphic novels from "Outlaw: The Legend of Robin Hood: A Graphic Novel"	855–860
Drama: Includes one-act and multi-act plays, both in written form and on film	
one-act plays *The Dying Detective* from *A Woman Called Truth* from *Pygmalion*	619 738 740
multi-act plays *The Diary of Anne Frank* *Sorry, Right Number*	640 714
Poetry: Includes the subgenres of narrative poems, lyrical poems, free verse poems, sonnets, odes, ballads, and epics	
narrative poems "O Captain! My Captain!" "Oranges" "Bats" "Casey at the Bat" "Paul Revere's Ride" "Birdfoot's Grampa" "The Cremation of Sam McGee"	74 84 551 566 571 590 594
lyrical poems "I Was Born at the Wrong Time" "Jerusalem" "Night Clouds" "Dreams" "A Dream Deferred" "Pretty Words" "The New Colossus" "The Other Pioneers" "Ceremony" "If I can stop one heart from breaking"	322 370 478 481 484 493 498 505 509 512
free verse poems "Grandma Ling"	582
sonnets "The New Colossus"	498
odes "Ode to My Socks"	561
ballads "John Henry Blues"	804–807

epics "Paul Revere's Ride" from "Tales of a Wayside Inn"	571
Nonfiction: Includes the subgenres of exposition, argument, and functional text in the form of personal essays, speeches, opinion pieces, essays about art or literature, biographies, memoirs, journalism, and historical, scientific, technical, or economic accounts (including digital sources) written for a broad audience	
personal essays "The Story of Iqbal Masih" "Good Housekeeping" "The Struggle to Be an All-American Girl" from "Chac"	238 302 335 448
speeches "Our Struggle Is Against All Forms of Racism"	354
opinion pieces "Soul of a Citizen: Living with Conviction in a Cynical Time" "Proclamation of the Indians of Alcatraz" "Appearances Are Destructive" from "Do not ask us to give up the buffalo for sheep"	312 341 376 390
essays about art or literature "The Ole Feller Recollects How Joe Fournier Became Paul Bunyan"	818
biographies from *Harriet Tubman: Conductor on the Underground Railroad* from *Paul Revere and the World He Lived In*	347 578
memoirs "Working on the Moon" "Epiphany: The Third Gift" "Counting Coup on a Wounded Buffalo" from *To Be or Not to Bop*	208 325 419 470
journalism from *Echoes of Shiloh* "Yana People to Receive Ishi's Brain"	61 299
historical, scientific, technical, or economic accounts (including digital sources) written for a broad audience from *Reluctant Witnesses: Children's Voices from the Civil War* "A Tale of Two Rocks" "On the Relativity of Time" "Indian Cattle" "Murder and More Mushroom Mayhem" "How to Use a Compass" "Industrial Light and Magic, Part 1: History" from *Immigrant Kids*	388 396 410 414 423 433 445 501

EMC *Mirrors & Windows,* Correlation to Common Core State Standards, Grade 8

Texts Illustrating the Complexity, Quality, and Range of Student Reading

NOTE: *Mirrors & Windows* offers high-quality literary works that were carefully chosen to enrich and enhance students' understanding of themselves and their world. Each unit in the program presents a diverse body of rich and relevant selections related to a particular theme or topic. The following texts represent the complexity, quality, and range of those selections.

Literature: Stories, Drama, Poetry	
"The Tell-Tale Heart" by Edgar Allan Poe (1843)	146–151
"Paul Revere's Ride" by Henry Wadsworth Longfellow (1861)	573–577
"If I can stop one Heart from breaking" by Emily Dickinson (1890)	513
"The Ransom of Red Chief" by O. Henry (1910)	189–197
"A Dream Deferred" by Langston Hughes (1926)	484
The Diary of Anne Frank (1955)	641–707
"Raymond's Run" by Toni Cade Bambara (1972)	96–103

Informational Texts: Literary Nonfiction	
from *The Autobiography of Malcolm X* (1965)	372–375
"Proclamation of the Indians of Alcatraz" (1969)	343–344
"Mrs. Flowers" from *I Know Why the Caged Bird Sings* by Maya Angelou (1969)	282–288
"Our Struggle Is Against All Forms of Racism" by Nelson Mandela (1990)	354–357
from *Harriet Tubman: Conductor on the Underground Railroad* by Ann Petry (2001)	348–353

–Program Overview–

Grades 6–12

Fiction • Nonfiction • Poetry • Drama • Folk Literature • Independent Reading

Great Expectations! Great Results!

Engage students to reflect on and connect personally with literature.

Motivate students to maximize their potential through the **gradual release of responsibility** reading model.

Challenge students to become independent readers, writers, and thinkers.

Try an Innovative Program That's More

Grades 6-8

Grades 9-12

More than great literature.

The student edition is also a resource rich with activities and reading support to motivate students to meet their goals.

- Diverse, interesting, and relevant selections teach the genres and literary elements and engage students in learning.

- Scaffolded instructional approach gradually releases responsibility to the students.

- Independent readings provide students with the opportunity to practice skills and read more on their own.

- Cross-Curricular and Text-to-Text Connections give relevance to literature by linking it to other subjects and students' lives.

(See pages T28–T37, T44–T45.)

More than a Teacher's Edition.

This easy-to-use, flexible management tool will fit your teaching style, and provide daily solutions to your classroom challenges.

- Consistent lesson plans address state standards and provide ongoing assessment opportunities.

- Lesson-planning tools are just a click away to save preparation time.

- Ideas for whole-group and flexible-group instruction provide practical options.

(See pages T38–T39.)

Grade 6

Grade 9

Teacher Editions

Grade 11

Than Just Another Literature Anthology!

More than "stuff" in a box.

This program offers just the right amount of the print and technology resources you need, when you need them, to ensure standards mastery.

- A variety of components provide differentiated materials to meet a range of student abilities and to support English language learners.

- Components are easily stored and available to preview and use.

- State-of-the art technology allows for customization to state standards.

(See pages T22–T27.)

More than scope and sequence.

Concepts, strategies, and activities are taught, practiced, and applied in meaningful contexts for all students.

- The *gradual release of responsibility* reading model provides three levels of reading support to scaffold instruction and develop independent readers.

- Differentiated Instruction focuses on Reading Proficiency, Enrichment, Learning Styles, and English Language Learning.

- Workshops for Vocabulary & Spelling, Grammar & Style, Writing, Speaking & Listening, and Test Practice provide wonderful opportunities for in-depth exploration.

(See pages T18–T19, T30–T37.)

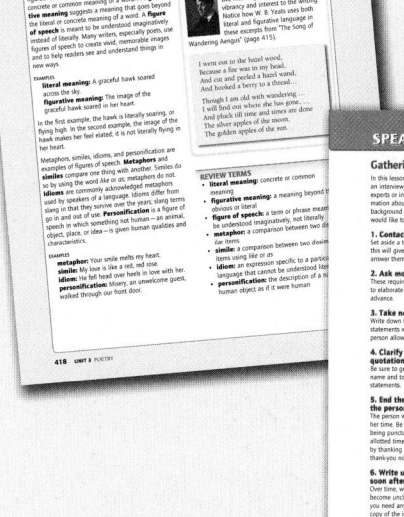

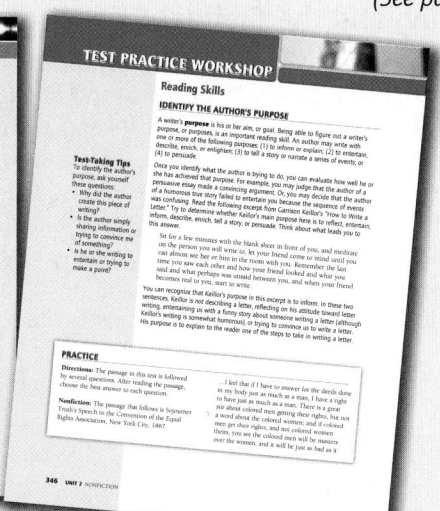

–Program Philosophy and Instructional Design–

"The whole purpose of education is to turn mirrors into windows."

—Sydney J. Harris

Program Overview and Philosophy

Mirrors & Windows: Connecting with Literature, EMC's new literature program for grades 6–12, presents a wide variety of literature to help students reflect on themselves and their world and to connect that understanding to people from other times and places.

Mirrors & Windows responds to the call for increased academic *rigor* that continues to be heard across the nation. Given the lack of rigor in many school programs, today's students are often not engaged in learning and fail to acquire even the most basic skills and knowledge. Using a scaffolded approach, *Mirrors & Windows* provides instruction in essential content and skills and then transfers responsibility for learning to the student.

Program Research and Instructional Design

Scaffolded instruction with the *gradual release of responsibility* model is applied within each unit and across the grades. This approach is based on research that supports the practice of leading students from guided, to directed, to independent reading. Three levels of reading support are provided to gradually transfer responsibility from the teacher and the textbook to the student. The reading support throughout the unit progresses from guided to directed to independent reading.

Guided Reading at the beginning of the unit (Grades 6–10) provides the framework for the teacher to guide students through the reading process. Reading Models walk students through the selections and demonstrate how to analyze literature and apply reading skills and strategies to each genre.

Directed Reading (Grades 6–12), begins the gradual release of responsibility process as the teacher begins to transfer responsibility to the students. Students are directed through explicit pre- and post-reading instruction, but during-reading support is reduced to encourage students to practice reading skills and monitor comprehension on their own.

Independent Reading (Grades 6–12), advances the total release of responsibility from the teacher to the students, who can now apply the skills and knowledge required to read increasingly more difficult selections on their own.

Scaffolding and the Gradual Release of Responsibility

"Since its introduction 25 years ago, the concept of instructional scaffolding has been investigated, elaborated, related to other instructional concepts, and strongly endorsed by virtually every major reading authority. Although different authors define scaffolding slightly differently, three closely related features are essential attributes of effective scaffolding. First, there is the scaffold itself, the temporary and supportive structure that helps a student or group of students accomplish a task they could not accomplish — or could not accomplish as well — without the scaffold. Second, the scaffold must place the learner in what Vygotsky (1978) has termed the zone of proximal development. As explained by Vygotsky, at any particular point in time, children have a circumscribed zone of development or range within which they can learn...Third, over time the teacher must gradually dismantle the scaffold and transfer the responsibility for completing tasks to students..."

Michael F. Graves
Program Reviewer
Professor Emeritus
University of Minnesota

Michael Graves, from *Adolescent Literacy Research and Practice,* ed. Tamara L. Jetton, Janice A. Dole. 2004 Guildford Press.

–Applying Gradual Release of Responsibility–

The *gradual release of responsibility* reading model emphasizes instruction that mentors students into becoming capable thinkers and learners when handling the tasks with which they have not yet developed expertise. Through gradual release, students are:

- exposed to repeated modeling of expert behavior through teacher think-alouds and discussions of effective strategies for learning.

- provided with ongoing guided practice before they are asked to be independent learners.

- encouraged to learn from one another in the context of large group, small group, or independent classroom activities as they experiment with the thinking necessary to succeed in a variety of learning tasks.

Gradual Release of Responsibility Reading Model

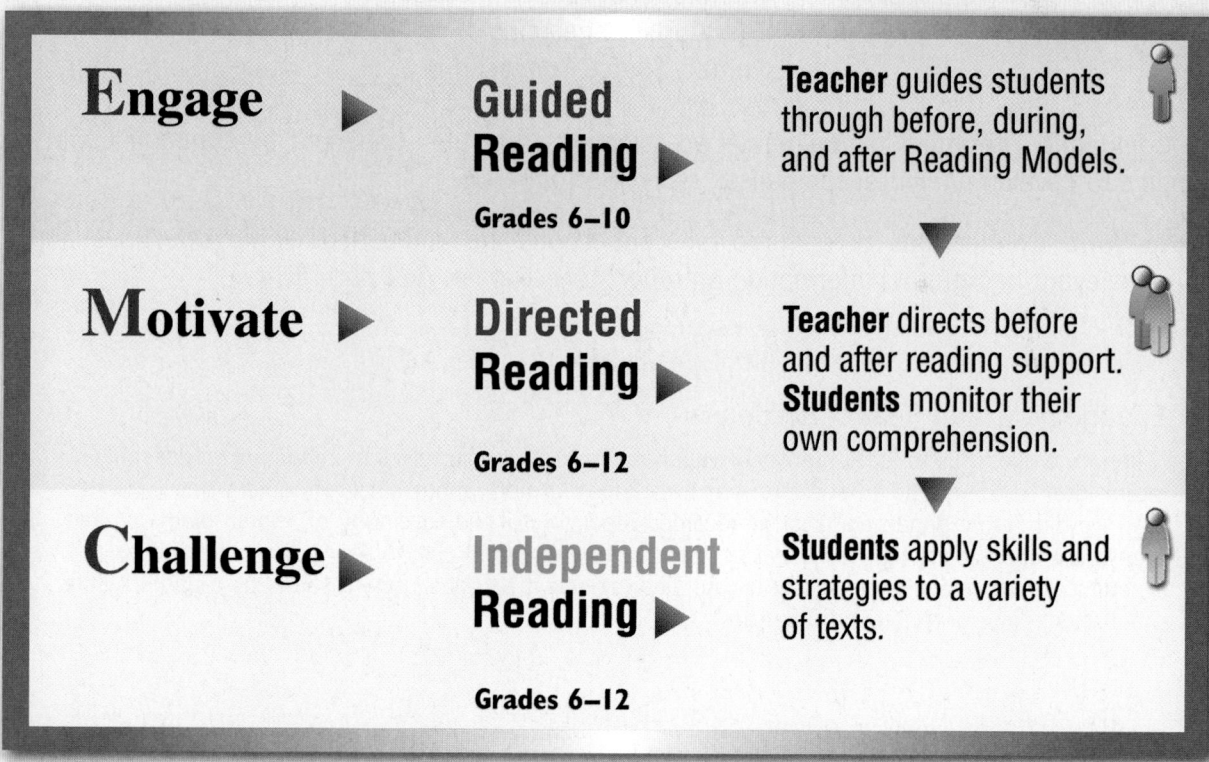

Engage ▶ **Guided Reading** ▶
Grades 6–10

Teacher guides students through before, during, and after Reading Models.

Motivate ▶ **Directed Reading** ▶
Grades 6–12

Teacher directs before and after reading support. **Students** monitor their own comprehension.

Challenge ▶ **Independent Reading** ▶
Grades 6–12

Students apply skills and strategies to a variety of texts.

* Adapted from Pearson, P.D., and Gallagher, M.C. (1983)

–Connecting with Literature–

Connecting with the Text

Mirrors & Windows provides multiple opportunities for students to make important connections, including text-to-self, text-to-text, and text-to-world connections.

Text-to-Self Connections Reader's Context questions before reading and *Mirrors & Windows* questions after reading ask essential questions that encourage students to make connections to their own lives and the world around them.

Text-to-Text Connections Connections to a variety of primary sources and informational readings give relevance to literature by helping students to see relationships between literature and other content areas and texts. *(See page T33.)* The three types of text-to-text connections are:

- Informational Text Connections
- Literature Connections
- Primary Source Connections

The Comparing Literature feature pairs two selections that are connected by common literary elements to develop analytical comparison skills. *(See page T32.)*

Text-to-World Connections Cross-Curricular Connections are embedded within selections and provide relevant background information on other subject areas. *(See page T34.)*

Engagement and Reader Response

"...literature allows us to leave the world we inhabited to invest ourselves in imaginary worlds, only to return later to the quotidian events of our lives knowing more about our environment and ourselves than we did before departing. It is the recorded repository of the continuity of human emotions and events, the one subject that can speak across time to evoke from each of us comparable feelings and experiences. Therefore, let us select it carefully and put it to good use — to draw us together while simultaneously respecting our differences."

Edmund J. Farrell
Senior Consultant
Professor Emeritus
University of Texas at Austin

Edmund J. Farrell, from "Tracks in the Sand: On Literary Inclusion." *English in Texas*, Fall/Winter Issue (Vol. 32:2).

–Developing Critical Thinking Skills–

The *Mirrors & Windows* post-reading questions are based on Bloom's Taxonomy of Educational Objectives.

In grades 6–8, **Find Meaning** questions assess students' comprehension of the selections. **Make Judgments** questions address higher level reasoning skills. Questions are paired to build from literal questions to interpretation through synthesis.

In grades 9–12, **Refer to Text** questions that ask students to recall facts from the selections are paired with **Reason with Text** questions that ask students to apply higher level thinking skills. These questions are explicitly labeled based on Bloom's taxonomy, using terminology updated by Lorin Anderson for classroom application. (See chart below.)

Bloom's Original Taxonomy	Anderson's Revised Taxonomy
Knowledge	Remembering
Comprehension	Understanding
Application	Applying
Analysis	Analyzing
Synthesis	Evaluating
Evaluation	Creating

–Extending Learning–

The post-reading material for each selection offers extensive opportunities for students to respond to the literature and to extend their learning through writing and extension activities.

Writing Options Two writing prompts are provided that cover the major modes of writing: *creative, expository, narrative, descriptive,* and *persuasive.*

Extension Activities Two extension activities or projects are offered to expand students' skills in the following areas:

- Media Literacy
- Critical Literacy
- Collaborative Learning
- Lifelong Learning

–Extensive Program Components and Technology Tools–

Engage, Motivate, and Challenge Your Students

Student Edition
Meet All Your State Standards within the Student Edition

- Relevant, interesting, and diverse literature selections
- Three levels of reading support from guided to directed to independent
- Mix of easy, moderate, and challenging selections
- Cross-curricular and Text-to-Text Connections
- In-depth workshops for skills mastery
- Thought-provoking questions

Interactive Student Text on CD
In addition to containing everything in the printed text, the Student Text on CD includes highlighting, note-taking, and bookmarking.

Audio Library
Authentic, dramatic recordings with listening activities offer additional support for developing readers and English language learners, and expand listening skills.

Differentiated Instruction
Intensive instruction and activities provide student support; includes separate resource books for:

- English Language Learners
- Developing Readers
- Advanced Students

Differentiated instruction is also available in CD/DVD format.

Meet Your State Standards Every Day

Meeting the Standards Unit Resources
Practice and Apply Strategies and Skills for State Standards Mastery

- Unit Study Guide with Practice Test
- Active Reading Model Lessons
- Guided Reading Lessons
- Directed Reading Lessons
- Comparing Literature Lessons
- Independent Reading Lessons
- Cumulative Vocabulary Lists
- Available in print and CD/DVD formats

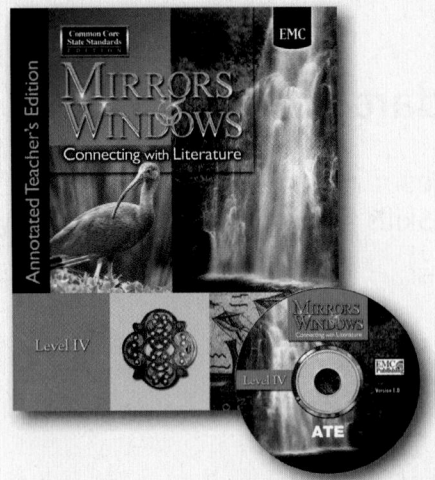

Save Valuable Classroom Planning Time

Annotated Teacher's Edition (ATE)
One location for accessing, previewing, and planning your use of all program resources.

- Visual Unit Planning Guides
- Complete lesson plans for all selections
- Differentiated instruction for all learners
- Ongoing assessment provided
- Teacher Notes add valuable information
- Extensive vocabulary instruction and resources
- Cross-curricular connections
- Broad range of skills activities

EMC Launchpad (Combined Desktop–Web-based technology)
Complete, customizable application for accessing, previewing, planning, posting, and grading all program resources.

- Include your personal resources
- Post personal lessons on class website
- Access the E-Lesson Planner and E-gradebook
- Access Training Modules for improving computer literacy

Visual Teaching Package
Unit-based lectures, games, art collections, writing workshops, and more, in PowerPoint format, E-Lesson Planner and Teacher Resources DVD.

Program Planning Guide and E-Lesson Planner
- Lesson Plans for all the selections in the unit
- Core Standards-Based Selections
- Reading Log and Evaluation Forms
- Lesson plans correlated to state standards in E-Lesson Planner
- Access to all program resources in E-Lesson Planner

Assess Students' Progress and Provide Feedback

 Criterion. Online Writing Evaluation
Publisher's Version

A Web-based tool for students to evaluate their essay writing online before submitting it for teacher review and final evaluation. It saves time in grading the mechanical areas and allows teachers to focus on voice, creativity, and organization.

This service provides these benefits:

- Students are provided with essay topics in key writing modes.
- Students write, submit, and receive annotated diagnostic feedback within 20 seconds.
- Students can revise essays based on feedback or use e-mail to communicate feedback to teachers.

(Grades 9–12)

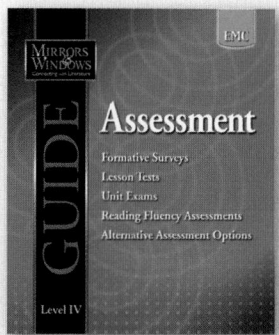

Assessment Guide

The *Assessment Guide* contains the following:

- Formative Surveys
- Lesson Tests
- Unit Exams
- Reading Fluency Assessments
- Alternative Assessment Options
- Remediation Rubrics

EXAMView® Assessment Suite on CD

Easy-to-use and Manage Testing Program

- Leveled multiple choice, short answer, and essay questions
- Ability to select, create, and edit questions to create personalized tests and exams
- Formative Survey test items keyed to state standards with customizable formats

 **Go Green!**

All print resources available on CD, on DVD, or online.

Enrich Students Beyond the Standards

Exceeding the Standards: Literature & Reading

Extended, unit-based lessons that integrate outside resources, varieties of media, and student creativity to analyze, compare, and fully appreciate literature and culture.

Exceeding the Standards: Test Practice

Timed, unit-based practice tests in formats most commonly found in standard achievement, state-specific, and high-stakes tests and exams. ACT and SAT format practice tests are included at each level.

Exceeding the Standards: Writing

- In-depth lessons to be used as extensions of the Writing Workshops in the student text.
- Developmental, in-depth writing lessons for each of the major writing modes—narrative, descriptive, expository, and persuasive.
- Lessons include models, examples, guidelines, writing checklist, and writing rubric.
- Writing lessons integrate grammar instruction.

Exceeding the Standards: Speaking & Listening

Detailed lessons with explicit instruction expand on the Speaking and Listening Workshops at the end of each unit to further develop speaking and listening skills.

Exceeding the Standards: Vocabulary & Spelling

- Comprehensive developmental Vocabulary and Spelling lessons build word study skills.
- In-depth instruction is modeled using words from the selections in each unit.

Exceeding the Standards: Special Topics

Extended lessons in technology, personal development, and career awareness provide students real-life, practical experience in applied communication skills.

Exceeding the Standards: Grammar & Style

A comprehensive, developmental grammar and style curriculum, taught within the context of selections in each unit.

Exceeding the Standards: Extension Activities

Extended lessons for each of the following catagories:
- Collaborative Learning
- Lifelong Learning
- Media Literacy
- Critical Literacy

Make Your Day Better with Online Resources!

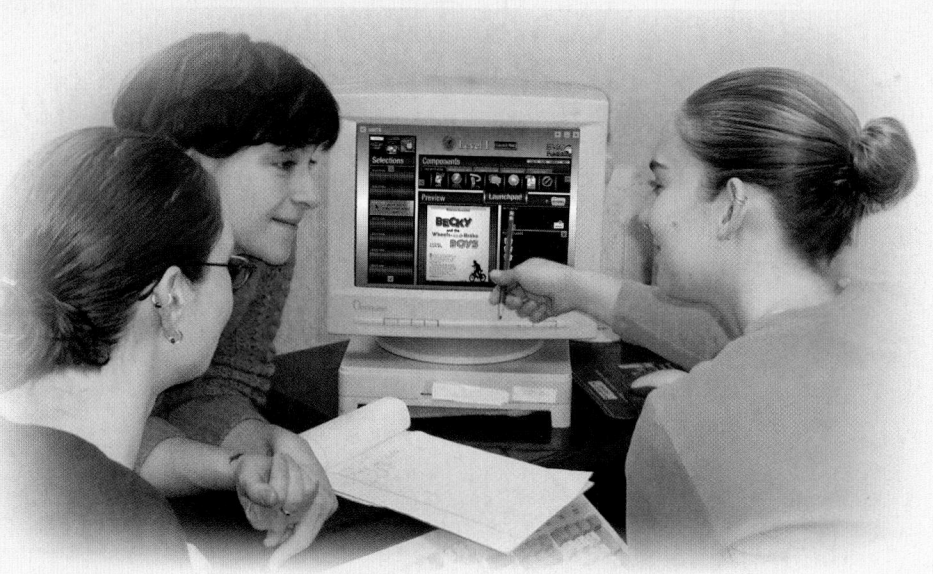

mirrorsandwindows.com
Open Up Your Classroom to a World of Possibilities!

Student and teacher resources, references, technology tools, and state-specific activities to enrich the program.

- Internet links and activities for most literature selections
- Literary links
- Professional development, scholarships, and grant opportunities
- Workshops
- Standardized test-preparation resources
- State-specific information
- Teaching tools
- Online reference materials
- Downloadable Audio Library
- Access to E-Library

EMC E-Library
Expand Your Classroom Library Instantly

- More than 20,000 pages of literary classics
- 120 long selections, including epic poems, novels, plays, nonfiction, and poetry
- 194 short selections, which include poetry and excerpts
- Ability to view on screen or print out individual selections to plan classes
- Electronic library guide with teaching suggestions, enrichment activities, and reading strategies guidesheets
- Accessed from mirrorsandwindows.com

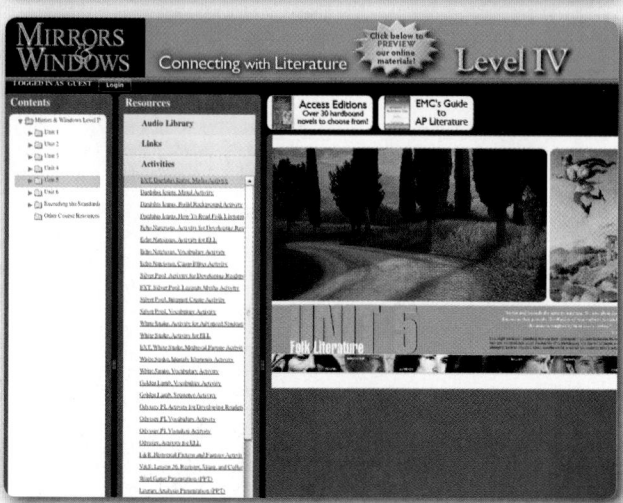

Audio Library
Authentic, dramatic recordings with listening activities expand students' listening skills and offer additional support for developing readers and English language learners. Accessed from mirrorsandwindows.com

Take a Walk Through
The Student Anthology

Great literature provides mirrors
that help students reflect on their world
and windows that lead them into new worlds.

–Motivate Students to Learn–

Unit Opener

- Introduces the genre and connects students to the literature
- Thought-provoking quote gives insight into literature
- Fine art and photographs connect with the unit theme
- Questions related to the unit theme generate interest and set the stage for learning

Defining Freedom
Nonfiction

unit 3

"*The only education we receive is English education. Surely we must show something for it. But suppose that we had been receiving during the past fifty years education through our vernaculars, what should we have today? We should have today a free India....*"
—MOHANDAS GANDHI, "There Is No Salvation for India"

What freedoms do you enjoy that people in other parts of the world do not? This speech was delivered by peace activist Mohandas Gandhi in his struggle to lead India to independence from British rule. As you read this unit, imagine how you would feel if your basic freedoms were challenged.

MOHANDAS GANDHI   AUNG SAN SUU KYI   GARY SOTO   ANNE FRANK   WALTER DEAN MYERS   ZITKALA-ŠA

259

Overview of grades 6–8. Pages shown from grade 6.

Mirrors & Windows

–Prepare Students for Success–

Introduction to Nonfiction

Fiction and Nonfiction

Leroy "Satchel" Paige appears in both of the following passages. Though the passages differ in several ways, the main difference is that the first selection is written in first-person point of view and describes an imaginary conversation, and the second is written in third-person point of view and tells facts about Paige and America's baseball leagues. In other words, Gutman's selection is fiction and Littlefield's is nonfiction.

> "Ya-hoooo!" shouted Laverne, "If you were white, you would be in the majors for sure."
> "Yeah," Satch said, "if."
> She meant well, but Laverne's comment seemed to take something out of Satch. I could see his shoulders sag and his head hang a little. I guess he had forgotten about his situation for the moment. Laverne had reminded him that he was the best pitcher in baseball but he was banned from playing at the highest level because of the color of his skin.

—DAN GUTMAN, *Satch & Me*

Everywhere these confrontations took place, Satchel Paige would hear the same thing: "If only you were white, you'd be a star in the big leagues." The fault, of course, was not with Satchel. The fault and the shame were with major league baseball, which stubbornly, stupidly clung to the same prejudice that characterized many institutions in the United States besides baseball.

—BILL LITTLEFIELD, "Satchel Paige"

Even though Gutman's fictional novel is about a boy who travels back in time to meet Satchel Paige, many of the novel's events and descriptions are historically accurate. Littlefield's nonfiction selection, on the other hand, is based on research and does not create any imagined situations or details.

Leroy R. Paige (1906–1982), American baseball player with the Kansas City Monarchs, 1941.

In the Introduction to Fiction (page 4), you learned that **fiction** includes any work of prose (writing that is not poetry or drama) that describes an invented or imaginary story. Typical forms of fiction are short stories and novels. **Nonfiction** is writing about real people, places, things, and events. Autobiographies, biographies, journals, essays, histories, and newspaper and magazine articles are all types of nonfiction.

Types of Nonfiction

Among the most common types of nonfiction are autobiography, memoir, biography, and essay.

Autobiography and Memoir

Writing is described as "autobiographical" when the writer presents part or all of his or her own life. There are many types of autobiographical writing, including autobiographies, memoirs, diaries, journals, and letters.

260 UNIT 3 NONFICTION

Introduction to Unit Genre

- The genre is introduced and defined before students read the unit selections.
- Detailed and extensive explanations of literary elements are followed by two selections that demonstrate the use of these elements.

An **autobiography** is the story of a person's life written by that person. It typically covers the whole of a person's life up to the time of writing. A more focused type of autobiography is the **memoir**, which usually deals with a specific period of a person's life, such as childhood. For example, Gary Soto's "The Jacket" (page 263) is a memoir about a period of Soto's adolescence.

> From my bed, I stared at the jacket. I wanted to cry because it was so ugly and so big that I knew I'd have to wear it a long time. I was a small kid, thin as a young tree, and it would be years before I'd have a new one.

—GARY SOTO, "The Jacket"

Biography

A **biography** is the story of a person's life told by another person. For example, Walter Dean Myers's *Abd al-Rahman Ibrahima* (page 270) is a biography about the son of an African chief who was captured and sold into slavery.

> As the son of a chief Ibrahima was expected to assume a role of political leadership when he came of age. He would also be expected to set a moral example, and to be well versed in his religion. When he reached twelve he was sent to Timbuktu to study.

—WALTER DEAN MYERS, *Abd al-Rahman Ibrahima*

Biographies are often told from the third-person point of view, though biographers may also include autobiographical materials, such as letters, diaries, or journals, so that the reader can gain firsthand knowledge about the subject of the biography.

Essay

An **essay** is a short nonfiction work that makes a point about a single subject. The point that the writer is making is called the **thesis**. For example, in an essay about school uniforms, the thesis might be that uniforms prevent personal expression.

There are many types of essays. A **personal essay** is a short nonfiction work on a single topic related to the life of the writer. The author of a personal essay may tell a story or an anecdote, or reflect on and share feelings about something in his or her life. For example, Carmen Tafolla's "Mi Familia" (page 355) describes her definitions for who makes up a family, and it's not always decided by bloodlines.

> The way I defined family was much like the old funerals I remember. In the front rows were the next of kin, the most greatly affected by the loss, behind them those close, behind them the friends, then the acquaintances and always, somewhere, the people of whom no one knew the exact relationship to the departed…

—CARMEN TAFOLLA, "Mi Familia"

In a **persuasive essay** the writer's goal is to persuade the reader to accept an opinion or point

Reading Model

- Each genre begins with a Reading Model, which introduces students to the *Before, During,* and *After* Reading process.
- Following the Reading Model are three Apply the Model selections that provide students with guidance in learning the *Before, During,* and *After* process.

Nonfiction Reading Model

BEFORE READING

Build Background
You need to apply two different types of background to read nonfiction effectively. One is the selection's historical, scientific, or cultural context. Read the **Build Background** and **Meet the Author** to get this kind of information. The other type of background is the personal knowledge you bring to your reading.

Set Purpose
A nonfiction writer writes to inform, describe, persuade, or entertain. Read **Set Purpose** to decide what you want to get out of a selection.

Analyze Literature
A nonfiction writer uses different techniques depending on the type of nonfiction he or she is writing. The **Analyze Literature** feature draws your attention to a key literary element.

Use Reading Skills
The **Use Reading Skills** feature will help you get the most out of your reading. Learn how to apply skills such as determining author's purpose and using context clues. Identify a graphic organizer that will help you apply the skill before and while you read.

DURING READING

Use Reading Strategies
- **Ask questions** about things that seem significant or interesting.
- **Make predictions** about what's going to happen next. As you read, gather more clues to confirm or change your prediction.
- **Visualize** the information. Form pictures in your mind to help you see what the writer is describing.
- **Make inferences,** or educated guesses, about what is not stated directly.
- **Clarify,** or check that you understand, what you read. Reread any difficult parts.

Analyze Literature
What literary elements stand out? Are the descriptions vivid or interesting? As you read, consider how these elements affect your enjoyment and understanding of the selection.

Make Connections
Notice where connections can be made between the selection and your life. What feelings or thoughts do you have while reading?

AFTER READING

Find Meaning
Recall the important details of the selection, such as the sequence of events and setting. Use this information to **interpret,** or explain, the meaning of the selection.

Make Judgments
- **Analyze** the text by examining significant details and determining what they contribute to the meaning.
- **Evaluate** the text by making judgments about how the author creates meaning.

Analyze Literature
Review how the use of literary elements increased your understanding of the selection. For example, did the author use sensory details? How did he or she help shape meaning?

Extend Understanding
Go beyond the text by exploring the selection's ideas through writing or other creative projects.

262 UNIT 3 NONFICTION

–Teach the Gradual Release of Responsibility–

Apply the Model
BEFORE READING
DURING READING
AFTER READING

The Jacket

A Memoir by Gary Soto

GUIDED READING

Build Background
Literary Context Although "The Jacket" reads like a short story, it is actually a memoir, a true story about something that happened to the author when he was in fifth and sixth grade. An autobiographical memoir is a primary, or eyewitness, account of events in the author's life and how he or she felt about them.

Reader's Context How does wearing a favorite item of clothing affect you? How could your clothes influence the way you experience events?

Set Purpose
Preview the memoir's title and first paragraph. As you read, look for ways Soto uses humor to reveal how the events affected him.

Analyze Literature
Memoir A **memoir** is a piece of nonfiction writing that tells a story from the writer's life. Memoirs are about a person's experiences and reactions to historical events. As you read "The Jacket," decide whether Gary Soto is using the memoir to tell about his own experiences or about a historical event that he lived through. Does knowing that the events actually happened to the writer make the story funnier or more interesting to you?

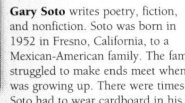

Meet the Author
Gary Soto writes poetry, fiction, and nonfiction. Soto was born in 1952 in Fresno, California, to a Mexican-American family. The family struggled to make ends meet when he was growing up. There were times when Soto had to wear cardboard in his shoes and pick grapes to make money. In college Soto discovered poetry. He began writing his own poems and soon won a national poetry award. Although Soto has written for adults, today he is best known for his writing for young people.

Use Reading Skills
Identify Sequence of Events Using a graphic organizer can help you achieve your purpose in reading. Identifying the sequence of events in a story can help you better understand the plot and allows you to analyze the possible meanings of the events. Create a story strip to record the events in the order in which they happened. Note that not all story events are of equal importance in the plot. Decide which events are significant enough to be recorded.

> Soto wants a black leather jacket. → Soto's mother buys him an ugly vinyl jacket.

Preview Vocabulary
vi·nyl (vī′ n'l) *adj.*, tough, shiny plastic
swoop (swüp) *v.*, descend quickly in a sweeping movement
vi·cious (vi′ shəs) *adj.*, cruel, fierce
mope (mōp) *v.*, be gloomy or in low spirits

Apply the Model
BEFORE READING
DURING READING
AFTER READING

Find Meaning
1. (a) What kind of jacket does the narrator want? (b) How does the jacket he receives compare to the jacket he wanted?
2. (a) List some of the unfortunate things that happen to the narrator during the years he wears the jacket. (b) How many of these things does the jacket cause?

Analyze Literature
Memoir In autobiographical writing, an author uses tone and word choice to express his or her feelings. How does Soto's use of humor affect the tone of this memoir? Use a cluster chart to record specific details or examples of Soto's word choice that contribute to the tone. Record each detail or example in the outer circles, and write in the center what you think is the overall tone.

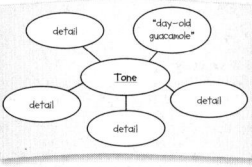

Make Judgments
3. (a) Why do you think the narrator teases his dog? (b) Does teasing Brownie help the situation? Explain.
4. Why doesn't the narrator tell his mother that he does not like the jacket?
5. At the end of the memoir, how have the narrator's feelings about the jacket changed?

Extend Understanding

Writing Options
Creative Writing Imagine that you are the narrator in "The Jacket." You have finally outgrown your jacket. Write a **diary entry** explaining how you feel about getting rid of the jacket at last. Add your own sensory details when describing the jacket and your feelings.

Expository Writing "The Jacket" vividly re-creates events in Soto's life and reveals his personal feelings. Write a **literary analysis** of how Soto's tone in this memoir reveals his true feelings about that time in his life. Support your thesis with details from your cluster chart.

Collaborative Learning
Compare Types of Nonfiction Both a memoir and an autobiography are forms of nonfiction written by an author about his or her life. Discuss with a partner the differences between a memoir and an autobiography. Work together to make a chart comparing the features of a memoir to the features of an autobiography. Refer to the Introduction to Nonfiction on page 260 for more information.

Critical Literacy
Read to Interpret In small groups, analyze how the story's meaning would change if the elements of humor were not present in the selection. What does Soto's inclusion of humor indicate about his character and personality?

 Go to www.mirrorsandwindows.com for more.

THE JACKET **269**

Guided Reading BEFORE

- Build Background, Set Purpose, Analyze Literature
- Meet the Author
- Use Reading Skills
- Preview Vocabulary

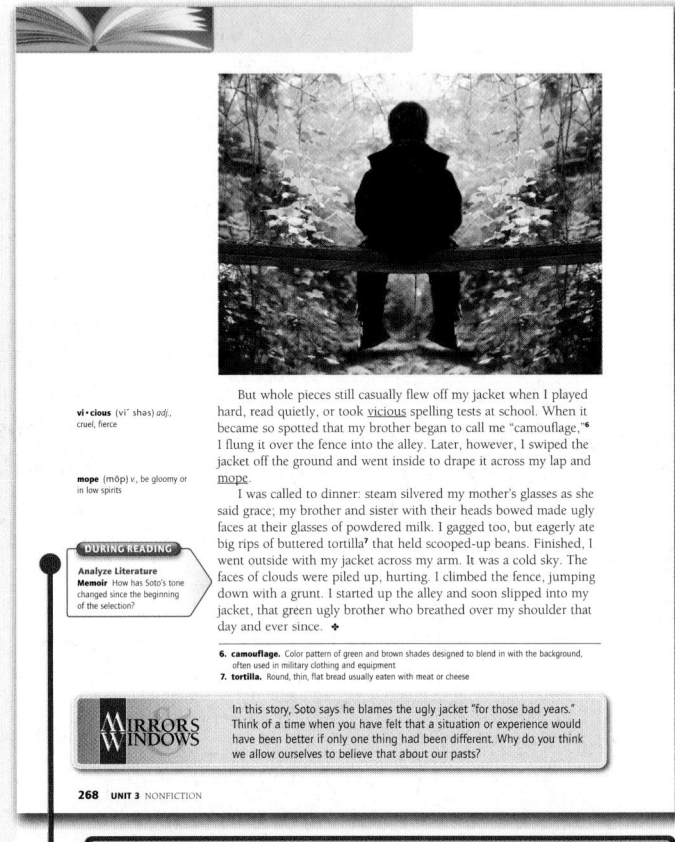

vi·cious (vi′ shəs) *adj.*, cruel, fierce

mope (mōp) *v.*, be gloomy or in low spirits

DURING READING
Analyze Literature
Memoir How has Soto's tone changed since the beginning of the selection?

But whole pieces still casually flew off my jacket when I played hard, read quietly, or took vicious spelling tests at school. When it became so spotted that my brother began to call me "camouflage,"[6] I flung it over the fence into the alley. Later, however, I swiped the jacket off the ground and went inside to drape it across my lap and mope.

I was called to dinner: steam silvered my mother's glasses as she said grace; my brother and sister with their heads bowed made ugly faces at their glasses of powdered milk. I gagged too, but eagerly ate big rips of buttered tortilla[7] that held scooped-up beans. Finished, I went outside with my jacket across my arm. It was a cold sky. The faces of clouds were piled up, hurting. I climbed the fence, jumping down with a grunt. I started up the alley and soon slipped into my jacket, that green ugly brother who breathed over my shoulder that day and ever since. ✦

6. **camouflage.** Color pattern of green and brown shades designed to blend in with the background, often used in military clothing and equipment
7. **tortilla.** Round, thin, flat bread usually eaten with meat or cheese

MIRRORS & WINDOWS
In this story, Soto says he blames the ugly jacket "for those bad years." Think of a time when you have felt that a situation or experience would have been better if only one thing had been different. Why do you think we allow ourselves to believe that about our pasts?

268 UNIT 3 NONFICTION

Guided Reading DURING

- Margin prompts help students analyze literature and develop reading strategies and skills.
- Vocabulary is identified and defined on the page.
- Mirrors & Windows questions encourage students to connect their personal experiences with the selection and the broader world around them.

Guided Reading AFTER

- Find Meaning and Make Judgments questions are based on Bloom's taxonomy.
- Analyze Literature explores literary elements.
- Extend Understanding provides two writing options and two extension projects.

Mirrors & Windows

–Develop Independent Learners–

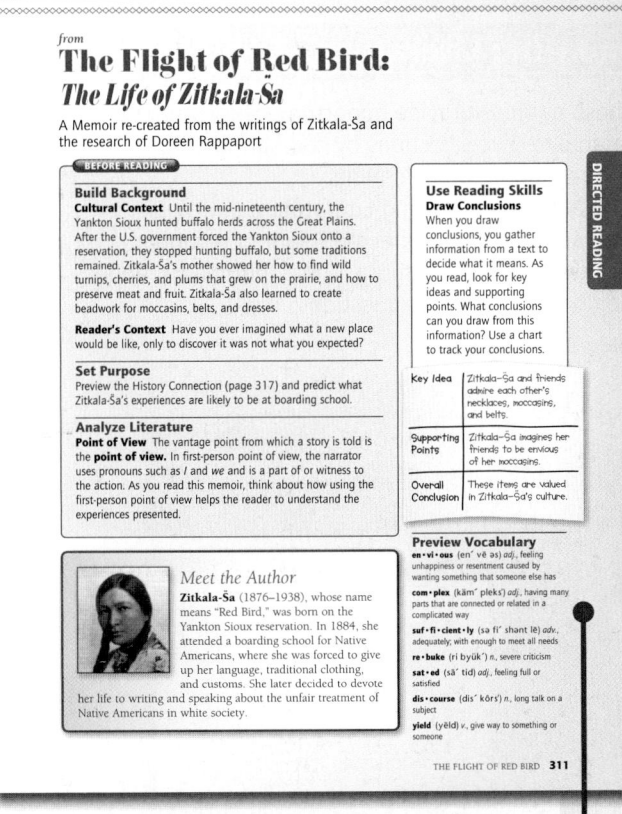

from
The Flight of Red Bird:
The Life of Zitkala-Ša

A Memoir re-created from the writings of Zitkala-Ša and the research of Doreen Rappaport

BEFORE READING

Build Background
Cultural Context Until the mid-nineteenth century, the Yankton Sioux hunted buffalo herds across the Great Plains. After the U.S. government forced the Yankton Sioux onto a reservation, they stopped hunting buffalo, but some traditions remained. Zitkala-Ša's mother showed her how to find wild turnips, cherries, and plums that grew on the prairie, and how to preserve meat and fruit. Zitkala-Ša also learned to create beadwork for moccasins, belts, and dresses.

Reader's Context Have you ever imagined what a new place would be like, only to discover it was not what you expected?

Set Purpose
Preview the History Connection (page 317) and predict what Zitkala-Ša's experiences are likely to be at boarding school.

Analyze Literature
Point of View The vantage point from which a story is told is the **point of view**. In first-person point of view, the narrator uses pronouns such as *I* and *we* and is a part of or witness to the action. As you read this memoir, think about how using the first-person point of view helps the reader to understand the experiences presented.

Meet the Author
Zitkala-Ša (1876–1938), whose name means "Red Bird," was born on the Yankton Sioux reservation. In 1884, she attended a boarding school for Native Americans, where she was forced to give up her language, traditional clothing, and customs. She later decided to devote her life to writing and speaking about the unfair treatment of Native Americans in white society.

Use Reading Skills
Draw Conclusions
When you draw conclusions, you gather information from a text to decide what it means. As you read, look for key ideas and supporting points. What conclusions can you draw from this information? Use a chart to track your conclusions.

Key Idea	Zitkala-Ša and friends admire each other's necklaces, moccasins, and belts.
Supporting Points	Zitkala-Ša imagines her friends to be envious of her moccasins.
Overall Conclusion	These items are valued in Zitkala-Ša's culture.

Preview Vocabulary
en·vi·ous (en′ vē əs) *adj.*, feeling unhappiness or resentment caused by wanting something that someone else has

com·plex (käm′ pleks′) *adj.*, having many parts that are connected or related in a complicated way

suf·fi·cient·ly (sə fi′ shənt lē) *adv.*, adequately; with enough to meet all needs

re·buke (ri byük′) *n.*, severe criticism

sat·ed (sā′ tid) *adj.*, feeling full or satisfied

dis·course (dis′ kôrs′) *n.*, long talk on a subject

yield (yēld) *v.*, give way to something or someone

THE FLIGHT OF RED BIRD **311**

DIRECTED READING

---

from
The Flight of Red Bird:
The Life of Zitkala-Ša

I heard wonderful stories about the strangers from my friend Judéwin.

A Memoir re-created from the writings of Zitkala-Ša and the research of Doreen Rappaport

---

Directed Reading

- Directed Reading begins the gradual release of responsibility from teacher to students.
- Students continue to be supported with before reading and after reading activities, but the during-reading margin prompts are omitted.
- Students begin to apply the during-reading comprehension skills on their own.

Independent Reading

- Two Independent Readings at the end of each unit provide students with the opportunity to practice skills on their own.

INDEPENDENT READING

from
Woodsong
A Memoir by Gary Paulsen

Whether I lived or died depended on him.

Fear comes in many forms but perhaps the worst scare is the one that isn't anticipated; the one that isn't really known about until it's here. A sudden fear. The unexpected.

And again, fire played a role in it.

We have bear trouble. Because we feed processed meat to the dogs there is always the smell of meat over the kennel. In the summer it can be a bit high[1] because the dogs like to "save" their food sometimes for a day or two or four—burying it to dig up later. We live on the edge of wilderness and consequently the meat smell brings any number of visitors from the woods.

Skunks abound, and foxes and coyotes and wolves and weasels—all predators.[2] We once had an eagle live over the kennel for more than a week, scavenging[3] from the dogs, and a crazy group of ravens has pretty much taken over the puppy pen. Ravens are protected by the state and they seem to know it. When I walk toward the puppy pen with the buckets of meat it's a toss-up to see who gets it—the pups or the birds. They have actually pecked the puppies away from the food pans until they have gone through and taken what they want.

Spring, when the bears come, is the worst. They have been in hibernation[4]

1. **a bit high.** Fairly strong
2. **predators.** Animals that live by preying on others
3. **scavenging.** Searching for usable material
4. **hibernation.** State of mental or physical inactivity

Gary Paulsen was born in 1939 in Minnesota. Paulsen learned to be self-sufficient at an early age, working as a trapper, farmer, soldier, truck driver, sailor, construction worker, field engineer, and magazine editor. When he decided to devote himself to writing, he moved to the remote woods of northern Minnesota and lived off the land, supporting himself by hunting and trapping. Paulsen draws on his own experiences to create novels and personal nonfiction that is noted for vivid descriptions of setting, themes of conflict with nature, and the struggle for survival.

351

–Compare Literature and Extend Reading–

Comparing Literature

Satchel Paige
A Biography by Bill Littlefield

THE SHUTOUT
Historical Nonfiction by Patricia C. and Fredrick McKissack Jr.

BEFORE READING

Build Background
Historical Context Patricia C. and Fredrick McKissack Jr.'s "The Shutout" describes the early history of baseball in the Negro leagues. Bill Littlefield's "Satchel Paige" tells the story of a star pitcher of the Negro leagues who became a star in the major leagues, too. African-American players formed the Negro leagues because they were banned from the major leagues until 1947.

Reader's Context Have you ever been excluded from an organization or activity you very much wanted to join? How did you feel? What did you do about it?

Set Purpose
Preview the Historical Context. Read to learn how black players reacted to discrimination by forming their own leagues, hosting their own championships, and developing legendary players.

Compare Literature:
Fact vs. Opinion
A **fact** is a statement that can be proven by direct observation or a reliable source. An **opinion** is a statement that expresses an attitude or feeling. As you read, distinguish between fact and opinion in these two selections.

Preview Vocabulary
po·ten·tial (pa ten[t]´ shal) adj., possible

con·fron·ta·tion (kän´ fran[t] tā´ shan) n., act of meeting face to face, especially in opposition

pre·ju·dice (pre´ ja das) n., opinion or judgment formed without sufficient knowledge of a person or group of people

wan·ing (wān´ iŋ) adj., approaching the end

ex·ploit (ek´ sploit) n., bold deed

an·ec·dote (a´ nik dōt) n., short, amusing narrative

e·volve (ē vŏlv´) v., develop from something else

di·verse (dī vurs´) adj., possessing different elements or qualities

in·te·grat·ed (in´ ta grāt´ ad) adj., characterized by equal membership in society

in·fa·mous (in´ fa mas) adj., possessing an extremely bad reputation

Meet the Authors

 Bill Littlefield has written numerous news articles, reviews, and essays. He currently hosts National Public Radio's "Only a Game," a weekly program about sports. He teaches writing and literature courses at Curry College.

 **Patricia C. and Fredrick McKissack Jr.** are a mother-and-son author team who have written about African-American history. "The Shutout" is from their book *Black Diamond: The Story of the Negro Baseball Leagues.* The book records the relationship between baseball and race and highlights heroes of the Negro leagues.

332 UNIT 3 NONFICTION

(Opposite page) Pitcher Satchel Paige warming up.

DIRECTED READING

Comparing Literature

- These pairings provide opportunities for students to analyze two selections by comparing and contrasting literary elements.
- At least one Comparing Literature pairing per unit appears in the Directed Reading section, followed by Find Meaning, Make Judgments, and Comparing Literature questions.

For Your Reading List

The Race to Save the Lord God Bird
by Phillip Hoose
 Although once found throughout the southeastern United States, the Ivory-billed Woodpecker has since become a modern endangered species. It was last spotted in 1987 in Cuba. This book details the bird's history through the accounts of people who followed its decline, from artists to scientists to avid bird watchers.

The Land I Lost: Adventures of a Boy in Vietnam
by Huynh Quang Nhuong
 This memoir focuses on Nhuong's life as a boy growing up in the Vietnam countryside. Divided into sections that describe individuals as well as animals in the area, the book depicts the importance of animals in Nhuong's lifestyle, such as his water buffalo and the crocodiles that live nearby. The author recalls many interesting encounters between the people of his village and the neighboring animals.

Team Moon: How 400,000 People Landed Apollo 11 on the Moon
by Catherine Thimmesh
When humans first landed on the moon in 1969, it wasn't just the result of the astronauts' hard work. This Sibert Award-winning book tells the story of the moon landing from the perspective of everyone behind the scenes, including workers at Kennedy Space Center, designers who built the spacecraft, and the people responsible for broadcasting the video. The book's photographs and firsthand accounts make the moon landing come to life from a fresh perspective.

Boy
by Roald Dahl
 A famous children's author, Roald Dahl has written such classic books as *Matilda, Charlie and the Chocolate Factory,* and *The BFG.* He tells his own story in this memoir. Dahl focuses on his childhood adventures, such as the "Great Mouse Plot." Fans of Dahl's work will be interested to see where he found inspiration for some of his characters, and those less familiar with Dahl's fiction will enjoy his tales of mischief.

Invisible Allies: Microbes That Shape Our Lives
by Jeanette Farrell
 In this award-winning book, Farrell describes the tiny microbes that help us survive. After a brief introduction to these microscopic creatures, she describes how microbes help us digest and break down food, and how they play a part in the processes of preserving and producing foods such as bread and cheese.

Good Brother, Bad Brother: The Story of Edwin Booth and John Wilkes Booth
by James Cross Giblin
Edwin and John Wilkes Booth were brothers and aspiring actors until John became famous for assassinating President Abraham Lincoln. The book chronicles the events leading up to Lincoln's assassination, as well as Edwin's later attempts to become a famous actor. The firsthand accounts paint an accurate and engaging picture.

FOR YOUR READING LIST 361

For Your Reading List

Independent reading suggestions:
- Appear at the end of each unit.
- Extend the unit theme with relevant, diverse titles.
- Encourage application of reading strategies and skills.

Mirrors & Windows

–Make Text-To-Text Connections–

Text-to-Text Connections add relevance to the literature selections by providing students with background information and context, and by helping them see relationships between literature, informational texts, and primary source materials.

Literature Connection

Primary Source Connection

LITERATURE ▶▶ CONNECTION

In the essay from *All I Really Need to Know I Learned in Kindergarten*, Robert Fulghum uses games as metaphors for the way people interact with each other. Fulghum sees that the world is not always perfect and that people need each other to survive. The following selection is a poem by **Nikki Giovanni** (b. 1943) from her book *My House*. Giovanni grew up in Tennessee and Ohio. Her poetry collections are about civil rights, equality, children, and families. Besides being a poet, Giovanni is an essayist and speaker who teaches writing and literature. As you read, think about the title and theme of the poem and how they connect to Fulghum's main idea.

The World Is Not a Pleasant Place to Be

A Lyric Poem by Nikki Giovanni

the world is not a pleasant place
to be without
someone to hold and be held by

5 a river would stop
its flow if only
a stream were there
to receive it

an ocean would never laugh
10 if clouds weren't there
to kiss her tears

the world is not
a pleasant place to be without
someone

[17 feb 72] ✦

TEXT ←TO→ TEXT CONNECTION Both Robert Fulghum's essay and Nikki Giovanni's poem make a statement about the importance of being with others. If Fulghum uses comparisons to games to support what he believes, what does Giovanni use as evidence? Is Giovanni trying to persuade? Explain.

296 UNIT

PRIMARY SOURCE ▶▶ CONNECTION

Since the 1960s, the National Aeronautics and Space Administration (NASA) has sent astronauts into space. The earliest—and most famous—of the photographs from space were taken by the *Apollo 16* crew, which explored the Moon in the *Lunar Rover*. In 1981, NASA launched the first space shuttle. The photographs in this selection were taken from various satellites and imaging modules orbiting Earth. Study these photographs to imagine the new perspectives astronomers have gained from the space program.

Earth from Space

Photographs from NASA

This true-color image shows North and South America as they would appear from space 35,000 km (22,000 miles) above Earth. The image is a combination of data from two satellites. NASA Goddard Space Flight Center.

386 UNIT 4 NONFICTION

Informational Text Connection

INFORMATIONAL TEXT ▶▶ CONNECTION

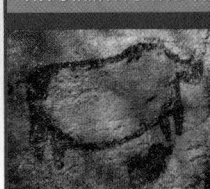

In "There Is No Salvation for India," Gandhi explains why he believes that Indians should be educated in their native languages. The following article is from *Tales from the Times*, a book of stories by the staff of the *New York Times*. This article describes the struggle of the Wayeyi people of Botswana in Africa to keep their native language from dying out. As you read, note why members of the Wayeyi tribe work so hard to preserve their language and customs.

Bushmen paintings at Tsodilo Hills, Botswana.

An Old Language Lives

An Article from *Tales from the Times,* by Rachel L. Swarns

In the beginning, there were the rushing rivers, the whispering reeds, the "Kwa! Kwa!" of shrieking herons and the rumble of lions. When the Wayeyi people drifted here some 200 years ago, they thought they had found paradise.

They settled in huts along the green marshes and built canoes to glide through the twisting streams. They fished, harvested water lilies and named the animals, flowers and stars in their language—Shiyeyi.

"First, first people to come here are Wayeyi and Bushmen,"[1] said Baagi Letsapa, as he guided his canoe through the sleepy waterways.

He is a leathery man who still remembers the teachings of his father. He knows that the boiled roots of the sage plant help ease indigestion, that papyrus[2] makes the best sleeping mats and that the ukayi plant produces a poison that kills fish, but not people. This knowledge is disappearing as young people abandon the rivers, the canoes and the old ways. But not without a fight.

Here in the swamps of northern Botswana,[3] the Wayeyi are battling not to disappear. They are just a tiny group in a country dominated by the Tswana people, and for generations tribes like theirs have been discouraged from practicing the traditions that make them different from each other so that there is only one national way. But a few years ago the Wayeyi decided their traditions were too important to fade away. They took the government to court and demanded that their tribe be officially recognized and that their all but forgotten language—a language only the elders of the tribe still speak—be taught in schools.

Critics said they were asking for trouble and that they would pit one tribe against another. Young people are not interested in the old ways, the critics also said. All across southern Africa, young people have left small villages and moved to the cities. Urban

---

1. **Bushmen.** Group of nomadic hunters in southern Africa
2. **papyrus.** Plant that can be made into a material like paper
3. **Botswana.** Country in southern Africa

306 UNIT 3 NONFICTION

–Integrate Cross-Curricular Connections–

Cross-Curricular Connections are embedded within the selections to provide related background information and to connect with other content areas.

Social Studies Connection

SOCIAL STUDIES ▶▶ CONNECTION

there is no way we can win. It has been more than forty years since Burma gained independence.[1] If we ask what progress has been made in these more than forty years, only depressing answers appear. When I visited Myikyina[2] over thirty years ago, there was no problem of electricity—it was always available. Now there is not even enough electricity and we find power in short supply. So we see that in these past thirty years and more there has been not only no progress but actual decline. We must ask ourselves, then: Why has this decline occurred? Most will answer that it is because the BSPP[3] was bad. I won't argue with that, but we must ask again: Why was the BSPP able to last so long, then? I think the answer to this has to do with the people at large. Because we, the citizens, simply stood by and watched, the system was able to last as long as it did. When the time came to take up independence, I think that the BSPP gained control of the government because the citizens failed to carry out the duties of citizenship. If we want a stable democracy in the future, every single one of us must bear this responsibility conscientiously. We must

Aung San Suu Kyi Aung San Suu Kyi received the Nobel Peace Prize in 1991 for her nonviolent struggle for democracy and human rights in Myanmar. Suu Kyi was not able to attend the awards ceremony in person to receive her prize because she was under house arrest in Myanmar. Although Suu Kyi was released in 1995, the military government severely restricted her words and actions. Suu Kyi continued writing and speaking in support of democracy for Myanmar until she was again placed under house arrest from 2000 to 2002. In May 2003, she was once again arrested, and as of the printing of this book, she remains under house arrest. Many people in Myanmar and in the international community support her struggle and continue to call for her release.

Human rights activists in Manila, Philippines, marched to the Burmese embassy with heart-shaped placards and balloons to symbolize their demand to free Aung San Suu Kyi from house arrest. February, 2007.

understand that there is great merit in sacrificing for others and that by so doing we live the full life.

It's not by living to the age of ninety or one hundred that one lives the full life. Some

1. **since Burma gained independence.** Burma won its independence from Great Britain in 1948.
2. **Myikyina.** Capital city of Kachin State in northern Myanmar. Kachin State is one of seven states and seven divisions in Myanmar.
3. **BSPP.** The Burma Socialist Program Party, a political party formed by the military regime that seized power in Burma in 1962 and lasted until 1988
4. **sacrifice.** Give something up for the benefit of something or someone else

de·cline (di klīn´) n., gradual loss of power, health, or prosperity; process of worsening

con·sci·en·tious·ly (kän[t]ʹ shē en[t]ʹ shəs lē) adv., guided by a sense of what is right; carefully

mer·it (merʹ ət) n., worthiness, virtue

History Connection

HISTORY ▶▶ CONNECTION

Native American Boarding Schools In the late nineteenth century, many white educators believed that Native Americans' lives would be better if they learned white culture and lived like white people. By 1884, there were forty-nine boarding schools for Native Americans across the country. Here, students were forbidden to speak their native languages or wear native dress. They learned English and trades like carpentry and agriculture. The students were shocked and angered at being forced to give up their traditional culture. Many had a difficult time adjusting to the white system of education. After graduation, many students returned to the reservations, but some found they had forgotten their traditional language and way of life. For others, education at these schools led to successful careers. Most boarding schools were gradually replaced by day schools on the reservations. How did Zitkala-Ša react to losing aspects of her culture at boarding school?

The First Day at School

The first day in the land of red apples was a bitter-cold one. Snow still covered the ground, and the trees were bare. A large bell rang for breakfast, its loud metallic voice crashing through the belfry[17] overhead into our sensitive ears several hours before sunrise. The annoying clatter of shoes gave us no peace. The constant clash of harsh noises, with many voices murmuring an unknown tongue, made a bedlam[18] within which I was securely tied. And though my spirit tore itself in struggling for its lost freedom, all was useless.

A woman with white hair came for us. We were placed in a line with other Indian girls dressed in stiff shoes and closely clinging dresses. The small girls wore sleeved aprons and had shingled (close-cropped and layered) hair.

I felt like sinking to the floor, for my blanket had been stripped from my shoulders. I looked hard at the Indian girls who had been here awhile. They seemed not to care that they were even more immodestly dressed than I in their tight-fitting clothes.

In the dining room I spied the three boys from home, looking as uncomfortable as I felt.

A small bell was tapped and each pupil drew a chair from under the table. I assumed this meant we should sit, so pulled out my chair and slipped into it. But when I turned

older Indian girls at the table whispered to me, "Wait until you are alone."

"I want my mother and my brother. I want my aunt!" I pleaded in my language, but the ears of the palefaces could not hear me.

We were taken up an incline of wooden boxes, which I later learned to call a stairway. At the top was a quiet, dimly lighted hall. Many narrow beds, with sleeping brown faces peeping out of the coverings, lined the wall. I was tucked into bed with one of the tall girls. She talked to me in my mother tongue, and it soothed me.

I had arrived in the wonderful land of rosy skies, but I was not happy, as I had thought I would be. My long travel and the bewildering sights had exhausted me.

I fell asleep, heaving deep, tired sobs. My tears were left to dry themselves in streaks, because neither my aunt nor my mother was there to wipe them away.

17. **belfry.** Tower for a bell
18. **bedlam.** Disturbing scene of confusion and uproar

homeland in twenty years. The people there were still being captured by slave traders. He would have to send a messenger who knew the countryside, and who knew the Fula. Where would he find such a man?

For a long time Ibrahima did nothing. Finally, some time after the death of Dr. Cox in 1816, Ibrahima wrote the letter that Marschalk suggested. He had little faith in the procedure but felt he had nothing to lose. Marschalk was surprised when Ibrahima appeared with the letter written neatly in Arabic. Since one place in Africa was the same to Marschalk, he sent the letter not to Fouta Djallon but to Morocco.

The government of Morocco did not know Ibrahima but understood from his letter that he was a Moslem. Moroccan officials, in a letter to President James Monroe, pleaded for the release of Ibrahima. The letter reached Henry Clay, the American Secretary of State.

The United States had recently ended a bitter war with Tripoli in north Africa, and welcomed the idea of establishing good relations with Morocco, another north African country. Clay wrote to Foster about Ibrahima.

Foster resented the idea of releasing Ibrahima. The very idea that the government of Morocco had written to Clay and discussed

DURING READING

Analyze Literature Biography Would Ibrahima's letter be a primary or a secondary source? Why?

Geography Connection

GEOGRAPHY ▶▶ CONNECTION

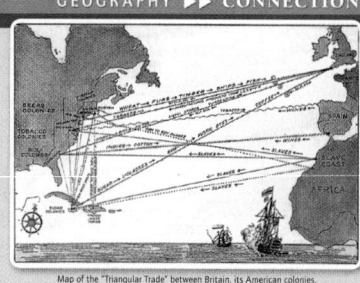

Map of the "Triangular Trade" between Britain, its American colonies, and Africa in the 17th and 18th centuries.

The Triangular Trade West Africa is the area of Africa closest both to Europe and to the Americas. As a result, European trading ships seeking captured Africans often stopped along the coast of West Africa to pick up their human cargo. There were many ports of call along the coast, but Goree Island off the coast of present-day Senegal was the most active port. From there ships sailed west across the Atlantic Ocean. In North America, the enslaved Africans were traded for sugar, rum, and lumber, which were then taken to be sold in Europe. Because this trading route touched on three continents, it was known as the Triangular Trade.

–Master Language Arts Skills–

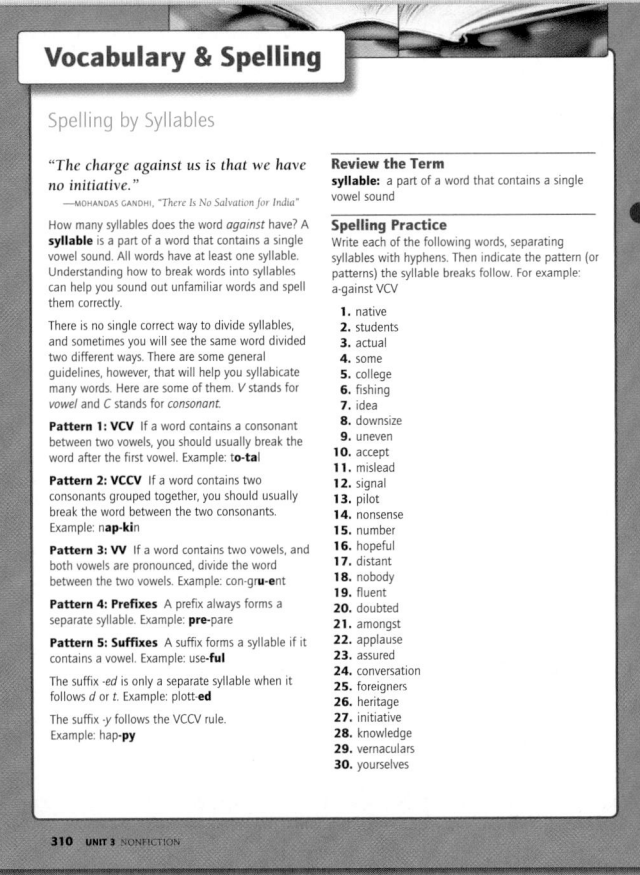

Vocabulary & Spelling

Spelling by Syllables

"The charge against us is that we have no initiative."
—MOHANDAS GANDHI, *"There Is No Salvation for India"*

How many syllables does the word *against* have? A **syllable** is a part of a word that contains a single vowel sound. All words have at least one syllable. Understanding how to break words into syllables can help you sound out unfamiliar words and spell them correctly.

There is no single correct way to divide syllables, and sometimes you will see the same word divided two different ways. There are some general guidelines, however, that will help you syllabicate many words. Here are some of them. *V* stands for *vowel* and *C* stands for *consonant*.

Pattern 1: VCV If a word contains a consonant between two vowels, you should usually break the word after the first vowel. Example: **to-tal**

Pattern 2: VCCV If a word contains two consonants grouped together, you should usually break the word between the two consonants. Example: **nap-kin**

Pattern 3: VV If a word contains two vowels, and both vowels are pronounced, divide the word between the two vowels. Example: **con-gru-ent**

Pattern 4: Prefixes A prefix always forms a separate syllable. Example: **pre-pare**

Pattern 5: Suffixes A suffix forms a syllable if it contains a vowel. Example: **use-ful**

The suffix *-ed* is only a separate syllable when it follows *d* or *t*. Example: **plott-ed**

The suffix *-y* follows the VCCV rule. Example: **hap-py**

Review the Term
syllable: a part of a word that contains a single vowel sound

Spelling Practice
Write each of the following words, separating syllables with hyphens. Then indicate the pattern (or patterns) the syllable breaks follow. For example: a-gainst VCV

1. native
2. students
3. actual
4. some
5. college
6. fishing
7. idea
8. downsize
9. uneven
10. accept
11. mislead
12. signal
13. pilot
14. nonsense
15. number
16. hopeful
17. distant
18. nobody
19. fluent
20. doubted
21. amongst
22. applause
23. assured
24. conversation
25. foreigners
26. heritage
27. initiative
28. knowledge
29. vernaculars
30. yourselves

310   UNIT 3 NONFICTION

Vocabulary & Spelling

- Concise vocabulary and spelling lessons follow one or two of the literature selections in each unit.
- The lessons incorporate words from the preceding selection.
- Each lesson contains instruction, followed by practice exercises.

Grammar & Style

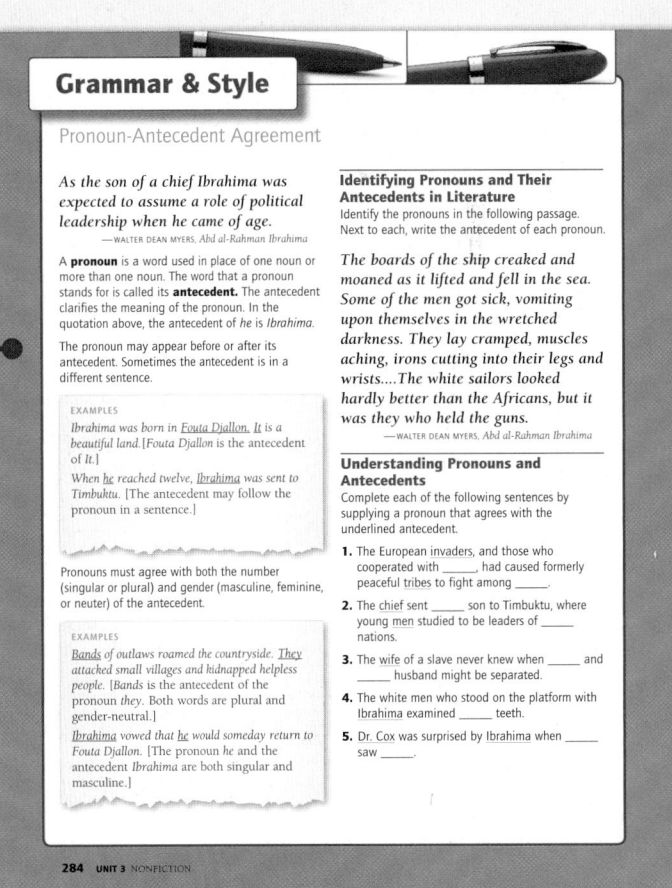

Pronoun-Antecedent Agreement

As the son of a chief Ibrahima was expected to assume a role of political leadership when he came of age.
—WALTER DEAN MYERS, *Abd al-Rahman Ibrahima*

A **pronoun** is a word used in place of one noun or more than one noun. The word that a pronoun stands for is called its **antecedent.** The antecedent clarifies the meaning of the pronoun. In the quotation above, the antecedent of *he* is *Ibrahima*.

The pronoun may appear before or after its antecedent. Sometimes the antecedent is in a different sentence.

> EXAMPLES
> *Ibrahima was born in Fouta Djallon. It is a beautiful land.* [Fouta Djallon is the antecedent of It.]
>
> *When he reached twelve, Ibrahima was sent to Timbuktu.* [The antecedent may follow the pronoun in a sentence.]

Pronouns must agree with both the number (singular or plural) and gender (masculine, feminine, or neuter) of the antecedent.

> EXAMPLES
> *Bands of outlaws roamed the countryside. They attacked small villages and kidnapped helpless people.* [Bands is the antecedent of the pronoun they. Both words are plural and gender-neutral.]
>
> *Ibrahima vowed that he would someday return to Fouta Djallon.* [The pronoun he and the antecedent Ibrahima are both singular and masculine.]

Identifying Pronouns and Their Antecedents in Literature
Identify the pronouns in the following passage. Next to each, write the antecedent of each pronoun.

The boards of the ship creaked and moaned as it lifted and fell in the sea. Some of the men got sick, vomiting upon themselves in the wretched darkness. They lay cramped, muscles aching, irons cutting into their legs and wrists....The white sailors looked hardly better than the Africans, but it was they who held the guns.
—WALTER DEAN MYERS, *Abd al-Rahman Ibrahima*

Understanding Pronouns and Antecedents
Complete each of the following sentences by supplying a pronoun that agrees with the underlined antecedent.

1. The European <u>invaders</u>, and those who cooperated with _____, had caused formerly peaceful <u>tribes</u> to fight among _____.

2. The <u>chief</u> sent _____ son to Timbuktu, where young <u>men</u> studied to be leaders of _____ nations.

3. The <u>wife</u> of a slave never knew when _____ and _____ husband might be separated.

4. The white men who stood on the platform with <u>Ibrahima</u> examined _____ teeth.

5. <u>Dr. Cox</u> was surprised by <u>Ibrahima</u> when _____ saw _____.

284   UNIT 3 NONFICTION

Grammar & Style

- As with vocabulary and spelling, concise grammar and style lessons appear several times in each unit.
- These lessons are also paired with the preceding literature selections.
- Students learn and reinforce their skills in context, as they study literature.

–Extend Learning with End-of-Unit Workshops–

Writing Workshop

The Writing Workshops provide one extended writing lesson for each unit. All lessons:

- Connect to the unit theme.
- Include a student model.
- Incorporate a fully developed, five-step writing process.
  - Prewrite
  - Draft
  - Revise
  - Edit and Proofread
  - Publish and Present

Writing Workshop

Persuasive Writing

Persuasive Essay

Assignment: Write a persuasive essay in which I present and support a clearly stated opinion.

Goal: Persuade my audience to accept or act on my opinion.

Strategy: Present clear reasons for my opinion, support my reasons, and anticipate and address counterarguments.

Writing Rubric: My persuasive essay should include the following:

- an introduction that clearly states my opinion
- reasons for my opinion
- support for my reasons
- thoughtful answers to counterarguments
- a conclusion with a call to action

Reading and Writing

In this unit, you read several pieces of persuasive writing. Topics ranged from personal advice, such as letting oneself be "found," to political issues, such as bearing responsibility for life in a democracy. No matter what the topic, writing that presents an opinion or argument is persuasive writing. Standardized tests will often ask you to write persuasively. You will also need persuasive skills in other areas of your life—from getting what you want from a brother or sister to achieving success in the workplace.

In this workshop, you will learn how to write a **persuasive essay.** You will present a clear opinion in a **thesis** or **opinion statement** and back it up with reasons and support. You will also anticipate and address **counterarguments,** which are arguments that oppose your own. The following summary shows a typical persuasive essay assignment. It includes requirements and standards that might not always be stated in an assignment but that you should consider when writing a persuasive essay.

What Great Writers Do
Mawi Asgedom came to the United States from Ethiopia. In this passage, he reflects on his journey and his mother's wise advice. What is his opinion? How does he support and explain it?

My mother's advice in childhood was to pull the covers over my head—that had been the easy part. But her later advice meant, I now realize, that I should know when to pull the covers down and stick my neck out. That's the hard part. Too many of us go through life with the covers over our heads. We want to reach out, but we fear to make ourselves vulnerable. And we are also busy....We race through a world of demands. And then we ask ourselves almost helplessly, "What can we do as individuals?"

—MAWI ASGEDOM, *Of Beetles & Angels*

362 UNIT 3 NONFICTION

Speaking & Listening Workshop

Each unit also includes one complete speaking and listening lesson.

- Students learn and practice oral presentation skills. Topics are related to both school and work.
- Rubrics are provided for evaluation.

Speaking & Listening Workshop

Delivering and Listening to a Persuasive Speech

People are always trying to persuade you to do something. Food companies want you to eat or drink their products. Clothing makers want you to wear their clothes. Now it's your turn. The goal of a **persuasive speech** is to convince others to believe, think, or do something. Actively listening to persuasive speeches helps you make up your own mind based on facts, not emotion.

Planning Your Persuasive Speech

Choose a Topic and Position Think about something you'd like to see changed. Is your weekend curfew too early? Should your teacher give less homework? Select a topic on which people have different opinions. Sum up your position in a strong statement, such as "Students who spend all day in school should have time to socialize with family and friends, earn extra money, or just relax instead of doing hours of homework."

Identify Your Audience Who are you trying to convince? Arguments you use to persuade fellow students might be different from those you use to convince teachers or parents. After identifying your audience, ask yourself, "What kind of arguments will convince these people to agree with me and take action?"

Outline and Research Your Arguments Begin by outlining your arguments. Stating your opinion isn't enough. What facts, statistics, expert opinions, anecdotes, examples, or other details will support your arguments? Consider your own point of view as well as possible arguments that those who disagree might use.

Position: Teachers should give less homework.

Point 1: Describe hours spent getting ready for school, getting to and from school, and at school as a percentage of waking hours.

Point 2: Describe total hours of homework assigned by all teachers. How much time is left in the day?

Point 3: Counterargument: homework is a necessary part of learning—why? Homework only covers school subjects; we learn social skills by associating with others.

Plan Your Opening Grab your audience's interest by telling a short dramatic story related to your point of view; by asking the audience a question, such as "Should people spend all their waking hours working?"; or by using a metaphor (*Feeding your mind only with schoolwork is like feeding your body with only one kind of food*).

Speaking Rubric

Your presentation will be evaluated on these elements:

Content

- ☐ presentation is clear and well-organized
- ☐ arguments are strong and well-supported
- ☐ opposing arguments are addressed

Delivery and Presentation

- ☐ tone is moderate and reasonable
- ☐ nonverbal communication effectively supports content
- ☐ questions are answered completely and politely

Listening Rubric

As a peer reviewer or audience member, I should do the following:

- ☐ listen quietly and attentively
- ☐ maintain eye contact with speaker
- ☐ ask appropriate questions
- ☐ (as peer reviewer) provide constructive feedback

368 UNIT 3 NONFICTION

Test Practice Workshop

Writing Skills

Persuasive Essay

Read the following excerpt and the writing assignment that follows. Before writing, think about what task the assignment is asking you to perform. Then create an outline to guide your writing.

from "The Fan Club" by Rona Maynard

Rachel crouched on her knees and began very clumsily to gather her scattered treasures. Papers and boxes lay all about, and some of the boxes had broken open, spilling their contents in wild confusion. No one went to help. At last she scrambled to her feet and began fumbling with her notes.

"My—my speech is on shells."

A cold and stony silence had settled upon the room.

"Lots of people collect shells, because they're kind of pretty—sort of, and you just find them on the beach."

"Well, whaddaya know!" It was Steve's voice, softer this time, but all mock amazement. Laura jabbed her notebook with her pencil. Why were they so cruel, so thoughtless? Why did they have to laugh?

Then, suddenly, chairs were shoved aside at the back of the room and there was the sound of many voices whispering. They were standing now, whole rows of them, their faces grinning with delight. Choked giggles, shuffling feet—and then applause—wild, sarcastic, malicious applause. That was when Laura saw that they were all wearing little white cards with a fat, frizzy-haired figure drawn on the front. What did it mean? She looked more closely. "HORTENSKY FAN CLUB," said the bright-red letters.

So that was what the whispering had been all morning. She'd been wrong. They weren't out to get her after all. It was only Rachel.

Diane was nudging her and holding out a card. "Hey, Laura, here's one for you to wear."

For a moment Laura stared at the card. She looked from Rachel's red, frightened face to Diane's mocking smile, and she heard the pulsing, frenzied rhythm of the claps and the stamping, faster and faster. Her hands trembled as she picked up the card and pinned it to her sweater. And as she turned, she saw Rachel's stricken look.

"She's a creep, isn't she?" Diane's voice was soft and intimate.

And Laura began to clap.

Assignment: In the passage you just read, Laura encounters peer pressure and makes a choice. Plan and write a **persuasive essay** in which you **state and support a thesis** about the effects of peer pressure on young people and how it should be handled. Include evidence from the passage and your own experience to support your thesis.

Revising and Editing Skills

Each sentence below has one or two blanks. Each blank indicates that a word has been omitted. Choose the word or set of words that, when inserted in the sentence, *best* fits the meaning of the sentence as a whole. Record your answers on a separate sheet of paper.

1. I ___ it my duty to take the ___ in raising funds for the class gift to the teacher.
   A. badgered...privilege
   B. considered...initiative
   C. instilled...potential
   D. destined...techniques
   E. exploited...character

2. The politician's ___ drove him to ___ hundreds of workers for his campaign.
   A. character...instill
   B. privilege...badger
   C. mastery...merit
   D. initiative...swoop
   E. ambition...recruit

3. The coach made his decision based on the ___ that the quarterback's injury would quickly improve.
   A. premise
   B. initiative
   C. tactics
   D. potential
   E. mastery

4. The students were very vocal in their ___ of the professor's ___ lectures.
   A. confirmation...undulating
   B. desegregation...lavish
   C. provision...distorted
   D. condemnation...pedantic
   E. prejudice...sufficient

5. Boats bobbed like corks on the ___ waves.
   A. berserk
   B. undulating
   C. waning
   D. diverse
   E. infamous

6. The author of the biography made it clear that the protagonist's ___ was ___.
   A. conscience...vernacular
   B. anecdote...berserk
   C. tactic...envious
   D. mastery...lavish
   E. character...unimpeachable

7. The actress was ___ for rambling on in the ___ of her Southern roots.
   A. lavish...discourse
   B. distorted...surplus
   C. infamous...vernacular
   D. reasonable...principle
   E. envious...tactics

8. The scientist delivered a ___ lecture about the ___ of space-time.
   A. complex...principle
   B. lavish...democracy
   C. berserk...ambition
   D. vicious...bondage
   E. waning...anecdotes

9. The slave ___ the courage to break free from his ___.
   A. merited...ambition
   B. destined...discourse
   C. badgered...democracy
   D. summoned...bondage
   E. integrated...privilege

10. Because of his ___ attacks on his opponent, support for the candidate was ___.
   A. evolved...sufficient
   B. crucial...vinyl
   C. vicious...waning
   D. conscientious...undulating
   E. diverse...infamous

Test Practice Workshop

- Students practice standardized test formats such as ACT and SAT at the end of each unit.
- The lessons emphasize writing skills, revising and editing skills, and reading skills.
- Topics are related to standard test-prep materials.

Language Arts Handbook

- Complete, easy-to-use student resource at the back of each text to answer questions, provide valuable information, and support the development of students' language arts skills.
- Encourages independent learning.

Language Arts Handbook

Take a Walk Through
The Annotated Teacher's Edition

The Mirrors & Windows Interactive Annotated Teacher's Edition (Desktop or Web-based) provides the instructional tools necessary to enhance the learning experience for all students.

—Choose the Resources You Need—

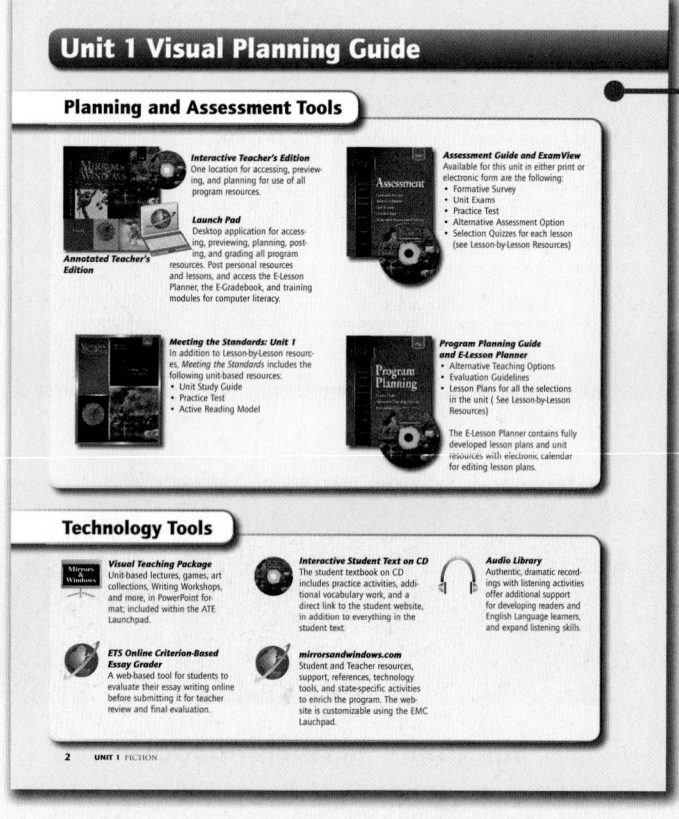

Unit-based Resources

- Unique, at-a-glance teacher planner for efficient decision-making.
- Planning and assessment tools and *Exceeding the Standards* Unit Resources are shown. Technology Tools are displayed for easy reference.

Lesson Resources

- Lesson-by-lesson resource options are pictured.
- Reading level is provided.
- Pacing guidelines are included.

Mirrors & Windows

–Plan Your Day the Easy Way–

Scope & Sequence Guide

- At-a-glance overview of unit selections. For each selection this guide provides information such as genre, reading level, reading skills taught, literary elements taught, themes, and cross-curricular connections.
- Information is organized to make planning easy and efficient.

–Teach Vocabulary Development–

Building Vocabulary

- Overview of all unit vocabulary words and Key Terms.
- Word lists are also referenced at point-of-use with each selection.

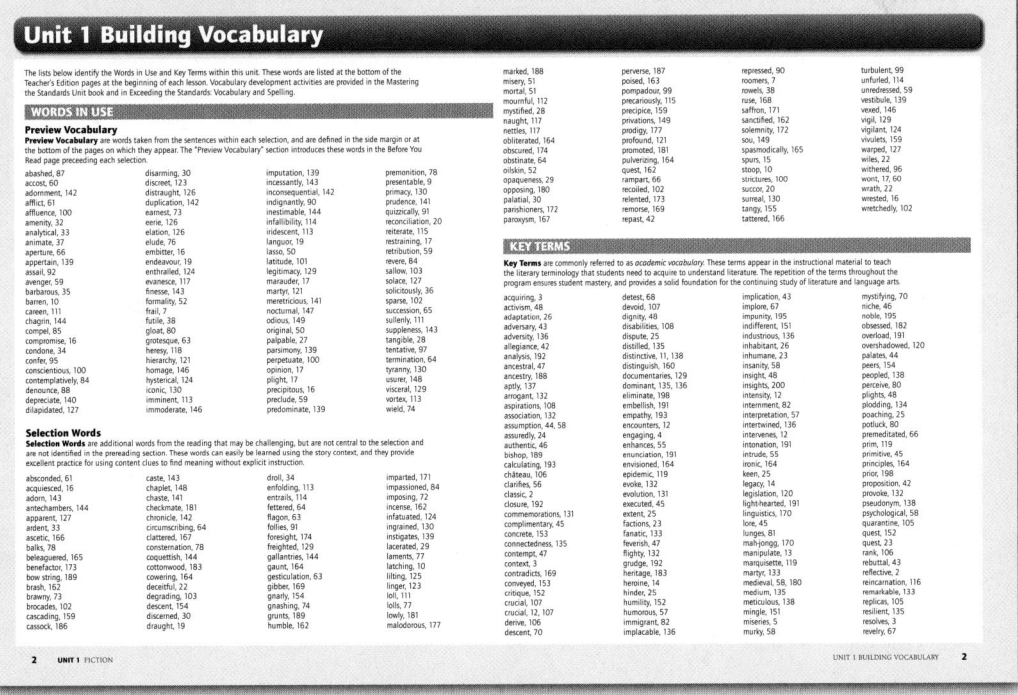

Mirrors & Windows

−Prepare Students *for the* Unit Genre *and* Theme−

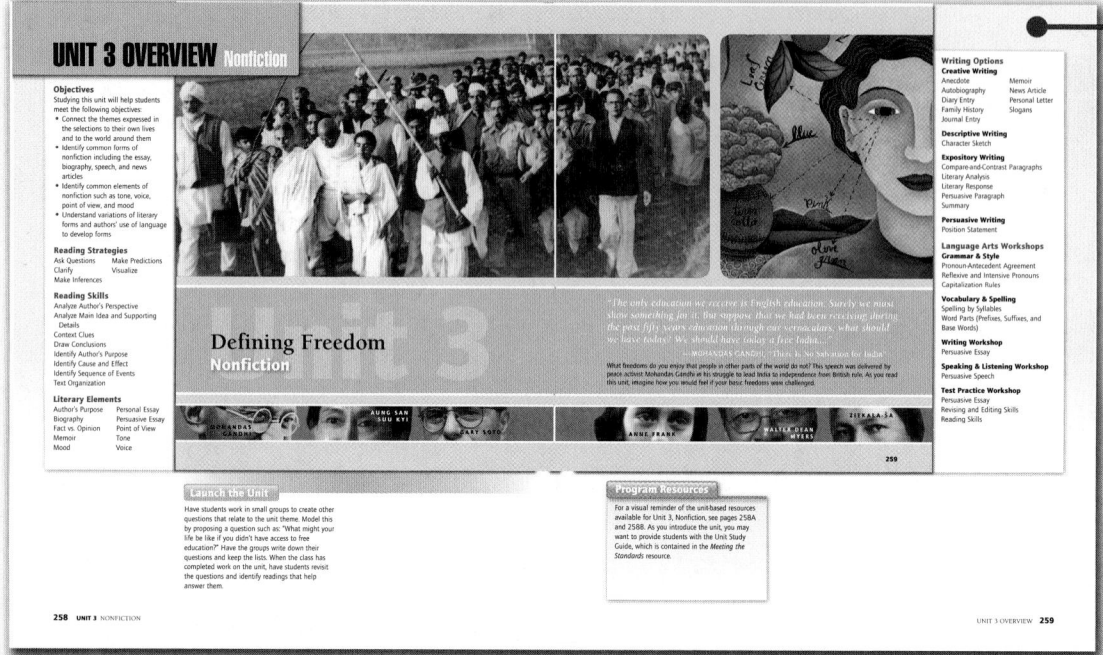

- Important information ensures a successful launch for new and experienced teachers.
- Clear objectives are outlined.
- Launch the Unit strategies for whole class and small groups are provided.

Introduction to Genre

- Launch the Lesson builds on prior knowledge.
- Differentiated Instruction focuses on Reading Proficiency, Enrichment, Learning Styles, and English Language Learners.
- Words in Use and Key Terms are listed for additional vocabulary development.

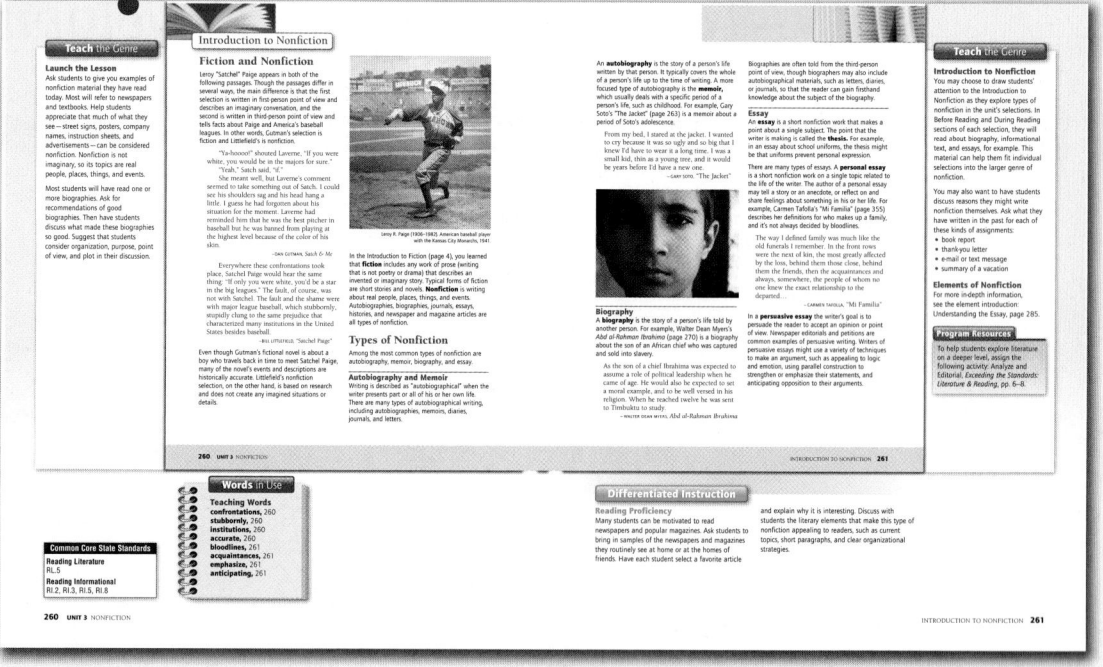

T40

–Introduce and Preview the Unit Genre Reading Model–

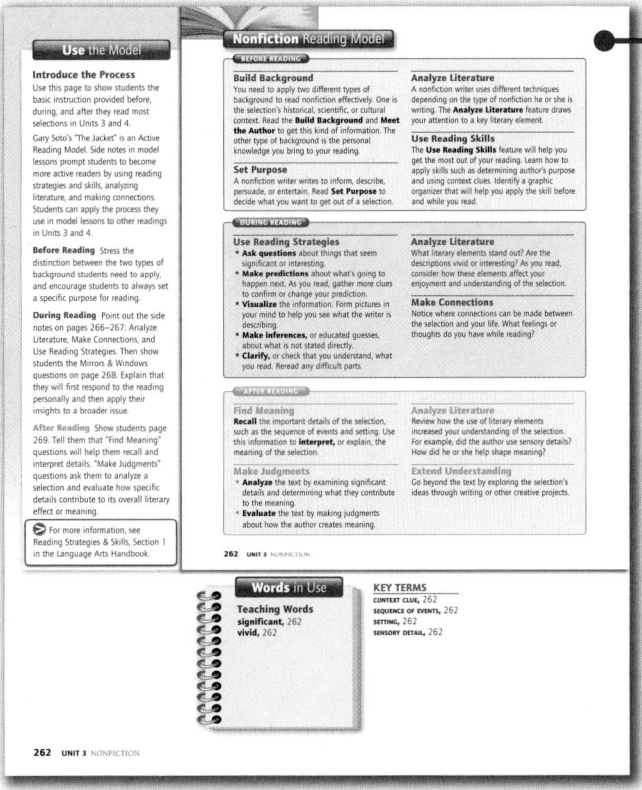

Unit Genre Reading Model

- The Genre Reading Model is taught before the first selection and applied throughout the unit.

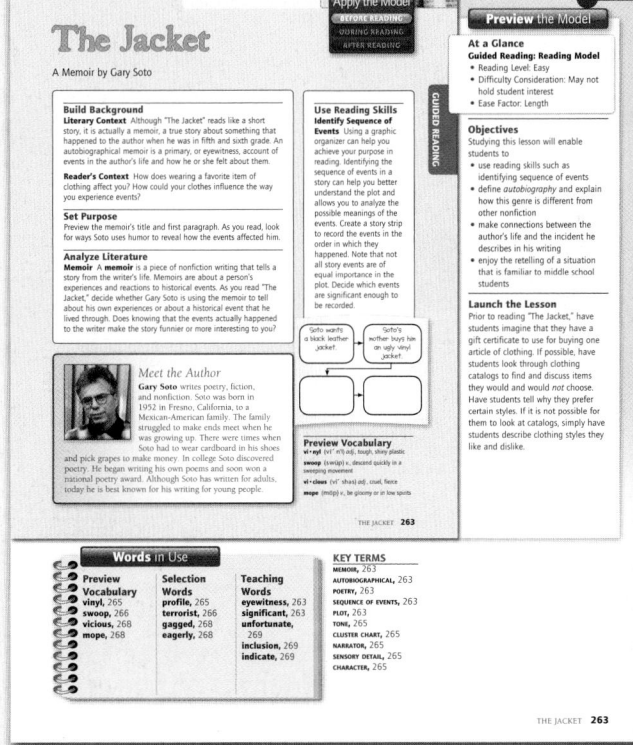

Before Reading

- Guided Reading– teacher guides students (Directed and Independent Reading follow later in the unit).
- At-a Glance provides Reading Level, Difficulty Considerations, and Ease Factors for each selection.
- Lesson objectives are clearly stated.
- Three categories of Words in Use and Key Terms are outlined with page references.

–Teach and Apply the Unit Genre Reading Model–

During Reading

- The *Mirrors & Windows* questions are previewed to prepare students to respond.
- Program Resources are conveniently listed.
- During Reading prompts ask students to Analyze Literature and Use Reading Strategies.

After Reading

- After Reading activities require students to recall and interpret detail, analyze and evaluate, and extend understanding.
- Rubrics for Writing Options are provided.
- Teaching Notes are packed with ideas and activities to stimulate discussion and add new information.

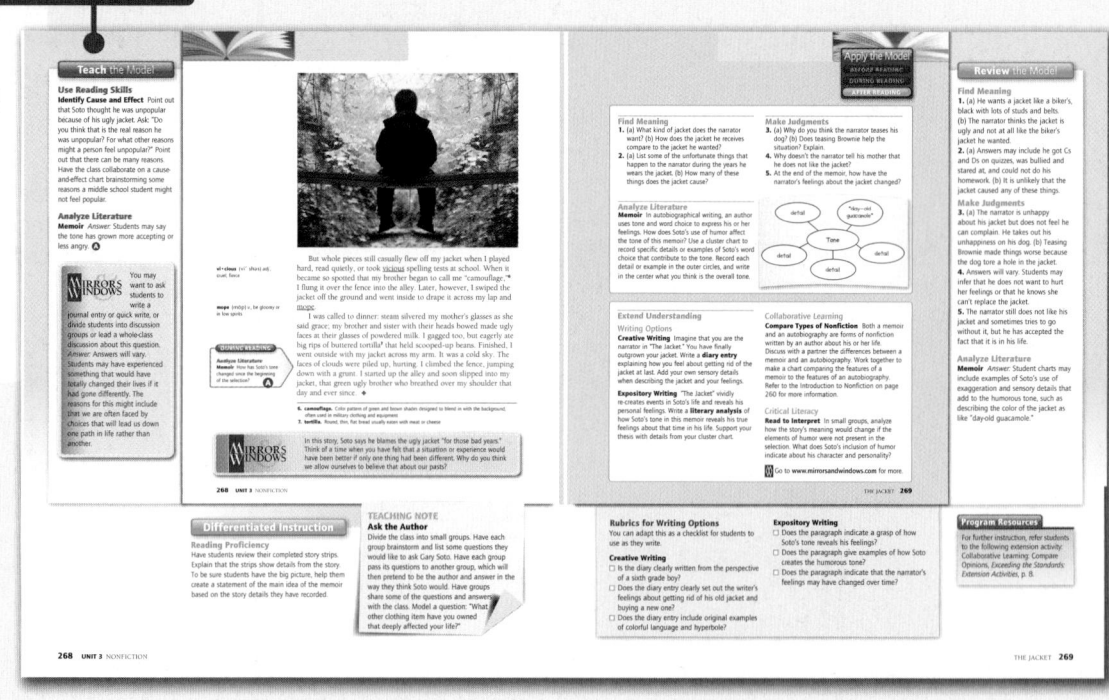

–Practice and Assess Language Arts Skills–

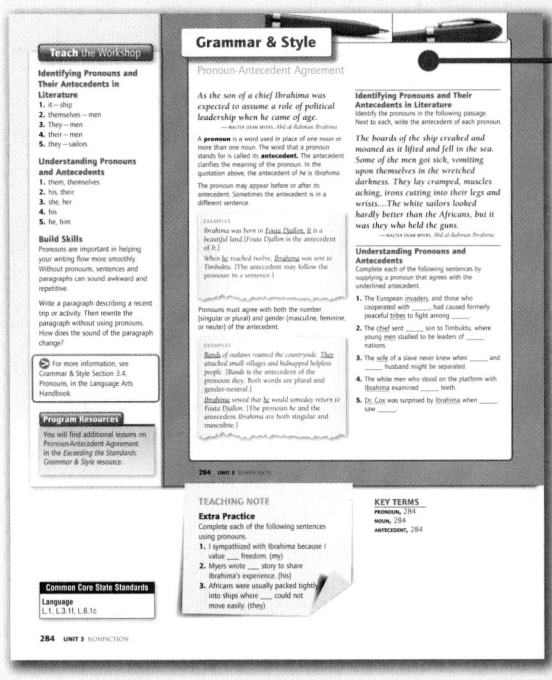

Grammar & Style

- Build Skills activities link grammar and writing instruction.
- Teaching Notes provide Extra Practice.
- Additional instruction is found in the Language Arts Handbook at the end of the text.
- Program Resources are listed.

Test Practice Workshop

- Rubric is provided for the Writing Activity.
- Test-taking tips and standardized test practice activities extend the lesson.

Additional Workshops Not Shown

- Vocabulary & Spelling
- Writing
- Speaking & Listening

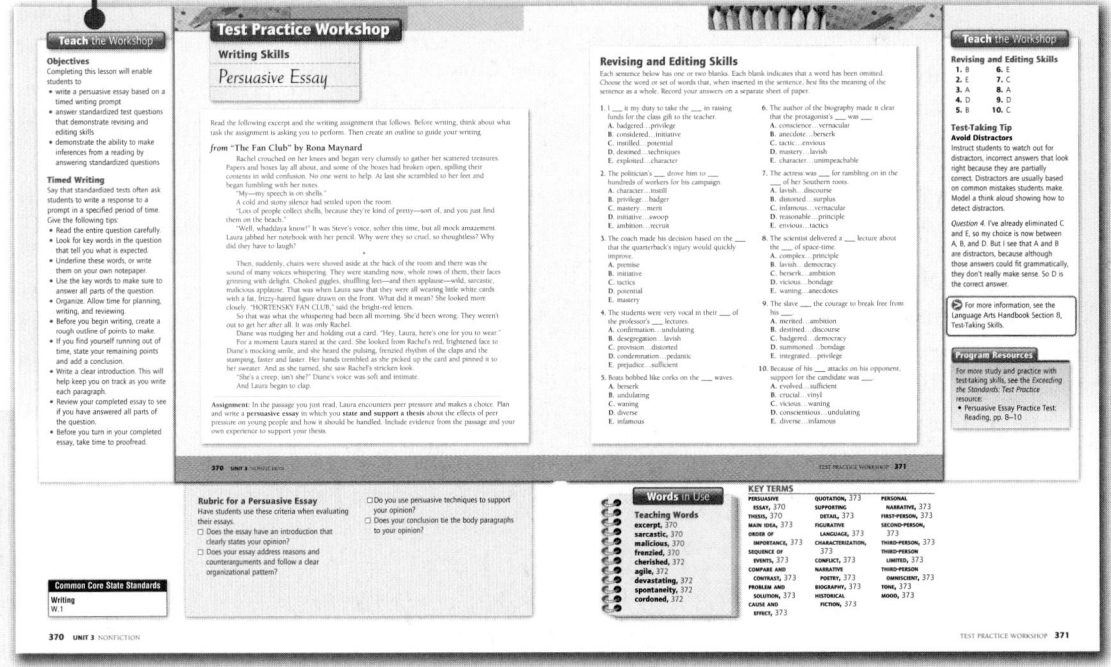

Mirrors & Windows

–Selections by Genre–

–Professional Resources and Research Base–

Teaching Literature

Applebee, A. N. (1993). *Literature in secondary schools: Studies of curriculum and instruction in U.S. schools*. Urbana, IL: National Council of Teachers of English.

Appleman, D. (2000). *Critical encounters in high school English*. Urbana, IL: National Council of Teachers of English.

Raphael, T., and Au, K. H., eds. (1998). *Literature-based instruction: Reshaping the curriculum*. Norwood, MA: Christopher-Gordon.

Rosenblatt, L. (1938, 1996). *Literature as exploration*, 5th ed. New York: MLA.

Teaching Reading Comprehension

Allen, J. (2000). *Yellow brick roads: Shared and guided paths to independent reading 4–12*. Portland, ME: Stenhouse Publishers.

Burke, J. (2000). *Reading reminders: Tools, tips, and techniques*. Portsmouth, NH: Boynton/Cook.

Gallagher, K. (2004). *Deeper reading: Comprehending challenging texts, 4-12*. Portland, ME: Stenhouse Publishers.

Graves, M. F., and Graves, B. B. (1994). *Scaffolding reading experiences: Designs for student success*. Norwood, MA: Christopher-Gordon.

Harvey, S., and Goudvis, A. (2001). *Strategies that work: Teaching comprehension to enhance understanding*. York, ME: Stenhouse Publishers.

Marzano, R. J., Pickering, D. J., and Pollock, J. E. (2001). *Classroom instruction that works: Research-based strategies for increasing student achievement*. Alexandria, VA: Association for Supervision and Curriculum Development.

Pearson, P. D., Roehler, L. R., Dole, J. A., and Duffy, G. G. (1992). Developing expertise in reading comprehension. In J. Samuels and A. Farstrup, eds., *What research has to say about reading instruction*. Newark, DE: International Reading Association.

Rosenblatt, L. (1938, 1996). *Literature as exploration*, 5th ed. New York: MLA.

Tovani, C. (2000). *I read it, but I don't get it: Comprehension strategies for adolescent readers*. Portland, ME: Stenhouse Publishers.

Teaching Vocabulary and Word Study

Anderson, R., and Nagy, W. (1991). Word meanings. In R. Barr, M. Kamil, P. Monsenthal, and P. D. Pearson, eds., *Handbook of reading research*, vol. 2, pp. 690–724. New York: Longman.

Baker, S. K., Simmons, D. C., and Kameenui, E. J. (1995a). *Vocabulary acquisition: Synthesis of the research*. Technical Report No. 13. University of Oregon; National Center to Improve the Tools for Educators

Bos, C. S., and Anders, P. L. (1990). Effects of interactive vocabulary instruction on the vocabulary learning and reading comprehension of junior-high learning-disabled students. *Learning Disability Quarterly*, 13(1), 31–42.

Nagy, W. E. (1988). *Teaching vocabulary to improve reading comprehension*. Urbana, IL: National Council of Teachers of English.

Teaching Grammar and Writing

Behrens, L., and Rosen, L. J. (2002). *Writing and reading across the curriculum*, 8th ed. New York: Addison Wesley.

Fowler, H. W. (1983). *Modern English usage*, 2nd ed. New York: Oxford University Press.

Garner, B. A. (1998). *A dictionary of modern American usage*. New York: Oxford University Press

University of Chicago Pr.ess, The (2003). *The Chicago manual of style: The essential guide for writers, editors, and publishers*, 15th ed. Chicago, IL: University of Chicago Press.

Weaver, C. (1996). *Teaching grammar in context*. Portsmouth, NH: Heinemann

Lesson Planning and Differentiating Instruction

Burke. J. (1999). *The English teacher's companion: A complete guide to classroom, curriculum, and the profession*. Portsmouth, NH: Heinemann.

Daniels, H. (2002). *Literature circles: Voice and choice in the student-centered classroom*, 2nd ed. York, ME: Stenhouse Publishers.

Gallagher, K. (2003). *Reading reasons: Motivational mini-lessons for middle and high school*.

Portland, ME: Stenhouse Publishers.

Gregory, G. H., and Chapman, C. (2002). *Differentiated instructional strategies: One size doesn't fit all*. Thousand Oaks, CA: Corwin Press.

Strickland, D.S. and Alvermann, D. E., eds. (2004). *Bridging the literacy achievement gap grades 4-12*. New York: Teachers College Press.

Vacca, R. T., and Vacca, J. A. (1999). *Content area reading: Literacy and learning across the curriculum*. New York: Longman.

Facilitating Transfer of Learning

Boriarsky, C. (2001). Learning to transfer knowledge from one assignment to the next. Talk delivered at Recreating the Classroom: 91st Annual NCTE Convention, Baltimore, November 16.

Salomen, G. and Perkins, D. N. (1994). Rocky roads to transfer: Rethinking mechanisms of a neglected phenomenon. *Educational Psychologist*, 24(2), 113–142.

Rigor in the Classroom

American Diploma Project, *Ready or Not: Creating a high school diploma thatcounts*. Achieve, Inc., 2004.

Expectations Gap: A 50-state review of high school graduation requirements. Achieve, Inc., 2004.

Jago, C. *With rigor for all*. (2000). Portsmouth, NH: Heinemann.

Assessment

Langer, J. A., ed. (1992). *Literature instruction: A focus on student response*. Urbana, IL: National Council of Teachers of English.

Barr, R., Blachowicz, C. Z., Katz, C., and Kaufman, B. (2001). *Reading diagnosis for teachers: An instructional approach*. New York: Allyn and Bacon.

Gillet, J. W., and Temple, C. (1990). *Understanding reading problems: Assessment and instruction*. New York: HarperCollins.

Johnston, P. (1984). Prior knowledge and reading comprehension test bias. *Reading Research Quarterly*, 19, 219–228.

Sadler, C. R. (2001). *Comprehension strategies for middle grade learners: A handbook for content area teachers*. New York: International Reading Association.

Partial List. Complete list available on request.

MIRRORS & WINDOWS

Connecting with Literature

"The whole purpose of education
is to turn mirrors into windows."

— Sydney J. Harris

Common Core
State Standards
EDITION

MIRRORS & WINDOWS

Connecting with Literature

Level III

EMC
Publishing

ST. PAUL • INDIANAPOLIS

Staff Credits

Senior Editor: Brenda Owens
Editor: Nancy Papsin
Associate Editor: Carley Bomstad
Editorial Assistants: Erin Saladin, Lindsay Ryan
Permissions Coordinator: Valerie Murphy
Photo Researcher: Brendan Curran
Marketing Managers: Bruce Ayscue, Laurie Skiba
Cover Designer: Leslie Anderson

Text Designer: Ronan Design
Page Layout Designers: Jack Ross, Matthias Frasch
Production Editor: Courtney Kost
Production Specialist: Petrina Nyhan
Project Manager: Sara Dovre Wudali, Buuji, Inc.
Editorial Development and Production: Nieman Inc.

Literary Acknowledgments: Literary Acknowledgments appear following the Glossary of Vocabulary Words. We have made every effort to trace the ownership of all copyrighted material and to secure permission from copyright holders. In the event of any question arising as to the use of any material, we will be pleased to make the necessary corrections in future printings. Thanks are due to the authors, publishers, and agents for permission to use the materials indicated.

Art and Photo Credits: Art and Photo Credits appear following the Literary Acknowledgments.

ISBN 978-0-82196-033-2

Consultants, Reviewers, and Focus Group Participants

Tracy Pulido
Language Arts Instructor
West Valley High School
Fairbanks, Alaska

Jean Martorana
Reading Specialist/English Teacher
Desert Vista High School
Phoenix, Arizona

Cindy Johnston
English Teacher
Argus High School
Ceres, California

Susan Stoehr
Language Arts Instructor
Aragon High School
San Mateo, California

John Owens
Reading Specialist
St. Vrain Valley Schools
Longmont, Colorado

Fred Smith
Language Arts Instructor
St. Bernard High School
Uncasville, Connecticut

Penny Austin-Richardson
English Department Chair
Seaford Senior High School
Seaford, Delaware

Cecilia Lewis
Language Arts Instructor
Mariner High School
Cape Coral, Florida

Jane Feber
Teacher
Mandarin Middle School
Jacksonville, Florida

Dorothy Fletcher
Language Arts Instructor
Wolfson Senior High School
Jacksonville, Florida

Tamara Doehring
English/Reading Teacher
Melbourne High School
Melbourne, Florida

Patti Magee
English Instructor
Timber Creek High School
Orlando, Florida

Margaret J. Graham
Language Arts/Reading Teacher
Elizabeth Cobb Middle School
Tallahassee, Florida

Elizabeth Steinman
English Instructor
Vero Beach High School
Vero Beach, Florida

Wanda Bagwell
Language Arts Department Chair
Commerce High School
Commerce, Georgia

Betty Deriso
Language Department Chairperson
Crisp County High School
Cordele, Georgia

Dr. Peggy Leland
English Instructor
Chestatee High School
Gainsville, Georgia

Matthew Boedy
Language Arts Instructor
Harlem High School
Harlem, Georgia

Patty Bradshaw
English Department Chair
Harlem High School
Harlem, Georgia

Dawn Faulkner
English Department Chair
Rome High School
Rome, Georgia

Carolyn C. Coleman
AKS Continuous Improvement
    Director
Gwinnett County Public Schools
Suwanee, Georgia

Elisabeth Blumer Thompson
Language Arts Instructor
Swainsboro High School
Swainsboro, Georgia

Toi Walker
English Instructor
Northeast Tifton County High
    School
Tifton, Georgia

Jeanette Rogers
English Instructor
Potlatch Jr.-Sr. High School
Potlatch, Idaho

Gail Taylor
Language Arts Instructor
Rigby High School
Rigby, Idaho

Carey Robin
Language Arts Instructor
St. Francis College Prep
Brookfield, Illinois

Patricia Meyer
English Department Chair
Glenbard East High School
Lombard, Illinois

Liz Rebmann
Language Arts Instructor
Morton High School
Morton, Illinois

Helen Gallagher
English Department Chair
Main East High School
Park Ridge, Illinois

Rosemary Ryan
Dean of Students
Schaumburg High School
Schaumburg, Illinois

Donna Cracraft
English Department Co-Chair/IB
    Coordinator
Pike High School
Indianapolis, Indiana

Consultants, Reviewers, and Focus Group Participants (cont.)

K. C. Salter
Language Arts Instructor
Knightstown High School
Knightstown, Indiana

Lisa Broxterman
Language Arts Instructor
Axtell High School
Axtell, Kansas

Shirley Wells
Language Arts Instructor
Derby High School
Derby, Kansas

Karen Ann Stous
Speech & Drama Teacher
Holton High School
Holton, Kansas

Martha-Jean Rockey
Language Arts Instructor
Troy High School
Troy, Kansas

Shelia Penick
Language Arts Instructor
Yates Center High School
Yates Center, Kansas

John Ermilio
English Teacher
St. Johns High School
Shrewsbury, Massachusetts

James York
English Teacher
Waverly High School
Lansing, Michigan

Mary Spychalla
Gifted Education Coordinator
Valley Middle School
Apple Valley, Minnesota

Shari K. Carlson
Advanced ILA Teacher
Coon Rapids Middle School
Coon Rapids, Minnesota

Rebecca Benz
English Instructor
St. Thomas Academy
Mendota Heights, Minnesota

Michael F. Graves
Professor Emeritus
University of Minnesota
330A Peik Hall
Minneapolis, Minnesota

Kathleen Nelson
English Instructor
New Ulm High School
New Ulm, Minnesota

Adonna Gaspar
Language Arts Teacher
Cooper High School
Robbinsdale, Minnesota

Sara L. Nystuen
English Department Chair; AP
    Instructor
Concordia Academy
Roseville, Minnesota

Tom Backen
English Teacher
Benilde-St. Margaret's School
St. Louis Park, Minnesota

Daniel Sylvester
Jr. High English & American
    Experience Teacher
Benilde-St. Margaret's School
St. Louis Park, Minnesota

Jean Borax
Literacy Coach
Harding High School
St. Paul, Minnesota

Erik Brandt
English Teacher
Harding High School
St. Paul, Minnesota

Kevin Brennan
High School English Teacher
Cretin-Derham Hall
St. Paul, Minnesota

Anna Newcombe
English Instructor
Harding High School
St. Paul, Minnesota

Rosemary Ruffenach
Language Arts Teacher, Consultant,
    and Writer
St. Paul, Minnesota

Nancy Papsin
English Teacher/Educational
    Consultant
White Bear Lake, Minnesota

Shannon Umfleet
Communication Arts Instructor
Northwest High School
Cedar Hill, Missouri

Ken Girard
Language Arts Instructor
Bishop LeBlond High School
St. Joseph, Missouri

Jessica Gall
Language Arts Instructor
Fremont High School
Fremont, Nebraska

Michael Davis
Language Arts Instructor
Millard West High School
Omaha, Nebraska

Lisa Larnerd
English Teacher
Basic High School
Henderson, Nevada

Jo Paulson
Title I Reading Teacher
Camino Real Middle School
Las Cruces, New Mexico

Stacy Biss
Language Arts Instructor
Hackensack High School
Hackensack, New Jersey

J. M. Winchock
Reading Specialist, Adult Literacy
    Instructor
Hillsborough High School
Hillsborough, New Jersey

Consultants, Reviewers, and Focus Group Participants (cont.)

Matthew Cahn
Department of English & Related
 Arts Supervisor
River Dell High School
Oradell, New Jersey

Jean Mullooly
Language Arts Instructor
Holy Angels High School
Trenton, New Jersey

Fenice Boyd
Assistant Professor, Learning and
 Instruction
State University of New York at
 Buffalo
Buffalo, New York

Michael Fedorchuk
Assistant Principal
Auburn High School
Auburn, New York

Robert Balch
English Instructor
Beacon High School
Beacon, New York

Rene A. Roberge
Secondary English/AP English
 Instructor
Hudson Falls High School
Hudson Falls, New York

Melissa Hedt
Literacy Coach
Asheville Middle School
Asheville, North Carolina

Jane Shoaf
Educational Consultant
Durham, North Carolina

Kimberly Tufts
Department Chair for ELA
Cranberry Middle School
Elk Park, North Carolina

Cheryl Gackle
English Instructor
Kulm High School
Kulm, North Dakota

Barbara Stroh
English Department Chair
Aurora High School
Aurora, Ohio

Mary Jo Bish
Language Arts Instructor
Lake Middle School
Millbury, Ohio

Judy Ellsesser-Painter
Language Arts Instructor
South Webster High School
South Webster, Ohio

Adele Dahlin
English Department Chair
Central Catholic High School
Toledo, Ohio

Joshua Singer
English Instructor
Central Catholic High School
Toledo, Ohio

Debbie Orendorf
Language Arts Instructor
Berlin Brothers Valley High School
Berlin, Pennsylvania

Dona Italiano
English Teacher/Language Arts
 Coordinator
Souderton Area High School
Souderton, Pennsylvania

Tina Parlier
Secondary English Instructor
Elizabethton High School
Elizabethton, Tennessee

Wayne Luellen
English Instructor
Houston High School
Germantown, Tennessee

Ed Farrell
Senior Consultant
Emeritus Professor of English
 Education
 University of Texas at Austin
Austin, Texas

Terry Ross
Secondary Language Arts
 Supervisor
Austin Independent School District
Austin, Texas

Angelia Greiner
English Department Chair
Big Sandy High School
Big Sandy, Texas

Sharon Kremer
Educational Consultant
Denton, Texas

E. J. Brletich
Supervisor of English/Language
 Arts
Spotsylvania City School
Fredericksburg, Virginia

Jeffrey Golub
Educational Consultant
Bothell, Washington

Clifford Aziz
Language Arts Instructor
Washington High School
Tacoma, Washington

Becky Palmer
Reading Teacher
Madison Middle School
Appleton, Wisconsin

Mary Hoppe
English Teacher
Bonduel High School
Bonduel, Wisconsin

Lou Wappel
English, Humanities & Guidance
 Instructor
St. Lawrence Seminary High School
Mount Calvary, Wisconsin

Gregory R. Keir
Language Arts Instructor
East Elementary School
New Richmond, Wisconsin

CONTENTS IN BRIEF

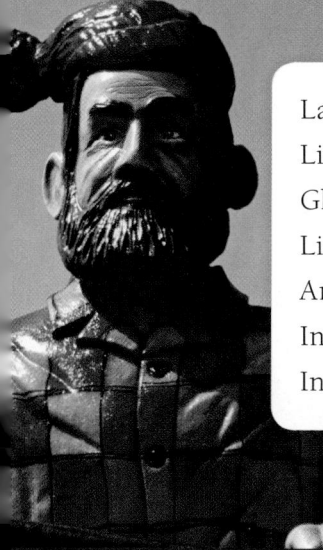
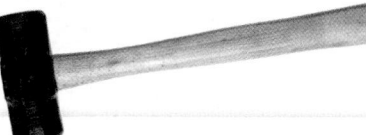

Unit 1 Finding Ourselves
Fiction

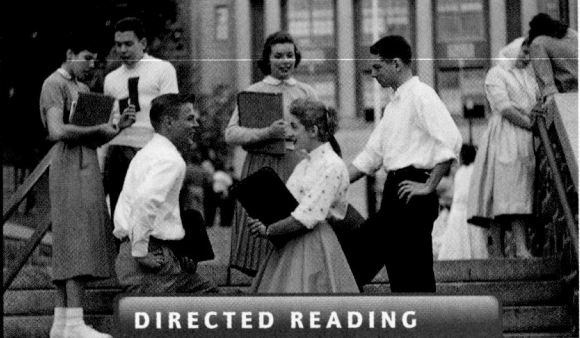

INDEPENDENT READING

Unit 2 Differing Perspectives
Fiction

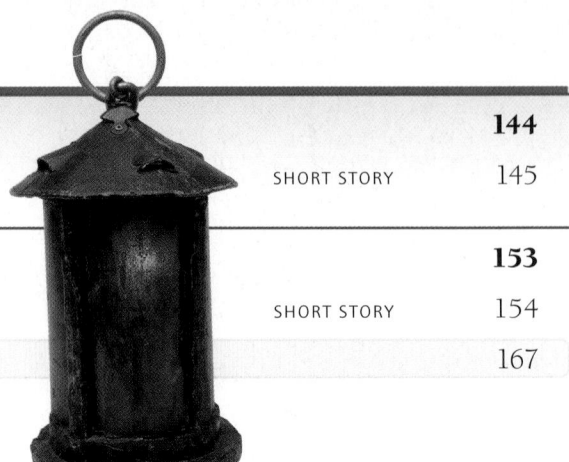

INDEPENDENT READING

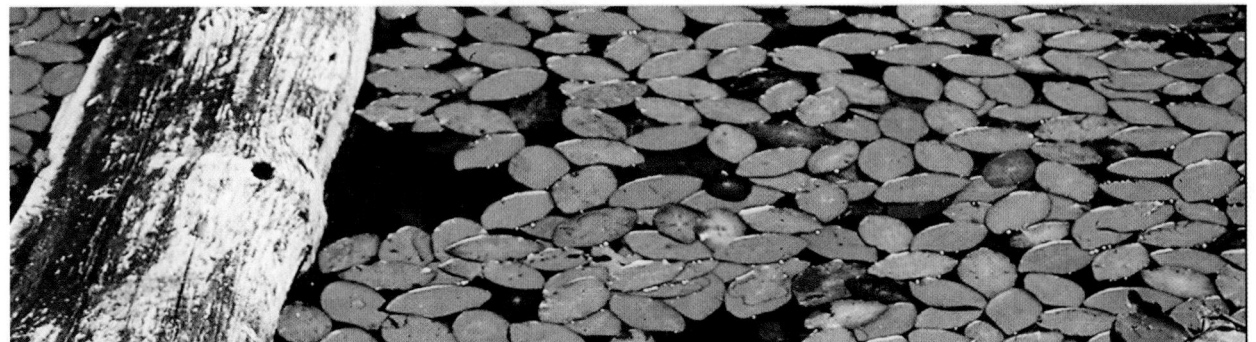

Unit 6 Reaching Out
Poetry

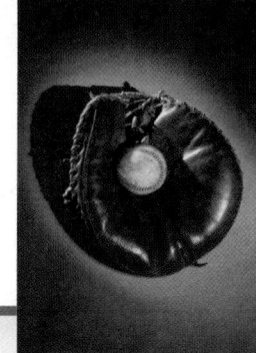

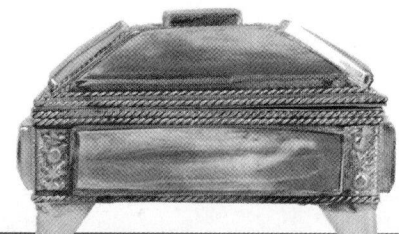

INDEPENDENT READING

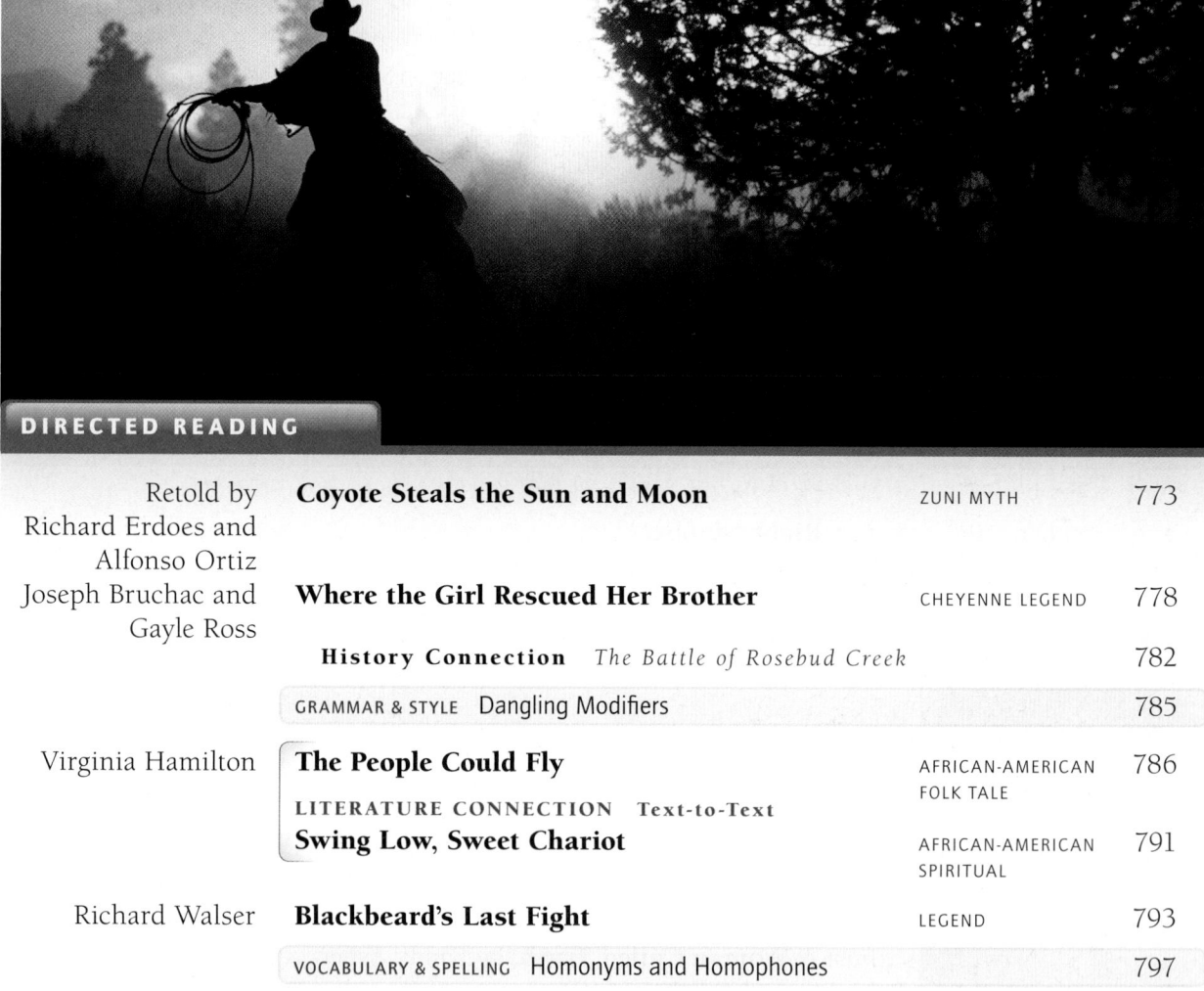

INDEPENDENT READING

LANGUAGE ARTS RESOURCES

LANGUAGE ARTS WORKSHOPS

Grammar & Style

Vocabulary & Spelling

Speaking & Listening

Writing

Viewing

Test Practice

INDEPENDENT READINGS

Fiction

Nonfiction

Poetry

Drama

Folk Literature

TO THE STUDENT

> ## "The whole purpose of education is to turn mirrors into windows."
> — Sydney J. Harris

Think about when you were young and about to start school for the first time. When you stood in front of the mirror, your view was focused on your own reflection and limited by your own experience. Then the windows of learning began to open your mind to new ideas and new experiences, broadening both your awareness and your curiosity.

As you discovered reading, you learned to connect with what you read and to examine your own ideas and experiences. And the more you read, the more you learned to connect with the ideas and experiences of other people from other times and other places. Great literature provides *mirrors* that help you reflect on your own world and *windows* that lead you into new worlds. This metaphor for the reading experience expresses the power of words to engage and transform you.

EMC's literature program, *Mirrors & Windows: Connecting with Literature,* provides opportunities for you to explore new worlds full of people, cultures, and perspectives different from your own. This book contains stories, essays, plays, and poems by outstanding authors from around the globe. Reading these selections will expand your appreciation of literature and your world view. Studying them will help you examine universal themes such as honesty, integrity, and justice and common emotions such as fear, pride, and belonging. You may already have thought about some of these ideas and feelings yourself.

As you read the selections in this book, try to see yourself in the characters, stories, and themes. Also try to see yourself as a citizen of the world—a world from which you have much to learn and to which you have much to offer.

Planning and Assessment Tools

Annotated Teacher's Edition

Annotated Teacher's Edition
One location for accessing, previewing, and planning for use of all program resources.

EMC Launchpad
Desktop application for accessing, previewing, planning, posting, and grading all program resources. Post personal resources and lessons, and access the E-Lesson Planner, the E-Gradebook, and training modules for computer literacy.

Assessment Guide and ExamView
A variety of assessments are available for this unit in print and electronic forms, including:
- Formative Survey
- Lesson Tests
- Unit Exams
- Alternative Assessment Options
- Reading Fluency Assessments

Meeting the Standards: Unit 1
In addition to lesson-by-lesson resources, *Meeting the Standards* includes the following unit-based resources:
- Unit Study Guide
- Practice Test
- Active Reading Model
- Selection Quizzes

Program Planning Guide and E-Lesson Planner
- Lesson Plans for all the selections in the unit
- Core Standards-Based Selections
- Reading Log and Evaluation Forms

The E-Lesson Planner contains fully developed lesson plans and unit resources with an electronic calendar for editing lesson plans.

Technology Tools

Visual Teaching Package
This package contains unit-based lectures, games, art collections, and Writing Workshops in PowerPoint format; included within the EMC Launchpad.

Interactive Student Text on CD
The student textbook on CD includes highlighting, note-taking, bookmarking, and a direct link to the student website, in addition to everything in the student text.

Audio Library
Authentic, dramatic recordings with listening activities expand listening skills and offer additional support for developing readers and English Language Learners.

ETS Online Criterion-Based Essay Grader (Grades 9–12)
Students can use this ETS web-based tool to evaluate their essays online before submitting them for teacher review and final evaluation.

mirrorsandwindows.com
Student and teacher resources, support, references, technology tools, and state-specific standards are available at **mirrorsandwindows.com.** The website is customizable using the EMC Launchpad.

Unit-Based Resources

Exceeding the Standards Unit Resources

Each of the *Exceeding the Standards* resources provides fully developed lessons to help you extend the textbook lessons and to expand upon the themes and skills covered in the unit. You can also download these lessons from **mirrorsandwindows.com**.

Grammar & Style
This resource contains:
* Five lessons on the Sentence and Parts of Speech, pp. 1–18

Literature & Reading
This resource contains:
* Independent Novel Study: Setting, pp. 1–5

Special Topics
This resource contains:
* Career Skills Development: Career Exploration Survey, pp. 1–2
* Lifelong Learning: Where Are You Now? pp. 3–4

Test Practice
This resource contains:
* Literary Response Practice Test: Reading, pp. 5–6

Writing
This resource contains:
* Narrative Writing: Tell About a Conflict, pp. 1–10

Speaking & Listening
This resource contains the following lesson to expand on the Speaking & Listening Workshop:
* Giving and Actively Listening to Literacy Presentations, pp. 1–3

Vocabulary & Spelling
This resource contains:
* Four lessons on the Word Study Notebook and Word Parts, pp. 1–8

Extension Activities
This resource contains:
* Collaborative Learning: Role-Play, pp. 1–2
* Media Literacy: Study Photographs, pp. 3–4

Unit 1 Visual Planning Guide

 Reading Level: Easy
Pacing: 3 days

Meeting the Standards,
Reading Model,
pp. 19–25

Advanced Students,
Author Study, pp. 1–3

English Language Learners,
Analyze Sequence of
Events, pp. 1–11

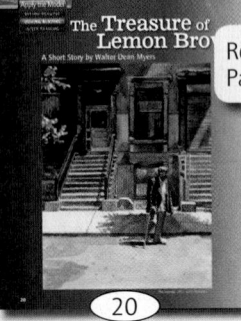

 Reading Level: Easy
Pacing: 3 days

Meeting the Standards,
Guided Reading,
pp. 26–31

Advanced Students,
Cultural Research
Project, p. 4

 Reading Level: Moderate
Pacing: 3 days

Meeting the Standards,
Guided Reading,
pp. 32–36

*English Language
Learners,* Use Context
Clues, pp. 12–25

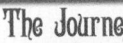 

 Reading Level: Moderate
 Pacing: 2 days

Meeting the Standards,
Directed Reading,
pp. 37–41

Advanced Students,
Theme Study, p. 5

 Reading Level: Challenging
 Pacing: 3 days

Meeting the Standards,
Directed Reading,
pp. 42–47

Developing Readers,
Visualize, pp. 1–3

 Interactive Student
Text on CD-ROM

 Selection
Lesson Plan

 Web-based
Resources

Lesson-by-Lesson Resources

64

Reading Level: Moderate
Pacing: 3 days

Meeting the Standards,
Directed Reading,
pp. 48–53

Developing Readers,
Make Connections,
pp. 4–6

79

84

Reading Level: Moderate; Easy
Pacing: 2 days

Meeting the Standards,
Comparing Literature,
pp. 54–61

87

Reading Level: Easy
Pacing: 3 days

Meeting the Standards,
Directed Reading,
pp. 62–67

96

Reading Level: Easy
Pacing: 2 days

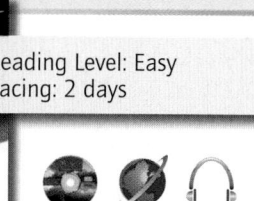   

Meeting the Standards,
Independent Reading,
pp. 68–73

Developing Readers,
Set Purpose, pp. 7–9

Advanced Students,
Independent Reading
Activity, pp. 6–7

Flowers for Algernon

105

Reading Level: Moderate
Pacing: 2 days

Meeting the Standards,
Independent Reading,
pp. 74–79

 Lesson Test

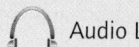 Audio Library

Unit 1 Scope & Sequence Guide

	Selection or Feature	Genre	Reading Support/ Reading Level	Word Count	Reading Skill	Graphic Organizer	
GUIDED READING	**Introduction to Fiction** pp. 4–5						
	Understanding Plot, pp. 6–7						
	Fiction Reading Model, p. 8						
	Charles Shirley Jackson pp. 9–17	Short Story	Guided Reading: Reading Model/Easy	1,604	Compare and Contrast	Compare and Contrast Chart; Conflict and Resolution Chart	
	Understand Character p. 18						
	The Treasure of Lemon Brown Walter Dean Myers pp. 19–30	Short Story	Guided Reading: Reading Model/Easy	3,391	Draw Conclusions	Drawing Conclusions Chart; Character Chart	
	Understanding Setting p. 32						
	A Mother in Mannville Marjorie Kinnan Rawlings pp. 33–44	Short Story	Guided Reading: Reading Model/ Moderate	3,035	Context Clues	Details Map	
DIRECTED READING	**The Journey** Duane BigEagle pp. 46–53	Short Story	Directed Reading/ Moderate	2,039	Analyze Cause and Effect	Cause and Effect Chart; Plot Diagram	
	The Drummer Boy of Shiloh Ray Bradbury pp. 54–62	Short Story	Directed Reading/ Challenging	1,984	Context Clues	Sensory Details Chart	
	Informational Text Connection: Echoes of Shiloh Shelby Foote p. 61	Article	Moderate	324			
	Gary Keillor Garrison Keillor pp. 63–76	Short Story	Directed Reading/ Moderate	4,493	Sequence of Events	Sequence of Events Map; Tone Map	
	Literature Connection: O Captain! O Captain! Walt Whitman pp. 74–75	Narrative Poem	Easy	211			

Literary Element	*Mirrors & Windows* Theme	Cross-Curricular Connection	Writing Options	Extension Activities
Types of Fiction Elements of Fiction				
What is Plot? The Elements of Plot Plot and Conflict External and Internal Conflicts Plot and Organization				
Plot	Maturation		Creative: Dialogue Expository: Paragraph	Collaborative Learning: Role-Play Critical Literacy: Hold a Panel Discussion
What are Characters? Characterization and Motivation Types of Characters				

Character	Legacy	Cultural Connection:
		Delta Blues
			Creative: Review
			Expository: Essay
				Collaborative Learning: Have a
				  Small Group Discussion
				Lifelong Learning: Create Concert
				  Posters

What is Setting? Setting in Fiction Setting and Community Setting and Mood				
Setting	Truth		Creative: Diary Entry Expository: Brief Essay	Media Literacy: Study Photographs; Write a Brief Essay Critical Literacy: Role-play

Plot	Life Journeys	Cultural Connection:
		Vision Quest
			Creative: Letter
			Expository: Problem-
			  Solution Essay
				Critical Literacy: Hold a Panel
				  Discussion
				Media Literacy: Conduct Internet
				  Research

Description	Courage in the Face of
	  Danger
			Creative: Narrative
			  Paragraph
			Expository: Character
			  Analysis
				Critical Literacy: Perform Reader's
				  Theater
				Media Literacy: Conduct Internet
				  Research

Tone	Peer Relations		Creative: Personal Narrative
			Expository: Literary
			  Response
				Collaborative Learning: Have a
				  Small Group Discussion
				Lifelong Learning: Research

Unit 1 Scope & Sequence Guide

	Selection or Feature	Genre	Reading Support/ Reading Level	Word Count	Reading Skill	Graphic Organizer	
DIRECTED READING	**Comparing Literature: Checkouts** Cynthia Rylant pp. 78–85	Short Story	Directed Reading/ Moderate	1,487			
	Oranges Gary Soto pp. 78–85	Narrative Poem	Directed Reading/Easy	263			
	Last Night Fae Myenne Ng pp. 86–94	Short Story	Directed Reading/Easy	2,329	Monitor Comprehension	Note-Taking Chart; Cause-and-Effect Chart	
INDEPENDENT READING	**Raymond's Run** Toni Cade Bambara pp. 96–103	Short Story	Independent Reading/ Easy	3,743	Make Inferences		
	Flowers for Algernon Daniel Keyes pp. 104–128	Short Story	Independent Reading/ Moderate	12,180	Make Predictions		

Unit 1 Language Arts Workshops

Grammar & Style	Vocabulary & Spelling	Writing	Speaking & Listening	Test Practice
Subject-Verb Agreement, p. 31 Pronoun-Antecedent Agreement, p. 77	Prefixes, Roots, and Suffixes, p. 45 Spelling by Syllables, p. 95	Expository Writing: Responding to a Short Story, pp. 130–135	Giving and Actively Listening to Literary Presentations, pp. 136–137	Writing Skills: Literary Response from "An Hour with Abuelo" by Judith Ortiz Cofer, p. 138 Revising and Editing Skills, p. 139 Reading Skills: from "The Osage Orange Tree" by William Stafford, pp. 140–141

Literary Element	*Mirrors & Windows* Theme	Cross-Curricular Connection	Writing Options	Extension Activities
Compare Literature: Motivation	Trust		Creative: Dialogue Expository: Short Essay	Collaborative Learning: Have a Small Group Discussion Lifelong Learning: Research
	Milestones			
Conflict	Solidarity	History Connection: *Chinese History*	Creative: Newspaper Article Descriptive: Character Sketch	Critical Literacy: Work in Groups Media Literacy: Conduct Internet Research
Description	Ambition		Expository: Short Essay	Media Literacy and Collaborative Learning: Rewrite One Scene as a Dramatic Dialogue
Character	Intelligence		Creative: Diary Entry	Critical Literacy: Hold a Debate

Unit 1 Building Vocabulary

The lists below identify the Words in Use and Key Terms within this unit. These words are listed at the bottom of the Teacher's Edition pages at the beginning of each lesson. Vocabulary development activities are provided in the *Meeting the Standards* unit book and in *Exceeding the Standards: Vocabulary & Spelling.*

WORDS IN USE

Preview Vocabulary

Preview Vocabulary are words taken from the sentences within each selection. These words are defined in the side margin or at the bottom of the pages on which they appear. The "Preview Vocabulary" section introduces these words in the Before Reading page preceding each selection.

ajar, 21	deftly, 82	intuition, 81	prevail, 66
anomalous, 42	delirium, 48	involuntary, 23	resolute, 59
askew, 56	elaborately, 11	legitimately, 58	sallow, 49
beckon, 25	erratic, 88	matronly, 15	sensation, 88
benediction, 56	flutter, 90	meager, 50	solitary, 81
brazen, 82	gravity, 69	mindful, 11	stoop, 21
churn, 90	haggard, 15	nausea, 48	strewn, 57
clarity, 37	inadequate, 36	omen, 90	sufficient, 39
coma, 51	inflection, 69	pandemonium, 72	tedious, 82
commune, 66	insolently, 11	predicated, 38	tentatively, 22

Selection Words

Selection Words are additional words from the reading that may be challenging but are not central to the selection and are not identified in the prereading section. These words can easily be learned using the story context, and they provide excellent practice for using content clues to find meaning without explicit instruction.

adventuress, 88	extolling, 70	jarring, 82	reputation, 99
agony, 35	feebleminded, 116	keel, 75	rhythmic, 87
awed, 15	finicky, 64	mangled, 36	sash, 99
barred, 92	fluorescent, 88	miraculous, 49	solemn, 56
basting, 56	garment, 87	miraculously, 56	solemnly, 13
brittle, 23	gnarled, 25	mystified, 48	specialization, 119
cassock, 65	grim, 75	neurosurgeons, 117	specter, 119
casualties, 61	grimly, 14	opportunist, 117	suffused, 37
commence, 24	halo, 23	organdy, 99	tangible, 119
corsages, 100	harried, 81	perverse, 83	trill, 75
crescent, 51	hemlocks, 35	petition, 118	vaulted, 22
deprived, 12	imbedded, 51	port, 75	ventriloquist dummy, 99
derives, 61	immeasurable, 61	primly, 16	weather'd, 75
evocative, 61	incredulity, 67	prodigy, 98	wedge, 119
evokes, 61	inferiority complex, 120	psyching, 101	
exalt, 75	interminable, 70	reliably, 81	

Teaching Words

Teaching Words consist of vocabulary that is used in the directions about the lessons. Teaching words explain to students what to focus on within the selection, help establish the story context, clarify the meaning of literary terms, and define the goals or instructional purpose.

acclaimed, 61	barrier, 94	components, 130	distinguished, 18
activist, 96	biographical, 30	concrete, 78	distress, 40
adapted, 105	casualties, 54	confirm, 8	documentary, 96
affection, 132	chapel, 54	conform, 49	dwindle, 140
annotations, 133	chronicles, 105	depression, 33	elated, 52
anxiousness, 17	combat, 54	descriptive, 32	elements, 32
assertions, 17	communion, 44	determining, 8	empathy, 132
atmosphere, 53	compelling, 30	devoting, 105	encounter, 6
attributes, 17	complexities, 18	dialogue, 8	engaging, 133

envious, 60
episode, 7
establish, 11
ethnic, 93
eventual, 46
evoke, 61
excel, 103
exclusion, 92
gender, 77
grim, 9
hallucination, 53
hijo, 138
hostility, 92
immigrants, 92
impact, 17, 134
implied, 5
indicate, 24
induce, 49
infatuated, 78

inferred, 5
inhabited, 86
initial, 17
intensified, 6
isolation, 49
landscapes, 32
lighthearted, 9
monetary, 28
monitor, 86
motivation, 60
mute, 94
navigate, 132
neuter, 77
omniscient, 5
oppression, 96
orphanages, 33
paraphrased, 130
perspective, 18
portrays, 54

primarily, 86
principal, 6
prolonged, 49
promote, 30
quest, 49
realistic, 30
reassuring, 53
relevant, 92
reluctant, 9
repealed, 92
representation, 78
rural, 33
savagery, 9
sensory, 33
significant, 8
span, 7
speculate, 62
strategy, 130
subgenres, 4

surname, 96
suspense, 6
tenement, 5
textual, 130
thesis, 44
threatening, 7
thugs, 26
traits, 18
transformation, 128
transition, 46
ultimately, 19
vantage, 5
varied, 133
vinyl, 138
vivid, 8
watershed, 77

KEY TERMS

Key Terms are commonly referred to as *academic vocabulary.* These terms appear in the instructional material to teach the terminology that students need to acquire to understand literature. The repetition of the terms throughout the program ensures student mastery and provides a solid foundation for the continuing study of literature and language arts.

adjective, 103
analyze, 8
antagonist, 5, 6, 18
antecedent, 77
audience, 130, 137
base word, 45
cause and effect, 46
character analysis, 62
character sketch, 94
character trait, 85
character, 5, 18
characterization, 18
chronological order, 7, 132
clarify, 8
clause, 77
climax, 5, 6, 46
cluster chart, 44, 76
compare and contrast, 9, 85
comprehension, 86
conclusions, 19
conflict, 6, 9, 46, 86
consonant, 95
context clue, 33, 54
context, 9, 141
description, 54, 138
dialect, 141

dialogue, 17, 32, 85, 103
dynamic character, 19
essay, 30, 103
evaluate, 8
exposition, 5, 6, 141
external conflict, 17
falling action, 6
fiction, 4
figurative language, 86, 141
figure of speech, 86
flashback, 7
foreshadowing, 7, 138
freewrite, 131
image, 78
imagery, 32
inference, 8
internal conflict, 17
interpret, 8
key idea, 19, 136
literary fiction, 4
literary response, 76
main point, 130
major character, 18
metaphor, 85
minor character, 18
mood, 32, 103, 130

motivation, 18, 78, 138
narrative, 4, 62, 78
narrator, 44
nonverbal expression, 137
noun, 77
novel, 4
oral summary, 136
order of importance, 132
organizational pattern, 132
outline, 132
pacing, 137
personal narrative, 76
plot summary, 136
plot, 5, 6, 9, 44, 46, 86
point of view, 5, 128
popular fiction, 4
prediction, 8, 46
prefix, 45, 95
prepositional phrase, 31
preview, 46
pronoun, 77
prose, 4
protagonist, 5, 18, 141
purpose, 8
recall, 8
resolution, 5, 6, 9, 44, 46

response, 130
review, 30
rising action, 6
root, 45
sensory detail, 44, 54, 141
sentence variety, 134
sequence, 63
setting, 5, 33, 32, 141, 130
short story, 4
simile, 85
skim, 19, 63
static character, 19
subject, 31
suffix, 45, 95
syllable, 95
theme, 5, 131
thesis, 130
thesis statement, 85
time line, 63
tone, 63, 103, 132, 137, 138
topic sentence, 132
topic, 131
verb tense, 137
verb, 31
visualize, 8
vowel, 95

Objectives

Studying this unit will help students meet the following objectives:

- Make connections from themes expressed in the selections to their own lives and the world around them
- Identify common forms of fiction
- Understand different elements of fiction, including *plot, character, setting, point of view*, and *theme*
- Understand variations of literary forms and author's use of language to develop forms

Reading Strategies

Ask Questions	Make Predictions
Clarify	Visualize
Make Inferences	

Reading Skills

Analyze Cause and Effect
Analyze Sequence of Events
Compare and Contrast
Determine Importance of Details
Distinguish Fact from Opinion
Draw Conclusions
Identify Author's Purpose
Identify Point of View
Monitor Comprehension
Use Context Clues

Literary Elements

Character	Plot
Figurative Language	Setting
Irony	Suspense
Motivation	Tone

Finding Ourselves
Fiction

CYNTHIA RYLANT   GARY SOTO   GARRISON KEILLOR

Launch the Unit

Have students work in small groups to create other questions that might relate to the theme of this unit. Model this by proposing such a question: "How do our dreams and ambitions help shape our process of self-discovery?" Have the class write down these questions and keep the list. When the class has completed work on the unit, have them take another look at these questions and discuss which selections provide insights about them.

> "It is odd how we sometimes deny ourselves the very pleasure we have longed for and which is finally within our reach."
>
> —CYNTHIA RYLANT, "Checkouts"

Have you ever had an experience that taught you something significant about who you are? As we grow up, we make such discoveries in a variety of ways. In her short story "Checkouts," Cynthia Rylant explores a clumsy but delicate emotional encounter between two young people that helps them in the process of finding themselves. As you read the short stories in the unit, use the imaginary experiences of the characters to enrich your own real process of self-discovery.

SHIRLEY JACKSON   RAY BRADBURY   MARJORIE KINNAN RAWLINGS

3

Writing Options

Creative Writing
Dialogue   Narrative Paragraph
Diary Entry   Newspaper Article
Informal Letter   Personal Narrative
Music Review

Expository Writing
Character Analysis
Character Sketch
Compare-Contrast Essay
Descriptive Writing
Exemplary Paragraph
Literary Response
Persuasive Essay
Persuasive Writing
Problem-Solution Essay

Language Arts Workshops

Grammar & Style
End Punctuation
Pronoun-Antecedent Agreement
Subject-Verb Agreement

Vocabulary & Spelling
Prefixes, Roots, and Suffixes
Spelling by Syllables

Writing Workshop
Responding to a Short Story

Speaking & Listening Workshop
Giving and Actively Listening to
   Literary Presentations

Test Practice Workshop
Literary Response
Revising and Editing Skills
Reading Skills

Program Resources

For a visual reminder of the unit-based resources available for Unit 1, Fiction, see pages 2A and 2B. As you introduce the unit, you may want to provide students with the Unit Study Guide, which is contained in the *Meeting the Standards* resource.

You may choose to direct students to the Introduction to Fiction pages later on, as they begin to explore the elements of fiction in the Before Reading and After Reading sections of each selection.

Instead of reading through all the text at once, you may want to begin by having students discuss the pros and cons of choosing popular or literary fiction for use in the following situations:

- reading on a beach or on a plane
- recommending reading to a friend
- reading for writing a paper in literature class
- reading for answering an essay on a standardized test

Launch the Lesson

Ask students to help you create a fiction "Top Ten" list by identifying the best stories they know. (In addition to conventional short stories and novels, accept folk and fairy tales, movie and TV plots, comic books, and other nonliterary fictions.) After you have gathered at least ten works, have students attempt to identify elements common to several of the stories. Exciting plots and memorable characters will probably stand out.

Introduction to Fiction

"We left the home place behind, mile by slow mile, heading for the mountains, across the prairie where the winds blew forever."

—DOROTHY M. JOHNSON, "Too Soon a Woman"

What happens next? The lure of narrative is one of the most basic attractions of literature and is an essential part of what draws readers to fiction. The very broad category of literature known as **fiction** includes any work of prose (writing other than poetry and drama) that tells an invented or imaginary story.

Types of Fiction

Short Stories and Novels

The two main forms of fiction are the short story and the novel. The **short story** is a brief prose narrative that usually presents only a single plot, one or two main characters, and one important setting. ("Brief" has often been defined to mean what can be read in a single sitting, but some longer stories often require more.) A **novel** is a long work of prose fiction. Novels often have several plots, many major and minor characters, and numerous settings.

Popular Fiction and Literary Fiction

Popular fiction includes subgenres such as mystery, horror, science fiction, fantasy, and Westerns. The works of writers in this book such as Ray Bradbury (famous for his science fiction and fantasy fiction) and Dorothy M. Johnson (famous for her Westerns) are examples of popular fiction.

Literary fiction does not fit into one of these categories. Writers in this book such as Tomás Rivera and Toshio Mori are considered writers of literary fiction. The dividing line between popular and literary fiction is not clear-cut. For example, some writers of highly "literary" fiction are known for their popular fiction as well.

Types of Popular Fiction

Here are some of the most widely read types of popular fiction and their common formulas or elements.

- **Mystery:** The main character usually takes on a detective role and tries to uncover clues to a crime or some baffling event.

- **Horror:** Ghosts, monsters, or other dangerous characters may lurk within these stories, whose purpose is to provide a good fright.

- **Science Fiction:** Often the setting is outer space, but it doesn't need to be, as long as advanced technology is a strong element in the story.

Pegasus, a winged-horse, is often written about in fantasy stories.

- **Fantasy:** Often confused with science fiction, fantasy relies on magic and magical beings instead of technology. Fantasy is often set in another age or world.

- **Westerns:** The setting is important here—the West. The main character is usually a cowboy, often fighting for survival against the wilderness or evildoers.

Teaching Words

subgenres, 4
tenement, 5
vantage, 5
omniscient, 5
implied, 5
inferred, 5

KEY TERMS

NARRATIVE, 4
FICTION, 4
PROSE, 4
SHORT STORY, 4
NOVEL, 4
POPULAR FICTION, 4
LITERARY FICTION, 4
PLOT, 5
EXPOSITION, 5

CLIMAX, 5
RESOLUTION, 5
CHARACTER, 5
PROTAGONIST, 5
ANTAGONIST, 5
SETTING, 5
POINT OF VIEW, 5
THEME, 5

Common Core State Standards

Reading Literature
RL.2, RL.3, RL.5, RL.6

Elements of Fiction

An artist uses such elements as line and color to create a painting. In a similar way, a writer uses various elements—plot, characters, setting, point of view, and theme—to create a work of fiction.

Plot

The plot of a work of fiction is the series of events related to a central conflict, or struggle. The plot typically introduces a conflict, develops it, and eventually resolves it. A typical plot contains exposition, rising action, climax, falling action, and resolution. For an explanation of these terms, see Understanding Plot on pages 6–7.

Characters

The characters are the individuals who take part in the action of a story. The **protagonist** is the most important character in the story. This character is sometimes opposed by an **antagonist** who is in conflict with the protagonist. In O. Henry's "The Ransom of Red Chief" (page 188), the two con men are the protagonists and the nine-year-old boy they kidnap is their antagonist.

Major characters play significant roles in the action, and **minor characters** play lesser roles. In Duane BigEagle's "The Journey" (page 46), the narrator, Raoul, is a major character because the story is told from his point of view. His cousin Alejandro, the train conductor, is a minor character because he appears only in the scenes on the train.

Setting

The **setting** of a story is the time, place, and environment in which the events take place. The setting can include:

- geographic location
- specific sites (such as a building or room)
- time period
- cultural, social, or economic conditions

Setting is important in helping to establish mood, or atmosphere, the emotion created in the reader by part or all of the story. The setting of Walter Dean Myers's "The Treasure of Lemon Brown" (page 19) includes both the geographic location of New York's African-American Harlem neighborhood and the specific site of an abandoned tenement building.

Point of View

Point of view is the vantage point from which the story is told—in other words, who is telling the story.

- In *first-person* point of view, the story is told by someone who participates in or witnesses the action; this person, called the *narrator*, uses words such as *I* and *we* in telling the story.
- In *third-person* point of view, the narrator usually stands outside the action and observes; the narrator uses such words as *he, she, it,* and *they*.
- In a *third-person omniscient* point of view, the thoughts of all the characters are revealed. Cynthia Rylant's "Checkouts" (page 78) is told from a third-person omniscient point of view.
- In a *third-person limited* point of view, the thoughts of only the narrator or a single character are revealed. Ray Bradbury's "The Drummer Boy of Shiloh" (page 54) is told from a third-person limited point of view.

Theme

The **theme** is the central idea or perception about life that is revealed through a literary work. A *stated theme* is presented directly, but an *implied theme* must be inferred by the reader. Many works of fiction do not have a stated theme, but rather one or more implied themes. A story may also have a stated theme and an implied theme. A stated theme of "Checkouts" is that young people in love do not act rationally. An implied theme is that time heals the wounds of love—often quite rapidly.

Understanding Plot

Reading strategies and skills that can help students understand plot include analyzing cause and effect, making predictions, and summarizing.

Use Reading Skills

Analyze Cause and Effect Point out to students that in any piece of fiction, as in life, the story develops as one event leads to another. Mention a current movie or TV program, or a popular novel with which your students might be familiar, and have them identify the causes and effects that create the plot.

Use Reading Strategies

Make Predictions Have pairs of students work together to make a prediction about something that will happen in school this year. Remind them that a prediction should be made on evidence. Model a possible response: "I predict that our soccer team will have a better season than last year. I'm basing my prediction on watching our first practice sessions." Tell students they can also make predictions to appreciate a story's plot. They can anticipate events based on what they learn about characters and previous events in their lives. Encourage students to make — and to revise — predictions as they read the selections in this unit.

Understanding Plot

What Is Plot?

When people ask us to describe a work of fiction we have read, they will often say, "What is it about?" What they are asking us to describe is the plot. The **plot** is a series of related events that drive a short story or novel. It is plot that first draws us to fiction as children, often in the form of adventure stories such as *Robinson Crusoe.*

The Elements of Plot

A typical plot contains the following elements: exposition, rising action, climax, falling action, and resolution as shown in the diagram below.

- The **exposition,** or introduction, sets the tone or mood, introduces the characters and setting, and provides necessary background information.
- In the **rising action,** the conflict is developed and intensified.
- The **climax** is the point of highest interest or suspense.
- The **falling action** consists of all the events that follow the climax.
- The **resolution** is the point at which the central conflict is resolved, or ended. It is sometimes referred to as the *denouement* (dā' nü' mä ⁿ), which is French for "untying."

Plot Diagram

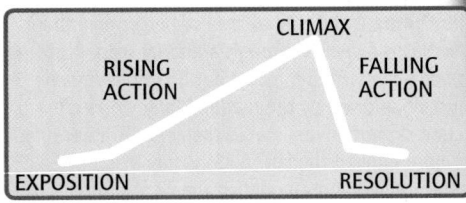

Plot and Conflict

A plot revolves around some type of **conflict,** or struggle. Usually, throughout the course of a story, a central conflict is introduced, developed, and resolved. In units 1 and 2, you will read stories in which characters encounter different kinds of conflict. There are two basic types of conflict, external and internal.

External and Internal Conflicts

An *external conflict* is a struggle that takes place between a character and some outside force. These outside forces are of three principal types:

- against another character, or **antagonist** (see Understanding Characters, page 18)
- against nature
- against society

> *It happened one day about noon going towards my boat, I was exceedingly surprised with the print of a man's naked foot on the shore, which was very plain to be seen in the sand. I stood like one thunderstruck, or as if I had seen an apparition.*
>
> —DANIEL DEFOE, *Robinson Crusoe*

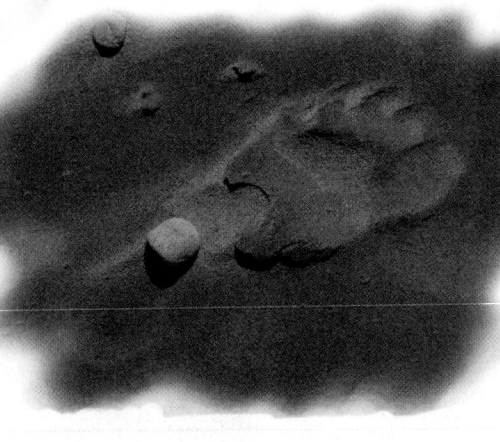

Teaching Words
intensified, 6
suspense, 6
encounter, 6
principal, 6
threatening, 7
span, 7
episode, 7

KEY TERMS

PLOT, 6
EXPOSITION, 6
RISING ACTION, 6
CLIMAX, 6
FALLING ACTION, 6
RESOLUTION, 6
CONFLICT, 6
ANTAGONIST, 6
CHRONOLOGICAL ORDER, 7
FLASHBACK, 7
FORESHADOWING, 7

Common Core State Standards

Reading Literature
RL.3

Conflict with Another Character In Gary Soto's "Born Worker" (page 154) the hard-working main character José is taken advantage of by his lazy, fast-talking cousin Arnie.

> José walked away from Arnie's jabbering. He walked away, and realized that there were people like his cousin, the liar, and people like himself, someone he was getting to know.

Conflict with Nature In Duane BigEagle's "The Journey" (page 46) the struggle is between the main character and a force of nature, the mysterious illness that is threatening his life.

Conflict with Society The main character in Toshio Mori's "Miss Butterfly" (page 180) is an elderly Japanese man living in the United States, who longs for the traditional culture of his homeland.

> "Please Sachi-chan, wear your beautiful kimono tonight and perform one dance for me. Just one, that is all I ask. I want to capture my lost memories and dream. Dance for an old man and let him enter his old world for several minutes."

The other principal type of conflict is *internal conflict,* a struggle that goes on within the main character. In Ray Bradbury's "The Drummer Boy of Shiloh" (page 54), the struggle goes on between the main character, a drummer boy, and his own doubts and fears on the night before the great Civil War battle of Shiloh.

Robinson Crusoe faced external conflict when his boat shipwrecked.

Plot and Organization

A story has a beginning, middle, and end. A story's plot, therefore, is often organized by time. Some stories may present a single day in a character's life, or even an hour, whereas others may span many years.

Many stories are told in **chronological order,** that is, the events are presented in the order in which they occur in time. Other stories start with an event and then go back in time.

Sometimes writers play with time. They use **flashbacks** to tell about something that happened in the past. In Fae Myenne Ng's "Last Night" (page 86), the narrator introduces an episode that took place a week earlier to help develop the relationship between the main characters and their landlady. This is a flashback.

Another way in which writers play with time is through the use of **foreshadowing,** giving hints or clues about what is going to happen in the future. In O. Henry's "The Ransom of Red Chief" (page 188), the first-person narrator hints about trouble to come.

> It looked like a good thing; but wait till I tell you. We were down South, in Alabama—Bill Driscoll and myself—when this kidnapping idea struck us. It was, as Bill afterward expressed it, "during a moment of temporary mental apparition"; but we didn't find that out till later.

As you read, pay attention to the way a writer reveals conflict in the story to better understand the plot.

Teach the Element

Use Reading Skills
Summarize After covering this material in class, have students work in three small groups to summarize what they have learned. Assign a segment of the introduction to each group: have one group summarize what the class has discussed about each element of the plot, one group summarize the types of conflict, and one group summarize how plot relates to organization. Ask each group to elect a spokesperson to share the group's summary with the class.

Analyze Literature
Antagonist and Protagonist This introduction identifies an antagonist as a character with whom someone has a conflict. You might want to introduce the term *protagonist* (main character) as well. Tell students they will learn more about protagonists and antagonists later in the unit (when they study character).

TEACHING NOTE
Conflict
Write down the principal types of conflicts on the board:
- External (against another character)
- External (against nature)
- External (against society)
- Internal (within character)

Divide the class into four groups, and assign each group one type of conflict. Ask each group to come up with several examples of stories from any media that show this type of conflict. Students can then discuss the various stories, deciding which is the best example of each type of conflict.

Differentiated Instruction

Enrichment
Ask students if any of them recall the plot of Defoe's novel *Robinson Crusoe.* Explain that the conflict in the novel is a castaway's struggle to survive alone on a small island. Write down on a board the following events from *Robinson Crusoe,* and work with the class to assign them to their correct places in a plot diagram:
- Crusoe and Friday leave the island. (resolution)
- Crusoe is cast away on uninhabited island. (rising action)
- Crusoe rescues a native from the cannibals. (climax)
- Crusoe is introduced and his early life described. (exposition)
- Crusoe discovers that cannibals sometimes visit the island. (rising action)

Use the Model

Introduce the Process
Use this page to walk students through the reading process. Shirley Jackson's short story "Charles" is an Active Reading Model. Side notes in the Active Reading Models provide point-of-use questions about applying reading strategies and skills, analyzing literature, and making connections. Students can apply the same process they use in reading "Charles" to the rest of the stories in Units 1 and 2.

Before Reading Stress the distinction between the two types of background students need to apply. Distinguish the broad purposes of reading—information, entertainment, experience—and setting a specific purpose for reading an individual work of fiction such as "Charles."

During Reading The four different types of side notes in "Charles" are designed to help students become more active readers. The Mirrors & Windows questions that precede and conclude the story ask them to respond first to the story as individuals and then to apply the experience they have gained in reading to some broader issue.

After Reading "Find Meaning" questions are designed to help students recall important details of a selection and interpret their meaning. "Make Judgments" questions ask students to analyze the selection and evaluate how specific details contribute to its overall literary effect or meaning.

Fiction Reading Model

BEFORE READING

Build Background
You need to apply two types of background to read fiction effectively. One type is the story's literary and historical context. Read the **Build Background** and **Meet the Author** features to get this information. The other type of background is the personal knowledge and experience you bring to your reading.

Set Purpose
A fiction writer presents characters and actions to say something about life. Read **Set Purpose** to decide what you want to get out of the story.

Analyze Literature
A fiction writer uses literary techniques, such as plot and setting, to create meaning. The **Analyze Literature** feature draws your attention to a key literary element in the story.

Use Reading Skills
The **Use Reading Skills** feature will show you skills to help you get the most out of your reading. Learn how to apply skills such as determining author's purpose and using context clues. Identify a graphic organizer that will help you apply the skill before and while you read.

DURING READING

Use Reading Strategies
- **Ask questions** about things that seem significant or interesting.
- **Make predictions** about what's going to happen next. As you read, gather more clues to confirm or change your prediction.
- **Visualize** the story. Form pictures in your mind to help see the characters and settings.
- **Make inferences,** or educated guesses, about what is not stated directly.
- **Clarify,** or check that you understand, what you read. Reread any difficult parts.

Analyze Literature
What literary elements stand out? Are the characters vivid and interesting? Is there a strong central conflict? As you read, consider how these elements affect your enjoyment and understanding of the story.

Make Connections
Notice where connections can be made between the story and your life or the world outside the story. What feelings or thoughts do you have while reading the story?

AFTER READING

Find Meaning
Recall the important details of the story, such as the sequence of events and characters' names. Use this information to **interpret,** or explain, the meaning of the story.

Make Judgments
- **Analyze** the text by examining significant details and deciding what they contribute to the overall meaning.
- **Evaluate** the text by making judgments about how the author creates meaning.

Analyze Literature
Review how the author's use of literary elements increased your understanding of the story. For example, did the author use dialogue? How did it help shape the story's meaning?

Extend Understanding
Go beyond the text by exploring the story's ideas through writing or other creative projects.

8 UNIT 1 FICTION

Words in Use

Teaching Words
determining, 8
significant, 8
confirm, 8
vivid, 8
dialogue, 8

KEY TERMS
PURPOSE, 8
PREDICTION, 8
VISUALIZE, 8
INFERENCE, 8
CLARIFY, 8
RECALL, 8
INTERPRET, 8
ANALYZE, 8
EVALUATE, 8

CHARLES

A Short Story by Shirley Jackson

GUIDED READING

Build Background

Literary Context Shirley Jackson's work tends to focus on the darker side of human experience and shows that things are not always what they seem. Her most famous short story, "The Lottery," is a grim fantasy with a shocking conclusion that exposes the hidden savagery of a small American town. "Charles" is a far more lighthearted story, but it also contains a surprise ending.

Reader's Context Have you ever been reluctant to take responsibility for your behavior? How did you finally resolve this situation?

Set Purpose

Preview the story by skimming the text and writing down any unfamiliar words. See if the context—the words and sentences around the unfamiliar words—provides any clues to their meanings. Consult a dictionary for words you can't figure out from the context clues alone.

Analyze Literature

Plot A **plot** is a series of events related to a central **conflict,** or struggle. A plot usually involves the introduction of a conflict, its development, and its eventual **resolution,** the point at which the central conflict is ended.

Meet the Author

Shirley Jackson (1919–1965) and her husband, the well-known literary critic Stanley Edgar Hyman, lived in North Bennington, Vermont, with their four children. Jackson's writing ranges from light, humorous accounts of family life to dark, often disturbing, fiction in which ordinary life is overshadowed by evil.

Use Reading Skills

Compare and Contrast When you compare one thing to another, you describe similarities between the two things. When you contrast two things, you describe their differences. As you read "Charles," use a Venn Diagram to note the similarities and differences between Laurie and Charles.

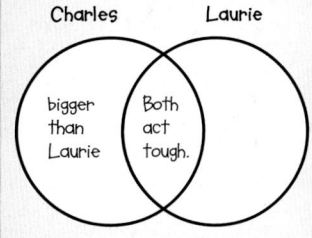

Charles — Laurie

bigger than Laurie | Both act tough.

Preview Vocabulary

in·so·lent·ly (in s[e]´ lent lē) *adv.,* exhibiting boldness or contempt; insultingly

e·lab·o·rate·ly (i la´ b[ə] rət lē) *adv.,* involving many details; lengthy or exaggerated

mind·ful (mīn[d] ´ fəl) *adj.,* bearing in mind; aware

ma·tron·ly (mā´ trʉn lē) *adv.,* relating to motherhood

hag·gard (ha´ gərd) *adj.,* worn or wild in appearance; tired

At a Glance
Guided Reading: Reading Model
- Reading Level: Easy
- Difficulty Consideration: Vocabulary
- Ease Factors: Simple plot, conversational tone

Objectives

Studying this lesson will enable students to

- use reading skills, such as comparing and contrasting
- define the plot elements *conflict* and *resolution,* and identify those elements in this story
- describe the literary accomplishments of Shirley Jackson and her use of personal experience in her fiction
- appreciate a story with a surprise ending

Launch the Lesson

Tell students that they are about to read "Charles," a story about mischief that takes place in a kindergarten classroom. Ask them to share any experiences they have had with mischievous little brothers and sisters. How might that type of mischief be similar to that of five-year-olds? What might make a kindergarten teacher's job difficult? Have them read to find out what happens in this kindergarten classroom.

Preview Vocabulary
- elaborately, 11
- insolently, 11
- mindful, 11
- matronly, 15
- haggard, 15

Selection Words
- deprived, 12

- solemnly, 13
- grimly, 14
- awed, 15
- primly, 16

Teaching Words
- grim, 9
- savagery, 9
- lighthearted, 9
- reluctant, 9

- establish, 11
- initial, 17
- anxiousness, 17
- impact, 17
- attributes, 17
- assertions, 17

KEY TERMS
- **CONTEXT,** 9
- **PLOT,** 9
- **CONFLICT,** 9
- **RESOLUTION,** 9
- **COMPARE AND CONTRAST,** 9
- **EXTERNAL CONFLICT,** 17
- **INTERNAL CONFLICT,** 17
- **DIALOGUE,** 17

Summary

When the narrator's young son, Laurie, comes home after his first day at kindergarten, he reports on the bad behavior of a classmate named Charles. Each day thereafter, the reports continue, astounding the narrator and her husband. They grow both curious and alarmed about Charles and his influence on Laurie. Finally, the narrator decides to go to a PTA meeting, hoping to confront Charles's mother. At the end of the meeting, the narrator introduces herself to Laurie's teacher. The teacher says that Laurie is doing well in class after an adjustment period. Finally, when the narrator asks about Charles, the teacher replies that there is no one named Charles in the class.

MIRRORS & WINDOWS

The Mirrors & Windows questions at the end of this selection focus on the theme of maturity. Before reading the story, ask students how Laurie's perception of Charles evolves from the beginning of the story through the end. As we grow older, how do we alter our concepts of good and bad behavior?

Apply the Model

BEFORE READING

DURING READING

AFTER READING

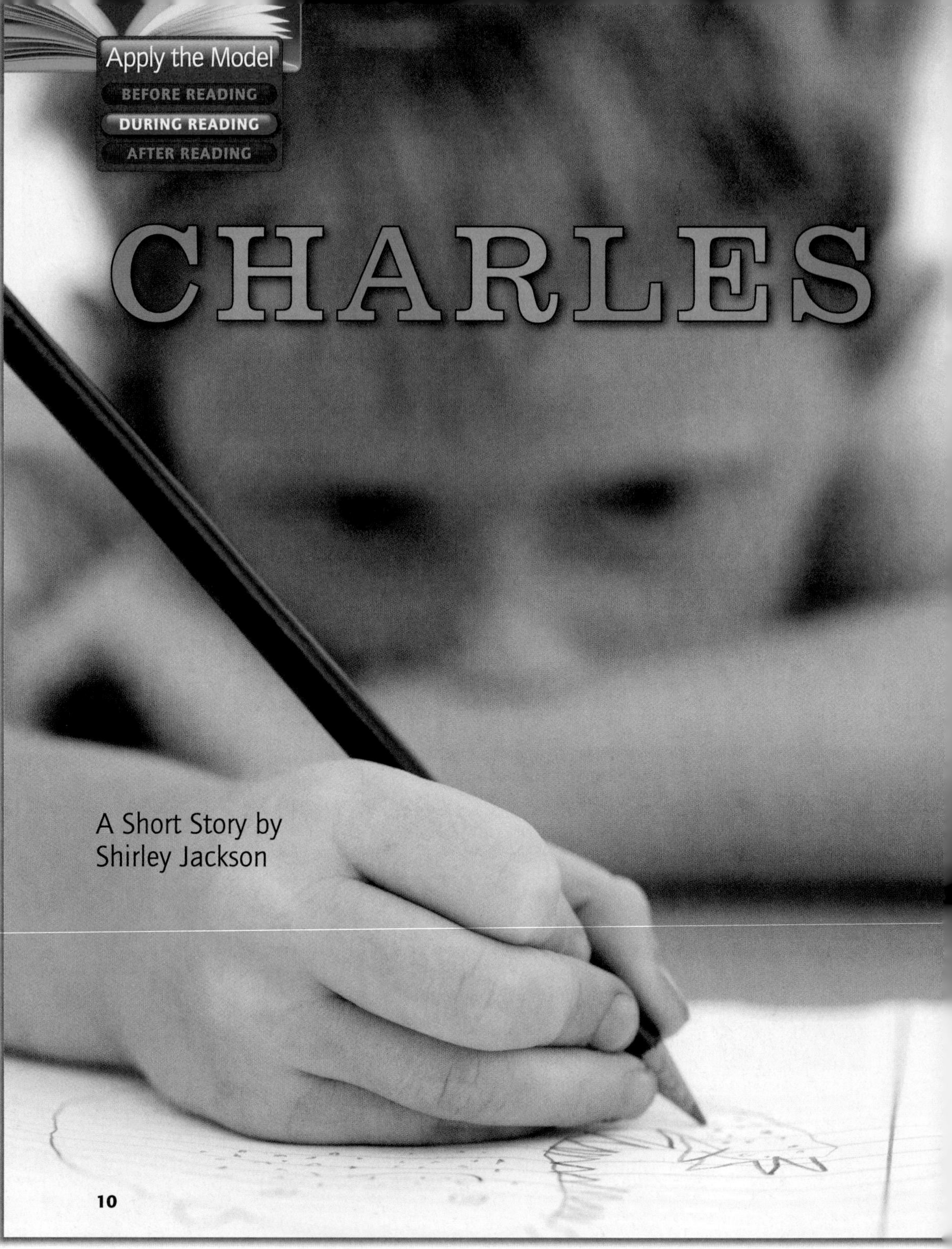

CHARLES

A Short Story by
Shirley Jackson

10

Program Resources

Planning and Assessment
Program Planning Guide, Selection Lesson Plan
E-Lesson Planner
Assessment Guide, Lesson Test
ExamView

Technology Tools
Interactive Student Text on CD
Visual Teaching Package
Audio Library
mirrorsandwindows.com

Meeting the Standards
Fiction: Unit 1, Reading Model, pp. 19–25

Differentiating Instruction
Advanced Students, Author Study, pp. 1–3
English Language Learners, Analyze Sequence
of Events, pp. 1–11

"Well, Charles was bad again today."

The day my son Laurie started kindergarten he renounced[1] corduroy overalls with bibs and began wearing blue jeans with a belt; I watched him go off the first morning with the older girl next door, seeing clearly that an era of my life was ended, my sweet-voiced nursery-school tot replaced by a long-trousered, swaggering[2] character who forgot to stop at the corner and wave good-bye to me.

He came home the same way, the front door slamming open, his cap on the floor, and the voice suddenly become raucous[3] shouting, "Isn't anybody *here?*"

At lunch he spoke <u>insolently</u> to his father, spilled his baby sister's milk, and remarked that his teacher said we were not to take the name of the Lord in vain.

"How *was* school today?" I asked, <u>elaborately</u> casual.

"All right," he said.

"Did you learn anything?" his father asked.

Laurie regarded his father coldly. "I didn't learn nothing," he said.

"Anything," I said. "Didn't learn anything."

"The teacher spanked a boy, though," Laurie said, addressing his bread and butter. "For being fresh," he added, with his mouth full.

"What did he do?" I asked. "Who was it?"

Laurie thought. "It was Charles," he said. "He was fresh. The teacher spanked him and made him stand in a corner. He was awfully fresh."

"What did he do?" I asked again, but Laurie slid off his chair, took a cookie, and left, while his father was still saying, "See here, young man."

The next day Laurie remarked at lunch, as soon as he sat down, "Well, Charles was bad again today." He grinned enormously and said, "Today Charles hit the teacher."

"Good heavens," I said, <u>mindful</u> of the Lord's name, "I suppose he got spanked again?"

"He sure did," Laurie said. "Look up," he said to his father.

"What?" his father said, looking up.

---

1. **renounced.** Gave up
2. **swaggering.** Walking with a boastful, arrogant air; strutting
3. **raucous.** Harsh, rowdy

> **DURING READING**
>
> **Use Reading Strategies**
> **Make Inferences** How do you think the narrator is really feeling? **B**

in・so・lent・ly
(in s[e]´ lent lē) *adv.*, exhibiting boldness or contempt; insultingly

e・lab・o・rate・ly
(i la´ b[ə] rət lē) *adv.*, involving many details; lengthy or exaggerated

> **DURING READING**
>
> **Analyze Literature**
> **Plot** How does this detail establish the conflict in the story? **C**

mind・ful (mīn[d]´ fəl)
adj., bearing in mind; aware

Use Reading Strategies

Ask Questions *Answer:* Students might feel that Laurie's claim is hard to believe, since children of his age rarely disobey their teachers. They might also feel that Laurie's claim is true because Charles is the kind of student who can get his peers to do what he wants. **Ⓐ**

Analyze Literature

Conflict Point out to students that this piece of dialogue reveals a central conflict in the story. Ask them to put the conflict into their own words and challenge them to identify other methods that Jackson uses to reveal it. **Ⓑ**

Use Reading Skills

Determine Importance of Details Direct students' attention to this sentence. Ask them to explain why it is or is not an important detail. **Ⓒ**

"Look down," Laurie said. "Look at my thumb. Gee, you're dumb." He began to laugh insanely.

"Why did Charles hit the teacher?" I asked quickly.

"Because she tried to make him color with red crayons," Laurie said. "Charles wanted to color with green crayons so he hit the teacher and she spanked him and said nobody play with Charles but everybody did."

The third day—it was Wednesday of the first week—Charles bounced a see-saw on to the head of a little girl and made her bleed, and the teacher made him stay inside all during recess. Thursday Charles had to stand in a corner during story-time because he kept pounding his feet on the floor. Friday Charles was deprived of blackboard privileges because he threw chalk.

DURING READING

Use Reading Strategies
Ask Questions What is your opinion of this claim by Laurie? **Ⓐ**

Ⓑ On Saturday I remarked to my husband, "Do you think kindergarten is too unsettling for Laurie? All this toughness, and bad grammar, and this Charles boy sounds like such a bad influence."

"It'll be all right," my husband said reassuringly. "Bound to be people like Charles in the world. Might as well meet them now as later."

Ⓒ On Monday Laurie came home late, full of news. "Charles," he shouted as he came up the hill; I was waiting anxiously on the front steps. "Charles," Laurie yelled all the way up the hill, "Charles was bad again."

"Come right in," I said, as soon as he came close enough. "Lunch is waiting."

Reading Skills

Understand Literary Elements

Point out to students that *italics* are often used to show emphasis. As an example, read aloud Laurie's question from page 11, "Isn't anybody *here*?" using appropriate emphasis. Discuss the intended meaning of emphasizing *here*. Then call on a volunteer to read aloud the narrator's question "How *was* school today?" Again, discuss the effect of emphasizing *was*. In the following sentences,

have students select a word to emphasize. Then have them explain how their choices affect the meaning of their sentences.

1. Jeremy loves peaches. (answers will vary)
2. Only you can prevent forest fires. (answers will vary)
3. Is that my red sweater you're wearing? (answers will vary)

"What are they going to do about Charles, do you suppose?"

"You know what Charles did?" he demanded, following me through the door. "Charles yelled so in school they sent a boy in from first grade to tell the teacher she had to make Charles keep quiet, and so Charles had to stay after school. And so all the children stayed to watch him."

"What did he do?" I asked.

"He just sat there," Laurie said, climbing into his chair at the table. "Hi, Pop, y'old dust mop."

"Charles had to stay after school today," I told my husband. "Everyone stayed with him."

"What does this Charles look like?" my husband asked Laurie. "What's his other name?"

"He's bigger than me," Laurie said. "And he doesn't have any rubbers and he doesn't ever wear a jacket."

Monday night was the first Parent-Teachers meeting, and only the fact that the baby had a cold kept me from going; I wanted passionately to meet Charles's mother. On Tuesday Laurie remarked suddenly. "Our teacher had a friend come to see her in school today."

"Charles's mother?" my husband and I asked simultaneously.[4]

"Naaah," Laurie said scornfully. "It was a man who came and made us do exercises, we had to touch our toes. Look." He climbed down from his chair and squatted down and touched his toes. "Like this," he said. He got solemnly back into his chair and said, picking up his fork, "Charles didn't even *do* exercises."

"That's fine," I said heartily. "Didn't Charles want to do exercises?"

"Naaah," Laurie said. "Charles was so fresh to the teacher's friend he wasn't *let* do exercises."

"Fresh again?" I said.

"He kicked the teacher's friend," Laurie said. "The teacher's friend told Charles to touch his toes like I just did and Charles kicked him."

"What are they going to do about Charles, do you suppose?" Laurie's father asked him. **E**

DURING READING

Analyze Literature
Plot How do you think the narrator's concern about her son is leading to the climax of the story? **D**

---

4. **simultaneously.** At the same time

Ask Questions *Answer:* Laurie's claim is hard to believe because it is unlikely that his teacher would make the whole class suffer the consequences of Charles's actions. Students might suggest that it is becoming clear that Laurie is telling lies, or at least stretching the truth. **A**

Cultural Connection

Eponym Point out to students that Laurie's family begins to employ the name *Charles* as a kind of eponym for "troublemaker." Some words in the English language are derived from people's names. Such words, called *eponyms,* reflect a characteristic or accomplishment of that person. As examples, write the words *sandwich, maverick, leotard, derrick,* and *zinnia* on the board. Model using a dictionary to find the meaning of each eponym, pointing out that *sandwich* was named after John Montagu, the fourth earl of Sandwich, who liked to play cards so much that he asked his servant to make him a meal that he could eat right at the card table, without a knife and fork. The servant made him the world's first sandwich! Have volunteers look up the meanings of the remaining eponyms. **B**

"Charles was so good today the teacher gave him an apple."

> **DURING READING**
> **Use Reading Strategies**
> **Ask Questions** How believable are Laurie's claims? What do you think is really happening? **A**

Laurie shrugged elaborately. "Throw him out of school, I guess," he said.

Wednesday and Thursday were routine;[5] Charles yelled during story hour and hit a boy in the stomach and made him cry. On Friday Charles stayed after school again and so did all the other children.

B With the third week of kindergarten Charles was an institution[6] in our family; the baby was being a Charles when she cried all afternoon; Laurie did a Charles when he filled his wagon full of mud and pulled it through the kitchen; even my husband, when he caught his elbow in the telephone cord and pulled the telephone, ashtray, and a bowl of flowers off the table, said, after the first minute, "Looks like Charles."

During the third and fourth weeks it looked like a reformation[7] in Charles; Laurie reported grimly at lunch on Thursday of the third week. "Charles was so good today the teacher gave him an apple."

"What?" I said, and my husband added warily, "You mean Charles?"

"Charles," Laurie said. "He gave the crayons around and he picked up the books afterward and the teacher said he was her helper."

"What happened?" I asked incredulously.[8]

"He was her helper, that's all," Laurie said, and shrugged.

"Can this be true, about Charles?" I asked my husband that night. "Can something like this happen?"

"Wait and see," my husband said cynically.[9] "When you've got a Charles to deal with, this may mean he's only plotting."

He seemed to be wrong. For over a week Charles was the teacher's helper; each day he handed things out and he picked things up; no one had to stay after school.

---

5. **routine.** Customary, regular, habitual
6. **institution.** Familiar, long-established person, thing, or practice; fixture
7. **reformation.** Improvement, betterment
8. **incredulously.** With doubt or disbelief
9. **cynically.** With disbelief about another person's honesty

Reading Skills

Analyze Text Organization

Like most stories with surprise endings, this story has an interesting structure, in which the climax and the resolution of the conflict occur together, at the very end, when the narrator learns the true identity of Charles. Before students read the final page, advise them to look for ways in which the characters try to face and address the conflict. Then, as they read, pause to discuss the element of suspense, as the narrator looks around the room, searching for a woman who looks "haggard enough" to be Charles's mother. When they have finished reading, lead them to identify the climax and evaluate the conflict resolution. Did they enjoy the surprise ending and the way in which the conflict is resolved, or do they feel the story would be better with a different ending?

"The PTA meeting's next week again," I told my husband one evening. "I'm going to find Charles's mother there."

"Ask her what happened to Charles," my husband said. "I'd like to know."

"I'd like to know myself," I said.

On Friday of that week things were back to normal. "You know what Charles did today?" Laurie demanded at the lunch table, in a voice slightly awed. "He told a little girl to say a word and she said it and the teacher washed her mouth out with soap and Charles laughed."

"What word?" his father asked unwisely, and Laurie said, "I'll have to whisper it to you, it's so bad." He got down off his chair and went around to his father. His father bent his head down and Laurie whispered joyfully. His father's eyes widened.

"Did Charles tell the little girl to say *that?*" he asked respectfully.

"She said it *twice,*" Laurie said. "Charles told her to say it *twice.*"

"What happened to Charles?" my husband asked.

"Nothing," Laurie said. "He was passing out the crayons."

Monday morning Charles abandoned the little girl and said the evil word himself three or four times, getting his mouth washed out with soap each time. He also threw chalk.

My husband came to the door with me that evening as I set out for the PTA meeting. "Invite her over for a cup of tea after the meeting," he said. "I want to get a look at her."

"If only she's there," I said prayerfully.

"She'll be there," my husband said. "I don't see how they could hold a PTA meeting without Charles's mother."

At the meeting I sat restlessly, scanning each comfortable <u>matronly</u> face, trying to determine which one hid the secret of Charles. None of them looked to me <u>haggard</u> enough. No one stood up in the meeting and apologized for the way her son had been acting. No one mentioned Charles.

After the meeting I identified and sought out Laurie's kindergarten teacher. She had a plate with a cup of tea and a piece of chocolate cake; I had a plate with a cup of tea and a piece of marshmallow cake. We maneuvered up to one another cautiously, and smiled.

"I've been so anxious to meet you," I said. "I'm Laurie's mother."

"We're all so interested in Laurie," she said.

"Well, he certainly likes kindergarten," I said. "He talks about it all the time."

DURING READING

Use Reading Skills
Compare and Contrast
What differences does Laurie note here? **D**

ma·tron·ly (mā´ trʉn lē)
adv., relating to motherhood

hag·gard (ha´ gərd) *adj.,*
worn or wild in appearance;
tired

CHARLES **15**

Analyze Literature
Characterization Discuss the ups and downs of Charles's behavior. Ask students why he might lapse into bad behavior after his "reformation" and reward to act as the teacher's helper. Have students use their own experiences with children to discuss whether such behavior swings are realistic. Then ask "What goals might Charles have for acting mischievously?" **C**

Use Reading Skills
Compare and Contrast *Answer:* Laurie notes that although Charles's behavior improved for some time, it has again become a problem. Now, however, it appears that Charles's actions are an even bigger problem than before because he seems to be convincing others to break rules, too. **D**

Vocabulary Skills

Idioms
Define *idiom* as a common expression that has come to have a different meaning than what its individual words literally mean. As an example, write "Charles was fresh" on the chalkboard. Explain that *fresh* has many literal meanings, including "new," as in *fresh paint,* and "not preserved or canned," as in *fresh vegetables.* However, used idiomatically, it means "rude." Ask students to give the meaning of the following idioms from "Charles."

1. see here (give me your attention)
2. good heavens (exclamation of surprise or frustration)
3. to deal with (to be responsible for)
4. set out for (left for)
5. have your hands full (be very busy)

You may want to ask students to write a journal entry or quick write, or divide students into discussion groups or lead a whole-class discussion about this question. *Answer:* At the beginning of the story, Laurie seems in awe of Charles's boldness and fresh behavior. Then, by the third or fourth week of kindergarten, Laurie reports that Charles has changed. He is now a classroom helper. Laurie does not seem impressed with Charles's change; in fact, when Charles has a lapse and uses a bad word, Laurie reports the incident "joyfully." Answers will vary regarding students' conceptions of attractive behavior. They might suggest that as we mature, we tend to find behavior that shows compassion, confidence, or a sense of justice attractive.

"We had a little trouble adjusting, the first week or so," she said primly, "but now he's a fine little helper. With occasional lapses,[10] of course."

"Laurie usually adjusts very quickly," I said. "I suppose this time it's Charles's influence."

"Charles?"

"Yes," I said laughing, "you must have your hands full in that kindergarten, with Charles."

"Charles?" she said. "We don't have any Charles in the kindergarten." ❖

DURING READING

Use Reading Strategies
Make Predictions What do you think the narrator would have said to Charles's mother if she had found her? **A**

10. **lapses.** Slips, temporary failures

What seems to be Laurie's attitude toward Charles at the beginning of the story? How does it change? How does our idea of what is good behavior change as we mature?

16　UNIT 1 FICTION

Enrichment

Once students have finished the story, review what they have learned about eponyms and how the characters in this story used *Charles* as an eponym. Then encourage interested students to work with partners or in small groups to imagine *Laurie* as an eponym and discuss how it might be used in sentences, based on the words and actions of that character. Finally, have partners or group members work together to create new eponyms based on the characteristics or accomplishments of current public figures, familiar fictional characters, and historical figures they have studied. Provide time for groups to present their new eponyms to the class.

Find Meaning

1. (a) What does Laurie tell his parents about his kindergarten class? (b) How do his parents react to Laurie's stories about school?

2. (a) How does Laurie describe Charles? (b) What does this description suggest about Laurie's feelings toward him?

3. (a) How does Laurie describe the change in Charles's behavior? (b) What is Laurie's initial reaction to Charles's new attitude?

Analyze Literature

Plot A plot revolves around some type of conflict, or struggle. How would you describe the major conflict in "Charles"? How is this conflict resolved, and how do the qualities of the main characters help to influence this resolution?

Make Judgments

4. (a) How would you describe the narrator's attitude toward her son's school at the beginning of the story? (b) How do the narrator's feelings change by the end?

5. *Suspense* is a feeling of anxiousness or curiosity. (a) How does the author build suspense in this story? (b) How would the impact of the story have changed if the author had moved the action to Laurie's classroom earlier?

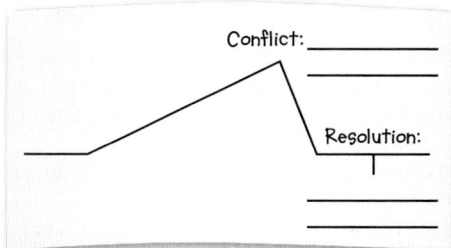

Conflict: _____

Resolution: _____

Extend Understanding

Writing Options

Creative Writing Imagine what happens to the characters after the ending of the story. How do you think Laurie's father reacts when he hears what the kindergarten teacher said? Write a brief **dialogue** between Laurie and his father that takes place after the father learns the truth about Charles. Share the dialogue with your classmates.

Expository Writing Foreshadowing is the act of hinting at events that will happen later. Now that you know how "Charles" ends, reread it to determine which details foreshadow the outcome. Then write a **paragraph** in which you present and explain your examples. Compare your examples with a partner.

Collaborative Learning

Role-Play Working in a group of four students, role-play a parent-teacher conference between Charles's teacher, his parents, and Charles. What advice might the teacher have for Charles's parents? How might the situation have been dealt with more directly earlier in the school year? Write a plan for Charles to help him adjust to school.

Critical Literacy

Hold a Panel Discussion Discuss the story as a class. Are the actions Laurie attributes to Charles actually things Laurie does? Or, are some of those actions simply from Laurie's imagination? Provide evidence from the story to support your assertions.

Go to **www.mirrorsandwindows.com** for more.

Find Meaning

1. (a) Laurie enjoys telling his parents about the misdeeds of a boy named Charles. (b) Laurie's parents are concerned that Charles may be having a bad effect on their son.

2. (a) Laurie describes Charles as "fresh," bigger than he, and lacking proper outdoor clothing. (b) Laurie clearly admires Charles.

3. Laurie reports that Charles seems to be adjusting to school. (b) Laurie seems disappointed.

Make Judgments

4. (a) The narrator seems worried about the negative impact that kindergarten is having on her son. (b) She realizes that Laurie had problems adjusting to school and discovers how he has coped.

5. (a) By presenting the classroom through Laurie's descriptions. (b) It would have dramatically reduced the impact of the ending on readers.

Analyze Literature

Plot *Answer:* The major conflict in the story is the impact that Laurie's parents think a classmate named Charles is having on their son. The resolution occurs at the very end of the story when the narrator realizes that Charles is actually Laurie. The qualities of the main characters cause the resolution to be delayed. Laurie's trickiness and his parents' trusting nature prevent them from realizing Charles's true identity sooner.

Rubrics for Writing Options

You can adapt this as a checklist for students to use as they write.

Creative Writing

☐ Does the student use dialogue form correctly?

☐ Does the dialogue accurately reflect the characters of Laurie and his father from the story?

☐ Does the dialogue imaginatively extend the narrative?

Expository Writing

☐ Does the paragraph correctly identify details in the story that foreshadow the ending?

☐ Does the paragraph reasonably explain how these details foreshadow the ending?

For further instruction, refer students to the following extension activity: Collaborative Learning: Role-Play, *Exceeding the Standards: Extension Activities*, pp. 1–2.

Understanding Characters

Reading strategies that can help students understand characterization and motivation include visualizing and making inferences.

Use Reading Strategies

Visualize Point out to students that among the key strategies of characterization is showing how characters look, move, and speak. "How does the narrator's use of first-person pronouns such as *my* and *me* reveal her character?"

Use Reading Strategies

Make Inferences Remind students that making inferences involves combining clues in the story with their own experiences. Model this behavior by making inferences about the motivation of the narrator in "Charles": "In her words and actions, she is clearly motivated by a growing anxiety about the influence of kindergarten on Laurie."

TEACHING NOTE

Graphic Organizer

Students might benefit from creating a cluster chart to organize the different types of characters. Have them draw a central oval in which they write the word *characters*. Have them draw eight smaller ovals connected by lines to the central one. In these they should write the terms *protagonist, antagonist, major characters, minor characters, flat character, rounded character, static character*, and *dynamic character*. Finally, in each of these outer ovals, have them write a key word or phrase to help them remember what the term means.

Literary Element

Understanding Characters

What Are Characters?

In this portrait, the photographer has created a character by capturing the perspective and physical traits of the subject. Writers also create characters. A **character** is an imaginary person or animal who takes part in the action of a literary work.

Characterization and Motivation

In the passage below right, how does the writer create character? **Characterization** is the act of creating or describing a character. Writers create character using three major techniques:

- Showing what characters say, do, or think
- Showing what other characters (and the narrator) say or think about them
- Describing what physical features, dress, and personality the characters display

In real life, people do not act for no reason at all. A need, a feeling, or some other force causes them to act. Characters respond in the same way. A **motivation** is a force that moves a character to think, feel, or behave in a certain way.

Types of Characters

The main character in a literary work is called the **protagonist.** A character who struggles against the main character is called an **antagonist.** Characters can also be classified as major characters or minor characters. **Major characters** are ones who play important roles in a work. **Minor characters** are ones who play less important roles.

Another way to classify characters is by how fully the writer develops them. A *flat character* is one-dimensional and exhibits only a single quality or trait. A *round character* is three-dimensional and seems to have all the complexities of an actual human being.

Finally, characters can be distinguished by whether they develop in the course of a literary work or remain the same. A *static character* does not change in the course of a work. A *dynamic character* changes as a result of the story's events.

Drummer boy, age ten, from the Civil War battle of Shiloh.

> *His face, alert or at rest, was solemn. It was indeed a solemn time and a solemn night for a boy just turned fourteen in the peach field near the Owl Creek not far from the church at Shiloh.*
>
> —RAY BRADBURY, "The Drummer Boy of Shiloh"

Words in Use

Teaching Words
perspective, 18
traits, 18
complexities, 18
distinguished, 18

KEY TERMS

CHARACTER, 18
CHARACTERIZATION, 18
MOTIVATION, 18
PROTAGONIST, 18
ANTAGONIST, 18
MAJOR CHARACTER, 18
MINOR CHARACTER, 18

Common Core State Standards

Reading Literature
RL.1, RL.6

The Treasure of Lemon Brown

A Short Story by Walter Dean Myers

GUIDED READING

At a Glance
Guided Reading: Reading Model
- Reading Level: Easy
- Difficulty Consideration: Length
- Ease Factors: Suspense, vivid description

Build Background
Cultural Context Homelessness is a problem in many American cities. Lemon Brown is an elderly blues singer who has fallen on hard times and is now homeless. Fourteen-year-old Greg Ridley had seen Lemon Brown before, picking through trash in the neighborhood, but never dreamed that the old man had such a fascinating history. The blues singer ultimately teaches Greg an important lesson about what really matters in life.

Reader's Context When have you talked to elderly family members, friends, or neighbors about their experiences? What types of lessons did you learn from them?

Set Purpose
Skim the title and the first few pages of the story to predict what Lemon Brown's "treasure" might be.

Analyze Literature
Character A **character** is a person or animal who takes part in the action of a story. Distinguish characters by noticing how much they develop or change by the end of the story. A *static character* stays mostly the same. A *dynamic character* changes as a result of the story's events. As you read, determine which characters are static and which are dynamic.

Meet the Author
Walter Dean Myers was born in West Virginia in 1937 but spent most of his childhood in Harlem, the location of many of his stories. Myers developed a love of reading and began writing poetry and short stories at an early age. His young readers can identify with the lives, dreams, and interests of his realistic characters.

Use Reading Skills
Draw Conclusions
As you read, you draw conclusions by gathering information that supports key ideas. During reading, keep a drawing conclusions log to help you track information in the story. Determine a few key ideas from the text and record the supporting ideas.

Key Idea:	Key Idea:	Key Idea:
Greg is upset about not being able to play on the basketball team.		
Support: He avoids going home.	Support:	Support:
Conclusion About Overall Message:		

Preview Vocabulary
stoop (stüp) *n.*, front steps or entrance

a·jar (ə jär´) *adj.*, slightly open

ten·ta·tive·ly (ten´ tə tiv lē) *adv.*, in an uncertain or hesitant way

in·vol·un·tar·y (in vä´ lən ter ē) *adj.*, done without conscious control

beck·on (be´ kən) *v.*, make a gesture to encourage someone to follow

Objectives
Studying this lesson will enable students to
- use reading skills such as drawing conclusions
- distinguish types of *characters*, including dynamic and static and round and flat
- describe the literary accomplishments of Walter Dean Myers and appreciate the history and culture of Harlem
- enjoy a story about values and goals

Launch the Lesson
Prior to reading "The Treasure of Lemon Brown," ask students to define *treasure*. Point out that common examples of treasure include gold, jewels, and other things of intrinsic value. Ask students to name things that have more subjective values such as a happy memory, a pet, or a first-place blue ribbon. Have them read to find out what Lemon Brown's treasure is.

THE TREASURE OF LEMON BROWN **19**

Words in Use

Preview Vocabulary	Selection Words	Teaching Words
stoop, 21	vaulted, 22	ultimately, 19
ajar, 21	brittle, 23	indicate, 24
tentatively, 22	halo, 23	thugs, 26
involuntary, 23	commence, 24	monetary, 28
beckon, 25	gnarled, 25	compelling, 30
		realistic, 30
		biographical, 30
		promote, 30

KEY TERMS
SKIM, 19
STATIC CHARACTER, 19
DYNAMIC CHARACTER, 19
CONCLUSIONS, 19
KEY IDEA, 19
REVIEW, 30
ESSAY, 30

Common Core State Standards
Reading Literature
RL.1, RL.3
Writing
W.9, W.10
Language
L.6

Summary

Greg Ridley loves to play basketball. However, when the school principal sends a letter home saying that Greg will probably fail math, Greg's father puts his foot down. Greg cannot play basketball on the school team until he improves his math grade. Angry and tired of his father's lectures, Greg goes for a walk in his neighborhood one night and ends up at a deserted tenement building. There, he meets an elderly homeless man, Lemon Brown, who claims to have a treasure. When three thugs come to rob Lemon, he and Greg work together to fend them off. In the process, Greg learns an important lesson about values and comes to an understanding about his father's goals for him.

The Mirrors & Windows questions at the end of this selection focus on the theme of legacy. Before reading the story, ask students what objects they would include in a "treasure" that symbolized their life thus far. For what purpose do people create, keep, and pass on such treasures?

The Treasure of Lemon Brown

A Short Story by Walter Dean Myers

The Journey, 2002. Colin Bootman.

20

Program Resources

Planning and Assessment
Program Planning Guide, Selection Lesson Plan
E-Lesson Planner
Assessment Guide, Lesson Test
ExamView

Technology Tools
Interactive Student Text on CD
Visual Teaching Package
Audio Library
mirrorsandwindows.com

Meeting the Standards
Fiction: Unit 1, Guided Reading, pp. 26–31

Differentiating Instruction
Advanced Students, Cultural Research Project, p. 4

The dark sky, filled with angry, swirling clouds, reflected Greg Ridley's mood as he sat on the <u>stoop</u> of his building. His father's voice came to him again, first reading the letter the principal had sent to the house, then lecturing endlessly about his poor efforts in math.

"I had to leave school when I was thirteen," his father had said; "that's a year younger than you are now. If I'd had half the chances that you have, I'd..."

Greg had sat in the small, pale-green kitchen listening, knowing the lecture would end with his father saying he couldn't play ball with the Scorpions. He had asked his father the week before, and his father had said it depended on his next report card. It wasn't often the Scorpions took on new players, especially fourteen-year-olds, and this was a chance of a lifetime for Greg. He hadn't been allowed to play high school ball, which he had really wanted to do, but playing for the Community Center team was the next best thing. Report cards were due in a week, and Greg had been hoping for the best. But the principal had ended the suspense early when she sent that letter saying Greg would probably fail math if he didn't spend more time studying.

"And you want to play *basketball?*" His father's brows knitted over deep-brown eyes. "That must be some kind of a joke. Now you just get into your room and hit those books."

That had been two nights before. His father's words, like the distant thunder that now echoed through the streets of Harlem, still rumbled softly in his ears.

It was beginning to cool. Gusts of wind made bits of paper dance between the parked cars. There was a flash of nearby lightning, and soon large drops of rain splashed onto his jeans. He stood to go upstairs, thought of the lecture that probably awaited him if he did anything except shut himself in his room with his math book, and started walking down the street instead. Down the block there was an old tenement that had been abandoned for some months. Some of the guys had held an impromptu[1] checkers tournament there the week before, and Greg had noticed that the door, once boarded over, had been slightly <u>ajar</u>.

Pulling his collar up as high as he could, he checked for traffic and made a dash across the street. He reached the house just as another flash of lightning changed the night to day for an instant,

---

A **stoop** (stüp) *n.,* front steps or entrance

DURING READING

Analyze Literature
Character How do you think the father's past experiences influence the way he disciplines his son? **B**

DURING READING

Use Reading Strategies
Make Predictions How do you think Greg will react to his father's harsh attitude? **C**

"You mean you ain't **never** heard of **Sweet Lemon Brown?**"

a•jar (ə jär´) *adj.,* slightly open

---

1. impromptu. Made or done without preparation

Teach the Model

Use Reading Strategies
Make Predictions Work with students to summarize the information contained in the first paragraph. Then, based on that information, have students jot down predictions about what the story's central conflict will be. Finally, have them read further to find more information that they can use to verify or change their predictions. **A**

Analyze Literature
Character *Answer:* Since Greg's father had to leave school when he was young and didn't have many of the opportunities that Greg has, he feels very strongly that Greg's studies must come first. **B**

Use Reading Strategies
Make Predictions *Answer:* Greg is upset about his father's position on schoolwork. Students might speculate that Greg will rebel against his father's insistence that he not join the basketball team. **C**

Differentiated Instruction

English Language Learning
Students learning English may need help in understanding Lemon Brown's dialect. Explain that dialect is a form of language used by people of specific regions or groups. It often has structures and sounds that are different from standard English. Write the following examples on the board, and discuss their meanings with students. Urge students to note the slang (*ain't*, double negatives) and the structural changes (*nothin'/nothing*) and use them, as they read this story, to unlock meaning.

1. Don't try nothin'
2. 'cause
3. Ain't you got no home?
4. They's bad men
5. Best you stay awhile

Analyze Literature

Plot *Answer:* Myers paints an ominous portrait of the abandoned building with descriptions of mysterious sounds and the rooms obscured in darkness. Based on the information in the story, students might suggest that the tenement was once a thriving apartment full of families. **Ⓐ**

History Connection

Harlem The setting of this story is Harlem, a large neighborhood of New York City's Manhattan borough. First settled by the Dutch in 1658, this area was originally named for the Dutch city of Haarlem. At the turn of the twentieth century, African Americans began moving into Harlem, and the neighborhood thrived. During its golden era, the Harlem Renaissance of the 1920s, African-American writers, musicians, and artists gained widespread attention. These included writers Zora Neale Hurston and Langston Hughes, musicians Eubie Blake and Duke Ellington, and artists Aaron Douglas and Augusta Savage.

Analyze Literature

Suspense Point out that the author uses different sensory details—both sights and sounds—in this passage in order to build suspense. Give one example, and then ask students to offer others. Ask them why such details create tension. **Ⓑ**

---

ten·ta·tive·ly
(ten′ tə tiv lē) *adv.,* in an uncertain or hesitant way

> **DURING READING**
> **Analyze Literature**
> **Plot** How does the author's description of the building create suspense for readers? **Ⓐ**

then returned the graffiti-scarred building to the grim shadows. He vaulted over the outer stairs and pushed <u>tentatively</u> on the door. It was open, and he let himself in.

The inside of the building was dark except for the dim light that filtered through the dirty windows from the street lamps. There was a room a few feet from the door, and from where he stood at the entrance, Greg could see a squarish patch of light on the floor. He entered the room, frowning at the musty smell. It was a large room that might have been someone's parlor at one time. Squinting, Greg could see an old table on its side against one wall, what looked like a pile of rags or a torn mattress in the corner, and a couch, with one side broken, in front of the window.

He went to the couch. The side that wasn't broken was comfortable enough, though a little creaky. From this spot he could see the blinking neon sign over the bodega² on the corner. He sat awhile, watching the sign blink first green, then red, allowing his mind to drift to the Scorpions, then to his father. His father had been a postal worker for all Greg's life and was proud of it, often telling Greg how hard he had worked to pass the test. Greg had heard the story too many times to be interested now.

For a moment Greg thought he heard something that sounded like a scraping against the wall. He listened carefully, but it was gone.

Ⓑ Outside, the wind had picked up, sending the rain against the window with a force that shook the glass in its frame. A car passed, its tires hissing over the wet street and its red taillights glowing in the darkness.

Greg thought he heard the noise again. His stomach tightened as he held himself still and listened intently. There weren't any more scraping noises, but he was sure he had heard something in the darkness—something breathing!

He tried to figure out just where the breathing was coming from; he knew it was in the room with him. Slowly he stood, tensing. As he turned, a flash of lightning lit up the room, frightening him with its sudden brilliance. He saw nothing, just the overturned table, the pile of rags, and an old newspaper on the

---

2. **bodega.** Small grocery store (Spanish)

Reading Skills

Use Graphic Organizers

Remind students that the plot of a story is the series of events that take place. Most plots contain a central conflict, or problem, that one or more of the characters must face. As the character or characters take action to solve the problem, the tension rises to the climax, the point of highest tension. Then the tension falls to the resolution, when the problem is solved.

On the board, draw a plot diagram like the one on page 6. Have students copy the diagram on paper. As they read, have them note the major plot events, the climax, and the resolution. To model the process, note the first plot event: "Greg's father won't let him play basketball because of poor grades."

floor. Could he have been imagining the sounds? He continued listening, but heard nothing and thought that it might have just been rats. Still, he thought, as soon as the rain let up he would leave. He went to the window and was about to look out when he heard a voice behind him.

"Don't try nothin', 'cause I got a razor here sharp enough to cut a week into nine days!"

Greg, except for an <u>involuntary</u> tremor in his knees, stood stock-still. The voice was high and brittle, like dry twigs being broken, surely not one he had ever heard before. There was a shuffling sound as the person who had been speaking moved a step closer. Greg turned, holding his breath, his eyes straining to see in the dark room.

The upper part of the figure before him was still in darkness. The lower half was in the dim rectangle of light that fell unevenly from the window. There were two feet, in cracked, dirty shoes from which rose legs that were wrapped in rags.

"Who are you?" Greg hardly recognized his own voice.

"I'm Lemon Brown," came the answer. "Who're you?"

"Greg Ridley."

"What are you doing here?" The figure shuffled forward again, and Greg took a small step backward.

"It's raining," Greg said.

"I can see that," the figure said.

The person who called himself Lemon Brown peered forward, and Greg could see him clearly. He was an old man. His black, heavily wrinkled face was surrounded by a halo of crinkly white hair and whiskers that seemed to separate his head from the layers of dirty coats piled on his smallish frame. His pants were bagged to the knee, where they were met with rags that went down to the old shoes. The rags were held on with strings, and there was a rope around his middle. Greg relaxed. He had seen the man before, picking through the trash on the corner and pulling clothes out of a Salvation Army box. There was no sign of the razor that could "cut a week into nine days."

"What are you doing here?" Greg asked.

"This is where I'm staying," Lemon Brown said. "What you here for?"

"Told you it was raining out," Greg said, leaning against the back of the couch until he felt it give slightly.

"Ain't you got no home?"

DURING READING

Use Reading Strategies
Make Inferences How do you think Greg feels at this point? **C**

in·vol·un·tar·y
(in vă´ lən ter ē) *adj.,* done without conscious control

Use Reading Strategies
Make Inferences *Answer:* Students might suggest that Greg is terrified and sorry that he wandered into the tenement building. **C**

Analyze Literature
Characterization Ask students what this physical characterization of Lemon Brown reveals about his situation. Challenge them to determine why Myers reveals it in this manner. Model an answer such as "Myers seems to want to show rather than tell the reader what Lemon's circumstances are." **D**

Use Reading Strategies
Visualize Ask students to use the vivid details in this passage to visualize Lemon Brown. Mention one detail—"crinkly white hair"—and call on students to add further details. **E**

Differentiated Instruction

English Language Learners
Students learning English might need help with the following words and idioms.
hit the books—study hard, 21
made a dash—ran quickly, 21
parlor—formal living room, 22

Enrichment
Students compelled by the history and culture of Harlem might be interested in researching and reporting on the lives and accomplishments of some of its celebrities, many of whom gained fame performing at the historic Apollo Theater. Examples include Ella Fitzgerald, Billie Holiday, Count Basie, Marvin Gaye, Aretha Franklin, and Michael Jackson (then performing as a member of the Jackson 5). Additionally, students interested in sports might enjoy researching and reporting on the Harlem Globetrotters.

Use Reading Strategies

Make Predictions *Answer:* Lemon Brown might have a treasure that is very valuable to him, but not worth much money. **Ⓐ**

Analyze Literature

Characterization Remind students that authors develop characters in many ways—using what the character says and does and how other characters react to him or her. Point out the movements of Lemon Brown, such as "pulling back his shoulders" as he speaks. Lead them to understand that this gesture indicates pride. **Ⓑ**

Use Reading Strategies

Make Inferences *Answer:* Lemon Brown's use of dialect and colorful phrases suggests that he comes from another part of the country (the deep South) and has an interesting history. **Ⓒ**

"I got a home," Greg answered.

"You ain't one of them bad boys looking for my treasure, is you?" Lemon Brown cocked his head to one side and squinted one eye. "Because I told you I got me a razor."

"I'm not looking for your treasure," Greg answered, smiling. "*If* you have one."

> **DURING READING**
> **Use Reading Strategies**
> **Make Predictions** What kind of treasure might Lemon Brown have?
> **Ⓐ**

"What you mean, *if* I have one," Lemon Brown said. "Every man got a treasure. You don't know that, you must be a fool!"

"Sure," Greg said as he sat on the sofa and put one leg over the back. "What do you have, gold coins?"

"Don't worry none about what I got," Lemon Brown said. "You know who I am?"

"You told me your name was orange or lemon or something like that."

Ⓑ "Lemon Brown," the old man said, pulling back his shoulders as he did so, "they used to call me Sweet Lemon Brown."

"Sweet Lemon?" Greg asked.

"Yessir. Sweet Lemon Brown. They used to say I sung the blues so sweet that if I sang at a funeral, the dead would commence to rocking with the beat. Used to travel all over Mississippi and as far as Monroe, Louisiana, and east on over to Macon, Georgia. You mean you ain't never heard of Sweet Lemon Brown?"

"Afraid not," Greg said. "What...what happened to you?"

> **DURING READING**
> **Use Reading Strategies**
> **Make Inferences** What do these details and his manner of speaking indicate about the character of Lemon Brown?
> **Ⓒ**

"Hard times, boy. Hard times always after a poor man. One day I got tired, sat down to rest a spell and felt a tap on my shoulder. Hard times caught up with me."

"Sorry about that."

"What are you doing here? How come you didn't go on home when the rain come? Rain don't bother you young folks none."

"Just didn't." Greg looked away.

"I used to have a knotty-headed boy just like you." Lemon Brown had half walked, half shuffled back to the corner and sat down against the wall. "Had them big eyes like you got. I used to call them moon eyes. Look into them moon eyes and see anything you want."

"How come you gave up singing the blues?" Greg asked.

"Didn't give it up," Lemon Brown said. "You don't give up the blues; they give you up. After a while you do good for yourself, and it ain't nothing but foolishness singing about how hard you got it. Ain't that right?"

"I guess so."

Differentiated Instruction

Auditory Learning

Students who have difficulty "hearing" the rhythms and flow of Lemon Brown's dialect might benefit from role-playing. Have pairs of students take turns playing the roles of Greg and Lemon Brown, reading lines of dialogue. Encourage students reading Lemon's lines to experiment with different tones of voice and emphases on certain words. For example,

lead them to emphasize the italicized words in this line:

"Didn't *give* it up. "You don't *give up* the blues. They give *you* up."

"What's that noise?" Lemon Brown asked, suddenly sitting upright.

Greg listened, and he heard a noise outside. He looked at Lemon Brown and saw the old man was pointing toward the window.

Greg went to the window and saw three men, neighborhood thugs,[3] on the stoop. One was carrying a length of pipe. Greg looked back toward Lemon Brown, who moved quietly across the room to the window. The old man looked out, then <u>beckoned</u> frantically for Greg to follow him. For a moment Greg couldn't move. Then he found himself following Lemon Brown into the hallway and up darkened stairs. Greg followed as closely as he could. They reached the top of the stairs, and Greg felt Lemon Brown's hand first lying on his shoulder, then probing down his arm until he finally took Greg's hand into his own as they crouched in the darkness.

D

beck·on (be´ kən) v., make a gesture to encourage someone to follow

"They's bad men," Lemon Brown whispered. His breath was warm against Greg's skin.

"Hey! Ragman!" a voice called. "We know you in here. What you got up under them rags? You got any money?"

E

Silence.

"We don't want to have to come in and hurt you, old man, but we don't mind if we have to."

Lemon Brown squeezed Greg's hand in his own hard, gnarled fist.

There was a banging downstairs and a light as the men entered. They banged around noisily, calling for the ragman.

"We heard you talking about your treasure." The voice was slurred. "We just want to see it, that's all."

"You sure he's here?" One voice seemed to come from the room with the sofa.

"Yeah, he stays here every night."

"There's another room over there; I'm going to take a look. You got that flashlight?"

"Yeah, here, take the pipe too."

Greg opened his mouth to quiet the sound of his breath as he sucked it in uneasily. A beam of light hit the wall a few feet opposite him, then went out.

"Ain't nobody in that room," a voice said. "You think he gone or something?"

"I don't know," came the answer. "All I know is that I heard him talking about some kind of treasure. You know they found that

---

3. thugs. Violent people; criminals

THE TREASURE OF LEMON BROWN **25**

Analyze Literature

Conflict Remind students that on the first page of the story, they made predictions about what the central conflict of the story would be. Now, as they read this paragraph, ask them if they would like to revise their ideas. Have them make any necessary changes. **D**

Cultural Connection

Homelessness In the United States, more than 3 million people are homeless, and that number is rising. Although there are many factors that can lead to homelessness, the main reason is economic. Like Lemon Brown, many homeless people are victims of "hard times." It is often a temporary situation resulting from a lost job, a lack of affordable housing, illness, or disability. The fastest-growing homeless population—about 35 percent—is made up of parents with children. Twenty percent are military veterans, and 30 percent are victims of domestic violence. Charitable organizations attempt to help the situation by providing free meals and overnight shelter. Many school groups help too, with food drives, blanket collections, and volunteer shifts at soup kitchens. You might ask students what they could do to help. **E**

Grammar Skills

Reflexive and Intensive Pronouns

Point out that a reflexive pronoun refers back to a noun or pronoun previously used and adds -self or -selves to another pronoun form. An intensive pronoun uses the same forms but immediately follows a noun or pronoun and is used only to add emphasis.

EXAMPLES

John bought *himself* a new jacket. (reflexive pronoun)

The president *himself* met with the students. (intensive pronoun)

Have students decide whether the italicized pronoun is reflexive or intensive.

1. I heard *myself* humming a familiar song. (reflexive)
2. If we *ourselves* do not take care of the environment, who will? (intensive)

Analyze Literature

Climax Review with students that the climax in a plot is the point of highest tension. As they read this page, ask them to be on the lookout for the climax. Once they have finished the page, discuss what events comprise the climax.

Use Reading Strategies

Make Predictions *Answer:* They will look for valuables in his "treasure," hurting the old man to get them if necessary. **A**

Use Reading Skills

Identify Author's Purpose Point out the all-capitals format of this line. Explain that authors sometimes use all capitals to indicate emphasis, and other times they use this format to indicate loudness. Then point out the use of italics (*could*) in the following paragraph. Lead students to understand that Myers uses the all-capital format to indicate that the men are shouting, and he uses the italic format to show emphasis. Model how each example might be spoken. **B**

Use Reading Strategies

Visualize Ask students to visualize this scene and explain what gave Greg the idea to howl like a ghost. **C**

Use Reading Skills

Draw Conclusions *Answer:* While Greg howls, Lemon Brown throws himself down the stairs directly at the thugs. Students may suggest that this was a very courageous move, but also reckless, since he could have seriously hurt himself. **D**

> **DURING READING**
> **Use Reading Strategies**
> **Make Predictions** What do you think the neighborhood thugs would do if they found Lemon Brown? **A**

Lemon Brown didn't move. Greg felt himself near panic.

> **DURING READING**
> **Use Reading Skills**
> **Draw Conclusions** What scares away the neighborhood thugs? How would you describe Lemon Brown's actions? **D**

shopping-bag lady with that money in her bags."

"Yeah. You think he's upstairs?"

B "HEY, OLD MAN, ARE YOU UP THERE?"

Silence.

"Watch my back, I'm going up."

There was a footstep on the stairs, and the beam from the flashlight danced crazily along the peeling wallpaper. Greg held his breath. There was another step and a loud crashing noise as the man banged the pipe against the wooden banister. Greg could feel his temples throb as the man slowly neared them. Greg thought about the pipe, wondering what he would do when the man reached them—what he *could* do.

Then Lemon Brown released his hand and moved toward the top of the stairs. Greg looked around and saw stairs going up to the next floor. He tried waving to Lemon Brown, hoping the old man would see him in the dim light and follow him to the next floor. Maybe, Greg thought, the man wouldn't follow them up there. Suddenly, though, Lemon Brown stood at the top of the stairs, both arms raised high above his head.

"There he is!" a voice cried from below.

"Throw down your money, old man, so I won't have to bash your head in!"

Lemon Brown didn't move. Greg felt himself near panic. The

C steps came closer, and still Lemon Brown didn't move. He was an eerie sight, a bundle of rags standing at the top of the stairs, his shadow on the wall looming over him. Maybe, the thought came to Greg, the scene could be even eerier.

Greg wet his lips, put his hands to his mouth, and tried to make a sound. Nothing came out. He swallowed hard, wet his lips once more, and howled as evenly as he could.

"*What's that?*"

As Greg howled, the light moved away from Lemon Brown, but not before Greg saw him hurl his body down the stairs at the men who had come to take his treasure. There was a crashing noise, and then footsteps. A rush of warm air came in as the downstairs door opened; then there was only an ominous[4] silence.

Greg stood on the landing. He listened, and after a while there was another sound on the staircase.

"Mr. Brown?" he called.

"Yeah, it's me," came the answer. "I got their flashlight."

---

4. ominous. Threatening; seeming to indicate that something bad will happen

---

Differentiated Instruction

English Language Learning

Help students learning English by asking language-proficient students to identify the meaning of the following phrases:

Watch my back, I'm going up—Be ready to protect me, because I'm going up the stairs., 26

bash your head in—wound you by hitting your head with a heavy object, 26

What's that?—What is that noise?, 26

You'd better leave—You should leave, 27

getting their nerve up to—gathering their courage to, 27

Greg exhaled in relief as Lemon Brown made his way slowly back up the stairs.

"You OK?"

"Few bumps and bruises," Lemon Brown said.

"I think I'd better be going," Greg said, his breath returning to normal. "You'd better leave, too, before they come back."

"They may hang around outside for a while," Lemon Brown said, "but they ain't getting their nerve up to come in here again. Not with crazy old ragmen and howling spooks. Best you stay awhile till the coast is clear. I'm heading out west tomorrow, out to East St. Louis."

"They were talking about treasures," Greg said. "You *really* have a treasure?"

"What I tell you? Didn't I tell you every man got a treasure?" Lemon Brown said. "You want to see mine?"

"If you want to show it to me," Greg shrugged.

"Let's look out the window first, see what them scoundrels be doing," Lemon Brown said.

They followed the oval beam of the flashlight into one of the rooms and looked out the window. They saw the men who had tried to take the treasure sitting on the curb near the corner. One of them had his pants leg up, looking at his knee.

"You sure you're not hurt?" Greg asked Lemon Brown.

"Nothing that ain't been hurt before," Lemon Brown said. "When you get as old as me, all you say when something hurts is, 'Howdy, Mr. Pain, sees you back again.' Then when Mr. Pain see he can't worry you none, he go on mess with somebody else."

Greg smiled.

> **DURING READING**
>
> **Use Reading Skills**
> **Draw Conclusions** What evidence is there in the story that Lemon Brown has begun to trust Greg? **E**

> **DURING READING**
>
> **Analyze Literature**
> **Character** What does this comment suggest about Lemon Brown's attitude about life? **F**

CULTURAL ▶▶ CONNECTION

Delta Blues The fictional musician Sweet Lemon Brown comes out of a real musical tradition known as Delta Blues, which originated in the Mississippi Delta, a region that lies in the northwest part of the state of Mississippi between the Mississippi and Yazoo rivers. The Delta Blues style appeared in the first decades of the twentieth century and then spread to other parts of the United States, such as Chicago and Detroit. Research the development and influence of the Delta Blues style. How were the lives of historical Delta Blues performers, such as Robert Johnson, Leadbelly, Muddy Waters, and Howlin' Wolf, similar to that of the fictional Sweet Lemon Brown? **G**

THE TREASURE OF LEMON BROWN **27**

Make Connections

Have students summarize the contents of Lemon Brown's "treasure." Are they surprised? Why might these things be so valuable to him? **A**

Use Reading Skills

Draw Conclusions *Answer:* Lemon Brown wanted to share with his son a part of his life that meant a lot to him and for which he had a measure of success and fame. Even though he wasn't able to always be there when his son was growing up, he wanted his son to understand who he was and to be proud of him. **B**

Use Reading Strategies

Make Inferences Ask students what Lemon Brown means, and have them suggest reasons why Greg doesn't really understand. **C**

Make Connections

Answer: Students should describe an item that has sentimental or emotional value. They should explain why this item was meaningful to the person who gave it to them. **D**

"Here, you hold this." Lemon Brown gave Greg the flashlight. He sat on the floor near Greg and carefully untied the strings that held the rags on his right leg. When he took the rags away, Greg saw a piece of plastic. The old man carefully took off the plastic **A** and unfolded it. He revealed some yellowed newspaper clippings and a battered harmonica.

"There it be," he said, nodding his head. "There it be."

Greg looked at the old man, saw the distant look in his eye, then turned to the clippings. They told of Sweet Lemon Brown, a blues singer and harmonica player who was appearing at different theaters in the South. One of the clippings said he had been the hit of the show, although not the headliner. All of the clippings were reviews of shows Lemon Brown had been in more than fifty years ago. Greg looked at the harmonica. It was dented badly on one side, with the reed holes on one end nearly closed.

"I used to travel around and make money for to feed my wife and Jesse—that's my boy's name. Used to feed them good, too. Then his mama died, and he stayed with his mama's sister. He growed up to be a man, and when the war come, he saw fit to go off and fight in it. I didn't have nothing to give him except these things that told him who I was, and what he come from. If you know your pappy did something, you know you can do something too.

"Anyway, he went off to war, and I went off still playing and singing. 'Course by then I wasn't as much as I used to be, not **C** without somebody to make it worth the while. You know what I mean?"

"Yeah," Greg nodded, not quite really knowing.

"I traveled around, and one time I come home, and there was this letter saying Jesse got killed in the war. Broke my heart, it truly did.

"They sent back what he had with him over there, and what it was is this old mouth fiddle and these clippings. Him carrying it around with him like that told me it meant something to him. That was my treasure, and when I give it to him, he treated it just like that, a treasure. Ain't that something?"

"Yeah, I guess so," Greg said.

"You *guess* so?" Lemon Brown's voice rose an octave[5] as he started to put his treasure back into the plastic. "Well, you got to guess, 'cause you sure don't know nothing. Don't know enough to get home when it's raining."

---

5. octave. Series of eight notes occupying the interval between (and including) two notes

> **DURING READING**
>
> **Use Reading Skills**
> **Draw Conclusions** What do you think Lemon Brown was trying to pass on to his son by giving him those articles? **B**

> **DURING READING**
>
> **Make Connections**
> What have you received that you consider a "treasure" even though it may not have great monetary value? **D**

Dialect

Point out to students that Lemon Brown uses dialect, a way of speaking that differs from standard English and is usually associated with a specific geographical area or group of people. Dialect has its own vocabulary, punctuation, grammar, and expressions. As an example, write this sentence on the board: "Don't try nothin', 'cause I got a razor here sharp enough to cut a week into nine days!"

Model rewording the sentence: "Don't try anything because I have a really sharp razor!" Then, discuss the reworded sentence's effect on tone.

"I guess ... I mean, you're right."

"You OK for a youngster," the old man said as he tied the strings around his leg, "better than those scalawags[6] what come here looking for my treasure. That's for sure."

"You really think that treasure of yours was worth fighting for?" Greg asked. "Against a pipe?"

"What else a man got 'cepting what he can pass on to his son, or his daughter, if she be his oldest?" Lemon Brown said. "For a big-headed boy, you sure do ask the foolishest questions."

Lemon Brown got up after patting his rags in place and looked out the window again.

"Looks like they're gone. You get on out of here and get yourself home. I'll be watching from the window, so you'll be all right."

Lemon Brown went down the stairs behind Greg. When they reached the front door, the old man looked out first, saw the street was clear, and told Greg to scoot on home.

"You sure you'll be OK?" Greg asked.

"Now, didn't I tell you I was going to East St. Louis in the morning?" Lemon Brown asked. "Don't that sound OK to you?"

"Sure it does," Greg said. "Sure it does. And you take care of that treasure of yours."

"That I'll do," Lemon said, the wrinkles about his eyes suggesting a smile. "That I'll do."

The night had warmed and the rain had stopped, leaving puddles at the curbs. Greg didn't even want to think how late it was. He thought ahead of what his father would say and wondered if he should tell him about Lemon Brown. He thought about it until he reached his stoop, and decided against it. Lemon Brown would be OK, Greg thought, with his memories and his treasure.

Greg pushed the button over the bell marked "Ridley," thought of the lecture he knew his father would give him, and smiled. ❖

DURING READING

Analyze Literature
Character Why do you think Greg smiled when he thought of the lecture he'd get from his father? **F**

---

6. **scalawags.** People who behave badly

The fact that Lemon Brown's son had kept his "treasure" with him meant a lot to the old man. If you had a family member who was going off to war and wanted to give him or her some kind of treasure, what would it be? Why? What makes such "treasure" valuable?

Analyze Literature
Characterization Lead students to understand the difference between the two characters in this passage. Greg doesn't initially see the treasure's value. He's not sure it is worth fighting for. Have them analyze Lemon's response and describe why it is so valuable to him. **E**

Analyze Literature

Character *Answer:* Students may suggest that after hearing Lemon Brown's story, Greg has become more appreciative of his relationship with his father and his father's concerns for his future. Because of the changes he has undergone by the end of the story, Greg is clearly a dynamic character. **F**

MIRRORS & WINDOWS *Answer:* Students will probably list personal items or mementoes that are of significance to them. They should explain why they consider such items as "treasures" and why they believe it would help people to remember them.

Writing Skills

Audience Awareness

Before students begin the Writing Options projects, review the importance of planning one's writing so that it effectively targets one's audience.

For the Creative Writing project, explain that the audience is made up of newspaper readers with knowledge of and interest in music. Guide students to think about what the audience might already know about blues music and would be interested in learning about Lemon Brown's music. Ask them how they might get their ideas across and what type of language would be most appropriate.

For the Expository Writing project, explain that the audience is the writer's classmates. Guide students in planning and writing effective compare-and-contrast essays that specifically deal with each character and that use appropriate language to hold the interest of their intended audience.

Review the Model

Find Meaning

1. He feels that improving Greg's grades is more important and worries about Greg's poor math grade.
2. (a) He wants to avoid his father's disapproval and insistence that he study math. (b) He hears a noise that he can't identify, and then he hears someone breathing.
3. Lemon Brown challenges Greg because he is fearful that Greg might want to hurt him.
4. (a) The thugs want the "treasure" they have heard about. (b) He throws himself down the stairs toward them.

Make Judgments

5. (a) Greg is wary of the old man. (b) Greg feels sympathetic toward Lemon Brown and is inspired by his outlook on life.
6. The items in his "treasure" represent a much happier time in his life. He was very moved that his son kept these items with him until he died. Now they are all he has left of his past and his son.
7. Lemon Brown's character is enriched by his regional dialect and colorful expressions.

Analyze Literature

Character *Answer:* Students should include examples of the author's descriptions of Lemon Brown's appearance, behavior (including his colorful language), and relationships with other people (including the change in his perception of Greg). Make sure students describe how their impressions of Lemon Brown changed by the end of the story.

Find Meaning

1. Why doesn't Greg's father want him to play on the basketball team?
2. (a) Why does Greg go into the abandoned tenement building? (b) What makes him nervous inside the tenement?
3. Why does Lemon Brown claim to have a razor that could "cut a week into nine days"?
4. (a) What do the neighborhood thugs want from Lemon Brown? (b) What does Lemon Brown do to scare them away?

Analyze Literature

Character Author Walter Dean Myers has a gift for creating compelling, realistic characters. In "The Treasure of Lemon Brown," he uses physical descriptions, dialogue, and action to develop his characters. Create a character chart for Sweet Lemon Brown. Skim the story and note any vivid descriptions of the character or dialogue that help you understand Lemon Brown.

Make Judgments

5. (a) How would you describe Greg's attitude about Lemon Brown when they first meet? (b) How do Greg's feelings about him change by the end of the story?
6. Why is Lemon Brown's treasure so meaningful to the old man?
7. How does the author use dialogue to make Lemon Brown a more interesting character?

	Appearance	Behaviors	Relationships with Others
Description	Old, black wrinkly face with white crinkly hair; dressed in layers of coats and rags		
Analysis			

Extend Understanding

Writing Options

Creative Writing Imagine you are a music reviewer for a newspaper at the time when Lemon Brown was playing the blues. Write a **review** of one of his performances. Include photographs and biographical information. Share the review with the class.

Expository Writing Lemon Brown had many tough experiences in his life, as had Greg's father. Write an **essay** in which you compare and contrast the experiences and attitudes of the two men. Share your essay with the class.

Collaborative Learning

Homelessness in America Working in small groups, discuss the problem of homelessness in this country. Find some ways you can address this problem. Share your research with the class.

Lifelong Learning

Create Concert Posters Use the Internet to locate blues musicians from the early twentieth century. Create posters that could have been used to promote the performers.

MW Go to www.mirrorsandwindows.com for more.

Rubrics for Writing Options

You can adapt this as a checklist for students to use as they write.

Creative Writing

☐ Does the review appear in an appropriate form?
☐ Does it contain details from the story regarding Lemon Brown?
☐ Does it contain factual information related to the time period and type of music reviewed?

Expository Writing

☐ Does the essay accurately identify similarities between the experiences of Lemon Brown and Greg's father?
☐ Does the essay clearly contrast the differences between the two men?

Grammar & Style

Subject-Verb Agreement

Identifying Subject-Verb Agreement

The old man named Lemon Brown lives in an abandoned building.

In the sentence above, the subject "man" is singular. A verb must agree with the subject in number. Number refers to whether the subject is singular or plural. If the subject is singular, the verb must also be singular. If the subject is plural, the verb must also be plural. Therefore, the singular subject "man" needs the singular verb "lives."

> EXAMPLE
> *The walls of the building are covered with graffiti.*

In this example, the subject and verb are separated by a prepositional phrase. The prepositional phrase "of the building" modifies the subject, "walls." The subject is plural, so the verb, "are," is also plural. If you are not sure of the subject-verb agreement in a sentence with a prepositional phrase, try rewriting the sentence without it.

Fixing Subject-Verb Agreement

> INCORRECT
> *One of the three men carry a length of pipe.*

In the sentence above, the verb "carry" agrees with "men," the noun it follows. "Men" is not the subject of the sentence, however, but is part of a prepositional phrase, "of the three men." The subject of the sentence is "one," which is singular. The verb "carry" is plural. To fix the sentence, change the verb to "carries," the singular form.

> CORRECT
> *One of the three men <u>carries</u> a length of pipe.*

> EXAMPLE
> *Lemon Brown frighten͜ the three men away.* ^s

In this example, the subject, "Lemon Brown," is singular, but the verb, "frighten," is plural. To fix the sentence, change the verb to "frightens," the singular form.

Sentence Improvement

For each of the following sentences, select the response that indicates the best revision.

1. Gusts of wind makes bits of paper dance between the parked cars.
   A. Gusts of wind make bits of paper dance between the parked cars.
   B. Gust of wind make bits of paper dance between the parked cars.
   C. Gusts of winds makes bits of paper dance between the parked cars.
   D. no change

2. Old newspaper clippings and a harmonica are the treasure of Lemon Brown.
   A. Old newspaper clippings and a harmonica is the treasure of Lemon Brown.
   B. Old newspaper clipping and a harmonica is the treasure of Lemon Brown.
   C. Old newspaper clippings and a harmonica is the treasures of Lemon Brown.
   D. no change

For each of the following sentences, select the subject that agrees with the verb.

3. The (light/lights) from the street lamps shines through the dirty windows.
4. The (tire/tires) of a car hiss over the wet street.
5. Some (rope/ropes) around his middle holds up Lemon Brown's ragged clothes.
6. The old newspaper (clipping/clippings) tells of blues singer Sweet Lemon Brown.

Sentence Improvement
1. A. Gusts of wind make bits of paper dance between the parked cars.
2. D. no change
3. light
4. tires
5. rope
6. clipping

> For more information, see Grammar & Style Section 3.7, Agreement, in the Language Arts Handbook.

Program Resources

You will find additional lessons on Subject-Verb Agreement in the *Exceeding the Standards: Grammar & Style* resource.

Build Skills

Some students might think that the *s* in third-person singular verbs creates a "plural verb." Tell students that a verb with an *s* almost always goes with a singular subject. As examples, run through several examples of first-person, second-person, and third-person singular and plural regular verbs. Have students listen for the *s*. For instance:
- I sing, you sing, he sings; we sing, you sing, they sing
- I eat, you eat, she eats; we eat, you eat, they eat

KEY TERMS
SUBJECT, 31
VERB, 31
PREPOSITIONAL PHRASE, 31

TEACHING NOTE

Extra Practice

Each of the following sentences has a prepositional phrase between the subject and the verb. Give students the sentences, and have them choose the correct form of the verb.

1. The guards at the museum (<u>protect</u>/protects) the collection.
2. The librarian, along with two aides, (hope/<u>hopes</u>) to attend the workshop.
3. The students in this school (<u>love</u>/loves) putting on shows.
4. The chapters at the beginning of this book (<u>grab</u>/grabs) a reader's attention.

Common Core State Standards
Reading Literature
RL.1
Language
L.3.1f

Understanding Setting
Reading strategies and skills that can help students understand setting include visualizing and drawing conclusions.

Use Reading Strategies

Visualize Point out to students that in many stories, the details of the physical setting create a powerful visual impression. Ask them to describe the main visual effect of the following passage from Joseph Conrad's short story "The Lagoon":

"The narrow creek was like a ditch: tortuous, fabulously deep; filled with gloom under the thin strip of pure and shining blue of the heaven. Immense trees soared up, invisible behind the festooned draperies of creepers. Here and there, near the glistening blackness of the water, a twisted root of some tall tree showed amongst the tracery of small ferns, black and dull, writhing and motionless, like an arrested snake."

Use Reading Skills

Draw Conclusions Ask students to consider how the plot of a story might be conditioned by the setting. Ask them to imagine a possible plot for a story that had the following settings:
- an arctic wasteland
- a rundown city street
- a tropical rain forest
- an airplane in flight

Understanding Setting

What Is Setting?
Where was this picture taken? What season or time of day does it show? What details in the picture are you using to answer these questions? These details relate to the setting of the picture. In the same way, writers use details of setting to tell a reader when and where the events of a story are taking place. The **setting** of a literary work is the time and place in which it happens. Setting can affect elements in the story such as tone and mood.

Setting in Fiction
Writers create setting in many different ways. Setting can be revealed through imagery in descriptive passages, but it can also be developed through action and dialogue. In fiction, setting is most often revealed through descriptions of the following:

- seasons and weather
- landscapes, cities, and towns
- buildings and vehicles
- furniture and clothing

In the passage at right, what type of details does the writer use to create setting?

Setting and Community
Setting can also be revealed by how characters talk and behave. Note details that characters reveal through their dialogue. Note also *how* characters talk to identify where and when the story occurs.

Setting and Mood
Setting is an important element in the creation of **mood,** or atmosphere, which is the feeling or emotion created by a literary work. How would you describe the mood created by the details of setting in the passage from "A Mother in Mannville"?

> *The orphanage is high in the Carolina mountains. Sometimes in winter the snowdrifts are so deep that the institution is cut off from the village below, from all the world. Fog hides the mountain peaks, the snow swirls down the valleys, and a wind blows so bitterly that the orphanage boys who take the milk twice daily to the baby cottage reach the door with fingers stiff in an agony of numbness.*
>
> —MARJORIE KINNAN RAWLINGS, "A Mother in Mannville"

32 UNIT 1 FICTION

To help students explore literature on a deeper level, assign the following activity: Independent Novel Study: Setting, *Exceeding the Standards: Literature & Reading*, pp. 1–5.

Common Core State Standards

Reading Literature
RL.4

Words in Use

Teaching Words
elements, 32
descriptive, 32
landscapes, 32

KEY TERMS
SETTING, 32
IMAGERY, 32
DIALOGUE, 32
MOOD, 32

A Mother in Mannville

A Short Story by Marjorie Kinnan Rawlings

Apply the Model
- BEFORE READING
- DURING READING
- AFTER READING

Preview the Model

At a Glance
Guided Reading: Reading Model
- Reading Level: Moderate
- Difficulty Consideration: Vocabulary
- Ease Factor: Tangible descriptions

Build Background
Historical Context During the Great Depression of the 1930s, people throughout the world suffered terrible financial losses. Therefore, if parents could not provide for their children, they often sent them to orphanages. Many children grew up there. Others were luckier. When their parents found jobs and could care for their children, they came and reclaimed them.

Reader's Context Most orphanages at this time were crowded, and life there was often grim. Try to imagine yourself in such conditions. What would be your greatest needs and hopes for the future?

Set Purpose
Skim the first two paragraphs. Watch for sensory details that help you to "see and hear" important details about the characters and the setting.

Analyze Literature
Setting The **setting** of a story is the time and place in which it happens. The **time** of this story is the 1930s, during the Great Depression. The **place** is rural North Carolina. As you read, think about how the setting affects the plot events and the thoughts, feelings, and needs of the characters.

Use Reading Skills
Context Clues Preview the vocabulary words from this selection as they are used in the sentences below. Try to unlock the meaning of each word, using the context clues provided in each sentence.

1. The image of my favorite park appeared in my mind with such <u>clarity</u> that I could see every detail.
2. Fifteen minutes is not a <u>sufficient</u> amount of time to study for a unit test.
3. Since he had just won the game, Sam's sad reaction seemed <u>anomalous</u>.

Preview Vocabulary
in·ad·e·quate (in ad´ e kwət) *adj.*, lacking in quality; not equal to what is required

clar·i·ty (kler´ e tē) *n.*, state of being clear

pred·i·cat·ed (pred´ i kāt əd) *adj.*, affirmed, or based, on given facts or conditions

suf·fi·cient (sə fi´ shənt) *adj.*, as much as is needed; enough

a·nom·a·lous (ə nä´ mə ləs) *adj.*, strange, abnormal, or irregular

Objectives
Studying this lesson will enable students to
- use reading skills such as context clues
- define *setting* as the time and place in which a story takes place, and understand how setting affects plot
- describe the literary accomplishments of Marjorie Kinnan Rawlings and the role of regionalism in her writing
- appreciate a story about friendship, truth, and giving

Launch the Lesson
Tell students that they are about to read "A Mother in Mannville," a story about a friendship between a young orphan boy and a woman who hires him to do odd jobs. Draw a circle for the center of a cluster diagram and label it *give-and-take*. Point out that this expression stands for the sharing that takes place between friends. Ask students to give you examples of "give-and-take" in their friendships. Offer a model such as "listening carefully to each other." Then, have them read to find other examples in the story.

Meet the Author
Marjorie Kinnan Rawlings (1896–1953) wrote her first story at the age of eleven and published it in the *Washington Post*, a large metropolitan newspaper. In 1928, she moved to a remote farmhouse and orange grove in Cross Creek, Florida, where she wrote fiction that focuses on the characters and rural settings she had come to love. In 1939, Rawlings won the Pulitzer Prize for her novel *The Yearling*.

Words in Use

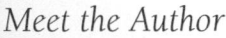

Preview Vocabulary	Selection Words	Teaching Words
inadequate, 36	agony, 35	depression, 33
clarity, 37	hemlocks, 35	orphanages, 33
predicated, 38	mangled, 36	sensory, 33
sufficient, 39	suffused, 37	rural, 33
anomalous, 42		distress, 40
		communion, 44
		thesis, 44

KEY TERMS
SETTING, 33
CONTEXT CLUE, 33
SENSORY DETAIL, 44
CLUSTER CHART, 44
NARRATOR, 44
PLOT, 44
RESOLUTION, 44

Common Core State Standards
Reading Literature
RL.1, RL.3
Writing
W.9, W.10
Language
L.6

Summary

When she comes to live in a rustic cabin in the North Carolina mountains, a writer becomes friendly with Jerry, a young boy from a local orphanage, whom she pays to do odd jobs. She admires Jerry for his hard work and honesty and for the sweet and gentle friendship that develops between him and her dog. Jerry comes to the cabin often and finds excuses to spend quiet, friendly time with her. Then, one day, he tells her that he has a mother living in a nearby town. The writer becomes extremely angry that a mother would desert her son. However, when she stops by the orphanage as she is leaving town, she learns that Jerry has made up the story.

MIRRORS & WINDOWS

The Mirrors & Windows questions at the end of this selection focus on the theme of truth. Before reading the story, ask students what emotions they might experience upon learning that a friend's life is not what he or she made it out to be. What do they imagine could drive a person to lie about his or her circumstances?

Apply the Model

BEFORE READING

DURING READING

AFTER READING

A Mother in Mannville

A Short Story by Marjorie Kinnan Rawlings

34

Program Resources

Planning and Assessment
Program Planning Guide, Selection Lesson Plan
E-Lesson Planner
Assessment Guide, Lesson Test
ExamView

Technology Tools
Interactive Student Text on CD
Visual Teaching Package
Audio Library
mirrorsandwindows.com

Meeting the Standards
Fiction: Unit 1, Guided Reading, pp. 32–36

Differentiating Instruction
English Language Learners, Use Context Clues, pp. 12–25

The orphanage is high in the Carolina mountains. Sometimes in winter the snowdrifts are so deep that the institution is cut off from the village below, from all the world. Fog hides the mountain peaks, the snow swirls down the valleys, and a wind blows so bitterly that the orphanage boys who take the milk twice daily to the baby cottage reach the door with fingers stiff in an agony of numbness.

"Or when we carry trays from the cookhouse for the ones that are sick," Jerry said, "we get our faces frostbit, because we can't put our hands over them. I have gloves," he added. "Some of the boys don't have any."

He liked the late spring, he said. The rhododendron[1] was in bloom, a carpet of color, across the mountainsides, soft as the May winds that stirred the hemlocks. He called it laurel.

"It's pretty when the laurel blooms," he said. "Some of it's pink and some of it's white."

I was there in the autumn. I wanted quiet, isolation, to do some troublesome writing. I wanted mountain air to blow out the malaria[2] from too long a time in the subtropics. I was homesick, too, for the flaming of maples in October, and for corn shocks and pumpkins and black-walnut trees and the lift of hills. I found them all, living in a cabin that belonged to the orphanage, half a mile beyond the orphanage farm. When I took the cabin, I asked for a boy or man to come and chop wood for the fireplace. The first few days were warm, I found what wood I needed about the cabin, no one came, and I forgot the order.

I looked up from my typewriter one late afternoon, a little startled. A boy stood at the door, and my pointer dog,[3] my companion, was at his side and had not barked to warn me. The boy was probably twelve years old, but undersized. He wore overalls and a torn shirt, and was barefooted.

He said, "I can chop some wood today."

I said, "But I have a boy coming from the orphanage."

"I'm the boy."

"You? But you're small."

"Size don't matter, chopping wood," he said. "Some of the big boys don't chop good. I've been chopping wood at the orphanage a long time."

---

1. **rhododendron.** Type of shrub or tree with alternate leaves and large clusters of bright flowers
2. **malaria.** Serious disease transmitted by the bite of a certain type of mosquito
3. **pointer dog.** Short-haired, muscular hunting dog, known for its ability to help a human hunter find prey by standing erect, with its head and body pointed in the direction of the prey

A MOTHER IN MANNVILLE **35**

> **DURING READING**
> **Analyze Literature**
> **Setting** How do the location and the time of year affect the characters? **A**

> A boy stood at the door, and my pointer dog, my companion, was at his side and had not barked to warn me.

> **DURING READING**
> **Use Reading Strategies**
> **Visualize** What picture do you have of the boy, based on the sensory details that describe him? **C**

> **DURING READING**
> **Analyze Literature**
> **Characterization** What do the boy's words suggest about his feelings? **D**

Teach the Model

Analyze Literature
Setting *Answer:* The opening paragraphs are set high in the mountains in the winter. It is very cold, with swirling snow. The orphans are rarely warm, and their fingers and faces often get frozen. **A**

Analyze Literature
Foreshadowing Point out to students that foreshadowing is the act of hinting at events or situations that will occur later on. Readers can use foreshadowing to make predictions. Model by drawing attention to the highlighted passage. Point out that it gives a hint that the dog and the boy have instantly established a sense of trust. This helps readers predict that they will develop a deep friendship. **B**

Use Reading Strategies
Visualize *Answer:* He is about twelve, but he is small for his age. He wears ragged clothes, and he is barefooted. **C**

Analyze Literature
Characterization *Answer:* He is proud of his abilities, and he feels that being short is not a problem. He can chop better than the bigger boys. **D**

Differentiated Instruction

Reading Proficiency
Students may benefit from hearing the story read aloud. Ask them to listen for descriptions of setting. Then instruct students to read the selection on their own.

English Language Learning
Students learning English may need help understanding words and expressions such as these:
cut off — separated from, 35
flaming of maples — brightly colored leaves of the maple trees in the fall, 35
a little blunt — abrupt or impolite, 36

Analyze Literature

Characterization Direct students' attention to this passage. Ask them to determine if what they are reading is direct or indirect characterization (indirect) and to explain why. Point out that the narrator is revealing certain aspects of herself through her description of her own thoughts, actions, and words. Model a response such as "The narrator's description of her thoughts reveals that, at this point, she doesn't expect much from people." Remind students that while some characters maintain the same outlook throughout a story, others gain new perspective. **(A)**

Geography Connection

Appalachian Mountains Part of the Appalachian mountain chain, the Blue Ridge Mountains and the Great Smoky Mountains tower over the western portion of North Carolina. Both ranges have rugged, densely forested peaks. Mt. Mitchell, the highest (6,684 feet), is the tallest mountain east of the Mississippi River. Winter in the mountains is often severe, but springtime brings an abundance of flowering trees and shrubs, including rhododendron, dogwood, redbud, and mountain laurel. **(B)**

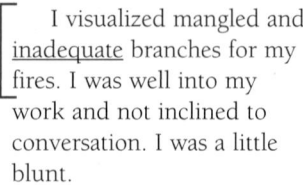

in·ad·e·quate
(in ad′ e kwət) *adj.*, lacking in quality; not equal to what is required

(A) I visualized mangled and inadequate branches for my fires. I was well into my work and not inclined to conversation. I was a little blunt.

"Very well. There's the ax. Go ahead and see what you can do."

I went back to work, closing the door. At first the sound of the boy dragging brush annoyed me. Then he began to chop. The blows were rhythmic and steady, and shortly I had forgotten him, the sound no more of an interruption than a consistent rain. I suppose an hour and a half passed, for when I stopped and stretched, and heard the boy's steps on the cabin stoop, **(B)** the sun was dropping behind the farthest mountain, and the valleys were purple with something deeper than the asters.

The boy said, "I have to go to supper now. I can come again tomorrow evening."

I said, "I'll pay you now for what you've done," thinking I should probably have to insist on an older boy. "Ten cents an hour?"

"Anything is all right."

We went together back of the cabin. An astonishing amount of solid wood had been cut. There were cherry logs and heavy roots of rhododendron, and blocks from the waste pine and oak left from the building of the cabin.

36 UNIT 1 FICTION

Auditory Learning

Ask students to describe the sounds that they "hear" in this passage. Why might the sound of the boy dragging brush annoy the writer? Why might the "rhythmic and steady" blows of his axe seem like the sounds of steady rain? Then ask students to think about background noises that they have encountered while trying to concentrate on writing or some other task. Which sounds were annoying? Which sounds could they gradually get used to and even ignore?

"But you've done as much as a man," I said. "This is a splendid pile."

I looked at him, actually, for the first time. His hair was the color of the corn shocks and his eyes, very direct, were like the mountain sky when rain is pending—gray, with a shadowing of that miraculous blue. As I spoke, a light came over him, as though the setting sun had touched him with the same suffused glory with which it touched the mountains. I gave him a quarter.

"You may come tomorrow," I said, "and thank you very much."

He looked at me, and at the coin, and seemed to want to speak, but could not, and turned away.

"I'll split kindling[4] tomorrow," he said over his thin, ragged shoulder. "You'll need kindling and medium wood and logs and backlogs."

At daylight I was half-wakened by the sound of chopping. Again it was so even in texture that I went back to sleep. When I left my bed in the cool morning, the boy had come and gone, and a stack of kindling was neat against the cabin wall. He came again after school in the afternoon and worked until time to return to the orphanage. His name was Jerry; he was twelve years old, and he had been at the orphanage since he was four. I could picture him at four, with the same grave gray-blue eyes and the same—independence? No, the word that comes to me is "integrity."

The word means something very special to me, and the quality for which I use it is a rare one. My father had it—there is another of whom I am almost sure—but almost no man of my acquaintance possesses it with the <u>clarity</u>, the purity, the simplicity of a mountain stream. But the boy Jerry had it. It is bedded on courage, but it is more than brave. It is honest, but it is more than honesty. The ax handle broke one day. Jerry said the woodshop at the orphanage would repair it. I brought money to pay for the job and he refused it.

---

4. kindling. Sticks and other thin pieces of wood used to start a fire

> **DURING READING**
>
> **Use Reading Skills**
> **Context Clues** What does the word *pending* mean? **D**

clar·i·ty (kler´ e tē) *n.,* the state of being clear

> **DURING READING**
>
> **Use Reading Skills**
> **Context Clues** What do the narrator's words suggest about the meaning of *integrity*? **E**

A MOTHER IN MANNVILLE **37**

Vocabulary Skills

Examples as Context Clues

Remind students that an author sometimes indicates the meaning of a word by providing an example. Ask them to use example clues to define the boldfaced words in the following sentences.

1. Attending the banquet were several *dignitaries*, including political leaders and movie personalities. (people considered important because of their position in society)

2. Of Benjamin Franklin's many *adages*, my favorite is "A penny saved is a penny earned." (short declarations that express general truths)

3. Manny has many *idiosyncrasies*, such as humming while he eats. (behaviors specific to individuals)

Use Context Clues Direct students' attention to this passage. Ask them to infer the meaning of the phrase "He was standing back of his own carelessness," based on the text surrounding it. Then challenge them to do the same with the phrase "He was a free-will agent." **A**

Use Reading Strategies

Visualize Ask students to describe the picture that they have in their minds regarding the cubbyhole and its contents. **B**

Make Connections

Answer: Students will probably say that he wants affection and warmth; he wants the narrator to act like a mother. **C**

TEACHING NOTE

Collaborative Learning

Have students work with partners. Ask partners to work together to reread the story to this point. Have them ask questions about the relationship between the narrator and Jerry. Model by suggesting such questions as, "How did the relationship begin? What were the narrator's initial thoughts about Jerry? What surprised her and changed her mind? What new task did Jerry just complete, all on his own?" Have partners work together to ask and answer questions. Then have them summarize how the relationship between the narrator and Jerry has grown and changed.

pred•i•cat•ed
(pred´ i kāt əd) *adj.*, affirmed, or based on given facts or conditions

"I'll pay for it," he said. "I broke it. I brought the ax down careless."

"But no one hits accurately every time," I told him. "The fault was in the wood of the handle. I'll see the man from whom I bought it."

A It was only then that he would take the money. He was standing back of his own carelessness. He was a free-will agent and he chose to do careful work, and if he failed, he took the responsibility without subterfuge.[5]

And he did for me the unnecessary thing, the gracious thing, that we find done only by the great of heart. Things no training can teach, for they are done on the instant, with no predicated experience. **B** He found a cubbyhole beside the fireplace that I had not noticed. There, of his own accord, he put kindling and "medium" wood, so that I might always have dry fire material ready in case of sudden wet weather. A stone was loose in the rough walk to the cabin. He dug a deeper hole and steadied it, although he came, himself, by a short cut over the bank. I found that when I tried to return his thoughtfulness with such things as candy and apples, he was wordless. "Thank you" was, perhaps, an expression for which he had had no use, for his courtesy was instinctive. He only looked at the gift and at me, and a curtain lifted, so that I saw deep into the clear well of his eyes, and gratitude was there, and affection, soft over the firm granite of his character.

He made simple excuses to come and sit with me. I could no more have turned him away than if he had been physically hungry. I suggested once that the best time for us to visit was just before supper, when I left off my writing. After that, he waited always until my typewriter[6] had been some time quiet. One day I worked until nearly dark. I went outside the cabin, having forgotten him. I saw him going up over the hill in the twilight toward the orphanage.

> **DURING READING**
>
> **Make Connections**
> What feelings lead Jerry to make excuses to sit near the narrator? **C**

---

5. subterfuge. Deception; dishonesty
6. typewriter. Machine for creating written materials in printed form, used prior to the invention of computers and word processing

Grammar Skills

To, Two, and *Too*

Remind students that *to* is a preposition that can mean "in the direction of." *Two* is the spelling of the number 2. *Too* is an adverb that means both "extremely" and "also." Have students complete each of these sentences correctly, using *to, two,* or *too.*

1. We moved to Texas when I was (two).
2. Is it (too) cold for a picnic today?
3. Al is invited, and Sharon is, (too).
4. Please take this gift (to) Ramon.

When I sat down on my stoop, a place was warm from his body where he had been sitting.

He became intimate, of course, with my pointer, Pat. There is a strange communion between a boy and a dog. Perhaps they possess the same singleness of spirit, the same kind of wisdom. It is difficult to explain, but it exists. When I went across the state for a weekend, I left the dog in Jerry's charge. I gave him the dog whistle and the key to the cabin, and left <u>sufficient</u> food. He was to come two or three times a day and let out the dog, and feed and exercise him. I should return Sunday night, and Jerry would take out the dog for the last time Sunday afternoon and then leave the key under an agreed hiding place.

My return was belated and fog filled the mountain passes so treacherously that I dared not drive at night. The fog held the next morning, and it was Monday noon before I reached the cabin. The dog had been fed and cared for that morning. Jerry came early in the afternoon, anxious.

"The superintendent said nobody would drive in the fog," he said. "I came just before bedtime last night and you hadn't come. So I brought Pat some of my breakfast this morning. I wouldn't have let anything happen to him."

"I was sure of that. I didn't worry."

"When I heard about the fog, I thought you'd know."

He was needed for work at the orphanage and he had to return at once. I gave him a dollar in payment, and he looked at it and went away. But that night he came in the darkness and knocked at the door.

"Come in, Jerry," I said, "if you're allowed to be away this late."

"I told maybe a story," he said. "I told them I thought you would want to see me."

"That's true," I assured him, and I saw his relief. "I want to hear about how you managed with the dog."

He sat by the fire with me, with no other light, and told me of their two days together. The dog lay close to him, and found

---

Teach the Model

Use Reading Skills
Context Clues *Answer:* In this sentence *communion* means "a deep, warm sense of understanding and friendship." **D**

Analyze Literature
Setting *Answer:* The fog prevents the narrator from getting home on time. Without being asked to do so, Jerry steps in to take care of the dog until she returns home. This action draws Jerry closer to the narrator, leading to his revelation about his mother. **E**

Analyze Literature
Characterization Remind students that a character's words, actions, and thoughts often reveal information about the character. Model this by pointing out that Jerry told a lie at the orphanage in order to be allowed to visit the narrator late at night. This action shows that he felt a great need to see her. Then have students read her response and his reaction to it. What do these words suggest about the narrator, and what does Jerry's reaction suggest about him? **F**

Reading Skills

Draw Conclusions

Remind students that drawing conclusions means gathering pieces of information and then deciding to what truth, or conclusion, that information leads. For example, point out Jerry's words: "I'll pay for it," he said. "I broke it. I brought the ax down careless." Model a conclusion based on this piece of information: "Jerry is very responsible and honest." Then ask students to tell what conclusions can be drawn about Jerry, and about the writer's feelings for Jerry, from information in the following sentence: "And he did for me the unnecessary thing, the gracious thing, that we find done only by the great of heart."

Analyze Literature

Rising Action Help students understand that Jerry's statement about having a mother and the narrator's strong response are significant to the rising action of this story. The relationship has grown to a point that Jerry now treats the narrator as a mother and the narrator cares for him as a mother would. Therefore, the revelation that he has a real mother, who has deserted him, creates great tension in the story. Ask students to identify other examples of tension in the story's rising action. **Ⓐ**

Analyze Literature

Character Motivation *Answer:* She is furious that a woman would desert her child. **Ⓑ**

> I was filled with a passionate resentment that any woman should go away and leave her son.

DURING READING

Analyze Literature
Character Motivation
What causes the narrator to feel such distress and anger?
Ⓑ

a comfort there that I did not have for him. And it seemed to me that being with my dog, and caring for him, had brought the boy and me, too, together, so that he felt that he belonged to me as well as to the animal.

"He stayed right with me," he told me, "except when he ran in the laurel. He likes the laurel. I took him up over the hill and we both ran fast. There was a place where the grass was high and I lay down in it and hid. I could hear Pat hunting for me. He found my trail and he barked. When he found me, he acted crazy, and he ran around and around me, in circles."

We watched the flames.

"That's an apple log," he said. "It burns the prettiest of any wood."

We were very close.

He was suddenly impelled[7] to speak of things he had not spoken of before, nor had I cared to ask him.

"You look a little bit like my mother," he said. "Especially in the dark, by the fire."

"But you were only four, Jerry, when you came here. You have remembered how she looked, all these years?"

"My mother lives in Mannville," he said.

For a moment, finding that he had a mother shocked me as greatly as anything in my life has ever done, and I did not know why it disturbed me. Then I understood my distress. I was filled with a passionate resentment[8] that any woman should go away and leave her son. A fresh anger added itself. A son like this one—The orphanage was a wholesome place, the executives were kind, good people, the food was more than adequate, the boys were healthy, a ragged shirt was no hardship, nor the doing of clean labor. Granted, perhaps, that the boy felt no lack, what blood fed the bowels of a woman who did not yearn over this child's lean body that had come in parturition[9] out of her own? At four he would have looked the same as now. Nothing, I thought, nothing in life could change those eyes. His quality must be apparent to an idiot, a fool. I burned with

---

7. **impelled.** Urged or driven, as if by strong moral or emotional feelings
8. **passionate resentment.** Very strong feelings of anger or annoyance
9. **parturition.** Childbirth

Differentiated Instruction

English Language Learning

Students learning English may need extra help understanding this sentence: "The human mind scatters its interests as though made of thistledown, and every wind stirs and moves it." You might display a picture of a thistle, milkweed, or dandelion seedpod, pointing out the many feathery seeds that easily scatter away on the wind. Have students share their knowledge of that process. Then make the connection between it and the author's image of scattered thoughts and interests.

questions I could not ask. In any case, I was afraid, there would be pain.

"Have you seen her, Jerry—lately?"

"I see her every summer. She sends for me."

I wanted to cry out, "Why are you not with her? How can she let you go away again?"

He said, "She comes up here from Mannville whenever she can. She doesn't have a job now."

His face shone in the firelight.

"She wanted to give me a puppy, but they can't let any one boy keep a puppy. You remember the suit I had on last Sunday?" He was plainly proud. "She sent me that for Christmas. The Christmas before that"—he drew a long breath, savoring the memory—"she sent me a pair of skates."

"Roller skates?"

My mind was busy, making pictures of her, trying to understand her. She had not, then, entirely deserted or forgotten him. But why, then—I thought, "I must not condemn her without knowing."

"Roller skates. I let the other boys use them. They're always borrowing them. But they're careful of them."

What circumstance other than poverty—

"I'm going to take the dollar you gave me for taking care of Pat," he said, "and buy her a pair of gloves."

I could only say, "That will be nice. Do you know her size?" **D**

"I think it's 8½," he said.

He looked at my hands.

"Do you wear 8½?" he asked.

"No. I wear a smaller size, a 6."

"Oh! Then I guess her hands are bigger than yours."

I hated her. Poverty or no, there was other food than bread, and the soul could starve as quickly as the body. He was taking his dollar to buy gloves for her big stupid hands, and she lived away from him, in Mannville, and contented herself with sending him skates.

"She likes white gloves," he said. "Do you think I can get them for a dollar?"

"I think so," I said.

> **Poverty or no, there was other food than bread, and the soul could starve as quickly as the body.**

DURING READING

Use Reading Skills
Context Clues What is the meaning of the word *condemn*? **C**

DURING READING

Use Reading Strategies
Make Inferences What does the narrator refer to in the phrase *other food than bread*? **E**

A MOTHER IN MANNVILLE **41**

Teach the Model

Use Reading Skills
Context Clues *Answer:* Condemn means "to judge guilty; to blame." **C**

Science Connection
Glove Measurement Explain to students that they can easily measure their own glove sizes by following these steps (they will need a measuring tape):
1. Make sure to measure, in inches, your dominant hand (the one with which you do the most work). If you are ambidextrous, measure either one.
2. Use the measuring tape to measure around the fullest, or widest, part of your dominant hand.
3. Next, measure from the base of your hand (just above the wrist) to the tip of your middle finger.
4. The larger of the two measurements is your glove size. **D**

Use Reading Strategies
Make Inferences *Answer:* Students will probably say that she means love and motherly care. **E**

Grammar Skills

Appositives and Appositive Phrases

Remind students that an appositive is a noun that is placed near another noun to identify it or to add information about it. An appositive phrase is a group of words that contains an appositive and other words that modify it. In the following sentences, have students identify appositives and appositive phrases.

1. My grandfather, a tall man with huge hands, could play any sport well. (appositive: man; appositive phrase: a tall man with huge hands)

2. The poet Walt Whitman wrote *Leaves of Grass*. (appositive: poet; appositive phrase: The poet)

3. The goldendoodle, a cross between a poodle and a golden retriever, is a very friendly dog. (appositive: cross; appositive phrase: a cross between a poodle and a golden retriever)

A MOTHER IN MANNVILLE **41**

Make Connections

Discuss the sudden change in the narrator's thoughts and feelings. Begin the discussion by asking, "The writer has busied herself with tasks and details and seems to be distancing herself from Jerry. Why might she be doing this?" **Ⓐ**

Analyze Literature

Setting *Answer:* Fall is turning into winter, and the weather is cold. Jerry often comes into the house and lies by the fire with the dog. He feels a sense of comfort that is abruptly shattered when the narrator announces that she is leaving. **Ⓑ**

Literary Connection

Regionalism Regionalism is an intellectual and literary movement that stresses the settings and values of a particular geographic area. Beginning in the 1920s and 1930s, a number of important Southern writers, such as William Faulkner, Robert Penn Warren, Eudora Welty, and Marjorie Kinnan Rawlings, wrote regionalist stories that stressed what they saw as uniquely Southern aspects of culture and character, including humor, dialect, a kinship with nature, and the simple comforts of home.

I decided that I should not leave the mountains without seeing her and knowing for myself why she had done this thing.

The human mind scatters its interests as though made of thistledown,[10] and every wind stirs and moves it. I finished my work. It did not please me, and I gave my thoughts to another field. I should need some Mexican material.

I made arrangements to close my Florida place. Mexico immediately, and doing the writing there, if conditions were favorable. Then, Alaska with my brother. After that, heaven knew what or where.

Ⓐ I did not take time to go to Mannville to see Jerry's mother, nor even to talk with the orphanage officials about her. I was a trifle abstracted about the boy, because of my work and plans. And after my first fury at her—we did not speak of her again—his having a mother, any sort at all, not far away, in Mannville, relieved me of the ache I had had about him. He did not question the <u>anomalous</u> relation. He was not lonely. It was none of my concern.

He came every day and cut my wood and did small helpful favors and stayed to talk. The days had become cold, and often I let him come inside the cabin. He would lie on the floor in front of the fire, with one arm across the pointer, and they would both doze and wait quietly for me. Other days they ran with a common ecstasy through the laurel, and since the asters were now gone, he brought me back vermilion[11] maple leaves, and chestnut boughs dripping with imperial yellow. I was ready to go.

I said to him, "You have been my good friend, Jerry. I shall often think of you and miss you. Pat will miss you too. I am leaving tomorrow."

He did not answer. When he went away, I remember that a new moon hung over the mountains, and I watched him go in silence up the hill. I expected him the next day, but he did not come. The details of packing my personal belongings, loading my car, arranging

---

10. **thistledown.** Fine, feathery seedlings from a thistle plant
11. **vermilion.** Vivid reddish orange

a·nom·a·lous
(ə nä′ mə ləs) *adj.*, strange, abnormal, or irregular

DURING READING

Analyze Literature
Setting What change is occurring in the setting? How is this change affecting the plot? **Ⓑ**

Differentiated Instruction

Enrichment

Point out that the narrator seems to move to different locations when the seasons change. At the opening of the story, she moves to North Carolina in the fall to get away from the heat and malaria of the subtropics. Have students track her plans to travel farther at this point in the story. Have them find facts and details about climate and seasonal changes among such destinations as Alaska, the subtropics, and Mexico. Then have them use those facts and details to explain why the writer might choose her series of destinations.

the bed over the seat, where the dog would ride, occupied me until late in the day. I closed the cabin and started the car, noticing that the sun was in the west and I should do well to be out of the mountains by nightfall. I stopped by the orphanage and left the cabin key and money for my light bill with Miss Clark.

"And will you call Jerry for me to say goodbye to him?"

"I don't know where he is," she said. "I'm afraid he's not well. He didn't eat his dinner this noon. One of the other boys saw him going over the hill into the laurel. He was supposed to fire the boiler[12] this afternoon. It's not like him; he's unusually reliable."

I was almost relieved, for I knew I should never see him again, and it would be easier not to say good-bye to him.

I said, "I wanted to talk with you about his mother—why he's here—but I'm in more of a hurry than I expected to be. It's out of the question for me to see her now too. But here's some money I'd like to leave with you to buy things for him at Christmas and on his birthday. It will be better than for me to try to send him things. I could so easily duplicate—skates, for instance."

She blinked her honest spinster's eyes.

"There's not much use for skates here," she said.

Her stupidity annoyed me.

"What I mean," I said, "is that I don't want to duplicate things his mother sends him. I might have chosen skates if I didn't know she had already given them to him."

She stared at me.

"I don't understand," she said. "He has no mother. He has no skates." ❖

---

12. **boiler.** Furnace or large heating element, fueled by wood, oil, or natural gas, in which heat is produced by boiling water

 **M**IRRORS & **W**INDOWS

How would you feel if you were the narrator and had just learned that Jerry did not have a mother in Mannville? Why might someone in Jerry's position decide to tell such a lie?

DURING READING

Use Reading Strategies
Ask Questions Why did Jerry lie about his mother? **D**

A MOTHER IN MANNVILLE **43**

Review the Model

Find Meaning

1. (a) The dog senses that the boy is a friend. (b) This prepares the reader for their deep friendship.

2. (a) He seems too small to be able to chop wood well. (b) He expertly chops a huge pile of wood for her.

3. (a) She is shocked, saddened, and angry. (b) She feels that he is a good, hardworking boy who should not have been deserted.

Make Judgments

4. (a) He offers to pay for the broken ax handle. He loads the cubbyhole with kindling. He takes care of the dog. (b) Answers will vary but should be supported by specific story details.

5. Possible answers: Jerry is saddened that the narrator and the dog are leaving him. He had come to depend on them for comfort and companionship. He disappears because he wants to be alone with his thoughts and his sadness.

Analyze Literature

Setting *Answer:* Examples of "see" details: fog and snow in the high mountains; the white and pink rhododendrons; "flaming" maple trees; logs that Jerry cuts; the hill at twilight when Jerry returns each night; Jerry and the dog playing together and lying by the fire. Examples of "hear" details: rhythmic chopping; tap of narrator's typewriter keys; the sound of quiet conversations by the fire. Examples of "feel" details: icy cold fingers of the orphans doing their chores during winter; warmth of the fire; warm, sunny fall days and the colder days as winter comes on.

Find Meaning

1. (a) When Jerry arrives at the cabin for the first time, the narrator's dog does not bark. Why? (b) How does this prepare the reader for the "strange communion" between Jerry and the dog later in the story?

2. (a) At first, why does the narrator think that Jerry will be unable to chop wood effectively? (b) Why does she change her mind?

3. (a) How does the narrator feel when Jerry tells her that he has a mother in Mannville? (b) Why does she feel this way?

Analyze Literature

Setting What sensory details does the narrator use to help readers "see," "hear," and "feel" elements in the setting—both the place and the time of day and year? Use a cluster chart to jot down such details. Then use those details to write a paragraph to describe the setting of this story.

Make Judgments

4. (a) What specific details and story events lead the narrator to say that Jerry has *integrity*? (b) What words would you use to describe him? Use details from the story to support your choices.

5. At the end of the story, Jerry doesn't answer the narrator when she tells him that she is leaving. Then, he disappears from the orphanage. What do these actions suggest about his feelings? Explain your answer.

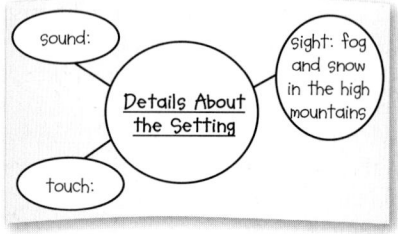

Extend Understanding

Writing Options

Creative Writing Imagine you are Jerry and have just learned the narrator and her dog are leaving. Write a **diary entry** in which you describe your feelings.

Expository Writing Using your cluster chart, write a brief **essay** in which you explain how the setting influenced the story's plot and resolution. Deliver your essay to an audience of classmates. State your main idea in your thesis, and support your thesis with details and examples from the story.

Media Literacy

Study Photographs Dorothea Lange was a photographer during the Great Depression. Find books containing her photographs. Choose one to write a brief essay about, expressing what it reveals about the Great Depression. Share your essay with the class.

Collaborative Learning

Role-Playing With a partner, take on the roles of Jerry and the narrator as they sit in front of the fire. If possible, tape-record or videotape your role-playing to share with the class.

Go to www.mirrorsandwindows.com for more.

44 UNIT 1 FICTION

Program Resources

For further instruction, refer students to the following extension activity: Media Literacy: Study Photographs, *Exceeding the Standards: Extension Activities*, pp. 3–4.

Rubrics for Writing Options

You can adapt this as a checklist for students to use as they write.

Creative Writing

☐ Does the entry clearly identify the situation of the narrator and the dog leaving him?

☐ Does it effectively express his feelings?

☐ Does it suggest what he would have liked to say and do with them before they left?

Expository Writing

☐ Does the essay contain specific details from the story?

☐ Does it contain details from the students' cluster charts?

☐ Does it effectively explain how the setting influenced the story's plot and resolution?

Vocabulary & Spelling

Prefixes, Roots, and Suffixes

The orphanage is high in the Carolina mountains.

—MARJORIE KINNAN RAWLINGS, "A Mother in Mannville"

Many words are formed by adding prefixes and suffixes, referred to as **affixes**, to base words. These affixes often originate from Greek, Latin, or other languages. In the sentence above, the word *orphanage* is an example of a word formed by the addition of a suffix. The suffix *-age,* meaning "residence of," added to the root, or base word *orphan,* creates *orphanage,* meaning "a residence for orphans."

A **root** or **base word** is a word to which a prefix or suffix is added. A **prefix** is a letter or group of letters added to the beginning of a base word to change its meaning. A **suffix** is a letter or group of letters added to the end of a base word to change its meaning.

> **EXAMPLES**
>
> *dis + similar = dissimilar*
>
> *un + happy = unhappy*
>
> *even + ness = evenness*
>
> *wonder + full = wonderful*

Common Prefixes

Prefix	Meaning	Origin
anti-	"against"	Greek
dis-	"not, opposite"	Latin
in-	"not"	Latin
post-	"after"	Latin
re-	"again"	Latin
under-	"beneath"	Latin

Common Suffixes

Suffix	Meaning	Origin
-ate	"characterized by"	Latin
-er, -or	"one who"	Anglo-Saxon
-ful	"full of"	Anglo-Saxon
-ive	"tending toward"	Latin
-less	"without"	Anglo-Saxon
-ment	"act of, state of"	Latin
-ness	"state of"	Anglo-Saxon
-tion	"act or state of"	Latin

Vocabulary Practice

Identify the origin and meaning of the roots, prefixes, and suffixes for each of the following academic terms. Then write the meaning of each term in your own words.

1. dermatology
2. bioscience
3. chloroform
4. instinctive
5. telescope
6. ambidextrous
7. universe
8. astronomy
9. democracy
10. pediatrics

Spelling Practice

Words with Prefixes, Roots, and Suffixes

The academic terms in the following list contain word parts from Greek, Latin, and other languages. Determine which word roots and affixes have been used in each word and use them to help you find its definition. To help you with this task, refer to the Language Arts Handbook 2.2, Breaking Words into Base Words, Word Roots, Prefixes, and Suffixes.

accurately	cyclone	legible
antibody	duplicate	photography
antonym	geode	psychology
asteroid	hydrogen	subterfuge
bibliography	imperial	transfer
biology	irrigate	visual

Vocabulary Practice

Sample response:

1. **dermatology** prefix *derma-*: Greek, "skin"; suffix *-ology:* Greek, "study"; meaning: "the branch of medicine that deals with the skin and diseases of the skin"

> ⊚ For more information, see the Vocabulary & Spelling Section 2.2, Breaking Words into Base Words, Word Roots, Prefixes, and Suffixes, in the Language Arts Handbook. Refer to Section 2.7, Spelling, for additional information on spelling rules.

TEACHING NOTE

Extra Practice

Have students identify the base word and the prefix or suffix for each of the following words. Then have them give the meaning and use the word in a sentence.

1. troublesome (base word: *trouble;* suffix: *-some;* meaning: "difficult")
2. thoughtful (base word: *thought;* suffix: *-ful;* meaning: "concerned for others")

KEY TERMS

ROOT, 45

BASE WORD, 45

PREFIX, 45

SUFFIX, 45

Program Resources

You will find additional lessons on Prefixes, Roots, and Suffixes in the *Exceeding the Standards: Vocabulary & Spelling* resource.

Common Core State Standards

Language

L.4

At a Glance
Directed Reading
- Reading Level: Moderate
- Difficulty Consideration: Specific cultural references
- Ease Factor: Familiar point of view

Objectives
Studying this lesson will enable students to
- use reading skills such as analyzing cause and effect
- define *plot* and recognize the effect of this literary technique in the selection
- describe the literary accomplishments of Duane BigEagle and explain the influence of Native American culture on his writing
- appreciate a story of self-discovery

Launch the Lesson
Prior to reading "The Journey," students might enjoy sharing accounts of various experiences that they feel have functioned as "rites of passage" in their own lives or those of family members and friends. The class could then identify what features these experiences have in common.

KEY TERMS
PREVIEW, 46
PREDICTION, 46
PLOT, 46
CONFLICT, 46
CLIMAX, 46
RESOLUTION, 46
CAUSE AND EFFECT, 46

Common Core State Standards

Reading Literature
RL.1

Writing
W.9

Language
L.6

DIRECTED READING

The Journey
A Short Story by Duane BigEagle

BEFORE READING

Build Background
Cultural Context Because a mysterious illness threatens his life, Raoul, the young narrator in "The Journey," undergoes an experience that seems to mark the end of his childhood. Such experiences, occurring at periods of transition from one stage of life to another, are often called "rites of passage."

Reader's Context Have you had any experience in your life thus far that seems to fit the definition of a "rite of passage"? How did you feel before, during, and after the experience?

Set Purpose
Previewing the title and the first two paragraphs of "The Journey" will enable you to make predictions about what the narrator will do and why he will do it. Read to determine how accurate your predictions are.

Analyze Literature
Plot A **plot** is a series of events related to a central **conflict,** or struggle. A plot usually involves the introduction of a conflict, its development, and its eventual resolution. The **climax** is the highest point of interest or suspense in a plot. The **resolution** is the point at which the central conflict is ended, or resolved. As you read "The Journey," identify the conflict, the climax, and the resolution.

Meet the Author
Duane BigEagle was born in 1946, the son of a Cherokee mother and an Osage father. Growing up on an Indian reservation in Oklahoma, he says that he "learned early on that individuality, creativity, self-expression, and love of beauty are essential to the survival of a whole person." He has expressed these values in his writing, teaching, and in performing traditional Native American dances.

Use Reading Skills
Analyze Cause and Effect In fiction, writers often explain *why* an event takes place. Such an event is an effect; the *why* is a cause. Understanding cause-and-effect relationships is vital to grasping the meaning of a story. Sometimes a single cause has several effects, and sometimes an effect has several causes. As you read "The Journey," use a chart to keep track of causes and effects.

Cause:	Effect:
Narrator has a mysterious illness doctors can't cure.	His father decides to send him to his aunt, a medicine woman.

Preview Vocabulary
de·lir·i·um (di lir´ ē əm) *n.*, temporary mental condition marked by confusion, excitement, wild talk, and hallucinations

nau·se·a (no´ zē ə) *n.*, feeling that one is about to vomit

sal·low (sa´ lō) *adj.*, having a yellowish, sickly color

mea·ger (mē´ gər) *adj.*, lacking in quantity or quality

co·ma (kō´ mə) *n.*, long, and very deep state of unconsciousness caused by injury, disease, or poison

46 **UNIT 1** FICTION

Words in Use

Preview Vocabulary	**Selection Words**	**Teaching Words**	
delirium, 48	mystified, 48	transition, 46	hallucination, 53
nausea, 48	miraculous, 49	eventual, 46	atmosphere, 53
sallow, 49	imbedded, 51	quest, 49	reassuring, 53
meager, 50	crescent, 51	isolation, 49	
coma, 51		prolonged, 49	
		induce, 49	
		conform, 49	
		elated, 52	

The Journey

A Short Story by Duane BigEagle

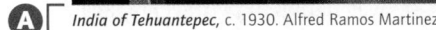
India of Tehuantepec, c. 1930. Alfred Ramos Martinez.

I began my journey upside down in a heap on top of my crumpled cardboard suitcase.

47

Summary

The narrator, a young Native American living in Mexico, is suffering from a mysterious illness that threatens his life. His parents send him on a long train journey alone to a relative in the United States, a medicine woman named Rosalie Stands Tall. During his journey, the boy suffers from fever and delirium, seeing strange visions, including one of a beautiful young girl in a dark red dress. When he reaches the home of Rosalie Stands Tall, she performs a ritual that cures him. Recovering, he again sees the beautiful young woman of his vision.

 The Mirrors & Windows questions at the end of this selection focus on the theme of life journeys. Before reading the story, ask students if the prospect of an extensive, solo journey exciting or unsettling to you? What similarities exist between a geographical journey and a new course in one's life?

Art Connection

The Mexican painter Alfred Ramos Martinez (1872–1946) was also an art teacher. Among his students was the great Mexican painter David Alfaro Siquieros. Ⓐ

Use Reading Skills

Analyze Cause and Effect Ask students to identify the different reasons given by the narrator for his father's plan to walk all the way from Mazatlán to Oklahoma. Model a response by indicating one reason: "One reason is that the family is too poor to afford more than a child's fare for the train." **Ⓐ**

Cultural Connection

Native Traditions You may want to mention to students that all of the Native American peoples mentioned in the story—the Yaqui, Papago, and Huichol—retain significant elements of traditional culture in their beliefs and rituals. For example, the Yaqui maintain the belief that four separate worlds exist: the world of animals, the world of people, the world of flowers, and the world of death.

I had known the train all my life. The wailing roar rushed through my dreams as through a tunnel and yet I had never even been on one. Now I was to take one on a two-thousand-kilometer journey halfway into a foreign country!

This particular adventure was my fault, if you can call being sick a fault. Mama says finding fault is only a way of clouding a problem and this problem was clouded enough. It began when I was thirteen and I still have tuberculosis[1] scars on my lungs but this illness was more than tuberculosis. The regular doctors were mystified by the fevers and <u>delirium</u> that accompanied a bad cough and <u>nausea</u>. After six months of treatment without improvement they gave up.

Papa carried me on his back as we left the doctor's office and began our walk to the barrio[2] that was our home. Mama cried as she walked and Papa seemed weighted by more than the weight of my thinned-down frame. About halfway home Papa suddenly straightened up. I was having a dizzy spell and almost slipped off his back but he caught me with one hand and shouted, "Aunt Rosalie! What a fool I am! Aunt Rosalie Stands Tall!" Papa started to laugh and to dance around and around on the dirt path in the middle of a field.

"What do you mean?" cried Mama as she rushed around with her hands out, ready to catch me if I fell. From the look on her face,

> "You can do anything in the world if you take it little by little and one step at a time."

the real question in her mind was more like, Have you gone mad? "Listen, woman," said Papa, "there are some people who can cure diseases the medical doctors can't. Aunt Rosalie Stands Tall is a medicine woman of the Yaqui[3] people and one of the best! She'll be able to cure Raoul! The only problem is she's married to an Indian in the United States. But that can't be helped, we'll just have to go there. Come on, we have plans to make and work to do!"

The planning began that day. We had very little money, but with what we had and could borrow from Papa's many friends there was just enough for a child's ticket to the little town in Oklahoma where Rosalie lived. I couldn't be left alone in a foreign country so Papa decided simply to walk. "I'll take the main highway north to the old Papago[4] trails that go across the desert. They'll also take me across the border undetected. Then I'll head east and north to Oklahoma. It should be easy to catch occasional rides once I get to the U.S. When I arrive I'll send word for Raoul to start."

Papa left one fine spring morning, taking only a blanket, a few extra pairs of shoes, bow and arrows to catch food, and a flintstone for building fires. Secretly I believe he was happy to be traveling again. Travel

Ⓐ

de·lir·i·um (di lir´ ē əm) *n.*, temporary mental condition marked by confusion, excitement, wild talk, and hallucinations

nau·se·a (no´ zē ə) *n.*, feeling that one is about to vomit

1. **tuberculosis.** Infectious disease that primarily affects the lungs
2. **barrio.** City neighborhood (Spanish); Mazatlán is a city on the west coast of Mexico
3. **Yaqui.** Native American people who live on the west coast of Mexico
4. **Papago.** Native American people of northern Mexico and southern Arizona

48 UNIT 1 FICTION

Understand Literary Elements

Point out to students that a symbol is a thing that stands for or represents both itself and something else. Some traditional symbols include doves for peace and lions for courage; the colors green for jealousy and purple for royalty; the seasons spring for youth and winter for old age. A writer may also create a nontraditional symbol to convey a special meaning in a literary work. As they read, have students keep note of the following elements in "The Journey" and decide if (a) they are traditional or nontraditional symbols and (b) what meaning(s) they convey.

• the train journey
• the girl in the red dress

had always been in his blood. As a young man, Papa got a job on a sailing ship and traveled all over the world. This must have been how he learned to speak English and also how he met Mama in the West Indies. Myself, I was still sixty kilometers from the town I was born in and even to imagine the journey I was about to take was more than my fevered brain could handle. But as Mama said, "You can do anything in the world if you take it little by little and one step at a time." This was the miraculous and trusting philosophy our family lived by, and I must admit it has usually worked.

CULTURAL ▶▶ CONNECTION

Vision Quest Among some Native American peoples, such as the Great Plains tribes, the rite of passage for young men took the form of a vision quest. Through isolation, prolonged fasting, and sometimes self-inflicted injuries, a young man sought to induce a vision in which a spirit, usually combining animal and human natures, would appear. The "spirit power" the young man obtained from this vision would safeguard him in adult life. How does the experience of the narrator in "The Journey" conform to the Native American tradition of the vision quest? **B**

Still, the day of departure found me filled with a dread that settled like lead in my feet. If I hadn't been so lightheaded from the fevers, I'm sure I would have fallen over at any attempt to walk. Dressed in my best clothes which looked shabby the minute we got to the train station, Mama led me into the fourth-class carriage and found me a seat on **C**

sal·low (sa´ lō) *adj.*, having a yellowish, sickly color

a bench near the windows. Then she disappeared and came back a minute later with a thin young man with <u>sallow</u> skin and a drooping Zapata mustache.[5] "This is your second cousin, Alejandro. He is a conductor on this train and will be with you till you get to Juarez; you must do whatever he says." **D**

At that time, the conductors on trains in Mexico were required to stay with a train the entire length of its journey which perhaps accounted for Alejandro's appearance. He did little to inspire my confidence in him. In any case, he disappeared a second later and it was time for Mama to go too. Hurriedly, she reminded me that there was money in my coat to buy food from the women who came onto the train at every stop and that there was a silver bracelet sewn into the cuff of my pants to bribe the guards at the border. With one last tearful kiss and hug, she was gone and I was alone. The train started with a jerk which knocked me off my bench and I began my journey upside down in a heap on top of my crumpled cardboard suitcase. I didn't even get a chance to wave goodbye.

I soon got used to the jerking starts of the train, and unsmiling Alejandro turned out to be a guardian angel which was fortunate because my illness began to get worse as the journey went along. Many times I awoke to find Alejandro shuffling some young thief

5. **Zapata mustache.** Thick, black, drooping mustache such as worn by Emiliano Zapata (1879–1919), a leader of the Mexican Revolution

THE JOURNEY **49**

Teach the Selection

Cultural Connection
Vision Quest *Answer:* Students may feel that the experience of the narrator conforms to the Native American tradition of the vision quest in several ways: He is isolated, he experiences visions, he is aided by various spirits in animal form, and his ordeal marks the end of his childhood. **B**

Use Reading Strategies
Ask Questions Model for students questions that this sentence might prompt a reader to ask: "Why does the narrator feel shabby when he arrives at the station?" "What does traveling 'fourth-class' mean?" **C**

Analyze Literature
Symbolism Remind students that a symbol is a person, place, or thing that represents a larger idea. Ask them to focus on the relationship between the narrator and his second cousin, Alejandro, and challenge them to posit theories as to what Alejandro might symbolize within the narrator's life journey. **D**

Differentiated Instruction

Enrichment
Interested students might enjoy preparing an oral reading of "The Journey." In addition to dividing up the parts, the students might use sound and lighting effects to heighten the dramatic impact of their reading.

Visual Learning
Duane BigEagle provides vivid physical descriptions of several characters in "The Journey," including the narrator's cousin Alejandro and the young girl in the red dress. Invite interested students to create imaginary portraits of these characters in any medium they choose (or to find pictures that they feel resemble these characters).

Hallucinations Point out to students that during his journey the narrator seems to be suffering at times from hallucinations, which are false visions, sounds, smells, or other sensory impressions that may result from physical or mental illness, as well as by the action of certain drugs. **A**

Analyze Literature
Plot Remind students that there are four main types of conflict (man v. man, man v. society, man v. nature, and man v. himself). Ask them what conflict the narrator is describing here, and discuss which type of conflict it represents. **B**

Use Reading Strategies
Make Predictions Discuss with students the emphasis that the author places on the narrator's visions of the girl in the red dress. Ask them to make predictions as to what future role she will have in the story. **C**

away from my <u>meager</u> possessions or buying me food at the last stop before a long stretch of desert. He would bring me things too, fresh peaches and apples and leftover bread and pastries from the first-class carriages where he worked. Once, in the middle of the desert he brought me a small ice-cold watermelon, the most refreshing thing I'd ever tasted—who knows where he got it?

A
B To this day, I'm not sure exactly which of the things I saw through the window of the train were real and which were not. Some of them I know were not real. In my delirium, a half-day's journey would pass in the blink of an eye. Often I noticed only large changes in the countryside, from plains to mountains to desert. Broad valleys remain clearly in my mind and there were many of these. Small scenes, too, remain—a family sitting down to dinner at a candle-lit table in a hut by a river. And a few more sinister ones—once between two pine trees I caught a glimpse of one man raising a large club to strike another man whose back was turned. I cried out but there

> **mea·ger** (mē´ gər) *adj.*, lacking in quantity or quality

was nothing to be done, the train was moving too fast on a downgrade and probably couldn't have been stopped. But then, did I really see them at all? My doubt was caused by the girl in the dark red dress.

C I think I began to see her about halfway through the journey to Juarez. She was very beautiful, high cheekbones, long black hair and very dark skin. She was about my height and age or maybe a little older. Her eyes were very large and her mouth seemed to have a ready smile. The first time I saw her, at a small station near a lake, she smiled and waved as the train pulled away. Her sensuality embarrassed me and I didn't wave back. I regretted it immediately. But she was back again the next day at a station in the foothills of the mountains, this time dressed in the white blouse and skirt that the Huichol[6] women wear.

She became almost a regular occurrence. Sometimes she was happy, sometimes serious and most of the time she was wearing the dark red dress. Often I would only see her in passing; she'd be working in a field and raise

---

6. **Huichol.** Native American people of western Mexico

Foreign Words in English
"Papa carried me on his back as we left the doctor's office and began our walk to the *barrio* that was our home."

Point out to students that many foreign words have entered the English language. The passage above from "The Journey" includes the Spanish word *barrio*, meaning "neighborhood." Have students use

dictionaries to identify the foreign languages that are the sources of the following words.
1. motto (Latin)
2. bungalow (Hindi)
3. coup (French)
4. arroyo (Spanish)
5. yogurt (Turkish)

up to watch the train go by. Gradually, my condition grew worse. My coughing fits grew longer and I slept more so I began not to see the girl so much, but the last time I saw her really gave me a shock. The mountains of the Sierra Madre Oriental[7] range are very rugged and are cut in places by deep gorges called barrancas. The train was in one of these gorges on a ledge above the river and was about to go around a bend. For some reason, I looked back the way we had come and there, imbedded in the mountain with her eyes closed, was the face of the girl, thirty feet high! For the first time, I noticed the small crescent-shaped scar in the middle of her lower lip. **E**

D The vision, or whatever it was, quickly disappeared as the train rounded the curve. I sank back on to the bench with a pounding heart and closed my eyes. I must have slept or perhaps I fell into a <u>coma</u> because I remember very little of the last part of the trip. I awoke once while Alejandro was carrying me across the border and delivering me to a friend of his on the train to Dallas. How I got from Dallas to Oklahoma I may never know because I remember nothing. But it happened. And finally, I awoke for a minute in my father's arms as he carried me off the train. **F**

> She was very beautiful,
> high cheekbones, long black hair
> and very dark skin.

7. **Sierra Madre Oriental.** Eastern range of Mexico's main mountain system

co•ma (kō′ mə) *n.*, long, and very deep state of unconsciousness caused by injury, disease, or poison

THE JOURNEY **51**

Use Reading Skills

Analyze Cause and Effect Direct students' attention to this section of the story. Discuss the repeating cause-effect relationship (each time a new animal appears, the pain rises higher in the narrator's body). **A**

Analyze Literature

Plot Remind students that the rising action of a plot culminates in the climax, the highest point of suspense in the narrative. Ask students which event in "The Journey" seems to them to be the climax of the story. Most students will probably feel that the healing of the narrator is the climax of the story. **B**

 **MIRRORS & WINDOWS**

Answer: Some students will see such a journey as an exciting opportunity; others will regard it as a daunting challenge. Both types of students may feel that this is why a journey makes an effective symbol of a passage in life. Students might enjoy holding a panel discussion to explore these questions.

Then, there was a sharp pain in the center of my chest. And a pounding. Rhythmic pounding. A woman's voice began to sing in a very high pitch. My eyes opened of themselves. At first I couldn't make it out, arched crossing lines, flickering shadows. I was in the center of an oval-shaped lodge built of bent willow limbs covered with skins and lit by a small fire. A tall woman came into view; she was singing and dancing back and forth. Somehow I knew this was Rosalie Stands Tall, the medicine woman. The pain hit me again and I wanted to get away but hands held me still.

Papa's voice said in my ear, "She is calling her spirit helpers, you must try and sit up." I was sitting up facing the door of the lodge. **A** There was a lizard there and he spoke in an old man's voice, words I couldn't understand. Rosalie sang again and there was a small hawk there. The pain rose up higher in my chest. There was a coyote in the door and his words were tinged with mocking laughter. The pain rose into my throat. There was a small brown bear in the door, his fur blew back and forth in the wind. The pain rose into the back of my mouth. I felt I needed to cough. Rosalie put two porcupine quills together and bound them with leather to make a pair of tweezers. She held my lips closed with them, painfully tight. A pair of wings beat against the top of the lodge. I needed badly to cough. There was something hot in my mouth, it was sharp, it was hurting my mouth, it needed to come out! IT WAS OUT! **B**

> "...I've come on a journey out of childhood."

I awoke in bed in a small room lit by a coal-oil lamp. There was a young woman with her back to me preparing food by the side of the bed. She had very long black hair. She put the tray down on the table beside the bed. As she turned to leave the room, I saw a small crescent-shaped scar in the middle of her lower lip. I started to call her back but there was no need. I knew who she was. An immense peacefulness settled over me. It was warm in the bed. Papa sat on the other side of the bed. He seemed very happy when I turned and looked at him. He said softly, "Raoul, you have changed completely. You're not anymore the young boy left in Mazatlán." I wanted to tell him everything! There was so much to say! But all I could get out was, "Yes, I know, Papa, I've come on a journey out of childhood." And then I went to sleep again. ❖

 **MIRRORS & WINDOWS**

If you had to take an important—or simply very long—journey alone, like the narrator, would you feel elated or anxious? Why do you think a journey is an effective symbol to represent a passage in life?

Differentiated Instruction

Reading Proficiency
Students may have trouble understanding the portion of the story describing the healing ceremony. Have them reread this section to grasp all the details. Ask them to describe the cause-effect relationships in the ceremony (Example: Rosalie Stands Tall sings > the narrator has a vision of an animal spirit > the illness comes closer to leaving his body).

English Language Learning
You might ask students who have come from other countries to describe religious rituals or social customs that function as rites of passage for young people in these cultures. To get them started, offer other rites of passage that occur in the United States, such as the Jewish Bar/Bat Mitzvah and the Latin American Quinceañera.

Find Meaning

1. (a) Why does the narrator say that his adventure was his fault? (b) What do you think his mother means when she says that finding fault is only a way of clouding a problem?

2. (a) Who is the girl in the dark red dress? (b) Is she a real person or a hallucination?

3. (a) How does Aunt Rosalie cure the narrator? (b) Why do you think Aunt Rosalie's cure is effective?

Analyze Literature

Plot Usually, the intensity of the conflict increases until the action reaches the climax, then the intensity decreases as the plot moves toward the resolution. On a plot diagram, indicate what event is the climax of "The Journey" and what is the resolution of the conflict. Also indicate how the qualities of the central characters influence this resolution.

Make Judgments

4. (a) What is the attitude of the narrator's father toward modern medicine? (b) What is your opinion of his attitude?

5. (a) How would you describe the narrator's experiences on the train? (b) What overall mood or atmosphere do these experiences create?

6. Why do you think the narrator's experience has caused him to grow up?

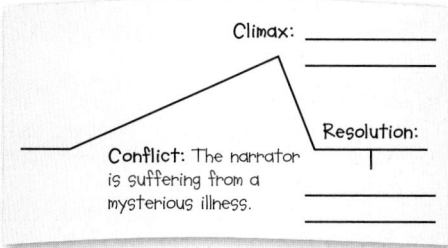

Climax: _____

Conflict: The narrator is suffering from a mysterious illness.

Resolution: _____

Extend Understanding

Writing Options

Creative Writing Imagine that you are Raoul. You and your father are going to stay with Aunt Rosalie Stands Tall until you are fully recovered. Write a **letter** to your mother in Mazatlán, telling her briefly about your train journey and cure, describing your return trip home, and concluding by reassuring her about your plans.

Expository Writing The narrator's mother observes, "You can do anything in the world if you take it little by little and one step at a time." In the introductory paragraph of a brief **problem-solution essay,** identify the problems faced by the narrator and his family. In the body paragraphs, show how they solved these problems. In the concluding paragraph, evaluate the effectiveness of Raoul's mother's advice. Share your work with the class.

Critical Literacy

Hold a Panel Discussion With fellow students, hold a panel discussion on the "girl in the dark red dress." Are any of her appearances to the narrator real or is she entirely a product of his delirium? Whether or not she is real, what does she seem to symbolize, or represent, in the story?

Media Literacy

Conduct Internet Research During his journey, the narrator travels from Mazatlán on Mexico's Pacific Coast, passes through the Sierra Madre Mountains, crosses the U.S.-Mexican border at Ciudad Juarez on the Rio Grande, travels on to Dallas, Texas, and finally reaches Oklahoma. Use the Internet to research a travel diary of this journey to present to your classmates.

 Go to **www.mirrorsandwindows.com** for more.

Find Meaning

1. (a) It is his illness that makes his journey necessary. (b) Finding fault doesn't solve a problem.

2. (a) She is the young girl the narrator sees many times during his journey. (b) The first time she appears to him she may be a real person. Her subsequent appearances seem less likely to be real.

3. (a) Enlisting various "spirit helpers" in the form of animals to help her, she causes the narrator to expel whatever is making him ill. (b) Students may feel that she is successful because the narrator and his father believe in her power to bring about a cure.

Make Judgments

4. (a) He believes there are conditions that modern medicine cannot cure. (b) Some students may feel that his belief in traditional medicine has merit; others may feel it is dangerous.

5. (a) His experiences are a jumbled mixture of actual events and visions caused by his illness. (b) They give the journey a dreamlike atmosphere.

6. Students may offer a variety of reasons, including the proximity of death, the movement away from his mother and the scenes of his childhood, and the encounter with the girl in the dark red dress.

Analyze Literature

Plot *Answer:* The climax of the story comes with Aunt Rosalie's extraction of whatever has been causing the narrator's illness. The resolution, which follows immediately, is the mutual recognition by the narrator and his father that he has grown up.

Rubrics for Writing Options

You can adapt this as a checklist for students to use as they write.

Creative Writing

☐ Does the letter adopt the personality of the narrator?

☐ Does it clearly outline the events of the journey and the cure?

☐ Does it indicate the plan for the return trip?

☐ Does it offer the narrator's mother reassurance about his health and his plans?

Expository Writing

☐ Does the introduction identify the problems faced by the narrator and his family?

☐ Do the body paragraphs clearly present the solutions they found?

☐ Does the conclusion evaluate the effectiveness of the advice?

The Drummer Boy of Shiloh

A Short Story by Ray Bradbury

DIRECTED READING

At a Glance
Directed Reading
- Reading Level: Challenging
- Difficulty Consideration: Vocabulary
- Ease Factor: Length

Objectives
Studying this lesson will enable students to
- use reading skills such as context clues
- analyze *description* and recognize the important role played by sensory details
- describe the literary achievement of Ray Bradbury
- compare historical fiction and nonfiction about the American Civil War

Launch the Lesson
You might ask students to think about how soldiers and other military personnel might feel, knowing that a battle is forthcoming. Ask them if they think a commanding general would have feelings different from those of his men. Then have them read "The Drummer Boy of Shiloh" to find out the feelings of both a general and a young drummer boy just before battle.

BEFORE READING

Build Background
Historical Context "The Drummer Boy of Shiloh" is historical fiction based on an event from the Civil War. Historical fiction combines actual events with imagined ones. On April 6, 1862, Confederate soldiers launched a surprise attack on Union troops, beginning a bloody two-day combat known as the Battle of Shiloh. The name came from a chapel near the battlefield. The huge casualties suffered by both sides at Shiloh shocked both North and South.

Reader's Context Have you ever spent an anxious, restless night, unable to sleep because of what you had to face the next day? What sort of thoughts went through your mind? How did you try to calm your fears?

Set Purpose
Use Build Background, the story title, and the first paragraph to preview "The Drummer Boy of Shiloh." Based on your preview, what do you think the story will focus on?

Analyze Literature
Description Writing that portrays a character, object, or scene through details is **description.** Descriptions make use of **sensory details,** words and phrases that describe how things look, sound, smell, taste, or feel. As you read "The Drummer Boy of Shiloh," be aware of how sensory details help describe the boy, the general, and the setting.

Meet the Author

Ray Bradbury is one of the best-known American writers of science fiction and fantasy. Born in Waukegan, Illinois, in 1920, he published his first stories at nineteen. Describing his inspiration for writing, Bradbury says, "My stories run up and bite me in the leg—I respond by writing down everything that goes on during the bite. When I finish, the idea lets go and runs off."

Use Reading Skills
Context Clues Preview the vocabulary words from this selection as they are used in the sentences below. Try to unlock the meaning of each word using the context clues provided in the sentences.

1. Jim wore his cap <u>askew</u>, with the bill turned to the side.
2. The priest gave a <u>benediction</u> before the meal last night.
3. The children's toys were always <u>strewn</u> about the room.
4. He was arrested for driving without a <u>legitimate</u> driver's license.
5. I tried to change Jamie's mind, but he was <u>resolute</u>.

Preview Vocabulary
as·kew (ə skyü´) *adv.*, crookedly

ben·e·dic·tion (be nə dik´ shən) *n.*, blessing

strewn (strün) *adj.*, spread about here and there as by sprinkling

le·git·i·mate·ly (li ji´ tə mət lē) *adv.*, conforming to laws, rules, or accepted standards

re·sol·ute (re´ ze lüt) *adj.*, having or showing a fixed, firm purpose

54 UNIT 1 FICTION

Words in Use

Preview Vocabulary
askew, 56
benediction, 56
strewn, 57
legitimately, 58
resolute, 59

Selection Words
miraculously, 56
solemn, 56
basting, 56

Teaching Words
combat, 54
chapel, 54
casualties, 54
portrays, 54
motivation, 60
envious, 60
acclaimed, 61
evoke, 61
speculate, 62

KEY TERMS
DESCRIPTION, 54
SENSORY DETAIL, 54
CONTEXT CLUE, 54
NARRATIVE, 62
CHARACTER ANALYSIS, 62

Common Core State Standards

Reading Literature
RL.4

Language
L.4, L.6

The Drummer Boy of Shiloh

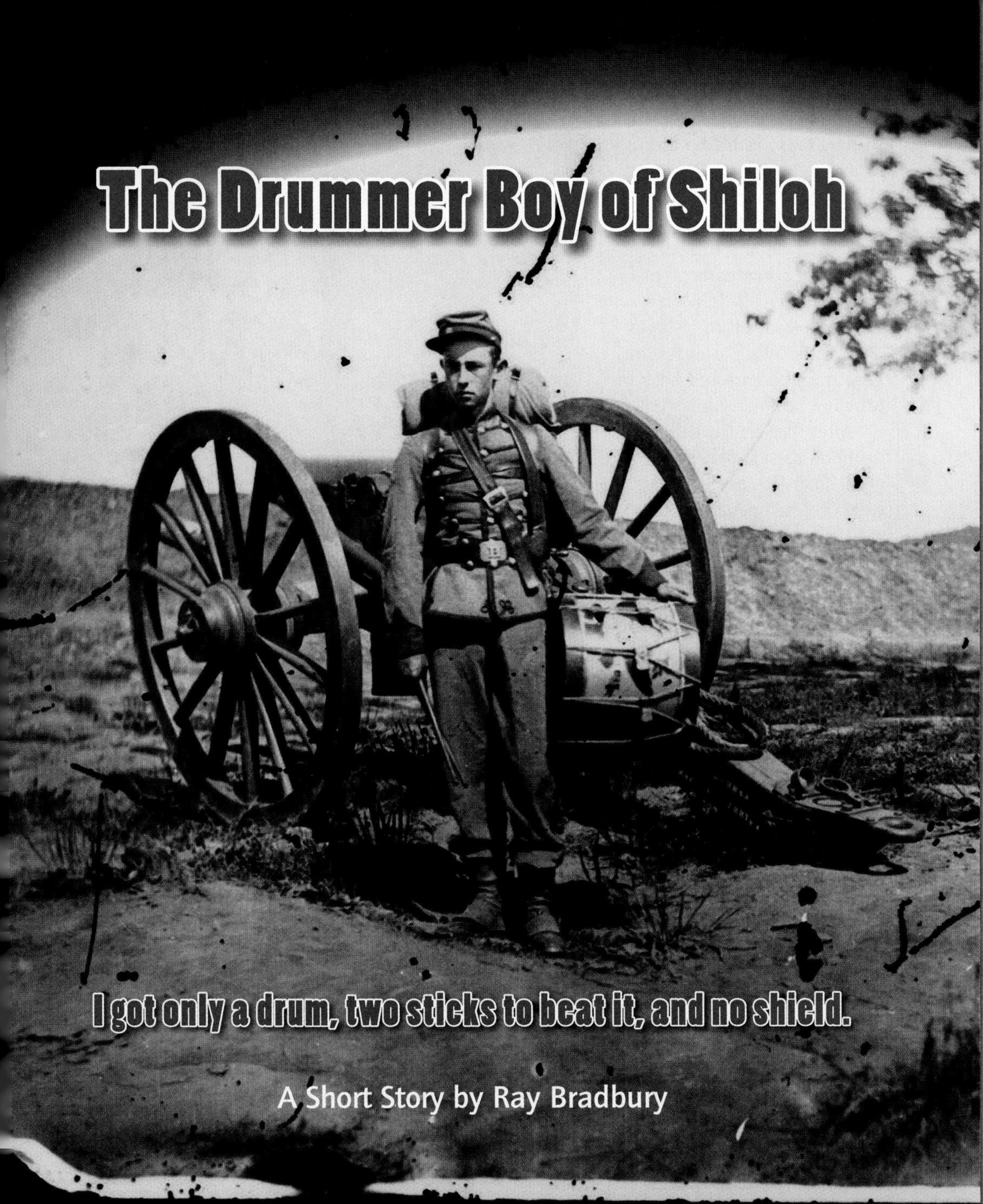

I got only a drum, two sticks to beat it, and no shield.

A Short Story by Ray Bradbury

Union soldier from the U.S. Civil War.

55

Teach the Selection

Summary

During the night before the battle of Shiloh, a young drummer boy can't sleep. He fears the battle ahead, in which he will serve without a weapon. The general, also unable to sleep, notices the boy and shares his own fears. Then the general asks the boy to be his partner, protecting the men as best he can by beating his drum rapidly, in order to force the men forward with a sense of courage and strength. This encounter calms the boy as he lies back down and waits for the day to begin.

MIRRORS & WINDOWS The Mirrors & Windows questions at the end of this selection focus on the theme of courage in the face of danger. Before reading the story, ask students how they would react to receiving a great responsibility from someone they admire and respect. What helps drive people to act bravely in the face of great danger?

Program Resources

Planning and Assessment
Program Planning Guide, Selection Lesson Plan
E-Lesson Planner
Assessment Guide, Lesson Test
ExamView

Technology Tools
Interactive Student Text on CD
Visual Teaching Package
Audio Library
mirrorsandwindows.com

Meeting the Standards
Fiction: Unit 1, Directed Reading, pp. 42–47

Differentiating Instruction
Developing Readers, Visualize, pp. 1–3

Analyze Literature

Description Ask students to use the details of sight and sound to identify the setting—both where and when the opening scene takes place. Then point out the meaning of Bradbury's metaphor, in which he compares the round, light skin of the drum with the face of the moon. **Ⓐ**

History Connection

Battle of Shiloh The Civil War battle that the drummer boy awaits is Shiloh, which took place in southwestern Tennessee on April 6 and 7, 1862. The battle was fought by largely inexperienced troops, and the heavy casualties shocked both North and South. After the battle, both sides realized the war would be long and bloody. (Ironically, the Hebrew word *Shiloh* means "place of peace.") **Ⓑ**

TEACHING NOTE

Self-Generated Questioning

Have students discuss any questions they have after reading the first two pages of the story. Model this by asking: "How old is the drummer boy?" "Why does Bradbury mention the gentle falling of the peach blossoms?" "What does the drummer boy hope will happen when the soldiers go off to battle?"

In the April night, more than once, blossoms fell from the orchard trees and lit with rustling taps on the drumskin. At midnight a peach stone left miraculously on a branch through winter, flicked by a bird, fell swift and unseen, struck once, like panic, which jerked the boy upright. In silence he listened to his own heart ruffle away, away, at last gone from his ears and back in his chest again.

Ⓐ After that, he turned the drum on its side, where its great lunar face peered at him whenever he opened his eyes.

Ⓑ His face, alert or at rest, was solemn. It was indeed a solemn time and a solemn night for a boy just turned fourteen in the peach field near the Owl Creek not far from the church at Shiloh.

"…thirty-one, thirty-two, thirty-three…"

Unable to see, he stopped counting.

Beyond the thirty-three familiar shadows, forty thousand men, exhausted by nervous expectation, unable to sleep for romantic dreams of battles yet unfought, lay crazily <u>askew</u> in their uniforms. A mile yet farther on, another army was strewn helter-skelter,[1] turning slow, basting themselves with the thought of what they would do when the time came: a leap, a yell, a blind plunge their strategy, raw youth their protection and <u>benediction</u>.

Now and again the boy heard a vast wind come up, that gently stirred the air. But he

knew what it was—the army here, the army there, whispering to itself in the dark. Some men talking to others, others murmuring to themselves, and all so quiet it was like a natural element arisen from south or north with the motion of the earth toward dawn.

---

1. **helter-skelter.** In haste and confusion

as·kew (ə skyü´) *adv.*, crookedly
ben·e·dic·tion (be nə dik´ shən) *n.*, blessing

56 UNIT 1 FICTION

Grammar Skills

Simple and Compound Predicates

Remind students that a sentence may contain either a simple predicate (one verb) or a compound predicate (two or more verbs that share the same subject). In the following sentences, have students indicate the predicates and identify them as simple or compound.

1. The drummer boy <u>awoke</u> and <u>looked</u> around. (compound)
2. The two armies <u>encamped</u> near the Tennessee River. (simple)
3. The general <u>talked</u> to Joby, <u>calmed</u> his fears, and <u>gave</u> him a mission. (compound)

Battle of Shiloh, c. 1888. Thure Thulstrup.

bones of their rifles, with bayonets fixed like eternal lightning lost in the orchard grass.

Me, thought the boy, I got only a drum, two sticks to beat it, and no shield. **C**

There wasn't a man-boy on this ground tonight did not have a shield he cast, riveted or carved himself on his way to his first attack, compounded of remote but nonetheless firm and fiery family devotion, flag-blown patriotism and cocksure[3] immortality strengthened by the touchstone[4] of very real gunpowder, ramrod, minnieball[5] and flint. But without these last the boy felt his family move yet farther off away in the dark, as if one of those great prairie-burning trains had chanted them away never to return, leaving him with this drum which was worse than a toy in the game to be played tomorrow or some day much too soon. **D**

The boy turned on his side. A moth brushed his face, but it was a peach blossom. A peach blossom flicked him, but it was a moth. Nothing stayed put. Nothing had a name. Nothing was as it once was. **E**

What the men whispered the boy could only guess, and he guessed that it was: Me, I'm the one, I'm the one of all the rest won't die. I'll live through it. I'll go home. The band will play. And I'll be there to hear it.

Yes, thought the boy, that's all very well for them, they can give as good as they get!

For with the careless bones of the young men harvested by night and bindled[2] around campfires were the similarly <u>strewn</u> steel

---

2. **bindled.** Bundled (slang)
3. **cocksure.** Absolutely sure and certain
4. **touchstone.** Any test of genuineness or value
5. **minnieball.** Minié ball. Cone-shaped rifle bullet that expands when fired

> **strewn** (strün) *adj.*, spread about here and there as by sprinkling

Writing Skills

Use Sensory Details

To prepare students for the Creative Writing activity on page 62, have them note sensory details that Bradbury uses to develop the setting, the characters, and the growing suspense related to the forthcoming battle. Have students work with partners to discuss how the Union and Confederate soldiers might be feeling, lying out in the darkness. What thoughts might be going through their heads?

What scenes might they be visualizing? What sounds and smells might they be experiencing? Encourage students to visualize characters and situations other than those involving the general and Joby. Have them jot down notes, pointing out that they will have a chance to use those notes later on for a writing activity.

Analyze Literature

Description Draw students' attention to the way in which Bradbury uses sensory details here both to evoke the night and to present the general from the drummer boy's point of view. Ask: "Why do most of the details appeal to the sense of smell rather than sight?" "What one visible detail is included?" "Why might the drummer boy compare the general to fathers?" **A**

Analyze Literature

Characterization Ask students what admission the general makes to Joby. Then ask, "Why did he cry, and what does this action suggest about his character?" **B**

History Connection

Ulysses S. Grant Remind students that although his story is fiction, Bradbury based it on historical events and people. Point out that the general is based on the real Union commander at Shiloh, Ulysses S. Grant, who had recently won the first major Union victory of the Civil War, the capture of the Confederates' Fort Donelson in Tennessee. After the terrible loss of life at Shiloh, Grant's reputation was damaged for a time, but his capture of the Confederate stronghold of Vicksburg in July of 1863 led to his appointment as commander of all Union forces. **C**

If he lay very still, when the dawn came up and the soldiers put on their bravery with their caps, perhaps they might go away, the war with them, and not notice him lying small here, no more than a toy himself.

"Well, now," said a voice.

The boy shut up his eyes, to hide inside himself, but it was too late. Someone, walking by in the night, stood over him.

"Well," said the voice quietly, "here's a soldier crying *before* the fight. Good. Get it over. Won't be time once it all starts."

And the voice was about to move on when the boy, startled, touched the drum at his elbow. The man above, hearing this, stopped. The boy could feel his eyes, sense him slowly bending near. A hand must have come down out of the night, for there was a little *rat-tat* as the fingernails brushed and the man's breath fanned his face.

"Why, it's the drummer boy, isn't it?"

The boy nodded, not knowing if his nod was seen. "Sir, is that you?" he said.

"I assume it is." The man's knees cracked as he bent still closer.

A He smelled as all fathers should smell, of salt sweat, ginger tobacco, horse and boot leather, and the earth he walked upon. He had many eyes. No, not eyes—brass buttons that watched the boy.

He could only be, and was, the general.

"What's your name, boy?" he asked.

"Joby," whispered the boy, starting to sit up.

"All right, Joby, don't stir." A hand pressed his chest gently, and the boy relaxed. "How long you been with us, Joby?"

"Three weeks, sir."

"Run off from home or joined legitimately, boy?"

Silence.

"Fool question," said the general. "Do you shave yet, boy? Even more of a fool. There's

your cheek, fell right off the tree overhead. And the others here not much older. Raw, raw, the lot of you. You ready for tomorrow or the next day, Joby?"

"I think so, sir."

B "You want to cry some more, go on ahead. I did the same last night."

"*You*, sir?"

"It's the truth. Thinking of everything ahead. Both sides figuring the other side will just give up, and soon, and the war done in weeks, and us all home. Well, that's not how it's going to be. And maybe that's why I cried."

"Yes, sir," said Joby.

The general must have taken out a cigar now, for the dark was suddenly filled with the smell of tobacco unlit as yet, but chewed as the man thought what next to say.

C "It's going to be a crazy time," said the general. "Counting both sides, there's a hundred thousand men, give or take a few thousand out there tonight, not one as can spit a sparrow off a tree, or knows a horse clod from a Minié ball. Stand up, bare the breast, ask to be a target, thank them and sit down, that's us, that's them. We should turn tail and train four months, they should do the same. But here we are, taken with spring fever and thinking it blood lust, taking our sulfur with cannons instead of with molasses,[6] as it should be, going to be a hero, going to live forever. And I can see all of them over there nodding agreement, save the other way around. It's wrong, boy, it's wrong as a head put on hindside front and a man marching backward through life. More innocents will get shot out of pure enthusiasm than ever got shot before. Owl

---

6. **sulfur...molasses.** Sulfur and molasses were mixed to make a home remedy; sulfur is also emitted when cannons are fired.

le·git·i·mate·ly (li ji′ tə mət lē) *adv.*, conforming to laws, rules, or accepted standards

Differentiated Instruction

Visual Learning

Help students to "see" the scene that the general describes to Joby—the soldiers marching rapidly, emboldened by the steady, rapid beat of Joby's drum. Contrast it to how the soldiers would move if Joby beat a slower pace. Use visualization to strengthen understanding of the general's intent—to strengthen each man's sense of courage and to keep casualties at a minimum.

Vocabulary Skills

Consonant Clusters

Explain to students that a consonant cluster is a group of consonants that occur within the same syllable in a word without any vowels between them. The grouping *spr* in the word *spring* is an example of a consonant cluster. Ask students to point out and pronounce the new vocabulary word for this selection that contains a consonant cluster (*strewn*).

Creek was full of boys splashing around in the noonday sun just a few hours ago. I fear it will be full of boys again, just floating, at sundown tomorrow, not caring where the tide takes them."

The general stopped and made a little pile of winter leaves and twigs in the darkness, as if he might at any moment strike fire to them to see his way through the coming days when the sun might not show its face because of what was happening here and just beyond.

The boy watched the hand stirring the leaves and opened his lips to say something, but did not say it. The general heard the boy's breath and spoke himself.

"Why am I telling you this? That's what you wanted to ask, eh? Well, when you got a bunch of wild horses on a loose rein somewhere, somehow you got to bring order, rein them in. These lads, fresh out of the milkshed, don't know what I know, and I can't tell them: men actually die, in war. So each is his own army. I got to make *one* army of them. And for that, boy, I need you."

"Me!" The boy's lips barely twitched.

E "Now, boy," said the general quietly, "you are the heart of the army. Think of that. You're the heart of the army. Listen, now."

And, lying there, Joby listened. And the general spoke on.

F If he, Joby, beat slow tomorrow, the heart would beat slow in the men. They would lag by the wayside. They would drowse in the fields on their muskets. They would sleep forever, after that, in those same fields—their hearts slowed by a drummer boy and stopped by enemy lead.

But if he beat a sure, steady, ever faster rhythm, then, then their knees would come up in a long line down over that hill, one knee after the other, like a wave on the ocean shore! Had he seen the ocean ever? Seen the waves rolling in like a well-ordered cavalry[7] charge to the sand? Well, that was it, that's what he wanted, that's what was needed! Joby was his right hand and his left. He gave the orders, but Joby set the pace!

So bring the right knee up and the right foot out and the left knee up and the left foot out. One following the other in good time, in brisk time. Move the blood up the body and make the head proud and the spine stiff and the jaw <u>resolute</u>. Focus the eye and set the teeth, flare the nostrils and tighten the hands, put steel armor all over the men, for blood moving fast in them does indeed make men feel as if they'd put on steel. He must keep at it, at it! Long and steady, steady and long! Then, even though shot or torn, those wounds got in hot blood—in blood he'd helped stir—would feel less pain. If their blood was cold, it would be more than

> # If he, Joby, beat slow tomorrow, the heart would beat slow in the men.

---

7. **cavalry.** Combat troops mounted on horses

re•sol•ute (reʹ ze lüt) *adj.,* having or showing a fixed, firm purpose

Use Reading Strategies
Visualize Ask students to describe the contrasting pictures that form in their minds involving young men in Owl Creek. Ask: "Why might the general be making such a contrast?" (to share his horror about what will happen) **D**

Use Reading Strategies
Ask Questions Ask students what the general means when he says that Joby is "the heart of the army." **E**

Use Reading Skills
Analyze Cause and Effect Ask students to express in their own words what the general wants Joby to do, and why. Use this passage to point out the importance of the drummer boy in nineteenth-century armies. He set the pace for the advancing march, and he also, with the bugler, created signals to tell the soldiers of changes in plans or movements. Discuss what a terrible responsibility this was, particularly since drummer boys were unarmed, and many were as young as ten years old. **F**

Speaking & Listening Skills

Interpersonal Communication
Discuss with students the following guidelines for communicating with another person.
- Make eye contact and maintain a relaxed posture.
- Provide feedback as you listen. Try not to interrupt or to finish the other person's sentences.
- If you are in doubt about what the other person means, restate it to him or her to make sure you understand.
- Control your emotions. Think before making a statement out of anger or excitement.
- Distinguish between facts and opinions.

Pair students, and explain that they will conduct an informal dialogue on the topic of young people in battle. Have them jot down preliminary thoughts, opinions, and questions and then discuss the issue with the communication guidelines in mind.

Answer: Students might say that they would either be frightened or be emboldened by the general's words. Regarding motivation, students might say that patriotism, the instinct to survive, and comradeship with fellow soldiers would be strong factors.

Find Meaning

1. (a) The sleeping soldiers are reassuring themselves that they will not be the ones to die. (b) They already visualize themselves back home, being treated as heroes.
2. The drummer boy is envious of the soldiers' weapons and their "shields," his metaphor for their self-protective attitude derived from loyalty and a youthful sense of immortality.
3. (a) The general tells the drummer boy that it is good he is crying now, because he won't have a chance to cry once the battle begins. He also admits that he himself cried the night before. (b) He wants to reassure him.

Make Judgments

4. (a) Most of the soldiers are young and untrained. (b) The result might be a very high level of casualties.
5. The drummer boy provides the beat that will quicken the army in combat.
6. Most students will probably feel that the general's kindly, inspiring words would have reassured them.

---

slaughter, it would be murderous nightmare and pain best not told and no one to guess.

The general spoke and stopped, letting his breath slack off. Then, after a moment, he said, "So there you are, that's it. Will you do that, boy? Do you know now you're general of the army when the general's left behind?"

The boy nodded mutely.[8]

"You'll run them through for me then, boy?"

"Yes, sir."

"Good. And, maybe, many nights from tonight, many years from now, when you're as old or far much older than me, when they ask you what you did in this awful time, you will tell them—one part humble and one part proud—'I was the drummer boy at the battle of Owl Creek,' or the Tennessee River. Or maybe they'll just name it after the church there. 'I was the drummer boy at Shiloh.' Good grief, that has a beat and sound to it fitting for Mr. Longfellow.[9] 'I was the drummer boy at Shiloh.' Who will ever hear

those words and not know you, boy, or what you thought this night, or what you'll think tomorrow or the next day when we must get up on our legs and move!"

The general stood up. "Well, then. Bless you, boy. Good night."

"Good night, sir." And tobacco, brass, boot polish, salt sweat and leather, the man moved away through the grass.

Joby lay for a moment, staring but unable to see where the man had gone. He swallowed. He wiped his eyes. He cleared his throat. He settled himself. Then, at last, very slowly and firmly, he turned the drum so that it faced up toward the sky.

He lay next to it, his arm around it, feeling the tremor, the touch, the muted thunder as, all the rest of the April night in the year 1862, near the Tennessee River, not far from the Owl Creek, very close to the church named Shiloh, the peach blossoms fell on the drum. ❖

---

8. **mutely.** Silently; without speaking
9. **Mr. Longfellow.** Henry Wadsworth Longfellow (1807–1882), celebrated American poet

---

MIRRORS & WINDOWS

How would you feel at the end of the story if you were the drummer boy? What do you think is the most effective motivation for soldiers facing the dangers of combat?

Find Meaning

1. (a) According to the drummer boy, what are the soldiers murmuring to themselves? (b) Why might some soldiers believe that they will not die in battle?
2. Why is the drummer boy at times envious of the soldiers?
3. (a) How does the general react to the drummer boy's tears? (b) Why do you think he responds this way?

Make Judgments

4. (a) What is the level of experience of most of the soldiers at Shiloh? (b) What results might this condition produce?
5. Why does the general call the drummer boy "the heart of the army"?
6. Would the general's words have made you feel more at ease? Explain your answer.

Differentiated Instruction

English Language Learning

Help students to understand Foote's sensory details, particularly his images and idioms. For example, clarify:

bluff—a high, steep bank or cliff, 61
cock an ear—listen closely, 61
grass-carpeted lip—grassy edge of the bluff, 61

blue and gray—the Union and Confederate troops who wore blue and gray, respectively, 61
singing of the bone saws—The high-pitched whine of saws cutting through the bone of limbs being amputated, 61

In "The Drummer Boy of Shiloh," Ray Bradbury imagines the night before one of the bloodiest battles of the Civil War. The following selection is an excerpt from "Echoes of Shiloh," an article by **Shelby Foote** (1916–2005). Born in Greenville, Mississippi, Foote was an acclaimed novelist and Civil War historian. As you read, notice how Foote uses sensory detail to evoke the battle.

from Echoes of Shiloh

An Article by Shelby Foote

The great Battle of Shiloh was over, with both armies in their original camps: one at Corinth, the other at Pittsburg Landing.

But not in the same numbers. In the war's bloodiest encounter to that time, 23,741 of the 100,000 troops engaged had been killed or wounded or were missing; close to 11,000 Confederates and just over 13,000 Federals. Casualties came to roughly 24 percent—the same as at Waterloo,[1] nearly fifty years before. Yet Waterloo had marked the end of something, whereas Shiloh was more of a beginning, with other Waterloos to follow. From Shiloh on, Grant[2] said later, "I gave up all idea of saving the Union except by complete conquest."

What remains is the field itself, those six square miles of green, evocative landscape stretching back from the Tennessee River bluff—Shiloh and the memory it evokes of those who fought here, with courage as immeasurable as the suffering. Cock an ear some calm day in the woods or fields or on the grass-carpeted lip of that tall bluff, and

you may hear, behind the stillness, the cries of battle mingling the deep-throated Union roar with the weird halloo[3] of the Rebel yell, the boom of guns and the rattle of musketry, fading to give way at last to the groans of the wounded, blue and gray, and the singing of the bone saws.

All this is there for those who know how to listen for it. One of the great satisfactions a historian, professional or amateur, derives from his work, provided he has done it truthfully and well, comes after he has put the work behind him. Once he has studied and written of an event in relation to the ground on which it happened, that scrap of earth belongs to him forever. To some extent he even feels he owns it. In that sense, Shiloh can be yours too, if you want it. ❖

---

1. **Waterloo.** Battle fought in Belgium on June 18, 1815, between the French under Napoleon and the Allies under Wellington; Napoleon's final defeat
2. **Grant.** Ulysses S. Grant (1822–1885), commander of the Union armies (1864–1865) and eighteenth president of the United States (1869–1877)
3. **halloo.** Shout or hunting call

TEXT ◀→ TEXT CONNECTION
Both Ray Bradbury's story and Shelby Foote's article deal with the Battle of Shiloh. How does each writer use sensory details to describe the scene?

ECHOES OF SHILOH **61**

Reading Skills

Synthesize Content from Several Texts
Remind students that this selection is historical fiction. For facts, readers should rely on nonfiction articles, books, and reliable Internet sources. You might divide the class into small groups and assign each group a different research source. Have students research facts about the battle of Shiloh. Then have each group present their findings to the class.

Words in Use

from "Echoes of Shiloh"

Selection Words
casualties, 61
evocative, 61
evokes, 61
immeasurable, 61
derives, 61

Teach the Connection

Use Reading Skills
Compare and Contrast Have students note the difference between each author's methods of describing the volume of men involved in the battle. While Bradbury uses imagery, such as an ocean wave, to convey the great numbers, Foote provides actual figures. **A**

Use Reading Skills
Distinguish Fact from Opinion
Ask students to point out facts in this selection (the return to original camps, the statistics regarding casualties, etc.). Then point out the opinion that the soldiers' courage was as immeasurable as their suffering. Remind students that people cannot agree or disagree with facts; however, people can choose to agree or disagree with opinions. Based on what they read in "The Drummer Boy of Shiloh," as well as the facts that Foote presents, ask students whether they agree or disagree with Foote's opinion. **B**

Text-to-Text Connection
Answer: In a very specific way, Bradbury uses sensory details to describe the quiet April night, the falling blossoms, the sounds made by the sleeping soldiers, and the way the general looks and smells. Foote uses sensory details in a more general way to describe the look of the battlefield today but also includes some specific details to evoke the sounds of battle.

Common Core State Standards

Reading Literature
RL.1

Reading Informational
RI.4

Writing
W.3, W.7, W.8, W.9

Language
L.6

Analyze Literature

Description *Answer:* Students' sensory details and effects charts might include the following: blossoms, peach stone tapping the drum (startling, frightening), moonlike appearance of drum (watchful, calming), soldiers' sleeping formation (chaotic, childlike), sweeping wind and moths and peach blossoms brushing Joby's face (temporary, transforming), the general's scent (strong, reassuring), soldiers described as wild horses (disorganized, untamed), beating of the soldiers' hearts (encouraging, anxious), and/or muted thunder (anticipatory, ominous). Students' characterizations of the story's overall mood might include *still, vigilant, dreamlike, ominous, daring, courageous,* and/or *tragic*.

Analyze Literature

Description A writer's use of sensory details helps to shape the mood or atmosphere, the feeling or emotion created by a literary work. Use a chart to analyze the effect of specific sensory details in "The Drummer Boy of Shiloh." Then characterize the overall mood of the story using two or three key words.

Sensory Detail	Effect
falling peach blossoms	softness, gentleness

Extend Understanding

Writing Options

Creative Writing Extend the events described in "The Drummer Boy of Shiloh" in a **narrative paragraph.** You might explore the same night scene from the perspective of another sleepless soldier, either Union or Confederate. You might imagine Joby's feelings and impressions as the Union troops hastily prepared for battle in the morning. (The Confederate forces launched a surprise attack at 6 AM.) However you extend the narrative, use dialogue and sensory details to create a realistic effect.

Expository Writing Bradbury's fictional drummer boy is based on a historical figure, Johnny Clem, who was just ten years old at the time he participated in the Battle of Shiloh. Bradbury made his character Joby four years older. Write a brief **character analysis** in which you speculate on why Bradbury might have made his character older than the historical Johnny Clem and evaluate how Joby's greater age affects the feeling created by the story. Share your work with the class.

Collaborative Learning

Perform Reader's Theater In reader's theater, two or more actors create a performance by reading a script based on a literary work. With two classmates, create a reader's theater version of "The Drummer Boy of Shiloh." Assign the parts of the narrator, the drummer boy, and the general. Create your script by highlighting photocopies of the text with the portions each actor is to deliver. Rehearse and perform your reader's theater version of the story for the class.

Media Literacy

Conduct Internet Research Perform keyword searches with a search engine or an electronic library database to locate further information about the battle of Shiloh. Evaluate the sources you encounter and create a list of the most reliable and the least reliable. Describe your evaluation process.

MW Go to **www.mirrorsandwindows.com** for more.

Rubrics for Writing Options

You can adapt this as a checklist for students to use as they write.

Creative Writing

☐ Does the narrative paragraph clearly indicate the perspective from which it is written?

☐ Does it clearly develop the setting of the battlefield?

☐ Does it make effective use of dialogue and sensory details?

Expository Writing

☐ Does the student's character analysis clearly describe Joby?

☐ Does it evaluate the effect of Joby's age?

☐ Does it offer an opinion as to why Bradbury made Joby older than Johnny Clem?

Gary Keillor

A Short Story by Garrison Keillor

BEFORE READING

Build Background

Cultural Context The story "Gary Keillor" takes place in the late 1950s. Keillor refers to several musicians and musical groups, including Elvis Presley, The Big Bopper, and the Conquistadores. These performers played a big part in the imagination of America's youth.

Reader's Context If you were going to be in a talent show, what would you do? Do you like to perform in public? Why or why not?

Set Purpose

Skim the text and view the images to preview "Gary Keillor." Based on your preview, what do you think the story will be about? What grabs your interest? What do you want to learn from reading the story? Jot down your initial impressions.

Analyze Literature

Tone A writer's or speaker's attitude toward the subject or the reader is **tone.** For example, a writer might use a lighthearted tone when writing about something happy or funny. A writer accomplishes tone through word choice and sentence structure. As you read "Gary Keillor," decide what the overall tone of the story is. Jot down words or sentences that reveal the tone.

Meet the Author

Garrison Keillor was born in Anoka, Minnesota, in 1942. He graduated from the University of Minnesota in 1966. Keillor is the host and creator of *A Prairie Home Companion*, a long-running and humorous radio show about the mythic town of Lake Wobegon, Minnesota. In addition to his radio show, Keillor has written many books, including a collection of short stories.

Use Reading Skills

Sequence of Events
Sequence refers to the order in which things happen. Keeping track of a story's sequence of events can help you to better understand what is happening and when it is happening in the story. You can keep track of events by creating a time line like the one below.

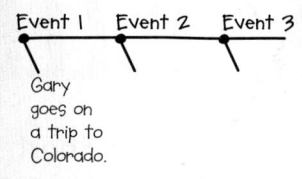

Event 1 Event 2 Event 3

Gary goes on a trip to Colorado.

Preview Vocabulary

pre•vail (pri vāl´) *v.*, succeed or win out in spite of difficulties

com•mune (kə myün´) *v.*, converse or talk together

grav•i•ty (gra´ və tē) *n.*, seriousness, importance

in•flec•tion (in flek´ shən) *n.*, change in pitch or tone of voice

pan•de•mon•i•um
(pan də mō´ nē əm) *n.*, chaos or confusion

At a Glance
Directed Reading
- Reading Level: Moderate
- Difficulty Consideration: Length
- Ease Factor: Sympathetic character

Objectives
Studying this lesson will enable students to
- use reading skills such as sequence of events
- define *tone* and recognize how an author develops tone through word choice, sentence structure, and imagery.
- describe the work of Garrison Keillor and appreciate a story containing his humor
- relate the story to the Walt Whitman poem "O Captain! My Captain!"

Launch the Lesson
You might ask students how they feel about reciting poems in front of a class or an audience. What might they do to make the poem more interesting, dramatic, or even humorous? Tell them that as they read "Gary Keillor," they will find out what one student did to add drama and humor to his poetry recitation.

Words in Use

Preview Vocabulary	Selection Words	Teaching Words
prevail, 66	finicky, 64	justified, 73
commune, 66	cassock, 65	humorous, 74
gravity, 69	incredulity, 67	commemorates, 74
inflection, 69	extolling, 70	assassinated, 74
pandemonium, 72	interminable, 70	tragedy, 75
		specific, 76

KEY TERMS
SKIM, 63
TONE, 63
SEQUENCE, 63
TIME LINE, 63
CLUSTER CHART, 76
PERSONAL NARRATIVE, 76
LITERARY RESPONSE, 76

Common Core State Standards
Reading Literature
RL.1, RL.4
Writing
W.9
Language
L.6

Summary

In this humorous personal narrative, Garrison Keillor recalls thoughts, feelings, and experiences he had as a junior in high school during the late 1950s. An entrant in a school talent show, Gary must follow the act of a more popular boy and romantic rival, who lip-synchs an Elvis Presley song. Gary's performance is to be the recital of the Whitman poem "O Captain! My Captain!" Inspired by listening to recorded poetry readings by British actor Sir John Gielgud, Gary decides to deliver the poem in a wildly exaggerated British accent to create a humorous effect. His performance is a smashing success.

MIRRORS & **W**INDOWS

The Mirrors & Windows questions at the end of this selection focus on the theme of peer relations. Before reading the story, ask students why they think a person who is well liked by his peers would feel the need to make fun of someone else. What are some potential results of ridicule like this?

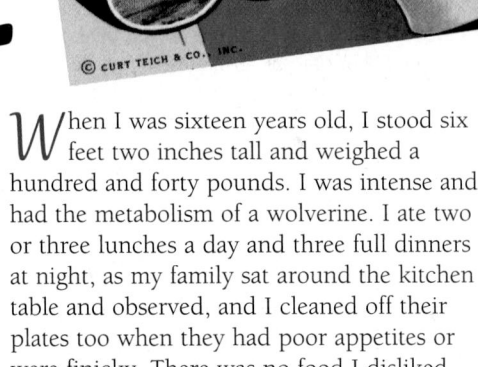

Gary Keillor

A Short Story by Garrison Keillor

When I was sixteen years old, I stood six feet two inches tall and weighed a hundred and forty pounds. I was intense and had the metabolism of a wolverine. I ate two or three lunches a day and three full dinners at night, as my family sat around the kitchen table and observed, and I cleaned off their plates too when they had poor appetites or were finicky. There was no food I disliked

64

Trips to Colorado don't fall in your lap. You've got to go out and earn Colorado.

except muskmelon, which smelled rotten and loathsome. Everything else I ate. (It was Minnesota so we didn't have seafood, except fish sticks, of course.) I was a remarkable person. I was a junior in high school, Class of 1960. I was smart, so smart that poor grades didn't bother me in the slightest; I considered them no reflection on my intelligence. I read four books a week, and I sometimes walked home from school, all twelve miles, so I could relive favorite chapters out loud, stride along the shoulder

of the highway past the potato farms, and say brilliant and outrageous things, and sing in a big throbbing voice great songs like "Til There Was You" and "Love Me Tender."

I had no wish to sing in front of an audience, songs were a private thing with me. I was an intense person, filled with powerful feelings, and I assumed that I **A** would live alone for the rest of my life, perhaps in a monastery, silent, swishing around in a cassock, my heart broken by a tragic love affair with someone like Natalie Wood,[1] my life dedicated to God.

I was a lucky boy. I had learned this two **B** years before on a car trip to Colorado. My Uncle Earl and Aunt Myrna drove there that summer—he had been stationed in Colorado Springs during the war—along with my cousins Gordon and Mel, and I got to go too. I won that trip by dropping over to their house and being extremely nice. I'd say, "Here, let me wash those dishes." I'd say, "Boy I'm sure in a mood to mow a lawn." And then she'd offer me a glass of nectar and a piece of angel food cake and I'd eat it and say, "Boy, I was looking at *National Geographic* the other night and they had a big article on Colorado. It was so interesting. Just the different rock formations and things.

---

1. **Natalie Wood.** Movie star of the 1950s and 1960s

GARY KEILLOR **65**

Teach the Selection

Cultural Connection
A Prairie Home Companion In 1969, Garrison Keillor went to work for Minnesota Public Radio as the host of a morning program called *A Prairie Home Companion*. A few years later, he decided to launch a radio program with musical guests and ads for imaginary products, and he named it after his original show. On July 6, 1974, Keillor hosted the first live broadcast. Today, *A Prairie Home Companion* is aired each week on more than 580 public radio stations and is heard all over the world by millions of listeners.

Analyze Literature
Characterization Work with students to create a character web in which you use the narrator's details on the first two pages of the story to summarize his character traits as a sixteen-year-old student. Then discuss what he means by the statement "I was an intense person." **A**

Use Reading Skills
Identify Sequence of Events Remind students that a flashback is a shift to an earlier time period. Often, authors interrupt the natural sequence of events to use a flashback to provide background information. What clues can the students find in this passage to indicate that the author has inserted a flashback? **B**

Differentiated Instruction

Reading Proficiency
Encourage students to preview the story. Read the Before Reading page, as well as the quotes within the story, and examine the illustrations. Point out that the story is a personal reflection about the author's experiences as a high school student in the late 1950s. Ask them to think about how their school experiences might be similar to, and different from, those of a student fifty years ago.

English Language Learning
Students learning English may need extra help with the following idioms:
Boy (used as an exclamation) — Wow!, 65
fit to be tied — very annoyed, 66
fall in your lap — come to you easily, without effort, 66
in a nutshell — in a very brief summarized form, 66
the cream of — best of, 66

Use Reading Skills

Identify Sequence of Events Direct students' attention to the gap in time that occurs at this point. Ask them why they think this gap exists. Point out that the author has concluded the flashback and has returned to the present time. **A**

Analyze Literature

Tone Ask students to use details from Keillor's description of Dede and Bill to describe their characters. Additionally, what do we learn about the narrator's character, based on his descriptions and his humorous, almost mocking tone? Why might he have used the word *intense* to describe both Bill and himself? Use this as a catalyst for a discussion of sarcasm. **B**

Use Reading Strategies

Make Predictions Ask students what the narrator's feelings are for Dede and what he might do next, in order to try to please her. **C**

I don't see how people can look at those mountains and not know there's a God." And she'd smile at me, a good boy who mowed lawns and whose faith was pure, and I got to go. Of course my brothers and sisters were fit to be tied. "How come he gets to go? We never get to go. Oh no, we have to stay here all summer and work in the garden while he goes riding out to Colorado." They just didn't get it. Trips to Colorado don't fall in your lap. You've got to go out and earn Colorado.

We took off on the trip, and I was a very good passenger. I sat in the favored front seat between my aunt and uncle, looking at the scenery for hours, no stains on my clothes, my face clean, a good strong bladder, never got carsick, and had a subtle sideways technique for picking my nose—you'd never see it even if you looked straight at me. Far off, the mountains appeared, shining on the horizon for almost a whole day, and then we rose up into them—snowcapped peaks, like the last scene in a western in which justice and romance <u>prevail</u>, and when we reached Denver (*EL. 5280*, the sign said, exactly a mile), we ate dinner at a Chinese restaurant and my fortune cookie said: "You are enterprising²—take advantage of it." Well, there it was in a nutshell.

The mountains were startling in their whiteness and steepness, the valleys dark in the late afternoon, the peaks glittering in **B** pure sunlight, beautiful stands of light gray-green aspen floating like fog, and my aunt took a picture of me with trees and mountains behind me. Just me, tall and intense. You would never guess I was from Minnesota. I thought, "This is my lucky picture. I'll keep it the rest of my life."

A My family lived in the country, along the Mississippi River between Minneapolis and Tryon, and I attended New Tryon High School, which was bulging under a tidal wave of children from new subdivisions on the other side of the river, places with names like Riverview Estates and Woodlawn and Forest Hills. Our side, South Tryon Township, along the West River Road, was still rural, truck farms, and scattered houses on big rolling tracts, and we West River Roaders were the cream of the school. The editor of the school paper, *The Beacon*, Elaine Eggert, was one of us; so were the stars of the debate team and the speech team, three of the class officers, and the chairperson of the spring talent show, Dede Petersen, who rode on my bus.

I had been in love with Dede for two years, in an intense and secret way. She had bouncy blonde hair and wore soft sweaters, plaid skirts, penny loafers and knee socks. One winter day I wrote her a fourteen-page letter (single-spaced) saying that she was my ideal of womanhood, a person of pure taste, excellent judgment, stunning beauty, and natural intelligence, a woman to whom I could pledge myself in a spiritual friendship that would last forever no matter what. If the friendship should turn into physical love, good, and if not, fine. We would be friends for the rest of our lives, our souls <u>communing</u> over vast distances.

I did not, after long thought, give her the letter. I guessed that she might laugh at it and also that her boyfriend Bill Swenson **B** might pound me into the ground. He was an intense person too.

One afternoon riding home on the bus, sitting behind her, I heard her complain to **C** her pal Marcy about the miseries of planning the April talent show. Bill Swenson would be

---

2. **enterprising.** Ready to take on difficult, untried, or important projects

---

pre·vail (pri vāl´) *v.*, succeed or win out in spite of difficulties
com·mune (kə myün´) *v.*, converse or talk together

Personal Pronouns

Remind students that a personal pronoun is used in place of the name of a person or thing. Personal pronouns can be singular, plural, or possessive. Have students rewrite the following sentence or sentence pairs, using personal pronouns in place of any repetitive nouns or groups of nouns.

1. Anna asked Anna's father if Anna's father would like more cake. (Anna asked her father if he would like more cake.)

2. Jim and Helen finally finished Jim and Helen's quilt. Jim and Helen's quilt hangs in the front hall of Jim and Helen's school. (Jim and Helen finally finished their quilt. It hangs in the front hall of their school.)

3. Dad and I spent Dad's and my vacation in San Diego. San Diego is Dad's and my favorite city. (Dad and I spent our vacation in San Diego. It is our favorite city.)

in it lip-synching "All Shook Up," and he was terrific, but there wasn't much other talent around, nothing compared to last year, when all those guys sang "Bali Hai" with the coconuts on their chests, and the skit about school lunch when the kids pretended to vomit and out came green confetti, and of course last year there had been Barbara Lee. Barbara Lee was the most talented person ever to graduate from our school. She danced, she sang, she did the splits, and she played the marimba. She was Broadway bound, no doubt about it.

I leaned forward and said, "Well, I think we have lots of talent." Oh? like who, for example? she said. I said, "Well, I could do something." *You?* she said. "Or I could get together with some other kids and we could do a skit." *Like what?* she said. I said, "Oh, I don't know. Something about the school burning down. It all depends."

"That doesn't sound funny to me," she said. Marcy didn't think it was funny either.

What burned my toast was her saying *"You?"* when I volunteered to be in her talent show. I was only being helpful, I was not claiming to be another Barbara Lee. I had no interest in the stage at all until I heard her incredulity and amusement—*"You?"*—and then I was interested in being interested. A spiritual friendship with Dede was out of the question, if she thought I was the sort of guy you could say *"You?"* to.

No one in our family sang or performed for entertainment, only for the glory of God and only in groups, never solo. We were Christian people; we did not go in for show. But I was an intense young man. Intensity was my guiding principle. And when I thought about joining that monastery after Natalie Wood rejected me and spending my life in the woodshop making sturdy chairs and tables, I thought that perhaps I ought to get in the talent show at New Tryon High

first, get a whiff of show business before I give my life to God.

It was one of those ugly and treacherous springs in the Midwest, when winter refuses to quit, like a big surly drunk who heads for home and then staggers back for another round and a few more songs that everyone has heard before. It was cold and wet, and we sat day after day in dim airless classrooms, the fluorescent lights turned on at midday, the murky sky and bare trees filling the big classroom windows, pools of oil-slicked rain in the parking lot, the grass in front dead, the Stars and Stripes hanging limp and wet like laundry. In plane geometry, I was lost in the wilderness, had been lost since Christmas, and in history, we were slogging through World War I, and in English class, we were memorizing poems. "These are treasures you will carry with you

Use Reading Strategies
Clarify Point out that the italicized words are spoken with emphasis. Call on volunteers to read the sentences aloud. Then ask them why Dede's use of such emphasis "burned [the] toast" of the narrator. **D**

Make Connections
Ask students what the narrator means by the clause *and then I was interested in being interested.* What changed his mind about being interested in the stage? Model questions: "Why do people sometimes abruptly change course when someone hurts their feelings? Does Gary see this as a challenge? Does he want to prove something?" **E**

Analyze Literature
Tone Ask students to paraphrase Keillor's description of the "ugly and treacherous" spring. If possible, have them draw on their own experiences of cold, dark weather that prolongs winter when everyone is eager for spring. Discuss the simile that Keillor uses, having students visualize how lingering, dark, and unpleasant winter weather is similar to the big, surly man who lingers and sings songs that everyone's already heard. Ask what overall effect these descriptions have on the passage's tone. **F**

Identify Author's Approach
Discuss other familiar stories or poems about romance and affection, particularly those with serious tones. Then ask students to compare and contrast the tones of those pieces of literature with that of this passage. Lead them to understand that Keillor uses a light, almost mocking tone here to make fun of his "intensity." Stress that he is making fun of himself, not all "teenagers in love." Lead students to understand that he uses overblown drama (his infatuation with Natalie Wood, a glamorous movie star of the era) and exaggeration (the details in his letter) to create humor. As they read on, urge them to find further examples of Keillor's use of exaggeration and overblown drama.

Literary Connection

"Oh Captain! My Captain!" Point out to students that Keillor will make many references in this story to Walt Whitman's poem "O Captain! My Captain!" If you feel greater background would be useful at this point, discuss the information provided in the Literary Connection on page 74. **A**

Analyze Literature

Character Discuss why the mother's response seems out of character. Then discuss the meaning of the idiom *watershed moment*. Ask students why the narrator was proud of his mother and what lesson her actions taught him. Why did it lead him to "open the door to show business"? **B**

Use Reading Skills

Compare and Contrast Ask students how Miss Rasmussen's reaction to the poem recitation is different from that of the narrator's classmates. Have them use their own knowledge and experiences to suggest why these different reactions take place. Then have them speculate about the narrator's feelings. Based on the reactions of his classmates, do they think he is eager to recite the poem in front of the whole school at the talent show? **C**

forever," said Miss Rasmussen, a big woman in a blue knit suit. In her wanderings around the classroom as she talked about poetry and metaphor, she often stopped in the aisle and stood looming above me, her voice overhead, her hand resting on my desk, her puffy white hand and red knuckles and short ringless fingers. Her stopping there indicated, I knew, her fondness for me. I was the only student of hers who wrote poems. She had even suggested that I memorize and recite one of my own poems. I declined. Part of the memorization assignment was reciting the poem in front of the class. My poems were far too intense and personal to be said out loud in front of people. I was memorizing Whitman's elegy on the death of Abraham Lincoln, "O Captain! My Captain!" I walked home through the rain one cold day crying out, "O Captain! my Captain! our fearful trip is done, / The ship has weather'd every rack, the prize we sought is won."

One day a fuel oil truck backed into our driveway and got stuck in the mud and the driver put it into forward gear and got dug in deeper. He gunned it in reverse and gunned it forward and rocked the truck loose and pulled forward and unwound his hose and started filling our fuel oil tank, but meanwhile he had left deep ruts in my mother's garden and the front yard. She was home alone, washing clothes. She heard the grinding and roaring from down in the laundry room and came outdoors to find her garden dug up and the tulips and irises destroyed, and the driver looked at her and said, "You ought to do something about your driveway." Not a word of apology, acted like it was the driveway's fault. My mother was the quietest, politest person ever, she felt that raising your voice indicated a flawed character, but she put her hands on her hips and said, "Mister, if you can't figure out how to drive a truck, then they oughta find you a

job you'd be able to handle." And she told him to get out and she would be sending the company a bill for the flower garden. And he did. And she did. And the company sent us a check and an apology from the general manager, a Harold L. Bergstrom.

It was the first time in my memory that my mother had fought back and raised her voice to a stranger, a watershed[3] moment for me. I heard the story from our neighbor, Mr. Couture, and I admired her so much for standing up to the jerk and defending our family's honor. Her principles had always told her to be quiet and polite and turn the other cheek and never make trouble, but there comes a time to let go of principle and do the right thing. To me, this seemed to open the door to show business.

And then, about a week before the talent show, suddenly I was in. The real power behind the show wasn't Dede, it was Miss Rasmussen, my teacher, the adviser to the talent show, and the day I stood before the class and recited "O Captain! My Captain!" she told Dede to put me in the show. The next day, Miss Rasmussen had me stand up in class and recite it again. It was one of the finest pieces of oral interpretation she had ever seen, she said. She sat in a back corner of the room, her head bowed, her eyes closed, as I stood in front and with dry mouth launched the Captain's ship again, and she did not see the kids smirking and gagging and retching and pulling long invisible skeins of snot from their nostrils and when my Captain died and I got to "O the bleeding drops of red, / Where on the deck my Captain lies, / Fallen cold and dead," they rolled their eyes and clutched at their hearts and died. Then, when she stood up, her eyes moist, and clapped, they all clapped too. "Wasn't that good!" she cried.

---

3. **watershed.** Moment where an important change takes place

Reading Proficiency

Keillor uses many images that some readers may find difficult. Have students work with partners to question, analyze, and "translate" the meanings of such passages as:

1. "And when I thought about joining the monastery . . . get a whiff of show business before I give my life to God." (page 67)

2. "In plane geometry, I was lost in the wilderness . . . we were memorizing poems." (page 67)

Provide time for partners to share and discuss their results with the class.

"You really liked it, didn't you! Oh, I'm glad you did! He's going to recite it in the talent show, too! Won't that be nice!" A couple of boys in front clapped their hands over their mouths and pretended to lose their lunch. They seemed to speak for most of the class.

So I was in the talent show, which I wanted to be, but with an inferior piece of material. I suggested to Miss Rasmussen that "O Captain! My Captain!" might not be right for the talent show audience, that maybe I could find a humorous poem, and she said, "Oh, it'll be just fine," not realizing the gravity of the situation. "Never give up on beauty," she said. "Never compromise your standards out of fear that someone may not understand." Teachers were full of useless advice like that.

I tried not to think about "O Captain." I experimented with combing my hair a new way, with the part on the right. I was handsome at certain angles, I thought, and a right-hand part would emphasize a good angle. I stood at the bathroom mirror, a small mirror in my hand, and experimented holding my head cocked back and aimed up and to the right, a pose favored by seniors in their graduation pictures, which looked good from either side, and reciting "O Captain" with my head at that angle. I had good skin except when it flared up, which it did two days before the show, and it took a long time to repair the damage. There were six children in our family and only one bathroom, but I spent fifteen minutes behind a locked door doing surgery and applying alcohol and cold packs and skin-toned cream. The little kids stood banging on the door, pleading to use the toilet. I said, "Well, how bad do you have to go?" I was the one in show business, after all.

I worked on "O Captain" so that every line was set in my head. I recited it to myself in the mirror ("O Captain! O Captain! the fateful day is done, / Your blemishes have disappeared, the skin you sought is won") and for my mother, who said I was holding my head at an unnatural angle, and then, the Friday night before the show, I recited it at a party at Elaine Eggert's house, and there my interpretation of "O Captain! My Captain!" took a sharp turn toward the English stage.

Miss Rasmussen loved a recording of Sir John Gielgud reading "Favourites of English Poetry" and she played it once for our class, a whole hour of it, and from that day, all the boys in the class loved to do English accents. A little lisp, endless dramatic pauses, fruity inflections including shrill birdlike tones of wonderment, and instead of the vowel *o* that delicious English *aaoooww*, a bleating sound not found anywhere in American speech. In the cafeteria, when my friend Ralph Moody came to the table where all of us West River Road rats sat, he stood holding his tray, peering down at us and the welter[4] of milk cartons and comic books and ice cream wrappers and uneaten macaroni-cheese lunches, and after a long pause he cried "Aaaaoooooww," with a shudder, a great man forced to sit among savages. So at the party, surrounded by kids from the debate team and the newspaper, the cream of West River Road society, when Elaine had said for the sixth time, "Do the poem you're going to do on Monday," I reached back for Ralph's *Aaoooww* and did "O Captain" as Sir John might have done it:

---

4. **welter.** State of wild disorder; chaos

grav•i•ty (gra′ və tē) *n.*, seriousness, importance
in•flec•tion (in flek′ shən) *n.*, change in pitch or tone of voice

Teach the Selection

Analyze Literature
Point of View Ask students how Keillor creates humor in this passage by describing the differences between the narrator's point of view and that of Miss Rasmussen. What generational statement might he be making? **D**

Make Connections
Ask students why the narrator seems suddenly so concerned about his appearance. What feelings might he have as he prepares for the talent show? **E**

Cultural Connection
Sir John Gielgud Sir John Gielgud (1904–2000) was a British actor, producer, and director. Most critics and scholars consider him to be among the greatest actors of his generation, particularly in Shakespearean drama. In 1953, he was knighted for services to the theater. Along with live theater, Gielgud appeared in many films. In 1981, he received the Academy Award for best supporting actor for his work in the film *Arthur*, starring Dudley Moore. Gielgud had a classic and dignified way of speaking, with a crisp English accent. There are many recordings in which he recites poems and Shakespearean monologues. If possible, play a recording for the class so that they can hear the accent to which Keillor refers. **F**

Grammar Skills

Punctuate Adverb Clauses
Point out to students that an adverb clause at the beginning of a sentence is followed by a comma, whereas one at the end of a sentence does not need to be set off by a comma.

EXAMPLES
Any time he could, Jim played basketball.
Trent is older *than I am.*

Ask students to write two sentences, each containing an adverb clause. One sentence should begin with the clause, and the other sentence should end with the clause.

Use Reading Strategies

Clarify Point out that the phrase *burst a blood vessel* is a hyperbole, a figure of speech that contains an exaggeration. Its meaning is similar to *blow her top*. Then discuss why Elaine used this hyperbole to describe Miss Rasmussen's reaction to Gary's new way of reciting the poem. **Ⓐ**

Cultural Connection

Elvis Presley Combining elements of blues, country, and gospel music in his performing style and repertoire, Elvis Presley was an instant hit in the mid-1950s. One of his early hits, "All Shook Up" reached the top of the pop, rhythm & blues, and country music charts in April and May 1957. **Ⓑ**

Cultural Connection

The Big Bopper Another pop star of the 1950s, the Big Bopper was known for his deep voice. His real name was J. P. Richardson, but he took on his stage name when he worked as a disk jockey in Beaumont, Texas, early in his career. The Big Bopper died in 1959 in a plane crash that also killed pop stars Ritchie Valens and Buddy Holly. The words that Bill says here (*Helllllllooo baby!* and *You knowwwwwwwww what I like!*) are from the Big Bopper's biggest hit song, "Chantilly Lace." It was one of the most popular songs of 1958. **Ⓒ**

Aoowww Cap-tin, myyyy Cap-tin,
Aower--------feeah-fool twip eez done!
Th' sheep has wethah'd--------eviddy rack!
th' priiiiiiize we sot------------eez won!
But--------aaaoooooooowwwww
th' bleeeeeeeding drrrops-------of rrred----
wheahhhh--------
on th' deck---------myyyy Captin liiiiiiiies----
fallin-----------
caaaooooowwwwld------------
and------------------------------ded!

It was a good party poem. I recited it in the basement, and then everyone upstairs had to come down and hear it, and then Elaine had to call up a friend of hers in the city and I did it on the phone. It got better.

Ⓐ "Miss Rasmussen is going to burst a blood vessel," said Elaine. She was a true rebel, despite the editorials she wrote extolling the value of team play and school spirit. I was starting to see some of the virtues in her that I had previously imagined in Dede Petersen.

Ⓑ Bill Swenson had worked for weeks on "All Shook Up," and he looked cool and capable backstage before the curtain went up. His hair was slicked down, and he wore heavy eye makeup, and he was dressed in a white suit with gold trim, without a single wrinkle in it. He stood, holding his arms out to the sides, avoiding wrinkling, and practiced moving his lips to "A-wella bless my soul, what'sa wrong with me? I'm itching like a man on a fuzzy tree." Dede knelt, shining his black shoes.

He pretended to be surprised to see me. "What are you doing here? You running the p.a. or what?"

I told him I would be in the show, reciting a poem by Walt Whitman.

"Who? Twitman?" No. Whitman, I said.

"Well, I'm glad I don't have to follow that," he said, with heavy sarcasm. He glanced at my outfit, brown corduroy pants, a green plaid cotton shirt, a charcoal gray sweater vest, and said, "You better change into your stage clothes though."

"These are my stage clothes," I said.

"Oh," he said, his eyebrows raised. "Oh." He smiled. "Well, good luck." He did not know how much luck I had. I had my lucky picture in my pocket, the one of me in the mountains.

Dede brushed his forehead with face powder and poofed up his hair. She gave him a light kiss on the lips. "You're going to be great," she said. He smiled. He had no doubt about that. She had put him high on the program, right after "America the Beautiful," a dramatic choral reading from *Antigone*, a solo trumpet rendition of "Nobody Knows the Trouble I've Seen," and a medley of Rodgers and Hammerstein songs performed on the piano by Cheryl Ann Hansen. Then Bill would electrify the crowd with "All Shook Up," and then I would do "O Captain."

He was Mr. Cool. After Cheryl Ann Hansen's interminable medley, which kids clapped and cheered for only because they knew that her mother had recently died of cancer, Bill grinned at Dede and bounced out **Ⓒ** on stage and yelled, "Helllll-ooo baby!" in a Big Bopper voice, and the audience clapped and yelled "Helllooo baby!" and he yelled, "You knowwwwwwwww what I like!" and he was a big hit in the first five seconds. He said it again, "Helllllllooo baby!" and the audience yelled back, "Hellllllllooo baby!" And then Dede carefully set the phonograph needle on the record of "All Shook Up" and Elvis's hoody voice blasted out in the auditorium and Bill started shimmying across the stage and tossing his head like a dustmop. "My friends say I'm acting queer as a bug, I'm in love—huh! I'm all shook up," and on the *huh* he stuck both arms in the air and threw his hip to the left, *huh*, and the audience sang along on the "hmm hmm hmm—oh—yeah yeah"—he was the star of the show right there. Dede ran to look out through a hole in the curtain, leaving me standing by

Differentiated Instruction

Auditory Learning

You might want to refer students to the poem "O Captain! My Captain!," beginning on page 75, to illustrate the differences between the actual words of the poem *(O)* and Keillor's exaggerated pronunciations *(Aoowww)*. Additionally, as suggested above, you might play a recording of Gielgud reciting this or another poem so that students can relate the actual accent to Keillor's exaggerated version. Finally, students might enjoy reading Keillor's auditory version aloud, mimicking the accent that he suggests.

Elvis Presley.

fateful decision. He went out and did his other number. **D**

It was "Vaya con Dios"[5] by the Conquistadores. Dede put the needle down and the guitars throbbed, and the audience clapped, but Bill hadn't worked as hard on "Vaya con Dios," as on "All Shook Up" and his lips didn't synch very well, but the main problem was that "Vaya con Dios" was "Vaya con Dios," and after "All Shook Up" it seemed like a joke, especially since the Conquistadores were a trio and Bill wasn't. Kids started to laugh, and Bill got mad—perhaps "Vaya con Dios" meant a lot to him personally— and his grim face and his clenched fists made "Vaya con Dios" seem even zanier. Dede ran to the hole in the curtain to see where the hooting and light booing were coming from, and there, standing by the record player, I thought I would help poor Bill out by lightly touching the record with my finger and making the music go flat and sour for a moment. **F**

It was miraculous, the effect this had, like pressing a laugh button. I touched the black vinyl rim and the music warbled, and fifty feet away, people erupted in fits of happiness. I did it again. How wonderful to hear people laugh! and to be able to give them this precious gift of laughter so easily. Then I discovered a speed control that let me slow it down and speed it up. The singers sounded demented,[6] in love one moment, carsick the next. The audience thought this was a stitch. But Bill sort of went to pieces. One prime qualification for a show business career, I would think, is the ability to improvise[7] and go with the audience, but

the record player. She was so thrilled, she hopped up and down and squealed.

I could see part of him out there, his white suit hanging loose, the red socks flashing, him pulling out the red satin hanky and tossing it into the audience, *hmmm hmmm hmmm oh yeah yeah,* and at the end the whole auditorium stood up and screamed. He came off stage bright with sweat, grinning, and went back out and made three deep bows, and threw his hip, *huh,* and came off and Dede wiped his face with a towel and kissed him, and the audience was still screaming and whistling and yelling, "More! More!" and right then Bill made his

5. **"Vaya Con Dios."** Title of a popular song
6. **demented.** Crazy, insane
7. **improvise.** In acting, this means to make up material on the spot.

GARY KEILLOR **71**

Use Reading Skills

Analyze Sequence of Events
Discuss the sequence of events here. Bill's second performance turns into a comic failure, followed by Gary's appearance on stage. Discuss with students how Gary's success is at least partially an effect of Bill's failure. The audience is ready for a laugh, and Gary uses that to his advantage. Thus, he solves both his conflict with Bill and his conflict involving the success of his own performance. **A**

Use Reading Skills

Identify Cause and Effect Ask students what Gary means by this sentence. What caused him to decide against an encore? **B**

Bill Swenson did not have that ability. Here he was, rescued from his drippy encore, magically transformed into comedy, and he was too rigid to recognize what a hit he was. His lips stopped moving. He shook his fist at someone in the wings, perhaps me, and yelled a common vulgar expression at someone in the crowd, and wheeled around and walked off.

I didn't care to meet him, so I walked fast right past him onto the stage, and coming out of the bright light into the dark, he didn't

A see me until I was out of reach. There was still some heavy booing when I arrived at the microphone, and I made a deep English-actor type of bow, with princely flourishes and flutters, and they laughed, and then they were mine all the way. I held on to them for dear life for the next two minutes. I sailed into "O Captain," in my ripest and fruitiest accent, with roundhouse gestures, outflung arms, hand clapped to the forehead----------I cried:

AOOWWW CAP-TIN, MYYYY CAP-TIN, AOWER-------FEEAH-FOOL TWIP EEZ DONE!

TH' SHEEP HAS WETHAH'D-----------EFIDDY RACK!

TH' PRIIIIIIIIZE WE SOT-----------EEZ WON!

BUT------------
AAAAOOOOOOOOWWWWW

TH' BLLEEEEEEEEDING DRRROPS-------
OF RRRED--------------------
WHEAHH-------
ON TH' DECK-----------
BEEEL SWEN-SON
LIIIIIIIIES----------------------
FALLIN------------------------------------
CAAAOOOOWWWLD
------------------------AND--------------
-----------DED!

B It wasn't a kind or generous thing to do, but it was successful, especially the "AAAAAOOOOOOOOWWWWW" and also the part about Bill Swenson, and at the end there was shouting and whistling and pandemonium, and I left the stage with the audience wanting more, but I had witnessed the perils of success, and did not consider an encore. "Go out and take a bow," said Miss Rasmussen, and out I went, and came back off. Dede and Bill were gone. Dede was not feeling well, said Miss Rasmussen.

I watched the rest of the show standing at the back of the auditorium. The act after me was a girl from the wrong side of the river who did a humorous oral interpretation entitled "Granny on the Phone with Her Minister." The girl had painted big surprise eyebrows and a big red mouth on her so

> **pan·de·mon·i·um** (pan də mō´ nē əm) *n.*, chaos or confusion

---

Differentiated Instruction

Auditory Learning

If possible, play recordings of Elvis Presley singing "All Shook Up," the Big Bopper singing "Chantilly Lace," and the Conquistadores or another group singing "Vaya con Dios." Encourage students to visualize Bill's performances and to "hear" him imitate Elvis and the Big Bopper singing the lines that appear in the story. Students might enjoy imitating the sounds themselves. Then, based on

what they have heard, ask them to compare and contrast the two numbers that Bill performed. Why was the first one such a success and the second one a letdown?

we would know it was comedy and as the sketch went on, she shrieked to remind us that it was humorous. The joke was that Granny was hard-of-hearing and got the words wrong. Then came an accordionist, a plump young man named David Lee, Barbara's cousin, who was a little overambitious with "Lady of Spain" and should have left out two or three of the variations, and a tap dancer who tapped to a recording of "Nola" and who made the mistake of starting the number all over again after she had made a mistake. I enjoyed watching these dogs, strictly from a professional point of view. And then the choir returned to sing "Climb Every Mountain," and then Miss Rasmussen stood and spoke about the importance of encouraging those with talent and how lucky we should feel to have them in our midst to bring beauty and meaning to our lives. And then the lights came up, and my classmates piled into the aisles and headed for the door and saw me standing in back, modest me, looking off toward the stage. Almost every one of them said how good I was as they trooped past—clapped my shoulder, said, hey, you were great, you should've done more, that was funny—and I stood and patiently endured their attention until the auditorium was empty and then I went home.

"You changed the poem a little," Miss Rasmussen said the next day. "Did you forget the line?" "Yes," I said. "Your voice sounded funny," she said. I told her I was nervous. "Oh well," she said, "they seemed to like it anyway."

"Thank you," I said, "thank you very much." ❖

Do you think that what Gary did to Bill was justified? Why do you think a boy like Bill might make fun of someone like Gary? What are possible effects of one person or a group of people ridiculing another person?

Find Meaning

1. (a) What is the effect on Gary of his mother's encounter with the truck driver?
   (b) Why does Gary respond this way?
2. (a) What happens the first time Gary recites the poem? (b) How does this relate to what happens when he recites the poem in the talent show?
3. (a) What is Gary's reaction to the photo taken in Colorado? (b) What does this tell you about him?

Make Judgments

4. (a) How would you describe Gary? Use examples from the text to support your description. (b) Would you like Gary for a friend? Explain.
5. (a) How does the author let the reader know how Bill feels about Gary? (b) How is Bill portrayed in the story?
6. Gary starts out in the story by saying that he is a lucky boy. Given the events and the ending of the story, do you agree with that statement? Explain.

GARY KEILLOR **73**

Writing Skills

Personal Narrative

Before students begin to plan their personal narratives in the Extend Understanding creative writing activity, review some of the techniques that Garrison Keillor used successfully in his personal narrative.

- A clear sequence of events, with a flashback to provide important background information
- A light, humorous tone that pokes good-natured fun at many situations and characters, including himself
- Vivid descriptions of settings, situations, characters, and feelings
- Clear identification of a central conflict, with action rising to a climax and then falling to a resolution

▶ More About the Author

The Civil War gave Walt Whitman a deep love for President Abraham Lincoln. Whitman wrote several poems about Lincoln and included them in his collection *Leaves of Grass.* Throughout the collection, he addresses the citizens of the United States directly, urging them to be generous and kind, to value the beauty of the natural world, and to respect the power and strength of the individual.

Analyze Literature

Figurative Language Students may not be familiar with the spelling *O*. Point out that this is a figure of speech called an apostrophe. The apostrophe is used to address a person, spirit, or thing, usually one that is not present. As in this poem, the apostrophe *O* is usually used in an exclamation.

Use Reading Skills

Compare and Contrast Ask students to identify specific ways in which the battered ship returning to port is like the United States coming to the end of the Civil War. Additionally, have them compare and contrast the feelings of the "swaying mass" standing on the pier to welcome the ship with the feelings of people at the end of a war. Finally, have them note that the speaker in the poem twice refers to the captain as "father." Ask them to suggest what these names suggest about Whitman's feelings for Abraham Lincoln.

LITERATURE ▶▶ CONNECTION

In "Gary Keillor," the narrator recites the poem "O Captain! My Captain!" for the talent show. Although Gary recites the poem in a humorous manner, the poem itself is serious. Written by **Walt Whitman** in 1865, the poem commemorates the death of President Abraham Lincoln, who was assassinated as the Civil War was ending. In the poem, the dead captain of the ship represents Lincoln. Walt Whitman (1819–1892) is considered one of America's greatest poets.

74 UNIT 1 FICTION

Differentiated Instruction

Enrichment

Students might enjoy learning more about Walt Whitman and *Leaves of Grass,* particularly his other poems related to Abraham Lincoln ("When Lilacs Last in the Dooryard Bloom'd," "Hush'd Be the Camps To-day," and "This Dust Was Once the Man"). Have them select poems to analyze and recite.

Common Core State Standards

Reading Literature
RL.1, RL.4

Writing
W.9

Language
L.6

O Captain! My Captain!

A Narrative Poem by Walt Whitman

O Captain! my Captain! our fearful trip is done,
The ship has weather'd every rack, the prize we sought is won,
The port is near, the bells I hear, the people all exulting,[1]
While follow eyes the steady keel, the vessel grim and daring;
5   But O heart! heart! heart!
          O the bleeding drops of red,
            Where on the deck my Captain lies,
              Fallen cold and dead.

O Captain! my Captain! rise up and hear the bells;
10 Rise up—for you the flag is flung—for you the bugle trills,
For you bouquets and ribbon'd wreaths—for you the shores a-crowding,
For you they call, the swaying mass, their eager faces turning;
        Here Captain! dear father!
          This arm beneath your head!
15   It is some dream that on the deck,
              You've fallen cold and dead.

My Captain does not answer, his lips are pale and still,
My father does not feel my arm, he has no pulse nor will,
The ship is anchor'd safe and sound, its voyage closed and done,
20 From fearful trip the victor ship comes in with object won;
        Exult O shores, and ring O bells!
          But I with mournful tread,
            Walk the deck my Captain lies,
              Fallen cold and dead. ❖   *1865–1866*

---

1. **exulting.** Acting joyful and proud

TEXT ← TO → TEXT CONNECTION

The poem "O Captain! My Captain!" tells of a tragedy. In some instances, humor can be a way a way of dealing with tragedy. How does that idea play a role in "Gary Keillor"?

Analyze Literature

Tone Lead students to note the shift in tone within the first stanza. The first four lines have a joyful tone of triumph. However, the tone suddenly shifts to horror and then sadness, with the appearance of the dead Captain. Remind them that writers often achieve tone through word choice and sentence structure. Have students cite elements that contribute to each tone in this stanza. **Ⓐ**

Analyze Literature

Figurative Language Discuss the meaning of these lines, leading students to understand that the speaker has put his arm under the head of the captain to support it. *It is some dream* suggests that the speaker wishes that he has only imagined, or dreamed, that the captain is dead. This disbelief relates to the nation's shock and horror regarding Lincoln's sudden death. **Ⓑ**

Text-to-Text Connection

Answer: Some students might say that the events in the poem happened a long time ago and are far away from the students' actual lives. Additionally, the students probably aren't paying attention to what the poem says. Gary makes the poem funny by distorting the words in a fake English accent and by reminding the audience of Bill's gaffe. This further distances the poem from any sense of tragedy.

TEACHING NOTE

Revision

Students who dislike the process of revising and proofreading drafts may be interested to know that Walt Whitman continued to revise his poems even after they were published. For a photograph of "O Captain! My Captain!" showing Whitman's handwritten revisions, suggest that students search on the Internet using a search term such as "Whitman O Captain manuscript."

Words in Use

"O Captain! My Captain!"

Selection Words
weather'd, 75
port, 75
keel, 75
grim, 75
trill, 75
exalt, 75

Review the Selection

Analyze Literature

Tone *Answer:* Students should choose humorous examples from the text, such as the word "intense," the sentence "I was intense and had the metabolism of a wolverine," the image of him writing a fourteen-page letter, and the instance of Gary's performance.

TEACHING NOTE

Self-Generated Questioning

Have students work with partners or in small groups to explain what makes Gary a dynamic character. To stimulate thought, review how he felt about himself early in the story—intense but unwilling to risk embarrassment, and resentful of Bill Swenson's "coolness." Then have students work together to outline the change that occurs in his feelings about himself.

Analyze Literature

Tone The tone in "Gary Keillor" is meant to be humorous. Use a cluster chart to write examples of words, sentences, images, and incidents that set the tone of the story. What in the story did you find the most funny?

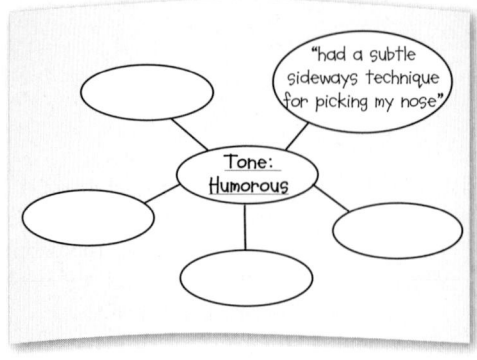

Extend Understanding

Writing Options

Creative Writing Write a short **personal narrative** telling about an experience you had that was embarrassing and how you dealt with it. Or, write about a triumph, a time when you or others were happy about what you did. Use specific images and details and tell events in chronological order. Share your narrative with a partner.

Expository Writing Write a **literary response** to "Gary Keillor." In your essay, discuss the tone of the story. Did you find the story funny? Why? State your main idea in a thesis. Use examples from your cluster chart to illustrate what is meant to be humorous in the story. Did the tone of the story affect how you felt about Gary and his actions? How might you have felt if the tone had been more serious? Share your essay with the class.

Collaborative Learning

Have a Discussion In small groups, discuss how Bill could have handled the situation that occurred on stage differently. How do you think Gary might have reacted to a similar situation? How would you have reacted? Express your opinions clearly and succinctly so that everyone in the group has a chance to speak. Summarize your group's responses in a single paragraph.

Lifelong Learning

Research Use the library or Internet to find out more about Garrison Keillor. Include information on how he started performing on the radio and his feelings about radio performance. Locate a transcript from his show or an excerpt from some of his other writing. Present your information and Keillor's work to the class.

Go to **www.mirrorsandwindows.com** for more.

Rubrics for Writing Options

You can adapt this as a checklist for students to use as they write.

Creative Writing

☐ Is the experience clearly described?

☐ Are the narrator's emotions clear to the reader?

☐ Do the details and images help the reader to visualize the event?

Expository Writing

☐ Does the literary response explain why the story is funny or not funny?

☐ Does it include specific examples from the story?

☐ Does it discuss how the tone of the story affected the reader's feelings about Gary?

☐ Does it include thoughts on how a different tone might affect the reader differently?

Grammar & Style

Pronoun-Antecedent Agreement

It was the first time in my memory that my mother had fought back and raised her voice to a stranger, a watershed moment for me.

—GARRISON KEILLOR, "Gary Keillor"

In the passage above, the pronoun *her* refers to the noun *mother*. Pronouns must always agree with their antecedents in number (singular or plural) and gender (masculine, feminine, or neuter). Since *mother* is singular and feminine, the singular feminine pronoun *her* is correct.

> **EXAMPLE**
> *The mountains were startling in their whiteness and steepness.*

In this example, the plural neuter pronoun *their* refers to *mountains*.

> **EXAMPLE**
> *The talent show took place in the school auditorium, which was a common meeting place for the students.*

In this example, the pronoun *which* refers to *auditorium* in the first clause. Avoid using pronouns such as *which*, *it*, *this*, and *that* without a clear antecedent.

> **EXAMPLE**
> *Gary and the West River Road kids were sitting at their table in the cafeteria.*

In this example, the pronoun *their* refers to *Gary and the West River Road kids*. The antecedent is plural so the pronoun is plural.

> **EXAMPLES**
> *Some of the town was left in its original condition.*
>
> *Some of the buildings were left in their original condition.*

The pronouns *any, some, all,* or *none* may be singular or plural, depending on how they are used. In the first example, *some* refers to *town*, so the pronoun *its* is singular. In the second example, *some* refers to *buildings,* so the pronoun *their is* plural.

Sentence Improvement

For each of the following sentences, select the response that indicates the best revision.

1. All of the students in the audience clapped its hands.
   A. All of the students in the audience clapped his hands.
   B. All of the students in the audience clapped their hands.
   C. All of the students in the audience clapped her hands.
   D. no change

2. Gary recited a Walt Whitman poem he was his teacher's favorite.
   A. Gary recited a Walt Whitman poem who was his teacher's favorite.
   B. Gary recited a Walt Whitman poem whom was his teacher's favorite.
   C. Gary recited a Walt Whitman poem that was his teacher's favorite.
   D. no change

Sentence Improvement

1. B. All of the students in the audience clapped their hands.
2. C. Gary recited a Walt Whitman poem that was his teacher's favorite.

Build Skills

Another common error students make is to use a pronoun, such as *this* or *that,* without a clearly stated antecedent. For example:

Many people like Garrison Keillor's radio program, and *this* is why *A Prairie Home Companion* was later made into a movie.

The pronoun *this* has no clear antecedent. Tell students they can often make an antecedent clearer by adding a noun after the pronoun *this* or *that*. For example:

Many people like Garrison Keillor's radio program, and *this popularity* is why *A Prairie Home Companion* was later made into a movie.

> For more information, see Grammar & Style Section 3.4, Pronouns, in the Language Arts Handbook.

Program Resources

You will find additional lessons on Pronoun-Antecedent Agreement in the *Exceeding the Standards: Grammar & Style* resource.

Words in Use

Teaching Words
watershed, 77
gender, 77
neuter, 77

KEY TERMS
PRONOUN, 77
NOUN, 77
ANTECEDENT, 77
CLAUSE, 77

Common Core State Standards

Language
L.3.1f

CHECKOUTS
A Short Story by Cynthia Rylant

ORANGES
A Narrative Poem by Gary Soto

Preview the Selections

At a Glance
Directed Reading
"Checkouts"
- Reading Level: Moderate
- Difficulty Consideration: Elaborate descriptions
- Ease Factor: Sympathetic character

"Oranges"
- Reading Level: Easy
- Difficulty Consideration: Verse format
- Ease Factors: Simple vocabulary, informal tone

DIRECTED READING

Objectives
Studying this lesson will enable students to
- compare literary selections of different genres
- use reading strategies such as making predictions
- define *motivation* and compare the effects of this literary technique in these selections
- describe the literary accomplishments of Cynthia Rylant and Gary Soto
- discuss how people sometimes "wear masks" to hide their real thoughts

Launch the Lesson
Explain to students that the following two selections are about young people about their age who meet and are attracted to one another. Note that both have very different circumstances surrounding these relationships. Ask students to think about why certain people seem more interesting than others.

BEFORE READING

Build Background
Literary Context Both "Checkouts" and "Oranges" are realistic narratives. A **narrative** is a story. A realistic narrative has events, characters, and settings that could be real.

Reader's Context Have you known someone who was infatuated with someone? How did that person behave toward the person he or she liked?

Set Purpose
An **image** is language that creates a concrete representation of an object or experience. As you read, think about how the images, characters, places, and events contribute to the realistic nature of the texts.

Meet the Authors

Cynthia Rylant was born in Virginia in 1954. She is the author of numerous children and young adult books and has won many writing awards including the Newbery Medal.

Gary Soto was born in 1952 in Fresno, California. He is the author of more than twenty books and has won numerous awards for his poetry and short stories. Much of Soto's writing focuses on the Mexican-American experience. He lives in Berkeley, California.

Compare Literature: Motivation
A **motivation** is a force that moves a character to think, feel, or behave in a certain way. As you read the selections, try to figure out the characters' and speakers' motivations for the way they behave. Decide if the authors give clear motivations for behavior, thoughts, and feelings of the characters and speakers.

Preview Vocabulary
in•tu•i•tion (in' tü i´ shən) *n.*, feeling or sense about something that can't be logically explained

sol•i•tar•y (sä´ lə ter ē) *adj.*, being alone or isolated

bra•zen (brā´ zən) *adj.*, bold and showing disregard for rules

deft•ly (def[t] lē) *adv.*, in a skillful and quick manner

te•di•ous (tē´ dē əs) *adj.*, tiring and boring

Words in Use

"Checkouts"

Preview Vocabulary	Selection Words	Teaching Words
intuition, 81	reliably, 81	infatuated, 78
solitary, 81	harried, 81	concrete, 78
brazen, 82	jarring, 82	representation, 78
deftly, 82	perverse, 83	
tedious, 82		

Common Core State Standards

Reading Literature
RL.3

Writing
W.9

Language
L.6

KEY TERMS

CHECKOUTS

A Short Story by Cynthia Rylant

The bag boy dropped her jar of mayonnaise and that is how she fell in love.

Her parents had moved her to Cincinnati, to a large house with beveled glass[1] windows and several porches and the *history* her mother liked to emphasize. You'll love the house, they said. You'll be lonely at first, they admitted, but you're so nice you'll make friends fast. And as an impulse tore at her to lie on the floor, to hold to their ankles and tell them she felt she was dying, to offer anything, anything at all, so they might allow her to finish growing up in the town of her childhood, they firmed their mouths and spoke from their chests and they said, It's decided.

---

1. **beveled glass.** Glass with edges cut at an angle, as in window glass

79

> **More About the Author**

Cynthia Rylant, the author of this story, has written numerous critically acclaimed books for young readers. In 1993, she won the prestigious Newbery Medal for her novel *Missing May*. The Newbery Medal, named for eighteenth-century British bookseller John Newbery, is awarded each year by the American Library Association to the author of the most distinguished contribution to American literature for children.

Art Connection

Largely self-taught as an artist, the American painter Fairfield Porter (1907–1975) focused on landscapes and scenes of everyday life.

Art Activity Discuss the mood of this painting with students. Model a process of questioning: "Does the girl seem lonely or simply alone? How do the colors used by the artist help shape the mood? How does the composition (with its placement of the girl at the center) affect the mood created by the painting? What words would best describe the mood?" **A**

A *Girl on Screen Porch*, 1962. Fairfield Porter.

Differentiated Instruction

English Language Learning

Be sure that students understand the meanings of the following phrases and idioms.

spoke from their chests—spoke in deep, firm voices, 79

bag boy—supermarket employee who puts the customers' purchases in bags, 81

checkout line—place in supermarket where customers pay for their purchases, 81

brown depression—deep sadness, 81

looked a fool—seemed foolish, 81

They moved her to Cincinnati, where for a month she spent the greater part of every day in a room full of beveled glass windows, sifting through photographs of the life she'd lived and left behind. But it is difficult work, suffering, and in its own way a kind of art, and finally she didn't have the energy for it anymore, so she emerged from the beautiful house and fell in love with a bag boy at the supermarket. Of course, this didn't happen all at once, just like that, but in the sequence of things that's exactly the way it happened.

She liked to grocery shop. She loved it in the way some people love to drive long country roads, because doing it she could think and relax and wander. Her parents wrote up the list and handed it to her and off she went without complaint to perform what they regarded as a great sacrifice of her time and a sign that she was indeed a very nice girl. She had never told them how much she loved grocery shopping, only that she was "willing" to do it. She had an <u>intuition</u> which told her that her parents were not safe for sharing such strong, important facts about herself. Let them think they knew her.

Once inside the supermarket, her hands firmly around the handle of the cart, she would lapse[2] into a kind of reverie[3] and wheel toward the produce. Like a Tibetan monk in <u>solitary</u> meditation,[4] she calmed to a point of deep, deep happiness; this feeling came to her, reliably, if strangely, only in the supermarket.

Then one day the bag boy dropped her jar of mayonnaise and that is how she fell in love.

He was nervous—first day on the job—and along had come this fascinating girl, standing in the checkout line with the unfocused stare one often sees in young children, her face turned enough away that he might take several full looks at her as he packed sturdy bags full of food and the goods of modern life. She interested him because her hair was red and thick, and in it she had placed a huge orange bow, nearly the size of a small hat. That was enough to distract him, and when finally it was her groceries he was packing, she looked at him and smiled and he could respond only by busting her jar of mayonnaise on the floor, shards of glass and oozing cream decorating the area around his feet.

She loved him at exactly that moment, and if he'd known this perhaps he wouldn't have fallen into the brown depression he fell into, which lasted the rest of his shift. He believed he must have looked a fool in her eyes, and he envied the sureness of everyone around him: the cocky cashier at the register, the grim and harried store

> It is reason enough to be alive, the hope you may see again some face which has meant something to you.

B

C

2. **lapse.** Pass into a specified state or condition
3. **reverie.** Daydream
4. **meditation.** Act of relaxing one's mind and body; act of deep thinking

> in·tu·i·tion (in' tü i′ shən) *n.*, feeling or sense about something that can't be logically explained
>
> sol·i·tar·y (sä′ lə ter ē) *adj.*, being alone or isolated

CHECKOUTS / ORANGES **81**

Teach the Selection

Analyze Literature
Motivation Remind students that motivations are the reasons why characters act in certain ways. As an example, point out that the girl's motivation for leaving the house was to get over her "suffering"—her loneliness. Then ask them to tell what her motivation was for grocery shopping and for not sharing her thoughts with her parents. **B**

Use Reading Skills
Compare and Contrast Ask students what led to the boy breaking the jar of mayonnaise. Then have them compare and contrast the girl's reaction to him and his own reaction—how are the characters' points of view different? **C**

Vocabulary Skills

Multiple-Meaning Words

Remind students that many words have more than one meaning. Some words, like *breaks,* can be used as either a verb or a noun. Write example sentences on the board, such as *The boy breaks the jar. The bag boys take breaks from their work.* Then have students work with partners to write pairs of sentences for each of the following words found in this story. In one sentence, they should use the word as a noun, and in the other sentence, have them use it as a verb.

1. sign
2. wheel
3. produce
4. point
5. bow
6. rest
7. shift
8. check

Use Reading Strategies

Make Inferences Ask students what "perfect contrast" the boy represents to the protagonist. Prompt responses by asking, "What bothers her about her current situation? How is the boy's appearance and behavior different from this situation?" What inferences can they make about why this contrast made him so attractive to her? **A**

Make Connections

Ask students to analyze the emotions described in this paragraph. Lead them to identify and explain the sources of the opposing feelings of "disappointment" and "ecstasy" by asking, "How can expectation of an event be even more exciting than the event itself?" Do they think those opposing feelings are realistic? **B**

---

manager, the bland butcher, and the brazen bag boys who smoked in the warehouse on their breaks. He wanted a second chance. Another chance to be confident and say witty things to her as he threw tin cans into her bags, persuading her to allow him to help her to her car so he might learn just a little about her, check out the floor of the car for signs of hobbies or fetishes and the bumpers for clues as to beliefs and loyalties.

But he busted her jar of mayonnaise and nothing else worked out for the rest of the day.

Strange, how attractive clumsiness can be. She left the supermarket with stars in her eyes, for she had loved the way his long nervous fingers moved from the conveyor belt to the bags, how deftly (until the mayonnaise) they had picked up her items and placed them into her bags. She had loved the way the hair kept falling into his eyes as he leaned over to grab a box or a tin. And the tattered brown shoes he wore with no socks. And the left side of his collar turned in rather than out.

A The bag boy seemed a wonderful contrast to the perfectly beautiful house she had been forced to accept as her home, to the *history* she hated, to the loneliness she had become used to, and she couldn't wait to come back for more of his awkwardness and dishevelment.

Incredibly, it was another four weeks before they saw each other again. As fate would have it, her visits to the supermarket

> Strange, how attractive clumsiness can be.

never coincided with his schedule to bag. Each time she went to the store, her eyes scanned the checkouts at once, her heart in her mouth. And each hour he worked, the bag boy kept one eye on the door, watching for the red-haired girl with the big orange bow.

B Yet in their disappointment these weeks there was a kind of ecstasy. It is reason enough to be alive, the hope you may see again some face which has meant something to you. The anticipation of meeting the bag boy eased the girl's painful transition into her new and jarring life in Cincinnati. It provided for her an anchor amid all that was impersonal and unfamiliar, and she spent less time on thoughts of what she had left behind as she concentrated on what might lie ahead. And for the boy, the long and often tedious hours at the supermarket which provided no challenge other than that of showing up the following workday...these hours became possibilities of mystery and romance for him as he watched the electric doors for the girl in the orange bow.

And when finally they did meet up again neither offered a clue to the other that he, or she, had been the object of obsessive thought for weeks. She spotted him as soon as she came into the store, but she kept her eyes strictly in front of her as she pulled out a cart

---

bra·zen (brā´ zən) *adj.,* bold and showing disregard for rules

deft·ly (def[t] lē) *adv.,* in a skillful and quick manner

te·di·ous (tē´ dē əs) *adj.,* tiring and boring

Differentiated Instruction

English Language Learning

There are several examples of figurative language on this page that students might find difficult. Help them by calling on language-proficient students to explain their meanings.

stars in her eyes — bright, happy feelings, 82

as fate would have it — as it turned out, 82

her heart in her mouth — in a jittery, nervous way, 82

one eye on the door — half his attention on the entrance to the supermarket, 82

provided for her an anchor — gave her comfort or strength, 82

swallow back the fear in his throat — relax and overcome his immediate fears, 83

and wheeled it toward the produce. And he, too, knew the instant she came through the door—though the orange bow was gone, replaced by a small but bright yellow flower instead—and he never once turned his head in her direction but watched her from the corner of his vision as he tried to swallow back the fear in his throat.

It is odd how we sometimes deny ourselves the very pleasure we have longed for and which is finally within our reach. For some perverse reason she would not have been able to articulate, the girl did not bring her cart up to the bag boy's checkout when her shopping was done. And the bag boy let her leave the store, pretending no notice of her.

This is often the way of children, when they truly want a thing, to pretend that they don't. And then they grow angry when no one tries harder to give them this thing they so casually rejected, and they soon find themselves in a rage simply because they cannot say yes when they mean yes. Humans are very complicated. (And perhaps cats, who have been known to react the same

way, though the resulting rage can only be guessed at.)

The girl hated herself for not checking out at the boy's line, and the boy hated himself for not catching her eye and saying hello, and they most sincerely hated each other without having ever exchanged even two minutes of conversation.

Eventually—in fact, within the week—a kind and intelligent boy who lived very near her beautiful house asked the girl to a movie and she gave up her fancy for the bag boy at the supermarket. And the bag boy himself grew so bored with his job that he made a desperate search for something better and ended up in a bookstore where scores of fascinating girls lingered like honeybees about a hive. Some months later the bag boy and the girl with the orange bow again crossed paths, standing in line with their dates at a movie theater, and, glancing toward the other, each smiled slightly, then looked away, as strangers on public buses often do, when one is moving off the bus and the other is moving on. ❖

 In "Checkouts" the girl feels that her parents "were not safe for sharing... important facts about herself." Do you agree? Why might teenagers feel this way? What overall point about love do you think the story makes?

Find Meaning
1. How does the girl feel about moving to Cincinnati? Support your answer by using examples from the text.
2. (a) How does the boy feel about himself after meeting the girl? Why? (b) What does he think she thinks about him? (c) How is that different from how she actually sees him?

Make Judgments
3. What is the effect of the boy and girl remaining unnamed?
4. Do you agree or disagree that "we sometimes deny ourselves the very pleasure we have longed for and which is finally within our reach"? Explain.

Teach the Selection

Make Connections
The narrator states that "Humans are very complicated." Ask students what story events and character traits and actions lead the narrator to make this statement. Do the feelings and actions of the characters seem realistic to them? Discuss. **C**

 Answer: Students may say that teenagers feel they will have more emotional and physical freedom if they keep parts of themselves private from their parents or that adults can't really understand their feelings. Students may say that the overall point about love is that it is mysterious, that it happens in strange ways, or that it can flare up and then fade.

Find Meaning
1. She is unhappy and lonely.
2. (a) He is depressed and envies the sureness of everyone else. (b) He thinks she finds him a fool. (c) She finds his clumsiness attractive.

Make Judgments
3. It gives the sense that the characters could be anyone and that their feelings and actions are universal.
4. Students may say that the boy and girl are disappointed that the other didn't approach him/her. Also, they don't like the feelings of self-hate they have for not approaching, so they project those feelings onto the other.

Reading Skills

Summarize
When students finish reading "Checkouts," ask them to summarize the story by writing descriptions of each of the following.
1. **exposition:** The setting and the girl's feelings at the beginning of the story
2. **first meeting:** How the characters meet; how they feel about each other; what motivates their feelings
3. **second meeting:** How the characters feel as they await a second meeting; what they do when it occurs; what feelings this event causes them to have
4. **third meeting:** How the characters meet; how they act when they meet; what motivates these actions

ORANGES

A Narrative Poem by Gary Soto

The first time I walked
With a girl, I was twelve,
Cold, and weighted down
With two oranges in my jacket.
5 December. Frost cracking
Beneath my steps, my breath
Before me, then gone,
As I walked toward
Her house, the one whose
10 Porch light burned yellow
Night and day, in any weather.
A dog barked at me, until
She came out pulling
At her gloves, face bright
15 With rouge.[1] I smiled,
Touched her shoulder, and led
Her down the street, across
A used car lot and a line
Of newly planted trees,
20 Until we were breathing
Before a drugstore. We
Entered, the tiny bell
Bringing a saleslady
Down a narrow aisle of goods.
25 I turned to the candies
Tiered like bleachers,
And asked what she wanted—
Light in her eyes, a smile
Starting at the corners

30 Of her mouth. I fingered
A nickel in my pocket,
And when she lifted a chocolate
That cost a dime,
I didn't say anything.
35 I took the nickel from
My pocket, then an orange,
And set them quietly on
The counter. When I looked up,
The lady's eyes met mine,
40 And held them, knowing
Very well what it was all
About.
    Outside,
A few cars hissing past,
45 Fog hanging like old
Coats between the trees.
I took my girl's hand
In mine for two blocks,
Then released it to let
50 Her unwrap the chocolate.
I peeled my orange
That was so bright against
The gray of December
That, from some distance,
55 Someone might have thought
I was making a fire in my hands. ❖

---

1. **rouge.** Blush, a kind of make-up that reddens the cheeks

The speaker of "Oranges" chooses to tell about the first time he experienced a date with a girl. If you were to write a poem about the first time you experienced something important, what would you write about and why? Why is a first date such an important event in a person's life?

84

Comparing Literature

Find Meaning

1. (a) How does the speaker react when the girl wants the chocolate that costs a dime? (b) What happens? Why do you think it happens?
2. How does the speaker feel at the end of the poem? Explain.

Compare Literature

Motivation In order for characters in narratives to seem realistic, they have to have **motivations,** or reasons, for doing, thinking, or feeling things. Do you feel that the authors of "Checkouts" and

Make Judgments

3. How does the speaker feel about the girl in the poem? Use evidence from the text to support your answer.
4. Tone is the speaker's attitude toward the subject matter. How would you describe the overall tone of "Oranges"? Explain.

"Oranges" gave their characters clear and realistic motivations for the way they act and feel? Explain your answer.

Extend Understanding

Writing Options

Creative Writing Imagine and write a **dialogue** between the characters in either "Checkouts" or "Oranges." Use what you know about the characters, their motivations, and character traits to make the dialogue sound like something the characters would actually say. Include the context and setting for the dialogue. Share your work with the class.

Expository Writing Compare and contrast the motivations of the speaker in "Oranges" and the main character of "Checkouts" in a short **essay.** How are they similar? How are they different? State your main idea in a thesis statement and make sure to use specific examples from the texts. Share your work with the class.

Collaborative Learning

Group Discussion In small groups, discuss the use of metaphors and similes in the poem and story. A metaphor is a figure of speech in which one thing is written or spoken about as if it were another. A simile also compares one thing to another, but uses the word *like* or *as*. Metaphors and similes help readers see things in new ways. Analyze how they affected your appreciation and understanding of the texts.

Lifelong Learning

Research The boy in "Checkouts" has a job bagging groceries. What sorts of jobs are available where you live? Use the Internet, newspaper classifieds, library, or talk to people to research job opportunities in your school, neighborhood, or town. Collect information about these opportunities in a journal. Include which jobs you would most like to do and why.

Go to www.mirrorsandwindows.com for more.

Find Meaning

1. (a) He tries to pay for it with an orange and a nickel. He doesn't want her to know that he doesn't have enough money. (b) The clerk lets the girl have the chocolate. Students may say that the clerk wants to protect the boy's pride.
2. Students may say that he feels a sense of power from having experienced a magical moment. The brightness of the remaining orange seems as powerful as fire in his hands.

Make Judgments

3. He likes her very much. He brings her an orange, he buys her candy, and he holds her hand. He calls her "my girl."
4. Students may say that the tone is one of wonder, of recalling a moment of magic.

Compare Literature

Motivation Rylant clearly explains why the boy and girl are attracted to each other. She makes their later behavior believable by acknowledging that people pretend not to want things they really do want. Soto makes it clear that the boy likes the girl but is proud and doesn't want her to know that he doesn't have enough money to buy her a chocolate. He bravely and silently "makes a deal" with the clerk, who accepts the offer because she is sympathetic and protective.

Rubrics for Writing Options

You can adapt this as a checklist for students to use as they write.

Creative Writing

☐ Does the dialogue reflect the characters' traits and motivations?
☐ Does it accurately relate to the setting and situations of the original text?
☐ Is the context of the dialogue clear?

Expository Writing

☐ Does the essay identify what will be compared and contrasted?
☐ Does the essay explain how the characters' motivations are similar and different?
☐ Is each point supported by details from the text?

At a Glance

Directed Reading
- Reading Level: Easy
- Difficulty Consideration: Vocabulary
- Ease Factor: Engaging plot

Objectives

Studying this lesson will enable students to
- use reading skills such as monitoring comprehension
- define *conflict* and recognize the elements of an external conflict within a story
- describe the literary work of Fae Myenne Ng and the effect of Chinese-American culture on her writing
- appreciate a story set in an ethnic neighborhood

Launch the Lesson

Ask students what they or their family might do to help a friendly neighbor who needed medical assistance. Have them read "Last Night," a short story by Fae Myenne Ng, to find out what the main characters in this story decide to do to solve the problem.

KEY TERMS

FIGURE OF SPEECH, 86
FIGURATIVE LANGUAGE, 86
CONFLICT, 86
PLOT, 86
COMPREHENSION, 86
CHARACTER SKETCH, 94

DIRECTED READING

BEFORE READING

Build Background

Cultural Context In this selection, the main characters live in an area of San Francisco called Chinatown. Chinatown refers to a section of a city that is primarily inhabited by people of Chinese ancestry. In these communities, stores, restaurants, houses of worship and organizations specialize in serving Chinese Americans.

Reader's Context Have you, or someone you know, ever been in a situation where it was necessary to communicate in another language? How can people communicate if they don't speak the same language?

Set Purpose

A **figure of speech** is writing or speech meant to be understood with your imagination instead of literally. Writers use figures of speech, called **figurative language,** to help readers see things in new ways. Figurative speech includes metaphors and similes. As you read, watch for figurative language and how it affects the story. Discuss your observations with a partner.

Analyze Literature

Conflict A **conflict** is a struggle between two people or things. A **plot,** or events in a story, is formed around conflict. An *external conflict* is a struggle that takes place between a character and another character, a condition, society, or nature. As you read, look for external conflict in the story.

Meet the Author

Fae Myenne Ng (fā myən əng) was born in San Francisco's Chinatown in 1957, where she grew up speaking Cantonese. Much of her experience living in Chinatown has influenced her writing, as seen in "Last Night."

Use Reading Skills

Monitor Comprehension To monitor comprehension means to be constantly aware of your understanding of the text. Monitoring your comprehension will help you to know when the text makes sense to you and when it does not. Sometimes a text won't make sense because a reader has forgotten important information or details. Use a note-taking chart like the one below to help you check your understanding of the ideas in "Last Night."

Page	Main Ideas	My Reactions
87	You Thin and Hang Fong rarely leave Chinatown.	I wonder how this will affect the events in the story.

Summary of My Notes

Preview Vocabulary

sen•sa•tion (sen sā´ shun) *n.,* feeling
er•rat•ic (i ra´ tik) *adj.,* irregular
flut•ter (flü tər´) *v.,* move rapidly
o•men (ō´ mən) *n.,* sign or warning
churn (churn) *v.,* move roughly

Common Core State Standards

Reading Literature
RL.1, RL.4

Writing
W.7, W.8, W.9

Language
L.6

Words in Use

Preview Vocabulary
sensation, 88
erratic, 88
flutter, 90
omen, 90
churn, 90

Selection Words
rhythmic, 87
garment, 87
adventuress, 88
fluorescent, 88
barred, 92

Teaching Words
primarily, 86
inhabited, 86
monitor, 86
immigrants, 92
hostility, 92
exclusion, 92
repealed, 92
relevant, 92

ethnic, 93
mute, 94
barrier, 94

Last Night

A Short Story by Fae Myenne Ng

"So, why do you sit around the Square now?"

When Hang Fong Toy finally awakens, she can't tell if the rhythmic pounding is one of her headaches or just the water pipes banging again. She looks around the room, listening. The street light falls through the Venetian blinds; the slanting lines make the room seem larger.

You Thin Toy sleeps curled toward the wall, a brush stroke on the wide bed. He's a retired merchant marine[1] and has sailed the world. Now he spends afternoons at Portsmouth Square, playing chess and telling stories about himself as a young man. "Like a seagull," he says, "I went everywhere, saw everything."

His old-timer friends like to tease him. "So, why do you sit around the Square now?"

"Curiosity," he says. "I want to see how you fleabags have been living."

You Thin knows all the terms for docking a ship; Hang Fong can name the parts and seams of a dress the way a doctor can name bones.

 Hang Fong sews in a garment shop. She's only been outside Chinatown for official business: immigration, unemployment and social security. When the children were

---

1. **merchant marine.** Sailor on a commercial ship

87

Teach the Selection

Summary
Hang Fong Toy and her husband, You Thin Toy, a Chinese-American couple living in San Francisco's Chinatown, discover their landlord, an elderly Italian woman, lying on the floor in her apartment. Because they have no common language with her, they try to comfort her in Chinese. You Thin then rushes out to find the landlord's mute son, who works the night shift. Somehow, he communicates the message and the son rushes home to his mother. Then You Thin calls an ambulance, doing the best he can to provide the vital information.

MIRRORS & WINDOWS The Mirrors & Windows questions at the end of this selection focus on the theme of solidarity. Before reading the story, ask students if they are familiar with any homogeneous communities. What are the benefits and drawbacks to people of similar ethnic backgrounds settling in isolated communities?

Analyze Literature
Setting Have students use clues in the two opening paragraphs to tell where, and at what time of day, the story is set. **A**

Program Resources

Planning and Assessment
Program Planning Guide, Selection Lesson Plan
E-Lesson Planner
Assessment Guide, Lesson Test
ExamView

Technology Tools
Interactive Student Text on CD
Visual Teaching Package
Audio Library
mirrorsandwindows.com

Meeting the Standards
Fiction: Unit 1, Directed Reading, pp. 62–67

Use Reading Strategies
Make Inferences Ask students how Hang Fong's life has changed now that her children are grown. Lead them to understand that she no longer goes out shopping because her children, who grew up in San Francisco and speak English, cannot translate for her. Make sure they understand the main idea that she does not speak English. **A**

Use Reading Skills
Monitor Comprehension Have students think about what they have read about You Thin that helps them to understand why Ah-Boy's anchor tattoo makes You Thin feel that they are "comrades of sorts." Then have them use information in the following paragraph to understand why Hang Fong is worried. **B**

Analyze Literature
Conflict Ask students what this passage indicates about the nature of the conflict in this story. **C**

Use Reading Strategies
Make Inferences Ask students to use what they know about the landlord, Hang Fong, and You Thin to understand why You Thin says, "She don't know what you say." **D**

young, they took her to Market Street, the Emporium and J. C. Penney's, but now, without translators, she's not an adventuress.

There was a time when her desire to return to China was a <u>sensation</u> in her belly, like hunger. Now she only dreams of it, almost tasting those dishes she loved as a young girl. Sometimes she says to You Thin before falling asleep, maybe a visit, eh?

A ⌜ After raising their children, Chinatown has become their world. They feel lucky to have an apartment on Salmon Alley. Louie's Grocery is around the corner on Taylor, and Hang Fong's sewing shop is just down the block. Their apartment is well situated in the back of the alley, far from the traffic fumes of Pacific Avenue.

Hang Fong and You Thin like their landlord, an old Italian lady, and her mute[2] son so much that they have given them Chinese names. Fay-Poah, Manager Lady, and Ah-Boy, Mute-Son. Manager Lady wears printed pastel dresses that Hang Fong, a sewing lady, admires very much. Ah-Boy, a big man with a milky smell, works as a porter at the Oasis Club, but during the day he works around the building. When Hang Fong hears his broom on the stairs or the garbage cans rattling in the airshaft, she feels safe. It's good to have a strong man like Ah-Boy nearby. She tells You Thin, Ah-Boy is a good son, and You Thin nods. He likes to

B ⌜ think that the anchor tattoo on Ah-Boy's arm makes them comrades of sorts.

Hang Fong thinks maybe Manager Lady left her window open. But then the sound becomes <u>erratic</u> and sharp. Hang Fong gets up, leans toward the wall. You Thin lets out a long breath.

C ⌜ Hang Fong presses her ear against the wall, listening. Her eyes are wide open. Suddenly she rushes toward her sleeping husband and shakes him. "Get up! Get up! It's the Manager Lady, she's in trouble!"

You Thin stretches out and props himself up on one elbow. He rubs his eyes, trying to wake up. The banging comes again, and the old couple stare at each other. Outside, a car screeches to an urgent stop. They listen to the faint bubbly hum of the fish tank in the other room, and then hear the rumbling icebox motor shut off with a final click. You Thin and Hang Fong look at each other; the silence feels big.

The pounding comes again. Once. Twice.

"Something's wrong! Manager Lady is trying to tell us that!" Hang Fong throws off her covers. In one motion, her legs whip out and her slippers make a swishing noise as she moves across the room. The overhead fluorescent light flickers and snaps and then is quiet. The room is bright, glaring.

You Thin squints, reaches over, and raps sharply, one-two-three on the wall.

A sound knocks back in return.

Hang Fong slaps the wall with her open palm; the sound is flat and dull. She presses palm and cheek into the wall, and shouts, "Manager, Manager, are you all right? Nothing's wrong, is there?"

"SSHHH!!!" You Thin yanks her away.

D ⌜ "Don't talk loud like that, she don't know what you say, maybe she thinks that you yell at her."

You Thin is out of bed, pacing. Hang Fong sits; she pulls her sweater closer around her neck. The sleeves hang limply at her sides.

"Let's see...wait a minute, where's Ah-Boy?"

"It's Tuesday; he's got the night shift."

"Oh. Tuesday. Right."

---

2. mute. Unable to speak

sen•sa•tion (sen sā´ shun) *n.*, feeling
er•rat•ic (i ra´ tik) *adj.*, irregular

Differentiated Instruction

Reading Proficiency
Some students may have trouble recognizing the shifts in time that occur during this story. Point out to them there are two principal flashbacks. One occurs on page 88 and presents background information on the main characters; the other takes place on page 90 and describes the discovery of the Chinese pot.

Enrichment
Interested students might enjoy researching the city of San Francisco and using a city map to find Chinatown, Portsmouth Square, Market Street, Broadway, Pacific Avenue, and other locations mentioned in this story.

> After raising their children, Chinatown has become their world.

Teach the Selection

Art Connection

The buildings in this photograph of San Francisco's Chinatown reflect the structural style of traditional Chinese architecture. The large roofs with upturned eaves extending well beyond the walls of the buildings show the strong emphasis on the horizontal that is a basic feature of traditional Chinese structures. The ornamental dragons on the street lamp in the foreground are widely used decorative motifs.

Art Activity Incorporate images of traditional Chinese buildings into a travel poster urging tourists to visit San Francisco's Chinatown.

Writing Skills

Consistent Verb Tense

Point out to students that the author uses present-tense verbs in the passages that occur in the present time, and then she shifts to past-tense verbs for the flashbacks. Explain that using consistent verb tense is important for clarity. It tells readers *when* things happen. Have students rewrite the following sentences, using a consistent verb tense in each one.

1. We walked to the park and then Jim buys (bought) me an ice cream cone.
2. My mother is (was) born in Japan and then moved to Texas.
3. At the craft show we bought a vase, eat (ate) lunch, and watched a man who is (was) drawing portraits.

A Last week, when You Thin was at Manager Lady's paying the rent, he looked out her kitchen window while waiting for her to come back with the receipt. He saw a Chinese pot beneath a pile of chipped plates. So the next day he returned with a blue vase, its floral pattern similar to many of Manager Lady's dresses.

"I see?" he asked, pointing out the window.

Manager Lady opened her mouth wide, as her hand <u>fluttered</u> toward the window.

"Oh. Si, si," she said.

You Thin pulled the window open. He moved the cream-colored plates and lifted the pot for Manager Lady to see. She nodded, cradling the blue vase to her bosom.

With both hands, You Thin carried the pot back across the hall. Under the running faucet, Hang Fong scrubbed hard. Red, green and yellow, the palace ladies and plum blossoms came clean. You Thin scraped away the last of the dirt with a toothpick. The characters came clear. Good Luck and Long Life. You Thin and Hang Fong laughed, feeling lucky.

"Well, you think I could make that big step across to their fire escape?"

"Worth a lot of money, in time," You Thin said.

"Something to pass on to the children," Hang Fong added.

You Thin told everyone on the Square that the pot belonged to a hard-working old-timer who died alone. Hang Fong said that it was a good <u>omen</u> that they were chosen to house this valuable object. "It's very old," she told her sewing-lady friends.

"So, should we call the Rescue Car?" Hang Fong asks.

You Thin looks out the window, distracted. He shakes his head. "Even if they **B** get here in two minutes, best we could do is stand in front of the door with our mouths open."

Hang Fong knows that he wants to climb the fire escape and get inside Manager Lady's apartment. It's risky, she thinks. You Thin isn't a young man and his step isn't always steady. She won't say anything, because the **C** long years of marriage have taught her one thing: he likes his way.

"Well, what do we do?" Hang Fong asks. On the fire escape, a pigeon sleeps, its beak in its chest feathers. Hang Fong watches it. She hears the big engines of the garbage trucks <u>churning</u> up the hill. Foghorns sound in the distance, like help on the way.

You Thin asks, "Well, you think I could make that big step across to their fire escape?"

Hang Fong shrugs her shoulders. "Don't know; how do you feel?"

You Thin raises the window, looks out and snaps back in. Before Hang Fong can speak, he's run to the bathroom and clattered his way out carrying the long wooden board they use as a shelf over the bathtub.

"This is how..." He slaps the board. "This will reach from our fire escape to theirs. You hold this end, just in case, and the rest I can do."

D Hang Fong grips hard, but she keeps a harder eye on him. Inside, she repeats over and over, "Be careful...be safe...be careful...be safe..." You Thin is a brave man, she thinks; You Thin is a good man.

---

flut·ter (flü′ tər′) *v.*, move rapidly

o·men (ō′ mən) *n.*, sign or warning

churn (churn) *v.*, move roughly

---

90 UNIT 1 FICTION

One leg, then the other, and he is over there. He peers through the window, knocks, and then tries to lift it open. Shut tight. He has to pull hard, two, three times before it comes open.

You Thin feels along the wall for the light switch. All along the way, he speaks to Manager Lady, softly, in Chinese, "You're all right, nothing's wrong, don't be frightened..." You Thin believes in the power of the voice: a well-meaning word spoken in the face of ill fortune can turn luck around. **E**

Manager Lady is a wide figure on the floor. Everything around her speaks of her age: the faded covers, the cluttered nightstand, the bottles of lotions and pills. You Thin takes her hands; he's happy hers are warm.

Hang Fong knocks in quick, urgent raps, and You Thin opens the door for her. She moves quickly through the entryway, kneels and takes Manager Lady's head onto her lap, whispering, "Don't be scared, don't be scared." Manager Lady's eyes open. She says something in Italian; the long vowels reach forth and hang heavy in the air. Hang Fong and You Thin look at each other. They understand. **F**

You Thin says, "I go. Go to get Ah-Boy."

"You know where it is then?"

"Uh. Let me think...where Lee's Rice Shop used to be?"

"No! Across from Chong's Imports."

"Yes, right, I know, I know."

The air outside is sharp. The street lamps cast an orange glow to the empty alley. You Thin moves quickly through Salmon Alley. But when he turns onto Pacific, he rests a moment. The long road before him is marked with globes of light. He runs his hand along the walls for support. On the steep hill, his legs feel strangely heavy when they land on the pavement and oddly light when they

LAST NIGHT **91**

Teach the Selection

Use Reading Strategies
Make Inferences Ask students why You Thin believes here, and may have come to believe over the years, in the power of the voice (meaning appropriate *tone* of voice). Lead them to understand that he is trying to soothe and comfort the landlord but that she speaks only Italian and he speaks only Chinese. **E**

Use Reading Strategies
Ask Questions Ask students how they understand what Manager Lady is saying. You might model how she uses her voice to show urgency by speaking in gibberish but moaning or elongating the tones in a dramatic way to show intent. Invite students to show how she might have spoken. Use this activity to stress that people can use tone of voice to express meaning. Ask: "What else might these people use to communicate without words?" Lead students to understand that they could use dramatic facial expressions, gestures, and body language. Invite students to model examples appropriate for this scene. **F**

Grammar Skills

Quotation Marks
Use the dialogue in "Last Night" to review the use of quotation marks to set off direct quotations. Then have students rewrite the following sentences, inserting quotation marks correctly.

1. I'd like to visit San Francisco someday, Kate. ("I'd like to visit San Francisco someday, Kate.")

2. Kate asked, How would you travel to San Francisco? (Kate asked, "How would you travel to San Francisco?")

3. I'd probably go by plane, I answered, because it is really far away. ("I'd probably go by plane," I answered, "because it is really far away.")

Analyze Literature

Character Lead students to understand the challenges involved in this communication. You Thin cannot speak Italian, and Ah-Boy can't speak at all. Then ask: "How do You Thin's gestures and words get the point across? How does Ah-Boy communicate that he understands and is worried?" **A**

Use Reading Skills

Identify Cause and Effect Ask students to infer how Hang Fong's memory of a similar scene causes her to be concerned, leading to You Thin's call for help. **B**

History Connection

Chinese Immigration *Answer:* Students will probably say that because the law unfairly limited the types of Chinese people who could enter, it created resentment within the Chinese-American community. The law and the underlying situation are relevant to today's society in that certain factions in this country are fighting the same battle—this time involving illegal immigrants and low-cost laborers from Mexico. **C**

---

bounce off. He chants to himself, "Hurry. Important. Faster."

When he reaches Powell, he leans against the fire hydrant for a moment, glad that he's halfway there. He can see Broadway; it's still brightly lit. He's breathing hard by the time he gets to The Oasis. This late, it's been long closed. You Thin stands outside, banging on the big wooden doors and rapping on the windows. He cups his hands to the barred window, trying to see in. But with the glare from the street lamps, it's like looking into a mirror.

He takes a deep breath. "Ah-Boy, AAHHH-Boy-AAAHH!..."

Silence. Then the sound of flapping slippers, and Ah-Boy opens the door, mop in hand.

A You Thin throws his arms about, waving toward Pacific. He slaps the restaurant wall, shouting, "Mah-mah. Be sick. Be sick."

Ah-Boy opens his mouth; his head jerks back and forth, but there is no sound. He lets his broom fall with a clatter. The heavy door slams shut.

Ah-Boy is a big man and You Thin can't keep up for long. At Pacific, You Thin waves him on.

You Thin watches for a moment as Ah-Boy moves up the hill. Yes, he nods. Ah-Boy is a good son.

When You Thin gets to the apartment, Ah-Boy is sitting on the floor with his mother's head on his lap, her gray hair loosened from its bun. She is speaking to Ah-Boy in a low voice.

B You Thin and Hang Fong stand under the door frame, watching. "Just like last year," Hang Fong says, "just like Old Jue."

HISTORY ▶▶ CONNECTION

Chinese Immigration Large numbers of Chinese immigrants started coming to the United States in 1848, when gold was discovered in California. Many Chinese immigrants found work and settled in San Francisco, where "Last Night" takes place. However, in the 1870s a downturn in the economy left many Americans without jobs. White Americans saw Chinese immigrants as taking away jobs. Moreover, the immigrants were often willing to work for lower pay, causing wages to go down, and thus further fueling the hostility of white laborers. This hostility, along with racism, led to the Chinese Exclusion Act of 1882. Under this law, Chinese laborers were not allowed to come to the United States. Only officials, teachers, students, merchants, and travelers were allowed to enter. This law wasn't repealed until 1943. How do you think this affected racial tension in America? How is it relevant to today's society? **C**

On the phone You Thin speaks loud. He pronounces the syllables as if each sound were a single character. "Numbah Two. Sah-moon Alley. Old Lady. Sick. You be the come. Now, sabei? I stand by downdaire, sabei? Numbah Two, Sah-moon Alley."

Hang Fong stands next to him, listening hard. She whispers something to him.

You Thin raises his head, and speaks even louder. "One minute. You know, Old Lady, she be...uh, uh...Old Lady she be come from Italy. You sabei? Lady not from China."

Visual Learning

Visual learners might enjoy sketching the scene referred to in the "Analyze Literature: Setting" note, on page 93. Discuss, as a group, possible approaches to depicting sights and sounds. When students are finished sketching, allow time for evaluation of volunteers' approaches.

Kinesthetic Learning

Have volunteers enact the scene between You Thin and Ah-Boy in the doorway of The Oasis. Then call on others to enact You Thin's telephone call. Urge them to use tone of voice, facial expressions, and physical gestures to add meaning and emphasis to the message.

Many of the sewing ladies went to hear Hang Fong's story, but missing a sentence here or there, they can't follow the drama.
Is it a story or is it real?

At the square the next day, You Thin challenges the Newspaper Man to a chess game. You Thin plays with one leg raised on the cement stool. "My Car over your lousy paper Gun, and you're eaten." The Newspaper Man's children fold *The Chinese Times* on the next table. Lame-Leg Fong tries to tell You Thin which pieces to move. The #15 Kearney bus inches down Clay, its brakes squeaking and hissing. Cars honk.

You Thin tells his story about last night in between chess moves. He describes the distance between Salmon Alley and Broadway. His running motions make his blue sleeves go vlop-vlop in the wind. He repeats all the English words he used, tries to use the ones he'd heard, and makes all the faces Ah-Boy made. He walks the line

on the ground to show what he did in midair. Little boys run by on their way to the water fountain.

Hang Fong tells the story without looking up. The ladies listen with rounded backs and moving hands. Sheets of fabric run from the machines to the floor. Clumps of thread knot around the chair legs; spools of color ripple above the ladies' bent heads. The overlock machines click; the steam irons hiss. Some ladies sing along with the drum and gong beat of the Cantonese opera playing on the radio. A voice booms over the intercom system, "LAST CHANCE TO HAND IN THOSE TICKETS, RIGHT NOW!" No one looks up. Some ladies cluck their tongues and roll their eyes. Others shake their heads and curse under their breath.

Many of the sewing ladies went to hear Hang Fong's story, but missing a sentence here or there, they can't follow the drama. Is it a story or is it real? The women become heavy-footed; the needles stamp urgent stitches into the fabric. Trousers fly over the work tables; the colorful mounds of clothing clutter the floor.

Eventually the grumble of the machines drowns out the story. A young girl runs in to ask her mother for money as the fish peddler arrives, singing out her catch in a breath as long as thread. ❖

Would you like to live, or do you like living, in a community where most of the people have the same ethnic or racial background as yourself? What is the effect of people of the same ethnic or racial backgrounds living in their own separate communities?

Analyze Literature
Setting Remind students that setting involves time and place and often involves the feelings and situations that the setting imparts to the characters. Ask them to identify the settings in which You Thin and Hang Fong find themselves the following day. Help them recognize that these settings represent "back to normal." **D**

Cultural Connection
Cantonese Opera The Cantonese Opera is a traditional Chinese art form begun more than three hundred years ago. Based on Chinese history and tradition, some operas are tales of warriors and others are dramas about scholars and royal figures. The singing is accompanied by traditional Chinese instruments, while drums and gongs create the overall rhythm and pace. **E**

Answer: Some students may feel that living in an ethnic community limits one's experience. Others may feel that there are fewer tensions in such communities and that communication and understanding are easier. Some students may feel that ethnic communities foster misunderstanding of other groups. Others may feel that they bolster the power of ethnic groups and grant better opportunities.

Research Skills

Key Word Searches on the Internet
Before students begin the Media Literacy activity on page 94, review how to use key words to facilitate Internet searches.
- Use a reliable search engine such as Google or Yahoo.
- Use a specific key word or word phrase such as *Chinatown; Chinatowns in California; United States Chinatowns.*

- Remember that search engines typically present links in descending order of importance or relevancy. The most useful sites will appear at the top of the list.
- If you aren't getting the desired results, check your input. Common mistakes include misspelled keywords or URLs. Correct any errors, including those involving misused capital or lowercase letters.

Review the Selection

Find Meaning

1. (a) They like them. Hang Fong admires the landlady's dresses, and You Thin feels a comradeship because the son has an anchor tattoo. (b) They give them Chinese names; they worry that something bad has happened to their landlady.
2. He doesn't speak English and feels unable to explain the problem.
3. They use broken English, facial expressions, voice tones, and physical gestures.

Make Judgments

4. (a) He is not completely honest because he doesn't tell the landlady that the pot is valuable. (b) Although he is not completely honest, he is caring and resourceful. He cares about his landlady, finds a way into her house, and communicates with her son.
5. A possible response is that a theme of this story is the ability to communicate without understanding the precise meaning of a language.
6. A possible response is that thread holds clothes together much like communication holds people together.

Analyze Literature

Conflict *Answer:* The conflicts in "Last Night" all arise out of the fact that the situations call for the characters to be able to communicate in a common language, and that is something the characters cannot do. The effect of this is that the characters have to find other means of communicating.

Find Meaning

1. (a) How do You Thin and Hang Fong feel about their landlady and her son? (b) How do they show this feeling?
2. Why does You Thin decide to go into the landlady's home instead of calling an ambulance?
3. How do the characters who speak different languages communicate in "Last Night"?

Analyze Literature

Conflict The plot of a story is shaped by the conflict that the characters face. What basic conflict arises again and again in "Last Night"? What other conflicts are caused by this basic conflict? How do these conflicts affect the events of the story? Use a chart like the one here to help you identify the causes of the conflicts and their effects.

Make Judgments

4. (a) What do the scenes involving You Thin and the Chinese pot suggest about You Thin? Explain. (b) Overall, how would you describe You Thin? Give examples from the text.
5. Why do you think the author chose to make the character of Ah-boy mute?
6. Reread the last sentence of "Last Night." What is the effect of the phrase, "singing out her catch in a breath as long as thread"?

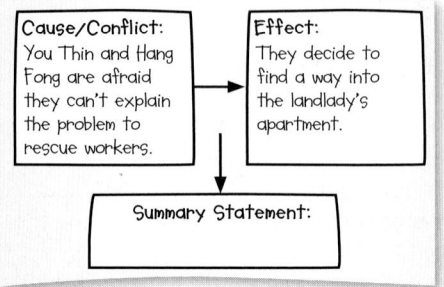

Cause/Conflict: You Thin and Hang Fong are afraid they can't explain the problem to rescue workers. → Effect: They decide to find a way into the landlady's apartment. → Summary Statement:

Extend Understanding

Writing Options

Creative Writing Imagine that you are a reporter and you have interviewed You Thin about the events in "Last Night." Write a **newspaper article** telling the story of what happened. Remember that newspaper articles answer the questions *who, what, when, where,* and *how* or *why.*

Descriptive Writing Create a **character sketch.** Reread the story, and then write a brief sketch of one of the characters. Use sensory details and precise and figurative language to help your audience better visualize the character, including his or her physical characteristics, behaviors, and personality.

Collaborative Learning

Work in Groups Work with fellow students in small groups. Discuss how language acts both as a barrier and as a bridge in "Last Night." Record your ideas and present them to the class. Afterwards, compare your group's opinions with those of other groups in your class.

Media Literacy

Conduct Internet Research Use the Internet to locate famous Chinatowns throughout the United States. Create a map, or other visual media, and present it to the class. Include information on population, landmarks, and any interesting or important history about the individual Chinatowns.

Go to **www.mirrorsandwindows.com** for more.

Rubrics for Writing Options

You can adapt this as a checklist for students to use as they write.

Creative Writing

☐ Does the article reflect the events in the story as You Thin would tell them?
☐ Does it fully cover the event (including *who, what, when, where, how,* and *why*)?
☐ Is the information presented in a vivid and interesting manner?

Descriptive Writing

☐ Does the sketch clearly identify the character and accurately reflect his or her qualities?
☐ Does it include sensory details and precise and figurative language that help the reader visualize the character and any traits or physical characteristics?

Vocabulary & Spelling

Spelling by Syllables

He's breathing hard by the time he gets to The Oasis.

—FAE MYENNE NG, "Last Night"

How many syllables does the word *oasis* have? A **syllable** is a part of a word that contains a single vowel sound. All words have at least one syllable. Understanding how to break words into syllables can help you sound out unfamiliar words and spell them correctly.

There is no single correct way to divide syllables, and sometimes you will see the same word divided two different ways. There are some general guidelines, however, that will help you syllabicate many words. Here are some of them. *V* stands for *vowel* and *C* stands for *consonant*.

Pattern 1: VCV If a word contains a consonant between two vowels, you should usually break the word after the first vowel.

> **EXAMPLE**
> *pro-ceed*

Pattern 2: VCCV If a word contains two consonants grouped together, you should usually break the word between the two consonants.

> **EXAMPLE**
> *mud-dy*

Pattern 3: VV If a word contains two vowels, and both vowels are pronounced, divide the word between the two vowels.

> **EXAMPLE**
> *cli-ent*

Pattern 4: Prefixes A prefix always forms a separate syllable.

> **EXAMPLE**
> *un-sent*

Pattern 5: Suffixes A suffix forms a syllable if it contains a vowel.

> **EXAMPLE**
> *sense-less*

The suffix *-y* follows the VCCV rule.

> **EXAMPLE**
> *hear-ty*

If you are still having trouble determining how many syllables a word has, try looking it up in a **dictionary**.

Spelling Practice

Write each of the following words, separating syllables with hyphens. Then indicate the pattern (or patterns) the syllable breaks follow. Look each word up in a dictionary to check your work.

1. armor
2. vital
3. dogma
4. riot
5. carry
6. embitter

Vocabulary Practice

Use a dictionary to find the syllabication for each of the following words from "Last Night."

1. rhythmic
2. immigration
3. erratic
4. challenge

Teach the Workshop

Spelling Practice
1. ar-mor VCCV
2. vi-tal VCV
3. dog-ma VCCV
4. ri-ot VV
5. car-ry VCCV
6. em-bit-ter Prefix/VCCV

Vocabulary Practice
1. rhyth-mic
2. im-mi-gra-tion
3. er-rat-ic
4. chal-lenge

> For additional instruction on spelling rules, see the Vocabulary & Spelling Section 2.7, Spelling, in the Language Arts Handbook.

Program Resources

You will find additional lessons on Spelling by Syllables in the *Exceeding the Standards: Vocabulary & Spelling* resource.

Build Skills

Point out to students that the suffix *-ed* is only a separate syllable when it follows a *d* or *t*.
Examples:
Two syllables   dott-ed
One syllable   planed

TEACHING NOTE

Extra Practice

Write each of the following words, separating syllables with hyphens. Then indicate the pattern (or patterns) the syllable breaks follow.

1. polar (po-lar VCV)
2. pesky (pes-ky Suffix/VCCV)
3. turbid (tur-bid VCCV)
4. unholy (un-ho-ly Prefix/VCV)
5. brier (bri-er VV)

KEY TERMS

SYLLABLE, 95
VOWEL, 95
CONSONANT, 95
PREFIX, 95
SUFFIX, 95

Common Core State Standards

Language
L.2

Preview the Selection

At a Glance
Independent Reading
- Reading Level: Easy
- Difficulty Consideration: Length
- Ease Factor: Formatting aids

Objectives
Reading this selection will enable students to do the following:
- read with developing fluency
- read silently with comprehension for a sustained period of time

Launch the Lesson
Point out to students that Squeaky, the protagonist of "Raymond's Run," competes in track events. She usually wins, but a new student has arrived who might give her competition. Have them read to find out how Squeaky feels about this conflict and what happens.

▶ More by This Author
Students who like "Raymond's Run" might enjoy other short stories in Bambara's collection *Gorilla, My Love*.

TEACHING NOTE
Although this selection is presented in the student edition as an independent reading, teaching support has been provided should you choose to cover it in class.

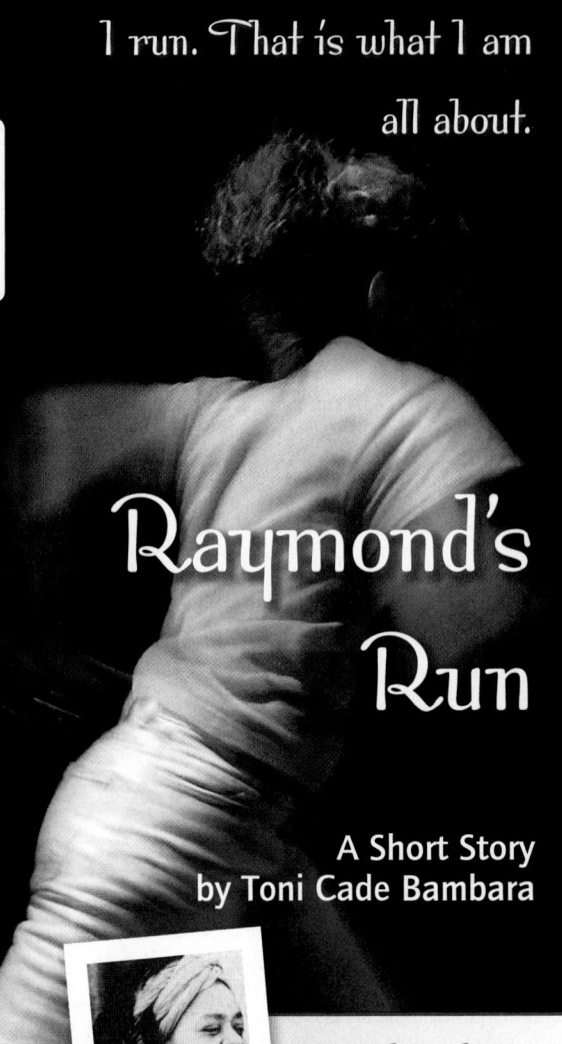

I run. That is what I am all about.

Raymond's Run

A Short Story by Toni Cade Bambara

Toni Cade Bambara (1939–1995) was an active writer, filmmaker, and activist. Born Miltona Mirkin Cade, she decided at the age of five that she wanted to change her name to Toni. As an adult, she added the surname Bambara. Her stories often feature tough, young females with a sassy attitude, such as the narrator of "Raymond's Run."

Bambara earned a degree from Queens College in New York and later traveled to Europe, studying in both Italy and France. She returned to America in 1964 to earn a master's degree from the City University of New York. It was then she published her first collection of stories *Gorilla, My Love* in 1972. Her novel *The Salt Eaters* earned the American Book Award in 1980. In addition to writing, Bambara worked on several documentary films about African-American oppression. She died in 1995 at the age of fifty-six.

I don't have much work to do around the house like some girls. My mother does that. And I don't have to earn my pocket money by hustling; George runs errands for the big boys and sells Christmas cards. And anything else that's got to get done, my father does. All I have to do in life is mind my brother Raymond, which is enough.

Sometimes I slip and say my little brother Raymond. But as any fool can see he's much bigger and he's older too. But a lot of people call him my little brother cause he needs looking after cause he's not quite right. And a lot of smart mouths got lots to say about that too, especially when George was minding him. But now, if anybody has anything to say to Raymond, anything to say about his big head, they have to come by me. And I don't play the dozens[1] or believe in standing around with somebody in my face doing a lot of talking. I'd much rather just knock you down and take my

---
1. **play the dozens.** Exchange insults

96

Program Resources

Planning and Assessment
Program Planning Guide, Selection Lesson Plan
E-Lesson Planner
Assessment Guide, Lesson Test
ExamView

Technology Tools
Interactive Student Text on CD
Visual Teaching Package
Audio Library
mirrorsandwindows.com

Meeting the Standards
Fiction: Unit 1, Independent Reading, pp. 68–73

Differentiating Instruction
Developing Readers, Set Purpose, pp. 7–9
Advanced Students, Independent Reading Activity, pp. 6–7

Common Core State Standards
Reading Literature
RL.10
Writing
W.9

chances even if I am a little girl with skinny arms and a squeaky voice, which is how I got the name Squeaky. And if things get too rough, I run. And as anybody can tell you, I'm the fastest thing on two feet.

There is no track meet that I don't win the first-place medal. I used to win the twenty-yard dash when I was a little kid in kindergarten. Nowadays, it's the fifty-yard dash. And tomorrow I'm subject to run the quarter-meter relay all by myself and come in first, second, and third. The big kids call me Mercury[2] cause I'm the swiftest thing in the neighborhood. Everybody knows that—except two people who know better, my father and me. He can beat me to Amsterdam Avenue with me having a two-fire hydrant head start and him running with his hands in his pockets and whistling. But that's private information. Cause can you imagine some thirty-five-year-old man stuffing himself into PAL[3] shorts to race little kids? So as far as everyone's concerned, I'm the fastest and that goes for Gretchen, too, who has put out the tale that she is going to win the first-place medal this year. Ridiculous. In the second place, she's got short legs. In the third place, she's got freckles. In the first place, no one can beat me and that's all there is to it.

I'm standing on the corner admiring the weather and about to take a stroll down Broadway so I can practice my breathing exercises, and I've got Raymond walking on the inside close to the buildings, cause he's subject to fits of fantasy and starts thinking he's a circus performer and that the curb is a tightrope strung high in the air. And sometimes after a rain he likes to step down off his tightrope right into the gutter and slosh around getting his shoes and cuffs wet. Then I get hit when I get home. Or sometimes if you don't watch him he'll dash across traffic to the island[4] in the middle of Broadway and give the pigeons a fit. Then I have to go behind him apologizing to all the old people sitting around trying to get some sun and getting all upset with the pigeons fluttering around them, scattering their newspapers and upsetting the waxpaper lunches in their laps. So I keep Raymond on the inside of me, and he plays like he's driving a stagecoach which is OK by me so long as he doesn't run me over or interrupt my breathing exercises, which I have to do on account of I'm serious about my running, and I don't care who knows it.

Now some people like to act like things come easy to them, won't let on that they practice. Not me. I'll high-prance down 34th Street like a rodeo pony to keep my knees strong even if it does get my mother uptight so that she walks ahead like she's not with me, don't know me, is all by herself on a shopping trip, and I am somebody else's crazy child. Now you take Cynthia Procter for instance. She's just the opposite. If there's

---

2. **Mercury.** Figure in Roman mythology known for his quickness
3. **PAL.** Police Athletic League
4. **island.** Stretch of concrete in the middle of the road, where pedestrians can wait to cross the street

Teach the Selection

Summary

Squeaky's household chore is to watch her mentally deficient brother, Raymond. Her great interest, and talent, is running. Usually, the chore and the interest are manageable, as Raymond is happy to run along with her as she trains for races. Gretchen, a new girl at school, may provide competition in the May Day race. Beating her becomes Squeaky's most important goal, until halfway through the race, when she spies Raymond on the sidelines, running along with her. Suddenly she realizes that if she trained Raymond to run, he might win races and have something to be proud of. Winning becomes secondary as she embraces this new goal.

MIRRORS & WINDOWS

The Mirrors & Windows questions at the end of this selection focus on the theme of ambition. Before reading the story, ask students what activities inspire them to dedicate their time and passion to it. Why do people strive for progress in the things to which they are devoted?

Words in Use

Selection Words
prodigy, 98
reputation, 99
ventriloquist-dummy, 99
organdy, 99
sash, 99
corsages, 100
psyching, 101

Teaching Words
activist, 96
surname, 96
documentary, 96
oppression, 96
excel, 103

KEY TERMS

Cultural Connection

Track Events Point out to students that Squeaky runs in different types of track events. In this story, the races are measured in yards; in many track events, they are measured in meters. A dash (also called a sprint) is a short race run by individual runners. Dashes often range from 55 to 400 meters. Runners begin from a crouched position and take off at the sound of a pistol shot. A relay race is run by a team of usually four runners. Each runner runs a section ("leg") of the race and then passes a baton—a hollow cylinder of wood or plastic—on to the next team member. Each leg is the same distance, often 100 or 400 meters. However, in a medley relay race, team members run different distances. For example, in a distance medley relay, the legs might be 1,200, 400, 800, and 1,600 meters.

Analyze Literature

Description Ask students to describe Gretchen and her "sidekicks." Ask them what probably leads Squeaky to describe the other girls as "sidekicks." **A**

a test tomorrow, she'll say something like, "Oh, I guess I'll play handball this afternoon and watch television tonight," just to let you know she ain't thinking about the test. Or like last week when she won the spelling bee for the millionth time, "A good thing you got 'receive,' Squeaky, cause I would have got it wrong. I completely forgot about the spelling bee." And she'll clutch the lace on her blouse like it was a narrow escape. Oh, brother. But of course when I pass her house on my early morning trots around the block, she is practicing the scales on the piano over and over and over and over. Then in music class she always lets herself get bumped around so she falls accidentally on purpose onto the piano stool and is so surprised to find herself sitting there that she decides just for fun to try out the ole keys. And what do you know— Chopin's[5] waltzes just spring out of her fingertips and she's the most surprised thing in the world. A regular prodigy. I could kill people like that. I stay up all night studying the words for the spelling bee. And you can see me any time of day practicing running. I never walk if I can

trot, and shame on Raymond if he can't keep up. But of course he does, cause if he hangs back someone's liable to walk up to him and get smart, or take his allowance from him, or ask him where he got that great big pumpkin head. People are so stupid sometimes.

So I'm strolling down Broadway breathing out and breathing in on counts of seven, which is my lucky number, and here comes Gretchen and her sidekicks: Mary Louise, who used to be a friend of mine when she first moved to Harlem from Baltimore and got beat up by everybody till I took up for her on account of her mother and my mother used to sing in the same choir when they were young girls, but people ain't grateful, so now she hangs out with the new girl Gretchen and talks about me like a dog; and Rosie, who is as fat as I am skinny and has a big mouth where Raymond is concerned and is too stupid to know that there is not a big deal of difference between herself and **A** Raymond and that she can't afford to throw stones. So they are steady coming up Broadway and I see right away that it's going to be one of those Dodge City scenes[6] cause

---

5. **Chopin's.** Frederic Francois Chopin (1810–1849), Polish composer
6. **Dodge City scenes.** "Showdowns" in the style of the Old West

English Language Learning

Students learning English may have difficulty with the following idioms and expressions:

not quite right—lacking in intelligence, 96
smart mouths—rude or sassy people, 96
put out the tale—started the rumor; let it be known, 97
won't let on—won't admit, 97

get my mother uptight—worry, concern, or embarrass my mother, 97
sidekicks—assistants (in this case, friends who are not quite as popular or important), 98
took up for her—looked out for her; protected her, 98
throw stones—criticize or gossip about someone, 98
all salty—in a sassy, overly confident way, 99

the street ain't that big and they're close to the buildings just as we are. First I think I'll step into the candy store and look over the new comics and let them pass. But that's chicken and I've got a reputation to consider. So then I think I'll just walk straight on through them or even over them if necessary. But as they get to me, they slow down. I'm ready to fight, cause like I said I don't feature a whole lot of chit-chat, I much prefer to just knock you down right from the jump and save everybody a lotta precious time.

"You signing up for the May Day races?" smiles Mary Louise, only it's not a smile at all. A dumb question like that doesn't deserve an answer. Besides, there's just me and Gretchen standing there really, so no use wasting my breath talking to shadows.

"I don't think you're going to win this time," says Rosie, trying to signify[7] with her hands on her hips all salty, completely forgetting that I have whupped her behind many times for less salt than that.

"I always win cause I'm the best," I say straight at Gretchen who is, as far as I'm concerned, the only one talking in this ventriloquist-dummy routine. Gretchen smiles, but it's not a smile, and I'm thinking that girls never really smile at each other because they don't know how and don't want to know how and there's probably no one to teach us how, cause grown-up girls don't know either. Then they all look at Raymond who has just brought his mule team to a standstill. And they're about to see what trouble they can get into through him.

"What grade you in now, Raymond?"

"You got anything to say to my brother, you say it to me, Mary Louise Williams of Raggedy Town, Baltimore."

"What are you, his mother?" sasses Rosie.

"That's right, Fatso. And the next word out of anybody and I'll be their mother too." So they just stand there and Gretchen shifts from one leg to the other and so do they. Then Gretchen puts her hands on her hips and is about to say something with her freckle-face self but doesn't. Then she walks around me looking me up and down but keeps walking up Broadway, and her sidekicks follow her. So me and Raymond smile at each other and he says, "Gidyap" to his team and I continue with my breathing exercises, strolling down Broadway toward the iceman on 145th with not a care in the world cause I am Miss Quicksilver[8] herself.

I take my time getting to the park on May Day because the track meet is the last thing on the program. The biggest thing on the program is the May Pole dancing, which I can do without, thank you, even if my mother thinks it's a shame I don't take part and act like a girl for a change. You'd think my mother'd be grateful not to have to make me a white organdy dress with a big satin sash and buy me new white baby-doll shoes that can't be taken out of the box till the big day. You'd think she'd be glad her daughter ain't out there prancing around a May Pole getting the new clothes all dirty and sweaty and trying to act like a fairy or a flower or whatever you're supposed to be when you should be trying to be yourself, whatever that is, which is, as far as I am concerned, a poor black girl who really can't afford to buy shoes and a new dress you only wear once a lifetime cause it won't fit next year.

I was once a strawberry in a Hansel and Gretel pageant when I was in nursery school and didn't have no better sense than to dance

---

7. **signify.** Slang that means to insult another
8. **Quicksilver.** Mercury, a type of liquid metal

Vocabulary Skills

Etymology
Point out to students that many words in the English language come from the languages of other cultures. As examples, have students use dictionaries to find the meanings and etymologies of the following words from the selection.

1. organdy (French; a delicate, thin cotton fabric with a crisp finish)

2. corsage (French; a small bouquet worn by a woman, often on the shoulder or wrist)

3. glockenspiel (German; a musical instrument made of steel bars and a frame and played with hammers)

4. bongo (Lokele; a small drum played with the fingers and palms)

Use Reading Strategies

Visualize Ask students to use the vivid details in this paragraph to describe the people and various activities at the park. **A**

Analyze Literature

Description Have students identify the two clues regarding why Mr. Pearson "sticks out in a crowd," leading them to see that *he's on stilts* and *Jack and the Beanstalk* suggest that he is very tall. (Later on this page, be sure that students also understand the meaning of the simile *like a periscope in a submarine movie.*) **B**

Use Reading Skills

Draw Conclusions Have students conclude what Mr. Pearson wants Squeaky to do and why it makes her angry. **C**

---

on tiptoe with my arms in a circle over my head doing umbrella steps and being a perfect fool just so my mother and father could come dressed up and clap. You'd think they'd know better than to encourage that kind of nonsense. I am not a strawberry. I do not dance on my toes. I run. That is what I am all about. So I always come late to the May Day program, just in time to get my number pinned on and lay in the grass till they announce the fifty-yard dash.

A I put Raymond in the little swings, which is a tight squeeze this year and will be impossible next year. Then I look around for Mr. Pearson, who pins the numbers on. I'm really looking for Gretchen if you want to know the truth, but she's not around. The park is jam-packed. Parents in hats and corsages and breast-pocket handkerchiefs peeking up. Kids in white dresses and light-blue suits. The parkees unfolding chairs and chasing the rowdy kids from Lenox[9] as if they had no right to be there. The big guys with their caps on backwards, leaning against the fence swirling the basketballs on the tips of their fingers, waiting for all these crazy people to clear out the park so they can play. Most of the kids in my class are carrying bass drums and glockenspiels[10] and flutes. You'd think they'd put in a few bongos or something for real like that.

B Then here comes Mr. Pearson with his clipboard and his cards and pencils and whistles and safety pins and fifty million other things he's always dropping all over the place with his clumsy self. He sticks out in a crowd because he's on stilts. We used to call him Jack and the Beanstalk to get him mad. But I'm the only one that can outrun him and get away, and I'm too grown for that silliness now.

"Well, Squeaky," he says, checking my name off the list and handing me number seven and two pins. And I'm thinking he's got no right to call me Squeaky, if I can't call him Beanstalk.

"Hazel Elizabeth Deborah Parker," I correct him and tell him to write it down on his board.

C "Well, Hazel Elizabeth Deborah Parker, going to give someone else a break this year?" I squint at him real hard to see if he is seriously thinking I should lose a race on purpose just to give someone else a break. "Only six girls running this time," he continues, shaking his head sadly like it's my fault all of New York didn't turn out in sneakers. "That new girl should give you a run for your money." He looks around the park for Gretchen like a periscope in a submarine movie. "Wouldn't it be a nice gesture if you were...to ahhh..."

I give him such a look he couldn't finish putting that idea into words. Grown-ups got a lot of nerve sometimes. I pin number seven to myself and stomp away, I'm so burnt. And I go straight for the track and stretch out on the grass while the band winds up with "Oh, the Monkey Wrapped His Tail Around the Flag Pole," which my teacher calls by some other name. The man on the loudspeaker is calling everyone over to the track and I'm on my back looking at the sky, trying to pretend I'm in the country, but I can't, because even grass in the city feels hard as sidewalk, and there's just no pretending you are anywhere but in a "concrete jungle" as my grandfather says.

---

9. Lenox. Lenox Avenue, a major road in Harlem, New York
10. glockenspiels. Musical instruments that produce a bell-like sound when struck

---

Participles

Remind students that participles are verb forms that act as adjectives. There are both present participles and past participles.

EXAMPLES:

crying (present participle)
cooked (past participle)

For each of the verbs below, have students write a pair of sentences. In the first sentence, they should use the verb as a present participle; in the second sentence, they should use it as a past participle.

1. hike
2. grow
3. crack

The twenty-yard dash takes all of two minutes cause most of the little kids don't know no better than to run off the track or run the wrong way or run smack into the fence and fall down and cry. One little kid, though, has got the good sense to run straight for the white ribbon up ahead so he wins. Then the second-graders line up for the thirty-yard dash and I don't even bother to turn my head to watch cause Raphael Perez always wins. He wins before he even begins by psyching the runners, telling them they're going to trip on their shoelaces and fall on their faces or lose their shorts or something, which he doesn't really have to do since he is very fast, almost as fast as I am. After that is **D** the forty-yard dash which I used to run when I was in first grade. Raymond is hollering from the swings cause he knows I'm about to do my thing cause the man on the loudspeaker has just announced the fifty-yard dash, although he might just as well be giving a recipe for angel food cake cause you can hardly make out what he's sayin for the static. I get up and slip off my sweat pants

and then I see Gretchen standing at the starting line, kicking her legs out like a pro. Then as I get into place I see that ole Raymond is on line on the other side of the fence, bending down with his fingers on the ground just like he knew what he was doing. I was going to yell at him but then I didn't. It burns up your energy to holler.

Every time, just before I take off in a race, I always feel like I'm in a dream, the kind of dream you have when you're sick with fever and feel all hot and weightless. I dream I'm flying over a sandy beach in the early morning sun, kissing the leaves of the trees as I fly by. And there's always the smell of apples, just like in the country when I was little and used to think I was a choo-choo train, running through the fields of corn and chugging up the hill to the orchard. And all the time I'm dreaming this, I get lighter and lighter until I'm flying over the beach again, **E** getting blown through the sky like a feather that weighs nothing at all. But once I spread my fingers in the dirt and crouch over the Get on Your Mark, the dream goes and I am solid again and am telling myself, Squeaky you must win, you must win, you are the fastest thing in the world, you can even beat your father up Amsterdam if you really try. And then I feel my weight coming back just behind my knees then down to my feet then into the earth and the pistol shot explodes **F** in my blood and I am off and weightless again, flying past the other runners, my arms pumping up and down and the whole world is quiet

Make Connections

Have students use their own experiences at sporting events to analyze and respond to this passage, explaining the effect that static and echoes have on the clarity of public address announcements. **D**

Analyze Literature

Description Have students describe the daydream that Squeaky has before a race, and how her feelings change as soon as she goes into her starting-position crouch. **E**

Analyze Literature

Figurative Language Lead students to understand that the hyperbole in the metaphor *the pistol shot explodes in my blood* appeals to both the sense of hearing and the sense of touch. Squeaky uses the cue of the pistol shot to burst into motion. **F**

Run-ons

Remind students that a run-on is made up of two or more sentences that have been run together as though they were just one complete thought. Although such sentences are technically incorrect, authors sometimes use them to develop a character's personality. In this story, Bambara often has Squeaky use run-ons. Point out the example on this page beginning "Raymond is hollering from the swings. ..."

Discuss why this run-on adds personality and humor to Squeaky's character. Then work with students to separate it into sentences so that each expresses only one complete thought. You might challenge students to find other examples of run-ons in the story and then have them work with partners to edit the run-ons for clarity.

Analyze Literature

Figurative Language Pause here and have a volunteer read this sentence aloud, while students close their eyes and envision the scene. When the volunteer has finished reading, ask students what type of sensory experience Squeaky's encounter with the white ribbon provides (visual, tactile). Next, ask students what type of figurative language Bambara employs with Squeaky's feet (personification). How does this approach to the description inform the reader of Squeaky's mindset as she draws near to and crosses the finish line? **A**

Use Reading Strategies

Ask Questions Ask students to express in their own words what new thoughts Squeaky has about Gretchen and Raymond. Model possible questions: "What causes her to have these thoughts? How do they change her attitude about herself and her goals?" **B**

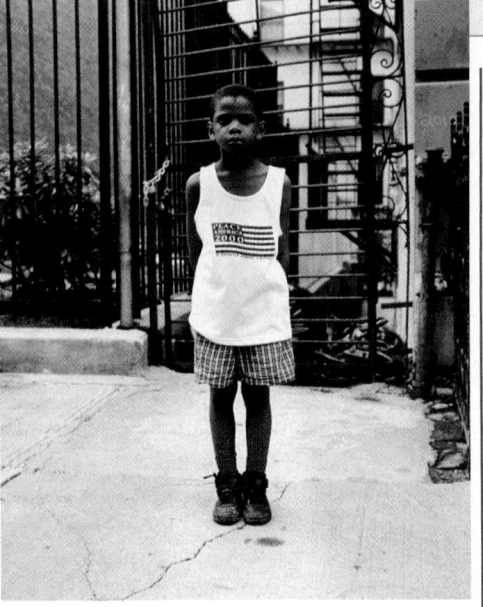

except for the crunch as I zoom over the gravel in the track. I glance to my left and there is no one. To the right, a blurred Gretchen, who's got her chin jutting out as if it would win the race all by itself. And on the other side of the fence is Raymond with his arms down to his side and the palms tucked up behind him, running in his very own style, and it's the first time I ever saw that and I almost stop to watch my brother Raymond on his first run. But the white ribbon is bouncing toward me and I tear past it, racing into the distance till my feet with a mind of their own start digging up footfuls of dirt and brake me short. Then all the kids standing on the side pile on me, banging me on the back and slapping my head with their May Day programs, for I have won again and everybody on 151st Street can walk tall for another year.

"In first place..." the man on the loudspeaker is clear as a bell now. But then he pauses and the loudspeaker starts to whine. Then static. And I lean down to catch my breath and here comes Gretchen walking back, for she's overshot the finish line too, huffing and puffing with her hands on her hips taking it slow, breathing in steady time like a real pro and I sort of like her a little for the first time. "In first place..." and then three or four voices get all mixed up on the loudspeaker and I dig my sneaker into the

grass and stare at Gretchen who's staring back, we both wondering just who did win.

I can hear old Beanstalk arguing with the man on the loudspeaker and then a few others running their mouths about what the stopwatches say. Then I hear Raymond yanking at the fence to call me and I wave to shush him, but he keeps rattling the fence like a gorilla in a cage like in them gorilla movies, but then like a dancer or something he starts climbing up nice and easy but very fast. And it occurs to me, watching how smoothly he climbs hand over hand and remembering how he looked running with his arms down to his side and with the wind pulling his mouth back and his teeth showing and all, it occurred to me that Raymond would make a very fine runner. Doesn't he always keep up with me on my trots? And he surely knows how to breathe in counts of seven cause he's always doing it at the dinner table, which drives my brother George up the wall. And I'm smiling to beat the band cause if I've lost this race, or if me and Gretchen tied, or even if I've won, I can always retire as a runner and begin a whole new career as a coach with Raymond as my champion. After all, with a little more study I can beat Cynthia and her phony self at the spelling bee. And if I bugged my mother, I could get piano lessons and become a star. And I have a big

Reading Proficiency

Struggling readers may have difficulty understanding Squeaky's language, sentence fragments, and run-on sentences. You might have them read with proficient partners, or have them read along silently while you or a volunteer reads the story aloud. Then pause from time to time to ask questions that will enable you to monitor their comprehension.

Enrichment

Point out that this story, like "The Treasure of Lemon Brown," takes place in Harlem, a large section of New York City. Interested students may enjoy using maps of New York City to find locations mentioned in this story, including Amsterdam Avenue, Lenox Avenue, and Squeaky's training route down Broadway to 145th Street.

rep as the baddest thing around. And I've got a roomful of ribbons and medals and awards. But what has Raymond got to call his own?

So I stand there with my new plans, laughing out loud by this time as Raymond jumps down from the fence and runs over with his teeth showing and his arms down to the side, which no one before him has quite mastered as a running style. And by the time he comes over I'm jumping up and down so glad to see him—my brother, Raymond, a great runner in the family tradition. But of course everyone thinks I'm jumping up and down because the men on the loudspeaker have finally gotten themselves together and compared notes and are announcing "In first place—Miss Hazel Elizabeth Deborah Parker." (Dig that.) "In second place—Miss Gretchen P. Lewis." And I look over at Gretchen wondering what the "P" stands for. And I smile. Cause she's good, no doubt about it. Maybe she'd like to help me coach Raymond; she obviously is serious about running, as any fool can see. And she nods to congratulate me and then she smiles. And I smile. We stand there with this big smile of respect between us. It's about as real a smile as girls can do for each other, considering we don't practice real smiling every day, you know, cause maybe we too busy being flowers or fairies or strawberries instead of something honest and worthy of respect... you know...like being people.

 What is an activity or sport at which you feel you excel? What is it about this activity that makes it appealing to you? Why do you think people strive to be the best at something? How is competition both helpful and harmful?

Analyze and Extend

1. (a) What is Squeaky's one responsibility? (b) Why is she responsible for this?
2. (a) What are some adjectives you would use to describe Squeaky? (b) How does Squeaky's personality affect the mood, or atmosphere, of the story?
3. What does Squeaky realize about Raymond at the end of the story? How has this also changed her views on competition?

Expository Writing The tone of a story is the writer or speaker's attitude toward the subject or the reader. For example, a writer might use a lighthearted tone when writing about something happy or funny, and a heavier one when writing about something sad. In a short **essay,** describe the tone of "Raymond's Run." Provide evidence in support of your claim by referring to specific details and passages in the text. When you are finished, exchange your work with a partner and provide each other feedback on the essay.

Media Literacy & Collaborative Learning Working with other students, rewrite one scene of this story as a dramatic **dialogue** between the characters. Think about what dialogue, body language, and actions would be realistic for each character. Then practice the dialogue and perform it for your classmates.

Go to www.mirrorsandwindows.com for more.

Use Reading Skills

Compare and Contrast Have students reread Squeaky's earlier comments on page 99 about the ways in which girls smile. Have them compare and contrast that point of view with the new point of view she has gained. Ask: "What caused her to change her opinion?" **C**

 *Answer:* Students should give reasons to support their choices of favorite activities. They might mention love of teamwork, competition, or the sense of achievement. Possible reasons for striving to be the best include having a sense of achievement, meeting a tough challenge, and feeling pride. Students might suggest that competition drives us to succeed but can also cause negative feelings toward others.

Analyze and Extend

1. (a) She is responsible for taking care of her brother Raymond. (b) Raymond is unable to care for himself and Squeaky protects him well.
2. (a) Students might describe Squeaky as sassy, tough, or street-smart. (b) Her attitude makes the mood of the story more humorous and urban.
3. Squeaky realizes that Raymond is a good runner and more important to her than the race; that competition can be friendly and helpful.

Rubric for Expository Writing

You can adapt this as a checklist for students to use as they write.

☐ Does the essay indicate the student's understanding of the tone of the story?

☐ Does it clearly present the student's opinion about how Toni Cade Bambara creates tone in "Raymond's Run"?

☐ Does the essay offer examples from the story to support this opinion?

At a Glance
Independent Reading
- Reading Level: Moderate
- Difficulty Consideration: Vocabulary
- Ease Factor: Sympathetic character

Objectives
Reading this selection will enable students to do the following:
- read with developing fluency
- read silently with comprehension for a sustained period of time

Launch the Lesson
Point out to students that in "Flowers for Algernon" a man of very limited intelligence suddenly grows smarter and smarter. Ask them if they believe geniuses are happier than most people. Then have them read to find out how this man's life changes, for better and for worse, as his intelligence grows.

▶ More by This Author
Students who like "Flowers for Algernon" might enjoy watching the 1968 film version of this story, *Charly*. Cliff Robertson won an Academy Award for his portrayal of Charly Gordon.

TEACHING NOTE
Although this selection is presented in the student edition as an independent reading, teaching support has been provided should you choose to cover it in class.

104

Program Resources

Planning and Assessment
Program Planning Guide, Selection Lesson Plan
E-Lesson Planner
Assessment Guide, Lesson Test
ExamView

Technology Tools
Interactive Student Text on CD
Visual Teaching Package
Audio Library
mirrorsandwindows.com

Meeting the Standards
Fiction: Unit 1, Independent Reading, pp. 74–79

Common Core State Standards
Reading Literature
RL.1, RL.3, RL.10

Speaking and Listening
SL.1

Flowers for Algernon

A Short Story by
Daniel Keyes

**Its very hard to be smart.
They said you know it will
probly be tempirery.**

Daniel Keyes Born in New York, Daniel Keyes held many careers before devoting his time to writing. He worked in the U.S. Maritime Service, as a fiction editor, as a fashion photographer, and as an English teacher. He eventually earned a bachelor's and master's degree from Brooklyn College in New York and went on to teach creative writing at the university level. "Flowers for Algernon," Keyes's most famous work, was published first as a short story in 1959 and later as a novel in 1966. The novel was adapted into a stage play and later into an Oscar-winning film. Keyes's latest book, *Algernon, Charlie and I: A Writer's Journey* chronicles his writing of the story. Keyes currently lives in South Florida.

1

progris riport 1—martch 5 1965
Dr. Strauss says I shud rite down what I think and evrey thing that happins to me from now on. I dont know why but he says its importint so they will see if they will use me. I hope they use me. Miss Kinnian says maybe they can make me smart. I want to be smart. My name is Charlie Gordon. I am 37 years old and 2 weeks ago was my brithday. I have nuthing more to rite now so I will close for today.

progris riport 2—martch 6
I had a test today. I think I faled it. and I think that maybe now they wont use me. What happind is a nice young man was in the room and he had some white cards with ink spillled all over them. He sed Charlie what do you see on this card. I was very skared even tho I had my rabits foot in my pockit because when I was a kid I always faled tests in school and I spillled ink to.

I told him I saw a inkblot. He said yes and it made me feel good. I thot that was all but when I got up to go he stopped me. He said now sit down Charlie we are not thru yet. Then I dont remember so good but he wantid me to say what was in the ink. I dint see nuthing in the ink but he said there was picturs there other pepul saw some picturs. I coudnt see any picturs. I reely tryed to see.

Teach the Selection

Summary
Charlie Gordon has an IQ of 68 when he is selected for a neurosurgical and psychological experiment regarding increases in intelligence. Charlie begins by competing in various tests with a laboratory mouse named Algernon, which has already had the surgery. Algernon always wins. Throughout the following five months, Charlie's intelligence grows to the point of genius. However, he soon observes Algernon's rapid decline, followed by his own.

 The Mirrors & Windows questions at the end of this selection focus on the theme of intelligence. Before reading the story, ask students how they think intelligence should be measured. What importance does society place on a person's "intelligence"?

Analyze Literature
Character Work with students to summarize the information about Charlie that Keyes provides on this opening page. Model this process by asking, "How old is Charlie? What do his words suggest about his abilities, his eagerness to please, and his motivation?"

Words in Use

Selection Words

feebleminded, 116
neurosurgeons, 117
opportunist, 117
petition, 118
wedge, 119
tangible, 119
specter, 119
specialization, 119
inferiority complex, 120

Teaching Words

devoting, 105
adapted, 105
chronicles, 105
transformation, 128

KEY TERMS
POINT OF VIEW, 128

Science Connection

Rorschach Test The Rorschach test that Charlie takes is named after its inventor, Hermann Rorschach (1884–1922). It is used by psychologists to analyze the emotional and intellectual functioning of a subject as he or she analyzes and interprets ten inkblot designs. The test is termed "projective" because the subject is supposed to project his or her personality into the inkblot via the shapes and situations he or she "sees." At the beginning of Charlie's story, he cannot see anything other than the inkblot itself. Later, his increased intelligence allows him to perceive definite shapes and situations. Work with students to compare and contrast Charlie's two experiences with the Rorschach inkblots, discussing why they are so different. **A**

I held the card close up and then far away. Then I said if I had my glases I coud see better I usally only ware my glases in the movies or TV but I said they are in the closit in the hall. I got them. Then I said let me see that card agen I bet Ill find it now.

I tryed hard but I still coudnt find the picturs I only saw the ink. I told him maybe I need new glases. He rote somthing down on a paper and I got skared of faling the test. I told him it was a very nice inkblot with littel points all around the eges. He looked very sad so that wasnt it. I said please let me try agen. Ill get it in a few minits becaus Im not so fast somtimes. Im a slow reeder too in Miss Kinnians class for slow adults but I'm trying very hard.

He gave me a chance with another card that had 2 kinds of ink spillled on it red and blue.

A He was very nice and talked slow like Miss Kinnian does and he explained it to me that it was a *raw shok.*[1] He said pepul see things in the ink. I said show me where. He said think. I told him I think a inkblot but that wasnt rite eather. He said what does it remind you—pretend something. I closd my eyes for a long time to pretend. I told him I pretned a fowntan pen with ink leeking all over a table cloth. Then he got up and went out.

I dont think I passd the *raw shok* test.

progris report 3—martch 7

Dr Strauss and Dr Nemur say it dont matter about the inkblots. I told them I dint spill the ink on the cards and I coudn't see anything in the ink. They said that maybe they will still use me. I said Miss Kinnian never gave me tests like that one only spelling and reading. They said Miss Kinnian told that I was her bestist pupil in the adult

---

1. **raw shok.** Rorschach test, used in psychology, where participants view inkblots and describe what images come to mind

Differentiated Instruction

Kinesthetic Learning

Work with students to create inkblots by spilling a small amount of ink or paint on a piece of paper and then folding the paper to make a symmetrical shape. Have them take turns interpreting the shapes as people, animals, objects, and so on. Then display pictures of people interacting. Use them to replicate the Thematic Apperception Test. Finally, have students complete a maze. Point out that for them, such tests are fun. Discuss why they might be very challenging and frustrating for Charlie.

nite scool becaus I tryed the hardist and I reely wantid to lern. They said how come you went to the adult nite scool all by yourself Charlie. How did you find it. I said I askd pepul and sumbody told me where I shud go to lern to read and spell good. They said why did you want to. I told them becaus all my life I wantid to be smart and not dumb. But its very hard to be smart. They said you know it will probly be tempirery. I said yes. Miss Kinnian told me. I dont care if it herts.

Later I had more crazy tests today. The nice lady who gave it me told me the name and I asked her how do you spellit so I can rite it in my progris riport. THEMATIC APPERCEPTION TEST. I dont know the frist 2 words but I know what *test* means. You got to pass it or you get bad marks. This test lookd easy becaus I coud see the picturs. Only this time she dint want me to tell her the picturs. That mixd me up. I said the man yesterday said I shoud tell him what I saw in the ink she said that dont make no difrence. She said make up storys about the pepul in the picturs.

I told her how can you tell storys about pepul you never met. I said why shud I make up lies. I never tell lies any more becaus I always get caut.

She told me this test and the other one the raw-shok was for getting personalty. I laffed so hard. I said how can you get that thing from inkblots and fotos. She got sore and put her picturs away. I dont care. It was sily. I gess I faled that test too.

B Later some men in white coats took me to a difernt part of the hospitil and gave me a game to play. It was like a race with a white mouse. They called the mouse Algernon.

Algernon was in a box with a lot of twists and turns like all kinds of walls and they gave me a pencil and a paper with lines and lots of boxes. On one side it said START and on the other end it said FINISH. They said it was *amazed* and that Algernon and me had the same *amazed* to do. I dint see how we could have the same *amazed* if Algernon had a box and I had a paper but I dint say nothing. Anyway there wasnt time because the race started.

One of the men had a watch he was trying to hide so I wouldnt see it so I tryed not to look and that made me nervus.

Anyway that test made me feel worser than all the others because they did it over 10 times with difernt *amazeds* and Algernon won every time. I dint know that mice were so smart. Maybe thats because Algernon is a white mouse. Maybe white mice are smarter then other mice.

progris riport 4—Mar 8

Their going to use me! Im so exited I can hardly write. Dr Nemur and Dr Strauss had a argament about it first. Dr Nemur was in the

> Their going to use me! Im so exited I can hardly write. **C**

Analyze Literature

Character Ask students what Charlie's attitude suggests about his perceptions of himself and the world around him and the motivation that stems from these perceptions. Model a response: "Charlie seems to perceive himself as lacking the intelligence of those around him and is, thereby, highly motivated to achieve what he thinks he lacks." **B**

Science Connection

Thematic Apperception Test The next psychological test that Charlie takes is the Thematic Apperception Test, in which subjects view thirty-one pictures of people interacting and are asked to describe what is happening in each one. It is designed to reveal people's subconscious characteristics, motives, needs, and abilities. **C**

Reading Skills

Sequence of Events

Point out that this story is told from Charlie's point of view and contains a series of diary entries. As they read, have students use the entries to create time lines that summarize the sequence of events. Model the procedure by working with them to create an entry for March 5, 1965.

March 5, 1965
—————————|—————————
Dr. Strauss
tells Charlie
to start his
progress report.

Ask Questions Model this strategy by stopping at the end of this passage and asking: "What type of operation will Charlie have? How might it make him smart?" Then have students read on and ask questions about the differing opinions of Dr. Strauss and Dr. Nemur. **Ⓐ**

Science Connection

IQ Point out that Charlie has an IQ (Intelligence Quotient) of 68. This figure is used to estimate a person's intelligence. A person with an IQ below 80 is considered to have low intelligence, a score of 100 is considered to show average intelligence, and a figure above 200 is considered to show genius. IQ is computed through multiple-choice tests. However, differing perspectives about what intelligence means and how to measure it have made these tests controversial. One problem with IQ tests is that they are often culturally biased, so subjects who share a culture with those who created the test tend to receive higher test scores than subjects from other cultures. Challenge students to come up with concrete examples of culturally biased test questions. **Ⓑ**

---

office when Dr Strauss brot me in. Dr Nemur was worryed about using me but Dr Strauss told him Miss Kinnian rekemmended me the best from all the people who she was teaching. I like Miss Kinnian becaus shes a very smart teacher. And she said Charlie your **Ⓐ** going to have a second chance. If you volenteer for this experament you mite get smart. They dont know if it will be perminint but theirs a chance. Thats why I said ok even when I was scared because she said it was an operashun. She said dont be scared Charlie you done so much with so little I think you deserv it most of all.

So I got scaird when Dr Nemur and Dr Strauss argud about it. Dr Strauss said I had something that was very good. He said I had a good *motor-vation.*[2] I never even knew **Ⓑ** I had that. I felt proud when he said that not every body with an eye-q of 68 had that thing. I dont know what it is or where I got it but he said Algernon had it too. Algernons *motor-vation* is the cheese they put in his box. But it cant be that because I didnt eat any cheese this week.

Then he told Dr Nemur something I dint understand so while they were talking I wrote down some of the words.

He said Dr Nemur I know Charlie is not what you had in mind as the first of your new brede of intelek** (coudnt get the word) superman. But most people of his low ment** are host** and uncoop** they are usualy dull apath** and hard to reach. He has a good natcher hes intristed and eager to please.

Dr Nemur said remember he will be the first human beeng ever to have his intelijence trippled by surgicle meens.

Dr Strauss said exakly. Look at how well hes lerned to read and write for his low

mentel age its as grate an acheve** as you and I lerning einstines therey of **vity[3] without help. That shows the intenss motor-vation. Its comparat** a tremen** achev** I say we use Charlie.

I dint get all the words and they were talking to fast but it sounded like Dr Strauss was on my side and like the other one wasnt.

Then Dr Nemur nodded he said all right maybe your right. We will use Charlie. When he said that I got so exited I jumped up and shook his hand for being so good to me. I told him thank you doc you wont be sorry for giving me a second chance. And I mean it like I told him. After the operashun Im gonna try to be smart. Im gonna try awful hard.

progris ript 5—Mar 10
Im skared. Lots of people who work here and the nurses and the people who gave me the tests came to bring me candy and wish me luck. I hope I have luck. I got my rabits foot and my lucky penny and my horse shoe. Only a black cat crossed me when I was comming to the hospitil. Dr Strauss says dont be supersitis Charlie this is sience. Anyway Im keeping my rabits foot with me.

I asked Dr Strauss if Ill beat Algernon in the race after the operashun and he said maybe. If the operashun works Ill show that mouse I can be as smart as he is. Maybe

---

2. **motor-vation.** Motivation; desire to achieve something
3. **einstines therey of **vity.** Einstein's theory of relativity, developed by physicist Albert Einstein (1879–1955), which describes the relation of space and time

---

Differentiated Instruction

Reading Proficiency
Some students might benefit from working with partners to edit one of Charlie's early diary entries, identifying and correcting the errors in grammar, punctuation, and spelling.

Enrichment
Students might enjoy researching IQ tests and finding sample questions. Then they might use the facts and questions they gather to hold a debate regarding the relevance, accuracy, and fairness of IQ testing. (They have been shown to be culturally biased.)

smarter. Then Ill be abel to read better and spell the words good and know lots of things and be like other people. I want to be smart like other people. If it works perminint they will make everybody smart all over the wurld.

They dint give me anything to eat this morning. I dont know what that eating has to do with getting smart. Im very hungry and Dr Nemur took away my box of candy. That Dr Nemur is a grouch. Dr Strauss says I

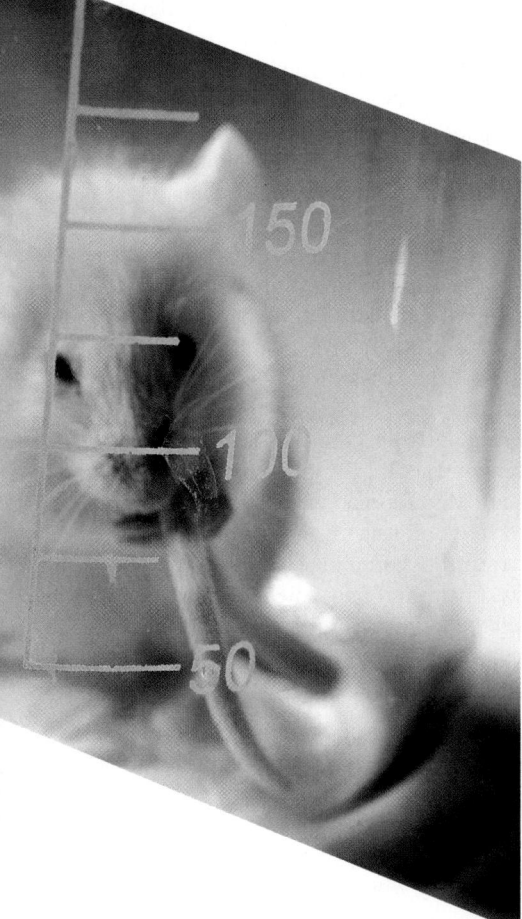

can have it back after the operashun. You cant eat befor a operashun…

Progress Report 6—Mar 15
The operashun dint hurt. He did it while I was sleeping. They took off the bandijis from my eyes and my head today so I can make a PROGRESS REPORT. Dr Nemur who looked at some of my other ones says I spell PROGRESS wrong and he told me how to spell it and REPORT too. I got to try and remember that.

I have a very bad memary for spelling. Dr Strauss says its ok to tell about all the things that happin to me but he says I shoud tell more about what I feel and what I think. When I told him I dont know how to think he said try. All the time when the bandijis were on my eyes I tryed to think. Nothing happened. I dont know what to think about. Maybe if I ask him he will tell me how I can think now that Im support to get smart. What do smart people think about. Fancy things I suppose. I wish I knew some fancy things alredy. **C**

Progress Report 7—mar 19
Nothing is happining. I had lots of tests and different kinds of races with Algernon. I hate that mouse. He always beats me. Dr Strauss said I got to play those games. And he said some time I got to take those tests over again. Thse inkblots are stupid. And those pictures are stupid too. I like to draw a picture of a man and a woman but I wont make up lies about people. **D**

I got a headache from trying to think so much. I thot Dr Strauss was my frend but he dont help me. He dont tell me what to think or when Ill get smart. Miss Kinnian dint come to see me. I think writing these progress reports are stupid too.

Teach the Selection

Make Connections
Ask students how they responded to Charlie's difficulty with thinking. Have them close their eyes, pretending that they have bandages over their eyes, like Charlie. Ask them what pictures or thoughts come to mind. Lead them to understand the difference between Charlie and people of normal intelligence. He does not have the ability to create thoughts or to remember thoughts. How would their lives be different if they were like Charlie? **C**

Use Reading Strategies
Clarify Ask students what Charlie means by "make up lies about people." Lead them to understand that this is his perception of fiction. He can't imagine a story about people in a picture because he thinks that that would be lying. **D**

Vocabulary Skills

Commonly Misspelled Words
Remind students that words that have similar sounds but different spellings and meanings are often confused, resulting in spelling errors. Offer this example from the story: "Their really my friends and they like me." Remind students that *their* is a possessive pronoun showing ownership, as in "Their car is blue." The correct word to use in the sentence from the story is *They're*, which is a contraction meaning "they are." Have students identify other examples in the story where the narrator confuses such words.

Make Predictions Lead students to understand that Charlie's goal is to beat Algernon at the maze. Have students predict whether or not this will actually happen and whether Charlie, like Algernon, will really become "3 times smarter" than he is now. **A**

Use Reading Strategies

Make Inferences Ask students to use clues in this passage to decide what leads the factory workers to make these jokes about Charlie. (He must have bruising and scars on his head from the brain surgery.) Then ask students whether they think these men are really Charlie's friends. Why do they make fun of him? Why doesn't this bother Charlie? **B**

Literary Connection

Eponym Remind students that an **eponym** is a term derived from a person's name. Point out the use of the eponym *Charlie Gordon* and discuss its meaning. Then have students use dictionaries to define other eponyms, such as *maverick, leotard, bloomers, Geiger counter,* and *Achilles' heel.* **C**

Progress Report 8—Mar 23

Im going back to work at the factery. They said it was better I shud go back to work but I cant tell anyone what the operashun was for and I have to come to the hospitil for an hour evry night after work. They are gonna pay me mony every month for lerning to be smart.

Im glad Im going back to work because I miss my job and all my frends and all the fun we have there.

Dr Strauss says I shud keep writing things down but I dont have to do it every day just when I think of something or something speshul happins. He says dont get discoridged because it takes time and it happins slow. He says it took a long time with Algernon before he got 3 times smarter then he was before. Thats why Algernon beats me all the time because he had that operashun too. That makes me feel better. I coud probly do that *amazed* faster than a reglar mouse. Maybe some day Ill beat Algernon. Boy that would be something. So far Algernon looks like he mite be smart perminent.

A

Mar 25 We had a lot of fun at the factery today. Joe Carp said hey look where Charlie had his operashun what did they do Charlie put some brains in. I was going to tell him but I remembered Dr Strauss said no. Then Frank Reilly said what did you do Charlie forget your key and open your door the hard way. That made me laff. Their really my friends and they like me.

B

Sometimes somebody will say hey look at Joe or Frank or George he really pulled a Charlie Gordon. I don't know why they say that but they always laff. This morning Amos Borg who is the 4 man at Donnegans used

C

my name when he shouted at Ernie the office boy. Ernie lost a packige. He said Ernie for godsake what are you trying to be a Charlie Gordon. I dont understand why he said that. I never lost any packiges.

Mar 28 Dr Strauss came to my room tonight to see why I dint come in like I was suppose to. I told him I dont like to race with Algernon any more. He said I dont have to for a while but I shud come in. He had a present for me only it wasnt a present but just for lend. I thot it was a little television but it wasnt. He said I got to turn it on when I go to sleep. I said your kidding why shud I turn it on when Im going to sleep. Who ever herd of a thing like that. But he said if I want to get smart I got to do what he says. I told him I dint think I was going to get smart and he put his hand on my sholder and said Charlie you dont know it yet but your getting smarter all the time. You wont notice for a while. I think he was just being nice to make me feel good because I dont look any smarter.

Oh yes I almost forgot. I asked him when I can go back to the class at Miss Kinnians school. He said I wont go their. He said that soon Miss Kinnian will come to the hospitil to start and teach me speshul. I was mad at her for not comming to see me when I got the operashun but I like her so maybe we will be frends again.

Mar 29 That crazy TV kept me up all night. How can I sleep with something yelling crazy things all night in my ears. And the nutty pictures. Wow. I dont know what it says when Im up so how am I going to know when Im sleeping.

Dr Strauss says its ok. He says my brains are lerning when I sleep and that will help

---

Differentiated Instruction

Reading Proficiency

Summarizing Point out to students that summarizing is a skill that can help them to read and enjoy fiction—particularly complicated stories like this one, which is told through a series of diary entries. Remind them that when we summarize, we retell in our own words only the main events. Ask them to use their own words to summarize the main events that have taken place so far in the story. They might refer to their time lines for guidance.

me when Miss Kinnian starts my lessons in the hospitl (only I found out it isnt a hospitil its a labatory). I think its all crazy. If you can get smart when your sleeping why do people go to school. That thing I dont think will work. I use to watch the late show and the late late show on TV all the time and it never made me smart. Maybe you have to sleep while you watch it.

PROGRESS REPORT 9—April 3

Dr Strauss showed me how to keep the TV turned low so now I can sleep. I dont hear a thing. And I still dont understand what it says. A few times I play it over in the morning to find out what I lerned when

I was sleeping and I dont think so. Miss Kinnian says Maybe its another langwidge or something. But most times it sounds american. It talks so fast faster then even Miss Gold who was my teacher in 6 grade and I remember she talked so fast I coudnt understand her.

I told Dr Strauss what good is it to get smart in my sleep. I want to be smart when Im awake. He says its the same thing and I have two minds. Theres the *subconscious*[4] and the *conscious* (thats how you spell it). And one dont tell the other one what its doing. They don't even talk to each other. Thats why I dream. And boy have I been having crazy dreams. Wow. Ever since that night TV. The late late late late late show.

I forgot to ask him if it was only me or if everybody had those two minds.

(I just looked up the word in the dictionary Dr Strauss gave me. The word is *subconscious. adj. Of the nature of mental operations yet not present in consciousness; as, subconscious conflict of desires.*) Theres more but I still dont know what it means. This isnt a very good dictionary for dumb people like me.

Anyway the headache is from the party. My frends from the factery Joe Carp

---

4. **subconscious.** Activity in the brain that one is not fully aware of, unlike the conscious, or thoughts one is aware of

---

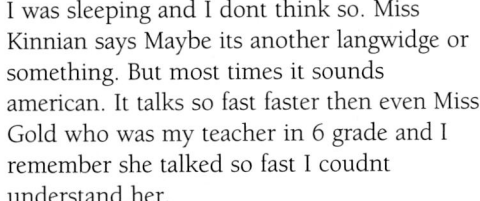

Teach the Selection

Science Connection
The Subconscious Mind Explain to students that Dr. Strauss is attempting to have Charlie learn through his subconscious mind. While it is widely debated what qualifies as being conscious, it is generally someone who is awake and/or aware of surroundings. The subconscious mind, then, is everything that operates or exists outside of the conscious mind. The two do not exist separately, however. For while we cannot be completely aware of the subconscious part of our minds, this part does influence our conscious thoughts and actions. Furthermore, some psychologists believe that people can learn through the subconscious mind when asleep or hypnotized. As Charlie sleeps, the tape recorder sends out information. Dr. Strauss believes that Charlie's subconscious mind is absorbing and gaining knowledge of the facts presented by the tape recording. **D**

Vocabulary Skills

Learn and *Teach*

Point out to students that *learn* and *teach* are related words that are sometimes confused. *Learn* means "to gain knowledge," and *teach* means "to give knowledge." These words cannot be used interchangeably.

EXAMPLES
Carrie is *learning* how to ski.
The instructor is *teaching* Carrie how to ski.

Have students copy and complete these sentences, inserting either *learn* or *teach*.
1. Sam (learned, <u>taught</u>) me to paint.
2. Henry (learns, <u>teaches</u>) kids about safety.
3. Let's (<u>learn</u>, teach) how to make ice cream.
4. I (learned, <u>taught</u>) myself how to knit.

Analyze Literature

Character Ask students to use the words and actions of Joe Carp and Frank Reilly to describe their personalities. **A**

Analyze Literature

Plot and Character Ask students to identify the major plot event that takes place here. (Charlie beats Algernon.) What does this event suggest? (Charlie is gaining in intelligence.) How do Charlie's feelings about Algernon change, and why? (He feels friendship and sympathy for the mouse because now Charlie feels superior.) **B**

Science Connection

B. F. Skinner Algernon is now undergoing a different type of test. Before, he learned to go through the maze in order to find a piece of cheese at the end. Now he must do different tasks each time. He might, for example, have to learn to step on a lever or undo a latch in order to get the cheese. This type of puzzle box is called a Skinner box, named after its inventor, the behavioral psychologist B. F. Skinner (1904–1990), who believed that human behavior develops as a reaction to environmental stimuli. Through his experiments, Skinner trained laboratory animals like Algernon to do complex tasks. For example, he taught pigeons to play table tennis in order to win a reward. **C**

and Frank Reilly invited me to go with them to Muggsys Saloon for some drinks. I dont like to drink but they said we will have lots of fun. I had a good time.

Joe Carp said I shoud show the girls how I mop out the toilet in the factory and he got me a mop. I showed them and everyone laffed when I told that Mr Donnegan said I was the best janiter he ever had because I like my job and do it good and never come late or miss a day except for my operashun.

I said Miss Kinnian always said Charlie be proud of your job because you do it good.

Everybody laffed and we had a good time and they gave me lots of drinks and Joe said Charlie is a card when hes potted. I dont know what that means but everybody likes me and we have fun. I cant wait to be smart like my best frends Joe Carp and Frank Reilly.

I dont remember how the party was over but I think I went out to buy a newspaper

and coffe for Joe and Frank and when I came back there was no one their. I looked for them all over till late. Then I dont remember so good but I think I got sleepy or sick. A nice cop brot me back home. Thats what my landlady Mrs Flynn says.

But I got a headache and a big lump on my head and black and blue all over. I think maybe I fell but Joe Carp says it was the cop they beat up drunks some times. I don't think so. Miss Kinnian says cops are to help people. Anyway I got a bad headache and Im sick and hurt all over. I dont think Ill drink anymore.

April 6 I beat Algernon! I dint even know I beat him until Burt the tester told me. Then the second time I lost because I got so exited I fell off the chair before I finished. But after that I beat him 8 more times. I must be getting smart to beat a smart mouse like Algernon. But I dont *feel* smarter.

I wanted to race Algernon some more but Burt said thats enough for one day. They let me hold him for a minit. Hes not so bad. Hes soft like a ball of cotton. He blinks and when he opens his eyes their black and pink on the eges.

I said can I feed him because I felt bad to beat him and I wanted to be nice and make frends. Burt said no Algernon is a very specshul mouse with an operashun like mine, and he was the first of all the animals to stay smart so long. He told me Algernon is so smart that every day he has to solve a test to get his food. Its a thing like a lock on a door that changes every time Algernon goes in to eat so he has to lern something new to get his food. That made me sad because if he couldnt lern he would be hungry.

I dont think its right to make you pass a

English Language Learning

Students learning English may have difficulty with Charlie's thoughts and experiments regarding commas and other punctuation marks. Use the money figures $10,000 and $1,000 to illustrate what Charlie means about someone losing money if the comma were misplaced. Then help students to understand the passages in which he sprinkles in commas in unusual places. Make sure that they understand that these are not correct uses of punctuation marks.

test to eat. How woud Dr Nemur like it to have to pass a test every time he wants to eat. I think Ill be frends with Algernon.

April 9 Tonight after work Miss Kinnian was at the laboratory. She looked like she was glad to see me but scared. I told her dont worry Miss Kinnian Im not smart yet and she laffed. She said I have confidence in you Charlie the way you struggled so hard to read and right better than all the others. At werst you will have it for a littel wile and your doing somthing for sience.

We are reading a very hard book. I never read such a hard book before. Its called *Robinson Crusoe* about a man who gets merooned on a dessert Iland. Hes smart and figers out all kinds of things so he can have a house and food and hes a good swimmer. Only I feel sorry because hes all alone and has no frends. But I think their must be somebody else on the iland because theres a picture with his funny umbrella looking at footprints. I hope he gets a frend and not be lonely.

April 10 Miss Kinnian teaches me to spell better. She says look at a word and close your eyes and say it over and over until you remember. I have lots of truble with *through* that you say *threw* and *enough* and *tough* that you dont say *enew* and *tew*. You got to say *enuff* and *tuff*. Thats how I use to write it before I started to get smart. Im confused but Miss Kinnian says theres no reason in spelling.

April 14 Finished *Robinson Crusoe*. I want to find out more about what happens to him but Miss Kinnian says thats all there is. *Why*

April 15 Miss Kinnian says Im lerning fast. She read some of the Progress Reports and

she looked at me kind of funny. She says Im a fine person and Ill show them all. I asked her why. She said never mind but I shoudnt feel bad if I find out that everybody isnt nice like I think. She said for a person who god gave so little to you done more then a lot of people with brains they never even used. I said all my frends are smart people but there good. They like me and they never did anything that wasnt nice. Then she got something in her eye and she had to run out to the ladys room.

April 16 Today, I lerned, the *comma,* this is a comma (,) a period, with a tail, Miss Kinnian, says its importent, because, it makes writing better, she said, sombeody, coud lose, a lot of money, if a comma, isnt, in the, right place, I dont have, any money, and I dont see, how a comma, keeps you from losing it,

But she says, everybody, uses commas, so Ill use, them too,

April 17 I used the comma wrong. Its punctuation. Miss Kinnian told me to look up long words in the dictionary to lern to spell them. I said whats the difference if you can read it anyway. She said its part of your education so now on Ill look up all the words Im not sure how to spell. It takes a long time to write that way but I think Im remembering. I only have to look up once and after that I get it right. Anyway thats how come I got the word *punctuation* right. (Its that way in the dictionary). Miss Kinnian says a period is punctuation too, and there are lots of other marks to lern. I told her I thot all the periods had to have tails but she said no.

You got to mix them up, she showed? me" how. to mix! them(up,. and now; I can!

Literary Connection
Robinson Crusoe British author Daniel Defoe (1660–1731) wrote the novel *Robinson Crusoe* in 1719. Based on a true story, it tells of the adventures of a shipwrecked Englishman and his native helper, Friday. It was an immediate success. Defoe then wrote a sequel, *The Farther Adventures of Robinson Crusoe* later that same year. A third volume, *Serious Reflections during the Life and Surprizing Adventures of Robinson Crusoe,* appeared the following year. Unlike the first two books, this one was a collection of moral essays. Although the sequels are rarely read today, the initial novel remains a popular adventure story. Several print editions and film versions are available. **D**

Use Reading Strategies
Ask Questions Model this strategy by asking: "Why does Charlie think that Miss Kinnian got something in her eye? What was actually happening, and why?" **E**

Grammar Skills

Contractions

Remind students that in his early Progress Reports, Charlie did not punctuate contractions correctly, omitting the apostrophes. Then point out that now that he has read the grammar book, he is beginning to use them correctly. Ask students to complete the following sentences, substituting a correctly punctuated contraction for the italicized words.

1. *I have not* seen Charlie today. (haven't)
2. *It is* a beautiful day. (It's)
3. *Let us* go on a hike together. (Let's)
4. *She has* taught Charlie to write. (She's)
5. *She is* a great teacher. (She's)

Analyze Literature

Character Discuss the change in Charlie that is evidenced by details in this passage. He can read a grammar book, he can identify errors in his past writing, and he can solve problems ("the whole thing straightened out in my mind"). Compare and contrast this passage with earlier ones in which Charlie said that he couldn't think. Then ask: "Why do you think that Charlie and Algernon no longer race?" (Charlie has reached a stage where he easily wins every time.) **A**

Make Connections

Ask students how they feel about the way that Joe and Frank treat Charlie. Then lead them to see that Charlie's feelings are changing. He's beginning to understand that they are cruel to him and make fun of him because of his low intelligence. Suddenly, he understands what a "Charlie Gordon" is. How do students think he feels? **B**

---

mix up all kinds" of punctuation, in! my writing? There, are lots! of rules? to lern; but Im gettin'g them in my head.

One thing I? like about, Dear Miss Kinnian: (thats the way it goes in a business letter if I ever go into business) is she, always gives me' a reason" when—I ask. She's a gen'ius! I wish! I cou'd be smart" like, her;

(Punctuation, is; fun!)

April 18 What a dope I am! I didn't even understand what she was talking about. I read the grammar book last night and it explanes the whole thing. Then I saw it was the same way as Miss Kinnian was trying to tell me, but I didn't get it. I got up in the middle of the night, and the whole thing straightened out in my mind.

Miss Kinnian said that the TV working in my sleep helped out. She said I reached a plateau. Thats like the flat top of a hill.

After I figgered out how punctuation worked, I read over all my old Progress Reports from the beginning. Boy, did I have crazy spelling and punctuation! I told Miss Kinnian I ought to go over the pages and fix all the mistakes but she said, "No, Charlie, Dr. Nemur wants them just as they are. That's why he let you keep them after they were photostated, to see your own progress. You're coming along fast, Charlie."

That made me feel good. After the lesson I went down and played with Algernon. We don't race anymore.

April 20 I feel sick inside. Not sick like for a doctor, but inside my chest it feels empty like getting punched and a heartburn at the same time.

I wasn't going to write about it, but I guess I got to, because it's important. Today

was the first time I ever stayed home from work.

Last night Joe Carp and Frank Reilly invited me to a party. There were lots of girls and some men from the factory. I remembered how sick I got last time I drank too much, so I told Joe I didn't want anything to drink. He gave me a plain Coke instead. It tasted funny, but I thought it was just a bad taste in my mouth.

We had a lot of fun for a while. Joe said I should dance with Ellen and she would teach me the steps. I fell a few times and I couldn't understand why because no one else was dancing besides Ellen and me. And all the time I was tripping because somebody's foot was always sticking out.

Then when I got up I saw the look on Joe's face and it gave me a funny feeling in my stomack. "He's a scream," one of the girls said. Everybody was laughing.

Frank said, "I ain't laughed so much since we sent him off for the newspaper that night at Muggsy's and ditched him."

"Look at him. His face is red."

"He's blushing. Charlie is blushing."

"Hey, Ellen, what'd you do to Charlie? I never saw him act like that before."

I didn't know what to

Differentiated Instruction

Kinesthetic and Auditory Learning
Students might enjoy experimenting with Dr. Strauss's methods of subconscious learning. Encourage them to listen to tapes in the classroom while doing other tasks that require concentration. They might also experiment at home while napping or doing chores. Have them report on their findings. as to whether or not they were able to learn and retain information through their subconscious minds.

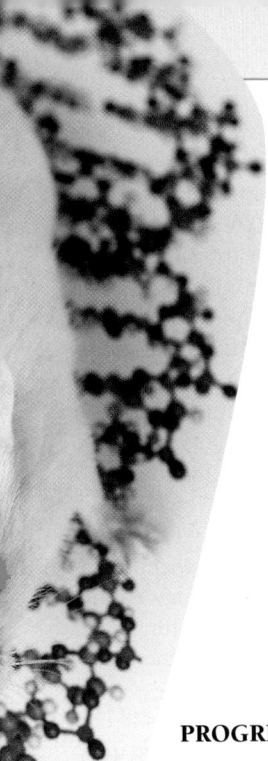

do or where to turn. Everyone was looking at me and laughing and I felt naked. I wanted to hide myself. I ran out into the street and I threw up. Then I walked home. It's a funny thing I never knew that Joe and Frank and the others liked to have me around all the time to make fun of me.

Now I know what it means when they say "to pull a Charlie Gordon."

I'm ashamed.

PROGRESS REPORT 10

April 21 Still didn't go into the factory. I told Mrs. Flynn my landlady to call and tell Mr. Donnegan I was sick. Mrs. Flynn looks at me very funny lately like she's scared of me.

I think it's a good thing about finding out how everybody laughs at me. I thought about it a lot. It's because I'm so dumb and I don't even know when I'm doing something dumb. People think it's funny when a dumb person can't do things the same way they can.

Anyway, now I know I'm getting smarter every day. I know punctuation and I can spell good. I like to look up all the hard words in the dictionary and I remember them. I'm reading a lot now, and Miss Kinnian says I read very fast. Sometimes I even understand what I'm reading about, and

it stays in my mind. There are times when I can close my eyes and think of a page and it all comes back like a picture. **C**

Besides history, geography, and arithmetic, Miss Kinnian said I should start to learn a few foreign languages. Dr. Strauss gave me some more tapes to play while I sleep. I still don't understand how that conscious and unconscious mind works, but Dr. Strauss says not to worry yet. He asked me to promise that when I start learning college subjects next week I wouldn't read any books on psychology—that is, until he gives me permission. **D**

I feel a lot better today, but I guess I'm still a little angry that all the time people were laughing and making fun of me because I wasn't so smart. When I become intelligent like Dr. Strauss says, with three times my I.Q. of 68, then maybe I'll be like everyone else and people will like me and be friendly.

I'm not sure what an I.Q. is. Dr. Nemur said it was something that measured how intelligent you were—like a scale in the drugstore weighs pounds. But Dr. Strauss had a big argument with him and said an I.Q. didn't weigh intelligence at all. He said an I.Q. showed how much intelligence you could get, like the numbers on the outside of a measuring cup. You still had to fill the cup up with stuff. **E**

Then when I asked Burt, who gives me my intelligence tests and works with Algernon, he said that both of them were wrong (only I had to promise not to tell them he said so). Burt says that the I.Q. measures a lot of different things including some of the things you learned already, and it really isn't any good at all.

So I still don't know what I.Q. is except that mine is going to be over 200 soon.

FLOWERS FOR ALGERNON **115**

Teach the Selection

Science Connection
Eidetic Memory Charlie has *eidetic*, or photographic, memory. It is the ability to recall images, sounds, or objects with great accuracy, almost as though the brain takes a photograph that stays in the mind. Chess players, orchestra conductors, and landscape painters have been known to have and use eidetic memory to perfect their talents. **C**

Use Reading Strategies
Make Predictions Ask students why Dr. Strauss might have made Charlie promise that he won't study psychology. (Possible answers: He doesn't want Charlie to understand what is happening to him; he doesn't want Charlie to outshine him.) Have students read on to check their predictions. **D**

Analyze Literature
Description Refer to the Science Connection information on IQ on page 108 and Rorschach testing to review with students that when Charlie's IQ reaches 200, he will be considered a genius. **E**

Grammar Skills

Commas in Compound Sentences
Remind students that a compound sentence contains two independent clauses connected by a comma and a coordinating conjunction *(and, but, or, nor, for, yet, so)*. Ask students to rewrite each pair of sentences as a compound sentence, using the coordinating conjunction shown in italics.

1. In the talent show, Hal sang a song. I presented a skit. (*and*)
2. I was really thirsty. There was no more lemonade. (*but*)
3. I might watch television tonight. I might read a book. (*or*)
4. Jim was carrying a huge carton of books. I held the door open for him. (*so*)

FLOWERS FOR ALGERNON **115**

Analyze Literature

Character Discuss why Charlie has such an angry response to Dr. Nemur. Then lead students to understand that Charlie has gained so much intelligence that he can't believe — or remember — that he was "feebleminded." Then have students compare and contrast Charlie's past and current reactions to the Rorschach inkblots. **A**

TEACHING NOTE

Identify Motivation

Have students work with partners. Have each pair work together to create a question regarding the motivation behind a character's thoughts, feelings, words, or actions. Model examples of these questions for them: "Why does Charlie feel lonely? Why are the doctors arguing? Why are the factory workers suddenly hostile to Charlie?" Have them trade papers with another set of partners. Have partners then work together to write an answer to the question they received. Use the questions and completed answers as the base for a classroom discussion.

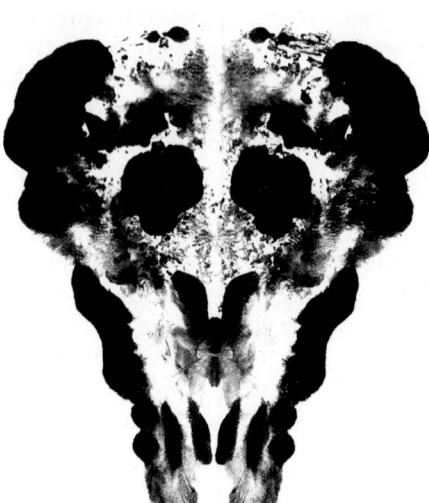

I didn't want to say anything, but I don't see how if they don't know *what it is*, or *where it is*—I don't see how they know *how much* of it you've got.

Dr. Nemur says I have to take a *Rorschach Test* tomorrow. I wonder what *that* is.

April 22 I found out what a *Rorschach* is. It's the test I took before the operation— the one with the inkblots on the pieces of cardboard. The man who gave me the test was the same one.

I was scared to death of those inkblots. I knew he was going to ask me to find the pictures and I knew I wouldn't be able to. I was thinking to myself, if only there was some way of knowing what kind of pictures were hidden there. Maybe there weren't any pictures at all. Maybe it was just a trick to see if I was dumb enough to look for something that wasn't there. Just thinking about that made me sore at him.

"All right, Charlie," he said, "you've seen these cards before, remember?"

"Of course I remember."

The way I said it, he knew I was angry, and he looked surprised. "Yes, of course. Now I want you to look at this one. What might this be? What do you see on this card? People see all sorts of things in these inkblots. Tell me what it might be for you— what it makes you think of."

I was shocked. That wasn't what I had expected him to say at all. "You mean there are no pictures hidden in those inkblots?"

He frowned and took off his glasses. "What?"

"Pictures. Hidden in the inkblots. Last time you told me that everyone could see them and you wanted me to find them too."

He explained to me that the last time he had used almost the exact same words he was using now. I didn't believe it, and I still have the suspicion that he misled me at the time just for the fun of it. Unless—I don't know any more—could I have been *that* feebleminded?

We went through the cards slowly. One of them looked like a pair of bats tugging at something. Another one looked like two men fencing with swords. I imagined all sorts of things. I guess I got carried away. But I didn't trust him any more, and I kept turning them around and even looking on the back to see if there was anything there I was supposed to catch. While he was making his notes, I peeked out of the corner of my eye to read it. But it was all in code that looked like this:

WF + A DdF-Ad orig. WF-A SF + obj

The test still doesn't make sense to me. It seems to me that anyone could make up lies about things that they didn't really see.

Reading Skills

Take Notes

This story contains many difficult scientific terms. Encourage students to jot down any terms that are unfamiliar and then use dictionaries and other reference sources to find the meanings. Use the Build Background materials, as well as your own classroom reference sources, to help them. Then have them take notes to show the relevance of these terms to Charlie's story. Additionally, have them note how Charlie's progress can be measured through his gradual understanding, and then mastery, of scientific terms and theories.

How could he know I wasn't making a fool of him by mentioning things that I didn't really imagine? Maybe I'll understand it when Dr. Strauss lets me read up on psychology.

April 25 I figured out a new way to line up the machines in the factory, and Mr. Donnegan says it will save him ten thousand dollars a year in labor and increased production. He gave me a twenty-five-dollar bonus.

I wanted to take Joe Carp and Frank Reilly out to lunch to celebrate, but Joe said he had to buy some things for his wife, and Frank said he was meeting his cousin for lunch. I guess it'll take a little time for them to get used to the changes in me. Everybody seems to be frightened of me. When I went over to Amos Borg and tapped him on the shoulder, he jumped up in the air.

People don't talk to me much anymore or kid around the way they used to. It makes the job kind of lonely.

April 27 I got up the nerve today to ask Miss Kinnian to have dinner with me tomorrow night to celebrate my bonus.

At first she wasn't sure it was right, but I asked Dr. Strauss and he said it was okay. Dr. Strauss and Dr. Nemur don't seem to be getting along so well. They're arguing all the time. This evening when I came in to ask Dr. Strauss about having dinner with Miss Kinnian, I heard them shouting. Dr. Nemur was saying that it was *his* experiment and *his* research, and Dr. Strauss was shouting back that he contributed just as much, because he found me through Miss Kinnian and he performed the operation. Dr. Strauss said that someday thousands of neurosurgeons might be using his technique all over the world.

Dr. Nemur wanted to publish the results of the experiment at the end of this month. Dr. Strauss wanted to wait a while longer to be sure. Dr. Strauss said that Dr. Nemur was more interested in the Chair of Psychology at Princeton than he was in the experiment. Dr. Nemur said that Dr. Strauss was nothing but an opportunist who was trying to ride to glory on *his* coattails.

When I left afterwards, I found myself trembling. I don't know why for sure, but it was as if I'd seen both men clearly for the first time. I remember hearing Burt say that Dr. Nemur had a shrew of a wife who was pushing him all the time to get things published so that he could become famous. Burt said that the dream of her life was to have a big shot husband.

Was Dr. Strauss really trying to ride on his coattails?

April 28 I don't understand why I never noticed how beautiful Miss Kinnian really is. She has brown eyes and feathery brown hair that comes to the top of her neck. She's only thirty-four! I think from the beginning I had the feeling that she was an unreachable genius—and very, very old. Now, every time I see her she grows younger and more lovely.

We had dinner and a long talk. When she said that I was coming along so fast that soon I'd be leaving her behind, I laughed.

"It's true, Charlie. You're already a better reader than I am. You can read a whole page at a glance while I can take in only a few lines at a time. And you remember every single thing you read. I'm lucky if I can recall the main thoughts and the general meaning."

"I don't feel intelligent. There are so many things I don't understand."

Grammar Skills

Infinitive Phrases
Remind students that an infinitive is a verb preceded by the word *to*. Then explain that an infinitive phrase contains an infinitive and all its modifiers and complements. Point out that this infinitive phrase serves as the direct object of the sentence. Have students complete each of the following sentences by adding an infinitive phrase.

1. Manny wanted ___. (to pitch in the last inning)
2. The team's strategy is ___. (to play defensively)
3. ___ would make me proud. (to win fairly)
4. It's fun ___ when you go to the ballpark. (to cheer with the crowd)
5. I congratulated Ana on her efforts ___. (to catch pop flies)

Analyze Literature

Similes Ask students to identify two similes in this passage (*like a giant sponge, like steps on a giant ladder*). Ask them to analyze them, explaining in their own words what each one means. **Ⓐ**

Use Reading Strategies

Make Predictions Ask students to suggest what "possibility" Charlie refers to here. Why might he compare that possibility to old people and death? Ask them to make predictions about what might happen to Algernon and Charlie. Then have them read on to check, confirm, or revise their predictions. **Ⓑ**

Analyze Literature

Motivation Discuss what feelings might have led the workers to sign the petition. **Ⓒ**

Ⓐ She took out a cigarette and I lit it for her. "You've got to be a *little* patient. You're accomplishing in days and weeks what it takes normal people to do in half a lifetime. That's what makes it so amazing. You're like a giant sponge now, soaking things in. Facts, figures, general knowledge. And soon you'll begin to connect them, too. You'll see how the different branches of learning are related. There are many levels, Charlie, like steps on a giant ladder that take you up higher and higher to see more and more of the world around you.

"I can see only a little bit of that, Charlie, and I won't go much higher than I am now, but you'll **Ⓒ** keep climbing up and up, and see more and more, and each step will open new worlds that you never even knew existed." She frowned. "I hope...I just hope to God—"

"What?"

"Never mind, Charles. I just hope I wasn't wrong to advise you to go into this in the first place."

I laughed. "How could that be? It worked, didn't it? Even Algernon is still smart."

We sat there silently for a while and I knew what she was thinking about as she watched me toying with the chain of my **Ⓑ** rabbit's foot and my keys. I didn't want to think of that possibility any more than elderly people want to think of death. I knew that this was only the beginning. I knew what she meant about levels because I'd seen some of them already. The thought of leaving her behind made me sad.

I'm in love with Miss Kinnian.

PROGRESS REPORT 11

April 30 I've quit my job with Donnegan's Plastic Box Company. Mr. Donnegan insisted that it would be better for all concerned if I left. What did I do to make them hate me so?

The first I knew of it was when Mr. Donnegan showed me the petition. Eight hundred and forty names, everyone **Ⓒ** connected with the factory, except Fanny Girden. Scanning the list quickly, I saw at once that hers was the only missing name. All the rest demanded that I be fired.

Joe Carp and Frank Reilly wouldn't talk to me about it. No one else would either, except Fanny. She was one of the few people I'd known who set her mind to something and believed it no matter what the rest of the world proved, said, or did—and Fanny did not believe that I should have been fired. She had been against the petition on principle and despite the pressure and threats she'd held out.

"Which don't mean to say," she remarked, "that I don't think there's something mighty strange about you, Charlie. Them changes. I don't know. You used to be a good, dependable, ordinary man—not too bright maybe, but honest. Who knows what you done to yourself to get so smart all of a

---

Reading Proficiency

Remind students that summarizing is a skill that can help them keep track of long works of fiction. Ask them to summarize the previous section of "Flowers for Algernon" (from Charlie's report of April 25 through his report of April 30).

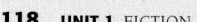

sudden. Like everybody around here's been saying, Charlie, it's not right."

"But how can you say that, Fanny? What's wrong with a man becoming intelligent and wanting to acquire knowledge and understanding of the world around him?"

She stared down at her work and I turned to leave. Without looking at me, she said: "It was evil when Eve listened to the snake and ate from the tree of knowledge. It was evil when she saw that she was naked. If not for that none of us would ever have to grow old and sick, and die." **D**

Once again now I have the feeling of shame burning inside me. This intelligence has driven a wedge between me and all the people I once knew and loved. Before, they laughed at me and despised me for my ignorance and dullness; now, they hate me for my knowledge and understanding. What in God's name do they want of me? **E**

They've driven me out of the factory. Now I'm more alone than ever before...

2

May 15 Dr. Strauss is very angry at me for not having written any progress reports in two weeks. He's justified because the lab is now paying me a regular salary. I told him I was too busy thinking and reading. When I pointed out that writing was such a slow process that it made me impatient with my

> ### Once again now I have the feeling of shame burning inside me.

poor handwriting, he suggested that I learn to type. It's much easier to write now because I can type nearly seventy-five words a minute. Dr. Strauss continually reminds me of the need to speak and write simply so that people will be able to understand me. **F**

I'll try to review all the things that happened to me during the last two weeks. Algernon and I were presented to the American Psychological Association sitting in convention with the World Psychological Association last Tuesday. We created quite a sensation. Dr. Nemur and Dr. Strauss were proud of us.

I suspect that Dr. Nemur, who is sixty—ten years older than Dr. Strauss—finds it necessary to see tangible results of his work. Undoubtedly the results of pressure by Mrs. Nemur.

Contrary to my earlier impressions of him, I realize that Dr. Nemur is not at all a genius. He has a very good mind, but it struggles under the specter of self-doubt.

He wants people to take him for a genius. Therefore, it is important for him to feel that his work is accepted by the world. I believe that Dr. Nemur was afraid of further delay because he worried that someone else might make a discovery along these lines and take the credit from him.

Dr. Strauss on the other hand might be called a genius, although I feel that his areas of knowledge are too limited. He was educated in the tradition of narrow specialization; the broader aspects of

Literary Connection
Adam and Eve Fanny refers to the biblical story of the fall of Adam and Eve. According to the story, when God created Adam and Eve, they were innocent and free of sin. God gave them the Garden of Eden, a paradise in which to live out their lives. He forbid them to eat the fruit of one specific tree, but a serpent persuaded Eve to take a bite of its fruit. When she did, she gained knowledge and shared it with Adam. God, angry at their actions, banished them from the Garden of Eden. The Bible deems Eve's action the original sin from which all other sins generate. Fanny compares this biblical "evil" to whatever power she believes Charlie must have used to forge such a dramatic change ("Who knows what you done to yourself to get so smart . . ."). **D**

Use Reading Skills
Compare and Contrast Discuss how Charlie's life is different from what it was and how it is the same. **E**

Analyze Literature
Irony Point out the irony that exists here. Before, Charlie spoke and wrote simply because he had limited intelligence. Now that he has grown so intelligent, he must scale down his language so that others can understand him. **F**

Synonyms
Remind students that synonyms are words with similar meanings. As an example, use the pair *intelligent* and *smart*. Call on volunteers to suggest other synonym pairs. Then review the use of dictionaries and thesauruses to find synonyms. Have students find synonyms for the following words.

1. confused (bewildered)
2. energy (drive)
3. mean (cruel)
4. coworker (associate)
5. concept (idea)
6. seldom (rarely)

Analyze Literature

Conflict Pause to discuss with students Charlie's initial conflict with the people around him. Guide them in recalling that he felt alienated because he considered himself "dumb" compared to them. Next, examine the conflict between Charlie and those around him illustrated on this page. How is this conflict different from the initial one? How is it similar? Help students understand that Charlie's alienation has come full circle, since he now feels alienated because he is *more* intelligent than those with whom he comes in contact. **A**

Use Reading Skills

Determine Importance of Details Charlie expresses dismay at Miss Kinnian's lack of understanding of a mathematical aspect of Dorbermann's Fifth Concerto. However, Dorbermann is a fictitious composer. Ask students if they think this fictitious element is purposeful on Keyes's part. If they think so, does Charlie's mention of it affect his credibility? How or how not? If they think not, does it affect Keyes's credibility? How or how not? **B**

---

background were neglected far more than necessary—even for a neurosurgeon.

I was shocked to learn that the only ancient languages he could read were Latin, Greek, and Hebrew, and that he knows almost nothing of mathematics beyond the elementary levels of the calculus of variations. When he admitted this to me, I found myself almost annoyed. It was as if he'd hidden this part of himself in order to deceive me, pretending—as do many people, I've discovered—to be what he is not. No one I've ever known is what he appears to be on the surface.

Dr. Nemur appears to be uncomfortable around me. Sometimes when I try to talk to him, he just looks at me strangely and turns away. I was angry at first when Dr. Strauss told me I was giving Dr. Nemur an inferiority complex. I thought he was mocking me and I'm oversensitive at being made fun of.

How was I to know that a highly respected psychoexperimentalist like Nemur was unacquainted with Hindustani and Chinese? It's absurd when you consider the work that is being done in India and China today in the very field of his study.

I asked Dr. Strauss how Nemur could refute Rahajamati's attack on his method and results if Nemur couldn't even read them in the first place. That strange look on Dr. Strauss's face can mean only one of two things. Either he doesn't want to tell Nemur what they're saying in India, or else—and this worries me—Dr. Strauss doesn't know either. I must be careful to speak and write clearly and simply so that people won't laugh.

May 18 I am very disturbed. I saw Miss Kinnian last night for the first time in over a week. I tried to avoid all discussions of intellectual concepts and to keep the conversation on a simple, everyday level, but she just stared at me blankly and asked me what I meant about the mathematical variance equivalent in Dorbermann's Fifth Concerto.

When I tried to explain she stopped me and laughed. I guess I got angry, but I suspect I'm approaching her on the wrong level. No matter what I try to discuss with her, I am unable to communicate. I must review Vrostadt's equations on *Levels of Semantic Progression*.

I find that I don't communicate with people much anymore. Thank God for books and music and things I can think about. I am alone in my apartment at Mrs. Flynn's boardinghouse most of the time and seldom speak to anyone.

May 20 I would not have noticed the new dishwasher, a boy of about sixteen, at the corner diner where I take my evening meals

---

Differentiated Instruction

Enrichment

Point out to students that "Flowers for Algernon" was made into an award-winning movie, *Charly*. Students may enjoy working with partners to write a script for one of the important scenes they have read. For example, they might write a scene in which Charlie quits his job after Mr. Donnegan shows him the petition and then has the conversation with Fanny. Or they might write a scene reflecting what takes place at the diner. Have them refer to *The Diary of Anne Frank* to copy the format of scripts. Provide time for volunteers to present their scenes to the class.

if not for the incident of the broken dishes.

They crashed to the floor, shattering and sending bits of white china under the tables. The boy stood there, dazed and frightened, holding the empty tray in his hand. The whistles and catcalls from the customers (the cries of "Hey, there go the profits!"… "Mazel tov!"…and "Well, *he* didn't work here very long…" which invariably seem to follow the breaking of glass or dishware in a public restaurant) all seemed to confuse him.

When the owner came to see what the excitement was about, the boy cowered as if he expected to be struck and threw up his arms as if to ward off the blow.

"All right! All right, you dope," shouted the owner, "don't just stand there! Get the broom and sweep that mess up. A broom…a broom, you idiot! It's in the kitchen. Sweep up all the pieces."

The boy saw that he was not going to be punished. His frightened expression disappeared and he smiled and hummed as he came back with the broom to sweep the floor. A few of the rowdier customers kept up the remarks, amusing themselves at his expense.

"Here, sonny, over here there's a nice piece behind you…"

"C'mon, do it again…"

"He's not so dumb. It's easier to break 'em than to wash 'em…"

As his vacant eyes moved across the crowd of amused onlookers, he slowly mirrored their smiles and finally broke into an uncertain grin at the joke which he obviously did not understand.

I felt sick inside as I looked at his dull, vacuous smile, the wide, bright eyes of a child, uncertain but eager to please. They were laughing at him because he was mentally retarded.

And I had been laughing at him too.

Suddenly, I was furious at myself and all those who were smirking at him. I jumped up and shouted, "Shut up! Leave him alone! It's not his fault he can't understand! He can't help what he is! But for God's sake … he's still a human being!"

The room grew silent. I cursed myself for losing control and creating a scene. I tried not to look at the boy as I paid my check and walked out without touching my food. I felt ashamed for both of us.

How strange it is that people of honest feelings and sensibility, who would not take advantage of a man born without arms or legs or eyes—how such people think nothing of abusing a man born with low intelligence. It infuriated me to think that not too long ago I, like this boy, had foolishly played the clown.

And I had almost forgotten.

I'd hidden the picture of the old Charlie Gordon from myself because now that I was intelligent it was something that had to be pushed out of my mind. But today in looking at that boy, for the first time I saw what I had been. *I was just like him!*

Only a short time ago, I learned that people laughed at me. Now I can see that unknowingly I joined with them in laughing at myself. That hurts most of all.

I have often re-read my progress reports and seen the illiteracy, the childish naiveté,[5] the mind of low intelligence peering from a dark room, through the keyhole, at the dazzling light outside. I see that even in my dullness I knew that I was inferior, and that

---

5. **naiveté.** Childlike innocence

Teach the Selection

Analyze Literature
Motivation Discuss what feelings lead Charlie to "feel sick" about the incident at the diner and why he loses his temper "creating a scene." Ask students if they think Charlie felt sympathy for the dishwasher. Why or why not? Do they think he was justified in his actions? **C**

Make Connections
Ask students to paraphrase Charlie's feelings. Why had he "played the clown"? Why was it so important to be liked and accepted? What does Charlie say "hurts most of all"? Do these feelings ring true, based on students' knowledge of people? Can they offer real-life examples of this behavior and explain how it affects peoples' self concepts? **D**

Vocabulary Skills

Comparison of Adjectives
Remind students that most one-syllable and a few two-syllable adjectives form their comparative and superlative degrees by adding *-er* or *-est*. Other two-syllable adjectives and all adjectives with more than two syllables use *more* or *most*.

Positive	Comparative	Superlative
smart	smarter	smartest
intelligent	more intelligent	most intelligent

Have students find examples of both comparative and superlative adjectives in the story.

Use Reading Strategies

Make Predictions Ask students why the incident at the diner causes Charlie to decide on future work. Then have them make predictions. Will he follow through on this plan? Will he be successful? Have them read on to find out. Then, ask them to revisit their predictions to see if they were right. **A**

Use Reading Skills

Identify Sequence of Events Point out to students that Charlie comes up with his plan on May 20. Ask them to summarize what happens on May 23, 24, and 25. What shift occurs?

other people had something I lacked—something denied me. In my mental blindness, I thought that it was somehow connected with the ability to read and write, and I was sure that if I could get those skills I would automatically have intelligence too.

Even a feeble-minded man wants to be like other men.

A child may not know how to feed itself, or what to eat, yet it knows of hunger.

This then is what I was like. I never knew. Even with my gift of intellectual awareness, I never really knew.

Even a feeble-minded man wants to be like other men.

This day was good for me. Seeing the past more clearly, I have decided to use my knowledge and skills to work in the field of increasing human intelligence levels. Who is better equipped for this work? Who else has lived in both worlds? These are my people. Let me use my gift to do something for them.

Tomorrow, I will discuss with Dr. Strauss the manner in which I can work in this area. I may be able to help him work out the problems of widespread use of the technique which was used on me. I have several good ideas of my own.

There is so much that might be done with this technique. If I could be made into a genius, what about thousands of others like myself? What fantastic levels might be achieved by using this technique on normal people? On *geniuses*?

There are so many doors to open. I am impatient to begin.

PROGRESS REPORT 12

May 23 It happened today. Algernon bit me. I visited the lab to see him as I do occasionally, and when I took him out of his cage, he snapped at my hand. I put him back and watched him for a while. He was unusually disturbed and vicious.

May 24 Burt, who is in charge of the experimental animals, tells me that Algernon is changing. He is less cooperative, he refuses to run the maze any more; general motivation has decreased. And he hasn't been eating. Everyone is upset about what this may mean.

May 25 They've been feeding Algernon, who now refuses to work the shifting-lock problem. Everyone identifies me with Algernon. In a way we're both the first of our kind. They're all pretending that Algernon's behavior is not necessarily significant for me. But it's hard to hide the fact that some of the other animals who were used in this experiment are showing strange behavior.

Dr. Strauss and Dr. Nemur have asked me not to come to the lab anymore. I know what they're thinking but I can't accept it. I am going ahead with my plans to carry their research forward. With all due respect to both of these fine scientists, I am well aware of their limitations. If there is an answer, I'll

Enrichment

Interested students might enjoy discussing how Dr. Strauss and Dr. Nemur might respond to Charlie's letter. Encourage students to work with partners to create either a dialogue between the doctors, in which they express their feelings, or a letter, in which they might jointly write to respond to Charlie. Urge students to keep in mind the conflicts that exist between the two doctors and to write accurately from each doctor's point of view.

have to find it out for myself. Suddenly, time has become very important to me.

May 29 I have been given a lab of my own and permission to go ahead with the research. I'm on to something. Working day and night. I've had a cot moved into the lab. Most of my writing time is spent on the notes which I keep in a separate folder, but from time to time I feel it necessary to put down my moods and my thoughts out of sheer habit.

I find the *calculus of intelligence* to be a fascinating study. Here is the place for the application of all the knowledge I have acquired. In a sense it's the problem I've been concerned with all my life.

May 31 Dr. Strauss thinks I'm working too hard. Dr. Nemur says I'm trying to cram a lifetime of research and thought into a few weeks. I know I should rest, but I'm driven on by something inside that won't let me stop. I've got to find the reason for the sharp regression in Algernon. I've got to know *if* and *when* it will happen to me.

June 4
LETTER TO DR. STRAUSS (*copy*)
Dear Dr. Strauss:
Under separate cover I am sending you a copy of my report entitled, "The Algernon-Gordon Effect: A Study of Structure and Function of Increased Intelligence," which I would like to have you read and have published.

As you see, my experiments are completed. I have included in my report all of my formulae, as well as mathematical analysis in the appendix. Of course, these should be verified.

B Because of its importance to both you and Dr. Nemur (and need I say to myself, too?) I have checked and rechecked my results a dozen times in the hope of finding an error. I am sorry to say the results must stand. Yet for the sake of science, I am grateful for the little bit that I here add to the knowledge of the function of the human mind and of the laws governing the artificial increase of human intelligence.

I recall your once saying to me that an experimental *failure* or the *disproving* of a theory was as important to the advancement of learning as a success would be. I know now that this is true. I am sorry, however, that my own contribution to the field must rest upon the ashes of the work of two men I regard so highly.

C

Yours truly,
Charles Gordon
encl.: rept

June 5 I must not become emotional. The facts and the results of my experiments are clear, and the more sensational aspects of my own rapid climb cannot obscure the fact that the tripling of intelligence by the surgical technique developed by Drs. Strauss and Nemur must be viewed as having little or no practical applicability (at the present time) to the increase of human intelligence.

As I review the records and data on Algernon, I see that although he is still in his physical infancy, he has regressed mentally. Motor activity is impaired; there is a general reduction of glandular activity; there is an accelerated loss of coordination.

There are also strong indications of progressive amnesia.

As will be seen by my report, these and other physical and mental deterioration

---

Teach the Selection

Analyze Literature
Motivation Discuss the meaning of this statement. Link Charlie's new concern with time to the changes in Algernon. Ask: "What might Charlie fear?" Have students read on to find out and encourage them to return to and evaluate their predictions. **B**

Use Reading Skills
Summarize Work with students to identify the main ideas in Charlie's letter. What was his purpose for writing? What is the meaning of his final sentence? **C**

Speaking & Listening Skills

Unfamiliar Words
Point out to students that when they listen to a speech or a lecture, they can use context clues to figure out the meanings of unfamiliar words. Model this strategy by reading the sentence from the June 5 entry, "As I review the records and data on Algernon, I see that although he is still in his physical infancy, he has regressed mentally." Ask students what *regressed* means. Ask what context clues the sentence provides. Call on volunteers to use this process to find the meanings of other unfamiliar words in other sentences on this page.

Ask Questions Based on Charlie's research and Algernon's rapid decline, what will probably happen to Algernon? What will probably happen to Charlie? **A**

Science Connection

Brain Terrain Algernon's brain has shrunk, an indication of the death of brain cells. Additionally, its surface has become smooth. A healthy, full-functioning brain contains many deep folds, or convolutions. Therefore, Charlie's examination shows the physical signs of Algernon's loss of brain functioning, leading to a loss of intelligence. **B**

Literary Connection

Paradise Lost Point out to students that John Milton (1608–1674) was a major English poet whose most famous work, the epic poem *Paradise Lost,* tells the biblical story of the fall from grace of Adam and Eve. One of the masterpieces of English literature, Milton's poem is remarkable for its sympathetic treatment of the rebel angel Lucifer, who aspires to equality with God and is condemned to Hell. Ask students why they think Charlie might have found *Paradise Lost* so powerful. **C**

Use Reading Skills

Identify Cause and Effect Ask students what might lead Charlie to think about the boy in the restaurant. **D**

A syndromes can be predicted with statistically significant results by the application of my formula.

The surgical stimulus to which we were both subjected has resulted in an intensification and acceleration of all mental processes. The unforeseen development, which I have taken the liberty of calling the *Algernon-Gordon Effect,* is the logical extension of the entire intelligence speed-up. The hypothesis here proven may be described simply in the following terms: Artificially increased intelligence deteriorates at a rate of time directly proportional to the quantity of the increase.

I feel that this, in itself, is an important discovery.

As long as I am able to write, I will continue to record my thoughts in these progress reports. It is one of my few pleasures. However, by all indications, my own mental deterioration will be very rapid.

I have already begun to notice signs of emotional instability and forgetfulness, the first symptoms of the burnout.

June 10 Deterioration progressing. I have become absent-minded. Algernon died two **B** days ago. Dissection shows my predictions were right. His brain had decreased in weight and there was a general smoothing out of cerebral convolutions as well as a deepening and broadening of brain fissures.[6]

I guess the same thing is or will soon be happening to me. Now that it's definite, I don't want it to happen.

I put Algernon's body in a cheese box and buried him in the backyard. I cried. **D**

---

6. **brain fissures.** Grooves on the brain's surface
7. **fugues of amnesia.** Brief flashes of amnesia, or forgetting one's surroundings

---

June 15 Dr. Strauss came to see me again. I wouldn't open the door and I told him to go away. I want to be left to myself. I have become touchy and irritable. I feel the darkness closing in. It's hard to throw off thoughts of suicide. I keep telling myself how important this introspective journal will be.

It's a strange sensation to pick up a book that you've read and enjoyed just a few months ago and discover that you don't **C** remember it. I remembered how great I thought John Milton was, but when I picked up *Paradise Lost* I couldn't understand it at all. I got so angry I threw the book across the room.

I've got to try to hold on to some of it. Some of the things I've learned. Oh, God, please don't take it all away.

June 19 Sometimes, at night, I go out for a walk. Last night I couldn't remember where I lived. A policeman took me home. I have the strange feeling that this has all happened to me before—a long time ago. I keep telling myself I'm the only person in the world who can describe what's happening to me.

June 21 Why can't I remember? I've got to fight. I lie in bed for days and I don't know who or where I am. Then it all comes back to me in a flash. Fugues of amnesia.[7] Symptoms of senility—second childhood. I can watch them coming on. It's so cruelly logical. I learned so much and so fast. Now my mind is deteriorating rapidly. I won't let it happen. **D** I'll fight it. I can't help thinking of the boy in the restaurant, the blank expression, the silly smile, the people laughing at him. No—please—not that again...

Differentiated Instruction

Visual Learners

Students may benefit from creating sequence charts, time lines, or original graphics to chart the various aspects of Charlie's decline. For example, to show the "last things learned, first things forgotten" process he describes in the first paragraph of his June 22 report, they might create a chart such as this one.

Things learned	Things forgotten
1. scientific concepts	1. motor skills
2.	2.
3.	3.
4.	4.

June 22 I'm forgetting things that I learned recently. It seems to be following the classic pattern—the last things learned are the first things forgotten. Or is that the pattern? I'd better look it up again...

I re-read my paper on the *Algernon-Gordon Effect* and I get the strange feeling that it was written by someone else. There are parts I don't even understand.

Motor activity impaired. I keep tripping over things, and it becomes increasingly difficult to type.

June 23 I've given up using the typewriter completely. My coordination is bad. I feel that I'm moving slower and slower. Had a terrible shock today. I picked up a copy of an article I used in my research, Krueger's *Uber psychische Ganzheit*, to see if it would help me understand what I had done. First I thought there was something wrong with my eyes. Then I realized I could no longer read German. I tested myself in other languages. All gone.

June 30 A week since I dared to write again. It's slipping away like sand through my fingers. Most of the books I have are too hard for me now. I get angry with them because I know that I read and understood them just a few weeks ago.

I keep telling myself I must keep writing these reports so that somebody will know what is happening to me. But it gets harder to form the words and remember spellings. I have to look up even simple words in the dictionary now and it makes me impatient with myself.

Dr. Strauss comes around almost every day, but I told him I wouldn't see or speak to anybody. He feels guilty. They all do. But

I don't blame anyone. I knew what might happen. But how it hurts.

July 7 I don't know where the week went. Todays Sunday I know becuase I can see through my window people going to church. I think I stayed in bed all week but I remember Mrs. Flynn bringing food to me a few times. I keep saying over and over Ive got to do something but then I forget or maybe its just easier not to do what I say Im going to do.

I think of my mother and father a lot these days. I found a picture of them with me taken at a beach. My father has a big ball under his arm and my mother is holding me by the hand. I dont remember them the way they are in the picture. All I remember is my father drunk most of the time and arguing with mom about money.

He never shaved much and he used to scratch my face when he hugged me. My mother said he died but Cousin Miltie said he heard his mom and dad say that my father

FLOWERS FOR ALGERNON **125**

Motivation Ask students what might motivate Charlie to place flowers on Algernon's grave. Model a possible response: "Algernon suffered a fate that Charlie is now suffering, and he feels sorry for the mouse." **A**

Make Connections
Ask students to describe the feelings that lead Charlie to get very angry with the doctor. How would they feel in the same situation? What might they say to Charlie? To the doctor? **B**

Use Reading Skills
Make Judgments Ask students if they think Charlie's response to Miss Kinnian is fair. Do they think she would laugh at him? Why or why not? If Charlie's reaction is unfair, what feelings are behind it? **C**

---

ran away with another woman. When I asked my mother she slapped my face and said my father was dead. I dont think I ever found out which was true but I don't care much. (He said he was going to take me to see cows on a farm once but he never did. He never kept his promises...)

July 10 My landlady Mrs Flynn is very worried about me. She says the way I lay around all day and dont do anything I remind her of her son before she threw him out of the house. She said she doesn't like loafers. If Im sick its one thing, but if Im a loafer thats another thing and she wont have it. I told her I think Im sick. **B**

I try to read a little bit every day, mostly stories, but sometimes I have to read the same thing over and over again because I dont know what it means. And its hard to write. I know I should look up all the words in the dictionary but its so hard and Im so tired all the time.

Then I got the idea that I would only use the easy words instead of the long hard ones. That saves time. I put flowers on Algernons grave about once a week. Mrs Flynn thinks Im crazy to put flowers on a mouses grave but I told her that Algernon was special. **A**

July 14 Its sunday again. I dont have anything to do to keep me busy now because my television set is broke and I dont have any money to get it fixed. (I think I lost this months check from the lab. I dont remember)

I get awful headaches and asperin doesnt help me much. Mrs Flynn knows Im really sick and she feels very sorry for me. Shes a wonderful woman whenever someone is sick.

July 22 Mrs Flynn called a strange doctor to see me. She was afraid I was going to die. I told the doctor I wasnt too sick and that I only forget sometimes. He asked me did I have any friends or relatives and I said no I dont have any. I told him I had a friend called Algernon once but he was a mouse and we used to run races together. He looked at me kind of funny like he thought I was crazy.

He smiled when I told him I used to be a genius. He talked to me like I was a baby and he winked at Mrs Flynn. I got mad and chased him out because he was making fun of me the way they all used to. **B**

July 24 I have no more money and Mrs Flynn says I got to go to work somewhere and pay the rent because I havent paid for over two months. I dont know any work but the job I used to have at Donnegans Plastic Box Company. I dont want to go back there because they all knew me when I was smart and maybe theyll laugh at me. But I dont know what else to do to get money.

July 25 I was looking at some of my old progress reports and its very funny but I cant read what I wrote. I can make out some of the words but they dont make sense.

Miss Kinnian came to the door but I said go away I dont want to see you. She cried and I cried too but I wouldnt let her in because I didn't want her to laugh at me. I told her I didn't like her any more. I told her I didnt want to be smart any more. Thats not true. I still love her and I still want to be smart but I had to say that so shed go away. She gave Mrs Flynn money to pay the rent. I dont want that. I got to get a job. **C**

English Language Learning
Students learning English may have particular difficulties understanding Charlie's phonetic spellings, such as *reed* for *read* and *agen* for *again*. Make sure that they can differentiate between his errors and the correct way to spell and punctuate.

Please...please let me not forget how to read and write...

July 27 Mr Donnegan was very nice when I came back and asked him for my old job of janitor. First he was very suspicious but I told him what happened to me then he looked very sad and put his hand on my shoulder and said Charlie Gordon you got guts.

Everybody looked at me when I came downstairs and started working in the toilet sweeping it out like I used to. I told myself Charlie if they make fun of you dont get sore because you remember their not so smart as you once thot they were. And besides they were once your friends and if they laughed at you that doesnt mean anything because they liked you too.

One of the new men who came to work there after I went away made a nasty crack he said hey Charlie I hear your a very smart fella a real quiz kid. Say something intelligent. I felt bad but Joe Carp came over and grabbed him by the shirt and said leave him alone you lousy cracker or Ill break your neck. I didn't expect Joe to take my part so I guess hes really my friend.

Later Frank Reilly came over and said Charlie if anybody bothers you or trys to take advantage you call me or Joe and we will set em straight. I said thanks Frank and I got choked up so I had to turn around and go into the supply room so he wouldnt see me cry. Its good to have friends.

July 28 I did a dumb thing today I forgot I wasnt in Miss Kinnians class at the adult center any more like I use to be. I went in and sat down in my old seat in the back of the room and she looked at me funny and she said Charles. I dint remember she ever called me that before only Charlie so I said hello Miss Kinnian Im redy for my lesin today only I lost my reader that we was using. She startid to cry and run out of the room and everybody looked at me and I saw they wasnt the same pepul who used to be in my class.

Then all of a suddin I rememberd some things about the operashun and me getting smart and I said holy smoke I reely pulled a Charlie Gordon that time. I went away before she come back to the room.

Thats why Im going away from New York for good. I dont want to do nothing like that agen. I dont want Miss Kinnian to feel sorry for me. Evry body feels sorry at the factery and I dont want that eather so Im going someplace where nobody knows that Charlie Gordon was once a genus and now he cant even reed a book or rite good.

D Im taking a cuple of books along and even if I cant reed them Ill practise hard and maybe I wont forget every thing I lerned. If I try reel hard maybe Ill be a littel bit smarter then I was before the operashun. I got my

...he looked very sad and put his hand on my shoulder and said Charlie Gordon you got guts.

E

Teach the Selection

Analyze Literature
Motivation Have students summarize ways in which Joe Carp and Frank Reilly have changed in their attitudes and actions toward Charlie. Discuss why these changes may have taken place. Why do they suddenly defend him? Challenge students to find and discuss parallel situations in their lives. **D**

Make Connections
Ask students what feelings have led Charlie to decide to go away from New York. Do they think it's a good idea? Why or why not? What would they say to him if they had the chance? **E**

Grammar Skills

Run-ons

Remind students that a run-on is made up of two or more sentences that have been run together as though they were just one complete thought. Stress that such sentences are not correct. Keyes has Charlie use them to show his rambling thoughts. For example, "I did a dumb thing today I forgot I wasnt in Miss Kinnians class at the adult center any more like I use to be." Have students work with partners to find other examples of run-on sentences on this page. Have them rewrite each example, correcting both its structure and its errors in punctuation and spelling.

Analyze Literature

Irony Point out the irony here. When Charlie let people laugh at him, they were nice to him because they felt superior to him. When he became a genius, he made people uncomfortable. **Ⓐ**

Answer: Students may suggest that IQ is a measure of a person's intelligence but not necessarily a measure of how well he or she uses that intelligence. Students may suggest that society treats people with a higher intelligence with more respect and judges people's intelligence based on behavior and appearance.

Analyze and Extend

1. (a) Charlie has an operation that increases his intelligence. (b) The Rorschach test shows his ability to comprehend the world around him.
2. (a) Miss Kinnian regrets what has happened to Charlie. (b) She looks after him, pays his rent, and cries when he returns to the special needs class.
3. (a) Without Charlie's point of view, readers would probably not understand fully Charlie's reactions to his environment during his different mental states. (b) The point of view is effective because it reveals Charlie's emotions and inner thoughts and reflects the ups and downs of his intelligence.

rabits foot and my luky penny and maybe they will help me.

If you ever reed this Miss Kinnian dont be sorry for me Im glad I got a second chanse to be smart becaus I lerned a lot of things that I never even new were in this world and Im grateful that I saw it all for a littel bit. I dont know why Im dumb agen or what I did wrong maybe its becaus I dint try hard enuff. But if I try and practis very hard maybe Ill get a littl smarter and know what all the words are. I remember a littel bit how nice I had a feeling with the blue book that has the torn cover when I red it. Thats why Im gonna keep trying to get smart so I can have that feeling agen. Its a good feeling to know things and be smart. I wish I had it rite now **Ⓐ**

if I did I would sit down and reed all the time. Anyway I bet Im the first dumb person in the world who ever found out somthing importent for sience. I remember I did somthing but I dont remember what. So I gess its like I did it for all the dumb pepul like me.

Good-by Miss Kinnian and Dr Strauss and evreybody. And P.S. please tell Dr Nemur not to be such a grouch when pepul laff at him and he woud have more frends. Its easy to make frends if you let pepul laff at you. Im going to have lots of frends where I go.

P.P.S. Please if you get a chanse put some flowrs on Algernons grave in the bakyard… ❖

 Throughout the story, several different characters provide their definitions of *I.Q.* What does the term mean to you? How do we judge other people based on their intelligence and appearance?

Analyze and Extend

1. (a) What kind of experiment is Charlie Gordon participating in? (b) How does his experience with the Rorschach test show his changes?
2. (a) How do you think Miss Kinnian feels about the experiment? (b) What evidence in the text leads you to believe this?
3. (a) How might have the story been different had it been told from another character's point of view? (b) What was the effect of telling the story from Charlie's point of view?

Creative Writing The events of "Flowers for Algernon" take place through a series of journal entries, or "progress reports." Pretend you are Charlie Gordon. Add an additional **diary entry** to Charlie's report. The entry may be from any point in time throughout the story. When you are finished, share your work with your classmates.

Critical Literacy Many of the characters in "Flowers for Algernon" have conflicting opinions on Charlie's transformation. Hold a debate in which you discuss whether or not Charlie should have participated in the experiment. State your ideas clearly, using eye contact, enunciation, speaking rate, and gestures to convey your position.

Go to **www.mirrorsandwindows.com** for more.

Rubric for Creative Writing
You can adapt this as a checklist for students to use as they write.

☐ Does the entry indicate the student's understanding of Charlie's current mental state?

☐ Does it have a voice that is consistent with the rest of Charlie's entries?

☐ Does it clearly present Charlie's responses to his environment?

For Your Reading List

The Outside Shot
by Walter Dean Myers

Lonnie Jackson is a talented basketball player who leaves his hometown of Harlem, New York, to attend a Midwestern college on scholarship. He encounters many obstacles, but also finds many new friends, including Sherry, a determined track star, and becomes a mentor to a child in need. Lonnie knows college is his shot at having a successful future—but does he have what it takes?

Missing May
by Cynthia Rylant

Summer, a twelve-year-old foster child, is struck with grief when her foster mother May suddenly dies while gardening. May's husband Ob is also devastated and Summer worries that she alone is not enough reason for Ob to keep on living. The two are brought closer together when they befriend Cletus, a smart, eccentric boy in Summer's class. The three decide to leave their rural home in West Virginia and take a trip to find the legacy of Aunt May.

Tunes for Bears to Dance To
by Robert Cormier

After his brother dies, Henry's family moves to a new town to escape the memories, but his father remains too depressed to work. Henry takes a job at a corner market to help out, meanwhile keeping an eye on the curious doings of an old neighbor man. Following the old man, Henry discovers he is carving a replica of his former village, which was destroyed in the Holocaust. Soon afterward, Henry's employer makes a surprising offer that it is hard to turn down. But there is a terrible price to pay.

Dandelion Wine
by Ray Bradbury

One day while out grape-picking with his father and brother, Douglas Spaulding realizes that he is alive, and awakens to the natural wonder of everything around him. He also realizes that he must deal with inevitable loss, and comes to terms with his best friend moving away. Many literary critics believe this story to be semi-autobiographical, telling the story of Ray Bradbury's childhood in Waukegan, Illinois.

A Tree Grows in Brooklyn
by Betty Smith

In turn-of-the-century Brooklyn, Francie Nolan lives in the slums with her family—including a harsh but realistic mother, a kind and gentle father, and her brother, who seems to be the favorite child of her parents. Francie is just beginning to learn that life can sometimes be cruel, but also beautiful.

Siddhartha
by Hermann Hesse

Siddhartha, an old ferryman, sits listening to the river. Once a handsome, wealthy, young man, he gave up his riches to become a poor wanderer. After meeting the Buddha, he decides that the life of an ascetic won't bring enlightenment and falls back into a life of pleasure. He becomes a child-person driven by his desires, until, almost despairing, he leaves everything to learn what the river has to teach. This novel, which describes the search for personal truth, has become a classic.

Program Resources

EMC Access Editions
For additional independent reading, you may wish to refer students to one of EMC's Access Edition titles such as Lois Lowry's *The Giver* or Mark Twain's *The Adventures of Tom Sawyer*. Each Access Edition contains a thorough study apparatus, including background information, literal comprehension questions, footnotes, vocabulary definitions, critical thinking questions, and related projects and activities. An Assessment Manual offering worksheets is available for each Access Edition.

Independent Reading

Independent Reading Activity
Help students link their reading to the unit theme, Finding Ourselves. Ask how fiction can help readers expand their understanding of themselves. You might try this as an in-class activity: Have students read silently in class a fiction work of their choosing for at least twenty minutes. Then have students identify what this short story or novel can teach a reader about themselves.

TEACHING NOTE

Book Club
Point out to students that one of the pleasures of independent reading is sharing these experiences with other readers. Suggest that students form classroom literature circles or book clubs, in which small groups meet to exchange insights, interpretations, and questions about the books they read. Have them select one of the books suggested here (or another book chosen by the members of the group) as the subject for a discussion. Follow these discussion guidelines.

- Summarize and repeat your ideas when necessary.
- Give reasons for your opinions.
- Answer questions other participants ask.
- Encourage others to talk.
- Listen politely and ask follow-up questions.

EMC E-Library
The EMC E-Library contains more than twenty thousand pages of literary classics that can be used for students' independent reading. An Electronic Library Guide provides teaching suggestions, enrichment activities, and reading strategy guidesheets.

Common Core State Standards

Reading Literature
RL.10

Objectives

Participating in this lesson will help students to write a response to a short story that

- has an effective opening
- has a clear thesis statement
- has a body with a clear organizational pattern
- uses textual evidence in support of the main ideas
- has an effective conclusion that restates the thesis in a new way

Workshop Launch

To stimulate students' thinking about a response to a short story, ask them what qualities are the most important to them in the fiction they read on their own. Are they primarily interested in plot? Do they read one or another type of genre fiction such as science fiction or fantasy? Do they prefer stories with characters their own age?

Program Resources

Additional writing workshops are available in the *Exceeding the Standards: Writing* resource.

⊳ More About the Author

Point out to students that Chaim Potok (1929–2002) was an American writer who used his fiction to portray the cultural conflicts experienced by Orthodox Jews in a secular society. The child of Polish immigrants, Potok became a Jewish rabbi before he began his career as a writer.

Expository Writing

Responding to a Short Story

Reading and Writing

Think about the characters and places you've read about in this unit's short stories. Why do you think Laurie lied about Charles? What new ideas about "treasures" occurred to you after meeting Lemon Brown? How does the setting of "Last Night" shape the mood of the story?

By organizing your impressions into ideas and turning your ideas into support for a thesis statement, you can compose a **response to a piece of literature** that is clear, informative, and unique. This workshop will help you brainstorm about the most memorable components of a story and create an original thesis statement with supporting evidence. The following summary, which includes a description of your assignment, your goal, strategy, and a writing rubric, will help you build a strong response.

Assignment: Use my critical thinking skills to write a response to a short story I have read.

Goal: Present a clear and engaging response to a story or an aspect of a story.

Strategy: Organize my main points and support them with evidence from the story.

Writing Rubric: My response to literature should include the following:

- an introduction that grabs the reader's attention and sets up my thesis statement
- a clear organizational pattern
- textual evidence (paraphrased and quoted) that supports my main ideas
- an awareness of my audience and an appropriate tone
- a conclusion that restates my thesis in a new way

What Great Writers Do

Chaim Potok was a novelist, essayist, and poet. In this interview excerpt, Potok discusses how reading influenced his writing. Consider how your own reading experiences inspire you.

I think it was...the realization that you could really create the world out of language...I figured if these writers could get me to be interested in two different... worlds that there was something about this form of communication that I wanted to be part of. That it captivated me the way it did, that it worked its magic on me, made me realize how powerful this medium is. And I wanted to become part of it.

Common Core State Standards

Writing
W.2, W.4, W.5, W.6, W.10

Language
L.4.1g, L.6.3a, L.6.3b

Words in Use

Teaching Words

components, 130	**varied,** 133
strategy, 130	**engaging,** 133
textual, 130	**impact,** 134
paraphrased, 130	
navigate, 132	
affection, 132	
empathy, 132	
annotations, 133	

KEY TERMS

SETTING, 130	**ORDER OF**
MOOD, 130	**IMPORTANCE,** 132
RESPONSE, 130	**CHRONOLOGICAL**
AUDIENCE, 130	**ORDER,** 132
THESIS, 130	**OUTLINE,** 132
MAIN POINT, 130	**TOPIC SENTENCE,** 132
TOPIC, 131	**TONE,** 132
FREEWRITE, 131	**SENTENCE VARIETY,** 134
THEME, 131	
ORGANIZATIONAL	
PATTERN, 132	

1. PREWRITE

Narrowing Your Topic

Think of the stories from the unit that stand out in your mind. Which stories surprised you? Which affected you strongly or changed your ideas about something? Think about which aspects of the story most influenced your reaction. As you consider stories to write about, choose one that interests you and that will give you enough to discuss in your response.

Gathering Details

Once you have chosen a story to write about, freewrite to gather ideas. When you freewrite, you write without pausing, reflecting, correcting mistakes, or changing ideas. In freewriting, you simply write. Begin by setting in front of you a pen and a clean sheet of paper. Think about your favorite story so far. Before touching pen to paper, consider: *Why is this your favorite? What is the best thing about it? Who are the most important characters? What deeper meaning might the story have? How does the story affect you?* Next, begin writing. Continue for five straight minutes.

The next step is to read over what you've just written. Your writing should give you some insight into what kinds of things you can focus on in your response. *Circle* each thing that seems like an important detail from the story. *Underline* anything that might be a good idea to expand. Trust your own observations.

In Charles I like ⟨ the surprise ending. ⟩ I like the twist. I think Laurie is a very bad kid. His parents are tricked. Jackson makes you think Laurie's mom will meet Charles's mom. The <u>ending is confusing</u>. I don't know what to make of it. It's my favorite because <u>it is weird</u>. And I like the mom. I think ⟨ the mom is the narrator. ⟩ I am not sure why. The story <u>reminded me of little kids using their imaginations</u>. They <u>forget what's real. None of the characters are who you thought they were.</u>

Deciding on Your Thesis

Now that you have gotten some of your impressions onto paper, organize them into ideas that can be used to build a response. Make a list of what you have circled and underlined. These ideas should become part of your thesis or evidence to support the thesis. In order to get your ideas in order, skim the story. This will help you remember the themes of the story, recall details, and answer any questions you have. Reread any parts of the story that are unclear and ask a classmate or teacher if you have additional questions.

the ending is confusing

it is unexpected

reminded me of little kids using their imaginations

characters weren't the people I thought they were

Thesis:

"Charles" is an interesting story because its unexpected ending makes you reconsider what you thought you knew about the characters.

Prewrite

Decide on a Story Model the process of determining which story to write about by modeling: "Even though I've read Marjorie Kinnan Rawlings's 'A Mother in Mannville' more than once, it always affects me. The character of the boy seems to me to reveal something very deep in human nature."

Use a Cluster Chart Point out to students that another way to gather details about a short story is to use a cluster chart. Write the title of the short story they have chosen in a circle at the center of a sheet of paper. Draw branches from the central circle ending in other circles, with such labels as "Why It Held My Interest" and "How It Made Me Feel," and so on. Fill in details from the story related to each of these categories.

Test the Thesis Have student pairs test the strength of their theses by analyzing their textual support.

What Great Writers Do

"Of Mr. Hawthorne's Tales we would say, emphatically, that they belong to the highest region of Art. . . . As Americans, we feel proud of the book. Mr. Hawthorne's distinctive trait is invention, creation, imagination, originality—a trait which, in the literature of fiction, is positively worth all the rest."

— EDGAR ALLAN POE,
REVIEW OF NATHANIEL HAWTHORNE'S
Twice-Told Tales

WRITING WORKSHOP **131**

Differentiated Instruction

English Language Learning

You might invite students who are learning English to base their essays on stories that they read in their native languages.

Enrichment

Ask the class to brainstorm a list of short stories and novels they like. Write these titles on the board, and then invite individual students to deliver an extemporaneous "review" of one of these works of fiction, giving reasons for an evaluation of its strengths (or weaknesses).

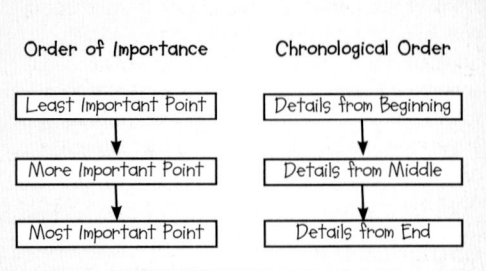

Teach the Workshop

Draft

Drafting an Introduction Point out to students that the purpose of an introduction is to capture the reader's attention and clearly establish the thesis of the essay. Urge them to think about the kinds of things that capture their attention when they're reading and provide a "hook" to hold their interest. Some effective hooks include a quote, question, anecdote, fact, or description.

Testing the Organization Suggest that students test the effectiveness of their organizational pattern by explaining the plan of their essays aloud to a partner. Students could also read their drafts to a partner and ask them to briefly summarize the main idea(s) of their essays. Point out to students that both these methods are good tests to check if they have expressed their ideas clearly.

What Great Writers Do

"All modern American literature comes from one book by Mark Twain called Huckleberry Finn. There was nothing before. There has been nothing as good since."

— ERNEST HEMINGWAY,
Green Hills of Africa

2. DRAFT

Organizing Ideas

After you have a strong thesis and have gathered enough ideas to write about, decide how to organize your ideas. Choose the **organizational pattern** that will help you express and connect your ideas clearly and effectively. To emphasize your strongest points, organize your points by **order of importance.** That is, place your most important point either first or last for the most impact. Or, you may prefer to use **chronological order,** in which you discuss details in the order they appear in the story. Whatever you decide, the order of paragraphs should be clear and logical to the reader.

Order of Importance	Chronological Order
Least Important Point	Details from Beginning
↓	↓
More Important Point	Details from Middle
↓	↓
Most Important Point	Details from End

Putting Your Thoughts on Paper

Now create an outline to show you how you will "navigate" your response from introduction to conclusion. Your outline should include the three basic parts of your essay: introduction, body, and conclusion. Effective introductions grab the reader's attention and introduce the thesis statement. The thesis is usually the last sentence of the introductory paragraph. Each of your body paragraphs should begin with a topic sentence that expresses the main idea of that paragraph. These main ideas should, in turn, support your thesis. In the supporting sentences of each paragraph, give evidence from the text to support your main idea. Evidence from the story should include examples, direct quotes, and paraphrased material. In your conclusion, sum up your main points and restate your thesis in new words.

Intro
- Identify the story "Charles" by Shirley Jackson.
- Include my thesis statement.

Body
- Discuss details from the beginning and support my point with evidence.
- Discuss details from the middle and support my point with evidence.
- Discuss details from the end and support my point with evidence.

Conclusion
- Sum up my main points.
- Restate my thesis.

Tone and Audience

There are two important terms to keep in mind as you plan and write: tone and audience. In order to be clear in your response, maintain an appropriate **tone,** or attitude toward your subject. Tone communicates the writer's emotions toward the subject, such as humor, affection, dislike, empathy, or sadness. Your tone can be formal or informal. For your response, try to sound natural, but not too informal.

Your **audience** includes whoever will read your essay. Most likely your audience will be your classmates, your teacher, and other readers of the story. As you write, be sure you have enough background information for your audience to follow your points. If your audience has also read the story, you should be able to summarize it in a few brief sentences rather than retelling every part.

Writing Skills

Audience

Point out to students that an audience is the intended person or group of people who will read what you write. For example, they might write for themselves, a friend, a relative, your classmates, or a teacher. Point out that choosing a specific audience will help them make important decisions about how they write. Discuss with them how selecting each of the following audiences would affect how they write.

1. young children
2. a potential employer
3. people interested in a particular sport or hobby
4. a friend or family member
5. someone in another country

3. REVISE

Evaluating Your Draft

Evaluate your draft. Mark any areas that sound awkward or unclear. Conduct a **peer review** in which you trade drafts with a classmate and have him or her look for any problems. Discuss strengths and weaknesses, and how to make improvements.

Below is the first part of a draft. The annotations in the right column explain the changes marked in the draft.

Revising Checklist

☐ Does the introduction grab the reader's attention and set up the thesis statement?

☐ Is the organizational pattern clear?

☐ Are the main ideas supported with specific details and examples?

☐ Are the sentences varied and engaging?

Introduction

Can you think of some unusual situations you found yourself in as a child? Children will do very strange things to avoid getting in trouble.

One such child is Laurie in Shirley Jackson's story "Charles." Laurie lies to his parents by imagining a bad child who does terrible things at school. The bad child turns out to be Laurie himself. "Charles" is an interesting story because ~~of~~ its unexpected ending. makes you reconsider what you thought you knew about the characters.

> Make your introduction interesting to your reader.

> In your thesis, specify what parts of the story made you respond the way you did.

Body

What makes "Charles" so good is its twist ending. When the teacher says there is no Charles in the class, suddenly you realize that Laurie has been lying all along. In addition, Laurie makes Charles, in his imaginary stories, "bigger" than he is. He says Charles is "bigger than me" and "he doesn't ever wear a jacket." You never know how much of Charles is really Laurie, and how much is exaggeration.

> Make sure each body paragraph has a topic sentence that states your main idea.

> Include evidence from the story and explain how it supports your thesis.

Teach the Workshop

Revise

Evaluating a Draft Discuss with students the following tips for delivering and receiving helpful criticism:

Delivering a Peer Review

- **Be focused.** Concentrate on content, organization, and style. Leave spelling and punctuation for the proofreading stage.
- **Be positive.** Respect the writer's feelings and genuine writing efforts.
- **Be specific.** Give the writer concrete ideas for improving his or her work.

Receiving a Peer Review

- **Be specific.** Tell your peer reviewer your specific concerns and questions.
- **Ask questions.** Make sure you understand your reviewer's comments.
- **Be selective.** Accept your reviewer's suggestions graciously, but you don't have to use all—or any—of them.

Differentiated Instruction

Reading Proficiency

To help students understand the lesson, tell them what the assignment will be and show them the student model. Point out that the lesson is organized into five steps. Then have students read and summarize the instructions for each step before they begin the assignment.

▶ Edit and Proofread

Students may want to use proofreader's marks when correcting their work. Refer them to page 945 of the Language Arts Handbook, Writing Section 4.1, Proofreader's Symbols.

What Great Writers Do

"Cooper's art has some defects. In one place in The Deerslayer, *and in the restricted space of two-thirds of a page, Cooper has scored 114 offenses against literary art out of a possible 115. It breaks the record."*

— MARK TWAIN
"Fenimore Cooper's Literary Offenses"

▶ Publish and Present

Before students begin their final version, they might benefit from reading the Language Arts Handbook, Writing Section 4.1, Writing Follow-up.

---

4. EDIT AND PROOFREAD

Focus: Sentence Variety

Include a variety of sentences in your response to make your writing more fluid and interesting. As you revise your draft, check that your sentences vary in length and type. For example, use questions to grab your reader's attention.

> ~~Children find themselves in some unusual situations.~~ *Can you think of some unusual situations you found yourself in as a child?* Children will do very strange things to avoid getting in trouble.

If many of your sentences start or end the same way, revise them to add variety. Add introductory phrases or change the order of the clauses in complex sentences. If you have several long, complex sentences in a row, include a short sentence to create impact. If you have several short, choppy sentences in a row, combine some of them with conjunctions to create compound and complex sentences.

Focus: Commonly Confused Words

Some words can be confusing when you are writing. Review words such as *whose and who's* carefully when you are revising your draft. If you are still confused, use a dictionary to find out which word you should use.

> The story makes you wonder about who's who, and if there are any other Charles-es out there.

If you substitute the words *who is* for the contraction *who's* you will notice that the correction from the first draft makes sense. The word *whose* is the possessive form of the word *who*, as in, "Whose umbrella is this in my backpack?"

Proofreading

Quality Control Although you can always look for mistakes as you draft and revise, set aside a last step in which you check your essay for errors in grammar, punctuation, and spelling. Use proofreader's marks to highlight any errors you find and correct them for your final draft. (See the Language Arts Handbook, section 4.1, for a list of proofreader's marks.)

5. PUBLISH AND PRESENT

Final Draft

Clean Copy Now that you have revised, edited, and proofread your essay, make a clean copy for presentation. Handwritten papers should be neat and legible. If you are working with a word processing program, double space the lines of text and use a readable typeface. Follow the presentation guidelines before submitting your work.

Writing Skills

Key Details

Point out to students that writing can often be improved by adding details or examples. Discuss the following examples:

Tragically, some of Lincoln's sons died in childhood. (draft)
Tragically, three of Lincoln's four sons died in childhood. (revision)

Have students work in pairs to propose revisions for the following sentences.

1. The home team tied the game in the last of the ninth.
2. I showed up late for my family's Thanksgiving dinner.
3. The zookeeper came in carrying a snake.

Student Model

Laurie and Charles
by Anne Fleming

Can you think of some unusual situations you found yourself in as a child? Children will do very strange things to avoid getting in trouble. One such child is Laurie in Shirley Jackson's story "Charles." Laurie lies to his parents by imagining a bad child who does terrible things at school. The bad child turns out to be Laurie himself. "Charles" is an interesting story because its unexpected ending makes you reconsider what you thought you knew about the characters.

Throughout the story, Laurie tells his parents all the bad things "Charles" does during his first few weeks of kindergarten. On his first day, Charles gets spanked "for being fresh." On the second day, Charles hits the teacher. He kicks the gym teacher and hits a boy in the stomach. Laurie continues to report to his parents how bad Charles is. Laurie's parents are surprised by Charles's behavior, and they wonder if he's a bad influence on Laurie. When Laurie's mom meets his teacher, she seems more interested in Charles than in Laurie.

What makes "Charles" so good is its twist ending. When the teacher says there is no Charles in the class, suddenly you realize that Laurie has been lying all along. Since the story is told from his mom's perspective, it feels like he has actually been lying to you, too. In addition, Laurie makes Charles, in his imaginary stories, "bigger" than he is. He says Charles is "bigger than me" and "he doesn't ever wear a jacket." You never know how much of Charles is really Laurie, and how much is exaggeration.

Once it becomes clear that Laurie made up Charles, even Laurie's parents don't seem to be the same characters. There are hints throughout the story that Laurie is having problems in kindergarten. Laurie speaks "insolently" to his father, calls him "dumb," and rarely listens to his parents. Yet, his parents hardly notice his bad behavior as they become more and more fascinated by the stories about Charles. When Laurie's mother wants to attend the PTA meeting, it's not to discuss Laurie. She wants to meet Charles's mother. After Laurie's mother and his teacher meet, his teacher says, "We're all so interested in Laurie." Ironically, Laurie's own parents have been much more interested in Charles.

This story is fun to read because it ends so unexpectedly. None of the characters are who they seem at first. Laurie's parents are so much more interested in Charles that they don't see the truth. The story makes you wonder about who's who, and if there are any other Charles-es out there.

Engages the reader

Names the story and its author

Presents a clear thesis statement that responds to one aspect of the story

Organized in chronological order

Includes clear topic sentences for body paragraphs

Supports the thesis by providing clear explanations

Supports main ideas with specific details and quoted evidence from the story

Sums up the main points without repeating the thesis exactly

Teach the Workshop

Objectives

Participating in this lesson will help students deliver an oral summary of a short story that

- has a clear order of events
- summarizes the main themes and conflicts
- exhibits appropriate volume and pacing
- exhibits effective nonverbal expression

Launch the Workshop

Point out to students that to do an effective oral summary of a short story, one needs to be a good storyteller. Ask them what kinds of literary, verbal, and nonverbal skills an effective storyteller needs. Ask them what experiences they have had of oral storytelling—either as performer or audience member.

> ▶ For more information see the Language Arts Handbook Section 7, Speaking & Listening.

Literary Connection

Oral Tradition Point out to students that behind every written literary tradition is a far longer tradition of oral storytelling. The Greek poet Homer, for example, was the inheritor of a long tradition of oral storytelling stretching back centuries to the time of the Trojan War.

Giving and Actively Listening to Oral Summaries

Without thinking about it, you have probably delivered many oral summaries in the past. Sometimes it might have been a response to a friend's request to tell him or her "what happened" in a movie or television program. Sometimes it may have been a response to a teacher. In this lesson, you will deliver an oral summary of a short story to an audience. An effective **oral summary** should discuss elements of a story's plot, setting, and characters. When you give and actively listen to oral summaries, you share information about a literary work and exchange ideas with your peers. By responding to others' oral summaries, you help others think of ways to improve their work and also improve your own speaking and listening skills.

Planning An Oral Summary

Choose a Story Before you can develop an oral summary, you must first select a story. Choose a story that you feel strongly about, since you need to convey your enthusiasm (or lack of) to your audience. Don't choose a story that is so brief your presentation will seem skimpy. However, don't pick a story that is so long that your oral summary becomes difficult for your audience to understand.

Select Key Ideas Using the story you have selected, outline the main ideas from your response on note cards. Do not copy your entire response word for word onto the cards. Instead, use brief key words and phrases. Being able to recall key ideas from your response will prove more helpful than simply memorizing an oral summary. You may also want to create a plot summary for your reference. A plot summary includes all the main events of the narrative without the minor details. For example, a key word plot summary for the story "Charles" might look something like this:

- Laurie begins kindergarten.
- Laurie tells his family about Charles, who behaves badly at school.
- The family begins to refer to anyone making a mess as pulling a "Charles."
- Laurie reports that Charles behaves well at school and is the teacher's special helper.
- Laurie's mother attends the PTA meeting and is anxious to meet Charles's mother and Laurie's teacher.
- Laurie's mother learns there is no Charles in the class.

Program Resources

To expand upon this workshop lesson, Giving and Actively Listening to Literary Presentations, see the *Exceeding the Standards: Speaking & Listening* resource.

Common Core State Standards

Speaking and Listening
SL.1, SL.3, SL.6

KEY TERMS

ORAL SUMMARY, 136	TONE, 137
KEY IDEA, 136	PACING, 137
PLOT SUMMARY, 136	NONVERBAL
AUDIENCE, 137	EXPRESSION, 137
VERB TENSE, 137	

Differentiated Instruction

Enrichment

Invite students to do extemporaneous oral storytelling based on some narrative with which they are familiar. Such narratives might include personal stories, family or historical anecdotes, jokes, urban legends, and other brief narratives.

Identify Your Audience After you select a story and decide which key ideas to summarize, you must then decide who your audience is. Is the audience familiar with the short story? Will you need to provide background information? Be prepared to answer questions from the audience about your presentation, regardless of how familiar they are with the story.

Use the Proper Verb Tense In any kind of summary, the writer or speaker needs to decide whether to use past or present tense. Most often, literature is discussed in the present tense. Keep your verb tense consistent throughout the entire summary.

Rehearse Your Summary Next, rehearse your oral summary. Try practicing in front of a mirror or use a video recorder to monitor your communication and delivery. Know that if you have practiced and are prepared to present, everything should go smoothly.

Evaluating Your Oral Summary

Working with partners or in a small group, rehearse your oral summary. Then, provide constructive feedback to your partner on what he or she did well and what could be improved. Constructive feedback means that you are respectful and polite whether you give criticism or praise. Follow the listening and speaking rubric on this page in order to evaluate each oral summary.

Delivering Your Oral Summary

Nonverbal communication is an important part of listening and speaking. As you deliver your oral summary, remember to make eye contact with the audience. Try to stand still and avoid any movements that can distract those you are speaking to. Varying the tone and volume of your voice can keep an audience focused and interested.

Just as it is important to be an effective speaker, it is also necessary to be an effective listener. To listen effectively, maintain eye contact with the speaker. Remain silent during the presentation, and ask questions when appropriate.

Speaking Rubric

Your presentation will be evaluated on these elements:

Content

☐ includes clear order of events—beginning, middle, and end

☐ includes introduction and conclusion

☐ main ideas are supported with text evidence

☐ main themes and conflicts of story are summarized

Delivery and Presentation

☐ appropriate volume

☐ appropriate pacing

☐ effective nonverbal expression

Listening Rubric

As a peer reviewer or audience member, you should do the following:

☐ listen quietly and attentively

☐ ask appropriate questions

☐ (as peer reviewer) provide constructive feedback

Evaluating an Oral Summary

Have students create a feedback checklist to use as they work with their partners in preparing their oral summaries. This checklist should relate to the literary qualities of their summaries and to both the verbal and nonverbal aspects of their deliveries.

Delivering an Oral Summary

Point out to students that if they use their normal conversational level of speaking, their oral summaries may not be heard by everyone in the audience. Like actors, they need to project their voices. This does not mean that they need to shout but rather to effectively focus their voices. Students can establish an appropriate volume by delivering a portion of their summary to a partner standing at the back of the classroom to determine if their projection is sufficient.

What Great Speakers Do

"I am a griot. . . . We are vessels of speech, we are the repositories which harbor secrets many centuries old. The art of eloquence has no secrets for us; without us the names of kings would vanish into oblivion, we are the memory of mankind; by the spoken word we bring to life the deeds and exploits of kings for younger generations."

—DJELI MAMADOU KOUYATÉ,
IN *Sundiata, an Epic of Old Mali*

Speaking & Listening Skills

Inflection

Point out to students that in order to deliver an effective oral summary, they need to speak with expression. This means introducing inflection, or variety, into their voices. Inflection can come through changes in pitch (how high or low a voice is) or volume (how loud or soft a it is). Inflection also comes from changes in pacing and emphasis.

Have students test the effect of inflection by examining how emphasizing the italicized word changes the meaning of each of the following sentences.

He can't order you to stay here.
He can't *order* you to stay here.
He can't order you to stay *here.*

Objectives

Completing this lesson will enable students to

- write a literary response
- answer standardized test questions that demonstrate revising and editing skills
- demonstrate the ability to make inferences from a reading by answering standardized questions

Timed Writing

Explain to students that standardized tests often ask students to write a response to a prompt in a specified period of time. Give the following tips:

- Read the entire question carefully.
- Look for key words in the question that tell you what is expected.
- Underline these words or write them on your own notepaper.
- Use the key words to make sure to answer all parts of the question.
- Organize. Allow time for planning, writing, and reviewing.
- Before you begin writing, create a rough outline of points to make.
- If you find yourself running out of time, state your remaining points and add a conclusion.
- Write a clear introduction. This will help keep you on track as you write each paragraph.
- Review your completed essay to see if you have answered all parts of the question.
- Before you turn in your completed essay, take time to proofread it.

Test Practice Workshop

Writing Skills

Literary Response

Read the following short excerpt and the writing assignment that follows. Before you begin writing, think carefully about what task the assignment is asking you to perform. Then create an outline to help guide your writing.

from "An Hour with Abuelo" by Judith Ortiz Cofer

She drops me off in front. She wants me to go in alone and have a "good time" talking to Abuelo.

I tell her to be back in one hour or I'll take the bus back to Paterson. She squeezes my hand and says, *"Gracias, hijo,"* in a choked-up voice like I'm doing her a big favor.

I get depressed the minute I walk into the place. They line up the old people in wheelchairs in the hallway as if they were about to be raced to the finish line by orderlies who don't even look at them when they push them here and there. I walk fast to room 10, Abuelo's "suite." He is sitting up in his bed writing with a pencil in one of those old-fashioned black hardback notebooks. It has the outline of the island of Puerto Rico on it. I slide into the hard vinyl chair by his bed. He sort of smiles and the lines on his face get deeper, but he doesn't say anything. Since I'm supposed to talk to him, I say, "What are you doing, Abuelo, writing the story of your life?"

It's supposed to be a joke, but he answers, "Sì, how did you know, Arturo?" His name is Arturo too. I was named after him. I don't really know my grandfather. His children, including my mother, came to New York and New Jersey (where I was born) and he stayed on the Island until my grandmother died. Then he got sick, and since nobody could leave their jobs to go take care of him, they brought him to this nursing home in Brooklyn. I see him a couple of times a year, but he's always surrounded by his sons and daughters.

Assignment: What do you think the details from this passage (including the narrator's **description**, **tone**, and **motivation**, and his interaction with other characters) **foreshadow**? Plan and write several paragraphs in which you describe what you believe these details foreshadow. Include evidence from this passage in your response.

Rubric for Literary Response

Have students use these criteria when evaluating their literary responses.

- ☐ Do your paragraphs follow your outline?
- ☐ Do your paragraphs offer an opinion of what the passage's description, tone, and motivation foreshadow?
- ☐ Do your paragraphs include details from the passage as evidence for your opinion?

Revising and Editing Skills

For each of the following questions, choose the *best* revision of the underlined portion of the sentence. If you feel that the underlined portion should not be changed, choose option (A), which repeats the phrasing of the original. Record your answers on a separate sheet of paper.

1. I can't decide whose the best player on their team.
   A. whose the best player on their team.
   B. whose the best player on they're team.
   C. who's the best player on their team.
   D. whose the greatest player on their team.
   E. who's the best player. On their team.

2. John and Mitch, after class, was unhappy with the homework the teacher assigned.
   A. John and Mitch, after class, was unhappy
   B. John and Mitch, after class, were unhappy
   C. John and Mitch, after class, is unhappy
   D. John and Mitch, after class, has been unhappy
   E. John and Mitch, after class, has unhappy

3. What is the outcome if neither team is able to score in overtime.
   A. is able to score in overtime.
   B. are able to score in overtime.
   C. were able to score in overtime.
   D. is able to score in overtime?
   E. is able to score in overtime!

4. Though they didn't like the work, Ron and Li were happy that their rooms were clean.
   A. were happy that their rooms were clean.
   B. were happy that their rooms were clean?
   C. is happy that their rooms were clean.
   D. were happy that there rooms were clean.
   E. were happy that their rooms is clean.

5. Rachel was unsure of who's bottle of water was in the kitchen.
   A. who's bottle of water was in the kitchen.
   B. who's bottle of water is in the kitchen.
   C. whose bottle of water was in the kitchen.
   D. who's bottle of water was in the kitchen?
   E. who's bottle of water were in the kitchen.

6. Instead of sweaters, Tara and Royce wore her flannels to the park.
   A. wore her flannels to the park.
   B. wears her flannels to the park.
   C. wearing their flannels to the park.
   D. were wearing her flannels to the park.
   E. wore their flannels to the park.

7. Mrs. Ramirez asked her class why no one had finished the homework?
   A. had finished the homework?
   B. had finished the homework.
   C. has finished the homework?
   D. have finished the homework?
   E. had finished their homework?

8. Pamela, without the help of her friends, are cleaning the basement of Mrs. Trent.
   A. are cleaning the basement of Mrs. Trent.
   B. are cleaning Mrs. Trent's basement.
   C. are gonna clean the basement of Mrs. Trent.
   D. were cleaning the basement of Mrs. Trent.
   E. is cleaning the basement of Mrs. Trent.

9. The student newspaper, though overseen by two teachers, were wrong about the scores.
   A. were wrong about the scores.
   B. are wrong about the scores.
   C. was wrong about the scores.
   D. about the scores, were wrong.
   E. have been wrong about the scores.

Reading Comprehension Tests

Point out to students that reading comprehension questions give you a short piece of writing and then ask you several questions about it. The questions may ask you to figure out something based on information in the passage. Urge them to keep the following tips in mind:

- Read all the questions quickly.
- Read the passage with the questions in mind.
- Reread the first question carefully.
- Scan the passage, looking for key words. When you find a key word, slow down and read carefully.
- Answer the first question.
- Repeat this process to answer all the rest of the questions.

Reading Skills

Carefully read the following passage. Then, on a separate piece of paper, answer each question.

from "The Osage Orange Tree" by William Stafford

On that first day of high school in the prairie town where the tree was, I stood in the sun by the flagpole and watched, but pretended not to watch, the others. They stood in groups and talked and knew each other, all except one—a girl though—in a faded blue dress, carrying a sack lunch and standing near the corner
5   looking everywhere but at the crowd.

I might talk to her, I thought. But of course it was out of the question.

That first day was easier when the classes started. Some of the teachers were kind; some were frightening. Some of the students didn't care, but I listened and waited; and at the end of the day I was relieved, less conspicuous from then on.
10   But that day was not really over. As I hurried to carry my new paper route, I was thinking about how in a strange town, if you are quiet, no one notices, and some may like you, later. I was thinking about this when I reached the north edge of town where the scattering houses dwindle. Beyond them to the north lay just openness, the plains, a big swoop of nothing. There, at the last house, just as I cut
15   across a lot and threw to the last customer, I saw the girl in the blue dress coming along the street, heading on out of town, carrying books. And she saw me.

"Hello."

"Hello."

And because we stopped we were friends. I didn't know how I could stop, but
20   I didn't hurry on. There was nothing to do but to act as if I were walking on out too. I had three papers left in the bag, and I frantically began to fold them—box them, as we called it—for throwing. We had begun to walk and talk. The girl was timid; I became more bold. Not much, but a little.

"Have you gone to school here before?" I asked.
25   "Yes, I went here last year."

A long pause. A meadowlark sitting on a fencepost hunched his wings and flew. I kicked through the dust of the road.

I began to look ahead. Where could we possibly be walking to? I couldn't be walking just because I wanted to be with her.
30   Fortunately, there was one more house, a gray house by a sagging barn, set two hundred yards from the road.

"I thought I'd see if I could get a customer here," I said, waving toward the house.

"That's where I live."
35   "Oh."

Differentiated Instruction

English Language Learning

Students learning English will need help with the academic vocabulary used in standardized tests. Explain the meaning of the following terms used in this workshop:

outline — short summary or description, usually arranged as a series of key points, 138
evidence — facts offered in support of an argument, 138

conclusion — judgment or decision reached by reasoning from evidence, 141
definition — explanation of the meaning of a word, 141

Common Core State Standards

Writing
W.4, W.5

1. Based on the narrator's statement in line 6, what conclusion might you draw about him?
   A. He is outgoing.
   B. He is shy.
   C. He is mean spirited.
   D. He is new in town.
   E. He has many friends.

2. Based on the context, which of the following is the best definition of the word *strange* in line 11?
   A. small
   B. old
   C. unfamiliar
   D. unpleasant
   E. unusual

3. Based on the context, which of the following is the best definition of the word *timid* in line 23?
   A. walking quickly
   B. showing courage
   C. talking loudly
   D. lacking courage
   E. having boldness

4. The paragraph beginning on line 26 mostly contains
   A. dialect.
   B. figurative language.
   C. conflict.
   D. plot.
   E. description.

5. The protagonist of this passage
   A. is the girl in the blue dress.
   B. are the frightening teachers.
   C. is the narrator.
   D. are the other students.
   E. are the girl's parents.

6. Which of the following is an example of sensory detail?
   A. "first day of high school," in line 1
   B. "That first day was easier," in line 7
   C. "And she saw me," in line 16
   D. "I began to look ahead," in line 28
   E. "a gray house by a sagging barn," in line 30

7. This passage most likely occurs during
   A. the exposition and rising action.
   B. the climax and falling action.
   C. the falling action.
   D. the falling action and the resolution.
   E. the resolution.

8. Which of the following best describes the narrator's motivation for following the girl in the blue dress to her house?
   A. He wants to sell her a newspaper.
   B. He wants to get to know her.
   C. He is interested in her parents.
   D. He is curious about her house.
   E. He is wasting time after school.

9. The setting of this passage is best described as a
   A. small town.
   B. high school.
   C. big city.
   D. house in the country.
   E. grove of oranges.

10. The overall tone of this passage can best be described as
    A. angry.
    B. panicked.
    C. humorous.
    D. overjoyed.
    E. thoughtful.

Reading Skills
1. B
2. C
3. D
4. E
5. C
6. E
7. B
8. B
9. A
10. B

Test-Taking Skills

Elimination of Incorrect Responses
Point out to students that a key skill in working with multiple-choice questions is eliminating incorrect responses. Demonstrate this skill by modeling a think aloud for one question in the Reading Skills section.

Question 1. Possible Think Aloud: The narrator says talking to the girl was "out of the question." That seems to eliminate A and E. Line 6 doesn't offer any evidence for C or D, so B is probably correct.

Select another question, and have the class work as a group to eliminate the incorrect responses.

Unit 2 Visual Planning Guide

Planning and Assessment Tools

Annotated Teacher's Edition

Annotated Teacher's Edition
One location for accessing, previewing, and planning for use of all program resources.

EMC Launchpad
Desktop application for accessing, previewing, planning, posting, and grading all program resources. Post personal resources and lessons, and access the E-Lesson Planner, the E-Gradebook, and training modules for computer literacy.

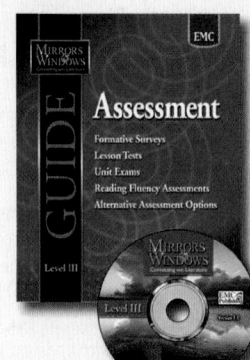

Assessment Guide and ExamView
A variety of assessments are available for this unit in print and electronic forms, including:
- Formative Survey
- Lesson Tests
- Unit Exams
- Alternative Assessment Options
- Reading Fluency Assessments

Meeting the Standards: Unit 1
In addition to lesson-by-lesson resources, *Meeting the Standards* includes the following unit-based resources:
- Unit Study Guide
- Practice Test
- Active Reading Model
- Selection Quizzes

Program Planning Guide and E-Lesson Planner
- Lesson Plans for all the selections in the unit
- Core Standards-Based Selections
- Reading Log and Evaluation Forms

The E-Lesson Planner contains fully developed lesson plans and unit resources with an electronic calendar for editing lesson plans.

Technology Tools

Visual Teaching Package
This package contains unit-based lectures, games, art collections, and Writing Workshops in PowerPoint format; included within the EMC Launchpad.

Interactive Student Text on CD
The student textbook on CD includes highlighting, note-taking, bookmarking, and a direct link to the student website, in addition to everything in the student text.

Audio Library
Authentic, dramatic recordings with listening activities expand listening skills and offer additional support for developing readers and English Language Learners.

ETS Online Criterion-Based Essay Grader (Grades 9–12)
Students can use this ETS web-based tool to evaluate their essays online before submitting them for teacher review and final evaluation.

mirrorsandwindows.com
Student and teacher resources, support, references, technology tools, and state-specific standards are available at **mirrorsandwindows.com.** The website is customizable using the EMC Launchpad.

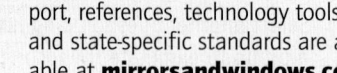

Unit-Based Resources

Exceeding the Standards Unit Resources

Each of the *Exceeding the Standards* resources provides fully developed lessons to help you extend the textbook lessons and to expand upon the themes and skills covered in the unit. You can also download these lessons from **mirrorsandwindows.com**.

Grammar & Style
This resource contains:
- Four lessons on Nouns, pp. 19–34
- Five lessons on Pronouns, pp. 35–51

Literature & Reading
This resource contains:
- Independent Novel Study: Character Development, pp. 6–8

Special Topics
This resource contains:
- Career Skills Development: Career Research Activity, pp. 5–6
- Lifelong Learning: Where Do You Want to Be? pp. 7–8

Test Practice
This resource contains:
- Literary Response Practice Test: Timed Writing, p. 7

Writing
This resource contains:
- Expository Writing: Write a Coherent Expository Essay, pp. 11–20

Speaking & Listening
This resource contains the following lesson to expand on the Speaking & Listening Workshop:
- Giving and Actively Listening to Literary Presentations, pp. 4–7

Vocabulary & Spelling
This resource contains:
- Five lessons on Word Parts and Spelling, pp. 11–20

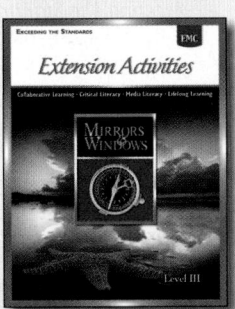

Extension Activities
This resource contains:
- Critical Literacy: Perform a Monologue, pp. 5–6
- Media Literacy: Compare Stories, p. 7

Unit 2 Visual Planning Guide

146

 Reading Level: Moderate
Pacing: 3 days

Meeting the Standards,
Reading Model,
pp. 19–30

Advanced Students,
Author's Style Activity,
pp. 8–9

English Language Learners,
Understand Literary
Elements, pp. 26–36

155

  Reading Level: Moderate
Pacing: 2 days

Meeting the Standards,
Guided Reading, pp.
25–30

*English Language
Learners,* Compare and
Contrast, pp. 37–52

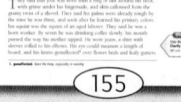

169

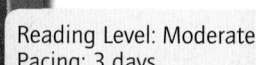 Reading Level: Moderate
Pacing: 3 days

Meeting the Standards,
Directed Reading,
pp. 31–37

181

  Reading Level: Challenging
Pacing: 2 days

Meeting the Standards,
Directed Reading,
pp. 38–44

Advanced Students,
Cultural Connection
Project, pp. 10–11

189

 Reading Level: Challenging
Pacing: 2 days

Meeting the Standards,
Directed Reading,
45–53

 Interactive Student
Text on CD-ROM

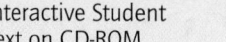  Selection
Lesson Plan

 Web-based
Resources

Lesson-by-Lesson Resources

201

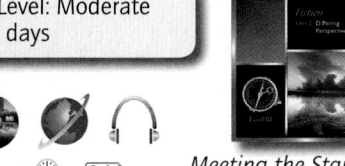
Reading Level: Moderate
Pacing: 3 days

Meeting the Standards,
Directed Reading,
pp. 54–61

Advanced Students,
Primary Source Project,
pp. 12–13

212

220

Reading Level: Moderate; Easy
Pacing: 3 days

Meeting the Standards,
Comparing Literature,
pp. 62–69

*English Language
Learners,* Visualize,
pp. 53–67

223

Reading Level: Challenging
Pacing: 5 days

Meeting the Standards,
Directed Reading,
pp. 70–76

Developing Readers,
Make Predictions,
pp. 10–12

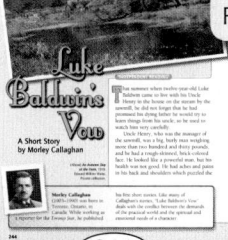

244

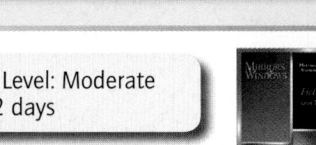
Reading Level: Moderate
Pacing: 2 days

Meeting the Standards,
Independent Reading,
pp. 77–84

Advanced Students,
Independent Reading
Study, p. 14

*English Language
Learners,* Analyze Cause
and Effect, pp. 78–95

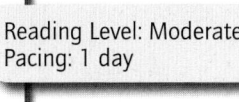

254

Reading Level: Moderate
Pacing: 1 day

Meeting the Standards,
Independent Reading,
pp. 85–92

Developing Readers,
Take Notes, pp. 13–15

 Lesson Test   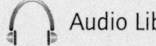 Audio Library

Unit 2 Scope & Sequence Guide

	Selection or Feature	Genre	Reading Support/ Reading Level	Word Count	Reading Skill	Graphic Organizer	
GUIDED READING	**Understanding Point of View,** p. 144						
	The Tell-Tale Heart Edgar Allan Poe pp. 145–152	Short Story	Guided Reading: Reading Model/ Moderate	2,150	Context Clues	Point of View Chart	
	Understanding Theme p. 153						
	Born Worker Gary Soto pp. 154–166	Short Story	Guided Reading: Reading Model/ Moderate	3,440	Compare and Contrast	Venn Diagram; Cluster Chart	
DIRECTED READING	**Sweet Potato Pie** Eugenia Collier pp. 168–178	Short Story	Directed Reading/ Moderate	3,931	Draw Conclusions	Draw Conclusions Chart; Characterizations Chart	
	Miss Butterfly Toshio Mori pp. 180–187	Short Story	Directed Reading/ Challenging	1,710	Activate Prior Knowledge	Prior Knowledge Chart	
	The Ransom of Red Chief O. Henry pp. 188–198	Short Story	Directed Reading/ Challenging	4,145	Analyze Cause and Effect	Cause and Effect Chart; Cluster Chart	
	Men on the Moon Simon Ortiz pp. 200–210	Short Story	Directed Reading/ Moderate	2,757	Monitor Comprehension	Note-Taking Chart; Characterization Chart	
	Primary Text Connection: Working on the Moon Edwin Aldrin, Jr. pp. 208–209	Primary Source	Moderate	665			
	Comparing Literature: The Medicine Bag Virginia Driving Hawk Sneve pp. 211–221	Short Story	Directed Reading/ Moderate	3,524		Cluster Chart	
	The Old Grandfather and His Little Grandson Leo Tolstoy pp. 211–221	Folk Tale	Directed Reading/Easy	260			

Literary Element	*Mirrors & Windows* Theme	Cross-Curricular Connection	Writing Options	Extension Activities
What is Point of View? Point of View in Fiction				
Point of View	Culpability		Creative: Letter Expository: Statement of Opinion	Collaborative Learning: Hold a Mock Trial Media Literacy: Conduct Internet Research
What is Theme? Themes and Topics Stated and Implied Themes				
Theme	Labor		Creative: Scene Expository: Comparison-and-Contrast Essay	Collaborative Learning: Make a List of Jobs Critical Literacy: Create a Set of Questions
Characterization	Nourishment		Creative: Dialogue Expository: Literary Response Paragraph	Collaborative Learning: Hold a Small Group Discussion Media Literacy: Conduct a Literature Review
Point of View	Acclimation	Cultural Connection: *Japanese Kimonos*	Creative: Diary Entry Expository: Summary	Lifelong Learning: Plan a Research Report Collaborative Learning: Foreign Words in English
Tone	Literary Elements		Creative: News Story Expository: Paragraph	Collaborative Learning: Discuss with a Partner Critical Literacy: Perform a Monologue
Characterization	Tradition		Creative: Description Expository: Essay	Critical Literacy: Research and Present Critical Literacy: Hold a Panel Discussion
Compare Literature: Theme	Generational Differences Generational Differences	Cultural Connection: *Sioux Nation*	Creative: Personal Essay Expository: Compare-and-Contrast Essay	Collaborative Learning: Work with a Partner Media Literacy: Compare Stories

Unit 2 Scope & Sequence Guide

	Selection or Feature	Genre	Reading Support/ Reading Level	Word Count	Reading Skill	Graphic Organizer	
DIRECTED READING	**Moon** Chaim Potok pp. 222–242	Short Story	Directed Reading/ Challenging	6,841	Context Clues	Cluster Chart	
	Informational Text Connection: The Story of Iqbal Masih David L. Parker pp. 238–241	Essay	Moderate	1,751			
INDEPENDENT READING	**Luke Baldwin's Vow** Morley Callaghan pp. 244–253	Short Story	Independent Reading/ Moderate	5,334	Make Predictions		
	Lose Now, Pay Later Carol Farley pp. 254–260	Short Story	Independent Reading/ Moderate	2,477	Make Inferences		

Unit 2 Language Arts Workshops

Grammar & Style	Vocabulary & Spelling	Writing	Speaking & Listening	Test Practice
Comma Use, p. 167 Pronoun Use, p. 199 Independent and Dependent Clauses, p. 243	Denotation and Connotation, p. 179	Narrative Writing: Writing a Short Story, pp. 262–269	Giving and Actively Listening to Literary Presentations, pp. 270–271	Writing Skills: Literary Response, p. 272 Revising & Editing Skills, p. 273 Reading Skills: from "Be-ers and Doers" by Budge Wilson, pp. 274–275

Literary Element	*Mirrors & Windows* Theme	Cross-Curricular Connection	Writing Options	Extension Activities
Character	Responsibility		Creative: Petition Applied: Set of Instructions	Lifelong Learning: Research Critical Literacy: Ask Questions
Character	Integrity		Creative: Contract	Collaborative Learning: Have a Small Group Discussion
Point of View	Conformity		Creative: Advertisement	Media Literacy and Collaborative Learning: Create a Jingle

Unit 2 Building Vocabulary

The lists below identify the Words in Use and Key Terms within this unit. These words are listed at the bottom of the Teacher's Edition pages at the beginning of each lesson. Vocabulary development activities are provided in the *Meeting the Standards* unit book and in *Exceeding the Standards: Vocabulary & Spelling.*

WORDS IN USE

Preview Vocabulary
Preview Vocabulary are words taken from the sentences within each selection. These words are defined in the side margin or at the bottom of the pages on which they appear. The "Preview Vocabulary" section introduces these words in the Before Reading page preceding each selection.

admiration, 184	emphatically, 183	lumber, 206	saunter, 174
audacity, 150	fatigue, 214	nimbly, 182	sheepishly, 215
bounded, 204	flaunt, 184	nuance, 171	stifle, 148
collage, 172	futilely, 172	pervade, 193	symmetrical, 184
concealment, 150	gaunt, 171	phase, 203	unseemly, 214
conceive, 147	guidance, 205	plaintive, 183	vex, 149
decry, 194	impudent, 197	prologue, 235	wearily, 213
defiantly, 234	intently, 203	pulsate, 227	
demeanor, 224	jovial, 225	radius, 190	
diatribe, 190	kimono, 183	rouse, 215	

Selection Words
Selection Words are additional words from the reading that may be challenging but are not central to the selection and are not identified in the prereading section. These words can easily be learned using the story context, and they provide excellent practice for using content clues to find meaning without explicit instruction.

affectionate, 245	disquiet, 226	literally, 258	sacred, 219
antiquity, 171	emit, 191	lonesome, 218	scaffolding, 238
array, 158	emitting, 203	martyrs, 195	sensible, 245
assessing, 245	frail, 215	negotiation, 253	shanty, 170
authentic, 213	gruesome, 254	perseverance, 240	somber, 185
bade, 150	headdress, 202	plight, 241	stagnant, 163
bondage, 241	hearkening, 148	porous, 197	tattoo, 149
burly, 244	hobbled, 246	precise, 224, 245	transaction, 245
calloused, 155	humbly, 183	publicity, 256	undeterred, 205
clamor, 224	hypocritical, 151	pummeled, 225	unheeding, 185
compacted, 209	impressions, 255	pungent, 209	veranda, 246
contiguous, 193	instability, 208	regulate, 257	whittling, 171
deployed, 208	irritant, 224	reposed, 150	
descendants, 215	lackadaisical, 190	resistance, 249	
detection, 260	leverage, 208	reverently, 176	

Teaching Words
Teaching Words consist of vocabulary that is used in the directions about the lessons. Teaching words explain to students what to focus on within the selection, help establish the story context, clarify the meaning of literary terms, and define the goals or instructional purpose.

accessible, 266	chasms, 222	desperadoes, 188	generations, 211
advocating, 211	complexities, 222	distinctness, 271	grasp, 266
agricultural, 154	comprehension, 266	diverse, 262	grime, 154
alternatives, 273	conclude, 152	drawbacks, 219	habitually, 266
ancestral, 178	concrete, 241	dynamic, 275	heritage, 168
ancestry, 211	constructive, 271	elaborate, 183	insane, 145
antagonist, 275	contend, 188	eludes, 254	internment, 180
attributes, 166	convey, 270	enlisted, 188	jingle, 260
bleak, 271	debating, 145	factual, 238	legible, 266

logical, 264
marathon, 270
marital, 183
marrow, 271
mock, 152
mythic, 178
negate, 260
nonverbal, 271
obligation, 220

omniscient, 275
opinion, 152
pacing, 270
perceive, 254
petition, 242
philosopher, 211
plead, 152
position, 272
precise, 266

principled, 272
propose, 166
protagonist, 275
protest, 211
quaver, 274
refute, 145
rustlers, 188
sensory, 275
sharecroppers, 168

somber, 271
static, 275
tenant, 168
universal, 263
unsanitary, 222
vague, 266
validity, 145
vivid, 154, 241, 266

KEY TERMS

Key Terms are commonly referred to as *academic vocabulary.* These terms appear in the instructional material to teach the terminology that students need to acquire to understand literature. The repetition of the terms throughout the program ensures student mastery and provides a solid foundation for the continuing study of literature and language arts.

adjective clause, 243
adjective, 188
adverb clause, 243
bandwagon, 260
cause and effect, 188
central conflict, 198
character trait, 237
character, 263, 270, 272
characterization, 168, 200
chronological order, 264
cluster chart, 198
comma, 167
compare and contrast, 154, 209
compound object, 199
compound sentence, 167
compound subject, 199
comprehension, 200
conclusion, 168
conflict, 263, 270, 275
conjunction, 167
connotation, 179

context clue, 145, 222
context, 275
coordinating conjunction, 167
denotation, 179
dependent clause, 243
description, 154, 210
dialogue, 178, 211, 265, 270, 275
direct characterization, 168
draft, 273
first-person point of view, 144, 145, 178
flat character, 222
foreshadow, 198, 221
image, 237
imagery, 237
implied theme, 153
independent clause, 243
inferred, 153
limited point of view, 144
limited, 270

main character, 144
main clause, 167
main idea, 200, 272
monologue, 198
mood, 145
motive, 152
narration, 211
narrator, 144, 270
near-synonym, 179
object pronoun, 199
omniscient, 270
omniscient point of view, 144
personal pronoun, 199
plot, 210, 263, 270
point of view, 144, 145, 178, 264, 270, 275
predicate, 243
preview, 200
pronoun, 199
propaganda, 260
purpose, 207

reliable narrator, 144
resolution, 198
round character, 222
sensory detail, 154, 210, 270
sequence, 211
setting, 207, 263, 270
skim, 188
stated theme, 153
subject pronoun, 199
subject, 243
suspense, 145
synonym, 179
theme, 153, 154, 210, 211, 263, 272
third-person narrator, 152
third-person point of view, 144
tone, 188, 270, 275
topic, 153
vantage point, 144, 145
verb tense, 266

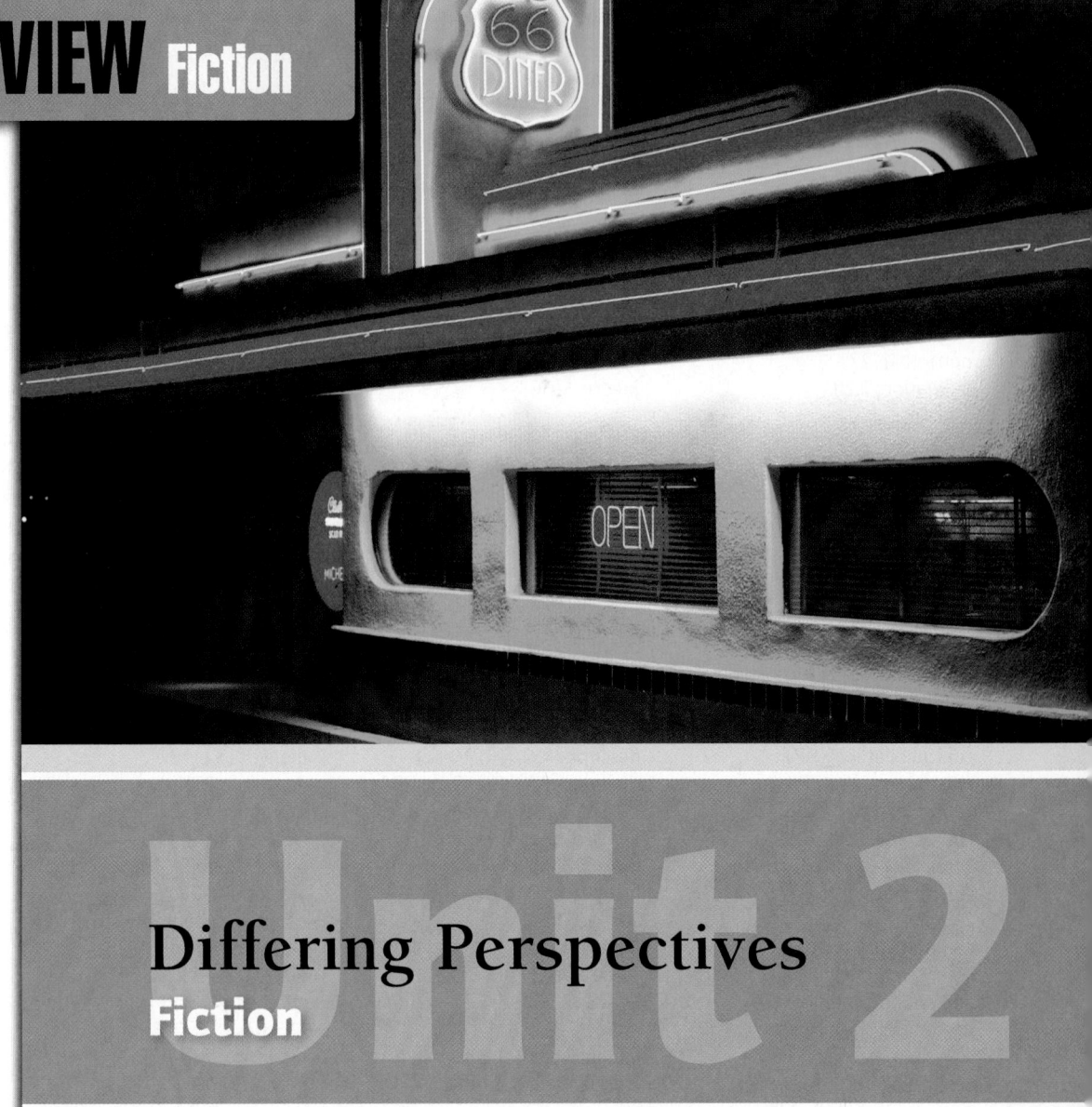

Objectives

Studying this unit will help students meet the following objectives:

- Make connections from themes expressed in the selections to their own lives and the world around them
- Identify common forms of fiction
- Understand different elements of fiction, including *plot, character, setting, point of view,* and *theme*
- Understand variations of literary forms and author's use of language to develop forms

Reading Strategies

Ask Questions
Clarify
Make Inferences
Make Predictions
Visualize

Reading Skills

Activate Prior Knowledge
Analyze Cause and Effect
Compare and Contrast
Draw Conclusions
Monitor Comprehension
Skim and Scan
Use Context Clues

Literary Elements

Character
Characterization
Point of View
Theme
Tone

Differing Perspectives
Fiction

Unit 2

LEO TOLSTOY   EUGENIA COLLIER   SIMON ORTIZ

Launch the Unit

Have students work in small groups to create other questions that might relate to the theme of this unit. Model this by proposing a question such as: "Which influences our perspective more: upbringing or experience?" Have the class write down these questions and keep the list. When the class has completed work on the unit, have them take another look at these questions and discuss which selections provide insights about them.

> *"Charley was taller than anybody in the world, including, I was certain, God. From his shoulders, where I spent considerable time in the earliest years, the world had a different perspective."*
>
> —EUGENIA COLLIER, "Sweet Potato Pie"

What we see is affected by the position from which we see it. In "Sweet Potato Pie," two brothers, Buddy and Charley, both began life as sharecroppers. Buddy has achieved far more than Charley, but these achievements were built on Charley's love and unselfish support. Buddy sees the world from Charley's shoulders. As you read this unit, think of how your own perspective is shaped by your experiences.

GARY SOTO   EDGAR ALLAN POE   VIRGINIA DRIVING HAWK SNEVE

143

Writing Options

Creative Writing

Advertisement	News Story
Description	Personal Essay
Dialogue	Petition
Diary	Scene
Letter	

Applied Writing
Set of Instructions

Expository Writing
Compare-and-Contrast Essay
Essay
Literary Response
Paragraph

Persuasive Writing
Statement of Opinion

Language Arts Workshops

Grammar & Style
Comma Use
Independent and Dependent Clauses
Pronoun Use

Vocabulary & Spelling
Denotation and Connotation

Writing Workshop
Writing a Short Story

Speaking & Listening Workshop
Giving and Actively Listening to
   Literary Presentations

Test Practice Workshop
Literary Response
Revising and Editing Skills
Reading Skills

Program Resources

For a visual reminder of the unit-based resources available for Unit 2, Fiction, see pages 142A and 142B. As you introduce the unit, you may want to provide students with the Unit Study Guide, which is contained in the *Meeting the Standards* resource.

Understanding Point of View

Reading strategies that can help students understand point of view include visualizing and making predictions.

Use Reading Strategies

Visualize Point out to students that the selection of details in a story is strongly affected by the point of view of the narrator. To help students grasp this effect, ask them to contrast the details presented in the two illustrations on this page. Encourage them to keep this effect of point of view in mind as they read the stories in this unit.

Use Reading Strategies

Make Predictions Ask students to consider how the plot of a story changes if it is told from a different point of view. Model this by saying, "If the story of Cinderella is told from the first-person point of view by one of the wicked stepsisters, it isn't a 'rags to riches' story anymore; it has an unhappy ending." Ask them to consider the effect of point of view on plot as they read the stories in this unit.

KEY TERMS

POINT OF VIEW, 144
MAIN CHARACTER, 144
NARRATOR, 144
VANTAGE POINT, 144
FIRST-PERSON POINT OF VIEW, 144
RELIABLE NARRATOR, 144
THIRD-PERSON POINT OF VIEW, 144
OMNISCIENT POINT OF VIEW, 144
LIMITED POINT OF VIEW, 144

Common Core State Standards

Reading Literature
RL.6

Literary Element

Understanding Point of View

What Is Point of View?

Each of these photographs shows the same subject—fly-fishing on a mountain stream. What is chiefly different about them is the point of view, the perspective from which the photograph was taken. One photograph shows the fisherman from the point of view of another person; the other shows the scene from the point of view of the fisherman himself. Point of view is an important element in fiction as well as photography.

Point of View in Fiction

Each of the passages on the right gives an account of the birth of the main character of a work of fiction. Who is the narrator in the first passage? In other words, who is telling the story? Who is the narrator in the second passage? How do you know? The vantage point from which a writer presents the events and characters of a story is called the **point of view.**

First-Person Point of View In the passage from *David Copperfield*, the story is told from a *first-person point of view*. In other words, the narrator is a character in the story and describes the events. You can tell that a story is told from a first-person point of view because the narrator uses such pronouns as *I* and *we*. In a story told from the first-person point of view, the information must be limited to what the character experiences or knows. Readers must decide whether the narrator is reliable or not.

Third-Person Point of View In the passage from "Born Worker," the story is told from a third-person point of view. The *third-person point of view* is indicated by the narrator's use of such pronouns as *he, she, it,* and *they*. If a story is told from a *third-person omniscient* ("all-knowing") point of view, the narrator is able to relate everything about all the characters—their experiences, thoughts, and feelings. In a *third-person limited* point of view, however, the narrator chiefly presents the perspective of only one character.

> To begin my life with the beginning of my life, I record that I was born (as I have been informed and believe) on a Friday, at twelve o'clock at night. It was remarked that the clock began to strike, and I began to cry, simultaneously.
>
> —CHARLES DICKENS, *David Copperfield*

> They said that José was born with a ring of dirt around his neck, with grime under his fingernails, and skin calloused from the grainy twist of a shovel.
>
> —GARY SOTO, "Born Worker"

Differentiated Instruction

English Language Learning

Students who are learning English may need additional help in using the personal pronouns as indications of whether a work of fiction is told from the first-person or the third-person point of view. Show them passages of first-person narration, pointing out the pronouns *I, me, my, mine, we,* and *our*. Then show them passages of third-person narration, indicating the literary pronouns *he, him, his, she,* *her, it, its, they, their,* and *them*. Point out that a story told from the third-person point of view might still have first-person pronouns in dialogue.

The Tell-Tale Heart

A Short Story by Edgar Allan Poe

Build Background
Historical Context The narrator of "The Tell-Tale Heart" is a murderer who—though showing clear signs of madness—protests that he is not insane. When Edgar Allan Poe wrote this short story in the early 1840s, Americans were seriously debating for the first time the validity of the insanity defense in cases of murder.

Reader's Context How does the effect of a sound depend on the circumstances under which it is heard? Imagine you are alone in a house at night and you hear the creak of a door opening. How does such a sound affect your emotions?

Set Purpose
Previewing the first paragraph of the story will show you that the narrator is telling his story to refute the charge that he is insane. Read to determine what he has done to be judged insane.

Analyze Literature
Point of View The vantage point from which a story is told is the **point of view.** If the story is told from the first-person point of view, the narrator (the person or character who tells the story) uses words such as *I* and *we* and is a part of or a witness to the action. As you read "The Tell-Tale Heart," think about how using the first-person point of view influences both the way information is conveyed and the mood, or atmosphere, created by the story.

Meet the Author
Edgar Allan Poe (1809–1849) was an American poet, fiction writer, and literary critic. As a critic, Poe shaped the modern short story, arguing that every detail in a well-constructed narrative must help create a single effect on the reader. In his brilliant stories of psychological horror, such as "The Tell-Tale Heart," Poe created vivid effects of suspense, dread, and terror.

Use Reading Skills
Context Clues Preview the vocabulary words from this selection as they are used in the sentences below. Try to unlock the meaning of each word using the context clues provided in the sentences.

1. He could not <u>conceive</u> what the answer to the question was.
2. They barely heard his <u>stifled</u> gasp.
3. Please don't <u>vex</u> me with your problems.
4. They agreed on the <u>concealment</u> of the house key under the doormat.

Preview Vocabulary
con·ceive (kən sēv´) *v.*, form or develop in the mind

sti·fled (stī´ fəld) *adj.*, held back; smothered

vex (veks) *v.*, bother; trouble

con·ceal·ment (kən sēl´ mənt) *n.*, hiding

au·dac·i·ty (ô das´ ə tē) *n.*, bold courage; daring

At a Glance
Guided Reading: Reading Model
- Reading Level: Moderate
- Difficulty Consideration: Sentence structure
- Ease Factor: Engaging plot

Objectives
Studying this lesson will enable students to
- use reading skills such as context clues
- define *point of view* and recognize the effect of this literary technique in the selection
- describe the literary accomplishments of Edgar Allan Poe and explain the historical significance of his writing

Launch the Lesson
Tell students that they are about to read "The Tell-Tale Heart," a story about a madman. Write the word *Madman* on the board. Underneath the word put these headings: "Physical Qualities," "Emotional Qualities," "Moral Qualities." Ask students to give you words or phrases describing characteristics that would go under these headings. Model an example for each heading: *uncontrolled actions, paranoid, detached from moral reasoning.* After students have listed enough characteristics, ask them which ones seem the most frightening.

Words in Use

Preview Vocabulary	Selection Words	Teaching Words
conceive, 147	hearkening, 148	insane, 145
stifle, 148	tattoo, 149	debating, 145
vex, 149	bade, 150	validity, 145
concealment, 150	reposed, 150	refute, 145
audacity, 150	hypocritical, 151	conclude, 152
		plead, 152
		opinion, 152
		mock, 152

KEY TERMS
POINT OF VIEW, 145

VANTAGE POINT, 145

FIRST-PERSON POINT OF VIEW, 145

MOOD, 145

SUSPENSE, 145

CONTEXT CLUE, 145

MOTIVE, 152

THIRD-PERSON NARRATOR, 152

Common Core State Standards
Reading Literature
RL.1, RL.6

Writing
W.9

Language
L.4

Summary

The first-person narrator is a confessed murderer who is describing his brutal killing of an old man. Denying he is insane, the murderer still admits he had no other motive than ridding himself of the victim's "vulture" eye. After he has killed, dismembered, and buried the old man under the floorboards, three policemen, alerted by a neighbor who had heard a shriek, visit the murderer. Becoming convinced that he hears his victim's heart still beating and that the policemen must hear the sound as well, the frenzied murderer confesses his crime.

 The Mirrors & Windows questions at the end of this selection focus on the theme of culpability. Before reading the story, ask students if they think the mentally insane should be incarcerated for violent crimes. How should our legal system approach this issue?

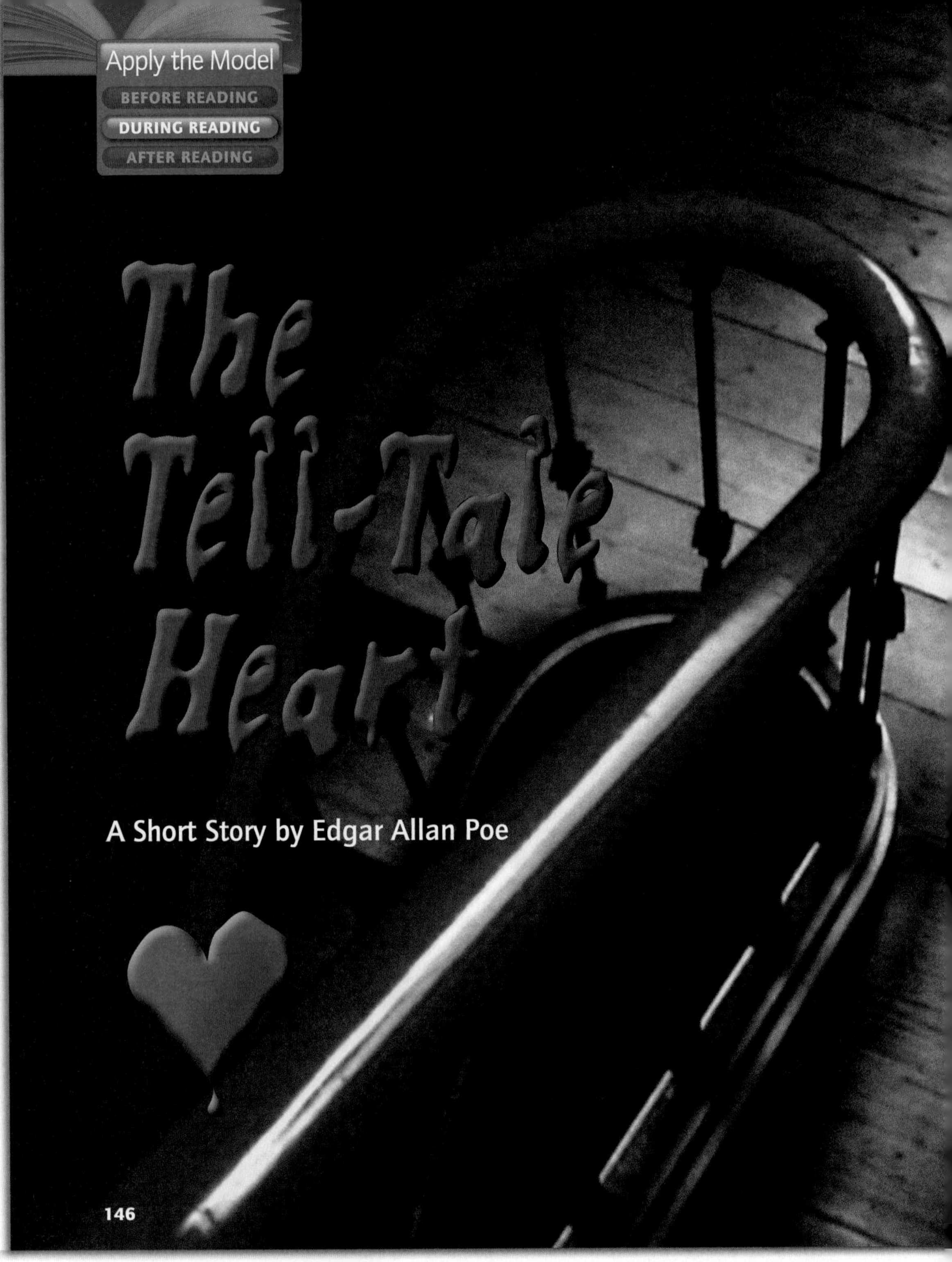

The Tell-Tale Heart

A Short Story by Edgar Allan Poe

146

Program Resources

Planning and Assessment
Program Planning Guide, Selection Lesson Plan
E-Lesson Planner
Assessment Guide, Lesson Test
ExamView

Technology Tools
Interactive Student Text on CD
Visual Teaching Package
Audio Library
mirrorsandwindows.com

Meeting the Standards
Fiction: Unit 2, Reading Model, pp. 19–30

Differentiating Instruction
Advanced Students, Author's Style Activity, pp. 8–9
English Language Learners, Understand Literary Elements, pp. 26–36

T rue!—nervous—very, very dreadfully nervous I had been and am; but why *will* you say that I am mad? The disease had sharpened my senses—not destroyed—not dulled them. Above all was the sense of hearing acute. I heard all things in the heaven and in the earth. I heard many things in hell. How, then, am I mad? Hearken![1] and observe how healthily—how calmly I can tell you the whole story.

It is impossible to say how first the idea entered my brain; but once <u>conceived</u>, it haunted me day and night. Object there was none. Passion there was none. I loved the old man. He had never wronged me. He had never given me insult. For his gold I had no desire. I think it was his eye! Yes, it was this! One of his eyes resembled that of a vulture—A pale blue eye, with a film over it. Whenever it fell upon me, my blood ran cold; and so by degrees— very gradually—I made up my mind to take the life of the old man, and thus rid myself of the eye forever.

Now this is the point. You fancy me mad. Madmen know nothing. But you should have seen *me*. You should have seen how wisely I proceeded—with what caution—with what foresight—with what dissimulation[2] I went to work! I was never kinder to the old man than during the whole week before I killed him. And every night, about midnight, I turned the latch of his door and opened it—oh, so gently! And then, when I had made an opening sufficient for my head, I put in a dark lantern,[3] all closed, closed, so that no light shone out, and then I thrust in my head. Oh, you would have laughed to see how cunningly[4] I thrust it in! I moved it slowly—very, very slowly, so that I might not disturb the old man's sleep. It took me an hour to place my whole head within the opening so far that I could see him as he lay upon his bed. Ha!—would a madman have been so wise as this? And then, when my head was well in the room, I undid the lantern cautiously—oh, so cautiously—cautiously (for the hinges creaked)—I undid it just so much that a single thin ray fell upon the vulture eye. And this I did for seven long nights—every night just at midnight—but I found the eye always closed; and so it was impossible to do the work; for it was not the old man who vexed me, but his Evil Eye. And every morning, when the day broke, I went boldly into the

---

1. **Hearken.** Listen carefully
2. **dissimulation.** Act of hiding; pretending
3. **dark lantern.** Lantern with a single opening that can be closed to block the light
4. **cunningly.** Skillfully or cleverly

Ha!—would a madman have been so wise as this?

con·ceive (kən sēv´) *v.*, form or develop in the mind

> **DURING READING**
> **Use Reading Strategies**
> **Ask Questions** What is unusual about the narrator's motivation?
> **A**

Use Reading Strategies
Ask Questions Point out to students that good readers ask lots of questions as they work their way through a text. Model for students other questions that these first paragraphs might prompt a reader to ask: "What does the narrator look like? Who is the narrator talking to? Does the narrator actually hear voices?"

Use Reading Strategies
Ask Questions *Answer:* The narrator lacks the ordinary motives for murder—such as greed and hatred. Instead, he fears the old man's "vulture" eye. **A**

Cultural Connection
Insanity Defense Several years before "The Tell-Tale Heart," Poe had written a magazine article in which he reacted to the trial of a man named James Wood, who had killed his daughter. The jury acquitted Wood of the charge of murder for reasons of insanity, partly because of the seeming absence of motive in his act. Poe may have incorporated this element into his portrait of the murderer in "The Tell-Tale Heart." **B**

Differentiated Instruction

Reading Proficiency
Have students read along while listening to the dramatic recording in the Audio Library. See also the English Language Learning instruction on page 148.

Visual Learning
Poe does not provide any physical details about the narrator. We do not even know whether the narrator is a man or a woman. Some students might like to create an imaginary portrait of the narrator. Others might prefer to storyboard some critical sequence in the action of the story such as the climax.

Analyze Literature

Point of View *Answer:* The narrator's sense of his power and cunning suggests delusions of grandeur. **A**

Analyze Literature

Point of View Point out to students that Poe was one of the first writers to use the technique of the *unreliable narrator,* one whose honesty or accuracy cannot be trusted by the reader. Model a response for students to such a narrator: "To what extent can I rely on the narrator's account of the events?" **B**

Make Connections

Answer: Students might say that this observation makes them feel that the narrator is cold or unfeeling. **C**

Cultural Connection

Treatment of the Mentally Ill At the time Poe wrote "The Tell-Tale Heart," treatment of the mentally ill in the United States was often very brutal. Reporting to the Massachusetts state legislature in 1841, the reformer Dorothea Dix described "the present state of insane persons confined in this Commonwealth, in cages, closets, cellars, stalls, pens! Chained, naked, beaten with rods, and lashed into obedience."

---

chamber, and spoke courageously to him, calling him by name in a hearty tone, and inquiring how he had passed the night. So you see he would have been a very profound old man, indeed, to suspect that every night, just at twelve, I looked in upon him while he slept.

Upon the eighth night I was more than usually cautious in opening the door. A watch's minute hand moves more quickly than did mine. Never before that night, had I *felt* the extent of my own powers—of my sagacity.[5] I could scarcely contain my feelings of triumph. To think that there I was, opening the door, little by little, and he not even to dream of my secret deeds or thoughts. I fairly chuckled at the idea; and perhaps he heard me; for he moved on the bed suddenly, as if startled. Now you may think that I drew back— but no. His room was as black as pitch with the thick darkness, (for the shutters were close fastened, through fear of robbers), and so I knew that he could not see the opening of the door, and I kept pushing it on steadily, steadily.

I had my head in, and was about to open the lantern, when my thumb slipped upon the tin fastening, and the old man sprang up in bed, crying out—"Who's there?"

I kept quite still and said nothing. For a whole hour I did not move a muscle, and in the meantime I did not hear him lie down. He was still sitting up in the bed, listening;—just as I have done, night after night, hearkening to the deathwatches[6] in the wall.

Presently I heard a slight groan, and I knew it was the groan of mortal terror. It was not a groan of pain or of grief—oh, no!—it was the low <u>stifled</u> sound that arises from the bottom of the soul when overcharged with awe. I knew the sound well. Many a night, just at midnight, when all the world slept, it has welled up from my own bosom, deepening, with its dreadful echo, the terrors that distracted me. I say I knew it well. I knew what the old man felt, and pitied him, although I chuckled at heart. I knew that he had been lying awake ever since the first slight noise, when he had turned in the bed. His fears had been ever since growing upon him. He had been trying to fancy them causeless, but could not. He had been saying to himself—"It is nothing but the wind in the chimney—it is only a mouse crossing the floor," or "It is merely a cricket which has made a single chirp." Yes, he has been trying to comfort himself with these suppositions:[7] but he had found all in vain. *All in vain; because*

DURING READING

Analyze Literature
Point of View What does this suggest about the narrator's sanity?
A

B

sti•fled (stī′ fəld) *adj.,* held back; smothered

DURING READING

Make Connections
How does this observation affect your feelings about the narrator?
C

---

5. **sagacity.** Wisdom; intelligence
6. **deathwatches.** Wood-boring beetles that make a tapping sound in the wood they invade. According to folklore, they are thought to predict death.
7. **suppositions.** Assumptions

Differentiated Instruction

English Language Learning

Students learning English may need help with the following key words in order to grasp the character of the narrator.

nervous—fearful, tense, 147
acute—sharp, intense, 147
dissimulation—act of hiding, pretending, 147

cunning—tricky, crafty, 147
chuckled—laughed inwardly or quietly, 148
raved—talked wildly, 151

Death, in approaching him, had stalked with his black shadow before him, and enveloped the victim. And it was the mournful influence of the unperceived shadow that caused him to feel—although he neither saw nor heard—to *feel* the presence of my head within the room.

When I had waited a long time, very patiently, without hearing him lie down, I resolved to open a little—a very, very little crevice in the lantern. So I opened it—you cannot imagine how stealthily,[8] stealthily—until, at length, a single dim ray, like the thread of the spider, shot from out the crevice and fell upon the vulture eye.

It was open—wide, wide open—and I grew furious as I gazed upon it. I saw it with perfect distinctness—all a dull blue, with a hideous veil over it that chilled the very marrow in my bones; but I could see nothing else of the old man's face or person: for I had directed the ray as if by instinct, precisely upon the damned spot. **E**

And now have I not told you that what you mistake for madness is but overacuteness of the senses?—now, I say, there came to my ears a low, dull, quick sound, such as a watch makes when enveloped in cotton. I knew *that* sound well, too. It was the beating of the old man's heart. It increased my fury, as the beating of a drum stimulates the soldier into courage.

But even yet I refrained and kept still. I scarcely breathed. I held the lantern motionless. I tried to see how steadily I could maintain the ray upon the eye. Meantime the hellish tattoo of the heart increased. It grew quicker and quicker, and louder and louder every instant. The old man's terror *must* have been extreme! It grew louder, I say, louder every moment!—do you mark me well? I have told you that I am nervous: so I am. And now at the dead hour of the night, amid the dreadful silence of that old house, so strange a noise as this excited me to uncontrollable terror. Yet, for some minutes longer I refrained and stood still. But the beating grew louder, louder! I thought the heart must burst. And now a new anxiety seized me—the sound would be heard by a neighbor! The old man's hour had come! With a loud yell, I threw open the lantern and leaped into the room. He shrieked once—once only. In an instant I dragged him to the floor, and pulled the heavy bed over him. I then smiled gaily, to find the deed so far done. But, for many minutes, the heart beat on with a muffled sound. This, however, did not <u>vex</u> me; it would not be heard through the wall. At length it ceased. The old man

8. **stealthily.** Quietly

D

DURING READING

Use Reading Strategies
Make Predictions Recall the title of the story. At this point, what do you think will be the outcome? **F**

DURING READING

Use Reading Skills
Context Clues What context is there for the meaning of *vex*? **G**

vex (veks) *v.*, bother; trouble

Teach the Model

Art Connection
Painted about 1818 and attributed to the French painter Théodore Géricault (1791–1824), *After Death: A Study of a Severed Head* depicts the decapitated head of a criminal who has been executed by the guillotine. Géricault painted a number of grotesque subjects, including severed heads and limbs and portraits of insane people. **D**

Art Activity Have students use the Internet or library to research Géricault's paintings of insane people, and discuss whether these portraits display sympathy for their subjects or are simply objective.

Use Reading Strategies
Visualize Ask students to consider what the scene with the lantern conveys about the character of the narrator. Model a possible response: "It emphasizes his obsession with the old man's 'vulture eye.'" **E**

Use Reading Strategies
Make Predictions *Answer:* Considering the title, it seems as if the narrator's growing fear of the sound of the beating heart will reveal his crime. **F**

Use Reading Skills
Context Clues *Answer:* The narrator's presentation of the sound of the beating heart as a potential problem provides context for *vex*. **G**

Writing Skills

Commas with Quotations
Point out to students that when a quotation is followed by a phrase indicating who is speaking, the comma setting off the quotation is enclosed within the quotation marks. For example: "Many of Poe's stories first appeared in magazines," Sean told her.

In the following sentences, decide whether the comma is correctly placed.

1. "I have no idea what you mean", the women said angrily. (incorrect)
2. "A house divided," Abraham Lincoln observed, "cannot stand." (correct)
3. "Don't drive so fast on this narrow street", he cautioned her. (incorrect)

Use Reading Strategies

Make Inferences Poe uses italics throughout "The Tell-Tale Heart" for emphasis as well as effect. Direct students' attention to Poe's use of italics in this sentence. Ask them what the italicized *now* implies about the narrator's prior fear. If he believes that he has nothing to fear at this point, what was the singular fear plaguing him prior to this stage in the plot? Guide them in inferring that he feared only the old man's eye, and discuss why it is such a relief for the narrator to be free of it. **A**

History Connection

Police Force Organized, professional police forces in the modern sense were coming into existence in American cities, such as Philadelphia, Boston, and New York, during the time that Poe was writing the first detective stories. The New York City Police Department, for example, was established in 1845. **B**

Analyze Literature

Point of View *Answer:* The narrator has his own insanity to fear. **C**

Use Reading Skills

Context Clues *Answer:* The narrator's use of the word *wild* and his description of the act of placing his chair right over the corpse of his victim provide context for *audacity*. **D**

---

con·ceal·ment
(kən sēl′ mənt) *n.,* hiding

---

au·dac·i·ty (ô das′ ə tē)
n., bold courage; daring

DURING READING

Analyze Literature
Point of View What does the narrator have to fear? **C**

DURING READING

Use Reading Skills
Context Clues What context is there for the meaning of *audacity*? **D**

---

was dead. I removed the bed and examined the corpse. Yes, he was stone, stone dead. I placed my hand upon the heart and held it there many minutes. There was no pulsation. He was stone dead. His eye would trouble me no more.

If still you think me mad, you will think so no longer when I describe the wise precautions I took for the <u>concealment</u> of the body. The night waned, and I worked hastily, but in silence. First of all I dismembered the corpse. I cut off the head and the arms and the legs.

I then took up three planks from the flooring of the chamber, and deposited all between the scantlings.[9] I then replaced the boards so cleverly, so cunningly, that no human eye—not even *his*—could have detected any thing wrong. There was nothing to wash out—no stain of any kind—no blood-spot whatever. I had been too wary for that. A tub had caught all—ha! ha!

When I had made an end of these labors, it was four o'clock— still dark as midnight. As the bell sounded the hour, there came **A** a knocking at the street door. I went down to open it with a light heart—for what had I *now* to fear? There entered three men, who **B** introduced themselves, with perfect suavity,[10] as officers of the police. A shriek had been heard by a neighbor during the night; suspicion of foul play had been aroused; information had been lodged at the police office, and they (the officers) had been deputed to search the premises.

I smiled—for *what* had I to fear? I bade the gentlemen welcome. The shriek, I said, was my own in a dream. The old man, I mentioned, was absent in the country. I took my visitors all over the house. I bade them search—search *well*. I led them, at length, to *his* chamber. I showed them his treasures, secure, undisturbed. In the enthusiasm of my confidence, I brought chairs into the room, and **D** desired them *here* to rest from their fatigues, while I myself, in the wild <u>audacity</u> of my perfect triumph, placed my own seat upon the very spot beneath which reposed the corpse of the victim.

The officers were satisfied. My *manner* had convinced them. I was singularly at ease. They sat, and while I answered cheerily, they chatted of familiar things. But, ere long, I felt myself getting pale and wished them gone. My head ached, and I fancied a ringing in my ears: but still they sat and still they chatted. The ringing became more distinct—it continued and became more distinct: I talked more

---

9. **scantlings.** Small beams or timbers
10. **suavity.** Smoothness; gracefulness; politeness

Differentiated Instruction

Enrichment

Interested students could research what might happen if a person, such as the narrator, were arrested for murder today. How would such a prisoner be evaluated as to his competence to stand trial? If he were put on trial, how might a lawyer conduct his defense on a plea of insanity?

English Language Learners

Verify that students recognize the directionality of English reading. Students should work from left to right and top to bottom. Also, point out to students that the During Reading boxes are included to support reading comprehension and are not part of the original text.

freely to get rid of the feeling: but it continued and gained definitiveness—until, at length, I found that the noise was *not* within my ears.

No doubt I now grew *very* pale—but I talked more fluently, and with a heightened voice. Yet the sound increased—and what could I do? It was *a low, dull, quick sound—much such a sound as a watch makes when enveloped in cotton.* I gasped for breath—and yet the officers heard it not. I talked more quickly—more vehemently;[11] but the noise steadily increased. I arose and argued about trifles, in a high key and with violent gesticulations;[12] but the noise steadily increased. Why *would* they not be gone? I paced the floor to and fro with heavy strides, as if excited to fury by the observations of the men—but the noise steadily increased. Oh God! what *could* I do? I foamed—I raved—I swore! I swung the chair upon which I had been sitting, and grated it upon the boards, but the noise arose over all and continually increased. It grew louder—louder—*louder!* And still the men chatted pleasantly, and smiled. Was it possible they heard not? Almighty God!—no, no! They heard!—they suspected!—they *knew!*—they were making a mockery of my horror!—this I thought, and this I think. But anything was better than this agony! Anything was more tolerable than this derision![13] I could bear those hypocritical smiles no longer! I felt that I must scream or die!—and now—again!—hark! louder! louder! *louder!*—

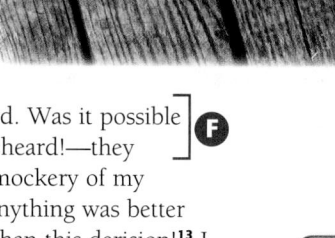

"Villains!" I shrieked, "dissemble no more! I admit the deed!—tear up the planks—here, here!—it is the beating of his hideous heart!" ❖

DURING READING

Use Reading Strategies
Make Inferences What does this detail indicate about the narrator?

---

11. **vehemently.** Violently; eagerly; forcefully
12. **gesticulations.** Energetic gestures or movements
13. **derision.** Contempt or ridicule

If the narrator were tried for murder and you were a member of the jury, would you vote to acquit him by reason of insanity? What basis should courts use for an insanity defense?

Research Skills

Primary and Secondary Sources
Point out that in researching the life and career of a writer, such as Poe, students can make use of both primary and secondary sources. A primary source is a firsthand account of an event; for example, a letter of Poe's would be a primary source for his life. Secondary sources are written by people who did not directly experience an event; for example, an encyclopedia article about Poe would be a secondary source. Have students identify which of the following materials related to Poe would be primary sources and which would be secondary sources.

1. A diary entry about Poe by someone who met him (primary)
2. A modern biography of Poe (secondary)
3. A book review by Poe (primary)

Find Meaning

1. (a) The narrator is speaking to someone who has given the opinion he is insane. (b) The narrator is defending himself against this charge.

2. (a) He is obsessed with the old man's "vulture" eye. (b) The narrator is very emotionally disturbed.

3. (a) He keeps hearing the beating of the old man's heart. (b) Since the police officers apparently hear nothing, they might conclude the narrator is mad.

Make Judgments

4. (a) His clear account and awareness of his actions and ability to interact with the police. (b) His obsession with the old man's eye, his spying, and his conviction that he can hear the beating of the old man's heart.

5. (a) He seems confident and reflective. (b) His state is one of panic and delusion.

6. (a) Poe creates an effect of ever-increasing tension leading to a breaking point. (b) He has his narrator describe how his obsessions led him first to commit a horrible murder and then to reveal it.

Analyze Literature

Point of View *Answer:* Poe can present information about the narrator's state of mind directly. The effect is to heighten the tension created by the story. A third-person narrator would have produced a more detached narrative.

Apply the Model

BEFORE READING
DURING READING
AFTER READING

Find Meaning

1. (a) To whom is the narrator speaking? (b) Why do you think the narrator gives this account of his crime?

2. (a) What motive does the narrator give for murdering the old man? (b) What does this suggest about the narrator's mental state?

3. (a) What sound does the narrator hear while he is talking to the police? (b) What might the police conclude from the visit?

Make Judgments

4. (a) What characteristics of the narrator make him seem sane? (b) What characteristics make him seem insane?

5. (a) What do you think is the narrator's mental state at the beginning of the story? (b) What is his mental state at the end of the story?

6. (a) What overall effect do you think Poe was trying to create in "The Tell-Tale Heart"? (b) How does he create this effect?

Analyze Literature

Point of View How does Poe's use of a first-person point of view affect the way information is conveyed in "The Tell-Tale Heart"? How does this point of view affect the mood created by the story? Use a chart to compare the differences between the effects of a first-person narrator and a third-person narrator.

	First-person Narrator	Third-person Narrator
How Story Conveys Information	Presents narrator's state of mind directly	
Mood Created by the Story		

Extend Understanding

Writing Options

Creative Writing Imagine that you are the narrator's lawyer and a trial is set. Write a **letter** advising your client how to plead.

Persuasive Writing The poet Walt Whitman wrote that Poe was "brilliant and dazzling, but with no heat." Write a brief **statement of opinion** in which you agree or disagree with Whitman's evaluation of Poe. Give support for your opinion.

Collaborative Learning

Hold a Mock Trial With classmates, put the narrator of "The Tell-Tale Heart" on trial. Choose who will take on the various roles in court and present evidence for and against the narrator.

Media Literacy

Conduct Internet Research Research the life and works of Edgar Allan Poe on the Internet. Decide which of his other works you might like to read.

 Go to **www.mirrorsandwindows.com** for more.

Rubrics for Writing Options

You can adapt this as a checklist for students to use as they write.

Creative Writing

☐ Does the letter clearly identify the writer as a lawyer?

☐ Does it clearly set out the client's legal options?

☐ Does it offer effective arguments in support of the writer's advice?

Persuasive Writing

☐ Does the paragraph indicate a grasp of the meaning of Whitman's observation?

☐ Does it clearly present the writer's opinion about the validity of the observation?

☐ Does it offer evidence for the writer's opinion based on "The Tell-Tale Heart"?

Understanding Theme

What is Theme?

What is the main point being made in the familiar fable from Aesop below? In answering this question, you are identifying the theme. A **theme** is the central idea of a literary work.

Themes and Topics

The theme is not the same as the topic. A topic is the subject of a literary work, or what it is about. For example, the topic of this fable is a race. The theme is a general observation based on that topic. Literary works can share the same topic but have different themes because each work is the basis for a different observation. For example, you might have two stories that are both on the topic of summer jobs. One story's theme might be stated: "Summer jobs are often a wonderful opportunity to broaden your experience of life." The other story's theme might be stated: "Summer jobs are usually boring, but necessary." The topic is the same, but the themes are very different.

Stated and Implied Themes

Sometimes the central idea of a literary work is presented directly. This is called a *stated theme*. What is the stated theme of the fable of the Hare and the Tortoise? More often, however, the theme of a literary work is not presented directly and must be inferred by the reader, using details from the story such as the qualities or actions of the characters. This is an *implied theme*. Some works can have both a stated theme and an implied theme, or even several themes, either stated or implied.

The Hare and the Tortoise, 1929. Milo Winter.

> The Tortoise never for a moment stopped, but went on with a slow but steady pace straight to the end of the course. The Hare, lying down by the wayside, fell fast asleep. At last waking up, and moving as fast as he could, he saw the Tortoise had reached the goal, and was comfortably dozing after her fatigue. Slow but steady wins the race.

Understanding Theme

Reading strategies that can help students understand theme include asking questions and making inferences.

Use Reading Strategies

Ask Questions Point out to students that they can ask themselves questions about a work of literature from the moment they decide to read it. To determine a theme, they can ask such questions as what details mean, what the author's purpose is, how many levels of meaning a work is supposed to have, what conflict the plot involves, and how characters change over the course of a story. The answers to all of these questions can help them determine a theme.

Use Reading Strategies

Make Inferences Review with students the difference between the verbs *imply* and *infer*. Point out that an implied theme is a quality of the work they read; they must infer the theme from their reading. Remind them that making inferences relies as much on their personal experience as it does on the information in the reading.

KEY TERMS

THEME, 153
TOPIC, 153
STATED THEME, 153
INFERRED, 153
IMPLIED THEME, 153

Writing Skills

Explore Themes through Freewriting

Tell students that freewriting is a prewriting activity that can help them select a topic for a report or essay. Through freewriting, they can explore their thoughts on a subject; they write ideas as they come, without pausing to edit or embellish.

Help students identify different themes suggested by the characters and events in "The Hare and the Tortoise," such as diligence, pride, natural talent, and the rewards of hard work. Then have students freewrite for ten minutes on one or more of these themes.

Common Core State Standards

Reading Literature
RL.2

Preview the Model

At a Glance
Guided Reading: Reading Model
- Reading Level: Moderate
- Difficulty Consideration: Theme
- Ease Factor: Vocabulary

Objectives
Studying this lesson will enable students to
- use reading strategies such as comparing and contrasting two characters
- define *theme* and recognize the effect of this literary technique in the selection
- describe the literary accomplishments of Gary Soto and the significance of Mexican-American experience in his writing
- understand different perspectives on the value of work

Launch the Lesson
Before reading "Born Worker," students may enjoy the chance to get together in small groups to discuss their own work experiences. Ask students to share their best and worst experiences. What have they learned about themselves from their work experiences?

Born Worker
A Short Story by Gary Soto

Build Background
Geographical Context California's Central (or San Joaquin) Valley lies between the Sierra Nevada Mountains and the Coast Range. Because of its rich soil, the valley is home to many farms and agricultural businesses. Many Mexican immigrants move there in search of jobs. Author Gary Soto draws from his own experience growing up in California's Central Valley and writes largely about the Mexican Americans who live there.

Reader's Context José takes jobs to earn money. What kinds of work should people your age be allowed to do?

Set Purpose
In the first sentence of "Born Worker," the author introduces José by using sensory details such as "grime under his fingernails" and "skin calloused from the grainy twist of a shovel." These vivid descriptions help the reader to see José clearly. As you read, watch for the sensory details and description. Think about how they help you picture the action of the story.

Analyze Literature
Theme A **theme** is a central idea in a literary work. A theme is not the same as a topic. A topic is the subject of a literary work, such as "helping others." A theme is a broad statement about a topic, such as "helping others is one of the best ways to feel good about yourself." Stories can share the same topic, but have different themes. There can also be more than one theme in a story. As you read, look for possible themes in "Born Worker."

Use Reading Skills
Compare and Contrast When you compare things, you describe their similarities. When you contrast them, you describe their differences. Create a Venn diagram like the one below to compare and contrast José and Arnie, the two central characters in "Born Worker." In the outer parts of each circle note the characteristics that distinguish José and Arnie. Use the overlapping part of both circles to note the characteristics the two boys share.

Meet the Author

Gary Soto was born in 1952 in Fresno, California. He is the author of more than twenty books and has won numerous awards for his poetry, short stories, and nonfiction. Much of Soto's writing focuses on the Mexican-American experience. He won an American Book Award in 1985 for his memoir *Living Up the Street*.

154 UNIT 2 FICTION

Words in Use

Selection Words
call**oused**, 155
array, 158
stagnant, 163

Teaching Words
agricultural, 154
grime, 154
vivid, 154
propose, 166
attributes, 166

KEY TERMS
SENSORY DETAIL, 154
DESCRIPTION, 154
THEME, 154
TOPIC, 154
COMPARE AND CONTRAST, 154

Common Core State Standards
Reading Literature
RL.1, RL.2
Writing
W.9
Language
L.6

Born Worker

A Short Story by Gary Soto

He was a good worker, honest, and always on time.

They said that José was born with a ring of dirt around his neck, with grime under his fingernails, and skin calloused from the grainy twist of a shovel. They said his palms were already rough by the time he was three, and soon after he learned his primary colors, his squint was the squint of an aged laborer. They said he was a born worker. By seven he was drinking coffee slowly, his mouth pursed the way his mother sipped. He wore jeans, a shirt with sleeves rolled to his elbows. His eye could measure a length of board, and his knees genuflected[1] over flower beds and leafy gutters.

---

1. **genuflected.** Bent the knee, especially in worship

> **DURING READING**
>
> **Use Reading Strategies**
> **Clarify** What do these details tell you about José?
> **A**

155

Teach the Model

Summary
The main character in the story is José, a junior high school student. José is strong and believes in working hard, as his parents do. His mother operates a sewing machine, and his father repairs wires for the telephone company. José's cousin, Arnie, is middle-class and more affluent. Arnie proposes a work deal to José, in which Arnie will find jobs and José will do the work. On one job, José is cleaning an almost-empty swimming pool when the elderly owner falls in and hits his head. José stays to help the man, but Arnie runs away. A little while later Arnie returns and tells the police an untrue version of the events that is more favorable to him. José realizes how different he and Arnie are.

MIRRORS & WINDOWS
The Mirrors & Windows questions at the end of this selection focus on the theme of labor. Before reading the story, ask students what their notions are of physical laborers. Can applied labor enrich the spirit?

Use Reading Strategies
Clarify *Answer:* As a child, José already acted like an adult. He was used to work and behaved as a laborer from an early age. **A**

Program Resources

Planning and Assessment
Program Planning Guide, Selection Lesson Plan
E-Lesson Planner
Assessment Guide, Lesson Test
ExamView

Technology Tools
Interactive Student Text on CD
Visual Teaching Package
Audio Library
mirrorsandwindows.com

Meeting the Standards
Fiction: Unit 2, Guided Reading, pp. 25–30

Differentiating Instruction
English Language Learners, Compare and Contrast, pp. 37–52

Use Reading Strategies

Ask Questions Model for students other questions that these first paragraphs might prompt a reader to ask: "What does José's father mean when he says he sees years of work from the tops of the telephone poles?" **A**

Analyze Literature

Theme *Answer:* Students may say that that this suggests that a possible theme is the value of doing hard physical work. **B**

Use Reading Skills

Compare and Contrast *Answer:* Arnie comes from a middle-class background. José's parents have much less money, and his parents struggle more to make ends meet. Arnie gets pretty much everything he wants. José's parents do not have enough to give him many extras. **C**

Analyze Literature

Stated and Implied Themes Remind students that themes can be stated or implied. A stated theme is provided in plain words (Hard work pays off in the end), while one must infer the meaning of an implied theme (She looked around the house she had just purchased and forgave her boss for demanding that she work more hours). Direct students' attention to the sentence *Arnie's family had never climbed a telephone pole to size up the future.* Tell them that the author is revealing an important theme in this statement. Is it stated or implied (implied)? What theme can they infer from the statement? **D**

They said lots of things about José, but almost nothing of his parents. His mother stitched at a machine all day, and his father, with a steady job at the telephone company, climbed splintered, sun-sucked poles, fixed wires and looked around the city at tree level.

A "What do you see up there?" José once asked his father.

"Work," he answered. "I see years of work, *mi'jo.*"[2]

José took this as a truth, and though he did well in school, he felt destined to labor. His arms would pump, his legs would bend, his arms would carry a world of earth. He believed in hard work, believed that his strength was as ancient as a rock's.

> **DURING READING**
>
> **Analyze Literature**
> **Theme** What does this suggest about a possible theme for the story? **B**

"Life is hard," his father repeated from the time José could first make out the meaning of words until he was stroking his fingers against the grain of his sandpaper beard.

His mother was an example to José. She would raise her hands, showing her fingers pierced from the sewing machines. She bled on her machine, bled because there was money to make, a child to raise, and a roof to stay under.

One day when José returned home from junior high, his cousin Arnie was sitting on the lawn sucking on a stalk of grass. José knew that grass didn't come from his lawn. His was cut and pampered, clean.

> **DURING READING**
>
> **Use Reading Skills**
> **Compare and Contrast** How is Arnie's life different from José's? **C**

"José!" Arnie shouted as he took off the earphones of his CD Walkman.

"Hi, Arnie," José said without much enthusiasm. He didn't like his cousin. He thought he was lazy and, worse, spoiled by the trappings of being middle class. His parents had good jobs in offices and showered him with clothes, shoes, CDs, vacations, almost **D** anything he wanted. Arnie's family had never climbed a telephone pole to size up the future.

> **He believed in hard work, believed that his strength was as ancient as a rock's.**

Arnie rose to his feet, and José saw that his cousin was wearing a new pair of high-tops. He didn't say anything.

"Got an idea," Arnie said cheerfully. "Something that'll make us money."

José looked at his cousin, not a muscle of curiosity twitching in his face.

Still, Arnie explained that since he himself was so clever with words, and his best cousin in the whole world was good at working with his hands, that maybe they might start a company.

---

2. *mi'jo.* My son (Spanish)

Differentiated Instruction

Reading Proficiency

You may want to help students by summarizing the information on the Before Reading page before they read the selection. Once they have finished reading "Born Worker," have them reread page 154 to increase their understanding.

Enrichment

Encourage students to write a description of their work ethic. How do they hope to utilize these values in their future careers? How does their work ethic help to define them as people? Challenge students to express their work ethics in poems, editorials, or essays.

"What would you do?" José asked.

"Me?" he said brightly. "Shoot, I'll round up all kinds of jobs for you. You won't have to do anything." He stopped, then started again. "Except—you know—do the work."

"Get out of here," José said.

"Don't be that way," Arnie begged. "Let me tell you how it works."

The boys went inside the house, and while José stripped off his school clothes and put on his jeans and a T-shirt, Arnie told him that they could be rich.

"You ever hear of this guy named Bechtel?" Arnie asked. **E**

José shook his head.

"Man, he started just like us," Arnie said. "He started digging ditches and stuff, and the next thing you knew, he was sitting by his own swimming pool. You want to sit by your own pool, don't you?" Arnie smiled, waiting for José to speak up.

"Never heard of this guy Bechtel," José said after he rolled on two huge socks, worn at the heels. He opened up his chest of drawers and brought out a packet of Kleenex.

Arnie looked at the Kleenex.

"How come you don't use your sleeve?" Arnie joked.

José thought for a moment and said, "I'm not like you." He smiled at his retort.

"Listen, I'll find the work, and then we can split it fifty-fifty." José knew fifty-fifty was a bad deal.

"How about sixty-forty?" Arnie suggested when he could see that José wasn't going for it. "I know a lot of people from my dad's job. They're waiting for us."

José sat on the edge of his bed and started to lace up his boots. He knew that there were agencies that would find you work, agencies that took a portion of your pay. They're cheats, he thought, people who sit in air-conditioned offices while others work.

"You really know a lot of people?" José asked.

"Boatloads," Arnie said. "My dad works with this millionaire—honest—who cooks a steak for his dog every day."

He's a liar, José thought. No matter how he tried, he couldn't picture a dog grubbing on steak. The world was too poor for that kind of silliness.

"Listen, I'll go eighty-twenty," José said.

"Aw, man," Arnie whined. "That ain't fair."

José laughed.

"I mean, half the work is finding the jobs," Arnie explained, his

> **DURING READING**
> **Make Connections**
> How do you feel about Arnie so far? How does your opinion of him differ from your opinion of José? **F**

BORN WORKER **157**

Teach the Model

History Connection
Warren Bechtel Warren Bechtel was born in 1872 and lived in Illinois until he was twelve, when his family moved to a farm in Kansas. He began a musical career but was not successful. Bechtel moved back to the family farm and then began using his mule team to grade roadbeds for the new train lines that were being built in the Midwest and West. He saved money and eventually started his own construction company. The Bechtel Company got the contract to build the Hoover Dam, as well as many other roads and dams. Bechtel's company eventually became the largest construction and engineering firm in the United States. Bechtel died in 1933. Members of his family still run the company. **E**

Make Connections
Answer: Responses will vary, though most students will probably be repelled by Arnie's laziness, self-centeredness, and opportunism. **F**

Grammar Skills

Capitalization
Remind students they should capitalize names of family members and words showing family relationships when used as titles or subsitiues for a name. They should not capitalize words for family relationships when preceded by a possessive noun or pronoun. For example:

name	Arnie
title	Cousin Arnie
possessive noun	José's cousin

Have students correct the capitalization in the following items. If the item is correct as written, have them write *correct*.

1. my father (correct)
2. uncle Tito (Uncle Tito)
3. José's Mother (José's mother)
4. her aunt and two cousins (correct)

Cultural Connection

Work Ethic Going back to the colonial period of U.S. history, the "work ethic"—often called the "Protestant" or "Puritan" work ethic—has helped define the American character. The emphasis on constant labor as an index of an individual's virtue was expressed in writings such as Benjamin Franklin's *Poor Richard's Almanac:* "Sloth makes all things difficult, but industry all easy." Ask students if the U.S. maintains this historical work ethic today. How or how not? **A**

Use Reading Skills

Compare and Contrast *Answer:* José is a conscientious and hard worker. Arnie is lazy and doesn't do much physical work. **B**

---

palms up as he begged José to be reasonable.

José knew this was true. He had to go door-to-door, and he **A** disliked asking for work. He assumed that it should automatically be his since he was a good worker, honest, and always on time.

"Where did you get this idea, anyhow?" José asked.

"I got a business mind," Arnie said proudly.

"Just like that Bechtel guy," José retorted.

"That's right."

José agreed to a seventy-thirty split, with the condition that Arnie had to help out. Arnie hollered, arguing that some people were meant to work and others to come up with brilliant ideas. He was one of the latter. Still, he agreed after José said it was that or nothing.

In the next two weeks, Arnie found an array of jobs. José peeled off shingles from a rickety garage roof, carried rocks down a path to where a pond would go, and spray-painted lawn furniture. And while Arnie accompanied him, most of the time he did nothing. He did help occasionally. He did shake the cans of spray paint and kick aside debris so that José didn't trip while going down the path carrying the rocks. He did stack the piles of shingles, but almost cried when a nail bit his thumb. But mostly he told José what he had missed or where the work could be improved. José was bothered because he and his work had never been criticized before.

But soon José learned to ignore his cousin, ignore his comments about his spray painting, or about the way he lugged rocks, two in each arm. He didn't say anything, either, when they got paid and Arnie rubbed his hands like a fly, muttering, "It's payday."

Then Arnie found a job scrubbing a drained swimming pool. The two boys met early at José's house. Arnie brought his bike. José's own bike had a flat that grinned like a clown's face.

"I'll pedal," José suggested when Arnie said that he didn't have much leg strength.

With Arnie on the handlebars, José tore off, his pedaling so strong that tears of fear formed in Arnie's eyes.

"Slow down!" Arnie cried.

José ignored him and within minutes they were riding the bike up a gravel driveway. Arnie hopped off at first chance.

"You're scary," Arnie said, picking a gnat from his eye.

José chuckled.

When Arnie knocked on the door, an old man still in pajamas appeared in the window. He motioned for the boys to come around to the back.

> **DURING READING**
>
> **Use Reading Skills**
> **Compare and Contrast**
> How are the responses to their work different? **B**

Differentiated Instruction

English Language Learning

Point out the following vocabulary words and expressions:

high-tops—kind of sneakers that come up above the ankle, 156

grubbing—eating, 157

compensate—pay, 160

pumice stone—volcanic rock; rough stone used for cleaning, 161

blazing—hot, 161

loquat—small yellow fruit, 162

"Let me do the talking," Arnie suggested to his cousin. "He knows my dad real good. They're like this." He pressed two fingers together.

José didn't bother to say OK. He walked the bike into the **C** backyard, which was lush with plants—roses in their last bloom,

Use Reading Skills
Determine Importance of Details
Discuss this sentence with students. What does José's omission reveal about his character and/or that of his cousin? **C**

Cultural Connection
Child Labor Laws In all fifty states, there are laws that govern teenage and young adult workers. A person must be at least fourteen years old to be hired for most jobs, unless he or she babysits, delivers newspapers, works on a farm, or is an actor. Jobs done as household chores or other simple jobs for friends and family are also allowed. For some hazardous or difficult jobs, such as operating machinery or driving large trucks, the person has to be eighteen or older.

Writing Skills

Transitions in Comparisons

Explain that when students compare two things, they should use transition words such as *also, and, both, like, same as,* and *similarly.* When they contrast things, they should use words such as *but, however, unlike, different from, on the other hand,* and *in contrast.* For example: "José's parents struggle to survive; *however,* Arnie's parents make a lot of money." Remind students that when they complete the Expository Writing exercise on page 166, they should include transition words to compare and contrast the two boys.

Teach the Model

Analyze Literature

Motivation Ask students to recall José's condition for accepting the seventy-thirty split of profits (Arnie must do some of the work). How does Arnie respond to this condition (He explains that some people [Arnie] are meant to labor and others [himself] are meant to think)? Next, discuss with students Arnie's initial interaction with Mr. Clemens. What motivates him to reveal his and José's "division of labor"? Based on his demeanor, which of the aforementioned two types of people does Arnie think Mr. Clemens is? Finally, examine Mr. Clemens's reaction to Arnie's explanation and demeanor. Does it reinforce or negate Arnie's assessment of the man? **Ⓐ**

Use Reading Strategies

Visualize *Answer:* The author uses words and phrases that appeal to the sense of sight. These phrases include "filthy with grime," "grayish water shimmered," and "leaves floated as limp as cornflakes." **Ⓑ**

> **DURING READING**
>
> **Use Reading Strategies**
> **Visualize** What sensory details does the author use to help you picture the setting? **Ⓑ**

---

geraniums, hydrangeas, pansies with their skirts of bright colors. José could make out the splash of a fountain. Then he heard the hysterical yapping of a poodle. From all his noise, a person might have thought the dog was on fire.

"Hi, Mr. Clemens," Arnie said, extending his hand. "I'm Arnie Sanchez. It's nice to see you again."

José had never seen a kid actually greet someone like this. Mr. Clemens said, hiking up his pajama bottoms, "I only wanted one kid to work."

"Oh," Arnie stuttered. "Actually, my cousin José really does the work and I kind of, you know, supervise."

Ⓐ Mr. Clemens pinched up his wrinkled face. He seemed not to understand. He took out a pea-sized hearing aid, fiddled with its tiny dial, and fit it into his ear, which was surrounded with wiry gray hair.

"I'm only paying for one boy," Mr. Clemens shouted. His poodle click-clicked and stood behind his legs. The dog bared its small crooked teeth.

"That's right," Arnie said, smiling a strained smile. "We know that you're going to compensate only one of us."

Mr. Clemens muttered under his breath. He combed his hair with his fingers. He showed José the pool, which was shaped as round as an elephant. It was filthy with grime. Near the bottom some grayish water shimmered and leaves floated as limp as cornflakes.

"It's got to be real clean," Mr. Clemens said, "or it's not worth it."

"Oh, José's a great worker," Arnie said. He patted his cousin's shoulders and said that he could lift a mule.

Mr. Clemens sized up José and squeezed his shoulders, too.

"How do I know you, anyhow?" Mr. Clemens asked Arnie, who was aiming a smile at the poodle.

"You know my dad," Arnie answered, raising his smile to the old man. "He works at Interstate Insurance. You and he had some business deals."

160 UNIT 2 FICTION

Reading Skills

Understand Literary Elements

Explain that a simile is a comparison using *like* or *as* such as this example from the story: "The black algae came up like a foamy monster." Point out that writers often use similes to help readers see things in new ways. Have students identify the two items that are being compared and explain what they visualize as they read these similes from the story.

1. Mr. Clemens's scalp was as pink as a crab. (*scalp* and *crab*)
2. Arnie rubbed his hands like a fly. (*Arnie* and *fly*)
3. José's own bike had a flat that grinned like a clown's face. (*flat* and *face*)

Mr. Clemens thought for a moment, a hand on his mouth, head shaking. He could have been thinking about the meaning of life, his face was so dark.

"Mexican fella?" he inquired.

"That's him," Arnie said happily.

José felt like hitting his cousin for his cheerful attitude. Instead, he walked over and picked up the white plastic bottle of bleach.

Next to it were a wire brush, a pumice stone, and some rags. He set down the bottle and, like a surgeon, put on a pair of rubber gloves.

"You know what you're doing, boy?" Mr. Clemens asked.

José nodded as he walked into the pool. If it had been filled with water, his chest would have been wet. The new hair on his chest would have been floating like the legs of a jellyfish.

"Oh yeah," Arnie chimed, speaking for his cousin. "José was born to work."

José would have drowned his cousin if there had been more water. Instead, he poured a bleach solution into a rag and swirled it over an area. He took the wire brush and scrubbed. The black algae came up like a foamy monster.

"We're a team," Arnie said to Mr. Clemens.

Arnie descended into the pool and took the bleach bottle from José. He held it for José and smiled up at Mr. Clemens, who, hands on hips, watched for a while, the poodle at his side. He cupped his ear, as if to pick up the sounds of José's scrubbing.

"Nice day, huh?" Arnie sang.

"What?" Mr. Clemens said.

"Nice day," Arnie repeated, this time louder. "So which ear can't you hear in?" Grinning, Arnie wiggled his ear to make sure that Mr. Clemens knew what he was asking.

Mr. Clemens ignored Arnie. He watched José, whose arms worked back and forth like he was sawing logs.

"We're not only a team," Arnie shouted, "but we're also cousins."

Mr. Clemens shook his head at Arnie. When he left, the poodle leading the way, Arnie immediately climbed out of the pool and sat on the edge, legs dangling.

"It's going to be blazing," Arnie complained. He shaded his eyes with his hand and looked east, where the sun was rising over a sycamore, its leaves hanging like bats.

José scrubbed. He worked the wire brush over the black and green stains, the grime dripping like tears. He finished a large area.

DURING READING

Analyze Literature
Conflict Why might José feel like hitting Arnie? **C**

Analyze Literature

Characterization Ask students how this small detail reveals a great deal about Arnie's character. What do his actions and words convey about his priorities? What do they expose about his work ethic? What does the question he poses to José tell you about his understanding of others with different lifestyles? **Ⓐ**

Cultural Connection

Loquat The loquat, also known as Japanese medlar and Nispero, is a rare and delicate fruit in the same family as apples, pears, and quinces. Its flesh can be orange, yellow, or off-white in color, and many describe its taste as a combination of apricot, plum, and cherry. Loquats are indigenous to southeastern China and became popular in California in the 1870's. Because they grow on rounded trees that have an average height of ten feet and display dense, almost palm-shaped leaves, they are often used to shade outdoor seating areas, such as patios. The fruit is very delicate and decays quickly after being picked, so loquats are rarely shipped to commercial markets. In California's Central Valley and its coastal area between Los Angeles and San Diego, where loquats flourish, they are generally sold in farmer's markets. **Ⓑ**

"Why don't you Ⓐ be quiet and let me work?" Ⓑ

He hopped out of the pool and returned hauling a garden hose with an attached nozzle. He gave the cleaned area a blast. When the spray got too close, his cousin screamed, got up, and, searching for something to do, picked a loquat from a tree.

"What's your favorite fruit?" Arnie asked.

José ignored him.

Arnie stuffed a bunch of loquats into his mouth, then cursed himself for splattering juice on his new high-tops. He returned to the pool, his cheeks fat with the seeds, and once again sat at the edge. He started to tell José how he had first learned to swim. "We were on vacation in Mazatlán. You been there, ain't you?"

José shook his head. He dabbed the bleach solution onto the sides of the pool with a rag and scrubbed a new area.

"Anyhow, my dad was on the beach and saw this drowned dead guy," Arnie continued. "And right there, my dad got scared and realized I couldn't swim."

Arnie rattled on about how his father had taught him in the hotel pool and later showed him where the drowned man's body had been.

"Be quiet," José said.

"What?"

"I can't concentrate," José said, stepping back to look at the cleaned area.

Arnie shut his mouth but opened it to lick loquat juice from his fingers. He kicked his legs against the swimming pool, bored. He looked around the backyard and spotted a lounge chair. He got up, dusting off the back of his pants, and threw himself into the cushions. He raised and lowered the back of the lounge. Sighing, he snuggled in. He stayed quiet for three minutes, during which time José scrubbed. His arms hurt but he kept working with long strokes. José knew that in an hour the sun would drench the pool with light. He hurried to get the job done.

Arnie then asked, "You ever peel before?"

José looked at his cousin. His nose burned from the bleach. He scrunched up his face.

"You know, like when you get sunburned."

"I'm too dark to peel," José said, his words echoing because he had advanced to the deep end. "Why don't you be quiet and let me work?"

Arnie babbled on that he had peeled when on vacation in Hawaii. He explained that he was really more French than Mexican,

TEACHING NOTE

Self-Generated Questioning

Urge students to ask as many questions as they can about the selection, such as "How did José and Arnie's lifestyles turn out so differently?" and record their responses on the board or on an overhead. Then place a star next to each question students consider important and two stars next to each question they consider hard to answer. As a class, discuss the starred questions.

and that's why his skin was sensitive. He said that when he lived in France, people thought that he could be Portuguese or maybe Armenian, never Mexican.

José felt like soaking his rag with bleach and pressing it over Arnie's mouth to make him be quiet.

Then Mr. Clemens appeared. He was dressed in white pants and a flowery shirt. His thin hair was combed so that his scalp, as pink as a crab, showed.

"I'm just taking a little rest," Arnie said.

Arnie leaped back into the pool. He took the bleach bottle and held it. He smiled at Mr. Clemens, who came to inspect their progress.

"José's doing a good job," Arnie said, then whistled a song.

Mr. Clemens peered into the pool, hands on knees, admiring the progress.

"Pretty good, huh?" Arnie asked.

Mr. Clemens nodded. Then his hearing aid fell out, and José turned in time to see it roll like a bottle cap toward the bottom of the pool. It leaped into the stagnant water with a plop. A single bubble went up, and it was gone.

"Dang," Mr. Clemens swore. He took shuffling steps toward the deep end. He steadied his gaze on where the hearing aid had sunk. He leaned over and suddenly, arms waving, one leg kicking out, he tumbled into the pool. He landed standing up, then his legs buckled, and he crumbled, his head striking against the bottom. He rolled once, and half of his body settled in the water.

"Did you see that!" Arnie shouted, big-eyed.

José had already dropped his brushes on the side of the pool and hurried to the old man, who moaned, eyes closed, his false teeth jutting from his mouth. A ribbon of blood immediately began to flow from his scalp.

"We better get out of here!" Arnie suggested. "They're going to blame us!"

José knelt on both knees at the old man's side. He took the man's teeth from his mouth and placed them in his shirt pocket. The old man groaned and opened his eyes, which were shiny wet. He appeared startled, like a newborn. "Sir, you'll be all right," José cooed, then snapped at his cousin. "Arnie, get over here and help me!"

"I'm going home," Arnie whined.

DURING READING
Use Reading Strategies
Make Inferences What can you infer about Arnie's attitude toward his ethnic identity? **C**

DURING READING
Use Reading Skills
Compare and Contrast
How's does Arnie's response differ from José's? **E**

Cultural Connection

911 The three-digit telephone number 9-1-1 is the "Universal Emergency Number" for United States citizens. Just who developed the concept of a phone number designated exclusively for emergencies is debatable, but it is widely accepted that Great Britain employed the first three-digit emergency number (999) in 1937. In 1957, the United States' National Association of Fire Chiefs recommended the implementation of a single number in reporting fire emergencies. Ten years later, President Johnson's Commission on Law Enforcement and Administration of Justice echoed the previous recommendation, extending it to all emergencies. The Federal Communications Commission (FCC) met with the American Telephone and Telegraph Company (AT&T) and, in 1968, established the digits 9-1-1 as the nationwide emergency code. **Ⓐ**

Make Connections

Answer: Responses will vary, but most students will probably admire José's calmness and compassion. **Ⓑ**

Ⓐ "You punk!" José yelled. "Go inside and call 911."

Arnie said that they should leave him there.

"Why should we get involved?" he cried as he started for his bike. "It's his own fault."

José laid the man's head down and with giant steps leaped out of the pool, shoving his cousin as he passed. He went into the kitchen and punched in 911 on a telephone. He explained to the operator what had happened. When asked the address, José dropped the phone and went onto the front porch to look for it.

"It's 940 East Brown," José breathed. He hung up and looked wildly about the kitchen. He opened up the refrigerator and brought out a plastic tray of ice, which he twisted so that a few of the cubes popped out and slid across the floor. He wrapped some cubes in a dish towel. When he raced outside, Arnie was gone, the yapping poodle was doing laps around the edge of the pool, and Mr. Clemens was trying to stand up.

"No, sir," José said as he jumped into the pool, his own knees almost buckling. "Please, sit down."

Mr. Clemens staggered and collapsed. José caught him before he hit his head again. The towel of ice cubes dropped from his hands. With his legs spread to absorb the weight, José raised the man up in his arms, this fragile man. He picked him up and carefully stepped toward the shallow end, one slow elephant step at a time.

"You'll be all right," José said, more to himself than to Mr. Clemens, who moaned and struggled to be let free.

> **DURING READING**
>
> **Make Connections**
> How does this make you feel about José? **Ⓑ**

Differentiated Instruction

Kinesthetic Learning

Have several students prepare a pantomime based on "Born Worker." Remind students that a pantomime tells a story without words. The pantomime should have a beginning, middle, and end, with specific characters and actions. Have students rehearse their pantomime and perform it for the class.

The sirens wailed in the distance. The poodle yapped, which started a dog barking in the neighbor's yard.

"You'll be OK," José repeated, and in the shallow end of the pool, he edged up the steps. He lay the old man in the lounge chair and raced back inside for more ice and another towel. He returned outside and placed the bundle of cubes on the man's head, where the blood flowed. Mr. Clemens was awake, looking about. When the old man felt his mouth, José reached into his shirt pocket and pulled out his false teeth. He fit the teeth into Mr. Clemens's mouth and a smile appeared, something bright at a difficult time.

"I hit my head," Mr. Clemens said after smacking his teeth so that the fit was right.

José looked up and his gaze floated to a telephone pole, one his father might have climbed. If he had been there, his father would have seen that José was more than just a good worker. He would have seen a good man. He held the towel to the old man's head. The poodle, now quiet, joined them on the lounge chair.

A fire truck pulled into the driveway and soon they were surrounded by firemen, one of whom brought out a first-aid kit. A fireman led José away and asked what had happened. He was starting to explain when his cousin reappeared, yapping like a poodle.

"I was scrubbing the pool," Arnie shouted, "and I said, 'Mr. Clemens, you shouldn't stand so close to the edge.' But did he listen? No, he leaned over and…Well, you can just imagine my horror."

José walked away from Arnie's jabbering. He walked away, and realized that there were people like his cousin, the liar, and people like himself, someone he was getting to know. He walked away and in the midmorning heat boosted himself up a telephone pole.

He climbed up and saw for himself what his father saw—miles and miles of trees and houses, and a future lost in the layers of yellowish haze. ✤

> **DURING READING**
>
> **Analyze Literature**
> **Theme** What does this convey about the theme of the story?
> **C**

 How would you describe José's views on people that do hard, physical work? How might hard work be related to strength of character?

Media Skills

Assess Media Messages

All forms of media—both print and electronic—communicate messages about the subjects they present. This is just as true of entertainment as it is of informational media. Sometimes the message is conveyed directly (as in much advertising); sometimes the message is implicit (as in most works of art). Have students collect some examples of media dealing with work and discuss the messages about the value of work that these media convey.

Find Meaning

1. (a) He was used to hard work at an early age. (b) José's parents had to work hard to survive.

2. (a) His father works for the phone company as a lineman; his mother is a seamstress. (b) Work is hard, but it is something that must be done in order to take care of one's family.

3. (a) Arnie proposes that he will find work for José and they will split what the jobs bring in. (b) Students may say that Arnie is good at putting together ideas and is outgoing with people but that he doesn't like to do physical labor. Others may say that it shows that Arnie exploits people.

Make Judgments

4. Students' perception of José will be both as a person to respect and a person to have sympathy for.

5. (a) The narrator clearly respects José. (b) José is presented in a very positive way (partly by contrast with Arnie, who is cowardly and selfish).

6. (a) José sees himself becoming a man like his father, a future that combines hard work and self-respect. (b) He imagines how his father would view his son's action in helping Mr. Clemens.

Analyze Literature

Theme *Answer:* Students might bring up one or more of the following themes: the value of hard work and self-respect, the difference between people who give and people who take, and the importance of self-knowledge.

Find Meaning

1. (a) What was José like as a child?
(b) Why do you think he was like that?

2. (a) What do José's parents do for a living?
(b) What are their attitudes about working?

3. (a) What business deal does Arnie propose to José? (b) What does this tell you about Arnie?

Analyze Literature

Theme As you read "Born Worker," what themes did you notice? In fiction, most themes tend to be unstated, and you need to infer them from the details in the story, such as the qualities or actions of the main characters. Use a theme map to gather the details that support a central theme in the story. Write a possible theme in the center circle, and provide supporting details in the smaller circles.

Make Judgments

4. The narrator describes José as being born with the attributes of a man who has already worked for many years. How does this affect your perception of José?

5. (a) How does the narrator of the story feel about Arnie? (b) How can you tell?

6. (a) What does José hope for the future?
(b) How does the author let you know José's feelings about the future?

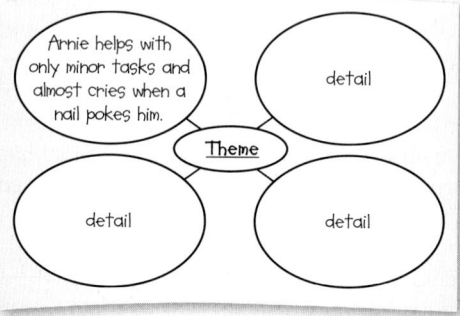

Extend Understanding

Writing Options

Creative Writing Write a new **scene** for this story that changes the ending. What happens to Mr. Clemens, Arnie, and José in your new scene? Share your work with the class.

Expository Writing Use the Venn diagram you created to write a short **comparison-and-contrast essay** to describe José and Arnie. Remember to include an introduction, main body, and conclusion. State your main idea in a thesis, and include details that support your statements about each character. Share your work with a partner when you are done.

Collaborative Learning

Lifelong Learning Use the Internet, newspapers, or other resources to learn about summer jobs in your area. Make a list of jobs appropriate for someone your age. Decide which of the jobs you would most like to do. Present your findings to the class.

Critical Literacy Imagine you could ask a character in "Born Worker" any question you like. How do you think the character would answer the questions? Create a set of questions for the character, and then write the answers you think the character might give.

Go to **www.mirrorsandwindows.com** for more.

Rubrics for Writing Options

You can adapt this as a checklist for students to use as they write.

Creative Writing

☐ Does the new scene make sense within the context of the established plot?

☐ Does it follow the established characterization and tone of the story?

☐ Does it bring effective closure to the story?

Expository Writing

☐ Does the essay show ways that the characters are alike as well as how they are different?

☐ Does it include details and examples that support statements about the characters?

☐ Does it use appropriate transitions?

Grammar & Style

Comma Use

Commas and Compound Sentences

His eye could measure a length of board, and his knees genuflected over flower beds and leafy gutters.

—GARY SOTO, "Born Worker"

In this sentence, two main clauses are joined by a coordinating conjunction *and*. (Other coordinating conjunctions are *but, or, nor, for,* and *yet*.) You should usually use a comma before the conjunction. Writers use commas and compound sentences to impact the reader. In this example, Jose's respect and skill are made to seem equally important.

> EXAMPLE
> *Arnie found the jobs, but José did the work.*

Even if a compound sentence is brief, add a comma if it would be confusing otherwise. The first sentence below is confusing. Add a comma to make it clear.

> EXAMPLES
> *Arnie greeted Mr. Clemens and José was startled by his manner.*
>
> *Arnie greeted Mr. Clemens, and José was startled by his manner.*

Commas in a Series

Use commas to separate items in a series. Three or more words make a series.

> EXAMPLE
> *The garden had roses, geraniums, hydrangeas, and pansies.*

It is not necessary to use commas if the items in the series are linked by conjunctions.

> EXAMPLE
> *José peeled shingles and carried rocks and spray-painted lawn furniture.*

Sentence Improvement

For each of the following sentences, select the response that indicates the best revision.

1. Arnie stacked piles of shingles but, he almost cried when he hurt his thumb on a nail.
   A. Arnie stacked piles of shingles, but, he almost cried when he hurt his thumb on a nail.
   B. Arnie stacked piles of shingles, but he almost cried when he hurt his thumb on a nail.
   C. Arnie stacked piles of shingles but he almost cried when he hurt his thumb on a nail.
   D. no change

2. Arnie talked about his father and José had to listen.
   A. Arnie talked about his father, and José had to listen.
   B. Arnie talked about his father, and, José had to listen.
   C. Arnie talked about his father and, José had to listen.
   D. no change

3. To clean the pool, José used bleach a wire brush a pumice stone, and some rags.
   A. To clean the pool, José used bleach, a wire brush, a pumice stone and some rags.
   B. To clean the pool, José used bleach, a wire brush a pumice stone and some rags.
   C. To clean the pool, José used bleach, a wire brush, a pumice stone, and some rags.
   D. no change

GRAMMAR & STYLE **167**

Teach the Workshop

Sentence Improvement

1. B. Arnie stacked piles of shingles, but he almost cried when he hurt his thumb on a nail.
2. A. Arnie talked about his father, and José had to listen.
3. C. To clean the pool, José used bleach, a wire brush, a pumice stone, and some rags.

> For more information, see Grammar & Style Section 3.15, Punctuation, in the Language Arts Handbook.

Program Resources

You will find additional lessons on Comma Use in the *Exceeding the Standards: Grammar & Style* resource.

Build Skills

Some students may need guidance about when a short compound sentence needs a comma. Emphasize that they should use a comma between clauses when the comma helps them avoid any possible confusion. Consider reading the first Extra Practice example aloud, without inflection. Then discuss whether adding a comma would clarify this sentence.

KEY TERMS

MAIN CLAUSE, 167
COORDINATING CONJUNCTION, 167
COMMA, 167
CONJUNCTION, 167
COMPOUND SENTENCE, 167

TEACHING NOTE

Extra Practice

Have students determine which of the following compound sentences need commas, and, if so, where the comma belongs.

1. You can take Arnie and José can go with his parents. (comma after *Arnie*)
2. Arnie looked around spotted a lounge chair and lay down. (commas after *around* and *chair*)
3. José agreed to a seventy-thirty split but insisted that Arnie help out. (correct)
4. Arnie got nice clothes and CDs and vacations and whatever he wanted. (correct)

Common Core State Standards

Language
L.2, L.5.2a

Preview the Selection

At a Glance
Directed Reading
- Reading Level: Moderate
- Difficulty Consideration: Cultural references
- Ease Factor: Simple plot

Objectives
Studying this lesson will enable students to
- use reading skills such as drawing conclusions
- define *characterization* and recognize how the author uses both direct and indirect characterization
- describe the literary accomplishments of Eugenia Collier and the influence of African-American culture on her writing
- appreciate the different perspectives of various members of the same family

Launch the Lesson
Tell students they are about to read "Sweet Potato Pie," a story in which the narrator shares memories of his childhood while recounting a very recent visit with his brother. Invite students to tell about either a childhood memory or a recent interaction with a family member. Model a response: "When I was six, my older brother scared off a dog that was growling at me."

Sweet Potato Pie

A Short Story by Eugenia Collier

BEFORE READING

Build Background
Historical Context Buddy, the narrator in "Sweet Potato Pie," grew up in a family of southern sharecroppers, tenant farmers who pay part of the crops they raise to their landlord as rent. After the Civil War, many former slaves became sharecroppers on plantations now split up into small farms. Landlords often took advantage of their tenants by paying them poorly for their crops.

Reader's Context What does it mean to "be somebody" today? How do our families and friends help us to achieve our goals?

Set Purpose
Skim the text and preview the images in "Sweet Potato Pie." Predict how Buddy, the narrator, feels about his brother Charley, and read to confirm or revise your prediction.

Analyze Literature
Characterization The act of creating or describing a character is **characterization.** Writers describe characters' physical features, dress, personality, speech, actions, and thoughts, and what other characters say or think about them. In *direct characterization,* the reader is "told" about the character. In *indirect characterization,* the reader is shown things about the character and must draw conclusions. As you read, look for examples of both direct and indirect characterization.

Meet the Author
Eugenia Collier (b. 1928) is an award-winning poet, fiction writer, and essayist. Her short story "Marigolds" won a Gwendolyn Brooks Award for Fiction in 1969. "Sweet Potato Pie" is one of Collier's most well-known stories and appears in many anthologies. "The richness, the diversity, the beauty of my black heritage," are the sources she credits for her creativity. Collier lives and writes in Baltimore.

Use Reading Skills
Draw Conclusions
Gathering pieces of information while you read and deciding what that information means are steps in drawing a conclusion. As you read "Sweet Potato Pie," use a drawing conclusions log like the one below to keep track of key ideas, points that relate to the ideas, and the conclusions you draw from them.

> **Key Idea:**
> Charley is important to Buddy.

> **Supporting Points:**
> - Buddy thinks "Charley never had a childhood."
> - Buddy remembers "clinging to Charley's neck."

> **Overall Conclusion:**

Preview Vocabulary
nu·ance (nü´ än[t]s) *n.,* slight difference or variation

gaunt (gônt) *adj.,* thin and bony

fu·tile·ly (fyu´ til lē) *adv.,* having no useful result

col·lage (ko läzh´) *n.,* combination of different things

saun·ter (son´ tər) *v.,* walk in a leisurely way

Words in Use

Preview Vocabulary	Selection Words	Teaching Words
nuance, 171	shanty, 170	sharecroppers, 168
gaunt, 171	antiquity, 171	
futilely, 172	whittling, 171	tenant, 168
collage, 172	reverently, 176	heritage, 168
saunter, 174		mythic, 178
		ancestral, 178

Common Core State Standards

Reading Literature
RL.1, RL.2
Writing
W.9
Language
L.6

KEY TERMS
CHARACTERIZATION, 168
DIRECT CHARACTERIZATION, 168
CONCLUSION, 168
DIALOGUE, 178
POINT OF VIEW, 178
FIRST-PERSON POINT OF VIEW, 178

Jim, 1930. William H. Johnson. Smithsonian American Art Museum, Washington, DC.

Sweet Potato Pie

A Short Story by Eugenia Collier

Eventually the family's hopes for learning fastened on me, the youngest.

169

Summary
The story starts out in present time, then rapidly moves to a flashback. The first-person narrator, Buddy, an African-American man, is attending a professional meeting in New York City. While he is there, he makes a surprise visit to his older brother Charley's home in Harlem. The visit stirs up memories of Buddy's humble beginnings as the child of sharecroppers. Buddy comments that he feels like he is coming to the ancestral home when he visits Harlem. Charley and his wife and children are glad to see Buddy, and the family spends an enjoyable evening together. As he is leaving, his sister-in-law gives Buddy a piece of sweet potato pie in a brown bag. Since Charley is a taxi driver, he drives Buddy back to his Fifth Avenue hotel. Charley refuses to let Buddy carry the paper bag into the hotel. Instead, Charley carries the bag into the hotel for Buddy.

The Mirrors & Windows questions at the end of this selection focus on the theme of nourishment. Before reading the story, ask students if any food item holds special significance in their homes. What role, apart from sustenance, does food play in society?

Program Resources

Planning and Assessment
Program Planning Guide, Selection Lesson Plan
E-Lesson Planner
Assessment Guide, Lesson Test
ExamView

Meeting the Standards
Fiction: Unit 2, Directed Reading, pp. 31–37

Technology Tools
Interactive Student Text on CD
Visual Teaching Package
Audio Library
mirrorsandwindows.com

Use Reading Skills

Draw Conclusions Ask students why they think the narrator feels such love for his brother. Model a response by indicating one conclusion: "Buddy realizes how much Charley did for him and the rest of the family." Remind students to add this information to their logs. **Ⓐ**

Analyze Literature

Flashback Point out that most of the story is told in flashback. Explain that in a flashback, the narrator often starts in the present time and then goes back in time to relate something that has already happened. Have students identify the point in the story where the flashback begins (the beginning of the third paragraph). Suggest that as they read, they determine which parts of the story are told in flashback, and if and when the story changes back to present time. **Ⓑ**

Analyze Literature

Characterization Read aloud mama's lines in dialect as they are written. Discuss with students how the narrator's use of dialect for his mother's words helps portray her. Ask students what they think of when they hear the dialect. **Ⓒ**

Ⓐ From up here on the fourteenth floor, my brother Charley looks like an insect scurrying among other insects. A deep feeling of love surges through me. Despite the distance, he seems to feel it, for he turns and scans the upper windows, but failing to find me, continues on his way. I watch him moving quickly—gingerly[1], it seems to me—down Fifth Avenue and around the corner to his shabby taxicab. In a moment he will be heading back uptown.

I turn from the window and flop down on the bed, shoes and all. Perhaps because of what happened this afternoon or maybe just because I see Charley so seldom, my thoughts hover over him like hummingbirds. The cheerful, impersonal tidiness of this room is a world away from Charley's walk-up flat in Harlem and a hundred worlds from the bare, noisy shanty where he and the rest of us spent what there was of childhood. I close my eyes, and side by side I see the Charley of my boyhood and the Charley of this afternoon, as clearly as if I were looking at a split TV screen. Another surge of love, seasoned with gratitude, wells up in me.

Ⓑ As far as I know, Charley never had any childhood at all. The oldest children of sharecroppers never do. Mama and Pa were shadowy figures whose voices I heard vaguely in the morning when sleep was shallow and whom I glimpsed as they left for the field before I was fully awake or as they trudged wearily into the house at night when my lids were irresistibly heavy.

They came into sharp focus only on special occasions. One such occasion was the day when the crops were in and the sharecroppers were paid. In our cabin there was so much excitement in the air that even I, the "baby," responded to it. For weeks we had been running out of things that we could neither grow nor get on credit. On the evening of that day we waited anxiously for our parents' return. Then we would cluster around the rough wooden table—I on Lil's lap or clinging to Charley's neck, little Alberta nervously tugging her plait,[2] Jamie crouched at Mama's elbow, like a panther about to spring, and all seven of us silent for once, waiting. Pa would place the money on the table—gently, for it was made from the sweat of their bodies and from their children's tears. Mama would count it out in little piles, her dark face stern and, I think now, beautiful. Not with the hollow beauty of well-modeled features but with the strong radiance of one who has suffered and never yielded.

Ⓒ "This for store bill," she would mutter, making a little pile. "This for c'llection. This for piece o'gingham..."[3] and so on, stretching the money as tight over our collective needs as Jamie's outgrown pants were stretched over my bottom. "Well, that's the crop." She would look up at Pa at last. "It'll do." Pa's face would relax, and a general grin flitted from child to child. We would survive, at least for the present.

The other time when my parents were solid entities[4] was at church. On Sundays we would don our threadbare Sunday-go-to-meeting clothes and tramp, along with neighbors similarly attired, to the Tabernacle Baptist Church, the frail edifice[5] of bare boards held together by God knows what, which was all that my parents ever knew of security and future promise.

Being the youngest and therefore the most likely to err, I was plopped between my

---

1. **gingerly.** Carefully or delicately
2. **plait.** Braid of hair
3. **gingham.** Cotton fabric, often checkered, striped, or plaid
4. **entities.** People or things that exist
5. **edifice.** Building

Differentiated Instruction

Enrichment

Encourage students to research some aspect of traditional African-American culture in the South. Topics might include spirituals, folk tales, proverbs, food, music, and arts and crafts.

Visual Learning

Eugenia Collier creates vivid physical descriptions of several places in "Sweet Potato Pie," including Lenox Avenue and Charley's apartment. Invite students to illustrate these scenes either by drawing them or by creating collages of photographs they find.

father and my mother on the long wooden bench. They sat huge and eternal like twin mountains at my sides. I remember my father's still, black profile silhouetted against the sunny window, looking back into dark recesses of time, into some dim antiquity, like an ancient ceremonial mask. My mother's face, usually sternly set, changed with the varying <u>nuances</u> of her emotion, its planes shifting, shaped by the soft highlights of the sanctuary, as she progressed from a subdued "amen" to a loud "Help me, Jesus" wrung from the depths of her <u>gaunt</u> frame.

My early memories of my parents are associated with special occasions. The contours of my everyday were shaped by Lil and Charley, the oldest children, who rode herd on the rest of us while Pa and Mama toiled in fields not their own. Not until years later did I realize that Lil and Charley were little more than children themselves.

Lil had the loudest, screechiest voice in the county.

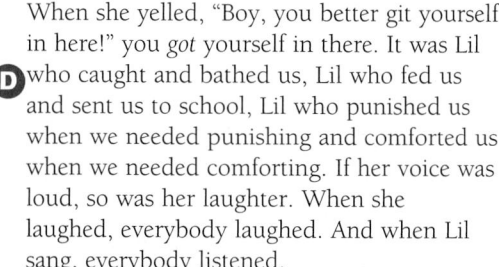

When she yelled, "Boy, you better git yourself in here!" you *got* yourself in there. It was Lil who caught and bathed us, Lil who fed us and sent us to school, Lil who punished us when we needed punishing and comforted us when we needed comforting. If her voice was loud, so was her laughter. When she laughed, everybody laughed. And when Lil sang, everybody listened.

Charley was taller than anybody in the world, including, I was certain, God. From his shoulders, where I spent considerable time in the earliest years, the world had a different perspective. I looked down at tops of heads rather than at the undersides of chins. As I grew older, Charley became more father than brother. Those days return in fragments of splintered memory: Charley's slender, dark hands whittling a toy from a chunk of wood, his face thin and intense, brown as the loaves Lil baked when there was flour. Charley's quick fingers guiding a stick of charred kindling over a bit of scrap paper, making a wondrous picture take shape—Jamie's face or Alberta's rag doll or the spare figure of our bony brown dog. Charley's voice low and terrible in the dark, telling ghost stories so delightfully dreadful that later in the night the moan of the wind through the chinks in the wall sent us scurrying to the security of Charley's pallet,[6] Charley's sleeping form.

Some memories are more than fragmentary. I can still feel the *whap* of the wet dishrag across my mouth. Somehow I developed a stutter, which Charley was determined to cure. Someone had told him that an effective cure was to slap the stutterer across the mouth with a sopping wet dishrag. Thereafter, whenever I began, "Let's g-g-g—,"

---

6. pallet. Narrow, hard bed

nu•ance (nü´ än[t]s) *n.,* slight difference or variation
gaunt (gônt) *adj.,* thin and bony

Cultural Setting Point out to students that the narrator gives background about the cultural setting of his childhood. Ask them to describe the image of the narrator's family they get by reading the simile "which hunted us like hawks." Have them point out additional words and phrases that help them understand the cultural setting and then summarize the cultural setting in their own words. **Ⓐ**

Cultural Connection
Education The education available to the children of African American sharecroppers was very limited. Schools were strictly segregated and black schools had very poor resources. Since most children had to work in the fields, the school year was often interrupted so children could help their families plant and gather crops. In many areas, black children could only go to school through the eighth grade. **Ⓑ**

Use Reading Skills
Draw Conclusions Point out that the narrator has forgotten the content of his valedictory address but remembers the commotion in the family cabin before they left for the graduation as well as the looks on the faces of his family members. Ask students what they can tell about the narrator from this revelation. Remind them to include this information in their logs. **Ⓒ**

---

whap! from nowhere would come the ubiquitous[7] rag. Charley would always insist, "I don't want hurt you none, Buddy—" and *whap* again. I don't know when or why I stopped stuttering. But I stopped.

Ⓐ Already laid waste by poverty, we were easy prey for ignorance and superstition, which hunted us like hawks. We sought education feverishly—and, for most of us, <u>futilely</u>, for the sum total of our combined energies was required for mere brute survival. Inevitably each child had to leave school and bear his share of the eternal burden.

Eventually the family's hopes for learning fastened on me, the youngest. I remember—I *think* I remember, for I could not have been more than five—one frigid day Pa huddled on a rickety stool before the coal stove, took me on his knee and studied me gravely. I was a skinny little thing, they tell me, with large, solemn eyes.

"Well, boy," Pa said at last, "If you got to depend on your looks for what you get out'n this world, you just as well lay down right now." His hand was rough from the plow, **Ⓑ** but gentle as it touched my cheek. "Lucky for you, you got a *mind*. And that's something ain't everybody got. You go to school, boy, get yourself some learning. Make something out'n yourself. Ain't nothing you can't do if you got learning."

Charley was determined that I would break the chain of poverty, that I would "be somebody." As we worked our small vegetable garden in the sun or pulled a bucket of brackish[8] water from the well, Charley would tell me, "You ain gon be no poor farmer, Buddy. You gon be a teacher or

> *Charley was determined that I would break the chain of poverty, that I would "be somebody."*

maybe a doctor or a lawyer. One thing, bad as you is, you ain gon be no preacher."

I loved school with a desperate passion, which became more intense when I began to realize what a monumental struggle it was for my parents and brothers and sisters to keep me there. The cramped, dingy classroom became a battleground where I was victorious. I stayed on top of my class. With glee I outread, outfigured, and outspelled the country boys who mocked my poverty, calling me "the boy with eyes in back of his head"— the "eyes" being the perpetual holes in my hand-me-down pants.

As the years passed, the economic strain was eased enough to make it possible for me to go on to high school. There were fewer mouths to feed, for one thing. Alberta went North to find work at sixteen; Jamie died at twelve.

I finished high school at the head of my class. For Mama and Pa and each of my brothers and sisters, my success was a personal triumph. One by one they came to me the week before commencement, bringing crumpled dollar bills and coins long hoarded, uttering, "Here, Buddy, put this on your gradiation clothes." My graduation suit was the first suit that was all my own.

Ⓒ On graduation night our cabin (less crowded now) was a frantic <u>collage</u> of frayed nerves. I thought Charley would drive me mad.

---

7. ubiquitous. Present or seeming to be present everywhere at the same time
8. brackish. Somewhat salty

fu‧tile‧ly (fyu′ til lē) *adv.*, having no useful result
col‧lage (ko läzh′) *n.*, combination of different things

Differentiated Instruction

English Language Learning
Students learning English may need help with the following figurative language in order to fully comprehend the text.
the chain of poverty—a lack of money and material goods that continues for one or more generations, 172
drop in on them—to visit someone without calling ahead to let them know you are coming, 174

shook loose—got away from an obligation or event to do something else, 174
look a mess—is untidy, 175
Whyn't—Why didn't, 175
"You're a nut"—acting in a silly or crazy manner, 176
eat and run—eat a meal and leave right after the meal, with no time for conversation, 176

"Buddy, you ain pressed out them pants right...Can't you git a better shine on them shoes?...Lord, you done messed up that tie!"

Overwhelmed by the combination of Charley's nerves and my own, I finally exploded. "Man, cut it out!" Abruptly he stopped tugging at my tie, and I was afraid I had hurt his feelings. "It's okay, Charley. Look, you're strangling me. The tie's okay."

Charley relaxed a little and gave a rather sheepish chuckle. "Sure, Buddy." He gave my shoulder a rough joggle. "But you gotta look good. You *somebody*."

My valedictory address[9] was the usual idealistic, sentimental nonsense. I have forgotten what I said that night, but the sight of Mama and Pa and the rest is like a lithograph[10] burned on my memory; Lil, her round face made beautiful by her proud smile; Pa, his head held high, eyes loving and fierce; Mama radiant. Years later when her shriveled hands were finally still, my mind kept coming back to her as she was now. I believe this moment was the apex[11] of her entire life. All of them, even Alberta down from Baltimore—different now, but united with them in her pride. And Charley, on the end of the row, still somehow the protector of them all. Charley, looking as if he were in the presence of something sacred.

As I made my way through the carefully rehearsed speech, it was as if part of me were standing outside watching the whole thing—their proud, work-weary faces, myself wearing the suit that was their combined strength and love and hope: Lil with her lovely, low-pitched voice, Charley with the hands of an artist, Pa and Mama with God knows what potential lost with their sweat in the fields. I realized in that moment that I

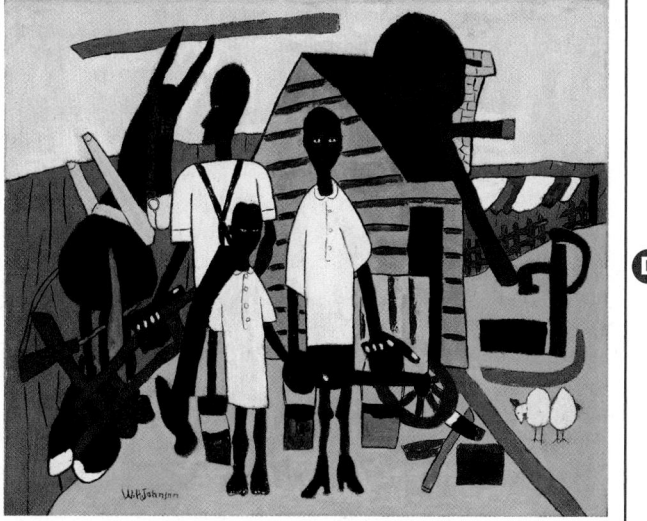

Early Morning Work, c. 1940. William H. Johnson. Smithsonian American Art Museum, Washington, DC.

wasn't necessarily the smartest—only the youngest. And the luckiest. The war came along, and I exchanged three years of my life (including a fair amount of my blood and a great deal of pain) for the GI Bill[12] and a college education. Strange how time can slip by like water flowing through your fingers. One by one the changes came—the old house empty at last, the rest of us scattered; for me, marriage, graduate school, kids, a professorship, and by now a thickening waistline and thinning hair. My mind spins off the years, and I am back to this afternoon and today's Charley—still long and lean, still gentle-eyed, still my greatest fan, and still determined to keep me on the ball.

I didn't tell Charley I would be at a professional meeting in New York and would surely visit, he and Bea would have spent days in fixing up, and I would have had to be

---

9. **valedictory address.** Closing or farewell statement or speech, usually delivered at graduation ceremonies by the top student in the graduating class
10. **lithograph.** Type of art print
11. **apex.** Highest point, peak
12. **GI Bill.** U.S. government program to help veterans get higher education, home loans, and so forth, at the government's expense

SWEET POTATO PIE **173**

Reading Skills

Sequence of Events
Point out to students that the author uses a fluid sense of time in the story. No specific dates are mentioned; the reference to "the war" and the GI Bill place the piece any time after World War II. The first several paragraphs of the flashback section describe general events that happened many times during the narrator's life. Then, once the narrator establishes his age as about five when Pa tells him

he should go to school, the flashback continues sequentially. The author brings the reader full circle, ending the story back at the hotel where it began. Ask students how the use of memory shapes the theme.

Use Reading Strategies

Clarify Ask students to clarify the different reasons given by the narrator for his decision to drop in on Charley rather than call ahead. Model a response by indicating one reason: "One reason is that the narrator didn't want Charley and his family to 'stiffen up' or act unnaturally polite and formal." **A**

Analyze Literature

Setting Point out to students the details the narrator uses to describe his walk along Lenox Avenue. Ask what the narrator's comment that he "savored the panorama" reveals about his character. **B**

A company. No, I would drop in on them, take them by surprise before they had a chance to stiffen up. I was eager to see them—it had been so long. Yesterday and this morning were taken up with meetings in the posh Fifth Avenue hotel—a place we could not have dreamed in our boyhood. Late this afternoon I shook loose and headed for Harlem,[13] hoping that Charley still came home for a few hours before his evening run. Leaving the glare and glitter of downtown, I entered the subway that lurks like the dark, inscrutable *id*[14] beneath the surface of the city. When I emerged, I was in Harlem.

B Whenever I come to Harlem I feel somehow as if I were coming home—to some mythic ancestral home. The problems are real, the people are real—yet there is some mysterious epic quality about Harlem, as if all black people began and ended there, as if each had left something of himself. As if in Harlem the very heart of Blackness pulsed its beautiful, tortured rhythms. Joining the throngs of people that <u>saunter</u> Lenox Avenue late afternoons, I headed for Charley's apartment. Along the way I savored the panorama of Harlem—women with shopping bags trudging wearily home; little kids flitting saucily through the crowd; groups of adolescent boys striding boldly along—some boisterous, some ominously silent; tables of merchandise spread on the sidewalks with hawkers singing their siren songs of irresistible bargains; a blaring microphone sending forth waves of words to draw passersby into a restless bunch around a slender young man whose eyes have seen Truth; defeated men standing around on street corners or sitting on steps, heads down, hands idle; posters announcing

---

13. Harlem. New York City neighborhood, known as a center of African-American culture

14. id. In psychoanalysis, the part of the mind that is the source of instinctual impulses and primitive urges

saun•ter (sȯn´ tər) *v.*, walk in a leisurely way

Reading Proficiency

Some students may have difficulty following the flow of the story. Write a phrase to describe each topic at the top of a piece of paper; for example, *Payday for the Sharecroppers* and *Going to Church*. Have students write words or draw simple pictures to describe each event. Then arrange the papers in sequential order, and have students use them to retell the events in the story.

Garvey Day;[15] "Buy Black" stamped on [C] pavements; store windows bright with things African; stores still boarded up, a livid scar from last year's rioting. There was a terrible tension in the air; I thought of how quickly dry timber becomes a roaring fire from a single spark.

I mounted the steps of Charley's building—old and in need of paint, like all the rest—and pushed the button to his apartment. The graffiti on the dirty wall recorded the fantasies of past visitors. Some of it was even a dialogue of sorts. Someone had scrawled, "Call Lola" and a telephone number, followed by a catalog of Lola's friends. Someone else had written, "I called Lola and she is a Dog." Charley's buzzer rang. I pushed open the door and mounted the urine-scented stairs.

"Well, do Jesus—it's Buddy!" roared Charley as I arrived on the third floor. "Bea! Bea! Come here, girl, it's Buddy!" And somehow I was simultaneously shaking Charley's hand, getting clapped on the back, and being buried in the fervor of Bea's gigantic hug. They swept me from the hall into their dim apartment.

"Lord, Buddy, what you doing here? Whyn't you tell me you was coming to New York?" His face was so lit up with pleasure that in spite of the inroads of time, he still looked like the Charley of years gone by, excited over a new litter of kittens.

"The place look a mess! Whyn't you let us know?" put in Bea, suddenly distressed.

"Looks fine to me, girl. And so do you!"

And she did. Bea is a fine-looking woman, plump and firm still, with rich brown skin and thick black hair.

"Mary, Lucy, look, Uncle Buddy's here!" Two neat little girls came shyly from the TV. Uncle Buddy was something of a celebrity in this house. [E]

I hugged them heartily, much to their discomfort. "Charley, where you getting all these pretty women?"

We all sat in the warm kitchen, where Bea was preparing dinner. It felt good there. Beautiful odors mingled in the air. Charley sprawled in a chair near mine, his long arms and legs akimbo.[16] No longer shy, the tinier girl sat on my lap, while her sister darted here and there like a merry little water bug. Bea bustled about, managing to keep up with both the conversation and the cooking.

[D] I told them about the conference I was attending, and, knowing it would give them pleasure, I mentioned that I had addressed the group that morning. Charley's eyes glistened.

"You hear that, Bea?" he whispered. "Buddy done spoke in front of all them professors!" [F]

"Sure I hear," Bea answered briskly, stirring something that was making an aromatic steam. "I bet he weren't even scared. I bet them professors learnt something, too."

We all chuckled. "Well anyway," I said, "I hope they did."

We talked about a hundred different things after that—Bea's job in the school cafeteria, my Jess and the kids, our scattered family.

"Seem like we don't git together no more, not since Mama and Pa passed on," said Charley sadly. "I ain't even got a Christmas card from Alberta for three-four year now."

"Well, ain't no two a y'all in the same city. An' everybody scratchin' to make ends meet," Bea replied. "Ain't nobody got time to git together." [G]

"Yeah, that's the way it goes, I guess," I said.

---

15. **Garvey Day.** Annual celebration of the birthday (August 17) of Marcus Garvey (1887–1940), a black leader for racial equality
16. **akimbo.** Bowed outward

Speaking & Listening Skills

Dialogue
Have small groups of students work together on dialogues drawn from the story. Each member of the group takes a different character. Suggest that students first read their character's lines of dialogue aloud to get a feel for the language and dialect. Students should use learning strategies, such as requesting assistance from you or their peers, to decipher any words or phrases that are not familiar to them. Groups may wish to tape-record themselves performing their dialogues.

Soul Food The meal the narrator describes is traditional soul food. African slaves found foods in America that were similar to the ones they ate in Africa, such as collard greens and sweet potatoes. They often made a quick bread from their allowance of corn meal. The use of these foods continued well after slavery. During the Civil Rights movement in the 1960s, the word "soul" was often used to refer to anything to do with African Americans. The term "soul food" was used to describe traditional African-American foods, including watermelon, sweet potatoes, ham hocks, and corn bread. **Ⓐ**

Use Reading Strategies

Make Inferences Ask students why they think Charley would have been embarrassed to discuss the incident further with Buddy. **Ⓑ**

Analyze Literature

Setting Remind students that setting can also be revealed by how characters talk and behave. Ask them how the author uses cultural details to develop the setting. Model a response by indicating some cultural details such as the contrast in the way Charley and Buddy speak and the traditional Southern dinner that Bea serves.

"But it sure is good to see you, Buddy. Say, look, Lil told me bout the cash you sent the children last winter when Jake was out of work all that time. She sure 'preciated it."

"Lord, man, as close as you and Lil stuck to me when I was a kid, I owed her that and more. Say, Bea, did I ever tell you about the time—" and we swung into the usual reminiscences.

They insisted that I stay for dinner. **Ⓐ** Persuading me was no hard job: fish fried golden, ham hocks and collard greens, corn bread— if I'd *tried* to leave, my feet wouldn't have taken me. It was good to sit there in Charley's kitchen, my coat and tie flung over a chair, surrounded by soul food and love.

"Say, Buddy, a couple months back I picked up a kid from your school."

"No stuff."

"I axed him did he know you. He say he was in your class last year."

"Did you get his name?"

"No, I didn't ax him that. Man he told me you were the best teacher he had. He said you were one smart cat!"

"He told you that cause you're my brother."

"Your *brother*—I didn't tell him I was your brother. I said you was a old friend of mine."

I put my fork down and leaned over. "What you tell him *that* for?"

Charley explained patiently as he had explained things when I was a child and had missed an obvious truth. "I didn't want your students to know your brother wasn't nothing but a cab driver. You *somebody*."

"You're a nut," I said gently. "You should've told that kid the truth." I wanted to

> "Man he told me you were the best teacher he had. He said you were one smart cat!"

Ⓑ say, I'm proud of you, you've got more on the ball than most people I know, I wouldn't have been anything at all except for you. But he would have been embarrassed.

Bea brought in the dessert—home made sweet potato pie! "Buddy, I must of knew you were coming! I just had a mind I wanted to make sweet potato pie."

There's nothing in this world I like better than Bea's sweet potato pie! "Lord, girl, how you expect me to eat all that?"

The slice she put before me was outrageously big— and moist and covered with a light, golden crust—I ate it all.

"Bea, I'm gonna have to eat and run," I said at last.

Charley guffawed.[17]

"Much as you et, I don't see how you gonna *walk*, let alone *run*." He went out to get his cab from the garage several blocks away.

Bea was washing the tiny girl's face. "Wait a minute, Buddy, I'm gon give you the rest of that pie to take with you."

"Great!" I'd eaten all I could hold, but my *spirit* was still hungry for sweet potato pie.

Bea got out some waxed paper and wrapped up the rest of the pie. "That'll do you for a snack tonight." She slipped it into a brown paper bag.

I gave her a long goodbye hug. "Bea, I love you for a lot of things. Your cooking is one of them!" We had a last comfortable laugh together. I kissed the little girls and went outside to wait for Charley, holding the bag of pie reverently.

In a minute Charley's ancient cab limped to the curb. I plopped into the seat next to him, and we headed downtown. Soon we

---

17. guffawed. Laughed heartily

Differentiated Instruction

Kinesthetic Learning

Have volunteers create a pantomime based on one of the key scenes of the story (such as counting out the money from the crop). Remind them that pantomime is telling a story with gestures and movements.

English Language Learning

You might ask students who have come from other countries to describe traditional foods that their families enjoy. If these foods are associated with special occasions, such as national holidays or religious or cultural observances, have them describe these events.

were assailed by the garish[18] lights of New York on a sultry spring night. We chatted as Charley skillfully managed the heavy traffic. I looked at his long hands on the wheel and wondered what they could have done with artists' brushes.

We stopped a bit down the street from my hotel. I invited him in, but he said he had to get on with his evening run. But as I opened the door to get out, he commanded in the old familiar voice, "Buddy, you wait!"

For a moment I thought my coat was torn or something. "What's wrong?"

"What's that you got there?"

I was bewildered. "That? You mean this bag? That's a piece of sweet potato pie Bea fixed for me."

"You ain't going through the lobby of no big hotel carrying no brown paper bag."

"Man, you *crazy!* Of course I'm going— Look, Bea fixed it for me—*That's my pie*—"

Charley's eyes were miserable. "Folks in that hotel don't go through the lobby carrying no brown paper bags. That's *country*. And you can't neither. You *somebody*, Buddy. You got to be *right*. Now gimme that bag."

"I want that pie, Charley. I've got nothing to prove to anybody—"

I couldn't believe it. But there was no point in arguing. Foolish as it seemed to me, it was important to him.

"You got to look *right*, Buddy. Can't nobody look dignified carrying a brown paper bag."

So finally, thinking how tasty it would have been and how seldom I got a chance to eat anything that good, I handed over my bag of sweet potato pie. If it was that important to him— **E**

I tried not to show my irritation. "Okay, man—take care now." I slammed the door harder than I had intended, walked rapidly to the hotel, and entered the brilliant, crowded lobby.

"That Charley!" I thought. Walking slower now, I crossed the carpeted lobby toward the elevator, still thinking of my lost snack. I had to admit that of all the herd of people who jostled each other in the lobby, not one was carrying a brown paper bag. Or anything but expensive attaché cases or slick packages from exclusive shops. I suppose we all operate according to the symbols that are meaningful to us, and to Charley a brown paper bag symbolizes the humble life he thought I had left. I was *somebody*.

D I don't know what made me glance back, but I did. And suddenly the tears of laughter, toil, and love of a lifetime burst around me like fireworks in a night sky.

For there, following a few steps behind, came Charley, proudly carrying a brown paper bag full of sweet potato pie. ✤

18. **garish.** Brightly colored or excessive

What is one of your favorite foods that your family shares? What purpose does food have in the lives of families and communities?

Find Meaning

1. (a) Buddy is a professor.
(b) Charley feels that Buddy's work makes him an important person.
2. Buddy does not want to be "company." He wants to be family.
3. (a) Bea is Buddy's sister-in-law.
(b) Bea is warm and loving toward Buddy. She is like a mother to him.

Make Judgments

4. (a) Buddy grew up in extreme poverty. His family were sharecroppers, which kept his parents busy most of the time working. He was raised largely by his oldest brother, Charley. (b) Knowing something about Buddy's childhood helps us understand his relationship with Charley.
5. They would probably agree that education and opportunity are important. However, they might disagree about whether Charley is *a somebody.*
6. Sweet potato pie is soul food, family food, and suggests the sweet comfort of nourishment, family love, and belonging.

Analyze Literature

Characterization *Possible answers:*
Physical Appearance: long, lean, gentle-eyed; hands of an artist
Habits/Mannerisms/Behaviors: helped Buddy dress for his valedictory speech
Relationships with Others: "somehow the protector of them all"
Direct Characterization: Charlie is paternal, sacrificing, and protective.

Find Meaning

1. (a) What does Buddy do as a career? (b) How does Charley feel about Buddy's work?
2. Why did Buddy drop in on Charley rather than letting him know in advance that he would be coming?
3. (a) What is Bea's relationship to Buddy? (b) How would you describe that relationship?

Analyze Literature

Characterization A character is a person (or sometimes an animal) who figures in the action of a literary work. Scan "Sweet Potato Pie" for examples of Buddy's characterization of Charley. Complete a character chart for Charley. Then, in one sentence, give a direct characterization of Charley.

Make Judgments

4. (a) How would you describe Buddy's childhood? (b) Why do you think his childhood was included in this story?
5. How might Buddy's and Charley's ideas about "being somebody" be the same and different?
6. Why do you think the author chose the title "Sweet Potato Pie"?

Character	Physical Appearance	Habits/ Mannerisms/ Behaviors	Relationships with Others
Charlie	long, lean, gentle—eyed; hands of an artist		

Extend Understanding

Writing Options

Creative Writing Suppose that Buddy called Charley from his hotel—after his visit to Harlem and before leaving New York City. Write a **dialogue** in which Buddy thanks Charley for the visit. Let the conversation begin with the visit, and then decide what else these two brothers might want to talk about. Decide whether they would talk openly about the nature of their relationship. Try to capture Collier's characterizations of Buddy and Charley in your dialogue.

Expository Writing Discuss the use of first-person point of view in "Sweet Potato Pie" in a **literary response paragraph.** State your main idea in your thesis, and use quotes from the text to show how the point of view contributes to the story. Write the same examples in third-person point of view and explain to a sixth grade reader, in each case, how first-person point of view is more effective.

Collaborative Learning

Small Group Discussion Reread the final paragraphs of "Sweet Potato Pie." Discuss the following questions: Why doesn't Charley want Buddy to take the pie? How is it consistent with Collier's characterization of Buddy that he gives in to Charley? How is Charley carrying in the pie an example of indirect characterization? Why does the sight of Charley carrying sweet potato pie make Buddy cry? After you discuss these questions with your group, discuss them as a class.

Media Literacy

Conduct a Literature Review In this story, Charley has settled in Harlem, the "mythic ancestral home." Suppose you are preparing to write a report about the history of Harlem. Your first step is to find out what books have been written on this subject. Use a library database to create your list. Note book titles and authors.

Go to **www.mirrorsandwindows.com** for more.

To help students explore literature on a deeper level, assign the following activity: Independent Novel Study: Character Development, *Exceeding the Standards: Literature & Reading*, pp. 6–8.

Rubrics for Writing Options

You can adapt this as a checklist for students to use as they write.

Creative Writing

☐ Is the writing a dialogue between Buddy and Charley?
☐ Does the writer make a decision about whether Buddy and Charley would openly discuss the nature of their relationship?

☐ Does the writer capture Collier's characterizations of Buddy and Charley?

Expository Writing

☐ Does the literary response use examples from the text?
☐ Does the writer give effective examples of third-person point of view?
☐ Does the writer create a paragraph appropriate for a sixth-grade audience?

Vocabulary & Spelling

Denotation and Connotation

Bea is a fine-looking woman, plump and firm still, with rich brown skin and thick black hair.

—EUGENIA COLLIER, "Sweet Potato Pie"

In the passage above, the narrator describes his sister-in-law as *plump*. In addition to its dictionary meanings, *plump* also has emotional associations.

Every word has a **denotation,** or dictionary definition. In the passage above, *plump* denotes "having a full and rounded form." *Plump* also has **connotations,** or emotional associations, suggesting a pleasing appearance.

> EXAMPLES
>
> *portly*
>
> *obese*
>
> *chubby*
>
> *stout*

In this example, each word shares the denotation of "fat," but each also connotes a different quality of fatness. You might think of these words as **synonyms,** or words that have basically the same meaning. However, these are **near-synonyms,** words that have somewhat different meanings. *Portly,* for example, means "heavy and dignified"; *obese* means "dangerously overweight."

> EXAMPLES
>
> *delicate / frail*
>
> *thin / gaunt*

In these examples, each pair of words denotes the same meaning. However, one has positive connotations, and the other negative connotations. *Delicate* and *thin* are positive, whereas *frail* and *gaunt* are negative.

Vocabulary Practice

For each of the following words from "Sweet Potato Pie," choose a word with a more positive connotation. Use a dictionary or thesaurus if you need to.

1. garish	**5.** insist
2. shanty	**6.** stutter
3. boisterous	**7.** gaunt
4. sentimental	**8.** nosy

Identify the denotation of each of the following words from "Sweet Potato Pie." Then note whether each word has a positive, neutral, or negative connotation.

9. frigid	**13.** feverishly
10. superstition	**14.** skinny
11. slender	**15.** posh
12. chuckled	**16.** guffawed

Spelling Practice

Commonly Misspelled Words

The following words from "Sweet Potato Pie" present a challenge to spellers. Study the list and see if you can figure out a spelling rule to help you remember how to spell each word. Also look up the syllabications of the words in a dictionary to help you break them into smaller parts that are easier to spell.

adolescent	necessarily
ancient	occasion
anxiously	outrageously
beautiful	patiently
commencement	reminiscences
desperate	simultaneously
embarrassed	ubiquitous
irresistible	

Vocabulary Practice

1. garish — vivid
2. shanty — cottage
3. boisterous — lively
4. sentimental — warm-hearted
5. insist — encourage
6. stutter — falter
7. gaunt — slender
8. nosy — inquisitive
9. frigid — negative
10. superstition — negative
11. slender — positive
12. chuckled — positive
13. feverishly — negative
14. skinny — negative
15. posh — positive
16. guffawed — negative

> For more information, see Vocabulary & Spelling Section 2.6, Understanding Denotation and Connotation, in the Language Arts Handbook.

Program Resources

You will find additional lessons on Denotation and Connotation in the *Exceeding the Standards: Vocabulary & Spelling* resource.

KEY TERMS

DENOTATION, 179
CONNOTATION, 179
SYNONYM, 179
NEAR-SYNONYM, 179

TEACHING NOTE

Extra Practice

The three words in each of these sets are near synonyms. Write each set, scrambled, on the board, and then have students put the words in each set in the order shown, from negative connotation to neutral connotation to positive connotation.

1. penny-pinching, economical, frugal
2. stiff, rigid, firm
3. rash, daring, intrepid
4. frail, fragile, delicate

Common Core State Standards

Reading Informational
RI.4

Language
L.5

Preview the Selection

At a Glance
Directed Reading
- Reading Level: Challenging
- Difficulty Consideration: Theme
- Ease Factor: Length

Preview the Selection

At a Glance
Directed Reading
- Reading Level: Challenging
- Difficulty Consideration: Theme
- Ease Factor: Length

DIRECTED READING

Objectives
Studying this lesson will enable students to
- use reading strategies such as connecting to prior knowledge
- define *point of view* and recognize the effect of this literary technique in the selection
- describe the literary accomplishments of Toshio Mori and the influence of Japanese and Japanese-American culture on his writing
- appreciate a story about conflict within a family

Launch the Lesson
Prior to reading "Miss Butterfly," ask students to share personal accounts of times that they have been requested by other family members to do things, and how they handled the requests. They may also enjoy sharing accounts of times they performed traditional dances or other traditional rituals.

BEFORE READING

Build Background
Historical Context Toshio Mori wrote "Miss Butterfly" around 1940 as part of his short story collection *Yokohama, California*. Yokohama is a large port city in Japan. In the years before World War II, Yokohama was Japan's most international city and had long been heavily influenced by Western culture and technology.

Reader's Context Do you ever feel as if fitting in with your family and fitting in with your friends is pulling you in two different directions? What kinds of situations bring about this feeling? What might you do?

Set Purpose
Skim the first few paragraphs of "Miss Butterfly." As you skim, preview the footnotes to help you clarify unfamiliar vocabulary. Revise your predictions as the plot of "Miss Butterfly" unfolds.

Analyze Literature
Point of View The perspective from which a story is told is **point of view.** "Miss Butterfly" is told from a *third-person point of view*. The narrator is outside the action and identifies characters with pronouns such as *he, she,* and *they*. As you read "Miss Butterfly," think how the story would have been different if it had been told in first-person by Sachi or Hamada-*san*.

Meet the Author
Toshio Mori (1910–1980) was born in Oakland, California. He was a *Nisei* ("second generation"), an American-born child of Japanese immigrants to the United States. Publication of his short story collection *Yokohama, California* was postponed when the United States entered World War II, due to hostility toward Japanese Americans. Mori, along with another 110,000 Japanese-American citizens, was relocated to an internment camp from 1941 to 1944. It was 1949 before his first book was finally published.

Use Reading Skills
Activate Prior Knowledge Prior knowledge is what you already know or have experienced before reading something. "Miss Butterfly" deals with a conflict between older and younger generations of Japanese Americans about loyalty to traditional Japanese culture versus the lure of American culture. Before you read the story, jot down what have read or experienced about such cultural conflicts involving newcomers to the United States.

What I Know
- My immigrant grandparents often said they missed the traditional culture of their Czech homeland.

Preview Vocabulary
nim・bly (nim´ blē) *adv.,* quickly and carefully

ki・mo・no (kə mō´ nō) *n.,* long-sleeve robe traditionally worn by Japanese women

plain・tive (plān´ tiv) *adj.,* sounding slightly sad

em・phat・i・cal・ly (im fa´ tik [ə] lē) *adv.,* done or said in a strong way

sym・met・ric・al (sə me´ tri kəl) *adj.,* evenly balanced

flaunt (flont) *v.,* display something boldly

ad・mir・a・tion (ad´ mə rā´ shun) *n.,* feeling of approval or deep respect

Common Core State Standards

Reading Literature
RL.1

Writing
W.7, W.9

Language
L.6

Words in Use

Preview Vocabulary
nimbly, 182
kimono, 183
plaintive, 183
emphatically, 183
symmetrical, 184
flaunt, 184
admiration, 184

Selection Words
humbly, 183
somber, 185
unheeding, 185

Teaching Words
internment, 180
elaborate, 183
marital, 183

KEY TERMS
POINT OF VIEW, 180
THIRD-PERSON POINT OF VIEW, 180
PRIOR KNOWLEDGE, 180
LIMITED NARRATOR, 187
OMNISCIENT NARRATOR, 187
SUMMARY, 187

Miss Butterfly

A Short Story by Toshio Mori

"Please, Sachi-chan. Please, this is my special request."

181

Teach the Selection

Summary

Sachi and Yuki, two Japanese-American girls, are on their way to a school dance. An elderly Japanese-American friend, Hamada-*san*, comes to the house and asks the girls to wear their kimonos and perform a traditional dance for him. At first Sachi refuses but then agrees. She and Yuki perform two dances. Hamada-*san* is initially pleased with the performances but then seems very sad. The girls leave for the dance. Hamada-*san* remains in the house, listening to the clock ticking.

 **MIRRORS & WINDOWS** The Mirrors & Windows questions at the end of this selection focus on the theme of acclimation. Before reading the story, pose the idea of students' families having to move to a different country. Would they try to fit in? Does age have anything to do with people's ability to acclimate to new situations?

Art Connection

This geisha performs at a festival in the Japanese city of Kyoto.

Art Activity Discuss with students the Japanese cultural ideals of beauty and femininity that are reflected in the appearance of the geisha.

Program Resources

Planning and Assessment
Program Planning Guide, Selection Lesson Plan
E-Lesson Planner
Assessment Guide, Lesson Test
ExamView

Technology Tools
Interactive Student Text on CD
Visual Teaching Package
Audio Library
mirrorsandwindows.com

Meeting the Standards
Fiction: Unit 2, Directed Reading, pp. 38–44

Differentiating Instruction
Advanced Students, Cultural Connection
Project, pp. 10–11

Use Reading Skills

Activate Prior Knowledge Ask students share something they know about Japanese immigrants to America or about the Japanese culture. Model a response by indicating one fact: "Japanese immigrants began coming to the United States over one hundred years ago."

Analyze Literature

Point of View Remind students that the point of view is the perspective from which a story is told. Point out that "Miss Butterfly" is told from the third-person omniscient point of view, where the narrator describes the thoughts and feelings of many of the characters. Have students find words, such as *she,* that indicate third-person point of view.

Use Reading Strategies

Ask Questions Remind students that asking questions as they read will help them keep track of characters and events and make predictions about the story. Model asking a question: "What is the relationship between Hamada-*san* and Sachi's family?" **Ⓐ**

The doorbell rang and Sachi ran <u>nimbly</u> to the door. "Yuki!" she called to her younger sister. "I think they're here!"

"I'll be out in a moment," Yuki answered from the bedroom.

Sachi opened the door and found an old man standing on the porch. "Oh hello, Hamada-*san*,"[1] she said, her face plainly revealing disappointment.

"Good evening, Sachi-*chan*,"[2] greeted Hamada-*san*, entering the hall. "Is your father home?"

Sachi looked up and down the street and then closed the door. "Yes. Hamada-*san*. He's in the living room. Go right in."

The old man looked admiringly at her, pausing for a word with her. "My, you are growing prettier every day. Is Yuki-*chan* home too?"

She smiled and nodded. "We're going to the dance tonight with our boy friends," she added eagerly.

Hamada-*san*'s face fell but brightened quickly. "Do you still have those Japanese records—the festival music, I mean?"

"Yes," Sachi replied, looking puzzled. "We still have them."

"And is your phonograph in good condition?" he asked.

She nodded impatiently, anxious to return to her dressing.

"Good!" cried the old man, clapping his **Ⓐ** hand. "Please come into the living room. I wish to have a talk with you and your father."

"But I will be late for the dance!" she protested. "I must dress now."

Hamada-*san* looked pleadingly at her. "Please, Sachi-*chan*. Please, this is my special request."

The old man led her into the living room where her father sat reading the Japanese daily. "Saiki-*san*, how are you?"

Saiki-*san* dropped his paper and took off his glasses. "Good evening, Hamada-*san*. Anything new?"

---

1. **-san.** In Japanese, used at the end of a name to show respect
2. **-chan.** In Japanese, used to address familiar children

nim·bly (nim´ blē) *adv.,* quickly and carefully

Differentiated Instruction

English Language Learning

You might ask students who have come from other countries to describe traditional costumes or dances that serve as expressions of their heritage.

Reading Proficiency

Students may have trouble understanding the portion of the story describing the traditional dances. Have them reread this section to grasp all the details.

Hamada-*san* dropped into the easy chair, leaning forward eagerly. "Saiki-*san*, I have one special request to make of your daughters tonight. It will bring me much happiness, and I shall forget that I am a lonely man for a short while. Please ask Sachi-*chan* and Yuki-*chan* to do it for an old man's sake."

"What is it you want?" asked Saiki-*san*.

"You may recall my repeated request in the past. I want to see the cherry blossom, the *taiko*[3] bridge, and hear the Japanese paper houses hum when the wind blows. I want

CULTURAL ▶▶ CONNECTION

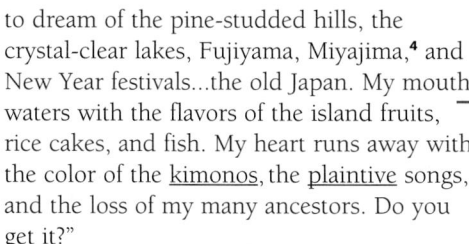

Japanese Kimonos The kimono is a traditional garment of Japan, worn by both men and women. Women's kimonos are usually more elaborate and beautiful. There are many styles of kimono for various occasions, from formal to casual. The choice of which type of kimono to wear is related to a woman's age, marital status, and the level of formality of the occasion. Young women's kimonos have longer sleeves and tend to be more detailed than older women's kimonos. Describe how Hamada-*san* and Sachi-*chan* feel differently about kimonos. **E**

to dream of the pine-studded hills, the crystal-clear lakes, Fujiyama, Miyajima,[4] and New Year festivals...the old Japan. My mouth waters with the flavors of the island fruits, rice cakes, and fish. My heart runs away with the color of the <u>kimonos</u>, the <u>plaintive</u> songs, and the loss of my many ancestors. Do you get it?"

Sachi groaned and waved her hands protestingly.

"So you wish them to perform Japanese folk dances," Saiki-*san* said, smilingly.

Hamada-*san* beamed and eagerly added, "Odori[5]—that's what I mean. Please, Sachi-*chan*, wear your beautiful kimono tonight and perform one dance for me. Just one, that is all I ask. I want to capture my lost memories and dream. Dance for an old man and let him enter his old world for several minutes." **C**

"No, I won't," she said <u>emphatically</u>," standing impatiently by the door. "I won't."

"Daughter, what are you saying?" Saiki-*san* said. "Make Hamada-*san* happy tonight. Wear your kimono and dance."

"One dance, Sachi-*chan*," begged the old man, humbly bowing. "For your father's old friend. He is poor and cannot reward you. Otherwise, he would shower you with gifts."

"I don't want anything," said Sachi, and looking at her father added, "I hate to wear kimono." **D**

Hamada-*san* looked horrified. "Ah, Sachi-*chan*!" he cried. "Please do not say that. Don't you Nisei[6] girls realize the truth? When you wear your bright, colorful kimono you are the most beautiful women in the world. Your eyes brighten up, your figure becomes

---

3. **taiko.** Japanese drum
4. **Fujiyama, Miyajima.** Fujiyama is a dormant volcano, the highest mountain in Japan; Miyajima is a Japanese island, the site of a famous shrine.
5. **Odori.** Japanese folk dance
6. **Nisei.** Someone born and raised in the United States whose parents emigrated from Japan

> **ki•mo•no** (kə mōʹ nō) *n.*, long-sleeve robe traditionally worn by Japanese women
>
> **plain•tive** (plānʹ tiv) *adj.*, sounding slightly sad
>
> **em•phat•i•cal•ly** (im faʹ tik [ə] lē) *adv.*, done or said in a strong way

---

Teach the Selection

Geography Connection
Mount Fuji You may want to mention to students that Fujiyama, also known as Mount Fuji, is the tallest mountain in Japan as well as an active volcano. The name Fuji is thought to have come from the ancient Ainu word for "deity of fire." The Buddhist and Shinto religions of Japan believe the mountain is sacred. Pilgrims regularly climb Fujiyama and worship at altars and shrines along the way. **B**

Analyze Literature
Conflict Have students identify the conflict in the story. Ask them to predict how the conflict might be resolved. **C**

Analyze Literature
Characterization Discuss what Sachi's admission about wearing her kimono tells about her. **D**

Cultural Connection
Japanese Kimonos *Answer:* Hamada-*san* loves the color of the kimonos. He says when the girls wear them they are the most beautiful women in the world. Hamada-*san* believes the kimono makes a woman's figure look symmetrical and helps her move more naturally. Sachi-*chan* does not like wearing the kimono. She says it takes a long time to put on and makes her feel clumsy and stiff. **E**

Reading Skills

Use Graphic Organizers
Point out to students that using a KWL chart is an effective way to help them connect their prior knowledge to information they learn in the selection. Suggest they create a KWL chart for the information in "Miss Butterfly." On a separate sheet of paper, have them draw a three-column chart like this one. Have them use the left column for facts they already know, the center column for information they want to find out, and the right column for what they learned. Complete the first two columns before reading and the third column after reading the selection.

K	W	L
Dance is a Japanese tradition.	What types of traditional dance are most popular?	

Explain to students that the Japanese-Americans use three terms to differentiate the generations who immigrated to other countries. Issei were the first-generation immigrants. The Nisei were the second generation, and embraced both Japanese and American culture. The Sansei are the U.S.-born grandchildren of the Issei.

Use Reading Strategies
Visualize Remind students to visualize the scenes and actions as they read. Have them reread Hamada-*san's* description of the day in autumn and tell what they see, hear, smell, and how things might feel. **Ⓐ**

TEACHING NOTE

Long and Short Vowels

Help students learn to pronounce the new vocabulary in this selection by reviewing the concept of long and short vowels. Provide them with examples of both types of vowels (short: *tap, pin, bet*; long: *tape, pine, beet*), and then have them identify the long and short vowels in the following vocabulary words from the selection. Students should copy the words into their notebooks and label each vowel with an *L* or an *S*. They should then practice pronouncing each word.

1. phonograph
2. capture
3. humbly
4. deliberation
5. indicating
6. parasols

symmetrical, your gestures move naturally. Don't you see, Sachi-*chan?*"

Sachi stood speechless, hesitating whether to laugh or smile.

"Sachi, why don't you like to wear kimono?" her father asked.

"It takes so much time, and I feel clumsy and stiff," she replied.

Hamada-*san* smiled and shook his head. "You don't look it when you wear it. You are merely saving that for an excuse. I don't believe it."

She looked at her watch and cried, "I've lost five minutes already."

"What time does the dance begin?" Saiki-*san* asked her.

"At eight sharp," Sachi answered eagerly. "Papa, may I go now?"

"Saiki-*san!* Please remember your old-time friend," cried Hamada-*san.*

From the bedroom came the younger sister in her glittering white evening gown. "I heard what you said about Nisei girls, Hamada-*san*," Yuki said, smiling. "Sachi, let's do one odori for him. It won't take but ten minutes, dressing and all, and it'll make him happy. I have your gown and the rest of your things out, all ready for you to slip them on."

Sachi thought for a moment. "All right. I'll do it," she said suddenly. "Papa, please select the record and be ready when we come out."

"I'll do that," Hamada-*san* said, beaming. "Saiki-*san*, just sit and relax."

Eagerly he began sorting out the record albums. The girls rushed into the bedroom. After much deliberation the old man selected two records and went to the phonograph.

"This is my favorite," Hamada-*san* said to

> "Sachi-chan, Yuki-chan, one more!
> The parasol dance! Please, just one more. Please!"

his friend, holding up one record. "This is about a day in autumn in Japan. The wind blows and the leaves fall. The sky is clear and the air is beginning to cool. The chants of the insects are dying out and late harvest is about over. The flowers shrivel and the last of the leaves flaunt their brilliant colors in the wind, and the day awaits the icy blast of winter."

The girls' father sat silently, lit his pipe, and blew smoke. He watched his old friend poring over the words of another record and wished he had some kind of an answer for him.

"It's a beautiful piece," Hamada-*san* informed, indicating the first record. "Especially when dancers perform skillfully as Sachi-*chan* and Yuki-*chan*."

The two girls hurriedly skipped into the room. They wore their best kimono, a colorful design on silk, enhancing their youthful beauty.

"Are you ready with the music, Hamada-*san*?" asked Yuki. "We're all set."

At that sight of the girls in kimono Hamada-*san* sat up, his eyes wide with open admiration. "Beautiful, beautiful! The whole world should see you now."

Sachi laughed it off, and Yuki smiled happily. They went over to the phonograph and inspected the record. Satisfied with the selection they rushed Hamada-*san* to a seat.

"Sit down and enjoy yourself," Sachi said. "We'll watch the record. Hamada-*san*, there will be positively one performance tonight."

"Two?" the old man asked timidly.

> **sym·met·ric·al** (sə me´ tri kəl) *adj.*, evenly balanced
> **flaunt** (flont) *v.*, display something boldly
> **ad·mir·a·tion** (ad´ mə rā´ shun) *n.*, feeling of approval or deep respect

Vocabulary Skills

Foreign Words in English

Point out to students that many foreign words have entered the English language. "Miss Butterfly" includes the Japanese word *kimono*, which defines a traditional floor-length Japanese robe with wide sleeves that wraps in the front. Have students use dictionaries to identify the meanings of following Japanese words.

1. samurai (a member of the Japanese aristocratic warrior class)
2. sushi (rice topped or rolled with raw seafood)
3. tofu (soybean curd)
4. tsunami (a massive wave caused by a seaquake or underwater volcanic activity)
5. bonsai (a dwarfed tree or shrub shaped by pruning)

"Positively one," Sachi repeated.

The music began, and the girls waited alertly for their cue. Hamada-*san* poked Saiki-*san* in the ribs as the two girls performed. He clapped his hands, keeping time with the music. His eyes, round with excitement, twinkled. His body swayed this way and that way. Then he forgot his friend, the time and place. Long after the music stopped and the girls paused by the phonograph, Hamada-*san* sat fixedly.

"Good night, Hamada-*san*," called the girls at the door.

"Wait!" cried Hamada-*san* springing to his feet. "Sachi-*chan*, Yuki-*chan*, one more! The parasol[7] dance! Please, just one more. Please!"

The girls looked at each other, hesitating. Hamada-*san* ran to the phonograph and started the record going. "Hurry, girls. Get your parasols!" he cried.

The high notes of a *samisen*[8] and the mixed instruments cut the air. The girls ran to get their parasols. Hamada-*san* beamed and clapped his hands in tune with the music. Saiki-*san* sat comfortably in his chair, his eyes closed, and sucked his pipe.

The girls returned and instantly snapped into the dance. Their parasols opened and twirling, they leaped over imaginary puddles and worried about their slippers. They looked up at the sky, their hands out to see if the rain was falling. Their faces bright with smiles they twirled their parasols with happy abandonment.[9] The sun is out once again, and they forget the puddles, the mud, and discomfort. Their bodies, minds, and hearts join to greet the sunny day, their somber aliveness increasing to gay abandon.

Once more Hamada-*san* sat motionlessly, unheeding the end of the music and the dance. Sachi stopped the phonograph.

---

7. **parasol.** Light umbrella used to shade the sun
8. *samisen.* A Japanese stringed instrument with a long neck
9. **abandonment.** Without restraint or moderation

MISS BUTTERFLY **185**

Analyze Literature

Conflict The conflict is resolved to Hamada-*san's* satisfaction. Discuss with students if their predictions were correct and if they were satisfied with the resolution. Model a response: "My prediction was correct. I liked the resolution, because the girls showed their respect for Hamada-*san* by granting his wish, and they were still able to get ready for the dance on time." **Ⓐ**

Analyze Literature

Theme Remind students that the theme is the overall message of the story. When they understand the theme, they can also understand what the author thinks or feels about a topic. Model thinking about the theme: "Hamada-*san*, who was born in Japan, is homesick for his first country and culture. Sachi, who was born in the United States, is more attached to U.S. culture and customs. It is sometimes difficult for different generations to understand one another's feelings about their shared heritage."

Answer: Students might talk about places they like to visit, such as camping or holiday locations, friends they would miss, favorite foods, music, celebrations, and other elements of American culture.

"Wonderful! Wonderful!" cried **Ⓐ** Hamada-*san*, becoming alive. "I shall never forget this performance."

"Yuki, how much time have we?" asked Sachi hurriedly.

"Exactly ten minutes," Yuki said. "Let's hurry."

The girls dashed into their room.

"Wasn't it wonderful, Saiki-*san*? Wasn't it?" asked Hamada-*san*.

"Yes, they were pretty good," replied Saiki-*san*.

When the girls returned to the room their father was reading the paper. Hamada-*san* sat silently by himself in the corner, his eyes staring in the distance.

"How do we look, Papa?" Sachi asked, the two girls showing off their evening gowns.

"Swell," Saiki-*san* said, looking up.

"What do you think of them, Hamada-*san*?" Yuki asked the old man. "Hamada-*san*!"

"Please don't ask me such a question, Yuki-*chan*. Not tonight," Hamada-*san* said sadly.

Sachi looked puzzled. "What's happened to you, Hamada-*san*? Are you ill?"

"Nothing is the matter with me. I'm all right," he said, cheering up with an effort. Then he added, "Sachi-*chan* and Yuki-*chan*, please be careful with your kimono. Don't let the moths get into them."

"We'll be very careful with them," Sachi promised.

"And don't you forget the odori. Keep brushing up."

The girls nodded obediently. Outside a horn blared.

"Oh, they're here!" cried Sachi, running to the window.

"Isn't it exciting?" Yuki cried, moving to her sister's side. "We're going to have a good band tonight."

The girls waved their hands, and the horn tooted again. "Good night, Hamada-*san*. Good night, Papa," they said.

"What is this dance? What kind?" the old man asked his friend, watching the girls skip out of the house.

"A social dance. Popular American pastime," answered Saiki-*san*, without looking up from his paper.

In the living room Saiki-*san* smoked incessantly and the place became stuffy. He continued to read the paper. Hamada-*san* sat mutely in the corner, his eyes smarting with smoke. He could have gone outside for a bit of fresh air but did not move. His eyes took in the phonograph, the record albums, the spots where the girls danced, and the room that was now empty. In the silence he heard the clock in the hall ticking. ❖

MIRRORS & WINDOWS

How would you feel if your family had to move to another country? What are some difficulties you might face? Why might people of different generations respond differently when adjusting to a new culture?

Differentiated Instruction

Kinesthetic Learning

Have volunteers enact one of the scenes in the story. The performers should choose the scene, then everyone in the class should reread it to review the words, gestures, emotions, and expressions involved. After the performers enact the scene, discuss as a class if they incorporated the main verbal and nonverbal components from that scene.

English Language Learners

Since much of the story is told through dialogue, English language learners might benefit from reading the selection aloud. Assign parts and have students use sticky notes or some other means to highlight their lines. Have students read the selection aloud, reminding them to adjust their fluency if they encounter difficult or unfamiliar language.

Find Meaning

1. (a) What are Sachi and Yuki excited about at the beginning of "Miss Butterfly"? (b) Why do you think the author chose these plans for the girls?

2. (a) What does Sachi say about kimonos? (b) Why does Hamada-*san* react with horror?

3. (a) How does Hamada-*san* react to the girls' performances of the festival dances? (b) What does this reveal about his values?

Make Judgments

4. (a) What is the attitude of the sisters Yuki and Sachi toward American and Japanese culture? (b) What is Hamada-*san's* attitude?

5. (a) What does Hamada-*san* seem to be suffering from? (b) What advice would you give him?

6. Why do you think "Miss Butterfly" ends with a ticking clock?

Analyze Literature

Point of View The third-person point of view can be limited or omniscient ("all-knowing"). A third-person limited narrator can enter the thoughts of only one character. Readers see the other characters in the story only from the outside.

A third-person omniscient narrator can enter the thoughts of any character in the story. What kind of third-person narrator tells the story of "Miss Butterfly"? Skim the story for evidence that supports your answer. Provide at least two examples. Then tell why you think Mori chose to tell the story this way.

Extend Understanding

Writing Options

Creative Writing Imagine that you are Hamada-*san*. You have come home from watching Sachi and Yuki dance the festival dances. You keep a personal diary that no one ever reads but you. In this diary you write about your private thoughts and feelings. Write a **diary entry** about your evening with Sachi and Yuki. Write the memories the evening evoked as well as the thoughts and reflections it brought to mind.

Expository Writing Imagine you want to pitch to a film producer the idea of making "Miss Butterfly" into a movie. Write a **summary** to sell the producer on your idea. Give descriptions of the setting and the characters. Include an outline of the plot to give the movie producer an idea of the actions that will occur in the movie. Make sure to fully explain the conflicts present in the story.

Lifelong Learning

Plan a Research Report Imagine your class has been assigned to write research reports on Japanese culture as a preparation to welcome Japanese exchange students to your school. Research at the library to see what books and other sources are available on your topic. Make a list of works that you might use. Include the titles and authors' names for your report.

Collaborative Learning

Foreign Words in English Many words from foreign languages have entered into the English language. In small groups, use a dictionary to find the definitions, pronunciations, and part-of-speech labels of the following Japanese words that have entered the English language: *kimono*, *samurai*, *sushi*, *tofu*, *tsunami*, and *bonsai*. Then brainstorm a list of other words that you think came to English from other languages. Use a dictionary to check your work.

 Go to www.mirrorsandwindows.com for more.

MISS BUTTERFLY **187**

Find Meaning

1. (a) They are waiting for their boyfriends to take them to a social dance. (b) The author may have wanted to directly contrast characters' feelings about American and Japanese culture through dance.

2. (a) Sachi says she hates to wear her kimono. (b) Hamada-*san* strongly identifies with Japanese culture.

3. (a) Hamada-*san* seems to be carried outside of time and space. (b) His reaction shows his nostalgia for Japan.

Make Judgments

4. (a) Yuki and Sachi are comfortable with and excited by American culture. They are familiar with Japanese culture, but not attracted to it. (b) Hamada-*san* seems the opposite.

5. (a) Hamada-*san* seems homesick for Japan and concerned that Nisei children preserve Japanese culture. (b) Students might suggest that Hamada-*san* start a Japanese cultural preservation society.

6. Students may say that the ticking clock emphasizes that change is occurring quickly in Japanese-American culture.

Analyze Literature

Point of View *Answer:* "Miss Butterfly" is told from the third-person omniscient point of view. Students may give examples such as "In the silence he heard the clock in the hall ticking," as evidence of third-person omniscient narration. Students may say that Mori wanted to use an objective point of view to give a balanced view of cultural perspectives.

Rubrics for Writing Options

You can adapt this as a checklist for students to use as they write.

Creative Writing

☐ Does the tone and content suggest a private diary?

☐ Does the diary entry discuss the evening spent with Sachi and Yuki?

☐ Does the writer imagine beyond "Miss Butterfly" to memories and thoughts Hamada-*san* might have?

Expository Writing

☐ Does the summary explain the conflicts present in "Miss Butterfly"?

☐ Does the summary describe the setting and characters as they occur in the story?

☐ Does the summary include an accurate overview of the plot?

At a Glance
Directed Reading
- Reading Level: Challenging
- Difficulty Consideration: Vocabulary
- Ease Factors: Engaging plot, sympathetic character

Objectives

Studying this lesson will enable students to

- use reading strategies such as analyzing cause and effect
- define *tone* and recognize the effect of this literary technique in the selection
- describe the literary accomplishments of O. Henry and the influence of the Old West on his writing
- appreciate a humorous story

Launch the Lesson

Before students read "The Ransom of Red Chief," ask them to share accounts of times when they or others they know have been tempted by easy money. The class could then identify what features these experiences have in common.

Common Core State Standards

Reading Literature
RL.1, RL.4

Language
L.6

DIRECTED READING

The Ransom of RED CHIEF

A Short Story by O. Henry

BEFORE READING

Build Background

Historical Context The "Old West" suggests a time and place in American History around 1865 to 1900. Elizabeth Roe, a woman living in 1870s Texas, said about her life in the Old West, "After my husband enlisted [in the Texas Rangers] I again lived in fear. The rangers had to contend with cattle rustlers, fights between cattlemen and between ranchers and sheep men, and with desperadoes." Read to see how the Old West influenced O. Henry in "The Ransom of Red Chief."

Reader's Context Have you ever been tempted by easy money? What happened?

Set Purpose

Skim the text and preview the images in "The Ransom of Red Chief" to predict what kind of story you are going to read. As you read, revise your predictions.

Analyze Literature

Tone A writer's attitude toward the subject or the reader is **tone.** For example, a writer might use a lighthearted tone when writing about something happy or funny, and a heavier one when writing about something sad. As you read, identify O. Henry's attitude toward the subject, and try to find adjectives to describe that tone.

Meet the Author

O. Henry (1862–1910) was born William Sydney Porter in Greensboro, North Carolina. At twenty, he moved to a ranch in Texas, where he herded sheep, cooked for ranch hands, and listened to stories of rugged outlaws, which likely influenced "The Ransom of Red Chief." His short stories met with great success, and he took on the pen name O. Henry.

Use Reading Skills

Analyze Cause and Effect In fiction, writers often explain *why* an event takes place. The event is an effect; *why* it happened is a cause. Understanding cause-and-effect relationships is vital to grasping the meaning of a story. Sometimes a single cause has several effects, and an effect can have several causes. As you read "The Ransom of Red Chief," use a chart to keep track of causes and effects.

Cause:	Effect:
Bill and Sam need $2,000.	They come up with a kidnapping idea to raise the money.

Preview Vocabulary

ra•di•us (ra´ dē us) *n.*, circular area

di•a•tribe (dī´ ə trīb) *n.*, angry and mean attack on a person's character

per•vade (pər vād´) *v.*, be present everywhere

de•cry (de krī) *v.*, openly express strong disapproval

im•pu•dent (im pyu̇ dənt) *adj.*, offensively bold

188 UNIT 2 FICTION

Words in Use

Preview Vocabulary	Selection Words	Teaching Words
radius, 190	lackadaisical, 190	enlisted, 188
diatribe, 190	emit, 191	contend, 188
pervade, 193	contiguous, 193	rustlers, 188
decry, 194	martyrs, 195	desperadoes, 188
impudent, 197	porous, 197	

KEY TERMS

SKIM, 188
TONE, 188
ADJECTIVE, 188
CAUSE AND EFFECT, 188
FORESHADOW, 198
CLUSTER CHART, 198
RESOLUTION, 198
CENTRAL CONFLICT, 198
MONOLOGUE, 198

The Ransom of
RED CHIEF

A Short Story by O. Henry

We selected for our victim the only child of a prominent citizen named Ebenezer Dorset.

189

Teach the Selection

Summary

The narrator is one of a pair of two scoundrels. The men need money to execute a fraud scheme, so they kidnap the young son of a wealthy businessman. The young boy proves to have a temper and a vivid imagination. Apparently undisturbed by his kidnapping, the boy tells the men he is "Red Chief" and enacts an extended game of playing Indian. The men's plan backfires when they send the ransom note to the boy's father. Instead of paying the ransom, the father asks the men for money for the privilege of returning the uncontrollable boy. In desperation the men agree to the terms.

MIRRORS & WINDOWS The Mirrors & Windows questions at the end of this selection focus on the theme of literary elements. Before reading the story, ask students what literary elements help to make a story humorous. What elements do people in general find funny?

Program Resources

Planning and Assessment
Program Planning Guide, Selection Lesson Plan
E-Lesson Planner
Assessment Guide, Lesson Test
ExamView

Technology Tools
Interactive Student Text on CD
Visual Teaching Package
Audio Library
mirrorsandwindows.com

Meeting the Standards
Fiction: Unit 2, Directed Reading, pp. 45–53

Literary Connection

Malapropism A malapropism is the humorous misuse of a word in speaking or in writing. The word was coined by playwright Richard Sheridan, whose character Mrs. Malaprop said things such as, "He is the very *pine-apple* of politeness!" She means *pinnacle*. Explain that Bill uses *apparition* instead of *aberration*. Continue to point out and discuss other malapropisms in the story. **A**

Analyze Literature

Point of View Point out that the use of the pronouns *me* and *we* in this sentence indicate a first-person point of view. The narrator is one of the con artists. Explain that since the character tells the story as if it happened to him, readers will only find out the things he knows. **B**

Analyze Literature

Tone Remind students that tone is the author's attitude toward the subject or reader. Ask students to identify or describe O. Henry's tone toward con artists and rural communities. **C**

Analyze Literature

Foreshadowing Ask students what they might expect to happen after reading the comparison of the boy to a bear. Model a possible response: "I think the men will continue to have problems with the boy. " **D**

A ⎡ It looked like a good thing; but wait till I tell you. We were down South, in Alabama—Bill Driscoll and myself—when this kidnapping idea struck us. It was, as Bill afterward expressed it, "during a moment of temporary mental apparition";[1] but we didn't find that out till later.

There was a town down there, as flat as a flannel-cake, and called Summit, of course. It contained inhabitants of as undeleterious[2] and self-satisfied a class of peasantry[3] as ever clustered around a Maypole.[4]

B ⎡ Bill and me had a joint capital of about six hundred dollars, and we needed just two thousand dollars more to pull off a fraudulent town-lot scheme in Western Illinois. We talked it over on the front steps of the hotel. Philoprogenitiveness,[5] says we, is strong in semi-rural communities; therefore, and for other reasons, a kidnapping project ought to do better there than in the <u>radius</u> of newspapers that send reporters out in plain clothes to stir up talk about such things. We knew that Summit

C ⎡ couldn't get after us with anything stronger than constables and, maybe, some lackadaisical bloodhounds and a <u>diatribe</u> or two in the Weekly Farmers' Budget. So, it looked good.

We selected for our victim the only child of a prominent citizen named Ebenezer Dorset. The father was respectable and tight, a mortgage[6] fancier and a stern, upright collection plate passer and forecloser.[7] The kid was a boy of ten, with bas-relief[8] freckles and hair the color of the cover of the magazine you buy at the newsstand when you want to catch a train. Bill and me figured that Ebenezer would melt down for a ransom of two thousand dollars to a cent. But wait till I tell you.

About two miles from Summit was a little mountain, covered with a dense cedar brake.[9] On the rear elevation of this mountain was a

---

cave. There we stored provisions.

One evening after sundown, we drove in a buggy past old Dorset's house. The kid was in the street, throwing rocks at a kitten on the opposite fence.

"Hey, little boy!" says Bill, "would you like to have a bag of candy and a nice ride?"

The boy catches Bill neatly in the eye with a piece of brick.

"That will cost the old man an extra five hundred dollars," says Bill, climbing over the wheel.

D ⎡ That boy put up a fight like a welterweight cinnamon bear; but, at last, we got him down in the bottom of the buggy and drove away. We took him up to the cave, and I hitched the horse in the cedar brake. After dark I drove the buggy to the little village, three miles away, where we had hired it, and walked back to the mountain.

Bill was pasting court plaster[10] over the scratches and bruises on his features.

There was a fire burning behind the big rock at the entrance of the cave, and the boy was watching a pot of boiling coffee, with two buzzard tail feathers stuck in his red hair. He points a stick at me when I come up, and says: "Ha! cursed paleface, do you dare to enter the camp of Red Chief, the terror of the plains?"

---

1. **apparition.** Sudden or unusual sight
2. **undeleterious.** Invented word meaning "harmless"
3. **peasantry.** Group of country people
4. **Maypole.** Pole with streamers held by dancers celebrating May Day
5. **philoprogenitiveness.** Invented word meaning "love for one's own children"
6. **mortgage.** Promise of property to insure a loan
7. **forecloser.** Invented word suggesting real estate dealings, perhaps meaning a person who resolves things ahead of time
8. **bas-relief.** Sculptural feature slightly raised from the background
9. **brake.** Thick grouping of trees or undergrowth
10. **court plaster.** Adhesive cloth used to cover cuts or scratches

---

ra•di•us (ra´ dē us) *n.*, circular area

di•a•tribe (dī´ ə trīb) *n.*, angry and mean attack on a person's character

---

190 UNIT 2 FICTION

Differentiated Instruction

English Language Learning

Give students learning English a definition and context sentence to help them understand unfamiliar words and phrases in the story.
lackadaisical—lazy, without energy, 190
The lackadaisical bloodhounds did not try to pick up the scent of the kidnappers.

tight—very careful and thrifty with money, 190
The man was so tight that he did not spend any money on entertainment or vacations.
melt down—give in or give up, 190
The kidnappers thought Ebenezer would melt down and pay the ransom.

"He's all right now," says Bill, rolling up his trousers and examining some bruises on his shins. "We're playing Indian. We're making Buffalo Bill's show look like magic-lantern views[11] of Palestine[12] in the town hall. I'm Old Hank, the Trapper, Red Chief's captive, and I'm to be scalped at daybreak. By Geronimo! that kid can kick hard." **E**

Yes, sir, that boy seemed to be having the time of his life. The fun of camping out in a cave had made him forget that he was a captive himself. He immediately christened me Snake-eye, the Spy, and announced that when his braves returned from the warpath, I was to be broiled at the stake at the rising of the sun.

Then we had supper; and he filled his mouth full of bacon and bread and gravy and began to talk. He made a during-dinner speech something like this:

"I like this fine. I never camped out before; but I had a pet possum once, and I was nine last birthday. I hate to go to school. Rats ate up sixteen of Jimmy Talbot's aunt's speckled hen's eggs. Are there any real Indians in these woods? I want some more gravy. Does the trees moving make the wind blow? We had five puppies. What makes your nose so red, Hank? My father has lots of money. Are the stars hot? I whipped Ed Walker twice, Saturday. I don't like girls. You dassent[13] catch toads unless with a string. Do oxen make any noise? Why are oranges round? Have you got beds to sleep on in this cave? Amos Murray has got six toes. A parrot can talk, but a monkey or a fish can't. How many does it take to make twelve?"

Every few minutes he would remember that he was an Indian, and pick up his stick rifle and tiptoe to the mouth of the cave to search for the scouts of the hated paleface. Now and then he would let out a war whoop that made Old Hank the Trapper shiver. That boy had Bill terrorized from the start.

"Red Chief," says I to the kid, "would you like to go home?"

"Aw, what for?" says he. "I don't have any fun at home. I hate to go to school. I like to camp out. You won't take me back home again, Snake-eye, will you?"

"Not right away," says I. "We'll stay here in the cave awhile."

"All right!" says he. "That'll be fine. I never had such fun in all my life." **F**

> It's an awful thing to hear a strong, desperate, fat man scream...

G We went to bed about eleven o'clock. We spread down some wide blankets and quilts and put Red Chief between us. We weren't afraid he'd run away. He kept us awake for three hours, jumping up and reaching for his rifle and screeching: "Hist! pard," in mine and Bill's ears, as the fancied crackle of a twig or the rustle of a leaf revealed to his young imagination the stealthy approach of the outlaw band. At last, I fell into a troubled sleep, and dreamed that I had been kidnapped and chained to a tree by a ferocious pirate with red hair.

Just at daybreak, I was awakened by a series of awful screams from Bill. They weren't yells, or howls, or shouts, or whoops, or yawps, such as you'd expect from a manly set of vocal organs—they were simply indecent, terrifying, humiliating screams, such as women emit when they see caterpillars. It's an awful thing to hear a

---

11. **magic-lantern views.** Slide-show images
12. **Palestine.** Historical region also called "the Holy Land"
13. **dassent.** Regional, southern pronunciation of "dare not"

Teach the Selection

History Connection
Buffalo Bill Buffalo Bill was a real person whose deeds and exploits became legendary. Born William Cody in 1846, he participated in the settlement of the West during the 1800s. He got his nickname as a scout during the Civil War. During the late 1800s he created a traveling show, Buffalo Bill's Wild West Show, loosely based on his experiences. The show included events, such as cowboy-and-Indian battles and buffalo hunts, and included Native Americans as actors. Cody's show heavily influenced people's perception of the Wild West. **E**

Use Reading Skills
Analyze Cause and Effect Ask students to identify the reasons given by the narrator that the boy had forgotten that he was a captive. Model a response by indicating one reason: "One reason is that the boy had never camped out before." **F**

Analyze Literature
Stereotypes Ask students to explain how the boy's during-dinner speech is a stereotype. Possible response: "Many young children talk a lot and switch topics frequently. This speech exaggerates a normal speech and serves as a stereotype for such speeches." **G**

Research Skills

Allusions
Point out to students that the story they are about to read contains several allusions, references to famous people and events in history, literature, and other areas. Suggest that they conduct research to find out more about these references. Assign small groups one of the following allusions in the story: Buffalo Bill, King Herod, Geronimo, David and Goliath, Bedlam, and *The Pirates of Penzance.*

Suggest that students use print references, such as encyclopedias and dictionaries, or do an Internet search of the name. Ask students to present their findings to the class.

Use Reading Skills
Determine Importance of Details
Direct students' attention to the scene in which the narrator comes upon Red Chief attempting to scalp Bill. Ask them whether this detail is important to the plot. Model a response: "This action by Red Chief squanders any hope Bill had of the kidnapping working to his benefit." **A**

Analyze Literature
Characterization Discuss with students the author's portrayal of Bill, a grown man and something of an outlaw, being broken by a ten-year-old boy. Ask students why they think Bill did not defend himself or take actions against the boy. Model a possible response: "Perhaps Bill did not have any experience with children, so he really didn't know how to handle the situation." **B**

---

strong, desperate, fat man scream incontinently[14] in a cave at daybreak.

A ⌐ I jumped up to see what the matter was. Red Chief was sitting on Bill's chest, with one hand twined in Bill's hair. In the other he had the sharp case knife we used for slicing bacon; and he was industriously and realistically trying to take Bill's scalp, according to the sentence that had been pronounced upon him the evening before.

B ⌐ I got the knife away from the kid and made him lie down again. But, from that moment, Bill's spirit was broken. He laid down on his side of the bed, but he never closed an eye again in sleep as long as that boy was with us. I dozed off for a while, but along toward sunup I remembered that Red Chief had said I was to be burned at the stake at the rising of the sun. I wasn't nervous or afraid; but I sat up and leaned against a rock.

"What you getting up so soon for, Sam?" asked Bill.

"Me?" says I. "Oh, I got a kind of pain in my shoulder. I thought sitting up would rest it."

"You're a liar!" says Bill. "You're afraid. You was to be burned at sunrise, and you was afraid he'd do it. And he would, too, if he could find a match. Ain't it awful, Sam? Do you think anybody will pay out money to get a little imp like that back home?"

"Sure," said I. "A rowdy kid like that is just the kind that parents dote[15] on. Now,

---

14. **incontinently.** Without control
15. **dote.** Show excessive fondness or love

Differentiated Instruction

Visual Learning
O. Henry creates vivid scenes in "The Ransom of Red Chief," including the scene where Red Chief attempts to scalp Bill and the descriptions of Bill's bruises. Suggest that students draw pictures of the scenes or find magazine pictures that remind them of the scenes.

English Language Learning
You might want to explain to students that young children in the United States often enjoy pretending to be characters from the days of the Old West in American history. Ask students if children from their native countries enjoy pretending to be characters from an earlier historical period.

you and the Chief get up and cook breakfast, while I go up on the top of this mountain and reconnoiter."[16]

I went up on the peak of the little mountain and ran my eye over the contiguous vicinity. Over toward Summit I expected to see the sturdy yeomanry[17] of the village armed with scythes and pitchforks beating the countryside for the dastardly kidnappers. But what I saw was a peaceful landscape dotted with one man plowing with a dun[18] mule. Nobody was dragging the creek; no couriers dashed hither and yon, bringing tidings of no news to the distracted parents. There was a sylvan[19] attitude of somnolent[20] sleepiness pervading that section of the external outward surface of Alabama that lay exposed to my view. "Perhaps," says I to myself, "it has not yet been discovered that the wolves have borne away the tender lambkin from the fold. Heaven help the wolves!" says I, and I went down the mountain to breakfast.

When I got to the cave, I found Bill backed up against the side of it, breathing hard, and the boy threatening to smash him with a rock half as big as a coconut.

"He put a red-hot boiled potato down my back" explained Bill, "and then mashed it with his foot; and I boxed his ears. Have you got a gun about you, Sam?"

I took the rock away from the boy and kind of patched up the argument. "I'll fix you," says the kid to Bill. "No man ever yet struck the Red Chief but he got paid for it. You better beware!" After breakfast the kid takes a piece of leather with strings wrapped around it out of his pocket and goes outside the cave unwinding it.

"What's he up to now?" says Bill, anxiously. "You don't think he'll run away, do you, Sam?"

"No fear of it," says I. "He don't seem to be much of a homebody. But we've got to fix up some plan about the ransom. There don't seem to be much excitement around Summit on account of his disappearance; but maybe they haven't realized yet that he's gone. His folks may think he's spending the night with Aunt Jane or one of the neighbors. Anyhow, he'll be missed today. Tonight we must get a message to his father demanding the two thousand dollars for his return."

Just then we heard a kind of war whoop, such as David might have emitted when he knocked out the champion Goliath. It was a sling that Red Chief had pulled out of his pocket, and he was whirling it around his head.

I dodged, and heard a heavy thud and a kind of a sigh from Bill, like a horse gives out when you take his saddle off. A rock the size of an egg had caught Bill just behind his left ear. He loosened himself all over and fell in the fire across the frying pan of hot water for washing the dishes. I dragged him out and poured cold water on his head for half an hour.

By and by, Bill sits up and feels behind his ear and says: "Sam, do you know who my favorite Biblical character is?"

"Take it easy," says I. "You'll come to your senses presently."

"King Herod,"[21] says he. "You won't go away and leave me here alone, will you, Sam?"

I went out and caught that boy and shook him until his freckles rattled.

"If you don't behave," says I, "I'll take you straight home. Now, are you going to be good, or not?"

---

16. **reconnoiter.** Military expedition to gather information
17. **yeomanry.** Class of people who are farmers
18. **dun.** Brownish-grey
19. **sylvan.** Characteristic of woods or forests
20. **somnolent.** Drowsy or sleepy
21. **King Herod.** Herod ruled Judea from 37 ʙᴄ to 4 ʙᴄ. The reference here is to his decree to execute all the boys in Bethlehem younger than two years old.

per•vade (pər vād´) v., be present everywhere

THE RANSOM OF RED CHIEF **193**

Teach the Selection

Use Reading Strategies
Visualize Point out that the narrator contrasts what he imagined the village would look like with what he actually saw. The image of the quiet, sleepy town should give the readers a clue that the boy's disappearance may not be that much of a concern to the townsfolk. **C**

Use Reading Strategies
Make Inferences Point out that the narrator makes an inference about the reasons no one in the town has seemed to notice the boy's disappearance. Ask students if they agree with the narrator's inference. If they disagree, ask them to make their own inference. Model a response: "The boy's parents may be enjoying the peace and quiet with the boy gone. Perhaps they will start looking in another day." **D**

History Connection
King Herod Explain to students that Herod was the King of the Jews under Roman Emperor Augustus. Bill's saying the Herod is his favorite Biblical character may refer to Herod's decree that all Jews return to the town of their birth for a census, or it may refer to the Gospel of Matthew where he says that Herod had all male children under the age of two executed. The story does not give any more clues about this reference. **E**

Reading Skills

Understand Literary Elements
Explain that alliteration is the repetition of consonant sounds at the beginnings of words. Point out that the repetition of the *s* sound at the beginning of the words *sylvan, somnolent, sleepiness, section* and *surface* in the following excerpt gives the sentence a quiet, peaceful tone.

There was a sylvan attitude of somnolent sleepiness pervading that section of the external outward surface of Alabama that lay exposed to my view.

Analyze Literature

Tone Discuss with students the emotions that O. Henry has the two characters express. Ask them to read the discussion between Bill and Sam aloud and to use the tone of voice they think each character would use. **Ⓐ**

Analyze Literature

Metaphor Direct students to the metaphor Bill uses to describe Red Chief. Ask them what a wildcat and Red Chief have in common. Why would Bill choose this metaphor to describe the boy? How does the use of this metaphor affect the characterization of Red Chief and Bill, and how does it impact the selection's tone? Guide students in understanding that the metaphor paints Red Chief as wild or untamed, Bill as a helpless victim, and the tone as humorous. **Ⓑ**

"I was only funning," says he, sullenly. "I didn't mean to hurt Old Hank. But what did he hit me for? I'll behave, Snake-eye, if you won't send me home and if you'll let me play the Scout today."

"I don't know the game," says I. "That's for you and Mr. Bill to decide. He's your playmate for the day. I'm going away for a while, on business. Now, you come in and make friends with him and say you are sorry for hurting him, or home you go, at once." **Ⓑ**

> **I never lost my nerve yet till we kidnapped that two-legged skyrocket of a kid.**

I made him and Bill shake hands, and then I took Bill aside and told him I was going to Poplar Grove, a little village three miles from the cave, and find out what I could about how the kidnapping had been regarded in Summit. Also, I thought it best to send a peremptory[22] letter to old man Dorset that day, demanding the ransom and dictating how it should be paid.

"You know, Sam," says Bill, "I've stood by you without batting an eye in earthquakes, fire, and flood—in poker games, dynamite outrages, police raids, train robberies, and cyclones. I never lost my nerve yet till we kidnapped that two-legged **Ⓐ** skyrocket of a kid. He's got me going. You won't leave me long with him, will you, Sam?"

"I'll be back sometime this afternoon," says I. "You must keep the boy amused and quiet till I return. And now we'll write the letter to old Dorset."

Bill and I got paper and pencil and worked on the letter while Red Chief, with a blanket wrapped around him, strutted up and down, guarding the mouth of the cave. Bill begged me tearfully to make the ransom fifteen hundred dollars instead of two thousand. "I ain't attempting," says he, "to decry the celebrated moral aspect of parental affection, but we're dealing with humans, and it ain't human for anybody to give up two thousand dollars for that forty-pound chunk of freckled wildcat. I'm willing to take a chance at fifteen hundred dollars. You can charge the difference up to me."

So, to relieve Bill, I acceded, and we collaborated[23] a letter that ran this way:

Ebenezer Dorset, Esq.:

We have your boy concealed in a place far from Summit. It is useless for you or the most skillful detectives to attempt to find him. Absolutely the only terms on which you can have him restored to you are these: We demand fifteen hundred dollars in large bills for his return; the money to be left at midnight tonight at the same spot and in the same box as your reply—as hereinafter described. If you agree to these terms, send your answer in writing by a solitary messenger tonight at half-past eight o'clock. After crossing Owl Creek on the road to Poplar Grove, there are three large trees about a hundred yards apart, close to the fence of the wheat field on the right-hand side. At the bottom of the fence post, opposite the third tree, will be found a small pasteboard box.

The messenger will place the answer in this box and return immediately to Summit.

---

22. **peremptory.** Not allowing contradiction
23. **collaborated.** Worked together on

de•cry (de krī) v., openly express strong disapproval of

Differentiated Instruction

Reading Proficiency

Students may have some difficulty reading some of the longer sentences that contain multiple clauses and phrases. Write them on the board, and break them down into simple sentences. Have students read the simple sentences aloud and explain the meaning of each one. Then have them read the longer sentences again and summarize them.

Auditory Learning

Since "The Ransom of Red Chief" includes a lot of dialogue, students may benefit from oral reading of the story. Remind students to include sound effects for Bill's cries at various times, as well as the sounds of leaves rustling, and writing and opening the ransom letter.

If you attempt any treachery or fail to comply[24] with our demand as stated, you will never see your boy again.

If you pay the money as demanded, he will be returned to you safe and well within three hours. These terms are final, and if you do not accede to them, no further communication will be attempted.

—Two Desperate Men

I addressed this letter to Dorset and put it in my pocket. As I was about to start, the kid comes up to me and says:

"Aw, Snake-eye, you said I could play the Scout while you was gone."

"Play it, of course," says I. "Mr. Bill will play with you. What kind of game is it?"

"I'm the Scout," says Red Chief, "and I have to ride to the stockade[25] to warn the settlers that the Indians are coming. I'm tired of playing Indian myself. I want to be the Scout."

"All right," says I. "It sounds harmless to me. I guess Mr. Bill will help you foil the enemy."

"What am I to do?" asks Bill, looking at the kid suspiciously.

"You are the hoss,"[26] says Scout. "Get down on your hands and knees. How can I ride to the stockade without a hoss?"

"You'd better keep him interested," said I, "till we get the scheme going. Loosen up."

Bill gets down on his all fours, and a look comes in his eye like a rabbit's when you catch it in a trap.

"How far is it to the stockade, kid?" he asks, in a husky manner of voice.

"Ninety miles," says the Scout. "And you have to hurry to get there on time. Whoa, now!"

The Scout jumps on Bill's back and digs his heels in his side.

"For Heaven's sake," says Bill, "hurry back, Sam, as soon as you can. I wish we hadn't made the ransom more than a thousand. Say, you quit kicking me or I'll get up and warm you good."

I walked over to Poplar Grove and sat around the post office and store, talking with the chaw-bacons[27] that came in to trade. One whiskerando[28] says that he hears Summit is all upset on account of Elder Ebenezer Dorset's boy having been lost or stolen. That was all I wanted to know. I referred casually to the price of black-eyed peas, posted my letter surreptitiously[29] and came away. The postmaster said the mail carrier would come by in an hour to take the mail to Summit.

When I got back to the cave, Bill and the boy were not to be found. I explored the vicinity of the cave and risked a yodel or two, but there was no response.

So I sat down on a mossy bank to await developments.

In about half an hour I heard the bushes rustle, and Bill wabbled out into the little glade in front of the cave. Behind him was the kid, stepping softly like a scout, with a broad grin on his face. Bill stopped, took off his hat, and wiped his face with a red handkerchief. The kid stopped about eight feet behind him. "Sam," says Bill, "I suppose you think I'm a renegade,[30] but I couldn't help it. I'm a grown person with masculine proclivities[31] and habits of self-defense, but there is a time when all systems of egotism and predominance fail. The boy is gone. I sent him home. All is off. There was martyrs in old times," goes on Bill, "that suffered death rather than give up the particular graft they enjoyed. None of 'em ever was

---

24. **comply.** Follow a command, request, or order
25. **stockade.** Defensive barrier made of poles
26. **hoss.** Regional, southern pronunciation of "horse"
27. **chaw-bacons.** Invented word suggesting people who eat bacon
28. **whiskerando.** Invented word suggesting a man with a beard
29. **surreptitiously.** In a sneaky way
30. **renegade.** Outlaw; rebel
31. **proclivities.** Natural inclinations

THE RANSOM OF RED CHIEF **195**

Analyze Literature

Setting Point out that although the author has not gone into great detail to describe the physical setting, he does give clues through dialogue. When Bill says that sand is not a substitute for oats, we learn that the ground around the cave is sandy. **Ⓐ**

Analyze Literature

Characterization Ask students what they can tell about Ebenezer Dorset from his letter. Model a possible response supported by textual evidence: "Based on his counteroffer, which suggests that the kidnappers pay him, I can tell that he is a shrewd businessman who also knows his son well." **Ⓑ**

subjugated to such tortures as I have been. I tried to be faithful to our articles of depredation;[32] but there came a limit."

"What's the trouble, Bill?" I asks him.

"I was rode," says Bill, "the ninety miles to the stockade, not barring an inch. Then, when the settlers was rescued, I was given **Ⓐ** oats. Sand ain't a palatable[33] substitute. And then, for an hour I had to try to explain to him why there was nothin' in holes, how a road can run both ways, and what makes the grass green. I tell you, Sam, a human can only stand so much. I takes him by the neck of his clothes and drags him down the mountain. On the way he kicks my legs black and blue from the knees down; and I've got to have two or three bites on my thumb and hand cauterized.[34]

"But he's gone"—continues Bill—"gone home. I showed him the road to Summit and kicked him about eight feet nearer there at one kick. I'm sorry we lose the ransom; but it was either that or Bill Driscoll to the madhouse."

Bill is puffing and blowing, but there is a look of ineffable[35] peace and growing content on his rose-pink features.

"Bill," says I, "there isn't any heart disease in your family, is there?"

"No," says Bill, "nothing chronic except malaria and accidents. Why?"

"Then you might turn around," says I, "and have a look behind you."

Bill turns and sees the boy, and loses his complexion and sits down plump on the ground and begins to pluck aimlessly at grass and little sticks. For an hour I was afraid of his mind. And then I told him that my scheme was to put the whole job through immediately and that we would get the ransom and be off with it by midnight if old Dorset fell in with our proposition.[36] So Bill braced up enough to give the kid a weak sort of a smile and a promise to play the Russian

in a Japanese war with him as soon as he felt a little better.

I had a scheme for collecting that ransom without danger of being caught by counterplots that ought to commend itself to professional kidnappers. The tree under which the answer was to be left—and the money later on—was close to the road fence, with big, bare fields on all sides. If a gang of constables[37] should be watching for anyone to come for the note, they could see him a long way off crossing the fields or in the road. But no, sirree! At half past eight I was up in that tree as well hidden as a tree toad, waiting for the messenger to arrive.

Exactly on time, a half-grown boy rides up the road on a bicycle, locates the pasteboard box at the foot of the fence post, slips a folded piece of paper into it, and pedals away again back toward Summit.

I waited an hour and then concluded the thing was square. I slid down the tree, got the note, slipped along the fence till I struck the woods, and was back at the cave in another half an hour. I opened the note, got near the lantern, and read it to Bill. It was written with a pen in a crabbed hand,[38] and the sum and substance of it was this:

Two Desperate Men

Gentlemen: I received your letter today by post, in regard to the ransom you ask for the return of my son. I think you are a little high in your demands, and I hereby make you a counterproposition, which I am inclined to believe you will accept. You **Ⓑ**

---

32. depredation. Attack on another for personal gain
33. palatable. Agreeable to the taste
34. cauterized. Burned a wound in order to stop bleeding or to promote healing
35. ineffable. Indescribable
36. proposition. Suggested plan
37. constables. Officers with less power than sheriffs
38. crabbed hand. Handwriting that is difficult to read

196 UNIT 2 FICTION

Differentiated Instruction

Enrichment

Interested students might enjoy preparing an alternate ending to "The Ransom of Red Chief." Suggest that students think about what might have happened had Dorset refused to pay the ransom, or if the kidnappers had refused to agree to Dorset's terms for returning the boy. Have students read their endings aloud.

bring Johnny home and pay me two hundred and fifty dollars in cash, and I agree to take him off your hands. You had better come at night, for the neighbors believe he is lost, and I couldn't be responsible for what they would do to anybody they saw bringing him back.

Very respectfully,

Ebenezer Dorset

"Great Pirates of Penzance," says I; "of all the <u>impudent</u>—"

But I glanced at Bill, and hesitated. He had the most appealing look in his eyes I ever saw on the face of a dumb or a talking brute.

"Sam," says he, "what's two hundred and fifty dollars, after all? We've got the money. One more night of this kid will send me to a bed in Bedlam.[39] Besides being a thorough gentleman, I think Mr. Dorset is a spendthrift[40] for making us such a liberal offer. You ain't going to let the chance go, are you?"

"Tell you the truth, Bill," says I, "this little he-ewe lamb has somewhat got on my nerves too. We'll take him home, pay the ransom, and make our getaway."

We took him home that night. We got him to go by telling him that his father had bought a silver-mounted rifle and a pair of moccasins for him and we were to hunt bears the next day.

It was just twelve o'clock when we knocked at Ebenezer's front door. Just at the moment when I should have been

abstracting[41] the fifteen hundred dollars from the box under the tree, according to the original proposition, Bill was counting out two hundred and fifty dollars into Dorset's hand.

When the kid found out we were going to leave him at home, he started up a howl like a calliope[42] and fastened himself as tight as a leech to Bill's leg. His father peeled him away gradually, like a porous plaster.

"How long can you hold him?" asks Bill.

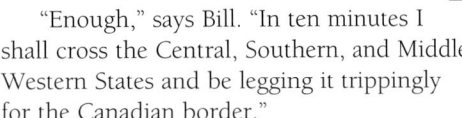

> One more night of this kid will send me to a bed in Bedlam.

"I'm not as strong as I used to be," says old Dorset, "but I think I can promise you ten minutes."

"Enough," says Bill. "In ten minutes I shall cross the Central, Southern, and Middle Western States and be legging it trippingly for the Canadian border."

And as dark as it was, and as fat as Bill was, and as good a runner as I am, he was a good mile and a half out of Summit before I could catch up with him. ❖

---

39. **Bedlam.** Insane asylum
40. **spendthrift.** Person who spends money recklessly
41. **abstracting.** Taking away, removing
42. **calliope.** Musical instrument with whistles blown by steam released by playing a keyboard

---

im·pu·dent (im pyʉ dənt) *adj.,* offensively bold

What parts of "The Ransom of Red Chief" seemed the funniest to you? In general, which literary elements—such as character, plot, and dialogue—do you think contribute most to making a story humorous?

Review the Selection

Find Meaning

1. (a) Red Chief is the play name of young Johnny Dorset, the kidnap victim of the narrator and his partner, Bill. (b) Students may say the story's title foreshadows the story's climax and suggests the Old West.

2. (a) He is throwing rocks at a kitten. (b) It immediately shows that this character is ruthless, mean, and nasty.

3. (a) Ebenezer Dorset sends a note that says he will accept Johnny's return if paid 250 dollars. (b) This is unexpected because the kidnappers expected to make money, not to lose it.

Make Judgments

4. Students may say the narrator's vocabulary suggests he wants to make a good impression on his listener by using big words.

5. (a) He is the devoted sidekick who takes the brunt of the abuse. (b) Students might mention Watson (Sherlock Holmes), Igor (Dr. Frankenstein), Robin (Batman), or R2D2 (C3PO).

6. Students will say it is not easy to live with Johnny. They may give as evidence that Ebenezer was confident the outlaws would pay to give Johnny back, that he suggested the kidnappers return him at night to avoid being attacked by the neighbors, and any of Johnny's abusive behaviors.

Analyze Literature

Tone *Answer:* Student's examples and adjectives will likely focus on O. Henry's humor. Adjectives such as *lighthearted, bemused,* and *ironic* would be appropriate.

Find Meaning

1. (a) Who is Red Chief? (b) Why do you think this story is called "The Ransom of Red Chief"?

2. (a) What is the Dorset boy doing the first time we see him in the story? (b) How does this foreshadow what is going to happen?

3. (a) How does Ebenezer Dorset respond to the ransom note? (b) Why is his response unexpected?

Analyze Literature

Tone Authors create tone through the words they choose and in the way they put those words together. Skim "The Ransom of Red Chief" for words, phrases, and sentences that help convey O. Henry's tone. Enter these words in the outer circles of a cluster chart like the one shown here. Then, think of your own adjective or adjectives to describe O. Henry's tone and enter it in the center circle.

Make Judgments

4. What can you gather from the narrator's use of words such as *undeleterious, philoprogenitiveness,* and *bas-relief*?

5. (a) How would you describe the character Bill to someone who has not read this story? (b) Of what other characters from literature and movies does he remind you?

6. How would you describe Ebenezer Dorset's experience of living with Johnny Dorset?

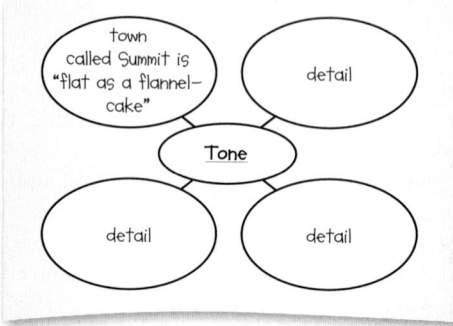

Extend Understanding

Writing Options

Creative Writing Imagine that you are a journalist writing for the *Summit Star.* You have been assigned to cover the story of the kidnapping and return of Johnny Dorset. Write a **news story** that covers all of the events. Include a headline and a catchy opening paragraph, and explain the *who, what, where, when, why,* and *how* of the story.

Expository Writing Use your cluster chart to write a **paragraph** analyzing O. Henry's tone in "The Ransom of Red Chief." State what you think the tone is in your thesis. Use details from the text to support your thesis. Write your paragraph to a friend whom you would like to convince to read, or not read, the story.

Collaborative Learning

Partner Discussion With a partner, discuss the resolution of "The Ransom of Red Chief." Resolution is the point in the story where the central conflict ends. Describe the central conflict and discuss what makes the resolution humorous. After your discussion, write a paragraph summarizing your discussion.

Critical Literacy

Perform a Monologue Work in a small group to prepare a portion of "The Ransom of Red Chief" to be performed as a short dramatic monologue. Write your monologue together. Then divide it into pieces and choose members of your group to read it aloud. Those who are not performing will the directors. Present your monologue to the class.

 Go to **www.mirrorsandwindows.com** for more.

Rubrics for Writing Options

You can adapt this as a checklist for students to use as they write.

Creative Writing

☐ Is the news story comprehensive in covering the events of the story?

☐ Does it include an attention-grabbing headline?

☐ Does it include an effective opening paragraph?

Expository Writing

☐ Does the paragraph indicate an understanding of tone?

☐ Does it offer an offer an opinion about the tone of the story?

☐ Is it persuasive?

☐ Does it use evidence from the chart?

Grammar & Style

Pronoun Use

Subject and Object Pronouns

We took him up to the cave, and I hitched the horse in the cedar brake.

—O. HENRY, "The Ransom of Red Chief"

A **pronoun** is a word that takes the place of a noun. A **personal pronoun** is used in place of the name of a person or thing. In the sentence above, the personal pronoun *we* takes the place of the names of two kidnappers; the personal pronoun *him* is used instead of the name of their victim.

Personal pronouns are sometimes used as the subjects of sentences. Personal pronouns are also used as the objects of verbs or prepositions. A **subject pronoun** is used as the subject of a sentence. An **object pronoun** is used as the object of a verb or a preposition.

EXAMPLES

subject pronoun	The narrator and Bill need money. <u>They</u> decided to kidnap a boy. [subject of sentence]
object pronoun	The kidnappers put <u>him</u> in the bottom of the buggy. [direct object of the verb *put*]
object pronoun	Mr. Dorset sent <u>them</u> a letter demanding money to take Johnny back. [indirect object of the verb *sent*]
object pronoun	The kidnappers left Johnny with <u>him</u> and ran away. [object of the preposition *with*]

	Singular	Plural
Used as Subjects	*I*	*we*
	you	*you*
	he, she, it	*they*
Used as Objects	*me*	*us*
	you	*you*
	him, her, it	*them*

Subject and object pronouns are also used in compound subjects and compound objects.

EXAMPLES

Johnny and the kidnappers camped out in a cave.

<u>He</u> and <u>they</u> camped out in a cave.

[*He* and *they* form the compound subject.]

Mr. Dorset opened the door and saw Johnny and the kidnappers.

Mr. Dorset opened the door and saw <u>him</u> and <u>them</u>.

[*Him* and *them* form the compound object.]

Identifying Subject and Object Pronouns

For each of the following sentences, identify the form of the pronoun that would correctly go in the blank.

1. The president welcomed the king and queen and then chatted with (he/him) and (she/her).
2. My brother and (I/me) drove from Boston to Chicago.
3. Winning the playoffs meant a great deal to (we/us).
4. We wrote (they/them) a letter of acceptance.
5. (She/Her) and (I/me) ran after the departing bus.

Teach the Workshop

Identifying Subject and Object Pronouns

1. him; her
2. I
3. us
4. them
5. she; I

> For more information, see the Grammar & Style Section 3.4, Pronouns, in the Language Arts Handbook.

Program Resources

You will find additional lessons on Pronoun Use in the *Exceeding the Standards: Grammar & Style* resource.

Build Skills

Remind students to use subject pronouns after linking verbs. Offer these examples:

The person at the door was he. (Think: He was the person at the door.)

The lacrosse champions were Anna and I. (Think: Anna and I were the lacrosse champions.)

KEY TERMS

PRONOUN, 199
PERSONAL PRONOUN, 199
SUBJECT PRONOUN, 199
OBJECT PRONOUN, 199
COMPOUND SUBJECT, 199
COMPOUND OBJECT, 199

TEACHING NOTE

Extra Practice

Give students these sentences, and have them choose the correct pronouns. Be sure students watch out for prepositions and linking verbs.

1. Seeing the film the first weekend it opened was important to (we/<u>us</u>).
2. (<u>They</u>/Them) drove together and met (we/<u>us</u>) at the movie theater.
3. Mark and (<u>she</u>/her) both liked the sequel better than the original movie.
4. The reaction from Katie and (I/<u>me</u>) was very different.
5. The actor in the original film was not (<u>he</u>/him).

Common Core State Standards

Language
L1

MEN ON THE MOON

A Short Story by Simon Ortiz

At a Glance
Directed Reading
- Reading Level: Moderate
- Difficulty Consideration: Unconventional style
- Ease Factors: None

Objectives
Studying this lesson will enable students to
- use reading skills such as monitoring comprehension
- define *characterization* and recognize the effect of this literary technique in the selection
- describe the work of Simon Ortiz and how his Native American heritage and the landscape of New Mexico influence his works
- appreciate a story showing differing perspectives of a historical event

Launch the Lesson
Before reading "Men on the Moon," you might ask students to think about what it must have been like for people watching the first moon landings and how those events changed their lives. You may also ask students to think about dreams they have had that mirrored real life, and how interpreting the dreams helped them understand real events.

BEFORE READING

Build Background
Historical Context This story deals with the reaction of an aged Acoma Indian to seeing the *Apollo 12* moon landing on television. On November 19, 1969, *Apollo 12* became the second manned landing on the moon. The mission was televised, and millions of people around the world watched.

Reader's Context Do you ever have dreams about unsettling events from real life? How might your dreams help you better understand your feelings?

Set Purpose
Use Build Background, the story title, and the first paragraph to preview "Men on the Moon." Based on your preview, what do you think the story will focus on?

Analyze Literature
Characterization The act of creating or describing a character is **characterization.** A character is a person or animal who takes part in the action of a literary work. Writers create characters by showing what they say, do, or think; by showing what other characters say or think about them; and by describing their physical features and personality. As you read, note how the author characterizes Faustin.

Meet the Author
Simon Ortiz has published more than a dozen books including poetry, memoir, short stories, nonfiction, and children's books. He was born in New Mexico in 1941 and is a member of the Acoma Pueblo people, a Native American tribe. Ortiz grew up speaking Keres, the language of the Acoma people, and did not learn to speak English until he was six. ("Men on the Moon" contains many Keres words.) Ortiz was greatly influenced by the Acoma oral storytelling tradition and the New Mexico landscape. Both of these influences are seen in "Men on the Moon."

Use Reading Skills
Monitor Comprehension
Monitoring comprehension means to be aware of your understanding of a text. Taking notes while you read helps you clarify and remember the main ideas in a selection. If you come across information or ideas that don't make sense to you, read on further to see if they become clearer. Create a note-taking chart like the one below. As you read, write down your reactions to the text and summarize the main ideas.

Section or Page	Main Ideas	My Reaction
Page 202	The family is watching a new TV.	Faustin, the grandfather, doesn't seem to understand TV.
Summary of My Notes		

Preview Vocabulary
phase (fāz) *n.*, part of a cycle

in·tent·ly (en tənt´ lē) *adv.*, with firm concentration

bound (baund) *v.*, move by leaping

gui·dance (gī´ dənts) *n.*, advice given to someone, often a student or child

lum·ber (lᴜm´ bər) *v.*, move slowly

Words in Use

Preview Vocabulary
phase, 203
intently, 203
bounded, 204
guidance, 205
lumber, 206

Selection Words
headdress, 202
emitting, 203
undeterred, 205

Common Core State Standards
Reading Literature
RL.1
Writing
W.9
Language
L.6

MEN ON THE MOON

A Short Story by Simon Ortiz

It's a dream, but it's the truth.

201

Teach the Selection

Summary

Faustin, an elderly Acoma Indian, watches the *Apollo 12* moon landing on television with his grandson. Faustin questions his grandson about the authenticity of the space flight as well as the purpose of the moon exploration. That night he has a dream in which a Pueblo hero has an encounter with a giant machine. He describes the dream to his grandson. The grandfather insists that the dream is the truth, and the grandson says he believes him.

The Mirrors & Windows questions at the end of this selection focus on the theme of tradition. Before reading the story, ask students how cultural traditions can enhance our experience in this technological age. What importance does our society place on cultural values?

Art Connection

This photograph of *Apollo 11* astronaut Edwin Aldrin on the moon was taken by fellow astronaut Neil Armstrong (who is reflected in Aldrin's visor). Point out that no humans have visited the moon for more than 35 years (since the *Apollo 17* mission in December 1972). Ask students how they react to this image. Does it seem heroic and exciting (as it did to most of those who first viewed it) or does it now seem merely "historic"?

Program Resources

Planning and Assessment
Program Planning Guide, Selection Lesson Plan
E-Lesson Planner
Assessment Guide, Lesson Test
ExamView

Technology Tools
Interactive Student Text on CD
Visual Teaching Package
Audio Library
mirrorsandwindows.com

Meeting the Standards
Fiction: Unit 2, Directed Reading, pp. 54–61

Differentiating Instruction
Advanced Students, Primary Source Project, pp. 12–13

Use Reading Skills

Monitor Comprehension Give students a few minutes after reading the page to record information on their note-taking charts. Ask them to share some of the information they have recorded. They may say that a main idea for the page is that the daughter and grandson take good care of Faustin. **Ⓐ**

Analyze Literature

Characterization Have students look back at the Analyze Literature: Characterization feature (page 200) and review the ways the author creates or describes a character. Ask them to consider which methods the author uses here to describe Faustin and what they learn about him from the descriptions. Model a response: "Faustin lives a simple life, as described by the worn couch and the old coat. He may be reluctant to accept changes." **Ⓑ**

Cultural Connection

The Pueblo People The Pueblo people mostly live in one of nineteen communities located mainly in New Mexico, but with some in Colorado and Arizona. There are two primary languages, Keres and Tano. Many people also speak English and/or Spanish. The Pueblo people are deeply spiritual and believe strongly in the sacredness of the natural world.

Ⓐ Joselita brought her father, Faustin, the TV on Father's Day. She brought it over after Sunday mass[1] and she had her son hook up the antenna. She plugged the TV into the wall socket.

Ⓑ Faustin sat on a worn couch. He was covered with an old coat. He had worn that coat for twenty years.

It's ready. Turn it on and I'll adjust the antenna, Amarosho told his mother. The TV warmed up and then it flickered into dull light. It was snowing. Amarosho tuned it a bit. It snowed less and then a picture formed.

Look, Naishtiya,[2] Joselita said. She touched her father's hand and pointed at the TV.

I'll turn the antenna a bit and you tell me when the picture is clear, Amarosho said. He climbed on the roof again.

After a while the picture turned clearer. It's better, his mother shouted. There was only the tiniest bit of snow falling.

That's about the best it can get I guess, Amarosho said. Maybe it'll clear up on the other channels. He turned the selector. It was clearer on another.

There were two men struggling with each other. Wrestling, Amarosho said. Do you want to watch wrestling? Two men are fighting, Nana. One of them is Apache Red. Chiseh tsah, he told his grandfather.

The old man stirred. He had been staring intently into the TV. He wondered why there

> *Faustin wondered if the men had run out of places to look for knowledge on the earth.*

was so much snow at first. Now there were two men fighting. One of them was Chiseh, an Apache, and the other was a Mericano.[3] There were people shouting excitedly and clapping hands within the TV.

The two men backed away from each other once in a while and then they clenched. They wheeled mightily and suddenly one threw the other. The old man smiled. He wondered why they were fighting.

Something else showed on the TV screen. A bottle of wine was being poured. The old man liked the pouring sound and he moved his mouth. Someone was selling wine.

The two fighting men came back on the TV. They struggled with each other and after a while one of them didn't get up and then another person came and held up the hand of the Apache who was dancing around in a feathered headdress.

It's over, Amarosho announced. Apache Red won the fight, Nana.

The Chiseh won. Faustin watched the other one, a light-haired man who looked totally exhausted and angry with himself. He didn't like the Apache too much. He wanted them to fight again.

After a few moments something else appeared on the TV.

What is that? Faustin asked. There was an object with smoke coming from it. It was standing upright.

---

1. **Sunday mass.** Roman Catholic religious service
2. **Naishtiya.** Father (Keres)
3. **Mericano.** American (Keres)

Differentiated Instruction

Reading Proficiency
Encourage students to preview the story. Have them read the Before Reading page, as well as the quotes within the story, and examine the photos and art. Discuss what they think the story will be about. What do they want to learn?

Enrichment
Interested students may research the history of the United States space exploration programs and present a short report. They could include a visual time line, NASA photographs, and information about websites that students could access.

Men are going to the moon, Nana, his grandson said. It's Apollo. It's going to fly three men to the moon.

That thing is going to fly to the moon?

Yes, Nana.

What is it called again?

Apollo, a spaceship rocket, Joselita told her father.

The Apollo spaceship stood on the ground emitting clouds of something that looked like smoke.

A man was talking, telling about the plans for the flight, what would happen, that it was almost time. Faustin could not understand the man very well because he didn't know many words in Mericano.

He must be talking about that thing flying in the air? he said.

Yes. It's about ready to fly away to the moon.

Faustin remembered that the evening before he had looked at the sky and seen that the moon was almost in the middle <u>phase</u>. He wondered if it was important that the men get to the moon.

Are those men looking for something on the moon? he asked his grandson.

They're trying to find out what's on the moon, Nana, what kind of dirt and rocks there are, to see if there's any life on the moon. The men are looking for knowledge, Amarosho told him.

Faustin wondered if the men had run out of places to look for knowledge on the earth. Do they know if they'll find knowledge? he asked.

They have some information already. They've gone before and come back. They're going again.

Did they bring any back?

They brought back some rocks.

Rocks. Faustin laughed quietly. The scientist men went to search for knowledge on the moon and they brought back rocks.

He thought that perhaps Amarosho was joking with him. The grandson had gone to Indian School for a number of years and sometimes he would tell his grandfather some strange and funny things.

C The old man was suspicious. They joked around a lot. Rocks—you sure that's all they brought back?

That's right, Nana, only rocks and some dirt and pictures they made of what it looks like on the moon.

The TV picture was filled with the rocket, close up now. Men were sitting and moving around by some machinery and the voice had become more urgent. The old man watched the activity in the picture <u>intently</u> but with a slight smile on his face.

Suddenly it became very quiet, and the voice was firm and commanding and curiously pleading. Ten, nine, eight, seven, six, five, four, three, two, liftoff. The white **D** smoke became furious and a muted rumble shook through the TV. The rocket was trembling and the voice was trembling.

---

phase (fāz) *n.*, part of a cycle

in·tent·ly (en tənt′ lē) *adv.*, with firm concentration

MEN ON THE MOON **203**

Teach the Selection

Use Reading Strategies
Visualize Remind students that visualizing a scene will help them appreciate and understand the story at deeper levels. Ask students to describe what they see when they read about Faustin watching the rocket on the television and remembering looking at the moon. Ask how he looks, what he is wearing, what sounds he might hear, and what the moon looks like. **C**

History Connection
The Apollo Program NASA ran the Apollo program from 1963 to 1972. In six of the missions, astronauts landed on the moon and returned to Earth with a total of more than 400 kilograms of samples of soil and rocks. This achievement is considered a milestone in planetary science. The availability of the moon samples on Earth has allowed scientists to continue studying them with increasingly sophisticated scientific equipment. **D**

Analyze Literature
Point of View Remind students that since the story is told from a third-person omniscient point of view, the reader learns about the thoughts and feelings of many of the characters. Ask students what they learn about Faustin in this part of the story. Model a response. "Faustin does not seem to have much background in science, because he does not understand the value of studying the moon rocks. He may not even believe that the moon exploration is real." **E**

Vocabulary Skills

Words from Myths

Point out to students that NASA and other scientific organizations often use the names of mythological characters to name space-related programs and objects. The Apollo program was named for the Roman god Apollo, who was associated with healing, light, and truth. The Mercury program was named for the Roman god of trade, profit, and travel. The planets were also named for Greek and Roman gods. Invite students to suggest other objects or programs that were named for mythological characters. Possible example: Atlas rockets used to launch U.S. spacecraft—named for Greek Titan who carried the world on his shoulders.

Analyze Literature

Conflict Tell students that one type of conflict is that between two characters. Ask students to read the section of text that identifies the conflict between Faustin and Amarosho. Ask students if they think Amarosho is aware of the conflict and to support their opinions. **A**

Use Reading Strategies

Make Predictions Remind students that when they make a prediction, they use information from the selection plus their own knowledge to make an intelligent guess about what might happen. Invite students to discuss what they think might happen next in the story and to explain how they arrived at the prediction. **B**

Analyze Literature

Setting Remind students that the setting usually includes time, place, and location. In "Men on the Moon," culture also plays an important part in the setting. Point out that Faustin's dream is based on characters from Native American legends and takes place in an area similar to where he lives. **C**

Using Reading Strategies

Ask Questions Model for students a few questions that they might ask about this section of the story: "Has Faustin had dreams like this before? Why is the coyote afraid of the machine?" Invite students to share some of their own questions with the class. **D**

It was really happening, the old man marvelled. Somewhere inside of that cylinder with a point at its top and long slender wings were three men who were flying to the moon.

The rocket rose from the ground. There were enormous clouds of smoke and the picture shook. Even the old man became tense and he grasped the edge of the couch. The rocket spaceship rose and rose.

There's fire coming out of the rocket, Amarosho explained. That's what makes it go.

Fire. Faustin had wondered what made it fly. He'd seen pictures of other flying machines. They had long wings and someone had explained to him that there was machinery inside which spun metal blades which made them fly. He had wondered what made this thing fly. He hoped his grandson wasn't joking him.

After a while there was nothing but the sky. The rocket Apollo had disappeared. It hadn't taken very long and the voice from the TV wasn't excited anymore. In fact the voice was very calm and almost bored.

I have to go now, Naishtiya, Joselita told her father. I have things to do.

Me, too, Amarosho said.

Wait, the old man said, wait. What shall I do with this thing. What is it you call it?

TV, his daughter said. You watch it. You turn it on and you watch it.

I mean how do you stop it. Does it stop like the radio, like the mahkina?[4] It stops?

This way, Nana, Amarosho said and showed his grandfather. He turned the dial and the picture went away. He turned the dial again and the picture flickered on again. Were you afraid this one-eye would be looking at you all the time? Amarosho laughed and gently patted the old man's shoulder.

Faustin was relieved. Joselita and her son left. He watched the TV for a while. A lot of activity was going on, a lot of men were

moving among machinery, and a couple of men were talking. And then it showed the rocket again.

He watched it rise and fly away again. It disappeared again. There was nothing but the sky. He turned the dial and the picture died away. He turned it on and the picture came on again. He turned it off. He went outside and to a fence a distance from his home. When he finished he studied the sky for a while.

II

That night, he dreamed.

Flintwing Boy[5] was watching a Skquuyuh[6] mahkina come down a hill. The mahkina made a humming noise. It was walking. It shone in the sunlight. Flintwing Boy moved to a better position to see. The mahkina kept on moving. It was moving towards him.

The Skquuyuh mahkina drew closer. Its metal legs stepped upon trees and crushed growing flowers and grass. A deer bounded away frightened. Tshushki[7] came running to Flintwing Boy.

Anaweh,[8] he cried, trying to catch his breath.

The coyote was staring at the thing which was coming towards them. There was wild fear in his eyes.

What is that, Anaweh? What is that thing? he gasped.

It looks like a mahkina, but I've never seen one like it before. It must be some kind of Skquuyuh mahkina.

Where did it come from?

---

4. **mahkina.** Machine (Keres)
5. **Flintwing Boy.** Hero from Pueblo oral tradition
6. **Skquuyuh.** Giant, powerful (with the added sense of monstrous, evil) (Keres)
7. **Tshushki.** Coyote, hero from Pueblo oral tradition (Keres)
8. **Anaweh.** Nephew (Keres)

bound (baund) v., move by leaping

Differentiated Instruction

English Language Learning

Giving students learning English a definition may help them understand unfamiliar terms.

snow — white specs on a television screen caused by interference with the signal, 202

middle phase — portion of the moon's cycle in which the moon is full, 203

Reading Proficiency

Encourage students to summarize the story at the end of Part I. Have them respond to the following questions: Who are the characters? What is the setting? What are the conflicts? What are the main events? Then ask them what they think will happen in the rest of the story.

I'm not sure yet, Anaweh, Flintwing Boy said. When he saw that Tshushki was trembling with fear, he said gently, Sit down, Anaweh. Rest yourself. We'll find out soon enough.

The Skquuyuh mahkina was undeterred. It walked over and through everything. It splashed through a stream of clear water. The water boiled and streaks of oil flowed downstream. It split a juniper tree in half with a terrible crash. It crushed a boulder into dust with a sound of heavy metal. Nothing stopped the Skquuyuh mahkina. It hummed.

Anaweh, Tshushki cried, what shall we do? What can we do?

Flintwing Boy reached into the bag at his side. He took out an object. It was a flint arrowhead. He took out some cornfood.

Come over here, Anaweh. Come over here. Be calm, he motioned to the frightened coyote. He touched the coyote in several places of his body with the arrowhead and put cornfood in the palm of his hand.

This way, Flintwing Boy said and closed Tshushki's fingers over the cornfood gently. And they faced east. Flintwing Boy said, We humble ourselves again. We look in your direction for guidance. We ask for your protection. We humble our poor bodies and spirits because only you are the power and the source and the knowledge. Help us then—that is all we ask.

They breathed on the cornfood and took in the breath of all directions and gave the cornfood unto the ground.

Now the ground trembled with the awesome power of the Skquuyuh mahkina. Its humming vibrated against everything. Flintwing Boy reached behind him and took several arrows from his quiver.[9] He inspected them carefully and without any rush he fit one to his bowstring.

And now, Anaweh, you must go and tell everyone. Describe what you have seen. The people must talk among themselves and decide what it is about and what they will do. You must hurry but you must not alarm the people. Tell them I am here to meet it. I will give them my report when I find out. **E**

Coyote turned and began to run. He stopped several yards away. Hahtrudzaimeh,[10] he called. Like a man of courage, Anaweh, like a man.

The old man stirred in his sleep. A dog was barking. He awoke and got out of his bed and went outside. The moon was past the midpoint and it would be morning light in a few hours.

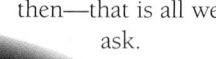

Later, the spaceship reached the moon.

Amarosho was with his grandfather. They watched a replay of two men walking on the moon.

So that's the men on the moon, Faustin said.

Yes, Nana, that's it.

There were two men inside of heavy clothing and equipment. The TV picture showed a closeup of one of them and indeed there was a man's face inside of glass. The face moved its mouth and smiled and spoke

---

9. **quiver.** Case for carrying arrows
10. **Hahtrudzaimeh.** Act with courage (Keres)

gui•dance (gī′ dənts) *n.,* advice given to someone, often a student or child

Cultural Connection

Dreams In Native North American cultures, dreams hold a great deal of significance. Dreams are considered to be true and another form or dimension of reality. Native Americans pay close attention to information presented in dreams.

Make Connections

Ask students how they might respond to a dream such as Faustin's. Have them share their ideas with the class.

Use Reading Strategies

Make Inferences Remind students that making an inference involves combining new information with what they already know. Ask students why Flintwing Boy told Anaweh to tell the people but not alarm them, and why he said he would give them a report. **E**

Use Reading Skills

Monitor Comprehension Review with students the information they have recorded on their charts so far. Discuss the main ideas for each page and their reactions to the story. Suggest that students keep adding to the chart until they finish reading the story and then write their summary.

Writing Skills

Textual Evidence

Review with students the criteria for the Expository Writing option on page 210. Suggest that they make a chart to keep track of information about the characters, setting, and plot. They should write down examples of each element from the story as well as the page numbers where they found the information. Tell students to state the theme early in the first paragraph of their essay. They might want to use separate paragraphs to explain how the characters, setting, and plot influence the theme. Remind them to use the examples from their list as textual evidence to support the theme. The last paragraph should restate the theme and summarize their ideas.

Science Connection

Gravity Gravity on the moon is one-sixth of what it is on Earth. For example, someone who weighs 90 pounds on Earth would weigh 14.9 pounds on the moon. Someone who weighs 125 pounds on Earth would weigh 20.8 pounds on the moon. The lower gravity allowed the astronauts to jump long distances. **A**

Analyze Literature

Point of View Discuss with students what Faustin's thoughts tell about him. What might be Faustin's definition of knowledge? Do they think he believes the astronauts will find knowledge on the moon? **B**

Analyze Literature

Characterization Point out that Faustin wonders if the moon landing vehicle will cause fear. However, he does not want to share his thoughts with his grandson. Ask students what these two situations reveal about Faustin's character. **C**

Analyze Literature

Tone Point out that word choice is important in establishing the tone. Ask students what tone the author's use of the word *knowledge* conveys. How would the tone be different if the author used words like *information* or *data* when talking about the rock samples from the moon? **D**

but the voice seemed to be separate from the face.

It must be cold. They have heavy clothing on, Faustin said.

It's supposed to be very cold and very hot. They wear the clothes and other things for protection from the cold and heat, Amarosho said.

The men on the moon were moving slowly. One of them skipped and he floated alongside the other.

The old man wondered if they were underwater. They seem to be able to float, he said.

A The information I have heard is that a man weighs less than he does on earth, Amarosho said to his grandfather. Much less, and he floats. And there is no air on the moon for them to breathe, so those boxes on their backs contain air for them to breathe.

He weighs less, the old man wondered, and there is no air except for the boxes on their backs. He looked at Amarosho but his grandson didn't seem to be joking with him.

The land on the moon looked very dry. It looked like it had not rained for a long, long time. There were no trees, no plants, no grass. Nothing but dirt and rocks, a desert. **D**

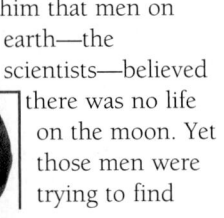

B Amarosho had told him that men on earth—the scientists—believed there was no life on the moon. Yet those men were trying to find knowledge on the moon. He wondered perhaps they had special tools with which they could find knowledge even if they believed there was no life on the moon desert.

The mahkina sat on the desert. It didn't make a sound. Its metal feet were planted flat on the ground. It looked somewhat awkward. Faustin searched vainly around the mahkina but there didn't seem to be anything except **C** the dry land on the TV. He couldn't figure out the mahkina. He wasn't sure whether it could move and could cause fear. He didn't want to ask his grandson that question.

After a while, one of the bulky men was digging in the ground. He carried a long thin hoe with which he scooped dirt and put it into a container. He did this for a while.

Is he going to bring the dirt back to earth too? Faustin asked.

I think he is, Nana, Amarosho said. Maybe he'll get some rocks too. Watch.

Indeed several minutes later the man <u>lumbered</u> over to a pile of rocks and gathered several handsize ones. He held them out proudly. They looked just like rocks from around anyplace. The voice from the TV seemed to be excited about the rocks.

They will study the rocks too for knowledge?

Yes, Nana.

What will they use the knowledge for, Nana?

They say they will use it to better mankind, Nana. I've heard that. And to learn more about the universe we live in. Also some of them say that the knowledge will be useful in finding out where everything began and how everything was made.

Faustin smiled at his grandson. He said, You are telling me the true facts aren't you?

lum • ber (lŭm´ bər) *v.*, move slowly

Identify Multiple Levels of Meaning

Remind students that an author often has more than one level of meaning in a passage. They can usually identify the factual meaning just by reading the passage. However, they may need to make inferences to arrive at the deeper level of meaning. Call attention to the scene early in the story where Faustin is watching the fight. He wonders why the Apache and the Mericano were wrestling. On the surface level, he is watching a wrestling match. Ask students what other significance this scene might have.

Why yes, Nana. That's what they say. I'm not just making it up, Amarosho said.

Well then—do they say why they need to know where everything began? Hasn't anyone ever told them?

I think other people have tried to tell them but they want to find out for themselves and also I think they claim they don't know enough and need to know more and for certain, Amarosho said.

The man in the bulky suit had a small pickaxe in his hand. He was striking at a boulder. The breathing of the man could clearly be heard. He seemed to be working very hard and was very tired.

Faustin had once watched a crew of Mericano drilling for water. They had brought a tall mahkina with a loud motor. The mahkina would raise a limb at its center to its very top and then drop it with a heavy and loud metal clang. The mahkina and its men sat at one spot for several days and finally they found water.

The water had bubbled out weakly, gray-looking and didn't look drinkable at all.

And then they lowered the mahkina, put their equipment away and drove away. The water stopped flowing.

After a couple of days he went and checked out the place. There was nothing there except a pile of gray dirt and an indentation in the ground. The ground was already dry and there were dark spots of oil-soaked dirt.

He decided to tell Amarosho about the dream he had.

After the old man finished, Amarosho said, Old man, you're telling me the truth now? You know that you have become somewhat of a liar. He was teasing his grandfather.

Yes, Nana. I have told you the truth as it occurred to me that night. Everything happened like that except that I might not have recalled everything about it.

That's some story, Nana, but it's a dream.

It's a dream, but it's the truth, Faustin said.

I believe you, Nana, his grandson said. ❖

What does this story suggest about the function of dreams in Native American tradition? What do you think are some of the important roles for traditional values in modern society?

Find Meaning

1. (a) What did Faustin know of the first manned landing on the moon? (b) What does that tell you about him?
2. (a) What is the setting of the dream? (b) What does this setting tell you about the conflict in the story?
3. (a) How does Faustin react to his grandson telling him that the knowledge found from data on the moon will be "useful in finding out where everything began and how everything was made"? (b) Why do you think Faustin reacts that way?

Make Judgments

4. What purpose does the character Amarosho serve in the story?
5. Why do you think Faustin dreams that Tshushki and Flintwing Boy are uncertain as to what to do about the Skquuyuh mahkina?
6. Coyote is instructed to tell the people about the Skquuyuh mahkina. How does this relate to the ending of the story?

Writing Skills

Media Literacy

Suggest to students that they create a multimedia presentation for the information they find about the *Apollo 11* mission. Discuss different formats they could use: a computer presentation done with presentation software that includes audio and video clips, a poster with accompanying video and/or audio recordings, a video they create of themselves acting as news reporters, a dramatic reading with background music and props. Students may also have other ideas. Remind them to use reliable Internet sources for their research such as the official NASA website and other sites that end with *.org* or *.edu*.

History Connection
"Buzz" Aldrin Edwin "Buzz" Aldrin was a member of the third group of astronauts that NASA formed in 1963. Aldrin was the lunar module pilot for *Apollo 11*, from July 16 to 24, 1969. He was the second human to ever walk on the moon, leaving the module soon after Neil Armstrong made the first historic step. During his career as an astronaut, Aldrin spent 289 hours and 53 minutes in space.

History Connection
The Space Race The Space Race took place between 1957 and 1969. As a part of the Cold War, the United States and the Soviet Union were both trying to establish their superiority through rocket launches and spaceflight. The Soviet Union was initially ahead when it launched *Sputnik I,* the first artificial satellite, in 1957. When the American astronauts landed on the moon in 1969, however, the United States effectively won the Space Race. Later, the Americans and Russians began working together in space exploration.

PRIMARY SOURCE ▶▶ CONNECTION

"Men on the Moon" shows a manned moon landing as seen through the eyes of an old Acoma man who is watching the event on television. In "Working on the Moon," you will read a firsthand account of what it was like to actually be on the moon. "Working on the Moon" is an account by astronaut **Edwin Aldrin, Jr.** Aldrin and Neil Armstrong were two members of the *Apollo 11* mission. They became the first humans to walk on the moon. As you read, compare Aldrin's firsthand account of his experiences on the moon with Faustin's reaction to watching men walk on the moon.

Working on the Moon

A Primary Source by Edwin Aldrin, Jr.

Other astronauts have walked on the moon since Neil Armstrong and Edwin Aldrin, and scientists have sent dozens of spacecraft to probe the mysteries of the solar system. But none of these missions has captured the popular imagination as did Apollo 11, *carrying the first explorers on the moon. In the following selection, Aldrin explains what it was like to work on the moon.*

Ⓐ The moon was a very natural and very pleasant environment in which to work. It had many of the advantages of zero-gravity [weightlessness], but it was in a sense less *lonesome* than zero G, where you always have to pay attention to securing attachment points to give you some means of leverage. In one-sixth gravity, on the moon, you had a distinct feeling of being *somewhere,* and you had a constant, though at many times ill defined, sense of direction and force.

One interesting thing was that the horizontal reference on the moon is not at all well defined. That is, it's difficult to know when you are leaning forward or backward and to what degree. This fact, coupled with the rather limited field of vision from our helmets, made local features of the moon appear to change slope, depending on which way you were looking and how you were standing. The weight of the backpack tends to pull you backward, and you must consciously lean forward just a little to compensate.[1] I believe someone has described the posture as "tired ape"—almost erect[2] but slumped forward a little. It was difficult sometimes to know when you were standing erect. It felt as if you could lean farther in any direction, without losing your balance, than on earth. By far the easiest and most natural way to move on the surface of the moon is to put one foot in front of the other. The kangaroo hop did work, but it led to some instability; there was not so much control when you were moving around.

As we deployed our experiments on the surface we had to jettison[3] things like lanyards [short cords], retaining fasteners, etc., and some of these we tossed away. The

---

1. **compensate.** Make up for something
2. **erect.** Standing up straight
3. **jettison.** Get rid of things

208 UNIT 2 FICTION

Common Core State Standards

Reading Literature
RL.3

Reading Informational
RI.1, RI.9

Writing
W.7, W.8, W.9, W.10

Language
L.6

Differentiated Instruction

Enrichment
Interested students might enjoy researching the kinds of tools the Apollo astronauts used on the moon. Others might want to identify consumer items that are offshoots of the space industry (Teflon, Velcro).

Words in Use

"Working on the Moon"

Selection Words
leverage, 208
instability, 208
deployed, 208
compacted, 209
pungent, 209

objects would go away with a slow, lazy motion. If anyone tried to throw a baseball back and forth in that atmosphere he would have difficulty, at first, acclimatizing[4] himself to that slow, lazy trajectory [path]; but I believe he could adapt to it quite readily.

Technically the most difficult task I performed on the surface was driving those core samplers into the ground to get little tubes of lunar material for study. There was a significant and surprising resistance just a few inches down. But this resistance was not accompanied by a strong supporting force on the sides. What this meant, quite simply, was that I had to hold on to the top of the core tube extension while I was hitting it with the hammer to drive it down into the ground. I actually missed once or twice. It wasn't a question of visibility. In bringing the hammer down, I tended to disturb my own body position and my balance. One explanation

for the strange degree of resistance may be that, having already been compressed by the lack of atmosphere, it has been continually pounded by meteorites. This pounding probably has compacted that lower material much further, to a point where additional compacting—like that of forcing a cutting tool and tube through it—requires significant applications of force....

Odor is very subjective [personal], but to me there was a distinct smell to the lunar material—pungent, like gunpowder or spent cap-pistol caps. We carted a fair amount of lunar dust back inside the vehicle with us, either on our suits and boots or on the conveyor system we used to get boxes and equipment back inside. We did notice the odor right away.

It was a unique, almost mystical environment up there. ❖

---
4. **acclimatizing.** Getting used to a different surrounding

TEXT →TO← TEXT
CONNECTION

Both Simon Ortiz's short story and Edwin Aldrin's nonfiction account deal with lunar landings. Compare and contrast what each writer presents and their purposes. How does Aldrin's account of his experience differ from Faustin's reaction to the lunar mission? Is any of the information in the two texts the same or similar?

Teach the Connection

Use Reading Strategies
Visualize Point out to students that Aldrin's description of the moon includes details about how its surface looked, how it smelled, and how its lower gravity affected him physically. Ask them to review the article and pick out two or three strong descriptions of Aldrin's experience on the moon. Model a possible answer such as "to me there was a distinct smell to the lunar material — pungent, like gunpowder or spent cap-pistol caps." **B**

Use Reading Skills
Compare and Contrast Ask students why they think Ortiz wrote "Men on the Moon" and why Aldrin wrote "Working on the Moon." Engage them in a discussion to compare the authors' purposes. Model a possible response: "Ortiz wanted to show how a modern event could affect someone from a traditional culture who is not familiar with modern technology. Aldrin wanted to share his real and exciting experiences with others."

Text-to-Text Connection
Answer: Students may say that Aldrin gives the reader a close-up, firsthand view of the experience, described in clear, scientific detail. Faustin experiences the walk from a distance, but he gives a more vivid description of what the moon looks like and how the astronauts appear in their suits.

Vocabulary Skills

Acronyms
Remind students that an acronym is a word formed from the initials or other parts of several words. For example, NASA is an acronym that stands for National Aeronautics and Space Administration. Write the following NASA acronyms on the board:

- *CM*—command module
- *LM*—lunar module
- *EVA*—extra-vehicular activity

Explain these acronyms are related to NASA's lunar missions. Ask students to guess their meanings. Students may want to discuss how the acronyms employed in text messaging are changing communication.

Review the Selection

Analyze Literature

Characterization *Answer:* Faustin doesn't know how to work a television, which suggests he has lived a life somewhat isolated from the modern world. Faustin questions the purpose, value, and outcome of the moonwalk. This suggests he doesn't have the need for new knowledge about the universe because he is content with his belief system. The moon mission also causes him to have a disturbing dream revealing Faustin's concerns about the effects of technology on the natural world. The fact that his dream contains traditional Pueblo heroes shows that Faustin has a close connection to traditional ways.

Analyze Literature

Characterization Authors will often give information about a character by showing how the character reacts to events or situations. Use the chart to describe how Faustin reacts to certain events. What do these reactions tell you about Faustin?

Event	Reaction
Watching television	
Apollo 12 mission	

Extend Understanding

Writing Options

Creative Writing In "Men on the Moon," Faustin has a vivid dream that greatly affects him. Think about a vivid dream that you've had. Write a **description** of your dream. Descriptions should include sensory details and precise language. Sensory details are words and phrases that describe how things look, sound, smell, taste, or feel. If the dream has a change of setting or character, include a transition so that the reader is aware of the change. Share your work with a partner.

Expository Writing A theme is a central idea in a literary work. In a short story, a theme is developed and conveyed, or shown, through the elements of character, setting, and plot. Write a brief **essay** analyzing the theme of "Men on the Moon." State your main idea about the theme in your thesis. In the body, be sure to include details from the story that support your claims. Make sure your essay is structured in a way that makes it easy for the reader to follow your ideas. Share your work with the class.

Media Literacy

Multimedia Presentation With a partner, research the *Apollo 11* mission and create a multimedia presentation of your findings. In your presentation, include background on the Space Race and the political reasons for sending humans to the moon. Also include examples of new technologies that came out of the mission. Your presentation might also include a discussion of Neil Armstrong's famous words, "That's one small step for [a] man, one giant leap for mankind."

Critical Literacy

Hold a Panel Discussion Work with a group of classmates to discuss the meaning of Faustin's dream. The discussion should include what the characters and actions represent. Remember that these elements can have more than one meaning, or can be interpreted differently. Give reasons for your interpretation of the dream and support your position with textual evidence. Use speaking rate, enunciation, volume, eye contact, gestures, and language conventions to communicate your ideas effectively.

Go to www.mirrorsandwindows.com for more.

THE MEDICINE BAG

A Short Story by Virginia Driving Hawk Sneve

The Old Grandfather and His Little Grandson

A Folk Tale retold by Leo Tolstoy

Preview the Selections

At a Glance
Directed Reading
"The Medicine Bag"
- Reading Level: Moderate
- Difficulty Consideration: Unfamiliar subject matter
- Ease Factor: Author's style

"The Old Grandfather and His Little Grandson"
- Reading Level: Easy
- Difficulty Consideration: May not hold interest of all students
- Ease Factors: Length, simple plot, language

BEFORE READING

Build Background
Cultural Context "The Medicine Bag" and "The Old Grandfather and His Little Grandson" deal with younger generations caring for older family members. In most cultures, adult children care for their elderly parents.

Reader's Context How do you relate to different generations in your family?

Set Purpose
Dialogue Conversation involving two or more people or characters is **dialogue. Narration** is writing that tells about an event or sequence of events. As you read, notice when information comes through dialogue and when it comes through narration.

Meet the Authors

Virginia Driving Hawk Sneve often writes about her Sioux ancestry. Born in 1933 on the Rosebud Reservation in South Dakota, she studied at South Dakota State College. "The Medicine Bag" was inspired by the personal experience of one of Sneve's friends.

Leo Tolstoy (1828–1910) was a Russian novelist and philosopher. He is considered by many to be one of the world's greatest novelists. Tolstoy is also known for advocating the principles of nonviolence and nonviolent protest, themes which play a large part in his writing.

Compare Literature: Theme
A **theme** is a central idea in a literary work. As you read "The Medicine Bag" and "The Old Grandfather and His Little Grandson," note details that relate to what you think is the central idea of each work. For example:

Preview Vocabulary
wear·i·ly (wir´ ə lē) *adv.*, in an exhausted way

fa·tigue (fə tēg´) *n.*, extreme weariness or exhaustion

un·seem·ly (un sēm´ lē) *adj.*, not decent or proper

sheep·ish·ly (shē´ pish lē) *adv.*, in an awkwardly, shy, or embarrassed manner

rouse (rauz) *v.*, stir up, as to anger or action

Objectives
Studying this lesson will enable students to
- compare literary selections of different genres
- use reading strategies such as visualizing
- define *theme* and compare the effects of this literary technique in these selections
- describe the literary accomplishments of Virginia Driving Hawk Sneve and Leo Tolstoy
- appreciate different perspectives on elderly people

Launch the Lesson
Students might enjoy sharing an interesting story from their own lives dealing with caring for or visiting an elderly relative. Ask students what they would do if they saw a younger child imitating one of their actions and realized that the action was unkind or otherwise unacceptable.

Words in Use

"The Medicine Bag"

Preview Vocabulary	Selection Words	Teaching Words
wearily, 213	authentic, 213	generations, 211
fatigue, 214	frail, 215	ancestry, 211
unseemly, 214	descendants, 215	philosopher, 211
sheepishly, 215	lonesome, 218	advocating, 211
rouse, 215	sacred, 219	protest, 211
		drawbacks, 219
		obligation, 220

KEY TERMS

Common Core State Standards
Reading Literature
RL.2
Language
L.6

Summary

Martin and his sister, Cheryl, are Sioux on their mother's side. Each summer they visit their mother's grandfather on the reservation and come back home with exciting stories. However, they don't show their grandfather's picture because he does not look like a TV Indian. When he unexpectedly comes to visit, Cheryl eagerly welcomes him and invites her friends over. Martin is embarrassed and does not invite his friends. When he finally does and the friends accept Grandpa, Martin realizes his mistake. When Grandpa offers the traditional family medicine bag to Martin, he is not sure he wants to accept it. He does accept it and gains a new respect for Grandpa, shortly before Grandpa dies.

 The Mirrors & Windows questions at the end of these selections focus on the theme of generational differences. Before reading the story, ask students to discuss how our society, familial and governmental, feels about and treats the elderly.

Art Connection

Artist Joseph Henry Sharp lived in a cabin on the Little Bighorn River, where he recorded Native American life in works such as this portrait.

THE MEDICINE BAG

A Short Story by Virginia Driving Hawk Sneve

212

Program Resources

Planning and Assessment
Program Planning Guide, Selection Lesson Plan
E-Lesson Planner
Assessment Guide, Lesson Test
ExamView

Technology Tools
Interactive Student Text on CD
Visual Teaching Package
Audio Library
mirrorsandwindows.com

Meeting the Standards
Fiction: Unit 2, Comparing Literature,
   pp. 62–69

Differentiating Instruction
English Language Learners, Visualize,
   pp. 53–67

...WHEN GRANDPA CAME TO VISIT US, I WAS SO ASHAMED AND EMBARRASSED I COULD'VE DIED.

My kid sister Cheryl and I always bragged about our Sioux grandpa, Joe Iron Shell. Our friends, who had always lived in the city and knew about Indians only from movies and TV, were impressed by our stories. Maybe we exaggerated and made Grandpa and the reservation sound glamorous, but when we'd return home to Iowa after our yearly summer visit to Grandpa we always had some exciting tale to tell.

We always had some authentic Sioux article to show our listeners. One year Cheryl had new moccasins that Grandpa had made. On another visit he gave me a small, round, flat, rawhide drum which was decorated with a painting of a warrior riding a horse. He taught me a real Sioux chant to sing while I beat the drum with a leather-covered stick that had a feather on the end. Man, that really made an impression.

We never showed our friends Grandpa's picture. Not that we were ashamed of him, but because we knew that the glamorous tales we told didn't go with the real thing. Our friends would have laughed at the picture, because Grandpa wasn't tall and stately[1] like TV Indians. His hair wasn't in braids, but hung in stringy, gray strands on his neck and he was old. He was our great-grandfather, and he didn't live in a tipi but all by himself in a part log, part tar-paper shack on the Rosebud Reservation in South Dakota. So when Grandpa came to visit us, I was so ashamed and embarrassed I could've died.

There are a lot of yippy poodles and other fancy little dogs in our neighborhood, but they usually barked singly at the mailman from the safety of their own yards. Now it

sounded as if a whole pack of mutts were barking together in one place.

I got up and walked to the curb to see what the commotion was. About a block away I saw a crowd of little kids yelling, with the dogs yipping and growling around someone who was walking down the middle of the street.

I watched the group as it slowly came closer and saw that in the center of the strange procession was a man wearing a tall black hat. He'd pause now and then to peer at something in his hand and then at the houses on either side of the street. I felt cold and hot at the same time as I recognized the man. "Oh, no!" I whispered. "It's Grandpa!"

I stood on the curb, unable to move even though I wanted to run and hide. Then I got mad when I saw how the yippy dogs were growling and nipping at the old man's baggy pant legs and how <u>wearily</u> he poked them

---

1. **stately.** Dignified

wear·i·ly (wirʹ ə lē) *adv.*, in an exhausted way

(Opposite page) *Ogalalla Sioux 'Indian Scout' Sioux,* 1913.
Joseph Henry Sharp. Butler Institute of American Art, Youngstown, Ohio.

History Connection

The Great Sioux Nation The Great Sioux Nation originated as an alliance of seven bands—the *Oceti Sakowin*, or "Seven Council fires"—that spoke three different dialects: Dakota, Nakota, and Lakota. The name *Sioux*, which means "little snakes," came from the Chippewa, a nation that historically was at odds with the seven bands. The people of the Great Sioux Nation prefer to be called Dakota, Nakota, or Lakota, according to their language group. **Ⓐ**

Analyze Literature

Setting Remind students that the setting usually includes a time and place, and these are usually described. In this story, the reservation is part of the setting. Although the reservation is not described, students can get some idea of what it is like by the way the narrator describes Grandpa's clothes as being out of place in the neighborhood. **Ⓑ**

Use Reading Strategies

Make Inferences Point out that Mom sighed when she was talking with Martin. Ask students what they can infer from this. Possible response: "Mom is surprised and does not know how to handle having Grandpa in her house." **Ⓒ**

---

away with his cane. "Stupid mutts," I said as I ran to rescue Grandpa.

When I kicked and hollered at the dogs to get away, they put their tails between their legs and scattered. The kids ran to the curb where they watched me and the old man.

"Grandpa," I said and felt pretty dumb when my voice cracked. I reached for his beat-up old tin suitcase, which was tied shut with a rope. But he set it down right in the street and shook my hand.

Ⓐ "*Hau, Takoza,* Grandchild," he greeted me formally in Sioux.

All I could do was stand there with the whole neighborhood watching and shake the hand of the leather-brown old man. I saw how his gray hair straggled from under his big black hat, which had a drooping feather in its crown. His rumpled black suit hung like a sack over his stooped frame. As he shook my hand, his coat fell open to expose a bright red satin shirt with a beaded bolo **Ⓑ** tie[2] under the collar. His getup wasn't out of place on the reservation, but it sure was here, and I wanted to sink right through the pavement.

"Hi," I muttered with my head down. I tried to pull my hand away when I felt his bony hand trembling, and looked up to see <u>fatigue</u> in his face. I felt like crying. I couldn't think of anything to say so I picked up Grandpa's suitcase, took his arm, and guided him up the driveway to our house.

Mom was standing on the steps. I don't know how long she'd been watching, but her hand was over her mouth and she looked as if she couldn't believe what she saw. Then she ran to us.

"Grandpa," she gasped. "How in the world did you get here?"

She checked her move to embrace Grandpa and I remembered that such a display of affection is <u>unseemly</u> to the Sioux and would embarrass him.

"*Hau*, Marie," he said as he shook Mom's hand. She smiled and took his other arm.

As we supported him up the steps the door banged open and Cheryl came bursting out of the house. She was all smiles and was so obviously glad to see Grandpa that I was ashamed of how I felt.

ALL I COULD DO WAS STAND THERE WITH THE WHOLE NEIGHBORHOOD WATCHING AND SHAKE THE HAND OF THE LEATHER-BROWN OLD MAN.

"Grandpa!" she yelled happily. "You came to see us!"

Grandpa smiled and Mom and I let go of him as he stretched out his arms to my ten-year-old sister, who was still young enough to be hugged.

"*Wicincala*, little girl," he greeted her and then collapsed.

He had fainted. Mom and I carried him into her sewing room, where we had a spare bed.

After we had Grandpa on the bed Mom stood there helplessly patting his shoulder.

"Shouldn't we call the doctor, Mom?" I suggested, since she didn't seem to know what to do.

Ⓒ "Yes," she agreed with a sigh. "You make Grandpa comfortable, Martin."

---

2. bolo tie. Cord with ornamental fastening, worn as a necktie

fa·tigue (fə tēg′) *n.,* extreme weariness or exhaustion
un·seem·ly (un sēm′ lē) *adj.,* not decent or proper

Differentiated Instruction

English Language Learning

Use this part of the story to help English language learners distinguish between dialogue and narration. Explain that dialogue is a conversation involving two or more people or characters. The dialogue is enclosed in quotation marks and is often accompanied by tag lines—words and phrases such as *he said* or *she answered*. Narration is writing that tells about an event or a sequence of events. Model reading a few lines of dialogue for students. Tell them to try to sound the way they think the characters would sound. Assign parts, and have students read the dialogue and narration.

I reluctantly moved to the bed. I knew Grandpa wouldn't want to have Mom undress him, but I didn't want to, either. He was so skinny and frail that his coat slipped off easily. When I loosened his tie and opened his shirt collar, I felt a small leather pouch that hung from a thong[3] around his neck. I left it alone and moved to remove his boots. The scuffed old cowboy boots were tight and he moaned as I put pressure on his legs to jerk them off. **D**

I put the boots on the floor and saw why they fit so tight. Each one was stuffed with money. I looked at the bills that lined the boots and started to ask about them, but Grandpa's eyes were closed again.

Mom came back with a basin of water. "The doctor thinks Grandpa is suffering from heat exhaustion," she explained as she bathed Grandpa's face. Mom gave a big sigh, "Oh, *hinh*, Martin. How do you suppose he got here?"

We found out after the doctor's visit. Grandpa was angrily sitting up in bed while Mom tried to feed him some soup.

"Tonight you let Marie feed you, Grandpa," spoke my dad, who had gotten home from work just as the doctor was leaving. "You're not really sick," he said as he gently pushed Grandpa back against the pillows. "The doctor said you just got too tired and hot after your long trip."

Grandpa relaxed, and between sips of soup he told us of his journey. Soon after our visit to him Grandpa decided that he would like to see where his only living descendants lived and what our home was like. Besides, he admitted <u>sheepishly</u>, he was lonesome after we left.

I knew everybody felt as guilty as I did—especially Mom. Mom was all Grandpa had left. So even after she married my dad, who's a white man and teaches in the college in our city, and after Cheryl and I were born, Mom

made sure that every summer we spent a week with Grandpa.

I never thought that Grandpa would be lonely after our visits, and none of us noticed how old and weak he had become. But Grandpa knew and so he came to us. He had ridden on buses for two and a half days. When he arrived in the city, tired and stiff from sitting for so long, he set out, walking, to find us.

He had stopped to rest on the steps of some building downtown and a policeman found him. The cop, according to Grandpa, was a good man who took him to the bus stop and waited until the bus came and told the driver to let Grandpa out at Bell View Drive. After Grandpa got off the bus, he started walking again. But he couldn't see the house numbers on the other side when he walked on the sidewalk, so he walked in the middle of the street. That's when all the little kids and dogs followed him.

I knew everybody felt as bad as I did. Yet I was proud of this 86-year-old man, who had never been away from the reservation, having the courage to travel so far alone.

"You found the money in my boots?" he asked Mom.

"Martin did," she answered, and <u>roused</u> herself to scold. "Grandpa, you shouldn't have carried so much money. What if someone had stolen it from you?"

Grandpa laughed. "I would've known if anyone had tried to take the boots off my feet. The money is what I've saved for a long time—a hundred dollars—for my funeral. But you take it now to buy groceries so that I won't be a burden to you while I am here." **E**

---

3. **thong.** Narrow strip of leather

sheep·ish·ly (shē´ pish lē) *adv.*, in an awkwardly, shy, or embarrassed manner

rouse (rauz) *v.*, stir up, as to anger or action

THE MEDICINE BAG / THE OLD GRANDFATHER **215**

Teach the Selection

Analyze Literature
Foreshadowing Remind students that foreshadowing is a device that an author uses to give clues about events that will happen later in a narrative. Ask students what the author might be foreshadowing when Martin is the one to see the medicine bag. If necessary, model a possible response: "Since Martin is the one to see the medicine bag, later on he and Grandpa might talk more about its meaning." **D**

Use Reading Strategies
Make Inferences Point out that Grandpa had given his granddaughter the money he had been saving for his funeral. Ask students what they can infer from his actions. **E**

TEACHING NOTE

Ask the Narrator
As they read, have students jot down two or three questions they would like to ask the narrator of this selection such as "Why does the narrator feel like disappearing when his grandfather arrives?" When students are done with the selection, have them work in small groups to identify the most interesting of these questions. List them on the board and have the class explore the answers.

Vocabulary Skills

Etymologies of Native American Terms
Explain to students that many familiar English words came from various Native American languages. Present the following words and their languages of origin. Ask students to tell which of the words below are familiar to them.

chipmunk — Ojibwa
moccasin — Chippewa
moose — Algonquian

muskrat — Abenaki
opossum — Algonquian
squash — Natick
succotash — Narragansett
tipi — Dakota
toboggan — Algonquian
tomahawk — Algonquian
wigwam — Abenaki

Analyze Literature

Theme Remind students that the theme is the central idea in a literary work. Ask students how Dad's response to Grandpa fits in with the theme of the story. If necessary, model a possible response: "Dad understands the importance of treating elderly family members with love and respect." **A**

Use Reading Strategies

Clarify Have students review the reasons that Martin has not brought his friends home yet to see Grandpa, and compare his actions with those of his sister, Cheryl. Tell them to work in pairs to make sure they get the details correct. Suggest that they ask each other questions to clarify what they have read. **B**

Analyze Literature

Characterization Point out that the author develops the character of Grandpa by describing his appearance and dress. Ask students what the description reveals about Grandpa. Model a possible response: "Grandpa is proud of his heritage and traditional dress. He senses that Martin is unsure and not as proud, so he takes an action to help Martin." **C**

A "That won't be necessary, Grandpa," Dad said. "We are honored to have you with us and you will never be a burden. I am only sorry that we never thought to bring you home with us this summer and spare you the discomfort of a long trip."

Grandpa was pleased. "Thank you," he answered. "But do not feel bad that you didn't bring me with you for I would not have come then. It was not time." He said this in such a way that no one could argue with him. To Grandpa and the Sioux, he once told me, a thing would be done when it was the right time to do it, and that's the way it was.

"Also," Grandpa went on, looking at me, "I have come because it is soon time for Martin to have the medicine bag."

We all knew what that meant. Grandpa thought he was going to die and he had to follow the tradition of his family to pass the medicine bag, along with its history, to the oldest male child.

"Even though the boy," he said still looking at me, "bears a white man's name, the medicine bag will be his."

I didn't know what to say. I had the same hot and cold feeling that I had when I first saw Grandpa in the street. The medicine bag was the dirty leather pouch I had found around his neck. "I could never wear such a thing," I almost said aloud. I thought of having my friends see it in gym class, at the swimming pool, and could imagine the smart things they would say. But I just swallowed hard and took a step toward the bed. I knew I would have to take it.

But Grandpa was tired. "Not now, Martin," he said, waving his hand in dismissal, "it is not time. Now I will sleep."

> "NOT NOW, MARTIN," HE SAID, WAVING HIS HAND IN DISMISSAL, "IT IS NOT TIME."

So that's how Grandpa came to be with us for two months. My friends kept asking to come see the old man, but I put them off. I told myself that I didn't want them laughing at Grandpa. But even as I made excuses I knew it wasn't Grandpa that I was afraid they'd laugh at.

B Nothing bothered Cheryl about bringing her friends to see Grandpa. Every day after school started there'd be a crew of giggling little girls or round-eyed little boys crowded around the old man on the patio, where he'd gotten in the habit of sitting every afternoon.

Grandpa would smile in his gentle way and patiently answer their questions, or he'd tell them stories of brave warriors, ghosts, animals, and the kids listened in awed silence. Those little guys thought Grandpa was great.

Finally, one day after school, my friends came home with me because nothing I said stopped them. "We're going to see the great Indian of Bell View Drive," said Hank, who was supposed to be my best friend. "My brother has seen him three times so he oughta be well enough to see us."

When we got to my house Grandpa was sitting on the patio. He had on his red shirt, but today he also wore a fringed leather vest that was decorated with beads. Instead of his usual cowboy boots he had solidly beaded moccasins on his feet that stuck out of his black trousers. Of course, he had his old black hat on—he was seldom without it. But it had been brushed and the feather in the beaded headband was proudly erect, its tip a brighter white. His hair lay in silver strands over the red shirt collar.

I stared just as my friends did and I heard one of them murmur, "Wow!"

Differentiated Instruction

Auditory Learning

Point out that to the boys, the Sioux word *Hau* that Grandpa said sounded like *how,* which is the way one of the boys responded to Grandpa. Have students practice saying the other Sioux words in the story.

Enrichment

Interested students might create visual representations of medicine bags. Some students might construct re-creations of bags from brown cotton, velvet, or other fabric. Others might prefer to produce sketches, drawings, or paintings of medicine bags. You might wish to create a medicine bag display to showcase the students' creations.

Grandpa looked up and when his eyes met mine they twinkled as if he were laughing inside. He nodded to me and my face got all hot. I could tell that he had known all along I was afraid he'd embarrass me in front of my friends. **D**

"*Hau, hoksilas,* boys," he greeted and held out his hand.

My buddies passed in a single file and shook his hand as I introduced them. They were so polite I almost laughed. "How, there,

Grandpa," and even a "How-do-you-do, sir."

"You look fine, Grandpa," I said as the guys sat on the lawn chairs or on the patio floor.

"*Hanh,* yes," he agreed. "When I woke up this morning it seemed the right time to dress in the good clothes. I knew that my grandson would be bringing his friends."

"You guys want some lemonade or something?" I offered. No one answered. They were listening to Grandpa as he started telling how he'd killed the deer from which his vest was made.

Grandpa did most of the talking while my friends were there. I was so proud of him and amazed at how respectfully quiet my buddies were. Mom had to chase them home at supper time. As they left they shook Grandpa's hand again and said to me:

"Martin, he's really great!"

"Yeah, man! Don't blame you for keeping him to yourself." **F**

"Can we come back?"

But after they left, Mom said, "No more visitors for a while, Martin. Grandpa won't admit it, but his strength hasn't returned. He likes having company, but it tires him."

That evening Grandpa called me to his room before he went to sleep. "Tomorrow," he said, "when you come home, it will be time to give you the medicine bag."

I felt a hard squeeze from where my heart is supposed to be and was scared, but I answered, "OK, Grandpa."

All night I had weird dreams about thunder and lightning on a high hill. From a distance I heard the slow beat of a drum. When I woke up in the morning I felt as if I hadn't slept at all. At school it seemed as if the day would never end and, when it finally did, I ran home.

Grandpa was in his room, sitting on the bed. The shades were down, and the place was dim and cool. I sat on the floor in front of Grandpa, but he didn't even look at me. After what seemed a long time he spoke.

"I sent your mother and sister away. What you will hear today is only for a man's ears. What you will receive is only for a

CULTURAL ▶▶ CONNECTION

Sioux Nation The Sioux are a group of Native Americans who lived in the Great Lakes Region. The Sioux were considered great warriors. Shortly after the Civil War, the United States government began to drive the Sioux away from their reservations. Many tribes resisted, and a Sioux uprising was led by the chiefs Sitting Bull, Crazy Horse, and Gall, although they later surrendered after fierce battles. How does Grandpa maintain Sioux heritage? **E**

Teach the Selection

Analyze Literature
Conflict Ask students how Martin's realization that Grandpa knew of his discomfort might affect the conflict in the story. Model a possible response: "Now that Martin realizes that Grandpa understands his embarrassment, it may be easier for Martin to accept his Grandpa the way he is." **D**

Cultural Connection
Sioux Nation *Answer:* Students might mention the moccasins and rawhide drum Grandpa made for the children or that he taught the narrator to do Sioux chants. He speaks the Sioux language and tells traditional stories. He wears a medicine bag which he will pass to his grandson. **E**

Make Connections
Have students stop reading for a moment and discuss the way that Martin's friends related to Grandpa. Ask them how they relate to different generations in their family and to older family members when they visit friends. **F**

Writing Skills

Brainstorming Techniques
Remind students that before they begin their creative writing assignments they should brainstorm ideas. They may want to make a list of experiences they have had, rank them according to interest, and then choose one from the list to write about. Once they choose their topic, they can make a chart like this one to help them brainstorm ideas specifically related to their topic.

Experience	My grandmother taught me to make Czechoslovakian holiday breads.
Background	She was from Czechoslovakia and enjoyed traditional foods at holidays.
Understanding	I learned the importance of family heritage.

Analyze Literature

Flashback Point out that this section of the story is a flashback, told by Grandpa. Explain that a flashback is a literary device that authors use to fill in information that happened at a previous time. The narrator may describe the flashback, or as in this story, the narrator relates the flashback that is told by another character. Ask students how the flashback adds to their enjoyment and understanding of the story. If necessary, model a response: "I learned more about Sioux traditions" or "I learned more about Grandpa and came to understand him better." **A**

man's hands." He fell silent and I felt shivers down my back.

A "My father in his early manhood," Grandpa began, "made a vision quest[4] to find a spirit guide for his life. You cannot understand how it was in that time when the great Teton Sioux were first made to stay on the reservation. There was a strong need for guidance from *Wakantanka,* the Great Spirit. But too many of the young men were filled with despair and hatred. They thought it was hopeless to search for a vision when the glorious life was gone and only the hated confines[5] of a reservation lay ahead. But my father held to the old ways.

"He carefully prepared for his quest with a purifying[6] sweat bath and then he went alone to a high butte[7] top to fast and pray. After three days he received his sacred dream—in which he found, after long searching, the white man's iron. He did not understand his vision of finding something belonging to the white people, for in that time they were the enemy. When he came down from the butte to cleanse himself at the stream below, he found the remains of a

campfire and the broken shell of an iron kettle. This was a sign which reinforced[8] his dream. He took a piece of the iron for his medicine bag, which he had made of elk skin years before, to prepare for his quest.

"He returned to his village, where he told his dream to the wise old men of the tribe. They gave him the name *Iron Shell,* but neither did they understand the meaning of the dream. The first Iron Shell kept the piece of iron with him at all times and believed it gave him protection from the evils of those unhappy days.

"Then a terrible thing happened to Iron Shell. He and several other young men were taken from their homes by the soldiers and sent far away to a white man's boarding school. He was angry and lonesome for his parents and the young girl he had wed before he was taken away. At first Iron Shell resisted the teachers' attempts to change him and he did not try to learn. One day it was his turn to work in the school's blacksmith shop. As he walked into the place he knew that his medicine had brought him there to learn and work with the white man's iron.

"Iron Shell became a blacksmith and worked at the trade when he returned to the reservation. All of his life he treasured the medicine bag. When he was old and I was a man, he gave it to me, for no one made the vision quest any more."

Grandpa quit talking and I stared in disbelief as he covered his face with his hands. His shoulders were shaking with quiet sobs and I looked away until he began to speak again.

"I kept the bag until my son, your mother's father, was a man and had to

---

4. **vision quest.** Spiritual journey
5. **confines.** Limits or boundaries
6. **purifying.** Cleansing
7. **butte.** Isolated hill or mountain
8. **reinforced.** Strengthened

Differentiated Instruction

Kinesthetic Learning

Have groups of volunteers enact the flashback scene. The performers should reread it to review the words, gestures, emotions, and expressions involved. Each group should choose a narrator and actors. Tell them they can create additional dialogue if they want to. After each performance, have classmates tell the group one way in which their performance was good and one area where they might improve.

leave us to fight in the war across the ocean. I gave him the bag, for I believed it would protect him in battle, but he did not take it with him. He was afraid that he would lose it. He died in a faraway place."

Again Grandpa was still and I felt his grief around me.

"My son," he went on after clearing his throat, "had only a daughter and it is not proper for her to know of these things."

He unbuttoned his shirt, pulled out the leather pouch, and lifted it over his head. He held it in his hand, turning it over and over as if memorizing how it looked.

"In the bag," he said as he opened it and removed two objects, "is the broken shell of the iron kettle, a pebble from the butte, and a piece of the sacred sage."[9] He held the pouch upside down and dust drifted down.

"After the bag is yours you must put a piece of prairie sage within and never open it again until you pass it on to your son." He replaced the pebble and the piece of iron, and tied the bag.

I stood up, somehow knowing I should. Grandpa slowly rose from the bed and stood upright in front of me holding the bag before my face. I closed my eyes and waited for him to slip it over my head. But he spoke.

"No, you need not wear it." He placed the soft leather bag in my right hand and closed my other hand over it. "It would not be right to wear it in this time and place where no one will understand. Put it safely away until you are again on the reservation. Wear it then, when you replace the sacred sage."

Grandpa turned and sat again on the bed. Wearily he leaned his head against the pillow. "Go," he said. "I will sleep now."

"Thank you, Grandpa," I said softly and left with the bag in my hands.

That night Mom and Dad took Grandpa to the hospital. Two weeks later I stood alone on the lonely prairie of the reservation and put the sacred sage in my medicine bag. ✤

---

9. **sage.** Type of fragrant plant

How would you have felt in Martin's position? What do you think are the benefits and drawbacks of having different generations of one family living together?

Find Meaning

1. (a) What do Martin and Cheryl tell their friends about their visits to Rosebud Reservation? (b) What do they show their friends? (c) What do they not show them? Why?
2. (a) What does Iron Shell dream? (b) What does he find? (c) How does this dream and discovery later affect him?

Make Judgments

3. (a) What is the effect of including Martin's dream in the story? (b) How does Martin's dream reflect other details in the story?
4. How do you think Martin feels about the medicine bag by the end of the story?

Research Skills

Possible Research Topics

Ask students to work in pairs or groups of three to research and write a brief paper about some aspect of the Dakota, Lakota, or Nakota. Students can focus on their daily lives, their arts and crafts, their spiritual beliefs, or their struggles against the U.S. government. Encourage students to share their information, pictures, or other material with the class.

Summary

When a young boy imitates his parents' poor treatment of their elderly father, the parents are ashamed and treat the elderly man better.

Analyze Literature

Theme Remind students that the theme is the central idea in a story. Explain that even such a short story will have a theme. Ask students what they think the theme is. Possible responses: "Children learn from watching their parents. Younger family members should treat older members with love and respect." **A**

Answer: Students might say they would feel humiliated, embarrassed, resentful, sad, or angry if they were the grandfather. Some students may say that older people, especially if they are poor, are often left to fend for themselves and that society has an obligation to do more to help the elderly. Others may say it is up to the families of the elderly to take better care of them.

The Old Grandfather and His Little Grandson

A Folk Tale retold by Leo Tolstoy

The grandfather had become very old. His legs would not carry him, his eyes could not see, his ears could not hear, and he was toothless. When he ate, bits of food sometimes dropped out of his mouth. His son and his son's wife no longer allowed him to eat with them at the table. He had to eat his meals in the corner near the stove.

One day they gave him his food in a bowl. He tried to move the bowl closer; it fell to the floor and broke. His daughter-in-law scolded him. She told him that he spoiled everything in the house and broke their dishes, and she said that from now on he would get his food in a wooden dish. The old man sighed and said nothing.

A few days later, the old man's son and wife were sitting in their hut, resting and watching their little boy playing on the floor. They saw him putting together something out of small pieces of wood. His father asked him, "What are you making, Misha?"

The little grandson said, "I'm making a wooden bucket. When you and Mama get old, I'll feed you out of this wooden dish." **A**

The young peasant and his wife looked at each other and tears filled their eyes. They

An Old Man And His Dog Seated By A Road Side. Sir Edwin Landseer.

were ashamed because they had treated the old grandfather so meanly, and from that day they again let the old man eat with them at the table and took better care of him. ❖

How would you feel if you were the grandfather in "The Old Grandfather and His Little Grandson"? What do you think about the way modern American society treats the elderly? What is the government's obligation to care for the elderly? What is the family's responsibility?

Differentiated Instruction

Reading Proficiency

Students may have difficulty understanding the culture and terms surrounding the Oceti Sakowin culture. Have them read the Prereading page and footnotes carefully before they begin reading the selection.

Visual Learning

Ask students to skim the selection looking for visual details. When they have done this, ask them what gives them the strongest impression, the descriptions of the different dishes, the grandfather's physical movements, the actions of the peasant couple, or the little boy's actions.

Comparing Literature

Find Meaning

1. (a) How does the old man react to learning that he will get his food in a wooden dish? (b) Why do you think he reacts this way?

2. (a) What does Misha make? (b) How does this affect his parents?

Compare Literature

Theme A theme is a central idea in a story. Using the notes you took about the themes in "The Medicine Bag" and "The Old Man and His Little Grandson," answer the following questions.

Make Judgments

3. Tolstoy does not describe the son or daughter-in-law. What is the effect of this?

4. How does the narrator immediately gain the reader's sympathy for the grandfather?

5. How do the son and daughter-in-law change during the story?

1. What is the theme of "The Medicine Bag"?

2. What is the theme of "The Old Grandfather and His Little Grandson"?

3. How do the themes of the two stories differ?

Extend Understanding

Writing Options

Creative Writing Write a short **personal essay** about a meaningful experience you've had with a family member that you found enlightening or that helped you to better understand who you are as a person. Be sure to describe the situation in which the experience took place and include any important background information. Include details that help your reader picture the family member. Share your work with the class.

Expository Writing Write a brief **compare-and-contrast essay** comparing the actions and beliefs of Martin from "The Medicine Bag" with the actions and beliefs of the son and wife in "The Old Grandfather and His Little Grandson." State your main idea in the thesis. Your body should include examples from the stories to support your thesis. Your conclusion should sum up the comparisons. Present your work to your classmates.

Collaborative Learning

Work with a Partner Foreshadowing is the act of hinting at events that will happen later in a selection. Discuss with a partner how elements from "The Medicine Bag" foreshadow the story's ending. Look for foreshadowing clues in this story in the gifts the grandfather has given Martin, Martin's attitude towards his great-grandfather, and the dreams. Make a list of examples. Present this list to the class and explain how these elements help foreshadow the ending.

Media Literacy

Compare Stories Locate another short story by Leo Tolstoy. Look for the story in the library or online. Write a paragraph comparing the story to "The Old Grandfather and His Little Grandson." Include information about the elements the stories share, how the stories are different, and which story you prefer. Give reasons for your preference.

 Go to www.mirrorsandwindows.com for more.

Find Meaning

1. (a) He sighs and says nothing. (b) Some students may say that he has no choice but to accept what he is told.

2. (a) Misha makes a wooden bucket for his parents to eat out of when they are old. (b) Some students might say that the parents realize they could one day be in the same position as the old man and that this shocks them into seeing how they have been treating the old man.

Make Judgments

3. Some students might say that this lack of description makes them seem anonymous and gives the story a universal appeal. They might also say that this helps the reader focus solely on the characters' behavior.

4. The grandfather is introduced as helpless and poorly treated.

5. Their attitude changes from cold, uncaring and selfish toward the grandfather to shameful of their behavior and deciding to treat him with decency.

Compare Literature

Theme

1. The theme of "The Medicine Bag" is the value of tradition in strengthening love and understanding between generations in families.

2. The theme of "The Old Grandfather and His Little Grandson" is the disgrace of mistreating the elderly.

3. In "The Medicine Bag," the older generation educates the younger; in "The Old Grandfather and His Little Grandson," this process is reversed.

Rubrics for Writing Options

You can adapt this as a checklist for students to use as they write.

Creative Writing

☐ Does the essay set up the situation for the experience or give meaningful background?

☐ Do the details help the reader to clearly see the family member and understand the circumstances or experience?

☐ Does the essay explain why the experience was meaningful?

Expository Writing

☐ Does the introduction identify what is being compared and contrasted?

☐ Does the body include examples from the stories to back up statements about the characters' beliefs and actions?

☐ Does the essay clearly show what is similar about the characters' actions and beliefs and what is different?

☐ Does the conclusion sum up the comparison?

Program Resources

For further instruction, refer students to the following extension activity: Media Literacy: Compare Stories, *Exceeding the Standards: Extension Activities*, p. 7.

A Short Story by Chaim Potok

Preview the Selection

At a Glance
Directed Reading
- Reading Level: Challenging
- Difficulty Consideration: Vocabulary
- Ease Factor: Engaging characters

Objectives

Studying this lesson will enable students to

- use reading skills such as context clues to determine meaning
- define *character* and recognize the effect of this literary technique in the selection
- describe the works of Chaim Potok and David L. Parker, and discuss how real events influence their work
- appreciate what it might be like to experience a loss

Launch the Lesson

Prior to reading "Moon," point out to students that some groups have attempted to organize boycotts of products produced in foreign countries by child labor. Ask students if they think this is the best way to stop the exploitation of young workers overseas.

BEFORE READING

Build Background
Cultural Context In "Moon," the main character has a moving encounter with a child laborer visiting from Pakistan, where more than 25 percent of factory workers are children under the age of fourteen. These children are forced to work long hours in dark, cramped, unsanitary conditions.

Reader's Context Think of a cause or issue you feel strongly about. What are three possible ways of changing the situation?

Set Purpose
Read the title and skim the text to preview "Moon." Based on Build Background and your preview, what do you predict the story will be about?

Analyze Literature
Character A **character** is a person or animal who takes part in the action of a literary work. A *flat character* is one who exhibits a single quality, or character trait. A *round character* is one who seems to have all the complexities of an actual human being. As you read, note how the characters react to other people, how they are described, and how they behave. Do the characters seem like they could be real people?

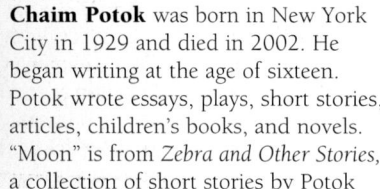

Meet the Author
Chaim Potok was born in New York City in 1929 and died in 2002. He began writing at the age of sixteen. Potok wrote essays, plays, short stories, articles, children's books, and novels. "Moon" is from *Zebra and Other Stories,* a collection of short stories by Potok published in 1998. In "Moon," two of the main characters play the drums. Potok observes, "Playing the drums is ... one of the oldest forms of communication, of people talking to each other across chasms of separation."

Use Reading Skills
Context Clues Preview the vocabulary words from this selection. Try to unlock the meaning of each word using the context clues.

1. The orderly woman chose the kitten with the calmest <u>demeanor</u>.

2. The department store was looking for a <u>jovial</u> man to play Santa.

3. After her brisk workout, her heart <u>pulsated</u> very fast.

4. A few drops of rain were the <u>prologue</u> to the devastating storm.

5. The captives were <u>defiant</u> and refused to follow the rules of their captors.

Preview Vocabulary
de•mean•or (di mē´ nər) *n.,* behavior toward others, outward manner

jo•vi•al (jō´ vē al) *adj.,* jolly, merry

pul•sate (pʉl´ sāt) *v.,* throb rhythmically

de•fi•ant•ly (de fī´ ənt lē) *adv.,* showing resistance

pro•logue (prō´ log) *n.,* preface, introduction

Common Core State Standards

Reading Literature
RL.1, R.3, RL.4

Writing
W.9

Language
L.4, L.6

Words in Use

Irinaland Ueber Dem Balkan—Irinaland Over The Balkans, 1966.
Friedensreich Hundertwasser. Private collection, Vienna, Austria.

Moon

A Short Story by Chaim Potok

"Why did he work in that factory?
Why didn't he just run away?"

oon Vinten, recently turned thirteen, was short for his age and too bony, too thin. He had a small pale face, dark angry eyes, and straight jet-black hair. A tiny silver ring hung from the lobe of his right ear, and a ponytail sprouted below the thick band at the nape of his neck and ran between his angular shoulder blades. The ponytail, emerging like a waterfall from the flat-combed dark hair, was dyed the clear blue color of a morning sky.

Moon marched into the family den one autumn evening and announced to his parents that he wanted to build a recording studio for himself and his band.

His parents, short, slender people in their late forties, had been talking quietly on the sofa. Moon's father, annoyed by his son's brusque[1] interruption of the conversation, thought: First, those drums; then the earring

---

1. **brusque.** Abrupt; blunt in manner or speech

Teach the Selection

Summary

Morgan "Moon" Vinten is a thirteen-year-old boy who has difficulty controlling his anger. His passion is playing his drums. When his parents, who are both doctors, tell him that a boy his age from Pakistan named Ashraf will be an overnight houseguest, Moon is not pleased. During a school assembly where Ashraf describes his life as a laborer in a carpet factory, Moon becomes interested in Ashraf's story. Later at the house, while Moon is practicing his drums, Ashraf asks to play them. He prefers the bongos, and Moon records Ashraf as he plays. Ashraf returns to Pakistan to crusade for other child laborers. Moon later learns that he has been killed. During a school memorial assembly, Moon plays the recording of Ashraf's bongo playing and accompanies it on his own drums.

MIRRORS & WINDOWS The Mirrors & Windows questions at the end of this selection focus on the theme of responsibility. Before reading the story, ask students if they perform any service work. Do they feel a responsibility to those they serve? Why or why not? How involved in the future welfare of those they serve should service organizations be?

Program Resources

Planning and Assessment
Program Planning Guide, Selection Lesson Plan
E-Lesson Planner
Assessment Guide, Lesson Test
ExamView

Technology Tools
Interactive Student Text on CD
Visual Teaching Package
Audio Library
mirrorsandwindows.com

Meeting the Standards
Fiction: Unit 2, Directed Reading, pp. 70–76

Differentiating Instruction
Developing Readers, Make Predictions, pp. 10–12

Analyze Literature

Conflict Remind students that one type of literary conflict is between characters. Ask them to identify the conflict here and the characters involved in it. Model a possible response: "Moon is having a conflict with his parents. He wants to build a recording studio in the house or the garage, but they are against it and want him to save his money for college." **Ⓐ**

Make Connections

Ask students to describe a situation that would make them angry. Then ask students to write down three distinct ways of dealing with the situation. What would the consequences of each be? **Ⓑ**

Ⓐ and the ponytail. And now a *recording studio?* In a restrained tone, he asked, "What, exactly, does that involve?"

"A big table, microphones, stands, extension cords, rugs or carpets for soundproofing, a mixing board,"[2] said Moon.

"And how will you pay for all that?"

"With the money I got for my birthday."

Patience is the desired mode here, Moon's father told himself. "I'll remind you again. That money has been put away for your college tuition."

> ### He felt the rage like a scalding second skin.

"The band will make lots of money, Dad."

"Then buy the equipment with that money."

"We'll need money to buy the equipment so we can make really high-quality recordings," said Moon, trying to keep himself calm. "We'll demo the recordings and send them out, and start making money from the gigs we'll get. It takes money to make money, Dad."

Moon's father turned to Moon's mother. "Where is he learning these things, Julia?"

"He's your son, too, Kenneth," said Moon's mother. "Why don't you ask him?" Her mind at that moment was on another matter: the face of a boy in Pakistan.

"He's only thirteen years old, for God's sake," Moon's father said.

Moon hated it when they talked about him as if he weren't there. His parents, who were physicians, spoke often to each other clinically about their patients, and at times about Moon as if he were a patient. It was one more irritant in the list of things that made him angry. **Ⓑ**

"We shouldn't attach an 'only' to a thirteen-year-old," said his mother, still seeing the face of the Pakistani boy, whose photograph had come to her office in the morning mail. "A thirteen-year-old is not a child."

Moon's father, a precise man with a dry, intimidating manner, looked at Moon and asked, "Where, exactly, do you plan to put all that equipment?"

"In the garage," Moon replied.

His parents stared at him. Calm is called for, his father thought, and remained silent. Inside Moon's mother, an unassuming woman of gentle <u>demeanor</u>, the picture of the gaunt,[3] brown-faced Pakistani boy—dry thin lips, small straight nose, enormous frightened eyes—abruptly winked out.

She said quietly to Moon, "Dear, we keep our cars in the garage."

Moon said, "Then I'll put it in the basement."

"We've been through all that," said Moon's father—the clamor erupting from the basement and streaming through the air ducts and filling the house with that booming drumming twanging pandemonium[4] they called music. "Let's talk about it another time."

"When, Dad?"

"Soon."

"But when?"

---

2. **mixing board.** Device with controls for balancing musical sounds for recording
3. **gaunt.** Excessively thin
4. **pandemonium.** Wild uproar

de·mean·or (di mē´ nər) *n.*, behavior towards others, outward manner

---

Differentiated Instruction

English Language Learning
Point out the following vocabulary words and expressions:
demo — make a recording to show off a song or a performer to a record producer, 224
gigs — jobs playing music, 224
winked out — vanished, 224
call waiting — service activated when a person is using the phone that indicates a second incoming phone call, 225

raked — scolded, 228
reedy — having the tone quality of a reed instrument, 228
deft precision — skilled accuracy, 231

His father said, "Morgan, I have very important calls to make." Morgan was Moon's given name, first on the list of things that made him angry. A <u>jovial</u> older cousin had called him Moon some years ago, for a reason Moon could no longer remember. His parents and his teachers still called him Morgan.

"I need the phone to call the guys in the band," said Moon.

"Whoever is on the phone, if an overseas call comes in on call waiting, please tell me immediately," said Moon's mother.

"I need the phone," said Moon again.

"Don't you have any homework?" his father asked.

"Dad, I really really really need to talk to the guys in my band," said Moon.

Moon's parents sat very quietly on the couch, looking at their son. Even excited or angered, his face retained its pallid[5] look. But his dark eyes glittered, and his thin lips drew back tight over his small white teeth as if keeping a seal on a poisonous boil of words.

The telephone rang.

Moon's father picked up the receiver and said crisply, "Dr. Vinten." He listened and handed the receiver to Moon's mother. "Pakistan," he said.

Moon, his hands clenched, turned and left the den.

He took the carpeted stairs two at a time to the second floor, and as he threw open the door to his room, the anger erupted. His heart raced, his hands shook. He felt the rage like a scalding second skin. He slammed the door shut. The large color photograph of the Beatles, tacked loosely to the inside of the door, fluttered briefly; the Beatles seemed to be dancing and undulating[6] in their costumes.

He flopped down on his bed.

C Always with the fury came fear. Occasional tantrums had accompanied him through childhood and in recent years had become too-frequent fits of rage that rose suddenly from deep inside him and sometimes took possession of his body. He lay on his back, tight and quivering. "When you feel it coming, stop what you're doing," Mrs. Graham, the school counselor, had advised. "Take deep breaths and count slowly." He counted: One...two...three...Mrs. Graham was a round-faced, goodhearted woman. "If you feel you're losing control, walk out of the classroom. I've told your teachers it's all right for you to do that." Four...five...six...It was after his fight with Tim Wesley two weeks before, when they pummeled each other and tumbled down the

---

5. **pallid.** Dull, lacking liveliness or color
6. **undulating.** Moving in waves

jo•vi•al (jō´ vē al) *adj.*, jolly, merry

Analyze Literature
Characterization Remind students that one way writers create characters is by describing what physical features, dress, and personality the characters display. Ask students what the description reveals about Moon. If necessary, model a response: "Moon has a pale face and often looks angry; Moon looks like he's trying to stay calm when he's upset inside." **C**

Use Reading Strategies
Visualize Encourage students to visualize the routine that Moon uses to calm himself down. Ask volunteers to demonstrate what they think he looks like. **D**

Vocabulary Skills

Jargon

Jargon is the specialized vocabulary that members of a particular group or profession use. Jargon can make writing more specific and authentic. "Moon" includes some musical jargon that students may not understand. Remind students to use context clues to uncover meaning. They may not know what *jam* means, but the context of the sentence and the paragraph explains that it refers to practicing music.

Have students use context and a dictionary to find the meaning of the following musical terms: *demo, gig, recording studio, stroke, beat, Hi-Hat,* and *bongos.* Also ask students with musical backgrounds to explain the meanings of the terms.

Use Reading Skills

Use Context Clues Remind students that they can use context clues to unlock the meaning of an unfamiliar word. Ask students what they think the word *moralizing* means and to find the context clues that helped them figure out the meaning. If necessary, model a response: "*Moralizing* means criticizing or giving advice about someone's behavior. Moon's mother's reminder to keep his door open is moralizing." Ask students to find other examples of moralizing in the selection. **Ⓐ**

Use Reading Strategies

Make Inferences Remind students that when they make an inference, they use clues in the story plus things they already know to understand an action or event in the story. Ask why they think Moon's mother told him to be nice to the boy from Pakistan. Model a possible response: "Moon's mother knows that he has trouble controlling his temper. Since he is already upset that his parents have not agreed to let him have a music studio, she may think he will be unkind or rude to the boy." **Ⓑ**

---

wide staircase into the school's main entrance hall. Seven...eight... nine...Later, Moon couldn't remember why the fight had begun. His parents and Mrs. Graham had discussed the possibility of Moon getting help. A therapist, a total stranger. Everything he'd say would be written down, probably recorded. Ten...eleven...twelve...Maybe go up to the third floor and play the drums awhile. But he needed the telephone.

> "I keep reminding you, if you close your door, we can't communicate with you."

Was that someone at the door?

He got down off the bed and pulled the door open and saw his mother standing in the hallway.

Ⓐ She said gently, "I keep reminding you, if you close your door, we can't communicate with you. Closed doors often turn into stone walls."

His mother's frequent moralizing was definitely on the list of things that made Moon angry. "Can I use the phone now?" he asked.

She sighed. "I came up to tell you that we'll be having a guest."

"Who?" asked Moon.

"A boy from Pakistan."

Children with rare diseases came to his parents from all over the world for diagnosis and treatment. But always to the hospital, never to the house.

He asked, "Why is he staying with us if he's sick?"

His mother said, "He's not sick, dear. An organization your father and I belong to is bringing him into the country. You'll hear about it in school."

"He's coming to my school?"

Ⓑ "Yes. Be nice to him, dear."

But Moon was imagining the boy wandering around the house and coming upon the small room on the third floor. He took a deep breath and said, "Can I use the phone now, Mom?"

Moon's mother remembered when her second son had gone off to college the year before. "It's difficult to let go, but it's much worse to hold on," she had said to Moon's father, and Moon, listening nearby, had suddenly and unaccountably run up to his room and slammed his door shut with such force that, to the disquiet of his father, the paint cracked near the ceiling on the hallway wall. She now gazed sadly at her youngest son, so different from the ambitious older ones: Andrew in engineering and football; Colin in pre-med and crew. And Morgan—so edgy and sullen,[7] so fixed upon himself.

"Yes, dear, you may use the phone," she said. She was still standing in the hallway, looking at Moon, when he closed the door.

He sat at his cluttered desk and dialed the telephone. Pete's father answered. "Peter is doing his homework," he said.

"This won't take long, Mr. Weybridge. I promise," said Moon.

"You just make sure of that," said Pete's father.

While waiting for Pete to come to the phone, Moon sat looking at the large photographs on the wall across from his bed: John Bonham and Stewart Copeland, playing the drums. And at the photographs on the

---

7. **sullen.** Gloomy, somber

Differentiated Instruction

Kinesthetic Learning

In groups of three, students can take on the roles of Mom, Dad, and Moon. Ask students to work together to rewrite the dialogue covering the discussion of the recording studio. Encourage students to incorporate their own opinions on how Moon could have presented his request or how Mom and Dad could have reacted. Discuss differences in communication skills and how

presentation — being polite, respectful, calm, and willing to compromise — can bring on different results than being short-tempered, rude, irrational, and unwilling to compromise.

wall near his bed: George and Paul with their guitars; Ringo at his drums; John singing. He imagined himself sauntering[8] over to them and taking the sticks from Ringo and starting with a light *tik tik tik tik* on the Hi-Hat,[9] and then—

"Hey, hey," came Pete's voice over the phone. "How you doin', Moon?"

"We can jam after school tomorrow, Pete."

"That's cool."

"Hey, Pete, there's a kid from Pakistan who's going to be staying in my house."

"He's stayin' with *you?* Hey, that's real cool!"

"You know about him?"

"Everybody knows."

"How come I never heard anything about him?"

"Hey, you're asleep half the time. And the other half, you're so angry you don't know what's happenin'."

"I need to call Ronnie and John about tomorrow." **C**

"Stay cool, Moon," said Pete.

Moon called Ronnie Klein and then John Wood. Just as he was telling John the time of their jam session, he heard the beep of the call waiting and told John to hang up. Another item on the list of things that angered him: the way call waiting broke into his conversations with his only friends, the members of his band. The low beep, once, twice; most of the calls were for his parents. They wouldn't give him his own telephone; they didn't want him talking on it hours on end; his brothers hadn't had their own telephones, and neither would he.

"This is Dr. Moraes," a voice said in a strange accent. "I am phoning from Pakistan for Dr. Julia Vinten."

"Just a minute, please," said Moon, and

he opened his door and called downstairs. "Mom, it's for you."

"Thank you, dear." His mother's voice came to him from the den.

When he returned to his desk, he put the receiver to his ear and heard: "Yes, Dr. Vinten, the boy will arrive early tomorrow. He will no doubt be tired, but he is—"

Moon hung up the telephone.

He had not thought to ask his mother where the boy would sleep. In Andy's room? In Colin's room? He feared the dusky silences in the house that enlarged the absence of his brothers and magnified invisible presences like the noises the squirrels made scampering inside the walls. Moon imagined he heard his brothers' voices: they were teaching him to hold a bat, catch a hardball, throw a football, dribble a basketball; they were teasing him, calling him the skinny runt of the family; they were helping him with his homework; they were bickering with Mom and Dad over cars and girls and late nights out. The thought of the boy from Pakistan staying in the room of one of his brothers...

Feeling an outrage at his very center, Moon began counting. One...two...three...four...He inserted a Pearl Jam CD into his player—five...six...seven—and put on his earphones, then opened one of the textbooks on the desk. He tapped his index and middle fingers on the desk, *doom-d-d-ka-doom-doom-d-ka-doom-d-d-ka-doom-doom-d-ka,* playing as if he were at a drum and snare. The words in the book flickered and <u>pulsated</u> in the torrent of drums and music. **D**

Moon sat slumped in the seat, dimly aware of the TV cameras and crews in the back of the crowded auditorium, the empty

---

8. sauntering. Moving in a leisurely manner
9. Hi-Hat. Pair of cymbals operated by a foot pedal

---

pul·sate (pʉl′ sāt) *v.,* throb rhythmically

Analyze Literature
Character Point out that Pete is basically a flat character because the reader does not find out much about him, and he does not exhibit a variety of traits. However, his comment to Moon shows that he is willing to accept Moon the way he is. **C**

Cultural Connection
Grunge Music Grunge music, also referred to as the Seattle Sound, is a style of alternative rock that became popular in the early 1990s. The group Pearl Jam is one of the bands associated with grunge music. The lyrics of many of their songs contain themes of social alienation, apathy, and freedom. **D**

Reading Skills

Characters and Conflict
Point out to students that the methods the characters in "Moon" use to deal with conflict provide clues to their overall personalities. Suggest students make a chart to help them keep track of these methods. After students have finished reading the selection and have recorded their information, discuss how the characters' actions are in keeping with their personalities.

Character	Conflict	Method
Moon	anger	plays drums
Father		
Mother		

Use Reading Strategies
Visualize Ask students to draw pictures of Mrs. Woolsten or to find magazine pictures that resemble her description. Discuss how the author's use of descriptive adjectives that appeal to the senses of sight and sound creates a vivid picture of her. **A**

Use Reading Skills
Use Context Clues Have students use context clues to find the meaning of the word *gaunt*. Remind them to use a dictionary to check the accuracy of their definitions. **B**

Analyze Literature
Point of View Remind students that the story is told from the third-person omniscient point of view, so the reader learns things about the characters that they themselves do not reveal. However, in this section of the story where Ashraf speaks, the reader only learns information that Ashraf himself tells.

chairs on the stage, and the whispering among the students and teachers. School assemblies—almost always full of monotonous,[10] preachy fake talk—were high on the list of things that annoyed Moon and made him angry.

The boy said that he himself had been bought at the age of five, for twelve dollars.

He was especially angry that morning. Mrs. Woolsten had raked him for not handing in the weekly English essay. She was a fat, ugly woman, with thick glasses and a voice like ice water. She wanted the essay tomorrow, and absolutely no excuses. He'd sensed the smirks of his classmates and saw out of the corner of his eye Pete's sympathetic look. He hadn't been able to think of anything to write about and, listening to Mrs. Woolsten's public scolding, had felt heat rise to his face. He'd considered walking out of the room, but instead he'd remained at his desk, counting to himself, fingers tapping silently on his knees...until the assistant principal's reedy voice came over the public address system, announcing the special assembly.

The crowd in the auditorium had fallen silent. Moon, still slumped in his seat, watched as some people emerged from the dark right wing of the stage and walked toward the chairs. The first was Dr. Whatley,

the school principal; then came two men Moon didn't know, both dressed in dark suits; then a tall, brown-skinned man with glasses and wearing a baggy light-brown suit, followed by a brown-skinned boy about Moon's age but an inch or two shorter than Moon. He looked gaunt. His eyes were dark and enormous. He wore dark trousers and a sky-blue woolen sweater, a white shirt and a tie. His neck stuck out from the collar of the shirt like the neck of a plucked bird.

Behind the boy walked Moon's mother and father.

Moon watched as they all sat down in the chairs on the stage. The boy, looking tense and fearful, seemed not to know what to do with his hands. He sat on the edge of his chair, leaning forward and staring apprehensively[11] at the crowded auditorium.

Dr. Whatley approached the podium and began to speak. Moon closed his eyes and wondered how he could convince his parents to let him build a recording studio. Maybe ask them for an addition to the garage. How much would that cost? Dr. Whatley droned on, his words amplified.

Moon felt itchy, impatient. There was a scattering of applause and some more talk.

A moment later, an odd-sounding voice filled the air, small and breathless and high, and Moon opened his eyes and saw the boy standing behind the podium, only his face and neck visible. Alongside the boy stood the brown-skinned man.

Moon vaguely recalled having heard that the boy's name was Ashraf.

The boy said something in a foreign language, and the man, who had been introduced as Mr. Khan, translated.

---

10. monotonous. Marked by unvarying pitch and intensity
11. apprehensively. Fearfully, anxiously

Differentiated Instruction

Reading Proficiency
To help students keep track of the characters in "Moon," have them use separate index cards to write the name of each character, draw a picture as they think the character looks, and write two descriptive words or phrases for each character. After students have completed their cards, work with them to separate the cards into two stacks, one each for flat and round characters.

The boy spoke again. He was talking about someone named Mr. Malik and the dozen boys who worked in his carpet factory. He said the boys had been bought by Mr. Malik from their parents.

Bought? thought Moon. *Bought?*

The boy said that he himself had been bought at the age of five, for twelve dollars. He told of sitting on a bench fifteen hours a day as a carpet weaver with the others in a long, airless room, two weak lightbulbs burning from a ceiling fixture and the temperature often over one hundred degrees and the mud walls hot when he put his hands to them and the single window closed against carpet-eating insects. But that was better than working in a quarry, hauling and loading stones onto carts for the building of roads, or in the sporting goods factory owned by one of the many nephews of Mr. Malik, making soccer balls by hand eighty hours a week in silence and near darkness. At the carpet looms,[12] he'd worked from six in the morning to eight at night, and sometimes around the clock, tying short lengths of thin thread to a lattice[13] of heavy white threads. His fingers often bled, and the blood mixed with the colors of the threads.

"Look," he said, thrusting his hands palms upward across the podium, his thin wrists jutting like chicken bones from the sleeves of his sweater, and Moon—listening to the quavery[14] words of the boy and the deep voice of Mr. Khan—tried to make out the fingers from across the length of the auditorium and could not, and he gazed at his own long, bony fingers and tapped them restlessly on his knees.

The audience was silent.

The boy went on talking in his high, breathless voice. Three weeks ago, in the village where he worked, two men in suits accompanied by two uniformed policemen

Children are forced to work long hours in sweatshops such as this one.

had entered Mr. Malik's carpet factory and taken him away, along with four younger boys and three older ones. What a shouting Mr. Malik had raised! How dare they take away his workers, his boys? All legally acquired from their parents—he had the papers to prove it, documents signed and recorded with the proper authorities! The boy paused and then said, Was it right that children were made to labor at carpet factories, at brick and textile factories, at tanneries[15] and steelworks? He said, People in America shouldn't buy the carpets made in his country. If the carpet makers couldn't sell their carpets, they wouldn't have any reason to use children as cheap labor.

---

12. **looms.** Weaving machines
13. **lattice.** Framework of crossed metal or wooden strips
14. **quavery.** Trembling
15. **tanneries.** Places where animal skins are darkened and hardened

Teach the Selection

Cultural Connection
Child Labor in Pakistan In Pakistan, more than 25 percent of factory workers are children under the age of fourteen. These children are forced to work long hours and live and work in dark, cramped, unsanitary conditions. They are separated from their families and deprived of an education. It is estimated that 500,000 to one million children aged four to fourteen currently work under these conditions in Pakistan and other countries. **C**

Analyze Literature
Setting Point out to students that the setting for this part of the story changes to the factory in Pakistan where Ashraf worked. Discuss with students the stark contrast between the setting of Ashraf's daily life with the setting of Moon's daily life. **D**

Use Reading Strategies
Make Predictions Ask students the following questions: "Do you think Ashraf was successful in educating the students about child labor in Pakistan? Why or why not?" Possible answers: Responses will vary. Most students will agree that Ashraf was successful. Some students will point out that the fact that Moon was listening to the talk was a sign that it was engaging, since Moon doesn't generally pay attention to school assemblies.

Research Skills

Topics for Research
Tell students that "Moon" was first published in 1998 and is set in that time period. Have students work in pairs or small groups to brainstorm questions about local, national, and world events during the late 1990s. Suggest that they browse through the story again to get some ideas. Tell students to use *who, what, when, where, why,* and *how* questions. Explain that they will eventually identify a single topic for further research. Invite groups to share their questions with the class. Record the questions on the board or on chart paper. Have each pair or small group choose one of the questions for further research. Keep track of the students and the questions they choose to avoid repetition.

History Connection

Child Labor in the U.S. Child labor also has an appalling history in the United States. In the 1850s, industrialization in America increased, and children as young as six years old worked in mills and mines from early in the morning to late in the evening with no time for play or school. Injury, disease, and even death in factory accidents were common occurrences. In the 1900s, crusaders such as Mother Jones and groups such as the National Child Labor Committee drew attention to the plight of child laborers. In 1938, legislation was passed regulating the wages, ages, and hours worked of children in the workplace. Unfortunately, some companies still use illegal and dangerous child labor behind closed doors. **A**

Use Reading Strategies

Make Predictions Point out to students that Moon is paying attention to Ashraf's drumming. Ask them to make predictions about how their common interest in drumming might be a connection for the boys. Model a possible response: "Since Ashraf is staying at Moon's house, Moon might allow him to play his drums." **B**

He stopped, peering uncertainly at Mr. Khan, who nodded and smiled. The boy thanked the audience for listening to him and walked back to his chair and sat down. He put his hands on his knees and gazed at the floor. All the adults on the stage were looking at him.

There was an uneasy stirring in the audience and nervous, scattered applause.

Moon sat very still looking at the boy.

Dr. Whatley stepped to the podium and introduced one of the two strangers, who turned out to be the governor of the state. The second stranger was the head of the organization that had brought the boy to the United States. Moon didn't listen to them. Nor did he pay much attention to the brief **A** talks given by his parents; each said something about the need to raise the consciousness of Americans. He was watching the boy, who sat on the edge of his chair, leaning forward and appearing a little lost—and wasn't it strange how right there on the stage, in front of everyone, as first the governor and then the head of the organization and then Moon's parents spoke, wasn't it strange how Ashraf had begun to tap with his fingers on his knees, lightly and silently tapping in small movements to some inner music he seemed to be hearing? Moon watched the rhythm and pattern of Ashraf's tapping, an odd sort of tempo, unlike anything Moon had ever seen before, and found himself tapping along with him. A one one one and a two and a one and a two and...

In the school lunchroom later that day, Moon was at a table with Pete and the two other members of his band when Ashraf entered with Mr. Khan. He saw them go along the food line and then carry their trays to a table and sit with some other students. Moon watched Ashraf eating and heard him respond to questions put to him by the students and translated by Mr. Khan. Where had he been born? What sort of food did he like? Had he ever heard of McDonald's or Walt Disney or Tom Hanks? Did he like rock and roll?

As the last question was translated, Ashraf's eyes grew wide and bright, and he nodded. What was his favorite band? He said radiantly, smiling for the first time, "The Beatles," pronouncing it "Bee-ah-tles."

"He says," Mr. Khan translated, "that someone near the carpet factory played recordings of the Beatles very often and very loud." Students crowded around the table, blocking Moon's view. Someone asked who was Ashraf's favorite Beatle, and Moon heard the eager, high-voiced answer: "Ringo."

Minutes later, the crowd around Ashraf thinned, and Moon saw him drumming lightly on the table surface with a knife and fork. Next to him sat Mr. Khan, finishing his meal. About a half-dozen students stood near the table, watching Ashraf's drumming.

"Hey, man," Moon heard Pete say. "You **B** talk to your mom and dad about the recording studio?"

"Yeah," said Moon, looking at Ashraf.

"What'd they say?"

"They're thinking about it."

"Man that'd be so cool," said Pete. "Our own studio and everything."

Moon wished Pete would be quiet so he could see and hear more clearly Ashraf's oddly rhythmed drumming.

"What's up, man?" said Pete into the telephone later that afternoon. "I got one foot out the door."

"We can't jam today, Pete," said Moon.

"What's happenin'?"

"The kid from Pakistan and his interpreter, they're in my house, sleeping. We can't make any noise."

"He must be tired, man."

Vocabulary Skills

Homophones

Remind students that homophones are words that have the same pronunciation but different spellings and meanings. *There, their,* and *they're* are homophones.

- *There* points out a place or introduces an independent clause.
- *Their* is the possessive form of *they.*
- *They're* is the contraction for *they are.*

Read these sentences from the selection. Tell whether to add *their, there,* or *they're* to complete the sentence.

1. Moon hated it when they talked about him as if he weren't (there).

2. Moon's parents sat very quietly on the couch, looking at (their) son.

3. "(They're) saying it was an accident, but no one believes it for a minute," said Pete.

"I don't like him sleeping in Andy's bed. And the man, he's in Colin's bed."

"Hey, you know what my dad once said to me? He said, 'You have your own house, you can decide who sleeps there.' "

"We'll jam tomorrow."

"Tomorrow I got my guitar lesson. The day after."

"Okay, Pete."

"Stay cool, man." **C**

Moon called the other two members of the band. Then he sat at the desk in his room, listening to the silence in the house. Two hours at the drums—gone. He thought of Ashraf's head on Andy's pillow. Did they carry diseases? Mom would know about that. His parents were at the hospital; and that evening they were to have dinner with Ashraf and Mr. Khan, along with the governor and the mayor. Moon would eat alone at home, as he did on occasion. He would put a CD into the stereo player in the den, fill the air with swelling, pounding music that drove away the ominous silences and muffled the occasional chittering and scurrying of the squirrels inside the walls of the house. **D**

A noise took him from his thoughts: barely audible voices in the next room. Ashraf and Mr. Khan. Moon rose and left his room. He walked past his parents' bedroom to the door at the end of the hallway and climbed the wooden staircase to the third floor.

The sloping roof of the large stone-and-brick house left space for three small rooms beneath the angled beams: a cedar closet; a storage area for his parents' files; and, the third, the room where Moon played his drums and jammed with his band. There was barely enough space for the chairs and the music stands and the table with the CD player and the small cassette recorder they used to tape some of their sessions. The crowded room was the only place in the house where his parents would permit Moon and his band to play.

He removed the covers from his drums, sat down, popped The Police into the CD player, put on the earphones, and took up his sticks. He knew by heart Stewart Copeland's stroke and beat, and he played with deft precision. The blue-dyed ponytail moved from side to side and bobbed on his shoulders and back. **E**

He played for some time, felt himself gliding off into the surge and crash of the drums and lifted into the cascades of thumping rhythms—and then he sensed an alien presence behind him, and he stopped and turned.

Ashraf and Mr. Khan were in the room.

Moon stared at them. He turned off the CD player and removed his earphones.

"We apologize if we are disturbing you," said Mr. Khan very politely.

"It's okay," said Moon, trying to keep the anger out of his voice. This was what he had feared most: an invasion of his most secret place! Slow, deep breaths...

...One...two...

Mr. Khan said, "Ashraf has asked me to tell you that your walls make sounds. He heard noises that woke him."

"Those are squirrels," said Moon. "Sometimes they get inside our walls. Usually we only hear them at night." Three...four ...five...

Mr. Khan spoke to Ashraf, who nodded and responded.

"He says to tell you the walls of the factory where he worked were filled with insects and sometimes he would hear them at night."

Moon said, "We once had a nest of honeybees in one of our walls. My parents had to bring in a man who raised bees to

Teach the Selection

Use Reading Strategies

Make Inferences Ask students the following question: "Do you think Pete is a good friend for Moon? Why or why not?" **C**

Analyze Literature

Tone Explain that tone is the author's way of speaking in a story and carries the author's attitude or feeling toward characters, events, or information. The tone may change for different characters. Point out that word choice is important in establishing the tone. Ask students what tone the author's use of the word *diseases* implies. Model a possible response: "The word *diseases* implies that Moon thinks Ashraf and Mr. Kahn might be dirty or possibly even dangerous to him." Have students demonstrate the tone Moon might use if he asked the question, "Did they carry diseases?" aloud to his parents. **D**

Cultural Connection

The Police The Police was a popular rock group in the 1970s and 1980s. Its members were singer/bassist Sting, guitarist Andy Sommers, and drummer Stuart Copeland. Copeland was the founder of the band. In 1983 their song "Every Breath You Take" won the Grammy Award for Song of the Year. The band broke up in the mid-1980s but reunited in 2007 for a performance at the Grammy Awards. **E**

Speaking & Listening Skills

Interviewing Techniques

Have students brainstorm a list of questions that they would like to ask author Chaim Potok. Urge them to propose open-ended questions that cannot be answered by a simple "yes" or "no" or a brief statement of fact. Model a question such as, "What type of problems did you have as an adolescent?" After the brainstorming activity, divide the class into small groups, and have each group hold mock interviews with the writer. They can choose one person to be the interviewer, one to be Potok, and the rest of the group to be observers. Tell groups to change roles so each member has a chance to be the interviewer and Potok.

Make Connections

Ask students why they think Ashraf is fascinated with Moon's hair. Have they ever experienced great wonder at a style choice of another culture? What did they do to try to understand it? How does this action compare to or contrast with Ashraf's? **A**

Analyze Literature

Theme Remind students that the theme is the central idea in a literary work. Discuss how Ashraf's comment ties in to the theme of the story. Model a possible response: "Moon often gets angry and feels like hitting things, so he plays his drums. The two boys connect over their feelings of anger and the one way they both deal with the feelings." **B**

TEACHING NOTE

Self-Generated Questioning

Invite students to write down any questions they have about the selection. Gather the questions into a container. Choose four students to come to the front of the room. Select a question from the container. Have the students in front of the room answer the question one word per person at a time. For example, to answer "What did Moon ask his parents for" the four students could say, one by one, "He/wanted/a /recording/studio." Call four new students to the front of the class for the next question, and continue as time allows.

---

take away the nest with the bees still in it." Why am I telling him this? Six...seven...

Ashraf listened attentively to the translation, nodding, then spoke softly.

"He says he does not know your name," said Mr. Khan.

"My name is Moon."

Mr. Khan looked puzzled.

"M-o-o-n," said Moon, spelling his name.

"Ah, yes?" said Mr. Khan. "Moon." He spoke to Ashraf, who responded.

"He asks why are you named Moon."

"It's my name, that's all," said Moon.

Mr. Khan spoke to Ashraf, who gazed intently at Moon. Dark, glittering pupils inside enormous, curious, eager eyes.

"Ashraf says he was drawn here by the sound of your drums and asks if he may speak frankly and put certain—um, how to say—personal questions to you."

"Personal? What do you mean, personal?"

"He says he will not be hurt if you do not answer."

"What questions?"

"First, he wishes to ask why you wear a ring in your ear."

"Why I wear the earring? I just do, that's all."

"Ashraf says he does not understand your answer."

"It makes me feel different. You know, not like everyone else."

"He asks why you dye your long hair blue."

"I saw it in a magazine."

"He says if you saw it in a magazine and are doing what others do, how does it make you different?"

Moon felt heat rising to his face. "No one else in my school does it."

A "He asks if he may touch your hair."

"What?"

"May he touch your hair?"

Moon took a deep breath. All those questions, and now this. Touch my hair. Well, why not? He turned his head to the side. The ponytail swayed back and forth, dangling blue and loose from its roots of raven hair. Ashraf leaned forward, ran his fingers gently through the ponytail, touching and caressing the sky-blue strands, a look of wonder on his thin face. Then he withdrew his hand. Moon saw him examining his fingers and heard him speak softly to Mr. Khan.

"He says he likes the way your hair looks and feels," Mr. Khan said to Moon.

Moon looked at Ashraf, who smiled back at him shyly and spoke again to Mr. Khan.

B "Now he asks why you play the drums."

Moon said, after a brief hesitation, "I just like to."

"He says to tell you that he plays drums because it is sometimes a good feeling to hit something."

"Yeah, I feel that way, too....sometimes."

Differentiated Instruction

Auditory Learning

Find a student, a professional musician, a DVD, or an audiotape to demonstrate different drumming patterns or rhythms to the class. Students may be especially interested to hear recordings by Pearl Jam or the Police or Indian music by Ravi Shankar.

Once students have heard a pattern several times, ask them to accompany the recording by beating out the same rhythm on their desks. Then discuss how the physical act of drumming makes them feel.

Moon had never before talked about these matters with anyone. **C**

"He says to thank you for your answers."

"Can I ask a question?"

"Of course."

"Why did he work in that factory? Why didn't he just run away?"

Mr. Khan translated, and Ashraf lowered his eyes as he responded.

"He says there was nowhere to run. He was hundreds of miles from his home and would have starved to death or been caught and brought back to his master and very severely beaten and perhaps chained to his workbench or sold off to work in the quarries."

"Why did his parents sell him?"

Ashraf listened to the translation and seemed to fill with shame.

"They needed the money to feed themselves and their other children."

"Does he have to go back?"

"Oh, yes. He feels obligated to return. Our organization will send him to school, and he will continue in the struggle to help other boys like him."

"Please say that I wish him good luck."

Mr. Khan translated, and Ashraf replied.

"He thanks you and asks if he may request of you a small favor."

"Sure."

"He asks if he may play your drums."

Moon, surprised, was silent. His drums! No one touched his drums, ever. He looked at Ashraf, who, after a moment, spoke again.

"He says he will not damage them," said Mr. Khan.

"Well, okay," Moon said.

Ashraf's eyes lit up as he extended his fingers toward Moon. Moon handed him his sticks and slid off the chair. Ashraf took the sticks, sat in Moon's chair, and tapped on **D**

Moon's drums. He tapped on the drums and the Hi-Hat, a bit awkwardly and with no apparent rhythm, and after a while he put down the sticks and picked up the bongos from the floor near the Hi-Hat. Holding the bongos between his knees, he began to tap out with his callused[15] fingers and palms the odd rhythm he had played in the auditorium and lunchroom, a one one one and a two and a one and a two and... **E**

> *Moon, standing next to him, felt the power and pull of the strange rhythm.*

Moon reached over and switched on the tape recorder.

Ashraf drummed on. Moon, standing next to him, felt the power and pull of the strange rhythm. Ashraf played for some while, *dum dat, dum dat, dum dat,* and sweat formed on his brow and beads of sweat flecked off his face as he played and his fingers became a blur, *dum dat, dum dat, dum dat*—and abruptly he stopped. His eyes were like glowing coals. Sweat streamed down his brown face. He placed the bongos on the floor.

Moon switched off the recorder.

There was a silence before Ashraf spoke.

"He thanks you for the opportunity to play your drums," said Mr. Khan.

"Well, sure, it's okay, you're welcome," said Moon.

___

16. **callused.** Hardened

Teach the Selection

Analyze Literature

Character Discuss with students what this sentence reveals about Moon. Also discuss why Moon would make such a revelation to a total stranger. **C**

Use Reading Strategies

Make Predictions Have students refer to the predictions they made on page 222. They can verify or change their prediction now. **D**

History Connection

Bongos The African drums that were the ancestors of bongos reached the Americas a result of the slave trade. The first bongo drums were produced in Cuba around 1900 for use in dance bands. During the 1950s–1960s, bongos became associated with Beatnik poets who used them as accompaniment for poetry readings. **E**

Writing Skills

Onomatopoeia

Remind students that onomatopoeia is the use of words or phrases that imitate sounds. Give them some examples from the story such as *dum dat,* and *doom-do'ak-doom-d'doom-ak.* Ask students to work in pairs to create a character sketch of either Moon or Ashraf. Tell them to draft, revise, and finalize a sketch of one to three paragraphs. At least once in each paragraph—but as often as they want—have them use onomatopoeia as they describe their character. When students have finished, have each pair read their sketch aloud to the class.

Use Reading Strategies

Visualize The author creates a vivid image of Ashraf's hand. Ask students to imagine they are Moon shaking Ashraf's hand. How does it feel to them? To what might students compare his hand? If necessary, model a possible response: "Ashraf's hand feels small and rough, like holding on to a small tree branch." **Ⓐ**

Use Reading Strategies

Clarify Have students review what Ashraf had been doing in the United States and then summarize the final paragraph from the essay titled "Blunt Reply to Crusading Boy." Tell them to work in pairs to make sure they get the details correct. Suggest that they ask each other questions to clarify what they have read. **Ⓑ**

"He says you and he will probably never see each other again, but he will remember you."

Moon looked at Ashraf, who briefly spoke again.

"He says we must now leave and prepare for this evening's dinner," said Mr. Khan.

Ⓐ Ashraf extended his hand. Moon took it and was startled by its boniness, its coarse, woodlike callus covering. Smiling shyly, Ashraf shook Moon's hand and then turned and left the small room, followed by Mr. Khan.

Moon rewound a portion of the tape, checked to see that it had recorded properly, and took it down to his room.

Pete asked, "Hey, you see him on TV?" "See who?" replied Moon. They were walking up the crowded stairs to their English class.

"That kid, what's his name, Ashraf."

"Was he on TV?"

"Man, what planet you livin' on? He was on the news last night and on the *Today* show this mornin'."

"I was writing that essay for Mrs. Woolsten."

"Is he still at your house?"

"He left before I woke up," said Moon.

That evening, he sat with his parents in the den, watching a national news report that showed Ashraf speaking at a high school in Baltimore. He looked small and frightened behind the podium, but he thrust out his hands <u>defiantly</u> to show his fingers. Mr. Khan stood beside him, translating.

The next evening, Ashraf was seen on television appearing before a committee of Congress. He wore a dark suit and a tie, and his neck protruded from the shirt collar. He sat at a long table with Mr. Khan. Moon saw Ashraf's fingers tapping silently from time to time on the edge of the table.

One of the congressmen asked a question. Moon saw Ashraf thrust his hands toward the members of the committee, showing his fingers.

"Spunky kid," said Moon's father. "He's going back to a bad situation."

"Nothing will happen to him, Kenneth. Too many eyes are watching," said Moon's mother.

When Moon came down to breakfast the following morning, he found his father at the kitchen table, tense and upset. His mother, almost always too cheerful for Moon in the early hours of the day, looked troubled.

"What's happening?" Moon asked.

"See for yourself," said his father, and, handing Moon the morning newspaper, pointed to the final paragraph of an essay titled "Blunt Reply to Crusading Boy," on the op-ed page.

Moon read the paragraph:

Ⓑ In conclusion, we hold that there is room for improvement in any society. But we feel that the present situation is acceptable the way it is. The National Assembly must not rush through reforms without first evaluating their impact on productivity and sales. Our position is that the government must avoid so-called humanitarian measures that harm our competitive advantages.

The essay was signed by someone named Imram Malik.

Moon asked, "What does it mean, Dad?"

"You're thirteen years old—what do you think it means?"

"I don't know," said Moon, afraid he understood it too well.

"They would not dare harm him," said his mother.

Moon felt a coldness in his heart, and the

---

de·fi·ant·ly (de fī′ ənt lē) *adv.*, showing resistance

Differentiated Instruction

Reading Proficiency

Students may have difficulty understanding the final paragraph from "Blunt Reply to Crusading Boy." Go through the passage sentence by sentence and simplify the language. Then ask questions such as the following to help students summarize the paragraph and demonstrate their comprehension:

- Should the society do better?
- Will the situation change soon?
- What will the National Assembly do before they make any changes?
- Will the government stop using child labor if it means it might lose money?

impotence[17] that was the prologue to rage.

In the weeks that followed he played the recording often, at times taking it upstairs to the third floor and listening to it and remembering the darkly glittering blaze in Ashraf's eyes when he'd played the bongos. And that's where Moon was the winter night the portable telephone rang on the table where he'd set it, near the tape recorder. It was someone from Washington, D.C., calling his mother. His parents weren't home, he said, and wrote down an unfamiliar name and number. He turned off the telephone, and immediately it rang again, and a man's voice asked for his father. Moon was writing down the man's name and number when he heard the beep of the call waiting and felt himself growing angry. What was he, his parents' secretary or something? He'd come upstairs to play the drums, not to take their phone calls one after the other like that.

"Hey, Moon." It was Pete.

"Hey, Pete. What's up?"

"You heard the news, man?"

"What news?"

"It was just on TV. That Ashraf kid. He's dead."

"What?"

"He's dead, man. Run down on his bike by a truck. Hit and run."

Moon's hands began to shake.

"They're sayin' it was an accident, but no one believes it for a minute," said Pete.

A fury was boiling in Moon's stomach and flaring red in his eyes. Breathe slowly...

"I'm tellin' you, man, they should've burned down all those factories," Pete said, loud and angry. "Only language some people understand."

Moon remained quiet. One...two... three... four...

"Hey, man," said Pete. "You there?"

"Yeah," said Moon.

"Your parents home?"

"No." Five...six...seven...

"You want me to come over?"

"No."

"You sure you're okay?"

"Yeah." Eight...nine...Ten...

"I gotta go. It's late. We'll talk tomorrow."

> "They would not dare harm him," said his mother.

Moon turned off the telephone and the tape recorder and sat for a while in the silent room. He removed the tape from the recorder, brought it down to his room, and placed it in his desk drawer. Then he sat at his desk and began to tap a rhythm on its surface with his hands. He played rudiments and patterns and flames.[18] Right right left left right right left left...right left right right...left right left left...flamadiddle paradiddle...

Was that someone at his door? He got up and opened the door and saw his parents in the hallway. They were in dinner clothes.

Moon and his parents looked at one another a moment.

"I see you know what happened," said his father.

"Pete called me," said Moon.

"It's horrible," his mother said. Her eyes were red, her face was pale.

---

17. **impotence.** Powerlessness, helplessness
18. **rudiments and patterns and flames.** Practice exercises for drummers

pro • logue (prō´ log) *n.*, preface, introduction

Use Reading Strategies
Make Predictions Ask students what they think might happen to Ashraf and why they think so. Model a possible response: "The agency that brought him to America might be able to keep him safe again at home, but if the business owners think he is causing problems, they may try to hurt him." **C**

Make Connections
Ask students how they might feel and react if they had been students at the school where Ashraf spoke and now heard of his death. **D**

Use Reading Strategies
Ask Questions Point out to students that good readers ask many questions as they read. Model for students a few questions that they might ask about this section of the story: "What happened to Ashraf? How did Moon find out about it? What was Moon's reaction to the news? What was Pete's reaction to the news?" Have students work in small groups to ask additional questions and then answer them.

Writing Skills

Similes

Remind students that a simile is a comparison that contains the word *like* or *as*. Memorable similes usually compare two things that are not alike—for example, Potok compares Moon's ponytail to a waterfall. Similes can help a writer with characterization. Point out the two similes on page 225: " . . . his thin lips drew back tight over his small white teeth as if keeping a seal on a poisonous boil of words" and "He felt the rage like a scalding second skin." Ask students what these similes reveal about Moon's character. Have students find and discuss the other similes in the selection. Ask students to pick an interesting person in their lives. Then give them several minutes to write a description of the person using one or more similes.

Use Reading Strategies

Make Inferences Ask students why they think Moon's parents glanced at each other and then why his mother said, "Oh, you poor dear." If necessary, model possible responses: "They don't seem aware that Moon might have liked Ashraf, or that he would express his feelings about anyone or anything." **A**

Use Reading Strategies

Visualize The author does not describe the audience as they listen to the principal's speech and then to the recording of Ashraf playing the bongos. Ask students to describe how they think the students in the audience looked and felt. **B**

Analyze Literature

Character Ask students how this description helps portray Moon as a round character. **C**

Analyze Literature

Plot Point out that although the story has ended, the original conflict between Moon and his parents has not been resolved. Ask students if the family's recent experience with Ashraf might influence further discussions about the recording studio.

"Did they really kill him?" asked Moon.

"Our people in Washington are investigating it," said his father.

"We were up on the third floor together," said Moon. "I made a tape recording of him playing my bongos."

"You did?" said his father, looking surprised.

"I liked him," said Moon.

A Moon saw his parents glance at each other.

"Oh, you poor dear," said his mother.

"We had no idea at all those people would do something that extreme," said his father.

Moon's heart pounded and his skin burned. He stepped back into his room, closing the door. The poster of the Beatles flapped briefly.

The telephone rang twice, and stopped. A moment later someone tapped on his door again.

It was his mother. "Dear, I keep reminding you, if you keep your door closed, we can't communicate with you. Your English teacher is on the phone."

Moon left the door open and went over to the desk and lifted the receiver. "Hello," he said.

B Moon's English teacher, Mrs. Woolsten, said, "Morgan, the essay you handed in about your meeting with Ashraf is very good. You wrote that you made a tape recording of him playing the bongos. Is that right?"

"Yeah," said Moon.

"Please bring it with you next Monday."

"Bring the recording to school?"

"Will you do that?"

"Sure," Moon heard himself say.

"And will you bring your drums?"

"My drums?"

"There will be a memorial service for Ashraf."

"Well, yeah, sure, I'll bring my drums," Moon said.

He sat for a while at the desk, then went downstairs and asked if he could borrow his father's tape recorder. Back in his room, he duplicated the tape of Ashraf playing the bongos.

The following Monday morning, he and his father loaded the drums into the car. Moon sat in the back while his parents rode in front, his father behind the wheel. It was a cold, windy day, the sky ice blue. They said nothing to one another during the trip to the school.

Pete met them in the parking lot and helped Moon carry his drums into the auditorium and set them up on the stage near the podium.

Later that morning, the entire school filed silently into the auditorium. From the dark right wing of the stage emerged Dr. Whatley, followed by the mayor, Moon's parents, and Moon. They sat down in chairs on the stage. Dr. Whatley stepped up to the podium and said that they had assembled to honor the memory of the brave boy named Ashraf who had spoken in their school some weeks before and been killed in a recent accident in Pakistan. He talked about how some people left behind records of their lives—books and music, works of art, deeds. He said that Ashraf had decided to live a life of deeds on behalf of young people his age. He announced that a special school fund would be set up in his memory.

Moon sat in his chair on the stage, listening.

The mayor spoke; then Moon's parents. Then, at a nod from Dr. Whatley, Moon went over to his drums and sat down.

A moment passed, and then over the public address system came the sound of the bongos being played by Ashraf.

Differentiated Instruction

Enrichment

Suggest that students work in small groups to research photographs portraying child labor. Students can check out library books that show examples of such photographs. Interested students may wish to create a collage or a bulletin board displaying photocopies of the photographs. As a class, discuss the impact of seeing photographs of children working in unhealthy conditions.

Moon waited a minute or two and then began to play an accompaniment to the bongos inside the spaces of Ashraf's beat, a one e and a two e and a three e. His Hi-Hat played the ands, and the snare did two and four, and he added ghost notes to the snare, to make it dance, and then added the bell and slipped into the Seattle sound, *doom-do'ak-doom-d'doom-ak,* and the bongos went *dum dat, dum dat, dum dat,* in that strange rhythm, and then Moon took the drums higher in volume and then was taking them higher still, his sticks beating a frenzied cadence,[19] a rhythm of scalding outrage, and he was thumping, driving, throbbing, tearing through his instruments, pouring onto the world a solid waterfall of sound, and he felt the outrage in his arms, and shoulders and heart and the sublime[20] sensation of secret power deep in the very darkest part of his innermost soul.

The bongos fell silent. With a crashing flurry, Moon climaxed the drumming, washed in sweat, strands of his blue-dyed hair clinging to his face and neck. He sat with his head bowed, breathing hard and feeling an exhilaration that he knew would be too quickly gone.

C A void followed, a gap in time, and utter silence from the audience. Moon, slowly raising his head, saw his parents staring at him, their faces like suddenly illumined[21] globes. Over the public address system came the hollow hissing sound that signaled the end of the recording of Ashraf playing the bongos. ❖

---

19. **cadence.** Rhythmic sequence
20. **sublime.** Lofty, grand
21. **illumined.** Bright or shining

If you were in Ashraf's position, would you have wanted to go back to Pakistan? What is your opinion on the organization's decision to have Ashraf give speeches about child labor and then return to Pakistan? What responsibility should organizations have toward people they are trying to help?

Find Meaning

1. (a) What does Moon want to build? (b) Why is this important to Moon?
2. (a) What does Moon do to control his anger? (b) How well does this technique work for Moon? Explain.
3. (a) What do Moon and Ashraf have in common? (b) How do their similarities draw them together?

Make Judgments

4. An image creates a vivid mental picture in the reader's mind of an object or experience. The images in a literary work, when considered together, are referred to as imagery. In "Moon," imagery is often used to show the reader how Moon is feeling or how he appears to others. (a) Find two examples. (b) What is the effect of using imagery rather than just saying that Moon is angry?
5. (a) What emotions and character traits does Moon reveal at the end of the story? (b) How are they different from his emotions and character traits at the beginning of the story? How do they influence the resolution of the story?
6. (a) How much information does Moon offer about the life of Ashraf? (b) How much does the story say about the culture and economy of Pakistan? (c) What value is there in offering this kind of information in a fictional story?

MIRRORS & WINDOWS *Answer:* Some students would feel an obligation to go back and speak up for other child laborers. Others would prefer to stay in America and seek a better life for themselves. Some students may feel the organization put Ashraf at risk.

Find Meaning

1. (a) A recording studio. (b) He wants the space and freedom to drum.
2. (a) He breathes deeply and counts. (b) It helps him control his anger.
3. (a) They like to drum. (b) The boys connect on a level that others cannot.

Make Judgments

4. (a) Possible example: "But his dark eyes glittered, and his thin lips drew back tight over his small white teeth as if keeping a seal on a poisonous boil of words." (b) It allows the reader to experience what the characters sense.
5. (a) He reveals outrage at Ashraf's death. He shows he can connect with someone else. (b) In the beginning, Moon is self-involved and destructive. At the end, his traits help him to channel his anger through music.
6. (a) Most students will point out the story offers a glimpse into the life of Ashraf. Much of this information reflects on Pakistan. (b) A story can educate as it entertains.

Reading Skills

Use Graphic Organizers

Remind students that writers create characters using three major techniques: by showing what characters say, do, or think; by showing what other characters (and the narrator) say or think about them; and by describing what physical features, dress, and personality the characters display. Have students use a chart to record examples of characterization in the story. After they have completed their charts, have students discuss their work in small groups.

Technique	Character	Example
showing what characters do	Moon	drums along to the recording of Ashraf

Teach the Connection

Analyze Literature

Essay Remind students that an essay is a nonfiction writing form that can vary greatly in length, style, and topic. Ask students to evaluate the style of this essay. How would they describe its tone? Is it formal or informal? Is it humorous or serious? Is it opinionated or informational? Discuss with students whether or not the essay could have been written in a different style. How would a different style affect the essay's tone?

Analyze Literature

Setting Point out that the details the author gives help the reader get a clear picture of the setting. Ask students to identify some of these details. Possible responses: the time of day, the number of children, the name of the country, description of roads. **Ⓐ**

TEACHING NOTE

Distinguish Fact from Opinion

Remind students that they should not believe an argument for or against a topic until they evaluate it for themselves. Tell students there are some questions they should answer for themselves when they analyze and evaluate an argument.

- Does the writer/speaker have factual evidence to back up the argument?
- Can the facts be verified?
- Is the chain of evidence clear?
- Does the writer/speaker draw a logical conclusion from the facts?

In his short story "Moon," Chaim Potok writes of a boy who is a child laborer in Pakistan. The following selection, "The Story of Iqbal Masih" by **David L. Parker,** is a factual account of a child laborer in Pakistan. Parker spent five years photographing children as they performed a variety of jobs in India, Nepal, Bangladesh, Thailand, Indonesia, Mexico, and the United States. As you read "The Story of Iqbal Masih," look for similarities between the lives of Iqbal and Ashraf.

The Story of Iqbal Masih

Essay by David L. Parker

Ⓐ Each morning, six days a week, more than half a million children between the ages of four and fourteen rise before dawn and make their way along dark country roads leading to Pakistan's carpet factories. Most of these children must be at work by 6:00 AM. If they are late, they may be punished—hit with a wooden cane, or worse, hung upside down, their ankles tightly bound with rope. The carpet weavers work 14 hours a day, with only a 30-minute break for lunch.

Iqbal Masih was one of these workers. He started working in a carpet factory when he was just four years old. His parents were poor farmers living near Lahore, the largest city in Pakistan. Because they did not have enough money to feed their children or buy them clothes, Iqbal's parents made a very difficult choice. In exchange for a small sum of money, about $16, they agreed to send their son to work in a nearby carpet factory until he had earned enough money to pay back the loan. Iqbal was told he would be paid three cents a day for his work.

A man named Arshad owned the factory. Inside, the only light came from two bare light bulbs that hung in the middle of the room like dragon's eyes. Only a few flecks of paint dotted the walls. The carpet looms looked as though they were a hundred years old. Two strong wooden beams ran across the top and bottom of each loom's frame, which had been created by driving four large stakes into the ground.

In front of each loom sat a small child on a piece of wood scaffolding. The young weaver would tie short lengths of brightly colored thread to a warp[1] of heavier white threads. To make just one carpet, workers had to tie more than a million small knots into a colorful rhythm of circles, squares, and other intricate designs. In the United States, hand-knotted carpets such as these sell for more than $2,000 each.

The scaffold bench could be moved up or down as the child worked on the rug, so the rug did not have to be moved. Except for a rare and forbidden whisper, the children never spoke to one another. "If I let them talk, I know they will start making mistakes,"

---
1. **warp.** Pile

Words in Use

"The Story of Iqbal Masih"

Selection Words
scaffolding, 238
perseverance, 240
bondage, 241
plight, 241

Common Core State Standards

Reading Informational
RI.3, RI.4

Writing
W.7, W.8

Language
L.6

Iqbal's boss said. "And when they make mistakes, I lose money."

If the children complained about how they were treated, they were beaten. Over the years, Iqbal received many cuts and bruises from Arshad's punishments. And Iqbal found out what would happen if he talked back or tried to force Arshad to stop treating the workers so badly.

One night, when Iqbal was 10 years old, Arshad pulled him out of bed at 3:00 AM and ordered him to repair some carpets. Iqbal went to the local police to complain. He told them that his boss had beat him up and showed them the bruises on his arms. One of the police officers glared at Iqbal. He told him he had no right to complain—he'd better stick to his work and do what he was told. The officer grabbed Iqbal by his sore arm and led him back to the factory. "If he tries this again, chain him to his loom," the officer told Arshad.

Arshad did chain Iqbal to his loom. Even when Iqbal hurt so much he could hardly move, he fought back. He believed that what Arshad was doing was wrong.

At 10 years old, Iqbal was just under 4 feet tall, the normal size of a child who is two or three years younger. He weighed less than 60 pounds. From years of sitting hunched in front of the loom, his spine curved like that of an old man. When Iqbal walked, his feet shuffled slowly, as though he were wearing slippers that were too big.

Arshad told Iqbal that the harder he worked, the faster the loan made to his parents would be paid off. But no matter what Iqbal did, the loan just got bigger and bigger. Iqbal's father left home, and his mother was forced to borrow more money from Arshad. By the time Iqbal was 11 years old, his loan had increased to $419—more than 25 times the original amount. When

Iqbal heard this, he knew he would be trapped forever unless he found a way to escape.

In the summer of 1992, Iqbal heard about a meeting to be held in a nearby town. A man named Essan Ulla Khan was going to speak about a new law forbidding carpet factories to employ children. Iqbal decided he must go to this meeting.

On the day of the meeting, Iqbal had worked almost 10 hours. In Arshad's factory there were no fans and no open windows. In the summer, the heat climbed to 120 degrees Fahrenheit. When Iqbal finally made it to the meeting, he was exhausted and very hot. He managed to push his way through the crowd to the front. He sat on the floor below the platform where Khan was speaking.

Khan talked about an organization called the Bonded Labor Liberation Front (BLLF). Its goal was to free Pakistan's bonded laborers. Like Iqbal, they were treated as slaves. The companies they worked for owned them just as they owned property or buildings. The workers were not free to leave their jobs. Khan said that thousands of children worked in bondage in Pakistan's textile and brick factories, tanneries, and steelworks. Under the new law, bonded laborers did not have to work if they did not want to.

When Khan finished speaking, several people jumped up to ask questions. Finally Khan noticed Iqbal's small raised hand and told the audience to let the boy speak. After a pause, Iqbal asked quietly, "How can I stop working and go to school?" Khan explained that Iqbal had new rights under the law. He could show Arshad some legal papers and Arshad would have to let Iqbal go. Khan also told Iqbal about the schools that the BLLF sponsored for children who had been bonded laborers.

THE STORY OF IQBAL MASIH **239**

Use Reading Strategies
Visualize Point out that the author describes Arshad's face but does not describe how Iqbal looks as he is showing Arshad the papers. Ask students to draw or dramatize the scene. **A**

Analyze Literature
Theme Remind students that the theme is the central idea in a literary work. Point out that like the author, Iqbal wants to make others aware of the suffering of child laborers. **B**

Iqbal Masih in 1994.

The next morning, when Iqbal returned to the carpet factory, he took the legal papers with him. He told Arshad he would no longer work, nor would he pay his debt, **A** because bonded labor was illegal. Arshad's face grew red with anger. He cursed at Iqbal and beat him. But Iqbal escaped and ran out of the factory.

Two days later, Arshad came to Iqbal's home, demanding that Iqbal return to the factory or pay the money he said the family owed. Iqbal stood his ground. He knew he could count on his new friend for help.

Khan did help Iqbal get away from the factory. He threatened to have Arshad arrested if he protested. Khan greatly admired Iqbal's courage and perseverance. He found Iqbal a place in a BLLF primary school in Lahore.

B Iqbal told his teachers that he wanted to become a lawyer and fight for children's rights. He did not want any child to suffer the way he had. Some of the other kids at school teased him by calling him "Chief Justice," but he didn't care. He worked hard at school and was a good student. Every night after school, he brought a book to bed and read late into the night.

Other children were not as lucky. Many did not hear about the new law. Factory

240 UNIT 2 FICTION

Differentiated Instruction

Reading Proficiency
Since the information about Iqbal's life is presented sequentially, students will benefit from remembering the details in order. Work with them to create a time line with the main events in Iqbal's life. Tell them to include dates and places wherever possible.

Enrichment
Some students might enjoy researching people (such as the nineteenth-century American labor leader Mother Jones) or groups (such as the National Child Labor Committee) who have worked to put an end to child labor. Encourage students to work in small groups to find information about such a person or group and to share their findings with the class.

owners kept workers from talking to people from the BLLF. The police did not enforce the labor law, and factories just ignored it.

Iqbal and Khan started traveling together to talk about the new law and to free young bonded laborers. One day Khan took Iqbal to visit a carpet factory in a village called Kasur. Because Iqbal was so small, the guards let him in the gate, thinking he was just another worker. But once he was inside, Iqbal started asking the children questions. How often were they beaten? How often did they have to work overtime? How were they treated?

Khan used the information that Iqbal gathered to write an investigative report. Because of the report, police raided the factory and found 300 children who had been tortured and beaten. They were all between the ages of four and ten.

When Iqbal was 12 years old, he began speaking to huge crowds in Pakistan and India. He inspired 3,000 child workers to break away from their masters. He encouraged adults to demand better working conditions. People in Europe and the United States heard about Iqbal and invited him to come speak in their countries. He told audiences that the colorful carpets some of them had in their homes were made by children who lived as slaves. In the United States, Iqbal was featured on ABC News as "Person of the Week." The Reebok Corporation honored him with an award for his work. **C**

When people learned how their carpets were being made, they did not want to buy **D**

any more. In 1992, factories in Pakistan sold fewer carpets to foreign countries than in previous years. At first, the decline was slight, but two years later sales fell sharply. **D**

Carpet factory owners and managers were furious. The Pakistan Carpet Manufacturers and Exporters Association blamed "subversive organizations" and "the child revolutionary." Threats were made on Iqbal's life.

On Easter Sunday in 1995, Iqbal went to visit relatives in a rural village. After spending some time with his aunt, he and two cousins rode their bicycles to see Iqbal's uncle, who was working in a nearby field. As the boys bounced along the dirt path, someone suddenly fired a shotgun at them from a short distance. Iqbal was instantly killed. He was 12 years old.

No one knows exactly what happened or who killed Iqbal. Some people say it was an accident. Others say it was a murder arranged by the carpet manufacturers. The real facts may never be known. Many human rights groups accused the police of failing to investigate the crime thoroughly.

At Iqbal's funeral, 800 mourners crowded into the small village cemetery. A week later, 3,000 protesters—half of them under the age of 12—marched through the streets of Lahore. For many children working under harsh conditions, Iqbal Masih provided a voice. He gave them the courage to follow him out of bondage. His story brought attention to the plight of the world's working children. ✤

TEXT ◄ **TO** ► **TEXT**
CONNECTION

Both Chaim Potok's story and David L. Parker's article deal with a child laborer in Pakistan. Compare and contrast what each writer presents about the child and his circumstances. What information is the same? What is different? How does each writer use concrete, vivid images to create a strong picture in the readers' minds?

Writing Skills

Persuasive Appeals
Explain to students that persuasive writing tries to convince the reader to think like the writer or to take an action the writer suggests. Tell them there are things they can do to make sure their petition is persuasive:
- Choose an issue or topic that can be argued or debated. The issue of child labor can be argued.
- Make sure that solid factual evidence to support the topic is easily available.

- Explain how the changes requested will help the readers.
- Use accurate, concise language.
- Recommend one or two actions.
- Ask for a response by a certain date.

After students have written their petitions, have them exchange petitions and read them to check for clarity.

Review the Selection

Analyze Literature

Character *Answer:* Moon exhibits many realistic qualities and reacts as a real person; therefore he is a rounded character. Sample description: He seems selfish and self-involved but at the end of the story is able to connect to and care about another's plight. He gets angry easily but understands he must control his temper. He has a passion for music, and that is how he best communicates. His manner of appearance shows he cares what others think about him. Students should explain why they would or would not like Moon for a friend. Some may say that despite his temper, he is an interesting and, underneath it all, caring person. Others may be put off by his temper and self-involvement.

Analyze Literature

Character A flat character is a one who is one-dimensional, exhibiting only a single quality or trait. A round character is one who is three-dimensional and seems to have all the complexities of an actual human being. Is Moon a round or flat character? To decide this question, use a cluster chart like this one to write down details that relate to his character.

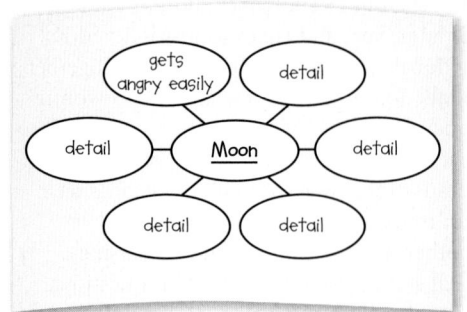

Extend Understanding

Writing Options

Creative Writing Write a **petition** to the government of Pakistan, voicing your concern for child laborers and requesting changes to the system that forces them to work under substandard conditions. Use the information from Build Background and "The Story of Iqbal Masih" to help you write the petition. Your petition should describe the situation and why it needs to be changed. Write it in the most persuasive, concise, and clear way possible. Try to make it no longer than half a page.

Applied Writing Write a **set of instructions** for a writing assignment Mrs. Woolsten might give her class the day of the memorial school assembly. What should the students write about? Is it creative or critical writing? What information should the students include? Read your instructions out loud to a partner, and listen as your partner reads his or her instructions. Exchange feedback on your work.

Lifelong Learning

Research Use the Internet to find information about child labor laws. What laws govern child labor in Pakistan? Are those laws enforced? Compare the Pakistani child labor laws to those of the United States. What is the history of child labor in the United States? Make sure you are using reliable sources. Write notes on your findings and present your information to the class.

Critical Literacy

Ask Questions Based on the story and Meet the Author Feature, create a set of questions you would like to ask Chaim Potok. The questions can be about what happens in "Moon," about the characters in the story, the writing process, the author's life, or anything else you feel is relevant and appropriate. Ask at least five questions. Afterward, share and compare your questions with your classmates.

Go to **www.mirrorsandwindows.com** for more.

Rubrics for Writing Options

You can adapt this as a checklist for students to use as they write.

Creative Writing

☐ Does the petition describe the situation that needs to be changed?
☐ Does it state why it needs to be changed?
☐ Does the writing contain persuasive, concise language appropriate to the audience?
☐ Are the grammar, spelling, and punctuation correct?

Applied Writing

☐ Do the instructions contain a purpose for the writing?
☐ Do they clearly state what form the writing should be in?
☐ Do they contain clear ideas to help students get started on their assignments?

Grammar & Style

Independent and Dependent Clauses

> "Even though the boy...bears a white man's name, the medicine bag will be his."

—VIRGINIA DRIVING HAWK SNEVE, "The Medicine Bag"

An **independent** (or main) clause has a subject and a predicate and can function as a complete sentence. A **dependent** (or subordinate clause) also has a subject and a predicate, but cannot stand alone. In the passage above, *Even though the boy bears a white man's name* is a dependent clause. It cannot stand by itself as a complete sentence.

Dependent clauses can function as several parts of speech. Two common types of dependent clauses are adjective clauses and adverb clauses.

Adverb Clauses

An **adverb clause** is a dependent clause that functions as an adverb. Like adverbs, adverb clauses answer such questions as when, where, why, and how an action took place.

> EXAMPLE
>
> *The boy ran outside, so that he could meet his grandfather.*

In this example, the dependent clause *so that he could meet his grandfather* modifies the verb *ran* and tells why the action took place.

Adjective Clauses

An **adjective clause** is a dependent clause that functions as an adjective. Like adjectives, adjective clauses modify nouns or pronouns.

> EXAMPLE
>
> *The narrator's family lives in a town that has very little knowledge of Native American culture.*

In this example, the adjective clause *that has very little knowledge of Native American culture* modifies the noun *town*.

> EXAMPLE
>
> *They who arrive first will get the best seats.*

In this example, the adjective clause *who arrive first* modifies the pronoun *they*.

Identifying Dependent Clauses

For each of the following sentences, identify the dependent clause and determine whether it is an adjective clause or an adverb clause.

1. After my mother dropped me off, Grandpa taught me a Sioux chant.
2. The boy wanted the medicine bag that his grandfather had saved.
3. Grandpa told Eugene about the medicine bag because it was time.
4. The two children stood where they could see the old man.
5. The narrator listened to stories about a man that he had never met.
6. He held the medicine bag as if it belonged to him.
7. After the old man crossed the street, he fainted.
8. He fainted because he was sick from the sun.
9. The girls' mother arrived outside after the boy greeted his grandfather.
10. When their grandfather visited, the children would listen to his stories.

Teach the Workshop

Identifying Dependent Clauses

1. After my mother dropped me off; adverb clause
2. that his grandfather had saved; adjective clause
3. because it was time; adverb clause
4. where they could see the old man; adverb clause
5. that he had never met; adjective clause
6. as if it belonged to him; adverb clause
7. After the old man crossed the street; adverb clause
8. because he was sick from the sun; adverb clause
9. after the boy greeted his grandfather; adverb clause
10. When their grandfather visited; adverb clause

> For more information, see the Grammar & Style Section 3.12, Clauses, in the Language Arts Handbook.

Program Resources

You will find additional lessons on Independent and Dependent Clauses in the *Exceeding the Standards: Grammar & Style* resource.

KEY TERMS

INDEPENDENT CLAUSE, 243

DEPENDENT CLAUSE, 243

SUBJECT, 243

PREDICATE, 243

ADVERB CLAUSE, 243

ADJECTIVE CLAUSE, 243

TEACHING NOTE

Extra Practice

For each of the following sentences, identify the dependent clause and determine whether it is an adjective clause or an adverb clause.

1. After Grandpa greeted my sister, he fainted. (After Grandpa greeted my sister, adverb clause)
2. I was embarrassed because Grandpa doesn't look like a TV Indian. (because Grandpa doesn't look like a TV Indian, adverb clause)
3. I had a strange dream that I wanted to tell Grandpa about. (that I wanted to tell Grandpa about, adjective clause)

Common Core State Standards

Language
L.1

At a Glance
Independent Reading
- Reading Level: Moderate
- Difficulty Consideration: Vocabulary
- Ease Factor: Familiar subject matter

Objectives
Reading this selection will enable students to do the following:
- read with developing fluency
- read silently with comprehension for a sustained period of time

Launch the Lesson
Point out to students that in "Luke Baldwin's Vow" there is a conflict of opinions about what is truly valuable. Ask them if they have ever had a difference of opinion with someone over the value of an item or perhaps a pet. Encourage students to explain how they might go about settling such a conflict.

TEACHING NOTE
Although this selection is presented in the student edition as an independent reading, teaching support has been provided should you choose to cover it in class.

(Above) *An Autumn Day at the Farm*, 1919. Edward Wilkins Waite. Private collection.

Luke Baldwin's Vow

A Short Story
by Morley Callaghan

Morley Callaghan (1903–1990) was born in Toronto, Ontario, in Canada. While working as a reporter for the *Toronto Star*, he published

INDEPENDENT READING

That summer when twelve-year-old Luke Baldwin came to live with his Uncle Henry in the house on the stream by the sawmill, he did not forget that he had promised his dying father he would try to learn things from his uncle; so he used to watch him very carefully.

Uncle Henry, who was the manager of the sawmill, was a big, burly man weighing more than two hundred and thirty pounds, and he had a rough-skinned, brick-colored face. He looked like a powerful man, but his health was not good. He had aches and pains in his back and shoulders which puzzled the

his first short stories. Like many of Callaghan's stories, "Luke Baldwin's Vow" deals with the conflict between the demands of the practical world and the spiritual and emotional needs of a character.

244

Program Resources

Planning and Assessment
Program Planning Guide, Selection Lesson Plan
E-Lesson Planner
Assessment Guide, Lesson Test
ExamView

Technology Tools
Interactive Student Text on CD
Visual Teaching Package
Audio Library
mirrorsandwindows.com

Meeting the Standards
Fiction: Unit 2, Independent Reading, pp. 77–84

Differentiating Instruction
Advanced Students, Independent Reading Study, p. 14
English Language Learners, Analyze Cause and Effect, pp. 78–95

Common Core State Standards

Reading Literature
RL.3, RL.10

Writing
W.4

Speaking and Listening
SL.1

"Maybe you should make him a practical proposition."

doctor. The first thing Luke learned about Uncle Henry was that everybody had great respect for him. The four men he employed in the sawmill were always polite and attentive when he spoke to them. His wife, Luke's Aunt Helen, a kindly, plump, straightforward woman, never argued with him. "You should try and be like your Uncle Henry," she would say to Luke. "He's so wonderfully practical. He takes care of everything in a sensible, easy way."

Luke used to trail around the sawmill after Uncle Henry not only because he liked the fresh clean smell of the newly cut wood and the big piles of sawdust, but because he was impressed by his uncle's precise, firm tone when he spoke to the men.

Sometimes Uncle Henry would stop and explain to Luke something about a piece of timber. "Always try and learn the essential facts, son," he would say. "If you've got the facts, you know what's useful and what isn't useful, and no one can fool you."

He showed Luke that nothing of value was ever wasted around the mill. Luke used to listen, and wonder if there was another man in the world who knew so well what was needed and what ought to be thrown away. Uncle Henry had known at once that Luke needed a bicycle to ride to his school, which was two miles away in town, and he bought him a good one. He knew that Luke needed good, serviceable clothes. He also knew exactly how much Aunt Helen needed to run the house, the price of everything, and how much a woman should be paid for doing the family washing. In the evenings Luke used to sit in the living room watching his uncle making notations in a black notebook which he always carried in his vest pocket, and he knew that he was assessing the value of the smallest transaction that had taken place during the day.

Luke promised himself that when he grew up he, too, would be admired for his good, sound judgment. But, of course, he couldn't always be watching and learning from his Uncle Henry, for too often when he watched him he thought of his own father; then he was lonely. So he began to build up another secret life for himself around the sawmill, and his companion was the eleven-year-old collie, Dan, a dog blind in one eye and with a slight limp in his left hind leg. Dan was a fat slow-moving old dog. He was very affectionate and his eye was the color of amber. His fur was amber too. When Luke left for school in the morning, the old dog followed him for half a mile down the road, and when he returned in the afternoon, there was Dan waiting at the gate.

Sometimes they would play around the millpond or by the dam, or go down the stream to the lake. Luke was never lonely when the dog was with him. There was an old rowboat that they used as a pirate ship in the stream, and they would be pirates together, with Luke shouting instructions to Captain Dan and with the dog seeming to understand and wagging his tail enthusiastically. Its amber eye was alert, intelligent and approving. Then they would plunge into the brush on the other side of the stream, pretending they were hunting tigers. Of course, the old dog was no longer much good for hunting; he was too slow and too lazy. Uncle Henry no longer used him for hunting rabbits or anything else.

Teach the Selection

Summary

Luke Baldwin is a twelve-year-old boy who lives with his Uncle Henry. Luke quickly learns that Uncle Henry is a practical man who never wastes anything of value. Luke becomes quite fond of Uncle Henry's eleven-year-old dog, Dan. When Uncle Henry decides the old dog has no more practical value, he arranges to have the dog drowned. Heartbroken, Luke defies Uncle Henry and saves Dan. He then appeals to an elderly neighbor, Mr. Kemp, for help in keeping the dog. Mr. Kemp suggests a practical business proposition: Luke will work for Mr. Kemp and pay his wages to Uncle Henry for Dan's upkeep. Uncle Henry agrees. From this transaction, Luke vows to always have enough money to protect truly valuable things from practical people.

The Mirrors & Windows questions at the end of this selection focus on the theme of integrity. Before reading the story, ask students if they have ever decided to do something contrary to their instructions because they believed the instructions were wrong. How can people make correct decisions in the face of opposition?

Words in Use

Selection Words

burly, 244
sensible, 245
precise, 245
assessing, 245
transaction, 245
affectionate, 245
veranda, 246
hobbled, 246

resistance, 249
negotiation, 253

KEY TERMS
CHARACTER, 253

Analyze Literature

Character Remind students that a character is an animal or a person who takes part in the action of a literary work. A round character has many traits and seems real. A flat character only exhibits one quality or trait. Point out that the dog, Dan, is an important character. Tells students to look for clues as they read that tell them whether Dan is a flat or a round character. **A**

Analyze Literature

Setting Ask students what these details of setting contribute to the mood of the story at this point. **B**

Use Reading Strategies

Make Predictions Remind students that Uncle Luke is very practical. Ask what he might want with the dog. List students' predictions on the board. Have them continue reading until they can confirm or change their predictions. **C**

A When they came out of the brush, they would lie together on the cool, grassy bank being affectionate with each other, with Luke talking earnestly, while the collie, as Luke believed, smiled with the good eye. Lying in the grass, Luke would say things to Dan he could not say to his uncle or his aunt. Not that what he said was important: it was just stuff about himself that he might have told to his own father or mother if they had been alive. Then they would go back to the house for dinner, and after dinner Dan would follow him down the road to Mr. Kemp's house, where they would ask old Mr. Kemp if they could go with him to round up his four cows. The old man was always glad to see them. He seemed to like watching Luke and the collie running around the cows, pretending they were riding on a vast range in the foothills of the Rockies.

Uncle Henry no longer paid much attention to the collie, though once when he tripped over him on the veranda, he shook his head and said thoughtfully, "Poor old fellow, he's through. Can't use him for anything. He just eats and sleeps and gets in the way."

B One Sunday during Luke's summer holidays when they had returned from church and had had their lunch, they had all moved out to the veranda where the collie was sleeping. Luke sat down on the steps, his back against the veranda post. Uncle Henry took the rocking chair, and Aunt Helen stretched herself out in the hammock, sighing contentedly. Then Luke, eying the collie, tapped the step with the palm of his hand, giving three little

> "The time comes when you have to get rid of any old dog."

taps like a signal and the old collie, lifting his head, got up stiffly with a slow wagging of the tail as an acknowledgment that the signal had been heard, and began to cross the veranda to Luke. But the dog was sleepy, his bad eye was turned to the rocking chair; in passing, his left front paw went under the rocker. With a frantic yelp, the dog went bounding down the steps and hobbled around the corner of the house, where he stopped, hearing Luke coming after him. All he needed was the touch of Luke's hand. Then he began to lick the hand methodically, as if apologizing.

C "Luke," Uncle Henry called sharply, "bring that dog here."

When Luke led the collie back to the veranda, Uncle Henry nodded and said, "Thanks, Luke." Then he took out a cigar, lit it, put his big hands on his knees and began to rock in the chair while he frowned and eyed the dog steadily. Obviously he was making some kind of an important decision about the collie.

"What's the matter, Uncle Henry?" Luke asked nervously.

"That dog can't see any more," Uncle Henry said.

"Oh, yes, he can," Luke said quickly. "His bad eye got turned to the chair, that's all, Uncle Henry."

"And his teeth are gone, too," Uncle Henry went on, paying no attention to what Luke had said. Turning to the hammock, he called, "Helen, sit up a minute, will you?"

When she got up and stood beside him, he went on. "I was thinking about this old dog the

246 **UNIT 2** FICTION

Differentiated Instruction

Auditory Learning

The narrator describes the sounds of the sawmill as well as the tones that the various characters use when speaking. For example, Uncle Henry uses a precise, firm tone; the employees are polite; the saws screech. Have small groups find recordings of voices/sounds that they think are similar to the voices and sounds in the story, or have them record their own voices and make sound effects. Invite each group to play their sounds for the class.

Kinesthetic Learning

Have small groups of students prepare oral interpretations of different scenes from "Luke Baldwin's Vow." Have them practice reading with emotion, pausing, varying volume and pace, emphasizing certain words and phrases, and using gestures and facial expressions.

other day, Helen. It's not only that he's just about blind, but did you notice that when we drove up after church he didn't even bark?"

"It's a fact he didn't, Henry."

"No, not much good even as a watchdog now."

"Poor old fellow. It's a pity, isn't it?"

"And no good for hunting either. And he eats a lot, I suppose."

"About as much as he ever did, Henry."

"The plain fact is the old dog isn't worth his keep any more. It's time we got rid of him."

"It's always so hard to know how to get rid of a dog, Henry."

"I was thinking about it the other day. Some people think it's best to shoot a dog. I haven't had any shells for that shotgun for over a year. Poisoning is a hard death for a dog. Maybe drowning is the easiest and quickest way. Well, I'll speak to one of the mill hands and have him look after it."

Crouching on the ground, his arms around the old collie's neck, Luke cried out, "Uncle Henry, Dan's a wonderful dog! You don't know how wonderful he is!"

"He's just a very old dog, son," Uncle Henry said calmly. "The time comes when you have to get rid of any old dog. We've got to be practical about it. I'll get you a pup, son. A smart little dog that'll be worth its keep. A pup that will grow up with you."

"I don't want a pup!" Luke cried, turning his face away. Circling around him, the dog began to bark, then flick his long pink tongue at the back of Luke's neck. **D**

Aunt Helen, catching her husband's eye, put her finger on her lips, warning him not to go on talking in front of the boy. "An old dog like that often wanders off into the brush and sort of picks a place to die when the time

comes. Isn't that so, Henry?"

"Oh sure," he agreed quickly. "In fact, when Dan didn't show up yesterday, I was sure that was what had happened." Then he yawned and seemed to forget about the dog.

But Luke was frightened, for he knew what his uncle was like. He knew that if his uncle had decided that the dog was useless and that it was sane and sensible to get rid of it, he would be ashamed of himself if he were diverted by any sentimental considerations. **E** Luke knew in his heart that he couldn't move his uncle. All he could do, he thought, was keep the dog away from his uncle, keep him out of the house, feed him when Uncle Henry wasn't around.

Next day at noontime Luke saw his uncle walking from the mill toward the house with old Sam Carter, a mill hand. Sam Carter was a dull, stooped, slow-witted man of sixty with an iron-gray beard, who was wearing blue overalls and a blue shirt. He hardly ever spoke to anybody. Watching from the veranda, Luke noticed that his uncle suddenly gave Sam Carter a cigar, which Sam put in his pocket. Luke had never seen his uncle give Sam a cigar or pay much attention to him.

Then, after lunch, Uncle Henry said lazily that he would like Luke to take his bicycle and go into town and get him some cigars.

"I'll take Dan," Luke said.

"Better not, son," Uncle Henry said. "It'll take you all afternoon. I want those cigars. Get going, Luke."

His uncle's tone was so casual that Luke tried to believe they were not merely getting rid of him. Of course he had to do what he was told. He had never dared to refuse to obey an order from his uncle. But when he had taken his bicycle and had ridden down **F**

Make Connections

Ask students how they responded to Luke's reaction to Uncle Henry's statement about drowning the dog and also to his offer to buy a new puppy for Luke instead. Would they have had a similar reaction? What would they have said to Uncle Henry? **D**

Analyze Literature

Conflict Point out that there can be more than one conflict in a story. Conflict can be internal—one character having a conflict with his/her own thoughts, emotions, or actions. Conflict can also occur between two characters. Ask students to identify the two conflicts here. Model a response: "Luke is in conflict with Uncle Henry about the decision to drown the dog. Uncle Henry has an internal conflict. Since he values practicality, he cannot allow any emotion to influence him to keep the dog." **E**

Use Reading Strategies

Make Predictions Ask students to predict what Luke might do. Then have them continue reading to confirm or change their predictions. **F**

Denotation and Connotation

Remind students that words often have a denotation, or dictionary meaning, as well as a connotation, or additional suggested meaning. The connotation is subjective and may differ from person to person. The connotation may be associated with other events. Have students create a chart to keep notes about the denotation and connotation of certain words in "Luke Baldwin's

Vow." Use the word *practical* to demonstrate finding denotation and connotation. Have students find denotations and connotations for the words *sentimental, sane, sensible,* and *weak.*

Word	Denotation	Connotation in Story
practical	sensible	unfeeling

Analyze Literature

Setting Point out that the author gives extensive details about the setting, including the measurement of distances. Discuss how this detail adds to students' understanding of the story. Have students work in pairs or in small groups to find pictures that resemble the setting, or suggest that they illustrate the setting themselves. Have students show their work to the class and discuss its accuracy. **A**

Use Reading Strategies

Clarify Have students review the problem with Dan, what Uncle Henry has ordered done about it, what his reasons are, and what Luke thinks of the idea. Tell them to work in pairs to make sure they get the details correct. Suggest that they ask each other questions to clarify what they have read. **B**

---

the path that followed the stream to the town road and had got about a quarter of a mile along the road, he found that all he could think of was his uncle handing old Sam Carter the cigar.

Slowing down, sick with worry now, he got off the bike and stood uncertainly on the sunlit road. Sam Carter was a gruff, aloof old man who would have no feeling for a dog. Then suddenly Luke could go no farther without getting some assurance that the collie would not be harmed while he was away. Across the fields he could see the house.

A Leaving the bike in the ditch, he started to cross the field, intending to get close enough to the house so Dan could hear him if he whistled softly. He got about fifty yards away from the house and whistled and waited, but there was no sign of the dog, which might be asleep at the front of the house, he knew, or over at the saw-mill. With the saws whining, the dog couldn't hear the soft whistle. For a few minutes Luke couldn't make up his mind what to do, then he decided to go back to the road, get on his bike and go back the way he had come until he got to the place where the river path joined the road. There he could leave his bike, go up the path, then into the tall grass and get close to the front of the house and the sawmill without being seen.

B He had followed the river path for about a hundred yards, and when he came to the place where the river began to bend sharply toward the house his heart fluttered and his legs felt paralyzed, for he saw the old

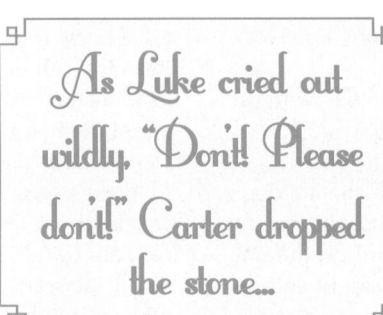

As Luke cried out wildly, "Don't! Please don't!" Carter dropped the stone...

rowboat in the one place where the river was deep, and in the rowboat was Sam Carter with the collie.

The bearded man in the blue overalls was smoking the cigar; the dog, with a rope around its neck, sat contentedly beside him, its tongue going out in a friendly lick at the hand holding the rope. It was all like a crazy dream picture to Luke: all wrong because it looked so lazy and friendly, even the curling smoke from Sam Carter's cigar. But as Luke cried out, "Dan, Dan! Come on, boy!" and the dog jumped at the water, he saw that Sam Carter's left hand was hanging deep in the water, holding a foot of rope with a heavy stone at the end.

As Luke cried out wildly, "Don't! Please don't!" Carter dropped the stone, for the cry came too late; it was blurred by the screech of the big saws at the mill. But Carter was startled, and he stared stupidly at the riverbank, then he ducked his head and began to row quickly to the bank.

But Luke was watching the collie take what looked like a long, shallow dive, except that the hind legs suddenly kicked up above the surface, then shot down, and while he watched, Luke sobbed and trembled, for it was as if the happy secret part of his life around the sawmill was being torn away from him. But even while he watched, he seemed to be following a plan without knowing it, for he was already fumbling in his pocket for his jackknife, jerking the blade open, pulling off his pants, kicking his shoes

---

Differentiated Instruction

English Language Learning

Students learning English may have difficulty with Callaghan's use of adjectives, particularly multiple adjectives such as "rough-skinned, brick-colored face," "sensible, easy way" and "good, serviceable clothes." Suggest that students identify adjectives that give them trouble, and have them work in pairs to identify their meanings.

Reading Proficiency

Have students read along while listening to the dramatic recording in the Audio Library. Then have them work in small groups and take turns reading the story aloud by paragraphs.

off while he muttered fiercely and prayed that Sam Carter would get out of sight.

It hardly took the mill hand a minute to reach the bank and go slinking furtively¹ around the bend as if he felt that the boy was following him. But Luke hadn't taken his eyes off the exact spot in the water where Dan had disappeared. As soon as the mill hand was out of sight, Luke slid down the bank and took a leap at the water, the sun glistening on his slender body, his eyes wild with eagerness as he ran out to the deep place, then arched his back and dived, swimming under water, his open eyes getting used to the greenish-gray haze of the water, the sandy bottom and the embedded rocks.

His lungs began to ache, then he saw the shadow of the collie floating at the end of the taut rope, rock-held in the sand. He slashed at the rope with his knife. He couldn't get much strength in his arm because of the resistance of the water. He grabbed the rope with his left hand, hacking with his knife. The collie suddenly drifted up slowly, like a water-soaked log. Then his own head shot above the surface, and while he was sucking in the air he was drawing in the rope, pulling the collie toward him and treading water. In a few strokes he was away from the deep place and his feet touched the bottom.

Hoisting the collie out of the water, he scrambled toward the bank, lurching and stumbling in fright because the collie felt like a dead weight.

He went on up the bank and across the path to the tall grass, where he fell flat, hugging the dog and trying to warm him with his own body. But the collie didn't stir, the good amber eye remained closed. Then suddenly Luke wanted to act like a resourceful, competent man. Getting up on

Companions. James Charles.

C his knees, he stretched the dog out on its belly, drew him between his knees, felt with trembling hands for the soft places on the flanks just above the hipbones, and rocked back and forth, pressing with all his weight, then relaxing the pressure as he straightened up. He hoped that he was working the dog's lungs like a bellows. He had read that men **D** who had been thought drowned had been saved in this way.

"Come on, Dan. Come on, old boy," he pleaded softly. As a little water came from the collie's mouth, Luke's heart jumped, and he muttered over and over, "You can't be dead, Dan! You can't, you can't! I won't let you die, Dan!" He rocked back and forth

---

1. furtively. Sneakily

LUKE BALDWIN'S VOW **249**

Teach the Selection

Use Reading Strategies
Visualize Point out that this simile helps a reader visualize the dog's movements. Ask students what additional effects this comparison has. If necessary, model a response: "I think it heightens the suspense by suggesting that Dan might be dead already." **C**

Use Reading Strategies
Ask Questions Model some questions for students: "What is a bellows? How does it work? How will working the lungs like a bellows help? How does Luke know what to do?" **D**

Vocabulary Skills

Homophones
Point out that the words *principal* and *principle* are homophones. *Principal* as a noun means "the person in charge" and as an adjective means "first in importance." *Principle* is a noun that means "a standard of moral decision making." Have students tell which word to use in each of the following sentences and to explain their reasoning.

1. It was Uncle Henry's (principle) to not waste things.
2. Luke's (principal) concern was for Dan.
3. Luke developed his own (principle) to always have money for truly valuable things.
4. Uncle Henry's position as manager of the sawmill could be compared to the job of a school (principal).

Analyze Literature

Characterization Remind students that characterization is the act of creating or describing a character. Writers create characters by describing what they say and do, by showing what other characters think about them, and by describing their physical features and personalities. Ask students which techniques the author uses to characterize Dan and Luke. Model a response: "The author describes what Dan is saying and what both of them are doing."

Use Reading Strategies

Make Predictions Have students predict what Luke will do next. Have them continue reading until they can confirm their prediction or need to change it. Ⓐ

On a Sussex Farm. James Charles.

tirelessly, applying the pressure to the flanks. More water dribbled from the mouth. In the collie's body he felt a faint tremor. "Oh gee, Dan, you're alive," he whispered. "Come on, boy. Keep it up."

With a cough the collie suddenly jerked his head back, the amber eye opened, and there they were looking at each other. Then the collie, thrusting his legs out stiffly, tried to hoist himself up, staggered, tried again, then stood there in a stupor. Then he shook himself like any other wet dog, turned his head, eyed Luke, and the red tongue came out in a weak flick at Luke's cheek.

"Lie down, Dan," Luke said. As the dog lay down beside him, Luke closed his eyes, buried his head in the wet fur and wondered why all the muscles of his arms and legs began to jerk in a nervous reaction, now that it was all over. "Stay there, Dan," he said softly, and he went back to the path, got his clothes and came back beside Dan and put them on. "I think we'd better get away from this spot, Dan," he said. "Keep down, boy. Come on." And he crawled on through the

tall grass till they were about seventy-five yards from the place where he had undressed. There they lay down together.

Ⓐ In a little while he heard his aunt's voice calling, "Luke. Oh, Luke! Come here, Luke!"

"Quiet, Dan," Luke whispered. A few minutes passed, and then Uncle Henry called, "Luke, Luke!" and he began to come down the path. They could see him standing there, massive and imposing, his hands on his hips as he looked down the path, then he turned and went back to the house.

As he watched the sunlight shine on the back of his uncle's neck, the exultation Luke had felt at knowing the collie was safe beside him turned to bewildered despair, for he knew that even if he should be forgiven for saving the dog when he saw it drowning, the fact was that his uncle had been thwarted. His mind was made up to get rid of Dan, and in a few days' time, in another way, he would get rid of him, as he got rid of anything around the mill that he believed to be useless or a waste of money.

As he lay back and looked up at the hardly moving clouds, he began to grow frightened. He couldn't go back to the house, nor could he take the collie into the woods and hide him and feed him there unless he tied him up. If he didn't tie him up, Dan would wander back to the house.

"I guess there's just no place to go, Dan," he whispered sadly. "Even if we start off along the road, somebody is sure to see us."

Grammar Skills

Predicate Adjectives

Remind students that predicate adjectives modify, or describe, the subject of a sentence that employs a linking verb. For example: "Luke was never lonely when the dog was with him." *Lonely* is the predicate adjective that describes *Luke,* the subject of the sentence. Write the following sentences on the board. Then ask students to identify the predicate adjective in each sentence.

1. Uncle Henry's tone was very <u>casual</u>.
2. Luke became <u>nervous</u> as he watched Sam Carter and the dog.
3. Luke felt <u>exultant</u> after rescuing Dan.

But Dan was watching a butterfly that was circling crazily above them. Raising himself a little, Luke looked through the grass at the corner of the house, then he turned and looked the other way to the wide blue lake. With a sigh he lay down again, and for hours they lay there together, until there was no sound from the saws in the mill and the sun moved low in the western sky.

B

> "I can't seem to think of a place to take you."

"Well, we can't stay here any longer, Dan," he said at last. "We'll just have to get as far away as we can. Keep down, old boy," and he began to crawl through the grass, going farther away from the house. When he could no longer be seen, he got up and began to trot across the field toward the gravel road leading to town.

On the road, the collie would turn from time to time as if wondering why Luke shuffled along, dragging his feet wearily, his head down. "I'm stumped, that's all Dan," Luke explained. "I can't seem to think of a place to take you."

When they were passing the Kemp place they saw the old man sitting on the veranda, and Luke stopped. All he could think of was that Mr. Kemp had liked them both and it had been a pleasure to help him get the cows in the evening. Dan had always been with them. Staring at the figure of the old man on the veranda, he said in a worried tone, "I wish I could be sure of him, Dan. I wish he was a dumb, stupid man who wouldn't know or care whether you were worth anything.... Well, come on." He opened the gate bravely, but he felt shy and unimportant.

"Hello, son. What's on your mind?" Mr. Kemp called from the veranda. He was a thin, wiry man in a tan-colored shirt. He had a gray, untidy mustache, his skin was wrinkled and leathery, but his eyes were always friendly and amused.

"Could I speak to you, Mr. Kemp?" Luke asked when they were close to the veranda.

"Sure. Go ahead."

"It's about Dan. He's a great dog, but I guess you know that as well as I do. I was wondering if you could keep him here for me."

"Why should I keep Dan here, son?"

"Well, it's like this," Luke said, fumbling the words awkwardly: "My uncle won't let me keep him any more...says he's too old." His mouth began to tremble, then he blurted out the story.

"I see, I see," Mr. Kemp said slowly, and he got up and came over to the steps and sat down and began to stroke the collie's head. "Of course, Dan's an old dog, son," he said quietly. "And sooner or later you've got to get rid of an old dog. Your uncle knows that. Maybe it's true that Dan isn't worth his keep."

"He doesn't eat much, Mr. Kemp. Just one meal a day."

"I wouldn't want you to think your uncle was cruel and unfeeling, Luke," Mr. Kemp went on. "He's a fine man...maybe just a little bit too practical and straightforward."

"I guess that's right," Luke agreed, but he was really waiting and trusting the expression in the old man's eyes.

"Maybe you should make him a practical proposition."

C

D

Teach the Selection

Use Reading Strategies

Visualize Have students compare the peaceful, idyllic setting with Luke's inner turmoil. **B**

Use Reading Strategies

Make Inferences Ask students why they think Luke is willing to trust Mr. Kemp. Remind them to use information from the story as well as their own background knowledge to make inferences. Model a possible response: "Luke and Mr. Kemp have become friendly, and Mr. Kemp has also been kind to Dan. Luke knows that Mr. Kemp has known Uncle Harry for a long time." **C**

Analyze Literature

Plot Point out that there is a twist in the plot here. Discuss with students how this new development moves the plot along. **D**

Writing Skills

Write a Contract

Explain to students that a contract is a legal document that is binding on both parties. Many times one party will draft a proposed contract and then the two parties will negotiate the terms in the contract. Suggest that students make a chart listing the details from the story that need to be agreed on, what they think Luke would want, and what they think Uncle Henry would want. Have half of the students write up the contract from Luke's point of view and the other half write it from Uncle Henry's point of view. Remind them that they need to use clear, specific language such as, "I will pay Uncle Henry seventy-five cents per week, payable every Sunday evening. The money will cover the cost of food for the dog." Then pair them and have the two sides negotiate an agreement.

Use Reading Strategies

Clarify Review with students the suggestion that Mr. Kemp made and why he thinks it will work. Ask students for their own responses as to whether Uncle Henry will accept the proposal. **A**

Use Reading Strategies

Make Inferences Ask students why they think Aunt Helen fled into the house. Model a possible response: "I think she is not used to challenging Uncle Henry and was afraid of what he might say back to her." **B**

"I—I don't know what you mean."

"Well, I sort of like the way you get the cows for me in the evenings," Mr. Kemp said, smiling to himself. "In fact, I don't think you need me to go along with you at all. Now, supposing I gave you seventy-five cents a week. Would you get the cows for me every night?"

"Sure I would, Mr. Kemp. I like doing it, anyway."

A "All right, son. It's a deal. Now I'll tell you what to do. You go back to your uncle, and before he has a chance to open up on you, you say right out that you've come to him with a business proposition. Say it like a man, just like that. Offer to pay him the seventy-five cents a week for the dog's keep."

"But my uncle doesn't need seventy-five cents, Mr. Kemp," Luke said uneasily.

"Of course not," Mr. Kemp agreed. "It's the principle of the thing. Be confident. Remember that he's got nothing against the dog. Go to it, son. Let me know how you do," he added, with an amused smile. "If I know your uncle at all, I think it'll work."

"I'll try it, Mr. Kemp," Luke said. "Thanks very much." But he didn't have any confidence, for even though he knew that Mr. Kemp was a wise old man who would not deceive him, he couldn't believe that seventy-five cents a week would stop his uncle, who was an important man. "Come on, Dan," he called, and he went slowly and apprehensively back to the house.

When they were going up the path, his aunt cried from the open window, "Henry, Henry, in heaven's name, it's Luke with the dog!"

"Oh. Oh, I see," Uncle Henry said, and gradually the color came back to his face.

"You fished him out, eh?" he asked, still looking at the dog uneasily. "Well, you shouldn't have done that. I told Sam Carter to get rid of the dog, you know."

"Just a minute, Uncle Henry," Luke said, trying not to falter. He gained confidence as Aunt Helen came out and stood beside her husband, for her eyes seemed to be gentle, and he went on bravely. "I want to make you a practical proposition, Uncle Henry."

"A what?" Uncle Henry asked, still feeling insecure, and wishing the boy and the dog weren't confronting him.

"A practical proposition," Luke blurted out quickly. "I know Dan isn't worth his keep to you. I guess he isn't worth anything to anybody but me. So I'll pay you seventy-five cents a week for his keep."

"What's this?" Uncle Henry asked, looking bewildered. "Where would you get seventy-five cents a week, Luke?"

"I'm going to get the cows every night for Mr. Kemp."

B "Oh, for heaven's sake, Henry," Aunt Helen pleaded, looking distressed, "let him keep the dog!" and she fled into the house.

"None of that kind of talk!" Uncle Henry called after her. "We've got to be sensible about this!" But he was shaken himself, and overwhelmed with a distress that destroyed all his confidence. As he sat down slowly in the rocking chair and stroked the side of his big face, he wanted to say weakly, "All right, keep the dog," but he was ashamed of being so weak and sentimental. He stubbornly refused to yield to this emotion: he was trying desperately to turn his emotion into a bit of good, useful common sense, so he could justify his distress. So he rocked and pondered. At last he smiled. "You're a smart

---

TEACHING NOTE

Self-Generated Questioning

Instruct students to each create two or more questions about the selection. Model a question such as "Why does everyone at Uncle Henry's work respect him?" Instruct a student to ask the class one of his or her questions. Call on someone who signals that he or she knows the answer. If the answer is right, give the responder a point and have

him or her ask a new question. If the answer is wrong, invite a new responder to create a question for the wrong answer, give him or her a point, and then tell him or her to ask a new question.

little shaver, Luke," he said slowly. "Imagine you working it out like this. I'm tempted to accept your proposition."

"Gee, thanks, Uncle Henry."

"I'm accepting it because I think you'll learn something out of this," he went on ponderously. **C**

"Yes, Uncle Henry."

"You'll learn that useless luxuries cost the smartest of men hard-earned money."

"I don't mind."

"Well, it's a thing you'll have to learn sometime. I think you'll learn, too, because you certainly seem to have a practical streak in you. It's a streak I like to see in a boy. O.K., son," he said, and he smiled with relief and went into the house.

Turning to Dan, Luke whispered softly, "Well, what do you know about that?"

As he sat down on the step with the collie beside him and listened to Uncle Henry talking to his wife, he began to glow with exultation. Then gradually his exultation began to change to a vast wonder that Mr. Kemp should have had such a perfect understanding of Uncle Henry. He began to dream of someday being as wise as old Mr. Kemp and knowing exactly how to handle people. It was possible, too, that he had already learned some of the things about his uncle that his father had wanted him to learn.

Putting his head down on the dog's neck, he vowed to himself fervently that he would always have some money on hand, no matter what became of him, so that he would be able to protect all that was truly valuable from the practical people in the world. ❖ **D**

Have you ever done something because you felt that not doing it would be wrong? How did you decide what to do? What were the results of your decision? What do you feel motivates people to make the right decision?

Analyze and Extend

1. (a) Why is Luke staying with Uncle Henry and Aunt Helen? (b) What is Uncle Henry like?

2. (a) With whom does Luke spend most of his time? (b) Why is this companion so important to Luke?

3. (a) What does Luke do to save Dan? (b) Do you think that Luke was right to save Dan, even though his actions were against his uncle's wishes?

Creative Writing Luke and his uncle are able to reach an agreement when Luke uses powers of negotiation. Think about what Uncle Henry wanted, and then think about what Luke

wanted. With this in mind, write a **contract** between Luke and Uncle Henry. Mention specific details from the story and decide upon terms that both characters would likely agree upon. Share your work with your classmates.

Collaborative Learning What does each character in "Luke Baldwin's Vow" find valuable? What do you find valuable in your own life? Work in groups to discuss your answers to this question, making sure everyone gets a chance to speak. Take notes and discuss these ideas with the rest of the class.

Ⓜ Go to **www.mirrorsandwindows.com** for more.

Analyze Literature

Plot Point out that the conflict between Uncle Henry and Luke is resolved here. Ask students how Uncle Henry seems to resolve his inner conflict. **C**

Analyze Literature

Theme Remind students that the theme is the central idea in a story. Ask them what they think the theme of the story is. **D**

Answer: Students' experiences will vary. They may feel that a desire to help others motivates many people.

Analyze and Extend

1. (a) Luke's father has died. (b) Uncle Henry is practical and widely respected.

2. (a) Luke spends most of his time with the old dog, Dan. (b) Luke is comfortable talking to Dan.

3. (a) Luke pulls Dan from the water and negotiates a business proposition with Uncle Henry in order to keep Dan. (b) Students may feel that Luke was right to save Dan because he cared about his friend.

Rubric for Creative Writing

You can adapt this as a checklist for students to use as they write.

☐ Does the student show knowledge of what both Uncle Henry and Luke wanted?

☐ Does the contract come to a plausible agreement?

☐ Does the contract make references to specific examples from the text?

Preview the Selection

At a Glance
Independent Reading
- Reading Level: Moderate
- Difficulty Consideration: Unfamiliar subject matter
- Ease Factors: Language, length

Objectives
Reading this selection will enable students to do the following:
- read with developing fluency
- read silently with comprehension for a sustained period of time

Launch the Lesson
Students might enjoy illustrating a scene from the selection. Remind them to use details from the text as well as their own mental picture of how they view the scene.

Independent Reading
Students who like "Lose Now, Pay Later" might enjoy other alternative reality stories, such as Isaac Asimov's "The Fun They Had" and H. G. Wells's "The Door in the Wall."

TEACHING NOTE
Although this selection is presented in the student edition as an independent reading, teaching support has been provided should you choose to cover it in class.

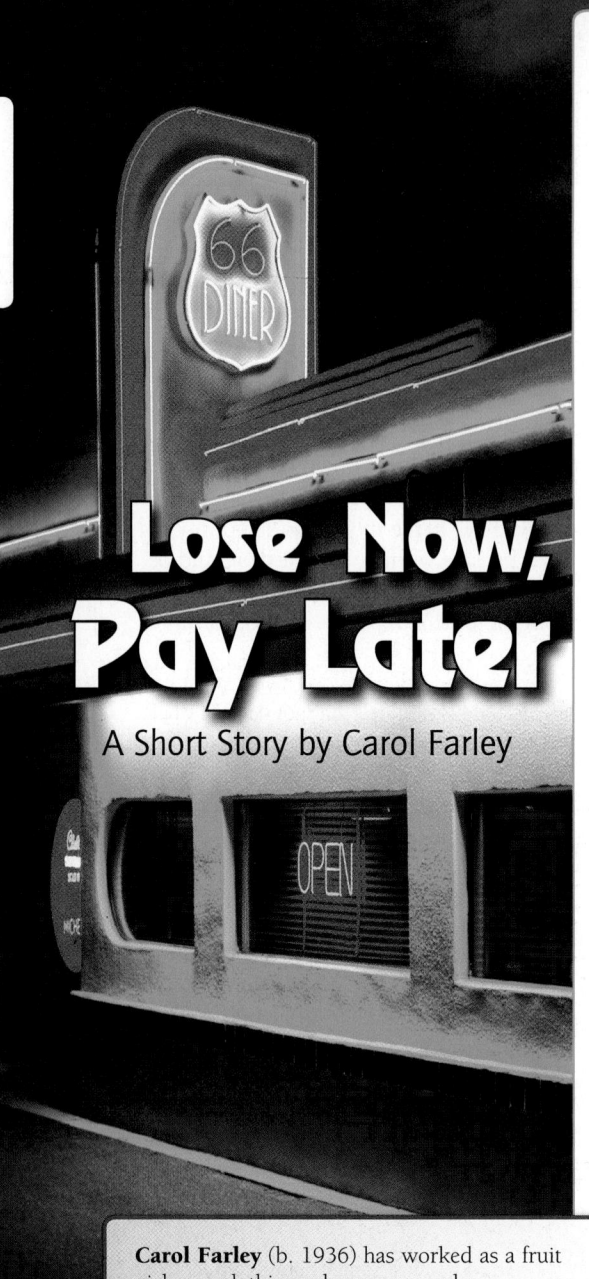

Lose Now, Pay Later

A Short Story by Carol Farley

Carol Farley (b. 1936) has worked as a fruit picker, a clothing salesperson, and a school teacher, as well as a writer. While she was in school, her favorite classes were literature classes because she enjoyed discussing what she had read. Farley believes that children often perceive the obvious, even when it eludes the adults around them.

254

I think my little brother is crazy. At least I hope he is. Because if his looney idea is right, then all of us are being used like a flock of sheep, and that's a pretty gruesome thought. Humans just can't be that stupid. My brother has a dumb idea, that's all. It's just a dumb idea.

This whole situation started about eight months ago. That's when I first knew anything about it, I mean. My best friend, Trinja, and I were shopping when we noticed a new store where an old insurance office used to be. It was a cubbyhole, really, at the far end of the mall where hardly anybody ever goes. We were there because we'd used that entrance as we came home from school.

"Swoodies!" Trinja said, pointing at the letters written across the display window. "What do you think they are, Deb?"

I stared through the glass. The place had always looked dim and dingy before, full of desks, half-dead plants, and bored-looking people; but now it was as bright and glaring as a Health Brigade Corp office. There weren't any people inside at all, but there were five or six gold-colored machines lining the walls. Signs were hung everywhere.

SWEETS PLUS GOODIES = SWOODIES, one said. Flavors were posted by each machine; peanut-butter-fudge-crunch...butter-rum-pecan...chocolate-nut-mint…

Things like that. The biggest sign of all simply said FREE.

I have to admit that the place gave me the creeps that first time I saw it. I don't know

Program Resources

Planning and Assessment
Program Planning Guide, Selection Lesson Plan
E-Lesson Planner
Assessment Guide, Lesson Test
ExamView

Technology Tools
Interactive Student Text on CD
Visual Teaching Package
Audio Library
mirrorsandwindows.com

Meeting the Standards
Fiction: Unit 2, Independent Reading, pp. 85–92

Differentiating Instruction
Developing Readers, Take Notes, pp. 13–15

Common Core State Standards
Reading Literature
RL.10

Speaking and Listening
SL.6

why. It just looked so bare and bright, so empty and clean, without any people or movement. The glare almost hurt my eyes. And I guess I was suspicious about anything that was completely free. Still, though, there was a terrific aroma drifting out of there—sort of a combination of all those flavors that were listed on the signs.

"Let's go in," Trinja said, grabbing my arm. I could see that the smell was getting to her too. She's always on a diet, so she thinks about food a lot.

"But it's so empty in there," I said, drawing away.

"They've just opened, that's all," she told me, yanking my arm again. "Besides, machines and robots run lots of the stores. Let's go inside and see what's in there."

Do you know that wonderful spurt of air that rushes out when you first open an expensive box of candy? The inside of that store smelled just like the inside of one of those boxes. For a few seconds we just stood there sniffing and grinning. My salivary glands¹ started swimming.

Trinja turned toward the nearest machine. "Coconut-almond marshmallow." She was almost drooling. "I've got to try one, Deb." She pressed the button, and a chocolate cone dropped down, like a coffee cup from a kitcho machine. Then a mixture, similar to the look of soft ice cream, filled it. "Want to try it with me?" she asked, reaching for the cone. We both took a taste.

It was absolutely the neatest sensation I've had in my whole life. Swoodies aren't

We tried every flavor before we finally staggered out into the mall again.

cold like ice cream or warm like cooked pudding, but they're a blending of both in temperature and texture. The flavor melts instantly, and your whole mouth and brain are flooded with tastes and impressions. Like that first swoodie I tried, coconut-almond-marshmallow; suddenly, as my mouth separated the individual tastes, my brain burst into memories associated with each flavor. I felt as if I were lying on a warm beach, all covered with coconut suntan oil—then I heard myself giggling and singing as a group of us roasted marshmallows around a campfire—then I relived the long-ago moments of biting into the special Christmas cookies my grandmother made with almonds when I was little.

"Wow!" Trinja looked at me, and I could see that she had just experienced the same kind of reactions. We scarfed up the rest of that swoodie in just a few more bites, and we moved on to another flavor. With each one it was the same. I felt a combination of marvelous tastes and joyous thoughts. We tried every flavor before we finally staggered out into the mall again.

"I'll have to diet for a whole year now," Trinja said, patting her stomach.

"I'll feel like a blimp myself," I told her, but neither one of us cared. We both felt terrific. "Go ahead in there," I called to some

---

1. **salivary glands.** Glands in the mouth that make saliva or spit

Teach the Selection

Summary

The story is set in the year 2041 and is narrated by Deb, one of the characters. Deb and her friend discover a new store at the mall that gives out free swoodies, which are described as a combination of sweets plus goodies. The swoodies become immensely popular, but people begin gaining weight from them. Then another store opens with machines that create instant weight loss, and people are able to eat all the swoodies they want and then lose weight. After each weight loss treatment, the machine's operator puts a small blue mark on the user's wrist. Deb's younger brother, Trevor, thinks the swoodies and slimmers are run by aliens who are using the energy from the fat burned off in the slimmers as fuel on their planet. Deb ridicules Trevor's idea, but at the end of the story she is still wondering if he might be correct.

MIRRORS & WINDOWS The Mirrors & Windows questions at the end of this selection focus on the theme of conformity. Before reading the story, ask students if they think they are susceptible to propaganda. How does propaganda help shape a society?

Words in Use

Selection Words
gruesome, 254
impressions, 255
publicity, 256
regulate, 257
literally, 258
detection, 260

Teaching Words
perceive, 254
eludes, 254
negate, 260
jingle, 260

KEY TERMS
PROPAGANDA, 260
BANDWAGON, 260

Literary Connection

Science Fiction Science fiction is imaginative literature based on scientific principles, discoveries, or laws. This genre allows writers to change certain elements of reality in order to create interesting and instructive alternatives. Science fiction stories are often set in the future or on distant planets. Guide students to look for story elements in "Lose Now, Pay Later" that are grounded in reality and others that demonstrate a twist on reality.

Analyze Literature

Point of View Remind students that point of view is the angle from which the author tells the story. Ask students to identify the point of view in this selection. Next, challenge them to determine its impact on the story's structure and theme.

Analyze Literature

Setting Explain that authors often use specific words to help readers understand the setting of the story. Ask students what they learn about the setting from the word *heliobiles*. Model a possible response: "I've never heard the word before, and it sounds like something from science fiction. Since it's in the parking lot, I think it's some kind of futuristic car." Ⓐ

grade-school kids who were looking at the store. "You'll love those swoodies."

"It's a publicity stunt, we think," Trinja told them. "Everything is free in there."

In no time at all the news about the swoodie shop had spread all over town. But days passed, and still everything was absolutely free. Nobody knew who the new owners were or why they were giving away their product. Nobody cared. The mall directors said a check arrived to pay for the rent, and that was all they were concerned about. The Health Brigade Corp said swoodies were absolutely safe for human consumption.[2]

Swoodies were still being offered free a month later, but the shop owners had still not appeared. By then nobody cared. There were always long lines of people in front of the place, but the swoodies tasted so good nobody minded waiting for them. And the supply was endless. Soon more shops like the first one began opening in other places around the city, with machines running in the same quiet, efficient way. And everything was still absolutely free.

Soon all of us were gaining weight like crazy.

"It's those darn swoodies," Trinja told me as we left the mall after our daily binge.[3] "I can't leave them alone. Each one must have a thousand calories, but I still pig out on them."

I sighed as I walked out into the sunshine. "Me too. If only there was some easy way to eat all the swoodies we want and still not gain any weight!"

---

2. **consumption.** Act of eating and drinking
3. **binge.** Spree of unrestrained eating

The words were hardly out of my mouth when I noticed a new feature in the mall parking lot. Among all the usual heliobiles there was a tall white plastic box, sort of like those big telephone booths you see in old pictures. A flashing sign near the booth said THE SLIMMER. A short, thin woman was standing beside it. She was deeply tanned, and her head was covered with a green turban almost the

Differentiated Instruction

English Language Learning

Students learning English may need a definition to help them understand the following words and expressions.

looney — crazy or foolish, 254
cubbyhole — small place for storage or hiding, 254
aroma — scent, 255
blimp — derogatory term for an overweight person, 255

publicity stunt — action taken to gain attention, 256
scam — dishonest strategy for making a quick profit, 257
wacko — person who acts very oddly, 258

same color as the jumpsuit she was wearing.

Trinja looked at the sign, then glanced at the woman. "What's that mean?"

"It means that this machine can make you slimmer," the woman answered. She had a deep, strange-sounding voice. "Just step inside, and you'll lose unwanted fat."

She seemed so serious and confident that I was startled. In the old days people thought they could lose weight in a hurry, but those of us who live in 2041 aren't that gullible.[4] No pills or packs or wraps or special twenty-four-hour diets can work. There isn't any easy way to get rid of fat, and that's all there is to it. I knew this booth was a scam or a joke of some kind, but the woman acted as if it were a perfectly respectable thing. Her seriousness sort of unnerved[5] me. I looked into the booth half expecting someone to jump out laughing. But it was empty, stark[6] white, and, except for some overhead grill work, it was completely smooth and bare. **B**

"How can a thing like this make you slimmer?" I asked.

The woman shrugged. "A new process. Do you care to try? Twenty-five yen to lose one pound of body fat."

Trinja and I both burst into laughter. "And how long is it before the pound disappears?" she asked.

The woman never even cracked a smile. "Instantly. Body fat is gone instantly." She gestured to a small lever on the side nearest to her. "I regulate the power flow according to your payment."

My mouth dropped open. "But that's impossible! No exercise? No chemicals? No starving on a retreat week?" **C**

"No." The woman folded her arms and leaned against the smooth white sides of her cubicle, as if she didn't much care whether we tried her new process or not. Trinja and I stared at each other. I was wondering if the

---

4. **gullible.** Easily cheated or tricked
5. **unnerved.** Caused to lose one's courage
6. **stark.** Bleak; barren

Vocabulary Skills

Blended Words

Explain to students that blended words are created by combining some of the letters from two words into one new word. As examples, show them the following blended words from the selection:

*swoodies = sw*eets + g*oodies*
*bodivision = bod*y + tele*vision*

Write the following blended words on the board. Ask students if they know the two original words, and then show the words if necessary.

1. cyborg = *cyb*ernetic + *org*anism
2. smog = *sm*oke + f*og*
3. pixel = *pi*cture + *el*ement
4. moped = *mo*tor + *ped*al
5. squiggle = *squi*rm + *wiggle*

Use Reading Strategies
Visualize Point out that the description of Deb's experience in the slimmer involves a detailed account of her thoughts and feelings as well as the machine's actions and the results. **Ⓐ**

Use Reading Strategies
Ask Questions Have pairs of students pause briefly in their reading and ask each other questions to make sure they understand the conflicts in the story and to determine whether or not the main events have taken place yet. Model one possible question such as "What is the conflict in the story?" **Ⓑ**

Use Reading Strategies
Make Predictions As students if they think the tiny pinpricks will have any significance later on. Possible answers: "Yes, they indicate some type of record of the weight loss. Yes, the people with the most pinpricks will have some misfortune later on." **Ⓒ**

woman had tried her machine herself—she didn't have an ounce of fat.

"You got any money?" I asked Trinja. As she was shaking her head, I was rummaging through my pack. "I've got a hundred and thirty yen."

"Five pounds then," the woman said, taking my money with one hand and setting her lever with the other. She literally pushed me into the booth, and the door slammed behind me.

Ⓐ At first I wanted to scream because I was so scared. The whole thing had happened too fast. I wanted to prove that this woman and her slimmer were a big joke, but suddenly I was trapped in a coffinlike structure as bare and as bright as an old microwave oven. My heart was hammering, and the hair on the back of my neck stood up straight. I opened my mouth, but before I could scream, there was a loud humming sound, and instantly the door flew open again. I saw Trinja's frightened face peering in at me.

"Are you all right, Deb? Are you okay? I guess she decided not to do anything after all. You ought to get your money back."

Ⓒ "Five pounds are gone," the woman said in her strange voice.

Trinja pulled me away. "I'll just bet!" she shouted back at the woman. "Somebody ought to report you and that phony machine! We might even call the Health Brigade Corp!" She leaned closer to me. "Are you really okay, Deb?"

> ### "The only thing slimmer after a treatment like that is your bank account."

I took a deep breath. "My jeans feel loose."

Frowning, Trinja shook her head. "It's just your imagination, that's all. What a fake! I think that woman was wacko, Debbie, really weird. The only thing slimmer after a treatment like that is your bank account. Nobody but nobody can lose weight that easily. We'll go to my house, and you can weigh yourself. You haven't lost an ounce."

Ⓑ But Trinja was wrong. I really *was* five pounds lighter. I know it sounds impossible, but Trinja's calshow[7] is never wrong. The two of us hopped and howled with joy. Then we ravaged her bedroom trying to find some more money. We ran all the way back to the mall, worrying all the way that the woman and her miracle machine might have disappeared. But the slimmer was still there. Within minutes Trinja had used up her three hundred yen, and she looked terrific.

"I can't believe it! I just can't believe it!" she kept saying as she notched her belt tighter. "Twelve pounds gone in seconds!"

Ⓒ "For safety's sake I'll have to prick your wrist, my dear," the woman said. "For every ten pounds you lose we give a tiny little mark. Nobody will ever notice it."

"It didn't even hurt," Trinja said as we walked home. And neither of us could see the tiny blue pinprick unless we looked closely. We were both so happy about the

7. **calshow.** Scale

Differentiated Instruction

Reading Proficiency
Explain to students that sensory details are words and phrases that describe how things look, sound, smell, taste, or feel. Sensory details enhance description by revealing a variety of information that readers may react to in a positive way – such as with "the rich, cool, chocolatey ice cream"– or in a negative way – such as with "the hot, painful, swollen bee sting." Have students look for sensory details in "Lose Now, Pay Later" and record them on a chart like the one below.

Sensory Detail	Sense	Positive or Negative?
chocolate ice cream	taste	positive

weight loss that we almost floated. All our worries and problems about calories and fat and diets were over forever.

In no time at all the slimmers were all over the city, near all the swoodie stores. They've been a real blessing. Everybody says so. Now there's hardly a fat person left on the streets. A few people have so many blue marks on their wrists that you can see them, but most have just four or five pinpricks.

Nobody really understands how these slimmers work. The attendants, all just as strange sounding as the woman in our mall, get so technical in their explanations that none of us can follow the principles they're talking about, so we don't much worry about it. The process has something to do with invisible waves that can change fat cells into

energy, which then radiates away from the body.

"I don't care how the slimmers work," Trinja says happily. "Now I can eat swoodies all day long if I want, and I never gain an ounce. That's all I care about."

Everybody feels that way, I guess. We're too happy to want to upset anything by asking questions. Maybe that's why you don't hear about the swoodies or slimmers on the fax or the bodivision or read about them anywhere. Nobody understands them well enough to sound very intelligent about them. But people all over Earth are beginning to use them. My cousin in Tokyo faxed to say that they have them in her area now and people there are just as happy as we are.

Except for my brother, Trevor. He's not the least bit happy, he says. Of course, few ten-year-olds worry about weight, so he doesn't know the joy of being able to eat everything in sight and still stay thin.

"Suppose the swoodies and the slimmers are run by aliens from outer space," he says. "From lots farther than we've been able to go. Maybe they have big starships posted around Earth, and they're gathering up the energy from human fat that's sent up from the slimmers. Maybe the swoodies are here so people will get fat quicker so that there'll be more to harvest through the slimmer machines. Then they'll take the fat back to their planet and use it as fuel."

> **"Suppose the swoodies and the slimmers are run by aliens from outer space..."**

D

E

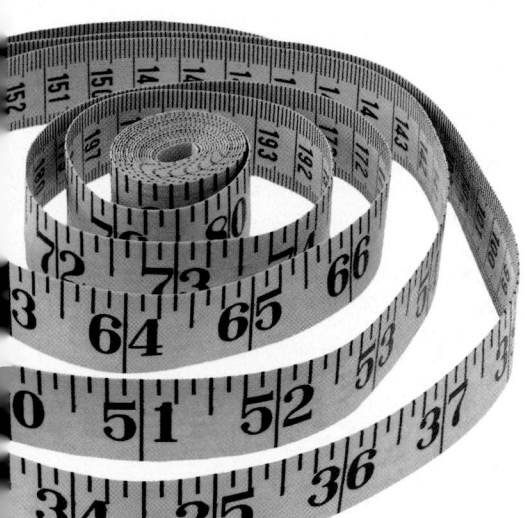

Use Reading Strategies

Make Inferences Ask students why they think the attendants use technical explanations instead of telling the people in simple terms how the slimmers work. Model a possible response: "The workers don't want the people to know how the machines work. If they make the explanation difficult, no one will ask questions." **D**

Use Reading Strategies

Make Inferences Ask students whether or not they agree with Trevor. Suggest that students write down how they think the story will end and then compare their ending with the actual one after they finish the story. **E**

TEACHING NOTE

Self-Generated Questioning

Fasten four or five large pieces of paper to walls around the room. Divide students into small groups, and assign each group to a piece of paper. Ask each group to write on its sheet as many questions about the text as possible. Model a question such as "Why does the narrator think her brother's idea is dumb?" Ask volunteers to answer the questions. When they answer, have them tell if they found the answer in the text or if they had to make inferences or draw their own conclusions to arrive at an answer.

Writing Skills

Personal Essay

Themes addressing body image in "Pay Now, Lose Later" are particularly important to discuss with and encourage responses from adolescent students. Ask students to spend a few minutes freewriting their thoughts and feelings concerning adolescent body image in the United States. Next, have students discuss their ideas in small groups. Remind students to adapt their language appropriately for an informal discussion—they should state their opinions without making long speeches or personal attacks. After the discussion, challenge students to revise and develop their prewriting into an informal essay with a clear thesis and ample support.

Analyze Literature

Conflict Ask students to summarize the conflict. Point out that the conflict is not resolved at the end of the story. **A**

Make Connections

Ask students what they think of Trevor. How might he try to get others to take his ideas seriously? **B**

Answer: Propaganda encourages people to think and act in certain ways. It can cause negative feelings about personal appearance and other feelings of inferiority.

Analyze and Extend

1. (a) They find a new shop that gives away a type of dessert called swoodies. (b) Swoodies evoke wonderful memories and make people happy.

2. (a) No one knows exactly how the slimmers work, but they transform excess fat into energy. (b) People are eager to use them because they are gaining weight from eating swoodies.

3. (a) Humans are getting fat and then using the machine to take it off. There are hardly any fat people left on Earth. (b) Humans have not been culled due to having a certain number of blue marks.

A

"That's the dumbest thing I ever heard of!" Trinja has told him. "Why don't we hear about the spaceships, then? Why doesn't the Health Brigade Corp tell us to stop doing this if it isn't good for us?"

B

Trevor thinks he has the answers. He says the spaceships are invisible to human detection, and he says the aliens have hypnotized our leaders into being as calm and placid as we all are. The blue marks on our wrists play a big role. He says maybe after each of us has had so many blue marks, we'll be culled[8] from the flock because our fat content won't be as good anymore.

He's crazy, isn't he? He must think we all have the brains of sheep. Ten-year-old brothers can be a real pain. He simply doesn't know people yet, that's all. Humans would never sacrifice their freedom and dignity just so they could eat and still be thin. Even aliens ought to know that.

I could quit eating swoodies and using those slimmers any time I want to.

But all those little blue marks Trinja and I have are beginning to look like delicate tattooed bracelets, and we both think they look really neat on our wrists. ❖

---

8. culled. Plucked from

How would you have reacted in Deb or Trinja's position? What is the purpose of propaganda, or the use of misleading language to influence people's thoughts and actions? How is propaganda harmful?

Analyze and Extend

1. (a) What do Deb and Trinja discover at the far end of the mall? (b) Why does their discovery become so popular?
2. (a) How do the slimmers work? (b) Why are people so eager to use them?
3. (a) What examples of human behavior from the story support the explanation offered by Deb's brother? (b) What examples of human behavior negate this view?

Creative Writing Advertisements often use forms of propaganda. For example, seeing a popular film star use a product in an advertisement may convince you to buy that product. Another type of propaganda—jumping on the bandwagon—appeals to people's desire to belong to a group. Advertising that uses this approach tries to convince you that because everyone else is buying a product or service, you should too. With this in mind, write an **advertisement** for a swoodie. Try to convince others why they should buy the product. Share with your classmates when you are finished.

Media Literacy & Collaborative Learning "Jingles" are a form of advertisement intended to make the listener remember a product through a catchy song or phrase. Why do you think jingles are effective? Work with a partner to create a jingle to sell a fictional product.

Go to **www.mirrorsandwindows.com** for more.

Rubric for Creative Writing

You can adapt this as a checklist for students to use as they write.

☐ Does the student appeal to others and persuade others to try the product?

☐ Does the advertisement make use of persuasive techniques?

☐ Does the advertisement make use of color and other visual appeals?

For Your Reading List

The Face on the Milk Carton
by Caroline B. Cooney

Fifteen-year-old Janie Johnson never paid much attention to the faces of lost or missing children that appeared on her milk cartons—until the face she was looking at was her own! She can't believe that her own loving parents would kidnap her—but who is the mysterious face on the milk carton?

Dragon's Gate
by Laurence Yep

Dragon's Gate tells the story of Chinese immigrants living in California. The story takes place in 1867, and opens with fourteen-year-old Otter, as he prepares to leave his village in China to live in America with his father and uncle. The book not only tells of an important time in history, but is also an exciting tale of adventure and family.

So Yesterday
by Scott Westerfeld

A 'cool hunter' is someone who roams the streets in search of the latest trends, and seventeen-year-old Hunter Braque is one. He and companion Jen, a true innovator who doesn't wear name brands, are hired by a shoe company market analyst for a special mission. When she disappears, the two start investigating and find the most amazing shoes ever. The shoes lead them into a plot to undermine the marketing machine that decides what is cool.

Nothing But the Truth
by Avi

Philip Malloy, a high school freshman and class clown, is punished by his homeroom teacher for humming during the recitation of "The Star Spangled Banner." The story is told through letters and journal entries, providing an interesting perspective on an already unique story.

Under the Baseball Moon
by John H. Ritter

Andy Ramos is a teenager living in Ocean Beach, California. He dreams of making it big as a musician, along with his band, FuChar Skool. He meets a strange and foreboding character named Max Lucero, who promises to help Andy make it. Shortly after Andy meets Max, things start to mysteriously go well for Andy's band. The story is told through Andy's point of view, showing his laid-back attitude and bright spirit.

The Watcher
by James Howe

Margaret is a teenage girl who lives a troubled life. She dreams of better times, when she can be free from the abuse and loneliness she experiences each day. She makes two close friends, Chris and Evan, and records her thoughts and experiences in a journal.

Program Resources

EMC Access Editions
For additional independent reading, you may wish to refer students to one of EMC's Access Edition titles such as Jerry Spinelli's *Stargirl*. Each Access Edition contains a thorough study apparatus, including background information, literal comprehension questions, footnotes, vocabulary definitions, critical thinking questions, and related projects and activities. An Assessment Manual offering worksheets is available for each Access Edition.

Independent Reading

Independent Reading Activity
Help students link their reading to the unit theme, Differing Perspectives. Ask how fiction can help readers appreciate the varying ways in which other people view the world. You might try this as an in-class activity: Have students read silently in class a fiction work of their choosing for at least twenty minutes. Then have students identify what this short story or novel can teach a reader about understanding other people's perspectives.

TEACHING NOTE

Reflect on Developing Literacy
Offer students an opportunity to evaluate their own development as readers. Write the word *Reflect* on the board, and ask for definitions. After you hear several possible meanings, tell students you would like them to recall and think about the reading they have done in the past year. If you wish, prompt them with questions: "How much fiction have you read in the past year? How much nonfiction? What is your favorite kind of reading now, and how does that compare to last year?" Provide several minutes for quiet thinking. Then either ask volunteers to tell how their reading habits have changed over the past year, or give students time to write one-paragraph summaries of how their reading has developed in the past year.

⊚ EMC E-Library
The EMC E-Library contains more than twenty thousand pages of literary classics that can be used for students' independent reading. An Electronic Library Guide provides teaching suggestions, enrichment activities, and reading strategy guidesheets.

Common Core State Standards
Reading Literature
RL.10

Objectives

Participating in this lesson will help students to write a short story that

- has complex and believable characters
- has a detailed setting
- has a logically organized plot
- has a consistent point of view
- exhibits colorful language and precise word choice

Motivation

To stimulate students' thinking about writing a short story, divide the class into two groups. Have one group brainstorm several conflicts that could be the basis for a short story. Have the other group brainstorm several characters who might be the protagonists of a short story. Have the two groups present their conflicts and characters. Discuss whether any of the conflicts could be creatively combined with the characters.

For a full writing rubric, go to **www.mirrorsandwindows.com.** Additional writing workshops are available in Exceeding the Standards: Writing.

▶ More About the Author

Latino writer Gary Soto was born in 1952 in Fresno, California. The setting for much of his fiction, nonfiction, and poetry is Fresno's Mexican-American neighborhood.

Narrative Writing

Writing a Short Story

Reading and Writing

In this unit, you have read stories by writers as diverse as Eugenia Collier, Toshio Mori, Gary Soto, and Virginia Driving Hawk Sneve, and you have considered the values presented in each story. As you read these stories, you also learned about theme, characterization, tone, mood, and conflict. When writing your own short stories, you will need to keep these elements in mind.

In this workshop you will learn how to write a short story. A short story is similar to a novel, but it is on a much smaller scale, with fewer characters, a less complicated plot, and often a single setting. Most short stories center on a main character who faces a conflict that is resolved by the end of the story. One way to plan this assignment is to ask yourself about your main character. What conflict might such a character face? How would the character solve this conflict? You will also want to consider the narrator of the story. Is the narrator part of the action or outside of it? This workshop includes a writing rubric, a set of standards by which to judge your story. You will use this rubric as you draft and revise your story.

- **Assignment:** Write a short story that develops true-to-life characters, setting, and plot.

- **Goal:** Write an interesting story that my audience will enjoy reading.

- **Strategy:** Create believable characters and a vivid setting. Create a plot in which a conflict builds tension, rises to a climax, and is resolved.

- **Writing Rubric:** My short story should include the following:

  - complex and believable characters
  - a detailed setting
  - a logically organized plot that includes a conflict, rising action, climax, and resolution
  - a consistent point of view
  - colorful language and precise word choice

What Great Writers Do

Gary Soto writes about subjects he knows well. Read what he says he tries to accomplish in his writing and apply it to your own:

To me the finest praise is when a reader says, I can see your stories. This is what I'm always working for, a story that becomes alive and meaningful in the reader's mind. That's why I write so much about growing up in the barrio. It allows me to use specific memories that are vivid for me.

Teaching Words

diverse, 262	**comprehension,** 266
universal, 263	
logical, 264	**habitually,** 266
precise, 266	**legible,** 266
vague, 266	
vivid, 266	
accessible, 266	
grasp, 266	

KEY TERMS

Common Core State Standards

Writing
W.3, W.4, W.5, W.6, W.10

Language
L.5.1d

1. PREWRITE

Choosing Your Topic

One way to begin developing your story is to ask yourself questions about story elements such as character, conflict, plot, and setting.

Character: Who is your main character? Is this character based on someone you know, have heard about, or have read about? Have you seen a character like this on television or in a movie? Ask yourself what this character is like. What interests does this character have? Your answers to these questions will help you develop a believable character.

Setting: How important is the setting in your story? Some conflicts would never occur in a particular setting; other conflicts are caused or magnified by the setting of the story. When looking for story ideas, consider starting with the setting. The setting might suggest particular problems and conflicts that can lead to a plot idea.

Conflict: What is bothering the character? What problem or difficult situation must the character face? Does the conflict involve another person or outside force, or is it a conflict within the character? You might choose a conflict you have experienced or imagined yourself. Perhaps the conflict is driven by a strong emotion, such as love, jealousy, grief, envy, ambition, compassion, or loyalty.

Plot: The plot is determined by the conflict and how the character deals with it. After the conflict is introduced, the conflict develops with each event until it reaches a climax or turning point. After the climax, the conflict must somehow be resolved.

Now that you've considered the basic elements of your story, you can work out the characters, conflict, plot, and setting in greater detail.

1. Reveal your characters through their physical actions, words, and thoughts, and through what others say about them.

2. Establish mood through descriptions of the setting.

3. Develop the plot by bringing the conflict to a critical point. Resolve the conflict by the end.

4. Consider whether you want your narrator to be a part of the action or an outside observer. Maintain consistent point of view throughout.

Gathering Details

To help develop your characters, setting, and plot, use a story map.

Element	My Story
Characters	Sophia, the narrator Kevin, Uncle Jason, and Josh
Setting	Uncle Jason's photography shop, Sophia and Kevin's home (present-day)
Conflict	Sophia's brother's bike is stolen, and no one can comfort him.
Plot	Sophia works in her uncle's photography shop. When her brother Kevin's bike is stolen, he is very upset. Then Sophia sees a picture of the bike in a roll of film she develops. They start the process of tracking down the bike. Kevin starts feeling better.

Deciding on Your Purpose

Determining Theme Once you have decided on the main parts of your story, think about the message or **theme** you want it to express. Consider what universal idea or insight you want to leave with your readers.

Prewrite

Decide on a Topic Model the process of choosing a topic: "I would like to write a story about a character who wants to be liked by co-workers but feels like an outsider. I want to make up believable characters by combining things I've experienced with what I can imagine."

Gather Details Point out that students can make separate cluster charts for plot, characters, and setting. Suggest they begin by putting the conflict into words. Continue to model: "The conflict is internal one. The main character feels he can only be accepted by pretending to be someone he isn't."

Determine Theme Suggest that students work in pairs. One student describes the main parts of his or her narrative. The other attempts to infer from this the theme that the story intends to convey.

What Great Writers Do

Many writers keep notebooks containing ideas for stories. The following ideas come from Nathaniel Hawthorne's notebooks:

"A stove possessed by a Devil"

"A physician for the cure of moral diseases"

"The print in blood of a naked foot to be traced through the street of a town"

"A person who has all the qualities of a friend, except that he invariably fails you at the pinch"

Differentiated Instruction

English Language Learning

You might invite English learners to plan their stories in their native languages and then describe them to you verbally. Encourage them to talk through their ideas in English—particularly the plot—so you can judge how well they understand that element of fiction.

Visual Learning

Some students might benefit from using visual aids to help them imagine the characters and plot of their stories. One technique is to cut pictures out of magazines or newspapers that seem to capture each of the characters and create a collage. Have students place the collage so they can see it as they write. Another technique is storyboarding, drawing the events of the plot in panels like a comic strip.

Draft

Organizing Ideas Point out that chronological order is easy and logical, but students can include foreshadowing and flashbacks in their stories. You might model one of these interruptions of chronological order: "My character might recall his sense of not fitting in when his family moved to a new neighborhood." As students follow the recommendations in the text, assure them that they can outline their stories in any order. Beginning with the climax might be easiest for some. Then they can think through the steps that would lead up to it and make sure the exposition introduces the proper elements for building the conflict.

TEACHING NOTE

Self-Generated Questioning

Students might benefit from extending the guidelines in the rubric on page 262. Have them work in groups to create questions about the assignment that might be the basis for additional guidelines. Model a possible question: "How much explanation needs to be provided at the beginning of the story?"

---

2. DRAFT

Organizing Ideas

Now that you have determined the main elements of your story, begin organizing your ideas about how the plot will develop. Often, the most logical and effective way to organize events is by the order they occurred, or **chronological order.** Now study the main parts of a story and how the conflict develops chronologically.

1. **Exposition** The main character(s) and setting are introduced, as well as any necessary background. The conflict is hinted or introduced.

2. **Rising Action** The conflict is developed and complicated through a series of events.

3. **Climax or Turning Point** This is the point of highest tension, when a decision or realization occurs.

4. **Falling Action** The consequences of the climax unfold and tension eases.

5. **Resolution** The conflict is resolved.

Putting Your Thoughts on Paper

When writing your first draft, organize your characters, setting, conflict, and plot in a logical plan like that shown here. Focus mainly on developing the main parts of the conflict. Use your story plan as a starting point, but feel free to change your plan as your ideas develop.

I. **Exposition:** Sophia works in her uncle's camera shop.

II. **Rising Action**
   1. Sophia's brother Kevin's bike is stolen.
   2. Kevin becomes depressed and inconsolable.
   3. Sophia sees Kevin's bike in a picture.

III. **Climax:** She enlarges the picture and is sure it's Kevin's bike.

IV. **Falling Action:** Sophia, Kevin, and their dad go to the address and get a list of the party guests.

V. **Resolution:** Kevin is feeling much better.

Consistent Point of View

The **point of view** is the perspective from which a story is told.

Once you decide on a point of view for your story, stick with it. As you edit and proofread your work, check to make sure you have maintained the same point of view throughout. If you decide halfway through the story that a different point of view would work better, go back and change it from the beginning.

Point of View	Characteristics
First-person	Narrator uses pronouns such as I, me, and my.
Third-person limited	Narrator reports on the words and actions of other characters, using pronouns such as he, him, she, and her.
Third-person omniscient	All-knowing narrator reports on the words and actions of other characters using pronouns, such as he, him, she, and her.

Writing Skills

Similes

Remind students that a simile is a comparison that contains the word *like* or *as*. Point out that similes can help a writer with characterization. Have students create a series of similes for one of the main characters in their stories, describing how that character looks, speaks, and moves. Model this activity by offering some examples:

Appearance: "She had the wide-eyed look of a child opening a present."
Voice: "Her voice was as faint as the squeak of a tired mouse."
Movement: "She moved with a curious hopping walk, like a sparrow."

Evaluating Your Draft

Reread your draft, looking for areas that can be improved. Does the dialogue sound like real speech? Is the setting vivid? To get a second opinion, exchange papers with a classmate for a **peer review.** Use the checklist as a guide.

Below is part of a draft of a short story. Changes have been made and reasons for the changes are given on the right.

Revising Checklist

☐ Are the characters believable?

☐ Is the setting described in detail?

☐ Is the story well organized?

☐ Is the point of view consistent?

☐ Does the story include colorful language?

I spend most of my time taking pictures. I'm pretty good at it. Usually, I take pictures of beautiful scenery. I also like to get up close to interesting things in my own backyard, such as a grasshopper or a single rosebud. Most of all, I like to take pictures of people: *whose faces are showing a flicker of emotion, like a shy smile or the hint of a laugh.* My little brother, Kevin, started calling me "Miss Camera." He thought he was teasing me, but I consider the title a compliment.

> *Add colorful language and use precise word choice to give your reader a vivid picture of what you're describing.*

On weekends, ~~Sophia works~~ *I work* at ~~her~~ *my* Uncle Jason's tiny photography shop. ~~She helps~~ *I help* him develop film that other people bring in. It's true—many people out there still don't use digital cameras. They prefer the old-fashioned kind.

> *Maintain a consistent point of view.*

My little brother, Kevin, doesn't care a bit about photography. He is too engrossed in his own passion. Saturdays, Sundays, and every weekday evening he spends riding his bike or working on it. *Every Saturday he takes the thing apart, cleaning all the pieces, one by one, until the paint shines like new and the chrome flashes. He even wipes the grease from the chain. Then he puts the whole thing back together again.*

> *Add details to develop complex, believable characters.*

Teach the Workshop

Revise

Evaluate Dialogue Remind students that characters and the plot develop together. Suggest that they evaluate each exchange of dialogue in the story to see if it advances the plot.

Evaluate a Draft Remind students to listen for a consistent point of view and believable tone as they review their own work. When they have done as much as they can in the available time, suggest that they conduct a peer review. Be sure they understand the rubric. Allow ample time for students to read the story they receive to review. Schedule peer review exchanges when each student will have several minutes to deliver his or her review and when each writer will have time to thoughtfully absorb the comments and ask questions for clarification.

What Great Writers Do

Point out to students that an arresting first sentence will grab a reader's attention. Offer a famous example:

"When Gregor Samsa awoke one morning from uneasy dreams he found himself in his bed transformed into a giant insect."

— FRANZ KAFKA, "The Metamorphosis"

Writing Skills

Wordy Sentences

Point out to students that wordy sentences slow down the pace of their narrative:

Kevin was very upset *because of the fact that* his bike was stolen. (wordy)

Kevin was very upset *because* his bike was stolen. (revised)

Have students rewrite the following sentences to eliminate wordiness.

1. A few weeks ago when we had gathered for dinner, Dad offered to buy Kevin a new bike.
2. In the photograph I saw something disturbed me a whole lot.
3. Taking pictures is just the sort of activity that I like.

Edit and Proofread

Students may want to use proofreader's marks when correcting their work. Refer them to the Language Arts Handbook, Writing Section 4.1, Proofreader's Symbols.

Literary Connection

Simon Ortiz Simon Ortiz (author of "Men on the Moon," a short story in this unit) has published more than a dozen books including poetry, memoir, short stories, nonfiction, and children's books. Ortiz was born in New Mexico in 1941 and is a member of the Acoma Pueblo people, a Native American tribe. Ortiz was greatly influenced by the Acoma oral storytelling tradition.

 Publish and Present

Before students begin their final version, they might benefit from reading the Language Arts Handbook, Writing Section 4.1, Writing Follow-up.

---

4. EDIT AND PROOFREAD

Focus: Word Choice

In the drafting stage, writers often focus on establishing characters and developing plot. As you revise your draft, however, pay close attention to the words you use. Is the language rich and precise, or is it vague and general? Do your descriptions give the reader a vivid picture of your setting and characters? As you revise, replace vague, dull language with specific nouns, verbs, and modifiers to make your descriptions interesting and memorable. Compare the following descriptions:

> *He coated the base of the bike in fluorescent green, and then he streaked red and yellow flames up the sides.*
> ~~He painted the base and sides of his bike.~~

Use specific nouns to give your reader a clear picture of who or what is involved in the sentence. Replace vague, general verbs with more vivid verbs to describe the specific action in the sentence and how the action is performed.

What Great Writers Do

This is what Simon Ortiz had to say about the responsibility of a writer regarding language. How can you apply his ideas to your own writing?

Making language familiar and accessible to others, bringing it within their grasp and comprehension, is what a writer, teacher, and storyteller does or tries to do. I've been trying for over thirty years.

—SIMON J. ORTIZ, *Woven Stone*

Focus: Consistent Verb Tense

A verb indicates an action, and a verb's tense indicates when in time that action takes place. Most short stories are written in the past tense. As you edit your story, check that you maintain the same tense throughout.

> Once the picture was enlarged, I ~~am~~ *was*
>
> absolutely sure that it ~~is~~ *was* Kevin's bike in the
>
> background at that party.

Note, however, that the present tense does more than tell what happens in the present. It also tells when something is universally or habitually true. When writing in the past tense, statements about what is universal or habitually true should be in the present tense.

> I *know* a great deal about lighting, framing,
>
> focusing, and all the rest.

Proofreading

Correcting Errors Proofread your story for errors in punctuation, capitalization, and spelling. Use proofreader's marks to highlight errors you find and then correct them.

---

5. PUBLISH AND PRESENT

Final Draft

Presentation Make a clean, final version of your story. Make handwritten stories neat and legible. If you are using a word-processing program, use double spacing and a typeface or font that is easy to read. Check with your teacher about any additional presentation guidelines.

Differentiated Instruction

Enrichment

Have interested students use library and Internet resources to learn about the writing habits of their favorite fiction authors. Ask them to share useful tips with the class.

Auditory Learning

Point out to students that reading their drafts aloud is often a good way to locate errors.

Student Model

Photographic Evidence
by Isabelle Jackson

I spend most of my time taking pictures. I'm pretty good at it. Usually, I take pictures of beautiful scenery. I also like to get up close to interesting things in my own backyard, such as a grasshopper or a single rosebud. Most of all, I like to take pictures of people whose faces are showing a flicker of emotion, like a shy smile or the hint of a laugh. My little brother, Kevin, started calling me "Miss Camera." He thought he was teasing me, but I consider the title a compliment.

> *Introduces the main characters and the setting in vivid detail*

I know a great deal about lighting, framing, focusing, and all the rest. Once I even won a photography contest at school. I love to manipulate and improve pictures after they've been taken. I use my computer to crop pictures and enhance images.

On weekends, I work at my Uncle Jason's tiny photography shop. I help him develop film that other people bring in. It's true—many people out there still don't use digital cameras. They prefer the old-fashioned kind.

I like working at my uncle's shop. I was glad when he suggested it. After the first two weeks on the job, I asked my uncle, "Don't you sometimes feel strange when you look at strangers' photographs? Doesn't it seem like you're invading their privacy?"

He said, "Not really. You'll find that most people take the same kinds of pictures. Some weekends you'll see more people blowing out birthday candles than most people see in a lifetime."

I realized Uncle Jason was right. Looking at other people's photos could be dull, but every now and then, I saw an outstanding photo. That more than made up for all the boring ones showing frosted birthday cakes and colored balloons. Nothing excites me more than seeing a unique moment perfectly caught on film. Just the right composition combined with just the right lighting—it gives me shivers.

> *Gives background to develop the characters*

My little brother, Kevin, doesn't care a bit about photography. He is too engrossed in his own passion. Saturdays, Sundays, and every weekday evening he spends riding his bike or working on it. Every Saturday he takes the thing apart, cleaning all the pieces, one by one, until the paint shines like new and the chrome flashes. He even wipes the grease from the chain. Then he puts the whole thing back together again.

Teach the Workshop

Student Model
Use the Model Direct students' attention to the model. Point out the side notes that identify the major parts of the short story such as exposition, conflict, rising action, dialogue, climax, falling action, and resolution. Some students might benefit from outlining the model to grasp the how the writer has developed her narrative.

What Great Writers Do

"The beginning of human knowledge is through the senses, and the fiction writer begins where human perception begins. He appeals through the senses, and you cannot appeal to the sense with abstractions."

—FLANNERY O'CONNOR,
"The Nature and Aim of Fiction"

Writing Skills

Active Voice

Point out to students that in narrative writing such as a short story, they should generally use the active voice to create stronger, more exciting writing and to clarify who is performing an action. Ask students to change the following sentences from passive to active voice.

1. Sophia was cautioned by Uncle Jason about invading other people's privacy.
2. The door was opened by a friendly, smiling woman.
3. Pictures of birthday parties were brought in by many customers.

Use the Model Point out to students that the writer introduces detail about Kevin's passion for his bike both to develop his character and to foreshadow the appearance of the conflict when his bike is stolen.

What Great Writers Do

Point out to students that a short story's title can often arouse a reader's interest. Offer some famous examples:

Richard Connell, "The Most Dangerous Game"

Arthur Conan Doyle, "The Red-Headed League"

James Thurber, "The Secret Life of Walter Mitty"

F. Scott Fitzgerald, "A Diamond as Big as the Ritz"

Graham Greene, "A Shocking Accident"

Rudyard Kipling, "The Man Who Would Be King"

Student Model CONTINUED

Includes precise word choice and specific details to develop a believable, interesting character

Begins the rising action by introducing the conflict

One weekend, he spent about ten hours designing a personalized license plate. After he chose the numbers, he designed an intricate, geometric border around the edges. The weekend after that, he repainted the frame of his bike. He coated the base of the bike in fluorescent green, and then he streaked red and yellow flames up the sides. To me, it was an eyesore, but Kevin was proud of it. I used to kid him about that flame business. After last month, though, I didn't joke about it anymore. He was too upset about what happened.

Last month, his bike was stolen outside the Hillsdale Mall. He started wearing dark glasses after that. I think he was trying to hide his swollen eyes. He refused to even consider getting another bicycle.

Uses natural, believable dialogue to develop the characters and plot

A few weeks ago at dinner, Dad offered to take him shopping for a new one. Kevin looked up from his steaming chicken stir-fry and said, "Dad, what's the point in caring for something if it hurts so much when you lose it? I'm just wondering. What's the point? Can you tell me?"

Mom looked at Dad sadly. She seemed a bit perplexed. Then she turned to Kevin and said, "Kevin, it's just a bicycle. It's not a person! You can replace a bicycle."

"You just don't understand, Mom," Kevin replied, "how much that bike meant to me."

None of us knew what to do. We just sat there at the table. None of us really had an appetite, but we sat there anyway. I know I'd probably feel the same as Kevin if I had lost my camera.

Yesterday, at Uncle Jason's photo lab, I saw something that really disturbed me. Well, it disturbed me, but it also got my adrenaline racing! What I saw looked typical at first. It seemed like just another photo of some kids at a birthday party in a park. I've seen enough photos of kids at birthday parties, but this one was unusual. In the background, some bicycles were leaned against a bush. One of them was painted fluorescent green with red and yellow flames running up the frame.

Builds tension toward a climax

I looked at the rest of the pictures on the roll. That same bicycle was in two other photos. One of the photos showed part of the license plate. I asked Uncle Jason if I could use the enlarger. My hands were shaking. I told him that I might have found Kevin's missing bike.

"Sophia," he said in a stern voice. "Developing pictures is one thing. Enlarging them and studying each detail is another. That *would* be an invasion of someone's privacy."

"But Uncle Jason, this is a special case," I pleaded. "You don't know how upset Kevin is. I might be able to get his bike back!"

Differentiated Instruction

English Language Learning
Use this opportunity to reinforce teaching with English learners. Have them show you their editing and proofreading to see how well they have absorbed spelling and grammar lessons you have given. Take time to correct and discuss any consistent problems in these areas before students prepare final drafts.

Finally, Uncle Jason relented. He said, "Okay, Sophia. You can enlarge one picture."

Once the picture was enlarged, I was absolutely sure that it was Kevin's bike in the background at that party. The enlargement showed the numbers 7, 18, and 364 on the license plate. The first two were Kevin's birth date. The last one was our street address. The chances of anyone else having the same personalized license plate were about a billion to one. Add the fluorescent paint with the flames, and chances were about two billion to one.

"Uncle Jason, I need to write down the address on this envelope," I said, holding up the envelope the film had been in.

"Be my guest," he said. By now, Uncle Jason agreed with me that this was a special case. All I had to do was track down the bike and prove that it was Kevin's.

Dad came with us when we went over to the address on the photo. It was only a few miles from our house. We rang the bell and waited patiently for a few moments. A friendly, smiling woman opened the door. I recognized her as one of the regular customers at the photo shop. She listened patiently as we explained why we were there.

"Won't you come in?" she asked. "I'll get my son. Maybe he can help you. After all, he was the birthday boy in those pictures."

A few minutes later, her son came downstairs.

"Hey, Kevin," he said as he saw my brother.

"Hey, Josh," said Kevin. It turned out that Josh had been in Kevin's class last year. He was glad to give us a list of all the kids from his party.

As we left Josh's house, I saw that Kevin was already feeling better. We didn't have the bike yet, but the trail was hot, and we had photographic evidence. I smiled as Kevin patted me on the back and said, "Thanks, Miss Camera!"

Maintains consistent verb tense

Begins resolving conflict with falling action

Resolves the conflict and brings the story to a satisfying close

Student Model

Use the Model Point out to students that they can use the final sentences of their stories for a lot of different purposes, including the following:

- to resolve the action
- to add a final touch to a character
- to state the theme
- to create a surprise

What Great Writers Do

Here is how Mark Twain wrapped up one his best known stories, "The Man That Corrupted Hadleyburg":

"It is an honest town once more, and the man will have to rise early that catches it napping again."

Ask students what function this sentence seems to serve.

Punctuating Dialogue

Remind students that a direct quotation should always begin with a capital letter. Separate a direct quotation from the rest of the sentence with a comma, quotation mark, or exclamation point. Do not separate the direct quotation from the rest of the sentence with a period. In the following sentences, have students decide whether the quotations are punctuated correctly.

1. "Do you know what happened to Kevin's bike?" Uncle Jason asked. (correct)
2. Mom told Kevin, "it's just a bicycle." (incorrect)
3. "Enlarging those photos would be an invasion of privacy." Uncle Jason cautioned Sophia. (incorrect)

Teach the Workshop

Objectives

Participating in this lesson will help students deliver literary presentations that

- are appropriate for their audience
- contain vivid sensory details and descriptive words
- exhibit appropriate pacing for tone and purpose
- have engaging dialogue
- employ effective nonverbal expression

Motivation

Ask students why we willingly listen to one person tell a story and not to another person. Ask students to identify what qualities really hold their attention as listeners. Point out that these are many of the same qualities that contribute to an effective literary presentation. Tell them they will learn effective tools for reading aloud by studying this workshop.

> ▶ For more information, see the Language Arts Handbook Section 7, Speaking & Listening.

Program Resources

To expand upon this workshop lesson, Giving and Actively Listening to Literary Presentations, see the *Exceeding the Standards: Speaking & Listening* resource.

Common Core State Standards

Speaking and Listening
SL.1, SL.6

Giving and Actively Listening to Literary Presentations

Plan a Literary Presentation

Literary presentations are a way to share your writing, or writing you admire, with an audience. When giving a **literary presentation,** you convey elements of a story through speech rather than the written word. In this lesson, you will deliver a literary presentation to an audience of your classmates.

Elements of a Short Story Since you are delivering a literary presentation, you must include the basic elements of a story, such as plot, characters, setting, and tone. Your presentation should also have effective dialogue and engaging conflicts between the characters. What other elements might an effective literary presentation include?

Review Your Story You can present on either a story that you have read and enjoyed, or a story that you have written on your own. However, you must be familiar with the story you are presenting in order to convey the important ideas to your audience. As you prepare to present, reread the story. Try reading it aloud, either in front of a mirror, video camcorder, or a friend. Decide what kind of emotion you will use to read the dialogue and key passages to your audience.

Point of View You should also examine the story's point of view. If it's in first-person, you will need to decide how to convey the personality of the narrator. If the story is told in third-person, you must then decide if the narrator is omniscient or has limited knowledge about the events of the story. The narrator and the story's point of view can affect how you develop your literary presentation and present the material to your audience.

Punctuation and Pacing Pay attention to punctuation in the story, as this will affect the pacing of your presentation. Certain kinds of punctuation, such as a dash, mean that a reader or speaker should move more quickly; while other kinds of punctuation, such as periods or semicolons can slow down the pace of a story.

Provide Sensory Details One way to keep the attention of an audience and fully explain the main ideas of a story is to develop sensory details in your presentation. **Sensory details** are descriptive words that appeal to the five senses and help your listeners "see" the story. Most people have the use of five major senses: sight, sound, touch, taste, and smell. The larger the number of these sense you use to observe something, the more you will notice about it. For example, to describe a marathon race you might note such sensory details as *crowds clapping, stinging sun, sore feet,* or *hot asphalt.*

Words in Use

Teaching Words

convey, 270	**constructive,** 271
pacing, 270	**nonverbal,** 271
marathon, 270	
somber, 271	
bleak, 271	
distinctness, 271	
marrow, 271	

KEY TERMS

PLOT, 270
CHARACTER, 270
SETTING, 270
TONE, 270
DIALOGUE, 270
CONFLICT, 270
POINT OF VIEW, 270
NARRATOR, 270
OMNISCIENT, 270
LIMITED, 270
SENSORY DETAIL, 270

Creating Mood and Tone Sensory details also help to set the mood and tone of your story, based upon the words you choose to describe the setting and characters. For example, if you wanted to create a dark and somber tone, you might describe the setting as *bleak, cold, foggy,* or *silent.* In the story "The Tell-Tale Heart," Edgar Allan Poe writes the sentence "I saw it with perfect distinctness—all a dull blue, with a hideous veil over it that chilled the very marrow in my bones." The words *dull blue, hideous veil, chilled,* and *bones* help to set an eerie tone of suspense. Working with a partner, brainstorm a list of words that would create a particular mood. Then, see if your classmates can guess the mood you were trying to create.

Rehearse and Evaluate Next, before presenting, rehearse your oral summary. Practice your literary presentation with a small group of classmates. Evaluate each other's presentations based on the rubric here. Take notes to summarize each other's presentations, and remember that feedback should be constructive. This means that your comments are helpful, not hurtful, and are intended to make the presentation stronger.

Delivering Your Literary Presentation

When delivering your literary presentation, use nonverbal communication to emphasize elements of your presentation. Use pauses where appropriate to keep your audience in suspense. Highlight the action of the story with gestures. You might want to mimic movements that a character in your story makes. Be creative. As with any presentation, maintain eye contact with the audience to keep them interested in what you are saying.

Speaking Rubric

Your presentation will be evaluated on these elements:

Content

☐ story includes plot, setting, and characters
☐ vivid sensory details
☐ descriptive word choice
☐ clear order of events—beginning, middle, and end

Delivery and Presentation

☐ appropriate volume
☐ maintain eye contact
☐ use of gestures and nonverbal communication

Listening Rubric

As a peer reviewer or audience member, you should do the following:

☐ listen quietly and attentively
☐ try to interpret the speaker's purpose by taking notes that summarize the content of the presentation
☐ analyze the images that are presented
☐ ask appropriate questions
☐ (as peer reviewer) provide constructive feedback

Dramatize

Tell students that making a literary presentation is similar to acting in a play. If they are reading fiction, encourage them to think through what their plot, setting, and characters mean, and to consider ways to bring those literary elements alive.

Prepare for Presentations

Give students opportunities to practice their presentations alone and with peer reviewers. Offer these tips:

- If the story is long, consider creating a cutting or selecting a portion of the story to read.
- Decide whether the presentation will be clearer with or without speech tags (such as "she said").
- Make sure the material will be easy to see when reading in front of an audience.
- Prepare a short introduction to the work, especially if the audience will be unfamiliar with the writer or type of literature.

TEACHING NOTE

Literary Devices

Tell students that their first job as an audience for literary presentations is to enjoy what they hear. Remind them to listen attentively and try to appreciate the literature rather than focusing on the presenter. Suggest, however, that they listen for how the writer has used such literary devices as figurative language, dialect, and suspense. Ask students to create a checklist for possible literary devices to detect during an oral presentation.

Differentiated Instruction

English Language Learning

Invite students from other countries to tell short stories or poems in their native languages. Encourage them to model appropriate pacing, tone, and expression. As a class, identify the nonverbal elements that make strong impressions on listeners.

Enrichment

Tell students that high schools often teach "oral interpretation" in speech classes. Many college communications and theater departments teach oral interpretation courses as well. Some people have careers reading literature aloud. Encourage interested students to find examples of college course descriptions and/or biographies of professional storytellers to share with the class.

Objectives

Completing this lesson will enable students to

- write a literary response based on a timed writing prompt
- answer standardized test questions that demonstrate revising and editing skills
- demonstrate the ability to make inferences from a reading by answering standardized questions

Timed Writing

Say that standardized tests often ask students to write a response to a prompt in a specified period of time. Give the following tips:

- Read the entire question carefully.
- Look for key words in the question that tell you what is expected.
- Underline these words, or write them on your own note paper.
- Use the key words to make sure you answer all parts of the question.
- Organize. Allow time for planning, writing, and reviewing.
- Before you begin writing, create a rough outline of points to make.
- If you find yourself running out of time, state your remaining points and add a conclusion.
- Write a clear introduction. This will help keep you on track as you write each paragraph.
- Review your completed essay to see if you have answered all parts of the question.
- Before you turn in your completed essay, take time to proofread.

Common Core State Standards

Reading Literature
RL.2

Writing
W.1, W.5

Language
L.4

Test Practice Workshop

Writing Skills

Literary Response

Carefully read the following writing prompt. Before you begin writing, think carefully about what task the assignment is asking you to perform. Then create an outline to help guide your writing.

> In Morley Callaghan's short story "Luke Baldwin's Vow," the main character Luke resists his Uncle Henry's decision to have their dog Dan, which has gone blind, put to sleep. Luke defies his uncle repeatedly in order to save the dog and do what he feels is right. Was Luke correct in taking a principled stand to keep his dog alive? Or should Luke have agreed to his Uncle's wishes? Does it matter that Luke's uncle was the actual owner of the dog?

In your essay, take a position on Luke's decision. Also, state the theme of the work and describe how Luke's actions relate to this theme. Use evidence from the story, including direct quotations in support of your position. As you write, be sure to:

- Organize your essay in a logical and consistent way
- Include introductory and concluding paragraphs
- Introduce your position in the first paragraph
- Support your main idea in each body paragraph

Rubric for Literary Response

You can adapt this as a checklist for students to use as they write.

Have students use these criteria when evaluating their literary responses:

- ☐ Does your response have an introductory paragraph that clearly states your position?
- ☐ Is your response organized logically and consistently?
- ☐ Does each body paragraph have material that supports your main idea, including such evidence as direct quotations from the story?
- ☐ Does your essay have a concluding paragraph?

Revising and Editing Skills

In the following excerpt from the first draft of a student's paper, words and phrases are underlined and numbered. Alternatives to the underlined words and phrases appear in the right hand column. Choose the one that best corrects any grammatical or style errors in the original. If you think that the original is error-free, choose "NO CHANGE."

Some questions might also be asked about a section of the passage or the entire passage. These do not refer to a specific underlined phrase or word, and are identified by a number in a box. Record your answers on a separate sheet of paper.

José, the main character in Gary Soto's short story "Born Worker," unfairly judges his cousin Arnie. At the beginning of the story, Arnie proposes <u>that him and José work together</u>: Arnie

$\underline{\qquad}$

1

will find and arrange jobs, and José will perform the physical labor. José thinks of Arnie as lazy and a <u>"liar".</u> José does not recognize the

2

importance of Arnie's work. Without Arnie, and people like him, the Josés of the world would not necessarily be able to find any work at all. ③

José is an excellent physical worker, he is very

4

dedicated to the work he does. The opening sentence of the story reads: "José was born with a ring of dirt around his neck, with grime under his fingernails, <u>and skin calloused from the grainy</u>

5

<u>twist of a shovel".</u> However, physical labor is not the only kind of work. Work can also be <u>mental,</u>

<u>artistic, or verbal.</u>

6

1. **A.** NO CHANGE
   B. that he and José work together
   C. that they and José work together
   D. that José and him work together

2. **A** NO CHANGE
   B. "liar";
   C. "liar."
   D. "liar"

3. The last sentence of this paragraph is the:
   A. topic sentence.
   B. plot.
   C. thesis.
   D. conflict.

4. **A.** NO CHANGE
   B. José is an excellent physical worker he is very dedicated to the work he does.
   C. He is very dedicated to the work he does, José is an excellent physical worker.
   D. José is an excellent physical worker. He is very dedicated to the work he does.

5. **A.** NO CHANGE
   B. and skin calloused from the grainy twist of a shovel.
   C. and skin calloused from the grainy twist of a shovel"
   D. and skin calloused from the grainy twist of a shovel."

6. **A.** NO CHANGE
   B. mental; artistic; or verbal
   C. mental. Artistic, or verbal
   D. mental, and artistic, or verbal

Teach the Workshop

Revising and Editing Skills
1. B	**4.** D
2. C	**5.** D
3. C	**6.** A

Test-Taking Skills
Revising and Editing Skills Tests
Tell students that in a revising and editing skills test, they should keep the following guidelines in mind:

- Read the passage through once before attempting to answer any questions.
- Read each question quickly to get an idea of the type of information you will have to consider. Some questions will refer to a brief section, but others may refer to the whole passage.
- Answer the questions in any order.
- When you are through, review all your answers to make sure they still seem best.

Ask students which questions refer to single sections and which to the whole passage.

> ⊳ For more information, see the Language Arts Handbook Section 8, Test-Taking Skills.

Program Resources
For more study and practice with test-taking skills, see the *Exceeding the Standards: Test Practice* resource:
- Literary Response Practice Test: Timed Writing, p. 7

Words in Use

Teaching Words
principled, 272	**protagonist,** 275
position, 272	**omniscient,** 275
alternatives, 273	
quaver, 274	
sensory, 275	
antagonist, 275	
static, 275	
dynamic, 275	

Tell students that reading comprehension questions give a short piece of writing and then ask several questions about it. The questions may ask students to figure out something based on information in the passage. Urge students to keep the following tips in mind:

- Read all the questions quickly.
- Read the passage with the questions in mind.
- Reread the first question carefully.
- Scan the passage, looking for key words. When you find a key word, slow down and read carefully.
- Answer the first question.
- Repeat this process to answer all the rest of the questions.

Reading Skills

Carefully read the following passage. Then, on a separate piece of paper, answer each question.

from "Be-ers and Doers" by Budge Wilson

"Albert!" she breathed. "We all thank you!" You've saved the house, the baby, all of us, even our Christmas presents. I'm proud, proud, *proud* of you."

Albert just stood there, smiling quietly, but very pale. His hands were getting red and sort of puckered looking.

5 Mom took a deep breath. "And *that*," she went on, "is what I've been looking for, all of your life. Some sort of a sign that you were one hundred percent alive. And now we all know you are. Maybe even a lick more alive than the rest of us. So!" She folded her arms, and her eyes bored into him. "I'll have no more excuses from you now. No one who can put out a house fire single-handed and rescue a niece and a sister and organize us all into

10 a fire brigade is gonna sit around for the rest of his life gatherin' dust. No siree! Or leanin' against no hoe. Why, you even had the fire department number tucked away in your head. Just imagine what you're gonna be able to do with them kind o' brains! I'll never, never rest until I see you educated and successful. Doin' what you was meant to do. I'm just proud of you, Albert. So terrible proud!"

15 Members of the fire department were starting to arrive at the front door, but Albert ignored them. He was white now, like death, and he made a low terrible sound. He didn't exactly pull his lips back from his teeth and growl, but the result was similar. It was like the sound a dog makes before he leaps for the throat. And what he said was "*You jest leave me be, woman!*"

20 We'd never heard words like this coming out of Albert, and the parlor was as still as night as we all listened.

"You ain't proud o' me, Mom," he whispered, all his beautiful grammar gone. "Yer jest proud o' what you want me t'be. And I got some news for you. Things I shoulda tole you years gone by. *I ain't gonna be what you want.*" His voice was starting to quaver now, and

25 he was trembling all over. "*I'm gonna be me*. And it seems like if that's ever gonna happen, it'll have t'be in some other place. And I plan t'do somethin' about that before the day is out."

Then he shut his eyes and fainted right down onto the charred carpet. The firemen carried him off to the hospital, where he was treated for shock and second-degree burns.

30 He was there for three weeks.

My dad died of a stroke when he was sixty-six. "Not enough exercise," said Mom, after she'd got over the worst part of her grief. "Too much sittin' around watchin' the lilacs grow. No way for his blood to circulate good." Me, I ask myself if he just piled up his silent tensions until he burst wide open. Maybe he wasn't all that calm and peaceful after

35 all. Could be he was just waiting, like Albert, for the moment when it would all come pouring out. Perhaps that wasn't the way it was; but all the same, I wonder.

Differentiated Instruction

English Language Learning
Students learning English will need help with the academic vocabulary used in standardized tests. Explain the following terms used in this workshop:
writing prompt — detailed instructions for a writing project, 272
outline — short summary or description, usually arranged as a series of key points, 272

position — opinion or point to be discussed, 272
evidence — facts that support an argument, 272

1. The sentence "His hands were getting red and sort of puckered looking" that begins in line 3 is an example of
   A. sensory detail.
   B. motivation.
   C. conflict.
   D. theme.

2. The description of Albert in the paragraph beginning on line 3 is an example of
   A. flat character.
   B. internal conflict.
   C. theme.
   D. characterization.

3. Which of the following best describes the tone of the dialogue in the paragraph beginning on line 5?
   A. indifferent
   B. angry and confused
   C. proud but condescending
   D. humorous

4. What can you conclude about Albert's reaction to his mother based on the narrator's observation in line 22 that his grammar had changed?
   A. Albert was confused by all of the commotion.
   B. Albert was afraid of the fire.
   C. Albert was very angry.
   D. Albert was distracted.

5. Based on the context, which of the following is the best definition of the word *quaver* in line 24?
   A. to speak more loudly
   B. to shake in speaking
   C. to yell
   D. to speak with clarity

6. Which of the following best describes Albert?
   A. He is the narrator.
   B. He is the antagonist.
   C. He is a static character.
   D. He is a dynamic character.

7. Which of the following best describes the theme of this passage?
   A. People should always listen to their elders' opinions.
   B. People should avoid conflict with their families at all cost.
   C. People should express themselves instead of repressing their feelings.
   D. In general, people should try to be more relaxed, and work less.

8. The conflict in this passage is primarily
   A. internal.
   B. external.
   C. antagonist.
   D. protagonist.

9. The father of the family as described in this passage is
   A. a round character.
   B. a flat character.
   C. the protagonist.
   D. an antagonist.

10. This story is written from which point of view?
    A. first person
    B. second person
    C. third person limited
    D. third person omniscient

Test-Taking Skills

Eliminate Incorrect Responses

Tell students that a key skill in answering multiple-choice questions is eliminating incorrect responses. Demonstrate this skill by modeling a think aloud for one question in the Reading Skills section.

Question 4. Possible Think Aloud: Albert was clearly not afraid of the fire, so B is not that answer. He seems neither confused nor distracted, so that probably eliminates A and D. That leaves C.

Select another question and have the class work as a group to eliminate the incorrect responses.

Unit 3 Visual Planning Guide

Planning and Assessment Tools

Annotated Teacher's Edition

Annotated Teacher's Edition
One location for accessing, previewing, and planning for use of all program resources.

EMC Launchpad
Desktop application for accessing, previewing, planning, posting, and grading all program resources. Post personal resources and lessons, and access the E-Lesson Planner, the E-Gradebook, and training modules for computer literacy.

Assessment Guide and ExamView
A variety of assessments are available for this unit in print and electronic forms, including:
- Formative Survey
- Lesson Tests
- Unit Exams
- Alternative Assessment Options
- Reading Fluency Assessments

Meeting the Standards: Unit 1
In addition to lesson-by-lesson resources, *Meeting the Standards* includes the following unit-based resources:
- Unit Study Guide
- Practice Test
- Active Reading Model
- Selection Quizzes

Program Planning Guide and E-Lesson Planner
- Lesson Plans for all the selections in the unit
- Core Standards-Based Selections
- Reading Log and Evaluation Forms

The E-Lesson Planner contains fully developed lesson plans and unit resources with an electronic calendar for editing lesson plans.

Technology Tools

Visual Teaching Package
This package contains unit-based lectures, games, art collections, and Writing Workshops in PowerPoint format; included within the EMC Launchpad.

Interactive Student Text on CD
The student textbook on CD includes highlighting, note-taking, bookmarking, and a direct link to the student website, in addition to everything in the student text.

Audio Library
Authentic, dramatic recordings with listening activities expand listening skills and offer additional support for developing readers and English Language Learners.

ETS Online Criterion-Based Essay Grader (Grades 9–12)
Students can use this ETS web-based tool to evaluate their essays online before submitting them for teacher review and final evaluation.

mirrorsandwindows.com
Student and teacher resources, support, references, technology tools, and state-specific standards are available at **mirrorsandwindows.com.** The website is customizable using the EMC Launchpad.

Unit-Based Resources

Exceeding the Standards Unit Resources

Each of the *Exceeding the Standards* resources provides fully developed lessons to help you extend the textbook lessons and to expand upon the themes and skills covered in the unit. You can also download these lessons from **mirrorsandwindows.com**.

Grammar & Style
This resource contains:
- Seven lessons on Verbs, pp. 52–75
- Two lessons on Subject-Verb Agreement and Usage, pp. 76–82

Literature & Reading
This resource contains:
- Reading and Analyzing Biographical and Autobiographical Nonfiction, pp. 9–11

Special Topics
This resource contains:
- Career Skills Development: Using the Internet to Search for Jobs, pp. 9–10
- Lifelong Learning: How Will You Get There? pp. 11–12

Test Practice
This resource contains:
- Expository Essay Practice Test: Revising and Editing, pp. 8–9

Writing
This resource contains:
- Descriptive Writing: Describe a Character, pp. 21–28

Speaking & Listening
This resource contains the following lesson to expand on the Speaking & Listening Workshop:
- Giving and Actively Listening to Informative Presentations, pp. 8–10

Vocabulary & Spelling
This resource contains:
- Four lessons on Academic Language, Reference Material, and Synonyms and Antonyms, pp. 23–31

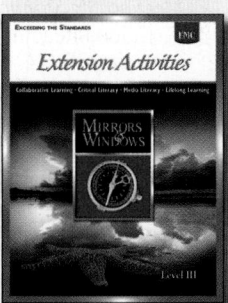

Extension Activities
This resource contains:
- Lifelong Learning: Internet Research, p. 8
- Media Literacy
- Critical Literacy: Hold a Debate, pp. 9–10

Unit 3 Visual Planning Guide

282

Reading Level: Moderate
Pacing: 2 days

Meeting the Standards,
Reading Model,
pp. 19–26

Advanced Students,
Author Study,
pp. 15–16

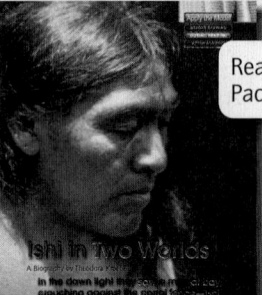
291

Reading Level: Challenging
Pacing: 3 days

Meeting the Standards,
Guided Reading,
pp. 27–32

*English Language
Learners,* Author's
Perspective, pp. 96–107

303

Reading Level: Moderate
Pacing: 2 days

Meeting the Standards,
Guided Reading,
pp. 33–38

Developing Readers,
Visualize, pp. 16–18

313

Reading Level: Challenging
Pacing: 3 days

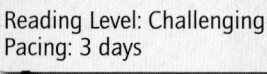

Meeting the Standards,
Guided Reading,
pp. 39–44

Developing Readers,
Unlock Word Meaning,
pp. 19–21

326

Reading Level: Moderate
Pacing: 2 days

Meeting the Standards,
Directed Reading,
pp. 45–50

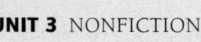 Interactive Student
Text on CD-ROM

 Selection
Lesson Plan

 Web-based
Resources

Lesson-by-Lesson Resources

Reading Level: Easy
Pacing: 1 day

Meeting the Standards,
Directed Reading,
pp. 51–55

Advanced Students,
Cultural Context
Project, p. 17

*English Language
Learners,* Take Notes,
pp. 108–116

336

Reading Level: Easy
Pacing: 1 day

Meeting the Standards,
Directed Reading,
pp. 56–61

Advanced Students,
Historical Connection
Project, p. 18

343

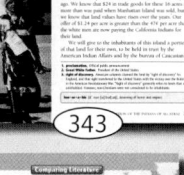

Reading Level: Easy; Challenging
Pacing: 4 days

Meeting the Standards,
Comparing Literature,
pp. 62–69

Developing Readers,
Set Purpose,
pp. 22–24

348

354

Reading Level: Challenging
Pacing: 3 days

Meeting the Standards,
Directed Reading,
pp. 70–75

360

Reading Level: Moderate
Pacing: 1 day

Meeting the Standards,
Independent Reading,
pp. 76–83

Developing Readers,
Use Text Organization,
pp. 25–27

372

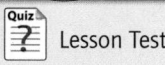 Lesson Test

 Audio Library

376

Reading Level: Easy
Pacing: 1 day

Meeting the Standards,
Independent Reading,
pp. 84–91

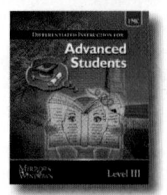
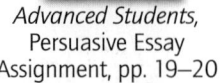

Advanced Students,
Persuasive Essay
Assignment, pp. 19–20

*English Language
Learners,* Identify Main
Idea, pp. 117–124

Unit 3 Scope & Sequence Guide

	Selection or Feature	Genre	Reading Support/ Reading Level	Word Count	Reading Skill	Graphic Organizer	
GUIDED READING	**Introduction to Nonfiction** pp. 278–279						
	Nonfiction Reading Model p. 280						
	Mrs. Flowers Maya Angelou pp. 281–289	Autobiography	Guided Reading: Reading Model/ Moderate	2,477	Distinguish Fact from Opinion	Fact or Opinion Chart; Timeline	
	Ishi in Two Worlds Theodora Kroeber pp. 290–300	Biography	Guided Reading: Reading Model/ Challenging	2,470	Author's Perspective	Timeline	
	Informational Text Connection: Yana People to Receive Ishi's Brain Robert Fri p. 299	Newspaper Article	Moderate	315			
	Understanding the Essay p. 301						
	Good Housekeeping Baily White pp. 302–311	Narrative Essay	Guided Reading: Reading Model/ Moderate	2,254	Analyze Cause and Effect	Cause and Effect Chart; Personal Essay Chart	

Literary Element	*Mirrors & Windows* Theme	Cross-Curricular Connection	Writing Options	Extension Activities
Fiction and Nonfiction Types of Nonfiction				
Autobiography	Power of Literature		Creative: Letter Expository: Essay	Lifelong Learning: Write a Biography Critical Literacy: Ask Questions
Biography	Compassion	Science Connection: *National Museum of the American Indian Act of 1989*	Creative: List Expository: Hypothesis	Collaborative Learning: Hold a Small Group Discussion Media Literacy: Compare and Contrast Perspectives
What is an Essay? Elements of an Essay Types of Essays				
Personal Essay	Perspective		Creative: Dialogue Applied: To-Do List	Collaborative Learning: Hold a Small Group Discussion Lifelong Learning: Conduct Internet Research

Unit 3 Scope & Sequence Guide

	Selection or Feature	Genre	Reading Support/ Reading Level	Word Count	Reading Skill	Graphic Organizer	
GUIDED READING	**Soul of a Citizen: Living with Conviction in a Cynical Time** Paul Rogat Loeb pp. 312–323	Persuasive Essay	Guided Reading: Reading Model/ Challenging	2,907	Summarize	Summary Chart; Persuasive Essay Chart	
	Literature Connection: I Was Born at the Wrong Time Angela Shelf Medearis p. 322	Lyric Poem	Easy	121			
DIRECTED READING	**Epiphany: The Third Gift** Lucha Corpi pp. 325–333	Memoir	Directed Reading/ Moderate	2,915	Analyze Text Structure	Cluster Chart	
	The Struggle to Be an All-American Girl Elizabeth Wong pp. 335–339	Personal Essay	Directed Reading/Easy	801	Take Notes	Note Taking Log; Conflict Chart	
	Proclamation of the Indians of Alcatraz Jay David, Editor pp. 341–345	Persuasive Essay	Directed Reading/Easy	458	Identify Author's Purpose	Author's Purpose Chart; Cluster Chart	
	Comparing Literature: Harriet Tubman: Conductor on the Underground Railroad Ann Petry pp. 347–358	Biography	Directed Reading/Easy	1,752			
	from **Our Struggle Is Against All Forms of Racism** Nelson Mandela pp. 347–358	Speech	Directed Reading/ Challenging	614			
	If You Could Be My Friend Litsa Boudalika pp. 359–371	Letters	Directed Reading/ Challenging	3,786	Fact and Opinion	Fact and Opinion Chart; Setting Chart	
	Literature Connection: Jerusalem Naomi Shihab Nye p. 370	Lyric Poem	Moderate	207			

Literary Element	*Mirrors & Windows* Theme	Cross-Curricular Connection	Writing Options	Extension Activities
Persuasive Essay	Social Obligation		Creative: Slogan Applied: List	Collaborative Learning: Create an Action Plan Critical Literacy: Analyze Speeches
Setting	Gender Expectation		Creative: Brief Narrative Expository: Analysis	Lifelong Learning: Research Careers Collaborative Learning: Create a Chart
Conflict	Maturation		Creative: Diary Entry Expository: Literary Response	Lifelong Learning: Create a Chinese Phrasebook Critical Literacy: Create a Dialogue
Tone	Protest	History Connection: *American Indian Movement*	Creative: Article Expository: Brief Essay	Collaborative Learning: Plan a Movie Shoot Critical Literacy: Hold a Debate
Compare Literature: Author's Purpose	Character		Creative: Newspaper Article Expository: Brief Essay	Lifelong Learning: Research and Take Notes Critical Literacy: Create Interview Questions
Setting	Perspective		Creative: Letter Expository: Compare and Contrast Essay	Lifelong Learning: Conduct Internet Research Critical Literacy: Write an Explanation

Unit 3 Scope & Sequence Guide

	Selection or Feature	Genre	Reading Support/ Reading Level	Word Count	Reading Skill	Graphic Organizer	
INDEPENDENT READING	from **The Autobiography of Malcolm X** Malcolm X and Alex Haley pp. 372–375	Autobiography	Independent Reading/ Moderate	1,250	Ask Questions		
	Appearances are Destructive Mark Mathabane pp. 376–378	Essay	Independent Reading/ Easy	583	Identify Author's Purpose		

Unit 3 Language Arts Workshops

Grammar & Style	Vocabulary & Spelling	Writing	Speaking & Listening	Test Practice
Punctuation: Dashes, Colons, and Semicolons, p. 324 Prepositional and Participial Phrases, p. 334 Consistent Verb Tense, p. 340	Synonyms and Antonyms, p. 346	Expository Writing: Cause-and-Effect Essay, pp. 380–385	Giving and Actively Listening to Informative Presentations, pp. 386–387	Writing Skills: Expository Essay, from "Reluctant Witnesses: Children's Voices from the Civil War" by Emmy Werner, p. 388 Revising and Editing Skills, p. 389 Reading Skills: from "Do not ask us to give up the buffalo for sheep" by Chief Ten Bears, pp. 390–391

Literary Element	*Mirrors & Windows* Theme	Cross-Curricular Connection	Writing Options	Extension Activities
Autobiography	Educating Oneself		Creative: Memo	Media Literacy and Collaborative Learning: Practice Nonverbal Communication in Small Groups
Tone	Dress Codes		Creative: Letter	Media Literacy and Collaborative Learning: Collect and Evaluate Different Advertisements

Unit 3 Building Vocabulary

The lists below identify the Words in Use and Key Terms within this unit. These words are listed at the bottom of the Teacher's Edition pages at the beginning of each lesson. Vocabulary development activities are provided in the *Meeting the Standards* unit book and in *Exceeding the Standards: Vocabulary & Spelling*.

WORDS IN USE

Preview Vocabulary
Preview Vocabulary are words taken from the sentences within each selection. These words are defined in the side margin or at the bottom of the pages on which they appear. The "Preview Vocabulary" section introduces these words in the Before Reading page preceding each selection.

adequate, 344	emaciate, 292	inculcate, 331	proliferation, 317
adjacent, 294	embroidery, 362	indicted, 362	protestation, 306
admonishingly, 331	enclave, 366	infuse, 286	refuge, 313
amicably, 366	foresight, 356	isolated, 344	solidarity, 355
benign, 283	groundless, 293	kinship, 355	taut, 282
chagrin, 327	honorable, 343	magnitude, 315	unwonted, 292
commemorate, 327	implication, 314	memorabilia, 307	
competently, 285	incentive, 352	perpetuity, 344	
degradation, 314	incomprehensible, 351	persistently, 283	

Selection Words
Selection Words are additional words from the reading that may be challenging but are not central to the selection and are not identified in the prereading section. These words can easily be learned using the story context, and they provide excellent practice for using content clues to find meaning without explicit instruction.

acquire, 372	embodiment, 320	iridescent, 304	qualms, 332
adhered, 299	fanatical, 338	lecherous, 306	redress, 314
antidote, 304	functional, 372	leer, 305	rehabilitation, 374
aristocrat, 282	gait, 283	leered, 287	repatriate, 299
articulate, 372	garnering, 317	militant, 365	revolt, 356
cascading, 288	gaudy, 377	miscellaneous, 295	riffling, 373
compelling, 376	heirloom, 307	obligation, 299	sacred, 299
cornea, 327	homely, 376	ogling, 377	squalor, 357
derailed, 376	immigrant, 362	overseer, 349	succeeding, 373
descendants, 299	indomitable, 355	patrimonial, 299	taunted, 376
disassociate, 337	inevitable, 373	perfunctorily, 331	terseness, 327
dissident, 319	innate, 319	posterity, 294	unceremonious, 283
dissuade, 337	intolerable, 356	preoccupied, 376	uncomprehendingly, 293
distraught, 376	invariably, 349	promote, 376	unconcealed, 352

Teaching Words
Teaching Words consist of vocabulary that is used in the directions about the lessons. Teaching words explain to students what to focus on within the selection, help establish the story context, clarify the meaning of literary terms, and define the goals or instructional purpose.

alter, 341	conveys, 371	engagement, 278	ghetto, 376
annotations, 383	correspondence, 369	enlistment, 388	hinder, 390
anthropologist, 290	cremated, 293	enraged, 293	incident, 294
anthropology, 301	deficiency, 278	epiphany, 325	indigenous, 344
apartheid, 347, 376	demonstration, 312	estimate, 388	influential, 372
appropriate, 380	differentiate, 359	excerpt, 281	innate, 353
assimilation, 341	disservice, 321	expository, 388	insignificant, 369
comrades, 358	division, 278	figurative, 308	investigative, 312
constitutions, 341	dynamic, 386	fluently, 387	legible, 384
constructive, 387	element, 278	fugitive, 353	mainstream, 290
controversial, 372	empowered, 321	gender, 332	memorandum, 375

mentor, 281
monotonous, 387
multiculturalism, 335
naïve, 391
objectionable, 346
omitted, 389
oppression, 281
orthodox, 372

outpouring, 290
overwhelmed, 290
perceptions, 380
perpetual, 346
playwright, 335
proclamation, 341
pro-democracy, 312
relatively, 371

relevant, 381
reluctant, 388
repatriate, 293
segregation, 281
sentimental, 311
skimming, 325
solidarity, 358
tourism, 335

transient, 346
unceasing, 346
unique, 301
vantage point, 301
withered, 380

KEY TERMS

Key Terms are commonly referred to as *academic vocabulary*. These terms appear in the instructional material to teach the terminology that students need to acquire to understand literature. The repetition of the terms throughout the program ensures student mastery and provides a solid foundation for the continuing study of literature and language arts.

adjective, 334
adverb, 334
anecdote, 279, 321, 386
antonym, 346
audience, 301, 358, 386, 391
author's perspective, 290
author's purpose, 301
autobiography, 278, 281, 372, 391
bias, 323
biography, 278, 290, 347, 391
body, 301
cause, 302, 388
cause-and-effect essay, 380
cause-and-effect order, 325
cause-and-effect organization, 382
character, 340
characterization, 289, 302
characterize, 391
chronological order, 325
climax, 302
compare and contrast, 371
comparison-and-contrast order, 325
conclusion, 301, 380, 387
conflict, 302, 335

consistent verb tense, 340
context clue, 280
context, 391
description, 290
descriptive essay, 391
dialogue, 311, 339
documentary, 359
effect, 302, 388
essay, 278, 301, 376
excerpt, 388
expository essay, 301
external conflict, 335
fact, 359
feedback, 387
fiction, 278
first-person point of view, 301
future tense, 340
grammar, 384
hypothesis, 300
informative presentation, 386
internal conflict, 335
introduction, 301, 380, 386
literary element, 280
main idea, 323, 358, 386
memo, 375
memoir, 278, 325
mood, 371

narrative essay, 302
narrative, 278, 289
nonfiction, 278, 280, 359
noun, 334
opinion, 359, 391
order of importance, 325
organizational pattern, 380
outline, 382, 386, 388
participial phrase, 334
past tense, 340
peer review, 383
personal essay, 279, 301, 302, 335, 391
persuasive essay, 279, 301, 312, 341
phrase, 334
plot, 340
point of view, 278, 301, 302
preposition, 334
prepositional phrase, 334
present tense, 340
proofread, 384
prose, 278
punctuation, 384
resolution, 302, 339
rhetorical technique, 323
rising action, 302

sensory detail, 280, 339
sensory language, 391
sentence structure, 301
sequence of events, 280
setting, 325, 340, 359, 391
situational irony, 311
slogan, 323
spatial order, 325
speech, 347, 391
subject, 334, 347
summary, 312, 380
supporting detail, 323, 382, 386
symbol, 358, 378
synonym, 346
theme, 335, 378
thesaurus, 346
thesis, 279, 345, 380, 388
thesis statement, 339, 381
third-person point of view, 279, 301
tone, 281, 301, 341, 346, 347
topic, 386
topic sentence, 383
transition, 383
verb, 334, 340
viewpoint, 323
voice, 301

Objectives

Studying this unit will help students meet the following objectives:

- Make connections from themes expressed in the selections to their own lives and the world around them
- Identify common forms of nonfiction
- Understand different elements of nonfiction, including *autobiography, character, personal essay, persuasive essay, setting, conflict,* and *tone*
- Understand variations of literary forms and author's use of language to develop forms

Reading Strategies

Ask Questions   Make Predictions
Clarify   Visualize
Make Inferences

Reading Skills

Analyze Cause and Effect
Analyze Text Structure
Distinguish Fact from Opinion
Identify Author's Perspective
Identify Author's Purpose
Summarize
Take Notes

Literary Elements

Autobiography   Personal Essay
Biography   Persuasive Essay
Conflict   Setting
Narrative Essay   Tone

Looking Back
Nonfiction

MAYA ANGELOU

THEODORA KROEBER

LUCHA CORPI

Launch the Unit

Have students work in small groups to create other questions that might relate to the theme of this unit. Model this by proposing such a question: "How does examining past situations help us improve upon our present circumstances?" Have the class write down their questions and keep the list. When the class has completed work on the unit, have them take another look at these questions and discuss which selections provide insights about them.

> "*As a child I didn't understand why everyone around me insisted on giving me dolls, especially since I had made it clear that I really didn't like to play with them.*"

—LUCHA CORPI, "Epiphany: The Third Gift"

When you look at your life five years ago, what stands out? In her essay "Epiphany: The Third Gift," Lucha Corpi recalls what she liked and disliked in childhood and how these tastes influenced the person she became. Nonfiction such as autobiography and biography take a backward look at the events of a person's life. As you read the nonfiction selections in this unit, relate the insights they offer to your own recollections.

MARK MATHABANE

ELIZABETH WONG

NELSON MANDELA

277

Writing Options

Creative Writing
Dialogue
Diary Entry
Letter
List
Memo
Narrative
Article
Slogan

Applied Writing
List
To-Do List

Expository Writing
Analysis
Compare-and-Contrast Essay
Essay
Hypothesis

Language Arts Workshops
Grammar & Style
Consistent Verb Tense
Prepositional and Participial Phrases
Punctuation: Dashes, Colons, and
   Semicolons

Vocabulary & Spelling
Synonyms and Antonyms

Writing Workshop
Cause-and-Effect Essay

Speaking & Listening Workshop
Giving and Actively Listening to
   Informative Presentations

Test Practice Workshop
Expository Essay
Reading Skills
Revising and Editing Skills

Program Resources

For a visual reminder of the unit-based resources available for Unit 3, Nonfiction, see pages 276A and 276B. As you introduce the unit, you may want to provide students with the Unit Study Guide, which is contained in the *Meeting the Standards* resource.

Teach the Genre

Introduction to Nonfiction

You may choose to direct students to the Introduction to Nonfiction pages later on, as they begin to explore the elements of nonfiction in the Before Reading and After Reading sections of each selection.

Instead of reading through all the text at once, you may want to begin by having students discuss the most desirable forms of nonfiction for use in the following situations:

- reading silently in class
- reading to a friend or family member
- reading in preparation for an oral presentation
- reading to locate information for an expository essay
- reading to recall details on a standardized test

Launch the Lesson

Ask students to freewrite about events in their past that have been fundamental in shaping who they are today. Next, create a chart on a board or overhead with the following categories: family, friends, decisions, accomplishments, disappointments, and self-reflection. Invite students to record their events under an appropriate category. Discuss why certain categories have been more significant to their growth as human beings than others.

Fiction and Nonfiction

Both of the following passages deal with the Civil War battle of Shiloh. How do they differ?

> Now and again the boy heard a vast wind come up, that gently stirred the air. But he knew what it was—the army here, the army there, whispering to itself in the dark. Some men talking to others, others murmuring to themselves, and all so quiet it was like a natural element arisen from South or North with the motion of the earth toward dawn.
>
> —RAY BRADBURY, "The Drummer Boy of Shiloh"

> Some two or three miles from Pittsburg landing was a log meeting-house called Shiloh. It stood on the ridge which divides the waters of Snake and Lick creeks, the former emptying into the Tennessee just north of Pittsburg landing, and the latter south. This point was the key to our position and was held by Sherman. His division was at that time wholly raw, no part of it ever having been in an engagement; but I thought this deficiency was more than made up by the superiority of the commander.
>
> —ULYSSES S. GRANT, "Personal Memoirs"

These two passages differ in several ways, including point of view and writing style. But one very important difference is that Bradbury's re-creation of these people and events is basically imaginary whereas Grant's is an eyewitness account. To put it another way, Bradbury's short story is fiction and Grant's autobiography is nonfiction.

Fiction is often highly realistic. In order to provide realistic details for his story, Bradbury did research on the Civil War, reading accounts about real people and events. But his narrative is still invented. On the other hand, Grant was the Union commander at Shiloh and in his autobiography he presented the actual events of the battle as he remembered them.

In the Introduction to Fiction (page 4), you learned that **fiction** includes any work of prose (writing that is not poetry or drama) that tells an invented or imaginary story. Typical forms of fiction are short stories and novels. **Nonfiction** is writing about real people, places, things, and events. Autobiographies, biographies, journals, essays, histories, and newspaper and magazine articles are all types of nonfiction.

Maya Angelou

Types of Nonfiction

Among the most common types of nonfiction are autobiography, biography, and essay.

Autobiography and Memoir

Writing is described as "autobiographical" when the writer presents parts or the whole of his or her own life. There are many types of autobiographical writing, including autobiographies, memoirs, diaries, journals, and letters.

An **autobiography** is the story of a person's life written by that person. It typically covers the whole of a person's life up to the time of writing. A more focused type of autobiography is the **memoir,** which usually deals with a specific period of a person's life, such as childhood. For example, Maya Angelou's *I Know Why the Caged Bird Sings* (page 281) is a memoir about her childhood.

Words in Use

Teaching Words
element, 278
division, 278
engagement, 278
deficiency, 278

KEY TERMS

POINT OF VIEW, 278	**MEMOIR,** 278
NARRATIVE, 278	**THIRD-PERSON POINT OF**
FICTION, 278	**VIEW,** 279
PROSE, 278	**THESIS,** 279
NONFICTION, 278	**PERSONAL ESSAY,** 279
BIOGRAPHY, 278	**ANECDOTE,** 279
ESSAY, 278	**PERSUASIVE ESSAY,** 279
AUTOBIOGRAPHY, 278	

Common Core State Standards

Reading Literature
RL.5

Reading Informational
RI.2, RI.3, RI.5, RI.6, RI.8, RI.10

Biography

A **biography** is the story of a person's life told by another person. For example, Theodora Kroeber's *Ishi in Two Worlds* (page 290) is a biography about a Native American who was the last surviving member of his people.

> The story of Ishi begins for us early in the morning of the twenty-ninth day of August in the year 1911 and in the corral of the slaughter house.
>
> —THEODORA KROEBER, *Ishi in Two Worlds*

Biographies are told from the third-person point of view, although writers of biography may also include autobiographical materials, such as letters, diaries, or journals, so that the reader may gain firsthand knowledge about the person whose life story is being told.

Essay

An **essay** is a short nonfiction work that makes a point about a single subject. The point that the writer is making is the **thesis.** For example, in an essay about highway billboards, the thesis might be that such outside advertising destroys the beauty of many American landscapes.

There are many types of essay. A **personal essay** is a short nonfiction work on a single topic related to the life of the writer. The author of a personal essay may tell a story or an anecdote or reflect on and share thoughts and feelings about something in his or her life. For example, Elizabeth Wong's "The Struggle to Be an All-American Girl" (page 335) describes the difficulty of growing up in two cultures—Chinese and American.

> Every day at 5 P.M., instead of playing with our fourth- and fifth-grade friends or sneaking out to the empty lot to hunt ghosts and animal bones, my brother and I had to go to Chinese school.
>
> —ELIZABETH WONG, "The Struggle to Be an All-American Girl"

In a **persuasive essay** the writer's goal is to persuade the reader to accept a point of view. For example, Paul Rogat Loeb (page 312) tries to push his readers in the direction of social activism on behalf of the causes in which they believe. Newspaper editorials and petitions are common examples of persuasive writing.

> There is no perfect time to get involved in social causes, no ideal circumstances for voicing our convictions. Instead, each of us faces a lifelong series of imperfect moments in which we must decide what to stand for.
>
> —PAUL ROGAT LOEB, "Soul of a Citizen"

Essays can have more than one purpose. A writer may use a personal anecdote in the course of an essay whose purpose is basically to persuade. Paul Rogat Loeb, for example, uses several personal experiences to help make his point about social activism.

Speaking & Listening Skills

Group Discussion

Students who read widely might like to discuss the following:

- whether nonfiction can be entirely objective
- why certain nonfiction topics are very popular among teen readers
- what current events tell us about whether decision makers are studying the past

Allow students time to support their opinions, absorb the different views of their classmates, and then modify their original positions, if they so choose.

Understand Autobiography and Biography

Introducing the Process This page is an overview of the basic instruction provided for students before, during, and after reading the majority of the nonfiction selections in Unit 3. Maya Angelou's memoir "Mrs. Flowers" is an Active Reading Model. Side notes in Active Reading Models provide point-of-use questions about applying reading strategies and skills, analyzing literature, and making connections.

Before Reading Distinguish for students the broad purposes of reading—information, entertainment, experience—and setting a specific purpose for reading a specific work, such as "Mrs. Flowers."

During Reading Point out that using the four different types of side notes in "Mrs. Flowers"—Use Reading Strategies, Use Reading Skills, Analyze Literature, and Make Connections—helps them become more active readers. Explain that the Mirrors & Windows questions that conclude the memoir ask them to respond to the memoir personally and to consider its meaning in the world around them.

After Reading Explain that the first group of questions, labeled "Find Meaning," helps them recall important details of a selection and interpret what they mean. The second group of questions, labeled "Make Judgments," asks them to analyze the selection and evaluate how specific details contribute to the overall literary effect or meaning of the work.

Nonfiction Reading Model

BEFORE READING

Build Background
You need to apply two types of background to read a piece of nonfiction effectively. One is the selection's historical, scientific, or cultural context. Read the **Build Background** and **Meet the Author** features to get this kind of information. The other type of background is the personal knowledge you bring to your reading.

Set Purpose
A nonfiction writer writes to inform, describe, persuade, or entertain. Read **Set Purpose** to decide what you want to get out of the selection.

Analyze Literature
A nonfiction writer uses different techniques depending on the type of nonfiction he or she is writing. The **Analyze Literature** feature draws your attention to a key literary element.

Use Reading Skills
The **Use Reading Skills** feature will show you skills to help you get the most out of your reading. Learn how to apply skills such as determining author's purpose and using context clues. Identify a graphic organizer that will help you apply the skill before and while you read.

DURING READING

Use Reading Strategies
- **Ask questions** about things that seem significant or interesting.
- **Make predictions** about what's going to happen next. As you read, gather more clues to confirm or change your prediction.
- **Visualize** the information. Form pictures in your mind to help you see what the writer is describing.
- **Make inferences,** or educated guesses, about what is not stated directly.
- **Clarify,** or check that you understand, what you read. Reread any difficult parts.

Analyze Literature
What literary elements stand out? Are the descriptions vivid and interesting? As you read, consider how these elements affect your enjoyment and understanding of the nonfiction.

Make Connections
Notice where connections can be made between the information presented in the selection and your life. What thoughts do you have while reading?

AFTER READING

Find Meaning
Recall the important details of the selection, such as the sequence of events and settings. Use this information to **interpret,** or explain, the meaning of the selection.

Make Judgments
- **Analyze** the text by examining details and deciding what they contribute to the meaning.
- **Evaluate** the text by making judgments about how the author creates meaning.

Analyze Literature
Review how the use of literary elements increased your understanding of the selection. For example, did the author use sensory details? How did they help shape meaning?

Extend
Go beyond the text by exploring the selection's ideas through writing or other creative projects.

Differentiated Instruction

English Language Learning
Students learning English may need help with the vocabulary used throughout the selection lessons. Explain the meaning of the following terms to them:
analyze—take something apart in order to understand what it is or how it works, 280
strategy—technique intended to accomplish a goal, 280
preview—look something over as a preparation to working with it, 281

KEY TERMS
NONFICTION, 280
LITERARY ELEMENT, 280
CONTEXT CLUE, 280
SEQUENCE OF EVENTS, 280
SENSORY DETAIL, 280

Mrs. Flowers

from *I Know Why the Caged Bird Sings*

Autobiography by Maya Angelou

GUIDED READING

At a Glance
Guided Reading: Reading Model
- Reading Level: Moderate
- Difficulty Consideration: Vocabulary
- Ease Factor: Sympathetic character

Objectives
This lesson will enable students to
- use reading skills such as distinguishing fact from opinion
- define *autobiography* and recognize that Maya Angelou is telling a true story about her own life
- describe the literary accomplishments of Maya Angelou and explain the historical significance of her writing

Launch the Lesson
Before students read "Mrs. Flowers," have them think about an adult who had a positive influence on their sense of self-worth. How was that adult influential? What qualities in that adult would they like to imitate? Write their answers on the board. Then tell them that the selection they are about to read describes an adult that the author admires. As they read, have them compare her qualities with the ones you have written on the board.

Build Background
Historical Context The excerpt "Mrs. Flowers" takes place in Stamps, Arkansas, in the 1930s, during segregation. "Mrs. Flowers" tells of Maya Angelou's upbringing and her experience with a mentor.

Reader's Context Who has had a big effect on your life? What did he or she do? How did he or she affect you?

Set Purpose
Skim the first paragraph to preview the narrator's attitude toward Mrs. Flowers. Based on Build Background and your preview, what do you predict might happen in the story?

Analyze Literature
Autobiography An **autobiography** is the story of a person's life, written by that person. The writer conveys his or her story through facts, opinions, and tone. **Tone** is the writer's attitude toward the subject. As you read, pay attention to the tone Angelou creates.

Meet the Author
Maya Angelou was born Marguerite Johnson on April 4, 1928, in St. Louis, Missouri. She spent much of her childhood with her grandmother in rural Stamps, Arkansas, which is the setting for the excerpt. "Mrs. Flowers" tells the story of how Maya Angelou gained self-confidence and a love of literature. Angelou's written works include autobiographies, poetry, and essays. Much of her work deals with both economic and racial oppression.

Use Reading Skills
Distinguish Fact from Opinion A fact can be proven true. An opinion expresses an attitude or desire. Create a chart to help distinguish fact from opinion as you read. If the evidence to support a fact is not in the text, list what are most likely facts and how they could be proven.

Fact or Opinion Chart

Fact: Mrs. Flowers didn't belong to our church.	Opinion: Momma had a strange relationship with Mrs. Flowers.
Proof: Could check church records	Support: Mrs. Flowers called Momma "Mrs. Henderson"; Momma called Mrs. Flowers "Sister Flowers."

Preview Vocabulary
taut (tot) *adj.*, tense, tight

be•nign (bi nīn´) *adj.*, harmless

per•sist•ent•ly (pər sis´ tənt lē) *adv.*, repeatedly

com•pe•tent•ly (käm´ pə tənt lē) *adv.*, capably

in•fuse (in fyüs´) *v.*, introduce gradually; cause to penetrate; instill

MRS. FLOWERS **281**

Words in Use

Preview Vocabulary
taut, 282
benign, 283
persistently, 283
competently, 285
infuse, 286

Selection Words
aristocrat, 282
unceremonious, 283
gait, 283
leered, 287
cascading, 288

Teaching Words
excerpt, 281
segregation, 281
mentor, 281
oppression, 281

KEY TERMS
AUTOBIOGRAPHY, 281
TONE, 281
NARRATIVE, 289
CHARACTERIZATION, 289

Common Core State Standards
Reading Literature
RL.1
Reading Informational
RI.4, RI.10
Writing
W.9, W.10
Language
L.6

Summary

In the black neighborhood of Stamps, Arkansas, where Maya Angelou grew up, Mrs. Bertha Flowers was the most elegant, refined, and well-educated resident. When she invited Angelou to her home one day, the young girl was beside herself. As they visited, Mrs. Flowers said things that changed Angelou's life. Maya Angelou still credits Mrs. Flowers with awakening in her a sense of the importance of spoken, as well as written, language.

The Mirrors & Windows questions at the end of this selection focus on the theme of the power of literature. Before reading, ask students to think about the books and poems they have read. Have any struck a chord in them? Why might some books and poems have a more widespread effect on people than others?

Independent Reading

Direct interested students to the following titles mentioned in "Mrs. Flowers":
Beowulf by Anonymous
Oliver Twist by Charles Dickens
A Tale of Two Cities by Charles Dickens

Analyze Literature

Autobiography *Answer:* It takes place in Stamps, Arkansas, which was divided along racial lines. **Ⓐ**

Apply the Model
BEFORE READING
DURING READING
AFTER READING

Mrs. Flowers

from

I Know Why the Caged Bird Sings

Autobiography by Maya Angelou

Blue Woman with Mirror, 1954. Hyacinth Manning. Private collection.

DURING READING

Analyze Literature
Autobiography What does this tell you about where the narrative takes place? **Ⓐ**

taut (tot) *adj.,* tense, tight

Mrs. Bertha Flowers was the aristocrat of Black Stamps. She had the grace of control to appear warm in the coolest weather, and on the Arkansas summer days it seemed she had a private breeze which swirled around, cooling her. She was thin without the <u>taut</u> look of wiry people, and her printed voile[1]

---

1. **voile.** Light, cotton fabric

282

Program Resources

Planning and Assessment
Program Planning Guide, Selection Lesson Plan
E-Lesson Planner
Assessment Guide, Lesson Test
ExamView

Technology Tools
Interactive Student Text on CD
Visual Teaching Package
Audio Library
mirrorsandwindows.com

Meeting the Standards
Nonfiction: Unit 3, Guided Reading, pp. 19–26

Differentiating Instruction
Advanced Students, Author Study, pp. 15–16

She was our side's answer to the richest white woman in town.

dresses and flowered hats were as right for her as denim overalls for a farmer. She was our side's answer to the richest white woman in town.

Her skin was a rich black that would have peeled like a plum if snagged, but then no one would have thought of getting close enough to Mrs. Flowers to ruffle her dress, let alone snag her skin. She didn't encourage familiarity. She wore gloves too.

I don't think I ever saw Mrs. Flowers laugh, but she smiled often. A slow widening of her thin black lips to show even, small white teeth, then the slow effortless closing. When she chose to smile on me, I always wanted to thank her. The action was so graceful and inclusively[2] <u>benign</u>.

She was one of the few gentlewomen I have ever known, and has remained throughout my life the measure of what a human being can be.

Momma had a strange relationship with her. Most often when she passed on the road in front of the Store, she spoke to Momma in that soft yet carrying voice, "Good day, Mrs. Henderson." Momma responded with "How you, Sister Flowers?"

Mrs. Flowers didn't belong to our church, nor was she Momma's familiar. Why on earth did she insist on calling her Sister Flowers? Shame made me want to hide my face. Mrs. Flowers deserved better than to be called Sister. Then, Momma left out the verb. Why not ask, "How *are* you, *Mrs.* Flowers?" With the unbalanced passion of the young, I hated her for showing her ignorance to Mrs. Flowers. It didn't occur to me for many years that they were as alike as sisters, separated only by formal education.

Although I was upset, neither of the women was in the least shaken by what I thought an unceremonious greeting. Mrs. Flowers would continue her easy gait up the hill to her little bungalow, and Momma kept on shelling peas or doing whatever had brought her to the front porch.

Occasionally, though, Mrs. Flowers would drift off the road and down to the Store and Momma would say to me, "Sister, you go on and play." As I left I would hear the beginning of an intimate conversation. Momma <u>persistently</u> using the wrong verb, or none at all.

"Brother and Sister Wilcox is sho'ly the meanest—" "Is,"

---

2. **inclusively.** In a way that includes everyone and everything

be·nign (bi nīn´) *adj.*, harmless

DURING READING

Make Connections
How does Marguerite's reaction to Momma's greeting affect your feelings about the characters?
D

---

per·sist·ent·ly (per sis´ tənt lē) *adv.*, repeatedly

Teach the Model

Use Reading Strategies
Visualize Have students take a moment to visualize Mrs. Bertha Flowers. Ask: "What details can you add to Maya Angelou's description that would be consistent with it? For example, what kind of shoes might she be wearing? How might she hold her head? What is her posture like?" **B**

Analyze Literature
Characteristics Ask students to recall a person they have known who could be called a "gentlewoman" or a "gentleman." Ask: "What characteristics set him or her apart from others? Do good manners earn a person this title, or does it require a certain attitude toward other people?" **C**

Make Connections
Answer: Some students might relate to being embarrassed by an adult's actions, while others might think that Marguerite is an ungrateful child. Her attitude might make them feel sorry for Momma. **D**

Vocabulary Skills

Standard English and Dialect
Point out to students the difference between Standard English and English dialects. Remind them that while dialects do not necessarily observe patterns of Standard English, they do follow a specific traceable system. Explain that when words or phrases within a certain dialect are unfamiliar or difficult to understand, an examination of context might help bring to light their meaning.

EXAMPLE:
Dialect: "How you, Sister Flowers?"
Standard English: "How are you, Sister Flowers?"
Context clue: Momma is responding to Mrs. Flowers salutation, "Good day, Mrs. Henderson."

Use Reading Skills
Distinguish Fact from Opinion
Answer: Mrs. Flowers had a slow dragging smile, she made Marguerite's name sound beautiful, the looks given were "age-group," and the statement "My name was beautiful when she said it" are all opinions. **A**

▶ More About the Author
Tell students how Maya Angelou got her name. Her brother Bailey, who was about a year and a half older than Marguerite, nicknamed her Maya when they were very young. Later, she took the professional name Maya Angelou, using a form of her first husband's last name, Angelos. **B**

TEACHING NOTE
If you give students definitions and context sentences, they might find it easier to understand unfamiliar words in the story.
familiarity—friendly closeness, 283
The easy familiarity between them was clear from the way they laughed together.
merging—joining; combining, 284
Due to construction, traffic is merging from four lanes into two.
incessantly—constantly, 284
It's difficult to have a conversation with someone who talks incessantly.

Momma? "Is"? Oh, please, not "is," Momma, for two or more. But they talked, and from the side of the building where I waited for the ground to open up and swallow me, I heard the soft-voiced Mrs. Flowers and the textured voice of my grandmother merging and melting. They were interrupted from time to time by giggles that must have come from Mrs. Flowers (Momma never giggled in her life). Then she was gone.

She appealed to me because she was like people I had never met personally. Like women in English novels who walked the moors[3] (whatever they were) with their loyal dogs racing at a respectful distance. Like the women who sat in front of roaring fireplaces, drinking tea incessantly from silver trays full of scones and crumpets. Women who walked over the "heath" and read morocco-bound books and had two last names divided by a hyphen. It would be safe to say that she made me proud to be Negro, just by being herself.

She acted just as refined[4] as whitefolks in the movies and books and she was more beautiful, for none of them could have come near that warm color without looking gray by comparison.

It was fortunate that I never saw her in the company of powhitefolks.[5] For since they tend to think of their whiteness as an evenizer, I'm certain that I would have had to hear her spoken to commonly as Bertha, and my image of her would have been shattered like the unmendable Humpty-Dumpty.

One summer afternoon, sweet-milk fresh in my memory, she stopped at the Store to buy provisions. Another Negro woman of her health and age would have been expected to carry the paper sacks home in one hand, but Momma said, "Sister Flowers, I'll send Bailey up to your house with these things."

B She smiled that slow dragging smile, "Thank you, Mrs. Henderson. I'd prefer Marguerite, though." My name was beautiful when she said it. "I've been meaning to talk to her, anyway." They gave each other age-group looks.

Momma said, "Well, that's all right then. Sister, go and change your dress. You going to Sister Flowers's."

The chifforobe[6] was a maze. What on earth did one put on to go to Mrs. Flowers' house? I knew I shouldn't put on a Sunday dress. It might be sacrilegious.[7] Certainly not a house dress, since I was

> ### DURING READING
> **Use Reading Skills**
> **Distinguish Fact from Opinion** What opinions are stated in this paragraph? **A**

---

3. **moors.** Open, grassy areas
4. **refined.** Polite; with elegant manners
5. **powhitefolks.** Poor white families
6. **chifforobe.** Closet for clothing
7. **sacrilegious.** Showing disrespect for something holy or very important

Differentiated Instruction

Auditory Learning
Guide students toward the realization that they employ a teen dialect of their own. Ask them to pinpoint words and expressions that are particular to their "teen-speak" and might be difficult for younger or older people to understand. Request that student volunteers write classroom-generated examples of teen dialect on the board. Then moderate a whole-class discussion of differences in the tone, purpose, and effect of each example and its Standard English equivalent.

already wearing a fresh one. I chose a school dress, naturally. It was formal without suggesting that going to Mrs. Flowers' house was equivalent to attending church.

I trusted myself back into the Store.

"Now, don't you look nice," I had chosen the right thing, for once.

"Mrs. Henderson, you make most of the children's clothes, don't you?"

"Yes, ma'am. Sure do. Store-bought clothes ain't hardly worth the thread it take to stitch them."

"I'll say you do a lovely job, though, so neat. That dress looks professional."

Momma was enjoying the seldom-received compliments. Since everyone we knew (except Mrs. Flowers, of course) could sew <u>competently</u>, praise was rarely handed out for the commonly practiced craft.

"I try, with the help of the Lord, Sister Flowers, to finish the inside just like I does the outside. Come here, Sister."

I had buttoned up the collar and tied the belt, apronlike, in back. Momma told me to turn around. With one hand she pulled the strings and the belt fell free at both sides of my waist. Then her large hands were at my neck, opening the button loops. I was terrified. What was happening?

"Take it off, Sister." She had her hands on the hem of the dress.

"I don't need to see the inside, Mrs. Henderson, I can tell..." But the dress was over my head and my arms were stuck in the sleeves. Momma said, "That'll do. See here, Sister Flowers, I French-seams around the armholes." Through the cloth film, I saw the shadow approach. "That makes it last longer. Children these days would bust out of sheet-metal clothes. They so rough."

"That is a very good job, Mrs. Henderson. You should be proud. You can put your dress back on, Marguerite."

"No ma'am. Pride is a sin. And 'cording to the Good Book, it goeth before a fall."

"That's right. So the Bible says. It's a good thing to keep in mind."

I wouldn't look at either of them. Momma hadn't thought that taking off my dress in front of Mrs. Flowers would kill me stone dead. If I had refused, she would have thought I was trying to be "womanish" and might have remembered St. Louis. Mrs. Flowers had known that I would be embarrassed and that was even worse.

com • pe • tent • ly
(käm´ pə tənt lē) *adv.*, capably

```
┌─ DURING READING ─┐
│ Use Reading Strategies │
│ Make Inferences What do │
│ Momma's actions tell you │
│ about her?          Ⓔ │
└──────────────────┘
```

MRS. FLOWERS **285**

Teach the Model

Analyze Literature
Characterization Ask students what this statement reveals about Maya's self-esteem. Ask: "Is she confident?" **Ⓒ**

Analyze Literature
Setting In this time and place, most people could not afford store-bought clothes. It was common for women to do a lot of sewing. **Ⓓ**

Use Reading Strategies
Make Inferences *Answer:* She is proud of her work. Also, she believes that Marguerite should not feel ashamed about taking off her clothes in front of Mrs. Flowers. **Ⓔ**

Writing Skills

Personal Letter
Remind students that a personal letter is a form of personal writing that you share with a friend, acquaintance, or family member. As such, its style is less formal than that of a business letter.

In the following example, select the form that is appropriate for a personal letter.

1. Salutation:
   a. Dear Mrs. Hasan:
   b. Hi Uncle Bobo, *(personal)*
2. Complimentary close:
   a. Your favorite niece, *(personal)*
   b. Sincerely,

MRS. FLOWERS **285**

Earlier in her autobiography, Maya Angelou tells of a traumatic childhood event that occurred when she was about seven and a half. Afterward, she became mute for about five years. She was able to speak but chose not to. Apparently, Mrs. Flowers has an idea to get her to talk again. **A**

Use Reading Skills
Distinguish Fact from Opinion
Answer: Angelou's memorization of Mrs. Flowers's words may be a fact. However, it can't be proven that Mrs. Flowers actually said them. **B**

I picked up the groceries and went out to wait in the hot sunshine. It would be fitting if I got a sunstroke and died before they came outside. Just dropped dead on the slanting porch.

There was a little path beside the rocky road, and Mrs. Flowers walked in front swinging her arms and picking her way over the stones.

A She said, without turning her head, to me, "I hear you're doing very good school work, Marguerite, but that it's all written. The teachers report that they have trouble getting you to talk in class." We passed the triangular farm on our left and the path widened to allow us to walk together. I hung back in the separate unasked and unanswerable questions.

"Come and walk along with me, Marguerite." I couldn't have refused even if I wanted to. She pronounced my name so nicely. Or more correctly, she spoke each word with such clarity that I was certain a foreigner who didn't understand English could have understood her.

"Now no one is going to make you talk—possibly no one can. But bear in mind, language is man's way of communicating with his fellow man and it is language alone which separates him from the lower animals." That was a totally new idea to me, and I would need time to think about it.

"Your grandmother says you read a lot. Every chance you get. That's good, but not good enough. Words mean more than what is set down on paper. It takes the human voice to <u>infuse</u> them with the shades of deeper meaning."

I memorized the part about the human voice infusing words. It seemed so valid and poetic.

She said she was going to give me some books and that I not only must read them, I must read them aloud. She suggested that I try to make a sentence sound in as many different ways as possible.

"I'll accept no excuse if you return a book to me that has been badly handled." My imagination boggled at the punishment I would deserve if in fact I did abuse a book of Mrs. Flowers'. Death would be too kind and brief.

The odors in the house surprised me. Somehow I had never connected Mrs. Flowers with food or eating or any other common experience of common people. There must have been an outhouse, too, but my mind never recorded it.

The sweet scent of vanilla had met us as she opened the door.

"I made tea cookies this morning. You see, I had planned to

> **DURING READING**
>
> **Use Reading Skills**
> **Distinguish Fact from Opinion** What in this paragraph is most likely fact? Can this fact be proven? **B**

in·fuse (in fyüs´) *v.*, introduce gradually, cause to penetrate; instill

---

Differentiated Instruction

Enrichment
Some students might enjoy researching the literary works mentioned here, *Beowulf* and *Oliver Twist.* They can read all or part of these works and report their findings to the class. You might suggest that they find out why Angelou mentions a cup of mead in reference to *Beowulf* and a cup of tea and milk in reference to *Oliver Twist.*

Reading Proficiency
Some students might benefit from working with a partner to review the selection. As they reread each paragraph, partners can discuss its meaning and determine its main idea.

invite you for cookies and lemonade so we could have this little chat. The lemonade is in the icebox."

It followed that Mrs. Flowers would have ice on an ordinary day, when most families in our town bought ice late on Saturdays only a few times during the summer to be used in the wooden ice-cream freezers.

She took the bags from me and disappeared through the kitchen door. I looked around the room that I had never in my wildest fantasies imagined I would see. Browned photographs leered or threatened from the walls and the white, freshly done curtains pushed against themselves and against the wind. I wanted to gobble up the room entire and take it to Bailey, who would help me analyze and enjoy it.

"Have a seat, Marguerite. Over there by the table." She carried a platter covered with a tea towel. Although she warned that she hadn't tried her hand at baking sweets for some time, I was certain that like everything else about her the cookies would be perfect.

They were flat round wafers, slightly browned on the edges and butter-yellow in the center. With the cold lemonade they were sufficient for childhood's lifelong diet. Remembering my manners, I took nice little lady-like bites off the edges. She said she had made them expressly for me and that she had a few in the kitchen that I could take home to my brother. So I jammed one whole cake in my mouth and the rough crumbs scratched the insides of my jaws, and if I hadn't had to swallow, it would have been a dream come true.

As I ate she began the first of what we later called "my lessons in living." She said that I must always be intolerant of ignorance but understanding of illiteracy.[8] That some people, unable to go to school were more educated and even more intelligent than college professors. She encouraged me to listen carefully to what country people called mother wit. That in those homely sayings was couched the collective wisdom of generations.

When I finished the cookies she brushed off the table and brought a thick, small book from the bookcase. I had read *A Tale of Two Cities*[9] and found it up to my standards as a romantic novel. She opened the first page and I heard poetry for the first time in my life.

"It was the best of times and the worst of times..." Her voice slid in and curved down through and over the words. She was nearly singing. I wanted to look at the pages. Were they the same that I had

---

8. **illiteracy.** Inability to read or write
9. ***A Tale of Two Cities.*** Novel by Charles Dickens about English people who get caught up in the French Revolution

---

DURING READING

Literary Element
Autobiography What sort of tone does Angelou use when describing things associated with Mrs. Flowers? **C**

Teach the Model

Analyze Literature
Autobiography *Answer:* She uses a tone that expresses awe and wonder. **C**

Literary Connection
A Tale of Two Cities *A Tale of Two Cities* is a historical novel by Charles Dickens that played against the backdrop of the French Revolution. Its opening lines, read by Mrs. Flowers, and its closing lines, quoted by Angelou later, are among the most famous lines in English literature. **D**

Use Reading Strategies
Visualize Many readers, young and old alike, breeze over or entirely skip descriptive portions of stories, claiming that they slow down or interrupt the action. However, if these readers are able to tap into their own sensory experiences, the importance of description in story writing and its connection to plot becomes more apparent and palpable. This section of the story is packed with imagery and sensory details. In order to foster appreciation of their significance to the character development of Mrs. Flowers and Marguerite (and thereby the plot), ask students to recall specific scents, sights, or sounds that made an impression on them.

Speaking & Listening Skills

Oral Tradition
Allow students the opportunity to appreciate "Mrs. Flowers" in the way that Marguerite learned to appreciate literature—by telling it aloud and listening to the power of its words. Pair students, and have them read to each other parts of the story that are particularly poignant to them. Remind them to employ pacing, expression, and tone to aid their partners in grasping the import of their selections.

After each student reads his or her part, the pairs should discuss and take notes on both the explicit and implicit ideas in the passage. Did reading the passage aloud cause students to notice anything they may have missed when reading it silently? Students should share their findings with the class.

Use Reading Skills
Distinguish Fact from Opinion
Is this statement an opinion or a universal truth? Responses will vary. Some students might say that the statement is an opinion, since it cannot be scientifically proven. Others might believe it to be a universal truth that could be proven with a comprehensive poll of children and adults. Students should provide reasons to back up their statements. **Ⓐ**

 You may want to ask students to write a journal entry or quick write, or divide students into discussion groups or lead a whole-class discussion about this question. *Answer:* Students should give concrete and specific text-related personal reasons why they were affected by written and spoken language. Explanation for how texts in general can affect readers may include greater understanding of self and others, different ways of looking at issues, awareness of cultures, and ways to solve problems.

read? Or were there notes, music, lined on the pages, as in a hymn book? Her sounds began cascading gently. I knew from listening to a thousand preachers that she was nearing the end of her reading, and I hadn't really heard, heard to understand, a single word.

"How do you like that?"

It occurred to me that she expected a response. The sweet vanilla flavor was still on my tongue and her reading was a wonder in my ears. I had to speak.

I said, "Yes, ma'am." It was the least I could do, but it was the most also.

"There's one more thing. Take this book of poems and memorize one for me. Next time you pay me a visit, I want you to recite."

I have tried often to search behind the sophistication of years for the enchantment I so easily found in those gifts. The essence[10] escapes but its aura[11] remains. To be allowed, no, invited, into the private lives of strangers, and to share their joys and fears, was a chance to exchange the Southern bitter wormwood for a cup of mead with Beowulf[12] or a hot cup of tea and milk with Oliver Twist.[13] When I said aloud, "It is a far, far better thing that I do, than I have ever done..." tears of love filled my eyes at my selflessness.

On that first day, I ran down the hill and into the road (few cars ever came along it) and had the good sense to stop running before I reached the Store.

I was liked, and what a difference it made. I was respected not as Mrs. Henderson's grandchild or Bailey's sister but for just being Marguerite Johnson.

Ⓐ Childhood's logic never asks to be proved (all conclusions are absolute). I didn't question why Mrs. Flowers had singled me out for attention, nor did it occur to me that Momma might have asked her to give me a little talking to. All I cared about was that she had made tea cookies for *me* and read to *me* from her favorite book. It was enough to prove that she liked me. ❖

---

10. **essence.** Most important quality of something that makes it what it is; something in its purest form
11. **aura.** Distinctive quality or atmosphere coming from a person, place, or thing
12. **Beowulf.** Famous character from literature
13. **Oliver Twist.** Famous character from literature

 Marguerite is very moved by the language of poetry and novels and by the lives of characters in books. What books or poems have had that effect on you? In general, how can the reading of novels and poems expand and affect the reader's world?

TEACHING NOTE

Ask the Author
Place students in pairs, and ask them to brainstorm questions for a hypothetical interview with a young Maya Angelou. Direct them to focus their queries on how her experience with the spoken word, both in literature and in the oral tradition of her community, has altered her perception of herself and the world around her. Model a question such as: "How has the spoken word affected the way you write?" Then challenge them to answer the questions as Marguerite might. Finally, invite pairs to choose the role of either interviewer or Marguerite and conduct mock interviews for a class audience.

Find Meaning

1. (a) Why does Marguerite find Mrs. Flowers so appealing? (b) Why do you think she compares her to white people? (c) What does this tell you about how Marguerite views most of the people she knows?

2. (a) What does Mrs. Flowers teach Marguerite in her first "lesson in living"? (b) How might that lesson affect how Marguerite views her Grandmother?

Analyze Literature

Autobiography An autobiography tells the story of person's life in his or her own words. Sometimes writers include present-day comments on what is happening in their narrative. A time line can help you keep track of what events are actually taking place within the timeframe of the narrative. Use a time line to record the events in "Mrs. Flowers." Remember that events can be emotional as well as physical. On your time line, include Marguerite's reactions to the events. How does Marguerite change from the beginning of the story to the end?

Make Judgments

3. From the beginning of the story, the author focuses on how Mrs. Flowers speaks and the sound of her voice. What is the effect of this?

4. What is the overall effect of the author's description of what Marguerite is given to eat and drink at Mrs. Flowers's house?

5. (a) Why is the attention Marguerite gets from Mrs. Flowers so important? (b) What does that tell you about how Marguerite usually sees herself in relationship to other people?

Mrs. Flowers stops to buy provisions at Momma's store.

Extend Understanding

Writing Options

Creative Writing Imagine you are Marguerite. Write a **letter** to Mrs. Flowers, thanking her for the cookies, lemonade, and books.

Expository Writing Locate a speech given by Maya Angelou. Write a short **essay** analyzing the words, phrases, and literary devices she uses and why she might have chosen them to appeal to the audience.

Lifelong Learning

Write a Biography Locate more information on Maya Angelou. Then write a short biography and present it to the class.

Critical Literacy

Ask Questions Create a series of questions to ask Maya Angelou about the excerpt. What would you like to know more about? Compare your questions with those of a classmate.

MW Go to **www.mirrorsandwindows.com** for more.

Find Meaning

1. (a) She is elegant and educated. (b) Marguerite has only seen white people portrayed elegantly in movies and books. (c) She views them as unrefined and unintelligent.

2. (a) People without formal education are often intelligent and wise. (b) Marguerite might be less judgmental about the way her grandmother speaks and seek to learn from her, too.

Make Judgments

3. It foreshadows Marguerite finding her own voice. It also shows that Marguerite is acutely aware of the spoken word's importance.

4. The effect is a moment in which Marguerite is overjoyed and feels special. The author uses positive sensory details like butter-yellow to show Marguerite's delight.

5. (a) Mrs. Flowers makes Marguerite feel liked and respected. (b) She thinks people don't see her individuality and don't like her for who she is.

Analyze Literature

Autobiography *Answer:* Marguerite starts speaking and realizes the power of oral expression. She learns that she is appreciated for who she is and that she should appreciate the intelligence of those who are not formally educated.

Rubrics for Writing Options

You can adapt this as a checklist for students to use as they write.

Creative Writing

☐ Does the letter reflect Marguerite's personality?

☐ Does the letter reflect the details of the experience?

☐ Does the letter explain why the visit was important?

Expository Writing

☐ Does the essay analyze the choice of words, phrases, and literary devices in a speech by Maya Angelou?

☐ Does the essay discuss why Angelou might have chosen to use these techniques to appeal to the audience?

Ishi in Two Worlds

A Biography by Theodora Kroeber

Preview the Model

At a Glance
Guided Reading: Reading Model
- Reading Level: Challenging
- Difficulty Consideration: Vocabulary
- Ease Factor: Intriguing plot

Objectives
Studying this lesson will enable students to
- use reading strategies such as analyzing author's perspective
- define *biography* and recognize that Kroeber is recounting a person's life
- describe the literary accomplishments of Theodora Kroeber and explain the historical significance of her writing
- appreciate the story of a man adapting to the modern world

Launch the Lesson
Have students do an Internet search on Ishi, looking for answers to these questions: "When was Ishi born? What did Ishi do while living at the university museum in San Francisco? What prompted the Smithsonian to return Ishi's brain to the Yana? Who else has studied Ishi's story, and what insights do they offer?" Once they gather information, encourage students to share their findings with the whole class.

Build Background
Historical Context This selection tells the story of Ishi, a Native American from the Yahi tribe, who encountered mainstream America in 1911. Upon his arrival in California, he was unable to communicate with anyone and was placed in jail. Later Ishi was brought to the museum at the University of California, where he lived until his death in 1916.

Reader's Context How could you communicate to someone if you had no common language or common experiences?

Set Purpose
Description Writing that portrays a character, object, or scene is **description.** Descriptions make use of **sensory details,** words and phrases that describe how things look, sound, smell, taste, or feel. As you read, be aware of how the author uses sensory details in descriptions of people, events, and setting.

Analyze Literature
Biography A **biography** is the story of a person's life told by another person. Sometimes the author includes background information on the subject of the biography. As you read, pay attention to the order in which things happened to Ishi. Note how events that Ishi might not have experienced directly still had an effect on his life.

Use Reading Skills
Author's Perspective A perspective is a way of looking at or regarding a subject or topic. As you read this biography, think about the author's perspective on her subject. How did the author's background, knowledge, and opinions shape her telling of the events in Ishi's life?

Preview Vocabulary
e•ma•ci•ate (i mā´shē āt´) *v.*, cause to lose flesh and become very thin

un•wont•ed (ən wôn´ təd) *adj.*, rare, unusual

ground•less (groun[d]´ ləs) *adj.*, not justified; having no real basis

ad•ja•cent (ə jā´ sənt) *adj.*, next to; adjoining

Meet the Author
Theodora Kroeber (1897–1979) was the wife of famous American anthropologist Alfred Kroeber (1876–1960). Alfred Kroeber, who knew and studied Ishi, provided much of the information for his wife's biography of Ishi. Theodora Kroeber felt that it was her responsibility to write a biography of Ishi. After publishing the book in 1961, a year after her husband's death, Theodora Kroeber was overwhelmed by the number of emotional responses to Ishi's story. She called the outpouring in response to Ishi's story "the greatest human experience of my life."

(Opposite page) Ishi, the last Native American from the Yahi tribe.

Words in Use

Preview Vocabulary
emaciate, 292
unwonted, 292
groundless, 293
adjacent, 294

Selection Words
uncomprehend-
  ingly, 293

posterity, 294
miscellaneous, 295
pantomime, 296

Teaching Words
mainstream, 290
anthropologist, 290

overwhelmed, 290
outpouring, 290
cremated, 293
enraged, 293
repatriate, 293
incident, 294

KEY TERMS
DESCRIPTION, 290
BIOGRAPHY, 290
AUTHOR'S PERSPECTIVE, 290
HYPOTHESIS, 300

Common Core State Standards

Reading Literature
RL.1

Reading Informational
RI.2, RI.3, RI.6

Writing
W.9

Language
L.6

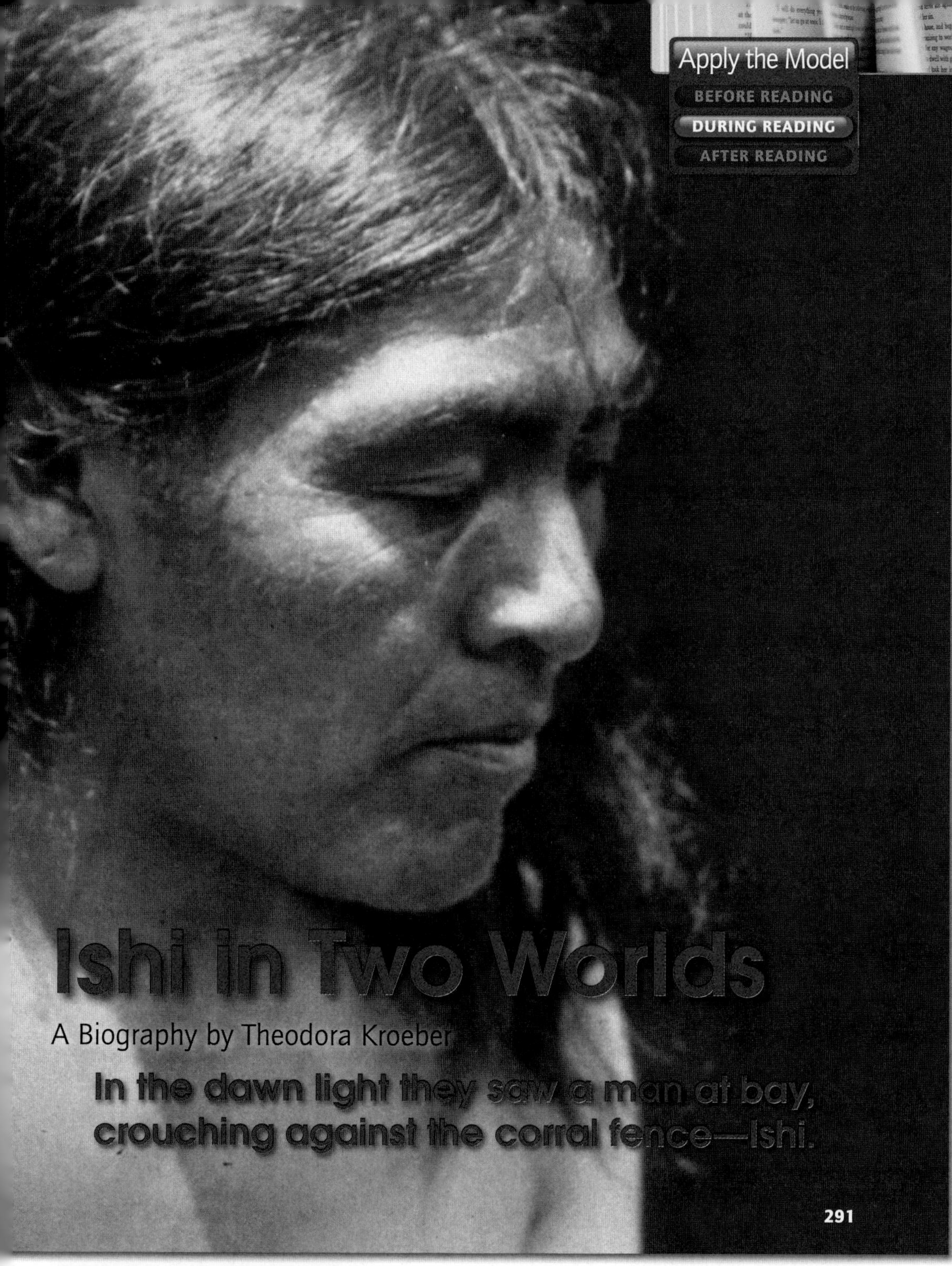

Ishi in Two Worlds

A Biography by Theodora Kroeber

In the dawn light they saw a man at bay, crouching against the corral fence—Ishi.

291

Teach the Model

Summary

On August 29, 1911, a man emerged from the wilderness and came to rest at a slaughterhouse in Oroville, California. The last living member of the Yahi Indians, he was frightened and starving. To protect him from prying eyes, the local sheriff placed him in a jail cell. Professor Waterman eventually succeeded in communicating with him. Waterman brought Ishi to the University of California's Museum of Anthropology, where he lived the remainder of his life. He taught those with whom he came in contact invaluable elements of the Yahi culture, including their history, language, skills, and beliefs.

 The Mirrors & Windows questions at the end of this selection focus on the theme of compassion. Before reading, ask students if they think it is right to isolate people for the purpose of studying them. Does the world today allow such practice?

Program Resources

Planning and Assessment
Program Planning Guide, Selection Lesson Plan
E-Lesson Planner
Assessment Guide, Lesson Test
ExamView

Technology Tools
Interactive Student Text on CD
Visual Teaching Package
Audio Library
mirrorsandwindows.com

Meeting the Standards
Nonfiction: Unit 3, Guided Reading, pp. 27–32

Differentiating Instruction
English Language Learners, Author's Perspective, pp. 96–107

Common Core State Standards

Reading Informational
RI.3, RI.6, RI.9
Writing
W.9
Language
L.6

Analyze Literature

Biography *Answer:* Ishi was found in a rural setting. **A**

Use Reading Skills

Author's Perspective *Answer:* It seems that she feels that the act was justified. She presents it as a way the sheriff tried to protect Ishi from curious townspeople and outsiders. **B**

Use Reading Strategies

Visualize Have students take a moment to visualize Ishi at the slaughterhouse. Ask: "If you were making a movie of the scene, how would you have Ishi react to the white men as they approached him? How would the dogs behave?" **C**

Analyze Literature

Biography *Answer:* It conveys that he has not eaten for a long time and that he is unwell and scared and probably has been confused and lost for a while. It also conveys that there is something agreeable, sensitive, and expressive about him, though that was not apparent when he was first found. **D**

Prologue: OUTSIDE THE SLAUGHTER HOUSE

> **DURING READING**
>
> **Analyze Literature**
> **Biography** What does this tell you about the setting where Ishi was first found? **A**

The story of Ishi begins for us early in the morning of the twenty-ninth day of August in the year 1911 and in the corral of a slaughter house. It begins with the sharp barking of dogs which roused the sleeping butchers. In the dawn light they saw a man at bay, crouching against the corral fence—Ishi.

They called off the dogs. Then, in some considerable excitement, they telephoned the sheriff in Oroville two or three miles away to say that they were holding a wild man and would he please come and take him off their hands. Sheriff and deputies arrived shortly, approaching the corral with guns at the ready. The wild man made no move to resist capture, quietly allowing himself to be handcuffed.

The sheriff, J. B. Webber, saw that the man was an Indian, and that he was at the limit of exhaustion and fear. He could learn nothing further, since his prisoner understood no English. Not knowing what to do with him, he motioned the Indian into the wagon with himself and his deputies, drove him to the county jail in Oroville, and locked him up in the cell for the insane. There, Sheriff Webber reasoned, while he tried to discover something more about his captive he could at least protect him from the excited curiosity of the townspeople and the outsiders who were already pouring in from miles around to see the wild man.

> **DURING READING**
>
> **Use Reading Skills**
> **Author's Perspective** What is the author's attitude about the sheriff locking up Ishi? **B**

e•ma•ci•ate
(i mā´shē āt´) *v.*, cause to lose flesh and become very thin

The wild man was <u>emaciated</u> to starvation, his hair was burned off close to his head, he was naked except for a ragged scrap of ancient covered-wagon canvas which he wore around his shoulders like a poncho. He was a man of middle height, the long bones, painfully apparent, were straight, strong, and not heavy, the skin color somewhat paler in tone than the full copper characteristic of most Indians. The black eyes were wary and guarded now, but were set wide in a broad face, the mouth was generous and agreeably molded. For the rest, the Indian's extreme fatigue and fright heightened a sensitiveness which was always there, while it masked the usual mobility and expressiveness of the features.

> **DURING READING**
>
> **Analyze Literature**
> **Biography** What does this description convey about Ishi? **D**

un•wont•ed
(ən wôn´ təd) *adj.*, rare, unusual

It should be said that the sheriff's action in locking Ishi up was neither stupid nor brutal given the circumstances. Until Sheriff Webber took the <u>unwonted</u> measure of keeping them out by force people filled the jail to gaze through the bars of his cell at the captive. Later, Ishi spoke with some diffidence[1] of this, his first contact with white men. He said that he was put up in a fine house

---

1. **diffidence.** Shyness; lack of self-confidence

Speaking & Listening Skills

Panel Discussion

Divide the class into groups of four or five. Tell them that they will be preparing a panel discussion to present to another group. The subject of the discussion will be whether a person like Ishi should be protected and studied like he was at the museum or encouraged to live his life freely, no matter the cost. Next, have groups work together, taking turns in speaking and listening roles. Remind speakers to use a variety of grammatical structures, sentence types and lengths, and connecting words to express their views in an interesting and cohesive way. Also remind listeners of their responsibilities: to pay attention to speakers, focus on the discussion's content, listen for main ideas, and ask questions when the speakers are finished.

where he was kindly treated and well fed by a big chief. That he would eat nothing and drink nothing during his first days of captivity Ishi did not say. Such was the case; nor did he allow himself to sleep at first. Quite possibly it was a time of such strain and terror that he suppressed all memory of it. Or he may have felt that it was unkind to recall his suspicions which proved in the event groundless, for Ishi expected in those first days to be put to death. He knew of white men only that they were the murderers of his own people. It was natural that he should expect, once in their power, to be shot or hanged or killed by poisoning.

Meanwhile, local Indians and half-breeds as well as Mexicans and Spaniards tried to talk to the prisoner in Maidu, Wintu, and Spanish. Ishi listened patiently but uncomprehendingly, and when he spoke it was in a tongue which meant no more to the Indians there than to the whites.

The story of the capture of a wild Indian became headline news in the local valley papers, and reached the San Francisco dailies in forms more or less lurid[2] and elaborated. The story in the *San Francisco Call* was accompanied by a picture, the first of many to come later. In another newspaper story, a Maidu Indian, Conway by name, "issued a statement" that he had conversed with the wild man. Conway's moment of publicity was brief since the wild man understood nothing of what he said.

These accounts were read by Professors Kroeber and Waterman, anthropologists at the University of California, who were at once alerted to the human drama behind the event and to its possible importance, the more particularly because it recalled to them an earlier episode on San

---

ground·less
(groun[d]′ ləs) *adj.*, not justified; having no real basis

DURING READING
Use Reading Strategies
Clarify What did Ishi expect might happen during his first days in captivity? Why? **E**

SCIENCE ▶▶ CONNECTION

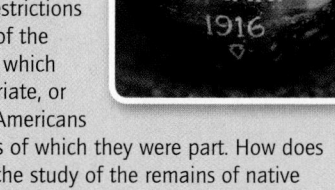

National Museum of the American Indian Act of 1989 After Ishi died, his body was cremated and his brain was sent to the Smithsonian Institution for study. At that time, scientists commonly studied the remains of native peoples, a practice that enraged many Native American groups. This opposition eventually led to restrictions and to the National Museum of the American Indian Act of 1989, which required the museum to repatriate, or return, the remains of Native Americans to the Native American groups of which they were part. How does the attitude that encouraged the study of the remains of native peoples reflect the way that Ishi was treated when he was alive? **F**

---

2. **lurid.** Startling; sensational

Teach the Model

Use Reading Strategies
Clarify *Answer:* Ishi expected to be put to death. His only knowledge of white people was that they killed his people. **E**

Science Connection
National Museum of the American Indian Act of 1989
Answer: The view that American Indians were physically and mentally different than people of European backgrounds promoted the study of American Indian remains and determined how Ishi was to be treated under museum supervision. While it seems that Ishi was well cared for, in terms of his basic needs, it is apparent that researchers treated him more as an experiment and a chance for historical and scientific breakthroughs than as a person. It is unclear, however, if Ishi was entirely taken advantage of or if he agreed with their methods. **F**

Cultural Connection
Yahi Taboo Yahi tradition forbade any member of the society to say his or her own name or ask it of another. Because Ishi was the last of his people, he was morally bound to keep his real name secret, even from those closest to him. Had a friend or family member been alive, he or she would have been able to tell anyone what Ishi's people named him at birth. Therefore, researchers at the museum gave him the name *Ishi*, which simply means *man*.

Differentiated Instruction

English Language Learning
Point out the following words and expressions:
half-breed — derogatory term for a person of mixed descent, 293
Maidu — Native American language, 293
Wintu — Native American language, 293
padre — priest or chaplain, 294
Yana — Native American people, 295
siwini — Yana term for "yellow pine," 295

Reading Skills

Use Graphic Organizers
Remind students that using a graphic organizer is a good way to keep track of the similarities and differences between important figures in literary works. Have them create a graphic organizer, such as a Venn diagram or a character map, to keep notes about similarities and differences between Ishi and Professor Waterman. Discuss the effectiveness, or lack thereof, of their chosen organizer.

History Connection

California Missions Inform students about the relationship between the California missions and the Native Americans. The chain of 21 missions, established between 1769 and 1823, intended to bring Christianity to the Native Americans. The padres initiated a system similar to serfdom, in which the Native Americans were largely exploited—they were forced to work for little compensation. **A**

Use Reading Strategies

Make Inferences *Answer:* They were devalued and their lives were not considered important. **B**

Analyze Literature

Description *Answer:* Responses will vary. The use of the phrase "skeletal outline" evokes the image of a skeleton, which has no personality. This reinforces the fact that not much was known about the woman or her people. The allusion to a skeleton also reinforces the tragedy of the woman's way of life. **C**

Analyze Literature

Biography *Answer:* The anthropologists remember that the surveyors had surprised and routed a small tribe of Native American people. The anthropologists think that maybe Ishi could belong to these people. **D**

DURING READING

Use Reading Strategies
Make Inferences What does this tell you about attitudes towards Native Americans in 1835? **B**

DURING READING

Analyze Literature
Description What is the effect of this description? **C**

DURING READING

Analyze Literature
Biography What incident three years earlier do the anthropologists remember? How does that incident relate to Ishi? **D**

ad·ja·cent (ə jā´ sənt)
adj., next to; adjoining

Nicolas Island, one of the Channel Islands of the Pacific Ocean some seventy miles offshore from Santa Barbara.

A In 1835, the padres of Mission Santa Barbara transferred the San Nicolas Indians to the mainland. A few minutes after the boat, which was carrying the Indians, had put off from the island, it was found that one baby had been left behind. It is not easy to land a boat on San Nicolas; the captain decided against returning for the baby; the baby's mother jumped overboard, and was last seen swimming toward the island. Half-hearted efforts made to find her in subsequent weeks were unsuccessful: it was believed that she had drowned in the rough surf. In 1853, eighteen years later, seal hunters in the Channel waters reported seeing a woman on San Nicolas, and a boatload of men from Santa Barbara went in search of her. They found her, a last survivor of her tribe. Her baby, as well as all her people who had been removed to the Mission, had died. She lived only a few months after her "rescue" and died without anyone having been able to communicate with her, leaving to posterity this skeletal outline of her grim story, and four words which someone remembered from her lost language and recorded as she said them. It so happens that these four words identify her language as having been Shoshonean, related to Indian languages of the Los Angeles area, not to those of Santa Barbara.

Another reason for the anthropologists' particular interest in the wild man was that three years earlier, in 1908, some surveyors working a few miles north of Oroville had surprised and routed a little band of Indians. After hearing of this incident, Waterman with two guides had spent several weeks in an unsuccessful search for the Indians: the wild man of Oroville might well be one of them.

On August 31, 1911, Kroeber sent the following telegram: "Sheriff Butte County. Newspapers report capture wild Indian speaking language other tribes totally unable to understand. Please confirm or deny by collect telegram and if story correct hold Indian till arrival Professor State University who will take charge and be responsible for him. Matter important account aboriginal[3] history."

The sheriff's office must have confirmed the report promptly: Waterman took the train to Oroville the same day. That he and Kroeber correctly "guessed" Ishi's tribe and language was no *tour de force*[4] of intuition. The guess was based on field work with Indians all up and down California; they knew that Oroville was <u>adjacent</u> to

---

3. **aboriginal.** Native
4. ***tour de force.*** Feat of skill, strength, or brilliance (French)

Differentiated Instruction

Enrichment

Encourage students to research the Yana. Ask them to try to answer the following questions:

1. What are the subgroups of the Yana?
2. In what part of the country do the Yana live?
3. What kinds of food do the Yana eat?
4. What spiritual beliefs do they follow?
5. What is their history of relations with the United States government?

Challenge students to summarize their findings in a report or put their findings in a visual display such as a poster or bulletin board.

country which formerly belonged to the Yana Indians; presumably the strange Indian would be a Yana. He might even be from the southernmost tribe of Yana, believed to be extinct. If this were true, neither they nor anyone so far as they knew could speak his language. But if he were a Northern or Central Yana, there were files of expertly recorded vocabularies for those dialects from two old Yanas, Batwi, called Sam, and Chidaimiya, called Betty Brown.

With a copy of Batwi's and Chidaimiya's vocabularies in his pocket, Waterman arrived in Oroville where he identified himself to Sheriff Webber and was taken to visit the wild man. Waterman found a weary, badgered Indian sitting in his cell, wearing the butcher's apron he had been given at the slaughter house, courteously making what answer he could in his own language to a barrage[5] of questions thrown at him in English, Spanish, and assorted Indian from a miscellaneous set of visitors. **E**

Waterman sat down beside Ishi, and with his phonetically[6] transcribed list of Northern and Central Yana words before him, began to read from it, repeating each word, pronouncing it as well as he knew how. Ishi was attentive but unresponding until, discouragingly far down the list, Waterman said *siwini* which means yellow pine, at the same time tapping the pine framework of the cot on which they sat. Recognition lighted up the Indian's face. Waterman said the magic word again; Ishi repeated it after him, correcting his pronunciation, and for the next moments the two of them banged at the wood of the cot, telling each other over and over, *siwini, siwini!* **F**

With the difficult first sound recognition achieved, others followed. Ishi was indeed one of the lost tribe, a Yahi; in other words, he was from the southernmost Yana. Waterman was learning that the unknown Yahi dialect differed considerably but not to the point of unintelligibility[7] from the two northern ones of his list. Together he and Ishi tried out more and more words and phrases: they were beginning to communicate. After a while Ishi ventured to ask Waterman, *I ne ma Yahi?* "Are you an Indian?" Waterman answered that he was. The hunted look left Ishi's eyes—here was a friend. He knew as well as did his friend that Waterman was not an Indian. The question was a tentative[8] and subtle way of reassuring and being reassured, not an easy thing to do when the

---

5. **barrage.** Heavy attack
6. **phonetically.** Concerning spoken language
7. **unintelligibility.** Not being understandable
8. **tentative.** Hesitant; uncertain

> Waterman said *siwini* which means yellow pine... Recognition lighted up the Indian's face.

Teach the Model

Use Reading Strategies
Make Predictions Ask students to predict what will happen when Waterman meets Ishi. Model a response: "Waterman will try to communicate with Ishi in the Yana dialects he is familiar with but will encounter some difficulty with this method." **E**

Literary Connection
The Kroeber Family Ursula K. Le Guin (b. 1929), the daughter of Alfred and Theodora Kroeber, has carried on their literary tradition. She is a writer of science fiction, fantasy, poetry, and essays. Among her best-known books are *The Earthsea Cycle,* *The Left Hand of Darkness,* and the *Catwings* series.

Use Reading Strategies
Make Inferences What inferences can students make about Waterman's phonetically transcribed list of Yana words? Model a response that suggests that Waterman's sources, Batwi and Chidaimiya, either pronounced the words differently than the way Ishi did or that Waterman's phonetic transcriptions were not accurate. **F**

Grammar Skills

Collective Nouns
Remind students that collective nouns are groups made up of individuals. They may be singular or plural, depending on whether the group acts as a whole or individually.

Discuss collective nouns in this paragraph.

The film showed a <u>herd</u> of elephants doing different tasks to raise young family members. Once, a <u>pack</u> of hyenas hunted an elephant. The filming <u>crew</u> shot terrific footage of animals on the African plains.

History Connection

Demise of the Yahi The fate of Yahi culture was one of many tragic consequences spawned by western settlement. The Yahi were a subgroup of the Yana, whose numbers fluctuated around three thousand prior to the arrival of white settlers. The Yana relocated to California's Mount Lassen foothills and remained there for close to three thousand years. Miners and ranchers moved into the foothills after James Marshall discovered gold in 1848, swiftly polluting streams and eventually depleting the Yana's natural resources. Fighting between the Yana and settlers ensued, and by 1861, the Southern Yana were annihilated. Three years later, the Northern and Central Yana population dropped from two thousand to less than fifty. The Three Knolls Massacre of 1865 left thirty Yahi alive, half of whom were murdered later by cattlemen. The surviving band of about fifteen individuals managed to cloak themselves in silence and their surroundings for nearly forty years. Ishi's mother died early in 1911, and he lived by himself until his discovery at the butchers' corral in Oroville.

Use Reading Strategies

Make Inferences *Answer:* These actions might reveal that the Yahi valued open expression of important experiences and the emotions with which they are tied. **A**

DURING READING

Use Reading Strategies
Make Inferences What do these actions reveal about Ishi's culture? **A**

meaningful shared sounds are few. Between meetings with Ishi, Waterman wrote to Kroeber from Oroville:

This man [Ishi] is undoubtedly wild. He has pieces of deer thong[9] in place of ornaments in the lobes of his ears and a wooden plug in the septum[10] of his nose. He recognizes most of my Yana words and a fair proportion of his own seem to be identical [with mine]. Some of his, however, are either quite different or else my pronunciation of them is very bad, because he doesn't respond to them except by pointing to his ears and asking to have them repeated. "No!" *k'u'i*—it is not—is one. "Yes!" *aha*, pleases him immensely. I think I get a few endings that don't occur in Northern Yana on nouns, for example. Phonetically, he has some of the prettiest cracked consonants I ever heard in my life. He will be a splendid informant, especially for phonetics, for he speaks very clearly. I have not communicated with him successfully enough to get his story, but what can I expect? He has a yarn to tell about his woman, who had a baby on her back and seems to have been drowned, except that he is so *cheerful* about it.

Waterman misunderstood. In the excitement and relief of having someone to talk to, Ishi poured out confidences and recollections which Waterman could by no means comprehend even with the aid of an elaborate pantomime. Ishi's seeming pleasure was not in the recollected event, but was rather a near hysteria[11] induced by human interchange of speech and feelings too long denied.

Waterman's letters continue:

We had a lot of conversation this morning about deer hunting and making acorn soup, but I got as far as my list of words would take me. If I am not mistaken, he's full of religion—bathing at sunrise, putting out pinches of tobacco where the lightning strikes,

---

9. **thong.** Strip of leather
10. **septum.** Membrane between nostrils
11. **hysteria.** Outbreak of wild, uncontrolled excitement

Differentiated Instruction

Reading Proficiency

Encourage students to use context clues to define difficult terms such as *phonetics* and *induced*. Model this strategy by saying: "I can determine the approximate meaning of *phonetics* by looking at words surrounding the term. Prior to using it, he says that Ishi 'will be a splendid informant.' So I know that *phonetics* informs people of something. Waterman then qualifies his thought by explaining that Ishi 'speaks very clearly.' Now I know that *phonetics* informs people about language and can assume that it is a type of language study."

etc. I'll try rattlesnake on him when I go back after lunch. It was a picnic to see him open his eyes when he heard Yana from me. And he looked over my shoulder at the paper in a most mystified way. He knew at once where I got my inspiration....We showed him some arrows last night, and we could hardly get them away from him. He showed us how he flaked the points, singed[12] the edges of the feathering, and put on the sinew wrappings.

B

Even before Waterman had established a thin line of communication with Ishi, the sheriff had become convinced that his prisoner was neither insane nor dangerous. There were no charges against him; he did not properly belong in jail. The question was, what in place of the shelter of the jail was there for him? Waterman offered to take him to San Francisco. Phones and telegraph wires were kept busy for the next forty-eight hours between Oroville and San Francisco, where the University's Museum of Anthropology then was, and between the museum and Washington, D.C.

DURING READING

C **Make Connections**
How does this passage affect your feelings for Ishi?

While these negotiations were going forward, the sheriff, at Waterman's suggestion, sent a deputy to Redding to find and bring back with him the old man, Batwi, to act as interpreter-companion to Ishi. Batwi came, and although he patronized[13] Ishi outrageously, he was for the present a help. He and Ishi could communicate in Yana, not without some difficulty, but quite fully. Meanwhile, the Indian Bureau in Washington telegraphed permission for Ishi to go to the University's museum whose staff was to be responsible for him at least until there was opportunity for fuller investigation. The sheriff of Butte County was greatly relieved; he at once made out a receipt of release from the jail to the University. This remarkable document seems not to have survived the years of moving and storing in odd corners which has been the fate of the museum files and specimens.[14]

D

In any case, Waterman, Batwi, and Ishi, with the release and government permission, left Oroville on Labor Day, September 4, arriving in San Francisco somewhat before midnight. There remained to Ishi four years and seven months of life, years which were to pass within the shelter of the museum walls at the Affiliated Colleges, or in the hospital next door when he was sick.

Ishi was the last wild Indian in North America, a man of Stone Age culture subjected for the first time when he was past middle age

---

12. **singed.** Burned
13. **patronized.** Acted helpful, but in a snobbish way
14. **specimens.** Artifacts

Teach the Model

Science Connection
Ishi's Bloodline Recent studies by archaeologists suggest that Ishi was of mixed heritage and most likely learned his stonework skills from a relative in the Wintu or Nomalki tribe. Ishi's adaptive skills support this theory. The presumption would add to the tragic nature of Ishi's circumstances, as it would highlight the ancient Yahi's necessity to intermarry with members of other groups, due to dwindling numbers and a cultural taboo against marrying relatives. Most importantly, the theory enriches our notion of Ishi and the Yahis. It casts him not as a cultural, linguistic, and historical phenomenon but as a complex person whose family adapted, contrary to social ideology, to forestall their eventual extinction. **B**

Make Connections
Answer: Responses will vary. Some students might say that it completely humanizes Ishi and makes them feel empathy for his situation. **C**

Analyze Literature
Cultural Setting What does the Indian Bureau in Washington's involvement in Ishi's situation imply about the government's attitude toward American Indians at this time? Model an answer that suggests American Indians seem to have been viewed like wards of the state. **D**

Reading Skills

Understand Sequence of Events
Have students put these events into proper chronological order and then transfer the information to a time line.

- Waterman communicates with Ishi. (3)
- Ishi is taken to San Francisco. (4)
- Ishi is found crouching at the corral. (1)
- Seal hunters find a woman on San Nicolas. (2)

- Surveyors rout a group of natives. (3)
- Padres of Mission Santa Barbara transfer the San Nicolas Indians to the mainland. (1)
- Waterman goes to Oroville. (2)

IRRORS & WINDOWS

Answer: Students might think the decision inhumane and that the anthropologists should have helped him return to a setting similar to that of the Yahi. If Ishi were discovered today, he would probably still be a sensation, but he would not have been isolated for study.

Find Meaning

1. (a) He was taken into custody. (b) He may have been exhausted or afraid.
2. (a) It means "yellow pine." (b) It broke the language barrier.
3. (a) He asked him if he was an Indian. (b) He replied yes. (c) He asked to determine if Waterman was hostile. (d) He was relieved.
4. (a) He went to the University Museum of Anthropology. (b) The sheriff let Ishi go, so other arrangements needed to be made.

Make Judgments

5. (a) He tells his thoughts and feelings through body language. (b) His fear of sleeping near whites shows that his encounters with them have been harmful.
6. They might have confirmed a belief that whites thought of American Indians as less than human.
7. The author seems to feel it was positive. She refers to it as a "shelter" and makes it clear that there was a hospital next door for his care.

---

to twentieth-century culture. He was content that it should be so, participating as fully as he could in the new life. Before examining more closely those astounding few years and what one Stone Age man contributed in so short a time to our understanding of man as such, let us go back to the years of childhood, young manhood, and middle age—almost a whole lifetime. These were years spent by him without experience or understanding of a way of life other than that of a tiny fugitive[15] band of fewer than a dozen souls at most, opposing their ancient Yahi skills and beliefs to an unknown but hostile outside world.

There came the time—months, perhaps two or three years before August, 1911—when Ishi was the only one remaining of the little band, violence from without, old age and illness from within, having brought death to the others. ✣

---

15. fugitive. Someone who has fled from danger or repression

IRRORS & WINDOWS

How would you evaluate the anthropologists' decision to bring Ishi to the university? How would Ishi be treated if he had been discovered today?

Find Meaning

1. (a) What happened to Ishi during his first encounter with the "civilized world"? (b) Why do you think Ishi made no move to resist capture?
2. (a) What does the word *siwini* mean? (b) Why did this word mean so much to Ishi? To Waterman?
3. (a) What was the first question Ishi asked Waterman? (b) How did Waterman respond? (c) Why did Ishi ask Waterman this question? (d) Why did Ishi respond the way he did?
4. (a) Where did Ishi end up going? (b) Why was this decision made?

Make Judgments

5. (a) In what ways does Ishi reveal his thoughts and feelings? (b) What clues does he give about his past experiences with white Americans?
6. In what ways might Ishi's experiences in Oroville and in San Francisco have reinforced his negative thoughts and feelings about white Americans?
7. Evaluate the author's perspective on Ishi being kept in a museum.

Differentiated Instruction

Enrichment

Students captivated by Ishi's stories might be pleased to know that he has not been forgotten. In addition to countless studies of the affair, Jed Riffe and Pamela Roberts produced an award-winning documentary in 1992 called *Ishi: The Last Yahi*. The film includes prudent narration, telling photographs, archival footage, and Ishi's recorded voice. The story that the film presents tracks Ishi's life from childhood through his stay at the university museum. It is available in public libraries throughout the United States.

The article "Yana People to Receive Ishi's Brain" by **Robert Fri** tells of Ishi's remains being returned to the Yana people. Robert Fri is the director of the Smithsonian Institution's National Museum of History. As you read, note how Fri's attitude differs from that of Kroeber's.

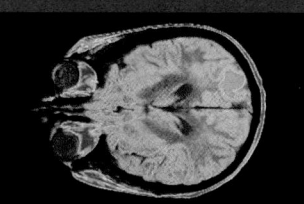

Yana People to Receive Ishi's Brain

A Newspaper Article by Robert Fri

Monday, May 10, 1999

This past week, the Smithsonian Institution announced that Ishi is coming home to Northern California. Ishi's brain will be returned to his closest living relatives, the Yana people of the Redding Rancheria and Pit River Tribe. The Yana will then determine how to proceed with a proper burial. This will conclude a process of repatriation[1] that has been guided by the Smithsonian's legal obligation and moral commitment to return Ishi's remains to his descendants.

When the Smithsonian was first contacted three months ago about Ishi, we knew of no living members of his tribe. In fact, although he has been described as "the last Yahi," Ishi always identified himself as a Yahi-Yana Indian. During the Smithsonian's consultations with Native American groups in Northern California, the Redding Rancheria and Pit River tribe came forward and asked us to repatriate Ishi's remains to the Yana.

In returning Ishi's remains to the Yana,

the Smithsonian has followed both the letter and the spirit of the National Museum of the American Indian Act of 1989. This law, together with the Native American Graves Protection and Repatriation Act of 1990, reflects the moral principle that American Indians and Native Alaskans have a right to determine the destiny of their ancestral remains, sacred objects, funerary offerings and cultural patrimonial objects conserved in museums throughout the United States. The Smithsonian's National Museum of Natural History has adhered to this principle in returning more than 4,000 human remains and nearly 1,000 cultural objects, and we continue to follow it as we repatriate other Native American remains and objects still found in the museum's collections.

Returning native remains to Indian hands does not absolve non-natives of responsibility for having taken them. But the process of repatriation worked for Ishi. And the Smithsonian is committed to seeing that it continues to work. ❖

1. **repatriation.** Returning to homeland

TEXT ◀ TO ▶ TEXT CONNECTION
Compare the attitudes revealed in the Kroeber biography with those expressed in "Yana People to Receive Ishi's Brain." What do you think of the policy described in the article and the way the Smithsonian Institution abided by the policy?

YANA PEOPLE TO RECEIVE ISHI'S BRAIN **299**

Independent Reading

Further Reading on Ishi Countless books, essays, and articles have been written about Ishi since Kroeber's publication in 1961. Additional academic materials, edited by Theodora Kroeber and R. F. Heizer, highlight a 1981 book called *Ishi the Last Yahi: A Documentary History.* More recently, Lawrence Holcolm published *The Last Yahi: A Novel About Ishi* in 2000. The Kroeber's sons and anthropologists Clifton and Carl edited *Ishi in Three Centuries* in 2003, achieving the status of the first academic book on Ishi to include American Indian essays, though native writers have expounded on the story for decades. Anthropologist Orin Starn presented a restructured version of Ishi's story, *Ishi's Brain: In Search of America's Last "Wild" Indian,* in 2004.

Analyze Literature

Biography *Answer:* Students will recall that the incident on San Nicolas Island occurred in 1853 and that the padres moved the island's residents to the mainland eighteen years earlier, in 1835. They might also include in their timeline September 4, 1911, when Ishi arrived in San Francisco, or 1916, when Ishi died.

Analyze Literature

Biography A biography is the story of a person's life told by another person. An author may include events that didn't happen to the main subject, but that nonetheless impacted the events of the subject's life. A time line can help you organize the sequence of events and clarify the impact of one event on another. Create a time line that reflects the order in which the events occurred. Consider, for example, at what point in her narrative did Kroeber include information about the earlier episode on San Nicolas Island? When did the actual event take place? Why do you think the information was included?

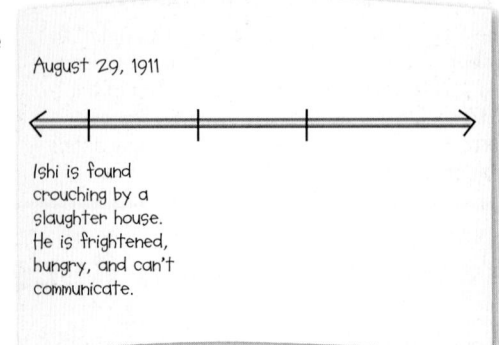

August 29, 1911

Ishi is found crouching by a slaughter house. He is frightened, hungry, and can't communicate.

Extend Understanding

Writing Options

Creative Writing Write a **list** of biographical information about a friend or family member. Include important dates, personal events, people, and places in that person's life. If outside events had an important impact on the person's life, include the events and a brief note explaining their effect.

Expository Writing Use information from this biography to create a **hypothesis,** or theory, about why Ishi was found near Oroville's slaughter house. Include the reasoning behind your hypothesis as well as details, facts, and examples from the selection to support your hypothesis.

Collaborative Learning

Discuss Ideas In small groups, discuss ideas about "civilization" and "wildness." Work together to agree upon a definition of both words. Discuss how definitions of what is "civilized" and what is "wild" can impact how different people are treated and viewed.

Media Literacy

Compare Perspectives Compare and contrast the perspectives of the authors of *Ishi in Two Worlds* and "Yana People to Receive Ishi's Brain." Discuss the social and political attitudes toward Native Americans in 1911 (when Ishi was discovered), in 1961 (when the biography was published), and in 1999 (when the newspaper article was published). How do you think these attitudes may have affected the perspectives of the two authors?

 Go to **www.mirrorsandwindows.com** for more.

Rubrics for Writing Options

You can adapt this as a checklist for students to use as they write.

Creative Writing

☐ Does it give details about the subject's life?
☐ Does it include the impact of outside events?

Expository Writing

☐ Does the paragraph clearly state an argument?
☐ Is the theory based on facts from the selection, as well as the student's own prior knowledge?

Literary Element

Understanding the Essay

What Is an Essay?

An essay is a short nonfiction work that expresses a writer's thoughts about a single subject. A well-written essay clearly presents information and usually has an introduction, body, and conclusion.

Elements of an Essay

Although there are several types of essays, they all share similar elements. These are:

An **author's purpose** is the goal or aim the writer wants to accomplish with his or her essay. For example, an author might write to inform, explain, entertain, tell a story, or persuade.

The **audience** is the person or group of people for whom the author is writing. Different audiences affect the way an author writes an essay. For example, an essay intended for an audience unfamiliar with the essay's subject would contain less technical vocabulary than an essay intended for a group familiar with the subject.

Tone is the writer's attitude toward the subject or the reader. A writer might use a lighthearted, informal tone when writing about something happy or funny, and a formal tone when writing about something more serious.

Voice is the way a writer uses language to reflect his or her unique personality and attitude toward topic, form, and audience. A writer expresses voice through tone, word choice, and sentence structure.

Point of View is the vantage point from which a story is told. Most essays are written in either first- or third-person point of view. If a story is told from the first-person point of view, the narrator uses the pronouns *I* and *we* and is a part of or a witness to the action. When a story is told from a third-person point of view, the narrator is outside the action and uses pronouns such as *he, she, it,* and *they*.

> *The essay is a literary device for saying almost everything about almost anything.*
>
> —ALDOUS HUXLEY

Types of Essays

There are three main types of essays.

A **personal essay** is a short nonfiction work on a single topic related to the life of the writer. A personal essay is written from the author's point of view and often uses the pronouns *I* and *me.* Maya Angelou's "Mrs. Flowers" (page 281) is an example of a personal essay.

An **expository essay** is written to communicate facts. Since the main purpose is to inform, the tone is usually formal. "Indian Cattle" (page 414) is an expository essay because it's intended to communicate information about anthropology.

A **persuasive essay** presents an argument in order to persuade or convince a reader. The writer supports his or her argument with evidence such as reasons and facts. Paul Rogat Loeb's "Soul of a Citizen" (page 312) is an example of a persuasive essay.

LITERARY ELEMENT **301**

Teach the Element

Understanding the Essay

Reading skills and strategies that can help students understand the essay include analyzing the author's purpose.

Use Reading Skills

Analyze Author's Purpose Explain to students that an author has a specific objective in mind when writing an essay. He or she might want to inform, explain, entertain, or persuade his or her audience. Make a chart of these purposes, and ask students to volunteer possible topics for each. Next, decide through discussion three topics to keep in each purpose column.

TEACHING NOTE

Identify Audience

Certain purposes and topics will appeal to certain audiences, while others might be too technical or too informal for a particular reader. For example, a story about a monkey who rides a bicycle might appeal to a younger audience reading for pleasure, while an explanation of a biological process might appeal to a student interested in learning a concept. Pair students, direct them to choose one topic from each column, and guide them in determining who might be the best audience for each choice. Remind them to provide explanations for their decisions as they share their thought processes.

Words in Use

Teaching Words
unique, 301
vantage point, 301
anthropology, 301

Common Core State Standards

Reading Informational
RI.4, RI.6, RI.10

At a Glance
Guided Reading: Reading Model
- Reading Level: Moderate
- Difficulty Consideration: Terminology
- Ease Factor: Author's style

Objectives
Studying this lesson will enable students to
- use reading strategies such as analyzing cause and effect
- define *narrative essay* and recognize that Bailey White is telling a true story that reveals her mother's character
- describe the literary accomplishments of Bailey White and explain how her writing reflects her time and place
- value an essay about an unusual mother

Launch the Lesson
Students might enjoy writing a personal essay on their views about cleanliness and orderliness. Brainstorm ideas as a class, and organize them in a graphic organizer. Steer their focus toward issues such as sanitation, organization, benefits, and consequences. When they are ready to draft, suggest that they discuss the advantages and disadvantages of diverse approaches.

Common Core State Standards
Reading Informational
RI.1, RI.4, RI.10
Writing
W.9
Language
L.6

GUIDED READING

Apply the Model
- BEFORE READING
- DURING READING
- AFTER READING

Good Housekeeping
A Narrative Essay by Bailey White

Build Background
Literary Context In "Good Housekeeping" Bailey White tells a story of preparing her mother's home to welcome extended family to Thanksgiving dinner. Because it follows a story form, with a conflict, rising action, climax, and resolution, the selection is called a "narrative essay," a true story that makes a point.

Reader's Context What can you tell about a person by visiting his or her home? What would a visitor learn about you by visiting your dream home or dream bedroom?

Set Purpose
Skim "Good Housekeeping" to preview the main characters. Read some of the quotes to get a sense of White's characterization of herself, her sister, and her mother. Read to deepen your understanding of these characters.

Analyze Literature
Personal Essay In addition to being a **narrative essay,** the selection is a **personal essay.** A personal essay is a short work of nonfiction on a single topic related to the life of the writer. It is told in the first person from the writer's point of view. As you read "Good Housekeeping," think about how this story might have been told differently had Mama narrated it.

Meet the Author
Bailey White was born in Thomasville, Georgia, in 1950, and she still lives in the house in which she grew up. White's father was a writer, and her mother was a farmer. A former first-grade teacher, White now writes full time. She is a frequent contributor to National Public Radio where every Thanksgiving since 1995 she has read a Thanksgiving Day story. She is also the author of two story collections, *Mama Makes Up Her Mind* and *Sleeping at the Starlite Motel,* and a novel, *Quite a Year for Plums.*

Use Reading Skills
Analyze Cause and Effect When you analyze cause and effect, you look for a relationship between a cause and one or more effects. *Effects* are what happens in a story, and *causes* explain why these things happen. Keep track of what happens in "Good Housekeeping" and why in a cause-and-effect chart.

Cause ⟶ Effect

Cause	Effect
There will be a wedding in the family, and Mama feels the family needs to meet "on her ground."	"Mama announced that she was going to invite the family of our cousin's bride to Thanksgiving dinner..."

Summary Statement

Mama's announcement is the source of conflict in this story.

Preview Vocabulary
pro•tes•ta•tion (prä´ təs tā´ shən) *n.,* strong expression of dissent

mem•o•ra•bil•i•a (me´ mə rə bi´ lē ə) *n. pl.,* things tied to past events that are worth remembering

302 UNIT 3 NONFICTION

Words in Use

Preview Vocabulary
protestation, 306
memorabilia, 307

Selection Words
iridescent, 304
antidote, 304
leer, 305
lecherous, 306
heirloom, 307

Teaching Words
figurative, 308
sentimental, 311

KEY TERMS
CONFLICT, 302
RISING ACTION, 302
CLIMAX, 302
RESOLUTION, 302
NARRATIVE ESSAY, 302
CHARACTERIZATION, 302
PERSONAL ESSAY, 302
POINT OF VIEW, 302
CAUSE, 302
EFFECT, 302
SITUATIONAL IRONY, 311
DIALOGUE, 311

Good Housekeeping

A Narrative Essay by Bailey White

Somehow, until this moment, it had not seemed odd to have a bowl of night crawlers getting their thrills in the kitchen.

303

Teach the Model

Summary

White's mother decides to invite future family members to Thanksgiving dinner so that they can become better acquainted. The author and her sister, all too aware of the home's clutter and disarray, are appalled at the idea. The two spend an entire weekend cleaning, polishing, and throwing out what they consider to be junk, while their mother tries to defend the value of discarded objects. When the guests arrive, they are impressed by how clean the house is, but Mr. Mitchell, the father of the bride-to-be, is astonished by the mother's spectacular garden, as he is a horticulture expert himself. They find common ground while discussing rare plants and the daughters begin to appreciate their mother's approach to "housekeeping."

MIRRORS & WINDOWS The Mirrors & Windows questions at the end of this selection focus on the theme of perception. Before reading, ask students how their perspectives on life differ from those of other family members. Is there a noticeable gap in how people of different generations go about their daily lives?

Program Resources

Planning and Assessment
Program Planning Guide, Selection Lesson Plan
E-Lesson Planner
Assessment Guide, Lesson Test
ExamView

Technology Tools
Interactive Student Text on CD
Visual Teaching Package
Audio Library
mirrorsandwindows.com

Meeting the Standards
Nonfiction: Unit 3, Guided Reading, pp. 33–38

Differentiating Instruction
Developing Readers, Visualize, pp. 16–18

Composting Making garden compost is a great way to recycle, avoid contamination, and save money. Chemical fertilizers are expensive and often contain fluorine, which can contaminate soil, water, and food. Plus, many households already contain the necessary ingredients for compost. *Vermicomposting* takes advantage of the red worm's ability to turn food waste into a rich fertilizer. These worms will eat close to their own body weight in food scraps daily. Their castings serve as fertilizer for healthy plants throughout the growing season. **A**

Use Reading Skills

Analyze Cause and Effect *Answer:* Mother has announced that she will invite extended family for Thanksgiving dinner, and the house looks different when White imagines how someone else will see it. **B**

Analyze Literature

Personal Essay *Answer:* The pronoun *I* and the adjective *my* tell me this is a personal essay. **C**

It was the middle of November, just a month before the wedding, when my mother announced that she was going to invite the family of our cousin's bride to Thanksgiving dinner at our house.

"They need to get to know us on our own ground," she said. She rared[1] back in her reclining chair. "You girls can help with the cooking. Let's see, there will be ten of us, and six of those Mitchells" (the bride's family).

My mother was sitting in the kitchen, dammed in by stacks of old *Natural History* magazines. Behind her a bowl of giant worms, night crawlers, was suspended from the ceiling. She uses worm castings[2] as an ingredient in her garden compost,[3] and she keeps the worms in the kitchen so she can feed them food scraps.

My sister and I didn't say anything for a while. I watched the worms. Every now and then one of them would come up to the edge of the bowl, loop himself out, swag[4] down—where he would hang for an instant, his coating of iridescent slime gleaming—and then drop down like an arrow into another bowl on the floor. My mother had an idea that the worms missed the excitement of a life in the wild, and she provided this skydiving opportunity as an antidote for boredom.

My sister was eyeing the jars of fleas on the kitchen counter, part of an ongoing experiment with lethal[5] herbs.

Those worms, or their ancestors, had been there my whole life, but somehow, until this moment, it had not seemed odd to have a bowl of night crawlers getting their thrills in the kitchen.

"Worms," I whispered to myself.

"Fleas," my sister whispered.

My eyes fell on a rusty 1930s Underwood typewriter under the kitchen sink. It had been there as long as I could remember, the G key permanently depressed, the strike arm permanently erect. My sister and I exchanged a look.

"What is that typewriter doing under the sink?" I asked flatly.

"Why on our own ground?" said my sister.

"Let's see, we'll have your Aunt Thelma's sweet potato crunch, and Corrie Lou's cranberry mold," my mother said.

> **DURING READING**
>
> **Use Reading Skills**
> **Analyze Cause and Effect**
> Why does it suddenly seem odd to have night crawlers in the kitchen? **B**

> **DURING READING**
>
> **Analyze Literature**
> **Personal Essay** Which words tell you this is a personal essay? **C**

---

1. **rared.** Southern expression for *reared*, raised to an upright position
2. **castings.** Excrement
3. **compost.** Mixture containing decaying organic matter such as leaves and manure that is used to nourish plants
4. **swag.** Lurch or sway
5. **lethal.** Deadly

Differentiated Instruction

Reading Proficiency

Suggest that students preview the story. As a group, examine the Before You Read page and note that Bailey currently lives in the house in which she spent her childhood. Then direct their attention to the photograph on the following page. Discuss what it might suggest about the essay's plot. Generate interest in the essay by asking "What do you predict is Bailey White's definition of 'good housekeeping'?"

Writing Skills

Spatial Order in Description

Explain to students that when they write descriptively, one good way to arrange details is in spatial order. Suggest that they write a description of a location of their choice. Model a description by saying, "I want to describe the classroom starting with what's closest to me and moving outward . . ." Have small groups read their descriptions aloud and determine what sort of spatial order was used.

Beside the typewriter was a guide to the vascular flora[6] of the Carolinas, a turtle skull, and a dog brush. There were hairs in the dog brush, black hairs. Our dog Smut had died fifteen years ago. I thought about the typewriter, the turtle skull, and the dog brush. I thought about the worms. I thought about the bride's family—nice people, we were told, from Bartow County—walking into this house on Thanksgiving Day. **D**

"Welcome to our home," my mother would say. And she would lead them over the stacks of books, through the musty main hall, and into a twilight of clutter. They would clamp their arms to their sides and creep behind her with their tight lips and furtive[7] eyes, past rooms with half-closed doors through which they would glimpse mounds of moldy gourds, drying onions spread on sheets of newspaper, broken pottery in stacks, and, amazingly preserved, my grandfather's ship model collection. From one room a moth-eaten stuffed turkey would blindly leer out at them. "Storage!" my mother would explain cheerfully.

The guests would be settled on the front porch, where they would gaze hollowly down into the garden while our mother explained the life cycle of the solitary wasp who made his home in one of the porch columns. My sister and I would pass around plates of olives and cheese brightly, trying to keep a lilt[8] in our voices and making the guests feel "at home."

"You can't do it!" my sister exploded. "We can never get ready in time!" **F**

"What is there to get ready?" our mother asked innocently. "Just the food, and we'll do that ahead of time. You should always do the food ahead of time, girls," she instructed us. "Then you can enjoy your guests."

"Mama!" my sister wailed. "Just look at this place!" She gestured wildly.

"What's wrong with it?" My mother peered out at the room through a haze of dust. Behind her, another worm dropped.

"Just look!" Louise threw her arms wide. "The clutter, the filth..." She spied the rows of jars on the counter. "...The fleas!"

"Don't worry about the fleas, Louise," our mother reassured her.

---

6. **vascular flora.** Plants that have vessels or ducts that support the plant, store food, and conduct water and minerals
7. **furtive.** Characterized by stealth, quiet caution, or secrecy
8. **lilt.** Cheerful or lively manner of speaking

DURING READING

Use Reading Strategies
Visualize Picture the Mitchells entering the Whites' home. What words and phrases did White choose that help you see what she imagined? **E**

Teach the Model

Geography Connection
Bartow County Created from the Cherokee lands of the Cherokee County territory and formerly called Cass County, Bartow County is situated in the foothills of the Appalachian Mountains in northeastern Georgia. Some of its geographic features are Allatoona Lake, the Etowah Indian Mounds, and the Red Top Mountain State Park. Bartow is a safe haven for an endangered plant, the Jeffersonia Diphylia, or Twin Leaf, as well as three endangered animals including the Indian bat, the red-cockaded woodpecker, and the southern bald eagle. **D**

Use Reading Strategies
Visualize *Answer:* Students will notice visual details such as *stacks of books, twilight of clutter, clamp their arms, creep, tight lips, furtive eyes, rooms with half-closed doors, mounds of moldy gourds, drying onions spread on sheets of newspaper, broken pottery in stacks, ship model collection, moth-eaten stuffed turkey, gaze hollowly, plates of olives and cheese.* **E**

Use Reading Skills
Analyze Cause and Effect Ask students to consider what caused White's sister, Louise, to have this reaction to her mother's plan. **F**

Grammar Skills

Prepositional Phrases
Remind students that a prepositional phrase is a group of words that begins with a preposition and includes the object of the preposition and any modifiers. Explain that a prepositional phrase can be used as an adverb or as an adjective.

Have students identify the prepositional phrases in this sentence and tell how each one functions—as an adjective or an adverb.

Much <u>of the junk</u> <u>from the house</u> was taken <u>to the dump</u>. (adjective, adjective, adverb)

Analyze Literature

Conflict Ask students what they think Bailey means and why she chose the following plan. Model a response: "Maybe Bailey foresees consequences of the house's condition and makes a decision about how to deal with the conflict." **A**

Cultural Connection

Grits Grits are widely known as "Southern oatmeal," since they are a staple breakfast item in this region. American Indians introduced the dish of boiled corn porridge into colonists' diets in 1607, when the British arrived on the coast of what later became Jamestown, Virginia. The Indians offered bowls of the piping hot mush, seasoned with animal fat and salt, and called it "rockahominie." Grits are often credited with the region's survival during the Depression, as they were plentiful and inexpensive. The dish is traditionally served with butter and milk but is also fashioned from complex recipes in some of the finest restaurants in the country. **B**

Use Reading Strategies

Make Inferences *Answer:* Students might say that Mama is passionate about gardening, as well as conservative and protective of objects seen as "old" and therefore of little value. **C**

"I am working on a new concoction,[9] based on myrtle[10] and oil of pennyroyal.[11] I may have the fleas under control by Thanksgiving."

Louise sank into a chair and looked our mother in the eye. "Mama," she began, "it's not just the fleas. It's..."

But I had come to my senses.

A "Stop, Louise," I said. "Get up. We've got a weekend. We'll start on Saturday."

Louise arrived at dawn, the Saturday before Thanksgiving, loaded down with vacuum cleaners, extra bags and filters, brooms, mops, and buckets.

Mama was sitting in her chair in the kitchen, eating grits[12] and making feeble <u>protestations.</u> "You girls don't have to do this, Bailey. I'll sweep up Wednesday afternoon. Then on Thursday there will just be the cooking."

pro·tes·ta·tion
(prä′ təs tā′ shən) *n.,* strong expression of dissent

"I know, Mama," I said, "but we want to do a good job. We want to really straighten up. You'll be glad when it's all **B** done. Eat your grits." I didn't want her to see Louise staggering out with the first load for the dump: a box of rotten sheets, some deadly appliances from the early days of electricity, and an old mechanical milking machine with attachments for only three teats.

Mama would not let us throw out a box of old photographs we found under the sofa—"I may remember who those people are some day"—or the lecherous old stuffed turkey with his hunched-up back and his bad-looking feet. "It was one of Ralph's earliest taxidermy[13] efforts," she said, fondly stroking the turkey's bristling feathers down. And she let us haul off boxes of back issues of the *Journal of the American Gourd Growers' Association* only if we promised to leave them stacked neatly beside the dumpster for others to find. But she got suspicious when she caught Louise with the typewriter.

"Where are you going with that typewriter, Louise?" she asked.

"We're going to throw it away, Mama."

"You can't throw it away, Louise. It's a very good typewriter!"

> **DURING READING**
>
> **Use Reading Strategies**
> **Make Inferences** Why do you think Mama wants others to find the journals? **C**

---

9. **concoction.** Mixture of ingredients
10. **myrtle.** Fragrant evergreen shrub
11. **pennyroyal.** Fragrant plant with leaves that yield an oil used as an insect repellent
12. **grits.** Cornmeal, a popular Southern breakfast
13. **taxidermy.** Process of preparing and stuffing the skins of dead animals

---

Differentiated Instruction

English Language Learning

This might be a good opportunity for students from other countries to explore the American tradition of Thanksgiving. The Smithsonian Institution's *Encyclopedia Smithsonian* provides a comprehensive and judicious history of the holiday's origins, myths, realities, and current practices. Preview the site for ideas on how to present this complex and controversial tradition.

Louise was getting edgy. "Mama, it's frozen up with rust and clogged with dust. None of the moving parts moves. And they don't make ribbons to fit those old typewriters anymore."

"Nonsense," said Mama. "You put that typewriter down, Louise. It just needs a little squirt of oil. Bring me the WD-40."

Louise put the typewriter down with a clunk. I brought a can of WD-40, with the little red straw to aim the spray. Mama put on her glasses, pursed her lips, and peered into the typewriter. *Skeet! Skeet!* She went to work with the WD-40 and a tiny, filthy rag. "You girls are throwing away too much," she said.

By midafternoon we began to feel that we were making progress. We could see out the windows, and we had several rooms actually in order. We had found our brother's long-lost snakeskin collection and the shoes our great-aunt Bertie had worn at her wedding; a dusty aquarium containing the skeletons of two fish; and under a tangle of dried rooster-spur peppers and old sneakers, a rat trap with an exquisitely preserved rat skeleton, the tiny bright-white neck bones delicately pinched. "Just like Pompeii,"[14] Mama marveled.

By the end of the day we had cleared the house out. What had not been thrown away was in its place. I had dropped a drawer on my foot, and Louise was in a bad mood. Mama's glasses were misted with WD-40. We sat down in the kitchen and drank tea.

"What I want to know is, where are the priceless heirlooms?"[15] asked Louise. "You read about people cleaning out their attics and finding 200-year-old quilts in perfect condition, old coins, cute kitchen appliances from the turn of the century, Victorian floral scenes made of the hair of loved ones. What kind of family are we? All we find is bones of dead animals and dried-up plants. Where are the Civil War <u>memorabilia</u>, the lost jewels, the silk wedding dresses neatly packed away in linen sheets and lavender?"

"Well," said Mama, "you found your brother's snakeskins. And I think this rat skeleton is fascinating. How long must it have been there?"

"Don't ask," moaned Louise. "I'm going home."

On Sunday we dusted everything, swept, vacuumed and mopped the floors, washed the windows, and laundered the curtains, rugs, and slipcovers. By nightfall the house was ready.

---

14. Pompeii. Ancient Italian city largely preserved in stunning completeness under the molten lava and hot ash of the volcano that destroyed it in AD 79

15. heirlooms. Things of special value passed from one generation to another

> **DURING READING**
>
> **Analyze Literature** E
> **Personal Essay** If Mama had written this essay, how might this sentence have read?

mem·o·ra·bil·i·a
(me´ mə rə bǐ´ lē ə) *n. pl.*,
things tied to past events that
are worth remembering

> **DURING READING**
>
> **Use Reading Skills**
> **Analyze Cause and Effect**
> What causes can you give for
> Louise's moan? F

Grammar Skills

Hyphens

Remind students that compound adjectives are singular descriptors made up of two or more words. The words that make up the adjective are joined with a hyphen when placed before a noun. Point out instances of compound descriptions on this page, *including long-lost snakeskin collection, 200-year-old quilts,* and *dried-up plants.* Ask students to come up with several more illustrations of this punctuation, have them write their examples on a board or overhead projector, and discuss any necessary revision.

Analyze Literature

Figurative Language *Answer:*
Students should say that the mother
uses a simile in her statement: "This
place is as clean as a morgue." They
should explain that they can tell this
because she compares two unlike
things and uses *as*. **A**

Analyze Literature

Setting Have students describe the
setting for the Thanksgiving dinner.
How is it different from the setting at
the beginning of the narrative? Model
a response by saying that the house is
clean, polished, and decorated with
flowers. It is different from the setting
at the beginning because the house
is now fit for company, in the girls'
eyes. **B**

Science Connection

Wasps Unlike organized social
groups of insects, such as
yellowjackets and honeybees, the
solitary female wasp mates, creates a
nest, and lives alone for the remainder
of her life. Social insects, including the
paper wasp, can afford to attack
potential threats, like people, because
they have many workers whose
purpose is to protect the queen.
However, a solitary female wasp
cannot risk injury from confrontation,
as she is the sole protector of her nest
and must continue to reproduce. **C**

DURING READING

Analyze Literature
Figurative Language What
type of figurative language is
in this passage? How can you
tell?
A

"You girls have certainly struck a blow," Mama congratulated us.
"This place is as clean as a morgue."[16] We left her sitting in her
chair with the worms, the typewriter, and the last three surviving
fleas.

I walked out with Louise. "She looks a little forlorn,"[17] I said.

"She'll get used to it," Louise declared. "And the Mitchells will
never dream that we are peculiar!"

Thanksgiving morning, Louise and I divided up the cooking.
She made the sweet potato soufflé and the squash casserole, and
I cooked the turkey and made bread. Mama spent the morning in
her garden picking every last English pea, even the tiniest baby
ones, because we knew we would have our first freeze that night.

B At ten o'clock we set the table. For a centerpiece Mama put
some pink and white sasanquas[18] to float in a crystal bowl, and the
low autumn light came slanting in through the windows onto the
flowers and the bright water. We had built a fire in the stove, and
the heat baked out the hay-field fragrance of the bunches of
Artemisia[19] hung to dry against the walls. The floors gleamed.
The polished silverware shone. Beneath the sweet fall smells of
baking bread and sasanquas and drying herbs I could just detect
the faintest whiff of Murphy Oil Soap. Louise and I stood in the
middle of the living room and gazed.

"The furniture looks startled," Louise said.

"It's beautiful," I said. "And here they are."

"Welcome to our home. We're so glad you could come,"
Mama was saying to the Mitchells. "Come out onto the porch.
C You will be interested to see the wasp who lives there. It's a solitary
wasp, quite rare…I know it looks a bit cleared out in here;
my girls have been cleaning. Bailey, Louise, come and meet these
Mitchells."

We sat on the porch for a while, bundled in coats, and watched
the last petals of the sasanquas drift to the ground. Mr. Mitchell
examined the neat, round hole of the solitary wasp with some
interest.

"Do you have a knowledge of the hymenoptera,[20] Mr. Mitchell?"
Mama asked. And she was off.

---

16. **morgue.** Place where the bodies of people found dead are kept until released for burial
17. **forlorn.** Sad because of isolation or desertion
18. **sasanquas.** Camellias, flowering shrubs with dark green shiny foliage and blooms that range in color
from white to hues of red or pink
19. **Artemisia.** Any of many species of fragrant herbs and shrubs, such as sagebrush, that grow in dry
areas
20. **hymenoptera.** Any of a group of highly specialized insects that includes bees, wasps, and ants

308 UNIT 3 NONFICTION

Differentiated Instruction

Enrichment

Encourage students to write descriptive essays
about what their families eat at Thanksgiving. Ask
them to choose appropriate organizational
structures, perhaps moving spatially from one end
of the table to the other. Suggest that they connect
each food item to a person, memory, or feeling.

Mrs. Mitchell had smiley eyes and a knowing look. She leaned over to Louise and me. "It's the cleanest house I've ever seen," she whispered. We were friends. Louise and I took her to the kitchen to help with the food.

Other guests arrived—our brother and his family, aunts and uncles, and the bridal couple. The house was full of talk and laughter. We brought out food and more food. Everyone sat down.

Then, "Where's Daddy?" asked the bride.

Sure enough, an empty chair...two empty chairs.

"Where's Mama?" asked Louise.

"On the porch?"

No.

"In the kitchen?"

No.

"Everyone please start. The food will get cold," I said. "I'll go find them."

Outside, the temperature was dropping. This was the last day the garden would be green. I wandered along the path, following the scent of bruised basil[21] until I heard voices way in the back of the yard.

Mr. Mitchell: "...and this is?"

"*Franklinia altamaha*, Mr. Mitchell, and quite a spectacular specimen, if I do say so."

"The famous Lost Franklinia of John Bartram,"[22] Mr. Mitchell] **E** murmured reverently, gazing up into its branches. I have never seen one."

The sun shining through the crimson leaves of the Franklinia lit up the air with a rosey glow. Mr. Mitchell was holding her arm in his and gesturing with her walking stick. She was cradling some stalks of red erythrina berries in their black pods.

Mr. Mitchell turned slowly and looked over the garden.

"Silver bell, shadbush,[23] euonymous,[24] bloodroot, trillium"[25]—he named them off. "Mrs. White, I've been collecting rare plants and heirloom seeds all my life, and I've never seen anything to equal this."

---

21. **basil.** Fragrant herb in the mint family
22. **The famous Lost Franklinia of John Bartram.** Small flowering tree discovered in 1765 by John and William Bartram, named for the river in Georgia it was found near and in honor of Benjamin Franklin, a friend of the Bartrams. The Franklinia has long been extinct in the world. All Franklinia today trace back to plants and seeds the Bartrams carried back to Philadelphia from Georgia in 1765.
23. **shadbush.** Any of various North American shrubs or trees that produce an edible fruit
24. **euonymous.** Shrub sometimes called "burning bush" because of its red bloom
25. **trillium.** Any of various plants characterized by having clusters of three leaves and flowers of three petals

DURING READING

Make Connections
What is Bailey's reaction to Mrs. Mitchell? When did someone put you at ease in a social situation? **D**

Teach the Model

Make Connections

Answer: Students might say Bailey realizes that Mrs. Mitchell understands the conflict and relaxes after her compliment. They might volunteer situations like a friend coming over to talk to them at a party where they don't know anybody or a fellow student explaining what's going on in class. **D**

Science Connection

John and William Bartram Share with students the following information about John and William Bartram: William (1739–1823) was the fifth son of noted botanist John Bartram (1699–1777). Together, they took a scientific tour of east Florida between 1775 and 1766, collecting specimens. In 1773, William began a four-year odyssey across the Southeast, keeping a journal with beautiful illustrations of plants, birds, and other animals. In 1803, William was asked by President Thomas Jefferson to join Lewis and Clark in their exploration of the Louisiana Territory. A 1999 33-cent postage stamp honors the 300th birthday of John Bartram by featuring a branch and flower from the *Franklinia alatamaha,* the tree they discovered and named after their friend Benjamin Franklin. **E**

Vocabulary Skills

Botanical Terminology

Share with students these facts about botanical terminology:

- Plants have a scientific name and a common name. The scientific name is in Latin and is always printed in italics (or underlined in handwriting). The common name is in the language of the writer and written in regular type.

- The scientific name has two parts: the genus (capitalized) and the species (lowercase).

Have students make a list of the plants named in this narrative and determine whether the word is a scientific name or a common name.

Analyze Literature

Narrative Essay *Answer:* Students may say Mama is vindicated somewhat in that the typewriter works well and that she is making this point by using the typewriter rather than handwriting the note. White's point may be to concede to Mama, by letting her have the last word and admitting the value of saving items. **A**

Answer: Students who would clean might say the place could have been offensive to the Mitchells and that they would not have understood Mama's collections. Students who would not clean might say Mama has a right to live in her own way and that it is disrespectful to take away her belongings. Students may say that it is okay to make decisions for any person who is a risk to himself or herself or others.

DURING READING

Analyze Literature
Narrative Essay What point does White make by ending with a typewritten note from Mama? **A**

"It's an old lady's pleasure, Mr. Mitchell," said my mother. "Now wait till I take you to the dump and show you my bones. Louise threw them out," she whispered hoarsely, "but I know right where they are. We'll get them tomorrow, if you're interested. You will be kind enough not to mention it to my girls."

"It would be my extreme pleasure to see your collection of bones, Mrs. White," said Mr. Mitchell. And slowly he led her out of the pink glow and back to the party.

The next day Louise came over, and we went to sit in the kitchen and drink hot chocolate with Mama and congratulate ourselves on a job beautifully done. But Mama was not in her chair. There was a note on the kitchen table. It was typewritten. Every letter was clear and black and even.

Sorry I missed you girls. Mr. Mitchell and I have gone on a little errand. Make yourselves some hot chocolate.

Love,
Mama ❖

If you were one of the sisters, what would you have done in her situation? What does the essay's ending reveal about Mama's perspective of the world as opposed to that of her daughters?

Differentiated Instruction

Kinesthetic Learning

Guide students in devising a dramatic interpretation of how Bailey and her sister might react to their mother's typewritten note. Ask preliminary questions to get them started like: "What would the girls' initial reaction be to the discovery that Mama had actually fixed the typewriter they thought was irreparable? Would the girls gain new perspectives immediately after reading the note, or would it take some time for their mother's lesson to sink in?"

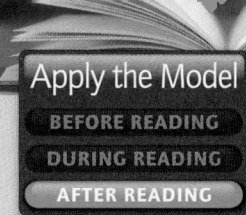
Find Meaning

1. What is the relationship between the author and the narrator?

2. (a) What kinds of objects do Bailey and Louise find in Mama's house? (b) Why does Mama value these objects? (c) What kinds of objects does Louise wish they had found?

3. What is the climax of the narrative?

4. How is the Mitchells' visit the same and different from how Bailey imagined it?

Analyze Literature

Personal Essay White chose to tell this story as a personal essay. She could have fictionalized this account and written her essay in the third person. Look at the features of a personal essay in the chart. Analyze "Good Housekeeping" to see how these features are used by White. Then make a statement about why you think White chose to write about the events in a personal essay rather than a short story or another kind of essay.

Make Judgments

5. What two meanings of the word *heirloom* did White use in "Good Housekeeping"?

6. Situational irony occurs when the outcome of a situation is the opposite, or nearly opposite, of what is expected. How is the ending of "Good Housekeeping" an example of situational irony?

Features of a Personal Essay	Features of "Good Housekeeping"
Short nonfiction work	A true story
Expresses the writer's thoughts about a single topic	
Topic related to the writer's life	

Extend Understanding

Writing Options

Creative Writing Imagine that you meet Mama. Write a **dialogue** between yourself and Mama using the style White used in writing "Good Housekeeping."

Applied Writing Skim the story to create a **to-do list** for Mama. What do you think Bailey and Louise would have put on the list if they were going to have Mama do all the cleaning herself? Mama is your audience.

Collaborative Learning

Examine Characterization Form small groups to discuss White's characterization of her mother. Discuss specifically how White used sentimental objects in her characterization.

Lifelong Learning

Internet Research On the Internet, search for "Bailey White sound files" to locate recordings of White's National Public Radio Thanksgiving Day broadcasts. Listen to and discuss the broadcast with your partner.

 Go to www.mirrorsandwindows.com for more.

Find Meaning

1. The author is the narrator.

2. (a) They find objects related to natural history and gardening. (b) Mama values these objects because she is a natural history buff and a gardener. (c) Louise wished they had found objects related to family and social history or with monetary value.

3. The Mitchells' arrival is the climax.

4. It is the same since Mama does present some unusual objects but is different since the company is contented and Bailey is relaxed.

Make Judgments

5. White uses "a family possession handed down from generation to generation" and "being an old variety that is being cultivated again: *heirloom vegetables and fruits.*"

6. One of the people they try to impress by clearing out Mama's possessions was most interested in those possessions.

Analyze Literature

Personal Essay *Answer:* By writing a personal essay, White combined story structure with opportunities to reveal character traits through dialogue. Since this is a personal essay, we feel we have grown closer to real people rather than characters. There is an intimacy to the personal essay.

Program Resources

For further instruction, refer students to the following extension activity: Lifelong Learning: Internet Research, *Exceeding the Standards: Extension Activities*, p. 8.

Preview the Model

At a Glance
Guided Reading: Reading Model
- Reading Level: Challenging
- Difficulty Consideration: Vocabulary
- Ease Factor: Organization

Objectives
Studying this lesson will enable students to
- use reading strategies such as summarizing
- define *persuasive essay* and recognize the argument for social action
- describe the literary accomplishments of Paul Rogat Loeb and explain how his writing reflects current issues

Launch the Lesson
Students probably have an idea of how they could become more socially active. Prior to reading "Soul of a Citizen: Living with Conviction in a Cynical Time," discuss as a class how the group could organize efforts and effect change in their community.

Common Core State Standards

Reading Informational
RI.2, RI.3, RI.4, RI.5, RI.6, RI.7

Writing
W.9

Speaking and Listening
SL.1

Language
L.6

Apply the Model
- BEFORE READING
- DURING READING
- AFTER READING

Soul of a Citizen: Living with Conviction in a Cynical Time
A Persuasive Essay by Paul Rogat Loeb

Build Background
Historical Context This essay discusses the idea that ordinary people can create extraordinary change in society. Two such people include Lois Gibbs, a housewife who fought to clean up a chemical dump in Niagara Falls, and Wei Jingshen, who helped inspire the Tiananmen Square pro-democracy demonstration in China.

Reader's Context What changes would you like to see in your community, in the country, or in the world at large?

Set Purpose
In persuasive writing, the writer may use appeals to logic and appeals to emotion. **Appeals to logic** use well-reasoned and well-supported arguments. **Appeals to emotion** speak to the readers' feelings. As you read, note when these devices are used.

Analyze Literature
Persuasive Essay In a **persuasive essay,** the author's purpose is to persuade readers to agree with a position or to perform an action. Read to find out the purpose of Loeb's essay.

Meet the Author
Paul Rogat Loeb was born in California in 1952. He is an investigative reporter and author of several books. A scholar with Seattle's Center of Ethical Leadership, Loeb frequently shares his ideas on citizen involvement through the *New York Times, The Washington Post, Psychology Today, CNN,* and *NPR.*

Use Reading Skills
Summarize A summary retells the main ideas of a text. Summarizing can help readers remember important information from a text. After reading, write a summary of that section. Then use your section summaries to write a summary of the essay.

Summary of Section 1: Many people feel helpless about their abilities to affect positive social and environmental changes. However, despite the odds, affecting change is possible.

Summary of Section 2: _____

Summary of Section 3: _____

Summary of Section 4: _____

Summary of the Selection: _____

Preview Vocabulary
ref•uge (re′ fyüj′) *n.,* shelter or protection from danger or difficulty

im•pli•ca•tion (im plə kā′ shən) *n.,* something indicated indirectly, from which something can be inferred

deg•ra•da•tion (deg′ rə dā′ shən) *n.,* lowering of rank or state

mag•ni•tude (mag′ nə tüd′) *n.,* great size or importance

pro•lif•er•a•tion (prə li′ fə rā′ shən) *n.,* growth or increase

---

Words in Use

Preview Vocabulary	Selection Words	Teaching Words
refuge, 313	redress, 314	pro-democracy, 312
implication, 314	garnering, 317	demonstration, 312
degradation, 314	innate, 319	investigative, 312
magnitude, 315	dissident, 319	empowered, 321
proliferation, 317	embodiment, 320	disservice, 321

KEY TERMS

Soul of a Citizen: Living with Conviction in a Cynical Time

A Persuasive Essay by Paul Rogat Loeb

Teach the Model

Summary

Loeb argues that public participation is the heart of a democratic society and that although most Americans are willing to help those in their own communities, they are morally obligated to extend this gesture to the rest of the country and the world. He admits that in a world whose issues, like worldwide extreme poverty, are so huge and complicated, we feel that we cannot, as individuals, make a real difference. However, he provides a moving account of the change effected by one man. Loeb claims that we have learned, incorrectly, that change occurs instantly. The reality, he argues, is that the change we read and hear about is the result of many people's efforts over long periods of time. If we gain patience, we will see the fruits of our labor ripen.

 The Mirrors & Windows questions at the end of this selection focus on the theme of social obligation. Before reading, ask students if they feel obligated to help improve society. Do people have an innate calling to make the world a better place?

Most Americans are thoughtful, caring, generous. We try to do our best by family and friends. We'll even stop to help a fellow driver stranded by a roadside breakdown, or give spare change to a stranger. But increasingly, a wall separates each of us from the world outside, and from others who have taken <u>refuge</u> in their own private sanctuaries. How can we renew the public participation that's the very soul of democratic citizenship?

ref•uge (reˊ fyüj) *n.*, shelter or protection from danger or difficulty

313

Program Resources

Planning and Assessment
Program Planning Guide, Selection Lesson Plan
E-Lesson Planner
Assessment Guide, Lesson Test
ExamView

Technology Tools
Interactive Student Text on CD
Visual Teaching Package
Audio Library
mirrorsandwindows.com

Meeting the Standards
Nonfiction: Unit 3, Guided Reading, pp. 39–44

Differentiating Instruction
Developing Readers, Unlock Word Meaning, pp. 19–21

Cultural Connection

Child Labor The June 1996 issue of *Life* magazine featured a piece on child labor in Pakistan. The article carried a photo of a twelve-year-old boy named Tariq stitching together pieces of leather to form soccer balls. The finished balls at his feet wore the "swoosh" symbol of the Nike Corporation. The reporter explained that Tariq earned sixty cents per ball, each of which took the majority of his long workday to complete. Many organizations now work to hold companies liable for their workers' safety and livelihood. **Ⓐ**

Use Reading Skills

Summarize *Answer:* Our challenge is not just to choose good causes but to trust that what we do as individuals for these causes makes a difference. **Ⓑ**

Use Reading Skills

Analyze Cause and Effect Ask students what caused large industrial interests to work against small family fishing operations. Model a response by saying: "They wanted to get them out of the industry so they would stop pushing for measures that might raise electric costs or otherwise cut big companies' profits." **Ⓒ**

---

im·pli·ca·tion
(im plə kā´ shən) *n.,* something indicated indirectly, from which something can be inferred

Ⓐ

> **DURING READING**
>
> **Use Reading Skills**
> **Summarize** How would you summarize this paragraph? **Ⓑ**

deg·ra·da·tion
(deg´ rə dā´ shən) *n.,* lowering of rank or state

To be sure, the issues we face are complex. It's hard to comprehend the moral <u>implications</u> of a world in which Nike pays Michael Jordan millions to appear in its ads while workers at its foreign shoe factories toil away for pennies a day. The 500 richest people on the planet now control more wealth than the poorest 3 billion, half the human population. Is it possible even to grasp this extraordinary imbalance? And, more important, how do we begin to redress it?

Certainly we need to decide for ourselves whether particular causes are wise or foolish. But we also need to believe that our individual involvement is worthwhile, that what we might do in the public sphere will not be in vain. The challenge is as much psychological as political. As the Ethiopian proverb says, "He who conceals his disease cannot be cured."

We need to understand our cultural diseases—callousness, shortsightedness, denial—and learn what it will take to heal our society and our souls. How did so many of us become convinced that we can do nothing to affect the future our children and grandchildren will inherit? And how have others managed to work powerfully for change?

Pete Knutson is one of my oldest friends. During 25 years as a commercial fisherman in Washington and Alaska, he has been forced to respond to the steady <u>degradation</u> of salmon spawning grounds.[1] He could have accepted this as fate and focused on getting a maximum share of the dwindling fish populations. Instead, he gradually built an alliance between Washington fishermen, environmentalists, and Native American tribes, and persuaded them to demand that habitat be preserved and restored.

Cooperation didn't come easily. Washington's fishermen are historically individualistic and politically mistrustful. But with their new allies, they pushed for cleaner spawning streams, preservation of the Endangered Species Act, and increased water flow over regional dams to help boost salmon runs. Fearing that these measures would raise electricity costs or restrict development opportunities, aluminum companies and other large industrial interests bankrolled a statewide referendum,[2] Initiative 640, to regulate fishing nets in a way that would eliminate small family operations.

At first, those who opposed 640 thought they had no chance of success: They were outspent, outstaffed, outgunned. Similar initiatives backed by similar corporate interests had already passed in

---

1. spawning grounds. Places where young are spread forth
2. referendum. Submission of proposed law to direct vote by the people

---

Reading Skills

Reread

Remind students that when they read something that they don't initially understand, they can reread to clarify. As they reread passages to gain understanding, have them consider these questions:
1. What is it that I don't understand? Does slowing down when I read help me better understand the passage?

2. Do I understand all the words in the passage? If not, do context clues help me determine meaning?

Florida, Louisiana, and Texas. But the opponents refused to give up. Pete and his coworkers enlisted major environmental groups to campaign against the initiative. They worked with the media to explain the larger issues at stake and focus public attention on the measure's powerful financial backers. On election day in November 1995, Initiative 640 was defeated. White fishermen, Native American activists, and Friends of the Earth[3] staffers threw their arms around each other in victory. "I'm really proud of you, Dad," Pete's 12-year-old son kept repeating. Pete was stunned.

We often think of social involvement as noble but impractical. Yet it can serve enlightened self-interest and the interests of others simultaneously, giving us a sense of connection and purpose nearly impossible to find in private life. "It takes energy to act," says Pete. "But it's more draining to bury your anger, convince yourself you're powerless, and swallow whatever's handed to you."

We often don't know where to start. Most of us would like to see people treated more justly and the earth accorded the respect it deserves. But we mistrust our own ability to make a difference. The <u>magnitude</u> of the issues at hand has led too many of us to conclude that social involvement isn't worth the cost.

Such resignation isn't innate[4] or inevitable. It's what psychologists call learned helplessness, a systematic way of ignoring the ills we see and leaving them for others to handle. We find it unsettling even to think about crises as profound as the extinction of species, depletion of the ozone layer, destruction of the rainforests, and desperate urban poverty. We're taught to doubt our voices, to feel that we lack either the time to learn about and articulate the issues or the standing to speak out and be heard. To get socially involved, we believe, requires almost saintlike judgment, confidence, and character—standards we can never meet. Our impulses toward involvement are dampened by a culture that demeans idealism, enshrines[5] cynicism, and makes us feel naive for caring about our fellow human beings or the planet we inhabit.

CHANGE *Happens* —*Slowly*

A few years ago, on Martin Luther King Day, I was interviewed on CNN along with Rosa Parks. "Rosa Parks was the woman who

---

3. **Friends of the Earth.** Environmental group
4. **innate.** Existing naturally
5. **enshrines.** Makes sacred or cherished

> **DURING READING**
>
> **Analyze Literature**
> **Persuasive Writing** What is Loeb arguing in this paragraph? **D**

mag • ni • tude
(mag´ nə tüd´) *n.*, great size or importance

We...need to believe that our individual involvement is worthwhile...

Teach the Model

Science Connection
Endangered Species Human and natural factors have diminished certain wild salmon stocks to the point of extinction and have reduced many other stocks so severely as to designate them under the Endangered Species Act. While this loss immediately threatens the livelihood of fishing families, it eventually affects the health of the entire ecosystem. In every stage of development, salmon serve as a major source of nutrients for animals and plants, as they transport energy and nutrients between rivers, estuaries, and the ocean. More than 137 species of Washington wildlife depend on them for survival, and as the salmon population decreases, so do populations of other fish, reptiles, birds, and mammals.

Analyze Literature
Persuasive Writing *Answer:* Social involvement can give one a sense of connection and purpose that one doesn't find in ordinary life. **D**

Analyze Literature
Evaluate Author's Purpose Ask: "What is the author suggesting here about his purpose in writing?" Model a response by suggesting that he wants to persuade his readers that an individual can make a difference and that social involvement is worth the cost. **E**

Differentiated Instruction

Auditory Learning
Have student pairs work together to read each paragraph aloud and discuss its meaning. Auditory learners will also benefit from listening to a taped recording of the selection as they read.

Reading Proficiency
Help students activate their prior knowledge about Rosa Parks, Dr. Martin Luther King Jr., the boycott, and the Civil Rights Movement by asking what they have already learned about these leaders and issues.

History Connection

Montgomery Bus Boycott In the years and months preceding Parks's act of civil disobedience, several people refused to give up their bus seats to white riders, including Aurelia Browder, Susie McDonald, Claudette Colvin, and Mary Louise Smith. Soon after the Montgomery bus boycott began, civil rights attorney Fred Gray asked the four women to act as plaintiffs in a Civil Action challenging Montgomery, Alabama's segregation codes. In February of 1956, *Browder v. Gale* was filed in a U.S. District Court. Four months later, the three-panel judge ruled the codes unconstitutional, and the bus boycott came to a successful close. **A**

Make Connections

Answer: Some students may feel that they have been encouraged to try and make things better. Others may feel that idealism or the goal of caring for others is not valued in our consumer-oriented society. Students should give examples to back up their ideas. **B**

Use Reading Skills

Summarize *Answer:* Rosa Parks did not make a spur-of-the-moment decision. She was a conscious part of a movement for change. **C**

---

wouldn't go to the back of the bus," said the host. "That set in motion the yearlong bus boycott in Montgomery. It earned Rosa Parks the title of 'mother of the civil rights movement.' "

The host's description—the standard rendition of the story—stripped the boycott of its context. Before refusing to give up her bus seat to a white person, Parks had spent 12 years helping to lead the local NAACP chapter. The summer before, she had attended a 10-day training session at the Highlander Center, Tennessee's labor and civil rights organizing school, where she'd met older activists and discussed the Supreme Court decision banning "separate but equal" schools. Parks had become familiar with previous challenges to segregation: another Montgomery bus boycott, 50 years earlier; a bus boycott in Baton Rouge two years before Parks was arrested; and an NAACP dilemma the previous spring, when a young Montgomery woman had also refused to move to the back of the bus. The NAACP had considered a legal challenge but decided the unmarried, pregnant woman would be a poor symbol for a campaign.

In short, Parks didn't make a spur-of-the-moment decision. She was part of a movement for change at a time when success was far from certain. This in no way diminishes her historical importance, but it reminds us that this powerful act might never have taken place without the humble, frustrating work that preceded it.

We elevate a few people to hero status—especially during times of armed conflict—but most of us know next to nothing of the battles ordinary men and women fought to preserve freedom, expand democracy, and create a more just society. Many have remarked on America's historical amnesia, but its implications are hard to appreciate without recognizing how much identity dissolves in the absence of memory. We lose the mechanisms that grassroots social movements have used successfully to shift public sentiment and challenge entrenched[6] institutional power. Equally lost are the means by which participants eventually managed to prevail.

Think about how differently one can frame Rosa Parks' historic action. In the prevailing myth, Parks—a holy innocent—acts almost on a whim, in isolation. The lesson seems to be that if any of us suddenly got the urge to do something heroic, that would be great. Of course most of us wait our entire lives for the ideal moment.

The real story is more empowering: It suggests that change is the product of deliberate, incremental[7] action. When we join together to

DURING READING

Make Connections
How accurate is Loeb's view about people's impulses toward involvement? **B**

DURING READING

Use Reading Skills
Summarize What is the main idea of Parks's story? **C**

6. **entrenched.** Firmly situated, unchanging
7. **incremental.** In small amounts

Reading Skills

Identify Main Idea

Have pairs of students work together to identify the main idea of each section in the essay. Suggest that they use these strategies as they work:

1. Note key details. Is an important word or phrase repeated throughout a passage? Does one sentence tie all the other sentences together?

2. Determine which details are important and which are less important. The important details support the main idea.

shape a better world, sometimes our struggles will fail or bear only modest fruits. Other times they will trigger miraculous outpourings of courage and heart. We can never know beforehand what the consequences of our actions will be.

Not for SAINTS
—Only

"It does us all a disservice," says Atlanta activist Sonya Tinsley, "when people who work for social change are presented as saints. We get a false sense that from the moment they were born they were called to act, never had doubts, were bathed in a circle of light. But I'm much more inspired learning how people succeeded despite their failings and uncertainties." **D**

Enshrining our heroes makes it hard for mere mortals to measure up. Because we can't imagine that an ordinary human being might make a critical difference in a worthy social cause, many of us have developed what I call the "perfect standard": Before we take action on an issue, we must be convinced not only that the issue is the world's most important, but also that we have perfect knowledge of it, perfect moral consistency, and perfect eloquence[8] with which to express our views.

As a result, we refrain from tackling environmental issues because they're technically complex. We don't address homelessness because we aren't homeless. Though we're outraged when moneyed interests corrupt our political system, we believe we lack the authority to insist that campaign financing be reformed.

<u>Proliferation</u> of information makes it even more likely that we'll use the perfect standard to justify detachment rather than seek the knowledge we need to get involved. Now we can spend our lives garnering information from books, magazines, newspapers, the Internet, satellite cable channels, and radio talk shows, yet we don't dare speak out unless we feel prepared to debate Henry Kissinger or Trent Lott[9] on *Nightline*.

Eloquence, however, is not as important as kindness, concern, and a straightforward declaration of belief. Will Campbell has been a Baptist preacher, civil rights activist, farmer, writer, and volunteer cook for his friend Waylon Jennings.[10] Years ago, he was invited to

> **DURING READING**
> **Analyze Literature**
> **Persuasive Writing** What is Loeb's argument here? **E**

pro·lif·er·a·tion
(prə li′ fə rā′ shən) *n.*, growth or increase

> **DURING READING**
> **Use Reading Strategies**
> **Make Inferences** What is a negative effect of so much information, according to the author? **F**

---

8. **eloquence.** Graceful, persuasive power
9. **Henry Kissinger or Trent Lott** Kissinger was secretary of state from 1973 to 1977, and Lott became the majority leader in the U.S. Senate in 1996.
10. **Waylon Jennings.** Grammy Award-winning country singer

Teach the Model

Analyze Literature

Tone What tone, or attitude, does the author express toward Will Campbell? Model a response by saying that the author has adopted a tone of admiration toward Campbell for speaking his mind in plain, truthful language. **A**

Analyze Literature

Persuasive Writing *Answer:* He is refuting the notion that people have to be experts or great speakers in order to argue against something they feel is wrong. **B**

Analyze Literature

Aphorism Share with students this definition: An aphorism is a short saying that expresses a wise or clever observation. Ask: "What do you think Rabindranath Tagore means by this aphorism? Do you agree?" Then ask students to look for and discuss other aphorisms in this essay, as well as any they might already know. An example from the essay is the Ethiopian proverb, "He who conceals his disease cannot be cured." An example from students' own experience might include, "You can't fool Mother Nature." **C**

---

participate in a student conference on capital punishment at Florida State University. At the last minute he discovered that he was supposed to formally debate an erudite[11] scholar, who delivered a long philosophical argument in favor of the death penalty as a

A means of buttressing[12] the legitimacy of the state. When Campbell got up to present the opposing view, nothing equally weighty came to mind. So he said, slowly and deliberately, "I just think it's tacky," and sat down.

The audience laughed.

"Tacky?" the moderator asked.

"Yessir," Campbell repeated. "I just think it's tacky."

"Now, come on," the moderator said, "tacky is an old Southern word, and it means uncouth, ugly, lack of class."

"Yessir. I know what it means," said Campbell. "And if a thing is

DURING READING

Analyze Literature
Persuasive Writing By giving the example of Will Campbell, what possible argument is Loeb challenging? **B**

ugly, well, ugly means there's no beauty there. And if there is no beauty in it, there is no truth in it. And if there is no truth in it, there is no good in it. Not for the victim of the crime. Certainly not for the one being executed. Not for the executioner, the jury, the judge, the state. For no one. And we were enjoined by a well-known Jewish prophet to love them all."

I'm not lobbying for disdaining reasoned arguments. But modern society, by virtue of its complexity and sophistication, makes moral engagement difficult; we don't need to compound the problem by demanding perfection. Simple can still be forceful and eloquent. Social change always proceeds in the absence of absolute knowledge, so long as people are willing to follow their convictions, to act despite their doubts, and to speak even at the risk

C of making mistakes. As the philosopher and poet Rabindranath Tagore once wrote, "If you shut your door to all errors, truth will be shut out."

THERE ARE NO *natural leaders or followers,*
—no people who by virtue of superior
genetic traits become activists.

According to another version of the perfect standard, we shouldn't begin working for social change until the time is ideal—when our kids are grown, say, or when our job is more secure. We wait for when our courage and wisdom will be greatest, the issues clearest, and our supporters and allies most steadfast.

---

11. erudite. Showing wide knowledge, scholarly
12. buttressing. Supporting; propping up

TEACHING NOTE

Self-Generated Questioning

Ask students to formulate two or more questions about the reading, along with ideas about how to answer them. Model this: "I want to know with which causes the author is involved. I can infer the answer by rereading the causes on which he focuses." Have students arrange themselves in a circle, and give a ball to one student. Instruct this student to ask the class one of his or her questions and to gently toss the ball to someone who signals that he or she knows the answer. This activity provides a framework for calm, organized discussion. Encourage students to control the discussion without your aid.

Hesitation is reasonable; we are subject to real pressures and constraints. Yet when will we not be subject to pressures?

There is no perfect time to get involved in social causes, no ideal circumstances for voicing our convictions. Instead, each of us faces a lifelong series of imperfect moments in which we must decide what to stand for. We may have to seek them out consciously, sometimes in discouraging contexts or when we don't feel ready. The wonder is that when we do begin to act, we often gain the knowledge, confidence, and strength that we need to continue.

LEADERS *Are Born*
—And Made, Too

I've heard countless people say they'd like to do more but are just not "the kind of person who gets involved." The suggestion here is that the ability to make a difference is innate and immutable,[13] either part of our character or not. But if developmental psychology theories are correct, there are no natural leaders or followers, no people who by sole virtue of superior genetic traits become activists. There are only individuals whose voices and visions through happenstance or habit have been sufficiently encouraged. Being able to stand up for our beliefs is a learned behavior, not an inherited disposition.

In fact, seemingly powerless people may be in a better position to change history than their more fortunate counterparts. Consider Martin Luther King Jr. early in his career, a 26-year-old preacher heading into Montgomery, Alabama, uncertain of what, if anything, he might achieve. Indeed, King's campaigns failed as often as they succeeded. Lech Walesa was a shipyard electrician before events thrust him into the forefront of Poland's Solidarity movement.[14] Wei Jingshen, the long-imprisoned dissident who helped inspire the Tiananmen Square protest by placing his democracy essay on a public wall, was a technician at the Beijing Zoo. Lois Gibbs was an ordinary housewife until she organized her neighbors at Love Canal, then founded Citizens Clearinghouse for Hazardous Waste. These people were not fulfilling a preordained destiny. They were developing character—their own unique character—by speaking out for what they believed. As the 18th-century Hasidic rabbi Susya once put it, "God will not ask me why I was not Moses. He will ask me why I was not Susya."

---

13. immutable. Never changing
14. Poland's Solidarity Movement. Labor movement led by Lech Walesa

> **DURING READING**
>
> **Make Connections**
> When have you had a moment such as the one Loeb describes? **D**

> **DURING READING**
>
> **Analyze Literature**
> **Persuasive Writing** Is this an appeal to logic or to emotion? **E**

> **DURING READING**
>
> **Use Reading Strategies**
> **Clarify** What is Loeb trying to do in this paragraph? How does he accomplish this effect? **G**

> **DURING READING**
>
> **Use Reading Strategies**
> **Make Inferences** What does this saying by Susya mean? **H**

Teach the Model

Make Connections
Answer: Students should give examples of a moment when they had to decide that for which they stood. **D**

Analyze Literature
Persuasive Writing *Answer:* Logic. Loeb uses psychology theories to make his point that leaders and followers are not born; they are made. **E**

History Connection
Solidarity Tell students that Lech Walesa (b. 1943) was a leader of a movement in Poland to form the first non-Communist trade union in the Soviet bloc. This union was called Solidarity. He served as its chairman and later became president of Poland (1990–1995). He was awarded the Nobel Peace Prize in 1983. Today, he is retired from politics. **F**

Use Reading Strategies
Clarify *Answer:* Loeb is trying to convince the reader that ordinary and seemingly powerless people can make an extraordinary difference and that these people learned how to create change by doing it—they weren't born knowing how to do it. Loeb accomplishes his purpose by giving examples. **G**

Use Reading Strategies
Make Inferences *Answer:* Most responses will include the idea that one doesn't have to be one of the greatest leaders who ever lived but that each person should instead do the best that he or she can do. **H**

Speaking & Listening Skills

Brainstorming
Share with students these brainstorming techniques to help with the Collaborative Learning activity on page 323:

- One group member takes the role of "recorder" and writes down every idea that is offered.
- Encourage all ideas, no matter how wild or wrong you think they are.

- Ask a participant to give reasons why he or she likes an idea. This will encourage discussion about the idea and spark new ones.

Make Connections
Answer: Taking to heart differing opinions helps us challenge, alter, and strengthen our own perspectives. **A**

Use Reading Skills
Identify Main Idea Ask students what the main idea of this paragraph is. Model a response: "You can't always be perfect in your methods and approaches, but you just do the best you can." **B**

Analyze Literature
Supporting Details Ask students to list the details the author uses to support his main idea that we "learn to live with contradictions in our personal lives." **C**

EXPERIMENTS *in Truth*
—Leave Room for Error

If participation in public life is a developmental process, then taking action is also an experiment in self-education. Sociologist Todd Gitlin argues that learning often takes place precisely when we enter "that difficult, rugged, sometimes impassable territory where arguments are made, points weighed, counters considered, contradictions faced, and where honest disputants[15] have to consider the possibility of learning something that might change their minds." Social activism, in other words, is as much a matter of learning how to listen, especially to those who disagree with us, as it is of learning how to voice our beliefs.

> **DURING READING**
>
> **Make Connections**
> Why should we listen to opinions different from our own? **A**

How do we know the changes we're promoting will do more good than harm? Advocates for the perfect standard would have us believe that uncertainty is an insurmountable obstacle, but it can also be a blessing. "The fact that we don't get it could be the best news of all," writes Sister Mary Smith of Portland's Franciscan Renewal Center, "because in not getting it we are opened up to a new way of seeing, a new way of hearing, and possibly a new way of living."

B Those of us who work for social justice often have no choice but to pursue our fundamental goals by means that are unclear, ad hoc,[16] half-baked, contradictory, and sometimes downright surreal.[17] I remember going to one Vietnam-era demonstration that focused on the role of major oil companies in promoting the war; my friends and I drove to the demonstration because there was no other cheap and efficient way to get there. As we stopped to fill up at a gas station along the way, it dawned on us that we were financially supporting one of the companies we would soon be vocally opposing. We felt more than a little absurd, but it was the best choice available.

C We learn to live with contradictions in our personal lives. A lonely few wait indefinitely for partners who match their romantic ideals, but most of us fall in love with people who, like ourselves, fall short of faultlessness. Children are the embodiment of unpredictability; we can influence but not control them. We respond to those dear to us moment by moment, as lovingly and mindfully as possible, improvising as we go. We embrace uncertain human bonds because the alternative is isolation.

15. **disputants.** People involved in a dispute
16. **ad hoc.** Relevant only to specific people
17. **surreal.** Difficult to accept as reality

Differentiated Instruction

Kinesthetic Learning
Invite students to choose one of the heroes mentioned by the author or anyone they believe fits the description. Then encourage them to stage a historical re-enactment of an incident for which the hero is remembered. Students might want to further research Pete Knutson, Rosa Parks, Sonya Tinsley, or Gandhi and put together a dramatic presentation based on something he or she accomplished.

English Language Learning
Point out the following words and expressions:
toil away—work extremely hard, 314
bankrolled—supported with money, 314
boycott—refusal to buy certain goods or use certain services, 316
ad hoc—improvised; impromptu, 320
half-baked—lacking adequate planning; unrealistic, 320

Public involvement demands a similar tolerance for mixed feelings, doubts, and contradictory motives. When we act, some may view us as heroic knights riding in to save the day, but we're more like knights on rickety tricycles, clutching our fears and hesitations as we go. Gandhi called his efforts "experiments in truth," because their results could come only through trial and error.

How then shall we characterize those who participate in our society as active citizens? They are persons of imperfect character, acting on the basis of imperfect knowledge, for causes that may be imperfect as well. That's a profile virtually any of us could match, given a willingness to live with ambiguity,[18] occasional failure, and frustration. Imperfection may not be saintly, but wielding[19] it in the service of justice is a virtue. Whoever we are, we can savor our imperfect journey of commitment. Learning as we go, we can discover how much our actions matter. ❖

---

18. **ambiguity.** Uncertainty
19. **wielding.** Handling and using

DURING READING

Use Reading Skills
Summarize How would you summarize Loeb's view about social activism?

D

> **MIRRORS & WINDOWS**
>
> What makes you feel helpless or empowered to make change in the world? How did this essay affect your feelings on the subject? How do you feel about the opinion that people have a social obligation to try and work for change in society?

Find Meaning

1. (a) What did Peter Knutson do to get involved with a cause he felt was important? (b) What do you think led him to this involvement?

2. (a) What story about Rosa Parks is widely told? (b) What is usually left out of her story? (c) Why is the missing information important?

3. (a) What contradictions do we learn to live with in our personal lives? (b) What are the consequences of this?

Make Judgments

4. (a) Identify five reasons that often keep people from getting socially involved. (b) What do these reasons have in common?

5. How do you feel about the statement, "It does us all a disservice when people who work for social change are presented as saints"? Explain.

6. An anecdote is a brief story, usually told to make a point. Identify two anecdotes in the selection. (a) What purpose do they serve? (b) What points do they make?

Teach the Model

Use Reading Skills
Summarize *Answer:* Social activism is a learning experience in which people must act under circumstances that are not always clear. **D**

 *Answer:* It might have inspired students by showing how ordinary citizens create change. They might feel that people who want the benefits of living in a just world need to participate in it.

Find Meaning
1. (a) He built an alliance. (b) He felt great concern for the cause.
2. (a) She sparked the bus boycott by her refusal to move seats. (b) She spent years working for change. (c) It shows that social change takes time.
3. (a) We learn to live with contradictions such as influencing children but not being able to control them. (b) People can apply action with fear or hesitation.

Make Judgments
4. (a) People see social involvement as impractical, feel the issues are too complex. (b) These are all based on fear of the unknown.
5. Enshrining heroes makes it hard for others to feel up to the task.
6. Answers will vary.

Reading Skills

Compare and Contrast

Have pairs of students work together to compare the two genres represented in this pairing. Suggest that they answer the following questions as they make their comparisons:

1. What are the characteristics of each genre?

2. What do the pieces have in common? How do they differ?

You might suggest that students create a Venn diagram to compare the two pieces.

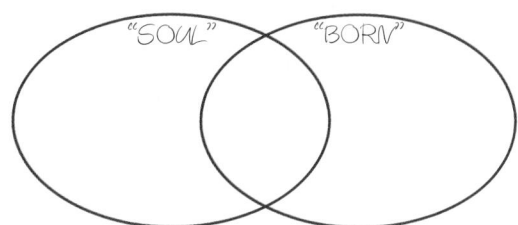

History Connection

Sit-ins A sit-in is a form of protest in which one or more persons occupy an area in a nonviolent manner in order to protest an injustice or promote social, political, or economic change. Participants usually seat themselves and stay seated until they are forcefully moved or until their requests have been met. When the peaceful protesters are removed by physical means, public sympathy is aroused, thus increasing the protesters' chances of achieving their goals. Sit-ins were first used by Mahatma Gandhi in the Indian independence movement. Later, they were widely used in the United States during the American Civil Rights Movement, beginning with sit-ins at the lunch counters in Greensboro, North Carolina, in 1960. **A**

Make Connections

Ask students to comment on the idea of being "born at the wrong time." If they could choose a historical period in which to live, which one would it be? Why? What could they do in their chosen period that they cannot do now? **B**

LITERATURE ▶▶ CONNECTION

In "Soul of a Citizen," Paul Rogat Loeb discusses social activism. The following poem by author **Angela Shelf Medearis** (b. 1956) also deals with this concept. The speaker in the poem is a young person who tells of having a mother who was active in the Civil Rights movement of the 1960s. As you read, think about what the speaker means when she says, "I was born at the wrong time."

I Was Born at the Wrong Time

A Lyric Poem by Angela Shelf Medearis

A
I had to ask
my mom
to define
a "sit in."[1]
5 You know, they sit in a place
to protest something,
carry signs, and get arrested.
I had to ask about it
B because I was born at the wrong time.
10 All the excitement is over with.
My mom had already marched for civil rights,
sung WE SHALL OVERCOME,[2]
shouted BLACK POWER,
MARCHED ON WASHINGTON,
15 had a basketball-sized Afro,
sang sweet soul music,
and cried over
Martin Luther King Jr. and both Kennedys[3]
long before my first birthday.
20 I wonder if there will be any causes left
to believe in
by the time I'm old enough
to join in the fight? ❖

1. **sit in.** Organized protest demonstration in which the participants seat themselves in an appropriate place and refuse to move
2. **WE SHALL OVERCOME.** Anthem of the Civil Rights movement
3. **both Kennedys.** President John F. Kennedy who was assassinated on November 22, 1963, and his brother Robert Kennedy, a United States senator who was assassinated in June 1968 while campaigning for the Democratic presidential nomination

---

Differentiated Instruction

Reading Proficiency

Remind students that when they read poetry, they need to observe the punctuation or lack thereof at the ends of lines, adjusting their rhythm to match the sense of each sentence. Have students reread the poem aloud, paying special attention to punctuation.

Common Core State Standards

Language
L.6

TEXT TO TEXT CONNECTION

Both Loeb's essay and Medearis's poem deal with social activism. Give at least two examples of how an idea in "I Was Born at the Wrong Time" relates to an idea or argument in "Soul of a Citizen." Support each example with textual evidence.

AFTER READING

Analyze Literature

Persuasive Essay When analyzing a persuasive essay, look at the writer's use of logical and rhetorical techniques to convince the reader of the writer's viewpoint. Be aware of bias to help separate fact from opinion. Look back over "Soul of a Citizen." Find examples of an appeal to logic and an appeal to emotion. Cite examples from the text.

Appeal to Logic	Appeal to Emotion
It's more inspiring to learn how people succeed acting for social change by overcoming their uncertainties than to be told they are saints who never had doubts.	"Though we're outraged when moneyed interests corrupt our political system, we believe we lack the authority to insist that campaign financing be reformed."

Extend Understanding

Writing Options

Creative Writing A slogan is a phrase or motto used to express a goal or belief. Think about a cause you care about. Write a few sentences to explain what the cause is. Then write a **slogan** to help rally people around that specific cause. Your slogan should be brief and catchy.

Expository Writing Choose a section of "Soul of a Citizen." Use your summary chart to decide what the main idea of the section is. Then create a **list** of all the supporting details in the section. Identify which of those details are the most essential and effective. Also indicate whether each detail is a fact or an opinion and explain how this impacts their effectiveness. Discuss your list with the class.

Collaborative Learning

Address Issues Individuals can make a difference, but a small group can often do even more. Work in small groups to come up with a short list of social or environmental issues you would like to address. Choose one of the issues and brainstorm ways you could take action. Create a plan with specific goals and deadlines. Make sure everyone in the group has a role.

Critical Literacy

Analyze Speeches Use the Internet to locate a passage from a speech by a famous social activist. Analyze the author's choice of words and phrases and use of literary devices. How do these elements help the activist appeal to an audience and motivate others to support the cause?

 Go to **www.mirrorsandwindows.com** for more.

Text-to-Text Connection

Answer: Students should use examples from both texts to show how the ideas relate. Sample examples: Loeb argues that ordinary people working together can create great change. The speaker's mother was one such person who joined others in protest and change. The poem references the March on Washington, where hundreds of thousands of people came together to make their voices heard. This relates to Loeb's assertion that people look for the perfect moment to join a cause.

Analyze Literature

Persuasive Essay *Answers:* Responses and examples will vary. Sample examples:

Appeal to logic: The first paragraph of the section entitled "Not for Saints."

Appeal to emotions: In the section "Not for Saints": *Though we're outraged when moneyed interests corrupt our political system, we believe we lack the authority to insist that campaign financing be reformed.*

Bias: Social activism is important and valuable. It is something everyone can and should do. Some students might also say that Loeb has a politically liberal bias.

Rubrics for Writing Options

You can adapt this as a checklist for students to use as they write.

Creative Writing

- ☐ Is it clear what the cause is?
- ☐ Is the slogan brief?
- ☐ Is the slogan catchy?

Expository Writing

- ☐ Is the main idea stated? Is it correct?
- ☐ Do the details support the main idea?
- ☐ Does the student evaluate which ideas are the most effective and most essential?
- ☐ Does the student evaluate which ideas are the least effective and least essential?

Teach the Workshop

Understanding Dashes, Semicolons, and Colons

1. We need to understand our flaws: callousness, shortsightedness, and denial.

2. *Correct*

3. The movement requires powerful leaders; they must have strong convictions.

4. Rosa Parks will be remembered — years after her death — for her great courage.

5. *Correct*

> For more information, see Grammar & Style Section 3.15, Punctuation, in the Language Arts Handbook.

Program Resources

You will find additional lessons on Punctuation: Dashes, Semicolons, and Colons in the *Exceeding the Standards: Grammar & Style* resource.

KEY TERMS

DASH, 324
PUNCTUATION, 324
PERIODS, 324
COMMAS, 324
SEMICOLON, 324
CONJUNCTIONS, 324
COLON, 324

Punctuation: Dashes, Semicolons, and Colons

Dashes

They were developing character—their own unique character—by speaking out for what they believed.

—PAUL ROGAT LOEB, "Soul of a Citizen"

A **dash** [–] is used to show a sudden break or change in thought. Dashes sometimes replace other marks of punctuation, such as periods, semicolons, or commas. In the quotation above, the dashes indicate a change in thought.

Semicolons

But modern society, by virtue of its complexity and sophistication, makes moral engagement difficult; we don't need to compound the problem by demanding perfection.

—PAUL ROGAT LOEB, "Soul of a Citizen"

A semicolon [;] joins two closely related sentences. The semicolon signals a longer pause than that of a comma, but shorter than the pause at a period.

> **EXAMPLE**
>
> *Most Americans are caring; they do what they can for friends.*

Conjunctions such as *and, but, so, or, nor, for,* and *yet* are often used to combine two related sentences. A semicolon can replace the comma and the conjunction. This adds emphasis to the second clause. Only use semicolons when the sentences are very closely related.

> **EXAMPLES**
>
> *Pete Knutson built an alliance, and he persuaded people that habitat could be restored.* [joined with a comma and conjunction]
>
> *Pete Knutson built an alliance; he persuaded people that habitat could be restored.* [joined with a semicolon]

Colons

A colon [:] introduces a list of items. Colons are also used between numbers that tell time and after the greeting in a business letter.

> **EXAMPLES**
>
> *The alliance had a broad base: fishermen, environmentalists, and Native Americans.*
>
> *The meeting on Initiative 640 is at 10:00 A.M.*
>
> *Dear Sir: Please join our alliance.*

Understanding Dashes, Semicolons, and Colons

Rewrite the following sentences, correcting the punctuation where necessary. If no changes are needed, write *correct*.

1. We need to understand our flaws; callousness, shortsightedness, and denial.

2. The five hundred richest people control more wealth than half the human population—a frightening statistic.

3. The movement requires powerful leaders: they must have strong convictions.

4. Rosa Parks will be remembered; years after her death; for her great courage.

5. Fear of failure should not stop us; we only fail if we don't try.

TEACHING NOTE

Extra Practice

Ask students to rewrite the following sentences, correcting punctuation where necessary. If no changes are needed, have them write *correct*.

1. Americans are generous, they try to help those who are close to them. (change the comma to a semicolon)

2. The following people affected social change—Pete Knutson, Rosa Parks, and Gandhi. (change the dash to a colon)

3. Parks didn't make her decision on the spot; she had studied public participation for years. (correct)

4. Don't wait for someone else to start a movement, do it yourself! (change the comma to a dash)

5. Dear Mr. Campbell, (change the comma to a colon)

Common Core State Standards

Language
L.2, L.4.3b, L.6.2a

EPIPHANY: THE THIRD GIFT

A Memoir by Lucha Corpi

Build Background

Literary Context In "Epiphany: The Third Gift," the author tells how she received a doll and a book, *The Arabian Nights*. *The Arabian Nights* tells the story of Scheherazade, a woman whose husband plots to kill her. Scheherazade saves herself from death by telling him stories every night without revealing the climax until the next day. Both the doll and the book play an important role in Lucha Corpi's memoir.

Reader's Context Of all the gifts you have ever received, which one has most influenced your life? Why?

Set Purpose

The word *epiphany* refers to the sudden insight or understanding of the meaning of something. Preview the selection by skimming the text and looking at the images. What do you think the selection will be about?

Analyze Literature

Setting The **setting** of a literary work is the time and place in which it happens. Writers create setting in different ways. In fiction and in memoirs, setting is often revealed through descriptions of landscape, scenery, buildings, furniture, clothing, weather, and seasons. It can also be revealed by how characters or people talk and behave. As you read "Epiphany: The Third Gift," note how the setting affects the people and the events in the memoir.

Meet the Author

Lucha Corpi was born in 1945 in the small town of Jáltipan in Mexico. When she was nineteen, she moved to the San Francisco Bay area. She has published books of poetry, novels, and children's books. Many of her works feature Latina characters, including her mystery novel, *Eulogy for a Brown Angel* and her novel *Delia's Song*. Lucha Corpi currently lives and teaches in Oakland, California.

Use Reading Skills

Analyze Text Structure Writing can be organized in different ways. When you analyze something, you break it down into parts and think about how the parts are related to each other and to the whole. The following are some methods of text organization:

- chronological, or time order
- spatial or location order
- order of importance
- comparison-and-contrast order
- cause-and-effect order

As you read "Epiphany: The Third Gift," decide how the text is primarily structured and how the structure affects your understanding of the memoir.

Preview Vocabulary

cha • grin (shə grin´) *n.,* feeling of irritation or shame due to a disappointment about something

com • mem • o • rate (kə me´ mə rāt´) *v.,* honor the memory of something or somebody in a ceremony

in • cul • cate (in kəl kāt´) *v.,* teach through frequent repetitions of something

ad • mon • ish • ing • ly (ad mä´ ni shiŋ lē) *adv.,* in a scolding or disapproving way

At a Glance
Directed Reading
- Reading Level: Moderate
- Difficulty Consideration: Vocabulary
- Ease Factor: Plot

Objectives
Studying this lesson will enable students to
- use reading strategies such as analyzing text structure
- define *setting* and recognize its importance in the selection
- describe the literary accomplishments of Corpi and explain the influence of Mexican culture on her writing
- appreciate a story of self-discovery

Launch the Lesson
Ask students how they would feel if a parent or mentor told them what to do with their life. Would they take this advice or resist it? Encourage them to describe the internal and external conflicts involved in this struggle.

The Mirrors & Windows questions at the end of this selection focus on the theme of gender. Before reading, ask students if they think their gender helps determine the way in which people treat them. Are men and women treated differently than in the past?

Words in Use

Preview Vocabulary	Selection Words	Teaching Words
chagrin, 327	cornea, 327	epiphany, 325
commemorate, 327	terseness, 327	skimming, 325
inculcate, 331	perfunctorily, 331	gender, 332
admonishingly, 331	qualms, 332	

KEY TERMS
MEMOIR, 325
SETTING, 325
CHRONOLOGICAL ORDER, 325
SPATIAL ORDER, 325
ORDER OF IMPORTANCE, 325
COMPARISON-AND-CONTRAST ORDER, 325
CAUSE-AND-EFFECT ORDER, 325

Common Core State Standards

Reading Literature
RL.2

Reading Informational
RI.1, RI.3

Writing
W.3, W.7, W.8, W.9, W.10

Speaking and Listening
SL.1

Language
L.6

Teach the Selection

Summary

The women in Lucha Corpi's life insistently gift her with dolls, despite her lack of interest in them. She prefers climbing trees and swinging on vines, but her greatest pleasure is reading. Her absorption in *The Arabian Nights* leads to an incident that cements her parents' concerns for her future. They dissuade her from pursuing careers they believe will impair her ability to maintain a family. Later she rediscovers literature and begins to write poetry that reflects the course of her life.

Art Connection

Jean Puy, who painted "Little Girl with Her Doll," was a student of a group of artists called Les Fauves. They invented a style of painting that conveyed emotion through color and valued originality over precision. Return to the painting after reading and ask students to relate elements of Fauvism to themes in the story.

TEACHING NOTE

Visualize

Repeat the painting's name, "Little Girl with Her Doll." Challenge students to discern and discuss whether the title captures what is going on in the painting. Guide them by asking questions such as "At what is the girl's attention directed?" After they form responses, invite students to predict the story's conflict.

EPIPHANY: THE THIRD GIFT

A Memoir by Lucha Corpi

Little Girl with her Doll. Jean Puy. Musée Antoine Lecuyer, Saint-Quentin, France.

326

Program Resources

Planning and Assessment
Program Planning Guide, Selection Lesson Plan
E-Lesson Planner
Assessment Guide, Lesson Test
ExamView

Technology Tools
Interactive Student Text on CD
Visual Teaching Package
Audio Library
mirrorsandwindows.com

Meeting the Standards
Nonfiction: Unit 3, Directed Reading, pp. 45–50

But most of all I preferred reading.

Ever since I was four years old, women insisted on giving me dolls. By age seven I had an assortment of them, made of papier-mâché, clay, and cloth. Using my older cousin's torn silky stockings, my grandmother had also made a few of them for me. And one of my mother's friends had brought me a porcelain "little lady" from Mexico City, which was kept in my mother's wardrobe so I wouldn't break or damage it.

As a child I didn't understand why everyone around me insisted on giving me dolls, especially since I had made it clear that I really didn't like to play with them.

I much more enjoyed climbing trees and running around with the boys—my older brother, a cousin, and their friends. I loved playing marbles, spinning tops until they hummed. Playing walk-the-high-wire on a narrow brick fence or, in Tarzan-like fashion, swinging on long vines from the rubber tree to the fence thrilled me no end. But most of all I preferred reading.

During recess and after school, I would go into the area in the principal's office that doubled as the school library. There I would look at the illustrations and read over and over the few natural sciences and biology books on the table. At home, after doing my homework, I would avidly consume any text lying around.

At the time, my father, who worked for the Mexican National Telegraph Company, had undergone a cornea transplant and had to wear a patch over one of his eyes for a while. Straining his other eye, he slowly read the daily reports coming into his office, but by the time he went home, that eye burned inside its lid.

Since I could read well, he asked me to read selections to him after supper from *La Opinión*, the region's daily newspaper. I was happy to do something for my father, whom I loved very much, but reading to him also gave me an opportunity to learn new words, for my father would patiently explain anything I didn't understand.

(A) Although I didn't fully grasp the issues reported in the news articles, my world nonetheless expanded, for I also began to learn about international, national, and regional politics, geography, and literature.

Naturally, reading and looking at my small tropical world from high above the tallest trees became more exciting activities for me than playing with those cute celluloid[1] creatures that could do nothing but stare into empty space. Every so often I'd rub my face against the silky surface of the cloth dolls, feel the warm terseness of the papier-mâché under my fingers or the smooth coolness of the porcelain whenever my mother allowed me to hold the doll in her wardrobe. But most of the time, to my **(B)** mother's <u>chagrin</u>, the dolls rested one upon the other like fallen dominoes alongside a wall in my room.

(C) For a few months after my seventh birthday, no one—including my mother—had given me any dolls, and I thought the adults around me had finally gotten over their need to do so. But I was wrong, for the sixth of January neared.

Like millions of children in Mexico, at home we received presents on the Twelfth Night after the birth of Jesus Christ—Epiphany—a time to <u>commemorate</u>

---

1. **celluloid.** Type of plastic

cha·grin (shə grin´) *n.*, feeling of irritation or shame due to a disappointment about something

com·mem·o·rate (kə me′ mə rāt´) *v.*, honor the memory of something or somebody in a ceremony

---

Teach the Selection

Make Connections

Corpi's dilemma will be familiar to many students. Ask: "Has anyone important in your life ever given you a gift that you didn't want? How did you react?" Discuss the pros and cons of diverse reactions such as pretending to enjoy the gift and politely refusing it. **A**

Literary Connection

The Arabian Nights The narrator's literary focus in "Epiphany" is a book called *The Arabian Nights,* also known as *The Thousand and One Nights.* While the stories were originally written in Arabic, countless versions exist in both Arabic and English today. The book is controversial since no one is in agreement as to which version accurately captures the original stories. It seems that the *Nights* are a compilation of many pieces of fiction that were once independent of one another, and certain versions leave out or include stories that others do not. There are, however, certainly three layers to the *Nights,* including Persian stories that integrate Indian stories, stories from Baghdad, and stories from Cairo. **B**

Use Reading Strategies

Visualize Ask students to picture the scene described here. Have them consider what the author's solution reveals about her character. **C**

---

the revealing of baby Jesus to the Magi and their offering to him of myrrh, incense, and gold.

On that January 6, 1952, my parents gave me three gifts: a doll (no great surprise!), a doll's house, and a book—a children's version of *The Arabian Nights,* which came wrapped in red tissue paper.

I used the wrapping tissue as a book cover and was just getting ready to read when my mother walked into my room.

"Isn't your doll just beautiful?" my mother asked. I looked at the doll—I'll have to call her "She" because I never gave her a name. *She* was a fair celluloid creature with light brown hair and blue eyes that matched the color of her ruffled dress. Her apron and socks were white.

A I puckered my lips and raised my eyebrows, not really knowing how to let my mother down easily.

"But this one is different," my mother explained, trying to talk me into playing with the toy. "Look," my mother emphasized, "this doll talks; she says, 'Mommy.'"

Then my mother turned the doll over, raised her tiny dress, and pulled on a chain to wind the doll's voice mechanism.

Something must have been wrong with the mechanism, because the noises *She* made sounded more like a cat's cries than a baby's babbles. My grandmother had often told me that our neighbor's cat cried like that because it needed love.

"*Anda buscando amor*—it's looking for love," my grandmother would explain, purposely neglecting to elaborate on the kind of love a cat in heat desires.

Interpreting my grandmother's comment literally, on several occasions I had tried to hug the cat to give it love, but it had scratched me and run away. Sure,

328   UNIT 3 NONFICTION

"And why is this doll hanging from the tree?"

nonetheless, that the doll needed love, I hugged her tightly for a long time. Useless, I said to myself finally, for the doll kept making the cat-looking-for-love noises. I decided to play instead with the doll's house, which my father had set down on the front porch, where it was cool in the afternoon. I went out to play with it. But since inspecting and rearranging the tiny furniture seemed to be the only activity possible, I quickly lost interest.

I could hear my friends in the yard talking and egging each other on to walk the high wire. Bending over or squatting to play with the doll's house had left my body and spirit in need of physical activity. So I went into my room to put on my shoes to **B** join my friends in the yard. I was tying my shoelaces when I saw again the third of my gifts—*The Arabian Nights*—wrapped in the red tissue paper, and I began to read it. From that moment on, the doll and the doll's house began to collect dust, and *Scheherazada* became my constant companion.

Every day, after doing my homework, I climbed the guava tree my father had planted a few years before. Nestled among its branches, during the next three weeks, I read and reread the stories in *The Arabian Nights* to my heart's content. But I was unaware that my mother had become concerned as she noticed that I wasn't playing with either the doll or the little house.

C My parents had always encouraged us to read. My mother wouldn't have dreamed of asking me to give up my reading session, but she began to insist that I take the doll up the tree with me.

Differentiated Instruction

English Language Learning

Students learning English may need help with the following words from the story.

insist—demand firmly; to be resolute, 327
avidly—with great enthusiasm; eagerly, 327
emphasized—stressed; pointed out for special notice, 328
inevitable—certain; unable to be avoided, 329
significant—important; noteworthy, 330
impeccable—flawless; free from fault, 331

Reading Proficiency

Have students read along while listening to the dramatic recording in the Audio Library. Also, survey the English Language Learning instruction at left.

Trying to read on a branch fifteen feet off the ground while holding on to the silly doll was not an easy feat. Not even for an *artist of the high wire and the flying trapeze.* After nearly falling off the branch twice, I finally had to devise a way to please my mother and keep my neck intact. Cutting two thin vines off a tree, I removed their skin and tied them together into one long rope; then I tied one end around the doll's neck and the opposite one around the branch. This way I could just let the doll hang in midair while I read.

I was always looking out for my mother, though. I sensed that my playing with the doll was of great importance to her. So every time I heard my mother coming, I lifted  **D** the doll up and hugged her. The smile in my mother's eyes told me my plan worked. Before suppertime, I entered the house through the kitchen so my mother could see me holding the doll.

During the next few days, my mother, the doll, and I were quite happy. But the inevitable happened one afternoon. Totally absorbed in the reading, I did not hear my mother calling me until she was right under the tree. When I looked down, I saw my mother, her mouth open in disbelief, staring at the dangling doll. Fearing the worst of scoldings, I climbed down in a flash, reaching the ground just as my mother was untying the doll.

"What is *this?*" she asked as she smoothed out the doll's dress.

My mother always asked me that or a similar rhetorical question when she wanted me to admit to some wrongdoing.

The Princess Consulting the Bird Bulbulhezar, from *The Arabian Nights*, 1939. Roger Broders. Private collection. **E**

From that point on, we would both follow an unwritten script. After my giving the appropriate answer for the particular situation we faced—"It's a doll, hanging," in this case—my mother would then ask me a second question. In this case, she would have asked, "And why is this doll hanging from the tree?"

To my surprise, on this occasion my mother wasn't following the script. Dumbfounded,[2] she kept on staring at the

---

2. **dumbfounded.** So amazed one cannot speak

Teach the Selection

Analyze Literature

Point of View First, ask students to consider the situation from the mother's point of view. If she were the narrator, what might she say about her daughter's behavior? Model a response that indicates concern that her daughter is not behaving in the manner expected of girls in that culture and time. Next, challenge students to imagine the father as narrator. How might his opinion of Corpi's behavior differ from that of his wife? Model a response that demonstrates his complex feelings about his daughter's behavior and future. **D**

Art Connection

Direct students' attention to the illustration from *The Arabian Nights* story "The Two Jealous Sisters." It is called "The Princess Consulting the Bird Bulbulhezar" and portrays Scheherazade situated before a wall carved in a linked pattern of six-pointed stars. The stars are a symbol of David, a prophet in Judaism, Christianity, and Islam, and are frequently found in this fundamental element of Islamic art, the arabesque. The arabesque is a repetition of geometric forms that symbolize the infinite nature of Allah. This arresting artwork has graced the walls of Islamic buildings throughout the world, and the master storyteller Scheherazade likely walked alongside them in the Sultan's palace. **E**

Writing Skills

Connecting Words

Remind students that in both writing and speaking, too many short sentences can sound choppy. Connecting words, such as *instead*, *otherwise*, *although*, and *while*, are a good way to combine sentences and make content flow more smoothly. Different sentence lengths and patterns create a pleasing rhythm that holds the audience's interest.

Have students work with a partner to revise and read aloud the following paragraph, using connecting words to help vary the sentence lengths and patterns.

Lucha Corpi wrote about her childhood. She said women were always giving her dolls. She didn't like dolls. She liked to be outside climbing trees. She also liked to read. Her parents worried about her. They thought she might grow up to be unhappy. Her mother told her to conform. Her mother said she would suffer if she didn't.

Teach the Selection

Use Reading Strategies

Make Predictions Ask students, based on what they already know of the narrator's relationship with her father, what they think will happen when he comes home after this incident. Then have them compare their predictions to what actually happens. **Ⓐ**

Use Reading Strategies

Make Inferences The Spanish phrase *jalón de orejas* is not translated. Ask students to make inferences about what it might mean based on its context. Next, explain that *oreja* means "ear," that the phrase translates literally to "tug of the ears," and that this punishment has the North American equivalent of "boxing of the ears." The phrase can indicate a simultaneous smacking of the ears against the head (imagine the hands as cymbals) or, when used metaphorically, implies a general reprimand. **Ⓑ**

Analyze Literature

Conflict Remind students that conflict in a story can be external or internal. How would they characterize the conflict experienced by the narrator's mother? Model a response: "Because of the hanging-doll incident, the narrator's mother felt an internal conflict concerning her daughter: She worried that she lacked a maternal instinct and would not have a happy family life." **Ⓒ**

doll, then she glanced at me. I swallowed hard. At that moment, I realized I had just accomplished the impossible: *I had rendered[3] my mother speechless!*

I also sensed for the first time in my seven years that I had done something *terribly, terribly* wrong—perhaps even unforgivable.

Ⓐ Making me carry the doll in my arms, my mother led me back to the house, still without a reprimand.[4] But I was sure that I would be paying for my transgression[5] by nightfall when my father came home. By suppertime, I feared, the storm would hover right above my head. But my father came home, and supper came and went, and I went to bed at my usual time with my ears, hands, and butt untouched.

The day after the hanging-doll incident, my father came home early and suggested that he and I play with the doll's house. He had stopped by my grandmother's house a block away and had picked up some tiny clay bowls, glasses, and pots she had bought for me. Among the kitchenware there was even a tiny metate,[6] in case we wanted to grind *masa*[7] to make tortillas, he said.

Already dust had collected on the little house's roof and on the tiny furniture, and it took us fifteen minutes to wipe everything clean before we could begin to put the kitchenware and the furniture back in the rooms.

A short while later I realized that playing with the doll's house this second time was just as boring as the first time. But my father seemed to be having so much fun I didn't have the heart to inform him I wasn't in the least interested. So quietly I slipped out of the room and picked up *Scheherazada* on my way to the yard. Absorbed as he was in arranging and rearranging the tiny furniture, he didn't even take notice of my quick exit.

Ⓑ At suppertime, again, I expected a good *jalón de orejas*. Instead, waving a finger but laughing, my father said, "Ah, *mi chaparrita traviesa* (my naughty little woman)."

"Miguel Angel, you're spoiling this child," my mother mildly objected.

My father's only reply was a chuckle.

Almost twenty years passed before I found out from both my parents why the hanging-doll episode had been so significant for them. By then I had already moved to California, my father had been diagnosed with terminal cancer, and I was a parent myself.

Ⓒ After recounting the episode of the hanging doll amid my father's and my laughter, my mother, teary eyed and sentimental, confessed that all those years she had been afraid I would turn out to be an unnatural mother because, as a child, I had hung the doll from the branch. She was delighted I had turned out to be a most loving and understanding mother to my three-year-old son Arturo.

---

3. **rendered.** Made or caused
4. **reprimand.** Punishment
5. **transgression.** Something that is not allowed
6. **metate.** Stone used to grind flour
7. *masa.* Corn flour

Differentiated Instruction

Enrichment

Some students might enjoy reading about Scheherazade as they investigate the frame story around *The Thousand and One Nights* (also called *The Arabian Nights*). Suggest that they read a few tales and report back to the class on why they think Corpi was so engrossed by the book.

Kinesthetic/Visual Learning

Place students in groups, have them choose roles, and direct them to act out parts of the selection. One good scene to enact would be the moments between the author and her mother during and immediately after the hanging-doll incident. If a student would prefer to work on his or her own, suggest that he or she dramatically represent the scene in which Corpi attempts to play with the doll that "talks" (p. 328).

During my nineteen years at home, neither my father nor my mother ever gave up trying to socialize me—"civilize" me, my mother would often say.

Throughout those years, they <u>inculcated</u> in me that intellectually and artistically I was as capable as my brothers. So they provided me with the best education they could afford. They made clear to me, nonetheless, that all this was being done not just to satisfy my own needs as an individual; above all, I was being educated to serve the needs of the family I would one day have. **D**

"When you educate a man," my father would often tell my younger sister and me, "you educate an individual. But when you educate a woman, you educate the whole family." Then he would caress my sister's cheek and mine as he added, "I don't remember who said that a child's education begins twenty years before he's born. But whoever said it was surely right. My grandchildren's education begins with yours, *mis chaparritas.*"

It wasn't unusual for Mexican fathers—almost regardless of class—to deny their daughters the advantages of formal schooling on the false premise that as women they would always be supported and protected by their husbands. The important thing was, then, my uncles perfunctorily stated, to get as successful a husband as could be found for the girls in the family. Problem solved.

My father was not quite the typical Mexican father in this respect. But even this atypical man, who has been and will continue to be one of the most influential people in my life, was subject to the social norms and pressures that made the education of a woman a separate (if equal) experience. **E**

Consistently throughout my life I was convinced by both my father and my mother

> ## During my nineteen years at home, neither my father nor my mother ever gave up trying to socialize me—"civilize" me...

that what I truly wanted—a career as either a medical doctor or an astronomer—was not what was best for me.

"As a medical doctor you will have to care for and examine male patients; you will be subject to men's low designs," my father warned every time I brought up the subject.

"You will suffer," my mother added, waving her finger <u>admonishingly</u>, to emphasize what she really wanted to say: "*Conform.*"

With impeccable[8] logic my father would state the advantages for a woman of a career in dentistry: independence (not working for a man), flexibility of schedule (time to take care of the children as well), and great financial rewards.

Relentlessly I would plead for a second wish, a career in astronomy. My father would caress my cheek gently and say, "But, my little woman, an astronomer has to work at night. When would you spend time with your children? And your husband? Surely, he would find someone else to keep him company at night."

"And you will suffer," my mother would interject in her usual manner. "Your children will grow up having a zombie for a mother, and you'll die young," she would state to

---

8. **impeccable.** Free from fault

---

in·cul·cate (in kəl kāt´) *v.*, teach through frequent repetitions of something

ad·mon·ish·ing·ly (ad mä´ ni shiŋ lē) *adv.*, in a scolding or disapproving way

---

Analyze Literature
Setting Remind students that setting refers not only to the time and place but to the cultural milieu as well. What does this passage reveal about the cultural milieu in which Lucha Corpi was raised? Model a response by saying the milieu features a prevalent attitude that a woman's place is in the home with her children—not in the workplace. Discuss with students how this environment might be difficult in any time period, especially for a woman who wishes to or must support herself. **D**

Use Reading Strategies
Ask Questions Students might ask themselves whether this attitude—that women's educational opportunities should be separate from men's—still prevails in Mexico or other places. They might also ask how one can resist social norms and pressures that they don't agree with. **E**

Parentheses
Explain that parentheses are used to enclose nonessential information in sentences. This nonessential information might include explanations, examples, and minor digressions that may help the reader understand the material but are not necessary to the meaning. Have students find some examples of parentheses in the selection. Ask: "Are they enclosing explanations, examples, or minor digressions?"

Clarify Point out that writing is so important to the author that she equates it with life itself. Would she have felt the same way about her work if she had gone on to become a dentist? **A**

Analyze Literature

Theme Remind students that theme is a central message about life that is revealed in a literary work. Theme can be stated or implied, and a literary work can have more than one theme. Ask what they think the main theme of this selection is. Model a response: "The theme might be that a person will never be happy trying to fulfill someone else's ambitions—he or she has to pursue his or her own interests."

Answer: Both sexes might talk about expectations of how they should act, dress, perform athletically and in school, etc. Students should give specific examples. Students might point out that although women today have more opportunities than in the 1950s, it is still not equal. They may point to government, big businesses, or what is reflected in their own lives. They may also point out that in most families the mother is still the primary caregiver.

strengthen her argument, with a stern and sad face, as if I were already the victim of an ancient curse.

Because I wanted to pursue a career, I eventually agreed to attend the school of dentistry in San Luis. I was happy the first two years, since my classmates and I carried the same subjects as first-year medical students, in addition to dental labs. But when I stared into a real open mouth for the first **A** time, I began to suspect that I was not cut out to be a good dentist. The first time I sweated out the extraction of a molar, my suspicions were confirmed. After the first ten tooth fillings, I knew I would surely go insane one day.

For a couple of years I had been going steady with Guillermo, who was preparing to move to Berkeley, where he hoped to attend the University of California. As painful as it was to leave my family and my country, I had no qualms in quitting dentistry school, marrying him, and moving to California.

Through my relationship with my husband I rediscovered the pleasure of reading for my own enjoyment. Although I would not start writing poetry for another five years after my arrival in Berkeley, I knew I wanted to make the study of literature my life's pursuit.

By the time I began to write poetry, I was already undergoing a painful separation from my husband, feeling cut off from the cultural and emotional support of family and friends, working as a bilingual secretary to support my son and put myself through college at Berkeley, grieving for my late father and expressing my daily thoughts and experiences in a language not yet my own.

For the next few years, in an almost manic manner, I wrote at least one poem a day, possessed by the terrifying notion that if I stopped writing I would stop breathing as well.

Every so often, when I visit my mother in Mexico, she recalls the incident of the hanging doll and thanks God aloud for making me a good parent. Then she sighs as she inventories my vicissitudes[9] in life, pointing out that I would be a rich dentist and a happily married woman now, living still in Mexico, instead of being a divorced woman, a poor schoolteacher, and a Chicana poet in California.

I look back at that same childhood incident, recall my third gift, the book I wrapped in red tissue paper, and for a fleeting instant I, too, take inventory of the experiences that have made me who and what I am. I pause to marvel at life's wondrous ironies. ❖

9. **vicissitudes.** Difficulties because of a way of life, career, or actions

When have you ever felt expected to do or like something because of your gender? How did that make you feel? How have opportunities for men and women changed in today's society?

Differentiated Instruction

Reading Proficiency

Students will benefit from a discussion of Corpi's return to literature, described on this page. Ask them how a new relationship might prompt one to "rediscover" the pleasure of reading for enjoyment. How might the failure of a relationship and the feelings that accompany that failure, such as anger, loneliness, or guilt, trigger a flood of writing inspiration? How can reading and writing serve as forms of healing?

Find Meaning

1. (a) As a child, and then as an adult, how do Lucha's interests differ from her parents' expectations of her? (b) How are they the same?

2. (a) Why did Lucha's hanging of the doll concern her mother? (b) How did her mother express that concern?

3. How was Lucha's father's view of education for girls unusual?

Analyze Literature

Setting Setting is the time and place in which the events of a narrative occur. An author's description of a setting, as well as the setting itself, can give a reader insight into the characters' traits, feelings, and viewpoints. In "Epiphany: The Third Gift," how does the setting of Jáltipan, Mexico, during the 1950s affect Lucha Corpi's childhood experiences? What do the details of the setting reveal about her? Use a cluster chart to record information about the setting and how it affects Lucha or reveals something about her.

Make Judgments

4. Why do Lucha's parents want her to play with the doll and the dollhouse?

5. Review the information about *The Arabian Nights* from Build Background. What is the connection between Scheherazade in *The Arabian Nights* and Lucha's choice of careers?

6. (a) In the end, how does Lucha's mother feel about the choices Lucha has made? (b) How are Lucha's feelings different?

Most women were not expected to have careers.

Main Setting: Jáltipan, Mexico, 1950s

Extend Understanding

Writing Options

Creative Writing Write a brief **narrative** from the perspective of either Lucha's mother or father about the doll hanging incident. Use precise and vivid language to help the reader better picture the events. Share your narrative with other members of the class.

Expository Writing Write an **analysis** of the arguments Lucha's family makes about her career choices. Discuss which points you feel are valid and which are not. State your opinion in your thesis statement, and support it with examples. Share your work with the class.

Lifelong Learning

Research Careers "Epiphany: The Third Gift" mentions many different careers. With a partner, research one of these careers. Create a list of the pros and cons for entering the profession.

Collaborative Learning

Discuss Setting With a partner, discuss the setting of this essay. Compare your cluster charts and discuss how they are alike and different. Use the information from your discussion to create a new chart.

Go to www.mirrorsandwindows.com for more.

Find Meaning

1. (a) Lucha prefers a more physical type of play as a child. As an adult, she is expected to choose a career compatible with raising a family. Lucha wants a career that follows her interests. (b) Both Lucha and her parents value reading. Both think it is okay for women to have a career.

2. (a) Her mother felt it meant Lucha would be an "unnatural" or bad mother. (b) Her mother tries to get Lucha to admit to wrongdoing.

3. Her father wants her to have a career that will allow her to be somewhat independent and believed that an educated mother would raise educated children.

Make Judgments

4. They think it will prepare her for motherhood.

5. Scheherazade tells stories to stay alive, and Lucha writes poetry to stay alive.

6. (a) Her mother is relieved that Lucha is a good mother, but she is disappointed that Lucha isn't married. (b) Lucha likes who she has become.

Analyze Literature

Setting *Answer:* Growing up in Mexico in the 1950s, Lucha Corpi was expected to conform to traditional expectations of what a girl of that time and place should do. She should play with dolls and choose a career compatible with being a mother and wife. Some of the setting details, like the high tree that Lucha likes to climb, show that she was a fearless child.

Rubrics for Writing Options

You can adapt this as a checklist for students to use as they write.

Creative Writing

☐ Does the student adopt the parent's persona?
☐ Does the narrative reflect the event?
☐ Does the narrative use precise language?

Expository Writing

☐ Does the essay clearly restate the arguments?
☐ Does the essay clearly discuss why the points of the arguments are valid or invalid?

Teach the Workshop

Teach the Workshop

Understanding Prepositional and Participial Phrases

1. <u>Inspecting and rearranging the tiny furniture</u>, I briefly played <u>with the doll's house</u>. The participial phrase is an adjective that modifies the noun *I*. The prepositional phrase is an adverb that modifies the verb *played*.

2. <u>Using his one good eye</u>, my father read the daily reports that came <u>into his office</u>. The participial phrase is an adjective modifying the noun *father*. The prepositional phrase is an adverb that modifies the verb *came*.

3. I left the dolls <u>against the wall</u>, <u>resting like fallen dominoes</u>. The prepositional phrase is an adverb that modifies the verb *left*. The participial phrase is an adjective that modifies the noun *dolls*.

4. The third gift, <u>wrapped in red tissue paper</u>, sat <u>on the table</u>. The participial phrase is an adjective that modifies the noun *gift*. The prepositional phrase is an adverb that modifies the verb *sat*.

> For more information, see Grammar & Style Section 3.11, Phrases, in the Language Arts Handbook.

KEY TERMS

PHRASE, 334	**ADJECTIVE,** 334
SUBJECT, 334	**ADVERB,** 334
VERB, 334	**NOUN,** 334
PREPOSITIONAL	**PARTICIPIAL PHRASE,**
PHRASE, 334	334
PREPOSITION, 334	

Prepositional and Participial Phrases

Phrases

A **phrase** is a group of words used as a single part of speech. Phrases are not sentences because they lack a subject, a verb, or both.

Prepositional Phrases

Relentlessly I would plead for a second wish, a career in astronomy.

—LUCHA CORPI, "Epiphany: The Third Gift"

A **prepositional phrase** consists of a preposition, its object, and any modifiers of that object. A prepositional phrase adds information to a sentence by modifying another word in the sentence. It may function as an adjective or an adverb. In the quotation above, *in astronomy* is a prepositional phrase that acts as an adjective modifying the noun *career*.

EXAMPLES

adjectives *It was a month <u>before my wedding.</u>* [*Before my wedding* is a prepositional phrase that modifies the noun *month*.]

She was blocked by stacks <u>of old magazines.</u> [*Of old magazines* modifies the noun *stacks*.]

adverbs *Mother said she was inviting the family <u>to our house.</u>* [The prepositional phrase *to our house* tells *where* the family was invited. It acts as an adverb modifying the verb *inviting*.]

You girls can help <u>with the cooking.</u> [The prepositional phrase *with the cooking* tells *what* the girls can help with. It acts as an adverb modifying the verb *help*.]

Participial Phrases

When I looked down, I saw my mother, her mouth open in disbelief, staring at the dangling doll.

—LUCHA CORPI, "Epiphany: The Third Gift"

A **participial phrase** consists of a participle, its object, and any modifiers of that object. The participle may end in *-ing*, *-ed*, or *-en*. A participial phrase always acts as an adjective in a sentence. In the quotation above, *staring at the dangling doll* is a participial phrase that modifies the noun *mother*.

EXAMPLES

She arrived at dawn, <u>loaded down with cleaning equipment.</u> [modifies the pronoun *she*]

The typewriter keys, <u>frozen with rust,</u> refused to move. [modifies the noun *keys*]

Understanding Prepositional and Participial Phrases

Rewrite each of the following sentences. Underline once any prepositional phrases and underline twice any participial phrases. Identify the function of each phrase and the word that it modifies.

1. Inspecting and rearranging the tiny furniture, I briefly played with the doll's house.
2. Using his one good eye, my father read the daily reports that came into his office.
3. I left the dolls against the wall, resting like fallen dominoes.
4. The third gift, wrapped in red tissue paper, sat on the table.

Program Resources

You will find additional lessons on Prepositional and Participial Phrases in the *Exceeding the Standards: Grammar & Style* resource.

Common Core State Standards

Language
L.1

TEACHING NOTE

Extra Practice

Ask students to carefully read each of the following sentences. Have them underline once any prepositional phrases and twice any participial phrases. Instruct them to identify the function of the phrase and the word it modifies.

1. Brendan played guitar <u>in the attic</u>, <u>explaining that the acoustics were best there</u>. The prepositional phrase is an adverb that modifies the verb *practiced*. The participial phrase is an adjective that modifies the noun *Brendan*.

2. <u>Burdened by her guilt</u>, Carla buried the memory deep <u>within her mind</u>. The participial phrase acts is an adjective and modifies the noun *Carla*. The prepositional phrase is an adverb and modifies the verb *buried*.

The Struggle to Be an All-American Girl

A Personal Essay by Elizabeth Wong

BEFORE READING

Build Background
Cultural Context In the United States, Chinatowns began as locations where large numbers of Chinese people either lived or ran businesses. Today those neighborhoods have become celebrated centers for tourism and multiculturalism. However, in the author's childhood, Chinatowns around the United States were often seen as neighborhoods to be avoided.

Reader's Context What do you think it means to be an all-American girl?

Set Purpose
Skim the text and art of "The Struggle to Be an All-American Girl" in order to make predictions about the essay's **theme.** Read to evaluate whether or not your predictions are correct.

Analyze Literature
Conflict A **conflict** is a struggle that occurs in a literary work. A conflict can be internal or external. A struggle that takes place between a character and some outside force such as another character, society, or nature is called an *external conflict.* A struggle that takes place within a character is called an *internal conflict.* As you read "The Struggle to Be an All-American Girl," pay attention to conflicts that the author faced and how they were resolved.

Use Reading Skills
Take Notes You will enjoy reading more if you engage with the text as you read. Take notes on what you read in order to recall events and understand what is happening in the selection. You can also respond to what you've recorded. As you read "The Struggle to Be an All-American Girl," use a log to keep track of your notes.

> **Note–taking Log**
>
> **Notes**
> Wong attended Chinese school.
>
> **Reactions**
> She might have resented spending every evening there.

Meet the Author

Elizabeth Wong was born in the Los Angeles Chinatown in 1958. She was a journalist for the *Hartford Courant* and the *San Diego Tribune* before she entered the Tisch School of the Arts at New York University to become a playwright. She is successful today not only as an award-winning playwright, but as a television screenwriter. Wong received writing credits for two episodes of the ABC sitcom *All American Girl* starring Margaret Cho. Describing her own work, she has said, "my work is about response." As you read, determine what Wong may be responding to in her essay.

Preview the Selection

At a Glance
Directed Reading
- Reading Level: Easy
- Difficulty Consideration: Cultural references
- Ease Factor: Plot

Objectives
Studying this lesson will enable students to
- use reading strategies such as asking questions
- define *conflict*, both internal and external, and recognize the importance of conflict in a literary work
- describe the literary accomplishments of Elizabeth Wong and explain the influence of her heritage on her writing

Launch the Lesson
Prior to reading "The Struggle to Be an All-American Girl," ask students how they would feel if they were forced to take lessons in the culture of their ancestors. Would they welcome this as an opportunity to enrich their own lives, or would they resent the time lost in activities that interest them now?

Words in Use

Selection Words	Teaching Words
dissuade, 337	tourism, 335
disassociate, 337	multiculturalism, 335
fanatical, 338	playwright, 335

KEY TERMS
PERSONAL ESSAY, 335
THEME, 335
CONFLICT, 335
INTERNAL CONFLICT, 335
EXTERNAL CONFLICT, 335
SENSORY DETAIL, 339
RESOLUTION, 339
THESIS STATEMENT, 339
DIALOGUE, 339

Common Core State Standards
Reading Literature
RL.2
Reading Informational
RI.1, RI.3, RI.4, RI.6
Writing
W.9
Language
L.6

Teach the Selection

Summary

The narrator relates her experiences as a ten-year-old in Los Angeles's Chinatown, where her mother makes her and her brother to go to Chinese school every afternoon. Wishing instead to play with friends after school, Wong resents the time she spends learning the Chinese language, customs, and culture that her mother values. She dislikes everything about the experience—the teacher, the odors, the environment, and the lessons. Wong explains her embarrassment at her grandmother's speech patterns and the behavior of the residents of Chinatown. She tells how her brother criticizes their mother for mispronunciations and misuses of English. After two years of Chinese lessons, Wong is allowed to stop attending. In retrospect, she regrets that she didn't learn more about her heritage.

 **MIRRORS & WINDOWS** The Mirrors & Windows questions at the end of this selection focus on the theme of maturity. Before reading, ask students if their perspectives or feelings about anything have changed since they were younger. What causes people to change their minds as they mature?

The Struggle to Be an All-American Girl

A Personal Essay by Elizabeth Wong

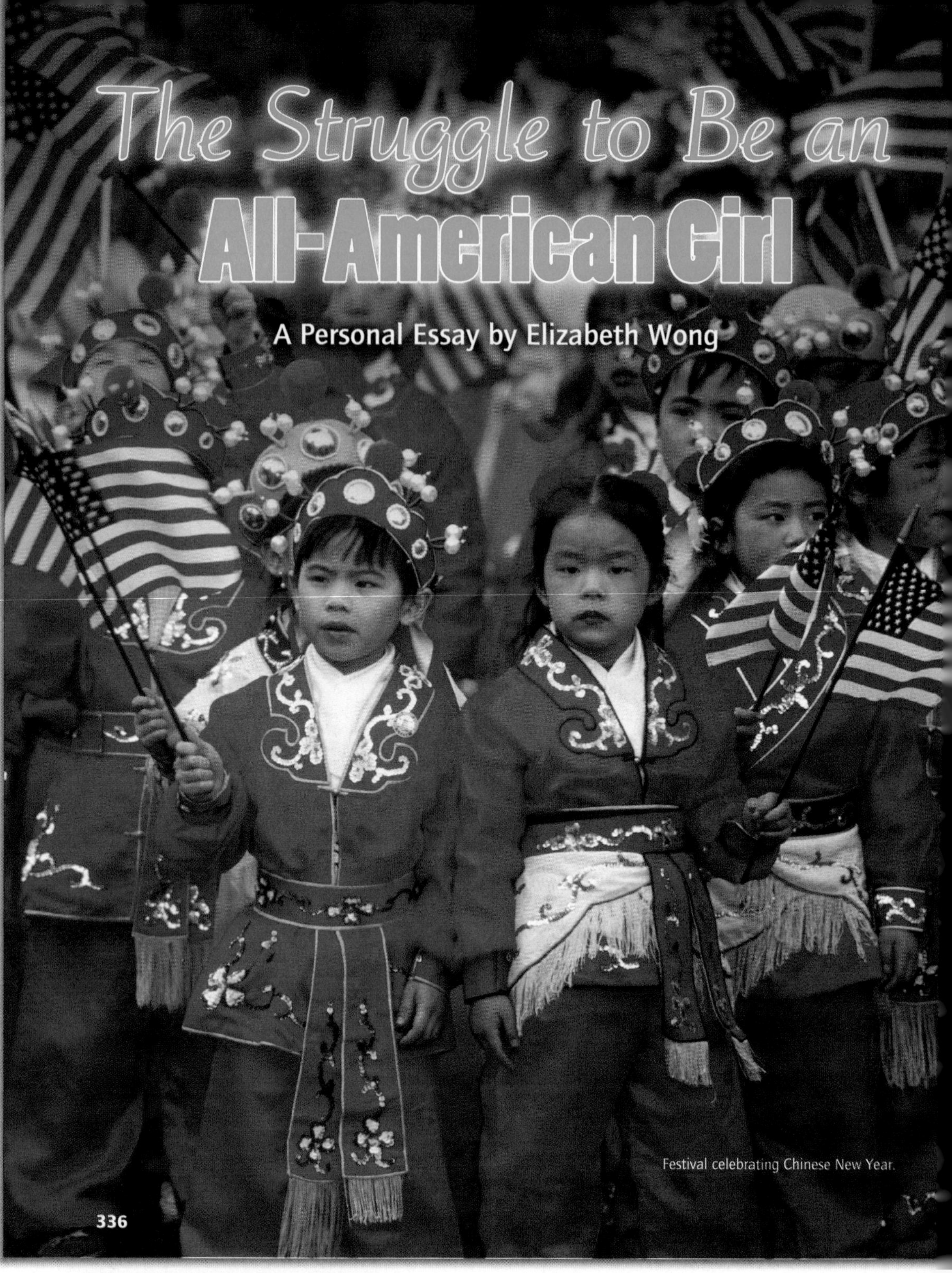

Festival celebrating Chinese New Year.

336

Program Resources

Planning and Assessment
Program Planning Guide, Selection Lesson Plan
E-Lesson Planner
Assessment Guide, Lesson Test
ExamView

Technology Tools
Interactive Student Text on CD
Visual Teaching Package
Audio Library
mirrorsandwindows.com

Meeting the Standards
Nonfiction: Unit 3, Directed Reading, pp. 51–55

Differentiating Instruction
Advanced Students, Cultural Context Project, p. 17
English Language Learners, Take Notes, pp. 108–116

It's still there, the Chinese school on Yale Street where my brother and I used to go. Despite the new coat of paint and the high wire fence, the school I knew 10 years ago remains remarkably, stoically[1] the same.

Every day at 5 P.M., instead of playing with our fourth- and fifth-grade friends or sneaking out to the empty lot to hunt ghosts and animal bones, my brother and I had to go to Chinese school. No amount of kicking, screaming, or pleading could dissuade my mother, who was solidly determined to have us learn the language of our heritage.[2]

Forcibly, she walked us the seven long, hilly blocks from our home to school, depositing our defiant tearful faces before the stern principal. My only memory of him is that he swayed on his heels like a palm tree, and he always clasped his impatient twitching hands behind his back. I recognized him as a repressed maniacal child killer, and knew that if we ever saw his hands we'd be in big trouble.

A

We all sat in little chairs in an empty auditorium. The room smelled like Chinese medicine,[3] an imported faraway mustiness.[4] Like ancient mothballs or dirty closets. I hated that smell. I favored crisp new scents. Like the soft French perfume that my American teacher wore in public school.

There was a stage far to the right, flanked by an American flag and the flag of the Nationalist Republic of China, which was also red, white and blue but not as pretty.

Although the emphasis at the school was mainly language—speaking, reading, writing—the lessons always began with an exercise in politeness. With the entrance of the teacher, the best student would tap a bell and everyone would get up, kowtow,[5] and chant, "Sing san ho," the phonetic for "How are you, teacher?"

Being ten years old, I had better things to learn than ideographs[6] copied painstakingly in lines that ran right to left from the tip of a *moc but,* a real ink pen that had to be held in an awkward way if blotches were to be avoided. After all, I could do the multiplication tables, name the satellites of Mars, and write reports on *Little Women* and *Black Beauty.* Nancy Drew, my favorite book heroine, never spoke Chinese.

B

The language was a source of embarrassment. More times than not, I had tried to disassociate myself from the nagging loud voice that followed me wherever I wandered in the nearby American supermarket outside Chinatown. The voice belonged to my grandmother, a fragile woman in her seventies who could outshout the best of the street vendors. Her humor was raunchy, her Chinese rhythmless, patternless. It was quick, it was loud, it was unbeautiful. It was not like the quiet, lilting romance of French or the gentle refinement of the American South. Chinese sounded pedestrian. Public.

In Chinatown, the comings and goings of

> In Chinatown, the comings and goings of hundreds of Chinese on their daily tasks sounded chaotic and frenzied.

---

1. **stoically.** Seemingly unaffected by emotion
2. **heritage.** Practices handed down from one's past
3. **Chinese medicine.** Ancient system of herbal medicine
4. **mustiness.** Quality of smelling or tasting old, stale, or moldy
5. **kowtow.** Touch the forehead to the floor while kneeling to show respect
6. **ideographs.** Characters or symbols that stand for ideas or things rather than sounds; characters in Chinese written language

THE STRUGGLE TO BE AN ALL-AMERICAN GIRL **337**

Cultural Connection

Chinese Calligraphy Share with students these facts about Chinese calligraphy:

- In China, calligraphy is an ancient art form.
- It is also called *brush calligraphy* to distinguish it from Western calligraphy, which often uses metal-tipped pens.
- Chinese calligraphy requires special tools and techniques.
- Each artist expresses individuality by the way he or she controls the concentration of ink.

Analyze Literature

Conflict Ask students to give examples of both internal and external conflict in this narrative. Model a response by suggesting that Wong's attitude toward anything connected with Chinatown and her Chinese heritage is an example of internal conflict and that arguments between Wong and her mother are examples of external conflict.

Answer: Students might say the author valued her heritage more as she grew older. They might remember turning away from family and toward friends. They might mention that as people grow older, they grow more independent.

hundreds of Chinese on their daily tasks sounded chaotic and frenzied. I did not want to be thought of as mad, as talking gibberish. When I spoke English, people nodded at me, smiled sweetly, said encouraging words. Even the people in my culture would cluck and say that I'd do well in life. "My, doesn't she move her lips fast," they would say, meaning that I'd be able to keep up with the world outside Chinatown.

My brother was even more fanatical than I about speaking English. He was especially hard on my mother, criticizing her, often cruelly, for her pidgin[7] speech—smatterings of Chinese scattered like chop suey in her conversation. "It's not 'What it is,' Mom," he'd say in exasperation. "It's 'What *is* it, what *is* it, what *is* it!'" Sometimes Mom might leave out an occasional "the" or "a," or perhaps a verb of being. He would stop her in mid-sentence: "Say it again, Mom. Say it right." When he tripped over his own tongue, he'd blame it on her: "See, Mom, it's all your

fault. You set a bad example."

What infuriated my mother most was when my brother cornered her on her consonants, especially "r." My father had played a cruel joke on Mom by assigning her an American name that her tongue wouldn't allow her to say. No matter how hard she tried, "Ruth" always ended up "Luth" or "Roof."

After two years of writing with a *moc but* and reciting words with multiples of meanings, I finally was granted a cultural divorce. I was permitted to stop Chinese school.

I thought of myself as multicultural. I preferred tacos to egg rolls; I enjoyed Cinco de Mayo more than Chinese New Year.

At last, I was one of you; I wasn't one of them.

Sadly, I still am. ❖

---

7. **pidgin.** Simplified form of speech that is usually a mixture of two or more languages

 How did the author's feelings change as she grew older? What things did you feel very different about when you were ten? Why do you think people's feelings change as they grow older?

Differentiated Instruction

Enrichment

Students might enjoy doing further research about Chinese calligraphy and other elements of Chinese culture. Suggest that they exhibit their findings in the form of an oral presentation with visual aids.

Reading Proficiency

Discuss the title of the selection and ask students what it implies about the author's point of view. Examine the photograph with students to decide if it helps them predict the subject of the essay. Ask: "Why do you think the author might find being 'all-American' a struggle?"

Find Meaning

1. (a) How did Wong feel about Chinese school when she was ten? (b) What details from the text support your answer?
2. (a) What subject was mainly taught at Chinese school? (b) How does Wong say she felt about the subject?
3. (a) How does Wong describe the sound of her grandmother's Chinese? (b) How does she describe other languages, and what does this comparison show?

Analyze Literature

Conflict Wong's essay describes both internal and external conflicts. In nonfiction as well as fiction, conflict is what keeps an audience reading. Readers want to see how conflicts will be resolved. Make a list of conflicts and their resolutions in "The Struggle to Be an All-American Girl." Scan the text for conflicts and resolutions to refresh your memory as you make your list.

Make Judgments

4. How does Wong use sensory details in her essay? Give examples.
5. Why do you think Wong included the description of an "exercise in politeness"?
6. "Chop suey" translates as "mixed pieces" and is not an authentic Chinese dish, but rather a dish that was invented in the United States. Why do you think Wong used "chop suey" in her description of her mother's speech?

Conflict	Resolution
Wong wants to feel like an all-American girl.	She leaves Chinese school.

Extend Understanding

Writing Options

Creative Writing Imagine that you are Elizabeth Wong when she was a child and you have been permitted to stop Chinese school. Write a **diary entry** that discusses the events of your day. Describe your own feelings on this day and the reactions of others, such as your principal, grandmother, and mother.

Expository Writing Write an analysis of the last line of "The Struggle to Be an All-American Girl." What does the author mean by "Sadly, I still am"? Plan a **literary response.** Create an outline for your response that introduces your interpretation in a thesis statement and supports it with evidence from the text. Conclude by commenting on the significance of Wong's essay in the context of modern American culture. Read your essay to the class.

Lifelong Learning

Create a Chinese Phrasebook Imagine that you and your family are relocating to China. Brainstorm a list of phrases you would be sure you wanted to learn before arriving in China. At your library, locate a Chinese language phrasebook. Translate into Chinese the phrases you think would be the most useful from your list.

Critical Literacy

Create a Dialogue Wong and her mother were very different people. Make a list of questions Wong's mother might ask about the English language. Then, make a list of questions Wong might ask about Chinese. Work with a partner. Use your lists of questions to create a dialogue about language between Wong and her mom. Read your dialogue aloud in front of your class with your partner. One of you will be Wong, and one will be Wong's mother.

 Go to www.mirrorsandwindows.com for more.

Review the Selection

Find Meaning

1. (a) She resented it. (b) She went "kicking, screaming, or pleading" and describes the principal as "a repressed maniacal child killer."
2. (a) The emphasis at the school was on speaking, reading, and writing Chinese. (b) Wong says she found the language to be a source of embarrassment.
3. (a) She describes it as loud and ugly. (b) She describes other languages as gentle and refined. The comparison shows her desire to leave behind her Chinese heritage.

Make Judgments

4. Wong uses the principal's "impatient twitching hands" to evoke an anxious mood. She uses the smell of Chinese medicine as a metaphor for her heritage, which she thinks has little to offer her.
5. Kowtowing might be uncomfortable to a ten-year-old.
6. "Chop suey" captures the mixed languages of pidgin speech. It comments on the issues of an imported culture.

Analyze Literature

Conflict *Answer:* Wong wants to feel like an all-American girl./ She leaves Chinese school.
Wong dislikes her grandmother's voice./She disassociates herself.
Wong didn't want to stand out by speaking Chinese./She spoke English and people praised her.
Wong did not want to think of herself as Chinese./She thought of herself as multicultural.

Rubrics for Writing Options

You can adapt this as a checklist for students to use as they write.

Creative Writing

☐ Does the entry discuss Chinese school?
☐ Does the entry reveal the author's feelings and explore the reactions of others?

Expository Writing

☐ Does the essay interpret the story's last line?
☐ Does it comment on the essay's significance in the context of modern American culture?

Understanding Consistent Verb Tense

1. insisted
2. begins
3. be able
4. blames
5. preferred

▶ For more information, see Grammar & Style Section 3.5, Verbs, in the Language Arts Handbook.

Program Resources

You will find additional lessons on Consistent Verb Tense in the *Exceeding the Standards: Grammar & Style* resource.

KEY TERMS

VERBS, 340
PRESENT TENSE, 340
PAST TENSE, 340
FUTURE TENSE, 340
CONSISTENT VERB TENSE, 340
CHARACTER, 340
SETTING, 340
PLOT, 340

Grammar & Style

Consistent Verb Tense

My brother was even more fanatical than I about speaking English.

— ELIZABETH WONG, "The Struggle to Be an All-American Girl"

Verbs have different forms called tenses, which tell the time in which an action takes place.

The **present tense** tells that an action happens now—in the present time.

The **past tense** tells that an action happened prior to the present time. The verb *was* in the quotation above is a past tense verb.

The **future tense** tells that an action will happen in the future.

> **EXAMPLES**
>
> **Present tense:** *My brother is even more fanatical than I about speaking English. He criticizes my mother.*
>
> **Past tense:** *My brother was even more fanatical than I about speaking English. He criticized my mother.*
>
> **Future tense**: *My brother will be even more fanatical than I about speaking English. He will criticize my mother.*

When writing about the same event (or group of events), use a **consistent verb tense,** whether it is past, present, or future.

> **EXAMPLES**
>
> **Incorrect:** *I swing my arms and will pick my way over the stones.*
>
> **Correct:** *I swing my arms and pick my way over the stones.*
>
> **Correct:** *I will swing my arms and pick my way over the stones.* [Will goes with both swing and pick.]

> **Incorrect:** *Each afternoon we went to the Chinese school, while our friends play.*
>
> **Correct:** *Each afternoon we go to the Chinese school, while our friends play.*
>
> **Correct:** *Each afternoon we went to the Chinese school, while our friends played.*

Keep in mind that you can change the tense in a sentence if you are indicating an event that occurred at a different time.

> **EXAMPLE**
>
> *I will never forget how it happened.*

When writing a literary analysis essay, maintain the present tense. Because the author is writing to a present reader in the present moment, refer to characters, settings, plots, and the author in present tense.

> **EXAMPLE**
>
> *Elizabeth Wong uses vivid detail in her description of Chinese school.*

Understanding Consistent Verb Tense

Select the correct verb in parentheses that is consistent with the underlined verb.

1. My brother and I pleaded with my mother, but she (insists, insisted, will insist) that we attend Chinese school.
2. The emphasis at Chinese school is language, but the lesson always (begins, began, will begin) with an exercise in politeness.
3. I will speak English well and (am able, was able, be able) to succeed outside Chinatown.
4. When my brother trips over his own tongue, he (blames, blamed, will blame) it on my mother.
5. I thought of myself as multicultural and (prefer, preferred, will prefer) tacos to egg rolls.

TEACHING NOTE

Extra Practice

Ask students to choose the verb in parentheses whose tense is consistent with the underlined verb.

1. I asked Denver who (choose, chose, would choose) her unusual name. (chose)
2. We will bring a fruit salad, since the weather (would be, is, will be) hot and humid. (will be)
3. Although Nasrin is the fastest runner on the team, she still (should practice, practices, practiced) more than any of us. (practices)
4. Their teacher would treat them with respect and they, in turn, (produced, would produce, would have produced) superior work. (would produce)
5. If Jaime had met her sooner, his outlook (will have been, will be, would have been) sunnier. (would have been)

Proclamation of the Indians of Alcatraz

A Persuasive Essay by the Indians of Alcatraz

At a Glance
Directed Reading
- Reading Level: Easy
- Difficulty Consideration: Satire
- Ease Factor: Length

BEFORE READING

Build Background
Historical Context For nineteen months, Native Americans from different tribes held a protest in which they overtook Alcatraz, an island with a closed federal prison, from the U.S. government. They protested the assimilation policy of the U.S. government, which was dissolving tribes, closing reservations, and forcing Native Americans to move into big cities. The protest helped change the direction of government policies that forced Native Americans to leave their reservations.

Reader's Context In 1796, George Washington, our country's first president, said, "The basis of our political systems is the right of the people to make and to alter their constitutions of government." What does this statement mean?

Set Purpose
Notice how an argument is constructed in "Proclamation of the Indians of Alcatraz." How do the writers appeal to your emotions? How do the writers appeal to logic? Read to find out.

Analyze Literature
Tone A writer's or speaker's attitude toward the subject or the reader is **tone.** As you read "Proclamation of the Indians of Alcatraz," notice clues that point to the writers' attitude toward "The Great White Father and All His People."

Meet the Authors
Richard Oakes, a leader of the occupation of Alcatraz, presented "Proclamation of the Indians of Alcatraz" to federal agency workers on November 9, 1969. Dr. LaNada Boyer, another occupation leader, said, "Alcatraz was symbolic in the rebirth of Indian people to be recognized as a people, as human beings, whereas before, we were not."

Use Reading Skills
Identify Author's Purpose Authors write for a reason, such as to inform, explain, entertain, reflect, or persuade. As you read, use the chart below to analyze the authors' purpose and how the ideas in the essay fulfill this purpose.

Before Reading	Identify the authors' purpose, the type of writing the authors use, and the ideas the authors want to communicate.
During Reading	Gather ideas that the authors communicate to readers.
After Reading	Summarize the ideas. Explain how these ideas help fulfill the authors' purpose.

Preview Vocabulary
hon·or·a·ble (ä´ nər [ə] bəl) *adj.*, deserving of honor and respect

per·pe·tu·i·ty (pʉr' pə tü´ ə tē) *n.*, condition of lasting for eternity

i·so·lat·ed (ï' sə lā´ tid) *adj.*, set apart from others

ad·e·quate (äd´ ə kwət) *adj.*, good enough to meet a need

DIRECTED READING

Objectives
Studying this lesson will enable students to
- use reading strategies such as identifying author's purpose
- define *persuasive essay* and recognize its purpose to influence the reader's way of thinking
- describe the literary accomplishments of the authors
- appreciate a proclamation expressing a position

Launch the Lesson
Place students in groups of three or four, and ask them to create a list of injustices they believe they suffer as young people. Request that a volunteer from each group offer one of their ideas, and write them on a board. Discuss possible avenues for addressing injustices and obstacles that require sacrifice. Tell them that the selection they are about to read, titled "Proclamation of the Indians of Alcatraz," claims injustices and demands reparation. Have them compare their ideas and obstacles with those of the authors.

Words in Use

Preview Vocabulary
honorable, 343
perpetuity, 344
isolated, 344
adequate, 344

Teaching Words
proclamation, 341
assimilation, 341
alter, 341
constitutions, 341
indigenous, 344

KEY TERMS

Common Core State Standards

Reading Literature
RL.4

Reading Informational
RI.1, RI.4, RI.6, RI.7, RI.8

Writing
W.6, W.7, W.8, W.9, W.10

Language
L.6

Summary

In November of 1969, a group of American Indian activists who came to call themselves Indians of All Tribes crafted a proclamation to accompany their occupation of Alcatraz Island. The document was addressed to the president of the United States and declared their reclamation of this land, which their ancestors inhabited before the arrival of Europeans in California. The authors portray injustices carried out against American Indians since the inception of European colonialism through bitter, ironic language. They justify their claim to the island by describing its negative attributes, which mirror those of the land to which native peoples were forced to relocate. The occupation unified members of different tribes, returned pride to an oppressed people, shined national attention on their cause, and turned the tide of U.S. policy toward American Indians.

MIRRORS & WINDOWS The Mirrors & Windows questions at the end of this selection focus on the theme of protest. Before reading, ask students if they have ever felt compelled to fight against great odds for a cause. What about the human spirit drives people to risk harm and loss for their beliefs?

342

Program Resources

Planning and Assessment
Program Planning Guide, Selection Lesson Plan
E-Lesson Planner
Assessment Guide, Lesson Test
ExamView

Technology Tools
Interactive Student Text on CD
Visual Teaching Package
Audio Library
mirrorsandwindows.com

Meeting the Standards
Nonfiction: Unit 3, Directed Reading, pp. 56–61

Differentiating Instruction
Advanced Students, Historical Connection
Project, p. 18

Proclamation[1]
of the Indians
of Alcatraz

A Persuasive Essay by the Indians of Alcatraz

Protestors march at Alcatraz.

We, the native Americans, reclaim the land known as Alcatraz Island.

Proclamation: To the Great White Father[2] and All His People

We, the native Americans, reclaim the land known as Alcatraz Island in the name of all American Indians by right of discovery.[3]

We wish to be fair and <u>honorable</u> in our dealings with the Caucasian inhabitants of this land, and hereby offer the following treaty:

We will purchase said Alcatraz Island for twenty-four dollars ($24) in glass beads and red cloth, a precedent set by the white man's purchase of a similar island about 300 years ago. We know that $24 in trade goods for these 16 acres is more than was paid when Manhattan Island was sold, but we know that land values have risen over the years. Our offer of $1.24 per acre is greater than the 47¢ per acre that the white men are now paying the California Indians for their land.

We will give to the inhabitants of this island a portion of that land for their own, to be held in trust by the American Indian Affairs and by the bureau of Caucasian

1. **proclamation.** Official public announcement
2. **Great White Father.** President of the United States
3. **right of discovery.** American colonists claimed the land by "right of discovery" for England, and that right transferred to the United States with the victory over the British in the American Revolutionary War. "Right of discovery" generally refers to lands that are uninhabited. However, non-Christians were not considered to be inhabitants.

hon·or·a·ble (ä´ nər [ə] bəl) *adj.,* deserving of honor and respect

PROCLAMATION OF THE INDIANS OF ALCATRAZ **343**

Cultural Connection

Thanksgiving Many Native Americans do not celebrate Thanksgiving. They instead consider the day one of sorrow, and have deemed it their National Day of Mourning. Thanksgiving intends to celebrate what some histories claim was the peaceful coexistence of natives and colonists upon the arrival of Europeans in America. Many Native Americans and non-natives, however, are working to correct this depiction and expose the reality of the circumstances, which include theft from and eventual extermination of thousands of indigenous peoples.

History Connection
American Indian Movement
Answer: Most students will note that the 1969 proclamation brought additional attention to the American Indian Movement. **Ⓐ**

Answer: Students might feel that the request was justified based on America's poor treatment of American Indians. They might suggest that these actions shed light on the real issues and history behind a cause of which people would not otherwise be aware.

Affairs[4] to hold in <u>perpetuity</u>, for as long as the sun shall rise and the rivers go down to the sea. We will further guide the inhabitants in the proper way of living. We will offer them our religion, our education, our life-ways, in order to help them achieve our level of civilization and thus raise them and all their white brothers up from their savage and unhappy state. We offer this treaty in good faith and wish to be fair and honorable in our dealings with all white men.

We feel that this so-called Alcatraz Island is more than suitable for an Indian Reservation,[5] as determined by the white man's own standards. By this we mean that this place resembles most Indian reservations in that:

1. It is <u>isolated</u> from modern facilities, and without <u>adequate</u> means of transportation.
2. It has no fresh running water.
3. It has inadequate sanitation facilities.
4. There are no oil or mineral rights.[6]
5. There is no industry and so unemployment is very great.
6. There are no health care facilities.
7. The soil is rocky and non-productive; and the land does not support game.[7]
8. There are no educational facilities.
9. The population has always exceeded the land base.
10. The population has always been held as prisoners and kept dependent upon others.

Based on your knowledge of history, how would you evaluate the requests of the writers? How might organizing protests and giving an official announcement help people take a cause seriously?

Further, it would be fitting and symbolic that ships from all over the world, entering the Golden Gate, would first see Indian land, and thus be reminded of the true history of this nation. This tiny island would be a symbol of the great lands once ruled by free and noble Indians. ✣

HISTORY ▶▶ CONNECTION

American Indian Movement
In the 1960s, the American Indian Movement (AIM) formed with the goal of protecting the rights and well-being of Native Americans living in urban centers. Inspired by the seizure of Alcatraz, AIM was involved in occupations of seventy-four federal facilities through the early to mid-1970s. Political action by Native Americans in the late 1960s and early 1970s resulted in Indian studies programs, tribal museums, and recognition by the United Nations of an international indigenous rights movement. How was the 1969 proclamation successful? **Ⓐ**

4. **bureau of Caucasian Affairs.** Imagined government office devoted to the affairs of white people that references the Bureau of Indian Affairs; at times widely considered to be a corrupt government organization
5. **Indian Reservation.** Tract of land set aside by the U.S. government for use by a Native American people
6. **mineral rights.** Rights to benefit from the valuable minerals that could be mined from land. Such rights have often been denied to Native Americans.
7. **game.** Wild animals that can be hunted for food

per•pe•tu•i•ty (pʉr′ pə tü′ ə tē) *n.,* condition of lasting for eternity

i•so•lat•ed (ī′ sə lā′ tid) *adj.,* set apart from others

ad•e•quate (ăd′ ə kwət) *adj.,* good enough

Differentiated Instruction

Visual Learning
John Trudell was one of the first and most active participants in the Alcatraz occupation. Students might benefit from examining the documentary film *Trudell*, which starts with the occupation, documents the subject's rise to national spokesman for the American Indian Movement, and details his shift from organized activism to poetic expression.

Enrichment
Students who have an affinity for American history might benefit from researching the history of Alcatraz Island, from its use by indigenous peoples prior to European arrival, through its various military and prison stages, to its current status as part of the Golden Gate National Recreation Area. Encourage students to reread the selection with this gained context in mind in order to enrich understanding.

Find Meaning

1. (a) What price did the Indians of Alcatraz offer to pay for the island? (b) How did they arrive at this price?

2. (a) How did the Indians of Alcatraz propose to "guide the inhabitants in the proper way of living"? (b) Why do you think they included this statement in the proclamation?

3. What opinion do the Indians of Alcatraz hold on the subject of Indian reservations?

Analyze Literature

Tone Authors convey their attitude toward an audience through the words they choose and how they put those words together. Skim "Proclamation of the Indians of Alcatraz" for words, phrases, and sentences that help convey the writers' tone. Enter these words in the outer circles of a cluster chart. Then, think of your own adjectives to describe the tone and enter them in the center circle.

Make Judgments

4. In what sense is the treaty offered by the Indians of Alcatraz "fair and honorable"?

5. Why do you think the writers refer to the price white men "are now paying the California Indians for their land"?

6. How did the writers use imagery effectively at the end of the essay? Explain your answer using examples from the text.

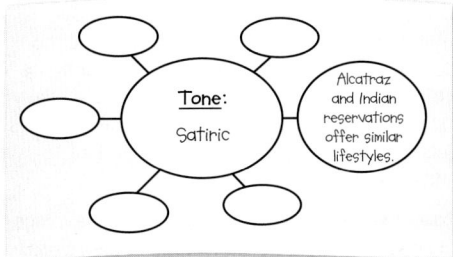

Tone: Satiric

Alcatraz and Indian reservations offer similar lifestyles.

Extend Understanding

Writing Options

Creative Writing On the Internet, research the media coverage of the occupation of Alcatraz. Look for articles or essays with many different viewpoints. Write a news article in which you explain the situation and objectively compare and contrast the perspectives of all parties involved.

Expository Writing "Proclamation of the Indians of Alcatraz" is a persuasive essay. Were you persuaded? Take a position on whether you agree or disagree with the proclamation. Write a brief **essay** in which you evaluate the effectiveness of "Proclamation of the Indians of Alcatraz." State whether or not the essay was effective in your thesis and cite at least two reasons. Discuss the essay's use of logical and emotional appeals and how they affected your opinion.

Collaborative Learning

Plan a Movie Shoot In a small group, plan a scene for a movie about the occupation of Alcatraz. Imagine you are going to film the scene in which Richard Oakes leads the successful crossing to Alcatraz Island at night. Begin with maps of California. Imagine that you are writing for your production company which has no knowledge of Alcatraz. Describe the challenges your group anticipates in shooting this scene and how to solve them.

Critical Literacy

Hold a Debate Prepare yourself for a class discussion about "Proclamation of the Indians of Alcatraz." Do you agree or disagree with the proclamation? With all or with parts? Be prepared to support your claims with evidence, such as anecdotes or other examples, from outside sources. When you are ready, begin the discussion.

 Go to www.mirrorsandwindows.com for more.

Find Meaning

1. (a) They paid twenty-four dollars in glass beads and red cloth. (b) The proclamation does not say.

2. (a) They proposed to teach them their religion, education, and lifestyles to help them achieve a higher level of civilization. (b) Students may be aware that this statement refers to Christianizing of Indians and forcing native children into boarding schools where they were alienated from their family, language, and cultural identity.

3. They are inadequate in every conceivable way.

Make Judgments

4. The treaty offered by the Indians of Alcatraz is neither fair nor honorable, but neither are the treaties offered by the United States government to Native Americans. They may say the treaty is fair and honorable because it is equivalent to a treaty offered by the United States.

5. The writers wish to bring this injustice to people's attention in order to bring about change.

6. Responses will vary. The island itself would greet those "entering the Golden Gate" and possibly symbolized the arrival of settlers to Native American land.

Analyze Literature

Tone *Answer:* Students might offer adjectives like *defiant, self-righteous, demanding, superior, sarcastic,* and *well-informed.*

Rubrics for Writing Options

You can adapt this as a checklist for students to use as they write.

Creative Writing

☐ Did the student research media coverage of the occupation of Alcatraz?

☐ Does the news article explain the situation and objectively compare the viewpoints of all parties involved?

Expository Writing

☐ Does the essay have an introduction, body, and conclusion?

☐ Does the essay clearly present the writer's position on the proclamation?

☐ Does the writer discuss the use of rhetorical devices that appeal to both logic and emotion?

For further instruction, refer students to the following extension activity: Critical Literacy: Hold a Debate, *Exceeding the Standards: Extension Activities*, pp. 9–10.

Vocabulary Practice

1. **white** synonyms: colorless, bleached; antonym: black; **savage** synonyms: wild, brutal; antonym: tame; **unhappy** synonyms: sad, miserable; antonym: cheerful; **good** synonyms: fine, wonderful; antonym: bad; **fair** synonyms: just, honorable; antonym: biased; **honorable** synonyms: righteous, decent; antonym: crooked

2. **offer** synonym: extend; **savage** synonym: wild; **faith** synonym: belief

3. **offer** antonym: withhold; **savage** antonym: tamed; **faith** antonym: mistrust

4. Paragraphs will vary according to students' chosen synonyms and antonyms.

5. Responses will vary, but students should recognize that their word choices affect the connotation or tone of the sentences.

6. Responses will vary, but students should suggest that the authors chose words to create a desired connotation or tone. Example response: *Savage* evokes a sense of irony, since U.S. policy makers had referred to American Indians in this derogatory way. It also reveals the author's view of white Americans' supposedly "cultured" lifestyles.

> For more information, see Vocabulary & Spelling Section 2.3, Using a Dictionary, in the Language Arts Handbook.

Synonyms and Antonyms

It is isolated from modern facilities, and without adequate means of transportation.

—"Proclamation of the Indians of Alcatraz"

How would the above quotation change if it said, "It is cut off from up-to-date services, and lacks enough ways to get around"? The words have the same meaning, but the tone is much different. **Synonyms** are words that have the same, or nearly the same, meaning. The synonym an author chooses depends on the author's style, as well as the intended tone or mood of the selection.

Antonyms are words that have opposite meanings. In the quotation, *nearby* is an antonym for *isolated*, *old-fashioned* is an antonym for *modern*, and *insufficient* is an antonym for *adequate*. Synonyms and antonyms must be the same part of speech as the original word.

A **thesaurus** is a reference containing synonyms for common words. Antonyms or contrasted words are often included.

EXAMPLES

Word	Synonyms	Antonyms
perpetual	*continual* *endless* *unceasing*	*temporary* *transient*
honorable	*noble* *high-principled*	*dishonorable* *unjust*
pleasant	*enjoyable* *likable* *agreeable*	*distasteful* *objectionable*

Review the Terms

Synonyms: words that have the same, or nearly the same, meaning

Antonyms: words that have opposite meanings

Thesaurus: reference containing synonyms for common words

Vocabulary Practice

Use a thesaurus and the following quote from "Proclamation of the Indians of Alcatraz" to complete the questions.

"We will offer them our religion, our education, our lifeways, in order to help them achieve our level of civilization and thus raise them and all their white brothers up from their savage and unhappy state. We offer this treaty in good faith and wish to be fair and honorable in our dealings with all white men."

1. List two synonyms and one antonym for each of the adjectives above.
2. Rewrite the quote using synonyms for one noun, one verb, and one adjective.
3. Rewrite the quote using antonyms for one noun, one verb, and one adjective.
4. Working with a partner, write a short paragraph using the synonyms and antonyms you created.
5. How do the different synonyms each change the meaning of the sentence? How do the different antonyms?
6. Why might the Native Americans at Alcatraz have chosen each adjective or adverb used in the above quote? What meanings or associations do they evoke?

Words in Use

Teaching Words
perpetual, 346
unceasing, 346
transient, 346
objectionable, 346

KEY TERMS
TONE, 346
SYNONYM, 346
ANTONYM, 346
THESAURUS, 346

Program Resources

You will find additional lessons on Synonyms and Antonyms in the *Exceeding the Standards: Vocabulary & Spelling* resource.

Common Core State Standards

Language
L.4

from **Harriet Tubman:** Conductor on the Underground Railroad

A Biography by Ann Petry

▲
▼

from **Our Struggle Is Against All Forms of Racism**

A Speech by Nelson Mandela

At a Glance
Directed Reading
from *Harriet Tubman: Conductor on the Underground Railroad*
- Reading Level: Easy
- Difficulty Consideration: Historical content
- Ease Factor: Formatting aids

from *Our Struggle Is Against All Forms of Racism*
- Reading Level: Challenging
- Difficulty Consideration: Historical content
- Ease Factor: Length

BEFORE READING

Build Background
Historical Context In different centuries and on different continents, Harriet Tubman and Nelson Mandela dedicated their lives to securing freedom and justice for blacks. An escaped slave in the American South, Harriet Tubman personally guided more than three hundred runaway slaves to freedom in Canada, along a secret network of "safe houses" known as the Underground Railroad. In South Africa, Nelson Mandela worked to end *apartheid,* a political and social order that enforced racial segregation and economic discrimination.

Reader's Context What problems create injustice in the world today? How can people fight against them? What risks would be involved? What strengths would people need to fight effectively?

Set Purpose
Preview the titles and images to predict each author's purpose.

Meet the Authors

Ann Petry (1908–1997) published her first novel, *The Street,* in 1946. It became a national bestseller, the first such success for an African-American woman.

Nelson Mandela was born in 1918 in South Africa. His teachings and writings helped to end apartheid in South Africa. He was awarded the Nobel Peace Prize in 1993.

Compare Literature: Author's Purpose
An **author's purpose** may be to entertain, explain, reflect, inform, or persuade. To identify each author's purpose, examine the subject, tone, and details of the selection. Ask yourself if the author is simply presenting information or is trying to persuade a reader, for example.

Preview Vocabulary
in·com·pre·hen·si·ble
(in' käm' pri hen´ sə bəl) *adj.,* impossible to understand

in·cen·tive (in sen´ tiv) *n.,* something that stimulates or encourages someone to take action

sol·i·dar·i·ty (sä´ lə da' rə tē) *n.,* complete unity and agreement within a group regarding opinions, purposes, goals, and feelings

kin·ship (kin´ ship') *n.,* very close relationship, as in a family or a group of people who share common opinions and outlooks

fore·sight (fôr' sīt´) *n.,* act or ability to see into the future with wisdom and knowledge

---

Objectives
Studying this lesson will enable students to
- compare literary selections of different genres
- use reading strategies such as previewing texts
- define *author's purpose* and explain the effect this has on a piece of writing
- describe the literary accomplishments of Ann Petry and Nelson Mandela
- recognize skills that help people achieve challenging goals

Launch the Lesson
Tell students that each selection is about a courageous person who fought for freedom for his or her people. Ask students what they would say to these people if they were able to meet them.

Words in Use

from *Harriet Tubman: Conductor on the Underground Railroad*

Preview Vocabulary	Selection Words	Teaching Words
incomprehensible, 351	overseer, 349	apartheid, 347
incentive, 352	invariably, 349	innate, 353
	unconcealed, 352	fugitive, 353
		comrades, 358
		solidarity, 358

KEY TERMS
BIOGRAPHY, 347
SPEECH, 347
SUBJECT, 347
TONE, 347
SYMBOL, 358
MAIN IDEA, 358
AUDIENCE, 358

Common Core State Standards

Reading Informational
RI.1, RI.2, RI.3, RI.6

Writing
W.9

Language
L.6

Teach the Selection

Summary

Soon after the Fugitive Slave Law passed, Maryland slave owners began hearing rumors about a man named Moses who helped slaves escape. Unbeknownst to them, the person they would in turn search for was actually Harriet Tubman, who, in December 1851, led a group of eleven slaves toward Canada and freedom. She managed to maintain her companions' courage and faith through inclement weather, little sleep, and fear of capture with descriptions of her own escape and the feeling of liberty. After a Quaker man and his wife welcome, feed, outfit, and house the travelers for a night, they continue on northward.

MIRRORS **W**INDOWS The Mirrors & Windows questions at the end of this selection focus on the theme of character. Before reading, ask students if they think that freedom fighters are destined to have great courage or gain it through experience. Are people born with a certain character, or do they build it as they mature?

from Harriet Tubman:
Conductor on the Underground Railroad

A Biography by Ann Petry

The Life of Harriet Tubman, #9: Harriet Tubman dreamt of freedom, 1940. Jacob Lawrence. Hampton University Museum.

348

Program Resources

Planning and Assessment
Program Planning Guide, Selection Lesson Plan
E-Lesson Planner
Assessment Guide, Lesson Test
ExamView

Technology Tools
Interactive Student Text on CD
Visual Teaching Package
Audio Library
mirrorsandwindows.com

Meeting the Standards
Nonfiction: Unit 3, Comparing Literature, pp. 62–69

Differentiating Instruction
Developing Readers, Set Purpose, pp. 22–24

She was determined that more and more slaves should know what freedom was like.

Along the Eastern Shore of Maryland, in Dorchester County, in Caroline County, the masters kept hearing whispers about the man named Moses, who was running off slaves. At first they did not believe in his existence. The stories about him were fantastic, unbelievable. Yet they watched for him. They offered rewards for his capture.

They never saw him. Now and then they heard whispered rumors to the effect that he was in the neighborhood. The woods were searched. The roads were watched. There was never anything to indicate his whereabouts. But a few days afterward, a goodly number of slaves would be gone from the plantation. Neither the master nor the overseer had heard or seen anything unusual in the quarter.[1] Sometimes one or the other would vaguely remember having heard a whippoorwill[2] call somewhere in the woods, close by, late at night. Though it was the wrong season for whippoorwills.

Sometimes the masters thought they had heard the cry of a hoot owl, repeated, and would remember having thought that the intervals between the low moaning cry were wrong, that it had been repeated four times in succession instead of three. There was never anything more than that to suggest that all was not well in the quarter. Yet, when morning came, they invariably discovered that a group of the finest slaves had taken to their heels.

Unfortunately, the discovery was almost always made on a Sunday. Thus a whole day was lost before the machinery of pursuit could be set in motion. The posters offering rewards for the fugitives[3] could not be printed until Monday. The men who made a living hunting for runaway slaves were out of reach, off in the woods with their dogs and their guns, in pursuit of four-footed game, or they were in camp meetings saying their prayers with their wives and families beside them.

Harriet Tubman could have told them that there was far more involved in this matter of running off slaves than signaling the would-be runaways by imitating the call

---

1. **quarter.** Area in a plantation where slaves lived; such areas often consisted of windowless, one-room cabins made of logs and mud.
2. **whippoorwill.** Bird that hunts for insects at night; the whippoorwill's name echoes its low, melodic call.
3. **fugitives.** People fleeing from danger or capture

HARRIET TUBMAN / OUR STRUGGLE IS AGAINST ALL FORMS OF RACISM **349**

History Connection

Moses Clarify with students why Harriet Tubman was called Moses. Explain that Moses is a religious figure considered by many to have been a great leader, lawgiver, and prophet. He was born in Egypt, where the Hebrews lived as slaves. According to religious beliefs, when the pharaoh ordered male children of Hebrews killed, Moses' mother put him in a small boat and floated him down the Nile River. The pharaoh's daughter found and adopted the child. As a grown man, Moses led the Hebrews out of Egypt by crossing the Red Sea on a journey that is known as the Exodus. They wandered in the wilderness for forty years, and just as they were within sight of the Promised Land, Moses died.

Use Reading Strategies

Make Inferences Have students infer why these people tied ashcake and salt herring in old bandannas. Model a response: "When they departed, they couldn't be sure when they'd eat next. They were taking along provisions." **A**

of a whippoorwill, or a hoot owl, far more involved than a matter of waiting for a clear night when the North Star[4] was visible.

In December, 1851, when she started out with the band of fugitives that she planned to take to Canada, she had been in the vicinity of the plantation for days, planning the trip, carefully selecting the slaves that she would take with her.

She had announced her arrival in the quarter by singing the forbidden spiritual[5]—"Go down, Moses, 'way down to Egypt Land"—singing it softly outside the door of a slave cabin, late at night. The husky voice was beautiful even when it was barely more than a murmur borne on the wind.

Once she had made her presence known, word of her coming spread from cabin to cabin. The slaves whispered to each other, ear to mouth, mouth to ear, "Moses is here." "Moses has come." "Get ready. Moses is back again." The ones who had agreed to go North **A** with her put ashcake[6] and salt herring in an

---

4. **North Star.** Runaways fleeing north used the North Star (Polaris) to help them stay on course.
5. **forbidden spiritual.** Spirituals are religious songs, some of which are based on the biblical story of the Israelites' escape from slavery in Egypt. Plantation owners feared that if slaves were allowed to sing such songs, they might rebel.
6. **ashcake.** Cornmeal bread baked in hot ashes

Differentiated Instruction

Reading Proficiency

As students activate their prior knowledge about the Underground Railroad, record their thoughts on a board. Students can add to the list as they learn more from the selection.

English Language Learning

Define *idiom*, an expression having a meaning different from the meaning of its individual words, and explain the meaning of one example from the selection, like "taken to their heels." Ask students for examples and explanations of idioms from their own cultures.

Harriet Tubman (far left) stands with family.

old bandanna,[7] hastily tied it into a bundle, and then waited patiently for the signal that meant it was time to start.

There were eleven in this party, including one of her brothers and his wife. It was the largest group that she had ever conducted, but she was determined that more and more slaves should know what freedom was like.

She had to take them all the way to Canada. The Fugitive Slave Law[8] was no longer a great many <u>incomprehensible</u> words written down on the country's lawbooks. The new law had become a reality. It was Thomas Sims, a boy, picked up on the streets of Boston at night and shipped back to Georgia. It was Jerry and Shadrach, arrested and jailed with no warning.

She had never been in Canada. The route beyond Philadelphia was strange to her. But she could not let the runaways who accompanied her know this. As they walked along she told them stories of her own first flight, she kept painting vivid word pictures of what it would be like to be free.

But there were so many of them this time. She knew moments of doubt, when she was half-afraid, and kept looking back over her shoulder, imagining that she heard the sound of pursuit. They would certainly be pursued. Eleven of them. Eleven thousand dollars' worth of flesh and bone and muscle that belonged to Maryland planters. If they were caught, the eleven runaways would be whipped and sold South, but she—she would probably be hanged.

---

7. **bandanna.** Square of fabric, often worn as a head scarf
8. **Fugitive Slave Law.** Harsh federal law passed in 1850 stating that fugitives who escaped from slavery to free states could be forced to return to their owners. As a result, slaves who escaped were not safe until they reached Canada. The law also made it a crime for a free person to help escaped slaves or to prevent their return to their owners.

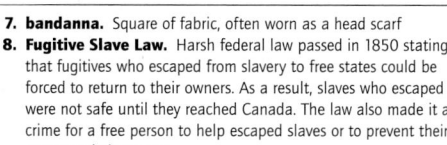

in·com·pre·hen·si·ble (in' käm' pri hen´ sə bəl) *adj.,* impossible to understand

Teach the Selection

Cultural Connection
Anthony Cohen Anthony Cohen grew up with accounts of Harriet Tubman and the Railroad, but a university research paper assignment prompted his desire to gain a real sense of the scope of Tubman's and other fugitives' experiences. In May of 1996, Cohen departed on foot from Sandy Springs, Maryland, on an eight-hundred-mile trek north. Students across the country charted his progress throughout the six-week expedition, sharing in his firsthand, real-world education.

Analyze Literature
Characterization Remind students that characterization is the way in which an author reveals characters' traits. Methods of characterization include revealing the inner thoughts of the character. What do Harriet Tubman's thoughts presented here uncover about her character? **B**

Make Connections
Ask students what they think about the fact that their government passed the Fugitive Slave Law, which would send the fugitives back to the South and resulted in the death of Harriet Tubman. Model a response such as: "The threat of violence between the North and South must have been very strong to allow for passage of this act." **C**

Writing Skills

Descriptive Language
Explain that good writers use words that convey their exact meaning. Use of precise nouns and verbs and modifiers makes writing more interesting.

Have students revise these sentences, replacing each underlined word with a more colorful, precise word.

1. He <u>took</u> the pitcher and <u>drank</u> its contents. (snatched, chugged)

2. The <u>cold</u> wind blew <u>strongly</u>. (icy, stoutly)

3. "It's not safe," he <u>said</u> as he <u>closed</u> the door. (whispered, latched)

Use Reading Strategies

Visualize Have students visualize this scene. What other fitting details can they imagine that are not described in this paragraph? For instance, what is the man's wife doing? Can furniture, children, or pets be seen through the door or windows? How does the house appear? Is the moon bright, or are they shrouded in darkness? What details of the man's face are visible? **Ⓐ**

Analyze Literature

Point of View Ask students how they can determine the narrator's point of view (limited third-person). Model a response: "The narrator stands outside the action and is not a part of it, using third-person pronouns to refer to the characters. The narrator gets into the thoughts of only one character, Harriet Tubman. All the reader knows about the other characters is what Harriet Tubman sees." **Ⓑ**

Use Reading Skills

Analyze Cause and Effect Ask students what caused the fugitives to have such poor sleep when they were outside. Why would they jump if a twig snapped or the wind sighed? Model a response that includes their fear of being discovered and the thought that a twig snapped because a pursuer stepped on it. **Ⓒ**

They tried to sleep during the day but they never could wholly relax into sleep. She could tell by the positions they assumed, by their restless movements. And they walked at night. Their progress was slow. It took them three nights of walking to reach the first stop. She had told them about the place where they would stay, promising warmth and good food, holding these things out to them as an <u>incentive</u> to keep going.

When she knocked on the door of a farmhouse, a place where she and her parties of runaways had always been welcome, **Ⓒ** always been given shelter and plenty to eat, there was no answer. She knocked again, softly. A voice from within said, "Who is it?" There was fear in the voice.

She knew instantly from the sound of the voice that there was something wrong. She said, "A friend with friends," the password on the Underground Railroad.

Ⓐ The door opened, slowly. The man who stood in the doorway looked at her coldly, looked with unconcealed astonishment and fear at the eleven disheveled[9] runaways who were standing near her. Then he shouted, "Too many, too many. It's not safe. My place was searched last week. It's not safe!" and slammed the door in her face.

She turned away from the house, frowning. She had promised her passengers food and rest and warmth, and instead of that, there would be hunger and cold and more walking over the frozen ground. Somehow she would have to instill courage into these eleven people, most of them strangers, would have to feed them on hope and bright dreams of freedom instead of the fried pork and corn bread and milk she had promised them.

Ⓑ They stumbled along behind her, half-dead for sleep, and she urged them on, though she was as tired and as discouraged as they were. She had never been in Canada

but she kept painting wondrous word pictures of what it would be like. She managed to dispel[10] their fear of pursuit, so that they would not become hysterical, panic-stricken. Then she had to bring some of the fear back, so that they would stay awake and keep walking though they drooped with sleep.

Yet during the day, when they lay down deep in a thicket, they never really slept, because if a twig snapped or the wind sighed in the branches of a pine tree, they jumped to their feet, afraid of their own shadows, shivering and shaking. It was very cold, but they dared not make fires because someone would see the smoke and wonder about it.

She kept thinking, eleven of them. Eleven thousand dollars' worth of slaves. And she had to take them all the way to Canada. Sometimes she told them about Thomas Garrett, in Wilmington.[11] She said he was their friend even though he did not know them. He was the friend of all fugitives. He called them God's poor. He was a Quaker[12] and his speech was a little different from that of other people. His clothing was different, too. He wore the wide-brimmed hat that the Quakers wear.

She said that he had thick white hair, soft, almost like a baby's, and the kindest eyes she had ever seen. He was a big man and strong, but he had never used his strength to harm anyone, always to help people. He would give all of them a new pair of shoes. Everybody. He always did. Once they reached his house in Wilmington, they would be safe. He would see to it that they were.

---

9. **disheveled.** Untidy or rumpled
10. **dispel.** Scatter or drive away
11. **Wilmington.** Large city in Delaware
12. **Quaker.** Member of the Society of Friends, a religious group active in the movement to end slavery

in·cen·tive (in sen´ tiv) *n.*, something that stimulates or encourages someone to take action

Kinesthetic Learning

Some students might benefit from performing one of the scenes from the story. Groups should choose a scene and ask classmates to review its descriptions of gestures, expressions, and emotions. After groups perform the scene, discuss as a class whether they successfully captured the mood in the passage. If you wish, use this discussion to reinforce the concept of mood.

English Language Learning

Students learning English may need help with the following key words in order to understand the story.
vaguely—not clearly, 349
pursuit—act of chasing in an attempt to capture, 349
disheveled—rumpled and untidy, 352
instill—introduce gradually, as by teaching, 352
reluctance—feeling of unwillingness, 353

She described the house where he lived, told them about the store where he sold shoes. She said he kept a pail of milk and a loaf of bread in the drawer of his desk so that he would have food ready at hand for any of God's poor who should suddenly appear before him, fainting with hunger. There was a hidden room in the store. A whole wall swung open, and behind it was a room where he could hide fugitives. On the wall there were shelves filled with small boxes—boxes of shoes—so that you would never guess that the wall actually opened.

While she talked, she kept watching them. They did not believe her. She could tell by their expressions. They were thinking, New shoes, Thomas Garrett, Quaker, Wilmington—what foolishness was this? Who knew if she told the truth? Where was she taking them anyway?

That night they reached the next stop—a farm that belonged to a German. She made the runaways take shelter behind trees at the edge of the fields before she knocked at the door. She hesitated before she approached the door, thinking, suppose that he, too, should refuse shelter, suppose—Then she thought, Lord, I'm going to hold steady on to You and You've got to see me through—and knocked softly.

She heard the familiar guttural[13] voice say, "Who's there?"

She answered quickly, "A friend with friends."

He opened the door and greeted her warmly. "How many this time?" he asked.

"Eleven," she said and waited, doubting, wondering.

He said, "Good. Bring them in."

He and his wife fed them in the lamp-lit kitchen, their faces glowing, as they offered food and more food, urging them to eat, saying there was plenty for everybody, have more milk, have more bread, have more meat.

They spent the night in the warm kitchen. They really slept, all that night and until dusk the next day. When they left, it was with reluctance.[14] They had all been warm and safe and well-fed. It was hard to exchange the security offered by that clean warm kitchen for the darkness and the cold of a December night. ✤

---

13. guttural. Deep and low, often with harsh or raspy tones
14. reluctance. Sadness or regret

 Do you think that Harriet Tubman was born with a courageous spirit? Is courage innate or something shaped by life experiences?

Find Meaning
1. What was the Fugitive Slave Law, and why did it make it necessary for Harriet Tubman to take the runaway slaves all the way to Canada?
2. (a) On what day of the week did the slave owners usually discover that slaves were missing? (b) What made Harriet's timing particularly clever?

Make Judgments
3. (a) What different reactions did Harriet experience at the two homes where she stopped for the night? (b) What might have led people to have these different reactions?
4. (a) How did Harriet use creative and persuasive language to urge the runaways onward? (b) In your opinion, why was her language so successful?

Teach the Selection

Answer: Students might say that she was born with a courageous spirit because few people could accomplish what she did, even if they wanted to. Others might say that her courage had to develop in order to preserve her safety and that of those in her charge.

Find Meaning
1. It stated that slaves who escaped to free states would be returned to their owners. She took them to a country with different laws.
2. (a) Sunday (b) The hunt was delayed because people did not work on Sundays. By escaping on Saturday night, the slaves had a great head start.

Make Judgments
3. (a) One man slammed the door in her face, and the other one welcomed her in. (b) The first man was afraid that the large number of slaves would endanger him, and slave hunters had searched his home the previous week. The second man was a Quaker. Maybe his convictions helped him overcome fear. Maybe he knew it was worth the risk.
4. (a) She recounts stories of her own flight, urges them on with descriptions of good things ahead, and explains the feeling of freedom. (b) Students will probably say that her tone, her "vivid word pictures," her confidence, and her strength of will successfully encouraged them.

Research Skills

Note Card Preparation
Have students follow these steps in preparing note cards for their research:
- Identify sources at the top right corner of cards. (Use source numbers from your bibliography cards.)
- Identify the subject or topic of the note on the top line of the card.
- Use a separate card for each fact or quotation.
- Write the pertinent source page number or numbers after the note.

Teach the Selection

Summary

Nelson Mandela gives a speech in Harlem on June 21, 1990. He relates how, when he was in prison in South Africa, he closely followed the struggle against racial discrimination and economic inequality in the United States. Mandela expresses that the African National Congress feels a kinship with the people of Harlem, not solely because of skin color. Instead, it is a kinship of shared historical experience. He praises various "antiracist freedom fighters" in America's history. He admits that the struggle is not over and that societies all over the world still endure the evils of racism. Although South Africa still suffers under apartheid, Mandela believes the system is nearing its end.

TEACHING NOTE

Research South Africa

Encourage students to make a bulletin board dedicated to South Africa's political history. Students might want to sketch drawings of famous people or a map of the country, compose reports on certain aspects of politics or government, or create South African arts and crafts.

from

Our Struggle Is Against All Forms of Racism

(Below) *Nelson Mandela*, 1990.
Cheik Ledy. Private collection.

A Speech by Nelson Mandela

354

Common Core State Standards

Reading Informational
RI.1, RI.2, RI.3, RI.6

Writing
W.7, W.8, W.9, W.10

Language
L.6

Words in Use

from *Our Struggle Is Against All Forms of Racism*

Preview Vocabulary	Selection Words
solidarity, 355	indomitable, 355
kinship, 355	intolerable, 356
foresight, 356	revolt, 356
	squalor, 357

...out of resistance to injustice comes renaissance, renewal, and rebirth.

Speech in Harlem,[1] New York, June 21, 1990

Chairman; distinguished guests:
We are very happy to be here this evening and it gives me immense pleasure to greet all of you on behalf of the leaders and members of the African National Congress[2] and the Mass Democratic Movement.[3]

It is with great joy that I speak to you this evening. My only regret is that I am not able to embrace each and every one of you.

Whilst[4] my comrades and I were in prison,[5] we followed closely your own struggle against the injustices of racist discrimination and economic inequality. We were and are aware of the resistance of the people of Harlem and continue to be inspired by your indomitable fighting spirit.

I am able to speak to you because of the mass resistance of our people and the unceasing <u>solidarity</u> of millions throughout the world. It is you, the working people of Harlem, that helped to make it happen. It is you, the clergy[6] and believers, who helped to make it happen. It is you, the professionals and the intellectuals, that helped to make it happen. It is you, the struggling women, who helped to make it happen.

The <u>kinship</u> that the ANC feels for the people of Harlem goes deeper than skin color. It is the kinship of our shared historical experience and the kinship of the solidarity of the victims of blind prejudice and hatred. To our people, Harlem symbolizes the strength and beauty in resistance, and you have taught us that out of resistance to injustice comes renaissance,[7] renewal, and rebirth.

From the beginning of this century, we have been inspired by great antiracist freedom fighters like W. E. B. DuBois,[8]

Rosa Parks.

---

1. **Harlem.** Large district within New York City; residential and commercial area populated predominantly by African Americans
2. **African National Congress (ANC).** Oldest black political organization in South Africa. Under Nelson Mandela's leadership, the ANC negotiated with the South African government to end apartheid. In 1994, the ANC became a registered political party, and for the first time, people of all races were allowed to vote. The ANC won 60 percent of the vote, and Mandela was elected president of South Africa.
3. **Mass Democratic Movement.** Group of people and organizations devoted to ending apartheid in South Africa
4. **Whilst.** While
5. **my comrades and I were in prison.** In 1960, the South African government banned the ANC, and in 1964, Nelson Mandela and many of his ANC colleagues were sentenced to life in prison. They were released in 1990.
6. **clergy.** Religious leaders
7. **renaissance.** Period of great intellectual, literary, and artistic activity
8. **W. E. B. DuBois.** (1868–1963) African-American sociologist and leading Civil Rights advocate; co-founder of the NAACP

---

sol·i·dar·i·ty (sä′ lə da′ rə tē) *n.*, complete unity and agreement within a group regarding opinions, purposes, goals, and feelings

kin·ship (kin′ ship′) *n.*, very close relationship, as in a family or a group of people who share common opinions and outlooks

Literary Connection

The Souls of Black Folk W. E. B. Du Bois (1868–1963) wrote numerous pieces detailing the arduous history of African Americans and prescribing methods for the eradication of racism. He published *The Souls of Black Folk* in 1909, which contains essays on race and the black experience in America. Many scholars argue that this work is part of the foundation for the Civil Rights movement, as it provides a line of reasoning for the black freedom struggle and rationalizes the African-American aim for higher education. **Ⓐ**

Analyze Literature

Metaphor Direct students to examine Mandela's metaphor "cancer of racism." Ask them why they think he relates these two things and how the metaphor affects the tone of his message. Model a response: "Cancer is a disease that often grows for some time before being detected. It can spread throughout the body and result in death. Racism also often goes undetected, or unchecked, until it infects all aspects of a society." **Ⓑ**

Make Connections

Ask if students agree with Mandela's statement about the importance of the issue of racism. Have they noticed instances of racism in their own neighborhoods, or do people of all ethnicities get along in their neighborhoods? **Ⓒ**

Martin Luther King, Jr.

Sojourner Truth,[9] Paul Robeson,[10] Rosa Parks,[11] Martin Luther King,[12] Marcus Garvey,[13] Fannie Lou Hamer,[14] Adam Clayton Powell,[15] Malcolm X,[16] Harriet Tubman,[17] and many others.

Ⓐ At the turning of this century, W. E. B. DuBois, with great <u>foresight</u>, predicted that "the problem of the twentieth century is the problem of the color line." As we enter the last decade of the twentieth century, it is intolerable and unacceptable that the cancer of racism is still eating away at the fabric of societies in different parts of our planet.

Ⓑ It remains one of the most important global issues confronting all humanity, black and white. It is a struggle that must involve people of all walks of life. It is a struggle that must involve people of different colors, religions, and creeds....[18]

Ⓒ The revolt of our people continues in the land of apartheid. Our struggle is the struggle

9. **Sojourner Truth.** (1797–1883) Daughter of slaves who later became an inspiring preacher and reformer, a leader in the fight to end slavery and obtain civil rights for women
10. **Paul Robeson.** (1898–1976) Famous African-American singer, actor, and Civil Rights activist
11. **Rosa Parks.** (1913–2005) Celebrated Civil Rights activist who gained international fame in 1955 in the segregated South when she refused to give up her seat on a bus to a white man
12. **Martin Luther King.** (1929–1968) Baptist minister who became leader of the Civil Rights movement in the United States from the 1950s until he was assassinated in 1968. In 1964, he was awarded the Nobel Prize for Peace.
13. **Marcus Garvey.** (1887–1940) Inspirational African American who led a Civil Rights organization based in Harlem in the 1920s
14. **Fannie Lou Hamer.** (1917–1977) Civil Rights activist who publicized incidents of violence and injustice in Mississippi and worked to desegregate the local Democratic Party.
15. **Adam Clayton Powell.** (1908–1972) Baptist minister whose work to bring jobs and better housing to Harlem led to his being elected to the House of Representatives, where he served eleven terms.
16. **Malcolm X.** (1925–1965) African-American militant leader who fought for civil rights and a sense of "black pride." He was assassinated in 1965.
17. **Harriet Tubman.** (1820–1913) Escaped slave who became a leading abolitionist, guiding hundreds of fugitive slaves to freedom along the Underground Railroad
18. **creeds.** Sets of fundamental beliefs or guiding principles

fore•sight (fôr′ sīt′) *n.*, act or ability to see into the future with wisdom and knowledge

Differentiated Instruction

Auditory Learning

Students might gain an increased appreciation for Mandela's speaking skills by listening to a recorded speech. His last public statement before being jailed for twenty-seven years was remastered in 2001 on the eleventh anniversary of his release. You can find the entire speech on CD or listen to a stirring excerpt at CNN's Web site.

English Language Learning

Point out the following expressions:
walks of life—backgrounds, 356
apartheid—racial segregation, 357
is trigger-happy—acts rashly, 357

to erase the color line that all too often determines who is rich and who is poor; that all too often decides who lives in luxury and who lives in squalor; that all too often determines who shall get food, clothing, and health care; and that all too often decides who will live and who will die.

We continue to live in a country enslaved by apartheid. The vote, the land, economic wealth, and power remain a monopoly of the white minority. The only monopoly blacks have is the monopoly of ghettoes, of deprived and suffering children, the monopoly of millions of unemployed, the monopoly of urban slums, rural starvation, low wages, and the bullets and clubs of too many trigger-happy police.

But, my dear brothers and sisters, comrades and friends, I am here to report to you that due to the enormous sacrifices of our people and the solidarity and support of people like you and the international community, apartheid is nearing its end.... ❖

NAACP members protest segregation laws in Houston, Texas. **D**

HARRIET TUBMAN / OUR STRUGGLE IS AGAINST ALL FORMS OF RACISM **357**

Review the Selections

Find Meaning

1. (a) They followed Harlem's struggle for racial equality and justice. (b) The issue had much in common with his battle.

2. (a) Harlem symbolizes strength and resistance to injustice. (b) The symbol has given him a sense of solidarity with others who have fought against injustice.

3. (a) He predicted that the main problem of the century would be the division of black people and white people. (b) Racism still exists.

Make Judgments

4. All spoke or acted out against injustice.

5. (a) He mentions working people, clergy and religious followers, professionals and intellectuals, and struggling women. (b) He mentions a broad range of people to stress that although they are different, they share beliefs, goals, and commitment.

Compare Literature

Author's Purpose

1. Her main purpose was to inform readers about Tubman's work, the plight of runaway slaves, and the stations along the Railroad.

2. Mandela's main purpose was to stress the theme of solidarity and encourage his listeners to fight against racism.

3. Petry and Mandela used strong, encouraging language to build a sense of solidarity.

AFTER READING

Find Meaning

1. (a) What did Mandela and his comrades follow closely while they were in prison? (b) Why was this issue particularly interesting to Mandela?

2. (a) According to Mandela, what does Harlem symbolize? (b) Why is this symbol particularly appropriate?

3. (a) At the beginning of the twentieth century, what did W. E. B. DuBois predict? (b) According to Mandela, why did this prediction remain accurate at the end of the twentieth century?

Make Judgments

4. Mandela mentions the names of many "antiracist freedom fighters." Based on the information in the footnotes, as well as your own knowledge, what common bond did these people share? Give examples to support your answer.

5. (a) What specific groups of people in Harlem does Mandela mention as workers for solidarity? (b) What purpose might he have for mentioning them?

Compare Literature

Author's Purpose An author's purpose is his or her aim or goal. An author may write with one or more purposes—such as to entertain, inform, or persuade. Review the main ideas and the tones of these two selections. Then answer these questions.

1. What was Ann Petry's main purpose for writing the biography of Harriet Tubman?

2. What was Nelson Mandela's main purpose for writing and giving his speech? Use details from the selection to support your answer.

3. Both Ann Petry and Nelson Mandela used strong, encouraging language. What overall purpose did they share?

Extend Understanding

Writing Options

Creative Writing Reread the Build Background and Meet the Authors material regarding Nelson Mandela, focusing on his work to end apartheid in South Africa. Then imagine that you are a newspaper reporter in the audience as Mandela delivers the speech you just read. Write a **newspaper article** in which you explain to your readers who Mandela is and why he is an important man, and then summarize the main ideas that he delivered in his speech.

Expository Writing Write a brief essay in which you analyze Nelson Mandela's choice of words, phrases, and literary devices in the passage from his "Our Struggle..." speech. Explain how these choices help him appeal to his audience. Use examples from the text to support your ideas.

Lifelong Learning

Research and Take Notes Choose one of the "antiracist freedom fighters" that Mandela mentions in his speech. Research to expand on the information provided in the footnote. Take notes on the person you chose and share your notes with the class.

Critical Literacy

Create Interview Questions Imagine that you have the chance to interview either Harriet Tubman or Nelson Mandela. To prepare for that interview, write a list of questions you would like to ask her or him.

MW Go to **www.mirrorsandwindows.com** for more.

Rubrics for Writing Options

You can adapt this as a checklist for students to use as they write.

Creative Writing

☐ Did the students use prereading facts?
☐ Did they show Mandela's importance?

Expository Writing

☐ Does the essay analyze Mandela's choice of words, phrases, and literary devices in the speech?
☐ Are the ideas in the essay supported by examples from the text?

FROM IF YOU COULD BE MY FRIEND

Letters presented by Litsa Boudalika

Build Background

Historical Context Since ancient times, Arabs and Jews have struggled and fought over the Middle Eastern region that has historically been known as Palestine. Both groups claim the region as their native homeland. Violent regional wars have continued to the present day.

Reader's Context Imagine that you met someone whose beliefs and family background were different from yours. How might you be able to find things that you could agree about and respect in each other?

Set Purpose

Use the title and Build Background to preview the text. Based on your preview, how might the girls find "common ground"?

Analyze Literature

Setting The **setting** of a selection is the time and place in which it happens. In this nonfiction selection, Mervet and Galit exchanged their letters during 1989, a time of great violence and conflict between the Arab Palestinians and the Jewish Israelis. In real life as in stories, the setting often has a great impact on what happens and how people view their present situation and their hopes for the future. As you read the letters, think about how the time and place affected the girls' thoughts and feelings.

Meet the Author

Litsa Boudalika is a producer of documentary films, or nonfiction movies that show real-life people, settings, and events. On a trip to Israel in 1988, she met Mervet and Galit and suggested that they write to each other. After they had written back and forth to each other for a while, the two girls finally met in person. Boudalika produced a documentary film about their relationship, called *Duo*.

Use Reading Skills

Fact and Opinion A fact is a statement that can be proven true or false. An example of a fact is *Dogs have four legs.* By contrast, an opinion is a person's attitude or feeling on a subject. It cannot be proven true or false. An example is *Dogs are better pets than cats.* As you read, create a chart to help you differentiate between facts and opinions.

Fact: The village was called Zakariya.	Opinion: From the terrace, there is a nice view of Dheisheh and the road.
How to Prove True: Check a map of the area.	Support: Mervet thinks the view is nice, but others might disagree.

Preview Vocabulary

in•dict•ed (in dī´ təd) *adj.*, accused or charged with a crime

em•broi•der•y (im brôi´ d[ə] rē) *n.*, decorative needlework on cloth

en•clave (en´ klāv') *n.*, distinct territorial, cultural, or social unit enclosed within a foreign territory

am•i•ca•bly (a´ mi kə blē) *adv.*, friendly in feeling; showing goodwill

---

Preview the Selection

At a Glance
Directed Reading
- Reading Level: Challenging
- Difficulty Consideration: Setting
- Ease Factor: Footnotes

Objectives

Studying this lesson will enable students to
- use reading strategies such as distinguishing fact and opinion
- define *setting*, both cultural and physical, and recognize the importance of setting in the selection
- describe the literary accomplishments of Litsa Boudalika and explain her influence on the two letter writers
- appreciate a series of letters between people on opposite sides of a conflict

Launch the Lesson

Students might especially enjoy writing their own letter to an imaginary student in another country with a very different background from their own. Encourage students to come up with a description of their correspondents. Then ask students to write a letter that introduces them, asks questions about their correspondent's life, and describes their own life.

Words in Use

Preview Vocabulary	**Selection Words**	**Teaching Words**
indicted, 362	immigrant, 362	differentiate, 359
embroidery, 362	militant, 365	insignificant, 369
enclave, 366		correspondence, 369
amicably, 366		conveys, 371
		relatively, 371

KEY TERMS

SETTING, 359
NONFICTION, 359
DOCUMENTARY, 359
FACT, 359
OPINION, 359
MOOD, 371
COMPARE AND CONTRAST, 371

Common Core State Standards

Reading Literature
RL.2

Reading Informational
RI.1, RI.2, RI.3, RI.6, RI.9

Writing
W.7, W.9

Language
L.6

Summary

Between August 1988 and March 1991, two young girls, whose countries are at war, exchange letters. One girl is Palestinian and lives in an Israeli refugee camp; the other is a Jewish girl living in Jerusalem. As the girls write, they learn much about each other and the significant disparities between their communities. However, they come to realize through their growing friendship that they are not so different after all. Side notes provide the reader with historical background concerning what was being reported in the newspapers at the time.

The Mirrors & Windows questions at the end of this selection focus on the theme of perspective. Before reading, ask students how gaining compassion for differing perspectives might enrich their own. How do positive relationships between apparent rivals challenge our notions of good and evil, right and wrong?

FROM IF YOU COULD

I NEVER WOULD HAVE IMAGINED YOUR LIFE THE WAY YOU DESCRIBED IT.

360

January 1, 1989

The first of January is the birthday of the creation of Fatah.[1] But it's not a festive occasion. Under the occupation, this event, like other celebrations and religious holidays, has become a day of conflict with the army. Nine wounded Palestinians[2] are hospitalized before nightfall. At night, thirteen Palestinians, including Ibraham Faraj, a twenty-five-year-old neighbor of Mervet's, are deported from the occupied territories[3] into Lebanon.

Dheisheh[4]
1 January 1989

My dear Galit,

I am so happy: they reopened our school and my grandfather will be released from prison this year! He was thrown in jail because they discovered explosives buried in our garden three years ago.

I have a ton of homework these days because we have to catch up all the time we lost these last few months. Every night we are buried in our books. The house has never been so quiet.

I promised to tell you the story of my family. My grandparents lived in a village near Hebron. They told me that they napped

---

1. **Fatah.** Principal military and political group in the Palestinian Liberation Organization (PLO)
2. **Palestinians.** Arabs currently or formerly living in Palestine who support the establishment of an Arab homeland there
3. **occupied territories.** Former Arab territories taken by Israel and patrolled by the Israeli army
4. **Dheisheh.** Refugee camp near Bethlehem and Jerusalem

Program Resources

Planning and Assessment
Program Planning Guide, Selection Lesson Plan
E-Lesson Planner
Assessment Guide, Lesson Test
ExamView

Technology Tools
Interactive Student Text on CD
Visual Teaching Package
Audio Library
mirrorsandwindows.com

Meeting the Standards
Nonfiction: Unit 3, Directed Reading, pp. 70–75

BE MY FRIEND

Letters Presented by Litsa Boudalika

on the lawn, grew their own vegetables, and made their own clothes. The village was called Zakariya, but it doesn't exist anymore. **A** In 1948 the Palestinians had to leave their land because they were driven out by the Jews.[5] Dheisheh was a barren hillside and they settled there with other refugees. In the beginning they didn't have a house or water or shelter. UNRWA[6] gave them tents to sleep in. When it rained the streets were flooded and filled with mud. In the winter the babies screamed from the cold, and the wind sometimes carried away the tents. My grandmother had to walk more than a mile to get firewood and water. The water container had to last a week for the whole family. They cooked the food they received **B** from UNRWA on a campfire because that was all they had. The poorest families in Dheisheh still get food from the UN.

After 1950 they started to build small houses. They had one room for households of five or less and two rooms for bigger families. After fifteen years my parents were able to build a big three-room house with a kitchen, running water, and electricity.

My favorite place in the house is the terrace. From there, there is a nice view of

---

5. **...they were driven out by the Jews.** The Jewish people did not settle in Hebron until after 1949. When Mervet's grandparents were forced out of Hebron in 1948, the British governed the area, and Jordanian authorities were in the process of taking control.
6. **UNRWA.** United Nations Relief and Works Agency, created to offer aid to Palestinian refugees

Geography Connection

Khirbet Zakariyya The Palestinian village of Zakariya, also called Khirbet Zakariyya, was leveled during the 1948 Arab-Israeli War and absorbed by the State of Israel after the 1949 Armistice Agreements. Although a small minority of Arabs still inhabit its few decaying buildings and makeshift tents, Khirbet Zakariyya is not recognized by the Israeli government, which established the Jewish settlement of Zekharya on its grounds in 1950. The majority of its residents were settled in the Dheeisheh and al-Aroub refugee camps. The ancient village has a rich history. The Bible declares that King David fought Goliath on the plain to its east. During the Roman Empire, Khirbet Zakariyya was part of the Syria Palaestinia province and called Caper Zachariah after the Hebrew prophet. **A**

Use Reading Strategies

Ask Questions An active reader forms the habit of asking questions as he or she reads. This strategy will be especially helpful with this selection, as it involves personal and diverse opinions about a shared history. Model questions that might be generated by this paragraph: "Why did one water container have to last a week for the whole family?" **B**

Monitor Comprehension

Remind students that voice is the unique way a writer has of "speaking" on the page. Elements that affect voice include word choice, tone, sound devices, rhythm, and pace.

Use an adjective to describe the writer's voice in each of these examples.

1. "I am so happy: they reopened our school and my grandfather will be released from prison this year!" (hasty)
2. "In the winter the babies screamed from the cold, and the wind sometimes carried away the tents." (downhearted)

Determine Sequence Remind students that sequence is the order in which events occur. The order provided, however, does not always match the actual time line of events. For example, this paragraph starts with al-Husseini being freed, then flashes back to tell what his father did, and then jumps ahead in time to tell what he would do years later. **Ⓐ**

History Connection

Intifada Inform students that *intifada* is an Arabic term that means "uprising." Palestinians use the word to describe two uprisings in the Israeli-Palestinian conflict, which many consider to be at the heart of the Arab-Israeli conflict. The first intifada began in 1987 and ended in 1993 with the signing of the Oslo Accord. A second intifada began in September 2000, apparently in reaction to Ariel Sharon's visit to the Temple Mount in Jerusalem, the site of the Al-Aqsa Mosque and a place disputed by Israelis and Palestinians. **Ⓑ**

Dheisheh and the road. I can also see when the soldiers are coming.

You haven't written me about what Jerusalem is like.

In your last letter there is a word I didn't understand. It was "Ashkenazi."

Mervet

January 30, 1989

Ⓐ *Faisal al-Husseini was freed after six months of administrative detention.[7] Fifty years old, he lives in the Arab section of Jerusalem. He is the son of the legendary Abdel-Kader al-Husseini, commander in chief of the Palestinian forces at the beginning of the Israeli-Palestinian war of 1947, who was killed in combat in April 1948. Faisal "the Moderate" is the most important individual in the occupied territories. Later, he would be a leader in the peace negotiations with Israel.*

Ⓑ *In the meantime the intifada[8] has intensified: in Bethlehem, Palestinians threw stones at several military vehicles and cars owned by settlers,[9] while in Gaza, five hundred youths organized a march waving Palestinian flags.*

According to representative A. Rubinstein, about twenty-nine thousand Palestinians have been arrested since the beginning of the uprising; however, this does not include the eight thousand indicted leaders and four thousand found guilty.

Jerusalem
30 January 1989

Dear Mervet,

"Ashkenazi" means to be from Poland, Russia, Romania, Germany, or Czechoslovakia like my grandmother in Haifa. It is mainly the Jews from Europe. Not all the Jews who live in Israel were born here. For two thousand years our people have lived in different countries. Before Israel, in many countries, we were hated and we were chased out simply because we were Jewish.

There is another very big community of Jews known as Sephardic Jews [Jews of ancient Spanish origin], like my grandparents on my mother's side. They come from Morocco. When an Israeli is born in an Arab country, he is Sephardic. I am neither. I am a "Sabra" because I was born here.

Today there are Jews on every continent in the world. They have different names depending on where they come from. One day, at the bus stop, I saw Ethiopian Jews who are black. They are called "Falashas." When they decide to live in Israel, the government helps them to make a life here and to learn Hebrew. My grandmother Ninette, from Morocco, told me that it isn't easy to be a new immigrant here.

When they arrived in Israel, they began their lives over with nothing. They sometimes tell me about how they had to find a house and a job when they knew no one. I often spend the weekend with them. When Grandma works I help her in the store. I love to wrap gifts. It's a store that sells souvenirs and embroidery on Jaffa Road in the center of the city. The embroidery is very beautiful. In addition to the linens and bags, she also sells hand-embroidered dresses. The patterns are very similar to your Arab dresses.

---

7. **administrative detention.** Practice of arresting someone for an unspecified amount of time without normal judicial process
8. **intifada.** Form of Palestinian revolt expressed by strikes, demonstrations, and terrorist attacks
9. **settlers.** Jewish citizens of Israel who live in territories occupied by Israel since the Six-Day War of 1967—the Gaza Strip, the Sinai Desert, East Jerusalem, the West Bank, and the Golan Heights

---

in·dict·ed (in dī′ təd) *adj.*, accused or charged with a crime
em·broi·der·y (im brôi′ d[ə] rē) *n.*, decorative needlework on cloth

---

Differentiated Instruction

Reading Proficiency

Encourage students to preview the selection. Read and discuss the Before You Read page, and draw their attention to the quotes within the selection. Examine the art, and take note of the italicized text alongside the letters, which was written by the author to include the historical context of the girls' correspondence.

Auditory Learning

Pair each student with a partner. Allow them to determine who will read Mervet's and Galit's words, and ask them to read the letters aloud. Students might also benefit from reading along with a recorded version of the text.

The women who know how to do this embroidery are old Jews from Yemen. I have visited two of them who live in one small room. Grandma Ninette sent me one day to bring them some new work. They are really old and poor. I gave them my package, but we didn't speak. I am so shy with older people that I didn't dare ask them their stories and how old they were when they learned to do this complicated embroidery. It seems that when they die, no one in Israel will know how to embroider the way they do. **C**

I GUESS THERE ARE THINGS IN YOUR PLACE THAT I KNOW NOTHING ABOUT.

Grandma has already teased me that it surely won't be me who will replace them.

Do you know how to embroider? I am terrible. I do a little better with knitting. Grandma is teaching me. Besides, I like it. I have started a dark green scarf for my father. I really want it to come out well. When my stitches are uneven, I undo them and I redo them. I bet my grandmother a movie ticket that I would finish before next winter!

In any case, what I like best is fashion and elegant clothes. When I grow up, I would like to be a designer or a model. Actually I can't decide between lots of things. I could also be a sketch artist because I love that.

When I have a bad dream or when I am sad, I take a pencil and, like Daddy, I draw. I try to put all my sadness in my drawings. Afterward I feel much better. Better than when my best friend comforts me. Last **D**

Saturday I was thinking about my grandmother in Haifa. So I drew a crying woman. Daddy told me I was getting much better.

I also draw when I am happy, but then I make collages with happier things: flowers, fish, clouds, or beautiful rainbows.

I also like to watch TV. And you? Do you watch *Dynasty*?

By chance I saw a show on the refugee camps. The people slept on the ground. I have slept on the ground twice in my life when my father was building the second floor in our house. I was afraid that the walls were going to fall down on top of me. I asked my mother how you manage, and she said it was a question of customs and of habit. **E**

I won't hide from you that, personally, I would be bored if I lived there. I prefer to live in the city because there are stores, movies, and video arcades. My favorite part of Jerusalem is the Old City.[10] But I guess there are things in your place that I know nothing about. In the beginning, for example, I imagined that you didn't even have a kitchen in your house. Do you have stores? Don't forget to tell me what your favorite TV show is.

Your friend,
Galit

February 22, 1989

After four Arab-Israeli wars since 1948, Egypt is the only Arab country to have signed a peace treaty with Israel. Egypt is now making an effort to help the other Arab countries, and especially the Palestinians, make peace with Israel. In Cairo, the capital of Egypt, a first significant step

---

10. Old City. Old quarter of Jerusalem where Judaism, Christianity, and Islam have sacred sites

Teach the Selection

Use Reading Strategies
Visualize Remind students that good readers try to visualize details that they read about. If they try to visualize the embroidery these old women do on linens, bags, and dresses, what do they imagine? **C**

Make Connections
Discuss with students various coping mechanisms people, including Galit, have for dealing with nightmares and sadness. Model possible responses by suggesting that some people get involved in physical activity like a walk or an exercise session. Others might do something creative like write, cook, or draw. **D**

Use Reading Strategies
Make Inferences Ask students to make inferences about what Galit's mother's reaction says about her and her attitudes toward the Palestinians. Model a response: "Galit's mother apparently thinks that the Palestinians deal with their substandard living conditions by continuing to observe their customs and maintaining resourceful habits." **E**

TEACHING NOTE
Students learning English may need help with the following words and expressions:
barren — not yielding fruit or crops, 361
sketch artist — person who draws or paints a rough picture, 363

Vocabulary Skills

Etymology
Explain that researching a word's etymology often uncovers interesting facts about it. The word *sabra* comes from the Arabic word for an Israeli prickly pear. Native-born Israelis are called Sabras because they are thought to share the same makeup: tough and prickly on the outside and sweet on the inside.

Have students study the etymologies of these words from the selection:
1. intifada, 362 (Arabic)
2. Sephardic, 362 (modern Hebrew)

Use Reading Strategies

Ask Questions This passage might prompt students to ask questions like these: "Why are the two camps so adamant against negotiating? What has happened in the past to make them not trust each other? What are other countries doing to help make these negotiations possible?" **A**

Analyze Literature

Characterization Mervet demonstrates that her character is evolving as a result of her correspondence with Galit. She appears to be willing to change her attitude concerning Israelis as she learns more about the situation's complexity and gains familiarity and a feeling of endearment toward Galit. **B**

Analyze Literature

Conflict Remind students that conflict in a work of literature can be internal or external. This is an example of external conflict (person against person). Discuss examples of external, as well as other examples of internal, conflict students have noted thus far in the selection. **C**

---

has been taken in this direction: *for the first time, the Soviet Union has joined the United States to open a discussion between the Palestinians and the Israelis. Eduard Shevardnadze, Soviet minister of foreign affairs, met his Israeli counterpart, Moshe Arens, and the head of the PLO, Yasir Arafat. Shevardnadze had no*

A *success. Despite increasing international pressure, the two camps refuse to sit down at the negotiating table.*

Dheisheh
22 February 1989

Dear Galit,
   Your letter made me happy. I know you better

B now. What you write me changes my thinking a little.
   You see, I would like to live with you, and you're especially lucky not to live a life as hard as ours.
   There are more and more arrests, and the curfew now lasts several days in a

C row. The soldiers arrest boys for nothing. They want to prevent the intifada. So the men who distribute political pamphlets go out in secret at night. They all wear a "kaffiyeh"[11] over their faces so no one will know who they are. But there isn't just the police to watch out for. We also have traitors, like in all wars.
   One time you wrote me that I was wrong to hate the Israelis. I wouldn't say that anymore because, for example, you are an Israeli and we get along.

But I swear to you that the soldiers here are horrible. They treat us badly and beat us like donkeys. One day, in the school courtyard, a little boy lost his eye when he was hit with a rubber bullet. I fainted. I will never be able to forget this.
   Last night we took in a wounded man. From the window I saw the *chababs*[12] arrive. They were carrying a body and they came to ask us for first aid. The man was covered with blood because he had been shot in the stomach. My father couldn't do much. He works at the hospital, but he isn't a doctor. He tried anyway to find the wound. Soldiers

Jerusalem X, c. 20th century. Elizabeth Barakah Hodges.

---

11. **kaffiyeh.** Palestinian traditional head scarf
12. **chababs.** Palestinian militants of the intifada between the ages of twelve and twenty-five

364 UNIT 3 NONFICTION

Differentiated Instruction

Enrichment
Interested students might enjoy preparing a report on the history of the conflict between the Palestinians and the Israelis. They could have the choice of presenting their findings orally to the class or writing an expository or persuasive essay on the subject.

Reading Proficiency
Some students might benefit from oral partner reading. Partners can take turns reading sections of the letters aloud, stopping frequently to paraphrase what they have just read.

rang the doorbell, and my mother went outside and said there was no one in the house. Once they left, she ran next door to use the phone. Fifteen minutes later a car came and took the wounded man to a hospital. This afternoon we heard he was operated on and is out of danger. The whole family was relieved to hear the good news.

Before, the young people in the camp weren't as bored, because there was more to do. There were tennis courts, a basketball court, and a youth club. It's been years since the military closed all of them because our camp is well known for its political activism. In addition to poor people, we also have lots of prisoners because the residents have remained very militant here.

Since the intifada, they built a very high barricade to stop us from throwing stones on the cars in the road. The army had closed all the entrances to the camp except for one. It is right near our school, but it's not the one closest to our house. I have to walk twice as far. When there are heavy rains, like we've had recently, the big hill that leads to the house is transformed into a mud slide.

Another big problem at Dheisheh is the sewers. The camp is so over-populated that the dirty water overflows and runs in the gutter all day long.

D You asked me if we have stores. Yes, but not many. Only about ten. Here the stores are only open in the morning. When there is a general strike[13] in support of the intifada, they stay shut all day long. At Dheisheh, we buy vegetables and food. If we need shoes or clothes, Daddy brings them back from Bethlehem. Abou-Roulouz's grocery store is at the bottom of our street. When I was younger, I went to play hide-and-seek in front of his store every day after school.

Abou-Roulouz often scolded us because we made too much noise. He is an old man who is seventy years old. He likes children, but like all old people, he gets annoyed if he is disturbed. To calm us down, he would tell us stories about how life used to be in Palestine.

He knows everyone in the camp and where each family comes from. He played guessing games with us. He asked each of us our last names and then said, "You come from Zakariya. Your grandfather was born in Beit Itab and your grandmother in Albourej." My sister Manaal, who was only six, thought he was a magician.

It's like another life when you're little. When I was five I thought we lived in Zakariya. I was afraid of the soldiers, and, I admit, I was more afraid than Manaal. I didn't dare go out into the street. Now I give stones to the *chababs*, and the army is just part of normal life. I almost never play anymore. I spend my time reading or I plant flowers. Knitting is not at all my thing. You are surely better at it than I am. There is one thing I want to learn how to do—to make a Palestinian bracelet. Tomorrow I am going to my neighbor Fatia, who is fifteen. She has promised to teach me how to weave it with the three colors of our flag. If it is not too hard, I will be able to make at least three; that way all my sisters can have one. I already have a bracelet like this, but when I go to school, I don't want the soldiers to see it. It is forbidden like the flags that the boys tie onto the electrical wires. **E**

I don't watch much television. Only once in a while. My father, who speaks Hebrew, watches the news on Israeli TV almost every day.

---

13. **general strike.** Cessation of all activity by the Palestinians following important events in the Palestinian-Israeli conflict

Teach the Selection

Make Connections
What would it be like to live under conditions like these? Have students imagine that they are living in Dheisheh, where they can't depend on the few stores that exist to be open when they need even the most essential items. How would families manage? Model a response: "Families would have to plan ahead and make sure they had enough provisions for desperate times. They would have to live much more simply than they did in their former towns and come to terms with the fact that they cannot possess amenities of the modern world." **D**

Use Reading Skills
Compare and Contrast Here, Mervet tells how her attitudes have changed since she was little. In what ways is she different as an adolescent? Model a response by saying: "Mervet has become somewhat desensitized to the restrictions of her surroundings and bolder in the face of military control. While she used to be afraid of the soldiers, she now views their presence as a part of everyday life. While she was once afraid to go out into the streets, she now provides stones for the *chababs* to throw at the soldiers." **E**

Grammar Skills

Brackets

Explain that brackets enclose:
- comments inserted into a quote
- parenthetical remarks that are already within parentheses
- stage directions in plays

Explain each use of brackets below.

1. *[Enter Servant]*
   Servant: Master, dinner is served. (stage directions)

3. The ad read: "These shorts [designed by Isaac Mizrahi] are on sale till May 6." (comments inserted into a quote)

5. "This incident (described in Chapter 8 of the text [2007 edition]) occurred 100 years ago." (parenthetical remark within parentheses)

Use Reading Strategies
Make Inferences Ask students to consider what this sentence implies. Does Mervet trust everything that Galit tells her? Or does she suspect that Galit might withhold truths that might be uncomfortable? Is there a similar hesitation on Galit's part to trust Mervet? Why or why not? **Ⓐ**

Analyze Literature
Setting What does this paragraph reveal about the setting in which Mervet and Galit live? Model a response by saying that even though symbolic acts of peace take place (like the returning of Taba to Egypt), the situation is very volatile. It also reveals that Palestinian resistance comes not just from militants but schoolgirls as well. **Ⓑ**

Use Reading Skills
Compare and Contrast Here, Galit elaborates in a more personal way on the situation described in the author's commentary about this day. Have students compare and contrast the descriptions of the violence that takes place every day. **Ⓒ**

CAN YOU BELIEVE IT? WE ARE FIFTEEN MINUTES AWAY FROM EACH OTHER, AND IT'S AS IF WE WERE ON TWO DISTANT PLANETS.

I sometimes watch the Arab soap opera, but I couldn't tell you the story because I miss at least half the shows. The only show I like is the *Tom and Jerry* cartoons. Their games and their funny actions make me laugh. It's funny to see that, for once, a cat and mouse get along.

I hope I haven't bored you with my long letter.

Do you know any Arabs in Jerusalem? You are so lucky to be able to live in Jerusalem.

Ⓐ I hope none of your cousins is doing military service in our camp. Tell me the truth, please.

Mervet
March 14, 1989

On the beach in Taba, at the head of the Gulf of Aqaba in the Sinai,[14] a Tsahal[15] officer carefully folds the blue-and-white Israeli flag. An Egyptian officer, in a white uniform, raises the flag of his country.

Ⓑ *Taba, a tiny <u>enclave</u> on the Red Sea, which the two countries have fought over for years, has returned to Egypt. The last of the disputes between the two former enemies has been <u>amicably</u> resolved.*

This symbolic act of peace has not stopped the daily violence: a Palestinian girls' school organized a demonstration during which an Israeli bank was bombarded with rocks, and traffic was stopped with trash cans and paving

stones. *A group of settlers from the group "Committee for Safe Travel," affiliated with Kach, vandalized the market in Hebron, turning over tables, breaking windows, destroying merchandise, and shooting guns.*

Jerusalem
14 March 1989

My dear Mervet,
Your letter didn't bore me at all. To the contrary, I am very happy because I never would have imagined your life the way you described it. Can you believe it? We are fifteen minutes away from each other, and it's as if we were on two distant planets. The worst is, you and I are so insignificant. I often ask myself why the Arabs and the Jews are always at war. I know that a long time ago the Arabs invaded our land and then we took it back. Now everyone wants the land.

I asked my father about the army. No one in the family is doing his *milouim*[16] in the occupied territories. By the way, can you explain to me how the curfew works for you?

Ⓒ I may be lucky to live in Jerusalem, but, believe me, it's not paradise either. It's true that Jerusalem is a beautiful city with a magnificent view, museums, and plenty of stores, but you feel the war here too. Now, in the Old City, people are being stabbed. I heard that, there, Arab women help the men kill Israelis. I learned that a lot of soldiers have been killed. If only the Arabs and the

---

14. **the Sinai.** Sinai Desert
15. **Tsahal.** Israeli army
16. *milouim.* Military reserve service that each Israeli must complete once a year, every year, until age fifty-four

---

en·clave (en′ klāv′) *n.*, distinct territorial, cultural, or social unit enclosed within a foreign territory

am·i·ca·bly (a′ mi kə blē) *adv.*, friendly in feeling; showing goodwill

---

(Right) Two boys stand near the Wailing Wall in Jerusalem.

TEACHING NOTE

Self-Generated Questioning
Ask students which parts of the selection have generated the most questions for them so far. Encourage them to mark those parts and jot down their questions. Model a question such as: "Why have Galit's parents forbidden her from visiting the Old City?" Then, as a class, reread the parts they have marked and locate answers to their questions.

Teach the Selection

History Connection

Al-Aqsa Mosque *Al Aqsa* is an Arabic word that means "farthest mosque," a term that refers to Muhammad's life, during which he told Muslims they should visit not only the mosque in Mecca but also the "farthest mosque," which at that time was two thousand kilometers north in Jerusalem. Al-Aqsa Mosque is the second oldest mosque in Islam, after the Ka'ba in Mecca. Following the mosques in Mecca and Medina, it rates third in holiness and importance. Al-Aqsa Mosque is large enough to accommodate up to forty thousand worshippers at one time, which allows enough room for each one to adopt the submissive kneeling position.

Dome of the Rock Jerusalem's most famous Islamic site is the Dome of the Rock. Constructed from 688 to 691 AD, this shrine is built over a rock that has sacred meaning to Jews, Christians, and Muslims. According to Judaism, the rock is the very place where Abraham prepared to sacrifice his son Isaac. Christians and Muslims of the Middle Ages believed that the dome was the Temple of Solomon. During the Crusades, the Knights Templar made it their headquarters. According to Islam, the rock is the place from which Muhammad ascended during his famous journey to heaven. The dome was originally made of gold but was later replaced by copper and then aluminum. It is now covered with gold leaf donated by the late King Hussein of Jordan.

Speaking & Listening Skills

Panel Discussion

Have students participate in a panel discussion based on issues raised in this selection. Students should follow these guidelines:

- As in an informal discussion, participants volunteer facts, ask questions, and state opinions without making speeches or personal attacks.
- Participants show respect for one another's contributions.
- After a predetermined time (perhaps twenty minutes), the panel answers questions from the rest of the class.

Geography Connection

Wailing Wall Also called the Western Wall, "Kotel," or the Wall of Lamentations, this is the only remaining structure related to the Second Temple built by King Herod in 20 BC. It is part of the retaining wall that enclosed the western part of the Temple Mount. In AD 70, the Romans destroyed Jerusalem and its Temple, leaving only this portion of the wall. Beginning in the sixteenth century, the Jews came to this wall to mourn the loss of the Temple. For centuries, the Western Wall was located in a narrow alley that could accommodate only a few hundred worshippers at once. However, in 1967, the Israelis leveled the surrounding Arab district, creating the Western Wall Plaza. Now tens of thousands of pilgrims visit the wall at the same time. The extreme right of the Western Wall has an area reserved for women, who, according to Orthodox Jewish tradition, are not allowed in the men's section. **Ⓐ**

Use Reading Strategies

Make Inferences Ask students to infer how Galit's grandfather was able to live side by side with Arabs in Morocco. Model a response: "Jews and Arabs in Morocco must have a history of peaceful coexistence." **Ⓑ**

Jews would stop fighting. For months I haven't dared go into the Old City. My parents have strictly forbidden it.

Ⓐ It is awful not to be free. I used to go to the "Kotel"[17] almost every week. You can put a message with a prayer that means a lot to you between the stones in the wall. If God agrees, your hope will become reality. Of course, you have to be patient! I have put in dozens of wishes that Daddy would stop smoking, but it hasn't worked! My grandfather Yaakov, the one from Morocco, sometimes goes to pray at the wall because it brings good luck. I give him my wishes. He is the only one in the family who can do errands in the Old City. He often brings us fruit and vegetables. Mom and Grandma are always afraid something awful will happen to him. Grandpa always calms them down because he says he knows the Arabs. He lived **Ⓑ** with them in Morocco. He also speaks Arabic, and so, if something happened, he could speak to them to defend himself.

I don't know many Arabs other than our gardener and a woman who sells fruit in our neighborhood. The only other ones are people I meet in Daddy's factory.

Before the intifada, my father had an Arab friend who worked at the factory with him. He would come to say hello to us, and sometimes we went to visit his family on Saturdays. They lived on a farm with an orchard, where they raised all kinds of animals: chickens, rabbits, goats. When his children showed me the farm it was really funny. We smiled a lot and talked with our hands. Now the place where they live has become too dangerous. We would have stones thrown at our car. It's too bad that we can never see them again. They were always so nice to us. I remember how they used to serve us coffee in tiny cups like dollhouse

cups. You don't drink the same coffee that we do. Israeli coffee is weaker and is served in big cups. In our house we put coffee powder in hot water, while you boil the two together, right?

I went to a restaurant in Haifa with my father once. The waiter was a young Arab boy, and he was so nice! Not like the ones who throw stones or bottle bombs. Do you know that when the police stop them, they say they haven't done anything.

The TV news is on and I'm going to turn off the TV because I can't stand hearing every day about the dead, the wounded, and the suffering.

Besides Ayala is coming soon. She is my best friend. Since my parents are going out tonight she is coming to help me take care of Irit and Yael. Ayala is the sweetest person in my class. We have known each other since kindergarten. Outside of school we walk in town, and in the summer, we go to the swimming pool together. When I told her our story she understood. The others don't know that I am writing to you. Who knows, maybe they would be jealous or they would pretend not to believe me just to annoy me. They annoy me so much that I don't care if they never know that I have an Arab friend.

I wanted to tell you about my neighborhood. I already told you that I live on Bethlehem Road. It's the old road that leads to Bethlehem, right near you. We have nice neighbors and here everyone helps each other. When my father has a migraine,[18] for example, they are happy to give us aspirin. If I see an old lady walking by with her groceries, I immediately offer to help her.

---

17. **"Kotel."** ("The Wall" in Hebrew) Wall of lamentation, the most sacred place for Jews because it is the last remaining piece of the Second Temple, destroyed by the Romans in AD 70
18. **migraine.** Severe headache

Differentiated Instruction

Kinesthetic Learning

Pair students and have them research prayer methods of both Israeli Jews and Muslims. Encourage them to determine and record the importance and/or symbolic nature of the diverse positions and movements involved. Then ask them to demonstrate aspects of a Jewish and a Muslim

prayer for the class. Ask the class to guess at the meaning of the prayer aspects each pair demonstrates. Then have the performers explain their research findings.

The only one who bugs me is our grocer. Yours sounds like a nice old grandfather, while ours always makes me mad. I hate his jokes that no one thinks are funny. Plus, I've noticed that he cheats his customers. If I complain about it he'll tell me I'm stupid and that I don't understand anything. Anyway, as my grandmother says, "It takes all kinds to make a world." My grandmother Ninette also lives in Baka. It is very handy because I only have a five-minute walk to see her.

I'm going tomorrow afternoon. She promised to help me with a costume for Purim[19] next Sunday. It's my favorite Jewish holiday. That day we eat cookies called hamantaschen, or "Haman's ear." In the legend, Haman was a mean man in Persia who tried to hurt the Jews. It's a kind of

vengeance[20] to say now that we are eating his ear. What customs do you have? I like Purim because we put on costumes. I also use disguises when we play. In the summer, in our garden, Irit, Yael, and I play a game we call "the royal court." Irit and Yael dress up like princesses and I am the queen. I make a bun with my hair and I use a scarf as a crown. When we do this I think maybe I will be an actress someday. I hear the doorbell.

Write soon, Mervet.
Galit

P.S. Don't forget to write me about what you want to be when you grow up. ❖

---

19. **Purim.** Jewish holiday that celebrates the thwarting of royal minister Haman's plans to exterminate the Jews in ancient Persia
20. **vengeance.** Revenge

How might you benefit from befriending someone with a vastly different perspective from your own? How might relationships such as Mervet and Galit's change people's feelings about "friends" and "enemies"?

Find Meaning

1. (a) What cartoon does Mervet enjoy? (b) Why might she especially enjoy watching a cat and a mouse get along as friends?
2. Mervet writes to Galit, "I hope none of your cousins is doing military service in our camp. Tell me the truth, please." What events have led Mervet to have such strong feelings about the Israeli soldiers?
3. (a) Galit writes to Mervet, "The worst is, you and I are so insignificant." What does she mean? (b) What result might she imagine happening if she and Mervet were more significant people?

Make Judgments

4. (a) Where do Mervet and Galit live? (b) In your opinion, which girl lives in a more challenging setting? Explain your answer.
5. (a) When Galit asked her mother about how Mervet and the other Palestinians "manage," her mother said that "it was a question of customs and of habit." What does that answer suggest about Galit's mother's feelings for the Palestinians? (b) What would you say to her or ask her if you had the opportunity to do so? Explain your answer.
6. (a) Why might Galit have told her best friend about her correspondence with Mervet, but no one else? (b) If you were Galit, who might you tell (or not tell) about the correspondence?

IF YOU COULD BE MY FRIEND **369**

 *Answer:* Students might say that a different perspective will challenge them to assess, strengthen, and/or alter their own perspectives. Relationships like the one between Mervet and Galit might help people understand that the distinction between a friend and an enemy is often simply a difference in perspective.

Find Meaning

1. (a) She likes *Tom and Jerry*.
(b) They are traditional enemies.
2. Some soldiers are cruel to people in the camps. A boy is shot in the eye.
3. (a) They are just two young people, not political or military leaders. (b) Galit envisions a chance for peace if she and Mervet were more influential.

Make Judgments

4. (a) Mervet lives in a Palestinian refugee camp, and Galit lives in Jerusalem. (b) Mervet's living conditions are rough, and there are few activities.
5. (a) She seems unsympathetic toward the Palestinians. (b) Students' answers will vary.
6. (a) She was afraid that others might criticize her for corresponding with an "enemy." She wanted to keep this friendship to herself. (b) Answers will vary.

Writing Skills

Persuasive Essay

Challenge students to write persuasive essays in which they present a solution to the Israeli-Palestinian conflict. Encourage them to research political progress toward and setbacks to this effort since Galit and Mervet's exchange.

Provide them with the following checklist:
- Do you present a clear argument?
- Does your argument involve themes present in the girls' letters?
- Do you provide specific evidence to support your argument?
- Do you prompt the audience to think independently about the matter?

Teach the Connection

Use Reading Skills

Activate Prior Knowledge Return to the Vocabulary Skills lesson on page 363. Review the word history of *sabra,* and discuss its use as a term for native-born Israelis. Then examine the function of pears within the poem. Does anything about their description reinforce or reject the use of the term in the prior selection? **Ⓐ**

Make Connections

Discuss the idea of a person "growing wings." What might the wings symbolize? Why is their growth necessary? What might happen as a result of this symbolic occurrence? Then ask students to recall incidents or situations in their lives that made them feel as if they had grown wings. **Ⓑ**

Text-to-Text Connection

Answer: Student comparisons will vary. The poem's statement about hate relates to Galit's incredulity and exasperation over the banishment of Jews from other countries "simply because we were Jewish" and to Mervet's increased understanding of Galit's perspective: "What you write changes my thinking a little."

The following selection is a poem entitled "Jerusalem," by **Naomi Shihab Nye,** who was born in 1952 in the United States to a Palestinian father and an American mother. As you read, think about how the speaker's thoughts and feelings are similar to those expressed by Mervet and Galit.

Jerusalem

A Lyric Poem by Naomi Shihab Nye

Let's be the same wound if we must bleed.
Let's fight side by side, even if the enemy
is ourselves: I am yours, you are mine.
　　　　　　　—Tommy Olofsson, Sweden

I'm not interested in
who suffered the most.
I'm interested in
people getting over it.

5　Once when my father was a boy
a stone hit him on the head.
Hair would never grow there.
Our fingers found the tender spot
and its riddle: the boy who has fallen
Ⓐ[10　stands up. A bucket of pears
in his mother's doorway welcomes him home.
The pears are not crying.
Later his friend who threw the stone
says he was aiming at a bird.
Ⓑ[15　And my father starts growing wings.

Each carries a tender spot:
something our lives forgot to give us.
A man builds a house and says,
"I am native now."
20　A woman speaks to a tree in place
of her son. And olives come.
A child's poem says,
"I don't like wars,
they end up with monuments."
25　He's painting a bird with wings
wide enough to cover two roofs at once.

Why are we so monumentally slow?
Soldiers stalk a pharmacy:
big guns, little pills.
30　If you tilt your head just slightly
it's ridiculous.

There's a place in my brain
where hate won't grow.
I touch its riddle: wind, and seeds.
35　Something pokes us as we sleep.

It's late but everything comes next. ❖

TEXT ◄—TO—► TEXT
CONNECTION

Compare and contrast the feelings that are expressed in these selections. How does the statement, "There's a place in my brain where hate won't grow," connect to statements written by the girls?

Differentiated Instruction

Reading Proficiency

Remind students that effective readers often reread passages in order to clarify meaning. Have them reread the poem and then answer these questions about it:

1. (a) What happened to the speaker's father when he was a boy? (his friend hit him with a stone) (b) How did this incident help her father grow? (he learned to heal, forgive)

2. What might be the symbolism behind the image of a bird with wings "wide enough to cover two roofs at once"? (a land large enough for two cultures)

3. What won't grow in a certain place in the speaker's brain? (hate)

Common Core State Standards

Language
L.6

Analyze Literature

Setting The setting of a literary work is the time and place in which it occurs. Often the setting has a strong influence on the mood—the atmosphere or emotions that the work conveys. The mood might be dark, peaceful, happy, serious, or mysterious. Use a chart to analyze the effect of setting on the mood conveyed by the letters in this selection.

Setting	Specific Details in Setting	Mood Conveyed by These Details
Mervet's setting: the Palestinian refugee camp	1. her favorite place, the terrace, with a nice view but the chance to see oncoming soldiers 2.	1. peaceful view, but always the threat of oncoming violence 2.
Galit's setting: the Jewish section within city of Jerusalem	1. She thinks she would be bored in Mervet's setting. She prefers the stores, movies, and video arcades of the city. 2.	1. happy, busy, peaceful activities in a relatively "normal" setting 2.

Extend Understanding

Writing Options

Creative Writing Reread the last letter written by Galit. Then, pretend you are Mervet. Write a **letter** that she might write to answer Galit. Use specific details from her experiences and descriptions.

Expository Writing Through their letters, the girls share similar and different experiences. Write a brief **compare and contrast essay** in which you compare and contrast their experiences and ideas. How are the girls alike? How are they different? Support your statements with specific details from their letters.

Lifelong Learning

Conduct Internet Research Use reliable Internet sources such as newspapers or encyclopedias to research the history of the founding of Israel. Use facts from your research to create a time line of the events that led directly to its creation. Share your completed time line with the class.

Critical Literacy

Write an Explanation How might Mervet and Galit's parents and grandparents respond if they found out that the girls were communicating? Write an essay to describe how the girls might explain their correspondence to older family members. Include details of what the girls have learned.

 Go to **www.mirrorsandwindows.com** for more.

IF YOU COULD BE MY FRIEND **371**

Review the Selection

Analyze Literature

Setting *Answer:* Most of the details in Mervet's setting (the closed school; the grandfather in jail; the soldiers; the lack of sports activities) convey a gloomy, dangerous, serious mood. Although Galit's setting has stores and other entertainments that convey a busy, happy mood, there are also details that convey a gloomy, dangerous, serious mood (her knowledge of Jews being despised; people being stabbed in Jerusalem; her fears for her grandfather's safety).

Rubrics for Writing Options

You can adapt this as a checklist for students to use as they write.

Creative Writing

☐ Do students adopt Mervet's persona?

☐ Does the letter contain specific details from Mervet's descriptions?

☐ Does the letter show that the student has connected with Mervet's feelings?

Expository Writing

☐ Is the essay organized effectively, with clear comparisons and contrasts?

☐ Are the comparisons and contrasts based on specific details in the letters?

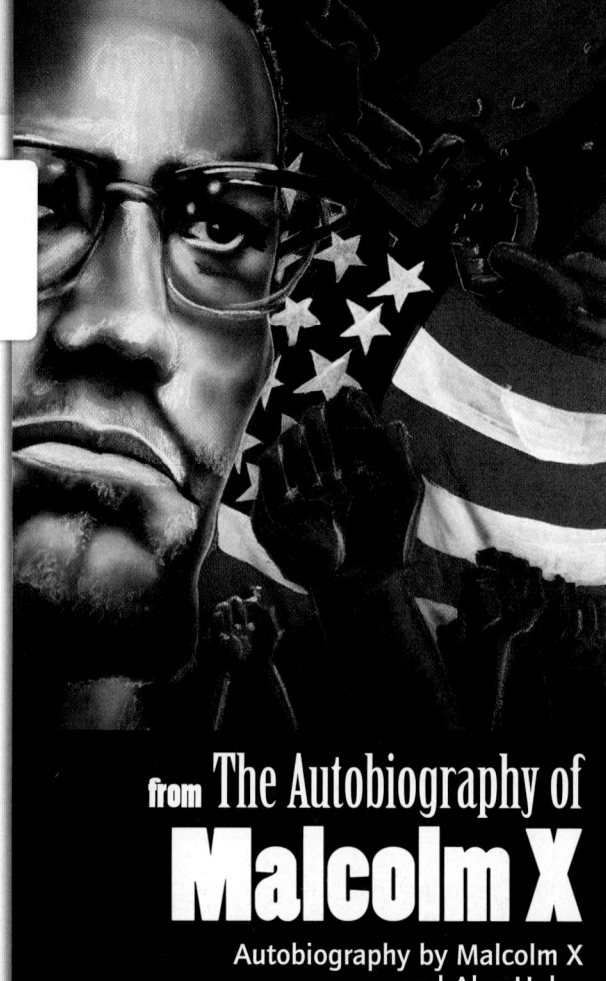

Preview the Selection

At a Glance
Independent Reading
- Reading Level: Moderate
- Difficulty Consideration: Vocabulary
- Ease Factor: Length

Objectives
Reading this selection will enable students to do the following:
- read with developing fluency
- read silently with comprehension for a sustained period of time

Launch the Lesson
Initiate discussion with this prompt: "Imagine that you are the lightkeeper at a lighthouse in a remote area. You rarely come in contact with other people and you don't have anything to do other than make sure that the light is working. However, the lighthouse company is willing to supply you with books on any subject. What would you choose to learn about? Malcolm X said, 'Months passed without my even thinking about being imprisoned. In fact, up to then, I never had been so truly free in my life.' What does isolation feel like to you? What would make the time pass quickly if you were alone for a long period of time?"

TEACHING NOTE
Although this selection is presented in the student edition as an independent reading, teaching support has been provided should you choose to cover it in class.

from The Autobiography of
Malcolm X
Autobiography by Malcolm X and Alex Haley

Malcolm X Malcolm Little was born in 1925, in Omaha, Nebraska. While he was in prison for burglary in 1946, he converted to the Black Muslim faith, changed his name to Malcolm X, and taught himself to read and write. He became an influential leader for many African Americans but also a controversial figure in the Civil Rights movement due to his powerful views. He later adopted orthodox Islam over the Black Muslim faith. He was assassinated at a rally in 1965.

Alex Haley (b. 1921) is best known for his 1977 Pulitzer Prize-winning book *Roots*, which was made into an epic film. He assisted Malcolm X in writing *The Autobiography of Malcolm X*, which was published in 1965. A member of the Coast Guard, he served as editor of *Out Post*, the official Coast Guard publication.

372

It was because of my letters that I happened to stumble upon starting to acquire some kind of a homemade education.

I became increasingly frustrated at not being able to express what I wanted to convey in letters that I wrote, especially those to Mr. Elijah Muhammad. In the street, I had been the most articulate hustler out there—I had commanded attention when I said something. But now, trying to write simple English, I not only wasn't articulate, I wasn't even functional. How would I sound writing in slang, the way I would *say* it, something such as, "Look, daddy, let me pull your coat about a cat, Elijah Muhammad—"

Many who today hear me somewhere in person, or on television, or those who read something I've said, will think I went to school far beyond the eighth grade. This impression is due entirely to my prison studies.

It had really begun back in the Charlestown Prison, when Bimbi first made me feel envy of his stock of knowledge. Bimbi had always taken charge of any conversation he was in, and I had tried to emulate him. But every book I picked up had few sentences which didn't contain anywhere from one to nearly all of the words that might as well have been in Chinese. When I

Program Resources

Planning and Assessment
Program Planning Guide, Selection Lesson Plan
E-Lesson Planner
Assessment Guide, Lesson Test
ExamView

Technology Tools
Interactive Student Text on CD
Visual Teaching Package
mirrorsandwindows.com

Meeting the Standards
Nonfiction: Unit 3, Independent Reading, pp. 76–83

Differentiating Instruction
Developing Readers, Use Text Organization, pp. 25–27

Common Core State Standards

Reading Literature
RL.10

Reading Informational
RI.2, RI.6, RI.10

Writing
W.10

Language
L.6

just skipped those words, of course, I really ended up with little idea of what the book said. So I had come to the Norfolk Prison Colony still going through only book-reading motions. Pretty soon, I would have quit even these motions, unless I had received the motivation that I did.

I saw that the best thing I could do was get hold of a dictionary—to study, to learn some words. I was lucky enough to reason also that I should try to improve my penmanship. It was sad. I couldn't even write in a straight line. It was both ideas together that moved me to request a dictionary along with some tablets and pencils from the Norfolk Prison Colony school.

I spent two days just riffling uncertainly through the dictionary's pages. I'd never realized so many words existed! I didn't know *which* words I needed to learn. Finally, just to start some kind of action, I began copying.

In my slow, painstaking, ragged handwriting, I copied into my tablet everything printed on that first page, down to the punctuation marks.

I believe it took me a day. Then, aloud, I read back, to myself, everything I'd written on the tablet. Over and over, aloud, to myself, I read my own handwriting.

I woke up the next morning, thinking about those words—immensely proud to realize that not only had I written so much at one time, but I'd written words that I never knew were in the world. Moreover, with a little effort, I also could remember what many of these words meant. I reviewed the words whose meanings I didn't remember. Funny thing, from the dictionary first page right now, that "aardvark" springs to my mind. The dictionary had a picture of it, a

I woke up the next morning, thinking about those words . . .

long-tailed, long-eared, burrowing African mammal, which lives off termites caught by sticking out its tongue as an anteater does for ants.

I was so fascinated that I went on—I copied the dictionary's next page. And the same experience came when I studied that. With every succeeding page, I also learned of people and places and events from history. Actually the dictionary is like a miniature encyclopedia. Finally the dictionary's A section had filled a whole tablet—and I went on into the B's. That was the way I started copying what eventually became the entire dictionary. It went a lot faster after so much practice helped me to pick up handwriting speed. Between what I wrote in my tablet, and writing letters, during the rest of my time in prison I would guess I wrote a million words.

I suppose it was inevitable that as my word-base broadened, I could for the first time pick up a book and read and now begin to understand what the book was saying. Anyone who has read a great deal can imagine the new worlds that opened. Let me tell you something: from then until I left that prison, in every free moment I had, if I was not reading in the library, I was reading on my bunk. You couldn't have gotten me out of books with a wedge. Between Mr. Muhammad's teachings, my correspondence, my visitors—usually Ella

THE AUTOBIOGRAPHY OF MALCOLM X **373**

Teach the Selection

Summary

While in jail, Malcolm X was frustrated by his inability to express himself in letters. Inspired by a fellow inmate who was very knowledgeable on a number of subjects, Malcolm began to study the dictionary. Eventually, he copied every page of the dictionary into tablets, improving his vocabulary and his handwriting in the process. When he finished that, he started to read books on many subjects from the prison library. During this time, even though he was imprisoned, he felt a sense of intellectual freedom never experienced outside of jail.

The Mirrors & Windows questions at the end of this selection focus on the theme of educating oneself. Before reading, ask students if they feel especially passionate about a certain skill or hobby they have taught themselves. How does teaching yourself a skill help you appreciate it more than skills taught to you by another person?

Words in Use

Selection Words
acquire, 372
articulate, 372
functional, 372
riffling, 373
succeeding, 373
inevitable, 373
rehabilitation, 374

Teaching Words
influential, 372
controversial, 372
orthodox, 372
memorandum, 375

KEY TERMS
AUTOBIOGRAPHY, 372
MEMO, 375

Analyze Literature

Point of View Point out to students that Malcolm X uses the pronoun *I* to refer to himself as he writes. Later, he uses the pronouns *me*, *my*, and *myself*. Ask them what this tells them about the point of view of the narrative. Model a response: "The use of the first-person pronouns indicates that the narrative is written from the first-person point of view." Discuss the fact that an autobiography, by definition, requires this point of view. **A**

History Connection

Nation of Islam Malcolm X was a leader in the Black Muslim religious movement who attracted many followers with his speeches and writings. Fard Muhammad established the Nation of Islam, in the United States in the early 1930s. The key principle that separated Black Muslims from Orthodox, or traditional, Muslims was a belief in separation of the black and white races. After the disappearance in 1934 of Fard Muhammad, Elijah Muhammad further developed the movement, which gained popularity by the end of World War II.

Use Reading Strategies

Ask Questions Remind students that active readers are constantly asking themselves questions about what they read and seeking the answers as they read on. Model for them what kinds of questions might be generated by this page: "Did Malcolm X participate in the debates?

A and Reginald[1]—and my reading of books, months passed without my even thinking about being imprisoned. In fact, up to then, I never had been so truly free in my life.

The Norfolk Prison Colony's library was in the school building. A variety of classes was taught there by instructors who came from such places as Harvard and Boston universities. The weekly debates between inmate teams were also held in the school building. You would be astonished to know how worked up convict debaters and audiences would get over subjects like "Should Babies Be Fed Milk?"

Available on the prison library's shelves were books on just about every general subject. Much of the big private collection that Parkhurst had willed to the prison was still in crates and boxes in the back of the library—thousands of old books. Some of them looked ancient: covers faded, old-time parchment-looking binding. Parkhurst, I've mentioned, seemed to have been principally interested in history and religion. He had the money and the special interest to have a lot of books that you wouldn't have in general circulation. Any college library would have been lucky to get that collection.

As you can imagine, especially in a prison where there was heavy emphasis on rehabilitation, an inmate was smiled upon if he demonstrated an unusually intense interest in books. There was a sizable number of well-read inmates, especially the popular debaters. Some were said by many to be practically walking encyclopedias. They were almost celebrities. No university would ask any student to devour literature as I did

1. **Ella and Reginald.** Half-sister and brother of Malcolm X

374 UNIT 3 NONFICTION

Differentiated Instruction

Reading Proficiency

Explain to students that summarizing main ideas in a text can aid in comprehension. Have them work together to summarize the main idea of each of the following subjects:

1. the influence Bimbi had on Malcolm's ambitions (spurs his desire for literacy)

2. the role the dictionary played in Malcolm's education (copying improves handwriting, increases vocabulary)

3. how he felt while he was reading (free)

4. how he managed to read late into the night (by the corridor light)

when this new world opened to me, of being able to read and *understand*.

I read more in my room than in the library itself. An inmate who was known to read a lot could check out more than the permitted maximum number of books. I preferred reading in the total isolation of my own room.

When I had progressed to really serious reading, every night at about ten P.M. I would be outraged with the "lights out." It always seemed to catch me right in the middle of something engrossing.

Fortunately, right outside my door was a corridor light that cast a glow into my room. The glow was enough to read by, once my eyes adjusted to it. So when "lights out" came, I would sit on the floor where I could continue reading in that glow.

I never had been so truly free in my life.

At one-hour intervals the night guards paced past every room. Each time I heard the approaching footsteps, I jumped into bed and feigned sleep. And as soon as the guard passed, I got back out of bed onto the floor area of that light-glow, where I would read for another fifty-eight minutes—until the guard approached again. That went on until three or four every morning. Three or four hours of sleep a night was enough for me. Often in the years in the streets I had slept less than that. ❖

 Do you value one skill more than another because you taught it to yourself? Why might learning a skill be more rewarding if it is self-taught?

Analyze and Extend

1. (a) What leads Malcolm X to the idea that he ought to study a dictionary? (b) Once he got the dictionary, how did he use it to learn reading and writing?
2. While he was still in prison, what opportunities did Malcolm have to use his new skills and knowledge?
3. (a) How did people perceive inmates who read many books? (b) Why did people think this way?

Creative Writing Within single organizations or companies, employees often communicate with each other by writing memorandums, called "memos" for short. Memos can contain formal announcements, important notes, or proposals. Write a **memo** from a prison employee to the prison director, requesting funding for the prison library and explaining the importance of your request.

Collaborative Learning Form groups of four or five students. Imagine that each person in the group speaks a different language. Try to think of ways to communicate the following circumstances: one of the members of your group has had an accident and needs medical assistance; someone has stolen your luggage; you have lost one of the members of your group.

 Go to www.mirrorsandwindows.com for more.

THE AUTOBIOGRAPHY OF MALCOLM X **375**

Appearances are Destructive

Essay by Mark Mathabane

As public schools reopen for the new year, strategies to curb school violence will once again be hotly debated. Installing metal detectors and hiring security guards will help, but the experience of my two sisters makes a compelling case for greater use of dress codes as a way to protect students and promote learning.

Shortly after my sisters arrived here from South Africa I enrolled them at the local public school. I had great expectations for their educational experience. Compared with black schools under apartheid, American schools are Shangri-Las,[1] with modern textbooks, school buses, computers, libraries, lunch programs and dedicated teachers.

But despite these benefits, which students in many parts of the world only dream about, my sisters' efforts at learning were almost derailed. They were constantly taunted for their homely outfits. A couple of times they came home in tears. In South Africa students were required to wear uniforms, so my sisters had never been preoccupied with clothes and jewelry.

They became so distraught that they insisted on transferring to different schools, despite my reassurances that there was nothing wrong with them because of what they wore.

---

1. **Shangri-Las.** Perfect, imaginary places

Mark Mathabane was born in Alexandra, Gauteng, South Africa, in 1960. He lived in Alexandra with his mother, his father, and six younger siblings. The family lived in a ghetto that was home to two hundred thousand other blacks. Encouraged by his mother, Mathabane focused on his education as a way to survive in South Africa under apartheid. Mathabane also focused on his passion for tennis, which helped him leave South Africa. In 1978, Mathabane received a tennis scholarship to attend Dowling College in Oakland, New York. He graduated from Dowling at the top of his class, and he then went on to study at Poynter Media Institute and the Columbia Graduate School of Journalism. In addition to *Kaffir Boy*, Mathabane is the author of five other books.

376

Program Resources

Planning and Assessment
Program Planning Guide, Selection Lesson Plan
E-Lesson Planner
Assessment Guide, Lesson Test
ExamView

Technology Tools
Interactive Student Text on CD
Visual Teaching Package
Audio Library
mirrorsandwindows.com

Meeting the Standards
Nonfiction: Unit 3, Independent Reading, pp. 84–91

Differentiating Instruction
Advanced Students, Persuasive Essay Assignment, pp. 19–20
English Language Learners, Identify Main Idea, pp. 117–124

We observe dress codes in nearly every aspect of our lives without any diminution of our freedoms...

I have visited enough public schools around the country to know that my sisters' experiences are not unique. In schools in many areas, Nike, Calvin Klein, Adidas, Reebok and Gucci are more familiar names to students than Zora Neale Hurston, Shakespeare and Faulkner. Many students seem to pay more attention to what's on their bodies than in their minds.

Teachers have shared their frustrations with me at being unable to teach those students willing to learn because classes are frequently disrupted by other students ogling themselves in mirrors, painting their fingernails, combing their hair, shining their gigantic shoes or comparing designer labels on jackets, caps and jewelry.

The fiercest competition among students is often not over academic achievements, but over who dresses most expensively. And many students now measure parental love by how willing their mothers and fathers are to pamper them with money for the latest fads in clothes, sneakers and jewelry.

Those parents without the money to waste on such meretricious² extravagances are considered uncaring and cruel. They

often watch in dismay and helplessness as their children become involved with gangs and peddle drugs to raise the money.

When students are asked why they attach so much importance to clothing, they frequently reply that it's the cool thing to do, that it gives them status and earns them respect. And clothes are also used to send sexual messages, with girls thinking that the only things that make them attractive to boys are skimpy dresses and gaudy looks, rather than intelligence and academic excellence.

---

2. **meretricious.** Superficial

APPEARANCES ARE DESTRUCTIVE **377**

Teach the Selection

Summary

The author argues that dress codes would help protect students and promote learning. His sisters, newly arrived from South Africa, were taunted in school for their simple style of dressing. Other students were preoccupied with style rather than academic excellence. Mathabane claims the argument that dress codes would infringe on personal freedom is misleading because we observe dress codes in every aspect of our lives.

Mirrors & Windows

The Mirrors & Windows questions at the end of this selection focus on the theme of dress codes. Before reading, ask students how much thought they put into their choice of clothing each day. What are some positive and negative effects of school dress codes?

TEACHING NOTE

Discuss Media Bias

Review with students some of the methods used by the media to influence the public:

Bandwagon—"Everyone is doing it, so you should, too."

Snob appeal—"All the cool/rich/smart people are doing it, so you should, too."

Testimonial—"This well-known person recommends the product, so you should buy it."

Either-or Fallacy—"You have only two choices, and this one is the only right one."

Words in Use

Selection Words
compelling, 376
promote, 376
derailed, 376
taunted, 376
homely, 376
preoccupied, 376
distraught, 376
ogling, 377
gaudy, 377

Teaching Words
ghetto, 376
apartheid, 376

KEY TERMS
ESSAY, 376
SYMBOL, 378
THEME, 378

IRRORS & WINDOWS

Answer: Students should be able to analyze their motivations for wearing particular outfits, and they should be able to list positive and negative effects of a dress code.

Analyze and Extend

1. (a) The sisters are taunted because their clothes are ugly by American standards. (b) The sisters and the author did not expect this because in South Africa they always wore uniforms.

2. (a) Skimpy dresses and gaudy looks—rather than better qualities like intelligence—make them attractive. (b) The author thinks students will focus on academics and learn better.

3. (a) The author calls these people "civil libertarians." (b) Civil libertarians believe that free dress is a part of the right to freedom of expression.

Rubric for Creative Writing
You can adapt this as a checklist for students to use as they write.

☐ Is the letter addressed to the author's sisters?

☐ Does the letter give the sisters information about American schools to help them feel better?

☐ Does the letter follow the proper format for a friendly letter?

The argument by civil libertarians[3] that dress codes infringe on freedom of expression is misleading. We observe dress codes in nearly every aspect of our lives without any diminution of our freedoms—as demonstrated by flight attendants, bus drivers, postal employees, high school bands, military personnel, sports teams, Girl and Boy Scouts, employees of fast-food chains, restaurants, and hotels.

In many countries where students outperform their American counterparts academically, school dress codes are observed as part of creating the proper learning environment. Their students tend to be neater, less disruptive in class and more disciplined, mainly because their minds are focused more on learning and less on materialism. It's time Americans realized that the benefits of safe and effective schools far outweigh any perceived curtailment of freedom of expression brought on by dress codes. ❖

---

3. **civil libertarians.** People who believe in little government authority

IRRORS & WINDOWS

Students often disagree on whether or not they think dress codes are necessary or helpful. When you get dressed in the morning, how important is your outfit? What are some pros and some cons of enforcing school dress codes?

Analyze and Extend

1. (a) What happens to the author's sisters at school? (b) When they started school, why didn't the author and his sisters anticipate this problem?

2. (a) According to the author, what are some negative messages that schools without dress codes send to female students? (b) What messages does Mathabane believe students learn at schools with dress codes?

3. (a) What does the author call people who are against dress codes? (b) According to the passage, what are this group's reasons for favoring free dress?

Creative Writing If you were in the situation of the author's sisters, what type of advice would you like to hear? What sort of things would make you feel better? Write a **letter** to the author's sisters giving them information about American schools and how they are similar or different. Share your work with the class.

Media Literacy Is the author correct about the messages sent by American clothing and jewelry? Collect advertisements for different products and evaluate them. What are common symbols, messages, and themes?

Go to **www.mirrorsandwindows.com** for more.

Differentiated Instruction

Enrichment
Students might enjoy writing a persuasive essay about a dress code that they think would be appropriate for their own school. Have them list rules and guidelines not only for clothing, but also for hairstyles, makeup, and accessories. They should include the reasoning behind their recommendations and employ persuasive techniques, such as "feel good" wording, emotional appeal, and testimonials.

English Language Learning
Students may need help with the following words in order to better understand the essay:
compelling—convincing, 376
taunted—ridiculed; made fun of, 376
distraught—extremely upset, 376
unique—one of a kind, 377
pamper—coddle; spoil, 377
infringe—trespass on; violate, 378

For Your Reading List

The Voice That Challenged a Nation: Marian Anderson and the Struggle for Equal Rights

by Russell Freedman

This award-winning book gives a biography of the famous African-American singer's life. In addition to being a professional vocalist, she battled segregation and played a key role in the Civil Rights movement. Freedman also vividly describes her famous 1939 concert at the Lincoln Memorial. Historical photographs help Anderson's story come to life.

Something Out of Nothing: Marie Curie and Radium

by Carla Killough McClafferty

This biography tells the story of Marie Curie, the woman who discovered radium. McClafferty follows her career, from her beginning at a Poland university to her death from radiation exposure. The book also discusses the issues that arose when Curie did not patent her work and other people claimed her research as their own, as well as the health dangers of radiation.

Close to Shore: The Terrifying Shark Attacks of 1916

by Michael Capuzzo

In the summer of 1916, people vacationing on the East Coast were terrified by attacks in the water. It was determined to be a shark that had swum inland along a New Jersey river. Capuzzo discusses the culture, the biology of sharks, and the details of that summer's events.

Escape! The Story of the Great Houdini

by Sid Fleischman

Harry Houdini, the famous magician, began as a poor boy named Ehrich Weiss. This biography tells of his rise to fame, from his first escape tricks to his later famous public stunts. The author had a personal friendship with Houdini's wife and stage partner, and he includes some of this firsthand information in telling Houdini's story.

Secrets of a Civil War Submarine: Solving the Mysteries of the *H.L. Hunley*

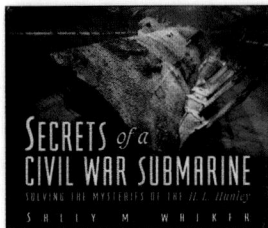

by Sally M. Walker

During the Civil War, one American wanted to invent a submarine to sneak up on enemy ships and destroy them. In 1864 the *H.L. Hunley* successfully sank another vessel, but the submarine never returned to land. The book chronicles the submarine from the original idea through its construction.

The Poet Slave of Cuba: A Biography of Juan Francisco Manzano

by Margarita Engle

Manzano was born a slave in Cuba in the late 1700s. As a child, he secretly learned to read and write. Although he had many difficult experiences, Manzano persevered by writing poetry. This book reveals Manzano's incredible story despite growing up in slavery.

Independent Reading

Independent Reading Activity

Help students link their reading to the unit theme, Looking Back. Ask how reading nonfiction can expand their understanding of the past. You might try this as a library activity: Have each student identify the person from the past that he or she would most like to meet. Another approach would be to identify the historical period each student would most like to visit. Then have students locate library books about the persons or periods they identified. After allowing time for students to read these books independently, ask volunteers to describe, in two or three minutes, how this reading gave them an experience of looking back.

EMC E-Library

The EMC E-Library contains over twenty thousand pages of literary classics that students may read independently. An Electronic Library Guide provides teaching suggestions, enrichment activities, and reading strategy guidesheets.

TEACHING NOTE

Author Bias

Point out to students that although nonfiction is primarily the presentation of facts—a reader must be alert to the possibility of bias. Bias refers to an attitude that prejudices a person for or against something. Ask students to provide examples of bias from selections in this and the following unit.

Program Resources

EMC Access Editions

For additional independent reading, you may wish to refer students to one of EMC's Access Edition titles. Each Access Edition contains a thorough study apparatus, including background information, literal comprehension questions, footnotes, vocabulary definitions, critical thinking questions, and related projects and activities. An Assessment Manual offering worksheets and exams is available for each Access Edition.

Common Core State Standards
Reading Literature RL.10
Reading Informational RI.10

Objectives

Participating in this workshop will help students write a cause-and-effect essay that

- has an introduction with a clear thesis that states a cause-and-effect relationship
- explains the relationship between each cause and its effect or effects
- has a clear organizational pattern
- uses textual evidence

Launch the Workshop

Ask students why they think some people choose writing as a profession. Prompt discussion with such questions as: "What are the rewards of being a writer? What kinds of childhood experiences would make someone want to be a writer?" Lead students to recognize that a person's career choice can have various causes. Tell them they now have an opportunity to explore significant cause-and-effect relationships through writing.

What Great Writers Do

Point out that Carson begins the passage with a series of effects. This buildup makes the statement of cause at the end come almost as a shock.

Program Resources

For a full writing rubric, go to **www.mirrorsandwindows.com.** Additional writing workshops are available in Exceeding the Standards: Writing.

Expository Writing

Cause-and-Effect Essay

Reading and Writing

In this unit, you have read many essays that detail changes in people's lives and argue for change in the world. These changes are rooted in perceptions, actions, interactions with others, and beliefs. Consider the relationship between Maya Angelou (Marguerite) and Mrs. Flowers. Think about the messages and examples from "Appearances are Destructive" and "Soul of a Citizen." Even in Angela Shelf Medearis's poem there is change. Change comes from events. An event is part of a cause-and-effect relationship. Sometimes causes and effects are easy to identify. Other times, a cause can lead to an effect, which, in turn, becomes a cause of something else.

In this workshop, you will learn how to write a **cause-and-effect essay.** In cause-and-effect writing, you analyze an event and the reasons why it occurred or you consider the relationship between an event and its results. Your essay will examine a cause-and-effect relationship in one of the selections from the unit. The following summary, which includes a description of your assignment, goal, strategy, and a writing rubric, will help you develop a strong essay.

- **Assignment:** Write an essay that identifies cause-and-effect relationships in a chosen selection.

- **Goal:** To identify a relationship between an event and the reasons why it occurred or the effects that occurred as a result.

- **Strategy:** Organize my ideas into a clear and appropriate pattern, and explain the relationship between the causes and effects of an event or outcome.

- **Writing Rubric:** My cause-and-effect essay should include the following:
  - an introduction that states the cause-and-effect relationship in a clear thesis
  - an explanation of the relationship between each cause and its effect(s)
  - a clear organizational pattern
  - textual evidence (paraphrased or quoted)
  - a conclusion that restates my thesis

What Great Writers Do

Rachel Carson was an essayist and environmentalist. Her book Silent Spring changed the way people thought about the natural world. How does Carson suggest a cause-and-effect relationship in the passage below?

The roadsides, once so attractive, were now lined with browned and withered vegetation as though swept by fire. These, too, were silent, deserted by all living things. Even the streams were now lifeless.

No witchcraft, no enemy action had silenced the rebirth of new life in this stricken world. The people had done it themselves.

Words in Use

Teaching Words
perceptions, 380
appropriate, 380
withered, 380
relevant, 381
annotations, 383
legible, 384

KEY TERMS

Common Core State Standards

Writing
W.2, W.3, W.4, W.5, W.6, W.10

Language
L.4.1g

Choosing Your Topic

First, choose which selection to analyze for cause and effect. Think of which selections interested you, particularly those with unexpected or memorable events and outcomes. Then, choose a selection in which you can easily find key events, or events that are important to the message, outcome, or thesis of the selection. Finally, make sure the selection you choose will give you enough to analyze in terms of cause-and-effect relationships.

Gathering Details

When you decide on a selection, identify the event or outcome you want to analyze and at least three causes or effects. Once you determine the important events, decide whether you want to focus on the reasons for the event or the results of it. You can analyze cause-and-effect relationships in one of three ways:

1. Analyze an event (effect) and the reasons why it occurred (causes).
2. Analyze an event (cause) and its results (effects).
3. Analyze a chain reaction in which a cause produces an effect, which becomes a cause for another effect, and so on.

Keep in mind that you will need to create a thesis that ties the causes and effects together. In addition, you will need to make judgments on your own about how the causes and effects are connected.

Distinguishing Cause and Effect Note that causes and effects can be either simple or complex. For example, if you break a rule (cause), you will get in trouble (effect). But what if breaking the rule was the effect of not reading a sign because it was in a language you did not know? Is the cause of getting in trouble your lack of knowledge about the language? Are there multiple causes? Are there multiple effects? These are the kinds of relationships you will determine as you identify the causes and effects within a selection. To gather details, look back at the selection and note relevant passages. Be open-minded. As you analyze the selection more in-depth, you may change your mind about which events are causes and which are effects.

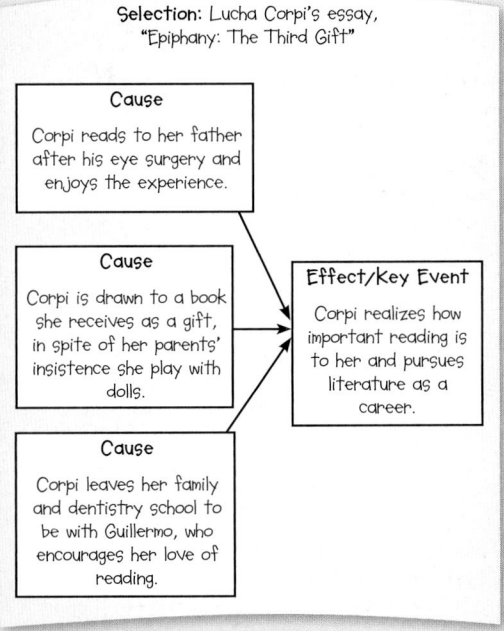

Selection: Lucha Corpi's essay, "Epiphany: The Third Gift"

Cause
Corpi reads to her father after his eye surgery and enjoys the experience.

Cause
Corpi is drawn to a book she receives as a gift, in spite of her parents' insistence she play with dolls.

Cause
Corpi leaves her family and dentistry school to be with Guillermo, who encourages her love of reading.

Effect/Key Event
Corpi realizes how important reading is to her and pursues literature as a career.

Creating a Thesis Statement

Evaluate your causes and effects and how they are connected. Then state the relationship between the causes and effects in a thesis statement.

Teach the Workshop

Prewrite

Gathering Details Once students choose the selections about which to write, give them ample time to reread. Encourage them to read several times, each time with a different purpose. First, they should read to make sure the selection is as engaging as they recall. Second, they should read to be sure they can identify and understand the main events. In subsequent readings, they can look for details to support their descriptions of causes and effects.

Creating a Thesis Statement If a student needs help devising a thesis statement, suggest trying to state the theme of the selection. Articulating the main idea may help a student decide whether to emphasize causes or effects in the thesis statement.

Have students work in pairs to test their thesis statements. Each student should read his or her statement and then ask for feedback on whether it is interesting and can be supported with details, facts, and examples.

TEACHING NOTE

Select a Subject

Be sure students understand that they will be writing about one of the literary works in Unit 3. Help them review their reading and choose a piece that engaged their interest. Check their choices and, if necessary, remind students that their choices should have obvious cause-and-effect relationships.

Writing Skills

Write for an Audience

Remind students that an audience is the person or group of people who will read their essay. Say that choosing a specific audience will help them make decisions as they write. To give students practice focusing on an audience, tell them to imagine they are writing an essay about Mathabane's "Appearances Are Destructive" for a group of fashion executives. Ask:

1. How much does this audience already know about school dress codes?
2. What background does the audience need in order to appreciate the essay's main point?

Draft

Organizing Ideas Be sure students have a clear organizational pattern in mind before they begin writing. For most students, the literary selection and thesis statement will lead to an easy choice. If a student has trouble choosing one of the patterns described in the text, suggest that he or she review previous decisions.

- Are causes and effects simple or complex?
- Which events dominate the selection?
- What relationship have I emphasized in my thesis statement?

Modeling a Plan Assure students that they can draft their essays in whatever order feels natural to them. Model thinking through this process: "I know that two main events have persuaded Mathabane that school fashion culture should change: his sisters' experience and visits to schools. I can write a paragraph about each event. Then I can connect the events to my thesis statement in the introduction: Two powerful experiences cause Mark Mathabane to advocate for school uniforms."

2. DRAFT

Organizing Ideas

When organizing your essay, use **cause-and-effect organization.** Choose which type of cause-and-effect order fits the relationship you will explain. If you focus on an event and its causes, use effect-to-cause organization. If you focus on an event and its effects, use cause-to-effect organization. Review the organizational models here.

In some cases, a cause-and-effect chain may be the clearest way to organize your essay. Use a cause-and-effect chain if your cause leads to an effect, which in turn causes a new effect, and so on, as in a chain reaction. Be sure to state the causes and effects in the order they occur.

Effect-to-Cause	Cause-to-Effect
State the Effect	State the Cause
Cause 1	Effect 1
detail	detail
detail	detail
Cause 2	Effect 2
detail	detail
detail	detail
Cause 3	Effect 3
detail	detail
detail	detail

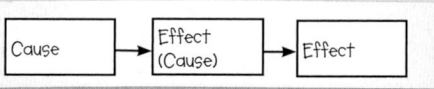

Putting Your Thoughts on Paper

Creating an Outline Now that you have chosen the cause-and-effect relationship to discuss, apply the information you gathered to one of the cause-and-effect organizational methods to create an outline. Include as many supporting details from the text as you can.

Once you have outlined each section of your essay, you should be able to fill in each section as you draft, adding details and explanation as necessary. Focus mainly on content and organization.

Introduction
- "Epiphany: The Third Gift" by Lucha Corpi
- Thesis

Body
- Cause 1: Corpi reads to her father.
- Cause 2: Corpi receives a book and dolls.
- Cause 3: Corpi leaves Mexico with Guillermo.

Conclusion

Making Connections

Elaborate and Explain When you discuss your causes and effects, give specific details to support the relationship you are trying to prove between causes and effects. Then explain how the details support your claim about a cause-and-effect relationship.

Corpi loved helping her father, and when she didn't know a word, he would patiently explain it to her. As a result, reading to him expanded Corpi's knowledge of the world and showed her how reading could expand her own world.

Differentiated Instruction

Visual Learning

Encourage visual learners to diagram their outlines. Using boxes, they can show the hierarchy of paragraph organization and structure the drafting process. Model this using a possible paragraph about Mathabane's essay. Sketch a large rectangle on the board. Write in it a topic sentence: "Mathabane's sisters nearly failed in school because of their clothes." Under it, sketch four smaller rectangles. Point out that each can contain a detail to support the topic sentence. Tell students that using a diagram will help them rearrange parts by erasing and refilling the shapes to see how the ideas flow.

3. REVISE

Evaluating Your Draft

Now that your draft is complete, look at what you have done. First, read your response aloud to yourself. Mark anything that needs to be fixed. Then, trade responses with one of your classmates to conduct a **peer review.** Your classmate will read your response and look for other parts to be improved. Use the checklist here as a guide.

Below is a draft of a cause-and-effect essay. The annotations to the right indicate the reasons for the changes marked in the draft.

> **Revising Checklist**
> ☐ Does the introduction identify the selection and state the thesis?
> ☐ Is the relationship between each cause and its effect(s) explained?
> ☐ Is the essay organized logically?
> ☐ Does the essay include supporting evidence from the text?

In Lucha Corpi's essay, *"Epiphany: The Third Gift,"* she recounts three presents she received from her parents as a girl. Though she frequently disagreed with her parents, Corpi learned important lessons from her interactions with them. Corpi's childhood interactions with her parents ~~were sometimes supportive and sometimes not.~~ —*whether supportive or not*—*led her to pursue her love of literature as an adult.*

An important moment in Corpi's life was when she realized how important reading was to her. After eye surgery, Corpi's father needed assistance reading. He could use only one eye, which became tired from work all day, so he needed her to read the newspaper to him in the evenings. Corpi loved helping her father, and when she didn't know a word, he would patiently explain it to her. *As a result,* reading to him expanded Corpi's knowledge of the world and showed her how reading could expand her own world.

> *Include the name of the selection you focus on.*
>
> *Make sure your thesis states the cause-and-effect relationship clearly.*

> *State each cause in a topic sentence.*
>
> *Use transitions and signal words to point out cause-and-effect relationships.*

Revise

Evaluating a Draft Give students tips for delivering and receiving helpful criticism:

Delivering a Peer Review
- **Be focused.** Concentrate on content, organization, and style. Leave spelling and punctuation for the proofreading stage.
- **Be positive.** Respect the writer's feelings and genuine writing efforts.
- **Be specific.** Give the writer concrete ideas for improving his or her work.

Receiving a Peer Review
- **Be specific.** Tell your peer reviewer your specific concerns and questions.
- **Ask questions.** Make sure you understand your reviewer's comments.
- **Be selective.** Accept your reviewer's suggestions graciously, but you don't have to use all—or any—of them.

Evaluating Tone Remind students that a cause-and-effect essay is expository, so it should have a formal tone. As they review and revise their work, have them check for a consistent, formal tone.

Writing Skills

Incorporate Suggestions

Encourage students to evaluate the feedback they receive from peer reviewers to determine how useful it is. Offer criteria for evaluation:
- Does the feedback focus on how well I express cause-and-effect relationships?
- Does the feedback include strong opinions?
- Is the feedback objective or subjective?

Tell students to improve their essays with objective suggestions and discard suggestions that would make the essay seem to be written by someone else.

Edit and Proofread

Students may want to use proofreader's marks when correcting their work. Refer them to the Language Arts Handbook Writing Section 4.1, Proofreader's Symbols.

TEACHING NOTE

Homophones

As students consider commonly confused words, point out that many such words are homophones—they sound alike. If you are going to have students read their essays aloud in class, advise them to be especially alert for homophones. Suggest they try to use context clues to clarify which meaning they intend.

 Publish and Present

Before students begin their final versions, suggest that they read the Language Arts Handbook, Writing Section 4.1, Writing Follow-up.

---

4. EDIT AND PROOFREAD

Focus: Transitions

In your essay, use transitions and other signal words and phrases to identify cause-and-effect relationships.

> He could use only one eye, which became tired from work all day, *so* he needed her to read the newspaper to him in the evenings.
>
> When her boyfriend Guillermo moved to California, Corpi went with him, married him, and had a son. Ironically, *as a result* of the marriage, Corpi gave up dentistry and pursued her love of literature and reading.

Here is a list of signal words and phrases that indicate cause-and-effect relationships.

after this	*since*
as a result	*so*
because	*then*
consequently	*therefore*
if	*thus*
in order that	*while*

Focus: Commonly Confused Words

Some words can be confusing when you are writing. Review carefully your usage of words such as *effect* and *affect* when you are revising your draft. If you are still confused, remember to use a dictionary to find out which word you should use.

An easy way to remember the difference between *effect* and *affect* is to consider what part of speech each word is. *Effect* is a thing, so it is a noun. *Affect* is a verb. An *effect* must have a *cause*. You can link the *e* in each word. If you are trying to talk about an action, then you want to use *affect*.

> *affected*
> The book ~~effected~~ her deeply, but she found the doll and dollhouse boring.

Proofreading

Quality Control Although you can always look for mistakes as you write, read, and rewrite, set aside time to proofread your essay in which you look primarily for errors in grammar, punctuation, and spelling. Use proofreader's marks to highlight any errors you find. (See the Language Arts Handbook, section 4.1, for a list of proofreader's marks.)

---

5. PUBLISH AND PRESENT

Final Draft

Clean Copy Now that you have revised, edited, and proofread your paper, it is time to make a clean copy for presentation. Handwritten papers should be neat and legible. If you are working with a word processing program, double space the lines of text and use a readable typeface. Follow your teacher's presentation guidelines before submitting your work.

Differentiated Instruction

Reading Proficiency

Review cause-and-effect signal words and phrases with students. Use each in a sentence, and have students tell you the causes and effects. Encourage them to use complete sentences.

English Language Learning

Students learning English might appreciate extra practice with commonly confused English words. When these students have completed their drafts, pair them with fluent native speakers as peer reviewers to help them identify and clarify any commonly confused words.

Student Model

The Third Gift: The First Love
by Anton Davis

In Lucha Corpi's essay, "Epiphany: The Third Gift," she recounts three presents she received from her parents as a girl. Though she frequently disagreed with her parents, Corpi learned important lessons from her interactions with them. Corpi's childhood interactions with her parents—whether supportive or not—led her to pursue her love of literature as an adult.

An important moment in Corpi's life was when she realized how important reading was to her. After eye surgery, Corpi's father needed assistance reading. He could use only one eye, which became tired from work all day, so he needed her to read the newspaper to him in the evenings. Corpi loved helping her father, and when she didn't know a word, he would patiently explain it to her. As a result, reading to him expanded Corpi's knowledge of the world and showed her how reading could expand her own world.

When Corpi received three presents from her parents, she clearly preferred one to the others, to her parents' dismay. She received a doll that cried, a dollhouse with furniture, and a book of stories. The book affected her deeply, but she found the doll and dollhouse boring. Her parents did encourage her reading, because, as Corpi's father explained, "When you educate a man, you educate an individual. But when you educate a woman, you educate the whole family." Corpi's parents felt that education was important, but it should not be an end in itself, at least not for women. Therefore, they grew upset when they realized that Corpi liked books instead of dolls because they thought that playing with dolls would cause Corpi to become a good mother. Her focus on reading was appreciated, so long as it did not interfere with her developing a family.

Corpi dreamed of a career as a doctor or astronomer, but her parents felt that neither was fit for a woman raising a family. So, Corpi attended dentistry school in order to please her parents. When her boyfriend Guillermo moved to California, Corpi went with him, married him, and had a son. Ironically, as a result of the marriage, Corpi gave up dentistry and pursued her love of literature and reading. Yet, through her parents' teaching, Corpi learned to be a good mother while also pursuing her love of literature.

Corpi's life did not work out how she might have expected. Yet, although she struggled with her parents over her focus on reading rather than on family, they helped her to see the importance of both.

Introduces the topic, the selection, and the author

Clearly states the cause-and-effect relationship in the thesis

Uses a logical order in which each cause is stated in the body and supported with details, quotations, and examples

Includes transitions and signal words to show cause-and-effect relationships

Summarizes the main points of the essay

Restates the thesis in a new way

Student Model
Using the Model Direct students' attention to the model. Point out the side notes that describe the thesis statement, the logical order and transitions, and the restatement in the last paragraph. Suggest that students outline the model to grasp the writer's organization and use of supporting material.

What Great Writers Do

Help students reflect on the writing process by asking what they might be able to use from it. Give them an example. Here, author Julia Alvarez tells interviewer Kathy Tarr how moving to a new country and reading books encouraged her to become a writer:

"And you know how it is: Read a wonderful book that stirs you and then you want to try to do that too. And having to learn a language, of course, really makes you pay attention to why people are saying things one way as opposed to another. And that's what we do when we're writers—we have to relearn the language and do that kind of listening to the language that happens when you're also learning a new language in order to survive."

Reading Skills

Using Emotional Appeals
Use this opportunity to refresh students' memories about recognizing emotional appeals in nonfiction writing. Such appeals are common in persuasive writing, but they can also appear in cause-and-effect essays. Read students these excerpts from the student model, and have them tell you which word or words—if any—appeal to the reader's emotion.

1. Corpi dreamed of a career as a doctor or astronomer. (dreamed)
2. Ironically, as a result of the marriage, Corpi gave up dentistry. (ironically, gave up)

Teach the Workshop

Objectives

Participating in this workshop will help students deliver an informative presentation with

- an attention-grabbing introduction and a satisfying conclusion
- content that will appeal to a particular audience
- a clear, concise main idea and effective supporting details

Launch the Workshop

Create a two-column chart with the headings "effective" and "ineffective" on a board or overhead projector. Next, ask volunteers to describe infomercials they have seen on television or heard on the radio. Request examples of those that they would describe as engaging and/or informative, as well as those they consider boring and/or meaningless. Chart the elements that students offer, and discuss the differences between effective and ineffective infomercials.

> For more information, see the Language Arts Handbook Section 7, Speaking & Listening.

Program Resources

To expand upon this workshop lesson, Giving and Actively Listening to Informative Presentations, see the *Exceeding the Standards: Speaking & Listening* resource.

Common Core State Standards

Speaking and Listening
SL.1, SL.3, SL.4, SL.5, SL.6

Giving and Actively Listening to Informative Presentations

If you've ever described an event you've witnessed, given instructions about how to do something, or explained a story or movie, you've presented information. In this lesson, you will give an **informative presentation** to an audience. A successful informative presentation delivers factual information to an audience in an interesting and dynamic manner. When giving informative presentations, you communicate and share ideas with your audience. Sharing also requires active listening on the part of the audience.

Planning an Informative Presentation

Choose a Topic The first step in planning an informative presentation is choosing a topic. Select a topic that interests you and about which you are well-informed. Decide which parts of the topic are most important for your audience to know. Narrow your topic enough so that you can explain it effectively in the time you have. For example, you might begin with a broad topic, such as computers, and narrow it to computers as a form of entertainment. You might then narrow it further to game-playing on the computer.

Identify Your Audience To what audience are you presenting your information? How old are they? How much do they already know about the topic? The answers to these questions will determine the kind of language you will use and the amount of background you will need to provide. For example, if your audience knows little about computer gaming, you might avoid or explain game-related jargon such as *game master*, *co-op mode*, and *avatar*.

Gather Information Once you have identified your topic and audience, you can begin doing research. First, outline the points you want to make, placing the strongest ideas first. As you gather information on each point, record it on a note card. Each card should have one main idea and at least three supporting details. Highlight the main idea so that you can find it easily when you present. Use your outline to organize the note cards.

Effective Introductions and Closings Pay particular attention to your introduction. Grab your audience's attention by using little-known and interesting facts, quotations, or anecdotes. Or make the audience a part of your presentation by opening with a question, such as *How could you play a game in real time with a friend in Africa?* Involve your audience in your presentation to make them more attentive and open to what you are going to explain.

Words in Use

Teaching Words
dynamic, 386
constructive, 387
monotonous, 387
fluently, 387

KEY TERMS

INFORMATIVE PRESENTATION, 386
AUDIENCE, 386
TOPIC, 386
OUTLINE, 386
MAIN IDEA, 386
SUPPORTING DETAIL, 386
INTRODUCTION, 386
ANECDOTE, 386
CONCLUSION, 387
FEEDBACK, 387

Conclude your presentation in a clear, concise, and satisfying way. Sum up the ideas you have presented by making a prediction, restating the main idea in a fresh way, or commenting on a statement or question you included earlier. Try to leave your audience wanting to know more about your topic.

Evaluating Your Informative Presentation

Working in small groups, rehearse your informative presentation. After each turn, the group should offer the speaker both positive and negative feedback in a constructive and polite way. What was good about the presentation? Where might it be strengthened? Use the speaking and listening rubrics on this page to evaluate each informative presentation.

Delivering Your Informative Presentation

Your voice communicates in many ways other than through the words you speak. Your tone, pitch, volume, rhythm, and inflection all influence your presentation and the way your audience receives it. If you sound bored, or have a monotonous tone, your audience will be bored too. Your main purpose is to deliver factual information, so use body movements only to emphasize points. Adjust your voice so that your entire audience can easily hear you. Look enthusiastic about your topic and maintain eye contact with your audience. Use charts, graphs, or other visual aids to enhance or clarify information rather than as frills or background.

Listen Actively Listeners play an equally important role in an informative presentation. To listen actively and effectively, maintain eye contact with the speaker and think about what he or she is saying. Ask questions when appropriate.

Speaking Rubric

Your informative presentation will be evaluated on the following elements:

Content

☐ includes an attention-grabbing introduction and a satisfying conclusion

☐ adapts content to the specific audience and purpose

☐ presents clear and concise content with a main idea and adequate, but not excessive, supporting details

Delivery and Presentation

☐ speaks fluently and expressively

☐ uses appropriate volume, enunciation, tone, and eye contact

☐ uses effective nonverbal cues

☐ responds to audience questions appropriately

Listening Rubric

As a peer reviewer or audience member, I should do the following:

☐ listen quietly and attentively

☐ maintain eye contact with speaker

☐ ask appropriate questions

☐ (as peer reviewer) provide constructive feedback

Evaluating Informative Presentations

Have students create a feedback checklist to use as they rehearse with their partners or small groups. This checklist should relate to the strength of introductions, how appropriate the content is for the audience, the clarity of information expressed, the effectiveness of the conclusion, and both verbal and nonverbal aspects of delivery. Tell students to use the checklist consistently so that they can recognize improvements in their ability to speak and listen.

Delivering Informative Presentations

Remind students that like actors, they need to project their voices. This means that they need to effectively focus their voices. Students can establish an appropriate volume by rehearsing with a partner standing at the back of the classroom.

TEACHING NOTE

Practice

Invite students to give brief extemporaneous speeches in small groups and ask for feedback. Students should choose topics about which they already know a great deal. Tell them not to use notes but instead to try grabbing attention with a strong introduction. They should follow this with two or three informative examples, and conclude with a simple summary of the main idea or message they tried to convey.

Speaking & Listening Skills

Self-Evaluation

As students rehearse, encourage them to stay alert for nonverbal feedback from the group. Point out that sometimes people are shy about verbalizing criticism, but their nonverbal cues communicate it anyway. Suggest that students reverse the listening rubric to recognize nonverbal clues that a speech needs work:

- People talk among themselves or read something while you are speaking.
- People look around the room or out the window, instead of at you.
- No one has any questions when you finish.

Objectives

Completing this workshop will enable students to

- write a literary response based on a timed writing prompt
- answer standardized test questions that demonstrate revising and editing skills
- demonstrate the ability to make inferences from a reading by answering standardized questions

Timed Writing

Point out that standardized tests often ask students to write a response to a prompt in a specified period of time. Give the following tips:

- Read the entire question carefully.
- Look for key words in the question that tell you what is expected.
- Underline these words or write them on your own note paper.
- Use the key words to make sure to answer all parts of the question.
- Organize. Allow time for planning, writing, and reviewing.
- Before you begin writing, create a rough outline of points to make.
- If you find yourself running out of time, state your remaining points and add a conclusion.
- Write a clear introduction. This will help keep you on track as you write each paragraph.
- Review your completed essay to see if you have answered all parts of the question.
- Before you turn in your completed essay, take time to proofread.

Common Core State Standards

Reading Information
RI.3, RI.4, RI.6
Writing
W.4, W.5
Language
L.4

Test Practice Workshop

Writing Skills

Expository Essay

Read the following short excerpt and the writing assignment that follows. Before you begin writing, think carefully about what task the assignment is asking you to perform. Then create an outline to help guide your writing.

from "Reluctant Witnesses: Children's Voices from the Civil War" by Emmy Werner

Historians estimate that anywhere between 250,000 and 420,000 boy soldiers, many in their early teens or even younger, served in the armies of the Union and the Confederacy between 1861 and 1865. Their experience in battle, seen from their vantage point, bears a striking resemblance to the eyewitness reports of contemporary child soldiers in Angola, Ethiopia, Liberia, Mozambique, Central America, and the Middle East. Some fifteen percent were seriously wounded or died from battle wounds, diarrhea, infections, or malnutrition. Others spent tortured months in prisons like Andersonville, whose conditions resembled the concentration camps of World War II.

Southern boys sought adventure and glory in the Confederate Army. They joined "to fight the Yankees—all fun and frolic." But they also wanted to defend their homes against an invading army. North or South, the process of enlistment was relatively simple, especially if parents supported the boy's decision to volunteer.

William Bircher was fifteen years old when he ran away from home to the recruiting depot in St. Paul, Minnesota. William remembered: "The happiest day of my life was when I put on my blue uniform for the first time and received my drum."

Assignment: What **caused** so many young men to become "boy soldiers"? What **effects** did joining the world of adults in so difficult a time have on their lives? Plan and write several paragraphs for an **expository essay** in which you state and support a **thesis** about the **causes** and **effects** of children becoming soldiers. Include evidence from the passage to support your thesis.

Rubric for Expository Essay
You can adapt this as a checklist for students to use as they write.

- ☐ Do your paragraphs follow your outline?
- ☐ Do your paragraphs present a thesis about the causes and effects of children becoming soldiers?
- ☐ Do your paragraphs include evidence from the passage in support of your thesis?

Revising and Editing Skills

Each sentence below has one or two blanks. Each blank indicates that a word has been omitted. Beneath the sentence are five words or sets of words labeled A through E. Choose the word or set of words that, when inserted in the sentence, best fits the meaning of the sentence as a whole.

1. Much to the candidate's ___, he later found that his accusations of fraud against his opponent were ___.
   A. degradation…sullen
   B. chagrin…groundless
   C. foresight…honorable
   D. solidarity…benign
   E. protestation…emaciated

2. The attorney ___ failed to help his clients reach agreement in an ___ manner.
   A. tautly…unwonted
   B. honorably…sullen
   C. benignly…honorable
   D. competently…isolated
   E. persistently…amicable

3. After going without food for several days, the dog began to look ___.
   A. unwonted
   B. amicable
   C. emaciated
   D. groundless
   E. honorable

4. Despite the ___ of the defendant, the jury ___ her for the crime.
   A. protestation…indicted
   B. chagrin…devised
   C. foresight…inculcated
   D. degradation…infused
   E. solidarity…disclosed

5. The student resented the ___ attack on his honesty.
   A. benign
   B. amicable
   C. honorable
   D. unwonted
   E. emaciated

6. Despite her mother's attempts to ___ Luisa with the love of truth, her lies continued to grow in ___.
   A. indict…enclave
   B. admonish…kinship
   C. devise…chagrin
   D. commemorate…foresight
   E. inculcate…magnitude

7. The clothing, books, and papers in my room seem to ___, which explains why it's so difficult to keep it clean.
   A. admonish
   B. commemorate
   C. proliferate
   D. inculcate
   E. infuse

8. The ___ done by the young pioneer girl was still ___ in its frame.
   A. embroidery…taut
   B. enclave…honorable
   C. kinship…benign
   D. solidarity…isolated
   E. memorabilia…groundless

9. Both candidates for the job completed their work ___, although one had a ___ expression on her face the whole time.
   A. benignly…groundless
   B. honorably…adjacent
   C. tautly…emaciated
   D. competently…sullen
   E. persistently…groundless

Words in Use

Teaching Words
reluctant, 388
estimate, 388
enlistment, 388
expository, 388
omitted, 389
hinder, 390
naïve, 391

KEY TERMS

Reading
Comprehension Tests

Point out to students that reading comprehension questions give you a short piece of writing and then ask you several questions about it. The questions may ask you to figure out something based on information in the passage. Urge them to keep the following tips in mind:

- Read all the questions quickly.
- Read the passage with the questions in mind.
- Reread the first question carefully.
- Scan the passage, looking for key words. When you find a key word, slow down and read carefully.
- Answer the first question.
- Repeat this process to answer all the rest of the questions.

Reading Skills

Carefully read the following passage. Then, on a separate piece of paper, answer each question.

from "Do not ask us to give up the buffalo for sheep"
by Chief Ten Bears

The Comanches are not weak and blind, like the pups of a dog when seven sleeps old. They are strong and farsighted, like grown horses. We took their road and we went on it. The white women cried, and our women laughed. But there are things which you have said to me which I do not like. They were not sweet
5 like sugar, but bitter like gourds. You said that you wanted to put us upon a reservation, to build us houses and to make us Medicine lodges. I do not want them.

I was born upon the prairie, where the wind blew free, and there was nothing to break the light of the sun. I was born where there were no enclosures, and
10 where everything drew a free breath. I want to die there, and not within walls. I know every stream and every wood between the Rio Grande and the Arkansas. I have hunted and lived over that country. I lived like my fathers before me, and like them, I lived happily.

When I was at Washington, the Great Father told me that all the Comanche
15 land was ours, and that no one should hinder us in living upon it. So why do you ask us to leave the rivers, and the sun, and the wind, and live in houses? Do not ask us to give up the buffalo for the sheep. The young men have heard talk of this, and it has made them sad and angry. Do not speak of it more. I love to carry out the talk I get from the Great Father. When I get goods and presents, I and my
20 people feel glad since it shows that he holds us in his eye. If the Texans had kept out of my country, there might have been peace. But that which you now say we must live on is too small.

Differentiated Instruction

English Language Learning

Students learning English will need help with the academic vocabulary used in standardized tests. Explain the meaning of the following terms used in this workshop:

outline — short summary or description, usually arranged as a series of key points, 386

expository essay — writing that explains or informs, 388

evidence — facts offered in support of an argument, 388

1. Based on the context, what is the meaning of "seven sleeps old" in lines 1–2?
   A. seven years old
   B. seven months old
   C. seven weeks old
   D. seven days old
   E. seven minutes old

2. What can you infer about the narrator's purpose and audience?
   A. He is telling a story to his people.
   B. He is writing a history of his people for the future.
   C. He is explaining his position to representatives of the government.
   D. He is telling Texans that he will wage war against them.
   E. He is trying to persuade the President to build them more houses.

3. In line 4, to what does the word *they* refer?
   A. the people to whom the Chief is talking
   B. things the Indians regularly eat
   C. things the Chief wants for the tribe
   D. things the Indians grow on their land
   E. things white people have said to the Chief

4. What is the purpose of paragraph 2?
   A. to persuade white people that houses are bad
   B. to explain why Indians don't want to live on a reservation
   C. to persuade the Comanches to accept the government's offer
   D. to entertain the children of the tribe with stories from the past
   E. to explain the history of the Comanche to the Ute

5. Based on the context, what is the meaning of the word *break* in line 9?
   A. interrupt
   B. destroy
   C. tear apart
   D. come into being
   E. take place

6. What is the most probable setting in which the Chief said these words?
   A. at a celebration on the Comanche reservation
   B. in a boat on the Rio Grande
   C. at the White House in Washington
   D. in the House of Representatives in Washington
   E. at a meeting between the Chief and representatives of the government

7. What words best characterize the speaker?
   A. weak and naive
   B. strong and reasonable
   C. submissive and gentle
   D. sullen and angry
   E. frightened and obedient

8. How would you describe the sentence in lines 14–15?
   A. persuasive thesis
   B. sensory language
   C. an opinion
   D. a statement of fact
   E. a statement of purpose

9. This passage is best described as
   A. a personal essay.
   B. an autobiography.
   C. a speech.
   D. a descriptive essay.
   E. a biography.

Teach the Workshop

Reading Skills
1. D
2. C
3. E
4. B
5. A
6. E
7. B
8. D
9. C

Test-Taking Skills

Use Context Clues

Point out to students that in reading skills tests they will frequently encounter questions about the meanings of words in context. Using context clues is vital in answering such questions. Model using this skill:

Question 5. Possible Think-Aloud: Break can mean several things depending on context. When dawn breaks it "comes into being" or "takes place," but though the speaker is talking about sunlight, this meaning is probably not intended. Break can also mean "destroy" or "tear apart," but light is unbreakable. So the answer must be A.

Unit 4 Visual Planning Guide

Planning and Assessment Tools

Annotated Teacher's Edition

Annotated Teacher's Edition
One location for accessing, previewing, and planning for use of all program resources.

EMC Launchpad
Desktop application for accessing, previewing, planning, posting, and grading all program resources. Post personal resources and lessons, and access the E-Lesson Planner, the E-Gradebook, and training modules for computer literacy.

Assessment Guide and ExamView
A variety of assessments are available for this unit in print and electronic forms, including:
- Formative Survey
- Lesson Tests
- Unit Exams
- Alternative Assessment Options
- Reading Fluency Assessments

Meeting the Standards: Unit 1
In addition to lesson-by-lesson resources, *Meeting the Standards* includes the following unit-based resources:
- Unit Study Guide
- Practice Test
- Active Reading Model
- Selection Quizzes

Program Planning Guide and E-Lesson Planner
- Lesson Plans for all the selections in the unit
- Core Standards-Based Selections
- Reading Log and Evaluation Forms

The E-Lesson Planner contains fully developed lesson plans and unit resources with an electronic calendar for editing lesson plans.

Technology Tools

Visual Teaching Package
This package contains unit-based lectures, games, art collections, and Writing Workshops in PowerPoint format; included within the EMC Launchpad.

Interactive Student Text on CD
The student textbook on CD includes highlighting, note-taking, bookmarking, and a direct link to the student website, in addition to everything in the student text.

Audio Library
Authentic, dramatic recordings with listening activities expand listening skills and offer additional support for developing readers and English Language Learners.

ETS Online Criterion-Based Essay Grader (Grades 9–12)
Students can use this ETS web-based tool to evaluate their essays online before submitting them for teacher review and final evaluation.

mirrorsandwindows.com
Student and teacher resources, support, references, technology tools, and state-specific standards are available at **mirrorsandwindows.com.** The website is customizable using the EMC Launchpad.

Unit-Based Resources

Exceeding the Standards Unit Resources

Each of the *Exceeding the Standards* resources provides fully developed lessons to help you extend the textbook lessons and to expand upon the themes and skills covered in the unit. You can also download these lessons from **mirrorsandwindows.com**.

Grammar & Style
This resource contains:
- Three lessons on Complements, pp. 83–92
- Five lessons on Modifiers, pp. 93–111

Literature & Reading
This resource contains:
- Reading and Analyzing Historical and Scientific Nonfiction, pp. 12–15

Special Topics
This resource contains:
- Career Skills Development: Create a Resumé, pp. 13–14
- Lifelong Learning: What Do You Need to Do? pp. 15–16

Test Practice
This resource contains the following:
- Descriptive Essay Practice Test: Reading, pp. 10–12

Writing
This resource contains:
- Persuasive Writing: Persuade Using Examples, pp. 29–38

Speaking & Listening
This resource contains the following lesson to expand on the Speaking & Listening Workshop:
- Critical Viewing, pp. 11–13

Vocabulary & Spelling
This resource contains:
- Four lessons on Word Origins, pp. 34–40

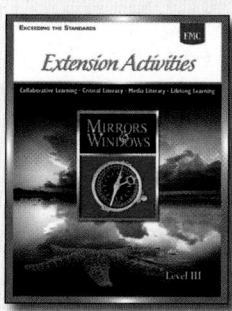

Extension Activities
This resource contains:
- Media Literacy: Sources of Scientific Data, p. 11
- Collaborative Learning: Research the Oregon Trail, pp. 12–13

Unit 4 Visual Planning Guide

397

Reading Level: Challenging
Pacing: 2 days

Meeting the Standards,
Guided Reading,
pp. 19–23

Developing Readers,
Take Notes, pp. 28–30

Advanced Students,
Historical Context
Project, p. 21

408

Reading Level: Easy
Pacing: 3 days

Meeting the Standards,
Guided Reading,
pp. 24–29

Indian Cattle
An Informational Text by Eugene Rachlis

415

Reading Level: Easy
Pacing: 3 days

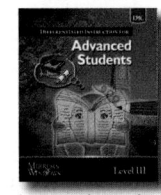

Meeting the Standards,
Directed Reading,
pp. 30–34

Advanced Students,
Cultural Context
Research Project, p. 22

Murder and More Mushroom Mayhem
An Informational Text by Elio Schaechter

424

Too Soon a Woman
A Short Story by Dorothy M. Johnson

426

Reading Level: Easy
Pacing: 3 days

Meeting the Standards,
Comparing Literature,
pp. 35–43

Advanced Students,
Literary Connection
Activity, pp. 23–24

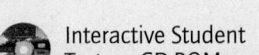
Interactive Student
Text on CD-ROM

Selection
Lesson Plan

Web-based
Resources

Lesson-by-Lesson Resources

HOW TO USE A COMPASS
A How-To Article by Kjetil Kjernsmo

(434)

Reading Level: Easy
Pacing: 2 days

Meeting the Standards,
Directed Reading,
pp. 44–48

Obi-Wan Kenobi:
Jedi Knight
from Star Wars Episode 1:
The Visual Dictionary
A Visual Dictionary by Dr. David West Reynolds

(441)

Reading Level: Easy
Pacing: 1 day

Meeting the Standards,
Directed Reading,
pp. 49–54

---

from **CHAC**
An Essay by Alan Rabinowitz

(448)

Reading Level: Moderate
Pacing: 2 days

Meeting the Standards,
Independent Reading,
pp. 55–61

Developing Readers,
Make Connections,
pp. 31–33

London Underground Map
A Visual Selection by Harry Beck

(456)

Reading Level: Easy
Pacing: 1 day

Meeting the Standards,
Independent Reading,
pp. 62–67

Advanced Students,
Visual Media Project,
pp. 25–26

Quiz ? Lesson Test   ∩ Audio Library

Unit 4 Scope & Sequence Guide

	Selection or Feature	Genre	Reading Support/ Reading Level	Word Count	Reading Skill	Graphic Organizer	
GUIDED READING	**Introduction to Informational Text and Visual Media,** pp. 394–395						
	A Tale of Two Rocks Valerie Jablow pp. 396–405	Science Article	Guided Reading: Reading Model/ Challenging	1,808	Analyze Main Idea and Supporting Details	Main Idea Map; K-W-L Chart	
	Scale of Geologic Time pp. 407–413	Scientific Chart	Guided Reading: Reading Model/Easy		Drawing Conclusions	Drawing Conclusions Chart; Visual Media Chart	
	Informational Text Connection: On the Relativity of Time Wolfgang F. Pauli pp. 410–412	Article	Moderate	1,047			
DIRECTED READING	**Indian Cattle** Eugene Rachlis pp. 414–421	Informational Text	Directed Reading/Easy	1,965	Summarize	Summary Chart; Cluster Chart	
	Primary Source Connection: Counting Coup on a Wounded Buffalo Chief Plenty-Coups pp. 419–420	Memoir	Easy	759			
	Comparing Literature: Murder and More Mushroom Mayhem Elio Schaechter pp. 423–431	Informational Text	Directed Reading/Easy	661	Sensory Details Chart		
	Too Soon a Woman Dorothy M. Johnson pp. 423–431	Short Story	Easy	1,849			
	How to Use a Compass Kjetil Kjernsmo pp. 433–439	How-To Article	Directed Reading/Easy	880	Monitor Comprehension	Comprehension Chart; Author's Purpose Chart	
	Informational Text Connection: Orienteering: The Thinking Sport David LaRochelle pp. 437–438	Informational Article	Moderate	650			

Literary Element	*Mirrors & Windows* Theme	Cross-Curricular Connection	Writing Options	Extension Activities
Purposes of Nonfiction Types of Informational Text Types of Visual Media				
Informational Text	Science and Beliefs		Creative: Screenplay Applied: Glossary	Collaborative Learning: Discuss, Research, and Present Media Literacy: Research and Present
Visual Media	Geologic History	Science Connection: *Dinosaur Fossils*	Creative: Myth Expository: Summary	Lifelong Learning: Conduct Research Media Literacy: Research and Evaluate Charts
Author's Purpose	Community		Creative: Transcript Expository: Informative Paragraph	Lifelong Learning: Conduct Internet and Library Research Critical Literacy: Hold a Panel Discussion
Compare Literature: Description	Safety		Creative: Diary Entry Applied: List	Collaborative Learning: Conduct Internet Research Critical Literacy: Role-Play a Scene
	Decisions			
Author's Purpose	Navigation		Creative: Advertisement Persuasive: Persuasive Paragraph	Collaborative Learning: Interview an Expert Critical Literacy: Give and Follow Directions

Unit 4 Scope & Sequence Guide

	Selection or Feature	Genre	Reading Support/ Reading Level	Word Count	Reading Skill	Graphic Organizer	
DIRECTED READING	**Obi-Wan Kenobi: Jedi Knight** Dr. David West Reynolds pp. 440–447	Visual Dictionary	Directed Reading/Easy	683	Activate Prior Knowledge	K-W-L Chart; Visual Media Chart	
	Informational Text Connection: Industrial Light & Magic, Part 1: History Dr. David West Reynolds pp. 445–446	Internet Article	Moderate	851			
INDEPENDENT READING	**Chac** Alan Rabinowitz pp. 448–455	Essay	Independent Reading/ Moderate	2,934	Use Context Clues		
	London Underground Map Harry Beck pp. 456–458	Visual Selection	Independent Reading/ Easy				

Unit 4 Language Arts Workshops

Grammar & Style	Vocabulary & Spelling	Writing	Speaking & Listening	Test Practice
Simple, Compound, and Compound-Complex Sentences, p. 406 Adjective and Adverb Clauses, p. 422	Reference: Using Dictionaries and Thesauruses, p. 432	Descriptive Writing: Descriptive Essay, p. 460–465	Critical Viewing, pp. 456–457	Writing Skills: Descriptive Essay, p. 468 Revising and Editing Skills, p. 469 Reading Skills: from *To Be or Not To Bop* by Dizzy Gillespie with Al Fraser, p. 470–471

Literary Element	*Mirrors & Windows* Theme	Cross-Curricular Connection	Writing Options	Extension Activities
Visual Media	Creating a Character	Cultural Connection: *Star Wars and Mythology*	Creative: Visual Dictionary Entry Persuasive: Movie Review	Collaborative Learning: Discuss Science Fiction Media Literacy: Write a Brief Compare-and-Contrasts Essay
Setting	Respect for Animals		Creative: Journal Entry	Media Literacy: Research and Present
	Maps		Applied: Set of Instructions	Collaborative Learning: Research and Display

Unit 4 Building Vocabulary

The lists below identify the Words in Use and Key Terms within this unit. These words are listed at the bottom of the Teacher's Edition pages at the beginning of each lesson. Vocabulary development activities are provided in the *Meeting the Standards* unit book and in *Exceeding the Standards: Vocabulary & Spelling*.

WORDS IN USE

Preview Vocabulary

Preview Vocabulary are words taken from the sentences within each selection. These words are defined in the side margin or at the bottom of the pages on which they appear. The "Preview Vocabulary" section introduces these words in the Before Reading page preceding each selection.

bewildered, 417	disrepute, 425	geologic, 408	resplendent, 424
composition, 402	elapse, 400	migration, 415	specimen, 424
delectable, 424	epoch, 408	period, 408	straggle, 418
derive, 398	era, 408	pulverize, 398	

Selection Words

Selection Words are additional words from the reading that may be challenging but are not central to the selection and are not identified in the prereading section. These words can easily be learned using the story context, and they provide excellent practice for using content clues to find meaning without explicit instruction.

ante, 446	elongated, 450	intermittently, 449	sauté, 424
apprentice, 442	everlasting, 410	intriguing, 401	savoring, 429
array, 398	formidable, 443	involuntarily, 450	scrawny, 449
caressed, 450	froth, 420	junction, 438	stampeded, 417
concede, 425	garnered, 446	modulator, 442	stonemasons, 298
coup, 419	gaunt, 427	ordeal, 419	transgressions, 442
definitively, 425	hefts, 428	overtones, 442	uniform, 412
depression, 438	homesteaders, 427	plodded, 428	unresponsive, 410
deprived, 403	hypothetical, 403	reckoned, 418	valor, 417
disbanded, 446	innovative, 446	recollection, 450	
dissipated, 449	innumerable, 415	renowned, 445	

Teaching Words

Teaching Words consist of vocabulary that is used in the directions about the lessons. Teaching words explain to students what to focus on within the selection, help establish the story context, clarify the meaning of literary terms, and define the goals or instructional purpose.

abundant, 409	engineered, 445	interprets, 394	radical, 400
ambassador, 419	episode, 460	inventory, 431	resources, 414
anecdotes, 421	essential, 469	inverted, 394	rubric, 460, 467
annotations, 462	expository, 460	line, 456	sedimentary, 466
archaeologist, 440	extensively, 448	livestock, 421	sensitive, 395
box-office, 440	extinct, 396, 404	metamorphic, 466	sequence, 407
collage, 467	extinction, 448	mortalities, 425	skim, 396
communal, 418	forays, 394	multimedia, 467	species, 396
consensus, 431	fossil, 396	mute, 460	subdivided, 407
conservation, 448	geologic, 407	mythologies, 444	testified, 419
constructive, 467	graphically, 458	negotiator, 419	traces, 413
consumers, 421	grasp, 410	objective, 394	transparencies, 467
conveyed, 395	harmonic, 470	perceived, 440	underpinnings, 444
coup, 468	highlight, 407	persecution, 423	upward, 394
depicts, 423	igneous, 466	perspective, 407, 447	urban, 458
draftsman, 458	incorporate, 470	plentiful, 469	verdant, 469
emeritus, 423	indirectly, 396	prop, 445	vital, 395
emigrated, 423	indulge, 396	psychological, 444	yardstick, 407

KEY TERMS

Key Terms are commonly referred to as *academic vocabulary*. These terms appear in the instructional material to teach the terminology that students need to acquire to understand literature. The repetition of the terms throughout the program ensures student mastery and provides a solid foundation for the continuing study of literature and language arts.

Objectives

Studying this unit will help students meet the following objectives:

- Make connections from themes expressed in the selections to their own lives and the world around them
- Identify common forms of nonfiction
- Understand different elements of nonfiction, including *informational text, author's purpose, description,* and *visual media*
- Understand variations of literary forms and author's use of language to develop forms

Reading Strategies

Ask Questions
Clarify
Make Inferences
Make Predictions
Visualize

Reading Skills

Activate Prior Knowledge
Analyze Main Idea and
  Supporting Details
Draw Conclusions
Monitor Comprehension
Summarize

Literary Elements

Author's Purpose
Description
Informational Text
Visual Media

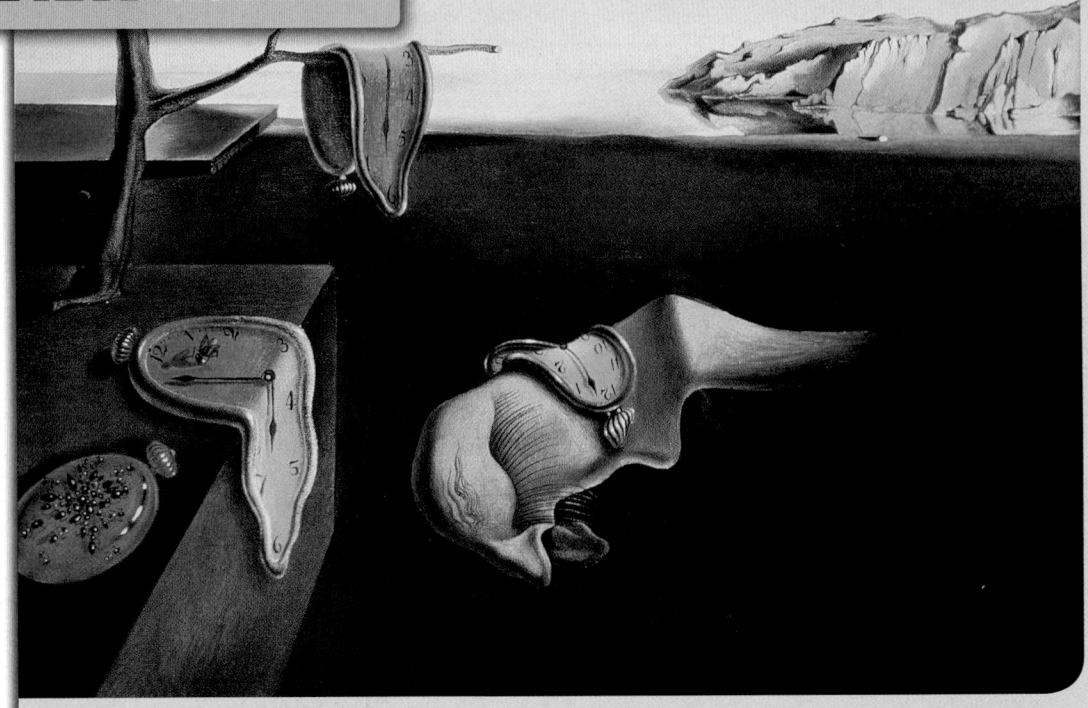

Expanding Horizons
Nonfiction

HARRY BECK   ALAN RABINOWITZ   DAVID WEST REYNOLDS

Launch the Unit

Place students into small groups, and have them read the quotation and introductory paragraph on page 393. Ask groups to develop additional questions about when, how, and why people cultivate their views, as Wolfgang F. Pauli does in his article. Model a possible question: "How does a person feel when he or she realizes that his or her views are changing?" Have groups keep their questions. After you complete the unit, return to the questions and try to answer them as a class.

"In the tempo of everyday life, a thousand years may seem a long time. But to someone who studies paleontology, thirty thousand years may seem but an instant..."

—WOLFGANG F. PAULI, "On the Relativity of Time"

Have you ever tried to imagine the vastness of geologic time or space? In his article, scientist Wolfgang F. Pauli helps us broaden our viewpoint by showing the passage of time from two extremes: the very fast and the very slow. One goal of informational texts is to enable us to expand our horizons. As you explore the texts and visual media in this unit, try to expand the limits of your understanding.

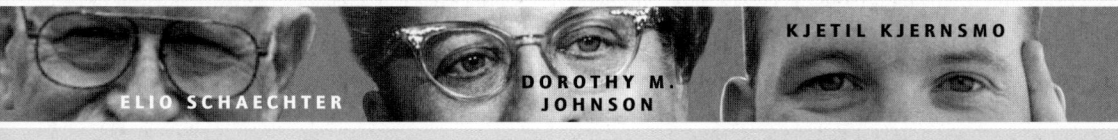

ELIO SCHAECHTER   DOROTHY M. JOHNSON   KJETIL KJERNSMO

393

Program Resources

For a visual reminder of the unit-based resources available for Unit 4, Nonfiction, see pages 392A and 392B. As you introduce the unit, you may want to provide students with the Unit Study Guide, which is contained in the *Meeting the Standards* resource.

Teach the Genre

Introduction to Informational Text and Visual Media

Most students will have experienced informational text and visual media. Try to draw on their past experience as you teach this lesson. Encourage them also to explore the elements of informational text and visual media in the Before Reading and After Reading sections of each selection in Unit 4.

Launch the Lesson

Divide the class into several groups, and provide each group with several different examples of a particular type of informational text—such as a newspaper, magazine, encyclopedia article, or how-to book. Have each group compare and contrast the examples, determining what features each has in common and how their presentations of information differ. Discuss what factors—such as intended audience—might affect this presentation. Explore with students the different ways in which reading informational texts will help them practice their analyzing and critical thinking skills. Suggest that studying informational text and visual media will also give them models of effective communication they can imitate in both words and images.

Program Resources

To help students explore literature on a deeper level, assign the following activity: Reading and Analyzing Historical and Scientific Nonfiction: *Exceeding the Standards: Literature & Reading*, pp. 12–15.

Common Core State Standards

Reading Literature
RL.5

Reading Informational
RI.5, RI.6, RI.7

Purposes of Nonfiction

In Unit 3, you read several types of nonfiction, including autobiography, biography, and essay. One of the characteristics these types of nonfiction share is a subjective approach, or an emphasis on the writer's personal response to his or her subject. There are many other types of nonfiction, however, in which the writer's approach to the subject is much more objective. To help understand this distinction, read the following passages. Both deal with Harriet Tubman, a runaway slave who in the years before the Civil War helped others fleeing slavery reach freedom in Canada via the Underground Railroad (page 347). How do the two passages differ?

> She had never been in Canada. The route beyond Philadelphia was strange to her.
>
> But she could not let the runaways who accompanied her know this. As they walked along she told them stories of her own first flight, she kept painting vivid word pictures of what it would be like to be free. But there were so many of them this time. She knew moments of doubt when she was half-afraid, and kept looking back over her shoulder, imagining that she heard the sound of pursuit.
>
> —ANN PETRY, *Harriet Tubman: Conductor on the Underground Railroad*

> In 1849, on the strength of rumors that she was about to be sold, Tubman fled to Philadelphia. In December 1850 she made her way to Baltimore, Maryland, whence she led her sister and two children to freedom. That journey was the first of some 19 increasingly dangerous forays into Maryland in which, over the next decade, she conducted upward of 300 fugitive slaves along the Underground Railroad to Canada.
>
> —"Harriet Tubman," *Encyclopaedia Britannica Online*

The two passages differ in several ways, including the style of the writing and the level of detail that is presented. Another major difference is in the basic purpose of the two passages. Ann Petry

dramatizes and interprets the facts, using the techniques of fiction to help the reader imagine Tubman's experience. By contrast, the basic purpose of the encyclopedia article is to present the facts about Tubman's life in a straightforward and objective way. An encyclopedia article is a common type of informational text.

Harriet Tubman. Paul Collins.

Types of Informational Text

An **informational text** is a type of nonfiction whose basic purpose is to inform or explain, rather than to entertain or persuade. Among the most common types of informational texts are articles of various kinds.

News Article

A **news article** is an informational text about a particular topic, issue, event, or series of events. News articles can be found in newspapers, magazines, and on Internet sites. Broadcast news stories on radio and television are also news articles. The main purpose of such articles is to convey information. This is particularly evident in the newspaper story, where the traditional structure is the "inverted pyramid." The most important facts are presented first, followed by less important supporting details. Valerie Jablow's "A Tale of Two Rocks" (page 396), is an example of a news article.

Words in Use

Teaching Words
objective, 394
forays, 394
upward, 394
interprets, 394
inverted, 394
vital, 395
conveyed, 395
sensitive, 395

KEY TERMS

NONFICTION, 394	VISUAL MEDIA, 395
AUTOBIOGRAPHY, 394	PHOTOGRAPH, 395
BIOGRAPHY, 394	ILLUSTRATION, 395
ESSAY, 394	CHART, 395
PURPOSE, 394	TIME LINE, 395
INFORMATIONAL TEXT, 394	FLOW CHART, 395
NEWS ARTICLE, 394	PIE CHART, 395
SUPPORTING DETAIL, 394	CIRCLE CHART, 395
HOW-TO ARTICLE, 395	DIAGRAM, 395
WEB PAGE, 395	MAP, 395

How-To Article

A familiar type of article is the **how-to article,** which explains the steps in a process. The main goal of a how-to article is to provide all the information that a reader will need to understand the process the writer is describing. Simplicity is vital, however, since too much information on minor details can make the directions confusing. Kjetil Kjernsmo's article "How to Use a Compass" (page 433) and David LaRochelle's "Orienteering: The Thinking Sport" (page 437) are both examples of how-to articles.

Web Page

A **web page** is the basic unit of the World Wide Web, an organizational structure that includes a large part of what is offered on the Internet. One of the main purposes of web pages is to provide information. Web pages can contain "links," or connections to other pages within the site or completely different sites altogether. David West Reynolds's "Industrial Light & Magic, Part 1: History" (page 445) is an example of a web page.

Types of Visual Media

In addition to written language, information is conveyed through **visual media,** pictorial or other graphic forms of communication. There is a wide variety of visual media, including photographs, illustrations, charts, graphs, diagrams, and maps.

Photograph

A **photograph** is an image typically created by light acting on a sensitive material. Photography is one of the primary visual methods of providing information. Like an informational text, a photograph needs to be "read" carefully. This might include identifying the overall subject, focusing on specific details, and checking the title, label, caption, or other accompanying text.

Illustration

An **illustration** is a photograph, drawing, or diagram that serves to make a concept clearer by providing a visual example. "Obi-Wan Kenobi: Jedi Knight" (page 440), an entry from a *Star Wars* visual dictionary, includes several illustrations.

Chart

A **chart** is a visual representation of data that is intended to clarify, highlight, or put a certain perspective on the information presented. There are many types of charts, each with a different purpose. Here are some common examples:

- A **time line** shows the relative order of a series of events, such as dates in a period of history. A time line can be organized either vertically or horizontally. The "Scale of Geologic Time" (page 407) is an example of a time line.
- A **flow chart** is a graphic representation of a process. For example, a flow chart might show how a bill becomes a law.
- A **pie chart** or **circle chart** shows the parts that make up the whole of something. For example, a pie chart might show what proportion of the world's fresh water exists on each of the different continents.

Diagram

A **diagram** is an illustration that serves to explain a concept or process, including the arrangement and relations of the various parts of the concept, object, or process. Harry Beck's "London Underground Map" (page 456), which shows London's subway system as it existed in the early 1930s, is an example of a diagram.

Map

A **map** is a representation, usually on a flat surface such as a sheet of paper, of a certain geographic area, showing various significant features. These features vary with the purpose of the map. For example, a *political map* includes such features as the boundaries of countries and the location of cities and towns. A *physical map* includes such features as mountain ranges and bodies of water.

Media Literacy Skills

Photo Exhibit

Ask students to bring in several examples of what they consider to be good photography. These can be photographs they have taken or ones they find. Have a group of student volunteers serve as curators to select the photographs they consider the best and create a small exhibit. Have them present to the class the following:

- what standards they used in selecting the photographs they included (in other words, what makes a good photograph)
- what different themes and styles the chosen photographs represent

Preview the Model

At a Glance
Guided Reading: Reading Model
- Reading Level: Challenging
- Difficulty Consideration: Scientific information
- Ease Factor: Length

Objectives
Studying this lesson will enable students to
- use reading strategies such as analyzing the main idea and supporting details
- define *informational text* and recognize the features of this literary technique in the selection
- describe the literary accomplishments of Valerie Jablow and explain why an author might choose a specific literary form
- appreciate an informative text about expanding horizons of understanding

Launch the Lesson
Prior to reading "A Tale of Two Rocks," ask students if they enjoy mystery stories or television shows in which scientists use forensic evidence to solve a crime. Have them explain what they like about the stories. Point out that clues sometimes come from unexpected places. Tell students that scientists often use clues and evidence in unexpected places to help them solve mysteries about events that occurred long ago.

Common Core State Standards

Reading Informational
RI.1, RI.2, RI.5

Writing
W.9

Speaking and Listening
SL.1

Language
L.6

GUIDED READING

A TALE OF TWO ROCKS
A Science Article by Valerie Jablow

Build Background
Scientific Context Using fossil evidence, scientists believe that many species became extinct at the end of the Cretaceous period, about sixty-five million years ago. Among the species that died out were the dinosaurs. There has been much debate regarding what events and conditions caused their extinction.

Reader's Context Based on what you know about dinosaurs, what is your theory concerning why they became extinct?

Set Purpose
Skim the text, looking for unfamiliar terms. Use context clues, vocabulary definitions, and footnotes to find the meanings of these terms. Then, make predictions regarding what "tale" the two rocks suggested to the scientists.

Analyze Literature
Informational Text is a category of nonfiction that uses facts, statistics, and details to inform readers on a specific topic or issue. As you read, try to determine the main idea of this selection and the ways in which the author communicates this idea.

Meet the Author
Valerie Jablow (b. 1965) has worked as a magazine writer and editor at *Science*, *Smithsonian*, and *Trial*. While at *Smithsonian*, she wrote "A Tale of Two Rocks." Of her career as a nonfiction writer, she says, "I feel quite lucky in all this—writing has always been fun for me. It gives me a chance to indulge my interests and curiosities, while giving others the opportunity to see something new. For me, it's like going to the finest school in the world—and the homework is always fun. Who could ask for anything better?"

Use Reading Skills
Analyze Main Idea and Supporting Details The main idea is a brief statement of what you think the author wants the reader to know or think after reading each paragraph. The author expresses the main idea indirectly, often in the first or last sentence of the paragraph. Frequently, however, the author does not directly state the main idea. To find it, gather details on a main idea map like the one below.

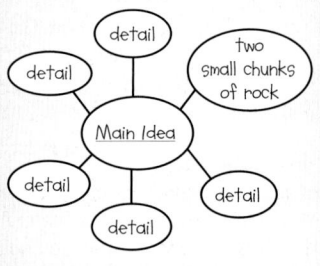

Preview Vocabulary
de•rive (di rīv´) *v.*, get from a source

pul•ver•ize (pəl´ və rīz) *v.*, crush into a powder or dust; demolish

e•lapse (i´ laps) *v.*, pass or go by, in the sense of time

com•po•si•tion (käm´ pə zi´ shun) *n.*, mixture containing many parts or materials

(Opposite page) Artist's depiction of asteroid crashing into Earth, which scientists believe occurred in the Cretaceous and Tertiary periods about sixty-five million years ago.

Words in Use

Preview Vocabulary	Selection Words	Teaching Words
derive, 398	array, 398	fossil, 396
pulverize, 398	stonemasons, 398	species, 396
elapse, 400	intriguing, 401	extinct, 396
composition, 402	hypothetical, 403	skim, 396
	deprived, 403	indirectly, 396
		indulge, 396
		radical, 400

KEY TERMS
SCIENCE ARTICLE, 396
CONTEXT CLUE, 396
FOOTNOTE, 396
INFORMATIONAL TEXT, 396
NONFICTION, 396
MAIN IDEA, 396
SUPPORTING DETAIL, 396
K-W-L CHART, 405
SCREENPLAY, 405
JARGON, 405
GLOSSARY, 405
THESIS, 405

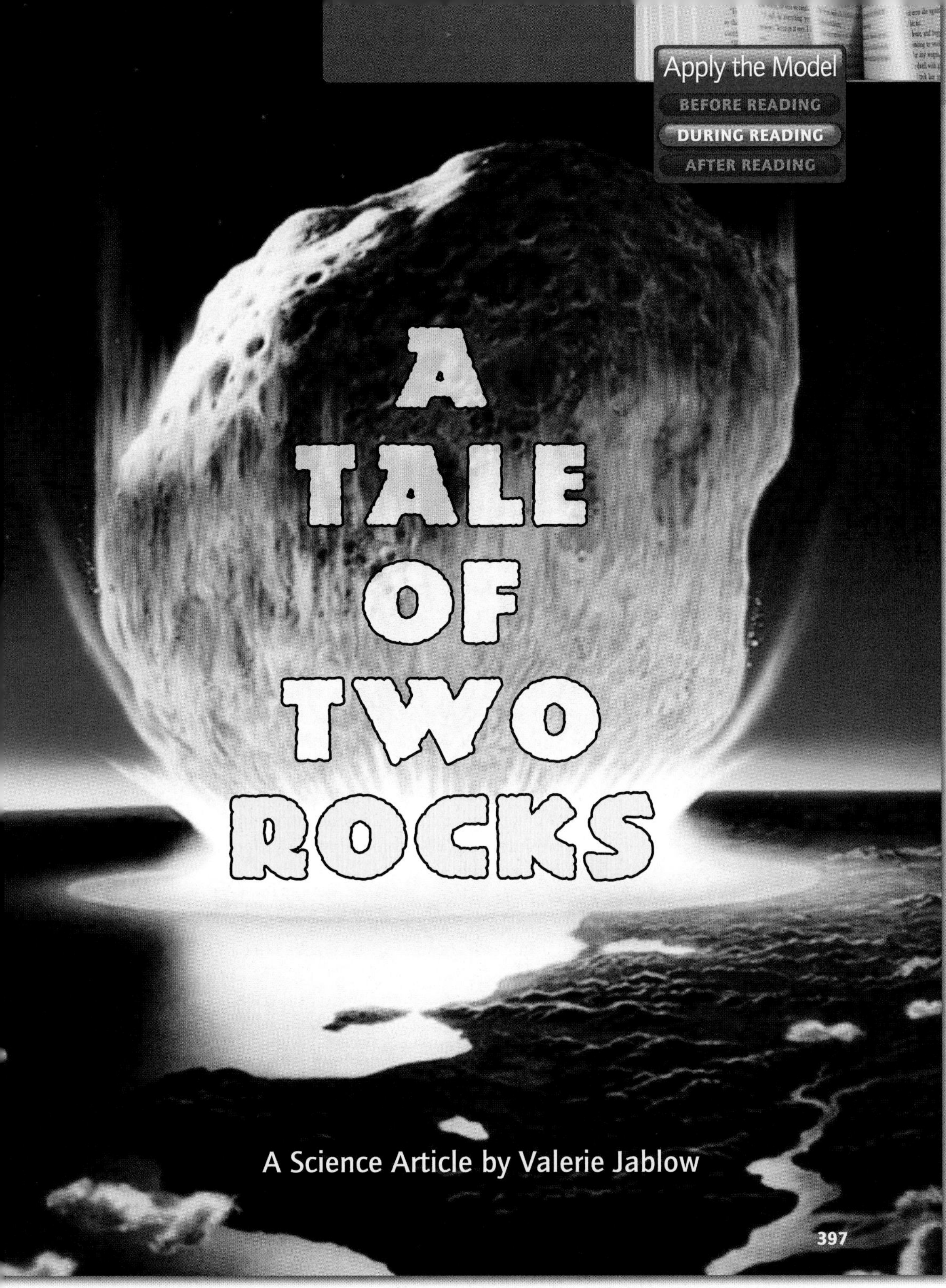

A TALE OF TWO ROCKS

A Science Article by Valerie Jablow

397

Teach the Model

Summary

This informational article demonstrates how evidence collected by scientists in various fields can combine to explain events in the past. Scientists using fossil records have long disagreed about how and why the dinosaurs disappeared. Many were skeptical of the idea that a huge asteroid strike on Earth created conditions for extinction until geologists looking for oil discovered a massive crater in the Gulf of Mexico. Further evidence proved that the crater was not a volcano but was caused by an extraterrestrial object striking Earth some sixty-five million years ago.

MIRRORS & WINDOWS The Mirrors & Windows questions at the end of this selection focus on the theme of science and beliefs. Before reading, ask students if they have ever found evidence that supports a belief they hold, and if so, how did that discovery make them feel? How does discovery further scientific progress?

Independent Reading

Students who like "A Tale of Two Rocks" might enjoy other texts about dinosaur extinction, such as *T. Rex and the Crater of Doom* by Walter Alvarez, one of the scientists mentioned in the selection.

Program Resources

Planning and Assessment
Program Planning Guide, Selection Lesson Plan
E-Lesson Planner
Assessment Guide, Lesson Test
ExamView

Technology Tools
Interactive Student Text on CD
Visual Teaching Package
Audio Library
mirrorsandwindows.com

Meeting the Standards
Nonfiction: Unit 4, Guided Reading, pp. 19–23

Differentiating Instruction
Developing Readers, Take Notes, pp. 28–30
Advanced Students, Historical Context Project, p. 21

Geography Connection

Yucatán Peninsula The Yucatán Peninsula is located in southeastern Mexico and separates the Caribbean Sea from the Gulf of Mexico. It sits to the east of the Isthmus of Tehuantepec, which serves as a natural border between Central America and North America. The peninsula includes the Mexican states of Campeche, Yucatán, and Quintana Roo, as well as northern portions of Belize and Guatemala. Cozumel Island and Isla Mujeres are just to the east of the Great Maya Reef, which stretches six hundred miles from the tip of the peninsula to the Bay of Honduras. The crater, Chicxulub, acquired its name from the modern town just to its south. The peninsula contains many ancient Mayan archaeological sites, including Chichen Itza, which houses the famous Temple of Kukulcan. **Ⓐ**

Use Reading Skills

Analyze Main Idea and Details

Answer: The huge object zoomed toward Earth, crashed into its surface, blasted rocks into dust, and created a huge hole. **Ⓑ**

Use Reading Skills

Identify Main Idea Point out that the main idea in the paragraph beginning "The crater, now known as Chicxulub . . ." is not directly stated. After reading the paragraph, invite several students to write on the board a sentence containing the paragraph's main idea. **Ⓒ**

... an object more or less the size of Washington, D.C. crashed to earth near what is now Mexico's Yucatán Peninsula.

de·rive (di rīv´) *v.*, get from a source

They are two small chunks of humble gray rock. Amid the glittering array of exhibits in the Hall of Geology, Gems and Minerals at the National Museum of Natural History (NMNH)[1] they are easy to overlook. Yet they bear witness to a shattering event in the life of our planet, and to one of the hottest scientific debates of this century—exactly what did (or did not) do in the dinosaurs.

The rocks are breccias, their name <u>derived</u> from the word Italian stonemasons use to describe bits of broken stone held together like pebbles in concrete. Today we know they were blasted into existence about 65 million years ago when an object more or less the size of Washington, D.C. crashed to earth near what is now Mexico's **Ⓐ** Yucatán Peninsula.[2]

The asteroid (or comet—scientists aren't sure which) weighed as much as one trillion tons and traveled at up to 35 miles per second—the record for a jet is only a little more than half a mile per second. Plunging several miles into the earth's crust after crashing into a shallow sea, it blasted billions of tons of sand, rock, dust and seabed through the atmosphere and all around the world. It vaporized, ejected, melted or <u>pulverized</u> the rock beneath it, creating a crater more than 120 miles in diameter. Left behind in the crater were hundreds of cubic miles of shattered and melted rocks, including these breccias.

pul·ver·ize (pəl´ və rīz) *v.*, crush into a powder or dust; demolish

DURING READING

Use Reading Skills
Analyze Main Idea and Details Use the details in this paragraph to summarize the main idea regarding the impact. **Ⓑ**

The crater, now known as Chicxulub[3] (CHEEK-shoe-lube), was not the only effect. There were fires worldwide, a tsunami[4] more than half a mile high and storms of acid rain. In the resulting devastation, the sky went dark. The sun did not shine through for perhaps a year because of a killing cloud cover of dust. As much as

---

1. **National Museum of Natural History (NMNH).** One of several museums of the Smithsonian Institution, a national museum in Washington, DC; the Hall of Geology, Gems and Minerals contains more than 375,000 specimens of rocks and precious stones collected from all over the world
2. **Yucatán Peninsula.** Thumblike land mass in southeastern Mexico that juts out into the sea, separating the Caribbean Sea from the Gulf of Mexico
3. **Chicxulub.** Word of the Mayans, an ancient people who lived in this region of Mexico. The word can be roughly translated as "tail of the devil."
4. **tsunami.** Huge wave caused by a major disturbance under the ocean, such as an earthquake

398 UNIT 4 NONFICTION

Differentiated Instruction

English Language Learning

English language learners may be more familiar with metric measurements. Help them convert Fahrenheit temperatures to Celsius using the formula $[°C = 5/9 \times (°F - 32)]$. Then tell students that one mile equals 1.6 kilometers so that they can convert those values as they come across them in the text. Conversely, students who are not very familiar with the metric system can practice opposite conversions: To determine temperatures in Fahrenheit, direct them to use the formula $[°F = 9/5 \times °C + 32]$.

70 percent of all plant and animal species on earth appear to have been wiped out—including, most spectacularly, the dinosaurs, whose disappearance would long puzzle modern scientists. The two breccias are pieces of evidence of that earthwrenching but only lately understood event. And they have figured in the great scientific detective story that resulted: the discovery of the crater itself, some 65 million years after it was formed. **D**

Breccias are fairly uncommon. They can be created slowly on the earth's surface over eons during which rock fragments are cemented together in the sediment[5] in which they lie. Volcanoes can do the job somewhat faster, as rocks are caught up in molten lava heated to nearly 2,000 degrees F. But when asteroids (or comets) collide with the earth, they manufacture instant breccias on impact. At Chicxulub, the impact produced pressures in the rock several million times greater than what we are experiencing right now in the

5. **sediment.** Matter that settles to the bottom of a liquid

A TALE OF TWO ROCKS **399**

Teach the Model

Analyze Literature
Tone Invite students to explain how the author's use of the "detective story" metaphor affects the tone of the article. **D**

Art Connection
Aerial Photography In 1858, Félix Nadar shot the first aerial photo from a hot-air balloon. M. Arthur Batut captured images by attaching a camera to a kite in 1888. Photos became clear and sharp when George Eastman invented rolled paper film the next year. During WWI, pilots of two-seater planes snapped shots of enemy territory, and camera quality improved significantly. Sherman M. Fairchild soon developed a camera whose shutter rested inside the lens, and this invention was the most popular aerial camera system for the next fifty years. This development helped rocket aerial photography into outer space and it accompanied the missions of *Apollo 15, 16,* and *17.* Today, aerial photographs are taken from aircraft, balloons, kites, rockets, and even skydivers. Aerial photography is used in fields as diverse as cartography, archaeology, film production, and art.

Reading Skills

Identify Main Idea
Remind students that the main idea of a paragraph may be implied. Explain that to *imply* is to suggest or state indirectly. Use the paragraph on page 400 that begins, "At that time only a few scientists . . ." to model identification of an implied main idea. The opening sentence suggests that scientists disagreed. Several theories are mentioned in the paragraph.

Ask students what sentence they might use as a topic sentence that would imply all this information. (Few scientists bought into the impact theory, as many were convinced of other manners of extinction and others thought it improbable.)

Analyze Literature

Informational Text *Answer:* It shows that the impact caused such an extreme temperature as to instantly form breccias. **A**

Science Connection

The Great Dying The extinction of about 70 percent of life on Earth described in this article took place at the end of the Cretaceous Period— about 65 million years ago. About 250 million years ago, at the end of the Permian Period, Earth was teeming with plant and animal life, including early mammals. At that time, a combination of factors caused an extinction, called The Great Dying, that nearly wiped out life on Earth. About 90 percent of marine plants and animals and 70 percent of land species disappeared. At that time, tectonic plates were pushing the continents together into a single giant continent surrounded by one massive ocean. As a result, weather patterns and ocean currents shifted; coastlines and their shallow marine ecosystems vanished. Sea levels dropped and volcanic activity increased. In the midst of all this, evidence suggests that an asteroid struck Earth. **B**

Use Reading Strategies

Clarify *Answer:* Some scientists believed that dinosaurs became extinct by a change in climate or sea level. Others thought that it was unlikely that an asteroid would strike Earth, given the huge size of the solar system. **C**

DURING READING

Analyze Literature
Informational Text How does the author's use of temperature measurements help you understand what happened to the rocks? **A**

e·lapse (i´ laps) *v.*, pass or go by, in the sense of time

DURING READING

Use Reading Strategies
Clarify What two beliefs led many scientists to consider the "impact theory" radical? **C**

---

air around us. Temperatures may have reached 18,000 degrees F— by comparison, the sun's surface is a chilly 10,000 degrees F. The rocks that were hit directly were instantly vaporized,[6] and the underlying rock was rapidly melted or pulverized.

To understand the story that the two NMNH breccias tell about the crater and its significance, you have to go back in time about 20 years, hardly more than an instant compared with the 65 million that have <u>elapsed</u> since the asteroid did its work.

At that time only a few scientists theorized that the massive biological extinctions (suggested by fossil remains) at the end of the Cretaceous period were caused by the impact of an extraterrestrial[7] object. It was regarded as a radical theory. Most scientists figured that the dinosaurs had been done in by a change of climate or a change in sea level. Others thought it unlikely that in such a large, empty solar system, an asteroid or comet could actually have managed to hit the earth—much less have wreaked[8] global destruction on impact.

---

6. **vaporized.** Destroyed beyond recognition; turned into tiny particles impossible to detect
7. **extraterrestrial.** Originating, occurring, or existing outside Earth or its atmosphere
8. **wreaked.** Caused

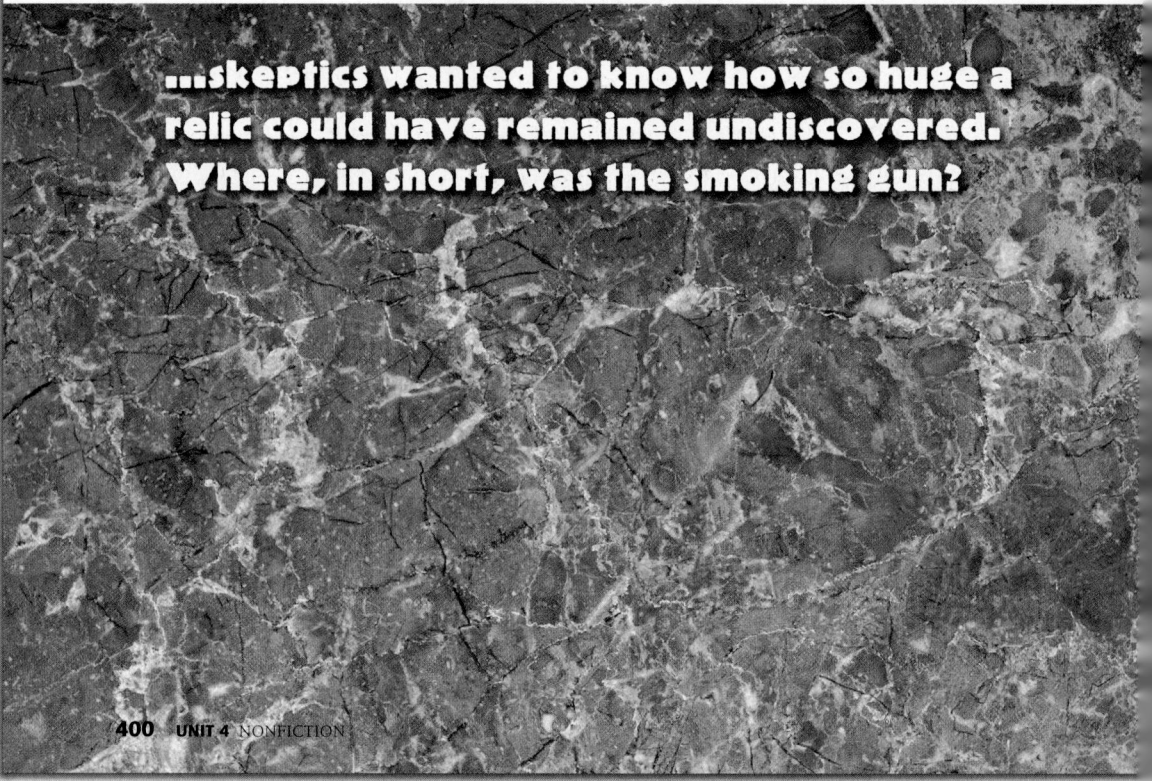

...skeptics wanted to know how so huge a relic could have remained undiscovered. Where, in short, was the smoking gun?

400 UNIT 4 NONFICTION

Vocabulary Skills

Jargon

Jargon is specialized vocabulary that members of a particular profession or group use. It makes writing more specific and authentic, but it can also make an informational article hard to read.

"A Tale of Two Rocks" includes a number of scientific terms that have specific meanings when used in relation to geologic process such as *ejected, sediment, magnetometer, pulverized,* and

anomalous. Remind students to use a word's part of speech, context clues, and previous knowledge to uncover meaning.

Of course, there were intriguing clues and searches in support of the monster asteroid theory. One involved iridium,[9] an element rare on the earth's surface but more abundant in asteroids. By examining the amount of iridium in rock layers in Italy, Denmark and New Zealand, the Alvarezes, a now famous father and son research team, were able to deduce[10] that a huge asteroid had struck the earth somewhere. Luis Alvarez, a physicist, and his son Walter, a geologist, had combined their knowledge, along with that of others, and released what amounted to a scientific bombshell. It was 1980, and the Alvarezes' asteroid theory suggested that somewhere there should be an enormous crater at least 100 miles in diameter. The impact sites[11] of many smaller asteroids were well known. Even allowing for changes in the earth's crust, which could have obliterated[12] the crater if the asteroid had fallen in the ocean, or buried it under 65 million years of sediment if it had fallen on land, skeptics[13] wanted to know how so huge a relic could have remained undiscovered. Where, in short, was the smoking gun?[14]

Curiously enough, the two NMNH breccia samples had already been wrested[15] from the earth and stored in Mexico, not for science but for purposes of commerce.[16] They came from sample cores drilled during the 1950s and '60s by the Mexican national oil company, PEMEX, not far from the northern Yucatán hamlets of Chicxulub Pueblo and Sacapuc.

They looked a lot like breccias of volcanic origin: melted rock holding together angular chunks of unmelted rock. Their presence in the drill cores did not bode well for the oil company's exploration of the area, since volcanic rock usually means that oil, even if present, is not easy to extract. The area from which the cores were taken did show a strange feature unlike that of a volcano—it was apparently part of a huge, semicircular ring with a high gravity field at the center. But because so few scientists took seriously the likelihood of a large asteroid's impact on earth, it seemed eminently sensible to assume the breccias were the products of a volcano.

In 1978 a young geophysicist named Glen Penfield, who was working with PEMEX, found himself assigned to fly over the Gulf of

DURING READING

Use Reading Skills
Analyze Main Idea and Details What is the main idea of this paragraph? **D**

E

---

9. **iridium.** Rare silver-white, brittle metallic element
10. **deduce.** Reason or draw a conclusion, based on known facts
11. **impact sites.** Locations where asteroids or other extraterrestrial objects struck Earth
12. **obliterated.** Erased
13. **skeptics.** People who doubt that a certain theory or point of view is accurate or true
14. **smoking gun.** Absolute and final evidence that an event truly happened
15. **wrested.** Dug
16. **commerce.** Business or trade

A TALE OF TWO ROCKS **401**

Use Reading Skills
Analyze Main Idea and Details
Answer: Skeptics didn't believe that a crater at least one hundred miles in diameter could remain undetected and wanted more proof. **D**

Analyze Literature
Metaphor Direct students to the metaphor "smoking gun." Discuss with them whether the image captures the idea of evidence in a vivid, yet sensible manner. Ask students where they have seen or heard this metaphor before. Provide students with other examples of its use in fiction and nonfiction. Challenge them to decide if "smoking gun" is a "dying metaphor," meaning that it is so commonly used that it is worn out to the point of being cliché, or if it still evokes a strong and useful image. **E**

TEACHING NOTE

Kinesthetic Activity
Have students observe what happens as they drop a large rock from various heights into a pan full of sand. Next, have them drop the rock into another pan filled with sand and water. Discuss how the effects change due to the water coverage, and hypothesize different effects if the rock were superheated by friction as it dropped through Earth's atmosphere.

Research Skills

Internet Sources
Help students evaluate Internet sources they might use for the Media Literacy extension on page 405. Explain that anyone can post information on the Internet. Point out that what they see in print isn't necessarily factual or accurate. Model evaluating informational websites, working with students to check URLs and web pages for names of respected encyclopedias, magazines, museums, colleges, and universities. Explain that .org extensions or the word "society" in an organization's name doesn't necessarily mean that a source is scientifically reliable.

Use Reading Strategies

Ask Questions *Answer:* Students might want to know what created the huge ring. **Ⓐ**

Use Reading Strategies

Ask Questions Challenge students to formulate questions and possible answers about the PEMEX oil company and its reluctance to share data about the discovered impact crater. Model questions such as: "Why would a company hold information that could help further scientific progress? What could it gain by keeping the data secret?" **Ⓑ**

com·po·si·tion
(käm´ pə zi' shun) *n.*,
mixture containing many parts
or materials

DURING READING

Use Reading Skills
Ask Questions What information would you like to know about this discovery? **Ⓐ**

Mexico. Using a magnetometer,[17] he was to measure the magnetic field of rocks on the Gulf floor—specifically off the coast near Chicxulub Pueblo. Like the findings of earlier PEMEX geologists, Penfield's were intended to map out the rock <u>composition</u> beneath the surface and determine the likelihood of finding oil.

But what Penfield's magnetometer let him see was very odd. More than a mile below the surface of the Yucatán Peninsula, and for 70 miles out into the Gulf of Mexico, was a saucer-shaped underground structure with a magnetic field different from that of any known volcanic terrain. It also had a most un-volcano-like symmetry.[18] Put together, the old land data and the new underwater data indicated the existence of a huge ring, about 120 miles in diameter, half on land, half under the Gulf of Mexico. It was ten times the size of any volcano, with an upward bulge at its center similar to those seen on known—though much smaller—impact craters.

Penfield and PEMEX geophysicist Antonio Camargo-Zanoguera concluded that it could not be the result of a volcano; it was probably an impact crater. But proving that scientifically was a major problem. For one thing, the data upon which their conclusion rested **Ⓑ** were held in confidence by the oil company. Worse yet, the warehouse in Mexico where all the core samples were supposed to have been stored and catalogued had burned down, apparently destroying everything.

Just why those core samples and the breccias they contained were so important was the result of some relatively recent research involving the effects of known asteroid impacts upon assorted rocks. It was only in the 1960s that scientists discovered that one of the most important of these effects is the production of what is known as "shocked" quartz.[19] Common in earth's crust, quartz is present in most impact breccias (including the ones on display at NMNH). Normally, quartz crystals are unmarked. But when an asteroid hits the ground, its powerful shock waves, passing through the tiny quartz grains at a rate of three to six miles per second, leave a unique, indelible mark: microscopic parallel lines scored through the quartz, like three-dimensional cross-hatching. The presence of these features provides certain proof of an asteroid impact.

It wasn't until spring of 1990 that Penfield got a call from a graduate student, Alan Hildebrand, who had examined a

---

17. magnetometer. Instrument for measuring magnetic forces
18. symmetry. Equal on both sides
19. quartz. Common mineral found in Earth's crust

Differentiated Instruction

Enrichment

Challenge students who are interested in geology to theorize and then research the connection between economic geology, whose main purpose is to excavate earthly materials for economic or industrial use, and historical geology, which aims to gain understanding of Earth's history. A preliminary question for students to consider might be: "Are the two branches at odds, or can they aid each other in their individual pursuits?" Guide them in considering the geologic paths crossed in this selection and the result of this "meeting of minds."

... imagine the Earth with the sun blocked out for a year ...

65-million-year-old rock layer in Haiti, only 300 miles from the Yucatán, and determined that the still-hypothetical asteroid impact of that time must have occurred somewhere around the Caribbean. Now Hildebrand wanted to see if he and Penfield could complete the puzzle by locating rock samples from Penfield's Chicxulub structure.

Working determinedly, they began their search for samples. By marvelous chance, they found that a few breccia samples, part of the original oil drill cores, had been distributed here and there in Mexico and the United States, thus escaping destruction in the Mexican warehouse fire. Penfield and Hildebrand were fortunate enough to get hold of a few of these, including one breccia from the 14th core of the PEMEX drill site called Yucatán 6. And that did it. Shocked quartz samples from the Yucatán 6 breccia clinched the fact that Penfield's underground saucer was not a volcano, but rather an asteroid impact crater—the elusive smoking gun.

Within a year, it turned out that many of the supposedly destroyed Chicxulub area cores were available. In the kind of coincidence that one might expect in an Indiana Jones adventure, a scientist at PEMEX, intrigued by the anomalous[20] structure from which the cores were taken, had stored the cores in an office in Mexico City for eventual study. The breccias on display at NMNH are from that cache.[21]

Today, most of those scientists who still think that the decline of the dinosaurs occurred gradually also grant that the great asteroid hastened the end of their existence—and the sudden birth of a very different world.

To understand why, you have only to imagine the effect on the modern world of a similar asteroid impact. Apart from the incredible physical destruction—and the human violence that might ensue—imagine the Earth with the sun blocked out for a year: there would be no harvests, and deprived of the warmth of the sun, the earth would grow dramatically colder, perhaps by as much as 30 degrees.

---

20. **anomalous.** Inconsistent; not following a general rule or pattern
21. **cache.** Collection of items stored in a safe place

DURING READING

**Use Reading Skills
Analyze Main Idea and Details** How do the details from this paragraph support the author's main idea about "the elusive smoking gun"?

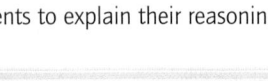
Use Reading Strategies

Make Inferences Ask students if they agree with the author's inference that humans and other large mammals wouldn't have evolved if dinosaurs hadn't become extinct. Encourage students to explain their reasoning. **Ⓐ**

You may want to ask students to write a journal entry or quick write, or divide students into discussion groups or lead a whole-class discussion about this question. *Answer:* Students might mention discoveries that confirmed beliefs in religion, historical occurrences, and opinions about contemporary issues. They might say this made them trust their instincts more. Students might say that the act of discovery challenges current scientific beliefs and enriches our knowledge.

Ⓐ The extremes of temperature and pressure that created these breccias literally changed the earth. Millions of years later, the breccias are a reminder of the new kind of life that resulted, one in which large mammals like us could evolve because dinosaurs were extinct. Like these rocks, we might not be here today if it weren't for the asteroid that formed the Chicxulub crater. ❖

MIRRORS & WINDOWS Have you ever discovered something that confirmed a belief that you had previously held? How did this feel? In what ways is the act of discovery important to science?

TEACHING NOTE

Self-Generated Questioning

Direct students to skim over the passage when they are finished reading, marking sections, phrases, and words that they would like to better understand. When they have had ample time to complete this task, generate, from their work, a list of questions as a class and write them on a board. Model a question such as, "What is a drill core?"

Choose several questions to answer through discussion, and provide support for students to answer remaining questions on their own or in groups.

Find Meaning

1. (a) What "two rocks" are at the center of this article? (b) What information is provided in the "tale" of these rocks?

2. (a) Where is the Chicxulub crater? (b) According to this article, how was it formed?

3. (a) What information did Glen Penfield's magnetometer uncover? (b) What did his findings suggest?

Analyze Literature

Informational Text Create a K-W-L chart like the one at right. Use your chart to analyze the information in "A Tale of Two Rocks." Then write a brief analysis of the article. Did it answer all your questions? If not, what questions remain? How might you find the answers?

What I Know	What I Want to Know	What I Learned
Dinosaurs became extinct millions of years ago.		

Make Judgments

4. (a) What "scientific bombshell" did Luis and Walter Alvarez offer? (b) Why did many scientists remain "skeptics"? (c) Would you have been a skeptic? Explain.

5. (a) What was the "smoking gun" that some scientists believe is the proof of the impact theory? (b) Do you believe this "smoking gun" truly supports this theory? Explain.

6. (a) At the end of the article, how does the author describe what the modern world would be like if another giant asteroid hit Earth? (b) What makes this description effective?

Extend Understanding

Writing Options

Creative Writing Write a **screenplay** for a scene in a science fiction movie or a nonfiction film about an asteroid hitting Earth. Base your screenplay on facts from Jablow's article.

Applied Writing *Jargon* is a term for the technical language of a special activity or group. Examples include *breccia* and *iridium*. Work with a partner to create a **glossary** of the scientific jargon appearing in this article. List the words in alphabetical order and include definitions.

Collaborative Learning

Discuss the Thesis According to many scientists, the impact of the asteroid was the catalyst for "the sudden birth of a very different world," changing the planet's appearance and its inhabitants. Work in groups to uncover other possible theories that suggest explanations about global warming. Present your research findings.

Media Literacy

Sources of Scientific Data Work with a partner to research the Chicxulub crater. When you are done, present your findings to the class.

MW Go to **www.mirrorsandwindows.com** for more.

A TALE OF TWO ROCKS **405**

Rubrics for Writing Options

You can adapt this as a checklist for students to use as they write.

Creative Writing

☐ Does it factually or creatively present a scene that occurs during or after an asteroid impact?

☐ Does it contain stage directions and/or visual descriptions of what the viewers will see?

Applied Writing

☐ Does it reflect an understanding of *jargon*?

☐ Does it contain an alphabetical listing of scientific jargon appearing in the article?

☐ Does each entry include an accurate definition of the term?

Understanding Different Types of Sentences

1. compound-complex
2. simple
3. compound
4. simple
5. simple

> For more information, see Grammar & Style Section 3.1, The Sentence, in the Language Arts Handbook.

Build Skills

Some students may need help distinguishing between a simple sentence with a compound predicate and a compound sentence. Point out that a simple sentence may have more than one predicate connected by a conjunction such as *and, or, neither, nor,* or *but.* In a compound sentence, each predicate has its own subject.

KEY TERMS

SIMPLE SENTENCE, 406
INDEPENDENT CLAUSE, 406
SUBORDINATE CLAUSE, 406
SUBJECT, 406
VERB, 406
PHRASE, 406
COMPOUND SUBJECT, 406
COMPOUND VERB, 406
COMPOUND SENTENCE, 406
COMMA, 406
COORDINATING CONJUNCTION, 406
COMPOUND-COMPLEX SENTENCE, 406

Simple, Compound, and Compound-Complex Sentences

Simple Sentences

They are two small chunks of humble gray rock.

—VALERIE JABLOW, "A Tale of Two Rocks"

Sentences are classified according to the types and number of clauses they contain. A **simple sentence** contains one independent clause and no subordinate clauses. Remember that a clause must have both a subject and verb. A simple sentence may have any number of phrases, a compound subject, or a compound verb. The quotation above is a simple sentence.

> EXAMPLES
>
> *The asteroid caused a large crater in the desert.*
>
> *Dinosaurs and other species disappeared.*
>
> *The asteroid vaporized and crushed the rocks.*

Compound Sentences

Their presence in the drill cores did not bode well for the oil company's exploration…since volcanic rock usually means that oil…is not easy to extract.

—VALERIE JABLOW, "A Tale of Two Rocks"

A **compound sentence** consists of two or more independent clauses joined with a comma and a coordinating conjunction such as *and, but, or, nor, for, yet, since, while,* or *so.* The quotation above uses the coordinating conjunction *since* to join the independent clauses *Their presence in the drill cores did not bode well for the oil company's exploration* and *volcanic rock usually means that oil…is not easy to extract.*

> EXAMPLES
>
> *Penfield received a call from a graduate student, but the student didn't explain what he had found.*
>
> *The quartz samples were collected, and the lab examined them.*

Compound-Complex Sentences

A **compound-complex sentence** consists of a compound sentence with one or more dependent clauses.

> EXAMPLE
>
> *The asteroid caused the sun to be blocked for a year, yet some species survived because they had unique life cycles.*

The asteroid caused the sun to be blocked for a year, yet some species survived is a compound sentence. *Because they had unique life cycles* is a dependent clause.

Understanding Different Types of Sentences

Identify each of the following sentences as simple, compound, or compound-complex.

1. Penfield decided that it was probably an impact crater, so it could not be the result of a volcano, which others had previously thought.
2. The breccias and cores on display are from Chicxulub.
3. One group studied the volcano, while another studied the crater.
4. The students excavated the crater and took samples back to the laboratory.
5. Millions of years later, the rocks offer clues to what happened.

You will find additional lessons on Simple, Compound, and Compound-Complex Sentences in the *Exceeding the Standards: Grammar & Style* resource.

Common Core State Standards

Language
L.6.3a

TEACHING NOTE

Extra Practice

Have students identify each of the following sentences as simple, compound, or compound-complex.

1. Luis Alvarez and his son Walter combined their knowledge with other scientists and released a scientific bombshell. (simple)
2. Although dinosaurs were a dominant species during the Mesozoic Era, many dinosaur species disappeared at its close and others evolved into birds. (compound-complex)
3. There have been several mass extinctions in Earth's history, and the one that killed off the dinosaurs was not even the most destructive. (compound)

Scale of Geologic Time
A Scientific Chart

Apply the Model

BEFORE READING

DURING READING

AFTER READING

GUIDED READING

At a Glance
Guided Reading: Reading Model
- Reading Level: Easy
- Difficulty Consideration: None
- Ease Factor: Visual appeal

Build Background
Scientific Context Scientists base their organization of the history of Earth on fossils, the hardened remains of plants and animals found in layers of rocks, or strata. In general, lower strata contain older fossils than the layers above them. The sequence of the layers of rocks and the fossils found in them form what scientists call the "fossil record." Using the fossil record as a yardstick, they have developed a system of time units to describe Earth's history. The largest division of geologic time is the *eon*. This is the time covered by the "Scale of Geologic Time" presented here. An eon is divided into units called *eras*. An era is subdivided into *periods*, which are in turn subdivided into *epochs*.

Reader's Context If you were creating a time chart for the history of the community in which you live, into what periods would you divide it?

Set Purpose
Preview the title, labels, and illustrations on this chart to get a general idea of its purpose. Read to determine how it organizes Earth's history.

Analyze Literature
Visual Media Pictorial or other graphic forms of communication are **visual media.** There is a wide variety of visual media, including photographs, illustrations, charts, graphs, diagrams, and maps. A **chart** is a visual representation of data that is intended to clarify, highlight, or present a certain perspective on the information presented. One type of chart is a **time line,** which shows the relative order of a series of events, such as dates in a period of history. As you read "Scale of Geologic Time," be aware of how it uses visual elements to present information.

Use Reading Skills
Drawing Conclusions
When you draw conclusions, you gather pieces of information and then decide what the information means. Create a conclusions chart to record evidence. Use this evidence to reach conclusions about the "Scale of Geologic Time."

> Evidence: Organisms in lower portions seem to be less complex.
>
> Evidence:
>
> Conclusion:

Preview Vocabulary
ge•o•log•ic (jē´ ə lä jik) *adj.*, relating to geology, the science that studies the origin, history, and structure of Earth

er•a (er´ ə) *n.*, unit of time; specifically, a unit of geologic time smaller than an eon and larger than a period

per•i•od (pir´ ē əd) *n.*, unit of time; specifically, a unit of geologic time smaller than an era and larger than an epoch

e•poch (e´ päk) *n.*, unit of time; specifically, a unit of geologic time smaller than a period and larger than an age

Objectives
Studying this lesson will enable students to
- use reading strategies such as drawing conclusions
- define *visual media* and identify the type and features of the visual media used in the selection
- appreciate how the chart represents the expanding horizon of geologic time

Launch the Lesson
Prior to reading "Scale of Geologic Time," invite students to think about how they might divide their lives into different periods. Have several students share their ideas. Point out that most people tend to begin with their birth. Ask students how they might divide up the life of the planet Earth. Where would they begin? How would they decide where one period ends and another begins? Have students explain their thinking.

Words in Use

Preview Vocabulary
geologic, 408
era, 408
period, 408
epoch, 408

Teaching Words
sequence, 407
yardstick, 407
geologic, 407
subdivided, 407
highlight, 407
perspective, 407
extinct, 409
abundant, 409

grasp, 410
traces, 413

KEY TERMS
SCIENTIFIC CHART, 407
TIME CHART, 407
PURPOSE, 407
VISUAL MEDIA, 407
CHART, 407
TIME LINE, 407
MYTH, 413
SUMMARY, 413

Common Core State Standards
Reading Informational
RI.1. RI.2, RI.7

Writing
W.9

Language
L.6

MIRRORS & WINDOWS The questions at the end of this selection focus on the theme of geologic history. Before reading, ask students how a geologist might view history differently than a historian.

Analyze Literature

Visual Media *Answer:* It shows a typical kind of animal that lived during this period. **A**

Use Reading Skills

Draw Conclusions *Answer:* The name links it to very early life-forms. **B**

Science Connection

Earth's Eons An eon is the largest formal unit of geologic time. Geologists divide geologic time on Earth into three eons: the Archean Eon begins about 3.8 billion years ago with the oldest known rocks on Earth—the time of the formation of Earth's crust. The only life on Earth during this eon was anaerobic one-celled bacteria. The Proterozoic Eon began about 2.5 billion years ago. Stable continents formed. Oxygen appeared in the atmosphere killing anaerobic bacteria, but aerobic organisms and primitive multi-cellular organisms appeared. The Phanerozoic Eon began roughly 545 million years ago with the rapid expansion of visible life-forms with unique ecological niches. The "eon of visible life" extends to the present day.

Scale of Geologic Time
A Scientific Chart

Era	Period	Epoch	Millions of Years Ago
CENOZOIC	QUATERNARY	HOLOCENE	0.01
		PLEISTOCENE	1.8
	TERTIARY	PLIOCENE	5
		MIOCENE	24
		OLIGOCENE	38
		EOCENE	54
		PALEOCENE	65
MESOZOIC	CRETACEOUS		145
	JURASSIC		210
	TRIASSIC		250
PALEOZOIC	PERMIAN		290
	PENNSYLVANIAN (CARBONIFEROUS)		365
	MISSISSIPPIAN (CARBONIFEROUS)		
	DEVONIAN		415
	SILURIAN		465
	ORDOVICIAN		510
	CAMBRIAN		575

PRECAMBRIAN

DURING READING

Analyze Literature
Visual Media Why do you think the illustration below appears there? **A**

DURING READING

Use Reading Skills
Drawing Conclusions
Paleozoic comes from Greek roots meaning "ancient life." Why do you think this era was given that name? **B**

ge·o·log·ic (jē´ ə lä jik) *adj.*, relating to geology, the science that studies the origin, history, and structure of Earth

er·a (er´ ə) *n.*, unit of time; specifically, a unit of geologic time smaller than an eon and larger than a period

per·i·od (pir´ ē əd) *n.*, unit of time; specifically, a unit of geologic time smaller than an era and larger than an epoch

e·poch (e´ päk) *n.*, unit of time; specifically, a unit of geologic time smaller than a period and larger than an age

408

SCIENCE ▶▶ CONNECTION

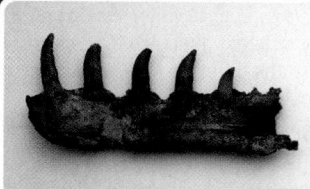

Dinosaur Fossils Fossil bones of huge, unknown animals had been found since ancient times. It was not until the 1800s, however, that scientists identified these fossils as the remains of extinct reptiles. In 1842, the British scientist Richard Owen gave the name *dinosaur* (from Greek words meaning "terrible lizard") to three species of these reptiles whose fossils had been discovered in several sites in southern England. These dinosaurs included *Megalosaurus,* whose jawbone is shown here. Before scientists identified fossils such as this one as the remains of extinct reptiles, what do you think people imagined they were? **C**

 **MIRRORS & WINDOWS** What information on this chart did you find the most surprising? What does this chart suggest about how a geologist views history?

Find Meaning

1. (a) In this chart, what information do you get by reading across? (b) What information do you get by reading down?
2. (a) In what section of the chart are the time units the largest? (b) In what section are they the smallest?
3. How many millions of years ago was the Devonian Period?
4. Use a dictionary to look up the definitions, origins, and pronunciations of the names of the different eras and periods included in the chart. How does this information add to your understanding of the chart?

Make Judgments

5. (a) Judging by the illustrations, in what period do land animals become abundant? (b) In what period do mammals become important?
6. What seem to be some differences between the Cenozoic Era, the Mesozoic Era, and the Paleozoic Era?
7. Why might there be more periods in the Paleozoic Era than the Cenozoic Era?

SCALE OF GEOLOGIC TIME **409**

Media Literacy Skills

Evaluate Media

Tell students that while a chart such as this makes large amounts of information easier to visualize, it leaves out many details. Have students create a large bulletin board copy of the chart. Assign pairs of students to find out more about the information appearing in each square of the chart. Other students can research each of the animals shown.

Have students write their information on index cards and place them in the matching squares on the bulletin board. When they are finished, have students compare and evaluate the pros and cons of the original versus the expanded chart.

The "Scale of Geologic Time" is a chart that presents the units of Earth's geologic history. In the following article, which originally appeared in *The World of Life: A General Biology*, science writer **Wolfgang F. Pauli** takes a very different approach to helping non-scientists grasp the different scales of time.

On the Relativity of Time

An Article by Wolfgang F. Pauli

A We may begin with a scene as it appears to us, a pond surrounded by pines. It is night, and the stars are out in space. With their great speeds so far away, they look like motionless, brilliant pinpoints in the familiar constellations. Fireflies weave against the pines and the sky, and all these patterns, still or moving, are reflected in the pond. A frog is croaking and mosquitoes whine. The Earth is solid underfoot, and the world seems stable and peaceful.

These are things we hear, see and feel with our senses. But how much of this is an extension of our minds? The interpretation of time, as of space, depends upon the viewpoint. In the tempo of everyday life, a thousand years may seem a long time. But to someone who studies paleontology,[1] thirty thousand years may seem but an instant, and this amount in a geologic era is no time at all. It seems quite certain, though, that the length of our life largely determines whether we consider something slow or fast.

To see how this may be, let us invent imaginary people with exaggeratedly brief and long life spans and call them *Minim* and *Chronos*, respectively. Minim's life span shall be as fast as the fraction of a thought. While we wink an eye, four or five of his

generations pass. If he stood by the pond, here is how he might describe what he saw:

"The universe is an immense black expanse of space, studded with many specks of life. Some of these specks are nestled among the spearlike, still matter called grass. Others are suspended in the air all about me, held there by an invisible force, while still others appear to be suspended far out in space, no doubt held there by the same mysterious force. Huge dark masses of inert[2] and apparently everlasting matter, called *trees*, surround me. A peculiarly formed, still, and motionless lump of matter called *man* forms a mound beneath the trees. No sign of motion or life has ever been detected in any of these objects. All of them are as unchanging and unresponsive as the things called *stones* which also lie all about. In fact, the world is motionless, unchanging. We, the Minims, appear to be the only creatures who have life and motion."

Thus Minim might describe his universe, and what a different universe he sees! His world is black because his life span happens to come at night. To him the fireflies are as

---

1. **paleontology.** Science that studies fossils and ancient forms of life
2. **inert.** Motionless

Teach the Connection

Summary
The "Scale of Geologic Time" displayed the age of Earth in terms of changes in rock structure and the earliest presence of various life-forms. "On the Relativity of Time" demonstrates that, while the chart may work for those of us who live in "human" time, Earth and the universe would appear very different to "people" who had much shorter or longer life spans. Pauli postulates the existence of Minim, whose life passes in a fraction of a second, and Chronos, whose life span encompasses the formation of the solar system and all changes on Earth. Pauli points out that the timing of the same events appears completely different depending on the life span of the observer.

Analyze Literature
Setting Invite students to give examples of how they know that time has passed. Then explain that although this is an informational article about time, the setting is extremely important because changes in our environmental setting influence our perception of time. **A**

Use Reading Skills
Compare and Contrast After students read the first paragraph, invite them to compare and contrast the information presented in the "Scale of Geologic Time" and in the beginning of this article. Which elements are the same? Which elements are different?

Common Core State Standards
Reading Informational RI.2, RI.3, RI.9
Writing W.9
Language L.6

Words in Use

"On the Relativity of Time"

Selection Words
everlasting, 410
unresponsive, 410
uniform, 412

Differentiated Instruction

Reading Proficiency
Students may need help with the following words in order to grasp the meaning of the article.
relativity—change, dependence on other factors, 410
constellations—groups of stars named by ancient people, 410
interpretation—explanation, meaning, 410
exaggeratedly—enlarged far beyond normal, 410

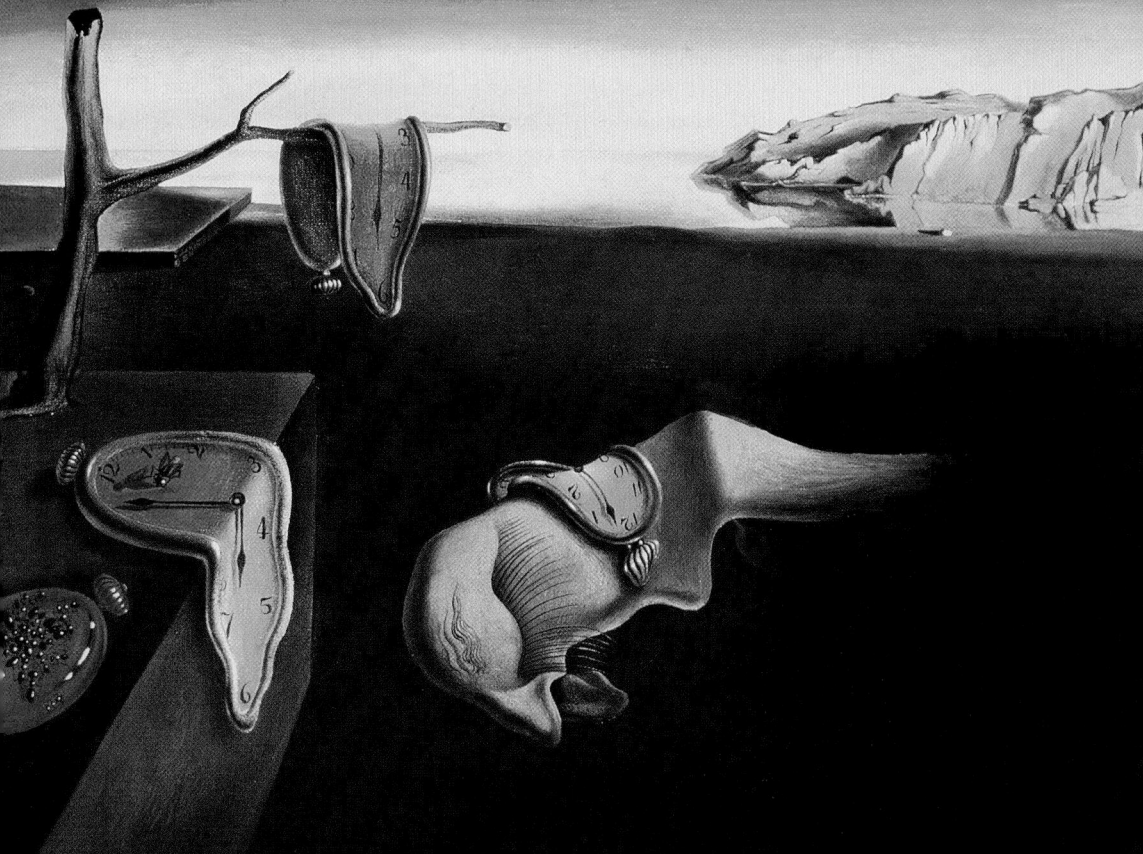

The Persistence of Memory, 1931. Salvador Dalí. Museum of Modern Art, New York.

Science Connection
Relativity To help students understand relativity, explain that the observed motion of objects is "relative to," or dependent on, the position of both the object and the observer. For example, a person seated on a bus observes himself at rest. An observer on the sidewalk sees the person moving forward at the speed of the bus. An observer on the moon can see Earth rotate, whereas an observer on Earth senses no rotational motion.

Use Reading Strategies
Visualize Encourage students to visualize what Minim and Chronos might see as they look at Earth and the moon from a position in outer space. Have students describe what they see. **B**

motionless as the stars, because in the 1/100 part of a second that he lives, the streaking fireflies do not move enough for their motion to be noticed. Wind, the quivering of a leaf, or of a blade of grass, don't exist for Minim. No sound within the range of human hearing would be heard by him. Stories of the far-off period when the world was in sunlight would not, even in the form of myth, come down to the night-living Minim generations. There is no more motion in such a world than in a photograph.

Now imagine a time far slower than human time, and a person as sluggish and long-lived to man as man is to Minim. We shall call this creature of near eternity

Chronos, and just one of his slow-moving hours would in our reckoning[3] be twenty-five million years. This is how the same pond might look to him: **B**

"Everything in the universe flashes and squirms with great speed. Most things exist but a moment and flash out of existence. There is no fixed, firm point on which to rest the eye. A moment ago as I sat down (it took him fifteen thousand of our years to do so) there was one of those ephemeral[4] things called a *pond* before me. By the time I was seated it had disappeared, as such mirages do. The Earth is a thick fluid that moves

---

3. **reckoning.** Estimation
4. **ephemeral.** Short-lived

ON THE RELATIVITY OF TIME **411**

Dramatize an Informational Article
Have students work in small groups to brainstorm how to dramatically compare the experience of Minim, a human, and Chronos. Have each group prepare props, costumes, scenery, and any other media they need to produce their dramatic scene. Students should then rehearse their dramatic production. When they are ready, have each group present their scene to the class. As they are speaking, students should employ learning strategies such as using nonverbal cues, synonyms, and circumlocution to convey ideas when they do not know the exact words to use. When each group is finished, other groups can offer constructive feedback about how effectively the drama demonstrated, compared, and contrasted the experience of Minim, a human, and Chronos.

Text-to-Text Connection

Answer: The chart's approach and organization are visual and chronological, while the article is organized by ideas rather than time periods. The approach and organization of each work seems appropriate—the chart conveys factual information while the article provokes thought.

Analyze Literature

Setting Remind students that setting includes both location and time. Point out that this article uses the same location in space, but it changes the setting in time relative to the life span of the observers. Ⓐ

Make Connections

Remind students that life-forms on Earth have very different life spans. For example, some insects and tiny aquatic creatures have an adult life span of less than a week. The Galapagos land tortoise may live nearly two hundred years. Invite students to describe and compare how the world might look like to these creatures.

---

constantly in a series of waves or hills. Valleys are dangerous with wicked writhing[5] streams that tear into the land. Most of the surface of this heaving Earth is covered with a turbulent[6] green stuff, which may persist some minutes and then disappear completely, only to flash back again for an instant the next second. A few minutes ago, the world was covered briefly with a white fluff, but this too faded away. Overhead is a great expanse of space, divided into distinct halves. One half is a uniform gray; the other is bright and shining. In the gray area I dimly see a squirming pattern of spirals and circles. The shining half of the sky is bright and unchanging, and a warm light comes from it. On the Earth I see no moving object, no organized creature with a life span or any life such as mine."

Ⓐ This is the world of Chronos, to whom seven thousand years are but a second. How could his world be the same as man's or Minim's? Actually, all three worlds have the same setting in space, but are differently set in time. Hence the three subjective impressions are totally different. To us a pond is as lasting as the light of the firefly is

to Minim, but for Chronos it would probably have vanished as soon as he glimpsed it. The average tree germinates,[7] matures, decays, and dies in less than 1/50 of one of his seconds. He would not even see the long-lived sequoia;[8] only the green haze which spreads and then disappears.

To Chronos, the slow process of erosion, the grinding away of mountains by wind and water, frost and heat, would be a visible flowing and sliding. Night and day and the seasons would not exist for him. In one of his seconds the sun rises and sets two million times. He would have lived through the last ice age[9] in a moment, but it would not have lasted long enough to produce a chill in his frame. He would not see the sun, but an arched band of light; or the stars, but weaving spirals.

Finally, to Chronos, all the life that populates the Earth is less than fleeting shadows, invisible and beyond the range of his senses. ❖

---

5. **writhing.** Weaving
6. **turbulent.** In violent motion
7. **germinates.** Produces seeds
8. **sequoia.** Type of tree that lives about two thousand years
9. **ice age.** Period of intense cold when ice sheets covered large parts of Earth's surface

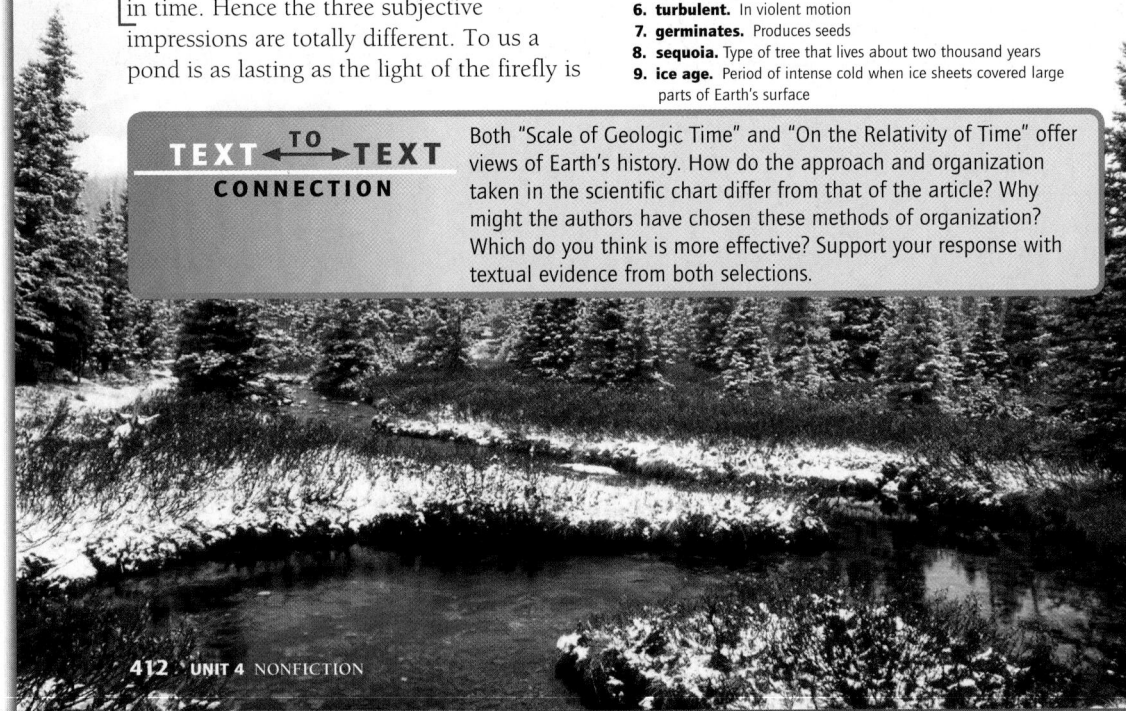

TEXT ← TO → TEXT CONNECTION
Both "Scale of Geologic Time" and "On the Relativity of Time" offer views of Earth's history. How do the approach and organization taken in the scientific chart differ from that of the article? Why might the authors have chosen these methods of organization? Which do you think is more effective? Support your response with textual evidence from both selections.

412 **UNIT 4** NONFICTION

Differentiated Instruction

Reading Proficiency

Have students read the article in pairs. Partners should take turns reading aloud a paragraph while the other partner reads along silently. The reading partner should then paraphrase or summarize the main idea of the paragraph.

Enrichment

Students who enjoy thinking about how perceptions of "reality" change may enjoy reading "Flatland" by Edwin A. Abbot—a story about what life would be like if one lived in a two-dimensional, rather than a three-dimensional world. You may also wish to show the movie adaptation to the class.

Analyze Literature

Visual Media "Scale of Geologic Time" is a time line that uses graphic elements to present information about Earth's history. Create a chart to record the different graphic elements of this time line and what specific information each presents.

Graphic Element	Information Presented
three different colors	three different time periods

Extend Understanding

Writing Options

Creative Writing The Mesozoic Era, sometimes called the Age of Dinosaurs, saw the rise and disappearance of these reptiles. Scientists have offered various explanations for the extinction of the dinosaurs, which took place rather suddenly—in geologic terms—about sixty-five million years ago. A currently popular theory traces the mass extinction to climate change caused by an asteroid striking Earth. Use the literary form of **myth** to offer your own explanation. A myth is a story that explains objects or events in the natural world. Share your work with the class.

Expository Writing "Scale of Geologic Time" presents information in the form of a chart. Imagine you want to translate that information into a **summary** for a fellow student. Identify the key points being made in the chart, for example, how geologic time is organized into units. Present each of these key points in your summary.

Lifelong Learning

Research a Geologic Era Research one of the eras, periods, or epochs listed in "Scale of Geologic Time." Find out what Earth's climate was like at that time, what kinds of plants and animals existed, how the continents were shaped, and other interesting information. Some possibilities might be the Cretaceous Period (when *Tyrannosaurus Rex* lived) or the Pleistocene Epoch (the Ice Age).

Media Literacy

Evaluate Charts "Scale of Geologic Time" is one example of a time line of Earth's history. Locate other examples on the Internet or in books. Select one of these and compare it to "Scale of Geologic Time," evaluating the effectiveness of visual presentation of data for each.

 Go to www.mirrorsandwindows.com for more.

Review the Model

Analyze Literature

Visual Media *Answer:* Student charts will vary.

Graphic Element	Information Presented
Picture of animal	Typical animal that lived during that period
Columns	Separates information into increasingly smaller segments of time
Rows	Shows relationships among era, period, epoch, dates, and living things

Rubrics for Writing Options

You can adapt this as a checklist for students to use as they write.

Creative Writing

☐ Does it present an interesting narrative?
☐ Does it offer an explanation for extinction?

Expository Writing

☐ Does the summary identify key points of the chart?
☐ Does the summary clearly present all the key points?

Preview the Selection

At a Glance
Directed Reading
- Reading Level: Easy
- Difficulty Considerations: Description, length
- Ease Factors: Vocabulary, familiarity

Objectives
Studying this lesson will enable students to
- use reading skills, such as summarizing, in order to retain details
- define *author's purpose* as a literary term and determine the purpose of this selection
- recognize the significance of the buffalo to Native American way of life in the nineteenth century
- appreciate an informational nonfiction essay

Launch the Lesson
Before reading "Indian Cattle," tell students that they are about to read a historical article about an animal that no longer exists as it did in the context of the period described. Ask students if they have ever seen a buffalo and, if so, where they saw it. Encourage students to imagine what it might have been like to see these animals in vast herds.

Common Core State Standards

Reading Informational
RI.1, RI.2, RI.6

Writing
W.9

Language
L.6

Indian Cattle
An Informational Text by Eugene Rachlis

BEFORE READING

Build Background
Cultural Context "Indian Cattle" tells of the Plains Indians' relationship to the buffalo. It is estimated that when Europeans first landed in America, there were thirty to sixty million buffalo. By the 1880s, there were fewer than one thousand. As white settlers moved westward, they hunted buffalo not only for food and for hides to sell, but also for sport. Railroads offered tourists the chance to shoot buffalo from the windows of the railroad cars. Moreover, the destruction of the buffalo was seen by some United States officials as a way to defeat Native Americans who resisted giving up their lands.

Reader's Context What resources, natural or otherwise, are most important to you? What makes these resources valuable?

Set Purpose
Before you begin reading, scan the text for unfamiliar words. Use the footnotes, Preview Vocabulary, and a dictionary if necessary to define these unfamiliar terms.

Analyze Literature
Author's Purpose An **author's purpose** is his or her aim or goal. Authors may have one or several purposes for writing. For example, a writer might write to inform, tell a story, persuade, or entertain. As you read "Indian Cattle," try to determine what the author's purpose was in writing this selection.

Meet the Author
Eugene Rachlis (1920–1986) was the author of many nonfiction articles and books, including "They Came to Kill," which describes the events surrounding the landing of Nazi forces on the Atlantic Coast during World War II. Rachlis was a book publisher as well as a senior editor of the *New York Times Magazine*.

Use Reading Skills
Summarize Summarize the information in a text to help you check your understanding of what you are reading. Summarizing can also help you remember important information from a text. A summary is a brief statement that gives the main ideas of a text. "Indian Cattle" gives information about the Plains Indians and their relationship to the buffalo. Use a summary chart to summarize the main ideas in "Indian Cattle." Add sections to the chart as necessary.

| Main Idea: Buffalo was an important food source for the Plains Indians. | Main Idea: |

Summary:

Preview Vocabulary
mi·gra·tion (mī grā´ shən) *n.*, movement from one location to another.

be·wil·dered (be wil´ dərd) *adj.*, confused

strag·gle (stra´ gəl) *v.*, follow slowly behind; wander or stray

Words in Use

Preview Vocabulary
migration, 415
bewildered, 417
straggle, 418

Selection Words
innumerable, 415
stampeded, 417
valor, 417
reckoned, 418

Teaching Words
resources, 414
communal, 418
negotiator, 419
ambassador, 419
testified, 419
anecdotes, 421
consumers, 421
livestock, 421

KEY TERMS
INFORMATIONAL TEXT, 414
AUTHOR'S PURPOSE, 414
NONFICTION, 414
SUMMARY, 414
SUMMARY CHART, 414
MAIN IDEA, 414
MEMOIR, 419
FIRST-PERSON POINT OF VIEW, 420
TONE, 421
SUPPORTING DETAIL, 421
THESIS STATEMENT, 421
PARAPHRASE, 421

Instead of Plains Indians, Americans might better have called them the Buffalo Indians.

Indian Cattle

An Informational Text by Eugene Rachlis

Of all the things the horse put within reach of the Plains Indians, none was as important as the buffalo. The big, ugly, shaggy animal represented life itself. He provided all that was needed for food, clothing, and shelter. His <u>migrations</u> decided where and how the Indians were to live.

Instead of Plains Indians, Americans might better have called them the Buffalo Indians. Their time of glory was simply the time when they hunted buffalo. When the buffalo disappeared, the roving life of the Plains Indians also disappeared.

In the days of plenty, it was hard to believe that a time would come when there would not be enough buffalo. As long ago as Coronado's[1] first appearance, men had wondered at the size of the herds. Coronado wrote the King of Spain that he saw so many

"it is impossible to number them, for while I was journeying through these plains...there was not a day that I lost sight of them."

Three hundred years later he was echoed by Captain Benjamin Bonneville, an American soldier: "As far as the eye could see the country seemed absolutely blacked by innumerable herds." Eye-witness accounts told how it took one herd of buffalo three days to swim the Missouri; how herds of two million, three million, even four million buffalo covered the earth. Sometimes, the mass of animals was ten miles long and eight miles wide.

---

1. **Coronado.** Francisco Vázquez de Coronado (1510–1544), a Spaniard who led an exploration of the North American interior

mi·gra·tion (mī grä´ shun) *n.*, movement from one location to another

415

Teach the Selection

Summary
Roaming the Great Plains in vast numbers, buffalo were an essential part of Native American life and culture. Their meat was used for food all year long, whether fresh or in the dried form, *pemmican*. Buffalo hides were used for many purposes. The buffalo hunt was an exciting time when whole tribes gathered to feast, play games, and tell stories.

MIRRORS & WINDOWS The Mirrors & Windows questions at the end of this selection focus on the theme of community. Before reading, ask students in what kinds of activities their communities participate as a group. How do these activities benefit their communities and those outside of them?

Use Reading Strategies
Ask Questions Remind students that good readers ask lots of questions as they work their way through a text. Model for students a question that the beginning of this excerpt might prompt: "I wonder how Native Americans hunted buffalo before they had horses?"

Program Resources

Planning and Assessment
Program Planning Guide, Selection Lesson Plan
E-Lesson Planner
Assessment Guide, Lesson Test
ExamView

Technology Tools
Interactive Student Text on CD
Visual Teaching Package
Audio Library
mirrorsandwindows.com

Meeting the Standards
Nonfiction: Unit 4, Directed Reading, pp. 30–34

Differentiating Instruction
Advanced Students, Cultural Context Research Project, p. 22

Use Reading Skills

Summarize Remind students that summarizing can help them retain important information from the text. Ask them to read and summarize the information given in this paragraph about preserving buffalo meat. **A**

Make Connections

At this point, you might ask students to respond to the description of the Plains Indians' lives thus far. Do their lives seem overly difficult or enjoyable? Encourage students to discuss what it might have been like to live this kind of life. **B**

TEACHING NOTE

Students may need help with the following words in order to better grasp the meaning of this selection.

roving — moving from place to place without a goal, 415

moccasin — shoe made of soft leather, 416

rawhide — untanned skin of cattle or other animals, 416

tepee — cone-shaped tent made from animal skins and long poles, 416

helter-skelter — in a disorderly manner, 417

The Indians were no less impressed than the white men by the size of the herds. There always had been buffalo: there always would be buffalo. The Plains Indians could ask no more. Some tribes even spoke of the buffalo as their cattle.

Even as a child the Indian knew the importance of buffalo. Before they had teeth, children sucked bits of buffalo meat. As they grew older, they learned to know that the meat from the cow made better eating than that from the bull. Buffalo tongue was a special treat, and served as a sacred food in many ceremonies. Great feasts followed successful hunts. Large pieces of the newly-killed buffalo were roasted over an open fire, and handed out to feed all who were hungry.

A It was not surprising that the Indians held tribal celebrations when they feasted on fresh buffalo meat. For, during most of the year, the Plains Indians ate preserved meat, which had been saved for use during the long periods when fresh meat was impossible to find. The most popular form of preserving buffalo meat was as pemmican. This was made by pounding the sun-dried meat with a stone hammer until it became a pulp. The pulp was then mixed with buffalo fat and stored in bags made of buffalo skin. Meat was also preserved by drying long, thin strips in the sun. These were then packed with alternate layers of uncooked buffalo fat and berries. It was kept in a buffalo skin packet (called a parfleche) which looked like a giant envelope. Food was only one of the many things the buffalo contributed to the Plains Indians. Buffalo skin was used in innumerable ways. The hides of the buffalo killed in winter were covered with heavy fur. From these winter hides the Indians made mittens, caps, moccasins, and robes, which could be used as blankets or as a kind of overcoat. The animals killed in the spring

and fall did not have heavy fur. Their skins were used as shirts, leggings, and dresses, when skins of deer, elk, and mountain sheep were not available. The even thinner skins of buffalo calves were used as underclothes.

The buffalo skin was tough and waterproof and, with care, lasted for years. The bull's hide was tougher than the hide of the cow. This made it useful for almost all the gear needed for the horse, and especially for attaching the travois.[2]

Wet thongs of rawhide were used to tie the heads of hammers and clubs to handles. When the rawhide dried it shrank and held the head firmly in place. The thick skin from around the buffalo bull's neck made an excellent shield when dried and hardened. Summer skins of the cows were used for making tepees.

But the Indians had use for more than the skin. The bones of the buffalo were used as tools for farming; the sinews were used as thread and, when twisted, made excellent bowstrings; the horns were used as spoons, ladles, and cups; the stomach was cleaned and made into a bag for carrying food or water; sometimes it served as a cooking pot. The dung of the buffalo—called "buffalo chips"—was used as fuel.

When the Plains Indians discovered that the white men valued buffalo hides, they set up a trading operation. And thus the buffalo was able to provide them with some of the things the white men offered—kettles for cooking; iron for arrow heads; guns and ammunition.

B And so the buffalo hunt took on vast importance for the Plains tribes. Around it were developed many of the Indian rituals, in which entire tribes would join, to pray for a world in which there would always be buffalo.

---

2. travois (trə voi´). Vehicle used by Plains Indians made of two trailing poles bearing a net or platform for the load

Grammar Skills

Proper Adjectives

Point out to students that a **proper adjective** is often formed by adding an ending, such as *–n*, *–an*, *–ian*, *–ese*, or *–ish* to a proper noun. They, like proper nouns, are always capitalized.

Have students review the sentences below, correcting any mistakes in capitalization.

1. The buffalo is also known as the american bison. (American)
2. Among the first Europeans to see buffalos were spanish explorers. (Spanish)

When the cold winter had passed, when the pemmican was all but used up, the Indians knew that the annual migration of the herds would start again. Small hunting bands which had spent the winter in separate shelters came together as a tribe. Tepees were set up, and in the days which followed, as scouts scattered to find the buffalo herd, there would be games and songs.

When the herd was sighted, a camp was selected, and the entire group moved to it in an orderly fashion. There was great excitement on the day of the hunt, as the men put their gear in order and the women and girls prepared for their chores—the skinning, cooking, and stripping of the meat for drying.

Before the Plains Indians became horsemen, the buffalo hunt took various forms, all of them based on the fact that the buffalo is not a very intelligent animal and has poor eyesight. One method was called "the surround" and consisted simply of many hunters forming a circle around part of a herd, and forcing the animals to move about in helter-skelter fashion. The <u>bewildered</u> animals then became easy targets for a good shot with a bow and arrow.

Sometimes the buffalo herd was stampeded over the edge of a cliff. They were driven by men shouting and waving robes from behind a line of stones leading to the cliff. The animals would either fall to their deaths, or be so crippled that they could be easily killed.

Another form of buffalo hunt was called impounding. This method was preferred by the Cree and Assiniboin, although the Blackfoot and Crow also used it.

First, a corral had to be built. Leading to the opening were fences which narrowed in toward the corral in the shape of a large V. After scouts found the buffalo herd, it was lured toward the corral, sometimes by an

C Indian who covered his body with a calf skin and imitated the bleating of a young buffalo; sometimes fire was used. Once the herd started on its way, other members of the tribe would move in from behind to keep the buffalo headed in the right direction.

> There was great excitement on the day of the hunt...

Despite these methods, the Plains Indian **D** did not fully gain the upper hand until he began hunting buffalo on horseback. With the horse, far greater numbers of buffalo could be killed on one hunt.

The horse also permitted the Plains Indian to show his valor while hunting. Astride a well-trained horse, the Indian could rush close to an animal, shoot it with a bow and arrow, and then continue on to the next and the next, until the racing herd thundered beyond his reach. Afterwards it was easy to tell which hunter had killed a particular buffalo. Each Indian's arrows could be identified by the way he tied the arrowhead to the shaft or by the color of the feathers. Some courageous hunters preferred to use a short lance with an iron head; killing a buffalo with this weapon while riding a fast-moving horse took even more skill than using a bow and arrow.

Buffalo hunting depended, of course, on the skill of a man's horse. A well-trained hunting horse—fast, alert, intelligent—was

be·wil·dered (be wil´ durd) *adj.*, confused

Teach the Selection

Analyze Literature
Setting Point out to students that setting can be important in nonfiction as well as fiction. Ask why setting is significant here. **C**

Cultural Connection
Horses in North America During the Spanish expeditions of Coronado and DeSoto, these explorers either lost or abandoned a number of their horses in the Plains region. Some of these horses came into the possession of the Plains Indians, but there is disagreement over whether the Plains Indians began to widely employ horses at this time or over a century later. At first look, the Plains Indians saw horses as "big dogs," animals to pull a travois, but soon recognized in the animals the great potential for hunting and war. Horses became vital to the Plains Indians' way of life, and much value was placed on the ownership and mastery of horses. In particular, bravery was measured by the theft of horses from rival tribes, and the man who could capture the most horses gained great honor. **D**

Vocabulary Skills

Etymology
Tell students that etymology is the study of the origins of words and how they developed their present meaning. In many dictionary entries, an etymology indicates the language from which the entry word originated. Dictionary etymologies often appear in brackets. Sometimes the etymology precedes the definition; sometimes it follows it.

EXAMPLE: ***parfleche*** [Canadian French, from French *parer* "to ward off" + *fleche* "arrow"]

Students should give examples of activities they do with people in their community. Some might say communal activities bring people closer together and allow people to use their talents to help others.

Find Meaning

1. (a) They would surround the buffalo, drive them over the edge of a cliff, or build a corral and lure the buffalo toward it. (b) They could get closer to the animals and kill them faster.

2. Small hunting bands came together as a tribe. The men worked together to hunt the buffalo; the women and girls worked together to skin, cook, and strip the meat for drying. The tribes celebrated the buffalo hunt together.

3. (a) No man could start hunting on his own or even disturb the herds. (b) Most likely, this rule was made to ensure the best outcome of the hunt.

Make Judgments

4. Buffalo herds were crucial to the Plains Indians' way of life. They provided food, clothing, tools, and utensils, among other things.

5. The Plains Indians used every part of the buffalo. They not only ate the meat and used the hides but also used the bones, sinews, horns, stomach, and dung to make things they needed every day. Today most people just use the meat and hide of animals.

---

worth two or three pack horses. But even the best horse might be knocked over by a charging buffalo, or might trip in a hole and throw his rider into the mass of stampeding buffalo. The hunt was a dangerous business, but that only made it more enjoyable to the Plains Indians.

No matter which hunting method was used, there were strict rules for a large tribal hunt. No man could start hunting on his own, or even disturb the herds. The penalties were heavy for those who broke the rules: their weapons were destroyed, their clothing torn, and they were disgraced before the entire group. Young men of proven bravery in battle acted as policemen during a hunt and made sure that the chief's instructions were carried out.

Despite the seriousness with which the rules were taken, a buffalo hunt was a happy and exciting event. Little boys on their colts followed the older hunters, to shoot the <u>straggling</u> buffalo calves. The poor and the old never went hungry. There was always someone generous enough to share his catch with those who had neither the horses nor the strength to capture buffalo for themselves.

When the hunt was over, the women moved in with sharp knives and pack horses. Swiftly they cut up the animals, and loaded them on horses. In the summer, when there were plenty of buffalo, only the best parts of the meat were kept. In the fall or winter, nearly every edible part of the animal was saved. Not counting the bones, this would amount to about five hundred pounds of freshly butchered meat—a much greater load than any single horse could carry.

But the results of a buffalo hunt were reckoned in more than meat and bones and hides. All winter long the Indians had fed on pemmican, occasionally shooting small game or a winter buffalo, but mainly trying to stay alive until the warm days came again. But with the hunt, came a time of games, feasting and singing, dancing and storytelling, of tracking down the vast buffalo herds, of making plans for battle with traditional enemies—a time of renewal for the entire tribe. ❖

> **strag•gle** (straˊ gəl) *v.*, follow slowly behind; wander or stray

The buffalo hunt and making use of the dead buffalo was something that the Plains Indians did as a community. What kind of communal activities do you do? What are the advantages of communal activities?

Find Meaning

1. (a) Before Plains Indians became horsemen, how did they hunt buffalo? (b) How did the use of horses change the buffalo hunt?

2. In what ways was buffalo hunting a communal activity?

3. (a) What were the rules for hunters on a large tribal hunt? (b) Why do you think these rules were made?

Make Judgments

4. Why do you think the Plains Indians prayed for a world in which there would always be buffalo?

5. How is the use of buffalo by the Plains Indians different from how most modern Americans use animals that are raised for food?

Differentiated Instruction

Enrichment

Some students may enjoy researching other aspects of the Plains Indians' lives. What was their culture like? Did they have a system of government? Ask interested students to research these questions and share their findings with the class in the form of an oral report.

Chief Plenty-Coups (1848–1932) was one of the last traditional Crow chiefs. During his early life, he was known as a brave warrior. Later, he became a negotiator and ambassador for his people, making many important visits to Washington, DC, where he testified on behalf of the Crows in front of Congress. In "Counting Coup on a Wounded Buffalo," Chief Plenty-Coups tells the story of participating in a buffalo hunt as a young boy. As you read the selection, think how the information it contains adds to your understanding of the role of the buffalo in the life of the Plains Indians.

Counting Coup on a Wounded Buffalo

A Memoir by Chief Plenty-Coups

One day when the chokecherries were black and the plums red on the trees, my grandfather rode through the village, calling twenty of us older boys by name. The buffalo-runners had been out since daybreak, and we guessed what was before us. "Get on your horses and follow me," said my grandfather, riding out on the plains.

We rode fast. Nothing was in sight until Grandfather led us over a hill. There we saw a circle of horsemen about one hundred yards across, and in its center a huge buffalo bull. We knew he had been wounded and tormented until he was very dangerous, and when we saw him there defying the men on horseback we began to dread the ordeal that was at hand. **A**

The circle parted as we rode through it, and the bull, angered by the stir we made, charged and sent us flying. The men were laughing at us when we returned, and this made me feel very small. They had again surrounded the bull, and I now saw an arrow sticking deep in his side. Only its feathers were sticking out of a wound that dripped blood on the ground.

"Get down from your horses, young men," said my grandfather. "A cool head, with quick feet, may strike this bull on the root of his tail with a bow. Be lively, and take care of yourselves. The young man who strikes, and is himself not hurt, may count coup." **B**

I was first off my horse. Watching the bull, I slipped out of shirt and leggings, letting them fall where I stood. Naked, with only my bow in my right hand, I stepped away from my clothes, feeling that I might never see them again. I was not quite nine years old.

The bull saw me, a human being afoot! He seemed to know that now he might kill, and he began to paw the ground and bellow as I walked carefully toward him.

COUNTING COUP ON A WOUNDED BUFFALO **419**

Teach the Connection

Use Reading Strategies
Visualize Have students identify the visual details the narrator uses to describe this scene. Ask them what effect is created by these details. **A**

Cultural Connection
Coup Among the Plains Indians, striking a live enemy—human or animal—was called *coup*, from a French word meaning "hit." Plains Indian warriors used special sticks, called *coup sticks*, to perform these feats. "Counting coup," the record of such achievements, was an important measure of a warrior's courage and greatly affected his status among his people. **B**

TEACHING NOTE

Visualize
Students might benefit from creating a storyboard, a visual treatment of the narrative arranged in panels, like a comic strip. Have interested students create a storyboard of the event described in the selection and then retell the story in their own words by describing each illustration.

Words in Use

"Counting Coup on a Wounded Buffalo"

Selection Words
ordeal, 419
coup, 419
froth, 420

Common Core State Standards

Reading Informational
RI.6, RI.9

Writing
W.2, W.7, W.8

Language
L.6

Analyze Literature
Point of View Ask students to describe their impression of Plenty-Coups created by his first-person account. How might this impression have changed in a third-person account? **A**

Make Connections
Ask students if they, like the young Plenty-Coups, have ever done something that was very brave but very frightening? How did they feel after this event was over? Encourage students to share these experiences with the rest of class. **B**

Text-to-Text Connection
Answer: Students will probably feel that Plenty-Coups' first-person account provides a close-up and rather bloody view on how it felt to be part of the hunt, including feelings of fear and bravery.

Suddenly he stopped pawing, and his voice was still. He came to meet me, his eyes green with anger and pain. I saw blood dropping from his side, not red blood now, but mixed with yellow.

I stopped walking and stood still. This seemed to puzzle the bull, and he too stopped in his tracks. We looked at each other, the sun hot on my naked back. Heat from the plains danced on the bull's horns and head; his sides were panting, and his mouth was bloody.

I knew that the men were watching me. I could feel their eyes on my back. I must go on. One step, two steps. The grass was soft and thick under my feet. Three steps. "I am a Crow. I have the heart of a grizzly bear," I said to myself. Three more steps. And then he charged!

A cheer went up out of a cloud of dust. I had struck the bull on the root of his tail! But I was in even greater danger than before.

Two other boys were after the bull now, but in spite of them he turned and came at me. To run was foolish. I stood still, waiting. The bull stopped very near me and bellowed, blowing bloody froth from his nose. The other boys, seeing my danger, did **A** not move. The bull was not more than four bows' lengths from me, and I could feel my heart beating like a war-drum.

Two large gray wolves crossed the circle just behind him, but the bull did not notice them, did not move an eye. He saw only me, and I was growing tired from the strain of watching him. I must get relief, must tempt him to come on. I stepped to my right. Instantly he charged—but I had dodged back to my left, across his way, and I struck him when he passed. This time I ran among the horsemen, with a lump of bloody froth on **B** my breast. I had had enough.

The End ❖

Both "Indian Cattle" and "Counting Coup on a Wounded Buffalo" give information about the Plains Indians' buffalo-hunting rituals and rules. However, unlike "Indian Cattle," "Counting Coup on a Wounded Buffalo" is written from the first-person point of view. What do you learn from this first-hand perspective that you did not learn in "Indian Cattle"?

420   UNIT 4 NONFICTION

Writing Skills

Intentional Sentence Fragments
Point out to students that writers sometimes use sentence fragments intentionally for effect. Write the following excerpt from "Counting Coup":

"One step, two steps. The grass was soft and thick under my feet. Three steps. 'I am a Crow. I have the heart of a grizzly bear,' I said to myself. Three more steps."

Ask a student to rewrite the fragment sentences in proper sentences on a board. Ask students how this changes the effect of the passage.

Then have students use both intentional sentence fragments and complete sentences to write a paragraph about a topic of their choosing. What effect do the varying sentence patterns create?

Analyze Literature

Author's Purpose By examining elements such as the tone, word choice, and the main idea and supporting details of a text, you should be able to determine the author's purpose. Use a web to organize the information. In the outer ovals, list details from the text that suggest the purpose. Then in the center oval list the author's purpose.

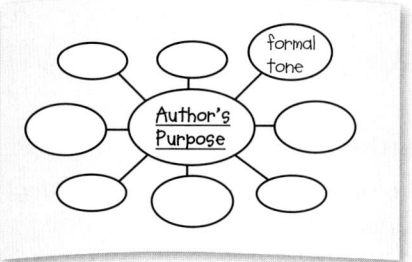

Extend Understanding

Writing Options

Creative Writing Imagine you are a reporter writing an article about buffalo, and you need to call a buffalo rancher to obtain information. With a partner, write a **transcript** of that hypothetical telephone conversation. Remember that you are calling for business purposes, so you should speak in a formal and respectful manner. Make sure to introduce yourself and to state your questions clearly. Conduct research to write the rancher's responses. When you are finished, present your transcript to the class.

Expository Writing Using "Indian Cattle" and the library as sources, write an **informative paragraph** explaining the relationship between the Plains Indians and the buffalo. Include a thesis statement as well as supporting paraphrases, direct quotations, and summaries of your research. Once you have finished, share your paragraph with the class.

Lifelong Learning

Research With a partner, research the decline of the American buffalo. Use both Internet and library resources to gather information. Record facts, statistics, anecdotes, and other relevant information on note cards. Then use these note cards to present your findings to the class. Include visual aids such as photographs and charts in your presentation.

Critical Literacy

Discuss Gather into groups and hold a panel discussion about the relationship between the Plains Indians and the buffalo. What were the most important elements of this relationship? How does this relationship differ from that between present day consumers and livestock? As you state your opinions, support your claims with evidence from the selection.

Go to **www.mirrorsandwindows.com** for more.

Review the Selection

Analyze Literature

Author's Purpose *Answer:* Students' responses might include a variety of specific details supporting the main idea of the article, which is the importance of the buffalo to the Plains Indians. The author's purpose is to support this main idea by providing information about the life and culture of the Plains Indians.

Rubrics for Writing Options

You can adapt this as a checklist for students to use as they write.

Creative Writing

☐ Does the transcript include lines for both the student and the buffalo rancher?

☐ Does the student use an appropriate tone for a business call?

☐ Did the partners conduct research to write the buffalo rancher's responses?

Expository Writing

☐ Does the informative paragraph describe the relationship between the Plains Indians and the buffalo?

☐ Does the paragraph include paraphrases, direct quotes, and summaries from the selection?

Identifying Adjective and Adverb Clauses

1. *Before the white man came* (adverb clause); *when buffalo were scarce* (adjective clause)

2. *When Coronado first explored the West* (adverb clause); *that he traveled across the plains* (adjective clause)

3. *which were once plentiful* (adjective clause); *after people began hunting them with guns* (adverb clause)

4. *When I read about the Plains Indians* (adverb clause); *because the topics are similar* (adverb clause)

> ► For more information, see Grammar & Style Section 3.8, Modifiers, in the Language Arts Handbook.

Build Skills

Point out to students that, in general, they should use the relative pronoun *that* to introduce an essential clause and the relative pronoun *which* to introduce a nonessential clause.

KEY TERMS

CLAUSE, 422	**MODIFY,** 422
ADJECTIVE CLAUSE, 422	**VERB,** 422
NOUN, 422	**ADJECTIVE,** 422
PRONOUN, 422	**ADVERB,** 422
COMMA, 422	**SUBORDINATING CONJUNCTION,** 422
ADVERB CLAUSE, 422	
DEPENDENT CLAUSE, 422	

Adjective and Adverb Clauses

Adjective Clauses

In the summer, when there were plenty of buffalo, only the best parts of the meat were kept.

—EUGENE RACHLIS, "Indian Cattle"

A **clause** is a group of words that acts as a single part of speech. An **adjective clause** is a dependent clause that acts as an adjective by modifying a noun or pronoun. In the quotation above, *when there were plenty of buffalo* is an adjective clause that modifies, or provides information about, the noun *summer*. Adjective clauses follow the word they modify and are generally introduced with words such as *that, which, who, whom, whose, after, before, since, than, when, why,* and *where.*

When an adjective clause is essential to the meaning of a sentence, it should not be set off from the rest of the sentence with commas.

> EXAMPLE
> The buffalo <u>that lived near the Indian village</u> were the easiest targets.

When an adjective clause is nonessential, it is set off with commas.

> EXAMPLE
> The buffalo, <u>which numbered in the millions</u>, provided the Indians with food and clothing.

Adverb Clauses

When the Plains Indians discovered that the white men valued buffalo hides, they set up a trading operation.

—EUGENE RACHLIS, "Indian Cattle"

An **adverb clause** is a dependent clause that functions as an adverb. It modifies a verb, an adjective, or another adverb. The quotation above contains two adverb clauses. *When the Plains Indians discovered* is an adverb clause that modifies the verb *set. That the white men valued buffalo hides* is an adverb clause that modifies the verb *discovered.* Adverb clauses often start with a subordinating conjunction such as *after, although, because, before, if, so that, unless, when, whether,* and *while.*

As in the above quotation, when an adverb clause begins a sentence, it is set off by a comma.

Identifying Adjective and Adverb Clauses

On a separate sheet of paper identify the adjective and adverb clauses found in the following sentences.

1. Before the white man came, it was hard to believe that there would come a time when buffalo were scarce.

2. When Coronado first explored the West, he saw buffalo every day that he traveled across the plains.

3. Yet the buffalo, which were once plentiful, all but disappeared after people began hunting them with guns.

4. When I read about the Plains Indians, it made me want to read about modern day exploration, because the topics are similar.

You will find additional lessons on Adjective and Adverb Clauses in the *Exceeding the Standards: Grammar & Style* resource.

Common Core State Standards

Language
L.1

TEACHING NOTE

Extra Practice

Have students identify the adjective and adverb clauses found in the following sentences.

1. When he was in battle (adverb clause), the Crow warrior struck his enemy with a coup stick, which was a type of ornamental club (adjective clause).

2. After he underwent a vision quest (adverb clause), which usually involved solitude, prayer, and fasting (adjective clause), a young Crow warrior often made contact with a guardian spirit.

3. Crow women sometimes went on raids against other tribes if they needed to avenge the death of a relative (adverb clause).

Murder and More Mushroom Mayhem

An Informational Text by Elio Schaechter

Too Soon a Woman

A Short Story by Dorothy M. Johnson

At a Glance
Directed Reading
"Murder and More Mushroom Mayhem"
- Reading Level: Easy
- Difficulty Consideration: Subject matter
- Ease Factors: Length, language

"Too Soon a Woman"
- Reading Level: Easy
- Difficulty Consideration: Dialect
- Ease Factor: Length

BEFORE READING

Build Background
Scientific Context Both "Murder and More Mushroom Mayhem" and "Too Soon a Woman" reference the danger in eating wild mushrooms, especially the deadly members of the *amanita* family. Johnson's "pumpkin with no color" may have been *Calvatia gigantea*, which grows up to fifty pounds.

Reader's Context What wild or garden-grown foods have you tasted? How would you compare them with supermarket foods?

Set Purpose
Skim the selections to identify the author's purpose. Note how each author accomplishes this purpose.

Compare Literature: Description
Writing that portrays a character, object, or scene is **description.** Descriptions make use of **sensory details,** words and phrases that describe how things look, sound, smell, taste, or feel. As you read, use a chart like the one below to record sensory details.

	"Murder and More Mushroom Mayhem"	"Too Soon a Woman"
Sight		
Sound		
Smell		
Taste		
Feel		

Preview Vocabulary
re·splend·ent (ri splen´ dənt) *adj.,* splendid or dazzling to look at

spec·i·men (spes´ ə mən) *n.,* item which is part of a scientific grouping

de·lect·a·ble (di lək´ tə bəl) *adj.,* delicious

dis·re·pute (dis´ ri pyüt´) *n.,* lack or decline of good reputation

Objectives
Studying this lesson will enable students to
- compare literary selections of different genres
- use reading strategies such as asking questions and visualizing
- define *description* and compare the effect of this literary technique in these selections
- describe the literary accomplishments of Elio Schaechter and Dorothy Johnson
- observe skills that help people identify potential danger and make difficult decisions

Launch the Lesson
Tell students that "Murder and More Mushroom Mayhem" is about a food that is consumed by millions of people but could be fatal if proper precautions are not taken. Ask students if they can think of foods that they enjoy that could possibly be dangerous. Prior to reading "Too Soon a Woman" ask students to consider the dangers that faced pioneers headed west such as starvation, hypothermia, and injury.

Meet the Authors

Elio Schaechter was born in Milan, Italy. His Polish Jewish family emigrated to Ecuador in 1940 to escape persecution. Schaechter is now Distinguished Professor of Molecular Biology and Microbiology, Emeritus, at Tufts University School of Medicine.

Dorothy M. Johnson (1905–1984) was born in Iowa and grew up in Montana. She wrote many books about frontier days, and three of her stories were made into movies: "The Hanging Tree," "The Man Who Shot Liberty Valance," and "A Man Called Horse." Her book *Buffalo Woman* depicts life in the 1800s in the American West from the perspective of an Oglala Sioux woman.

MURDER AND MORE MUSHROOM MAYHEM / TOO SOON A WOMAN **423**

Words in Use

"Murder and More Mushroom Mayhem"

Preview Vocabulary	Selection Words	Teaching Words
resplendent, 424	sauté, 424	emigrated, 423
specimen, 424	concede, 425	persecution, 423
delectable, 424	definitively, 425	emeritus, 423
disrepute, 425		depicts, 423
		mortalities, 425
		inventory, 431
		consensus, 431

KEY TERMS
INFORMATIONAL TEXT, 423
SHORT STORY, 423
AUTHOR'S PURPOSE, 423
DESCRIPTION, 423
SENSORY DETAILS, 423

Common Core State Standards

Reading Informational
RI.1, RI.2, RI.4

Writing
W.9

Language
L.6

Teach the Selection

Summary
The author describes his hobby of enjoying wild mushrooms. Though they can be enjoyed if one follows safety rules, he explains that the result of breaking these rules could result in mushroom poisoning. Mushroom poisoning is rare these days, but it was a real danger in ancient Rome. After the death of the Roman emperor Claudius, believed to be a victim of mushroom poisoning, Romans became mistrustful of the mushroom and, without the food regulations that we have today, some decided to avoid them altogether.

The Mirrors & Windows questions at the end of this selection focus on the theme of safety. Before reading, ask students if they would eat plants growing in the wild. Should people eat wild plants?

Analyze Literature

Description Ask students whether the description the author provides of the chicken mushroom is concrete or abstract. To help them grasp the distinction, ask if, on the basis of the details he provides, they can picture the mushroom. **Ⓐ**

Fly Agaric. Martin du Mesnil. Private collection.

Murder and More Mushroom Mayhem

An Informational Text
by Elio Schaechter

A dozen or so people in the United States are severely poisoned from eating wild mushrooms every year. A few of them die. Although the exact number is not known—the Centers for Disease Control[1] do not keep records of mushroom poisoning—it is less than the number of deaths due to bee stings or lightning. These cases represent a minority of all the mushroom poisonings; most poisonings are not nearly that severe. In most instances, the person who eats a poisonous mushroom suffers an unpleasant but relatively mild and short-lived intestinal disorder, much like the symptoms caused by food poisoning. Nevertheless, each poisoning is a surprise, for there is a strong taboo[2] in this country against eating mushrooms not bought in a store. Nearly everyone seems to know that wild mushrooms can be dangerous and should be avoided at all costs.

Some of my friends think I am playing with fire when I indulge in a plateful of wild mushrooms. I tell them that I always obey the rules of only eating mushrooms I know for sure are safe and only sampling one or two bites when trying out a new species.[3] However, I recognize that it may be tempting to break these rules. Imagine finding a <u>resplendent</u> twenty-pound <u>specimen</u> of the chicken mushroom (*Laetiporus sulphureus*) and proudly bringing it home. You've eaten this species of mushroom plenty of times, so has your family, and you believe it is as safe as mother's milk. That evening you have a party at your house, and you sauté a whole mess of the mushroom and pass it around to your guests as a <u>delectable</u> and novel finger food. You are sharing the delights of your hobby with your friends and want to prove to them that it is safe and enjoyable. Sure enough, your skills as a gatherer are much admired.

Ⓐ

---

1. **Centers for Disease Control.** Agency of the federal government that works to prevent and control infectious and chronic diseases
2. **taboo.** Inhibition resulting from social custom
3. **species.** Scientific category in biology

> **re·splend·ent** (ri splen´ dənt) *adj.*, splendid or dazzling to look at
>
> **spec·i·men** (spes´ ə mən) *n.*, item which is part of a scientific grouping
>
> **de·lect·a·ble** (di lək´ tə bəl) *adj.*, delicious

424 UNIT 4 NONFICTION

Program Resources

Planning and Assessment
Program Planning Guide, Selection Lesson Plan
E-Lesson Planner
Assessment Guide, Lesson Test
ExamView

Technology Tools
Interactive Student Text on CD
Visual Teaching Package
Audio Library
mirrorsandwindows.com

Meeting the Standards
Nonfiction: Unit 4, Comparing Literature, pp. 35–43

Differentiating Instruction
Advanced Students, Literary Connection Activity, pp. 23–24

There is a strong taboo in this country against eating mushrooms not bought in a store.

Some people just have a small bite but others like the mushroom so much that they eat a lot of it. Probably nothing will happen, but what if some of your guests are allergic or otherwise sensitive to this mushroom?

Mushroom poisoning is hardly new. It is mentioned in the earliest writings on mycology[4] by the ancient Greeks and Romans. To quote Pliny the Elder:[5] "Among those foods that are eaten carelessly, I would place mushrooms. Although mushrooms taste wonderful, they have fallen in <u>disrepute</u> because of a shocking murder. They were the means by which the emperor Tiberius Claudius[6] was poisoned by his wife Agrippina. Thus, she gave the world a poison worse still—her own son Nero."[7]

In defense of mushrooms, some historians proclaim their innocence as the agent of death but concede that they could be used as a handy vehicle for some other poison. Pliny himself states that mushrooms were an accommodating instrument for other poisons (*venenis accommodatissimi*), which for him was reason enough to avoid them altogether. Perhaps that is why mushrooms were the only food that was prepared by the host at Roman banquet tables. This practice did not ensure safety, but at least it might

cast suspicion on a possible perpetrator.

Mithridates VI (also known as the Great), king of Pontus in Asia Minor in the first century BC, tried to become resistant to poisons by taking them in gradually increasing doses. It is not known if mushroom poisons were included in the menu, but the method may well have worked. In 1976, the Swiss biochemist G. Floersheim discovered that injecting mice with small amounts of an extract of deadly mushroom (*Amanita phalloides*) protected the animals from a later injection of a usually lethal dose. The reason for this acquired drug tolerance has not been definitively established, but the immune system is not responsible for it. No one would suggest that someone who enjoys wild mushrooms should emulate[8] Mithridates and eat increasing "doses" of poisonous varieties—unless, perhaps, they have as many enemies as he did. ❖

4. **mycology.** Study of fungi
5. **Pliny the Elder.** Roman scholar and naturalist
6. **Tiberius Claudius.** Emperor of Rome from AD 14 to AD 37
7. **Nero.** Cruel and irresponsible Emperor of Rome from AD 54 to AD 68
8. **emulate.** Imitate in order to equal or excel

dis·re·pute (dis' ri pyüt´) *n.*, lack or decline of good reputation

 What would you tell a friend who was interested in trying to hunt and eat wild mushrooms? Do you think it is generally wise for people to eat mushrooms in the wild?

Find Meaning
1. (a) What historical examples did Schaechter use? (b) Why do you think he included these?
2. (a) What does Schaechter suggest could happen when wild mushrooms are served at a party? (b) Does this seem likely? Explain.

Make Judgments
3. Why do you think Schaechter includes the annual number of mortalities that result from mushrooms?
4. What do you think the main idea of "Murder and More Mushroom Mayhem" is?

Teach the Selection

 Some students would remind this friend that some wild mushrooms are deadly. Most will agree that only people who have been properly trained should pick and eat wild mushrooms.

Find Meaning
1. (a) The author describes the murder of Claudius by Agrippina, the practice of Roman hosts, and the tolerance that Mithridates the Great developed to mushrooms. (b) Students may say that Schaechter wants to show the long, deadly, and complex history of mushrooms.
2. (a) Schaechter suggests that partygoers could become unexpectedly ill. (b) Many students will claim that this outcome is unlikely if the party's host is an expert.

Make Judgments
3. Many students will claim that the author presents this figure to show that the number of deaths caused by mushrooms is relatively small.
4. The main idea is that though the danger may be overblown in the minds of some, mushrooms can be deadly and should be dealt with cautiously.

Grammar Skills

Abbreviations with Dates
Explain to students that the abbreviation BC ("Before Christ") is used to indicate how many years before the birth of Christ a specific event occurred. The abbreviation BC is placed after the date. The time abbreviation AD (from the Latin phrase *Anno Domini*, "In the year of Our Lord") is used to indicate how many years after the birth of Christ a specific date occurred. The abbreviation AD is placed before the date. Both BC and AD are always capitalized.

EXAMPLES: Julius Caesar was dictator of Rome in 44 BC. The Roman emperor Nero died in AD 68. Write the following sentences on the board and have students determine whether BC and AD are used correctly.
1. Cleopatra VII became queen of Egypt in BC 51. (incorrect, 51 BC)
2. The Declaration of Independence was signed in 1776 AD. (incorrect, AD 1776)
3. The Battle of Hastings was fought in AD 1066. (correct)

Teach the Selection

Summary

The narrator travels west with his family to a new home in the mountains. Along the trail, they encounter Mary, a runaway, and the father allows her to travel with them. Two weeks later, their food supply is nearly exhausted, and the father goes out on his own, leaving the children in Mary's care. When he still has not returned after four days, the children are starving. Mary finds a large mushroom in the forest but is unsure whether or not it is poisonous. She tests it herself and, after sitting up all night she is still alive and healthy. The children eat and the father later returns with supplies. The narrator reveals that Mary becomes his stepmother.

The Mirrors & Windows questions at the end of this selection focus on the theme of decisions. Before reading the story, ask students if they've ever had to decide something of great importance. How does making tough decisions affect character?

Use Reading Strategies

Visualize Ask students to identify details in the opening paragraphs that help them visualize the setting and the situation of the narrator's family. **A**

Common Core State Standards

Reading Literature
RL.1, RL.4

Speaking and Listening
SL.1

Language
L.6

Seeking the New Home. Newell Convers Wyeth. Private collection.

Too Soon a Woman

A Short Story
by Dorothy M. Johnson

"Mushrooms ain't good eating," I said. "They can kill you."

A We left the home place behind, mile by slow mile, heading for the mountains, across the prairie where the wind blew forever.

At first there were four of us with the one-horse wagon and its skimpy load. Pa and I walked, because I was a big boy of eleven. My two little sisters romped and trotted until they got tired and had to be boosted up into the wagon bed.

That was no covered Conestoga,[1] like Pa's folks came West in, but just an old farm wagon, drawn by one weary horse, creaking

---

1. **Conestoga.** Heavy covered wagon with broad wheels

426 UNIT 4 NONFICTION

Words in Use

"Too Soon a Woman"

Selection Words
homesteaders, 427
gaunt, 427
plodded, 428
hefts, 428
savoring, 429

Differentiated Instruction

English Language Learning
Point out to students that the dialogue used by the characters in this selection is written in dialect and is not proper English. Dialect is the version of language spoken by the people of a particular place, time, or group. The dialect used here is that of the rural United States in the 1800s.

and rumbling westward to the mountains, toward the little woods town where Pa thought he had an old uncle who owned a little two-bit[2] sawmill.

Two weeks we had been moving when we picked up Mary, who had run away from somewhere that she wouldn't tell. Pa didn't want her along, but she stood up to him with no fear in her voice.

"I'd rather go with a family and look after the kids," she said, "but I ain't going back. If you won't take me, I'll travel with any wagon that will."

Pa scowled at her, and her wide blue eyes stared back.

"How old are you?" he demanded.

"Eighteen," she said. "There's teamsters[3] come this way sometimes. I'd rather go with you folks. But I won't go back."

"We're prid'near out of grub,"[4] my father told her. "We're clean out of money. I got all I can handle without taking anybody else." He turned way as if he hated the sight of her. "You'll have to walk," he said.

So she went along with us and looked after the little girls, but Pa wouldn't talk to her.

On the prairie, the wind blew. But in the mountains, there was rain. When we stopped at little timber claims[5] along the way, the homesteaders said it had rained all summer. Crops among the blackened stumps were rotted and spoiled. There was no cheer anywhere and little hospitality. The people we talked to were past worrying. They were scared and desperate.

So was Pa. He traveled twice as far each day as the wagon. He ranged through the woods with his rifle, but he never saw game. He had been depending on venison,[6] but we never got any except as a grudging[7] gift from the homesteaders.

He brought in a porcupine once; that was fat meat and good. Mary roasted it in chunks

over the fire, half crying with the smoke. Pa and I rigged up the tarp sheet for shelter to keep the rain from putting the fire clean out.

The porcupine was long gone, except for some of the tired-out fat that Mary had saved, when we came to an old, empty cabin. Pa said we'd have to stop. The horse was wore out, couldn't pull anymore up those grades[8] on the deep-rutted roads in the mountains.

At the cabin, at least there was shelter. We had a few potatoes left and some corn meal. There was a creek that probably had fish in it, if a person could catch them. Pa tried it for half a day before he gave up. To this day I don't care for fishing. I remember my father's sunken eyes in his gaunt, grim face.

He took Mary and me outside the cabin to talk. Rain dripped on us from branches overhead.

"I think I know where we are," he said. "I calculate to get to old John's and back in about four days. There'll be grub in the town, and they'll let me have some whether old John's still there or not."

He looked at me. "You do like she tells you," he warned. It was the first time he had admitted Mary was on earth since we picked her up two weeks before.

"You're my pardner," he said to me, "but it might be she's got more brains. You mind what she says."

He burst out with bitterness, "There ain't anything good left in the world, or people to care if you live or die. But I'll get grub in the town and come back with it."

He took a deep breath and added, "If you

---

2. **two-bit.** Unimportant
3. **teamsters.** People who haul loads as work
4. **grub.** Food
5. **timber claims.** Small villages
6. **venison.** Deer meat used as food
7. **grudging.** Unwilling
8. **grades.** Degrees of slope

Teach the Selection

History Connection
The Oregon Trail The route the narrator and his family travel resembles the Oregon Trail, by which American pioneers crossed the Great Plains and Rocky Mountains. Two thousand miles long, the trail began in Missouri and ended in Oregon's Willamette Valley. Starting in the 1840s, an estimated 350,000 emigrants attempted this journey in hopes of finding fertile lands and a better life in Oregon. Most traveled in simple wagons drawn by oxen. The terrain was rough, and food was scarce. Diseases such as cholera and dysentery killed many. It is estimated that 20,000 emigrants died along the Oregon Trail.

Analyze Literature
Characterization Show students three basic techniques to develop characters: (1) show what characters do, say, or think; (2) show what other characters say or think about them; (3) describe physical features. Write these three techniques on the board, and have students think of examples of each technique used to describe Pa. Explore Pa's character further by asking students what kind of character he is, and what his role is in "Too Soon a Woman." Is Pa a major or minor character? **B**

Make Connections
Have students pause in their reading to discuss why Pa behaves as he does toward Mary. Why do they think he ignores her? What motivates him to act this way? **C**

Visual Literacy

Study a Painting
Point out to students that they can "read" a painting by paying close attention to details of subject, composition, color, and style. Write those words on the board, and use the bulleted questions below as starting points for analysis of the painting on the prior page.

subject
- What is pictured in the painting on this page?
- How do the people relate to each other?

color
- What colors stand out in this painting?
- What kind of mood do these colors create?

style
- Would you describe this painter's style as realistic or idealized? Why?
- What "comment" does this painting make about American pioneers?

Use Reading Strategies
Ask Questions Ask students why they think the writer marks the passage of time so carefully in this section of the story. **A**

Analyze Literature
Description Remind students that writers use sensory details—details that appeal to the senses of sight, hearing, smell, taste, and touch—to create description. What kind of details does the author use in "Too Soon a Woman" to describe the mushroom that Mary finds? **B**

Analyze Literature
Characterization Ask students what Mary's response to the narrator indicates about her character. **C**

> **More by This Author**
Students who like "Too Soon a Woman" might also enjoy other Western fiction by Dorothy M. Johnson, such as the short stories in her collection *Indian Country*.

get too all-fired hungry, butcher the horse. It'll be better than starvin'."

He kissed the little girls good-bye and plodded off through the woods with one blanket and the rifle.

The cabin was moldy and had no floor. We kept a fire going under a hole in the roof, so it was full of blinding smoke, but we had

B Mary didn't have the horse—we never saw hide nor hair of that old horse again—but she was carrying something big and white that looked like a pumpkin with no color to it.

She didn't say anything, just looked around and saw Pa wasn't there yet, at the end of the fifth day.

That was the day we ate up the last of the grub.

to keep the fire so as to dry out the wood.

The third night, we lost the horse. A bear scared him. We heard the racket, and Mary and I ran out, but we couldn't see anything in the pitch dark.

In gray daylight I went looking for him, and I must have walked fifteen miles. It seemed like I had to have that horse at the cabin when Pa came or he'd whip me. I got plumb[9] lost two or three times and thought maybe I was going to die there alone and nobody would ever know it, but I found the way back to the clearing.

That was the fourth day, and Pa didn't come. That was the day we ate up the last of the grub.

A The fifth day, Mary went looking for the horse. My sisters whimpered, huddled in a quilt by the fire, because they were scared and hungry.

I never did get dried out, always having to bring in more damp wood and going out **C** to yell to see if Mary would hear me and not get lost. But I couldn't cry like the little girls did, because I was a big boy, eleven years old.

It was near dark when there was an answer to my yelling, and Mary came into the clearing.

"What's that thing?" my sister Elizabeth demanded.

"Mushroom," Mary answered. "I bet it hefts ten pounds."

"What are you going to do with it now?" I sneered. "Play football here?"

"Eat it—maybe," she said, putting it in a corner. Her wet hair hung over her shoulders. She huddled by the fire.

My sister Sarah began to whimper again. "I'm hungry!" she kept saying.

"Mushrooms ain't good eating," I said. "They can kill you."

"Maybe," Mary answered. "Maybe they can. I don't set up to know all about everything, like some people."

"What's that mark on your shoulder?" I asked her. "You tore your dress on the brush."

"What do you think it is?" she said, her head bowed in the smoke.

"Looks like scars," I guessed.

C "'Tis scars. They whipped me. Now mind your own business. I want to think."

Elizabeth whimpered, "Why don't Pa come back?"

---

9. **plumb.** Completely

Kinesthetic Learning
Ask volunteers to enact a conversation from the story, such as Mary and Pa's first meeting. Have the class review the chosen conversation to understand the words, gestures, and emotions involved. After the performers have enacted the conversation, remind students what they have learned about characterization. Ask the class how the performers made use of the three techniques of characterization.

Enrichment
Encourage interested students to use library or Internet sources to further research different species of mushrooms. Ask them to try to find examples of mushrooms from different regions and how they are used in the diet and cooking of the peoples who live there. Let them share their findings with the class.

"He's coming," Mary promised. "Can't come in the dark. Your pa'll take care of you soon's he can."

She got up and rummaged around in the grub box.

"Nothing there but empty dishes," I growled. "If there was anything, we'd know it."

Mary stood up. She was holding the can with the porcupine grease. "I'm going to have something to eat," she said coolly. "You kids can't have any yet. And I don't want any squalling,[10] mind."

It was a cruel thing, what she did then. She sliced that big, solid mushroom and heated grease in a pan.

The smell of it brought the little girls out of their quilt, but she told them to go back in so fierce a voice that they obeyed. They cried to break your heart.

The little girls stared at her as she ate. Sarah was chewing an old leather glove.

When Mary crawled into the quilts with them, they moved away as far as they could get.

I was so scared that my stomach heaved, empty as it was. **D**

Mary didn't stay in the quilts long. She took a drink out of the water bucket and sat down by the fire and looked through the smoke at me.

She said in a low voice, "I don't know how it will be if it's poison. Just do the best you can with the girls. Because your pa will come back, you know....You better go to bed, I'm going to sit up."

And so would you sit up. If it might be your last night on earth and the pain of death might seize you at any moment, you would sit up by the smoky fire, wide-awake, **E**

I was so scared that my stomach heaved, empty as it was.

I didn't cry. I watched, hating her.

I endured the smell of the mushroom frying as long as I could. Then I said, "Give me some."

"Tomorrow," Mary answered. "Tomorrow, maybe. But not tonight." She turned to me with a sharp command: "Don't bother me! Just leave me be."

She knelt there by the fire and finished frying the slice of mushroom.

If I'd had Pa's rifle, I'd have been willing to kill her right then and there.

She didn't eat right away. She looked at the brown, fried slice for a while and said, "By tomorrow morning, I guess you can tell whether you want any."

remembering whatever you had to remember, savoring life.

We sat in silence after the girls had gone to sleep. Once I asked, "How long does it take?"

"I never heard," she answered. "Don't think about it."

I slept after a while, with my chin on my chest. Maybe Peter dozed that way at Gethsemane[11] as the Lord knelt praying.

Mary's moving around brought me wide-awake. The black of night was fading.

"I guess it's all right," Mary said. "I'd be

---

10. **squalling.** Crying or screaming loudly and harshly
11. **Gethsemane.** Garden east of Jerusalem where Jesus was betrayed

Teach the Selection

Use Reading Strategies
Make Inferences Ask students what the narrator has now realized. **D**

Make Connections
Ask students if they agree with the narrator's view of how someone would spend his or her last night alive. **E**

Research Skills

Primary and Secondary Sources

Point out to students that in researching her Western fiction, a writer such as Dorothy Johnson uses both primary and secondary sources. A primary source is a firsthand account of an event; for example, a diary kept by an emigrant on the Oregon Trail. Secondary sources are written by people who did not directly experience an event; for example, an encyclopedia article about the Oregon Trail would be a secondary source. Have students identify which of the following materials related to the Oregon Trail would be primary sources and which would be secondary sources.

1. A letter from an emigrant to someone back home (primary)
2. A history of the emigrant routes (secondary)
3. A newspaper article from the 1840s about the Oregon Trail (primary)
4. An autobiography by a nineteenth-century Plains Indian chief (primary)

Use Reading Strategies

Ask Questions Ask students why they think Mary doesn't eat any more of the mushroom. Model some possible responses: "Is she just not hungry? Has the fear associated with testing whether the mushroom was poisonous made her unwilling to eat any more?" **A**

Analyze Literature

Conflict Ask students if they think this final line suggests that the conflict in the story was more than merely a struggle to survive. **B**

able to tell by now, wouldn't I?"

I answered gruffly, "I don't know."

Mary stood in the doorway for a while, looking out at the dripping world as if she found it beautiful. Then she fried slices of the mushroom while the little girls danced with anxiety.

We feasted, we three, my sisters and I, until Mary ruled, "That'll hold you," and would not cook any more. She didn't touch

He glanced at us anxiously as he tore at the ropes that bound the pack.

"Where's the other one?" he demanded.

Mary came out of the cabin then, walking sedately.[12] As she came toward us, the sun began to shine.

B My stepmother was a wonderful woman. ❖

---

12. **sedately.** In a manner that is serene, deliberate, composed, and dignified

In the afternoon we heard a shout, and my sisters screamed, and I ran ahead of them across the clearing.

any of the mushroom herself.

That was a strange day in the moldy cabin. Mary laughed and was gay; she told stories, and we played "Who's Got the Thimble?" with a pine cone.

In the afternoon we heard a shout, and my sisters screamed, and I ran ahead of them across the clearing.

The rain had stopped. My father came plunging out of the woods leading a packhorse—and well I remember the treasures of food in that pack.

MIRRORS & WINDOWS Have you ever been in a situation where you had to make an unpleasant or even frightening decision? Describe that experience. What effect do you think such experiences have on people?

430 UNIT 4 NONFICTION

TEACHING NOTE

Ask the Author

Divide the class into small groups, and have the groups brainstorm and jot down questions they would like to ask Dorothy Johnson. Model a question such as: "How did you gather information about frontier life?"

Instruct each group to pass its questions to another group, and then have each group pretend it is Johnson and attempt to answer the questions it receives. Have the groups share some of their questions and answers as a class.

Find Meaning

1. (a) Who is traveling at the beginning of the story? (b) What is this group's relationship?

2. (a) How old is the narrator? (b) What is your opinion on the narrator's maturity?

3. (a) Why does Pa leave Mary and the children alone? (b) How do they react to his departure?

Make Judgments

4. How would you describe Pa? Give evidence from the text to support your description.

5. What does the narrator mean by "My stepmother was a wonderful woman"?

Compare Literature

Description Descriptions make use of sensory details—words and phrases that describe how things look, feel, sound, smell, or taste. Review the sensory details from both selections that you recorded in your chart. Then answer the following questions, using textual evidence to support your responses.

1. What words and phrases does Schaechter use to describe his imaginary chicken mushroom?

2. What words and phrases does Johnson use to describe Mary's mushroom?

3. Which mushroom, Schaechter's chicken mushroom or Mary's mushroom, would you rather try? Why do you feel this way?

Extend Understanding

Writing Options

Creative Writing Imagine you are on a wagon train heading west to California. Write a **diary entry** about an experience you had along the way involving a chicken mushroom. Imagine you are keeping a diary because you intend to write a book about your journey someday.

Applied Writing Create a **list** of the items you think a frontier family would need if they were journeying west. Think about the most basic necessities: food, clothing, and shelter. What other kinds of things might they bring to help them pass the time? Once you have completed your list, locate a source, either online or in the library, to expand or reduce your inventory.

Collaborative Learning

Research the Oregon Trail Use the Internet to look up information about the Oregon Trail. As you research, ask yourself: Where did the trail begin and end, and what route did it take? How

many people traveled westward on the trail, and how many used it to go back east? What was the most common form of transportation on the trail? Find answers to the questions above and report your findings to your class.

Critical Literacy

Perform a Role-Play In small groups, role-play the following scene. You and your partners are traveling on the Oregon Trail. You are worried because it is getting late in the season and snow and cold weather may soon block your path. Also, your food supply is very low. Some group members think you should continue ahead, hoping you will find food along the way. Others think you should stop and hunt for a few days to make sure you don't run out of food. Argue your points and discuss the issues while remembering to keep an open mind. Finally, take a group vote on which course of action to follow.

Go to **www.mirrorsandwindows.com** for more.

Find Meaning

1. (a) Pa, the narrator, and the narrator's two little sisters, Elizabeth and Sarah. (b) This group is a family.

2. (a) He is eleven. (b) Students might say the narrator has a lot of responsibility for someone so young and that he handles himself as someone much older.

3. (a) Pa leaves Mary and the children after he is unable to catch fish in the river by the cabin. He is going to get food. (b) Mary and the children are frightened but resolute. As the days pass and Pa does not return, they grow more hungry and desperate.

Make Judgments

4. Students might describe Pa as poor, gruff, desperate, or scared. They might also describe him as caring and strong, citing his efforts to save his children.

5. The narrator implies that Pa married Mary.

Compare Literature

Description

1. *resplendent, twenty-pound, safe as mother's milk, delectable, novel finger food*

2. *big, white, like a pumpkin with no color to it, ten pounds, solid, the smell of it brought the little girls out of their quilt*

3. Some students might feel safer with Mary's mushroom, since she has eaten it herself; but Schaechter's mushroom sounds like it is safe, and he describes it as delectable.

Rubrics for Writing Options

You can adapt this as a checklist for students to use as they write.

Creative Writing

☐ Does the diary entry describe the experience of a person heading west in a wagon?

☐ Does the diary entry describe the experience of eating a chicken mushroom?

Applied Writing

☐ Does the list include the most necessary items?

☐ Does the list also include things used to pass the time?

☐ Does the list only include objects available in the nineteenth century?

Program Resources

For further instruction, refer students to the following extension activity: Collaborative Learning: Research the Oregon Trail, *Exceeding the Standards: Extension Activities*, pp. 12–13.

Vocabulary Practice

1. may·hem, (n): needless or willful damage or violence; synonyms: violence, damage

2. in·dulge (v): take unrestrained pleasure in; to yield to the desire of; synonyms: pamper, spoil

3. de·lec·ta·ble (adj): highly pleasing; synonyms: delightful, delicious

4. pro·claim (v): declare publicly; synonyms: announce, broadcast

5. per·pe·tra·tor (n): one who brings about or carries out (as a crime); synonyms: criminal, wrongdoer

6. ex·tract (n): product obtained from a substance; synonyms: essence, concentrate

7. em·u·late (v): attempt to equal or surpass another; synonyms: imitate, mimic

8. de·li·cious (adj): very pleasing, particularly to the sense of taste or smell; synonyms: appetizing; delectable

9. un·der·stand (v): grasp the nature or significance of; synonyms: comprehend; recognize

10. mon·i·tor (v): watch over or direct; synonyms: oversee, supervise

11. achieve (v): to succeed in doing or gaining something; synonyms: accomplish, realize

12. strive (v): to struggle or fight with great effort; synonyms: endeavor, contend

---

> For more information, see Vocabulary & Spelling Section 2.3, Using a Dictionary, in the Language Arts Handbook. Refer to Section 2.7, Spelling, for additional instruction on spelling rules.

Vocabulary & Spelling

Reference: Using Dictionaries and Thesauruses

Although mushrooms taste wonderful, they have fallen in disrepute because of a shocking murder.

—ELIO SCHAECHTER,
"Murder and More Mushroom Mayhem"

Although the context clues in the above quotation suggest that *disrepute* has a negative meaning, what exactly does the word mean? To understand its meaning, you might first look in a dictionary.

A **dictionary** is a reference source that provides one or more **definitions,** or meanings, of a word. Dictionaries also provide the **pronunciation** of the word—or the way the word is usually spoken—the **syllabication** of the word—the number and arrangement of syllables it contains—and a word's etymology. A word's **etymology** is its history or origin, including the root or base words from which it is formed. Etymology is usually provided for the simplest present tense form of the word. A dictionary entry will also contain a word's **part-of-speech** label, which tells how the word can be used.

> **EXAMPLE**
>
> **dis·re·pute** (dis' ri pyüt´) *n.* lack or decline of good reputation; a state of being held in low esteem
>
> [Latin *dis-* meaning "lack of" + *reputatio* meaning "consideration"]

A **thesaurus** is a reference source that contains synonyms rather than definitions. Synonyms are words that have the same, or nearly the same, meaning as another word.

> **EXAMPLE**
>
> resplendent: *adj.* SPLENDID: glorious, magnificent, superb

Vocabulary Practice

Use a dictionary to define each of the following words and note their syllabications, pronunciations, and part-of-speech labels. Then use a thesaurus to list two synonyms for each word.

1. mayhem (noun)
2. indulge
3. delectable
4. proclaim
5. perpetrator
6. extract (noun)
7. emulate
8. delicious
9. understand
10. monitor
11. achieve
12. strive

Spelling Practice

Words with *-able/-ible* or *-ance/-ence*
One of the most confusing things about spelling is knowing when a word ends with *-able* or *-ible*, *-ance* or *-ence*. A general rule is that *-able* is attached to whole words, whereas the *-ible* is added to word parts. Notice these examples:

peace + able = peaceable
incred + ible = incredible

However, there are many exceptions to this rule. For *-ance/-ence,* it helps to study the words as a group (words that end in *-ance* or *-ence*). Try to remember the spelling of these words from "Murder and More Mushroom Mayhem."

delectable	resistant
enjoyable	resplendent
innocence	responsible
instance	tolerance
possible	unpleasant

Program Resources

To expand upon this lesson, Reference: Using Dictionaries and Thesauruses, see the *Exceeding the Standards: Vocabulary & Spelling* resource.

Common Core State Standards

Language
L.4

HOW TO USE A COMPASS

A How-To Article by Kjetil Kjernsmo

BEFORE READING

Build Background

Scientific Context A magnetic compass has a needle, which is the magnet, balanced on a pivot point. The needle's red point always points north, no matter which way the compass is turned, because it is attracted to Earth's magnetic North Pole. People use compasses to orient themselves in many different situations: hiking, orienteering, sailing, and exploring. Orienteering is a sport in which competitors use maps and compasses to reach a series of goals or checkpoints in the shortest time possible.

Reader's Context What situations can you remember in which you have needed to find your way to an unfamiliar destination? How did you find your way?

Set Purpose

Use Build Background, the story title, and the illustrations to preview "How to Use a Compass." Based on your preview, what do you think is the author's purpose?

Analyze Literature

Author's Purpose Authors write with a **purpose.** Some possible purposes are to inform, describe, and entertain. As you read "How to Use a Compass," notice details that might be clues to the author's purpose.

Meet the Author

Kjetil Kjernsmo was born on August 14, 1973, in Oslo, Norway, and has lived there his whole life. He holds a master's degree in theoretical astrophysics. In his current position as senior knowledge engineer with Computas AS, Kjernsmo specializes in Semantic Web technologies, a future direction for the Web. When not working, one of his favorite hobbies is to spend the night in the mountains, sleeping in tents or snow-caves, or if the conditions are right, under the open skies. He has climbed to 20,000 feet in Peru and is also a glacier guide.

Use Reading Skills

Monitor Comprehension This how-to article teaches the steps in the process of reading a compass. As you read "How to Use a Compass," imagine that you are following the instructions with a real compass. Monitor your comprehension using the chart below. Write your own summary of the process, and keep track of your questions about the process as you go along.

Step	My Summary	My Questions
Step 1	Identify the four points on a compass.	What is the purpose of a compass?

Preview Vocabulary

or·i·en·teer (ôr' ē en tēr´) *n.,* person who takes part in a running sport with directions and maps

tu·tor·i·al (tü tôr´ ē əl) *n.,* instruction in how to do something

suf·fi·cient (sə fi´ shənt) *adj.,* well enough, satisfactory

ter·rain (ter´ ān) *n.,* landscape

At a Glance
Directed Reading
- Reading Level: Easy
- Difficulty Consideration: Subject matter
- Ease Factor: Language

Objectives

Studying this lesson will enable students to
- use reading strategies, such as monitoring comprehension, by taking notes
- define *author's purpose* and analyze details that help you determine the author's purpose in this literary selection
- explain why Kjetil Kjernsmo wrote this selection
- expand their horizons by learning how to use a compass

Launch the Lesson

Before reading "How to Use a Compass," invite students to think about how people might have found their way through unfamiliar territory before the invention of the compass. Have students explain their ideas. Encourage students to think about travel at sea, as well as on land.

Words in Use

Preview Vocabulary
orienteer, 434
tutorial, 434
sufficient, 436
terrain, 436

Teaching Words
magnetic, 433
pivot, 433
orient, 433
theoretical astrophysics, 433
semantic, 433
substantial, 437
generate, 439

KEY TERMS

Common Core State Standards

Reading Informational
RI.1, RI.6

Writing
W.9

Language
L.6

Summary

The article describes the steps in using a baseplate or protractor compass to determine direction of travel. The author names and describes the parts of the compass and then explains how to use the housing, needle, orienteering bars, and direction of travel arrow to go in a chosen direction.

MIRRORS & **W**INDOWS

The Mirrors & Windows questions at the end of this selection focus on the theme of navigation. Before reading, ask students in what types of situations they would find a compass useful. How does the compass aid exploration and navigation?

TEACHING NOTE

Process Writing

Although the article contains a series of steps, they aren't numbered. As students read, encourage them to create a list of numbered steps. When they are finished, they can compare and modify their lists.

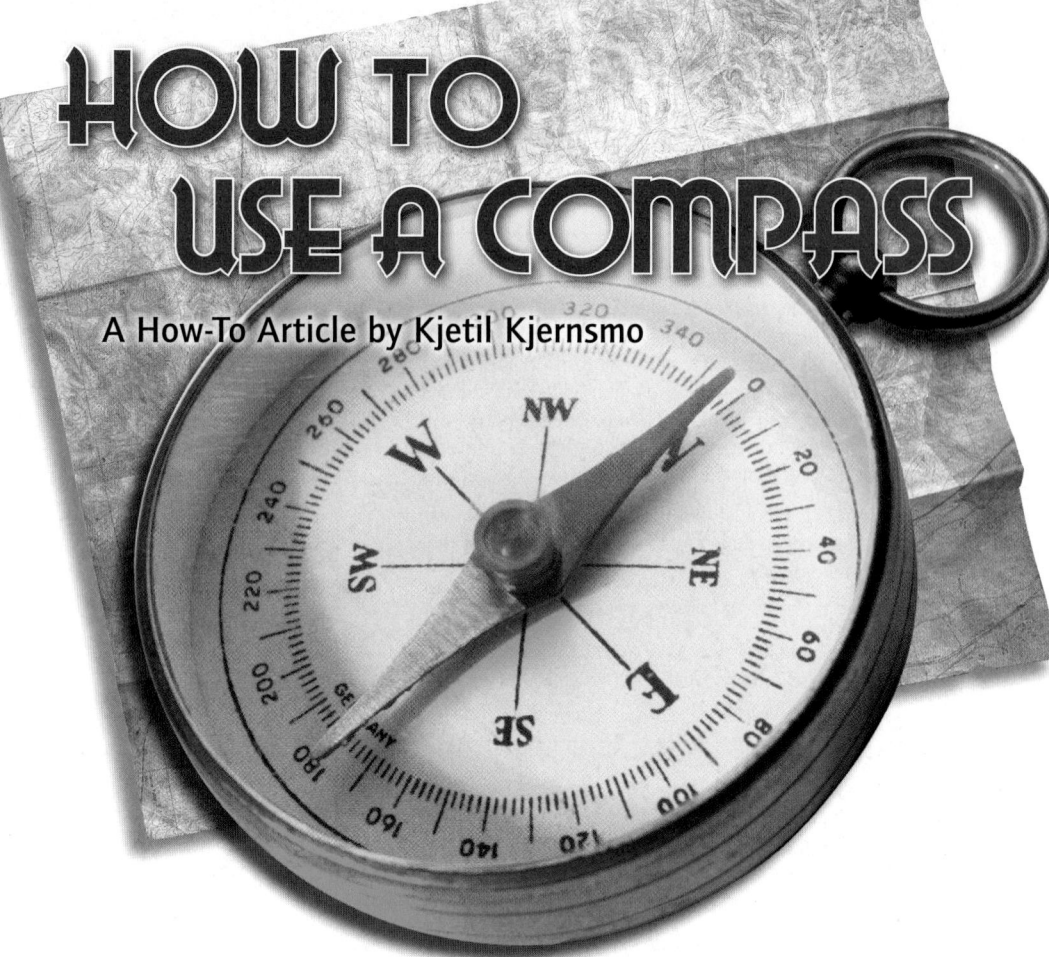

HOW TO USE A COMPASS

A How-To Article by Kjetil Kjernsmo

The first thing you need to learn are the directions. North, South, East and West. Look at the figure and learn where they are. North is the most important.

There are several kinds of compasses—one kind to attach to the map, one kind to attach to your thumb. The thumb-compass is used mostly by <u>orienteers</u> who just want to run fast, and this is the kind of compass I normally use.

But not in this <u>tutorial</u>. I would recommend the third kind of compass. Let's take a look at it.

A You see this red and black arrow? We call it the *compass needle*. Well, on some compasses it might be red and white, for instance, but the red part of it is always pointing towards the earth's magnetic north pole. Got that? That's basically what you need to know. It's as simple as that.

But what if you don't want to go north, but a different direction? Hang on and I'll tell you.

or‧i‧en‧teer (ôr' ē en tēr´) *n.,* person who takes part in a running sport with directions and maps

tu‧tor‧i‧al (tü tôr´ ē əl) *n.,* instruction in how to do something

Program Resources

Planning and Assessment

Program Planning Guide, Selection Lesson Plan
E-Lesson Planner
Assessment Guide, Lesson Test
ExamView

Technology Tools

Interactive Student Text on CD
Visual Teaching Package
Audio Library
mirrorsandwindows.com

Meeting the Standards

Nonfiction: Unit 4, Directed Reading, pp. 44–48

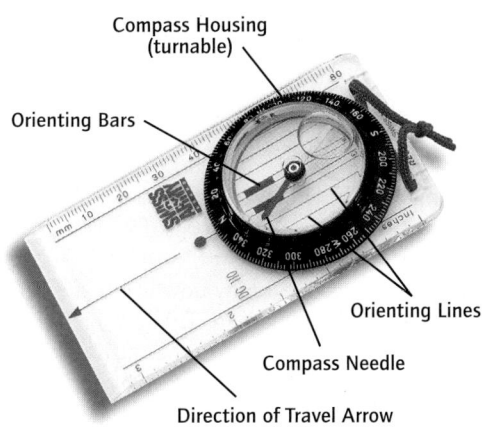

Compass Housing (turnable)

Orienting Bars

Orienting Lines

Compass Needle

Direction of Travel Arrow

You've got this turnable thing on your compass. We call it the *compass housing*. On the edge of the compass housing, you will probably have a scale, from 0 to 360 or from 0 to 400. Those are the degrees or the *azimuth*[1] (or you may also call it the bearing in some contexts). And you should have the letters N, S, W and E for North, South, West and East. If you want to go in a direction between two of these, you would combine them. If you would like to go in a direction just between North and West, you simply say: "I would like to go Northwest."

Let's use that as an example: You want to go northwest. What you do is find out where on the compass housing northwest is. Then you turn the compass housing so that northwest on the housing comes exactly to where the large *direction of travel arrow* meets the housing.

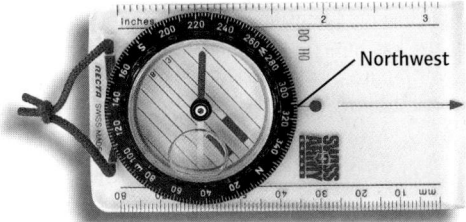

Northwest

Hold the compass in your hand—and you'll have to hold it quite flat, so that the compass needle can turn. Then turn yourself, your hand, the entire compass (just make sure the compass housing doesn't turn) and turn it until the compass needle is aligned with the lines inside the compass housing.

Now, time to be careful! It is *extremely* important that the red, north part of the compass needle points at north in the compass housing. If south points at north, you would walk off in the exact opposite direction of what you want! And it's a very common mistake among beginners. So always take a second look to make sure you did it right!

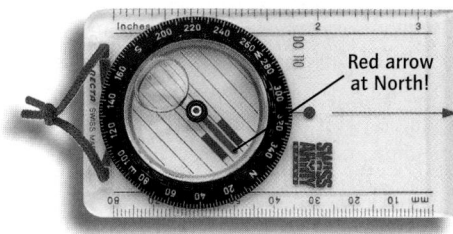

Red arrow at North!

A second problem might be local magnetic attractions. If you are carrying something made of iron or something like that, it might disturb the arrow. Even a staple in your map might be a problem. Make sure there is nothing of the sort around. There is a possibility for magnetic attractions in the soil as well, which might cause "magnetic deviation,"[2] but they are rare. This might occur if you're in a mining district.

When you are sure you've got it right, walk off in the direction the *direction of travel arrow* is pointing. To avoid getting off the

---

1. **azimuth.** Arc of the horizon all around a person as measured from true north all the way through 360 degrees
2. **magnetic deviation.** Magnetic pull that causes the compass needle to move in the wrong direction

Answer: Students might suggest situations such as finding a location in an unknown area or exploring nature in uninhabited land. This discovery allowed people to create an instrument that tells direction under most circumstances.

Find Meaning

1. The first step is locating the directions north, south, east, and west, indicated as N, S, E, and W.

2. (a) The moving arrow is called the compass needle. (b) The fixed arrow is called the direction of travel arrow.

3. (a) You will walk in the direction opposite of the one you intend. (b) Beginners might only look at the lines inside the compass housing without reviewing the directions.

Make Judgments

4. (a) Kjernsmo organized his article in sequential order. (b) Students might say this organization was helpful because it taught the steps in the same order that a compass user would do them.

5. Answers will vary. Some students may say that it isn't clear in the first paragraph where they are to "learn the directions."

---

course, make sure to look at the compass quite frequently, say every hundred meters at least.

But you shouldn't stare down at the compass. Once you have the direction, aim at some point in the distance, and go there. But this gets more important when you use a map.

There is something you should look for to avoid going in the opposite direction: The Sun. At noon, the sun is roughly in the south (or in the north on the southern hemisphere), so if you are heading north and have the sun in your face, it should set off a bell.

When do you need this technique?

When you are out there without a map, and you don't know where you are, but you know that there is a road, trail, stream, river or something long and big you can't miss if you go in the right direction. And when you know in what direction you must go to get there, at least approximately what direction.

Then all you need to do is to turn the compass housing, so that the direction you want to go in is where the direction of travel-arrow meets the housing. And follow the above steps.

But why isn't this technique <u>sufficient</u>? It is not very accurate. You are going in the right direction, and you won't go around in circles, but you're very lucky if you hit a small spot this way.

If you are taking a long hike in unfamiliar <u>terrain</u>, you should always carry a good map that covers the terrain—especially if you are leaving the trail.

You also need to know how to use a compass along with a map. This can be somewhat more complicated, because of something called *magnetic declination*.[3] I'm not going to talk about declination here, because that is only connected to the use of maps. But you may wish to learn about it if you are serious about using a compass, because it is in the interaction between the map and a compass that the compass becomes really valuable. ❖

---

3. magnetic declination. Angle between true north and magnetic north at a particular place

---

suf·fi·cient (sə fiʹ shənt) *adj.,* well enough, satisfactory
ter·rain (terʹ ān) *n.,* landscape

When might you use a compass? How do you think the discovery of Earth's magnetic north pole changed exploration and navigation?

Find Meaning

1. What is the first step in using a compass?
2. (a) What is the moving arrow called? (b) What is the fixed arrow called?
3. (a) What could happen if the compass housing is positioned so the compass needle points at *S*? (b) Why do you think this happens to beginners?

Make Judgments

4. (a) How did Kjernsmo organize his article? (b) How was this organization helpful?
5. Which parts of the article do you think could have been written more clearly?

Differentiated Instruction

English Language Learning

Discuss the meaning of the following expressions: "hang on," 435; "take a second look," 435; "aim on some point," 436; "ring a bell," 436; and "you're lucky if you hit a small spot," 436.

Enrichment

Students might want to learn more about compasses and using them. After reading Kjernsmo's explanations, have students locate several websites about compasses in order to compare and contrast the information they find.

Teach the Connection

Analyze Literature
Author's Purpose Have students locate clues and draw conclusions about the author's purpose in writing the article. How does the title reflect the author's feeling about orienteering? **A**

TEACHING NOTE

Explain a Process
Have students share their expertise by explaining a process they already know how to do. Each student should plan his or her presentation by:

1. identifying a process
2. breaking the process into steps
3. identifying terms that need definitions
4. selecting visual aids to explain their process
5. preparing a graphic organizer, such as the one shown on page 433, to organize their presentation.

Have students take turns presenting their explanations in small groups.

In "How to Use a Compass," Kjetil Kjernsmo mentions the "thumb-compass" that is used by orienteers. The following selection, "Orienteering: The Thinking Sport," is an article that explains orienteering by **David LaRochelle** (b. 1960). LaRochelle has been a member of the Minnesota Orienteering Club for the past fourteen years. At his first meet, he got lost while still in the parking lot but has made substantial improvement since then. He is a frequent artist- and writer-in-residence at elementary and middle schools. His young adult novel *Absolutely, Positively Not* received the 2005 Sid Fleischman Award for excellence in humor writing, and his books for younger readers include *The End* and *The Best Pet of All*.

Orienteering: The Thinking Sport

An Informational Article by David LaRochelle

Nature hike, treasure hunt, cross-country track race—the sport of orienteering is a little of each. Using a compass and a highly detailed topographical map,[1] participants visit a series of checkpoints called controls. These controls, marked by orange and white flags, are placed throughout the site of the event, which is usually a park or forest.

Everyone is welcome at an O-meet (short for orienteering event). You'll find participants ranging from young children to senior citizens, first-timers to seasoned athletes. The only special equipment needed is a compass, which can usually be borrowed or rented at the site. Suitable clothing includes a long-sleeved shirt and long pants to prevent scratches from branches, and a pair of comfortable outdoor shoes.

When you arrive at a meet you'll find plenty of people to help you get started. After paying a registration fee (usually only a few dollars) you'll be asked to select the course you'd like to try. Each O-meet offers a variety of courses, varying in length and difficulty. The easiest is typically only a few kilometers (1 or 2 miles) in length with easy-to-find controls placed along well-marked trails. The more challenging courses may be 10 or more kilometers with controls in out-of-the-way locations.

Once you've decided on your course you'll be given three things: a map of the area, a clue card to help you locate the controls, and a control card to keep track of your progress. An official will record your starting time and signal you to proceed to the master map for your course. This map shows the specific locations of all your controls, circled and numbered in the order in which they'll need to be found. Carefully copy their locations onto your map. A careless slip here can send you hunting in the wrong area!

---

1. **topographical map.** Map showing natural and man-made features that has lines to indicate the steepness of slopes

ORIENTEERING: THE THINKING SPORT **437**

Words in Use

"Orienteering: The Thinking Sport"

Selection Words
depression, 438
junction, 438

Common Core State Standards

Reading Informational
RI.1, RI.6
Writing
W.4
Language
L.6

Illustration by David LaRochelle.

Teach the Connection

Make Connections

Have students think about whether they would enjoy orienteering and explain their thinking. Ask students to describe whether they would go fast, or slowly and carefully, to complete the course. **A**

Use Reading Skills

Monitor Comprehension After students complete the selection, invite a volunteer to write on the board the main idea of the work. After discussing and refining the main idea, invite other volunteers to add details that support the main idea.

Text-to-Text Connection

Answer: Students might say that the LaRochelle article helped them understand why a person even today might enjoy using a compass. They might say the Kjernsmo article helped them understand the challenges of orienteering.

---

and enjoy the scenery along the way. A leisurely walker with a carefully chosen route, however, may actually find a control faster than a runner who blindly heads from one point to the next.

If you've read your map carefully and planned your route well you'll reach the control with no problem. Hanging from the orange and white flag will be a device similar to a paper punch to mark your control card as an indicator that you reached that spot.

Once you've found all your checkpoints, head to the finish. An official will take your control card and record the time that you returned. Finding all the controls is a satisfying accomplishment, whether or not you finished faster than other participants.

There are many variations on the standard O-meet. Depending on the season and location, orienteering can be done using skis, snowshoes, mountain bikes, or canoes. For the truly adventurous there is even nighttime orienteering!

Check the Internet or a sporting goods or camping store for information on local orienteering clubs. They'll let you know about O-meets in your area. Then grab a compass and get ready to join others for a map-reading adventure out in the woods. ❖

You are now ready to locate your first control. Find the first circle you copied onto your map. The clue card you were given when you registered will give an added description of where that control will be found (on top of a hill, in a depression, at a trail junction). It is up to you to decide the best route to reach that control. Does it make more sense to take a short route over a hill or take a longer route that avoids steep changes in elevation? Is there terrain that would be difficult to traverse? It is this ability to read a map and make smart route selections that gives orienteering the name "The Thinking Sport," or "Cunning Running."

A Some people choose to race from one control to the next. Others take a slower approach, content to move at a relaxed pace

TEXT ⟷ TEXT CONNECTION

While Kjetil Kjernsmo's article is about compasses and mentions orienteering, David LaRochelle's article is about orienteering and mentions compasses. Paraphrase each text, stating the main ideas and the evidence supporting them. How does each article help you understand the other? Which one do you recommend reading first? Why?

Differentiated Instruction

Visual Learning

Display a topographic and relief map of a region that has mountains and water features. Have students compare and contrast how the maps display slope of mountains and location of water features. Ask students why orienteering uses topographical maps rather than relief maps.

Enrichment

Interested students may wish to organize an orienteering course and plan an orienteering event. Encourage students to write press releases for the event and post them around their school to spur greater interest and participation.

Analyze Literature

Author's Purpose Authors write for many different purposes, including to inform, entertain, and persuade. Sometimes writers write for more than one purpose. List details from "How to Use a Compass" that seem to be clues to the author's purpose. Then write what you believe the author's purpose to be in your own words.

Detail	Purpose
"this tutorial"	

Extend Understanding

Writing Options

Creative Writing The Rockies, a mountaineering club, is trying to attract new members. They are planning a hike in one month. You have been given the task of writing an **advertisement** for the trip that will generate excitement and increase enrollment in the club. First decide to write a radio, newspaper, or Internet ad. Use what you learned from the article to discuss the safety of hiking with experienced wilderness guides.

Persuasive Writing When navigating a new city, it is important to have tools such as a map or compass. Choose one tool you might like to have if you were exploring a new city. Write a **persuasive paragraph** explaining your reasons and how this tool would help you in an unfamiliar place. Share your paragraph with classmates.

Collaborative Learning

Interview an Expert In small groups, make a plan to learn more about orienteering meets near you. Working together, brainstorm a list of questions. Then, ask a physical education or science teacher in your school for help finding an orienteering expert. Conduct an interview and share your findings with your class.

Critical Literacy

Give and Follow Directions Work with a partner to follow the directions described in "How to Read a Compass." Take turns reading the directions out loud while the other person follows them. As you work through the directions, discuss any questions the arise regarding content, new vocabulary, or new expressions. Seek help from your teacher as needed.

 Go to www.mirrorsandwindows.com for more.

Analyze Literature

Author's Purpose *Answer:* Students should fill in a chart such as this, using their own language to provide details leading to the conclusion that Kjernsmo writes to teach, or inform.

Detail	Purpose
"this tutorial"	instruction
"thing you need to learn"	instruction
"what you do . . ."	instruction

Rubrics for Writing Options

You can adapt this as a checklist for students to use as they write.

Creative Writing

☐ Does it effectively promote The Rockies and the upcoming hike?

☐ Does it use information from the articles to discuss the safety of hiking with The Rockies' experienced wilderness guides?

Persuasive Writing

☐ Does the paragraph focus on one navigational tool?

☐ Does it argue for the tool's navigational effectiveness?

☐ Does it contain support for its argument?

Preview the Selection

At a Glance
Directed Reading
- Reading Level: Easy
- Difficulty Considerations: Subject matter, vocabulary
- Ease Factors: Topic, visual appeal

Objectives
Studying this lesson will enable students to
- use reading strategies such as activating prior knowledge
- explain *author's purpose* and use details from the selection to identify its purpose
- draw conclusions about why archaeologist David West Reynolds became an expert on *Star Wars*
- appreciate a story about expanding perspectives to include other worlds and future time periods

Launch the Lesson
Ask students what science fiction books they have read and/or movies they have seen. What do they like/ dislike about them? Which characters are their most and least favorite? Have students explain their answers.

Obi-Wan Kenobi: Jedi Knight
from Star Wars Episode 1: The Visual Dictionary

A Visual Dictionary by Dr. David West Reynolds

BEFORE READING

Build Background
Cultural Context The first *Star Wars* movie came out in 1977. Written and directed by George Lucas, it broke all box-office records and won seven Academy Awards. *Star Wars Episode 1: The Phantom Menace* was released in 1999. These films have had a major impact on the way science fiction is perceived by Hollywood and the filmgoing public.

Reader's Context Science fiction books and movies typically deal with other worlds, other galaxies, or the distant future. What aspects of the genre do you find most interesting?

Set Purpose
Skim the text, images, labels, and captions to preview "Obi-Wan Kenobi: Jedi Knight." Based on your preview, what do you think you will learn about Jedi Knights?

Analyze Literature
Visual Media Pictorial or other graphic forms of communication are **visual media.** There is a wide variety of visual media, including photographs, illustrations, charts, graphs, diagrams, and maps. A **visual dictionary** is a dictionary with pictorial entries. Descriptive captions and labels explain the visual item in writing. As you read, be aware of how information is presented both visually and with text.

Meet the Author
Dr. David West Reynolds is an archaeologist who has been on field expeditions and has authored several scientific archaeological publications. The world of *Star Wars* interests Reynolds as it is "a culture from another time and place to explore" in a world not entirely different from the worlds of ancient Rome or Egypt, which he has studied as an archaeologist. Dr. Reynolds lives in Marin County, California.

440 UNIT 4 NONFICTION

Use Reading Skills
Activate Prior Knowledge Prior knowledge is what a reader knows about a given topic, gathered from reading and from personal experience. Connect prior knowledge to a new text to help comprehend the text. Connect what you already know about the Jedi Knights and *Star Wars* and what you want to know by filling in the first two columns before you read the selection. Fill in the last column after you read the selection.

What I Know
Jedi Knights are characters in the *Star Wars* movies.

What I Want to Learn

What I Have Learned

Common Core State Standards

Reading Informational
RI.1, RL.3

Writing
W.9

Language
L.6

Words in Use

Selection Words	Teaching Words
apprentice, 442	box-office, 440
transgressions, 442	perceived, 440
overtones, 442	archaeologist, 440
modulator, 442	mythologies, 444
formidable, 443	psychological, 444
	underpinnings, 444
	prop, 445
	engineered, 445
	perspective, 447

KEY TERMS
DICTIONARY, 440
GENRE, 440
VISUAL MEDIA, 440
VISUAL DICTIONARY, 440
MYTHOLOGY, 444
PLOT, 444
SETTING, 444
FAIRY TALE, 444
STORYTELLING, 444

Obi-Wan Kenobi:
Jedi Knight

from Star Wars Episode 1:
The Visual Dictionary

A Visual Dictionary by Dr. David West Reynolds

441

Summary

The selection is part of a visual dictionary that provides background about characters and unique objects associated with the movie *Star Wars Episode 1: The Phantom Menace.* This excerpt describes the personality and character of Obi-Wan Kenobi, a Jedi Knight. Articles of clothing and equipment are explained and described in pictures with labels and captions.

 The Mirrors & Windows questions at the end of this selection focus on the theme of creating a character. Before reading, ask students what would be some traits and actions of their ideal science fiction character. Why do *Star Wars* characters still resonate with audiences?

► More by This Author

Students who like "Obi-Wan Kenobi: Jedi Knight" might enjoy reading other *Star Wars Visual Dictionaries* by the same author such as *Incredible Cross-Sections of Star Wars* and *Episodes IV, V & VI: The Ultimate Guide to Star Wars Vehicles and Spacecraft.*

Program Resources

Planning and Assessment
Program Planning Guide, Selection Lesson Plan
E-Lesson Planner
Assessment Guide, Lesson Test
ExamView

Technology Tools
Interactive Student Text on CD
Visual Teaching Package
Audio Library
mirrorsandwindows.com

Meeting the Standards
Nonfiction: Unit 4, Directed Reading, pp. 49–54

Use Reading Skills
Activate Prior Knowledge As students read the description of Obi-Wan, have them think about people in their own lives who have similar characteristics. Discuss their ideas. **Ⓐ**

Cultural Connection
Myth *Star Wars* has been referred to as a modern myth. A myth is a story that explains the worldview of a culture. Myths resonate with people because they reflect deeply held beliefs about our purpose and what people are capable of achieving. The most enduring myths employ archetypes—plots or character elements that recur in cultural or cross-cultural myths. In the original *Star Wars* trilogy, Luke Skywalker is transformed in the archetype of the hero's journey, which begins with separation from a life of drudgery and a quest for a higher calling. Mentors or father-figures, such as Yoda and Obi-Wan, guide the fledgling hero through a series of trials to test whether he has what it takes to achieve the task. Once the hero has proven himself, he must endure a series of trials that help him evolve to his full potential.

Obi-Wan Kenobi
JEDI KNIGHT

Ⓐ OBI-WAN KENOBI has followed a responsible path on his journey toward Jedi knighthood as the Padawan apprentice to Jedi Master Qui-Gon Jinn. Strongly influenced by other leading Jedi as well as by Qui-Gon, Obi-Wan is more brooding and cautious than his teacher. He is careful to weigh the consequences of his actions and is reluctant to entangle himself unnecessarily in transgressions against the will of the Jedi High Council. A serious, quiet man possessed of a dry sense of humor, Obi-Wan strives to be worthy of his order and feels honored to be Qui-Gon's student, although he worries about his Master's tendency to take risks in defiance of the Council. Nevertheless, Obi-Wan follows Qui-Gon Jinn's example and develops an independent spirit of his own.

Short hair
Padawan apprentice
Apprentice's long braid
Tunic
Hooded

UTILITY BELT   *Belt fastener*   *Fastener band*   *Utility belt*

Traditional leather   *Food and tool pouches*

UTILITY POUCHES
On field missions, Jedi carry a basic kit consisting of food capsules, medical supplies, multitools, and other essential devices.

BREATHER POUCH

FOOD AND ENERGY CAPSULES

Jedi Gear
The basic Jedi clothing of belted tunic, travel boots, and robe speaks of the simplicity vested in Jedi philosophy and carries overtones of their mission as travelers. Individual Jedi keep utility belt field gear to a minimum. As initiates are taught in the great Temple, Jedi reputations are based on their spirits and not on material trappings.

A99 Aquata Breather
In this era, Jedi Knights usually carry various high-tech devices concealed in their robes or in belt pouches. On their mission to Naboo, Obi-Wan and Qui-Gon Jinn carry A99 Aquata breathers, knowing that much of the planet's surface is water. Breathers allow the Jedi to survive underwater for up to two hours. In other times, Jedi have avoided such technological devices in order to minimize their dependence on anything but their own resourcefulness.

Rugged travel boots
Regulator
Hinges for storage
Mouthpiece   *Compressed air tanks*

442   **UNIT 4** NONFICTION

Differentiated Instruction

English Language Learners
Have students skim the text and identify unfamiliar terms such as *brooding, transgressions, modulators,* and *unobtrusive.* Help students use context clues to determine meaning. For example, have students use the context of the sentences following the description of Obi-Wan as *brooding* to draw conclusions about the word's meaning.

Kinesthetic Learning
Invite interested students to act out Obi-Wan's positions shown on the pages. Tell students to begin with the stance on the left and then draw their lightsaber as they shift into battle stance. Have students describe how it feels to have "centered awareness" and explain why Obi-Wan holds the lightsaber in two hands instead of one.

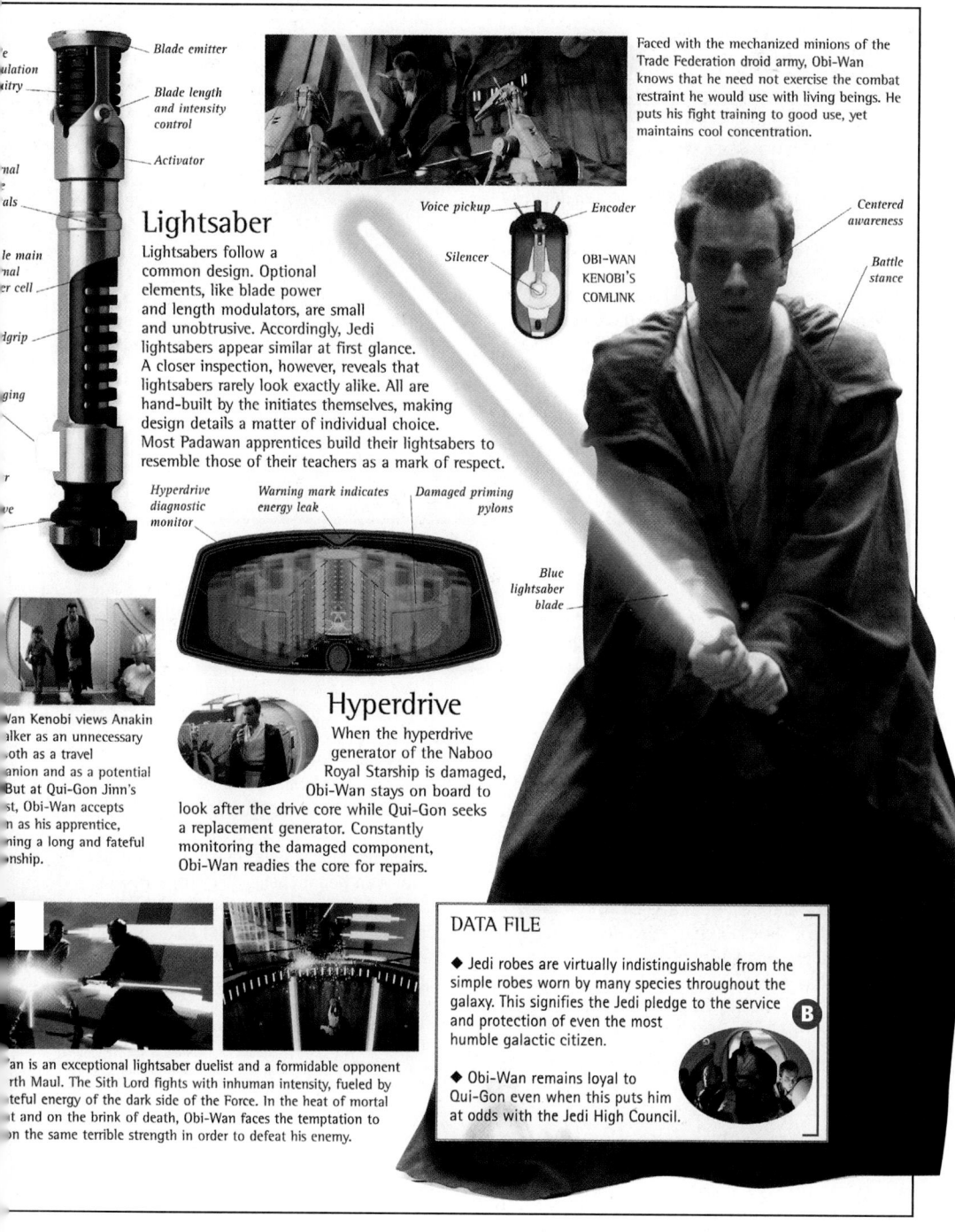

Blade emitter

Blade length and intensity control

Activator

Faced with the mechanized minions of the Trade Federation droid army, Obi-Wan knows that he need not exercise the combat restraint he would use with living beings. He puts his fight training to good use, yet maintains cool concentration.

Voice pickup

Silencer

Encoder

Centered awareness

Battle stance

OBI-WAN KENOBI'S COMLINK

Lightsaber

Lightsabers follow a common design. Optional elements, like blade power and length modulators, are small and unobtrusive. Accordingly, Jedi lightsabers appear similar at first glance. A closer inspection, however, reveals that lightsabers rarely look exactly alike. All are hand-built by the initiates themselves, making design details a matter of individual choice. Most Padawan apprentices build their lightsabers to resemble those of their teachers as a mark of respect.

Hyperdrive diagnostic monitor

Warning mark indicates energy leak

Damaged priming pylons

Blue lightsaber blade

Hyperdrive

When the hyperdrive generator of the Naboo Royal Starship is damaged, Obi-Wan stays on board to look after the drive core while Qui-Gon seeks a replacement generator. Constantly monitoring the damaged component, Obi-Wan readies the core for repairs.

...Wan Kenobi views Anakin ...lker as an unnecessary ...oth as a travel ...anion and as a potential ...But at Qui-Gon Jinn's ...st, Obi-Wan accepts ...n as his apprentice, ...ning a long and fateful ...nship.

...an is an exceptional lightsaber duelist and a formidable opponent ...rth Maul. The Sith Lord fights with inhuman intensity, fueled by ...teful energy of the dark side of the Force. In the heat of mortal ...t and on the brink of death, Obi-Wan faces the temptation to ...n the same terrible strength in order to defeat his enemy.

DATA FILE

◆ Jedi robes are virtually indistinguishable from the simple robes worn by many species throughout the galaxy. This signifies the Jedi pledge to the service and protection of even the most humble galactic citizen.

◆ Obi-Wan remains loyal to Qui-Gon even when this puts him at odds with the Jedi High Council.

B

Use Reading Skills

Draw Conclusions Have each student write a question that requires a conclusion such as "Why is Obi-Wan's lightsaber blue, while the Sith Lord's is red?" Tell students to exchange questions and answer the question they receive.

Analyze Literature

Identify Author's Purpose Review the possible purposes for writing such as to inform, persuade, entertain, enlighten, or share a point of view. Ask students which of these purposes is achieved by the author's use of features such as verbal descriptions and explanations, pictures, labels, captions, and "facts" in the Data File. **B**

Make Connections

Invite students to think about a character they might create for a science fiction story. Have them describe the philosophy and code of conduct of their character and how they would reflect these traits in the character's personality and behavior.

TEACHING NOTE

Read Aloud

Some students might benefit from working with a partner as they read the selection aloud. Remind them to adjust their reading fluency rate based on the nature of the text and their purpose for reading. Also encourage them to ask each other questions if they don't understand part of the reading.

Media Literacy Skills

Visual Dictionary

Have students create their own visual dictionary. Invite students to choose a topic related to the theme of this unit. Possible topics include asteroids, geologic time, American Indians, mushrooms, orienteering, jaguars, and science fiction. Tell students to compose ten to fifteen entries related to the topic they will explain. Students should research the definitions and then draw or locate pictures to accompany the definitions. Encourage students to use features similar to the selection in their visual dictionary such as explanatory paragraphs, captions, labeled diagrams, and brief facts.

Cultural Connection
***Star Wars* and Mythology** *Answer:* Elements of *Star Wars* might remind students of the legend of King Arthur, biblical stories, or the mythological Oedipus. **A**

MIRRORS & WINDOWS *Answer:* Responses will vary.

Find Meaning

1. (a) Obi-Wan is Qui-Gon's apprentice. (b) Obi-Wan is more brooding and cautious.

2. (a) Jedi clothing includes a belted tunic, travel boots, and robe. (b) The basic kit includes food capsules, medical supplies, and multitools. (c) The clothing reflects the simplicity of Jedi philosophy. The purpose is to survive with as little as possible.

3. (a) Obi-Wan carries an Aquata breather and a lightsaber. (b) The Aquata breather allows Jedis to survive underwater. The lightsaber is for battle and protection. (c) Their spirits, rather than their devices, build their reputations.

Make Judgments

4. Jedi are respectful, minimalist, resourceful, well-trained, and caring.

5. (a) Lucas has given Obi-Wan rounded character traits such as a brooding and cautious nature. (b) Although some of his physical feats are unlikely, they could be attributed to a human who has discipline and practiced skills.

CULTURAL ▶▶ CONNECTION

***Star Wars* and Mythology** George Lucas had many inspirations for his *Star Wars* series. One of these was *The Hero with a Thousand Faces*, a book by anthropologist Joseph Campbell. In this book, Campbell traces the common patterns in the stories of the hero's journey in many mythologies from around the world. According to Lucas, "There was no modern mythology to give kids a sense of values, to give them a strong mythological fantasy life. Westerns were the last of that genre for Americans. Nothing was being done for young people with real psychological underpinnings." In what ways do the plots, settings, or characters from the *Star Wars* movies remind you of classical mythology, fairy tales, or other kinds of traditional storytelling? **A**

MIRRORS & WINDOWS If you were going to create a character for a science fiction movie, what would that character be like? How would the character act? Why do you think the characters from *Star Wars* movies are so popular?

Find Meaning

1. (a) What is Obi-Wan Kenobi's relationship to Jedi Master Qui-Gon Jinn? (b) What personality traits does Obi-Wan have that make him different from Qui-Gon?

2. (a) What is the basic Jedi clothing? (b) What basic kit and gear does a Jedi carry? (c) How does Jedi basic clothing reflect Jedi philosophy and lifestyle?

3. (a) What high-tech devices does Obi-Wan carry with him? (b) What is the purpose of each of these devices? (c) Why have Jedi sometimes avoided using technological devices?

Make Judgments

4. Based on the information provided in the selection, write a list of the principles of Jedi philosophy and code of conduct.

5. (a) In your opinion, what makes the character of Obi-Wan Kenobi believable? (b) Based on the information you are given about his personality and skills, which of his characteristics resemble those of a real human being? Explain.

444 UNIT 4 NONFICTION

Writing Skills

Movie Review

After reviewing the following features of a movie review, have students write a review about a *Star Wars* film or other science fiction movie they've seen.

The introduction includes the title, the director and/or stars, and the reviewer's opinion. The body includes a brief summary of the movie; details about character, setting, and plot; and examples from the movie that support the reviewer's opinion.

The conclusion sums up the reviewer's main points and leaves the reader with a memorable impression of the movie.

For his work on this visual dictionary, Dr. David West Reynolds spent several weeks at the headquarters of Lucas films, Skywalker Ranch. There he talked with prop makers, special effects technicians, and scriptwriters who worked on the *Star Wars* movies. Dr. Reynolds became an expert on *Star Wars*. In addition to various books on *Star Wars*, Dr. David West Reynolds also wrote the following article for www.starwars.com. The article tells the history of Industrial Light & Magic, the company that engineered special effects on the *Star Wars* series. As you read the article, think about how special effects might have been used to make the Jedi, their devices, and their actions seem more real.

Industrial Light & Magic, Part 1: History

An Internet Article by Dr. David West Reynolds

Founded by George Lucas in 1975 to create the special effects for *Star Wars*, Industrial Light & Magic quickly became internationally renowned for the quality and originality of its work. The history of ILM had yet to be written, but the small group of creative minds that had successfully transported excited audiences to the far reaches of space and back knew that they were standing at a turning point in the development of movie special effects. They were heirs to a long, proud tradition, and were building an important legacy for the generations to come.

Legend has it that the very first special effect was discovered completely by accident **A** at the end of the 19th century. While French filmmaker Georges Méliès was shooting a street scene, his camera jammed for a few seconds before resuming its operation. Upon reviewing the footage, Méliès saw that since the street traffic had kept moving during the camera jam, the result on screen was the remarkable transformation of a man into a woman, and a bus into a hearse. Movie special effects were born. Recognizing the tremendous potential of these "camera tricks," Méliès never ceased to experiment with them and develop inventive techniques to bring the impossible to the silver screen.

Three quarters of a century later, George Lucas set out to bring to life his space-opera vision of a group of righteous rebels fighting the evil Galactic Empire. When it came time to tackle the extensive special effects essential to the story the young filmmaker wanted to tell, Lucas looked around for special effects workshops—only to discover that they didn't exist anymore. During the previous fifteen years, special effects had almost completely disappeared from cinema, with a few exceptions such as Stanley Kubrick's *2001: A Space Odyssey*. Thus no studio was equipped to produce the seemingly impossible visuals required for *Star Wars*, let alone handle the overwhelming number of effects required to sustain Lucas' wild imagination. So Lucas did the only thing he could do: build his own special effects house from scratch. John Dykstra, a young

---

Text-to-Text Connection

Answer: Responses will vary. Most students will probably agree that the goal was accomplished. The Jedi have working lasers; fantastic starships that seem real; devices, such as the Aquata breather, that appear real when used in the movie. Students may say that special effects make an unreal world feel real and allow the viewer to experience things they would never see in real life.

Use Reading Skills

Activate Prior Knowledge Invite students to describe movie or television special effects that they have particularly enjoyed such as computer-generated characters (Jar Jar Binks in *Star Wars* and Gollum in *Lord of the Rings*). Discuss problems in making such characters seem real. **A**

Make Connections

Ask students why they think George Lucas called his company "Industrial Light & Magic." **B**

---

designer who had experimented with cameras controlled by a computer, was hired to put together the original ILM team, located in the San Fernando Valley, California, just north of Hollywood.

Lucas' vision for *Star Wars* included a large array of visuals that had never been attempted before, forcing the small group of wizards at ILM not only to refine existing special effects techniques, but also to create new ones. Starting with tricks taken right out of Méliès' repertoire,[1] ILM perfected traditional tools like model construction, photography using matte paintings and blue screens,[2] and optical compositing,[3] and then went on to invent and develop brand-new techniques such as motion control cameras (where the camera movements are controlled by a computer). Once work on *Star Wars* was completed, everybody expected ILM to be dissolved, joining in oblivion the "camera tricks" workshops of the past. But the unexpected success of *Star Wars* allowed Lucas to start work on *The Empire Strikes Back*, which, in turn, ensured the survival of the group of movie magicians who had made it all possible. In order to have his film editing and special effects facilities closer together, Industrial Light & Magic was relocated to San Rafael, in northern California. That was in 1978.

Since then, ILM has thrived. Far from being disbanded, the ever-growing team has continued to push the envelope and pioneer new ways to bring effects no one dared imagine within the reach of filmmakers. Even before completing the *Star Wars* Trilogy, ILM was handed other projects:

Raiders of the Lost Ark, Star Trek II: The Wrath of Khan, and *E.T.: The Extra-Terrestrial,* among others. Consistently breaking new ground, ILM has led the digital revolution that brought computer imaging into feature films. From the famous "morphing" effect in *Willow* to the revolutionary, lifelike dinosaurs in *Jurassic Park,* the creative minds gathered in the San Rafael installations have never ceased to up the ante. To date, the company's innovative work has garnered 14 Academy Awards for Best Visual Effects and 14 Technical Achievement Awards. With *Star Wars Episode I: The Phantom Menace,* ILM went full circle and returned to the world that gave it birth, in a galaxy far, far away. And once again, the movie wizards broke through the barriers of conventional wisdom by creating the first completely computer-generated main characters, and by perfecting digital effects traditionally very difficult to master, such as cloth simulation, terrain generation (earth, grass, and so on).

At the dawn of a new millennium, ILM stands ready to conquer new digital realms and to continue pushing back the limits of an art that was born almost at the same time as cinema itself. From Georges Méliès (who was a magician before he became a filmmaker) to Industrial Light & Magic (whose original logo depicted a magician superimposed on a gear) the tradition of special effects has undergone quite an evolution. But its main goal remains the same: to surprise, to amaze, to make the impossible, quite simply, come true. ❖

1. **repertoire.** Routine
2. **blue screens.** Blank screens actors stand in front of; special effects are added to screens in editing
3. **optical compositing.** Film technique in which several different shots are merged into one

In the article, Dr. Reynolds says that the goal of Industrial Light & Magic is "...to make the impossible, quite simply, come true." Given what you learned in the visual dictionary entry, would you say that goal was accomplished? How do special effects add to the moviegoer's experience? Support your response with textual evidence.

Writing Skills

Clichés

Tell students that a cliché is an overused expressed such as "cute as a button." Most clichés begin as vivid, colorful examples of figurative language but become uninteresting because of overuse.

Have students locate examples of clichés in the Informational Text Connection. (Possible responses include "push the envelope," "up the ante," "breaking new ground," and "went full circle.")

Challenge students to reword these figures of speech. When they are finished, have students read aloud the original sentence and then read it again with their new wording.

AFTER READING

Analyze Literature

Visual Media Captions explain a visual item in writing. Labels—simple headings or titles with a graphic that give names to different parts—also assist readers in reading and understanding the graphic. Create a list of the information given in the captions, labels, and photographs of the visual dictionary entry. How do these details affect your understanding of the images?

Dictionary Entry	Details	Effect
Obi-Wan Kenobi	Apprentice's long braid	Hair signifies character's status

Extend Understanding

Writing Options

Creative Writing Write a **visual dictionary entry** for an imaginary tool or device that has not yet been invented. Draw a diagram of the tool, and then use captions and labels to point out and name each of its parts. Include a paragraph describing what the device does. Share your entry with the class.

Persuasive Writing Science fiction is imaginative storytelling based on scientific principles, discoveries, or laws. Often science fiction deals with the future, the distant past, or with worlds other than our own. Write a **movie review** about a *Star Wars* film or another science fiction film you have seen. Be sure to include the full title of the movie and a summary of the plot and characters. Give your opinion of the movie, and make sure to support it with details. Share your review with the class.

Collaborative Learning

Discuss Science Fiction In small groups, discuss how science fiction can help shed light on real life problems, situations, and even on history. Give examples of science fiction that you think accomplish this. As you discuss, consider these questions: What is the theme of the story? In what ways does this story offer a unique perspective on real life?

Media Literacy

Compare Movies George Lucas had many influences in the creation of *Star Wars.* One of these influences was Japanese filmmaker Akira Kurosawa and his film *The Seven Samurai.* If possible, locate and watch *The Seven Samurai.* Then watch or re-watch the original *Star Wars* film. What elements do these movies share? In what ways are they different? Write a brief compare-and-contrast essay about these two films.

Go to **www.mirrorsandwindows.com** for more.

Review the Selection

Analyze Literature

Visual Media *Answer:* Students should complete a chart by filling in other details about Obi-Wan and his equipment from the selection. Examples might include the *lightsaber*, whose details show the weapon's complexity, or *Jedi gear,* whose utility belt details affect one's understanding of its simplicity.

Rubrics for Writing Options

You can adapt this as a checklist for students to use as they write.

Creative Writing

- ☐ Does the diagram show what the item is?
- ☐ Do labels and captions name each of its parts?
- ☐ Does the entry explain what the device does?
- ☐ Is the device original?

Persuasive Writing

- ☐ Is it clear what film is being reviewed?
- ☐ Is the student's opinion clearly stated?
- ☐ Is the student's opinion backed up by details?
- ☐ Is the grammar, punctuation, and spelling correct?
- ☐ Did the student clearly communicate his or her position when presenting the review?

OBI-WAN KENOBI: JEDI KNIGHT 447

448

Preview the Selection

At a Glance
Independent Reading
- Reading Level: Moderate
- Difficulty Consideration: Setting
- Ease Factor: Compelling plot

Objectives
Reading this selection will enable students to do the following:
- define *anecdote* and *external conflict* and provide examples of each from the selection
- briefly explain Alan Rabinowitz's reasons for his trip to Belize in 1983
- read silently with comprehension for a sustained period of time
- recognize the importance of expanding the horizons of our understanding of nature and other cultures

Launch the Lesson
Have students think about animals they have seen in a natural setting, such as the woods or a naturalized zoo. Which animals do they most like to watch? Which animals do they not like? Invite students to explain why they prefer some animals over others. Discuss the importance of the preservation of certain animals for the survival of all animals in their ecological niche.

TEACHING NOTE

Although this selection is presented in the student edition as an independent reading, teaching support has been provided should you choose to cover it in class.

Growling Jaguar, 2000. John Bunker.

from CHAC

An Essay by Alan Rabinowitz

Dr. Alan Rabinowitz (b. 1953) has traveled extensively over the last two decades, concentrating his research efforts in Belize, Borneo, Taiwan, Thailand, Laos, and Myanmar (Burma). He has studied jaguars, leopards, tigers, and other large mammal species. Dr. Rabinowitz has made many exciting discoveries, including the leaf deer in Myanmar, currently the smallest, most primitive deer in the world. He also made contact with the Taron, a group of Burmese pygmies who are near extinction and virtually unknown by the outside world. Dr. Rabinowitz currently oversees a tiger survey team in Myanmar and has helped initiate a jaguar conservation program which, he hopes, will ensure this magnificent cat's survival.

448

Program Resources

Planning and Assessment
Program Planning Guide, Selection Lesson Plan
E-Lesson Planner
Assessment Guide, Lesson Test
ExamView

Technology Tools
Interactive Student Text on CD
Visual Teaching Package
Audio Library
mirrorsandwindows.com

Meeting the Standards
Nonfiction: Unit 4, Guided Reading, pp. 55–61

Differentiating Instruction
Developing Readers, Make Connections, pp. 31–33

Common Core State Standards

Reading Informational
RI.1, RI.6, RI.10

My problems with the Maya were to take many forms, one of the more serious being their attitude toward the wild cats. One afternoon, when I was trying to get a few hours of sleep, Adriana came over with Agapita and Formenta in tow. At first I ignored them, hoping they'd be gone when I awoke. Just as I began drifting off, Adriana called my name and started talking about a tiger-cat, the local name for the smaller spotted cats. Now I listened, though I still feigned[1] sleep.

"Our dog chase tiger-cat up de tree near de house," she repeated.

I jumped out of bed. "Where is it?" I asked, starting to gather my equipment.

"Ignacio shoot it. It dead; we got skin. You want see it?"

I thought this must be another joke. Her face said it wasn't. I ran out of the house to find Ignacio.

Their hut was apart from the main body of the Indian village. It stood at the edge of the forest about a hundred yards west of the timber camp. While I slept, the cat had been treed by a scrawny little Indian dog that it could have killed and eaten as a snack. Ignacio was tacking the skin to the side of their hut when I got there. I recognized it immediately as a male ocelot.[2] When Ignacio saw me, he waved me over to see his prize.

I had brought several small radio collars with me to Belize in case I came across some of the smaller cats. I had told all the Indians that I'd pay them if in any way they helped me catch a cat alive: Bze$100 for a small cat and Bze$400 for a jaguar. It was much more than they could have sold the skins for.

"Ignacio, why'd you kill that cat?" I asked.

"My dog, he tree it, so I kill it."

"Ignacio, don't you remember I said I'd pay you a lot of money if you help me catch a cat like this?"

"Yes."

"Why didn't you come tell me?" I was starting to get frustrated.

"My dog, he tree it, you sleep. I no want wake you, so I shoot it. It no kill my chickens now."

"Was it killing your chickens?"

"No, but it want kill chicken. Tiger-cat always want kill chicken. It look pretty hanging in house, no?"

"Didn't you want a hundred dollars?"

"Yes, dat nice," he replied.

"Why didn't you come get me, wake me up?" Now I was shouting.

"The cat in de tree, it near de house, it pretty. I shoot it."

That was the end of our conversation. My anger quickly dissipated and in its place there was only frustration. Would any of my work ever mean anything? Could attitudes change before it was too late?

> I thought this must be another joke. Her face said it wasn't.

---

1. **feigned.** Pretended
2. **ocelot.** Medium-sized American wildcat with a golden or gray coat and black dots and stripes

Summary

"Chac" relates Alan Rabinowitz's attempt to study and protect the jaguars of Belize. He describes his frustration with the local people who regularly kill the jungle cats. Rabinowitz traps and drugs a large jaguar, who he names *Chac*. After measuring the animal, he attaches a radio collar so that he can follow the jaguar's movements.

The Mirrors & Windows questions at the end of this selection focus on the theme of respect for animals. Before reading, ask students if the animals they like match those that their cultures value. Are there any animals that their cultures dislike?

▶ More by This Author

Students who like "Chac" by Alan Rabinowitz might enjoy reading more about his efforts to save the jaguar in Belize in *Jaguar: One Man's Struggle to Establish the World's First Jaguar Preserve.*

Words in Use

Selection Words
scrawny, 449
dissipated, 449
elongated, 450
caressed, 450
recollection, 450
involuntarily, 450
intermittently, 451

Teaching Words
extensively, 448
extinction, 448
conservation, 448

KEY TERMS
ESSAY, 448
VISUAL AID, 455

Make Connections

Direct students' attention to the sentence, "They feared these cats, yet no one to their recollection had ever been hurt by them." Invite students to think about something they may fear without apparent reason or because it is something their culture sees as frightening. Have students describe their fears and discuss their reasons. **A**

Use Reading Strategies

Ask Questions Point out that asking questions as they read helps students develop a better understanding of the subject by thinking more deeply about it. For example, they might ask: "How did the Indians figure out how to make jaguar callers? Why did the man spend so much time calling jaguars to his little shack?" **B**

Analyze Literature

Point of View Explain that an author may directly or indirectly state his or her point of view about a topic. Model identifying clues that reflect the author's point of view, such as ". . . he saw little difference between live and dead beauty." Have students locate other clues to the author's point of view and list them on the board. **C**

I rubbed my hand through the black-spotted white fur of the ocelot, then pulled the measuring tape from my pocket. The total length of the skin was fifty inches, including the tail, which measured fifteen inches. The elongated spots almost gave the appearance of black lines in the fur. Ignacio watched me as I caressed it. He walked over, took the skin down, and handed it to me.

"You like, you take," he said, thinking it would please me. I took it, knowing it was offered as an act of friendship. He had not killed the animal to sell or keep the skin. He killed it because it was pretty and he saw little difference between live and dead beauty.

During my initial jaguar survey I had been told that I wouldn't find jaguars around Maya villages. A Creole[3] snake doctor had said that the Maya "do something" around their villages to keep cats away. Now I realized that that "something" was not magic. It was killing any cat that came near. **A** They feared these cats, yet no one to their recollection had ever been hurt by them. I learned that some Indians collected the jaguar's fat, which they would then either melt down and spread or burn in the milpa[4] to keep other pest species away from the corn.

B People serious about killing jaguars had little trouble given the cat's curiosity. I met a man south of Cockscomb, Irenayo Chinchia, who claimed to have killed over one hundred jaguars by calling them in. In his little shack he showed me a strange-looking instrument that looked like a drum. It was made from a large calabash,[5] one end of which was covered by deerskin. A piece of banana peel hardened by beeswax hung inside the gourd,

one end knotted through the deerskin. It was a jaguar caller, he told me, and could be "played" by gently rubbing two fingers down the banana peel. I had heard of such callers when I first came to Belize. It was said that an expert could simulate the calls of either sex and thus attract either males or females.

He showed me the technique and I tensed involuntarily. It was the deep, guttural[6] grunting of a jaguar. It sounded as if one were in the room with us. He played it for several minutes, subtly changing the tonal[7] qualities and the rate with which the **C** sounds were made. It was too easy, I thought. I wondered if the cats had a chance.

The proper technique is important in using jaguar callers, but often a cat may come in simply out of curiosity upon hearing the sound. One man claimed to have called in and shot a jaguar by putting a bucket over his head and grunting. I was also to see callers made of plastic milk jugs and cardboard boxes. Whatever was used, it was always advisable to stay up in a tree when calling, I was told. Often, hunters said, a male jaguar will come in very angry thinking another male is in his area.

The hunting of jaguars in this fashion is well documented throughout their entire range. Such a hunt, the experience of a man who lived among the Indians of the upper Amazon in Peru, is vividly described in Bruce Lamb's *Wizard of the Upper Amazon* (1971). In that case the jaguar caller was in the form of a small earthenware[8] jug.

3. **Creole.** Person of European descent born in the West Indies or Central or South America
4. **milpa.** Small, temporary field
5. **calabash.** Type of gourd
6. **guttural.** Made in the throat
7. **tonal.** Relating to musical pitch
8. **earthenware.** Clay

Differentiated Instruction

Visual/Auditory/Kinesthetic Learning

Encourage interested students to act out the scene between Ignacio and the author. Students can work with a partner to decide how they will portray the characters and how they will use their voices and bodies to portray emotions. Have three sets of partners join in a group and take turns presenting their skit. After all three teams have finished, the group can compare and contrast the presentations and decide which team best represented the scene.

It was necessary for the caller to get above the forest canopy if his calls were to reach any distance. Soon a wavering, wailing call of a wild cat floated out over the forest from our treetop caller with his jug. This weird sound made one's spine tingle and stopped every other sound for some minutes. The call was repeated intermittently for an hour or more, and as time passed the tension built up in our bodies as we perched in the low trees.

Suddenly from nowhere a tremendous spotted animal was in an open spot just below us, looking up into the trees and growling. Almost in unison the bowstrings twanged from different directions.

The week after we set the trap, Cirillo didn't want to work, so I checked the trap myself every morning. I carried a cup of black coffee in one hand, while with the other I tried to negotiate the ravines.[9] It was several days before I was able to drink more coffee than I spilled on myself.

During the first four days, no jaguars came near the trap. I started to worry. On the fifth day I pulled up in front of the trap as usual, and looked out the passenger window to check on the pig. I found myself staring once again into the eyes of a jaguar.

It had rained hard during the night and the cat was covered with mud. When he saw me, he roared and lunged at the door of the trap, paws against the bars, claws extended.

Mud splashed through the open window and into my face as I fell back against the steering wheel.

The trap works! was my first thought as I threw the truck into reverse and backed quickly out of sight of the jaguar. I raced back to camp to get the drugging equipment and to find Cirillo. "It works!" I yelled out loud. "The project will work!"

I sent a passing Indian boy to get Cirillo while I loaded the truck. He returned to tell me that Cirillo had gone off to his milpa. I'd have to work with the jaguar alone. I was frightened and excited. Within thirty minutes I was back at the trap. It was 6 AM. I parked about fifty feet away, around a bend in the road. I got out of the truck and grabbed my three-foot-long jab pole with a syringe attached to one end. Ideally, all I had to do was walk up to the trap and inject the cat.

I walked through the forest to within twelve feet of the trap, then got on my hands and knees and started to crawl the rest of the distance. The jaguar, a large male, was not so easily fooled, and I saw two eyes peering at me through the cohune leaves as I reached the side of the trap. I was sweating profusely and took several deep breaths to calm myself while looking at the angry eyes peeking through the leaves.

Suddenly from nowhere a tremendous spotted animal was in an open spot just below us, looking up into the trees and growling.

---

9. **ravines.** Small, narrow, steep-sided valleys

Teach the Selection

Science Connection

Rain Forest Canopy The rain forest canopy is the thick covering of closely spaced trees and their branches that act as a "ceiling" to the remaining forest. Dense green leaves of the canopy convert sunlight into energy through photosynthesis at a much higher rate than lower parts of the forest, which are shaded by the canopy. Therefore, the canopy contains many more fruits, seeds, flowers, and leaves that attract and support a great diversity of animal life. Scientists estimate that 70-90 percent of life in the rain forest exists in the canopy. The canopy also regulates the exchange of heat, water vapor, and gases between the forest floor and the atmosphere, shielding the lower levels of the forest from harsh sunlight and drying winds. This lets the lower plant layers retain moisture and produces a much more stable environment for animals and plants that thrive on the forest floor. **D**

Analyze Literature

Tone Invite students to describe the author's tone as he writes about trapping the jaguar. Point out clues, such as "The trap works!" and ask students what word they would use to describe the author's feelings at the time. Have students suggest how the writing would differ if the author were angry, bored, or depressed. **E**

Differentiated Instruction

Reading Proficiency

Remind students to use context and footnotes to help them determine the meaning of unfamiliar words. Before reading, have students skim the text and identify unfamiliar words that are not explained in footnotes, such as *treed, gourd,* and *toucan.*
treed—trapped in a tree with no escape, 449. *The treed cat snarled at the dogs.*

gourd—hard-rinded inedible fruits of plants that are often used for bowls or utensils, 450. *She used a hollowed-out gourd to scoop water.*
toucan—tropical bird with bright feathers and a large beak, 455. *The toucan uses its large beak to pluck small fruits and insects from the trees.*

Make Connections

Ask students what would motivate them to approach an animal such as a trapped jaguar alone. What knowledge and abilities would they want to have before attempting it? **A**

Use Reading Skills

Context Clues Review the types of context clues that hint at the meaning of underlined words:

definitions: "The man used melted jaguar fat to protect his milpa, or small farm field."

description: The hunter hung a dried banana peel inside the hollowed-out calabash.

comparison: The sound was guttural, like an elephant clearing its throat.

contrasts: Unlike the steady hum of the jungle, the jaguar's calls were intermittent.

Alexander von Humboldt, a German explorer-naturalist traveling throughout the American tropics in the early nineteenth century, found himself unexpectedly face to face with a jaguar. "No tiger had ever appeared to me so large," he had said. I had similar feelings now.

I judged the jaguar to be about a hundred and twenty pounds, so I loaded the syringe with a gram of Ketaset.[10] I could see his footprints in the trap and knew this was one of the jaguars I'd been following east of the camp. Five inches long and nearly four and a half inches wide, the prints were the largest I'd yet seen in the area.

A I got to my feet and he leaped at the bars as if they weren't there. I jumped back, nearly jabbing myself with the syringe. I looked at the pig and saw that he had turned over the water bucket and had hidden his head underneath it, his rear end facing the jaguar.

As I moved, the jaguar followed, lunging at me constantly. This was an angry jaguar. I needed to jab him in his hindquarters, but he wouldn't allow me to maneuver around him easily. Finally, I grabbed a branch and banged it on the door. As the jaguar swerved toward the noise, I pushed the syringe through the bars and injected him in the rump.

Within five minutes he was asleep and I pulled him out of the trap. His nose was scraped and bleeding from banging into the bars. I opened his mouth to examine his dentition,[11] and his tongue licked my hand.

---

10. **Ketaset.** Sedative
11. **dentition.** Development or characteristics of a set of teeth
12. **papillae.** Small nubs on the surface of the tongue
13. **canines.** Cone-shaped pointed teeth

It felt like someone was rubbing sandpaper against my skin. The upper surface of a cat's tongue has sharpened papillae,[12] directed toward the back and used for cleaning the fur or removing remnants of flesh from bones. The jaguar's teeth were cream-colored and the tips of the canines[13] were just barely flattened, characteristics of a mature adult. The canines in these cats serve to hold and often kill larger prey by crushing their bones. Another more sharpened pair of teeth toward the rear of the mouth, called the carnassial teeth, are adapted for cutting into the meat.

Mayan sculpture.

Differentiated Instruction

Enrichment

Some students may wish to find out more about how people who study wild animals safely trap and handle the animals. Encourage students to research the methods these people use to humanely drug, measure, and treat large wild animals. Point out that some veterinarians have to treat sick or injured animals that are much larger or stronger than humans or that could be dangerous. Students can share what they learn with the class.

These teeth are the reason cats often turn their heads sideways when feeding.

I took his measurements:

Sex—male
Age—mature adult
Total length—72 inches
Tail length—21 inches
Head circumference[14]—22 inches
Height to shoulder—23 inches
Height to hip—22 inches
Weight—110 pounds

Although he appeared in excellent condition, there were numerous breathing holes of botfly larvae[15] in his coat. I squeezed several out, each of them one and a half inches long, and dropped them in alcohol.

The hardest part of working on the cat alone was trying to weigh him. I fashioned a harness around his chest and attached it to a scale tied to a long pole. Jamming one end of the pole between the top bars of the trap,

I pushed up on the other end until the jaguar barely cleared the ground.

I attached a radio collar around his neck and tested the signal with my receiver. He was still sleeping soundly when I treated the abrasions on his nose with antibiotic[16] and then placed him back in the trap. I tied the door of the trap so that it was slightly ajar, about eighteen inches. I wanted him recovered enough to maneuver out the narrow opening. I packed up the equipment, went over to the side of the road, and sat down on a rock to wait.

I was covered with mud, sweat, and insect bites, which now began to itch. The cat had been walking the road during one of the heaviest rainfalls so far this season when he got trapped. I decided to name him Chac, after the ancient Maya rain god. Chac was a prominent figure in the Maya pantheon,[17] a benevolent[18] deity associated with creation and life. His intervention was sought more frequently by the Maya than that of all the other gods combined.

Chac tried to get to his feet, swayed, and lay back down. It was sad to see an animal like this so vulnerable. I thought of Ah Puch somewhere out in the forest, maybe close by. The sites where Ah Puch and Chac were captured were only a few miles apart. I wondered if the animals were neighbors.

An hour passed and Chac finally crawled out of the trap and started walking down the road. He was unsteady but had recovered

---

14. **circumference.** Distance around something
15. **botfly larvae.** Type of immature insect that burrows into the skin of mammals
16. **antibiotic.** Substance that inhibits or kills a harmful bacteria or fungus
17. **pantheon.** Officially recognized gods of a people
18. **benevolent.** Marked by doing good

Ask Questions What did the author learn after he attached the radio collars to the jaguars? (Possible response: He learned that the jaguars probably slept on the ground rather than in trees.) **A**

Analyze Literature

Setting Invite student to think about the author's purpose in using a lot of sensory language to describe the setting throughout the story. Encourage students to explain how being able to visualize the setting of the story contributes to their understanding of jaguars and the work of scientists who study them. **B**

---

most of his muscle coordination. He was walking toward me, his head down. Remembering his anger, I stood up, wondering how close I should let him come and what I could do anyway if I decided he **A** was too close. My boots scraped the rock and he stopped and looked up at me.

"Hello, Chac," I said nervously, not knowing what else to do. He turned, stumbled, and fell, then stood up and started walking away from me. I followed him down the road, staying about thirty feet behind. I wanted to keep him moving away from camp. I would not have followed so close had he not been partially drugged.

Occasionally he'd stop and look back at me. Once, I watched as he clawed at the dirt, making a scrape that I was later to find was part of a whole system of communication among these cats. Why did he do it then? I later wondered. Finally, he walked to the side of the road, rolled in the grass, and lay quietly, his eyes fuzzy with the drug but watching me as I watched him.

It was the first opportunity I had to observe jaguars make what I'd been calling beds, areas of flattened grass where they apparently rested. I'd been finding beds averaging forty inches in length and twenty-two inches in width along the roadsides where jaguars walked. These beds

seemed to indicate that jaguars in Cockscomb rested mainly on the ground instead of up in trees, as they are thought to do elsewhere. Later, when I was unable to pick up the radio **A** signals of resting jaguars, I became more certain of this. Had they been resting in trees, the radio signals should have become stronger, not weaker.

I almost started to drift off, listening to the clicking of some red-capped manakins[19] nearby and watching **B** the occasional group of toucans fly overhead. A noise in back of me made me jump, and I swung around. There stood Cirillo with his bicycle, the characteristic smile gone from his face. He was looking past me to where the jaguar lay. I wondered what he was thinking.

"You been there long, Cirillo?" I asked quietly.

"No, not so long," he replied, still keeping his eyes glued to the cat.

"See the radio around its neck, Cirillo?" I asked.

"I see radio," he said. "What dat for? You talk to cat with dat radio?"

I hadn't thought of it that way, but it made more sense than many other explanations. "The cat talk to me with that radio," I answered, glad that Cirillo was even curious about such things. "He tell me if he

I watched as he clawed at the dirt, making a scrape that I was later to find was part of a whole system of communication among these cats.

19. **red-capped manakins.** Type of bird

Differentiated Instruction

Enrichment

Students may enjoy planning and creating a media campaign to educate the public about endangered species, such as the jaguar, and efforts being made to protect endangered animals. Encourage students to plan their campaign as a class, focusing on educating others about what they can do to assist conservation programs. Students can then complete portions of the campaign in small groups such as researching topics, creating advertisements, and making a commercial. Some students might enlist the aid of the community in making their campaign public.

sleep, he tell me if he awake."

I looked back at Chac, who was now watching us both. Then I looked at Cirillo watching Chac. Two worlds so intertwined yet so foreign to each other, I thought. You're not as far apart as you think. And I'm right in the middle.

"Let's go back to camp and leave Chac alone," I said, confident that the jaguar would now be all right.

Cirillo looked at me strangely and I realized he hadn't heard the cat's new name.

"That's Chac," I said, pointing to the jaguar. "Chac, the old Maya god of rain." My finger pointed toward the sky. For an instant Cirillo's eyes followed my hand, then quickly returned to the jaguar.

"Chac," he repeated slowly, almost as if he were savoring the words. From his mouth the name sounded better than ever.

Word soon spread around camp that I could talk to the jaguars with my radios. It was not what I had originally intended them to think, but I knew that if Cirillo continued to work with me, he would eventually come to understand. For now, however, I decided to use that belief for my own ends. ❖

 Different cultures praise different animals. What animals do you especially like? Which animals does your culture generally appreciate? What kinds of animals are not respected in your culture? How have these attitudes come about?

Analyze and Extend

1. How does the author differ from the Maya in his view of jaguars in the wild?
2. (a) What does the name "Chac" mean? (b) Why do you think Rabinowitz chose this particular name?
3. Rabinowitz describes the belief of many in the camp that he can talk to jaguars. At the end of the selection the author writes: "I decided to use that belief for my own ends." How would you evaluate Rabinowitz's decision? Explain.

Creative Writing Write a **journal entry** that describes your dream job. What is it, and why would you most like to do it? What would this job allow you to accomplish? What challenges might this position present? As you complete the entry, reevaluate your choice. Is this job still your dream job? Explain.

Media Literacy Conduct basic research on the Maya of ancient times and the Maya of today. Consider the following questions as you do your research: What are some of the most impressive accomplishments of ancient Mayan society? What was everyday life like for the ancient Maya? What is everyday life like for the Maya of today? Explain your findings to your class. You may also use visual aids, such as pictures or drawings.

 Go to **www.mirrorsandwindows.com** for more.

MIRRORS & **W**INDOWS

Answer: Students should give reasons to support their choice of their favorite animals. Students may suggest that Americans like animals, such as dogs, cats, and horses, because they are tame and friendly but not animals, such as rats or snakes, because they have a reputation for being dirty or dangerous. Some students may know that certain cultures think animals, such as monkeys or cattle, are sacred and won't injure them.

Analyze and Extend

1. The author values and wants to protect them, but the Maya see them as a threat.
2. (a) Chac is the ancient Mayan rain god. (b) The author gives the jaguar a name that has a lot of positive significance to the Maya to show them that jaguars are not always enemies.
3. The author sees himself in the middle of Cirillo's and Chac's world. Therefore, his decision is logical, since he can use it to bridge the gap between his perspective and that of the Maya.

Rubric for Creative Writing

You can adapt this as a checklist for students to use as they write.

☐ Does the journal entry clearly describe the job and why the author wishes to do it?

☐ Does the writer offer thoughtful reasons about what the job would help him or her accomplish?

☐ Is the writer realistic in describing challenges and rewards of the job?

Preview the Selection

At a Glance
Independent Reading
- Reading Level: Easy
- Difficulty Consideration: Background
- Ease Factor: Reference key

Objectives
Reading this selection will enable students to do the following:
- make inferences based on a diagram
- evaluate the effectiveness of a diagram

Launch the Lesson
Ask students how they like to have people give them directions to get from one place to another. Do they like compass directions such as "Go west one block and then turn north" or landmark directions such as "Go past three stoplights and turn left at the gas station on the corner"? Do they prefer looking at a map? Discuss why they find one type of direction easier than another.

TEACHING NOTE

Reference Key
Before students read the diagram, discuss the reference key. Be sure students understand what each of the colors and symbols means in reference to the diagram.

London Underground Map

A Visual Selection by Harry Beck

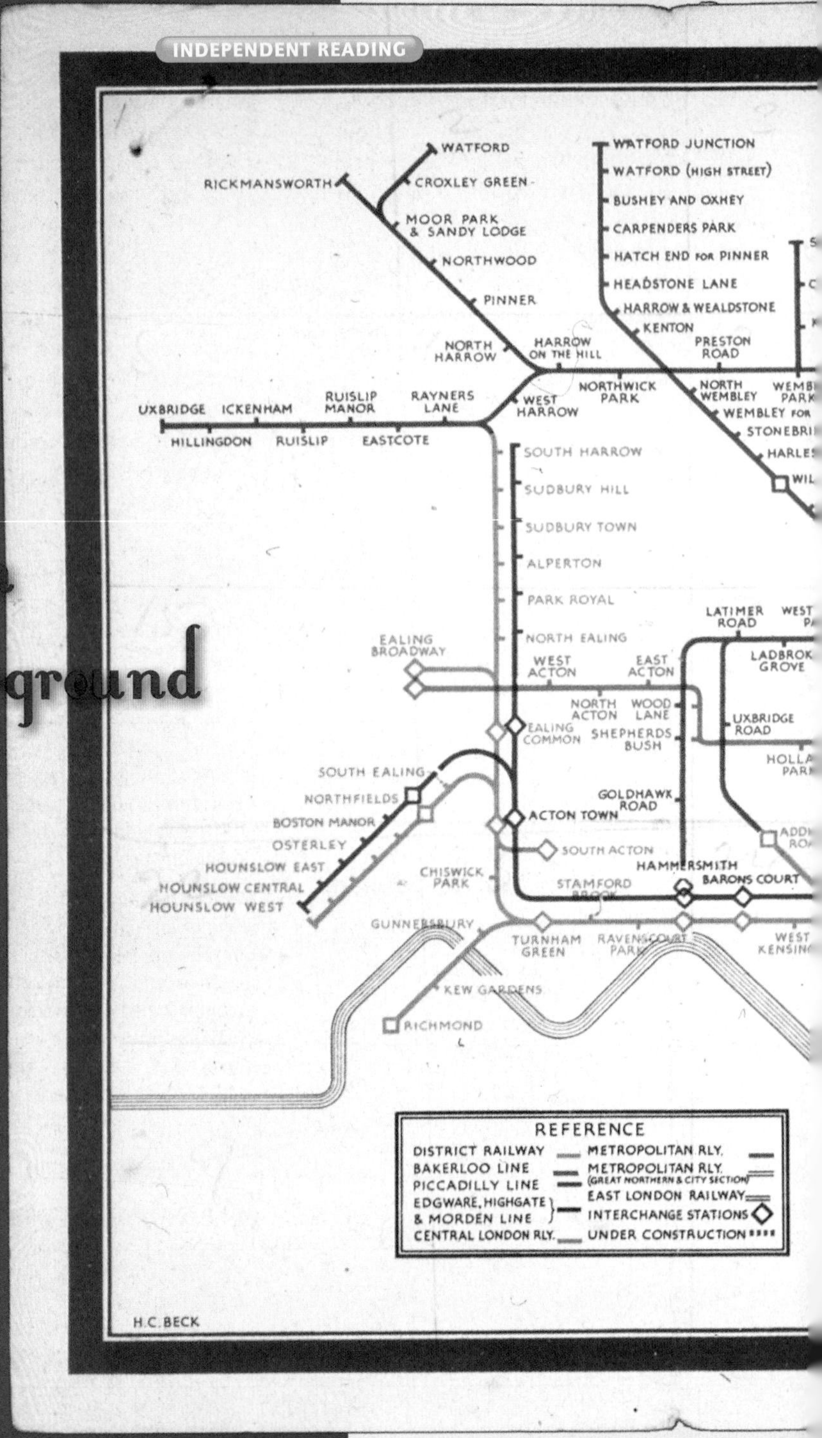

456

Common Core State Standards
Writing
W.7, W.8

Program Resources

Planning and Assessment
Program Planning Guide, Selection Lesson Plan
E-Lesson Planner
Assessment Guide, Lesson Test
ExamView

Technology Tools
Interactive Student Text on CD
Visual Teaching Package
Audio Library
mirrorsandwindows.com

Meeting the Standards
Nonfiction: Unit 4, Independent Reading, pp. 62–67

Differentiating Instruction
Advanced Students, Visual Media Project, pp. 25–26

The London Underground map with station names:

COCKFOSTERS
OPEN MIDSUMMER 1933
ENFIELD WEST
SOUTHGATE
ARNOS GROVE
BOUNDS GREEN
WOOD GREEN
TURNPIKE LANE
MANOR HOUSE
EDGWARE
BURNT OAK (WATLING)
COLINDALE
HIGHGATE
HENDON CENTRAL
BRENT
GOLDERS GREEN
DEN GREEN
TUFNELL PARK
HAMPSTEAD
KENTISH TOWN
BURN & BRONDESBURY
WEST HAMPSTEAD
BELSIZE PARK
FINSBURY PARK
FINCHLEY ROAD
CHALK FARM
ARSENAL (HIGHBURY HILL)
DRAYTON PARK
SWISS COTTAGE
CAMDEN TOWN
HOLLOWAY ROAD
HIGHBURY & ISLINGTON
MARLBORO ROAD
MORNINGTON CRESCENT
CALEDONIAN ROAD
CANONBURY & ESSEX ROAD
ST JOHNS WOOD
K AVENUE
MARYLEBONE
KINGS CROSS ST. PANCRAS
EUSTON
OLD STREET
ANGEL
EDGWARE ROAD
BAKER STREET
GREAT PORTLAND ST. REGENTS PARK
EUSTON SQUARE
WARREN STREET
FARRINGDON
ALDERSGATE
MOORGATE
TON
PRAED STREET
GOODGE STREET
RUSSELL SQUARE
CASTER ATE
BOND STREET
TOTTENHAM COURT ROAD
BRITISH MUSEUM
CHANCERY LANE
POST OFFICE
BANK
LIVERPOOL STREET
HOLBORN
MARBLE ARCH
OXFORD CIRCUS
ALDWYCH
COVENT GARDEN
MANSION HOUSE
SHOREDITCH
PICCADILLY
ALDGATE
DOVER STREET
LEICESTER SQUARE
STRAND
MONUMENT
ST. MARYS
STEPNEY GREEN
HYDE PARK CORNER
BLACKFRIARS
CANNON STREET
MARK LANE
ALDGATE EAST
WHITECHAPEL
MILE END
KNIGHTSBRIDGE
BROMPTON ROAD
TRAFALGAR SQUARE
TEMPLE
CHARING CROSS
SHADWELL
WESTMINSTER
WATERLOO
LONDON BRIDGE
WAPPING
VICTORIA
LAMBETH NORTH
BOROUGH
SOUTH ENSINGTON
SLOANE SQUARE
ST JAMES PARK
ELEPHANT & CASTLE
ROTHERHITHE
EEN
SURREY DOCKS
KENNINGTON
DGE
OVAL
EY
STOCKWELL
CLAPHAM NORTH
NEW CROSS GATE
NEW CROSS
OS
CLAPHAM COMMON
CLAPHAM SOUTH
PARK
BALHAM
TRINITY ROAD (TOOTING BEC)
TOOTING BROADWAY
COLLIERS WOOD
SOUTH WIMBLEDON (MERTON)
MORDEN

TO
BOW ROAD
BROMLEY
WEST HAM
PLAISTOW
UPTON PARK
EAST HAM
BARKING
UPNEY
BECONTREE
HEATHWAY
DAGENHAM
HORNCHURCH
UPMINSTER
& SOUTHEND

UNDERGROUND

LONDON UNDERGROUND MAP **457**

Teach the Selection

MIRRORS & WINDOWS The Mirrors & Windows questions at the end of this selection focus on the theme of maps. Before reading, ask students what maps they find most useful. What characterizes a useful map?

History Connection

Development of the London Underground The first section of the London Underground was the world's premier underground railway and carried its first load of forty thousand passengers on January 10, 1863. By 1880, the "Met" transported forty million people per year. An American businessman named Charles Yerkes bought and joined five railways to form the Underground Electric Railways of London Company, Limited (UERL), in 1902, which reduced or eliminated travel time between lines and lowered fare cost. Several railways were transformed into surface lines during the 1930s and 1940s. Today, more than half of the Underground is actually above ground. The system has 275 stations and travels over 250 combined miles.

Use Reading Strategies

Make Inferences Have students analyze the diagram and make inferences about questions such as "Why did the artist use different colors?" "Why isn't the diagram drawn to scale?"

Words in Use

Teaching Words
line, 456
urban, 458
draftsman, 458
graphically, 458

KEY TERMS
CHART, 458
DIAGRAM, 458
MAP, 458
GUIDELINE, 458

Answer: Students might be reminded of electrical wiring diagrams or other kinds of technical diagrams. Students might mention such characteristics as accuracy, ease of use, and simplicity.

Analyze and Extend

1. Students might mention the stylized design and use of color.

2. You would travel on the Bakerloo Line and the District Railway.

3. (a) Students' responses to the map will vary. (b) Students will probably feel that the more graphically appealing a diagram is, the more likely people will be to use it.

TEACHING NOTE

London Underground

Interested students might research the history of the London Underground and the influence of the Art Deco movement on its design and construction. Encourage students to create a time line that illustrates some of the major incidents in its history such as the date of its groundbreaking. Students can illustrate their time line with pictures copied from books or articles.

Beginning operations on January 10, 1863, the London Underground was the world's first urban passenger-carrying subway system. Known to Londoners as "the Tube," it served as a model for subway systems in other big cities around the world. In 1931 **Harry Beck** (1903–1974), a draftsman employed by the London Underground, used his free time to create a diagram mapping the entire system. His diagram presented the same basic information (such as the order of stations) as existing Underground maps. Beck's innovation was to ignore geographic factors (such as accurate distance between stations) in favor of ease of use. Initially rejected by the London Underground Publicity Office, Beck's map was eventually accepted. His basic idea has been copied for transit maps around the world.

Of what other types of charts or diagrams does Harry Beck's London Underground map remind you? What do you think are the most important characteristics of a successful map?

Analyze and Extend

1. What features of this London Underground map do you find particularly striking?

2. If you had to go from Baker Street to Victoria on the Underground, on what different lines would you travel?

3. (a) How do you feel about the design of Beck's Underground map? (b) How important do you think it is for a diagram of this type to be graphically appealing? Explain.

Applied Writing Working with a group, discuss and decide on a **set of instructions** for the creation of a map of your school. Vote on what landmarks should be represented, the basic graphic style, and any special features. Explain your instructions orally to another group, and listen as they explain theirs. Both groups should create maps from the other's instructions and then meet to discuss the results.

Collaborative Learning Harry Beck's London Underground Map is a classic example of the twentieth-century artistic movement known as Art Deco. Work with other students to research Art Deco and create a visual display showing some of the key features of its approach to design. Show how these features are embodied in Beck's London Underground Map.

Go to **www.mirrorsandwindows.com** for more.

Rubrics for Applied Writing

You can adapt this as a checklist for students to use as they complete the activity.

☐ Do the guidelines include the major landmarks of the area, the basic graphic style of the map, and any special features?

☐ Were these elements decided on as a group?

☐ Were the guidelines explained orally to another group?

☐ Did the group listen to another group's instructions and create a map accordingly?

☐ Did the groups meet to discuss the results?

For Your Reading List

Write Your Own Fantasy Story
by Tish Farrell

Do you believe that the beginnings of a fantasy story exist somewhere inside your head? This book will help you explore the "lost corners of your imagination" and show you how to express your thoughts and ideas on paper. Learn about other fantasy stories, myths, and fairy tales to read for inspiration, how to describe your fantasy world, create interesting characters, and craft a compelling story.

e.guides Rock and Mineral
by John Farndon

Amazing photographs of rocks, minerals, and gemstones fill this book, along with fascinating descriptions of stones ranging from space rocks to star sapphires to watermelon tourmaline. This book has its own website where readers can go for more information, games and activities, and downloadable images.

September 11, 2001: Attack on New York City
by Wilborn Hampton

The *New York Times* editor Wilborn Hampton provides eyewitness accounts of people escaping the World Trade Center after the planes hit: a blind man and his guide dog, and the firefighters of Ladder Company No. 6 who helped an elderly woman down the stairs of the North Tower as it collapsed. Hampton addresses the following questions: How did the people nearby respond? What was it like on the streets outside? What may have been the motivations of the attackers? Photos throughout show the extent of the devastation.

Peanut Butter, Milk, and Other Deadly Threats: What You Should Know About Food Allergies

by Sherri Mabry Gordon

Allergies to common foods like peanuts and milk are increasing. The author profiles young people with severe food allergies who describe in vivid detail what it is like to suffer a severe allergic reaction. The book follows their daily struggles to avoid certain foods in restaurants, school cafeterias, or at a friend's house. You will learn how to help a friend with a food allergy avoid "trigger" foods, and what to do if a friend suffers an allergic reaction.

Understanding the Holy Land: Answering Questions About the Israeli-Palestinian Conflict
by Mitch Frank

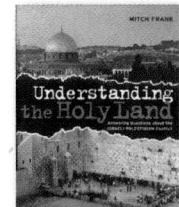

How did the Israeli-Palestinian conflict begin? Why has it lasted for so long? Author Mitch Frank answers these and other questions about this complicated situation that has received extensive media coverage over the years. This book is an invaluable resource for anyone wanting to better understand a fundamental conflict of our time.

Harlem Stomp: A Cultural History of the Harlem Renaissance
by Laban Carrick Hill

Between 1900 and 1924, Harlem, New York, exploded in a dizzying display of creativity in perhaps the most important cultural movement in U.S. history. Beautifully illustrated with photographs and art of the period, this book offers a fine introduction to an amazing time.

Independent Reading Activity

Help students link independent reading to the unit theme, Expanding Horizons. Have students select a book from the list here, or go to the library and find a similar nonfiction work that has many illustrations. They might also seek out books featuring time lines, diagrams, and other types of informational visuals. When students have brought their selections to class, allow time for everyone to examine the books. Each student should then choose one image to which to respond. Ask students to write an essay of several paragraphs that describes the image and their thoughts and feelings about it. Students may read their essays to the class, exchange them with partners for feedback, or simple keep them in their journals or portfolios.

⊳ EMC E-Library

The EMC E-Library contains over twenty thousand pages of literary classics that students may read independently. An Electronic Library Guide provides teaching suggestions, enrichment activities, and reading strategy guidesheets.

TEACHING NOTE

Distinguish Fact from Opinion

Remind students that in reading nonfiction, it is important to distinguish between facts and opinions. A fact is a statement that can be proved (or disproved). An opinion can be supported, but not proved.

Program Resources

EMC Access Editions

For additional independent reading, you may wish to refer students to one of EMC's Access Edition titles. Each Access Edition contains a thorough study apparatus, including background information, literal comprehension questions, footnotes, vocabulary definitions, critical thinking questions, and related projects and activities. An Assessment Manual offering worksheets and exams is available for each Access Edition.

Common Core State Standards
Reading Informational
RI.10

Teach the Workshop

Objectives

Participating in this workshop will help students write a descriptive essay that

- illustrates an impression in its introduction
- has a clear organizational pattern
- uses figurative language and sensory details in its body paragraphs to support the impression
- reinforces the impression with personal thoughts and feelings
- has a conclusion that summarizes and conveys a new insight

Launch the Workshop

Give students several minutes to practice using sensory details and figurative language. Ask them to verbally describe a particular corner or other small section of the classroom. Challenge them with such questions as: "How does that area look, smell, and sound? What mood does that area have, and why? What kind of story can you imagine happening with that area as a setting?" After students offer ideas, tell them they will be writing about a personally meaningful place, object, or event in this workshop.

Program Resources

For a full writing rubric, go to **www.mirrorsandwindows.com.** Additional writing workshops are available in Exceeding the Standards: Writing.

Common Core State Standards

Writing
W.2, W.4, W.5, W.6, W.10

Descriptive Writing

Descriptive Essay

Reading and Writing

Consider the way you have used your imagination in this unit. Every selection contains an element of description. To describe something is to create an account that includes important or interesting details about the subject, often from the five senses. In "On the Relativity of Time," the author uses two very different descriptions of a pond in order to contrast them. In "Indian Cattle," it is easy to picture the hunting of buffalo because of the author's detailed descriptions. The same goes for the accounts of controversial rocks found in Mexico, poisonous mushrooms, and fear of starvation on the frontier.

In this workshop you will learn how to write a **descriptive essay.** This is an expository essay that gives an account of someone or something using sensory details, figurative language, and personal thoughts and feelings. The following summary includes your assignment, goal, strategy, and writing rubric. These tools will help you develop a strong descriptive essay.

Assignment: Write a descriptive essay about a meaningful subject or event.

Goal: Vividly describe a subject or episode so that my audience can share in the experience.

Strategy: Use a clear organizational pattern, clear sensory details and figurative language, and my own thoughts and feelings.

Writing Rubric: My descriptive essay should include the following:

- an introduction that illustrates my impression of a subject or event
- a clear organizational pattern appropriate to the subject or event I'm describing
- body paragraphs that support my impression through the use of sensory details and figurative language
- personal thoughts and feelings to help reinforce my overall impression
- a conclusion that sums up my impression and adds an additional insight

What Great Writers Do

Stuart Dybek recalls writing one of his first essays and what excited him about it.

By the light of snow, I wrote about the heat and flies and the jungle. When I tried to describe how tall the trees were I was stuck for a moment, mute with awe. Grasping for a comparison, I thought of the tallest things I'd ever seen, which were the skyscrapers downtown, and I wrote the phrase *the tree-scraped skies*…It was as if a bolt shot through me—the spark that leaps between opposite poles in the laboratories of mad doctors intent on creating life.

Words in Use

Teaching Words

controversial, 460
expository, 460
rubric, 460
episode, 460
mute, 460
annotations, 462

KEY TERMS

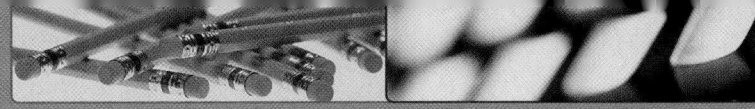

1. PREWRITE

Choosing Your Topic

The first thing you need to do is to choose a subject to describe. You want to choose something for which you can identify many interesting details. Consider places, people, events, and things you see in everyday life. You are an expert on these subjects and you can go observe them as part of your prewriting. Or think of a trip you have taken. What was your favorite site? Do you have pictures to work from? Or perhaps you have an unusual memory of something you saw when you were a child. How about an important meal? What strange plants or animals have you touched? What smells comfort you? What sounds scare you? Begin by making a list of the most interesting and memorable ideas.

1. Trip to Grand Canyon
2. Favorite park bench by the river
3. My backyard in spring
4.
5.

Gathering Your Details

When you have a list of ideas, you can use those ideas to create cluster charts. Begin by placing your idea in the middle of your page. From there, brainstorm possible sub-ideas (details and related topics). The sub-ideas stretch like branches from your first idea. Try to make new branches for different categories.

Choose your favorite ideas from your list. For each one, make a cluster chart. This will help you to identify which topic will provide the most material. Choose the topic with the fullest cluster chart.

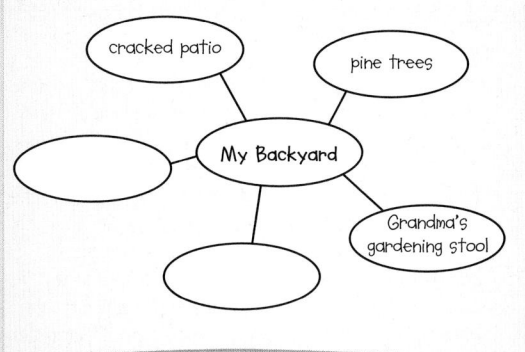

Deciding on Your Purpose

For a descriptive essay, your purpose is to describe. The goal of your descriptions is to make the readers feel as if they are there, sharing the experience with you. Create a thesis statement that conveys the overall impression or significance of the subject or event you're describing.

Each year when spring rushes in, I am startled as if seeing my backyard for the first time.

Prewrite

Choosing Your Topic Reinforce the value of choosing a personally significant topic. Tell students that they can tap into emotions and impressions they may have had when they first experienced this object or event. Model recalling details and emotions about a possible topic: "I once had to wait alone in the Miami airport for hours on my way to a summer study program. I was already on edge because I had never flown alone before. I arrived on time and was supposed to meet the program leader, but no one was there and no one came for hours. Hundreds of jumbled thoughts ricocheted through my head."

Deciding on Your Purpose Suggest that students use an unusual verb or adjective in their thesis statements. Point out that in the sample, it is unusual for someone to be "startled" by his or her backyard.

What Great Writers Do

Author Louise Erdrich tried to learn the language of her ancestors, Ojibwe. Ask students to note the images in this quote.

"The language bit deep into my heart, but it was an unfulfilled longing. I had nobody to speak it with, nobody who remembered my grandfather's standing with his sacred pipe in the woods next to a box elder tree, talking to the spirits."

Writing Skills

Precise Language

When students have narrowed their topic to one or two ideas, suggest that they revisit each cluster chart to make the language more precise. Explain that this means changing broad terms to specific ones and adding adjectives or adverbs. If you have used the "My Backyard" model, give them the example of changing "pine trees" to "fragrant pine trees at various stages of growth."

Draft

Organizing Ideas Help students distinguish between organization of the entire essay and organization of paragraphs. Explain that the overall essay may be chronological, but individual paragraphs may have chronological, spatial, compare-contrast, or cause-effect organization.

Putting Your Thoughts on Paper

This assignment asks for personal impressions and feelings. Gauge how reflective your students are, and consider giving them some guidance on describing an emotion. Suggest that they can imagine what someone else would look like as they experienced the same feeling. Model an example: "I was angry and scared at the same time, but I didn't want anyone to know I was feeling that way. I can picture a person in a chair jiggling a leg and biting fingernails. I'll say 'As the hours wore on, I chewed my nails and kept having to stop my leg's insane jiggling.'"

2. DRAFT

Organizing Ideas

You now have your subject, a cluster chart that tells you some important details, and a thesis statement. Before you write, choose an organizational pattern to follow. If you are describing a particular episode or event, you might use **chronological order,** and tell the events in the order they occurred. If you are describing a person or place, you might use **spatial order** to shift your focus from one area to the next.

Chronological Order	Spatial Order
First Event ↓	1. Top ↕ Bottom
Second Event ↓	2. Left ⟷ Right
Third Event (and so on) ↓	3. Near ⟷ Far
Final Event	

Putting Your Thoughts on Paper

Now that you have a pattern to follow, take a second look at your cluster chart. This chart provides some of your details. Take a minute to mark where these details will fall in your organizational pattern. Then consider what other details you will add. The first step is to create an introductory paragraph. The introduction should introduce your topic in an interesting way and set up your thesis. The next step is to structure the body of your essay. In this case, the body will be made of paragraphs that fit each part of your organizational pattern. Remember that each paragraph should have a topic sentence at the start. The final step is to create a conclusion. A good conclusion summarizes your main ideas, restates your thesis, and adds a final insight.

Introduction
- Introduce the subject I will describe and state my overall impression.

Body
- Organize by chronological or spatial order.
- Include sensory details and figurative language.
- Include my personal thoughts and feelings to support my overall impression.

Conclusion
- Sum up my overall impression and add additional insight.

Staying Focused

You already know that each body paragraph should have a topic sentence. Each sentence in a paragraph should work to support that topic sentence. When every sentence in a paragraph is working to support the topic sentence, then that paragraph is said to have **unity.** For the body paragraphs of your descriptive essay, support the impression you gave in the introduction with sensory details, figurative language, and your own thoughts and feelings.

Topic Sentence
1. Detail (sensory details)
2. Detail (figurative language)
3. Detail (personal thoughts and feelings)

Differentiated Instruction

Reading Proficiency

Help struggling readers translate their cluster charts into organizational patterns. Have each student name three categories into which the chart details might fall. Then have the student make a table to place details into those categories. Finally, ask students to put the categories in a logical order and then try to write a paragraph based on each category.

English Language Learners

You may wish to explain that an insight is a new perception or understanding of a situation. (Other languages have words for this, such as the Spanish word *perspicacia*.)

Evaluating Your Draft

Read your response aloud to yourself and mark anything that needs to be fixed. Then read the response silently. Lastly, trade responses with one of your classmates for a **peer review**. He or she will read your response and look for other things to improve. Use the revising checklist here as a guide.

Below is a draft of a descriptive essay. The annotations to the right indicate the reasons for the changes marked in the draft.

Revising Checklist

☐ Does the introduction illustrate my impression of a subject or event?

☐ Is the essay organized in a logical way?

☐ Do I use figurative language and sensory details?

☐ Do I include personal thoughts and feelings?

My backyard is as ordinary as they come. All winter I nearly forget there is any backyard at all. *Yet, each year when spring rushes in, I am startled as if seeing my backyard for the first time.*

When I first open the back door, I step onto a cracked stone patio that looks almost new. Here up close, everything is wet. The eaves drip onto the patio *in quick, steady plops.* The rust-colored bricks of the patio floor gleam from all the melting. In March, the patio always looks as smooth and slick as strawberry glaze.

Beside the patio, a splash of yellow catches my eye. It isn't a flower, but my grandmother's painted garden stool. *In the summertime, she is always sitting on the stool, pulling weeds or watering flowers with a dented aluminum watering can.* Today the legs of the stool are sunk half into the muddy yard. When I walk over to pick it up out of the mud, my shoes stick and squish in the muck. The smell of fresh, cool mud tickles my nostrils.

State your impression in your thesis.

Add sensory details.

Include transitions to help your reader follow your organization.

Add vivid details to help your reader picture your descriptions.

Teach the Workshop

Revise

Evaluating a Draft Have students read the tips below for delivering and receiving constructive criticism.

Delivering Criticism

- **Be focused.** Concentrate on content, organization, and style. Leave spelling and punctuation for the proofreading stage.
- **Be positive.** Respect the writer's feelings and writing efforts.
- **Be specific.** Give concrete ideas for improving the essay.

Receiving Criticism

- **Ask questions.** Make sure you understand your reviewer's comments.
- **Be specific.** Ask your reviewer to clarify comments and suggestions.
- **Be selective.** Accept your reviewer's time and suggestions graciously. When you revise your essay, you can use just some—or none—of the suggestions.

What Great Writers Do

Point out that most people are their own harshest critics. Novelist Allegra Goodman describes making choices about listening to that "inner critic."

"Ultimately every writer must choose between safety and invention; between life as a literary couch potato and imaginative exercise. You must decide which you like better, the perfectionist within or the flawed pages at hand."

Writing Skills

Revision

Review four of the main ways to revise as stated below. Ask volunteers for examples of times they used each technique. (You may also model examples, as in the parentheses with Item 1.)

1. Adding or expanding: Adding transitions or examples to connect ideas or make images more vivid. ("I needed to add a transition to connect the empty waiting room and my loneliness.")

2. Cutting or condensing: Deleting unrelated details, replacing wordy sentences with shorter ones, and eliminating repetition.

3. Replacing: Using active, concrete, vivid, and precise words instead of passive, abstract, boring, and imprecise words.

4. Moving: Putting related images and ideas closer to each other.

➤ Edit and Proofread

Students may want to use proofreader's marks when correcting their work. Refer them to the Language Arts Handbook, Writing Section 4.1, Proofreader's Symbols.

Figurative Language This may be a good point for revisiting the writing goal on page 460: "Vividly describe a subject or episode so that my audience can share in the experience." Tell students to try to stand "outside" their work when they edit and proofread. Have them imagine that they are readers experiencing the work for the first time. Ask them to notice places where metaphors, similes, and personification could make the episode more immediate or real to the average reader.

➤ Publish and Present

Before students begin their final versions, they might benefit from reading the Language Arts Handbook, Writing Section 4.1, Writing Follow-up.

---

4. EDIT AND PROOFREAD

Focus: Description

To support your impression, use plenty of descriptive details, such as sensory details and figurative language. **Sensory details** are details based on your five senses. Any sight, smell, sound, taste, or texture is sensory. **Figurative language** is writing or speech meant to be understood imaginatively instead of literally. Two of the most important kinds of figurative language are metaphors and similes. A **metaphor** compares or equates two unlike things. A **simile** is a comparison between two unlike things using the word *like* or *as.*

Look at how a simile can make the following sentence more vivid.

> In March, the patio always looks smooth.
>
> In March, the patio always looks *as smooth and slick as strawberry glaze.*

Personification is another kind of figure of speech. In **personification,** a nonhuman thing is given human characteristics. See how personification makes the following sentence more interesting.

> Here our backyard is bordered by woods, and a few pine trees grow in our yard.
>
> Here our backyard is bordered by woods, and a few *stray* pine trees *have wandered in.*

Focus: Comparatives and Superlatives

Adjectives and adverbs can help make your descriptions more colorful or precise. The form of an adjective or adverb is often changed to show the extent or degree to which a certain quality is present.

> The maple tree is <u>tall.</u>
> **Comparative:** The pine tree is <u>taller.</u>
> **Superlative:** The redwood is <u>tallest.</u>

Each modifier has a **comparative** and **superlative** form of comparison. Most one-syllable modifiers and some two-syllable modifiers form their comparative and superlative degrees by adding -*er* or -*est.* Other two-syllable modifiers and all modifiers of more than two syllables use *more* and *most.*

Use comparatives and superlatives to indicate a form of comparison.

> I let them alone and follow the fence, laced with dried, curled grapevines, to the *farthest* spot in the yard.

Proofreading

Quality Control Use proofreader's marks to highlight any errors you find, then correct them. (See the Language Arts Handbook, section 4.1, for a list of proofreader's marks.)

---

5. PUBLISH AND PRESENT

Final Draft

Clean Copy Now that you have revised, edited, and proofread your paper, make a clean copy for presentation. Handwritten papers should be neat and legible. If you are working with a word processing program, double space the text and use a readable typeface. Follow your teacher's presentation guidelines before submitting your work.

TEACHING NOTE

Self-Generated Questioning

Have students form groups of three or four. Ask each group to generate a list of five questions they have about the process of revising, editing, and proofreading. Model a question such as: "Should proofreading be done in one step?" Encourage students to share their writing experiences at each of these steps and to identify questions that arise from their different experiences.

When groups have completed their lists, have a representative of each come to the front of the class. Have representatives read one question apiece until there are no more new questions. Finally, ask the class when and how they would go about finding answers to the questions.

Student Model

Startling March
by Loretta Yevich

My backyard is as ordinary as they come. During winter, it nearly disappears under mountains of snow and ice. Each March, the snow melts into harmless mounds, and the icicles on the eaves drip until there's nothing left. All winter I nearly forget there is any backyard at all. Yet, each year when spring rushes in, I am startled as if seeing my backyard for the first time.

Illustrates the writer's impression of the subject

When I first open the back door, I step onto a cracked stone patio that looks almost new. Here up close, everything is wet. The eaves drip onto the patio in quick, steady plops. Rivers flood the cracks and stream into the yard. The rust-colored bricks of the patio floor gleam from all the melting. The floor is badly in need of repair, and another winter probably hasn't helped matters. Yet, in March, the patio always looks as smooth and slick as strawberry glaze.

Beside the patio, a splash of yellow catches my eye. It isn't a flower, but my grandmother's painted garden stool. In the summertime, she is always sitting on the stool, pulling weeds or watering flowers with a dented aluminum watering can. Today the legs of the stool are sunk half into the muddy yard. When I walk over to pick it up out of the mud, my shoes stick and squish in the muck. After months of walking on packed snow, the ground feels soft and buoyant under foot. The smell of fresh, cool mud tickles my nostrils.

Organized logically and clearly using spatial order

Supports the writer's impression through sensory details and figurative language

Farther out in the yard, a lone maple tree stretches upward. From a distance, it looks as bald and bare as it did all winter. On closer inspection, however, tiny emerald buds speckle the tips of its branches. Its trunk is bumpy and rough like toad skin.

Includes personal thoughts and feelings to help reinforce the overall impression

In a sunny spot by the fence, two brave crocuses have shot up already. Their closed, milky petals feel like firm pudding, and their thin, fragile stems shiver in the cool wind. I let them alone and follow the fence, laced with dried, curled grapevines, to the farthest spot in the yard.

Here our backyard is bordered by woods, and a few stray pine trees have wandered in. Their boughs droop, heavy with moisture. I inhale, and their evergreen scent brings back faint memories of Christmas. In a day or two, all traces of winter will have vanished.

Every year, winter hangs on and spring seems as though it will never come. Only when I step into my backyard do I notice March pushing winter out. Every year, I'm startled by the change.

Sums up the impression and adds an additional insight

Teach the Workshop

Student Model
Using the Model Direct students' attention to the model. Point out the side notes that identify the writer's impression in the first paragraph, the observations and feelings in the body paragraphs, and the insight in the concluding paragraph. Some students might benefit from outlining the model to grasp the writer's plan of organization and use of evidence.

Titles Use this opportunity to discuss titles. Point out that the title of the model relates to the thesis statement—how startling the backyard is every spring.

If your students have titled their essays, ask how they made their title decisions. If they have not yet titled their essays, hold a general discussion about choosing titles. Bring out these points:

- Titles can be written last, when the writer knows what he or she has said.
- Titles can be written first, to lead and remind the writer of the essay's focus.
- The title makes the first impression. If it's weak, the reader will go elsewhere.
- The title should not mislead. Its tone and its promise should be matched by the qualities of the essay.

Writing Skills

Review and Reflect
Students have now completed several Writing Workshops and have offered each other constructive criticism. Have small groups meet to review and reflect on the writing process.

- First, review the process. Give students five minutes—one minute per step in the process—to list the easiest and hardest parts of each step. (The steps are Prewriting, Drafting, Revising,

Editing and Proofreading, and Publishing and Presenting.)
- Second, reflect on the process. Tell students to reach a consensus on three topics: the most enjoyable part of the process, the most difficult step (these could be the same), and the step on which they would most like to strengthen their skills. Let each group report results to the class.

Objectives
Participating in this workshop will help students plan and deliver a visual presentation that
- is clear and well-organized
- effectively employs visuals to enhance audience understanding
- adequately explains the topic
- exhibits appropriate volume and pacing and effective nonverbal expression
- employs an interesting, engaging tone

Launch the Workshop
Ask students to reminisce about science classes they have taken. Ask them to describe memorable demonstrations and videos. Prompt them to agree on two or three key features of effective, informative visual presentations. List these features on the board. You may use the list to guide a discussion after students make their presentations.

History Connection
Presentation Software Note that many people use computers to generate visuals for presentations. The well-known PowerPoint program was developed in 1987, and the first Microsoft Windows version was released in 1990. Today people have many presentation software packages from which to choose.

Viewing Workshop

Critical Viewing

How do you decide whether you like or don't like a television program? **Critical viewing** means to carefully evaluate or judge something by combining what you already know with what you see and hear. You can then compare the quality of what you are viewing against similar things you've seen or experienced. In this workshop, you'll select visuals to enhance a presentation and critically evaluate the effectiveness of your speech.

Planning Your Visual Presentation
Choose an Idea Do you build models or collect coins, stamps, or rocks? What do you know a lot about that you could share with others? Choose a topic that would make a good visual presentation. For example, if you collect rocks, you could explain how to identify sedimentary, metamorphic, and igneous rocks as you display pictures, drawings, or actual rock samples.

Identify Your Audience Does your audience already know a lot about the topic, or will you have to explain key terms and use visuals that focus on the basics? For a knowledgeable audience, you may be able to go into more detail or choose an unusual aspect of the topic. Identify your audience to help you anticipate questions you might have to answer during your presentation.

Select Key Ideas and Visuals Make an outline of your presentation. Use the outline to research your topic in books, magazines, or on the Internet. Think critically about what objects, photographs, diagrams, or film clips would enhance your presentation and make it more effective and easier for your audience to understand. You might choose to record film clips from television shows or documentaries on your subject. If you choose photographs, will you mount them on poster board, display them as slides, or give a computer presentation? Determine what effect you want the visuals to have on your audience. You may want to set up a storyboard to organize your presentation. Each box contains visuals and information on one major point of your presentation.

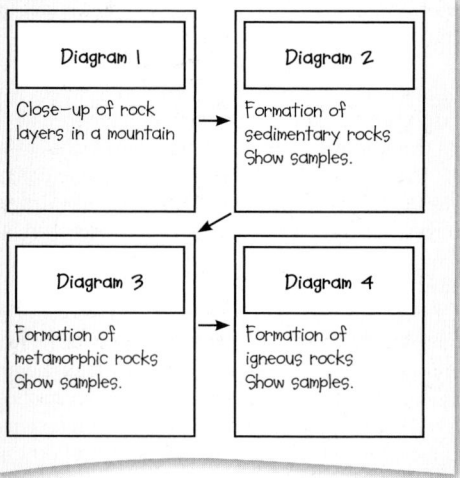

Words in Use

Teaching Words
sedimentary, 466
metamorphic, 466
igneous, 466
transparencies, 467
collage, 467
multimedia, 467
rubric, 467
constructive, 467

KEY TERMS

Common Core State Standards

Reading Informational
RI.7

Speaking and Listening
SL.5

Organizing Your Presentation

Use note cards to help you remember the order of your presentation. For each point in your outline, write a main idea and several details on a note card. Indicate where you will use visuals. You can organize your presentation in several ways:

- **Overhead transparencies or PowerPoint presentation:** use for diagrams, bullet points, or outlines
- **Slide show:** use to display photographs
- **Poster board:** make a collage of pictures, diagrams, and real objects
- **Real objects:** display or pass around examples for each point in your outline
- **Multimedia presentation:** If your visuals include video clips, still pictures, and diagrams, a multimedia presentation using the computer may be more efficient and less confusing to your audience than switching between pieces of display equipment.

DO: Use visuals that add to or enhance, rather than simply repeat, the verbal part of your presentation.

DON'T: Use more than one presentation format other than real objects.

Evaluating Your Presentation

Work in teams of three or four. Group members critically view each presentation, and then offer constructive, polite, and respectful criticism aimed at helping the presenter make the presentation stronger and more effective. Use the rubric on this page to evaluate the presentations.

Delivering Your Presentation

The purpose of your presentation is to provide information orally and visually in an effective way. Involve your audience by making eye contact and speaking directly to them rather than reading from your note cards. Look and act enthusiastic about your topic. When you refer to your visuals, point to them. Give your viewers time to study your visuals before you begin talking again. Make sure your visuals are large enough and placed so your audience can see them. Give your audience an opportunity to ask questions.

Audience members should listen actively and be courteous to the speaker. Connect information from the speaker's words to the visuals. When invited, ask questions on ideas or visuals that need clarification.

Speaking Rubric

Your presentation will be evaluated on these elements:

Content

- ☐ presentation is clear and well organized
- ☐ visuals are interesting and enhance understanding of presentation
- ☐ topic is adequately and effectively explained

Delivery and Presentation

- ☐ uses appropriate volume and pacing
- ☐ speaks in an interesting and engaging tone of voice
- ☐ effectively uses nonverbal communication

Listening and Viewing Rubric

As a peer reviewer or audience member, you should do the following:

- ☐ listen quietly and attentively
- ☐ maintain eye contact with speaker
- ☐ ask appropriate questions
- ☐ (as peer reviewer) provide constructive feedback

Organizing Presentations

Tell students that even though they need to focus on the main message of each of their visual images, they must also know the details. Encourage them to devise ways to keep detailed information close at hand in case an audience member asks for it. For example, if a photograph shows layers of sedimentary rock in the Grand Canyon, the presenter should be ready with such details as how old some of the layers are thought to be, what different rock colors indicate, and where a person could find similar rocks formations today.

Delivering and Responding to Presentations

Allow time for a question-and-answer period after each student presentation. Try to control this period by giving each audience member an opportunity to speak once before permitting any individual to ask a second question. If there are no questions about an individual presentation, prompt students to tell what, in particular, made it so clear and interesting.

TEACHING NOTE

Managing Visual Information

Ask interested students to research presentation software and software for managing visual information—such as photo and animation programs—and present an overview to the class. Students can work in pairs or small groups, using classroom or school computers, to find examples of the software programs.

Speaking & Listening Skills

Audience Questions

Tell students that as they rehearse their presentations, they can also practice responding to audience questions. Point out that speakers often pause to absorb a question and decide if it calls for giving a definition, elaborating with examples, or offering to seek additional information. Assure students that speakers do not have to have an answer for every question.

Read these questions, and have students suggest responses that would be appropriate.

1. Why did you choose this picture?
2. What research did you do to make this visual?
3. What did you leave out?
4. How is this relevant to me and my family?
5. When will more information be available?

Objectives

Completing this workshop will enable students to

- write a literary response based on a timed writing prompt
- answer standardized test questions that demonstrate revising and editing skills
- demonstrate the ability to make inferences from a reading by answering standardized questions

Timed Writing

Point out that standardized tests often ask students to write a response to a prompt in a specified period of time. Give the following tips:

- Read the entire question carefully.
- Look for key words in the question that tell you what is expected.
- Underline these words or write them on your own note paper.
- Use the key words to make sure to answer all parts of the question.
- Organize. Allow time for planning, writing, and reviewing.
- Before you begin writing, create a rough outline of points to make.
- If you find yourself running out of time, state your remaining points and add a conclusion.
- Write a clear introduction. This will help keep you on track as you write each paragraph.
- Review your completed essay to see if you have answered all parts of the question.
- Before you turn in your completed essay, take time to proofread.

Test Practice Workshop

Writing Skills

Descriptive Essay

Read the following writing prompt. Before you begin writing, think carefully about what task the assignment is asking you to perform. Then create an outline to help guide your writing.

> In his memoir, "Counting Coup on a Wounded Buffalo," Chief Plenty-Coups describes a "rite of passage" for young men learning to hunt for their people. What rites of passage must young people today experience before they are seen as contributing members of society? In what ways are these experiences similar to and different from the experiences of young people in earlier cultures? How do these experiences expand the horizons of a young person?

In your essay, use descriptive, sensory, and figurative language to describe a "rite of passage" young people today must experience as they grow into adulthood. Include comparisons from "Counting Coup," practices you have read or heard about, and evidence from your own life. As you write, be sure to:

- Organize your essay in a logical and consistent way
- Include introductory and concluding paragraphs
- Introduce your position in the first paragraph
- Support your main idea in each body paragraph

Common Core State Standards

Reading Informational
RI.3, RI.4, RI.6

Writing
W.2, W.4, W.5

Language
L.4

Rubrics for Descriptive Essay

You can adapt this as a checklist for students to use as they write.

Rubric for Descriptive Essay

Have students use these criteria when evaluating their descriptive essays.

- ☐ Does your essay follow your outline?
- ☐ Does your essay use descriptive, sensory, and figurative language to describe a "rite of passage"?
- ☐ Does your essay include comparisons to "Counting Coup," other rites of passage you have read or heard about, and your own experience?

Revising and Editing Skills

In the following excerpt from the first draft of a student's paper, words and phrases are underlined and numbered. Alternatives to the underlined words and phrases appear in the right hand column. Choose the one that best corrects any grammatical or style errors in the original. If you think that the original is error-free, choose "NO CHANGE."

Some questions might also focus on a section of the passage or the entire passage. These do not refer to a specific underlined phrase or word, and are identified by a number in a box. Record your answers on a separate sheet of paper.

The term, "The American Dream" was first
_____
1
used to describe the seemingly endless

possibilities for individuals in a new land. In the
_____
2
1700s, prairies extended as far as the eye could
_____
3
see, and the rich earth cried out for the plow,
_____

assuring abundance to all. Verdant forests
_____
4
promised plentiful lumber for homes, barns, and
_____

businesses. Fur, fish, and fowl, which filled the
⑤
woods and streams, were available for the price

of a trap, a rod, or a gun.

People flocking to America saw it as the pot of
⑥
gold at the end of the rainbow. Their dreams

included achieving fame and fortune, escaping

from social, ethnic, or class boundaries, owning

land, cattle, or starting a thriving business to

serve the growing population. For many, the

American Dream was simply a fulfilling life.

1. **A.** NO CHANGE
   B. The term "The American Dream"
   C. The term "The American Dream,"
   D. The term, "The American Dream,"

2. The sentence beginning *In the 1700s* is a
   A. simple sentence.
   B. complex sentence.
   C. compound sentence.
   D. compound-complex sentence.

3. **A.** NO CHANGE
   B. as far as the eye could see the rich earth
   C. as far as the eye could see, but the rich earth
   D. as far as the eye could see: the rich earth

4. **A.** NO CHANGE
   B. Verdant, forests promised plentiful lumber
   C. Verdant, forests, promised plentiful lumber
   D. Plentiful lumber was promised by verdant forests

5. The clause *which filled the woods and streams* is an
   A. essential adjective clause.
   B. essential adverb clause.
   C. adverb clause.
   D. adjective clause.

6. The sentence beginning *People flocking* is a
   A. simple sentence.
   B. complex sentence.
   C. compound sentence.
   D. compound-complex sentence.

Teach the Workshop

Revising and Editing Skills
1. B
2. D
3. A
4. A
5. D
6. A

Test-Taking Tip
Eliminate Incorrect Responses

Point out to students that a key skill in working with multiple-choice questions is eliminating some incorrect responses. Demonstrate this skill by modeling a think-aloud for one question in the Revising and Editing Skills section.

Question 2. Possible Think-Aloud: The sentence contains two subjects and two verbs, so neither A nor B is correct. It's either a compound or a compound-complex sentence. The answer is either C or D.

Select another question and have the class work as a group to eliminate the incorrect responses.

> For more information, see the Language Arts Handbook, Section 8, Test-Taking Skills.

Program Resources

For more study and practice with test-taking skills, see the *Exceeding the Standards: Test Practice* resource:
• Descriptive Essay Practice Test: Reading, pp. 10–12

Words in Use

Teaching Words
coup, 468
verdant, 469
plentiful, 469
essential, 469
harmonic, 470
incorporate, 470

KEY TERMS
OUTLINE, 468
MEMOIR, 468
ESSAY, 468
FIGURATIVE
   LANGUAGE, 468
MAIN IDEA, 468
EXCERPT, 469
CONTEXT, 471
CONFLICT, 471
CHARACTERIZATION, 471
SETTING, 471
DESCRIPTION, 471

EXTERNAL CONFLICT, 471
INTERNAL CONFLICT, 471
THEME, 471
FIRST-PERSON
   POINT OF VIEW, 471
SECOND-PERSON
   POINT OF VIEW, 471
THIRD-PERSON LIMITED
   POINT OF VIEW, 471
THIRD PERSON OMNISCIENT
   POINT OF VIEW, 471
TONE, 471

Point out to students that reading comprehension questions give you a short piece of writing and then ask you several questions about it. The questions may ask you to figure out something based on information in the passage. Urge them to keep the following tips in mind:

- Read all the questions quickly.
- Read the passage with the questions in mind.
- Reread the first question carefully.
- Scan the passage, looking for key words. When you find a key word, slow down and read carefully.
- Answer the first question.
- Repeat this process to answer all the rest of the questions.

Reading Skills

Carefully read the following passage. Then, on a separate piece of paper, answer each question.

from *To Be or Not To Bop* by Dizzy Gillespie with Al Fraser

"Now the way that word bebop came about to my way of thinking is when Dizzy would be trying to explain something or show you how to play it, he would hum it to you. And he would say, 'No, no, it goes like this—umpde-be-de-bop-be-bop-be-doo-dop-de-debop.' So they would come up to Dizzy and say, 'Hey, play
5 some more of that bebop music,' because he would be scatting like that. See, and they just picked up that word and they'd say, 'Play some more of that bebop music.' This was the description, you know, this was the way—the only way they could identify it and tell him what they wanted to hear him play. And of course Dizzy, being as intelligent as he is, he just kept it going. So this thing went on and
10 made him a fortune....

"When you have a lot of knowledge of music, and understand the theory and the new harmonic devices and everything, it's not very difficult to come out with a sound. But with a style of music, it's very very difficult, man, because it's hard to play something that somebody has never played before. But, I mean, see this is what
15 Diz had on all of these musicians. And he could sit down and play the piano so well. Even today, Dizzy says, 'Dig this, this little thing I wrote.' And the beautiful simplicity to it and with the way he is going harmonically, you say, 'Oh, wow, man isn't that pretty!' It's something that you haven't heard before. And of course, now, with his wide, wide world of traveling and picking up different sounds from
20 different countries and really understanding their music, he can incorporate that into what he already knows and always have something new to present....

"On 'Salt Peanuts' he had that all set up. The drum part worked like part of a jigsaw puzzle 'Bop-be-da' the little figures. He had little parts in there that had to work together, and this was all going a mile a minute, man.

Differentiated Instruction

English Language Learning

Students learning English will need help with the academic vocabulary used in standardized tests. Explain the meaning of the following terms used in this workshop:

descriptive essay—writing that describes something using visual and other sensory details, 468
sensory language—language that appeals to one or more of the five senses, 468

1. What is the main idea of the passage?
   A. Dizzy traveled around the world a lot and listened to music.
   B. The speaker liked to listen to Dizzy play.
   C. Dizzy was a musical genius who invented a new style of music called bebop.
   D. The speaker played the piano in Dizzy's band.

2. Based on the context, what is the most likely meaning of *scatting* in line 5?
   A. going away quickly
   B. dancing around
   C. talking in nonsense syllables
   D. improvising music

3. From the first paragraph, what can you conclude about the way other musicians felt about Dizzy?
   A. They admired him.
   B. They envied him.
   C. They disliked him.
   D. They were confused by his music.

4. Lines 8–9 are an example of which of the following?
   A. conflict
   B. characterization
   C. setting
   D. figurative language

5. What does the speaker contrast in lines 11–15?
   A. a theory and a sound
   B. a sound and a style
   C. harmonic devices and theory
   D. knowledge and a sound

6. What can you infer from lines 17–20?
   A. Dizzy had more training in music than other musicians.
   B. Dizzy taught a lot of other musicians how to play bebop.
   C. Dizzy appreciated the music of other cultures.
   D. Dizzy made records with musicians in other countries.

7. The sentence that begins *The drum part* in line 22 contains
   A. description.
   B. external conflict.
   C. internal conflict.
   D. theme.

8. The purpose of this passage is mainly
   A. to entertain.
   B. to persuade.
   C. to instruct.
   D. to inform.

9. This passage is written from
   A. the first-person point of view.
   B. the second-person point of view.
   C. the third-person limited point of view.
   D. the third-person omniscient point of view.

10. What is the tone of the passage?
    A. admiring
    B. critical
    C. sarcastic
    D. humorous

Teach the Workshop

Reading Skills
1. C
2. D
3. A
4. B
5. B
6. C
7. A
8. D
9. A
10. A

Test-Taking Skills

Distractors

Instruct students to watch out for distractors, incorrect answers that look right because they are partially correct. Distractors are usually based on common mistakes students make. Model a think aloud showing how to detect distractors.

Question 2. Possible Think Aloud: I've already eliminated A and B, so my choice is now between C and D. But I see that C is a distractor, because although it's correct that scatting does employ nonsense syllables, that's not its purpose, which is to improvise music. So D is the correct answer.

Unit 5 Visual Planning Guide

Planning and Assessment Tools

Annotated Teacher's Edition

Annotated Teacher's Edition
One location for accessing, previewing, and planning for use of all program resources.

EMC Launchpad
Desktop application for accessing, previewing, planning, posting, and grading all program resources. Post personal resources and lessons, and access the E-Lesson Planner, the E-Gradebook, and training modules for computer literacy.

Assessment Guide and ExamView
A variety of assessments are available for this unit in print and electronic forms, including:
- Formative Survey
- Lesson Tests
- Unit Exams
- Alternative Assessment Options
- Reading Fluency Assessments

Meeting the Standards: Unit 1
In addition to lesson-by-lesson resources, *Meeting the Standards* includes the following unit-based resources:
- Unit Study Guide
- Practice Test
- Active Reading Model
- Selection Quizzes

Program Planning Guide and E-Lesson Planner
- Lesson Plans for all the selections in the unit
- Core Standards-Based Selections
- Reading Log and Evaluation Forms

The E-Lesson Planner contains fully developed lesson plans and unit resources with an electronic calendar for editing lesson plans.

Technology Tools

Visual Teaching Package
This package contains unit-based lectures, games, art collections, and Writing Workshops in PowerPoint format; included within the EMC Launchpad.

Interactive Student Text on CD
The student textbook on CD includes highlighting, note-taking, bookmarking, and a direct link to the student website, in addition to everything in the student text.

Audio Library
Authentic, dramatic recordings with listening activities expand listening skills and offer additional support for developing readers and English Language Learners.

ETS Online Criterion-Based Essay Grader (Grades 9–12)
Students can use this ETS web-based tool to evaluate their essays online before submitting them for teacher review and final evaluation.

mirrorsandwindows.com
Student and teacher resources, support, references, technology tools, and state-specific standards are available at **mirrorsandwindows.com.** The website is customizable using the EMC Launchpad.

Unit-Based Resources

Exceeding the Standards Unit Resources

Each of the *Exceeding the Standards* resources provides fully developed lessons to help you extend the textbook lessons and to expand upon the themes and skills covered in the unit. You can also download these lessons from **mirrorsandwindows.com**.

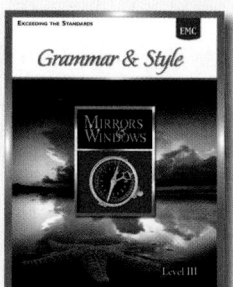

Grammar & Style
This resource contains:
- Three lessons on Linkers and Joiners, pp. 112–120
- Three lessons on Interrupters, pp. 121–128

Literature & Reading
This resource contains:
- Interpreting Contemporary Poet Laureates, pp. 16–17

Special Topics
This resource contains:
- Career Skills Development: Design and Complete a Job Application, pp. 17–18
- Media Literacy: Formatting and Publishing a Document, pp. 19–20

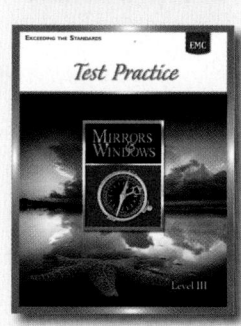

Test Practice
This resource contains:
- Expository Essay Practice Test: Timed Writing, p. 13

Writing
This resource contains:
- Expository Writing: Explain Using Details, pp. 39–48

Speaking & Listening
This resource contains the following lesson to expand on the Speaking & Listening Workshop:
- Giving and Actively Listening to Expository Presentations, pp. 14–17

Vocabulary & Spelling
This resource contains:
- Four lessons on Word Parts and Meaning, pp. 43–49

Extension Activities
This resource contains:
- Critical Literacy: Ask Questions, pp. 14–15
- Collaborative Learning: Group Activity, pp. 16–17

Unit 5 Visual Planning Guide

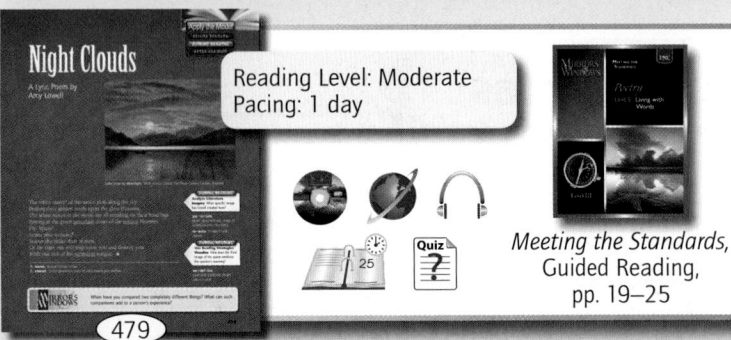

Night Clouds
A Lyric Poem by
Amy Lowell

479

Reading Level: Moderate
Pacing: 1 day

Meeting the Standards,
Guided Reading,
pp. 19–25

482

Reading Level: Easy
Pacing: 2 days

Meeting the Standards,
Guided Reading,
pp. 26–30

*English Language
Learners,* Identify Main
Idea, pp. 125–131

The Naming of Cats
A Humorous Poem
by T. S. Eliot

489

Reading Level: Easy
Pacing: 2 days

Meeting the Standards,
Guided Reading,
pp. 31–35

Developing Readers,
Use Text Organization,
pp. 34–36

494

Reading Level: Moderate
Pacing: 1 day

Meeting the Standards,
Guided Reading,
pp. 36–40

The New Colossus
A Lyric Poem by
Emma Lazarus

499

Reading Level: Easy
Pacing: 3 days

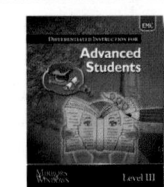

Meeting the Standards,
Directed Reading,
pp. 41–45

Advanced Students,
Genre Activity,
pp. 27–28

 Interactive Student
Text on CD-ROM

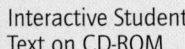 Selection
Lesson Plan

 Web-based
Resources

Lesson-by-Lesson Resources

The Other Pioneers

A Lyric Poem
by Roberta Félix Salazar

506

Reading Level: Easy
Pacing: 1 day

Meeting the Standards,
Directed Reading,
pp. 46–50

Advanced Students,
Historical Connection
Project, p. 29

Ceremony
A Lyric Poem by Leslie Marmon Silko

510

Reading Level: Easy
Pacing: 1 day

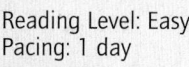

Meeting the Standards,
Directed Reading,
pp. 51–56

Advanced Students,
Cultural Context
Activity, p. 30

If I can stop one Heart from breaking

A Lyric Poem by Emily Dickinson

513

Reading Level: Moderate
Pacing: 1 day

Meeting the Standards,
Directed Reading,
pp. 57–64

He ate and drank the precious words

A Lyric Poem by Emily Dickinson

514

Reading Level: Moderate
Pacing: 1 day

Meeting the Standards,
Directed Reading,
pp. 57–64

Developing Readers,
Make Connections,
pp. 37–39

Legacies

A Lyric Poem by Nikki Giovanni

517

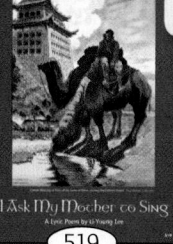

I Ask My Mother to Sing
A Lyric Poem by Li-Young Lee

519

Reading Level: Moderate
Pacing: 2 days

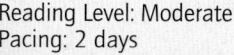

Meeting the Standards,
Comparing Literature,
pp. 65–72

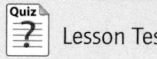 Lesson Test

 Audio Library

Meeting the Standards,
Independent Reading,
pp. 73–78

Advanced Students,
Independent Author
Study, p. 31

Unit 5 Scope & Sequence Guide

Selection or Feature	Genre	Reading Support/ Reading Level	Word Count	Reading Skill	Graphic Organizer	
Introduction to Poetry pp. 474–475						
Understanding Imagery and Figurative Language p. 476						
Poetry Reading Model p. 477						
Night Clouds Amy Lowell pp. 478–480	Lyric Poem	Guided Reading: Reading Model/ Moderate	76	Take Notes	Sensory Details Chart; Imagery Chart	
Dreams Langston Hughes pp. 481–485	Lyric Poem	Guided Reading: Reading Model/Easy	33	Identify Main Idea	Main Idea Map; Figurative Language Chart	
Literature Connection: A Dream Deferred Langston Hughes p. 484	Lyric Poem	Easy	56			
Understanding Sound Devices, pp. 486–487						

(left margin) GUIDED READING

Reading Level: Easy
Pacing: 1 day

Meeting the Standards,
Independent Reading,
pp. 79–84

Literary Element	*Mirrors & Windows* Theme	Cross-Curricular Connection	Writing Options	Extension Activities
Types of Poetry Poetic Forms Elements of Poetry				
What is Imagery? What is Figurative Language?				
Imagery	Comparisons		Creative: Imagist Poem Expository: Analysis	Lifelong Learning: Research and Present Critical Literacy: Make Observations
Metaphor and Simile	Aspiration		Creative: Personal Letter Persuasive: Persuasive Speech	Collaborative Learning: Conduct Research and Write a Report Critical Literacy: Ask Questions
What are Sound Devices? Rhyme Rhythm Alliteration, Consonance, and Assonance Onomatopoeia				

Unit 5 Scope & Sequence Guide

Selection or Feature	Genre	Reading Support/ Reading Level	Word Count	Reading Skill	Graphic Organizer
GUIDED READING					
The Naming of Cats T.S. Eliot pp. 488–491	Humorous Poem	Guided Reading: Reading Model/Easy	261	Analyze Effects of Form on Meaning	Effects Chart; Rhyme Chart
Pretty Words Elinor Wylie pp. 493–496	Lyric Poem	Guided Reading: Reading Model/ Moderate	114	Analyze Text Organization	Text Organization Chart; Sound Devices Chart
DIRECTED READING					
The New Colossus Emma Lazarus pp. 498–504	Lyric Poem	Directed Reading/Easy	111	Monitor Comprehension	Comprehension Chart
Informational Text Connection: from Immigrant Kids Russell Freedman pp. 501–503	Historical Nonfiction	Easy	1,247		
The Other Pioneers Roberto Félix Salazar pp. 505–508	Lyric Poem	Directed Reading/Easy	93	Identify Author's Purpose	Author's Purpose Chart; Description Chart
Ceremony Leslie Marmon Silko pp. 509–511	Lyric Poem	Directed Reading/Easy	129	Identify Author's Purpose	Author's Purpose Chart; Metaphor Chart
If I can stop one Heart from breaking Emily Dickinson pp. 512–515	Lyric Poem	Directed Reading/ Moderate	52	Identify Main Idea	Main Idea Map; Cluster Chart
He ate and drank the precious words Emily Dickinson pp. 514–515	Lyric Poem	Directed Reading/ Moderate	58		
Comparing Literature: Legacies Nikki Giovanni pp. 516–521	Lyric Poem	Directed Reading/ Moderate	108		
I Ask My Mother to Sing Li-Young Lee pp. 516–521	Lyric Poem	Directed Reading/ Moderate	110		

Literary Element	*Mirrors & Windows* Theme	Cross-Curricular Connection	Writing Options	Extension Activities
Rhyme	Portrayal	Cultural Connection: *Musical: Cats*	Creative: Personal Narrative Expository: Literary Response	Critical Literacy: Perform a Poetry Reading Media Literacy: Compare Literary Forms
Alliteration and Onomatopoeia	Connotation		Creative: Poem Expository: Literary Analysis	Collaborative Learning: Hold a Small Group Discussion Critical Literacy: Perform a Poetry Reading
Rhyme Scheme	Adjustment & Acceptance	Cultural Connection: *A Symbol of Freedom*	Creative: Poem Expository: Essay	Media Literacy: Compare and Contrast Sonnets Lifelong Learning: Recite Poetry and Hold a Discussion
Description	Ancestors	History Connection: *New Spain*	Creative: Descriptive Essay Expository: Biography	Critical Literacy: Hold a Panel Discussion Media Literacy: Use a Map and Make a List
Metaphor	Tradition		Creative: Short Story Expository: Literary Response	Lifelong Learning: Conduct Internet or Library Research Critical Literacy: Hold a Panel Discussion
Lyric Poetry	Resonance		Creative: Personal Letter Expository: Expository Essay	Collaborative Learning: Hold a Small Group Discussion and Create a Diagram Media Literacy: Conduct Library or Internet Research
Compare Literature: Diction and Tone	Heritage		Creative: Personal Narrative Expository: Compare-and-Contrast Essay	Lifelong Learning: Research Media Literacy: Compare Poetry Styles
	Music			

Unit 5 Scope & Sequence Guide

	Selection or Feature	Genre	Reading Support/ Reading Level	Word Count	Reading Skill	Graphic Organizer	
INDEPENDENT READING	**your little voice Over the wires came leaping** E.E. Cummings pp. 523–524	Lyric Poem	Independent Reading/ Easy	100		Analyze Text Organization	
	Lyric 17 José Garcia Villa pp. 525–526	Lyric Poem	Independent Reading/ Easy	95		Visualize	

Unit 5 Language Arts Workshops

Grammar & Style	Vocabulary & Spelling	Writing	Speaking & Listening	Test Practice
Nouns: Proper, Plural, Possessive, and Collective, p. 492 Simple and Compound Subjects, p. 522	Figurative Language: Similes, Metaphors, Analogies, and Idioms, p. 497	Expository Writing: Compare-and-Contrast Essay, p. 528–533	Giving and Actively Listening to Expository Presentations, pp. 534–535	Writing Skills: Expository Essay, "At the Library" by Nikki Grimes, "The First Book" by Rita Dove, p. 536 Revising and Editing Skills, p. 537 Reading Skills: "Cat" by J.R.R. Tolkien, pp. 538–539

Literary Element	*Mirrors & Windows* Theme	Cross-Curricular Connection	Writing Options	Extension Activities
Imagery	Communication		Narrative: Personal Narrative	Media Literacy: Compare and Present Findings
Figurative Language	Enrichment		Expository: Essay	Collaborative Learning: Create a Definition

Unit 5 Building Vocabulary

The lists below identify the Words in Use and Key Terms within this unit. These words are listed at the bottom of the Teacher's Edition pages at the beginning of each lesson. Vocabulary development activities are provided in the *Meeting the Standards* unit book and in *Exceeding the Standards: Vocabulary & Spelling*.

WORDS IN USE

Preview Vocabulary

Preview Vocabulary are words taken from the sentences within each selection. These words are defined in the side margin or at the bottom of the pages on which they appear. The "Preview Vocabulary" section introduces these words in the Before Reading page preceding each selection.

bequest, 514	dingy, 514	jostling, 523	sway, 520
brazen, 499	docile, 495	luminous, 495	teeming, 499
command, 499	exquisite, 523	pomp, 499	vermilion, 479
conquering, 499	gilded, 495	porcelain, 479	wee, 523
courtesied, 523	ineffable, 490	remote, 479	
dappled, 495	inscrutable, 490	robust, 514	

Selection Words

Selection Words are additional words from the reading that may be challenging but are not central to the selection and are not identified in the prereading section. These words can easily be learned using the story context, and they provide excellent practice for using content clues to find meaning without explicit instruction.

abnormalities, 502	din, 502	pawing, 479	teeming, 503
astride, 499	etched, 501	peculiar, 489	yearning, 499
clustered, 502	imprisoned, 499	profound, 490	
detained, 502	overturn, 520	steerage, 501	
dignified, 489	particular, 489	strain, 479	

Teaching Words

Teaching Words consist of vocabulary that is used in the directions about the lessons. Teaching words explain to students what to focus on within the selection, help establish the story context, clarify the meaning of literary terms, and define the goals or instructional purpose.

abstract, 497	distinguished, 488	legacies, 518	rebelled, 512
advocate, 498	docile, 497	legibly, 532	refined, 512
almanac, 480	emigrated, 525	literal, 497	reinforces, 500
aloof, 488	engage, 505	literally, 476	representation, 476
ancestry, 509	enlighten, 505, 509	luminous, 476	reservation, 509
anthologized, 505	enlightenment, 500	mechanical errors, 532	rubric, 528, 535
associated, 478	evoke, 520	missions, 507, 509	signature style, 523
cinders, 478	excerpt, 476	multitalented, 525	signifying, 500
Civil Rights movement, 516	generated, 529	opalescent, 476, 497	sluggish, 529
collective memory, 509	gory, 538	originating, 474	somber, 516
conservative, 512	heritage, 521	origins, 534	spinster, 478
constructive, 535	hesitant, 512	outward manifestation, 516	unbowed, 538
consumed, 478	impact, 521	passionate, 512	unconventional, 523
context, 539	incorporate, 526	persecuted, 498	unique, 474, 529
convey, 478, 535	indigenous, 511	precise, 478	vain, 515
cultivate, 525	inscribed, 498	prestigious, 525	widow, 490
dappled, 497	intense, 512	prose, 474	
derived, 508	kin, 538	prosperous, 498	

KEY TERMS

Key Terms are commonly referred to as *academic vocabulary*. These terms appear in the instructional material to teach the terminology that students need to acquire to understand literature. The repetition of the terms throughout the program ensures student mastery and provides a solid foundation for the continuing study of literature and language arts.

Objectives

Studying this unit will enable students to

- Connect the themes expressed in poems to their own lives and to the world around them
- Identify common forms of poetry
- Understand different elements of nonfiction, including *alliteration, description, diction, humorous poetry, imagery, lyric poetry,* and *metaphor and simile, onomatopoeia, rhyme and rhyme scheme, sonnet,* and *tone*

Reading Strategies

Ask Questions   Make Predictions
Clarify   Visualize
Make Inferences

Reading Skills

Analyze Effects of Form on Meaning
Analyze Text Organization
Identify Author's Purpose
Identify Main Idea
Monitor Comprehension
Take Notes

Literary Elements

Alliteration
Description
Imagery
Lyric Poetry
Metaphor and Simile
Onomatopoeia
Rhyme and Rhyme Scheme
Sensory Details

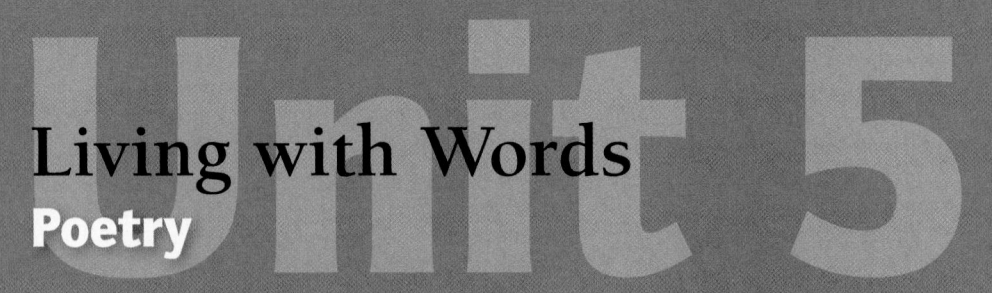

Living with Words
Poetry

Unit 5

T. S. ELIOT

LANGSTON HUGHES

ELINOR WYLIE

Launch the Unit

Have small groups create other questions that relate to the unit theme, Living with Words. Suggest that they choose one of two possible topics: Experiencing Words and Employing Words. Model this by proposing two questions: "How do words affect me when I'm on my way to school?" and "How do words help me change gears as I leave school for home?" Give groups three to five minutes to list their questions. Tell students to choose one person who will keep the list for the group. When you complete the unit, have groups gather again and revisit their lists. Ask groups to identify selections that provide insight about how to answer their questions.

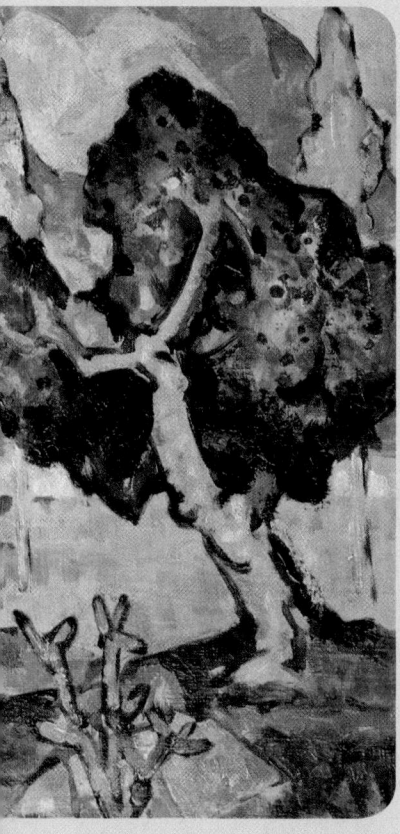

"*I love bright words, words up and singing early;*
Words that are luminous in the dark, and sing…"

—ELINOR WYLIE, "Pretty Words"

What do words mean to you? Do you take pleasure in both the sound and sense of the language you use? As Elinor Wylie observes, poets make "pets" of words, enjoying the play of language. As you read the poems in this unit, enjoy the texture of the language as well as the poem's meaning.

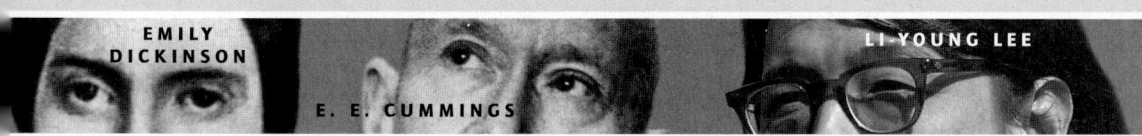

EMILY DICKINSON
E. E. CUMMINGS
LI YOUNG LEE

473

Program Resources

For a visual reminder of the unit-based resources available for Unit 5, Poetry, see pages 472A and 472B. As you introduce the unit, you may want to provide students with the Unit Study Guide, which is contained in the *Meeting the Standards* resource.

Teach the Genre

Introduction to Poetry

You may use these "Introduction to Poetry" pages at any point in the unit, as students explore the elements of poetry in the Before Reading and After Reading sections of each selection.

Launch the Lesson

Write these opening lines of Matthew Arnold's "Dover Beach" on the board, and then read them aloud to the class:

The sea is calm to-night.
The tide is full, the moon lies fair
Upon the straits; – on the French
   coast the light
Gleams and is gone; the cliffs of
   England stand,
Glimmering and vast, out in the
   tranquil bay.
Come to the window, sweet is the
   night-air!

Have students work in pairs or groups of three. Ask each set of students to take a minute to read the lines again and then respond to these questions:

- What do the poem's lines look like?
- What does the poem sound like?
- How do these lines make us feel?
- Do any phrases or sentences in this poem sound familiar?

Ask students to share their responses to the questions. When you have heard from all the pairs or groups, tell them they will continue to explore the structure, sound, and meaning of poems in this lesson.

Common Core State Standards

Reading Literature
RL.4
Language
L.5

Introduction to Poetry

Hold fast to dreams
For if dreams die
Life is a broken-winged bird
That cannot fly.

— LANGSTON HUGHES, "Dreams"

Types of Poetry

The language of **poetry** is musical and the word choices exact. As a result, poetry is often best experienced when read aloud. Poets use imagery, metaphor, simile, and other kinds of figurative language, as well as sound devices such as rhyme and alliteration.

There are two main kinds of poetry: **lyric** and **narrative.** A lyric poem expresses the emotions of the poem's speaker. Often lyric poetry focuses on a single moment, image, or idea. Narrative poetry tells a story. Long narrative poems that describe the deeds of heroes, gods, or goddesses are called **epics.** Many epic poems offer insights into the culture from which they originate.

Poetic Forms

Within these two broad categories exist many different poetic forms. A poem's form is determined by its individual elements. Here is a list of some poetic forms:

- **Sonnet:** A sonnet is a fourteen-line poem that usually explores the theme of romantic love. Sonnets are rhymed and use a regular rhythm.
- **Haiku:** Originating in Japan, haikus are short, three-line poems that describe a single image or scene from nature. Traditionally, the first and third lines of a haiku have five syllables, while the second line is made up of seven.

- **Concrete Poem:** A concrete poem is a poem that is shaped like the thing it describes. For example, if a poem describes a tree, the words on the page would be organized to visually resemble a tree.
- **Blank Verse:** Blank verse is the form most commonly used by Shakespeare in his plays. Blank verse does not rhyme, but each line has five stressed syllables, or beats.
- **Free Verse:** Free verse does not use consistent rhymes or rhythms. Free verse can take any shape and address any subject.

Elements of Poetry

Every poem is unique, but most poems use some of the elements listed below. Knowing these elements will help you better understand poetry in general.

Line

One of the major distinctions between poetry and prose is the use of the **line.** A line of poetry is a single row of words. In prose, sentences are the basic unit with which writers work. Poets, however, work with both the sentence and the line.

Stanza

Stanzas are made up of lines in the same way that paragraphs are made up of sentences. In a poem, each stanza is separated from the next by a space. The number of lines in a stanza helps to determine the kind of stanza it is. Some of the most common kinds of stanzas include the *couplet,* which is a two-line stanza, the *tercet,* which is a three-line stanza, and the *quatrain,* which is a four-line stanza.

Words in Use

Teaching Words
originating, 474
unique, 474
prose, 474

KEY TERMS

Sound Devices

Some **sound devices** include *rhyme, rhythm,* and *repetition.* Sound devices make poetry more exciting, more musical, and can affect its meaning. Before the printing press, sound devices even had a practical application. Poetry is more easily memorized and passed from place to place and generation to generation if it rhymes and uses a consistent rhythm.

Rhyme is the repetition of sounds at the ends of words. For example, the word *soon* rhymes with *moon.* Sometimes a rhyme is not completely exact, like *step* and *stop.* This is called a slant rhyme.

Rhythm is the pattern of beats, or stressed syllables, in a line of poetry. If this pattern is regular, it is called **meter.**

Alliteration is the repetition of consonant sounds at the beginnings of words. For example, the repetition of the *b* sounds in <u>b</u>right <u>b</u>lue <u>b</u>ottle is alliteration.

Figurative Language and Imagery

Nearly all poems use figurative language and imagery. **Figurative language** is anything written or spoken that is not meant to be taken literally. Figurative language includes metaphors and similes. A **metaphor** is a figure of speech in which one thing is spoken or written about as if it were another. For example, in "Dreams" (page 481), the speaker uses a metaphor to compare life to a bird: "Life is a broken-winged bird / That cannot fly." A **simile** also compares one thing to another, but it uses the word *like* or *as.*

Other common kinds of figurative language include hyperbole and personification. **Hyperbole** is an exaggeration used for effect or to make a point. **Personification** is a figure of speech in which something not human is described as if it were human. In "Pretty Words" (page 493), the speaker uses personification to describe words as "up and singing early."

Meaning in Poetry

Finding meaning in poetry is slightly different from finding meaning in short stories or essays. Poems can have many different layers of meaning that make it difficult to identify a single main idea or purpose. In part, this is because poets express their ideas, experiences, and feelings with imagery, figurative language, and symbols. A **symbol** is a thing that stands for itself and something else. Some traditional symbols include doves for peace and owls for wisdom. Symbols can also be unique to a particular piece of literature, author, or culture.

Types of Poetry

Instead of reading through all the text at once, you may want to begin by having students read the explanations of the poetic forms. Ask them to name other poetic forms they know such as limericks, nursery rhymes, advertising jingles, folk songs, and rap. Work with the class to identify common features of all these forms such as repetition, rhythm, and figurative language.

Elements of Poetry

For more in-depth information, see the element introductions in Units 5 and 6:
Understanding Imagery and Figurative Language, page 476
Understanding Sound Devices, pages 486–487
Understanding Meaning in Poetry, page 542

TEACHING NOTE

Collaborative Learning

Invite students to collaborate on a performance of famous poems in other languages. Ask students to choose short poems, consulting with family members or using the library and Internet as appropriate. Allow students to work individually, in pairs, or as a group to rehearse the chosen poems. After each reading, have the class name the sound devices (such as rhythm, rhyme, and alliteration) they heard and sum up the emotional impact of each poem. Conclude by noting that, even when one does not understand their meaning, the sound of words alone can convey a great deal.

INTRODUCTION TO POETRY **475**

Writing Skills

Poetry

Reinforce the distinction between lyric and narrative poetry for students: lyric poems express ideas and emotions, while narrative poems tell a story. Say that in writing poems, their first goal should be to get the emotion, idea, or story down on paper. Then, they can arrange the material into lines and stanzas and add rhyme and other sound devices.

Ask students to write three-line poems. Have them choose one of these topics:
- cars on an assembly line
- a crowded swimming pool
- the first day of eighth grade

If some students do not want to write new poems, have them turn excerpts of their own prose into three-line poems.

Program Resources

To help students explore literature on a deeper level, assign the following activity: Interpreting the Works of Contemporary Poets Laureate: *Exceeding the Standards: Literature & Reading*, pp. 16–17.

Understanding Imagery and Figurative Language

Reading strategies and skills that can help students understand imagery and figurative language include visualizing and identifying multiple levels of meaning.

Use Reading Strategies

Visualize Because images are concrete and almost always incorporate at least one sensory detail, encourage students to let pictures form in their minds—as well as to imagine smells, sounds, feelings, and tastes that relate to these pictures. Tell students that poets intend for them to take time to fully experience imagery, even just a few words or lines at a time.

Use Reading Skills

Identify Multiple Levels of Meaning Help students understand that poems evoke feelings and trigger associations for many readers. This is true of both lyric and narrative poems. Also point out that, by their nature, various figures of speech bring together different meanings. Walk through an example of multiple meanings: "'Warm lazy words' has meanings related to feeling cozy and satisfied. It also suggests that words, which aren't alive, can have the qualities of something that is alive (personification)." Encourage students to notice associations that come to them while reading a poem, and explain that they can use these associations to help interpret a poem's overall meaning.

Understanding Imagery and Figurative Language

What Is Imagery?

An **image** is language that creates a concrete representation of an object or an experience. When considered together, the images in a literary work are referred to as **imagery.**

In the passage below from Elinor Wylie's "Pretty Words," the poet uses sensory details to create the poem's imagery. For example, "white cattle under trees," "midsummer moths," and "honied words like bees" are all examples of imagery. Writers can use imagery to create a setting or character, to express an idea or emotion, or to affect the mood, or atmosphere, of a piece of literature.

What Is Figurative Language?

Figurative language is writing or speech meant to be understood imaginatively instead of literally. Many writers use figures of speech to help readers see things in new ways.

A **metaphor** is a figure of speech in which one thing is spoken or written about as if it were another. Metaphors invite the reader to make a comparison between these two things. A **simile** is like a metaphor. However, similes use the word *like* or *as* when making a comparison. For example, in the excerpt, the speaker enjoys "honied words like bees." The word *like* in this passage compares words to bees.

When a writer uses **personification,** he or she is describing something that is not human as if it were. For example, Wylie writes that she likes words that are "up and singing early."

Hyperbole is exaggeration. Writers use hyperbole to make a point or to have an effect on the reader.

Beehives, 14th century. Italian School. Osterreichische Nationalbibliothek, Vienna, Austria.

> I love bright words, words up and
>   singing early;
> Words that are luminous in the dark,
>   and sing;
> Warm lazy words, white cattle under
>   trees;
> I love words opalescent, cool, and
>   pearly,
> Like midsummer moths, and honied
>   words like bees,
> Gilded and sticky, with a little sting.
>
> —ELINOR WYLIE, "Pretty Words"

Teaching Words
representation, 476
literally, 476
excerpt, 476
luminous, 476
opalescent, 476

KEY TERMS
IMAGE, 476
IMAGERY, 476
SENSORY DETAIL, 476
SETTING, 476
CHARACTER, 476
MOOD, 476
FIGURATIVE LANGUAGE, 476
METAPHOR, 476
SIMILE, 476
PERSONIFICATION, 476
HYPERBOLE, 476

Common Core State Standards

Reading Literature
RL.4

Language
L.5

Poetry Reading Model

Build Background
You need to apply two types of background to read a poem effectively. One type is the poem's literary and historical context. Read the **Build Background** and **Meet the Author** features to get this information. The other type of background is the personal knowledge and experience you bring to your reading.

Set Purpose
Read **Set Purpose** to decide what you want to get out of the poem. Before reading the poem, preview how the lines are arranged.

Analyze Literature
Poets use different techniques in writing different types of poems. **Analyze Literature** draws your attention to the type of poem or a literary element important to a particular poem.

Use Reading Skills
The **Use Reading Skills** feature will show you skills to help you get the most out of your reading. Learn how to apply skills such as determining author's purpose and using context clues. Identify a graphic organizer that will help you apply the skill before and while you read.

DURING READING

Use Reading Strategies
- **Ask questions** about things that seem significant or interesting.
- **Make predictions** about what's going to happen next. As you read, gather more clues to confirm or change your prediction.
- **Visualize** the images. Form pictures in your mind to help you see the descriptions.
- **Make inferences,** or educated guesses, about what is not stated directly.
- **Clarify,** or check that you understand, what you read. Reread any difficult parts.

Analyze Literature
What is the purpose of the poem, and what literary elements achieve that purpose? For example, how does imagery or rhyme add to the meaning? Note how these elements affect your understanding of the poem.

Make Connections
Notice where connections can be made between the poem and your life or the world outside the poem. What feelings or thoughts do you have while reading the poem?

AFTER READING

Find Meaning
Recall the important details of the poem, such as images, figurative language, and rhyme scheme. Use this information to **interpret,** or explain, the meaning of the poem.

Make Judgments
- **Analyze** the poem by examining details and deciding what they contribute to the meaning.
- **Evaluate** the poem by making judgments about how the author creates meaning.

Analyze Literature
Review how the use of literary elements increases your understanding of the poem. For example, how might figurative language shape a poem's meaning?

Extend Understanding
Go beyond the text by exploring the poem's ideas through writing or other creative projects.

Use the Model

Introduce the Process
Use this page to show students the basic instruction provided for them before, during, and after reading most poems in Units 5 and 6.

"Night Clouds" is an Active Reading Model. Side notes in these lessons prompt students to become more active readers by using reading strategies and skills, analyzing literature, and making connections. Students can apply the process they use to read "Night Clouds" to other poems in Units 5 and 6.

Before Reading Stress the distinction between the two types of background students need to apply, and encourage students to always set a specific purpose for reading.

During Reading Point out the side notes in "Night Clouds": Analyze Literature and Use Reading Strategies. Then show students the Mirrors & Windows questions. Explain that they will respond to the poem personally and then apply their insights to a broader issue.

After Reading Show students page 480. Tell them that Find Meaning questions ask them to recall and interpret details. Make Judgments questions ask them to analyze a poem and evaluate how specific details contribute to its overall literary effect or meaning.

Speaking & Listening Skills

Dramatic Reading
Tell students that poetry is a spoken art form. Like songs or dramas, poems have meaning that comes from sound. Assign each student to read one line from Elinor Wylie's poem on page 493. Assure students that there is no one right way to read each line. Give them a minute to rehearse saying the line, aloud or silently, and then ask each student to say his or her line aloud. Note how each reading conveys something different about the words. After reading his or her line, each student should verbally summarize what he or she thinks it means. As they speak, students should employ learning strategies to improve their speaking skills, such as using nonverbal cues, synonyms, or circumlocution when they do not know the exact word, or requesting assistance if they are stuck.

KEY TERMS
AUTHOR'S PURPOSE, 477
CONTEXT CLUE, 477
IMAGERY, 477
RHYME, 477
FIGURATIVE LANGUAGE, 477
RHYME SCHEME, 477

Night Clouds

A Lyric Poem by Amy Lowell

Preview the Model

At a Glance
Guided Reading: Reading Model
- Reading Level: Moderate
- Difficulty Consideration: Poetic technique
- Ease Factor: Selection length

Objectives
Studying this lesson will enable students to
- use reading strategies such as visualizing
- define *imagery* and *metaphor* and recognize the effects of these literary techniques in the selection
- describe the accomplishments of Amy Lowell and explain her role as a member of the Imagist movement
- analyze a poem about the night sky

Launch the Lesson
Tell students that this poem is about the sky. Ask them to think about how sunlight and moonlight cast different types of light and shadows. Have them think about how the light changes at sunrise and sunset.

The Mirrors & Windows questions at the end of the selection focus on comparisons. Ask students if they have ever encountered similarities between two very different things. How do these discoveries enhance their knowledge?

Common Core State Standards

Reading Literature
RL.1, RL.4

Writing
W.9

Language
L.6

Build Background
Literary Context Amy Lowell is associated with an American literary movement known as Imagism, which was popular in the early 1900s. Imagists attempted to use clear, precise images to reveal a feeling rather than to directly describe the feeling.

Reader's Context When you look up into the clouds, what do you see? Describe the shapes and pictures you imagine.

Set Purpose
Look at the line lengths in this poem. How do you think the line lengths will affect the poem?

Analyze Literature
Imagery An **image** is language that creates a picture of an object or an experience. Taken together, the images in a poem are called its **imagery**. "Night Clouds" uses metaphors as part of its imagery. A **metaphor** compares one thing to another by describing it as if it were the other. As you read the poem, identify the images and ask yourself how they convey the author's feelings about the night sky.

Meet the Author
Amy Lowell (1874–1925) was born to a distinguished New England family. An Imagist poet, Lowell filled her writing with clear, precise images. On her death, journalist Heywood Broun wrote: "She was upon the surface of things a Lowell, a New Englander and a spinster. But inside everything was molten like the core of the earth…. Given one more gram of emotion, Amy Lowell would have burst into flame and been consumed to cinders."

Use Reading Skills
Take Notes Like many poems, "Night Clouds" is filled with sensory details to help you form mental pictures. As you read, take notes to record the sensory details and their effect on your understanding of the poem.

Sensory Detail	Effect
"rush along the sky"	This gives the poem a quick pace and establishes setting.

Preview Vocabulary
por·ce·lain (pȯr´ s[ə] lən) *adj.*, made of a hard ceramic, like china

re·mote (ri mōt´) *adj.*, distant

ver·mil·ion (vər mil' yən) *adj.*, bright red or scarlet

Words in Use

Preview Vocabulary	Selection Words	Teaching Words
porcelain, 479	pawing, 479	associated, 478
remote, 479	strain, 479	precise, 478
vermilion, 479		convey, 478
		spinster, 478
		consumed, 478
		cinders, 478
		almanac, 480

KEY TERMS

Night Clouds

A Lyric Poem by
Amy Lowell

Lake Scene by Moonlight, 1879. Arthur Gilbert. The Maas Gallery, London, England.

The white mares[1] of the moon rush along the sky
Beating their golden hoofs upon the glass Heavens;
The white mares of the moon are all standing on their hind legs
Pawing at the green <u>porcelain</u> doors of the <u>remote</u> Heavens.
Fly, Mares!
Strain your utmost,[2]
Scatter the milky dust of stars,
Or the tiger sun will leap upon you and destroy you
With one lick of his <u>vermilion</u> tongue. ✣

---

1. **mares.** Mature female horses
2. **utmost.** To the greatest or most of one's powers and abilities

> **DURING READING**
> **Analyze Literature**
> **Imagery** What specific image has Lowell created here? **A**

> **por•ce•lain**
> (por´ s[ə] lən) *adj.,* made of a hard ceramic, like china
>
> **re•mote** (ri mōt´) *adj.,* distant

> **DURING READING**
> **Use Reading Strategies**
> **Visualize** How does the final image of the poem reinforce the speaker's warning? **B**

> **ver•mil•ion**
> (vər mil' yən) *adj.,* bright red or scarlet

MIRRORS & WINDOWS

When have you compared two completely different things? What can such comparisons add to a person's experience?

479

Review the Model

Find Meaning

1. (a) The speaker describes white mares. (b) The speaker wants to associate the movement of clouds with the power and beauty of horses.

2. (a) The mares rush along the sky, beat their hooves, stand on their hind legs, and paw against the doors of the heavens. (b) They create feelings of wonder and power.

3. (a) The speaker urges the mares to work their hardest. (b) They will be destroyed by the sun. (c) It is nighttime. (d) "The milky dust of stars" is still present, and the warning about the "tiger sun" is expressed in future tense.

Make Judgments

4. (a) They are far away and fragile. (b) Students might say that it makes them feel helpless or restless.

5. (a) The speaker seems to feel that the nighttime is powerful. (b) Students might say they can tell this by the speaker's delicate and forceful images, like "porcelain doors" and "vermilion tongue."

6. The speaker uses vivid and active phrases such as *rush along the sky, Beating their golden hoofs,* and *Scatter the milky dust of stars.*

Analyze Literature

Imagery *Answer:* Metaphors and qualities might include remote, glass heavens with green porcelain doors as the sky (distant, fragile, confined) and milky dust that can be scattered as stars (white, fine, powdery).

Find Meaning

1. (a) What creatures does the speaker describe in lines 1–4? (b) Why might the speaker have chosen this metaphor?

2. (a) What actions occur in lines 1–4? (b) What feeling or mood do these lines create?

3. (a) What action does the speaker urge the mares to take? (b) What does the speaker say will happen if the mares don't follow this advice? (c) What time of day is the speaker describing in lines 5–9? (d) What evidence supports your answer?

Analyze Literature

Imagery Amy Lowell uses several metaphors to create the imagery in the poem "Night Clouds." Use the chart to identify the metaphors. Then list the qualities that these metaphors suggest.

Make Judgments

4. (a) How are the Heavens described in the poem? (b) How does this description make you feel?

5. (a) How does the speaker seem to feel about the scene and time of day he or she is describing? (b) How can you tell?

6. How does the speaker create a feeling of action and movement in the night sky?

Metaphor	Qualities
White mares with golden hoofs are compared to clouds.	beautiful, strong, feminine, fast, magical

---

Extend Understanding

Writing Options

Creative Writing Write your own Imagist **poem** about the night sky. Use vivid imagery, repetition, and precise language. Check to see that your images communicate the mood and feeling you want to convey. Read your poem aloud for the class.

Expository Writing Analysis is the act of examining parts of something and then thinking about how the parts are related. Write an **analysis** of Lowell's use of imagery in "Night Clouds." Your audience is a friend who has read the poem and doesn't quite understand it. Use evidence from the text to support your thesis.

Lifelong Learning

Research Use a field manual or weather almanac to learn more about different kinds of clouds. Present your findings to the class using visual media.

Critical Literacy

Make Observations Using the information you collected about clouds, go outdoors over the course of several days and record your observations about the clouds you see. Compare your observations and determine how the clouds related to the weather of each day.

Go to **www.mirrorsandwindows.com** for more.

Rubrics for Writing Options

You can adapt this as a checklist for students to use as they write.

Creative Writing

☐ Is the poem about the night sky?

☐ Does it contain vivid imagery, repetition, and precise language?

☐ Does it clearly communicate a specific mood?

Expository Writing

☐ Does the analysis clearly address the imagery in "Night Clouds"?

☐ Does the student use evidence from the text to discuss the poem's meaning?

☐ Is the language appropriate for a peer audience?

Dreams

A Lyric Poem by Langston Hughes

Preview the Model

At a Glance
Guided Reading: Reading Model
- Reading Level: Easy
- Difficulty Consideration: Figurative language
- Ease Factors: Familiar subject, simple sentence structure

Build Background
Historical Context Langston Hughes was one of the major poets of the Harlem Renaissance, a movement in the 1920s that brought national fame to many African-American poets, playwrights, and authors. The movement also drew greater attention to the problems that existed for African Americans.

Reader's Context What are your dreams? What would you do and how would you feel if they came true?

Set Purpose
Preview the poem "Dreams" to see how it is structured. How many stanzas are there? How many lines are in each stanza? What else do you notice about the poem's form?

Analyze Literature
Metaphor and Simile Both **metaphors** and **similes** are figures of speech that invite the reader to make a comparison between two unlike things and to note a surprising characteristic they share. A simile always includes the word *like* or *as*. Note how Hughes uses both figures of speech in "Dreams."

Meet the Author
Langston Hughes (1902–1967) spent his early life with his grandmother in Lawrence, Kansas. He later lived with his mother in Lincoln, Illinois, where his classmates elected him class poet. Hughes's writing focuses on themes related to the African-American experience. Today, Hughes is recognized as one of the most outstanding writers of the Harlem Renaissance.

Use Reading Skills
Identify Main Idea The overall point the author wants a reader to understand after reading a selection is its main idea. To find the main idea, gather the important details into a main idea map. Then use details from the poem to form a short summary statement. This statement is the main idea.

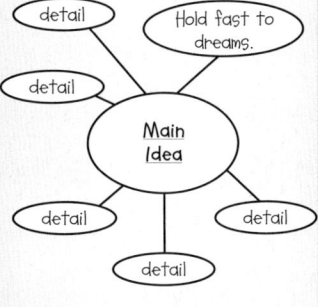

Objectives
Studying this lesson will enable students to
- use reading strategies such as identifying main idea
- define *metaphor* and *simile* and recognize the effect of these literary techniques in the selection
- describe the literary accomplishments of Langston Hughes and appreciate his role as one of the major poets of the Harlem Renaissance
- analyze a poem about determination

Launch the Lesson
Ask student volunteers to name and discuss some goals they have set for themselves but are not sure they can achieve. How does this situation make them feel? Tell students that the poem they are about to read warns of what happens when goals fall by the wayside. As they read, have them think about how the speaker's advice might influence their outlooks toward their futures.

Summary
The speaker implores readers to hold onto their dreams. Once a dream is gone, life is cold and unbearable.

DREAMS **481**

Reading Strategies

Make Predictions
Have students make predictions regarding the topic and theme of "Dreams," based on its title and the information provided by the Build Background and Meet the Author sections on page 481. Then, after they have read the poem, ask them to confirm or revise their predictions.

KEY TERMS
LYRIC POEM, 481
PLAYWRIGHT, 481
STANZA, 481
METAPHOR, 481
SIMILE, 481
MAIN IDEA, 481
SUMMARY, 481
FIGURATIVE LANGUAGE, 485

Common Core State Standards
Reading Literature
RL.1, RL.2
Writing
W.9
Language
L.6

Teach the Model

The Mirrors & Windows questions at the end of the selection focus on the theme of aspiration. Before reading the poem, ask students what their aspirations are for the near and distant future and whether they think they will attain them. Then ask them why literature that involves this theme is often presented to young people.

The Falling Star, 1909 (oil on canvas). James Hamilton Hay. Walker Art Gallery, National Museums Liverpool / The Bridgeman Art Library.

482

Program Resources

Planning and Assessment
Program Planning Guide, Selection Lesson Plan
E-Lesson Planner
Assessment Guide, Lesson Test
ExamView

Technology Tools
Interactive Student Text on CD
Visual Teaching Package
Audio Library
mirrorsandwindows.com

Meeting the Standards
Poetry: Unit 5, Guided Reading, pp. 26–30

Differentiating Instruction
English Language Learners, Identify Main Idea, pp. 125–131

Dreams

A Lyric Poem by Langston Hughes

Hold fast to dreams
For if dreams die
Life is a broken-winged bird
That cannot fly.

Hold fast to dreams
For when dreams go
Life is a barren field
Frozen with snow. ❖

DURING READING

Analyze Literature
Metaphor and Simile Is the author using a metaphor or a simile in this stanza? What is being compared? **A**

DURING READING

Use Reading Skills
Identify Main Idea What is the main idea of this stanza? Explain. **B**

People often dream of things they want in their lives or in life in general: a great job or world peace, for example. What are your dreams? Why do you think the poem "Dreams" is included in many books for young people?

Find Meaning

1. (a) In the first stanza, what does the speaker urge the reader to do? (b) What argument does the speaker use to convince the reader of this action?
2. (a) What image is used in the first stanza? (b) Why might the author have chosen this image?
3. (a) What image is used in the second stanza? (b) Why might the author have chosen this image?

Make Judgments

4. The word *dreams* has more than one meaning. What meaning do you think is being used in "Dreams"? Explain.
5. (a) How effective are the figures of speech used in this poem? (b) Do they make for convincing arguments? In your answer, explain why the comparisons do or do not have power to persuade a reader.
6. How did this poem affect you? Explain.

DREAMS **483**

Teach the Connection

Analyze Literature
Metaphor and Simile Work with students to identify and discuss the five similes in this poem, noting the intent of each comparison. Then, point out that the final line contains a metaphor: A dream that is not acted on might cause an explosion within one's spirit, involving such strong emotions as rage, disappointment, and depression.

Use Reading Skills
Identify Main Idea Guide students in paraphrasing the main idea of this poem: that a dream that is postponed or never acted on can cause a person terrible pain and sadness.

Text-to-Text Connection
Answer: Both poems warn of the consequences of not following through, or being allowed to follow through, with dreams. Both rely on figurative language to express main ideas. Both use negative images to reinforce what could happen. Both poems contain rhyme. They differ in that "Dreams" uses metaphors and "A Dream Deferred" primarily uses similes. "Dreams" expresses that if dreams "die" or "go," you are left with lack of fulfillment and growth. The last line of "A Dream Deferred" suggests that a thwarted dream might "explode," which connotes negative and violent results.

Langston Hughes knew that, in his time, many African Americans felt the only things they had were their dreams. Hughes knew that people's dreams are a source of hope and that to deny them their dreams is to deny them hope for a better future. He originally called this poem "Harlem" after a district in New York City that was, and still is, primarily occupied by African Americans. As you read "A Dream Deferred," look for the warning Hughes is giving to the people of Harlem.

A Dream Deferred

A Lyric Poem by Langston Hughes

Harlem

What happens to a dream deferred?[1]

Does it dry up
like a raisin in the sun?
Or fester like a sore—
5   And then run?
Does it stink like rotten meat?
Or crust and sugar over—
like a syrupy sweet?

Maybe it just sags
10   like a heavy load.

Or does it explode? ❖

---

1. deferred. Delayed, postponed

TEXT—TO—TEXT CONNECTION What similarities do you see between the poems "Dreams" and "A Dream Deferred"? How are the poems different? Use evidence from the poems to support your answers.

TEACHING NOTE

Self-Generated Questioning
Ask students which poem or image generated the most questions for them as they read. Encourage them to note those parts and jot down their questions. Model a question such as: "Did an unrealized dream encourage Hughes to write this poem?" As a class, reread the parts that have generated the most questions, deciding whether each question requires them to recall parts of the text or to infer meaning. Focus on working through answers for the latter type of question.

Common Core State Standards
Writing
W.7, W.8
Language
L.6

Analyze Literature

Metaphor and Simile Metaphors and similes are figures of speech, or figurative language. A figure of speech is meant to be understood imaginatively instead of literally. Create a chart to explore the figurative language in "Dreams." What images do you picture in response to the language?

Figurative Language	What I Envision
"Life is a broken-winged bird / That cannot fly."	I picture a bird hopping along the ground flapping its wings, but it can't get off the ground.

Extend Understanding

Writing Options

Creative Writing Write a **personal letter** to Langston Hughes telling him about your dreams for your life. Explain why these dreams are important to you and how you think you might accomplish them. Begin with a connection between his poem and your thoughts.

Persuasive Writing Write a short **persuasive speech** that will convince people that it is possible to have a better future. In order to prepare your arguments, think of why people might need to be persuaded of this idea. Anticipate and answer arguments or questions your audience might have.

Collaborative Learning

Conduct Research Work with a partner to research the history of the Harlem Renaissance. Include information on who belonged to the movement and why the movement was important. Write a brief report and share your findings with the class.

Critical Literacy

Ask Questions Imagine you could interview Langston Hughes. Based on what you read in Meet the Author, Build Background, and the poems, write a list of questions you would like to ask him.

 Go to www.mirrorsandwindows.com for more.

DREAMS **485**

Review the Model

Literary Connection

A Raisin in the Sun African American playwright Lorraine Hansberry (1930-1965) employed Hughes's image of a raisin in the sun for the title of her award-winning play, *A Raisin in the Sun,* which was first produced on Broadway in 1959. *New York Times* drama critic Frank Rich wrote that the play "changed American theater forever [by forcing] both blacks and whites to re-examine the deferred dreams of black America." In 1961, a movie version appeared, starring Sidney Poitier. Hansberry's illustrious career as a playwright was cut short by her premature death at the age of thirty-four.

Analyze Literature

Metaphor and Simile *Answer:* Students should identify both the broken-winged bird and the barren, frozen, snow-covered field. Their imaginative response should have a logical connection to Hughes's figurative language.

Program Resources

For further instruction, refer students to the following extension activity: Critical Literacy: Ask Questions, *Exceeding the Standards: Extension Activities,* pp. 14–15.

Rubrics for Writing Options

You can adapt this as a checklist for students to use as they write.

Creative Writing

☐ Does the letter follow the standard form and conventions of a personal letter?

☐ Does it begin by connecting the poem to the student's thought?

☐ Does it clearly state the student's dreams?

☐ Does it explain why these dreams are important and how they might be accomplished?

Persuasive Writing

☐ Does the speech clearly state a position?

☐ Does it promote the possibility of a better future?

☐ Does it anticipate and address possible arguments from its intended audience?

Understanding Sound Devices

Reading skills that can help students understand sound devices include reading aloud and determining the importance of details.

Use Reading Skills

Read Aloud Demonstrate that reading aloud reveals sound devices and is especially helpful for hearing internal rhyme and the rhythm of each line. Read the excerpt from Eliot's poem, and tell students to listen for the short *a* sound in words such as *cats, matter, mad, hatter,* and *family.* Read the excerpt aloud a second time, and adjust your tone and pace to emphasize end rhymes. Then, ask students how they would read the line in capital letters. Elicit the observation that a person would probably have to start at the beginning of this sentence and then emphasize the capitalized words in some way.

Use Reading Skills

Determine Importance of Details

Tell students that, although a poet may not think through absolutely every sound and punctuation mark as he or she writes a poem, these can all be significant when it comes to interpreting a poem. Have students tell you what they think of the names Eliot suggests for cats. Ask: "How do the names sound? Do you think the names are important details? Are the sounds important or just the look of each name?"

Literary Element

Understanding Sound Devices

What Are Sound Devices?

Poetry is often musical, having rhythms, rhymes, and other sound devices. **Sound devices** are elements that writers use to appeal to the ears of listeners or readers. In what ways does the excerpt below from "The Naming of Cats" appeal to your ear?

Sound devices can impact the mood and tone of a poem. Certain sound devices might contribute to a lighthearted mood or convey feelings of gloom. Also, sound devices can influence a poem's meaning by suggesting the way in which a line is meant to be read.

Rhyme

Rhyme is the repetition of sounds at the ends of words. For example, the word *games* at the end of the second line in the excerpt from "The Naming of Cats" rhymes with the word *names* in the fourth line. Because these words appear at the ends of their lines, the rhyme is referred to as an *end rhyme.* When a poem has a consistent pattern of end rhymes, it is said to have a **rhyme scheme.** You can identify the rhyme scheme by assigning a new letter to each new rhyme. For example:

> The Naming of Cats is a difficult matter,   *a*
>
> It isn't just one of your holiday games;   *b*
>
> You may think at first I'm as mad as a hatter,   *a*
>
> When I tell you, a cat must have
>
>   THREE DIFFERENT NAMES.   *b*

At times, a word in the middle of a line rhymes with either a word at the end of a line or with a word in the middle of another line. This is called *internal rhyme.* For example, when Eliot writes, "His ineffable effable / Effanineffable / Deep and inscrutable singular Name," *ineffable* and *effable* are internal rhymes. Also, rhymes are not always completely exact. Sometimes words are used that only partially rhyme. If a rhyme is close, but not exact, it is called a *slant* or *half rhyme.*

Olympia, 1863. Edouard Manet. Musée d'Orsay, Paris, France.

> The Naming of Cats is a difficult
>   matter,
> It isn't just one of your holiday
>   games;
> You may think at first I'm as
>   mad as a hatter
> When I tell you, a cat must have
>   THREE DIFFERENT NAMES.
> First of all, there's the name that the
>   family use daily,
> Such as Peter, Augustus, Alonzo or
>   James,
> Such as Victor or Jonathan, George
>   or Bill Bailey—
> All of them sensible everyday names.
>   —T. S. ELIOT, "The Naming of Cats"

Differentiated Instruction

Enrichment

Students interested in reading and writing poetry can explore some details of meter. Encourage them to learn about the four most common metrical feet in English: the iamb, the trochee, the dactyl, and the anapest. Have students collaborate on a visual aid that defines each term, shows how a person would mark it as part of scanning a poem, and gives an example of lines of poetry using each metrical foot. As an extension, ask students to give examples of one or more metrical feet in tetrameter (four-foot), pentameter (five-foot), and hexameter (six-foot) lines. (You can demonstrate iambic pentameter as an example: "The Inuit have fifteen words for snow.")

Common Core State Standards

Reading Literature
RL.4

Rhythm

The pattern of stressed and unstressed syllables in a line of poetry is its **rhythm.** Stressed syllables are referred to as beats. A regular and predictable pattern of stressed and unstressed syllables is called **meter.** Reading a poem aloud can help you better hear its rhythm and determine whether or not it is written in meter. For example, read this line from "The New Colossus" aloud.

 I lift my lamp beside the golden door!

Can you hear the rhythm? Is the pattern of stressed and unstressed syllables regular and predictable? One way to help you determine whether a poem has a regular rhythm is by scanning it. Scanning is the process of marking / over stressed syllables, and ˘ over unstressed syllables.

  ˘ / ˘ / ˘ / ˘ / ˘   /
  I lift my lamp beside the golden door!

In this case, the pattern is regular. These lines are metered. Every meter is made up of feet. A **foot** is a group of two or more stressed or unstressed syllables. There are different kinds of feet. In the above passage, the poem's meter is made up of feet called iambs. An *iamb* contains a single unstressed syllable followed by a single stressed syllable. The first two words in the scanned lines above, *I lift,* make up a single iambic foot.

Alliteration, Consonance, and Assonance

Writers sometimes repeat the same consonant or vowel sound in two or more nearby words. In Amy Lowell's poem "Night Clouds" (page 478), for example, the *m* sound is repeated several times in a line: "The white mares of the moon rush along the sky." When a consonant sound is repeated at the beginnings of words, as it is in Lowell's poem, it is called **alliteration.**

If a consonant sound is repeated at the ends or in the middles of words, it is called **consonance.** When a writer repeats vowel sounds, it is called **assonance.** In "Night Clouds," Lowell writes: "The white mares of the moon are all standing on their hind legs." In this line, the *a* sound is repeated throughout the line.

Onomatopoeia

When a writer uses a word or phrase that sounds like the thing it names, then the writer is using **onomatopoeia.** Words like *pow, crash,* and *meow* are all examples of onomatopoeia. This device can add excitement and an additional layer of sensory experience to a description.

Snowdown by Moonlight, 1792. Joseph Wright of Derby. University of Liverpool Art Gallery & Collections, Liverpool, England.

LITERARY ELEMENT **487**

Analyze Literature

Rhythm Tap out the rhythm of the first four Eliot lines, and make sure students can hear the anapests. Ask if they know any songs or dances with this rhythm (it sounds a lot like the rhythm of a waltz).

Cultural Connection

Onomatopoeia This word comes from Greek roots that together mean "name maker." Every known language has onomatopoeia. The simplest onomatopoeic words are usually animal sounds—*meow* and *oink,* for example. Challenge students to give you examples of onomatopoeic words. Encourage English learners to give examples from their first languages. You might also have students tell you how each word "names" the thing to which it refers.

Use Reading Skills

Read Aloud Have students work in groups of three or four. Let each group select a poem from this text and practice reading it aloud. Ask group members to take turns reading and listening for rhythm, rhyme, onomatopoeia, alliteration, assonance, and consonance.

KEY TERMS

SOUND DEVICE, 486	**STRESSED SYLLABLE,** 487
MOOD, 486	**UNSTRESSED SYLLABLE,** 487
TONE, 486	**RHYTHM,** 487
RHYME, 486	**METER,** 487
REPETITION, 486	**FOOT,** 487
END RHYME, 486	**IAMB,** 487
RHYME SCHEME, 486	**ALLITERATION,** 487
INTERNAL RHYME, 486	**CONSONANCE,** 487
SLANT RHYME, 486	**ASSONANCE,** 487
HALF RHYME, 486	**ONOMATOPOEIA,** 487

Multiple-Meaning Words

Using the excerpt from "The Naming of Cats" on page 486, have students choose the best meaning for each of these multiple-meaning words.

1. mad: angry / hilarious / <u>insane</u>
2. sensible: perceptible to the senses / sensitive / conscious / <u>reasonable</u> / practical

Point out that the simile "mad as a hatter" refers to a time when mercury was used in making hats. Mercury causes nervous system damage when ingested, and people who became jittery from making hats were considered insane. As noted in the text on page 489, Eliot is probably alluding to Lewis Carroll's Mad Hatter.

The Naming of Cats

A Humorous Poem by T. S. Eliot

Preview the Model

At a Glance
Guided Reading: Reading Model
- Reading Level: Easy
- Difficulty Consideration: Pronunciation of names
- Ease Factor: Humorous

Objectives
Studying this lesson will enable students to
- use reading strategies such as analyzing the effects of form on meaning
- define *rhyme, end rhyme,* and *rhyme scheme* and recognize the effect of rhyme on the overall tone of the poem
- describe the literary accomplishments of T. S. Eliot

Launch the Lesson
Tell students that in this poem, "The Naming of Cats," the speaker states that naming a cat is a very complicated thing to do. Have them predict why it might be so complicated. Then have them read to find out how their ideas are similar to, and different from, those of the speaker.

Summary
The poem explains that cats have three names, including a common name used by the family, a peculiar and dignified name, and a secret name that no human would know.

Build Background
Cultural Context Unlike most dogs, who seem born to serve and please their owners, cats often tend to be aloof, reserved, and mysterious. According to this poem, cats will accept the names that people give them, but they reserve the right to pick "secret" names that only they recognize.

Reader's Context What name might you give to a cat, and what "secret" name might the cat choose for itself?

Set Purpose
Preview the poem, noting the rhythm and the rhyme scheme. As you read, take notes on how these elements affect your understanding of the poem.

Analyze Literature
Rhyme Many poems include **rhyme,** which is the repetition of the same, or similar, sounds at the ends of words. In Eliot's poem, *end rhymes*—rhymes at the ends of lines—form the **rhyme scheme,** or consistent patterns of end rhymes, of *abab.* As you read the poem, note the *abab* rhyme scheme.

Use Reading Skills
Analyze Effects of Form on Meaning The form, or structure, of a poem, as well as the words and rhyme scheme, affect the poem's tone and meaning. As you read this poem, use a chart to keep track of the effects of form, language, and rhymes.

Element in Poem	Effect on Tone and Meaning
rhythm	
abab rhyme scheme	
alliteration, consonance, assonance	

Preview Vocabulary
in·ef·fa·ble (i ne´ fə bəl) *adj.,* too awesome to be spoken

in·scru·ta·ble (in skrü´ tə bəl) *adj.,* extremely puzzling or mysterious

Meet the Author
T. S. Eliot (1888–1965), like the cats in his poem, had a secret made-up name: George Pushdragon. He used it when he entered crossword puzzle competitions. It was also the name of one of his cats. (Wiscus and Pittipaws were others.) Born in the United States, Eliot moved to England in 1915 and became a British citizen in 1927. He quickly became distinguished as a serious poet, playwright, essayist, and critic. In 1948, he was awarded the Nobel Prize for Literature. "The Naming of Cats" is from a lighthearted volume of poems titled *Old Possum's Book of Practical Cats,* which Eliot wrote for his godchildren.

488 UNIT 5 POETRY

Words in Use

Preview Vocabulary
ineffable, 490
inscrutable, 490

Selection Words
particular, 489
peculiar, 489
dignified, 489
profound, 490

Teaching Words
aloof, 488
distinguished, 488
widow, 490

KEY TERMS
RHYTHM, 488
RHYME SCHEME, 488
RHYME, 488
END RHYME, 488
PLAYWRIGHT, 488
TONE, 488
ALLITERATION, 488
CONSONANCE, 488

ASSONANCE, 488
NARRATIVE, 491
RISING ACTION, 491
CLIMAX, 491
RESOLUTION, 491
CHRONOLOGICAL ORDER, 491

Common Core State Standards

Reading Literature
RL.1, RL.5

Writing
W.7, W.8, W.9

Language
L.6

The Naming of Cats

A Humorous Poem
by T. S. Eliot

The Naming of Cats is a difficult matter,
    It isn't just one of your holiday games;
You may think at first I'm as mad as a hatter[1]
When I tell you, a cat must have THREE DIFFERENT NAMES.
5 First of all, there's the name that the family use daily,
    Such as Peter, Augustus, Alonzo or James,
Such as Victor or Jonathan, George or Bill Bailey—
    All of them sensible everyday names.
There are fancier names if you think they sound sweeter,
10   Some for the gentlemen, some for the dames:
Such as Plato, Admetus, Electra, Demeter—
    But all of them sensible everyday names.
But I tell you, a cat needs a name that's particular,
    A name that's peculiar, and more dignified,
15 Else how can he keep up his tail perpendicular,[2]
    Or spread out his whiskers, or cherish his pride?
Of names of this kind, I can give you a quorum,[3]
    Such as Munkustrap, Quaxo, or Coricopat,

---

1. **mad as a hatter.** A *hatter* is a person who makes hats. *Mad* is an informal synonym for *crazy*. The phrase *mad as a hatter* is an allusion to the Mad Hatter, a silly character in *Alice's Adventures in Wonderland*, by Lewis Carroll.
2. **keep up his tail perpendicular.** *Perpendicular* means "at a right angle to an adjoining surface or line." A happy, healthy cat often walks and runs with its tail upright, perpendicular to the surface of its back.
3. **quorum.** Select group

DURING READING

Use Reading Skills
Analyze Effects of Form on Meaning How does the repetition of names affect the sound and meaning? **A**

DURING READING

Analyze Literature
Rhyme In lines 13–16, what four words does the poet use to create the *abab* rhyme scheme? **B**

489

Teach the Model

The **Mirrors & Windows** questions at the end of the selection focuses on the theme of portrayal. Before reading the poem, ask students for their personal descriptions of cats. How do other cultures view cats?

History Connection
Animal Domestication More than ten thousand years ago, humans began domesticating wild animals. Birds provided humans with eggs, feathers, and meat. Sheep, pigs, and goats provided food and materials from which to make clothing. Originally trained to hunt, herd, and protect, dogs quickly also became companions and pets. So did cats. Domesticated for its beauty and elegance, the cat was also useful as a rat catcher. The ancient Egyptians revered cats and often mummified them to accompany royal humans in the afterlife.

Use Reading Skills
Analyze Effects of Form on Meaning *Answer:* The repetition of *names* makes the poem sound sort of like a nursery rhyme. It affects the poem's meaning by making the main idea overly clear, adding to the poem's humor and sarcasm. **A**

Analyze Literature
Rhyme *Answer: particular, dignified, perpendicular,* and *pride* **B**

Program Resources

Planning and Assessment
Program Planning Guide, Selection Lesson Plan
E-Lesson Planner
Assessment Guide, Lesson Test
ExamView

Technology Tools
Interactive Student Text on CD
Visual Teaching Package
mirrorsandwindows.com

Meeting the Standards
Poetry: Unit 5, Guided Reading, pp. 31–35

Differentiating Instruction
Developing Readers, Use Text Organization, pp. 34–36

Use Reading Skills

Analyze Effects of Form on Meaning *Answer:* The use of all capital letters gives emphasis to the words. It leads the reader toward Eliot's purpose for writing the poem and the poem's main idea. **Ⓐ**

Cultural Connection

Musical: *Cats* *Answer:* Students may say that the success of the musical would make the cats spread out their whiskers or cherish their pride, because they were the inspiration for the material. Others might say that the cat would not show how it felt because it is secretive, or because it simply does not care what people think about it.

Answer: Students might describe a pompous and regal cat, an energetic and playful cat, or a reclusive, temperamental cat. They might say that, based on their experience, Eliot's description of cats as dignified and proud is accurate. They might also say that he is providing them with unrealistic human qualities.

Such as Bombalurina, or else Jellylorum—
20   Names that never belong to more than one cat.
But above and beyond there's still one name left over,
        And that is the name that you never will guess;
The name that no human research can discover—
        But THE CAT HIMSELF KNOWS, and will never confess.
25 When you notice a cat in profound meditation,[4]
        The reason, I tell you, is always the same;
His mind is engaged in a rapt contemplation[5]
        Of the thought, of the thought, of the thought of his name:
            His <u>ineffable</u> effable
30   Effanineffable
Deep and <u>inscrutable</u> singular Name. ❖

DURING READING

Use Reading Skills
Analyze Effects of Form on Meaning How does the use of capitalization influence your reading of the poem? **Ⓐ**

in·ef·fa·ble (i neˊ fə bəl) *adj.,* too awesome to be spoken

in·scru·ta·ble (in skrüˊ tə bəl) *adj.,* extremely puzzling or mysterious

---

4. **profound meditation.** State of deep thinking
5. **rapt contemplation.** State of concentrated, focused study or inspection of various options

CULTURAL ▶▶ CONNECTION

Musical: *Cats* In 1977, composer Andrew Lloyd Webber put several poems from Eliot's *Old Possum's Book of Practical Cats* to music. In 1980, he presented a concert that Valerie Eliot, the poet's widow, attended. She was so happy with his work that she gave Webber additional "cat" poems never before published. Working with theatrical director Trevor Nunn, Webber developed the poems into a musical play. In 1981, the musical *Cats* was first performed in London and was instantly a smash hit. *Cats* has been produced all over the world, has been translated into ten languages, and has won every major theater award. How might this success make one of Eliot's made-up cats act? Explain your response.

Describe a cat that you have known or read about. Does Eliot's description of cats seem accurate in general?

Differentiated Instruction

Enrichment

Students might enjoy watching a recording of highlights from the musical *Cats* or listening to the original cast recording on CD. Display the famous logo on the cover of the DVD and CD. Students might also enjoy doing research on the Internet to find reviews and articles about *Cats*, especially in regards to the imaginative use of makeup, wardrobe, and props.

Grammar Skills

Synonyms and Connotation

Point out that part of the humor of this poem comes from the poet's use of sophisticated language to describe the "secret lives" of cats. Then explain that some synonyms carry different connotations, or feelings. Have students use dictionaries or thesauruses to find synonyms for words from this poem. Discuss whether the synonyms carry positive, negative, or neutral feelings.

Find Meaning

1. In line 1, the poet states that the naming of cats is a "difficult matter." What details and opinions does he offer to support that statement?

2. (a) Give an example of a cat's name that the poet considers "more dignified." (b) Why might such names "never belong to more than one cat"?

3. Why can human research never discover a cat's third name?

Analyze Literature

Rhyme Words that rhyme end in the same vowel and consonant sounds. They may have the same number of syllables, as in *cat* and *hat*. Or, they may have different numbers of syllables, as in *prevent* and *went*. Beginning at line 5 of the poem, pick an eight-line section. Use a chart to analyze the rhyme and rhyme scheme of these lines. In the chart, the first four lines of the poem have been used as an example.

Make Judgments

4. (a) What leads the poet to suggest that readers may think that he is "mad as a hatter"? (b) Do you think the ideas expressed in the poem show that he is "mad as a hatter"? Explain.

5. Of all the names that the poet suggests, which do you think is the best one for a cat? Explain.

Lines of Poem	Pairs of Rhyming Words	Number of Syllables in Each	Rhyme Scheme of Stanza
lines 1–4	1. matter, hatter	1. matter = 2, hatter = 2	abab
	2. games, names	2. games = 1, names = 1	

Find Meaning

1. It is complicated because the cat must have three names—a "sensible one" for everyday, a "dignified one" to make it proud, and a secret one that it chooses for itself.

2. (a) Munkustrap, Quaxo, Coricopat, Bombalurina, or Jellylorum. (b) Such names are unique, just as each cat is unique.

3. It is a secret name that the cat made up itself and will not—or cannot—reveal to humans.

Make Judgments

4. (a) He believes that naming a cat is of great importance and that a cat requires three distinct names.
(b) Answers will vary, but should be supported by the text.

5. Answers will vary, but should be supported by logic.

Analyze Literature

Rhyme *Answer:* Students should use their charts to identify the lines of two different stanzas, list the rhyming pairs, show accurate syllable counts, and correctly identify the rhyme scheme as *abab* (or, for the last seven lines, *ababccb*).

Extend Understanding

Writing Options

Creative Writing Write a short **personal narrative** about a pet you have had or known. Include your personal thoughts and feelings. Remember that a narrative should have rising action, a climax, and resolution and should be told in chronological order.

Expository Writing In a **literary response,** a writer analyzes literature. Write an analysis of Eliot's use of rhyme. Support your thesis with examples. How does it affect the tone and theme present in the poem?

Critical Literacy

Poetry Reading With a partner, practice reading different stanzas of this poem aloud. Experiment with the tone of your voice and the pacing of your reading. Perform the poem for the class.

Media Literacy

Comparing Literary Forms Find a recording of the music from *CATS*. Listen to various songs, including "The Naming of Cats." Which are your favorites? How do they relate to the themes in "The Naming of Cats"? Discuss the music in small groups.

MW Go to **www.mirrorsandwindows.com** for more.

THE NAMING OF CATS **491**

Rubrics for Writing Options

You can adapt this as a checklist for students to use as they write.

Creative Writing

☐ Does the narrative identify a pet by name and express the writer's feelings for it?

☐ Does it clearly relate a personal experience that the writer shared with the animal?

☐ Does it include all basic narrative elements and follow chronological order?

Expository Writing

☐ Does it clearly and effectively analyze Eliot's use of rhyme?

☐ Does it identify the rhyme scheme as *abab*?

☐ Does it offer logical and appropriate ideas concerning how the rhyme scheme adds to the lighthearted, humorous tone of the poem?

Recognizing Nouns

1. girl (singular), family (collective), cat's (singular possessive), games (plural)
2. people (plural), Quaxo (proper), Munkustrap (proper), names (plural), neighbors' (plural possessive), cats (plural)
3. Thomas (proper), cats' (plural possessive), beds (plural), vacation (singular)
4. Peter's (singular possessive), expressions (plural)

> For more information, see Grammar & Style Section 3.3, Nouns, in the Language Arts Handbook.

Program Resources

You will find additional lessons on Nouns: Proper, Plural, Possessive, and Collective in the *Exceeding the Standards: Grammar & Style* resource.

KEY TERMS

PROPER NOUN, 492
PLURAL NOUN, 492
POSSESSIVE NOUN, 492
SINGULAR NOUN, 492
APOSTROPHE, 492
COLLECTIVE NOUN, 492
SINGULAR VERB, 492

Grammar & Style

Nouns: Proper, Plural, Possessive, and Collective

Proper and Plural Nouns

Some for the gentlemen, some for the dames:

Such as Plato, Admetus, Electra, Demeter—

— T. S. ELIOT, "The Naming of Cats"

A **proper noun** names a specific person, place, or thing and begins with a capital letter. In the quotation above, *Plato, Admetus, Electra,* and *Demeter* are names for cats. Proper nouns include names, dates, places, and things.

If a noun represents more than one thing, it is a **plural noun.** In the quotation above, *dames* is a plural noun formed by adding -*s* to the end of the word *dame.* Here are several other rules for forming plural nouns.

Rule	Examples
If a noun ends in *s*, *sh*, *ch*, *x*, or *z*, add -*es*.	pass = passes dish = dishes catch = catches fox = foxes
If a noun ends in *o* preceded by a consonant, add -*es*.	hero = heroes
If a noun ends in *y* preceded by a consonant, change the *y* to *i* and add -*es*.	berry = berries
For some nouns that end in *f* or *fe*, change the *f* to *v* and add -*es* or -*s*.	loaf = loaves life = lives

Possessive Nouns

Possessive nouns show ownership. To form the possessive of a singular noun, add an apostrophe and an -*s* to the end of the word.

> **EXAMPLE**
> The *cat's* name is Alonzo.

There are several ways to form the possessive of a plural noun. If the plural noun does not end in *s*, add an apostrophe and an -*s* to the end of the word. If the plural noun ends with an *s*, add only an apostrophe.

> **EXAMPLES**
> The *men's* cats had strange names.
> The *cats'* tails were all different lengths.

Collective Nouns

Collective nouns name groups that are made up of individuals. A collective noun takes a singular verb when the group acts together and a plural verb when individuals within the group act differently.

> **EXAMPLES**
> **singular**   The *family* calls the cat Plato.
> **plural**   The *family* disagree on the cat's name.

Recognizing Nouns

On another sheet of paper, rewrite each of the following sentences. Then, underline each noun, and write its type above the word.

1. The girl and her family played the cat's games.
2. The people thought that Quaxo and Munkustrap were strange names for the neighbors' cats.
3. Thomas had to decide whether to take the cats' beds on vacation.
4. Peter's expressions were meditative.

TEACHING NOTE

Extra Practice

Each of these sentences has a collective noun. Have students tell you why the verb is either singular or plural in each case.

1. The committee elects an outside advisor. (Singular- the committee functions as a single unit)
2. After the committee heard the lecture, they had a lot of questions. (Plural- the committee asks questions as individuals)
3. The dance troupe is learning its steps (Singular- the troupe moves as a single unit)
4. The children applaud wildly as the dance troupe take another bow. (Plural- troupe members bow separately)

Common Core State Standards

Language
L.1

Pretty Words

A Lyric Poem by Elinor Wylie

At a Glance
Guided Reading: Reading Model
- Reading Level: Moderate
- Difficulty Consideration: Vocabulary
- Ease Factor: Selection length

Build Background

Literary Context This lyric poem expresses the narrator's thoughts and feelings about words. In the twentieth century, many writers and poets wrote about the craft of writing. Such literature gives the reader a glimpse of how a specific writer approached his or her craft. As you read, think about the attitude that Wylie reveals about the art of writing poetry.

Reader's Context In your opinion, what are some words that have interesting sounds?

Set Purpose

Preview the poem, reading the vocabulary and footnotes. As you read, note the rhyme scheme in each stanza.

Analyze Literature

Alliteration and Onomatopoeia The repetition of consonant sounds at the beginning of words is **alliteration.** The phrase *sail the salty sea* contains alliteration, formed by the repetition of the *s* sound. **Onomatopoeia** is the use of words that imitate sounds. Examples include *meow, crash,* and *beep.* As you read, note how the speaker uses alliteration and onomatopoeia.

Meet the Author

Elinor Wylie (1885–1928) grew up in Washington, DC. She began to write poetry as a teenager, but it was not until her thirties that she turned to sonnets. Her literary career blazed brightly, but it was brief. In December 1928, at the age of forty-three, she put the finishing touches on her last volume of poems and died of a stroke the following day.

Use Reading Skills

Analyze Text Organization This poem is a Petrarchan sonnet. Named for its originator, the Italian poet Francesco Petrarca (1304–1374), this type of sonnet has fourteen lines, divided into two stanzas. Petrarchan sonnets are difficult to compose, due to the strict requirements of their rhyme schemes. As you read, use this chart to note the different features of each stanza.

Stanza	Number of Lines	Rhyme Scheme
First Stanza		
Second Stanza		

Preview Vocabulary

doc•ile (dä´ səl) *adj.,* gentle; agreeable; obedient

dap•pled (dap´ p[ə]ld) *adj.,* spotted

lu•mi•nous (lü´ mə nəs) *adj.,* shiny; glowing; bright

gild•ed (gild´ əd) *adj.,* covered with a thin layer of gold

Objectives

Studying this lesson will enable students to
- use reading strategies such as analyzing text organization
- define *alliteration* and *onomatopoeia,* find examples, and recognize the effects of these literary techniques
- describe the literary accomplishments of Elinor Wylie and her use of the Petrarchan sonnet

Launch the Lesson

Remind students that many words carry connotations (positive or negative shadings). As examples, discuss the similarities and differences of *inexpensive* and *cheap.* Then, as students read "Pretty Words," urge them to look for connotative words.

Summary

This poem describes words as pets that belong to poets. The poem describes types of words as different types of creatures.

Preview Vocabulary
docile, 495
dappled, 495
luminous, 495
gilded, 495

Common Core State Standards

Reading Literature
RL.1

Writing
W.9

Speaking and Listening
SL. 1

Language
L.6

The Mirrors & Windows questions at the end of the selection focus on the theme of connotation. Ask students to name some words that they consider appealing and some they think are unattractive? What effect do words that have "pretty" or "ugly" connotations have on an audience?

History Connection

The Roaring Twenties Elinor Wylie lived and wrote in the 1920s, a period in which relief from the horrors of World War I brought new ideas and freedoms. Often called "the Roaring '20s," this was a brash, lighthearted era that came to a screeching halt when the stock market crashed in 1929, ushering in the Great Depression. However, while the post-war exuberance lasted, many American women gained their first glimpses of liberation from traditional "roles." Popular literature gave support. By becoming literary editor of *Vanity Fair*, Wylie was an influential force, as were other "Bohemian lady poets of the '20s," including Marianne Moore at *Dial* and Louise Bogan at *The New Yorker*. Similarly influential voices rose up years later, during the Women's Liberation movement of the 1960s, led by such feminist poets as Sylvia Plath, Anne Sexton, and Audre Lorde.

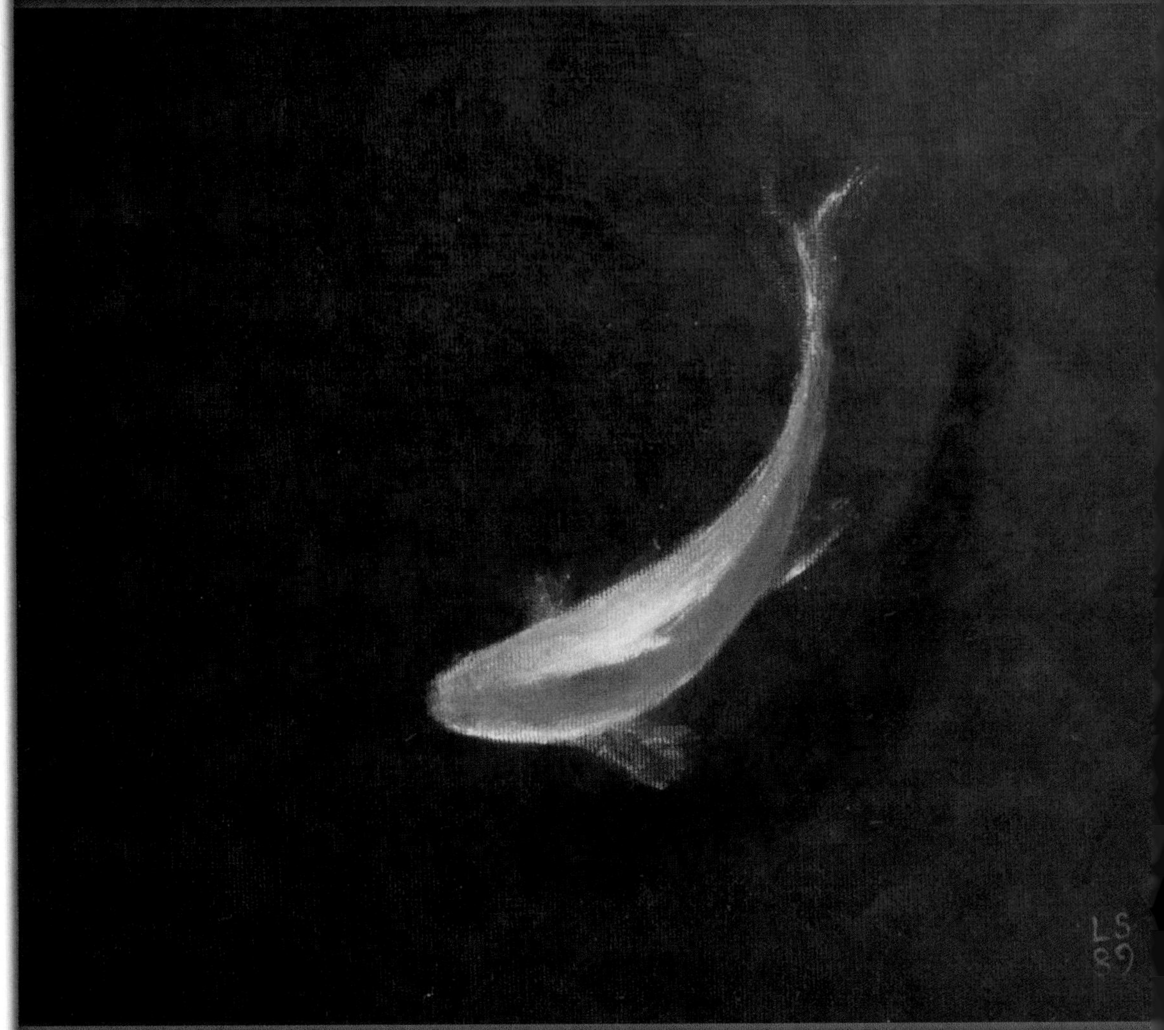

Apply the Model

BEFORE READING

DURING READING

AFTER READING

Goldfish. Lincoln Seligman. Private collection.

494

Program Resources

Planning and Assessment
Program Planning Guide, Selection Lesson Plan
E-Lesson Planner
Assessment Guide, Lesson Test
ExamView

Technology Tools
Interactive Student Text on CD
Visual Teaching Package
Audio Library
mirrorsandwindows.com

Meeting the Standards
Poetry: Unit 5, Guided Reading, pp. 36–40

Pretty Words

A Lyric Poem by Elinor Wylie

Poets make pets of pretty, <u>docile</u> words:
I love smooth words, like gold-enameled[1] fish
Which circle slowly with a silken swish,[2]
And tender ones, like downy-feathered[3] birds:
5 Words shy and <u>dappled</u>, deep-eyed[4] deer in herds,
Come to my hand, and playful if I wish,
Or purring softly at a silver dish,
Blue Persian[5] kittens, fed on cream and curds.

I love bright words, words up and singing early;
10 Words that are <u>luminous</u> in the dark, and sing;
Warm lazy words, white cattle under trees;
I love words opalescent,[6] cool, and pearly,
Like midsummer moths, and honied[7] words like bees,
<u>Gilded</u> and sticky, with a little sting. ❖

---

1. **gold-enameled.** Covered with a hard, protective layer of gold
2. **swish.** Light sweeping or brushing sound
3. **downy-feathered.** Most baby birds have soft, fluffy feathers known as *down*.
4. **deep-eyed.** Deer are known for their large, gentle, deep brown eyes.
5. **Blue Persian.** Long-haired domestic cat with bluish gray fur. Elegant and expensive, these cats are often pampered pets.
6. **opalescent** (o' pə le´ sənt). Reflecting iridescent light, meaning the rainbow display of colors that can be seen in soap bubbles
7. **honied.** Covered or filled with honey

doc•ile (dä´ səl) *adj.*, gentle; agreeable; obedient

dap•pled (dap´ p[ə]ld) *adj.*, spotted

> **DURING READING**
> **Use Reading Skills**
> **Analyze Text Organization** **A** What is the rhyme scheme of this stanza?

lu•mi•nous (lü´ mə nəs) *adj.*, shiny; glowing; bright

> **DURING READING**
> **Analyze Literature**
> **Alliteration and Onomatopoeia** **B** Does the final line contain alliteration or onomatopoeia?

gild•ed (gild´ əd) *adj.*, covered with a thin layer of gold

Which of the descriptions of "pretty words" did you enjoy the most? What are the consequences and benefits of words having associations such as "pretty" or "ugly"?

Review the Model

Find Meaning

1. (a) It means that poets nurture these words by employing them well. (b) It suggests that Wylie loves to "play" with words as she creates her poems.

2. (a) The phrase brings to mind the image of a bird. (b) High-energy or vivid words, like *sparkling* and *flaming*.

3. Responses will vary.

Make Judgments

4. (a) She compares them to downy-feathered birds, deep-eyed deer, and Blue Persian kittens. (b) The comparisons are effective because each animal is a gentle, soft creature.

5. Answers will vary, but should all be supported with logic.

6. The main difference is in the types of words. The first stanza mentions docile, tender words, and the second stanza mentions bright, warm, "stinging" words.

Analyze Literature

Alliteration and Onomatopoeia
Answer: Examples of alliteration: Poets, pets, pretty; circle, slowly, swish; dappled, deep-eyed deer; cream, curds; warm, words, white; midsummer, moths; sticky, sting. Examples of assonance: Poets, docile; which, circle, silken, swish; tender, feathered; shy, eyed; silver dish; Persian, curds, words, early; are, dark; gilded, sticky, little, sting. Examples of consonance: Poets, pets; dappled, deep-eyed; Or, silver.

Find Meaning

1. (a) According to the first line, "Poets make pets of pretty, docile words." What does this line mean? (b) What does this line suggest about the poet's feelings about words?

2. (a) In line 9, what image does the phrase "words up and singing early" bring to mind? (b) What type of word is suggested by this phrase? Give an example.

3. In line 11, Wylie compares "warm lazy words" with "white cattle under trees." Write a brief analogy describing another object that "warm, lazy words" could be compared to. Include the function of the object.

Analyze Literature

Alliteration and Onomatopoeia Alliteration is the repetition of consonant sounds at the beginning of words, as in the phrase *cantering colt*. Assonance is the repetition of the same or similar vowel sounds, as in the phrase *the sound of an owl*. Consonance is the repetition of consonant sounds, as in the phrase *a black rake*. Look at the poem. Use this chart to list examples of alliteration, assonance, and consonance.

Make Judgments

4. (a) To what three animals does the poet compare "tender" words? (b) Do you feel the comparisons are effective? Explain.

5. Which examples of figurative language in Wylie's poem do you feel make words seem the most "pretty"? Why?

6. In a Petrarchan sonnet, the second stanza often expresses a different concept or attitude than the first stanza. How are the concepts in Wylie's first and second stanzas different?

Words from Poem	Type of Sound Device
silver dish (line 7)	assonance

Extend Understanding

Writing Options

Creative Writing Make a list of as many groups of alliterative words as you can. Then, write a **poem** using those words.

Expository Writing In a **literary analysis,** a writer studies the parts of a selection to determine something about the whole. Write an analysis of the extended metaphor in this poem. In your thesis, state what the metaphor is and why it is or is not effective. Support your opinion with examples from the poem.

Collaborative Learning

Group Activity With a small group, discuss the meaning of this poem. What are the major themes and ideas it presents? Share your conclusions with those of other groups.

Critical Literacy

Poetry Reading With a partner, practice reading this poem aloud. Use appropriate volume and pacing. Read the poem to the class.

Go to **www.mirrorsandwindows.com** for more.

Rubrics for Writing Options

You can adapt this as a checklist for students to use as they write.

Creative Writing
☐ Does the poem contain words that are truly alliterative?
☐ Do the alliterative words effectively relate to the topic of the poem?

Expository Writing
☐ Does the literary analysis attempt to analyze the poem effectively?
☐ Does it identify the extended metaphor as the physical beauty of words, or the sense of words as both docile and energetic animals?
☐ Does the writing effectively explain why or why not the metaphor is effective?

Vocabulary & Spelling

Figurative Language: Similes, Metaphors, Analogies, and Idioms

I love smooth words, like
gold-enameled fish

Which circle slowly with a silken
swish,...

— ELINOR WYLIE, "Pretty Words"

Figurative language is language that expresses more than the literal meaning of the words. Poets often use figurative language to express emotions or abstract ideas. In the above quotation, Wylie uses a **simile,** a comparison between seemingly unrelated things using the word *like* or *as.* The simile compares smooth words to the movement of fish.

Similarly, a **metaphor** compares unrelated things, but without the words *like* or *as.*

> **EXAMPLE**
> *Warm lazy words, white cattle under trees;*

An **analogy** is an extended comparison between two different things. In "Pretty Words," the author describes types of words by comparing them to fish, birds, insects, and other animals.

Idioms are expressions that mean something other than the literal meaning of the words. For example, *I'm in the doghouse* means "I'm in trouble." *Don't get your nose out of joint* means "Don't take things so seriously."

Vocabulary Practice
Identify the type of figurative speech in each example from "Pretty Words."

1. "Poets make pets of pretty, docile words:"
2. "And tender ones, like downy-feathered birds:"
3. "I love words opalescent, cool, and pearly, / Like midsummer moths,"
4. "Words shy and dappled, deep-eyed deer in herds,"

What is the meaning of the following idioms?

5. The ball is in your court.
6. It's all water under the bridge.
7. I'll be there rain or shine.
8. A house divided against itself cannot stand.

Complete the following analogies that describe objects and their functions.

9. Paint is to walls as carpet is to _____.
10. Wood is to a fire as _____ is to a lamp.
11. Mud is to sticky as _____ is to slippery.
12. Canaries are to yellow as crows are to _____.

Working with a partner, create your own examples of figurative language. Create at least two similes, metaphors, analogies, and idioms. Share your work with the class. As you listen to other students' examples, write down any vocabulary or expressions you do not understand and ask your teacher or classmates about them later.

Spelling Practice
Words with the "s" Sound
The sound of the letter *s* is one of the most frequently occurring sounds in the English language. Part of the reason for its frequency is that it can be spelled by different letters or combinations of letters. Examine these words from "Pretty Words" to see the different ways the *s* sound is created.

circle	midsummer
docile	opalescent
luminous	silken

Vocabulary Practice
1. metaphor
2. simile
3. simile
4. metaphor
5. It's your turn to take action.
6. Everything is past; let's move on.
7. I'll be there no matter what.
8. Any group with internal bickering will fall apart.
9. floors
10. electricity or oil
11. ice
12. black

> For additional instruction on spelling rules, see the Vocabulary & Spelling Section 2.7, Spelling, in the Language Arts Handbook.

TEACHING NOTE
Extra Practice
Have students turn these similes into metaphors.
1. Her words pierced the armor of my soul like poison arrows. (Her poison arrows pierced my soul.)
2. The speech was as long as a hot summer day. (The speech was a hot summer day.)

Have students turn these metaphors into similes.
3. Dusk was a comma in the sentences of the day. (Place *like* after *was.*)
4. The song was a waterfall trickling over my head. (The song was as refreshing as a waterfall trickling over my head.)

Words in Use

Teaching Words
literal, 497
abstract, 497
docile, 497
opalescent, 497
dappled, 497

Program Resources

You will find additional lessons on Figurative Language: Similes, Metaphors, Analogies, and Idioms in the *Exceeding the Standards: Vocabulary & Spelling* resource.

KEY TERMS

FIGURATIVE LANGUAGE, 497	**ANALOGY,** 497
SIMILE, 497	**IDIOM,** 497
METAPHOR, 497	

Common Core State Standards
Reading Literature
RL.4
Language
L.5

The New Colossus
A Lyric Poem by Emma Lazarus

At a Glance
Directed Reading
- Reading Level: Easy
- Difficulty Considerations: Metaphor, line breaks, symbolism
- Ease Factor: Guiding questions

Objectives
Studying this lesson will enable students to
- use reading strategies such as rereading and asking questions to monitor reading comprehension
- define *rhyme scheme* and *Petrarchan sonnet* and analyze the structure and content of an example
- describe the work of Emma Lazarus and understand why her poem was chosen to be inscribed on the Statue of Liberty
- learn about Ellis Island and its role in the nineteenth-century wave of immigration

Launch the Lesson
Have students picture themselves as young immigrants in 1890, standing on the deck of a ship steaming into New York Harbor. What would be their goals and feelings? Have them read the poem to find out how the Statue of Liberty will try to welcome them.

Summary
The poem describes the Statue of Liberty as a "mighty woman with a torch" who guides people to freedom.

BEFORE READING

Build Background
Historical Context The Statue of Liberty is located in New York City Harbor, near Ellis Island, which was once the main immigrant processing center for the United States. In 1903, the poem "The New Colossus" was chosen to be inscribed on the base of the Statue of Liberty. In the poem, Lazarus compares the Statue of Liberty to the Colossus of Rhodes, an enormous ancient Greek statue of the sun god, Helios.

Reader's Context The Statue of Liberty's formal name is "Liberty Enlightens the World." What does liberty mean to you?

Set Purpose
As you read, visualize the images in the poem.

Analyze Literature
Rhyme Scheme The pattern of end rhymes used in a poem is the **rhyme scheme,** usually represented with letters. For example, if every other line rhymes, the rhyme scheme is *abab*. The poem "The New Colossus" is considered a *Petrarchan sonnet,* also known as an Italian sonnet. A *sonnet* is a fourteen-line poem. A Petrarchan sonnet is divided into two sections: an eight-line octave and a six-line sestet. As you read, note the rhyme scheme.

Meet the Author
Emma Lazarus (1848–1887) was born in New York. Lazarus came from a Sephardic (Spanish-Jewish) background and was well educated by her prosperous parents. As an adult, she became an essayist and poet. In the 1880s, Lazarus grew concerned about news of Jews being persecuted in Russia and Eastern Europe. She became an advocate for Jewish immigrants and wrote numerous essays protesting anti-Semitism, or discrimination against Jews.

Use Reading Skills
Monitor Comprehension To monitor comprehension means to be constantly aware of one's understanding of the text. If you have problems understanding what you are reading, go back and reread the difficult parts, read more slowly, ask questions, or take and review notes. Use a note-taking chart to monitor your understanding of the ideas in "The New Colossus."

Lines	Main Ideas	My Reactions
Lines 1–2	contrasts the Statue of Liberty with a Greek statue that is a symbol of conquest	

Summary of My Notes:

Preview Vocabulary
bra•zen (brā´ zən) *adj.*, bold

con•quer•ing (kän´ k[e]rin) *adj.*, strong and overpowering

com•mand (kə mand´) *v.*, call to attention

pomp (pämp) *n.*, show of magnificence; splendor

teem•ing (tē´ min) *adj.*, being very full of

Words in Use

Preview Vocabulary	Selection Words	Teaching Words
brazen, 499	**astride,** 499	**inscribed,** 498
conquering, 499	**imprisoned,** 499	**prosperous,** 498
command, 499	**yearning,** 499	**persecuted,** 498
pomp, 499		**advocate,** 498
teeming, 499		**enlightenment,** 500
		reinforces, 500
		signifying, 500

KEY TERMS
LYRIC POEM, 498
RHYME SCHEME, 498
END RHYME, 498
PETRARCHAN SONNET, 498
SONNET, 498
OCTAVE, 498
SESTET, 498
POINT OF VIEW, 504
VENN DIAGRAM, 504

Common Core State Standards

Reading Literature
RL.1

Writing
W.9

Language
L.6

The New Colossus

A Lyric Poem by
Emma Lazarus

Not like the <u>brazen</u> giant of Greek fame,
With <u>conquering</u> limbs astride from land to land;
Here at our sea-washed, sunset gates shall stand
A mighty woman with a torch, whose flame
5 Is the imprisoned lightning, and her name
Mother of Exiles. From her beacon¹-hand
Glows world-wide welcome; her mild eyes <u>command</u>
The air-bridged harbor that twin cities² frame.
"Keep, ancient lands, your storied <u>pomp</u>!" cries she
10 With silent lips. "Give me your tired, your poor,
Your huddled masses yearning to breathe free,
The wretched refuse³ of your <u>teeming</u> shore.
Send these, the homeless, tempest-tost⁴ to me.
I lift my lamp beside the golden door!" ❖

*The Unveiling of the Statue of Liberty,
Enlightening the World*, 1886. Edward Moran.
Museum of the City of New York, New York.

---

1. **beacon.** Light used as a signal; source of light or inspiration
2. **twin cities.** Manhattan and Brooklyn
3. **refuse.** Things that are thrown away because they have no value or use
4. **tempest-tost.** *Tempest* means "storm." *Tempest-tost* means "tossed by a storm."

---

bra•zen (brā´ zən) *adj.*, bold

con•quer•ing (kän´ k[e]riŋ) *adj.*, strong and overpowering

com•mand (kə mand´) *v.*, call to attention

pomp (pämp) *n.*, show of magnificence; splendor

teem•ing (tē´ miŋ) *adj.*, being very full of

499

Teach the Selection

Cultural Connection

A Symbol of Freedom Responses will vary. **Ⓐ**

Answer: Students may fear leaving behind the familiar or welcome the chance to start over. Some might say that Americans welcome immigrants; others may say that immigrants are negatively stereotyped.

Find Meaning

1. (a) Mother of Exiles. (b) The word *Mother* implies that they will be cared for in their new land.
2. (a) The torch contains "imprisoned lightning." (b) The effect is a sense of potential energy.
3. (a) Possible responses include *shout* or *yell*. (b) Possible responses include *soldier* or *cadet*. (c) Possible responses include *surrendering* or *yielding*.

Make Judgments

4. (a) The old Colossus is a harsh male who imposes his will on others; the new Colossus is a gentle female who "welcomes" the "huddled masses" home. (b) The speaker might be comparing the "pomp" and persecution in Europe at the time with the freedom and acceptance that America offered.
5. Responses should be supported with details from the poem.
6. Responses will vary.

A Symbol of Freedom The sculptor of the Statue of Liberty, Frederic-Auguste Bartholdi, included many symbols in the monument, such as the torch, crown, and tablet, among others. The torch was the first part of the statue to be built. The torch recalls the name of the statue, "Liberty Enlightens the World" and symbolizes the idea that light, or enlightenment, is essential to freedom. The seven points of the crown symbolize the seven continents and seven seas of the world. The crown reinforces the concept that the need for liberty is universal. The Statue holds a tablet in her left hand, which is a book of law signifying the founding principles of the United States. The writing on the tablet gives the date July 4, 1776, the date the United States won independence. After reading "The New Colossus," what do you think the Statue of Liberty represents? What might an immigrant feel seeing the statue for the first time? **Ⓐ**

How would you feel if you had to leave your country and start life in a new land? How would you describe the overall attitude of Americans toward immigrants in the United States today? Do you agree with that attitude?

Find Meaning

1. (a) What name does the speaker give the statue in line 6? (b) Why might the speaker have used that name?
2. (a) How is the torch described? (b) What is the effect of that image?
3. The following analogies describe objects and their functions using new vocabulary from the selection. Complete them by filling in the blanks. (a) Timid is to whisper as brazen is to _____. (b) A general is to command as a _____ is to obey. (c) Conquering is to the winning team as _____ is to the losing team.

Make Judgments

4. (a) Give an example of how the speaker contrasts the new and old Colossus. (b) Why might the speaker have chosen to refer to the Colossus of Rhodes?
5. What sort of image or picture do you visualize when you read lines 9–14? Explain.
6. What is the overall meaning of lines 9–14?

Differentiated Instruction

Auditory Learning

To fully grasp the spirit of "The New Colossus," students should prepare and perform a choral reading of this poem. Model a tone of voice that expresses the statue's offering of nurture and promise to the "homeless" and the "tempest-tost."

Enrichment

Interested students might enjoy writing a letter or a journal entry that someone their age could use to describe his or her feelings upon arriving in New York Harbor and laying eyes on the Statue of Liberty.

In the poem "The New Colossus," Emma Lazarus gives readers a poetic glimpse of the immigrants coming to America in the late 1880s. In "Immigrant Kids," a historical nonfiction text, writer **Russell Freedman** explains the actual experience of immigrants entering the country through Ellis Island. "Immigrant Kids" includes primary source information told by the immigrants themselves. As you read "Immigrant Kids," compare the ideas and information in the selection to those in "The New Colossus."

from **Immigrant Kids**

Historical Nonfiction by Russell Freedman

In the years around the turn of the century, immigration to America reached an all-time high. Between 1880 and 1920, 23 million immigrants arrived in the United States. They came mainly from the countries of Europe, especially from impoverished[1] towns and villages in southern and eastern Europe. The only thing they had in common was a fervent[2] belief that in America, life would be better.

Most of these immigrants were poor. Somehow they managed to scrape together enough money to pay for their passage to America. Many immigrant families arrived penniless. Others had to make the journey in stages. Often the father came first, found work, and sent for his family later.

Immigrants usually crossed the Atlantic as steerage passengers. Reached by steep, slippery stairways, the steerage lay deep down in the hold of the ship. It was occupied by passengers paying the lowest fare.

Men, women, and children were packed into dark, foul-smelling compartments. They slept in narrow bunks stacked three high. They had no showers, no lounges, and no dining rooms. Food served from huge kettles was dished into dinner pails provided by the steamship company. Because steerage conditions were crowded and uncomfortable, passengers spent as much time as possible up on deck.

The voyage was an ordeal, but it was worth it. They were on their way to America.

The great majority of immigrants landed in New York City, at America's busiest port. They never forgot their first glimpse of the Statue of Liberty.

Edward Corsi, who later became United States Commissioner of Immigration, was a ten-year-old Italian immigrant when he sailed into New York harbor in 1907:

> My first impressions of the New World will always remain etched in my memory, particularly that hazy October morning when I first saw Ellis Island. The steamer *Florida*, fourteen days out of Naples, filled to capacity with 1,600 natives of Italy, had weathered one of the worst storms in our captain's memory; and glad we were, both children and grown-ups, to leave the open sea and come at last through the Narrows into the Bay.

---

1. **impoverished.** Poor
2. **fervent.** Having or showing extreme passion and enthusiasm

Teach the Connection

History Connection

U.S. Immigration Beginning around 1840, millions of immigrants flooded into the United States each year. Immigration peaked between 1890 and 1910, when between 8 million and 9 million immigrants arrived each year. During that period, most immigrants hailed from Austria, Hungary, Italy, and Russia. America offered jobs in its factories and mills and promised freedom from religious and ethnic persecution. Additionally, America offered a social structure that was far more lenient than the restricting class systems of Europe. People arrived with the notion that hard work really could lead to the "American dream" of success and the American promise of "the pursuit of happiness."

Analyze Literature

Point of View Point out that this article contains both a nonfiction factual frame and personal narratives from primary sources—people who actually arrived at Ellis Island. The nonfiction frame of the article is written in third-person point of view, by the narrator. It contains such third-person pronouns as *they, he,* and *his.* The personal narratives are written in first-person point of view. They contain such first-person pronouns as *I, my, us,* and *we.* As students read, have them pause from time to time to identify the point of view in certain passages.

Words in Use

from
Immigrant Kids

Selection Words
steerage, 501
etched, 501
clustered, 502
din, 502
detained, 502
abnormalities, 502
teeming, 503

Common Core State Standards

Reading Literature
RL.5
Reading Informational
RI. 3
Writing
W.10
Language
L.6

Use Reading Skills
Compare and Contrast Discuss with students the feelings that Edward Corsi describes as the ship steams into the harbor. Then have them compare and contrast those feelings to emotions the immigrants might have had as they were herded, forced to stand in long lines, and then examined. How might the reality of Ellis Island have affected the joy and hope they felt when they saw the Statue of Liberty?

Analyze Literature
Tone Ask students what conditions might have led the immigrants to nickname Ellis Island "Heartbreak Island." What tone is created by the facts that the author presents in the paragraphs that follow that statement? **A**

My mother, my stepfather, my brother Giuseppe, and my two sisters, Liberta and Helvetia, all of us together, happy that we had come through the storm safely, clustered on the foredeck for fear of separation and looked with wonder on this miraculous land of our dreams.

Giuseppe and I held tightly to Stepfather's hands, while Liberta and Helvetia clung to Mother. Passengers all about us were crowding against the rail. Jabbered conversation, sharp cries, laughs and cheers—a steadily rising din filled the air. Mothers and fathers lifted up babies so that they too could see, off to the left, the Statue of Liberty....

Finally the *Florida* veered to the left, turning northward into the Hudson River and now the incredible buildings of lower Manhattan came very close to us.

The officers of the ship…went striding up and down the decks shouting orders and directions and driving the immigrants before them. Scowling and gesturing, they pushed and pulled the passengers, herding us into separate groups as though we were animals. A few moments later we came to our dock, and the long journey was over.

But the journey was not yet over. Before they could be admitted to the United States, immigrants had to pass through Ellis Island, which became the nation's chief immigrant processing center in 1892. There they would be questioned and examined. Those who could not pass all the exams would be detained; some would be sent back to Europe. And so their arrival in America **A** was filled with great anxiety. Among the immigrants, Ellis Island was known as "Heartbreak Island."

When their ship docked at a Hudson River pier, the immigrants had numbered identity tags pinned to their clothing. Then they were herded onto special ferryboats that carried them to Ellis Island. Officials hurried them along, shouting "Quick! Run! Hurry!" in half a dozen languages.

Filing into an enormous inspection hall, the immigrants formed long lines separated by iron railings that made the hall look like a great maze.

Now the examinations began. First the immigrants were examined by two doctors of the United States Health Service. One doctor looked for physical and mental abnormalities. When a case aroused suspicion, the immigrant received a chalk mark on the right shoulder for further inspection: L for lameness, H for heart, X for mental defects, and so on.

The second doctor watched for contagious and infectious diseases. He looked especially for infections of the scalp and at the eyelids for symptoms of trachoma, a blinding disease. Since trachoma caused more than half of all medical detentions, this doctor was greatly feared. He stood directly in the immigrant's path. With a swift movement, he would grab the immigrant's eyelid, pull it up, and peer beneath it. If all was well, the immigrant was passed on.

Those who failed to get past both doctors had to undergo a more thorough medical exam. The others moved on to the registration clerk, who questioned them with the aid of an interpreter: What is your name? Your nationality? Your occupation? Can you read and write? Have you ever been in prison? How much money do you have with you? Where are you going?

Some immigrants were so flustered that they could not answer. They were allowed to sit and rest and try again.

About one immigrant out of every five or six was detained for additional examinations or questioning.

Differentiated Instruction

Visual and Kinesthetic Learning
Students who have seen the movie *Titanic* will be at an advantage in understanding the cramped conditions in steerage, the hopes and courageous spirits of the immigrant families, and the often pompous and disrespectful attitudes of ship officials toward the steerage passengers. Consider showing poignant and telling clips from the movie. Lead them to discuss details from the movie and relate them to the facts and personal narratives in this article.

The writer Angelo Pellegrini has recalled his own family's detention at Ellis Island:

> We lived there for three days—Mother and we five children, the youngest of whom was three years old. Because of the rigorous physical examination that we had to submit to, particularly of the eyes, there was this terrible anxiety that one of us might be rejected. And if one of us was, what would the rest of the family do? My sister was indeed momentarily rejected; she had been so ill and had cried so much that her eyes were absolutely bloodshot, and Mother was told, "Well, we can't let her in." But fortunately, Mother was an indomitable[3] spirit and finally made them understand that if her child had a few hours' rest and a little bite to eat she would be all right. In the end we did get through.

Most immigrants passed through Ellis Island in about one day. Carrying all their worldly possessions, they left the examination hall and waited on the dock for the ferry that would take them to Manhattan, a mile away. Some of them still faced long journeys overland before they reached their final destination. Others would head directly for the teeming immigrant neighborhoods of New York City....

B Immigrants still come to America. Since World War II, more than 8 million immigrants have entered the country. While this is a small number compared to the mass migrations at the turn of the century, the United States continues to admit more immigrants than any other nation.

Many of today's immigrants come from countries within the Western Hemisphere, and from Asia and Africa as well as Europe. When they reach the United States, they face many of the same problems and hardships that have always confronted newcomers. And they come here for the same reason that immigrants have always come: to seek

C a better life for themselves and their children. ❖

---

3. indomitable. Brave, determined, and impossible to defeat

Teach the Connection

Use Reading Skills
Make Judgments Ask students to use details in Angelo Pellegrini's narrative to describe how the family members felt. What do they think the mother would have done if one of her children were rejected? What would students have done? How is the mother in this passage like "Mother of Exiles," the Statue of Liberty? How are the two mothers different in spirit? **B**

Make Connections
Point out that the author states that the immigrants carried "all their worldly possessions" to America with them. Have students step into the shoes of the immigrants. If they could take only what they could carry, what would they choose? **C**

An immigrant family arrives at Ellis Island.

IMMIGRANT KIDS **503**

Vocabulary Skills

Homonyms
Point out to students that the vocabulary word *teeming* appears in both the poem and in the final sentence of the paragraph on this page beginning "Most immigrants passed through . . ." Explain that *teem* means "to be full of." Then, write the word *team* on the board. Identify *teem* and *team* as homonyms—two words that sound alike but have different spellings and meanings. Point out that homonyms are tricky words that can cause confusion and mistakes to both readers and writers.

Review the Selection

Text-to-Text Connection

Answer: The poem gives the impression that immigrants seen as "wretched refuse" in other countries will be welcomed here. The nonfiction piece "Immigrant Kids" makes it clear that there were difficult requirements for passing through the "golden doors." The immigrants also had to pass certain medical requirements and fit certain standards. However, the idea that the impoverished immigrants came because of hopes of a better future is clear in both the poem and the article.

Analyze Literature

Rhyme Scheme *Answer:* The rhyme scheme is *abbaabbacdcdcd*. The scheme changes its pattern after the eighth line. This reflects a change in perspective in the poem, which is a standard feature of a Petrarchan sonnet. In this shift, the description of the statue stops, and the statue begins to "speak."

TEXT TO TEXT CONNECTION

How does the welcome given to immigrants in Ellis Island in "Immigrant Kids" compare or contrast with ideas in "The New Colossus"? In what ways does the information in "Immigrant Kids" reinforce that in the poem?

Analyze Literature

Rhyme Scheme A rhyme scheme is the pattern of end rhymes used in a poem. To find end rhymes, look for the last word in each line. Recall that the rhyme scheme is usually represented with letters, and a new letter is assigned to each new rhyme sound. For example, if every other line rhymes, the rhyme scheme is *abab*. What is the rhyme scheme of "The New Colossus"? What does the rhyme scheme add to the tone of the poem?

Extend Understanding

Writing Options

Creative Writing Write a **poem** that uses the idea of immigration as its main theme. You can write it from the point of view of an immigrant, from the point of view of someone who stayed behind in the immigrant's country, or from that of someone who already lives in the country in which the immigrant is arriving. In your poem, use the rhyme scheme used in "The New Colossus."

Expository Writing Use the Internet to find a speech written about the Statue of Liberty. Write a short **essay** comparing and contrasting the speech with "The New Colossus." Analyze the choice of words and phrases in both works, as well as the use of literary devices. Which one is more appealing?

Media Literacy

Compare Sonnets This poem is a sonnet. Locate another sonnet and compare and contrast the two. How are the poems similar in tone and structure? How are they different? How does the sonnet form help emphasize the content of each poem? Use a Venn diagram to organize details about the poems.

Lifelong learning

Recite Poetry Locate another example of a poem used to dedicate an important object, person, or event. Read it aloud to the class. Discuss whether or not you feel the poem captures the intent or spirit of the object, person, or event.

Go to **www.mirrorsandwindows.com** for more.

Rubrics for Writing Options

You can adapt this as a checklist for students to use as they write.

Creative Writing
☐ Does the poem use immigration as its theme?
☐ Does the student adapt an appropriate point of view?
☐ Did the student attempt to follow the rhyme scheme of "The New Colossus"?

Expository Writing
☐ Did the student locate a speech written about the Statue of Liberty?
☐ Does the essay compare and contrast the word and phrase choice and use of literary devices in the speech and the poem?
☐ Does the essay assess which work is more appealing?

The Other Pioneers

A Lyric Poem by Roberto Félix Salazar

BEFORE READING

Build Background
Historical Context In the early 1800s, Spanish and Mexican pioneers established ranches and towns on the land now known as Texas, California, Arizona, and New Mexico. Many place names in the Southwest still reflect their Spanish influence. San Diego, Rio Grande, and the Sangre de Cristos are just three among many examples.

Reader's Context What do you imagine life was like in Texas for early settlers? Would you have wanted to live in this time period?

Set Purpose
Preview the title of the poem, the length of the lines, and the capitalized words. Predict what the theme of the poem will be. Read to determine how accurate your prediction is.

Analyze Literature
Description Writing that portrays a character, object, or scene through details is known as **description.** Descriptions make use of **sensory details,** or words and phrases that describe how things look, sound, smell, taste, or feel. As you read "The Other Pioneers," pay attention to words that engage your senses. How does the poet make you feel as if you are there?

Meet the Author
Roberto Félix Salazar (b. 1913) is a Mexican-American writer from Laredo, Texas. Salazar was one of the earliest Chicano authors to write in English. He wrote both poetry and short stories. "The Other Pioneers" was first published in 1939. It has been anthologized many times, among them a 1973 collection of Mexican-American literature titled *We Are Chicanos.*

Use Reading Skills
Identify Author's Purpose Authors write for a reason, or a combination of reasons, such as to inform, explain, entertain, enlighten, persuade, or reflect. As you read "The Other Pioneers," use the chart below to identify the author's purpose and how the ideas in the poem fulfill this purpose.

Before Reading	Identify the author's purpose, the type of writing the author uses, and the ideas the author wants to communicate.
During Reading	Gather ideas that the author communicates to readers.
After Reading	Summarize the ideas the author communicates. Explain how these ideas help fulfill the author's purpose.

At a Glance
Directed Reading
- Reading Level: Easy
- Difficulty Considerations: None
- Ease Factor: Length

Objectives
Studying this lesson will enable students to
- use reading strategies such as identifying author's purpose
- define *sensory details,* recognize examples in context, and understand their effect on descriptions
- describe the literary accomplishments of Roberto Félix Salazar
- appreciate a poem about pride

Launch the Lesson
Ask students to use what they already know about history to define the word *pioneer.* Then point out that this poem expresses thoughts about the "other" pioneers. Have students predict who these "others" are and read to confirm or alter their predictions.

Summary
The poem honors Spanish and Mexican pioneers who built towns and ranches in the Southwest.

KEY TERMS
LYRIC POEM, 505
DESCRIPTION, 505
SENSORY DETAIL, 505
AUTHOR'S PURPOSE, 505
TONE, 508
THEME, 508
BIOGRAPHY, 508

Words in Use

Teaching Words
engage, 505
anthologized, 505
enlighten, 505
missions, 507
derived, 508

Vocabulary Skills

Spanish-English Words
As students read the poem, urge them to read footnotes to clarify unfamiliar terms. After they have read the poem, direct attention to footnote 3, and point out that the English names of many places and objects came from the Spanish language. Other Spanish words continue to enrich the English language, brought by modern Spanish speakers.

Common Core State Standards
Reading Literature
RL.1
Writing
W.9
Language
L.6

The Other Pioneers

Teach the Selection

Use Reading Skills

Identify Author's Purpose After students have read the poem, have them use its main ideas and details to suggest the author's main purpose or purposes for writing. Model by pointing out the message in lines 1-3, using the phrases *must write* and *long before* to suggest that one of the poet's main reasons for writing is to pay respect to his ancestors, who settled this land long before the English and Irish arrived. Ask students to use details to suggest other purposes he may have had for writing.

Analyze Literature

Sensory Details Call on volunteers to identify descriptive phrases containing words that appeal to the reader's sense of hearing. Model by pointing out that "soft-woven Spanish names" makes you think of the soft sounds of such names as *Los Angeles, Laredo,* and *Santa Fe.*

Road to Taos at the Rio Grande. William Penhallow Henderson. Fred Jones Jr. Museum of Art, University of Oklahoma, Norman, Oklahoma.

A Lyric Poem
by Roberto Félix Salazar

506

Now I must write
Of those of mine who rode these plains
Long years before the Saxon[1] and the Irish came.
Of those who plowed the land and built the towns
5 And gave the towns soft-woven Spanish names.
Of those who moved across the Rio Grande[2]
Toward the hiss of Texas snake and Indian yell.
Of men who from the earth made thick-walled homes[3]
And from the earth raised churches to their God.
10 And of the wives who bore them sons
And smiled with knowing joy. ❖

---

1. **Saxon.** English
2. **Rio Grande.** River that forms today's U.S.-Mexico border
3. **thick-walled homes.** Homes built of adobe bricks

HISTORY ▶▶ CONNECTION

New Spain Spanish exploration of the region known as the Southwest began with Francisco Vasquez de Coronado's quest for the fabled Seven Cities of Cibola around 1540. The seven cities were supposed to be rich in gold and silver. Spanish missionaries, soldiers, and colonists followed, building missions, forts, and towns. Santa Fe, the capital of what is today New Mexico, was founded around 1610, Albuquerque around 1706, and Taos around 1780. At the time, this region was known as New Spain. What Spanish influences do you recognize in the poem? **A**

 What information do you know about your distant ancestors? What contributions have your native or immigrant ancestors made to the culture of the United States?

THE OTHER PIONEERS **507**

Review the Model

Find Meaning

1. Answers should fall somewhere between 1540 and 1840–before the Mexican-American War and after Spanish exploration.

2. The poem describes riding, plowing, building towns, naming towns, crossing the Rio Grande, facing snakes and yelling Indians, building homes, raising churches, having sons, smiling, and knowing.

3. (a) Women are wives of men and mothers of boys. (b) Students might say this poem was written in an earlier era, when women's roles were more limited.

Make Judgments

4. (a) The tone is proud, reverent, and reflective. (b) Examples might include *those of mine* and *raised churches to their God.*

5. The speaker is a descendent of Spanish pioneers of the Southwest. The phrases *those of mine, these plains,* and *toward the hiss of Texas snake* support this statement.

6. (a) Students may say the theme is the sometimes-forgotten Spanish history of many places in the United States. (b) The title best supports this answer.

Analyze Literature

Description *Answer:* Students will probably conclude that the mood of the poem is proud and happy.

Find Meaning

1. What is the time period of "The Other Pioneers"?

2. What actions are described in the poem?

3. (a) What roles do women have in this poem? (b) What does that detail suggest about when this poem was written?

Analyze Literature

Description Descriptions that appeal to a reader's senses, whether seeing, hearing, feeling, tasting, or smelling, help establish mood. Mood is the feeling or atmosphere the writer creates in a literary work. Use the chart below to analyze the use of description in "The Other Pioneers." Notice which sense or feeling the author is appealing to, and analyze the effect the description has on the mood of the poem. When you are finished, use the chart to come to a conclusion about the overall mood of the poem.

Make Judgments

4. (a) How would you describe the tone of "The Other Pioneers"? (b) What words or phrases support your description?

5. Who is the speaker in this poem? Explain.

6. (a) What is the theme of "The Other Pioneers"? (b) What words or phrases support your answer?

Description	Effect
must/feeling	urgency

Extend Understanding

Writing Options

Creative Writing Write a short **descriptive essay** about the region of the country in which you live. Like the author of "The Other Pioneers," include details about the people, activities, towns, place names, natural landscape, and architecture, as well as other specific details. Remember to use language that appeals to the five senses.

Expository Writing The narrator of "The Other Pioneers" writes about his Spanish ancestors. Write a brief **biography** about one of your own ancestors. You may not know about an ancestor from long ago, but you can write about an aunt, grandparent, or great uncle. Write about a contribution that person made to his or her country, community, or family.

Critical Literacy

Hold a Panel Discussion With fellow students, hold a panel discussion on the importance of different cultures' contributions to the history of the United States. What cultures have particularly influenced the history of your region? What evidence do you find of a Native American influence in your region?

Media Literacy

Use a Map Salazar refers to towns with "soft-woven Spanish names" in "The Other Pioneers." In your library, or on the Internet, locate a map of the southwestern United States. Identify as many Spanish derived place names as you can in this region. Look at natural features as well as cities and towns. Make a list of the place names you find.

 Go to **www.mirrorsandwindows.com** for more.

Rubrics for Writing Options

You can adapt this as a checklist for students to use as they write.

Creative Writing

☐ Does the descriptive essay identify the student's region and include specific details about it?

☐ Does it effectively use sensory details?

Expository Writing

☐ Did the student write about an ancestor?

☐ Does the biography focus on a contribution made by this person?

Ceremony

A Lyric Poem by Leslie Marmon Silko

Preview the Selection

At a Glance
Directed Reading
- Reading Level: Easy
- Difficulty Consideration: Pronoun-antecedent relationship
- Ease Factor: Familiar vocabulary

Objectives
Studying this lesson will enable students to

- use reading strategies such as identifying author's purpose
- define *metaphor*, identify examples in context, and recognize the effect of this literary technique
- describe the literary accomplishments of Leslie Marmon Silko and understand how her heritage as a Laguna Pueblo is reflected in her work
- analyze a poem about oral tradition

Launch the Lesson
Tell students that in this poem, a man speaks about the stories that have been passed down from generation to generation. Ask them to think about why those stories might be very important to him.

The Mirrors & Windows questions at the end of the selection focus on the theme of tradition. Ask students which song lyrics, poems, and stories they have valued memorizing at different stages in their youth.

BEFORE READING

Build Background
Cultural Context Folk literature is the works, ideas, or customs passed by word of mouth from generation to generation. Native American nations have oral traditions thousands of years old that still exist today. Leslie Marmon Silko discussed the communal nature of the oral tradition, noting, "It is a collective memory and depends upon the whole community."

Reader's Context What stories are told in your family that have never been written down? What customs do you practice year after year for which there are no written instructions?

Set Purpose
Preview the title of the poem. Based on the title, predict what the theme of the poem will be. Read to determine how accurate your prediction is.

Analyze Literature
Metaphor A **metaphor** is a figure of speech in which one thing is spoken or written about as if it were another. Metaphors do not use *like* or *as* to compare. This figure of speech invites the listener or reader to make a comparison between two unlike things. A metaphor works because the things compared have one or more qualities in common. Pay attention to the use of figurative language as you read "Ceremony."

Use Reading Skills
Identify Author's Purpose Authors write for a reason, or a combination of reasons, such as to inform, explain, entertain, enlighten, persuade, describe, or reflect. As you read "Ceremony," use the chart below to identify the author's purpose and how the details in the poem contribute to this purpose.

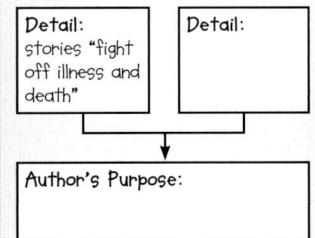

| Detail: stories "fight off illness and death" | Detail: |

Author's Purpose:

Meet the Author
Leslie Marmon Silko (b. 1948) is a writer of mixed ancestry, part Laguna Pueblo, part Mexican, and part European. She was born in Albuquerque, New Mexico, and learned the oral traditions of the Laguna Pueblo people from her Laguna grandmother on the reservation in New Mexico. "Ceremony" was published in 1981, in a collection titled *Storyteller*. About growing up Laguna, she says, "The education of the children is done within the community, this is in the old times before the coming of the Europeans. Each adult works with every child, children belong to everybody and the way of teaching is to tell stories."

CEREMONY **509**

Common Core State Standards

Reading Literature
RL.1
Writing
W.9, W.10
Language
L.6

Teach the Selection

Summary
The speaker of this poem listens to a man describing the importance of stories. Stories fight off illness and death. Evil tries to destroy or confuse stories. The man explains that rituals and ceremonies (the belly of these stories) are still growing.

Use Reading Skills
Identify Author's Purpose Lead students in identifying the antecedent of *their* and *they*. Then ask them to suggest the author's underlying purpose for writing this stanza. **A**

Answer: Encourage students to explain why they have memorized certain songs, poems, or stories. They might say that they think people consider traditions and ceremonies very important because it reminds them of their history or ancestry, improves their personal lives, or keeps them connected with others in their culture.

Ceremony
A Lyric Poem by Leslie Marmon Silko

Interior of a Cree Indian Tent. John Franklin. Newberry Library, Chicago.

> I will tell you something about stories,
> [he said]
> They aren't just entertainment.
> Don't be fooled.
> 5 They are all we have, you see,
> all we have to fight off
> illness and death.
>
> You don't have anything
> if you don't have the stories.
>
> **A**
> 10 Their evil is mighty
> but it can't stand up to our stories.
> So they try to destroy the stories
> let the stories be confused or forgotten.
> They would like that
> 15 They would be happy
> Because we would be defenseless then.
>
> He rubbed his belly.
> I keep them here
> [he said]
> 20 Here, put your hand on it
> See, it is moving.
> There is life here
> for the people.
>
> And in the belly of this story
> 25 the rituals[1] and the ceremony[2]
> are still growing. ❖

---

1. **rituals.** Social or religious rites or customs
2. **ceremony.** Formal acts done in a customary way

What poems, stories, or songs can you recite by memory? Why do you think people place such special importance on traditions and ceremonies?

Program Resources

Planning and Assessment
Program Planning Guide, Selection Lesson Plan
E-Lesson Planner
Assessment Guide, Lesson Test
ExamView

Technology Tools
Interactive Student Text on CD
Visual Teaching Package
Audio Library
mirrorsandwindows.com

Meeting the Standards
Poetry: Unit 5, Directed Reading, pp. 51–56

Differentiating Instruction
Advanced Students, Cultural Context Activity, p. 30

Find Meaning

1. What is the theme of "Ceremony"?
2. What attributes does Silko give to stories?
3. (a) Which phrases do you find in brackets in the poem? (b) How do you interpret the phrases and the punctuation used to set them off from the rest of the poem?

Analyze Literature

Metaphor Review "Ceremony" for the use of metaphor. A metaphor is a comparison that does not use *like* or *as.* It is an example of figurative language, language that is interpreted through the imagination rather than being interpreted literally. Use a chart to help you analyze the use of metaphor in "Ceremony."

Make Judgments

4. (a) What do you see in the shape of "Ceremony"? (b) Why do you think Silko chose to shape the poem this way?
5. (a) What conflict do you find in the third stanza? (b) How do you interpret the use of "their" and "our"?
6. To what is Silko comparing a man who keeps a story in his belly?

Metaphor	What Is Compared?	What I Envision
"all we have to fight off illness and death"	Stories are compared to medicine.	

Extend Understanding

Writing Options

Creative Writing Write a **short story** that does more than entertain. For example, you could write a story that conveys a message about how to live a happy life or avoid an unhappy one. Or, you could write a story based on an event in your family that you would like to remember for future generations. Whatever kind of story you choose to write, share it with your class.

Expository Writing Write a brief **literary response** for your school newspaper based on your experience of reading "Ceremony." In your response, discuss the relationship between Silko's use of metaphor and the meaning of the poem. State your opinion in a clear thesis statement. Support your opinion with evidence from the poem, including quotations, details, and examples.

Lifelong Learning

Research Oral Tradition On the Internet or at the library, research to find a story that you enjoy that comes from the oral tradition of an indigenous culture. Focus your research on the continent that holds the most interest for you. Find out something about the culture as well as the story. Then present the story and your research to your class.

Critical Literacy

Hold a Panel Discussion With fellow students, hold a panel discussion on the importance of storytelling. Share personal examples of how stories have affected your lives, but also address broader questions. Why are stories important? How can they affect or improve our lives?

M W Go to **www.mirrorsandwindows.com** for more.

Find Meaning

1. Students might say the theme is stories, or the oral traditions, of cultures indigenous to the Americas.
2. Students may mention some of the following: the capacity to fight off illness and death, the power to defend against evil, the power to give life, the capacity to carry ritual and ceremony.
3. (a) The phrase *he said* is set off in brackets in the first and fourth stanzas. (b) Students might say this phrase makes it clear that the stanzas are being spoken by a man, or that the speaker wants to clarify that these are the thoughts of someone else, perhaps a revered elder.

Make Judgments

4. (a) Students might mention vessels or curves or might see a human-like form with a belly in the middle. (b) Students might say it is pleasing to the eye, or that the belly in the middle of the poem reinforces the poem's main metaphor.
5. (a) Students may say there is conflict between "them" and "us" and that the culture is under attack by an outside force. (b) Students might interpret "their" to be conquerors or colonizers and "us" to be indigenous populations.
6. Silko compares a man who keeps a story in his belly to a woman who carries a baby in her womb.

Analyze Literature

Metaphor *Answer:* Point out the middle column text and suggest that the speaker may also be comparing stories to the human immune system.

Rubrics for Writing Options

You can adapt this as a checklist for students to use as they write.

Creative Writing

☐ Does the short story convey a message or reflect on an important personal event?
☐ Is it interesting and enjoyable to read?

Expository Writing

☐ Does the literary response begin with an effective thesis statement?
☐ Does the student support his or her thesis statement with specific details from the poem?
☐ Does the response provide a logical and accurate analysis of the poem's central metaphor?

At a Glance
Directed Reading
- Reading Level: Moderate
- Difficulty Consideration: Vocabulary
- Ease Factor: Length

Objectives

Studying this lesson will enable students to
- use reading strategies such as identifying main idea
- define *lyric poem* and analyze the structure and content of two examples
- describe the work of Emily Dickinson and recognize her as one of America's leading poets
- appreciate two poems that reveal the poet's inner thoughts and feelings

Launch the Lesson

Have students share their thoughts about helping others. What might they do to help a friend who is sad? Have them keep these thoughts in mind as they read these poems.

Summary

The first Dickinson poem explains that one would not have lived in vain if they are able to help the broken-hearted or the weary. The second poem describes how books can free minds from day-to-day problems.

DIRECTED READING

If I can stop one Heart from breaking

He ate and drank the precious words

Lyric Poems by Emily Dickinson

BEFORE READING

Build Background

Historical Context Emily Dickinson lived in an era when most young women were expected to be "proper"—polite, refined, and obedient. Emily's father attempted to protect her from reading any books that might challenge the family's conservative values. Emily rebelled somewhat from these strict rules and limitations by turning inward and writing clever, passionate poetry.

Reader's Context Have you ever felt hesitant to share your deepest thoughts? How might it help to put them in writing?

Set Purpose

Preview the first few lines of the poems. What themes do the poems share? Read to find out.

Analyze Literature

Lyric Poetry A **lyric poem** is verse that reveals the feelings and attitudes of the speaker. Most lyric poems are short and musical, somewhat similar to the lyrics of a song. Though lyric poems were originally written to be sung, that is no longer the case. As you read, note the poems' musical qualities.

Meet the Author

Emily Dickinson (1830–1886) is considered one of America's great poets. She was born and died at her parents' home in Amherst, Massachusetts, and, except for one year in college and a few travels to Boston and Washington, DC, she rarely left home. Lacking outside relationships and experiences, Dickinson lived an intense inward life and captured her reflections in brief yet explosive lyric poems. Perhaps her life motto can best be summed up by a line from one of her poems: "I dwell in Possibility."

Use Reading Skills

Identify Main Idea The main idea of a poem is its theme, or central concept. Readers can often find the theme by thinking about the poem's topic and details. As you read, use a main idea map to find the theme.

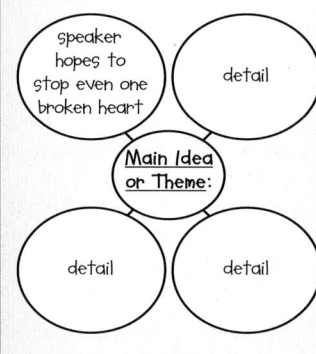

Poem 1: "If I can stop one Heart from breaking"

Topic:

- speaker hopes to stop even one broken heart
- detail

Main Idea or Theme:

- detail
- detail

Preview Vocabulary

ro·bust (rō bust´) *adj.*, strong and healthy

din·gy (din´ jē) *adj.*, dirty or discolored

be·quest (bē´ kwest) *n.*, gift or inheritance

512   UNIT 5 POETRY

Common Core State Standards

Reading Literature
RL.1, RL.2

Writing
W.9

Language
L.6

Words in Use

"He ate and drank the precious words"

Preview Vocabulary
robust, 514
dingy, 514
bequest, 514

Teaching Words
refined, 512
conservative, 512
rebelled, 512
passionate, 512
hesitant, 512
intense, 512
vain, 515

KEY TERMS

LYRIC POEM, 512
VERSE, 512
MAIN IDEA, 512
THEME, 512
CLUSTER CHART, 515
TONE, 515
MEANING, 515
RHYTHM, 515
RHYME, 515
THESIS, 515
VENN DIAGRAM, 515

If I can stop one Heart from breaking

A Lyric Poem by Emily Dickinson

If I can stop one Heart from breaking
I shall not live in vain[1]
If I can ease one Life the Aching
Or cool one Pain

Or help one fainting Robin
Unto his Nest again
I shall not live in Vain. ❧

---

1. **in vain.** Without success

(Above) *Robin,* c. 1816. Joseph Mallord William Turner. City Art Gallery, Leeds, England.

513

Use Reading Skills

Identify Main Idea Ask students why Dickinson chose to associate a book with the gift of wings. Lead them to understand that Dickinson feels that literature is a gift that brings freedom and self-reliance through new knowledge and ideas.

▶ More About the Author

Rarely going outside her home, Emily Dickinson gained most of her knowledge of the world through reading books and maintaining correspondence with friends and literary figures. Many of her poems, like this one, extol the pleasures and benefits of reading.

Answer: Answers will vary, but they should be supported by reasons. Students might respond to the second question by stating that Dickinson writes about universal notions that many people still believe in today.

Program Resources

Meeting the Standards
Poetry: Unit 5, Directed Reading

Differentiating Instruction
Developing Readers, Take Notes

Common Core State Standards

Reading Literature
RL.1, RL.2, RL.5

Writing
W.9

Language
L.6

He ate and drank the precious words

A Lyric Poem by Emily Dickinson

He ate and drank the precious words,
His spirit grew <u>robust</u>;
He knew no more that he was poor,
Nor that his frame[1] was dust.
He danced along the <u>dingy</u> days,
And this <u>bequest</u> of wings
Was but a book. What liberty
A loosened spirit brings! ❖

---

1. frame. Human body

ro•bust (rō bust´) *adj.*, strong and healthy
din•gy (din´ jē) *adj.*, dirty or discolored
be•quest (bē´ kwest) *n.*, gift or inheritance

 Some people feel that Dickinson's poems are like riddles or puzzles. What might lead them to think that way? Do you agree?

(Above) *The Day of Rest*, c. 1926. Frederick Cayley Robinson. Bury Art Gallery and Museum, Lancashire, England.

Differentiated Instruction

Enrichment

Have interested students work with school or local officials to find schools and libraries that would benefit from the donation of books. Possible sites include those devastated by natural disasters or those in urban or rural districts with very limited budgets. Organize a book drive, in which students ask family members and neighbors to donate used books to send to these locations.

Reading Skills

Identify Author's Purpose

Remind students that the theme of a piece of literature is the main message the author or poet wants to express. Relaying that message often becomes the author's main purpose for writing. After they have read each poem, have students use their main idea maps to express the message, or theme, of each poem. Ask students what these themes suggest about Dickinson's purpose for writing these poems.

Find Meaning

1. In the first poem, what four specific things will prevent the speaker from living in vain?

2. In the first poem, how would you sum up what the speaker hopes to accomplish in life?

3. (a) In the second poem, what makes the man feel strong and happy? (b) What did the experience help him to forget?

4. (a) What does the phrase "this bequest of wings" mean? (b) Paraphrase the sentence "What liberty a loosened spirit brings."

Analyze Literature

Lyric Poetry A lyric poem is verse that reveals the feelings and attitudes of the speaker. Look back at the poems. In one or two sentences, describe the overall feelings and attitudes that the speaker expresses in each poem. Use a cluster chart to record your details and their overall effect.

Make Judgments

5. Look back at the first poem and think about what the speaker wants to accomplish in life. (a) What does the poem suggest about the type of person the speaker is? (b) What does it suggest about Dickinson's values?

6. Reread the Build Background and Meet the Author sections. Based on that information, and the theme of the second poem, explain why books might have been particularly important to Dickinson.

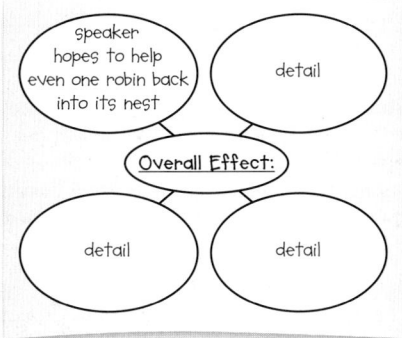

Extend Understanding

Writing Options

Creative Writing What questions do you have about these poems? Pick one poem as the topic of a **personal letter** to Emily Dickinson. Include your thoughts and questions in the letter. Then share those thoughts and questions with classmates. Discuss possible answers.

Expository Writing Write a brief **expository essay** in which you compare and contrast the two poems. Explain how they are similar and different. Include facts and details about each poem's structure, tone, meaning, rhythm, and use of rhyme. In your thesis, state your main point. In your body, cite examples, quotes, and details to support your thesis.

Collaborative Learning

Group Activity With a small group of classmates, discuss the elements of these two poems, including themes, structures, and tones. Work together to create a Venn diagram to show how such elements in the poems are similar and different.

Media Literacy

Dickinson Poems Using library or Internet sources, locate, analyze, and evaluate several more of Dickinson's poems. Select the one that you like best. Share the poem and your recommendation with a classmate.

Go to www.mirrorsandwindows.com for more.

I Ask My Mother to Sing
A Lyric Poem by Li-Young Lee

Preview the Selections

At a Glance
Directed Reading
"Legacies"
- Reading Level: Moderate
- Difficulty Consideration: Poetic style
- Ease Factors: Length, vocabulary

"I Ask My Mother to Sing"
- Reading Level: Moderate
- Difficulty Consideration: Geographical allusions
- Ease Factors: Length, author's style

DIRECTED READING

Objectives
Studying this lesson will enable students to
- compare two poems with similar topics
- use reading strategies such as comparing and contrasting
- define *tone* and understand how a poet's diction affects a poem's tone
- describe the literary accomplishments of Nikki Giovanni and Li-Young Lee

Launch the Lesson
Tell students that this first poem is about the relationship between a grandmother and a young girl. As they read, urge them to think about how they feel about their own grandparents or other older family members.

Before reading the second poem ask students if they have special songs that family members sing at get-togethers and celebrations. Ask: "When you hear certain songs, do they bring back memories or pictures in your mind of experiences you have had?"

BEFORE READING

Build Background
Literary Context Both Giovanni's "Legacies" and Li-Young Lee's "I Ask My Mother to Sing" are lyric poems. A **lyric poem** is verse that expresses the emotions of the speaker and does not typically tell a story, unlike **narrative poems,** which do tell a story. As you read, pay attention to the emotions they express.

Reader's Context What traditions have you acquired from older people in your life?

Set Purpose
Preview the poems' titles and skim the text. Predict the theme of each poem.

Meet the Authors

Nikki Giovanni (b. 1943) is a poet, professor, lecturer, and essayist. She was also one of the most outspoken voices of the Civil Rights movement in the 1960s. She writes, "Nobody ever got married reading the latest rap record. They turn to poetry. So poetry has its place. It offers comfort; it's celebratory and joyful."

Li-Young Lee (b. 1957) was born in Jakarta, Indonesia. Lee wandered through Hong Kong, Macau, and Japan before finally settling in the United States. Lee has said, "I feel as if [my family's] experience may be no more than an outward manifestation of a homelessness that people in general feel."

Compare Literature: Diction and Tone
The writer's or speaker's attitude toward the subject or the reader is called **tone.** For example, a writer might use a lighthearted tone when writing about something happy or funny, and a somber tone when writing about something sad.
Diction is the writer's choice of words. Diction affects the voice and tone of a poem. For example, the diction of a text can be formal, informal, or conversational. As you read the poems "Legacies" and "I Ask My Mother to Sing," notice how diction affects each poem's voice and tone.

Preview Vocabulary
sway (swā) *v.*, swing back and forth

Words in Use

Teaching Words
Civil Rights movement, 516
outward manifestation, 516
somber, 516
legacies, 518
evoke, 520
heritage, 521
impact, 521

KEY TERMS
LYRIC POEM, 516
NARRATIVE POEM, 516
TONE, 516
DICTION, 516
STANZA, 521
THESIS STATEMENT, 521
FEEDBACK, 521
STRUCTURE, 521
LINE LENGTH, 521
PUNCTUATION, 521
CAPITALIZATION, 521

Common Core State Standards
Reading Literature
RL.1
Language
L.6

Can I Have the Bowl? 1994. Jessie Coates. Private collection.

Legacies[1]

A Lyric Poem by Nikki Giovanni

---

1. **Legacies.** Things that are handed down from the past

517

Summary

A grandmother calls her granddaughter in to learn how to make rolls. The granddaughter refuses, afraid that if her grandmother dies she'll be less dependent on her spirit. Both refuse to acknowledge their eventual separation.

MIRRORS & WINDOWS The Mirrors & Windows questions at the end of the selection focus on the theme of heritage. Before reading, ask students which features of their heritage they would like to preserve through future generations. Why are these features important to them? Why do people place great importance on sustaining heritage?

Analyze Literature

Diction and Tone Call attention to the direct quotations by both the grandmother and the girl. Point out that the girl's words *yes* and *ma'am* create a tone of friendly respect, and that the grandmother speaks her words "proudly." Model aloud how she might have spoken, pointing out how the diction ("chu") creates an informal tone. Repeat with the girl's "i don't want . . ." line, including her gesture ("with her lips poked out"), and the grandmother's final line. Discuss how word choice and gestures help to create tone and develop meaning.

Planning and Assessment
Program Planning Guide, Selection Lesson Plan
E-Lesson Planner
Assessment Guide, Lesson Test
ExamView

Technology Tools
Interactive Student Text on CD
Visual Teaching Package
Audio Library
mirrorsandwindows.com

Meeting the Standards
Poetry: Unit 5, Comparing Literature, pp. 65–72

Answer: Some students may say that legacies are an important way to stay connected to past events and people. Others may feel constrained by legacies.

Find Meaning

1. (a) The grandmother wants to teach her to make rolls. (b) She wants to teach her because she is proud of the tradition.

2. (a) The girl tells her grandmother she doesn't want to know how to make the rolls. (b) The girl feels that if she knows how to make the rolls, she won't need to remember her grandmother as much after she dies.

Make Judgments

3. It gives the interaction between the grandmother and granddaughter and the emotions that powered the interaction a universal feel. It calls attention to the fact that many people don't always say what they really feel or think.

4. (a) The title refers to learning to make the grandmother's rolls, but it also may refer to the legacy of not saying what one actually thinks. (b) The author likely used this title so that she could explain the grandmother's desire to pass along her knowledge to her granddaughter, as well as to suggest that the avoidance of revealing one's feelings is also passed down through generations.

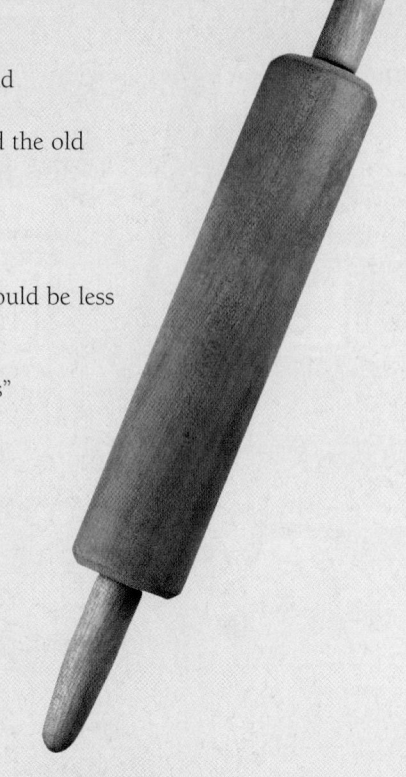

her grandmother called her from the playground
    "yes, ma'am"
    "i want chu to learn how to make rolls" said the old
woman proudly
5 but the little girl didn't want
to learn how because she knew
even if she couldn't say it that
that would mean when the old one died she would be less
dependent on her spirit so
10 she said
    "i don't want to know how to make no rolls"
with her lips poked out
and the old woman wiped her hands on
her apron saying "lord
15   these children"
and neither of them ever
said what they meant
and i guess nobody ever does ✤

What legacies do you hope to one day pass on to your children or other family members? Why? What is the value in passing on legacies?

Find Meaning

1. (a) What does the grandmother want to teach the girl? (b) Why does she want to teach that to her grandchild?

2. (a) How does the girl respond to the grandmother's request? (b) In your own words, explain the girl's reason for responding this way.

Make Judgments

3. What is the effect of the last line in the poem?

4. (a) To what does the title "Legacies" refer? (b) Why might the author have chosen that title?

Vocabulary Skills

Letter-Sound Correspondence

Point out that the word *chu* is dialect, a form of language spoken by people of certain regions. Explain that readers who are unfamiliar with a dialect can often figure out the meanings of its terms by examining context clues and thinking about the sounds that the letters make.

Differentiated Instruction

Reading Proficiency

Help struggling readers compare and contrast the grandmother's and granddaughter's points of view. Both want to preserve traditions but are unable to say what they really mean. Discuss whether this situation seems realistic. Have students base their answers on their own experiences, as well as their knowledge of people and the world.

Camels Watering in Front of the Gates of Pekin—Visiting the Extreme Orient. Paul Bremen Collection.

I Ask My Mother to Sing

A Lyric Poem by Li-Young Lee

519

Teach the Selection

Summary
The speaker's mother and grandmother sing about China, and the speaker, who has never visited, loves to hear them. The women cry, but never stop singing.

MIRRORS & WINDOWS The Mirrors & Windows questions at the end of the selection focus on the theme of music. Ask students what music evokes strong emotions in them. How do they explain this phenomenon?

Analyze Literature
Lyric Poetry After students have finished reading the poem, discuss what characteristics make it a lyric poem. Lead them to understand that it expresses the feelings of the speaker related to a personal experience.

Words in Use

"I Ask My Mother to Sing"

Preview Vocabulary
sway, 520

Selection Words
overturn, 520

Research Skills

Interviews
Ask students to interview family members or friends about traditional songs that bring memories or physical sites to mind.

Prepare students for interviews by having them draft a series of questions for their subject. Discuss the use of follow-up questions to clarify the meanings of the subject's responses. Provide class time for students to report their interview results.

Common Core State Standards

Reading Literature
RL.1, RL.4, RL.5
Writing
W.9, W.10
Language
L.6

Use Reading Strategies

Visualize Ask students to describe the pictures that form in their mind of the mother and grandmother singing, the father swaying like a boat, and the sites in Peking (Beijing) that are mentioned in their song. **A**

Use Reading Strategies

Visualize Call on volunteers to use details in the poem, as well as what they know about waterlilies, to describe the picture that comes to mind after reading these lines. **B**

Answer: Students should identify the music or song and tell what emotion it evokes and how. Some students may say that hearing a song might remind people of what they were doing when they first heard it. Others may say that the words and music connect to, reinforce, or explain emotions and feelings that people have.

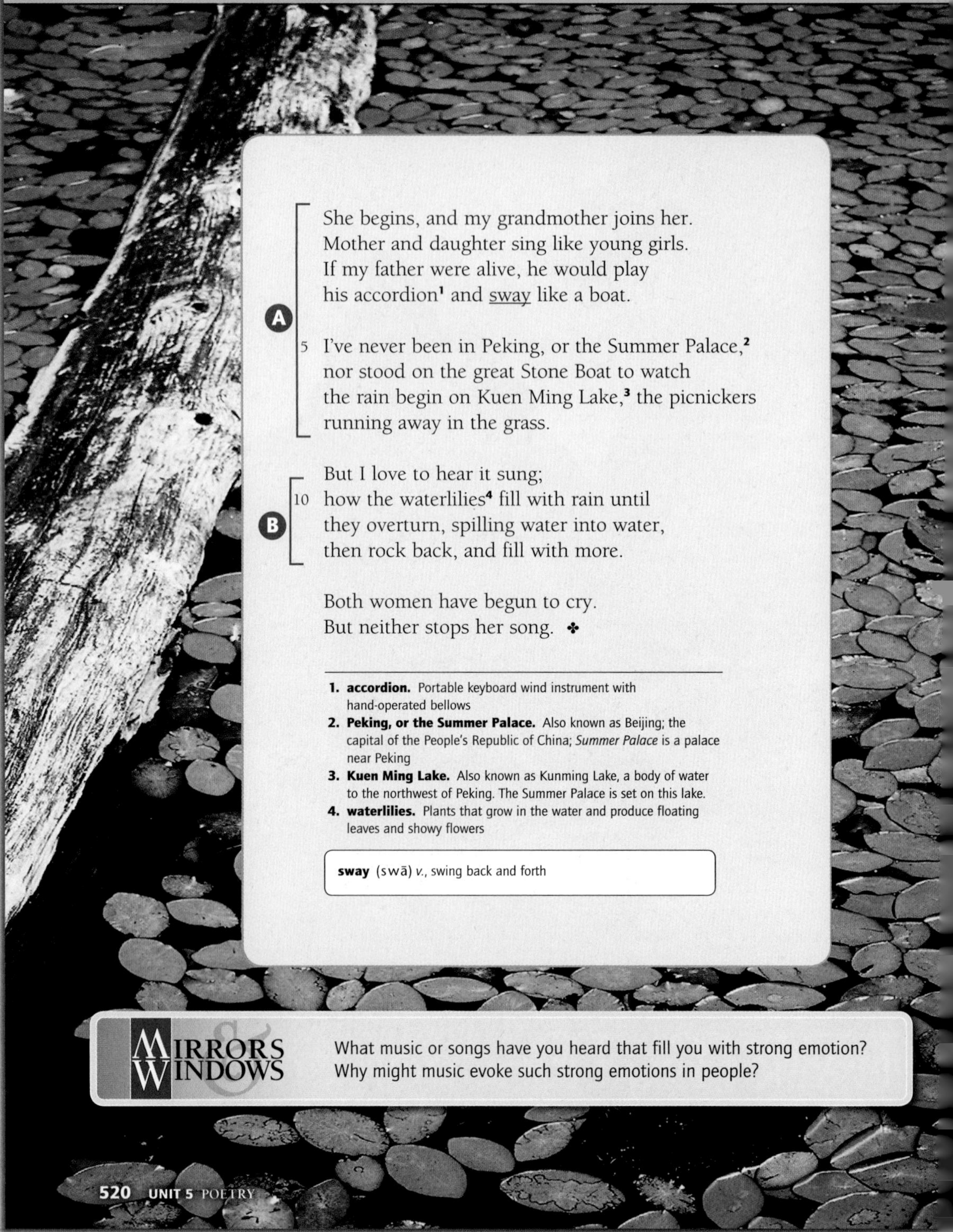

A

She begins, and my grandmother joins her.
Mother and daughter sing like young girls.
If my father were alive, he would play
his accordion[1] and <u>sway</u> like a boat.

5 I've never been in Peking, or the Summer Palace,[2]
nor stood on the great Stone Boat to watch
the rain begin on Kuen Ming Lake,[3] the picnickers
running away in the grass.

B

But I love to hear it sung;
10 how the waterlilies[4] fill with rain until
they overturn, spilling water into water,
then rock back, and fill with more.

Both women have begun to cry.
But neither stops her song. ❖

---

1. **accordion.** Portable keyboard wind instrument with hand-operated bellows
2. **Peking, or the Summer Palace.** Also known as Beijing; the capital of the People's Republic of China; *Summer Palace* is a palace near Peking
3. **Kuen Ming Lake.** Also known as Kunming Lake, a body of water to the northwest of Peking. The Summer Palace is set on this lake.
4. **waterlilies.** Plants that grow in the water and produce floating leaves and showy flowers

sway (swā) *v.*, swing back and forth

What music or songs have you heard that fill you with strong emotion? Why might music evoke such strong emotions in people?

Differentiated Instruction

Enrichment

Students might enjoy writing a song or a lyric poem about a special place. Encourage them to include specific details about the place and to express their thoughts and feelings about it.

Visual Learning

Display pictures of sites in Beijing to help students understand why their beauty and antiquity might cause the women to weep—from homesickness, perhaps, or as a pure reaction to beauty.

AFTER READING

Find Meaning

1. (a) Whom does the speaker ask to sing? (b) Who is unable to join in? (c) What would that person do if he or she could join in?

2. (a) What does the first stanza (lines 1–4) reveal about the speaker's family situation? (b) How does the speaker's family seem to feel about music?

3. (a) Where has the speaker never been? (b) What is the song the speaker's mother and grandmother sing about? (c) What does the song reveal about the speaker's heritage? (d) Why do you think the speaker enjoys listening to this song?

4. (a) What happens to the waterlilies in the rain? (b) What happens to the mother and grandmother as they sing? (c) What might this suggest about the waterlilies and the speaker's mother and grandmother?

Make Judgments

5. (a) How is the image of a "boat" used in the poem? (b) How does this use connect to possible feelings the speaker has about his father?

6. Why do the speaker's mother and grandmother cry as they sing?

Compare Literature

Diction and Tone Diction, the writer's choice of words, affects the tone of a poem. Tone is the writer's or speaker's attitude towards the subject of the poem. Compare the diction and tone in "Legacies" with that in "I Ask My Mother to Sing."

1. How are the diction and tone similar in both poems?

2. How are they different?

3. How does the diction affect the tone differently in each poem?

Extend Understanding

Writing Options

Creative Writing Write a short personal **narrative** about a family member who has had an impact on your life. In your narrative, it should be clear what the impact was and why that was so important to you. Share your narrative with the class.

Expository Writing Write a brief **compare and contrast** essay. How is the tone of each poem similar or different to the other? State your opinion in a thesis statement. Use evidence from the poems to support your thesis. You may organize your essay by examining tone first in one poem and then in the other, or by directly comparing lines from the poems to show how the tone is conveyed. Share your essay with a classmate and incorporate his or her feedback.

Lifelong Learning

Research Use an encyclopedia or the Internet to locate information on one of the places mentioned in Li-Young Lee's poem. Use the information you find to give a brief informative speech about the location.

Media Literacy

Compare Poetry Styles Compare the styles of "Legacies" and "I Ask My Mother to Sing." Analyze the use of structure, line length, punctuation, and capitalization. How do these elements influence your reading of each poem? Why might the authors have made the choices they did?

Go to www.mirrorsandwindows.com for more.

Find Meaning

1. (a) The speaker asks his or her mother to sing. (b) The father is unable to join in. (c) He would play his accordion and sway.

2. (a) It reveals that the speaker has a living mother and grandmother and that his or her father is dead. (b) The family values and cherishes music.

3. (a) The speaker has never been to China. (b) The song is about a rainy day on Kuen Ming Lake. (c) It reveals important places and scenes in China. (d) The speaker enjoys it because it connects him or her to his or her heritage.

4. (a) The waterlilies fill with rain, empty, and fill again. (b) The mother and grandmother begin to cry. (c) They all spill over—the flowers with water and the women with emotion.

Make Judgments

5. (a) The image of a boat is echoed later in the poem as the flowers rock back and forth. (b) This reflects the speaker's notion that his or her father was in harmony with the world around him.

6. The mother and grandmother are filled with longing for their homeland and their husband/son.

Compare Literature

Diction and Tone

Both poems have serious tones. In "Legacies," the use of conversational diction creates an informal tone. "I Ask My Mother to Sing" uses more formal diction, so its tone is slightly more distant than in "Legacies."

Rubrics for Writing Options

You can adapt this as a checklist for students to use as they write.

Creative Writing

☐ Does the narrative clearly identify the family member?

☐ Does the student describe the impact and its importance?

☐ Does the writing follow the format of a narrative?

Expository Writing

☐ Does the essay note both similarities and differences in the tones of the two poems?

☐ Does it begin with an effective and clear thesis statement?

☐ Is the thesis statement effectively supported with evidence from the text?

If one subject is listed, the sentence is simple. If more than one subject is listed, the sentence has a compound subject.

1. Tired of arguing, the old <u>woman</u> wiped her hands on her apron.
2. <u>Nikki Giovanni</u> is a poet, professor, and lecturer.
3. Neither <u>the girl nor the grandmother</u> said what they felt.
4. Although the <u>girl</u> loved her grandmother, <u>she</u> didn't want to depend on her.
5. <u>Legacies</u> are skills or ideas passed along from ancestors.
6. As I listened, <u>my grandmother and her daughter</u> began to cry.
7. If my <u>father</u> were alive, <u>he</u> would have taken me to Peking.
8. <u>Colorful waterlilies, tumbling waterfalls, and sparkling streams</u> are some appealing features of the park.
9. Like carefree young girls, my <u>mother and grandmother</u> love to sing.
10. After listening for a while, my <u>sister and I</u> began to daydream.

> For more information, see Grammar & Style Section 3.1, The Sentence, in the Language Arts Handbook.

Program Resources

You will find additional lessons on Simple and Compound Subjects in the *Exceeding the Standards: Grammar & Style* resource.

Simple and Compound Subjects

Simple Subjects

her grandmother called her from the playground…

—NIKKI GIOVANNI, "Legacies"

In a sentence, the **simple subject** is the key word or words in the subject of the independent clause. The simple subject is usually a noun or a pronoun and does not include any modifiers. A subject that is a proper name may have more than one word. The simple subject in the quotation above is the noun *grandmother*.

> EXAMPLES
>
> *<u>Grandma Grace</u> wanted to teach her granddaughter to make rolls.* [The proper noun *Grandma Grace* is the simple subject.]
>
> *"<u>I</u> don't want to learn," said the girl.* [The pronoun *I* is the simple subject.]

Compound Subjects

Mother and daughter sing like young girls.

—LI-YOUNG LEE, "I Ask My Mother to Sing"

A sentence with a **compound subject** has two or more simple subjects that share the same predicate. The subjects are joined by the conjunction *and, or, nor,* or *but.* In the quotation above, the compound subject is *mother and daughter.*

> EXAMPLES
>
> *My <u>father and I</u> watched the picnickers in the park.* [*Father* and *I* share the verb *watched.*]
>
> *<u>Peking, the Summer Palace, and Kuen Ming Lake</u> are places that I'd like to visit when I have time.* [*Peking, Summer Palace,* and *Kuen Ming Lake* form the compound subject of the independent clause in the sentence.]

Identifying Simple and Compound Subjects

Rewrite the following sentences. Underline once the simple subjects in the sentences. Underline twice any compound subjects.

1. Tired of arguing, the old woman wiped her hands on her apron.
2. Nikki Giovanni is a poet, professor, and lecturer.
3. Neither the girl nor her grandmother said what they meant.
4. Although the girl loved her grandmother, she didn't want to depend on her.
5. Legacies are skills or ideas passed along from ancestors.
6. As I listened, my grandmother and her daughter began to cry.
7. If my father were alive, he would have taken me to Peking.
8. Colorful waterlilies, tumbling waterfalls, and sparkling streams are some appealing features of the park.
9. Like carefree young girls, my mother and grandmother love to sing.
10. After listening for a while, my sister and I began to daydream.

TEACHING NOTE

Extra Practice

Have students identify the sentences with compound subjects that share the same predicate.

1. Lonnie took the bat and Fred threw the ball.
2. <u>Egbert and Ethelred</u> both led England to war.
3. Marnie danced and Jim sat and sulked.
4. <u>Orla and Dulce</u> finally boarded the boat.

KEY TERMS

SIMPLE SUBJECT, 522

INDEPENDENT CLAUSE, 522

NOUN, 522

PRONOUN, 522

MODIFIER, 522

COMPOUND SUBJECT, 522

PREDICATE, 522

CONJUNCTION, 522

Common Core State Standards

Language
L.1

your little voice
Over the wires
came leaping

Preview the Selection

At a Glance
Independent Reading
• Reading Level: Easy
• Difficulty Consideration: Format
• Ease Factor: Subject matter

INDEPENDENT READING

Woman on the Telephone, 1948. Milton Clark Avery. Private collection.

A Lyric Poem
by E. E. Cummings

your little voice
    Over the wires came leaping
and i felt suddenly
dizzy
  With the jostling and shouting of merry flowers   **A**
wee skipping high-heeled flames
courtesied before my eyes
      or twinkling over to my side
Looked up
with impertinently[1] exquisite faces
floating hands were laid upon me
I was whirled and tossed into delicious dancing
up
Up
with the pale important
      stars and the Humorous
         moon
dear girl
How i was crazy how i cried when i heard
       over time
and tide and death
leaping
Sweetly
   your voice ❖

---

1. **impertinently.** Rudely or disrespectfully

E. E. Cummings (1894–1962) is an American poet best known for the unusual grammar and style in his poems. Cummings was born in Cambridge, Massachusetts, and he spent a large portion of his life living in the northeastern part of the United States. He developed a signature style based on his unconventional use of capital letters, punctuation, and sentence structure. In addition to writing poetry, Cummings wrote plays and experimental stories. He was also a trained painter.

523

Objectives
Reading this selection will enable students to:
• read with developing fluency
• read silently with comprehension for a sustained period of time

Launch the Lesson
Prior to reading "your little voice Over the wires came leaping," ask students to think about a time when they might have been sad or worried until a friend's call cheered them up. Point out that remembering this situation as they read will help them relate to the speaker's thoughts and feelings.

Summary
The speaker describes how delighted he feels when he speaks to someone he cares about on the phone.

Analyze Literature
Imagery Ask students what picture comes to mind when they read these lines. Then ask: "Why did the speaker choose to use such imagery? What feelings is he describing?" **A**

KEY TERMS
LYRIC POEM, 523
PUNCTUATION, 523
SENTENCE STRUCTURE, 523
PERSONAL NARRATIVE, 524
CHRONOLOGICAL ORDER, 524
SENSORY DETAIL, 524
FIGURATIVE LANGUAGE, 524

The Mirrors & Windows questions at the end of the selection focus on the theme of communication. Ask students if anyone in their life speaks in a manner that affects their emotions. How does this voice impact them? *Answer:* Students should identify the person, describe their reactions to the person's voice, and describe the situations in which this reaction occurs. They might say that technology helps us communicate more quickly and regularly, but with less thought and care.

Analyze and Extend

1. Students will probably say that the speaker is overjoyed to hear the person's voice.

2. (a) The speaker hears it over the telephone. (b) Receiving her voice over the telephone is probably special because she is away from him and has perhaps interrupted a sad experience or mood.

3. The speaker had felt totally separated from the girl, and he is delighted that she initiated contact.

Is there one person in your life whose voice makes you feel a certain way? How do you feel when you hear this one person speak? How does technology affect our relationships with people?

Analyze and Extend

1. How would you describe in your own words the speaker's emotions?

2. (a) How is the speaker from the poem hearing his dear girl's voice? (b) Why is their mode of communication significant?

3. The poem states the speaker and his girl were separated by many factors that do not necessarily go together. What is the effect of grouping these factors together and how does it change your understanding of the poem's meaning?

Narrative Writing Write a short **personal narrative** about a time when you were excited or pleased to be in contact with someone you hadn't heard from in a while. Write your narrative in chronological order. Include sensory details, figurative language, and personal thoughts and feelings.

Media Literacy Find another Cummings poem. Compare it to this poem. How do the typographical elements in both influence each poem's meaning? Present your findings to the class.

 Go to **www.mirrorsandwindows.com** for more.

Words in Use

Preview Vocabulary
jostling, 523
wee, 523
courtesied, 523
exquisite, 523

Teaching Words
signature style, 523
unconventional, 523

Rubric for Narrative Writing
You can adapt this as a checklist for students to use as they write.

☐ Does the personal narrative present an experience similar to that described in the poem?

☐ Is the chronological order clear?

☐ Does the narrative include sensory details, figurative language, and personal thoughts and feelings?

Lyric 17

A Lyric Poem by
José Garcia Villa

First, a poem must be magical,
Then musical as a sea-gull.
It must be a brightness moving
And hold secret a bird's flowering.
5 It must be slender as a bell,
And it must hold fire as well.
It must have the wisdom of bows
And it must kneel like a rose.
It must be able to hear
10 The luminance[1] of dove and deer.
It must be able to hide
What it seeks, like a bride.
And over all I would like to hover
God, smiling from the poem's cover. ✤

---

1. **luminance.** Visible light

(Left) *Fawn*, c. 1805–1818. Chinese School. Royal
Asiatic Society, London, England.

José Garcia Villa
(1908–1997) was a
multitalented artist known
especially for his poetry.
Born in Manila,
Philippines, in 1908, Villa later emigrated to
the United States in 1929. He attended the
University of New Mexico, where he founded
and edited a literary magazine, *Clay*. Villa
began his career as a published poet in the
Philippines, though his work was deemed
inappropriate and too racy. In the United
States, however, he quickly gained the
support of noted American poets. Villa
received prestigious American awards and
went on to cultivate an impressive reputation.

525

Preview the Selection

At a Glance
Independent Reading
- Reading Level: Easy
- Difficulty Consideration: Literary elements
- Ease Factor: Length

Objectives
Reading this selection will enable students to do the following:
- read with developing fluency
- read silently with comprehension for a sustained period of time

Launch the Lesson
Ask students to define the literary term *poem*. Then ask them what they like best about poetry and how they would describe its effect on them. Have them read "Lyric 17" to find out how this poet describes what a poem should be.

Summary
Using metaphors, similes, and other figurative language, the speaker describes what a poem must be.

Use Reading Strategies
Visualize Have students describe how they visualize such images as "brightness moving." Model by pointing out that "slender as a bell" refers to the very thin metal of orchestral bells, which enables the instruments to have a pure, high tone when rung.

Program Resources

Planning and Assessment
Program Planning Guide, Selection Lesson Plan
E-Lesson Planner
Assessment Guide, Lesson Test
ExamView

Technology Tools
Interactive Student Text on CD
Visual Teaching Package
Audio Library
mirrorsandwindows.com

Meeting the Standards
Poetry: Unit 5, Independent Reading, pp. 79–84

The Mirrors & Windows question at the end of the selection focuses on the theme of enrichment. Before reading the poem, ask students how poems and stories affect their lives. Why is this the case for so many people? *Answer:* Students should describe the importance of poems and stories in their lives. Students might say that poetry is very meaningful because it expresses people's innermost feelings.

Analyze and Extend

1. It calls on the sense of hearing ("musical as a sea-gull") and sight ("brightness moving").

2. Sample response: The words of a poem should make you "hear" the beauty of a dove or deer. The words should make their beauty shine.

3. Answers will vary. Students should list and evaluate each item, describing how each one contributes to the overall description of a poem.

Rubric for Expository Writing

You can adapt this as a checklist for students to use as they write.

☐ Does the essay begin with a clear thesis statement that expresses the writer's point of view?

☐ Is the thesis statement supported by reasons that are based on examples and quotations from the poem?

☐ Is the essay free of errors in punctuation, grammar, and spelling?

In what ways are poems and stories important in your life? Why do you think poetry is so meaningful in so many people's lives?

Analyze and Extend

1. How does the poem call on human senses to express its message?
2. What might the speaker mean by stating a poem "must be able to hear the luminance of dove and deer"? Explain.
3. Evaluate each item the poem mentions. How does each item help build a single overall description of a poem?

Expository Writing Do you agree with Villa's definition of poetry? Write a brief **essay** stating your position and your reasons. State your position in a clear thesis statement and use examples and quotes from the poem to support each reason.

Collaborative Learning An *analogy* is an extended comparison between two things. In small groups, create a list of analogies that describe what a poem is and what its function should be. Discuss images and themes to compare with a poem. Present your analogies to the class. Finally, incorporate class responses into your list of analogies.

 Go to **www.mirrorsandwindows.com** for more.

Words in Use

Teaching Words
multitalented, 525
emigrated, 525
prestigious, 525
cultivate, 525
incorporate, 526

KEY TERMS
LYRIC POEM, 525
THESIS STATEMENT, 526
IMAGE, 526
THEME, 526

Common Core State Standards

Reading Literature
RL.10

Writing
W.10

Language
L.6

For Your Reading List

This Same Sky: A Collection of Poems from Around the World
by Naomi Shihab Nye

The poems in this anthology come from a wide variety of countries across the world. The poems cover several topics, from cultural and political issues to more general subjects, such as the beauty of nature and the importance of family. The poems are indexed by country, making it easy to investigate the differences in poetry between cultures and regions.

Here in Harlem: Poems in Many Voices
by Walter Dean Myers

In this award-winning collection, Myers gives each poem a distinct style and each character a unique voice, from schoolchildren to preachers. As a result, he makes Harlem come alive in verse. Specifically, he focuses on the different people that live in the urban setting and the wide variety of personal experiences they go through on a daily basis.

The Complete Collected Poems
by Maya Angelou

Maya Angelou is one of today's most famous poets, as well as the writer of the autobiography *I Know Why The Caged Bird Sings*. This collection includes all of Angelou's poems, from her earliest works written in 1971 through the poem she delivered at President Clinton's inauguration in 1993.

Poems from Homeroom: A Writer's Place to Start
by Kathi Appelt

In the first half of this book, Appelt includes her own poetry about common topics in teenage life, such as worrying about dances, passing notes in class, and dealing with friends. In the second half, she discusses her poems and inspiration. She also provides questions and suggestions for young poets.

My America: A Poetry Atlas of the United States
by Lee Bennett Hopkins

In this book, forty different poets write about the various regions of the United States, and many of the poems were commissioned especially for this collection. Classic and contemporary poets are featured, from Carl Sandburg to Myra Cohn Livingston. The book also includes paintings depicting the geography of the area, maps, and lists of facts about the regions and states.

It's a Woman's World: A Century of Women's Voices in Poetry
by Neil Philip

In this collection, poems from around the world focus on women's views in different cultures during the twentieth century. The collection includes works by famous poets, such as Dorothy Parker and Sylvia Plath, as well as lesser known poets. Black-and-white photographs add an interesting visual element to the pages.

Independent Reading

Independent Reading Activity

Help students form literature circles. Create groups of five or six students each, in combinations you think will facilitate fruitful discussions. Ask each group to choose a poetry anthology devoted to a single theme such as Walter Dean Myers's Harlem collection. Students may wish to consult a librarian to find an anthology.

When a group has chosen its book, help members locate enough copies for everyone to read. Give groups a week to read books outside of class. Then ask groups to meet for ten minutes and select a topic for longer discussion. This can be a single poem, poems on a particular theme, poems of a specific length, and so on. Allow another week for students to prepare for discussion.

Finally, let literature circles meet during class. See the Skills lesson below for how students can establish their own rules of etiquette. Tell students to reflect on their experiences once they conclude their group discussion.

▶ EMC E-Library

The EMC E-Library contains over twenty thousand pages of literary classics that students may read independently. An Electronic Library Guide provides teaching suggestions, enrichment activities, and reading strategy guidesheets.

Program Resources

EMC Access Editions

For additional independent reading, you may wish to refer students to one of EMC's Access Edition titles. Each Access Edition contains a thorough study apparatus, including background information, literal comprehension questions, footnotes, vocabulary definitions, critical thinking questions, and related projects and activities. An Assessment Manual offering worksheets and exams is available for each Access Edition.

Common Core State Standards

Reading Literature
RL.10

Objectives

Participating in this lesson will help students write a compare-and-contrast essay that has

- an introduction that grabs a reader's interest
- a thesis statement and a clear, logical, effective organizational pattern
- transitions that signal comparisons and contrasts
- a closing that summarizes main points and restates the thesis

Launch the Lesson

Ask small groups to come up with five practical reasons for learning to write a compare-and-contrast essay. Model one reason: "I'd use an essay like this to describe my favorite music." Groups may list useful applications for various purposes such as persuading, informing, entertaining, and sharing. After groups devise their lists, have volunteers report ideas to the class.

What Great Writers Do

Answer: These people all bear responsibility for keeping other people safe.

Additional writing workshops are available in the *Exceeding the Standards: Writing* resource.

Writing Workshop

Expository Writing

Compare-and-Contrast Essay

Reading and Writing

In this unit, you read a poem by Emma Lazarus called "The New Colossus," which compares the ancient Colossus of Rhodes with the Statue of Liberty. One stands "with conquering limbs astride from land to land," while the other offers "world-wide welcome." What other features do these statues have in common? What is different about them? To answer these questions, you would use compare-and-contrast skills. You also use these skills in a variety of subject areas. You might use them in a science class to describe different types of stars, in language arts to compare characters in a novel, and in social studies to compare different historical periods.

In this workshop you will learn how to write a **compare-and-contrast essay,** a type of expository (or informational) writing that describes the similarities and differences between two or more subjects. Here's a summary of the assignment for a compare-and-contrast essay—what its goal is and a strategy for accomplishing that goal. This summary includes a writing rubric, a set of standards by which to judge your work. You will use this rubric as you draft and revise your essay.

- **Assignment:** Write a compare-and-contrast essay in which I identify similarities and differences between two or more things, people, places, or ideas.

- **Goal:** Make an overall point about these two subjects that my audience will find interesting.

- **Strategy:** Present evidence for this point by organizing details about my two subjects in a way that clearly shows their likenesses and differences.

- **Writing Rubric:** My compare-and-contrast essay should include the following:

  - an introduction that grabs my reader's interest
  - a thesis statement that expresses my overall point
  - a clear, logical, and effective pattern of organization
  - transitions that signal comparisons and contrasts
  - a closing that summarizes my main points and restates my thesis

What Great Writers Do

An effective technique in a compare-and-contrast essay is to show unexpected similarities between things that are otherwise very different. What is Tracy Kidder saying about stair-builders, crossing guards, and trainers of guide dogs?

A [poorly built] stair like that will never stop tripping people, even ones who know its flaw. Stair-making carpenters are like school crossing guards or trainers of seeing-eye dogs. They take on one of society's small sacred trusts.

—TRACY KIDDER, *House*

Teaching Words
rubric, 528
generated, 529
unique, 529
sluggish, 529
mechanical errors, 532
legibly, 532

KEY TERMS

COMPARE-AND-CONTRAST
  ESSAY, 528
CLUSTER CHART, 529
VENN DIAGRAM, 529
THESIS, 529
ORGANIZATIONAL PATTERN, 530
SUBJECT-BY-SUBJECT, 530
POINT-BY-POINT, 530
ANECDOTE, 530

TRANSITION, 530
PASSIVE VOICE, 532
ACTIVE VOICE, 532
APOSTROPHE, 532
POSSESSIVE, 532
SINGULAR POSSESSIVE, 532
PLURAL POSSESSIVE, 532
CONTRACTION, 532

Writing
W.2, W.3, W.4, W.5, W.6, W.10

1. PREWRITE

Choosing Your Topic

Choose a topic that has enough similarities between parts to make an effective comparison and enough differences to make a logical contrast. This topic should, of course, be something that you already know about or that you would enjoy researching. It should involve subjects that are neither completely alike nor completely different.

Here are some strategies you might use to generate topics:

Word Association Get together with a partner and make a list of pairs. These pairs can be subjects that are opposites or closely related. Take turns suggesting a person, an idea, a place, a product, or an animal. Your partner will then respond with the first word that comes to mind. After listing ideas, choose a pair that you think you could develop into a compare-and-contrast essay. Here's an example of a list generated by two partners:

Hummingbirds	Eagles
Eighth-grade	First-grade
Superman	Batman
Short story	Novel
e-mail	Snail mail
New York City	Honolulu
mammals	reptiles

Journal Look through your journal for ideas and experiences that you have thought about. Which of these ideas would you like to pursue further?

Library Look at books in your favorite section of the library, but browse in other sections, too. You'd be surprised at the good writing ideas that might present themselves.

Gathering Details

Once you have your topic, start gathering details. If you are comparing two experiences you have had, you might rely on your memory and make a cluster chart. If you are comparing products, ideas, places, or animals, you might need to do some research to get accurate information and identify the best details to compare and contrast. After gathering details for your essay, organize them in a logical manner. The best way to organize details for a compare-and-contrast essay is to make a Venn diagram. Such a diagram shows what both items have in common and what is unique about each one. Here's a Venn diagram that might be used to compare mammals and reptiles.

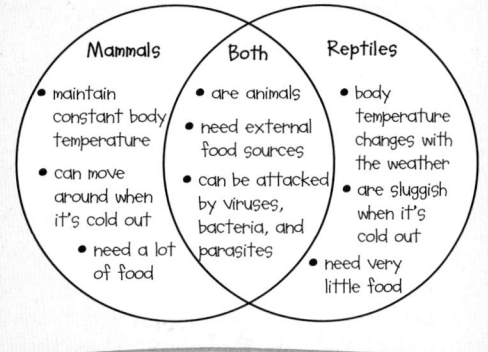

Deciding on Your Purpose

Now review your details to determine what the purpose of your essay will try. Decide the basic point you are trying to make and state it in your **thesis.** An essay comparing mammals and reptiles might include a thesis statement similar to this:

> One of the main differences between mammals and reptiles is the way they respond to the outside temperature.

WRITING WORKSHOP **529**

Teach the Workshop

Prewrite
Thesis Statements Tell students that a thesis statement has two parts: the topic and something particular about the topic. Demonstrate that the model in the book on page 533 has a topic—differences between mammals and reptiles—and a particular feature—how they respond to the outside temperature.

Have students work in pairs to test their thesis statements. Each student should read his or her statement and then ask for feedback on whether it promises an essay whose topic is narrow enough, whose points will be interesting, and whose ideas will be easy to support with details, facts, and examples.

What Great Writers Do

Remind students that topics can come from their personal experience. Author Julia Alvarez compared her family to other families in her native Dominican Republic:

We knew that Michelangelo's Sistine Chapel was a great work of art, but we didn't know why. It wasn't a literary family, but it was within a culture where 80 percent of the people couldn't read at all. So to have once read Shakespeare was a big deal.

Research Skills

Questions and Methods

Point out that there are two purposes for research during prewriting: to find an appropriate topic and to find supporting details. The first kind of research requires asking general questions of a variety of sources; the second kind of research requires asking specific questions of carefully selected sources. Ask students to categorize these questions as either topic oriented or supporting detail oriented:

1. How many tourists visit San Francisco and Los Angeles each year?
2. Where are the biggest U.S. zoos?
3. When did the city first allow fast-food restaurants to locate downtown?
4. How do airlines choose in-flight movies?

Draft

Organizing Ideas Tell students that the details they collect may suggest an organizational pattern. For example, details may reveal that the items are similar in all but two key ways; a point-by-point organization could highlight the differences. Also remind students that whichever pattern they use, they will summarize their main points in the essay's conclusion.

Making Connections Encourage students to clearly state what readers should notice. If they have a great idea that isn't coming through, tell them to stop and add a sentence that says plainly what they mean. The sentence may be long, but it must be clear. Remind them that they will be able to refine their sentences when they revise.

2. DRAFT

Organizing Ideas

Once you have decided on your subjects, gathered and organized details, and created your thesis statement, decide what kind of **organizational pattern** you want to use in your essay. For a compare-and-contrast essay, there are two basic ways to organize your information. If you choose the **subject-by-subject** (or block) method, you present all the information you plan to include about your first subject, followed by all the information about your second subject. In the **point-by-point** method, you present each feature in turn, looking at your first subject, then at the second subject. Here's how these two organizational patterns would look for an essay about mammals and reptiles:

Subject-by-Subject	Point-by-Point
Mammals	**How they deal with outside temperature**
• How they deal with outside temperature	• Mammals
• Amount of food they need	• Reptiles
• Advantages of being warm-blooded	**Amount of food they need**
Reptiles	• Mammals
• How they deal with outside temperature	• Reptiles
• Amount of food they need	**Advantages of method**
• Advantages of being cold-blooded	• Mammals
	• Reptiles

Putting Your Thoughts on Paper

As you write your draft, keep in mind that an essay has three basic parts: an introduction, a body, and a conclusion. Create a plan for your compare-and-contrast essay, such as the one on the right comparing and contrasting mammals and reptiles.

Many writers begin with the introduction, which may include an anecdote of some kind to grab the reader's interest, followed by the thesis statement. Then they write the body and conclusion. Others write the body first, and then insert the introduction and conclusion later. Whichever method works best for you, your goal is to get your ideas down on paper according to the plan you have chosen. At this stage, concentrate on content and organization.

Introduction
• Lead with an interesting fact, question, or anecdote.
• Present my thesis statement.

Body
• Write one paragraph dealing with each feature or compare and contrast the points about each animal.

Conclusion
• Rephrase my thesis statement in a way that refers back to the opening fact, question, or anecdote.
• Wrap up my essay.

Making Connections

As you draft, make connections between ideas by using **transitions,** or words and phrases that make it easier for the reader to see the comparisons and contrasts. Here are some examples of different types of transitional words and phrases that would be useful in a compare-and-contrast essay.

Transitions that Show Comparisons	Transitions that Show Contrasts
also	although
as	but
both	except
each	however
in the same way	in contrast
just	on the other hand
like	whereas
similarly	while
too	yet

Differentiated Instruction

English Language Learning

Have students work in pairs. Provide each pair with a sheet of paper that has a mixed list of compare and contrast transitions, such as *by comparison, also, instead, unlike, another, yet, in the same way, similarly, likewise, in contrast, differently, on the other hand, both, also, but, although, however, too,* and *the same.* Have one student read half of the transitions one at a time. For each transition, the other student should state whether it indicates comparison, contrast, or possibly either. Depending on his or her proficiency, the second student might also use the word in a sentence. Then have students switch roles and complete the list.

Evaluating Your Draft

A draft is just that; it is not your final copy. To polish your draft, you need to identify its strengths and weaknesses in terms of organization, content, and word choice. You can evaluate your essay on your own, or you can work with a **peer reviewer.** Exchange papers, and point out strengths and suggest improvements. Refer to the revising checklist on the right as you judge the essay.

Below is part of a draft. Changes have been made and reasons for the changes are given in the annotations on the right.

> **Revising Checklist**
> - ☐ Does the introduction grab the reader's interest?
> - ☐ Is there a thesis statement that expresses the overall point?
> - ☐ Is the organization clear and logical?
> - ☐ Are transitions included to signal comparisons and contrasts?

Darlene told the class about a ~~weird thing that happened~~ *frightening experience* she had during that cold snap last week. She had gone down to the hot tub area in her apartment complex, wanting to relax in the bubbles. ~~She brought along with her a big towel and a bottle of water.~~ Imagine her surprise when she found a few snakes curled up on the spa cover. After a sharp intake of breath, she dashed back to the apartment, called the animal control agency, and described the animals. Even though the agency assured her that the snakes were of a harmless variety, Darlene is now avoiding the hot tub area, at least until the weather warms up a bit.

Darlene's experience points out one of the main differences between mammals and reptiles: the way they respond to the outside temperature. Reptiles, cold-blooded creatures, take on the external temperature of the environment. When it's cold out, they get cold; when it's hot out, they get hot. Those snakes at the hot tub were just trying to get warm.

> *Reword opening sentence to include more precise word choice.*

> *Delete a sentence that has nothing to do with the topic.*

> *Clearly state the main point in a thesis statement.*

Teach the Workshop

Revise

Evaluating Your Draft Draw attention to the Revising Checklist. Show students that it relates directly to the rubric on page 528. As students check their own writing, suggest that they try starting at the bottom of the checklist and working their way up.

Interest-Grabbing Introductions
Tell students that readers often relate to personal anecdotes, so they should use an anecdote if they have one. An easier introduction to write is the leading question. For example: "Why can't snakes move fast in the cold?" If students have trouble with an introduction, encourage them to consult other students for ideas.

Peer Review Give students these tips for reviewing.

Delivering Criticism
- **Be focused.** Concentrate on the introduction, the organization, and transitions.
- **Be positive.** Respect the writer's feelings and writing efforts.
- **Be specific.** Give concrete ideas for improving the essay.

Receiving Criticism
- **Ask questions.** Make sure you understand your reviewer's comments. Ask your reviewer for clarification if necessary.
- **Be selective.** Accept your reviewer's time and suggestions graciously. When you revise your essay, you can use just some—or none—of the suggestions.

Speaking & Listening Skills

Monitor Comprehension While Listening

You can use the peer review process as an opportunity for students to practice listening skills. Have each student read his or her draft aloud for a peer reviewer. Tell reviewers to listen for and take notes on these things as they monitor their own comprehension.

1. What does the introduction make you think? Do you want to learn more?

2. Does the organization make sense to you? Does your mind wander at any point? If so, where?

3. Do you understand how the items in the essay are alike and different? If not, what is confusing about the organization or transition words and phrases?

Edit and Proofread

Students may want to use proofreader's marks when correcting their work. Refer them to the Language Arts Handbook Writing Section 4.1, Proofreader's Symbols.

What Great Writers Do

Tell students that it is fine to continue revising as they edit. If they allow some time to pass between revising and editing, they will probably see things they want to change or delete. Robert Louis Stevenson said

There is but one art, to omit.

Publish and Present

Before students begin their final versions, they might benefit from reading the Language Arts Handbook Writing Section 4.1, Writing Follow-up.

4. EDIT AND PROOFREAD

Focus: Passive and Active Voice

Sometimes you may find yourself writing sentences that use the **passive voice.** Passive voice is the act of telling who or what *receives* the action in a sentence, rather than showing who or what *performs* the action.

> **Passive Voice:**
> Much less energy is used by cold-blooded animals than warm-blooded animals, so less food is needed by them.
>
> **Change to Active Voice:**
> Cold-blooded animals use much less energy than warm-blooded animals, so they need less food.

Using the passive voice usually makes writing flat and uninteresting. It can also create awkward sentences. To recognize passive voice, look for phrases after the action verb that begin with *by* or *by the.* Watch out also for verb phrases that use forms of the verb *be.* Look over your writing and try to rewrite passive sentences so that they are in active voice. Strong verbs in the active voice will make your descriptions clearer and more effective.

Focus: Apostrophes and Possessives

Apostrophes are used to show possession. Pay careful attention to the use of apostrophes in your writing: *Miguel's hat, the boys' laughter.* Remember these rules about the use of apostrophes in possessives:

- To form the singular possessive noun, add an apostrophe and the letter *s* to the end of the noun: *Darlene's apartment, the reptile's body temperature.*
- To form the plural possessive noun, write it in its plural form and add the apostrophe after the *s: the mammals' characteristics, the puppies' noses.* For a noun whose plural form does not end in *s,* add and apostrophe and *s* to the end: *children's laughter, men's shoes.*

> Darlene's experience points out one of the main differences between mammals and reptiles: the way they respond to the outside temperature.

Apostrophes are also used in contractions, such as *don't, didn't, won't, should've, wouldn't, she's,* and *it's.* Note that the possessive form of *it* is *its; it's* is a contraction for *it is.*

Proofreading

Final Read-through After revising and editing your story for errors in grammar and style, look for mechanical errors, such as errors in punctuation, capitalization, and spelling. Use proofreader's marks to highlight any errors you find, and then correct them. (See the Language Arts Handbook, section 4.1, for a list of proofreader's symbols.)

5. PUBLISH AND PRESENT

Final Draft

It's Show Time! Make a clean, final version of your story. If you are handwriting your essay, do it neatly and legibly. If, on the other hand, you are using a word-processing program, double-space your essay and use an easy-to-read typeface or font. Ask your teacher about any presentation guidelines before you submit your work.

Differentiated Instruction

Reading Proficiency

Use this opportunity to review students' comprehension of the grammar and vocabulary skills in this unit. Review their handling of different kinds of nouns, especially plurals and possessives, and their grasp of similes. A compare-and-contrast essay is an excellent place to practice using similes.

Enrichment

Scientists often write in the passive voice to avoid implying that nonhumans can think or have motivations. However, most nature writers use active voice to involve readers in their narratives. Have students use their science textbooks to find examples of passive voice, and then have them rewrite the examples using active voice.

Student Model

Hot and Cold
by Jerome Chavez

Darlene told the class about a frightening experience she had during that cold snap last week. She had gone down to the hot tub area in her apartment complex, wanting to relax in the bubbles. Imagine her surprise when she found a few snakes curled up on the spa cover. After a sharp intake of breath, she dashed back to the apartment, called the animal control agency, and described the animals. Even though the agency assured her that the snakes were of a harmless variety, Darlene is now avoiding the hot tub area, at least until the weather warms up a bit.

Engages the reader's interest in the introduction with an anecdote

Darlene's experience points out one of the main differences between mammals and reptiles: the way they respond to the outside temperature. Reptiles, cold-blooded creatures, take on the external temperature of the environment. When it's cold out, they get cold; when it's hot out, they get hot. Those snakes at the hot tub were just trying to get warm.

Clearly states the main point in a thesis statement

Mammals, on the other hand, are warm-blooded creatures. Mammals and other warm-blooded animals are able to maintain a steady internal temperature almost regardless of the temperature outside. How do they do it? The main requirement is food—fuel to feed the fire inside. That is why warm-blooded animals spend so much time hunting and eating. Pound for pound, mammals eat at least ten times more than reptiles. Most of the mammal's meal will go toward fueling its constant body temperature, while most of the reptile's meal will go toward greater body mass.

What are the advantages to being warm-blooded? Well, for one thing, warm-blooded animals can move around in cold weather, looking for food and defending themselves when necessary. This means that warm-blooded animals can live almost anywhere on Earth.

Yet, there are advantages to being cold-blooded as well. Cold-blooded animals use much less energy than warm-blooded animals, so they need less food. Another advantage is that they are less susceptible to viruses, bacteria, and parasites. On the other hand, the immune systems of cold-blooded animals are far weaker than those of warm-blooded animals.

Uses point-by-point method of organization

Includes transitions to signal comparisons and contrasts

Warm-blooded animals and cold-blooded animals sometimes have to share the same space, as Darlene found out. So the next time you go out to dinner and have leftovers, remember to bring a doggie bag home for your warm-blooded friend; your pet snake can wait a while.

Sums up main points and refers back to introductory anecdote

Writing Skills

Management Time Lines

Tell students that analyzing the writing task at hand will help them make decisions about how long they spend on any step in the process. Point out that sometimes they will have several weeks to produce an essay; other times they will have a few days or will have to write on demand, as on a test. In quick-turnaround circumstances, they will have to adjust the time they spend prewriting or drafting. Ask students how they would manage their time in these situations:

- Your deadline for a school newspaper article on teacher vacations is two days from today.
- A test asks you for a three-paragraph comparison of two haikus.
- You must shorten an old essay on patriotism to enter a writing contest being judged next month.

Teach the Workshop

Objectives

Participating in this lesson will help students plan and deliver an expository presentation that

- is clear and well organized
- uses visuals effectively
- provides sufficient details and visuals to be informative

Launch the Lesson

Ask students to imagine they have to tell a group of fifth-graders about being a poet. Have students gather briefly in small groups to brainstorm what they could say about writing poetry as a profession. Then reconvene the class and ask groups to report. Finally, tell students they are about to learn how to structure and style informational presentations on the unit theme, Living with Words.

Program Resources

To expand upon this workshop lesson, Giving and Actively Listening to Expository Presentations, see the *Exceeding the Standards: Speaking & Listening* resource.

TEACHING NOTE

Listening Skills

Form a discussion group of students who learn best by hearing instruction. Have the students collaborate to write a checklist of good expository practices. Assure them that they know, as well as anyone, what kinds of presentations are most effective for good listeners.

Giving and Actively Listening to Expository Presentations

Have you ever watched a television show on how ancient people built the pyramids, or how a huge ocean liner is assembled? Programs such as these are called expository presentations. An **expository presentation** might explain, describe, give information, or instruct people about how to do something. By actively listening to an expository presentation, you gain new, interesting, and useful information.

Planning Your Expository Presentation

Choose a Topic Focus your attention on the topic of the unit—the use of words. You might choose to inform your audience about how new words are added to the dictionary, word origins, how various forms of poetry use words in different ways, or figures of speech. Choose a topic that both you and your audience will find interesting. Decide what portion of the topic you will be able to effectively explain in the time you have. For example, if you choose word origins, you might focus on blended words, such as *loudspeaker* or *eggshell;* or words that arise from proper names, such as *sandwich* or *boycott.*

Identify Your Audience For what audience will you give your presentation? What do they already know about the subject? What would they be interested in learning more about? Identifying the age and knowledge level of your audience lets you select appropriate language and content, as well as helping you anticipate questions they might ask.

Decide on Organization Expository presentations can be organized in a variety of ways. Use transitions to signal the type of organization you choose. Here are some examples:

- Use **compare and contrast order** to explain how lyric poetry and narrative poetry use words to create a mood. Signal words include *by comparison, similarly, in the same way, by contrast, on the other hand,* and *different from.*
- Use **cause and effect order** to explain how proper names become commonly-used words. Signal words include *because, as a result of, for this reason,* and *led to.*
- Use **chronological order** to explain how new words, such as *ringtone* or *supersized,* arise and are eventually added to the dictionary. Signal words include *first, next, later,* and *finally.*
- Use **classification order** to explain the different categories of figures of speech, such as *metaphor, simile, alliteration,* and *personification.* Signal words include *one type* and *another kind.*

Words in Use

Teaching Words
origins, 534
constructive, 535
rubric, 535
convey, 535

KEY TERMS

EXPOSITORY PRESENTATION, 534	CLASSIFICATION ORDER, 534
AUDIENCE, 534	METAPHOR, 534
COMPARE AND CONTRAST ORDER, 534	SIMILE, 534
CAUSE AND EFFECT ORDER, 534	ALLITERATION, 534
CHRONOLOGICAL ORDER, 534	PERSONIFICATION, 534
	SUPPORTING DETAIL, 535
	TRANSITION, 535
	TONE, 535

Common Core State Standards

Speaking and Listening
SL.1, SL.4, SL.6

Organizing Your Presentation

Draw a graphic organizer for the organization you have chosen. For example, you might draw a Venn diagram for compare-contrast, or a time line for chronological order. As you research your topic in books, magazines, or on the Internet, fill in the graphic organizer. Decide whether you will use any visuals to support your presentation.

Transfer the ideas you will include from the graphic organizer to index cards. Each card should have a main idea, several supporting details, and the name of any visual you will use with that point. Put your note cards in order and practice moving from one card to the next using transition words that signal your organization.

Evaluating Your Presentation

Work in teams of three or four to get and give feedback on your expository presentation. As each person finishes, the other group members should offer constructive, polite, and respectful criticism aimed at helping the presenter make the presentation more effective. Use the listening and speaking rubric on this page to evaluate the presentations.

Delivering Your Presentation

The key purpose of your presentation is to provide information in an effective and entertaining way. Use your index cards to help you remember all your points, but don't read your presentation. Involve your audience by making eye contact and speaking in a clear and engaging manner. Your facial expression, voice tone, and body language should convey enthusiasm about your subject. If you use visuals, give your viewers time to study them before continuing. From time to time, ask if anyone has questions. Answer questions completely, but don't start discussing other subjects.

Audience members should listen actively and be courteous to the speaker. Connect what the speaker says to what you already know. If you're unclear on something, ask questions at appropriate times.

Speaking Rubric

Your presentation will be evaluated on these elements:

Content

☐ presentation is clear and well-organized

☐ visuals are interesting and enhance understanding of presentation

☐ sufficient details and visuals are provided to understand the topic

Delivery and Presentation

☐ speaks in an interesting and engaging tone of voice

☐ responds to audience questions by clarifying and elaboration

☐ effectively uses nonverbal communication

Listening Rubric

As a peer reviewer or audience member, you should do the following:

☐ listen quietly and attentively

☐ analyze the images that are presented

☐ ask appropriate questions

☐ (as peer reviewer) provide constructive feedback

Develop Visuals

Students may want to consider refining their graphic organizers after they have rehearsed their presentations. This is because their organizers might serve as excellent visual aids. Point out that they will probably want to simplify the information included in the organizer to help the audience better understand what is shown. For instance:

- A Venn diagram that shows a key similarity and a key difference, such as a root word and two of its variations, can help the audience compare and contrast.
- A cause-and-effect chain can help people see how one thing leads to another. One example would be how an ancient Greek word was adapted in Latin and then in other languages.
- A time line will give the audience a sense of history. An example could be showing how a poet's style developed from early works to later works.
- A chart or table can show classifications such as parts of speech or types of poems.
- A simple map could show the places people encounter words on a daily basis such as in highway signs, grocery stores, and schools.

> For more information, see the Language Arts Handbook Section 7, Speaking & Listening.

Retelling and Summarizing

Use this opportunity to have students self-assess their listening skills. Devise a handout that asks these two questions and has space for students to write answers:

1. In one or two sentences, what was the speaker's topic and the main message the speaker wanted to convey?

2. Tell one example the speaker gave to help communicate the main message.

Give each student the handout, and instruct students to complete the handout just once, after a presentation of their own choosing. After all the presentations and self-assessments are complete, tell students to look at their handouts and decide how well they were able to listen.

Objectives

Completing this lesson will enable students to

- write a compare-and-contrast expository essay based on a timed writing prompt
- answer standardized test questions that demonstrate revising and editing skills
- demonstrate the ability to make inferences from a reading by answering standardized questions

Timed Writing

Remind students that standardized tests often ask for a response to a prompt in a specified period of time. Give the following tips:

- Read the entire assignment carefully.
- Look for key words that identify what is expected.
- Underline these words or write them on your own notepaper.
- Use the key words to make sure to answer all parts of the question.
- Organize. Allow time for planning, writing, and reviewing.
- Before you begin writing, create a rough outline of points to make.
- Write a clear introduction.
- If you find yourself running out of time, state your remaining points and add a conclusion.
- Review your completed essay to see if you have answered all parts of the question.
- Before you turn in your essay, take time to proofread it.

Test Practice Workshop

Writing Skills

Expository Essay

Read the following poems and the writing assignment that follows. Before you begin writing, think carefully about what task the assignment is asking you to perform. Then create an outline to help guide your writing.

"At the Library" by Nikki Grimes

I flip the pages of a book and slip inside,
Where crystal seas await and pirates hide.
I find a paradise where birds can talk,
Where children fly and trees prefer to walk.
Sometimes I end up on a city street.
I recognize the brownskin girl I meet.
She's skinny, but she's strong, and brave, and wise.
I smile because I see me in her eyes.

"The First Book" by Rita Dove

Open it.
Go ahead, it won't bite.
Well…maybe a little.
More a nip, like. A tingle.
It's pleasurable, really.
You see, it keeps on opening.
You may fall in.
Sure, it's hard to get started;
remember learning to use
knife and fork? Dig in:
you'll never reach bottom.
It's not like it's the end of the world—
just the world as you think
you know it.

Assignment: What do the two poems have in common? In what ways are they different? Plan and write several paragraphs for an **expository essay** in which you **compare** and **contrast** the poems. Use **transitions** that signal the organization of your essay. Include evidence from the poems to support your thesis.

Rubric for an Expository Essay

Have students use these criteria when evaluating their essays.

- ☐ Does the essay have an introduction that clearly states the thesis?
- ☐ Does the essay have both comparisons and contrasts?
- ☐ Do transitions signal a clear organizational pattern?
- ☐ Does the essay use evidence from the poems to support ideas?

Common Core State Standards

Reading Information
RI.1, RI.5

Writing
W.2, W.4, W.5

Language
L.4

Revising and Editing Skills

The following sentences test your ability to recognize grammar and usage errors. Each sentence contains either a single error or no error at all. No sentence contains more than one error. The error, if there is one, is underlined and lettered. If the sentence contains an error, select the one underlined part that must be changed to make the sentence correct. If the sentence is correct, select choice E. In choosing answers, follow the requirements of standard written English.

1. The national spelling bee (A) had one winner, a home-schooled boy (B) from Montana, and (C) several runners-up. (D) No error. (E)
2. The audience were (A) surprised when the actors (B) came (C) down from the stage and started talking (D) to people. No error. (E)
3. My mother gets (A) annoyed with my neighbor's (B) pet cat because it's (C) always digging up her flower beds. (D) No error. (E)
4. We wanted to try (A) a new Restaurant, so (B) we went to Luigi's Taco Stand, (C) even though the name seemed a bit strange. (D) No error. (E)
5. Twenty students, (A) three parents, and (B) one teacher is (C) on the field trip to the museum. (D) No error. (E)
6. Several books (A) sat on the desk that Jason had read, (B) but the one he is reading (C) is on his nightstand. (D) No error. (E)
7. When the teacher asked, "Do you like poetry," (A) most of the girls said (B) they did, but (C) few of the boys would (D) admit to enjoying it. No error. (E)
8. When the poet talks (A) about the people milling around like (B) ghosts, it (C) means that they seem to have (D) no purpose in life. No error. (E)
9. Your response (A) to the poem was quite (B) different from (C) that of most of the other students. (D) No error. (E)
10. When it (A) comes to choosing (B) a career, each (C) person should follow their (D) dreams. No error. (E)

Teach the Workshop

Revising and Editing Skills

1. A	**6.** B
2. A	**7.** A
3. E	**8.** C
4. B	**9.** E
5. C	**10.** D

Test-Taking Tip

Test Purpose Point out that people assign and take tests for specific reasons, including to learn how much students have understood, to assess a person's skill level, and to judge how well a person can find big ideas that underlie details. Tell students that if several test questions in a row seem unclear or otherwise hard to answer, they should take a minute to remind themselves of the purpose of the test. For instance, if a math test has word problems with grammar mistakes, they should remember that the test is looking for math answers, not English answers, and should focus on the math parts of the problem. Similarly, if an English test asks about spelling errors, they should ignore style issues and focus on spelling.

For more information, see the Language Arts Handbook Section 8, Test-Taking Skills.

Program Resources

For more study and practice with test-taking skills, see the *Exceeding the Standards: Test Practice* resource:

- Expository Essay Practice Test: Timed Writing, p. 13

Words in Use

Teaching Words

unbowed, 538
kin, 538
gory, 538
context, 539

KEY TERMS

EXPOSITORY ESSAY, 536
COMPARE, 536
CONTRAST, 536
TRANSITION, 536
THESIS, 536
HYPERBOLE, 539
SIMILE, 539
INTERNAL RHYME, 539
ALLITERATION, 539
ASSONANCE, 539
CONSONANCE, 539
IRONY, 539
METAPHOR, 539
RHYME SCHEME, 539

Tell students that reading comprehension tests give a short piece of writing and then ask questions about it. Urge them to keep the following tips in mind:

- Skim all the questions quickly.
- Read the passage with the questions in mind.
- Reread the first question carefully.
- Find the portion of the passage to which the question refers. Slow down and read carefully.
- Answer the first question.
- Repeat this process to answer all the rest of the questions.

Reading Skills

Carefully read the following passage. Then, on a separate piece of paper, answer each question.

"Cat" by J. R. R. Tolkien

The fat cat on the mat
   may seem to dream
of nice mice that suffice
   for him, or cream;
5 but he free, maybe,
   walks in thought
unbowed, proud, where loud
   roared and fought
his kin, lean and slim,
10   or deep in den
in the East feasted on beasts
   and tender men.
The giant lion with iron
   claw in paw,
15 and huge ruthless tooth
   in gory jaw;
the pard dark-starred,
   fleet upon feet,
that oft soft from aloft
20   leaps upon his meat
where woods loom in gloom—
   far now they be,
   fierce and free,
   and tamed is he;
25 but fat cat on the mat
   kept as a pet
   he does not forget.

Differentiated Instruction

English Language Learning

Give definitions to help students interpret this poem.

suffice — enough
ruthless — having no pity or kindness
pard — large cat such as a leopard or panther
fleet — fast
oft — often

loom — seem large
gloom — darkness or partial darkness
fierce — showing anger or being violent

1. Which types of sound devices are found in line 1?
   A. hyperbole and simile
   B. internal rhyme and alliteration
   C. alliteration and consonance
   D. assonance and internal rhyme
   E. simile and metaphor

2. In line 3, "nice mice that suffice" means
   A. mice that are easy to catch.
   B. friendly mice that play with the cat.
   C. mice that are fun to catch.
   D. mice that the cat has eaten.
   E. enough mice to satisfy the cat.

3. What can you infer from the words "he, free, maybe" in line 5?
   A. The author thinks the cat can walk around in its dreams.
   B. The cat wants to be free to catch mice.
   C. The author is guessing what the cat is dreaming about.
   D. The cat was once free to run around.
   E. The author thinks the cat looks like a free lion.

4. Which line contains an example of assonance?
   A. line 4
   B. line 5
   C. line 6
   D. line 8
   E. line 10

5. In line 8, who roared and fought?
   A. the cat's kin
   B. the pet
   C. the fat cat
   D. the mice in his dream
   E. the beasts

6. Which type of sound device is found in line 10?
   A. assonance
   B. consonance
   C. alliteration
   D. hyperbole
   E. internal rhyme

7. Lines 13 and 14 contain an example of
   A. irony.
   B. a simile.
   C. a metaphor.
   D. alliteration.
   E. hyperbole.

8. Which of the following represents the rhyme scheme in all but the last three lines of the poem?
   A. *abba*
   B. *aabb*
   C. *abca*
   D. *abcb*
   E. *abbc*

9. In line 17, the word *pard* is a name for a medieval beast. Based on the context, a "pard dark-starred" is probably most like
   A. a leopard.
   B. a cat.
   C. a zebra.
   D. a monkey.
   E. a lion.

10. What does the author mean by "far now they be" in line 22?
    A. The animals in the dream live outdoors.
    B. The animals in the dream are the cat's distant ancestors.
    C. The animals in the dream live far apart from one another.
    D. The animals in the dream were animals the cat knew when he was younger.
    E. The animals in the dream were made up by the cat.

Test-Taking Skills

Elimination of Incorrect Responses

Tell students that one way to find a multiple-choice answer is to methodically eliminate the incorrect responses. Model a think aloud for doing this, using a question on this page.

Question 1. I've already eliminated A and E because there aren't any comparisons in this line. That leaves B, C, and D. I can hear internal rhyme in the line, but I don't see any alliteration, so that eliminates B and C. That leaves D as the correct answer.

Select another question and have the class work as a group to eliminate the incorrect responses.

Planning and Assessment Tools

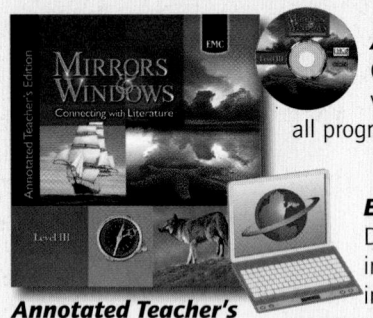

Annotated Teacher's Edition
One location for accessing, previewing, and planning for use of all program resources.

Annotated Teacher's Edition

EMC Launchpad
Desktop application for accessing, previewing, planning, posting, and grading all program resources. Post personal resources and lessons, and access the E-Lesson Planner, the E-Gradebook, and training modules for computer literacy.

Assessment Guide and ExamView
A variety of assessments are available for this unit in print and electronic forms, including:
- Formative Survey
- Lesson Tests
- Unit Exams
- Alternative Assessment Options
- Reading Fluency Assessments

Meeting the Standards: Unit 1
In addition to lesson-by-lesson resources, *Meeting the Standards* includes the following unit-based resources:
- Unit Study Guide
- Practice Test
- Active Reading Model
- Selection Quizzes

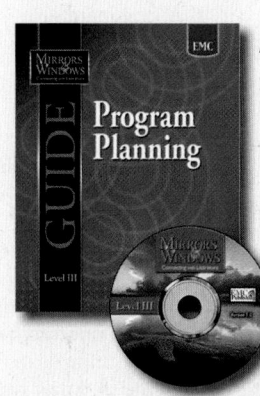

Program Planning Guide and E-Lesson Planner
- Lesson Plans for all the selections in the unit
- Core Standards-Based Selections
- Reading Log and Evaluation Forms

The E-Lesson Planner contains fully developed lesson plans and unit resources with an electronic calendar for editing lesson plans.

Technology Tools

Visual Teaching Package
This package contains unit-based lectures, games, art collections, and Writing Workshops in PowerPoint format; included within the EMC Launchpad.

Interactive Student Text on CD
The student textbook on CD includes highlighting, note-taking, bookmarking, and a direct link to the student website, in addition to everything in the student text.

Audio Library
Authentic, dramatic recordings with listening activities expand listening skills and offer additional support for developing readers and English Language Learners.

ETS Online Criterion-Based Essay Grader (Grades 9–12)
Students can use this ETS web-based tool to evaluate their essays online before submitting them for teacher review and final evaluation.

mirrorsandwindows.com
Student and teacher resources, support, references, technology tools, and state-specific standards are available at **mirrorsandwindows.com.** The website is customizable using the EMC Launchpad.

Exceeding the Standards Unit Resources

Each of the *Exceeding the Standards* resources provides fully developed lessons to help you extend the textbook lessons and to expand upon the themes and skills covered in the unit. You can also download these lessons from **mirrorsandwindows.com**.

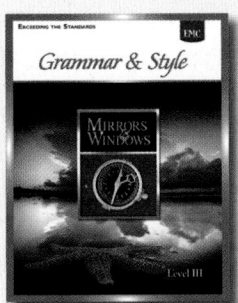

Grammar & Style
This resource contains:
• Seven lessons on Phrases and Clauses, pp. 129–150

Literature & Reading
This resource contains:
• Reading and Analyzing Cultural and Historical Essays, pp. 18–19

Special Topics
This resource contains:
• Career Skills Development: Be an Interviewer, pp. 21–22
• Media Literacy: Designing and Building a Website, pp. 23–24

Test Practice
This resource contains:
• Narrative Essay Practice Test: Revising and Editing, pp. 14–15

Writing
This resource contains:
• Narrative Writing: Write a Narrative Poem, pp. 49–58

Speaking & Listening
This resource contains the following lesson to expand on the Speaking & Listening Workshop:
• Giving and Actively Listening to Narrative Presentations, pp. 18–20

Vocabulary & Spelling
This resource contains:
• Five lessons on Word Study Skills and Context Clues, pp. 52–61

Extension Activities
This resource contains:
• Lifelong Learning: Research Dorothy Parker, pp. 18–19
• Collaborative Learning: Hold a Discussion, p. 20

Unit 6 Visual Planning Guide

Southbound on the Freeway
A Lyric Poem by May Swenson

(544)

Reading Level: Moderate
Pacing: 2 days

Meeting the Standards,
Guided Reading,
pp. 19–24

English Language Learners,
Analyze Text Organization,
pp. 142–148

Southern Mansion
A Lyric Poem by Arna Bontemps

(549)

Reading Level: Easy
Pacing: 2 days

Meeting the Standards,
Guided Reading,
pp. 25–30

Advanced Students,
Author Study, p. 32

Bats
A Narrative Poem by Randall Jarrell

(552)

Reading Level: Easy
Pacing: 3 days

Meeting the Standards,
Directed Reading,
pp. 31–35

Developing Readers,
Set Purpose,
pp. 40–42

The Choice
A Humorous Poem by Dorothy Parker

(558)

Reading Level: Easy
Pacing: 1 day

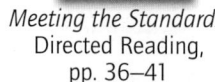

Meeting the Standards,
Directed Reading,
pp. 36–41

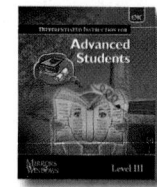

Advanced Students,
Poetic Form Activity,
pp. 33–34

Ode to My Socks

Oda a los calcetines
A Lyric Poem by Pablo Neruda

(561)

Reading Level: Moderate
Pacing: 2 days

Meeting the Standards,
Directed Reading,
pp. 42–47

English Language Learners,
Identifying Author's
Purpose, pp. 149–156

 Interactive Student
Text on CD-ROM

Selection
Lesson Plan

 Web-based
Resources

Lesson-by-Lesson Resources

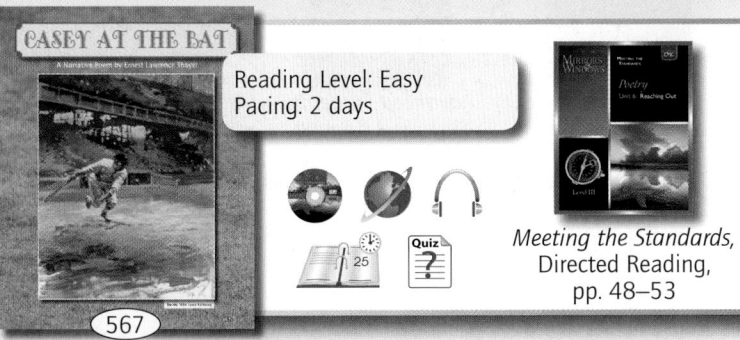

CASEY AT THE BAT
A Narrative Poem by Ernest Lawrence Thayer

Reading Level: Easy
Pacing: 2 days

Meeting the Standards,
Directed Reading,
pp. 48–53

567

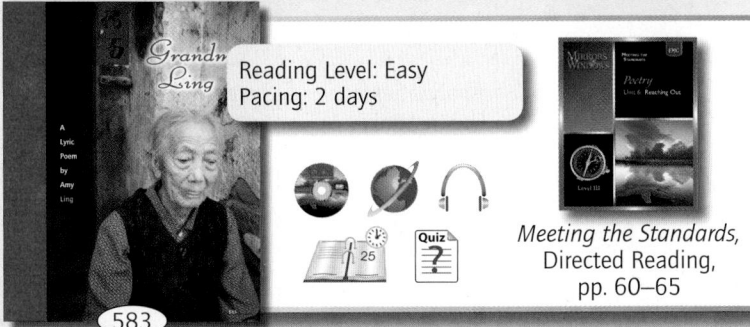

Paul Revere's Ride
A Narrative Poem by Henry Wadsworth Longfellow

Reading Level: Moderate
Pacing: 3 days

Meeting the Standards,
Directed Reading,
pp. 54–59

Developing Readers,
Unlock Word Meaning,
pp. 43–45

Advanced Students,
Author Biographical
Study, p. 35

572

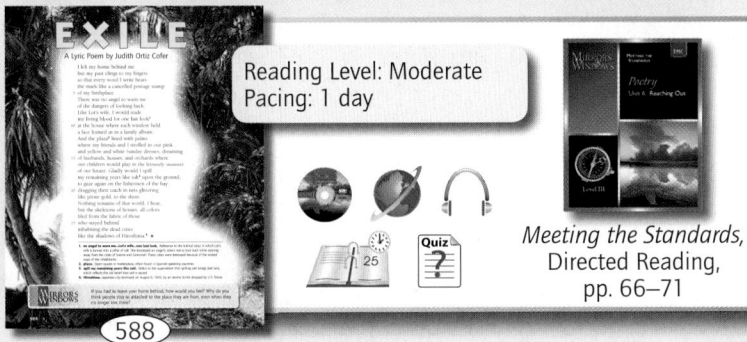

Grandma Ling
A Lyric Poem by Amy Ling

Reading Level: Easy
Pacing: 2 days

Meeting the Standards,
Directed Reading,
pp. 60–65

583

EXILE
A Lyric Poem by Judith Ortiz Cofer

Reading Level: Moderate
Pacing: 1 day

Meeting the Standards,
Directed Reading,
pp. 66–71

588

Birdfoot's Grampa
A Narrative Poem by Joseph Bruchac

The Time We Climbed Snake Mountain
A Lyric Poem by Leslie Marmon Silko

Reading Level: Easy
Pacing: 2 days

Meeting the Standards,
Comparing Literature,
pp. 72–80

*English Language
Learners,* Compare and
Contrast, pp. 157–162

591

592

 Lesson Test   Audio Library

Reading Level: Moderate
Pacing: 2 days

Meeting the Standards,
Independent Reading,
pp. 81–86

Developing Readers,
Make Predictions,
pp. 46–48

Advanced Students,
Historical Context
Project, pp. 36–37

594

Unit 6 Scope & Sequence Guide

Selection or Feature	Genre	Reading Support/ Reading Level	Word Count	Reading Skill	Graphic Organizer	
Understanding Meaning in Poetry, p. 542						
Southbound on the Freeway May Swenson pp. 543–546	Lyric Poem	Guided Reading: Reading Model/ Moderate	127	Analyze Text Organization	Sensory Detail Chart	
Southern Mansion Arna Bontemps pp. 548–550	Lyric Poem	Guided Reading: Reading Model/Easy	99	Analyze Author's Perspective	Author's Perspective Chart; Symbolism Chart	
Bats Randall Jarrell pp. 551–555	Narrative Poem	Directed Reading/Easy	240	Take Notes	Sensory Details Chart	
Literature Connection: The Bat Theodore Roethke p. 554	Lyric Poem	Easy	92			
The Choice Dorothy Parker pp. 557–559	Humorous Poem	Directed Reading/Easy	108	Monitor Comprehension	Comprehension Chart	
Ode to My Sock/Oda a los Calcentines Pablo Neruda pp. 560–564	Lyric Poem	Directed Reading/ Moderate	225	Identify Author's Purpose	Cluster Chart; Metaphor and Simile Chart	
Casey at the Bat Ernest Lawrence Thayer pp. 566–570	Narrative Poem	Directed Reading/Easy	580	Identify Main Idea	Main Idea Map; Suspense Chart	

GUIDED READING

DIRECTED READING

Nikki-Rosa
A Lyric Poem by Nikki Giovanni

Reading Level: Moderate
Pacing: 1 day

599

Meeting the Standards,
Independent Reading,
pp. 87–92

Literary Element	*Mirrors & Windows* Theme	Cross-Curricular Connection	Writing Options	Extension Activities
How Do Poems *Mean*? Speaker Symbolism				
Speaker	Instinct versus Intellect		Creative: Short Story Expository: Literary Response	Lifelong Learning: Conduct Internet Research and Design a Poster Critical Literacy: Debate
Symbolism	Disparity		Creative: Poem Expository: Literary Response	Collaborative Learning: Discuss with a Partner; Write a Paragraph Critical Literacy: Participate in a Panel Discussion; Research and Summarize
Imagery	Assumptions	Science Connection: *Navigating at Night*	Creative: Description Expository: Literary Response	Lifelong Learning: Use an Encyclopedia to Research Critical Literacy: Create a List of Questions
Rhythm	Choices		Creative: Poem Expository: Critical Analysis	Collaborative Learning: Discuss in Small Groups Lifelong Learning: Research and Write a Paragraph
Metaphor and Simile	Treasures		Creative: Personal Letter Expository: Review	Collaborative Learning: Create a Cluster Chart Media Literacy: Compare and Contrast Poems
Suspense	Heroes	Cultural Connection: *The History of Baseball*	Creative: Business Letter Expository: Summary	Media Literacy: Evaluate a Recording Critical Literacy: Read to the Class

Unit 6 Scope & Sequence Guide

	Selection or Feature	Genre	Reading Support/ Reading Level	Word Count	Reading Skill	Graphic Organizer	
DIRECTED READING	**Paul Revere's Ride** Henry Wadsworth Longfellow pp. 571–580	Narrative Poem	Directed Reading/ Moderate	993	Identify Sequence of Events	Time Line; Plot Diagram	
	Informational Text Connection: from **Paul Revere and the World He Lived In** Esther Forbes, pp. 578–579	Biography	Easy	702			
	Grandma Ling Amy Ling, pp. 582–586	Lyric Poem	Directed Reading/Easy	147	Draw Conclusions	Conclusions Chart; Cluster Chart	
	Literature Connection: My Mother Juggling Bean Bags James Mitsui, p. 585	Lyric Poem	Easy	213			
	Exile Judith Ortiz Cofer pp. 587–589	Lyric Poem	Directed Reading/ Moderate	180	Identify the Main Idea	Main Idea Map; Simile Chart	
	Comparing Literature: Birdfoot's Grampa Joseph Bruchac pp. 590–593	Narrative Poem	Directed Reading/Easy	92	Symbolism Chart		
	The Time We Climbed Snake Mountain Leslie Marmon Silko pp. 590–593	Lyric Poem	Directed Reading/Easy	67			
INDEPENDENT READING	**The Cremation of Sam McGee** Robert Service, pp. 594–597	Narrative Poem	Independent Reading/ Moderate	899		Summarize	
	Nikki-Rosa Nikki Giovanni, pp. 598–600	Lyric Poem	Independent Reading/ Moderate	160		Compare and Contrast	

Unit 6 Language Arts Workshops

Grammar & Style	Vocabulary & Spelling	Writing	Speaking & Listening	Test Practice
Personal and Possessive Pronouns, p. 547 Simple, Complete, and Compound Predicates, p. 556 Intensive and Reflexive Pronouns, p. 565	Context Clues, p. 581	Narrative Writing: Personal Narrative, pp. 602–607	Giving and Actively Listening to Narrative Presentations, pp. 608–609	Writing Skills: Narrative Essay, p. 610 Revising and Editing Skills, p. 611 Reading Skills: "Courage" by Robert Service, pp. 612–613

Literary Element	*Mirrors & Windows* Theme	Cross-Curricular Connection	Writing Options	Extension Activities
Narrative Poetry	American Spirit	History Connection: *Paul Revere*	Creative: Short Story Expository: Literary Response	Collaborative Learning: Analyze Rhyme Scheme Critical Literacy: Present a Poetry Reading
Free Verse	Communication		Creative: Personal Letter Applied: List	Lifelong Learning: Conduct Internet Research Critical Literacy: Interview a Classmate
Simile	Exile		Creative: Similes Expository: Literary Response	Collaborative Learning: Hold a Discussion Lifelong Learning: Conduct Internet or Library Research
Compare Literature: Symbolism	Wildlife Conservation Respect for Wildlife		Creative: Fable Persuasive: Persuasive Essay	Collaborative Learning: Have a Small-Group Discussion Critical Literacy: Research and Debate
Narrative Poetry	Integrity		Expository: Personal Essay	Critical Literacy: Perform a Choral Reading
Speaker	Reminiscence		Creative: Poem	Critical Literacy: Hold a Panel Discussion

Unit 6 Building Vocabulary

The lists below identify the Words in Use and Key Terms within this unit. These words are listed at the bottom of the Teacher's Edition pages at the beginning of each lesson. Vocabulary development activities are provided in the *Meeting the Standards* unit book and in *Exceeding the Standards: Vocabulary & Spelling*.

WORDS IN USE

Preview Vocabulary
Preview Vocabulary are words taken from the sentences within each selection. These words are defined in the side margin or at the bottom of the pages on which they appear. The "Preview Vocabulary" section introduces these words in the Before Reading page preceding each selection.

aloft, 573	gnat, 552	multitude, 568	sheen, 558
decrepit, 562	haughty, 569	rafter, 552	smolder, 558
defiance, 577	impulse, 563	recoil, 568	somber, 574
diagram, 544	lace, 558	remorse, 563	stricken, 568
flutter, 552	mooring, 573	sacred, 563	transparent, 544
glimmer, 558	muffled, 573	shade, 549	tumult, 569

Selection Words
Selection Words are additional words from the reading that may be challenging but are not central to the selection and are not identified in the prereading section. These words can easily be learned using the story context, and they provide excellent practice for using content clues to find meaning without explicit instruction.

abnormally, 578	gladdened, 568	ought, 558	stamina, 579
belfry, 573	grisly, 597	outlook, 568	surefooted, 578
billowing, 558	hearkened, 595	parsonage, 578	tax, 595
brawn, 595	homely, 595	ploughed, 578	tranquil, 575
burrowed, 596	immense, 562	rare, 558	twilight, 562
clings, 588	inhabiting, 588	sheepherder, 561	unacceptable, 562
cursèd, 595	leisurely, 588	sickly, 568	unheeded, 569
despised, 568	magnified, 573	skirt, 575	whirls, 552
fine, 558	mushing, 595	soaring, 552	
gaily, 558	nonchalant, 578	somersaulting, 552	
ghastly, 595	o'erhead, 595	spectral, 575	

Teaching Words
Teaching Words consist of vocabulary that is used in the directions about the lessons. Teaching words explain to students what to focus on within the selection, help establish the story context, clarify the meaning of literary terms, and define the goals or instructional purpose.

academic, 548	bleak, 612	echolocation, 553	hemlock, 547
accessibility, 594	boggy, 560	elaborate, 557	heritage, 587, 590
acclaimed, 578	bondmen, 542	emigration, 586	honorary, 599
activism, 599	bough, 547	encountered, 590	imaginative, 602
advocate, 599	captivity, 542	ensure, 592	imitate, 550
allude, 553	Civil Rights movement, 582, 599	evolved, 568	immigrant, 585
alternatives, 611	climate, 560	existence, 546	immigrated, 587
ambassador, 560	colonists, 571	experimental, 560	incorporate, 589
annotation, 605	colonize, 613	explicitly, 542, 587	inflection, 580
anxiousness, 566	commemorate, 564	extraterrestrials, 546	inhabitants, 546
association, 550	compiled, 548	exultant, 612	institutions, 599
assume, 542	concrete representation, 551	facial, 609	intent, 570
athirst, 612	contrast, 550	foundry, 576	interacting, 609
atmosphere, 589	courteous, 609	frequency, 553	interpret, 543
ballads, 594	courtesy, 547	glee, 612	interpretation, 542
beacon, 612	cremated, 594	gracious, 547	ironic, 613
bicultural, 587	disdain, 612	grale, 612	literally, 542
bilingual, 543, 587	dramatic intensity, 594	habitat, 590	lyre, 582
biographers, 600	dread, 612	Harlem Renaissance, 548	mammals, 551

memorable, 608
multiculturalism, 582
nocturnal, 553
Northern Lights, 594
pacing, 580
paternal, 586
perspective, 603
piping, 612
plantation, 542, 548
pollen, 551
prestigious, 578, 599

principal, 570
production, 548
prominent, 576
represent, 550, 590
republic, 566
rubric, 602
rural, 560
scheme, 559
sequence, 609
silversmith, 576
skim, 550

smoldering, 559
socially respectable, 602
spatial, 611
speculations, 559
strategy, 602
temptation, 564
thrush, 612
topography, 589
tourist, 543
traditional, 548, 590
typeface, 606

unconventional, 557, 582
unique, 542, 543
uniting, 585
urgency, 612
visualize, 593
voluntary, 589
women's movement, 582
wrath, 612

KEY TERMS

Key Terms are commonly referred to as *academic vocabulary.* These terms appear in the instructional material to teach the terminology that students need to acquire to understand literature. The repetition of the terms throughout the program ensures student mastery and provides a solid foundation for the continuing study of literature and language arts.

adjective, 606
adverb, 606
alliteration, 613
audience, 593, 602, 609
author's purpose, 560
ballad, 566, 594
biography, 548, 578
capitalization, 582
character, 542, 609
chronological order, 602
climax, 580, 608
cluster chart, 586, 603
complete predicate, 556
compound predicate, 556
concluding paragraph, 610
conclusion, 608
conflict, 580
conjunction, 556
couplet, 543
descriptive language, 602, 610
dialogue, 580, 603
fable, 593
falling action, 580
figurative language, 542, 593,
    603, 610
figure of speech, 560
first person, 547
first person point of view, 542
formal language, 570

free verse, 582
image, 551
imagery, 542, 551, 589, 593,
    605
intensive pronoun, 565
introduction, 550, 593, 608
introductory paragraph, 602, 610
irony, 559, 613
lyric poem, 543, 548, 560, 582,
    587, 590, 599
main idea, 566, 587, 610
metaphor, 560, 603
meter, 557
mood, 542, 564, 570, 571, 589
narrative poem, 551, 566, 571,
    590, 594
narrative presentation, 608
narrative, 610
narrator, 542, 543
nonverbal cue, 609
noun, 565, 606
octave, 557
ode, 560
outline, 610
paragraph, 604, 610
past tense, 604
peer reviewer, 609
personal narrative, 602
personal pronoun, 547

personification, 603, 613
plot, 542, 580, 609
plot diagram, 608
plural, 547
poem, 542
point of view, 613
possessive pronoun, 547
present tense, 550, 604
pronoun, 565, 606
proofreading, 606
punctuation, 582, 606
reflexive pronoun, 565
resolution, 580
rhyme, 557
rhyme scheme, 580, 613
rhythm, 557, 571, 594
second person, 547
sensory description, 593
sensory detail, 546, 551, 559,
    587
sensory language, 603, 609, 610
sequence, 571
setting, 542, 609
short story, 580
simile, 550, 560, 587, 603, 613
simple predicate, 556
singular, 547
sound device, 542

speaker, 542, 543, 547, 589,
    593, 600, 602
stanza, 543, 550, 557, 580, 582,
    613
subjective, 542
summarize, 553
summary, 570, 604
suspense, 566, 580
syllable, 557
symbol, 542, 548, 590
symbolism, 548, 579, 590, 613
text organization, 543
theme, 542, 557, 587, 593, 600
thesis, 546, 550
thesis statement, 593
third person, 547
third-person omniscient, 613
third-person point of view, 542
tone of voice, 609
tone, 542, 548, 554, 559, 593
topic, 554
transition word, 605
Venn diagram, 554, 579
verb, 556, 606
verb phrase, 556
verb tense, 604
verbal cue, 609

Objectives

Studying this unit will help students to meet the following objectives:

- Make connections from the themes expressed in the selections to their own lives and to the world around them
- Identify common forms of poetry
- Understand different elements and types of poetry, including *speaker, symbolism, rhythm, metaphor, suspense, narrative poem, free verse,* and *simile*
- Understand variations of literary forms and author's use of language to develop forms

Reading Strategies

Ask Questions
Clarify
Make Inferences
Make Predictions
Visualize

Reading Skills

Analyze Author's Perspective
Analyze Text Organization
Draw Conclusions
Identify Author's Purpose
Identify Main Idea
Identify Sequence of Events
Monitor Comprehension
Take Notes

Literary Elements

Free Verse	Simile
Imagery	Speaker
Metaphor	Suspense
Narrative Poem	Symbolism
Rhythm	

Reaching Out
Poetry

Unit 6

LESLIE MARMON SILKO
JOSEPH BRUCHAC
MAY SWENSON

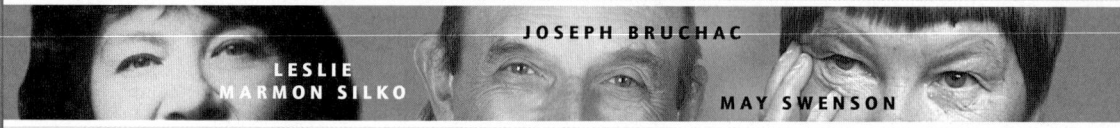

Launch the Unit

Draw a web diagram (a central oval with six or more radiating spokes) on the board with the phrase "Personal Communication" in the central oval. Ask students to use this diagram to identify various ways in which people communicate their feelings to others. Model the response by writing one possible way (for example, "gifts") at the end of one of the spokes. When the class has filled in the diagram, have them copy and save it. After they read the poems in the unit, have them review the diagram and see which of these methods of communication they express.

> "She spoke a tongue I knew no word of,
> and I was sad I could not understand,
> but I could hug her."
>
> —AMY LING, "Grandma Ling"

How do you communicate your emotions to others? In Amy Ling's poem "Grandma Ling," the speaker tells how she traveled to Taiwan to meet her grandmother for the first time. Though the two could not communicate through language, the speaker expresses herself with a hug. As you read the unit, consider how the poems communicate universal experiences in fresh and unexpected ways.

JUDITH ORTIZ COFER   RANDALL JARRELL   NIKKI GIOVANNI

541

Writing Options

Creative Writing
Business Letter
Description
Fable
Personal Letter
Poem
Short Story
Similes

Applied Writing
List

Expository Writing
Critical Analysis
Literary Response
Personal Essay
Review
Summary

Persuasive Writing
Persuasive Essay

Language Arts Workshops

Grammar & Style
Personal and Possessive Pronouns
Simple, Complete, and Compound Predicates
Intensive and Reflexive Pronouns

Vocabulary & Spelling
Context Clues

Writing Workshop
Personal Narrative

Speaking & Listening Workshop
Giving and Actively Listening to Narrative Presentations

Test Practice Workshop
Narrative Essay
Revising and Editing Skills
Reading Skills

Program Resources

For a visual reminder of the unit-based resources available for Unit 6, Poetry, see pages 540A and 540B. As you introduce the unit, you may want to provide students with the Unit Study Guide, which is contained in the *Meeting the Standards* resource.

Teach the Element

Understanding Meaning in Poetry

Reading strategies and skills that can help students understand poetry include clarifying and identifying multiple levels of meaning.

Use Reading Strategies

Clarify Urge students to read carefully to determine who is speaking in a poem. Begin by showing students examples of poems, such as "Southbound on the Freeway," where the speaker is clearly not the poet. Point out that use of the personal pronoun *I* does not equate the poet and the speaker. Poets often create a speaker to present a certain attitude toward life.

Use Reading Skills

Identify Multiple Levels of Meaning Point out that although poets do make extensive use of traditional symbols (for example, Robert Frost's use of diverging roads to represent life's choices in "The Road Not Taken"), they often invent new symbolism. Sometimes poets use a traditional symbol in a new way. For example, the butterfly traditionally represents fragile beauty or carefree living. But in his poem "Flying Crooked," Robert Graves creates a new symbolism for the butterfly, using its halting, uncertain flight to represent the odd, shifting process of the poetic imagination itself. Poets also use symbols that have no conventional association to what they represent. For example, in his poem "Ode to My Socks," Pablo Neruda employs the symbol of fish to represent feet.

Understanding Meaning in Poetry

How Do Poems *Mean?*

Poems frequently challenge readers to imagine something in a unique or unexpected way. Poets accomplish this with figurative language, sound devices, and imagery. In Arna Bontemps's poem "Southern Mansion," a plantation in the South is described as having ghosts of former slaves walking among the cotton fields. Why do you think Bontemps describes the plantation this way?

Speaker

In short stories and novels, the voice that describes the characters, setting, and plot is called the **narrator.** In poetry, the voice that narrates the poem is referred to as the **speaker.** The speaker sometimes participates in the action of the poem, using the first-person point of view. Other times, as in "Southern Mansion," the speaker narrates from the outside, using the third-person point of view.

The speaker's voice can be very much like the poet's voice, expressing beliefs or describing experiences similar to those of the poet. However, never assume that a poem's speaker is the same as the poet. Often, the speaker is a fictional character. A speaker can be a person, an animal, an object, or even an idea.

A poem's speaker sometimes explicitly states the theme, or central idea, of the poem. Generally, you must infer the theme by examining the tone, mood, description, and use of figurative language.

Symbolism

A **symbol** is a thing that stands for itself and something else. In "Southern Mansion," the word *chains* is used both literally and as a symbol for punishment and forced captivity.

> There is a sound of music echoing
> Through the open door
> And in the field there is
> Another sound tinkling in the cotton:
> Chains of bondmen dragging on the ground.
>
> —ARNA BONTEMPS, "Southern Mansion"

Some symbols are traditional, such as roses for love, roads for journeys, and doves for peace. Other symbols are unique to a piece of literature or an author.

Symbols can be subjective, having more than one interpretation. It is not always clear how a writer intends a reader to interpret his or her use of a symbol.

Words in Use

Teaching Words
unique, 542
plantation, 542
assume, 542
explicitly, 542
literally, 542
captivity, 542
bondmen, 542
interpretation, 542

KEY TERMS
POEM, 542
FIGURATIVE
  LANGUAGE, 542
SOUND DEVICE, 542
IMAGERY, 542
CHARACTER, 542
SETTING, 542
PLOT, 542
NARRATOR, 542
SPEAKER, 542

FIRST-PERSON
  POINT OF VIEW, 542
THIRD-PERSON
  POINT OF VIEW, 542
THEME, 542
TONE, 542
MOOD, 542
SYMBOL, 542
SUBJECTIVE, 542

Common Core State Standards
Reading Literature
RL.4

Southbound on the Freeway

A Lyric Poem by May Swenson

Preview the Model

At a Glance
Guided Reading: Reading Model
- Reading Level: Moderate
- Difficulty Consideration: Style
- Ease Factor: Vocabulary

GUIDED READING

Build Background

Historical Context A lyric poem is a short poem that expresses the thoughts and feelings of the speaker. In the first verse of "Southbound on the Freeway," the poet introduces the speaker, a tourist from another planet. When May Swenson wrote this lyric poem in the early 1960s, automobile travel was expanding enormously, and space travel was becoming a reality. Swenson's poem reflects America's growing interest in moving machines during that time.

Reader's Context When have you looked at something you did not understand? How did you interpret it?

Set Purpose

Read to find out what the tourist from Orbitville was looking at and how he or she interpreted it.

Analyze Literature

Speaker The **speaker** is the voice that speaks, or narrates, a poem. The speaker and the writer of a poem are not necessarily the same. As you read, think about whom the speaker might be talking to.

Use Reading Skills

Analyze Text Organization
Swenson chose to write this poem in couplets, or two-line stanzas. A stanza is not always a sentence. Notice when a couplet is a complete sentence. How does the emphasis change when a sentence continues into another couplet? Read the poem aloud. Pause at the ends of sentences. Give a shorter pause at the ends of couplets that do not end sentences. Pause slightly at dashes. Notice how reading this way helps you interpret the poem.

Preview Vocabulary

trans·par·ent (tränz per´ ənt) *adj.*, see-through

di·a·gram (dī´ ə gram) *n.*, chart or drawing that explains something

Meet the Author

May Swenson (1919–1989) was an American poet, teacher, and editor. Born in Logan, Utah, Swenson was the eldest of ten children. Her family spoke Swedish at home, and Swenson grew up bilingual. English was her second language. She is known for her imaginative use of language. "Southbound on the Freeway" was first published in 1963. Swenson's poetry is known for its wordplay, unique text arrangements, and riddles.

Objectives

Studying this lesson will enable students to

- use reading strategies such as text organization
- define *speaker* and recognize the effect of this literary technique in the selection
- describe the literary accomplishments of May Swenson and explain the appeal of her lyric poems
- use poetic structure as a tool for effective reading

Launch the Lesson

Tell students they are going to read a lyric poem that is also science fiction. Explain that science fiction is based on real scientific principles, laws, or discoveries but also has elements that twist reality. Have students identify the elements that are real and those that demonstrate a twist on reality as they read.

Summary

The speaker of the poem is an alien who believes that earth is populated with automobiles. The speaker wonders if the people inside the cars are guts or brains.

SOUTHBOUND ON THE FREEWAY **543**

Words in Use

Preview Vocabulary	**Teaching Words**
transparent, 544	tourist, 543
diagram, 544	bilingual, 543
	unique, 543
	interpret, 543
	inhabitants, 546
	existence, 546
	extraterrestrials, 546

Common Core State Standards

Reading Literature
RL.1, RL.4
Writing
W.9, W.10
Language
L.6

Teach the Model

MIRRORS & WINDOWS

The Mirrors & Windows questions at the end of the selection focus on the theme of instinct versus intellect. Before you read the poem, ask students if they act instinctually or use reason to make choices. Then, ask which is the case for people in general.

Use Reading Strategies

Make Inferences *Answer:* The tourist has some kind of flying spaceship. **A**

Analyze Literature

Speaker Remind students that the speaker is the voice that speaks, or narrates, the poem. This poem has two speakers: the narrator speaks in the first two lines, and then the tourist speaks throughout the rest of the poem.

Use Reading Skills

Analyze Text Structure *Answer:* The line length makes the images seem superficial or robotic. **B**

Use Reading Strategies

Make Inferences *Answer:* The five-eyed one is a police car on the highway. Its front and back headlights are four of its eyes, and the fifth one is the revolving light on top. This is revealed by the other creatures slowing down when they see it. **C**

Southbound on the Freeway

A Lyric Poem by May Swenson

> **DURING READING**
> **Use Reading Strategies**
> **Make Inferences** What kind of vehicle does the tourist have?
> **A**

A tourist came in from Orbitville,[1]
parked in the air, and said:

The creatures of this star
are made of metal and glass.

trans·par·ent
(tränz per´ ənt) *adj.,*
see-through

di·a·gram (dī´ ə gram) *n.,*
chart or drawing that explains
something

5 Through the <u>transparent</u> parts
you can see their guts.

Their feet are round and roll
on <u>diagrams</u> or long

> **DURING READING**
> **Use Reading Skills**
> **Analyze Text Structure**
> What does the use of the short lines in couplets suggest about the speaker?
> **B**

10 measuring tapes, dark
with white lines.

They have four eyes.
The two in the back are red.

> **DURING READING**
> **Use Reading Strategies**
> **Make Inferences** What is the five-eyed one? How can you tell?
> **C**

Sometimes you can see a five-eyed
one, with a red eye turning

15 on the top of his head.
He must be special—

---

1. **Orbitville.** Name of a fictional planet

Program Resources

Planning and Assessment
Program Planning Guide, Selection Lesson Plan
E-Lesson Planner
Assessment Guide, Lesson Test
ExamView

Technology Tools
Interactive Student Text on CD
Visual Teaching Package
Audio Library
mirrorsandwindows.com

Meeting the Standards
Poetry: Unit 6, Guided Reading, pp. 19–24

Differentiating Instruction
English Language Learners, Analyze Text
  Organization, pp. 142–148

Analyze Literature
Voice Ask students to describe the voice of the tourist narrator. Model a possible response: "The narrator's voice is matter-of-fact in that it gives details without judgment, but it is curious and sympathetic in its attempts to analyze the scene it views."

Analyze Literature
Speaker *Answer:* Some traits are curiosity, attention to detail, and fondness for adventure. Some perspective features are a lack of familiarity with Earth, a nonjudgmental attitude, and the formation of theories without facts. **D**

the others respect him
and go slow

when he passes, winding
20 among them from behind.

They all hiss as they glide,
like inches, down the marked

tapes. Those soft shapes,
shadowy inside

25 the hard bodies—are they
their guts or their brains? ✤

DURING READING
Analyze Literature
Speaker What do you learn about the speaker's traits and perspective, or viewpoint? **D**

You may want to ask students to write a journal entry or quick write, or divide students into discussion groups or lead a whole-class discussion about this question. *Answer:* Students might discuss the difference between intellect and instinct. They might give examples of a time they made a rational decision such as choosing to seek adult help in a time of trouble or consciously controlling their emotions. They may contrast that with a purely emotional response, as when one screams at seeing a mouse or a spider. Students may discuss the difficulty of living only by just one or the other.

MIRRORS & WINDOWS
How would you react if you lived by your brains? How would it differ if you lived by your guts? Are people in general driven by their brains or by their guts?

SOUTHBOUND ON THE FREEWAY **545**

Writing Skills

Onomatopoeia
Remind students that onomatopoeia is the use of words or phrases that sound like what they mean. As a class, brainstorm a list of additional onomatopoeic words that could be used to describe the creatures that the tourist sees. Then have pairs of students use some of the words as they write additional couplets for the poem. When students have finished, have each pair read their couplet aloud, emphasizing their onomatopoeic choices.

Find Meaning

1. The speaker is parked in the air over a freeway.

2. (a) The speaker says the creatures are made of metal and glass. (b) The feet are round and roll on diagrams.

3. (a) The creatures are rolling along on diagrams. (b) They hiss. (c) The speaker sees soft, shadowy shapes inside the creatures.

4. The speaker has never seen a car or a human; the speaker is too high above the scene to make out shapes.

Make Judgments

5. (a) The speaker seems to be talking to another member of its own race or possibly recording a voice log of the journey. (b) The listener is probably expressing amazement at the interesting creatures.

6. Students might say they would explain that humans are a combination of instinct and intellect.

7. Metal and glass with transparent parts, round feet that roll, four eyes, two red eyes in back, a red eye turning on the top, and hissing down the marked tapes are clues.

Analyze Literature

Speaker *Possible answer:*

Sight	Sound	Touch
metal	hiss	soft
glass		hard

The speaker investigates new situations like a scientist, basing predictions and assumptions on sensory evidence.

Apply the Model

BEFORE READING
DURING READING
AFTER READING

Find Meaning

1. Where is the speaker parked?

2. (a) What does the speaker say the creatures are made of? (b) How does the speaker describe the creatures' feet?

3. (a) What are the creatures doing? (b) What sound do the creatures make? (c) What does the speaker see inside the creatures?

4. Why doesn't the speaker recognize the things it sees?

Analyze Literature

Speaker May Swenson included many sensory details in her lyric poem. These details help a reader visualize what is being described. Identify the words and phrases that contain sensory details. Write each detail beneath the sense to which it appeals. What do these details help you understand about the speaker of the poem?

Make Judgments

5. (a) To whom is the speaker talking? (b) What might be the listener's response to the speaker's description of what it saw?

6. How would you answer the speaker's last question?

7. Suppose you did not see the title of the poem or the illustration on the page. What clues in the poem would help you understand what the speaker of the poem is describing?

Sight	Sound	Touch
metal	hiss	soft

Extend Understanding

Writing Options

Creative Writing Write a **short story** from the perspective of the poem's speaker. Include details that let the reader know what the inhabitants and their planet look like.

Expository Writing Write a brief **literary response** to "Southbound on the Freeway." State your opinion of the effect of the poem in your thesis, explaining what literary elements or devices contribute to the effect. Support your thesis with examples.

Lifelong Learning

Research a Star Use the Internet to find the star nearest our own sun and gather information about it. Design a poster with key facts.

Critical Literacy

Debate Hold a debate about the existence of extraterrestrials. Make an outline of the key facts you find. Present your evidence to the class.

Go to **www.mirrorsandwindows.com** for more.

Rubrics for Writing Options

You can adapt this as a checklist for students to use as they write.

Creative Writing

☐ Does the story clearly identify the narrator as the speaker from the poem?

☐ Does the short story include details about the speaker's home planet and its inhabitants?

☐ Is the short story imaginative?

Expository Writing

☐ Does the writer clearly present an opinion about the effectiveness of the speaker?

☐ Does the literary response explain the speaker's perspective?

☐ Does the response use examples from the poem to explain why the speaker is unreliable?

☐ Does the response offer suggestions to improve the speaker's credibility?

Grammar & Style

Personal and Possessive Pronouns

*Sometimes you can see a five-eyed
one, with a red eye turning
on the top of his head.*

— MAY SWENSON, "Southbound on the Freeway"

A **personal pronoun** is used in place of a person or thing. In the quotation above, *you* and *his* are personal pronouns. Personal pronouns may be singular, plural, or possessive.

A **possessive pronoun** shows ownership or possession. Possessive pronouns may be singular or plural.

> **EXAMPLES**
>
> *personal pronouns*
> **singular**   *I, me, you, he, she, it, him, her*
>
> **plural**   *we, us, you, they, them*
>
> **possessive**   *mine, yours, his, hers, its, ours, theirs*

Personal pronouns may refer to the speaker (first person), to the person or people to whom the speaker is talking (second person), or to other people, places, and things (third person).

> **EXAMPLES**
>
> *first person*   the speaker or speakers refer to themselves: *I, me, my, mine, we, us, our, ours*
>
> *second person*   the speaker refers to the person talked to: *you, your, yours*
>
> *third person*   the speaker refers to someone or something else: *he, him, his, she, her, hers, it, its, they, them, their, theirs*

In the quotation at left, *you* is singular and second person, and *his* is possessive, singular, and third person.

Identifying Personal Pronouns in Literature

Underline the ten personal pronouns in the following passage. Then state whether each pronoun is possessive, and if it is singular or plural. Finally, decide whether it is first, second, or third person.

*I often pass a gracious tree
  Whose name I can't identify,
But still I bow, in courtesy
  It waves a bough, in kind reply.*

*I do not know your name, O tree
  (Are you a hemlock or a pine?)
But why should that embarrass me?
  Quite probably you don't know mine.*

— CHRISTOPHER MORLEY, "Tit for Tat"

Understanding Personal and Possessive Pronouns

For each of the following sentences, choose the correct pronoun in parentheses.

1. (He, Him) came in from Orbitville and looked around.
2. (My, Mine) friend and (me, I) think (he, his, him) was rude for spying on (we, us, our).
3. (Our, Ours) new house was the first thing we owned that was truly (our, ours).
4. If (we, us) went to (they, them, their) world, we would probably think of (its, it) in terms of (ours, we, us).

Identifying Personal Pronouns in Literature

I is singular and first person in each case where it is used.

It is singular and third person.

Your is possessive, singular or plural, and second person.

You is singular and second person.

Me is singular and first person.

Mine is possessive, singular, and first person.

Understanding Personal and Possessive Pronouns

1. He
2. My, I, he, us
3. Our, ours
4. we, their, it, ours

> ⊳ For more information, see Grammar & Style Section 3.4, Pronouns, in the Language Arts Handbook.

Build Skills

Remind students not to confuse possessive pronouns and contractions. Some may sound alike, but they have different meanings and spellings. Possessive pronouns do not contain an apostrophe.

Pronoun	Contraction
your	*you're*
their	*they're*
theirs	*there's*
its	*it's*

Teaching Words
gracious, 547
courtesy, 547
bough, 547
hemlock, 547

You will find additional lessons on Personal and Possessive Pronouns in the *Exceeding the Standards: Grammar & Style* resource.

KEY TERMS

Language
L.6.1c

Southern Mansion

A Lyric Poem by Arna Bontemps

Preview the Model

At a Glance
Guided Reading: Reading Model
- Reading Level: Easy
- Difficulty Consideration: Symbolism
- Ease Factor: Language

Objectives
Studying this lesson will enable students to
- use reading strategies such as analyzing the author's perspective
- define *tone* and recognize the effect of this literary technique in the selection
- describe the literary accomplishments of Arna Bontemps and explain the historical significance of his writing
- identify the symbolism in the poem

Launch the Lesson
Tell students that they are about to read a poem about a southern mansion. Draw a word web with "southern mansion" in the center. Ask students to contribute words or phrases that relate to a southern mansion.

 The Mirrors & Windows questions at the end of the selection focus on the theme of disparity. Before reading the poem, ask students which modern circumstances reflect those described in the poem. Has the world changed since the time of slavery, or is it echoed in modern institutions?

GUIDED READING

Build Background
Historical Context In the 1800s, Southern plantations included a large main house, called a *mansion*. There the wealthy landowner and his family lived and entertained their friends. The landowner's wealth came from the sale of crops, such as cotton. New mass production methods had caused a rapid rise in the demand for cotton, and large Southern plantations used enslaved people to harvest these crops.

Reader's Context Many words have images and ideas associated with them. What images come into your mind when you read the word *mansion*?

Set Purpose
Tone describes an author's attitude toward a subject. Authors reveal tone through word choice, the images they choose, and other details. As you read, take notes on the author's tone.

Analyze Literature
Symbolism A **symbol** is a thing that stands for itself and something else. For example, traditional symbols include doves for peace and roads or paths for journeys.

Meet the Author
Arna Bontemps (1902–1973) was a writer, historian, and educator who was also an active member of the Harlem Renaissance. He wrote poetry, fiction, and nonfiction about many aspects of black experience. He compiled numerous collections of African-American literature. At a time when black history and culture were not often part of academic teachings, Bontemps wrote numerous works for children on these subjects, including biographies and a book of black history.

Use Reading Skills
Analyze Author's Perspective Every writer looks at the world in a certain way. That is his or her perspective. Create a chart to help you analyze Bontemps's perspective. In the first column, list several details from the poem that you believe reflect this author's perspective. In the second column, give reasons for your choices.

Detail that Reflects Author's Perspective	Reason for Choosing Detail
subject of the poem: Southern mansion	plantations were important in black history

Preview Vocabulary
shade (shād) *n.*, darkness

Words in Use

Preview Vocabulary
shade, 549

Teaching Words
plantations, 548
production, 548
traditional, 548
Harlem Renaissance, 548
compiled, 548
academic, 548

skim, 550
association, 550
represent, 550
contrast, 550
imitate, 550

KEY TERMS
LYRIC POEM, 548
TONE, 548
SYMBOLISM, 548
SYMBOL, 548
BIOGRAPHY, 548
SIMILE, 550
STANZA, 550
PRESENT TENSE, 550
INTRODUCTION, 550
THESIS, 550

Common Core State Standards

Reading Literature
RL.1, RL.4

Writing
W.9

Language
L.6

Southern Mansion

A Lyric Poem by Arna Bontemps

Poplars[1] are standing there still as death
And ghosts of dead men
Meet their ladies walking
Two by two beneath the <u>shade</u>
5 And standing on the marble steps.

There is a sound of music echoing
Through the open door
And in the field there is
Another sound tinkling in the cotton:
10 Chains of bondmen[2] dragging on the ground.

The years go back with an iron clank,
A hand is on the gate,
A dry leaf trembles on the wall.
Ghosts are walking.
15 They have broken roses down
And poplars stand there still as death. ❖

---

1. **poplars.** Tall, fast-growing hardwood trees of the willow family
2. **bondmen.** Male slaves

shade (shād) *n.*, darkness

DURING READING
Use Reading Skills
Analyze Author's Perspective What do details such as "chains" and "iron clank" suggest about the author's perspective? **A**

DURING READING
Analyze Literature
Symbolism What might roses symbolize here? **B**

How does this poem affect your idea of "mansions"? What situation today most mirrors the one that Bontemps describes in the poem?

549

Teach the Model

Summary
The poem recalls the past of a southern plantation, noting the contrasts between life in the mansion and life in the fields.

Analyze Literature
Tone Remind students that tone, in poetry, is the *speaker's* attitude toward the poem subject. Ask them to describe the tone of the poem. Model a possible response: "Words like *still*, *death*, *ghosts*, and *chains* indicate that the tone is mysterious and melancholy."

Use Reading Skills
Analyze Author's Perspective
Answer: The author feels that life at this mansion is not as pleasant as it seems. He contrasts the harsh sound of slavery's chains with the cheerful music of a party. **A**

Analyze Literature
Symbolism *Answer:* The roses might symbolize the beautiful outward appearance of southern life that is shamed and tainted by its past. **B**

Answer: Students might say that the poem challenges the notion of mansions as beautiful. Students might bring up sweatshops, where workers toil for low wages to create goods they cannot afford to buy or similar situations in which people suffer to create a luxurious world for others.

Program Resources

Planning and Assessment
Program Planning Guide, Selection Lesson Plan
E-Lesson Planner
Assessment Guide, Lesson Test
ExamView

Technology Tools
Interactive Student Text on CD
Visual Teaching Package
Audio Library
mirrorsandwindows.com

Meeting the Standards
Poetry: Unit 6, Guided Reading, pp. 25–30

Differentiating Instruction
Advanced Students, Author Study, p. 32

Find Meaning

1. (a) The simile that compares poplars with death. (b) The simile creates a somber tone.

2. (a) The mansion is shaded by trees and was once filled with people who enjoyed leisurely activities. (b) These details suggest a life of wealth and ease.

3. (a) The sound of music is described. (b) One is a beautiful sound that suggests parties or leisure, while the other is the clinking sound of chains that suggests bondage.

Make Judgments

4. (a) The words *ghosts, dead, echoing,* and "the years go back" all suggest the past. (b) The past's influence is very present.

5. (a) The word *tinkling* sounds light and musical, while the word *dragging* sounds heavy and tired. (b) The words emphasize the contrast between people who resided and those who labored on the property.

6. Students may mention a prison or an armed camp.

Analyze Literature

Symbolism *Answer:* By including such symbols as the poplars, which represent stability, and chains, which represent slavery, Bontemps is able to show his feelings toward the topic and to arouse feelings in his readers.

Find Meaning

1. (a) What simile is repeated in the first and last lines of the poem? (b) What effect does this have on the tone?

2. (a) What details do you learn about the mansion in the first six lines? (b) What do these details suggest about the people who lived in the mansion?

3. (a) What sounds are described at the beginning of the second stanza? (b) How do those sounds differ from those at the end of the stanza?

Analyze Literature

Symbolism Bontemps uses several examples of symbolism in "Southern Mansion." Skim the poem again to find at least three symbols. Make a chart to identify these symbols, to tell a few details about them, and to then explain what association each symbol might represent or suggest.

Make Judgments

4. (a) What words and phrases suggest the past? (b) What is the effect of using these words in a poem written in present tense?

5. (a) What feelings are associated with the words *tinkling* and *dragging?* (b) What effect does the contrast between the words have?

6. In the last stanza, the speaker mentions "an iron clank" and "the gate." What images are suggested by these words?

Symbol	Details	What It Means
the mansion		

Extend Understanding

Writing Options

Creative Writing Write a **poem** for a friend in which you imitate the tone in "Southern Mansion." Choose a subject that lends itself to such a tone.

Expository Writing Write a brief **literary response** about Bontemps's use of symbolism. In the introduction, state your thesis. In the body, provide support for your position. Include your reasons, examples from the text, and other details that support your thesis statement.

Collaborative Learning

Discuss Imagery With a partner, identify examples of imagery in "Southern Mansion." Then discuss what this imagery contributes to the meaning and tone of the poem. Write a paragraph that states your response.

Critical Literacy

Participate in a Panel Discussion Hold a panel discussion on the history and role of slavery in the United States. Then have individuals each research an issue related to slavery and summarize their findings.

Go to **www.mirrorsandwindows.com** for more.

Rubrics for Writing Options

You can adapt this as a checklist for students to use as they write.

Creative Writing

☐ Does the poem have a clear subject?

☐ Does the poem contain specific words and images that suggest a thoughtful approach?

☐ Does the tone of the poem reflect the tone of "Southern Mansion"?

Expository Writing

☐ Does the first paragraph of the essay include a clear thesis statement about the use of symbolism in "Southern Mansion"?

☐ Do the body paragraphs contain textual examples, reasons, and other supporting details?

☐ Does the concluding paragraph restate the thesis and urge readers to take action?

Bats

A Narrative Poem by Randall Jarrell

BEFORE READING

Build Background
Scientific Context Bats are the only mammals that fly. Mother bats care for their babies until the babies are strong enough to survive on their own. Throughout the world, there are nearly a thousand kinds of bats. Most sleep during the day and hunt for food at night. Some eat fruit, others eat flower pollen, and still others use their claws to catch fish. Most bats, however, eat insects.

Reader's Context Although bats are helpful to humans, many people fear them. How do you feel about bats?

Set Purpose
Poets often use sensory details—those that appeal to the reader's sense of sight, smell, taste, hearing, and touch—to create vivid descriptions. As you read this poem, watch for such details.

Analyze Literature
Imagery An **image** is language that creates a concrete representation of an object or an experience. The images in a poem or passage are collectively referred to as **imagery.** As you read "Bats," use the imagery to form vivid pictures in your mind.

Meet the Author
Randall Jarrell (1914–1965) was a poet, novelist, literary critic, and teacher. He also worked as a control tower operator in the army, which provided him with many experiences to explore in his poetry. Of all his talents, he seemed to enjoy teaching the most. In fact, he once said, "If I were a rich man, I'd pay money to teach."

Use Reading Skills
Take Notes Like many poems, "Bats" is filled with sensory details to help you form mental pictures. As you read, take notes to record the sensory details in the poem and their effect on your understanding of the poem.

Lines from Poem	Details	Effect
lines 1–2	a baby bat, naked, blind, and pale	The baby bat is small, weak, and dependent on its mother.

Preview Vocabulary
gnat (nät) *n.*, small flying insect

flut•ter (flət´ tər) *v.*, fly lightly, with rapidly beating wings

raf•ter (raf´ tər) *n.*, ceiling beam

Preview the Selection

At a Glance
Directed Reading
- Reading Level: Easy
- Difficulty Consideration: Subject matter
- Ease Factor: Language

Objectives
Studying this lesson will enable students to
- use reading strategies such as taking notes to record sensory details
- define *imagery* and recognize the effect of this literary technique in the selection
- describe the work of Randall Jarrell and how the scientific content adds to the imagery in the poem
- appreciate a poem about bats

Launch the Lesson
You might ask students to tell what they know about bats, including facts and legends. Invite them to describe any encounters they have had with bats. Ask for a show of hands of students who like or dislike bats, and ask for explanations that include sensory details.

Summary
The speaker describes a night for a mother bat and her baby. The mother spends the night flying and whirling about, while the child clings to her. At the end of night, she folds her baby in her arms and they sleep.

Words in Use

Preview Vocabulary
gnat, 552
flutter, 552
rafter, 552

Selection Words
soaring, 552
somersaulting, 552
whirls, 552

Teaching Words
mammals, 551
pollen, 551
concrete representation, 551
nocturnal, 553
echolocation, 553
frequency, 553
allude, 553

KEY TERMS
NARRATIVE POEM, 551
SENSORY DETAIL, 551
IMAGERY, 551
IMAGE, 551
SUMMARIZE, 553
TONE, 554
TOPIC, 554
VENN DIAGRAM, 554

Common Core State Standards
Reading Literature
RL.1
Writing
W.7, W.8, W.9
Language
L.6

Science Connection

Bat Populations in Danger

Indiana bats are found in the eastern United States. These small bats have hibernated in caves in groups of from twenty to fifty thousand bats. When the caves are opened to tourists, or are disturbed by construction, many bats die. Bats are also losing their habitats because of deforestation. Their food supplies are often poisoned by pesticides, and they sometimes drink contaminated water. Since 1973, the Indiana bat has been on the endangered species list, and a recovery plan is in place.

Use Reading Skills

Identify Author's Purpose Remind students that authors write to inform, entertain, or persuade. Ask them why they think Jarrell wrote "Bats." Model a possible response: "I think he wanted to inform people about the lifestyle and habits of bats, as well as to persuade them that bats aren't bad or evil as they are sometimes shown to be."

Bats

A Narrative Poem by Randall Jarrell

A bat is born
Naked and blind and pale.
His mother makes a pocket of her tail
And catches him. He clings to her long fur
5 By his thumbs and toes and teeth.
And then the mother dances through the night
Doubling and looping, soaring, somersaulting—
Her baby hangs on underneath.
All night, in happiness, she hunts and flies.
10 Her high sharp cries
Like shining needlepoints of sound
Go out into the night and, echoing back,
Tell her what they have touched.
She hears how far it is, how big it is,
15 Which way it's going:
She lives by hearing.
The mother eats the moths and <u>gnats</u> she catches
In full flight; in full flight
The mother drinks the water of the pond
20 She skims across. Her baby hangs on tight.
Her baby drinks the milk she makes him
In moonlight or starlight, in mid-air.
Their single shadow, printed on the moon
Or <u>fluttering</u> across the stars,
25 Whirls on all night; at daybreak
The tired mother flaps home to her <u>rafter</u>.
The others are all there.
They hang themselves up by their toes,
They wrap themselves in their brown wings.
30 Bunched upside-down, they sleep in air.
Their sharp ears, their sharp teeth, their quick sharp faces
Are dull and slow and mild.
All the bright day, as the mother sleeps,
She folds her wings about her sleeping child. ❖

gnat (nät) *n.*, small flying insect
flut·ter (flət´ tər) *v.*, fly lightly, with rapidly beating wings
raf·ter (raf´ tər) *n.*, ceiling beam

552

Program Resources

Planning and Assessment
Program Planning Guide, Selection Lesson Plan
E-Lesson Planner
Assessment Guide, Lesson Test
ExamView

Technology Tools
Interactive Student Text on CD
Visual Teaching Package
Audio Library
mirrorsandwindows.com

Meeting the Standards
Poetry: Unit 6, Directed Reading, pp. 31–35

Differentiating Instruction
Developing Readers, Set Purpose, pp. 40–42

SCIENCE ▶▶ CONNECTION

Navigating at Night The saying *blind as a bat* is based on a myth. Bats are not blind. In fact, those that are active during the day use their sharp eyes to find food. However, most bats are nocturnal. To find food in the darkness, they have developed a special ability called echolocation. As a bat flies along, it sends out high-frequency sound waves through its mouth or nose. These sounds bounce off objects and back to the bat's ears. The echoes provide the bat with lots of useful information, such as where an object is, which way it is traveling, and how big it is. In what lines of "Bats" does Randall Jarrell allude to echolocation, and why is *echolocation* a perfect name for this special sense? **A**

Science Connection
Navigating at Night *Answer:* Lines 10–16. It is a perfect name because the bat receives locations of food through echoes. **A**

 Students might say that the poem's emphasis on the mother-child relationship enabled them to see bats in a new way. People might be afraid of bats because they are associated with the dark and vampires.

Find Meaning
1. (a) It is hairless, blind, and pale. (b) She carries her baby as she hunts and feeds it with her milk. She wraps her wings around it to keep it safe and warm as they sleep.
2. (a) She uses echolocation to detect flying insects. (b) She depends on her hearing to help her find food.
3. They both eat and drink. The mother eats insects and drinks from the pond; the baby drinks its mother's milk.

Make Judgments
4. (a) At night, she carries her baby as she hunts. During the day, she wraps her wings around her baby and sleeps. (b) Bats make good mothers because the mother protects and feeds her baby carefully.
5. (a) The speaker has a sympathetic, positive attitude toward bats.
(b) Answers should be supported.

 Did the poem change your feelings about bats in any way? Why do you think people are afraid of bats?

Find Meaning
1. (a) Describe the appearance of a newborn bat. (b) What does a mother bat do to protect and care for her baby?
2. (a) How does a mother bat find food? (b) What does the poet mean by the line "She lives by hearing"?
3. What do both the mother and the baby do during the flight?

Make Judgments
4. (a) Summarize the nighttime and daytime activities of a mother bat. (b) Do you think bats are good mothers? Explain your answer.
5. (a) Based on details in the poem, how would you characterize the speaker's attitude toward bats? (b) How is the speaker's attitude toward bats similar to, and different from, yours? Explain your answers.

BATS **553**

Reading Skills

Identify Sequence of Events
"Bats" sequentially describes the actions of a mother and baby bat during a single night. Point out that a time line can help students keep track of when events in the poem took place. Draw a time line on the board, and suggest that students fill in the time line of events in "Bats." Students will find clues to the timing of events by looking for sequence words, such as *then,* and time indicators such as *night, moonlight, starlight,* and *day.*

Analyze Literature

Tone Point out that the tone of the poem changes. Ask students to describe the tone before and after the change. Possible response: "At first the tone is light and almost playful, but then it changes to more serious and scary." **Ⓐ**

Text-to-Text Connection

Answer: Venn diagrams should effectively compare and contrast the two poems. Sample responses: How they are alike: They have the same topic; they summarize the daytime and nighttime activities of bats; they describe what a bat looks like as it hangs upside down and as it "loops" in flight. Elements of "Bats" only: Description of newborn bat and the way in which the mother holds it and feeds it as she flies; description of echolocation; description of colony of bats asleep; gentle, positive tone. Elements of "The Bat" only: Comparison to mouse and to human face; description of pulse; action of brushing up against a screen and being seen by a human; spooky, scary tone. From the description of tone, students should contrast the positive attitude of "Bats" with the negative, frightened attitude of "The Bat." Answers will vary regarding which attitude is closer to their own.

The following selection is a poem entitled "The Bat," by **Theodore Roethke** (1908–1963). Like Jarrell, Roethke was both a writer and a teacher, who taught at several colleges and universities. His writing career began in high school when a speech he gave on the Junior Red Cross was published all over the world in twenty-six different languages. He published his first book of poetry, *Open House,* in 1941 and went on to publish several more volumes, including *The Waking* (1953), which won the Pulitzer Prize. Roethke's *Words for the Wind* (1957) won several literary prizes, including the National Book Award. As you read "The Bat," note how it differs in structure, mood, and tone from Randall Jarrell's poem "Bats."

The Bat

A Lyric Poem by Theodore Roethke

By day the bat is cousin to the mouse.
He likes the attic of an aging house.

His fingers make a hat about his head.
His pulse beat is so slow we think him dead.

5 He loops in crazy figures half the night
Among the trees that face the corner light.

Ⓐ But when he brushes up against a screen,
We are afraid of what our eyes have seen:

For something is amiss or out of place
10 When mice with wings can wear a human face. ❖

Both poems have the same topic—bats. They are alike in other ways, too, but they are also different. Use a Venn diagram to compare and contrast the poems. Then explain how the two speakers' attitudes toward bats differ. Which attitude is more like yours?

TEACHING NOTE

Self-Generated Questioning

Divide the class into pairs. Instruct each pair to create a question for the poem, based on their notes, and to draw a picture, a chart, or another graphic that answers the question as best they can. Model a question such as: "Why does the bat have such a low pulse?" Invite the pairs to share their questions and answers in small groups or as a class.

Common Core State Standards

Reading Literature
RL.4

Writing
W.9

Language
L.6

Analyze Literature

Imagery An image is language that creates a vivid picture in the reader's mind. Taken together, the images in a poem or passage are called its imagery. Look back at the chart you made about the pictures you visualized as you read "Bats." Add a new section to note images from the second poem, "The Bat." Then, when the chart is complete, find an image in "The Bat" that creates a similar picture as an image in "Bats." Finally, find an image in "The Bat" that creates a very different picture from an image in "Bats." Summarize your findings.

Lines from Poem	Details	Effect
lines 1–4	a sleeping bat, hanging upside down from a rafter in an attic	a mouse with wings

Extend Understanding

Writing Options

Creative Writing Complete the following analogies about animals:

- Mice are to owls as _____ are to lions.
- A lodge is to a beaver as a _____ is to a bird.
- Stripes are to zebras as _____ are to cheetahs.

Then write a **description** of an animal of your choice. To help readers visualize your animal, pack your description with sensory details—things a person might see, hear, taste, touch, or smell. Include at least one analogy in your writing. Do not identify the animal! When you have finished writing, exchange descriptions with a classmate and try to guess each other's topics.

Expository Writing Write a brief **literary response** in which you analyze the tone of "Bats." First, identify the tone, supporting your point of view with details from the poem. Examine how the tone shifts near the end of the poem. Then write responses to these questions:

- In what way or ways does the tone seem surprising?
- Do you think the tone is appropriate? Explain why or why not.

Lifelong Learning

Find the Facts Choose an animal that interests you. Using an encyclopedia, research the animal. Create a list of interesting facts about it. Share your results with classmates.

Critical Literacy

Ask Questions Create a list of questions you would like to ask Randall Jarrell about the sights and personal experiences that inspired this poem. For example, why did he decide to use a bat as his subject? What qualities of the bat most interested or amused him? What feelings led him to write about them?

 Go to www.mirrorsandwindows.com for more.

Analyze Literature

Imagery *Answer:* Charts should summarize and tell the effects of the images in each poem. Examples to show similar and different mental pictures will vary. Sample responses: Similar images: the bats asleep, hanging upside down; the "loopy" flight. Different images: newborn bat; bat brushing up against screen; mother bat wrapping her wings around baby; mother sending out signals to find insects.

Rubrics for Writing Options

You can adapt this as a checklist for students to use as they write.

Creative Writing

Possible analogy responses: antelope, zebra, or any other animal on which lions prey; nest; spots

- ☐ Does the description use vivid sensory details to describe an animal?
- ☐ Do the details provide effective clues?

Expository Writing

- ☐ Does it effectively and accurately identify the tone of the poem, supported by specific details?
- ☐ Does it state whether or not the tone seems surprising and appropriate, and are these points of view supported by details and reasons?

Simple, Complete, and Compound Predicates

Teach the Workshop

Identifying Simple, Complete, and Compound Predicates

1. Several of the bats | <u>had flown</u> into the cave and <u>were hanging</u> from the ceiling.
2. Many bats | <u>eat</u> insects or fruit.
3. Female bats | <u>like</u> to hide in dark places and usually <u>produce</u> only one newborn bat each year.

Using Simple, Complete, and Compound Predicates

Answers will vary.

1. Bats hang by their claws and sleep in branches.
2. Seven baby bats were born.
3. I would have been afraid of bats when I was younger.

> For more information, see Grammar & Style Section 3.1, The Sentence, in the Language Arts Handbook.

Program Resources

You will find additional lessons on Simple, Complete, and Compound Predicates in the *Exceeding the Standards: Grammar & Style* resource.

KEY TERMS

SIMPLE PREDICATE, 556
VERB, 556
VERB PHRASE, 556
COMPLETE PREDICATE, 556
COMPOUND PREDICATE, 556
CONJUNCTION, 556

Simple and Complete Predicates

He clings to her long fur
By his thumbs and toes and teeth.

— RANDALL JARRELL, "Bats"

The **simple predicate** in a sentence is the main verb or verb phrase that tells what the subject does, has, or is. The **complete predicate** includes the verb and all the words that modify it. In the quotation above, *clings* is the simple predicate and *clings to her long fur by his thumbs and toes and teeth* is the complete predicate.

In the following examples, a vertical line separates the subject from the predicate. The simple predicate or verb appears in boldface.

EXAMPLES

Almost all bats | **are** *social creatures, who roost together.*

All species of bats | **fly.** [*Fly* is both the simple and complete predicate.]

Verbs may have more than one word, and as many as four.

EXAMPLES

Some bats | **live** *in caves.*

Some bats | **were living** *in this cave.*

Some bats | **have been living** *in this cave.*

Some bats | **might have been living** *in this cave.*

Compound Predicates

His mother makes a pocket of her tail
And catches him.

— RANDALL JARRELL, "Bats"

A **compound predicate** has two or more simple predicates, or verbs, that share the same subject. The verbs are connected by the conjunction *and, or,* or *but.* In the quotation above, *makes* and *catches* share the subject *mother.*

EXAMPLES

During the day, the bat | <u>hides</u> *and* <u>rests.</u>

When some people see bats, they | <u>scream, cover</u> *their heads, and* <u>run</u> *away.*

Identifying Simple, Complete, and Compound Predicates

Draw a vertical line between the subject and complete predicate in each sentence. Then underline once the simple predicate. Underline twice each compound predicate.

1. Several of the bats had flown into the cave and were hanging from the ceiling.
2. Many bats eat insects or fruit.
3. Female bats like to hide in dark places and usually produce only one newborn bat each year.

Using Simple, Complete, and Compound Predicates

Write sentences containing the elements described in each of the directions below.

1. a compound predicate
2. a simple predicate that is also a complete predicate
3. a complete predicate containing more than three words

TEACHING NOTE

Extra Practice

Have students draw a vertical line between the subject and complete predicate in each sentence. Then underline the simple predicate once and each compound predicate twice.

1. The world's largest bats | <u>are found</u> in the region of the Indian Ocean and <u>are known</u> as flying foxes.
2. Some flying foxes | <u>have</u> a wingspan of about five feet.
3. These bats | <u>eat</u> fruit and <u>drink</u> nectar from flowers.
4. Flying foxes | <u>have</u> large eyes and <u>navigate</u> by sight rather than sound.
5. Flying foxes | <u>have been used</u> in horror films because of their size and spooky appearance.

Common Core State Standards

Language
L.6.3a

The Choice

A Humorous Poem by Dorothy Parker

Build Background

Literary Context Poets use stanzas, line lengths, meter, and rhyme to structure their poems. In Dorothy Parker's "The Choice," each of the two stanzas is an octave, that is, it has eight lines. The rhyming pattern in each stanza can be described as *ababcdcd*. This means the first and third lines, second and fourth lines, fifth and seventh lines, and sixth and eighth lines rhyme.

Reader's Context Have you ever admired someone unconventional? Explain.

Set Purpose

Preview the title of the poem. Predict what the theme of the poem will be. Read to determine how accurate your prediction is.

Analyze Literature

Rhythm The pattern of stressed syllables, or beats, that you hear when you read a line of poetry is called **rhythm**. A regular and predictable pattern of stressed and unstressed syllables is called **meter**. As you read "The Choice," notice the number of syllables in each line and which are stressed and unstressed.

Meet the Author

Dorothy Parker (1893–1967) was born Dorothy Rothschild in West End, New Jersey. She described herself as "a late unexpected arrival in a loveless family," and was just four years old when her mother died. Unlike the speaker of "The Choice," Parker chose a stock broker for her first husband. The marriage did not last long. She was married twice more later on, both times to actor Alan Campbell. Parker, a successful critic and writer of short stories, drama, poetry, and movie scripts, is particularly recognized for her wit.

Use Reading Skills

Monitor Comprehension As you read "The Choice," ask yourself questions to monitor comprehension about Parker's tone. You can ask questions about words, phrases, lines, stanzas, or the entire poem. For example, after reading the first stanza, ask yourself, What two things is Parker comparing? What is her attitude toward each? Write and answer at least two more questions of your own to help you recognize Parker's tone in "The Choice."

Questions	Answers
What are houses of marble?	elaborate, expensive homes

Preview Vocabulary

smol·der (smōl´ dər) *v.*, burn with little smoke and no flame

lace (lāce) *n.*, delicate fabric

glim·mer (gli´ mər) *v.*, emit a dim or flickering light

sheen (shēn) *n.*, glow

DIRECTED READING

Preview the Selection

At a Glance
Directed Reading
- Reading Level: Easy
- Difficulty Consideration: Unfamiliar subject matter
- Ease Factor: Rhyme scheme

Objectives

Studying this lesson will enable students to
- use reading strategies such as asking questions
- define *rhythm* and *stanza* and recognize the effect of these literary techniques in the selection
- describe the literary accomplishments of Dorothy Parker and explain the entertainment value of her writing
- identify the humorous tone in a poem

Launch the Lesson

Tell students that they are about to read a humorous poem about a woman who chooses between two men. Invite them to tell about a time they had to make a difficult choice and how they arrived at the choice.

MIRRORS & WINDOWS The Mirrors & Windows question at the end of this selection relates to choices. Prior to reading, discuss with students how they make decisions.

Preview Vocabulary
smolder, 558
lace, 558
glimmer, 558
sheen, 558

Selection Words
billowing, 558
rare, 558
fine, 558
gaily, 558
ought, 558

Teaching Words
unconventional, 557
elaborate, 557
speculations, 559
smoldering, 559
scheme, 559

KEY TERMS

Common Core State Standards

Reading Literature
RL.1, RL.3, RL.6
Writing
W.9
Language
L.6

Summary
The speaker in this poem describes two suitors: one wealthy, the other swift and strong. The speaker chooses the one without the wealth and decides that someone should examine her head.

Analyze Literature
Stanza Explain that a stanza is a poetic paragraph, usually offset by a line space. Ask students to point out the stanzas in "The Choice."

Analyze Literature
Rhythm Model reading the poem aloud so students can hear the rhythm. Then have partners read the poem aloud to each other, following the same rhythm.

Use Reading Strategies
Ask Questions Remind students that they should ask themselves questions as they read or when they finish reading. Model for students questions they might ask when they finish a first reading of the poem: "To whom is the narrator speaking? What was the person referred to as 'he' going to give her? What was the person referred to as 'you' going to give her?" Tell students to go back and reread if they cannot answer the questions.

Analyze Literature
Poetic Shift Direct students' attention to the poem's last line. Ask them what shift, or change in emphasis, direction, or focus, occurs in this line. **A**

The Choice
A Humorous Poem by Dorothy Parker

He'd have given me rolling lands,
  Houses of marble, and billowing farms,
Pearls, to trickle between my hands,
  <u>Smoldering</u> rubies, to circle my arms.
5 You—you'd only a lilting[1] song.
  Only a melody, happy and high,
You were sudden and swift and strong,—
  Never a thought for another had I.

He'd have given me <u>laces</u> rare,
10   Dresses that <u>glimmered</u> with frosty <u>sheen</u>,
Shining ribbons to wrap my hair,
  Horses to draw me, as fine as a queen.
You—you'd only to whistle low,
  Gaily I followed wherever you led.
15 I took you, and I let him go,—
  A Somebody ought to examine my head! ❖

1. **lilting.** Cheerful and rhythmic

smol•der (smōl´ dər) v., burn with little smoke and no flame
lace (lāce) n., delicate fabric
glim•mer (gli´ mər) v., emit a dim or flickering light
sheen (shēn) n., glow

558

Program Resources

Planning and Assessment
Program Planning Guide, Selection Lesson Plan
E-Lesson Planner
Assessment Guide, Lesson Test
ExamView

Technology Tools
Interactive Student Text on CD
Visual Teaching Package
Audio Library
mirrorsandwindows.com

Meeting the Standards
Poetry: Unit 6, Directed Reading, pp. 36–41

Differentiating Instruction
Advanced Students, Poetic Form Activity, pp. 33–34

 **MIRRORS & WINDOWS**

If you knew someone who could choose between a charming person and a wealthy one, what advice would you give? In love, is it better to follow your heart or your head?

AFTER READING

Find Meaning

1. What choice is Parker writing about?
2. (a) How would you describe the man the speaker addresses as "He"? (b) How would you describe the man addressed as "You"?
3. (a) How does the speaker feel about the choice she made? (b) How does she communicate this point of view to the reader?

Make Judgments

4. Consider Parker's choice of the words *rolling, billowing, trickle,* and *smoldering.* Why do you think Parker chose these words?
5. (a) Which sensory details did Parker include that describe sounds? (b) Why did Parker use these kinds of details in the lines about the second man and not in those about the first?
6. Irony exists when what actually happens is the opposite, or nearly the opposite, of what is expected. How is the poem ironic?

Analyze Literature

Rhythm The rhythm of a poem can affect its mood and tone. Reread "The Choice." Pay close attention to the even-numbered lines, and read only them aloud. What do you notice about the rhythm of these lines? Now read only the odd-numbered lines aloud. What do you notice about their rhythm? How many beats, or stressed syllables, occur in each line of the poem? How does the rhythm affect the poem's tone?

Extend Understanding

Writing Options

Creative Writing Write a **poem** borrowing the rhyme scheme from "The Choice." The audience for your poem should be a friend you like to make laugh, so keep your tone light and humorous. Use your rhythm and rhyme scheme to emphasize the content of your poem. Read the poem out loud for your friend.

Expository Writing Write a short **critical analysis** essay of the speaker's choice. In your thesis, state your opinion of that choice. In the body, give your reasons, examples, and other support. Quote lines from the poem as evidence and explain how they support your argument. In your conclusion, make speculations about the future of the speaker, and restate your opinion. Share your work with your class.

Collaborative Learning

Discuss in Small Groups Meet in small groups to talk about the tone of "The Choice." You should describe the tone in your own words and explain your reasoning. As a group, draw conclusions about Parker's tone, citing lines from the poem to support your conclusions. Then briefly discuss Parker's tone as a whole class.

Lifelong Learning

Research Dorothy Parker Suppose that your class has been invited to make a presentation at a celebration of Dorothy Parker's life. At the library, research Parker's life. Then write a paragraph that tells something about her life that you think may have influenced her writing of "The Choice." You may choose to discuss the content of the poem or its tone.

 Go to www.mirrorsandwindows.com for more.

THE CHOICE **559**

 **MIRRORS & WINDOWS**

Answer: Students might suggest that love will grow between them over time and that being financially secure is more important in the long run. Other students might suggest that people must follow their heart in matters of love in order to ensure happiness.

Find Meaning

1. She is writing about choosing between two kinds of sweethearts.
2. (a) "He" is a man who is rich and generous. (b) "You" is a man who is impulsive and strong.
3. (a) The speaker feels that she chose well. (b) She communicates this through the use of irony.

Make Judgments

4. They convey the sensual.
5. (a) "lilting song," "melody, happy and high," "whistle low" (b) Some students might say that sound is immaterial like passion is.
6. She thinks it's the right choice.

Analyze Literature

Rhythm *Answer:* Students might feel that the regular rhythm contributes to a conventional expectation: her advice to lovers will be "follow your heart." Thus, the rhythm makes the shift funny and surprising. Some students may find the rhythm reminiscent of children's poems and find humor in the adult mood of the last line of the poem.

Rubrics for Writing Options

You can adapt this as a checklist for students to use as they write.

Creative Writing

☐ Does the student's poem share some of the rhythm of "The Choice"?
☐ Is the rhyme scheme of the student's poem correct?
☐ Did the student compare the rhyme scheme of the two poems?

Expository Writing

☐ Is the writing a short essay with a topic sentence that states the writer's opinion?
☐ Does the analysis express an opinion of the speaker's choice and develop an argument in support of the writer's opinion?
☐ Does the analysis quote lines from the poem?
☐ Does the paragraph conclude with speculations about the speaker's future and a restatement of the writer's opinion?

Program Resources

For further instruction, refer students to the following extension activity: Lifelong Learning: Research Dorothy Parker, *Exceeding the Standards: Extension Activities*, pp. 18–20.

Preview the Selection

At a Glance
Directed Reading
- Reading Level: Moderate
- Difficulty Considerations: Vocabulary, Spanish terms
- Ease Factor: Subject matter

Objectives

Studying this lesson will enable students to
- use reading strategies such as making inferences
- define *simile* and *metaphor* and recognize the effect of these literary techniques in the selection
- describe the literary accomplishments of Pablo Neruda and explain the influence of Chilean culture on his writing
- identify the author's purpose in writing the poem
- appreciate the value of literature in its original language, as well as its translation

Launch the Lesson

Prior to reading "Ode to My Socks," students might enjoy describing a favorite article of clothing and explaining why it is a favorite. Allow students to bring in the article or a picture of it to show as they speak.

Summary

The speaker describes receiving a pair of woven socks and fighting the urge to put them away and not use them. The speaker eventually wears the bright socks, noting that they are doubly good as beautiful, useful socks.

Common Core State Standards

Reading Literature
RL.1

Writing
W.9

Language
L.6

DIRECTED READING

BEFORE READING

Build Background
Cultural Context Pablo Neruda grew up in a rural area of Chile. Summers were hot, but winters were rainy and icy cold. The wet climate made for green pastures for sheep and boggy areas for rice. Sheep farmers were fortunate. They had plenty of wool for warm socks, sweaters, and hats. Neruda first wrote this poem in his native language, Spanish.

Reader's Context What homemade gift have you received that seemed remarkable in some way? What made that gift special?

Set Purpose
An *ode* is a special type of lyric poem that celebrates a person, object, or event. Why might a person write an ode to a pair of socks? As you read, take notes on the answer to this question.

Analyze Literature
Metaphor and Simile A **metaphor** is a figure of speech in which one thing is spoken or written about as if it were another. Another figure of speech, the **simile,** uses *like* or *as* in its comparison. As you read, look for metaphors and similes. Analyze how they add meaning to what is described.

Meet the Author

Pablo Neruda (1904–1973) is considered by many to be the finest Latin American poet of the twentieth century. Born in Parral, Chile, he published his first poem at thirteen. At sixteen, he joined a group of experimental poets and contributed works to literary journals. From 1927 to 1943, he served as a Chilean ambassador, traveling to such faraway places as Singapore, Spain, and France. In 1945, he was elected senator of the Republic. Neruda wrote several volumes of poetry and, in 1971, was awarded the Nobel Prize in Literature.

Use Reading Skills
Identifying Author's Purpose An author's purpose is his or her aim or goal. An author may write to entertain, to inform, to describe, to tell a story, or to persuade. The author's word choices provide clues to the purpose. As you read "Ode to My Socks," look for clues to identify Pablo Neruda's purpose for writing. Create a chart to jot down your ideas.

Preview Vocabulary
de·crep·it (di kre´ pət) *adj.,* worn out; weakened by age or use

sa·cred (sā krəd´) *adj.,* holy or especially treasured

im·pulse (im´ pəls) *n.,* sudden force or action

re·morse (ri môrs´) *n.,* regret

Words in Use

Preview Vocabulary
decrepit, 562
sacred, 563
impulse, 563
remorse, 563

Selection Words
sheepherder, 561
twilight, 562
immense, 562
unacceptable, 562

Teaching Words
rural, 560
climate, 560
boggy, 560
experimental, 560
ambassador, 560
temptation, 564
commemorate, 564

KEY TERMS
LYRIC POEM, 560
ODE, 560
METAPHOR, 560
SIMILE, 560
FIGURE OF SPEECH, 560
AUTHOR'S PURPOSE, 560
MOOD, 564

Ode to My Socks

Silly Socks, 2006. Elin Pendleton.

Oda a los calcetines

A Lyric Poem by Pablo Neruda

Maru Mori brought me
a pair
of socks
which she knitted herself
5 with her sheepherder's hands,
two socks as soft
as rabbits.
I slipped my feet
into them
10 as though into
two

Me trajo Maru Mori
un par
de calcetines
que tejió con sus manos
5 de pastora,
dos calcetines suaves
como liebres.
En ellos
metí los pies
10 como en
dos

561

Teach the Selection

MIRRORS & WINDOWS The Mirrors & Windows questions at the end of this poem focus on the theme of treasures. Have you ever felt that a simple possession held great value? Should people be proud of simple things?

Literary Connection

Poetic Translation The well-known Italian expression "traduttore-traditore" ("translator equals traitor") encapsulates the attitude of some people toward literary translation. Robert Frost went so far as to say "Poetry gets lost in translation." While it is true that one can never *duplicate* a work of literature in another language, many modern translators consider their work to be to critically interpret originals rather than create carbon copies of them. Modern translators and their readers find value in honoring original versions by crafting a work true to its source but original in spirit. Furthermore, as none of us speaks every language on the planet, translations provide valuable insights into cultures apart from our own. Robert Pinsky's famous translation of Dante's "Inferno" affirms the notion that the literary world is coming to accept, and even admire, the work of literary translators.

Program Resources

Planning and Assessment
Program Planning Guide, Selection Lesson Plan
E-Lesson Planner
Assessment Guide, Lesson Test
ExamView

Technology Tools
Interactive Student Text on CD
Visual Teaching Package
Audio Library
mirrorsandwindows.com

Meeting the Standards
Poetry: Unit 6, Directed Reading, pp. 42–47

Differentiating Instruction
English Language Learners, Identifying Author's Purpose, pp. 149–156

Analyze Literature

Simile Ask students to identify the phrase (which begins on page 561) as a simile or metaphor and to tell what the narrator compares the socks to. Discuss the effectiveness of the simile. Possible responses: "Simile. The socks are compared to two cases. This is an effective simile because a case would completely enclose something, the way a sock encloses a foot." **A**

Analyze Literature

Metaphor Ask students to identify the phrase in lines 18–26 as a simile or metaphor and to tell what the narrator compares the feet to. Discuss the effectiveness of the metaphor. Possible responses: "Metaphor; fish, sharks, blackbirds, cannons. All of these metaphors compare the feet to things that move quickly, so they are effective." **B**

Use Reading Skills

Identify Author's Purpose Remind students to stop reading and record ideas on their author's purpose charts.

A cases
knitted
with threads of
15 twilight
and goatskin.
Violent socks,
my feet were
two fish made
20 of wool,
two long sharks
B sea-blue, shot
through
by one golden thread,
25 two immense blackbirds,
two cannons:
my feet
were honored
in this way
30 by
these
heavenly
socks.
They were
35 so handsome
for the first time
my feet seemed to me
unacceptable
like two <u>decrepit</u>
40 firemen, firemen
unworthy
of that woven
fire,
of those glowing
45 socks.

Nevertheless
I resisted
the sharp temptation
to save them somewhere
50 as schoolboys
keep
fireflies,

estuches
tejidos
con hebras del
15 crepúsculo
y pellejo de ovejas.
Violentos calcetines,
mis pies fueron
dos pescados
20 de lana,
dos largos tiburones
de azul ultramarino
atravesados
por una trenza de oro,
25 dos gigantescos mirlos,
dos cañones:
mis pies
fueron honrados
de este modo
30 por
estos
celestiales
calcetines.
Eran
35 tan hermosos
que por primera vez
mis pies me parecieron
inaceptables
como dos decrépitos
40 bomberos, bomberos,
indignos
de aquel fuego
bordado,
de aquellos luminosos
45 calcetines.

Sin embargo
resistí
la tentación aguda
de guardarlos
50 como los colegiales
preservan
las luciérnagas,

---

de·crep·it (di kreˊ pət) *adj.*, worn out; weakened by age or use

---

TEACHING NOTE

Nonverbal Messages

Help students understand that in poetry, the mere sound of words can communicate great meaning since all people, regardless of native tongue, convey the same array of tone and emotion through vocal expression. An example of this is sighing in relief or exasperation.

as learned men
collect
55 <u>sacred</u> texts,
I resisted
the mad <u>impulse</u>
to put them
into a golden
60 cage **C**
and each day give them
birdseed
and pieces of pink melon.
Like explorers **D**
65 in the jungle who hand
over the very rare
green deer
to the spit[1]
and eat it
70 with <u>remorse</u>,
I stretched out
my feet
and pulled on
the magnificent
75 socks
and then my shoes.

The moral
of my ode is this:
beauty is twice
80 beauty
and what is good is doubly
good
when it is a matter of two socks
made of wool
85 in winter. ❖ **E**

como los eruditos
coleccionan
55 *documentos sagrados,*
resistí
el impulso furioso
de ponerlos
en una jaula
60 *de oro*
y darles cada día
alpiste
y pulpa de melón rosado.
Como descubridores
65 *que en la selva*
entregan el rarísimo
venado verde
al asador
y se lo comen
70 *con remordimiento,*
estiré
los pies
y me enfundé
los bellos
75 *calcetines*
y luego los zapatos.

Y es ésta
la moral de mi oda:
dos veces es belleza
80 *la belleza*
y lo que es bueno es doblemente
bueno
cuando se trata de dos calcetines
de lana
85 *en el invierno.* ❖

---

sa•cred (sā krəd´) *adj.,* holy or especially treasured

im•pulse (im´ pəls') *n.,* sudden force or action

re•morse (ri môrs´) *n.,* regret

1. **spit.** Long, spearlike piece of metal used to cook large pieces of meat over a fire

MIRRORS & **W**INDOWS

When have you felt that something you owned deserved honor? Why is it special to you? Why might it be important to take pride in simple things?

Writing Skills

Write an Ode
Remind students that a poet writes an ode to show love or respect for a person or an object or to remember an event. Ask students to make a list of objects that they might like to write about and then to choose one for the topic of their ode. Remind them to include similes and metaphors in their odes. Suggest that they draw or find a picture of an object similar to theirs or, if possible, to bring the object to class and look at it while writing. When students have finished, invite them to read their odes to the class.

Review the Selection

Find Meaning

1. (a) He sees his feet as fish. (b) They make him imagine that his feet are violent sharks.

2. The socks are so handsome that he feels his feet don't deserve them.

3. (a) He resists the temptation to put his socks away and save them rather than wearing them. (b) Schoolboys trap and keep fireflies in closed jars. The speaker will not keep his socks trapped and unused.

4. Possible response: Real, tangible beauty is more valuable than the idea of beauty and twice as valuable when it comes in the form of two warm woolen socks in the winter.

Make Judgments

5. (a) The firemen are old and weak, not worthy of the "fire" of those colorful socks. (b) Acceptable answers demonstrate understanding of the metaphor.

6. The socks are colorful and warm; the speaker may be appreciative that someone made them for him. Answers should be supported by reasons.

7. Answers should be supported by reasons.

Analyze Literature

Metaphor and Simile *Answer:*
Similes: as though into two cases; like two decrepit firemen; as schoolboys keep fireflies; as learned men collect sacred texts; like explorers in the jungle
Metaphors: threads of twilight and goatskin; two fish made of wool; two long sharks; two immense blackbirds; two cannons; woven fire

---

Find Meaning

1. (a) When the speaker first puts on the socks, he sees his feet transformed into different animals. What is one example? (b) Why does he refer to the socks as "Violent socks"?

2. What makes the speaker think of his feet as "unacceptable"?

3. (a) What temptation does the speaker resist? (b) Why does he contrast himself to "schoolboys" who "keep fireflies"?

4. In your own words, express the moral that the speaker gives for his ode.

Analyze Literature

Metaphor and Simile Metaphors and similes are creative comparisons. In a metaphor, one thing is spoken or written about as if it were something else. A simile is a comparison that uses *like* or *as*. Look back at the poem. Use a figurative language chart to identify and analyze each simile and metaphor.

Make Judgments

5. (a) Why does the speaker compare his feet to "two decrepit firemen"? (b) Do you think that simile is effective? Why or why not?

6. Think about why the speaker so enjoys the socks. Is his main reason their beauty, their warmth, or the fact that someone made them for him? Explain.

7. Poets usually write odes to show deep love and respect for a person or to commemorate an important event, such as a triumphant battle. Why might an ode to a pair of socks be ironic?

Figurative Language	Simile or Metaphor?	Meaning
socks as soft as rabbits	simile	The socks were soft and fluffy.

Extend Understanding

Writing Options

Creative Writing The speaker in this poem is very thankful for the gift of socks. Think of a special gift that you received. Write a **personal letter** to thank the person who gave you the gift. In your letter, explain why the gift pleases you.

Persuasive Writing Write a **review** of this poem, in which you express your overall thoughts and feelings about it. Identify three to four elements of the poem that you liked or disliked. Support each opinion with clearly stated reasons, examples, and quotes from the poem.

Collaborative Learning

Mood Analysis The mood of a poem is the overall feeling or atmosphere that the poet tries to create for the reader. With a partner, create a cluster chart filled with details from the poem. Using those details, identify the poem's mood and explain your reasoning to a small group or to the class.

Media Literacy

More by Neruda Using library or Internet sources, locate another poem by Pablo Neruda. Compare and contrast it with "Ode to My Socks." Present your findings to the class.

Go to **www.mirrorsandwindows.com** for more.

Rubrics for Writing Options

You can adapt this as a checklist for students to use as they write.

Creative Writing

☐ Does the letter identify a special gift?
☐ Does it describe the gift and its significance?
☐ Does it follow the standard form and guidelines for personal letters?

Persuasive Writing

☐ Does the review effectively express an overall opinion regarding the poem?
☐ Does it support that point of view with at least three quoted details and elements in the poem?
☐ Is the review fair and accurate?

Grammar & Style

Intensive and Reflexive Pronouns

Intensive Pronouns

Maru Mori brought me
a pair
of socks
which she knitted herself...

 —PABLO NERUDA, "Ode to My Socks"

Intensive pronouns are used to emphasize a noun or pronoun. In the quotation above, the word *herself* emphasizes that Maru Mori knitted the socks rather than buying them. Intensive pronouns typically follow the word they are intended to emphasize, and they don't suggest any action on the part of the noun or pronoun.

> EXAMPLES
>
> **noun**   *the socks themselves, the thread itself*
>
> **pronoun**   *I myself, she herself, they themselves, we ourselves*

Occasionally, an intensive pronoun is placed several words away from the noun or pronoun it emphasizes.

> EXAMPLE
>
> *I prefer colorful socks myself.*

Reflexive Pronouns

> EXAMPLE
>
> *My feet slipped themselves into the socks.*

A **reflexive pronoun** refers back to a noun or pronoun previously used in the sentence. It signals that the subject has done something *to* or *for* itself. Reflexive pronouns are formed by adding the suffix *-self* or *-selves* to a pronoun. In the sentence

above, the reflexive pronoun *themselves* refers back to the noun *feet*. Reflexive pronouns may be either singular or plural.

> EXAMPLES
>
> *myself, herself, himself, ourselves, yourself, yourselves, themselves*

The subject of a reflexive pronoun may be implied.

Identifying Intensive and Reflexive Pronouns

Copy the following sentences. Underline once any reflexive pronouns and the noun or pronoun to which they refer. Underline twice any intensive pronouns and the nouns or pronouns to which they refer.

1. I reminded myself to put my socks away carefully.
2. The socks themselves seemed to glow with color.
3. Did you knit those socks yourself?
4. The threads wound themselves into colorful images.
5. He prided himself on his socks.

Using Intensive Pronouns

For each of the following sentences, choose the correct intensive pronoun.

1. The colors _____ were like a rainbow.
2. The poet _____ was very impressed with the socks.
3. When I go to school, I wear plain socks _____.

Using Reflexive Pronouns

For each of the following sentences, choose the correct reflexive pronoun.

1. Maru Mori lifted _____ from the chair.
2. I kept _____ from locking the socks in a golden cage.
3. Pick up after _____!

GRAMMAR & STYLE **565**

TEACHING NOTE

Extra Practice

Have students complete each of the following sentences using reflexive or intensive pronouns.

1. We listened to the novelist (herself) read from her latest work.
2. Her many fans yelled (themselves) hoarse when she appeared.
3. Do you (yourself) enjoy her fiction?

Identifying Reflexive and Intensive Pronouns

1. I reminded myself to put my socks away carefully.
2. The socks themselves seemed to glow with color.
3. Did you knit those socks yourself?
4. The threads wound themselves into colorful images.
5. He prided himself on his socks.

Using Intensive Pronouns

1. themselves
2. himself
3. myself

Using Reflexive Pronouns

1. herself
2. myself
3. yourself

> For more information, see Grammar & Style Section 3.4, Pronouns, in the Language Arts Handbook.

Program Resources

You will find additional lessons on Pronouns in the *Exceeding the Standards: Grammar & Style* resource.

Build Skills

Point out to students that reflexive and intensive pronouns should never be used as the subject of a sentence.

incorrect

My friends and myself enjoyed the film.

correct

My friends and I enjoyed the film.

Common Core State Standards

Language
L.1

At a Glance
Directed Reading
- Reading Level: Easy
- Difficulty Consideration: Length
- Ease Factors: Vivid description, familiar subject

Objectives
Studying this lesson will enable students to
- use reading strategies such as identifying the main idea
- define *suspense* and recognize the effect of this literary technique in the selection
- describe the literary accomplishments of Ernest Lawrence Thayer
- appreciate a humorous poem that has a twist at the end

Launch the Lesson
Before assigning "Casey at the Bat," ask students to share accounts of various experiences they have had at baseball games or other sports events. Ask them to describe a key moment at the game and how they felt at that time.

Summary
The poem describes a baseball game in Mudville, where all hope seems lost until Casey, the team's best player, comes up to bat. Everyone is confident that Casey will win the game, but he strikes out and the game is over.

Common Core State Standards
Reading Literature
RL.1, RL.6
Writing
W.7, W.8, W.9
Language
L.6

DIRECTED READING

CASEY AT THE BAT

A Narrative Poem by Ernest Lawrence Thayer

BEFORE READING

Build Background
Cultural Context "Casey at the Bat, a Ballad of the Republic" was first published on June 3, 1888, in the *San Francisco Examiner*. At first "Casey at the Bat" didn't receive much attention. Then in August 1888, a comedian named De Wolf Hopper, knowing there would be important baseball players in the audience that night, performed the ballad in a theater in New York City. The audience went wild, and Hopper went on to perform "Casey at the Bat" many times over.

Reader's Context How would you describe your feelings about baseball?

Set Purpose
Preview the title of the poem. What do you predict the poem will be about?

Analyze Literature
Suspense The feeling of anxiousness and curiosity while waiting to find out what will happen next is called **suspense.** Writers create suspense by using details that raise questions and alarm in the reader's mind. As you read "Casey at the Bat," notice the details that create suspense in the poem.

Meet the Author
Ernest Lawrence Thayer (1863–1940) attended Harvard University. There he met William Randolph Hearst, who later became publisher of the newspaper *The San Francisco Examiner*. Hearst hired his friend to write a humor column, and Thayer used his old college nickname, "Phin," as his byline. Under this name, Thayer penned "Casey at the Bat."

Use Reading Skills
Identify Main Idea The main idea is a brief statement of what the author wants you to know, think, or feel after reading the selection. A good way to find the main or overall idea of a selection is to gather details into a main idea map like the one here. Make a map and record details to determine the main idea of "Casey at the Bat."

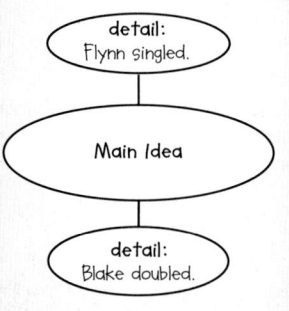

detail:
Flynn singled.

Main Idea

detail:
Blake doubled.

Preview Vocabulary
strick·en (stri′ kən) *adj.*, affected with strong emotions

mul·ti·tude (məl tə′ tüd′) *n.*, large quantity

re·coil (ri koi[e]l′) *v.*, spring back

haugh·ty (hô′ tē) *adj.*, snobby or boastful

tu·mult (tü′ məlt′) *n.*, loud noise and confusion

566 UNIT 6 POETRY

Words in Use

Preview Vocabulary	Selection Words	Teaching Words
stricken, 568	**outlook**, 568	**republic**, 566
multitude, 568	**sickly**, 568	**anxiousness**, 566
recoil, 568	**despised**, 568	**evolved**, 568
haughty, 569	**gladdened**, 568	**intent**, 570
tumult, 569	**unheeded**, 569	**principal**, 570

CASEY AT THE BAT

A Narrative Poem by Ernest Lawrence Thayer

The Hit, 1994. Lance Richbourg.

567

Teach the Selection

The Mirrors & Windows questions at the end of this selection focus on the theme of heroes. Before reading the poem, ask students to describe a sporting event they have witnessed in which fans have reacted emotionally to the game before them. Why do they think people put so much stock in sports and their players?

Cultural Connection

Sports are popular all over the United States. Some states have favorites, with many players and even more fans attending events:

- **Lacrosse** The Lacrosse Classic is held in August in Ocean City, Maryland. Lacrosse is a sports obsession in Maryland, although it is not played in many other states. About 1,000 players compete.
- **Mountain Biking** The mountain bike relay race in Moa, Utah, in October brings bikers from all over the country.
- **All-American Soap Box Derby** The derby, held in Akron, Ohio, has hundreds of participants.
- **Little League World Series** This is the largest youth sports program in the world, involving 3 million players in more than 100 countries. As many as 70,000 fans watch each game. It's held in Williamsport, Pennsylvania, each August.

Program Resources

Planning and Assessment
Program Planning Guide, Selection Lesson Plan
E-Lesson Planner
Assessment Guide, Lesson Test
ExamView

Technology Tools
Interactive Student Text on CD
Visual Teaching Package
Audio Library
mirrorsandwindows.com

Meeting the Standards
Poetry: Unit 6, Directed Reading, pp. 48–53

Use Reading Skills
Identify the Main Idea Ask students to identify the main idea in this verse. Remind them to fill in their main idea charts after reading. Possible response: "Casey is at bat and shows his confidence." **A**

Use Reading Skills
Summarize Ask students to work in pairs to summarize this portion of the reading. Possible response: "A few fans have given up on the Mudville nine, but the majority still think that Casey can save them." **B**

Analyze Literature
Suspense Ask students to identify the details that create suspense in this verse. Possible response: "The description of the failure of several batters ahead of Casey builds suspense." **C**

Cultural Connection
The History of Baseball *Answer:* Students should include examples from the text in their responses. **D**

A

The outlook wasn't brilliant for the Mudville nine that day;
The score stood four to two, with but one inning more to play;
And so, when Cooney died at first, and Burrows did the same,
A sickly silence fell upon the patrons of the game.

B

5 A straggling few got up to go in deep despair. The rest
Clung to the hope which springs eternal in the human breast;
They thought, if only Casey could but get a whack, at that,
They'd put up even money now, with Casey at the bat.

C

But Flynn preceded Casey, as did also Jimmy Blake,
10 And the former was a pudding, and the latter was a fake;
So upon that <u>stricken</u> <u>multitude</u> grim melancholy[1] sat,
For there seemed but little chance of Casey's getting to the bat.

But Flynn let drive a single, to the wonderment of all,
And Blake, the much-despised, tore the cover off the ball;
15 And when the dust had lifted, and they saw what had occurred,
There was Jimmy safe on second, and Flynn a-hugging third.

Then from the gladdened multitude went up a joyous yell;
It bounded from the mountaintop, and rattled in the dell;
It struck upon the hillside, and <u>recoiled</u> upon the flat;
20 For Casey, mighty Casey, was advancing to the bat.

There was ease in Casey's manner as he stepped into his place;
There was pride in Casey's bearing, and a smile on Casey's face;
And when, responding to the cheers, he lightly doffed[2] his hat,
No stranger in the crowd could doubt 'twas Casey at the bat.

---

strick • en (strĭ´ kən) *adj.*, affected with strong emotions
mul • ti • tude (məl tə´ tüd) *n.*, large quantity
re • coil (rĭ koi[e]l´) *v.*, spring back

1. **melancholy.** Gloomy sadness
2. **doffed.** Tipped

CULTURAL ▶▶ CONNECTION

The History of Baseball American baseball evolved from an English game called Rounders in the 1800s. In 1845, a New York baseball club, the Knickerbockers, developed formal rules for the game. That year they played what is considered the first modern baseball game against the New York Club. Over time baseball grew in popularity, and fans were willing to pay to watch it. In 1869, the Cincinnati Red Stockings paid their players, making them baseball's first professional team. The Red Stockings traveled around the country thrilling thousands of fans. To this day, baseball remains extremely popular. What details in "Casey at the Bat" help explain the sport's appeal? **D**

TEACHING NOTE

Self-Generated Questioning
Instruct students to each create two or more questions about the poem, along with answers on a separate piece of paper. Model a question such as: "Why did the crowd think Casey could save the game?" Divide the class into teams. Instruct a student to ask the class one of his or her questions and to toss a ball to someone who signals that he or she knows the answer. If the answer is correct, the responder asks the next question and tosses the ball again. If the answer is incorrect, the student tosses the ball to another student to answer. Play continues until all questions have been asked or until a determined amount of time is over.

25 Ten thousand eyes were on him as he rubbed his hands with dirt;
Five thousand tongues applauded when he wiped them on his shirt;
Then while the writhing[3] pitcher ground the ball into his hip,
Defiance gleamed in Casey's eye, a sneer curled Casey's lip.

And now the leather-covered sphere came hurtling through the air,
30 And Casey stood a-watching it in <u>haughty</u> grandeur there;
Close by the sturdy batsman the ball unheeded sped.
"That ain't my style," said Casey. "Strike one," the umpire said.

From the benches, black with people, there went up a muffled roar,
Like the beating of the storm waves on a stern and distant shore;
35 "Kill him! Kill the umpire!" shouted someone on the stand;
And it's likely they'd have killed him had not Casey raised his hand.

With a smile of Christian charity great Casey's visage[4] shone;
He stilled the rising <u>tumult</u>; he bade[5] the game go on;
He signaled to the pitcher, and once more the spheroid[6] flew;
40 But Casey still ignored it, and the umpire said, "Strike two."

"Fraud!" cried the maddened thousands, and the echo answered, "Fraud!"
But a scornful look from Casey, and the audience was awed;
They saw his face grow stern and cold, they saw his muscles strain,
And they knew that Casey wouldn't let that ball go by again.

45 The sneer is gone from Casey's lips, his teeth are clenched in hate,
He pounds with cruel violence his bat upon the plate;
And now the pitcher holds the ball, and now he lets it go,
And now the air is shattered by the force of Casey's blow.

Oh! somewhere in this favored land the sun is shining bright;
50 The band is playing somewhere, and somewhere hearts are light;
And somewhere men are laughing, and somewhere children shout,
But there is no joy in Mudville—mighty Casey has struck out! ❧

---

haugh·ty (hô′ tē) *adj.*, snobby or boastful
tu·mult (tü′ məlt') *n.*, loud noise and confusion

3. **writhing.** Twisting and turning in pain
4. **visage.** Face
5. **bade.** Commanded someone or something
6. **spheroid.** Ball-shaped object

What game can you recall where fans acted like those in the poem? How did the game turn out? What do you think makes sports fans take games so seriously?

Review the Selection

Find Meaning

1. (a) They are worried and hopeful. (b) Their team is losing and the next two players do not usually play well.
2. Flynn and Blake bat well, which means that Casey will bat.
3. (a) Casey is so confident that he lets the first two pitches go past without swinging. (b) When the umpire calls them strikes, the crowd goes wild with anger.

Make Judgments

4. (a) Students may point to the reality of details such as fans who leave early or others who shout "Kill the umpire!" (b) Students may cite details about the sound of the crowd, the changing expression on Casey's face, or the inclusion of baseball terminology.
5. Students may say that he is confident and aware of his status as a hero to the baseball fans. Evidence might include "ease in Casey's manner" and "haughty grandeur."

Analyze Literature

Suspense *Answer:* Details: Stanza 2: A few left in deep despair; the rest clung to hope. People would be willing to put money on Casey if he came up to bat.
Suspense Created: The words *If only Casey* suggest he could win for the team, but *if only* implies there's a reason why he may not come up to bat. Curiosity is aroused.

Find Meaning

1. (a) How do the Mudville fans feel at the beginning of the game? (b) Why?
2. What gives the people of Mudville hope that they can win the game?
3. (a) How does Casey act when he is at bat? (b) How does the crowd react to the first two pitches?

Analyze Literature

Suspense Suspense is a feeling of anticipation about what will happen next. The poem "Casey at the Bat" creates the suspense of watching a real baseball game. Create a chart in which you record details from the poem that create suspense. Then use your chart to summarize how Thayer creates suspense in the poem "Casey at the Bat."

Make Judgments

4. (a) How well does the poem capture the feeling of being at a game? (b) What details contribute to the reader's experience of the game?
5. How would you describe Casey? Use evidence from the text to support your description.

Details	Suspense Created
Stanza 1: It is the last inning of the game, and Mudville is behind 4 to 2 with two outs.	

Extend Understanding

Writing Options

Creative Writing Write a **business letter** of complaint to the manager of the Mudville team. A business letter uses formal language and is specific regarding its intent. Make sure to include exactly what you are complaining about and what actions you feel should be taken to address your complaint. Read your letter out loud to the class in a formal presentation. Leave time for questions after you are finished.

Expository Writing Write a **summary** of this poem. Your summary should include brief descriptions of the principal actions and characters, including the crowd. Make sure to describe the expectations, mood, and reaction of the crowd, players, and speaker.

Media Literacy

Evaluate a Recording Listen to a recording of this poem being read aloud. Evaluate the reading and the way in which the reading affected you. How did your reaction differ from that of reading the poem silently?

Critical Literacy

Read to the Class Practice reading this poem aloud by yourself and then present it to the class. Adjust your reading rate, volume, tone, and pitch to suit the action and mood of each stanza of the poem.

Go to **www.mirrorsandwindows.com** for more.

Rubrics for Writing Options

You can adapt this as a checklist for students to use as they write.

Creative Writing
☐ Does the letter opening and closing follow the conventions of a formal business letter?
☐ Is the complaint clearly stated?
☐ Does the letter include what actions the writer would like the manager to take?
☐ Did the student formally present his or her letter to the class?

Expository Writing
☐ Does the summary include all the principal actions?
☐ Does the summary include brief descriptions of the characters?
☐ Does the summary include the expectations, mood, and reaction of the crowd?

Paul Revere's Ride

A Narrative Poem by Henry Wadsworth Longfellow

DIRECTED READING

BEFORE READING

Build Background

Historical Context In 1775, tensions boiled between American colonists and the British government. Late at night on April 18, Paul Revere (1725–1818) and other messengers set out on horseback to warn colonists living along the route to Concord that the British were coming. Armed colonists then assembled in the village of Lexington. The next morning, when the British marched into Lexington, gunfire broke out. The American Revolution had begun.

Reader's Context What might the colonists have felt when they heard Paul Revere's warning that the British soldiers were coming?

Set Purpose

The pattern of beats in a line of poetry is known as **rhythm.** As you read, try to determine if the rhythm is regular and how it affects the mood.

Analyze Literature

Narrative Poetry A **narrative poem** is verse that tells a story. As you read "Paul Revere's Ride," note how Longfellow uses setting, plot, conflict, and character to make the story exciting.

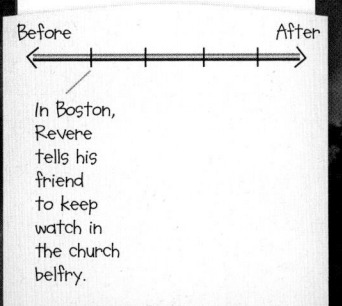

Meet the Author

Until **Henry Wadsworth Longfellow** (1807–1882) published his poems, many scholars and critics felt that the only "good" poetry came from Europe. Longfellow helped change that, becoming famous internationally as a great American poet. He had an exceptional ear for rhyme and rhythm, and he chose to write on American themes.

Use Reading Skills

Identify Sequence of Events The sequence of events in a selection refers to the order in which things happen. Keeping track of the sequence helps readers to understand when and why things happen. As you read this poem, use a time line to note the sequence of events.

Before ⟵|———|———|———|⟶ After

In Boston, Revere tells his friend to keep watch in the church belfry.

Preview Vocabulary

a·loft (ə lôft´) *adv.*, at or on a great height

muf·fled (mə´ fəld) *adj.*, wrapped or padded with thick material to keep out sound

moor·ing (môr´ iŋ) *n.*, device (such as a chain, rope, or anchor) that secures a boat or ship in place

som·ber (säm´ bər) *adj.*, dark and gloomy

de·fi·ance (di fī´ ən[t]s) *n.*, act or thoughts of rebellion, challenge, or a willingness to fight

Preview the Selection

At a Glance
Directed Reading
- Reading Level: Moderate
- Difficulty Considerations: Sentence length, archaic language
- Ease Factors: Rhyme, rhythm

Objectives

Studying this lesson will enable students to

- use reading strategies such as identifying sequence of events
- define *rhythm, stress,* and *meter* and analyze the effect of these poetic techniques on the tone and meaning of the poem
- understand that the purpose of a *narrative poem* is to tell a story
- describe the work of Henry Wadsworth Longfellow, appreciate his exceptional use of rhythm, and understand why people of his era considered him "the great American poet."
- enjoy a poem based on an important event in American history

Launch the Lesson

Have students picture themselves as young American patriots. What feelings would they have, knowing that the British army was marching toward their town? Have them read to find out how the suspense built along the route of Paul Revere's ride.

Summary

This narrative poem describes the events on the night Paul Revere alerted the colonists that the British were coming.

Words in Use

KEY TERMS

Preview Vocabulary
aloft, 573
muffled, 573
mooring, 573
somber, 574
defiance, 577

Selection Words
belfry, 573
magnified, 573
spectral, 575
tranquil, 575
skirt, 575

Teaching Words
colonists, 571
prominent, 576
silversmith, 576
foundry, 576
acclaimed, 578
prestigious, 578
pacing, 580
inflection, 580

Common Core State Standards

Reading Literature
RL.1

Language
L.6

Paul Revere's Ride

A Narrative Poem by Henry Wadsworth Longfellow

 The Mirrors & Windows questions at the end of this narrative poem focus on the theme of the American spirit. Prior to reading the narrative poem, discuss with students how they would define American spirit.

Literary Connection

Cultural Heroes and Legends

Every civilization, from ancient times, has had cultural heroes and legendary characters. The Greeks wrote tales about Prometheus, the man who brought fire from the gods. Native Americans told tales about Montezuma, Sitting Bull, and other great chiefs. The English had Robin Hood and King Arthur and his Knights of the Round Table. Henry Wadsworth Longfellow helped to create American legends out of real historical figures, including Paul Revere and Miles Standish. Other, less esteemed writers also played a role in creating American folklore. Beginning in 1860, "dime novels" were popular. Affordable precursors to comic books, they made such real-life figures as Buffalo Bill, Jesse James, and Wild Bill Hickock into legendary adventure heroes.

572

Program Resources

Planning and Assessment
Program Planning Guide, Selection Lesson Plan
E-Lesson Planner
Assessment Guide, Lesson Test
ExamView

Technology Tools
Interactive Student Text on CD
Visual Teaching Package
Audio Library
mirrorsandwindows.com

Meeting the Standards
Poetry: Unit 6, Directed Reading, pp. 54–59

Differentiating Instruction
Developing Readers, Unlock Word Meaning,
  pp. 43–45
Advanced Students, Author Biographical Study,
  p. 35

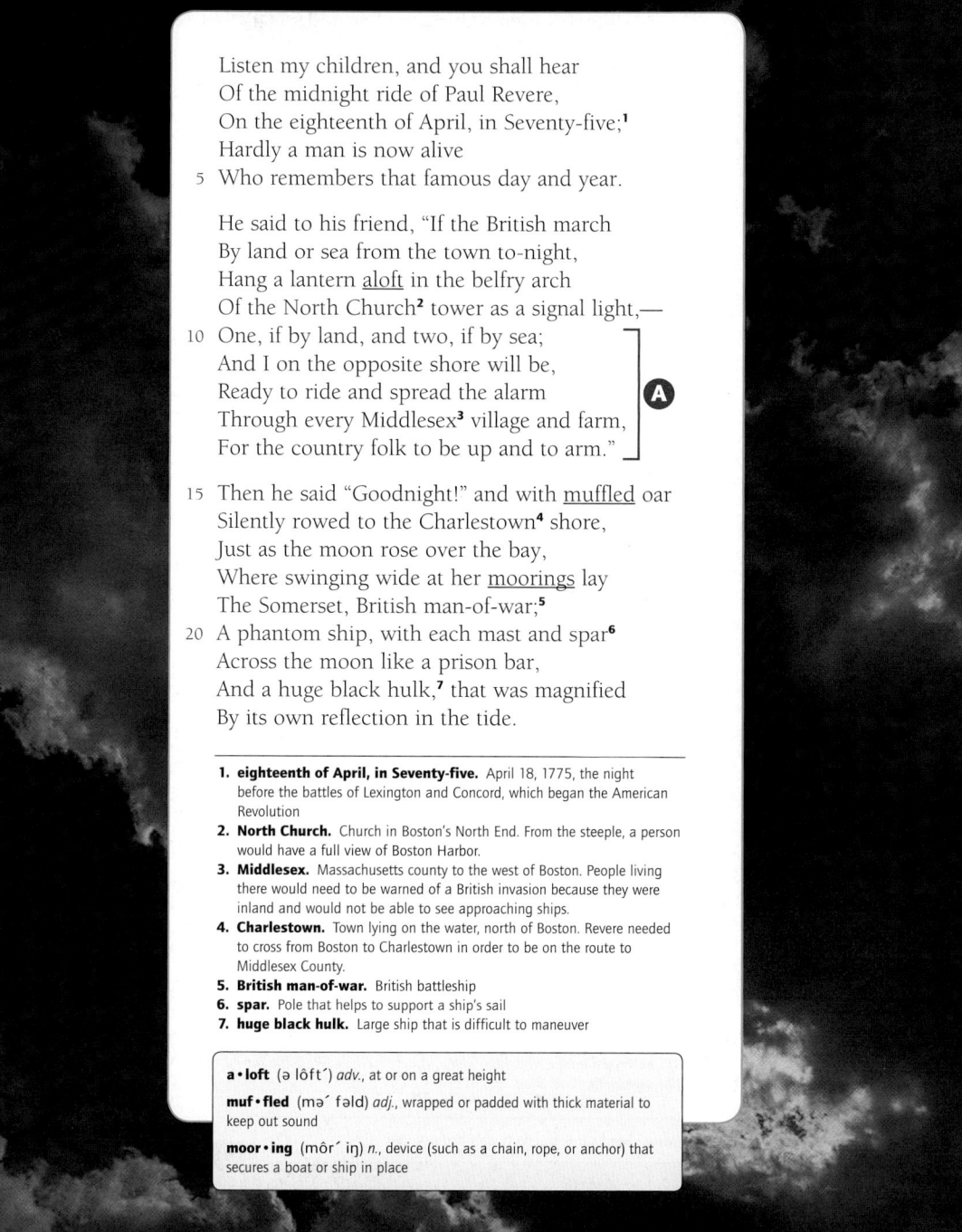

Listen my children, and you shall hear
Of the midnight ride of Paul Revere,
On the eighteenth of April, in Seventy-five;[1]
Hardly a man is now alive
5   Who remembers that famous day and year.

He said to his friend, "If the British march
By land or sea from the town to-night,
Hang a lantern <u>aloft</u> in the belfry arch
Of the North Church[2] tower as a signal light,—
10 One, if by land, and two, if by sea;
And I on the opposite shore will be,
Ready to ride and spread the alarm
Through every Middlesex[3] village and farm,
For the country folk to be up and to arm."

15 Then he said "Goodnight!" and with <u>muffled</u> oar
Silently rowed to the Charlestown[4] shore,
Just as the moon rose over the bay,
Where swinging wide at her <u>moorings</u> lay
The Somerset, British man-of-war;[5]
20 A phantom ship, with each mast and spar[6]
Across the moon like a prison bar,
And a huge black hulk,[7] that was magnified
By its own reflection in the tide.

---

1. **eighteenth of April, in Seventy-five.** April 18, 1775, the night before the battles of Lexington and Concord, which began the American Revolution
2. **North Church.** Church in Boston's North End. From the steeple, a person would have a full view of Boston Harbor.
3. **Middlesex.** Massachusetts county to the west of Boston. People living there would need to be warned of a British invasion because they were inland and would not be able to see approaching ships.
4. **Charlestown.** Town lying on the water, north of Boston. Revere needed to cross from Boston to Charlestown in order to be on the route to Middlesex County.
5. **British man-of-war.** British battleship
6. **spar.** Pole that helps to support a ship's sail
7. **huge black hulk.** Large ship that is difficult to maneuver

a·loft (ə lôft´) *adv.*, at or on a great height

muf·fled (məˊ fəld) *adj.*, wrapped or padded with thick material to keep out sound

moor·ing (môr´ iŋ) *n.*, device (such as a chain, rope, or anchor) that secures a boat or ship in place

PAUL REVERE'S RIDE **573**

Analyze Literature
Rhyme Scheme Ask students to identify the rhyme scheme in this stanza *(abbaccddeed)*. Does its rhythm inform the reader about a change in tone? **Ⓐ**

Use Reading Skills
Identify Sequence of Events Ask: "After the man climbs to the belfry tower, what does he look down upon? What thoughts go through his mind? What breaks the spell and draws his attention? Why is this important to the plot?" (He sees the British ships; he knows he must hang two lanterns.) **Ⓑ**

TEACHING NOTE

Set a Purpose
Point out that when it was published, this poem became instantly popular with people all over the world. It made them think of Paul Revere as the spirit of America. He became larger than life—like Davy Crockett, Zorro, Pecos Bill, and other figures of American history and folklore. As they read, have students identify elements of the poem that might have been particularly memorable, leading people to make Paul Revere almost a legendary character. When they have completed the poem, discuss their findings.

Meanwhile, his friend, through alley and street,
25 Wanders and watches with eager ears,
Till in the silence around him he hears
The muster[8] of men at the barrack[9] door,
The sound of arms, and the tramp of feet,
And the measured tread of the grenadiers,[10]
30 Marching down to their boats on the shore.

Then he climbed the tower of the Old North Church,
By the wooden stairs, with stealthy tread,
To the belfry-chamber[11] overhead,
And startled the pigeons from their perch
35 On the somber rafters, that round him made
Ⓐ Masses and moving shapes of shade,—
By the trembling ladder, steep and tall,
To the highest window in the wall,
Where he paused to listen and look down
40 A moment on the roofs of the town,
And the moonlight flowing over all.

Beneath, in the churchyard, lay the dead,
In their night-encampment on the hill,
Wrapped in silence so deep and still
45 That he could hear, like a sentinel's[12] tread,
The watchful night-wind, as it went
Creeping along from tent to tent,
And seeming to whisper, "All is well!"
A moment only he feels the spell
50 Of the place and the hour, and the secret dread
Of the lonely belfry and the dead;
For suddenly all his thoughts are bent
Ⓑ On a shadowy something far away,
Where the river widens to meet the bay,—
55 A line of black that bends and floats
On the rising tide, like a bridge of boats.

---

8. **muster.** Gathering of soldiers to prepare for battle
9. **barrack.** Hall where soldiers gather
10. **grenadiers.** Infantry soldiers
11. **belfry-chamber.** Enclosure within a church steeple where the bell hangs
12. **sentinel's.** Guard's

som·ber (säm´ bər) *adj.*, dark and gloomy

Differentiated Instruction

English Language Learning
Students who are new to American schools may not have enough background in American history to understand what is happening, why Revere is determined to warn the sleeping colonists, and what situations cause danger and suspense along his route. Provide them with a brief paragraph that describes the event before reading the poem. Then pause at the end of each page to discuss and clarify, and work with students to use the footnotes to aid comprehension.

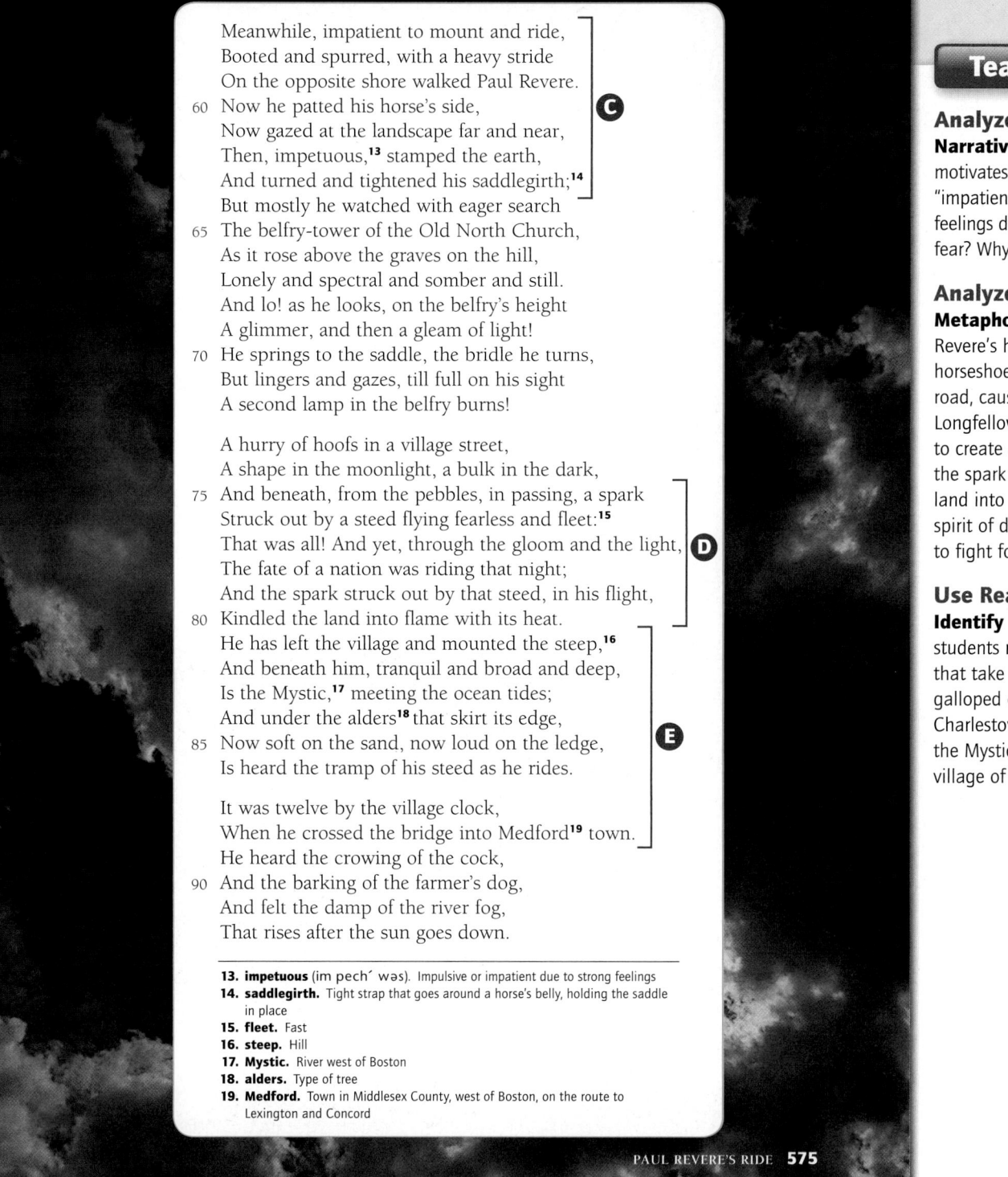

Meanwhile, impatient to mount and ride,
Booted and spurred, with a heavy stride
On the opposite shore walked Paul Revere.
60 Now he patted his horse's side, **C**
Now gazed at the landscape far and near,
Then, impetuous,[13] stamped the earth,
And turned and tightened his saddlegirth;[14]
But mostly he watched with eager search
65 The belfry-tower of the Old North Church,
As it rose above the graves on the hill,
Lonely and spectral and somber and still.
And lo! as he looks, on the belfry's height
A glimmer, and then a gleam of light!
70 He springs to the saddle, the bridle he turns,
But lingers and gazes, till full on his sight
A second lamp in the belfry burns!

A hurry of hoofs in a village street,
A shape in the moonlight, a bulk in the dark,
75 And beneath, from the pebbles, in passing, a spark
Struck out by a steed flying fearless and fleet:[15]
That was all! And yet, through the gloom and the light, **D**
The fate of a nation was riding that night;
And the spark struck out by that steed, in his flight,
80 Kindled the land into flame with its heat.
He has left the village and mounted the steep,[16]
And beneath him, tranquil and broad and deep,
Is the Mystic,[17] meeting the ocean tides;
And under the alders[18] that skirt its edge,
85 Now soft on the sand, now loud on the ledge, **E**
Is heard the tramp of his steed as he rides.

It was twelve by the village clock,
When he crossed the bridge into Medford[19] town.
He heard the crowing of the cock,
90 And the barking of the farmer's dog,
And felt the damp of the river fog,
That rises after the sun goes down.

---

13. **impetuous** (im pech´ wəs). Impulsive or impatient due to strong feelings
14. **saddlegirth.** Tight strap that goes around a horse's belly, holding the saddle in place
15. **fleet.** Fast
16. **steep.** Hill
17. **Mystic.** River west of Boston
18. **alders.** Type of tree
19. **Medford.** Town in Middlesex County, west of Boston, on the route to Lexington and Concord

Analyze Literature
Narrative Poem Discuss what motivates Paul Revere to be "impatient" and "impetuous." What feelings does he have? What might he fear? Why is he eager to get going? **C**

Analyze Literature
Metaphor Point out that as Paul Revere's horse gallops along, his iron horseshoes hit the pebbles on the road, causing sparks. However, Longfellow uses that physical image to create a metaphor. Discuss what the spark stands for as it "kindled the land into flame with its heat." (the spirit of defiance; the determination to fight for freedom; etc.) **D**

Use Reading Skills
Identify Sequence of Events Have students note the sequence of events that take place here. Revere has galloped out of the village of Charlestown, crossed the bridge over the Mystic River, and entered the village of Medford. It is midnight. **E**

Reading Skills

Understand Text Organization
Remind students that in many poems, the sentences do not always begin at the beginning of lines and end at the end of lines. Sentences that run on from one line to the next with little or no pause are called **enjambments.** Work with students to analyze and paraphrase complete sentences on this page.

Urge them to continue to do this as they read on, pointing out that paraphrasing the sentences will help them to understand and follow the plot events.

Identify Sequence of Events As students read this page, have them use Longfellow's noting of the times on the village clocks to keep clear the sequence of events and the stops along Revere's ongoing ride.

Analyze Literature

Foreshadowing Explain that most colonial villages had a grassy park in the center of town, called a "green" or a "common," because it was considered common ground, owned by all. It was a place where everyone could graze livestock. On one side of the common was the town meetinghouse, a place where the villagers gathered to discuss issues and make laws. Point out the personification that Longfellow employs here, regarding the meetinghouse windows, and the foreshadowing. Ask: "What bloody work would they look upon?" (They faced the Lexington Green, where the battle would take place the next morning.) **A**

History Connection

Paul Revere Student responses will vary. Students may comment on his role as a silversmith and wonder how well-known he became during his lifetime. **B**

It was one by the village clock,
When he galloped into Lexington.[20]
95 He saw the gilded weathercock[21]
Swim in the moonlight as he passed,
And the meeting-house windows, black and bare,
Gaze at him with a spectral glare,
As if they already stood aghast[22]
100 At the bloody work they would look upon.

It was two by the village clock,
When he came to the bridge in Concord[23] town.
He heard the bleating of the flock,
And the twitter of birds among the trees,
105 And felt the breath of the morning breeze
Blowing over the meadow brown.
And one was safe and asleep in his bed
Who at the bridge would be first to fall,
Who that day would be lying dead,
110 Pierced by a British musket-ball.

20. **Lexington.** Town west of Medford. The first shots—and deaths—of the American Revolution occurred on Lexington Green, a square in the middle of town.
21. **gilded weathercock.** Golden weathervane in the shape of a rooster. It swings in the wind to show the direction the wind is blowing.
22. **aghast** (ə gast´). Shocked
23. **bridge in Concord.** Old North Bridge in Concord, Massachusetts, site of the second battle

HISTORY ▶▶ CONNECTION

Paul Revere Prior to his midnight ride, Revere was well known as a prominent Boston silversmith. He continued this work after the war, and he also built an iron and brass foundry. There, he produced cannon, large church bells, and nails. Later, he built the first successful copper rolling mill in America. His copper sheets were used primarily to build ships. One of his customers was Robert Fulton, the man who invented the steamship. When Massachusetts became a state in 1788, its new state house in Boston was topped by a dome covered with Revere copper. How do these details affect your perception of Paul Revere? **B**

Differentiated Instruction

Enrichment

Review the information provided in the History Connection on page 576 of the student's book. Interested students might enjoy doing further research on Paul Revere as well as other heroes and important diplomats of the American Revolution such as Samuel Adams, John Hancock, Benjamin Franklin, George Washington, and Lafayette. Provide time for research and the delivery of oral or written reports.

You know the rest. In the books you have read,
How the British Regulars[24] fired and fled,—
How the farmers gave them ball for ball,
From behind each fence and farm-yard wall,
115 Chasing the red-coats[25] down the lane,
Then crossing the fields to emerge again
Under the trees at the turn of the road,
And only pausing to fire and load.

So through the night rode Paul Revere;
120 And so through the night went his cry of alarm
To every Middlesex village and farm,—
A cry of <u>defiance</u> and not of fear,
A voice in the darkness, a knock at the door,
And a word that shall echo forevermore!
125 For, borne on the night-wind of the Past,
Through all our history, to the last,
In the hour of darkness and peril[26] and need,
The people will waken and listen to hear
The hurrying hoof-beats of that steed,
130 And the midnight message of Paul Revere. ❖

---

24. **British Regulars.** Members of the British Army
25. **red-coats.** British soldiers, so named because their uniforms included red coats
26. **peril.** Danger

de•fi•ance (di fī´ ən[t]s) *n.*, act or thoughts of rebellion, challenge, or a willingness to fight

Do you think Paul Revere is a fitting subject for a poem? Why? Why did Paul Revere become a symbol of the American spirit?

Find Meaning

1. (a) Why does Revere's friend hang two lanterns in the belfry of North Church? (b) What does Revere do when he sees the lanterns?
2. What does the speaker mean when he says, "The fate of a nation was riding that night"?
3. As Revere rides on, how does the speaker show the passage of time?
4. What do Revere's actions imply about his character?

Make Judgments

5. (a) What is the overall mood of this poem? (b) What elements contribute to the mood?
6. (a) Reread the last six lines of the poem. Paraphrase these lines, using your own words. (b) In your opinion, what does the "midnight message of Paul Revere" symbolize?

PAUL REVERE'S RIDE **577**

Media Skills

Paul Revere in Art

Guide students in using library resources, history textbooks, and reliable Internet sources to find paintings of Paul Revere. There are many famous paintings such as those by artists A. L. Ripley and Grant Woods.

The following selection is an excerpt from a biography titled *Paul Revere and the World He Lived In* by **Esther Forbes** (1891–1967). Published in 1942, this biography of Paul Revere won the Pulitzer Prize for history. Forbes wrote many other highly acclaimed books. Perhaps her most famous was the award-winning *Johnny Tremain,* a fictional account of the American Revolution, told through the eyes of a young boy. It won the prestigious Newbery Medal for outstanding children's literature and was made into a Disney movie in 1957. As you read, note how the details and events compare to those in Longfellow's poem.

Teach the Connection

Analyze Literature
Setting Discuss the details that the author uses here to identify the setting as an April night in Boston and Charlestown. **Ⓐ**

Use Reading Skills
Compare and Contrast Discuss with students how this account of the beginning of Paul Revere's ride is similar to, and different from, the account provided in Longfellow's poem. Include in your discussion events, characters, and mood. Additionally, discuss what new dangers face Revere in this account. (There are already British troops patrolling the roads that he will take. He might be captured or killed.)

Use Reading Skills
Identify Cause and Effect Refer back to the Build Background material on page 571 in the pupil edition. Point out that Paul Revere and other Patriots depended on horseback as their only means of spreading word of the impending British attack. Use this information to ask students why it was important that Revere sense what he did about his horse. **Ⓑ**

from **Paul Revere and the World He Lived In** A Biography by Esther Forbes

Ⓐ All winter it had been abnormally warm and spring had come almost a month ahead of itself. Fruit trees were in blossom; the fields already ploughed. That night, however, was chill, and 'it was young flood, the ship was winding and the moon was rising,' as Paul Revere noticed. The muffled oars softly eased his little rowboat closer and closer to the Charlestown side. There had been neither hail nor shot from the *Somerset*. So he leaped to dry land close to the old Battery. Richardson and Bentley had done their work. Revere went on alone.

At Colonel Conant's he found a group waiting for him. Had they seen his signals? They had. He told them 'what was acting' and learned to his surprise that the roads towards Cambridge and on to Concord were already patrolled by British officers who had left Boston in the afternoon.

Richard Devens, of the Committee of Safety, said he had left Menotomy in his chaise[1] around sunset. And he had seen 'a great number of B.O. [British officers] and their servants on horseback.' As they were behaving in a suspiciously nonchalant manner and had asked where 'Clark's tavern was,' Devens had sent word to the Clark parsonage. It might be they were out to arrest the two rebel chiefs housed there. He knew this messenger might be picked up, as he was. Paul Revere himself might have better luck. He would need a good horse to slip through the cordon.[2] Probably he had as fine a mount as the luxurious town of Charlestown could produce. John Larkin was one of the wealthiest citizens. It was his best horse that was now turned over to Revere. Twenty-three years later, he gratefully remembered how good, how 'very good,' was **Ⓑ** this Larkin horse. It would be slender and nervous in the Yankee manner, small by modern standards, surefooted, tireless. Now for the remainder of the night Revere's success, perhaps his life and the lives of others, would depend upon this horse. He would adjust the stirrups carefully to his own length, test with a forefinger the

1. **chaise.** Horse-drawn vehicle
2. **cordon.** Line of troops

Words in Use

from *Paul Revere and the World He Lived In*

Selection Words
abnormally, 578
ploughed, 578
nonchalant, 578
parsonage, 578
surefooted, 578
stamina, 579

Common Core State Standards

Writing
W.10

Language
L.6

Differentiated Instruction

Reading Proficiency
Help struggling readers by reminding them that *Somerset* is the British ship mentioned in the poem and that the signals are the lanterns that are visible in Charlestown from the church steeple in Boston.

snugness of the girths. They must be tight, but not binding. The bit must hang exactly right. In that unhurried moment before mounting, he could measure the courage and stamina of his companion, catch the flash of white in the wild, soft eye, note the impatient stamp of the small hooves, feel under his hand the swelling of muscle along the neck, the strength in withers and loin, his touch and voice assuring the sensitive animal that he was his friend.

And now it was eleven o'clock. Only an hour before, he had stood in Joseph Warren's parlor knowing that the time had come. Then, by the bright cold moonlight everyone noticed that night, he swung to the saddle. Colonel Conant, Richard Devens, the light from the open door, were left behind. He eventually rode about twelve miles to get to Lexington and Concord was six miles farther on. Probably he would set a pace which he believed would last him through. With the hundreds of miles he had ridden the last few years, he would be able to judge well. Nor would he wish to fling himself headlong into any trap set for him by that advance guard of officers Devens had warned him of, with a jaded[3] mount. For such an emergency his horse must have an extra spurt of speed left in him. That he rode the Larkin horse with more care than he does on sugar boxes, American Legion posters, copper advertisements, and all known pictures and statues is proved by the excellent condition the animal was in five hours later.

So away, down the moonlit road, goes Paul Revere and the Larkin horse, galloping into history, art, editorials, folklore, poetry; the beat of those hooves never to be forgotten. The man, his bold, dark face bent, his hands light on the reins, his body giving to the flowing rhythm beneath him, becoming, as it were, something greater than himself—not merely one man riding one horse on a certain lonely night of long ago, but a symbol to which his countrymen can yet turn.

Paul Revere had started on a ride which, in a way, has never ended. ❖

---

3. jaded. Tired and unexcited due to repetition

C

TEXT ← TO → TEXT
CONNECTION

The poem and biography piece share the same topic. They are alike in other ways, too, but they are also different. Use a Venn diagram to compare and contrast the details and events that they present, as well as their moods and their uses of symbolism. Which selection did you enjoy more? Explain your choice.

Analyze Literature
Allegory Point out that Paul Revere has become such an American symbol that his image has been used on packaging for Revere Sugar and Revere Copper and on American Legion posters. Here, his ride becomes an **allegory,** a literary work in which the characters and events stand for ideas, qualities, or situations beyond themselves. The overall purpose of an allegory is to teach a moral lesson. Discuss the author's use of allegory and the moral lesson that she attempts to teach. **C**

Text-to-Text Connection
Answer: How they are alike: treatment of Revere as a hero; British ships in harbor. Elements of poem: Rhythm and rhyme; second-person point of view ("Listen, my children . . ."); hanging of the lanterns; specific mention of the towns and times at which he passes through. Elements of nonfiction piece: mentions other participants by name; includes scene at Colonel Conant's house and warning about British officers on the road; alludes to Adams and Hancock.

TEACHING NOTE

Research Project
Interested students might do research to find facts about Richardson, Bentley, and Colonel Conant—real-life figures who played a role in Paul Revere's midnight ride.

Writing Skills

Write a Description
Have students imagine that they are Paul Revere. It is two days before his historic ride, and he is writing a letter to John Larkin, asking for a horse to take him on his important ride. Based on details on this page, have them write the letter, describing exactly what characteristics the horse must have and why each characteristic is important.

Review the Selection

Analyze Literature
Narrative Poetry *Possible answer:*
Exposition: At midnight, April 18, 1775, British troops are advancing. Rising action: Revere instructs his friend in the lamp-lighting code, rows to shore, awaits the signal. Climax: The friend sees a ship in the distance and lights two lanterns in the church. Falling action: Revere gallops through villages warning townspeople of the coming invasion. Resolution: Revere becomes a legend.

Analyze Literature
Narrative Poetry A narrative poem is a verse that tells a story. Like a short story, a narrative poem has a plot with a conflict, climax, and resolution. The plot events rise to the climax and then fall to the resolution. Use a plot diagram to show the rising action, climax, falling action, and resolution of "Paul Revere's Ride."

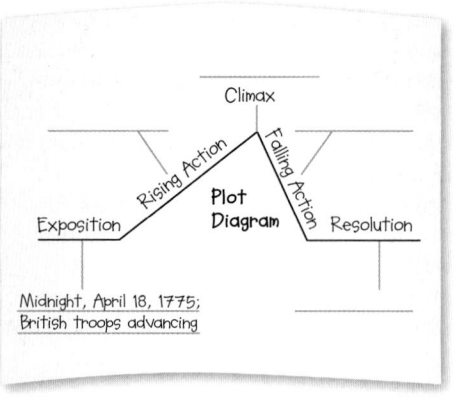

Extend Understanding

Writing Options
Creative Writing Using facts and details in this poem, write a **short story** about the historic ride of Paul Revere. Invent vivid details and dialogue to develop the character of Paul Revere, to show what motivates him, and to create an overall mood of suspense. Structure your story so that it has a clear beginning, middle, and end. Have the action rise toward a climax and then fall toward the resolution.

Expository Writing Write a brief **literary response** in which you analyze Longfellow's main purpose or purposes for writing this poem. Possible purposes include to entertain, to inform, to describe, to reflect, and to persuade. In your thesis statement, state what you believe to be Longfellow's purpose or purposes. Identify specific details in the poem that you used as clues to support your analysis.

Collaborative Learning
Analyze Rhyme Scheme Work with a small group to select the stanza of this poem that you consider the most interesting or exciting. Then work together to identify the stanza's rhyme scheme. Use letters such as *abc* to note the rhyme scheme, using a new letter for each new rhyme. Present your findings to the class.

Critical Literacy
Present a Poetry Reading This poem has a dramatic rhythm. Practice reading it aloud, taking turns with a partner. Give each other constructive feedback about delivery, pacing, and inflection. Once you feel comfortable reciting the poem aloud, present your dramatic reading to the class.

Go to **www.mirrorsandwindows.com** for more.

Rubrics for Writing Options
You can adapt this as a checklist for students to use as they write.

Creative Writing
☐ Does the story contain details and events appearing in the poem?
☐ Does it use actions, descriptions, and dialogue effectively to develop the character of Revere and to show what motivates him?
☐ Does it have a clear beginning, middle, and end, with action that rises toward a climax and then falls to the resolution?
☐ Do its elements work together to create suspense?

Expository Writing
☐ Does the response make a logical statement regarding Longfellow's main purpose or purposes for writing the poem?
☐ Does it support this analysis effectively, citing specific details from the poem?

Vocabulary & Spelling

Context Clues

And the measured tread of the grenadiers,

Marching down to their boats on the shore.

— HENRY WADSWORTH LONGFELLOW, "Paul Revere's Ride"

Context clues are words, phrases, or sentences that can help readers determine the meaning of an unfamiliar word. Combine context clues with what you already know to determine a word's meaning. For example, in the above quote, you can infer from the words *measured, tread,* and *marching* that *grenadiers* are some type of soldier.

Several types of context clues may help you understand the meaning of underlined words:

Comparisons: similarities between things

> EXAMPLE
>
> *"A phantom ship, with each <u>mast</u> and <u>spar</u> Across the moon <u>like a prison bar</u>,"*

Contrasts: differences between things

> EXAMPLE
>
> *"A cry of <u>defiance</u>, and <u>not of fear</u>,"*

Definitions: brief explanations of words

> EXAMPLE
>
> *"The Somerset, British <u>man-of-war</u>; A phantom <u>ship</u>."*

Descriptions: describing details or qualities

> EXAMPLE
>
> *"the secret <u>dread</u> Of the <u>lonely</u> belfry and the <u>dead</u>;"*

Examples: related terms or illustrations

> EXAMPLE
>
> *"Hang a <u>lantern</u> aloft in the belfry arch Of the North Church tower as a <u>signal light</u>,"*

Restatement: a synonym or related term

> EXAMPLE
>
> *"with <u>muffled</u> oar <u>Silently</u> rowed to the Charlestown shore,"*

Vocabulary Practice

For each of the following lines, use context clues to define the italicized word. Then describe the type of context clue you used to figure out the meaning.

1. Held by its *moorings*, the ship swung back and forth.
2. The *belfry*, or bell tower, was reached by a ladder.
3. *Weathercocks*, such as the one atop the barn, turn with the wind.
4. Their faces were *somber*, like mourners at a funeral.
5. The churchyard was *spectral*, ghostlike.
6. The *encampment* in a field was inhospitable compared to the grenadiers' lodging.

Teach the Workshop

Vocabulary Practice

1. *Moorings* are ropes that tie a ship to a dock or anchor. The context clue is description.
2. A *belfry* is a bell tower. The context clue is definition.
3. A *weathercock* is a weathervane that looks like a rooster. The context clue is example.
4. *Somber* means serious. The context clue is comparison.
5. *Spectral* means ghostlike. The context clue is restatement.
6. *Encampment* means a temporary campsite. The context clue is contrast.

> ▶ For more information, see Vocabulary & Spelling Section 2.1, Using Context Clues, in the Language Arts Handbook.

Build Skills

Point out to students that restatement clues are sometimes signaled by such words and phrases as *or, that is, in other words,* or *in short.*
Examples:
This dinosaur was a herbivore, or plant-eater.
They worried if the water was potable, in other words, fit to drink.

Program Resources

You will find additional lessons on Context Clues in the *Exceeding the Standards: Vocabulary & Spelling* resource.

KEY TERMS
CONTEXT CLUE, 581
COMPARISON, 581
CONTRAST, 581
DEFINITION, 581
DESCRIPTION, 581
EXAMPLE, 581
RESTATEMENT, 581
SYNONYM, 581

Common Core State Standards

Language
L.4

Preview the Selection

At a Glance
Directed Reading
- Reading Level: Easy
- Difficulty Considerations: None
- Ease Factor: Vocabulary

Objectives
Studying this lesson will enable students to
- use reading strategies such as drawing conclusions
- define *free verse* and analyze Amy Ling's blending of the elements of free verse and traditional lyric poetry
- describe the work of Amy Ling and James Mitsui, and compare and contrast the characters and themes of their poems

Launch the Lesson
Have students picture themselves meeting someone whom they had heard about for most of their lives. Now, at the moment they meet, they understand that they can't communicate with words. How would they demonstrate their thoughts and feelings? Have them read "Grandma Ling," a lyric poem about one person's experience with this situation.

Summary
The speaker describes going to Taiwan to meet her grandmother. She notes that they look alike. The two embrace, and while the speaker is unable to understand the language, she is able to hug the older woman.

DIRECTED READING

BEFORE READING

Build Background
Literary Context A lyric poem is a short poem that expresses the emotions of the speaker. You might notice the word *lyric* is also used to refer to the words of a song. Long ago, lyric poems were written to accompany music played on an instrument called a lyre.

Reader's Context What might it be like to meet a family member you had only heard about before? Describe the feelings you might have.

Set Purpose
Based on the title and the first stanza, make a prediction about the feeling that will be described in the poem. During reading, revise your prediction.

Analyze Literature
Free Verse Poetry that does not use regular rhyme, rhythm, or division into stanzas is known as **free verse.** Free verse also sometimes uses techniques such as unconventional spelling, punctuation, or capitalization to create effects. As you read "Grandma Ling," notice which poetic techniques Amy Ling uses, and ask yourself why she might have made these choices.

Meet the Author
Amy Ling (1939–1999) was born in China and moved to the United States with her mother and little brother as a young girl. During college, the literature Ling studied shared little with her own immigrant experience. During the Civil Rights movement of the 1960s and the women's movement of the 1970s, Ling became a pioneer of multiculturalism.

Use Reading Skills
Draw Conclusions
By paying close attention to what you read, you will be able to draw conclusions about what the writer is trying to communicate. Drawing conclusions means putting together the clues given in the text to determine what they mean. As you read "Grandma Ling," use the chart below to note details in the text and the conclusions you draw from them.

> Detail: "If you dig that hole deep enough, / you'll reach China, they used to tell me, / a child in a backyard in Pennsylvania."

> Detail:

> My Conclusions:

Words in Use

Teaching Words
lyre, 582
unconventional, 582
Civil Rights movement, 582
women's movement, 582
multiculturalism, 582
uniting, 585
immigrant, 585
paternal, 586
emigration, 586

KEY TERMS
LYRIC POEM, 582
STANZA, 582
FREE VERSE, 582
PUNCTUATION, 582
CAPITALIZATION, 582
CLUSTER CHART, 586

Common Core State Standards

Reading Literature
RL.1

Writing
W.9

Language
L.6

Grandma Ling

A
Lyric
Poem
by
Amy
Ling

583

The Mirrors & Windows questions at the end of this selection focus on the theme of communication. Before reading the poem, ask students to describe experiences with language barriers. What are some ways in which people communicate without words?

History Connection

When the California Gold Rush began in 1848, people from all over the world emigrated to California, seeking jobs and wealth. Among them were many Chinese laborers, willing to work for low wages. Conflicts arose with American workers, who saw their jobs at risk. To respond to growing pressures from these workers, Congress passed the Chinese Exclusion Act in 1882. Essentially, it banned Chinese laborers from entering the country for ten years. It was renewed in 1892 as the Geary Act but then was finally repealed in 1943, when the United States deemed China a very useful ally in its war against Japan. Suddenly, the doors were open again for Chinese people willing to work hard for the success offered by the "American dream." Like Amy Ling's father, many Chinese men emigrated, found jobs and housing, and then sent for their wives and children to join them.

Program Resources

Planning and Assessment
Program Planning Guide, Selection Lesson Plan
E-Lesson Planner
Assessment Guide, Lesson Test
ExamView

Technology Tools
Interactive Student Text on CD
Visual Teaching Package
Audio Library
mirrorsandwindows.com

Meeting the Standards
Poetry: Unit 6, Directed Reading, pp. 60–65

She spoke a tongue I knew no word of...

Answer: Students should describe situations in detail. Students might say people communicate through their facial expressions, actions, body language, tone of voice, and more.

If you dig that hole deep enough,
you'll reach China, they used to tell me,
a child in a backyard in Pennsylvania.
Not strong enough to dig that hole,
5   I waited twenty years,
then sailed back, half way around the world.

In Taiwan I first met Grandma.
Before she came to view, I heard
her slippered feet softly measure
10   the tatami[1] floor with even step;
the aqua paper-covered door slid open
and there I faced
my five foot height, sturdy legs and feet,
square forehead, high cheeks and wide-set eyes;
15   my image stood before me,
acted on by fifty years.

She smiled, stretched her arms
to take to heart the eldest daughter
of her youngest son a quarter century away.
20   She spoke a tongue I knew no word of,
and I was sad I could not understand,
but I could hug her. ❖

---

1. tatami. Straw floor covering in some Asian homes

Have you ever been in a situation where language failed you? How can people communicate without using words?

Find Meaning

1. Where does the speaker live?
2. Where did the speaker sail to?
3. What do Grandma Ling and the speaker do at the end of the poem?

Make Judgments

4. (a) Describe Grandma Ling's physical appearance. (b) Why do you think Ling included this information in the poem?
5. (a) In the last stanza, what is meant by "a quarter century away"? (b) Why do you think Ling used this phrase?

584   UNIT 6 POETRY

Find Meaning

1. The speaker lives in Pennsylvania.
2. The speaker sailed to Taiwan, a part of China.
3. They hug.

Make Judgments

4. (a) She is an Asian woman in her seventies, five feet tall with sturdy legs and feet, a square forehead, high cheeks, and wide-set eyes. (b) Students might note the impact of meeting someone who looks very much like you.
5. (a) Grandma Ling's youngest son, the speaker's father, has been in America about twenty-five years. (b) Students might say the word *century* adds to the emotional impact by making the separation seem much larger than mere geography.

Differentiated Instruction

Enrichment

Students might enjoy researching typical housing of the Taiwanese, including such features as tatami floors and paper-covered doors. Have them use their findings to explain how the grandmother's house was different from that of the speaker, who might have lived in a traditional American home in Pennsylvania.

In "Grandma Ling," Amy Ling evokes the feelings of finally uniting with a family member who lives far away. In "My Mother Juggling Bean Bags," by **James Mitsui** (b. 1940), the family relationship is a closer one. Mitsui is a Japanese American born to immigrant parents, a theme that often inspires his work. As you read, compare and contrast themes in "Grandma Ling" and "My Mother Juggling Bean Bags."

My Mother Juggling Bean Bags

A Lyric Poem by James Mitsui

At 71, my mother juggled three,
even four bean bags
while shouting *"yeeaaat"*[1]

and *"yoi-cho"*[2] between her gold
5 front teeth. My children
stooped to pick up

her mistakes. They watched,
mouths shaped like little *o's*,
as "Little Grandma"

10 laughed in a language
anyone could understand.
On visitation weekends

we visited her low-income apartment
and shared 7-UP, too many
15 British jelly cookies

and potato chips.
Now, over twenty years later,
I value my mother's humor.

As a child I had one-present
20 Christmases, but there was always
roast turkey on holidays,

jeans with no holes, and a first-base
glove from Montgomery Ward[3]
that they really couldn't afford.

25 I remember the night when two girls
from the Class of '59
had driven ten miles from Odessa

just to show my mother how to
short-sheet my bed. I can still hear
30 her laughter in the dark.

I can also remember my mother
chasing me with a stick of firewood
around the trash burner[4] in the parlor,

using my father's railroad swear words.
35 She always managed not
to catch me. Now I warn my children—

when I turn 71, I may turn from poetry
to juggling oranges. I owe it to my mother;
I owe it to my six grandchildren. ❖

---

1. **yeeaaat.** Enthusiastic expression like "Yes!" or "All right!" in Japanese
2. **yoi-cho.** Expression of exerting effort—something like "one, two, three" in Japanese
3. **Montgomery Ward.** American catalog and mail order sales company
4. **trash burner.** Heating and cooking unit that resembles a small wood burning stove

MY MOTHER JUGGLING BEAN BAGS **585**

Teach the Connection

Analyze Literature
Character Work with students to use details from this portion of the poem to describe the speaker's mother. Have them include words that describe her physical appearance, her personality, and her values as a parent and grandparent. Be sure to highlight the fact that the speaker always received a special Christmas gift, even though his mother and father could not really afford it.

Analyze Literature
Imagery Ask students why the speaker chose to describe the children's mouths as "shaped like little *o's*." (They are surprised by the actions of their grandmother.) **Ⓐ**

Use Reading Skills
Draw Conclusions Point out to students that both grandmothers, in the first and second poems, do not speak the language of the visiting grandchildren. Then ask students what the speaker means by "Grandma Little laughed in a language anyone could understand." (Even without words or explanation, anyone could understand her happiness and enthusiasm.) **Ⓑ**

Reading Skills

Identify Text Organization
Point out that at the beginning of the poem, the speaker talks about events that happened when his mother was seventy-one years old. Then the time shifts to the present, twenty years later. Have them use time lines or other graphic organizers to clarify the time scheme. Continue the use of the graphic organizer on the next page, when the speaker once again shifts the time to the past, with the girls from his class.

Grammar Skills

Compound Adjectives
Draw attention to the phrase *one-present Christmases.* Explain that *one-present* is a compound adjective, a modifier formed by combining two words. By understanding the meanings of each word, readers can understand the meaning of the compound adjective *(receiving only one present for Christmas)*. Point out that while some compound adjectives contain hyphens, many do not, such as *worldwide* and *halfhearted*).

Common Core State Standards
Language
L.6

Text-to-Text Connection

Answer: The subject matter of "Grandma Ling" is a grandmother/ granddaughter relationship. The subject matter of "My Mother Juggling Bean Bags" is a mother/son relationship. Some students may notice that Ling puts end stops at the ends of lines, while Mitsui puts end stops mid-line. Ling's stanzas begin with capital letters, while Mitsui's do not, but both writers use conventional sentences.

Analyze Literature

Free Verse *Answer:* Cluster charts should include details from Ling's poem, including images, ideas, and sounds. Students may say that free verse sounds modern or like spoken language.

TEXT ← TO → TEXT CONNECTION

Both Ling and Mitsui have written free verse poems about family relationships. Compare and contrast the relationships described in these poems and the techniques employed by each poet. What relationships are the subject matter of each poem? What is similar and different about how each writer uses lines, sentences, and stanzas?

AFTER READING

Analyze Literature

Free Verse Use the cluster chart to analyze the free verse poem "Grandma Ling." Write *Grandma Ling* in the center circle. In the outer circles, list details from the poem that contribute to the main idea. You can note images, ideas, and sounds the poet uses, and anything that helps you understand the poem.

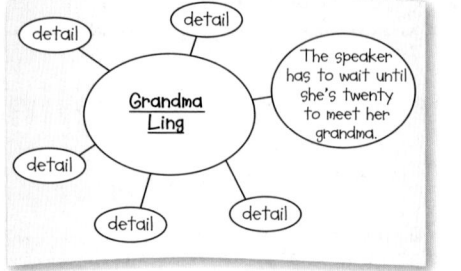

Extend Understanding

Writing Options

Creative Writing In "My Mother Juggling Bean Bags," James Mitsui writes about a talent his mother has that he would like to take up. Write a **personal letter** to an older person or grandparent in your life. Ask about one thing you would like to learn from him or her. Use a proper format for a personal letter. In the letter, explain why it is that you want to learn this particular thing.

Applied Writing In "Grandma Ling," Amy Ling lists physical traits she inherited from her paternal grandma. We inherit more than physical traits from our families, however. Create a **list** of traits or values you would like to pass on to your grandchildren or other younger people in your life. Write the list to be read to your imagined grandchildren or other young people.

Lifelong Learning

Research Taiwan Use the Internet to learn more about Taiwan. Present your findings to the class. Use visual aids, such as maps, time lines, or other graphic organizers. For example, you could create a graphic organizer to show emigration patterns from Taiwan or research Taiwanese architecture and do a photo presentation.

Critical Literacy

Interview a Classmate Both of these lyric poems portray a grandmother with certain unique characteristics. Working with a partner, ask each other questions that focus on unusual habits, mannerisms, and so on. Take interview notes and use this information to write a free verse poem that reveals your partner's distinct personality.

Go to **www.mirrorsandwindows.com** for more.

586 UNIT 6 POETRY

Rubrics for Writing Options

You can adapt this as a checklist for students to use as they write.

Creative Writing

☐ Does the letter address an older person or relative?

☐ Does it ask one thing the student would like to learn from the older person and explain why?

☐ Does it follow the standard form?

Applied Writing

☐ Is the writing in the form of a list?

☐ Does it show consideration of traits and values that the student feels are worth passing along?

☐ Is the writing appropriate for a younger audience?

EXILE

A Lyric Poem by Judith Ortiz Cofer

At a Glance
Directed Reading
- Reading Level: Moderate
- Difficulty Consideration: Figurative language
- Ease Factor: Syntax

BEFORE READING

Build Background
Cultural Context The speaker of the poem has left her home to move to a new land, which becomes a life-changing experience. Such experiences, occurring at periods of transition, are often called "rites of passage." The narrator moves from her old, familiar life to something new and unfamiliar.

Reader's Context Have you had any experience in your life where you needed to become part of a new and different group? How did you do this? What did you learn from the experience?

Set Purpose
Note the use of sensory details and other description to better appreciate and enjoy the poet's style and the speaker's message. Read to find out how the speaker felt about leaving her home and coming to a strange new place.

Analyze Literature
Simile A **simile** is a comparison using *like* or *as*. The two things being compared are unlike but have some feature or characteristic in common. *You are as beautiful as a rose* and *He is sly like a fox* are similes. Poets often use similes to create images that the reader can relate to. As you read "Exile," identify the similes. Think about how the similes affect your understanding and enjoyment of the poem.

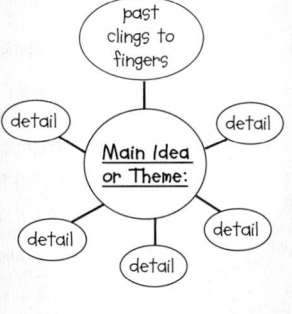

Meet the Author
Judith Ortiz Cofer was born in 1952 in Puerto Rico. She immigrated to the United States with her family when she was about two years old. She grew up in a bilingual, bicultural community in Paterson, New Jersey. Her father was in the Navy, and her mother did not speak much English. Cofer began telling stories at an early age, following in the oral tradition of the women of her family. Much of her work reflects her bilingual, bicultural heritage.

Use Reading Skills
Identify the Main Idea
The main idea is the most important message or idea in a selection. In fiction, the main idea is also referred to as the theme. In some selections, the main idea is stated explicitly. Most often, the main idea is not directly stated, so the reader must use details to identify it. As you read "Exile," use a main idea map to keep track of important details. Then use the details to determine the main idea of the poem.

Diagram: past clings to fingers — detail, detail, detail, detail, detail — Main Idea or Theme:

Objectives
Studying this lesson will enable students to
- use reading strategies such as identifying main idea
- define *simile*, recognize examples in context, and understand this literary device's impact on descriptions
- describe the literary accomplishments of Judith Ortiz Cofer
- appreciate a poem about looking back on a homeland left behind

Launch the Lesson
Ask students what part visual images of favorite places or experiences play in their memories. Model by sharing a "snapshot" you have in your mind related to a happy memory. Then have them read to find out what "snapshots" exist in the speaker's memory.

 **MIRRORS & WINDOWS** The Mirrors & Windows questions at the end of this selection focus on the theme of exile. Before reading the poem, ask students why people may maintain ties with their places of origin?

EXILE **587**

Words in Use

Selection Words
clings, 588
leisurely, 588
inhabiting, 588

Teaching Words
immigrated, 587
bilingual, 587
bicultural, 587
heritage, 587
explicitly, 587
voluntary, 589
atmosphere, 589
incorporate, 589
topography, 589

KEY TERMS
LYRIC POEM, 587
SENSORY DETAIL, 587
SIMILE, 587
MAIN IDEA, 587
THEME, 587
SPEAKER, 589
MOOD, 589
IMAGERY, 589

Common Core State Standards
Reading Literature
RL.1, RL.4
Writing
W.9
Speaking and Listening
SL.1
Language
L.6

Summary

The speaker uses similes to describe her desire to return to the past or visit the places of her youth, knowing that "nothing remains of that world."

History Connection

Although Judith Ortiz Cofer immigrated to the United States at the age of two, her mother took the family back to Puerto Rico whenever Cofer's father was on overseas naval missions. Cofer's birthplace, Hormigueros, was settled by the Spanish in the sixteenth century. Puerto Rico remained under Spanish rule until 1898, when Spain ceded it to the United States at the end of the Spanish-American War. A 1917 law made all Puerto Ricans U.S. citizens. In 1950, the island was named the Commonwealth of Puerto Rico, and in 1952 it officially adopted its current flag.

Answer: Some students might see it as an exciting opportunity; others may see it as devastating. They may want to remember special places, friends, and family members. They may be willing to work hard or give up things in order to return.

E-XILE

A Lyric Poem by Judith Ortiz Cofer

I left my home behind me
but my past clings to my fingers
so that every word I write hears
the mark like a cancelled postage stamp
5 of my birthplace.
There was no angel to warn me
of the dangers of looking back.
Like Lot's wife, I would trade
my living blood for one last look[1]
10 at the house where each window held
a face framed as in a family album.
And the plaza[2] lined with palms
where my friends and I strolled in our pink
and yellow and white Sunday dresses, dreaming
15 of husbands, houses, and orchards where
our children would play in the leisurely summer
of our future. Gladly would I spill
my remaining years like salt[3] upon the ground,
to gaze again on the fishermen of the bay
20 dragging their catch in nets glittering
like pirate gold, to the shore.
Nothing remains of that world, I hear,
but the skeletons of houses, all colors
bled from the fabric of those
25 who stayed behind
inhabiting the dead cities
like the shadows of Hiroshima.[4] ❖

---

1. **no angel to warn me...Lot's wife...one last look.** Reference to the biblical story in which Lot's wife is turned into a pillar of salt. She disobeyed an angel's orders not to look back while running away from the cities of Sodom and Gomorrah. These cities were destroyed because of the wicked ways of the inhabitants.
2. **plaza.** Open square or marketplace, often found in Spanish-speaking countries
3. **spill my remaining years like salt.** Refers to the superstition that spilling salt brings bad luck, which reflects the old belief that salt is sacred
4. **Hiroshima.** Japanese city destroyed on August 6, 1945, by an atomic bomb dropped by U.S. forces

MIRRORS & WINDOWS
If you had to leave your home behind, how would you feel? Why do you think people stay so attached to the place they are from, even when they no longer live there?

588

Program Resources

Planning and Assessment
Program Planning Guide, Selection Lesson Plan
E-Lesson Planner
Assessment Guide, Lesson Test
ExamView

Technology Tools
Interactive Student Text on CD
Visual Teaching Package
Audio Library
mirrorsandwindows.com

Meeting the Standards
Poetry: Unit 6, Directed Reading, pp. 66–71

Find Meaning

1. (a) What does the speaker say clings to her fingers? (b) What does the speaker see in the windows when she looks back?

2. What place does the speaker describe where she used to go with her friends?

3. What remains of the place where the speaker first lived?

Analyze Literature

Simile In a simile, the author compares two unlike things using the word *like* or *as*. Authors often use similes to make a reader think differently about each thing being compared. In a simile chart, list the similes in "Exile." Write your interpretation of each simile. Then with a small group, discuss how the similes influenced your response to the poem.

Simile	Interpretation
"like a cancelled postage stamp"	Something no longer useful

Make Judgments

4. (a) What is the attitude of the speaker about her move? (b) What does the title of the poem tell you about her attitude? (c) What is your opinion of her attitude?

5. (a) How would you describe the speaker's experience of her move? (b) Was the move voluntary or forced? (c) What overall mood or atmosphere does her description of this experience create?

Extend Understanding

Writing Options

Creative Writing Reread the poem "Exile." Imagine that you are the speaker. You have left your home behind, with no hope of returning. Create new **similes** for the things that Cofer describes. You may want to start by referring to the simile chart that you already created. For example, the narrator refers to Lot's wife in one simile. Is there another real person or a character from literature to whom you could compare the speaker?

Expository Writing In a short **literary response**, describe the main idea of "Exile." Present your opinion of the main idea in your thesis, and include evidence from the poem as support. Refer to your main idea map to help you. Explain how each detail relates to the main idea. Share your response with a classmate and incorporate his or her feedback.

Collaborative Learning

Hold a Discussion With a partner, discuss the use of imagery and sensory details in the poem. First, make a list of the images and the sensory details from the poem. Then, look at each detail individually and discuss how it adds to your understanding and enjoyment of the poem.

Lifelong Learning

Conduct Research Cofer immigrated to the United States from Puerto Rico. Using the Internet, an encyclopedia, or another resource, research the geography of Puerto Rico. Write a brief description of the island's topography. Include descriptions of the natural features such as mountains and rivers. You may want to include photographs or your own illustrations as well. Share your research with a group.

Go to www.mirrorsandwindows.com for more.

EXILE **589**

Find Meaning

1. (a) She says that her past clings to her fingers. (b) She sees the faces of her family members.

2. She describes the plaza lined with palm trees.

3. The skeletons of houses remain.

Make Judgments

4. (a) She seems to be very unhappy. (b) The title suggests that the move was a kind of forced punishment or banishment. (c) Students may agree that she has reasons to be unhappy, or they may say that she should give her new home a chance.

5. (a) This was a rather traumatic move. (b) She probably did not know that she was going to move. (c) It created a mood of anger and sadness.

Analyze Literature
Simile *Answer:*

Simile	Interpretation
like a cancelled postage stamp	something no longer useful
like Lot's wife	a tragic figure in a Bible story
as in a family album	faces in the windows that looked like photos in an album
like salt upon the ground	a sacrifice of something valuable
glittering like pirate gold	shiny, golden fish
like the shadows of Hiroshima	the charred remains of Hiroshima

Rubrics for Writing Options
You can adapt this as a checklist for students to use as they write.

Creative Writing
☐ Did the writer adopt the persona of the speaker?
☐ Does each simile contain *like* or *as*?
☐ Does each simile compare two dissimilar things that have a common characteristic?
☐ Are the similes effective?

Expository Writing
☐ Does the thesis statement clearly state the main idea of the poem?
☐ Is the thesis statement effectively supported by details from the poem?
☐ Does the essay explain how each detail relates to the main idea?

For further instruction, refer students to the following extension activity: Collaborative Learning: Hold a Discussion, *Exceeding the Standards: Extension Activities*, p. 20.

EXILE **589**

At a Glance
Directed Reading
"Birdfoot's Grampa"
- Reading Level: Easy
- Difficulty Considerations: None
- Ease Factors: Length, language

"The Time We Climbed Snake Mountain"
- Reading Level: Easy
- Difficulty Considerations: None
- Ease Factor: Length

Objectives
Studying this lesson will enable students to
- compare two poems with similar topics and themes
- use reading strategies such as comparing and contrasting
- define *symbolism*, analyze examples in context, and learn how symbolism can deepen the meaning of a piece of literature
- enjoy two poems about respect for, and preservation of, wild creatures and their habitats

Launch the Lesson
Tell students these poems are about encounters with animals. Have students share any "close encounters" they have had with wild animals while involved in outdoor activities.

Summary
The speaker describes a man who stops his car repeatedly to help toads that have wandered into the road. While the speaker protests, the man just smiles and explains that small creatures "have places to go to too."

Common Core State Standards
Reading Literature
RL.1, RL.4
Language
L.6

DIRECTED READING

Comparing Literature

Birdfoot's Grampa
A Narrative Poem by Joseph Bruchac

The Time We Climbed Snake Mountain
A Lyric Poem by Leslie Marmon Silko

BEFORE READING

Build Background
Cultural Context The poems "Birdfoot's Grampa" and "The Time We Climbed Snake Mountain" both deal with respect for animals and the coming together of two worlds. The authors of those poems, Joseph Bruchac and Leslie Marmon Silko, are of Native American descent. Many Native American cultures hold great regard for the natural world and believe in a respectful relationship with both the land and its creatures.

Reader's Context Have you ever encountered animals in their natural habitat? What was your experience?

Set Purpose
To preview the poems, examine the titles and the illustrations. What do you think the poems will be about?

Compare Literature: Symbolism
A **symbol** is a thing that stands for or represents both itself and something else. Some traditional symbols include doves for peace, roads or paths for journeys through life, and owls for wisdom. As you read the two poems, think about what the images and actions might represent. How might the symbolism add to the meanings of the poems?

Meet the Authors

Joseph Bruchac, born in 1942, is an Abenaki poet and writer who often draws on his heritage in developing his stories and poems. Bruchac grew up in the foothills of the Adirondack Mountains in New York. As a young adult, he began to seek out Native American stories, which he has retold in story collections. He has also written novels and a poetry collection.

Leslie Marmon Silko was born in 1948 in Albuquerque, New Mexico. She is of Laguna Pueblo, Mexican, and European descent. She grew up on a Laguna Pueblo reservation where she attended an Indian School. She later graduated from the University of New Mexico. Silko writes fiction, nonfiction, and poetry. Her work often draws on her Native American heritage and the issues that surround being a Native American in the United States.

590   UNIT 6 POETRY

Words in Use

Teaching Words
encountered, 590
habitat, 590
heritage, 590
represents, 590
traditional, 590
ensure, 592
visualize, 593

KEY TERMS

Birdfoot's Grampa

A Narrative Poem by Joseph Bruchac

The old man
must have stopped our car
two dozen times to climb out
and gather into his hands
5 the small toads blinded
by our lights and leaping,
live drops of rain.

The rain was falling,
a mist about his white hair
10 and I kept saying
you can't save them all,
accept it, get back in
we've got places to go.

But, leathery hands full
15 of wet brown life,
knee deep in the summer
roadside grass,
he just smiled and said
they have places to go to
20 *too.* ❖

Would you have acted the same way the grandfather does in the poem? Why might it be important to protect other forms of life, such as animals?

Find Meaning

1. (a) What does the Old Man in the poem do? (b) Why does he do this?
2. (a) How does the speaker of the poem respond to what the Old Man is doing? (b) Why might he respond that way?

Make Judgments

3. What do the Old Man's actions and words reveal about his character?
4. What do the images add to the poem's meaning?

591

Teach the Selection

Analyze Literature

Symbolism Ask students what larger concepts the car and the toads might symbolize (technology or human interference; wildlife, nature).

 The Mirrors & Windows questions at the end of this selection focus on the theme of wildlife conservation. Before reading the story, ask students if they feel it is important to protect all animals or certain ones over others. *Answer:* Responses should be supported by details from the poem. Students might say that protecting other forms of life ensures our own safety, health, and environment.

Find Meaning

1. (a) He takes toads off the road. (b) He wants to help them travel.
2. (a) He tells him that it's impossible to save them all and that they have places to get to. (b) He feels that his destination is more important than saving the toads.

Make Judgments

3. He is a deeply caring person who values nature's creatures' well-being as much as his own.
4. Some students may say that the mist around his white hair makes them see the old man as an angel. Students may say that the old man represents a guardian angel of nature.

Program Resources

Planning and Assessment
Program Planning Guide, Selection Lesson Plan
E-Lesson Planner
Assessment Guide, Lesson Test
ExamView

Technology Tools
Interactive Student Text on CD
Visual Teaching Package
Audio Library
mirrorsandwindows.com

Meeting the Standards
Poetry: Unit 6, Comparing Literature, pp. 72–80

Differentiating Instruction
English Language Learners, Compare and Contrast, pp. 157–162

Teach the Selection

Summary
The speaker sees a spotted yellow snake while climbing a mountain. She warns her companions not to step on him as this is his home and the climbers are visitors.

The Mirrors & Windows questions at the end of this selection focus on the theme of respect for wildlife. Before reading the poem, ask students if they are aware of and troubled by the state of an animal or its habitat in the world. Are we doing enough to protect our wildlife? *Answer:* Students may say that most people are not particularly concerned. Others may say that there are many people working to protect animals in reserves, national parks, zoos, etc. They may suggest actions like limiting building and access in wilderness areas, passing protective laws, and raising awareness.

Use Reading Skills
Compare and Contrast Ask students how the speaker in this poem is similar to the old man in the first poem.

The Time We Climbed Snake Mountain

A Lyric Poem by Leslie Marmon Silko

Seeing good places
    for my hands
I grab the warm parts of the cliff
    and I feel the mountain as I climb.
5 Somewhere   around here
    yellow spotted snake is sleeping   on his rock
    in the sun.
So
    please, I tell them
10   watch out,
    don't step on the spotted yellow snake
      he lives here.
The mountain is his. ❖

Are you concerned about animals and their habitats? What is being done to protect animals in the wild? What else might be done to ensure their survival?

Differentiated Instruction

Enrichment
Encourage students to research such national organizations as the World Wildlife Federation and the Nature Conservancy to find out how people might help in the preservation and protection of wildlife and their habitats. Additionally, steer them toward any local wildlife preservation and educational groups that might inspire them and help them to get involved.

Reading Proficiency
Each of these poems contains enjambments—long sentences that continue on many lines. Each of the three stanzas in "Birdfoot's Grampa" is a single sentence, and "The Time We Climbed Snake Mountain" contains four sentences. Help struggling readers to follow the sentences through, from beginning to end, in order to gain better comprehension.

Common Core State Standards

Reading Literature
RL.1, RL.4, RL.5
Writing
W.9
Language
L.6

AFTER READING

Find Meaning

1. (a) What is the speaker of the poem doing? (b) When you visualize the first four lines of the poem, what do you see? (c) What is the effect of this image?

2. (a) How do you know that the speaker is not alone, even before you read the poem? (b) What does the speaker tell the other climbers?

Compare Literature

Symbolism Both "Birdfoot's Grampa" and "The Time We Climbed Snake Mountain" describe specific events. At the same time, the events, the people, and the objects in the poem represent something other than themselves. This symbolism gives the poems larger meanings. To analyze the symbolism in these poems, create a three-column chart like the one on the right for each of the poems. Use your chart to answer the following questions.

1. What are the themes of the poems?

2. How are the symbols in the two poems related?

Make Judgments

3. (a) How would you describe the form of this poem? (b) What is the effect of the writer's use of line length in this poem? Use an example from the text to support your answer.

4. How would you describe the speaker's attitude toward the natural world?

5. What do you think the speaker means by the last line in the poem, "The mountain is his"?

"Birdfoot's Grampa"

Symbol	Details	What It Suggests
car	gives out a blinding light	It suggests the danger of human technologies on the natural world.

"The Time We Climbed Snake Mountain"

Symbol	Details	What It Suggests
mountain	has "warm parts"	The mountain is a living place.

Extend Understanding

Writing Options

Creative Writing Choose one of the poems you just read and decide what its theme is. Then turn the poem into a **fable** that uses that same theme. A fable is a brief story that frequently includes a lesson. Share your fable with the class.

Persuasive Writing Write a short **persuasive essay** in which you try to convince others to treat animals with respect. Decide who your audience is and why they need to be convinced. In your introduction, include a thesis statement that makes your position clear.

Collaborative Learning

Have a Small-Group Discussion In small groups, compare and contrast the two poems. How are they similar? How are they different? Consider each poem's form, imagery, tone, figurative language, and sensory descriptions.

Critical Literacy

Debate Hold a group debate about the importance of environmental protection in your community. Do research, using the library and the Internet, to gather facts about current environmental practices or issues.

 Go to **www.mirrorsandwindows.com** for more.

Find Meaning

1. (a) The speaker is climbing up a cliff. (b) The speaker is using his/her hands and feet to feel his/her way up the mountain. The cliff is described as having warm parts, which suggests that it is in the sun. (c) It gives a feeling of harmony between man and nature.

2. (a) The word *we* is in the title. (b) The speaker warns them to watch for, and not step on, the snake.

Make Judgments

3. (a) Some of the lines are shorter than others, and some contain just a few words. (b) This structure calls attention to and gives extra weight to what the speaker is saying.

4. The speaker is respectful of it.

5. The speaker is saying that the mountain does not belong to the people; it belongs to the creatures that live there.

Compare Literature

Symbolism

1. The theme of "Bird Foot's Grampa" is that human technology, carelessness, and self-importance endanger wildlife. The theme of "The Time We Climbed Snake Mountain" also draws attention to the fact that wild creatures have rights to be safe in their own environments.

2. The toads and the yellow spotted snake symbolize all wildlife. The old man and the speaker in the second poem symbolize the protective, conscientious humans. The speaker in the first poem represents careless, self-absorbed people.

Rubrics for Writing Options

You can adapt this as a checklist for students to use as they write.

Creative Writing

☐ Does the fable accurately and effectively reflect details in the poem?

☐ Do the fable and poem share the same theme?

☐ Is the theme accurately and clearly stated as a moral at the end of the fable?

Persuasive Writing

☐ Does the essay begin with a clearly stated thesis statement?

☐ Is the thesis statement effectively supported by evidence?

☐ Has the writer shown an ability to use persuasive language and techniques effectively?

The Cremation of Sam McGee

A Narrative Poem
by Robert Service

There are strange things done in the midnight sun
    By the men who moil[1] for gold
The Arctic trails have their secret tales
    That would make your blood run cold;
5 The Northern Lights have seen queer sights,
    But the queerest they ever did see
Was that night on the marge,[2] of Lake Lebarge
    I cremated Sam McGee.

---

1. **moil.** Search for
2. **marge.** Shores

Preview the Selection

At a Glance
Independent Reading
- Reading Level: Moderate
- Difficulty Consideration: Vocabulary
- Ease Factors: Narrative structure, rhyme

Objectives
Reading this selection will enable students to:
- read with developing fluency
- read silently with comprehension for a sustained period of time

Launch the Lesson
Discuss familiar tall tales such as those featuring Pecos Bill and Paul Bunyan. Urge students to think of these characters' exaggerated adventures as they read "The Cremation of Sam McGee."

Summary
The narrative poem tells the tale of Sam McGee, who hates the cold and made the speaker promise to cremate him, should he die while they traveled through the North Pole. He dies and the speaker honors his wish, only to discover Sam McGee, alive in the fire—much happier in the heat.

TEACHING NOTE
Although this selection is presented in the student edition as an independent reading, teaching support has been provided should you choose to cover it in class.

Robert Service
(1874–1958) was a popular verse writer known for his ballads. His poetry was well loved for its thrilling rhythms, dramatic intensity, and accessibility.

After driving an ambulance in World War I, Service settled in France briefly before moving to Vancouver. This area remained part of Service's life until his death in 1958. Much of his poetry, including "The Cremation of Sam McGee," is set in this region.

594

Program Resources

Planning and Assessment
Program Planning Guide, Selection Lesson Plan
E-Lesson Planner
Assessment Guide, Lesson Test
ExamView

Technology Tools
Interactive Student Text on CD
Visual Teaching Package
Audio Library
mirrorsandwindows.com

Meeting the Standards
Poetry: Unit 6, Independent Reading, pp. 81–86

Differentiating Instruction
Developing Readers, Make Predictions, pp. 46–48
Advanced Students, Historical Context Project, pp. 36–37

Common Core State Standards

Reading Literature
RL.3, RL.10
Language
L.6

Now Sam McGee was from Tennessee, where the cotton blooms and blows.
10 Why he left his home in the South to roam 'round the Pole, God only knows.
He was always cold, but the land of gold seemed to hold him like a spell;
Though he'd often say in his homely way that "he'd sooner live in hell."

On a Christmas Day we were mushing our way over the Dawson trail.
Talk of your cold! through the parka's fold it stabbed like a driven nail.
15 If our eyes we'd close, then the lashes froze till sometimes we couldn't see;
It wasn't much fun, but the only one to whimper was Sam McGee.

And that very night, as we lay packed tight in our robes beneath the snow,
And the dogs were fed, and the stars o'erhead were dancing heel and toe,
He turned to me, and "Cap," says he, "I'll cash in this trip, I guess;
20 And if I do, I'm asking that you won't refuse my last request."

Well, he seemed so low that I couldn't say no; then he says with a sort of moan:
"It's the cursèd cold, and it's got right hold till I'm chilled clean through to the bone.
Yet 'tain't being dead—it's my awful dread of the icy grave that pains;
So I want you to swear that, foul or fair, you'll cremate my last remains."

25 A pal's last need is a thing to heed, so I swore I would not fail;
And we started on at the streak of dawn; but God! he looked ghastly pale.
He crouched on the sleigh, and he raved all day of his home in Tennessee;
And before nightfall a corpse was all that was left of Sam McGee.

There wasn't a breath in that land of death, and I hurried, horror driven,
30 With a corpse half hid that I couldn't get rid, because of a promise given;
It was lashed to the sleigh, and it seemed to say: "You may tax your brawn and brains,
But you promised true, and it's up to you to cremate those last remains."

Now a promise made is a debt unpaid, and the trail has its own stern code.
In the days to come, though my lips were dumb, in my heart how I cursed that load.
35 In the long, long night, by the lone firelight, while the huskies, round in a ring,
Howled out their woes to the homeless snows—O God! how I loathed the thing.

And every day that quiet clay seemed to heavy and heavier grow;
And on I went, though the dogs were spent and the grub was getting low;
The trail was bad, and I felt half mad, but I swore I would not give in;
40 And I'd often sing to the hateful thing, and it hearkened with a grin.

Teach the Selection

The Mirrors & Windows questions at the end of this selection focus on the theme of integrity. Before reading the poem, ask students to describe a promise they have made in the past. Why is following through so important?

History Connection

Klondike Gold Rush Robert Service set many of his poems in the wilderness of northwest Canada. There, particularly in the autumn and winter, the Northern Lights (Aurora Borealis) flash, dance, and swirl in the nighttime sky. In 1897, the Klondike Gold Rush led thousands of men, like the speaker and Sam McGee in this poem, to rush to this area in search of gold. The work was brutal. Most of the gold was ten or more feet below the surface, and miners had to dig through permafrost (permanently frozen earth) to get to it. Many died due to freezing temperatures and lack of food.

Analyze Literature

Ballad Point out that this poem is very similar to a ballad—a narrative song that tells about heroes and adventures. Like a song, it has a chorus (the opening and closing stanzas) that acts as a frame for the verses. Be sure to point out the rhythm and the use of both end and internal rhyme.

Words in Use

Selection Words
homely, 595   burrowed, 596
mushing, 595   grisly, 597
o'erhead, 595
cursèd, 595
ghastly, 595
tax, 595
brawn, 595
hearkened, 595

Teaching Words
Northern Lights, 594
cremated, 594
ballads, 594
dramatic intensity, 594
accessibility, 594

KEY TERMS
NARRATIVE POEM, 594
BALLAD, 594
RHYTHM, 594

Visualize Have students describe
the setting. Ask them to explain why
the setting has such an impact on the
plot events.

Analyze Literature

Character Ask students why the
speaker refers to the body as a
"hateful thing." Then ask: "If he hated
the body that was tied to the dogsled,
why did he keep on going with it?"
Lead them to understand that he had
made a promise to his friend and was
determined to keep that promise.

Use Reading Skills

Summarize To monitor
comprehension, have students work
with partners or in small groups to
summarize important plot events.
They might use story maps to chart
the action leading up to, including,
and following the climax. If students'
climaxes differ, discuss the best
possible choice.

Till I came to the marge of Lake Lebarge, and a derelict[3] there lay;
It was jammed in the ice, but I saw in a trice it was called the "Alice May."
And I looked at it, and I thought a bit, and I looked at my frozen chum;
Then "Here," said I, with a sudden cry, "is my cre-ma-tor-eum."[4]

45 Some planks I tore from the cabin floor, and I lit the boiler fire;
Some coal I found that was lying around, and I heaped the fuel higher;
The flames just soared, and the furnace roared—such a blaze you seldom see;
And I burrowed a hole in the glowing coal, and I stuffed in Sam McGee.

Then I made a hike, for I didn't like to hear him sizzle so;
50 And the heavens scowled, and the huskies howled, and the wind began to blow.
It was icy cold, but the hot sweat rolled down my cheeks, and I don't know why;
And the greasy smoke in an inky cloak went streaking down the sky.

---

3. **derelict.** Abandoned ship
4. **cre-ma-tor-eum.** Crematorium. Place to cremate bodies of the deceased

Differentiated Instruction

Auditory Learning

Have students take turns reading a verse of the
poem aloud. Encourage them to accentuate the
rhythm and read with dramatic tones of voice.
Students might also enjoy listening to an audio
recording of the poem. Several are available.

Enrichment

Interested students might enjoy researching the
history of Canada's Northwest Territories to learn
about the Native Americans and Inuits who settled
there and to learn about the Klondike Gold Rush,
the Aurora Borealis, and the locations (Lake Lebarge,
Dawson trail) that Service mentions in his poem.

I do not know how long in the snow I wrestled with grisly fear;
But the stars came out and they danced about ere again I ventured near;
55 I was sick with dread, but I bravely said: "I'll just take a peep inside.
I guess he's cooked, and it's time I looked"…then the door I opened wide.

And there sat Sam, looking cool and calm, in the heart of the furnace roar;
And he wore a smile you could see a mile, and he said: "Please close that door.
It's fine in here, but I greatly fear you'll let in the cold and storm—
60 Since I left Plumtree, down in Tennessee, it's the first time I've been warm."

There are strange things done in the midnight sun
By the men who moil for gold;
The Arctic trails have their secret tales
That would make your blood run cold;
65 *The Northern Lights have seen queer sights,*
But the queerest they ever did see
Was the night on the marge of Lake Lebarge
I cremated Sam McGee.

 The speaker says that "a promise made is a debt unpaid." How is this true? Have you ever made a promise to someone? Why do you think it's important to keep promises to people?

Analyze and Extend

1. Where is Sam McGee from originally? What causes his death?
2. (a) Where does the speaker finally carry out his promise? (b) What surprising thing does the speaker see and hear when he decides to "take a peep inside"?
3. Explain how the poem might have been different if it had not contained its surprise.

Expository Writing Write a **personal essay** about a person in your own life—a family member, friend, or personal hero—who you believe has shown you something about the meaning of the word *courage*.

Critical Literacy A ballad is a simple poem that tells a story. Many ballads were meant to be sung. Working with a group of students, practice reading this poem aloud. Then give a choral reading of "The Cremation of Sam McGee." You do not need to sing, but be sure that your presentation is dramatic and interesting.

 Go to **www.mirrorsandwindows.com** for more.

Analyze Literature

Tall Tales Ask students if the end of the poem (Sam McGee's appearance) reminds them of plot events that take place in tall tales. Have them explain why or why not.

Answers: Students will probably say that once you make a promise, it is an unpaid debt until you follow through and keep that promise. They will also probably say that keeping promises is important because it is a measure of one's honesty and sense of commitment.

Analyze and Extend

1. He is from Tennessee. He freezes to death or becomes sick and weak because of the freezing temperatures.
2. (a) He burns the body in the boiler of an old boat he finds trapped in the ice of Lake Lebarge. (b) Sam McGee comes back to life and enjoys the warmth of the fire.
3. The poem would have lost its humor and its tall tale elements if the speaker had merely burned the body as promised.

Rubric for Expository Writing

You can adapt this as a checklist for students to use as they write.

☐ Does the essay clearly identify the person and state why he or she is courageous?
☐ Is the statement supported by details?
☐ Is the essay free of errors in punctuation, grammar, and spelling?

Preview the Selection

At a Glance

Independent Reading

- Reading Level: Moderate
- Difficulty Considerations: Structure, background
- Ease Factor: Straightforward language

Objectives

Reading this selection will enable students to

- read with developing fluency
- read silently with comprehension for a sustained period of time

Launch the Lesson

Ask students to think about what they might say if someone asked them this question: "What was it like when you were a little child?" Have them read "Nikki-Rosa" to find out what this speaker remembers.

Summary

The speaker briefly describes his or her childhood, noting that no biographer will understand that having little money did not affect the family's happiness. In fact, the speaker was quite happy.

TEACHING NOTE

Although this selection is presented in the student edition as an independent reading, teaching support has been provided should you choose to cover it in class.

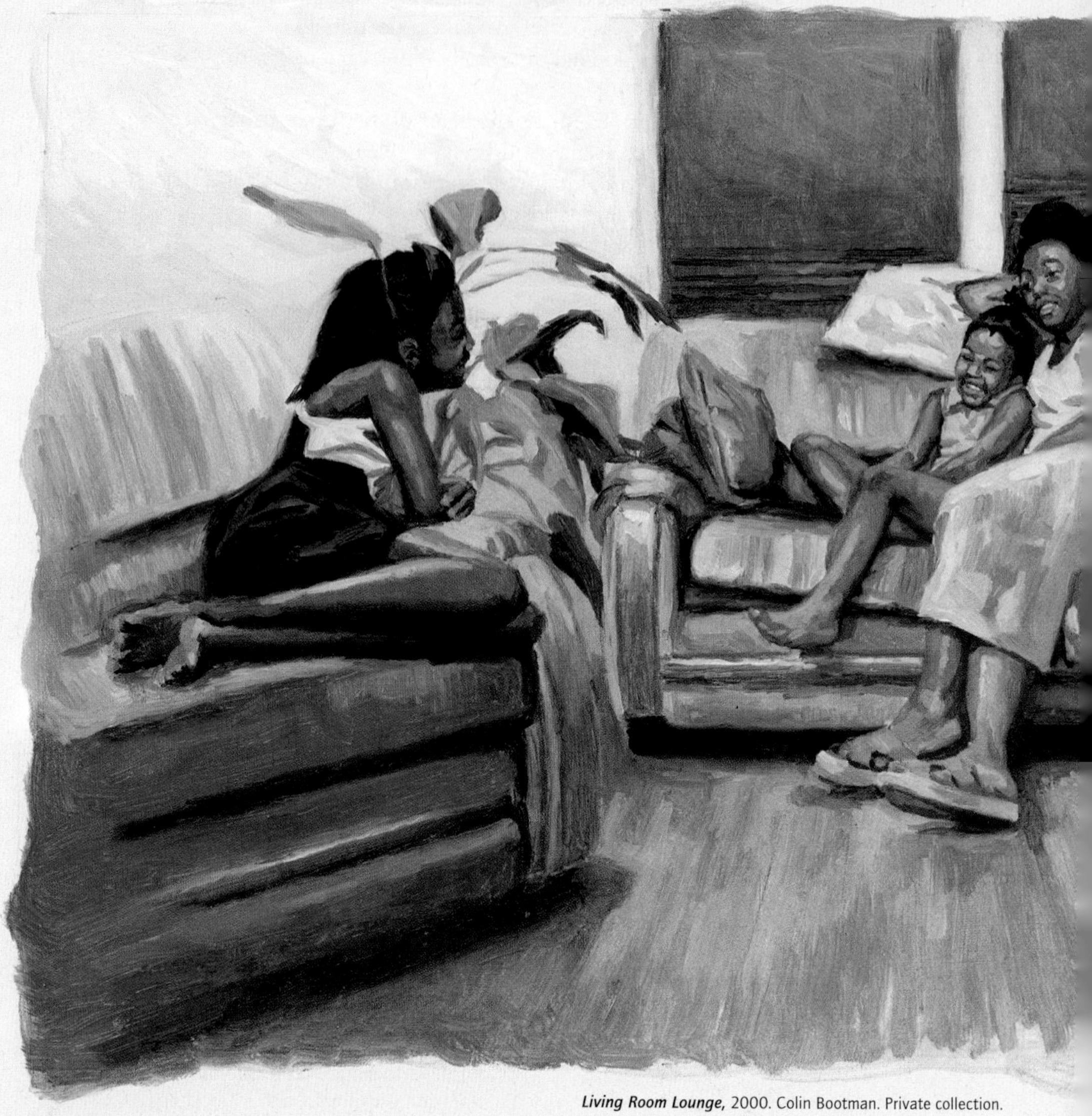

Living Room Lounge, 2000. Colin Bootman. Private collection.

598

Program Resources

Planning and Assessment

Program Planning Guide, Selection Lesson Plan
E-Lesson Planner
Assessment Guide, Lesson Test
ExamView

Technology Tools

Interactive Student Text on CD
Visual Teaching Package
Audio Library
mirrorsandwindows.com

Meeting the Standards

Poetry: Unit 6, Independent Reading, pp. 87–92

Common Core State Standards

Reading Literature
RL.1, RL.10

Nikki-Rosa

A Lyric Poem by Nikki Giovanni

childhood remembrances are always a drag
if you're Black
you always remember things like living in Woodlawn
with no inside toilet
5   and if you become famous or something
they never talk about how happy you were to have
your mother
all to yourself and
how good the water felt when you got your bath
10 from one of those
big tubs that folk in chicago barbecue in
and somehow when you talk about home
it never gets across how much you
understood their feelings
15 as the whole family attended meetings about Hollydale
and even though you remember
your biographers never understand

Nikki Giovanni
(b. 1943) is widely known
for both her poetry and
commitment to activism in
the 1960s and 1970s. She
was born in Knoxville, Tennessee, and grew
up near Cincinnati, Ohio. During the Civil
Rights movement, Giovanni was a vocal
advocate of Black Power, and she used her
poetry to convey her opinions. Giovanni has
received several honorary degrees from
universities and prestigious awards from
various institutions. Currently, Giovanni is a
professor at Virginia Tech in Blacksburg,
Virginia.

Teach the Selection

MIRRORS & WINDOWS The Mirrors & Windows questions at the end of this selection focus on the theme of childhood reminiscence. Before reading the story, ask students which events and experiences from their childhoods stand out in their memories. Are there "universal" childhood milestones that many people easily recall?

Use Reading Skills
Compare and Contrast As students read, have them compare and contrast how the speaker feels about her childhood and how others—interviewers and biographers—report her childhood.

Analyze Literature
Structure and Form Discuss the lack of capitalization and punctuation and the single run-on sentence. Compare this form to that of the e. e. cummings poem that students read on page 523. Ask them why Giovanni might have chosen this form. Discuss what it might suggest about her emotions (strong emotions, bubbling out very quickly) or about her thoughts (coming in a stream of consciousness, with related ideas strung together in memory).

Words in Use

Teaching Words
activism, 599
**Civil Rights
  movement,** 599
advocate, 599
honorary, 599
prestigious, 599
institutions, 599
biographers, 600

KEY TERMS
LYRIC POEM, 599
SPEAKER, 600
THEME, 600

Answer: Students should describe in detail one or more memories. They might suggest memories that include holidays, traditions, and family experiences.

Analyze and Extend

1. The speaker didn't seem to worry about the problems of her childhood—poverty, parental arguments, a home without indoor plumbing. In fact, she feels that her biographers tend to accentuate these problems and overlook that she felt happy and secure.

2. (a) She loved them, sympathized with their pain, and understood their feelings. (b) Yes. She loved having her mother all to herself, and the whole family went together to meetings.

3. (a) Despite the problems of her childhood, the speaker remembers love, togetherness, and happy holidays. Her interviewers seem focused on the problems instead of the happiness. (b) The speaker has the ability to look above the problems and find happiness. The interviewers seem to treat the speaker as a stereotype—a child of poverty. They focus on only the problems.

your father's pain as he sells his stock
and another dream goes
20 and though you're poor it isn't poverty that
concerns you
and though they fought a lot
it isn't your father's drinking that makes any difference
but only that everybody is together and you
25 and your sister have happy birthdays and very good christmasses
and I really hope no white person ever has cause
to write about me
because they never understand
Black love is Black wealth and they'll
30 probably talk about my hard childhood
and never understand that
all the while I was quite happy

 What are your most vivid childhood memories? What seem to be the most important memories people recall from childhood?

Analyze and Extend

1. What concerns does the speaker share?
2. (a) How does the speaker feel about her parents? (b) Based on the information given in the poem, did the speaker spend a lot of time with her parents? Explain your position.
3. (a) The poem contrasts what the speaker remembers with what possible interviewers want to know. Why is the difference important? (b) How does the contrast affect the depiction of the speaker and the interviewers?

Creative Writing Write a **poem** in response to Giovanni's. Address the themes she addresses, specifically, the difference between how others might see your life and how you see it. Include what you think biographers might ask, as well as what they might not ask, but that you would like people to know about your life.

Critical Literacy Hold a panel discussion in which you examine the ideas Giovanni suggests in this poem. Discuss in particular the poem's ending. How do the final lines affect the rest of the poem's meaning?

Go to **www.mirrorsandwindows.com** for more.

Differentiated Instruction

Reading Proficiency

Students may have difficulty due to the run-on sentence and lack of punctuation. You might want to suggest that they break the poem apart into sections. Then they can pause after reading each one to work with you or with partners to paraphrase the speaker's meaning. You may also wish to provide students with a copy of the poem to punctuate.

Rubric for Creative Writing

You can adapt this as a checklist for students to use as they write.

☐ Does the poem address the themes in Giovanni's poem?
☐ Does it describe what the speaker would like others to know about his or her life?
☐ Does it compare those thoughts with thoughts others might have about the speaker's life?

For Your Reading List

The Space Between Our Footsteps: Poems and Paintings from the Middle East
by Naomi Shihab Nye

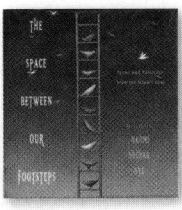 The poems and paintings in this anthology reveal a region very different from the Middle East sometimes portrayed on television news. The poets write about childhood, nature, love, homeland, war, family, and daily life, offering American readers a deeper understanding of the people and cultures of this region.

Heart to Heart: New Poems Inspired by Twentieth-Century American Art
by Jan Greenberg

 Discover poems inspired by great works of twentieth-century art, reprinted side-by-side with the works of art in this vibrant, colorful book. Find poems inspired by Grant Wood's *American Gothic,* Georgia O'Keeffe's *Poppy,* and Andy Warhol's images of Marilyn Monroe, among others.

William Butler Yeats
by Jonathan Allison

 Many of the poems in this anthology were inspired by the myths, folklore, and landscape of William Butler Yeats's native Ireland. In these poems, you will visit enchanted lands and places of great beauty, such as "The Lake Isle of Innisfree." Other poems describe the fairies who lure mortals to fairyland and other stories from Irish folklore.

The Rime of the Ancient Mariner
by Samuel Taylor Coleridge

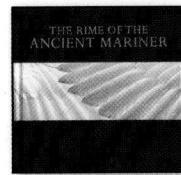 An ancient mariner describes supernatural events that occur on a disastrous sea voyage in this poem by Samuel Taylor Coleridge. The haunting verses of Coleridge's ballad are illustrated with dramatic and powerful images by artist Ed Young. Discover the mesmerizing power of the mariner's story in this well-known poem.

Step Lightly: Poems for the Journey
by Nancy Willard

 Since childhood, author and teacher Nancy Willard has saved copies and clippings of her favorite poems in a shoebox. These clippings now appear in *Step Lightly.* There is a mix of both themes and poets in *Step Lightly,* and it includes poetry from well-known as well as less established poets.

Imaginary Animals
by Charles Sullivan

 The Loch Ness Monster, the Jabberwocky, and the awe-inspiring Crackbeak make fearsome appearances in poems selected for this anthology, along with poems about real animals like cats and horses. These poems are all are illustrated with an imaginative selection of photographs, paintings, drawings, and sculpture.

Program Resources

EMC Access Editions
For additional independent reading, you may wish to refer students to one of EMC's Access Edition titles. Each Access Edition contains a thorough study apparatus, including background information, literal comprehension questions, footnotes, vocabulary definitions, critical thinking questions, and related projects and activities. An Assessment Manual offering worksheets and exams is available for each Access Edition.

Independent Reading

Independent Reading Activity
Help students link independent reading to the unit theme, Reaching Out. Have students select a book from the list here or go to the library and find other poetry collections. Remind students of the "Personal Communication" chart the class created before beginning the unit. Urge them to keep these different ways of reaching out in mind as they read the poems in one of these books or another that they choose.

▶ EMC E-Library
The EMC E-Library contains over twenty thousand pages of literary classics that students may read independently. An Electronic Library Guide provides teaching suggestions, enrichment activities, and reading strategy guidesheets.

TEACHING NOTE

Critical Viewing
Point out to students that several of the books recommended here make creative links between poems and works of art. As they read one of these collections, encourage them to respond actively to these pairings by asking themselves questions such as the following:
- What is the link between the poem and the image?
- How does the image clarify the meaning of the poem?
- How does the poem expand the meaning of the image?

Common Core State Standards
Reading Literature
RL.10

Objectives

Participating in this lesson will help students write a personal narrative that

- grabs a reader's attention
- clearly explains the controlling idea
- organizes the sequence of events
- employs descriptive language
- includes personal thoughts and feelings
- maintains consistent verb tense and point of view
- uses effective transitions
- makes an event's significance clear in a compelling conclusion

Launch the Workshop

Ask students what compels people to write autobiographies and memoirs. Is it merely egotism, or are they trying to connect with their audience? Then ask students why we value these writing forms. Are we looking for a bit of ourselves, or our lives, in these narratives? Do they help us relate to others with similar or dissimilar experiences? Do they teach us about the past or inspire us to influence the future? Remind them of personal narratives they have read for this class such as those by Lucha Corpi in Unit 3 and by Russell Freedman in Unit 5. Tell them that now they will have an opportunity to tell their own stories in short narratives.

Additional writing workshops are available in the *Exceeding the Standards: Writing* resource.

Writing Workshop

Narrative Writing

Personal Narrative

Reading and Writing

Every poem you read in this unit uses imaginative language to explain or describe. Many of the poems also tell stories. Some tell stories from a first-person point of view. Consider the opening line of "Exile": "I left my home behind me." Or think back to the images and ideas in "The Choice." In that poem the speaker compares rolling lands and pearl necklaces to songs and melodies. Think also of James Mitsui's description of an older woman juggling bean bags. Then there are poems like "Casey at the Bat" and "Paul Revere's Ride," which tell the stories of others, from a third-person point of view.

In this workshop, you will learn how to write a **personal narrative.** This is an essay that tells a true story. You can use some of the storytelling techniques from your favorite poems and stories. The point of view that you use and the way in which you order the events you describe will help make your story exciting. The following summary includes your assignment, goal, strategy, and writing rubric. These tools will allow you to develop a strong personal narrative.

- **Assignment:** Write a personal narrative about a subject of my choosing.

- **Goal:** Narrate an interesting and engaging story from my own life and reveal the significance of the story to my audience.

- **Strategy:** Choose a significant event from my life and use details, descriptive language, and chronological order to narrate the events.

- **Writing Rubric:** My personal narrative should include the following:

  - an introductory paragraph that grabs my reader's attention and introduces the story I will narrate
  - events organized in chronological order
  - consistent use of first-person point of view
  - descriptive details and personal thoughts and feelings
  - a conclusion that reveals the meaning or significance of my story

What Great Writers Do

Russell Baker is a newspaper writer. Consider how point of view increases the effectiveness of Baker's descriptions.

The topic on which my eye stopped was "The Art of Eating Spaghetti"...This title produced an extraordinary sequence of mental images...a vivid recollection of a night in Belleville when all of us were seated at the supper table...and Aunt Pat served spaghetti for supper. Spaghetti was an exotic treat in those days...I recalled the laughing arguments we had that night about the socially respectable method for moving spaghetti from plate to mouth.

Words in Use

Teaching Words
imaginative, 602
strategy, 602
rubric, 602
socially respectable, 602
perspective, 603
annotation, 605
typeface, 606

KEY TERMS

SPEAKER, 602	SIMILE, 603	PRESENT TENSE, 604
PERSONAL NARRATIVE, 602	METAPHOR, 603	PAST TENSE, 604
DESCRIPTIVE LANGUAGE, 602	PERSONIFICATION, 603	IMAGERY, 605
CHRONOLOGICAL ORDER, 602	SENSORY LANGUAGE, 603	TRANSITION WORD, 605
INTRODUCTORY PARAGRAPH, 602	DIALOGUE, 603	PRONOUN, 606
CONCLUSION, 602	CLUSTER CHART, 603	ADJECTIVE, 606
FIGURATIVE LANGUAGE, 603	PARAGRAPH, 604	NOUN, 606
	SUMMARY, 604	ADVERB, 606
	VERB TENSE, 604	VERB, 606
		PROOFREADING, 606
		PUNCTUATION, 606

Common Core State Standards

Writing
W.3, W.4, W.5, W.6, W.10

Language
L.5.1d

1. PREWRITE

Choosing Your Topic

The first thing you need to do is to brainstorm possible stories from your own life. A personal narrative can be something that happened to you or something that you observed. However, a narrative essay must have a controlling idea. You might want to relate a funny story about the worst day you ever had. Or you might want to tell a story about a grandparent's life from your perspective as a grandchild.

Gathering Details

Next you need to consider the details. As you know, stories are most interesting when writers use description. Remember that figurative language like similes, metaphors, and personification can be used with sensory language to create a vivid picture for your reader. Consider details such as weather, facial expressions, clothing, and important dialogue, for example. Be sure to include your own thoughts and feelings about the events as you narrate the story. Specific details and personal thoughts will make the narrative more fun to read and help the reader connect to your experience. They also help explain how elements of your story are connected. To gather and organize details, create a cluster chart.

Keep in mind your audience. What will they need to know in order to understand your narrative? Include enough background information so your audience can understand the events you are describing.

Deciding on Your Purpose

You now have a story to tell and a list of details to make that story come alive. At this point, you need a controlling idea. A controlling idea, like a thesis, is the main idea of your essay. It is the thing you want readers to know or feel after reading your personal narrative. You should write out a sentence that acts as a guide for what you will write.

> I want my personal narrative to tell the story of the never-ending peanut jar and to show what a good sense of humor my mom has.

Teach the Workshop

Prewrite
Brainstorm Stories Draw attention to the student cluster chart on this page. Suggest other details students might include in a story with this subject, reminding them that the details must be possible in real life: *We heard an explosive sneeze exit the library, followed by nearly ten more,* for example. Give students several minutes to determine categories for a narrative, such as humorous, moving, or enlightening, and to jot down any stories from their lives that fit these categories. If a student gets stuck, pair him or her with a partner and have them interview each other to identify interesting life events.

What Great Writers Do

Assure students that if they choose to write about an experience that made an impact on them and to which they still have strong emotions, their narrative will engage other people.

Speaking of personal experience as the driving force of writing, Pablo Neruda writes:

> *I grew up in this town, my poetry was born between the hill and the river, it took its voice from the rain, and like the timber, it steeped itself in the forests.*

Speaking & Listening Skills

Consistent Verb Tense

Explain to students that while they will write the majority of their narratives in the past tense, certain story elements, such as dialogue, may require them to switch momentarily to the present or future tense. Obtain an author's personal narrative, such as Nikki Giovanni's *Gemini*, and choose an excerpt that includes past tense narration and present or future tense dialogue. Instruct students to raise their hands when they note a shift in tense as you read the excerpt aloud to them. Discuss the author's methods for returning to the main, or past, tense.

Draft

Organizing Ideas Help students understand that, as in fiction, real life has its high and low points, spurred by conflicts and resolutions. Thus, they can apply their knowledge of plot elements to their narratives. Remind students that they can choose where to begin narrating in order to create the tension and relief necessary to hold their audience's attention.

Putting Your Thoughts on Paper Encourage students to see that if they provoke curiosity in their audience with an intriguing opening sentence, the audience is likely to satisfy that curiosity by reading on. When several students feel ready to analyze the effectiveness of their opening sentences with the class, read each one aloud (shielding the author's identity) and stop to ask: "Do you want to hear the next line?" Ask students why the sentence intrigues them or not, and have them provide suggestions for improvement.

Being Consistent Explain to students that sometimes, when writers feel particularly strongly about an incident within a narrative, they "enter the moment" and switch from past to present tense. While certain authors do this purposely for emotional effect, others do it unintentionally and confuse their reader in the process. Encourage them to read their narratives aloud before publishing and presenting them. They will catch accidental tense changes more readily than if they simply read them silently.

2. DRAFT

Organizing Ideas

Now that you have a controlling idea, you can decide how to arrange the narrative and its details. The easiest way to organize a story is in **chronological order.** This means that you tell the events and details in the order that they actually happened. You can connect things by using transition words like *first, second, next, then,* and *finally.* In order to best outline your draft, create a time line on which you plot events in the order they occurred.

> 1. My father bought a giant jar of peanuts.
>
> ↓
>
> 2. My mother bought a jar of peanuts and hid it.
>
> ↓
>
> 3. My father ate peanuts every night after dinner.
>
> ↓
>
> 4. My mother filled the peanut jar every morning.

Putting Your Thoughts on Paper

Now that you have a time line, details, and a controlling idea, begin writing your narrative. The introductory paragraph should introduce your story in a unique way. You might want to ask a question, use a quote, or describe something. Remember that it is your job as a writer to hook your reader and keep him or her interested. The next step is to organize the body of your essay. In this case, the body will be made of paragraphs that narrate or describe the various events on your time line. The final step is to create a conclusion. A good conclusion, like a good introduction, uses unique language. It might include a summary of your story or a dramatic final detail.

> **Introduction**
> - Begin my essay in an interesting way.
> - Write a sentence that explains my controlling idea.
>
> **Body**
> - Write a paragraph for each event on my time line.
> - Use transition words to connect events.
>
> **Conclusion**
> - Summarize the story.
> - End with an interesting detail.

Being Consistent

Be sure to use a consistent verb tense throughout your essay. Avoid any accidental changes to the verb tense as you tell your story. While some stories are told in the present tense, most stories are told in the past tense. Because your personal narrative tells a true story about something you experienced or observed, tell your events in the past tense.

If you narrate your events in past tense, keep in mind that statements that express something habitual or universally true always take the present tense.

> **Past tense words**
> ate
> read
> came
>
> **Present tense words**
> eat
> reads
> comes

Differentiated Instruction

Enrichment

Challenge students who have mastered the maintenance of consistent verb tense to experiment with deliberate changes in tense. Direct them to find moments in their narratives that heighten their emotional state, causing them to smile or furrow their brows, for instance. These are places where students can create dramatic effect by switching from the past to the present. When they have finished, encourage them to explain their changes, including how they decided when to switch *back* to the past tense.

3. REVISE

Evaluating Your Draft

Read your narrative and mark areas to improve. Then read the narrative aloud to a partner. This will help your partner hear what needs to be improved and what is successful. Have your partner take notes while listening. Use the checklist as a guide.

Below is a draft of a personal narrative. The annotations to the right indicate the reasons for the changes marked in the draft.

> **Revising Checklist**
> ☐ Is first-person point of view used?
> ☐ Is the organization chronological?
> ☐ Does the writer include descriptive details and personal thoughts?

Does this sound familiar? *We all stood in the kitchen, in the orange early evening light, laughing so hard we were crying. My father was laughing so much he could not eat even one peanut from the now amazing jar. My mother kept throwing a dishtowel up in the air, laughing so hard tears ran down her cheeks.* Has your family ever shared a joke that became a favorite story to tell? The day that my father realized that his "never-ending" jar of peanuts wasn't mysterious at all is a day my family will remember forever. *Because of my mother's great sense of humor and my father's good nature, the following story will live on.*

> *Include a sentence that explains the controlling idea.*

Every single night, my father eats peanuts after dinner while he reads. On a Tuesday night not long ago, my father came home from work with something special. He had stopped at the store to get the flour we needed for dinner. While there, a giant jar of peanuts ~~catches~~ caught his eye. *The jar was the size of a toddler.* The price was cheap. My father forgot all about the flour and bought the peanuts. When he got home, he was very excited. He made us look at the size of the jar and taste the delicious peanuts. *Then,* we watched as he put the jar on top of the red table where we kept our two fish in a little bowl.

> *Use consistent verb tense.*

> *Use description to create imagery.*

> *Use transition words.*

Speaking & Listening Skills

Retell and Summarize Points

Use the peer review process as an opportunity for students to practice listening skills. Ask reviewers to have their partners read their narratives aloud. Tell reviewers to use the Revising Checklist on this page as a rubric for listening. In addition, after listening, have each reviewer summarize the narrative he or she heard and retell the significance of the event in his or her own words.

Teach the Workshop

Revise

Evaluating Your Draft Explain the evaluative benefits of reading drafts aloud, as well as taking a break from them. If students read their work aloud or have a peer reviewer read it to them, they will notice many more mistakes than they would by reading silently. When they put aside an initial draft for a day or so, they will return to it with a fresh perspective and have a better chance of making meaningful revisions.

Take time to consider appropriate pairings for peer review based on your classroom's specific makeup. Pairing a highly skilled writer with a struggling one, for example, can prove extremely helpful to both students. Remind students to provide constructive criticism, which clearly indicates an issue and proposes a solution, rather than using empty phrases.

What Great Writers Do

Explain to students that their narratives, like all writing, are "living documents," meaning that they can always be altered and/or improved, even after the assignment is over. Remind them that our Constitution allows for indefinite revision, in the form of amendments:

"*The Congress, whenever two thirds of both houses shall deem it necessary, shall propose amendments to this Constitution.*"

Edit and Proofread

Consistent Point of View Ask students to revise the following sentences so that they maintain the initial point of view expressed. Then have them identify the point of view of each revised sentence.

1. Henrik talked in a calm, hushed voice, but he means (meant) business (past).
2. Before tomorrow morning, I will finish my math homework, bake brownies, and picked (pick) up my room (future).
3. Avani presents a confident attitude when she prepared (prepares) her speech in advance (present).

Adjectives and Adverbs Ask students to choose the correct word in parentheses, identify its part of speech, determine its antecedent, and identify that word's part of speech.

1. As she opened the door, a (horrendous, horrendously) stench assaulted her nose. (adjective, modifies *stench*, a noun)
2. Judy cleared the hurdles (effortless, effortlessly). (adverb, modifies *cleared*, a verb)
3. When did you start to speak so (proper, properly)? (adverb, modifies *speak*, a verb)

> **Proofreading Marks** Refer students to the Language Arts Handbook Writing Section 4.1, Proofreader's Symbols.

4. EDIT AND PROOFREAD

Focus: Consistent Point of View

You might remember that point of view is the vantage point from which a story is told. If the story is told from the first-person point of view, the narrator uses the pronouns *I* and *we* and is part of or a witness to the action. When a story is told from a third-person point of view, the narrator is outside the action and uses words such as *he, she, it,* and *they.* Be consistent in your point of view and the pronouns you use so your reader can follow your narrative. A personal narrative should be written using the first-person point of view. Here is the first-person point of view:

> As I stumbled into the kitchen, I saw my mother crouched over the two jars.

The third-person point of view would look like this:

> As he stumbled into the kitchen, he saw his mother crouched over two jars.

Focus: Adjectives and Adverbs

You know by now that words and phrases are tools for creating good descriptions and communicating events. It is also important to know when and how to use different parts of speech. An **adjective** is a word that describes a noun. In the draft on the previous page, *red* describes the table and *little* describes the bowl. **Adverbs** describe verbs in the same way that adjectives describe nouns. Adverbs frequently end in *-ly.* Choose adjectives and adverbs that enhance your descriptions. Consider this revision:

> Then, we all watched as he *ceremoniously* put the jar on top of the red table where we kept our two fish in a little bowl.

Be careful not to overuse adjectives and adverbs, however. Use vivid nouns and verbs as the basis of your descriptions and select specific adjectives and adverbs to enhance or modify those descriptions.

Proofreading

Quality Control As with any piece of writing, your personal narrative is not complete until you proofread. The purpose of proofreading is to correct errors in grammar, punctuation, and spelling. Use proofreader's marks to highlight any errors you find.

5. PUBLISH AND PRESENT

Final Draft

Clean Copy Now that you have revised, edited, and proofread your paper, make a clean copy for presentation. Handwritten papers should be neat and legible. If you are working with a word processing program, double-space the lines of text and use a readable typeface. Follow your teacher's presentation guidelines before submitting your work.

Differentiated Instruction

English Language Learning

Use this opportunity to gauge progress among English learners. Have them show you their editing and proofreading to see how well they have absorbed spelling and grammar lessons you have given. Choose one consistent problem in each student's draft, and respond to it verbally, in writing, or in a whole-class mini-lesson.

Enrichment

Offer confident writers the opportunity to proofread each other's work. Encourage them to practice using proofreader's marks.

Student Model

The Never-ending Jar of Peanuts
by Derrick Wood

Does this sound familiar? *We all stood in the kitchen, in the orange early evening light, laughing so hard we were crying. My father was laughing so much he could not eat even one peanut from the now amazing jar. My mother kept throwing a dishtowel up in the air, laughing so hard tears ran down her cheeks.* Has your family ever shared a joke that became a favorite story to tell? The day that my father realized that his "never-ending" jar of peanuts wasn't mysterious at all is a day my family will remember forever. Because of my mother's great sense of humor and my father's good nature, the following story will live on.

> Uses questions to create a compelling introduction. Sets up the controlling idea

Every single night, my father eats peanuts after dinner while he reads. On a Tuesday night not long ago, my father came home from work with something special. He had stopped at the store to get the flour we needed for dinner. While there, a giant jar of peanuts caught his eye. The jar was the size of a toddler. The price was cheap. My father forgot all about the flour and bought the peanuts. When he got home, he was very excited. He made us look at the size of the jar and taste the delicious peanuts. Then, we watched as he ceremoniously put the jar on top of the red table where we kept our two fish in a little bowl.

> Gives audience-appropriate background for the reader
>
> Uses adjectives, adverbs, and figurative language to create description

The following Wednesday night, my mother stopped at the store on her way home. She, too, saw the jar for sale. She bought it and drove home. Then she secretly hid the jar in her sewing closet. Before any of us got up, my mother would sneak into the kitchen with her secret jar and fill the empty space.

I did not know about any of this. About two weeks later, I woke up early. As I stumbled into the kitchen, I saw my mother crouched over the two jars. She was trying to hold her laughter in. When she saw me, she held her finger up to her mouth to hush me. I was in on the joke now.

Several days after my discovery, my father called from work to ask if he should stop at the store. My mother asked him to get some cauliflower. When he got home, he mentioned that the peanuts were on sale again but that he did not need to buy another. "In fact," he said as he glanced at the jar, "this jar is practically magical. It never seems to go down! It's full every night." My mother began to laugh. When she explained the joke, my father laughed. We laughed all through dinner.

> Uses transitional words to link ideas and events
>
> Maintains consistent first-person point of view
>
> Narrates events in chronological order

This story still makes us laugh. It demonstrates my mother's quirky sense of humor like no other story. I can still picture my father reading and eating his peanuts from his favorite glass dish, smiling.

> Concludes with a statement that reveals the significance of the story

Teach the Workshop

Student Model
Use the Model Give students several minutes to read the model. Then have them review it in detail. Point out the side notes that identify the compelling introduction, appropriate background, descriptive language, effective transitions, consistent point of view, logical order, and revealing conclusion.

Some students might benefit from outlining the model to grasp the writer's strategies. They may also create graphic organizers, such as cluster charts, to investigate the writer's development of character and setting.

▷ Publish and Present
Before students begin their final versions, they might benefit from reading the Language Arts Handbook Writing Section 4.1, Writing Follow-up.

Writing Skills

Refer to Prewriting Plan
When students have submitted their final narratives, ask them to take several minutes to review the writing process. Have them focus on the prewriting tools they used to choose a topic, gather details, and decide on a purpose. Ask them to answer these questions, keeping the responses in their journals for future reference.

1. What led you to choose the event about which you wrote?

2. As you wrote your draft, did you find that you had plenty of details to choose from, or did you have to add more?

3. How did your purpose change as you wrote and revised your draft, if at all?

4. What would you do differently the next time you prepare to write a personal narrative?

Objectives

Participating in this lesson will help students deliver and actively listen to narrative presentations that

- provide an engaging introduction
- present a clear order of events
- use sensory language to convey events
- build tension and resolve it
- employ vocal and facial expressions
- make attention-grabbing changes in tone and inflection
- use voice to convey feeling

Launch the Workshop

Ask several volunteers to take turns reading aloud Elizabeth Wong's personal essay "The Struggle to Be an All-American Girl" on pages 335-339. Instruct the rest of the class to note descriptive words of varied parts of speech that stand out to them. Ask them how Wong's description helps authenticate her experience. Explain that they will now have a chance to deliver their own narratives.

Planning a Narrative Presentation

Choose a Story Explain to students that while written narratives can more easily convey the impression of an intimate or intellectual experience, those that are tactile, or based on sensory experience, will be more accessible to the audience. Orally relating a sensory-based event allows the audience to grasp the speaker's impressions through their imaginations.

Giving and Actively Listening to Narrative Presentations

Do you have friends who are great storytellers? When they talk about something they've experienced, do they make you feel as if you're there with them? What makes one friend's stories so interesting, while other stories are boring? Another name for storytelling is a narrative presentation. In this workshop, you'll give and listen to **narrative presentations.** When you give and actively listen to a narrative presentation, you share information about yourself with others.

Planning a Narrative Presentation

Choose a Story Think about a memorable event in your life. It might be funny, happy, sad, serious, or simply interesting. Begin by brainstorming ideas about things that have happened to you alone; with friends, family, or animals; or in nature. Jot down events as they pop into your head. Continue until you have between five and ten memorable events.

Select one event from your list that you think will interest others. Then write down answers to these questions about the event you chose: What happened? Who was involved? Where did it happen? When did it happen? Why did it happen? What did I learn from it?

Finally, create a plot diagram to organize the events of your narrative.

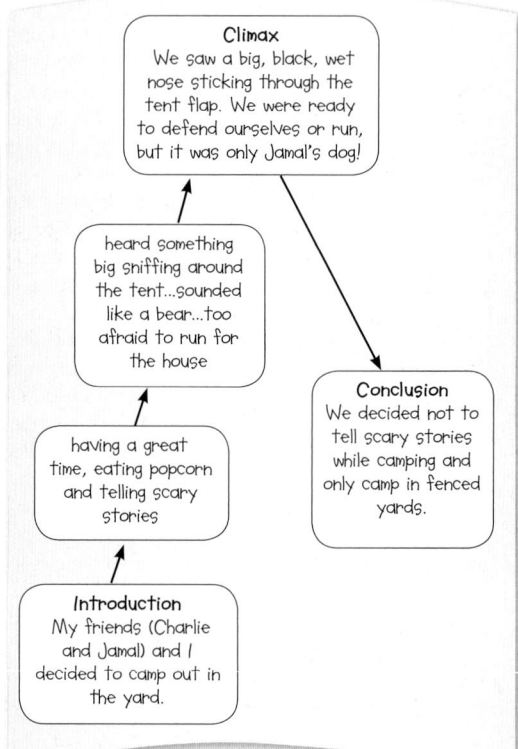

Climax
We saw a big, black, wet nose sticking through the tent flap. We were ready to defend ourselves or run, but it was only Jamal's dog!

heard something big sniffing around the tent...sounded like a bear...too afraid to run for the house

having a great time, eating popcorn and telling scary stories

Conclusion
We decided not to tell scary stories while camping and only camp in fenced yards.

Introduction
My friends (Charlie and Jamal) and I decided to camp out in the yard.

Teaching Words
memorable, 608
interacting, 609
facial, 609
courteous, 609
sequence, 609

KEY TERMS

NARRATIVE
  PRESENTATION, 608
PLOT DIAGRAM, 608
CLIMAX, 608
INTRODUCTION, 608
CONCLUSION, 608
AUDIENCE, 609
PLOT, 609

SETTING, 609
CHARACTER, 609
VERBAL CUE, 609
NONVERBAL CUE, 609
SENSORY LANGUAGE, 609
TONE OF VOICE, 609
PEER REVIEWER, 609

Common Core State Standards

Speaking and Listening
SL.1, SL.6

Sequence Your Story Think about how great storytellers keep the interest of their audience. Even if you are telling about a single event, your story should have a plot. Begin by setting the scene. Establish the setting and introduce the characters. Were you interacting with your own thoughts, other people, nature, or society? The amount of background you'll need to give depends on how well your audience knows you.

Building your story to a climax keeps your audience interested. Keep in mind that your climax may be serious, exciting, or funny, like the punch line of a joke. After the climax, bring your story to a satisfying conclusion. Use a diagram similar to the one below to sequence the events in your story.

Verbal and Nonverbal Cues Draw your audience into your story by using sensory language. Use words that help them experience how the popcorn smelled or tasted, what the sniffing sounded like, and how your body felt when you were afraid. Make everything as real for your audience as possible.

As you tell your story, your facial expressions, voice, tone, and body language are as important as the words you say. Build emotions and drama by varying your tone of voice as well as your facial expression. If you were excited or sad, look and sound excited or sad. Change the pitch and loudness of your voice to build suspense. Use your entire body to keep your audience wondering until you reveal the climax. Changes in emotional tone keep the audience interested and involved.

Evaluating Your Narrative Presentation

Work with a partner or a group to rehearse your narrative presentation. After each person finishes, provide constructive feedback in a courteous and helpful way. Tell the speaker what you enjoyed about the story as well as what could be improved. Use the Speaking and Listening Rubric on this page to evaluate each narrative presentation.

Delivering Your Narrative Presentation

To keep your story fresh, plan the sequence of the presentation, but not the words themselves. Imagine telling the story to a group of close friends. Use movement only for dramatic effect. If your audience laughs or reacts in other ways, wait until they are quiet again before continuing.

Active listening is as important as being an effective speaker. Concentrate on and react honestly to what the speaker says. Save comments to other audience members and questions until after the presentation to avoid breaking the flow of the narrative.

Speaking Rubric

Your presentation will be evaluated on these elements:

Content
- ☐ engaging introduction
- ☐ clear order of events from beginning to end
- ☐ sensory language used to convey events
- ☐ story builds to a climax and satisfying conclusion

Delivery and Presentation
- ☐ voice and facial expression supports the story
- ☐ interesting changes in tone and inflection
- ☐ good use of voice to portray feeling

Listening Rubric

As a peer reviewer or audience member, you should do the following:

- ☐ listen quietly and attentively
- ☐ ask appropriate questions
- ☐ (as peer reviewer) provide constructive feedback

Sequence Your Story Remind students that by building suspense they will maintain their audience's interest. Help students choose details that figures in the story would be concerned with, in order to authenticate the experience and draw the audience in.

Use Verbal and Nonverbal Clues Many times, when novice presenters see recordings of their delivery, they are surprised to discover that their body language communicates a completely different message than what they intended. If possible, allow students the opportunity to practice in front of a camera and then review the recording to adjust their nonverbal clues.

Delivering Your Narrative Presentation

Explain to students that they will want to maintain a comfortable level of eye contact with their audience and meet the eyes of as many audience members as possible. Remind students that no matter how much they prepare, they cannot predict the reaction of their audience. Encourage them to maintain their confidence, even in the face of an undesired reception.

> ⊳ For more information, see the Language Arts Handbook Section 7, Speaking & Listening.

Program Resources

To expand upon this workshop lesson, Giving and Actively Listening to Narrative Presentations, see the *Exceeding the Standards: Speaking & Listening* resource.

Rubrics for Presentation

You can adapt this as a checklist for students to use as they prepare and listen.

Speaking Rubric

- ☐ Does the speaker begin in an engaging way?
- ☐ Does he or she follow a clear order of events?
- ☐ Does he or she use sensory language?
- ☐ Does he or she build and resolve tension?
- ☐ Does he or she effectively use voice and body language to convey feeling?

Listening Rubric

- ☐ Does the student listen attentively?
- ☐ Does he or she ask appropriate questions?
- ☐ Does he or she provide constructive criticism in peer review?

Objectives

Completing this lesson will enable students to

- write a narrative essay based on a writing prompt
- answer standardized test questions that demonstrate revising and editing skills
- demonstrate the ability to make inferences from a reading by answering standardized questions

Timed Writing

Say that standardized tests often ask students to write a response to a prompt in a specified period of time. Give the following tips:

- Determine how much time you will need to plan, organize, outline, draft, review, revise, and proofread.
- Read the entire prompt to gain a sense of the subject matter with which you will be dealing. If time permits, jot down any words or phrases associated with that subject that come to mind, including how it relates to your life.
- Read it again, hunting for language that explains exactly what you must do with the prompt such as relate, analyze, interpret, discuss, compare, or persuade.
- Write a clear introduction that lays out the topics, or purposes, of your supporting paragraphs. This will help keep you on track as you write.
- If you find yourself running out of time, plainly state your remaining points and add a conclusion.

Common Core State Standards

Reading Literature
RL.1, RL.4, RL.5, RL.6
Writing
W.3, W.4
Language
L.4

Test Practice Workshop

Writing Skills

Narrative Essay

Carefully read the following writing prompt. Before you begin writing, think carefully about what task the assignment is asking you to perform. Then create an outline to help guide your writing.

> In her poem "Southbound on the Freeway," May Swenson describes what an alien might think when visiting Earth for the first time. Have you ever felt like an alien in unfamiliar surroundings, such as your first day in a new neighborhood or school? Have you ever misunderstood your surroundings or the actions of strangers?

Relate a story from your own life that describes what it is like to be in unfamiliar surroundings or a situation you've never before experienced. In your narrative, use descriptive, sensory, and figurative language. Concentrate on writing a compelling opening and closing for your story. As you write, be sure to:

- Organize your narrative in a logical and consistent way
- Include introductory and concluding paragraphs
- Introduce the story you will narrate in the first paragraph
- Support your main idea in each body paragraph

Rubrics for a Narrative Essay

Make sure students understand that they should follow the instructions *above* and *below* the first box in order to respond to the questions *inside* the box. The second box provides additional instruction in the form of a checklist. Use these criteria to evaluate their essays.

You can adapt this as a checklist for students to use as they prepare and listen.

- ☐ Does the student provide a gripping introduction that clearly states his or her controlling idea?
- ☐ Does the essay relate a personal story that supports this idea?
- ☐ Is the essay organized logically?
- ☐ Does each body paragraph support the controlling idea revealed in the introduction?
- ☐ Does the essay use descriptive, sensory, and figurative language?
- ☐ Does the essay have a compelling closing?

Revising and Editing Skills

In the following excerpt from the first draft of a student's paper, words and phrases are underlined and numbered. Alternatives to the underlined words and phrases appear in the right hand column. Choose the one that *best* corrects any grammatical or style errors in the original. If you think that the original is error-free, choose "NO CHANGE."

Some questions might also focus on a section of the passage or the entire passage. These do not refer to a specific underlined phrase or word, and are identified by a number in a box. Record your answers on a separate sheet of paper.

Toto…I've got a feeling we're not in Kansas anymore. Literally! <u>When my family and me</u> <u>moved</u> from our sleepy little Kansas town of [**1**]

Millville to <u>Chicago;</u> I knew just how Dorothy [**2**]

<u>would feel when</u> the tornado dropped her in Oz. [**3**]

In Millville, people strolled along Main Street, <u>waved at passing cars, and stopping</u> often to chat [**4**]

with a friend or neighbor…and everyone was a friend or neighbor! <u>In Chicago, throngs of people</u> [**5**]

rush around the streets, bouncing off one another and yakking at the tops of their voices on their cell-phones. [**6**]

1. **A.** NO CHANGE
   B. me and my family moved
   C. my family and I moved
   D. my family moved, with me

2. **A.** NO CHANGE
   B. Chicago…
   C. Chicago—
   D. Chicago,

3. **A.** NO CHANGE
   B. must have felt when
   C. feels when
   D. would feels when

4. **A.** NO CHANGE
   B. waving at passing cars, and stopped
   C. waved at passing cars, and stopped
   D. passing and waving at cars

5. **A.** NO CHANGE
   B. In Chicago throngs of people
   C. Throngs of people in Chicago
   D. In Chicago, throngs of people,

6. The organization of the passage is
   A. problem and solution.
   B. spatial order.
   C. cause and effect.
   D. compare and contrast.

Reading Comprehension Tests

Remind students that reading comprehension tests give a short piece of writing and then ask several questions about it. The questions often ask students to interpret the passage. Urge students to keep the following tips in mind:

- Begin by skimming all the questions.
- Read the passage with the questions in mind. If time permits, read the passage twice before answering any questions.
- Reread the first question carefully.
- Locate the portion of the passage to which the question refers. Read it slowly and carefully.
- Answer the first question.
- Repeat this process to answer all the rest of the questions.

Reading Skills

Carefully read the following passage. Then, on a separate piece of paper, answer each question.

"Courage" by Robert Service

Today I opened wide my eyes,
And stared with wonder and surprise,
To see beneath November skies
An apple blossom peer;
5 Upon a branch as bleak as night
It gleamed exultant on my sight,
A fairy beacon burning bright
Of hope and cheer.

"Alas!" said I, "poor foolish thing,
10 Have you mistaken this for Spring?
Behold, the thrush has taken wing,
And Winter's near."
Serene it seemed to lift its head:
"The Winter's wrath I do not dread,
15 Because I am," it proudly said,
"A Pioneer.

"Some apple blossom must be first,
With beauty's urgency to burst
Into a world for joy athirst,
20 And so I dare;
And I shall see what none shall see—
December skies gloom over me,
And mock them with my April glee,
And fearless fare.

25 "And I shall hear what none shall hear—
The hardy robin piping clear,
The Storm King gallop dark and drear
Across the sky;
And I shall know what none shall know—
30 The silent kisses of the snow,
The Christmas candles' silver glow,
Before I die.

"Then from your frost-gemmed window pane
One morning you will look in vain,
35 My smile of delicate disdain
No more to see;
But though I pass before my time,
And perish in the grale and grime,
Maybe you'll have a little rhyme
40 To spare for me."

Differentiated Instruction

English Language Learning

Students learning English will need help with the academic vocabulary used in standardized tests. Explain the following terms used in this workshop: *prompt*—cue, something to help one begin, 610. A "writing prompt" is usually a detailed paragraph of instruction.

outline—short summary or description, usually arranged as a series of key points, 610
compelling—attracting interest and attention, 610
narrative—story, 613

1. Based on the first stanza, the speaker's point of view is
   A. first-person.
   B. second-person.
   C. third-person limited.
   D. third-person omniscient.

2. Based on the context, what is the most likely meaning for the word *Pioneer* in line 16?
   A. first to colonize a new area
   B. first to experiment in a new field
   C. first to experience something
   D. first to farm in a new area

3. In line 30, "The silent kisses of the snow" can *best* be described as
   A. onomatopoeia.
   B. sensory detail.
   C. hyperbole.
   D. simile.

4. What is the rhyme scheme for the poem?
   A. *aaabcccb*
   B. *aabbccaa*
   C. *abababab*
   D. *abacabac*

5. Which of the following literary devices is present in lines 27–28?
   A. assonance
   B. onomatopoeia
   C. simile
   D. personification

6. This passage is an example of which type of poetry?
   A. meter
   B. concrete
   C. haiku
   D. narrative

7. Line 38 contains
   A. consonance.
   B. assonance.
   C. alliteration.
   D. onomatopoeia.

8. Why are the last two lines of the poem ironic?
   A. because you don't expect the apple blossom to die
   B. because "Courage" is the "little rhyme"
   C. because an apple blossom can speak
   D. because apple blossoms don't bloom in November

9. What is the speaker's attitude toward the apple blossom?
   A. The speaker thinks it is courageous.
   B. The speaker thinks it is too dumb to know when to bloom.
   C. The speaker envies it because it experiences new things.
   D. The speaker is afraid it will die.

10. What literary device does the poet use when he quotes the apple blossom?
    A. symbolism
    B. onomatopoeia
    C. hyperbole
    D. personification

Teach the Workshop

Reading Skills
1. A
2. C
3. D
4. A
5. D
6. D
7. C
8. B
9. A
10. D

Test-Taking Skills

Elimination of Incorrect Responses

Tell students that a key skill in answering multiple-choice questions is eliminating incorrect responses. Model a think-aloud for one question on this page.

Question 6. Meter is a poetic element, not a type of poetry, so I can eliminate choice A. A concrete poem has a recognizable shape, and a haiku is only three lines long, so I can eliminate choices B and C.

I know that narrative poetry tells a story with vivid description, so the answer must be D.

Select another question and have the class work as a group to eliminate the incorrect responses.

Planning and Assessment Tools

Annotated Teacher's Edition

Annotated Teacher's Edition
One location for accessing, previewing, and planning for use of all program resources.

EMC Launchpad
Desktop application for accessing, previewing, planning, posting, and grading all program resources. Post personal resources and lessons, and access the E-Lesson Planner, the E-Gradebook, and training modules for computer literacy.

Assessment Guide and ExamView
A variety of assessments are available for this unit in print and electronic forms, including:
- Formative Survey
- Lesson Tests
- Unit Exams
- Alternative Assessment Options
- Reading Fluency Assessments

Meeting the Standards: Unit 1
In addition to lesson-by-lesson resources, *Meeting the Standards* includes the following unit-based resources:
- Unit Study Guide
- Practice Test
- Active Reading Model
- Selection Quizzes

Program Planning Guide and E-Lesson Planner
- Lesson Plans for all the selections in the unit
- Core Standards-Based Selections
- Reading Log and Evaluation Forms

The E-Lesson Planner contains fully developed lesson plans and unit resources with an electronic calendar for editing lesson plans.

Technology Tools

Visual Teaching Package
This package contains unit-based lectures, games, art collections, and Writing Workshops in PowerPoint format; included within the EMC Launchpad.

Interactive Student Text on CD
The student textbook on CD includes highlighting, note-taking, bookmarking, and a direct link to the student website, in addition to everything in the student text.

Audio Library
Authentic, dramatic recordings with listening activities expand listening skills and offer additional support for developing readers and English Language Learners.

ETS Online Criterion-Based Essay Grader (Grades 9–12)
Students can use this ETS web-based tool to evaluate their essays online before submitting them for teacher review and final evaluation.

mirrorsandwindows.com
Student and teacher resources, support, references, technology tools, and state-specific standards are available at **mirrorsandwindows.com.** The website is customizable using the EMC Launchpad.

Unit-Based Resources

Exceeding the Standards Unit Resources

Each of the *Exceeding the Standards* resources provides fully developed lessons to help you extend the textbook lessons and to expand upon the themes and skills covered in the unit. You can also download these lessons from **mirrorsandwindows.com**.

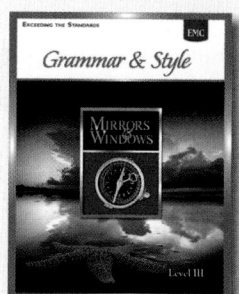

Grammar & Style
This resource contains:
- Seven lessons on Punctuation, pp. 151–168
- Five lessons on Capitalization, pp. 169–183

Literature & Reading
This resource contains:
- Analyzing Elements of Contemporary Drama, pp. 20–22

Special Topics
This resource contains:
- Career Skills Development: Practice an Interview, pp. 25–26
- Media Literacy: Multimedia: Pictures, Sound, and Video, pp. 27–28

Test Practice
This resource contains:
- Persuasive Essay Practice Test: Timed Writing, p. 16

Writing
This resource contains:
- Descriptive Writing: Reveal Character through Dialogue, pp. 59–69

Speaking & Listening
This resource contains the following lesson to expand on the Speaking & Listening Workshop:
- Giving and Actively Listening to Persuasive Presentations, pp. 21–23

Vocabulary & Spelling
This resource contains:
- Three lessons on Choosing Words, pp. 64–69

Extension Activities
This resource contains:
- Lifelong Learning: Analyze Elements of Theater, p. 21
- Media Literacy
- Critical Literacy: Present a Scene, pp. 22–23

Unit 7 Visual Planning Guide

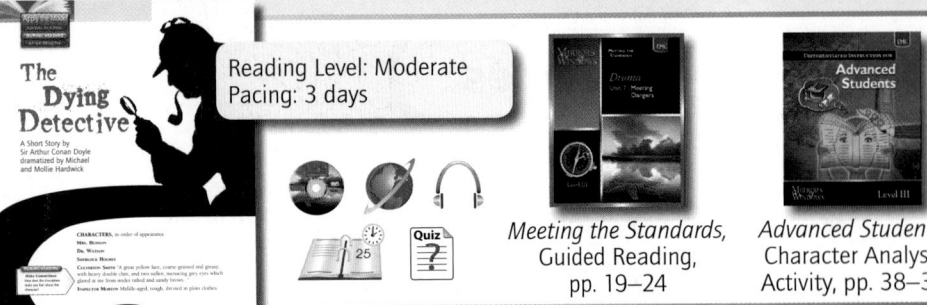

The Dying Detective
A Short Story by Sir Arthur Conan Doyle dramatized by Michael and Mollie Hardwick

(620)

Reading Level: Moderate
Pacing: 3 days

Meeting the Standards, Guided Reading, pp. 19–24

Advanced Students, Character Analysis Activity, pp. 38–39

The Diary of Anne Frank, Act 1
A Drama by Frances Goodrich and Albert Hackett

(641)

Reading Level: Moderate
Pacing: 5 days

Meeting the Standards, Directed Reading, pp. 25–31

Developing Readers, Take Notes, pp. 49–52

Advanced Students, Primary Source Project, pp. 40–41

Unit 7 Scope & Sequence Guide

Selection or Feature	Genre	Reading Support/ Reading Level	Word Count	Reading Skill	Graphic Organizer	
GUIDED READING						
Introduction to Drama pp. 616–617						
Drama Reading Model p. 618						
The Dying Detective Sir Arthur Conan Doyle pp. 619–638	Drama	Guided Reading: Reading Model/ Moderate	4,718	Determine the Importance of Details	Details Chart; Drama Chart	

 Interactive Student Text on CD-ROM

Selection Lesson Plan

 Web-based Resources

Lesson-by-Lesson Resources

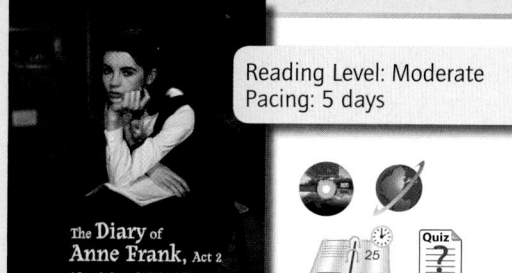

The Diary of
Anne Frank, Act 2
A Drama by Frances Goodrich and Albert Hackett
685

Reading Level: Moderate
Pacing: 5 days

Meeting the Standards,
Directed Reading,
pp. 32–35

Advanced Students,
Historical Context
Study, pp. 42–43

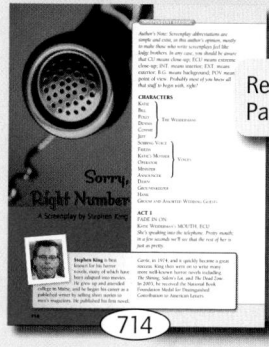

Sorry,
Right Number
A Screenplay by Stephen King
714

Reading Level: Challenging
Pacing: 2 days

Quiz
25

Meeting the Standards,
Independent Reading,
pp. 36–42

Advanced Students,
Independent Reading
Study, pp. 44–45

*English Language
Learners,* Sequence of
Events, pp. 163–187

Literary Element	*Mirrors & Windows* Theme	Cross-Curricular Connection	Writing Options	Extension Activities
Dramatic Forms Elements of Drama				
Drama	Friendship	Cultural Connection: *The Death of Sherlock Holmes*	Creative: News Article Expository: Literary Response Essay	Collaborative Learning: Classify and Identify Characters Media Literacy: Create a List

Quiz
Lesson Test

Audio Library

Unit 7 Scope & Sequence Guide

	Selection or Feature	Genre	Reading Support/ Reading Level	Word Count	Reading Skill	Graphic Organizer	
DIRECTED READING	**The Diary of Anne Frank, Act 1** Frances Goodrich and Albert Hackett pp. 640–683	Drama	Directed Reading/ Moderate	17,858	Summarize	Summary Chart; Plot Diagram	
	Primary Source Connection: from Anne Frank: the Diary of a Young Girl Anne Frank pp. 678–682	Diary Entries	Moderate	2,512			
	The Diary of Anne Frank, Act 2 Frances Goodrich and Albert Hackett pp. 685–712	Drama	Directed Reading/ Moderate	11,636		Plot Diagram	
	Primary Source Connection: from All But My Life Gerda Weissmann Klein pp. 708–711	Autobiography	Moderate	1,555			
INDEPENDENT READING	**Sorry, Right Number** Stephen King pp. 714–728	Screenplay	Independent Reading/ Challenging	6,013	Make Predictions		

Unit 7 Language Arts Workshops

Grammar & Style	Vocabulary & Spelling	Writing	Speaking & Listening	Test Practice
Verbals, p. 684 Sentence Fragments and Run-on Sentences, p. 713	Greek, Latin, and Anglo-Saxon Roots, p. 639	Persuasive Writing: Persusaive Essay, pp. 730–735	Giving and Actively Listening to Persuasive Presentations, pp. 736–737	Writing Skills: Persuasive Essay: from *A Woman Called Truth* by Sandy Asher, p. 738 Revising and Editing Skills, p. 739 Reading Skills: from *Pygmalion* by George Bernard Shaw, pp. 740–741

Literary Element	*Mirrors & Windows* Theme	Cross-Curricular Connection	Writing Options	Extension Activities
Plot	Music		Creative: Short Story Expository: Literary Response	Collaborative Learning: Draw a Diagram or Construct a Diorama Critical Literacy: Present a Scene
	Faith in Humanity		Creative: Personal Letter Applied: Bibliography	Critical Literacy: Hold a Small Group Discussion Lifelong Learning: Conduct Internet Research
Suspense	Familiarity		Expository: Essay	Collaborative Learning: Hold a Small Group Discussion

Unit 7 Building Vocabulary

The lists below identify the Words in Use and Key Terms within this unit. These words are listed at the bottom of the Teacher's Edition pages at the beginning of each lesson. Vocabulary development activities are provided in the *Meeting the Standards* unit book and in *Exceeding the Standards: Vocabulary & Spelling*.

WORDS IN USE

Preview Vocabulary
Preview Vocabulary are words taken from the sentences within each selection. These words are defined in the side margin or at the bottom of the pages on which they appear. The "Preview Vocabulary" section introduces these words in the Before Reading page preceding each selection.

agitated, 622
conspicuous, 644
corroborate, 633
dreadful, 621

foreboding, 689
implore, 626
improvise, 670
inarticulate, 688

ineffectually, 704
intimate, 692
ostentatiously, 672

pathological, 624
sparsely, 642

Selection Words
Selection Words are additional words from the reading that may be challenging but are not central to the selection and are not identified in the prereading section. These words can easily be learned using the story context, and they provide excellent practice for using content clues to find meaning without explicit instruction.

asylum, 625
battered, 717
bleakly, 720
condemn, 629
dejected, 716
depressive, 717
engaged, 715

exterior, 714
fade, 714
fidget, 625
idles, 715
interior, 714
loathe, 651
lodge brothers, 714

mediocre, 623
meticulously, 694
orthodontic, 716
poise, 698
radiant, 722
rummaging, 717
sanctified, 669

scrawny, 715
smite, 669
strenuous, 721
sullen, 620
tussling, 718
veteran, 718
wrought, 669

Teaching Words
Teaching Words consist of vocabulary that is used in the directions about the lessons. Teaching words explain to students what to focus on within the selection, help establish the story context, clarify the meaning of literary terms, and define the goals or instructional purpose.

abnormal, 639
absurd, 682
albeit, 679
annex, 707
annotations, 733
archenemy, 629
aspects, 616
assumptions, 731
barricaded, 708
behalf, 738
beloved, 619
brigade, 679
charred, 708
cited, 712
coarse, 741
collaboration, 616
condemning, 679
consistent, 683
constricted, 616
constructive, 737
contemptible, 741
context, 617

contracted, 639
courteous, 737
degrades, 730
derives, 639
diorama, 683
disregard, 730
distinguished, 714
dragletailed guttersnipe, 740
dramatized, 619
dreadful, 639
dynamic, 682
effective, 732
eliminated, 739
endure, 616
engaging, 617
envisions, 616
essential, 621
excerpt, 708
follies, 740
foundation, 714
gloated, 708
Hanukkah, 677

heighten, 625
insights, 682
interactions, 728
ironic, 707
irresistible, 740
liberated, 730
logical, 732
melancholy, 678
mishaps, 616
monstrous, 639
motive, 638
naïve, 708
Nazi Germany, 640
obsolete, 739
occupation, 728
omitted, 680
outraged, 629
parallel, 730
perturbed, 681
potential, 730
prominent, 738
props, 638

reinforce, 734
remonstrance, 639
revived, 629
rubric, 730, 737
screenplay, 640
segregation statutes, 730
simplified, 739
static, 617
strategy, 730
succession, 679
tension, 640
tragic flaw, 616
tranquility, 682
typeface, 734
unintentionally, 639
vague, 737
verified, 731
vibrant, 617
vindictive, 639

KEY TERMS

Key Terms are commonly referred to as *academic vocabulary*. These terms appear in the instructional material to teach the terminology that students need to acquire to understand literature. The repetition of the terms throughout the program ensures student mastery and provides a solid foundation for the continuing study of literature and language arts.

Objectives

Studying this unit will help students meet the following objectives:

- Connect the themes expressed in the selections to their own lives and to the world around them
- Identify common forms of drama
- Understand different elements of drama, including *plot, characters, dialogue, script, scenery,* and *stage directions*
- Understand variations of literary forms and authors' use of language to develop forms

Reading Strategies

Ask Questions
Clarify
Make Inferences
Make Predictions
Visualize

Reading Skills

Determine the Importance of Details
Summarize

Literary Elements

Characters
Dialogue
Drama
Plot
Script
Stage Directions

Meeting Dangers
Drama

ALBERT HACKETT

FRANCES GOODRICH

Have students read the introductory paragraph on page 615. Then ask them to develop additional questions related to the unit theme, Meeting Dangers. Prompt them to begin by asking them to write down any fears they harbor, including those that concern their own lives, people close to them, and the world at large. When they have finished, challenge them to recall literary figures that experience similar fears, guiding them on an individual basis. Next, direct them to form questions that address why they and others experience these fears and what they do, or might do, to overcome them. Model a possible question: "Why do I fear for my parents' health? Could improving my own health help alleviate this fear?" Have students keep their questions. After you complete the unit, return to the questions and try to answer them as a class.

"...*in spite of everything I still believe that people are really good at heart.*"

——ANNE FRANK, *Anne Frank: The Diary of a Young Girl*

Have you ever felt your life was at risk? How did the experience affect your values? Anne Frank and her family faced one of the greatest atrocities of the twentieth century, the Holocaust, in which the Nazis killed millions of Jews and other victims. The play based on Anne Frank's diary shows how humanity can survive even the worst evils.

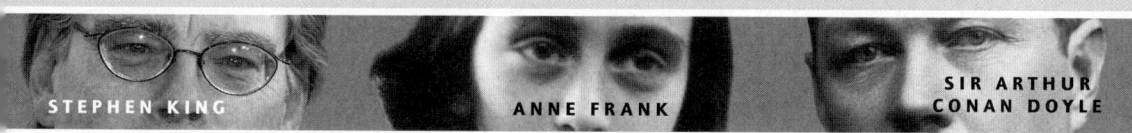

STEPHEN KING   ANNE FRANK   SIR ARTHUR CONAN DOYLE

615

Writing Options
Creative Writing
News Article
Personal Letter
Short Story

Applied Writing
Bibliography

Expository Writing
Bibliography
Essay
Literary Response

Language Arts Workshops
Grammar & Style
Sentence Fragments and Run-On
  Sentences
Verbals

Vocabulary & Spelling
Greek, Latin, and Anglo-Saxon Roots

Writing Workshop
Persuasive Essay

Speaking & Listening Workshop
Giving and Actively Listening to
  Persuasive Presentations

Test Practice Workshop
Persuasive Essay
Revising and Editing Skills
Reading Skills

Program Resources

For a visual reminder of the unit-based resources available for Unit 7, Drama, see pages 614A and 614B. As you introduce the unit, you may want to provide students with the Unit Study Guide, which is contained in the *Meeting the Standards* resource.

"The play was a great success, but the audience was a disaster."

—OSCAR WILDE

The art of performance has existed since the beginnings of human history. Modern theater can trace its roots back to prehistoric dance rituals, Native American healing ceremonies, African storytellers, and the dramatic productions of the ancient Greeks, to name a few. A **drama** is a piece of literature that is written to be performed for an audience.

Dramatic Forms

Plays for the Theater

A play is a type of drama written for the stage. The playwright envisions how the story will unfold and includes in the work specifics such as actors' locations on stage and details about props and sets. Unlike in fiction, the completed written work is not the final step. A director uses the written script, in collaboration with actors, to make the story come alive on stage.

Screenplays and Television

Dramas are not always performed on stage. When you go to the movie theater or watch a sitcom on television, you are watching a different kind of drama. Screenplays and television scripts are dramas written to be acted out on film and later shown to an audience on screen. Like plays, screenplays and TV scripts include stage directions that dictate how an actor should speak and move. They also include directions as to how a scene should be filmed.

Drama Versus Fiction

Drama and fiction share many similar elements, such as plot, characters, setting, and dialogue. A playwright's job, however, is much more constricted by aspects of time, place, and duration than that of a novelist. A typical play usually lasts a few hours, and all the action and plot development must take place within that time frame. Playwrights must always be conscious of time and space constrictions, as well as an audience's ability to endure and immediately understand what is taking place.

Types of Drama

Most modern Western theater descends from the style of the theatrical productions of the ancient Greeks.

- **Greek Tragedy:** There is usually a heroic protagonist, or main character, who struggles—with the gods, historically—and is ultimately brought down by a tragic flaw within himself or herself.

- **Comedy:** The plot often involves a series of mishaps and humorous situations.

- **Straight Drama:** Most modern plays fall into this category, characterized by realistic characters and situations in which the audience can often see themselves reflected. Frances Goodrich and Albert Hackett's *The Diary of Anne Frank* is an example of straight drama. Elements of tragedy or comedy may be involved, but usually not in extremes.

Elements of Drama

A drama, in its simplest form, is a story like any other piece of fiction. Unlike fiction, drama comprises various theatrical elements that allow the story to be performed and brought to life.

Plot

Just as in novels and short stories, the **plot** introduces a drama's central conflict, or struggle; develops the conflict through rising action; and resolves it after the climax.

Characters

The **characters** are the individuals who take part in the action of a drama. As in fiction, the **protagonist** is the most important character. Sometimes, another character takes on the role of the **antagonist,** who engages in conflict with the protagonist. Together, all of the characters form the drama's **cast.** The cast is usually listed at the beginning of a script, and it is the actions of and interactions between these characters that reveal the drama's plot.

Dialogue

In a drama, plot is mostly revealed through physical action and **dialogue,** or conversation between characters. Because of the performance format of drama, there is little room for narrative description as there is in most fiction. Thus, the audience learns the thoughts and feelings of characters, as well as the context for the story line, through what the characters do and say to each other. Sometimes information is presented to the audience through the speech of one character, which other characters may not hear. This is called a **monologue.**

Script

A **script** is a drama's actual text. It includes character names, setting, stage directions, and dialogue. **Stage directions** appear before and after lines of dialogue, and they indicate how a character should speak a certain line, what facial expressions to make, how to gesture, and so on.

Directions telling actors how and where to stand, move, or enter and exit the stage usually refer to this grid:

Up Right	Up Center	Up Left
Right Center	Center	Left Center
Down Right	Down Center	Down Left

Audience

Note that the parts of the stage are described from the actors' point of view, looking out at the audience. Just as a novel is sometimes divided into chapters, a script is usually divided into **acts** and **scenes.** Many plays have two to three acts, and each act is made up of a number of scenes.

Scenery

The scenery of a drama is called the **set.** The set includes the setting of each scene, the stage design, the lighting, and the props, or movable objects used by the characters. The playwright or screenwriter usually includes notes about stage design and the setting of each scene, but it is ultimately up to the production's director to interpret the scenery as he or she wishes.

Interpretations and Culture

Drama is a vibrant and engaging art form because it is never static. A playwright's script may always read the same on paper, but the playwright's words are only the beginning. Each interpretation and performance breathes new life into a drama. Today we are still reading the classic plays of the ancient Greeks and performing them around the world. A drama becomes something new in each theater, with each cast or director, and in each culture or time period in which it is performed and received.

Teach the Genre

Introduction to Drama

Emphasize that in a drama, actors convey ideas and emotions by interacting with each other in a limited amount of space: the stage. Create a grid like the one displayed on page 617 on the classroom floor with masking tape or string. Allow students time to explore the space and experiment moving and interacting within different parts of the stage, as described in the grid. Challenge them to realize the diverse effects they create by speaking or moving downstage and upstage. Return to this activity frequently throughout the unit, when reading stage directions and imagining or re-creating the action of each play.

Program Resources

To help students explore literature on a deeper level, assign the following activity: Analyzing Elements of Contemporary Drama: *Exceeding the Standards: Literature & Reading*, pp. 20–22.

Reading Skills

Take Notes

Ask students to recall what they have learned about using graphic organizers to take notes. Have volunteers come to the board and draw common graphic organizers — ones you have used in class — for keeping track of key elements of fiction. Possibilities include the plot diagram, character web, character chart, time line, story strip, cluster chart, cause-and-effect chart, and main idea map.

Once students have sketched the organizers, ask the class to suggest which ones would be most useful for taking notes about a drama. Elicit the observation that taking notes about drama will be very similar to taking notes about fiction.

Introduce the Process

Use this page to show students the basic instruction provided for them before, during, and after reading most dramas in Unit 7.

The Dying Detective is an Active Reading Model. Side notes in the lesson prompt students to become more active readers by using reading strategies and skills, analyzing literature, and making connections. Students can apply the process they use to read *The Dying Detective* to other selections in Unit 7.

Before Reading Stress the two types of background students need to apply, and encourage students to set a purpose for reading.

During Reading Point out the side notes on pages 620–621: Make Connections and Analyze Literature. Then show students the Mirrors & Windows questions on page 637. Explain that through these questions, they will respond to the drama personally and then apply their insights to a broader issue.

After Reading Show students page 638. Tell them that Find Meaning questions will help them recall and interpret details. Make Judgments questions ask them to analyze a play and evaluate how specific details contribute to its overall literary effect and meaning.

KEY TERMS

DRAMA, 618	**SETTING,** 618
PLAYWRIGHT, 618	**SEQUENCE OF**
PLOT, 618	**EVENTS,** 618
DIALOGUE, 618	**MONOLOGUE,** 618

Drama Reading Model

BEFORE READING

Build Background

You need to apply two types of background to read a drama effectively. One type is the drama's literary and historical context. Read the **Build Background** and **Meet the Author** features to get this information. The other type of background is the personal knowledge and experience you bring to your reading.

Set Purpose

A playwright presents characters and scenes to say something about life. Read **Set Purpose** to decide what you want to get out of the drama.

Analyze Literature

A playwright uses literary techniques, such as plot and dialogue, to create meaning. The **Analyze Literature** feature draws your attention to a key literary element in the drama.

Use Reading Skills

The **Use Reading Skills** feature will show you skills to help you get the most out of your reading. Learn how to apply skills such as drawing conclusions and summarizing. Identify a graphic organizer that will help you apply the skill before and while you read.

DURING READING

Use Reading Strategies

- **Ask questions** about things that seem significant or interesting.
- **Make predictions** about what's going to happen next. As you read, gather more clues to confirm or change your prediction.
- **Visualize** the drama. Form pictures in your mind to help you see the characters, actions, and settings.
- **Make inferences,** or educated guesses, about what is not stated directly.
- **Clarify,** or check that you understand, what you read. Reread any difficult parts.

Analyze Literature

What literary elements stand out? Are the characters vivid and interesting? Is there a strong central conflict? As you read, consider how these elements affect your enjoyment and understanding of the drama.

Make Connections

Notice where connections can be made between the drama and your life or the world outside the drama. What feelings or thoughts do you have while reading the drama?

AFTER READING

Find Meaning

Recall the important details of the drama, such as the sequence of events and characters' names. Use this information to **interpret,** or explain, the meaning of the drama.

Make Judgments

- **Analyze** the text by examining details and deciding what they contribute to the meaning.
- **Evaluate** the text by making judgments about how the author creates meaning.

Analyze Literature

Review how the use of literary elements increases your understanding of the story. For example, if the author uses monologue, how does it help to shape the drama's meaning?

Extend Understanding

Go beyond the text by exploring the drama's ideas through writing or other creative projects.

Differentiated Instruction

Visual and Kinesthetic Learning

Students who learn best in a visual or kinesthetic manner may find great success comprehending material and expressing themselves in this unit. Remind them of the power of movement in drama, and encourage them to articulate how movement can aid in understanding and composing literature. Challenge students to assume central roles throughout the unit and to record their experiences with the material in a journal.

Reading Proficiency

Use drama to help students develop fluency. Choose a play or excerpt based on its vocabulary level, which you can preview by scanning footnotes. Then gather readers and help them develop a frame of reference for reading. For example, you could say that Sir Arthur Conan Doyle's *The Dying Detective* is about a man who outwits a crafty enemy. Then pair students for cooperative reading.

The Dying Detective

A Short Story by Sir Arthur Conan Doyle
dramatized by Michael and Mollie Hardwick

Build Background

Literary Context Sherlock Holmes and Dr. Watson appear in four novels as well as dozens of short stories by the British writer Sir Arthur Conan Doyle. Doyle created his famous fictional detective in 1887, yet Sherlock Holmes is still so beloved worldwide that fans continue to write about him, discuss him, and quote him.

Reader's Context What would you do if one of your friends ordered you not to help even though he or she seemed in need?

Set Purpose

Preview the characters. Read to determine who the characters are and when and where the action takes place.

Analyze Literature

Drama A **drama**, or play, is a story told through **characters** who are played by actors. The **script** of a drama provides the characters' names; their **dialogue**, or what they say; and stage directions. **Stage directions** are notes to describe how something should look, sound, or be performed. When you read drama, try to picture in your mind the setting and characters.

Meet the Author

Sir Arthur Conan Doyle (1859–1930) was born in Scotland and originally studied to be a doctor. In fact, one of Doyle's teachers in medical school, Dr. Joseph Bell, was a model for Sherlock Holmes. For a time, Doyle combined his medical and literary careers, until an illness encouraged him to focus on writing. Although Doyle wrote many literary works besides those featuring Sherlock Holmes, his other fiction was never as popular.

Use Reading Skills

Determine the Importance of Details Writers include details to help readers determine a selection's theme, or main idea, as well as to focus attention on significant aspects of the selection. As you read, do a little detective work yourself. Determine which details are major, or particularly important, and which are minor, or less important. Think of the details as clues, and use them to unlock the meaning of the selection.

Major Details	Meaning or Significance
the title	suggests that a detective might die

Preview Vocabulary

dread·ful (dred´ fəl) *adj.*, causing terror or dread

ag·i·tat·ed (aj´ ə tāt´ əd) *adj.*, extremely disturbed; very upset

path·o·log·i·cal (pa´ thə lä´ ji kəl) *adj.*, caused by disease or the origins of disease

im·plore (im plôr´) *v.*, beg urgently

cor·rob·o·rate (kə rä´ bə rāt') *v.*, confirm; support with evidence

THE DYING DETECTIVE **619**

Preview the Model

At a Glance
Guided Reading: Reading Model
- Reading Level: Moderate
- Difficulty Considerations: Vocabulary, length
- Ease Factor: Compelling plot

Objectives

Studying this lesson will enable students to
- use reading strategies such as making predictions
- define *drama* and recognize that Sir Arthur Conan Doyle has dramatized a story about his character Sherlock Holmes
- describe the literary accomplishments of Sir Arthur Conan Doyle and explain the significance of his writing
- appreciate a play about a memorable character in the history of detective fiction

Launch the Lesson

Ask students to name qualities they think a good detective must have. Write their answers on the board. Then tell them that the selection they are about to read features one of the most famous fictional detectives of all time: Sherlock Holmes. As they read "The Dying Detective," have them compare his qualities with the ones you have written on the board.

Words in Use

Common Core State Standards

Reading Literature
RL.1, RL.3, RL.6

Writing
W.9

Language
L.6

Teach the Model

Summary
Sherlock Holmes lies prostrate in bed when Dr. Watson comes to visit. Holmes will not let Watson near him, claiming that his sickness is deadly and contagious. He urges Watson to fetch a man named Culverton Smith, and when Watson returns, Holmes tells him to hide behind the bed just before Smith is admitted. Holmes then accuses Smith of having killed his own cousin with a deadly poison on which Smith is an expert. Smith admits to the murder, thinking Holmes is dying from the same cause. Claiming to have trouble seeing, Holmes begs Smith to turn up the light, which Smith does. Inspector Morton enters on this cue and arrests Smith. Watson emerges from his hiding place and corroborates Holmes's claims. It turns out that Holmes had only been pretending to be sick in order to lure Smith to his room and get him to confess.

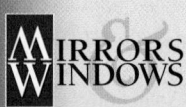

MIRRORS & WINDOWS The Mirrors & Windows questions at the end of this selection focus on the theme of friendship. Before reading the selection, ask students what they look for in a friend. What are universal elements of friendship?

Make Connections
Answer: The character description gives a negative impression about the character. (A)

Apply the Model
BEFORE READING
DURING READING
AFTER READING

The Dying Detective

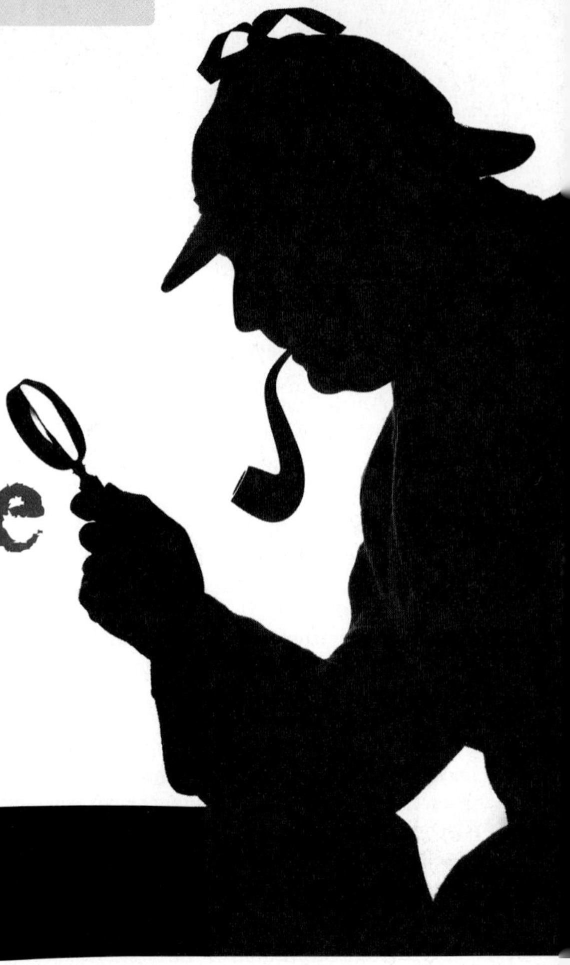

A Short Story by
Sir Arthur Conan Doyle
dramatized by Michael
and Mollie Hardwick

CHARACTERS, in order of appearance

Mrs. Hudson

Dr. Watson

Sherlock Holmes

Culverton Smith "A great yellow face, coarse-grained and greasy, with heavy double chin, and two sullen, menacing grey eyes which glared at me from under tufted and sandy brows..."

Inspector Morton Middle-aged, tough, dressed in plain clothes.

DURING READING
Make Connections
How does the description make you feel about this character? (A)

620

Program Resources

Planning and Assessment
Program Planning Guide, Selection Lesson Plan
E-Lesson Planner
Assessment Guide, Lesson Test
ExamView

Technology Tools
Interactive Student Text on CD
Visual Teaching Package
Audio Library
mirrorsandwindows.com

Meeting the Standards
Drama: Unit 7, Guided Reading, pp. 19–24

Differentiating Instruction
Advanced Students, Character Analysis Activity, p. 38–39

PLACE

SCENE 1: Sherlock Holmes's bedroom, afternoon

SCENE 2: The same, dusk

SCENE 3: The same, evening

SCENE 1

SHERLOCK HOLMES's *bedroom at 221B Baker Street. The essential features* **B** *are: a bed with a large wooden head, placed crosswise on the stage, the head a foot or two from one side wall; a small table near the bed-head, on the audience's side, on which stand a carafe of water and a glass, and a tiny metal or ivory box; a window in the back wall, the curtains parted; and, under the window, a table or chest of drawers, on which stand a green wine bottle, some wine-glasses, a biscuit-barrel, and a lamp. Of course there may be further lamps and any amount of furnishing and clutter:* HOLMES's *bedroom was adorned with pictures of celebrated criminals and littered with everything from tobacco pipes to revolver cartridges.*

There is daylight outside the window. SHERLOCK HOLMES *lies in the bed on his back, tucked up to the chin and evidently asleep. He is very pale.* MRS. HUDSON *enters followed by* DR. WATSON, *who is wearing his coat and hat and carrying his small medical bag.* MRS. HUDSON *pauses for a moment.*

MRS. HUDSON. He's asleep, sir.

They approach the bed. WATSON *comes round to the audience's side and looks down at* HOLMES *for a moment. He shakes his head gravely, then he and* MRS. HUDSON *move away beyond the foot of the bed.* WATSON *takes off his hat and coat as they talk and she takes them from him.*

WATSON. This is <u>dreadful</u>, Mrs. Hudson. He was perfectly hale and hearty when I went away only three days ago.

MRS. HUDSON. I know, sir. Oh, Dr. Watson, sir, I'm glad you've come back. If anyone can save Mr. Holmes, I'm sure you can.

WATSON. I shall have to know what is the matter with him first. Mrs. Hudson, please tell me, as quickly as you can, how it all came about.

MRS. HUDSON. Yes, sir. Mr. Holmes has been working lately on some case down near the river—Rotherhithe, I think.

WATSON. Yes, yes. I know.

MRS. HUDSON. Well, you know what he is for coming in at all hours. I was just taking my lamp to go to my bed on Wednesday night

---

> **DURING READING**
>
> **Analyze Literature**
> **C** **Drama** Why do the stage directions distinguish between essential features and others?

> **DURING READING**
>
> **Analyze Literature**
> **D** **Characterization** What do you learn about Holmes from Watson's reaction?

dread·ful (drĕd´ fəl) *adj.,* causing terror or dread

Analyze Literature

Dialogue Point out to students that dialogue has to sound natural, the way people actually talk. Here, Mrs. Hudson omits the subject in each sentence, in much the same way that people talk in informal situations. **A**

Analyze Literature

Drama *Answer:* The stage directions show that embarrassment is the reason for her pause. **B**

Analyze Literature

Stage Directions Point out that these stage directions describe the actions of each character. Have students notice that each time a character is mentioned, his or her name is printed in capital letters. This is partly to help the actors as they learn their parts and partly to help the reader follow the action.

Ask why it is important that Watson come to the audience's side of the bed. Model a response: "This way, the audience can see him better. If he sat on the other side of the bed, most of his body would be concealed from the audience." **C**

when I heard a faint knocking at the street door. I…I found Mr. Holmes there. He could hardly stand. Just muttered to me to help him up to his bed here, and he's barely spoken since.

WATSON. Dear me!

A **MRS. HUDSON.** Won't take food or drink. Just lies there, sleeping or staring in a wild sort of way.

WATSON. But, goodness gracious, Mrs. Hudson, why did you not send for another doctor in my absence?

MRS. HUDSON. Oh, I told him straightaway I was going to do that, sir. But he got so agitated—almost shouted that he wouldn't allow any doctor on the premises. You know how masterful he is, Dr. Watson.

ag·i·tat·ed (aj′ ə tāt′ əd) *adj.,* extremely disturbed; very upset

> **DURING READING**
>
> **Analyze Literature**
> **Drama** How do the stage directions help explain Mrs. Hudson's pause? **B**

WATSON. Indeed. But you could have telegraphed for me.

MRS. HUDSON *appears embarrassed.*

MRS. HUDSON. Well, sir…

WATSON. But you didn't. Why, Mrs. Hudson?

MRS. HUDSON. Sir, I don't like to tell you, but…well, Mr. Holmes said he wouldn't even have you to see him.

WATSON. What? This is monstrous! I, his oldest friend and…

HOLMES *groans and stirs slightly.*

Ssh! He's waking. You go along, Mrs. Hudson, and leave this to me. Whether he likes it or not, I shall ensure that everything possible is done.

MRS. HUDSON. Thank you, sir. You'll ring if I can be of help.

C *She exits with* WATSON'S *things.* HOLMES *groans again and flings out an arm restlessly.* WATSON *comes to the audience's side of the bed and sits on it.*

WATSON. Holmes? It's I—Watson.

HOLMES. [*Sighs.*] Ahh! Well, Watson? We…we seem to have fallen on evil days.

WATSON. My dear fellow!

He moves to reach for HOLMES'S *pulse.*

HOLMES. [*Urgently.*] No, no! Keep back!

WATSON. Eh?

HOLMES. Mustn't come near.

622   **UNIT 7** DRAMA

Differentiated Instruction

English Language Learning
If you give students learning English a definition and context sentence, they might find it easier to understand unfamiliar words and phrases in the story.
hale and hearty—strong and healthy, 621. *Madeline's daily walk keeps her hale and hearty.*
general practitioner—doctor who does not specialize in any particular field of medicine, 623.

The general practitioner referred Sam to an eye specialist.
merely—no more than; only, 623. *Sherri took merely one bite and then stopped eating.*
colleagues—fellow workers in the same profession, 624. *Mark's colleagues voted him the most valuable member of the team.*
urgent—calling for immediate action; insistent, 625. *"Come immediately. It is urgent!" cried Mona.*

Watson. Now, look here, Holmes…!

Holmes. If you come near…order you out of the house.

Watson. [*Defiantly.*] Hah!

Holmes. For your own sake, Watson. Contracted…a coolie disease—from Sumatra.[1] Very little known, except that most deadly. Contagious[2] by touch. So…must keep away. **D**

Watson. Utter rubbish, Holmes! Mrs. Hudson tells me she helped you to your bed. There's nothing the matter with her.

Holmes. Period of…incubation.[3] Only dangerous after two or three days. Deadly by now.

Watson. Good heavens, do you suppose such a consideration weighs with me? Even if I weren't a doctor, d'you think it would stop me doing my duty to an old friend? Now, let's have a good look at you.

He moves forward again.

Holmes. [*Harshly.*] I tell you to keep back!

Watson. See here, Holmes…

Holmes. If you will stay where you are, I will talk to you. If you will not, you can get out.

Watson. Holmes! [*Recovering.*] Holmes, you aren't yourself. You're sick and as helpless as a child. Whether you like it or not, I'm going to examine you and treat you.

Holmes. [*Sneering.*] If I'm to be forced to have a doctor, let him at least be someone I've some confidence in. **F**

Watson. Oh! You…After all these years, Holmes, you haven't… confidence in me?

Holmes. In your friendship, Watson—yes. But facts are facts. As a medical man you're a mere general practitioner, of limited experience and mediocre qualifications.

Watson. Well…! Well, really!

Holmes. It is painful to say such things, but you leave me no choice.

Watson. [*Coldly.*] Thank you. I'll tell you this, Holmes. Such a remark, coming from you, merely serves to tell me what state your nerves are in. Still, if you insist that you have no confidence in me,

---

1. **Contracted…from Sumatra.** Caught an exotic Indonesian disease
2. **contagious.** Catching or infectious
3. **incubation.** Period between catching a disease and developing symptoms

DURING READING

Use Reading Strategies
Make Predictions Based on what you have read, what do you think Watson will do? **E**

THE DYING DETECTIVE **623**

History Connection
Prejudice The reference to a "coolie" reflects the racism that existed in nineteenth-century England. The word was a derogatory term for an indentured worker from Asia and later became a racial slur directed mostly at Chinese and Indian laborers in England. **D**

Use Reading Strategies
Make Predictions *Answer:* Most students will predict that Watson will stay away in order to talk to Holmes. Some may suggest that since he is a doctor, he will ignore Holmes's request. **E**

Analyze Literature
Dialogue Explain to students that well-written dialogue wastes no time but rather serves to keep the plot rolling, even when providing background details and other seemingly nonessential information. Direct students' attention to Holmes's assessment of Watson's medical qualifications. Ask them, based on what they know about the two men's relationship, how might Holmes's assessment serve to further the plot, rather than just function as an insult? **F**

Dictionary
Remind students that a dictionary can provide them with not only the pronunciation, derivation, and part of speech of a word but also with an explanation of the nuances of meaning of various synonyms of the word.

Each of the following closely related words could be used to describe Sherlock Holmes at various times. In a dictionary, look up the precise meaning of each, and write a sentence about Holmes in which you use the word.

1. adamant
2. inflexible
3. obdurate
4. inexorable
5. unyielding

Tropical Diseases Tapanuli Fever and Black Formosa Corruption are names made up by Doyle. He based these words on real place names. Tapanuli is in the northern part of Sumatra, and Formosa is what the island of Taiwan used to be called, a name given to it by Portuguese sailors. Doyle concocted these names to suggest rare tropical diseases for which the average British citizen would have no immunities. **A**

Analyze Literature

Drama *Answer:* The dialogue reveals that Holmes has a greater knowledge of exotic diseases than Watson has. It also makes Watson's deference to Holmes's superiority and authority believable. **B**

I will not intrude my services. But what I shall do is to summon Sir Jasper Meek or Penrose Fisher, or any of the other best men in London.

HOLMES. [*Groans.*] My…dear Watson. You mean well. But do you suppose they—any of them—know of the Tapanuli Fever?

WATSON. The Tap…?

HOLMES. What do you yourself know of the Black Formosa Corruption?

WATSON. Tapanuli Fever? Black Formosa Corruption? I've never heard of either of 'em.

HOLMES. Nor have your colleagues. There are many problems of disease, many <u>pathological</u> possibilities, peculiar to the East. So I've learned during some of my recent researches. It was in the course of one of them that I contracted this complaint. I assure you, Watson, you can do nothing.

WATSON. Can't I? I happen to know, Holmes, that the greatest living authority on tropical disease, Dr. Ainstree, is in London just now.

HOLMES. [*Beseeching.*] Watson!

WATSON. All remonstrance[4] is useless. I am going this instant to fetch him. [*He gets up.*]

HOLMES. [*A great cry.*] No!

WATSON. Eh? Holmes…my dear fellow…

HOLMES. Watson, in the name of our old friendship, do as I ask.

WATSON. But…

HOLMES. You have only my own good at heart. Of course, I know that. You…you shall have your way. Only…give me time to…to collect my strength. What is the time now?

WATSON *sits and consults his watch.*

DURING READING **A**

Analyze Literature
Drama What information is revealed by this dialogue? **B**

path·o·log·i·cal
(pa´ thə lä' ji kəl) *adj.,*
caused by disease or the origins of disease

---

4. **remonstrance.** Statement of opposition; protest

Differentiated Instruction

Enrichment

Students might enjoy researching the history of the British monetary system. Suggest that they look for answers to these questions:

1. What is the basic monetary unit in Great Britain?
2. What are the most common coins in circulation?
3. What are the denominations of paper currency?
4. How was the British monetary system different before 1971?
5. What is the pound worth today, compared to the American dollar?

WATSON. Four o'clock.

HOLMES. Then at six you can go.

WATSON. This is insanity!

HOLMES. Only two hours, Watson. I promise you may go then.

WATSON. Hang it, this is urgent, man!

HOLMES. I will see no one before six. I will not be examined. I shall resist!

WATSON. [*Sighing.*] Oh, have it your own way, then. But I insist on staying with you in the meantime. You need an eye keeping on you, Holmes.

HOLMES. Very well, Watson. And now I must sleep. I feel exhausted. [*Drowsily.*] I wonder how a battery feels when it pours electricity into a non-conductor?

WATSON. Eh?

HOLMES. [*Yawning.*] At six, Watson, we resume our conversation.

He lies back and closes his eyes. WATSON *makes as though to move, but thinks better of it. He sits still, watching* HOLMES. *A slow black-out.*

SCENE 2

The stage lights up again, though more dimly than before, to disclose the same scene. Twilight is apparent through the window. HOLMES *lies motionless.* WATSON *sits as before, though with his head sagging, half-asleep. His chin drops suddenly and he wakes with a jerk. He glances round, sees the twilight outside, and consults his watch. He yawns, flexes his arms, then proceeds to glance idly about him. His attention is caught by the little box on the bedside table. Stealthily, he reaches over and picks it up.*

HOLMES. [*Very loudly and urgently.*] No! No, Watson, no!

WATSON. [*Startled.*] Eh? What?

HOLMES. Put it down! Down this instant! Do as I say, Watson!

WATSON. Oh! All right, then. [*Putting the box down.*] Look here, Holmes, I really think...

HOLMES. I hate to have my things touched. You know perfectly well I do.

WATSON. Holmes...!

HOLMES. You fidget me beyond endurance. You, a doctor—you're enough to drive a patient into an asylum!

> **DURING READING**
>
> **Analyze Literature**
> **Suspense** What questions does this dialogue raise in readers' minds that heighten suspense? **C**

> **DURING READING**
>
> **Analyze Literature**
> **Drama** What do you learn about Holmes from this stage direction and dialogue? **D**

THE DYING DETECTIVE **625**

Use Reading Skills

Determine the Importance of Details Ask students to consider this exchange between Holmes and Watson concerning the coins in Watson's pocket. Ask: "Why do you think Doyle included this dialogue in the story?" Model a response by suggesting that Holmes is trying to make Watson think he is so sick that he is getting delirious. **A**

Using Reading Skills

Connect to Prior Knowledge Ask students what they know about lighting in those days. Model a response: "Electricity was not in common use; people used fire for light and heat." You might want to point out that although Thomas Edison had perfected the lightbulb in 1879, electricity was not used to light homes until after World War I. The lamp Holmes refers to could be using oil, kerosene, or paraffin as a fuel source. **B**

Use Reading Skills

Determine the Importance of Details *Answer:* Clues include Holmes's repeated requests that Watson be careful about the lamp. **C**

WATSON. Really!

HOLMES. Now, for heaven's sake, sit still, and let me have my rest.

WATSON. Holmes, it is almost six o'clock, and I refuse to delay another instant.

He gets up determinedly.

HOLMES. Really? Watson, have you any change in your pocket?

WATSON. Yes.

HOLMES. Any silver?

WATSON. [*Fishing out his change.*] A good deal.

A **HOLMES.** How many half-crowns?

WATSON. Er, five.

HOLMES. [*Sighing.*] Ah, too few, too few. However, such as they are, you can put them in your watch-pocket—and all the rest of your money in your left trouser-pocket. It will balance you so much better like that.

WATSON. Balance…? Holmes, you're raving! This has gone too far…!

B **HOLMES.** You will now light that lamp by the window, Watson, but you will be very careful that not for one instant shall it be more than at half flame.

WATSON. Oh, very well.

WATSON goes to the lamp and strikes a match.

HOLMES. I <u>implore</u> you to be careful.

WATSON. [*As though humoring him.*] Yes, Holmes.

He lights the lamp, carefully keeping the flame low. He moves to draw the curtains.

HOLMES. No, you need not draw curtains.

WATSON leaves them and comes back round the bed.

WATSON. Well, thank heaven for that.

HOLMES. His name is Mr. Culverton Smith, of 13 Lower Burke Street.

WATSON. [*Staring.*] Eh?

HOLMES. Well, go on, man. You could hardly wait to fetch someone before.

WATSON. Yes, but…Culverton Smith? I've never heard the name!

im • plore (im plôr´) *v.,* beg urgently

DURING READING

Use Reading Skills
Determine the Importance of Details What details suggest that the lamp might be important later? **C**

Differentiated Instruction

English Language Learning

Point out the spelling of the word *enquired*, and tell students that this is the British spelling of *inquired*. Have students review this list showing the differences between American and British spelling of some other common words:

theater / theatre
color / colour
skillful / skilful

bank / banque
judgment / judgement
defense / defence
plow / plough
program / programme
traveling / travelling

Also, point out Doyle's use of the words *bed-head* and *bed-foot,* rather than the American *headboard* and *footboard.*

Holmes. Possibly not. It may surprise you to know that the one man who knows everything about this disease is not a medical man. He's a planter.

Watson. A planter!

Holmes. His plantation is far from medical aid. An outbreak of this disease there caused him to study it intensely. He's a very methodical man, and I asked you not to go before six because I knew you wouldn't find him in his study till then.

Watson. Holmes, I…I never heard such a…!]**D**

Holmes. You will tell him exactly how you have left me. A dying man.

Watson. No, Holmes!

Holmes. At any rate, delirious.[5] Yes, not dying, delirious. [*Chuckles.*] No, I really can't think why the whole ocean bed isn't one solid mass of oysters.

Watson. Oysters?

Holmes. They're so prolific, you know.

Watson. Great Heavens! Now, Holmes, you just lie quiet, and…

Holmes. Strange how the mind controls the brain. Er, what was I saying, Watson?

Watson. You were…

Holmes. Ah, I remember. Culverton Smith. My life depends on him, Watson. But you will have to plead with him to come. There is no good feeling between us. He has…a grudge. I rely on you to soften him. Beg, Watson. Pray. But get him here by any means.

Watson. Very well. I'll bring him in a cab, if I have to carry him down to it.

Holmes. You will do nothing of the sort. You will persuade him to come—and then return before him. [*Deliberately.*] Make any excuse so as not to come with him. Don't forget that, Watson. You won't fail me. You never did fail me.

Watson. That's all very well, Holmes, but…

Holmes. [*Interrupting.*] Then, shall the world be overrun by oysters? No doubt there are natural enemies which limit their increase. And yet…No, horrible, horrible!

<hr>

5. **delirious.** Suffering from a temporary state of mental confusion

> **DURING READING**
>
> **Use Reading Skills**
> **Determine the Importance of Details** What clues help you predict what Watson is likely to do? **E**

Teach the Model

Analyze Literature

Dialogue Remind students that good dialogue, or lack thereof, always serves to further the plot. Direct their attention to Watson's incomplete exclamation. Ask them what they think he would have said if he had had time to finish his thought. Guide them to see that he might have said something to the effect of "I never heard such a lie!" or "I never heard such a ridiculous statement!" Ask students why they think Watson would have felt this way about Holmes's claim and why they think Holmes cut Watson's thought short in the way he did. **D**

Use Reading Skills

Determine the Importance of Details *Answer:* The dialogue shows that Watson is a man who does what he says he will do. This information helps readers predict that Watson will do what Holmes asked. **E**

Writing Skills

Dynamic Dialogue

Define "dynamic dialogue" as dialogue that moves the plot along and reveals details about the characters. Point out to students a few examples of dynamic dialogue, such as the exchange between Smith and Holmes about Victor Savage's death. Have students find other examples of dynamic dialogue in the play. Then have them revise the following example of mundane dialogue to make it more dynamic.

HOLMES. Good morning, Watson.
WATSON. Good morning, Holmes.
HOLMES. I need your help on a puzzling case.
WATSON. Always happy to help. What can I do?

Analyze Literature

Scenes Point out to students that this play is divided into three scenes. Tell them that many plays are divided into acts, which are then subdivided into scenes. Other plays, like this one, do not have act divisions. Ask students why a playwright might divide a play into scenes rather than just show continuous action. Model a response: "A new scene can take place in a different setting, or it can indicate that time has passed in the same setting. In this play, all the action takes place in the same setting, but time elapses between each scene."

Use Reading Skills

Determine the Importance of Details Home in on Watson's description of Culverton Smith's attitude toward Holmes. Ask students if they think this description is important to the plot. Why? Lead them to understand that it alters the play's tone, causes the audience to wonder why Smith would bear a grudge against Holmes, and leads one to question the quality of treatment he will provide Holmes.

WATSON. [*Grimly.*] I'm going, Holmes. Say no more, I'm going!

He hurries out. HOLMES *remains propped up for a moment, staring after* WATSON, *then sinks back into a sleeping posture as the stage blacks out.*

SCENE 3

The stage lights up on the same scene. HOLMES *lies still. It is now quite dark outside. After a moment* WATSON *bustles in, pulling off his coat. He pauses to hand it to* MRS. HUDSON, *who is behind him.*

WATSON. Thank you, Mrs. Hudson. A gentleman will be calling very shortly. Kindly show him up here immediately.

MRS. HUDSON. Yes, sir. [*She exits.* WATSON *approaches the bed.*]

HOLMES. [*Drowsily.*] Watson?

WATSON. Yes, Holmes. How are you feeling?

HOLMES. Much the same, I fear. Is Culverton Smith coming?

WATSON. Should be here any minute. It took me some minutes to find a cab, and I almost expected him to have got here first.

HOLMES. Well done, my dear Watson.

WATSON. I must say, Holmes, I'm only doing this to humor you. Frankly, I didn't take to your planter friend at all.

HOLMES. Oh? How so?

WATSON. Rudeness itself. He almost showed me the door before I could give him your message. It wasn't until I mentioned the name, Sherlock Holmes…

HOLMES. Ah!

WATSON. Quite changed him—but I wouldn't say it was for the better.

HOLMES. Tell me what he said.

WATSON. Said you'd had some business dealings together, and that he respected your character and talents. Described you as an amateur of crime, in a way that he regards himself as an amateur of disease.

HOLMES. Quite typical—and surely, quite fair?

WATSON. Quite fair—if he hadn't put such sarcasm into saying it. No, Holmes, you said he bears you some grudge. Mark my words, as soon as he has left this house I insist upon calling a recognized specialist.

Differentiated Instruction

Kinesthetic Learning
Kinesthetic learners might benefit from acting out one or more of the scenes described in the play. Provide props that would be helpful, and invite students to perform for the class.

Reading Proficiency
Have students stop from time to time to monitor their comprehension of what they have just read. Partners can take turns summarizing the action as they go along.

HOLMES. My dear Watson, you are the best of messengers. Thank you again.

WATSON. Not at all. Holmes, Holmes—let me help you without any of this nonsense. The whole of Great Britain will condemn me otherwise. Why, my cabmen both enquired anxiously after you; and so did Inspector Morton…

HOLMES. Morton?

CULTURAL ▶▶ CONNECTION

The Death of Sherlock Holmes At one point, Arthur Conan Doyle grew tired of writing about the fictional Sherlock Holmes and decided to stop. In a story titled "The Final Problem," Holmes appears to fall to his death in hand-to-hand combat with his archenemy, Professor Moriarty. The public reaction was swift and outraged. Fans wore black bands to show that they were in mourning, and more than twenty thousand readers cancelled subscriptions to the magazine that often published stories about Holmes. Doyle bowed to public pressure and revived Holmes—who had escaped Moriarty, he now revealed. Sherlock Holmes was one of the first detective story heroes. Why do think this type of fiction has remained so popular? **B**

WATSON. Of the Yard.[6] He was passing our door just now as I came in. Seemed extremely concerned.

HOLMES. Scotland Yard concerned for me? How very touching! And now, Watson, you may disappear from the scene.

C

WATSON. Disappear! I shall do no such thing. I wish to be present when this Culverton Smith arrives. I wish to hear every word of this so-called medical expert's opinion.

HOLMES. [*Turning his head.*] Yes, of course. Then I think you will just find room behind the head of the bed.

WATSON. What? Hide?

HOLMES. I have reason to suppose that his opinion will be much more frank and valuable if he imagines he is alone with me.

---

6. **Yard.** Short form of Scotland Yard, the headquarters of London's Metropolitan Police

> ### DURING READING
> **Analyze Literature**
> **Drama** At what point in the play do you first learn that there is a space behind the head of the bed? **D**

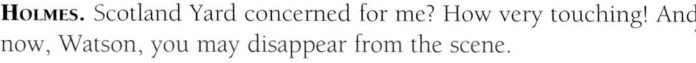

Speaking & Listening Skills

Dramatic Performance
Have a group of students perform the play for the class. Alternatively, you could have three different groups perform one scene each, if you want to actively involve more students. Scene 1 needs three actors (Mrs. Hudson, Watson, and Holmes), Scene 2 needs two actors (Holmes and Watson), and

Scene 3 needs five actors (Holmes, Watson, Mrs. Hudson, Smith, and Morton). Other roles might include director and prop person.

Allow sufficient time for rehearsals, and on the day of the performance, remind the audience of their responsibility to listen attentively.

Use Reading Strategies

Visualize Ask students to visualize this scene, in which Holmes and Smith converse and Watson hides. First, have students refer to the stage directions on page 621. Guide them in understanding that, based on the placement and positioning of the bed on the set, Watson is visible to the audience but not to the actors on the stage. What different approaches might the actor playing Watson take in silently responding to the action on the stage? How would each approach affect the tone of the scene? **A**

Analyze Literature

Tone Direct students' attention to the exchange between Smith and Mrs. Hudson. What tone does Smith's manner of addressing Mrs. Hudson and her physical and verbal response to this address create? **B**

We hear the murmur of MRS. HUDSON's *and* CULVERTON SMITH's *voices offstage.*

Listen! I hear him coming. Get behind the bed, Watson, and do not budge, whatever happens. *Whatever* happens, you understand?

WATSON. Oh, all right, Holmes. Anything to please you. But I don't like this. Not at all.

A *He goes behind the bed-head and conceals himself.* MRS. HUDSON *enters, looks round the room and then at* HOLMES. SMITH *enters behind her.*

MRS. HUDSON. [*To* SMITH.] Oh, Dr. Watson must have let himself out. No doubt he'll be back directly, sir.

B **SMITH.** No matter, my good woman. [MRS. HUDSON *bristles at this form of address.*] You may leave me alone with your master.

MRS. HUDSON. As you wish—sir.

She sweeps out. SMITH *advances slowly to the bed and stands at the foot, staring at the recumbent* HOLMES.

SMITH. [*Almost to himself.*] So, Holmes. It has come to this, then.

HOLMES *stirs.* SMITH *chuckles and leans his arms on the bed-foot and his chin on them, continuing to watch* HOLMES.

HOLMES. [*Weakly.*] Watson? Who…? Smith? Smith, is that you?

SMITH *chuckles.*

HOLMES. I…I hardly dared hope you would come.

SMITH. I should imagine not. And yet, you see, I'm here. Coals of fire,[7] Holmes—coals of fire!

HOLMES. Noble of you…

SMITH. Yes, isn't it?

HOLMES. I appreciate your special knowledge.

SMITH. Then you're the only man in London who does. Do you know what is the matter with you?

HOLMES. The same as young Victor—your cousin.

SMITH. Ah, then you recognize the symptoms. Well, then, it's a bad look-out for you. Victor was a strong, hearty young fellow—but a dead man on the fourth day. As you said at the time, it *was* rather surprising that he should contract an out-of-the-way Asiatic disease in the heart of London—a disease of which *I* have made very special

---

7. **Coals of fire.** Reference to a New Testament passage, Romans 12:20, "Therefore if thine enemy hunger, feed him; if he thirst, give him drink; for in so doing thou shalt heap coals of fire on his head."

Differentiated Instruction

Reading Proficiency

This page features punctuation that signals extended pauses key to grasping the tone and meaning of the scene ("As you wish—*sir*," "Watson? Who…?", "I…I hardly dared," "Coals of fire, Holmes—coals of fire!", "young Victor—your cousin"). To

ensure students' appreciation of the scene, discuss the purpose and effect of these and other instances of punctuation. Then allow them time to practice heeding the marks as they read aloud.

study. [*Chuckles.*] And now, you, Holmes. Singular coincidence, eh? Or are you going to start making accusations once again—about cause and effect, and so on.

HOLMES. I...I knew you caused Victor Savage's death.

SMITH *comes round the bed.*

SMITH. [*Snarling.*] Did you? Well, proving it is a different matter, Holmes. But what sort of a game is this, then—spreading lying reports about me one moment, then crawling to me for help the next?

HOLMES. [*Gasping.*] Give...give me water. For...pity's sake, Smith. Water!

SMITH *hesitates momentarily, then goes to the table and pours a glass from the carafe.*

SMITH. You're precious near your end, my friend, but I don't want you to go till I've had a word with you.

He holds out the glass to HOLMES *who struggles up feebly to take it and drinks.*

HOLMES. [*Gulping water.*] Ah! Thank...thank you. Please...do what you can for me. Only cure me, and I promise to forget.

SMITH. Forget what?

HOLMES. About Victor Savage's death. You as good as admitted just now that you had done it. I swear I will forget it.

SMITH. [*Laughs.*] Forget it, remember it—do as you like. I don't see you in any witness-box, Holmes. Quite another shape of box, I assure you. But you must hear first how it came about.

HOLMES. Working amongst Chinese sailors. Down at the docks.

SMITH. Proud of your brains, aren't you? Think yourself smart? Well, you've met a smarter one this time.

HOLMES *falls back, groaning loudly.*

Getting painful, is it?

HOLMES *cries out, writhing[8] in agony.*

SMITH. That's the way. Takes you as cramp, I fancy?

HOLMES. Cramp! Cramp!

---

8. **writhing.** Twisting as if in severe pain

DURING READING

Use Reading Skills
Determine the Importance of Details What important details does this dialogue reveal about Smith and the plot?

Teach the Model

Use Reading Strategies

Make Inferences As the play draws nearer to its climax, the reality of the situation begins to unfold. Doyle reveals essential information explicitly and implicitly. Direct students' attention to Smith's query. Ask, "What kind of accusation is Smith implying and how do you know?" Model a response: "Smith is implying that Holmes will accuse him of causing his infection. I can tell this because of the information I have gathered throughout the play about Smith's familiarity with the disease, as well as Holmes's curious way of approaching him." **C**

Use Reading Skills

Determine the Importance of Details *Answer:* The dialogue reveals that Victor died from contracting the same disease that Holmes seems to have, and that Smith is an expert in the disease. **D**

Use Reading Skills

Use Context Clues Ask students what kind of box Smith is talking about, and have them explain what context clues led them to this conclusion. Model a response: "Smith is obviously talking about a coffin; the context clues are the facts that Holmes appears very ill and Smith says, 'You're precious near your end.' " **E**

Research Skills

Primary and Secondary Sources

Remind students that when they research the life and career of a writer such as Doyle, both primary and secondary sources can be useful. A primary source is a firsthand account of an event. Secondary sources are written by people who did not directly experience an event. Have students identify which of the following materials related to Doyle would be primary sources and which would be secondary sources.

1. A magazine article based on a personal interview of Doyle
2. A book review about a new edition of Sherlock Holmes stories
3. A diary entry written by Doyle
4. A book report by an eighth-grade student on one of Doyle's books
5. A biography of Doyle at a website
6. A letter written by Doyle to a fan

Use Reading Strategies

Make Predictions *Answer:* Many students will predict that Holmes dies; others may suggest that he will plead for his life. **A**

Use Reading Skills

Analyze Cause and Effect Have students speculate on the cause of Smith's animosity toward Holmes and the effect of that animosity on their relationship. Model a response: "It appears that Holmes has interfered with some of Smith's evildoings in the past, and now Smith wants to not only get even with Holmes but stop his meddling altogether." **B**

Use Reading Skills

Activate Prior Knowledge Ask students where they have heard the phrase "valley of the shadow" before. What is its relevance here? Model a response by repeating the line "Yea, though I walk through the valley of the shadow of death" from the Twenty-Third Psalm and suggesting that Smith is sure that Holmes will die any minute. **C**

Analyze Literature

Drama *Answer:* The stage direction shows a surprising change in the condition of Holmes. **D**

DURING READING

Use Reading Strategies
Make Predictions What prediction can you make about Holmes based on these clues? **A**

SMITH. Well, you can still hear me. Now, can't you just remember any unusual incident—just about the time your symptoms began?

HOLMES. I...can't think. My mind is gone! Help me, Smith!

SMITH. Did nothing come to you through the post,[9] for instance?

HOLMES. Post? Post?

SMITH. Yes. A little box, perhaps?

HOLMES *emits a shuddering groan.*

SMITH. [*Closer; deadly.*] Listen! You *shall* hear me! Don't you remember a box—a little ivory box? [*He sees it on the table and holds it up.*] Yes, here it is on your bedside table. It came on Wednesday. You opened it—do you remember?

HOLMES. Box? Opened? Yes, Yes! There was...sharp spring inside. Pricked my finger. Some sort of joke...

B **SMITH.** It was no joke, Holmes. You fool! Who asked you to cross my path? If you'd only left me alone I would never have hurt you.

HOLMES. Box! Yes! Pricked finger. Poison!

SMITH. [*Triumphantly.*] So you do remember. Good, good! I'm glad indeed. Well, the box leaves this room in my pocket, and there's your last shred[10] of evidence gone. [*He pockets it.*] But you have the truth now, Holmes. You can die knowing that I killed you. You knew too much about what happened to Victor Savage, so you must share his fate. Yes, Holmes, you are very near your end now. I think I shall sit here and watch you die.

He sits on the bed.

HOLMES. [*Almost a whisper.*] The shadows...falling. Getting...so dark. I can't see Smith! Smith, are you there? The light...for charity's sake, turn up the light!

SMITH *laughs, gets up and goes to the light.*

C **SMITH.** Entering the valley of the shadow, eh, Holmes? Yes, I'll turn up the light for you. I can watch your face more plainly, then.

He turns the flame up full.

There! Now, is there any *further* service I can render you?

HOLMES. [*In a clear, strong voice.*] A match and my pipe, if you please.

He sits bolt upright, SMITH *spins round to see him.*

DURING READING

Analyze Literature
Drama Why is this stage direction important? **D**

---

9. **post.** Mail from a post office
10. **shred.** Tiny amount

Differentiated Instruction

Enrichment
Holmes's last line and stage direction on this page function as the play's climax, or turning point. Challenge students to come to this conclusion on their own by creating a plot diagram and mapping the exposition and rising action that lead to the climax. Invite students to share their completed maps with the class.

English Language Learners
Confirm that students recognize the directionality of reading English. Students should work from left to right and top to bottom. Also, point out that the During Reading and Cultural Connection boxes are included to provide background information for the reader and are not part of the original text.

Smith. Eh? What the devil's the meaning of this?

Holmes. [*Cheerfully.*] The best way of successfully acting a part is to *be* it. I give you my word that for three days I have neither tasted food nor drink until you were good enough to pour me out that glass of water. But it's the tobacco I find most irksome.

We hear the thud of footsteps running upstairs offstage.

Hello, hello! Do I hear the step of a friend.

Inspector Morton hurries in.

Morton. Mr. Holmes?

Holmes. Inspector Morton, this is your man.

Smith. What is the meaning of…?

Morton. Culverton Smith, I arrest you on the charge of the murder of one Victor Savage, and I must warn you that anything you say…

Smith. You've got nothing on me! It's all a trick! A pack of lies!

He makes to escape. Morton *restrains him.*

Morton. Keep still, or you'll get yourself hurt!

Smith. Get off me!

Morton. Hold your hands out!

They struggle. Morton *gets out handcuffs and claps them on* Smith's *wrists.*

That'll do.

Holmes. By the way, Inspector, you might add the attempted murder of one Sherlock Holmes to that charge. Oh, and you'll find a small box in the pocket of your prisoner's coat. Pray, leave it on the table, here. Handle it gingerly,[11] though. It may play its part at his trial.

Morton *retrieves the box and places it on the table.*

Smith. Trial! You'll be the one in the dock,[12] Holmes. Inspector, he asked me to come here. He was ill, and I was sorry for him, so I came. Now he'll pretend I've said anything he cares to invent that will corroborate his insane suspicions. Well, you can lie as you like, Holmes. My word's as good as yours.

Holmes. Good heavens! I'd completely forgotten him!

Morton. Forgotten who, sir?

---

11. **gingerly.** With great care
12. **dock.** Area in a courtroom where an accused person sits

cor·rob·o·rate
(kə rä′ bə rāt′) *v.*, confirm, support with evidence

Teach the Model

Analyze Literature
Drama Discuss with students the validity of this statement by Holmes. Point out that many actors try to take on the persona of the character they are playing so that their emotional state matches the state of the character. This is called *method acting.* **E**

Analyze Literature
Dialogue Have students comment on what Holmes really means here. Model a response: "What Holmes is saying is that it is the *lack* of tobacco that he finds most irksome." **F**

Analyze Literature
Climax This is the climax, or the high point, of the plot. It is what Holmes has been planning all along. Everything that follows is the falling action, or denouement, where all the loose ends are tied up. **G**

Writing Skills

Author's Purpose
Remind students that Doyle had a specific purpose for writing this story (to entertain his audience by presenting another witty triumph by Sherlock Holmes). The falling action, including Smith turning up the lamp and Inspector Morton entering the room to arrest him, helps Doyle achieve his set purpose. Ask students to alter the falling action to fit the following purposes:

1. To entertain the audience by having Holmes narrowly escape death.
2. To shock the audience by allowing Holmes's antagonist to achieve his objective.

Analyze Literature

Characterization Holmes's attitude toward Watson varies throughout the story. He is alternately manipulative, condescending, and praising. Discuss with students their opinions of Holmes's and Watson's relationship, paying attention to Watson's attitude as well. **A**

Use Reading Strategies

Make Predictions *Answer:* Most students will predict that Smith will be arrested and that Holmes will prove not to be ill at all. **B**

Use Reading Skills

Determine the Importance of Details Guide students to the realization that if Smith had not turned up the lamp, Inspector Morton would not have received his signal to enter. Ask students to imagine that Smith did not turn up the lamp, and have them offer alternative plot results. **C**

HOLMES. Watson, my dear fellow! Do come out!

WATSON emerges with cramped groans.

A I owe you a thousand apologies. To think that I should have overlooked you!

WATSON. It's all right, Holmes. Would have come out before, only you said, whatever happened, I wasn't to budge.

SMITH. What's all this about?

HOLMES. I needn't introduce you to my witness, my friend Dr. Watson. I understand you met somewhere earlier in the evening.

SMITH. You…you mean you had all this planned?

HOLMES. Of course. To the last detail. I think I may say it worked very well—with your assistance, of course.

SMITH. Mine?

C **HOLMES.** You saved an invalid trouble by giving my signal to Inspector Morton, waiting outside. You turned up the lamp.

SMITH and WATSON are equally flabbergasted. **¹³**

MORTON. I'd better take him along now, sir. [*To* SMITH.] Come on.

He bundles SMITH *roughly towards the door.*

We'll see you down at the Yard tomorrow, perhaps, Mr. Holmes?

HOLMES. Very well, Inspector. And many thanks.

WATSON. Goodbye, Inspector.

MORTON exits with SMITH.

WATSON. [*Chuckles.*] Well, Holmes?

DURING READING

Use Reading Strategies
Make Predictions What predictions can you make about the play's outcome based on this dialogue? **B**

---

13. **flabbergasted.** Totally astonished and surprised

Differentiated Instruction

Visual Learning

Students might further appreciate the humor of *The Dying Detective* if they watch and/or participate in an enactment of this section. Remind them that Watson has been hiding behind the bed's headboard throughout Holmes's dealings with Smith. Invite students to take turns playing Watson as he conceals himself, allowing them to explore what actions he might take while in hiding. Discuss the comedic effect of each student's portrayal.

Holmes. Well, Watson, there's a bottle of claret over there—it is uncorked—and some biscuits in the barrel. If you'll be so kind, I'm badly in need of both.

Watson. Certainly. You know, Holmes, all this seems a pretty, well, elaborate way to go about catching that fellow. I mean, taking in Mrs. Hudson—*and me*—like that. Scared us half to death. **D**

Holmes. It was very essential that I should make Mrs. Hudson believe in my condition. She was to convey it to you, and you to him.

Watson. Well…

Holmes. Pray do not be offended, my good Watson. You must admit that among your *many* talents, dissimulation[14] scarcely finds a place. If you'd shared my secret, you would never have been able to impress Smith with the urgent necessity of coming to me. It was the vital point of the whole scheme. I knew his vindictive[15] nature, and I was certain he would come to gloat over his handiwork.

Watson returns with the bottle, glasses and barrel.

Watson. But…but your appearance, Holmes. Your face! You really do look ghastly.

Holmes. Three days of absolute fast does not improve one's beauty, Watson. However, as you know, my habits are irregular, and such a feat means less to me than to most men. For the rest, there is nothing that a sponge won't cure. Vaseline to produce the glistening forehead; belladonna[16] for the watering of the eyes; rouge over the cheekbones and crust of beeswax round one's lips…

Watson. [*Chuckling.*] And that babbling oysters! [*He begins pouring the wine.*]

Holmes. Yes. I've sometimes thought of writing a monograph[17] on the subject of malingering.[18]

Watson. But why wouldn't you let me near you? There was no risk of infection.

Holmes. Whatever I may have said to the contrary in the grip of delirium, do you imagine that I have no respect for your medical talents? Could I imagine that you would be deceived by a dying man

---

14. **dissimulation.** Concealing of the truth
15. **vindictive.** Showing a great desire for revenge
16. **belladonna.** Drug that can change the appearance of the eyes
17. **monograph.** Scholarly piece of writing on one topic
18. **malingering.** Avoiding work by pretending to be ill

> **DURING READING**
>
> **Analyze Literature**
> **Drama** What important details do you learn about characters and plot from this dialogue? **E**

Literary Connection
Detective Fiction Since Doyle

Point out to students the influence that Doyle has had on the genre of detective fiction. Since Doyle's time, many writers have created a somewhat eccentric detective who seems to have an income independent of crime-solving and independent of a full-time job. (Dorothy Sayers's Lord Peter Wimsey and Agatha Christie's Hercule Poirot and Miss Jane Marple come to mind.) The less intelligent sidekick, like Dr. Watson, who asks questions for the famous detective to answer is also a stock character. Students can probably name many eccentric detectives, from literature's Encyclopedia Brown, Nancy Drew, and the Hardy Boys to television's Kojak, Monk, and Magnum, who exhibit some of the traits of Sherlock Holmes.

636 UNIT 7 DRAMA

Differentiated Instruction

Enrichment

The Sherlock Holmes Society of London was formed in 1951. Membership is international and does not discriminate by age. Society members pretend that Holmes, Watson, and all other characters are real people and that the stories deal with historical cases. Encourage students to research this society and other Holmesian groups. Then challenge them to take a position as to whether Doyle's work

deserves such consistent and widespread praise and attention, based on their reactions to varied elements of *The Dying Detective*. Have students present their arguments in essays or oral presentations.

with no rise of pulse or temperature? At four yards distance I *could* deceive you.

WATSON *reaches for the box.*

WATSON. This box, then…

HOLMES. No, Watson! I wouldn't touch it. You can just see, if you look at it sideways, where the sharp spring emerges as you open it. I dare say it was by some such device that poor young Savage was done to death. He stood between that monster and an inheritance, you know.

WATSON. Then it's true, Holmes! You… you might have been killed, too!

HOLMES. As you know, my correspondence is a varied one. I am somewhat on my guard against any packages which reach me. But I saw that by pretending he had succeeded in his design I might be enabled to surprise a confession from him. That pretense I think I may claim to have carried out with the thoroughness of a true artist.

WATSON. [*Warmly.*] You certainly did, Holmes. Er, a biscuit?

He holds out the barrel.

HOLMES. On second thoughts, Watson, no thank you. Let us preserve our appetite. By the time I have shaved and dressed, I fancy it will just be nice time for something nutritious at our little place in the Strand.

They raise their glasses to one another and drink. The curtain falls. ✣

DURING READING

Use Reading Strategies
Clarify How does Holmes tie up loose ends before the curtain falls? **B**

Would you rather have Holmes or Watson as a friend? What qualities would make that person a better friend than the other? What qualities are most important in a friend?

Use Reading Skills
Identify Cause and Effect This sentence explains why Culverton Smith wanted to kill his own nephew. Point out to students that greed is the motivation behind most crimes in detective stories. **A**

Use Reading Strategies
Clarify *Answer:* Holmes ties up loose ends by explaining how he made himself appear so ill, why he kept Watson away, and why he was not poisoned by the box that Smith sent. **B**

MIRRORS & WINDOWS You may want to ask students to write a journal entry or quick write, or divide students into discussion groups or lead a whole-class discussion about this question. *Answer:* Students might prefer Holmes because he was smart, analytical, and successful; they might prefer Watson because he was such a loyal and reliable friend and colleague.

TEACHING NOTE

Ask the Author
Divide the class into small groups, and have them brainstorm and jot down questions they would like to ask Sir Arthur Conan Doyle. Model a question such as: "How did you know which symptoms to portray?" Instruct each group to pass its questions to another group, and to then pretend it is the author and attempt to answer the questions it receives. Have the groups share some of their questions and answers as a class.

Review the Model

Find Meaning

1. (a) Mrs. Hudson. (b) Mrs. Hudson was probably easier to trick than Dr. Watson would have been.

2. (a) He begs him to wait until 6 PM to fetch him. (b) He would have known right away that Holmes was not ill. Also, Holmes had probably set up a prearranged time for Inspector Morton to be waiting outside.

Make Judgments

3. Because the title suggests that a detective is dying, students are likely to believe that Holmes is truly ill.

4. (a) Both are intelligent, crafty, and knowledgeable men. (b) Their even match makes Holmes's triumph even more amazing.

5. Holmes bases his plan on Watson's reliability, and he apologizes and compliments him on his medical skill.

6. Holmes is clever, interesting, possesses unusual and broad knowledge, judges people well, and seems like a decent friend.

Analyze Literature

Drama *Answer:* Essential characteristics include Holmes's intelligence, Smith's vindictiveness, and Watson's reliability. Essential dialogue might include the tale of contracting an exotic disease, the discussion of local doctors' lack of knowledge about these, or the instructions to light the lamp only halfway. Essential stage directions may include the opening list of essential features, the description of Watson reaching for the box, or Holmes's fake writhing in agony.

Apply the Model

BEFORE READING
DURING READING
AFTER READING

Find Meaning

1. (a) From whom does the audience first learn what happened to Holmes while Watson was away? (b) What motive might Holmes have had for waiting until Watson was out of town?

2. (a) What does Holmes do after Watson announces that the greatest authority on tropical diseases is in London? (b) Why was it important that Watson not ask that authority to examine Holmes?

Analyze Literature

Drama The elements of drama—characters, dialogue, and stage directions—work together to tell a story. Consider the personalities of each character, the information contained in dialogue, and the stage directions. What essential elements did each contribute to *The Dying Detective?* Provide additional examples of each.

Make Judgments

3. What effect does the title of the play have on your attitudes toward Holmes's behavior in the first two scenes?

4. (a) In what ways are Smith and Holmes similar? (b) What do these similarities add to the central conflict?

5. What details suggest that Holmes truly values his friend Watson?

6. What characteristics does Holmes exhibit that might make him so popular with readers?

Character	Dialogue	Stage Directions
Watson is a loyal friend.	Holmes won't allow any doctors to see him.	head of the bed is a foot or two from the side wall

Extend Understanding

Writing Options

Creative Writing Write a brief **news article** describing how Holmes solved the case. Remember that news stories answer the questions *who, what, when, where, why,* and *how.*

Expository Writing Use your details chart to write a brief **literary response essay** that discusses the most significant details and how they contributed to a particular theme or message in the play. State your opinion of the theme in a thesis. Support it with evidence.

Collaborative Learning

Identify Characters Work with a partner to classify the characters in the play *The Dying Detective.* Identify the protagonist, or main character, and the antagonist, or character who struggles with the main character. Provide reasons for each of your choices.

Lifelong Learning

Analyze Elements of Theater Independently create a list of all stage elements and props that a production of *The Dying Detective* would use. Afterward, compare your list with those of your classmates, creating a single complete list.

Go to **www.mirrorsandwindows.com** for more.

Rubrics for Writing Options

You can adapt this as a checklist for students to use as they write.

Creative Writing

☐ Does it explain how Holmes solved the case?
☐ Does it employ a pyramid structure?
☐ Does it answer the questions *who, what, where why,* and *how?*

Expository Writing

☐ Does the first paragraph of the literary response include a clear thesis statement about the theme of *The Dying Detective?*
☐ Do the body paragraphs contain examples of significant details and explain how they support the theme?
☐ Does the concluding paragraph sum up the arguments?

Vocabulary & Spelling

Greek, Latin, and Anglo-Saxon Roots

"This is dreadful, Mrs. Hudson. He was perfectly hale and hearty when I went away only three days ago."

—MICHAEL AND MOLLY HARDWICK, *The Dying Detective*

New words are added to the dictionary each year. However, thousands of common English words are formed from **Latin** or **Greek roots** or base words. Many others come from **Anglo-Saxon** or "Old English" roots—English spoken during the fifth through twelfth century. In the above quotation, the word *dreadful* derives from the Anglo-Saxon word *draeden,* meaning "to fear."

The meaning of some words is slightly different from their roots. For example, *hale* is an Old English word meaning "whole." In the quotation, the adjective *hale* means "healthy."

> **EXAMPLES**
>
> *pathological*—from the Greek words *pathos* meaning "suffering" and *logia* meaning "to study." *Pathological* refers to an illness or abnormal condition.
>
> *agitated*—from the Latin word *agito* meaning "to put in motion or move." *Agitated* means "disturbed."

Here are some common roots.

Root Word	Meaning	Origin	English Words
polis, polit	"citizen, city, state"	Greek	politics, polls
log	"idea, reason, speech"	Greek	logic, dialogue
tal/tall	"put into words"	Anglo-Saxon	tell, talk, tale

say	"speak or declare"	Anglo-Saxon	said, saying
port	"carry"	Latin	import, support
vert	"turn"	Latin	invert, convert

The dictionary provides information on word origin, or **etymology,** of the simplest form of a word. For example, you would look up *intend* rather than *unintentionally.*

Vocabulary Practice

Many academic terms are derived from Latin, Greek, and Anglo-Saxon. Look up the origin and the meaning of each of the words below. Then write down the connection between the word's origin and its current meaning.

1. mathematics
2. anthropology
3. barometer
4. participle
5. organism
6. playwright

Spelling Practice

Greek, Latin, and Anglo-Saxon Word Parts

Many academic terms are derived from Greek, Latin, or Anglo-Saxon word parts. Examine the words below and use the root words as well as the prefixes and suffixes (known as *affixes*) to help you determine the meaning of each term. To help you with this task, refer to the Language Arts Handbook 2.2, Breaking Words into Base Words, Word Roots, Prefixes, and Suffixes, as well as a dictionary.

aquatic	knowledge	plagiarism
bladder	liberal	spelling
conduct	logical	stereotype
evolution	nutritious	symptom
infinite	pathological	temperature

Vocabulary Practice

Sample response:

1. **mathematics** Origin: from Latin *mathematica* meaning learning or knowledge; Current Meaning: the science of numbers (a science of learning and knowledge)

> ▶ Refer to Section 2.7, Spelling, in the Language Arts Handbook for additional instruction on spelling rules.

Words in Use

Teaching Words

dreadful, 639
derives, 639
abnormal, 639
unintentionally, 639
monstrous, 639
contracted, 639
remonstrance, 639
vindictive, 639

Program Resources

You will find additional lessons on Greek, Latin, and Anglo-Saxon Roots in the *Exceeding the Standards: Vocabulary & Spelling* resource.

KEY TERMS

LATIN ROOT, 639
GREEK ROOT, 639
BASE WORD, 639
ANGLO-SAXON ROOT, 639
ETYMOLOGY, 639

Common Core State Standards

Language
L.4

At a Glance
Directed Reading
- Reading Level: Moderate
- Difficulty Consideration: Length
- Ease Factor: Sympathetic characters

Objectives
Studying this lesson will enable students to
- use reading strategies such as summarizing
- define *plot* and recognize the plot elements in Anne Frank's story
- describe the literary accomplishments of Frances Goodrich and Albert Hackett in putting Anne Frank's diary into drama form

Launch the Lesson
Ask students to imagine being told they were going to hide somewhere for an undetermined amount of time. They must decide what to take with them, and they must be able to get the items to the hiding place without drawing attention to themselves. As students name items, write them on the board. Then go through the list and determine how many of those items one person could wear or carry unobtrusively. Tell students that Anne Frank was in just such a position.

Common Core State Standards
Reading Literature
RL.1, RL.2, RL.3, RL.6
Writing
W.9
Language
L.6

DIRECTED READING

The Diary of Anne Frank, Act 1
A Drama by Frances Goodrich and Albert Hackett

BEFORE READING

Build Background
Historical Context Anne Frank and her family were Jews who fled Nazi Germany to Holland. After the Nazis occupied Holland in 1940, the Franks were no longer safe, and in 1942 they "disappeared" into a hideout, a tiny secret apartment in the warehouse where Anne's father worked. She recorded in her diary what her life was like in such cramped quarters and expressed her hopes for the future after the war.

Reader's Context What do you think would be the hardest part of "disappearing," as Anne did?

Set Purpose
Preview the selection. Write down your initial questions and what you would like to learn more about. Then read to discover the answers to your questions and to increase your understanding.

Analyze Literature
Plot The **plot** of a story or drama is the series of events that take place. Each plot usually begins with **exposition**—details that introduce the characters and setting. **Rising action** occurs as the conflict grows more complicated. The tension rises to its highest point at the **climax.** Once that occurs, **falling action** leads downward to the **resolution,** the final outcome. As you read Act 1, identify the exposition, conflict, and the events that lead up to the climax.

Meet the Authors
Husband-and-wife team **Frances Goodrich** (1890–1984) and **Albert Hackett** (1900–1995) spent two years transforming Anne Frank's diary into this play. During the course of their work, they met with Anne's father, Otto Frank. The play won the Pulitzer Prize in 1954. Goodrich and Hackett then wrote the screenplay for the movie version, which was produced in 1959.

640 UNIT 7 DRAMA

Use Reading Skills
Summarize To summarize a piece of literature is to give only the most important points or details. As you read this play, use a summary chart to jot down the main events.

	Summary of Main Events
Act 1	Mr. Frank finds Anne's diary.
Act 2	

Preview Vocabulary
sparse • ly (spärs´ lē) *adv.*, thinly; not full or densely

con • spic • u • ous (kən spi´ kyə wəs) *adj.*, easily seen or noticed

im • pro • vise (im´ prə vīz´) *v.*, make with materials easily at hand, usually to fulfill a sudden need

os • ten • ta • tious • ly (äs´ tən tā´ shəs lē) *adv.*, in a showy way; overly proudly or boastfully

in • ar • tic • u • late (i´ när ti´ kyə lət´) *adj.*, incapable of speech, especially under the stress of strong emotions

fore • bod • ing (fôr bō´ diŋ) *adj.*, prediction that something bad or harmful will happen

in • ti • mate (in´ tə mət) *adj.*, marked by close association, familiarity, and warm friendship

in • ef • fec • tu • al • ly (i´ nə fek´ chə[wə] lē) *adv.*, without success

Words in Use

Preview Vocabulary	Selection Words	Teaching Words
sparsely, 642	loathe, 651	Nazi Germany, 640
conspicuous, 644	sanctified, 669	tension, 640
improvise, 670	wrought, 669	screenplay, 640
ostentatiously, 672	smite, 669	Hanukkah, 677
		dynamic, 682
		insights, 682
		consistent, 683
		diorama, 683

KEY TERMS
DRAMA, 640
PLOT, 640
EXPOSITION, 640
CHARACTER, 640
SETTING, 640
RISING ACTION, 640
CLIMAX, 640
FALLING ACTION, 640
RESOLUTION, 640
SUMMARY, 640
DIALOGUE, 683
FIRST-PERSON POINT OF VIEW, 683
THIRD-PERSON POINT OF VIEW, 683

The Diary of Anne Frank, Act 1

A Drama by Frances Goodrich and Albert Hackett

Summary

As the play opens, Anne Frank's father and his dear friend Miep Gies visit the cramped attic above his old business. There, helped by Miep and Mr. Kraler, Otto Frank and his family, along with three other Jews, had lived for two years, hiding from the Nazis. Three years have passed since then. Miep gives Mr. Frank his daughter's diary, which she had found after the family had been captured. As Mr. Frank reads aloud from the diary, the offstage voice of Anne joins his, drawing us back to the past as the families begin their new life in the "secret annex." As the months of hiding drag on, tension among members of the group increases, caused by fear and lack of privacy. An eighth person joins them, adding to the tension and discomfort. As Act 1 ends, the group is celebrating Hanukkah. Their festivities are interrupted by the sounds of a thief below. After the thief leaves the building, the group tries to resume its celebration, even though they fear that they will soon be discovered.

Teach the Selection

The Mirrors & Windows questions at the end of this selection focus on the theme of music. Before reading the act, ask students if music positively affects them and, if so, in what ways? How can music uplift people in general?

641

Program Resources

Planning and Assessment
Program Planning Guide, Selection Lesson Plan
E-Lesson Planner
Assessment Guide, Lesson Test
ExamView

Technology Tools
Interactive Student Text on CD
Visual Teaching Package
mirrorsandwindows.com

Meeting the Standards
Drama: Unit 7, Directed Reading, pp. 25–31

Differentiating Instruction
Developing Readers, Take Notes, pp. 49–52
Advanced Students, Primary Source Project, pp. 40–41

Geography Connection

Amsterdam Point out the location of Amsterdam, Holland, on a map. Inform students that this is the location of the Anne Frank House, the building that included the secret annex, where she hid, along with seven others, for 25 months. The house has been turned into a museum highlighting Anne's diary and other memorabilia. It opened its doors in 1960.

Analyze Literature

Plot Remind students that a story's plot does not necessarily unfold chronologically and that author's sometimes choose to move backward and forward in time to create a certain effect. In *The Diary of Anne Frank*, Scene 1 opens in 1945, after the end of World War I and the Holocaust. Ask students what event launches Mr. Frank, as well as the audience, three years back to 1942, when the majority of the play's action occurs. Model a response: "When Miep hands Mr. Frank Anne's diary, he begins to read from the beginning, which leads the audience to the time she began writing."

CHARACTERS

MR. FRANK

MIEP

MRS. VAN DAAN

MR. VAN DAAN

PETER VAN DAAN

MRS. FRANK

MARGOT FRANK

ANNE FRANK

MR. KRALER

MR. DUSSEL

ACT 1

SCENE 1

The scene remains the same throughout the play. It is the top floor of a warehouse and office building in Amsterdam, Holland. The sharply peaked roof of the building is outlined against a sea of other rooftops, stretching away into the distance. Nearby is the belfry[1] of a church tower, the Westertoren, whose carillon[2] rings out the hours. Occasionally faint sounds float up from below: the voices of children playing in the street, the tramp of marching feet, a boat whistle from the canal.

The three rooms of the top floor and a small attic space above are exposed to our view. The largest of the rooms is in the center, with two small rooms, slightly raised, on either side. On the right is a bathroom, out of sight. A narrow steep flight of stairs at the back leads up to the attic. The rooms are sparsely *furnished with a few chairs, cots, a table or two. The windows are painted over, or covered with makeshift blackout curtains.[3] In the main room there is a sink, a gas ring for cooking and a wood-burning stove for warmth.*

The room on the left is hardly more than a closet. There is a skylight in the sloping ceiling. Directly under this room is a small steep stairwell, with steps leading down to a door. This is the only entrance from the building below. When the door is opened we see that it has been concealed on the outer side by a bookcase attached to it.

The curtain rises on an empty stage. It is late afternoon, November, 1945.[4]

The rooms are dusty, the curtains in rags. Chairs and tables are overturned.

The door at the foot of the small stairwell swings open. MR. FRANK *comes up the steps into view. He is a gentle, cultured European in his middle years. There is still a trace of a German accent in his speech.*

He stands looking slowly around, making a supreme effort at self-control. He is weak, ill. His clothes are threadbare.[5]

After a second he drops his rucksack[6] on the couch and moves slowly about. He opens the door to one of the smaller rooms, and then abruptly closes it again, turning away. He goes to the window at the back, looking off at the Westertoren as its carillon strikes the hour of six, then he moves restlessly on.

From the street below we hear the sound of a barrel organ[7] and children's voices at play. There is a many-colored scarf hanging from a nail. MR. FRANK *takes it, putting it around his neck.*

1. **belfry.** Bell tower
2. **carillon** (ker´ ə län´). Set of stationary bells, each producing one note of the musical scale
3. **blackout curtains.** Sheets or shades placed over the windows to prevent light from escaping in order to avoid detection by enemy troops and airplanes
4. **November, 1945.** World War II has ended, and Mr. Frank is returning to the apartment after being away. The main action of the play will unfold as a flashback, taking readers back to events that have already taken place.
5. **threadbare.** Worn out and thin, with holes or missing threads
6. **rucksack.** Knapsack or backpack
7. **barrel organ.** Hand organ, or an instrument played by turning a crank

sparse•ly (spärs´ lē) *adv.*, thinly; not full or densely

Grammar Skills

Sentence Fragments

Remind students that a sentence has a subject and a predicate and makes sense when it stands on its own. If any one of these elements is missing, it is a sentence fragment. Have students identify the sentences and the sentence fragments in these examples:

1. Anne Frank's diary.
2. Made her famous.
3. Her father published it.
4. After World War II had ended.
5. Mr. Frank survived the war.

As he starts back for his rucksack, his eye is caught by something lying on the floor. It is a woman's white glove. He holds it in his hand and suddenly all of his self-control is gone. He breaks down, crying.

We hear footsteps on the stairs. MIEP GIES *comes up, looking for* MR. FRANK. *MIEP is a Dutch[8] girl of about twenty-two. She wears a coat and hat, ready to go home. She is pregnant. Her attitude toward* MR. FRANK *is protective, compassionate.*

MIEP. Are you all right, Mr. Frank?

MR. FRANK. [*Quickly controlling himself.*] Yes, Miep, yes.

MIEP. Everyone in the office has gone home…It's after six. [*Then pleading.*] Don't stay up here, Mr. Frank. What's the use of torturing yourself like this?

MR. FRANK. I've come to say good-bye…I'm leaving here, Miep.

MIEP. What do you mean? Where are you going? Where?

MR. FRANK. I don't know yet. I haven't decided.

MIEP. Mr. Frank, you can't leave here! This is your home! Amsterdam is your home. Your business is here, waiting for you…You're needed here…Now that the war is over, there are things that…

MR. FRANK. I can't stay in Amsterdam, Miep. It has too many memories for me. Everywhere there's something…the house we lived in…the school…that street organ playing out there…I'm not the person you used to know, Miep. I'm a bitter old man. [*Breaking off.*] Forgive me. I shouldn't speak to you like this…after all that you did for us…the suffering…

MIEP. No. No. It wasn't suffering. You can't say we suffered. [*As she speaks, she straightens a chair which is overturned.*]

MR. FRANK. I know what you went through, you and Mr. Kraler. I'll remember it as long as I live. [*He gives one last look around.*] Come, Miep. [*He starts for the steps, then remembers his rucksack, going back to get it.*]

MIEP. [*Hurrying up to a cupboard.*] Mr. Frank, did you see? There are some of your papers here. [*She brings a bundle of papers to him.*] We found them in a heap of rubbish on the floor after…after you left.

MR. FRANK. Burn them. [*He opens his rucksack to put the glove in it.*]

MIEP. But, Mr. Frank, there are letters, notes…

MR. FRANK. Burn them. All of them.

MIEP. Burn *this?* [*She hands him a paperbound notebook.*]

MR. FRANK. [*Quietly.*] Anne's diary. [*He opens the diary and begins to read.*] "Monday, the sixth of July, nineteen forty-two." [*To* MIEP.] Nineteen forty-two. Is it possible, Miep?… Only three years ago. [*As he continues his reading, he sits down on the couch.*] "Dear Diary, since you and I are going to be great friends, I will start by telling you about myself. My name is Anne Frank. I am thirteen years old. I was born in Germany the twelfth of June, nineteen twenty-nine. As my family is Jewish, we emigrated to Holland when Hitler came to power."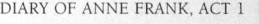

[*As* MR. FRANK *reads on, another voice joins his, as if coming from the air. It is* ANNE'S VOICE.]

MR. FRANK AND ANNE. "My father started a business, importing spice and herbs. Things went well for us until nineteen forty. Then the war came, and the Dutch capitulation,[9] followed by the arrival of the Germans. Then things got very bad for the Jews."

---

8. **Dutch.** People of Holland are known as the Dutch.
9. **capitulation.** Conditional surrender; act of giving up under prearranged terms

THE DIARY OF ANNE FRANK, ACT 1 **643**

Use Reading Skills

Evaluate Authors' Purpose Ask students to consider the authors' purpose in opening the play after the end of the war, rather than beginning at the same point that Anne Frank's diary begins. Model a response by suggesting that they wanted to show how Otto Frank came into possession of his daughter's diary.

Use Reading Skills

Summarize Have students summarize the events that are described in Scene 1.

Cultural Connection

Star of David The Star of David, a symbol of Judaism, is a six-pointed star (a hexagram) with two intertwining equilateral triangles, one pointing up and the other pointing down. Hitler forced all Jews age six and over to wear an identifying Star of David on their clothing. The Star of David is also called the Shield of David, or *Magen David* in Hebrew. According to legend, the star was placed on the shields of King David's soldiers to symbolize God's protection. Since 1948, the symbol has been part of Israel's flag. **Ⓐ**

MR. FRANK'S VOICE *dies out.* ANNE'S VOICE *continues alone. The lights dim slowly to darkness. The curtain falls on the scene.*

ANNE'S VOICE. You could not do this and you could not do that. They forced Father out of his business. We had to wear yellow stars.[10] I had to turn in my bike. I couldn't go to a Dutch school any more. I couldn't go to the movies, or ride in an automobile, or even on a streetcar, and a million other things. But somehow we children still managed to have fun. Yesterday Father told me we're going into hiding. Where, he wouldn't say. At five o'clock this morning Mother woke me and told me to hurry and get dressed. I was to put on as many clothes as I could. It would look too suspicious if we walked along carrying suitcases. It wasn't until we were on our way that I learned where we were going. Our hiding place was to be upstairs in the building where Father used to have his business. Three other people were coming in with us…the Van Daans and their son Peter…Father knew the Van Daans but we had never met them…

During the last lines the curtain rises on the scene. The lights dim on. ANNE'S VOICE *fades out.*

SCENE 2

It is early morning, July, 1942. The rooms are bare, as before, but they are now clean and orderly.

MR. VAN DAAN, *a tall, portly*[11] *man in his late forties, is in the main room, pacing up and down, nervously smoking a cigarette. His clothes and overcoat are expensive and well cut.*

MRS. VAN DAAN *sits on the couch, clutching her possessions, a hatbox, bags, etc. She is a pretty woman in her early forties. She wears a fur coat over her other clothes.*

PETER VAN DAAN *is standing at the window of the room on the right, looking down at the street below. He is a shy, awkward boy of sixteen. He*

wears a cap, a raincoat, and long Dutch trousers, like "plus fours."[12] *At his feet is a black case, a carrier for his cat.*

Ⓐ *The yellow Star of David is* <u>conspicuous</u> *on all of their clothes.*

MRS. VAN DAAN. [*Rising, nervous, excited.*] Something's happened to them! I know it!

MR. VAN DAAN. Now, Kerli!

MRS. VAN DAAN. Mr. Frank said they'd be here at seven o'clock. He said…

MR. VAN DAAN. They have two miles to walk. You can't expect…

MRS. VAN DAAN. They've been picked up.

---

10. **yellow stars.** Reference to the Star of David, the symbol of Judaism, which Germans forced Jews to sew onto their clothes so that they could be easily identified
11. **portly.** Large and heavy, in a dignified way
12. **"plus fours."** Loose knickers or short pants, stylish at the time

con•spic•u•ous (kən spiˊ kyə wəs) *adj.*, easily seen or noticed

---

Differentiated Instruction

Enrichment
Have students prepare character charts to record and keep track of traits exhibited by each character. As they read, they can add to their charts by using information from the stage directions and from the dialogue itself.

Reading Proficiency
Students might benefit from reading Act 1 in small sections, stopping from time to time to review what they have read and to summarize the content. This can be a partner activity, with students taking turns reading sections aloud.

That's what's happened. They've been taken…

Mr. Van Daan *indicates that he hears someone coming.*

Mr. Van Daan. You see?

Peter *takes up his carrier and his schoolbag, etc., and goes into the main room as* Mr. Frank *comes up the stairwell from below.* Mr. Frank *looks much younger now. His movements are brisk, his manner confident. He wears an overcoat and carries his hat and a small cardboard box. He crosses to the* Van Daans, *shaking hands with each of them.*

Mr. Frank. Mrs. Van Daan, Mr. Van Daan, Peter. [*Then, in explanation of their lateness.*] There were too many of the Green Police[13] on the streets…we had to take the long way around.

Up the steps come Margot Frank, Mrs. Frank, Miep (*not pregnant now*), *and* Mr. Kraler. *All of them carry bags, packages, and so forth. The Star of David is conspicuous on all of the* Franks' *clothing.* Margot *is eighteen, beautiful, quiet, shy.* Mrs. Frank *is a young mother, gently bred, reserved. She, like* Mr. Frank, *has a slight German accent.* Mr. Kraler *is a Dutchman, dependable, kindly.*

As Mr. Kraler *and* Miep *go upstage to put down their parcels,* Mrs. Frank *turns back to call* Anne.

Mrs. Frank. Anne?

Anne *comes running up the stairs. She is thirteen, quick in her movements, interested in everything, mercurial[14] in her emotions. She wears a cape, long wool socks and carries a schoolbag.*

Mr. Frank. [*Introducing them.*] My wife, Edith. Mr. and Mrs. Van Daan…[Mrs. Frank *hurries over, shaking hands with them.*] their son, Peter…my daughters, Margot and Anne.

Anne *gives a polite little curtsy as she shakes*

Mr. Van Daan's *hand. Then she immediately starts off on a tour of investigation of her new home, going upstairs to the attic room.*

Miep *and* Mr. Kraler *are putting the various things they have brought on the shelves.*

Mr. Kraler. I'm sorry there is still so much confusion.

Mr. Frank. Please. Don't think of it. After all, we'll have plenty of leisure to arrange everything ourselves.

Miep. [*To* Mrs. Frank.] We put the stores of food you sent in here. Your drugs are here… soap, linen here.

Mrs. Frank. Thank you, Miep.

Miep. I made up the beds…the way Mr. Frank and Mr. Kraler said. [*She starts out.*] Forgive me. I have to hurry. I've got to go to the other side of town to get some ration books[15] for you.

Mrs. Van Daan. Ration books? If they see our names on ration books, they'll know we're here.

Mr. Kraler. There isn't anything…

Miep. Don't worry. Your names won't be on them. [*As she hurries out.*] I'll be up later.

Mr. Frank. Thank you, Miep.

Mrs. Frank. [*To* Mr. Kraler.] It's illegal, then, the ration books? We've never done anything illegal.

Mr. Frank. We won't be living here exactly according to regulations.

As Mr. Kraler *reassures* Mrs. Frank, *he takes various small things, such as matches, soap, etc., from his pockets, handing them to her.*

---

13. **Green Police.** Nazi police officers wore green uniforms.
14. **mercurial.** Frequently changing, with a range from very high to very low
15. **ration books.** Books of coupons, distributed during wartime, that limited the amount of scarce items (fresh meat, eggs, sugar, shoes, etc.) a family could buy

Teach the Selection

Analyze Literature

Staging Tell students that one element of staging is "blocking," or the positioning of the actors on the stage. With effective blocking, no character is hidden from the audience's view by another actor, unless such hiding is a necessary plot detail. Have students visualize the blocking in this scene. **B**

Analyze Literature

Stage Directions How do these stage directions reveal details about Anne's character? Model a response: "They show that Anne is polite and respectful. She is also very curious about her new surroundings." **C**

Reading Skills

Suspension of Judgment

Remind students that it is important to suspend judgment of characters and situations until all information has been presented. Suggest that they use these strategies as they read:

1. Ask questions. Why does a character behave in a certain way? How do one character's actions affect the others? What kind of pressure does each character have to contend with?

2. Take notes. One way to take notes about characters is to make a character chart, with the character's name on the inside and traits, words, and actions on radiating lines.

3. Identify with the characters. Put yourself in the character's place. How would you feel? How would you act? Can you understand why the character is acting a certain way?

Staging Remind students that stage directions often indicate sound effects. Ask: "What effect does the sound of the carillon have on the audience's understanding of the play?" Model a response: "The sound of the carillon reminds the audience that time is passing. It also reminds the audience that the secret annex is in a specific city that has certain landmarks." **Ⓐ**

Use Reading Strategies

Visualize Have students take a moment to visualize Mrs. Frank as she shakes Mr. Kraler's hand. What would they add to the description? For example, what expression shows on her face? Is her body bent toward him or is she reserved? **Ⓑ**

Use Reading Strategies

Clarify Ask students why the characters are removing so many layers of clothes. Model a response by suggesting that they are wearing many layers of clothes because, if they carried suitcases through the streets of Amsterdam, it would look suspicious. **Ⓒ**

Make Connections

Ask students how they think they would feel if they had to follow rules like these every day. **Ⓓ**

MR. KRALER. This isn't the black market,[16] Mrs. Frank. This is what we call the white market…helping all of the hundreds and hundreds who are hiding out in Amsterdam.

Ⓐ *The carillon is heard playing the quarter-hour before eight.* MR. KRALER *looks at his watch.* ANNE *stops at the window as she comes down the stairs.*

ANNE. It's the Westertoren!

MR. KRALER. I must go. I must be out of here and downstairs in the office before the workmen get here. [*He starts for the stairs leading out.*] Miep or I, or both of us, will be up each day to bring you food and news and find out what your needs are. Tomorrow I'll get you a better bolt for the door at the foot of the stairs. It needs a bolt that you can throw yourself and open only at our signal. [*To* MR. FRANK.] Oh…You'll tell them about the noise?

MR. FRANK. I'll tell them.

MR. KRALER. Good-bye then for the moment. I'll come up again, after the workmen leave.

MR. FRANK. Good-bye, Mr. Kraler.

Ⓑ **MRS. FRANK.** [*Shaking his hand.*] How can we thank you?

The others murmur their good-byes.

MR. KRALER. I never thought I'd live to see the day when a man like Mr. Frank would have to go into hiding. When you think—

He breaks off, going out. MR. FRANK *follows him down the steps, bolting the door after him. In the interval before he returns,* PETER *goes over to* MARGOT, *shaking hands with her. As* MR. FRANK *comes back up the steps,* MRS. FRANK *questions him anxiously.*

MRS. FRANK. What did he mean, about the noise?

MR. FRANK. First let us take off some of these clothes.

They all start to take off garment after garment. On each of their coats, sweaters, blouses, suits, dresses, is another yellow Star of David. MR. *and* MRS. FRANK *are underdressed quite simply. The others wear several things, sweaters, extra dresses, bathrobes, aprons, nightgowns, etc.*

MR. VAN DAAN. It's a wonder we weren't arrested, walking along the streets… Petronella with a fur coat in July…and that cat of Peter's crying all the way.

ANNE. A cat?

Finally, as they have all removed their surplus clothes, they look to MR. FRANK, *waiting for him to speak.*

MR. FRANK. Now. About the noise. While the men are in the building below, we must have complete quiet. Every sound can be heard down there, not only in the workrooms, but in the offices too. The men come at about eight-thirty, and leave at about five-thirty. So, to be perfectly safe, from eight in the morning until six in the evening we must move only when it is necessary, and then in stockinged feet. We must not speak above a whisper. We must not run any water. We cannot use the sink, or even, forgive me, the w.c.[17] The pipes go down through the workrooms. It would be heard. No trash… **Ⓓ**

MR. FRANK *stops abruptly as he hears the sound of marching feet from the street below. Everyone is motionless, paralyzed with fear.* MR. FRANK *goes quietly into the room on the right to look down out of the window.* ANNE *runs after him, peering out with him. The tramping feet pass without stopping. The tension is relieved.* MR. FRANK, *followed by* ANNE, *returns to the main room and resumes his instructions to the group.*

…No trash must ever be thrown out which might reveal that someone is living up here… not even a potato paring. We must burn

---

16. **black market.** System for buying and selling scarce items illegally, often through secret deals and at inflated prices
17. **w.c.** Abbreviation for *water closet*, a European term for a toilet

---

Differentiated Instruction

Reading Proficiency

Some students might have difficulty with the time sequence. Point out that Scene 2 takes place prior to Scene 1 chronologically. Clues that indicate a different time include the fact that Miep is pregnant in one scene and not pregnant in the other. In addition, the rooms are tidy in one scene and messy in the other. Explain that this playing with time sequences is one way to introduce a story set in the past.

everything in the stove at night. This is the way we must live until it is over, if we are to survive.

There is silence for a second.

MRS. FRANK. Until it is over. **E**

MR. FRANK. [*Reassuringly.*] After six we can move about…we can talk and laugh and have our supper and read and play games…just as we would at home. [*He looks at his watch.*] And now I think it would be wise if we all went to our rooms, and were settled before eight o'clock. Mrs. Van Daan, you and your husband will be upstairs. I regret that there's no place up there for Peter. But he will be here, near us. This will be our common room, where we'll meet to talk and eat and read, like one family.

MR. VAN DAAN. And where do you and Mrs. Frank sleep?

MR. FRANK. This room is also our bedroom.

MRS. VAN DAAN. That isn't right. We'll sleep here and you take the room upstairs.

MR. VAN DAAN. It's your place.

MR. FRANK. Please. I've thought this out for weeks. It's the best arrangement. The only arrangement. **F**

MRS. VAN DAAN. [*To MR. FRANK.*] Never, never can we thank you. [*Then to MRS. FRANK.*] I don't know what would have happened to us, if it hadn't been for Mr. Frank.

MR. FRANK. You don't know how your husband helped me when I came to this country…knowing no one…not able to speak the language. I can never repay him for that. [*Going to VAN DAAN.*] May I help you with your things?

MR. VAN DAAN. No. No. [*To MRS. VAN DAAN.*] Come along, *liefje.*[18]

MRS. VAN DAAN. You'll be all right, Peter? You're not afraid?

PETER. [*Embarrassed.*] Please, Mother.

They start up the stairs to the attic room above. MR. FRANK *turns to* MRS. FRANK.

MR. FRANK. You too must have some rest, Edith. You didn't close your eyes last night. Nor you, Margot.

ANNE. I slept, Father. Wasn't that funny? I knew it was the last night in my own bed, and yet I slept soundly.

MR. FRANK. I'm glad, Anne. Now you'll be able to help me straighten things in here. [*To* MRS. FRANK *and* MARGOT.] Come with me…You and Margot rest in this room for the time being.

He picks up their clothes, starting for the room on the right.

MRS. FRANK. You're sure…? I could help… And Anne hasn't had her milk…

MR. FRANK. I'll give it to her. [*To* ANNE *and* PETER.] Anne, Peter…it's best that you take off your shoes now, before you forget.

He leads the way to the room, followed by MARGOT.

MRS. FRANK. You're sure you're not tired, Anne?

ANNE. I feel fine. I'm going to help Father.

MRS. FRANK. Peter. I'm glad you are to be with us.

PETER. Yes, Mrs. Frank.

MRS. FRANK *goes to join* MR. FRANK *and* MARGOT.

During the following scene MR. FRANK *helps* MARGOT *and* MRS. FRANK *to hang up their clothes. Then he persuades them both to lie down and rest. The* VAN DAANS *in their room above settle themselves. In the main room* ANNE *and* PETER *remove their shoes.* PETER *takes his cat out of the carrier.* **G**

18. *liefje.* "Little love" (Dutch)

THE DIARY OF ANNE FRANK, ACT 1 **647**

Teach the Selection

Use Reading Skills

Evaluate Authors' Purpose Draw students' attention to Mrs. Frank's words. Have them consider why the authors have her repeat her husband's words here. Model a response: "The authors want to emphasize the sense of optimism that the families have. Despite their situation, they still hope that everything will turn out well and that their suffering will soon be over." **E**

Use Reading Skills

Identify Main Idea The main idea in this exchange between Mr. Frank and Mrs. Van Daan is that each family owes the other a great debt. Mr. Frank is helping them in part because Mr. Van Daan helped him earlier, when he was new to the country. **F**

Analyze Literature

Plot Point out that stage directions can move a plot along, just as dialogue does. Ask: "What do the characters' actions in this scene tell the reader about how the plot is progressing?" Model a response by saying that the characters' actions show that the families are becoming familiar with their new home and are getting ready to settle into a regular daily routine. **G**

Vocabulary Skills

Word Parts

Remind students that when they encounter an unfamiliar word, they can decode it by focusing on prefixes, suffixes, and roots. Have students define these words, using the root word of each in the definition.

1. suspicious
2. possessions
3. explanation
4. dependable
5. investigation
6. various
7. illegal

Art Connection

Film Art Film is a complex art form that requires the collaboration of many specialized individuals. The 1959 film version of *The Diary of Anne Frank* won several Oscars in the art department: The Academy awarded Best Cinematography to William Mellor and presented the award for Best Art Direction and Best Set Direction to Lyle Wheelor, George Davis, Walter Scott, and Stuart Reiss. Cinematography involves making the right choices in cameras, film stock, laboratory work, filters, lenses, depth of field, focus, lighting, camera movement, and special effects for a film, the actual recording process, and the development of the film. Art direction is the command over all visual elements of a film. Set decoration is the art of dressing a film set with furnishings, wallpaper and paint, lighting fixtures, and most all other visible objects in a film.

648   UNIT 7 DRAMA

English Language Learning

Onomatopoeia Students learning English might be interested to know that onomatopoeia is the use of a word that sounds like what it means. The term *ping-pong*, used by Anne on this page, is an example. Give students this list of onomatopoeic words, and point out how each sounds like its meaning:

plop	boom
fizz	whisper
zip	tinkle
buzz	hiss

ANNE. What's your cat's name?

PETER. Mouschi.

ANNE. Mouschi! Mouschi! Mouschi! [*She picks up the cat, walking away with it. To* PETER.] I love cats. I have one...a darling little cat. But they made me leave her behind. I left some food and a note for the neighbors to take care of her...I'm going to miss her terribly. What is yours? A him or a her?

PETER. He's a tom. He doesn't like strangers. [*He takes the cat from her, putting it back in its carrier.*]

ANNE. [*Unabashed.*] Then I'll have to stop being a stranger, won't I? Is he fixed? **Ⓐ**

PETER. [*Startled.*] Huh?

ANNE. Did you have him fixed?

PETER. No.

ANNE. Oh, you ought to have him fixed—to keep him from—you know, fighting. Where did you go to school?

PETER. Jewish Secondary.

ANNE. But that's where Margot and I go! I never saw you around.

PETER. I used to see you...sometimes...

ANNE. You did?

PETER. ...in the school yard. You were always in the middle of a bunch of kids.

He takes a penknife from his pocket.

ANNE. Why didn't you ever come over?

PETER. I'm sort of a lone wolf. [*He starts to rip off his Star of David.*]

ANNE. What are you doing?

PETER. Taking it off.

ANNE. But you can't do that. They'll arrest you if you go out without your star.

He tosses his knife on the table.

PETER. Who's going out?

ANNE. Why, of course! You're right! Of course we don't need them any more. [*She picks up his knife and starts to take her star off.*] I wonder what our friends will think when we don't show up today?

PETER. I didn't have any dates with anyone.

ANNE. Oh, I did. I had a date with Jopie to go and play ping-pong at her house. Do you know Jopie de Waal?

PETER. No.

ANNE. Jopie's my best friend. I wonder what she'll think when she telephones and there's no answer?...Probably she'll go over to the house...I wonder what she'll think...we left everything as if we'd suddenly been called away...breakfast dishes in the sink...beds not made...[*As she pulls off her star, the cloth underneath shows clearly the color and form of the star.*] Look! It's still there! [PETER *goes over to the stove with his star.*] What're you going to do with yours?

PETER. Burn it.

ANNE. [*She starts to throw hers in, and cannot.*] It's funny, I can't throw mine away. I don't know why. **Ⓑ**

PETER. You can't throw...? Something they branded you with...? That they made you wear so they could spit on you?

ANNE. I know. I know. But after all, it *is* the Star of David, isn't it?

In the bedroom, right, MARGOT *and* MRS. FRANK *are lying down.* MR. FRANK *starts quietly out.*

PETER. Maybe it's different for a girl.

MR. FRANK *comes into the main room.*

MR. FRANK. Forgive me, Peter. Now let me see. We must find a bed for your cat. [*He goes to a cupboard.*] I'm glad you brought your cat. Anne was feeling so badly about hers. [*Getting a used small washtub.*] Here we are. Will it be comfortable in that?

PETER. [*Gathering up his things.*] Thanks.

THE DIARY OF ANNE FRANK, ACT 1 **649**

Teach the Selection

Use Reading Skills
Use Context Clues If students are not familiar with the word *unabashed*, they can use context clues to determine that it means "not embarrassed or confused." **Ⓐ**

History Connection
The "Final Solution" Hitler considered the Jewish population in Europe a problem. His goal was to rid Europe of all Jews. An early plan, called the Madagascar Plan, called for the forcible deportation of European Jews to the island of Madagascar, off the southeast coast of Africa. This plan had to be abandoned when Germany was unable to conquer England, for Hitler had planned to use the British naval ships to transport the Jews to Madagascar. When it became apparent that the war would last longer than expected, Hitler and his cohorts came up with the "final solution to the Jewish problem": genocide.

Use Reading Skills
Identify Multiple Levels of Meaning Point out to students the different attitudes that Anne and Peter seem to have toward the Star of David on their clothes. Ask: "What does the star mean to each character?" Model a response by suggesting that to Peter, the star represents the humiliation and degradation suffered by the Jews under the Nazi rule, and to Anne, the star represents Judaism. **Ⓑ**

Reading Skills

Text Organization
Point out to students that various features in the text (stage directions, recitations from Anne's diary, and dialogue) all contribute to our understanding of the play. Have them find an example of a text feature that clarifies each of the following elements:

- setting
- mood
- characters
- plot
- theme

Make Connections

How would you feel if you knew you were going to see only one other person your own age for an indeterminate period of time? How would you make sure that both of you would get the most benefit out of the situation? **A**

Analyze Literature

Rising Action Ask students to comment on the significance of Mr. Frank's gifts to Anne. Model a response by suggesting that the diary he gives her is the very one that was returned to him in the opening scene of the play. Without this gift, the world would never have heard of Anne Frank. **B**

Use Reading Skills

Monitor Comprehension Students should recognize that "going into hiding" means that Anne and the others will not be able to leave the secret annex for any reason, and they will have to be quiet most of the time. **C**

Use Reading Skills

Analyze Authors' Point of View Ask students to analyze the authors' point of view toward Mr. Frank. Do they admire him? Model a response: "The authors seem to admire Mr. Frank for his ability to lead the group, set down rules, and help the others find something positive about their situation."

MR. FRANK. [*Opening the door of the room on the left.*] And here is your room. But I warn you, Peter, you can't grow any more. Not an inch, or you'll have to sleep with your feet out of the skylight. Are you hungry?

PETER. No.

MR. FRANK. We have some bread and butter.

PETER. No, thank you.

MR. FRANK. You can have it for luncheon then. And tonight we will have a real supper…our first supper together.

PETER. Thanks. Thanks.

He goes into his room. During the following scene he arranges his possessions in his new room.

MR. FRANK. That's a nice boy, Peter.

ANNE. He's awfully shy, isn't he?

MR. FRANK. You'll like him, I know.

A **ANNE.** I certainly hope so, since he's the only boy I'm likely to see for months and months.

MR. FRANK *sits down, taking off his shoes.*

MR. FRANK. Anneke, there's a box there. Will you open it?

He indicates a carton on the couch. **ANNE** *brings it to the center table. In the street below there is the sound of children playing.*

ANNE. [*As she opens the carton.*] You know the way I'm going to think of it here? I'm going to think of it as a boarding house. A peculiar summer boarding house, like the one that we—[*She breaks off as she pulls out some photographs.*] Father! My movie stars! I was wondering where they were! I was looking for them this morning…and Queen Wilhelmina!**¹⁹** How wonderful!

MR. FRANK. There's something more. Go on. Look further.

He goes over to the sink, pouring a glass of milk from a thermos bottle.

B **ANNE.** [*Pulling out a pasteboard-bound book.*] A diary! [*She throws her arms around her father.*] I've never had a diary. And I've always longed for one. [*She looks around the room.*] Pencil, pencil, pencil, pencil. [*She starts down the stairs.*] I'm going down to the office to get a pencil.

MR. FRANK. Anne! No!

He goes after her, catching her by the arm and pulling her back.

ANNE. [*Startled.*] But there's no one in the building now.

MR. FRANK. It doesn't matter. I don't want you ever to go beyond that door.

ANNE. [*Sobered.*] Never…? Not even at nighttime, when everyone is gone? Or on Sundays? Can't I go down to listen to the radio?

MR. FRANK. Never. I am sorry, Anneke. It isn't safe. No, you must never go beyond that door.

C *For the first time* **ANNE** *realizes what "going into hiding" means.*

ANNE. I see.

MR. FRANK. It'll be hard, I know. But always remember this, Anneke. There are no walls, there are no bolts, no locks that anyone can put on your mind. Miep will bring us books. We will read history, poetry, mythology. [*He gives her the glass of milk.*] Here's your milk. [*With his arm about her, they go over to the couch, sitting down side by side.*] As a matter of fact, between us, Anne, being here has certain advantages for you. For instance, you remember the battle you had with your mother the other day on the subject of overshoes?**²⁰** You said you'd rather die than wear overshoes? But in the end you had to wear them? Well now, you see, for as long as

---

19. **Queen Wilhelmina.** Queen of Holland from 1890 to 1948
20. **overshoes.** Rubber boots that fit over shoes to protect shoes from puddles

Differentiated Instruction

Kinesthetic/Visual Learning

Have pairs of students work together to sketch diagrams of the set described in the stage directions. Have partners compare their diagrams with those of other sets of partners and decide which sketch most accurately depicts the set described. Have a volunteer enlarge that diagram on poster board and post it on a bulletin board. Students can refer to it as they continue to read the play.

we are here you will never have to wear overshoes! Isn't that good? And the coat that you inherited from Margot, you won't have to wear that any more. And the piano! You won't have to practice on the piano. I tell you, this is going to be a fine life for you!

Anne's panic is gone. Peter appears in the doorway of his room, with a saucer in his hand. He is carrying his cat.

Peter. I...I...I thought I'd better get some water for Mouschi before...

Mr. Frank. Of course.

As he starts toward the sink the carillon begins to chime the hour of eight. He tiptoes to the window at the back and looks down at the street below. He turns to Peter, indicating in pantomime[21] that it is too late. Peter starts back for his room. He steps on a creaking board. The three of them are frozen for a minute in fear. As Peter starts away again, Anne tiptoes over to him and pours some of the milk from her glass into the saucer for the cat. Peter squats on the floor, putting the milk before the cat. Mr. Frank gives Anne his fountain pen, and then goes into the room at the right. For a second Anne watches the cat, then she goes over to the center table, and opens her diary.

In the room at the right, Mrs. Frank has sat up quickly at the sound of the carillon. Mr. Frank comes in and sits down beside her on the settee,[22] his arm comfortingly around her.

Upstairs, in the attic room, Mr. and Mrs. Van Daan have hung their clothes in the closet and are now seated on the iron bed. Mrs. Van Daan leans back exhausted. Mr. Van Daan fans her with a newspaper.

Anne starts to write in her diary. The lights dim out, the curtain falls.

In the darkness Anne's Voice comes to us again, faintly at first, and then with growing strength.]

Anne's Voice. I expect I should be describing what it feels like to go into hiding. But I really don't know yet myself. I only know it's funny never to be able to go outdoors...never to breathe fresh air...never to run and shout and jump. It's the silence in the nights that frightens me most. Every time I hear a creak in the house, or a step on the street outside, I'm sure they're coming for us. The days aren't so bad. At least we know that Miep and Mr. Kraler are down there below us in the office. Our protectors, we call them. I asked Father what would happen to them if the Nazis found out they were hiding us. Pim said that they would suffer the same fate that we would...Imagine! They know this, and yet when they come up here, they're always cheerful and gay[23] as if there were nothing in the world to bother them...Friday, the twenty-first of August, nineteen forty-two. Today I'm going to tell you our general news. Mother is unbearable. She insists on treating me like a baby, which I loathe. Otherwise things are going better. The weather is...

As Anne's Voice is fading out, the curtain rises on the scene.

Scene 3

It is a little after six o'clock in the evening, two months later.

Margot is in the bedroom at the right, studying. Mr. Van Daan is lying down in the attic room above. The rest of the "family" is in the main room. Anne and Peter sit opposite each other at the center table, where they have been doing their lessons. Mrs. Frank is on the couch. Mrs. Van Daan is seated with her fur coat, on which she has been sewing, in her lap. None of them are wearing their shoes.

---

21. **pantomime.** Dramatic presentation, given without words, using only actions and gestures to express meaning
22. **settee** (se tē′). Small couch or sofa
23. **gay.** Showing a happy, optimistic attitude

Analyze Literature

Monologue Point out that Scene 2, like Scene 1, ends with a monologue by Anne. The monologue serves several functions: it fills the audience in on how Anne really feels, as she tells the diary things she would not tell Peter, her parents, or any of the others. It also provides dates, which help the audience understand how much time has passed. The monologue also has a practical effect from the standpoint of staging. Because Anne speaks in the darkness, the stage hands have a chance to rearrange any parts of the set that need to change for the next scene; in addition, the actors have a chance to change costumes if necessary. **D**

Use Reading Skills

Summarize Have students summarize what has happened in Scene 2.

Analyze Literature

Stage Directions Ask students to consider what these stage directions reveal about the people and their attitudes. Model a response by suggesting that the fact that Margot, Anne, and Peter are all studying indicates that they are looking forward to the day when their hiding will end. They want to keep up with their studies so they won't be behind when they go back to school. Also, the routine gives a sense of normalcy to their lives. **E**

Denotation and Connotation
Remind students that denotation is the literal meaning of a word, the definition found in a dictionary. Connotation is the suggested meaning of a word; it can be neutral, positive, or negative. For example, *slim, thin,* and *skinny* have similar denotative meanings, but *slim* has a positive connotation and *skinny* has a negative connotation.

Have pairs of students identify the connotation (neutral, positive, or negative) of each of these underlined words from the play:

1. "He doesn't like strangers."
2. "I didn't have any dates with anyone."
3. "Something they branded you with . . .?"
4. "Are you hungry?"
5. "He's awfully shy, isn't he?"

Use Reading Strategies

Make Inferences Based on this exchange between Peter and Anne, students should be able to infer that this is not the first time Anne has teased Peter by taking his shoes. **(A)**

Analyze Literature

Staging Ask students to consider what the stage directions reveal about the changing relationship between Anne and Peter. They should recognize that Anne and Peter have overcome their initial awkwardness and are now relating to each other in much the same way as a brother and sister might—they tease each other and become annoyed with each other over little things. **(B)**

Literary Connection

Pseudonyms Point out to students that some of the names used in Anne's diary were not the real names of the people in the secret annex, but rather pseudonyms, or fictitious names. She used real names for herself, her sister, and her parents. However, the real names of the Van Daans were Hermann van Pels (the father), Auguste van Pels (the mother), and Peter van Pels (the son). The other resident of the secret annex, Mr. Dussel, was named Fritz Pfeffer in real life.

Their eyes are on Mr. Frank, *waiting for him to give them the signal which will release them from their day-long quiet.* Mr. Frank, *his shoes in his hand, stands looking down out of the window at the back, watching to be sure that all of the workmen have left the building below.*

After a few seconds of motionless silence, Mr. Frank *turns from the window.*

Mr. Frank. [*Quietly, to the group.*] It's safe now. The last workman has left.

There is an immediate stir of relief.

Anne. [*Her pent-up energy explodes.*] WHEE!

Mrs. Frank. [*Startled, amused.*] Anne!

Mrs. Van Daan. I'm first for the w.c.

She hurries off to the bathroom. Mrs. Frank *puts on her shoes and starts up to the sink to prepare supper.* Anne *sneaks* Peter's *shoes from under the table and hides them behind her back.* Mr. Frank *goes in to* Margot's *room.*

Mr. Frank. [*To* Margot.] Six o' clock. School's over.

Margot *gets up, stretching.* Mr. Frank *sits down to put on his shoes. In the main room* Peter *tries to find his.*

(A) **Peter.** [*To* Anne.] Have you seen my shoes?

Anne. [*Innocently.*] Your shoes?

Peter. You've taken them, haven't you?

Anne. I don't know what you're talking about.

Peter. You're going to be sorry!

Anne. Am I?

Peter *goes after her.* Anne, *with his shoes in her hand, runs from him, dodging behind her mother.*

Mrs. Frank. [*Protesting.*] Anne, dear!

Peter. Wait till I get you!

Anne. I'm waiting!

(B) [Peter *makes a lunge for her. They both fall to the floor.* Peter *pins her down, wrestling with her to get the shoes.*] Don't! Don't! Peter, stop it. Ouch!

Mrs. Frank. Anne!…Peter!

Suddenly Peter *becomes self-conscious. He grabs his shoes roughly and starts for his room.*

Anne. [*Following him.*] Peter, where are you going? Come dance with me.

Peter. I tell you I don't know how.

Anne. I'll teach you.

Peter. I'm going to give Mouschi his dinner.

Anne. Can I watch?

Peter. He doesn't like people around while he eats.

Anne. Peter, please.

Peter. No! [*He goes into his room.* Anne *slams his door after him.*]

Mrs. Frank. Anne, dear, I think you shouldn't play like that with Peter. It's not dignified.[24]

Anne. Who cares if it's dignified? I don't want to be dignified.

Mr. Frank *and* Margot *come from the room on the right.* Margot *goes to help her mother.* Mr. Frank *starts for the center table to correct* Margot's *school papers.*

Mrs. Frank. [*To* Anne.] You complain that I don't treat you like a grown-up. But when I do, you resent it.

Anne. I only want some fun…someone to laugh and clown with…After you've sat still all day and hardly moved, you've got to have some fun. I don't know what's the matter with that boy.

Mr. Frank. He isn't used to girls. Give him a little time.

---

24. dignified. Showing proper manners; polite and refined

Differentiated Instruction

Visual Learning

Have student consider the personalities, interests, habits, and social skills of Anne and Peter, making a list of similarities and differences between them. Suggest that they complete a Venn diagram to organize the information in their lists.

English Language Learning

Designate various areas of the classroom as different parts of the set. Have volunteers mime the action described in the stage directions as others read the text aloud. Those doing the miming can perform in the appropriate areas of the "set." Whether they do the miming or the watching, their understanding of the play will be enhanced.

ANNE. Time? Isn't two months time? I could cry. [*Catching hold of* MARGOT.] Come on, Margot...dance with me. Come on, please.

MARGOT. I have to help with supper.

ANNE. You know we're going to forget how to dance...When we get out we won't remember a thing.

She starts to sing and dance by herself. MR. FRANK *takes her in his arms, waltzing with her.* MRS. VAN DAAN *comes in from the bathroom.*

MRS. VAN DAAN. Next? [*She looks around as she starts putting on her shoes.*] Where's Peter?

ANNE. [*As they are dancing.*] Where would he be!

MRS. VAN DAAN. He hasn't finished his lessons, has he? His father'll kill him if he catches him in there with that cat and his work not done. [MR. FRANK *and* ANNE *finish their dance. They bow to each other with extravagant*[25] *formality.*] Anne, get him out of there, will you?

ANNE. [*At* PETER'S *door.*] Peter? Peter?

PETER. [*Opening the door a crack.*] What is it?

ANNE. Your mother says to come out.

PETER. I'm giving Mouschi his dinner.

MRS. VAN DAAN. You know what your father says.

She sits on the couch, sewing on the lining of her fur coat.

PETER. For heaven's sake. I haven't even looked at him since lunch.

MRS. VAN DAAN. I'm just telling you, that's all.

ANNE. I'll feed him.

PETER. I don't want you in there.

MRS. VAN DAAN. Peter!

PETER. [*To* ANNE.] Then give him his dinner and come right out, you hear?

He comes back to the table. ANNE *shuts the door of* PETER'S *room after her and disappears behind the curtain covering his closet.*

MRS. VAN DAAN. [*To* PETER.] Now is that any way to talk to your little girlfriend?

PETER. Mother...for heaven's sake...will you please stop saying that?

MRS. VAN DAAN. Look at him blush! Look at him!

PETER. Please! I'm not...anyway...let me alone, will you?

MRS. VAN DAAN. He acts like it was something to be ashamed of. It's nothing to be ashamed of, to have a little girlfriend.

PETER. You're crazy. She's only thirteen.

MRS. VAN DAAN. So what? And you're sixteen. Just perfect. Your father's ten years older than I am. [*To* MR. FRANK.] I warn you, Mr. Frank, if this war lasts much longer, we're going to be related and then...

MR. FRANK. *Mazeltov!*[26]

MRS. FRANK. [*Deliberately changing the conversation.*] I wonder where Miep is. She's usually so prompt.

Suddenly everything else is forgotten as they hear the sound of an automobile coming to a screeching stop in the street below. They are tense, motionless in their terror. The car starts away. A wave of relief sweeps over them. They pick up their occupations again. ANNE *flings open the door of* PETER'S *room, making a dramatic entrance. She is dressed in* PETER'S *clothes.* PETER *looks at her in fury. The others are amused.*

ANNE. Good evening, everyone. Forgive me if I don't stay. [*She jumps up on a chair.*] I have a friend waiting for me in there. My friend Tom. Tom Cat. Some people say that we look alike. But Tom has the most beautiful

---

25. **extravagant.** Overdone; exaggerated; beyond usual limits
26. ***Mazeltov!*** In the Yiddish language of the Jews, "congratulations" or "good luck"

THE DIARY OF ANNE FRANK, ACT 1 **653**

Use Reading Skills
Monitor Comprehension Ask students why Anne's mother is so concerned about Anne's health. They should recognize the seriousness of any illness in the secret annex. A contagious disease could be a disaster, since no doctor can be called. **A**

Use Reading Skills
Use Context Clues Students should be able to infer that the term *w.c.* means the same as "bathroom." Inform students that the letters stand for "water closet," a British euphemism for the bathroom. **B**

History Connection
Air Raids During World War II, many European cities were under heavy attack from the air. This was the first major war in which this tactic was used. To make cities less visible from the air at night, residents used blackout curtains to block the light from inside their homes from escaping beyond their windows. Other defenses against air attack included radar, which had been recently developed. The sounds that Anne and the others are hearing were common sounds throughout Europe during the war. Often the drone of the bombers flying overhead was followed by the sound of bombs exploding or an airplane going down in flames. **C**

whiskers, and I have only a little fuzz. I am hoping…in time…

PETER. All right, Mrs. Quack Quack!

ANNE. [*Outraged—jumping down.*] Peter!

PETER. I heard about you…How you talked so much in class they called you Mrs. Quack Quack. How Mr. Smitter made you write a composition…"'Quack, quack,' said Mrs. Quack Quack."

ANNE. Well, go on. Tell them the rest. How it was so good he read it out loud to the class and then read it to all his other classes!

PETER. Quack! Quack! Quack…Quack… Quack…

ANNE *pulls off the coat and trousers.*

ANNE. You are the most intolerable,²⁷ insufferable boy I've ever met!

She throws the clothes down the stairwell. PETER *goes down after them.*

PETER. Quack, quack, quack!

MRS. VAN DAAN. [*To* ANNE.] That's right, Annele! Give it to him!

ANNE. With all the boys in the world… Why I had to get locked up with one like you!…

PETER. Quack, quack, quack, and from now on stay out of my room!

As PETER *passes her,* ANNE *puts out her foot, tripping him. He picks himself up, and goes on into his room.*

A **MRS. FRANK.** [*Quietly.*] Anne, dear…your hair. [*She feels* ANNE's *forehead.*] You're warm. Are you feeling all right?

ANNE. Please, Mother.

She goes over to the center table, slipping into her shoes.

MRS. FRANK. [*Following her.*] You haven't a fever, have you?

ANNE. [*Pulling away.*] No. No.

MRS. FRANK. You know we can't call a doctor here, ever. There's only one thing to do… watch carefully. Prevent an illness before it comes. Let me see your tongue.

ANNE. Mother, this is perfectly absurd.

MRS. FRANK. Anne, dear, don't be such a baby. Let me see your tongue. [*As* ANNE *refuses,* MRS. FRANK *appeals to* MR. FRANK.] Otto…?

MR. FRANK. You hear your mother, Anne.

ANNE *flicks out her tongue for a second, then turns away.*

MRS. FRANK. Come on—open up! [*As* ANNE *opens her mouth very wide.*] You seem all right…but perhaps an aspirin…

B **MRS. VAN DAAN.** For heaven's sake, don't give that child any pills. I waited for fifteen minutes this morning for her to come out of the w.c.

ANNE. I was washing my hair!

MR. FRANK. I think there's nothing the matter with our Anne that a ride on her bike, or a visit with her friend Jopie de Waal wouldn't cure. Isn't that so, Anne?

C MR. VAN DAAN *comes down into the room. From outside we hear faint sounds of bombers going over and a burst of ack-ack.²⁸*

MR. VAN DAAN. Miep not come yet?

MRS. VAN DAAN. The workmen just left, a little while ago.

MR. VAN DAAN. What's for dinner tonight?

MRS. VAN DAAN. Beans.

MR. VAN DAAN. Not again!

MRS. VAN DAAN. Poor Putti! I know. But what can we do? That's all that Miep brought us.

---

27. intolerable. Unbearable, terrible
28. ack-ack. Sound of antiaircraft machine-gun fire

English Language Learning
Have students who are proficient in English demonstrate the meaning of the following words and expressions by using facial expressions and body language:

- pent-up energy
- startled
- amused
- sneaks
- stretching
- innocently
- dodging behind her mother
- protesting
- lunge
- self-conscious
- dignified
- clown with
- extravagant formality
- blush
- motionless in their terror
- dramatic entrance

After each demonstration, have English learners explain the term in their own (English) words.

Use Reading Strategies
Make Inferences Ask students what Mr. Frank means by saying that Anne has "caught up" to him in algebra. Model a response: "Mr. Frank means that Anne now knows as much as he does about algebra." **D**

Use Reading Skills
Draw Conclusions Have students discuss the relationship between Anne and her father. What evidence indicates that they have a very close relationship? How does this relationship compare with Anne's relationship with her mother? Model a response by suggesting that Anne and her father are very close, as indicated by their dancing together, kidding around with each other, and both thinking that algebra is "vile." Anne's relationship with her mother, on the other hand, is distant and cold. Anne obviously prefers her father. **E**

[Mr. Van Daan *starts to pace, his hands behind his back.* Anne *follows behind him, imitating him.*]

Anne. We are now in what is known as the "bean cycle." Beans boiled, beans *en casserole,* beans with strings, beans without strings…

Peter *has come out of his room. He slides into his place at the table, becoming immediately absorbed in his studies.*

Mr. Van Daan. [*To* Peter.] I saw you…in there, playing with your cat.

Mrs. Van Daan. He just went in for a second, putting his coat away. He's been out here all the time, doing his lessons.

Mr. Frank. [*Looking up from the papers.*] Anne, you got an excellent in your history paper today…and very good in Latin.

Anne. [*Sitting beside him.*] How about algebra?

Mr. Frank. I'll have to make a confession. Up until now I've managed to stay ahead of you in algebra. Today you caught up with me. We'll leave it to Margot to correct. **D**

Anne. Isn't algebra *vile,*[29] Pim! **E**

Mr. Frank. Vile!

Margot. [*To* Mr. Frank.] How did I do?

Anne. [*Getting up.*] Excellent, excellent, excellent, excellent!

Mr. Frank. [*To* Margot.] You should have used the subjunctive[30] here…

---

29. **vile.** Awful; disgusting
30. **subjunctive.** Form of a verb

Brackets
Inform students that brackets are used to:
- enclose a comment that is inserted into a quoted passage
- add to a quoted passage
- insert a correction into quoted material or to enclose the word *sic* (Latin for "thus") for an error you choose not to correct
- enclose stage directions in some plays
- enclose parenthetical remarks that are already within parentheses

Identify the reason for these brackets:
1. Anne. [*At* Peter's *door*] Peter?
2. Diane wrote, "I am to [*sic*] tired!"
3. "Lincoln was born in Kentuky [Kentucky]."
4. "She was sentenced to thirty-five days [five weeks] in jail."
5. The teacher said, "Test tomorrow. [Groan!] But it will be open book."

Use Reading Skills

Identify Multiple Levels of Meaning Students might notice that Mrs. Van Daan's telling her husband, "Shut up!" is said in a "good-humored" way, according to the stage directions. They should recognize that this expression is usually considered rude, but if said in a certain tone, it can sound less rude and even friendly. **Ⓐ**

Make Connections

Ask students what they think of Mrs. Van Daan's flirtatious behavior with Mr. Frank here. Most will probably say that it is disrespectful not only to her husband but also to Mrs. Frank. **Ⓑ**

Use Reading Strategies

Ask Questions Students might ask themselves why Anne wants to listen to what is going on below. If they read ahead a bit, they will find out that she can hear a radio being played, and later she can hear a man's voice. They might speculate that the reason she wants to listen is to find out about the world beyond the secret annex, as the hiding place must have been very claustrophobic at times. **Ⓒ**

MARGOT. Should I?…I thought…look here…I didn't use it here…

The two become absorbed in the papers.

ANNE. Mrs. Van Daan, may I try on your coat?

MRS. FRANK. No, Anne.

MRS. VAN DAAN. [*Giving it to* ANNE.] It's all right…but careful with it. [ANNE *puts it on and struts with it.*] My father gave me that the year before he died. He always bought the best that money could buy.

ANNE. Mrs. Van Daan, did you have a lot of boyfriends before you were married?

MRS. FRANK. Anne, that's a personal question. It's not courteous to ask personal questions.

MRS. VAN DAAN. Oh I don't mind. [*To* ANNE.] Our house was always swarming with boys. When I was a girl we had…

MR. VAN DAAN. Oh, God. Not again!

Ⓐ **MRS. VAN DAAN.** [*Good-humored.*] Shut up! [*Without a pause, to* ANNE. MR. VAN DAAN *mimics* MRS. VAN DAAN, *speaking the first few words in unison with her.*] One summer we had a big house in Hilversum. The boys came buzzing round like bees around a jam pot. And when I was sixteen!…We were wearing our skirts very short those days and I had good-looking legs. [*She pulls up her skirt, going to* MR. FRANK.] I still have 'em. I may not be as pretty as I used to be, but I still have my legs. How about it, Mr. Frank?

Ⓑ

MR. VAN DAAN. All right. All right. We see them.

MRS. VAN DAAN. I'm not asking you. I'm asking Mr. Frank.

PETER. Mother, for heaven's sake.

MRS. VAN DAAN. Oh, I embarrass you, do I? Well, I just hope the girl you marry has as good. [*Then to* ANNE.] My father used to worry about me, with so many boys hanging round. He told me, if any of them gets fresh, you say to him…"Remember, Mr. So-and-So, remember I'm a lady."

ANNE. "Remember. Mr. So-and-So, remember I'm a lady."

She gives MRS. VAN DAAN *her coat.*

MR. VAN DAAN. Look at you, talking that way in front of her! Don't you know she puts it all down in that diary?

MRS. VAN DAAN. So, if she does? I'm only telling the truth!

Ⓒ ANNE *stretches out, putting her ear to the floor, listening to what is going on below. The sound of the bombers fades away.*

MRS. FRANK. [*Setting the table.*] Would you mind, Peter, if I moved you over to the couch?

ANNE. [*Listening.*] Miep must have the radio on.

PETER *picks up his papers, going over to the couch beside* MRS. VAN DAAN.

MR. VAN DAAN. [*Accusingly, to* PETER.] Haven't you finished yet?

PETER. No.

MR. VAN DAAN. You ought to be ashamed of yourself.

PETER. All right. All right. I'm a dunce.[31] I'm a hopeless case. Why do I go on?

MRS. VAN DAAN. You're not hopeless. Don't talk that way. It's just that you haven't anyone to help you, like the girls have. [*To* MR. FRANK.] Maybe you could help him, Mr. Frank?

MR. FRANK. I'm sure that his father…?

MR. VAN DAAN. Not me. I can't do anything with him. He won't listen to me. You go ahead…if you want.

---

31. dunce. Person who has limited intelligence

English Language Learning

Point out to students that the prefix *in-* in the words *intolerable* and *insufferable* makes the words mean the opposite of their root words. Tell them that the prefix *un-* has the same effect. Have students list other words in which the prefix *in-* or *un-* changes the meaning of the root word to its opposite. Possibilities include *injustice, inability, unjust,* and *unable.*

Enrichment

Obtain a recording of a waltz and have students listen to it. Encourage students to comment on the rhythm of the music. Interested students may wish to learn some waltz steps and demonstrate them for the class. Invite students to consider why the waltzing scene between Anne and her father was included in the play.

MR. FRANK. [*Going to* PETER.] What about it, Peter? Shall we make our school coeducational?[32]

MRS. VAN DAAN. [*Kissing* MR. FRANK.] You're an angel, Mr. Frank. An angel. I don't know why I didn't meet you before I met that one there. Here, sit down. Mr. Frank…[*She forces him down on the couch beside* PETER.] Now, Peter, you listen to Mr. Frank.

MR. FRANK. It might be better for us to go into Peter's room.

PETER *jumps up eagerly, leading the way.*

MR. VAN DAAN. That's right. You go in there, Peter. You listen to Mr. Frank. Mr. Frank is a highly educated man.

As MR. FRANK *is about to follow* PETER *into his room,* MRS. FRANK *stops him and wipes the lipstick from his lips. Then she closes the door after them.*

ANNE. [*On the floor, listening.*] Shh! I can hear a man's voice talking.

MR. VAN DAAN. [*To* ANNE.] Isn't it bad enough here without your sprawling all over the place?

ANNE *sits up.*

MRS. VAN DAAN. [*To* MR. VAN DAAN.] If you didn't smoke so much, you wouldn't be so bad-tempered.

MR. VAN DAAN. Am I smoking? Do you see me smoking?

MRS. VAN DAAN. Don't tell me you've used up all those cigarettes.

MR. VAN DAAN. One package. Miep only brought me one package.

MRS. VAN DAAN. It's a filthy habit anyway. It's a good time to break yourself.

MR. VAN DAAN. Oh, stop it, please.

MRS. VAN DAAN. You're smoking up all our money. You know that, don't you?

MR. VAN DAAN. Will you shut up? [*During this,* MRS. FRANK *and* MARGOT *have studiously kept their eyes down. But* ANNE, *seated on the floor, has been following the discussion interestedly.* MR. VAN DAAN *turns to see her staring up at him.*] **D**

And what are you staring at?

ANNE. I never heard grown-ups quarrel before. I thought only children quarreled.

MR. VAN DAAN. This isn't a quarrel! It's a discussion. And I never heard children so rude before.

ANNE. [*Rising indignantly.*[33]] I, rude!

MR. VAN DAAN. Yes!

MRS. FRANK. [*Quickly.*] Anne, will you get me my knitting? [ANNE *goes to get it.*] I must remember, when Miep comes, to ask her to bring me some more wool.

MARGOT. [*Going to her room.*] I need some hairpins and some soap. I made a list. [*She goes into her bedroom to get the list.*]

MRS. FRANK. [*To* ANNE.] Have you some library books for Miep when she comes?

ANNE. It's a wonder that Miep has a life of her own, the way we make her run errands for us. Please, Miep, get me some starch. Please take my hair out and have it cut. Tell me all the latest news, Miep. [*She goes over, kneeling on the couch beside* MRS. VAN DAAN.] Did you know she was engaged? His name is Dirk, and Miep's afraid the Nazis will ship him off to Germany to work in one of their war plants. That's what they're doing with some of the young Dutchmen…they pick them up off the streets—

MR. VAN DAAN. [*Interrupting.*] Don't you ever get tired of talking? Suppose you try keeping still for five minutes. Just five minutes.

---

32. **coeducational.** Having students of both sexes in classes together. Until this day, Mr. Frank was teaching only his two girls.
33. **indignantly.** With anger or resentment; with feelings of being treated unfairly

Cultural Connection
Anne as an Icon Inform students that when *Anne Frank: The Diary of a Young Girl* was published in the United States in 1953, it was an instant success. The horrors of the Holocaust had been known to the world for some time, but Anne's diary put a human face on the tragedy. Anne became a symbol for all the lives lost—especially those of children—and her hopeful voice throughout the text became an inspiration to all who read the diary. After the book came out, many people wanted to make it into a play. Kermit Bloomgarden won the rights to produce it, and he hired Frances Goodrich and Albert Hackett, a husband-and-wife writing team. They met with Otto Frank and visited the secret annex to see for themselves where the families had hidden from the Nazis. The play opened to rave reviews, and it won the Pulitzer Prize and three Tony awards in 1955.

Analyze Literature
Stage Directions Remind students that stage directions often reveal important details about characters. Ask students what these stage directions reveal about Mrs. Frank's and Margot's reaction to the argument between the Van Daans. Model a response by suggesting that Mrs. Frank and Margot are embarrassed by the way the Van Daans are arguing, and they are looking down to hide their embarrassment and discomfort. **D**

Ellipses
The ellipsis mark is made up of three periods (…). Remind students that ellipses are used
- to indicate omissions within quotations
- to indicate pauses and unfinished statements in quoted speech

Point out that if the ellipsis mark follows a sentence, four evenly spaced periods result: the sentence period (closed up to the last word of the sentence) and the three periods of the ellipsis mark.

Have students find three examples in the play of the use of ellipses to indicate pauses or unfinished statements. Then have students quote a passage in the play, omitting some material and using ellipses to indicate the omission.

Teach the Selection

Analyze Literature

Stage Directions Ask students what these stage directions reveal about the characters. Model a response by suggesting that the stage directions show that Mr. Van Daan is nervous and has trouble relaxing, Anne has fun mimicking him, and Mrs. Frank wants Anne to behave more respectfully to the Van Daans. **Ⓐ**

Make Connections

Point out that the attitude expressed by Mr. Van Daan is one that reflects the customs of that time. The feminist movement of the last half of the twentieth century has helped change this attitude in western society. Ask students what they think of this attitude. Do they think women's roles should be so narrow? Or do they think that everyone benefits if women have more opportunities? **Ⓑ**

Use Reading Skills

Compare and Contrast Students might notice how quickly Mrs. Van Daan's attitude toward Anne has changed. Earlier, she was happy to share information about her own youth with Anne and the others. Now, she is suddenly angry with Anne, for a reason that probably would not have bothered her under normal circumstances (in which she would have been able to get the coat cleaned). Students might realize that their close proximity and their tense situation might have contributed to Mrs. Van Daan's sudden change of mood. **Ⓒ**

Ⓐ *He starts to pace again. Again* ANNE *follows him, mimicking*[34] *him.* MRS. FRANK *jumps up and takes her by the arm up to the sink, and gives her a glass of milk.*

MRS. FRANK. Come here, Anne. It's time for your glass of milk.

MR. VAN DAAN. Talk, talk, talk. I never heard such a child. Where is my...? Every evening it's the same talk, talk, talk. [*He looks around.*] Where is my...?

MRS. VAN DAAN. What're you looking for?

MR. VAN DAAN. My pipe. Have you seen my pipe?

MRS. VAN DAAN. What good's a pipe? You haven't got any tobacco.

MR. VAN DAAN. At least I'll have something to hold in my mouth! [*Opening* MARGOT's *bedroom door.*] Margot, have you seen my pipe?

MARGOT. It was on the table last night.

ANNE *puts her glass of milk on the table and picks up his pipe, hiding it behind her back.*

MR. VAN DAAN. I know, I know. Anne, did you see my pipe?...Anne!

MRS. FRANK. Anne, Mr. Van Daan is speaking to you.

ANNE. Am I allowed to talk now?

MR. VAN DAAN. You're the most aggravating... The trouble with you is, you've been spoiled. What you need is a good old-fashioned spanking.

ANNE. [*Mimicking* MRS. VAN DAAN.] "Remember, Mr. So-and-So, remember I'm a lady." [*She thrusts the pipe into his mouth, then picks up her glass of milk.*]

MR. VAN DAAN. [*Restraining himself with difficulty.*] Why aren't you nice and quiet like your sister Margot? Why do you have to show off all the time? Let me give you a little

Ⓑ advice, young lady. Men don't like that kind of thing in a girl. You know that? A man likes a girl who'll listen to him once in a while...a domestic girl, who'll keep her house shining for her husband...who loves to cook and sew and...

ANNE. I'd cut my throat first! I'd open my veins! I'm going to be remarkable! I'm going to Paris...

MR. VAN DAAN. [*Scoffingly.*[35]] Paris!

ANNE. ...to study music and art.

MR. VAN DAAN. Yeah! Yeah!

ANNE. I'm going to be a famous dancer or singer...or something wonderful.

She makes a wide gesture, spilling the glass of milk on the fur coat in MRS. VAN DAAN's *lap.* MARGOT *rushes quickly over with a towel.* ANNE *tries to brush the milk off with her skirt.*

Ⓒ **MRS. VAN DAAN.** Now look what you've done...you clumsy little fool! My beautiful fur coat my father gave me...

ANNE. I'm so sorry.

MRS. VAN DAAN. What do you care? It isn't yours...So go on, ruin it! Do you know what that coat cost? Do you? And now look at it! Look at it!

ANNE. I'm very, very sorry.

MRS. VAN DAAN. I could kill you for this. I could just kill you!

MRS. VAN DAAN *goes up the stairs, clutching the coat.* MR. VAN DAAN *starts after her.*

MR. VAN DAAN. Petronella...liefje! Liefje!... Come back...the supper...come back!

MRS. FRANK. Anne, you must not behave in that way.

ANNE. It was an accident. Anyone can have an accident.

---

34. **mimicking.** Copying actions or gestures, usually in order to ridicule
35. **scoffingly.** In a mocking, ridiculing way

Differentiated Instruction

English Language Learning

Point out to students that Mrs. Van Daan uses several idiomatic expressions. When she tells her husband that it would be a good time to "break yourself," she means to break himself of the smoking habit. Breaking a habit means stopping it. When she says he is "smoking up all our money," she means that the money spent on cigarettes disappears forever. Give students practice with other idiomatic expressions, such as these, which appear in this scene:

- hanging around: occupying a space
- walk all over: take advantage of
- to leave in good hands: to leave with a capable person
- get everyone's back up: annoy everyone

MRS. FRANK. I don't mean that. I mean the answering back. You must not answer back. They are our guests. We must always show the greatest courtesy to them. We're all living under terrible tension. [*She stops as* MARGOT *indicates that* VAN DAAN *can hear. When he is gone, she continues.*] That's why we must control ourselves...You don't hear Margot getting into arguments with them, do you? Watch Margot. She's always courteous with them. Never familiar. She keeps her distance. And they respect her for it. Try to be like Margot.

ANNE. And have them walk all over me, the way they do her? No thanks!

MRS. FRANK. I'm not afraid that anyone is going to walk all over you, Anne. I'm afraid for other people, that you'll walk on them. I don't know what happens to you, Anne. You are wild, self-willed. If I had ever talked to my mother as you talk to me...

ANNE. Things have changed. People aren't like that any more. "Yes, Mother." "No, Mother." "Anything you say, Mother." I've got to fight things out for myself! Make something of myself!

MRS. FRANK. It isn't necessary to fight to do it. Margot doesn't fight, and isn't she...? **D**

ANNE. [*Violently rebellious.*] Margot! Margot! Margot! That's all I hear from everyone...how wonderful Margot is..."Why aren't you like Margot?"

MARGOT. [*Protesting.*] Oh, come on, Anne, don't be so...

ANNE. [*Paying no attention.*] Everything she does is right, and everything I do is wrong! I'm the goat around here!...You're all against me!...And you worst of all!

She rushes off into her room and throws herself down on the settee, stifling her sobs. MRS. FRANK *sighs and starts toward the stove.*

MRS. FRANK. [*To* MARGOT.] Let's put the soup on the stove...if there's anyone who cares to eat. Margot, will you take the bread out? [MARGOT *gets the bread from the cupboard.*] I don't know how we can go on living this way...I can't say a word to Anne...she flies at me...

MARGOT. You know Anne. In half an hour she'll be out here, laughing and joking.

MRS. FRANK. And...[*She makes a motion upward, indicating the* VAN DAANS.]...I told your father it wouldn't work...but no...no...he had to ask them, he said...he owed it to him, he said. Well, he knows now that I was right! These quarrels!...This bickering! **E**

MARGOT. [*With a warning look.*] Shush. Shush.

The buzzer for the door sounds. MRS. FRANK *gasps, startled.*

MRS. FRANK. Every time I hear that sound, my heart stops!

MARGOT. [*Starting for* PETER'S *door.*] It's Miep. [*She knocks at the door.*] Father?

MR. FRANK *comes quickly from* PETER'S *room.*

MR. FRANK. Thank you, Margot. [*As he goes down the steps to open the outer door.*] Has everyone his list?[36] **F**

MARGOT. I'll get my books. [*Giving her mother a list.*] Here's your list. [MARGOT *goes into her and* ANNE'S *bedroom on the right.* ANNE *sits up, hiding her tears, as* MARGOT *comes in.*] Miep's here.

MARGOT *picks up her books and goes back.* ANNE *hurries over to the mirror, smoothing her hair.*

MR. VAN DAAN. [*Coming down the stairs.*] Is it Miep?

MARGOT. Yes. Father's gone down to let her in.

MR. VAN DAAN. At last I'll have some cigarettes!

---

36. **Has everyone his list?** "Does everyone have a list of things for Miep to get?"

THE DIARY OF ANNE FRANK, ACT 1 **659**

Analyze Literature

Stage Directions Students might notice the contradiction between what the stage directions indicate and how Mrs. Frank interprets Mr. Kraler's visit. Ask students what might account for the discrepancy. Model a response by suggesting that Mr. Frank, having had a moment alone with him, has some idea about Mr. Kraler's mission. **Ⓐ**

Use Reading Strategies

Make Predictions Ask students to predict how each character will react to this request. Have them support their predictions with details that they already know about each character. Model a response by suggesting that Mr. and Mrs. Frank's kind and generous natures, Anne's sociability, and Margot's easy-going nature will lead them to accept the new lodger willingly. Mr. and Mrs. Van Daan seem to be selfish and accustomed to having much more space, so they will probably object. **Ⓑ**

Use Reading Skills

Summarize Ask students to summarize the reactions of the others to Mrs. Frank's question. What do their reactions reveal about their characters? Model a response by suggesting that Peter, Anne, and Margot's responses indicate that they are generous and helpful, even in circumstances that would make most people uncomfortable. Mr. and Mrs. Van Daan reveal themselves to be selfish and greedy. **Ⓒ**

MRS. FRANK. [*To* MR. VAN DAAN.] I can't tell you how unhappy I am about Mrs. Van Daan's coat. Anne should never have touched it.

MR. VAN DAAN. She'll be all right.

MRS. FRANK. Is there anything I can do?

MR. VAN DAAN. Don't worry.

He turns to meet MIEP. *But it is not* MIEP *who comes up the steps. It is* MR. KRALER, *followed by* MR. FRANK. *Their faces are grave.*[37] ANNE *comes from the bedroom.* PETER *comes from his room.*

Ⓐ **MRS. FRANK.** Mr. Kraler!

MR. VAN DAAN. How are you, Mr. Kraler?

MARGOT. This is a surprise.

MRS. FRANK. When Mr. Kraler comes, the sun begins to shine.

MR. VAN DAAN. Miep is coming?

MR. KRALER. Not tonight.

KRALER *goes to* MARGOT *and* MRS. FRANK *and* ANNE, *shaking hands with them.*

MRS. FRANK. Wouldn't you like a cup of coffee?...Or, better still, will you have supper with us?

MR. FRANK. Mr. Kraler has something to talk over with us. Something has happened, he says, which demands an immediate decision.

MRS. FRANK. [*Fearful.*] What is it?

MR. KRALER *sits down on the couch. As he talks he takes bread, cabbages, milk, etc., from his briefcase, giving them to* MARGOT *and* ANNE *to put away.*

MR. KRALER. Usually, when I come up here, I try to bring you some bit of good news. What's the use of telling you the bad news when there's nothing that you can do about it? But today something has happened... Dirk...Miep's Dirk, you know, came to me just now. He tells me that he has a Jewish

Ⓑ friend living near him. A dentist. He says he's in trouble. He begged me, could I do anything for this man? Could I find him a hiding place?...So I've come to you...I know it's a terrible thing to ask of you, living as you are, but would you take him in with you?

MR. FRANK. Of course we will.

MR. KRALER. [*Rising.*] It'll be just for a night or two...until I find some other place. This happened so suddenly that I didn't know where to turn.

MR. FRANK. Where is he?

MR. KRALER. Downstairs in the office.

MR. FRANK. Good. Bring him up.

MR. KRALER. His name is Dussel...Jan Dussel.

MR. FRANK. Dussel...I think I know him.

MR. KRALER. I'll get him.

He goes quickly down the steps and out. MR. FRANK *suddenly becomes conscious of the others.*

MR. FRANK. Forgive me. I spoke without consulting you. But I knew you'd feel as I do.

MR. VAN DAAN. There's no reason for you to consult anyone. This is your place. You have a right to do exactly as you please. The only thing I feel...there's so little food as it is...and to take in another person...

PETER *turns away, ashamed of his father.*

MR. FRANK. We can stretch the food a little. It's only for a few days.

MR. VAN DAAN. You want to make a bet?

Ⓒ **MRS. FRANK.** I think it's fine to have him. But, Otto, where are you going to put him? Where?

PETER. He can have my bed. I can sleep on the floor. I wouldn't mind.

MR. FRANK. That's good of you, Peter. But your room's too small...even for *you.*

---

37. grave. Very serious and concerned

Differentiated Instruction

Visual Learning

To better understand the differences and similarities between various characters, pairs of students might benefit from making Venn diagrams. They might compare the two Frank sisters in one diagram, Mrs. Frank and Mrs. Van Daan in another, and Mr. Frank and Mr. Van Daan in yet another. Make sure students apply the correct comparative or superlative forms learned in the Grammar Skills on page 659. Groups can then get together and compare the diagrams the various pairs have created.

ANNE. I have a much better idea. I'll come in here with you and Mother, and Margot can take Peter's room and Peter can go in our room with Mr. Dussel.

MARGOT. That's right. We could do that.

MR. FRANK. No, Margot. You mustn't sleep in that room…neither you nor Anne. Mouschi has caught some rats in there. Peter's brave. He doesn't mind.

ANNE. Then how about *this*? I'll come in here with you and Mother, and Mr. Dussel can have my bed.

MRS. FRANK. No. No. *No!* Margot will come in here with us and he can have her bed. It's the only way. Margot, bring your things in here. Help her, Anne.

MARGOT hurries into her room to get her things.

ANNE. [*To her mother.*] Why Margot? Why can't I come in here?

MRS. FRANK. Because it wouldn't be proper for Margot to sleep with a…Please, Anne. Don't argue. Please.

ANNE starts slowly away.

MR. FRANK. [*To* ANNE.] You don't mind sharing your room with Mr. Dussel, do you, Anne?

ANNE. No. No, of course not.

MR. FRANK. Good. [ANNE *goes off into her bedroom, helping* MARGOT. MR. FRANK *starts to search in the cupboards.*] Where's the cognac?[38]

MRS. FRANK. It's there. But, Otto, I was saving it in case of illness.

MR. FRANK. I think we couldn't find a better time to use it. Peter, will you get five glasses for me?

PETER goes for the glasses. MARGOT *comes out of her bedroom, carrying her possessions, which she hangs behind a curtain in the main room.* MR. FRANK *finds the cognac and pours it into the five*

glasses that PETER *brings him.* MR. VAN DAAN *stands looking on sourly.* MRS. VAN DAAN *comes downstairs and looks around at all the bustle.*[39]

MRS. VAN DAAN. What's happening? What's going on?

MR. VAN DAAN. Someone's moving in with us.

MRS. VAN DAAN. In here? You're joking.

MARGOT. It's only for a night or two…until Mr. Kraler finds him another place.

MR. VAN DAAN. Yeah! Yeah!

MR. FRANK *hurries over as* MR. KRALER *and* DUSSEL *come up.* DUSSEL *is a man in his late fifties, meticulous,[40] finicky…bewildered now. He wears a raincoat. He carries a briefcase, stuffed full, and a small medicine case.*

MR. FRANK. Come in, Mr. Dussel.

MR. KRALER. This is Mr. Frank.

DUSSEL. Mr. Otto Frank?

MR. FRANK. Yes. Let me take your things. [*He takes the hat and briefcase, but* DUSSEL *clings to his medicine case.*] This is my wife Edith… Mr. and Mrs. Van Daan…their son, Peter… and my daughters, Margot and Anne.

DUSSEL *shakes hands with everyone.*

MR. KRALER. Thank you, Mr. Frank. Thank you all. Mr. Dussel, I leave you in good hands. Oh…Dirk's coat.

DUSSEL *hurriedly takes off the raincoat, giving it to* MR. KRALER. *Underneath is his white dentist's jacket, with a yellow Star of David on it.*

DUSSEL. [*To* MR. KRALER.] What can I say to thank you…?

MRS. FRANK. [*To* DUSSEL.] Mr. Kraler and Miep…They're our life line. Without them we couldn't live.

---

38. **cognac** (kōn´ yak'). Very fine French brandy
39. **bustle.** Noisy, busy activity
40. **meticulous.** Very neat

Analyze Literature
Stage Directions Point out to students that these stage directions reveal a great deal about Mr. Dussel's personality. Based on the fact that he is "meticulous" and "finicky," students can probably predict that he will not adjust easily to life in the secret annex. **D**

Use Reading Strategies
Make Inferences Ask students why Mr. Dussel might have been wearing Dirk's coat. Model a response by suggesting that he wanted to hide the Star of David on his white dentist's jacket, to avoid being noticed by any Nazis or informers who might have seen him go into the building with Mr. Kraler. **E**

Vocabulary Skills

Difficult Words
The number of words that seem difficult will vary from student to student, but all students can benefit from these strategies to decode those words:
- Keep reading, looking for context clues that will clarify the meaning of the word.
- Break long words apart into syllables and pronounce each word aloud. Does it sound familiar?
- Break words down into root words, prefixes, and suffixes. Does this help in decoding meaning?
- Look the word up in a dictionary.

Use Reading Skills

Identify Main Idea Point out that Mr. Dussel's dialogue here reveals a great deal about Mr. Frank. The fact that Mr. Dussel is so surprised to find Mr. Frank here tells the reader that Mr. Frank had been well-known and highly regarded in Amsterdam. It is clear that many people have been talking about the Franks. The fact that Mr. Frank had put a piece of paper in the wastebasket with a Zurich address on it shows that Mr. Frank did some careful planning about going into hiding with his family. (A)

Cultural Connection

Swiss Neutrality Mr. Dussel's reference to Switzerland as a safe haven for Jews points out the fact that Switzerland was a neutral country during World War II and was one of the few European countries not occupied by the Germans at this time. Even though Switzerland welcomed many Jewish refugees, it was not easy to get there. In German-occupied countries, Jews were not allowed to use public transportation. To reach Switzerland, the Franks would have been forced to travel by foot and cross many borders. Along the way, they would have to hide from German troops in the occupied countries. Mr. Frank obviously thought his family would be safer hiding in the Netherlands. (B)

MR. KRALER. Please. Please. You make us seem very heroic. It isn't that at all. We simply don't like the Nazis. [*To* MR. FRANK, *who offers him a drink.*] No, thanks. [*Then going on.*] We don't like their methods. We don't like...

MR. FRANK. [*Smiling.*] I know. I know. "No one's going to tell us Dutchmen what to do with our Jews!"

MR. KRALER. [*To* DUSSEL.] Pay no attention to Mr. Frank. I'll be up tomorrow to see that they're treating you right. [*To* MR. FRANK.] Don't trouble to come down again. Peter will bolt the door after me, won't you, Peter?

PETER. Yes, sir.

MR. FRANK. Thank you, Peter. I'll do it.

MR. KRALER. Good night. Good night.

GROUP. Good night, Mr. Kraler. We'll see you tomorrow, *etc., etc.*

MR. KRALER *goes out with* MR. FRANK. MRS. FRANK *gives each one of the "grown-ups" a glass of cognac.*

MRS. FRANK. Please, Mr. Dussel, sit down.

MR. DUSSEL *sinks into a chair.* MRS. FRANK *gives him a glass of cognac.*

DUSSEL. I'm dreaming. I know it. I can't believe my eyes. Mr. Otto Frank here! [*To* MRS. FRANK.] You're not in Switzerland then? A woman told me...She said she'd gone to your house...the door was open, everything was in disorder, dishes in the sink. She said she found a piece of paper in the wastebasket with an address scribbled on it...an address in Zurich. She said you must have escaped to Zurich.

ANNE. Father put that there purposely...just so people would think that very thing!

DUSSEL. And you've been *here* all the time?

MRS. FRANK. All the time...ever since July.

ANNE *speaks to her father as he comes back.*

ANNE. It worked. Pim...the address you left! Mr. Dussel says that people believe we escaped to Switzerland.

MR. FRANK. I'm glad...And now let's have a little drink to welcome Mr. Dussel. [*Before they can drink,* MR. DUSSEL *bolts his drink.* MR. FRANK *smiles and raises his glass.*] To Mr. Dussel. Welcome. We're very honored to have you with us.

MRS. FRANK. To Mr. Dussel, welcome.

The VAN DAANS *murmur a welcome. The "grown-ups" drink.*

MRS. VAN DAAN. Um. That was good.

MR. VAN DAAN. Did Mr. Kraler warn you that you won't get much to eat here? You can imagine...three ration books among the seven of us...and now you make eight.

PETER *walks away, humiliated.[41] Outside a street organ is heard dimly.*

DUSSEL. [*Rising.*] Mr. Van Daan, you don't realize what is happening outside that you should warn me of a thing like that. You don't realize what's going on...[*As* MR. VAN DAAN *starts his characteristic pacing,* DUSSEL *turns to speak to the others.*] Right here in Amsterdam every day hundreds of Jews disappear...They surround a block and search house by house. Children come home from school to find their parents gone. Hundreds are being deported[42]...people that you and I know...the Hallensteins...the Wessels...

MRS. FRANK. [*In tears.*] Oh, no. No!

DUSSEL. They get their call-up notice...come to the Jewish theater on such and such a day and hour...bring only what you can carry in a rucksack. And if you refuse the call-up notice, then they come and drag you from

---

41. humiliated. Extremely embarrassed
42. deported. Sent away, out of the country

English Language Learning

Words with multiple meanings are especially challenging to students learning English. Here are some examples:

grave	turn
shaking	spoke
still	right
over	fine
down	mind

just	case
course	glasses

Have students write these words, along with definitions that match their use in the play. Then have partners use dictionaries to find additional definitions for each word.

Cultural Connection
Concentration Camps Mr. Dussel refers to Mauthausen, a concentration camp near Linz, Austria, that had forty-nine subcamps. In every country that was occupied by the Germans, concentration camps were set up, many of them with numerous subcamps. The following countries had concentration camps: Germany, Austria, Belgium, Czechoslovakia, Estonia, Finland, France, Great Britain, Holland, Italy, Latvia, Lithuania, Norway, Poland, Russia, and Yugoslavia. **C**

Make Connections
Mr. Dussel's answer to Anne's question is shocking. Put yourself in Anne's place. How would you feel upon hearing such news? **D**

your home and ship you off to Mauthausen.[43] The death camp!

MRS. FRANK. We didn't know that things had got so much worse.

DUSSEL. Forgive me for speaking so.

ANNE. [*Coming to* DUSSEL.] Do you know the de Waals?…What's become of them? Their daughter Jopie and I are in the same class. Jopie's my best friend.

DUSSEL. They are gone.

ANNE. Gone?

DUSSEL. With all the others.

ANNE. Oh, no. Not Jopie!

She turns away, in tears. MRS. FRANK *motions to*

MARGOT *to comfort her.* MARGOT *goes to* ANNE, *putting her arms comfortingly around her.*

MRS. VAN DAAN. There were some people called Wagner. They lived near us…?

MR. FRANK. [*Interrupting, with a glance at* ANNE.] I think we should put this off until later. We all have many questions we want to ask…But I'm sure that Mr. Dussel would like to get settled before supper.

DUSSEL. Thank you. I would. I brought very little with me.

MR. FRANK. [*Giving him his hat and briefcase.*] I'm sorry we can't give you a room alone. But I hope you won't be too uncomfortable.

---

43. **Mauthausen.** Site of a Nazi concentration camp in Austria

Grammar Skills

Subject-Verb Agreement

Remind students that a verb must agree with its subject in number. In other words, if the subject is plural, the verb must be plural; if the subject is singular, the verb must be singular. These distinctions apply only to verbs in the present tense that are used with third-person pronouns. Past-tense verbs do not change forms to indicate number, nor do verbs used with first-person and second-person pronouns. For example:

singular: I hide. You hide. He hides.

plural: We hide. You hide. They hide.
singular: I hid. You hid. He hid.
plural: We hid. You hid. They hid.

In the following sentences, have students select the verb that agrees in number with the subject.

1. Mr. Frank (search, searches) in the cupboards for the cognac.
2. Mr. Kraler and Mr. Dussel (come, comes) up the stairs.
3. Many Dutch people (help, helps) the Jews hide from the Nazis.

Use Reading Skills

Read Aloud Encourage pairs of students to read aloud the conversation between Anne and Mr. Dussel. As they read, suggest that they try to capture the personality of each character. They should also ask questions to clarify any parts of the conversation they do not understand.

Analyze Literature

Dialogue Ask: "In this bit of dialogue, what feature of the room does Anne say she likes the best, and what does that tell you about her?" Model a response: "Anne likes the idea that she can see part of the street and the canal from the window. The fact that she likes to watch the family with the baby shows that she is concerned about other people and wishes to interact with the world outside the secret annex." Ⓐ

We've had to make strict rules here…a schedule of hours…We'll tell you after supper. Anne, would you like to take Mr. Dussel to his room?

ANNE. [*Controlling her tears.*] If you'll come with me, Mr. Dussel?

She starts for her room.

DUSSEL. [*Shaking hands with each in turn.*] Forgive me if I haven't really expressed my gratitude to all of you. This has been such a shock to me. I'd always thought of myself as Dutch. I was born in Holland. My father was born in Holland, and my grandfather. And now…after all these years…[*He breaks off.*] If you'll excuse me.

DUSSEL *gives a little bow and hurries off after* ANNE. MR. FRANK *and the others are subdued.*

ANNE. [*Turning on the light.*] Well, here we are.

DUSSEL *looks around the room. In the main room* MARGOT *speaks to her mother.*

MARGOT. The news sounds pretty bad, doesn't it? It's so different from what Mr. Kraler tells us. Mr. Kraler says things are improving.

MR. VAN DAAN. I like it better the way Kraler tells it.

They resume their occupations, quietly. PETER *goes off into his room. In* ANNE's *room,* ANNE *turns to* DUSSEL.

ANNE. You're going to share the room with me.

DUSSEL. I'm a man who's always lived alone. I haven't had to adjust myself to others. I hope you'll bear with me until I learn.

ANNE. Let me help you. [*She takes his briefcase.*] Do you always live all alone? Have you no family at all?

DUSSEL. No one.

He opens his medicine case and spreads his bottles on the dressing table.

ANNE. How dreadful. You must be terribly lonely.

DUSSEL. I'm used to it.

ANNE. I don't think I could ever get used to it. Didn't you even have a pet? A cat, or a dog?

DUSSEL. I have an allergy for fur-bearing animals. They give me asthma.⁴⁴

ANNE. Oh, dear. Peter has a cat.

DUSSEL. Here? He has it here?

ANNE. Yes. But we hardly ever see it. He keeps it in his room all the time. I'm sure it will be all right.

DUSSEL. Let us hope so.

He takes some pills to fortify himself.

ANNE. That's Margot's bed, where you're going to sleep. I sleep on the sofa there. [*Indicating the clothes hooks on the wall.*] We cleared these off for your things. [*She goes over to the window.*] The best part about this room…you can look down and see a bit of the street and the canal. There's a houseboat…you can see the end of it…a bargeman lives there with his family…They have a baby and he's just beginning to walk and I'm so afraid he's going to fall into the canal some day. I watch him….

DUSSEL. [*Interrupting.*] Your father spoke of a schedule.

ANNE. [*Coming away from the window.*] Oh, yes. It's mostly about the times we have to be quiet. And times for the w.c. You can use it now if you like.

DUSSEL. [*Stiffly.*] No, thank you.

ANNE. I suppose you think it's awful, my talking about a thing like that. But you don't know how important it can get to be, especially when you're frightened…About

---

44. asthma. Disease that makes breathing difficult, often caused by allergies

---

Differentiated Instruction

Auditory Learning

Have small groups work together to read the dialogue aloud and discuss its meaning. Auditory learners will also benefit from listening to a taped recording of the selection as they read along.

Enrichment

Draw students' attention to the "etc., etc." line on page 662 as Mr. Kraler is leaving. Tell them that this line is not meant to be spoken. Instead, the authors expect the actors to make up a few parting words as Mr. Kraler leaves. Students might enjoy writing lines for each character that reflect the person's personality and fit the occasion. Have students share their lines with the class.

this room, the way Margot and I did it…she had it to herself in the afternoons for studying, reading…lessons, you know…and I took the mornings. Would that be all right with you?

DUSSEL. I'm not at my best in the morning. **B**

ANNE. You stay here in the mornings then. I'll take the room in the afternoons.

DUSSEL. Tell me, when you're in here, what happens to me? Where am I spending my time? In there, with all the people?

ANNE. Yes.

DUSSEL. I see. I see.

ANNE. We have supper at half past six.

DUSSEL. [*Going over to the sofa.*] Then, if you don't mind…I like to lie down quietly for ten minutes before eating. I find it helps the digestion.

ANNE. Of course. I hope I'm not going to be too much of a bother to you. I seem to be able to get everyone's back up.[45]

DUSSEL lies down on the sofa, curled up, his back to her.

DUSSEL. I always get along very well with children. My patients all bring their children to me, because they know I get on well with them. So don't you worry about that.

ANNE leans over him, taking his hand and shaking it gratefully.

ANNE. Thank you. Thank you, Mr. Dussel.

The lights dim to darkness. The curtain falls on the scene. ANNE'S VOICE *comes to us faintly at first, and then with increasing power.*

ANNE'S VOICE. …And yesterday I finished Cissy Van Marxvelt's latest book. I think she is a first-class writer. I shall definitely let my children read her. Monday the twenty-first of September, nineteen forty-two. Mr. Dussel and I had another battle yesterday. Yes, Mr. Dussel! According to him, nothing, **C**

I repeat…nothing, is right about me…my appearance, my character, my manners. While he was going on at me I thought… sometime I'll give you such a smack that you'll fly right up to the ceiling! Why is it that every grown-up thinks he knows the way to bring up children? Particularly the grown-ups that never had any. I keep wishing that Peter was a girl instead of a boy. Then I would have someone to talk to. Margot's a darling, but she takes everything too seriously. To pause for a moment on the subject of Mrs. Van Daan. I must tell you that her attempts to flirt with father are getting her nowhere. Pim, thank goodness, won't play. **D**

As she is saying the last lines, the curtain rises on the darkened scene. ANNE'S VOICE *fades out.*

SCENE 4

It is the middle of the night, several months later. The stage is dark except for a little light which comes through the skylight in PETER'S *room.*

Everyone is in bed. MR. *and* MRS. FRANK *lie on the couch in the main room, which has been pulled out to serve as a makeshift[46] double bed.*

MARGOT *is sleeping on a mattress on the floor in the main room, behind a curtain stretched across for privacy. The others are all in their accustomed rooms.*

From outside we hear two…soldiers singing "Lili Marlene." A girl's high giggle is heard. The sound of running feet is heard coming closer and then fading in the distance. Throughout the scene there is the distant sound of airplanes passing overhead.

A match suddenly flares up in the attic. We dimly see MR. VAN DAAN. *He is getting his bearings. He comes quickly down the stairs, and goes to the cupboard where the food is stored. Again the*

---

45. get everyone's back up. Annoy everyone
46. makeshift. Alternate; made to work as a replacement for the real thing

Use Reading Skills
Identify Multiple Meanings
Students might recognize that Mr. Dussel's statement here can be interpreted in several ways. He could be saying this assertively, to bully Anne into letting him have the room. Conversely, he could be saying this apologetically, sorry that this fact might inconvenience Anne. **B**

Literary Connection
Kitty Cissy Van Marxvelt (1889-1948) wrote a series of books that was popular among adolescent girls in Holland when Anne Frank lived there. In fact, the "Kitty" to whom Anne addressed her diary is based on the character of Kitty Francken from Van Marxvelt's books. The novels feature the headstrong Joop ter Heul and her adventures with her friends from girlhood to marriage. Van Marxveldt began writing after her marriage to Leo Beek, a reserve infantry officer. Her husband was active in the Dutch resistance against the Nazis; he was arrested in 1943 and killed in 1944 by firing squad in Westerbork, the same concentration camp that Anne Frank and the others were first sent to when they were discovered. Van Marxvelt learned of her husband's fate in 1947 and died a year later. **C**

Analyze Literature
Subplot Anne's relationship with Mr. Dussel is a subplot in the play. Have students describe the relationship and comment on how this subplot relates to the main plot. **D**

Balance
Have students use their research skills to find out more about the realities of life for European Jews during this time. As they discover historical facts about this period, encourage them to strive for an effective balance between verifiable facts and their own original ideas about how those facts impacted individual lives.

They might want to use a two-column chart like this one to keep track of which ones are original.

Verifiable Fact	Impact on My Imaginary Character
Typhus killed many people in the camps.	Severe muscle pain prevents her from working.

Literary Connection

Stage Adaptation Discuss with students the process of adapting a text for the stage. Remind them that the writers must consider how the scenes will look on the stage, so they have to think about set design and arrangement. Further, they often have to combine several characters into one or two, to avoid confusing the audience. In the case of *The Diary of Anne Frank,* the many Dutch people who helped the families were reduced to just Miep and Mr. Kraler.

Use Reading Skills

Identify Cause and Effect Have students speculate on the causes of Anne's nightmare. Model an answer: "The tensions of living in such close quarters with the others, not being able to have the life of a normal teenager, and being constantly worried about being discovered and sent to a concentration camp all contributed to her nightmare." **Ⓐ**

---

match flares up, and is as quickly blown out. The dim figure is seen to steal back up the stairs.

There is quiet for a second or two, broken only by the sound of airplanes, and running feet on the street below.

Suddenly, out of the silence and the dark, we hear ANNE *scream.*

Ⓐ **ANNE.** [*Screaming.*] No! No! Don't…don't take me!

She moans, tossing and crying in her sleep. The other people wake, terrified. DUSSEL *sits up in bed, furious.*

DUSSEL. Shush! Anne! Anne, for God's sake, shush!

ANNE. [*Still in her nightmare.*] Save me! Save me!

She screams and screams. DUSSEL *gets out of bed, going over to her, trying to wake her.*

DUSSEL. Quiet! Quiet! You want someone to hear?

In the main room MRS. FRANK *grabs a shawl and pulls it around her. She rushes in to* ANNE, *taking her in her arms.* MR. FRANK *hurriedly gets up, putting on his overcoat.* MARGOT *sits up, terrified.* PETER's *light goes on in his room.*

MRS. FRANK. [*To* ANNE, *in her room.*] Hush, darling, hush. It's all right. It's all right. [*Over her shoulder to* DUSSEL.] Will you be kind enough to turn on the light, Mr. Dussel? [*Back to* ANNE.] It's nothing, my darling. It was just a dream.

DUSSEL *turns on the light in the bedroom.* MRS. FRANK *holds* ANNE *in her arms. Gradually* ANNE *comes out of her nightmare, still trembling with horror.* MR. FRANK *comes into the room, and goes quickly to the window, looking out to be sure that no one outside has heard* ANNE's *screams.* MRS. FRANK *holds* ANNE, *talking softly to her. In the main room* MARGOT *stands on a chair, turning on the center hanging lamp. A light goes on in the*

VAN DAANS' *room overhead.* PETER *puts his robe on, coming out of his room.*

DUSSEL. [*To* MRS. FRANK, *blowing his nose.*] Something must be done about that child, Mrs. Frank. Yelling like that! Who knows but there's somebody on the streets? She's endangering all our lives.

MRS. FRANK. Anne, darling.

DUSSEL. Every night she twists and turns. I don't sleep. I spend half my night shushing her. And now it's nightmares!

MARGOT *comes to the door of* ANNE's *room, followed by* PETER. MR. FRANK *goes to them, indicating that everything is all right.* PETER *takes* MARGOT *back.*

MRS. FRANK. [*To* ANNE.] You're here, safe, you see? Nothing has happened. [*To* DUSSEL.] Please, Mr. Dussel, go back to bed. She'll be herself in a minute or two. Won't you, Anne?

DUSSEL. [*Picking up a book and a pillow.*] Thank you, but I'm going to the w.c. The one place where there's peace!

He stalks out. MR. VAN DAAN, *in underwear and trousers, comes down the stairs.*

MR. VAN DAAN. [*To* DUSSEL.] What is it? What happened?

DUSSEL. A nightmare. She was having a nightmare!

MR. VAN DAAN. I thought someone was murdering her.

DUSSEL. Unfortunately, no.

He goes into the bathroom. MR. VAN DAAN *goes back up the stairs.* MR. FRANK, *in the main room, sends* PETER *back to his own bedroom.*

MR. FRANK. Thank you, Peter. Go back to bed.

PETER *goes back to his room.* MR. FRANK *follows him, turning out the light and looking out the window. Then he goes back to the main room,*

Differentiated Instruction

Enrichment

Students might enjoy researching the history of the song "Lili Marlene," which is referred to in the stage directions for Scene 4. They will be interested to find out that the original words were written in 1915, during World War I, but that it was not set to music until 1938. Many online versions of the song are available, and students might like to learn how to sing the song themselves and perform it for the class.

and gets up on a chair, turning out the center hanging lamp.

MRS. FRANK. [*To* ANNE.] Would you like some water? [ANNE *shakes her head.*] Was it a very bad dream? Perhaps if you told me…?

ANNE. I'd rather not talk about it.

MRS. FRANK. Poor darling. Try to sleep then. I'll sit right here beside you until you fall asleep. [*She brings a stool over, sitting there.*]

ANNE. You don't have to.

MRS. FRANK. But I'd like to stay with you… very much. Really.

ANNE. I'd rather you didn't.

MRS. FRANK. Good night, then. [*She leans down to kiss* ANNE. ANNE *throws her arm up over her face, turning away.* MRS. FRANK, *hiding her hurt, kisses* ANNE'S *arm.*] You'll be all right? There's nothing that you want?

ANNE. Will you please ask Father to come.

MRS. FRANK. [*After a second.*] Of course, Anne dear.

[*She hurries out into the other room.* MR. FRANK *comes to her as she comes in.*] Sie verlangt nach Dir![47]

B **MR. FRANK.** [*Sensing her hurt.*] Edith, *Liebe, schau…*[48]

C **MRS. FRANK.** *Es macht nichts! Ich danke dem lieben Herrgott, dass sie sich wenigstens an Dich wendet, wenn sie Trost braucht! Geh hinein, Otto, sie ist ganz hysterisch vor Angst.*[49] [*As* MR. FRANK *hesitates.*] *Geh zu ihr.* [*He looks at her for a second and then goes to get a cup of water for* ANNE. MRS. FRANK *sinks down on the bed, her face in her hands, trying to keep from sobbing aloud.* MARGOT *comes over to her, putting her arms around her.*] She wants nothing of me. She pulled away when I leaned down to kiss her.

MARGOT. It's a phase…You heard Father…Most girls go through it… they turn to their fathers at this age…they give all their love to their fathers.

MRS. FRANK. You weren't like this. You didn't shut me out.

MARGOT. She'll get over it…

---

47. **Sie verlangt nach Dir!** "She's asking for you to come!" (German)
48. **Liebe, schau…** "Dear, look…" ("Try to understand….") (German)
49. **Es macht…vor Angst.** "It's all right. I thank dear God that at least she turns to you when she needs comfort. Go in, Otto. She is hysterical because of fear." (German)

THE DIARY OF ANNE FRANK, ACT 1 **667**

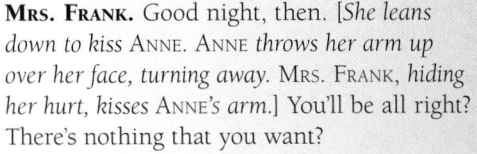

History Connection

Green Police The residents of the secret annex were in constant fear of being discovered by the "Green Police," or the Gestapo (an acronym for the Geheime Staatspolizei — the Secret State Police of Germany. The job of the Gestapo was to promote Hitler and Nazism by terrorizing those who were suspected of undermining the Third Reich. The Gestapo was also in charge of sending victims to the concentration camps. After the war, the International Military Tribunal at Nuremberg declared the Gestapo a criminal organization. **A**

Analyze Literature

Aside Tell students than an aside is the words of an actor spoken in such a way that they can be heard by the audience but supposedly not by the other actors on the stage. In this play, Anne Frank's voice-overs as she reads her diary can be seen as asides. In these asides, Anne reveals her private thoughts. **B**

She smooths the bed for MRS. FRANK *and sits beside her a moment as* MRS. FRANK *lies down. In* ANNE's *room* MR. FRANK *comes in, sitting down by* ANNE. ANNE *flings her arms around him, clinging to him. In the distance we hear the sound of ack-ack.*

A **ANNE.** Oh, Pim. I dreamed that they came to get us! The Green Police! They broke down the door and grabbed me and started to drag me out the way they did Jopie.

MR. FRANK. I want you to take this pill.

ANNE. What is it?

MR. FRANK. Something to quiet you.

She takes it and drinks the water. In the main room MARGOT *turns out the light and goes back to her bed.*

MR. FRANK. [*To* ANNE.] Do you want me to read to you for a while?

ANNE. No. Just sit with me for a minute. Was I awful? Did I yell terribly loud? Do you think anyone outside could have heard?

MR. FRANK. No. No. Lie quietly now. Try to sleep.

ANNE. I'm a terrible coward. I'm so disappointed in myself. I think I've conquered my fear...I think I'm really grown-up...and then something happens...and I run to you like a baby...I love you, Father, I don't love anyone but you.

MR. FRANK. [*Reproachfully.*] Annele!

ANNE. It's true. I've been thinking about it for a long time. You're the only one I love.

MR. FRANK. It's fine to hear you tell me that you love me. But I'd be happier if you said you loved your mother as well...She needs your help so much...your love...

ANNE. We have nothing in common. She doesn't understand me. Whenever I try to explain my views on life to her she asks me if I'm constipated.

MR. FRANK. You hurt her very much just now. She's crying. She's in there crying.

ANNE. I can't help it. I only told the truth. I didn't want her here...[*Then, with sudden change.*] Oh, Pim, I was horrible, wasn't I? And the worst of it is, I can stand off and look at myself doing it and know it's cruel and yet I can't stop doing it. What's the matter with me? Tell me. Don't say it's just a phase! Help me.

MR. FRANK. There is so little that we parents can do to help our children. We can only try to set a good example...point the way. The rest you must do yourself. You must build your own character.

ANNE. I'm trying. Really I am. Every night I think back over all of the things I did that day that were wrong...like putting the wet mop in Mr. Dussel's bed...and this thing now with Mother. I say to myself, that was wrong. I make up my mind, I'm never going to do that again. Never! Of course I may do something worse...but at least I'll never do that again!...I have a nicer side, Father...a sweeter, nicer side. But I'm scared to show it. I'm afraid that people are going to laugh at me if I'm serious. So the mean Anne comes to the outside and the good Anne stays on the inside, and I keep on trying to switch them around and have the good Anne outside and the bad Anne inside and be what I'd like to be...and might be...if only... only...

B *She is asleep.* MR. FRANK *watches her for a moment and then turns off the light, and starts out. The lights dim out. The curtain falls on the scene.* ANNE's VOICE *is heard dimly at first, and then with growing strength.*

ANNE'S VOICE. ...The air raids[50] are getting worse. They come over day and night. The noise is terrifying. Pim says it should be

---

50. air raids. Attacks by planes dropping bombs

Differentiated Instruction

Kinesthetic Learning

Students might benefit from analyzing the sounds that are heard from the outside at the beginning of Scene 4. For example, they will probably recognize that the two soldiers singing "Lili Marlene" are a reminder of the German Army occupying Amsterdam; the girl laughing is a reminder that other people are living normal, happy lives; the sound of running feet is a reminder that some people are still being chased; and the sounds of airplanes overhead are a reminder that the war continues.

music to our ears. The more planes, the sooner will come the end of the war. Mrs. Van Daan pretends to be a fatalist.[51] What will be, will be. But when the planes come over, who is the most frightened? No one else but Petronella!…Monday, the ninth of November, nineteen forty-two. Wonderful news! The Allies[52] have landed in Africa. Pim says that we can look for an early finish to the war. Just for fun he asked each of us what was the first thing we wanted to do when we got out of here. Mrs. Van Daan longs to be home with her own things, her needle-point chairs, the Beckstein piano her father gave her…the best that money could buy. Peter would like to go to a movie. Mr. Dussel wants to get back to his dentist's drill. He's afraid he is losing his touch. For myself, there are so many things…to ride a bike again…to laugh till my belly aches…to have new clothes from the skin out…to have a hot tub filled to overflowing and wallow in it for hours…to be back in school with my friends…

As the last lines are being said, the curtain rises on the scene. The lights dim on as ANNE'S VOICE *fades away.*

SCENE 5

It is the first night of the Hanukkah[53] celebration. MR. FRANK *is standing at the head of the table on which is the Menorah.[54] He lights the Shamos,[55] or servant candle, and holds it as he says the blessing. Seated listening is all of the "family," dressed in their best. The men wear hats,[56]* PETER *wears his cap.*

MR. FRANK. [*Reading from a prayer book.*] "Praised be Thou, oh Lord our God, Ruler of the universe, who has sanctified us with Thy commandments and bidden us kindle the Hanukkah lights. Praised be Thou, oh Lord our God, Ruler of the universe, who has wrought wondrous deliverances for our fathers in days of old. Praised be Thou, oh

Lord our God, Ruler of the universe, that Thou has given us life and sustenance and brought us to this happy season." [MR. FRANK *lights the one candle of the Menorah as he continues.*] "We kindle this Hanukkah light to celebrate the great and wonderful deeds wrought through the zeal with which God filled the hearts of the heroic Maccabees,[57] two thousand years ago. They fought against indifference, against tyranny and oppression, and they restored our Temple to us. May these lights remind us that we should ever look to God, whence cometh our help." Amen. [*Pronounced O-mayn.*]

ALL. Amen.

MR. FRANK *hands* MRS. FRANK *the prayer book.*

MRS. FRANK. [*Reading.*] "I lift up mine eyes unto the mountains, from whence cometh my help. My help cometh from the Lord who made heaven and earth. He will not suffer thy foot to be moved. He that keepeth thee will not slumber. He that keepeth Israel doth neither slumber nor sleep. The Lord is thy keeper. The Lord is thy shade upon thy right hand. The sun shall not smite thee by day, nor the moon by night. The Lord shall keep thee from all evil. He shall keep thy soul. The Lord shall guard thy going out and thy coming in, from this time forth and forevermore." Amen.

ALL. Amen.

---

51. **fatalist.** Someone who believes that "what will be will be"—that all events are determined by fate and thus cannot be changed
52. **Allies.** Allied Forces (Great Britain, France, Soviet Union, United States). People in Europe kept hoping that the Allies would get to Germany and defeat Hitler, bringing an end to the war. (The United States joined the Allies in December 1941, after the attack at Pearl Harbor.)
53. **Hanukkah** (hä´ nə kə). Annual Jewish holiday and celebration that lasts for eight days
54. **Menorah** (mə nor´ uh). Candle stand with nine candleholders and candles, used during Hanukkah
55. **Shamos** (shä´ məs). Candle used to light the others, each night during Hanukkah
56. **The men wear hats.** During religious ceremonies and celebrations, Jewish men cover their heads to show respect.
57. **Maccabees.** Followers of Judas Maccabaeus, whose rededication of the Temple in 165 BC is the origin of Hanukkah

Use Reading Strategies

Make Inferences Point out that Mr. Dussel's behavior is different from that of the others. Students should recognize the implications of this: Mr. Dussel does not practice his religion as seriously as the others do. **A**

Analyze Literature

Rising Action Students will probably recognize that Anne has multiple reasons for giving these gifts: First, she wants to carry on the Hanukkah tradition despite their trying circumstances. She wants everyone to enjoy the holiday. Second, she enjoyed using her creative talents to produce all the gifts. And third, perhaps she wants to make up to the others for her past behavior that might have been annoying to them. **B**

Use Reading Skills

Evaluate Authors' Purpose Ask students to consider how this sound effect contributes to the poignancy of the scene and why the authors might have included it. Model a response by suggesting that the passing streetcar reminds the characters (and the audience) that life outside is going on in a normal fashion, while the residents of the secret annex have their lives on hold, despite all their attempts to carry on. **C**

MRS. FRANK *puts down the prayer book and goes to get the food and wine.* MARGOT *helps her.* MR. FRANK *takes the men's hats and puts them aside.*

A **DUSSEL.** [*Rising.*] That was very moving.

ANNE. [*Pulling him back.*] It isn't over yet!

MRS. VAN DAAN. Sit down! Sit down!

ANNE. There's a lot more, songs and presents.

DUSSEL. Presents?

MRS. FRANK. Not this year, unfortunately.

MRS. VAN DAAN. But always on Hanukkah everyone gives presents...everyone!

DUSSEL. Like our St. Nicholas' Day.[58]

There is a chorus of "no's" from the group.

MRS. VAN DAAN. No! Not like St. Nicholas! What kind of a Jew are you that you don't know Hanukkah?

MRS. FRANK. [*As she brings the food.*] I remember particularly the candles...First one, as we have tonight. Then the second night you light two candles, the next night three...and so on until you have eight candles burning. When there are eight candles it is truly beautiful.

MRS. VAN DAAN. And the potato pancakes.

MR. VAN DAAN. Don't talk about them!

MRS. VAN DAAN. I make the best *latkes*[59] you ever tasted!

MRS. FRANK. Invite us all next year...in your own home.

MR. FRANK. God willing!

MRS. VAN DAAN. God willing.

MARGOT. What I remember best is the presents we used to get when we were little...eight days of presents...and each day they got better and better.

MRS. FRANK. [*Sitting down.*] We are all here, alive. That is present enough.

ANNE. No, it isn't. I've got something...

[*She rushes into her room, hurriedly puts on a little hat* improvised *from the lamp shade, grabs a* satchel[60] *bulging with parcels and comes running back.*]

MRS. FRANK. What is it?

B **ANNE.** Presents!

MRS. VAN DAAN. Presents!

DUSSEL. Look!

MR. VAN DAAN. What's she got on her head?

PETER. A lamp shade!

ANNE. [*She picks out one at random.*] This is for Margot. [*She hands it to* MARGOT, *pulling her to her feet.*] Read it out loud.

MARGOT. [*Reading.*]

"You have never lost your temper.

You never will, I fear,

You are so good.

But if you should,

Put all your cross words here."

[*She tears open the package.*] A new crossword puzzle book! Where did you get it?

ANNE. It isn't new. It's one that you've done. But I rubbed it all out,[61] and if you wait a little and forget, you can do it all over again.

MARGOT. [*Sitting.*] It's wonderful, Anne. Thank you. You'd never know it wasn't new.

C *From outside we hear the sound of a streetcar passing.*

ANNE. [*With another gift.*] Mrs. Van Daan.

---

58. **St. Nicholas' Day.** December 6, the day on which Christian children in Holland receive gifts. (In Holland, Christmas Day, December 25, is a religious day without presents.)
59. *latkes* (lät´ kəs). Potato pancakes that are traditionally served at Hanukkah (Yiddish)
60. **satchel.** Small bag or suitcase
61. **rubbed it all out.** Anne erased all the answers that Margot had written in the book of crossword puzzles. Therefore, Margot could start anew and do all the puzzles again.

im • pro • vise (im´ prə vīz´) *v.*, make with materials easily at hand, usually to fulfill a sudden need

Differentiated Instruction

English Language Learning

Pair students proficient in English with students who are English language learners. Invite them to make a two-column chart of unfamiliar words found in the prayer book. In the first column, they can write the words. In the second column, they can write the definitions, using a dictionary as necessary.

Enrichment

Suggest that students imagine themselves in the place of any one of the residents of the secret annex. Have them consider how they would answer Mr. Frank's question about what they would do first when they get out. Have students write brief essays answering Mr. Frank's question and giving reasons for their choices.

MRS. VAN DAAN. [*Taking it.*] This is awful...I haven't anything for anyone...I never thought...

MR. FRANK. This is all Anne's idea.

MRS. VAN DAAN. [*Holding up a bottle.*] What is it?

ANNE. It's hair shampoo. I took all the odds and ends of soap and mixed them with the last of my toilet water.

MRS. VAN DAAN. Oh, Anneke!

ANNE. I wanted to write a poem for all of them, but I didn't have time. [*Offering a large box to* MR. VAN DAAN.] Yours, Mr. Van Daan, is *really* something...something you want more than anything. [*As she waits for him to open it.*] Look! Cigarettes!

MR. VAN DAAN. Cigarettes!

ANNE. Two of them! Pim found some old pipe tobacco in the pocket lining of his coat...and we made them...or rather, Pim did.

MRS. VAN DAAN. Let me see...Well, look at that! Light it, Putti! Light it.

MR. VAN DAAN *hesitates.*

ANNE. It's tobacco, really it is! There's a little fluff in it, but not much.

Everyone watches intently as MR. VAN DAAN *cautiously lights it. The cigarette flares up. Everyone laughs.*

PETER. It works!

MRS. VAN DAAN. Look at him.

MR. VAN DAAN. [*Spluttering.*] Thank you, Anne. Thank you.

ANNE *rushes back to her satchel for another present.*

ANNE. [*Handing her mother a piece of paper.*] For Mother, Hanukkah greeting.

She pulls her mother to her feet.

MRS. FRANK. [*She reads.*] "Here's an I.O.U. that I promise to pay. Ten hours of doing

whatever you say. Signed, Anne Frank." [MRS. FRANK, *touched, takes* ANNE *in her arms, holding her close.*]

DUSSEL. [*To* ANNE.] Ten hours of doing what you're told? *Anything* you're told?

ANNE. That's right.

DUSSEL. You wouldn't want to sell that, Mrs. Frank?

MRS. FRANK. Never! This is the most precious gift I've ever had!

She sits, showing her present to the others. ANNE *hurries back to the satchel and pulls out a scarf, the scarf that* MR. FRANK *found in the first scene.*

ANNE. [*Offering it to her father.*] For Pim.

MR. FRANK. Anneke...I wasn't supposed to have a present!

He takes it, unfolding it and showing it to the others.

ANNE. It's a muffler...to put round your neck...like an ascot, you know. I made it myself out of odds and ends...I knitted it in the dark each night, after I'd gone to bed. I'm afraid it looks better in the dark!

MR. FRANK. [*Putting it on.*] It's fine. It fits me perfectly. Thank you, Annele.

ANNE *hands* PETER *a ball of paper with a string attached to it.*

ANNE. That's for Mouschi.

PETER. [*Rising to bow.*] On behalf of Mouschi, I thank you.

ANNE. [*Hesitant, handing him a gift.*] And...this is yours...from Mrs. Quack Quack. [*As he holds it gingerly in his hands.*] Well...open it... Aren't you going to open it?

PETER. I'm scared to. I know something's going to jump out and hit me.

ANNE. No. It's nothing like that, really.

MRS. VAN DAAN. [*As he is opening it.*] What is it, Peter? Go on. Show it.

Use Reading Strategies

Ask Questions Students might ask themselves why Mr. Dussel would want to buy Mrs. Frank's gift. Model a response to that question by suggesting that Mr. Dussel is annoyed by Anne's youthful exuberance, which disturbs his peace and quiet. If he could control her for ten hours, he would probably ask her to sit still and remain quiet. **D**

Analyze Literature

Plot Have students look back to the first scene of the play, in which Mr. Frank finds the scarf that Anne had given him for Hanukkah. Ask students to speculate about future plot developments that might have led to the scarf ending up in the secret annex three years later. Model a response by suggesting that the residents probably left in a big hurry, not taking time to pack important items like the scarf and the diary, which means that they were probably caught by the Green Police. **E**

Purpose

Remind students of the importance of communicating clearly the purpose of their writing and maintaining that purpose throughout the work.

For practice, have students determine which of these sentences would contribute to a diary entry that has the purpose of exploring the diarist's emotional state.

1. As we lit the candles, my eyes swelled with tears at the recollection of past Hanukkah celebrations.

2. Mother just upsets me so much with her constant complaints about me.

3. Mr. Dussel wants to get back to his dental practice.

4. I long to be outside, in the fresh air, taking deep breaths and getting exercise!

5. Mrs. Van Daan puts great importance on her fur coat.

Use Reading Strategies
Visualize If students take a moment to visualize the "beginning of a mustache" on Peter's upper lip, they will realize that he is maturing and that Anne has noticed it (which means that she is maturing as well). This is another indication of the passage of time in the secret annex. **A**

Use Reading Skills
Distinguish Between Major and Minor Details Students might notice this detail of a dog barking outside. Seemingly a minor detail, it nevertheless is suggestive of the situation in which the characters find themselves. The dog barks just as Peter goes looking for his cat. We know that dogs and cats are enemies; the parallel to the Nazis outside and the families inside can be drawn. **B**

Use Reading Strategies
Make Inferences Based on the thoughtfulness of Anne's gifts, students can make the inference that she has a generous personality. The fact that she makes something even for Mr. Dussel, who does not seem to like her (or anyone else) that much, is very touching. **C**

Use Reading Skills
Monitor Comprehension Ask students why Mr. Frank does not want the group to sing the Hannukah song. They should recognize that he is afraid they will become "too enthusiastic" and sing loudly enough to be heard outside. **D**

ANNE. [*Excitedly.*] It's a safety razor!

DUSSEL. A what?

ANNE. A razor!

MRS. VAN DAAN. [*Looking at it.*] You didn't make that out of odds and ends.

ANNE. [*To* PETER.] Miep got it for me. It's not new. It's second-hand. But you really do need a razor now.

DUSSEL. For what?

A   **ANNE.** Look on his upper lip…you can see the beginning of a mustache.

DUSSEL. He wants to get rid of that? Put a little milk on it and let the cat lick it off.

PETER. [*Starting for his room.*] Think you're funny, don't you?

DUSSEL. Look! He can't wait! He's going in to try it!

PETER. I'm going to give Mouschi his present!

He goes into his room, slamming the door behind him.

MR. VAN DAAN. [*Disgustedly.*] Mouschi, Mouschi, Mouschi.

B   *In the distance we hear a dog persistently barking.* ANNE *brings a gift to* DUSSEL.

ANNE. And last but never least, my roommate, Mr. Dussel.

C   **DUSSEL.** For me? You have something for me?

He opens the small box she gives him.

ANNE. I made them myself.

DUSSEL. [*Puzzled.*] Capsules! Two capsules!

ANNE. They're ear-plugs!

DUSSEL. Ear-plugs?

ANNE. To put in your ears so you won't hear me when I thrash around at night. I saw them advertised in a magazine. They're not real ones…I made them out of cotton and candle wax. Try them…See if they don't work…see if you can hear me talk…

DUSSEL. [*Putting them in his ears.*] Wait until I get them in…so.

ANNE. Are you ready?

DUSSEL. Huh?

ANNE. Are you ready?

DUSSEL.…Oh! They've gone inside! I can't get them out! [*They laugh as* MR. DUSSEL *jumps about, trying to shake the plugs out of his ears. Finally he gets them out. Putting them away.*] Thank you, Anne! Thank you!

MR. VAN DAAN. A real Hanukkah!

MRS. VAN DAAN. Wasn't it cute of her?

MRS. FRANK. I don't know when she did it.

MARGOT. I love my present.

} *Together.*

ANNE. [*Sitting at the table.*] And now let's have the song, Father…please…[*To* DUSSEL.] Have you heard the Hanukkah song, Mr. Dussel? The song is the whole thing! [*She sings.*] "Oh, Hanukkah! Oh, Hanukkah! The sweet celebration…"

D   **MR. FRANK.** [*Quieting her.*] I'm afraid, Anne, we shouldn't sing that song tonight. [*To* DUSSEL.] It's a song of jubilation, of rejoicing. One is apt to become too enthusiastic.

ANNE. Oh, please, please. Let's sing the song. I promise not to shout!

MR. FRANK. Very well. But quietly now…I'll keep an eye on you and when…

As ANNE *starts to sing, she is interrupted by* DUSSEL *who is snorting and wheezing.*

DUSSEL. [*Pointing to* PETER.] You…You!

[PETER *is coming from his bedroom,* <u>ostentatiously</u> *holding a bulge in his coat as if he were holding his cat, and dangling* ANNE'S *present before it.*] How many times…I told you…Out! Out!

> **os•ten•ta•tious•ly** (äs' tən tā´ shəs lē) *adv.*, in a showy way; overly proudly or boastfully

---

Differentiated Instruction

English Language Learning
Take this opportunity to instruct students about multiple-meaning words, such as Anne's use of the word *cross* in her poem for her sister. Give them several meanings, and make sure they understand the pun in the poem. Other multiple-meaning words on pages 670 and 671 include the following: *present, shade, back, label, temper, ends, last, flares,* and *show.*

Enrichment
Have students write the poems that Anne didn't have time to write. They should use Anne's poem for Margot as a model, and write verse that says something about the personality of the recipient, the gift Anne presented to him or her, and Anne's relationship to that person.

MR. VAN DAAN. [*Going to* PETER.] What's the matter with you? Haven't you any sense? Get that cat out of here.

PETER. [*Innocently.*] Cat?

MR. VAN DAAN. You heard me. Get it out of here!

PETER. I have no cat. [*Delighted with his joke, he opens his coat and pulls out a bath towel. The group at the table laugh, enjoying the joke.*]

DUSSEL. [*Still wheezing.*] It doesn't need to be the cat...his clothes are enough...when he comes out of that room...

MR. VAN DAAN. Don't worry. You won't be bothered any more. We're getting rid of it.

DUSSEL. At last you listen to me. [*He goes off into his bedroom.*]

MR. VAN DAAN. [*Calling after him.*] I'm not doing it for you. That's all in your mind...all of it! [*He starts back to his place at the table.*] I'm doing it because I'm sick of seeing that cat eat all our food.

PETER. That's not true! I only give him bones...scraps...

MR. VAN DAAN. Don't tell me! He gets fatter every day! [That] cat looks better than any of us. Out he goes tonight!

PETER. No! No!

ANNE. Mr. Van Daan, you can't do that! That's Peter's cat. Peter loves that cat.

MRS. FRANK. [*Quietly.*] Anne.

PETER. [*To* MR. VAN DAAN.] If he goes, I go.

MR. VAN DAAN. Go! Go!

MRS. VAN DAAN. You're not going and the cat's not going! Now please...this is Hanukkah...Hanukkah...this is the time to celebrate...What's the matter with all of you? Come on, Anne. Let's have the song.

ANNE. [*Singing.*] "Oh, Hanukkah! Oh, Hanukkah! The sweet celebration."

MR. FRANK. [*Rising.*] I think we should first blow out the candle...then we'll have something for tomorrow night.

MARGOT. But, Father, you're supposed to let it burn itself out.

E **MR. FRANK.** I'm sure that God understands shortages. [*Before blowing it out.*] "Praised be Thou, oh Lord our God, who hast sustained us and permitted us to celebrate this joyous festival."

He is about to blow out the candle when suddenly there is a crash of something falling below. They all freeze in horror, motionless. For a few seconds there is complete silence. MR. FRANK *slips off his shoes. The others noiselessly follow his example.* MR. FRANK *turns out a light near him. He motions to* PETER *to turn off the center lamp.* PETER *tries to reach it, realizes he cannot and gets up on a chair. Just as he is touching the lamp he loses his balance. The chair goes out from under him. He falls. The iron lamp shade crashes to the floor. There is a sound of feet below, running down the stairs.* **F**

MR. VAN DAAN. [*Under his breath.*] God Almighty! [*The only light left comes from the Hanukkah candle.* DUSSEL *comes from his room.* MR. FRANK *creeps over to the stairwell and stands listening. The dog is heard barking excitedly.*] Do you hear anything?

MR. FRANK. [*In a whisper.*] No. I think they've gone.

MRS. VAN DAAN. It's the Green Police. They've found us.

MR. FRANK. If they had, they wouldn't have left. They'd be up here by now.

MRS. VAN DAAN. I know it's the Green Police! They've gone to get help. That's all. They'll be back!

MR. VAN DAAN. Or it may have been the Gestapo,[62] looking for papers...

---

62. Gestapo. Nazi secret police, infamous for their cruelty and terrorism

---

Use Reading Strategies
Make Inferences Ask students what they can infer about Mr. Dussel's personality, based on his reaction to Peter's joke. Model a response by suggesting that Mr. Dussel is obviously highly suggestible: he starts wheezing because he thinks Peter has the cat under his coat. It isn't much of a leap to conclude that Mr. Dussel seems to be a hypochondriac who overreacts and exaggerates every little symptom he feels. **E**

Analyze Literature
Climax Students will probably recognize Peter's fall as the climax of this act. It is a moment that the residents have been dreading all along: the sound that will give them away. Of course, they will never know if this was the determining event, but they are aware of its seriousness. **F**

Diary Entry
Have students write a diary entry that one of the play's characters might have written. Share with students these points about diaries:
- A diary is an autobiographical account of experiences, thoughts, and emotions.
- Diaries are usually written in prose.
- Traditionally, diaries have been written by hand in a bound book of blank or lined pages.

- Most diaries are not written for publication; however, they can often give readers insights about historical periods or times of world crisis.

Analyze Literature

Staging Ask students what Peter's actions and those of his father reveal about their personalities and their relationship. Model a response by suggesting that Peter's father obviously has no patience or affection for his son. For some reason, he fails to comfort his son even in this extreme moment. Peter's response, picking up the chair as if to hit his father with it, reveals his deep anger at his father's treatment of him, but his restraint at putting the chair down shows that he has immense self-control. Point out that all this information is conveyed to the audience through staging—the actor's movements on the stage—rather than through any dialogue. **Ⓐ**

Use Reading Skills

Evaluate Authors' Purpose Point out that Mrs. Frank's prayer is the same one she recited at the beginning of Scene 5, when the Hanukkah celebration was beginning. Ask students what they think the authors' purpose is in repeating it here. Model a response: "The authors want to contrast the joy and happiness of the earlier part of the scene with the somber, serious feeling of this part of the scene. The fact that Mrs. Frank uses prayer to enhance each moment shows the importance of religion in her life." **Ⓑ**

MR. FRANK. [*Interrupting.*] Or a thief, looking for money.

MRS. VAN DAAN. We've got to do something… Quick! Quick! Before they come back.

MR. VAN DAAN. There isn't anything to do. Just wait.

MR. FRANK *holds up his hand for them to be quiet. He is listening intently. There is complete silence as they all strain to hear any sound from below. Suddenly* ANNE *begins to sway. With a low cry she falls to the floor in a faint.* MRS. FRANK *goes to her quickly, sitting beside her on the floor and taking her in her arms.*

MRS. FRANK. Get some water, please! Get some water!

MARGOT *starts for the sink.*

MR. VAN DAAN. [*Grabbing* MARGOT.] No! No! No one's going to run water!

MR. FRANK. If they've found us, they've found us. Get the water. [MARGOT *starts again for the sink.* MR. FRANK, *getting a flashlight.*] I'm going down.

MARGOT *rushes to him, clinging to him.* ANNE *struggles to consciousness.*

MARGOT. No, Father, no! There may be someone there, waiting…It may be a trap!

MR. FRANK. This is Saturday. There is no way for us to know what has happened until Miep or Mr. Kraler comes on Monday morning. We cannot live with this uncertainty.

MARGOT. Don't go, Father!

MRS. FRANK. Hush, darling, hush. [MR. FRANK *slips quietly out, down the steps, and out through the door below.*] Margot! Stay close to me.

MARGOT *goes to her mother.*

MR. VAN DAAN. Shush! Shush!

MRS. FRANK *whispers to* MARGOT *to get the water.*

MARGOT *goes for it.*

MRS. VAN DAAN. Putti, where's our money? Get our money. I hear you can buy the Green Police off, so much a head. Go upstairs quick! Get the money!

MR. VAN DAAN. Keep still!

MRS. VAN DAAN. [*Kneeling before him, pleading.*] Do you want to be dragged off to a concentration camp? Are you going to stand there and wait for them to come up and get you? Do something, I tell you!

MR. VAN DAAN. [*Pushing her aside.*] Will you keep still!

He goes over to the stairwell to listen. PETER *goes to his mother, helping her up onto the sofa. There is a second of silence, then* ANNE *can stand it no longer.*

ANNE. Someone go after Father! Make Father come back!

PETER. [*Starting for the door.*] I'll go.

MR. VAN DAAN. Haven't you done enough?

Ⓐ *He pushes* PETER *roughly away. In his anger against his father* PETER *grabs a chair as if to hit him with it, then puts it down, burying his face in his hands.* MRS. FRANK *begins to pray softly.*

ANNE. Please, please, Mr. Van Daan. Get Father.

MR. VAN DAAN. Quiet! Quiet!

ANNE *is shocked into silence.* MRS. FRANK *pulls her closer, holding her protectively in her arms.*

Ⓑ **MRS. FRANK.** [*Softly, praying.*] "I lift up mine eyes unto the mountains, from whence cometh my help. My help cometh from the Lord who made heaven and earth. He will not suffer thy foot to be moved…He that keepeth thee will not slumber…"

She stops as she hears someone coming. They all watch the door tensely. MR. FRANK *comes quietly in.* ANNE *rushes to him, holding him tight.*

Enrichment

Anne mentions that she saw earplugs advertised in a magazine. Interested students might enjoy researching magazines that were published during World War II and looking at the types of advertisements that Anne would have seen. If original magazines are unavailable, they might find samples on microfilm. Have students report their findings to the class.

MR. FRANK. It was a thief. That noise must have scared him away.

MRS. VAN DAAN. Thank goodness.

MR. FRANK. He took the cash box. And the radio. He ran away in such a hurry that he didn't stop to shut the street door. It was swinging wide open. [*A breath of relief sweeps over them.*] I think it would be good to have some light.

MARGOT. Are you sure it's all right?

MR. FRANK. The danger has passed. [MARGOT *goes to light the small lamp.*] Don't be so terrified, Anne. We're safe.

DUSSEL. Who says the danger has passed? Don't you realize we are in greater danger than ever?

MR. FRANK. Mr. Dussel, will you be still!

MR. FRANK *takes* ANNE *back to the table, making her sit down with him, trying to calm her.*

DUSSEL. [*Pointing to* PETER.] Thanks to this clumsy fool, there's someone now who knows we're up here! Someone now knows we're up here, hiding!

MRS. VAN DAAN. [*Going to* DUSSEL.] Someone knows we're here, yes. But who is the someone? A thief! A thief! You think a thief is going to go to the Green Police and say… I was robbing a place the other night and I heard a noise up over my head? You think a thief is going to do that?

DUSSEL. Yes. I think he will.

MRS. VAN DAAN. [*Hysterically.*] You're crazy!

She stumbles back to her seat at the table. PETER *follows protectively, pushing* DUSSEL *aside.*

DUSSEL. I think some day he'll be caught and then he'll make a bargain with the Green Police…if they'll let him off, he'll tell them where some Jews are hiding!

He goes off into the bedroom. There is a second of appalled silence.

MR. VAN DAAN. He's right.

ANNE. Father, let's get out of here! We can't stay here now…Let's go…

MR. VAN DAAN. Go! Where?

MRS. FRANK. [*Sinking into her chair at the table.*] Yes. Where?

MR. FRANK. [*Rising, to them all.*] Have we lost all faith? All courage? A moment ago we thought that they'd come for us. We were sure it was the end. But it wasn't the end. We're alive, safe.

MR. VAN DAAN *goes to the table and sits.* MR. FRANK *prays.*

"We thank Thee, oh Lord our God, that in Thy infinite mercy Thou hast again seen fit to spare us." [*He blows out the candle, then turns to* ANNE.] Come on, Anne. The song! Let's have the song! [*He starts to sing.* ANNE *finally starts falteringly to sing, as* MR. FRANK *urges her on. Her voice is hardly audible at first.*]

ANNE. [*Singing.*] "Oh, Hanukkah! Oh, Hanukkah!
The sweet…celebration…"

As *she goes on singing, the others gradually join in, their voices still shaking with fear.* MRS. VAN DAAN *sobs as she sings.*

GROUP. "Around the feast…we…gather
In complete…jubilation…
Happiest of sea…sons
Now is here.
Many are the reasons for good cheer."

DUSSEL *comes from the bedroom. He comes over to the table, standing beside* MARGOT, *listening to them as they sing.*

"Together we'll weather
Whatever tomorrow may bring."

As they sing on with growing courage, the lights start to dim.

THE DIARY OF ANNE FRANK, ACT 1 **675**

Analyze Literature
Universal Theme Ask: "In what way do Mr. Frank's lines here express the universal theme of Act 1?" Model a response: "Mr. Frank is saying that despite the danger, the group is still safe. As long as they're alive, they have much to be thankful for. This echoes the universal theme of the act: that life is infinitely precious, each day is a gift, and hope for a better future can overcome great difficulties." **C**

Make Connections
Have students consider how they would have responded to Mr. Frank's words if they had been there. Would they, like Anne, suggest leaving the secret annex immediately? Or would they agree with Mr. Frank that they are better off staying put? **D**

Analyze Literature
Resolution Remind students that the resolution is a plot element in which the loose ends are tied up and the characters find a way to deal with their problems. Students should recognize that the resolution of Act 1 takes place when the characters sing the Hanukkah song. Because the song refers to jubilation and good cheer, it suggests that the residents have not yet given up hope. They are determined to be together for "whatever tomorrow may bring." This display of courage is admirable and inspirational, despite our knowledge that Mr. Frank will return to this room alone in three years, "a bitter old man," in his own words. **E**

Types of Communication
Remind students that ideas can be communicated through spoken, written, and visual language. For example, the terror experienced by the residents in the secret annex is expressed through their conversation with one another, through Anne's written account, and through the performance of this play. Have students compare and contrast these different types of language. What is alike about them? What is different? Suggest that students create a three-way Venn diagram to answer these questions.

History Connection

Hitler's Rise to Power After World War I, Germany had suffered greatly. Forbidden by the Treaty of Versailles to rebuild their army, they were also saddled with huge war debts. Then the Great Depression hit, and things got worse. Unemployed and hungry Germans were ready to believe Adolf Hitler, who told them that they were a "super race." He promised to restore Germany's former glory and power. Anyone who was not white and Germanic was inferior, according to Hitler. And the worst of all, according to Hitler, were the Jewish people. He blamed the Jews for all of Germany's troubles. By 1933, the Germans were ready to accept Hitler as leader of the National Socialist (Nazi) Party and Chancellor of Germany.

Kinesthetic Learning
Students might enjoy acting out parts of Scene 5. Have them choose a section to perform, provide time for a brief rehearsal, and invite students to perform the scene for the class.

Reading Proficiency
Students might benefit from rereading Scene 5, from the moment the residents hear the noises below until the end of the scene. As they read, have them pay particular attention to each character's reaction to this new twist in the plot. They can make a three-column chart with the characters' names, their reaction to the new situation, and a comment on what the reaction reveals about the character.

"So hear us rejoicing
And merrily voicing
The Hanukkah song that we sing.
Hoy!"

The lights are out. The curtain starts slowly to fall.

"Hear us rejoicing
And merrily voicing
The Hanukkah song that we sing."

They are still singing, as the curtain falls.

Curtain. ❖

Why does Mr. Frank ask Anne to sing the Hanukkah song at the end of Act 1? How do you think the group could benefit from the song? What, in general, does music often inspire in a group?

Find Meaning

1. (a) Describe the relationships that Anne has with her mother and her father. (b) Why might Anne's mother get along better with Margot than with Anne?

2. (a) After the Franks and the Van Daans have been in hiding for a while, what request does Mr. Kraler express? (b) How do Mr. Frank and Mr. Van Daan respond to the request, and what do their responses suggest about their personalities?

3. Mrs. Frank says of Miep and Mr. Kraler, "They're our life line. Without them we couldn't live." What causes her to feel this way?

4. (a) What happens to Anne's friend Jopie? (b) What nightmare does Anne have after learning about Jopie?

5. (a) What schedule regarding making noise and being quiet must the characters follow? (b) Despite this schedule, what frightening thing happens on the first night of Hanukkah?

Make Judgments

6. Anne says, "I have a nicer side, Father...a sweeter, nicer side. But I'm scared to show it. I'm afraid that people are going to laugh at me if I'm serious." (a) What do these lines suggest about Anne's personality? (b) Do you think these feelings are somewhat common in teenagers? Explain.

7. (a) In your opinion, why does only Anne, with her father's help, make Hanukkah presents? (b) Pick one of the presents that she makes. Explain why it is a perfect gift for the person she gives it to.

8. Anne says of Mr. Dussel, "Why is it that every grown-up thinks he knows the way to bring up children? Particularly the grown-ups that never had any." Do you think her point of view is fair regarding Mr. Dussel? Use specific details from his actions and words to support your response.

Visual Skills

Design and Publish

Remind students that the final step in most writing projects is the publishing stage. Have students publish a sample of their own writing. Suggest that they use publishing software and graphic programs to enhance the quality of their publication. Have them consider the following details as they work with the software:

- Line length
- Font style and size for headings and text
- Graphic elements such as diagrams, tables, and art
- Border and background designs

Have students consider what they would write in a diary if they decided to keep one. Would they discuss their feelings, or would they simply write about the events of their days? Would they discuss the news and politics of the day and how these things affect (or don't affect) their own lives? As students read Anne Frank's diary, have them compare her attitudes with their own.

Use Reading Strategies

Set Purpose Suggest that students examine the art on this page. Discuss what they think the diary entries will be about. What do they want to learn about Anne Frank?

TEACHING NOTE

Letter to the Author

Interested students may write a letter, as if to Anne Frank. Suggest that they express their feelings about the situation in which she found herself. They might also address the question of whether they have had feelings similar to the ones Anne writes about.

Common Core State Standards

Reading Literature
RL.4, RL.7

Writing
W.7, W.8, W.10

Language
L.6

PRIMARY SOURCE ▶▶ CONNECTION

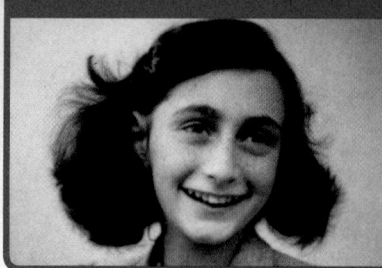

The following selection contains original diary entries by **Anne Frank.** Since her father first published it in 1947, Anne's diary, which she had named "Kitty," has been translated into more than thirty languages, and millions of copies have been sold all over the world. As you read these diary entries, note how Anne's vivid language enables readers to feel as if they know her as a friend.

from Anne Frank: The Diary of a Young Girl

Diary Entries by Anne Frank

Saturday, 20 June, 1942

I haven't written for a few days, because I wanted first of all to think about my diary. It's an odd idea for someone like me to keep a diary; not only because I have never done so before, but because it seems to me that neither I—nor for that matter anyone else—will be interested in the unbosomings of a thirteen-year-old schoolgirl. Still, what does that matter? I want to write, but more than that, I want to bring out all kinds of things that lie buried deep in my heart.

There is a saying that "paper is more patient than man"; it came back to me on one of my slightly melancholy days, while I sat chin in hand, feeling too bored and limp even to make up my mind whether to go out or stay at home. Yes, there is no doubt that paper is patient and as I don't intend to show this cardboard-covered notebook, bearing the proud name of "diary," to anyone, unless I find a real friend, boy or girl, probably nobody cares. And now I come to the root of

the matter, the reason for my starting a diary: it is that I have no such real friend.

Let me put it more clearly, since no one will believe that a girl of thirteen feels herself quite alone in the world, nor is it so. I have darling parents and a sister of sixteen. I know about thirty people whom one might call friends—I have strings of boy friends, anxious to catch a glimpse of me and who, failing that, peep at me through mirrors in class. I have relations, aunts and uncles, who are darlings too, a good home, no—I don't seem to lack anything. But it's the same with all my friends, just fun and joking, nothing more. I can never bring myself to talk of anything outside the common round. We don't seem to be able to get any closer, that is the root of the trouble. Perhaps I lack confidence, but anyway, there it is, a stubborn fact and I don't seem to be able to do anything about it.

Hence, this diary. In order to enhance in my mind's eye the picture of the friend for whom I have waited so long, I don't want to set down a series of bald facts in a diary like

678 UNIT 7 DRAMA

Words in Use

from *Anne Frank: The Diary of a Young Girl*

Teaching Words

melancholy, 678	**perturbed,** 681
albeit, 679	**absurd,** 682
succession, 679	**tranquility,** 682
condemning, 679	
brigade, 679	
omitted, 680	

most people do, but I want this diary itself to be my friend, and I shall call my friend Kitty. No one will grasp what I'm talking about if I begin my letters to Kitty just out of the blue, so, albeit unwillingly, I will start by sketching in brief the story of my life.

My father was thirty-six when he married my mother, who was then twenty-five. My sister Margot was born in 1926 in Frankfort-on-Main, I followed on June 12, 1929, and, as we are Jewish, we emigrated to Holland in 1933, where my father was appointed Managing Director of Travies N.V. This firm is in close relationship with the firm of Kolen & Co. in the same building, of which my father is a partner.

The rest of our family, however, felt the full impact of Hitler's anti-Jewish laws, so life was filled with anxiety. In 1938 after the pogroms, my two uncles (my mother's brothers) escaped to the U.S.A. My old grandmother came to us, she was then seventy-three. After May 1940 good times rapidly fled: first the war, then the capitulation, followed by the arrival of the Germans, which is when the sufferings of us Jews really began. Anti-Jewish decrees followed each other in quick succession. Jews must wear a yellow star, Jews must hand in their bicycles, Jews are banned from trams and are forbidden to drive. Jews are only allowed to do their shopping between three and five o'clock and then only in shops which bear the placard "Jewish shop." Jews must be indoors by eight o'clock and cannot even sit in their own gardens after that hour. Jews are forbidden to visit theaters, cinemas, and other places of entertainment. Jews may not take part in public sports. Swimming baths, tennis courts, hockey fields, and other sports grounds are all prohibited to them. Jews may not visit Christians. Jews must go to Jewish schools, and many more restrictions of a similar kind.

So we could not do this and were forbidden to do that. But life went on in spite of it all. Jopie used to say to me, "You're scared to do anything, because it may be forbidden." Our freedom was strictly limited. Yet things were still bearable.

Granny died in January 1942; no one will ever know how much she is present in my thoughts and how much I love her still.

In 1934 I went to school at the Montessori Kindergarten and continued there. It was at the end of the school year, I was in form 6B, when I had to say good-bye to Mrs. K. We both wept, it was very sad. In 1941 I went, with my sister Margot, to the Jewish Secondary School, she into the fourth form and I into the first.

So far everything is all right with the four of us and here I come to the present day.

Saturday, 15 July, 1944

Dear Kitty,

We have had a book from the library with the challenging title of: *What Do You Think of the Modern Young Girl?* I want to talk about this subject today.

The author of this book criticizes "the youth of today" from top to toe, without, however, condemning the whole of the young brigade as "incapable of anything good." On the contrary, she is rather of the opinion that if young people wished, they have it in their hands to make a bigger, more beautiful and better world, but that they occupy themselves with superficial things, without giving a thought to real beauty.

In some passages the writer gave me very much the feeling she was directing her criticism at me, and that's why I want to lay myself completely bare to you for once and defend myself against this attack.

I have one outstanding trait in my character, which must strike anyone who knows me for any length of time, and that is

Summary

The first entry in this excerpt is dated June 20, 1942, shortly after Anne's thirteenth birthday. She explains her reasons for writing in a diary: though she has many friends, she does not have meaningful conversations with them. She decides to address her diary as if it were her best friend and names it Kitty. She describes her life in Holland since 1933, after her family emigrated from Germany to avoid Hitler's anti-Jewish decrees. Hitler's policies were eventually implemented in Holland as well, and the freedom of all Jews there was severely restricted.

The next entry is dated July 15, 1944, two years after the family had gone into hiding. Anne analyzes the strengths in her character, her attitude toward her parents, her feelings about Peter, and her view that youth is a more difficult stage in life than old age. She closes on a hopeful note that she will someday be able to fully realize her ideals.

Use Reading Strategies

Clarify Have students consider the saying Anne quotes on the first page of the selection: "Paper is more patient than man." What does Anne wish to convey? Model a response: "Anne means that when she writes in her diary, no one is urging her to hurry up and get to the point. She can take the time to work out her thoughts until they are clear to her. Furthermore, the diary will not criticize her in any way. It will accept anything she says."

Reading Skills

Adjusting Reading Rate

Point out to students the importance of adjusting the rate at which they read, depending on the difficulty of the text. These are some of the situations where a slower reading rate would be useful:

- for text that presents difficult concepts
- for text that provides connections to previous ideas

- for text that includes new vocabulary
- for information-packed text

Have students find examples of each situation in these excerpts from Anne Frank's diary.

Literary Connection

Keeping a Journal The benefits of diary or journal writing are numerous. They include the benefit cited by Anne, "to bring out all kinds of things that lie buried deep in my heart." Remind students that diaries help us sort out our thoughts and feelings, acting as a friend in the way Anne's diary did. They also are a way to record the events of our lives, serving later to jog our memories of our past. For the person who idealizes the past, a diary can serve as a reminder that each age has its problems. Some people keep diaries of their diets, their workouts, their practice sessions, their reading, and other things that are important to them. These types of diaries serve a practical purpose, keeping the writer on track toward some accomplishment.

Analyze Literature

Memoir Anne's diary, like a memoir, is a description of a specific period in her life, told by Anne herself. Memoirs often provide insight into the historical forces that shaped the author's experience, and Anne's diary is no exception.

Anne Frank.

my knowledge of myself. I can watch myself and my actions, just like an outsider. The Anne of every day I can face entirely without prejudice, without making excuses for her, and watch what's good and what's bad about her. This "self-consciousness" haunts me, and every time I open my mouth I know as soon as I've spoken whether "that ought to have been different" or "that was right as it was." There are so many things about myself that I condemn; I couldn't begin to name them all. I understand more and more how true

Daddy's words were when he said: "All children must look after their own upbringing." Parents can only give good advice or put them on the right paths, but the final forming of a person's character lies in their own hands.

In addition to this, I have lots of courage, I always feel so strong and as if I can bear a great deal, I feel so free and so young! I was glad when I first realized it, because I don't think I shall easily bow down before the blows that inevitably come to everyone.

But I've talked about these things so often before. Now I want to come to the chapter of "Daddy and Mummy don't understand me." Daddy and Mummy have always thoroughly spoiled me, were sweet to me, defended me, and have done all that parents could do. And yet I've felt so terribly lonely for a long time, so left out, neglected, and misunderstood. Daddy tried all he could to check my rebellious spirit, but it was no use, I have cured myself, by seeing for myself what was wrong in my behavior and keeping it before my eyes.

How is it that Daddy was never any support to me in my struggle, why did he completely miss the mark when he wanted to offer me a helping hand? Daddy tried the wrong methods, he always talked to me as a child who was going through difficult phases. It sounds crazy, because Daddy's the only one who has always taken me into his confidence, and no one but Daddy has given me the feeling that I'm sensible. But there's one thing he's omitted: you see, he hasn't realized that for me the fight to get on top

680 UNIT 7 DRAMA

English Language Learning

Help students understand the selection by providing definitions of difficult words, such as these:

melancholy—sad, 678

confidence—feeling being sure of oneself, 678

enhance—increase; add to, 678

pogroms—organized massacres or attacks on a minority group, especially Jews, 679

capitulation—surrender, 679

placard—poster or sign publicly displayed, 679

prohibited—forbidden, 679

was more important than all else. I didn't want to hear about "symptoms of your age," or "other girls," or "it wears off by itself"; I didn't want to be treated as a girl-like-all-others, but as Anne-on-her-own-merits. Pim didn't understand that. For that matter, I can't confide in anyone, unless they tell me a lot about themselves, and as I know very little about Pim, I don't feel that I can tread upon more intimate ground with him. Pim always takes up the older, fatherly attitude, tells me that he too has had similar passing tendencies. But still he's not able to feel with me like a friend, however hard he tries. These things have made me never mention my views on life nor my well-considered theories to anyone but my diary and, occasionally, to Margot. I concealed from Daddy everything that perturbed me; I never shared my ideals with him. I was aware of the fact that I was pushing him away from me.

I couldn't do anything else. I have acted entirely according to my feelings, but I have acted in the way that was best for my peace of mind. Because I should completely lose my repose and self-confidence, which I have built up so shakily, if, at this stage, I were to accept criticisms of my half-completed task. And I can't do that even from Pim, although it sounds very hard, for not only have I not shared my secret thoughts with Pim but I have often pushed him even further from me, by my irritability.

This is a point that I think a lot about: why is it that Pim annoys me? So much so that I can hardly bear him teaching me, that his affectionate ways strike me as being put on, that I want to be left in peace and would really prefer it if he dropped me a bit, until I felt more certain in my attitude towards him. Because I still have a gnawing feeling of guilt over that horrible letter that I dared to write him when I was so wound up. Oh, how hard it is to be really strong and brave in every way!

Ⓐ   Yet this was not my greatest disappointment; no, I ponder far more over Peter than Daddy. I know very well that I conquered him instead of he conquering me. I created an image of him in my mind, pictured him as a quiet, sensitive, lovable boy, who needed affection and friendship. I needed a living person to whom I could pour out my heart; I wanted a friend who'd help to put me on the right road. I achieved what I wanted, and slowly but surely, I drew him towards me. Finally, when I had made him feel friendly, it automatically developed into an intimacy which, on second thought, I don't think I ought to have allowed.

We talked about the most private things, and yet up till now we have never touched on those things that filled, and still fill, my heart and soul. I still don't know quite what to make of Peter, is he superficial, or does he still feel shy, even of me? But dropping that, I committed one error in my desire to make a real friendship: I switched over and tried to get at him by developing it into a more intimate relation, whereas I should have explored all other possibilities. He longs to be loved and I can see that he's beginning to be more and more in love with me. He gets satisfaction out of our meetings, whereas they just have the effect of making me want to try Ⓑ it out with him again. And yet I don't seem able to touch on the subjects that I'm so longing to bring out into the daylight. I drew Peter towards me, far more than he realizes. Now he clings to me, and for the time being, I don't see any way of shaking him off and putting him on his own feet. When I realized that he could not be a friend for my understanding, I thought I would at least try to lift him up out of his narrow-mindedness

Analyze Literature
Conflict Remind students that conflict can be internal or external, but it is sometimes a combination of both. Here, Anne describes the way she wants her father to treat her, as well as the way she wishes to be viewed. Ⓐ

Analyze Literature
Characterization Remind students that characterization is the way an author reveals details about a character's personality. It can be done directly (simply stating facts) or indirectly (implying information through what a character says or does or what others say). Here, Anne indirectly characterizes herself through a description of how her father makes her feel. Ask students what she indirectly reveals about herself without being conscious of it. Ⓑ

Use Reading Skills
Paraphrase Remind students of the difference between paraphrasing and summarizing and that when they paraphrase, they reword a passage, using new language to express the same ideas. Have students paraphrase this paragraph expressing Anne's feelings about her relationship with Peter. Make sure they attend to appropriate connotation and figurative language. Ⓒ

Visual Skills

Found Object Sculpture

Inform students that "found objects" are everyday items that are usually recognized as having certain utilitarian purposes. They can be put together in unique ways that suggest something other than what they are. Suggest that they use found objects to make a sculpture that depicts Anne's emotions.

Cultural Connection

Adolescence Discuss with students the challenges of adolescence: to achieve a growing amount of independence from parental control while, at the same time, maintaining a loving relationship with parents and learning what one can from them. Suggest that one reason adolescence is often difficult is that physical changes, including hormonal development, might be confusing and frightening to the adolescent who is struggling with such things as schoolwork, extracurricular interests, and personal relationships. **Ⓐ**

Analyze Literature

Characterization This paragraph is an example of indirect characterization. Anne does not say outright that she is optimistic, hopeful, and positive, but her statements lead us to know that about her. **Ⓑ**

Text-to-Text Connection

Answer: Students may say that Anne provides much more detail about her father and mother, and about how the Jews are being persecuted. She also expresses her goals—and the goals that she sees in other young people—to make a better world. She speaks at length about her relationship with Peter, and she ends with optimistic statements about her future—after the war ends.

Anne at her desk.

and make him do something with his youth.

Ⓐ "For in its innermost depths youth is lonelier than old age." I read this saying in some book and I've always remembered it, and found it to be true. Is it true then that grown-ups have a more difficult time here than we do? No. I know it isn't. Older people have formed their opinions about everything, and don't waver before they act. It's twice as hard for us young ones to hold our ground,

and maintain our opinions, in a time when all ideals are being shattered and destroyed, when people are showing their worst side, and do not know whether to believe in truth and right and God.

Anyone who claims that the older ones have a more difficult time here certainly doesn't realize to what extent our problems weigh down on us, problems for which we are probably much too young, but which thrust themselves upon us continually, until, after a long time, we think we've found a solution, but the solution doesn't seem able to resist the facts which reduce it to nothing again. That's the difficulty in these times: ideals, dreams, and cherished hopes rise within us, only to meet the horrible truth and be shattered.

Ⓑ It's really a wonder that I haven't dropped all my ideals, because they seem so absurd and impossible to carry out. Yet I keep them, because in spite of everything I still believe that people are really good at heart. I simply can't build up my hopes on a foundation consisting of confusion, misery, and death. I see the world gradually being turned into a wilderness, I hear the ever approaching thunder, which will destroy us too, I can feel the sufferings of millions and yet, if I look up into the heavens, I think that it will all come right, that this cruelty too will end, and that peace and tranquility will return again.

In the meantime, I must uphold my ideals, for perhaps the time will come when I shall be able to carry them out.

Yours, Anne ❖

TEXT ←TO→ TEXT CONNECTION Both the drama and the diary entries present Anne as a full, dynamic character. What insights into Anne's personality and values did you have after reading the diary entries that you did not have after reading Act 1? Support your response with textual evidence.

Differentiated Instruction

Kinesthetic Learning

Some students might enjoy performing a role-play based on one or more of the relationships Anne touches on in this excerpt. They might act out a conversation between Anne and any one of the people she mentions.

Reading Proficiency

Some students might benefit from reviewing the selection with a partner. They can take turns rereading each paragraph and then discussing the main idea expressed in it.

Analyze Literature

Plot Use a plot diagram like the one here to show the exposition and rising action that occur in Act 1. Below the diagram, write one or two sentences to summarize the conflict that Anne and the other characters face. You can complete the diagram, showing the climax, falling action, and resolution, after you read Act 2.

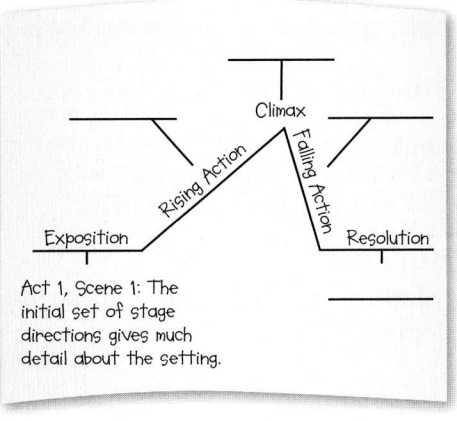

Act 1, Scene 1: The initial set of stage directions gives much detail about the setting.

Extend Understanding

Writing Options

Creative Writing Adapt a brief portion of Act 1—a scene or a particularly memorable interaction between two or more characters—into a **short story** of less than five hundred words. Fill out the dialogue of the drama with narration. Use sensory details and figurative language to make your descriptions, and your character development, vivid. Choose either first-person point of view, telling the story through the eyes of one of the characters, or third-person point of view, telling it through the eyes of a narrator. Be sure to keep your point of view consistent throughout your story.

Expository Writing In a paragraph, present a **literary response** in which you analyze how the stage directions in Act 1 helped you to better understand the characters. Use an outline or a cluster diagram to gather the details you need to write an effective response. State your position in a thesis, and support it with evidence and examples from the text.

Collaborative Learning

Diagram the Set Work with a small group to review details of the stage set and props found in the stage directions of Act 1. Then work together to draw a diagram or construct a diorama of how you visualize the stage. Be sure to include the staircase and all rooms in the apartment.

Critical Literacy

Present a Scene Work with a small group to practice and perform a scene from Act 1. Use the stage directions for guidance as to how to speak and move, as well as analyzing them for additional information about the personalities and values of the protagonists and antagonists. Experiment with tones of voice that effectively show the inner feelings of the characters. When your group is ready, present your scene to the class.

W Go to www.mirrorsandwindows.com for more.

1. *Having* — participle;
   to calm — infinitive
2. *Whispering* — participle,
   to silence — infinitive;
   crying — participle
3. *Writing* — gerund;
   unfinished — participle;
   to make — infinitive
4. *to dance* — infinitive
5. *helping* — gerund

> For more information, see Grammar & Style Section 3.11, Phrases, in the Language Arts Handbook.

Program Resources

You will find additional lessons on Verbals in the *Exceeding the Standards: Grammar & Style* resource.

KEY TERMS

VERBAL, 684
NOUN, 684
ADJECTIVE, 684
ADVERB, 684
VERB, 684
PARTICIPLE, 684
GERUND, 684
INFINITIVE, 684
PRONOUN, 684
PAST PARTICIPLE, 684
PREDICATE NOMINATIVE, 684
PREPOSITION, 684

Common Core State Standards

Language
L.1

Grammar & Style

Verbals

A **verbal** is a noun, adjective, or adverb formed from a verb. There are three different forms of verbals: participles, gerunds, and infinitives.

Participles

My father started a business, importing spice and herbs.

— FRANCES GOODRICH AND ALBERT HACKETT,
The Diary of Anne Frank

A **participle** is a verbal that acts as an adjective, modifying a noun or pronoun. There are two kinds of participles: *present participles* and *past participles*. Present participles, such as the word *importing* in the quotation above, are made by adding *-ing* to a verb. Past participles end in *-ed*, *-en*, *-d*, *-t*, or *-n*, as in the words *asked*, *eaten*, *saved*, *dealt*, and *seen*.

> EXAMPLES
>
> *Making* an effort to control his temper, he took a deep breath.
>
> The cat finished the *half-eaten* food.

Gerunds

Yesterday Father told me we're going into hiding.

— FRANCES GOODRICH AND ALBERT HACKETT,
The Diary of Anne Frank

A **gerund** is a verbal that ends in *-ing* and acts as a noun. Gerunds can act as the subject, direct object, predicate nominative, or object of a preposition. The gerund *hiding* in the quotation above acts as the object of the preposition *into*.

> EXAMPLES
>
> *Walking* along with suitcases made us look suspicious. [subject]
>
> Her favorite activity was *playing* ping-pong. [predicate nominative]

Infinitives

I'm going to think of it as a boarding house.

— FRANCES GOODRICH AND ALBERT HACKETT,
The Diary of Anne Frank

An **infinitive** is a verbal consisting of the word *to* plus a verb in its simplest form. An infinitive functions as a noun, adjective, or adverb in a sentence. In the quotation above, *to think* is an infinitive that acts as a noun.

> EXAMPLES
>
> He lacked the strength *to carry* the suitcase. [adjective]
>
> We must learn *to entertain* ourselves. [adverb]

Identifying Participles, Gerunds, and Infinitives

Write the verbals in the following sentences. Then label each one *participle*, *gerund*, or *infinitive*.

1. Having escaped, he took several deep breaths to calm himself.
2. Whispering, Peter tried to silence the crying cat.
3. Writing in her unfinished diary was a way to make the time go faster.
4. Anne wanted to dance with Peter.
5. Mr. Frank enjoyed helping others.

TEACHING NOTE

Extra Practice

Have students identify the underlined verbals in each of the following sentences.

1. Dani had a difficult time finding the motivation necessary <u>to achieve</u> her purpose. (infinitive)
2. <u>Planning</u> a course of action was imperative. (gerund)
3. <u>Knowing</u> her tendency to give up easily, she made a promise to follow through with her plan. (gerund)
4. As it turned out, Dani's plan was <u>half-baked</u>, so she momentarily lost her focus. (participle)
5. Luckily, she gritted her teeth and decided <u>to honor</u> her promise to herself. (infinitive)

Summary

As Act 2 opens, the two families and Mr. Dussel have been hiding in the secret annex for a year and a half. News of the long-awaited Allied invasion boosts their spirits, but tension among the group increases as a result of fear, hunger, crowding, and boredom. Despite these issues, Anne and Peter form a relationship that helps them endure the difficult days. The worst possible scenario plays out when the Nazis discover their hiding place. Anne's voice-over relates her last diary entry as the Nazis lead the group away. The play then returns to the opening scene in 1945, when Otto is given Anne's diary and comes to terms with his family's tragedy.

Launch the Lesson

Have students recall a time when they had to stay indoors longer than they wished. How did they feel about it? What did they do to entertain themselves? How did it feel to finally get outside? Remind them that Anne and the others were confined to their cramped indoor space for over two years.

KEY TERMS

AUTOBIOGRAPHY, 708
PLOT, 712
ACT, 712
SCENE, 712
DRAMA, 712
BIBLIOGRAPHY, 712
EXPOSITION, 712
CLIMAX, 712
RESOLUTION, 712
CONFLICT, 712

The Diary of Anne Frank, Act 2

A Drama by Frances Goodrich and Albert Hackett

685

Preview Vocabulary
inarticulate, 688
foreboding, 689
intimate, 692
ineffectually, 704

Teaching Words
annex, 707
ironic, 707
excerpt, 708
cited, 712

Selection Words
meticulously, 694
poise, 698

Meeting the Standards
Drama: Unit 7, Directed Reading, pp. 32–35

Differentiating Instruction
Advanced Students, Historical Context Study, pp. 42–43

Cultural Sensitivity

Remind students of the importance of being aware of cultural sensitivity when they participate in any speaking or listening activities. For example, they should be aware that all cultures do not have the same attitudes and customs, but this simply means that they are different, not inferior or superior. The views of all participants need to be respected.

Analyze Literature

Act Point out to students that the play is divided into two acts. Remind them that an act is a major division in a play. Acts are divided into scenes. Scene divisions often signal a change in location or time. **A**

History Connection

V for Victory During World War II, the "V for Victory" sign was a powerful propaganda tool. It started in 1940 when a refugee from Belgium, Victor de Laveleye, transmitted short-wave radio broadcasts from London to Belgium suggesting widespread public displays of the letter V for Victorie to show defiance of the German occupation. Other countries picked up the symbol, for the letter V stands for *freedom* in Dutch, *heroism* in Serbian, and *victory* in Czech. In Morse Code, the symbol for the letter v is dot-dot-dot-dash, so Miep's signal would have been three short buzzes and one long one. **B**

The Mirrors & Windows questions at the end of this selection focus on the theme of faith in humanity. Before reading the story, ask students to offer examples of cruel human actions in today's society. Does this behavior shake their faith in the good of humanity, or can they still maintain a belief in the natural goodness of people? How could the latter attitude be valuable in society?

Common Core State Standards

Reading Literature
RL.1, RL.2, RL.3, RL.6
Language
L.6

A **ACT 2**
SCENE 1

In the darkness we hear ANNE'S VOICE, *again reading from the diary.*

ANNE'S VOICE. Saturday, the first of January, nineteen forty-four. Another new year has begun and we find ourselves still in our hiding place. We have been here now for one year, five months, and twenty-five days. It seems that our life is at a standstill.

The curtain rises on the scene. It is late afternoon. Everyone is bundled up against the cold. In the main room MRS. FRANK *is taking down the laundry which is hung across the back.* MR. FRANK *sits in the chair down left, reading.* MARGOT *is lying on the couch with a blanket over her and the many-colored knitted scarf around her throat.* ANNE *is seated at the center table, writing in her diary.* PETER, MR. *and* MRS. VAN DAAN *and* DUSSEL *are all in their own rooms, reading or lying down.*

As the lights dim on, ANNE'S VOICE *continues, without a break.*

ANNE'S VOICE. We are all a little thinner. The Van Daans' "discussions" are as violent as ever. Mother still does not understand me. But then I don't understand her either. There is one great change, however. A change in myself. I read somewhere that girls of my age don't feel quite certain of themselves. That they become quiet within and begin to think of the miracle that is taking place in their bodies. I think that what is happening to me is so wonderful…not only what can be seen, but what is taking place inside. Each time it has happened I have a feeling that I have a sweet secret. [*We hear the chimes and then a hymn being played on the carillon outside.*] And in spite of any pain, I long for the time when I shall feel that secret within me again.

The buzzer of the door below suddenly sounds. Everyone is startled, MR. FRANK *tiptoes*

---

cautiously to the top of the steps and listens. **B** [*Again the buzzer sounds, in* MIEP'S *V-for-Victory signal.*

MR. FRANK. It's Miep!

He goes quickly down the steps to unbolt the door. MRS. FRANK *calls upstairs to the* VAN DAANS *and then to* PETER.

MRS. FRANK. Wake up, everyone! Miep is here! [ANNE *quickly puts her diary away.* MARGOT *sits up, pulling the blanket around her shoulders.* MR. DUSSEL *sits on the edge of his bed, listening, disgruntled.[1]* MIEP *comes up the steps, followed by* MR. KRALER. *They bring flowers, books, newspapers, etc.* ANNE *rushes to* MIEP, *throwing her arms affectionately around her.*] Miep…and Mr. Kraler…What a delightful surprise!

MR. KRALER. We came to bring you New Year's greetings.

MRS. FRANK. You shouldn't…you should have at least one day to yourselves.

She goes quickly to the stove and brings down teacups and tea for all of them.

ANNE. Don't say that, it's so wonderful to see them! [*Sniffing at* MIEP'S *coat*] I can smell the wind and the cold on your clothes.

MIEP. [*Giving her the flowers.*] There you are. [*Then to* MARGOT, *feeling her forehead.*] How are you, Margot?…Feeling any better?

MARGOT. I'm all right.

ANNE. We filled her full of every kind of pill so she won't cough and make a noise.

She runs into her room to put the flowers in water. MR. *and* MRS. VAN DAAN *come from upstairs. Outside there is the sound of a band playing.*

MRS. VAN DAAN. Well, hello, Miep. Mr. Kraler.

MR. KRALER. [*Giving a bouquet of flowers to*

---

1. **disgruntled.** Displeased; grumpy

Differentiated Instruction

Reading Proficiency

Have students preview Act 2. What does the art suggest about what will happen next? Students might want to make a K-W-L chart, indicating what they <u>Know</u> (based on what they have already read in Act 1), what they <u>Want</u> to know, and, later, what they <u>Learned</u>.

English Language Learning

Draw students' attention to the quotation marks around "discussions" when Anne describes what the Van Daans have been doing. Point out that the quotation marks signal an ironic tone. They indicate that this is what the Van Daans call their arguments. Since Anne doesn't consider their arguments to be discussions, she uses quotation marks to show that this is the Van Daans' expression, not hers.

MRS. VAN DAAN.] With my hope for peace in the New Year.

PETER. [*Anxiously.*] Miep, have you seen Mouschi? Have you seen him anywhere around?

MIEP. I'm sorry, Peter. I asked everyone in the neighborhood had they seen a gray cat. But they said no.

MRS. FRANK *gives* MIEP *a cup of tea.* MR. FRANK *comes up the steps, carrying a small cake on a plate.*

MR. FRANK. Look what Miep's brought for us!

MRS. FRANK. [*Taking it.*] A cake!

MR. VAN DAAN. A cake! [*He pinches* MIEP'S *cheeks gaily and hurries up to the cupboard.*] I'll get some plates. [DUSSEL, *in his room, hastily puts a coat on and starts out to join the others.*]

MRS. FRANK. Thank you, Miepia. You shouldn't have done it. You must have used all of your sugar ration[2] for weeks. [*Giving it to* MRS. VAN DAAN.] It's beautiful, isn't it?

MRS. VAN DAAN. It's been ages since I even saw a cake. Not since you brought us one last year. [*Without looking at the cake, to* MIEP.] Remember? Don't you remember, you gave us one on New Year's Day? Just this time last year? I'll never forget it because you had "Peace in nineteen forty-three" on it. [*She looks at the cake and reads.*] "Peace in nineteen forty-four!"

MIEP. Well, it has to come sometime, you know. [*As* DUSSEL *comes from his room.*] Hello, Mr. Dussel.

MR. KRALER. How are you?

MR. VAN DAAN. [*Bringing plates and a knife.*] Here's the knife, *liefie.* Now, how many of us are there?

MIEP. None for me, thank you.

MR. FRANK. Oh, please. You must.

MIEP. I couldn't.

MR. VAN DAAN. Good! That leaves one… two…three…seven of us.

DUSSEL. Eight! Eight! It's the same number as it always is!

MR. VAN DAAN. I left Margot out. I take it for granted Margot won't eat any.

ANNE. Why wouldn't she?

MRS. FRANK. I think it won't harm her.

MR. VAN DAAN. All right! All right! I just didn't want her to start coughing again, that's all.

DUSSEL. And please, Mrs. Frank should cut the cake.

MR. VAN DAAN. What's the difference? } *Together*

MRS. VAN DAAN. It's not Mrs. Frank's cake, is it, Miep? It's for all of us. }

DUSSEL. Mrs. Frank divides things better.

MRS. VAN DAAN. [*Going to* DUSSEL.] What are you trying to say? } *Together*

MR. VAN DAAN. Oh, come on! Stop wasting time! }

MRS. VAN DAAN. [*To* DUSSEL.] Don't I always give everybody exactly the same? Don't I?

MR. VAN DAAN. Forget it, Kerli.

MRS. VAN DAAN. No. I want an answer! Don't I?

DUSSEL. Yes. Yes. Everybody gets exactly the same…except Mr. Van Daan always gets a little bit more.

VAN DAAN *advances on* DUSSEL, *the knife still in his hand.*

MR. VAN DAAN. That's a lie!

DUSSEL *retreats before the onslaught[3] of the* VAN DAANS.

---

2. **sugar ration.** Sugar was scarce during wartime, and people were allowed to buy only a certain amount each week with their ration coupons.
3. **onslaught.** Violent advance or attack

Teach the Selection

Literary Connection
Other Adaptations Inform students that Anne's diary has been adapted to several versions of drama and film. In 1959, a motion picture of the Goodrich-Hackett play was made, with a screenplay by Goodrich and Hackett. Starring Millie Perkins as Anne and Shelley Winters as Mrs. Van Daan, it won three Oscars. In 2001, a movie called *Anne Frank: The Whole Story* was released; this made-for-TV movie stars Ben Kingsley as Otto Frank and Brenda Blethyn as Mrs. Van Daan. It differs from the Goodrich-Hackett version in that it includes scenes from the concentration camps after the group was discovered.

Use Reading Strategies
Visualize Ask students to visualize and then describe the scene in which Mr. Van Daan and Mr. Dussel argue about the cake. Particularly, ask them to focus on the facial expressions of the three men. Model a response by suggesting that Mr. Frank would probably have an embarrassed and apologetic expression on his face, Mr. Van Daan would be showing anger, and Mr. Dussel would likely appear self-righteous and a little frightened.

Reading Skills

Read Aloud
Remind students that it is important to read fluently and accurately when reading orally. Suggest that they pay particular attention to punctuation as they read aloud and adjust their intonations and pacing accordingly:

1. Slow down slightly at commas, slightly more at semicolons, and even more at periods.
2. Use appropriate intonations for questions and exclamations.
3. Hesitate when encountering ellipses.

Analyze Literature

Symbol Discuss with students the symbolic value of Mrs. Van Daan's fur coat. Point out that it symbolizes her former life of luxury; even though she has no use for it in the secret annex, it means a lot to her. Other symbols in the play include the Hanukkah gifts Anne gave at the end of Act 1, which symbolizes her affection and concern for the others, and Miep's cake, which symbolizes her desire to make life in the secret annex more bearable for the people.

Analyze Literature

Characterization Students will probably recognize how well the characterization crafted by the authors works here. This exchange between Mrs. Van Daan, Mr. Van Daan, and Miep reveals a great deal about each one. For example, Mrs. Van Daan appears very attached to luxury, Mr. Van Daan appears selfish, and Miep appears generous and helpful. **A**

MR. FRANK. Please, please! [*Then to* MIEP.] You see what a little sugar cake does to us! It goes right to our heads!

MR. VAN DAAN. [*Handing* MRS. FRANK *the knife.*] Here you are, Mrs. Frank.

MRS. FRANK. Thank you. [*Then to* MIEP *as she goes to the table to cut the cake.*] Are you sure you won't have some?

MIEP. [*Drinking her tea.*] No, really, I have to go in a minute.

The sound of the band fades out in the distance.

PETER. [*To* MIEP.] Maybe Mouschi went back to our house…they say that cats…Do you ever get over there…? I mean…do you suppose you could…?

MIEP. I'll try, Peter. The first minute I get I'll try. But I'm afraid, with him gone a week…

DUSSEL. Make up your mind, already someone has had a nice big dinner from that cat! [PETER *is furious,* _inarticulate_. He starts toward DUSSEL *as if to hit him.* MR. FRANK *stops him.* MRS. FRANK *speaks quickly to ease the situation.*]

MRS. FRANK. [*To* MIEP.] This is delicious, Miep!

MRS. VAN DAAN. [*Eating hers.*] Delicious!

MR. VAN DAAN. [*Finishing it in one gulp.*] Dirk's in luck to get a girl who can bake like this! **A**

MIEP. [*Putting down her empty teacup.*] I have to run. Dirk's taking me to a party tonight.

ANNE. How heavenly! Remember now what everyone is wearing, and what you have to eat and everything, so you can tell us tomorrow.

MIEP. I'll give you a full report! Good-bye, everyone!

MR. VAN DAAN. [*To* MIEP.] Just a minute. There's something I'd like you to do for me.

He hurries off up the stairs to his room.

MRS. VAN DAAN. [*Sharply.*] Putti, where are you going? [*She rushes up the stairs after him, calling hysterically.*] What do you want? Putti, what are you going to do?

MIEP. [*To* PETER.] What's wrong?

PETER. [*His sympathy is with his mother.*] Father says he's going to sell her fur coat. She's crazy about that old fur coat.

DUSSEL. Is it possible? Is it possible that anyone is so silly as to worry about a fur coat in times like this?

PETER. It's none of your darn business…and if you say one more thing…I'll, I'll take you and I'll…I mean it…I'll…

There is a piercing scream from MRS. VAN DAAN *above. She grabs at the fur coat as* MR. VAN DAAN *is starting downstairs with it.*

MRS. VAN DAAN. No! No! No! Don't you dare take that! You hear? It's mine! [*Downstairs* PETER *turns away, embarrassed, miserable.*] My father gave me that! You didn't give it to me. You have no right. Let go of it…you hear?

MR. VAN DAAN *pulls the coat from her hands and hurries downstairs.* MRS. VAN DAAN *sinks to the floor, sobbing. As* MR. VAN DAAN *comes into the main room the others look away, embarrassed for him.*

MR. VAN DAAN. [*To* MR. KRALER.] Just a little—discussion over the advisability of selling this coat. As I have often reminded Mrs. Van Daan, it's very selfish of her to keep it when people outside are in such desperate need of clothing…[*He gives the coat to* MIEP.] So if you will please to sell it for us? It should fetch a good price. And by the way, will you get me cigarettes. I don't care what kind they are…get all you can.

MIEP. It's terribly difficult to get them, Mr. Van Daan. But I'll try. Good-bye.

> **in·ar·tic·u·late** (i' när ti´ kyə lət') *adj.,* incapable of speech, especially under the stress of strong emotions

---

Differentiated Instruction

English Language Learning

Providing students with the following definitions will help them understand some of the more difficult vocabulary.

hastily—quickly, 687
retreats—goes back; withdraws, 687
hysterically—showing uncontrolled emotion, 688
piercing—loud or high-pitched, 688
miserable—very unhappy, 688

She goes. MR. FRANK *follows her down the steps to bolt the door after her.* MRS. FRANK *gives* MR. KRALER *a cup of tea.*

MRS. FRANK. Are you sure you won't have some cake, Mr. Kraler?

MR. KRALER. I'd better not.

MR. VAN DAAN. You're still feeling badly? What does your doctor say?

MR. KRALER. I haven't been to him.

MRS. FRANK. Now, Mr. Kraler!…

MR. KRALER. [*Sitting at the table.*] Oh, I tried. But you can't get near a doctor these days… they're so busy. After weeks I finally managed to get one on the telephone. I told him I'd like an appointment…I wasn't feeling very well. You know what he answers…over the telephone…Stick out your tongue! [*They laugh. He turns to* MR. FRANK *as* MR. FRANK *comes back.*] I have some contracts here…I wonder if you'd look over them with me…

MR. FRANK. [*Putting out his hand.*] Of course.

MR. KRALER. [*He rises.*] If we could go downstairs…[MR. FRANK *starts ahead,* MR. KRALER *speaks to the others.*] Will you forgive us? I won't keep him but a minute.

He starts to follow MR. FRANK *down the steps.*

MARGOT. [*With sudden <u>foreboding</u>.*] What's happened? Something's happened! Hasn't it, Mr. Kraler?

MR. KRALER *stops and comes back, trying to reassure* MARGOT *with a pretense of casualness.*

MR. KRALER. No, really. I want your father's advice…

MARGOT. Something's gone wrong! I know it!

MR. FRANK. [*Coming back, to* MR. KRALER.] If it's something that concerns us here, it's better that we all hear it.

MR. KRALER. [*Turning to him, quietly.*] But… the children…?

MR. FRANK. What they'd imagine would be worse than any reality.

As MR. KRALER *speaks, they all listen with intense apprehension.*[4] MRS. VAN DAAN *comes down the stairs and sits on the bottom step.*

MR. KRALER. It's a man in the storeroom… I don't know whether or not you remember him…Carl, about fifty, heavy-set, near-sighted…He came with us just before you left.

MR. FRANK. He was from Utrecht?

MR. KRALER. That's the man. A couple of weeks ago, when I was in the storeroom, he closed the door and asked me…how's Mr. Frank? What do you hear from Mr. Frank? I told him I only knew there was a rumor that you were in Switzerland. He said he'd heard that rumor too, but he thought I might know something more. I didn't pay any attention to it…but then a thing happened yesterday…He'd brought some invoices[5] to the office for me to sign. As I was going through them, I looked up. He was standing staring at the bookcase…your bookcase. He said he thought he remembered a door there…Wasn't there a door there that used to go up to the loft? Then he told me he wanted more money. Twenty guilders[6] more a week.

MR. VAN DAAN. Blackmail![7]

MR. FRANK. Twenty guilders? Very modest blackmail.

MR. VAN DAAN. That's just the beginning.

DUSSEL. [*Coming to* MR. FRANK.] You know what I think? He was the thief who was

---

4. **intense apprehension.** Strong worries or fears
5. **invoices.** Itemized lists of goods or services, with prices shown; bills
6. **guilders.** Once the unit of currency in Holland, worth just under a dollar
7. **blackmail.** Payment demanded in return for a promise not to reveal information that could be very dangerous or disgraceful

fore·bod·ing (fôr bō′ diŋ) *adj.*, prediction that something bad or harmful will happen

---

Analyze Literature
Parallel Episodes This speech by Mr. Kraler can be seen as relating a parallel episode, something that happened while the residents of the annex were busy doing other things. It can also be seen as rising action in the plot. The residents have been fearful of the very thing Mr. Kraler is describing. It's beginning to appear as if someone else besides their helpers knows about their whereabouts. **B**

Use Reading Skills
Monitor Comprehension Students will probably see that Mr. Kraler thinks the man has figured out their secret: that the bookcase hides the staircase leading to the annex. This heightens the drama, since it is essential that the hiding place remain a secret. **C**

Reading Skills

Make Connections
Point out to students that literature doesn't belong just in the English classroom. It spills over into the study of history, social studies, psychology, and so on. Consider these questions:

1. What facts about history are illuminated by this play?

2. What does this play teach us about the social interactions between the Dutch people and the Jews in hiding?

3. What do the actions and words of the annex residents and their helpers reveal about their psychological state of mind?

Use Reading Strategies

Ask Questions Students might ask themselves if Mr. Kraler is overreacting. Why should he be so nervous? They can answer their own question when they remember that Mr. Kraler is taking a great risk to help the people in the annex. If he is caught helping them, he will suffer their same fate: arrest, detention, concentration camp, and probable death. **A**

Make Connections

Point out to students that, up to now, Margot has said very little. When she finally speaks, she shocks her mother with her ideas. Ask them how they react to Margot's statement. Does it make sense, under the circumstances? Is it possible that Margot's recent illness has weakened her resolve to survive? **B**

Make Connections

Ask students to respond to what Anne says here. How do they deal with being miserable? Does thinking about people who are worse off help? Or is it better to think of other things besides their own misery and the misery of others? **C**

down there that night. That's how he knows we're here.

MR. FRANK. [*To* MR. KRALER.] How was it left? What did you tell him?

MR. KRALER. I said I had to think about it. What shall I do? Pay him the money?…Take a chance on firing him…or what? I don't know.

DUSSEL. [*Frantic.*] For God's sake don't fire him! Pay him what he asks…keep him here where you can have your eye on him.

MR. FRANK. Is it so much that he's asking? What are they paying nowadays?

MR. KRALER. He could get it in a war plant. But this isn't a war plant. Mind you, I don't know if he really knows…or if he doesn't know.

MR. FRANK. Offer him half. Then we'll soon find out if it's blackmail or not.

DUSSEL. And if it is? We've got to pay it, haven't we? Anything he asks we've got to pay!

MR. FRANK. Let's decide that when the time comes. **A**

MR. KRALER. This may be all my imagination. You get to a point, these days, where you suspect everyone and everything. Again and again…on some simple look or word, I've found myself…

The telephone rings in the office below.

MRS. VAN DAAN. [*Hurrying to* MR. KRALER.] There's the telephone! What does that mean, the telephone ringing on a holiday?

MR. KRALER. That's my wife. I told her I had to go over some papers in my office…to call me there when she got out of church. [*He starts out.*] I'll offer him half then. Good-bye… we'll hope for the best! [*The group call their good-byes half-heartedly.* MR. FRANK *follows* MR. KRALER, *to bolt the door below. During the following scene,* MR. FRANK *comes back up and stands listening, disturbed.*]

DUSSEL. [*To* MR. VAN DAAN.] You can thank your son for this…smashing the light! I tell you, it's just a question of time now.

He goes to the window at the back and stands looking out.

MARGOT. Sometimes I wish the end would come…whatever it is. **B**

MRS. FRANK. [*Shocked.*] Margot!

ANNE *goes to* MARGOT, *sitting beside her on the couch with her arms around her.*

MARGOT. Then at least we'd know where we were.

MRS. FRANK. You should be ashamed of yourself! Talking that way! Think how lucky we are! Think of the thousands dying in the war, every day. Think of the people in concentration camps.

ANNE. [*Interrupting.*] What's the good of that? What's the good of thinking of misery when you're already miserable? That's stupid! **C**

Auditory Learning

Some students will benefit from choral reading of parts of the play. Have them read aloud a section of the play chosen by you. It could be an entire scene or just part of one. As students read aloud, read aloud with them, setting the pace while you model proper pronunciation and intonation. You might wish to have smaller groups take the role of individual characters, rather than having the entire class read all roles aloud. Have students follow these guidelines:

- Speak loudly enough to be heard, but not so loud as to drown out others.
- Use appropriate intonation.
- Observe punctuation, pausing where indicated.
- Follow the pace set by the teacher.

MRS. FRANK. Anne!

As ANNE *goes on raging at her mother,* MRS. FRANK *tries to break in, in an effort to quiet her.*

ANNE. We're young, Margot and Peter and I! You grown-ups have had your chance! But look at us…If we begin thinking of all the horror in the world, we're lost! We're trying to hold onto some kind of ideals…when everything…ideals, hopes…everything, are being destroyed! It isn't our fault that the world is in such a mess! We weren't around when all this started! So don't try to take it out on us!

She rushes off to her room, slamming the door after her. She picks up a brush from the chest and hurls it to the floor. Then she sits on the settee, trying to control her anger.

MR. VAN DAAN. She talks as if we started the war! Did we start the war?

He spots ANNE'S *cake. As he starts to take it,* PETER *anticipates[8] him.*

PETER. She left her cake. [*He starts for* ANNE'S *room with the cake. There is silence in the main room.* MRS. VAN DAAN *goes up to her room, followed by* MR. VAN DAAN. DUSSEL *stays looking out the window.* MR. FRANK *brings* MRS. FRANK *her cake. She eats it slowly, without relish.[9]* MR. FRANK *takes his cake to* MARGOT *and sits quietly on the sofa beside her.* PETER *stands in the doorway of* ANNE'S *darkened room, looking at her, then makes a little movement to let her know he is there.* ANNE *sits up, quickly, trying to hide the signs of her tears.* PETER *holds out the cake to her.*] You left this.

ANNE. [*Dully.*] Thanks.

PETER *starts to go out, then comes back.*

PETER. I thought you were fine just now. You know just how to talk to them. You know just how to say it. I'm no good…I never can think…especially when I'm mad…That Dussel…when he said that about Mouschi…

someone eating him…all I could think is…I wanted to hit him. I wanted to give him such a…a…that he'd…That's what I used to do when there was an argument at school… That's the way I…but here…And an old man like that…it wouldn't be so good. **E**

ANNE. You're making a big mistake about me. I do it all wrong. I say too much. I go too far. I hurt people's feelings…

DUSSEL *leaves the window, going to his room.*

PETER. I think you're just fine…What I want to say…if it wasn't for you around here, I don't know. What I mean…

PETER *is interrupted by* DUSSEL'S *turning on the light.* DUSSEL *stands in the doorway, startled to see* PETER. PETER *advances toward him forbiddingly.* DUSSEL *backs out of the room.* PETER *closes the door on him.*

ANNE. Do you mean it, Peter? Do you really mean it?

PETER. I said it, didn't I?

ANNE. Thank you, Peter!

In the main room MR. *and* MRS. FRANK *collect the dishes and take them to the sink, washing them.* MARGOT *lies down again on the couch.* DUSSEL, *lost, wanders into* PETER'S *room and takes up a book, starting to read.*

PETER. [*Looking at the photographs on the wall.*] You've got quite a collection.

ANNE. Wouldn't you like some in your room? I could give you some. Heaven knows you spend enough time in there…doing heaven knows what…

PETER. It's easier. A fight starts, or an argument…I duck in there.[10]

ANNE. You're lucky, having a room to go to.

---

8. **anticipates.** Peter understands what his father is about to do and steps in to prevent it.
9. **without relish.** Without pleasure or enthusiasm
10. **I duck in there.** Peter quickly goes to his room to get away from troubling events.

Analyze Literature

Stage Directions Ask students what these stage directions reveal about how the characters interact. Model a response: "Mr. and Mrs. Van Daan do the same thing, sticking close together. Mr. Dussel remains alone, apparently unable or unwilling to form a close relationship with anyone. Mr. Frank takes care of his wife and daughter, showing affection by serving them and sitting close. Peter shows that he wants to have a close relationship with Anne." **D**

Analyze Literature

Style The writing style in this brief exchange between Peter and Anne demonstrates the differences in personality. Peter speaks hesitantly, as indicated by the ellipses, whereas Anne is more direct and sure of herself. **E**

Vocabulary Skills

Determine Meaning

Remind students that if a word seems unrecognizable, they can use letter/sound correspondence to sound it out. Sometimes hearing the word jogs auditory memory of it. Another technique is to break the word into syllables and then determine the meaning of each syllable to decode meaning. Suggest that they try these techniques with these words:

- imagination
- half-heartedly
- concentration
- miserable
- anticipates
- argument
- interrupted
- forbiddingly

Analyze Literature

Dialogue The dialogue between Anne and Peter introduces the subplot of the developing relationship between the two. Students will recognize that their conversation is, for the first time, about their personal feelings.

Use Reading Strategies

Ask Questions Students might ask themselves why Anne and Peter haven't sought out each other's company before this. A possible answer would involve Peter's shyness and the fact that his parents constantly criticize and embarrass him, making him want to withdraw. **A**

Cultural Connection

Music References The reference to Toscanini leading an orchestra in the "Ride of the Valkyries" brings up two interesting historical tidbits. Inform students that Arturo Toscanini (1867–1957) was considered the greatest conductor of his era. His interpretations of operas and symphonies are still revered today. As to Richard Wagner (1813–1883), whose "Ride of the Valkyries" is part of his masterpiece *The Ring of the Niebelungenleid*, controversy still surrounds his name. Long before the rise of Nazism, Wagner came up with the phrases "the Jewish problem" and "the final solution." His anti-Semitic views and pride in German nationalism had a great influence on the development of Nazism. Beloved by Hitler, Wagner is today considered a symbol of the Nazi era, even though he died fifty years before Hitler's rise to power. **B**

His lordship is always here…I hardly ever get a minute alone. When they start in on me, I can't duck away. I have to stand there and take it.

PETER. You gave some of it back just now.

ANNE. I get so mad. They've formed their opinions…about everything…but we…we're still trying to find out…We have problems here that no other people our age have ever had. And just as you think you've solved them, something comes along and bang! You have to start all over again.

PETER. At least you've got someone you can talk to.

ANNE. Not really. Mother…I never discuss anything serious with her. She doesn't understand. Father's all right. We can talk about everything…everything but one thing. Mother. He simply won't talk about her. I don't think you can be really <u>intimate</u> with anyone if he holds something back, do you?

PETER. I think your father's fine.

ANNE. Oh, he is, Peter! He is! He's the only one who's ever given me the feeling that I have any sense. But anyway, nothing can take the place of school and play and friends of your own age…or near your age…can it?

PETER. I suppose you miss your friends and all.

ANNE. It isn't just…[*She breaks off, staring up at him for a second.*] Isn't it funny, you and I? Here we've been seeing each other every minute for almost a year and a half, and this is the first time we've ever really talked. It helps a lot to have someone to talk to, don't you think? It helps you to let off steam.[11]

PETER. [*Going to the door.*] Well, any time you want to let off steam, you can come into my room.

ANNE. [*Following him.*] I can get up an awful lot of steam. You'll have to be careful how

you say that.

PETER. It's all right with me.

ANNE. Do you mean it?

PETER. I said it, didn't I?

He goes out. ANNE *stands in her doorway looking after him. As* PETER *gets to his door he stands for a minute looking back at her. Then he goes into his room.* DUSSEL *rises as he comes in, and quickly passes him, going out. He starts across for his room.* ANNE *sees him coming, and pulls her door shut.* DUSSEL *turns back toward* PETER'S *room.* PETER *pulls his door shut.* DUSSEL *stands there, bewildered, forlorn.*[12]

The scene slowly dims out. The curtain falls on the scene. ANNE'S VOICE *comes over in the darkness…faintly at first, and then with growing strength.*

ANNE'S VOICE. We've had bad news. The people from whom Miep got our ration books have been arrested. So we have had to cut down on our food. Our stomachs are so empty that they rumble and make strange noises, all in different keys. Mr. Van Daan's is deep and low, like a bass fiddle. Mine is high, whistling like a flute. As we all sit around waiting for supper, it's like an orchestra tuning up. It only needs Toscanini to raise his baton and we'd be off in the Ride of the Valkyries.[13] Monday, the sixth of March, nineteen forty-four. Mr. Kraler is in the hospital. It seems he has ulcers. Pim says we are his ulcers. Miep has to run the business and us too. The Americans have landed on the southern tip of Italy.[14] Father

---

11. **to let off steam.** Calm down; relieve tense feelings
12. **bewildered, forlorn.** Confused and very sad
13. **Toscanini…Ride of the Valkyries.** Anne is referring to Italian orchestra conductor Arturo Toscanini and an orchestral piece by German composer Richard Wagner.
14. **The Americans…Italy.** American troops landed in southern Italy to try to get a foothold in Europe and to defeat the Italians, who were one of the Axis Powers (with Germany and Japan).

in·ti·mate (in´ tə mət) *adj.*, marked by close association, familiarity, and warm friendship

692   UNIT 7 DRAMA

Visual Learning

Visual learners will benefit from drawing a picture of any part of Scene 1. Suggest that they take care to indicate expressions on characters' faces that reflect their emotions. Suggest also that they refer to stage directions to make accurate depictions of characters' positions on the stage.

Use Reading Strategies

Visualize Ask students to close their eyes during Anne's monologue on pages 692–694 and visualize what she describes. Then, pause for a moment in the reading to view the movie still on this page. Discuss with students its impact on their mental images of the characters. Do these actors and their surroundings correspond or conflict with student's personal images? What are some benefits and drawbacks of accompanying literature with artistic depictions?

Analyze Literature

Drama Guide students in understanding that, even with stage directions, a play's text cannot reveal as much as the performers who enact it on the stage. Have students study the facial expressions and body language of Anne and Peter in the movie still on this page. How does the expression on Anne's face expose her state of mind? What does Peter's body position in reference to Anne reveal about his feelings for her? How do these physical indicators reinforce the authors' message in the text?

Grammar Skills

Commas in Direct Address

Remind students of the use of commas in direct address. Tell them that a comma goes before, after, or before *and* after the name or title of the person being addressed, depending on how the sentence is set up. Here are some examples:

Before: That isn't true, Mr. Dussel.
After: Margot, do you think I'm pretty?
Both: Listen, Pim, I have something to tell you.

Have students rewrite these sentences correctly.
1. Exactly when Peter shall we meet? (commas before and after *Peter*)
2. Mrs. Van Daan stop flirting with Pim. (comma after *Daan*)
3. I disagree with you Mother. (comma before *Mother*)

Use Reading Skills
Identify Text Organization
Students should recognize that the text is always organized the same way: scenes open with a description of the set and the activities of the actors on the stage. This is followed by dialogue among the characters. Remind students that in a drama, the plot is moved along only through dialogue. There is no narrator to fill in details about the characters' motivations, innermost thoughts, or conflicts.

Use Reading Skills
Read Aloud By reading aloud the exchange between Anne and Margot, students will get a clearer idea that Anne is just like any typical teenager getting ready for a date. Her questions to her sister reveal that she is concerned with how others see her. **Ⓐ**

Use Reading Skills
Analyze Cause and Effect Have students reread the conversation between Mrs. Frank and Anne. Then ask them to analyze the cause of the strained relationship between the two. Model a response by suggesting that one reason Anne and her mother do not get along well is that Anne questions her mother's attitudes about her relationship with Peter. Her mother is concerned about appearances, thinking that young people should not be alone behind a closed door; Anne is not concerned about petty criticism by Mrs. Van Daan.

looks for a quick finish to the war. Mr. Dussel is waiting every day for the warehouse man to demand more money. Have I been skipping too much from one subject to another? I can't help it. I feel that spring is coming. I feel it in my whole body and soul. I feel utterly confused. I am longing…so longing…for everything…for friends…for someone to talk to…someone who understands…someone young, who feels as I do… **Ⓐ**

As these last lines are being said, the curtain rises on the scene. The lights dim on. ANNE'S VOICE *fades out.*

SCENE 2

It is evening, after supper. From outside we hear the sound of children playing. The "grown-ups," with the exception of MR. VAN DAAN, *are all in the main room.* MRS. FRANK *is doing some mending,* MRS. VAN DAAN *is reading a fashion magazine.* MR. FRANK *is going over business accounts.* DUSSEL, *in his dentist's jacket, is pacing up and down, impatient to get into his bedroom.* MR. VAN DAAN *is upstairs working on a piece of embroidery in an embroidery frame.*

In his room PETER *is sitting before the mirror, smoothing his hair. As the scene goes on, he puts on his tie, brushes his coat and puts it on, preparing himself meticulously for a visit from* ANNE. *On his wall are now hung some of* ANNE'S *motion picture stars.*

In her room ANNE *too is getting dressed. She stands before the mirror in her slip, trying various ways of dressing her hair.* MARGOT *is seated on the sofa, hemming a skirt for* ANNE *to wear.*

In the main room DUSSEL *can stand it no longer. He comes over, rapping sharply on the door of his and* ANNE'S *bedroom.*

ANNE. [*Calling to him.*] No, no, Mr. Dussel! I am not dressed yet. [DUSSEL *walks away, furious, sitting down and burying his head in his*

hands. ANNE *turns to* MARGOT.] How is that? How does that look?

MARGOT. [*Glancing at her briefly.*] Fine.

ANNE. You didn't even look.

MARGOT. Of course I did. It's fine.

ANNE. Margot, tell me, am I terribly ugly?

MARGOT. Oh, stop fishing.[15]

ANNE. No. No. Tell me.

MARGOT. Of course you're not. You've got nice eyes…and a lot of animation, and…

ANNE. A little vague, aren't you?

She reaches over and takes a brassière out of MARGOT'S *sewing basket. She holds it up to herself, studying the effect in the mirror. Outside,* MRS. FRANK, *feeling sorry for* DUSSEL, *comes over, knocking at the girls' door.*

MRS. FRANK. [*Outside.*] May I come in?

MARGOT. Come in, Mother.

MRS. FRANK. [*Shutting the door behind her.*] Mr. Dussel's impatient to get in here.

ANNE. [*Still with the brassière.*] Heavens, he takes the room for himself the entire day.

MRS. FRANK. [*Gently.*] Anne, dear, you're not going in again tonight to see Peter?

ANNE. [*Dignified.*] That is my intention.

MRS. FRANK. But you've already spent a great deal of time in there today.

ANNE. I was in there exactly twice. Once to get the dictionary, and then three-quarters of an hour before supper.

MRS. FRANK. Aren't you afraid you're disturbing him?

ANNE. Mother, I have some intuition.[16]

MRS. FRANK. Then may I ask you this much, Anne. Please don't shut the door when you go in.

---

15. **Oh, stop fishing.** "Oh, stop looking for compliments."
16. **intuition.** Natural ability to sense and understand what is right or true

Enrichment
What if Margot had also kept a diary? What would she have said about her conversations with Anne regarding Peter? Students might enjoy writing diary entries that Margot might have written about this topic and others. Have students share their diary entries with the class, comparing and contrasting the content.

ANNE. You sound like Mrs. Van Daan!

She throws the brassière back in MARGOT'S *sewing basket and picks up her blouse, putting it on.*

MRS. FRANK. No. No. I don't mean to suggest anything wrong. I only wish that you wouldn't expose yourself to criticism…that you wouldn't give Mrs. Van Daan the opportunity to be unpleasant.

ANNE. Mrs. Van Daan doesn't need an opportunity to be unpleasant!

MRS. FRANK. Everyone's on edge, worried about Mr. Kraler. This is one more thing…

ANNE. I'm sorry, Mother. I'm going to Peter's room. I'm not going to let Petronella Van Daan spoil our friendship.

MRS. FRANK *hesitates for a second, then goes out, closing the door after her. She gets a pack of playing cards and sits at the center table, playing solitaire. In* ANNE'S *room* MARGOT *hands the finished skirt to* ANNE. *As* ANNE *is putting it on,* MARGOT *takes off her high-heeled shoes and stuffs paper in the toes so that* ANNE *can wear them.*

MARGOT. [*To* ANNE.] Why don't you two talk in the main room? It'd save a lot of trouble. It's hard on Mother, having to listen to those remarks from Mrs. Van Daan and not say a word.

ANNE. Why doesn't she say a word? I think it's ridiculous to take it and take it.

MARGOT. You don't understand Mother at all, do you? She can't talk back. She's not like you. It's just not in her nature to fight back.

ANNE. Anyway…the only one I worry about is you. I feel awfully guilty about you.

She sits on the stool near MARGOT, *putting on* MARGOT'S *high-heeled shoes.*

MARGOT. What about?

ANNE. I mean, every time I go into Peter's room, I have a feeling I may be hurting you.

[MARGOT *shakes her head.*] I know if it were me, I'd be wild. I'd be desperately jealous, if it were me.

MARGOT. Well, I'm not.

ANNE. You don't feel badly? Really? Truly? You're not jealous?

MARGOT. Of course I'm jealous…jealous that you've got something to get up in the morning for…But jealous of you and Peter? No.

ANNE *goes back to the mirror.*

ANNE. Maybe there's nothing to be jealous of. Maybe he doesn't really like me. Maybe I'm just taking the place of his cat…[*She picks up a pair of short white gloves, putting them on.*] Wouldn't you like to come in with us?

MARGOT. I have a book. [*The sound of the children playing outside fades out. In the main room* DUSSEL *can stand it no longer. He jumps up, going to the bedroom door and knocking sharply.*]

DUSSEL. Will you please let me in my room!

ANNE. Just a minute, dear, dear Mr. Dussel. [*She picks up her Mother's pink stole*[17] *and adjusts it elegantly over her shoulders, then gives a last look in the mirror.*] Well, here I go…to run the gauntlet.[18]

She starts out, followed by MARGOT.

DUSSEL. [*As she appears—sarcastic.*] Thank you so much.

DUSSEL *goes into his room.* ANNE *goes toward* PETER'S *room, passing* MRS. VAN DAAN *and her parents at the center table.*

MRS. VAN DAAN. My God, look at her! [ANNE *pays no attention. She knocks at* PETER'S *door.*] I don't know what good it is to have a son. I never see him. He wouldn't care if I killed

---

17. **stole.** Short cape or wrap worn across the shoulders
18. **run the gauntlet.** Face a challenge. This expression refers to medieval prisoners who were forced to run past a line of knights, all wearing heavy spiked gloves (called "gauntlets"). As the prisoner ran, each knight would reach out and hit him.

THE DIARY OF ANNE FRANK, ACT 2 **695**

Teach the Selection

Use Reading Strategies
Visualize Ask students to visualize this scene: the audience can see both Mrs. Frank and the two girls. What is the effect of this staging? Model a response: "By visualizing the scene, the reader—and the audience—can see how all three characters react to the conversation between Anne and her mother. Mrs. Frank withdraws into solitaire, and Margot helps her sister get ready."

Analyze Literature
Parallel Episodes Draw students' attention to Anne's actions here. When she puts on the white gloves, are students reminded of the glove Mr. Frank picked up in the first scene of Act 1? They may recall that he dissolved in tears at that moment. Point out that the authors have used these parallel episodes to underscore Mr. Frank's sorrow and emphasize the innocence of the victims. **B**

Use Reading Skills
Identify Multiple Levels of Meaning Have students identify what Mr. Dussel is really saying here. Does he mean to express his gratitude here, or is he really expressing his exasperation and his sense of entitlement to the privacy of the room? **C**

Grammar Skills

Abbreviations

Remind students of these rules of capitalization for titles:

- Capitalize the titles or abbreviations that come before the names of people: Mayor Bradley, Mr. Jones.
- Capitalize a person's title when it is used as a proper noun: Hello, Grandfather.
- Capitalize words showing family relationships when used as titles or substitutes for a name: I had lunch with Aunt Jane.
- Do not capitalize occupations: She is the mayor of our town.
- Do not capitalize words for family relationships when they are preceded by a possessive noun or pronoun: I visited my uncle Raymond yesterday.

Have students write their own example for each rule.

Analyze Literature

Characterization Remind students that characterization is the way an author reveals details about characters. One way is by what the character says. Here, Anne's words reveal that she recalls enjoying typical activities of teenagers, but that she also realizes that she has matured during the many months of hiding. Point out that her situation no doubt contributed to her maturation. Had she enjoyed a normal life, she would probably not have been so serious at this age. **Ⓐ**

Literary Connection

Diary Revisions Inform students that Anne's diary is really a series of books and loose pages. The original diary was actually an autograph book with a red-and-green plaid cover and a simple keyless lock. This book was filled within six months, and she started writing in a second notebook, which was lost, and two more notebooks. These became called "version A." In May 1944, Anne heard a Dutch radio broadcast urging citizens to preserve their war memoirs. Anticipating publication, Anne then began revising her diary. She rewrote 324 pages; some say she meant to turn them into a novel. This became called "version B." "Version C," a heavily edited version of "B," was released in 1947 as the first publication of the diary. Since then, a "definitive edition" was published (in 1995), including 30 percent more material than Otto Frank had allowed in the 1947 edition.

---

myself. [PETER *opens the door and stands aside for* ANNE *to come in.*] Just a minute, Anne. [*She goes to them at the door.*] I'd like to say a few words to my son. Do you mind? [PETER *and* ANNE *stand waiting.*] Peter, I don't want you staying up till all hours tonight. You've got to have your sleep. You're a growing boy. You hear?

MRS. FRANK. Anne won't stay late. She's going to bed promptly at nine. Aren't you, Anne?

ANNE. Yes, Mother…[*To* MRS. VAN DAAN.] May we go now?

MRS. VAN DAAN. Are you asking me? I didn't know I had anything to say about it.

MRS. FRANK. Listen for the chimes,[19] Anne dear.

The two young people go off into PETER's *room, shutting the door after them.* **Ⓐ**

MRS. VAN DAAN. [*To* MRS. FRANK.] In my day it was the boys who called on the girls. Not the girls on the boys.

MRS. FRANK. You know how young people like to feel that they have secrets. Peter's room is the only place where they can talk.

MRS. VAN DAAN. Talk! That's not what they called it when I was young.

MRS. VAN DAAN *goes off to the bathroom.* MARGOT *settles down to read her book.* MR. FRANK *puts his papers away and brings a chess game to the center table. He and* MRS. FRANK *start to play. In* PETER's *room,* ANNE *speaks to* PETER, *indignant, humiliated.*

ANNE. Aren't they awful? Aren't they impossible? Treating us as if we were still in the nursery.

She sits on the cot. PETER *gets a bottle of pop and two glasses.*

PETER. Don't let it bother you. It doesn't bother me.

ANNE. I suppose you can't really blame them…they think back to what *they* were like at our age. They don't realize how much more advanced we are…When you think what wonderful discussions we've had!…Oh, I forgot. I was going to bring you some more pictures.

PETER. Oh, these are fine, thanks.

ANNE. Don't you want some more? Miep just brought me some new ones.

PETER. Maybe later.

He gives her a glass of pop and, taking some for himself, sits down facing her.

ANNE. [*Looking up at one of the photographs.*] I remember when I got that…I won it. I bet Jopie that I could eat five ice-cream cones. We'd all been playing ping-pong…We used to have heavenly times…we'd finish up with ice cream at the Delphi, or the Oasis, where Jews were allowed…there'd always be a lot of boys…we'd laugh and joke…I'd like to go back to it for a few days or a week. But after that I know I'd be bored to death. I think more seriously about life now. I want to be a journalist…or something. I love to write. What do you want to do? **Ⓐ**

PETER. I thought I might go off some place… work on a farm or something…some job that doesn't take much brains.

ANNE. You shouldn't talk that way. You've got the most awful inferiority complex.[20]

PETER. I know I'm not smart.

ANNE. That isn't true. You're much better than I am in dozens of things…arithmetic and algebra and…well, you're a million times better than I am in algebra. [*With sudden directness.*] You like Margot, don't you? Right from the start you liked her, liked her much better than me.

---

19. **Listen for the chimes.** Anne's mother wants her to leave Peter's room when the bells in the church tower strike nine o'clock.
20. **inferiority complex.** Lack of confidence in one's own abilities; a feeling that one's skills are inferior to the skills of others

---

Differentiated Instruction

Kinesthetic Learning

Students who learn best through physical activity will benefit from acting out a scene or scenes from the play. Encourage the use of props and sound effects, and invite students to perform their scenes for the class.

Enrichment

Have students prepare a dramatic monologue that the character of their choice might have performed. Remind them that a dramatic monologue is a speech that reveals the thoughts and feelings of the speaker. Allow time for rehearsal and revision, and encourage students to perform their monologues for the class.

PETER. [*Uncomfortably.*] Oh, I don't know.

In the main room MRS. VAN DAAN *comes from the bathroom and goes over to the sink, polishing a coffee pot.*

ANNE. It's all right. Everyone feels that way. Margot's so good. She's sweet and bright and beautiful and I'm not.

PETER. I wouldn't say that.

ANNE. Oh, no, I'm not. I know that. I know quite well that I'm not a beauty. I never have been and never shall be.

PETER. I don't agree at all. I think you're pretty.

ANNE. That's not true!

PETER. And another thing. You've changed… from at first, I mean.

ANNE. I have?

PETER. I used to think you were awful noisy.

ANNE. And what do you think now, Peter? How have I changed?

PETER. Well…er…you're…quieter.

In his room DUSSEL *takes his pajamas and toilet articles and goes into the bathroom to change.*

ANNE. I'm glad you don't just hate me.

PETER. I never said that.

ANNE. I bet when you get out of here you'll never think of me again.

PETER. That's crazy.

ANNE. When you get back with all of your friends, you're going to say…now what did I ever see in that Mrs. Quack Quack. **B**

PETER. I haven't got any friends.

ANNE. Oh, Peter, of course you have. Everyone has friends.

PETER. Not me. I don't want any. I get along all right without them.

ANNE. Does that mean you can get along without me? I think of myself as your friend.

PETER. No. If they were all like you, it'd be different.

He takes the glasses and the bottle and puts them away. There is a second's silence and then ANNE *speaks, hesitantly, shyly.*

ANNE. Peter, did you ever kiss a girl?

PETER. Yes. Once.

ANNE. [*To cover her feelings.*] That picture's crooked. [PETER *goes over, straightening the photograph.*] Was she pretty? **C**

PETER. Huh?

ANNE. The girl that you kissed.

PETER. I don't know. I was blindfolded. [*He comes back and sits down again.*] It was at a party. One of those kissing games.

ANNE. [*Relieved.*] Oh. I don't suppose that really counts, does it?

PETER. It didn't with me.

ANNE. I've been kissed twice. Once a man I'd never seen before kissed me on the cheek when he picked me up off the ice and I was crying. And the other was Mr. Koophuis, a friend of Father's who kissed my hand. You wouldn't say those counted, would you?

PETER. I wouldn't say so.

ANNE. I know almost for certain that Margot would never kiss anyone unless she was engaged to them. And I'm sure too that Mother never touched a man before Pim. But I don't know…things are so different now… What do you think? Do you think a girl shouldn't kiss anyone except if she's engaged or something? It's so hard to try to think what to do, when here we are with the whole world falling around our ears and you think…well…you don't know what's going to happen tomorrow and…What do you think?

PETER. I suppose it'd depend on the girl. Some girls, anything they do's wrong. But

Teach the Selection

Use Reading Skills
Recall Details This statement of Anne's will make more sense once students recall that in Act 1, Peter called her "Mrs. Quack Quack" because of the way she talked so much. They will also recall that it upset her then; the fact that it doesn't upset her now shows that Peter and Anne have become more comfortable with each other. **B**

Use Reading Strategies
Make Predictions Have students predict whether Anne's question will lead to a kiss between Anne and Peter. **C**

Analyze Literature
Dialogue Have volunteers read aloud this dialogue between Anne and Peter. Ask: "How does this dialogue move along the subplot of the growing relationship between the two?" Model a response by saying that they are being open with each other. They are discussing how their situation is forcing them to reassess their definitions of what constitutes moral behavior. They realize, no doubt, that their situation precludes the luxury of a traditional courtship.

Grammar Skills

Proper Nouns
Remind students of the difference between common nouns and proper nouns: common nouns name places, persons, things, or ideas and are not capitalized; proper nouns name specific places, persons, things, or ideas and are capitalized.

(*Park, boy, car,* and *religion* are common nouns. *Central Park, Jerome, Chevrolet,* and *Protestantism* are corresponding proper nouns.)

Have students provide a proper noun to correspond to each of the following common nouns: lake, teacher, school, book, mountain, city.

Teach the Selection

Use Reading Strategies

Make Inferences Ask students what Mrs. Van Daan knows and how she came to that conclusion. Model a response by saying that Mrs. Van Daan knows that Peter kissed Anne. The evidence that leads her to this realization is the fact that Anne looks dazed and is acting in an uncharacteristic way, by kissing her family and then Mrs. Van Daan. **Ⓐ**

History Connection

The Secret Annex The entrance to the secret annex was a single door, plain and gray, leading to a staircase. Some time after the residents moved in, a movable bookcase that moved like a door was built to hide the entrance. Have students imagine what it would be like if they had to block the only exit from their living quarters, and their only means of enjoying sunlight was through the windows or through the skylight. **Ⓑ**

Literary Connection

La Belle Nivernaise Anne is referring to a children's story written in 1887 by French writer Alphonse Daudet. The plot centers on bargeman Louveau, who takes in an abandoned boy named Victor and raises him as his own child, teaching him about life as a bargeman on the river. Ten years later, the boy and Louveau's daughter Clara are in love. **Ⓒ**

---

others…well…it wouldn't necessarily be wrong with them. [*The carillon starts to strike nine o'clock.*] I've always thought that when two people…

ANNE. Nine o'clock. I have to go.

PETER. That's right.

ANNE. [*Without moving.*] Good night. [*There is a second's pause, then* PETER *gets up and moves toward the door.*]

PETER. You won't let them stop you coming?

ANNE. No. [*She rises and starts for the door.*] Sometime I might bring my diary. There are so many things in it that I want to talk over with you. There's a lot about you.

PETER. What kind of things?

ANNE. I wouldn't want you to see some of it. I thought you were a nothing, just the way you thought about me.

PETER. Did you change your mind, the way I changed my mind about you?

ANNE. Well…You'll see…

For a second ANNE *stands looking up at* PETER, *longing for him to kiss her. As he makes no move she turns away. Then suddenly* PETER *grabs her awkwardly in his arms, kissing her on the cheek.* ANNE *walks out dazed. She stands for a minute, her back to the people in the main room. As she regains her poise she goes to her mother and father and* MARGOT, *silently kissing them. They murmur their good nights to her. As she is about to open her bedroom door, she catches sight of* MRS. VAN DAAN. *She goes quickly to her, taking her face in her hands and kissing her first on one cheek and then on the other. Then she hurries off into her room.* MRS. VAN DAAN *looks after her, and then looks over at* PETER's *room. Her suspicions are confirmed.*

Ⓐ ⎡MRS. VAN DAAN. [*She knows.*] Ah hah!

The lights dim out. The curtain falls on the scene. In the darkness ANNE'S VOICE *comes faintly at first and then with growing strength.*

698 UNIT 7 DRAMA

ANNE'S VOICE. By this time we all know each other so well that if anyone starts to tell a story, the rest can finish it for him. We're having to cut down still further on our meals. What makes it worse, the rats have been at work again. They've carried off some of our precious food. Even Mr. Dussel wishes now that Mouschi was here. Thursday, the twentieth of April, nineteen forty-four. Invasion fever[21] is mounting every day. Miep tells us that people outside talk of nothing else. For myself, life has become much more pleasant. I often go to Peter's room after supper. Oh, don't think I'm in love, because I'm not. But it does make life more bearable to have someone with whom you can exchange views. No more tonight. P.S.…I must be honest. I must confess that I actually **Ⓑ** ⎡live for the next meeting. Is there anything lovelier than to sit under the skylight and feel the sun on your cheeks and have a darling boy in your arms? I admit now that I'm glad the Van Daans had a son and not a daughter. I've outgrown another dress. That's the third. **Ⓒ** ⎡I'm having to wear Margot's clothes after all. I'm working hard on my French and am now reading *La Belle Nivernaise*.

As she is saying the last lines—the curtain rises on the scene. The lights dim on, as ANNE'S VOICE *fades out.*

SCENE 3

It is night, a few weeks later. Everyone is in bed. There is complete quiet. In the VAN DAANS' *room a match flares up for a moment and then is quickly put out.* MR. VAN DAAN, *in bare feet, dressed in underwear and trousers, is dimly seen coming stealthily[22] down the stairs and into the main room, where* MR. *and* MRS. FRANK *and*

---

21. **Invasion fever.** People of France and Holland eagerly awaited an Allied invasion, which they hoped would finally defeat the Germans and end the war. The Allies finally did invade, but not until June 6, 1944 ("D-Day")—about two months after Anne wrote this diary entry.
22. **stealthily.** In a sneaky, quiet way, to avoid detection

---

Differentiated Instruction

Enrichment

Students might enjoy holding a trial for Mr. Van Daan. They can assign the roles of prosecuting attorney, defense attorney, judge, witnesses, defendant, and jury. Have them present the trial to the class.

Visual Learning

Visual learners will benefit from creating a Venn diagram based on Mrs. Frank's character. They can compare and contrast the traits Mrs. Frank has shown in Act 1 and the first two scenes of Act 2 with those traits she exhibits after Mr. Van Daan is caught.

MARGOT *are sleeping. He goes to the food safe and again lights a match. Then he cautiously opens the safe, taking out a half-loaf of bread. As he closes the safe, it creaks. He stands rigid.* MRS. FRANK *sits up in bed. She sees him.*

MRS. FRANK. [*Screaming.*] Otto! Otto! *Komme schnell!*[23]

The rest of the people wake, hurriedly getting up.

MR. FRANK. *Was ist los? Was ist passiert?*[24]

DUSSEL, *followed by* ANNE, *comes from his room.*

MRS. FRANK. [*As she rushes over to* MR. VAN DAAN.] *Er stiehlt das Essen!*[25]

DUSSEL. [*Grabbing* MR. VAN DAAN.] You! You! Give me that.

MRS. VAN DAAN. [*Coming down the stairs.*] Putti…Putti…what is it?

DUSSEL. [*His hands on* VAN DAAN's *neck.*] You dirty thief…stealing food…you good-for-nothing…

MR. FRANK. Mr. Dussel! For God's sake! Help me, Peter!

PETER *comes over, trying, with* MR. FRANK, *to separate the two struggling men.*

PETER. Let him go! Let go!

DUSSEL *drops* MR. VAN DAAN, *pushing him away. He shows them the end of a loaf of bread that he has taken from* VAN DAAN.

DUSSEL. You greedy, selfish…

MARGOT *turns on the lights.*

MRS. VAN DAAN. Putti…what is it? [*All of* MRS. FRANK's *gentleness, her self-control, is gone. She is outraged, in a frenzy of indignation.*]

MRS. FRANK. The bread! He was stealing the bread!

DUSSEL. It was you, and all the time we thought it was the rats!

MR. FRANK. Mr. Van Daan, how could you!

MR. VAN DAAN. I'm hungry.

MRS. FRANK. We're all of us hungry! I see the children getting thinner and thinner. Your own son Peter…I've heard him moan in his sleep, he's so hungry. And you come in the night and steal food that should go to them…to the children! **D**

MRS. VAN DAAN. [*Going to* MR. VAN DAAN *protectively.*] He needs more food than the rest of us. He's used to more. He's a big man. **E**

MR. VAN DAAN *breaks away, going over and sitting on the couch.*

MRS. FRANK. [*Turning on* MRS. VAN DAAN.] And you…you're worse than he is! You're a mother, and yet you sacrifice your child to this man…this…this…

MR. FRANK. Edith! Edith!

MARGOT *picks up the pink woolen stole, putting it over her mother's shoulders.*

MRS. FRANK. [*Paying no attention, going on to* MRS. VAN DAAN.] Don't think I haven't seen you! Always saving the choicest bits for him! I've watched you day after day and I've held my tongue. But not any longer! Not after this! Now I want him to go! I want him to get out of here!

MR. FRANK. Edith!   } *Together.*
MR. VAN DAAN. Get out of here?

MRS. VAN DAAN. What do you mean?

MRS. FRANK. Just that! Take your things and get out!

MR. FRANK. [*To* MRS. FRANK.] You're speaking in anger. You cannot mean what you are saying.

MRS. FRANK. I mean exactly that!

MRS. VAN DAAN *takes a cover from the* FRANKS' *bed, pulling it about her.*

---

23. *Komme schnell!* Come quickly! (German)
24. *Was ist los? Was ist passiert?* What is wrong? What is going on? (German)
25. *Er stiehlt das Essen!* He's stealing food! (German)

THE DIARY OF ANNE FRANK, ACT 2   **699**

Teach the Selection

Analyze Literature
Characterization Students will probably recognize that Mr. Frank's words here reveal that he is a peacemaker, a person who wants everyone to get along. Unlike his wife, he is looking for a way to keep the group together; he is able to keep his anger under control. **A**

Science Connection
Psychology Inform students that there is often a connection between poor living conditions and poor behavior. Mr. Van Daan and Mrs. Frank both exhibit behavior that they would never exhibit under normal circumstances. But hunger, lack of privacy, boredom, stress, and worry have changed them. Remind students that desperate situations often lead to desperate behavior. **B**

A **MR. FRANK.** For two long years we have lived here, side by side. We have respected each other's rights...we have managed to live in peace. Are we now going to throw it all away? I know this will never happen again, will it, Mr. Van Daan?

MR. VAN DAAN. No. No.

MRS. FRANK. He steals once! He'll steal again! [MR. VAN DAAN, *holding his stomach, starts for the bathroom.* ANNE *puts her arms around him, helping him up the step.*]

MR. FRANK. Edith, please. Let us be calm. We'll all go to our rooms...and afterwards we'll sit down quietly and talk this out...we'll find some way...

MRS. FRANK. No! No! No more talk! I want them to leave!

MRS. VAN DAAN. You'd put us out, on the streets?

MRS. FRANK. There are other hiding places.

MRS. VAN DAAN. A cellar...a closet. I know. And we have no money left even to pay for that.

MRS. FRANK. I'll give you money. Out of my own pocket I'll give it gladly.

She gets her purse from a shelf and comes back with it.

MRS. VAN DAAN. Mr. Frank, you told Putti you'd never forget what he'd done for you when you came to Amsterdam. You said you could never repay him, that you...

MRS. FRANK. [*Counting out money.*] If my husband had any obligation to you, he's paid it, over and over.

B **MR. FRANK.** Edith, I've never seen you like this before. I don't know you.

MRS. FRANK. I should have spoken out long ago.

DUSSEL. You can't be nice to some people.

MRS. VAN DAAN. [*Turning on* DUSSEL.] There would have been plenty for all of us, if you hadn't come in here!

MR. FRANK. We don't need the Nazis to destroy us. We're destroying ourselves.

He sits down, with his head in his hands. MRS. FRANK *goes to* MRS. VAN DAAN.

MRS. FRANK. [*Giving* MRS. VAN DAAN *some money.*] Give this to Miep. She'll find you a place.

ANNE. Mother, you're not putting Peter out. Peter hasn't done anything.

Differentiated Instruction

Reading Proficiency
Have less proficient readers pair up with more proficient readers and reread Scene 3 together. Encourage them to pause at intervals and monitor their comprehension by summarizing what they have read or asking questions about it.

Enrichment
Interested students might like to research how much food people actually got in World War II through the American rationing system. They can compare this to today's food pyramid to determine how healthful this diet was. Remind students that the residents of the annex were living on far less food than this.

MRS. FRANK. He'll stay, of course. When I say I must protect the children, I mean Peter too.

PETER *rises from the steps where he has been sitting.*

PETER. I'd have to go if Father goes.

MR. VAN DAAN *comes from the bathroom.* MRS. VAN DAAN *hurries to him and takes him to the couch. Then she gets water from the sink to bathe his face.*

MRS. FRANK. [*While this is going on.*] He's no father to you…that man! He doesn't know what it is to be a father!

PETER. [*Starting for his room.*] I wouldn't feel right. I couldn't stay.

MRS. FRANK. Very well, then. I'm sorry.

ANNE. [*Rushing over to* PETER.] No, Peter! No! [PETER *goes into his room, closing the door after him.* ANNE *turns back to her mother, crying.*] I don't care about the food. They can have mine! I don't want it! Only don't send them away. It'll be daylight soon. They'll be caught…

MARGOT. [*Putting her arms comfortingly around* ANNE.] Please, Mother!

MRS. FRANK. They're not going now. They'll stay here until Miep finds them a place. [*To* MRS. VAN DAAN.] But one thing I insist on! He must never come down here again! He must never come to this room where the food is stored! We'll divide what we have…an equal share for each! [DUSSEL *hurries over to get a sack of potatoes from the food safe.* MRS. FRANK *goes on, to* MRS. VAN DAAN.] You can cook it here and take it up to him. [DUSSEL *brings the sack of potatoes back to the center table.*]

MARGOT. Oh, no. No. We haven't sunk so far that we're going to fight over a handful of rotten potatoes.

DUSSEL. [*Dividing the potatoes into piles.*] Mrs. Frank, Mr. Frank, Margot, Anne, Peter, Mrs. Van Daan, Mr. Van Daan, myself…Mrs.

Frank…

The buzzer sounds in MIEP'S *signal.*

MR. FRANK. It's Miep!

He hurries over, getting his overcoat and putting it on.

MARGOT. At this hour?

MRS. FRANK. It is trouble.

MR. FRANK. [*As he starts down to unbolt the door.*] I beg you, don't let her see a thing like this!

MR. DUSSEL. [*Counting without stopping.*]… Anne, Peter, Mrs. Van Daan, Mr. Van Daan, myself…

MARGOT. [*To* DUSSEL.] Stop it! Stop it!

DUSSEL. …Mr. Frank, Margot, Anne, Peter, Mrs. Van Daan, Mr. Van Daan, myself, Mrs. Frank…

MRS. VAN DAAN. You're keeping the big ones for yourself! All the big ones…Look at the size of that!…And that!…

DUSSEL *continues on with his dividing.* PETER, *with his shirt and trousers on, comes from his room.*

MARGOT. Stop it! Stop it!

We hear MIEP'S *excited voice speaking to* MR. FRANK *below.*

MIEP. Mr. Frank…the most wonderful news!…The invasion has begun! **C**

MR. FRANK. Go on, tell them! Tell them!

MIEP *comes running up the steps, ahead of* MR. FRANK. *She has a man's raincoat on over her nightclothes and a bunch of orange-colored flowers in her hand.*

MIEP. Did you hear that, everybody? Did you hear what I said? The invasion has begun! The invasion!

They all stare at MIEP, *unable to grasp what she is telling them.* PETER *is the first to recover his wits.*

Use Reading Strategies

Visualize Ask students to visualize the scene in which Mr. Dussel is dividing the potatoes. What is each character doing while he does this? Model a response: "All the characters are wearing their nightclothes. Mr. Frank is sitting in the main room, with his head in his hands. Mr. Van Daan is sitting on the couch, and Mrs. Van Daan is near him, bathing his face with water. Peter is in his room. Anne has turned toward her mother and is crying. Margot is trying to comfort Anne by putting her arms around her."

History Connection

D-Day In the early morning hours of June 6, 1944, American, British, and Canadian forces landed on Normandy Beach in France. The invasion from the English side of the English Channel to Normandy was in the planning stage for many months; most of the French coastline was filled with German troops, so the plan was complicated. But, somehow, the Allies managed to keep the time and place of their plan a secret. Allied casualties were greater than expected, but the troops were able to keep pushing ahead because Hitler, convinced that the "real" invasion would take place north of the Seine, refused to send reinforcements to the German troops. The liberation of Amsterdam was less than a year away at this point. If the residents of the annex had avoided detection just a little longer, they would have been saved. **C**

Alternate Ending

Have students imagine an alternate ending, one in which Anne lived a long life. While they're at it, they can go back and write a new beginning for this play, for Otto Frank's visit to the annex would have been a happy event rather than such a sad one. Propose these questions to get students' ideas going:

- What event precipitated the residents' release from the annex?

- Whose tread did they hear coming up the stairs on that final night?
- Where did they go after getting out?
- Where did Anne continue her education?
- How did Anne and Peter's relationship progress?
- What else did Anne write?
- What other interests did Anne pursue?
- What did Anne tell her children about her experiences?

Analyze Literature

Tone Pause to discuss with students the impact of Miep's announcement on the play's tone. Ask them what the tone was prior to her arrival. What sound, in the beginning of Scene 4, drastically changes the tone once again?

Use Reading Skills

Compare and Contrast Have volunteers read aloud the conversation between the residents after Miep leaves. Then have students comment on their reactions to Miep's news about the invasion, comparing the reactions of the characters. Model a response by saying that at first, everyone is excited, but then Mr. Van Daan feels ashamed for stealing the food. Margot reassures him, saying that the theft means nothing now. Mrs. Frank forgives Mr. Van Daan, and Anne is sorry for the way she treated her mother.

PETER. Where?

MRS. VAN DAAN. When? When, Miep?

MIEP. It began early this morning…[*As she talks on, the realization of what she has said begins to dawn on them. Everyone goes crazy. A wild demonstration takes place.* MRS. FRANK *hugs* MR. VAN DAAN.]

MRS. FRANK. Oh, Mr. Van Daan, did you hear that?

DUSSEL *embraces* MRS. VAN DAAN. PETER *grabs a frying pan and parades around the room, beating on it, singing the Dutch National Anthem.* ANNE *and* MARGOT *follow him, singing, weaving in and out among the excited grown-ups.* MARGOT *breaks away to take the flowers from* MIEP *and distribute them to everyone. While this* pandemonium[26] *is going on* MRS. FRANK *tries to make herself heard above the excitement.*

MRS. FRANK. [*To* MIEP.] How do you know?

MIEP. The radio…The B.B.C.![27] They said they landed on the coast of Normandy![28]

PETER. The British?

MIEP. British, Americans, French, Dutch, Poles, Norwegians…all of them! More than four thousand ships! Churchill spoke, and General Eisenhower! D-Day they call it!

MR. FRANK. Thank God, it's come!

MRS. VAN DAAN. At last!

MIEP. [*Starting out.*] I'm going to tell Mr. Kraler. This'll be better than any blood transfusion.

MR. FRANK. [*Stopping her.*] What part of Normandy did they land, did they say?

MIEP. Normandy…that's all I know now…I'll be up the minute I hear some more!

She goes hurriedly out.

MR. FRANK. [*To* MRS. FRANK.] What did I tell you? What did I tell you? [MRS. FRANK *indicates that he has forgotten to bolt the door*

after MIEP. *He hurries down the steps.* MR. VAN DAAN, *sitting on the couch, suddenly breaks into a* convulsive[29] *sob. Everybody looks at him, bewildered.*]

MRS. VAN DAAN. [*Hurrying to him.*] Putti! Putti! What is it? What happened?

MR. VAN DAAN. Please. I'm so ashamed.

MR. FRANK *comes back up the steps.*

DUSSEL. Oh, for God's sake!

MRS. VAN DAAN. Don't, Putti.

MARGOT. It doesn't matter now!

MR. FRANK. [*Going to* MR. VAN DAAN.] Didn't you hear what Miep said? The invasion has come! We're going to be liberated! This is a time to celebrate!

He embraces MRS. FRANK *and then hurries to the cupboard and gets the cognac and a glass.*

MR. VAN DAAN. To steal bread from children!

MRS. FRANK. We've all done things that we're ashamed of.

ANNE. Look at me, the way I've treated Mother…so mean and horrid to her.

MRS. FRANK. No, Anneke, no.

ANNE *runs to her mother, putting her arms around her.*

ANNE. Oh, Mother, I was. I was awful.

MR. VAN DAAN. Not like me. No one is as bad as me!

DUSSEL. [*To* MR. VAN DAAN.] Stop it now! Let's be happy!

MR. FRANK. [*Giving* MR. VAN DAAN *a glass of cognac.*] Here! Here! *Schnapps!*[30] *Locheim!*[31]

---

26. **pandemonium.** Wild uproar; loud celebration
27. **B.B.C.** British Broadcasting Corporation, a radio network
28. **Normandy.** Northwestern region of France. The Allied forces crossed the English Channel from England and landed on the Normandy beaches.
29. **convulsive.** Strong and uncontrolled
30. *Schnapps!* A drink! (German)
31. *Locheim!* To life! (Yiddish toast)

Differentiated Instruction

Enrichment

Interested students can research the history of the planning of D-Day. Suggest that they look up the Casablanca Conference, in which Roosevelt, Churchill, Giraud, and de Gaulle came to an agreement about the "unconditional surrender" of the Axis forces. They can also research the Tehran Conference in November 1943, in which Churchill, Roosevelt, and Stalin planned the invasion of

Western Europe in March of 1944, which turned into June 6 of that year. Suggest that they also research Eisenhower's role in the implementation of the plan. Have them present their findings to the class.

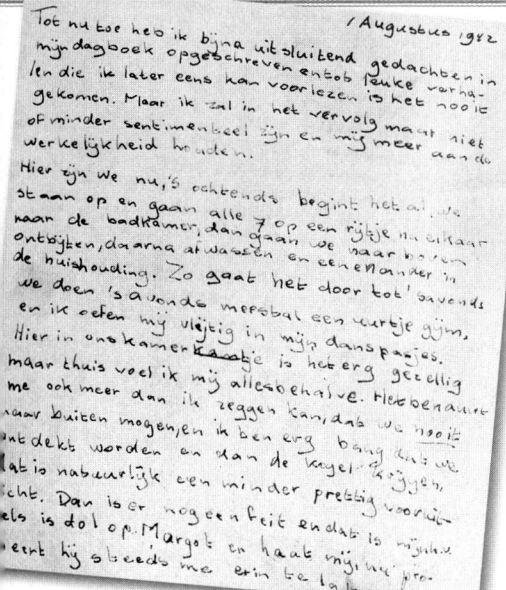
Page from Anne Frank's diary.

VAN DAAN *takes the cognac. They all watch him. He gives them a feeble smile.* ANNE *puts up her fingers in a V-for-Victory sign. As* VAN DAAN *gives an answering V-sign, they are startled to hear a loud sob from behind them. It is* MRS. FRANK, *stricken with remorse. She is sitting on the other side of the room.*

MRS. FRANK. [*Through her sobs.*] When I think of the terrible things I said…

MR. FRANK, ANNE *and* MARGOT *hurry to her, trying to comfort her.* MR. VAN DAAN *brings her his glass of cognac.*

MR. VAN DAAN. No! No! You were right!

MRS. FRANK. That I should speak that way to you!…Our friends! Our guests!

She starts to cry again.

DUSSEL. Stop it, you're spoiling the whole invasion!

As they are comforting her, the lights dim out. The curtain falls.

ANNE'S VOICE. [*Faintly at first and then with growing strength.*] We're all in much better spirits these days. There's still excellent news of the invasion. The best part about it is that I have a feeling that friends are coming. Who knows? Maybe I'll be back in school by fall. Ha, ha! The joke is on us! The warehouse man doesn't know a thing and we are paying him all that money! I…Wednesday, the second of July, nineteen forty-four. The invasion seems temporarily to be bogged down. Mr. Kraler has to have an operation, which looks bad. The Gestapo have found the radio that was stolen. Mr. Dussel says they'll trace it back and back to the thief, and then, it's just a matter of time till they get to us. Everyone is low. Even poor Pim can't raise their spirits. I have often been downcast myself…but never in despair. I can shake off everything if I write. But…and that is the great question…will I ever be able to write well? I want to so much. I want to go on living even after my death. Another birthday has gone by, so now I am fifteen. Already I know what I want. I have a goal, an opinion.

As this is being said—the curtain rises on the scene, the lights dim on, and ANNE'S VOICE *fades out.*

SCENE 4

It is an afternoon a few weeks later…Everyone but MARGOT *is in the main room. There is a sense of great tension.*

Both MRS. FRANK *and* MR. VAN DAAN *are nervously pacing back and forth,* DUSSEL *is standing at the window, looking down fixedly at the street below.* PETER *is at the center table, trying to do his lessons.* ANNE *sits opposite him, writing in her diary.* MRS. VAN DAAN *is seated on the couch, her eyes on* MR. FRANK *as he sits reading.*

The sound of a telephone ringing comes from the office below. They all are rigid,[32] *listening tensely.* MR. DUSSEL *rushes down to* MR. FRANK.

---

32. rigid. Stiff with tension and fear

THE DIARY OF ANNE FRANK, ACT 2   **703**

Teach the Selection

Analyze Literature
Aside Anne's voice acts as an aside—a direct address to the audience that the other characters on the stage supposedly cannot hear. In this aside, she seems confused about how the residents of the annex feel. At first, she says "We're all in much better spirits these days," and later she says "Everyone is low." Still, she is "never in despair." She seems to be optimistic about the future, despite Mr. Dussel's words of doom and gloom. **Ⓐ**

Analyze Literature
Irony Point out the irony of Anne's words: "But . . . and that is the great question . . . will I ever be able to write well? I want to so much. I want to go on living even after my death." Anne would probably have been very surprised to find out about the popularity of her book. **Ⓑ**

Analyze Literature
Plot Point out the importance of the ringing telephone in the development of the plot. It serves as a turning point, changing the somewhat upbeat mood of the previous scene into a mood of tension and fear. **Ⓒ**

Writing Skills

Revision

An important step in the writing process is revision. Have partners exchange the papers they started for the assignment on page 695 and conduct a peer review, answering questions like these:
- Does the paper follow a clear method of organization?
- Are the paragraphs arranged in logical order?
- Are sentences and paragraphs joined with adequate transitions?
- Does the paper have a balance in types of sentences—simple, compound, complex, compound-complex?
- Is the language lively?

Students can base their revisions on the answers to these questions.

Analyze Literature
Conflict Point out that the conflict faced by the residents is whether or not to pick up the phone. What argument does each person offer in favor or against the idea? **A**

Make Connections
Ask students to put themselves in the place of the residents of the annex. They might recall that Mr. Kraler has been sick and was scheduled for an operation. Would that explain the phone call? What would they have done if the phone started ringing on a Friday? Why? **B**

Analyze Literature
Resolution Point out that the fact that the phone stops ringing is the resolution of the conflict between the residents. **C**

DUSSEL. There it goes again, the telephone! Mr. Frank, do you hear?

MR. FRANK. [*Quietly.*] Yes. I hear.

A **DUSSEL.** [*Pleading, insistent.*] But this is the third time, Mr. Frank! The third time in quick succession! It's a signal! I tell you it's Miep, trying to get us! For some reason she can't come to us and she's trying to warn us of something!

MR. FRANK. Please. Please.

MR. VAN DAAN. [*To* DUSSEL.] You're wasting your breath.

B **DUSSEL.** Something has happened, Mr. Frank. For three days now Miep hasn't been to see us! And today not a man has come to work. There hasn't been a sound in the building!

MRS. FRANK. Perhaps it's Sunday. We may have lost track of the days.

MR. VAN DAAN. [*To* ANNE.] You with the diary there. What day is it?

DUSSEL. [*Going to* MRS. FRANK.] I don't lose track of the days! I know exactly what day it is! It's Friday, the fourth of August. Friday, and not a man at work. [*He rushes back to* MR. FRANK, *pleading with him, almost in tears.*] I tell you Mr. Kraler's dead. That's the only explanation. He's dead and they've closed down the building, and Miep's trying to tell us!

MR. FRANK. She'd never telephone us.

DUSSEL. [*Frantic.*] Mr. Frank, answer that! I beg you, answer it!

MR. FRANK. No.

MR. VAN DAAN. Just pick it up and listen. You don't have to speak. Just listen and see if it's Miep.

DUSSEL. [*Speaking at the same time.*] For God's sake…I ask you.

MR. FRANK. No. I've told you, no. I'll do nothing that might let anyone know we're in

the building.

PETER. Mr. Frank's right.

MR. VAN DAAN. There's no need to tell us what side you're on.

MR. FRANK. If we wait patiently, quietly, I believe that help will come.

There is silence for a minute as they all listen to the telephone ringing.

DUSSEL. I'm going down.

C [*He rushes down the steps.* MR. FRANK *tries* ineffectually *to hold him.* DUSSEL *runs to the lower door, unbolting it. The telephone stops ringing.* DUSSEL *bolts the door and comes slowly back up the steps.*] Too late. [MR. FRANK *goes to* MARGOT *in* ANNE's *bedroom.*]

MR. VAN DAAN. So we just wait here until we die.

MRS. VAN DAAN. [*Hysterically.*] I can't stand it! I'll kill myself! I'll kill myself!

MR. VAN DAAN. For God's sake, stop it!

In the distance, a German military band is heard playing a Viennese waltz.

MRS. VAN DAAN. I think you'd be glad if I did! I think you want me to die!

MR. VAN DAAN. Whose fault is it we're here? [MRS. VAN DAAN *starts for her room. He follows, talking at her.*] We could've been safe somewhere…in America or Switzerland. But no! no! You wouldn't leave when I wanted to. You couldn't leave your things. You couldn't leave your precious furniture.

MRS. VAN DAAN. Don't touch me!

She hurries up the stairs, followed by MR. VAN DAAN. PETER, *unable to bear it, goes to his room.* ANNE *looks after him, deeply concerned.* DUSSEL *returns to his post at the window.* MR. FRANK *comes back into the main room and takes a book,*

> **in·ef·fec·tu·al·ly** (iˈ nə fekˊ chə[wə] lē) *adv.*, without success

---

Differentiated Instruction

English Language Learning
Take this opportunity to discuss contractions with students. Tell them that a contraction is a shortened version of a word or words, with the apostrophe replacing the missing letter or letters. Here are a few examples that appear on pages 704 and 705:

   it's (it is)
   can't (cannot)
   she's (she is)

you're (you are)
don't (do not)
aren't (are not)
they've (they have)
you'd (you would)
we're (we are)

Have students find other contractions in the play and write their meanings.

trying to read. MRS. FRANK *sits near the sink, starting to peel some potatoes.* ANNE *quietly goes to* PETER's *room, closing the door after her.* PETER *is lying face down on the cot.* ANNE *leans over him, holding him in her arms, trying to bring him out of his despair.*

ANNE. Look, Peter, the sky. [*She looks up through the skylight.*] What a lovely, lovely day! Aren't the clouds beautiful? You know what I do when it seems as if I couldn't stand being cooped up for one more minute? I think myself out. I *think* myself on a walk in the park where I used to go with Pim. Where the jonquils and the crocus and the violets grow down the slopes. You know the most wonderful part about *thinking* yourself out? You can have it any way you like. You can have roses and violets and chrysanthemums all blooming at the same time…It's funny… I used to take it all for granted…and now I've gone crazy about everything to do with nature. Haven't you?

PETER. I've just gone crazy. I think if something doesn't happen soon…if we don't get out of here…I can't stand much more of it!

ANNE. [*Softly.*] I wish you had a religion, Peter.

PETER. No, thanks! Not me!

ANNE. Oh, I don't mean you have to be Orthodox…or believe in heaven and hell and purgatory[33] and things…I just mean some religion…it doesn't matter what. Just to believe in something! When I think of all that's out there…the trees…and flowers… and seagulls…when I think of the dearness of you, Peter…and the goodness of the people we know…Mr. Kraler, Miep, Dirk, the vegetable man, all risking their lives for us every day…When I think of these good things, I'm not afraid any more…I find myself, and God, and I…

PETER *interrupts, getting up and walking away.*

PETER. That's fine! But when I begin to think, I get mad! Look at us, hiding out for two years. Not able to move! Caught here like… waiting for them to come and get us…and all for what?

ANNE. We're not the only people that've had to suffer. There've always been people that've had to…sometimes one race…sometimes another…and yet…

PETER. That doesn't make me feel any better!

ANNE. [*Going to him.*] I know it's terrible, trying to have any faith…when people are doing such horrible…But you know what I sometimes think? I think the world may be going through a phase, the way I was with Mother. It'll pass, maybe not for hundreds of years, but some day…I still believe, in spite of everything, that people are really good at heart.

PETER. I want to see something now…Not a thousand years from now!

He goes over, sitting down again on the cot.

ANNE. But, Peter, if you'd only look at it as part of a great pattern…that we're just a little minute in the life…[*She breaks off.*] Listen to us, going at each other like a couple of stupid grown-ups! Look at the sky now. Isn't it lovely? [*She holds out her hand to him.* PETER *takes it and rises, standing with her at the window looking out, his arms around her.*] Some day, when we're outside again, I'm going to…

She breaks off as she hears the sound of a car, its brakes squealing as it comes to a sudden stop. The people in the other rooms also become aware of the sound. They listen tensely. Another car roars up to a screeching stop. ANNE *and* PETER

---

33. **purgatory.** According to some religions, the immediate but temporary place where one goes after death, in order to atone, or pay for, one's sins

THE DIARY OF ANNE FRANK, ACT 2 **705**

Teach the Selection

Use Reading Skills
Read Aloud Have students close their eyes and listen as two volunteers read this conversation between Anne and Peter. Then ask students to describe in their own words how Anne tries to help Peter cope with the situation. Model a response by saying that she tells Peter how she uses her imagination to escape the confines of the annex and suggests that he try it, too. Then she talks to him about the comfort religion offers her.

Analyze Literature
Mood Remind students that mood is the overall emotional atmosphere in a scene or a passage. Here, the mood suddenly changes. In one moment, Anne and Peter are enjoying, as much as possible, the elements of nature that they can see through the skylight. The next moment, the mood changes to one of fear and tension, as soon as the car comes to a screeching stop outside. **D**

Writing Skills

Peer Feedback
Peer feedback is a useful element in the revision process. Have students consider what their peer reviewers said in the activity on page 703. They can ask themselves questions like these:
- Do I agree with my partner's assessment?
- Will this change improve my paper?

Remind students that revision is perhaps the most important step in writing. In this stage, the writer rethinks his or her ideas to see if they hold up. The word itself comes from the Latin *vis*, meaning "to see," so the reviser takes a second, third, fourth, and fifth (maybe more!) look at the work to see if it can be improved.

THE DIARY OF ANNE FRANK, ACT 2 **705**

Analyze Literature

Flashforward Point out that the last scene of Act 2, like the first scene of Act 1, takes place three years beyond the events related in Anne's diary. In a sense, this can be seen as a flash-forward. Another way to look at it is to see Anne's reminiscences in the diary as a flashback from Mr. Frank's point of view in the first scene. **Ⓐ**

Analyze Literature

Tragedy Inform students of the definition of tragedy: a drama, in prose or verse, relating important events in the life of a person of significance, with those events ending in an unhappy catastrophe and the whole story being treated with great dignity and seriousness. Ask: "Does this play meet the definition of tragedy?"

---

come from PETER's *room.* MR. *and* MRS. VAN DAAN *creep down the stairs.* DUSSEL *comes out from his room. Everyone is listening, hardly breathing. A doorbell clangs again and again in the building below.* MR. FRANK *starts quietly down the steps to the door.* DUSSEL *and* PETER *follow him. The others stand rigid, waiting, terrified.*

In a few seconds DUSSEL *comes stumbling back up the steps. He shakes off* PETER's *help and goes to his room.* MR. FRANK *bolts the door below, and comes slowly back up the steps. Their eyes are all on him as he stands there for a minute. They realize that what they feared has happened.* MRS. VAN DAAN *starts to whimper.* MR. VAN DAAN *puts her gently in a chair, and then hurries off up the stairs to their room to collect their things.* PETER *goes to comfort his mother. There is a sound of violent pounding on a door below.*

MR. FRANK. [*Quietly.*] For the past two years we have lived in fear. Now we can live in hope. [*The pounding below becomes more insistent. There are muffled sounds of voices, shouting commands.*]

MEN'S VOICES. *Auf machen! Da drinnen! Auf machen! Schnell! Schnell! Schnell!*[34] *etc., etc.*

The street door below is forced open. We hear the heavy tread of footsteps coming up. MR. FRANK *gets two school bags from the shelves, and gives one to* ANNE *and the other to* MARGOT. *He goes to get a bag for* MRS. FRANK. *The sound of feet coming up grows louder.* PETER *comes to* ANNE, *kissing her good-bye, then he goes to his room to collect his things. The buzzer of their door starts to ring.* MR. FRANK *brings* MRS. FRANK *a bag. They stand together, waiting. We hear the thud of gun butts on the door, trying to break it down.*

ANNE *stands, holding her school satchel, looking over at her father and mother with a soft, reassuring smile. She is no longer a child, but a woman with courage to meet whatever lies ahead.*

The lights dim out. The curtain falls on the scene. We hear a mighty crash as the door is shattered. After a second ANNE's VOICE *is heard.*

ANNE'S VOICE. And so it seems our stay here is over. They are waiting for us now. They've allowed us five minutes to get our things. We can each take a bag and whatever it will hold of clothing. Nothing else. So, dear Diary, that means I must leave you behind. Good-bye for a while. P.S. Please, please, Miep, or Mr. Kraler, or anyone else. If you should find this diary, will you please keep it safe for me, because some day I hope…

Her voice stops abruptly. There is silence. After a second the curtain rises.

SCENE 5

Ⓐ *It is again the afternoon in November, 1945. The rooms are as we saw them in the first scene.* MR. KRALER *has joined* MIEP *and* MR. FRANK. *There are coffee cups on the table. We see a great change in* MR. FRANK. *He is calm now. His bitterness is gone. He slowly turns a few pages of the diary. They are blank.*

MR. FRANK. No more.

He closes the diary and puts it down on the couch beside him.

MIEP. I'd gone to the country to find food. When I got back the block was surrounded by police…

MR. KRALER. We made it our business to learn how they knew. It was the thief…the thief who told them.

MIEP *goes up to the gas burner, bringing back a pot of coffee.*

MR. FRANK. [*After a pause.*] It seems strange to say this, that anyone could be happy in a concentration camp. But Anne was happy in the camp in Holland where they first took us. After two years of being shut up in these

---

34. ***Auf machen! Da drinnen! Auf machen! Schnell! Schnell! Schnell!*** Open up! You in there! Open up! Hurry! Hurry! Hurry! (German)

TEACHING NOTE

Self-Generated Questioning

Invite students to generate questions about the selection, and gather the questions into a container. Model a question such as: "What did Mr. Frank do after returning to the annex?" Divide the class into two teams. Ask a student from Team A to select a question and then illustrate an answer to the question. If the other members of Team A can guess the question in two minutes, they get five points. If they are unable to guess correctly, invite the other team to make an attempt, and if it succeeds, it gets five points. Then invite a student from Team B to choose a question and illustrate the answer. Go back and forth between teams until all students have had a chance to illustrate an answer.

rooms, she could be out...out in the sunshine and the fresh air that she loved.

MIEP. [*Offering the coffee to* MR. FRANK.] A little more?

MR. FRANK. [*Holding out his cup to her.*] The news of the war was good. The British and Americans were sweeping through France. We felt sure that they would get to us in time. In September we were told that we were to be shipped to Poland...The men to one camp. The women to another. I was sent to Auschwitz.[35] They went to Belsen.[36] In January we were freed, the few of us who were left. The war wasn't yet over, so it took us a long time to get home. We'd be sent here and there behind the lines where we'd be safe. Each time our train would stop...at a siding, or a crossing...we'd all get out and go from group to group...Where were you? Were you at Belsen? At Buchenwald?[37] At Mauthausen? Is it possible that you knew my wife? Did you ever see my husband? My son? My daughter? That's how I found out about my wife's death...of Margot, the Van Daans...Dussel. But Anne...I still hoped... Yesterday I went to Rotterdam. I'd heard of a woman there...She'd been in Belsen with Anne...I know now.

He picks up the diary again, and turns the pages back to find a certain passage. As he finds it we hear ANNE'S VOICE.

ANNE'S VOICE. In spite of everything, I still believe that people are really good at heart.

MR. FRANK *slowly closes the diary.*

MR. FRANK. She puts me to shame. [*They are silent.*]

The Curtain Falls ✦

35. **Auschwitz.** Nazi concentration camp in Poland, where many Jews were killed
36. **Belsen.** Bergen-Belsen, a Nazi concentration camp in Germany, also a death camp
37. **Buchenwald.** Another Nazi concentration and death camp in Germany

Anne says, "In spite of everything, I still believe that people are really good at heart." Given the situation that she and her family—as well as many other Jews—are in, would you agree with her statement? What do you think is the value of such an outlook?

Find Meaning

1. (a) At the beginning of Act 2, what argument occurs regarding the cake that Miep brings? (b) What probably leads the people to argue over something that seems unimportant?

2. (a) What goals does Anne have for the future? (b) In what ways might having such goals be helpful to her?

3. (a) In Act 2, how does the relationship between Anne and Peter change? (b) Which characters are not pleased with this change, and why might they feel that way?

4. (a) What does Mr. Van Daan do that angers the other residents of the annex? (b) What does Mr. Frank mean when he says, "We don't need the Nazis to destroy us. We're destroying ourselves"?

5. (a) Toward the end of Act 2, Miep rushes in with the news of the Allied invasion on D-Day. How do the characters react? (b) How might this reaction prove to be ironic a few weeks later? Explain.

Make Judgments

6. Mr. Frank ends the drama with the line, "She puts me to shame." What does he mean?

7. How might this drama make a statement about younger and older generations? Explain.

THE DIARY OF ANNE FRANK, ACT 2   **707**

Teach the Selection

Answer: Her remark suggests that she somehow is able to hold optimistic, positive feelings about people in general, despite the tragic cruelty of the Holocaust.

Find Meaning

1. (a) They argue over who will cut the cake. (b) Their stressful living conditions.
2. (a) She wants to be a journalist. (b) They give her hope that she will survive the war.
3. (a) Their friendship deepens into a romance, and they enjoy sharing their thoughts and feelings. (b) Mrs. Van Daan might fear that Peter will be hurt, and Mrs. Frank may feel that it is not "ladylike."
4. (a) He steals food. (b) The anger and tension they create are destroying their friendships and sense of common good.
5. (a) Their spirits return and they believe they will survive. (b) All of them die except Mr. Frank.

Make Judgments

6. He refers to her optimistic attitude. Because he has lost his entire family and is aware of the cruelty of the Holocaust, he cannot share in her optimism.
7. Anne, by example, could have taught the adults many lessons about human behavior. She differs from the adults in that she has optimistic, generous feelings for others.

Grammar Skills

Run-ons

Remind students that a run-on is two sentences that are joined by a comma rather than by the correct punctuation of a period, a semicolon, or a comma and a coordinating conjunction. Have students identify the correct sentences and the run-ons in these examples:

1. Miep visited, she brought a cake.
2. Mr. Van Daan was hungry, so he started stealing food.
3. Mrs. Frank caught him, she wanted him to leave immediately.
4. Anne tried to help Peter; she told him how she coped.
5. Mr. Frank revisited the annex. He was overcome with grief.

Teach the Connection

Literary Connection
Literature by Holocaust Survivors
Although Anne Frank's diary is the most famous piece of literature to come out of the Holocaust, other works exist that describe that tragic time. Among the works written by Holocaust survivors are the autobiographical *Night* and *One Generation After* by Elie Weisel, the novel *The Painted Bird* by Jerzy Kosinski, the memoirs *Survival in Auschwitz* by Primo Levi and *The Lost Childhood* by Yehuda Nir, and, of course, this autobiography by Gerda Weissmann Klein.

Use Reading Strategies
Make Predictions Have students predict what happens next. What do they think the noise outside means? Have the liberators arrived, or is something bad about to happen? **Ⓐ**

History Connection
Frau Kuegler The author says elsewhere that at Bolkenhain she met a Nazi who saved her life. This woman, Frau Kuegler, was one of only two Nazis that Klein met in six years who exhibited any kindness or compassion. Klein was sick and at the camp hospital when Frau Kuegler dragged her out of bed and back to the factory, put her in front of her loom (Bolkenhain was a weaving plant), and started it. Even though Klein was "delirious with fever," she passed the inspection of the SS man who was looking for sick people to send to the gas chambers. **Ⓑ**

from All But My Life

An Autobiography by Gerda Weissmann Klein

The sirens began to howl more and more frequently. The Germans threw frightened glances toward the sky and hatefully looked at us. Let them worry now, we gloated. Let them sit on the charred remains of their homes. Let them see their families killed. Then will they shout "Heil Hitler!"? **Ⓐ**

"It's coming," whispered my heart. "Their downfall is coming!" But I was not naïve. I knew that it would not come without increased suffering on our part.

Christmas passed. There was no Christmas spirit that year. The new year came—the year of 1945.

In January the sirens blew almost daily. Less and less production was entered into the books. At noon one day the electricity went off. The supervisors stood talking excitedly. The SS women took us back to camp. Something drastic had happened. Perhaps the war was over.

That night we were ordered to take all our belongings and go into the dining hall. The door to our sleeping quarters was barricaded. After being given food we huddled together, waiting.

It was snowing heavily. After a time we heard the courtyard gates burst open. Every heart beat faster in expectation. There were shrieks and screams and cries outside. We could hear running feet and shouting from the other side of the barricaded doors. Those of us who sat next to the doors started calling to the newcomers in our sleeping quarters.

They were Jewish girls. They had come from another camp and had been walking for five days. Now we were to join them. They thought we were going to Oranienburg, a concentration camp like Auschwitz, to be gassed. Auschwitz, they said, had been captured by the Russians, who had reconquered Poland and were crossing the German frontier. The English and Americans were invading Germany from the West. Would a miracle happen before we reached the gas chambers?

And so the last stretch of the war began. Not in peaceful Bolkenhain, not in the coal cars of Märzdorf, the night shifts of Landeshut. Nor were we to endure it in **Ⓑ**

Words in Use

from *All But My Life*

Teaching Words
gloated, 708
charred, 708
naïve, 708
barricaded, 708

Common Core State Standards

Writing
W.10

Language
L.6

Differentiated Instruction

Enrichment
Interested students may wish to learn more about Gerda Weissmann Klein. The U.S. Holocaust Museum has a website where they can hear her voice as she recalls her experiences. They can also hear the voice of her husband, the man who was one of the first two liberators to arrive at the camp where she was being held. Have students report on their findings to the class.

tuberculosis-ridden Grünberg. I was certain that we would meet freedom somewhere in the open, and that we would meet it soon.

"You are crazy!" Suse said. "We will never see the liberation, for they will see to it. They would leave us here if they did not want us killed."

"We will be free," I insisted. "I know it, I feel it."

Ilse and Liesel sat in silence. Suse's big eyes filled with tears, the first tears that I ever saw her shed.

"How can you believe so strongly?" she murmured. "But then, you always believed. Remember when we met on the train?"

I nodded.

"Well, you lost that bet," she reminded me. **C**

"I know," I said.

"But you still believe?"

"I do!"

"Tell me, Gerda," Suse whispered urgently, "what is it? What makes you so sure?"

"I don't know. It's something I cannot explain, but I know somehow that we will be liberated." **D**

"And I feel," Suse stammered, "I feel that I will not be."

All that last night in Grünberg I coughed. I think I had a temperature. Ilse, Suse, Liesel, and I cuddled together closely.

"Gerda, don't get sick," they begged, as if I could decide.

At dawn we were given three portions of bread, which we carefully placed in our bundles. We saw the kitchen personnel pack big parcels of food in their bundles.

At the last moment before we assembled, the four of us decided to put on most of the

German soldiers.

ALL BUT MY LIFE **709**

Teach the Connection

TEACHING NOTE

Speculate
Ask students to speculate on the bet Suse is talking about. Model a response by suggesting that Klein might have bet that they would be liberated from the Nazis after just a short time or that none of the prisoners would be killed or that the prisoners would be given good food and provided with adequate sanitation facilities. Remind them that it has to be a bet that Klein would have lost. **C**

Analyze Literature
Narrator Ask students what this statement reveals about the narrator's personality and character. Model a response: "This statement by the narrator reveals that she has a positive outlook despite the dire circumstances under which she has been forced to live." **D**

Use Reading Skills
Read Aloud Have partners take turns reading sections of the selection aloud while the other reads along silently. Remind them that as they read aloud they should adjust their fluency rates based on the nature of the section of text they are reading and their purpose for reading it. They can stop at intervals to summarize the material, helping each other answer any questions they might have.

Reading Skills

Distinguish Fact from Opinion
Point out to students that good readers stop from time to time to evaluate the accuracy of what they are reading. Here are some questions they might ask themselves:
- Can I picture in my mind what the author is saying?
- What do I already know about the situation?
- Based on my prior knowledge, are the author's claims believable?
- Have other people told similar stories of the events of this time?
- Do we have historical evidence of the accuracy of the story?

Suggest that students use these guidelines as they evaluate the accuracy of what they read.

Polish women being led by soldiers through woods to execution.

Make Connections

Ask students to imagine being in the position of the girls who tried to shift from one group to the other. What criteria might they use to determine which is the better group? Would their choices be logical or emotional? **A**

Use Reading Skills

Compare and Contrast Ask students to consider how the girls who have just arrived compare with those who are already at the camp. What is alike about the two groups? What is different? Challenge students to recall specific physical differences from the text, as well as to infer mental and emotional differences. **B**

clothes we had intended to carry.

The SS women came for us. We lined up. Ilse was on my left, Liesel and Suse were on my right. We stood erect.

"Let us be strong," Liesel whispered.

"Yes," I answered.

"You be strong," Ilse whispered back to me. I was now the least fit of the group.

As we squeezed through the door, we gripped hands for a fleeting moment. Then we marched out into the bright snow.

The outer gates were open when we reached the courtyard. Stretching as far as we could see were columns of girls. I was shocked to see so many. We learned later there were about three thousand from other camps; with our contingent from Grünberg we totaled nearly four thousand. We were divided into two transports amidst much **A** whipping and screaming by the SS. Many girls tried to shift from one group to another, in the hope that it might be the better one.

We four were in the column which was doomed; out of two thousand only a hundred and twenty survived. The other column was liberated much sooner. Had I been part of it my fate would have been different. Less suffering, yes, but less happiness, too, I am sure.

Although I had seen misery, I was utterly unprepared for the picture that the girls who had already been marching for a week presented. Covered with gray blankets, they reminded me of drawings of Death when, **B** winged and garbed in loose sheets, he comes to collect the living. Some of them were barefoot, others wore crude wooden clogs. Many of them left a bloody trail in the fresh snow.

Suse looked at me and I looked at my feet—clad in the ski boots that Papa had insisted I wear on that hot summer day. Papa, Papa, how could he possibly have known. The boots were still in good shape, and I had precious things hidden in them: snapshots of Papa, Mama, Arthur, and Abek, wrapped in a piece of cloth, and the packet of poison. In Grünberg they had taken away all pictures, papers, and letters. Germany, we were told, needed all scrap paper she could get. Ilse and I had managed to hide our pictures. Our only worry now was that water might soak through our shoes and ruin them.

"Forward march!" shouted the SS *Wachtmeister* at the head of our column.

"Forward march!" echoed SS men.

710 **UNIT 7** DRAMA

English Language Learning

Help students understand the selection by providing definitions of difficult words, such as these:

drastic—very severe or forceful; extreme, 708
liberation—the act of setting free, 709
urgently—in a demanding or insistent manner, 709

contingent—group making up part of a larger group, 710
misery—condition of great suffering, 710
garbed—dressed, 710

Carrying rifles, they were stationed along our column at intervals of about thirty feet.

"Forward march!" came the high-pitched voices of the whip-armed SS women.

We took the first step. I thought: I am marching to death or to liberation. It was the morning of January 29, 1945.

We marched all day, with a break at noon. Ilse and I shared one of our portions of bread, guarding the rest carefully. At the head of the column we saw the commandant of the SS with a Hungarian-Jewish girl who, we were told, was his mistress. She and a few of her close friends knew no want; they had plenty to eat, and slept always in peasant houses, rather than in barns or in open fields as the others did.

"How could they?" I asked myself over and over again.

Toward evening, as it grew colder, we were herded off the road and into a huge barn. We huddled together in the darkness and again Ilse and I shared a portion of our bread. It wasn't enough.

"Ilse, I am terribly hungry," I confessed.

"So am I," Ilse admitted. "I would like something warm to drink. We can't eat any more bread, for who knows when they will give us more?"

"Careful, careful!" somebody called in the darkness. "The Magyars are after our bread."

Yes, the poor Hungarian girls were hungry. They had been marching a week already.

"My shoes, my shoes!" another voice cried. "They took them from right next to me!"

Many of the Hungarian girls had no shoes. To save their lives they stole shoes off the feet of those who slept. How much I learned that night!

When the doors of the dark barn were thrown open in the morning I could see a flood of wintry sunlight on the glittering snow. Two SS men stood at the entrance and with their rifles prodded us as we emerged four abreast.

A little distance away stood the SS commandant with his girl friend and her court of privileged friends. They were eating bread and drinking something steaming out of a large thermos. How good it must feel, I thought, the warm drink in that cold!

We assembled and were counted and recounted. A girl from Grünberg was missing. A few others were beaten bloody because of it, but either they did not know what had become of her or they would not tell.

We learned the story later. A German from the factory who was in love with the girl had followed our column, and under cover of darkness had snatched her quietly away.

We marched many miles that second day, often plowing through untouched snow. Again we rested at midday.

"I wonder when they will give us something to eat," Ilse said to the three of us as we nibbled our dry, frozen bread.

We did not answer.

Girls who had lagged behind that morning had been beaten by the SS men with the butts of their guns.

After the midday pause, a couple of girls just sat motionless on the snow, refusing to go. We marched on. Behind us there were pistol shots.

"God!" I said, "God!" looking up to the sky. The sky was blue, the snow was clean, the snowy pine trees were beautiful in the sunlight. ❖

History Connection

1945 Death March From January to April of 1945, thousands of prisoners were forced on marches of up to a thousand miles, insufficiently clothed for the extremely cold weather and already weakened by the terrible conditions of the concentration camps. Many died along the way from cold, disease, and exhaustion. Those who couldn't keep up with the others were shot on the spot and left by the side of the road. The Germans had several reasons for this forced march. First, the Allies were closing in on the German strongholds in Europe. As Britain and the United States approached from the west, the Soviet Union was coming from the east. The Nazis wanted to destroy evidence of the atrocities they had committed at the camps, so they moved prisoners and destroyed evidence. **C**

Use Reading Skills

Compare and Contrast What is the difference between what the author sees in nature and what she is experiencing at the hands of the Nazis? Model a response by suggesting that nature exhibits the beauty of a winter landscape, a visual delight under normal circumstances. But what is happening to the prisoners goes against the natural order; there is nothing natural or normal about the relationship between the prisoners and the SS guards. **D**

Graphic Organizers

Remind students that as they conduct research, it is helpful to organize it in appropriate ways. One way is to write information on separate index cards, which can then be arranged and rearranged in whatever order works best for the presentation. This method is effective when preparing a research paper. However, for a multi-media presentation, several other methods of organizing research work well. Here are some of them:

- Venn diagrams (for comparing and contrasting information)
- Pie charts
- Bar graphs
- Charts with columns
- Sequence charts
- K-W-L charts

Review the Selection

Text-to-Text Connection

Answer: How they are alike: They are both female Jewish teenagers. The Nazis sent both of them to concentration camps. Anne: She is German. She goes into hiding when the Nazis begin sending Jews to concentration camps. She does not survive the war. Gerda: She is Polish. Early in the war, she and her family are sent to a concentration camp. Her family dies, but she survives.

Analyze Literature

Plot Diagrams will vary.

<u>Climax:</u> Act 2, Scene 4. As Anne tries to comfort Peter, they hear a car stop outside. All those in the annex realize that German soldiers have discovered them.

<u>Falling Action:</u> Act 2, Scene 4. The characters prepare to be taken away, Peter kisses Anne goodbye, the soldiers break down the door.

<u>Resolution:</u> Act 2, Scene 5. The action returns to the present. Mr. Kraler joins Miep and Mr. Frank. Mr. Frank has come to terms with his loss. Anne's voice repeats the drama's theme: "In spite of everything, I still believe that people are really good at heart."

TEXT ←TO→ TEXT
CONNECTION

Gerda Weissmann Klein and Anne Frank were both young Jewish women caught in the tragedy of the Holocaust. Their situations were both similar and different. Using specific details and evidence from the text, create a Venn diagram to compare and contrast the events and experiences of their lives.

> **AFTER READING**

Analyze Literature

Plot Return to the plot diagram you began at the end of *The Diary of Anne Frank,* Act 1. What part or parts of the plot took place in Act 2? For each plot part you identify, write the act and scene number on your diagram. In addition, include a brief description of the action that occurred during that part of the plot.

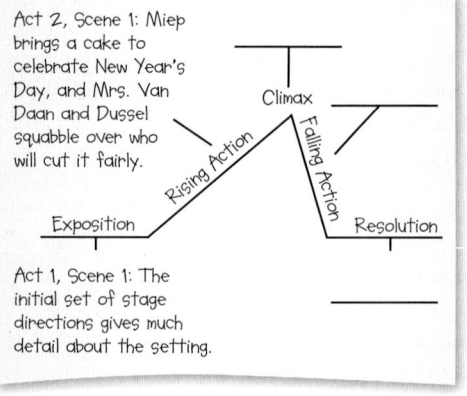

Act 2, Scene 1: Miep brings a cake to celebrate New Year's Day, and Mrs. Van Daan and Dussel squabble over who will cut it fairly.

Climax
Rising Action
Falling Action
Exposition
Resolution

Act 1, Scene 1: The initial set of stage directions gives much detail about the setting.

Extend Understanding

Writing Options

Creative Writing What are your thoughts and feelings toward Anne Frank, having read the drama and the excerpts from her diary? Write a **personal letter** to her to share your thoughts about her experiences and to comment on her diary.

Applied Writing Use Internet and library resources to find additional information about Anne Frank and the Anne Frank House in Amsterdam, Holland. Use a style guide to create a **bibliography** or Works Cited list.

Collaborative Learning

Analyze Conflict As you know, the plot of a piece of literature is the series of events that take place. The plot begins with exposition; then rises to a climax, the point of highest tension; and falls to the resolution, the final outcome. In small groups, identify and discuss the major and minor conflicts in the play. Determine if and how each conflict was resolved, and share your findings with the class.

Lifelong Learning

Research the Holocaust Visit the Holocaust Museum online. Use an Internet search engine to locate the site. Look at images, and read online materials related to the Holocaust. Then write a brief essay to relate your thoughts and feelings about what you saw and learned.

 Go to www.mirrorsandwindows.com for more.

Rubrics for Writing Options

You can adapt this as a checklist for students to use as they write.

Creative Writing
☐ Does the letter effectively express the student's thoughts and feelings regarding Anne's experiences?
☐ Does it include details from her life?

Applied Writing
☐ Does the bibliography or Works Cited list show evidence of a thorough effort to find sources of further information regarding Anne Frank?
☐ Does it contain both library and reliable Internet sources?
☐ Does each entry conform to the standard rules for bibliographies or Works Cited lists?

Grammar & Style

Sentence Fragments and Run-on Sentences

Sentence Fragments

MR. FRANK: *This is the way we must live until it is over, if we are to survive.*

MRS. FRANK: *Until it is over.*

— FRANCES GOODRICH AND ALBERT HACKETT,
The Diary of Anne Frank

A sentence contains a subject and a verb and should express a complete thought. A **sentence fragment** is a phrase or clause that does not express a complete thought but that has been punctuated as though it did. In the quotation above, *Until it is over* is a sentence fragment. The clause does not express a complete thought.

Writers sometimes use sentence fragments deliberately, as in the above quotation. Some sentences fragments, such as *Keep them* or *Pick that up!* have an implied subject (you). Questions such as *Where?* or *Why?* are sentence fragments that rely on context for their meaning. With exceptions such as these, sentence fragments should be avoided. Correct fragments by replacing the missing parts.

EXAMPLES	
complete sentence	*The curtain rises on an empty stage.*
sentence fragment	*Rises on an empty stage.* [missing subject]
sentence fragment	*The curtain on an empty stage.* [missing verb]

Run-On Sentences

A **run-on sentence** is made up of two or more sentences that have been run together as if they were one complete thought.

Correct run-on sentences as follows:

- Divide the sentence into separate sentences. Mark the end of each idea with a period, question mark, or exclamation point.
- If the two sentences are very closely related, use a semicolon to join them.

EXAMPLES	
run-on sentence	*Mr. Frank, did you <u>see</u> <u>there</u> are some of your papers here.*
corrected sentences	*Mr. Frank, did you <u>see?</u> <u>There</u> are some of your papers here.*
run-on sentence	*I'm not the person you used to know, <u>Miep</u> <u>I'm</u> a bitter old man.*
corrected sentence	*I'm not the person you used to know, Miep; I'm a bitter old man.*

Understanding Sentence Fragments and Run-ons

Identify each of the following as a sentence fragment or run-on sentence. Then rewrite each sentence correctly.

1. I feel fine I'm going to help Father.
2. In the school yard.
3. Go out at nighttime?
4. It isn't safe no, you must never go beyond that door.
5. Mr. Otto Frank?
6. The address that you left.
7. Mr. Dussel welcome we're very honored to have you with us.
8. To put in your ears so you won't hear me.

GRAMMAR & STYLE **713**

Preview the Selection

At a Glance
Reading model
- Reading Level: Challenging
- Difficulty Considerations: Vocabulary, length
- Ease Factor: Compelling plot

Objectives
Reading this selection will enable students to do the following:
- read with developing fluency
- read silently with comprehension for a sustained period of time

Launch the Lesson
Tell students that they are about to read "Sorry, Right Number," a screenplay about an impossible event. Ask students to give examples of impossible events that often form the basis of horror and science fiction tales. List their ideas on the board. Later, they can compare their list to the event dreamed up by Stephen King.

TEACHING NOTE

Although this selection is presented in the student edition as an independent reading, teaching support has been provided should you choose to cover it in class.

Author's Note: Screenplay abbreviations are simple and exist, in this author's opinion, mostly to make those who write screenplays feel like lodge brothers. In any case, you should be aware that CU means close-up; ECU means extreme close-up; INT. means interior; EXT. means exterior; B.G. means background; POV means point of view. Probably most of you knew all that stuff to begin with, right?

CHARACTERS

KATIE
BILL
POLLY
DENNIS   } THE WEIDERMANS
CONNIE
JEFF
SOBBING VOICE
FRIEDA
KATIE'S MOTHER
OPERATOR   } VOICES
MINISTER
ANNOUNCER
DAWN
GROUNDSKEEPER
HANK
GROOM AND ASSORTED WEDDING GUESTS

ACT 1
FADE IN ON:
KATIE WEIDERMAN'S MOUTH, ECU
She's speaking into the telephone. Pretty mouth; in a few seconds we'll see that the rest of her is just as pretty.

Stephen King is best known for his horror novels, many of which have been adapted into movies. He grew up and attended college in Maine, and he began his career as a published writer by selling short stories to men's magazines. He published his first novel, *Carrie,* in 1974, and it quickly became a great success. King then went on to write many more well-known horror novels including *The Shining, Salem's Lot,* and *The Dead Zone.* In 2003, he received the National Book Foundation Medal for Distinguished Contribution to American Letters.

714

Program Resources

Planning and Assessment
Program Planning Guide, Selection Lesson Plan
E-Lesson Planner
Assessment Guide, Lesson Test
ExamView

Technology Tools
Interactive Student Text on CD
Visual Teaching Package
Audio Library
mirrorsandwindows.com

Meeting the Standards
Drama: Unit 7, Independent Reading, pp. 36–42

Differentiating Instruction
Advanced Students, Independent Reading Study, pp. 44–45
English Language Learners, Sequence of Events, pp. 163–167

Common Core State Standards

Reading Literature
RL.1, RL.3

Writing
W.9

KATIE. Bill? Oh, he says he doesn't feel very well, but he's always like that between books, can't sleep, thinks every headache is the first symptom of a brain tumor…once he gets going on something new, he'll be fine.

SOUND. B.G: THE TELEVISION.

THE CAMERA DRAWS BACK. KATIE *is sitting in the kitchen phone nook, having a good gab with her sister while she idles through some catalogues. We should notice one not-quite-ordinary thing about the phone she's on: it's the sort with two lines. There are lighted buttons to show which ones are engaged. Right now only one—*KATIE's—*is. As* KATIE *continues her conversation,* THE CAMERA SWINGS AWAY FROM HER, TRACKS ACROSS THE KITCHEN, *and through the arched doorway that leads into the family room.*

KATIE. [*Voice, fading.*] Oh, I saw Janie Charlton today…yes! Big as a *house!…*

She fades. The TV gets louder. There are three kids: JEFF, *eight,* CONNIE, *ten, and* DENNIS, *thirteen. Wheel of Fortune is on, but they're not watching. Instead they're engaged in that great pastime, Fighting About What Comes On Later.*

JEFF. Come onnn! It was his first *book!*

CONNIE. His first *gross* book.

DENNIS. We're gonna watch *Cheers* and *Wings,* just like we do every week, Jeff.

DENNIS *speaks with the utter finality only a big brother can manage. "Wanna talk about it some more and see how much pain I can inflict on your scrawny body, Jeff?" his face says.*

JEFF. Could we at least tape it?

CONNIE. We're taping CNN for Mom. She said she might be on the phone with Aunt Lois for quite awhile.

JEFF. How can you tape CNN, for God's sake? It *never stops!*

DENNIS. That's what she likes about it.

CONNIE. And don't say God's sake, Jeffie— you're not old enough to talk about God except in church.

JEFF. Then don't call me Jeffie.

CONNIE. Jeffie, Jeffie, Jeffie.

JEFF *gets up, walks to the window, and looks out into the dark. He's really upset.* DENNIS *and* CONNIE, *in the grand tradition of older brothers and sisters, are delighted to see it.*

DENNIS. Poor Jeffie.

CONNIE. I think he's gonna commit suicide.

JEFF. [*Turns to them.*] It was his *first* book! Don't you guys even care?

CONNIE. Rent it down at the Video Stop tomorrow, if you want to see it so bad.

JEFF. They don't rent R-rated pictures to little kids and you know it!

CONNIE. [*Dreamily.*] Shut up, it's Vanna! I *love* Vanna!

JEFF. Dennis—

DENNIS. Go ask Dad to tape it on the VCR in his office and quit being such a totally annoying little booger.

JEFF *crosses the room, poking his tongue out at Vanna White as he goes.* THE CAMERA FOLLOWS *as he goes into the kitchen.*

KATIE.…so when he asked me if Polly had tested strep positive, I had to remind him she's away at prep school…and gosh, Lois, I miss her…

JEFF *is just passing through, on his way to the stairs.*

KATIE. Will you kids *please* be quiet?

JEFF. [*Glum.*] They'll be quiet. *Now.*

Teach the Selection

Summary

Katie Weiderman gets a desperate-sounding call, which is cut off in mid-sentence, and is sure she recognizes the voice of her older daughter. Later, she and her husband, Bill, a writer of horror stories that have been made into movies, decide it was a stranger who dialed incorrectly. That night, Bill dies of a heart attack. Five years later to the day, as she sits in Bill's old chair, she accidentally knocks the phone off the hook and hears the hum of an open line. Then she hears the voice of her dead husband, asking her who she would call, "if it wasn't too late." She calls her old number and hears her own voice, repeating the mysterious call of five years ago. She realizes that the complete message was a warning to take her husband to the hospital for immediate care.

 **MIRRORS & WINDOWS** The Mirrors & Windows questions at the end of this selection focus on the theme of familiarity. Before reading the story, ask students what voices in their life are most familiar. How are people able to recognize the voices of those close to them?

Words in Use

Selection Words
lodge brothers, 714
interior, 714
exterior, 714
fade, 714
idles, 715
engaged, 715
scrawny, 715
dejected, 716

orthodontic, 716
rummaging, 717
battered, 717
depressive, 717
veteran, 718
tussling, 718
bleakly, 720
strenuous, 721
radiant, 722

Teaching Words
foundation, 714
distinguished, 714
occupation, 728
interactions, 728

KEY TERMS
SCREENPLAY, 714
FORESHADOW, 728
PLOT, 728
THESIS STATEMENT, 728

Use Reading Skills

Activate Prior Knowledge Ask students what they already know about Dracula. Why is this poster of Dracula a fitting decoration for Bill Weiderman's office door? Bela Lugosi is an actor who played Count Dracula in the 1931 movie based on Bram Stoker's novel. This image is fitting for Bill Weideman's office door because Bill writes horror stories. **A**

Analyze Literature

Indirect Characterization When authors reveal details about characters without saying in so many words what those details are, it is called indirect characterization. This is an example of it: showing that Bill has photos of each member of his family in his office, we can infer that his family is very important to him. Thus, the author *shows* us this bit of information rather than *telling* us directly. Have students be on the lookout for other examples of indirect characterization in this screenplay. **B**

Use Reading Strategies

Ask Questions Students might wonder at first why Bill does not get scared when Jeff sneaks up on him. After all, the carpet has muffled the sound of Jeff's feet. Their answer to this question might be that Bill heard the door open when Jeff came in. **C**

He goes up the stairs, a little dejected. KATIE *looks after him for a moment, loving and worried.*

KATIE. They're squabbling again. Polly used to keep them in line, but now that she's away at school...I don't know...maybe sending her to Bolton wasn't such a hot idea. Sometimes when she calls home she sounds so unhappy...

A INT. BELA LUGOSI AS DRACULA, CU.

Drac's standing at the door of his Transylvanian castle. Someone has pasted a comic-balloon coming out of his mouth which reads: "Listen! My children of the night! What music they make!" The poster is on a door but we only see this as JEFF *opens it and goes into his father's study.*

INT. A PHOTOGRAPH OF KATIE, CU.

B THE CAMERA HOLDS, THEN PANS SLOWLY RIGHT. *We pass another photo, this one of* POLLY, *the daughter away at school. She's a lovely girl of sixteen or so. Past* POLLY *is* DENNIS...*then* CONNIE...*then* JEFF.

THE CAMERA CONTINUES TO PAN AND ALSO WIDENS OUT *so we can see* BILL WEIDERMAN, *a man of about forty-four. He looks tired. He's peering into the word-processor on his desk, but his mental crystal ball must be taking the night off, because the screen is blank. On the walls we see framed book-covers. All of them are spooky. One of the titles is Ghost Kiss.*

JEFF *comes up quietly behind his dad. The carpet muffles his feet.* BILL *sighs and shuts off the word-cruncher. A moment later* JEFF *claps his hands on his father's shoulders.*

C **JEFF.** BOOGA-BOOGA!

BILL. Hi, Jeffie.

He turns in his chair to look at his son, who is disappointed.

JEFF. How come you didn't get scared?

BILL. Scaring is my business. I'm case-hardened. Something wrong?

JEFF. Daddy, can I watch the first hour of *Ghost Kiss* and you tape the rest? Dennis and Connie are hogging *everything*.

BILL *swivels to look at the book-jacket, bemused.*

BILL. You sure you want to watch *that*, champ? It's pretty—

JEFF. Yes!

INT. KATIE, IN THE PHONE NOOK.

In this shot, we clearly see the stairs leading to her husband's study behind her.

KATIE. I *really* think Jeff needs the orthodontic work but you know Bill—

The other line rings. The other light stutters.

KATIE. That's just the other line, Bill will—

But now we see BILL *and* JEFF *coming downstairs behind her.*

BILL. Honey, where're the blank videotapes? I can't find any in the study and—

KATIE. [*To* BILL.] Wait! [*To* LOIS.] Gonna put you on hold a sec, Lo.

She does. Now both lines are blinking. She pushes the top one, where the new call has just come in.

KATIE. Hello, Weiderman residence.

SOUND. DESPERATE SOBBING.

SOBBING VOICE. [*Filter.*] Take...please take... t-t-

KATIE. Polly? Is that you? What's wrong?

SOUND. SOBBING...*It's awful, heartbreaking.*

SOBBING VOICE. [*Filter.*] Please—quick—

Differentiated Instruction

English Language Learning
Students learning English will benefit from reviewing the meaning of these key words and phrases:

symptom—sign or indication of illness, 715
tested strep positive—had a positive test result for strep throat germs, 715
dejected—low in spirits; unhappy, 716
squabbling—having petty arguments, 716
muffles—deadens the sound, 716

hogging—slang for taking more than one's proper share, 716
bemused—lost in thought, 716
orthodontic—having to do with teeth straightening, 716
bumming her out—slang for putting her in a bad mood, 717
frantically—wildly, 717
interludes—short intervals of time that interrupt something, 717

SOUND. SOBBING…*Then,* CLICK! *A broken connection.*

KATIE. Polly, calm down! Whatever it is can't be that b—

HUM OF AN OPEN LINE.

JEFF *has wandered toward the TV room, hoping to find a blank tape.*

BILL. Who was that?

Without looking at her husband or answering him, KATIE *slams the lower button in again.*

KATIE. Lois? Listen, I'll call you back. That was Polly, and she sounded very upset. No… she hung up. Yes. I will. Thanks.

She hangs up.

BILL. [*Concerned.*] It was Polly?

KATIE. Crying her head off. It sounded like she was trying to say "Please take me home"…I knew that…school was bumming her out…Why I ever let you talk me into it… **D**

She's rummaging frantically on her little phone desk. Catalogues go slithering to the floor around her stool.

KATIE. Connie did you take my address book?

CONNIE. [*Voice.*] No, Mom.

BILL *pulls a battered book out of his back pocket and pages through it.*

BILL. I got it. Except—

KATIE. I know,…dorm phone is always busy. Give it to me.

BILL. Honey, calm down.

KATIE. I'll calm down after I talk to her. She is sixteen, Bill. Sixteen-year-old girls are prone to depressive interludes. Sometimes they even k…just give me the…number!

BILL. 617-555-8641.

As she punches the numbers, THE CAMERA SLIDES IN TO CU.

KATIE. Come on, come on…don't be busy… just this once…

SOUND. CLICKS. *A pause. Then…the phone starts ringing.*

KATIE. [*Eyes closed.*] Thank You, God.

VOICE. [*Filter.*] Hartshorn Hall, this is Frieda. If you want Christine…, she's still in the shower, Arnie. **E**

KATIE. Could you call Polly to the phone? Polly Weiderman? This is Kate Weiderman. Her mother. **F**

VOICE. [*Filter.*] Oh, jeez! Sorry. I thought— hang on, please, Mrs. Weiderman.

SOUND. THE PHONE CLUNKS DOWN.

VOICE. [*Filter, and very faint.*] Polly? Pol?… Phone call!…It's your mother!

INT. A WIDER ANGLE ON THE PHONE NOOK, WITH BILL.

BILL. Well?

KATIE. Somebody's getting her. I hope.

JEFF *comes back in with a tape.*

JEFF. I found one, Dad. Dennis hid 'em. As usual.

BILL. In a minute, Jeff. Go watch the tube.

JEFF. But—

BILL. I won't forget. Now go *on.*

JEFF *goes.*

KATIE. Come on, come on, come on…

BILL. Calm down, Katie.

KATIE. [*Snaps.*] If you'd heard her, you wouldn't tell me to calm down! She sounded—

Use Reading Strategies

Visualize Have students close their eyes and visualize Katie as she rummages through the items on her desk. What is her facial expression like? What else is on her desk? What kinds of catalogues does she have? **D**

Use Reading Strategies

Make Inferences Ask students what this line of dialogue by Frieda indicates about the types of calls that the girls in the dorm usually get. Model a response by suggesting that Frieda's statement indicates that most of the calls to the dorm are from young men calling the young women for dates and that apparently Arnie calls Christine quite often. **E**

Use Reading Skills

Read Aloud Have students read aloud the section from the time Katie asks for Polly on the phone to the time Katie starts dialing her mother's phone number. Remind them to read with appropriate expression, to get a sense of Katie's feelings of urgency, Polly's feelings of excitement, and Katie's confusion about the mysterious phone call. **F**

Dashes

Remind students that the dash is an emphatic mark of punctuation that should be used sparingly. It is used for these reasons:

- to introduce or set off a word or group of words that you want to emphasize:
  He wanted one thing—a good job. I think—no, I am sure—you're right.

- to show a sudden break in thought:
  When we met—but I'm trying to forget that day.

- to separate a summarizing statement from that which precedes it:
  Liberty, equality, fraternity—these were the goals of the French Revolution.

- to indicate an unfinished statement or word:
  I wanted to buy the car, but—

Cultural Connection

Popular Literature Discuss with students the fact that Stephen King's work has enjoyed widespread popularity and that this very fact has led some to think that it is inferior to what critics generally consider "great literature." The argument is that if the masses like it, it can't be all that good. Ask students what they think about this argument. Model a response by suggesting that, while the idea has some truth, it does not apply to all popular authors. Charles Dickens was popular in his time, as was Mark Twain, and their work is still highly respected.

Tell students that Stephen King recognizes the dilemma of being a popular writer and still feeling outside "the club" of respected writers. When accepting an award from the National Book Foundation in 2003, he said this: "For far too long the so-called popular writers of this country and the so-called literary writers have stared at each other with animosity and a willful lack of understanding .... Bridges can be built between the so-called popular fiction and the so-called literary fiction. The first gainers in such a widening of interest would be the readers, of course...."

POLLY. [*Filter, cheery voice.*] Hi, mom!

KATIE. Pol? Honey? Are you all right?

POLLY. [*Happy, bubbling voice.*] Am I *all right?* I aced my bio exam, got a B on my Free Conversational Essay, and Ronnie Hansen asked me to the Harvest Ball. I'm so all right that if one more good thing happens to me today, I'll probably blow up like the *Hindenburg.*[1]

KATIE. You didn't just call me up, crying your head off?

We see by KATIE's *face that she already knows the answer to this question.*

KATIE. I'm glad about your test and your date, honey. I guess it was someone else. I'll call you back, okay?

POLLY. [*Filter.*] 'Kay. Say hi to Dad!

KATIE. I will.

INT. THE PHONE NOOK, WIDER.

BILL. She okay?

KATIE. Fine. I could have *sworn* it was Polly, but...*she's* walking on air.

BILL. So it was a prank. Or someone who was crying so hard she dialed a wrong number..."through a shimmering film of tears," as we veteran hacks like to say.

KATIE. It was not a prank and it was not a wrong number! It was someone in *my family.*

BILL. Honey, you can't know that.

KATIE. No? If Jeffie called up, just crying, would you know it was him?

BILL. [*Struck by this.*] Yeah, maybe. I guess I might.

She's not listening. She's punching numbers, fast.

BILL. Who you calling?

She doesn't answer him. SOUND: PHONE RINGS TWICE. *Then:*

OLDER FEMALE VOICE. [*Filter.*] Hello?

KATIE. Mom? Are you...[*She pauses.*] Did you call just a few seconds ago?

VOICE. [*Filter.*] No, dear...why?

KATIE. Oh...you know these phones. I was talking to Lois and I lost the other call.

VOICE. [*Filter.*] Well, it wasn't me. Kate, I saw the *prettiest* dress in La Boutique today, and—

KATIE. We'll talk about it later, Mom, okay?

VOICE. [*Filter.*] Kate, are you all right?

KATIE. I have...Mom, I think maybe I've got diarrhea. I have to go. 'Bye.

She hangs up. BILL *hangs on until she does, then he bursts into wild donkey-brays of laughter.*

BILL. Oh boy...diarrhea...I gotta remember that the next time my agent calls...oh Katie, that was so cool—

KATIE. [*Almost screaming.*] *This is not funny!*

BILL *stops laughing.*

INT. THE TV ROOM.

JEFF *and* DENNIS *have been tussling. They stop. All three kids look toward the kitchen.*

INT. IN THE PHONE NOOK WITH BILL AND KATIE.

KATIE. *I tell you it was someone in my family and she sounded—oh, you don't understand. I knew that voice.*

BILL. But if Polly's okay and your mom's okay...

---

1. *Hindenburg.* German airship that burst into flames while landing in Lakehurst, New York, in 1936

Differentiated Instruction

Visual Learning

Students who learn visually will benefit from drawing a sketch of the set. Have them include the kitchen with its phone nook, the family room with the TV, and Bill's study with his word-processor. They might also like to draw the characters, incorporating details about their appearance that are revealed in the stage directions. For example, all we know about Katie is that she is pretty—we don't know her hair color or anything else. All we know about the children are their ages and the fact that Jeff might need braces. All we know about Bill's appearance are his age and the fact that he appears tired.

KATIE. [*Positive.*] It's Dawn.

BILL. Come on, hon, a minute ago you were sure it was Polly.

KATIE. It *had* to be Dawn. I was on the phone with Lois and Mom's okay so Dawn's the only other one it *could* have been. She's the youngest…I could have mistaken her for Polly…and she's out there in that farmhouse alone with the baby!

BILL. [*Startled.*] What do you mean, alone?

KATIE. Jerry's in Burlington! It's Dawn! *Something's happened to Dawn!*

CONNIE *comes into the kitchen, worried.*

CONNIE. Mom? Is Aunt Dawn okay?

BILL. So far as we know, she's fine. Take it easy, doll. Bad to buy trouble before you know it's on sale.

KATIE *punches numbers and listens.* SOUND: *The DAH-DAH-DAH of a busy signal.* KATIE

hangs up. BILL *looks a question at her with raised eyebrows.*

KATIE. Busy.

BILL. Katie, are you sure—

KATIE. She's the only one left—it had to be her. Bill, I'm scared. Will you drive me out there?

BILL *takes the phone from her.*

BILL. What's her number?

KATIE. 555-6169.

BILL *dials. Gets a busy. Hangs up and punches 0.*

OPERATOR. [*Filter.*] Operator.

BILL. I'm trying to reach my sister-in-law, operator. The line is busy. I suspect there may be a problem. Can you break into the call, please?

INT. THE DOOR TO THE TV ROOM.

All three kids are standing there, silent and worried.

INT. THE PHONE NOOK, WITH BILL AND KATIE.

OPERATOR. [*Filter.*] What is your name, sir?

BILL. William Weiderman. My number is—

OPERATOR. [*Filter.*] Not the William Weiderman that wrote *Spider Doom?*

SORRY, RIGHT NUMBER, ACT 1 **719**

Teach the Selection

Analyze Literature
Suspense Point out to students that King is building the suspense here. The hint that something has happened to Katie's sister, who is alone in a farmhouse with a baby, conjures up all kinds of possibilities in the reader's mind. **A**

Analyze Literature
Sensory Details Have students consider the sensory details in these stage directions. Katie's punching numbers and then hearing the sound of a busy signal are details that appeal to the sense of hearing. Bill's raising his eyebrows as if to ask a question is a detail that appeals to the sense of sight. **B**

Use Reading Skills
Identify Author's Purpose Students will no doubt notice that William Weiderman has a great deal in common with Stephen King. They are both wildly popular writers of horror fiction. Do students think King is trying to show what it's like to be recognized by strangers, even when the stranger doesn't see him? Does this fame make it difficult to get everyday tasks done? **C**

Grammar Skills

Hyphens
Share with students these uses of hyphens:
- in compound nouns: mother-in-law
- with combining forms attached to a capitalized word: pro-American
- after a single letter joined to a noun: X-ray
- in numbers from 21 to 99 when spelled out: thirty-two
- in certain fractions: four-fifths
- between a number and its unit of measurement: a 10-day vacation
- usually when *ex* or *self* is the first element: ex-president; self-respect
- to divide a word at the end of the line: ap-ple

Have students find examples of hyphen use in the screenplay and indicate the reason for the hyphen in the word.

Use Reading Strategies

Make Predictions Have students make predictions about what Bill and Katie will find when they get to Dawn's house. Are Dennis's fears justified? **Ⓐ**

Use Reading Strategies

Visualize Have students imagine they are the director of this play. How would they make the phone on the wall look "like a snake ready to strike"? Remind students that at the time this screenplay was written (1987), cordless phones had only recently been introduced and were not in general use, due to their limitations and high cost. Cell phones were introduced in the mid-1980s, but their use was mostly confined to cars—in fact, they were called "car phones" because they relied on the car battery for their power. Portable cell phones were expensive and not nearly as popular as they are today. The phone in this screenplay was attached to its base with a cord, which could have been straight or coiled. Model a response to the question by suggesting that the director might want to focus in on the phone cord, perhaps showing its shadow against the wall. **Ⓑ**

Bill. Yes, that was mine. If—

Operator. [*Filter.*] Oh my God. I just *loved* that book! I love *all* your books! I—

Bill. I'm delighted you do. But right now my wife is very worried about her sister. If it's possible for you to—

Operator. [*Filter.*] Yes, I can do that. Please give me your number, Mr. Weiderman, for the records. [*She giggles.*] I *promise* not to give it out.

Bill. It's 555-4408.

Operator. [*Filter.*] And the call number?

Bill. [*Looks at* Katie.] Uh…

Katie. 555-6169.

Bill. 555-6169.

Operator. [*Filter.*] Just a moment, Mr. Weiderman…*Night of the Beast* was also great, by the way. Hold on.

SOUND. TELEPHONIC CLICKS AND CLACKS

Katie. Is she—

Bill. Yes. Just…

There's one final CLICK.

Operator. [*Filter.*] I'm sorry, Mr. Weiderman, but that line is not busy. It's off the hook. I wonder if I sent you my copy of *Spider Doom*—

Bill *hangs up the phone.*

Katie. Why did you hang up?

Bill. She can't break in. Phone's not busy. It's off the hook.

They stare at each other bleakly.

EXT. NIGHT. A LOW-SLUNG SPORTS CAR PASSES THE CAMERA.

INT. THE CAR, WITH Katie AND Bill.

Katie's *scared.* Bill, *at the wheel, doesn't look exactly calm.*

Katie. Hey, Bill—tell me she's all right.

Bill. She's all right.

Katie. Now tell me what you really think.

Bill. Jeff snuck up behind me tonight and put the old booga-booga on me. He was disappointed as hell when I didn't jump. I told him I was case-hardened. [*Pause.*] I lied.

Katie. Why did Jerry have to move out there when he's gone half the time? Just her and that little tiny baby? *Why*?

Bill. Shh, Kate. We're almost there.

Katie. Go faster.

EXT. THE CAR.

He does. That car is smokin.

INT. THE Weiderman TV ROOM.

The tube's still on and the kids are still there, but the horsing around has stopped.

Connie. Dennis, do you think Aunt Dawn's okay?

Ⓐ **Dennis.** [*Thinks she's dead, decapitated by a maniac.*] Yeah. Sure she is.

INT. THE PHONE, POV FROM THE TV ROOM.

Ⓑ *Just sitting there on the wall in the phone nook, lights dark, looking like a snake ready to strike.*

FADE OUT.

ACT 2

EXT. AN ISOLATED FARMHOUSE.

A long driveway leads up to it. There's one light on in the living room. Car lights sweep up the driveway. The Weiderman *car pulls up close to the garage and stops.*

Differentiated Instruction

Kinesthetic Learning

Students who learn by doing will benefit from acting out a scene from the screenplay. Provide any necessary props, allow time for rehearsal, and have students act out the scene for the class.

Enrichment

Have students write a letter to Stephen King in which they discuss this screenplay. They can either mail the letter to him directly or gather the letters into a notebook and put the notebook on display in the classroom.

INT. THE CAR, WITH Bill AND Katie.

Katie. I'm scared.

Bill *bends down, reaches under his seat, and brings out a pistol.*

Bill. [*Solemnly.*] Booga-booga.

Katie. [*Total surprise.*] How long have you had that?

Bill. Since last year. I didn't want to scare you or the kids. I've got a license to carry. Come on.

EXT. Bill AND Katie.

They get out. Katie *stands by the front of the car while* Bill *goes to the garage and peers in.*

Bill. Her car's here.

THE CAMERA TRACKS WITH THEM *to the front door. Now we can hear the* TV, PLAYING LOUD. Bill *pushes the doorbell. We hear it inside. They wait.* Katie *pushes it. Still no answer. She pushes it again and doesn't take her finger off.* Bill *looks down at:*

EXT. THE LOCK, Bill'S POV.

Big scratches on it.

EXT. Bill AND Katie.

Bill. [*Low.*] The lock's been tampered with.

Katie *looks, and whimpers.* Bill *tries the door. It opens. The* TV *is louder.*

Bill. Stay behind me. Be ready to run if something happens. God, I wish I'd left you home, Kate.

He starts in. Katie *comes after him, terrified, near tears.*

INT. Dawn AND Jerry'S LIVING ROOM.

From this angle we see only a small section of the room. The TV *is much louder.* Bill *enters the room, gun up. He looks to the right…and*

suddenly all the tension goes out of him. He lowers the gun.

Katie. [*Draws up beside him.*] Bill…what…

He points.

INT. THE LIVING ROOM, WIDE, Bill AND Katie'S POV.

The place looks like a cyclone hit it…but it wasn't robbery and murder that caused this mess; only a healthy eighteen-month-old baby. After a strenuous day of trashing the living room, Baby got tired and Mommy got tired and they fell asleep on the couch together. The baby is in Dawn's *lap. There is a pair of* Walkman *earphones on her head. There are toys—tough plastic* Sesame Street *and* PlaySkool *stuff, for the most part—scattered here to breakfast. The baby has also pulled most of the books out of the bookcase. Had a good munch on one of them, too, by the look.* Bill *goes over and picks it up. It is* Ghost Kiss.

Bill. I've had people say they just eat my books up, but this is ridiculous.

He's amused. Katie *isn't. She walks over to her sister, ready to be mad…but she sees how really exhausted* Dawn *looks and softens.*

INT. Dawn AND The Baby, Katie's POV.

Fast asleep and breathing easily, like a Raphael painting of Madonna and Child. THE CAMERA PANS DOWN TO: *the* Walkman. *We can hear the faint strains of Huey Lewis and the News.* THE CAMERA PANS A BIT FURTHER TO *a* Princess *telephone on the table by the chair. It's off the cradle. Not much; just enough to break the connection and scare people to death.*

INT. Katie.

She sighs, bends down, and replaces the phone. Then she pushes the STOP *button on the* Walkman.

Teach the Selection

Analyze Literature

Suspense Ask students to consider how Stephen King is building suspense here. Model an answer by suggesting that all the clues point to trouble inside. Because the car is there, they know Dawn is inside, but she doesn't answer the doorbell. The scratches on the lock hint that someone's been forcing it. The door being unlocked is not a good sign, either. **C**

Make Connections

Ask students if they have ever been so tired that they could fall asleep on a couch with the TV blaring in the background and music blasting through a pair of earphones. What were the circumstances? **D**

Analyze Literature

Sensory Details Point out the sensory details that make this scene easy to imagine: the sight of Dawn and the baby looking like a Raphael painting; the sounds of the music; the sight of the telephone "off the cradle" on the table. Students might be able to fill in other details by using their imaginations. How are the people dressed? What does the couch look like? **E**

Research Skills

Media Coverage

Have students choose a current news story and compare the way various forms of the media cover it. They might follow the story in the following sources:

- TV news programs
- newspapers
- Internet websites

Suggest that they ask these questions as they evaluate and compare the sources:

1. Does the report include visuals such as photographs, live footage, and interviews?
2. Does it cite sources for the information?
3. Does it cover different perspectives?
4. Does it seem complete? Are the 5 W's (*who, what, why, when,* and *where*) answered?

Literary Connection

Varied Media This screenplay was filmed as an episode of the TV series *Tales from the Darkside* and was first aired on November 22, 1987. Later, it was published in *Nightmares & Dreamscapes*, an anthology of Stephen King's short stories. This screenplay is certainly not the only one King has written (the list is long), but it is the only one that he included in any of his anthologies.

Use Reading Skills

Read Aloud Assign roles and have students read aloud the conversation between Dawn, Bill, and Katie while the rest of the class follows along. Remind the readers to use expressions that fit the words and communicate the emotions well.

Use Reading Skills

Identify Chronological Order

Have students make a time line that identifies the chronological order of the events in this screenplay. They can begin with this incident described by Dawn, and they can add to the time line as they go along. **A**

INT. DAWN, BILL, AND KATIE.

DAWN *wakes up when the music stops. Looks at* BILL *and* KATIE, *puzzled.*

DAWN. [*Fuzzed out.*] Well…hi.

She realizes she's got the Walkman phones on and removes them.

BILL. Hi, Dawn.

DAWN. [*Still half asleep.*] Shoulda called, guys. Place is a mess.

She smiles. She's radiant when she smiles.

KATIE. We *tried.* The operator told Bill the phone was off the hook. I thought something was wrong. How can you sleep with that music blasting?

DAWN. It's restful. [*Sees the gnawed book* BILL'S *holding.*] Oh, my God, Bill, I'm sorry! Justin's teething and—

BILL. There are critics who'd say he picked just the right thing to teethe on. I don't want to scare you, beautiful, but somebody's been at your front door lock with a screwdriver or something. Whoever it was forced it.

A **DAWN.** Gosh, no! That was Jerry, last week. I locked us out by mistake and he didn't have his key and the spare wasn't over the door like it's supposed to be. He was mad so he took the screwdriver to it. It didn't work, either—that's one tough lock.

BILL. If it wasn't forced, how come I could just open the door and walk in?

DAWN. [*Guiltily.*] Well…sometimes I forget to lock it.

KATIE. You didn't call me tonight, Dawn?

DAWN. Gee, no! I didn't call *anyone!* I was too busy chasing Justin around! He kept wanting to eat the fabric softener! Then he got sleepy and I sat down here and thought I'd listen to some tunes while I waited for your movie to come on, Bill, and I fell asleep—

At the mention of the movie BILL *starts visibly and looks at the book. Then he glances at his watch.*

BILL. I promised to tape it for Jeff. Come on, Katie, we've got time to get back.

KATIE. Just a second.

She picks up the phone and dials.

DAWN. Gee, Bill, do you think Jeffie's old enough to watch something like that?

BILL. It's network. They take out the blood-bags.

DAWN. [*Confused but amiable.*] Oh. That's good.

INT. KATIE, CU.

DENNIS. [*Filter.*] Hello?

KATIE. Just thought you'd like to know your Aunt Dawn's fine.

DENNIS. [*Filter.*] Oh! Cool. Thanks, Mom.

INT. THE PHONE NOOK, WITH DENNIS AND THE OTHERS.

He looks very relieved.

DENNIS. Aunt Dawn's okay.

INT. THE CAR, WITH BILL AND KATIE.

They drive in silence for awhile.

KATIE. You think I'm a hysterical idiot, don't you?

BILL. [*Genuinely surprised.*] No! I was scared, too.

KATIE. You sure you're not mad?

BILL. I'm too relieved. [*Laughs.*] She's sort of a scatterbrain, old Dawn, but I love her.

KATIE. [*Leans over and kisses him.*] I love *you.* You're a sweet man.

Differentiated Instruction

Reading Proficiency

Have pairs of students work together rereading Act 1 and paraphrasing passages as they go along, thus monitoring their comprehension. Do they agree on how best to paraphrase each section? If so, that means they understand it. If not, they can re-examine the text until they agree on a paraphrase. When they finish paraphrasing Act 1, have them write a one- or two-sentence summary.

BILL. I'm the *boogeyman!*

KATIE. I am not fooled, sweetheart.

EXT. THE CAR PASSES THE CAMERA AND WE DISSOLVE TO:

INT. JEFF, IN BED.

His room is dark. The covers are pulled up to his chin.

JEFF. You *promise* to tape the rest?

CAMERA WIDENS OUT *so we can see* BILL, *sitting on the bed.*

BILL. I promise.

JEFF. I especially liked the part where the dead guy ripped off the punk rocker's head.

BILL. Well…they *used* to take out all the blood-bags.

JEFF. What, Dad?

BILL. Nothing. I love you, Jeffie.

JEFF. I love you, too. So does Rambo.

JEFF *holds up a stuffed dragon of decidedly unmilitant aspect.* BILL *kisses the dragon, then* JEFF.

BILL. 'Night.

JEFF. 'Night. [*As* BILL *reaches the door.*] Glad Aunt Dawn was okay.

BILL. Me too.

He goes out.

INT. TV, CU.

A guy who looks like he died in a car crash about two weeks prior to filming (and has since been subjected to a lot of hot weather) is staggering out of a crypt. THE CAMERA WIDENS *to show* BILL, *releasing the VCR pause button.*

KATIE. [*Voice.*] Booga-booga.

BILL *looks around companionably.* THE CAMERA WIDENS OUT MORE *to show* KATIE, *wearing a nightgown.*

BILL. Same to you. I missed the first forty seconds or so after the break. I had to kiss Rambo.

KATIE. You sure you're not mad at me, Bill?

He goes to her and kisses her.

BILL. Not even a smidge.

KATIE. It's just that I could have sworn it was one of mine. You know what I mean? One of mine?

BILL. Yes.

KATIE. I can still hear those sobs. So lost…so heartbroken.

BILL. Kate, have you ever thought you recognized someone on the street, and called her, and when she finally turned around it was a total stranger? C

KATIE. Yes, once. In Seattle. I was in a mall and I thought I saw my old roommate. I…oh. I see what you're saying.

BILL. Sure. There are sound-alikes as well as look-alikes.

KATIE. But…*you know your own.* At least I thought so until tonight.

She puts her cheek on his shoulder, looking troubled.

KATIE. I was so *positive* it was Polly…

BILL. Because you've been worried about her getting her feet under her at the new school…but judging from the stuff she told you tonight, I'd say she's doing just fine in that department. Wouldn't you?

KATIE. Yes…I guess I would.

BILL. Let it go, hon.

Cultural Connection

Boogeyman The word *boogeyman* brings to mind a legendary monster of indeterminate appearance, feared by children who suspect that it lurks somewhere in the bedroom waiting to attack the sleeper. The word is also spelled *bogeyman, boogyman,* and *bogyman,* with origins in the word *bogey* or *bogy,* meaning "a person or thing much dreaded." It was originally a proper name, *Bogey* and *Old Bogey,* meaning the Devil. The word is of ancient Scottish origin. **B**

Use Reading Skills

Read Aloud Have two students read aloud this conversation between Bill and Katie as the rest of the class reads along. Remind them to follow the pacing indicated by the punctuation, pausing at the ellipses.

Make Connections

Students will probably remember having similar experiences. Ask how they felt when this happened to them. Model a response by suggesting that they were disappointed to find out the person wasn't who they thought it was. **C**

Writing Skills

Contemporary Horror Writers

Have students write a report in which they compare and contrast the work of two or more contemporary horror writers. Here are some authors they might consider researching:

Clive Barker	Mark Z. Danielewski
Jason Dark	William Hope Hodson
T.E.D. Klein	Dean Koontz
Akmal Shebl	R. L. Stine
Poppy Z. Brite	Melanie Tem

R. Patrick Gates	Bret Easton Ellis
Robert R. McCammon	

Suggest that they consider the following points in their reports:
- What is similar about the writers?
- What is unique about each writer?
- Do they use graphic descriptions of horror, or is the horror more psychological?

Analyze Literature

Foreshadowing Point out that this is not the first time Katie has mentioned how tired Bill looks. Suggest that this might be foreshadowing. **(A)**

Analyze Literature

Author's Purpose Point out that this is the third time the author has made reference to this scene. First, Jeff told his father it was his favorite scene. Second, Katie asked Bill to edit it out of the copy. And here it appears again. What is the author's purpose in emphasizing this scene? Model a response by suggesting that it hints at sudden death and might be another example of foreshadowing. **(B)**

Make Connections

The words of the minister remind us that most religions believe in the immortality of the soul. Students might wish to comment on how this belief comforts us when a loved one dies or when we contemplate our own deaths. **(C)**

(A) **KATIE.** [*Looks at him closely.*] I hate to see you looking so tired. Hurry up and have an idea, you.

BILL. Well, I'm trying.

KATIE. You coming to bed?

BILL. Soon as I finish taping this for Jeff.

KATIE. [*Amused.*] Bill, that machine was made by Japanese technicians who think of…near everything. It'll run on its own.

BILL. Yea, but it's been a long time since I've seen this one, and…

KATIE. Okay. Enjoy. I think I'll be awake for a little while. [*Pause.*] I've got a few ideas of my own.

BILL. [*Smiles.*] Yeah?

KATIE. Yeah.

She starts out, then turns in the doorway as something else strikes her.

KATIE. If they show that part where the punk's head gets—

BILL. [*Guiltily.*] I'll edit it.

KATIE. 'Night. And thanks again. For everything.

She leaves. BILL sits in his chair.

INT. TV, CU.

(B) *A couple is necking in a car. Suddenly the passenger door is ripped open by the dead guy and we DISSOLVE TO:*

INT. KATIE, IN BED.

It's dark. She's asleep. She wakes up…sort of.

KATIE. [*Sleepy.*] Hey, big guy—

She feels for him, but his side of the bed is empty, the coverlet still pulled up. She sits up. Looks at:

INT. A CLOCK ON THE NIGHT-TABLE, KATIE'S POV.

It says 2:03 AM. Then it flashes 2:04.

INT. KATIE.

Fully awake now. And concerned. She gets up, puts on her robe, and leaves the bedroom.

INT. THE TV SCREEN, CU.

Snow.

KATIE. [*Voice, approaching.*] Bill? Honey? You okay? Bill? Bi—

INT. KATIE, IN BILL'S STUDY.

She's frozen, wide-eyed with horror.

INT. BILL, IN HIS CHAIR.

He's slumped to one side, eyes closed, hand inside his shirt. DAWN was sleeping. BILL is not.

EXT. A COFFIN, BEING LOWERED INTO A GRAVE.

(C) **MINISTER.** [*Voice.*] And so we commit the earthly remains of William Weiderman to the ground, confident of his spirit and soul. "Be ye not cast down, brethren…"

EXT. GRAVESIDE.

All the WEIDERMANS are ranged here. KATIE and POLLY wear identical black dresses and veils. CONNIE wears a black skirt and white blouse. DENNIS and JEFF wear black suits. JEFF is crying. He has Rambo the Dragon under his arm for a little extra comfort.

CAMERA MOVES IN ON KATIE. *Tears course slowly down her cheeks. She bends and gets a handful of earth. Tosses it into the grave.*

KATIE. Love you, big guy.

EXT. JEFF.

Weeping.

EXT. LOOKING DOWN INTO THE GRAVE.

Scattered earth on top of the coffin.

Differentiated Instruction

English Language Learning

Students learning English might have trouble with some of the idioms and slang that appear in this screenplay. Share with them the meanings of these:

- "… they just eat my books up": To *eat something up* means to accept it eagerly.
- "Polly used to keep them in line": Being *in line* means doing what's expected or appropriate.
- "Go watch the tube": *The tube* is TV.
- "I aced my bio exam …": To *ace* something is to get a perfect score.
- "She's sort of a scatterbrain …": A *scatterbrain* is someone whose thoughts are not organized.

DISSOLVE TO:

EXT. THE GRAVE.

A groundskeeper pats the last sod into place.

GROUNDSKEEPER. My wife says she wishes you'd written a couple more before you had your heart attack, mister. [*Pause.*] I like Westerns, m'self.

The GROUNDSKEEPER *walks away, whistling.*

DISSOLVE TO:

EXT. DAY. A CHURCH.

TITLE CARD: FIVE YEARS LATER.

The Wedding March is playing. POLLY, *older and radiant with joy, emerges into a pelting shower of rice. She's in a wedding gown, her new husband by her side.*

Celebrants throwing rice line either side of the path. From behind the bride and groom come

others. Among them are KATIE, DENNIS, CONNIE, *and* JEFF…*all five years older. With* KATIE *is another man. This is* HANK. *In the interim,* KATIE *has also taken a husband.*

POLLY *turns and her mother is there.*

POLLY. Thank you, Mom.

KATIE. [*Crying.*] Oh doll, you're so welcome.

They embrace. After a moment POLLY *draws away and looks at* HANK. *There is a brief moment of tension and then* POLLY *embraces* HANK, *too.*

POLLY. Thank you too, Hank. I'm sorry I was such a creep for so long…

HANK. [*Easily.*] You were never a creep, Pol. A girl only has one father.

CONNIE. Throw it! Throw it!

After a moment, POLLY *throws her bouquet.*

EXT. THE BOUQUET, CU, SLOW MOTION.

Turning and turning through the air.

Analyze Literature

Repetition Point out that this dialogue between Katie and Hank parallels the language and suggestions of the last conversation Katie had with Bill. The author might have done this to suggest that Katie has gone on with her life, despite the fact that she still misses Bill.

Analyze Literature

Sensory Detail The sensory detail of this simile helps readers visualize the image. Can students think of other similes that would have worked as well? Model an example: "One tear rims one eye, threatening to spill like floodwaters over a dam." **A**

Analyze Literature

Metaphor Point out that King is using a metaphor here. He is comparing Katie's self-control up to now to a dam that has been holding back her emotions. Now, when the dam breaks, her sorrow spills out. **B**

DISSOLVES TO:

INT. NIGHT. THE STUDY, WITH KATIE.

The word-processor has been replaced by a wide lamp looming over a stack of blueprints. The book jackets have been replaced by photos of buildings. Ones that have first been built in HANK's mind, presumably.

KATIE is looking at the desk, thoughtful and a little sad.

HANK. [*Voice.*] Coming to bed, Kate?

She turns and THE CAMERA WIDENS OUT to give us HANK. He's wearing a robe over pajamas. She comes to him and gives him a little hug, smiling. Maybe we notice a few streaks of gray in her hair; her pretty pony has done its fair share of running since BILL died.

KATIE. In a little while. A woman doesn't see her first one get married every day, you know.

HANK. I know.

THE CAMERA FOLLOWS *as they walk from the work area of the study to the more informal area. This is much the same as it was in the old days, with a coffee table, stereo, TV, couch, and BILL's old easy-chair. She looks at this.*

HANK. You still miss him, don't you?

KATIE. Some days more than others. You didn't know, and Polly didn't remember.

HANK. [*Gently.*] Remember what, doll?

KATIE. Polly got married on the five-year anniversary of Bill's death.

HANK. [*Hugs her.*] Come on to bed, why don't you?

KATIE. In a little while.

HANK. Okay. Maybe I'll still be awake.

KATIE. Got a few ideas, do you?

HANK. I might.

KATIE. That's nice.

He kisses her, then leaves, closing the door behind him. KATIE sits in BILL's old chair. Close by, on the coffee table, is a remote control for the TV and an extension phone. KATIE looks at the blank TV, and THE CAMERA MOVES IN on her face. One tear rims one eye, sparkling like a sapphire.

KATIE. I *do* still miss you, big guy. Lots and lots. Every day. And you know what? It hurts.

The tear falls. She picks up the TV remote and pushes the ON button.

INT. TV, KATIE'S POV.

An ad for Ginsu Knives comes to an end and is replaced by a STAR LOGO.

ANNOUNCER. [*Voice.*] Now back to Channel 63's Thursday night Star Time Movie…*Ghost Kiss.*

The logo DISSOLVES INTO a guy who looks like he died in a car crash about two weeks ago and has since been subjected to a lot of hot weather. He comes staggering out of the same old crypt.

INT. KATIE.

Terribly startled—almost horrified. She hits the OFF button on the remote control. The TV blinks off.

KATIE's face begins to work. She struggles against the impending emotional storm, but the coincidence of the movie is just one thing too many on what must have already been one of the most emotionally trying days of her life. The dam breaks and she begins to sob…terrible heartbroken sobs. She reaches out for the little table by the chair, meaning to put the remote

---

Differentiated Instruction

English Language Learning

Explain to students that sometimes writers use words that aren't really words. Instead, they are words that sound like what people say when they are talking fast, or they are shortened versions of words. Here are some examples from the screenplay:

Example	Meaning
gonna	going to
wanna	want to
'em	them
I gotta	I have got to
smidge	smidgeon (tiny bit)
m'self	myself

control on it, and knocks the phone onto the floor.

SOUND: THE HUM OF AN OPEN LINE.

Her tear-stained face grows suddenly still as she looks at the telephone. Something begins to fill it…an idea? an intuition? Hard to tell. And maybe it doesn't matter.

INT. THE TELEPHONE, KATIE'S POV.

THE CAMERA MOVES IN TO ECU… MOVES IN *until the dots in the off-the-hook receiver look like chasms.*

SOUND OF OPEN-LINE BUZZ UP TO LOUD.

WE GO INTO THE BLACK…*and hear:*

BILL. [*Voice.*] Who are you calling? Who do you *want* to call? Who *would* you call, if it wasn't too late?

INT KATIE.

There is now a strange hypnotized look on her face. She reaches down, scoops the telephone up, and punches in numbers, seemingly at random.

SOUND. RINGING PHONE.

KATIE continues to look hypnotized. The look holds until the phone is answered…and she hears herself on the other end of the line.

KATIE. [*Voice; filter.*] Hello, Weiderman residence.

KATIE—our present-day KATIE with streaks of gray in her hair—goes on sobbing, yet an expression of desperate hope is trying to be born on her face. On some level she understands that the depth of her grief has allowed a kind of telephonic-time-travel. She's trying to talk, to force the words out.

KATIE. [*Sobbing.*] Take…please take…t-t-

INT. KATIE, IN THE PHONE NOOK, REPRISE.

It's five years ago. BILL *is standing beside her, looking concerned.* JEFF *is wandering off to look for a blank tape in the other room.*

KATIE. Polly? What's wrong?

INT. KATIE, IN THE STUDY.

KATIE. [*Sobbing.*] Please—quick—

SOUND. CLICK OF A BROKEN CONNECTION.

KATIE. [*Screaming.*] Take him to the hospital! If you want him to live, take him to the hospital! He's going to have a heart attack. He— **C**

SOUND. HUM OF AN OPEN LINE.

Slowly, very slowly, KATIE *hangs up the telephone. Then, after a moment, she picks it up again. She speaks aloud with no self-consciousness whatever. Probably doesn't even know she's doing it.*

KATIE. I dialed the old number. I dialed—

SLAM CUT TO:

INT. BILL, IN THE PHONE NOOK WITH KATIE BESIDE HIM.

He's just taken the phone from KATIE *and is speaking to the operator.*

OPERATOR. [*Filter, giggles.*] I *promise* not to give it out.

BILL. It's 555-

SLAM CUT TO:

INT. KATIE, IN BILL'S OLD CHAIR, CU.

KATIE. [*Finishes.*] -4408.

INT. THE PHONE, CU.

KATIE's trembling finger carefully picks out the number, and we hear the corresponding tones: 555-4408.

Literary Connection

The Horror Genre Although the element of horror has been a part of literature since ancient times (think *Beowulf* and *Sir Gawain and the Green Knight*), horror as a genre is generally regarded as having its roots in the Gothic novels of the eighteenth century, particularly with Horace Walpole's *The Castle of Otranto* (1764). Edgar Allan Poe, generally regarded as the father of modern horror literature, made invaluable contributions to the form during the nineteenth century. Works such as "The Telltale Heart," and "The Pit and the Pendulum," are good examples. Like Poe, Bram Stoker was a pioneer in the form. His *Dracula* (1897) began a trend in vampire literature that continues to this day. During the early part of the twentieth century, further strides in the field were made by H. P. Lovecraft (numerous short stories, such as "Dragon") and Gaston Leroux (*Phantom of the Opera*, 1910).

Analyze Literature

Resolution Explain that this is the point at which Katie realizes the nature of the call she received five years before. Ask students to respond to this moment of revelation. Is it a satisfying climactic moment? Model a response by suggesting that it requires a "suspension of disbelief" to accept the moment for what it is. **C**

Presentation

Have students present oral reports based on their research on contemporary horror writers on page 723. Review with students these pointers for speakers:

- Speak clearly and loudly enough for all to hear.
- Maintain a good pace—not too fast or too slow—pausing at appropriate times.
- Make eye contact with the audience.
- Use appropriate gestures, and move around.
- Use visual aids such as overhead transparencies, video, charts, drawings, photographs, models, props, or costumes.

Provide these tips for listeners:

- Pay attention courteously.
- Ask questions for clarification at the end.

Answer:
Students should name people whose voices they would recognize under any circumstance. They should also be able to name specific traits that people in their families share.

Analyze and Extend

1. When the voice on the line sounds so terribly upset, she jumps to the conclusion that her daughter is miserable at her new boarding school. In addition, it is possible that her voice and her daughter's voice are similar.

2. (a) She is a great fan of his work, she seems to idolize him, and she even wants his autograph on a book she owns. (b) In the context of the screenplay, Bill's occupation as a horror writer is significant because his family goes through a little horror story of their own.

3. The family still lives in the same house, and Bill's study is still used in this manner. Apparently the same extension telephone is in the study, but we don't know about the phone in the kitchen nook. We do know that the old number has been changed, even though Katie was able to reach it on the first try, if only in her imagination.

INT. KATIE, IN BILL'S OLD CHAIR, CU.

She closes her eyes as the PHONE BEGINS TO RING. Her face is filled with an agonizing mixture of hope and fear. If only she can have one more chance to pass the vital message on, it says…just one more chance.

KATIE. [*Low.*] Please…please…

RECORDED VOICE. [*Filter.*] You have reached a non-working number. Please hang up and dial again. If you need assistance—

KATIE hangs up again. Tears stream down her cheeks. THE CAMERA PANS AWAY AND DOWN to the telephone.

INT. THE PHONE NOOK, WITH KATIE AND BILL, REPRISE.

BILL. So it was a prank. Or someone who was crying so hard she dialed a wrong number…"through a shimmering film of tears," as we veteran hacks like to say.

KATIE. It was not a prank and it was not a wrong number! It was someone in *my family!*

INT. KATIE (PRESENT DAY) IN BILL'S STUDY.

KATIE. Yes. Someone in my family. Someone who is close. [*Pause.*] Me.

She suddenly throws the phone across the room. She starts to sob again and puts her hands over her face. CAMERA HOLDS on her for a moment, then DOLLIES ACROSS.

INT. THE PHONE.

It lies on the carpet, looking both bland and somber. CAMERA MOVES IN TO ECU—the holes in the receiver look like huge dark chasms. We HOLD, then

FADE TO BLACK.

MIRRORS & WINDOWS

Who are the people in your life whose voices you recognize regardless of the circumstance? What specific traits do people in a family share?

Analyze and Extend

1. What leads Katie to believe that her daughter Polly is calling her?

2. (a) Why does Bill receive special treatment from the telephone operator? (b) In the context of the screenplay, what is the significance of Bill's occupation?

3. Determine what remains the same at the end of the screenplay compared to five years earlier. What is the importance of these consistencies?

Expository Writing In a short **essay,** analyze how the characters' interactions foreshadow events in the plot. State your position in a clear thesis statement, and support your thesis with examples and direct evidence from the screenplay.

Collaborative Learning In small groups, discuss the ways in which the author builds suspense throughout this screenplay. With your group, list specific literary techniques King uses, and give at least one example from the text. Determine how these techniques, when used together, contribute to the overall effect of suspense. Share your list with the class once you finish.

Go to **www.mirrorsandwindows.com** for more.

Rubric for Expository Writing

You can adapt this as a checklist for students to use as they write.

☐ Does the essay analyze how the characters' interactions foreshadow events in the plot?

☐ Does the essay have a clear thesis statement?

☐ Is the thesis supported with examples and direct evidence from the screenplay?

For Your Reading List

The Glass Menagerie

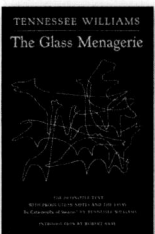

by Tennessee Williams

A mother's attempts to find a "gentleman caller" for her extremely shy daughter, Laura, is the focus of this play by one of the finest American playwrights. Laura fears the outside world and chooses to stay at home and play with her collection of glass animal figurines, while her mother worries about her future and criticizes her son for his selfish and restless behavior. This play is considered by many to be Williams's finest play.

Children of a Lesser God

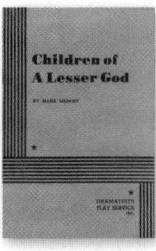

by Mark Medoff

This Tony award–winning play tells the story of a young deaf woman and her mentor. It gives readers a glimpse into the world of a deaf person as well as inspiring questions of how people interact with others with physical or mental challenges.

Backstage at a Play

by Kimberly M. Miller

This fascinating book takes you backstage for a look at the inner workings of a play in progress. Learn how plays are rehearsed and staged and also receive helpful tips for getting involved in the theater. A list of resources for further reading about theater is included. This book is part of a series that offers an insider's look at many types of entertainment.

An Actor on the Elizabethan Stage

by Stephen Currie

Take a closer look at Elizabethan theater through a description of the lives of the men and boys who made up a typical theater troupe. Learn how Elizabethan actors rehearsed and prepared plays, how the dramas were performed, and what skills an aspiring actor needed to have: singing, dancing, memorization, acrobatics, and swordplay, among others.

Shakespeare: His Work and His World

by Michael Rosen

This lively and compelling introduction to Shakespeare provides fascinating details about the playwright, his theater, the plays, and the period. The author looks closely at *A Midsummer Night's Dream, Romeo and Juliet, Macbeth, King Lear*, and *The Tempest*. He also investigates those parts of Shakespeare's life that still inspire curiosity, including his early education and marriage.

Break a Leg! The Kids' Guide to Acting and Stagecraft

by Lise Friedman

This introduction to acting and stage production provides information about every theater topic imaginable: acting skills, improvisation, voice projection, breathing exercises, script analysis, rehearsals, and performance. Also included is information on the technical aspects of theater production. Special sections cover clowning, juggling, stage combat, fainting, and death scenes. This volume ends with scenes and monologues for student actors.

Independent Reading

Independent Reading Activity

Dramas are unusual and provocative readings for student Literature Circles. Create groups of five or six students, in combinations you think will have fruitful discussions. Ask each group to choose a short drama from one of the collections here or from another collection. They may wish to consult a librarian. Allow ample time for students to collaborate on their group choices.

When a group has chosen its play, help members locate enough copies for everyone to read. Give groups a week to read the play outside of class. Then allow Literature Circles to meet during class. Encourage students to devise a focus question for their discussions, or prompt them with this question: "How is the play relevant to the modern world?"

See the Skills lesson below for how students can establish their own rules of etiquette. Tell students to reflect on their experiences once they conclude the group discussion.

 EMC E-Library

The EMC E-Library contains over twenty thousand pages of literary classics that students may read independently. An Electronic Library Guide provides teaching suggestions, enrichment activities, and reading strategy guide sheets.

Program Resources

EMC Access Editions

For additional independent reading, you may wish to refer students to one of EMC's Access Edition titles. Each Access Edition contains a thorough study apparatus, including background information, literal comprehension questions, footnotes, vocabulary definitions, critical thinking questions, and related projects and activities. An Assessment Manual offering worksheets and exams is available for each Access Edition.

Common Core State Standards

Reading Literature
RL.10

Reading Informational
RI.10

Objectives

Participating in this lesson will help students write a persuasive essay that has

- a topic that maintains student inspiration
- an effective introduction
- a clear thesis statement
- a clear and logical organizational pattern
- evidence that supports the thesis
- an effective conclusion that restates the thesis and adds an insight

Launch the Workshop

Tell students to imagine that their state government wants to pass a law that would disallow students from speaking in the classroom unless first spoken to by the teacher. Encourage initial emotional responses to this concept. Divide the class into two groups, one arguing for the law and one arguing against it. Ask groups to brainstorm for three minutes on arguments they would use to win people to their side. Then convene the class and ask volunteers to explain whether it was easy or difficult to come up with arguments. After several comments from students, tell the class that now they will learn how to draft convincing arguments to win people over, that is, to persuade.

Program Resources

For a full writing rubric, go to **www.mirrorsandwindows.com.** Additional writing workshops are available in Exceeding the Standards: Writing.

Common Core State Standards

Writing
W.1, W.4, W.5, W.6, W.10
Language
L.3.3a

Writing Workshop

Persuasive Writing

Persuasive Essay

Reading and Writing

In this unit, you read examples of drama and autobiography. Characters and writers were often in positions in which they had to persuade others to accept a certain idea or belief. Think about Anne Frank's journals: she tried to persuade her readers to disregard certain views about people in her age group. Gerda Weissmann Klein tried to persuade her friends to believe that they were going to be liberated. Writers often try to persuade readers to accept their ideas. In particular, persuasion can be found in advertisements, speeches, and newspapers.

In this workshop, you will learn how to write a **persuasive essay.** This is an essay that presents an argument and attempts to persuade the reader to agree with an idea or to take action. The following summary includes your assignment, goal, strategy, and writing rubric. These tools will help you develop a strong essay.

- **Assignment:** Write a persuasive essay about an issue that is important to me.

- **Goal:** Construct my argument with appeals to logic and emotion and by addressing potential counterarguments.

- **Strategy:** Create a clear thesis statement, follow an appropriate pattern of organization, and support my thesis with different types of evidence.

- **Writing Rubric:** My persuasive essay should include the following:

  - an introductory paragraph that sets up my issue and states my thesis
  - a clear organizational pattern
  - evidence, such as reasons, facts, and examples, to support my thesis
  - logical and emotional appeals as well as rhetorical devices
  - an effective conclusion that sums up my main points and restates my thesis

What Great Writers Do

Martin Luther King, Jr., is known today for his work as a Civil Rights activist. He was also an inspiring public speaker and an elegant writer. In a clip from one of his most famous works, "Letter from a Birmingham Jail," King emphasizes a point using two parallel sentences. How might parallel structure strengthen your points?

How does one determine whether a law is just or unjust?…Any law that uplifts human personality is just. Any law that degrades human personality is unjust. All segregation statutes are unjust because segregation…damages the personality.

Words in Use

Teaching Words

disregard, 730	**assumptions,** 731
liberated, 730	**verified,** 731
strategy, 730	**effective,** 732
rubric, 730	**logical,** 732
potential, 730	**annotations,** 733
parallel, 730	**reinforce,** 734
degrades, 730	**typeface,** 734
segregation statutes, 730	

KEY TERMS

PERSUASIVE ESSAY, 730	COUNTERARGUMENTS, 732
THESIS, 730	
RHETORICAL DEVICE, 730	FIGURATIVE LANGUAGE, 734
SUPPORTING DETAIL, 731	REPETITION, 734
LOGICAL APPEAL, 731	PARALLELISM, 734
EMOTIONAL APPEAL, 731	COORDINATING CONJUNCTION, 734
LOADED WORDS, 731	SUBORDINATING CONJUNCTION, 734
RHETORICAL QUESTION, 731	CORRELATIVE CONJUNCTION, 734
ORDER OF IMPORTANCE, 732	

1. PREWRITE

Choosing Your Topic

To write an effective persuasive essay, choose a topic about which you feel strongly. You might want to consider your audience. Is there an important topic at your school that you would like to bring to your principal's attention? Can you take a position about something you have seen in the news? Remember that your audience might disagree with you. You will need to have solid evidence to support your position.

Identifying a Position

Once you have an issue, write a clear statement of your position. Your position allows you to create your **thesis statement,** or the argument you will make in your essay. It is also your guide for finding supporting details.

> Issue: Recycling
>
> Position: I want my school to recycle and reuse paper.
>
> Thesis: Our school should have a program to reuse and recycle paper.

Gathering Details

Once you have an issue and a position, you will need to gather evidence to support your position. A good persuasive essay uses two kinds of evidence. Evidence that appeals to logic relies on assumptions about the reader's sense of reason.

A **logical appeal** presents facts, statistics, and examples that can be verified. That is, a logical appeal is a statement that can be proved. Most of your evidence should be logical appeals.

Evidence that appeals to emotion relies on assumptions about the reader's beliefs and feelings.

An **emotional appeal** draws forth feelings in the reader. Two types of emotional appeals are **loaded words** and **rhetorical questions.**

- **Loaded words** are words that have strong emotional content.
- **Rhetorical questions** are questions that the reader is not meant to answer because, according to the writer, the answer is obvious.

You will need both kinds of evidence. It is helpful to create a chart of your evidence.

Evidence	Appeal to Emotion	Appeal to Logic
Reusing paper saves money.		✔
A recycling and reusing program can build a sense of community.	✔	
Recycling and reusing help conserve trees, a precious natural resource.	✔	
Recycling reduces the garbage our facility creates.		✔

Draft

Organizing Ideas Students may also wish to explore using cause-and-effect, compare-and-contrast, or problem-solution organization patterns. Discuss each pattern of organization in detail, and determine, as a class, a few essay topics that might come across especially well when organized in each pattern.

Putting Thoughts on Paper Tell students that one strategy for beginning a persuasive essay is to establish rapport with the reader. They can achieve this by creating common ground—points on which most people agree. Model this technique: "I'm going to write an essay arguing that all our schools should teach music. I know some people think music instruction should be optional. I'll open with a quote: 'To paraphrase Henry Wadsworth Longfellow, Music is the language of humanity.'"

What Great Writers Do

Encourage students to welcome counterarguments, as they often serve to strengthen their arguments when effectively addressed. Andrei Sakharov wrote:

Profound insights arise only in debate, with a possibility of counterargument, only when there is a possibility of expressing not only correct ideas but also dubious ideas.

2. DRAFT

Organizing Ideas

Now organize your information in a clear and logical way for your topic. The easiest way to organize your persuasive essay is to list your pieces of evidence in **order of importance.** First, evaluate your evidence. Begin with your strongest piece of evidence. Then present your second strongest piece of evidence, and so on. Look at how the evidence generated during the prewriting stage is arranged according to the author's sense of order of importance.

Most important: Recycling and reusing help conserve trees, a precious natural resource.
↓
Second: Reusing paper saves money.
↓
Third: Recycling reduces the garbage our facility creates.
↓
Fourth: A recycling and reusing program can build a sense of community.

Putting Your Thoughts on Paper

A persuasive essay has three basic parts: an introduction, body, and conclusion. Create a plan for your essay by considering the main parts. Introduce your topic and state your position in a clear thesis in the introduction. Cite your reasons and evidence in the body paragraphs in order of importance. Be sure to include a topic sentence for each body paragraph as well as supporting sentences to develop and explain your reasons. Also, address and respond to any counterarguments in the body paragraphs. Finally, summarize your main points and restate your thesis in your conclusion.

Introduction
- Create a compelling introduction.
- Present my position.

Body
- In each paragraph, include a reason for my position or address a counterargument.
- Support each reason with evidence, including appeals to logic and emotion.

Conclusion
- Paraphrase my thesis.
- Restate the key points.

Addressing Counterarguments

To write an effective persuasive paper, consider both sides of your issue. Anticipate potential **counterarguments,** or opposing views, and respond to them in a way that strengthens your own argument. Use facts and details to show why your position should be viewed as the correct one. When addressing a counterargument, keep in mind your audience. Keep your tone respectful, but make your position clear. Your goal is to show your audience that your position is the most logical one.

Set up your counterargument like a supporting paragraph. Address the counterargument in your topic sentence and show its weaknesses through facts, details, and examples.

Supporting Paragraph

Topic Sentence: States a reason that supports your opinion statement

Supporting Sentences: Explanation and supporting facts, details, and examples

OR

Counterargument

Topic Sentence: Presents a counterargument

Supporting Sentence: Explanation of the counterargument and facts, details, and examples that reveal its weaknesses

Differentiated Instruction

Enrichment

Several approaches to teaching persuasive writing refer to the ancient art of rhetoric, or using language to please and persuade. One foundation of rhetoric is called the "three appeals": logos, ethos, and pathos. These Greek words refer to reason, to credibility of the speaker, and to emotion. Have students explore the three terms using library and Internet resources. Then ask them to summarize for the whole class what they learned and how it applies to writing a persuasive essay.

Evaluating Your Draft

One of the best ways to judge the effectiveness of your essay is to ask others to read your essay. First read it aloud to yourself. Use a pencil to mark anything that you think needs to be fixed. Then ask at least two of your peers to read it silently. Have them evaluate your argument.

Below is part of a draft of a persuasive essay. The annotations indicate reasons for the changes.

Revising Checklist

☐ Does the introduction grab the reader's attention?

☐ Does the thesis present the argument?

☐ Is there a clear organizational pattern?

☐ Are the points supported with evidence?

~~Our school should have a program to recycle and reuse paper.~~ Last week, I helped the school custodian take out the garbage from our classroom. She asked me to help because there were more than four bags at our door. Everything was piled up like last year's toys. Do you know what was in two of those bags? Paper. Recycling and reusing paper would save time, energy, money, and natural resources. *Our school should have a program to recycle and reuse paper.*

Move the thesis to the end of the paragraph to build a more compelling introduction.

The main reason to recycle and reuse paper is to help conserve trees, a precious natural resource. ~~People love trees.~~ *Most people at our school love the old elm trees in the playground. Several students have climbed the oak tree, and it continues to be a favorite gathering place.* What would happen if those trees had to be chopped down to satisfy our need for paper? *Local ecologists warn that within twenty years, the number of trees in our county would be reduced by 50% if the demand for paper continues at its current rate.* Reusing and recycling paper would help prevent this decline in trees and offer time for newly planted trees to grow.

Add emotional appeals that will affect your particular audience.

Include logical appeals, such as facts and statistics, to support the thesis and main points.

Revise

Evaluating a Draft Give students the following tips for delivering and receiving constructive criticism.

Delivering Criticism

- **Be focused.** Concentrate on the introduction, the organization, and transitions. Leave spelling and punctuation for later.
- **Be positive.** Respect the writer's feelings and writing efforts.
- **Be specific.** Give concrete ideas for improving the essay.

Receiving Criticism

- **Ask questions.** Make sure you understand your reviewer's comments. Ask your reviewer to clarify comments and suggestions if necessary.
- **Be selective.** Accept your reviewer's time and suggestions graciously. When you revise your essay, you can use just some—or none—of the suggestions.

Speaking Skills

Constructive Criticism

Explain to students that they should provide constructive criticism with care in a peer editing setting, as both parties are still new to the process and susceptible to emotional responses. Emphasizing areas for improvement without shaking a person's confidence is difficult, as is reinforcing areas of strength with practical praise. Provide students with the following tips:

1. Understand the difference between peer feedback and teacher feedback. Neither of you have rank over the other. In fact, you are colleagues with the same goal.
2. When providing constructive criticism, speak respectfully and ask your partner questions that will engage him or her in the process.
3. Balance criticism and praise, and treat them with equal importance.

Students may want to use proofreader's marks when correcting their work. Refer them to the Language Arts Handbook Writing Section 4.1, Proofreader's Symbols.

▶ **Publish and Present**

Before students begin their final versions, they might benefit from reading the Language Arts Handbook Writing Section 4.1, Writing Follow-up.

4. EDIT AND PROOFREAD

Focus: Rhetorical Devices

Rhetorical devices are tools you can use to persuade. Common rhetorical devices include figurative language, repetition, and parallelism.

Figurative language such as metaphors and similes can help a reader understand your point in a new way.

> Everything was piled up like last year's toys.

Repetition of words or phrases can create a dramatic effect or reinforce your point.

> There were newspaper clippings from social studies. There were pieces of scratch paper from math. There were observation sheets from science.

Parallelism is the expression of similar ideas in a similar way, whether between words, phrases, or sentences.

> Recycling and reusing paper would save time, energy, money, and natural resources.

Focus: Conjunctions

Conjunctions are words used to link words or phrases together.

Coordinating conjunctions connect two sentence elements of similar type and equal weight:

> Recycling *and* reusing paper can save our school some money.

Subordinating conjunctions connect two sentence parts of unequal weight, usually an independent clause and dependent clause:

> *Because* doing good things for the school makes people feel like teammates, a recycling and reusing program would help build community.

Correlative conjunctions are pairs of words:

> *Neither* recycling *nor* reusing will take more energy than is currently used to take out the excess garbage.

Proofreading

Quality Control As with any piece of writing, proofread your persuasive essay before you turn it in. The purpose of proofreading is to correct errors in grammar, punctuation, and spelling. Use proofreader's marks to highlight any errors you find. (See the Language Arts Handbook, section 4.1, for a list of proofreader's marks.)

5. PUBLISH AND PRESENT

Final Draft

Clean Copy Now that you have revised, edited, and proofread your paper, make a clean copy for presentation. Handwritten papers should be neat and legible. If you are working with a word processing program, double-space the lines of text and use a readable typeface. Follow the presentation guidelines of your class before submitting your work.

Differentiated Instruction

Enrichment

Tell students that there are many kinds of figurative language, in addition to similes and metaphors, that function as rhetorical devices, including alliteration, allusion, personification, symbol, and synecdoche, to name a few.

Challenge students to research these and other kinds of figurative language that are effective rhetorical devices. How do they persuade, dissuade, and/or produce sympathy and/or approval? Encourage students to share their research with others in the class and integrate their researched figurative language into their persuasive essays.

Student Model

That's Not Just Garbage!
By Maribel Ramos

Last week, I helped the school custodian take out the garbage from our classroom. She asked me to help because there were more than four bags at our door. Everything was piled up like last year's toys. Do you know what was in two of those bags? Paper. There were newspaper clippings from social studies. There were pieces of scratch paper from math. There were observation sheets from science. Recycling and reusing this paper would save time, energy, money, and natural resources. Our school should have a program to recycle and reuse paper.

The main reason to recycle and reuse paper is to help conserve trees, a precious natural resource. Most people at our school love the old elm trees in the playground. Several students have climbed the oak tree, and it continues to be a favorite gathering place. What would happen if those trees had to be chopped down to satisfy our need for paper? Local ecologists warn that within twenty years, the number of trees in our county would be reduced by 50% if the demand for paper continues at its current rate. Reusing and recycling paper would help prevent this decline in trees and offer time for newly planted trees to grow. We could both conserve the trees we have and plant more trees to satisfy our paper needs.

Secondly, recycling and reusing paper can save our school money. If we recycle enough paper, we'll be eligible for the Mayor's Responsible School Fund. We can use this money for maintenance expenses or to develop and expand more school programs. Also, if we reuse paper, we'll save money simply by reducing the amount of paper we need to buy.

Some decision-makers might object to a recycling plan because of the time, energy, and people needed to organize the process. However, if the custodian has so much garbage that she can't do it all herself, then recycling and reusing can only help. Neither recycling nor reusing will take more energy than is currently used to take out the excess garbage. Ultimately, recycling would reduce the total garbage our school creates. In addition, if we use student volunteers to organize the school recycling plan, the project will bring people together. The project would show how easy it is for individuals to make a difference.

Starting a serious recycling and reusing program would help students learn to protect natural resources, save our school's money, and learn how to organize to make a difference. In the meantime, check before you throw that piece of paper away. It's probably not just garbage!

> **Introduces issue and position in a compelling way and sets up thesis statement**
>
> **Uses rhetorical devices for effect**

> **Follows organizational pattern by beginning with most important evidence**
>
> **Includes both logical and emotional appeals**

> **Addresses a counterargument and responds to it in a way that strengthens the writer's own argument**

> **Restates thesis and summarizes evidence**
>
> **Uses parallelism for emphasis**

Writing Skills

Effective Conclusions

Lead students to see that advertisements aim to convince consumers not only that their product is good but also that they should go out and buy it. Encourage them to see the similarity in purpose between ads and their arguments. One of the purposes of their conclusion is to lead others to action concerning the issue.

Have students research possible courses of action that their readers might take. Recommend areas such as politics, business, law, and service work as fertile ground for activities that support the cause they are illustrating. Encourage them to recommend at least one of the activities they discover in their conclusions.

Objectives

Participating in this lesson will help students deliver persuasive presentations that

- open and close strongly
- promote a solid viewpoint
- use valid arguments
- present ideas clearly
- employ persuasive techniques convincingly
- incorporate effective pacing, volume, and nonverbal expression

Participating in this lesson will also help students achieve the following listening objectives:

- be courteous to the speaker
- listen attentively
- maintain eye contact
- sustain interest in the presentation
- ask suitable questions
- provide constructive verbal feedback

Launch the Workshop

Choose a student to help you illustrate the importance of speaking and listening well in a presentation situation. Create a short skit with the student, in which one person is the speaker and the other an audience member. Incorporate as many poor examples of presentation etiquette as possible. Present the skit to the classroom. Then discuss the problems with the mock delivery and reception and possible ways to remedy them.

Giving and Actively Listening to Persuasive Presentations

Have you ever tried to convince your parents to let you do something? The goal of a **persuasive presentation** is to convince others to believe something, to change their beliefs, or take some action. Learning to actively listen to and evaluate the arguments in a persuasive presentation, such as advertisements or political speeches, helps you make informed decisions rather than being influenced by emotion.

Planning Your Persuasive Speech

Choose a Topic and Position Think about attitudes or practices at school or in your community that you think should be changed. Is the dress code too strict? Should your community build a teen center? You may decide to present the persuasive essay you just wrote. Select a topic about which you feel strongly. Sum up your position in a strong statement, such as, "While our school recycles paper, we still waste many resources such as glass and plastic, so we should begin a broader recycling program."

Identify Your Audience The arguments you use to convince fellow students might be different from those you would use to convince school administrators. Once you identify your audience, ask yourself, "What kind of arguments will convince these people to take my side and act?"

Outline and Research Your Arguments Begin by outlining your arguments. Use concrete evidence from expert sources to back up your own opinions. Evaluate arguments *for* your position, as well as analyzing arguments that opponents might raise *against* your position. Look for statistics, expert opinions, anecdotes, examples, and other supporting details. You may also wish to use visuals to support your arguments. Use a table to outline the body of your speech.

My Arguments	Opponent's Arguments
• Statistics on number of glass and plastic containers used in school • Photo of garbage cans overflowing with glass/plastic • Expert opinion on recycling natural resources • Easy to do...separate containers	• Costs too much to buy separate containers and have them picked up by recycler. (Counter short-term costs with long-term benefits) • No place to put extra containers • No one will bother

To expand upon this workshop lesson, Giving and Actively Listening to Persuasive Presentations, see the *Exceeding the Standards: Speaking & Listening* resource.

Common Core State Standards

Speaking and Listening
SL.1, SL.2, SL.3, SL.4, SL.6

Teaching Words
vague, 737
rubric, 737
courteous, 737
constructive, 737

KEY TERMS

PERSUASIVE
  PRESENTATION, 736
TOPIC, 736
AUDIENCE, 736
OUTLINE, 736
ANECDOTE, 736
FIGURATIVE
  LANGUAGE, 737
REPETITION, 737
TRANSITION WORD, 737
BANDWAGON, 737
LOADED WORD, 737

CONNOTATION, 737
GLITTERING
  GERNERALITY, 737
POINT OF VIEW, 737
SUPPORTING DETAIL, 737

Attention Getters Grab your audience's interest by telling a related dramatic story; asking the audience a question, such as, "How would you like to live next to a landfill?"; or using figurative language (*If all the glass and plastic we use in a year were piled up, it would be as big as...*).

Persuasive Techniques Decide what persuasive techniques you will use in your speech.

Repetition and Transition Words Repeat a word or phrase to add emphasis. For example, you might end each argument with the words "Act now!" Use transition words to set apart your arguments from those of your opponents. (*Some may think* it will cost too much to recycle. *In reality,* it will cost far more in the long run if we don't recycle.)

Clinchers The clincher is the last sentence of the speech. It should be a powerful call to action but worded differently from the rest of your speech.

Avoid Deceptive Techniques Use facts rather than trickery to convince your audience. Some techniques attempt to persuade people by appealing to emotions rather than logic.

Every other school recycles. This **"bandwagon"** technique suggests that, because everyone else does it, you should too.

This is a criminal waste of resources. Criminal is a **"loaded word"**—a word with strong connotations that can influence the audience's emotions.

Taking an active role in recycling will make our school great! This is a **"glittering generality"**—a vague statement with no supporting evidence.

Evaluating Your Presentation

With a peer group, take turns delivering your speech. Take notes to summarize the main ideas of your peers' speeches. After each presentation, the group should offer helpful and polite feedback on how well the speech accomplished its purpose. Follow the listening and speaking rubric on this page in order to evaluate the presentation.

Delivering Your Presentation

The purpose of your presentation is to persuade the audience to adopt your point of view. Focus on a strong attention getter and then deliver your main arguments supported by factual details. Use a respectful and reasonable tone and avoid insulting people who don't agree with your position. Answer questions by elaborating rather than arguing.

As an active listener, be courteous to the speaker, even if you don't agree. Base your decisions on facts, not emotions. Ask questions when appropriate on the arguments or supporting details.

Speaking Rubric

Your presentation will be evaluated on these elements:

Content

❑ presentation is clear and organized

❑ arguments are strong and well-supported

❑ opposing arguments are addressed

Delivery and Presentation

❑ tone is moderate and reasonable

❑ nonverbal communication effectively supports content

❑ clarification and elaboration used to answer audience questions

---

Listening Rubric

As a peer reviewer or audience member, you should do the following:

❑ listen quietly and attentively

❑ maintain eye contact with speaker

❑ try to interpret the speaker's purpose by taking notes that summarize the content of the presentation

❑ ask appropriate questions

❑ (as peer reviewer) provide constructive feedback

Evaluating an Audience

Emphasize for students the value of developing rapport with an audience. (You can define *rapport* as a relationship based on understanding and sharing the same concerns.) Point out that people are persuaded when they identify with a speaker who has a particular point of view. For a concrete demonstration of relating to different listeners, ask students how they would present their arguments to each of these audiences:

- a group of politicians
- their extended family
- a group of recent immigrants
- a group of peers

What Great Writers Do

It is not enough to simply state ideas. Good speakers make their words come alive for the audience. Ben Johnson, a famous English poet, dramatist, and actor said:

To speak and to speak well are two things. A fool may talk, but a wise man speaks.

Rehearsing a Speech

Give students opportunities to practice their presentations alone and with peer reviewers. Offer these tips:

- Set a time limit, such as four or five minutes.
- Make sure your arguments are memorable. This may mean editing explanations and adding repetition or figurative language.
- Ask for feedback. If a listener is not persuaded, find out why.

Speaking & Listening Skills

Appropriate questions

Remind students that asking appropriate questions will help the listener understand the speaker's intentions, as well as provide the speaker with a chance to clarify his or her thoughts. Divide the class into pairs and instruct them to listen to each other's speeches, politely raise their hand when they have a useful question, and voice the question in a respectful manner. Discuss the benefits and drawbacks of the questions.

> ⊘ For more information, see the Language Arts Handbook Section 7, Speaking & Listening.

Objectives

Completing this lesson will enable students to

- write a persuasive essay based on a timed writing prompt
- answer standardized test questions that demonstrate revising and editing skills
- demonstrate the ability to make inferences from a reading by answering standardized questions

Timed Writing

Explain that standardized tests often ask students to write a response to a prompt in a specified period of time. Give the following tips:

- Read the entire prompt carefully.
- Look for key words in the prompt that tell you what is expected.
- Underline these words or write them on your own note paper.
- Use the key words to make sure you follow all the instructions.
- Organize. Allow time for planning, writing, and reviewing.
- Before you begin writing, create a rough outline of points to make.
- Write a clear introduction. This will help keep you on track as you write each paragraph.
- If you find yourself running out of time, state your remaining points and add a conclusion.
- Review your completed essay to see if you have responded completely to the instructions.
- Before you turn in your completed essay, take time to proofread it.

Test Practice Workshop

Writing Skills

Persuasive Essay

Read the following short excerpt and the writing assignment that follows. Before you begin writing, think carefully about what task the assignment is asking you to perform. Then create an outline to help guide your writing.

from *A Woman Called Truth* by Sandy Asher

SOJOURNER.....Master Gedney is madder than a hornet about bringing Pete back. He'll take it out on my boy. I must have my child. I must have him now.

CHIP. [*Losing patience.*] Do you have any idea how much trouble you've put us to? Do you think it's a simple matter to bring a case against a prominent citizen like Solomon Gedney? A case on behalf of a slave—and a woman? The least you can do now is to be reasonable and wait as I tell you to. There's nothing to be done until next session. Go home! [SOJOURNER *folds her arms and stays put.*] What do you think you are doing?

SOJOURNER. I won't leave until you bring Master Gedney to court. I'll stay right here all day every day until you bring Master Gedney to court.

CHIP. You can't do that.

SOJOURNER. Is there a law says I can't?

CHIP. No.

SOJOURNER. Then I can. And I will.

CHIP. [*Exasperated, but admiring her tenacity.*] Oh, very well. There is something I can do.

SOJOURNER. I thought maybe there was.

CHIP. I can call a special session of the court. But prepare yourself, Isabelle. It won't be an easy day....

SOJOURNER. I've never had an easy day in my life, and I don't expect any very soon. But I feel the power of a nation within me today. The law, Squire Chip, the law is for everybody.

CHIP. Let's hope so, Isabelle.

Assignment: Was Isabelle (Sojourner Truth) correct when she said, "the law is for everybody"? Plan and write a **persuasive essay** in which you state and support a **thesis** about whether the laws of the nation apply equally to everyone. Include **persuasive techniques** and **rhetorical devices,** as well as **counterarguments.**

Teaching Words

prominent, 738	**coarse,** 741
behalf, 738	**contemptible,** 741
simplified, 739	
obsolete, 739	
eliminated, 739	
irresistible, 740	
follies, 740	
draggletailed guttersnipe, 740	

KEY TERMS

OUTLINE, 738
PERSUASIVE ESSAY, 738
THESIS, 738
PERSUASIVE TECHNIQUE, 738
RHETORICAL DEVICE, 738
COUNTERARGUMENT, 738
SETTING, 739
ADAPTATION, 739
SUBPLOT, 739

Common Core State Standards

Reading Literature
RL.1, RL.3, RL.4, RL.6

Writing
W.5

Language
L.4

Revising and Editing Skills

The following passage is an early draft of an essay. Some parts of the passage need to be rewritten. Read the passage and select the best answers for the questions that follow. Some questions are about particular sentences or parts of sentences and ask you to improve sentence structure or word choice. Other questions ask you to consider organization and development. In choosing answers, follow the requirements of standard written English.

(1) People agree and disagree about adapting Shakespeare's plays. (2) Some say the language <u>is too old-fashioned and not understandable.</u> (3) It should be staged in a familiar setting, and the language must be simplified. (4) If this isn't done, no one will bother <u>reading or going to see it.</u> (5) Then you have the people on the other side. (6) Others say that changing any of Shakespeare's language weakens the play. (7) Shakespeare used verse and rhetorical devices that often get lost in adaptations. (8) Some adaptations focus on subplots rather than the main plot of Shakespeare's plays. (9) I think people should stop arguing about it. (10) Weighing these arguments, I think it's acceptable to adapt Shakespeare's plays if just the difficult words are changed to simpler ones.

1. In context, which is the best revision for the first sentence?
   A. Some people think it's O.K. to adapt Shakespeare's plays and others don't.
   B. Some believe that adapting Shakespeare's plays is sometimes necessary, whereas others argue against it.
   C. Adapting Shakespeare's plays often gets argued about.
   D. Whether people should adapt Shakespeare's plays is agreed and disagreed about.
   E. Arguments often happen about whether Shakespeare's plays should be adapted.

2. What change would improve the structure of the underlined part of sentence 2?
   A. is too weird and not familiar.
   B. is too old-fashioned and people can't understand it.
   C. is obsolete and difficult to understand.
   D. is too old-fashioned and you can't understand it.
   E. The sentence is fine as it is.

3. What problem in sentence 3 reduces clarity?
   A. It's not clear to what the pronoun *it* refers.
   B. *Should* must be changed to *must*.
   C. Break the sentence into two sentences.
   D. Replace *simplified* with *made simple*.
   E. Change *staged* to *played*.

4. Which of the following choices improves the underlined part of sentence 4?
   A. The sentence needs no change.
   B. reading it or going to see the play.
   C. reading it or going to see it.
   D. reading the play or going to watch it.
   E. reading or watching the play.

5. Which sentence should be eliminated to make the paragraph more focused?
   A. Sentence 4
   B. Sentence 5
   C. Sentence 6
   D. Sentence 7
   E. Sentence 8

Remind students that reading comprehension tests give a short piece of writing and then ask several questions about it. The questions often ask students to interpret the passage. Urge students to keep the following tips in mind:

- Begin by skimming all the questions.
- Read the passage with the questions in mind. If time permits, read the passage twice before answering any questions.
- Reread the first question carefully.
- Locate the portion of the passage to which the question refers. Read it slowly and carefully.
- Answer the first question.
- Repeat this process to answer all the rest of the questions.

Reading Skills

Carefully read the following passage. Then, on a separate piece of paper, answer each question.

from *Pygmalion* by George Bernard Shaw

PICKERING. Higgins: I'm interested. What about the ambassador's garden party? I'll say you're the greatest teacher alive if you make that good. I'll bet you all the
5 expenses of the experiment you can't do it. And I'll pay for the lessons.

LIZA. Oh, you are real good. Thank you, Captain.

HIGGINS. [*Tempted, looking at her.*] It's
10 almost irresistible. She's so deliciously low—so horribly dirty—

LIZA. [*Protesting extremely.*] Ah-ah-ah-ah-ow-ow-oo-oo!!! I ain't dirty: I washed my face and hands afore I come, I did.

15 **PICKERING.** You're certainly not going to turn her head with flattery, Higgins....

HIGGINS. [*Becoming excited as the idea grows on him.*] What is life but a series of inspired follies? The difficulty is to find
20 them to do. Never lose a chance: it doesn't come every day. I shall make a duchess of this draggletailed guttersnipe.

LIZA. [*Strongly deprecating this view of her.*] Ah-ah-ah-ow-ow-oo!

25 **HIGGINS.** [*Carried away.*] Yes: in six months—in three if she has a good ear and a quick tongue—I'll take her anywhere and pass her off as anything. We'll start today: now! this moment!

30 Take her away and clean her, Mrs. Pearce. Monkey Brand, if it won't come off any other way. Is there a good fire in the kitchen?

MRS. PEARCE. [*Protesting.*] Yes; but—

35 **HIGGINS.** [*Storming on.*] Take all her clothes off and burn them. Ring up Whiteley or somebody for new ones. Wrap her up in brown paper till they come.

40 **LIZA.** You're no gentleman, you're not, to talk of such things. I'm a good girl, I am; and I know what the like of you are, I do.

HIGGINS. We want none of your Lisson
45 Grove prudery here, young woman. You've got to learn to behave like a duchess. Take her away, Mrs. Pearce. If she gives you any trouble, wallop her.

LIZA. [*Springing up and running between*
50 PICKERING *and* MRS. PEARCE *for protection.*] No! I'll call the police, I will....

MRS. PEARCE. [*Resolutely.*] You must be reasonable, Mr. Higgins: really you must. You can't walk over everybody like this.

Differentiated Instruction

English Language Learning

Students may need help with some of the words and phrases in the *Pygmalion* passage.

flattery—extreme or dishonest praise
duchess—the wife or female equivalent of a duke
deprecating—showing disapproval of
ring up—call
wallop—hit someone or something with great force
resolutely—with determination

1. To what is Pickering referring when he says "you can't do it" in lines 5–6?
   A. dress Liza like a lady
   B. give Liza English lessons
   C. get Liza a job in a flower shop
   D. pass Liza off as a lady
   E. get an invitation to the ambassador's garden party

2. Based on the context, what does the word *low* in line 11 mean?
   A. amount less than normal
   B. near the ground
   C. coarse in character
   D. contemptible
   E. bottom

3. In lines 17–18, what do the italicized words "the idea grows on him" mean?
   A. Higgins begins to think seriously about the idea.
   B. Higgins is becoming convinced by Pickering's pleading.
   C. Higgins begins to feel sorry for Liza.
   D. Higgins likes the idea of being paid to work with Liza.
   E. Higgins is tired of arguing with Pickering and Liza.

4. What does Higgins mean.by *follies* in line 19?
   A. great opportunities
   B. unexpected events
   C. crazy accidents
   D. brilliant behavior
   E. foolish behavior

5. Based on the context, what does the word *deprecating* mean in line 23?
   A. being flattered by
   B. expressing a negative opinion about
   C. making fun of
   D. being complimented by
   E. feeling pleased by

6. What can you infer about Professor Higgins's reasons for working with Liza?
   A. He wants to help her get a better job.
   B. He wants to prove how good he is.
   C. He feels sorry for Liza.
   D. He wants to please Pickering.
   E. He wants to prove that Liza is smart.

7. In line 32, what can you infer about *Monkey Brand*?
   A. It is used to wash monkeys.
   B. It is a brand of shampoo.
   C. It is a very strong soap.
   D. It is usually used when bathing.
   E. It doesn't taste very good.

8. What conclusion can you draw about *Whiteley* mentioned in line 37?
   A. It is a company that collects old clothes.
   B. It is the name of Liza's family.
   C. It is a store that sells brown paper.
   D. It is a store that sells women's clothes.
   E. It is the name of the ambassador.

9. What can you infer about Lisson Grove, mentioned in lines 44–45?
   A. It is where Pickering lives.
   B. It is where Liza works.
   C. It is where the Queen lives.
   D. It is where Professor Higgins lives.
   E. It is where Liza lives or grew up.

10. What does Mrs. Pearce's last speech suggest about her attitude toward Liza?
    A. She is trying to protect Liza from Professor Higgins's rudeness.
    B. She doesn't want to have to work with Liza.
    C. She doesn't want Professor Higgins to work with Liza.
    D. She thinks Liza is too stupid for Professor Higgins to teach her.
    E. She thinks Liza's request is reasonable.

Reading Skills

1. D
2. C
3. A
4. E
5. B
6. B
7. C
8. D
9. E
10. A

Test-Taking Skills

Choose the Best Answer

Tell students that a key skill in answering multiple-choice questions is deciding which is the *best* answer available. Note that many times, they will be able to think of good answers to a question. However, not all of those answers will be offered as choices. Model this skill using a question from the sample.

Question 6. The question asks me to infer Professor Higgins's intentions. I'm not sure I know what they *are* after reading the passage, but I'm pretty sure of what they're *not*. Higgins seems to think of Liza as more of an animal than a person, and he speaks of her cruelly, so I know that A, C, and E are not correct. He doesn't seem interested in pleasing anyone but himself, so D is also incorrect. The best available answer, therefore, is B.

Planning and Assessment Tools

Annotated Teacher's Edition

Annotated Teacher's Edition
One location for accessing, previewing, and planning for use of all program resources.

EMC Launchpad
Desktop application for accessing, previewing, planning, posting, and grading all program resources. Post personal resources and lessons, and access the E-Lesson Planner, the E-Gradebook, and training modules for computer literacy.

Assessment Guide* and *ExamView
A variety of assessments are available for this unit in print and electronic forms, including:
- Formative Survey
- Lesson Tests
- Unit Exams
- Alternative Assessment Options
- Reading Fluency Assessments

Meeting the Standards: Unit 1
In addition to lesson-by-lesson resources, *Meeting the Standards* includes the following unit-based resources:
- Unit Study Guide
- Practice Test
- Active Reading Model
- Selection Quizzes

Program Planning Guide* and *E-Lesson Planner
- Lesson Plans for all the selections in the unit
- Core Standards-Based Selections
- Reading Log and Evaluation Forms

The E-Lesson Planner contains fully developed lesson plans and unit resources with an electronic calendar for editing lesson plans.

Technology Tools

Visual Teaching Package
This package contains unit-based lectures, games, art collections, and Writing Workshops in PowerPoint format; included within the EMC Launchpad.

Interactive Student Text on CD
The student textbook on CD includes highlighting, note-taking, bookmarking, and a direct link to the student website, in addition to everything in the student text.

Audio Library
Authentic, dramatic recordings with listening activities expand listening skills and offer additional support for developing readers and English Language Learners.

ETS Online Criterion-Based Essay Grader (Grades 9–12)
Students can use this ETS web-based tool to evaluate their essays online before submitting them for teacher review and final evaluation.

mirrorsandwindows.com
Student and teacher resources, support, references, technology tools, and state-specific standards are available at **mirrorsandwindows.com.** The website is customizable using the EMC Launchpad.

Unit-Based Resources

Exceeding the Standards Unit Resources

Each of the *Exceeding the Standards* resources provides fully developed lessons to help you extend the textbook lessons and to expand upon the themes and skills covered in the unit. You can also download these lessons from **mirrorsandwindows.com**.

Grammar & Style
This resource contains:
- Five lessons on Common Usage Problems, pp. 184–197
- Three lessons on Building Effective Sentences, pp. 198–206

Literature & Reading
This resource contains:
- Analyzing Historical Context, pp. 23–25

Special Topics
This resource contains:
- Career Skills Development: Film and Critique an Interview, pp. 29–30
- Media Literacy: Integrated Media Project, pp. 31–32

Test Practice
This resource contains:
- Research Report Practice Test: Revising and Editing, pp. 17–18
- SAT Practice Test: Critical Reading and Writing, pp. 19–22
- ACT Practice Test: English, Reading, and Writing, pp. 23–26

Writing
This resource contains:
- Narrative Writing: Write a Tall Tale, pp. 70–78

Speaking & Listening
This resource contains the following lesson to expand on the Speaking & Listening Workshop:
- Giving and Actively Listening to Research Presentations, pp. 24–26

Vocabulary & Spelling
This resource contains:
- Three lessons on Choosing and Collecting Words, pp. 72–79

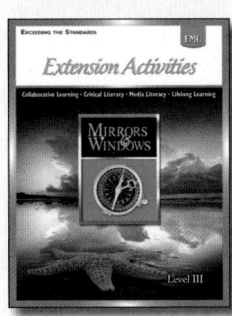

Extension Activities
This resource contains:
- Lifelong Learning: Events Over Time, p. 24
- Media Literacy: Research Urban Legends, pp. 25–26
- Critical Literacy

Unit 8 Visual Planning Guide

Reading Level: Moderate
Pacing: 3 days

Meeting the Standards,
Guided Reading,
pp. 19–23

748

Reading Level: Moderate
Pacing: 2 days

Meeting the Standards,
Guided Reading,
pp. 24–32

Developing Readers,
Take Notes, pp. 53–55

761

Reading Level: Easy
Pacing: 2 days

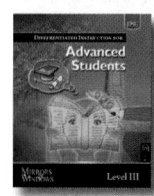

Meeting the Standards,
Directed Reading,
pp. 33–37

Advanced Students,
Theme Study,
pp. 46–47

Coyote Steals
the Sun and Moon

774

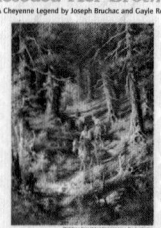

Reading Level: Moderate
Pacing: 1 day

Meeting the Standards,
Directed Reading,
pp. 38–42

*English Language
Learners,* Summarize,
pp. 188–197

779

Reading Level: Easy
Pacing: 3 days

Meeting the Standards,
Directed Reading,
pp. 43–49

Developing Readers,
Visualize, pp. 56–58

Advanced Students,
Genre Research
Project, pp. 48–49

The People Could Fly

787

 Interactive Student
Text on CD-ROM

 Selection
Lesson Plan

 Web-based
Resources

Lesson-by-Lesson Resources

794

Reading Level: Moderate
Pacing: 1 day

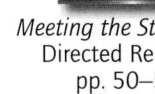

Meeting the Standards, Directed Reading, pp. 50–53

Developing Readers, Unlock Word Meaning, pp. 59–62

799

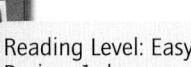
Reading Level: Easy
Pacing: 1 day

Meeting the Standards, Directed Reading, pp. 54–60

Advanced Students, Poetic Form Study, pp. 50–51

805

808

Reading Level: Challenging; Moderate
Pacing: 2 days

Meeting the Standards, Comparing Literature, pp. 61–68

English Language Learners, Understand/Compare, pp. 198–213

815

Reading Level: Moderate
Pacing: 2 days

Meeting the Standards, Directed Reading, pp. 69–72

English Language Learners, Author's Purpose, pp. 214–220

823

Reading Level: Moderate
Pacing: 2 days

Meeting the Standards, Directed Reading, pp. 73–78

Advanced Students, Cultural Context Activity, pp. 52–53

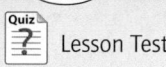 Lesson Test

 Audio Library

Reading Level: Challenging
Pacing: 1 day

Meeting the Standards,
Directed Reading,
pp. 79–82

830

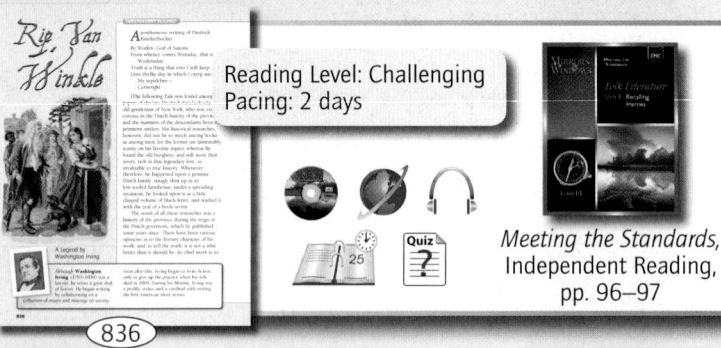

Reading Level: Challenging
Pacing: 2 days

Meeting the Standards,
Independent Reading,
pp. 96–97

836

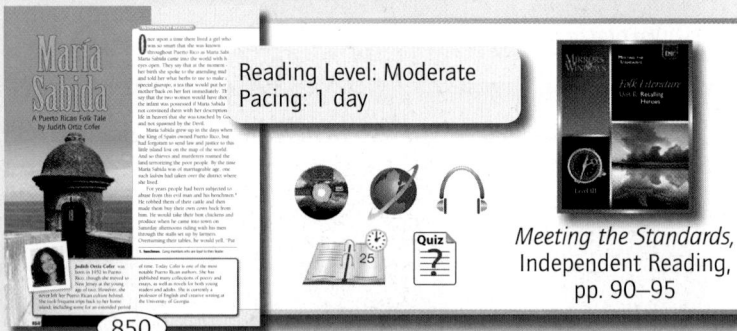

Reading Level: Moderate
Pacing: 1 day

Meeting the Standards,
Independent Reading,
pp. 90–95

850

Unit 8 Scope & Sequence Guide

	Selection or Feature	Genre	Reading Support/ Reading Level	Word Count	Reading Skill	Graphic Organizer	
GUIDED READING	**Introduction to Folk Literature,** pp. 744–745						
	Folk Literature Reading Model, p. 746						
	Legend of the Feathered Serpent Antonio Hernández Madrigal pp. 747–759	Aztec Legend	Guided Reading: Reading Model/ Moderate	2,984	Identify Sequence of Events	Time Line; Legend Chart	
	Pecos Bill Adrien Stoutenberg pp. 760–771	Tall Tale	Guided Reading: Reading Model/ Moderate	3,232	Activate Prior Knowledge	K-W-L Chart; Cluster Chart	
DIRECTED READING	**Coyote Steals the Sun and Moon** Richard Erdoes and Alfonso Ortiz pp. 773–777	Zuni Myth	Directed Reading/Easy	888	Analyze Cause and Effect	Cause and Effect Chart; Myth Chart	

855

Reading Level: Moderate
Pacing: 1 day

Meeting the Standards,
Independent Reading,
pp. 96–97

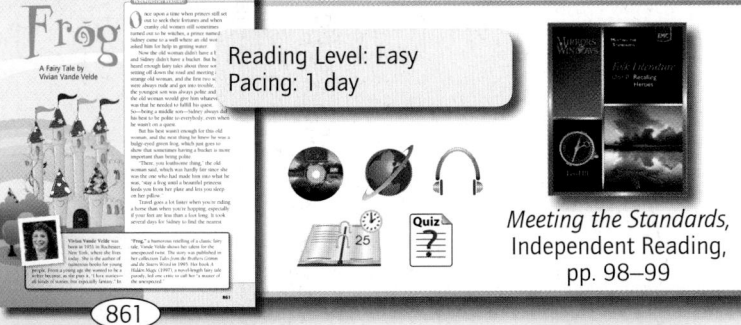

861

Reading Level: Easy
Pacing: 1 day

Meeting the Standards,
Independent Reading,
pp. 98–99

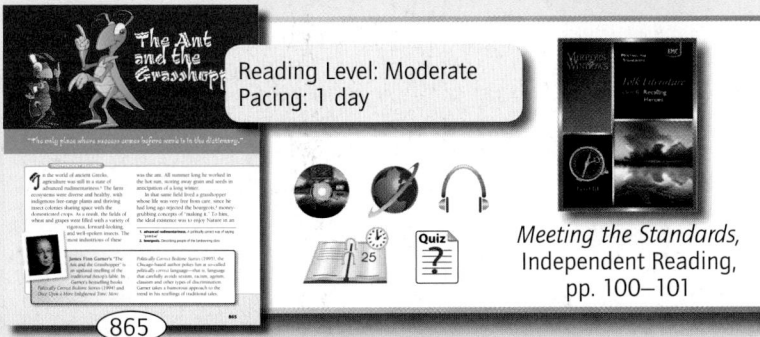

865

Reading Level: Moderate
Pacing: 1 day

Meeting the Standards,
Independent Reading,
pp. 100–101

Literary Element	*Mirrors & Windows* Theme	Cross-Curricular Connection	Writing Options	Extension Activities
Folk Literature				
Legend	Heroes	History Connection: *Cortés's Conquest*	Creative: Lyric Poem Expository: Essay	Lifelong Learning: Research and Make a Time Line Critical Literacy: Read and Analyze in Small Groups
Tall Tale	Heroes		Creative: Lyrics Expository: Summary	Collaborative Learning: Brainstorm in Small Groups Media Literacy: Conduct Library Research; Create a Diagram
Myth	Culpability		Creative: Myth Expository: Expository Essay	Lifelong Learning: Research and Present Media Literacy: Compare Themes Across Cultures

Unit 8 Scope & Sequence Guide

Selection or Feature	Genre	Reading Support/ Reading Level	Word Count	Reading Skill	Graphic Organizer	
Where the Girl Rescued her Brother Joseph Bruchac and Gayle Ross pp. 778–784	Cheyenne Legend	Directed Reading/ Moderate	1,759	Summarize	Summary Chart; Flashback Chart	
The People Could Fly Virginia Hamilton pp. 786–792	African-American Folk Tale	Directed Reading/Easy	1,230	Identify Author's Purpose	Cluster Chart; Dialect Chart	
Literature Connection: Swing Low, Sweet Chariot p. 791	African-American Spiritual	Easy	123			
Blackbeard's Last Fight Richard Walser pp. 793–796	Legend	Directed Reading/ Moderate	355	Context Clues	Characterization Chart	
Barbara Frietchie John Greenleaf Whittier pp. 798–803	Narrative Poem	Directed Reading/Easy	164	Find the Main Idea	Main Idea Map; Cause and Effect Chart	
Comparing Literature: John Henry pp. 804–813	Narrative Poem	Directed Reading/ Challenging	365			
Annie Christmas Walker Brents pp. 804–813	Tall Tale	Directed Reading/ Moderate	1,335			
Paul Bunyan of the North Woods Carl Sandburg pp. 814–821	Tall Tale	Directed Reading/ Moderate	686	Identify Author's Purpose	Author's Purpose Chart; Hyperbole Chart	
Informational Text Connection: The Ole Feller Recollects How Joe Fournier Became Paul Bunyan D. Laurence Rogers pp. 818–820	Essay	Directed Reading/ Moderate	1,550			
The Souls in Purgatory Retold by Guadalupe Baca-Vaughn pp. 822–828	Folk Tale	Directed Reading/ Moderate	1,645	Analyze Cause and Effect	Cause and Effect Chart; Cluster Chart	
Gatored Community Barbara and David P. Mikkelson pp. 829–835	Legend	Directed Reading/ Challenging	1,740	Analyze Text Organization	Tone Chart	

Literary Element	*Mirrors & Windows* Theme	Cross-Curricular Connection	Writing Options	Extension Activities
Flashback	Heroism	History Connection: *The Battle of Rosebud Creek*	Creative: Short Story Expository: Short Essay	Collaborative Learning: Discuss in Small Groups Critical Literacy: Create a Multimedia Presentation
Dialect	Hope		Creative: Drama Expository: Expository Essay	Lifelong Learning: Research and Create a Visual Presentation Media Literacy: Analyze a Vocal Performance
Characterization	Tyranny		Creative: Article Expository: Literary Analysis	Lifelong Learning: Conduct Research Critical Literacy: Create and Perform a Skit
Conflict	Conviction	Cultural Connection: *The Fireside Poets*	Creative: Ballad Expository: Short Essay	Collaborative: Discuss in Small Groups Media Literacy: Determine Historical Accuracy
Compare Literature: Character	Valor Determination		Creative: Eulogy Expository: Expository Essay	Lifelong Learning: Research Critical Literacy: Recite
Hyperbole	Hero Appeal		Creative: Tall Tale Expository: Expository Essay	Lifelong Learning: Research and Write a Journal Entry Media Literacy: Conduct an Interview
Mood	Helping Others		Creative: Personal Letter Expository: Literary Response	Critical Literacy: Hold a Panel Discussion Media Literacy: Compare and Contrast
Tone	Urban Legends		Creative: Newspaper Article Expository: Literary Response	Collaborative Learning: Write a Public Service Announcement Media Literacy: Conduct Internet Research

Unit 8 Scope & Sequence Guide

Selection or Feature	Genre	Reading Support/ Reading Level	Word Count	Reading Skill	Graphic Organizer	
Rip Van Winkle Washington Irving pp. 836–849	Legend	Independent Reading/ Challenging	6,755	Identify Cause and Effect		
María Sabida Judith Ortiz Cofer pp. 850–854	Puerto Rican Folk Tale	Independent Reading/ Moderate	1,697	Activate Prior Knowledge		
from Outlaw: The Legend of Robin Hood Tony Lee, Sam Hart, and Artur Fujita pp. 855–860	Legend, Graphic Novel	Independent Reading/ Moderate	371	Make Inferences		
Frog Vivian Vande Velde pp. 861–864	Fairy Tale	Independent Reading/ Easy	6,734	Make Connections		
The Ant and the Grasshopper James Finn Garner pp. 865–868	Fable	Independent Reading/ Moderate	5,832	Compare and Contrast		

(Side tab: INDEPENDENT READING)

Unit 8 Language Arts Workshops

Grammar & Style	Vocabulary & Spelling	Writing	Speaking & Listening	Test Practice
Misplaced Modifiers, p. 772 Dangling Modifiers, p. 785	Homonyms and Homophones, p. 797	Expository Writing: Research Report, pp. 870–877	Giving and Actively Listening to Research Presentations, pp. 878–879	Writing Skills: Research Report, p. 880 Revising and Editing Skills, p. 895 Reading Skills: from "William Tell," a Swiss Legend, pp. 882–883

Literary Element	*Mirrors & Windows* Theme	Cross-Curricular Connection	Writing Options	Extension Activities
Characterization	Time		Creative: News Article	Lifelong Learning: Write a Biography
Conflict	Conquering		Creative: Lyrics	Collaborative Learning: Role-Play and Interview
Setting, Characterization	Popularity of Legend		Persuasive: Petition	Critical Literary: Enact Trial
Parody	Humor		Creative: Fairy Tale Parody	Collaborative Learning: Panel Discussion
Satire	Moral		Expository: Critical Analysis	Collaborative Learning: Politically Correct Glossary

Unit 8 Building Vocabulary

The lists below identify the Words in Use and Key Terms within this unit. These words are listed at the bottom of the Teacher's Edition pages at the beginning of each lesson. Vocabulary development activities are provided in the *Meeting the Standards* unit book and in *Exceeding the Standards: Vocabulary & Spelling*.

WORDS IN USE

Preview Vocabulary

Preview Vocabulary are words taken from the sentences within each selection. These words are defined in the side margin or at the bottom of the pages on which they appear. The "Preview Vocabulary" section introduces these words in the Before Reading page preceding each selection.

cowed, 795	infestation, 834	pursuit, 776	shrivel, 776
croon, 788	inglorious, 831	quivering, 768	stir, 801
cyclone, 768	intercession, 824	ravage, 795	tendril, 811
determined, 781	lag, 776	reproach, 826	tread, 801
dumbfounded, 824	maneuver, 757	retreat, 783	tuft, 795
embroider, 826	mortal, 754	sacred, 775	veritable, 831
exquisite, 750	perpetrator, 755	scorned, 788	vibrant, 826
famished, 800	plume, 809	seize, 789	
homestead, 762	premises, 831	serenely, 833	
host, 802	prophecy, 750	shanty, 816	

Selection Words

Selection Words are additional words from the reading that may be challenging but are not central to the selection and are not identified in the prereading section. These words can easily be learned using the story context, and they provide excellent practice for using content clues to find meaning without explicit instruction.

abbey, 857	ecosystem, 865	loathsome, 861	retrieved, 795
aground, 811	exoskeleton, 866	maverick, 819	scheme, 824
amid, 816	exploits, 818	microfilm, 831	silhouette, 755
armored, 795	fearsome, 795	midwife, 850	skeptics, 818
bandido, 853	ferocity, 782	nobler, 801	sodden, 811
barometers, 837	fiancée, 851	obedient, 824	subjected, 850
barricaded, 852	follies, 837	ominous, 868	submerged, 811
behold, 809	gallantly, 837	oregano, 852	suffice, 834
beneficence, 866	hauled, 800	orifice, 866	toll, 856
burghers, 836	henpecked, 849	pandemonium, 811	torpor, 848
capriciousness, 867	hewer, 818	parish, 856	treacherous, 819
chivalrous, 837	hoax, 818	peril, 819	venerable, 849
clergy, 857	honorable, 780	pillar, 816	ventilation, 851
consent, 826	incriminate, 859	plodding, 765	vigorous, 865
contend, 818	industrious, 824, 865	posthumous, 836	vowed, 767
corrupt, 857	interfere, 834	precipice, 843	withdrawal, 783
deed, 801	intermarried, 816	pueblo, 851	woebegone, 842
deference, 837	irresistible, 852	quest, 861	wringing, 826
desisted, 842	karma, 867	quintessential, 866	yarns, 833
discontent, 751	lamentably, 836	rampaged, 851	yon, 801
dismembered, 837	lassoed, 765, 832	resounded, 751	

Teaching Words

Teaching Words consist of vocabulary that is used in the directions about the lessons. Teaching words explain to students what to focus on within the selection, help establish the story context, clarify the meaning of literary terms, and define the goals or instructional purpose.

acquire, 864	ancestor, 798	benefits, 878	compassion, 827
activist, 773	ancestral, 773	bolstered, 754	compelling, 849
adapted, 860	anecdotal, 817	buyouts, 782	compound, 881
ageism, 865	anthropologist, 773	cavalry, 782	constructive, 879
alliances, 754	appealing, 878	classism, 865	conveys, 792
alternatives, 881	authoritative, 883	collaborating, 836	courteous, 879

cravings, 753
debunking, 870
demonized, 796
depict, 745
discrimination, 865
documented, 793
emulate, 854
enlisted, 798
era, 786
exaggerate, 772
exaggerated, 760
exaggeration, 814
excerpt, 881
excessive, 855
explanatory, 777
feats, 804
folklore, 793
folkways, 814
freebooter, 744
frontier, 760
generation, 745

genres, 814
glamorized, 796
glamorous, 760
heritage, 778, 793
heroine, 813
inappropriate, 772
influential, 773
institutions, 773
ironically, 754
isolated, 814
legend, 778
lieutenant, 744
lumberjacks, 814
manipulation, 854
memorabilia, 821
memorial, 798
multivolumed, 814
musings, 836
mythic, 760
nonverbal, 879
notable, 850

notation, 871
notorious, 793
oppressed, 798
oral tradition, 778
outlandish, 829
overseer, 786
paraphrased, 870
particulars, 745
persistence, 835
physical phenomena, 880
pillar, 745
plundering, 796
portraying, 813
predicate, 881
prolific, 836
prosecute, 860
purgatory, 822
racism, 865
reciting, 744
reevaluate, 871
relevant, 812

reliable, 759, 870
relocated, 778
represented, 773
reservation, 778
romanticized, 796
rugged, 760
sadistic, 883
sexism, 865
siege, 754
spatial, 872
springboard, 871
supernatural, 744, 759, 773
suppress, 834
technique, 778
terrorized, 854
testimony, 860
textual, 759
traditional, 773
transparency, 879
unionist, 798
vivid, 772

KEY TERMS

Key Terms are commonly referred to as *academic vocabulary*. These terms appear in the instructional material to teach the terminology that students need to acquire to understand literature. The repetition of the terms throughout the program ensures student mastery and provides a solid foundation for the continuing study of literature and language arts.

adjective, 874
alliteration, 883
annotation, 873
antagonist, 804
appositive, 874
appositive phrase, 874
argument, 829
audience, 878
ballad, 745, 803, 807
bibliography, 870
biography, 849
cause, 773
character, 744, 773, 778, 786,
    793, 798, 804, 854
character trait, 784
characterization, 793
chronological order, 872
classification order, 872
clause, 772
cluster chart, 771, 828
compound predicate, 881
compound subject, 881
conclusion, 777, 858, 872, 879
conflict, 778, 798, 803
context clue, 793, 797
coordinating conjunction, 872
correlative conjunction, 872
counterargument, 829
creation myth, 744
critical analysis, 868

dangling modifier, 785
dialect, 786
dialogue, 777, 792, 828
draft, 881
drama, 792
effect, 773
essay, 803
eulogy, 813
external conflict, 798
fable, 865
fairy tale, 861
fiction, 836
figure of speech, 883
flashback, 778
folk hymn, 791
folk song, 745, 804
folk tale, 745, 786, 814, 822,
    850
folklore, 804, 822, 829
foreshadow, 807, 883
genre, 762
graphic novel, 855
hero myth, 744
homonym, 797
homophone, 797
hyperbole, 814, 883
internal conflict, 798
introduction, 821, 879
irony, 869
legend, 744, 747, 778, 793, 829,
    836, 854, 855, 880

line, 745
lyric poem, 759
lyrics, 771, 854
main idea, 777, 798, 880
misplaced modifier, 772, 785
mood, 792, 803, 813, 822
moral, 868
myth, 744, 759, 773, 804, 880
narrative poem, 798
narrator, 786, 817, 835
noun, 772
oral tradition, 744
order of importance, 872
organizational pattern, 870
origin myth, 744
outline, 813, 878, 880
paraphrase, 874
parodoy, 861
peer review, 873
petition, 860
phrase, 745, 772, 881
plagiarism, 874
plot, 773
prepositional phrase, 874
protagonist, 804
pun, 817
punctuation, 872
refrain, 745
research presentation, 878
research report, 870
rhyme scheme, 745, 798

rhymed couplet, 798
rhythm, 803
satire, 868
sequence of events, 747
setting, 803, 828
simple predicate, 881
simple subject, 881
situational irony, 759, 883
spatial order, 872
spiritual, 791
stage direction, 792
stanza, 745, 803, 807
subordinating conjunction, 872
summarize, 874
summary, 771, 835
tall tale, 745, 760, 804, 814
text organization, 829
theme, 777, 778, 854
thesis statement, 835
thesis, 759, 777, 792, 803, 870
tone, 803, 813, 821, 829, 854
topic, 878
transition, 879
understatement, 814
Venn diagram, 771, 813
verbal irony, 883
verse, 759, 798
visualization, 883
works cited, 870

Objectives

Studying this unit will help students meet the following objectives:

- Connect the themes expressed in the selections to their own lives and to the world around them
- Identify and understand common forms and elements of folk literature, including *legend, myth, folk tale, tall tale, folk songs, ballads, narrative poetry, flashback, dialect, characterization, conflict, character, hyperbole, mood*, and *tone*
- Understand variations of literary forms and authors' use of language to develop forms

Reading Strategies

Ask Questions	Make Predictions
Clarify	Visualize
Make Inferences	

Reading Skills

Activate Prior Knowledge
Analyze Cause and Effect
Analyze Text Organization
Identify Author's Purpose
Identify Main Idea
Identify Sequence of Events
Summarize
Use Context Clues

Literary Elements

Character	Legend
Characterization	Mood
Conflict	Myth
Dialect	Tall Tale
Flashback	Tone
Hyperbole	Understatement

Recalling Heroes
Folk Literature

Unit 8

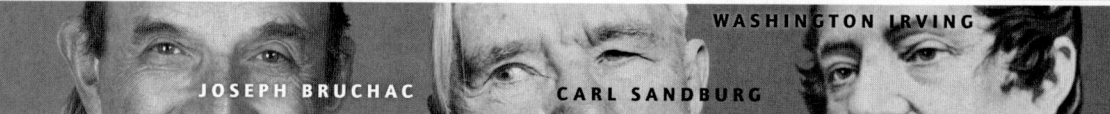

JOSEPH BRUCHAC   CARL SANDBURG   WASHINGTON IRVING

Launch the Unit

Have students work in small groups to generate lists of questions that relate to the theme of this unit, Recalling Heroes. Model several such questions: "How do we judge who can be called a hero? Are most heroes male or female? Why do people like to tell stories about heroes?" Encourage students to be creative and not to try to answer the questions at this point. Ask groups to write down their questions and keep the list. When the class has completed work on the unit, have groups reconvene to take a fresh look at the questions. Have representatives from each group share some sample questions with the class, and have the entire class identify selections from the unit that offer insights into answering each question.

"*They say the people could fly. Say that long ago in Africa, some of the people knew magic. And they would walk up on the air like climbin up on a gate.*"

—VIRGINIA HAMILTON, "The People Could Fly"

Who are your heroes? Why do you admire them? Human beings have always told tales—wild, wonderful, amazing tales—celebrating larger-than-life people and extraordinary deeds. In her retelling of an African-American legend, Virginia Hamilton gives us a glimpse of how enslaved people kept alive their dreams of freedom. As you read the unit, note what each tale reveals about the culture that created it.

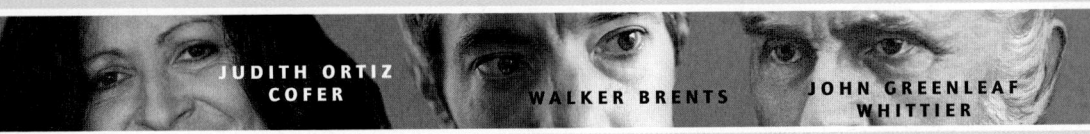

JUDITH ORTIZ COFER   WALKER BRENTS   JOHN GREENLEAF WHITTIER

743

Writing Options

Creative Writing

Article	Myth
Ballad	Newspaper
Drama	Article
Eulogy	Personal Letter
Lyric Poem	Short Story
Lyrics	Tall Tale

Expository Writing

Essay	Literary Response
Expository Essay	Short Essay
Literary Analysis	Summary

Language Arts Workshops

Grammar & Style
Misplaced Modifiers
Dangling Modifiers

Vocabulary & Spelling
Homonyms and Homophones

Writing Workshop
Research Report

Speaking & Listening Workshop
Giving and Actively Listening to
  Research Presentations

Test Practice Workshop
Research Report
Revising and Editing Skills
Reading Skills

Program Resources

For a visual reminder of the unit-based resources available for Unit 8, Folk Literature, see pages 742A and 742B. As you introduce the unit, you may want to provide students with the Unit Study Guide, which is contained in the *Meeting the Standards* resource.

Teach the Genre

Launch the Lesson

Read these three scenarios aloud to students (about the superhero Spider Man, President George Washington, and scientist George Washington Carver).

A radioactive spider bit Peter Parker, who developed superpowers. He learned to use his powers to protect his loved ones and society.

At nineteen George went to Barbados, where he caught and survived smallpox. Later, leading the Revolution, he would survive the smallpox epidemics that killed many other soldiers.

His mother was kidnapped when George was a baby, and plantation owners raised him. He was too sickly to do field chores, so he helped with gardening. This led to a career in agriculture. Before he died, he had created hundreds of products from peanuts and sweet potatoes.

Place students into small groups to answer this question: Which of these men do you think is the biggest hero and why? After several minutes, have groups report back to the class. When they are done, tell students they will read about a wide variety of heroes in this unit.

Folk Literature

Long before people invented writing, they were already telling stories, reciting poetry, and singing songs about their beliefs, dreams, and experiences. Much of this material formed part of the **folk literature,** or the works, ideas, or customs of a culture, passed by word of mouth from generation to generation. Eventually many of these stories, poems, and songs were written down, and they have become an important part of world literature. Works found in folk literature or the oral traditions of peoples around the world include legends, myths, folk tales, tall tales, folk songs, and ballads.

Legends

Which details in the following passage seem realistic? What details do not?

> The two ships touched, and vicious Blackbeard jumped aboard the sloop and faced the lieutenant. Maynard drew blood first with a bullet right through the pirate's body, but, the freebooter fought on. Finally, with a mighty swish of his sword, Maynard severed Blackbeard's head from his trunk. The head dropped into the water and circled the ship three times, crying out, "O crow, Cock! O crow, Cock!"

—RICHARD WALSER, "Blackbeard's Last Fight"

The details about the fight seem realistic. The detail about the severed head does not. The mixture of history and fantasy here indicates that the story is a legend. A **legend** is a story that has been passed down through time, often based on important real events and characters, such as the death of the pirate Blackbeard, which was a historical event involving real people. Yet, a legend often mixes into its history elements of the supernatural, such as the severed head circling the boat and crying out.

Words from American Folklore

Bunyanesque "gigantic"—reference to American tall tale hero Paul Bunyan

El Dorado "place of extraordinary wealth or opportunity"—reference to a legendary country in the Americas fabled for its riches

Paul Bunyan and Blue Ox.

Myths

How does a legend differ from a myth? Unlike a legend, a myth focuses on the supernatural. A **myth** is a traditional story that usually presents supernatural events involving gods and heroes. There are many different kinds of myths. Three common and widespread types are creation myths, origin myths, and hero myths. A **creation myth** tells how the world and human beings came to exist. An **origin myth** is a story that explains objects or events in the natural world. "Coyote Steals the Sun and Moon" (page 773), a Zuni tale about the origin of the seasons, is an example of an origin myth. A **hero myth** tells of the deeds and adventures of a hero.

Words in Use

Teaching Words
reciting, 744
lieutenant, 744
freebooter, 744
supernatural, 744
generation, 745
depict, 745
pillar, 745
particulars, 745

Common Core State Standards

Reading Literature
RL.5

Folk Tales and Tall Tales

Folk tales are stories passed by word of mouth from generation to generation. Although the term *folk tale* is often used to refer to any type of story in the folk literature, it also refers specifically to stories that could have taken place anywhere and at any time and that are considered anonymous (created by an unknown person). "Hansel and Gretel" and "Little Red Riding Hood" are two well-known folk tales. One common type of folk tale is the tall tale. A **tall tale** is a lighthearted or humorous story with many exaggerated elements. Many tall tales depict the wild adventures of North American folk heroes of the frontier. Some tall tales offer explanations for the way certain mountains, lakes, and other geographic features came to exist. Common characters in tall tales include Paul Bunyan, Calamity Jane, Pecos Bill, Davie Crockett, Annie Oakley, and Johnny Appleseed. Adrien Stoutenberg's "Pecos Bill" (page 760) and Carl Sandburg's "Paul Bunyan of the North Woods" (page 814) are both examples of American tall tales.

What elements of the passage below have exaggerated elements? How do they affect your view of the character?

> One year when it rained from St. Patrick's Day till the Fourth of July, Paul Bunyan got disgusted because his celebration on the Fourth was spoiled. He dived into Lake Superior and swam to where a solid pillar of water was coming down. He dived under this pillar, swam up into it and climbed with powerful swimming strokes, was gone about an hour, came splashing down, and as the rain stopped, he explained, "I turned the thing off." This is told in the Big North Woods and on the Great Lakes, with many particulars.
>
> —CARL SANDBURG, "Paul Bunyan of the North Woods"

West African storytellers called *griots* pass down family stories and tribal history.

Folk Songs and Ballads

Folk songs typically have structured stanzas, a refrain, and a relatively simple melody. They can be traditional or composed but often express a group's shared ideas or feelings. "Yankee Doodle" is an example of a folk song. Narrative folk songs often tell of adventure, war, or everyday life. **Ballads** are short narrative folk songs that often contain repeated words, lines, or phrases. Most ballads have four-line stanzas that have the rhyme scheme *abcb*. Sometimes the last line is repeated. The anonymous African-American song "John Henry Blues" (page 804) is an example of a ballad.

The Value of Folk Literature

Every early culture around the world creates its own folk literature. Learning about these tales and songs can help you better understand the cultures that produced them. An effective way to compare and contrast the beliefs and values of different cultures is to examine their folk literature. In addition, you can better understand your own culture by becoming familiar with its folk literature. Characters, events, and ideas from folk literature often appear in contemporary literature. Words derived from legendary characters and places also appear in modern English. Becoming familiar with folk literature from around the world will help you identify references in other works and in everyday life.

Introduction to Folk Literature

Reinforce definitions for students as necessary. Affirm that categories of folk literature overlap.

myth — story with supernatural beings that tells about creation, origins, and/or heroes

legend — story that mixes real history and supernatural elements

folk tale — story passed by word of mouth

tall tale — humorous folk tale with many exaggerated elements

folk song — simple tune with words that tell of a group's shared ideas, feelings, or history

ballad — narrative folk song with repeating lines and stanzas

You do not have to cover this entire introduction at one time. As students prepare to read selections in the unit, encourage them to return to these pages to learn about the different genres of the oral tradition.

TEACHING NOTE

Research Ballads

Have interested students find examples of classic and contemporary ballads. Ask each student to identify the typical subject matter of a ballad, name an example, and show how the example treats the subject matter.

Grammar Skills

Comma Splice

Remind students that they can join two independent clauses with a comma and a coordinating conjunction. Model an example: "George's father died when he was eleven, and George inherited a small estate." Tell students that a comma splice occurs when a writer joins independent clauses with a comma but leaves out the coordinating conjunction. The above example with a comma splice would be "George's father died when he was eleven, George inherited a small estate."

Have students tell you which of these sentences has a comma splice (the correct answer is 2).
1. Please come in, and make yourself at home.
2. Use this chair, don't let your coat drip on it.
3. I can see you need a hanger, so here's one.

Program Resources

To help students explore literature on a deeper level, assign the following activity: Analyzing Historical Context: *Exceeding the Standards: Literature & Reading*, pp. 23–25.

Introduce the Process

Use this page to show students the basic instruction provided for them before, during, and after reading most selections in Unit 8.

"Legend of the Feathered Serpent" is an Active Reading Model. Side notes in such lessons prompt students to become more active readers by using reading strategies and skills, analyzing literature, and making connections. Students can apply the process they use to read this legend to other selections in Unit 8.

Before Reading Stress the two types of background students need to apply, and encourage students always to set a purpose for reading.

During Reading Point out the side notes on pages 750–751: Use Reading Skills, Analyze Literature, and Use Reading Strategies. Then show students the Mirrors & Windows questions on page 758. Explain that they will first respond to a story personally and then apply their insights to a broader issue.

After Reading Show students page 759. Tell them that Find Meaning questions will help them recall and interpret details. Make Judgments questions ask them to analyze a selection and evaluate how specific details contribute to its overall literary effect and meaning.

BEFORE READING

Build Background
Apply two types of background to read myths, fables, and folk tales effectively. One type is the story's literary and cultural context. Read the **Build Background** and **Meet the Author** features to get this information. The other type of background is the personal knowledge and experience you bring to your reading.

Set Purpose
Folk literature presents characters and actions to say something about life. Read **Set Purpose** to decide what you want to get out of the story.

Analyze Literature
Folk literature includes literary techniques, such as plot and setting, to create meaning. The **Analyze Literature** feature draws your attention to key literary elements.

Use Reading Skills
The **Use Reading Skills** feature will show you skills to help you get the most out of your reading. Identify a graphic organizer to help you apply the skill before and while you read.

DURING READING

Use Reading Strategies
- **Ask questions** about things that seem significant or interesting.
- **Make predictions** about what's going to happen next. As you read, gather more clues to confirm or change your prediction.
- **Visualize** the story. Form pictures in your mind to help you see the characters, actions, and settings.
- **Make inferences,** or educated guesses, about what is not stated directly.
- **Clarify,** or check that you understand, what you read. Reread any difficult parts.

Analyze Literature
What literary elements stand out? Are the characters vivid and interesting? Is there a lesson or moral? As you read, consider how these elements affect your enjoyment and understanding of the story.

Make Connections
Notice where connections can be made between the story and your life or another story, myth, or legend. What feelings or thoughts do you have while reading the story?

AFTER READING

Find Meaning
Recall the important details of the story, such as the sequence of events and character traits. Use this information to help **interpret,** or explain, the meaning of the story.

Make Judgments
- **Analyze** the text by examining details and deciding what they contribute to the meaning.
- **Evaluate** the text by making judgments about how the author creates meaning.

Analyze Literature
Review how the use of literary elements increases your understanding of the story. For example, if the story includes dialogue, how does it help shape the story's meaning?

Extend Understanding
Go beyond the text by exploring the story through writing or other creative projects.

KEY TERMS
MYTH, 746
FABLE, 746
FOLK TALE, 746
FOLK LITERATURE, 746
PLOT, 746
SETTING, 746
LEGEND, 746
SEQUENCE OF EVENT, 746
CHARACTER TRAIT, 746
DIALOGUE, 746

Differentiated Instruction

Enrichment
During Reading questions in the text's Active Reading Models sometimes ask students to "make connections" by responding to events and characters or by relating those elements to their own experience and knowledge. As students read the legends, tales, and other stories in this unit, invite them to keep a log of personal connections.

Legend of the Feathered Serpent

An Aztec Legend by Antonio Hernández Madrigal

At a Glance
Guided Reading: Reading Model
- Reading Level: Moderate
- Difficulty Consideration: Aztec names
- Ease Factor: Vocabulary

Build Background
Historical Context In the 1400s and 1500s, the Aztecs controlled a vast, rich empire in the Valley of Mexico. According to legend, the god Quetzalcóatl, or "Feathered Serpent," had grown angry with the Aztecs and left them but would return in the year One Reed as a bearded white man. That year corresponds to 1519, when the Spanish conqueror Hernán Cortés arrived. Believing him to be the long-awaited god, the Aztec emperor Moctezuma II welcomed Cortés and his troops, sealing the fate of his empire.

Reader's Context When you learn of a prediction about an event, how does it affect your actions?

Set Purpose
Preview the selection, looking at the title and pictures. What would you like to learn from the text? Write down your purpose for reading this story.

Analyze Literature
Legend A **legend** is a story that is handed down from generation to generation. Legends are often based on real people and real historical events. As you read this legend, think about how it relates to real people and historical events.

Meet the Author

As a child growing up in Mexico, **Antonio Hernández Madrigal** enjoyed listening to the stories and legends told by his grandmother, a healer and storyteller. Gradually, he began to pursue his love of writing and has brought his grandmother's stories to many young readers.

Use Reading Skills
Identify Sequence of Events The sequence of events in a story refers to the order in which things happen. When you keep track of the sequence of events in a story, you gain understanding of when and why things happen. As you read this selection, use a time line to note the sequence of events.

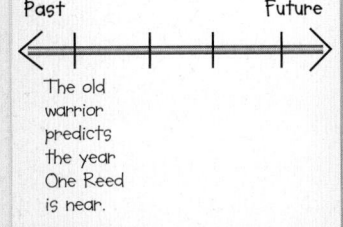

The old warrior predicts the year One Reed is near.

Preview Vocabulary
ex·qui·site (ek skwi´ zət) *adj.*, elegant or refined; pleasing because of beauty or perfection

proph·e·cy (präf´ ə sē) *n.*, prediction of something to come

mor·tal (môr´ tl) *n.*, human being (as opposed to a god)

per·pe·tra·tor (pər pə trāt´ ər) *n.*, criminal; person who commits harmful or illegal acts

ma·neu·ver (mə nü´ vər) *v.*, make a series of changes in direction and position for a specific purpose

Objectives
Studying this lesson will enable students to
- use reading skills such as identifying sequence of events
- define *legend* and recognize elements of the genre in this selection
- explain the historical significance of this selection in relation to the Spanish invasion of the Aztec empire
- appreciate a legend from an ancient culture

Launch the Lesson
Prior to reading "Legend of the Feathered Serpent," tell students that they are about to read a legend from a civilization that was destroyed by invaders largely motivated by greed. Write the word *greed* on the a board and ask students to think about what this word means. Ask them to give examples of greedy behavior and how it can negatively impact people's lives.

LEGEND OF THE FEATHERED SERPENT **747**

Words in Use

KEY TERMS

Common Core State Standards
Reading Literature
RL.1
Writing
W.7, W.8, W.9, W.10
Language
L.5. L6

Summary

Believing that the bearded leader of a group of strangers was the god Quetzalcoatl, the Aztec emperor Moctezuma sent him gifts of gold and jewels and allowed his followers to do as they pleased. Greedy for Aztec treasure, the strangers tortured, looted, and burned, destroying Moctezuma's great city of Tenochtitlan and its temples. The strangers later went to a nearby village and stole the jeweled statue of the god Xochipilli. Itauqui, keeper of Xochipilli's temple, led a group of villagers who pursued the thieves, reclaimed the statue, and buried it. Angry at the loss of their prize, the strangers captured and tortured Itauqui, but he died without revealing the statue's location. The villagers buried him beneath the altar of Xochiplli and preserved the memory of his courage.

MIRRORS & WINDOWS The Mirrors & Windows questions at the end of this selection focus on the theme of heroes. Which qualities of the legendary heroes that you have encountered in your reading have most impressed you? What about human nature makes people admire these extraordinary beings?

Apply the Model

BEFORE READING
DURING READING
AFTER READING

Legend of the

An Aztec Legend by Antonio Hernández Madrigal

748

Program Resources

Planning and Assessment
Program Planning Guide, Selection Lesson Plan
E-Lesson Planner
Assessment Guide, Lesson Test
ExamView

Technology Tools
Interactive Student Text on CD
Visual Teaching Package
Audio Library
mirrorsandwindows.com

Meeting the Standards
Drama: Unit 8, Guided Reading, pp. 19–23

Feathered Serpent

The end was near.

And in the last days

all lived in fear.

LEGEND OF THE FEATHERED SERPENT **749**

Cultural Connection
Worship of Quetzalcoatl The Aztecs had borrowed the worship of the god Quetzalcoatl from the Toltecs, a people who had ruled central Mexico about two centuries before the Aztecs. In Toltec legend, Quetzalcoatl was a wise and gentle ruler who represented all that was good. The Toltecs' god-king taught them how to grow corn and how to keep track of time with a calendar.

Art Connection
The sculpture on the prior page is a stone representation of Quetzalcoatl, the Feathered Serpent. It resides at the Temple of Quetzalcoatl at Teotihuacán, the ruins of an ancient Aztec city near present-day Mexico City. The sculpture depicts the serpent with its jaws fully extended, revealing large menacing teeth. The Aztecs did not create art to please the senses but rather to instruct citizens in the culture's religious, political, and military laws. Ask students how this sculpture might meet this objective. Which of its characteristics might have impressed the Aztecs and reminded them of their religious duty?

Vocabulary Skills

Aztec Words in English
Point out to students that some familiar words have entered the English language from Nahuatl, the language of the Aztecs. The best known of these is *chocolate*, which comes from the Nahuatl word *xocolatl*, meaning "bitter water." Have students use a dictionary to identify the Nahuatl words that are the origins of the following English words. Ask students what is common to all these Aztec words (the noun ending *–tl*).

1. avocado *(ahuacatl)*
2. tomato *(tomatl)*
3. ocelot *(ocelotl)*
4. coyote *(cóyotl)*
5. mesquite *(mizquitl)*

Use Reading Skills

Identify Sequence of Events
Answer: They listened very quietly, with fear. According to the prophecy, the end was near. **A**

Use Reading Skills

Identify Sequence of Events Point out to students that the sequence of events in a narrative can be compared to a chain. Each link in the chain is an event connected to a preceding or succeeding event. Ask students to link the event in this passage to the next event. Model a question such as: "How do you think the emperor Moctezuma will react to the prophecy?" **B**

History Connection

Moctezuma's Palace In the gardens of his palace, Moctezuma had large collections of birds, beasts, and reptiles. Bernal Díaz, one of the soldiers with Cortés, described the Aztec emperor's elaborate meals: "For each meal his servants prepared him more than thirty dishes. . . . Sometimes they brought him in cups of gold a drink made from the cocoa-plant . . . all frothed up, of which he would drink a little." **C**

Analyze Literature

Legend *Answer:* It includes comet or a meteor shower. **D**

DURING READING

Use Reading Skills
Identify Sequence of Events How do the children react after the old warrior gives his prediction? What causes this reaction? **A**

B

ex·qui·site
(ek skwi´ zət) *adj.*, elegant or refined; pleasing because of beauty or perfection

proph·e·cy (präf´ ə sē)
n., prediction of something to come

DURING READING

Analyze Literature
Legend Legends often include mythological elements—explanations of why natural events, such as a fierce storm, occur. What natural event does this legend include? **D**

---

he old warrior who had fought many battles sat by his earthen fire. The children knelt around him as he began the legend.

"The year One Reed is near," he said, "and Quetzalcóatl, the Feathered Serpent, God of Life and Learning, will fulfill his promise by returning to this, his land. He will soon come back from the sea in a floating raft and reclaim his power and his people." The children listened to his words without making a sound or movement. The mighty Feathered Serpent, the god of whom their parents and the people before them spoke about for so long, was finally coming. The end was near. And in the last days all lived in fear.

But no one in the Aztec empire knew of greater fear than Moctezuma, the mighty emperor. Moctezuma lived in a palace as large as a city. He was surrounded by forests and beautiful gardens in which quetzals,[1] parrots and other colorful birds flew about the bushes and trees. The grounds were covered with many kinds of flowers whose sweet scent spread with the wind.

Moctezuma rested every afternoon in his favorite courtyard where pumas, jaguars and tigers roamed inside large wooden cages. At mealtimes the servants paraded around his table with hundreds of different dishes. But now, in the last days, all of his pleasures were forgotten. The song of his beloved birds, the <u>exquisite</u> perfume from his gardens and the flavorful feasts no longer provided Moctezuma with joy or pleasure. The voices of the <u>prophecy</u> haunted his long days and sleepless nights.

One day a ball of fire[2] appeared across the sky and burned throughout the night. The noblemen, wizards and priests came to Moctezuma with concern. "Great Lord," a priest warned, "strange signs and omens[3] are appearing on earth and in the sky."

"The people are awakened at night by strange howls and cries," a nobleman reported.

"Our nights are plagued with horrible dreams and visions," a wizard complained. The mighty ruler listened as he sadly stared through the window at his beloved city of Tenochtitlan.[4] When the men finished speaking, Moctezuma remained silent for a long time.

"Do not be afraid," he finally said to them. "You must remember that all which begins also comes to an end. I, the ruler of this great empire, shall guide my people in the last days." Moctezuma knew

---

1. **quetzals.** Central American birds that have brilliant green feathers and red breasts
2. **a ball of fire.** This may have been a comet or a meteor shower. The people saw it as a sign that the god would soon arrive.
3. **omens.** Signs that something important or frightening is about to happen
4. **Tenochtitlan** (tā nôch´ tēt län). Capital city of the Aztec empire, on the site of Mexico City today

---

Differentiated Instruction

English Language Learning
Students learning English may heave difficulty with some of the words and phrases in this selection.

earthen fire—firepit in the ground, 750
fasting—not eating or drinking, 751
provoke his wrath—make him angry, 751
maddened—crazed, 758

his days of glory and power would soon be over, but his people must not witness his trembling.

Moctezuma stayed alone in his sleeping chamber. With sharp needles from the agave cactus, he pierced his body in sacrifice to the gods. He did not eat or drink, so that by fasting he could purify himself.

Many days later he sent for all of his helpers. When the servants and wizards, the priests and noblemen came to his calling, they saw that he looked very thin, and that he had not bathed for many days. "We shall prepare to welcome the Feathered Serpent, who will soon take my place," Moctezuma instructed.

At dawn the people were awakened by a call from conch shells[5] that resounded across and beyond Tenochtitlan. Everyone rose and hurried to the palace. "Why is it that we are awakened at this early hour?" they wondered along the way.

When the large crowds arrived at the palace doors, Moctezuma himself came out and said, "He who left to the east is coming back. And after the great Feathered Serpent returns, I, Moctezuma, shall no longer rule."

"Will he be angry at us and our children? Will he take revenge upon us?" the crowd asked. For according to the legend, the Feathered Serpent had left greatly displeased with the forefathers.[6] One day he grew angry at their ways of human sacrifices and wars.[7] With great discontent he went away on a raft of snakes and disappeared into the eastern waters.

Moctezuma again spoke to the crowds as he noticed fear in their words. "The Feathered Serpent must be loved and respected. We shall obey his ways and avoid all that may displease him or provoke his wrath," he warned.

As the year One Reed began, Moctezuma grew more anxious with each day that passed. One morning while he looked at the new blossoms in the gardens, a servant came to him. "One of your guardians of the water's shores has come to speak with you," he said. But before the man who had come from the coast spoke, Moctezuma already knew what his message would be.

"Oh, Great Lord," he said, "we have seen over the waters of the east floating rafts as big as many houses." As soon as the messenger left, Moctezuma called his noblemen.

---

5. **conch shells.** Large spiral seashells. People blow air into them to make a loud, trumpeting sound.
6. **forefathers.** Ancestors; generations of people who lived in the past
7. **human sacrifices and wars.** The Aztecs were fierce warriors and sometimes practiced human sacrifice.

DURING READING

Analyze Literature
Character Why does Moctezuma hide his trembling? **E**

"Will he take revenge upon us?" the crowd asked.

DURING READING

Use Reading Strategies
Ask Questions According to the legend, why did the Feathered Serpent leave? **F**

Teach the Model

Analyze Literature

Character *Answer:* He doesn't want his people to know how frightened he is about the returning god; he wants to hold onto the power he has until the god returns. **E**

Use Reading Strategies
Ask Questions *Answer:* He was angry at the Aztecs for their human sacrifices and their wars. **F**

Analyze Literature

Description Ask students what details they might have added to the description of Quetzalcoatl's departure. Model a response: "I think I might have included some descriptive words about the snake such as *writhing, twining, twisting, hissing.*" **G**

Reading Skills

Identify Multiple Levels of Meaning

Many fiction writers make use of hidden messages that demand the reader to dig a little deeper into the text to get the full meaning of the selection. Have students make a chart to keep track of the apparent and hidden messages in "Legend of the Feathered Serpent." Model a question to get them started: "If the apparent message is that the Spanish explorers were greatly pleased by the wealth of the Aztecs, a possible hidden message is that they were simply looking for wealth to begin with."

Cultural Connection

Aztec Craft Workers Special Aztec craft workers produced luxury items such gold and greenstone jewelry and brilliantly colored featherwork objects, including shields, fans, and capes. These luxury goods were created exclusively for the Aztec nobility. The craft workers were organized in a system like the medieval guilds of Europe. **A**

Analyze Literature

Legend *Answer:* The historical event is the meeting of Moctezuma with Cortés and the Spanish forces. **B**

Use Reading Strategies

Make Predictions Ask students to make predictions about these men and the impact they will have on the Aztec people.

Cultural Connection

Aztec Religion The Aztecs worshipped numerous gods and goddesses. Especially important were Tialoc, god of rain; Quetzalcoatl, god of civilization and order; and Tezcatlipoca, god of the underworld. Xochipilli, whose name means "Prince of Flowers," was the god of love, beauty, and the arts. Each part of Aztec life had one or more gods associated with it, and sacrifices were made to the god in order to achieve success in that area. The Aztecs believed that death was essential to the creation of life and expected humans and gods alike to sacrifice themselves to maintain harmony in the world.

A "You must find an offering worthy of the mighty Feathered Serpent," he ordered. Soon the best workers of jewels, metals, clothing and feathers were brought to him. For many days and nights, the jewelers created exquisite gifts of gems, turquoise and jade.[8] The goldsmiths carved bracelets and pendants adorned with mother-of-pearl. The weavers spun the finest clothes, and a crown of quetzal feathers was made for the returning one. Once the offerings were finished, Moctezuma led his helpers and noblemen to welcome the longawaited god.

After a tiring journey, the Aztec emperor finally came face to face with the bearded god and his followers.

The bearded god, guarded closely by his men, approached Moctezuma. Many of his men were mounted on four-legged beasts never before seen in the land.[9] The bearded god and his companions were dressed in strange clothing with metal parts.[10] They held their weapons as if they were ready to strike.

When Moctezuma and the bearded god stood within arm's length, the emperor's servants laid the offerings at the feet of the god. And they saw with relief that the gifts pleased him greatly, for his face lit up with a smile. Then Moctezuma, the owner of glory and

> **DURING READING**
>
> **Analyze Literature**
> **Legend** What real historical event does the legend speak about here?
> **B**

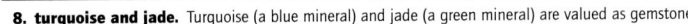

8. **turquoise and jade.** Turquoise (a blue mineral) and jade (a green mineral) are valued as gemstones.
9. **four-legged beasts never before seen in the land.** The Spanish introduced horses to the Americas.
10. **strange clothing with metal parts.** Armor

Spanish soldiers.

Differentiated Instruction

Enrichment
Interested students might enjoy researching more about Moctezuma, Tenochtitlán, and the Aztec people. Possible topics for research might include the following:
- Moctezuma's palace
- the markets of Tenochtitlán
- Tenochtitlán's neighborhood units (or *calpullis*)
- Aztec farming on reclaimed land (or *chinampas*)
- Aztec medicine
- Aztec schools
- Aztec warfare

power which had known no limits, spoke with a low and humble voice. "Oh, Mighty One, the long-awaited Feathered Serpent, I am your servant, the honored one who was chosen to guard your kingdom and your people. We cherish your return. May our gifts be to your pleasing. May you and your followers rest your tired feet from the long travel to this, your land."

The bearded one and his men did not understand the strange language of the leader who wore a large headdress of feathers and fancy clothing. But they spoke in their own words among one another. And all along their eyes preyed upon the gifts of precious metals and jewels, as the thirsty traveler craves water to quench his thirst.

Moctezuma and his men escorted the bearded one and his people back to the palace. Along the way the Aztec emperor instructed his helpers, "Behold the mighty one, and be assured that he and his companions are fed and clothed properly." And as they arrived, in the last days of peace, the wind grew still in the great Tenochtitlan. Many of the old women and men did not rejoice at the coming of the strangers. But they wept and prayed to the gods for the fate of their sons and daughters.

"What evil fate has fallen upon us?" the elders worried.

As the days passed the people became more trusting of the ones who had come in the floating rafts. They saw that the men greeted them with broad smiles and held their hands and patted their backs in a strange manner. But the more gifts and offerings the men received, the faster they changed their ways. They soon began to make more demands, and when not pleased, they lashed their whips upon the men and women.

Many of the people brought their complaints to Moctezuma. "Must you allow the unkindness of the bearded men toward us?" they asked.

"We should not anger the Feathered Serpent and his soldiers. But we shall please them and obey their ways," Moctezuma responded.

"Are you no longer our lord, the one who rules over us?"

"The mighty Quetzalcóatl now sits at my throne. He is the new lord and ruler of us all," he reminded them. The people turned their backs after he spoke. In great disappointment they returned to the city.

The bearded one now realized that Moctezuma regarded him as the longawaited god, and that he was greatly feared. He began

> **DURING READING**
>
> **Analyze Literature**
> **Simile** What meaning does the author intend by comparing the eyes of the men with the cravings of a thirsty traveler? **C**

> **DURING READING**
>
> **Use Reading Skills**
> **Identify Sequence of Events** How do the men change after they receive more and more gifts? Why might they have changed? **E**

> **DURING READING**
>
> **Use Reading Strategies**
> **Clarify** What change in Moctezuma causes the people to be disappointed in him? **F**

Teach the Model

Analyze Literature
Simile *Answer:* The author uses this simile to express how strong the desire of the men was to own the precious metals and jewels—they thirsted for them. **C**

Use Reading Skills
Read Aloud Students might find that reading a section of the text aloud will enable them to better comprehend the mood of a selection. Have a volunteer read aloud this section describing the introduction of Cortés and his followers to the people of Tenochtitlan. **D**

Use Reading Skills
Identify Sequence of Events *Answer:* They become rough, angry, violent, and destructive. The receipt of precious gifts only makes them greedy for more. **E**

Use Reading Strategies
Clarify *Answer:* Instead of being a powerful, aggressive ruler, he has become peaceful and submissive. He urges them to do whatever the bearded god asks. **F**

Vocabulary Skills

Context Clues
On our trip to Central America we saw beautifully colored *quetzals* flying among the treetops.

Remind students that using context clues to determine the meaning of an unfamiliar word can help them to be more efficient readers.

In the example above, the context indicates that a *quetzal* is a Central American bird. Have students use context clues to write definitions of the italicized words in the following sentences.

1. The sweet *scent* of the flowers was carried by the wind.
2. The stare in their eyes was that of the hungry snake looking for its *prey*.
3. The young man *scampered* up a tree and looked down the trail.

Teach the Model

Teach the Model

History Connection

Cortes's Conquest *Answer:* Students might say that the legend is of great help in understanding the cultural and political factors that contributed to the downfall of Aztec society, since history books rarely present this period from an Aztec point of view and often portray Aztecs as helpless victims. **Ⓐ**

Analyze Literature

Irony Remind students that irony is an outcome of events that is different from what is expected. Ask students how irony is used in "Legend of the Feathered Serpent." **Ⓑ**

Use Reading Strategies

Make Inferences *Answer:* The historical event is the death in captivity of Moctezuma. **Ⓒ**

---

instructing his men with his evil ways. Mounted on the fourlegged beasts, he led them into the city carrying heavy maces[11] and torches.

For many days and nights the evil men went into the temples and smashed their maces against the gods of stone. They broke into the houses of nobles and peasants and stuffed their saddlebags with gold and jewels. With their torches they burned every book that told the story of the Aztec people and the ones who came before them. They tortured and imprisoned the men and women who stood in their way. The great Tenochtitlan soon was ablaze. And of all that its people held sacred or holy, nothing was left standing or whole.

HISTORY ▶▶ CONNECTION

Cortés's Conquest Hernán Cortés sailed from Spain in February 1519 with eleven ships, more than five hundred soldiers, and sixteen horses. He landed on the Yucátan Peninsula a month later. Cortés made alliances with local natives, sometimes through trade and sometimes through force. Ironically, many groups joined with Cortés because of their hatred and fear of the Aztecs, who had often warred against them. With his army thus bolstered, Cortés marched on the Aztec city of Tenochtitlan in November 1519. His conquest of Moctezuma follows that related in the legend. The Aztecs briefly regained control of the city. However, Cortés marched again on Tenochtitlan in December 1520. After a lengthy siege, the Spanish defeated the Aztecs in August 1521. Now in complete control of a vast region that stretched from the Caribbean Sea to the Pacific Ocean, Cortés had Tenochtitlan rebuilt as Mexico City. How does the legend add to your understanding of Mexico's history? **Ⓐ**

mor·tal (môr´ tl) *n.*, human being (as opposed to a god) **Ⓑ**

> As the bearded one and his men created a path of destruction, the people understood that he was not a true god. He who was called the mighty Feathered Serpent by their ruler was but a mad and ruthless <u>mortal</u>.

DURING READING

Use Reading Strategies
Make Inferences What real historical event does the legend speak about here? **Ⓒ**

A priest soon brought sad news to the people. "Our lord Moctezuma has perished because of the invaders. Those men are no longer worthy of our trust," he warned. His words soon spread to the farmers in a village near the city.

11. maces. Clubs

754 UNIT 8 FOLK LITERATURE

TEACHING NOTE

Self-Generated Questioning

Divide the class into two groups, the Spanish invaders and the Aztecs. Have each group brainstorm to generate two or three questions for the other group. Model a question for the Aztecs such as: "Why have you left your homeland?" When finished, let the groups exchange questions and try to answer them as a group.

"We are at the mercy of the evil ones," cried a woman.

"We shall defend ourselves from the invaders!" a man shouted.

"But we can not fight their fire-spitting weapons," said another.

"Xochipilli is in great danger," the singers, poets and dancers realized. Word had come to them of how the bearded men were destroying all their gods and shrines. Everyone began to fear for Xochipilli, the God of Flowers and the Arts.

"Let us save our god," shouted Itauqui, or the devoted one. Itauqui, the young keeper of the temple of Xochipilli, vowed, "I shall guard his house day and night."

But it was not long before the evil men arrived in the village. One evening, Itauqui discovered the silhouette of the invaders creeping into the temple. He saw how the men sneaked silently, like thieves in the night.

Once the men were inside, they lit their torches and began searching. Soon they discovered the god of stone that was covered with flowers from its head to its feet. The men quickly raised their maces to crash them against the god.

Itauqui's body trembled with anger and he readied himself to strike against the <u>perpetrators</u>. Suddenly one of the men howled a strange cry. The others stopped and, lowering their maces, looked closer, circling tightly around Xochipilli. The men smiled wickedly as they saw what lay beneath the adorning flowers—The god's head was crowned with mother-of-pearl,[12] a large heart made of gold was encrusted in his chest, and his body was clothed with gems and turquoise. The bearded thieves pointed with their fingers at the precious jewels. They muttered strange words which Itauqui could not understand. But he saw that the stare in their eyes was that of the hungry snake looking upon its prey.

The men desperately tried to remove the treasures from the god's body, but none of them succeeded. They whispered to one another, and once again surrounded Xochipilli. Joining their strength, the evil ones tried to lift and drag the God of Flowers and the Arts away from his altar. But soon the men realized that the great statue of stone was much too heavy for them to carry. They went outside and quickly returned, bringing in their beasts along with thick ropes across their shoulders. They wrapped and knotted the ropes around the god and hitched the beasts to the statue and began tugging and pushing.

12. **mother-of-pearl.** Hard, white, shiny substance on the insides of certain seashells, such as oysters. This substance is often used to make jewelry and buttons.

per·pe·tra·tor
(pər pə trāt´ ər) *n.*, criminal, person who commits harmful or illegal acts

---

DURING READING

Analyze Literature
Figurative Language What does the Aztec mean by "fire-spitting weapons," and what does this language suggest about Aztec technology? **D**

DURING READING

Make Connections
When have you witnessed an attack on someone or something you hold dear? How did it make you feel? **E**

DURING READING

Use Reading Strategies
Ask Questions What do the men do to get the treasures off the god's body? **F**

Teach the Model

Analyze Literature
Figurative Language *Answer:* He refers to guns. This description suggests that the Aztecs used manual weapons, rather than gunpowder, in battle. **D**

Analyze Literature
Character Now that all of the major characters in "Legend of the Feathered Serpent" have been introduced, remind students of the distinction between round and flat characters. Ask them which of the major characters (Moctezuma, Cortés, and Itauqui) are round and which are flat.

Analyze Literature
Conflict Remind students that conflict is a struggle between two characters or things in a literary work. There are two types of conflict— *internal*, which occurs within a character, and *external*, which occurs between a character and another character or an outside force. Ask students what type of conflict is happening with Itaqui. How does this conflict affect the plot of the story?

Make Connections
Answer: Witnessing such an attack may have made them fearful or angry. **E**

Use Reading Strategies
Ask Questions *Answer:* They hitch the horses to the statue and drag it away. **F**

Reading Skills

Create a Time Line
Point out to students that creating a time line is sometimes a good way to visually organize the events in a selection. Have students create a time line to chart the events in "Legend of the Feathered Serpent." Suggest they start with Quetzalcoatl's departure from Mexico and the prophecy about his return.

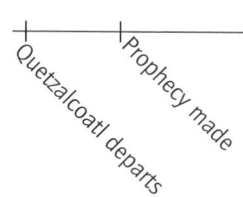

Use Reading Skills

Summarize Ask students to summarize the importance the musicians, poets, dancers, and farmers place on Xochipilli. *Answer:* They attribute all their successes—in poetry, music, dance, and farming—to his presence. Without him, they feel they will fail. **A**

Use Reading Skills

Examine Multiple Levels of Meaning Tell students that the characters in this story have both literal roles in the plot and moral roles. Have students pause in their reading to discuss what moral roles each character plays. Model a possible question: "How does Itauqui represent courage and honor?" **B**

Use Reading Skills

Identify Sequence of Events
Answer: They silently drag Xochipilli away and bury him. **C**

Hidden in one corner, Itauqui saw how the bearded ones and their beasts slowly pulled away the body of his beloved Xochipilli. As soon as the men disappeared into the darkness, he ran with all his might toward the village. "The evil ones are taking Xochipilli away! They are stealing the God of Flowers and the Arts!" he shouted from the cobblestone streets.

A The young men in the House of Poets rose from their beds. "Who will now inspire us to create our poems?" they asked one another.

"Without our god who will help us make our music?" the musicians also worried.

"For whom will we dance, if not for Xochipilli?" cried the maidens in the House of Dance.

Among the shadows of the night, the farmers and all the others came together. "Without Xochipilli our crops will be lost," the farmers told one another.

"But how can we fight the evil ones and their fire-spitting weapons?" a man asked.

B "Fear not their weapons or their beasts. We shall go after them and bring our Xochipilli back to where he belongs," Itauqui commanded.

"Let us do as the brave Itauqui says," the poets agreed. The musicians and the maidens also joined as Itauqui whirled around and set out down the road. They followed the invaders' footsteps and the tracks of their beasts.

When they reached the end of the road, the men and women spotted the invaders warming themselves around a fire. The tired men rested while Xochipilli's body lay nearby. Itauqui and the others patiently waited.

After the men fell asleep Itauqui whispered to his friends, "There is no time to waste." They swiftly sneaked through the shadows. Like night ghosts they began to pull with all their might on the ropes still attached to their god. And while the greedy men slept, the worshippers of Xochipilli slowly dragged its body back toward the village. For many hours all pushed and pulled. Their hands blistered and bled from the coarse ropes, but no one grumbled or complained.

Near dawn, when they had come close to the village, Itauqui stopped suddenly. "Listen," he whispered. Everyone stopped and turned to look at him. "I hear the pounding hooves of the beasts."

> **DURING READING**
>
> **Use Reading Skills**
> **Identify Sequence of Events** What do the people do after they find the invaders sleeping? **C**

Differentiated Instruction

Visual Learning

Students who are gifted visually might enjoy creating a storyboard based "Legend of the Feathered Serpent." Point out to them that a storyboard is a visual narrative arranged in cartoon-like panels. They can use some of the graphic conventions of cartooning—such as speech and thought balloons—in their storyboard.

English Language Learners

Confirm that students recognize the directionality of reading English. Students should work from left to right and top to bottom. Also, point out that the During Reading and History Connection boxes are included to provide background information for the reader and are not part of the original text.

A young man scampered up a tree and looked down the trail. 🅓 "They are coming! The bearded ones and their beasts are coming after us!" he warned.

The men and women's voices filled with panic. "How can we save Xochipilli?"

"How can we spare ourselves from the ruthless men?" they asked.

"Hurry!" Itauqui responded. "Help me dig a hiding place for Xochipilli." And quickly all joined him, digging with sharp wooden sticks and scooping out the ground with their bare hands.

After the hole was deep enough, Itauqui again commanded, "Let's now bury our god." The poets, musicians and dancers helped with their tired arms and bleeding hands until they <u>maneuvered</u> the statue into the hole. While they pushed back the soil to cover its body, the rumble of the beasts' hooves came closer and closer to their ears. Then Itauqui warned, "There is no more time. Go back to the village and save yourselves. Tell the people that our god is safe. Tell all that Xochipilli will never be taken away from our land."

ma•neu•ver (mə nü´ vər) *v.*, make a series of changes in direction and position for a specific purpose

Aztec village.

Use Reading Skills

Scan Tell students that scanning a text before and after reading can help with reading comprehension. Have students scan this section of the story for words indicating action. Model a possible response such as: "The word *scampered* indicates that there is some hurried action in this section." 🅓

Analyze Literature

Legend Remind students that legends often serve to reinforce the values of a culture or society. Direct their attention to the joint and valiant effort of poets, musicians, and dancers in this section. Ask students what cultural or societal values this endeavor highlights. Model a response: "This section highlights the values of cooperation, religious reverence, and respect for the arts."

Speaking & Listening Skills

Group Discussion

Have students discuss some significant recent events that are in the process of becoming legendary. Prompt students to focus on the event from a literary perspective—by identifying the protagonist, the conflict, and supporting characters. How do they think future generations will view the event? Possible topics could be the war in Iraq, Hurricane Katrina, or the "Green" movement.

Use Reading Strategies

Ask Questions *Answer:* They see his blistered, bleeding hands. **Ⓐ**

Analyze Literature

Symbolism Remind students that a literary symbol is a person, thing, or event that represents something else. Ask students how the death and burial of Itauqui might be symbolic. What might this event represent? **Ⓑ**

Analyze Literature

Legend *Answer:* He courageously gave his life to protect the statue of one of their most important gods. In so doing, he attempted to preserve an important part of the Aztec culture. **Ⓒ**

 You may want to ask students to write a journal entry or quick write, or divide students into discussion groups or lead a whole-class discussion about this question. Most students will identify Itauqui as the hero, because he sacrificed his life to protect the people of his village and the statue of Xochipilli.

While the men and women ran to the safety of the village, Itauqui stayed behind and finished covering the god with the loose soil. Then he set out on the road, toward the village.

But soon the men appeared. Their angry eyes searched around Itauqui. They rode on their beasts peeking up the road and into the forest. But the statue of stone had disappeared. The enraged men swarmed around Itauqui and noticed his blistered, bleeding hands. They screamed and yelled at him like maddened animals while their brutal lashes[13] fell mercilessly over his body. But the protector of Xochipilli silently stood still without giving away his secret.

The angered men soon realized that their captive would not tell where the god dressed with jewels lay hidden. Their chief instructed two men and sent them into the forest.

The men returned carrying logs of wood with which they built a fire. After they tied Itauqui's hands, the men placed his feet into the burning embers. But as the hours passed, the pain did not make him speak or beg for mercy. Only the chirping of the birds in the trees and the crackling of the burning coals below his feet broke the silence of the forest. When the pain became too intense to bear, Itauqui finally closed his eyes. He died with a peaceful smile on his face before the eyes of the frustrated men.

The next day after the invaders had gone, the villagers returned to the spot where they had buried Xochipilli. Nearby they found the lifeless body of Itauqui lying on the ground. The men and women wept for him. After unearthing their god, they carried to the village the bodies of both Xochipilli and Itauqui, back where the two belonged.

When the people arrived at the temple they dug a grave beneath the altar of Xochipilli. After burying Itauqui in it, they finally returned the God of Flowers and the Arts back to his place, above where the loyal Itauqui now rested.

In time, Itauqui became known as the courageous protector of Xochipilli. And his name and courage lived forever in the hearts of the Aztec people. ❖

13. lashes. Whips

DURING READING

Use Reading Strategies
Ask Questions What causes the invaders to be suspicious of Itauqui?
Ⓐ

DURING READING

Analyze Literature
Legend Why might Itauqui live on in legend as a symbol of the once mighty Aztecs?
Ⓒ

 Think back over your experience with legends of heroic and powerful historical figures. In your opinion, who is the hero of this legend, Moctezuma or Itauqui? Why are legends such as this one still passed on today?

Differentiated Instruction

Auditory and Kinesthetic Learning
Ask three student volunteers (one to play Itauqui and other two as the invaders) to pantomime the action in the section of the story when Itauqui observes the invaders stealing away Xochipilli. Let a student read this section aloud as the others act it out.

Find Meaning

1. (a) How does the priest react when the "ball of fire" appears in the night sky? (b) What probably leads the Aztecs to think that this event is part of the prophecy?

2. (a) Who is the Feathered Serpent, and why do the Aztecs fear him? (b) According to the prophecy, how will he return, and what will he look like?

3. (a) Why does Moctezuma think that Cortés is the Feathered Serpent? (b) How does this mistake lead to disaster?

4. (a) What do the Spanish do to the statue of Xochipilli? (b) What leads the Aztecs to fear the disappearance of Xochipilli?

Analyze Literature

Legend A legend is often based on real events and people. By contrast, a myth explains occurrences in the natural world as being caused by some supernatural force. Which parts of "Legend of the Feathered Serpent" are legend, and which parts are myth?

Make Judgments

5. (a) How does the "bearded god" begin to change? (b) Do you think that Moctezuma should have acted differently when the "bearded god" began to change? Explain.

6. From this legend and the factual background information that you read, how would you characterize the Aztec people?

7. How do you think that history might have changed if the Aztecs had not mistaken Cortés for their returning god?

Parts That Are Legend (based on real people and events)	Parts That Are Myth (explanations of events caused by supernatural forces or beings)
Aztec empire prior to the Spanish invasion	prophecy of Quetzalcóatl's return

Extend Understanding

Writing Options

Creative Writing A lyric poem is verse that expresses the emotions of a speaker and does not tell a story. Imagine you are a poet in Tenochtitlan. Write a **lyric poem** to honor the god Xochipilli.

Expository Writing Situational irony occurs when something happens that is very different from what is expected to happen. Write an **essay** for a student literary journal. In your essay, analyze the situational irony in this legend. Include a thesis and textual evidence.

Lifelong Learning

Events Over Time Using library and reliable Internet sources, research facts and events about the Aztec empire. Make a time line to show when important events took place.

Critical Literacy

Explore Legends Work with a small group of classmates to locate another legend. Read and discuss the plot events and what the legend suggests about the culture from which it came. Share your findings with the class.

Go to **www.mirrorsandwindows.com** for more.

Find Meaning

1. (a) He reacts with great fear. (b) The "ball of fire" is so unusual, and its arrival corresponds with the date of the prophecy.

2. (a) He is the god Quetzalcoatl. When he returns, he might punish them for the actions of their ancestors. (b) He will come back as a bearded man on a raft.

3. (a) Cortés comes on a ship and has a beard. (b) Moctezuma welcomes the invaders because he wants to show honor and dignity to the god.

4. (a) The Spanish plunder and drag the statue away. (b) The Aztecs attribute all their successes in poetry, music, dance, and farming to Xochipilli's presence. Without him, they fear failure.

Make Judgments

5. (a) He becomes destructive, greedy, and ruthless. (b) Students might say that Moctezuma should have fought back.

6. They had a great faith in their religion and their leader.

7. They might have fought off the invaders and preserved their culture.

Analyze Literature

Legend *Possible answer:*
Legend: Aztec empire prior to the Spanish invasion; death of Moctezuma; death of Itauqui
Myth: prophecy of Quetzalcoatl's return; "ball of fire"; strange four-legged creatures; fire-spitting weapons

---

Rubrics for Writing Options

You can adapt this as a checklist for students to use as they write.

Creative Writing

☐ Does the poem express the speaker's thoughts and feelings?

☐ Does it honor Xochipilli?

Expository Writing

☐ Does the essay accurately identify the elements of situational irony in the legend?

☐ Does it explain why each element fits the definition of situational irony?

☐ Is each explanation logically based and effectively expressed?

For further instruction, refer students to the following extension activity: Lifelong Learning: Events Over Time, *Exceeding the Standards: Extension Activities*, p. 24.

PECOS BILL

A Tall Tale by Adrien Stoutenberg

Preview the Model

At a Glance
Guided Reading: Reading Model
- Reading Level: Moderate
- Difficulty Consideration: Unfamiliar setting
- Ease Factors: Style, vocabulary

Objectives
Studying this lesson will enable students to
- use reading skills such as activating prior knowledge
- define *tall tale* and recognize elements of the genre in literature
- explain the cultural significance of American Old West tales
- appreciate an American tall tale

Launch the Lesson
Before reading "Pecos Bill," ask students to think about what it means to be a "cowboy." Do they think this occupation still exists, or has it become something of a legend?

Build Background
Cultural Context Americans have long held a glamorous view of the Old West. In the American imagination, the Old West was a mythic place of heroic men, rugged lifestyles, and adventure. The story of Pecos Bill and all the amazing things he can do reflects that view of the Old West. The original writer of the story was Edward O'Reilly. O'Reilly wrote the story for *The Century Magazine* in 1923.

Reader's Context Have you ever exaggerated, or heard someone exaggerate, while describing something? Explain.

Set Purpose
Think about what you already know about tall tales. What do you predict will happen in "Pecos Bill"?

Analyze Literature
Tall Tale A **tall tale** is a lighthearted or humorous story with exaggerated elements. Many tall tales depict the adventures of American folk heroes of the frontier and offer explanations as to how certain mountains, lakes, or other geographic features came to exist. As you read "Pecos Bill," note the exaggerated elements of the story.

Meet the Author
Adrien Stoutenberg (b. 1916) has written about forty books for children, including mysteries, biographies, and folk tales. "Pecos Bill" was taken from her book *American Tall Tales*. Born in Dafur, Minnesota, she studied at the Minneapolis School of Arts. In addition to writing, Stoutenberg has worked as a librarian and political reporter.

Use Reading Skills
Activate Prior Knowledge Prior knowledge is what a reader knows about a given topic, gathered from reading and from personal experience. Using related prior knowledge will help you to better understand a text. For the story "Pecos Bill," use the chart to help you apply what you already know of tall tales, Pecos Bill, and the Old West and what you want to know. Fill in the first two columns before you read the selection. Fill in the last column after you read the selection.

What I Know	What I Want to Know	What I Have Learned
"Pecos Bill" is a tall tale. Tall tales have exaggerated elements.		

Preview Vocabulary
home•stead (hōm´ sted) *n.*, house, especially a farmhouse, with adjoining buildings and land

cy•clone (sī´ klōn) *n.*, violent rotating windstorm, like a tornado

quiv•er•ing (kwiv´ ə ring) *adj.*, shaking with small rapid movements

Words in Use

Preview Vocabulary	Selection Words	Teaching Words
homestead, 762	plodding, 765	glamorous, 760
cyclone, 768	lassoed, 765	mythic, 760
quivering, 768	vowed, 767	rugged, 760
		exaggerated, 760
		frontier, 760

KEY TERMS

Common Core State Standards
Reading Literature
RL.1, RL.6
Writing
W.9
Language
L.6

Being human was a hard thing for Bill to face up to, but he realized that the cowboy must be right. He told his coyote friends goodbye and thanked them for all that they had taught him. Then he straddled a mountain lion he had tamed and rode with the cowboy toward the cowboy's ranch. On the way to the ranch, a big rattlesnake reared up in front of them. The cowboy galloped off, but Bill jumped from his mount and faced the snake.

"I'll let you have the first three bites, Mister Rattler, just to be fair. Then I'm going to beat the poison out of you until you behave yourself!"

That is just what Bill did. He whipped the snake around until it stretched out like a thirty-foot rope. Bill looped the rattler-rope in one hand, got back on his lion, and caught up with the cowboy. To entertain himself, he made a loop out of the snake and tossed it over the head of an armadillo plodding along through the cactus. Next, he lassoed several Gila monsters.

"I never saw anybody do anything like that before," said the cowboy.

"That's because nobody invented the lasso before," said Pecos Bill.

Before Pecos Bill came along, cowboys didn't know much about their job. They didn't know anything about rounding up cattle, or branding them, or even about ten-gallon hats. The only way they knew to catch a steer was to hide behind a bush, lay a looped rope on the ground, and wait for the steer to step into the loop.

Pecos Bill changed all that the minute he reached the Dusty Dipper Ranch. He slid off his mountain lion and marched up to the biggest cowboy there.

"Who's the boss here?" he asked.

The man took one look at Bill's lion and at the rattlesnake rope and said, "I was."

Young though he was, Bill took over. At the Dusty Dipper and at other ranches, Bill taught the cowboys almost everything they know today. He invented spurs for them to wear on their boots. He taught them how to round up the cattle and drive the herds to railroad stations where they could be shipped to market. One of the finest things Bill did was to teach the cowboys to sing cowboy songs.

Bill made himself a guitar. On a night when the moon was as reddish yellow as a ripe peach, though fifty times as large, he led some of the fellows at the ranch out to the corral and set himself down on the top rail.

Teach the Model

Make Connections

Answer: Responses will vary. Some students may say that the image is funny because it is so absurd. Others may be concerned about the animals and not think it is funny. **C**

Analyze Literature

Dialect Point out to students that a dialect is a version of a language spoken by people of a particular place, time, or group. Remind students that they, too, speak a dialect of American English. The characters in "Pecos Bill" also speak an American English dialect, but theirs is that of cowboys and other laborers in the western United States in the mid to late nineteenth century. Ask students to examine the dialogue and determine what words and phrases stand out as evidence of "cowboy dialect."

Use Reading Skills

Analyze Cause and Effect Remind students that analyzing cause and effect in literature can help the reader achieve a deeper level of understanding of the selection. Ask students to reread the paragraph beginning with "Young though he was, Bill took over," and think about what effect was caused by Bill teaching these things to the cowboys. A possible response is that the cowboys became more efficient at their jobs and happier on long cattle drives because they had songs to sing. **D**

DURING READING

Make Connections
Tall tales often contain humor. Do you think this image is funny? Explain.

Reading Skills

Death Valley Legends

Encourage students to expand their knowledge of Death Valley by reading and comparing "Pecos Bill" with another myth whose setting is this region. Provide students with a copy of "The Queen of Death Valley," a Shoshone myth that explains Death Valley's creation. When students finish reading, have them record the similarities and differences in a Venn diagram. As they read, have them pay close attention to details regarding nature and weather. If necessary, they may return to "Pecos Bill" to skim for details concerning natural events.

Art Connection

Frederick Remington helped define and cement this country's concept of the American West, just as its wide-open ranges began to close. Remington (1861-1909) was born and spent most of his life on the East Coast but traveled throughout the country as a young man and spent most of this time drawing people and places in frontier states like Montana, Kansas, Arizona, New Mexico, North Dakota, and Wyoming. Historians contend that this arrangement drove his romantic vision of the West and attracted the attention of eventual followers, who had little knowledge of the frontier's harsh realities. Remington's artwork centered on a singular theme, the individual's struggle against great odds, which aligned perfectly with eastern Americans' concepts of the West, as well as themselves. Direct students attention to *A Bucking Bronco*. Ask them what elements of the painting illustrate this theme. What elements of "Pecos Bill" and tall tales in general align with this notion of struggle and overcoming great obstacles?

"I don't want to brag," he told the cowhands, "but I learned my singing from the coyotes, and that's about the best singing there is."

He sang a tune the coyotes had taught him, and made up his own words:

"My seat is in the saddle,
*   and my saddle's in the sky,*
And I'll quit punchin' cows
*   in the sweet by and by."*

A Bucking Bronco.
F. Remington.

Differentiated Instruction

Reading Proficiency

To help students keep track of the many characters Pecos Bill encounters, ask them to write down the name or description of each character encountered and how that character influences Pecos Bill (or how he influences the character). Model this strategy by offering possible phrases for one character such as: "Widow-Maker—Pecos Bill's loyal horse. Rescued by Pecos Bill."

He made up many more verses and sang many other songs. When Bill was through, the roughest cowboy of all, Hardnose Hal, sat wiping tears from his eyes because of the beauty of Bill's singing. Lefty Lightning put his head down on his arms and wept. All the cowboys there vowed they would learn to sing and make up songs. And they did make up hundreds of songs about the lone prairie, and the Texas sky, and the wind blowing over the plains. That's why we have so many cowboy songs today.

Pecos Bill invented something else almost as useful as singing. This happened after a band of cattle rustlers came to the ranch and stole half a hundred cows.

"You boys," said Bill, "have to get something to protect yourselves with besides your fists. I can see I'll have to think up a six-shooter."

"What's a six-shooter?" asked Bronco-Busting Bertie. (Bill had taught horses how to buck and rear so that cowboys could learn bronco busting.)

"Why," said Bill, "that's a gun that holds six bullets."

Bill sat down in the shade of a yucca tree and figured out how to make a six-shooter. It was a useful invention, but it had its bad side. Some of the cowboys started shooting at each other. Some even went out and held up trains and stagecoaches.

One of the most exciting things Bill did was to find himself the wildest, strongest, most beautiful horse that ever kicked up the Texas dust. He was a mighty, golden mustang, and even Bill couldn't outrun that horse. To catch the mustang, Bill had the cowboys rig up a huge slingshot and shoot him high over the cactus and greasewood. When Bill landed in front of the mustang, the horse was so surprised he stopped short, thrusting out his front legs stiff as rifle barrels. The mustang had been going so fast that his hoofs drove into the ground, and he was stuck. Bill leaped on the animal's back, yanked on his golden mane, and pulled him free. The mustang was so thankful for being pulled from the trap that he swung his head around and gave Pecos Bill a smacking kiss. From then on, the horse was as gentle as a soft wind in a thatch of Jimson weed.

No one else could ride him, however. Most of the cowboys who tried ended up with broken necks. That's why Bill called his mustang "Widow-Maker."

Bill and Widow-Maker traveled all over the western range, starting new ranches and helping out in the long cattle drives. In stormy weather they often holed up with a band of coyotes. Bill would strum his guitar and the coyotes would sing with him.

PECOS BILL **767**

DURING READING

Use Reading Skills
Activate Prior Knowledge
Does the information here connect to what you already know about cowboys? How does your prior knowledge help you visualize the cowboys? **A**

DURING READING

Analyze Literature
Tall Tale How does the image of Bill in a slingshot reflect elements of a tall tale? **C**

Teach the Model

Use Reading Skills
Activate Prior Knowledge *Answer:* Responses will vary. Some students may say that they've seen images or read about cowboys singing or that they know "cowboy songs." They may say that that knowledge helps them to picture cowboys sitting around fires or riding on the trail, singing. **A**

History Connection
Old West Stagecoach Robbery
The stagecoach, a four-wheeled horse-drawn carriage, was used in the Old West for the purpose of transporting mail, passengers, and, at times, cash. Because they traveled alone with no method of communication, they were prime targets for robberies. An outlaw gang called the "Wild Bunch," consisting of Butch Cassidy and Tom "Black Jack" Ketchum, among others, made a living of preying on stagecoaches. **B**

Analyze Literature
Tall Tale *Answer:* It is a humorous image. The idea of someone being shot out of a slingshot in order to catch a horse is also an exaggerated element. **C**

Analyze Literature
Hyperbole Tell students that hyperbole is exaggeration made for effect. Ask students how the description of Pecos Bill rescuing Widow-Maker qualifies as hyperbole. **D**

Writing Skills

Tall Tale
Using their research from the Research Skills activity on page 763, have students write brief tall tales about their chosen landmarks. Encourage them to use creative and exaggerated details to explain the factual elements of the landmark, as well as larger-than-life characters that facilitate the events surrounding their formation. Allow time for students to share their work in pairs or with the entire class.

Use Reading Skills

Activate Prior Knowledge *Answer:* Responses may vary. Students may say that Pecos Bill will find a way to end the drought. They may want to know how he will do it. **Ⓐ**

Use Reading Skills

Take Notes Tell students that note-taking is an essential skill that they will use throughout their educations. Have students take notes on key action in the passage describing the wrangling of the cyclone—beginning at "Bill rode around on Widow-Maker, watching the clear, burning sky..." and finishing at "That was what made Death Valley." Remind students that in taking notes, they can use the summarizing skills they have learned to pick up the most essential details.

Use Reading Strategies

Visualize *Answer:* Responses will vary. Some students may guess a cyclone or other kind of storm. The image of the bees creates a mood of danger. **Ⓑ**

Analyze Literature

Tall Tale *Answer:* The fact that the cyclone is described as if it were a living creature ("feel its hot breath") gives the cyclone an exaggerated and even more dangerous feel. This, in turn, makes Pecos Bill an exaggerated hero. **Ⓒ**

> **DURING READING**
>
> **Use Reading Skills**
> **Activate Prior Knowledge**
> Think about what you know of tall tales and Pecos Bill. What do you think will happen next? What do you want to know? **Ⓐ**

cy·clone (sī´ klōn) *n.,* violent rotating windstorm, like a tornado

> **DURING READING**
>
> **Use Reading Strategies**
> **Visualize** What do you think the tall whirling tower of black bees is? What mood is created by comparing the object to the bees? **Ⓑ**

quiv·er·ing (kwiv´ ə ring) *adj.,* shaking with small rapid movements

> **DURING READING**
>
> **Analyze Literature**
> **Tall Tale** What in the description of the cyclone gives a tall tale feel? **Ⓒ**

Then came the year of the Terrible Drought. The land shriveled for lack of water, and the droves of cattle stood panting with thirst.

The cowboys and the ranch bosses from all around came to Bill, saying, "The whole country's going to dry up and blow away, Bill, unless you can figure out some way to bring us rain."

"I'm figuring," Bill told them, "but I've never tried making rain before, so I'll have to think a little."

While Bill thought, the country grew so dry it seemed that there would be nothing but bones and rocks left. Even cactus plants, which could stand a lot of dryness, began to turn brown. The pools where the cattle drank dried up and turned to cracked mud. All the snakes hid under the ground in order to keep from frying. Even the coyotes stopped howling, because their throats were too dry for them to make any sound.

Bill rode around on Widow-Maker, watching the clear, burning sky and hoping for the sight of a rain cloud. All he saw were whirls of dust, called dust devils, spinning up from the yellowing earth. Then, toward noon one day, he spied something over in Oklahoma that looked like a tall whirling tower of black bees. Widow-Maker reared up on his hind legs, his eyes rolling.

"It's just a <u>cyclone</u>," Pecos Bill told his horse, patting the golden neck.

But Widow-Maker was scared. The mighty horse began bucking around so hard that even Bill had a time staying in the saddle.

"Whoa there!" Bill commanded. "I could ride that cyclone as easy as I can ride you, the way you're carrying on."

That's when Bill had an idea. There might be rain mixed up in that cyclone tower. He nudged Widow-Maker with his spurs and yelled, "Giddap!"

What Bill planned to do was leap from his horse and grab the cyclone by the neck. But as he came near and saw how high the top of the whirling tower was, he knew he would have to do something better than that. Just as he and Widow-Maker came close enough to the cyclone to feel its hot breath, a knife of lightning streaked down into the ground. It stuck there, <u>quivering</u>, just long enough for Bill to reach out and grab it. As the lightning bolt whipped back up into the sky, Bill held on. When he was as high as the top of the cyclone, he jumped and landed astraddle its black, spinning shoulders.

By then, everyone in Texas, New Mexico, Arizona, and Oklahoma was watching. They saw Bill grab hold of that cyclone's shoulders and haul them back. They saw him wrap his legs around the cyclone's belly and squeeze so hard the cyclone started to pant.

Differentiated Instruction

Kinesthetic Learning

Students might more fully grasp the humor and absurdity of Pecos Bill's adventures through a reenactment of the Terrible Drought and Bill versus the cyclone. Invite students to assume the roles of Bill and Widow-Maker, as well as the cattle, cactus plants, coyotes, snakes, and the cyclone, emphasizing the personified elements of the plants, animals, and weather phenomenon.

Then Bill got out his lasso and slung it around the cyclone's neck. He pulled it tighter and tighter until the cyclone started to choke, spitting out rocks and dust. All the rain that was mixed up in it started to fall.

Down below, the cattle and the coyotes, the jack rabbits and the horned toads, stuck out their tongues and caught the sweet, blue falling rain. Cowboys on the ranches and people in town ran around whooping and cheering, holding out pans and kettles to catch raindrops. Bill rode the cyclone across three states. By the time the cyclone reached California, it was all out of steam and out of rain, too. It gave a big sigh, trembled weakly, and sank to earth. Bill didn't have time to jump off. He fell hard, scooping out a few thousand acres of sand and rock and leaving a big basin below sea level. That was what made Death Valley.

Bill was a greater hero than ever after that. Yet at times, he felt almost as lonely as on the day when he had bounced out of his folks' wagon and found himself sitting alone under the empty sky. Widow-Maker was good company most of the time, but Bill felt there was something missing in his life.

One day, he wandered down to the Rio Grande and stood watching the brown river flow slowly past. Suddenly, he saw a catfish as big as a whale jumping around on top of the water, its whiskers shining like broomsticks. On top of the catfish was a brown-eyed, brown-haired girl.

Somebody beside Bill exclaimed, "Look at Slue-Foot Sue ride that fish!"

Pecos Bill felt his heart thump and tingle in a way it had never done before. "That's the girl I want to marry!" he said. He waded out into the Rio Grande, poked the catfish in the nose, and carried Slue-Foot Sue to a church. "You're going to be my bride," he said.

"That's fine with me," said Sue, looking Pecos Bill over and seeing that he was the biggest, boldest, smartest cowboy who had ever happened to come along beside the Rio Grande.

That was the beginning of a very happy life for Bill. He and Sue raised a large family. All of the boys grew up to be cowboys, and the girls grew up to be cowgirls. The only time Bill and Sue had any trouble was when Bill wanted to adopt a batch of baby coyotes who were orphans.

D

> Down below, the cattle and the coyotes, the jack rabbits and the horned toads, stuck out their tongues and caught the sweet, blue falling rain.

DURING READING

Analyze Literature
Tall Tale What geographic feature of the West is Pecos Bill supposedly responsible for?

E

Teach the Model

Analyze Literature
Personification Remind students that personification is the literary technique of describing something not human as if it were human. Direct students to the passage describing the cyclone. Model a question for students to encourage them to identify examples of personification such as: "What descriptive details of the cyclone does the author use to make it possible for Pecos Bill to tame it?" **D**

Analyze Literature
Tall Tale *Answer:* He is responsible for Death Valley. **E**

Analyze Literature
Imagery Remind students that authors use imagery to create a vivid mental picture in the reader's mind. Ask students what details are used to create an image of Slue-Foot Sue.

Use Reading Skills
Read Aloud To help students understand the humorous mood of this selection, have a volunteer read aloud the two paragraphs where Pecos Bill decides to marry Slue-Foot Sue (beginning at "Pecos Bill felt his heart thump and tingle. . . .") **F**

Grammar Skills

Past Tense of Irregular Verbs
Remind students that while they can create the past tense of many verbs by adding *—ed* to the end, they must memorize the diverse past tense forms of irregular verbs. Examine the irregular past tense verb forms found on this page, including the following:

slung	caught
rode	was
fell	felt
found	stood
saw	said

Make Connections

Answer: Several of the coyotes were elected to public office. Some students may find it funny because it is saying that some politicians have the characteristics of coyotes—not to be trusted.

Analyze Literature

Characterization Remind students that a writer uses direct and indirect characterization to complete the image of a character. Ask students to identify what type of characterization the author uses to describe the character of Pecos Bill as an old man. **B**

Use Reading Skills

Identify Author's Purpose Remind students that authors have a purpose or goal when they write. Ask students why they think the author chose not to let the reader know how Pecos Bill dies. Would it change the feel of the story if the reader knew for certain how Pecos Bill dies? **C**

Answer: Responses will vary. Students' heroes should be able to do feats and have characteristics suited to tall tales. Students might say that like Pecos Bill, Superman (or another fantasy hero) comes to the rescue of those in need and has incredible strength or other superhuman abilities.

"We're human beings," Sue said, "and we can't be raising varmints."

"I was a varmint once myself," said Bill. He argued so much that Sue agreed to take the coyotes in and raise them as members of the family. Eventually, several of them were elected to public office.

Pecos Bill grew old, as everyone and everything does in time. Even so, there wasn't a bronco he couldn't bust, or a steer he couldn't rope, or a bear he couldn't hug to death faster and better than anyone else.

No one knows, for sure, how he died, or even if he did die. Some say that he mixed barbed wire in his coffee to make it strong enough for his taste, and that the wire rusted in his stomach and poisoned him. Others say that one day he met a dude cowboy, all dressed up in fancy clothes, who didn't know the front end of a cow from the side of a boxcar. The dude asked so many silly questions about cow punching that Pecos Bill lay down in the dust and laughed himself to death.

But the cowboys back in the Pecos River country say that every once in a while, when the moon is full and puffing its white cheeks out and the wind is crooning softly through the bear grass, Pecos Bill himself comes along and sits on his haunches and sings right along with the coyotes. ✤

DURING READING

Make Connections
What happens to several of the coyotes? What makes this humorous? **A**

MIRRORS **&** **W**INDOWS

If you were going to create a tall tale, what would the hero or heroine be able to do? How is a contemporary hero like Superman similar to Pecos Bill?

770 UNIT 8 FOLK LITERATURE

TEACHING NOTE

Self-Generated Questioning

Divide the class into pairs. Instruct the pairs to create a question for the selection such as: "Are there records of the story's oral tradition prior to its recording in 1923?" Next, have students draw a picture, a chart, or another graphic that answers the question. Invite the pairs to share their questions and answers in small groups or as a class.

Find Meaning

1. (a) What happens to Bill when he falls out of the wagon? (b) How believable do you think this is? Explain your answer.

2. (a) How does Bill react when he encounters the cowboy? (b) Why does Bill believe he is not human himself? (c) Why does he change his mind so easily?

3. (a) What about Slue-Foot Sue impresses Bill? (b) Why do Bill and Sue make a good couple?

Analyze Literature

Tall Tale "Pecos Bill" is a tall tale. A tall tale is a lighthearted or humorous story with many exaggerated elements. Tall tales contain larger-than-life heroes, exaggerated feats, and explanations for how things came into being. Use a cluster chart to show the tall tale elements of "Pecos Bill." What inventions and feats is Pecos Bill supposedly responsible for?

Make Judgments

4. What makes this story humorous?

5. Why do you think Pecos Bill is such a popular Old West character?

6. What purpose does this story serve?

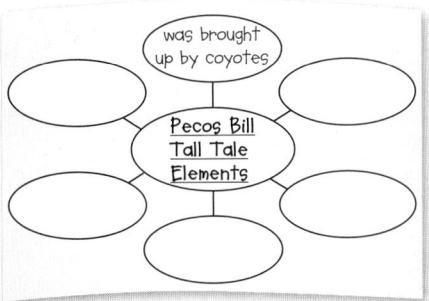

Extend Understanding

Writing Options

Creative Writing Cowboy songs are usually about the land, the work cowboys do, and the adventures they have. Think about what you know of the West and cowboys. Write **lyrics** for a cowboy song. Share your lyrics with the class.

Expository Writing In the tall tale "Pecos Bill," Bill was responsible for the creation of Death Valley. Write a **summary** that tells how that land formation actually came about. Share your summary with the class.

Collaborative Learning

Brainstorm Inventions In small groups, brainstorm inventions, either outlandish or practical. Decide why those inventions are needed and who would be most likely to use them. Name your invention and describe it in detail.

Media Literacy

Conduct Library Research At your library, locate another tall tale or fable from another culture. Compare it to "Pecos Bill." What are the similarities and differences between the two stories? Create a Venn diagram to express them.

 Go to www.mirrorsandwindows.com for more.

Find Meaning

1. (a) He goes to live with coyotes. (b) Students should give reasons to support their opinions.

2. (a) He's ready to fight him. (b) Bill doesn't think he's human because he's lived with coyotes as long as he can remember. He does all the things that coyotes do. (c) He changes his mind when he realizes that, unlike coyotes, he doesn't have a tail.

3. (a) Her ability to ride a giant catfish. (b) Sue was also bold and could perform unusual feats.

Make Judgments

4. The author tells of the most unlikely and impossible events in a very matter-of-fact tone. There is a lot of visual humor such as the image of Bill riding a cyclone. The audience never feels that Bill is in real danger so they are free to be amused by his antics and the outcomes.

5. Perhaps he is popular because he's likeable, he helps people, he's humorous, and he's able to conquer almost anything.

6. The story serves as a humorous tale to entertain readers. It also gives some information about cowboy life in the Old West. People find comfort in stories about heroes.

Analyze Literature

Tall Tale *Answer:* He was brought up by coyotes and could run faster and hunt better than they. He invented the lasso, spurs, cowboy songs, and the six-shooter. He saved the West from drought. He created Death Valley.

Rubrics for Writing Options

You can adapt this as a checklist for students to use as they write.

Creative Writing

☐ Do the lyrics reflect the cowboy song genre?
☐ Do the lyrics describe aspects of a cowboy's life?

Expository Writing

☐ Does the summary include the main ideas of how Pecos Bill created Death Valley?
☐ Does the summary leave out unimportant details?
☐ Are the grammar, spelling, and punctuation correct?

Correcting Misplaced Modifiers

These are sample answers.

1. Listening to Bill sing, the cowboys rested their heads on their saddles.

2. Put the meat that the coyote gave you in your mouth.

3. Bill, looking for a rain cloud, saw nothing but dust devils.

4. After they ate, the cowboys rounded up the cattle.

5. As it was getting light, Bill spotted the wild horse.

Understanding Misplaced Modifiers

1. Bill, who believed he was a coyote, learned that he was human from the cowboy.

2. Pecos Bill, who had made himself a guitar, taught the cowboys to sing.

3. Bill traveled to many other ranches with Widow-Maker, who no one else could ride.

4. Sue, who didn't want to adopt baby coyotes, raised a large family with Bill.

5. Stories about Pecos Bill are called tall tales, which exaggerate many things.

6. Tall tales that are fascinating have been around for many years.

7. Many people know the vivid and memorable story of Pecos Bill.

> For more information, see Grammar & Style Section 3.13, Common Usage Problems, in the Language Arts Handbook.

Misplaced Modifiers

> *When Bill was two weeks old, his father found a half-grown bear and brought the bear home.*
>
> —ADRIEN STOUTENBERG, "Pecos Bill"

A **misplaced modifier** is a phrase or clause that confuses the meaning of a sentence. The modifier is located so far from the word it should modify that it appears to be modifying an inappropriate word.

For example, in the quotation above, the clause *When Bill was two weeks old* modifies the verb *found*. What if the quotation said, *His father found a half-grown bear when he was two weeks old?* The placement of the clause now makes it appear to modify the noun *bear*.

To correct misplaced modifiers, move the modifier closer to the word it modifies.

EXAMPLES

misplaced modifier	The spurs sat on the table <u>that Bill had invented.</u> [This sounds as if Bill invented the table.]
corrected sentence	The spurs <u>that Bill had invented</u> sat on the table.
misplaced modifier	Bill was fed by a coyote <u>after he fell from the wagon.</u> [This sounds as if the coyote fell from the wagon.]
corrected sentence	<u>After he fell from the wagon</u>, Bill was fed by a coyote.

Correcting Misplaced Modifiers

Rewrite each sentence so that the underlined phrase or clause modifies the underlined word.

1. The <u>cowboys</u> rested their heads on their saddles <u>listening to Bill sing</u>.

2. Put the <u>meat</u> in your mouth <u>that the coyote gave you</u>.

3. <u>Bill</u> saw nothing but dust devils <u>looking for a rain cloud</u>.

4. The <u>cowboys</u> rounded up the cattle <u>after they ate</u>.

5. Bill <u>spotted</u> the wild horse <u>as it was getting light</u>.

Understanding Misplaced Modifiers

Combine each pair of sentences below by making one sentence into a modifier. Be sure your modifiers aren't misplaced.

EXAMPLE

Bill's family were pioneers.
They were Texas settlers.

combined sentence
Bill's family, Texas settlers, were pioneers.

1. Bill believed he was a coyote. The cowboy told him he was a human.

2. Pecos Bill taught the cowboys to sing. He made himself a guitar.

3. Bill and Widow-Maker traveled to many other ranches. No one else could ride him.

4. Bill and Sue raised a large family. Sue didn't want Bill to adopt baby coyotes.

5. Stories about Pecos Bill are called tall tales. They exaggerate many things.

6. Tall tales have been around for many years. They are fascinating.

7. Many people know the story of Pecos Bill. It is vivid and memorable.

Words in Use

Teaching Words
inappropriate, 772
exaggerate, 772
vivid, 772

KEY TERMS
MISPLACED MODIFIER, 772
PHRASE, 772
CLAUSE, 772
NOUN, 772

Program Resources

You will find additional lessons on Misplaced Modifiers in the *Exceeding the Standards: Grammar & Style* resource.

Common Core State Standards

Language
L.7.1c

Coyote Steals the Sun and Moon

A Zuni Myth retold by Richard Erdoes and Alfonso Ortiz

BEFORE READING

Build Background

Cultural Context The Zuni are North American Pueblo who live in New Mexico and Arizona. According to their traditional religion, Kachinas are powerful ancestral spirits who act as go-betweens for humans and gods. Each Kachina—and there are hundreds—has a distinct appearance and behavior. For half of each year, Kachinas are believed to live with a tribe. Humans can see them during ceremonies in which masked men wear Kachina costumes and perform dances and other rituals. The Kachina represented by each dancer is thought to be present with him during the ceremony. Although they are not worshipped, Kachinas are greatly respected.

Reader's Context Every society has certain institutions, people, or places that are greatly respected. How should individuals behave toward these things, and why?

Set Purpose

Use the title, illustrations, and Cultural Context to make predictions about the characters and plot of this myth. Then, as you read, determine how accurate your predictions are and adjust them accordingly.

Analyze Literature

Myth A **myth** is a story that explains objects or events in the natural world. These objects or events are explained as being caused by some supernatural force or being, often a god. Traditional myths often reflect the culture and values of the people who tell them.

Meet the Authors

Richard Erdoes was born in Frankfurt, Germany, and later moved to New Mexico. Both an award-winning photographer and author, Erdoes focuses much of his work on the American West and Native Americans.

Alfonso Ortiz (1939–1997) was born in San Juan Pueblo, New Mexico, to parents of Pueblo and Hispanic descent. Ortiz became an influential anthropologist and activist.

Use Reading Skills

Analyze Cause and Effect In stories, events often have a cause-and-effect relationship. In other words, one event (cause) makes something happen (effect). Often signal words, including *because, since,* or *therefore,* can help you identify causes and effects. As you read "Coyote Steals the Sun and Moon," use a chart to keep track of causes and effects.

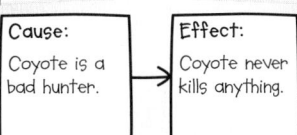

Cause:	Effect:
Coyote is a bad hunter.	Coyote never kills anything.

Preview Vocabulary

sa‧cred (sā´ krəd) *adj.,* believed to be holy; worthy of deep respect

lag (lag) *v.,* fall behind or fail to keep up with

shriv‧el (shri´ vəl) *v.,* become smaller in size because of dryness

pur‧suit (pər süt´) *n.,* act of chasing or pursuing

At a Glance
Directed Reading
- Reading Level: Easy
- Difficulty Considerations: Fantastic elements
- Ease Factor: Length

Objectives

Studying this lesson will enable students to

- use reading skills like analyzing cause and effect
- define *myth* and recognize elements of the genre in this selection
- explain the scientific function of feathers in flight
- appreciate a myth from a different culture

Launch the Lesson

Tell students that they are about to read a creation myth called "Coyote Steals the Sun and Moon." Based on the title, ask them to make predictions about what element of nature will be created and how.

COYOTE STEALS THE SUN AND MOON **773**

Words in Use

Preview Vocabulary
sacred, 775
lag, 776
shrivel, 776
pursuit, 776

Teaching Words
ancestral, 773
represented, 773
institutions, 773
supernatural, 773
traditional, 773
influential, 773
anthropologist, 773
activist, 773
explanatory, 777

KEY TERMS

Common Core State Standards

Reading Literature
RL.1, RL.5

Writing
W.9

Language
L.6

Summary

Coyote is having difficulty hunting in the dark, so he and Eagle journey to the land of the Kachinas looking for light. They steal their boxes containing the Sun and the Moon, and on the trip home Eagle foolishly allows Coyote to carry the boxes. Curious about the contents, Coyote opens the boxes, allowing the Sun and Moon to escape into the sky and create the seasons.

The Mirrors & Windows questions at the end of this selection focus on the theme of culpability. Before reading the story, ask students how they divide responsibilities associated with a task when multiple people are involved. How does our society, in general, share responsibility with others?

Zuni, 1895. Frank Reed Whiteside. David David Gallery, Philadelphia.

Coyote Steals the Sun and Moon

A Zuni Myth retold by Richard Erdoes and Alfonso Ortiz

774

Program Resources

Planning and Assessment
Program Planning Guide, Selection Lesson Plan
E-Lesson Planner
Assessment Guide, Lesson Test
ExamView

Technology Tools
Interactive Student Text on CD
Visual Teaching Package
mirrorsandwindows.com

Meeting the Standards
Drama: Unit 8, Directed Reading, pp. 33–37

Differentiating Instruction
Advanced Students, Theme Study, pp. 46–47

Coyote is a bad hunter who never kills anything. Once he watched Eagle hunting rabbits, catching one after another—more rabbits than he could eat. Coyote thought, "I'll team up with Eagle so I can have enough meat." Coyote is always up to something.

"Friend," Coyote said to Eagle, "we should hunt together. Two can catch more than one."

"Why not?" Eagle said, and so they began to hunt in partnership. Eagle caught many rabbits, but all Coyote caught was some little bugs.

At this time the world was still dark; the sun and the moon had not yet been put in the sky. "Friend," Coyote said to Eagle, "no wonder I can't catch anything; I can't see. Do you know where we can get some light?"

"You're right, friend, there should be some light," Eagle said. "I think there's a little toward the west. Let's try and find it."

And so they went looking for the sun and moon. They came to a big river, which Eagle flew over. Coyote swam, and swallowed so much water that he almost drowned. He crawled out with his fur full of mud, and Eagle asked, "Why don't you fly like me?"

"You have wings; I just have hair," Coyote said. "I can't fly without feathers."

At last they came to a pueblo,¹ where the Kachinas happened to be dancing. The people invited Eagle and Coyote to sit down and have something to eat while they watched the <u>sacred</u> dances. Seeing the power of the Kachinas, Eagle said, "I believe these are the people who have light."

Coyote, who had been looking all around, pointed out two boxes, one large and one small, that the people opened whenever they wanted light. To produce a lot of light, they opened the lid of the big box, which contained the sun. For less light they opened the small box, which held the moon.

Coyote nudged Eagle. "Friend, did you see that? They have all the light we need in the big box. Let's steal it."

"You always want to steal and rob. I say we should just borrow it."

"They won't lend it to us."

"You may be right," said Eagle. "Let's wait till they finish dancing and then steal it." **A**

After a while the Kachinas went home to sleep, and Eagle scooped up the large box and flew off. Coyote ran along trying to keep up, panting, his tongue hanging out. Soon he yelled up to Eagle, "Ho, friend, let me carry the box a little way."

"No, no," said Eagle, "you never do anything right."

He flew on, and Coyote ran after him. After a while Coyote shouted again: "Friend, you're my chief, and it's not right for you to carry the box; people will call me lazy. Let me have it."

"No, no, you always mess everything up." And Eagle flew on and Coyote ran along.

So it went for a stretch, and then Coyote started again. "Ho, friend, it isn't right for you to do this. What will people think of you and me?"

"I don't care what people think. I'm going to carry this box."

> ## "No, no," said Eagle, "you never do anything right."

---

1. **pueblo.** Traditional community in the Southwest created by certain native peoples

sa·cred (sā′ krəd) *adj.*, believed to be holy; worthy of deep respect

Teach the Selection

Science Connection

Flying Power Much like the wings of an aircraft, a bird's wings create lift and force when air flows over and under them, a phenomenon called airfoil. There are several sets of feathers on a bird's wing that create the airfoil. The shaft, called the rachis; the branches, called barbs; and the barbs' side branches, called barbules, determine the feather's tree-like shape. The barbules link together in flight to hold the airfoil, which maintains flight.

Use Reading Skills

Analyze Cause and Effect Remind students that it is important to think about the relationship between cause and effect in literature. Ask students to pause here in their reading to think about what caused Coyote and Eagle to resort to stealing the Sun and Moon. **A**

Research Skills

Zuni Kachinas

Remind students that there are hundreds of distinct Zuni Kachinas. They include, but are not limited to, animals (Antelope), weather phenomena (Rainbow Kachina), human figures (Warrior), and mythical creatures (Ogre). Ask each student to research reliable sources in order to find out as much as possible about one type of Zuni Kachina.

Challenge them to determine what their chosen Kachina represents, what it causes, and/or what it brings to or does for people. Encourage students to present their findings to the class or to small groups.

Analyze Literature

Myth Remind students that a myth is a story that explains objects or events in the natural world. Now that they have read the entire story, ask students to discuss together what other myths they have read or heard that explain the seasons or the presence of light and fire. (A possible response is the Greek myth of Prometheus stealing fire from the gods and giving it to humanity.)

MIRRORS & WINDOWS Some students will blame Eagle as well, since he agreed to steal the Sun and also knew that Coyote never did anything right; others will believe that Coyote alone is responsible. Students should state specific criteria for determining responsibility in joint activities.

Again Eagle flew on and again Coyote ran after him. Finally Coyote begged for the fourth time:[2] "Let me carry it. You're the chief, and I'm just Coyote. Let me carry it."

Eagle couldn't stand any more pestering. Also, Coyote had asked him four times, and if someone asks four times, you'd better give him what he wants. Eagle said, "Since you won't let up on me, go ahead and carry the box for a while. But promise not to open it."

"Oh, sure, oh yes, I promise." They went on as before, but now Coyote had the box. Soon Eagle was far ahead, and Coyote <u>lagged</u> behind a hill where Eagle couldn't see him. "I wonder what the light looks like, inside there," he said to himself. "Why shouldn't I take a peek? Probably there's something extra in the box, something good that Eagle wants to keep to himself."

And Coyote opened the lid. Now, not only was the sun inside, but the moon also. Eagle had put them both together, thinking that it would be easier to carry one box than two.

As soon as Coyote opened the lid, the moon escaped, flying high into the sky. At once all the plants <u>shriveled</u> up and turned brown. Just as quickly, all the leaves fell off the trees, and it was winter. Trying to catch the moon and put it back in the box, Coyote ran in <u>pursuit</u> as it skipped away from him. Meanwhile the sun flew out and rose into the sky. It drifted far away, and the peaches, squashes and melons shriveled up with cold.

Eagle turned and flew back to see what had delayed Coyote. "You fool! Look what you've done!" he said. "You let the sun and moon escape, and now it's cold." Indeed, it began to snow, and Coyote shivered. "Now your teeth are chattering," Eagle said, "and it's your fault that cold has come into the world."

It's true. If it weren't for Coyote's curiosity and mischief making, we wouldn't have winter; we could enjoy summer all the time. ❖

---

2. **for the fourth time.** The number four is important in many Native American cultures and appears in many stories and myths.

---

lag (lag) *v.*, fall behind or fail to keep up with

shriv•el (shriʹ vəl) *v.*, become smaller in size because of dryness

pur•suit (pər süt´) *n.*, act of chasing or pursuing

MIRRORS & WINDOWS Do you blame only Coyote for the outcome, or do you blame Eagle as well? How should someone determine responsibility when more than one person is involved?

Differentiated Instruction

Reading Proficiency

Students may have difficulty comprehending how Eagle ended up with both the Moon and the Sun. Direct their attention to the prior page, where it appears that Eagle took only the Sun in the large box. Then point out that, on this page, the authors explain that Eagle had placed the Moon inside this box as well in order to more easily carry the two. Discuss this inconsistency as a class. Did the authors purposely or accidentally leave out an explanation of how and when Eagle placed the Moon in the box with the Sun? Why might inconsistencies like this appear in retellings of traditional stories?

Find Meaning

1. (a) What does Eagle ask after Coyote swims across the big river? (b) What does this suggest about how well they know each other?

2. (a) What details do you learn about the Kachinas? (b) Which show their power, and which show their humanity?

3. (a) What does Coyote promise? (b) Why does he break his promise?

Analyze Literature

Myth A typical myth includes supernatural or magical elements to explain objects or events in the natural world. Skim "Coyote Steals the Sun and Moon," looking for such elements. List them in a chart. Then discuss with your class how each contributes to the explanatory function of this myth.

Make Judgments

4. (a) How are the people and animals alike in this story, and how are they different? (b) Which group is more powerful and why?

5. (a) What happens because Coyote opens the lid? (b) What message does this suggest about those who break rules?

6. (a) Why do you think Coyote appears in many stories? (b) What makes him both appealing and useful as a character?

Supernatural or Magical Elements

1. talking animals

2.

3.

4.

Extend Understanding

Writing Options

Creative Writing Write a retelling of this **myth,** suitable for a general audience, using a different setting and characters. You might begin by creating a simple plot map of this story and then changing the characters and setting. Include dialogue and enough details to make the story interesting.

Expository Writing The characters of Eagle and Coyote are the force behind the story; their desires put events in motion. Write a brief **expository essay** that compares and contrasts the two characters. In the introductory paragraph, identify the myth and the characters. In your thesis, state your main idea about how the characters are similar or different. In the body paragraphs, support your thesis with details that show how they are alike and different. Share your work with the class.

Lifelong Learning

Conduct Research on the Zuni The Zuni have a long and fascinating history and culture. Do research to learn more about them. Include information from multiple sources, such as the Internet, library texts, or encyclopedias. Then create a brief oral or visual presentation to share your findings. Include images or other graphics if possible.

Media Literacy

Compare Themes Across Cultures Locate a retelling of the Greek myth about Pandora's box. Identify themes that are present in that myth and the one you just read. What conclusions can you draw from comparing the themes? Write a brief essay explaining your conclusions. Include specific details from both myths.

W M Go to www.mirrorsandwindows.com for more.

Find Meaning

1. (a) Eagle asks why Coyote did not fly. (b) This suggests that Eagle does not know everything about Coyote.

2. (a) The Kachinas are powerful enough to control the Sun and the Moon. (b) Like humans, they sleep at night.

3. (a) He promises not to open the box. (b) He breaks his promises because he does not totally trust Eagle and is curious.

Make Judgments

4. (a) Both people and animals can communicate with each other, but only the people are given the light. (b) The Kachinas dance only for people, so people are probably more powerful.

5. (a) Plants shriveled and the world grew cold. (b) Those who break rules may cause problems for everyone.

6. (a) Students may offer a variety of reasons, including the fact that Coyote's quick mind and curiosity make things happen. (b) He has many human qualities.

Analyze Literature

Myth *Answer:* Students should identify at least the Sun and Moon in a box and the instant change of climate after the box was opened. These magical elements provide an explanation that is understandable by others and sounds reasonable.

Rubrics for Writing Options

You can adapt this as a checklist for students to use as they write.

Creative Writing

☐ Did the student choose new characters?

☐ Did the student choose a new setting?

☐ Do the student's choices assist in the retelling?

Expository Writing

☐ Does the introduction identify the characters and the myth?

☐ Do the body paragraphs use details to show similarities and differences?

Preview the Selection

At a Glance
Directed Reading
- Reading Level: Moderate
- Difficulty Consideration: Unfamiliar setting
- Ease Factors: Length, vocabulary

Objectives
Studying this lesson will enable students to
- use reading skills such as summarizing and clarifying
- recognize and explain the literary technique of flashback
- appreciate a story from another culture

Launch the Lesson
Prior to reading "Where the Girl Rescued Her Brother," ask students what they know about the Cheyenne, a people who populated North America long before us. Engage students in a group discussion about the Cheyenne. Model questions for them to discuss such as: "What was life like for them before and after European contact? How did it change them? Did their lives improve after Europeans settled there?"

DIRECTED READING

BEFORE READING

Build Background
Historical Context The Cheyenne nation once consisted of farmers and small-game hunters in what is today central Minnesota. During the 1600s and 1700s, they moved west—driven out by Dakota and Ojibway peoples—many of whom had already lost their land to white settlers. The Cheyenne nation eventually settled in the Black Hills of South Dakota but were again relocated to a reservation in Montana, which is still their land today.

Reader's Context Describe a time when you witnessed someone acting more bravely than you thought possible.

Set Purpose
Preview the title and images in "Where the Girl Rescued Her Brother" to make predictions about the theme of the legend. As you read, revise your predictions.

Analyze Literature
Flashback A **flashback** is part of a story, poem, or play that presents events that happened at an earlier time. As you read "Where the Girl Rescued Her Brother," identify when the authors use this technique. What makes the technique effective?

Meet the Authors

Joseph Bruchac (b. 1942) is a storyteller and poet of Native American, English, and Slovak descent. He often draws on this heritage to develop his stories and poems. Bruchac travels the country sharing stories as part of a long heritage of oral tradition.

Gayle Ross (b. 1951) is a storyteller and writer who describes her heritage as Scots-Cherokee. With Bruchac, Ross authored the collection *The Girl Who Married the Moon*, sixteen Native American stories with female heroes.

Use Reading Skills
Summarize When you summarize events from a text, you recall important ideas and information and retell them. Summarizing can help you to better remember events in a story. As you read "Where the Girl Rescued Her Brother," think about the major events of the text. Who are the major characters? What conflicts and challenges do they experience throughout the story? By recalling and retelling these important details, you are summarizing the events in the story.

Event #1: Buffalo Calf Road Woman rides out of her camp with her husband.
Event #2:
Summary:

Preview Vocabulary
al·ly (a´ lī) *n.*, person who is helpful; friend

de·ter·mined (di tər´ mənd) *adj.*, not easily moved or changed

re·treat (ri trēt´) *v.*, withdraw; back off

Words in Use

Preview Vocabulary
ally, 780
determined, 781
retreat, 783

Selection Words
honorable, 780
ferocity, 782
withdrawal, 783

Teaching Words
relocated, 778
reservation, 778

legend, 778
technique, 778
heritage, 778
oral tradition, 778
buyouts, 782
cavalry, 782

KEY TERMS
LEGEND, 778
THEME, 778
FLASHBACK, 778
CHARACTER, 778
CONFLICT, 778
CHARACTER TRAIT, 784

Common Core State Standards
Reading Literature
RL.1

Writing
W.7, W.8, W.9, W.10

Speaking and Listening
SL.5

Language
L.6

Where the Girl Rescued Her Brother

A Cheyenne Legend by Joseph Bruchac and Gayle Ross

Chief 'Crazy Horse.' Robert Ottokar Lindneux. Private collection.

This time, however, she was the one going into the fight.

779

Teach the Selection

Summary

Buffalo Calf Road Woman rides into battle with the men of her Cheyenne tribe. As a member of the Quilter's Society, a group of only the bravest women, she rides to war with pride. On this day her tribe is joining forces with their allies, the Lakota and Oglala, to drive out the white people who are taking their lands. During battle, Buffalo Calf Road Woman sees that her brother becomes surrounded by the enemy with no means of escape. Immediately she rides into the fight, surprising the enemy with her bravery, and carries her brother away to safety. This act turns the battle to her side's favor, and the enemy withdraws.

The Mirrors & Windows questions at the end of this selection focus on the theme of heroism. Before reading the story, ask students if anyone in their life has risked their safety for the well-being of another. Do heroes like this still exist?

Program Resources

Planning and Assessment
Program Planning Guide, Selection Lesson Plan
E-Lesson Planner
Assessment Guide, Lesson Test
ExamView

Technology Tools
Interactive Student Text on CD
Visual Teaching Package
Audio Library
mirrorsandwindows.com

Meeting the Standards
Drama: Unit 8, Directed Reading, pp. 38–42

Differentiating Instruction
English Language Learners, Summarize, pp. 188–197

Use Reading Skills

Determine the Importance of Details Ask students to explain why they think it is important for the author to describe what Buffalo Calf Road Woman and her brother and husband are wearing. Model a question for them such as: "What does this elaborate dress say about their character?" **Ⓐ**

Analyze Literature

Flashback Remind students that a flashback is part of a story that presents events that happened at an earlier time. Writers will either use flashback by beginning a work at a final event and then telling the rest of the story as a flashback, or beginning a story with a final event and using the flashback to fill in events that happened previously. Have students identify which technique is used here and to what purpose. **Ⓑ**

It was the moon when the chokecherries were ripe. A young woman rode out of a Cheyenne camp with her husband and her brother. The young woman's name was Buffalo Calf Road Woman. Her husband, Black Coyote, was one of the chiefs of the Cheyenne, the people of the plains who call themselves Tsis-tsis-tas, meaning simply "The People." Buffalo Calf Road Woman's brother, Comes-in-Sight, was also one of the Cheyenne chiefs, and it was well-known how close he was to his sister.

Like many of the other young women of the Cheyenne, Buffalo Calf Road Woman was respected for her honorable nature. Although it was the men who most often went to war to defend the people—as they were doing on this day—women would accompany their husbands when they went to battle. If a man held an important position among the Cheyenne, such as the keeper of the Sacred Arrows, then his wife, too, would have to be of the highest moral character, for she shared the weight of his responsibility.

Buffalo Calf Road Woman was well aware of this, and as she rode by her husband she did so with pride. She knew that today they were on their way to meet their old <u>allies</u>, the Lakota. They were going out to try to drive back the *veho*, the spider people who were trying to claim all the lands of the Native peoples.

The Cheyenne had been worried about the *veho*, the white people, for a long time. They had given them that name because, like the black widow spider, they were very beautiful but it was dangerous to get close to them. And unlike the Cheyenne, they seemed to follow a practice of making promises and not keeping them. Although their soldier chief Custer had promised to be friendly with the Cheyenne, now he and the others had come into their lands to make war upon them.

Buffalo Calf Road Woman wore a robe embroidered with porcupine quills. The clothing of her brother and her husband, Black Coyote, was also beautifully decorated with those quills, which had been flattened, dyed in different colors, folded, and sewed on in patterns. Buffalo Calf Road Woman was proud that she belonged to the Society of Quilters. As with the men's societies, only a few women—those of the best character—could join. Like the men, the women had to be strong, honorable, and brave. Buffalo Calf Road Woman had grown up hearing stories of how Cheyenne women would defend their families when the men were away. The women of the Cheyenne were brave, and those in the Society of Quilters were the bravest of all.

> "Grandfather," she said..."we do not wish to harm you, but we will protect our camp. Go back to your own home."

Buffalo Calf Road Woman smiled as she remembered one day when the women of the Society of Quilters showed such bravery. It was during the Moon of Falling Leaves. A big hunt had been planned. The men who acted as scouts had gone out and located the great buffalo herd. They had seen, too, that there were no human enemies anywhere near their camp. So almost none of the men remained behind.

On that day, when all the men were away, a great grizzly bear came into the

---

al·ly (a´ lï') *n.*, person who is helpful; friend

Differentiated Instruction

Reading Proficiency

Have students listen to you read the story aloud. When you are finished, ask students what values they associate with the Cheyenne from listening to the story. Then have students read through the selection on their own.

Reading Skills

Read Aloud

Note that fluent silent reading is an essential reading skill, but it may take a little time to accomplish. Have students focus on a single portion of the selection, such as the Buffalo Calf Road Woman's flashback. Have them write down an unknown word and try to figure out its meaning from context clues or by looking it up in the dictionary. Have students reread the section, two or three times if necessary, until they are able to read through the entire section fluently.

camp. Such things seldom happened, but this bear was one that had been wounded in the leg by a white fur-trapper's bullet. It could no longer hunt as it had before, and hunger brought it to the Cheyenne camp, where it smelled food cooking.

When the huge bear came walking into the camp, almost everyone scattered. Some women grabbed their little children. Old people shut the door flaps of their tepees, and the boys ran to find their bows and arrows. Only a group of seven women who had been working on the embroidery of an elk-skin robe did not run. They were members of the Society of Quilters, and Buffalo Calf Road Woman was among them. The seven women put down their work, picked up the weapons they had close to hand, and stood to face the grizzly bear.

Now of all of the animals of the plains, the only one fierce enough and powerful enough to attack a human was the grizzly. But confronted by that <u>determined</u> group of women, the grizzly bear stopped in its tracks. It had come to steal food, not fight. The head of the Society of Quilters stepped forward a pace and spoke to the bear.

"Grandfather," she said, her voice low and firm, "we do not wish to harm you, but we will protect our camp. Go back to your own home."

The grizzly shook its head and then turned and walked out of the camp. The women stood and watched it as it went down through the cottonwoods and was lost from sight along the bend of the stream.

Buffalo Calf Road Woman turned her mind away from her memories. They were close to Rosebud Creek. The scouts had told them that a great number of the *veho* soldiers would be there and that the Gray Fox, General George Crook, was in command. The Cheyenne had joined up now with the

> **de•ter•mined** (di tər´ mənd) *adj.*, not easily moved or changed

WHERE THE GIRL RESCUED HER BROTHER **781**

Teach the Selection

Analyze Literature
Character Remind students that a character is a person or animal who takes part in the action of a literary work. A one-dimensional character, flat character, or caricature is one who exhibits a single quality. A three-dimensional, full, or rounded character has all the complexities of a human being. Ask students to define which type of character the head of the Society of Quilters, the woman who stands up to the grizzly bear, is and why. **C**

Use Reading Strategies
Clarify Have students review the description of the beginning of the battle. Tell them to work in pairs or groups to make sure they understand exactly who was fighting on which side and why the battle was taking place. If they are unable to follow a part of the description, have them write a question to ask other pairs or groups so they can clarify what they have read. **D**

Grammar Skills

Coordinating and Subordinating Conjunctions
Point out to students that a coordinating conjunction is a word used to join words or groups of equal importance in a sentence. The most common coordinating conjunctions are *and, or, nor, for, but, yet,* and *so*.

A subordinating conjunction introduces a subordinate clause and joins it to an independent clause. Common subordinating conjunctions include *after, although, as, as if, because, before, if, since, unless, till, when,* and *where*.

Geography Connection
Rosebud Creek Southern Montana is home to Rosebud Creek, which flows just north of the Absaroka-Beartooth Wilderness Area. It runs only four miles, originating at the confluence of its two tributaries, the East Fork Rosebud Creek and the West Fork Rosebud Creek, and ending at the Stillwater River. The two forks wind through mountainous terrain before moving into the prarie. The creeks are flanked by trees, brush, and meadow.

Use Reading Skills
Summarize Point out to students that summarizing is a skill that can help them read fiction. Remind them that when you summarize, you retell the main events in a selection, or part of a selection, using your own words. Ask them to summarize the two paragraphs describing what Buffalo Calf Road Woman sees of the battle from the hilltop.

History Connection
The Battle of Rosebud Creek
Answer: Student responses will vary. **A**

Oglala,[1] led by Crazy Horse. The Lakota people were always friends to the Cheyenne, but this man, Crazy Horse, was the best friend of all. Some even said that he was one of their chiefs, too, as well as being a war leader of his Oglala.

There were Crow and Shoshone scouts with Crook, and the *veho* had many cannons. The Lakota and the Cheyenne were outnumbered by the two thousand men in Crook's command. But they were prepared to fight. They had put on their finest clothes, for no man should risk his life without being dressed well enough so that if he died, the enemy would know a great warrior had fallen. Some of the men raised their headdresses three times, calling out their names and the deeds they had done. Those headdresses of eagle feathers were thought to give magical protection to a warrior. Other men busied themselves painting designs on their war ponies.

Now they could hear Crook's army approaching. The rumble of the horses' hooves echoed down the valley, and there was the sound of trumpets. War ponies reared up and stomped their feet. Many of the Cheyenne men found it hard to put on the last of their paint as their hands shook from the excitement of the coming battle.

Crazy Horse vaulted onto his horse and held up one arm. "*Hoka Hey*," he cried. "It is a good day to die."

Buffalo Calf Road Woman watched from a hill as the two lines of men—the blue soldiers to one side, and the Lakota and

Cheyenne to the other—raced toward each other. The battle began. It was not a quick fight or an easy one. There were brave men on both sides. Two Moons, Little Hawk, Yellow Eagle, Sitting Bull, and Crazy Horse were only a few of the great warriors who fought for the Cheyenne and the Lakota. And Crook, the Gray Fox general of the whites, was known to be a tough fighter and a worthy enemy.

HISTORY ▶▶ CONNECTION

The Battle of Rosebud Creek In 1876, the U.S. government was under pressure to open up the Dakotas for white settlement and gold mining. The Lakota and Cheyenne peoples would not accept buyouts of their land, and full-scale war broke out. The Battle of Rosebud Creek was named for the location of the fight, forty miles south of the Little Bighorn site. Crazy Horse led the Lakota and Cheyenne into battle against the armed forces of Brigadier General George Crook. Crazy Horse's successful strategy of disrupting Crook's lines and isolating his cavalry led to his victory. This led to the later victory at Little Bighorn, when Crook was unwilling to join Custer's forces after his defeat by Crazy Horse. How does the legend affect your understanding of this famous historical conflict? **A**

Buffalo Calf Road Woman's husband, Black Coyote, and her brother, Comes-in-Sight, were in the thick of the fight. The odds in the battle were almost even. Although the whites had more soldiers and guns, the Lakota and the Cheyenne were better shots and better horsemen. Had it not been for the Crow and Shoshone scouts helping Crook, the white soldiers might have broken quickly from the ferocity of the attack.

---

1. **Oglala.** Principal branch of the Lakota nation

Differentiated Instruction

English Language Learning
Students learning English may benefit from the following definitions:
veho — white people, 780
scouts — soldiers sent ahead of a main military force to gather information about the opposing force's location, size, and capabilities, 781
headdress — often elaborate covering for the head, 782

From one side to the other, groups of men attacked and <u>retreated</u> as the guns cracked, cannons boomed, and smoke filled the air. The war shouts of the Lakota and the Cheyenne were almost as loud as the rumble of the guns. The sun moved across the sky as the fight went on, hour after hour, while the confusion of battle swirled below.

Then Buffalo Calf Road Woman saw something that horrified her. Her brother had been drawn off to one side, surrounded by Crow scouts. He tried to ride free of them, but his pony went down, struck by a rifle bullet and killed. Now he was on foot, still fighting. The Crow warriors were trying to get close, to count coup[2] on him. It was more of an honor to touch a living enemy, so they were not firing their rifles at him. And he was able to keep them away with his bow and arrows. But it was clear that soon he would be out of ammunition and would fall to the enemy.

Buffalo Calf Road Woman waited no longer. She dug her heels into her pony's sides and galloped down the hill. Her head low, her braids streaming behind her, she rode into the heart of the fight. Some men moved aside as they saw her coming, for there was a determined look in her eyes. She made the long howling cry that Cheyenne women used to urge on the warriors. This time, however, she was the one going into the fight. Her voice was as strong as an eagle's. Her horse scattered the ponies of the Crow scouts who were closing in on her brother, Comes-in-Sight. She held out a hand; her brother grabbed it and vaulted onto the pony behind her. Then she wheeled, ducking the arrows of the Crow scouts, and heading back up the hill.

That was when it happened. For a moment, it seemed as if all the shooting stopped. The Cheyenne and the Lakota, and even the *veho* soldiers, lowered their guns to watch this act of great bravery. A shout went up, not from one side but from both, as Buffalo Calf Road Woman reached the safety of the hilltop again, her brother safe behind her on her horse. White men and Indians cheered her.

> Her head low, her braids streaming behind her, she rode into the heart of the fight.

So it was that Buffalo Calf Road Woman performed the act for which the people would always remember her. Inspired by her courage, the Cheyenne and Lakota drove back the Gray Fox—Crook made a strategic withdrawal.

"Even the *veho* general was impressed," said the Cheyenne people. "He saw that if our women were that brave, he would stand no chance against us in battle." **B**

So it is that to this day, the Cheyenne and the Lakota people do not refer to the fight as the Battle of the Rosebud. Instead, they honor Buffalo Calf Road Woman by calling the fight Where the Girl Rescued Her Brother. ✤

---

2. **count coup.** Claim victory

re·treat (ri trēt´) *v.,* withdraw; back off

What risks would you take to save the life of someone you love? Do you believe the kind of heroism described in the story still exists today?

Research Skills

Create the Front Page of a Native American Newspaper
Have students work in pairs or small groups to research contemporary issues related to American Indians. Suggest possible research topics like the current state of American Indian reservations or the modern cultural significance of American Indians.

After they have researched several topics, have students design and fill the front page of a Native American newspaper. Allow each pair or group time to present their page to the class.

Review the Selection

Find Meaning

1. (a) The white men. (b) They make promises and break them.

2. (a) She belongs to the Society of Quilters. (b) A person must be of the best character—strong, honorable, and brave.

3. (a) The Cheyenne put on their finest clothes, perform rituals, and paint designs on their war ponies. (b) Students might say these preparations give the Cheyenne unity, confidence, and courage.

4. (a) She rides into the battle and rescues her brother. (b) Students may say the onlookers do not expect to see a woman risk her life in that way.

Make Judgments

5. Students may point to family, honor, honesty, and bravery as being the most important to the Cheyenne. (b) Honor, honesty, strength, bravery, and family are all worthy of their respect.

6. They might infer a more personal investment from the Cheyenne naming or infer values of family and courage.

7. Students might point to the fact that the tone of the story is different from nonfiction and the use of flashback.

Analyze Literature

Flashback *Answer:* Students should see parallels in Buffalo Calf Road Woman's participation and the example of a woman's brave and heroic actions.

Find Meaning

1. (a) What have the Cheyenne been worried about for a long time? (b) What cause do they have to be worried about this?

2. (a) To what society does Buffalo Calf Road Woman belong? (b) What character attributes must a person have to join the society?

3. (a) How do the Cheyenne prepare for the battle? (b) What importance do these preparations have?

4. (a) What does Buffalo Calf Road Woman do when she sees her brother in trouble? (b) Why do the onlookers react the way they do?

Analyze Literature

Flashback Authors sometimes use flashbacks to disclose parallel events that occurred in a time prior to the setting of a story. Reread the flashback from "Where the Girl Rescued Her Brother," looking for parallels to the main thread of the story. Use the two-column chart to note your findings.

Make Judgments

5. (a) What things in life are most important to the Cheyenne people? (b) What is worthy of their respect?

6. To the Cheyenne, the battle described in this story is known as Where the Girl Rescued Her Brother, whereas the U.S. Army named it the Battle of Rosebud Creek. What can you infer about differences between the Cheyenne culture and the culture of the U.S. Army based on these different names?

7. What elements in this story make it a legend rather than nonfiction?

Flashback	Main Thread
grizzly is injured by a veho bullet	threat is directly from veho bullets

---

Extend Understanding

Writing Options

Creative Writing Write a **short story** for children based on the events in the legend "Where the Girl Rescued Her Brother." Choose the most important events to retell in your story and make sure your writing fits the needs of a young audience.

Expository Writing Write a **short essay** describing the authors' purpose and perspective. In the first paragraph, speculate why the authors chose to share this legend. In the second paragraph, support your speculation about the authors' purpose with examples from the text that show the authors' perspective. In the last paragraph, imagine how the story would have been different if a descendant of Brigadier General Crook were the author. Share your essay with your class.

Collaborative Learning

Discuss in Small Groups The authors of "Where the Girl Rescued Her Brother" emphasize certain character traits of Buffalo Calf Road Woman and other characters to reveal cultural values. In small groups, discuss the values of the characters depicted in this legend. How do the values of the characters reflect those of the larger culture?

Media Literacy

Create a Multimedia Presentation Think of a question that interests you about the conflict you read about that might also interest your classmates. Do research at the library or on the Internet to find answers. Then prepare a presentation to share the answer with your class. You may include photos, artwork, or a sound recording to enhance your presentation.

Go to **www.mirrorsandwindows.com** for more.

Rubrics for Writing Options

You can adapt this as a checklist for students to use as they write.

Creative Writing
☐ Is the story based on the legend?
☐ Is the writing appropriate for a younger audience?

Expository Writing
☐ Does the author speculate as to why the authors chose to share this legend?
☐ Does the author support his or her speculation with evidence from the text that shows the authors' perspective?
☐ Does the author offer an alternate vision from the view of a descendant of General Crook?

Grammar & Style

Dangling Modifiers

They had put on their finest clothes, for no man should risk his life without being dressed well enough so that if he died, the enemy would know a great warrior had fallen.

—JOSEPH BRUCHAC AND GAYLE ROSS,
"Where the Girl Rescued Her Brother"

A **dangling modifier** seems to modify no word at all because the word it should modify does not appear in the sentence, unlike a misplaced modifier, which modifies an incorrect word. For example, imagine a sentence similar to the quotation above. *Having put on their finest clothes, the enemy would know they were great warriors.* The sentence is confusing because it appears that *the enemy* had put on their finest clothes.

To correct dangling modifiers, reword the sentence to include the modified word. For example, *The enemy would know they were great warriors because they were wearing their finest clothes.*

EXAMPLES

dangling modifier	*Expecting the battle to begin soon, headdresses were raised to the sun.* [This sounds as if the headdresses expected the battle to begin soon.]
corrected sentence	*Expecting the battle to begin soon, the warriors raised their headdresses to the sun.*
corrected sentence	*The warriors raised their headdresses to the sun in expectation of the battle.*

dangling modifier	*Lowering their guns, cheers for Buffalo Calf Road Woman went up on both sides.* [This sounds as if the cheers lowered their guns.]
corrected sentence	*The soldiers on both sides lowered their guns and cheered Buffalo Calf Road Woman.*
corrected sentence	*Lowering their guns, soldiers on both sides cheered Buffalo Calf Road Woman.*

Notice that there are several ways that a sentence may be reworded to correct a dangling modifier.

Understanding Dangling Modifiers
Identify the dangling modifier in each of the following sentences. Then revise the sentence to correct the dangling modifier.

1. Riding out of camp together, the chokecherries were ripe.
2. Dressed in clothing decorated with porcupine quills, it was easy to recognize a great warrior.
3. Honoring the women's bravery, a big hunt had been planned.
4. Growling and wounded, the women confronted the bear.
5. Riding from the field, cheers greeted her.

The People Could Fly

An African-American Folk Tale by Virginia Hamilton

At a Glance
Directed Reading
- Reading Level: Easy
- Difficulty Consideration: Dialect
- Ease Factor: Compelling plot

Objectives
Studying this lesson will enable students to
- use reading skills such as identifying the author's purpose and visualizing
- recognize and explain the literary significance of fantasy and dialect
- explain the cultural significance of slave folk tales

Launch the Lesson
Students might benefit from role-playing in pairs for the class. Ask students to pretend the year is 1925, and one student will interview the second student who will assume the role of a former slave, born in 1850. Have the interviewer ask the former slave about his life as a ten-year-old slave in 1860. Encourage the students to use what they have read in "The People Could Fly" to ask and answer the questions.

BEFORE READING

Build Background
Historical Context This folk tale emerged from the era prior to the Civil War, when slavery was legal in the United States. The master, or slave owner, often hired an overseer, usually a white man, to "oversee" and manage the slaves. He was often assisted by a driver, usually a black man who was a slave. Both the overseer and the driver carried whips to punish slaves whom they felt were not working hard or fast enough.

Reader's Context Slaves often created stories and songs to remind one another to never give up hope. When have you wanted to use magic words to solve a problem or bring about a dramatic change?

Set Purpose
Preview the title, first paragraph, and illustrations to predict the lessons and themes of this folk tale. As you read, write down reasons why this tale might have been helpful to slaves who longed for freedom.

Analyze Literature
Dialect A variation of language spoken by people in a particular region or group is a **dialect**. Often a dialect contains words, spellings, sentence structures, or punctuation patterns that are different from the standard and usual forms of language. As you read, note the dialect that the narrator and the characters use.

Meet the Author
"I've been a writer all my life," says award-winning author **Virginia Hamilton,** "since the time I was a child in grade school, when I first learned to scribble down sentences describing the pictures in my head." Hamilton has written numerous books for young readers, including *Zeely, The House of Dies Drear, The Planet of Junior Brown,* and *The People Could Fly: American Black Folktales,* in which this tale appears.

Use Reading Skills
Identify Author's Purpose An author's purpose is his or her aim or goal. Virginia Hamilton may have chosen to retell this traditional African-American folk tale for one or more purposes—such as to entertain, to inform, to describe, or to teach a lesson.

As you read the folk tale, look for clues to identify the author's purpose. Create a chart like this one to jot down your ideas.

Long ago in Africa, some of the people knew magic.

clue — Author's Purpose — clue / clue / clue / clue

Preview Vocabulary
scorned (skôrnd) *adj.,* treated with disrespect; rejected as unworthy

croon (krün) *v.,* sing or speak in a gentle manner

seize (sēz) *v.,* grasp suddenly and forcefully

Words in Use

Preview Vocabulary
scorned, 788
croon, 788
seize, 789

Teaching Words
era, 786
overseer, 786
conveys, 792

KEY TERMS

Common Core State Standards
Reading Literature
RL.1
Writing
W.9
Language
L.6

Dance, 1996. Francks Deceus. Private collection.

The People Could Fly

An African-American Folk Tale by Virginia Hamilton

They kept their secret magic in the land of slavery.

787

Summary

Told in a personal storytelling style, "The People Could Fly" is an African-American folk tale originally intended to give hope to those held in slavery. The narrator tells of a people in Africa who had magical powers and could fly but lost the ability when sold into slavery. One man, called Toby, retained the ability and encourages a young woman and mother called Sarah to remember how to fly so that she can escape death by the Overseer's hands. Once Sarah flies away, Toby speaks the magic words to the other slaves in the field and they all float into the air and fly away, escaping the brutality of slavery. Those who were left behind became the keepers of the story.

MIRRORS & WINDOWS The Mirrors & Windows questions at the end of this selection focus on the theme of hope. Before reading the story, ask students how they feel when they read or hear about people who have achieved what they have not yet been able to achieve. Why do those who strive for goals tell stories of those who have reached them?

Program Resources

Planning and Assessment
Program Planning Guide, Selection Lesson Plan
E-Lesson Planner
Assessment Guide, Lesson Test
ExamView

Technology Tools
Interactive Student Text on CD
Visual Teaching Package
Audio Library
mirrorsandwindows.com

Meeting the Standards
Folk Literature: Unit 8, Directed Reading,
   pp. 43–49

Differentiating Instruction
Developing Readers, Visualize, pp. 56–58
Advanced Students, Genre Research Project,
   pp. 48–49

Analyze Literature

Legend Remind students that a legend is a story rooted in the past that is based on real events or characters. Ask students why they think the character called Toby has become legendary. Is he a real or imaginary character? Possible responses are that Toby is based on a real person who helped other slaves escape, but most students might say that he is an imagined character—a powerful source of hope where there is none. **A**

Use Reading Strategies

Visualize Ask students to silently read this section several times. When they are finished, have them pin down an image from the section that particularly strikes them (The hungry, crying child/The Overseer's reaction / Sarah's pain and exhaustion). Ask students to pause, close their eyes, and let the image materialize in their minds. When they are ready, challenge them to open their eyes, record in words the sensory details that most clearly stand out to them, and then sketch the image, emphasizing those details.

They say the people could fly. Say that long ago in Africa, some of the people knew magic. And they would walk up on the air like climbin up on a gate. And they flew like blackbirds over the fields. Black, shiny wings flappin against the blue up there.

Then, many of the people were captured for Slavery. The ones that could fly shed their wings. They couldn't take their wings across the water on the slave ships. Too crowded, don't you know.

The folks were full of misery, then. Got sick with the up and down of the sea. So they forgot about flyin when they could no longer breathe the sweet scent of Africa.

Say the people who could fly kept their power, although they shed their wings. They kept their secret magic in the land of slavery. They looked the same as the other people from Africa who had been coming over, who had dark skin. Say you couldn't tell anymore one who could fly from one who couldn't.

A One such who could was an old man, call him Toby. And standin tall, yet afraid, was a young woman who once had wings. Call her Sarah. Now Sarah carried a babe tied to her back. She trembled to be so hard worked and scorned.

The slaves labored in the fields from sunup to sundown. The owner of the slaves callin himself their Master. Say he was a hard lump of clay. A hard, glinty coal. A hard rock pile, wouldn't be moved. His Overseer on horseback pointed out the slaves who were slowin down. So the one called Driver cracked his whip over the slow ones to make them move faster. That whip was a slice-open cut of pain. So they did move faster. Had to.

Sarah hoed and chopped the row as the babe on her back slept.

Say the child grew hungry. That babe started up bawling too loud. Sarah couldn't stop to feed it. Couldn't stop to soothe and

quiet it down. She let it cry. She didn't want to. She had no heart to croon to it.

"Keep that thing quiet," called the Overseer. He pointed his finger at the babe. The woman scrunched low. The Driver cracked his whip across the babe anyhow. The babe hollered like any hurt child, and the woman fell to the earth.

The old man that was there, Toby, came and helped her to her feet.

"I must go soon," she told him.

"Soon," he said.

Sarah couldn't stand up straight any longer. She was too weak. The sun burned her face. The babe cried and cried, "Pity me, oh, pity me," say it sounded like. Sarah was so sad and starvin, she sat down in the row.

"Get up, you black cow," called the Overseer. He pointed his hand, and the Driver's whip snarled around Sarah's legs. Her sack dress tore into rags. Her legs bled onto the earth. She couldn't get up.

Toby was there where there was no one to help her and the babe.

"Now, before it's too late," panted Sarah. "Now, Father!"

"Yes, Daughter, the time is come," Toby answered. "Go, as you know how to go!"

He raised his arms, holding them out to her. "*Kum…yali, kum buba tambe*," and more magic words, said so quickly, they sounded like whispers and sighs.

The young woman lifted one foot on the air. Then the other. She flew clumsily at first, with the child now held tightly in her arms. Then she felt the magic, the African mystery. Say she rose just as free as a bird. As light as a feather.

The Overseer rode after her, hollerin. Sarah flew over the fences. She flew over the

---

scorned (skôrnd) *adj.*, treated with disrespect; rejected as unworthy

croon (krün) *v.*, sing or speak in a gentle manner

Differentiated Instruction

English Language Learning

Students learning English may find the following definitions helpful as they make their way through the text:

up and down of the sea—rocking of the boat caused by waves, 788

bawling—crying persistently, 788

Reading Skills

Read Aloud

Point out to students that fluent and accurate oral reading is a useful skill that will enable them to better understand the text and maintain focus. Have students read a section of the text aloud and use their voice to create emphasis and expression. Remind them to adjust their reading fluency rate based on the nature of the text and their purpose for reading.

woods. Tall trees could not snag her. Nor could the Overseer. She flew like an eagle now, until she was gone from sight. No one dared speak about it. Couldn't believe it.

But it was, because they that was there saw that it was.

Say the next day was dead hot[1] in the fields. A young man slave fell from the heat. The Driver come and whipped him. Toby come over and spoke words to the fallen one. The words of ancient Africa once heard are never remembered completely. The young man forgot them as soon as he heard them. They went way inside him. He got up and rolled over on the air. He rode it awhile. And he flew away.

Another and another fell from the heat. Toby was there. He cried out to the fallen and reached his arms out to them. "*Kum kunka yali, kum…tambe!*" Whispers and sighs. And they too rose on the air. They rode the hot breezes. The ones flyin were black and shinin sticks, wheelin above the head of the Overseer. They crossed the rows, the fields, the fences, the streams, and were away.

"Seize the old man!" cried the Overseer. "I heard him say the magic words. Seize him!"

The one callin himself Master come runnin. The Driver got his whip ready to curl around old Toby and tie him up. The slaveowner took his hip gun[2] from its place. He meant to kill old, black Toby.

But Toby just laughed. Say he threw back his head and said, "Hee, hee! Don't you know who I am? Don't you know some of us in this field?" He said it to their faces. "We are ones who fly!"

And he sighed the ancient words that were a dark promise. He said them all around to the others in the field under the whip, "…*buba yali…buba tambe….*"

There was a great outcryin. The bent backs straighted up. Old and young who were called slaves and could fly joined hands.

---

1. **dead hot.** Very hot temperature with no breeze
2. **hip gun.** Gun held in a holster on one's hip

seize (sēz) *v.,* grasp suddenly and forcefully

Teach the Selection

Analyze Literature

Dialect Remind students that dialect is a version of language spoken by people of a particular time or region. Ask students to define the dialect spoken in "The People Could Fly." Why do they think the author chose to use dialect, and would the story have been as effective without it? (Without the use of dialect in the dialogue of "The People Could Fly," the characters would have been much less realistic.)

Analyze Literature

Fantasy Tell students that fantasy is an unrealistic or imaginative story. Point out that "The People Could Fly" has fantastical elements but is based in fact. Ask students if the story would have been as effective if it contained no fantasy—if the slaves escaped on foot instead of flying. Why is the slaves' power of flight significant to the story?

Speaking & Listening Skills

Persuasive Speech

Working on their own, have students prepare, organize, and present a persuasive speech concerning slavery. Remind them that persuasive speech attempts to convince listeners to agree with a position, take an action, change views on an issue, or reach an agreement. Model possible topics for the speeches such as: "Slavery in Other Countries" or "Repercussions of Slavery in Today's Society." Allow students time to research their topics and present them to the class. Each student should be aware of this as a listening exercise as well and should take notes on their classmates' speeches.

Students may say that these people felt great regret or sadness that they could not also fly away. Others may say that the people were given a sense of hope that someday they would be free, too.

Find Meaning

1. (a) They shed their wings. (b) There was no room on the slave ships.

2. They could fly.

3. He is harsh and unfeeling about the brutal conditions he imposes.

4. (a) She wants to fly away before she is killed. (b) He wants to catch her and bring her back.

Make Judgments

5. (a) They plan to kill him to prevent the escape of more slaves. (b) He laughs at them because he knows these men can't prevent it.

6. He doesn't have time to teach them to fly.

7. (a) The Driver says nothing. (b) The Master says it was an illusion. (c) The Driver doesn't want to get into trouble or doesn't want to reveal the secret. The Master denies it because the magic power defies his authority.

8. (a) He offers them the hope that when things get really terrible, they will be able to fly away. (b) It gives them hope that someday they will be free and gives them pride in their heritage.

Say like they would ring-sing.[3] But they didn't shuffle in a circle. They didn't sing. They rose on the air. They flew in a flock that was black against the heavenly blue. Black crows or black shadows. It didn't matter, they went so high. Way above the plantation, way over the slavery land. Say they flew away to *Freedom*.

And the old man, old Toby, flew behind them, takin care of them. He wasn't cryin. He wasn't laughin. He was the seer.[4] His gaze fell on the plantation where the slaves who could not fly waited.

"*Take us with you!*" Their looks spoke it but they were afraid to shout it. Toby couldn't take them with him. Hadn't the time to teach them to fly. They must wait for a chance to run.

"Goodie-bye!" The old man called Toby spoke to them, poor souls! And he was flyin gone.

So they say. The Overseer told it. The one called master said it was a lie a trick of the light.[5] The Driver kept his mouth shut.

The slaves who could not fly told about the people who could fly to their children. When they were free. When they sat close before the fire in the free land, they told It. They did so love firelight and *Free-dom*, and tellin.

They say that the children of the ones who could not fly told their children. And now, me, I have told it to you. ❖

---

3. **ring-sing.** Sing while holding hands in a circle
4. **seer.** One who sees or watches; also, one who can see the future
5. **a lie a trick of the light.** Something that didn't really happen, or something that appeared to happen due to shadows and shapes created by sunlight

How do you think the children of the slaves who could not fly—who were forced to remain in slavery—felt after hearing this folk tale? Why might this folk tale still be passed on today?

Find Meaning

1. (a) When the people who could fly left Africa on the slave ships, what happened to their wings? (b) Why did this happen?

2. According to the narrator, how were Toby and Sarah different from many of the other African slaves?

3. The narrator says that the Master was a "hard lump of clay." What is the intended meaning of this metaphor?

4. (a) What does Sarah mean when she pleads, "Now, before it's too late"? (b) Why does the Overseer ride after Sarah?

Make Judgments

5. (a) What do the Master, Overseer, and Driver plan to do to Toby? (b) How does Toby reply, and what leads him to react this way?

6. Why doesn't Toby take all the slaves away?

7. (a) After Toby and the people fly away, what does the Driver say about it? (b) What does the Master say about it? (c) What do their different responses suggest about each man? Explain your point of view.

8. (a) In what way does Toby bring hope to the slaves? (b) What does this folk tale offer to the slaves who could not fly and to their children?

Differentiated Instruction

Enrichment

Have interested students research other folk tales passed down from the era of slavery in the United States. Encourage them to interpret the stories' messages, or themes. In addition, what characteristics do the stories share with "The People Could Fly"? How do they differ from it? Invite students to share their discoveries with the class.

The following selection is a song entitled "Swing Low, Sweet Chariot." It is a spiritual, a folk hymn that slaves often sang to raise their spirits and confirm their religious faith. This spiritual was a favorite of Harriet Tubman, the former slave who risked her life many times to go back to the South and guide hundreds of other slaves along the Underground Railroad to freedom in the North and in Canada. The *chariot* mentioned in the spiritual may refer to wagons used to carry runaway slaves, or it may be a code word for a "train car" on the "railroad." As you read the spiritual, note how it, like the folk tale, is about a flight to freedom.

Swing Low, Sweet Chariot

An African-American Spiritual

Swing low, sweet chariot,
Coming for to carry me home,
Swing low, sweet chariot,
Coming for to carry me home.

5 I looked over Jordan[1] and what did I see,
Coming for to carry me home?
A band of angels coming after me,
Coming for to carry me home.

If you get there before I do,
10 Coming for to carry me home,
Tell all my friends I'm coming too;
Coming for to carry me home.

I'm sometimes up, I'm sometimes down,
Coming for to carry me home,
15 But still my soul feels heavenly bound;
Coming for to carry me home.

Swing low, sweet chariot,
Coming for to carry me home,
Swing low, sweet chariot,
20 Coming for to carry me home. ❖

---

1. Jordan. Jordan River. According to the Bible, when the Jews were fleeing from slavery in Egypt, they had to cross the Jordan River in order to reach their Promised Land.

TEXT ◀TO▶ **TEXT**
CONNECTION

Both the folk tale and the spiritual deal with slaves' flight to freedom. In both selections, the flight occurs on two levels. On one level, it refers to the physical disappearance of slaves—on their journey to a free, safe place to live. On a deeper level, what might the flight refer to?

Media Messages
Have students work in pairs or small groups to create a presentation to share with the rest of the class. Explain to them that different media, such as artwork, literature, and music, can communicate a singular theme, or tone. Using the Internet or library, have groups locate visual interpretations of

"Swing Low, Sweet Chariot" and compare the themes used in the artwork with those in the song. Possible artistic portrayals include those by William H. Johnson and Ruth Starr Rose.

Teach the Connection

Analyze Literature
Allusion Inform students that an allusion is a reference in literature to something famous. "Swing Low, Sweet Chariot" makes reference to God bringing those who suffer to heaven. Ask students how this allusion relates to "The People Could Fly."

Use Reading Strategies
Make Inferences Remind students that by reading closely, they will be able to infer what the author is trying to communicate. After reading "Swing Low, Sweet Chariot," ask students what they think the author is communicating with the lyrics "If you get there before I do/ Tell all my friends I'm coming to." (This line is a message to the other freed slaves, friends, and family that the singer will escape and meet them soon.) **A**

Text-to-Text Connection
Possible answer: In the spiritual, the slaves rely on what they have heard about the Underground Railroad. At a deeper level, they also rely on religious faith and redemption, as well as the promise of going to heaven after death. Students may see that on a deeper level, the flight of the slaves refers to death. After the brutality of slavery, they will finally be free when they fly away "home"—to heaven.

Common Core State Standards
Language
L.6

Review the Selection

Analyze Literature

Allegory Explain to students that while an allusion simply refers to a famous event or person, an allegory is a work in which every element in the selection is a symbol for something else. In the case of "Swing Low, Sweet Chariot," each element symbolizes a part of the Underground Railroad and those who helped runaway slaves escape. Have pairs of students work out the symbolism in the song.

Use Reading Skills

Identify Author's Purpose Ask students to compare the authors' purposes in "The People Could Fly" and "Swing Low, Sweet Chariot." Model a possible response by asking what idea is common in both selections.

Analyze Literature

Dialect *Answer:* Examples of dialect will vary. Most examples create a mood of mystery and wonder. Others, like *hard lump of clay* and *slice-open cut of pain*, create a mood of suffering and despair. Still others, such as *wheelin above the head of the Overseer* and *Hee, hee,* create a mood of defiance and independence.

Analyze Literature

Dialect Dialect is a variation of language spoken by people in a particular region or group. It often contains pronunciations, words, spellings, and sentence structures that are different from the standard forms of language. Often dialect has a strong influence on the mood—the atmosphere or emotions that the work conveys. The mood might be dark, peaceful, happy, serious, or mysterious, for example. Use a chart to analyze the effect of dialect on the mood of "The People Could Fly."

Example of Dialect	Mood Conveyed by Dialect
"...they would walk up on the air like climbin up on a gate."	

Extend Understanding

Writing Options

Creative Writing Rewrite this African-American folk tale in the form of a **drama,** to be performed on stage. Begin with a cast of characters. Use lines of dialogue to carry the plot events, and use stage directions to describe the stage set and props and to tell the actors how to speak and act. Before writing, you might turn back to *The Diary of Anne Frank* to review the form of a drama script.

Expository Writing Write a brief **expository essay** in which you analyze this folk tale, explaining why enslaved people would particularly relate to it and why it might have helped soothed their pain and struggles. State your main point in the thesis. Use specific details from the folk tale to support your point of view.

Lifelong Learning

Research and Present One of the shared themes of "The People Could Fly" and "Swing Low, Sweet Chariot" is the search for freedom. With a partner, use the Internet or library to find stories, songs, or poems from other cultures that also share this theme. Present your findings to the class.

Media Literacy

Analyze a Vocal Performance Locate an audio recording of "Swing Low, Sweet Chariot." Listen to it carefully, thinking about the mood of the music. Then write an analysis. In your analysis, describe the mood of the song and what elements contribute to that mood. State your main point in your thesis and support it with evidence. Finally, compare and contrast the mood of the song with that of the folk tale.

Go to **www.mirrorsandwindows.com** for more.

Rubrics for Writing Options

You can adapt this as a checklist for students to use as they write.

Creative Writing

☐ Does it follow the standards and forms of conventional drama scripts, as modeled in the script of *The Diary of Anne Frank*?

Expository Writing

☐ Does the essay effectively analyze the folk tale, explaining why enslaved people would relate to it?

☐ Is each point of analysis supported by facts and details in the folk tale?

Blackbeard's Last Fight

A Legend by Richard Walser

BEFORE READING

Build Background

Historical Context Blackbeard is said to have been the boldest and most notorious pirate living along the waters of England's North American colonies in the early 1700s. Legend has it that Blackbeard used scare tactics and mind games to frighten sailors into surrendering their ships and valuables. There is no evidence that Blackbeard killed anyone until the Battle of Ocracoke, off the coast of North Carolina, which is the focus of "Blackbeard's Last Fight." Very little is known of his early life on the sea. However, Blackbeard's actions from 1716 to 1718, when he lived along the coast of North Carolina, are well documented.

Reader's Context What would you do if you found yourself face to face with one of the most wicked pirates in history?

Set Purpose

Preview the title to make predictions about what the legend is about. Read to determine how accurate your predictions are.

Analyze Literature

Characterization The act of creating or describing a character is **characterization.** Writers create characters using three major techniques: by showing what characters say, do, or think; by showing what other characters say or think about them; and by describing what physical features, dress, and personality the characters display. As you read the story, pay attention to which techniques the author uses for characterization.

Use Reading Skills

Context Clues Preview the vocabulary words from this selection as they are used in the sentences below. Try to unlock the meaning of each word using the context clues provided in the sentences.

1. Blackbeard was known to <u>ravage</u> the ships he conquered, stealing all of their possessions.
2. Often Blackbeard could <u>cow</u> a man simply by his angry demeanor and gruff appearance.

Preview Vocabulary

rav•age (rav´ ij) v., ruin, destroy; commit destructive acts

tuft (təft) n., small cluster of longer, grown-out hair

cow (kau) v., destroy another's courage by intimidation

Meet the Author

Richard Walser was born in Lexington, North Carolina, in 1908. He was always fascinated with North Carolina's culture, literary heritage, and folklore. After completing high school, Walser attended the University of North Carolina. During his career, he taught English at both high schools and colleges. He also served in the U.S. Navy during World War II (1939–1945). Walser wrote and edited more than thirty books and was an active member of the North Carolina Folklore Society. He died in 1988.

Preview the Selection

At a Glance
Directed Reading
- Reading Level: Moderate
- Difficulty Consideration: Vernacular
- Ease Factor: Length

Objectives

Studying this lesson will enable students to

- use context clues to improve reading skills
- recognize and explain the literary technique of characterization
- understand important events in the history of English language
- think critically about the fascination of pirate literature

Launch the Lesson

Write the word "CRIMINAL" on the blackboard, and tell students that they are about to read "Blackbeard's Last Fight," a story about one of the most vicious criminals in American history. Ask students to discuss what they think a criminal is and if pirates fall in this category.

Words in Use

Preview Vocabulary
ravage, 795
tuft, 795
cowed, 795

Selection Words
fearsome, 795
armored, 795
retrieved, 795

Teaching Words
notorious, 793
documented, 793

heritage, 793
folklore, 793
plundering, 796
glamorized, 796
romanticized, 796
demonized, 796

KEY TERMS
LEGEND, 793
CHARACTERIZATION, 793
CHARACTER, 793
CONTEXT CLUE, 793

Common Core State Standards

Reading Literature
RL.1, RL.3, RL.9

Writing
W.7, W.8, W.9

Language
L.6

Teach the Selection

Summary

The legendary pirate Blackbeard is terrorizing the coast of North Carolina. He has no respect for authority and travels the coast as he wishes, since he has terrified North Carolinian officials. At last, Lieutenant Robert Maynard is sent to dispatch the pirate, and although the fight is a violent one, Maynard defeats Blackbeard by severing his head from his body.

 **MIRRORS & WINDOWS** The Mirrors & Windows questions at the end of this selection focus on the theme of tyranny. Before reading the story, ask students how they would respond to the appearance of an incredibly destructive bully as a new classmate. Why do stories about infamous characters often involve exaggeration?

TEACHING NOTE

Fluency

Students having difficulty with fluid reading might benefit from finding a quiet, private place to read the selection aloud to themselves. Have the students pause to identify each difficult word or phrase and then continue reading and rereading as necessary until they are able to read fluidly.

The Capture of the Pirate Blackbeard, 1718. Jean Leon Jerome Ferris. Private collection.

Blackbeard's Last Fight

A Legend by Richard Walser

794

Program Resources

Planning and Assessment
Program Planning Guide, Selection Lesson Plan
E-Lesson Planner
Assessment Guide, Lesson Test
ExamView

Technology Tools
Interactive Student Text on CD
Visual Teaching Package
Audio Library
mirrorsandwindows.com

Meeting the Standards
Folk Literature: Unit 8, Directed Reading, pp. 50–53

Differentiating Instruction
Developing Readers, Unlock Word Meaning, pp. 59–62

Of the many pirates who <u>ravaged</u> the coast of North Carolina during the early years of the eighteenth century, by far the most fearsome was Blackbeard. He had been born in England with a name such as Edward Teach or Thatch or Thach, but because of his grizzly hair the color of midnight, he soon was appropriately nicknamed Blackbeard. Sometimes to make himself even more horrible, he would attach slow-burning fuses to some ragged <u>tuft</u> of his inky beard to give the impression he was about to blow up. Not even heavy-armored men-o'-war[1] awed him, but when the odds became too great, he would retreat, through a shallow North Carolina inlet[2] and hide behind the sandbanks.

Governor Charles Eden was so <u>cowed</u> by this scurvy[3] villain that he let him roam at will along the coast. Tradition says the privateer[4] even gave the governor some of his booty.[5] Most of his treasures the pirate buried at one place or another on the shore. At his house in the town of Bath, Blackbeard settled briefly with his thirteenth wife, but he was restless and soon was back at sea, raiding vessels from Virginia and South Carolina. When Governor Eden couldn't, or wouldn't, do anything to stop him, the governor of Virginia sent Lieutenant Robert Maynard to catch the corsair.[6]

At Ocracoke[7] before daylight on November 22, 1718, they met: Maynard's sloop[8] and Blackbeard's *Adventure*. The two ships touched, and vicious Blackbeard jumped aboard the sloop and faced the lieutenant. Maynard drew blood first with a bullet right through the pirate's body, but, the freebooter[9] fought on. Finally, with a mighty swish of his sword, Maynard severed Blackbeard's head from his trunk. The head dropped into the water and circled the ship three times, crying out, "O crow, Cock! O crow, Cock!" The crowing of a cock signaled the coming of morning, and Blackbeard wanted enough light to find his body. But it was too late. Maynard's men counted twenty-five wounds in the pirate. They retrieved the head, swung it to the bowsprit[10] of Maynard's ship, and sailed from the island. ❖

Not even heavy-armored men-o'-war awed him....

(A)

1. **men-o'-war.** Navy warships
2. **inlet.** Recess in the shore or a narrow water passage leading inland
3. **scurvy.** Despicable
4. **privateer.** Pirate
5. **booty.** Stolen goods, plunder
6. **corsair.** Pirate
7. **Ocracoke.** Island off the coast of North Carolina
8. **sloop.** Boat with one mast and one sail
9. **freebooter.** Pirate
10. **bowsprit.** Large pole pointing out from the front of a ship

rav•age (rav´ ij) *v.*, ruin, destroy; commit destructive acts

tuft (təft) *n.*, small cluster of longer, grown-out hair

cow (kau) *v.*, destroy another's courage by intimidation

If you were the governor of North Carolina or Virginia, what would you have done about a pirate who was ravaging the coast, seizing ships and stealing treasures? Why are legends particularly suitable for describing larger-than-life people such as Blackbeard?

Literary Connection
Pirate Genre Since the height of piracy in the mid-17th century, there has been great interest in pirate literature. Although in reality, life as a pirate was miserable and food was usually scarce, literature has created a romantic swash-buckling world for pirates. *Treasure Island*, written in 1883 by Robert Louis Stevenson, is perhaps the best known of the pirate genre and responsible for creating the myths that surround piracy today. Other fictional piratical tales, like *Peter Pan* by James M. Barrie, soon followed, helping carve a niche for the pirate in classical literature.

Use Reading Skills
Use Context Clues Remind students that employing context clues can help them maintain fluidity in reading when they encounter an unfamiliar word. Have students pause here in their reading to focus on the word *privateer*. Discuss what elements of the surrounding passage provide clues to its meaning. **(A)**

Students might suggest that they would try to negotiate with the pirate in order to minimize the loss of life that occurs in a battle. Legends suit figures like Blackbeard because their characteristics are already larger than life.

Nautical Terminology in Common Speech
Point out to students that many nautical, or sailing, terms have entered common English language. Have students use the Internet or a dictionary to identify the nautical origins associated with the following words.

1. windfall
2. dismantle
3. skyscraper
4. aloof
5. hulk

Review the Selection

Find Meaning

1. (a) He attaches slow-burning fuses to his beard to make people think he is ablaze. (b) He retreats when the odds in battle with Navy warships are too great for him.

2. (a) He does most of his plundering along the Atlantic Coast, near North Carolina and Virginia. (b) He buries it along the shore. (c) Governor Eden of North Carolina.

3. (a) The governor of Virginia gives the order. (b) Lieutenant Robert Maynard cuts off Blackbeard's head.

Make Judgments

4. (a) Possible responses include attaching fuses to his beard, marrying thirteen times, calling out after his head has been detached from his body. (b) Answers should be supported with details.

5. (a) Students might mention sword fights, threatening ships, and robbery. (b) Students should point to specific passages and story elements to support their responses.

Analyze Literature

Characterization *Possible answer:* What He Says, Does, or Thinks (He hides behind sandbanks), What Others Think of Him (The governor is terrified of him), Appearance, Dress, and Personality (Grizzly hair)

Find Meaning

1. (a) What does Blackbeard do to make himself look even more horrible? (b) When does Blackbeard sometimes retreat and hide behind the sandbanks?

2. (a) Where does Blackbeard do most of his plundering? (b) What does the pirate do with most of his treasure? (c) Who is rumored to receive shares of the stolen goods?

3. (a) Who gives the order to have Blackbeard killed? (b) How is Blackbeard finally killed?

Analyze Literature

Characterization The act of creating or describing a character is characterization. Writers create characters using three major techniques: by showing what characters say, do, or think; by showing what other characters say or think about them; and by describing what physical features, dress, and personality the characters display. What techniques does the author use to characterize Blackbeard in the story you just read? Fill in a chart with details about Blackbeard's character.

Make Judgments

4. There are many myths surrounding pirates and pirate life. In order to attract an audience, fiction writers and others have glamorized, romanticized, and demonized pirates. (a) What elements in the legend you just read glamorize, romanticize, or demonize Blackbeard? (b) Do you think Blackbeard was as terrible as his reputation made him out to be?

5. (a) What ideas come to mind when you think about pirates? (b) How are these ideas included in "Blackbeard's Last Fight"?

	Blackbeard
What He Says, Does, or Thinks	He hides behind sandbanks.
What Others Think of Him	
Appearance, Dress, and Personality	Grizzly hair the color of midnight

---

Extend Understanding

Writing Options

Creative Writing Imagine that you are a reporter doing a story on the Battle of Ocracoke. Write a short **article** for a local newspaper describing the battle, its cause, and its outcome. Make sure to start with a catchy headline and include the *who, what, when, where, why,* and *how* of the story.

Expository Writing A legend is a story from the past, often based on important real events or people. Which elements of "Blackbeard's Last Fight" might be true? Write a brief **literary analysis** stating which parts you think are true, your reasons why, and what about Blackbeard makes him such a legendary figure.

Lifelong Learning

Conduct Research Blackbeard's sunken ship, *Queen Anne's Revenge,* was discovered in 1996. Use the following search terms to research new developments: *Queen Anne's Revenge, OAR Project, Blackbeard,* and *Ocracoke.* Take notes as you search and share your findings with the class.

Critical Literacy

Create a Skit Work in small groups to develop a skit of the Battle of Ocracoke about Lieutenant Maynard's sloop. Cast students to play the roles of Blackbeard, Maynard, and the others. After the group has practiced the skit several times, perform it for the class.

MW Go to www.mirrorsandwindows.com for more.

Rubrics for Writing Options

You can adapt this as a checklist for students to use as they write.

Creative Writing
☐ Does it have a captivating headline?
☐ Does it include the 5 Ws and H facts?
☐ Is it historically accurate?

Expository Writing
☐ Does the student support his or her reasoning with textual evidence?
☐ Does the student give a sufficient explanation of why Blackbeard is such a legendary figure?

Vocabulary & Spelling

Homonyms and Homophones

…he would retreat, through a shallow North Carolina inlet and hide behind the sandbanks.

—RICHARD WALSER, "Blackbeard's Last Fight"

The word *retreat* in the above quotation has several meanings: 1) a signal to withdraw troops; 2) a place of privacy; and 3) to move away from or backward. Words with the same spelling and sound but different meanings are called **homonyms.** Other words, such as *through* and *threw,* sound alike but are spelled differently and have different meanings. They are called **homophones.**

Use context clues to figure out the meaning of homonyms. In the quotation, *retreat* is a verb. *Move away* makes sense in the context of the quotation.

The context and part of speech determine which form of a homophone to use.

> EXAMPLES
>
> When *I* said <u>aye</u>, every <u>eye</u> turned to look at me.
>
> I told him to <u>seize</u> every ship he <u>sees</u> on the high <u>seas</u>.

Vocabulary Practice

Circle the correct homophone in each sentence.

1. "The (to, two, too) ships touched…"

2. "…when the odds became too (grate, great), he would retreat"

3. "…he was restless and soon was back at (see, sea)…"

4. "He had been (borne, born) in England…"

5. We didn't (sea, see) the jellyfish floating near the sandbar on our vacation to the (sea, see).

Select the correct meaning of the underlined word.

6. "…he let him roam at will along the <u>coast</u>."
   a. slide
   b. move effortlessly
   c. seashore

7. "Sometimes to make himself <u>even</u> more horrible…"
   a. to the full extent
   b. divisible by two
   c. smooth

8. "Governor Charles Eden was so cowed by this <u>scurvy</u> villain…"
   a. disease caused by a lack of vitamin C
   b. miserable
   c. type of grass

9. We didn't want to <u>rock</u> the boat; we might fall overboard.
   a. piece of stone
   b. shake
   c. type of music

10. After the battle, the ships <u>stole</u> away into the night.
    a. long wide scarf
    b. come or go secretly
    c. wrongfully take property

Spelling Practice
Homophones

Homophones are words that sound alike but are spelled differently and have different meanings. Homophones can pose a problem for spelling because, if you use the wrong spelling, a spellchecker program on your computer will not flag the word as being misspelled. Be sure you know the proper use of the homophones listed below from "Blackbeard's Last Flight."

awed—odd	one—won
been—bin	or—oar, ore
born—borne	right—rite, write
bury—berry	sail—sale
by—buy	sea—see
do—dew, due	so—sew
find—fined	some—sum
great—grate	through—threw
hair—hare	time—thyme
morning—mourning	to—too, two
not—knot, naught	would—wood

Vocabulary Practice

1. two
2. great
3. sea
4. born
5. see, sea
6. c
7. a
8. b
9. b
10. b

> For additional instruction on spelling rules, see Vocabulary & Spelling Section 2.7, Spelling, in the Language Arts Handbook.

Program Resources

You will find additional lessons on Homonyms and Homophones in the *Exceeding the Standards: Vocabulary & Spelling* resource.

KEY TERMS
HOMONYM, 797
HOMOPHONE, 797
CONTEXT CLUE, 797

TEACHING NOTE

Extra Practice

Have students identify the underlined words as homonyms or homophones.

1. She had to <u>wait</u> to find out if her <u>weight</u> had changed. (homophones)
2. Darla <u>ate</u> <u>eight</u> bananas. (homophones)
3. He had to <u>dart</u> to the left to escape the poison <u>dart</u>. (homonyms)
4. That <u>snake</u> can really <u>snake</u> through the grass. (homonyms)

Have students create logical sentences using each set of homonyms or homophones below.

5. would, wood (homophones)
6. new, knew (homophones)
7. class, class (homonyms)

Common Core State Standards

Language
L.4.1g

Barbara Frietchie

A Narrative Poem by John Greenleaf Whittier

At a Glance
Directed Reading
- Reading Level: Easy
- Difficulty Consideration: Subject matter
- Ease Factor: Rhyme scheme

Objectives
Studying this lesson will enable students to
- use reading skills such as connecting to prior knowledge and finding the main idea
- identify and explain the literary techniques *conflict, ballad,* and *internal rhyme*
- recognize the importance of Frederick to the Civil War
- appreciate elements of legend in a different literary genre

Launch the Lesson
Bring the students' attention to the United States flag. Ask students what they think the flag stands for and what the flag means to them. How would they feel if the flag were attacked?

KEY TERMS

NARRATIVE	VERSE, 798
POEM, 798	SETTING, 803
RHYME	STANZA, 803
SCHEME, 798	RHYTHM, 803
CONFLICT, 798	MOOD, 803
CHARACTER, 798	TONE, 803
EXTERNAL	CONFLICT, 803
CONFLICT, 798	BALLAD, 803
INTERNAL	ESSAY, 803
CONFLICT, 798	THESIS, 803
MAIN IDEA, 798	
RHYMED	
COUPLET, 798	

BEFORE READING

Build Background
Historical Context Whittier wrote "Barbara Frietchie" in 1864 during the American Civil War (1861–1865). Barbara Frietchie (1766–1862) was a real person, a unionist who lived in Frederick, Maryland, and she attended a memorial for our country's first president, George Washington, when he died. However, historians debate whether the event described in the poem actually took place.

Reader's Context Describe a time when you saw someone act out of loyalty. What did he or she do? Why did he or she do it?

Set Purpose
Preview "Barbara Frietchie" by examining the rhyme scheme. Predict whether the rhyme scheme will change as you read.

Analyze Literature
Conflict A **conflict** is a struggle between two people or things in a literary work. A struggle that takes place between a character and some outside force, such as another character, society, or nature is called an *external conflict*. A struggle that takes place within a character is called an *internal conflict*. As you read "Barbara Frietchie," analyze the conflict and identify whether it is internal or external and how it is resolved.

Meet the Author
John Greenleaf Whittier (1807–1892) was born in Haverhill, Massachusetts, in the home of his first American ancestor. The home had been built in the 1600s. Whittier was a member of the Quaker Church and noted, "As a member of the Society of Friends, I had been educated to regard slavery as a great and dangerous evil, and my sympathies were strongly enlisted for the oppressed slaves...."

Use Reading Skills
Find the Main Idea To determine the main idea or overall message of "Barbara Frietchie," gather important ideas into a main idea map and analyze what main idea or theme they suggest. You will notice that the poem is written in rhymed couplets, units of verse with two lines. Summarize the content of key groups of couplets in the details section. Then look at all the details and write the main idea in the center.

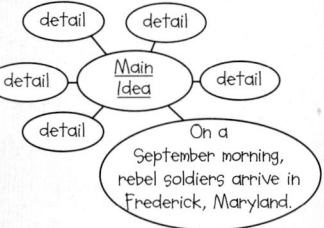

Preview Vocabulary
clus·tered (kləsʹ tərd) *adj.,* gathered together

fam·ished (faʹ misht) *adj.,* extremely hungry

tread (tred) *n.,* footsteps, or the sound of footsteps

stir (stər) *v.,* wake or rise

host (hōst) *n.,* person who entertains guests

Words in Use

Preview Vocabulary	Selection Words	Teaching Words
clustered, 800	**hauled,** 800	**unionist,** 798
famished, 800	**nobler,** 801	**memorial,** 798
tread, 801	**deed,** 801	**ancestor,** 798
stir, 801	**yon,** 801	**enlisted,** 798
host, 802		**oppressed,** 798

Common Core State Standards

Reading Literature
RL.1, RL.9

Writing
W.9, W.10

Language
L.6

Barbara Frietchie waves the Union flag above General "Stonewall" Jackson.

Barbara Frietchie

A Narrative Poem by John Greenleaf Whittier

799

Summary

Stonewall Jackson, Confederate general, is marching his troops through Frederick on his way to battle the Union army at Sharpsburg, Virginia. Frederick was in Union territory, and the Confederate army was not welcome. To underline this, old Barbara Frietchie hangs her flag outside her attic window. When Lee's troops shoot it down, Barbara catches it and waves it at them in disdain. Jackson is shamed by the old woman's pride of country and orders his troops to leave her alone as they march through the town and on to battle.

The Mirrors & Windows questions at the end of this selection focus on the theme of conviction. Before reading the story, ask students if they have any beliefs they would defend with their actions.

History Connection

The Real Barbara Frietchie The poem written in 1864 by John Greenleaf Whittier was based on a real person. She was a very patriotic woman who lived in Frederick, Maryland, at the time the Confederate troops passed through on their way to Antietam. She never laid eyes on Stonewall Jackson, but she did have a flag and she waved it as Confederate soldiers, led by Burnside, marched through town.

Program Resources

Planning and Assessment
Program Planning Guide, Selection Lesson Plan
E-Lesson Planner
Assessment Guide, Lesson Test
ExamView

Technology Tools
Interactive Student Text on CD
Visual Teaching Package
Audio Library
mirrorsandwindows.com

Meeting the Standards
Folk Literature: Unit 8, Directed Reading, pp. 54–60

Differentiating Instruction
Advanced Students, Poetic Form Study pp. 50–51

Analyze Literature

Rhyme Scheme Remind students that the rhyme scheme of a poem is the pattern of rhyming lines in a poem. This pattern is represented with letters. For example, in a poem with a rhyme scheme of *abba*, the first and fourth lines in a stanza would rhyme with each other, as would the second and third lines. Ask students to identify the rhyme scheme in "Barbara Frietchie."

Geography Connection

The Virginia Theater of War In May of 1862, near Richmond, Virginia, newly appointed Commander of the Confederate Army, General Robert E. Lee, attacked the Union armies under the command of General George McClellan. This meeting became known as the Seven Days Battle. After suffering heavy losses, McClellan withdrew his troops to Washington. On August 30, Generals Jackson and Longstreet defeated Union armies at Manassas Junction in northern Virginia, approximately 10 miles west of Washington. Meanwhile, Lee invaded the North with fifty thousand men and headed for Harper's Ferry, located fifty miles northwest of Washington, with McClellan and his army in pursuit. Both armies passed through Frederick, Maryland, and met for battle at Antietam Creek (also known as the Battle of Sharpsburg). This battle gained infamy as the deadliest of the Civil War.

Up from the meadows rich with corn,
Clear in the cool September morn,

The <u>clustered</u> spires of Frederick stand
Green-walled by the hills of Maryland.

5 Round about them orchards sweep,
Apple and peach tree fruited deep,

Fair as the garden of the Lord
To the eyes of the <u>famished</u> rebel horde,[1]

On that pleasant morn of the early fall
10 When Lee marched over the mountain wall;

Over the mountains winding down,
Horse and foot, into Frederick town.

Forty flags with their silver stars,
Forty flags with their crimson bars,

15 Flapped in the morning wind: the sun
Of noon looked down, and saw not one.

Up rose old Barbara Frietchie then,
Bowed with her fourscore years and ten;[2]

Bravest of all in Frederick town,
20 She took up the flag the men hauled down

In her attic window the staff she set,
To show that one heart was loyal yet.

---

1. horde. Large crowd
2. fourscore years and ten. Ninety years

clus·tered (kləs´ tərd) *adj.*, gathered together
fam·ished (fa´ misht) *adj.*, extremely hungry

Differentiated Instruction

Reading Proficiency

Some students may find it difficult to read poetry. Reading the poem aloud to students may help them to better interpret the details and get a sense of the poem's rhythm. Have students read along while you read, and model when to pause at the end of a line and when to continue straight on to the next.

Enrichment

Interested students might enjoy researching the evolution of the U.S. flag. From its conception in 1776, the flag has changed many times. Ask students to find pictures of each U.S. flag, making sure to include those of the Civil War, and share their findings with the class.

Up the street came the rebel[3] <u>tread</u>,
Stonewall Jackson riding ahead.

25 Under his slouched hat left and right
He glanced; the old flag met his sight.

"Halt!"—the dust-brown ranks stood fast.
"Fire!"—out blazed the rifle blast.

It shivered the window, pane and sash;
30 It rent[4] the banner with seam and gash.

Quick, as it fell, from the broken staff
Dame Barbara snatched the silken scarf.

She leaned far out on the windowsill,
And shook it forth with a royal will.

35 "Shoot, if you must, this old gray head,
But spare your country's flag," she said.

A shade of sadness, a blush of shame,
Over the face of the leader came;

The nobler nature within him <u>stirred</u>
40 To life at that woman's deed and word;

"Who touches a hair of yon gray head
Dies like a dog! March on!" he said.

All day long through Frederick street
Sounded the tread of marching feet:

---

3. **the rebel.** Having to do with Confederate General Stonewall Jackson
4. **rent.** Past tense of verb *rend;* ripped or torn

> **tread** (tred) *n.,* footsteps, or the sound of footsteps
> **stir** (stər) *v.,* wake or rise

Writing Skills

Haiku

Remind students that there are many fixed forms in poetry, including the ballad, sonnet, and haiku. A poet can take one subject and create very different poems with each of these forms. Remind students that "Barbara Frietchie" is a ballad, which has a simple *aabb* stanza form. A haiku does not use rhyming words, but instead is formed by syllables.

The haiku is made up of three lines—five syllables in the first line, seven in the second, and five in the third. Have students write a pair of haikus describing the events in "Barbara Frietchie." Point out to students that in haiku, every word counts, so they must choose their words carefully.

Analyze Literature

Personification Examine with students the personification in lines 48 and 59. Ask them what they think was the author's purpose in employing this type of figurative language in the poem. What is its effect on the poem?

Cultural Connection

The Fireside Poets *Answer:* Student responses will vary. Students may note that the simple rhyme scheme would appeal to young people and would be easier to memorize. Ⓐ

 *Answer:* Ask students to substantiate their personal responses with reasoning and comparisons to the selection. Students who think that most people would act as Barbara Frietchie did might explain that most people, whether naturally brave or not, would feel an increase in patriotism if their nation were under immediate threat. Students who think that most people would not act similarly might explain that Frietchie's action was dangerous or unnecessary, and that while people might defend themselves and their land, they would not be concerned with the preservation of a symbol such as a flag.

45 All day long that free flag tossed
Over the heads of the rebel <u>host</u>.

Ever its torn folds rose and fell
On the loyal winds that loved it well;

And through the hill gaps sunset light
50 Shone over it with a warm good night.

Barbara Frietchie's work is o'er,
And the Rebel rides on his raids no more.

Honor to her! and let a tear
Fall, for her sake, on Stonewall's bier.

55 Over Barbara Frietchie's grave,
Flag of Freedom and Union, wave!

Peace and order and beauty draw
Round thy symbol of light and law;

And ever the stars above look down
60 On thy stars below in Frederick town! ❖

---

host (hōst) *n.,* person who entertains guests

CULTURAL ▶▶ CONNECTION

The Fireside Poets John Greenleaf Whittier was among the first American poets to gain great popularity. As such, he is grouped with Henry Wadsworth Longfellow ("Paul Revere's Ride"), William Cullen Bryant ("To a Waterfowl"), James Russell Lowell ("The Vision of Sir Launfal"), and Oliver Wendell Holmes, Sr. ("The Autocrat of the Breakfast Table"), a group known as the Fireside Poets. The group is also sometimes called the Schoolroom Poets or the Household Poets. These names all come from the popularity of their works and the fact that they were memorized and recited in schools and homes for education and entertainment. What would make poems such as "Barbara Frietchie" appealing to young audiences? Ⓐ

 Would you have acted as Barbara Frietchie did in a similar situation? What do you passionately believe in? Would most people today act the way Barbara Frietchie did in the poem?

Grammar Skills

Semicolon

Remind students that a semicolon can join two closely related, independent clauses. This adds emphasis to the second half of the statement, making it equal in importance to the first.

Write this sentence on a board. Then ask students to add a semicolon where needed.

Barbara Frietchie was a very patriotic woman she took great pride in her nation's flag.

Find Meaning

1. (a) What is the setting, or time and place, for most of the poem? (b) How does the setting change near the end of the poem?
2. (a) What are the "Forty flags" in the seventh stanza? (b) What happens to the flags?
3. What do you think Whittier means by "the nobler nature" of the rebel leader?
4. What is the "symbol of light and law" in the second to last stanza?

Analyze Literature

Conflict Review the causes and effects in "Barbara Frietchie" to determine the central conflict. Remember that the *effects* are what happens in a narrative. *Causes* are the reasons why those things happen. Often an effect has multiple causes, and a cause can have multiple effects. Draw arrows to show which causes and effects are related.

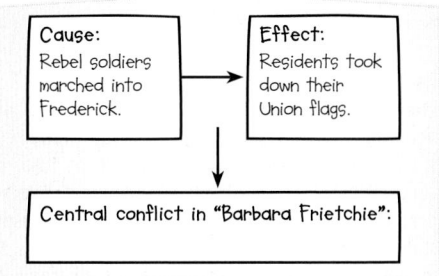

Cause:
Rebel soldiers marched into Frederick.

Effect:
Residents took down their Union flags.

Central conflict in "Barbara Frietchie":

Make Judgments

5. (a) How would you describe the rhythm of the poem? (b) How do you think the rhythm contributes to the mood of the poem?
6. (a) Why do you think Barbara Frietchie's actions were successful in changing the behavior of Stonewall Jackson? (b) Does this part of the poem seem realistic to you? Explain.
7. How would you describe the author's tone?

Extend Understanding

Writing Options

Creative Writing Write your own **ballad** that celebrates a person important to you or to your community. Mimic the rhythm and the form of "Barbara Frietchie." Write in rhyming couplets, and present a complete idea in each stanza. Write a poem that a third-grade student could memorize and recite in school. Then memorize part of your poem and recite it for your class.

Expository Writing Write a short **essay** describing the mood of the poem, in other words, how the poem made you feel. Focus on elements such as imagery and rhyme and how they contribute to the mood. Support your thesis with examples from the poem. Share your essay with your class.

Collaborative Learning

Discuss in Small Groups Reread the couplets that focus on Stonewall Jackson's response to Barbara Frietchie's courageous action. Then in small groups, discuss these questions: What did Stonewall Jackson do in response to Barbara Frietchie? What was his motivation for the actions he took? Share your conclusions with the class.

Media Literacy

Determine Historical Accuracy Use the library and the Internet to gather information about events described in this poem. Use the search terms "Barbara Frietchie" and "Stonewall Jackson." What facts are presented in the poem? What part of the poem is fiction? Share your findings with the class.

 Go to www.mirrorsandwindows.com for more.

Find Meaning

1. (a) A September day during the American Civil War in Frederick, Maryland. (b) The time of the poem changes to when Frietchie and Jackson have died.
2. (a) Forty Union flags that hung in Frederick. (b) The flags are removed as the Confederate army approaches, but Barbara Frietchie replaces one. Confederate soldiers shoot the flag, and Barbara Frietchie hangs what is left of it.
3. Students might say that his compassion and humanity were stirred or his loyalty to his country.
4. The flag on Frietchie's grave.

Make Judgments

5. (a) Students may hear marching footsteps or describe the rhythm as even and regimented. (b) Students might say the rhythm reinforces the military action in the poem and makes the mood more dramatic.
6. (a) Students might say her courage and loyalty were overwhelming or that she was so old and frail that she stirred compassion. (b) Students may feel it is unusual for shame to bring about a change in behavior, especially in the case of a group mentality that is bent on violence.
7. Students should choose from adjectives such as patriotic, passionate, celebratory, and so on.

Analyze Literature

Conflict *Answer:* Students should determine that the central conflict is the external conflict between Frietchie and Jackson.

Rubrics for Writing Options

You can adapt this as a checklist for students to use as they write.

Creative Writing

☐ Does the poem mimic the rhythm of "Barbara Frietchie"?
☐ Is the poem written in rhyming couplets?

Expository Writing

☐ Does the student describe the mood of the poem in the first paragraph?
☐ Does the student support his or her description with examples?

JOHN HENRY BLUES

A Folk Song

Annie Christmas

A Tall Tale by Walker Brents

Preview the Selections

At a Glance
Directed Reading
"John Henry Blues"
- Reading Level: Challenging
- Difficulty Consideration: Subject matter
- Ease Factor: Repetition

"Annie Christmas"
- Reading Level: Moderate
- Difficulty Consideration: Vocabulary
- Ease Factor: Length

Objectives
Studying this lesson will enable students to
- compare literary selections of different genres
- use reading strategies such as comparing and contrasting texts
- define *character* and compare the effects of this literary technique in these selections
- recognize a folk ballad and folk tale and identify the characteristics of both

Launch the Lesson
Tell students that "John Henry Blues" is a "working-class hero," meaning that he did physical labor and was considered lower on the societal and economic ladder than other people, and was noble and strong in character. Ask students to think about someone they know who would qualify as a "working-class hero."

As they read "Annie Christmas," have students develop a mental picture of Annie. When they are finished reading, have students sketch a picture of what they think Annie looks like.

BEFORE READING

Build Background
Historical Context The story of Annie Christmas tells of a fictional character and fictional events. Many believe that the story of John Henry, however, is based on historical circumstances, despite having the characteristics of a tall tale. In the 1800s, railroad companies hired men to use hammers and stakes to make holes in rocks to create tunnels. In order to save money, railroad companies started using steam drills. According to the legend, John Henry challenged the use of a steam drill in a contest to prove that a man was better than a machine.

Reader's Context What unusual feats would you like to accomplish?

Set Purpose
Preview the titles of the selections and skim the text. Predict what the selections will be about.

Meet the Author
The story of John Henry has been around since the 1800s and there are many versions of this traditional folk song. The lyrics to "John Henry Blues" were transcribed by Norm Cohen.

Walker Brents (b. 1959) is a poet and storyteller who has loved folklore and myths since he discovered at age five the myths of Hercules and the Greek gods. Brents is a teacher and has published poetry in a number of literary magazines.

Compare Literature:
Character A **character** is a person or animal who takes part in the action of a literary work. The main character is called the **protagonist.** A character who struggles against the main character is called an **antagonist.** As you read "John Henry" and "Annie Christmas," compare the protagonists' traits. Identify and compare the antagonists in each selection as well.

Preview Vocabulary
ca·pac·i·ty (kə pas´ ət ē) *n.*, ability; skill

bar·ri·cade (ber´ ə kād´) *n.*, barrier; obstacle

plume (plüm) *n.*, feather

buoy·ant (boi´ ənt) *adj.*, capable of floating

ten·dril (ten´ drəl) *n.*, slender spiral shoot of a climbing vine that attaches the vine to its support; anything looking like a tendril

804 UNIT 8 FOLK LITERATURE

Words in Use

Teaching Words
feats, 804
relevant, 812
portraying, 813
heroine, 813

KEY TERMS

Common Core State Standards
Reading Literature
RL.1
Language
L.6

JOHN HENRY BLUES

John Henry. Dan Dutton.

A Folk Song

805

Teach the Selection

Summary
John Henry, the steel-driving man, is born with exceptional strength and grows up to work on the railroads. When the captain brings in a steam drill, John Henry scoffs at it and challenges the drill to a competition. He wins, but he dies immediately after.

MIRRORS & WINDOWS The Mirrors & Windows questions at the end of this selection focus on the theme of valor. Before reading the story, ask students if they ever feel the need to prove their superiority in any area. What are some different reasons people have for proving their superiority?

Use Reading Skills
Author's Purpose Remind students that the ability to identify the author's purpose, or aim, is an important reading skill. Write examples of purpose on the board (to reflect; to entertain, enrich, or enlighten; to narrate a series of events; to inform or explain; to persuade), have students identify which best suits the author's purpose in writing "John Henry Blues" and discuss whether the author achieved that purpose.

Program Resources

Planning and Assessment
Program Planning Guide, Selection Lesson Plan
E-Lesson Planner
Assessment Guide, Lesson Test
ExamView

Technology Tools
Interactive Student Text on CD
Visual Teaching Package
Audio Library
mirrorsandwindows.com

Meeting the Standards
Folk Literature: Unit 8, Comparing Literature, pp. 61–68

Differentiating Instruction
English Language Learners, Understand Literary Elements/Compare and Contrast, pp. 198–213

John Henry and Railroad Expansion After the Civil War, the United States began to expand and railroads were recognized as an essential means of connecting the east and west coasts. Building railroads became a huge industry, and men like John Henry made their living on it. That John Henry was a real man, a former slave, and a steel-driver is undisputed, but the details of his life are uncertain. It is true that steam drills were introduced in order to reduce costs, putting many men out of work, but whether or not John Henry really did challenge the drill remains speculation.

Use Reading Skills

Compare and Contrast Remind students that when you compare one thing with another, you are describing similarities between the two things; when you contrast two things, you describe the differences. Have students compare and contrast John Henry and the steam drill, using a Venn diagram.

Analyze Literature

Protagonist Remind students that the protagonist is the main character in a story who faces some sort of struggle. Ask students to identify how John Henry is a protagonist. What are his struggles, and with what or whom does he struggle?

John Henry was a very small boy,
Fell on his mammy's[1] knee;
Picked up a hammer and a little piece of steel,
"Lord, a hammer'll be the death of me,
5 Lord, a hammer'll be the death of me."

John Henry went upon the mountain,
Come down on the side;
The mountain so tall, John Henry was so small,
Lord, he lay down his hammer and he cried, "Oh, Lord,"
10 He lay down his hammer and he cried.

John Henry was on the right hand,
But that steam drill was on the left;
"Before your steam drill beats me down,
Hammer my fool self to death,
15 Lord, I'll hammer my fool self to death."

The captain says to John Henry,
"Believe my tunnel's fallin' in."
"Captain, you needn't not to worry,
Just my hammer hawsing[2] in the wind,
20 Just my hammer hawsing in the wind."

"Look away over yonder, captain,
You can't see like me."
He hollered out in a low, lonesome cry,
"This hammer'll be the death of me,
25 Lord, this hammer'll be the death of me."

John Henry told his captain,
"Captain, you go to town,
Bring John back a twelve-pound hammer,
And he'll whup your steam drill down,
30 [And] he'll whup your steam drill down."

For the man that invented that steam drill
Thought he was mighty fine;
John Henry sunk a fo'teen foot,
The steam drill only made nine,
35 The steam drill only made nine.

1. **mammy's.** Mother's
2. **hawsing.** Falling forward

Differentiated Instruction

Enrichment

"John Henry Blues" is the best-known and most widely recorded American folk song. Challenge interested students to research and listen to some of the songs recorded about John Henry. This hero of folklore has been a subject for many jazz, blues, and folk artists—including Johnny Cash and Mississippi John Hurt.

John Henry told his shaker,[3]
"Shaker, you better pray;
For if I miss the six-foot steel,
Tomorrow'll be your buryin' day,
40 An' tomorrow'll be your buryin' day."

John Henry told his lovin' little woman,
"Sick and I want to go to bed;
Fix me a place to lay down, child,
Got a rollin' in my head,
45 Got a rollin' in my head."

John Henry had a lovely little woman,
Called her Polly Ann;
John Henry got sick and he had to go home,
But Polly broke steel like a man,
50 Polly broke steel like a man.

John Henry had another little woman,
The dress she wore was blue;
She went down the track and she never looked back,
"John Henry, I've been true to you." ❖

---

3. shaker. Person who holds the steam drill

 John Henry wants to prove that he can do better work than a machine. What would you like to prove that you can do better than someone or something else? How would you prove that? Why might John Henry be such a popular folk hero?

Find Meaning

1. (a) What was John Henry's reaction to the size of the mountain? (b) Why did he react that way?

2. (a) According to the ballad, what did the man who invented the steam drill think? (b) What does this imply? (c) How did John Henry prove him wrong?

Make Judgments

3. (a) How does the first stanza of the ballad foreshadow what will happen to John Henry? (b) What is the effect of this foreshadowing? Explain.

4. (a) What is the attitude of the speaker in the ballad toward John Henry? (b) How can you tell?

 Students should explain what they want to prove, why, and how they would do it. Students may say that John Henry proved that physical laborers are important and that he shows determination and skill.

Find Meaning

1. (a) He cried "Oh Lord," lay down his hammer, and cried. (b) John Henry realized that he was up against great odds.

2. (a) He thought he was "mighty fine." (b) He thought his machine would replace a man. (c) He makes a larger hole than the steam drill.

Make Judgments

3. (a) As a small boy, John Henry picks up a hammer and declares that it will be the death of him. At the end of the ballad John Henry has become fatally sick from the exhaustion of hammering. (b) Students might say that the foreshadowing adds to the tension and suspense because they know that something bad will happen to John Henry and want to find out what it is.

4. (a) The speaker admires John Henry. (b) The speaker portrays him as a man determined to succeed.

Speaking & Listening Skills

Recitation

Ask students to form groups of three, and have the members of each group choose a role—John Henry, captain, and narrator. Have the groups recite "John Henry Blues," paying careful attention to rhythm. Instruct students to listen to their group member as they recite.

Teach the Selection

Summary

Annie Christmas is the strongest woman in all of New Orleans and can outwork any man. After saving the city from flood by building a barricade, Anne rewards herself with a scarlet dress and a journey on a flatboat up the Big River. On her journey, she encounters the sinking ship *Natchez Belle* and single-handedly saves the crew and passengers. She receives a hero's welcome as she returns to New Orleans with her passengers, but it is short-lived, as the exertion of saving the *Natchez Belle* results in a mortal fever. When she dies, her body is placed on her flatboat, and she's set adrift on the Big River for eternity.

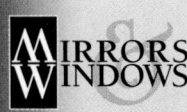

MIRRORS & WINDOWS

The Mirrors & Windows questions at the end of this selection focus on the theme of determination. Before reading the story, ask students for examples of people who are especially determined. Why do stories of determination inspire people?

Comparing Literature

Annie Christmas

A Tall Tale by Walker Brents

Blue, 1994. Elizabeth Heuer. Collection of the artist.

808

Common Core State Standards
Reading Literature RL.1, RL.9
Writing W.7, W.8, W.9
Language L.6

Words in Use

"Annie Christmas"

Preview Vocabulary	Selection Words
capacity, 809	**behold,** 809
barricade, 809	**pandemonium,** 811
plume, 809	**aground,** 811
buoyant, 811	**sodden,** 811
tendril, 811	**submerged,** 811

Differentiated Instruction

Reading Proficiency

There are a number of difficult vocabulary words in this selection. Have students get together with partners to read through the vocabulary words and practice them in sentences. Then have students read the story.

Annie Christmas was six feet eight inches tall, dark and beautiful to behold, and with the power to blow over boulders. In build she was neither muscle-bound nor skinny. It was the way she moved and used movement that made her able to lift and pull. Her mind was just as strong: she knew the Big River like the back of her hand.

She had twelve sons, each one tall as her, some say taller. They stood six on either side of her. No one took their photograph—there were no picture-takers then—but people of New Orleans, Natchez, and points between remembered them so vividly their stories survive to this day.

It was a bright sunny day when Annie, loading bales of cotton on a busy New Orleans dock, was approached by Mike Fink who, new in town, aggressively cast aspersions[1] on her <u>capacity</u> to work like a man. He told her out and out to go home. Said Annie casually, looking at her as she took off her gloves, "Seems to me we should be clear about who should be where." So saying she raised a half-ton cotton bale over her head with her bare hands and threw it into the river in such a way that it hit the water just in front of him. The splash it made generated a mighty wave that swept poor Mike Fink off the dock and carried him all the way to Natchez. It was one time in his life when he didn't know what to say. He was just carried away on the waves with his mouth open wide but no sound coming out. He never returned to New Orleans.

Big rains hammer the delta[2] at various times of the year. They threaten to fill the river past its banks and flood the lowlands where the crops are. That is why men were building a <u>barricade</u> to support the riverbank when Annie Christmas came by. Racing against time to beat the flood, the men called on her to help. Annie joined right in, working round the clock and long past it, finally sending the men on to other emergency work. She finished the barricade by herself in the nick of time to save the lowlands. When she was done, she went into town and bought herself a beautiful red velvet dress, some say scarlet satin, with matching red <u>plumes</u> which she placed in her shining black hair. She gathered her friends around her and they went on a journey in a flatboat up the river, stopping in every town along the way and having a good time. By and by her friends made friends in the towns where they stopped and stayed behind, leaving Annie Christmas all alone pulling her flatboat along on a rope. It just shows you how strong she was, pulling against that river. No one else could do that. One day she said, "It's just you and me, Boat, way up here on this big river. I'll call you *Big River's Daughter*. That will be

> **Said Annie casually, looking at him as she took off her gloves, "Seems to me we should be clear about who should be where."**

A

1. **cast aspersions.** Attacked with evil reports or false or harmful accusations
2. **delta.** Place where a river empties into a larger body of water; here it refers to the Mississippi River delta

> **ca·pac·i·ty** (kə pas′ ət ē) *n.*, ability; skill
>
> **bar·ri·cade** (ber′ ə kād′) *n.*, barrier; obstacle
>
> **plume** (plüm) *n.*, feather

Use Reading Skills

Compare and Contrast Now that students have become familiar with both John Henry and Annie Christmas, have them compare and contrast the two characters. Instruct students to use a Venn diagram to record the similarities and differences. Model an example for students such as: "Because Annie could memorize every detail of the Big River, she must be very clever. Is John Henry similar or different?"

Science Connection

Flatboats Flatboats, straight-prowed boats, and flat-bottomed boats, were used in the early nineteenth century to transport large freight along rivers. These boats were designed to travel downriver and were generally used for just one trip; once they reached their destination, they were disassembled for lumber. Flatboats became obsolete in the 1840s when the steamboat became a more efficient method of river travel.

your name. We'll float this river up and down and make it our own." And that's just what she did. She knew the swirls, the shadows and the brambles. She knew the currents and the shoals,[3] the snags and the tears. Her mind was a map of that river. The boat was like her second skin; the river to her was like a string of freshwater pearls of which she knew every bend and kink.

One cold rainy night she found herself close behind the great steamboat, *Natchez Belle*. Annie peered ahead through the driving hail. "She seems to be in trouble. Better have a look." Annie tied *Big River's Daughter* to the rail of the *Natchez Belle* and climbed up into

---

3. **shoals.** Shallows in water or sandbanks; sandbars that make the water shallow

Differentiated Instruction

English Language Learning

Students may find the following clarification useful as they make their way through the text.

bales of cotton — large bundles of cotton, 809
barricade — an obstruction built to keep something back, 809
nick of time — just in time; at the last possible moment, 809

flatboat — boat with a flat bottom used for transporting bulky freight, 809
brambles — prickly shrubs, 810
sandbar — ridge of sand built up by currents, 810

it to behold utter pandemonium. The steamboat had run aground on a sandbar. The deck was listing, small fires burning, scared sodden people running every which way. Worst of all the captain and crew were locked in the cabin. Annie broke open the lock with a shovel—some say her bare hands—and pulled the captain and crew to safety before they burned in a fire that started at that very spot. Annie started gathering all the people who hadn't jumped or fallen overboard. Far away bobbed *Big River's Daughter* upon the waves. She was too <u>buoyant</u> and steady-keeled[4] to sink or break apart, but that wasn't the danger: the rope tying her to the rail of the other vessel was frayed and ready to break. In some sections only one or two <u>tendrils</u> held the rope together. Annie reached out with her strong graceful arms. She placed her long supple[5] fingers around the frayed sisal[6] lifeline and began to draw the rope in, and her boat toward her. The rope stretched and more strands popped asunder. Hailstones stung her eyes. The people in their dripping clothes, teeth chattering, held their breath and watched. Slowly but surely Annie drew *Big River's Daughter* to her. The rope held together. She brought the boats toward each other so closely the captain and crew and passengers all stepped over to *Big River's Daughter,* with no one so much as stumbling. It was timely they got over when they did, for as soon as Annie poled them a safe distance away, the *Natchez Belle* split apart over the sandbar, rolled over twice, and cracked into pieces upon the jagged branches of submerged fallen trees. Annie navigated *Big River's Daughter,* now carrying about a hundred

> ## The rope stretched and more strands popped asunder.

people, and used her steering-pole to continue picking up what survivors she could. The passengers and crew helped with coils of rope they used as lifelines to grab onto, and they used tree branches as poles to help those in the water catch hold. As the rain lessened they neared home, Annie pulling them along in her mud-soaked scarlet dress.

As they approached New Orleans a funny thing happened, an early rising watcher saw them coming, and informed the whole city of the news. Soon the docks were full of people and they greeted Annie Christmas and the survivors of the *Natchez Belle* with a hero's welcome. Everyone acclaimed[7] her, but she was not to enjoy it long. A fever brought on by overexertion[8] soon laid her low. Upon her deathbed she gathered her twelve sons around her, six on either side of the bed. Her strong breath was fading from this world. She knew her time had come, and spoke her dying words.

"Dress me in my scarlet dress. Put the bright red plumes in my black hair. Walk on either side of me as you wear your black suits. Let the horse cart draw me down the road to the river on the darkest night of all. The river, my boat, and me: we were one. Put me on my boat; let me float upon my

---

4. **steady-keeled.** Level; the keel of a boat is the structure along the center of its bottom.
5. **supple.** Flexible; able to move without stiffness or awkwardness
6. **sisal.** Strong, durable fiber used to make rope
7. **acclaimed.** Applauded; praised
8. **overexertion.** Excessive effort

> **buoy·ant** (boi´ ənt) *adj.,* capable of floating
>
> **ten·dril** (ten´ drəl) *n.,* slender spiral shoot of a climbing vine that attaches the vine to its support; anything looking like a tendril

Answer: Responses will vary. Students should give reasons to support their opinions. Some students may say that the town will be different because when Annie was alive they knew they had someone special who could take care of difficult conditions, that they had a mythic person in their midst. Now the town just has ordinary people. Students may also say that Annie inspired the town's folk as demonstrated by the last line of the story.

river. Annie fades away, but Big River goes on and on."

It was a sad night when New Orleans said goodbye to Annie Christmas. The moon hid her face from grief. The stars sparkled in their own tears. The horses clip-clopped over the stones drawing her funeral coach. Her sons sang a song of farewell. The men she'd defeated in feats of strength joined in, then all the women, children, and men of New Orleans.

The night was dark as death when they loaded her body from the funeral coach to *Big River's Daughter*, which floated waiting at the docks. Her body in its dress and plumes was placed upon her planks and the boat pushed away. The river's current caught her and carried her to sea. All the people of New Orleans stood watching as she faded in the distance. At the very point upon the horizon where she disappeared from sight, the morning sun began to rise.

From then on, if ever a man demonstrated great might, people would say, "Why, he's as strong as Annie Christmas." ❖

> Think of a person you believe is as determined as Annie Christmas. What other qualities does that person have in common with Annie? How are they different from each other? How might this tale be relevant today?

TEACHING NOTE

Self-Generated Questioning

Encourage students to ask as many questions about the selection as they can such as: "How did Annie know the Big River so well?" and record their questions on a board or overhead projector. Place a star next to each question students deem essential to their understanding and two stars next to each question they consider difficult to answer. As a class discuss the starred questions and possible answers to them.

Comparing Literature

Find Meaning

1. (a) Describe Annie's physical qualities.
(b) Why does the storyteller compare her body to her mind?

2. (a) What does Mike Fink tell Annie Christmas at the dock? (b) Why do you think he tells her that?

3. (a) Where does Annie want to be buried? (b) Why do you think she wants to be buried there?

Compare Literature

Character John Henry and Annie Christmas are both the protagonists, or main characters, in their stories. A character who struggles against the main character is called an antagonist. An antagonist doesn't have to be a person; it can be a force such as nature or society.

Make Judgments

4. (a) What are three things that only Annie can do—things she does by herself? (b) What does this reveal about her character?

5. (a) Why might people say "Why, he's as strong as Annie Christmas"? (b) In other words, does the story do a good job of portraying Annie as a measure of strength against which others can be compared? Why or why not?

1. How are John Henry and Annie Christmas alike? How are they different? What do these protagonists represent?

2. Who or what is the antagonist in each selection? Explain.

Extend Understanding

Writing Options

Creative Writing A eulogy is a speech about a person usually given at that person's funeral. Write a **eulogy** for either John Henry or Annie Christmas. Tell what deeds he or she did and why those actions were important. Also talk about the kind of person he or she was. Read your eulogy to the class.

Expository Writing Write an **expository essay** in which you compare and contrast the characters in these two stories. How are they similar? How are they different? Use a graphic organizer, such as a Venn diagram or an outline, to plan your essay before writing it. Share your essay with the class.

Lifelong Learning

Research John Henry and Annie Christmas are both African-American folklore heroes. Use the Internet or library to research other African-American folklore heroes. Which hero or heroine interests you the most? Summarize the story in which that hero or heroine appears.

Collaborative Learning

Recite Practice reciting the ballad of John Henry. Adjust your tone and speaking rate to fit the tone, mood, and events in the ballad. Try memorizing a portion or all of it, and present it to the class.

Go to www.mirrorsandwindows.com for more.

Find Meaning

1. (a) She is tall, dark, and beautiful. (b) He does this to explain that her mind is strong like her body.

2. (a) He tells her to leave and go home. (b) Mike probably feels threatened by Annie because she is physically stronger than he.

3. (a) She wants the river to be her grave. (b) The river is her home.

Make Judgments

4. (a) She finishes the barricade, pulls her boat against the river's current, and saves a boat full of people. (b) Her body and mind are strong.

5. (a) To illustrate that "he" is incredibly strong. (b) Some students may say that the storyteller gives many examples of Annie's strength. Other may say that because her feats are so unlikely, it is impossible for other people to measure up.

Compare Literature
Character

1. They have superhuman strength, are very determined, and work themselves to death. In "Annie Christmas" the storyteller shows us that Annie cared about her appearance. There is nothing in "John Henry Blues" that tells the reader that appearance was important to him.

2. In "John Henry Blues" the antagonist is the steam drill, which represents man versus machine. In "Annie Christmas" the antagonist is the river, which represents the struggle between man and nature.

Rubrics for Writing Options

You can adapt this as a checklist for students to use as they write.

Creative Writing

☐ Does the eulogy name the character's deeds?

☐ Does it discuss the kind of person he or she was and why he or she will be missed?

Expository Writing

☐ Did the student create a graphic organizer or outline before writing the essay?

☐ Does the essay tell how the characters are alike?

☐ Does the essay tell how the characters are different?

☐ Is the essay logically organized?

A Tall Tale by Carl Sandburg

Preview the Selection

At a Glance
Directed Reading
- Reading Level: Moderate
- Difficulty Consideration: Vocabulary
- Ease Factor: Familiar story

Objectives

Studying this lesson will enable students to
- use reading strategies such as identifying and evaluating the author's purpose
- define *hyperbole* and recognize the effect of this literary technique in the selection
- describe the work of Carl Sandburg and explain how he is an influential American writer
- appreciate a tall tale

Launch the Lesson

Before reading "Paul Bunyan of the North Woods," have students create a comic strip with a superhero of their choice. Encourage them to focus their strip on situations that demonstrate the superhero's strengths and accomplishments.

DIRECTED READING

BEFORE READING

Build Background

Historical Context Many American folk tales, such as "Paul Bunyan of the North Woods," deal with people struggling against natural elements. This was a daily experience for American pioneers, particularly for lumberjacks who lived in isolated logging camps in the wilderness. The logging industry was booming as towns were being built.

Reader's Context Imagine being faced with a large and difficult task, such as building a new city or stopping a hurricane. What superhuman powers would help you complete such a task?

Set Purpose

Think about what you already know about Paul Bunyan. Based on your prior knowledge, what do you think the story will focus on?

Analyze Literature

Hyperbole An exaggeration made for effect is **hyperbole.** An **understatement** is a statement that treats something important as though it was not important. As you read, look for examples of hyperbole and understatement.

Meet the Author

Carl Sandburg (1878–1967) was born in Galesburg, Illinois. He wrote in a wide range of genres—poetry, fiction, nonfiction, and history. Much of his writing was based on his own personal experiences traveling around the country and holding a variety of jobs. Sandburg focused his interests on the history and folkways of the American people. His poetry often celebrates American people, places, and events. In addition, Sandburg wrote a multivolumed biography of Abraham Lincoln and won the Pulitzer Prize in history in 1940.

Use Reading Skills

Identify Author's Purpose An author writes with a purpose in mind. The main purposes are to inform, entertain, reflect, and persuade. The style of writing often reflects the purpose. A writer will use a news article or research report to inform. A writer may use a poem or short story to entertain. As you read "Paul Bunyan of the North Woods," use a chart to keep track of details related to the author's purpose.

Before Reading

Identify the author's purpose, the type of writing he or she uses, and the ideas he or she wants to communicate.

During Reading

Gather ideas that the author communicates to readers.

After Reading

Summarize the ideas the author communicates. Explain how these ideas help fulfill the author's purpose.

Preview Vocabulary

ap•pa•ri•tion (a' pə ri´ shən) *n.*, strange figure that appears suddenly

shanty (shan´ tē) *n.*, shack; hut

Common Core State Standards

Reading Literature
RL.1

Writing
W.9

Language
L.6

Words in Use

Preview Vocabulary
apparition, 816
shanty, 816

Selection Words
amid, 816
pillar, 816
intermarried, 816

Teaching Words
lumberjacks, 814
isolated, 814
exaggeration, 814
genres, 814
folkways, 814
multivolumed, 814

anecdotal, 817
memorabilia, 821

KEY TERMS

TALL TALE, 814
FOLK TALE, 814
HYPERBOLE, 814
UNDERSTATEMENT, 814
NARRATOR, 817
PUN, 817
TONE, 821
INTRODUCTION, 821

PAUL BUNYAN OF THE NORTH WOODS

A Tall Tale by Carl Sandburg

Paul is old as the hills, young as the alphabet.

Teach the Selection

Summary

The writer, Carl Sandburg, considers the origin of Paul Bunyan stories and recounts their many variations. The tall tales in which Paul Bunyan gave a winter party for his Seven Axmen and Paul's battle with the ravenous mosquitoes are recounted. Sandburg tells the story of Benny, Paul's ox—how he grew so large and that his appetite led to his end.

 **MIRRORS & WINDOWS** The Mirrors & Windows questions at the end of this selection focus on the theme of hero appeal. Before reading the story, ask students who some of their favorite heroes are, real or fictional. What draws them to these figures? Why do stories of heroic action stand the test of time?

815

Program Resources

Planning and Assessment
Program Planning Guide, Selection Lesson Plan
E-Lesson Planner
Assessment Guide, Lesson Test
ExamView

Technology Tools
Interactive Student Text on CD
Visual Teaching Package
Audio Library
mirrorsandwindows.com

Meeting the Standards
Folk Literature: Unit 8, Directed Reading, pp. 69–72

Differentiating Instruction
English Language Learners, Identify Author's Purpose, pp. 214–220

Use Reading Skills

Identify Author's Purpose Remind students that the ability to identify the author's purpose is an important reading skill. Have students pause here to discuss what they believe the author's purpose in writing this selection is. Model a question such as: "What does the author's description of Paul Bunyan as 'an apparition easing the hours of men amid axes and trees, saws, and lumber' hint to the reader about his purpose?" **A**

Analyze Literature

Hyperbole Explain to students that hyperbole is exaggeration used for effect. Have students make a list of the example of hyperbole in this selection such as the description of the granite floor in this section. How does this description qualify as a hyperbole? **B**

Science Connection

Modern-Day Logging The logging industry has, unfortunately, many negative impacts on the environment. The harvesting of the timber itself disrupts the structure of woodland species, and the loss of shade can alter the temperature of streams, which affects the life living in them. The machinery used in modern logging also has a large impact. Roads must often be built in order to transport the equipment, causing habitat fragmentation, and the use of this large equipment can cause landslides and soil erosion. Large machinery uses oil that can cause pollution. All of these factors result in a degraded habitat.

A ho made Paul Bunyan, who gave him birth as a myth, who joked him into life as the Master Lumberjack, who fashioned him forth as an <u>apparition</u> easing the hours of men amid axes and trees, saws and lumber? The people, the bookless people, they made Paul and had him alive long before he got into the books for those who read. He grew up in <u>shanties</u>, around the hot stoves of winter, among socks and mittens drying, in the smell of tobacco smoke and the roar of laughter mocking the outside weather. And some of Paul came overseas in wooden bunks below decks in sailing vessels. And some of Paul is old as the hills, young as the alphabet.

The Pacific Ocean froze over in the winter of the Blue Snow and Paul Bunyan had long teams of oxen hauling regular white snow over from China. This was the winter **B** Paul gave a party to the Seven Axmen. Paul fixed a granite[1] floor sunk two hundred feet deep for them to dance on. Still, it tipped and tilted as the dance went on. And because the Seven Axmen refused to take off their hobnailed[2] boots, the sparks from the nails of their dancing feet lit up the place so that Paul didn't light the kerosene[3] lamps. No women being on the Big Onion river at that time the Seven Axmen had to dance with each other, the one left over in each set taking Paul as a partner. The commotion of the dancing that night brought on an earthquake and the Big Onion river moved over three counties to the east.

One year when it rained from St. Patrick's Day till the Fourth of July, Paul Bunyan got disgusted because his celebration on the Fourth was spoiled. He dived into Lake Superior and swam to where a solid pillar of water was coming down. He dived under this pillar, swam up into it and climbed with powerful swimming strokes, was gone about

> **The Pacific Ocean froze over in the winter of the Blue Snow and Paul Bunyan had long teams of oxen hauling regular white snow over from China.**

an hour, came splashing down, and as the rain stopped, he explained, "I turned the thing off." This is told in the Big North Woods and on the Great Lakes, with many particulars.

Two mosquitoes lighted on one of Paul Bunyan's oxen, killed it, ate it, cleaned the bones, and sat on a grub shanty picking their teeth as Paul came along. Paul sent to Australia for two special bumblebees to kill these mosquitoes. But the bees and the mosquitoes intermarried; their children had stingers on both ends. And things kept getting worse till Paul brought a big boatload of sorghum[4] up from Louisiana and while all the bee mosquitoes were eating at the sweet sorghum he floated them down to the Gulf of Mexico. They got so fat that it was easy to drown them all between New Orleans and Galveston.[5]

1. **granite.** Very hard rock
2. **hobnailed.** Nailed with hobnails, short large-headed nails used to attach the sole of the shoe
3. **kerosene.** Flammable oil used for fuel
4. **sorghum.** Tropical grass grown and harvested to produce grain or syrup
5. **Galveston.** City in Texas on the Gulf of Mexico

ap·pa·ri·tion (a' pə ri´ shən) *n.*, strange figure that appears suddenly

shanty (shan´ tē) *n.*, shack, hut

Reading Proficiency

Students will benefit from hearing the story read aloud. After the students have listened to the story, discuss what traits Paul Bunyan had that made him a hero to the pioneers and why. Model a comment such as: "They might have admired his concern for those around them, exemplified in his Fourth of July party efforts, since pioneers had to work together to survive and prosper. Then have students read through the story on their own.

Research Skills

Scientific Research

In the tall tales, Paul Bunyan was said to have created many environmental changes due to his actions and adventures. For example, the footsteps of Paul and his blue ox, Benny, are said to have formed the Great Lakes. Using the library and the Internet, have students research the science behind these natural phenomena. They should record their findings in a one- or two-page paper.

Paul logged on the Little Gimlet in Oregon one winter. The cookstove at that camp covered an acre of ground. They fastened the side of a hog on each snowshoe and four men used to skate on the griddle[6] while the cook flipped the pancakes. The eating table was three miles long; elevators carried the cakes to the ends of the table where boys on bicycles rode back and forth on a path down the center of the table dropping the cakes where called for.

Benny, the Little Blue Ox of Paul Bunyan, grew two feet every time Paul looked at him, when a youngster. The barn was gone one morning and they found it on Benny's back: he grew out of it in a night. One night he kept pawing and bellowing for more pancakes, till there were two hundred men at the cook-shanty stove trying to keep him fed. About breakfast time Benny broke loose, tore down the cook-shanty, ate all the pancakes piled up for the loggers' breakfast. And after that Benny made his mistake: he ate a red hot stove; and that finished him. This is only one of the hot-stove stories told in the North Woods. ❖

---

6. **griddle.** Heavy, flat metal plate that is heated and used for cooking

 What heroes appeal to you? What qualities do they have that you find especially appealing? Why do stories about heroes remain popular?

Find Meaning

1. Look back at the narrator's opening question. What answer is given in the passage?
2. (a) What freezes over in the winter of the Blue Snow? (b) What threatens to spoil Paul's Fourth of July celebration? (c) How does Paul solve this problem?
3. How does Paul get rid of the bee mosquitoes?
4. (a) Who is Benny? (b) How fast does Benny grow? (c) What kills Benny?

Make Judgments

5. (a) Why does Sandburg include the introductory paragraph? (b) What does he mean by the "bookless people"? (c) What does he mean when he says that "Paul is old as the hills, young as the alphabet"?
6. (a) How effective is the use of an anecdotal style of writing in this selection? (b) A pun is a play on words. Explain the play on words in the phrase "hot-stove stories" in the last line of the paragraph about Benny. What is the double meaning? (Keep in mind that in frontier America, people often sat around a fire or stove in the evening, spinning yarns.)

 Some students may say that real-life heroes, such as police officers and firefighters, appeal to them. They may find the qualities of bravery, honesty, and service to others appealing. Students might say that these stories remain popular because they continue to inspire their listeners and readers.

Find Meaning

1. American people created Paul Bunyan before his stories were written down for the literate.
2. (a) The Pacific Ocean. (b) Rain. (c) Paul swims up a pillar of water and turns off the water at the source.
3. He drowns them in the Gulf of Mexico.
4. (a) Paul's blue ox, Benny. (b) Two feet each time Paul looks at him. (c) Benny eats a red-hot stove and dies.

Make Judgments

5. (a) Sandburg might include this to give the impression of a very old tale. (b) "Bookless people" could be people who are illiterate, can't afford books, or prefer oral tradition. (c) It could mean that he's been around as long as the hills have been, but only written about since the alphabet.
6. (a) Students should give reasons to support their opinions. (b) The play on the words "hot-stove story" is both the activity of sitting around listening to stories and Benny eating a hot stove.

Writing Skills

Legend

Challenge students to become legends by casting themselves as the protagonists of their own tall tales. Ask them to choose a natural landmark or phenomenon from their current region or the region of their homeland to explain. Then have students create a preliminary character sketch, including character traits that build on their actual makeup and that would aid the creation of their chosen natural occurrence. Allow them ample time to develop their prewriting into a complete tale, and have volunteers share their work with the class.

Some historians believe that Joe Fournier, a French-Canadian logger born around 1845, was the man on whom the Paul Bunyan stories are based. In "The Ole Feller Recollects How Joe Fournier Became Paul Bunyan," **D. Laurence Rogers** discusses the possible man behind the myth.

The Ole Feller Recollects How Joe Fournier Became Paul Bunyan

An Essay by D. Laurence Rogers

Ever think Paul Bunyan may have been a real, living man—not just a fictional character? Some academic skeptics contend that he was a hoax and ignore him as part of our national folklore. We don't agree with those so-called experts. Here's our side of the story, so you can judge for yourself about Joe and how he became the model for Paul.

There was a timber hewer and logging camp boss whose real life exploits mirrored early Paul Bunyan tales. Fabian "Joe" Fournier was the tough timber boss whose fame grew into fantastic stories.

Nobody ever heard of a lumberjack in those days. The timber hewers were called "fellers," because that's what they did: fell trees. Maine, Minnesota, Wisconsin, and even California claim Paul Bunyan, but Michigan, where he won fame, was his real home. Joe Fournier was born in Quebec, Canada, about 1845, and lived in the village of Bangor, or Banks, now part of Bay City, Michigan, with upriver Saginaw then the world's busiest lumber area and headquarters of Saginaw pine country.

Fournier's fame was forged by his exploits as he ranged the northern Michigan woods, in Saginaw River pine country and in the AuSable River region, from about 1865 to 1875.

Fournier, also called "Saginaw Joe," was the foreman, the boss logger, the big feller in the woods. The foreman cruised the property to pick the woods for the next day's cutting. Often he would be planning for the following day's work while the rest of the fellers had been in bed for hours. Then he'd be the first on his feet, sometimes at four o'clock in the blackness and chill of the morning. Then he'd try to be everywhere at the same time, keeping an eye on everything. He called the tune and if it wasn't right he'd have to answer to the camp owner.

Joe came to Michigan from Quebec after the Civil War when President Andrew Johnson opened up the state at a buck and a quarter an acre. Things weren't so good in Quebec, with the best jobs paying only about four dollars a month from the local "notaire," a kind of a boss clerk who worked for the landowner. Down in Saginaw country,

Ⓐ

Teach the Connection

Analyze Literature
Legend Remind students that a legend is a story rooted in the past that is often based on important real events or characters. Some parts of a legend can become exaggerated over time, creating tall tales. What characteristics of this legendary figure could have been exaggerated into characteristics of Paul Bunyan?

Cultural Connection
French Canadians In the nineteenth century, waves of French Canadians immigrated to the United States seeking better work situations. So many came that they created villages known as "Little Canada." Their impact on the United States is significant. They participated in the industrial movement, and a French-Canadian immigrant introduced the idea of the credit union. New words, such as *shanty* and *toboggan*, with French-Canadian origins made their way into the English language. **Ⓐ**

Common Core State Standards

Reading Literature
RL.5, RL.9

Writing
W.4

Language
L.6

Words in Use

"The Ole Feller Recollects How Joe Fournier Became Paul Bunyan"

Selection Words

skeptics, 818	**peril,** 819
contend, 818	**treacherous,** 819
hoax, 818	
hewer, 818	
exploits, 818	
maverick, 819	

timber hewers received a dollar a day, more than six times as much as they could earn in Quebec.

The smaller French Canadians became voyageurs,[1] paddling canoes and helping fur-trading companies get richer. Some liked being coureurs de bois (wood runners), free-lance traders and trappers. Many struck up friendships with Indians who helped them trap beaver. The big, strong French Canadians like Joe became timber hewers in the winter and worked in the mills, on the docks, or in the shipyards in the summer.

Joe was big enough, all right, standin' near six feet tall and weighin' 180 pounds, but he sure wasn't the giant in those tall stories they came out with later. The story tellers got crazy in the head—had him at twelve or thirteen feet tall and 888 pounds. Talk about tall stories! Most folks in Joe's times averaged only a little over five feet high, so they did all look up to him. But not that far up! **B**

Joe was sort of good looking for the mean cuss he was. He had a broad face, strong chin, wide-set eyes, and curly hair, but no beard or moustache as the drawings in the Paul Bunyan books always show.

Though uneducated, Joe was brilliant; a camp boss needed to be smart as well as tough to control a crew of maverick timber-fellers.

Some things about Joe were almost unnatural. Even other loggers marveled at the size of his hands, half again larger than most men's with thumbs as long as the average fingers. Those huge meat hooks could handle an axe like a matchstick. Strangest of all, but absolutely true, Joe had a double row of teeth. Two complete sets, uppers and lowers—cuspids, bicuspids and molars, as a dentist would say. No logger was better equipped to chow on stringy salt pork or bite hunks from wooden bar rails. More on that

weird habit Joe was noted for later.

Joe had sloping shoulders that fooled people about his strength, which some say was equal to three or four ordinary men. He was double-jointed, which made him very agile. Joe at age nine could climb the frame of a barn and catch a squirrel, or so they said.

That kind of speed and strength paid off for a boss logger in the North Woods, where danger awaited. You know what a widow-maker is? That's when an 80 or 100 foot-high white pine comes down the wrong way and clunks a logger on the head, making his wife—if he has one—a widow. Peril to life and limb lurked on the icy roads with a horse-drawn team and a shifting skid of sixteen footers[2] on the travois.[3] Many a river hog's luck ran out in treacherous jams on fast flowing spring streams. One river driver called for a double-bit axe and took his pal's leg off at the knee to get him out of a jam. Saved his life, though. Other river hogs weren't so "lucky," and their bodies, swallowed by the icy current, were never found. The run to the booming ground kept the drivers hopping on a river solid with logs from bank to bank. The rafting for the trip to the mill was easy.

When Joe first got to Saginaw Country he was the top feller in the woods. He could handle a double-bit axe or his end of a crosscut saw and, as the loggers used to say, make the pines whimper. When Joe was on the team of fellers the "timber-r-r-rs" echoed as fast as though two or three teams were working. He could flip logs with a peavey[4] and find the key log in a tangle on

---

1. **voyageurs.** World travelers
2. **skid of sixteen footers.** Load of sixteen-foot logs
3. **travois.** Type of sled first used by Plains Indians that was connected to the horses by two trailing poles with a platform or net for the load
4. **peavey.** Lumber cutter's lever that has a hook and a spike at one end

Use Reading Skills
Evaluate Author's Purpose Now that students are able to identify the author's purpose in writing a selection, have them evaluate the author's purpose. Has the author of "The Ole Feller Recollects How Joe Fournier Became Paul Bunyan" succeeded in his purpose? Model a question such as: "Does this description of Joe Fournier succeed in being informative as well as entertaining?"

Analyze Literature
Eponym Explain to students that an eponym is a person, real or imaginary, from whom something takes, or is said to take, its name. Have students locate the eponym *Bon Jean*, found on this page, and explain how it came about. **A**

the river to free a jam faster than any other river hog. Good timber was never splintered with dynamite when Joe was on the drive. He also was a topnotch cruiser who could spot and lay-out a stand of uppers[5] real quick. And his gangs of fellers, butters, buckers, and skidders always got their hundred logs each day. He made sure it was a full day—dawn to dusk.

Joe was tough on the camp rules: "No fighting on the river; no drinking on the river; and to bed at nine o'clock." But he freely joined in when the shanty boys were on the deacon's seat, with the camboose roarin' and the dulcey twangin',[6] for a song or two. Nobody ever got him to tie on the hanky, but Joe would jog right in there with 'em all. Yup, the shanty boys liked ole' Joe, and worked hard for him. He sure was worth his seventy-five greenbacks a month.

The name Bunyan comes from a French Canadian hero of the 1837 Papineau Rebellion,[7] "Bon Jean," whom loggers had admired for years. "Bon Jean" means "Good John" or "Brave John," and is pronounced in French something like "Bone, yaahn." The name first was used by writers as Bonion then Bunyon and finally, Bunyan. Loggers often called a strong, tough woodsman a "Bon Jean." By adding Paul, a common French name, our hero Joe Fournier became Paul Bunyan. We've always believed Fournier's feats were exaggerated and other exploits added to create Paul Bunyan. **A**

When you read more I think you'll agree: this real timber feller was hewn[8] into a real big feller—Paul Bunyan, a legend much larger than life—by storytellers and writers using their imaginations.

Fournier was a great logger—and brawler—until treachery ended his fighting days. He was murdered on the Third Street dock in Bay City the night of November 7, 1875. The villain surprised him in the dark behind his back and caved in his skull with a ship carpenter's mallet.

Strange as it may seem, that murder helped to begin one of America's greatest legends. You see, all the news about the murder and then about the trial of Blinky Robertson, who did the deed, got lots of people talking about Joe Fournier.

Tales were told of Joe's amazing strength and how he saved many of his men in tight spots in the woods and on the river. The amount of timber cut by Joe's crews seemed to grow as the stories were told and retold. Then the stories about Joe got all mixed up with other tales old timers told about the original Bon Jean, the big Frenchman who fought the Queen's troops in Canada and then headed a logging crew. Pretty soon you couldn't tell Bon Jean from Fournier.

As the years passed, it became impossible to separate the tales about Joe from those about Paul. Around thousands of campfires the tales were repeated over the years, and each storyteller added a little to the size of Paul Bunyan, the amount of timber his crews cut, and his exploits, making up most of it as they went along.

More than thirty years after Joe Fournier's murder a newspaper-man who had heard the tales as a boy in the lumber camps sat down to write the story for the first time. ❖

---

5. **lay-out a stand of uppers.** Chop down a grove of standing trees
6. **deacon's seat...camboose roarin'...dulcey twangin'.** A deacon's seat is a bench where the "shanty boys" might sit when they wanted to play their music; a camboose was a shanty, or shack, at the lumbering camp; "dulcey" refers to a dulcimer, a stringed instrument shaped like a trapezoid, played with light hammers held in the hands.
7. **Papineau Rebellion.** Rebellion of the French Canadians against the British government of Canada
8. **hewn.** Past participle of *hew*, meaning to chop down with an ax or to give form to something by chopping at it with an ax

Differentiated Instruction

English Language Learning
Giving students learning English a definition and context sentence may help them with unfamiliar words in the story.

hoax—trick played to deceive people, 818. *Dad set up a big hoax to trick Mom on April Fool's Day.*
exploits—act or deed, especially a brilliant or heroic one, 818. *Joey was famous in our town; his exploits were always talked about.*

lurked—laid in wait, 819. *The cat lurked behind the bush and waited for the mouse to come out of its hole.*
topnotch—first rate, excellent, 820. *Sarah is a topnotch basketball player.*

TEXT TO TEXT CONNECTION

Both Carl Sandburg's story and D. Laurence Rogers's essay deal with the legend of Paul Bunyan. Compare and contrast what each writer presents. How likely is it that Sandburg's retelling of the Paul Bunyan tall tale is based on stories about Fournier? Explain your answer.

AFTER READING

Analyze Literature

Hyperbole Hyperbole is exaggeration used for effect. In "Paul Bunyan of the North Woods," there are exaggerations of size and actions. Make a chart like the one here. On it, list at least eight examples of hyperbole in the selection. Next to each example, explain how the hyperbole contributes to the tone of the tall tale.

Hyperbole	How It Contributes to the Tone
• Paul had teams of oxen hauling regular white snow over from China.	• exaggeration of action adds to amusement
• The eating table was three miles long.	• exaggeration of size gives a comparison for the size of Paul Bunyan

Extend Understanding

Writing Options

Creative Writing Write a short **tall tale** with Paul Bunyan as the main character. Make sure to explain how Paul Bunyan influenced or interacted with a natural event. Include several examples of hyperbole as well. Include additional characters such as Benny the Little Blue Ox or the other loggers. You may also want to illustrate your tall tale.

Expository Writing Write a brief **expository essay** in which you compare and contrast "Paul Bunyan of the North Woods" with "The Ole Feller Recollects How Joe Fournier Became Paul Bunyan." State your position in the introduction. Then in the body use examples from both selections to support your position. End with a concluding statement that summarizes your position and main points.

Lifelong Learning

Write a Journal Entry Use the Internet or library resources to research the lives of pioneer Americans. Find out how they lived and worked. Research what their social customs were, what their children's education was like, the kinds of work they performed, and the tools they used. Then pretend to be one of the pioneers. Use your research to write a historically accurate journal entry explaining what your daily life is like.

Critical Literacy

Conduct an Interview Invite a classmate to interview you about a particular event in your family history. Explain how stories about the event have been passed down over many generations. Then interview your classmate about an event in his or her family history. Share old photographs or family memorabilia, if possible. Together, discuss the importance of remembering the past. Summarize your interview and discussion for the class.

 Go to **www.mirrorsandwindows.com** for more.

THE OLE FELLER RECOLLECTS / PAUL BUNYAN OF THE NORTH WOODS **821**

Review the Selection

Text-to-Text Connection
Answers: Sandburg presents the story of Paul Bunyan as a tall tale that grew as it was repeated, while Rogers claims that Paul Bunyan was really Joe Fournier, a Canadian "feller." Student responses will vary, but should contain examples from the selections.

Analyze Literature

Hyperbole *Answer:* Examples of hyperbole might include the following: "Paul fixed a granite floor sunk two hundred feet deep for them to dance on"; "the sparks from the nails of their dancing feet lit up the place so that Paul didn't light the kerosene lamps"; "the commotion of the dancing . . . brought on an earthquake . . ."; "it rained from St. Patrick's Day till the Fourth of July"; turning off the pillar of water in Lake Superior; "two mosquitoes lighted on one of Paul Bunyan's oxen, killed it, ate it, cleaned the bones"; and Benny growing two feet every time Paul looked at him. Students should include examples of hyperbole (as noted above) in their charts. The examples give the tone a light-hearted feeling.

Rubrics for Writing Options
You can adapt this as a checklist for students to use as they write.

Creative Writing
☐ Does it explain how Paul Bunyan influenced or interacted with a natural event?
☐ Does it use hyperbole and other characters?

Expository Writing
☐ Does the introduction clearly state the student's position?
☐ Do the body paragraphs use examples from both selections to support the position?
☐ Does the conclusion summarize the position?

THE OLD FELLER RECOLLECTS / PAUL BUNYAN OF THE NORTH WOODS **821**

Preview the Selection

DIRECTED READING

At a Glance
Directed Reading
- Reading Level: Moderate
- Difficulty Consideration: Spanish terminology
- Ease Factors: Humor, suspense

Objectives
Studying this lesson will enable students to
- use reading strategies such as analyzing cause and effect
- define *mood* and recognize the effect of this literary technique in the selection
- explain how the background of Guadalupe Baca-Vaughn relates to this selection
- appreciate a traditional story

Launch the Lesson
Before reading "The Souls in Purgatory," ask students to share experiences of when adults or family members tried to "help" them in ways they might have found embarrassing. The class could then discuss what these experiences had in common.

BEFORE READING

Build Background
Cultural Context Mexico has a rich heritage of folk tales. The folk tales often include communication with or assistance from spiritual beings. Many people in the country are very religious. They pray to God, to the saints, and sometimes to the souls in purgatory for assistance with everyday matters.

Reader's Context Have you had any experience in your life when someone bragged that you could do things that you knew you could not do? How did you handle the situation?

Set Purpose
Skim the text to make predictions about what will happen. Read to determine how accurate your predictions are.

Analyze Literature
Mood The **mood,** or atmosphere, of a selection is the feeling or emotion the writer creates in a literary work. As you read, identify the mood of the story. See if the mood changes and, if so, why.

Meet the Author
Guadalupe Baca-Vaughn was born in Las Vegas, New Mexico, on August 3, 1905. Her family traced its roots back more than four hundred years to the original Spanish settlers of the area. Baca-Vaughn taught elementary and secondary school in New Mexico for over thirty-three years. Her subjects included Spanish arts and crafts, Spanish folklore, and regular educational courses. She was the president of the New Mexico Folklore Society. Baca-Vaughn died in her home in New Mexico on January 8, 2001.

Use Reading Skills
Analyze Cause and Effect In fiction, writers often explain *why* an event takes place. Such an event is an effect; the *why* is a cause. Understanding cause-effect relationships is vital to grasping the meaning of a story. Sometimes a single cause has several effects, and an effect can have several causes. As you read "The Souls in Purgatory," use a chart to keep track of causes and effects.

Cause:	Effect:
An old woman wants her niece to be safely married so the old woman can die in peace.	The old woman lies to a gentleman about some of the girl's abilities.

Preview Vocabulary
in•ter•ces•sion (in' tər se´ shən) *n.*, request, appeal, or prayer on behalf of another person

dumb•found•ed (dəm faůnd´ əd) *adj.*, speechless with amazement; astonished

em•broi•der (im broi´ dər) *v.*, sew together with needlework; decorate with needlework

re•proach (ri prōch´) *v.*, criticize; blame

vi•brant (vī´ brənt) *adj.*, bright; energetic; alive-looking

(Opposite) *Vanitas.* Inez Nickmans.

Words in Use

Preview Vocabulary	Selection Words	Teaching Words
intercession, 824	obedient, 824	purgatory, 822
dumbfounded, 824	industrious, 824	compassion, 827
embroider, 826	scheme, 824	
reproach, 826	consent, 826	
vibrant, 826	wringing, 826	

KEY TERMS

Common Core State Standards
Reading Literature
RL.1

Writing
W.9

Language
L.6

THE SOULS IN PURGATORY

A Folk Tale retold by Guadalupe Baca-Vaughn

"Don't sell yourself short," the old lady replied with twinkling eyes.

823

Summary
The story tells of an old lady who was concerned about what would happen to her niece after the woman died. The aunt finds out about a rich merchant and tells him about her niece. The man tests the niece by asking her to spin, sew, and embroider. The girl can do none of these things but is helped by three souls from Purgatory. Their only request is that she invite them to her wedding. The girl worries about what will happen when the merchant finds she can't spin, sew, or embroider. But at the wedding, the souls turn up in an unexpected way and solve her problem.

MIRRORS & WINDOWS The Mirrors & Windows questions at the end of this selection focus on the theme of helping others. Before reading the story, ask students if anyone has ever intended to help them but actually made the situation more difficult. How do people show compassion toward each other? Is it always a positive, helpful action?

Program Resources

Planning and Assessment
Program Planning Guide, Selection Lesson Plan
E-Lesson Planner
Assessment Guide, Lesson Test
ExamView

Technology Tools
Interactive Student Text on CD
Visual Teaching Package
Audio Library
mirrorsandwindows.com

Meeting the Standards
Folk Literature: Unit 8, Directed Reading,
pp. 73–78

Differentiating Instruction
Advanced Students, Cultural Context Activity,
pp. 52–53

Use Reading Skills

Analyze Cause and Effect Ask students to identify the causes of several of the old lady's and the girl's actions. Model a response by suggesting one cause: "The old lady was worried about her niece (effect) because the girl was shy and timid (cause)." **A**

Cultural Connection

Afterlife Many ancient cultures believed that dead souls must be purified before entering heaven. For example, the Egyptians carefully prepared their dead and wrote spells and rituals on the walls of the tombs that must be completed before the soul could enter the realm of the gods. Purgatory as an actual place arose from medieval Christianity. In Buddhism, souls are reborn into other temporary forms depending on their actions in their former lives (karma). **B**

"Please," she prayed, "don't let my aunt do something rash to embarrass us both."

Si es verdad, allá va,
Si es mentira, queda urdida.

(If it be true, so it is.
If it be false, so it be.)

A There was once an old lady who had raised a niece since she was a tiny baby. She had taught the girl to be good, obedient, and industrious, but the girl was very shy and timid, and spent much time praying, especially to the Souls in Purgatory.

As the girl grew older and very beautiful, the old woman began to worry that when she died her niece would be left all alone in the world, a world which her niece saw only through innocent eyes. The old lady prayed daily to all the saints in heaven for their <u>intercession</u> to Our Lord that He might send some good man who would fall in love with her niece and marry her…then she could die in peace.

As it happens, the old woman did chores for a *comadre*[1] who had a rooming house. Among her tenants there was a seemingly rich merchant who one day said that he would like to get married if he could find a nice quiet girl who knew how to keep house, and be a good wife and mother to his children when they came.

The old lady opened her ears and began to smile and scheme in her mind, for she could imagine her niece married to the nice gentleman. She told the merchant that he could find all that he was looking for in her niece, who was a jewel, a piece of gold, and so gifted that she could even catch birds while they were flying!

The gentleman became interested and said that he would like to meet the girl, and would go to her house the next day.

The old woman ran home as fast as she could, she appeared to be flying. When she got home all out of breath, she called her niece and told her to straighten up the house and get herself ready for the next day, as there was a gentleman who would be calling. She told her to be sure to wash her hair and brush it until it shone like the sun, and to put on her best dress, for in this meeting her future was at stake.

B The poor timid girl was <u>dumbfounded</u>. She went to her room and knelt before her favorite *retablo*[2] of the Souls in Purgatory. "Please," she prayed, "don't let my aunt do something rash to embarrass us both."

The next day she obediently prepared herself for the meeting. When the merchant arrived, he asked her if she could spin.[3] "Spin?" answered the old woman, while the poor embarrassed girl stood by with bowed head. "Spin! The hanks[4] disappear so fast you would think she was drinking them like water."

1. **comadre.** Spanish word that refers to a godmother or to a female friend
2. **retablo.** Wooden panel painted or carved with religious pictures, often seen in Mexican homes, especially in the past (Spanish)
3. **spin.** Twist raw fibers of wool, silk, or cotton so they form a continuous yarn or thread
4. **hanks.** Bundles of raw fibers that are spun into yarn or thread

in·ter·ces·sion (in′ tər se´ shən) *n.*, request, appeal, or prayer on behalf of another person

dumb·found·ed (dəm faünd´ əd) *adj.*, speechless with amazement; astonished

---

Differentiated Instruction

Enrichment

Students will gain an understanding of universal concepts and shared notions by comparing "The Souls in Purgatory" to other tales that share its elements. Discuss with students the similarities between this selection and stories like "Snow White," "Rumpelstiltskin," and "Cinderella." Ask them to theorize how specific plot details, characters, and themes were composed in distinct and distant cultures. Challenge them to research this phenomenon and report their findings to the class.

The merchant left three hanks of linen to be spun by the following day. "What have you done Tía?"[5] the poor girl asked. "You know I can't spin!" "Don't sell yourself short," the old lady replied with twinkling eyes. "Where is your faith in God, the Souls in Purgatory? You pray to them every day. They will help you. Just wait and see!" Sobbing, the girl ran to her room and knelt down beside her bed and began to pray, often raising her head to the *retablo* of the Souls in Purgatory which hung on the wall beside her bed. After she quieted down, she thought she heard a soft sound behind her. She turned and saw three beautiful ghosts dressed in white, smiling at her. "Do not be concerned," they said, "we will help you in gratitude for all the good you have done for us." Saying this, each one took a hank of linen and in a wink spun the linen into thread as fine as hair.

The following day when the merchant came, he was astonished to see the beautiful linen, and was very pleased. "Didn't I tell you, Sir?" said the old lady with pride and joy. The gentleman asked the girl if she could sew. Before the surprised girl could answer, the old aunt cried. "Sew? Of course she can sew. Her sewing is like the cherries in the mouth of a dragon." The merchant then left a piece of the finest linen to be made into three shirts. The poor girl cried bitterly, but her aunt told her not to worry, that her devotion to the Poor Souls would get her out of this one too, as they had shown how much they loved her on the previous day.

5. *Tía.* "Aunt" (Spanish)

Teach the Selection

Analyze Literature
Simile Point out the old aunt's words, "Her sewing is like the cherries in the mouth of a dragon." Discuss the possible meaning of the simile. Then have students suggest other figurative language with the same meaning. **C**

Use Reading Skills
Activate Prior Knowledge Explain to students that folk tales, or elements of folk tales, sometimes cross cultures and eras. Ask them what other folk tales come to mind as they read this part of the selection. What universal ideas or themes do these similar elements evoke? What does the universality of these ideas and themes reveal about human nature?

TEACHING NOTE
Summarize
Have students read the selection on their own. Then have students work with a partner. Partners should take turns rereading parts of the selection. After each reading, tell students to stop and summarize or retell to their partner what they've read.

Grammar Skills

Infinitives

Almost at once the old woman went to her comadre to tell her the good news, and to ask her to help get ready for the wedding.

Reminds students that an infinitive is a verbal consisting of the word *to* plus a verb in its simplest form. In the above quotation, *to tell* and *to ask* are infinitives. An infinitive may function as a noun, adjective, or adverb, so it may be a subject, direct object, adjective, or adverb in a sentence. Point out that *to tell* and *to ask* are both objects of the verb *went*.

Analyze Literature

Mood Have students describe several places in the story where the mood changes. For example, at first the girl is miserable, but the mood changes when the ghosts offer to help her. Encourage students to point out specific examples of mood change.

Analyze Literature

Motivation Discuss with students the aunt's motivation for promising the merchant results of which her niece is incapable. Is the promise reckless or wise? Does her motivation warrant the responsibility she has placed upon her niece's shoulders? Challenge students to describe other situations in literature and/or their own lives in which someone has created a challenge for another, motivated by their desire for the other's welfare.

The three ghosts were waiting for the girl beside her bed when she went into her room, crying miserably. "Don't cry, little girl," they said. "We will help you again, for we know your aunt, and she knows what she is doing and why."

The ghosts went to work cutting and snipping and sewing. In a flash they had three beautiful shirts finished with the finest stitches and the tiniest seams.

The next morning when the gentleman came to see if the girl had finished the shirts, he could not believe his eyes. "They are lovely, they seem to have been made in heaven," he said.

This time the merchant left a vest of rare satin to be <u>embroidered</u>. He thought he would try this girl for the third and last time. The girl cried desperately, and could not even <u>reproach</u> her aunt. She had decided that she would not ask any more favors of the Souls. She went to her room and lay across the bed and cried and cried. When she finally sat up and dried her tears, she saw the three ghosts smiling at her. "We will help you again, but this time we have a condition, and that is that you will invite us to your wedding." "Wedding? Am I going to get married?" she asked in surprise. "Yes," they said, "and very soon."

The next day a very happy gentleman came for his vest, for he was sure that the lovely girl would have it ready for him. But he was not prepared for the beauty of the vest. The colors were <u>vibrant</u> and beautifully matched. The embroidery looked like a painting. It took his breath away. Without hesitation, he asked the old lady for her niece's hand in marriage. "For," he said, "this vest looks as if it was not touched by human hands, but by angels!"

> "Don't cry, little girl," they said. "We will help you again, for we know your aunt, and she knows what she is doing and why."

The old woman danced with joy, and could hardly contain her happiness. She gave her consent at once. The merchant left to arrange for the wedding. Wringing her hands, the poor girl cried, "But Tía, what am I going to do when he finds out that I can't do any of those things?" "Don't worry, my *Palomita*,[6] the Blessed Souls will get you out of this trouble too. You wait and see!"

Almost at once the old woman went to her *comadre* to tell her the good news, and to ask her to help get ready for the wedding. Soon everything was ready.

The poor girl did not know how to invite the Souls to her wedding. She timidly went and stood beside her bed and asked the *retablo* to come to her wedding.

The great day finally arrived. The girl looked beautiful in the gown which the merchant had brought as part of her *donas*.[7] Everyone in the village had been invited to the wedding.

---

6. **Palomita.** In Spanish, literally "little dove"; here used as a term of affection
7. **donas.** Gifts a groom gives to his bride when they marry (Spanish)

---

em·broi·der (im broi´ dər) *v.*, sew together with needlework; decorate with needlework

re·proach (ri prōch´) *v.*, criticize; blame

vi·brant (vī´ brənt) *adj.*, bright; energetic; alive-looking

Reading Skills

Evaluate an Author's Perspective

Point out that perspective is the author's attitude about the characters and/or story. Differentiate between attitude and the point of view from which the story is told (first- or third-person). Model identifying the author's perspective by analyzing the adjectives the author uses to describe a character

such as *industrious niece; twinkling eyes;* and *poor embarrassed girl.* Contrast those with phrases such as *lazy niece, cunning eyes,* and *silly girl.* As students read, have them jot down examples of how the author reveals her perspective about the characters.

During the fiesta when everyone was drinking *brindes*[8] to the bride and groom, and the music was playing, three ugly hags came to the *sala*[9] and stood waiting for the groom to come and welcome them in. One of the hags had an arm that reached to the floor and dragged; the other arm was short. The second hag was bent almost double, and had to turn her head sideways to look up. The third hag had bulging, bloodshot eyes like a lobster. "Jesús María," cried the groom. "Who are those ugly creatures?" "They are aunts of my father, whom I invited to my wedding," answered the bride, knowing quite well who they might be. The groom, being well bred, went at once to greet the ugly hags. He took them to their seats and brought them refreshments. Very casually, he asked the first hag, "Tell me, Señora,[10] why is one of your arms so long and the other one short?" "My son," she answered, "my arms are like that because I spin so much."

The groom went to his wife and said, "Go at once and tell the servants to burn your spinning wheel, and never let me see a spinning wheel in my house, never let me see you spinning ever!"

The groom went to the second hag and asked her why she was so humped over.

"My son," she replied, "I am that way from embroidering on a frame so much." The groom went to his wife and whispered, "Burn your embroidery frame at once, and never let me see you embroider another thing."

Next, the groom went to the third hag and asked, "Why are your eyes so bloodshot and bulging?" "My son, it is because I sew so much and bend over while sewing." She had hardly finished speaking when the groom went to his wife and said, "Take your needles and thread and bury them. I never want to see you sewing, never! If I see you sewing, I will divorce you and send you far away, for the wise man learns from others' painful experiences."

Well…so the Souls, in spite of being holy, can also be rascals.

Colorín, colorado,
ya mi cũento se ha acabado.
(Scarlet or ruby red,
my story has been said.) ✤

---

8. *brindes.* Offer of goodwill (Spanish)
9. *sala.* Living room or other large room for entertaining (Spanish)
10. *Señora.* "Mrs." or "Madam" (Spanish)

If someone were trying to help you and the help resulted in putting you in a dangerous or uncomfortable situation, what would you do? What does it mean to show compassion for others?

Teach the Selection

Use Reading Skills
Identify Parallel Structure
Remind students that repetition and parallel structure help readers follow a plot and know what to expect. Ask students what elements the author uses to create parallel structure. For example, the merchant asks each of the three old hags how she got that way. Ⓐ

 *Answer:* Some students might say they would ask the person to stop, or they might refuse to go along with the situation. Others might suggest asking a third person for assistance. Students might say that a show of real compassion takes into account the receiver's wants and needs.

Reading Skills

Visualize
Imagining unspoken thoughts of a story's character can aid comprehension of important plot events. Such is the case with the groom when he converses with the beneficent souls at his wedding. Some students will infer the groom's thoughts, as each soul explains that her physical deformity has been caused by the very tasks he has charged to his new wife. Others will benefit from a visual representation of these thoughts. Choose three students to assume the role of the new wife. Then, ask each one to act out the groom's imagination of her progression toward deformity caused by spinning, embroidering, and sewing. Afterward, discuss why the groom forbade his wife from ever doing these activities "again."

Review the Selection

Find Meaning

1. (a) She is obedient and timid. (b) She prays to the souls in Purgatory. (c) She lives with her aunt.
2. (a) She worries that she will die and leave her niece alone. (c) She prays that God will send a good man to look after the girl.
3. (a) Three ghosts who are souls in Purgatory help her. (b) They ask to be invited to her wedding.

Make Judgments

4. (a) The aunt probably thought the girl would not be attractive to a man on her own merits. (b) Some students might say the woman had a low opinion of her niece. Others might say the woman understood life in those times and was truly concerned for her niece's welfare.
5. (a) Some students might say the experiences were scary but turned out all right. Others might say she was relieved to get help. (b) Students might say he would feel angry and betrayed.
6. Students might agree that the woman was concerned for her niece's welfare, although her actions might have been less than ideal.

Analyze Literature

Mood *Answer:* Students should identify moods such as tense, hopeless, amusing, and happy. The chart should match each mood with examples from the story.

Find Meaning

1. (a) Describe the young girl's personality. (b) How does the young girl spend a lot of her time? (c) With whom does the young girl live?
2. (a) What situation worries the old woman as the girl grows older and more beautiful? (b) What does the old woman do about the situation?
3. (a) Who helps the girl when the gentleman asks her to spin, sew, and embroider? (b) What is the helpers' request when they say they will help her do the embroidery?

Analyze Literature

Mood The author conveys the mood of the story through dialogue as well as the setting and the characters' feelings and actions. One way to determine the mood is to take notes as you read. On a cluster chart, jot down examples of dialogue, setting, and the description of characters' actions and feelings that evoke emotion. Analyze the individual examples to determine the mood they create.

Make Judgments

4. (a) Why did the old woman think that she had to brag about things her niece could not do? (b) What does this say about the old woman's opinion of her niece?
5. (a) How would you describe the young girl's experience with the three tasks? (b) How do you think the gentleman would feel if he found out that he had been deceived?
6. Do you think the old woman was acting in the young girl's best interest? Explain your answer.

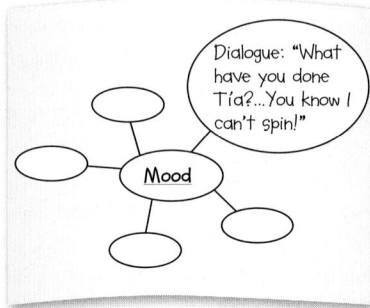

Extend Understanding

Writing Options

Creative Writing Write a **personal letter** to the three souls from the perspective of the young girl. Thank them for their efforts. Explain how their efforts have improved your life as well as your old aunt's life.

Expository Writing Write a short **literary response** discussing the mood of the story. In the introduction, tell what you think the mood is. Use the cluster chart you created to find examples that support your conclusion. Write these in the body of your essay. Explain if you think the mood changes, why you think so, and where you think it changes. Conclude with a summary and a restatement of the mood.

Critical Literacy

Hold a Panel Discussion With fellow students, discuss the actions of the girl and her aunt. Was it right of them to deceive the gentleman to get him to marry the girl? Defend your position, using eye contact, speaking rate, volume, enunciation, gestures, and conventions of language to clearly communicate your view.

Media Literacy

Compare and Contrast "The Souls in Purgatory" has many elements that are similar to the folk tale "Rumpelstiltskin." Read "Rumpelstiltskin" for the first time, or reread it if you have read it before. Compare and contrast the conflicts, characters, actions, and outcomes of these two tales.

Go to **www.mirrorsandwindows.com** for more.

Rubrics for Writing Options

You can adapt this as a checklist for students to use as they write.

Creative Writing

☐ Did the student adopt the persona of the young girl?
☐ Did the letter clearly say "thank you"?
☐ Did the letter explain how the efforts of the three Souls improved the writer's life?
☐ Did the letter explain how the efforts of the three Souls improved the aunt's life?

Expository Writing

☐ Does the introduction identify the mood of the story?
☐ Do the body paragraphs clearly present examples of the mood?
☐ Do the body paragraphs tell if mood changes? If the writer thinks the mood changes, are examples provided?
☐ Does the conclusion summarize the writer's opinion of the story's mood?

Gatored Community

A Legend by Barbara and David P. Mikkelson

Build Background

Cultural Context Urban legends are a type of folklore with certain characteristics. First, they appear mysteriously and spread in various forms. Next, they contain elements of humor or horror. The "horror" often punishes someone who ignores society's conventions. Third, urban legends make good stories. Finally, they do not have to be false, although most are. Some have a basis in fact, but over repeated tellings, they become more and more outlandish.

Reader's Context What stories have you heard that might be urban legends?

Set Purpose

Think about what you know about alligators, sewers, and New York City. Predict whether the claim will turn out to be true or false.

Analyze Literature

Tone A writer or speaker's attitude toward the subject or the reader is the writer's **tone.** A writer may have a tone of wonder, disgust, anger, awe, pride, or joy. As you read, decide what you think the tone of the selection is.

Meet the Authors

Barbara and **David P. Mikkelson** are a husband and wife team whose hobby is to collect urban legends and to investigate the truth behind each legend. David is a self-proclaimed public affairs officer for the mythical San Fernando Valley Folklore Society. He and his wife have developed an Internet site, Urban Legends Reference Pages, that provides an extensive collection of popular legends in various categories.

Use Reading Skills

Analyze Text Organization A piece of writing can be organized in different ways. Often persuasive writing is organized into arguments and counterarguments. An argument is a statement of a position that is supported by facts and other details. A counterargument is the opposing position, also supported by facts and other details. As you read "Gatored Community," try to identify the arguments and counterarguments.

Preview Vocabulary

in·glo·ri·ous (in' glôr´ ē əs) *adj.,* shameful; lacking fame or honor

ver·i·ta·ble (ver´ ə tə bəl) *adj.,* being in fact the thing named; not false or imaginary

prem·is·es (pre´ məs əs) *pl. n.,* area of land; grounds

se·rene·ly (sə rēn lē) *adv.,* calmly

in·fes·ta·tion (in' fes´ tā shən) *n.,* invasion or troublesome spread of a harmful pest

At a Glance
Directed Reading
- Reading Level: Challenging
- Difficulty Considerations: Structure, vocabulary
- Ease Factor: Author's style

Objectives

Studying this lesson will enable students to

- use reading strategies such as analyzing text organization
- evaluate arguments and counterarguments
- define *tone* and recognize the effect of this literary technique in the selection
- describe the literary accomplishments of Barbara and David P. Mikkelson and explain the influence of urban legends on their writing
- appreciate an urban legend

Launch the Lesson

Ask students to describe any long-standing rumors or urban legends that they know to be false. Why, when all evidence points to falsehood, do people maintain belief in these tales? Tell students that they will now read "Gatored Community," which describes an eighty-year-old rumor about our greatest metropolis.

GATORED COMMUNITY **829**

Words in Use

Preview Vocabulary	Selection Words	Teaching Words
inglorious, 831	microfilm, 831	outlandish, 829
veritable, 831	lassoed, 832	suppress, 834
premises, 831	yarns, 833	persistence, 835
serenely, 833	suffice, 834	
infestation, 834	interfere, 834	

KEY TERMS

Common Core State Standards

Reading Informational
RI.1, RI.4

Writing
W.6, W.9

Language
L.6

Teach the Selection

Summary

This selection explores the urban legend about a large group of alligators who live and thrive in the sewer system of New York City and in some of the nearby lakes and rivers. Dates, times, and other details are given for each sighting or capture of some of these alligators. Each sighting is countered by an explanation of what really happened and why the authors think the original legend could not be true. However, the reader is left to draw his/her own conclusion about the actual truth of the urban legend.

 **MIRRORS & WINDOWS** The Mirrors & Windows questions at the end of this selection focus on the theme of urban legends. Before reading the story, ask students if there are any urban legends that they think hold at least a grain of truth, and have them explain why. Why do urban legends persist?

Gatored Community

A Legend by Barbara and David P. Mikkelson

830

Program Resources

Planning and Assessment
Program Planning Guide, Selection Lesson Plan
E-Lesson Planner
Assessment Guide, Lesson Test
ExamView

Technology Tools
Interactive Student Text on CD
Visual Teaching Package
Audio Library
mirrorsandwindows.com

Meeting the Standards
Folk Literature: Unit 8, Directed Reading, pp. 79–82

> **Police organize alligator hunt in Westchester County after two boys bring in 3-foot dead alligator and claim the Bronx River is swarming with them.**

Claim: A thriving colony of large alligators lives deep in the bowels[1] of the New York City sewer system

Status: *False.*

Origins: It's long been rumored there are thriving colonies of alligators lurking in New York City's sewer system. Supposedly, baby alligators brought back as pets from Florida end up being dumped into the sewer system when they outgrow their young and innocent stage. From such an <u>inglorious</u> beginning, these discarded gators grow to immense size and daily terrorize all those foolish enough to risk a visit to the bowels of the city. **Ⓐ**

We've all heard it. And it ain't true.

It's amazing who believes in those invisible alligators too. As the Director of the New York Sea Grant Institute in Albany said to *The New York Times* in 1982: "No less a source than *All the News That's Fit to Print* reported a <u>veritable</u> rash of 'saurian[2] sightings' in the city sewers through the 1930s."

You know, if you stopped right there, you might walk away from all this convinced there are alligators down there. But it's amazing what a little digging will uncover (or, in this case, *not* uncover).

Figuring any "alligators in our sewers!" story would be considered newsworthy by the New York press, I went through *The New York Times* index from 1905 to 1993 in search of alligator stories. Then I located each story on microfilm. Here's a summary of what I found:

September 4, 1927:
A "good-sized Florida alligator" found in a storm-swollen stream in Middletown, NY. "It was later discovered that the alligator had escaped several months ago from a pen on the <u>premises</u> of Dr. F. E. Fowler."

July 3, 1929:
2-foot alligator found in the grass at someone's home in Port Jervis, NY.

May 22, 1931:
Another 2-foot gator found in the bushes on someone's estate in Pleasantville (Westchester), NY.

June 30, 1932:
Police organize alligator hunt in Westchester County after two boys bring in 3-foot dead alligator and claim the Bronx River is swarming with them. (See the end of this article for excerpts from this story—too funny to miss.)

July 2, 1932:
The alligator hunt was called off after it was decided the boys had seen snakes or lizards in the river, not gators. The dead "gator" they'd brought in was identified as a pet crocodile which had escaped from a neighbor's backyard a few weeks prior to all the excitement.

---

1. **bowels.** Deep or remote parts
2. **saurian.** Any animals belonging to the Sauria group of reptiles, including lizards, crocodiles, and dinosaurs

> **in·glo·ri·ous** (in' glôr´ ē əs) *adj.*, shameful; lacking fame or honor
>
> **ver·i·ta·ble** (ver´ ə tə bəl) *adj.*, being in fact the thing named; not false or imaginary
>
> **prem·is·es** (pre´ məs əs) *pl. n.*, area of land; grounds

> **Vocabulary Skills**

Alliteration
Write the phrase *saurian sightings* on the board, and underline the initial letter *s* in each word. Say the words aloud, and have students repeat them. Tell students that *saurian sightings* is an example of alliteration, where the sound at the beginning of words is repeated. Explain that authors often use alliteration to make their writing more lively and interesting.

Work with students to find more examples of alliteration in the selection.

EXAMPLE: *storm-swollen stream, sickly saurian, swum to shore, despite the dearth.*

Teach the Selection

Analyze Literature

Tone Ask students how the phrase *sickly saurian* is consistent with the authors' belief that the alligators are not a threat. **A**

Analyze Literature

Style Explain to students that style is the way a text is written. Word choice, imagery, and tone are all parts of a writer's style. Ask students how the image of boys killing a lassoed alligator with shovels contributes to the overall tone of the selection. **B**

Use Reading Skills

Analyze Text Organization Point out that the authors first present the evidence of the argument, that there were alligators in the sewers of New York City. Then, they present the counterargument, which explains why the alligators were there. **C**

September 12, 1933:
"A squadron of riflemen was organized here [Belleville, NY] today to hunt for alligators in the Passaic River…Belleville police said it is probable the alligators were some of the six reptiles which disappeared last year from a lagoon[3] in Military Park, Newark."

February 10, 1935:
Boys shoveling snow into a manhole discovered a 6-foot gator trying to make his escape from the sewer. The boys lassoed the **A** sickly saurian with a clothesline and dragged him up to street level. Because the gator snapped at the kids (and thus convinced **B** them he could indeed be dangerous), they attacked him with shovels and killed him. Speculation was the gator had fallen off a passing steamer, swum to shore and found the entrance to the sewer.

March 8, 1935:
A seal and two alligators turn up in Westchester County. "A 3-foot gator was found in Northern Yonkers by Joseph Domomico yesterday morning. Another twice that size was found, dead, on the east side of Grassy Sprain reservoir."[4]

June 1, 1937:
A barge captain captures a 4-foot alligator in the East River. The gator "was clearly exhausted and seemed in no humor to fight."

June 7, 1937:
"Passengers waiting on the eastbound platform of the Brooklyn Museum station of the I.R.T. subway just before midnight were startled by the sudden appearance of a 2-foot alligator which had emerged from a refuse[5] **C** can." As to how the beastie might have gotten in there, "Passengers on the station told the police that shortly before the alligator appeared a man put a large bundle in the refuse can."

August 16, 1938:
Five alligators caught in Huguenot Lake (Westchester, NY), the largest of which was 19 inches.

August 17, 1942:
A 4-foot alligator (thought to have escaped from an outdoor aquarium in a local home) was found in Lake Mindowaskin (Westfield, NJ).

August 12, 1982:
A 26-inch alligator was found swimming in Kensico Reservoir (in Westchester, NY), part of the New York City water supply system.

---

3. **lagoon.** Shallow pond or channel near or connected to a large body of water
4. **reservoir.** Artificial lake where water is collected and stored for human use
5. **refuse.** Garbage

Differentiated Instruction

Visual Learning

Use online or paper maps of the locations in the article where the alligators were sighted. Have students highlight the locations, noting their proximity to any bodies of water. Guide them to use an Internet search engine to find historical documents, including photographs, of the New York City sewer system in the 1930s, when the first alligator sightings took place. Students may be able to find online maps of portions of the sewer system as well. Online maps of the New York City subway system will also help students locate the bodies of water where the alligators were found, as well as to visualize what an underground system might look like.

All these alligators found in and around New York City, but only one had turned up in a sewer. (Mind you, Westchester County looks like a fine place to avoid if you're not saurianly inclined[6]—every second gator story seemed to come from there.) Not surprising either, for alligators thrive in Florida and it's hard to believe creatures that accustomed to a warm climate would survive in the NY sewer system. A New York winter is hard on native New Yorkers; I wouldn't think a colony of gators would stand a chance in that cold.

Nature writer Diane Ackerman has this to say about alligators' longevity under those conditions:

> But they couldn't survive for any length of time in the sewers, only a few months at the most, because they can't live long in salmonella or shigella or E. coli, organisms that one usually finds in sewage. Also, alligators live at temperatures between 78 and 90 degrees…

Despite the dearth[7] of news stories about NY alligators and in the face of what we know about how gators are put together, the "alligators in the New York sewer system" stories persist. Most of the blame for this tale's persistence should be assigned to Robert Daley's 1959 *The World Beneath the City*. In it, Daley passes along a tale from Teddy May, New York's superintendent of sewers until 1955. According to the book, sewer inspectors first reported seeing gators around 1935, but May did not believe them. He went himself into the sewers and afterwards:

> He sat at his desk screwing his fists into his eyes, trying to forget the sight of alligators <u>serenely</u> paddling around in his sewers. The beam of his own flashlight had spotted alligators whose length, on the average, was about two feet…The colony appeared to

have settled contentedly under the very streets of the busiest city in the world.

D The book then goes on to tell how the alligators were dispatched[8] by various means including being poisoned, being shot, or being herded into the trunk mains where currents washed them out to sea.

I'm left wondering why this massive alligator hunt wasn't reported in the popular press for, as we've seen, *The New York Times* will publish just about anything that has to do with alligators in or around New York. As well, *World Beneath The City* doesn't give a date for all this taking place; all it says is Teddy May first heard gator reports in 1935. The date of his visit to the sewers or the extermination of the alligators is not provided.

Daley spoke to May in 1959 (when May was 84 years old and 20-odd years after the alligators were supposedly discovered and dispatched down there). To my mind, the details are a bit too fuzzy and there's a decided lack of outside confirmation. May's story could easily be a fanciful tale and I, for one, am of that opinion. As for how seriously to take May, according to a 1992 magazine article, "…a sewer official told [folklorist Jan Harold] Brunvand that Teddy May was 'almost as much of a legend as the alligators,' a spinner of colorful yarns."

Each year at least half a dozen people ask New York City's Bureau of Sewers about those infamous gators. John T. Flaherty (Chief of Design) answers these inquiries routinely.

> I could cite you many cogent,[9] logical reasons why the sewer system is not a fit

---

6. **saurianly inclined.** Inclined to like saurians
7. **dearth.** Inadequate supply
8. **dispatched.** Killed; removed quickly
9. **cogent.** Relevant; persuasive

se·rene·ly (sə rēn lē) *adv.*, calmly

habitat for an alligator, but suffice it to say[10] that, in the 28 years I have been in the sewer game, neither I nor any of the thousands of men who have worked to build, maintain or repair the sewer system has ever seen one.

A Flaherty (whose sense of humor is of the dry yet deadly variety) added the one clear proof of the absence of alligators—not a single union official has ever advanced alligator <u>infestation</u> as a reason for a pay increase for sewer workers.

Even though it's next to impossible to prove something didn't happen, I would still suggest from the lack of credible sightings it's safe to assume there are no alligators down there. As a suitable finale, I present excerpts from a 1932 *New York Times* about police plans to stalk alligators they believed were living in a Bronx River lair:

…two small boys had appeared at headquarters last night to show the chief a dead alligator, about 36 inches long, which they said they had captured along the shore of the lake. The boys told the chief that the Bronx River, of which the lake is a part, had been 'swarming' with at least two or three other alligators.

The start of the explorers was delayed today because of fear on the part of the police chief that a species of human beings, known as baseball players, who congregate[11] on the shores of the lake, would interfere with the expedition.

The proper method of catching an alligator alive was the subject of a conference this afternoon between the police chief and his men. […] Someone

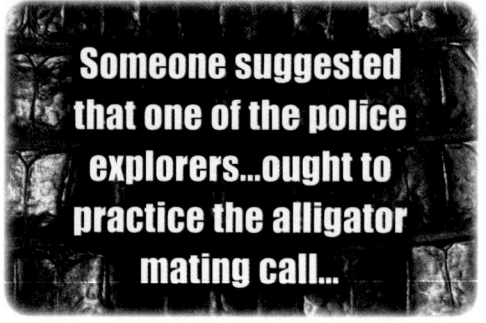

Someone suggested that one of the police explorers...ought to practice the alligator mating call...

suggested that one of the police explorers, who sings bass in the police quartet, ought to practice the alligator mating call, which the police chief learned was a cross between the bark of a dog and the grunt of a pig.

A hurried visitor to Police Headquarters told the police chief that a piece of liver would make an alligator literally walk across the water to shore and that it could be captured alive easily with the type of net generally used by butterfly chasers.

The police chief put in a requisition for enough liver to feed a good-sized alligator, and one of his men promised to lend the explorers a fishing net for the expedition.

Sightings: This legend shows up as the plot of the 1980 film *Alligator* and in the 1963 Thomas Pynchon novel *V.* ❖

10. **suffice it to say.** It is sufficient or enough to say
11. **congregate.** Gather

in•fes•ta•tion (in' fes´ tā shən) *n.,* invasion or troublesome spread of a harmful pest

MIRRORS & **W**INDOWS In what ways are stories about alligators in the sewers and other urban legends similar to or different from stories about visitors from outer space? Which type of story do you find easier to believe and why? Why are urban legends so difficult to stop or suppress?

Find Meaning

1. (a) Where does the narrator look to prove or disprove the rumors about alligators in the sewers? (b) Why choose that source?

2. What factors about climate and sewers make it impossible for alligators to survive for any length of time in New York?

3. In what ways did the book *The World Beneath the City* contribute to the persistence of the rumor?

Analyze Literature

Tone The tone an author uses in a text can reveal that author's purpose. An author's purpose may be to inform, entertain, or to persuade readers. Authors reveal tone and purpose by the way they describe events. What is the tone of "Gatored Community"? How does this reveal the author's purpose? Use a graphic organizer like the one at right to organize your thoughts.

Make Judgments

4. (a) Where are most alligators that are described in the *New York Times* stories discovered? (b) What conclusions can you draw from this?

5. Why do you think the narrator considers the *New York Times* story from 1932 a "suitable finale"?

6. (a) How would you describe the author's tone? (b) What details from the article helped you arrive at that judgment?

Description	Tone	Purpose
Description of the rumor of alligators loose in the city uses words like "lurking," "supposedly," "dumped," and "bowels of the city."	Dark, mysterious	Engage the reader emotionally with the legend

Extend Understanding

Writing Options

Creative Writing Write a **newspaper article** that describes an alligator sighting in your own community. Make up the details, including who first saw the alligator, when and where it was seen, and what happened next. Include a brief attention-getting headline.

Expository Writing The authors of "Gatored Community" include a great deal of evidence to support their position "there are no alligators down there." How convincing do you find their evidence? Write a brief **literary response** for your teacher and classmates that analyzes and evaluates the evidence. State your opinion in your thesis statement. Share your work with the class.

Collaborative Learning

Write a Public Service Announcement Work with a small group to create a brief public service announcement warning people of alligators in the sewers. First, decide whether your announcement will take the form of a poster, a twenty-second radio announcement, or a print advertisement. Then, decide what elements your announcement must have, such as graphics or a script. Share your announcement with your class.

Media Literacy

Research Urban Legends Use an Internet search engine to research additional urban legends. Find out what types of categories exist in these legends and what purpose they might serve. Then write a brief summary of one urban legend to share with classmates.

 Go to www.mirrorsandwindows.com for more.

Find Meaning

1. (a) In the index of the *New York Times* newspaper. (b) It is considered a reliable source.

2. Alligators live at temperatures between 78 and 90 degrees. New York winters are much colder.

3. It passed along a story by Teddy May, who reported that he had seen a colony of alligators in the sewers.

Make Judgments

4. (a) Streams, grass, bushes, and other places that are not sewers. (b) The sewers are not full of alligators.

5. The story appears in the *New York Times*, is somewhat ridiculous, and promises to solve the problem.

6. (a) The tone is humorous, lighthearted, conversational, relaxed, or friendly. (b) Examples might include diction and language levels ("And it ain't true."), author asides ("Mind you, Westchester County looks like a fine place. . . ."), and the inclusion of humorous details.

Analyze Literature

Tone *Answer:* <u>Description:</u> "Someone suggested that one of the police explorers, who sings bass in the police quartet, ought to practice the alligator mating call, which the police learned was a cross between the bark of a dog and the grunt of a pig."
<u>Tone:</u> sarcastic
<u>Purpose:</u> to make the people who believe there are alligators in the sewers seem silly

---

Rubrics for Writing Options

You can adapt this as a checklist for students to use as they write.

Creative Writing

☐ Does the article contain details that tell *who, when, where,* and *what*?

☐ Does the story contain an attention-grabbing headline?

Expository Writing

☐ Does the introduction identify the literary work and state the authors' main argument and the student's response?

☐ Do the body paragraphs include specific reasons and evidence for the response?

☐ Does the conclusion summarize the student's response to the evidence presented?

Program Resources

For further instruction, refer students to the following extension activity: Media Literacy: Research Urban Legends, *Exceeding the Standards: Extension Activities*, pp. 25–26.

Preview the Selection

At a Glance
Independent Reading
- Reading Level: Challenging
- Difficulty Considerations: Vocabulary, references
- Ease Factor: Compelling plot

Objectives
Reading this selection will enable students to:
- read with developing fluency
- read silently with comprehension for a sustained period of time

Launch the Lesson
Point out to students that "Rip Van Winkle" is a legend, which is a story that has been passed down as history but is probably not true. Ask them what some of their favorite legends are. Write the titles of several of these legends on the board, and ask students to summarize them.

TEACHING NOTE
Although this selection is presented in the student edition as an independent reading, teaching support has been provided should you choose to cover it in class.

Rip Van Winkle

A Legend by
Washington Irving

Although **Washington Irving** (1783–1859) was a lawyer, he wrote a great deal of fiction. He began writing by collaborating on a collection of essays and musings on society.

A posthumous writing of Diedrich Knickerbocker

By Woden, God of Saxons,
From whence comes Wensday, that is
  Wodensday.
Truth is a thing that ever I will keep
Unto thylke day in which I creep into
  My sepulchre—
Cartwright

[The following Tale was found among the papers of the late Diedrich Knickerbocker, an old gentleman of New York, who was very curious in the Dutch history of the province, and the manners of the descendants from its primitive settlers. His historical researches, however, did not lie so much among books as among men; for the former are lamentably scanty on his favorite topics; whereas he found the old burghers, and still more their wives, rich in that legendary lore, so invaluable to true history. Whenever, therefore, he happened upon a genuine Dutch family, snugly shut up in its low-roofed farmhouse, under a spreading sycamore, he looked upon it as a little clasped volume of black-letter, and studied it with the zeal of a book-worm.

The result of all these researches was a history of the province during the reign of the Dutch governors, which he published some years since. There have been various opinions as to the literary character of his work, and, to tell the truth, it is not a whit better than it should be. Its chief merit is its

Soon after this, Irving began to write fiction, only to give up the practice when his wife died in 1809. During his lifetime, Irving was a prolific writer and is credited with writing the first American short stories.

836

Program Resources

Planning and Assessment
Program Planning Guide, Selection Lesson Plan
E-Lesson Planner
Assessment Guide, Lesson Test
ExamView

Technology Tools
Interactive Student Text on CD
Visual Teaching Package
Audio Library
mirrorsandwindows.com

Meeting the Standards
Folk Literature: Unit 8, Independent Reading, pp. 83–89

Common Core State Standards
Reading Literature
RL.10

"Does nobody here know Rip Van Winkle?"

scrupulous[1] accuracy, which indeed was a little questioned on its first appearance, but has since been completely established; and it is now admitted into all historical collections, as a book of unquestionable authority.

The old gentleman died shortly after the publication of his work, and now that he is dead and gone, it cannot do much harm to his memory to say that his time might have been much better employed in weightier labors. He, however, was apt to ride his hobby his own way; and though it did now and then kick up the dust a little in the eyes of his neighbors, and grieve the spirit of some friends, for whom he felt the truest deference and affection; yet his errors and follies are remembered "more in sorrow than in anger," and it begins to be suspected, that he never intended to injure or offend. But however his memory may be appreciated by critics, it is still held dear by many folk, whose good opinion is well worth having; particularly by certain biscuit-bakers, who have gone so far as to imprint his likeness on their new-year cakes; and have thus given him a chance for immortality, almost equal to the being stamped on a Waterloo Medal, or a Queen Anne's Farthing.]

Whoever has made a voyage up the Hudson must remember the Kaatskill mountains. They are a dismembered branch of the great Appalachian family, and are seen away to the west of the river, swelling up to a noble height, and lording it over the surrounding country. Every change of season, every change of weather, indeed, every hour of the day, produces some change in the magical hues and shapes of these mountains,

and they are regarded by all the good wives, far and near, as perfect barometers. When the weather is fair and settled, they are clothed in blue and purple, and print their bold outlines on the clear evening sky; but, sometimes, when the rest of the landscape is cloudless, they will gather a hood of gray vapors about their summits, which, in the last rays of the setting sun, will glow and light up like a crown of glory.

At the foot of these fairy mountains, the voyager may have descried the light smoke curling up from a village, whose shingle roofs gleam among the trees, just where the blue tints of the upland melt away into the fresh green of the nearer landscape. It is a little village, of great antiquity, having been founded by some of the Dutch colonists, in the early times of the province, just about the beginning of the government of the good Peter Stuyvesant, (may he rest in peace!) and there were some of the houses of the original settlers standing within a few years, built of small yellow bricks brought from Holland, having latticed windows and gable fronts, surmounted with weather-cocks.

In that same village, and in one of these very houses (which, to tell the precise truth, was sadly time-worn and weather-beaten), there lived many years since, while the country was yet a province of Great Britain, a simple good-natured fellow, of the name of Rip Van Winkle. He was a descendant of the Van Winkles who figured so gallantly in the chivalrous days of Peter Stuyvesant, and accompanied him to the siege of Fort

---

1. **scrupulous.** Acting with strict consideration for what is right

---

Teach the Selection

Summary

Irving presents the legend as a tale found in the writings of another writer named Diedrich Knickerbocker, after his death. Rip Van Winkle lived in the Kaatskill (Catskill) Mountains area of New York in the mid-1700s, just before the Revolutionary War. Rip was henpecked by his wife and never did much work. During a walk in the mountains, he fell asleep. When he awoke he encountered group of small men dressed in an antique style of Dutch clothing. Rip drank some of the men's liquor. He fell asleep, and after he woke up he gradually realized that he had slept for twenty years. Some of the older people in his hometown recognized him. His wife had died, so he went to live with his daughter and her family, resuming the lifestyle that he had before his disappearance. The villagers agreed that Rip had met up with the ghosts of Hendrick Hudson and his crew of the *Half-Moon*.

The Mirrors & Windows questions at the end of this selection focus on the theme of time. Before reading the story, ask students to relate a situation in which they felt completely out of place. How would people prepare themselves for a journey to the future or the past?

Geography Connection

The Catskills The Catskill (Kaatskill) Mountains are located in upper New York State, northwest of New York City and southwest of Albany. Have students locate the Catskills on a map.

Analyze Literature

Legend Remind students that a legend is a story that has been passed down as history but is probably not true. "Rip Van Winkle" could be considered a legend within a legend. Irving wrote the legend, but starts out by presenting the tale as a legend written by Diedrich Knickerbocker.

Analyze Literature

Characterization Tell students that characterization is the act of creating or describing a character. Writers create character by describing what they say and do, by showing what other characters think about them, and by describing their physical features and personalities. In direct characterization, the author makes direct, clear statements about the character's personality. In indirect characterization, the author tells about the character by describing his interactions with others. Have students list the examples of direct and indirect characterization of Rip on this page. Model a response: Indirect: "The children shouted with joy when he approached." Direct: "He would never refuse to assist a neighbor." **Ⓐ**

Christina. He inherited, however, but little of the martial character of his ancestors. I have observed that he was a simple good-natured man; he was, moreover, a kind neighbor, and an obedient hen-pecked husband. Indeed, to the latter circumstance might be owing that meekness of spirit which gained him such universal popularity; for those men are most apt to be obsequious[2] and conciliating abroad, who are under the discipline of shrews at home. Their tempers, doubtless, are rendered pliant and malleable in the fiery furnace of domestic tribulation; and a curtain lecture is worth all the sermons in the world for teaching the virtues of patience and long-suffering. A termagant wife may, therefore, in some respects, be considered a tolerable blessing; and if so, Rip Van Winkle was thrice blessed.

Certain it is, that he was a great favorite among all the good wives of the village, who, as usual, with the amiable sex, took his part in all family squabbles; and never failed, whenever they talked those matters over in their evening gossipings, to lay all the blame on Dame Van Winkle. The children of the village, too, would shout with joy whenever he approached. He assisted at their sports, made their playthings, taught them to fly kites and shoot marbles, and told them long stories of ghosts, witches, and Indians. Whenever he went dodging about the village, he was surrounded by a troop of them, hanging on his skirts, clambering on his back, and playing a thousand tricks on him with impunity; and not a dog would bark at him throughout the neighborhood.

The great error in Rip's composition was an insuperable[3] aversion to all kinds of profitable labor. It could not be from the want of assiduity[4] or perseverance; for he would sit on a wet rock, with a rod as long and heavy as a Tartar's lance, and fish all day without a murmur, even though he should not be encouraged by a single nibble. He would carry a fowling-piece on his shoulder for hours together, trudging through woods and swamps, and up hill and down dale, to shoot a few squirrels or wild pigeons. He would never refuse to assist a neighbor even in the roughest toil, and was a foremost man at all country frolics for husking Indian corn, or building stone-fences; the women of the village, too, used to employ him to run their errands, and to do such little odd jobs as their less obliging husbands would not do for them. In a word Rip was ready to attend to anybody's business but his own; but as to doing family duty, and keeping his farm in order, he found it impossible.

In fact, he declared it was of no use to work on his farm; it was the most pestilent little piece of ground in the whole country; every thing about it went wrong, and would go wrong, in spite of him. His fences were continually falling to pieces; his cow would either go astray, or get among the cabbages; weeds were sure to grow quicker in his fields than anywhere else; the rain always made a point of setting in just as he had some out-door work to do; so that though his patrimonial estate had dwindled away under his management, acre by acre, until there was little more left than a mere patch of Indian corn and potatoes, yet it was the worst conditioned farm in the neighborhood.

His children, too, were as ragged and wild as if they belonged to nobody. His son Rip, an urchin begotten in his own likeness, promised to inherit the habits, with the old

---

2. **obsequious.** Flattering
3. **insuperable.** Incapable of being overcome
4. **assiduity.** Persistence; devotion

Differentiated Instruction

Visual Learning

Irving describes Rip Van Winkle's farm in great detail. Ask students to close their eyes while you read this paragraph aloud, allowing concrete images to form in their minds. When you are finished reading, ask students to sketch, draw, paint, or collage their image of the farm. Challenge students to opine whether the farm's state is simply bad luck or if Rip has something to do with its condition. Either way, encourage them to depict this opinion by including Rip in their piece.

clothes of his father. He was generally seen trooping like a colt at his mother's heels, equipped in a pair of his father's cast-off galligaskins, which he had much ado to hold up with one hand, as a fine lady does her train in bad weather.

Rip Van Winkle, however, was one of those happy mortals, of foolish, well-oiled dispositions, who take the world easy, eat white bread or brown, whichever can be got with least thought or trouble, and would rather starve on a penny than work for a pound. If left to himself, he would have whistled life away in perfect contentment: but his wife kept continually dinning in his ears about his idleness, his carelessness, and the ruin he was bringing on his family. Morning, noon, and night, her tongue was incessantly going, and every thing he said or did was sure to produce a torrent of household eloquence. Rip had but one way of replying to all lectures of the kind, and that, by frequent use, had grown into a habit. He shrugged his shoulders, shook his head, cast up his eyes, but said nothing. This, however, always provoked a fresh volley from his wife; so that he was fain to draw off his forces, and take to the outside of the house—the only side which, in truth, belongs to a hen-pecked husband.

Rip's sole domestic adherent was his dog Wolf, who was as much hen-pecked as his master; for Dame Van Winkle regarded them as companions in idleness, and even looked upon Wolf with an evil eye, as the cause of his master's going so often astray. True it is, in all points of spirit befitting an honorable dog, he was as courageous an animal as ever scoured the woods—but what courage can withstand the ever-during, and all-besetting terrors of a woman's tongue? The moment

Wolf entered the house his crest fell, his tail drooped to the ground, or curled between his legs, he sneaked about with a gallows air, casting many a sidelong glance at Dame Van Winkle, and at the least flourish of a broomstick or ladle, he would fly to the door with yelping precipitation.

Times grew worse and worse with Rip Van Winkle as years of matrimony rolled on; a tart temper never mellows with age, and a sharp tongue is the only edged tool that grows keener with constant use. For a long while he used to console himself, when driven from home, by frequenting a kind of perpetual club of the sages, philosophers, and other idle personages of the village; which held its sessions on a bench before a small inn, designated by a rubicund portrait of His Majesty George the Third. Here they used to sit in the shade through a long lazy summer's day, talking listlessly over village gossip, or telling endless sleepy stories about nothing. But it would have been worth any statesman's money to have heard the profound discussions that sometimes took place, when by chance an old newspaper fell into their hands from some passing traveler. How solemnly they would listen to the contents, as drawled out by Derrick Van Bummel, the schoolmaster, a dapper learned little man, who was not to be daunted by the most gigantic word in the dictionary; and how sagely they would deliberate upon public events some months after they had taken place.

The opinions of this junto were completely controlled by Nicholas Vedder, a patriarch of the village, and landlord of the inn, at the door of which he took his seat from morning till night, just moving sufficiently to avoid the sun and keep in the shade of a large tree; so that the neighbors

Analyze Literature

Character Explain to students that a dynamic character experiences some kind of important change during the course of a story. A static character does not undergo a major change. At this point in the story, Rip is a happy person who takes things easy. Students should watch to see if there are any major changes in his character as the story progresses. **B**

Use Reading Strategies

Visualize Point out to students that in "Rip Van Winkle," the author provides many visual details to help readers visualize interaction between characters as well as details of the physical surroundings. Ask them to identify some key details that help a reader visualize Dame Van Winkle's effect on Rip and Wolf. Possible response: Wolf sneaks around with his tail between his legs as though he is very scared.

Vocabulary Skills

Prefixes, Roots, and Suffixes

Point out to students they can use the meaning of a prefix, a root, or a suffix to understand the meaning of a word. Show students an example of each:

- incessantly: prefix *in-* meaning "not"; not ceasing or stopping
- colonists: suffix *-ist*, meaning "one who practices"; a colonist is a member of a colony
- patriarch: root *pater*, meaning "father"; an elder male leader of the family or community

Cultural Connection

Appalachian Folklore The Appalachian Mountain area is a rich source of folk tales. Most of these tales originated in Germany, the Netherlands, and the other native countries of the first inhabitants of the region. These first settlers brought their tales with them, and the tales took on the flavor of the local scenery. Students can use an Internet search engine or a reference librarian to help them find collections of Appalachian folk tales.

Analyze Literature

Foreshadowing Explain that authors use foreshadowing to give readers a clue about events that will happen later in the story. Ask students what they might expect to happen after reading Rip's pledge to stand by Wolf. Model a possible response: "I think that Rip may have the opportunity later to show his loyalty to Wolf, or Wolf may need to show his loyalty to Rip." **A**

Use Reading Strategies

Make Predictions Ask students who might be calling Rip and what might happen to Rip. Possible response: "The call might be from a neighbor or maybe from a ghost." **B**

---

could tell the hour by his movements as accurately as by a sun-dial. It is true he was rarely heard to speak, but smoked his pipe incessantly. His adherents, however (for every great man has his adherents), perfectly understood him, and knew how to gather his opinions. When any thing that was read or related displeased him, he was observed to smoke his pipe vehemently, and to send forth short, frequent and angry puffs; but when pleased, he would inhale the smoke slowly and tranquilly, and emit it in light and placid clouds; and sometimes, taking the pipe from his mouth, and letting the fragrant vapor curl about his nose, would gravely nod his head in token of perfect approbation.

From even this stronghold the unlucky Rip was at length routed by his termagant wife, who would suddenly break in upon the tranquility of the assemblage and call the members all to naught; nor was that august personage, Nicholas Vedder himself, sacred from the daring tongue of this terrible virago, who charged him outright with encouraging her husband in habits of idleness.

Poor Rip was at last reduced almost to despair; and his only alternative, to escape from the labor of the farm and clamor of his wife, was to take gun in hand and stroll away into the woods. Here he would sometimes seat himself at the foot of a tree, and share the contents of his wallet with Wolf, with whom he sympathized as a fellow-sufferer in persecution. "Poor Wolf," he would say, "thy mistress leads thee a dog's life of it; but never mind, my lad, whilst I live thou shalt never want a friend to stand by thee!" Wolf would wag his tail, look wistfully in his master's face, and if dogs can feel pity I verily believe he reciprocated the sentiment with all his heart.

In a long ramble of the kind on a fine autumnal day, Rip had unconsciously scrambled to one of the highest parts of the Kaatskill mountains. He was after his favorite sport of squirrel shooting, and the still solitudes had echoed and reechoed with the reports of his gun. Panting and fatigued, he threw himself, late in the afternoon, on a green knoll, covered with mountain herbage, that crowned the brow of a precipice. From an opening between the trees he could overlook all the lower country for many a mile of rich woodland. He saw at a distance the lordly Hudson, far, far, below him, moving on its silent but majestic course, with the reflection of a purple cloud, or the sail of a lagging bark, here and there sleeping on its glassy bosom, and at last losing itself in the blue highlands.

On the other side he looked down into a deep mountain glen, wild, lonely, and shagged, the bottom filled with fragments from the impending cliffs, and scarcely lighted by the reflected rays of the setting sun. For some time Rip lay musing on this scene; evening was gradually advancing; the mountains began to throw their long blue shadows over the valleys; he saw that it would be dark long before he could reach the village, and he heaved a heavy sigh when he thought of encountering the terrors of Dame Van Winkle.

As he was about to descend, he heard a voice from a distance, hallooing, "Rip Van Winkle! Rip Van Winkle!" He looked round, but could see nothing but a crow winging its solitary flight across the mountain. He thought his fancy must have deceived him, and turned again to descend, when he heard the same cry ring through the still evening air; "Rip Van Winkle! Rip Van Winkle!"—at the same time Wolf bristled up his back, and

---

TEACHING NOTE

Interdisciplinary Study

Explain to students that fictional writing often includes real or historic events. Point out the following historical people and events that are included in "Rip Van Winkle."

1. Peter Stuyvesant was the Dutch-born governor of the colony of New Netherland when the area was under Dutch rule.
2. Dutch colonists settled in what is now New York State from 1609 until around 1641. The area was called New Netherland. The Dutch lost the colony in a conflict with the British, and it was renamed New York.
3. The New York area was deeply involved in the Revolutionary War from 1775–1783.

giving a low growl, skulked to his master's side, looking fearfully down into the glen. Rip now felt a vague apprehension stealing over him; he looked anxiously in the same direction, and perceived a strange figure slowly toiling up the rocks, and bending under the weight of something he carried on his back. He was surprised to see any human being in this lonely and unfrequented place, but supposing it to be some one of the neighborhood in need of his assistance, he hastened down to yield it. **C**

On nearer approach he was still more surprised at the singularity of the stranger's appearance. He was a short square-built old fellow, with thick bushy hair, and a grizzled beard. His dress was of the antique Dutch fashion—a cloth jerkin strapped round the waist—several pair of breeches, the outer one of ample volume, decorated with rows of buttons down the sides, and bunches at the knees. He bore on his shoulder a stout keg, that seemed full of liquor, and made signs for Rip to approach and assist him with the load. Though rather shy and distrustful of this new acquaintance, Rip complied with his usual alacrity;[5] and mutually relieving one another, they clambered up a narrow gully, apparently the dry bed of a mountain torrent. As they ascended, Rip every now and then heard long rolling peals, like distant thunder, that seemed to issue out of a deep ravine, or rather cleft, between lofty rocks, toward which their rugged path conducted. He paused for an instant, but supposing it to be the muttering of one of those transient[6] thunder-showers which often take place in mountain heights, he proceeded. Passing through the ravine, they came to a hollow, like a small amphitheater, surrounded by perpendicular precipices, over the brinks of

In the Forest with a Barrel, 1905. Arthur Rackham.

which pending trees shot their branches, so that you only caught glimpses of the azure and the bright evening cloud. During the whole time Rip and his companion had labored on in silence; for though the former marveled greatly what could be the object of carrying a keg of liquor up this wild mountain, yet there was something strange and incomprehensible about the unknown, that inspired awe and checked familiarity.

On entering the amphitheater, new objects of wonder presented themselves. On a level spot in the center was a company of odd-looking personages playing at nine-pins. They were dressed in a quaint outlandish fashion; some wore short doublets,[7] others jerkins, with

---

5. **alacrity.** Enthusiasm or eagerness
6. **transient.** Passing through briefly
7. **doublets.** Close-fitting jackets for men

Teach the Selection

Art Note

In the Forest with a Barrel was painted in 1905 by the English painter Arthur Rackham (1867–1939). The painting was one of fifty-one color plates that Rackham created in 1905 for an illustrated version of "Rip Van Winkle." Rackham's illustrations all include some of his trademarks, such as sinewy tree roots and scary forests. Have students discuss how well they think this painting contributes to their visual imagery of "Rip Van Winkle."

Use Reading Skills

Analyze Cause and Effect Ask students to identify the reasons that Rip felt apprehensive. Model a response by indicating one reason: "Rip was surprised to see anyone in that section of the mountains." **C**

Use Reading Skills

Activate Prior Knowledge Ask students what they know about the early settlement of New York by the Dutch. Point out that when they connect their knowledge about historical events to events in fiction, they can better understand the fictional stories.

Grammar Skills

Analysis Paragraph

Remind students that a paragraph is a group of sentences about one main idea. The sentence that tells the main idea is called the topic sentence. In many paragraphs, the topic sentence is the first sentence in the paragraph, but the topic sentence may also be elsewhere in the paragraph. Sometimes the topic sentence is not present in the paragraph, and the reader must infer the topic. The first word in a paragraph is always indented. When writing a paragraph, students should state the main idea in a topic sentence, follow with supporting detail sentences, and write an ending sentence that clearly concludes the paragraph.

Washington Irving used the pen name "Diedrich Knickerbocker" when he first began writing. In 1809, he wrote *A History of New York,* which was a satire of the early Dutch settlers in and around Manhattan. The term "Knickerbocker" eventually became associated with residents of New York. Irving often wrote about the places he visited. Under his own name he wrote *Bracebridge Hall,* set in England, and *The Life and Voyages of Christopher Columbus. The Sketch-Book* was originally published under the name of "Geoffrey Crayon Gent." This book included "The Legend of Sleepy Hollow" and "Rip Van Winkle."

Use Reading Strategies
Make Predictions Ask students what they think might happen to Rip now that he has fallen asleep. Possible response: The men may carry him off somewhere.

Use Reading Strategies
Make Inferences Ask students what they think the villagers are thinking about Rip and what he is thinking about them. Model a possible response: "The villagers are probably wondering if this stranger is a crazy man from the mountains. Rip is probably wondering what happened to all of his friends."

long knives in their belts, and most of them had enormous breeches, of similar style with that of the guide's. Their visages, too, were peculiar: one had a large beard, broad face, and small piggish eyes: the face of another seemed to consist entirely of nose, and was surmounted by a white sugar-loaf hat, set off with a little red cock's tail. They all had beards, of various shapes and colors. There was one who seemed to be the commander. He was a stout old gentleman, with a weather-beaten countenance;[8] he wore a laced doublet, broad belt and hanger, high crowned hat and feather, red stockings, and high-heeled shoes, with roses in them. The whole group reminded Rip of the figures in an old Flemish painting, in the parlor of Dominie Van Shaick, the village parson, and which had been brought over from Holland at the time of the settlement.

What seemed particularly odd to Rip was, that though these folks were evidently amusing themselves, yet they maintained the gravest faces, the most mysterious silence, and were, withal, the most melancholy party of pleasure he had ever witnessed. Nothing interrupted the stillness of the scene but the noise of the balls, which, whenever they were rolled, echoed along the mountains like rumbling peals of thunder.

As Rip and his companion approached them, they suddenly desisted from their play, and stared at him with such fixed statue-like gaze, and such strange, uncouth, lackluster countenances, that his heart turned within him, and his knees smote together. His companion now emptied the contents of the keg into large flagons, and made signs to him to wait upon the company. He obeyed with fear and trembling; they quaffed the liquor in profound silence, and then returned to their game.

By degrees Rip's awe and apprehension[9] subsided. He even ventured, when no eye was fixed upon him, to taste the beverage, which he found had much of the flavor of excellent Hollands. He was naturally a thirsty soul, and was soon tempted to repeat the draught. One taste provoked another; and he reiterated his visits to the flagon so often that at length his senses were overpowered, his eyes swam in his head, his head gradually declined, and he fell into a deep sleep.

On waking, he found himself on the green knoll whence he had first seen the old man of the glen. He rubbed his eyes—it was a bright sunny morning. The birds were hopping and twittering among the bushes, and the eagle was wheeling aloft, and breasting the pure mountain breeze. "Surely," thought Rip, "I have not slept here all night." He recalled the occurrences before he fell asleep. The strange man with a keg of liquor—the mountain ravine—the wild retreat among the rocks—the woebegone party at nine-pins—the flagon—"Oh! that flagon! that wicked flagon!" thought Rip—"what excuse shall I make to Dame Van Winkle!"

He looked round for his gun, but in place of the clean well-oiled fowling-piece, he found an old firelock lying by him, the barrel incrusted with rust, the lock falling off, and the stock worm-eaten. He now suspected that the grave roysters of the mountain had put a trick upon him, and, having dosed him with liquor, had robbed him of his gun. Wolf, too, had disappeared, but he might have strayed away after a squirrel or partridge. He whistled after him and shouted his name, but all in vain; the echoes repeated his whistle

---

8. **countenance.** Facial expression
9. **apprehension.** Hesitation; nervousness

Differentiated Instruction

Enrichment
Encourage students to find other versions of "Rip Van Winkle" such as a retelling for younger children. They may also want to find scholarly interpretations of the legend. Students should use the Internet or go their school or local library to find the information. Suggest that they bring in any books or printouts of the websites and summarize their information for the class.

Reading Proficiency
Have students read along while listening to the dramatic recording in the Audio Library. Have them pause after each page and write down two things that they remember. Students should then check their work with the story and make any necessary corrections.

and shout, but no dog was to be seen.

He determined to revisit the scene of the last evening's gambol, and if he met with any of the party, to demand his dog and gun. As he rose to walk, he found himself stiff in the joints, and wanting in his usual activity. "These mountain beds do not agree with me," thought Rip, "and if this frolic should lay me up with a fit of the rheumatism, I shall have a blessed time with Dame Van Winkle." With some difficulty he got down into the glen: he found the gully up which he and his companion had ascended the preceding evening; but to his astonishment a mountain stream was now foaming down it, leaping from rock to rock, and filling the glen with babbling murmurs. He, however, made shift to scramble up its sides, working his toilsome way through thickets of birch, sassafras, and witch-hazel, and sometimes tripped up or entangled by the wild grapevines that twisted their coils or tendrils from tree to tree, and spread a kind of network in his path.

At length he reached to where the ravine had opened through the cliffs to the amphitheater; but no traces of such opening remained. The rocks presented a high impenetrable wall over which the torrent came tumbling in a sheet of feathery foam, and fell into a broad deep basin, black from the shadows of the surrounding forest. Here, then, poor Rip was brought to a stand. He again called and whistled after his dog; he was only answered by the cawing of a flock of idle crows, sporting high in air about a dry tree that overhung a sunny precipice; and who, secure in their elevation, seemed to look down and scoff at the poor man's perplexities. What was to be done? The morning was passing away, and Rip felt famished for want of his breakfast. He grieved to give up his dog and gun: he dreaded to meet his wife; but it would not do to starve among the mountains. He shook his head, shouldered the rusty firelock, and, with a heart full of trouble and anxiety, turned his steps homeward.

As he approached the village he met a number of people, but none whom he knew, which somewhat surprised him, for he had thought himself acquainted with everyone in the country round. Their dress, too, was of a different fashion from that to which he was accustomed. They all stared at him with equal marks of surprise, and whenever they cast their eyes upon him, invariably stroked their chins. The constant recurrence of this gesture induced Rip, involuntarily, to do the same, when, to his astonishment, he found his beard had grown a foot long!

He had now entered the skirts of the village. A troop of strange children ran at his heels, hooting after him, and pointing at his gray beard. The dogs, too, not one of which he recognized for an old acquaintance, barked at him as he passed. The very village was altered; it was larger and more populous. There were rows of houses which he had never seen before, and those which had been his familiar haunts had disappeared. Strange names were over the doors—strange faces at the windows—everything was strange. His mind now misgave him; he began to doubt whether both he and the world around him were not bewitched. Surely this was his native village, which he had left but the day before. There stood the Kaatskill mountains—there ran the silver Hudson at a distance—there was every hill and dale precisely as it had always been—Rip was sorely perplexed—"That flagon last night," thought he, "has addled my poor head sadly!"

Teach the Selection

Use Reading Skills
Monitor Comprehension Remind students that when they read, they should stop after every few paragraphs or pages to make sure they understand what they are reading. When they come to a reference about something that happened earlier in the story, they should summarize that event for themselves or go back and reread. Ask students to summarize Rip's thoughts as he wakes and attempts to retrace his steps.

Research Skills

Criticism

Explain to students that Washington Irving was critical of some aspects of American society, especially the War of 1812 and later on the government's treatment of American Indians. Tell students to conduct research about Irving's life and writings, with a focus on his criticism of American society. Suggest that they use both primary and secondary sources. Remind them that a primary source is a firsthand account of an event and a secondary source is written by people who did not directly experience an event.

Art Connection

Point out to students the tricorner hat on the young boy in the front of the illustration, which was in style around the time of the American Revolution. The other costumes are also indicative of the period. Discuss with students how Rip's tattered, out-of-style clothes are a contrast to the clothes of the others in the illustration. Ask students what image the artist is trying to convey with Rip's clothing and facial expression. Is the artist conveying his or her feelings about Rip or the sentiments of those in contact with him? Have students support their responses with details about how the other characters in the illustration respond to his presence and appearance.

Analyze Literature

Imagery Explain that authors use imagery, which is language that relates to the reader's five senses. Ask students which senses Irving appeals to with his imagery of Rip's house. Model a response: "The author appeals to the senses of sight and sound."

Rip Van Winkle.

Differentiated Instruction

Auditory Learning

Irving gives several detailed descriptions that involve sounds. Have students create sound effects for scenes such as the children shouting with joy when they saw Rip or Rip hearing what he thought were the peals of thunder in the ravine. Suggest that students tape-record their sound effects and play them for the class.

It was with some difficulty that he found the way to his own house, which he approached with silent awe, expecting every moment to hear the shrill voice of Dame Van Winkle. He found the house gone to decay—the roof fallen in, the windows shattered, and the doors off the hinges. A half-starved dog that looked like Wolf was sulking about it. Rip called him by name, but the cur snarled, showed his teeth, and passed on. This was an unkind cut indeed—"My very dog," sighed poor Rip, "has forgotten me!"

He entered the house, which, to tell the truth, Dame Van Winkle had always kept in neat order. It was empty, forlorn, and apparently abandoned. This desolateness overcame all his connubial[10] fears—he called loudly for his wife and children—the lonely chambers rang for a moment with his voice, and then all again was silence.

He now hurried forth, and hastened to his old resort, the village inn—but it too was gone. A large rickety wooden building stood in its place, with great gaping windows, some of them broken and mended with old hats and petticoats, and over the door was painted, "the Union Hotel, by Jonathan Doolittle." Instead of the great tree that used to shelter the quiet little Dutch inn of yore, there now was reared a tall naked pole, with something on the top that looked like a red night-cap, and from it was fluttering a flag, on which was a singular assemblage of stars and stripes—all this was strange and incomprehensible. He recognized on the sign, however, the ruby face of King George, under which he had smoked so many a peaceful pipe; but even this was singularly metamorphosed. The red coat was changed for one of blue and buff, a sword was held in the hand instead of a scepter, the head was decorated with a cocked hat, and underneath was painted in large characters, GENERAL WASHINGTON.

There was, as usual, a crowd of folk about the door, but none that Rip recollected. The very character of the people seemed changed. There was a busy, bustling, disputatious[11] tone about it, instead of the accustomed phlegm and drowsy tranquility. He looked in vain for the sage Nicholas Vedder, with his broad face, double chin, and fair long pipe, uttering clouds of tobacco-smoke instead of idle speeches; or Van Bummel, the schoolmaster, doling forth the contents of an ancient newspaper. In place of these, a lean, bilious-looking fellow, with his pockets full of handbills, was haranguing[12] vehemently about rights of citizens—elections—members of congress—liberty—Bunker's Hill—heroes of seventy-six—and other words, which were a perfect Babylonish jargon to the bewildered Van Winkle.

The appearance of Rip, with his long grizzled beard, his rusty fowling-piece, his uncouth dress, and an army of women and children at his heels, soon attracted the attention of the tavern politicians. They crowded around him, eyeing him from head to foot with great curiosity. The orator[13] bustled up to him, and, drawing him partly aside, inquired "on which side he voted?" Rip stared in vacant stupidity. Another short but busy little fellow pulled him by the arm, and, rising on tiptoe, inquired in his ear, "whether he was Federal or Democrat?" Rip was equally at a loss to comprehend the question;

---

10. **connubial.** Referring to marriage
11. **disputatious.** Suggesting a dispute or argument
12. **haranguing.** Lecturing
13. **orator.** Speaker

Teach the Selection

History Connection
The American Revolution The story takes place before and after the American Revolution. The fellow with the handbills is referring to new elements of American society and government—the Bill of Rights, the establishment of Congress, and the Declaration of Independence in 1776. The Battle of Bunker Hill took place near Boston on June 17, 1775. While the British defeated the Continental army, it showed that the Americans were willing and able to fight. **A**

Analyze Literature
Characterization Ask students if Irving uses direct or indirect characterization in his portrayal of the tavern politicians. Students should support their answer with examples from the text. Anticipated response: Direct, since Irving gives examples of how the politicians behave. **B**

Writing Skills

Freewriting
Remind students that some of the villagers doubted Rip's account of his meeting with the mysterious men. They thought he must have had a dream, and even Rip was not sure if he had dreamed it or the meeting was real. Ask students to freewrite about a vivid dream they had. Set a time limit or write beginning and ending times on the board. Give students between five and ten minutes to write. Tell them to write whatever comes to mind in whatever format they choose: they do not need to think about correct spelling, punctuation, or sentence or paragraph formation. Invite students who wish to share their writing to do so.

Make Connections

Ask students to think about a time when they or someone they know received news that was hard to understand and/or caused a change in their thinking. Invite students to share if they are comfortable.

Use Reading Skills

Identify Cause and Effect Ask students what effect Rip's description of his adventures had on the villagers. Anticipated response: The villagers indicated that they thought he was crazy.

when a knowing, self-important old gentleman, in a sharp cocked hat, made his way through the crowd, putting them to the right and left with his elbows as he passed, and planting himself before Van Winkle, with one arm akimbo,[14] the other resting on his cane, his keen eyes and sharp hat penetrating, as it were, into his very soul, demanded in an austere tone, "what brought him to the election with a gun on his shoulder, and a mob at his heels, and whether he meant to breed a riot in the village?"—"Alas! gentlemen," cried Rip, somewhat dismayed, "I am a poor quiet man, a native of the place, and a loyal subject of the king, God bless him!"

Here a general shout burst from the by-standers—"A tory! a tory! a spy! a refugee! hustle him! away with him!" It was with great difficulty that the self-important man in the cocked hat restored order; and, having assumed a tenfold austerity of brow, demanded again of the unknown culprit, what he came there for, and whom he was seeking? The poor man humbly assured him that he meant no harm, but merely came there in search of some of his neighbors, who used to keep about the tavern.

"Well—who are they?—name them."

Rip bethought himself a moment, and inquired, "Where's Nicholas Vedder?"

There was a silence for a little while, when an old man replied, in a thin piping voice, "Nicholas Vedder! why, he is dead and gone these eighteen years! There was a wooden tombstone in the churchyard that used to tell all about him, but that's rotten and gone too."

"Where's Brom Dutcher?"

"Oh, he went off to the army in the beginning of the war; some say he was killed at the storming of Stony Point—others say he was drowned in a squall at the foot of Antony's Nose. I don't know—he never came back again."

"Where's Van Bummel, the schoolmaster?"

"He went off to the wars too, was a great militia general, and is now in congress."

Rip's heart died away at hearing of these sad changes in his home and friends, and finding himself thus alone in the world. Every answer puzzled him too, by treating of such enormous lapses of time, and of matters which he could not understand: war—congress—Stony Point;—he had no courage to ask after any more friends, but cried out in despair, "Does nobody here know Rip Van Winkle?"

"O, Rip Van Winkle!" exclaimed two or three, "Oh, to be sure! that's Rip Van Winkle yonder, leaning against the tree."

Rip looked, and beheld a precise counterpart of himself, as he went up to the mountain: apparently as lazy, and certainly as ragged. The poor fellow was now completely confounded. He doubted his own identity, and whether he was himself or another man. In the midst of his bewilderment, the man in the cocked hat demanded who he was, and what was his name?

"God knows," exclaimed he, at his wit's end; "I'm not myself—I'm somebody else—that's me yonder—no—that's somebody else got into my shoes—I was myself last night, but I fell asleep on the mountain, and they've changed my gun, and every thing's changed, and I'm changed, and I can't tell what's my name, or who I am!"

The by-standers began now to look at each other, nod, wink significantly, and tap

---

14. **akimbo.** Having the hand on the hip and the elbow turned out

Differentiated Instruction

English Language Learning

Point out to students that many of the sentences in the story have multiple phrases. Break down some of the more detailed sentences into several small sentences. Read the sentences aloud with students, and have them rephrase them in their own words.

their fingers against their foreheads. There was a whisper, also, about securing the gun, and keeping the old fellow from doing mischief, at the very suggestion of which the self-important man in the cocked hat retired with some precipitation. At this critical moment a fresh comely woman pressed through the throng to get a peep at the gray-bearded man. She had a chubby child in her arms, which, frightened at his looks, began to cry. "Hush, Rip," cried she, "hush, you little fool; the old man won't hurt you." The name of the child, the air of the mother, the tone of her voice, all awakened a train of recollections in his mind. "What is your name, my good woman?" asked he.

"Judith Gardenier."

"And your father's name?"

"Ah, poor man, Rip Van Winkle was his name, but it's twenty years since he went away from home with his gun, and never has been heard of since—his dog came home without him; but whether he shot himself, or was carried away by the Indians, nobody can tell. I was then but a little girl."

Rip had but one question more to ask; but he put it with a faltering voice:

"Where's your mother?"

"Oh, she too had died but a short time since; she broke a blood-vessel in a fit of passion at a New-England peddler."

There was a drop of comfort, at least, in this intelligence. The honest man could contain himself no longer. He caught his daughter and her child in his arms. "I am your father!" cried he—"Young Rip Van Winkle once—old Rip Van Winkle now!—Does nobody know poor Rip Van Winkle?"

All stood amazed, until an old woman, tottering out from among the crowd, put her hand to her brow, and peering under it in his

New Year's Cakes, 1935. Arthur Rackham. Private collection.

face for a moment, exclaimed, "Sure enough! It is Rip Van Winkle—it is himself! Welcome home again, old neighbor—Why, where have you been these twenty long years?"

Rip's story was soon told, for the whole twenty years had been to him but as one night. The neighbors stared when they heard it; some were seen to wink at each other, and put their tongues in their cheeks: and the self-important man in the cocked hat, who, when the alarm was over, had returned to the field, screwed down the corners of his mouth, and shook his head—upon which there was a general shaking of the head throughout the assemblage.

It was determined, however, to take the opinion of old Peter Vanderdonk, who was seen slowly advancing up the road. He was a descendant of the historian of that name,

Teach the Selection

Art Connection

New Year's Cakes was also painted by Arthur Rackham. The title of the painting refers to special cakes that are traditionally eaten to celebrate the New Year. Remind students that on page 837 of the story, Irving refers to bakers who have imprinted the likeness of Diedrich Knickerbocker on their new-year cakes.

Use Reading Strategies

Make Inferences Ask students how they think Rip might feel now that he has found his daughter. Ask how the daughter might feel as well. Model a possible response: "Rip probably feels relieved that he has found her, and he may feel now that he is not crazy. His daughter may still feel confused or possibly happy that Rip has been found."

Use Reading Strategies

Ask Questions Have pairs of students briefly pause in their reading and ask each other questions to review the events since Rip awoke from his long sleep. Model one possible question such as: "Why are the neighbors winking and putting their tongues in their cheeks?" **A**

Analyze Literature

Legend Point out that Peter Vanderdonk is confirming the legend about the historical figures of Hendrick (Henry) Hudson and his crew. Vanderdonk's affirmation gives substance to Rip's story. **B**

Writing Skills

Narrative

Have students turn their dream description into a narrative about the importance of goals. After students write a first draft, have them work in groups to peer edit their essays. Also, review the narratives, and give suggestions for improvement. Then have students write a final draft of their narratives.

Science Connection

Dream Work According to scientists who study sleep and dreams, many changes go on in the body and mind when we dream. Some changes that occur during sleep are an increase in heart rate, rapid breathing, a slightly elevated temperature, and a change in brain waves. People experience many different kinds of dreams as well. Many scientists believe that dreams are related to the person's emotional state, although as yet there is no conclusive scientific evidence about the meaning of dreams.

Analyze Literature

Character Review with students the definitions of static and dynamic characters. Ask them if they think Rip is an example of a static or a dynamic character, and ask them to support their answer with examples from the text. Possible response: Rip is a static character because his experience did not change him; he resumes his old habits of sitting around gossiping and not doing any work.

Analyze Literature

Allegory Explain to students that an allegory is an extended metaphor, or a story with two meanings. The characters, actions, and things have their literal meaning in the story but also another political, moral, religious, or social meaning. Invite students to discuss the characters and events in "Rip Van Winkle" as allegory. Possible responses: Rip's may be an allegory for a lazy person or for a person who is politically unaware.

who wrote one of the earliest accounts of the province. Peter was the most ancient inhabitant of the village, and well versed in all the wonderful events and traditions of the neighborhood. He recollected Rip at once, and corroborated his story in the most satisfactory manner. He assured the company that it was a fact, handed down from his ancestor the historian, that the Kaatskill mountains had always been haunted by strange beings. That it was affirmed that the great Hendrick Hudson, the first discoverer of the river and country, kept a kind of vigil there every twenty years, with his crew of the Half-moon; being permitted in this way to revisit the scenes of his enterprise, and keep a guardian eye upon the river, and the great city called by his name. That his father had once seen them in their old Dutch dresses playing at nine-pins in a hollow of the mountain; and that he himself had heard, one summer afternoon, the sound of their balls, like distant peals of thunder.

To make a long story short, the company broke up, and returned to the more important concerns of the election. Rip's daughter took him home to live with her; she had a snug, well-furnished house, and a stout cheery farmer for a husband, whom Rip recollected for one of the urchins that used to climb upon his back. As to Rip's son and heir, who was the ditto of himself, seen leaning against the tree, he was employed to work on the farm; but evinced[15] an hereditary disposition to attend to any thing else but his business.

Rip now resumed his old walks and habits; he soon found many of his former cronies, though all rather the worse for the wear and tear of time, and preferred making friends among the rising generation, with

whom he soon grew into great favor.

Having nothing to do at home, and being arrived at that happy age when a man can be idle with impunity, he took his place once more on the bench at the inn door, and was reverenced as one of the patriarchs of the village, and a chronicle of the old times "before the war." It was some time before he could get into the regular track of gossip, or could be made to comprehend the strange events that had taken place during his torpor. How that there had been a revolutionary war—that the country had thrown off the yoke of old England—and that, instead of being a subject of his Majesty George the Third, he was now a free citizen of the United States. Rip, in fact, was no politician; the changes of states and empires made but little impression on him; but there was one species of despotism[16] under which he had long groaned, and that was petticoat government. Happily that was at an end; he had got his neck out of the yoke of matrimony, and could go in and out whenever he pleased, without dreading the tyranny of Dame Van Winkle. Whenever her name was mentioned, however, he shook his head, shrugged his shoulders, and cast up his eyes; which might pass either for an expression of resignation to his fate, or joy at his deliverance.

He used to tell his story to every stranger that arrived at Mr. Doolittle's hotel. He was observed, at first, to vary on some points every time he told it, which was, doubtless, owing to his having so recently awaked. It at last settled down precisely to the tale I have related, and not a man, woman, or child in the neighborhood, but knew it by heart.

---

15. **evinced.** Displayed clearly
16. **despotism.** Type of government where the ruler has unlimited power

TEACHING NOTE

Self-Generated Questioning

Tell students to write down two questions about the story and to include suggestions on how to answer the questions. Model a question such as: "Why does the narrator consider Dame Van Winkle so terrible?" Have one student ask a question and toss a soft ball to another student, who will answer the question. If the student answers correctly without one of the hints, give them two points. If they can't answer without the hint, have the student who asked the question give one of his or her hints. If the student answers correctly this time, they get one point. If they still can't answer, the student who wrote the question gives the answer and the student who caught the ball asks one of their questions.

Some always pretended to doubt the reality of it, and insisted that Rip had been out of his head, and that this was one point on which he always remained flighty. The old Dutch inhabitants, however, almost universally gave it full credit. Even to this day they never hear a thunderstorm of a summer afternoon about the Kaatskill, but they say Hendrick Hudson and his crew are at their game of nine-pins; and it is a common wish of all henpecked husbands in the neighborhood, when life hangs heavy on their hands, that they might have a quieting draught out of Rip Van Winkle's flagon.

Note

The foregoing Tale, one would suspect, had been suggested to Mr. Knickerbocker by a little German superstition about the Emperor Frederick *der Rothbart,* and the Kypphaüser mountain: the subjoined note, however, which he had appended to the tale,

shows that it is an absolute fact, narrated with his usual fidelity:

"The story of Rip Van Winkle may seem incredible to many, but nevertheless I give it my full belief, for I know the vicinity of our old Dutch settlements to have been very subject to marvellous events and appearances. Indeed, I have heard many stranger stories than this, in the villages along the Hudson; all of which were too well authenticated to admit of a doubt. I have even talked with Rip Van Winkle myself, who, when last I saw him, was a very venerable old man, and so perfectly rational and consistent on every other point, that I think no conscientious person could refuse to take this into the bargain; may, I have seen a certificate on the subject taken before a country justice and signed with a cross, in the justice's own handwriting. The story, therefore, is beyond the possibility of doubt."

D.K. ✤

 Describe a time when you felt out of place as Rip Van Winkle did. If one traveled to the future, what sort of changes might he or she expect?

Analyze and Extend

1. (a) Evaluate Rip Van Winkle's relationship with his wife. (b) How does Rip feel about her?
2. What event took place while Rip was absent?
3. (a) Who leads Rip to the amphitheater? (b) Who are the people he sees there? (c) Where do they come from, and how do you explain the ritual Rip witnesses?

Creative Writing Write a **news article** describing the incredible events of Rip Van Winkle's life. Include details about the changes in his life from before he went missing and after.

Think of a compelling headline and first paragraph. You should aim to interest the reader in the events of Van Winkle's life but also answer important questions such as *who, what, when, where,* and *why.*

Lifelong Learning Washington Irving was the first American writer to achieve international fame. He had many interests other than writing. Use the library to learn more about Washington Irving. Write a brief biography of the author, and share your findings with the class.

Ⓜ️Ⓦ Go to www.mirrorsandwindows.com for more.

Answer: Students should be able to give details about the future. Students may mention the use of personal airplanes, advanced Internet technology, or colonies on the moon or other planets. They might expect positive changes such as an end to wars or increased life expectancy. Clothing styles, vehicles, and buildings would all indicate the passage of time.

Analyze and Extend

1. (a) Rip and his wife do not seem to have a pleasant or loving relationship. (b) He seems to be afraid of her.
2. The Revolutionary War took place while Rip was absent.
3. (a) The short stranger leads Rip to the amphitheater. (b) The people are men who are dressed as Dutchmen from an old painting. (c) They are Hendrick Hudson and his crew from the ship Half-moon. The ritual is a vigil the men perform every twenty years to commemorate their discovery of the Hudson River.

Rubric for Creative Writing

You can adapt this as a checklist for students to use as they write.

☐ Does the news article answer the questions *who, what, when, where, why,* and *how?*

☐ Does the article have a compelling headline?

☐ Does the article have an interesting first paragraph?

Preview the Selection

At a Glance
Independent Reading
- Reading Level: Moderate
- Difficulty Consideration: Spanish terminology
- Ease Factor: Compelling plot

Objectives
Reading this selection will enable students to:
- read with developing fluency
- read silently with comprehension for a sustained period of time

Launch the Lesson
Point out to students that in "María Sabida" a young girl uses her intelligence and courage to defeat an evil man. Ask them to relate other tales or real-life stories about people who used a combination of intelligence and courage to overcome great odds or evil.

TEACHING NOTE

Although this selection is presented in the student edition as an independent reading, teaching support has been provided should you choose to cover it in class.

María Sabida

A Puerto Rican Folk Tale
by Judith Ortiz Cofer

Judith Ortiz Cofer was born in 1952 in Puerto Rico, though she moved to New Jersey at the young age of two. However, she never left her Puerto Rican culture behind. She took frequent trips back to her home island, including some for an extended period of time. Today Cofer is one of the most notable Puerto Rican authors. She has published many collections of poetry and essays, as well as novels for both young readers and adults. She is currently a professor of English and creative writing at the University of Georgia.

850

Once upon a time there lived a girl who was so smart that she was known throughout Puerto Rico as María Sabida. María Sabida came into the world with her eyes open. They say that at the moment of her birth she spoke to the attending midwife and told her what herbs to use to make a special *guarapo*, a tea that would put her mother back on her feet immediately. They say that the two women would have thought the infant was possessed if María Sabida had not convinced them with her descriptions of life in heaven that she was touched by God and not spawned by the Devil.

María Sabida grew up in the days when the King of Spain owned Puerto Rico, but had forgotten to send law and justice to this little island lost on the map of the world. And so thieves and murderers roamed the land terrorizing the poor people. By the time María Sabida was of marriageable age, one such *ladrón* had taken over the district where she lived.

For years people had been subjected to abuse from this evil man and his henchmen.[1] He robbed them of their cattle and then made them buy their own cows back from him. He would take their best chickens and produce when he came into town on Saturday afternoons riding with his men through the stalls set up by farmers. Overturning their tables, he would yell, "Put

---
1. **henchmen.** Gang members who are loyal to their leader

Program Resources

Planning and Assessment
Program Planning Guide, Selection Lesson Plan
E-Lesson Planner
Assessment Guide, Lesson Test
ExamView

Technology Tools
Interactive Student Text on CD
Visual Teaching Package
Audio Library
mirrorsandwindows.com

Meeting the Standards
Folk Literature: Unit 8, Independent Reading, pp. 90–95

Common Core State Standards

Reading Literature
RL.10

it on my account." But of course he never paid for anything he took. One year several little children disappeared while walking to the river, and although the townspeople searched and searched, no trace of them was ever found. That is when María Sabida entered the picture. She was fifteen then, and a beautiful girl with the courage of a man, they say.

She watched the chief *ladrón* the next time he rampaged through the pueblo. She saw that he was a young man: red-skinned, and tough as leather. *Cuero y sangre, nada más*, she said to herself, a man of flesh and blood. And so she prepared herself either to conquer or to kill this man.

María Sabida followed the horses' trail deep into the woods. Though she left the town far behind she never felt afraid or lost. María Sabida could read the sun, the moon, and the stars for direction. When she got hungry, she knew which fruits were good to eat, which roots and leaves were poisonous, and how to follow the footprints of animals to a waterhole. At nightfall, María Sabida came to the edge of a clearing where a large house, almost like a fortress,[2] stood in the forest.

"No woman has ever set foot in that house," she thought, "no *casa* is this, but a man-place." It was a house built for violence, with no windows on the ground level, but there were turrets[3] on the roof where men could stand guard with guns. She waited until it was nearly dark and approached the house through the kitchen side. She found it by smell.

In the kitchen which she knew would have to have a door or window for ventilation, she saw an old man stirring a huge pot. Out of the pot stuck little arms

...she prepared herself either to conquer or to kill this man.

and legs. Angered by the sight, María Sabida entered the kitchen, pushed the old man aside, and picking up the pot threw its horrible contents out of the window.

"Witch, witch, what have you done with my master's stew!" yelled the old man. "He will kill us both when he gets home and finds his dinner spoiled."

"Get, you filthy *viejo*."[4] María Sabida grabbed the old man's beard and pulled him to his feet. "Your master will have the best dinner of his life if you follow my instructions."

María Sabida then proceeded to make the most delicious *asopao* the old man had ever tasted, but she would answer no questions about herself, except to say that she was his master's fiancée.

When the meal was done, María Sabida stretched and yawned and said that she would go upstairs and rest until her *prometido*[5] came home. Then she went upstairs and waited.

---

2. **fortress.** Large area—sometimes even a whole town—that is surrounded by a wall to keep enemies out
3. **turrets.** Small towers on top of a building
4. *viejo.* Old man (Spanish)
5. *prometido.* Fiancé (Spanish)

Teach the Selection

Summary

The story is set in Puerto Rico during the time that Spain owned the island. María Sabida was a very smart girl. When she was born she could already talk and told the midwife how to help her mother recover quickly from childbirth. María's town was constantly terrorized by a cruel bandit. When María was fifteen, she snuck into his house, served him a drugged stew, beat him, and went home. Shortly after, the bandit came to María's home and married her. Realizing that he wanted to kill her, she again tricked him by making a doll with her clothes, covering it in honey, and putting it in their bed. When the bandit did stab the doll, he commented aloud on the sweet blood and said he should not have killed her. María, who had been hiding, revealed herself. The bandit became an honest man and they raised many children.

MIRRORS & WINDOWS

The Mirrors & Windows questions at the end of this selection focus on the theme of conquering. Before reading the story, ask students to relate incidents in which someone attempted to intimidate them. How do people generally respond to these situations?

Words in Use

Selection Words

midwife, 850
subjected, 850
rampaged, 851
pueblo, 851
ventilation, 851
fiancée, 851
irresistible, 852

oregano, 852
barricaded, 852
bandido, 853

Teaching Words

notable, 850
terrorized, 854
manipulation, 854
emulate, 854

KEY TERMS

FOLK TALE, 850
THEME, 854
LYRICS, 854
LEGEND, 854
CHARACTER, 854
TONE, 854

Cultural Connection

Midwifery A midwife is a woman who is trained to aid women through pregnancy, labor, and birth and is the most common birth assistant in the world today. Her practice has been integral to society throughout recorded history. In fact, the Torah and the Old Testament, as well as ancient Hindu records, refer to midwifery as a routine custom. The English term *midwife* is derived from the Middle English *mid* (with) and *wif* (woman). Her name translates the same in French (*sage-femme*), in German (*weise frau*), and in Spanish and Portuguese (*comadre*). The practice of midwifery traditionally involves the use of herbs and tonics and is passed from generation to generation through an apprentice system. Misunderstanding of the practice in some ancient societies led to fear and persecution of midwives. During medieval times, they were branded as witches and killed in great numbers. Today, many midwives are trained in modern medical practice, often as nurses, which has lessened their mystery and gained them more widespread acceptance.

Analyze Literature

Conflict Ask students to consider what the scene in which María paddles the chief *ladrón* conveys about the conflict in the story. Model a possible response: "María personalizes conflict between her and the *ladrón*, whereas earlier the conflict was between the group of thieves and the villagers." Ⓐ

The men came home and ate ravenously of the food María Sabida had cooked. When the chief *ladrón* had praised the old man for a fine meal, the cook admitted that it had been *la prometida* who had made the tasty chicken stew.

"My what?" the leader roared, "I have no *prometida*." And he and his men ran upstairs. But there were many floors, and by the time they were halfway to the room where María Sabida waited, many of the men had dropped down unconscious and the others had slowed down to a crawl until they too were overcome with irresistible sleepiness. Only the chief *ladrón* made it to where María

Sabida awaited him holding a paddle that she had found among his weapons. Fighting to keep his eyes open, he asked her, "Who are you, and why have you poisoned me?"

"I am your future wife, María Sabida, and you are not poisoned, I added a special sleeping powder that tastes like oregano to your *asopao*. You will not die."

"Witch!" yelled the chief *ladrón*, "I will kill you. Don't you know who I am?" And reaching for her, he fell on his knees, whereupon María Sabida beat him with the paddle until he lay curled like a child on the floor. Each time he tried to attack her, she beat him some more. When she was satisfied that he was vanquished,[6] María Sabida left the house and went back to town.

Ⓐ A week later, the chief *ladrón* rode into town with his men again. By then everyone knew what María Sabida had done and they were afraid of what these evil men would do in retribution.[7] "Why did you not just kill him when you had a chance, *muchacha*?"[8] many of the townswomen had asked María Sabida. But she had just answered mysteriously, "It is better to conquer than to kill." The townspeople then barricaded themselves behind closed doors when they heard the pounding of the thieves' horses approaching. But the gang did not stop until they arrived at María Sabida's house. There the men, instead of guns, brought out musical instruments: a *cuatro*, a *güiro*, *maracas*,[9] and a harmonica. Then they played a lovely melody.

6. **vanquished.** Defeated
7. **retribution.** Action motivated by revenge
8. **muchacha.** Girl (Spanish)
9. **cuatro...güiro...maracas.** These are all instruments native to Latin America. A *cuatro* is similar to the guitar. The *güiro* is a percussion instrument made from a gourd and played with a wooden stick. It is specific to Puerto Rico. The *maracas* are gourds filled with beans, and a player shakes them to make noise.

Differentiated Instruction

Reading Proficiency

Have students stop after reading each page and, for one minute, write down as many details as they can remember. Tell them to read their lists aloud with a partner and then to go back to the story, check the accuracy of what they wrote, and make any necessary corrections.

> **That evening, as she rode behind him on his horse, she felt the dagger concealed beneath his clothes.**

"María Sabida, María Sabida, my strong and wise María," called out the leader, sitting tall on his horse under María Sabida's window, "come out and listen to a song I've written for you—I call it *The Ballad of María Sabida*." **B**

María Sabida then appeared on her balcony wearing a wedding dress. The chief *ladrón* sang his song to her: a lively tune about a woman who had the courage of a man and the wisdom of a judge, and who had conquered the heart of the best *bandido* on the island of Puerto Rico. He had a strong voice and all the people cowering in their locked houses heard his tribute to María Sabida and crossed themselves at the miracle she had wrought.

One by one they all came out and soon María Sabida's front yard was full of people singing and dancing. The *ladrónes* had come prepared with casks of wine, bottles of rum, and a wedding cake made by the old cook from the tender meat of coconuts. The leader

of the thieves and María Sabida were married on that day. But all had not yet been settled between them. That evening, as she rode behind him on his horse, she felt the dagger concealed beneath his clothes. She knew then that she had not fully won the battle for this man's heart.

On her wedding night María Sabida suspected that her husband wanted to kill her. After their dinner, which the man had insisted on cooking himself, they went upstairs. María Sabida asked for a little time alone to prepare herself. He said he would take a walk but would return very soon. When she heard him leave the house, María Sabida went down to the kitchen and took several gallons of honey from the pantry. She went back to the bedroom and there she fashioned a life-sized doll out of her clothes and poured the honey into it. She then blew out the candle, covered the figure with a sheet and hid herself under the bed.

After a short time, she heard her husband climbing the stairs. He tip-toed into the dark room thinking her asleep in their marriage bed. Peeking out from under the bed, María Sabida saw the glint of the knife her husband pulled out from inside his shirt. Like a fierce panther he leapt onto the bed and stabbed the doll's body over and over with his dagger. Honey splattered his face and fell on his lips. Shocked, the man jumped off the bed and licked his lips. **C**

"How sweet is my wife's blood. How sweet is María Sabida in death—how sour in life and how sweet in death. If I had known she was so sweet, I would not have murdered her." And so declaring, he kneeled down on the floor beside the bed and prayed to María Sabida's soul for forgiveness.

History Connection
Spain and Puerto Rico Christopher Columbus first landed on the island of Boriken (or Boriquen) on November 19, 1492, and claimed the land for Spain. Spain ruled the island directly and then as a province with its own representative government. At the end of the Spanish-American War in 1898, Spain ceded the island to the United States. The name *Puerto Rico* means "rich port."

Analyze Literature
Ballad Explain to students that a ballad is a song that tells a story and is sung in a traditional style. A ballad usually has a slow tempo with romantic sounds to the instruments. **B**

Analyze Literature
Figurative Language Point out that the author uses a simile, comparing the thief to a fierce panther. Ask students to create an animal-related simile for María. Model a possible response: "María is like a sly fox." **C**

Writing Skills

Folk Tale
Review with students the elements of a folk tale: It is a narrative that explains something about a group's history; it is told as a true story and may mention a time and place, although its accuracy cannot be verified; it may include semi-magical beings. Have students write a folk tale based on elements of their culture. Invite students to read their folk tales aloud.

Reading Skills

Compare and Contrast Themes
Tell students that folk tales from many cultures often have similar themes, such as good triumphing over evil, honesty being rewarded, or generosity prevailing over greed. Suggest that students choose a folk tale from one country, analyze the theme, then search for a similar folk tale from another culture. Have them create a graphic organizer to compare and contrast the two tales.

Answer: Students may relate an incident such as being bullied by a sibling or another student. They may say that they responded by fighting back or by telling an adult about the problem. Knowing that they did something to help themselves may have made them feel better.

Analyze and Extend

1. (a) María was able to speak as soon as she was born. She knew which herbs would help her mother, and she was able to describe heaven in detail. (b) She believed she had been touched by God, so she would be an extraordinary person.

2. (a) She takes out the bodies of the children and puts in an herb to make the men sleep. (b) María has a special knowledge of herbs, plus she has the courage and wits to use her knowledge to her advantage.

3. His response shows that he was a foolish man because he did not suspect that she would be able to trick him twice.

At that moment María Sabida came out of her hiding place. "Husband, I have tricked you once more, I am not dead." In his joy, the man threw down his knife and embraced María Sabida, swearing that he would never kill or steal again. And he kept his word, becoming in later years an honest farmer. Many years later he was elected mayor of the same town he had once terrorized with his gang of *ladrónes*.

María Sabida made a real *casa* out of his thieves' den, and they had many children together, all of whom could speak at birth. But, they say, María Sabida always slept with one eye open, and that is why she lived to be one hundred years old and wiser than any other woman on the island of Puerto Rico, and her name was known even in Spain. ❖

Have you ever been in a situation where you felt terrorized by someone with more power? How did you respond in this situation? What other stories are you familiar with that share the theme, "It is better to conquer than to kill"?

Analyze and Extend

1. (a) What special qualities does María Sabida exhibit as a young child? (b) How do you know she will go on to be an extraordinary person?

2. (a) How does María change the stew? (b) How does her manipulation of the stew help you understand María's talents?

3. Evaluate María's husband's response to tasting the honey on his lips. What do you learn about him during this event?

Creative Writing Write **lyrics** to the song "The Ballad of María Sabida." Incorporate important parts of the legend, including the major events of the story, into the lyrics. In your lyrics, try to emulate Cofer's style and reveal the characters as well as the tone of the tale.

Collaborative Learning Create a set of questions you would like to ask María Sabida in an interview. With a partner, role-play the characters of María Sabida and interviewer. Then switch roles.

Go to **www.mirrorsandwindows.com** for more.

Rubric for Creative Writing
You can adapt this as a checklist for students to use as they write.

☐ Do the lyrics incorporate important events from the legend?

☐ Do the lyrics imitate Cofer's writing style?

☐ Do the lyrics reveal the characters as well as the tone of the legend?

from OUTLAW
THE LEGEND OF ROBIN HOOD

INDEPENDENT READING

A Graphic Novel by Tony Lee, Sam Hart, and Artur Fujita

Tony Lee is a comic-book writer who has worked on the titles *X-Men, Doctor Who Magazine,* and *Starship Troopers.* He lives in England. **Sam Hart** and **Artur Fujita** are comic book illustrators who live in Brazil. The three teamed up to create this graphic novel depicting the legend of Robin Hood. The story is set in England in 1192 under the rule of the wicked Prince John, who is bleeding the country dry through excessive taxes. While the Sheriff of Nottingham enforces the prince's unreasonable laws, Robin Hood emerges as a hero for the people. Hiding out with his band of outlaws in Sherwood Forest, he robs the rich and gives back to the poor. The book was chosen to be on the 2010 list of Great Graphic Novels for Teens by The American Library Association and Young Adult Library Services Association.

855

Preview the Selection

At a Glance
Independent Reading
- Reading Level: Moderate
- Difficulty Considerations: Vocabulary
- Ease Factor: Illustrations

Objectives
Reading this selection will enable students to do the following:
- read with developing fluency
- read silently with comprehension for a sustained period of time

Launch the Lesson
Before they open their books, ask students to discuss what they already know about Robin Hood. Are they familiar with him through books or movies?

TEACHING NOTE
Although this selection is presented in the student edition as an independent reading, teaching support has been provided should you choose to cover it in class.

Program Resources

Planning and Assessment
Program Planning Guide, Selection Lesson Plan
E-Lesson Planner
Assessment Guide, Lesson Test
ExamView

Technology Tools
Interactive Student Text on CD
Visual Teaching Package
Audio Library
mirrorsandwindows.com

Meeting the Standards
Folk Literature: Unit 8, Independent Reading

Common Core State Standards
Reading Literature
RL.1, RL.9, RL.10
Writing
W.1, W.10

Teach the Selection

Summary

Robin Hood and his accomplices stop a coach passing through Sherwood Forest. The passenger, a priest, says he has two bags of money, one for supplies for the abbey and one for the taxman. As the priest is honest, Robin Hood takes nothing. Later that evening, however, he robs the taxman and gives all the money back to the people.

 The Mirrors & Windows questions at the end of the selection focus on why the Robin Hood story has been so popular over the ages. Before they read, ask students what it means to be a legend.

Words in Use

Selection Words
toll, 856
abbey, 857
corrupt, 857
clergy, 857
parish, 857
incriminate, 859

Teaching Words
excessive, 855
adapted, 860
prosecute, 860
testimony, 860

KEY TERMS
GRAPHIC NOVEL, 855
LEGEND, 855
PETITION, 860

Teach the Selection

Analyze Literature

Graphic Tale Point out to students that in a graphic novel, the pictures are just as important as the words. Ask students: How do the pictures help you understand the story? When and why does the illustrator shift from close-ups to wider views? (For instance, in the first frame of this excerpt, a wide view is used to set the scene. On the following page, where Robin says "if we wait until he gives it to the taxman—," a close-up is used to place the focus on Robin's mischievous smile.)

Analyze Literature

Setting The story of Robin Hood is set in medieval England—that is, around 1192. As they read, ask students what clues they can find about the setting. For instance, the style of dress, the type of transportation, weaponry, and currency are all clues to the time period. The leadership role of the sheriff and the clergy are also clues that this story takes place in medieval times.

Analyze Literature

Legend Remind students that legends are passed down through generations and are often based on real events or characters. As they read, ask students to make note of place names. Later, they can look these up in an encyclopedia or atlas to connect the story to real places in England.

Differentiated Instruction

Reading Proficiency

Students may benefit from a review of words and phrases related to religion, such as the following:
abbey—a home for priests or nuns, 857
clergy—members of a religious order, 857
parish—local church community, 857

Teach the Selection

Analyze Literature

Characterization and Hero Ask students to explain how Robin Hood is characterized in this graphic novel. What kind of person is he? How do his words and actions in this excerpt establish him as a heroic character?

Use Reading Strategies

Make Inferences Remind students that in a story, not everything is stated directly. They will need to make inferences as they read. Ask them to infer the identity of the man whom Robin steals from. Where did this man get his gold? What did he say when Robin asked him how much money he was carrying? They should be able to infer from the context that the man is the taxman. He received the gold from the priest as payment of taxes collected from the people, but when Robin asked how much money he was carrying, he probably said he did not have any or lied about the amount.

Independent Reading

Students who enjoy this excerpt may wish to read the entire book *Outlaw: The Legend of Robin Hood.*

Differentiated Instruction

Auditory Learning

Stories like this one are from the oral tradition, meaning they were traditionally told aloud, not read in a book. Have students work in pairs to read the story aloud, or go around the room and have one student read each frame.

English Language Learning

Point out the words *whoosh* and *splash* and explain that these are examples of words that sound like what they mean. Other examples of onomatopoeic words include *buzz, click,* and *pop.* Ask English language learners to give examples of words in their language that sound like what they mean. See if other students can guess the meanings of the foreign words based on their sound.

Use Reading Skills

Evaluate Cause and Effect Ask students to explain why Robin waits until the taxman has collected the money before he steals it. What effect would it have on the poor of the area if he were to steal the money directly from the priest, and why? Also, why does Robin Hood toss the money on the ground rather than give it to the people by hand? What would happen if he were to give the money to them directly?

Analyze Literature

Tone Remind students that **tone** is the emotional attitude toward the reader or the subject implied by a literary work. Examples of the different tones include familiar, ironic, playful, and serious. Ask: What is the tone of this graphic novel excerpt? They may say that although the tone is serious, there is an element of playful humor in the story created by Robin's witty comments.

Vocabulary Skills

Use Word Parts

Remind students that if they encounter an unfamiliar word, they can sometimes decipher its meaning by examining the word parts. For instance, the word *incriminating* on page 859 contains the Latin word root *crimin,* which is related to *crime* and *criminal.* To *incriminate* oneself means to become guilty of a criminal act.

Answer: Students may say the legend is popular because it portrays a hero working against a corrupt government. Most people view government as corrupt and identify with the common people.

Analyze and Extend

1. (a) Robin asks how much money and jewels the traveler carries.
(b) Those who tell the truth pay a small toll. Those who lie are robbed of everything.

2. (a) The priest is honest, so Robin instead robs the taxman, who lies. By waiting to steal the money until after the priest has given it to the taxman, Robin ensures that the priest will not be responsible for recouping the loss.
(b) Robin gives the money back to the people.

3. (a) Responses will vary. The pictures may help them visualize the action. (b) Robin is similar to other comic-book heroes because he fights evil, wears a cape, and has an alias.

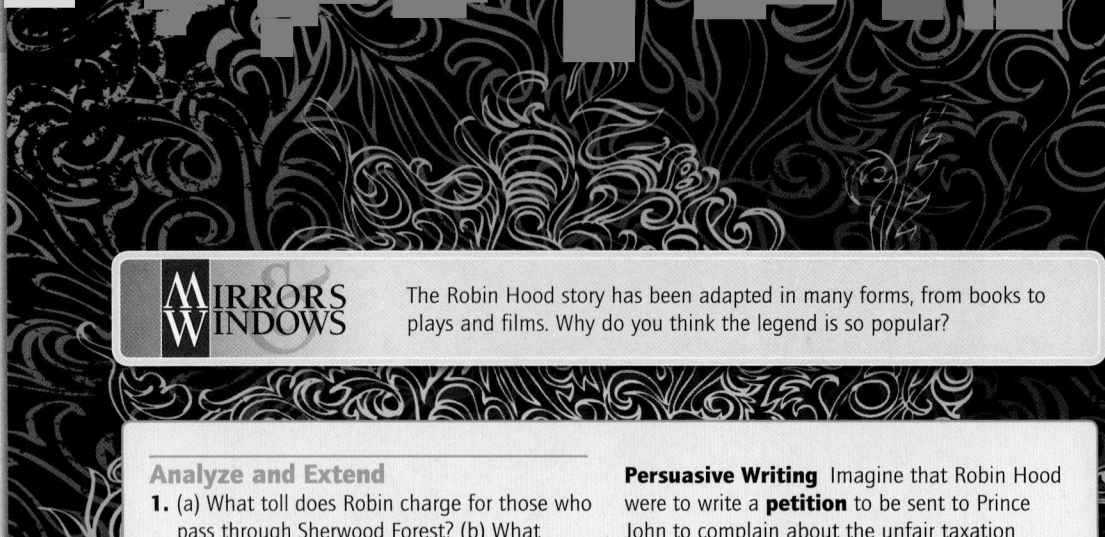

MIRRORS & WINDOWS The Robin Hood story has been adapted in many forms, from books to plays and films. Why do you think the legend is so popular?

Analyze and Extend

1. (a) What toll does Robin charge for those who pass through Sherwood Forest? (b) What happens to those who tell the truth, and what happens to those who lie to Robin?

2. (a) Why does Robin choose not to steal from the priest? (b) Whom does he take money from, and why? What does Robin do with the money?

3. A **graphic novel** is one that is told through pictures. (a) How do the pictures add to the story? (b) What qualities make Robin Hood similar to other comic-book heroes like Superman and Batman?

Persuasive Writing Imagine that Robin Hood were to write a **petition** to be sent to Prince John to complain about the unfair taxation system. Write the letter Robin might compose, using persuasive language to convince Prince John to change his laws.

Critical Literacy Imagine that Robin Hood is being put on trial for the crime of robbing people in Sherwood Forest. Act out the trial in class, with one student acting as the prosecuting attorney and one acting as Robin's defense. Testimony should be given by Robin, Robin's victims, and several witnesses. The teacher may play the role of judge, while the rest of the class should act as the jury.

Go to **www.mirrorsandwindows.com** for more.

Rubric for Persuasive Writing
You can adapt this as a checklist for students to use as they write.

☐ Does the petition clearly state a goal (a change in the tax laws)?
☐ Is it written in persuasive language, telling why the change is needed?
☐ Does it avoid errors in spelling, grammar, and mechanics?

Differentiated Instruction

Enrichment

Remind students that legends are stories that are passed down through generations and are often based on real events or characters from the past. Unlike myths, legends are usually considered to be historical, but may contain elements that are fantastic or unverifiable. Ask students to conduct research on the Robin Hood tale with the goal of identifying the history behind the legend. What was life like in England in 1192? What evidence is there that Robin Hood was a real person? Where is the real Sherwood Forest? Students may read some of the old ballads, which are the oldest form of the Robin Hood legends.

Frog

A Fairy Tale by
Vivian Vande Velde

Once upon a time when princes still set out to seek their fortunes and when cranky old women still sometimes turned out to be witches, a prince named Sidney came to a well where an old woman asked him for help in getting water.

Now the old woman didn't have a bucket and Sidney didn't have a bucket. But he'd heard enough fairy tales about three sons setting off down the road and meeting a strange old woman, and the first two sons were always rude and got into trouble, and the youngest son was always polite and then the old woman would give him whatever it was that he needed to fulfill his quest. So—being a middle son—Sidney always did his best to be polite to everybody, even when he wasn't on a quest.

But his best wasn't enough for this old woman, and the next thing he knew he was a bulgy-eyed green frog, which just goes to show that sometimes having a bucket is more important than being polite.

"There, you loathsome thing," the old woman said, which was hardly fair since she was the one who had made him into what he was, "stay a frog until a beautiful princess feeds you from her plate and lets you sleep on her pillow."

Travel goes a lot faster when you're riding a horse than when you're hopping, especially if your feet are less than a foot long. It took several days for Sidney to find the nearest

Vivian Vande Velde was born in 1951 in Rochester, New York, where she lives today. She is the author of numerous books for young people. From a young age she wanted to be a writer because, as she puts it, "I love stories—all kinds of stories, but especially fantasy." In

"**Frog**," a humorous retelling of a classic fairy tale, Vande Velde shows her talent for the unexpected twist. The story was published in her collection *Tales from the Brothers Grimm and the Sisters Weird* in 1995. Her book *A Hidden Magic* (1997), a novel-length fairy tale parody, led one critic to call her "a master of the unexpected."

861

Preview the Selection

At a Glance
Independent Reading
- Reading Level: Easy
- Difficulty Considerations: Ironic twist on original fairy tale
- Ease Factor: Familiar plot; humor

Objectives
Reading this selection will enable students to do the following:
- read with developing fluency
- read silently with comprehension for a sustained period of time

Launch the Lesson
Ask students to retell what they can remember of the fairy tale "The Frog Prince." Are they familiar with the saying, "You have to kiss a lot of frogs before you find your prince"?

TEACHING NOTE
Although this selection is presented in the student edition as an independent reading, teaching support has been provided should you choose to cover it in class.

Program Resources

Planning and Assessment
Program Planning Guide, Selection Lesson Plan
E-Lesson Planner
Assessment Guide, Lesson Test
ExamView

Technology Tools
Interactive Student Text on CD
Visual Teaching Package
Audio Library
mirrorsandwindows.com

Meeting the Standards
Folk Literature: Unit 8, Independent Reading

Common Core State Standards
Reading Literature
RL.1, RL.5, RL.9, RL.10
Writing
W.3, W.10
Speaking and Listening
SL.1

Summary

A prince named Sidney is turned into a frog by a witch, who tells him that the spell will be broken when a princess feeds him from her plate and lets him sleep on her pillow. He meets a beautiful princess and tries to make an exchange with her but she breaks her promise. At the king's insistence, the princess allows Sidney to eat a little lettuce from her plate but refuses to let him sit on her pillow. Instead she throws him against the wall, and then throws the pillow on top of him. As soon as the pillow touches him, Sidney regains his normal appearance as a handsome prince. The princess falls in love and proposes marriage, but Sidney angrily refuses.

The Mirrors & Windows questions at the end of the selection ask what parts of the story students find surprising or humorous. Before they begin reading, ask students to write down one or two predictions about how the story will turn out.

castle, and when he got there, he didn't even know whose castle it was. Everything looked different from grass level, but he was still pretty sure he didn't know the people who lived here. He hoped there was a princess.

Sidney hopped across the drawbridge and into the dusty courtyard. There were horses and dogs and chickens. People, too, way, way high up. And lots and lots of legs. Many of them were walking so fast that he knew he was in danger of getting stepped on. He saw a well in the courtyard, but Sidney had had quite enough of wells for the time being. Hurriedly, he hopped off to the side, where there was a quiet and well-tended garden.

In the garden was a lovely, cool-looking reflecting pool, with fresh, clear water and lily pads. Sidney jumped in and it felt like heaven.

Until something bonked him on the head and dunked him.

Sidney came up sputtering, just as a beautiful girl of about his own age came running up to the pool.

"Oh, no!" the girl cried. "My golden ball."

"Excuse me," Sidney said, "are you a princess?"

The girl didn't answer. She just flung herself onto the bench by the pool's edge and began to weep.

Sidney, in the middle of the pool, looked down and could see the ball just settling onto the soft mud below him. He paddled closer to the girl. "Excuse me," he said again, "are you a princess?"

"What a twit," the girl snapped, never even looking up. "Of course I am. Don't I look like one?"

"Yes, you do," Sidney admitted apologetically. "And a very lovely one at that. I think the two of us can help each other out."

"I don't want to help you out," the princess said. "I want to have my ball back."

"That's what I mean," Sidney said.

The princess finally looked at him. "You can get my ball?" she asked.

Sidney nodded.

"Well, then, do it."

"Yes," Sidney said, "but then, afterward, will you let me eat from your plate and sleep on your pillow? I'm a prince, you see, and I have a magic spell on me, and that's the only way to break it."

Travel goes a lot faster when you're riding a horse than when you're hopping, especially if your feet are less than a foot long.

The princess's lip curled in disgust. "I need that ball. It's my father's paperweight and I wasn't supposed to be playing with it."

"I don't have to eat a *lot* from your plate," Sidney told her, "and I can sleep *way over* on the side of the pillow and not take up much room at all."

"Oh, all right," the princess said.

Sidney dove into the water. The ball was heavy, but with a great deal of struggling he finally managed to get it up close enough that the princess could reach over and grasp it. As she turned the ball over in her hands to make sure it wasn't damaged, Sidney jumped onto the bench next to her. "Now," he said just as she shook the water off the ball, drenching

Words in Use

Selection Words
quest, 861
loathsome, 861

KEY TERMS
FAIRY TALE, 861
PARODY, 861

him all over again. He coughed a little bit, and when he looked up again, she was gone.

"Wait," he called, catching sight of her leaving the garden.

But she didn't.

By the time he made it out of the garden, across the courtyard, and into the castle, the princess was sitting down to dinner with her family.

Sidney kicked on the dining-room door. "Hey," he yelled. "Hey, princess!"

He heard the king ask, "What's that noise?"

"Nothing," the princess answered.

"Princess!" Sidney yelled. It's me, the frog prince. You accidentally left me behind."

The king's voice said, "He says he's a frog prince. What does he mean, you left him behind?"

"I don't know," the princess said.

"You promised you'd help me." Sidney wasn't used to yelling, and his throat was getting sore.

"You promised you'd help him?" the king asked.

"No," the princess said.

There was no other way. Sidney called out, "In return for getting back your father's golden ball paperweight that you were playing with and dropped into the pool in the garden."

"The gold paperweight that left a wet spot on my papers this afternoon?" the king asked.

"I don't know anything about it," the princess said.

The king must have brought his fist down on the table. Sidney could hear the dishes rattle. "A promise" the king said, "is a promise. Let the frog in."

Servants came and opened the big golden doors.

Sidney hopped into the dining room, which was decorated with mirrors and crystal chandeliers and hundreds of flickering candles. He hopped until he came to the princess's chair.

"What, exactly," the king asked his daughter, "did you promise him?"

"I can't remember," the princess said.

"That I could eat from your plate," Sidney reminded her. "That I could sleep on your pillow. I promised not to eat too much and to use only the corner of the pillow."

"A promise is a promise," the king repeated.

The princess lifted Sidney, not very gently, and plunked him down on the white linen tablecloth beside her china dish.

Sidney nibbled on a piece of lettuce that was hanging off the edge of the dish.

The princess put her napkin up to her mouth and made gagging sounds. "I'm all finished," she announced, shoving the plate away.

"Then you may leave the table," the king said. "Don't forget your little friend."

The princess scooped up Sidney and brought him up the stairs to her bedroom, stamping her feel all the way.

"Thank you," Sidney yelled back down the stairs to the king.

"You horrid beast," the princess growled at Sidney. "You told him about the paperweight. Now I'm going to be in trouble."

"It was your own fault for walking away so fast that I couldn't keep up," Sidney said. "Are you going to put me on your pillow now?"

"I'll put you on my pillow!" the princess shouted. "But I'll put you on my wall first."

She flung Sidney with all her might against the wall.

Analyze Literature

Fairy Tale and Parody To help students understand how Vande Velde parodies fairy tales in this selection, ask them to create a graphic organizer in which they compare "Frog" to the traditional tale "The Frog Prince" and other fairy tales. They may make notes such as the following:

Traditional Fairy Tale	Parody
People are cursed because of bad behavior	Sidney is cursed for no good reason
Serious tone	Humorous tone
Happy ending with marriage	Prince rejects princess

Analyze Literature

Humor Point out to students that some of the humor of this story comes from the author's use of updated language in a story with a medieval setting. For instance, the princess snaps, "What a twit," and Sidney says, "I can sleep *way over* on the side of the pillow." The author also creates humorous images by showing the frog's perspective; for instance, Sidney sees "lots and lots of legs" in the palace courtyard.

Differentiated Instruction

Visual Learning

Visual learners may enjoy drawing pictures of the major scenes of the story. For extra credit, ask them to put drawings and words together to create a picture book for children. They will need to simplify the text and edit it down to fewer words so that it can be easily read by children.

English Language Learning

English language learners may need help with some of the vocabulary in the tale:

drawbridge — a bridge that can be pulled up or let down in order to control entrance to a castle, 862

courtyard — an outdoor area enclosed on all four sides, 862

bonked — hit, 862

paperweight — a small, heavy object used to hold down papers on a desk, 862

gagging — choking, 863

Answer: Students may be surprised and amused by the changes made to the story, such as the change from a traditional happy ending to the prince's rejection of the princess.

Analyze and Extend

1. (a) A cranky old woman (actually a witch) turns him into a frog because he has no bucket to help her get water. (b) Sidney does not deserve his fate. Being a middle son, he did his best to be polite, but it wasn't enough for the old woman.

2. (a) The princess mistreats Sidney, breaking her promise to help him and then almost killing him by throwing him against a wall. (b) Sidney refuses to marry her because she is not a nice person.

3. (a) "Frog" is a parody because it pokes fun at elements of traditional fairy tales. (b) The traditional tale has a happy ending in which the prince and princess marry, but in this version, the prince rejects her.

"Ow!" Sidney cried, landing in a heap on the floor.

"Now here's the pillow," the princess said, throwing that on top of him.

But as soon as the pillow touched Sidney's head, he instantly regained his normal shape.

"Oh my!" the princess gasped. She was going to be in serious trouble with her father now, she thought. Here she had a man in her room and her father was never going to believe that this was the same person who had come into her room as a frog. Even now she could hear her father coming up the stairs, demanding, "What's all the commotion?"

But the prince—he was obviously a prince—who stood before her was incredibly handsome, and she was falling in love already, which surely would balance out the trouble she'd be in with her father.

"Oh" she said, clapping her hands together. "I'm so sorry. But my father will make it worth your while. We can get married, and he'll give you half the kingdom and—"

"Are you out of your mind?" Sidney said. "First you break your promise to me, then you lie about it until your father forces you to keep it, then you try to kill me. No, thank you, princess." He strode out of the door, out of the castle, out of the kingdom, returning home, where he eventually married the goose girl.

And the princess was right: her father didn't believe her story. ❖

What parts of the story surprised you? What parts did you find humorous? Discuss your reactions with your classmates.

Analyze and Extend

1. (a) How does Sidney get turned into a frog? (b) Does he do anything to deserve this fate? Explain.

2. (a) How is Sidney treated by the princess? (b) Why does he refuse to marry her at the end of the story?

3. A **parody** is a piece of writing that imitates another work in order to poke fun at it. (a) Explain why this selection can be considered a parody. (b) How is it different from the traditional Grimm brothers tale of the frog prince?

Creative Writing Vivian Vande Velde provides the following instructions on how to write a "fractured" fairy tale: "(1) Make the villain a hero. (2) Make the hero a villain. (3) Tell what really happened. (4) All of the above." Follow her instructions to create a **fairy tale parody** of your own. For best results, choose a familiar tale that most of your classmates will know and keep the same basic storyline, but give it a new spin.

Collaborative Learning Hold a panel discussion about the value of fairy tales in teaching values to young children. In preparation for the discussion, brainstorm a list of popular fairy tales and determine what messages, or morals, are communicated in each. For instance, what does "The Frog Prince" teach children about looking beyond appearances? What important lesson may be found in "Little Red Riding Hood"? Do the stories of princesses place too much emphasis on the value of beauty?

Go to **www.mirrorsandwindows.com** for more.

Rubric for Creative Writing

☐ You can adapt this as a checklist for students to use as they write.

☐ Does the story parody, or poke fun at, a well-known fairy tale?

☐ Does it give a new spin on the fairy tale, such as presenting the villain as a hero or the hero as a villain, or telling what really happened?

☐ Does it avoid errors in spelling, grammar, and mechanics?

Enrichment

The story "The Frog Prince" was collected by German scholars Jacob and Wilhelm Grimm and appeared in their collection of fairy tales in the early 1800s. Ask students to learn more about Jacob and Wilhelm Grimm, known as the Brothers Grimm, and how they collected their tales. They may also locate and read several versions of the tale of the frog prince and compare the various versions.

The Ant and the Grasshopper

A Fable by James Finn Garner

"The only place where success comes before work is in the dictionary."

Preview the Selection

At a Glance
Independent Reading
- Reading Level: Moderate
- Difficulty Considerations: Vocabulary; satirical tone
- Ease Factor: Familiar plot; humor

Objectives
Reading this selection will enable students to do the following:
- read with developing fluency
- read silently with comprehension for a sustained period of time

Launch the Lesson
In the 1980s and 1990s, terms like *people of color, differently-abled,* and *senior citizen* replaced the old, biased *colored people, disabled,* and *aged.* The term *womyn* arose as an alternative way to spell *women* without using the word *men.* Before reading the fable, ask students to think of other "politically-correct terms" that have replaced biased language.

TEACHING NOTE
Although this selection is presented in the student edition as an independent reading, teaching support has been provided should you choose to cover it in class.

INDEPENDENT READING

In the world of ancient Greeks, agriculture was still in a state of advanced rudimentariness.[1] The farm ecosystems were diverse and healthy, with indigenous free-range plants and thriving insect colonies sharing space with the domesticated crops. As a result, the fields of wheat and grapes were filled with a variety of vigorous, forward-looking, and well-spoken insects. The most industrious of these was the ant. All summer long he worked in the hot sun, storing away grain and seeds in anticipation of a long winter.

In that same field lived a grasshopper whose life was very free from care, since he had long ago rejected the bourgeois,[2] money-grubbing concepts of "making it." To him, the ideal existence was to enjoy Nature in an

---

1. **advanced rudimentariness.** A politically correct way of saying "primitive"
2. **bourgeois.** Describing people of the landowning class

James Finn Garner's "The Ant and the Grasshopper" is an updated retelling of the traditional Aesop's fable. In Garner's bestselling books *Politically Correct Bedtime Stories* (1994) and *Once Upon a More Enlightened Time: More Politically Correct Bedtime Stories* (1995), the Chicago-based author pokes fun at so-called *politically correct* language—that is, language that carefully avoids sexism, racism, ageism, classism and other types of discrimination. Garner takes a humorous approach to the trend in his retellings of traditional tales.

865

Program Resources

Planning and Assessment
Program Planning Guide, Selection Lesson Plan
E-Lesson Planner
Assessment Guide, Lesson Test
ExamView

Technology Tools
Interactive Student Text on CD
Visual Teaching Package
Audio Library
mirrorsandwindows.com

Meeting the Standards
Folk Literature: Unit 8, Independent Reading

Common Core State Standards
Reading Literature
RL.1, RL.3, RL.6, RL.10
Writing
W.3, W.10
Language
L.6

Summary

In ancient Greece, an ant and a grasshopper clash because of their differing lifestyles. The ant is an industrious "type-A personality" who works so hard at hoarding his grain that he develops an ulcer. The grasshopper enjoys sleeping, singing, and doing yoga. When winter arrives early, the grasshopper begins to starve, but the ant refuses to share his hoard. Just then a praying mantis arrives to audit the ant's finances. The ant's hoard is appropriated and redistributed and he is jailed, while the grasshopper receives government benefits.

The Mirrors & Windows questions at the end of the selection ask students to come up with a moral for this story. Before they begin reading, ask students familiar with Aesop's fables to retell what they can remember of "The Ant and the Grasshopper." What is the moral of the original tale?

TEACHING NOTE

The original Aesop's fable "The Ant and the Grasshopper" appears in *Mirrors & Windows* Level II on page 766. The grade 7 E-book can be accessed at **www.mirrorsandwindows.com**.

Analyze Literature

Tone Help students identify the satirical tone in this fable. For instance, point out the sentence "vigorous, forward-looking, and well-spoken insects." By describing insects in such positive terms, Garner is being satirical or sarcastic. He is making fun of the way so-called politically correct language is used to avoid offending different populations—in this case, bugs.

---

unstructured and playfully exploratory manner, and he often took advantage of His/Her/Its beneficence by sleeping most of the day. At other times, he would sing joyfully in the meadow, *churREEP churREEP*, thus keeping alive the rich oral tradition of the grasshoppers.

This alternative attitude did not go unnoticed by the ant, as he toiled in the heat and dust. When he saw the grasshopper enjoying life on his own terms, it made every orifice in his exoskeleton cinch up tight.

"Look at that grasshopper," the ant muttered to himself. "Sitting around on his abdomen all day, singing his blasted songs. When will he ever show some responsibility? To call him leech would be an insult to all the hardworking segmented worms in this country. He's just watching me, waiting for the chance to jump me and take everything I've worked so hard for. That's the way it is with his phylum."[3]

For his part, the grasshopper was also watching the ant, but with an entirely different train of thought. "Look at that ant," he mused, "working so hard to accumulate his little store of grain. And for what? If only he would try to be a little more Zen-like.[4] He might understand that, to the stone, one kernel of grain is the same as one thousand, and the rain never has to worry about its penmanship."

So the summer went. The ant, a quintessential type-A persunality,[5] worked

---

himself into a frenzy every day, but his selfish and socially irresponsible activity took its toll. He developed a peptic ulcer, had some scares with thorax pains, and lost most of the hair on the top of his head. In mid-September, his wife left him and took the pupae,[6] but he scarcely noticed. The ant became so obsessed with his store of grain that we went so far as to install an elaborate security system in and around his anthill, with video cameras and motion sensors to catch any would-be thief.

In between naps, the grasshopper watched all this with detached curiosity. He also studied hatha yoga, scoured the area for the perfect cup of cappuccino, taught himself to play the guitar (really only one song, a self-penned, quasi-blues number with three notes), and generally hung out. He tried to keep his leisure-centric lifestyle attuned to the passing of the seasons. When the weather turned less congenial, he planned to go to Australia and do a little surfing.

But winter arrived early that year (or summer left too soon, depending on your climatic orientation) and the fields were quickly barren. The unfortunate grasshopper found himself a victim of the capriciousness

What's the sound of one bug starving?

---

3. **phylum.** Biological type
4. **Zen-like.** Following the teachings of Japanese Zen Buddhism
5. **personality.** Garner is making fun of politically correct spelling, used in words like *womyn*. The spelling of *person* as *persun* removes the male word *son*, making the word gender-neutral.

Words in Use

Selection Words

ecosystem, 865
vigorous, 865
industrious, 865
beneficence, 866
orifice, 866
exoskeleton, 866
quintessential, 866
capriciousness, 867
karma, 867
ominous, 868

Teaching Words

sexism, 865
racism, 865
ageism, 865
classism, 865
discrimination, 865

KEY TERMS

FABLE, 865
MORAL, 868
SATIRE, 868
CRITICAL ANALYSIS, 868

of meteorological change. He went hopping about the field, looking for sustenance of any kind. He would have settled for a crumb, a husk, a bit of tofu—but nothing edible could be found.

Soon the grasshopper spotted the ant, lustily dragging a full cornstalk behind him. The grasshopper's hunger got the better of his pride, and he walked over, intending to ask the ant to share a little of his immense hoard. But as soon as he caught sight of the grasshopper, the ant began to scream.

"AAAHHHHH!!! What do you want? What are you doing here? You've come to take my cornstalk, haven't you? I know you've been plotting the day when you would snatch everything I own! Your type are all the same!"

The grasshopper tried to interrupt, but the ant raved on: "Don't say anything! Don't try to work your wiles on me, with your sob stories and empty promises! I've worked hard for what I have, even if that might not be fashionable in some circles."

The grasshopper said politely, "But surely, Brother Ant, you have more than you could ever possibly eat."

"That's my business," said the ant, "and we don't live in some blood-sucking socialist state[7]. . . yet! Get with the program, grasshopper! The only place where success comes before work is in the dictionary."

"I was planning to go to Australia, see, but the weather, like, *changed* and all the food has disappeared. . . ."

"That's how a free market works, pal. Take a lesson."

"Forgive me, Brother Ant, but I feel obliged to say, like, I think you need to work on your karma. The aura you're giving off is full of negative energy, which you could easily convert into positive by simply—"

"Look, you want to get all mystical on me, then tell me: What's the sound of one bug starving? Ha ha!"

The ant and the grasshopper were interrupted in their fruitless debate by the sound of a cough. They turned and saw a huge mantis bigger than the two of them put together! (The mantis was at one time a praying mantis but had been prohibited from such practices by court order. He did, however, retain a deeply spiritual side.) The ant and the grasshopper were frightened, not by the mantis's larger-than-proportionally-

---

6. **pupae.** Young insects in the state of development between larva and adult; that is, the ant's children

7. **socialist state.** A state similar to communism in which resources are shared

Teach the Selection

Reading Skills
Paraphrase In order to monitor their comprehension of the story, ask students to paraphrase passages as they go along, putting the story into simpler language in order to understand it at a literal level. For instance, the first paragraph of the story might be paraphrased as: "Many insects lived in ancient Greece, and the most hardworking was the ant, who worked all summer storing grain and seeds for winter."

Science Connection
Entomology Inform students that entomology is the study of insects. Ask students to skim the text for scientific terms related to entomology and create a mini-glossary. They may record words like *exoskeleton*, *abdomen*, *thorax*, *forelegs*, and *phylum*.

Analyze Literature
Personification Fables usually feature animals who are personified, or given human characteristics. Ask students to collect details about how the ant and the grasshopper are personified in this tale. For instance, the ant gets an ulcer and a divorce; the grasshopper plays the guitar and does yoga.

Vocabulary Skills

Word Parts
Remind students that prefixes are meaningful word parts that come at the beginnings of words, while suffixes are meaning word parts at the ends of words. Ask them to come up with definitions for the following words based on their prefix or suffix.
1. self-penned
2. quasi-blues
3. leisure-centric
4. redistribution

Answer: A possible moral might be: "Don't bother to work hard, as the government will provide."

Analyze and Extend

1. (a) The ant is hardworking, uptight, and miserly while the grasshopper is laid-back and irresponsible. (b) The ant represents a conservative capitalist while the grasshopper is like a socialist or left-wing radical.

2. (a) In the original fable the grasshopper is left to perish without any food stored up for the winter. In this version, the ant is jailed and his wealth is seized by the government and redistributed, and the grasshopper happily continues his lazy way of life. (b) The change suggests that in modern society, hard work is no longer valued.

3. (a) This fable is satirical because it offers a biting critique of modern society. Responses will vary. (b) Garner makes fun of type-A personalities who work hard to get ahead as well as hippie types who spout Eastern philosophy. He also makes fun of politically correct language.

average size but by the nonsense-free aspect of his appearance. He wore a gray polyester suit and brown loafers with tassels, and in his forelegs he carried a briefcase, a brown paper lunch bag, and a calculator.

"Ant?" the mantis asked, even though he knew exactly which one he was looking for. "Ant, I've come for an audit."[8]

With those six ominous words, the course of our story changes. Omitting the details of the audit, and the contested charges, and the suit and countersuit, and the ant's attempted flight to the Caymans,[9] suffice it to say that the greedy insect's hoard was appropriated[10] and put to more

responsible community uses after he was enrolled in the correctional system. The grasshopper, meanwhile, organized a program for young area insects eager for cultural interchange with countries with warmer climates. Thanks to government revenue redistribution (and the ant's estate), the grasshopper has been directing surfing expeditions from that day to this. ❖

---

8. audit. A detailed review of a person's finances to determine whether more taxes are owed
9. Caymans. The Cayman Islands, a British territory in the Caribbean Sea known as a haven for those who wish to avoid taxation
10. appropriated. Seized

A **fable** is a tale with a moral, or lesson. What might be the moral of this modern fable?

Analyze and Extend

1. (a) Describe the characters of the ant and the grasshopper. (b) What types of people and political beliefs do they represent?

2. (a) How is the ending of this tale different from that of the original fable "The Ant and the Grasshopper"? (b) What does the change suggest about the values of modern society?

3. Satire is humorous writing intended to point out human failings. (a) What makes this fable satirical? (b) What types of human behavior or thought is Garner criticizing?

Expository Writing Write a **critical analysis** of Garner's fable, explaining how Garner uses satire to make fun of contemporary American culture. What modern values does he make fun of? Do you agree or disagree with his criticism of modern society? Use quotations from the story to support your points.

Collaborative Learning Working in small groups, review the story "The Ant and the Grasshopper" and make a glossary of all the politically correct terms. Give a definition for each. For example: *advanced rudimentariness:* primitive state; *thriving insect colonies:* pests.

 Go to www.mirrorsandwindows.com for more.

Rubric for Expository Writing
You can adapt this as a checklist for students to use as they write.
☐ Does the essay examine the fable as a satire of modern culture?
☐ Are quotations from the story used to support the writer's points?
☐ Does the essay avoid errors in spelling, grammar, and mechanics?

Differentiated Instruction

Enrichment
The story "The Ant and the Grasshopper" compares socialism to free-market capitalism. In order to better understand the story, students will need to know the definitions of these two types of political economies. Ask students to do some research to come up with good definitions of these two terms. Which economic system is dominant in the U.S.? Which is preferable, in their opinion?

For Your Reading List

White Wolf Woman and Other Native American Transformation Myths

by Teresa Pijoan

This collection of Native American transformation myths includes tales about snakes, wolves, bears, and other animals. "Wolf Woman Running" is a powerful story about a Sioux woman who runs away from her abusive husband to live with the wolves. In "Spirit Eggs," a Cheyenne youth sees his friend transformed into Snake Man, protector of the Mississippi River.

Golden Tales: Myths, Legends, and Folktales from Latin America

by Lulu Delacre

These twelve tales from four native cultures, Taino, Zapotec, Muisca, and Inca, include folk tales, legends of the conquistadors, and traditional creation myths. The early folk tales in this volume present a picture of Latin American cultures before Columbus, and later tales show the Spanish influence in Mexico and the Caribbean.

The Legend of the Wandering King

by Laura Gallego García

Walid ibn Hujr, a prince of ancient Arabia, has riches and honor but dreams of becoming a great poet. When his poems repeatedly lose in competition to a humble carpet weaver, Hammad, the prince, punishes him by forcing him to weave a carpet containing the entire history of the human race. One glance at this magical carpet can drive viewers mad. When the carpet is stolen, it is up to the prince to find it and right the wrongs he committed.

Solomon and the Ant: And Other Jewish Folktales

by Sheldon Oberman

The folk tales in this collection reflect the wisdom and humor of the Jewish oral tradition. Tales include "Solomon's Ring of Wisdom," "The Seven Questions of Alexander the Great," "A Special Way of Thinking," and "Which One Was Blind?" arranged chronologically, with background information and commentary.

Spider Spins a Story: Fourteen Legends from Native America

by Jill Max

These tales from many different tribes, including the Navajo, Zuni, Cherokee, Hopi, Lakota, and Muskogee, feature a spider character. The spider occasionally plays the role of a trickster, but most often it appears as Spider Woman, "Grandmother of the Earth," who represents wisdom, light, or good fortune. Stunning paintings and drawings by Native American artists illustrate these legends.

The Legend of the White Buffalo Woman

by Paul Goble

This Native American legend describes a great flood that destroyed almost all life on the earth. The legend relates how the Lakota Nation came to life again from the union of a surviving woman and an eagle of the sky. The people fell on hard times, but the arrival of the powerful White Buffalo Woman, and her gift of the Sacred Calf Pipe, brought new hope to the Lakota people.

Program Resources

EMC Access Editions

For additional independent reading, you may wish to refer students to one of EMC's Access Edition titles such as Stephen Crane's *The Red Badge of Courage.* Each Access Edition contains a thorough study apparatus, including background information, literal comprehension questions, footnotes, vocabulary definitions, critical thinking questions, and related projects and activities. An Assessment Manual offering worksheets and exams is available for each Access Edition.

Independent Reading

Independent Reading Activity

Define the word *icon* as an emblem or image that comes to represent a large idea. Tell students that some of the figures in the oral tradition can be called *iconic*. Give them some examples such as Cinderella as an iconic underappreciated stepdaughter or Blackbeard as an iconic pirate.

Help students link their independent reading to the unit theme, Recalling Heroes, by asking them to identify some iconic figures in stories they have read. You might try an in-class activity: Have students read silently a tale from an ancient tradition for at least ten minutes. Then have students identify an iconic figure from the tale and describe what the figure conveys about the culture from which the story came.

◈ EMC E-Library

The EMC E-Library contains over twenty thousand pages of literary classics that students may read independently. An Electronic Library Guide provides teaching suggestions, enrichment activities, and reading strategy guidesheets.

Common Core State Standards

Reading Literature
RL.10

Objectives

Participating in this lesson will help students write a research report that

- clearly states a thesis or frames a question
- follows a logical organizational pattern
- relies on multiple sources of information
- accurately documents sources
- employs clear topic sentences and supporting details
- closes by summarizing main points and either restating the thesis or answering the opening question

Launch the Workshop

Have students take out a clean sheet of paper. Give them two minutes to describe, in writing, their current favorite topic to research and why it is so appealing. Tell them that they can consider informal research, such as checking out a new style of clothing, as well as academic topics.

Collect the papers and shuffle them. Read the topics out loud (students should remain anonymous), and ask for ideas on how to study them. Finally, tell students they will have a chance to pursue and present some exciting research in this workshop.

Program Resources

Additional writing workshops are available in the *Exceeding the Standards: Writing* resource.

Writing Workshop

Expository Writing

Research Report

In this unit, you read an article debunking the urban legend about crocodiles in the sewers of New York. The authors of "Gatored Community" cite sources in the *New York Times* to support their thesis. You might have noticed the use of quotation marks enclosing direct quotations, as in this example:

> September 4, 1927:
> A "good-sized Florida alligator" found in a storm-swollen stream in Middletown, NY. "It was later discovered that the alligator had escaped several months ago from a pen on the premises of Dr. F. E. Fowler."

Documenting sources of information is standard procedure when using someone else's ideas to back up your points: give credit where it is due. Even if you do not use someone else's exact words, give credit if you have summarized or paraphrased someone else's ideas.

In this workshop, you will learn how to write a **research report,** a type of expository (or informational) writing in which you take information from different sources and use it to support a thesis or answer a question. You also document your sources briefly within the paper and, in a more detailed fashion, in a bibliography or list of works cited. Here's a summary of the assignment for a research report. This summary includes a writing rubric, a set of standards by which you can evaluate your work. You will refer to this rubric as you draft and revise your report.

Assignment: Write a research report in which I support a thesis or answer a question.

Goal: Use reliable sources that I analyze, interpret, and evaluate, taking care to document them properly.

Strategy: Take notes as I research my topic and then organize them in a way that clearly supports my thesis.

Writing Rubric: My research report should include the following:

- a clearly stated thesis or well-framed question
- a logical organizational pattern
- information gathered from multiple sources as well as my own ideas and explanation
- accurately documented sources
- well-developed paragraphs with clear topic sentences and supporting details
- a closing that clearly summarizes my main points and restates my thesis or answers my question

What Great Writers Do

Here's what Virginia Hamilton has to say about the research she does for her stories and novels:

All of my books take research. There is always something I do not know or need to find out about. Research is vital. For the story collections, it may take six months. Novel research can take quite a long time.

Words in Use

Teaching Words

debunking, 870
paraphrased, 870
reliable, 870
springboard, 871
notation, 871
reevaluate, 871
spatial, 872

KEY TERMS

THESIS, 870	SPATIAL ORDER, 872	PEER REVIEW, 873
RESEARCH REPORT, 870	ORDER OF IMPORTANCE, 872	ANNOTATION, 873
BIBLIOGRAPHY, 870	CONCLUSION, 872	PARAPHRASE, 874
WORKS CITED, 870	PUNCTUATION, 872	SUMMARIZE, 874
ORGANIZATIONAL PATTERN, 870	COORDINATING CONJUNCTION, 872	PLAGIARISM, 874
CHRONOLOGICAL ORDER, 872	CORRELATIVE CONJUNCTION, 872	APPOSITIVE, 874
CLASSIFICATION ORDER, 872	SUBORDINATING CONJUNCTION, 872	APPOSITIVE PHRASE, 874
		ADJECTIVE, 874
		PREPOSITIONAL PHRASE, 874

Common Core State Standards

Writing
W.2, W.4, W.5, W.6, W.7, W.8, W.10

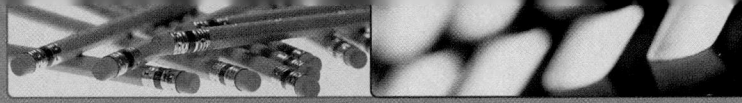

1. PREWRITE

Choosing Your Topic

A research paper is a time-consuming project, so you should choose a topic that you find interesting. If you are having trouble coming up with a topic, try some of these strategies.

Scan the News Browse through recent newspapers and magazines, tune in to news broadcasts on television and the radio, and scan news articles on your Internet browser. Make a list of people, places, events, or issues that you want to learn more about. Choose one of these items as a topic for your research.

Respond to Literature Reread a selection from this unit and use it as a springboard for new ideas. For example, does the Aztec "Legend of the Feathered Serpent" push you to want to learn more about Aztec culture? Do the two selections about Paul Bunyan suggest a paper on the lumber industry or environmental issues?

Gathering Information

You have chosen a topic that interests you, so you might already know quite a bit about it. Jot down what you already know, including as many details as you can recall. Then collect information from various sources to fill in any holes. You may already have a thesis (main point) in mind, so begin by looking for information that supports that thesis. As you research, keep an open mind. Expect that you may need to revise your thesis as you learn more about your topic. Get a stack of note cards and follow these guidelines for your note-taking:

- Write one note per card.
- Use quotation marks when you copy someone else's words exactly.
- Make sure you have spelled names and technical terms correctly.
- On each card, make a brief note of the title of the book or article and its page number, or the name of the website.

- Create a separate list giving complete information about each book, article, or website. For print sources, list the author, title, publisher, and place and date of publication. For Internet sources, list the sponsor, page name, date of last revision if given, date you visited it, and address.

Here's a sample note card:

> **Ellis Island**
>
> "Soon after the 1924 Immigration Act was adopted, traffic through Ellis Island subsided to a trickle."
>
> Bell, p. 95

Here's a sample notation that you might make on your separate list about this source:

> Bell, James B., and Richard I. Abrams. _In Search of Liberty: The Story of the Statue of Liberty and Ellis Island._ New York: Doubleday, 1984.

The reason you put all this information in a separate list is to avoid having to write it on each card as you take notes. You'll need this information later, when you write your list of works cited. Another way to gather information is to make photocopies of source material or print it from the Internet source. Highlight the information you plan to use.

Deciding on Your Purpose

What are you trying to prove in your paper? Reevaluate your thesis. Should you revise it, based on what you found out? A research paper on Ellis Island might include a thesis statement like this:

> For the poor immigrants entering the United States through Ellis Island, the experience was often frightening.

Teach the Workshop

Prewrite

Choose a Topic If you conducted the "Launch the Workshop" activity on page 856, encourage students to consider ideas they heard about as additional potential topics.

Gather Information Remind students that they may use both primary and secondary sources. Suggest that they use a graphic organizer to plan their research. For example, they can use a chart with columns for titles of primary and secondary sources. In their initial explorations of secondary sources, such as encyclopedias, they will probably read about primary sources they would like to consult.

Students can develop their organizers to keep track of source credibility. For example, they can note a source's date and the background of its author.

Internet Research Remind students to carefully check the credibility of any source they find on the Internet. A first step is to rely more on sources whose names end with .org, .gov, .edu, or .mil than on sources that include .com or .net. Caution them that even these sources can vary in quality. A student paper at an educational website (.edu) would be less reliable than an article by several professors from the same site, for example.

Writing Skills

Brainstorming

Remind students that brainstorming is a way of generating a lot of ideas without stopping to analyze them. Organize students into small groups based on similar interests, reading levels, or other appropriate factors. Have each group decide on a way to record its ideas before it begins. Provide the guidelines below, and allow groups to brainstorm for five minutes about interesting research topics.

When groups finish, tell students to note any great ideas they want to pursue.

1. For the first round of ideas, go around the group and let everyone speak. Then start generating ideas from the first round.
2. Do not comment on any idea. Just record it.
3. Repetition is OK.

Draft

Organizing Ideas Help students distinguish between organization of the entire essay and organization of paragraphs. Explain that the overall essay may be chronological, but particular paragraphs may have classification, spatial, compare-contrast, cause-effect, or order-of-importance organization. You may wish to give students sample transition words and phrases.

- Order-of-importance—*first, most, least, greater, greatest*
- Compare-contrast—*also, both, however, in contrast, in the same way*
- Cause-effect—*as a result, because*
- Classification—*among, one of, like, another, related*
- Spatial—*here, there, above, below, around, next to, together, apart*

Putting Thoughts on Paper Direct attention to the sample plan on this page. Point out that these instructions relate to all research papers, not just to the model paper about Ellis Island. Have volunteers read each bulleted item aloud. Ask students for examples of each item and/or questions about each one.

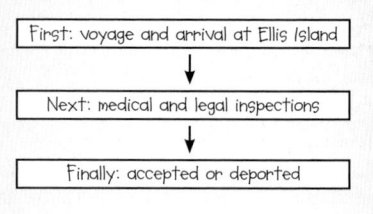

2. DRAFT

Organizing Ideas

Once you have a strong thesis and have gathered information from multiple sources, choose an organizational pattern for your paper. A paper on Ellis Island, for example, might best use **chronological order.** This type of organization would describe the immigrant's experience in the order in which events happened. Other topics might require different sorts of organization, such as classification order, spatial order, or order of importance. Choose the type of organization that works best with your topic.

> First: voyage and arrival at Ellis Island
> ↓
> Next: medical and legal inspections
> ↓
> Finally: accepted or deported

Putting Your Thoughts on Paper

As you write your draft, keep in mind that a research report has three basic parts: an introduction, body, and conclusion. Create a plan for your paper, such as the one on the right based on Ellis Island.

It doesn't really matter which section you write first. Some writers begin with the main body of their paper, writing the introduction and conclusion later. Some writers begin with the introduction, perhaps grabbing the reader's interest with an anecdote followed by the thesis statement. Then they write the body and conclusion. Use whichever method works best for you. Remember that your goal is to get your ideas down on paper according to the organizational plan you have chosen. At this point, focus your efforts on content and organization. You can check your punctuation, spelling, and grammar later, when you edit and proofread your work.

Introduction

- Open with an interesting fact, image, question, or anecdote to draw the reader in.
- Present my thesis statement.

Body

- State each main idea in a topic sentence.
- Support each main idea with paraphrased, summarized, and quoted information from multiple sources documented correctly.
- Explain how the research supports my thesis, and add my own ideas.

Conclusion

- Refer back to the opening idea or image as I summarize my main points.
- Wrap up the main ideas of my report.

Making Connections

As you draft your essay, use conjunctions to make connections between ideas. If the ideas are of equal importance in a sentence, use coordinating and correlative conjunctions. If one idea is subordinate to another, use subordinating conjunctions. Here are some examples of conjunctions that can be helpful in achieving clarity and sentence variety.

Coordinating Conjunctions	Correlative Conjunctions	Subordinating Conjunctions
and	both...and	although
but	either...or	because
for	neither...nor	if
nor	not only...but also	since
or	whether...or	though
so		unless
yet		until

Differentiated Instruction

Kinesthetic Learning

Offer kinesthetic learners the chance to arrange their material on the board or on a large sheet of paper. The paper can hang on the wall or lie on a tabletop. Invite students to use this space to experiment with putting their notes in different sequences and to map their reports in the form of time lines, cluster charts, and other organizers. When students are satisfied with how they have laid out their notes, encourage them to record their work before removing it.

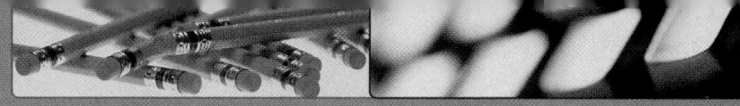

Evaluating Your Draft

When you revise, your goal is to identify the strengths and weaknesses in your writing. Consider the organization and content, and decide how to improve your draft. Evaluate your paper on your own, and then trade papers with a partner for a **peer review** to see how you can improve each other's work. Use the checklist as a guide.

Below is a draft of part of a research paper. Changes have been made within the body of the text, and reasons for the changes are given in the annotations on the right.

Revising Checklist

❑ Does the report contain a clear thesis?

❑ Is the organization clear?

❑ Is there information from multiple sources to support my thesis and main ideas?

❑ Are sources correctly documented?

❑ Do I include my own ideas and explanations?

Between 1892 and 1924, Ellis Island was the port of entry for over twelve million immigrants who were coming to the United States in search of a better life. Imagine what it must have felt like to see the Statue of Liberty holding her torch high in a gesture of welcome. ~~This statue had been a gift to the people of America from the people of France.~~ Behind her, the sight of the New York City skyline promised a new beginning. For the wealthier passengers, Ellis Island could indeed be called the "Island of Hope," but for many of the poorer passengers, Ellis Island became known as the "Island of Tears." *For the poor immigrants entering the United States through Ellis Island, the experience was often frightening.*

Their difficult journey began the day they stepped on the boat in their own countries. The voyage across the sea took anywhere from eight to fourteen days *(Burns 226)*. For those in steerage, the area "in the dark 'basement' of the boat near the steering equipment" *(Jango-Cohen 14)*, the trip was especially difficult.

> *Delete a sentence that does not support the topic sentence.*

> *Add a sentence that states the thesis of the paper.*

> *Document sources for any information from another source.*

Teach the Workshop

Revise

Evaluating a Draft Remind students to check for a clear organization and good transitions as they review their own work. When they have done as much as they can in the available time, suggest that they conduct a peer review. Be sure they understand the rubric.

Allow ample time for reviewers to read the report they receive. Schedule peer review exchanges when each student will have several minutes to deliver his or her review, and when each writer will have time to thoughtfully absorb the comments and ask questions for clarification.

Review the Thesis Statement Counsel students to double-check their thesis statements at this point. Remind them that a thesis statement identifies the topic and an aspect of or perspective on the topic that the writer will explore. In the model thesis statement (italicized), the topic is immigrants entering the United States through Ellis Island, and the perspective is how frightening the experience could be.

Writing Skills

Predicate Adjectives

Point to the word *poor* in the model thesis statement. Ask if this word can ever be used as an adverb. Most students will say no, and tell them they are right. Then ask what the word *poor* modifies in this sentence: "That child looks poor." Some may say it modifies *child,* and others may say it modifies *looks.*

Tell students that after linking verbs, such as *is* and *seems,* and after verbs related to the senses, such as *looks, smells, feels, tastes,* and *sounds,* a person should use an adjective instead of an adverb. This is called the predicate adjective. Examples include saying, "That looks good" instead of "That looks well," and "I feel bad" instead of "I feel badly."

Edit and Proofread

Students may want to use proofreader's marks when correcting their work. Refer them to the Language Arts Handbook 4.1, Proofreader's Symbols.

Editing

Purpose Remind students of the goal of editing their reports: to ensure clarity and to ensure accuracy. This means that they can remove unnecessary information, add missing information, and reorganize.

Citation Styles Instruct students to use the citation style you prefer. The one in the model gives an author and page number. If you wish, teach students how to use footnotes.

 Publish and Present

Before students begin their final drafts, they might benefit from reading the Language Arts Handbook 4.1, Writing Follow-up.

---

4. EDIT AND PROOFREAD

Focus: Citing Sources

Information from other sources can be incorporated in three ways: quoted directly, paraphrased, or summarized.

- **Quote** the exact words of the author only when you can't paraphrase them without losing their sense. Place quotation marks around direct quotes.
- **Paraphrase** information by rewriting others' ideas in your own words.
- **Summarize** paragraphs or pages of someone else's work by stating only the main ideas.

No matter how you incorporate research into your report, avoid plagiarism by citing your sources. When you include research in your paper from other sources, be sure to cite it accurately and consistently, both in the body of the paper and in a Works Cited page at the end of your paper. In the body, include the author's last name or agency and the page number in parentheses at the end of the clause or sentence containing the research, inside the punctuation. For a long quote, place the citation outside the punctuation.

> Fearing theft, some carried their belongings with them through the entire inspection process (Yans-McLaughlin 66).

Focus: Punctuating Appositives

An **appositive** is a noun that is placed next to another noun to identify it or add information about it. An **appositive phrase** is a group of words that includes an appositive and other words that modify it, such as adjectives and prepositional phrases. An appositive or appositive phrase that provides extra information about the noun is set off from the rest of the sentence with one or more commas.

> Ellis Island, _off the coast of New York City_, is now a tourist destination.

If, however, the appositive is needed to identify the noun, it is not set off with commas.

> People _who had left their home countries healthy_ often became sick on the voyage.

Proofreading

Polishing Your Work After correcting any errors in grammar and style, go through your work one more time to check for mechanical errors. These include errors in punctuation, capitalization, and spelling. Use proofreader's marks to highlight any errors you find, and then correct them.

---

5. PUBLISH AND PRESENT

Final Draft

May I Present? Make a clean final version of your research paper. If you are handwriting it, make it neat and legible. If you are using a word-processing program, double-space your work and use an easy-to-read typeface or font. Find out if your teacher has any presentation guidelines before you turn in your paper.

Differentiated Instruction

English Language Learning

Use this opportunity to gauge progress among English learners. Have them show you their editing and proofreading to see how well they have absorbed spelling and grammar lessons you have given. Evaluate how their vocabularies have grown or changed as a result of recent reading. Take time to correct and discuss any consistent problems in these areas before students prepare final drafts of their reports.

Student Model

Island of Hope, Island of Tears
by Erin Ahlich

Between 1892 and 1924, Ellis Island was the port of entry for over twelve million immigrants who were coming to the United States in search of a better life. Imagine what it must have felt like to see the Statue of Liberty holding her torch high in a gesture of welcome. Behind her, the sight of the New York City skyline promised a new beginning. If you were one of the wealthier immigrants who had been able to afford first- or second-class accommodations on the ship, you would soon be walking on the streets of New York, for you would not be subjected to the close scrutiny that the third-class passengers faced. For the wealthier passengers, Ellis Island could indeed be called the "Island of Hope," but for many of the poorer passengers, Ellis Island became known as the "Island of Tears." For the poor immigrants entering the United States through Ellis Island, the experience was often frightening.

> Includes an interesting introduction
>
> Clearly states the thesis

Their difficult journey began the day they stepped on the boat in their own countries. The voyage across the sea took anywhere from eight to fourteen days (Burns 226). For those in steerage, the area "in the dark 'basement' of the boat near the steering equipment" (Jango-Cohen 14), the trip was especially difficult. Unlike the first- and second-class passengers who had cabins with running water and were served well-prepared meals in comfortable dining rooms, the third-class passengers had no cabins. Instead, they slept in an open area in rows of bunks. Not only were they uncomfortable, but they were also deprived of any privacy. It was not until 1922 that third-class passengers had the luxury of cabins (Jango-Cohen 15), but even then, the steerage area was seldom cleaned, and the stench was almost unbearable. Imagine hundreds of people suffering from seasickness, unable to bathe, and with insufficient bathroom facilities. People who had left their home countries healthy often became sick on the voyage.

> Includes a main idea in the topic sentence of each paragraph and supporting details
>
> Includes information from multiple sources documented correctly and consistently

Upon arriving in New York Harbor, the ship would dock in Manhattan to let the wealthier passengers off. For the poorer passengers, however, the process was much more complicated. Once the wealthier passengers had debarked, the third-class passengers were brought back to Ellis Island by ferry. The only first- and second-class passengers who had to go to Ellis Island first were those who were sick or had legal problems (National Park Service 1).

Using One's Own Ideas

Remind students that the rubric for the research report suggests that they use their own ideas and explanations. Point out that a series of quotations or citations can be difficult for a reader to process. To help readers, writers can pause and summarize or interpret details.

Invite students to review the student model and try to identify the writer's personal opinions and explanations. Examples include the sentence beginning "Imagine what it" and the sentence that follows in the first paragraph. Encourage students to mention any difficulties they have identifying the writer's opinions. Suggest that they try to mentally rule out any "facts" they can identify and look at what remains to discern opinions.

Finally, ask students to describe the tone of the model report. Remind them that the tone reflects the writer's attitude toward the subject and the audience. Ask volunteers to propose words for the essay's tone such as *sympathetic, objective, informative, curious,* and so on.

Student Model CONTINUED

> *Follows a logical and effective organizational pattern (chronological order)*
>
> *Includes explanation of researched material as well as the writer's own ideas*

Once at Ellis Island, the long process of medical and legal inspection began. Men "were separated from women and children at once. They were lined up separately for inspection" (Coan *xv*). For about eighty percent of the immigrants, the process would take between three and five hours. The other twenty percent were detained overnight or longer until their cases could be cleared (National Park Service 4).

Upon entering the building, the immigrants were asked to leave their belongings in the Baggage Room. Most of them did so, but some were afraid to leave all their worldly possessions with strangers. Fearing theft, some carried their belongings with them through the entire inspection process (Yans-McLaughlin 66).

The next step was to walk up the grand staircase to the second floor. Medical officers observed them as they struggled up the stairs, some of them carrying small children and large suitcases. In what became known as the "six-second exam," the medical officers evaluated each immigrant. Was that person out of breath because of the heavy suitcase he was dragging, or did he have lung problems? Were that child's eyes red because he'd been crying, or does he have an eye infection? In six seconds or so, these medical officers could determine if a person had any obvious ailments. Such persons had their outer garments, front or back, marked with chalk. By 1917, there were fifty such possible marks: an *E* for eye problems, an *L* for lameness, an *X* for suspected mental problems, a circled *X* for definite mental problems, an *H* for possible heart problems, and so on (Yans-McLaughlin 66).

One woman remembers how frightened she was when her sister's coat was marked with chalk. She worried about where the sister would go if she were deported. A kind stranger had some good advice for her, though. The girl was wearing a coat with a fancy silk lining. The stranger told her to just turn her coat inside out, a trick that saved her from being pulled out of the line for further inspection (Jango-Cohen 25).

Once up the stairs and in the Registry Room, the immigrants faced a more formal medical examination. The most feared procedure was the eye exam. This was often done with a button hook, a metal instrument designed for buttoning gloves. The doctor would use this hook to pull the eyelids back to check for eye infections. If trachoma was detected, the immigrant was refused entry. This highly contagious disease is the leading cause of blindness worldwide. Trachoma was then, and still is, grounds for refusal of entry (Yans-McLaughlin 66).

For those immigrants who passed the medical exams, the ordeal was

TEACHING NOTE

Self-Generated Questioning

After students have read the model, have them gather in groups of three or four. Ask each group to generate five questions they would like to ask the model author, either about the content of the report or about the process she used to write it. Model some possible questions: "How did people find ships for traveling to the United States? What is trachoma?"

Have groups write their questions on a sheet of paper. Collect the sheets, and read the questions aloud one by one. For each question, have students suggest either an answer or a source they could consult to find an answer.

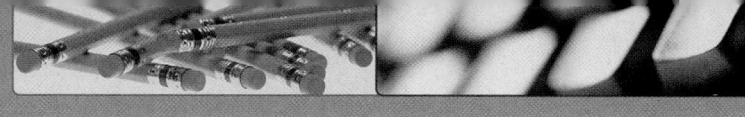

not yet over. The last step was the legal inspection, an interrogation designed to weed out any undesirables. "In rapid succession, each was asked to state his or her name, place of birth, destination, and occupation; how much money he or she had, whether he or she had ever been in jail, or had ever been an anarchist" (Burns 230).

Most immigrants eventually passed all the inspections and were allowed entry into the United States. Only two percent of those who came through Ellis Island between 1892 and 1924 were deported. After 1924, new immigration laws reduced traffic through Ellis Island dramatically. Immigrants were examined at U.S. consulates overseas before they sailed for New York; possession of a U.S. visa guaranteed admission to the country (Bell 95). By 1954, Ellis Island was closed completely, its buildings left to decay in the salty air.

The main building on Ellis Island was eventually restored and turned into a museum, which opened in 1990. Visitors to New York can take the ferry ride to Ellis Island. They can see all the rooms where people were examined and questioned. They can look at all the pictures and artifacts honoring the millions of immigrants who came through this place. Then they can take the ferry back to Manhattan, and just as every immigrant who came in through Ellis Island, they can marvel at the skyline.

> *Summarizes main points and restates the thesis in the conclusion*

Works Cited

Bell, James B., and Richard I. Abrams. *In Search of Liberty: The Story of the Statue of Liberty and Ellis Island.* New York: Doubleday, 1984. Print.

Burns, Ric, and James Sanders. *New York: An Illustrated History.* New York: Knopf, 1999. Print.

Coan, Peter Morton. *Ellis Island Interviews: In Their Own Words.* New York: Facts on File, 1997. Print.

Jango-Cohen, Judith. *Ellis Island.* New York: Children's Press, 2005. Print.

National Park Service, U.S. Department of the Interior. "Ellis Island National Monument: History and Culture." Last updated 4 September 2006. Web. 5 April 2009. <http://www.nps.gov/elis/historyculture/index.htm>

Yans-McLaughlin, Virginia, and Marjorie Lightman. *Ellis Island and the Peopling of America: The Official Guide.* New York: The New Press, 1997. Print.

> *Includes a Works Cited section correctly documenting all sources used*

Teach the Workshop

Concluding the Report

Have students compare the final paragraph to the introductory paragraph on page 861. Have them tell you how they think the conclusion related to the thesis statement (it does not reiterate it directly or, some may say, at all). Then ask them to connect other statements in the conclusion to the opening paragraph and to main points in the body of the report.

Works Cited

Tell students that the terms *bibliography* and *works cited* are often used interchangeably. Note that different teachers and different schools prefer different styles for citing sources. Encourage students to always ask for instructions about citing sources before they begin gathering data for a research report. That way, they can be sure to record all the necessary information as they take notes.

Reading Skills

Distinguish Fact from Opinion

Direct students to the Writing Rubric on page 856. It instructs them to use multiple sources. Challenge students to review their sources to distinguish facts from opinions. Offer these tips for identifying opinions.

1. Look for words that imply a judgment or conclusion on the writer's part, words such as *always, never, forever, must, cannot, worst, best, all,* and *none.*

2. Look for strong adjectives, especially those about feelings. Examples include *fantastic, horrifying, gorgeous, joyful, desperate, precious,* and *outrageous.*

3. Look for phrases that indicate personal opinion such as *I think* and *I believe.*

Objectives

Participating in this lesson will help students deliver research presentations that

- have strong introductions and conclusions
- follow clear organization
- cover material in depth
- support ideas with evidence
- incorporate photographs or objects
- demonstrate appropriate volume, pacing, eye contact, and nonverbal expression

Launch the Workshop

Have the class describe a time they have used research to find answers to a question. Point out examples within the school such as a science fair, informational bulletin board, or results of school elections. Ask students: "What makes for a good research presentation?"

Allow students time to think of how each situation used research to find an answer. Then have students describe what kinds of research resources might have been useful to the person creating the presentation. Encourage them to share resources they have used for their prior research.

> For more information, see the Language Arts Handbook Section 7, Speaking & Listening.

Speaking & Listening Workshop

Giving and Actively Listening to Research Presentations

When you research a topic, you become something of an expert on it. Your new knowledge benefits you, but it can also benefit others if you share what you have learned. When you give a **research presentation,** you present orally the information you have learned about a topic. Actively listening to research presentations is a way to acquire knowledge on a variety of subjects you might not have time to explore on your own.

Planning a Research Presentation

Focus Your Topic You have probably written a well-researched paper in science, history, or language arts. Your research presentation involves more than simply reading what you have written. The specific points you choose to explain depend on your audience's age, background, knowledge, and interests.

Identify Your Audience Who will listen to your research presentation? Even if your audience knows something about your topic, you probably know more because you have done research. What can you tell your audience that they don't already know? What will they find appealing or interesting? Think about the kinds of questions your audience might ask about the subject, and select your points accordingly.

Select Key Points Review the outline you made and the notes you took for your written research report. Select the points that would be of greatest interest to your audience. Did you discover any interesting facts that you didn't include in the written report? Would they make your oral presentation more interesting? Use all these sources to make an outline for your research presentation.

The History of Timekeeping

Introduction—Humans are often obsessed with keeping track of time. They've come a long way from the first sundials to today's atomic clocks.

Why Timekeeping Is Important
- brief overview of why people "keep" time from measuring seasons for agriculture to measuring nanoseconds for computers

Advances in Timekeeping (show time line)
- the sun and stars
- the Roman calendar
- water and sand clocks
- mechanical clocks
- crystal and atomic clocks

Words in Use

Teaching Words
benefits, 878
acquire, 878
appealing, 878
transparency, 879
courteous, 879
nonverbal, 879
constructive, 879

KEY TERMS

TOPIC, 878
RESEARCH
  PRESENTATION, 878
AUDIENCE, 878
OUTLINE, 878
TRANSITION, 879
INTRODUCTION, 879
CONCLUSION, 879

Program Resources

To expand upon this workshop lesson, Giving and Actively Listening to Research Presentations, see the *Exceeding the Standards: Speaking & Listening* resource.

When your outline is complete, turn it into more complete note cards you can use for your speech. Include the main heading and several supporting details for each point.

Organize Your Speech Organize your note cards in a way that presents the points you have selected logically. Select visuals that add to your presentation rather than just repeat something you have said. If your presentation is complex, you may want to help your audience by displaying a transparency with a simple outline. If you are describing how things changed throughout history, display a time line or show photos and drawings. Match your organization to your content, and consider what signal words and transitions you will use to help the audience follow your points.

Evaluating Your Research Presentation

Work with a partner to evaluate your research presentations. As you actively listen to your partner's presentation, take notes to summarize the main points. Jot down any questions you have. Use the speaking and listening rubrics on this page to remind you what to look for as you evaluate the presentation.

When the presentation is complete, offer constructive feedback on the subject matter, organization, and delivery of the material. Begin with the strong points and then politely suggest ways that your partner might make the presentation clearer or more interesting.

Delivering Your Research Presentation

Use the feedback you received to polish your research presentation. Before you begin, organize your note cards and have on hand any pictures or objects you want to display. Glance at your notes to stay on topic rather than reading from them.

Connect with your audience by making eye contact. If you see frowns or other indications that your audience is puzzled, check with them to see if they have questions. Expressing enthusiasm about your topic and using examples that show how the topic is relevant to their lives will keep your audience interested.

Audience members should be courteous and considerate. Demonstrate active listening by asking questions that allow the speaker to clarify or expand on what he or she has said.

Speaking Rubric

Your presentation will be evaluated on these elements:

Content
- ☐ clear organization of material
- ☐ strong introduction and conclusion
- ☐ interesting choice of information
- ☐ effective use of visuals

Delivery and Presentation
- ☐ appropriate volume and pacing
- ☐ effective interaction with audience
- ☐ appropriate use of nonverbal expression

Listening Rubric

As a peer reviewer or audience member, you should do the following:

- ☐ listen quietly and attentively
- ☐ maintain eye contact with speaker
- ☐ try to interpret the speaker's purpose by taking notes that summarize the content of the presentation
- ☐ ask appropriate questions
- ☐ (as peer reviewer) provide constructive feedback

Relate to an Audience
Explain that the purpose of a research presentation is to convey information to an audience. Have students think about other times they have presented information to an audience. Ask volunteers to share their responses. Point out that many speakers use famous quotes, historical events, or anecdotes to connect their ideas to something an audience is already familiar with. Model one possibility: "We have all read 'Coyote Steals the Sun and Moon' so I might refer to it when delivering my presentation on the development of Native American legends."

Peer Reviews
Allow students time to practice their research presentations alone and then with peer reviewers. Have students first review the rubric on page 865. Suggest that before they give feedback, peer reviewers write down something new that they learned from a presentation. They can incorporate this item into their positive feedback.

TEACHING NOTE

Research Report
Let students review the research reports they wrote for the Writing Workshop or another research report. Tell students to develop that report into a speech. Explain that the goal is to break the report down into a few main points, while leaving out unimportant details. Have students create an outline or note cards to use during their speech.

Speaking & Listening Skills

Visual Aids
The rubric calls for "effective use of visuals." Give students some guidance on effective and appropriate visuals based on the following broad topic categories:

- For research on a culture or a historical event, show a map or photograph to represent the people and places.
- For research on an author or historical figure, show a photograph or painting of the person.

- For research on a scientific discovery, begin the presentation by showing an object and describing how it works, or use a graphic with interesting data.

During peer reviews, have students discuss at least two visuals that could accompany their presentations.

Objectives

Completing this lesson will enable students to

- write a research report based on a timed writing prompt
- answer standardized test questions that demonstrate revising and editing skills
- demonstrate the ability to make inferences from a reading by answering standardized questions

Timed Writing

Tell students that standardized tests such as the SAT and ACT often require students to write a response in a limited amount of time. Give the following tips for timed tests:

- Read the prompt or questions carefully.
- Look for key words in the directions that tell you what is expected.
- Circle or underline these words or write them on your own note paper.
- Be sure to follow all instructions exactly. If you have questions, ask the moderator.
- Prewrite. Before you begin writing, create a rough outline or graphic organizer of points to make.
- Write a clear introduction that explains the points you intend to address in your answer.
- If time begins to runs out, briefly state your remaining points and add a one-sentence conclusion.
- Review your completed essay for major errors and to see if you have responded completely to the instructions.

Test Practice Workshop

Writing Skills

Research Report

Carefully read the following writing prompt. Before you begin writing, think carefully about what task the assignment is asking you to perform. Then create an outline to help guide your writing.

> In this unit, you have read several myths and legends that explain physical phenomena, such as Paul Bunyan creating Minnesota's lakes and Coyote's actions creating summer and winter. Why did people create stories such as these? Is it likely that similar stories would arise today?

Write an expository research report in which you examine myths that explain physical phenomena in different cultures. Focus on when these myths and legends began and why. Gather your information from several sources. Be sure to document each source, paraphrasing and using quotes as you write your report. As you write, be sure to:

> - Organize your report in a logical and consistent way
> - Include introductory and concluding paragraphs
> - Introduce your position in the first paragraph
> - Support your main idea in each body paragraph

Rubrics for a Research Report

Make sure students understand that they should use myths in this textbook as the sources for answering the writing prompt. Have students ask the following questions as they draft a report:

- ☐ Does the first paragraph state the thesis and introduce the main idea?
- ☐ Does each body paragraph support the main idea?
- ☐ Is the report organized logically and consistently?
- ☐ Does the report have a conclusion?

Common Core State Standards

Reading Literature
RL.3, RL.4

Writing
W.4, W.5

Language
L.4

Revising and Editing Skills

In the following excerpt from the first draft of a student's paper, words and phrases are underlined and numbered. Alternatives to the underlined words and phrases appear in the right-hand column. Choose the answer that *best* corrects any grammatical or style errors in the original. If you think that the original is error-free, choose "NO CHANGE."

Some questions might also be asked about a section of the passage or the entire passage. These do not refer to a specific underlined phrase or word and are identified by a number in a box. Record your answers on a separate sheet of paper.

Before <u>children were old enough</u> to understand
1
scientific explanations, they often ask questions

such as <u>"Why do rabbits have short tails"?</u> or
2
"Where does the sun go at night?" Long ago,

before people began to study nature scientifically,

they also <u>asked this type of questions.</u> Over time,
3
they <u>developed stories to answer these questions</u>
4
<u>called myths.</u> Some myths, called creation myths,

contain interesting <u>explanations about how</u>
5
<u>humans appeared on Earth.</u> Others, called

explanatory myths, explain natural phenomena.

Some myths and legends have been told and

retold for thousands of years. 6

1. **A.** NO CHANGE
   B. children is old enough
   C. children are old enough
   D. children would be old enough

2. **A.** NO CHANGE
   B. "Why do rabbits have short tails?"
   C. "Why do rabbits have short tails,"
   D. "Why do rabbits have short tails?",

3. **A.** NO CHANGE
   B. asked these types of questions.
   C. asked this types of questions.
   D. asked these type of questions.

4. **A.** NO CHANGE
   B. developed stories to answer these questions that are called myths.
   C. developed myths to explain these stories.
   D. developed stories, called myths, to answer these questions.

5. **A.** NO CHANGE
   B. explanations to tell how humans came to be present on Earth.
   C. explanations about how humans appeared there on Earth.
   D. ways to easily explain how humans appeared on Earth.

6. The last sentence of this passage contains
   A. a simple subject and simple predicate.
   B. a simple subject and compound predicate.
   C. a compound subject and compound predicate.
   D. a compound subject and simple predicate.

Reading Comprehension Tests

Direct students to the reading comprehension test on this page; give students a moment to look over the format of the test. Explain that a reading comprehension test gives a short piece of writing and then asks several questions about it. The questions usually ask students to interpret the meaning of the passage. Tell students to keep the following tips in mind:

- Begin by skimming the passage and all of the questions.
- Read the passage with the questions in mind. If time permits, read the passage twice before answering any questions.
- Carefully read the first question.
- Locate the portion of the passage to which the question refers. Read it slowly and carefully.
- Answer the first question.
- Repeat this process to answer all the rest of the questions.

Reading Skills

Carefully read the following passage. Then, on a separate piece of paper, answer each question.

from "William Tell," a Swiss legend

The Austrian Emperor…sent a cruel man named Gessler to rule Switzerland with an iron hand. Gessler was a hard ruler. When he passed through a town, all men had to salute him. Anyone who refused to salute was taken to a cold, damp prison. But even this was not enough for Gessler. He wanted people to salute him when he wasn't there. So he had one of
5 his hats placed on a pole. His soldiers were to make sure that the hat was saluted.

…One day [William] Tell walked from his home in the hills to the market town of Altorf. He carried his bow, a quiver of arrows, and some rabbits he had shot in the woods. Beside him walked his young son.

William Tell marched right past the pole that held Gessler's hat. He did not salute….In
10 no time at all, Austrian soldiers had grabbed both his arms.

"Didn't you see Gessler's hat?" asked the soldiers.

"Yes, I saw it," said William Tell.

"Then why didn't you salute it?" the soldiers barked.

Tell looked at the hat above him on the pole…."I would not salute that hat," he said,
15 "not even if it were sitting on top of Gessler's fat head!"

The soldiers…marched their prisoner and his son to Gessler's office in a nearby city…. Gessler was just finishing an enormous dinner at a sidewalk restaurant. Again William Tell refused to salute.

"This man needs to be taught a lesson," Gessler said, standing up. His lips twisted into a
20 cruel smile….He picked up an apple from a pile of fruit on the table. "I will have this apple placed on the head of your son. You are to walk a hundred steps up the street. Then you will hit the apple with one of your arrows"….

William Tell planted his feet firmly on the ground. He placed an arrow in his bow….He took careful aim. Zoom!
25 Crack! The apple split into two halves. They fell to the ground on either side of the boy. A cheer went up from the crowd….

Only one person was not happy. "You did it, but you were never too sure of yourself," shouted Gessler. "What's that second arrow I see there under your coat?"…

"This arrow," Tell said, "was to use in case I shot too low….It was meant for you,
30 Gessler."

"That's enough!" shouted Gessler. But no sooner had the words left his lips than Tell's second arrow hit his chest….

The crowd was too much for the few Austrian soldiers. By that evening the city was free.

Differentiated Instruction

Enrichment

Tell students who like this story that it comes from a famous Swiss legend. Encourage them to use library and Internet resources to find out more about William Tell and the culture and historical period it represents.

Reading Proficiency

As students read the legend, encourage them to visualize the setting and the action that is taking place. Then ask them to draw a picture of the image that this created from what they have read. Tell students that visualizing what you read will help you recall details about setting and plot during a test.

1. What figure of speech does the author use in lines 1 and 2?
A. irony
B. hyperbole
C. personification
D. alliteration

2. What is the most likely reason that Gessler wanted people to salute him?
A. He was a military officer.
B. He wanted to be treated like a general.
C. He wanted the Swiss to admit an Austrian was their ruler.
D. He didn't like Swiss people.

3. What was Tell's most likely reason for carrying the rabbits to Altorf?
A. to show them off to his friends
B. to brag about how good he was with the bow and arrow
C. to trade them for other goods at the market
D. to have them skinned and cooked for supper

4. What do Tell's actions in line 9 foreshadow?
A. that he will be captured by the soldiers
B. that he doesn't salute hats
C. that his hands were full and he couldn't salute
D. that he didn't want to drop the rabbits

5. What do Tell's words in lines 14–15 suggest about his attitude toward Gessler?
A. He thought Gessler looked funny wearing the hat.
B. He thought Gessler was too fat to be a ruler.
C. He didn't think the hat fit Gessler very well.
D. He had no respect for Gessler.

6. What word describes Gessler's behavior when he orders Tell to shoot an apple from his son's head?
A. confident
B. authoritative
C. virtuous
D. sadistic

7. Based on the context, what is the meaning of the word *planted* in line 23?
A. hid
B. buried
C. set securely
D. established

8. Which literary device is used when Gessler accuses Tell of having a second arrow because he isn't sure of himself?
A. hyperbole
B. situational irony
C. verbal irony
D. visualization

9. William Tell was considered a hero by the Swiss people because
A. he was very courageous in standing up for his beliefs.
B. he was very good with a bow and arrow.
C. he talked back to the soldiers.
D. he used his bow and arrow to kill a cruel leader.

10. What was the probable cause of the people's actions in the last paragraph?
A. They didn't want Tell to get mad at them.
B. They were tired of saluting the hat.
C. They weren't afraid because Gessler was dead.
D. They were inspired by Tell's actions.

Teach the Workshop

Reading Skills
1. B
2. C
3. C
4. A
5. D
6. D
7. C
8. B
9. A
10. D

Test-Taking Skills

Choose the Best Answer

Tell students that when answering multiple-choice questions, it is important to choose the *best* answer available. Explain that many times the test will provide two or more possible answers, but that the best answer is the one that completely answers the question asked. Model an example for students:

Question 10. The question asks for the probable cause of the people's actions in the last paragraph. The people were excited to be free. Therefore, they were likely inspired by Tell's actions. While answer B is also true, answer D most completely answers the question.

Language Arts Handbook

BUILD BACKGROUND

Each reader brings his or her own context to a selection based on prior knowledge and experiences. What do you know about the topic? What do you want to know? Before and during reading, think about what you already know about the topic or subject matter. By connecting to your prior knowledge, you will increase your interest in and understanding of what you read. Fill in the first two columns of a K-W-L Chart before you read. Fill in the last column after you finish reading.

K-W-L Chart

What I _Know_	What I _Want_ to Learn	What I Have _Learned_
Harriet Tubman helped many slaves escape.	How did Harriet Tubman make contact with the slaves to tell them it was time to escape?	Harriet Tubman sang the spiritual "Go down, Moses, 'way down to Egypt Land" to signal the slaves it was time to escape.

SET PURPOSE

Before you begin reading, think about your reason for reading the material. You might be reading from a textbook to complete a homework assignment, skimming a magazine for information about one of your hobbies, or reading a novel for your own enjoyment. Know why you are reading and what information you seek. Decide on your purpose for reading as clearly as you can. Be aware that the purpose of your reading may change as you read.

Preview the text to set a purpose for reading. Skim the first few paragraphs and glance through the selection to figure out what it's about and who the main characters are. What can you learn from the art or photos? Fill in a Reader's Purpose Chart at each stage of reading to set a purpose for reading and to help you attain it.

Reader's Purpose Chart

Before Reading
Set a purpose for reading
I want to read "The Treasure of Lemon Brown" to find out who Lemon Brown is and what his treasure is.
During Reading
Take notes on what you learn
After Reading
Reflect on your purpose and what you learned

ASK QUESTIONS

Think and reflect by asking questions to further your understanding of what you are reading. Asking questions helps you to pinpoint parts of the text that are confusing. You can ask questions in your head, or you may write them down. Ask questions about things that seem unusual or interesting, like why a character might have behaved in an unexpected way. What do you wonder about as you read the text? Use a Generate Questions Bookmark like the following to record your questions as you read.

Generate Questions Bookmark

Page #	What I Wonder About
21	Why does Greg want to go into the abandoned tenement building?

VISUALIZE

Reading is more than simply sounding out words. It is an active process that requires you to use your imagination. When you visualize, you form a picture or an image in your mind of the action and descriptions in a text. Each reader's images will be different based on his or her prior knowledge and experiences. Keep in mind that there are no "right" or "wrong" visualizations. Visualize by forming pictures in your mind to help you see the characters or actions. Use a Visualization Map to draw pictures that represent key events in a selection. Write a caption under each box that explains each event. Draw the events in the order they occur.

Visualization Map

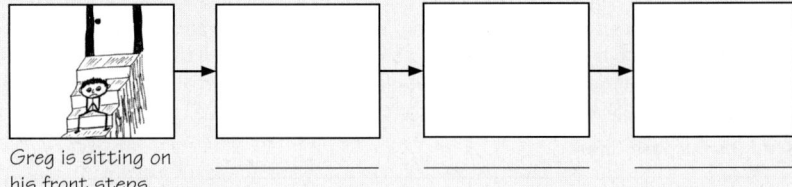

Greg is sitting on his front steps.

MAKE PREDICTIONS

When you **make predictions** during reading, you are making guesses about what the reading is going to be about or what might happen next. Before you read, make predictions based on clues from the page and from what you already know about the topic. As you read, gather more clues that will either confirm or change your predictions.

Prediction Chart

Guesses	Reasons	Evidence
The man will comfort the boy and help him be brave for the morning's battle of Shiloh.	The man is gentle and kind with the boy about his crying.	The man is described as smelling like a father, which would be comforting.

MAKE INFERENCES

Making an inference means putting together the clues given in the text with your own prior knowledge. Make inferences, or educated guesses, about what is not stated directly. Things may be implied or hinted at, or they may be left out altogether. By paying close attention to what you read, you will be able to make inferences about what the writer is trying to communicate. Use an Inference Chart to document your conclusions.

Inference Chart

Text	What I Infer
"You had better come at night, for the neighbors believe he is lost, and I couldn't be responsible for what they would do to anybody they saw bringing him back."	The boy is not well liked by his neighbors.
Detail from Text	Conclusions

CLARIFY

Check that you understand what you read and identify text that is confusing or unclear. If you encounter problems or lose focus, it may be helpful to use **Fix-Up Ideas,** such as rereading difficult parts, reading in shorter chunks, going back and reading aloud, or changing your reading rate. (See Monitor Comprehension on page 884 for more information.)

MAKE CONNECTIONS

Notice where there are **connections** between the story and your life or the world beyond the story. Be aware of feelings or thoughts you have while reading the story.

Connections Chart

Page #	Event	Reminds Me of
415	The narrator describes the importance of buffalo to the Plains Indians.	I saw a history program on TV about the hunting of buffalo.

1.3 Using Reading Skills

Using the following skills as you read helps you to become an independent, thoughtful, and active reader who can accomplish tasks evaluated on tests, particularly standardized tests.

Reading Skills

- Identify Author's Purpose and Approach
- Skim and Scan
- Find the Main Idea
- Determine Importance of Details
- Understand Literary Elements
- Meaning of Words
- Use Context Clues
- Take Notes
- Analyze Text Organization

- Identify Sequence of Events
- Compare and Contrast
- Evaluate Cause and Effect
- Classify and Reorganize Information
- Distinguish Fact from Opinion
- Identify Multiple Levels of Meaning
- Interpret Visual Aids
- Monitor Comprehension
- Summarize
- Draw Conclusions

IDENTIFY AUTHOR'S PURPOSE AND APPROACH

Author's Purpose

A writer's **purpose** is his or her aim or goal. Being able to figure out an author's purpose, or purposes, is an important reading skill. An author may write with one or more of the purposes listed in the following chart. A writer's purpose corresponds to a specific mode, or type, of writing. A writer can choose from a variety of forms while working within a mode.

Purposes of Writing

Mode of Writing	Purpose	Examples
expository	to inform	news article, research report
narrative	to express thoughts or ideas, or to tell a story	personal account, memoir
descriptive	to portray a person, place, object, or event	travel brochure, personal profile
persuasive	to convince people to accept a position and respond in some way	editorial, petition

Once you identify what the author is trying to do, you can evaluate, or judge, how well the author achieved that purpose. For example, you may judge that the author of a persuasive essay made a good and convincing argument. Or, you may decide that the novel you are reading has a boring plot.

Before Reading
Identify the author's purpose, the type of writing he or she uses, and the ideas he or she wants to communicate.
During Reading
Gather ideas that the author communicates to the readers.

After Reading
Summarize the ideas the author communicates. Explain how these ideas help fulfill the author's purpose.

Author's Approach

The literary elements, the terms and techniques used in literature, make up the **author's approach** to conveying his or her main idea or theme. Understanding the author's approach in fiction involves recognizing literary elements such as *point of view, tone,* and *mood.* What perspective, or way of looking at things, does the author have? What is his or her attitude toward the subject? Is the writing serious or playful in nature? What emotions is the writer trying to evoke in the reader? (See Understand Literary Elements on page 878.)

SKIM AND SCAN

When you **skim,** you glance through material quickly to get a general idea of what it is about. Skimming is an excellent way to get a quick overview of material. It is useful for previewing a chapter in a textbook, for surveying material to see if it contains information that will be useful to you, and for reviewing material for a test or an essay.

When you **scan,** you look through written material quickly to locate particular information. Scanning is useful when, for example, you want to find an entry in an index or a definition in a textbook chapter. To scan, simply run your eye down the page, looking for a key word. When you find the key word, slow down and read carefully.

To **skim** a text, preview the following:	When you **scan** a text, you may be looking for the following:
• titles • headings • bold or colored type • topic sentences • first/last paragraphs of sections • summaries • graphics	• specific information • key words • main ideas • answers to questions

FIND THE MAIN IDEA

The **main idea** is a brief statement of what you think the author wants you to know, think, or feel after reading the text. In some cases, the main idea will actually be stated. Check the first and last paragraphs for a sentence that sums up the entire passage. The author may not tell you what the main idea is, and you will have to infer it.

In general, nonfiction texts have main ideas; literary texts (poems, short stories, novels, plays, and personal essays) have themes. Sometimes, however, the term *main idea* is used to refer to the theme of a literary work, especially an essay or a poem. Both deal with the central idea in a written work.

A good way to find the main or overall idea of a whole selection (or part of a selection) is to gather important details into a Main Idea Map like the one below. Use the details to determine the main or overall thought or message.

Main Idea Map

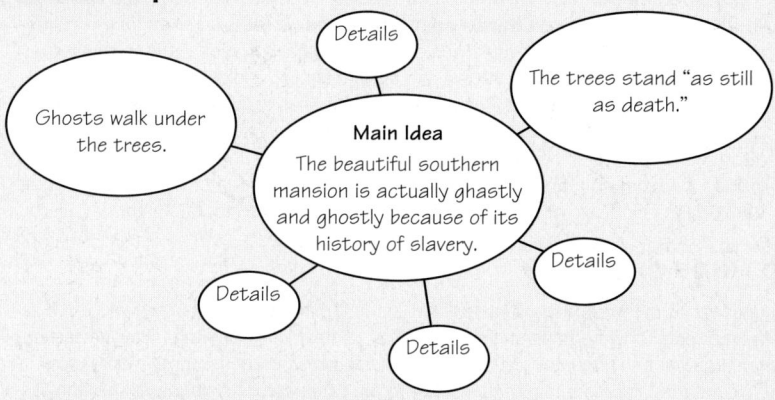

DETERMINE IMPORTANCE OF DETAILS

The main ideas are what the selection is about; the minor ideas and details provide support for the main ones. To identify supporting details, you need to do the following:
• **Locate basic facts,** such as names, dates, and events.
• **Determine the importance** of those facts to the understanding of the piece. Some facts or details will be more important than others.

- **Interpret** subtly stated details. These details can help clarify the author's stance or purpose, or they may give fuller meaning to the basic facts.
- **Understand the function** of a part of a passage. Is the author providing information, supporting a previously made point, presenting a conflicting argument, building suspense? Pay attention to how your understanding of a topic or your feelings toward it change as you read.
- **Make inferences,** or educated guesses, about how the author uses the supporting details to achieve his or her desired result. Put together clues from the text with your known prior knowledge to make inferences. A Main Idea Map or an Inference Chart can help you keep track of your ideas.

UNDERSTAND LITERARY ELEMENTS

Literary elements are the terms and techniques that are used in literature. When you read literature, you need to be familiar with the literary terms and reading skills listed below. These literary elements are explained in more detail in the Introduction to Fiction on page 4.

- **Recognize Mood and Tone** The atmosphere or emotion conveyed by a literary work is called **mood.** A writer creates mood by using concrete details to describe the setting, characters, or events. **Tone** is the writer's attitude toward the subject or toward the reader of a work. Examples of different tones that a work may have include familiar, ironic, playful, sarcastic, serious, and sincere.
- **Understand Point of View** The vantage point, or perspective, from which a story or narrative is told is referred to as **point of view.** Stories are typically written from the following points of view:

  first-person point of view: narrator uses words such as *I* and *we*
  second-person point of view: narrator uses *you*
  third-person point of view: narrator uses words such as *he, she, it,* and *they*

- **Analyze Character and Characterization** A **character** is a person (or sometimes an animal) who takes part in the action of a story. Characterization is the literary techniques writers use to create characters and make them come alive.
- **Examine Plot Development** The plot is basically what happens in a story. A **plot** is a series of events related to a central conflict, or struggle. A typical plot involves the introduction of a conflict, its development, and its eventual resolution. The elements of plot include the exposition, rising action, climax, falling action, and resolution. A graphic organizer called a Plot Diagram (page 6) can be used to chart the plot of a literature selection.

MEANING OF WORDS

To understand the **meaning of words** that are unfamiliar, use vocabulary skills, such as prior knowledge of word parts and word families, context clues (see the following section), and denotation and connotation. Other helpful resources include footnotes, glossaries, and dictionaries. For more information, refer to the Language Arts Handbook, section 2, Vocabulary & Spelling, page 886.

USE CONTEXT CLUES

You can often figure out the meaning of an unfamiliar word by using context clues. **Context clues** are words and phrases near a difficult word that provide hints about its meaning. The context in which a word is used may help you guess what it means without having to look it up in the dictionary.

Different types of context clues include the following:

- **comparison clue:** shows a comparison, or how the unfamiliar word is like something that might be familiar to you
- **contrast clue:** shows that something contrasts, or differs in meaning, from something else
- **restatement clue:** uses different words to express the same idea
- **examples clue:** gives examples of other items to illustrate the meaning of something
- **cause-and-effect clue:** tells you that something happened as a result of something else

TAKE NOTES

Taking or making notes helps you pay attention to the words on a page and remember important ideas. *Paraphrase,* or write in your own words, what you have read and put it into notes you can read later. Taking or making notes is also a quick way for you to retell what you have just read. Since you cannot write in, mark up, or highlight information in a textbook or library book, make a response bookmark like the one that follows and use it to record your thoughts and reactions. As you read, ask yourself questions, make predictions, react to ideas, identify key points, and/or write down unfamiliar words.

Response Bookmark

Page #	Questions, Predictions, Reactions, Key Points, and Unfamiliar Words
780	Will the Buffalo Calf Road Woman help to defeat the white people with her bravery?

Making notes in **graphic organizers** helps you organize ideas as you read. For instance, if you are reading an essay that compares two authors, you might use a Venn Diagram to collect information about each author. If you are reading about an author's life, you may construct a Time Line. As you read a selection, create your own method for gathering and organizing information. You might use your own version of a common graphic organizer or invent a new way to show what the selection describes.

Common Graphic Organizers

Cause-and-Effect Chart, page 881
Classification Chart, page 882
Connections Chart, page 875
Drawing Conclusions Log, page 885
Fact from Opinion Chart, page 882
Generate Questions Bookmark, page 874
Inference Chart, page 875
K-W-L Chart, page 873
Levels of Meaning Chart, page 883
Main Idea Map, page 877

Prediction Chart, page 874
Pro and Con Chart, page 881
Reader's Purpose Chart, page 873
Response Bookmark, above
Sequence Map, page 880
Summary Chart, page 885
Time Line, page 880
Venn Diagram, page 881
Visualization Map, page 874

ANALYZE TEXT ORGANIZATION

Text organization refers to the different ways a text may be presented or organized. If you are aware of the ways different texts are organized, you will find it easier to understand what you read. For example, familiarity with typical plot elements—the exposition, rising action, climax, falling action, and resolution—is important for understanding the events in a short story or novel. Focusing on signal words and text patterns is important for understanding nonfiction and informational text. For instance, transition words, such as *first, second, next, then,* and *finally,* might indicate that an essay is written in chronological, or time, order. Common methods of organization are shown in the following chart.

Methods of Organization

Chronological Order	Events are given in the order they occur.
Order of Importance	Details are given in order of importance or familiarity.
Comparison and Contrast Order	Similarities and differences of two things are listed.
Cause and Effect Order	One or more causes are presented followed by one or more effects.

IDENTIFY SEQUENCE OF EVENTS

Sequence refers to the order in which things happen. When you read certain types of writing, such as a short story, a novel, a biography of a person's life, or a history book, keep track of the sequence of events. You might do this by making a Time Line or a Sequence Map.

Time Line
To make a Time Line, draw a line and divide it into equal parts like the one below. Label each part with a date or a time. Then add key events at the right places along the Time Line.

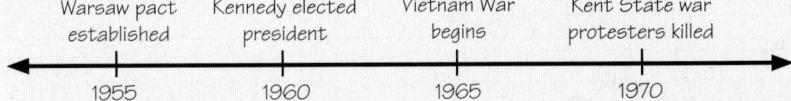

Warsaw pact established	Kennedy elected president	Vietnam War begins	Kent State war protesters killed
1955	1960	1965	1970

Sequence Map
In each box, draw pictures that represent key events in a selection. Then write a caption under each box that explains each event. Draw the events in the order in which they occur.

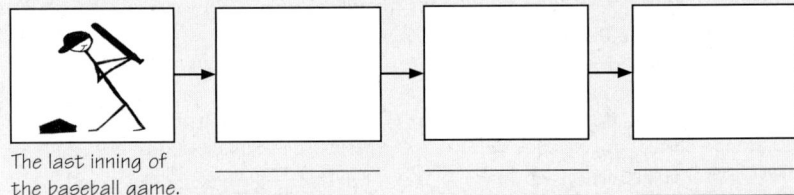

The last inning of the baseball game.

COMPARE AND CONTRAST

Comparing and contrasting are closely related processes. When you **compare** one thing to another, you describe similarities between the two things; when you **contrast** two things, you describe their differences. To compare and contrast, begin by listing the features of each subject. Then go down both lists and check whether each feature is shared or not. You can also show similarities and differences in a *Venn Diagram.* A Venn Diagram uses two slightly overlapping circles. The outer part of each circle shows what aspects of two things are different from each other. The inner, or shared, part of each circle shows what aspects the two things have in common.

Venn Diagram

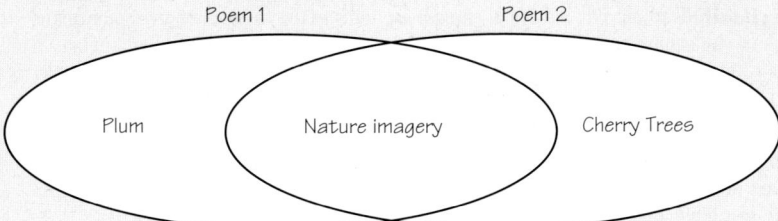

Another method for comparison and contrast is to use a Pro and Con Chart like the one below to take notes on both sides of an argument.

Pro and Con Chart

Arguments in Favor of American Indians' ownership of Alcatraz (PRO)	Arguments Against American Indians' ownership of Alcatraz (CON)
Argument 1: Alcatraz Island should belong to the American Indians. **Support:** American Indians should have the island because they discovered it.	**Argument 1:** **Support:**

EVALUATE CAUSE AND EFFECT

When you evaluate **cause and effect,** you are looking for a logical relationship between a cause or causes and one or more effects. A writer may present one or more causes followed by one or more effects, or one or more effects followed by one or more causes. Transitional, or signal, words and phrases that indicate cause and effect include *one cause, another effect, as a result, consequently,* and *therefore.* As a reader, you determine whether the causes and effects in a text are reasonable. A graphic organizer like the one below will help you to recognize relationships between causes and effects. Keep track of what happens in a story and why in a chart like the one below. Use cause-and-effect signal words to help you identify causes and their effects.

Cause-and-Effect Chart

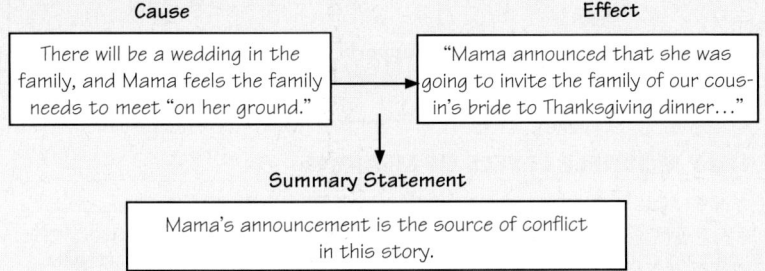

CLASSIFY AND REORGANIZE INFORMATION

To **classify** is to put into classes or categories. Items in the same category should share one or more characteristics. A writer may group things to show similarities and name the categories to clarify how one group is similar or different from another. For example, whales can be classified by their method of eating as *baleen* or *toothed*. Classifying or reorganizing the information into categories as you read increases your understanding.

The key step in classifying is choosing categories that fit your purpose. Take classification notes in a chart like the one that follows to help you organize separate types or groups and sort their characteristics.

Classification Chart

Category 1 Paleozoic	Category 2 Mesozoic	Category 3 Cenozoic
Items in Category	Items in Category	Items in Category
Details and Characteristics	Details and Characteristics	Details and Characteristics

DISTINGUISH FACT FROM OPINION

A **fact** is a statement that can be proven by direct observation. Every statement of fact is either true or false. The following statement is an example of fact:

> Many Greek myths deal with human emotion. (This statement is a fact that can be proven by examining the content of Greek myths.)

An **opinion** is a statement that expresses an attitude or a desire, not a fact about the world. One common type of opinion statement is a *value statement*. A value statement expresses an attitude toward something.

> Ancient Greece produced some **beautiful** and **inspiring** myths. (The adjectives used to describe myths express an attitude or opinion toward something that cannot be proven.)

Fact from Opinion Chart

Fact: Ishi was found on August 29, 1911. Proof: Historical records	Opinion: Support:

IDENTIFY MULTIPLE LEVELS OF MEANING

There is often more than one purpose to a story or nonfiction work. Though there is always a main idea or theme, other levels of meaning are nonetheless important in understanding the overall meaning of the selection. As you read, take note of the multiple levels of meaning, and record them in a Levels of Meaning Chart like the one on the following page.

Levels of Meaning Chart

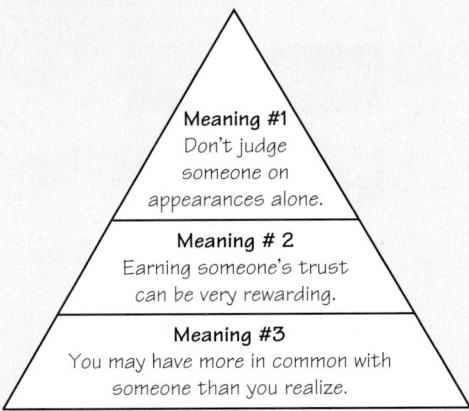

INTERPRET VISUAL AIDS

Visual aids are charts, graphs, pictures, illustrations, photos, maps, diagrams, spreadsheets, and other materials that present information. Many writers use visual aids to present data in understandable ways. Information visually presented in tables, charts, and graphs can help you find data, see trends, discover facts, and uncover patterns.

Pie Chart

A **pie chart** is a circle that stands for a whole group or set. The circle is divided into parts to show the divisions of the whole. When you look at a pie chart, you can see the relationships of the parts to one another and to the whole.

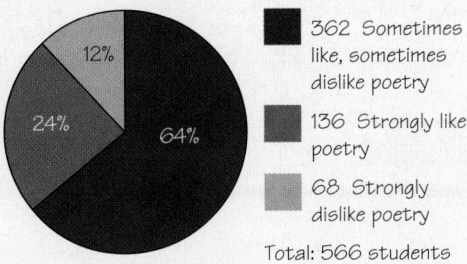

Bar Graph

A **bar graph** compares amounts of something by representing the amounts as bars of different lengths. In the bar graph shown on the next page, each bar represents the value in dollars of canned goods donated by several communities to a food drive. To read the graph, simply imagine a line drawn from the edge of the bar to the bottom of the graph. Then read the number. For example, the bar graph on the next page shows that the community of Russell Springs donated $600 worth of goods during the food drive.

DOLLAR VALUE OF DONATED GOODS TO CANNED FOOD DRIVE

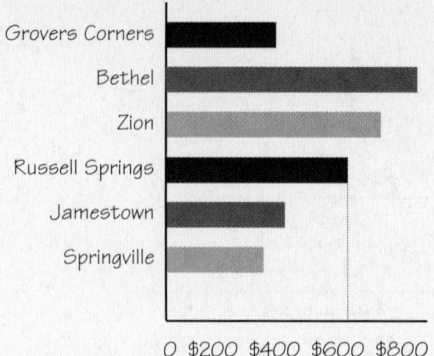

Map

A **map** is a representation, usually on a surface such as paper or a sheet of plastic, of a geographic area showing various significant features of that area.

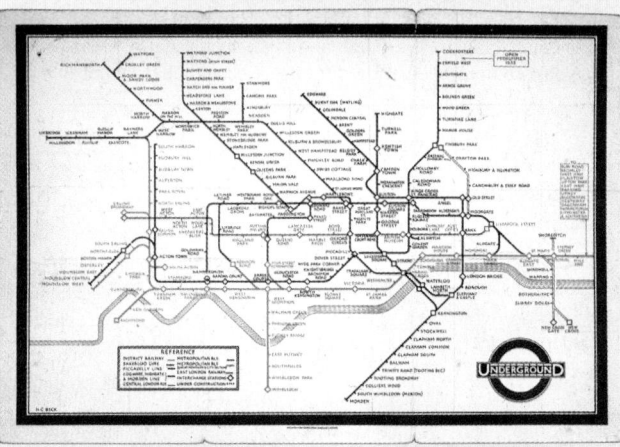

MONITOR COMPREHENSION

All readers occasionally have difficulty as they read. As you read, you should always **monitor,** or pay attention to, your progress, stopping frequently to check how well you are understanding what you are reading. If you encounter problems or lose focus, use a **fix-up idea** to get back on track. The following **fix-up ideas** can help you "fix up" any confusion or lack of attention you experience as you read. You probably use many of these already.

- **Reread** If you don't understand a sentence, paragraph, or section the first time through, go back and reread it. Each time you reread a text, you understand and remember more.
- **Read in shorter chunks** Break a long text into shorter chunks. Read through each "chunk." Then go back and make sure you understand that section before moving on.

- **Read aloud** If you are having trouble keeping your focus, try reading aloud to yourself. Go somewhere private and read aloud, putting emphasis and expression in your voice. Reading aloud also allows you to untangle difficult text by talking your way through it.
- **Ask questions** As you read, stop and ask yourself questions about the text. These questions may help you pinpoint things that are confusing you or things that you want to come back to later. You can ask questions in your head, or jot them down in the margins or on a piece of paper.
- **Change your reading rate** Your reading rate is how fast or slow you read. Good readers adjust their rate to fit the situation. In some cases, when you just need to get the general idea or main points of a reading, or if the reading is simple, you will want to read through it quickly and not get bogged down. Other times, such as when a text is difficult or contains a lot of description, you will need to slow down and read carefully.

SUMMARIZE

Summarizing is giving a shortened version of something that has been said or written, stating its main points. When you summarize a selection, you are **paraphrasing,** or restating something using other words in order to make it simpler or shorter. Summarizing what you have read will help you identify, understand, and remember the main and supporting points in the text. Read and summarize short sections of a selection at a time. Then write a summary of the entire work. Use a Summary Chart like the one below.

Summary Chart

Summary of Section 1: Although actual cases of mushroom poisoning aren't numerous, eating wild mushrooms can be dangerous.
Summary of Section 2: Serving wild mushrooms that appear to be safe to your guests at a party is risky, because people may react differently.
Summary of Section 3: The history of mushroom poisoning goes back as far as the ancient Greeks and Romans.
Summary of Section 4: It may be possible to develop a resistance to poisonous mushrooms by eating small doses, but it has not been proven.
Summary of the Selection: Eating unidentified wild mushrooms should be avoided because there is always a risk that they may cause death by poisoning.

DRAW CONCLUSIONS

When you **draw conclusions,** you are gathering pieces of information and then deciding what that information means. Drawing conclusions is an essential part of reading. It may be helpful to use a graphic organizer such as a chart or log to keep track of the information you find while you are reading and the conclusions you draw.

Drawing Conclusions Log

Key Idea Malcolm X was a determined man. Supporting Points He taught himself how to read and write much beyond his eighth grade education by copying pages from a dictionary and memorizing the words.	Key Idea Supporting Points	Key Idea Supporting Points
Overall Conclusion		

> For additional instruction and practice refer to the Vocabulary & Spelling Workshop, Context Clues, on page 581.

VOCABULARY & SPELLING

2 Vocabulary & Spelling

2.1 Using Context Clues

You can often figure out the meaning of an unfamiliar word by using context clues. Context clues, or hints you gather from the words and sentences around the unfamiliar word, prevent you from having to look up every unknown word in the dictionary. The chart below defines the types of context clues and gives you an example of each. It also lists words that signal each type of clue.

Context Clues	
comparison clue	shows a comparison, or how the unfamiliar word is like something that might be familiar to you
signal words	*and, like, as, just as, as if, as though*
EXAMPLE Joan was as nimble as a mountain goat as she hiked along the steep, rocky trail. (A mountain goat is extremely agile and sure on its feet. Nimble must mean "agile.")	
contrast clue	shows that something contrasts, or differs in meaning, from something else
signal words	*but, nevertheless, on the other hand, however, although, though, in spite of*
EXAMPLE Hsuan is very reflective, but his friend Ku Min is known for jumping into things without thinking about them. (The word *but* signals a contrast between Hsuan's and Ku Min's ways of doing things. If Ku Min jumps in without thinking, Hsuan must think things through more thoroughly. *Reflective* must mean "thoughtful, meditative.")	
restatement clue	uses different words to express the same idea
signal words	*that is, in other words, or*
EXAMPLE I know Kayesha will prevail in the student council election; I have no doubt that she's going to win! (As the information after the semicolon indicates, *prevail* means "win.")	
examples clue	gives examples of other items to illustrate the meaning of something
signal words	*including, such as, for example, for instance, especially, particularly*
EXAMPLE Trevor has always been interested in celestial bodies such as planets, stars, and moons. (If you know enough about the examples listed, you can tell that celestial bodies are visible bodies in the sky.)	
cause-and-effect clue	tells you that something happened as a result of something else
signal words	*if/then, when/then, thus, therefore, because, so, as a result of, consequently*
EXAMPLE I hadn't planned on going to the party, but the host invited me in such a cordial way that I felt welcome. (If the host's cordial invitation helped the speaker feel welcome, you can guess that *cordial* means "friendly.")	

Program Resources

For more study and practice with vocabulary and spelling, see the *Exceeding the Standards: Vocabulary & Spelling* resource.

2.2 Breaking Words Into Base Words, Word Roots, Prefixes, and Suffixes

Many words are formed by adding prefixes and suffixes to main word parts called base words (if they can stand alone) or word roots (if they can't). A prefix is a letter or group of letters added to the beginning of a word to change its meaning. A suffix is a letter or group of letters added to the end of a word to change its meaning.

> For additional instruction and practice refer to the Vocabulary & Spelling Workshop, Prefixes, Roots, and Suffixes, on page 45.

Word Part	Definition	Example
base word	main word part that can stand alone	form
word root	main word part that can't stand alone	struc
prefix	letter or group of letters added to the beginning of the word	pre—
suffix	letter or group of letters added to the end of the word	—tion

Common Prefixes		
Prefix	**Meaning**	**Examples**
anti–/ant–	against; opposite	antibody, antacid
bi–	two	bicycle, biped
circum–	around; about	circumnavigate, circumstance
co–/col–/com–/con–/cor–	together	cooperate, collaborate, commingle, concentrate, correlate
counter–	contrary; complementary; opposite	counteract, counterpart
de–	opposite; remove; reduce	decipher, defrost, devalue
dia–	through; apart	dialogue, diaphanous
dis–	not; opposite of	dislike, disguise
dys–	abnormal; difficult; bad	dysfunctional, dystopia
ex–	out of; from; away	explode, export, extend
extra–/extro–	outward; outside; beyond	extraordinary, extrovert
hyper–	too much, too many, extreme; above	hyperbole, hyperactive
hypo–	under	hypodermic, hypothermic
il–, im–, in–, ir–	not	illogical, impossible, inoperable, irrational
	in; within; toward; on	illuminate, imperil, infiltrate, irrigate
inter–	among; between	international, intersect
intra–/intro–	into; within; inward	introvert, intramural
mis–	wrongly	mistake, misfire
non–	not	nonsense, nonsmoker

Common Prefixes

Prefix	Meaning	Examples
out–	in a manner that goes beyond	outrun, outmuscle
over–	excessive	overdone, overkill
post–	after; later	postgame, postpone
pre–	before	prefix, premature
pro–	before; forward	proceed, prologue
re–	again; back	redo, recall
retro–	back	retrospect, retroactive
semi–	half; partly	semicircle, semidry
sub–/sup–	under	substandard, subfloor, support
super–	above; over; exceeding	superstar, superfluous
trans–	across; beyond	transatlantic, transfer, transcend
ultra–	too much; too many; extreme	ultraviolet, ultrasound
un–	not	unethical, unhappy
under–	below; short of a quantity or limit	underestimate, understaffed
uni–	one	unicorn, universe

Common Suffixes

Noun Suffixes	Meaning	Examples
–ance/–ancy/–ence/–ency	quality; state	defiance, independence, emergency
–age	action; process	marriage, voyage
–ant/–ent	one who	defendant, assistant, resident
–ar/–er/–or	one who	lawyer, survivor, liar
–dom	state; quality of	freedom, boredom
–ion/–tion	action; process	revolution, occasion
–ism	act; state; system of belief	plagiarism, barbarism, Buddhism
–ist	one who does or believes something	ventriloquist, idealist
–itude, –tude	quality of; state of	multitude, magnitude
–ity/–ty	state of	longevity, piety
–ment	action or process; state or quality; product or thing	development, government, amusement, amazement, ointment, fragment
–ness	state of	kindness, happiness

Common Suffixes

Adjective Suffixes	Meaning	Examples
–able/–ible	capable of	attainable, possible
–al	having characteristics of	personal, governmental
–er	more	higher, calmer, shorter
–est	most	lowest, craziest, tallest
–ful	full of	helpful, gleeful, woeful
–ic	having characteristics of	scientific, chronic
–ish	like	childish, reddish
–ive	performs; tends toward	creative, pensive
–less	without	hapless, careless
–ous	possessing the qualities of	generous, joyous
–y	indicates description	happy, dirty, flowery
Adverb Suffixes	**Meaning**	**Examples**
–ly	in such a way	quickly, studiously, invisibly
–ward, –ways, –wise	in such a direction	toward, sideways, crosswise
Verb Suffixes	**Meaning**	**Examples**
–ate	make or cause to be	fixate, activate
–ed	past tense of verb	walked, acted, fixed
–ify/–fy	make or cause to be	magnify, glorify
–ing	indicates action in progress (present participle); can also be a noun (gerund)	running, thinking, being
–ize	bring about; cause to be	colonize, legalize

Common Word Roots

Word Root	Meaning	Examples
act	do	actor, reaction
ann/annu/enni	year	annual, bicentennial
aqu	water	aquarium, aquatic
aster, astr	star	asteroid, astronomy
aud	hear	audition, auditorium
bene	good	beneficial, benefactor
bibl, bibli	book	Bible, bibliography
chron	time	chronic, chronological
cred	believe; trust	credit, credible
cycl	circle	bicycle, cyclone

Common Word Roots

Word Root	Meaning	Examples
dem/demo	people	democracy, demagogue
derm	skin	dermatologist, hypodermic
dic/dict	say	dictate, dictionary
fer	carry	transfer, refer
fin	end	finish, infinite
flect/flex	bend	deflect, reflex, flexible
hydra, hydro	water	hydrate, hydrogen
ign	fire	ignite, ignition, igneous
ject	throw	projector, eject
lect/leg	read; choose	lecture, election, legible
liber	free	liberate, liberal
log/logue	word; speech; discourse	logic, monologue
luc/lumin	shine; light	lucid, luminous
mal	bad	malevolent, malodorous
man/manu	hand	manufacture, manual
metr	measure	metric, metronome
ped	foot; child	pedal, pediatrics
phon/phony	sound; voice; speech	symphony, microphone
phot	light	photography, photon
physi	nature	physical, physics
pop	people	popular, populate
port	carry	transport, portable
psych	mind; soul	psychology, psychic
reg	rule	register, regulate
rupt	break	disrupt, interruption, rupture
scrib/script	write	describe, prescription
spec/spect/spic	look	speculate, inspect, specimen
ter/terr	earth	inter, terrestrial, terrain
therm	heat	thermal, hypothermia
vid/vis	see	video, visual
vol/volv	turn	evolution, revolve

2.3 Using a Dictionary

When you can't figure out a word using the strategies already described, or when the word is important to the meaning of the text and you want to make sure you have it right, use a dictionary. There are many parts to a dictionary entry.

pole¹ (pōl) *n.* [ME, from OE *pal,* from L *palus,* stake.] 1. a long, slender, generally rounded piece of wood 2. [Sports] the inside position on the starting line of a racetrack: *qualified in the time trials to start on the pole*

pole² (pōl) *n.* [ME, from L *polus,* from Gr *polos,* axis of the sphere.] 1. the extreme part of an axis through a sphere 2. either of two related opposites

labels: entry word, pronunciation, homograph indicator, part-of-speech label, etymology, second definition, first definition, usage note, usage illustration

The **pronunciation** is given immediately after the entry word. The dictionary's table of contents will tell you where you can find a complete key to pronunciation symbols. In some dictionaries, a simplified pronunciation key is provided at the bottom of each page.

An abbreviation of the **part of speech** usually follows the pronunciation. This label tells how the word can be used. If a word can be used as more than one part of speech, a separate entry is provided for each part of speech.

An **etymology** is the history of the word. In the first entry, the word *pole* can be traced back through Middle English (ME) and Old English (OE) to the Latin (L) word *palus,* which means "stake." In the second entry, the word *pole* can be traced back through Middle English to the Latin word *polus,* which comes from the Greek (Gr) word *polos,* meaning "axis of the sphere."

Sometimes the entry will include a list of **synonyms,** or words that have the same or very similar meanings. The entry may also include a **usage illustration,** which is an example of how the word is used in context.

2.4 Exploring Word Origins and Word Families

The English language expands constantly and gathers new words from many different sources. Understanding the source of a word can help you unlock its meaning.

One source of new words is the names of people and places associated with the thing being named. Words named for people and places are called **eponyms.**

EXAMPLES

hamburger Originally known as "Hamburg steak," the hamburger takes its name from the German city Hamburg.

spoonerism The slip of the tongue whereby the beginning sounds of words are switched is named after the Rev. William A. Spooner, who was known for such slips. For example, after a wedding, he told the groom, "It is kisstomary to cuss the bride."

> For additional instruction and practice refer to the Vocabulary & Spelling Workshop, Reference: Using Dictionaries and Thesauruses, on page 432.

VOCABULARY & SPELLING

Another source for new words is **acronyms.** Acronyms are words formed from the first letter or letters of the major parts of terms.

EXAMPLES

sonar, from sound navigation ranging

NATO, from North American Treaty Organization

Some words in the English language are borrowed from other languages.

EXAMPLES
deluxe (French), **Gesundheit** (German), **kayak** (Inuit)

Many words are formed by shortening longer words.

EXAMPLES

ad, from advertisement

lab, from laboratory

stereo, from stereophonic

Brand names are often taken into the English language. People begin to use these words as common nouns, even though most of them are still brand names.

EXAMPLES

Scotch tape   Xerox   Rollerblade

2.5 Understanding Multiple Meanings

Each definition in the entry gives a different meaning of the word. When a word has more than one meaning, the different definitions are numbered. The first definition in an entry is the most common meaning of the word, but you will have to choose the meaning that fits the context in which you have found the word. Try substituting each definition for the word until you find the one that makes the most sense. If you come across a word that doesn't seem to make sense in context, consider whether that word might have another, lesser known meaning. Can the word be used as more than one part of speech, for example, as either a noun or a verb? Does it have a broader meaning than the one that comes to your mind?

Keep in mind that some words not only have multiple meanings but also different pronunciations. Words that are spelled the same but are pronounced differently are called **homographs.**

2.6 Understanding Denotation and Connotation

The **denotation** of a word is its dictionary definition. Sometimes, in order to understand a passage fully, it is helpful to know the connotations of the words as well. A **connotation** of a word is an emotional association the word has in addition to its literal meaning. For example, the words *cheap* and *thrifty* both denote "tending to spend less money," but *cheap* has a negative connotation similar to "stingy," whereas *thrifty* has a positive connotation involving being responsible with money. The best way to learn the connotation of a word is to pay attention to the context in which the word appears or to ask someone more familiar with the word.

For additional instruction and practice refer to the Vocabulary & Spelling Workshop, Denotation and Connotation, on page 179.

Connotation Chart

Negative	Neutral	Positive
weird	unusual	unique
freakish	different	remarkable
bizarre	uncommon	extraordinary
abnormal	rare	unequaled
mob	group	congregation

2.7 Spelling

SPELLING RULES

Always check your writing for spelling errors, and try to recognize the words that give you more trouble than others. Use a dictionary when you find you have misspelled a word. Keep a list in a notebook of words that are difficult for you to spell. Write the words several times until you have memorized the correct spelling. Break down the word into syllables and carefully pronounce each individual syllable.

Some spelling problems occur when adding prefixes or suffixes to words or when making nouns plural. Other spelling problems occur when words follow certain patterns, such as those containing *ie/ei*. The following spelling rules can help you spell many words correctly.

PREFIXES AND SUFFIXES

Prefixes

A **prefix** is a letter or a group of letters added to the beginning of a word to change its meaning. When adding a prefix, do not change the spelling of the word itself.

EXAMPLES

mis– + perception = misperception   anti– + social = antisocial
im– + possible = impossible   al– + mighty = almighty
in– + conceivable = inconceivable

Suffixes

A **suffix** is a letter or a group of letters added to the end of a word to change its meaning.

The spelling of most words is not changed when the suffix –*ness* or –*ly* is added.

EXAMPLES

shy + –ness = shyness   strange + –ly = strangely
forgive + –ness = forgiveness   bad + –ly = badly
eager + –ness = eagerness   splendid + –ly = splendidly

If you are adding a suffix to a word that ends with *y* following a vowel, usually leave the *y* in place.

EXAMPLES

employ   employs   employing   employed
defray   defrays   defraying   defrayment
buoy   buoys   buoying   buoyancy

For additional instruction and practice refer to the Vocabulary & Spelling Workshop, Spelling by Syllables, on page 95.

2 VOCABULARY & SPELLING   **907**

If you are adding a suffix to a word that ends with *y* following a consonant, change the *y* to *i* before adding any ending except –*ing*.

EXAMPLES

bury	buried	burying
copy	copied	copying
supply	supplied	supplying
magnify	magnified	magnifying

Double the final consonant before adding a suffix beginning with a vowel (such as –*ed*, –*en*, –*er*, –*ing*, –*ence*, –*ance*, or –*y*) in words ending in a single consonant preceded by a single vowel if the word is either a single syllable or ends in a stressed syllable.

EXAMPLES

regret	regrettable	regretting
quit	quitter	quitting
fan	fanned	fanning
refer	referred	referring
plot	plotted	plotting
deter	deterrence	deterring
rot	rotten	rotting

If you are adding a suffix that begins with a vowel to a word that ends with a silent *e*, usually drop the *e*.

EXAMPLES

tune	tuning
oblige	obligation
pursue	pursuable
grieve	grievous

If you are adding a suffix that begins with a consonant to a word that ends with a silent *e*, usually leave the *e* in place.

EXAMPLES

spite	spiteful
achieve	achievement
state	stately
lame	lameness

EXCEPTIONS

awe	awful
wise	wisdom
nine	ninth
due	duly

If the word ends in a soft *c* sound (spelled *ce*) or a soft *g* sound (spelled *ge*), keep the *e* when adding the suffixes –*able* or –*ous*.

EXAMPLES

acknowledge	acknowledgeable
enforce	enforceable
outrage	outrageous

PLURAL NOUNS

Plural Nouns

Most noun plurals are formed by simply adding *–s* to the end of the word.

EXAMPLES

surface + –s = surfaces	platelet + –s = platelets
mouthful + –s = mouthfuls	refrigerator + –s = refrigerators

The plural of nouns that end in *o, s, x, z, ch,* or *sh* should be formed by adding *–es.*

EXAMPLES

tomato + –es = tomatoes	buzz + –es = buzzes
loss + –es = losses	inch + –es = inches
fox + –es = foxes	flash + –es = flashes

The exception to the rule above is that musical terms and certain other words that end in *o* are usually made plural by adding *–s.* Check a dictionary if you aren't sure whether to add *–s* or *–es.*

EXAMPLES

piano + –s = pianos	soprano + –s = sopranos
solo + –s = solos	vibrato + –s = vibratos

Form the plural of nouns that end in *y* following a consonant by changing the *y* to an *i* and adding *–es.*

EXAMPLES

democracy	democracies
fairy	fairies
fallacy	fallacies
fifty	fifties
filly	fillies

Nouns that end in *f* or *fe* must be modified, changing the *f* or *fe* to *v,* before adding *–es* to the plural form.

EXAMPLES

shelf	shelves
knife	knives
scarf	scarves
leaf	leaves
calf	calves

SPELLING PATTERNS

The ie/ei Spelling Pattern

A word spelled with the letters *i* and *e* and has a long *e* sound is usually spelled *ie* except after the letter *c.*

EXAMPLES

belief	conceive
piece	receive
field	deceit

EXCEPTIONS

leisure	either

Use *ei* when the sound is not long *e*.

EXAMPLES

forfeit   surfeit   foreign   height

EXCEPTIONS

science   mischief   sieve

If the vowel combination has a long *a* sound (as in *eight*), always spell it with *ei*.

EXAMPLES

weight   reign   vein

When two vowels are pronounced separately in a word, spell them in the order of their pronunciation.

EXAMPLES

siesta   patio   diode   transient

The "Seed" Sound Pattern

The "seed" ending sound has three spellings: *−sede*, *−ceed*, and *−cede*.

EXAMPLES

Only one word ends in *−sede: supersede*

Three words end in *−ceed: proceed, succeed, exceed*

All other words end in *−cede: accede, concede, recede, precede, secede*

Silent Letters

Some spelling problems result from letters written but not heard when a word is spoken. Becoming familiar with the patterns in letter combinations containing silent letters will help you identify other words that fit the patterns.

- Silent *b* usually occurs with *m*.

EXAMPLES

dumb   bomb   climb   lamb

- Silent *b* also appears in *debt* and *doubt*.

- Silent *c* often appears with *s*.

EXAMPLES

scissors   scent   scenic   science

- Silent *g* often appears with *n*.

EXAMPLES

design   resign   gnome   foreign

- Silent *gh* often appears at the end of a word, either alone or in combination with *t* (*−ght*).

EXAMPLES

fright   freight   sought   wrought

- Silent *h* appears at the beginning of some words.

EXAMPLES

hourly   heir   honestly   honor

- Silent *h* also appears in a few other words, as in *rhythm* and *ghost.*

- Silent *k* occurs with *n.*

EXAMPLES

knack   knight   knot   kneecap   knapsack

- Silent *n* occurs with *m* at the end of some words.

EXAMPLES

condemn   solemn   column   autumn

- Silent *p* occurs with *s* at the beginning of some words.

EXAMPLES

psyche   psychosis   psoriasis

- Silent *s* occurs with *l* in some words.

EXAMPLES

island   islet   aisle

- Silent *t* occurs with *s* in a few words.

EXAMPLES

listen   hasten   nestle

- Silent *w* occurs at the beginnings of some words.

EXAMPLES

wreak   wrong   wraith   wrapper

- Silent *w* also occurs with *s* in a few words, such as *sword* and *answer.*

Letter Combinations

Some letter combinations have a different pronunciation when combined and can cause spelling problems.

- The letters *ph* produce the *f* sound.

EXAMPLES

sphinx   photograph   alphanumeric   phosphate

- The letters *gh* produce the *f* sound usually at the end of a word. (Otherwise, they are silent.)

EXAMPLES

cough   enough   neigh   weigh

- The letter combination *tch* sounds the same as *ch.*

EXAMPLES

sketch   pitch   snitch   hatch
such   hunch   grouch   torch

If the letters *c* and *g* have soft sounds (of *s* and *j*), they will usually be followed by *e, i,* or *y.*

EXAMPLES

cyclone   circle   regent
giant   cent   gyroscope
outrageous   region

If the letters *c* and *g* have hard sounds (of *k* and *g*), they will usually be followed by *a*, *o*, or *u*.

EXAMPLES

candid	gasket	conjugate
congeal	garland	gun
convey	argument	cunning

Spelling Patterns of Borrowed Words

Many words borrowed from other languages follow the spelling patterns of the original language. For example, some English words borrowed from French, Spanish, and Italian follow letter patterns of the language of origin.

• The final *t* is silent in many words borrowed from French.

EXAMPLES

croquet   ballet

• The letter combinations *eur* and *eau* appear at the end of many words with French origin.

EXAMPLES

amateur	bureau	grandeur
chauffeur	plateau	tableau

• The letter combination *oo* appears in many words borrowed from the Dutch language.

EXAMPLES

roost	cooper	toot

Many plural Italian words end in *i*.

EXAMPLES

ravioli	manicotti	linguini

Many words of Spanish origin end in *o*.

EXAMPLES

machismo	tomato	patio

Compound Nouns

A **compound noun** consists of two or more nouns used together to form a single noun. Sometimes they are written as one word *(football, uptown)*; other times they are written separately *(picnic table, tennis shoes)*. Some compound nouns are connected with hyphens *(great-grandfather, fly-by-night)*. Consult a good dictionary when you are not sure of the form of compounds.

Numerals

Spell out numbers of *one hundred* or less and all numbers rounded to hundreds. Larger round numbers such as *seven thousand* or *three million* should also be spelled out.

EXAMPLES

Joe Morgan hit more than **twenty** home runs and stole at least **thirty** bases in the same season **four** times in his career.

Joe DiMaggio was the first baseball player to receive an annual salary of more than **a hundred thousand** dollars.

Use a hyphen to separate compound numbers from twenty-one through ninety-nine.

VOCABULARY & SPELLING

EXAMPLES

forty-two birds	one hundred soldiers
seventy-four candles	sixty thousand dollars

Use a hyphen in a fraction used as a modifier, but not in a fraction used as a noun.

EXAMPLES

The glass is **two-fifths full** of water.

After an hour, I had mowed **three fourths** of the backyard.

Use Arabic numerals for numbers greater than one hundred that are not rounded numbers.

EXAMPLES

Our company sent out **493,745** mailings in just **145** days this year.

My uncle boasted that he has read **1,323** books thus far in his life.

If a number appears at the beginning of a sentence, spell it out or rewrite the sentence.

EXAMPLES

incorrect
356 years ago, my ancestors moved to North America.
correct
Three hundred fifty-six years ago, my ancestors moved to North America.
correct
My ancestors moved to North America **356** years ago.

Use words to write the time unless you are writing the exact time (including the abbreviation AM or PM). When the word *o'clock* is used for time of day, express the number in words.

EXAMPLES

Our meeting will start at **a quarter after ten.**

At **eight-thirty,** the show will begin.

I was born at **5:22 PM** on a Monday.

You have until **three o'clock** to finish the proposal.

Use numerals to express dates, street numbers, room numbers, apartment numbers, telephone numbers, page numbers, exact amounts of money, scores, and percentages. Spell out the word *percent.* Round dollar or cent amounts of only a few words may be expressed in words.

EXAMPLES

May 27, 1962	three hundred dollars
(402) 555-1725	Apartment 655
5219 Perret Street	38 percent
pages 49–73	$1.6 billion (or $1,600,000,000)
seventy cents	$2,634

When you write a date, do not add *–st, –nd,* or *–th.*

EXAMPLES

incorrect	
August 17th, 1968	November 5th
correct	
August 17, 1968	November 5 or the fifth of November

COMMON SPELLING ERRORS

Pronunciation is not always a reliable guide for spelling because words are not always spelled the way they are pronounced. However, by paying attention to both letters that spell sounds and letters that are silent, you can improve some aspects of your spelling. Always check a dictionary for the correct pronunciations and spellings of words that are new to your experience.

Extra Syllables

Sometimes people misspell a word because they include an extra syllable. For example, *arthritis* is easily misspelled if it is pronounced *artheritis,* with four syllables instead of three. Pay close attention to the number of syllables in these words.

EXAMPLES

two syllables

foundry   carriage   lonely

three syllables

privilege   boundary   separate

Omitted Sounds

Sometimes people misspell a word because they do not sound one or more letters when pronouncing the word. Be sure to include the underlined letters of these words even if you don't pronounce them.

EXAMPLES

barbarous   candidate   drowned   mischievous   sophomore

gratitude   governor   grocery   quantity   literature

Homophones

Words that have the same pronunciation but different spellings and meanings are called **homophones.** An incorrect choice can be confusing to your readers. Knowing the spelling and meaning of these groups of words will improve your spelling.

EXAMPLES

allowed/aloud	coarse/course	compliment/complement
sole/soul	alter/altar	site/sight/cite
hear/here	some/sum	plain/plane
ascent/assent	lead/led	capital/capitol
threw/through	bear/bare	who's/whose
night/knight	wait/weight	peace/piece
brake/break	pair/pear	buy/bye/by
weak/week		

Commonly Confused Words

Some other groups of words are not homophones, but they are similar enough in sound and spelling to create confusion. Knowing the spelling and meaning of these groups of words will also improve your spelling.

EXAMPLES

access/excess	farther/further	nauseous/nauseated
accept/except	principle/principal	stationary/stationery
formally/formerly	passed/past	alternate/alternative
literal/literally	desert/dessert	loose/lose

COMMONLY MISSPELLED WORDS

Some words are often misspelled. Here is a list of 150 commonly misspelled words. If you master this list, you will avoid many errors in your spelling.

absence	enormous	parallel
abundant	enthusiastically	pastime
academically	environment	peasant
accessible	exhaust	permanent
accidentally	existence	persistent
accommodate	fascinating	phenomenon
accurate	finally	physician
acknowledgment	forfeit	pneumonia
acquaintance	fulfill	prestige
adequately	guerrilla	privilege
adolescent	guidance	procedure
advantageous	hindrance	prophesy
advisable	hypocrite	prove
ancient	independent	receipt
annihilate	influential	referred
anonymous	ingenious	rehearsal
answer	institution	relieve
apparent	interference	resistance
article	irrelevant	resources
attendance	irresistible	responsibility
bankruptcy	judgment	rhythm
beautiful	league	schedule
beggar	leisure	seize
beginning	license	separate
behavior	lightning	sergeant
biscuit	liquefy	siege
breathe	magnificent	significance
business	manageable	souvenir
calendar	maneuver	sponsor
camouflage	meadow	succeed
catastrophe	mediocre	surprise
cellar	miniature	symbol
cemetery	mischievous	synonymous
changeable	misspell	temperature
clothes	mortgage	tomorrow
colossal	mysterious	transparent
column	naïve	twelfth
committee	necessity	undoubtedly
conceivable	nickel	unmistakable
conscientious	niece	unnecessary
conscious	noticeable	vacuum
consistency	nucleus	vehicle
deceitful	nuisance	vengeance
descendant	nutritious	villain
desirable	obedience	vinegar
disastrous	occasionally	weird
discipline	occurrence	whistle
efficiency	orchestra	withhold
eighth	outrageous	yacht
embarrass	pageant	yield

For additional instruction and practice refer to the Grammar & Style Workshop, Simple, Compound, and Compound-Complex Sentences, on page 406.

3 Grammar & Style

3.1 The Sentence

THE SENTENCE

In the English language, the sentence is the basic unit of meaning. A **sentence** is a group of words that expresses a complete thought. Every sentence has two basic parts: a subject and a predicate. The **subject** tells whom or what the sentence is about. The **predicate** tells information about the subject.

EXAMPLE

> **sentence**
> The old professor | read the dusty manuscript.
>   **(subject)**   **(predicate)**

A group of words that does not have both a subject and a predicate is called a **sentence fragment.** A sentence fragment does not express a complete thought.

EXAMPLES

> **sentence fragment** The baker.
> (The fragment does not have a predicate. The group of words does not answer the question *What did the baker do?*)
> **sentence fragment** Frosted the chocolate cake.
> (The fragment does not have a subject. The group of words does not answer the question *Who frosted the chocolate cake?*)
> **sentence fragment** In his kitchen.
> (The fragment does not have a subject or predicate. The group of words does not tell what the sentence is about or tell what the subject does.)
> **complete sentence** The baker frosted the chocolate cake in his kitchen.

FUNCTIONS OF SENTENCES

There are four different kinds of sentences: *declarative, interrogative, imperative,* and *exclamatory*. Each kind of sentence has a different purpose. You can vary the tone and mood of your writing by using the four different sentence types.

- A **declarative sentence** makes a statement. It ends with a period.

EXAMPLE

> Your cat would like to eat her supper now.

- An **interrogative sentence** asks a question. It ends with a question mark.

EXAMPLE

> When will your cat eat her supper?

- An **imperative sentence** gives an order or makes a request. It ends with a period or an exclamation point. An imperative sentence has an understood subject, most often *you*.

EXAMPLES

> (You) Please feed your cat.
> (You) Look in the cupboard for the cat food.

Program Resources

You will find additional lessons on grammar and style in the *Exceeding the Standards: Grammar & Style* resource.

- An **exclamatory sentence** expresses strong feeling. It ends with an exclamation point.

EXAMPLE

Your cat is really hungry!

SIMPLE AND COMPLETE SUBJECTS AND PREDICATES

In a sentence, the **simple subject** is the key word or words in the subject. The simple subject is usually a noun or a pronoun and does not include any modifiers. The **complete subject** includes the simple subject and all the words that modify it.

The **simple predicate** is the key verb or verb phrase that tells what the subject does, has, or is. The **complete predicate** includes the verb and all the words that modify it.

In the following sentence, a vertical line separates the complete subject and complete predicate. The simple subject is underlined once. The simple predicate is underlined twice.

EXAMPLE

     (complete subject)   **(complete predicate)**

The large black <u>umbrella</u> | <u>shielded</u> my brother and sister from the rain.

Sometimes, the simple subject is also the complete subject, and the simple predicate or verb is also the complete predicate.

EXAMPLE

<u>Jesse Owens</u> | <u>ran</u>.

To find the simple subject and simple predicate in a sentence, first break the sentence into its two basic parts: complete subject and complete predicate. Then, identify the simple predicate by asking yourself, "What is the action of this sentence?" Finally, identify the simple subject by asking yourself, "Who or what is performing the action?" In the following sentences, the complete predicate is in parentheses. The simple predicate, or verb, appears in boldface.

EXAMPLES

one-word verb Three energetic monkeys (**climbed** up the tree.)
two-word verb Three energetic monkeys (**are climbing** up the tree.)
three-word verb Three energetic monkeys (**have been climbing** up the tree.)
four-word verb Three energetic monkeys (**might have been climbing** up the tree.)

COMPOUND SUBJECTS AND PREDICATES

A sentence may have more than one subject or predicate. A **compound subject** has two or more simple subjects that have the same predicate. The subjects are joined by the conjunction *and, or,* or *but.*

A **compound predicate** has two or more simple predicates, or verbs, that share the same subject. The verbs are connected by the conjunction *and, or,* or *but.*

EXAMPLES

compound subject

<u>Ice</u> and <u>snow</u> | <u>make</u> travel difficult in the winter.

compound predicate

Some <u>teachers</u> | <u>show</u> videos and <u>play</u> CDs during their classes.

For additional instruction and practice refer to the Grammar & Style Workshop, Simple, Complete, and Compound Predicates, on page 556.

For additional instruction and practice refer to the Grammar & Style Workshop, Simple and Compound Subjects, on page 522.

GRAMMAR & STYLE

The conjunctions *either* and *or* and *neither* and *nor* can also join compound subjects or predicates.

EXAMPLES

compound subject
Either <u>Peter</u> *or* <u>Paul</u> | <u>sings</u> the national anthem before each game.
Neither <u>yesterday</u> *nor* <u>today</u> | <u>seemed</u> like a good time to start the project.

compound predicate
Her <u>dogs</u> | *either* <u>heard</u> *or* <u>smelled</u> the intruder in the basement.
The police <u>inspector</u> | *neither* <u>visited</u> *nor* <u>called</u> last night.

A sentence may also have a compound subject and a compound predicate.

EXAMPLE

compound subject and compound predicate
John and Diane | drove to the lake and fished all afternoon.

SENTENCE STRUCTURES

A **simple sentence** consists of one independent clause and no subordinate clauses. It may have a compound subject and a compound predicate. It may also have any number of phrases. A simple sentence is sometimes called an independent clause because it can stand by itself.

EXAMPLES

Three bears emerged from the forest.

They spotted the campers and the hikers and decided to pay a visit.

The three bears enjoyed eating the campers' fish, sandwiches, and candy bars.

A **compound sentence** consists of two sentences joined by a semicolon or by a coordinating conjunction and a comma. Each part of the compound sentence has its own subject and verb. The most common coordinating conjunctions are *and, or, nor, for, but, so,* and *yet.*

EXAMPLES

compound sentence
Grover Cleveland served as president from 1885 to 1889**;** he served a second term in the White House from 1893 to 1897.

compound sentence
An economic downturn gripped the nation during Cleveland's second term**, and** his popularity with Americans dwindled.

A **complex sentence** consists of one independent clause and one or more subordinate clauses. The subordinate clauses in the examples below are underlined.

EXAMPLES

<u>When you finish your report</u>, remember to print it out on paper <u>that contains 25 percent cotton fiber</u>.

Jim will water the lawn <u>after he returns home from the baseball game</u>.

3.2 The Parts of Speech

IDENTIFYING THE PARTS OF SPEECH

Each word in a sentence performs a basic function or task. Words perform four basic tasks; they name, modify, express action or state of being, or link.

There are eight different parts of speech. Each part of speech is defined in the following chart.

Part of Speech	Definition	Example
noun	A **noun** names a person, place, thing, or idea.	**Apples, oranges,** and **potato chips** were the only **items** on the **list.**
pronoun	A **pronoun** is used in place of a noun.	Fanny whispered to **her** friend as **they** waited for **their** new teacher.
verb	A **verb** expresses action or a state of being.	Playful fox cubs **tumbled** out of the den and **chased** one another across the field.
adjective	An **adjective** modifies a noun or pronoun. The most common adjectives are the articles *a, an,* and *the.*	**Tattered** curtains hung in the **dark** windows of the **gray, sagging** house.
adverb	An **adverb** modifies a verb, an adjective, or another adverb.	**Sharply** turning to the left, the bicyclist **nearly** caused an accident.
preposition	A **preposition** shows the relationship between its object—a noun or a pronoun—and another word in a sentence. Common prepositions include *after, around, at, behind, beside, off, through, until, upon,* and *with.*	**During** winter, we often sit **by** the fireplace **in** the evening.
conjunction	A **conjunction** joins words or groups of words. Common conjunctions are *and, but, for, nor, or, so,* and *yet.*	**Neither** Grant **nor** Felix felt tired after two miles, **so** they ran another mile.
interjection	An **interjection** is a word used to express emotion. Common interjections are *oh, ah, well, hey,* and *wow.*	**Wow!** Did you see the dive he took from the high jump?

3.3 Nouns

NOUNS

A **noun** is a part of speech that names a person, place, idea, or thing. In this unit, you'll learn about the different kinds of nouns and what they name.

EXAMPLES

people Sidney, teacher, mother, photographer

places city, Wrigley Field, Kentucky

ideas admiration, addition, relief, plan

things checkerboard, butterfly, flight, ring

> For additional instruction and practice refer to the Grammar & Style Workshop, Nouns: Proper, Plural, Possessive, and Collective, on page 492.

Types of Nouns	Definition	Examples
common noun	names a person, place, idea, or thing	mother, garage, plan, flower
proper noun	names a specific person, place, or thing; begins with capital letter	John Adams, New York City, Monroe Doctrine
concrete noun	names a thing that can be touched, seen, heard, smelled, or tasted	ruler, mirror, giggle, garbage, banana
abstract noun	names an idea, a theory, a concept, or a feeling	approval, philosophy, faith, communism
singular noun	names one person, place, idea, or thing	governor, tree, thought, shoe
plural noun	names more than one thing	governors, trees, thoughts, shoes
possessive noun	shows ownership or possession of things or qualities	Jan's, Mrs. Wilson's, women's, intern's
compound noun	made up of two or more words	staircase, picnic table, brother-in-law
collective noun	names groups	organization, platoon, team

3.4 Pronouns

PRONOUNS

A **pronoun** is used in place of a noun. Sometimes a pronoun refers to a specific person or thing.

Pronouns can help your writing flow more smoothly. Without pronouns, your writing can sound awkward and repetitive.

The most commonly used pronouns are *personal pronouns*, *reflexive and intensive pronouns*, *demonstrative pronouns*, *indefinite pronouns*, *interrogative pronouns*, and *relative pronouns*.

Types of Pronouns	Definition	Examples
personal pronoun	used in place of the name of a person or thing	I, me, we, us, he, she, it, him, her, you, they, them
indefinite pronoun	points out a person, place, or thing, but not a specific or definite one	one, someone, anything, other, all, few, nobody
reflexive pronoun	refers back to a noun previously used; adds –self and –selves to other pronoun forms	myself, herself, yourself, themselves, ourselves
intensive pronoun	emphasizes a noun or a pronoun	me myself, he himself, you yourself, they themselves, we ourselves
interrogative pronoun	asks a question	who, whose, whom, what, which
demonstrative pronoun	points out a specific person, place, idea, or thing	this, these, that, those
relative pronoun	introduces an adjective clause	that, which, who, whose, whom
singular pronoun	used in place of the name of one person or thing	I, me, you, he, she, it, him, her
plural pronoun	used in place of more than one person or thing	we, us, you, they, them
possessive pronoun	shows ownership or possession	mine, yours, his, hers, ours, theirs

> For additional instruction and practice refer to the Grammar & Style Workshop, Pronoun Use, on page 199.

> For additional instruction and practice refer to the Grammar & Style Workshop, Personal and Possessive Pronouns, on page 547.

> For additional instruction and practice refer to the Grammar & Style Workshop, Reflexive and Intensive Pronouns, on page 565.

PRONOUNS AND ANTECEDENTS

The word that a pronoun stands for is called its **antecedent.** The antecedent clarifies the meaning of the pronoun. The pronoun may appear in the same sentence as its antecedent or in a following sentence.

EXAMPLES

Where is **Michael? He** is at the library.
(*Michael* is the antecedent of *He*.)

Amy's black **dog** barks loudly because **he** is hungry.
(*Dog* is the antecedent of *he*.)

A pronoun should agree in both number (singular or plural) and gender (masculine, feminine, or neutral) with its antecedent.

EXAMPLES

number

singular	**Robert Frost** wrote many poems. "Stopping by Woods on a Snowy Evening" is perhaps **his** most well-known poem.
plural	The visiting **poets** were asked if **they** would give a reading on Saturday night.

gender

masculine	**Robert Frost** was born in California, but **he** was raised in Massachusetts and New Hampshire.
feminine	**Toni Morrison** begins **her** writing day before dawn.
neutral	The **poem** is titled "Birches," and **it** is one of my favorites.

Singular pronouns are used with some nouns that are plural in form but singular in meaning, such as *economics, electronics, gymnastics, linguistics, mathematics, measles, news,* and *physics.*

EXAMPLES

My younger brother has the **measles.** I hope I don't catch **it.**
Would you like to try **gymnastics? It** is excellent exercise.

Plural pronouns are used with some nouns that are plural in form but refer to single items, such as *pliers, eyeglasses, pants, scissors,* and *shorts.*

EXAMPLES

I can't find my **eyeglasses.** Have you seen **them?**
The **pants** fit you well, but **they** need hemming.

Agreement between a relative pronoun—*who, whom, whose, which,* and *that*—and its antecedent is determined by the number of the antecedent.

EXAMPLES

Marie, who has always enjoyed **her** rural life, has surprisingly decided to move to the city. (*Who* is singular because it refers to the singular noun *Marie. Her* is used to agree with *who*.)

All who wish to vote by absentee ballot should complete **their** ballots and mail **them** to the county clerk's office. (*Who* is plural because it refers to the plural pronoun *All. Their* is used to agree with *who. Them* is used to agree with *ballots*.)

For additional instruction and practice refer to the Grammar & Style Workshop, Pronoun-Antecedent Agreement, on page 77.

GRAMMAR & STYLE

PRONOUN CASES

Personal pronouns take on different forms—called *cases*—depending on how they are used in sentences. Personal pronouns can be used as subjects, direct objects, indirect objects, and objects of prepositions. In the English language, there are three case forms for personal pronouns: *nominative, objective,* and *possessive.* The following chart organizes personal pronouns by case, number, and person.

Personal Pronouns

	Nominative Case	Objective Case	Possessive Case
Singular			
first person	I	me	my, mine
second person	you	you	your, yours
third person	he, she, it	him, her, it	his, her, hers, its
Plural			
first person	we	us	our, ours
second person	you	you	your, yours
third person	they	them	their, theirs

Indefinite Pronouns

An **indefinite pronoun** points out a person, place, or thing, but not a particular or definite one. The indefinite pronouns are listed below.

Singular	Plural	Singular or Plural
another	both	all
anybody	few	any
anyone	many	more
anything	others	most
each	several	none
each other		some
either		
everybody		
everyone		
everything		
much		
neither		
nobody		
no one		
nothing		
one		
one another		
somebody		
someone		
something		

EXAMPLES

singular

Something makes a ticking noise in the night.

Everyone is welcome to join us at the picnic.

plural

Many are eager to participate in the summer festival.

Several were missing the necessary information.

 **Verbs**

VERBS — PREDICATES

Every sentence can be divided into two parts: the **subject** and the **predicate.** The following sentence is divided between the complete subject and the complete predicate.

EXAMPLE

The barn **owl** | **glided** slowly over the cornfield.

The subject of a sentence names whom or what the sentence is about. The predicate tells what the subject does, is, or has. A **verb** is the predicate without any complements, linkers, or modifiers. In other words, the verb is the simple predicate.

Verbs are the **expressers** of the English language. Verbs are used to express action or a state of being. They tell whether the action is completed, continuing, or will happen in the future. Verbs also express all kinds of conditions for the action. Verbs in the English language can be from one to four words long. When a main verb is preceded by one or more helping verbs, it is called a **verb phrase.**

EXAMPLES

Dale **mows** his neighbors' lawns.

Dale **is mowing** his neighbors' lawns.

Dale **has been mowing** his neighbors' lawns.

Dale **might have been mowing** his neighbors' lawns.

The following chart lists the different types of verbs and their functions, along with examples of how they are used.

Type of Verb	Definition	Examples
action verb	names an action	howl, wobble, skitter, flutter, fly
helping verb	helps a main verb express action or a state of being	My dogs will howl when a siren sounds. A butterfly has been fluttering above the daisies.
linking verb	connects a noun with another noun, pronoun, or adjective that describes or identifies it; the most common linking verbs are formed from the verb *to be*	The butterfly is a monarch. It seems to float in the breeze.
transitive verb	has a direct object	The scientist remembered the secret code.
intransitive verb	does not have a direct object	My brother snores.
irregular verb	has a different past tense form and spelling	forget/forgot think/thought write/wrote

VERB TENSES

The Simple Tenses

Verbs have different forms, called **tenses,** which are used to tell the time in which an action takes place. The **simple tenses** of the verb are **present, past,** and **future.**

For additional instruction and practice refer to the Grammar & Style Workshop, Consistent Verb Tense, on page 340.

The **present tense** tells that an action happens now—in present time.

EXAMPLES

present tense singular	The green frog **jumps** into the pond.
present tense plural	The green frogs **jump** into the pond.
present tense singular	The teacher **walks** down the hall.
present tense plural	The teachers **walk** down the hall.

The **past tense** tells that an action happened in the past—prior to the present time. The past tense of a regular verb is formed by adding –*d* or –*ed* to the present verb form.

EXAMPLES

past tense singular	The green frog **jumped** into the pond.
past tense plural	The green frogs **jumped** into the pond.
past tense singular	The teacher **walked** down the hall.
past tense plural	The teachers **walked** down the hall.

The **future tense** tells that an action will happen in the future. The future tense is formed by adding the word *will* or *shall* before the present verb form.

EXAMPLES

future tense singular	The green frog **will jump** into the pond.
future tense plural	The green frogs **will jump** into the pond.
future tense singular	The teacher **shall walk** down the hall.
future tense plural	The teachers **shall walk** down the hall.

The Perfect Tenses

The **perfect tenses** of verbs also express present, past, and future time, but they show that the action continued and was completed over a period of time or that the action will be completed in the present or future. The perfect tense is formed by using *has, have,* or *had* with the past participle.

EXAMPLES

present perfect singular	Vera **has baked** the birthday cake. The birthday cake **has been baked** by Vera.
present perfect plural	Vera and Hans **have baked** the birthday cake. (have or has + past participle)
past perfect singular	Vera **had baked** the birthday cake. The birthday cake **had been baked** by Vera.
past perfect plural	Vera and Hans **had baked** the birthday cake. (had + past participle)
future perfect singular	Vera **will have baked** the birthday cake. The birthday cake **will have been baked** by Vera.
future perfect plural	Vera and Hans **will have baked** the birthday cake. (will have or shall have + past participle)

3.6 Complements

COMPLEMENTS FOR ACTION VERBS

A sentence must have a subject and a verb to communicate its basic meaning. In the following sentences, the subject and verb express the total concept. There is no receiver of the verb's action.

EXAMPLES

We talked.

I never lose.

The tree fell.

Many sentences that include action verbs, however, need an additional word or group of words to complete the meaning.

EXAMPLES

The soldiers climbed.

The soldiers climbed the wall.

The group of words *The musicians tuned* contains a subject *(musicians)* and a verb *(tuned).* Although the group of words may be considered a sentence, it does not express a complete thought. The word *instruments* completes the meaning expressed by the verb *tuned.* Therefore, *instruments* is called a **complement** or a completing word. The *completers* for action verbs are **direct objects** and **indirect objects.**

Direct Objects

A **direct object** receives the action in the sentence. It usually answers the question *what?* or *whom?* To find the direct object, find the action verb in the sentence. Then ask *what?* or *whom?* about the verb.

EXAMPLES

I **found** a **coin** in the pond. (*Found* is the action verb. What did I find? *Coin* is the direct object.)

The dog **jumped** the **fence.** (*Jumped* is the action verb. What did the dog jump? *Fence* is the direct object.)

Remember to use object pronouns for a direct object.

singular me, you, him, her, it
plural us, you, them

EXAMPLES

Betty told **us** to drive west.

Evan questioned **him** about the wallet.

Indirect Objects

Sometimes the direct object is received by someone or something. This receiver is called the **indirect object.** It comes before the direct object and tells *to whom* the action is directed or *for whom* the action is performed. Only verbs that have direct objects can have indirect objects.

EXAMPLE

Seth **sold** Karl a **car.** (*Sold* is the action verb. *Car* is the direct object because it tells what Seth sold. *Karl* is an indirect object. It tells to whom Seth sold a car.)

To identify the indirect object: (1) Look for a noun or a pronoun that precedes the direct object. (2) Determine whether the word you think is a direct object seems to be the understood object of the preposition *to* or *for*.

COMPLEMENTS FOR LINKING VERBS

A **linking verb** connects a subject with a noun, a pronoun, or an adjective that describes it or identifies it. Linking verbs do not express action. Instead, they express state of being and need a noun, a pronoun or an adjective to complete the sentence meaning.

In each of the following sentences, the subject and verb would not be complete without the words that follow them.

EXAMPLES

The chocolate cake **was** rich.
(The verb *was* connects the subject *cake* with a word that describes it — *rich*.)

The wind and rain **are** cold.
(The verb *are* connects the compound subject *wind and rain* with a word that describes it — *cold*.)

Most linking verbs are forms of the verb *to be*, including *am, are, is, was,* and *been*. Other words that can be used as linking verbs include *appear, feel, grow, smell, taste, seem, sound, look, stay, feel, remain,* and *become.* When *to be* verbs are part of an action verb, they are helpers.

3.7 Agreement

SUBJECT AND VERB AGREEMENT

A **singular** noun describes or stands for *one* person, place, thing, or idea. A **plural noun** describes or stands for *more than one* person, place, thing, or idea.

EXAMPLES

singular nouns	book	apple	rose	mouse	child
plural nouns	books	apples	roses	mice	children

In a sentence, a verb must be singular if its subject is singular and plural if its subject is plural. In other words, a verb must agree in number with its subject.

EXAMPLES

singular subject and verb	The apple seems ripe.
plural subject and verb	The apples seem ripe.
singular subject and verb	A rose smells lovely in the evening.
plural subject and verb	The roses smell lovely in the evening.
singular subject and verb	A mouse runs across the room.
plural subject and verb	The mice run across the room.

For additional instruction and practice refer to the Grammar & Style Workshop, Subject-Verb Agreement, on page 31.

COMPOUND SUBJECT AND VERB AGREEMENT

A **compound subject** consists of two or more subjects that share the same verb.

EXAMPLE

Frank and Wyatt ride horses in the corral. (The compound
subject—*Frank and Wyatt*—shares the verb *ride*.)

A compound subject must have either a singular or a plural verb, depending on how the
parts of the subject are connected.

Use a singular verb:
- when the compound subject is made up of singular nouns or pronouns connected by
  either/or or *neither/nor*.

EXAMPLES

singular verb

Either Tom or Jesse **looks** like a good choice to start the game.

Neither sword nor axe **prevents** me from finishing this quest.

Use a plural verb:
- when the compound subject is connected by the coordinating conjunction *and*.
- when the compound subject is formed from plural nouns or pronouns.

EXAMPLES

plural

Cars and trucks **park** in the field.

Either cats or dogs **provide** good companionship.

When a compound subject consists of a singular subject and a plural subject connected by *or*
or *nor*, use a verb that agrees in number with the subject that is closer to it in the sentence.

EXAMPLES

Either Kevin or his sisters **watch** the children in the park. (*sisters watch*—plural)

Neither the players nor their coach **endorses** the statement of the owner. (*coach
endorses*—singular)

INDEFINITE PRONOUN AND VERB AGREEMENT

An **indefinite pronoun** does not refer to a specific person, place, or thing. Some indefinite pronouns are always singular and take singular verbs: *anybody, anyone, anything,
each, either, everybody, everyone, everything, much, neither, nobody, no one, nothing, one,
somebody, someone, something.*

EXAMPLES

singular

Nobody knows the size of the universe.

Something occurs at noon every day.

Some indefinite pronouns are always plural and take plural verbs: *both, few, many, others,
several.*

EXAMPLES

plural

Many of our presidents **were** military officers.

Both understand that this must never happen again.

For additional instruction and practice refer to the Grammar & Style Workshop, Adjective and Adverb Clauses, on page 422.

3.8 Modifiers

ADJECTIVES

Adjectives modify nouns by telling specific details about them.

EXAMPLES

noun	a car
a little more specific	an orange car
more specific yet	the fast orange car
even more specific	a sporty, fast orange car

Some adjectives tell *how many* or *what kind* about the nouns or pronouns they modify.

EXAMPLES

There were **several** cars in the lot.

They chose the car with the **tinted** windows.

Other adjectives tell *which one* or *which ones*.

EXAMPLES

Our car has rust spots.

Those cars in the junkyard were once very expensive.

The **articles** *a, an,* and *the* are the most commonly occurring adjectives. *A* and *an* refer to any person, place, or thing in general. *The* refers to a specific person, place, or thing.

EXAMPLES

A fence can be made of wood or metal. (*A* refers to a fence in general.)

The gate on **the** fence is open. (*The* refers to a specific gate on a specific fence.)

A **proper adjective** is formed from a proper noun. Proper adjectives are capitalized and often end in *–n, –an, –ian, –ese,* or *–ish.*

EXAMPLES

African mahogany trees are valued for their hard, reddish brown wood.

Furniture and ships are often built with durable **Asian** teakwood.

Type of Adjective	Definition	Examples
adjective	modifies nouns and pronouns; answers the questions *what kind? which one? how many?* and *how much?*	**shiny** pennies **hieroglyphic** inscription **dozen** roses **one** mistake
article	*a* and *an* refer to an unspecified person, place, thing, or idea; *the* refers to a specific person, place, thing, or idea	**A** problem has developed. I peeled **an** orange. **The** tomatoes are ripe.
proper adjective	is formed from proper nouns; is capitalized; often ends in *–n, –an, –ian, –ese,* or *–ish*	**Serbian** restaurant **Victorian** England **Chinese** calendar **Jewish** tradition

ADVERBS

Adverbs modify verbs, adjectives, or other adverbs. Many times adverbs will tell us *how, when, where, why* or *to what extent.*

EXAMPLES

adverbs modify verbs
The children sing **cheerfully.** (*Cheerfully* tells how they sing.)

Eagles **usually** fly **high** in the summer sky. (*Usually* tells when they fly in the sky; high tells where they fly.)

adverbs modify adjectives
These noble birds are **especially** graceful. (*Especially* tells to what extent they are graceful.)

Some rare birds are **nearly** extinct. (*Nearly* tells to what extent the birds are extinct.)

adverbs modify adverbs
The eagles swoop down on their prey **very** quickly. (*Very* tells to what extent they swoop down on their prey quickly.)

The birds grip **so** strongly, few animals can escape their clutches. (*So* tells how strongly they grip.)

POSITION OF ADVERBS

An adverb can be placed before or after a verb it modifies. Sometimes an adverb can be separated from a verb by another word or words.

EXAMPLES

The coin collector **carefully examined** the rare silver coin.

Eager to find out when it was minted, he **looked carefully** through the magnifying glass.

He **polished** the coin **carefully** to reveal the embossed date.

Note, however, in the following examples, how changing the position of an adverb changes the meaning of the sentence.

EXAMPLES

He **only** worried about money. (He did nothing else but worry about money.)

He worried **only** about money. (He worried about nothing else but money.)

3.9 Prepositions and Conjunctions

PREPOSITIONS AND CONJUNCTIONS

Prepositions and conjunctions are the linkers of the English language. They are used to join words and phrases to the rest of a sentence. They also show the relationships between ideas. Prepositions and conjunctions help writers vary their sentences by connecting sentence parts in different ways.

A **preposition** is used to show how its object, a noun or a pronoun, is related to other words in the sentence. Some commonly used prepositions include *above, after, against, among, around, at, behind, beneath, beside, between, down, for, from, in, on, off, toward, through, to, until, upon,* and *with.*

EXAMPLES

> A whale swam **under** our boat.

> We had to crawl **through** the tunnel **between** the two buildings.

A **conjunction** is a word used to link related words, groups of words, or sentences. Like a preposition, a conjunction shows the relationship between the words it links. Some of the most commonly used conjunctions are *and, but, for, nor, or, yet, so, if, after, because, before, although, unless, while,* and *when.* Some conjunctions are used in pairs, such as *both/and, neither/nor,* and *not only/but also.*

EXAMPLES

> I found leaves **and** twigs in the yard.

> He stopped running **after** he twisted his ankle.

> **Neither** the plaintiffs **nor** the defendants understand the ruling.

3.10 Interjections

An **interjection** is a part of speech that expresses feeling, such as surprise, joy, relief, urgency, pain, or anger. Common interjections include *ah, aha, alas, bravo, dear me, goodness, great, ha, help, hey, hooray, hush, indeed, mercy, of course, oh, oops, ouch, phooey, really, say, see, ugh,* and *whew.*

EXAMPLES

> **Hey,** that's not fair!

> **Goodness,** you don't need to get so upset.

> **Hush!** You'll wake the baby.

> **Why, of course!** Please do join us for dinner.

3.11 Phrases

A **phrase** is a group of words used as a single part of speech. A phrase lacks a subject, a verb, or both; therefore, it cannot be a sentence. There are three common kinds of phrases: prepositional phrases, verbal phrases, and appositive phrases.

PREPOSITIONAL PHRASES

A **prepositional phrase** consists of a preposition, its object, and any modifiers of that object. A prepositional phrase adds information to a sentence by relating its object to another word in the sentence. It may function as an adjective or an adverb.

EXAMPLES

> **adjectives**
> Ted bought a car **with a sunroof.** (The prepositional phrase *with a sunroof* tells what kind of car Ted bought. The phrase is an adjective, modifying the noun *car.*)

> **adverbs**
> The fog drifted **over the hill.** (The prepositional phrase *over the hill* tells where the fog drifted. The phrase is an adverb, modifying the verb *drifted.*)

For additional instruction and practice refer to the Grammar & Style Workshop, Prepositional and Participial Phrases, on page 334.

VERBAL PHRASES

Verbals are verb forms that act as namers or modifiers.

A **participle** is a verb form ending in –*ing*, –*d*, or –*ed* that acts as an adjective, modifying a noun or a pronoun. A **participial phrase** is made up of a participle and all of the words related to the participle, which may include objects, modifiers, and prepositional phrases. The entire phrase acts as an adjective.

EXAMPLES

Climbing carefully up the tree, Elijah was able to reach the cat. (The participle *climbing*, the adverb *carefully*, and the prepositional phrase *up the tree* make up the participial phrase that modifies *Elijah*.)

Jim came up with the idea for the mural **painted on the building.** (The participle *painted* and the prepositional phrase *on the building* make up the participial phrase that modifies *mural*.)

A **gerund phrase** is a phrase made up of a gerund (a verb form ending in –*ing*) and all of its modifiers and complements. The entire phrase functions as a noun.

EXAMPLES

Waiting for the bus is boring for Tracy. (The gerund phrase functions as the subject of the sentence.)

Tracy hates **waiting for the bus** at the corner. (The gerund phrase functions as the direct object of the sentence.)

Sometimes the *to* of an infinitive phrase is left out; it is understood.

EXAMPLES

Jerry helped **[to]** paint the house.

I'll go **[to]** feed the cat.

APPOSITIVE PHRASES

An **appositive phrase** is a group of words made up of an appositive and all its modifiers. The phrase renames or identifies a noun or a pronoun.

EXAMPLES

Dr. George, **the former football coach,** is our new professor. (The appositive phrase renames the noun *Dr. George*.)

The television show **_Let's Make a Deal_** used to be very popular. (The appositive phrase identifies which show used to be very popular.)

The first example above, *the former football coach,* is a **nonessential,** or **nonrestrictive, appositive phrase.** It is not necessary to the meaning of the sentence; it is not needed to identify Dr. George, since we already know that he is our new professor. Therefore, it is set off with commas.

The second example, *Let's Make a Deal,* is an **essential,** or **restrictive, appositive phrase.** It is necessary for understanding the sentence because it identifies which particular television show, since we do not already know which one. This appositive phrase is not set off with commas.

For additional instruction and practice refer to the Grammar & Style Workshop, Verbals, on page 684.

> For additional instruction and practice refer to the Grammar & Style Workshop, Independent and Dependent Clauses, on page 243.

3.12 Clauses

A **clause** is a group of words that contains a subject and a verb and that functions as one part of speech. There are two types of clauses—independent and subordinate.

An **independent clause,** sometimes called a *main clause,* has a subject and a verb and expresses a complete thought. Since it can stand alone as a sentence, it is called *independent.*

EXAMPLE

Abraham Lincoln is often called the "Great Emancipator."

A **subordinate clause** or *dependent clause* has a subject and a verb, but it doesn't express a complete thought. It can't stand alone. It must be attached to or inserted into an independent clause. When you combine subordinate clauses with independent clauses, you form complete sentences.

EXAMPLES

When the bell rang, the students ran out of the room. (The subordinate clause *when the bell rang* is attached to an independent clause.)

The dog **that barked all night** slept throughout the day. (The subordinate clause *that barked all night* is inserted into the independent clause *The dog slept throughout the day.*)

3.13 Common Usage Problems

INCORRECT SUBJECT-VERB AGREEMENT

A subject and its verb must agree in number. Use singular verb forms with singular subjects and plural verb forms with plural subjects.

Intervening Words

A prepositional phrase that comes between a subject and a verb does not determine whether the subject is singular or plural.

EXAMPLES

The **captain** on the bridge **gazes** across the sea. (*captain gazes,* singular)

The **detective,** in addition to the police, **looks** for clues at the house. (*detective looks,* singular)

The **players** on the team **practice** diligently. (*players practice,* plural)

The **books** in the back of the store **are** only half price. (*books are,* plural)

In some cases, the *object* of the preposition controls the verb.

EXAMPLES

Jim and his brother **plan** strategy before each game.

Cars, trucks, and motorcycles **roar** past our house.

Compound Subjects

Use a plural verb with most compound subjects connected by *and.*

EXAMPLES

<u>Charlotte and her boss</u> **review** the budget once a month.

<u>Otters, beavers, and alligators</u> **live** near bodies of water.

INCORRECT USE OF APOSTROPHES

Use an apostrophe to replace letters that have been left out in a contraction.

EXAMPLES

it's = it is   don't = do not   I'll = I will

Use an apostrophe to show possession.

Singular Nouns

Use an apostrophe and an *s* ('*s*) to form the possessive of a singular noun, even if it ends in *s*, *x*, or *z*.

EXAMPLES

Rachel's notebook   Frank's lizard   Conan's ring
lynx's paw   jazz's history   boss's desk

Plural Nouns

Use an apostrophe and an *s* ('*s*) to form the possessive of a plural noun that does not end in *s*.

EXAMPLES

women's shirts   children's books   people's candidate

Use an apostrophe alone to form the possessive of a plural noun that ends in *s*.

EXAMPLES

rodents' food   the boys' locker room   the ships' sails

Do not add an apostrophe or '*s* to possessive personal pronouns: *mine, yours, his, hers, its, ours,* or *theirs.* They already show ownership.

EXAMPLES

Our cars are painted; **theirs** are still rusty.

The shark opened **its** mouth.

DOUBLE NEGATIVES

Make sure that you use only one of the following negatives in each sentence: *not, nobody, none, nothing, hardly, can't, doesn't, won't, isn't, aren't.* A **double negative** is the use of two negative words together when only one is needed. Correct double negatives by removing one of the negative words or by replacing one of the negative words with a positive word.

EXAMPLES

double negative
We won't hardly make it in time.

corrected sentence
We will hardly make it in time. We won't make it in time.

double negative

Nell wasn't never able to win the big prize.

corrected sentence

Nell was never able to win the big prize. Nell wasn't ever able to win the big prize.

DANGLING AND MISPLACED MODIFIERS

A **dangling modifier** has nothing to modify because the word it would logically modify is not present in the sentence. In the following sentence, the modifying phrase has no logical object. The sentence says that a whale was flying.

EXAMPLE

Flying above the ocean, a whale was spotted.

You can eliminate dangling modifiers by rewriting the sentence so that an appropriate word is provided for the modifier to modify. You can also expand a dangling phrase into a full subordinate clause.

EXAMPLES

Flying above the ocean, we saw a whale.

As we flew above the ocean, we spotted a whale.

A **misplaced modifier** is located too far from the word it should modify.

EXAMPLE

I found a penny during my morning jog on a park bench.

You can revise a misplaced modifier by moving it closer to the word it modifies.

EXAMPLES

I found a penny on a park bench during my morning jog.

On a park bench I found a penny during my morning jog.

During my morning jog, I found a penny on a park bench.

FORMS OF *WHO* AND *WHOM*

Who and *whom* can be used to ask questions and to introduce subordinate clauses. Knowing what form of *who* to use can sometimes be confusing. The case of the pronoun *who* is determined by the pronoun's function in a sentence.

nominative case   who, whoever

objective case   whom, whomever

EXAMPLES

Who wrote the novel *One Hundred Years of Solitude?* (Because *who* is the subject in the sentence, the pronoun is in the nominative case.)

Did you say **who** called? (Because *who* is the subject of the subordinate clause, the pronoun is in the nominative case.)

Whoever returns my wallet will receive a reward. (Because *whoever* is the subject in the sentence, the pronoun is in the nominative case.)

Whom did you visit? (Because *whom* is the direct object in the sentence, the pronoun is in the objective case.)

> For additional instruction and practice refer to the Grammar & Style Workshop, Dangling Modifiers, on page 785.

> For additional instruction and practice refer to the Grammar & Style Workshop, Misplaced Modifiers, on page 772.

The following chart contains an alphabetic list of words and phrases that often cause usage problems.

Word/Phrases	Correct Use	Examples
a, an	Use *a* before words beginning with a consonant sound. Use *an* before words beginning with a vowel sound, including a silent *h*.	While walking in the woods, Jonah saw **a** coyote. **An** orangutan has a shaggy, reddish brown coat and very long arms. It is hard to find **an** honest politician in this town.
accept, except	*Accept* is a verb meaning "to receive willingly" or "to agree." *Except* is a preposition that means "leaving out" or "but."	I wish you would **accept** this token of my appreciation. Everyone has apologized for the misunder- standing **except** the mayor.
affect, effect	*Affect* is a verb that means "to influence." The noun *effect* means "the result of an action." The verb *effect* means "to cause" or "to bring about."	You can't let the audience **affect** your concentration. We saw the **effect** of last night's storm throughout the town. Peter will **effect** the proposed reorganization when he takes office.
ain't	This word is nonstandard English. Avoid using it in speaking and writing.	**nonstandard:** I ain't going to study English this semester. **standard:** I **am not** going to study English this semester.
all ready, already	*All ready* means "entirely ready or prepared." *Already* means "previously."	Speaking with each team member, I deter- mined that they were **all ready** to play. Sandy **already** finished her homework before soccer practice.
all right	*All right* means "satisfactory," "unhurt," "correct," or "yes, very well." The word *alright* is not acceptable in formal written English.	**All right,** let's begin the meeting. Is your ill father going to be **all right?**
a lot	*A lot* means "a great number or amount" and is always two words. Because it is imprecise, you should avoid it except in informal usage. *Alot* is not a word.	We found **a lot** of seashells on the beach. Your brother had **a lot** of help planning the surprise party.
altogether, all together	*Altogether* is an adverb meaning "thoroughly." Something done *all together* is done as a group or mass.	He was **altogether** embarrassed after trip- ping on the sidewalk. The family members were **all together** when they heard the good news.
anywheres, everywheres, somewheres, nowheres	Use these words and others like them without the *s*: *anywhere, everywhere, somewhere, nowhere*.	The little gray dog was **nowhere** to be found. Yolanda never goes **anywhere** without her cell phone.
at	Don't use this word after *where*.	Where are your brothers hiding?
bad, badly	*Bad* is always an adjective, and *badly* is always an adverb. Use *bad* after linking verbs.	I developed a **bad** cold after shoveling the heavy, wet snow. Tom feels **bad** about losing your favorite CD. We **badly** need to find another relief pitcher.

Word/Phrases	Correct Use	Examples
beside, besides	*Beside* means "next to." *Besides* means "in addition to." *Besides* can also be an adverb meaning "moreover."	The yellow plant is sitting **beside** the purple vase. I bought socks and shoes **besides** a new shirt and jacket. There is nothing worth watching on TV tonight; **besides,** I have to study for a test.
between, among	Use *between* when referring to two people or things. Use *among* when you are discussing three or more people or things.	While on vacation, I divided my time **between** Paris and Brussels. The thoughtful pirate divided the loot **among** his shipmates.
bring, take	Use *bring* when you mean "to carry to." It refers to movement toward the speaker. Use *take* when you mean "to carry away." It refers to movement away from the speaker.	You need to **bring** your backpack home. Don't forget to **take** the garbage out to the curb tonight.
bust, busted	Do not use these nonstandard words as verbs to substitute for *break* or *burst*.	**nonstandard:** I busted my leg sliding into third base. The barrel busted after the extra batch was added. **standard:** I **broke** my leg sliding into third base. The barrel **burst** after the extra batch was added.
can, may	The word *can* means "able to do something." The word *may* is used to ask or give permission.	**Can** you speak a foreign language? You **may** borrow my red sweater.
choose, chose	*Choose* is the present tense, and *chose* is the past tense.	I **choose** to start work at 6:00 AM each day. Randy **chose** to quit his job after working only three days.
could of	Use the helping verb *have* (which may sound like *could of*) with *could, might, must, should, ought,* and *would.*	**nonstandard:** We could of won the game in overtime. **standard:** We **could have** won the game in overtime.
doesn't, don't	*Doesn't* is the contraction of *does not*. It is used with singular nouns and the pronouns *he, she, it, this,* and *that. Don't* is the contraction of *do not.* Use it with plural nouns and the pronouns *I, we, they, you, these,* and *those.*	Jason **doesn't** know what to make for lunch. We **don't** answer the phone during dinner.
farther, further	Use *farther* to refer to physical distance. Use *further* to refer to greater extent in time or degree or to mean "additional."	I walked **farther** today than I did yesterday. The board members will discuss this issue **further** at the meeting. The essay requires **further** revision before it can be published.
fewer, less	Use *fewer*, which tells "how many," to refer to things that you can count individually. *Fewer* is used with plural words. Use *less* to refer to quantities that you cannot count. It is used with singular words and tells "how much."	I see **fewer** fans coming out to the ballpark each year. Jasmine has more experience and thus needs **less** training than Phil.
good, well	*Good* is always an adjective. *Well* is an adverb meaning "ably" or "capably." *Well* is also a predicate adjective meaning "satisfactory" or "in good health." Don't confuse *feel good*, which means "to feel happy or pleased," with *feel well*, which means "to feel healthy."	Charles was a **good** pilot during the war. Leslie felt **good** [pleased] after bowling three strikes in a row. Shirley paints **well** for someone with no formal training. Not feeling **well,** Samuel stayed home from school today.

Word/Phrases	Correct Use	Examples
had ought, hadn't ought	The verb *ought* should never be used with the helping verb *had*.	**nonstandard:** Ted had ought to find another route into town. **standard:** Ted **ought** to find another route into town. **nonstandard:** She hadn't ought climb that tree. **standard:** She **ought** not climb that tree.
hardly, scarcely	Since both of these words have negative meanings, do not use them with other negative words such as *not, no, nothing*, and *none*.	**nonstandard:** That music is so loud I can't hardly hear myself think. **standard:** That music is so loud I can **hardly** hear myself think. **nonstandard:** Shane hadn't scarcely enough gas to make it back home. **standard:** Shane had **scarcely** enough gas to make it back home.
he, she, they	Do not use these pronouns after a noun. This error is called a double subject.	**nonstandard:** Jed's brother he is a famous actor. **standard:** Jed's brother is a famous actor.
hisself, their-selves	These are incorrect forms. Use *himself* and *themselves*.	**nonstandard:** Paul talks to hisself when mowing the lawn. **standard:** Paul talks to **himself** when mowing the lawn. **nonstandard:** The panel talked among theirselves about the Holy Roman Empire. **standard:** The panel talked among **themselves** about the Holy Roman Empire.
how come	Do not use in place of *why*.	**nonstandard: How come** you didn't call me last night? **standard: Why** didn't you call me last night?
in, into	Use *in* to mean "within" or "inside." Use *into* to suggest movement toward the inside from the outside.	The children were **in** the kitchen. The children raced **into** the kitchen.
its, it's	*Its* is a possessive pronoun. *It's* is the contraction for *it is*.	The radio station held **its** annual fundraiser. **It's** too late tonight to start another game.
kind, sort, type	Use *this* or *that* to modify the singular nouns *kind, sort*, and *type*. Use *these* and *those* to modify the plural nouns *kinds, sorts*, and *types*. *Kind* should be singular when the object of the preposition following it is singular. It should be plural when the object of the preposition is plural.	This **kind** of ice cream is my favorite. These **types** of problems are difficult to solve.
kind of, sort of	Do not use these terms to mean "somewhat" or "rather."	**nonstandard:** He feels kind of sluggish today. **standard:** He feels rather sluggish today.
lay, lie	*Lay* means "to put" or "to place." *Lay* usually takes a direct object. *Lie* means "to rest" or "to be in a lying position." *Lie* never takes a direct object. (Note that the past tense of *lie* is *lay*.)	Please **lay** the blanket on the bed. I **laid** the blanket on the bed. **Lie** down on the bed and take a nap. Mary **lay** down on the bed and took a nap.
learn, teach	*Learn* means "to gain knowledge." *Teach* means "to give knowledge." Do not use them interchangeably.	Betty took lessons to **learn** how to fly a small airplane. I would like to find someone to **teach** me how to sew.

Word/Phrases	Correct Use	Examples
like, as	*Like* is usually a preposition followed by an object. It generally means "similar to." *As, as if,* and *as though* are conjunctions used to introduce subordinate clauses. *As* is occasionally a preposition: *He worked as a farmer.*	The alligator was motionless **like** a rock on the riverbank. The spider spun its web **as** the unsuspecting fly flew into the silky trap. Roger looks **as though** he's not feeling well.
of	This word is unnecessary after the prepositions *inside, outside,* and *off.*	The feather pillow slid **off** the bed. People gathered **outside** the stadium before the game. Please put the chattering parrot **inside** its cage.
precede, proceed	*Precede* means "to go or come before." *Proceed* means "to go forward."	The calf-roping competition will **precede** the bull-riding event. If you hear the alarm, **proceed** down the stairs and out the exit.
quiet, quite	Although these words sound alike, they have different meanings. *Quiet* is an adjective that means "making little or no noise"; *quite* is an adverb meaning "positively" or "completely."	The house became **quiet** after the baby finally fell asleep. Unfortunately, our bill for the car repairs was **quite** large.
real, really	*Real* is an adjective meaning "actual." *Really* is an adverb meaning "actually" or "genuinely." Do not use *real* to mean "very" or "extremely."	The table is very sturdy because it is made of **real** oak. Heather was **really** (not *real*) excited about trying out for the play.
reason...because	*Reason is because* is both wordy and redundant. Use *reason is that* or simply *because.*	**nonstandard:** The reason I am in a good mood is because today is Friday. **standard:** The reason for my good mood is that it is Friday. **standard:** The reason for my good mood is that today is Friday. **standard:** I am in a good mood because today is Friday.
regardless, irre-gardless	Use *regardless, unmindful, heedless,* or *anyway. Irregardless* is a double negative and should never be used.	**nonstandard:** Irregardless of the rain, the concert will still be held as scheduled. **standard: Regardless** of the rain, the concert will still be held as scheduled.
rise, raise	*Rise* is an intransitive verb that means "to move upward." It is an irregular verb that does not take a direct object. *Raise* is a transitive verb that means "to lift or make something go upward." It is a regular verb that takes a direct object.	The sun **rises** and sets every day. Perry **raised** his hand to ask a question.
scratch, itch	*Scratch* means "to scrape lightly to relieve itching." *Itch* means "to feel a tingling of the skin, with the desire to scratch."	Please do not **scratch** the mosquito bites. The mosquito bites on my leg still **itch.**
set, sit	*Set* is a transitive verb meaning "to place something." It always takes a direct object. *Sit* is an intransitive verb meaning "to rest in an upright position." It does not take a direct object.	Please **set** the pitcher of milk on the table. Let's **sit** outside on the back deck.
some, somewhat	*Some* is an adjective meaning "a certain unspecified quantity." *Somewhat* is an adverb meaning "slightly." Do not use *some* as an adverb.	**nonstandard:** The pressure on her schedule has eased some. **standard:** The pressure on her schedule has eased **somewhat.** **standard:** I need to find **some** index cards before starting my report.

Word/Phrases	Correct Use	Examples
than, then	*Than* is a conjunction used in comparisons. *Then* is an adverb that shows a sequence of events.	Hank's lawn is greener **than** Dale's lawn is. We went to the post office and **then** drove to the mall.
that	*That* is used to refer either to people or things. Use it to introduce essential, or restrictive, clauses that refer to things or groups of people. Do not use a comma before *that* when it introduces an essential clause.	The tree **that** fell in the storm was more than one hundred years old. An automobile **that** never needs repairs is rare.
their, there, they're	*Their* is the possessive form of *they*. *There* points out a place or introduces an independent clause. *They're* is the contracted form of *they are*.	Our neighbors inspected **their** roof after the hailstorm. When you arrive at the airport, I will be **there** waiting. I don't think **they're** going to be visiting us this summer.
them	*Them* is a pronoun. It should never be used as an adjective. Use *those*.	**nonstandard:** Remember to return them books to the library. **standard:** Remember to return **those** books to the library.
this here, that there	Do not use. Simply say *this* or *that*.	**nonstandard:** This here is the best coffee shop in town. **standard: This** is the best coffee shop in town. **nonstandard:** That there is an antique rocking chair. **standard: That** is an antique rocking chair.
to, too, two	*To* is a preposition that can mean "in the direction of." *Too* is an adverb that means both "extremely, overly" and "also." *Two* is the spelling for the number 2.	Please carry the luggage **to** the car. Leah has **too** many boxes in the attic. Tony and Liz are excellent students, **too.** I bought **two** pairs of blue jeans.
try and	Use *try to* instead.	**nonstandard:** Try and find the umbrella before you leave. **standard: Try to** find the umbrella before you leave.
use to, used to	Be sure to add the *–d* to *use* to form the past participle.	**nonstandard:** Rory use to enjoy singing in the choir. **standard:** Rory **used to** enjoy singing in the choir.
way, ways	Do not use *ways* for *way* when referring to distance.	**nonstandard:** We traveled a long ways from home. **standard:** We traveled a long **way** from home.
when, where	When you define a word, don't use *when* or *where*.	**nonstandard:** A *perfect game* is when a bowler throws twelve strikes resulting in a score of 300. **standard:** A *perfect game* is twelve strikes resulting in a score of 300.
where, that	Do not use *where* to mean "that."	**nonstandard:** I read where school will start a week earlier in August. **standard:** I read **that** school will start a week earlier in August.

Word/Phrases	Correct Use	Examples
which, that, who, whom	*Which* is used to refer only to things. Use it to introduce nonessential, or nonrestrictive, clauses that refer to things or to groups of people. Always use a comma before *which* when it introduces a nonessential clause.	Our garage, **which** was built last year, is already showing signs of wear. The panel, **which** was assembled to discuss the election, will publish its conclusions.
who, whom	*Who* or *whom* is used to refer only to people. Use *who* or *whom* to introduce essential and nonessential clauses. Use a comma only when the pronoun introduces a nonessential clause.	Lyle is the man **who** rescued us from the fire. Abraham Lincoln, **whom** many admired, issued the Emancipation Proclamation.
who's, whose	*Who's* is a contraction for *who is* or *who has*. *Whose* is the possessive form of *who*.	**Who's** going to make dinner tonight? **Whose** pig is running loose in my garden?
without, unless	Do not use the preposition *without* in place of the conjunction *unless*.	**nonstandard:** I am not leaving without I have your endorsement. **standard:** I am not leaving **without** your endorsement. **standard:** I am not leaving **unless** I have your endorsement.
your, you're	*Your* is a possessive pronoun. *You're* is a contraction for the words *you are*.	Ron repaired **your** leaky kitchen faucet. **You're** very skilled at repairing things!

3.15 Punctuation

EDITING FOR PUNCTUATION ERRORS

When editing your work, correct all punctuation errors. Several common punctuation errors to avoid are the incorrect use of end marks, commas, semicolons, and colons.

Punctuation Reference Chart

Punctuation	Function	Examples
End Marks	tell the reader where a sentence ends and show the purpose of the sentence; periods are also used for abbreviations.	Our next-door neighbor is Mrs. Ryan.
Periods	with **declarative** sentences	The weather forecast predicts rain tonight.
	with **abbreviations**	
	personal names	**N.** Scott Momaday, **W. W.** Jacobs, Ursula **K.** Le Guin
	titles	**Mr.** Bruce Webber, **Mrs.** Harriet Cline, **Ms.** Steinem, **Dr.** Duvall, **Sen.** Hillary Clinton, **Gov.** George Pataki, **Capt.** Horatio Hornblower, **Prof.** Klaus
	business names	Tip Top Roofing **Co.**, Green **Bros.** Landscaping, Gigantic **Corp.**
	addresses	Oak **Dr.**, Grand **Blvd.**, Main **St.**, Kennedy **Pkwy.**, Prudential **Bldg.**
	geographical terms	Kensington, **Conn.**, San Francisco, **Calif.**, Canberra, **Aus.**
	time	2 **hrs.** 15 **min.**, **Thurs.** morning, **Jan.** 20, 21st **cent.**

Punctuation	Function	Examples
	units of measurement	3 **tbsp.** olive oil 1/2 **c.** peanut butter 8 **oz.** milk 5 **ft.** 4 **in.** 20 **lbs.**
	exceptions: metric measurements, state names in postal addresses, or directional elements	**metric measurements** cc, ml, km, g, L **state postal codes** MN, WI, IA, NE, CA, NY **compass points** N, NW, S, SE
Question Marks	with **interrogative** sentences	May I have another serving of spaghetti**?**
Exclamation Points	with **exclamatory** sentences	Hey, be careful**!**
Commas	to separate words or groups of words within a sentence; to tell the reader to pause at certain spots in the sentence	Casey was confident he could hit a home run**,** but he struck out.
	to separate items in a series	The magician's costume included a **silk scarf, black satin hat,** and **magic wand.**
	to combine sentences using *and, but, or, nor, yet, so,* or *for*	An infestation of beetles threatened the summer squash and zucchini crops**, yet** the sturdy plants thrived. I'll apply an organic insecticide, **or** I'll ignore the garden pest problem.
	after an introductory word, phrase, or clause	**Surprisingly,** fashions from the 1970s are making a come-back. **Frayed and tight-fitting,** denim bellbottoms remain a fashion hit.
	to set off words or phrases that interrupt sentences	Harpers Ferry**, a town in northeastern West Virginia,** was the site of John Brown's raid in 1859. The violent raid**, however,** frightened people in the North and South. **An abolitionist leader,** Brown was captured during the raid and later executed.
	between two or more adjectives that modify the same noun and that could be joined by *and*	A **warm,** [and] **spicy** aroma enticed us to enter the kitchen. Steaming bowls of chili satisfied the **tired,** [and] **hungry** travelers.
	to set off names used in direct address	**Olivia,** the zinnias and daisies need to be watered. Please remember to turn off the back porch light**, John.**
	to separate parts of a date	The United States Stock Exchange collapsed on October **28, 1929.** The stock market crash in October 1929 precipitated a severe economic crisis.
	to separate items in addresses	Gabriel García Márquez was born in **Aracataca, Colombia.** My brother will be moving to **1960 Jasmine Avenue, Liberty, Missouri 64068.**
Semicolons	to join two closely related sentences	It was a beautiful summer morning**;** we took advantage of it by going on a picnic.
	to join the independent clauses of a compound sentence if no coordinating conjunction is used	Marjory Stoneman Douglas was a pioneer conservationist. She formed a vigorous grassroots campaign to protect and restore the Everglades. Marjory Stoneman Douglas was a pioneer conservationist**;** she formed a vigorous grassroots campaign to protect and restore the Everglades.

> For additional instruction and practice refer to the Grammar & Style Workshop, Comma Use, on page 167.

> For additional instruction and practice refer to the Grammar & Style Workshop, Punctuation: Dashes, Semicolons, and Colons, on page 324.

Punctuation	Function	Examples
	between independent clauses joined by a conjunction if either clause contains commas	Douglas was a writer, editor, publisher, and tireless advocate for the protection of the Everglades**;** and President Clinton awarded her the Medal of Freedom in 1993 for her work.
	between items in a series if the items contain commas	Members of Friends of the Everglades **wrote petitions; contacted local groups, political organizations, and governmental agencies; and gathered public support** for the restoration of the Everglades.
	between independent clauses joined by a conjunctive adverb or a transitional phrase	**conjunctive adverb** Starting in 1948, the Central and Southern Florida Project ditched and drained the Everglades**; consequently,** the four million acre wetland was reduced by half. **transitional phrase** Douglas knew that restoration of the Everglades would be a daunting task**; in other words,** she knew that it would take the combined efforts of local, state, and federal groups working in unison.
Colons	to mean "note what follows"	Make sure you have all your paperwork in order**:** passport, visa, and tickets.
	to introduce a list of items	*The Tragedy of Romeo and Juliet* explores **these dominant themes:** civil strife, revenge, love, and fate. The main characters in the play are **as follows:** Romeo, Juliet, Paris, Mercutio, Tybalt, and Friar Lawrence. The role of Juliet has been played by **the following actresses:** Norma Shearer, Susan Shentall, and Olivia Hussey.
	to introduce a long or formal statement or a quotation	Shakespeare's prologue to *Romeo and Juliet* begins with **these memorable lines:** Two households, both alike in dignity, In fair Verona, where we lay our scene, From ancient grudge break to new mutiny, Where civil blood makes civil hands unclean. John Dryden made **the following remark about Shakespeare:** "He was the man who of all modern, and perhaps ancient poets, had the largest and most comprehensive soul." Nearly everyone recognizes **this line by Shakespeare:** "All the world's a stage."
	between two independent clauses when the second clause explains or summarizes the first clause	Shakespeare deserves the greatest of praise**:** his work has influenced and inspired millions of people over the centuries. For Romeo and Juliet, their love is star-crossed**:** If they tell their feuding parents of their love, they will be forbidden from seeing each other. On the other hand, by keeping their love secret, they follow a path that leads, tragically, to their deaths.
	between numbers that tell hours and minutes, after the greeting in a business letter, and between chapter and verse of religious works	Our English class meets Tuesdays and Thursdays from **9:00** AM to **10:00** AM Dear Juliet**:** Please meet me on the balcony at midnight. Ecclesiastes **3:1–8**

Punctuation	Function	Examples
	not after a verb, between a preposition and its object(s), or after *because* or *as*	**after a verb** **incorrect** Three of Shakespeare's most famous plays are: *Romeo and Juliet, Macbeth,* and *Hamlet.* **correct** These are three of Shakespeare's most famous plays: *Romeo and Juliet, Macbeth,* and *Hamlet.* **between a preposition and its object(s)** **incorrect** I have seen performances of Shakespeare's plays in: London, New York, and Chicago. **correct** I have seen performances of Shakespeare's plays in the following cities: London, New York, and Chicago. **after *because* or *as*** **incorrect** Shakespeare was a great playwright because: he had an extraordinary skill in depicting human nature and the universal struggles all people experience. **correct** Shakespeare was a great playwright because he had an extraordinary skill in depicting human nature and the universal struggles all people experience.
Ellipsis Points	to show that material from a quotation or a quoted passage has been left out	"Doing something does not require discipline**...**it creates its own discipline."
	if material is left out at the beginning of a sentence or passage	**...**The very thought of hard work makes me queasy.
	if material is left out in the middle of a sentence	The very thought**...**makes me queasy.
	if material is left out at the end of a sentence	It's hard work, doing something with your life**....**I'd rather die in peace. Here we are, all equal and alike and none of us much to write home about**....**
Apostrophes	to form the possessive case of a singular or plural noun	the **window's** ledge, **Carlos's** father, **jazz's** beginnings, **wolves'** howls, twenty-five **cents'** worth, **countries'** treaties, **students'** textbooks
	to show joint or separate ownership	**Zack and Josh's** experiment, **Lisa and Randall's** cabin, **Sarah's** and **Jason's** schedules, **Steve's and John's** trumpets
	to form the possessive of an indefinite pronoun	**anyone's** guess, **each other's** notes, **everybody's** dream
	to form a contraction to show where letters, words, or numerals have been omitted	**I'm** = I am **you're** = you are **she's** = she is **o'clock** = of the clock **they're** = they are
	to form the possessive of only the last word in a compound noun, such as the name of an organization or a business	brother-in-**law's** sense of humor; Teller, Teller, and **Teller's** law firm; Volunteer Nursing **Association's** office
	to form the possessive of an acronym	**NASA's** flight plan, **NATO's** alliances, **UNICEF's** contributions
	to form the plural of letters, numerals, and words referred to as words	two **A's**, **ABC's**, three **7's**, twelve **yes's**
	to show the missing numbers in a date	drought of **'02**, class of **'06**

Punctuation	Function	Examples
Underlining and Italics	with titles of books, plays, long poems, periodicals, works of art, movies, radio and television series, videos, computer games, comic strips, and long musical works and recordings	**books:** *To Kill a Mockingbird, Silent Spring, Black Elk Speaks* **plays:** *The Tragedy of Romeo and Juliet, The Monsters Are Due on Maple Street* **long poems:** *Metamorphoses, The Odyssey* **periodicals:** *Sports Illustrated, Wall Street Journal, The Old Farmer's Almanac* **works of art:** *The Acrobat, In the Sky, The Teacup* **movies:** *Il Postino, North by Northwest, Cast Away* **radio/television series:** *Fresh Air, West Wing, Friends, Animal Planet* **videos:** *Yoga for Strength, Cooking with Julia, Wizard of Oz* **computer games:** *Empire Earth, Age of Wonders II* **comic strips:** *Zits, Foxtrot, Overboard* **long musical works/recordings:** *Requiem, Death and the Maiden, La Traviata*
	with the names of trains, ships, aircraft, and spacecraft	**trains:** *Sunset Limited* **ships:** *Titanic* **aircraft:** *Air Force One* **spacecraft:** *Apollo 13*
	with words, letters, symbols, and numerals referred to as such	The word ***filigree*** has a Latin root. People in western New York pronounce the letter *a* with a harsh, flat sound. The children learned that the symbol *+* is used in addition. Your phone number ends with four *7*'s.
	to set off foreign words or phrases that are not common in English	Did you know the word ***amor*** means "love"? The first Italian words I learned were ***ciao*** and ***pronto***.
	to place emphasis on a word	Why is the soup ***blue***? You're not going to borrow ***my*** car.
Quotation Marks	at the beginning and end of a direct quotation	"Do you want to ride together to the concert?" asked Margaret. "Don't wait for me," sighed Lillian. "I'm running late as usual."
	to enclose the titles of short works such as short stories, poems, articles, essays, parts of books and periodicals, songs, and episodes of TV series	**short stories:** "Gwilan's Harp," "Everyday Use" **poems:** "Hanging Fire," "Mirror" **articles:** "Where Stars Are Born," "Ghost of Everest" **essays:** "Thinking Like a Mountain," "It's Not Talent; It's Just Work" **parts of books:** "The Obligation to Endure," "Best Sky Sights of the Next Century" **songs:** "At the Fair," "Johnny's Garden" **episodes of TV series:** "The Black Vera Wang," "Isaac and Ishmael"
	to set off slang, technical terms, unusual expressions, invented words, and dictionary definitions	We nicknamed our dog **"Monkey"** because he moves quickly and loves to play tricks. My mother says that **"groovy"** and **"cool"** were the slang words of her generation. Did you know that the word *incident* means **"a definite, distinct occurrence"**?

Punctuation	Function	Examples
Hyphens	to make a compound word or compound expression	**compound nouns:** great-grandfather Schaefer, great-uncle Tom **compound adjectives used before a noun:** best-known novel, down-to-earth actor, real-life adventure **compound numbers:** ninety-nine years, twenty-five cents **spelled-out fractions:** one-half inch, three-fourths cup
	to divide an already hyphenated word at the hyphen	Finally, after much coaxing, our **great-grandfather** told his stories.
	to divide a word only between syllables	**incorrect:** After hiking in the woods, the novice ca-mpers became tired and hungry. **correct:** After hiking in the woods, the novice **camp-ers** became tired and hungry.
	with the prefixes *all-*, *ex-*, *great-*, *half-* and *self-*, and with all prefixes before a proper noun or proper adjective	**all-**purpose, **ex-**husband, **pre-**Industrial age, **great-**grandparent, **half-**baked, **self-**expression
	with the suffixes *-free*, *-elect*, and *-style*	fragrance-**free** detergent, mayor-**elect** Kingston, Southern-**style** hospitality
Dashes	to show a sudden break or change in thought	"I say it did," replied the other. "There was no thought about it; I had just—What's the matter?"
	to mean *namely*, *that is*, or *in other words*	Our puppy knows only two commands—sit and stay. The hotel rates were surprisingly reasonable—less than a hundred dollars—for a double room.
Parentheses and Brackets	around material added to a sentence but not considered of major importance	Toni Cade Bambara (1939–1995) grew up in Harlem and Brooklyn, New York. The Taj Mahal (a majestic site!) is one man's tribute of love to his departed, beloved wife. More grocery stores are stocking natural food ingredients (for example, whole grains, soy products, and dried fruits).
	to punctuate a parenthetical sentence contained within another sentence.	When the quilt is dry (it shouldn't take long), please fold it and put it in the linen closet. The piping-hot funnel cakes (they were covered with powdered sugar!) just melted in our mouths. The vitamin tablets (aren't you supposed to take one every morning?) provide high doses of vitamins A and E.
	to enclose words or phrases that interrupt the sentence and are not considered essential to meaning.	They took pasta salad and fruit (how could we have forgotten dessert?) to the summer concert.
	to enclose information that explains or clarifies a detail in quoted material	A literary critic praised the author's new book, "She [Martha Grimes] never fails to delight her devoted fans with witty dialogue, elegant prose, and a cast of characters we'd like to consider our friends." Another literary critic wrote, "[Martha] Grimes is the queen of the mystery genre."

3.16 Capitalization

EDITING FOR CAPITALIZATION ERRORS

To avoid capitalization errors, check your draft for proper nouns and proper adjectives; geographical names, directions, and historical names; and titles of artworks and literary works.

Capitalization Reference Chart

Category/Rule	Examples
Proper Nouns and Proper Adjectives	
Proper Nouns	
Names of people	Sojourner Truth, Franklin D. Roosevelt, Martin Luther King Jr.
Months, days, and holidays	October, Wednesday, Memorial Day
Names of religions, languages, races, and nationalities	Baptist, Catholicism, Chilean, Buddhism, French, Hispanic, Greek, African American
Names of clubs, organization, businesses, and institutions	Little League, American Heart Association, Pratt-Read Company, Webster Bank
Names of awards, prizes, and medals	Emmy Award, Nobel Peace Prize, Purple Heart, Pulitzer Prize
Proper Adjectives	
Proper adjectives formed from proper nouns	Japanese gardening, English class, Caribbean music, Alaskan oil drilling
Proper nouns used as adjectives	Senate bill, Agatha Christie masterpiece, California coast, Franklin stove
I and First Words	
The pronoun *I*.	Next week **I** will leave on my trip to Yellowstone National Park.
First word of each sentence.	**T**he oldest of the U.S. national parks is noted for its beauty, wildlife, and geysers.
First word of a direct quotation.	"**T**hat mountain stands taller than any other in the state," the guide reported with pride to his group of tourists.
First lines of most poetry. (Follow the capitalization of the original poem.)	**A**nd far as the eye of God could see **D**arkness covered everything, **B**lacker than a hundred midnights **D**own in a cypress swamp.
First word in a letter salutation and the name or title of the person addressed.	**D**ear **D**ad, **M**y dear **A**unt **N**ola, **D**ear **M**adam
First word in letter closings.	**S**incerely yours, **Y**ours truly, **F**ondly, **W**arm wishes
Family Relationships and Titles of Persons	
Capitalize the titles or abbreviations that come before the names of people.	**A**dmiral Michael Chase, **M**s. Gloria Steinem, **S**enator Dodd, **M**r. and **M**rs. Douglas, **D**r. Watson, **C**hief **J**ustice Oliver Wendell Holmes
Person's title as a proper noun.	Can you meet us on Tuesday, **R**abbi? It's time to start rounds, **D**octor.
Words showing family relationships when used as titles or as substitutes for a name.	**U**ncle Fred, **G**randmother Parker, **F**ather, **C**ousin Sam
Abbreviations	
Social titles after a name.	My teacher is named **Mr.** Franks. Can't you ask **Prof.** Pardoe to help us in the soup kitchen?
Abbreviate the titles of organizations.	Northeastern **Mfg.** Connecticut Yard Workers **Assoc.**

Category/Rule	Examples
Parts of government, and business, with the initials of each word in the title.	**NATO** (North Atlantic Treaty Organization) **USMC** (United States Marine Corps) **IBM** (International Business Machines) **SNET** (Southern New England Telephone)
Abbreviate address titles.	Stoughton **St.**, Fort **Rd.**, Park **Ave.**
Time Designations	
Time abbreviations BCE (BC), CE (AD), AM, and PM	Hatshepsut, who lived from 1503 to 1482 **BCE**, was one of five women to reign as Queen of Egypt. The cruel Caligula ruled Rome until **CE** 41. My appointment was for 9:30 **AM**, and I'm not happy about waiting. We have a 7:00 **PM** dinner reservation at my favorite restaurant.
Geographical Names, Directions, and Historical Names	
Names of cities, states, countries, islands, and continents	**cities:** Honolulu, Moscow, Guatemala City **states:** Georgia, Iowa, New Mexico **countries:** Zimbabwe, Belgium, Ecuador **islands:** Tahiti, Cayman Islands, Cyprus **continents:** North America, Europe, Africa
Names of bodies of water and geographical features	Black Sea, Snake River, Sahara Desert, Mount McKinley
Names of buildings, monuments, and bridges	Woolsey Hall, Empire State Building, Vietnam Veterans Memorial, Golden Gate Bridge
Names of streets and highways	Railroad Avenue, New England Turnpike, Palm Drive, Route 153
Sections of the country	the Sunbelt, the Pacific Coast, the Southeast, the Midwest
Names of historical events, special events, documents, and historical periods	**historical events:** Battle of the Bulge, World War I **special events:** Summerfest, Boston Marathon **documents:** Magna Carta, Declaration of Independence **historical periods:** Reconstruction, Industrial Age
Titles of Artworks and Literary Works	
First and last words and all important words in the titles of artworks and literary works, including books, magazines, short stories, poems, songs, movies, plays, paintings, and sculpture	*Transworld Skateboarding* (magazine), *Too Close to the Falls* (book), "The Cask of Amontillado" (short story), Birches at Sunrise (painting), "Polka Dots and Moonbeams" (song), *The Lion in Winter* (movie)
Titles of religious works	Hebrew Bible, Koran, Old Testament

▶ For additional instruction and practice refer to the Grammar & Style Workshop, Sentence Fragments and Run-on Sentences, on page 713.

3.17 **Writing Effective Sentences**

SENTENCE FRAGMENTS

A sentence contains a subject and a verb and should express a complete thought. A **sentence fragment** is a phrase or clause that does not express a complete thought but that has been punctuated as though it did.

EXAMPLES

complete sentence   The gray fox ran across the field.

sentence fragment   Ran across the field. (The subject is missing.)

sentence fragment   The gray fox. (The verb is missing.)

sentence fragment   Across the field. (The subject and verb are missing.)

RUN-ON SENTENCES

Take a look at the following examples of run-on sentences. In the first run-on, no punctuation mark is used between the run-on sentences. In the second run-on, a comma is used incorrectly.

EXAMPLES

The umpire watched the two teams warm up before the game his headache had gone away.

At the start of the American Revolution, about three million people lived in the thirteen colonies, about one third of them supported the British government.

You can correct a run-on by dividing it into two separate sentences. Mark the end of each idea with a period, question mark, or exclamation point. Capitalize the first word of each new sentence.

EXAMPLE

The umpire watched the two teams warm up before the game. His headache had gone away.

You can also correct a run-on by using a semicolon. The second part of the sentence is not capitalized. Use a semicolon to join two sentences only if the thoughts are closely related.

EXAMPLE

At the start of the American Revolution, about three million people lived in the thirteen colonies; about one third of them supported the British government.

SENTENCE COMBINING AND EXPANDING

A series of short sentences in a paragraph can make your writing sound choppy and uninteresting. The reader might also have trouble understanding how your ideas are connected. By **combining and expanding sentences,** you can connect related ideas, make sentences longer and smoother, and make a paragraph more interesting to read.

One way to combine sentences is to take a key word or phrase from one sentence and insert it into another sentence.

short, choppy sentences
The girl rode a bicycle. It was pink.

combined sentence (with key word)
The girl rode a pink bicycle.

short, choppy sentences
We took a trip in the summer. We went to the Texas coast.

combined sentence (with key phrase)
We took a summer trip to the Texas coast.

Another way of combining sentences is to take two related sentences and combine them by using a coordinating conjunction—*and, but, or, so, for, yet,* or *nor.* By using a coordinating conjunction, you can form a compound subject, a compound verb, or a compound sentence. Be sure to use a comma before the coordinating conjunction that links two sentences.

EXAMPLES

two related sentences
Stephen lived close to the ocean. He often sailed on his boat in the summer.

combined sentence
Stephen lived close to the ocean, **and** he often sailed on his boat in the summer. (compound sentence)

two related sentences
Dandelions sprang up in the backyard. There were also broadleaf weeds.

combined sentence
Dandelions **and** broadleaf weeds sprang up in the backyard. (compound subject)

two related sentences
Rain beat down upon the trail. It drenched the weary travelers.

combined sentence
Rain beat down upon the trail **and** drenched the weary travelers. (compound verb)

VARYING SENTENCE STRUCTURE

Just as you probably wouldn't like to eat the same thing for breakfast every morning, your readers don't enjoy reading the same sentence pattern in every paragraph. By **varying sentence beginnings** you can give your sentences rhythm, create variety, and keep your readers engaged. Sentences often begin with a subject. To vary sentence beginnings, start some sentences with a one-word modifier, a prepositional phrase, a participial phrase, or a subordinate clause.

EXAMPLES

subject
She usually finishes her test before the rest of the class.

one-word modifier
Usually, she finishes her test before the rest of the class.

prepositional phrase
Before lunch he plans the following day's activities.

participial phrase
Humming a lively tune, the warden reviewed the parole cases.

subordinate clause
Since it rarely rains where he lives, Jeff leaves the top down on his convertible.

WORDY SENTENCES

A **wordy sentence** includes extra words and phrases that can be difficult, confusing, or repetitive to read. When you write, use only words necessary to make your meaning clear. Revise and edit your sentences so that they are not unnecessarily wordy or complicated.

Replace a group of words with one word.

EXAMPLES
wordy
I quit my job **because of the fact that** the company wanted me to work overtime each week.

revised
I quit my job **because** the company wanted me to work overtime each week.

Replace a clause with a phrase.

EXAMPLES
wordy
When the batter hit the ball over the fence into the stands, the crowd cheered wildly.

revised
When the batter hit the ball over the fence, the crowd cheered wildly.

Delete a group of unnecessary or repetitive words.

EXAMPLES
wordy
What I think is your book will appeal to children in grade school.

revised
I think your book will appeal to grade school children.

wordy
Joe suffers from insomnia, **and he doesn't sleep well at night.**

revised
Joe suffers from insomnia.

USING PARALLELISM

A sentence has **parallelism** when the same forms are used to express ideas of equal—or parallel—importance. Parallelism can add emphasis, balance, and rhythm to a sentence. Words, phrases, and clauses that have the same form and function in a sentence are called **parallel.**

EXAMPLES
not parallel
The singers **took** the stage, **dazzled** the crowd, and then **had returned** to their dressing rooms. (The highlighted verbs are not in the same tense.)

parallel

The singers **took** the stage, **dazzled** the crowd, and **returned** to their dressing rooms.

not parallel

The performers are **talented, lively,** and **dance.** (The three highlighted words include two adjectives and one verb.)

parallel

The performers are **talented, lively,** and **energetic** dancers.

MAKING PASSIVE SENTENCES ACTIVE

A verb is **active** when the subject of the verb performs the action. It is **passive** when the subject of the verb receives the action.

EXAMPLES

active

Lenny bought Rachel a scarf.

passive

A scarf was bought for Rachel by Lenny.

USING COLORFUL LANGUAGE

When you write, use words that tell your readers exactly what you mean. **Colorful language**—such as precise and lively nouns, verbs, and modifiers—tells your readers exactly what you mean and makes your writing more interesting.

Precise nouns give your reader a clear picture of who or what is involved in the sentence.

EXAMPLES

original sentence

The cat walked into the building.

revised sentence

The Siamese cat walked into the grocery **store.**

Colorful, vivid verbs describe the specific action in the sentence.

EXAMPLES

original sentence

Her brother ran across the yard.

revised sentence

Her brother darted across the yard.

Modifiers—adjectives and adverbs—describe the meanings of other words and make them more precise. Colorful or surprising modifiers can make your writing come alive for your readers.

EXAMPLES

original sentence

The tired farmer planted the last row of corn.

revised sentence

The exhausted farmer wearily planted the last row of corn.

> Refer to the following pages for the unit Writing Workshops:
Expository Writing, pp. 130–135
Narrative Writing pp. 262–269
Expository Writing, pp. 380–385
Expository Writing, pp. 460–465
Narrative Writing, pp. 602–607
Persuasive Writing, pp. 730–735
Expository Writing, pp. 870–877

WRITING

4 Writing

4.1 The Writing Process

All writers—whether they are beginning writers, famous published writers, or somewhere in between—go through a process that leads to a complete piece of writing. The specifics of each writer's process may be unique, but for every writer, writing is a series of steps or stages.

The Writing Process	
Stage	**Tasks**
1. Prewriting	Plan your writing: choose a topic, audience, purpose, and form; gather ideas; arrange them logically.
2. Drafting	Get your ideas down on paper.
3. Revising	Evaluate, or judge, the writing piece and suggest ways to improve it. Judging your own writing is called self-evaluation. Judging a classmate's writing is called peer evaluation.
	Work to improve the content, organization, and expression of your ideas.
	Proofread your writing for errors in spelling, grammar, capitalization, and punctuation. Correct these errors, make a final copy of your paper, and proofread it again.
Writing Follow-Up: Publish and Present	Share your work with an audience.
Reflect	Think through the writing process to determine what you learned as a writer, what you accomplished, and what you would like to strengthen the next time you write.

While writing moves through these stages, it is also a continuing cycle. You might need to go back to a previous stage before going on to the next step. Returning to a previous stage will strengthen your final work. Note also that you can take time to reflect on your writing between any of the other stages. The more you reflect on your writing, the better your writing will become.

1 PREWRITE

In the prewriting stage of the writing process, you decide on a purpose, audience, topic, and form. You also begin to discover your voice and gather and organize ideas.

Prewriting Plan	
Set Your Purpose	A **purpose,** or aim, is the goal that you want your writing to accomplish.
Identify Your Audience	An **audience** is the person or group of people intended to read what you write.
Find Your Voice	**Voice** is the quality of a work that tells you that one person wrote it.
Select Your Topic	A **topic** is simply something to write about. For example, you might write about a sports hero or about a cultural event in your community.
Select a Writing Form	A **form** is a kind of writing. For example, you might write a paragraph, an essay, a short story, a poem, or a news article.

Program Resources

Additional writing workshops are available in *Exceeding the Standards: Writing.*

Set Your Purpose

When you choose your mode and form of writing, think about what purpose or aim you are trying to accomplish. Your purpose for writing might be to inform, to tell a story, to describe something, or to convince others to see your viewpoint. Your writing might have more than one purpose. For example, a piece of writing might inform your readers about an important event while persuading them to respond in a specific way.

Mode of Writing	Purpose	Form
expository	to inform	news article, research report
narrative	to express thoughts or ideas, or to tell a story	personal account, memoir, short story
descriptive	to portray a person, place, object, or event	travel brochure, personal profile, poem
persuasive	to convince people to accept a position and respond in some way	editorial, petition, political speech

Identify Your Audience

An **audience** is the person or group of people intended to read what you write. For example, you might write for yourself, a friend, a relative, or your classmates. The best writing usually is intended for a specific audience. Choosing a specific audience before writing will help you make important decisions about your work. For an audience of young children, for example, you would use simple words and ideas. For an audience of your peers in an athletic group, you would use jargon and other specialized words that your peers already know. For an adult audience, you would use more formal language.

Use the following questions to help identify your audience.

- Who will be most interested in my topic?
- What are their interests and values?
- How much do they already know about the topic?
- What background information do they need in order to understand my ideas and point of view?
- What words, phrases, or concepts will I need to define for my audience?
- How can I capture my audience's interest from the very start?

Use Appropriate Language

Formal Versus Informal English To write effectively, you must choose your language according to your audience, purpose, and the occasion or situation. **Formal English** contains carefully constructed, complete sentences; avoids contractions; follows standard English usage and grammar; uses a serious tone; and uses sophisticated vocabulary. **Informal English** contains everyday speech and popular expressions, uses contractions, and may include sentence fragments.

Formal English is appropriate for school essays, oral or written reports, interviews, and debates. Informal English is appropriate for communication with friends, personal letters or notes, and journal entries.

EXAMPLES

formal English
I am very pleased that I received a perfect score on the math exam.

informal English
I'm so pumped that I aced that math exam!

Find Your Voice

Voice is the quality of a work that tells you that one person wrote it. Voice makes a person's writing unique. In your writing, you should strive to develop your own voice, not to imitate the voices of others. Be true to your own voice, and your experience will speak directly to the experience of others.

Select Your Topic

A **topic** is simply something to write about. For example, you might write about a sports hero or about a cultural event in your community. Here are some ideas that may help you find interesting writing topics:

Ways to Find a Writing Topic	
Check your journal	Search through your journal for ideas that you jotted down in the past. Many professional writers get their ideas from their journals.
Think about your experiences	Think about people, places, or events that affected you strongly. Recall experiences that taught you important lessons or that you felt strongly about.
Look at reference works	Reference works include printed or computerized dictionaries, atlases, almanacs, and encyclopedias.
Browse in a library	Libraries are treasure houses of information and ideas. Simply looking around in the stacks of a library can suggest good ideas for writing.
Use mass media	Newspapers, magazines, radio, television, and films can suggest good topics for writing. For example, a glance at listings for public television programs might suggest topics related to the arts, to history, or to nature.
Search the Internet	Search key words in a search engine or web browser to expand on your ideas. Make sure to keep your work original and avoid plagiarizing from websites.

Select a Writing Form

Another important decision that a writer needs to make is what form his or her writing will take. A form is a kind of writing. Once you've identified your topic, your purpose for writing, and your audience, a particular form of writing may become immediately obvious as the perfect one to convey your ideas. But, sometimes, an unexpected choice of form may be even more effective in presenting your topic. The following chart lists some of the many different forms of writing.

Forms of Writing

adventure	brochure	directions	fantasy
advertisement	character sketch	editorial	history
advice column	children's story	epitaph	human interest story
agenda	comedy	essay	instructions
apology	consumer report	eulogy	interview questions
autobiography	debate	experiment	itinerary
biography	detective story	fable	journal entry
book review	dialogue	family history	letter

magazine article	obituary	proposal	speech
memorandum	parable	radio or tv spot	sports story
minutes	paraphrase	recommendation	statement of belief
movie review	petition	research report	summary
mystery	play	résumé	tall tale
myth	police/accident	science fiction	tour guide
narrative	report	short story	want ad
newspaper article	poster	song lyrics	

Gather Ideas

After you have identified your purpose, audience, topic, and form, the next step in the prewriting stage is to gather ideas. There are many ways to gather ideas for writing.

- **Brainstorm** When you **brainstorm,** you think of as many ideas as you can, as quickly as you can, without stopping to evaluate or criticize them. Anything goes — no idea should be rejected in the brainstorming stage.
- **Freewrite Freewriting** is simply taking a pencil and paper and writing whatever comes into your mind. Try to write for several minutes without stopping and without worrying about spelling, grammar, usage, or mechanics.
- **Question** Ask the **reporting questions** *who, what, where, when, why,* and *how* about your topic. This questioning strategy is especially useful for gathering information about an event or for planning a story.
- **Create a Graphic Organizer** A good way to gather information is to create a **graphic organizer,** such as a Venn Diagram, Sensory Details Chart, Time Line, Story Map, or Pro-and-Con Chart. For examples, see the Language Arts Handbook, section 1, Reading Strategies and Skills, page 871.

Organize Your Ideas

Writing Paragraphs After you have gathered ideas for a piece of writing, the next step is to organize these ideas in a useful and reader-friendly way. The most basic organization of ideas occurs in forming paragraphs. A good paragraph is a carefully organized unit of writing. It develops a sequence in narrative writing or develops a particular topic in informational or persuasive writing.

Paragraphs with Topic Sentences Many paragraphs include a topic sentence that presents a main idea. The topic sentence can be placed at the beginning, middle, or end of the paragraph. Topic sentences usually appear early on in the paragraph and are commonly followed by one or more supporting sentences. Often these supporting sentences begin with transitions that relate them to the other sentences or to the topic sentence. This type of paragraph may end with a clincher sentence, which sums up what has been said in the paragraph.

EXAMPLE

> <u>Whether it's rock or Bach, music that's played too loud can put more than a temporary damper on your hearing</u>. At most rock concerts and many night clubs, the sound intensity is high enough to cause irreversible damage to the delicate sensor cells lining the inner ear. Car and home stereo equipment and headphones can also harm your hearing when the volume is cranked up too high.
>
> from "Hearing Under Seige"
> by Bob Ludlow

Paragraphs Without Topic Sentences Most paragraphs do not have topic sentences. In a narrative piece of writing, many paragraphs state a series of events, and no sentence in the paragraph sums up the events. In good narrative writing, the sequence of events appears in chronological order. Descriptive writing may contain paragraphs organized spatially—in the order in which the speaker or narrator sees, hears, feels, smells, and tastes things in a given situation.

Write Your Thesis Statement

One way to start organizing your writing, especially if you are writing an informative or persuasive essay, is to identify the main idea of what you want to say. Present this idea in the form of a sentence or two called a thesis statement. A **thesis statement** is simply a sentence that presents the main idea or the position you will take in your essay.

Example thesis for a persuasive essay

The development at Rice Creek Farm should be stopped because it will destroy one of the best natural areas near the city.

Example thesis for an informative essay

Wilma Rudolph was an athlete who succeeded in the elite sport of tennis before the world was willing to recognize her.

Methods of Organization

The ideas in your writing should be ordered and linked in a logical and easily understandable way. You can organize your writing in the following ways:

Methods of Organization	
Chronological Order	Events are given in the order they occur.
Order of Importance	Details are given in order of importance or familiarity.
Comparison-and-Contrast Order	Similarities and differences of two things are listed.
Cause-and-Effect Order	One or more causes are presented followed by one or more effects.

To link your ideas, use connective words and phrases. In informational or persuasive writing, *for example, as a result, finally, therefore,* and *in fact* are common connectives. In narrative and descriptive writing, words like *first, then, suddenly, above, beyond, in the distance,* and *there* are common connectives. In comparison-contrast organization, common phrases include *similarly, on the other hand,* and *in contrast.* In cause-and-effect organization, linkers include *one cause, another effect, as a result, consequently, finally,* and *therefore.*

Create an Outline An **outline** is an excellent framework for highlighting main ideas and supporting details. To create a rough outline, simply list your main ideas in some logical order. Under each main idea, list the supporting details set off by dashes.

EXAMPLE
What Is Drama?
Definition of Drama
—Tells a story
—Uses actors to play characters
—Uses a stage, properties, lights, costumes, makeup, and special effects
Types of Drama
—Tragedy
    —Definition: A play in which the main character meets a negative fate

—Examples: *Antigone, Romeo and Juliet, Death of a Salesman*
— Comedy
—Definition: A play in which the main character meets a positive fate
—Examples: *A Midsummer Night's Dream, Cyrano de Bergerac, The Odd Couple*

2 DRAFT

After you have gathered your information and organized it, the next step in writing is to produce a draft. A **draft** is simply an early attempt at writing a paper. Different writers approach drafting in different ways. Some prefer to work slowly and carefully, perfecting each part as they go. Others prefer to write a discovery draft, getting all their ideas down on paper in rough form and then going back over those ideas to shape and focus them. When writing a discovery draft, you do not focus on spelling, grammar, usage, and mechanics. You can take care of those details during revision.

Draft Your Introduction

The purpose of an introduction is to capture your reader's attention and establish what you want to say. An effective introduction can start with a quotation, a question, an anecdote, an intriguing fact, or a description that hooks the reader to keep reading. An effective introduction can open with a quotation, question, anecdote, fact, or description.

EXAMPLES

"That's one small step for man, one giant leap for mankind." With these words, Neil Armstrong signaled his success as the first man to set foot on the moon...

What would it be like if all the birds in the world suddenly stopped their singing?

When my brother was nineteen, he volunteered in a homeless shelter making sure people had a safe place to spend the night. He told me once that he would never forget the time he met...

Draft Your Body

When writing the body of an essay, refer to your outline. Each heading in your outline will become the main idea of one of your paragraphs. To move smoothly from one idea to another, use transitional words or phrases. As you draft, include evidence from documented sources to support the ideas that you present. This evidence can be paraphrased, summarized, or quoted directly. For information on proper documentation, see the Language Arts Handbook 5.5, Documenting Sources, page 954.

Draft Your Conclusion

In the conclusion, bring together the main ideas you included in the body of your essay and create a sense of closure to the issue you raised in your thesis. There is no single right way to conclude a piece of writing. Possibilities include:
• Making a generalization
• Restating the thesis and major supporting ideas in different words
• Summarizing the points made in the rest of the essay
• Drawing a lesson or moral
• Calling on the reader to adopt a view or take an action
• Expanding on your thesis or main idea by connecting it to the reader's own interests
• Linking your thesis to a larger issue or concern

3 REVISE

Evaluate Your Draft

Self- and Peer Evaluation When you evaluate something, you examine it carefully to find its strengths and weaknesses. Evaluating your own writing is called **self-evaluation.** A **peer evaluation** is an evaluation of a piece of writing done by classmates, or peers. The following tips can help you to become a helpful peer reader, to learn to give and receive criticism, and to improve your writing.

Tips for evaluating writing
- **Check for content** Is the content, including the main idea, clear? Have any important details been left out? Do unimportant or unrelated details confuse the main point? Are the main idea and supporting details clearly connected to one another?
- **Check for organization** Are the ideas in the written work presented in a logical order?
- **Check the style and language** Is the language appropriately formal or informal? Is the tone appropriate for the audience and purpose? Have any key or unfamiliar terms been defined?

Tips for delivering helpful criticism
- **Be focused** Concentrate on content, organization, and style. At this point, do not focus on proofreading matters such as spelling and punctuation; they can be corrected during the proofreading stage.
- **Be positive** Respect the writer's feelings and genuine writing efforts. Tell the writer what you like about his or her work. Answer the writer's questions in a positive manner, tactfully presenting any changes you are suggesting.
- **Be specific** Give the writer concrete ideas for improving his or her work.

Tips for benefiting from helpful criticism
- **Tell your peer evaluator your specific concerns and questions.** If you are unsure whether you've clearly presented an idea, ask the evaluator how he or she might restate the idea.
- **Ask questions to clarify comments that your evaluator makes.** When you ask for clarification, you make sure you understand your evaluator's comments.
- **Accept your evaluator's comments graciously.** Criticism can be helpful, but you don't have to use any or all of the suggestions.

Revise for Content, Organization, and Style

After identifying weaknesses in a draft through self-evaluation and peer evaluation, the next step is to revise the draft. Here are four basic ways to improve meaning and content:
- **Adding or Expanding** Sometimes writing can be improved by adding details, examples, or transitions to connect ideas. Often a single added adjective, for example, can make a piece of writing clearer or more vivid.

EXAMPLE

draft   Wind whistled through the park.

revised   The **bone-chilling** wind whistled through the park.

- **Cutting or Condensing** Often writing can be improved by cutting unnecessary or unrelated material.

EXAMPLE

draft   Will was firmly determined to find the structure of the DNA molecule.

revised   Will was determined to find the structure of the DNA molecule.

EXAMPLE

draft   Several things had been bothering Tanya.

revised   Several personal problems had been bothering Tanya.

- **Moving** Often you can improve the organization of your writing by moving part of it so that related ideas appear near one another.

After you've revised the draft, ask yourself a series of questions. Think of these questions as your "revision checklist."

REVISION CHECKLIST

Content

☐ Does the writing achieve its purpose?
☐ Are the main ideas clearly stated and supported by details?

Organization

☐ Are the ideas arranged in a sensible order?
☐ Are the ideas connected to one another within paragraphs and between paragraphs?

Style

☐ Is the language appropriate to the audience and purpose?
☐ Is the mood appropriate to the purpose of the writing?

Proofread for Errors

When you proofread your writing, you read it through to look for errors and to mark corrections. When you mark corrections, use the standard proofreading symbols as shown in the following chart.

Proofreader's Symbols

Symbol and Example	Meaning of Symbol	Symbol and Example	Meaning of Symbol
The very first time	Delete (cut) this material.	gebril	Change the order of these letters.
dog's life	Insert (add) something that is missing.	end. "Watch out," she yelled.	Begin a new paragraph.
George	Replace this letter or word.	Love conquers all.	Put a period here.
All the horses king's	Move this word to where the arrow points.	Welcome friends.	Put a comma here.
		Get the stopwatch	Put a space here.
french toast	Capitalize this letter.	Dear Madam	Put a colon here.
the vice-President	Lowercase this letter.	She walked he rode.	Put a semicolon here.
housse	Take out this letter and close up space.	name-brand products	Put a hyphen here.
		cats meow	Put an apostrophe here.
book keeper	Close up space.	cat's cradle	Let it stand. (Leave as it is.)

After you have revised your draft, make a clean copy of it and proofread it for errors in spelling, grammar, and punctuation. Use the following proofreading checklist.

Proofreading Checklist

Spelling
- ❏ Are all words, including names, spelled correctly?

Grammar
- ❏ Does each verb agree with its subject?
- ❏ Are verb tenses consistent and correct?
- ❏ Are irregular verbs formed correctly?
- ❏ Are there any sentence fragments or run-ons?
- ❏ Have double negatives been avoided?
- ❏ Have frequently confused words, such as *affect* and *effect,* been used correctly?

Punctuation
- ❏ Does every sentence end with an end mark?
- ❏ Are commas used correctly?
- ❏ Do all proper nouns and proper adjectives begin with capital letters?

WRITING FOLLOW-UP

Publish and Present

Some writing is done just for oneself—journal writing, for example. Most writing, however, is meant to be shared with others. Here are several ways in which you can publish your writing or present it to others:

- Submit your work to a local publication, such as a school literary magazine, school newspaper, or community newspaper.
- Submit your work to a regional or national publication.
- Enter your work in a contest.
- Read your work aloud to classmates, friends, or family members.
- Collaborate with other students to prepare a publication—a brochure, online literary magazine, anthology, or newspaper.
- Prepare a poster or bulletin board, perhaps in collaboration with other students, to display your writing.
- Make your own book by typing or word processing the pages and binding them together.
- Hold an oral reading of student writing as a class or school-wide project.
- Share your writing with other students in a small writers' group.

Reflect

After you've completed your writing, think through the writing process to determine what you learned as a writer, what you learned about your topic, how the writing process worked or didn't work for you, and what skills you would like to strengthen.

Reflection can be done on a self-evaluation form, in small-group discussion, or simply in silent reflection. By keeping a journal, however, you'll be able to keep track of your writing experience and pinpoint ways to make the writing process work better for you. Here are some questions to ask as you reflect on the writing process and yourself as a writer:

- Which part of the writing process did I enjoy most and least? Why? Which part of the writing process was most difficult? least difficult? Why?
- What would I change about my approach to the writing process next time?
- What have I learned in writing about this topic?
- What have I learned by using this form?
- How have I developed as a writer while writing this piece?
- What strengths have I discovered in my work?
- What aspects of my writing do I want to strengthen? How can I strengthen them?

4.2 Modes and Purposes of Writing

Types of writing generally fall within four main classifications or modes: expository, narrative, descriptive, and persuasive. Each of these modes has a specific purpose. See the Mode of Writing Chart on page 876.

Expository Writing

The purpose of **expository writing** is to inform, to present or explain an idea or a process. News articles and research reports are examples of informative expository writing. One function of expository writing is to define, since a definition explains what something is. Another function of expository writing is to analyze and interpret. For example, a book review is writing that analyzes and interprets a piece of literature to inform an audience about its worth. Similarly, a movie review evaluates and judges for its viewing audience how well a movie accomplishes its purpose.

Narrative Writing

Narrative writing tells a story or relates a series of events. It can be used to entertain, to make a point, or to introduce a topic. Narrating an event involves the dimension of action over time.

Narratives are often used in essays, reports, and other nonfiction forms because stories are entertaining and fun to read. Just as important, they are a good way to make a point. Biographies, autobiographies, and family histories are also forms of narrative writing.

Descriptive Writing

The purpose of **descriptive writing** is to entertain, enrich, and enlighten by using a form such as fiction or poetry to share a perspective. Descriptive writing is used to describe something, to set a scene, to create a mood, to appeal to the reader's senses. Descriptive writing is often creative and uses visual and other sensual details, emotional responses, and imagery. Poems, short stories, and plays are examples of descriptive writing.

Persuasive Writing

The purpose of **persuasive writing** is to persuade readers or listeners to respond in some way, such as to agree with a position, change a view on an issue, reach an agreement, or perform an action. Examples of persuasive writing are editorials, petitions, political speeches, and essays.

5.1 Research Skills

Learning is a lifelong process, one that extends far beyond school. Both in school and on your own, it is important to remember that your learning and growth are up to you. One good way to become an independent lifelong learner is to master research skills. Research is the process of gathering ideas and information. One of the best resources for research is the library.

How Library Materials Are Organized

Each book in a library is assigned a unique number, called a call number. The call number is printed on the spine (edge) of each book. The numbers serve to classify books as well as to help the library keep track of them. Libraries commonly use one of two systems for classifying books. Most school and public libraries use the Dewey Decimal System.

Dewey Decimal System	
Call Numbers	**Subjects**
000–099	Reference and General Works
100–199	Philosophy, Psychology
200–299	Religion
300–399	Social Studies
400–499	Language
500–599	Science, Mathematics
600–699	Technology
700–799	Arts
800–899	Literature
900–999	History, Geography, Biography[1]

1. Biographies (920s) are arranged alphabetically by the name of the person whose life is treated in each biography.

How to Locate Library Materials

If you know the call number of a book or the subject classification number you want, you can usually go to the bookshelves, or stacks, to obtain the book. Use the signs at the ends of the rows to locate the section you need. Then find the particular shelf that contains call numbers close to yours.

Library collections include many other types of publications besides books, such as magazines, newspapers, audio and video recordings, and government documents. Ask a librarian to tell you where to find the materials you need. To find the call numbers of books that will help you with your research, use the library's catalog. The catalog lists all the books in the library (or a group of libraries if it is part of a larger system).

Internet Libraries It is also possible to visit the Internet Public library online at **http://www.ipl.org/.** The Internet Public Library is the first public library of the Internet. This site provides library services to the Internet community by finding, evaluating, selecting, organizing, describing, and creating quality information resources; teaches what librarians have to contribute in a digital environment; and promotes the importance of libraries.

Computerized Catalogs Many libraries today use computerized catalogs. Systems differ from library to library, but most involve using a computer terminal to search through the library's collection. You can usually search by author, title, subject, or key word.

EXAMPLE COMPUTERIZED CATALOG SEARCHES

Search By	Example	Hints
Author	gould, stephen j	Type last name first. Type as much of the name as you know.
Title	mismeasure of man	Omit articles such as *a*, *an*, or *the* at the beginning of titles.
Subject	intelligence tests; ability-testing	Use the list of subjects provided by the library.
Key words	darwin; intelligence; craniology	Use related topics if you can't find anything in your subject.

If your library has a computerized catalog, you will need to learn how to use your library's particular system. A librarian can help you to master the system. The following is a sample book entry screen from a computerized catalog.

Author	Wallace, David Rains, 1945–
Title	The Quetzal and the Macaw: The Story of Costa Rica's National Parks
Publication info.	Sierra Club Books, 1992
No. of pages/size	xvi, 222 p. : maps : 24 cm.
ISBN	ISBN 0-87156-585-4
Subjects	National parks and reserves–Costa Rica–History
	Costa Rica. Servicio de Parques
	Nacionales–History
	Nature conservation–Costa Rica–History
Dewey call number	333.78

Interlibrary Loans Many libraries are part of larger library networks. In these libraries, the computerized catalog covers the collections of several libraries. If you want a book from a different library, you will need to request the book at the library's request desk or by using its computer. Ask your librarian to help you if you have questions. He or she will be able to tell you when the book will be shipped to your library.

Using Reference Works

Most libraries have an assortment of reference works in which knowledge is collected and organized so that you can find it easily. Usually, reference works cannot be checked out of the library.

Types of Dictionaries You will find many types of dictionaries in the library reference section. The most common is a dictionary of the English language. Examples include *Merriam Webster's Collegiate Dictionary*, the *American Heritage Dictionary*, and the multi-volume *Oxford English Dictionary*. Other word dictionaries focus on slang, abbreviations and acronyms, English/foreign language translation, and spelling. Biographical, historical, scientific, and world language dictionaries are also some of the works you will find in the reference section.

Using a Thesaurus A thesaurus is a reference book that groups synonyms, or words with similar meanings. Suppose that you are writing an essay and have a word that means almost but not quite what you want, or perhaps you find yourself using the same word over and over. A thesaurus can give you fresh and precise words to use. For example, if you look up the word *sing* in a thesaurus, you might find the following synonyms listed:

  sing (v.) carol, chant, croon, hum, vocalize, warble, yodel

Using Almanacs, Yearbooks, and Atlases Almanacs and **yearbooks** are published each year. An almanac provides statistics and lists, often related to recent events. In an almanac you can find facts about current events, countries of the world, famous people, sports, entertainment, and many other subjects. An overview of the events of the year can be found in a yearbook. Some of the more widely used almanacs and yearbooks are *The Guinness Book of World Records;* the *Information Please, Almanac, Atlas, and Yearbook;* the *World Almanac and Book of Facts;* and the *World Book Yearbook of Events.*

An **atlas** is a collection of maps and other geographical information. Some atlases show natural features such as mountains and rivers; others show political features such as countries and cities. If you need to locate a particular feature on a map in an atlas, refer to the gazetteer, an index that lists every item shown on the map.

Using Biographical References and Encyclopedias A **biographical reference** contains information on the lives of famous people. Examples include *Who's Who,* the *Dictionary of American Biography,* and *Contemporary Authors.*

Encyclopedias provide a survey of knowledge. General encyclopedias, such as *World Book,* contain information on many different subjects. Specialized encyclopedias, such as the *LaRousse Encyclopedia of Mythology,* contain information on one particular area of knowledge. The topics in an encyclopedia are treated in articles, which are usually arranged in alphabetical order. If you look up a topic and do not find it, check the index (usually in the last volume). The index will tell you where in the encyclopedia your topic is covered.

Using Indexes, Appendices, and Glossaries An **index** lists in alphabetical order the subjects mentioned in a book or collection of periodicals and pages where these subjects are treated. Indexes help you locate possible sources of information about your topic. An index can be at the back of a book of nonfiction, or it can be a published book itself. Indexes are available as bound books, on microfilm, and online on the Internet.

An **appendix** provides additional material, often in chart or table form, at the end of a book or other writing.

A **glossary** lists key words in a book and their definitions.

Primary and Secondary Sources

Primary sources are the original unedited materials created by someone directly involved in an event or speaking directly for a group. They may include firsthand documents such as diaries, interviews, works of fiction, artwork, court records, research reports, speeches, letters, surveys, and so on.

Secondary sources offer commentary or analysis of events, ideas, or primary sources. They are often written significantly later and may provide historical context or attempt to describe or explain primary sources. Examples of secondary sources include dictionaries, encyclopedias, textbooks, and books and articles that interpret or review original works.

	Primary Source	Secondary Source
Art	Painting	Article critiquing the artist's technique
History	Prisoner's diary	Book about World War II internment camps
Literature	Poem	Literary criticism on a particular form of poetry
Science	Research report	Analysis of results

See the Language Arts Handbook 5.3, Media Literacy, page 952, for information on using newspapers, periodicals, and other forms of media to document your research.

5.2 Internet Research

The Internet is an enormous collection of computer networks that can open a whole new world of information. With just a couple of keystrokes, you can access libraries, government agencies, high schools and universities, nonprofit and educational organizations, museums, user groups, and individuals around the world.

Keep in mind that the Internet is not regulated and everything you read online may not be verified or accurate. Confirm facts from the Internet against another source. In addition, to become a good judge of Internet materials, do the following:

- **Consider the domain name of the resource.** Be sure to check out the sites you use to see if they are commercial (.com or .firm), educational (.edu), governmental (.gov), or organizational (.org or .net). Ask yourself questions like these: What bias might a commercial site have that would influence its presentation of information? Is the site sponsored by a special-interest group that slants or spins information to its advantage?

Key to Internet Domains

.com	commercial entity
.edu	educational institution
.firm	business entity
.gov	government agency or department
.org or .net	organization

- **Consider the author's qualifications.** Regardless of the source, ask these questions: Is the author named? What expertise does he or she have? Can I locate other online information about this person? Evaluate the quality of information.
- **How accurate is the information?** Does it appear to be reliable and without errors? Is the information given without bias?
- **Check the date posted.** Is the information timely? When was the site last updated?

Keep Track of Your Search Process

❑ Write a brief statement of the topic of your research.

❑ Write key words or phrases that will help you search for this information.

❑ Note the search engines that you will use.

❑ As you conduct a search, note how many "hits" or Internet sites the search engine has accessed. Determine whether you need to narrow or expand your search. Write down new key words and the results of each new search.

❑ Write down all promising sites. As you access them, evaluate the source and nature of the information and jot down your assessment.

❑ As you find the information you need, document it carefully according to the directions in Citing Internet Sources, page 956.

❑ Keep a list of favorite websites, either in your research journal or in your browser software. This feature may be called bookmark or favorites. You can click on the name of the site in your list and return to that page without having to retype the URL (Uniform Resource Locator).

Search Tools

A number of popular and free search engines allow you to find topics of interest. Keep in mind that each service uses slightly different methods of searching, so you may get different results using the same key words.

All the Web	http://www.alltheweb.com
AltaVista	http://www.altavista.com
Go	http://www.go.com
Yahoo	http://www.yahoo.com
Excite	http://www.excite.com
HotBot	http://www.hotbot.com
WebCrawler	http://www.webcrawler.com
Google	http://www.google.com

Search Tips

- To make searching easier, less time consuming, and more directed, narrow your subject to a key word or a group of key words. These key words are your search terms. Key search connectors, or Boolean commands, can help you limit or expand the scope of your topic.

    AND (or +) narrows a search by retrieving documents that include both terms — for example: Ulysses Grant AND Vicksburg.

    OR broadens a search by retrieving documents that include any of the terms — for example: Ulysses Grant OR Vicksburg OR Civil War.

    NOT narrows a search by excluding documents containing certain words — for example: Ulysses Grant NOT Civil War.

- If applicable, limit your search by specifying a geographical area by using the word *near* — for example, golf courses near Boulder, Colorado.
- When entering a group of key words, present them in order, from the most important to the least important key word.
- If the terms of your search are not leading you to the information you need, try using synonyms. For example, if you were looking for information about how to care for your garden, you might use these terms: *compost, pest control,* and *watering*.
- Avoid opening the link to every page in your results list. Search engines typically present pages in descending order of relevancy or importance. The most useful pages will be located at the top of the list. However, skimming the text of lower order sites may give you ideas for other key words.
- If you're not getting the desired results, check your input. Common search mistakes include misspelling search terms and mistyping URLs. Remember that URLs must be typed exactly as they appear, using the exact capital or lowercase letters, spacing, and punctuation.

For information on citing Internet sources, see the Language Arts Handbook 5.6, Documenting Sources.

5.3 Media Literacy

The term **media,** in most applications, is used as a plural of *medium,* which means a channel or system of communication, information, or entertainment. *Mass media* refers specifically to means of communication, such as newspapers, radio, or television, which are designed to reach the mass of the people. *Journalism* is the gathering, evaluating, and disseminating, through various media, of news and facts of current interest. Originally, journalism encompassed only such printed matter as newspapers and periodicals. Today, however, it includes other media used to distribute news, such as radio, television, documentary or newsreel films, the Internet, and computer news services.

Newspapers are publications usually issued on a daily or weekly basis, the main function of which is to report the news. Newspapers also provide commentary on the news, advocate various public policies, furnish special information and advice to readers, and sometimes include features such as comic strips, cartoons, and serialized books.

Periodicals are publications released at regular intervals, such as journals, magazines, or newsletters. Periodicals feature material of special interest to particular audiences. The contents of periodicals can be unrelated to current news stories — however, when dealing with the news, periodicals tend to do so in the form of commentaries or summaries.

Technical writing refers to scientific or process-oriented instructional writing that is of a technical or mechanical nature. Technical writing includes instruction manuals, such as computer software manuals, how-to instructional guides, and procedural memos.

Electronic media include online magazines and journals, known as webzines or e-zines; computer news services; and many web-based newspapers that are available on the Internet. The web is by far the most widely used part of the Internet.

Multimedia is the presentation of information using the combination of text, sound, pictures, animation, and video. Common multimedia computer applications include games, learning software, presentation software, reference materials, and web pages. Most multimedia applications include links that enable users to switch between media elements and topics. The connectivity provided by these links transforms multimedia from static presentations with pictures and sound into a varied and informative interactive experience.

Visual media, such as fine art, illustrations, and photographs, are used extensively in today's visually stimulating world to enhance the written word. Visual arts offer insights into our world in a different way than print does. Critical viewing or careful examination of a painting or photograph can help you to comprehend its meaning and be able to compare and contrast the visual image with a literary work or other piece of writing.

5.4 Evaluating Sources

To conduct your research efficiently, you need to evaluate your sources and set priorities among them. Ideally, a source will be:

- **Unbiased** When an author has a personal stake in what people think about a subject, he or she may withhold or distort information. Investigate the author's background to see if she or he is liable to be biased. Using loaded language and overlooking obvious counterarguments are signs of author bias.
- **Authoritative** An authoritative source is reliable and trustworthy. An author's reputation, especially among others who conduct research in the same field, is a sign of authority. Likewise, periodicals and publishers acquire reputations for responsible or poor editing and research.
- **Timely** Information about many subjects changes rapidly. An astronomy text published last year may already be out of date. In other fields — for instance, algebra — older texts may be perfectly adequate. Consult with your teacher and your librarian to decide how current your sources must be.
- **Available** Borrowing through interlibrary loan, tracing a book that is missing, or recalling a book that has been checked out to another person takes time. Make sure to allow enough time for these materials.

- **Appropriate for your level** Find sources that present useful information that you can understand. Materials written for "young people" may be too simple to be helpful. Books written for experts may presume knowledge that you do not have. Struggling with a difficult text is often worth the effort, but if you do so, monitor your time and stay on schedule.

5.5 Documenting Sources

As you use your research in your writing, you must document your sources of information.
- Credit the sources of all ideas and facts that you use.
- Credit original ideas or facts that are expressed in text, tables, charts, and other graphic information.
- Credit all artistic property, including works of literature, song lyrics, and ideas.

Keeping a Research Journal A research journal is a notebook, electronic file, or other means to track the information you find as you conduct research. A research journal can include the following:
- A list of questions you want to research. (Such questions can be an excellent source of writing topics.)

EXAMPLES

How did the Vietnam Veterans Memorial come to be? Why is it one of the most visited memorials in America?

Where can I find more artwork by Faith Ringgold?

Why was Transcendentalism such an important literary movement in America but not in Europe?

Avoiding Plagiarizing Plagiarism is taking someone else's words or thoughts and presenting them as your own. Plagiarism is a very serious problem and has been the downfall of many students and professionals. Whenever you use someone else's writing to help you with a paper or a speech, you must be careful either to **paraphrase,** put the ideas in your own words; **summarize** the main ideas; or to use **quotation marks.** In any case, you must document your sources and give credit to the person whose ideas you are using. As you do research, make sure to include paraphrases, summaries, and direct quotations in your notes.

Informal and Formal Note-Taking

Informal Note-Taking Take informal notes when you want information for your own use only, and when you will not need to quote or document your sources. You would take informal notes when preparing materials to use in studying, for instance, as you watch a film or listen to a lecture.

Informal note-taking is similar to outlining. Use important ideas as headings, and write relevant details below. You will not be able to copy every word, nor is there any need to. Write phrases instead of sentences. You will also want to record information about the event or performance, including the date, time, place, speaker, and title, as applicable.

EXAMPLE
quotation
"Jerzy Kosinski came to the United States in 1957, and in 1958 he was awarded a Ford Foundation fellowship."

notes

Jerzy Kosinski
— came to US 1957
— Ford Foundation fellowship 1958

Formal Note-Taking Take formal notes when you may need to quote or document your sources. When you are keeping formal notes for a project—for instance, for a debate or a research paper—you should use 4" x 6" index cards.

Preparing Note Cards

1. Identify the source at the top right corner of the card. (Use the source numbers from your bibliography cards.)
2. Identify the subject or topic of the note on the top line of the card. (This will make it easier to organize the cards later.)
3. Use a separate card for each fact or quotation. (This will make it easier to organize the cards later.)
4. Write the pertinent source page number or numbers after the note.

EXAMPLE

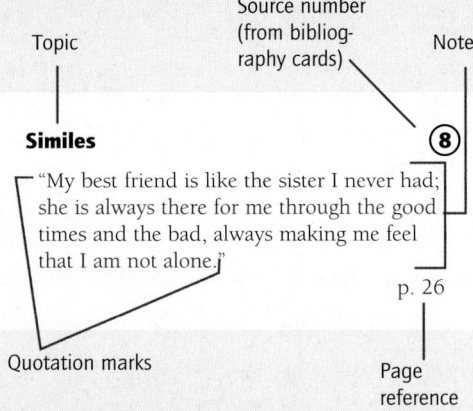

Topic

Source number
(from bibliog-
raphy cards)

Note

Similes ⑧

"My best friend is like the sister I never had; she is always there for me through the good times and the bad, always making me feel that I am not alone."

p. 26

Quotation marks

Page
reference

Bibliographies and Bibliography Cards

If you are writing a research paper, your teacher will ask you to include a bibliography to tell where you got your information. A bibliography is a list of sources that you used for your writing. A source is a book, a magazine, a film, or any other written or audiovisual material that you use to get information. As you work on your paper, you should be writing down on note cards the information for each source that you use.

EXAMPLE

2

Van Lawick-Goodall, Jane.

In the Shadow of Man

Boston: Houghton, 1971.

Peabody Institute Library

599.8

For each source used, prepare an index card with complete bibliographical information. Include all of the information in the following chart when preparing your cards.

Information to Include on a Bibliography Card	
Author(s)	Write the complete name(s) of all author(s), editor(s), and translator(s).
Title	Write the complete title. If the piece is contained in a larger work, include the title of the larger work. (For example, write the name of the encyclopedia as well as the name of the article you used.)
Publisher	Write exactly as it appears on the title page.
Place and date of publication	Copy this information from the title page or copyright page of a book. For a magazine, write the date of the issue that you used.
Location and call number	Note where you found the book. If it is in a library collection, write the call number.
Card number	Give each bibliography card that you prepare a number. Write that number in the top right-hand corner of the card and circle it. When you take notes from the source, include this number on each note card so that you will be able to identify the source of the note later on.

The following chart shows the correct form for citing different types of bibliography entries, following the *Modern Language Association (MLA) Style Manual*. Note that all citations should include the medium of the publication, such as *print*, *film*, or *Web*.

MLA Forms for Works Cited

Book	Douglass, Frederick. *Escape from Slavery: The Boyhood of Frederick Douglass in His Own Words*. New York: Alfred A. Knopf, 1994. Print.
Magazine article	Reston, James, Jr. "Orion: Where Stars Are Born." *National Geographic*. December 1995: 90–101. Print.
Encyclopedia entry	"Lewis and Clark Expedition." *Encyclopedia Americana*. Jackson, Donald. 1995 ed. Print.
Interview	Campbell, Silas. Personal interview. 6 February 2007.
Film	*The Big Heat*. Dir. Fritz Lang. With Glenn Ford and Gloria Grahame. Writ. Sidney Boehm. Based on the novel of the same title by William P. McGiven. 90 min. Columbia, 1953. Film.

Citing Internet Sources

To document your Internet sources, use your research journal to record each site you visit (See the Language Arts Handbook, 5.2 Internet Research, page 879) or make bibliography cards as you search. An Internet source entry should include the following general pieces of information:

- Name of the author, if available, last name first, followed by a period.
- Title of the source, document, file, or page in quotation marks, followed by a period.
- Date of the material if available, followed by a period.
- Name of the database or online source, underlined or italicized, and followed by a period.
- Medium of publication (Web).
- Date the source was accessed (day, month, year).

- Provide an electronic address, URL, only when needed to locate the source or if required by your instructor. Enclose the URL in angle brackets (< >), followed by a period. Avoid showing network and e-mail addresses as underlined hyperlinks. Note that when line length forces you to break a Web address, always break it after a slash mark.

The *Modern Language Association Style Manual* acknowledges that all source tracking information on the Internet may not be obtainable. Therefore, the manual recommends that if you cannot find some of this information, cite what is available.

EXAMPLES
Armstrong, Mark. "That's 'Sir' Mick Jagger to You." 17 June 2002. E! Online, Inc. Web. 17 June 2009 <http://www.eonline.com/News/Items/0,1,10110,00.html>.

For sites with no name of the database or online source:
Chachich, Mike. "Letters from Japan Vol 1" 30 March 1994. Web. 17 June 2009 <http://www.chachich.com/cgi-bin/catlfj?1>.

For sites with no author:
"The Science Behind the Sod." 13 June 2002. *MSU News Bulletin*. Web. 17 June 2009 <http://www.newsbulletin.msu.edu/june13/sod.html>.

For e-mail messages:
Daniel Akaka (senator@akaka.senate.gov). "Oceanic Exploration Grant." E-mail to Al Franken (senator@franken.senate.gov). 17 June 2009.

Parenthetical Documentation Parenthetical documentation is currently the most widely used form of documentation. To use this method to document the source of a quotation or an idea, you place a brief note identifying the source in parentheses immediately after the borrowed material. This type of note is called a parenthetical citation, and the act of placing such a note is called citing a source.

The first part of a parenthetical citation refers the reader to a source in your List of Works Cited or Works Consulted. For the reader's ease in finding the source in your bibliography, you must cite the work according to how it is listed in the bibliography.

EXAMPLES

For works listed by title, use an abbreviated title.

Sample bibliographic entry
"History." *Encyclopedia Britannica: Macropædia*. 1992 ed. Print.

Sample citation
Historians go through three stages in textual criticism ("History" 615).

For works listed by author or editor, use the author's or editor's last name.

Sample bibliographic entry
Brown, Dee. *Bury My Heart at Wounded Knee: An Indian History of the American West*. New York: Holt, 1970. Print.

Sample citation
"Big Eyes Schurz agreed to the arrest" (Brown 364).

When the listed name or title is stated in the text, cite only the page number.

Brown states that Big Eyes Schurz agreed to it (364).

For works of multiple volumes, use a colon after the volume number.

Sample bibliographic entry
Pepys, Samuel. *The Diary of Samuel Pepys.* Eds. Robert Latham and William Matthews. 10 vols. Berkeley: University of California Press, 1972. Print.

Sample citation
On the last day of 1665, Pepys took the occasion of the new year to reflect, but not to celebrate (6: 341–2).

For works quoted in secondary sources, use the abbreviation "qtd. in."

Sample citation
According to R. Bentley, "reason and the facts outweigh a hundred manuscripts" (qtd. in "History" 615).

For classic works that are available in various editions, give the page number from the edition you are using, followed by a semicolon; then identify the section of the work to help people with other editions find the reference.

Footnotes and Endnotes

In addition to parenthetical documentation, footnoting and endnoting are two other accepted methods.

Footnotes Instead of putting citations in parentheses within the text, you can place them at the bottom or foot of the page; hence the term *footnote.* In this system, a number or symbol is placed in the text where the parenthetical citation would otherwise be, and a matching number or symbol at the bottom of the page identifies the citation. This text-book, for example, uses numbered footnotes in its literature selections to define obscure words and to provide background information.

Endnotes Many books use endnotes instead of footnotes. Endnotes are like footnotes in that a number or symbol is placed within the text, but the matching citations are compiled at the end of the book, chapter, or article rather than at the foot of the page. Footnote and endnote entries begin with the author's (or editor's) name in its usual order (first name, then last) and include publication information and a page reference.

EXAMPLES

Book with one author
[1]Jean Paul-Sartre, *Being and Nothingness* (New York: The Citadel Press, 1966) 149–151. Print.

Book with one editor and no single author
[2]Shannon Ravenel, ed., *New Stories from the South: The Year's Best, 1992* (Chapel Hill, NC: Algonquin Books, 1992) 305. Print.

Magazine article
[3]Andrew Gore, "Road Test: The Apple Powerbook," *MacUser,* December 1996: 72. Print.

6.1 Workplace and Consumer Documents

Applied English is English in the world of work or business, or *practical* English. Entering a new school, writing a professional letter, applying for a job, reading an instructional manual—these are but a few of the many situations you may encounter that involve **workplace and consumer documents.** You can apply English skills to many real-world situations, using your reading, writing, speaking, and listening abilities to help you be successful in any field or occupation you choose to pursue.

6.2 Writing a Step-by-Step Procedure

A **step-by-step procedure** is a how-to or process piece that uses directions to teach someone something new. Written procedures include textual information and sometimes graphics. Spoken procedures can be given as oral demonstrations. They can include textual and graphic information and other props. Examples of step-by-step procedures include an oral demonstration of how to saddle a horse; instructions on how to treat a sprained ankle; a video showing how to do the perfect lay-up in basketball; and an interactive Internet site allowing the user to design and send a bouquet of flowers.

Guidelines for Writing a Step-by-Step Procedure

- Demonstrate the steps. If you are showing how to make something, create several different samples to show each step of the procedure. For example, if you are showing how to make a wooden basket, you might want to display the raw materials, the started basket, the basket halfway finished, and then the finished product.
- Be prepared. The best way to prevent problems is to anticipate and plan for them. Rehearse an oral demonstration several times. If you are preparing the procedure in written form, go through your directions as if you knew nothing about the process. Anticipate what it would be like to learn this procedure for the first time. See if you can follow your own directions, or have a friend work through the procedure and offer suggestions for improvement.
- Acknowledge mistakes. If you are sharing a procedure "live" as an oral demonstration and you can't talk around or correct a mistake, tell your audience what has gone wrong, and why. If you handle the situation in a calm, direct way, the audience may also learn from your mistake.
- Know your topic. The better you know it, the better you will be able to teach others.

6.3 Writing a Business Letter

A **business letter** is usually addressed to someone you do not know personally. Therefore, a formal tone is appropriate for such a letter. Following appropriate form is especially important when writing business letters. If you follow the correct form and avoid errors in spelling, grammar, usage, and mechanics, your letter will sound professional and make a good impression. Above the salutation, a business letter should contain the name and title of the person to whom you are writing and the name and address of that person's company or organization (see the model on the following page).

One common form for a business letter is the block form. In the **block form,** each part of the letter begins at the left margin. The parts are separated by line spaces.

Begin the salutation with the word *Dear,* followed by the courtesy or professional title used in the inside address, such as Ms., Mr., or Dr., and a colon. If you are not writing to a specific person, you may use a general salutation such as *Dear Sir or Madam.*

In the body of your letter, use a polite, formal tone and standard English. Make your points clearly, in as few words as possible.

End with a standard closing such as *Sincerely, Yours truly,* or *Respectfully yours.* Capitalize only the first word of the closing. Type your full name below the closing, leaving three or four blank lines for your signature. Sign your name below the closing in blue or black ink (never in red or green). Proofread your letter before you send it. Poor spelling, grammar, or punctuation can ruin an otherwise well-written business letter.

One of the most frequently used types of business letters is an **application letter,** which you would write to apply to a school or for a job. In an application letter, it is important to emphasize your knowledge about the business and the skills that you can bring to the position.

Guidelines for Writing a Business Letter

- Outline your main points before you begin.
- Word process your letter, if at all possible. Type or print it on clean 8 1/2" x 11" white or off-white paper. Use only one side of the paper.
- Use the block form or another standard business letter form.
- Single space, leaving a blank line between each part, including paragraphs.
- Use a standard salutation and a standard closing.
- Stick to the subject. State your main idea clearly at the beginning of the letter. Keep the letter brief and informative.
- Check your spelling, grammar, usage, and punctuation carefully.

6.4 Writing a Proposal

A **proposal** outlines a project that a person wants to complete. It presents a summary of an idea, the reasons why the idea is important, and an outline of how the project would be carried out. Because the proposal audience is people who can help carry out the proposal, a proposal is both informative and persuasive.

EXAMPLES

- You want funding for an art project that would benefit your community.
- Your student council proposes a clothing drive for disaster relief.
- You and a group of your friends want to help organize a summer program for teens your age.

Guidelines for Writing a Proposal

- Keep the tone positive, courteous, and respectful.
- State your proposal and rationale briefly and clearly.
- Give your audience all necessary information. A proposal with specific details makes it clear what you want approved, and why your audience—often a committee or someone in authority—should approve it.
- Use standard, formal English.
- Format your proposal with headings, lists, and schedules to make your proposed project easy to understand and approve.

6.5 Writing a Public Service Announcement

A **public service announcement,** or **PSA,** is a brief, informative article intended to be helpful to the community. PSAs are written by nonprofit organizations and concerned citizens for print in local newspapers, for broadcast by television and radio stations, and for publication on the Internet.

EXAMPLES

- an article by the American Cancer Society outlining early warning signs of cancer

- an announcement promoting Safety Week

- an informative piece telling coastal residents what to do during a hurricane

Guidelines for Writing a Public Service Announcement

- Know your purpose. What do you want your audience to know from reading or hearing your piece?
- State your information as objectively as possible.
- As with most informative writing, use the 5 *Ws* and an *H—who, what, where, why, when,* and *how—*questioning strategy to get your important information at the beginning of your story.
- Keep your announcement brief. Local media are more likely to publish or broadcast your piece if it is short and to the point.
- Include contact information in case the media representative has any questions. You might also include contact information in the PSA itself.
- Key or type your PSA in conventional manuscript form. Make sure the text is double-spaced and that you leave margins of at least an inch on all sides of the page.
- At the end of the PSA, key "END" to designate the end of the announcement.
- Be aware of print and broadcast deadlines and make sure your material is sent on time.

▶ Refer to the following pages for the unit Speaking and Listening Workshops:

Giving and Actively Listening to
  Literary Presentations,
    pp. 136–137
Giving and Actively Listening to
  Literary Presentations,
    pp. 270–271
Giving and Actively Listening to
  Informative Presentations,
    pp. 386–387
Giving and Actively Listening to
  Expository Presentations,
    pp. 534–535
Giving and Actively Listening to
  Narrative Presentations,
    pp. 608–609
Giving and Actively Listening to
  Persuasive Presentations,
    pp. 736–737
Giving and Actively Listening to
  Research Presentations,
    pp. 878–879

▶ Refer to the following pages for the unit Viewing Workshop:
Critical Viewing, pp. 466–467

SPEAKING & LISTENING

7 Speaking & Listening

7.1 Verbal and Nonverbal Communication

When a person expresses meaning through words, he or she is using verbal communication. When a person expresses meaning without using words, for example by standing up straight or shaking his or her head, he or she is using nonverbal communication. When we speak to another person, we usually think that the meaning of what we say comes chiefly from the words we use. However, as much as sixty percent of the meaning of a message may be communicated nonverbally.

Elements of Verbal Communication

Element	Description	Guidelines for Speakers
Volume	Loudness or softness	Vary your volume, but make sure that you can be heard.
Melody, Pitch	Highness or lowness	Vary your pitch. Avoid speaking in a monotone (at a single pitch).
Pace	Speed	Vary the speed of your delivery to suit what you are saying.
Tone	Emotional quality	Suit your tone to your message, and vary it appropriately as you speak.
Enunciation	Clearness with which words are spoken	When speaking before a group, pronounce your words more precisely than you would in ordinary conversation.

Elements of Nonverbal Communication

Element	Description	Guidelines for Speakers
Eye contact	Looking audience members in the eye	Make eye contact regularly with people in your audience. Try to include all audience members.
Facial expression	Using your face to show your emotions	Use expressions to emphasize your message—raised eyebrows for a question, pursed lips for concentration, eyebrows lowered for anger, and so on.
Gesture	Meaningful motions of the arms and hands	Use gestures to emphasize points. Be careful, however, not to overuse gestures. Too many can be distracting.
Posture	Position of the body	Keep your spine straight and head high, but avoid appearing stiff. Stand with your arms and legs slightly open, except when adopting other postures to express particular emotions.
Proximity	Distance from audience	Keep the right amount of distance between yourself and the audience. You should be a comfortable distance away, but not so far away that the audience cannot hear you.

976 LANGUAGE ARTS HANDBOOK

Program Resources

To expand upon speaking and listening skills, see the *Exceeding the Standards: Speaking & Listening* resource.

7.2 Listening Skills

Active Versus Passive Listening

Active listening requires skill and concentration. The mind of a good listener is focused on what a speaker is trying to communicate. In other words, an effective listener is an active listener. Ineffective listeners view listening as a passive activity, something that simply "happens" without any effort on their part. **Passive listening** is nothing more than hearing sounds. This type of listening can cause misunderstanding and miscommunication.

ADAPTING LISTENING SKILLS

Just as different situations require different types of listening, different tasks or goals may also require different listening strategies and skills.

Listening for Comprehension

Listening for comprehension means listening for information or ideas communicated by other people. For example, you are listening for comprehension when you try to understand directions to a friend's house or your teacher's explanation of how to conduct a classroom debate.

When listening for comprehension, your goal is to reach understanding, so it is important to recognize and remember the key information or ideas presented. Concentrate on getting the **main points or major ideas** of a message rather than all the supporting details. This can prevent you from becoming overwhelmed by the amount of information presented.

You might also use a technique called **clarifying and confirming** to help you better remember and understand information. This technique involves paraphrasing or repeating back to the speaker in your own words the key information presented to make sure that you have understood correctly. If the situation prevents you from using the technique—for instance, if there is no opportunity for you to respond directly to the speaker—it can still be helpful to rephrase the information in your own words in your head to help you remember and understand it.

Listening Critically

Listening critically means listening to a message in order to comprehend and evaluate it. When listening for comprehension, you usually assume that the information presented is true. Critical listening, on the other hand, includes **comprehending and judging** the arguments and appeals in a message in order to decide whether to accept or reject them. Critical listening is most useful when you encounter a persuasive message such as a sales pitch, advertisement, campaign speech, or news editorial.

When evaluating a persuasive message, you might consider the following:
- Is the speaker trustworthy and qualified to speak about this subject?
- Does the speaker present logical arguments supported by solid facts?
- Does the speaker use unproven assumptions to make a case?
- Does the speaker use questionable motivational appeals, such as appeals to fear or to prejudice?

These questions can help you decide whether or not to be convinced by a persuasive message.

Listening to Learn Vocabulary

Listening to learn vocabulary involves a very different kind of listening because the focus is on learning new words and how to use them properly. For instance, you have a conversation with someone who has a more advanced vocabulary and use this as an opportunity to learn new words. The key to listening in order to learn vocabulary is to **pay attention to how words are used in context.** Sometimes it is possible to figure out what an unfamiliar word means based simply on how the word is used in a sentence.

Once you learn a new word, try to use it several times so it becomes more familiar and you become comfortable using it. Also be sure to look up the word in a dictionary to find out whether it has other meanings or connotations of which you are not aware.

Listening for Appreciation

Listening for appreciation means listening purely for enjoyment or entertainment. You might listen appreciatively to a singer, a comedian, a storyteller, an acting company, or a humorous speaker. Appreciation is a very individual matter and there are no rules about how to appreciate something. However, as with all forms of listening, listening for appreciation requires attention and concentration.

7.3 Collaborative Learning and Communication

Collaboration is the act of working with one or more other people to achieve a goal. Many common learning situations involve collaboration.
- Participating in a small-group discussion
- Doing a small-group project
- Tutoring another student or being tutored
- Doing peer evaluation

Guidelines for Group Discussion

- **Listen actively.** Maintain eye contact with the speakers. Make notes on what they say. Mentally translate what they say into your own words. Think critically about whether you agree or disagree with each speaker, and why.
- **Be polite.** Wait for your turn to speak. Do not interrupt others. If your discussion has a group leader, ask to be recognized before speaking by raising your hand.
- **Participate in the discussion.** At appropriate times, make your own comments or ask questions of other speakers.
- **Stick to the discussion topic.** Do not introduce unrelated or irrelevant ideas.
- **Assign roles.** For a formal dicussion, choose a group leader to guide the discussion and a secretary to record the minutes (the main ideas and proposals made by group members). Also draw up an agenda before the discussion, listing items to be discussed.

Guidelines for Projects

- **Choose a group leader** to conduct the meetings of your project group.
- **Set a goal** for the group. This goal should be some specific outcome or set of outcomes that you want to bring about.
- **Make a list of tasks** that need to be performed.
- **Make a schedule** for completing the tasks, including dates and times for completion of each task.
- **Make an assignment sheet.** Assign certain tasks to particular group members. Be fair in distributing the work to be done.

- **Set times for future meetings** You might want to schedule meetings to evaluate your progress toward your goal as well as meetings to actually carry out specific tasks.
- **Meet to evaluate** your overall success when the project is completed. Also look at the individual contributions of each group member.

7.4 Asking and Answering Questions

There are many situations in which you will find it useful to ask questions of a speaker, or in which you will be asked questions about a presentation. Often a formal speech or presentation will be followed by a question-and-answer period. Keep the following guidelines in mind when asking or answering questions.

Guidelines for Asking and Answering Questions

- **Wait to be recognized.** In most cases, it is appropriate to raise your hand if you have a question and to wait for the speaker or moderator to call on you.
- **Make questions clear and direct.** The longer your question, the less chance a speaker will understand it. Make your questions short and to the point.
- **Do not debate or argue.** If you disagree with a speaker, the question-and-answer period is not the time to hash out an argument. Ask to speak with the speaker privately after the presentation is over, or agree on a later time and place to meet.
- **Do not take others' time.** Be courteous to other audience members and allow them time to ask questions. If you have a follow-up question, ask the speaker if you may proceed with your follow up.
- **Do not give a speech.** Sometimes audience members are more interested in expressing their own opinion than in asking the speaker a question. Do not give in to the temptation to present a speech of your own.
- **Come prepared for a question-and-answer period.** Although you can never predict the exact questions that people will ask you, you can anticipate many questions that are likely to be asked. Rehearse aloud your answers to the most difficult questions.
- **Be patient.** It may take some time for audience members to formulate questions in response to your speech. Give the audience a moment to do so. Don't run back to your seat the minute your speech is over, or if there is an awkward pause after you invite questions.
- **Be direct and succinct.** Be sure to answer the question directly as it has been asked, and to provide a short but clear answer.

7.5 Conducting an Interview

In an interview, you meet with someone and ask him or her questions. Interviewing experts is an excellent way to gain information about a particular topic. For example, if you are interested in writing about the art of making pottery, you might interview an art teacher, a professional potter, or the owner of a ceramics shop.

When planning an interview, you should do some background research on your subject and think carefully about questions you would like to ask. Write out a list of questions, including some about the person's background as well as about your topic. Other questions might occur to you as the interview proceeds, but it is best to be prepared. For guidelines on being a good listener, see Language Arts Handbook 7.2, Listening Skills, page 963. Guidelines for interviewing appear on the following page:

Guidelines for Conducting an Interview

- **Set up a time in advance.** Don't just try to work questions into a regular conversation. Set aside time to meet in a quiet place where both you and the person you are interviewing can focus on the interview.
- **Explain the purpose** of the interview. Be sure the person you are interviewing knows what you want to find out and why you need to know it. This will help him or her to answer your questions in a way that is more useful and helpful to you.
- **Ask mostly open-ended questions.** These are questions that allow the person you are interviewing to express a personal point of view. They cannot be answered with a simple "yes" or "no" nor a brief statement of fact. The following are all examples of open-ended questions:

   "Why did you become a professional potter?"
   "What is the most challenging thing about owning your own ceramics shop?"
   "What advice would you give to a beginning potter?"

   One of the most valuable questions to ask at the end of the interview is, "What would you like to add that I haven't asked about?" This can provide some of the most interesting or vital information of all.
- **Tape-record the interview** (if possible). Then you can review the interview at your leisure. Be sure to ask the person you are interviewing whether or not you can tape-record the session. If the person refuses, accept his or her decision.
- **Take notes** during the interview, whether or not you are also tape-recording it. Write down the main points and some key words to help you remember details. Record the person's most important statements word for word.
- **Clarify spelling and get permission** for quotations. Be sure to get the correct spelling of the person's name and to ask permission to quote his or her statements.
- **End the interview on time.** Do not extend the interview beyond the time limits of your appointment. The person you are interviewing has been courteous enough to give you his or her time. Return this courtesy by ending the interview on time, thanking the person for his or her help, and leaving.
- **Write up the results** of the interview as soon as possible after you conduct it. Over time, what seemed like a very clear note may become unclear or confusing. If you are unclear of something important that the person said, contact him or her and ask for clarification.
- **Send a thank-you note** to the person you interviewed as a follow-up.

7.6 Public Speaking

The nature of a speech, whether formal or informal, is usually determined by the situation or context in which it is presented. **Formal speeches** usually call for a greater degree of preparation, might require special attire such as a suit or dress, and are often presented to larger groups who attend specifically to hear the presentation. A formal speech situation might exist when presenting an assigned speech to classmates, giving a presentation to a community group or organization, or presenting a speech at an awards ceremony. **Informal speeches** are more casual and might include telling a story among friends, giving a pep talk to your team at halftime, or presenting a toast at the dinner table.

Types of Speeches

The following are four common types of speeches:
- **Extemporaneous:** a speech in which the speaker refers to notes occasionally and that has a specific purpose and message. An example would be a speech given at a city council meeting.

- **Informative:** a speech used to share new and useful information with the audience. Informative speeches are based on fact, not opinion. Examples would include a speech on how to do something or a speech about an event.
- **Persuasive:** a speech used to convince the audience to side with an opinion and adopt a plan. The speaker tries to persuade the audience to believe something, do something, or change their behavior. Persuasive speeches use facts and research to support, analyze, and sell an opinion and plan. Martin Luther King's famous "I Have a Dream" speech and Nelson Mandela's "Glory and Hope" speech are examples of persuasive speeches.
- **Commemorative:** a speech that honors an individual for outstanding accomplishments and exemplary character. Examples would be a speech honoring a historical figure, leader, teacher, athlete, relative, or celebrity.

Guidelines for Giving a Speech

A speech should always include a beginning, a middle, and an end. The **beginning,** or introduction, of your speech should spark the audience's interest, present your central idea, and briefly preview your main points. The **middle,** or body, of your speech should expand upon each of your main points in order to support the central idea. The **end,** or conclusion, of your speech should be memorable and should give your audience a sense of completion.

- **Be sincere and enthusiastic.** Feel what you are speaking about. Apathy is infectious and will quickly spread to your audience.
- **Maintain good but relaxed posture.** Don't slouch or lean. It's fine to move around a bit; it releases normal nervous tension. Keep your hands free to gesture naturally instead of holding on to note cards, props, or the podium so much that you will "tie up" your hands.
- **Speak slowly.** Oral communication is more difficult than written language and visual images for audiences to process and understand. Practice pausing. Don't be afraid of silence. Focus on communicating with the audience. By looking for feedback from the audience, you will be able to pace yourself appropriately.
- **Maintain genuine eye contact.** Treat the audience as individuals, not as a mass of people. Look at individual faces.
- **Speak in a genuine, relaxed, conversational tone.** Don't act or stiffen up. Just be yourself.
- **Communicate.** Focus on conveying your message, not "getting through" the speech. Focus on communicating with the audience, not speaking at or to it.
- **Use strategic pauses.** Pause briefly before proceeding to the next major point, before direct quotations, and to allow important or more complex bits of information to sink in.
- **Remain confident and composed.** Remember that listeners are generally "for you" while you are speaking, and signs of nervousness are usually undetectable. To overcome initial nervousness, take two or three deep breaths as you are stepping up to speak.

7.7 Oral Interpretation

Oral interpretation is the process of presenting a dramatic reading of a literary work or group of works. The presentation should be sufficiently dramatic to convey to the audience a sense of the particular qualities of the work. Here are the steps you need to follow to prepare and present an oral interpretation:

Guidelines for Oral Interpretation

1. **Choose a cutting,** which may be a single piece; a selection from a single piece; or several short, related pieces on a single topic or theme.
2. **Write** the introduction and any necessary transitions. The introduction should mention the name of each piece, the author, and, if appropriate, the translator. It should also present the overall topic or theme of the interpretation. Transitions should introduce and connect the parts of the interpretation.
3. **Rehearse,** using appropriate variations in volume, pitch, pace, stress, tone, gestures, facial expressions, and body language. If your cutting contains different voices (a narrator's voice and characters' voices, for example), distinguish them. Try to make your verbal and nonverbal expression mirror what the piece is saying. However, avoid movement—that's for drama. Practice in front of an audience or mirror, or use a video camera or tape recorder.
4. **Present** your oral interpretation. Before actually presenting your interpretation, relax and adopt a confident attitude. If you begin to feel stage fright, try to concentrate on the work you are presenting and the audience, not on yourself.

Interpreting Poetry

Here are some additional considerations as you prepare to interpret a poem. The way you prepare your interpretation of a poem will depend on whether the poem you have chosen is a lyric poem, a narrative poem, or a dramatic poem.

- A **lyric poem** has a single speaker who reports his or her own emotions.
- A **narrative poem** tells a story. Usually a narrative poem has lines belonging to the narrator, or person who is telling the story. The narrator may or may not take part in the action.
- A **dramatic poem** contains characters who speak. A dramatic poem may be lyrical, in which characters simply report emotions, or narrative, which tells a story. A dramatic monologue presents a single speaker at a moment of crisis or self-revelation and may be either lyrical or narrative.

Before attempting to dramatize any poem, read through the poem carefully several times. Make sure that you understand it well. To check your understanding, try to paraphrase the poem, or restate its ideas, line by line, in your own words.

7.8 Telling a Story

A story or narrative is a series of events linked together in some meaningful fashion. We use narratives constantly in our daily lives: to make a journal entry, to tell a joke, to report a news story, to recount a historical event, to record a laboratory experiment, and so on. When creating a narrative, consider all of the following elements:

Guidelines for Storytelling

- **Decide on your purpose.** Every story has a point or purpose. It may be simply to entertain or to share a personal experience, but it may have a moral or lesson.
- **Select a focus.** The focus for your narrative will depend largely on your purpose in telling it.
- **Choose your point of view.** The storyteller or narrator determines the point of view from which the story will be told. You can choose to speak in the *first person,* either as a direct participant in the events or as an observer (real or imagined) who witnessed the events firsthand, or in the *third person* voice to achieve greater objectivity.

- **Determine sequence of events.** The sequence of events refers to the order in which they are presented. Although it might seem obvious that stories should "begin at the beginning," this is not always the best approach. Some narratives begin with the turning point of the story to create a sense of drama and to capture the listeners' interest. Others begin at the end of the story and present the events leading up to this point in hindsight. Wherever you choose to begin the story, your narrative should present events in a logical fashion and establish a clear sense of direction for your listeners.

- **Determine duration of events.** Duration refers to how long something lasts. Everyone has experienced an event that seemed to last for hours, when in reality it only took minutes to occur. A good storyteller can likewise manipulate the duration of events in order to affect the way listeners experience them.

- **Select details carefully.** Make them consistent with your focus and make sure they are necessary to your purpose. A well-constructed story should flow smoothly, and should not get bogged down by irrelevant or unnecessary detail. Details can also establish the tone and style of the story and affect how listeners react to the events being described.

- **Choose characters.** All stories include characters who need to be developed so that they become real for listeners. Try to provide your listeners with vivid, concrete descriptions of the mental and physical qualities of important characters in the story. Remember that listeners need to understand and relate to the characters in order to appreciate their behavior.

- **Create dialogue.** Although it is possible to tell a story in which the characters do not speak directly, conversation and dialogue help to add life to a story. As with detail, dialogue should be used carefully. It is important that dialogue sound authentic, relate to the main action of the story, and advance the narrative.

7.9 Participating in a Debate

A debate is a contest in which two people or groups of people defend opposite sides of a proposition in an attempt to convince a judge or an audience to agree with their views. Propositions are statements of fact, value, or policy that usually begin with the word "resolved." The following are examples of typical propositions for debate:

RESOLVED	That lie detector tests are inaccurate. (proposition of fact)
RESOLVED	That imagination is more important than knowledge. (proposition of value)
RESOLVED	That Congress should prohibit the sale of handguns to private citizens. (proposition of policy)

The two sides in a debate are usually called the affirmative and the negative. The affirmative takes the "pro" side of the debate and argues in favor of the proposition, whereas the negative takes the "con" side and argues against the proposition. Using a single proposition to focus the debate ensures that the two sides argue or clash over a common topic. This allows the participants in the debate to develop their logic and ability to argue their positions persuasively.

Guidelines for Participating in a Debate

- **Be prepared.** In a debate, it will never be possible to anticipate all the arguments your opponent might make. However, by conducting careful and thorough research on both sides of the issue, you should be able to prepare for the most likely arguments you will encounter. You can prepare briefs or notes on particular issues in advance of the debate to save yourself preparation time during the debate.

- **Be organized.** Because a debate involves several speeches that concern the same basic arguments or issues, it is important that you remain organized during the debate. When attacking or refuting an opponent's argument, or when advancing or defending your own argument, be sure to follow a logical organizational pattern to avoid confusing the audience or the other team.
- **Take notes** by turning a long sheet of paper sideways. Draw one column for each speaker, taking notes on each speech going down one column, and recording notes about a particular argument or issue across the page as it is discussed in each successive speech.
- **Be audience-centered.** In arguing with your opponent, it is easy to forget the goal of the debate: to persuade your audience that your side of the issue is correct.
- **Prepare in advance** for the most likely arguments your opponents, will raise. Use time sparingly to organize your materials and think of responses to unanticipated arguments. Save time for the end of the debate, during rebuttal speeches, when it will be more valuable.

7.10 Preparing a Multimedia Presentation

Whether you use a simple overhead projector and transparencies or a PowerPoint presentation that involves graphics, video, and sound, multimedia technology can add an important visual element to a presentation. Consider the following guidelines to create a multimedia presentation:

Guidelines for a Multimedia Presentation

- **Use effective audiovisuals** that enhance understanding. The multimedia elements should add to the verbal elements, not distract from them. Be sure the content of the presentation is understandable, and that the amount of information — both verbal and visual — will not overwhelm audience members.
- **Make sure the presentation is clearly audible and visible.** Video clips or graphics may appear blurry on a projection screen or may not be visible to audience members in the back or on the sides of the room. Audio clips may sound muffled or may echo in a larger room or a room with different acoustics. When creating a multimedia presentation, be sure the presentation can be easily seen and heard from all parts of the room.
- **Become familiar with the equipment.** Well before the presentation, be sure you know how to operate the equipment you will need, that you know how to troubleshoot if the equipment malfunctions, and that the equipment you will use during the presentation is the same as that which you practiced with.
- **Check the room** to be sure it can accommodate your needs. Once you know where you will make your presentation, be sure the necessary electrical outlets and extension cords are available, that lights can be dimmed or turned off as needed, that the room can accommodate the equipment you will use, and so on.
- **Rehearse with the equipment.** Make sure that you can operate the equipment while speaking at the same time. Be sure that the multimedia elements are coordinated with other parts of your presentation. If you will need to turn the lights off in the room, make sure you can operate the equipment in the dark and can still see your note cards.

8 Test-Taking Skills

8.1 Preparing for Tests

Tests are a common part of school life. You take tests in your classes to show what you have learned in each class. In addition, you might have to take one or more standardized tests each year. Standardized tests measure your skills against local, state, or national standards and may determine whether you graduate, what kind of job you can get, or which college you can attend. Learning test-taking strategies will help you succeed on the tests you are required to take.

The following guidelines will help you to prepare for and take tests on the material you have covered in class.

Preparing for a Test
- **Know what will be covered on the test.** If you have questions about what will be covered, ask your teacher.
- **Make a study plan** to allow yourself time to go over the material. Avoid last-minute cramming.
- **Review the subject matter.** Use the graphic organizers and notes you made as you read as well as notes you took in class. Review any study questions given by your teacher.
- **Make lists** of important names, dates, definitions, or events. Ask a friend or family member to quiz you on them.
- **Try to predict questions** that may be on the test. Make sure you can answer them.
- **Get plenty of sleep** the night before the test. Eat a nutritious breakfast on the morning of the test.

Taking a Test
- **Survey the test** to see how long it is and what types of questions are included.
- **Read all directions and questions carefully.** Make sure you know exactly what to do.
- **Plan your time.** Answer easy questions first. Allow extra time for complicated questions. If a question seems too difficult, skip it and go back to it later. Work quickly, but do not rush.
- **Save time for review.** Once you have finished, look back over the test. Double-check your answers, but do not change answers too readily. Your first responses are often correct.

8.2 Strategies for Taking Standardized Tests

Standardized tests are given to large groups of students in a school district, a state, or a country. Statewide tests measure how well students are meeting the learning standards the state has set. Other tests, such as the SAT (Scholastic Aptitude Test) or ACT (American College Test), are used to help determine admission to colleges and universities. Others must be taken to enter certain careers. These tests are designed to measure overall ability or skills acquired so far. Learning how to take standardized tests will help you to achieve your goals.

You can get better at answering standardized test questions by practicing the types of questions that will be on the test. Use the Test Practice Workshop questions in this book and other sample questions your teacher gives you to practice. Think aloud with a partner or small group about how you would answer each question. Notice how other students tackle the questions and learn from what they do.

Refer to the following pages for the unit Test Practice Workshops:

Writing Skills:
Literary Response, p. 138
Literary Response, p. 272
Expository Essay, p. 388
Descriptive Essay, p. 468
Expository Essay, p. 536
Narrative Essay, p. 610
Persuasive Essay, p. 738
Research Report, p. 880

Revising and Editing Skills:
139, 273, 389, 469, 537, 611, 739, 867

Reading Skills:
140, 274, 390, 470, 538, 612, 740, 882

TEST-TAKING SKILLS

Program Resources

For more study and practice with test-taking skills, see the *Exceeding the Standards: Test Practice* resource.

In addition, remember these points:

- **Rule out some choices** when you are not sure of the answer. Then guess from the remaining possibilities.
- **Skip questions that seem too difficult** and go back to them later. Be aware, however, that most tests allow you to go back only within a section.
- **Follow instructions exactly.** The test monitor will read instructions to you, and instructions may also be printed in your test booklet. Make sure you know what to do.

8.3 Answering Objective Questions

An **objective question** has a single correct answer. The following chart describes the kinds of questions you may see on objective tests. It also gives you strategies for tackling each kind of question.

Description	Guidelines
True/False You are given a statement and asked to tell whether the statement is true or false.	• If any part of a statement is false, then the statement is false. • Words like *all, always, never,* and *every* often appear in false statements. • Words like *some, usually, often,* and *most* often appear in true statements. • If you do not know the answer, guess. You have a 50/50 chance of being right.
Matching You are asked to match items in one column with items in another column.	• Check the directions. See if each item is used only once. Also check to see if some are not used at all. • Read all items before starting. • Match those items you know first. • Cross out items as you match them.
Short Answer You are asked to answer the question with a word, phrase, or sentence.	• Read the directions to find out if you are required to answer in complete sentences. • Use correct spelling, grammar, punctuation, and capitalization. • If you cannot think of the answer, move on. Something in another question might remind you of the answer.

8.4 Answering Multiple-Choice Questions

On many standardized tests, questions are multiple choice and have a single correct answer. The guidelines below will help you answer these kinds of questions effectively.

- **Read each question carefully.** Pay special attention to any words that are bolded, italicized, written in all capital letters, or otherwise emphasized.
- **Read all choices** before selecting an answer.
- **Eliminate** any answers that do not make sense, that disagree with what you remember from reading a passage, or that seem too extreme. Also, if two answers have exactly the same meaning, you can eliminate both.
- **Beware of distractors.** These are incorrect answers that look attractive because they are partially correct. They might contain a common misunderstanding, or they might apply the right information in the wrong way. Distractors are based on common mistakes students make.
- **Fill in circles completely** on your answer sheet when you have selected your answer.

8.5 Answering Reading Comprehension Questions

Reading comprehension questions ask you to read a passage and answer questions about it. These questions measure how well you perform the essential reading skills. Many of the Reading Assessment questions that follow each literature selection in this book are reading comprehension questions. Use them to help you learn how to answer these types of questions correctly. Work through each question with a partner using a "think aloud." Say out loud how you are figuring out the answer. Talk about how you can eliminate incorrect answers and determine the correct choice. You may want to make notes as you eliminate answers. By practicing this thinking process with a partner, you will be more prepared to use it silently when you have to take a standardized test.

The following steps will help you answer the reading comprehension questions on standardized tests.

- **Preview the passage and questions** and predict what the text will be about.
- **Use the reading strategies** you have learned to read the passage. Mark the text and make notes in the margins.
- **Reread the first question carefully.** Make sure you know exactly what it is asking.
- **Read the answers.** If you are sure of the answer, select it and move on. If not, go on to the next step.
- **Scan the passage** to look for key words related to the question. When you find a key word, slow down and read carefully.
- **Answer the question** and go on to the next one. Answer each question in this way.

8.6 Answering Synonym and Antonym Questions

Synonym or antonym questions give you a word and ask you to select the word that has the same meaning (for a synonym) or the opposite meaning (for an antonym). You must select the best answer even if none is exactly correct. For this type of question, you should consider all the choices to see which is best. Always notice whether you are looking for a synonym or an antonym. You will usually find both among the answers.

8.7 Answering Sentence Completion Questions

Sentence completion questions present you with a sentence that has one or two words missing. You must select the word or pair of words that best completes the sentence. The key to questions with two words missing is to make sure that both parts of the answer you have selected work well in the sentence.

8.8 Answering Constructed-Response Questions

In addition to multiple-choice questions, many standardized tests include **constructed-response questions** that require you to write essay answers in the test booklet. Constructed-response questions might ask you to identify key ideas or examples from the text by writing a sentence about each. In other cases, you will be asked to write a paragraph in response to a question about the selection and to use specific details from the passage to support your answer.

Other constructed-response questions ask you to apply information or ideas from a text in a new way. Another question might ask you to use information from the text in a particular imaginary situation. As you answer these questions, remember that you are being evaluated based on your understanding of the text. Although these questions may offer opportunities to be creative, you should still include ideas, details, and examples from the passage you have just read.

The following tips will help you answer constructed-response questions effectively:

- **Skim the questions first.** Predict what the passage will be about.
- **Use reading strategies** as you read. Underline information that relates to the questions and make notes. After you have finished reading, you can decide which of the details you have gathered to use in your answers.
- **List the most important points** to include in each answer. Use the margins of your test booklet or a piece of scrap paper.
- **Number the points** you have listed to show the order in which they should be included.
- **Draft your answer to fit** in the space provided. Include as much detail as possible in the space you have.
- **Revise and proofread** your answers as you have time.

8.9 Answering Essay Questions

An essay question asks you to write an answer that shows what you know about a particular subject. A simplified writing process like the one below will help you tackle questions like this.

1. Analyze the Question

Essay questions contain clues about what is expected of you. Sometimes you will find key words that will help you determine exactly what is being asked. See the chart below for some typical key words and their meanings.

Key Words for Essay Questions	
analyze; identify	break into parts, and describe the parts and how they are related
compare	tell how two or more subjects are similar; in some cases, also mention how they are different
contrast	tell how two or more subjects are different from each other
describe	give enough facts about or qualities of a subject to make it clear to someone who is unfamiliar with it
discuss	provide an overview and analysis; use details for support
evaluate; argue	judge an idea or concept, telling whether you think it is good or bad, or whether you agree or disagree with it
explain	make a subject clearer, providing supporting details and examples
interpret	tell the meaning and importance of an event or concept
justify	explain or give reasons for decisions; be persuasive
prove	provide factual evidence or reasons for a statement
summarize	state only the main points of an event, concept, or debate

2. Plan Your Answer

As soon as the essay prompt is clear to you, collect and organize your thoughts about it. First, gather ideas using whatever method is most comfortable for you. If you don't immediately have ideas, try freewriting for five minutes. When you **freewrite,** you write whatever comes into your head without letting your hand stop moving. You might also gather ideas in a cluster chart like the one below. Then, organize the ideas you came up with. A simple outline or chart can help.

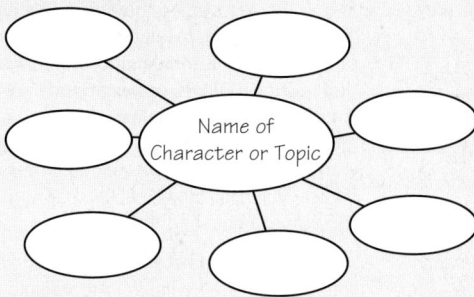

Name of Character or Topic

3. Write Your Answer

Start with a clear thesis statement in your opening paragraph. Your **thesis statement** is a single sentence that sums up your answer to the essay question. Then follow your organizational plan to provide support for your thesis. Devote one paragraph to each major point of support for your thesis. Use plenty of details as evidence for each point. Write quickly and keep moving. Don't spend too much time on any single paragraph, but try to make your answer as complete as possible. End your essay with a concluding sentence that sums up your major points.

4. Revise Your Answer

Make sure you have answered all parts of the question and included everything you were asked to include. Check to see that you have supplied enough details to support your thesis. Check for errors in grammar, spelling, punctuation, and paragraph breaks. Make corrections to your answer.

Literary Terms Handbook

ACT. An **act** is a major division of a play. There are two acts in *The Diary of Anne Frank* (Unit 7).

ALLEGORY. An **allegory** is a work in which characters, events, or settings symbolize, or represent, something else. Spirituals such as "Go Down, Moses" as sung by Harriet Tubman on the Underground Railroad (from *Harriet Tubman: Conductor of the Underground Railroad* by Ann Petry in Unit 3) are often allegorical. "Go Down, Moses" is on one level about Moses demanding freedom for the Jews from the Pharaoh in Egypt, but on another level it can be read as being about slaves seeking their freedom in the United States.

ALLITERATION. **Alliteration** is the repetition of initial consonant sounds. Though alliteration usually refers to sounds at the beginnings of words, it can also be used to refer to sounds within words. In Amy Lowell's poem "Night Clouds" (Unit 5), the *m* sound is repeated several times in a line:

> The white mares of the moon rush along
>   the sky.

ALLUSION. An **allusion** is a reference to a well-known person, event, object, or work from history or literature. For example, T. S. Elliot's poem "The Naming of Cats" (Unit 5) contains an allusion to to the Mad Hatter, a silly character in *Alice's Adventures in Wonderland,* by Lewis Carroll.

ANALOGY. An **analogy** is a comparison of two things that are alike in some ways but otherwise quite different. Often an analogy explains or describes something unfamiliar by comparing it to something more familiar.

ANECDOTE. An **anecdote** is usually a short account of an interesting, amusing, or biographical incident. Anecdotes are sometimes used in nonfiction writing as examples to help support an idea or opinion. In *"Soul of a Citizen"* (Unit 3), Paul Rogat Loeb, for example, uses several personal experiences to help make his point about social activism.

ANTAGONIST. An **antagonist** is a character or force in a literary work that is in conflict with a main character, or protagonist. The antagonist in O. Henry's story "The Ransom of Red Chief" (Unit 2), is a nine-year-old boy. *See* Character.

ARTICLE. An **article** is an informational piece of writing about a particular topic, issue, event, or series of events. Articles usually appear in newspapers, professional journals, or magazines, or on websites. An *editorial* is an article meant to give an opinion. A *review* is an article that is a critical evaluation of a work, such as a book, play, movie, or musical performance. Valerie Jablow's "A Tale of Two Rocks" (Unit 4), is an example of a news article.

ASSONANCE. **Assonance** is the repetition of vowel sounds in stressed syllables. An example is the repetition of the short *i* sound in the following line from Elinor Wylie's "Pretty Words" (Unit 5):

> Like midsummer moths, and honied words
>   like bees,
> Gilded and sticky, with a little sting.

ATMOSPHERE. *See* Mood.

AUTOBIOGRAPHY. An **autobiography** is the story of a person's life, written by that person. *The Autobiography of Malcolm X* (Unit 3) is an example of an autobiography. *See* Biography *and* Memoir.

BALLAD. A **ballad** is a poem that tells a story and is written in four- to six-line stanzas, usually meant to be sung. Most ballads have regular rhythms and rhyme schemes and feature a refrain, or repetition of lines. The anonymous African-American song "John Henry" (Unit 8) is an example of a ballad.

BIAS. **Bias** is a personal judgment about something, or a mental leaning in one direction or another.

BIOGRAPHY. A **biography** is the story of a person's life, told by someone other than that person. Ann Petry's "Harriet Tubman: Conductor on the Underground Railroad" (Unit 3) is a biography. *See* Autobiography.

BLANK VERSE. **Blank verse** is unrhymed poetry with a rhythmic pattern known as iambic pentameter. Shakespeare used blank verse in his plays. *See* Meter.

CHARACTER. A **character** is an individual that takes part in the action of a literary work. A character is usually a person but may also be a personified plant, animal, object, or imaginary creature. The main character, or protagonist, has the central role in a work and is in conflict with the antagonist.

Characters can also be classified in other ways. *Major characters* play significant roles in a work, and *minor characters* play lesser roles. A *flat character* shows only one quality, or character trait. The grandfather and grandson in the folktale "The Old Grandfather and His Little Grandson" by Leo Tolstoy (Unit 2) are flat characters. A *round character* shows the multiple character traits of a real person. A *static character* does not change during the course of the action. A *dynamic character* does change.

CHARACTERIZATION. Characterization is the act of creating or describing a character. Writers create characters using three major techniques: showing what characters say, do, or think; showing what other characters say or think about them; and describing what physical features, dress, and personalities the characters display. The first two methods may be considered examples of *indirect characterization,* in which the writer *shows* what a character is like and allows the reader to judge the character. The third technique is considered *direct characterization,* in which the writer *tells* what the character is like. *See* Character.

CHORUS. In drama, a **chorus** is a group of actors who speak directly to the audience between scenes, commenting on the action of the play. In classical Greek drama, the chorus conveyed its message through a series of *odes,* or serious poems, which it sang throughout the play.

CHRONOLOGICAL ORDER. When telling a story in **chronological order,** the writer unfolds events in the order in which they occurred.

CLIMAX. The **climax** is the high point of interest and suspense in a literary work. The term also is sometimes used to describe the turning point of the action in a story or play, the point at which the rising action ends and the falling action begins. The climax in *Charles* by Shirley Jackson (Unit 1) occurs when Laurie's mother discovers there is no one named Charles in Laurie's class. *See* Plot.

COMEDY. A **comedy** is any lighthearted or humorous literary work with a happy ending, especially one prepared for the stage or the screen. Comedy is often contrasted with tragedy, in which the hero meets an unhappy fate. Comedies typically show characters with human limitations, faults, and misunderstandings. The action in a comedy usually progresses from initial order to a humorous misunderstanding or confusion and back to order again. Standard elements of comedy include mistaken identities, word play, satire, and exaggerated characters and events. *See* Tragedy.

CONFLICT. A **conflict** is a struggle between two forces in a literary work. A plot introduces a conflict, develops it, and eventually resolves it. There are two types of conflict: external and internal. In an *external conflict,* the main character struggles against another character, against the forces of nature, against society or social norms, or against fate. In an *internal conflict,* the main character struggles against some element within himself or herself. In Ray Bradbury's "The Drummer Boy of Shiloh" (Unit 1), the conflict is between the main character, a drummer boy, and his own doubts and fears on the night before the great Civil War Battle of Shiloh. *See* Plot.

CONNOTATION. The **connotation** of a word is the set of ideas or emotional associations it suggests, in addition to its actual meaning. For example, the word *inexpensive* has a positive connotation, whereas the word *cheap* has a negative connotation, even though both words refer to "low cost." *See* Denotation.

CONSONANCE. Consonance is a kind of rhyme in which the consonant sounds of two words match, but the preceding vowel sounds do not, as in the words *wind* and *sound.* The following line from Elinor Wylie's poem "Pretty Words" (Unit 5) provides an example:

> Words shy and dappled, deep-eyed deer in
> herds,

CONTEXT. The conditions under which a literary work occurs make up its **context.** Context is closely related to setting but focuses more on the environment of the time and place. Two common types of context include historical and cultural.

COUPLET. A **couplet** is two lines of verse that rhyme. These lines from Theodore Roethke's "The Bat" (Unit 6) provide an example:

> For something is amiss or out of place
> When mice with wings can wear a human
> face.

A *closed couplet* is a pair of rhyming lines that present a complete statement. A pair of rhyming iambic pentameter lines is also known as a *heroic couplet.*

DENOTATION. The **denotation** of a word is its dictionary meaning without any emotional associations. For example, the words *dirt* and *soil* share a common denotation. However, dirt has a negative connotation of uncleanliness, whereas soil does not. *See* Connotation.

DÉNOUEMENT. *See* Plot.

DESCRIPTION. A **description** is a picture in words. *Descriptive writing* is used to portray a character, an object, or a scene. Descriptions include *sensory details*—words and phrases that describe how things look, sound, smell, taste, or feel. In his poem "Casey at the Bat" (Unit 6), Ernest Lawrence Thayer appeals to the sense of hearing by describing the sound of cheering in the following manner:

> Then from the gladdened multitude went
>   up a joyous yell;
> It bounded from the mountaintop, and
>   rattled in the dell;
> It struck upon the hillside, and recoiled
>   upon the flat;
> For Casey, mighty Casey, was advancing to
>   the bat.

DIALECT. A **dialect** is a version of a language spoken by the people of a particular place, time, or social group. A *regional dialect* is one spoken in a particular place. A *social dialect* is one spoken by members of a particular social group or class. The following is an example of dialect from Eugenia Collier's short story "Sweet Potato Pie" (Unit 2):

> "I axed him did he know you. He say he
> was in your class last year."
> "Did you get his name?"
> "No, I didn't ax him that. Man he told me
> you were the best teacher he had. He said
> you were one smart cat!"

DIALOGUE. **Dialogue** is conversation between two or more people or characters. Plays are made up of dialogue and stage directions. Fictional works are made up of dialogue, narration, and description. When dialogue is included in fiction or nonfiction, the speaker's words are enclosed in quotation marks.

DICTION. **Diction,** when applied to writing, refers to the author's choice of words. Much of a writer's style is determined by his or her diction, the types of words that he or she chooses. *See* Style.

DRAMA. A **drama** is a story told through characters played by actors. Dramas are divided into segments called *acts.* The script of a drama is made up of dialogue spoken by the characters and stage directions. Because it is meant to be performed before an audience, drama features elements such as lighting, costumes, makeup, properties, set pieces, music, sound effects, and the movements and expressions of actors.

Two major types of drama are comedy and tragedy. *See* Comedy, Dialogue, Stage Directions, *and* Tragedy.

DRAMATIC IRONY. *See* Irony.

DRAMATIC MONOLOGUE. A **dramatic monologue** is a poem written in the form of a speech of a single character to an imaginary audience.

DRAMATIC POEM. A **dramatic poem** relies heavily on literary devices such as *monologue* (speech by a single character) or *dialogue* (conversation involving two or more characters). Often dramatic poems tell stories. Types of dramatic poetry include the dramatic monologue and the soliloquy. *See* Dramatic Monologue *and* Soliloquy.

EPIC. An **epic** is a long story, often told in verse, involving heroes and gods. Grand in length and scope, an epic provides a portrait of an entire culture, of the legends, beliefs, values, laws, arts, and ways of life of a people. *The Odyssey* and *Beowulf* are examples of epics.

EPIPHANY. An **epiphany** is a moment of sudden insight in which the nature of a person, thing, or situation is revealed.

ESSAY. An **essay** is a short nonfiction work that presents a single main idea, or *thesis,* about a particular topic.

- An *expository,* or *informative, essay* explores a topic with the goal of informing or enlightening the reader.
- A *persuasive essay* aims to persuade the reader to accept a certain point of view. Paul Rogat Loeb's "Soul of a Citizen" (Unit 3) is an example of a persuasive essay.
- A *personal essay* explores a topic related to the life or interests of the writer. Personal essays are characterized by an intimate and informal style or tone. For example, Elizabeth Wong's "The Struggle to Be an All-American Girl" (Unit 3) describes the difficulty of growing up in two cultures—Chinese and American.

EXPOSITION. In a plot, the **exposition** provides background information, often about the characters, setting, or conflict. Exposition is also another word for *expository writing,* the type of writing that aims to inform or explain. *See* Plot.

EXTENDED METAPHOR. An **extended metaphor** is a point-by-point presentation of one thing as though it were another. The description is meant as an implied comparison, inviting the reader to associate the thing being described with something that is quite different from it.

FABLE. Fables are brief stories, often with animal characters, told to express morals. Famous fables include those of Aesop and Jean de La Fontaine.

FALLING ACTION. *See* Plot.

FANTASY. A fantasy is a literary work that contains highly unrealistic elements. Included as fantasy are stories that resemble fairy tales, involve the supernatural, or have imaginary characters and settings. *See* Magical Realism *and* Science Fiction.

FAIRY TALES. Fairy tales are stories that deal with mischievous spirits and other supernatural occurrences, often in medieval settings.

FICTION. Fiction is any work of prose that tells an invented or imaginary story. The primary forms of fiction are the novel and the short story. *See* Novel *and* Short Story.

FIGURATIVE LANGUAGE. Figurative language is writing or speech meant to be understood imaginatively instead of literally. Many writers, especially poets, use figurative language to help readers to see things in new ways. Types of figurative language, or **figures of speech,** include *hyperbole, metaphor, personification, simile,* and *understatement.*

FIGURES OF SPEECH. *See* Figurative Language.

FLASHBACK. A flashback interrupts the chronological sequence of a literary work and presents an event that occurred earlier. Writers use flashbacks most often to provide background information about characters or situations. In the short story "Last Night" (Unit 1), Fae Myenne Ng's narrator introduces an episode that took place a week earlier. This flashback helps develop the relationship between the main characters and their landlady.

FOLK LITERATURE. Folk literature, or *folklore,* refers to a body of cultural knowledge and beliefs passed from one generation to the next, both orally and in writing. Much of folk literature originated as part of the *oral tradition,* or the passing of a work, an idea, or a custom by word of mouth from generation to generation.

FOLK SONG. Folk songs are traditional or composed songs typically made up of stanzas, a refrain, and a simple melody. A form of folk literature, folk songs are expressions of commonly shared ideas or feelings and may be narrative or lyric in style. "Yankee Doodle" is an example of a folk song.

FOLK TALE. A folk tale is a brief story passed by word of mouth from generation to generation. Types of folk tales include fairy tales, tall tales, parables, and fables. "María Sabida" (Unit 8) is an example of a Puerto Rican folk tale.

FOOT. *See* Meter.

FORESHADOWING. Foreshadowing is the act of presenting hints to events that will occur later in a story. In the ballad "John Henry" (Unit 8), the baby John Henry's words, "Lord, a hammer'll be the death of me, / Lord, a hammer'll be the death of me" foreshadow his contest to the death against a steam drill.

FREE VERSE. Free verse is poetry that does not use regular rhyme, meter, or stanza division. Free verse may contain irregular line breaks and sentence fragments and tends to mimic the rhythm of ordinary speech. Most contemporary poetry is written in free verse. "Grandma Ling" by Amy Ling (Unit 6) is an example of poem written in free verse.

GENRE. A genre (zhän′ rə) is a type or category of literary composition. Major genres of literature include fiction, nonfiction, poetry, and drama. *See* Drama, Fiction, Poetry, *and* Prose.

HAIKU. A haiku is a traditional Japanese three-line poem containing five syllables in the first line, seven in the second, and five again in the third. The syllable pattern is often lost when a haiku is translated into English. A haiku presents a single vivid image, often of nature or the seasons, intended to evoke in the reader a specific emotional or spiritual response.

HERO. A hero is a character whose actions are inspiring and courageous. In early literature, a hero was often part divine and had remarkable abilities, such as magical power, superhuman strength, or great courage. Pecos Bill in the tall tale of that name by Adrien Stoutenberg (Unit 8) is one such hero. In contemporary literature, the term *hero* often refers to any main character. Squeaky is the hero of Toni Cade Bambara's story "Raymond's Run" (Unit 1).

HYPERBOLE. A **hyperbole** (hī pür´ bə lē´) is an overstatement, or exaggeration, used for dramatic effect.

IAMB. *See* Meter.

IAMBIC PENTAMETER. *See* Meter.

IDIOM. An **idiom** is an expression that cannot be understood from the meanings of its separate words but must be learned as whole.

IMAGE. An **image** is a picture formed in the mind of a reader.

IMAGERY. **Imagery** is language that creates pictures by appealing to the senses of sight, sound, touch, taste, and smell. *See* Description *and* Figurative Language.

INFORMATIONAL TEXT. An **informational text** is a form of nonfiction that aims to convey or explain information. Examples of informational texts include reference materials, articles, editorials, and how-to writing.

IRONY. **Irony** is the difference between appearance and reality—in other words, what seems to be and what really is. Types of irony include the following: *dramatic irony,* in which something is known by the reader or audience but unknown to the characters; *verbal irony,* in which a character says one thing but means another; and *irony of situation,* in which an event occurs that violates the expectations of the characters, the reader, or the audience. Irony of situation occurs in Bailey White's "Good Housekeeping" (Unit 3), when Mama leaves a note to Bailey and Louise written with the typewriter the daughters were convinced should be thrown out.

LEGEND. A **legend** is a story that is passed down through generations and is often based on real events or characters from the past. Unlike myths, legends are usually considered to be historical; however, they may contain elements that are fantastic or unverifiable.

LYRIC POEM. A **lyric poem** is a highly musical type of poetry that expresses the emotions of a speaker. Lyric poems are often contrasted with narrative poems, which have storytelling as their main purpose. "I Was Born at the Wrong Time" by Angela Shelf Medearis (Unit 3) is a lyric poem. *See* Poetry.

MEMOIR. A **memoir** is a type of autobiography that focuses on one incident or period in a person's life. Memoirs are often based on a person's memories of, and reactions to, historical events. Chief Plenty-Coups's *Counting Coup on a Wounded Buffalo* (Unit 4) is a memoir about his coming of age. *See* Autobiography.

METAPHOR. A **metaphor** is a comparison in which one thing is spoken or written about as if it were another. This figure of speech invites the reader to make a comparison between the writer's actual subject, the *tenor* of the metaphor, and another thing to which the subject is likened, the *vehicle* of the metaphor. For example, in "Dreams" by Langston Hughes (Unit 5), the speaker uses a metaphor to compare life to a bird:

> Life is a broken-winged bird
> That cannot fly.

See Extended Metaphor *and* Figurative Language.

METER. **Meter** is a regular rhythmic pattern in poetry. This pattern is determined by the number of beats, or stresses, in each line. Stressed and unstressed syllables are divided into rhythmical units called *feet.* Feet commonly used in poetry are as follows:

Type of Foot	Stress Pattern	Example
iamb (iambic)	an unstressed syllable followed by a stressed syllable	in**sist**
trochee (trochaic)	a stressed syllable followed by an unstressed syllable	**free**dom
anapest (anapestic)	two unstressed syllables followed by one stressed syllable	unim-**pressed**
dactyl (dactylic)	one stressed syllable followed by two unstressed syllables	**fe**verish
spondee (spondaic)	two stressed syllables	**baseball**

Terms used to describe the number of feet in a line include the following:

> *monometer* for a one-foot line
> *dimeter* for a two-foot line
> *trimeter* for a three-foot line
> *tetrameter* for a four-foot line
> *pentameter* for a five-foot line
> *hexameter,* or Alexandrine, for a six-foot line
> *heptameter* for a seven-foot line
> *octameter* for an eight-foot line

A complete description of the meter of a line includes both the term for the type of foot used most often in the line and the term for the number of feet in the line. The most common meters are iambic tetrameter and iambic pentameter. The following are examples of each:

iambic tetrameter

⏑ / ⏑ / ⏑ / ⏑ /
O slow | ly, slow | ly rose | she up

iambic pentameter

⏑ / ⏑ / ⏑ / ⏑ / ⏑ /
The cur | few tolls | the knell | of part | ing day

MOOD. Mood, or atmosphere, is the emotion created in the reader by part or all of a literary work. The writer can evoke in the reader an emotional response—such as fear, discomfort, longing, or anticipation—by working carefully with descriptive language and sensory details. "The Drummer Boy of Shiloh" (Unit 1) has a solumn mood.

MORAL. A **moral** is a lesson that relates to the principles of right and wrong and is intended to be drawn from a story or other work of literature.

MOTIF. A **motif** is any element that appears in one or more works of literature or art. Examples of common folk tale motifs found in oral traditions throughout the world include the granting of three wishes, the trial or quest, and the magical metamorphosis, or transformation of one thing into another. "Cinderella," "The Ugly Duckling," and the Arthurian "Sword in the Stone" are examples of the transformation motif, in which persons or creatures of humble station are revealed to be exceptional. Much can be revealed about a literary work by studying the motifs within it.

MOTIVATION. A **motivation** is a force that moves a character to think, feel, or behave in a certain way. Gary, in "Gary Keillor" (Unit 1), is motivated by adolescent love and by longing for fame to recite a poem in a school talent show.

MYTH. A **myth** is a traditional story, rooted in a particular culture, that deals with gods, goddesses, and other supernatural beings, as well as human heroes. Myths often embody religious beliefs and values and explain natural phenomena. Every early culture around the globe has produced its own myths. "Coyote Steals the Sun and Moon" (Unit 8) is a Zuni myth.

NARRATION. Narration is a type of writing that tells a story or describes events.

NARRATIVE POEM. A **narrative poem** is one that tells a story. "Barbara Frietchie" by John Greenleaf Whittier (Unit 8) is an example of a narrative poem. *See* Poetry.

NARRATOR. A **narrator** is a character or speaker who tells a story. The writer's choice of narrator is important to the story and determines how much and what kind of information readers will be given about events and other characters. The narrator in a work of fiction may be a major or minor character or simply someone who witnessed or heard about the events being related. A *reliable narrator* gives a trustworthy account of events. An *unreliable narrator,* such as the one in "Gary Keillor" (Unit 1), cannot be trusted because he or she comments on and offers opinions about events. *See* Point of View *and* Speaker.

NONFICTION. Nonfiction writing explores real people's lives, places, things, events, and ideas. Essays, autobiographies, biographies, and news articles are all types of nonfiction. *See* Prose.

NOVEL. A **novel** is a long work of fiction. Often novels have involved plots, many characters, and numerous settings.

ODE. An **ode** is a poem to honor or praise someone or something. Pablo Neruda's lyric poem "Ode to my Socks" (Unit 6) is an example of an ode.

ONOMATOPOEIA. Onomatopoeia is the use of words or phrases that sound like the things to which they refer. Examples of onomatopoeia include words such as buzz, click, and pop. The word "hiss" is an example of onomatopoeia from Roberto Félix Salazar's lyric poem "The Other Pioneers" (Unit 5),

> Toward the hiss of Texas snake and Indian
>   yell.

ORAL TRADITION. The **oral tradition** is the passing of a work, an idea, or a custom by word of mouth from generation to generation. Common works found in the oral traditions of peoples around the world include folk tales, fables, fairy tales, tall tales, nursery rhymes, proverbs, legends, myths, parables, riddles, charms, spells, and ballads. *See* Folk Tale, Legend, Myth, *and* Parable.

PARABLE. A **parable** is a very brief story told to teach a moral lesson. The most famous parables are those told by Jesus in the Bible.

PARALLELISM. Parallelism is a rhetorical device in which a writer emphasizes the equal value or weight of two or more ideas by expressing them in the same grammatical form. *See* Rhetorical Device.

PERSONIFICATION. Personification is a figure of speech in which an animal, a thing, a force of nature, or an idea is described as if it were human or is given human characteristics. For example, Elinor Wylie writes in her poem "Pretty Words" that she loves words that are "up and singing early."

PERSUASION. Persuasion, or *persuasive writing,* is intended to change or influence the way a reader thinks or feels about a particular issue or idea.

PLOT. A **plot** is the series of events related to a central conflict, or struggle. A plot typically introduces a conflict, develops it, and eventually resolves it. A plot often contains the following elements, although it may not include all of them and they may not appear in precisely this order:

- The **exposition,** or introduction, sets the tone or mood, introduces the characters and setting, and provides necessary background information.
- The **rising action** is where the conflict is developed and intensified.
- The **climax** is the high point of interest or suspense.
- The **falling action** consists of all the events that follow the climax.
- The **resolution,** or dénouement (dā' nü män´), is the point at which the central conflict is ended, or resolved.

POETRY. Poetry is a major type of literature. It features imaginative and musical language carefully chosen and arranged to communicate experiences, thoughts, or emotions. It differs from prose in that it compresses meaning into fewer words and often uses meter, rhyme, and imagery. Poetry is usually arranged in lines and stanzas as opposed to sentences and paragraphs, and it can be more free in the ordering of words and the use of punctuation. Types of poetry include narrative, dramatic, and lyric. *See* Dramatic Poem, Lyric Poem, Meter, Narrative Poem, *and* Rhyme.

POINT OF VIEW. Point of view is the vantage point, or perspective, from which the story is told—in other words, who is telling the story. In **first-person** point of view, the story is told by someone who participates in or witnesses the action; this person, called the narrator, uses words such as *I* and *we* in telling the story. **Second-person** point of view uses the word *you* and addresses the reader directly, positioning the reader in the story. In **third-person** point of view, the narrator usually stands outside the action and observes; the narrator uses words such as *he, she, it,* and *they.* There are two types of third-person point of view: limited and omniscient. In *limited point of view,* the thoughts of only the narrator or a single character are revealed. In *omniscient point of view,* the thoughts of all the characters are revealed. Cynthia Rylant's story "Checkouts" (Unit 1) is told from a third-person omniscient point of view. *See* Narrator.

PRIMARY SOURCE. *See* Source.

PROPAGANDA. The intentional use of false arguments to persuade others is called **propaganda.** Propaganda most often appears in nonfiction. There are many types of propaganda:

- A **glittering generality** is a statement given to make something sound more appealing than it actually is.
- **Spin** is a technique of creating manipulative and misleading statements in order to slant public perception of the news.
- **Circular reasoning** is the error of trying to support an opinion by restating it in different words.
- Words that stir up strong feelings, both positive and negative, are called **loaded words.**
- **Bandwagon appeal** is a statement that plays to a person's desire to be part of the crowd—to be like everyone else and do what everyone else is doing.
- A **stereotype** is an overgeneralization about a group of people based on a lack of knowledge or experience.

PROSE. Prose is the broad term used to describe all writing that is not drama or poetry, including fiction and nonfiction. Types of prose writing include novels, short stories, essays, and news stories. Most biographies, autobiographies, and letters are written in prose.

PROSE POEM. A **prose poem** is a passage of prose that makes such extensive use of poetic language that the line between prose and poetry becomes blurred.

PROTAGONIST. A **protagonist** has the central role in a literary work. In O. Henry's "The Ransom of Red Chief" (Unit 2), the two con men are the protagonists and the nine-year-old boy they kidnap is their antagonist. *See* Antagonist.

PROVERBS. Proverbs, or *adages,* are traditional sayings, such as "You can lead a horse to water, but you can't make it drink."

PUN. A **pun** is a play on words involving two words that sound alike but have different meanings or a word with two or more meanings. "Paul Bunyan of the North Woods" by Carl Sandburg (Unit 8) contains several puns. One example is the line "This is only one of the hot-stove stories told in the North Woods. Here "hot-stove" refers to both the subject of the story (Benney, the blue ox ate a hot stove) and the kind of story—a story that was told while sitting around a hot stove or fire.

PURPOSE. A writer's **purpose** is his or her aim, or goal. People usually write with one or more of the following purposes: to inform or explain *(expository writing)*; to portray a person, place, object, or event *(descriptive writing)*; to convince people to accept a position and respond in some way *(persuasive writing)*; and to express thoughts or ideas, or to tell a story *(narrative writing)*.

QUATRAIN. A **quatrain** is a stanza of poetry containing four lines. *See* Stanza.

REFRAIN. A **refrain** is a line or group of lines repeated in a poem or song. Many ballads contain refrains.

REPETITION. **Repetition** is a writer's intentional reuse of a sound, word, phrase, or sentence. Writers often use repetition to emphasize ideas or, especially in poetry, to create a musical effect. *See* Rhetorical Device.

RESOLUTION. *See* Plot.

RHETORICAL DEVICE. A **rhetorical device** is a technique used by a speaker or writer to achieve a particular effect, especially to persuade or influence. Common rhetorical devices include parallelism, repetition, and rhetorical questions. *See* Parallelism, Repetition, *and* Rhetorical Question.

RHETORICAL QUESTION. A **rhetorical question** is a question asked for effect but not meant to be answered. In his essay "Soul of a Citizen" (Unit 3), Paul Rogat Loeb asks rhetorical questions:

> The 500 richest people on the planet now control more wealth than the poorest 3 billion, half the human population. Is it possible even to grasp this extraordinary imbalance? And, more important, how do we begin to redress it?

RHYME. **Rhyme** is the repetition of sounds in words. Types of rhyme include the following:

- *end rhyme* (the use of rhyming words at the ends of lines)
- *internal rhyme* (the use of rhyming words within lines)
- *exact rhyme* (in which the rhyming words end with the same sound or sounds, as in *moon* and *June*)
- *slant rhyme* (in which the rhyming sounds are similar but not identical, as in *rave* and *rove*)
- *sight rhyme* (in which the words are spelled similarly but pronounced differently, as in *lost* and *ghost* or *give* and *thrive*)

RHYME SCHEME. A **rhyme scheme** is the pattern of end rhymes designated by assigning a different letter of the alphabet to each rhyme. In the following verse from "The Naming of Cats" by T. S. Elliot (Unit 5), the rhyme scheme is *abab*.

> The Naming of Cats is a difficult matter,
> It isn't just one of your holiday games;
> You may think at first I'm as mad as a
>   hatter
> When I tell you, a cat must have THREE
> DIFFERENT NAMES.

RHYTHM. **Rhythm** is the pattern of beats, or stresses, in a line poetry. Rhythm can be regular or irregular. A regular rhythmic pattern in a poem is called a *meter*. *See* Meter.

RISING ACTION. *See* Plot.

ROMANCE. **Romance** is a term used to refer to the following four types of literature:

- medieval stories about the adventures and loves of knights
- novels and other fiction involving exotic locations and extraordinary or mysterious events and characters
- nonrealistic fiction in general
- in popular, modern usage, love stories of all kinds

SATIRE. **Satire** is humorous writing or speech intended to point out errors, falsehoods, foibles, or failings. It is written for the purpose of reforming human behavior or human institutions.

SCENE. A **scene** is a short section of a play that usually marks changes of time and place.

SCIENCE FICTION. **Science fiction** is highly imaginative fiction containing fantastic elements based on scientific principles, discoveries, or laws. Daniel Keyes's short story "Flowers for Algernon" (Unit 1) is an example of science fiction.

SENSORY DETAILS. *See* Description.

SESTET. *See* Stanza.

SETTING. The **setting** of a literary work is the time and place in which it occurs, together with all the details used to create a sense of a particular time and place. Writers create setting by various means. In drama, the setting is often revealed by the stage set and the costumes, though it may be revealed through what the characters say about their environs. In fiction, setting is most often revealed by means of description of such elements as landscape, scenery, buildings, furniture, clothing, the weather, and the season. It can also be revealed by how characters talk and behave. The setting of Walter Dean Myers's "The Treasure of Lemon Brown" (Unit 1) includes both the geographic location of New York's African-American Harlem neighborhood and the specific site of an abandoned tenement building.

SHORT STORY. A **short story** is a brief work of fiction. Short stories are typically crafted carefully to develop a plot, a conflict, characters, a setting, a mood, and a theme, all within relatively few pages. *See* Fiction *and* Genre.

SIMILE. A **simile** is a comparison of two seemingly unlike things using the word "like" or "as." Pablo Neruda uses this figure of speech in "Ode to my Socks" (Unit 6):

> my feet seemed to me
> unacceptable
> like two decrepit
> firemen, firemen
> unworthy
> of that woven
> fire,
> of those glowing
> socks.

SONNET. A **sonnet** is a fourteen-line poem, usually in iambic pentameter, that follows one of a number of different rhyme schemes. The *English, Elizabethan,* or *Shakespearean* sonnet is divided into four parts: three quatrains and a final couplet. The rhyme scheme of such a sonnet is *abab cdcd efef gg.* Shakespeare's "Shall I compare thee to a summer's day?" and Edna St. Vincent Millay's "I know I am but summer to your heart" (Unit 3) are examples. The *Italian* or *Petrarchan* sonnet is divided into two parts: an octave and a sestet. The rhyme scheme of the octave is *abbaabba.* The rhyme scheme of the sestet can be *cdecde, cdcdcd,*

or *cdedce.* Elinor Wylie's "Pretty Words" (Unit 5) is a Petrarchan sonnet. *See* Stanza *and* Rhyme Scheme.

SOURCE. A **source** is evidence of an event, an idea, or a development. A *primary source* is direct evidence, or proof that comes straight from those involved. Primary sources include official documents as well as firsthand accounts, such as diaries, letters, photographs, and paintings done by witnesses or participants.

SPEAKER. The **speaker** is the character who speaks in, or narrates, a poem—the voice assumed by the writer. The speaker and the writer of a poem are not necessarily the same person. The speaker in Leslie Marmon Silko's poem "Ceremony" (Unit 5) is a Native American storyteller. *See* Narrator.

SPEECH. A **speech** is a public address that was original delivered orally. "Our Struggle Is Against All Forms of Racism" (Unit 3) is an example of a speech by Nelson Mandela.

SPIRITUALS. **Spirituals** are religious songs from the African-American folk tradition. In "Harriet Tubman: Conductor on the Underground Railroad" (Unit 5), Ann Petry describes Harriet Tubman singing the spiritual "Go Down, Moses" to announce her presence in the slave quarters.

STAGE DIRECTIONS. **Stage directions** are notes included in a play, in addition to the dialogue, for the purpose of describing how something should be performed on stage. Stage directions describe setting, lighting, music, sound effects, entrances and exits, properties, and the movements of characters. They are usually printed in italics and enclosed in brackets or parentheses.

STANZA. A **stanza** is a group of lines in a poem. The following are some types of stanza:

two-line stanza	couplet
three-line stanza	triplet or tercet
four-line stanza	quatrain
five-line stanza	quintain or quintet
six-line stanza	sestet
seven-line stanza	septet
eight-line stanza	octave

STEREOTYPE. A **stereotype** is an overgeneralization about a group of people based on a lack of knowledge and experience. *See* Propaganda.

STYLE. **Style** is the manner in which something is said or written. A writer's style is characterized by such elements as word choice (or *diction*), sentence structure and length, and other recurring features that distinguish his or her work from that of another. One way to think of a writer's style is as his or her written personality.

SUSPENSE. **Suspense** is a feeling of expectation, anxiousness, or curiosity created by questions raised in the mind of a reader or viewer.

SYMBOL. A **symbol** is anything that stands for or represents both itself and something else. Writers use two types of symbols—conventional, and personal or idiosyncratic. A *conventional symbol* is one with traditional, widely recognized associations. Such symbols include doves for peace; the color green for jealousy; winter, evening, or night for old age; wind for change or inspiration. A *personal* or *idiosyncratic symbol* is one that assumes its secondary meaning because of the special use to which it is put by a writer. In Duane BigEagle's "The Journey" (Unit 1), the narrator's journey to Oklahoma symbolizes a passage into adulthood.

TALL TALE. A **tall tale** is a story, often lighthearted or humorous, that contains highly exaggerated, unrealistic elements. Stories about Paul Bunyan are tall tales.

TANKA. A **tanka** is a traditional Japanese poem consisting of five lines, with five syllables in the first and third lines and seven syllables in the other lines (5-7-5-7-7). The syllable pattern is often lost when a tanka is translated into English. Tanka uses imagery to evoke emotions in the reader, but its images are often more philosophical and less immediate than those in a haiku. *See* Haiku.

THEME. A **theme** is a central message or perception about life that is revealed through a literary work. Themes may be stated or implied. A *stated theme* is presented directly, whereas an *implied theme* must be inferred. Most works of fiction do not have a stated theme but rather several implied themes. A *universal theme* is a message about life that can be understood by people of most cultures. A stated theme of "Checkouts" by Cynthia Rylant (Unit 1) is that young people in love do not act rationally. An implied theme is that time heals the wounds of love—often quite rapidly.

THESIS. A **thesis** is a main idea that is supported in a work of nonfiction. The thesis of "Soul of a Citizen" by Paul Rogat Loeb is stated below:

There is no perfect time to get involved in social causes, no ideal circumstances for voicing our convictions. Instead, each of us faces a lifelong series of imperfect moments in which we must decide what to stand for.

TONE. **Tone** is the emotional attitude toward the reader or toward the subject implied by a literary work. Examples of the different tones that a work may have include familiar, ironic, playful, sarcastic, serious, and sincere. In the short story "Gary Keillor" (Unit 1), Garrison Keillor employs a humorous tone.

TRAGEDY. A **tragedy** is a work of literature, particularly a drama, that tells the story of the fall of a person of high status. It celebrates the courage and dignity of a tragic hero in the face of inevitable doom. Sometimes that doom is made inevitable by a tragic flaw. Today, the term *tragedy* is used more loosely to mean any work that has an unhappy ending. *The Diary of Anne Frank* (Unit 7) by Frances Goodrich and Albert Hackett is a tragedy. *See* Comedy, Tragic Hero, *and* Tragic Flaw.

TRAGIC FLAW. A **tragic flaw** is a weakness of personality that causes the tragic hero to make unfortunate choices.

TRAGIC HERO. A **tragic hero** is the main character in a tragedy.

TRICKSTER. The **trickster,** who is either an animal or a shape-shifter, is more than an annoyance to the mythical gods: He or she is often responsible for bringing important gifts to humanity, such as fire.

UNDERSTATEMENT. An **understatement** is an ironic statement that de-emphasizes something important. One example can be found in Carl Sandberg's "Paul Bunyan of the North Woods." After it rains "from St. Patrick's Day till the Fourth of July," Paul dives into Lake Superior, climbs a solid pillar of water, and stops the rain. Paul's words are, "I turned the thing off."

VOICE. **Voice** is the way a writer uses language to reflect his or her unique personality and attitude toward topic, form, and audience. A writer expresses voice through tone, word choice, or diction, and sentence structure. *See* Diction *and* Tone.

Vowel Sounds

a	h**a**t	i	s**i**t	ü	bl**ue**, st**ew**	ə	**e**xtra
ā	pl**ay**	ī	m**y**	oi	b**oy**		**u**nder
ä	st**ar**	ō	g**o**	ou	w**ow**		c**i**v**i**l
e	th**e**n	ô	p**aw**, b**or**n	u	**u**p		hon**o**r
ē	m**e**	ù	b**oo**k, p**u**t	ʉ	b**ur**n		bog**u**s

Consonant Sounds

b	**b**ut	j	**j**ump	p	**p**op	th	**th**e
ch	wa**tch**	k	bri**ck**	r	**r**od	v	**v**alley
d	**d**o	l	**l**ip	s	**s**ee	w	**w**ork
f	**f**udge	m	**m**oney	sh	**sh**e	y	**y**ell
g	**g**o	n	o**n**	t	si**t**	z	plea**s**ure
h	**h**ot	ŋ	so**ng**, si**nk**	th	wi**th**		

A

ad•e•quate (äd′ ə kwət) *adj.*, good enough

ad•ja•cent (ə jā′ sənt) *adj.*, next to; adjoining

ad•mir•a•tion (ad′ mə rā′ shun) *n.*, feeling of approval or deep respect

ad•mon•ish•ing•ly (ad mä′ ni shiŋ lē) *adv.*, in a scolding or disapproving way

ag•i•ta•ted (a′ jə tā′ tid) *adj.*, extremely disturbed; very upset

a•jar (ə jär′) *adj.*, slightly open

a•loft (ə lôft′) *adv.*, at or on a great height

al•ly (a′ lī′) *n.*, person who is helpful; friend

am•i•ca•bly (a′ mi kə blē) *adv.*, friendly in feeling; showing goodwill

a•nom•a•lous (ə nä′ mə ləs) *adj.*, strange, abnormal, or irregular

ap•pa•rition (a′ pə ri′ shən) *n.*, strange figure that appears suddenly

as•kew (ə skyü′) *adv.*, crookedly

au•dac•i•ty (ô das′ ə tē) *n.*, bold courage; daring

B

bar•ri•cade (ber′ ə kād′) *n.*, barrier

beck•on (be′ kən) *v.*, make a gesture to encourage someone to follow

ben•e•dic•tion (be nə dik′ shən) *n.*, blessing

be•nign (bi nīn′) *adj.*, harmless

be•quest (bē′ kwest) *n.*, gift or inheritance

be•wil•dered (be wil′ dʉrd) *adj.*, confused

bound (baund) *v.*, move by leaping

bra•zen (brā′ zən) *adj.*, bold and showing disregard for rules

buoy•ant (boi′ ənt) *adj.*, capable of floating

C

ca•pac•i•ty (kə pas′ ət ē) *n.*, ability, skill

cha•grin (shə grin′) *n.*, feeling of irritation or shame due to a disappointment about something

churn (churn) *v.*, move roughly

clar•i•ty (kler′ e tē) *n.*, the state of being clear

clus•tered (klas′ tərd) *adj.*, gathered together

col•lage (ko läzh′) *n.*, combination of different things

co•ma (kō′ mə) *n.*, long, and very deep state of unconsciousness caused by injury, disease, or poison

com•mand (kə mand′) *v.*, call to attention

com•mem•o•rate (kə me′ mə rāt′) *v.*, honor the memory of something or somebody in a ceremony

com•mune (kə myün′) *v.*, converse or talk together

com•pe•tent•ly (käm′ pə tənt lē) *adv.*, capably

com•po•si•tion (käm′ pə zi′ shun) *n.*, mixture containing many parts or materials

con•ceal•ment (kən sēl′ mənt) *n.*, hiding

con•ceive (kən sēv′) *v.*, form or develop in the mind

con•quer•ing (käŋ′ k[e]riŋ) *adj.*, strong and overpowering

con•spic•u•ous (kən spi′ kyə wəs) *adj.*, easily seen or noticed

cor•rob•o•rate (kə rä′ bə rāt′) *v.*, confirm; support with evidence

cow (kau) *v.*, destroy another's courage by intimidation

croon (krün) *v.*, sing or speak in a gentle manner

cy•clone (sī′ klōn) *n.*, violent rotating windstorm, like a tornado

D

dap•pled (dap′ p[ə]ld) *adj.*, spotted

de•crep•it (di kre′ pət) *adj.*, worn out; weakened by age or use

de•cry (de krī) *v.*, openly express strong disapproval of

de•fi•ance (di fī′ ən[t]s) *n.*, act or thoughts of rebellion, challenge, or a willingness to fight

de•fi•ant•ly (de fī′ ənt lē) *adv.*, showing resistance

deft•ly (def[t] lē) *adv.*, in a skillful and quick manner

deg•ra•da•tion (deg′ rə dā′ shən) *n.*, lowering of rank or state

de•lect•a•ble (di lək′ tə bəl) *adj.*, delicious

de•lir•i•um (di lir′ ē əm) *n.*, temporary mental condition marked by confusion, excitement, wild talk, and hallucinations

de•mean•or (di mē′ nor) *n.*, behavior toward others, outward manner

de•rive (di riv′) *v.*, get from a source

de•ter•mined (di tər′ mənd) *adj.*, not easily moved or changed

di•a•gram (dī′ ə gram) *n.*, chart or drawing that explains something

di•a•tribe (dī′ ə trīb) *n.*, angry and mean attack on a person's character

din•gy (din′ jē) *adj.*, dirty or discolored

dis•re•pute (dis′ ri pyüt′) *n.*, lack or decline of good reputation

doc•ile (dä′ səl) *adj.*, gentle; agreeable; obedient

dread•ful (dred′ fəl) *adj.*, causing terror or dread

dumb•found•ed (dəm′ faùnd′ əd) *adj.*, speechless with amazement; astonished

E

e•lab•o•rate•ly (i la′ b[ə] rət lē) *adv.*, involving many details; lengthy or exaggerated

e•lapse (i′ laps) *v.*, pass or go by, in the sense of time

e•ma•ci•ate (i mā′shē āt′) *v.*, cause to lose flesh and become very thin

em·broi·der (im broi´ dər) v., sew together with needlework; decorate with needlework

em·broi·der·y (im brôi´ d[ə] rē) n., decorative needlework on cloth

em·phat·i·cal·ly (im fa´ tik [ə] lē) adv., done or said in a strong way

en·clave (en´ klāv') n., distinct territorial, cultural, or social unit enclosed within a foreign territory

e·poch (e´ päk) n., unit of time; specifically, a unit of geologic time smaller than a period and larger than an age

er·a (er´ ə) n., unit of time; specifically, a unit of geologic time smaller than an eon and larger than a period

er·rat·ic (i ra´ tik) adj., irregular

ex·qui·site (ek skwi´ zət) adj., elegant or refined; pleasing because of beauty or perfection

F

fam·ished (fa´ misht) adj., extremely hungry

fa·tigue (fə tēg´) n., extreme weariness or exhaustion

flaunt (flont) v., display something boldy

flut·ter (flü tər´) v., move rapidly

fore·bod·ing (fôr bō´ diŋ) adj., prediction that something bad or harmful will happen

fore·sight (fôr´ sīt´) n., act or ability to see into the future with wisdom and knowledge

fu·tile·ly (fyu´ til lē) adv., having no useful result

G

gaunt (gônt) adj., thin and bony

ge·o·log·ic (jē´ ə lä jik) adj., relating to geology, the science that studies the origin, history, and structure of Earth

gild·ed (gild´ əd) adj., covered with a thin layer of gold

glim·mer (gli´ mər) v., emit a dim or flickering light

gnat (nät) n., small flying insect

grav·i·ty (gra´ və tē) n., seriousness, importance

ground·less (groun[d]´ ləs) adj., not justified; having no real basis

gui·dance (gi´ dəns) n., advice given to someone, often a student or child

H

hag·gard (ha´ gərd) adj., worn or wild in appearance; tired

haugh·ty (hô´ tē) adj., snobby or boastful

home·stead (hōm´ sted) n., house, especially a farmhouse, with adjoining buildings and land

hon·or·a·ble (ä´ nər [ə] bəl) adj., deserving of honor and respect

host (hōst) n., person who entertains guests

I

im·pli·ca·tion (im plə kā´ shən) n., something indicated indirectly, from which something can be inferred

im·plore (im plôr´) v., beg urgently

im·pro·vise (im´ prə vīz') v., make with materials easily at hand, usually to fulfill a sudden need

im·pu·dent (im pyʉ dənt) adj., offensively bold

im·pulse (im´ pəls') n., sudden force or action

in·ad·e·quate (in ad´ e kwət) adj., lacking in quality; not equal to what is required

in·ar·tic·u·late (i' när ti´ kyə lət) adj., incapable of speech, especially under the stress of strong emotions

in·cen·tive (in sen´ tiv) n., something that stimulates or encourages someone to take action

in·com·pre·hen·si·ble (in' käm' pri hen´ sə bəl) adj., impossible to understand

in·cul·cate (in kəl´ kāt) v., teach through frequent repetitions of something

in·dict·ed (in dī´ təd) v., accused or charged with a crime

in·ef·fa·ble (i ne´ fə bəl) adj., too awesome to be spoken

in·ef·fec·tu·al·ly (i' nə fek´ chə[wə] lē) adv., without success

in·fes·ta·tion (in' fes´ tā shən) n., invasion or troublesome spread of a harmful pest

in·flec·tion (in flek´ shən) n., change in pitch or tone of voice

in·fuse (in fyüs´) n., introduce gradually, cause to penetrate; instill

in·glo·ri·ous (in' glôr´ ē əs) adj., shameful; lacking fame or honor

in·scru·ta·ble (in skrü´ tə bəl) adj., extremely puzzling or mysterious

in·so·lent·ly (in s[e] ´ lent lē) adv., exhibiting boldness or contempt; insultingly

in·tent·ly (en tənt´ lē) adv., with firm concentration

in·ter·ces·sion (in' tər se´ shən) n., request, appeal, or prayer on behalf of another person

in·ti·mate (in´ tə mət) adj., marked by close association, familiarity, and warm friendship

in·tu·i·tion (in' tü i´ shən) n., feeling or sense about something that can't be logically explained

in·vol·un·tar·y (in vä´ lən ter ē) adj., done without conscious control

i·so·lat·ed (ī´ sə lā´ tid) adj., set apart from others

J

jo·vi·al (jō´ vē al) adj., jolly, merry

K

ki·mo·no (kə mō´ nō) n., long-sleeved robe traditionally worn by Japanese women

kin·ship (kin´ ship') n., very close relationship, as in a family or a group of people who share common opinions and outlooks

L

lace (lāce) n., delicate fabric

lag (lag) v., fall behind or fail to keep up with

le·git·i·mate·ly (li ji´ tə mət lē) adv., conforming to laws, rules, or accepted standards

lum·ber (lʌm´ bər) v., move slowly

lu·mi·nous (lü´ mə nəs) adj., shiny; glowing; bright

M

mag·ni·tude (mag´ nə tüd') n., great size or importance

ma·neu·ver (mə nü´ vər) v., make a series of changes in direction and position for a specific purpose

ma·tron·ly (mä´ trʌn lē) adv., relating to a mature married woman

mea·ger (mē´ gər) adj., lacking in quantity or quality

mem·o·ra·bil·i·a (me´ mə rə bi' lē ə) n. pl., things tied to past events that are worth remembering

mi·gra·tion (mī grä´ shun) n., movement from one location to another.

mind·ful (mīn[d] ´ fəl) adj., bearing in mind; aware

moor·ing (môr´ iŋ) n., device (such as a chain, rope, or anchor) that secures a boat or ship in place

mor·tal (môr´ tl) n., human being (as opposed to a god)

muf·fled (mə´ fəld) adj., wrapped or padded with thick material to keep out sound

mul·ti·tude (məl tə´ tüd') n., large quantity

N

nau•se•a (no´ zē ə) *n.,* feeling that one is about to vomit

nim•bly (nim´ blē) *adv.,* quickly and carefully

nu•ance (nü´ än[t]s) *n.,* slight difference or variation

O

o•men (ō´ mən) *n.,* sign or warning

or•i•en•teer (ôr´ ē en tēr´) *n.,* person who takes part in a running sport with directions and maps

os•ten•ta•tious•ly (äs' tən tā´ shəs lē) *adv.,* in a showy way; overly proudly or boastfully

P

pan•de•mo•ni•um (pan də mō´ nē əm) *n.,* chaos or confusion

path•o•log•i•cal (pa´ thə lä' ji kəl) *adj.,* caused by disease or the origins of disease

per•i•od (pir´ ē əd) *n.,* unit of time; specifically, a unit of geologic time smaller than an era and larger than an epoch

per•pe•tra•tor (pər pə trāt´ ər) *n.,* criminal; person who commits harmful or illegal acts

per•pe•tu•i•ty (pʉr' pə tü´ ə tē) *n.,* condition of lasting for eternity

per•sist•ent•ly (per sis´ tənt lē) *adv.,* repeatedly

per•vade (pər vād´) *v.,* be present everywhere

phase (fāz) *n.,* part of a cycle

plain•tive (plān´ tiv) *adj.,* sounding slightly sad

plume (plüm) *n.,* feather

pomp (pämp) *n.,* show of magnificence; splendor

por•ce•lain (por´ s[ə] lən) *adj.,* made of a hard ceramic, like china

pred•i•cat•ed (pred´ ə kāt id) *adj.,* affirmed, or based on given facts or conditions

prem•is•es (pre´ məs əs) *pl. n.,* area of land; grounds

pre•vail (pri vāl´) *v.,* succeed or win out in spite of difficulties

pro•lif•er•a•tion (prə li´ fə rā´ shən) *n.,* growth or increase

pro•logue (prō´ lòg) *n.,* preface, introduction

proph•e•cy (präf´ ə sē) *n.,* prediction of something to come

pro•tes•ta•tion (prä´ təs tā' shən) *n.,* strong expression of dissent

pul•sate (pʉl´ sāt) *v.,* throb rhythmically

pul•ver•ize (pəl´ və rīz) *v.,* crush into a powder or dust; demolish

pur•suit (pər süt´) *n.,* act of chasing or pursuing

Q

quiv•er•ing (kwiv´ ə riŋ) *adj.,* shaking with small rapid movements

R

ra•di•us (rā´ dē us) *n.,* circular area

raf•ter (raf´ tər) *n.,* ceiling beam

rav•age (rav´ ij) *v.,* ruin, destroy; commit destructive acts

re•coil (ri koi[e]l´) *v.,* spring back

ref•uge (re´ fyüj) *n.,* shelter or protection from danger or difficulty

re•morse (ri môrs´) *n.,* regret

re•mote (ri mōt´) *adj.,* distant

re•proach (ri prōch´) *v.,* criticize; blame

res•o•lute (re´ ze lüt) *adj.,* having or showing a fixed, firm purpose

re•splend•ent (ri splen´ dənt) *adj.,* splendid or dazzling to look at

re•treat (ri trēt´) *v.,* withdraw; back off

ro•bust (rō bʉst´) *adj.,* strong and healthy

rouse (rauz) *v.,* stir up, as to anger or action

S

sa•cred (sā´ krəd) *adj.,* believed to be holy; worthy of deep respect

sal•low (sa´ lō) *adj.,* having a yellowish, sickly color

saun•ter (son´ tər) *v.,* walk in a leisurely way

scorned (skôrnd) *adj.,* treated with disrespect; rejected as unworthy

seize (sēz) *v.,* grasp suddenly and forcefully

sen•sa•tion (sen sā´ shun) *n.,* feeling

se•rene•ly (sə rēn lē) *adv.,* calmly

shade (shād) *n.,* darkness

shanty (shan´ tē) *n.,* shack, hut

sheen (shēn) *n.,* glow

sheep•ish•ly (shē´ pish lē) *adv.,* in an awkwardly, shy, or embarrassed manner

shriv•el (shri´ vəl) *v.,* become smaller in size because of dryness

smol•der (smōl´ dər) *v.,* burn with little smoke and no flame

sol•i•dar•i•ty (sä´ lə da' rə tē) *n.,* complete unity and agreement within a group regarding opinions, purposes, goals, and feelings

sol•i•tar•y (sä´ lə ter ē) *adj.,* being alone or isolated

som•ber (säm´ bər) *adj.,* dark and gloomy

sparse•ly (spärs´ lē) *adv.,* thinly; not full or densely

spec•i•men (spes´ ə mən) *n.,* item which is part of a scientific grouping

sti•fled (sti´ fəld) *adj.,* held back; smothered

stoop (stüp) *n.,* front steps or entrance

strag•gle (stra´ gəl) *v.,* follow slowly behind; wander or stray

strewn (strün) *adj.,* spread about here and there as by sprinkling

strick•en (stri´ kən) *adj.,* affected with strong emotions

suf•fi•cient (sə fi´ shənt) *adj.,* as much as is needed; enough

sway (swā) *v.,* swing back and forth

sym•met•ri•cal (sə me´ tri kəl) *adj.,* evenly balanced

T

taut (tot) *adj.,* tense, tight

te•di•ous (tē dē´ əs) *adj.,* tiring and boring

teem•ing (tē´ miŋ) *adj.,* being very full of

ten•dril (ten´ drəl) *n.,* slender spiral shoot of a climbing vine that attaches the vine to its support; anything looking like a tendril

ten•ta•tive•ly (ten´ tə tiv lē) *adv.,* in an uncertain or hesitant way

ter•rain (ter´ ān) *n.,* landscape

trans•par•ent (tränz per´ ənt) *adj.,* see-through

tread (tred) *n.,* footsteps, or the sound of footsteps

tuft (təft) *n.,* small cluster of longer, grown-out hair

tu•mult (tü´ məlt') *n.,* loud noise and confusion

tu•tor•i•al (tü tôr´ ē əl) *n.,* instruction in how to do something

U

un•seem•ly (un sēm´ lē) *adv.,* not decent or proper

un•wont•ed (ən wôn´ təd) *adj.,* rare, unusual

V

ver•i•ta•ble (ver´ ə tə bəl) *adj.,* being in fact the thing named; not false or imaginary

ver•mil•ion (vər mil' yən) *adj.,* bright red or scarlet

vex (veks) *v.,* bother; trouble

vi•brant (vī´ brənt) *adj.,* bright; energetic; alive-looking

W

wear•i•ly (wir´ ə lē) *adv.,* in an exhausted way

Miriam Altshular Literary Agency. "The Treasure of Lemon Brown" from *Boy's Life Magazine,* March 1983 by Walter Dean Myers. Copyright © 1983 by Walter Dean Myers. Reprinted by Miriam Altshuler Literary Agency, on behalf of Walter Dean Myers.

American Heritage Publishing. "Indian Cattle" from *Indians of the Plains* by Eugene Rachlis. Copyright © 1960 by American Heritage Publishing Company, Inc. Reprinted by permission of American Heritage Publishing.

Arté Publico Press. "Exile" by Judith Ortiz Cofer. Reprinted by permission of Arte Publico Press. "Maria Sabida" from *Tales Told Under the Mango Tree* by Judith Ortiz Cofer. Reprinted by permission of Arte Publico Press.

Duane BigEagle. "The Journey" by Duane BigEagle from *Earth Power Coming: Short Fiction in Native American Literature.* Reprinted by permission of the author.

Robert Bly. "Ode to My Socks" from *Neruda and Vallejo: Selected Poems* by Pablo Neruda, translated by Robert Bly. Reprinted by permission of Robert Bly.

BOA Editions, Ltd. "I Ask My Mother To Sing" from *Rose* by Li-Young Lee. Reprinted by permission of BOA Editions, Ltd.

Walker Brents. "The Tale of Annie Christmas" retold by Walker Brents. Reprinted by permission of the author.

Candlewick Press. OUTLAW: THE LEGEND OF ROBIN HOOD. Text copyright © 2009 by Tony Lee. Illustrations copyright © 2009 by Sam Hart. Reproduced by permission of the publisher, Candlewick Press, Somerville, MA on behalf of Walker Books, London.

Carmen Balcells Literary Agency. "Oda a los calcetines" from *Odas Elementales* by Pablo Neruda. Copyright © Fundacion Pablo Neruda, 2007. Reprinted by permission of Agencia Literaria Carmen Balcells S.A.

Curtis Brown, Ltd. "At the Library" from *It's Raining Laughter.* Copyright © 1997 by Nikki Grimes. Reprinted by permission of Curtis Brown, Ltd.

Chronicle Books. "Oranges" from *New and Selected Poems* by Gary Soto. Reprinted by permission of Chronicle Books.

Eugenia Collier. "Sweet Potato Pie" by Eugenia Collier from *Black World,* August 1972. Reprinted by permission of the author.

Don Congdon Associates. "The Drummer Boy of Shiloh" by Ray Bradbury. Copyright © 1960 by Curtis Publishing Company, renewed 1988 by Ray Bradbury. Reprinted by permission of Don Congdon Associates, Inc.

Donadio & Olson, Inc. "Last Night" by Fae Myenne Ng from *City Lights Review.* Copyright 1987 Fae Myenne Ng. Reprinted by permission of Donadio & Olson, Inc.

Rita Dove. "The First Book" from *On the Bus with Rosa Parks* by Rita Dove. Published by W. W. Norton & Co., Inc. Copyright © 1999 by Rita Dove. Reprinted by permission of the author.

Dramatic Publishing. From *A Woman Called Truth* by Sandra Fenichel Ashner. Reprinted by permission of Dramatic Publishing

Exile Editions. An excerpt from *Luke Baldwin's Vow* by Morley Callaghan. Reprinted by permission of Exile Editions.

Farrar, Straus and Giroux, LLC. Excerpt from *All But My Life* by Gerda Weissmann Klein. Copyright © 1957 and copyright renewed 1995 by Gerda Weissmann Klein. Reprinted by permission of Farrar, Straus & Giroux, LLC. "Bats" from *The Complete Poems* by Randall Jarrell. Copyright © 1969, renewed 1997 by Mary von S. Jarrell. Reprinted by permission of Farrar, Straus & Giroux, LLC. "Charles" from *The Lottery* by Shirley Jackson. Reprinted by permission of Farrar, Straus & Giroux, LLC.

Fitzhenry and Whiteside Publishing. "Be-ers and Doers" from *The Leaving and Other Stories.* Copyright © 1990 by Budge Wilson. Reprinted by permission of Fitzhenry and Whiteside Publishing.

Fulcrum Publishing. "Legend of the Feathered Serpent" from *The Eagle and the Rainbow: Timeless Tales from Mexico* by Antonio Hernandez Madrigal. Reprinted by permission of Fulcrum Publishing.

imprint of Scholastic Inc. "Checkouts" from *A Couple of Kooks and Other Stories about Love* by Cynthia Rylant. Copyright © 1990 by Cynthia Rylant. Reprinted by permission of Orchard Books, an imprint of Scholastic Inc. From *If You Could Be My Friend: Letters of Mervet Akram Sha'ban and Galit Fink* presented by Litsa Boudalika. Copyright © 1992 by Gallimard Publications. Translation copyright © 1998 by Orchard Books, New York. Reprinted by permission of Orchard Books, an imprint of Scholastic Inc.

Simon & Schuster, Inc. "A Mother in Mannville" from *When the Whippoorwill* by Marjorie Kinnan Rawlings. Copyright © 1936, 1940 by Marjorie Kinnan Rawlings; copyright renewed © 1964, 1968 by Norton Baskin. All rights reserved. "Epiphany: The Third Gift" by Lucha Corpi. Copyright © 1992 by Lucha Corpi. Reprinted by permission of Simon & Schuster, Inc. "The Grandfather and His Little Grandson" from *Twenty-Two Russian Tales for Young Children* by Leo Tolstoy, translated by Miriam Morton, English translation copyright © 1969 by Miriam Morton. Reprinted by permission of Simon & Schuster, Inc.

Virginia Driving Hawk Sneve. "The Medicine Bag" by Virginia Driving Hawk Sneve, published in *Boy's Life*, March 1975. Reprinted by permission of the author.

The Estate of William Stafford. An Excerpt from "The Osage Orange Tree" from *The Oregon Centennial Anthology* by William Stafford. Copyright © 1959 by William Stafford. Reprinted by permission of The Estate of William Stafford.

Literary Estate of May Swenson. "Southbound on the Freeway" from *The Complete Poems to Solve* by May Swenson. Reprinted by permission of Literary Estate of May Swensen.

University of California, Los Angeles. "Miss Butterfly" from *Chauvinist and Other Stories* by Toshio Mori. Reprinted by permission of UCLA Asian American Studies Center.

University of Illinois Press. "John Henry" from *Long Steel Rail: The Railroad in American Folksong* transcribed by Norm Cohen. Copyright © 2000 by Board of Trustees. Used with permission of the University of Illinois Press.

University of New Mexico Press. "The Souls in Purgatory" from *Voces; An Anthology of Nuevo Mexicano Writers* edited by Rudolfo Anaya. Reprinted by permission of University of New Mexico Press.

University of Oklahoma Press. From "Do not ask us to give up the buffalo for the sheep" by Chief Ten Bears from *Indian Oratory: Famous Speeches by Noted Indian Chiefs*. Reprinted by permission of University of Okhahoma Press.

University of Washington Press. "My Mother Juggling Bean Bags" from *From a Three-Cornered World* by James Mitsui. Reprinted by permission of University of Washington Press.

The Estate of Jose Garcia Villa. "Lyric 17" from *Have Come, Here Now* by Jose Garcia Villa. Reprinted by permission of John Edwin Cowen, literary agent.

Writers and Artists Agency, Inc. "The Struggle to Be an All-American Girl" by Elizabeth Wong. Reprinted by permission of Writers and Artists Agency, Inc.

The Wylie Agency. "The Time We Climbed Snake Mountain" from *Yellow Woman* by Leslie Marmon Silko. Copyright © 1981 by Leslie Marmon Silko, reprinted by permission of The Wylie Agency, Inc.

Art and Photo Credits

Cover (top left) © Images.com/CORBIS; (top right) Photo by foureyes (http://www.photo.net/photos/foureyes) copyright 2003; (bottom left) © Don Hammond/Design Pics/CORBIS (bottom right) © George H. H. Huey/CORBIS; **i:** Photo by foureyes (http://www.photo.net/photos/foureyes) copyright 2003; **iii** (top left) © Images.com/CORBIS; (top right) Photo by foureyes (http://www.photo.net/photos/foureyes) copyright 2003; (bottom left) © Don Hammond/Design Pics/CORBIS (bottom right) © George H. H. Huey/CORBIS; **viii** (top and middle right) Jupiter Unlimited; (middle full column and bottom) Jupiter Images; **ix** (top) Tom Jenz/ Jupiter Images; (middle) Jupiter Unlimited; (bottom left) © Lowell Georgia/CORBIS; (bottom right) Jupiter Images; **x** (top) © plainpicture/Klietz, T./Jupiter Images; (middle) © William Gottlieb/CORBIS; **xi** (top) Jupiter Images; (middle) iStockphoto; (bottom) Image Source; **xii** (top) Jupiter Unlimited; (middle) iStockphoto; (bottom) © SuperStock, Inc./SuperStock; **xiii** (top) © Tom Till/Alamy; (middle) PhotoDisc; (bottom) iStockphoto; **xiv** (top left and middle right) Jupiter Unlimited; (top right) PhotoDisc; (bottom) iStockphoto; **xv** (top) Nik Wheeler/CORBIS; (middle) Getty Images; (bottom) Jupiter Images; **xvi** (top and bottom) Jupiter Images; (middle) © Jerome Minet/Kipa/CORBIS; **xvii** (top) PhotoDisc; (middle) Jupiter Images; (bottom) Shutterstock; **xviii** Jupiter Unlimited; **xix** (top) Jupiter Unlimited; (middle) Jupiter Images; (bottom) Image Source; **xx** (top) Jupiter Unlimited; (middle left) PhotoDisc; **xxi** (top) © OscarWhite/CORBIS; (middle left) Jupiter Images; (middle right) Jupiter Unlimited; (bottom) © Stuart Abraham/Alamy; **xxii** (top) PhotoDisc; (middle left) © Hulton-Deutsch Collection/CORBIS (middle right) Shutterstock; (bottom) The Picture Desk; **xxiii** (top) Media Bakery; (middle and bottom) Jupiter Unlimited; **xiv** (top) Jupiter Unlimited; **xxv** (top and lower middle) Jupiter Unlimited; (upper middle) Jupiter Images; (bottom) © Lowell Georgia/CORBIS

Unit 1

2 (top) *The Journey,* 2002 (w/c on paper), Bootman, Colin (Contemporary Artist)/Private Collection/The Bridgeman Art Library; (bottom left) Courtesy of Cynthia Rylant; (bottom middle) Courtesy of Gary Soto; (bottom right) © Eddie Adams/Sygma/CORBIS;

3 (top) © William A. Bake/CORBIS; (bottom left) AP Images; (bottom middle) Ulf Andersen/Getty Images; (bottom right) Time & Life Pictures/Getty Images; **4** Jupiter Unlimited; **5** © Jochen Tack/Alamy; **6** © Magnus Rietz/Jupiter Images; **7** Courtesy of Library of Congress; **9** AP Images; **10** Jupiter Unlimited; **12** © plainpicture/Klietz, T./Jupiter Images; **14** Photodisc; **16** Jupiter Unlimited; **17** Photodisc; **18** Courtesy Library of Congress; **19** Courtesy of The Anacostia Museum Archives Smithsonian Institution; **20** *The Journey,* 2002 (w/c on paper), Bootman, Colin (Contemporary Artist)/Private Collection/The Bridgeman Art Library; **22** © Jochen Tack/Alamy; **27** © Michael Ochs Archives/CORBIS; **28** Photodisc; **32** Jupiter Unlimited; **33** Time & Life Pictures/Getty Images; **34** © William A. Bake/CORBIS; **36** (top) © CORBIS; **36—43** (bottom) Jupiter Unlimited; **46** Courtesy of Duane BigEagle; **47** © Christie's Images/CORBIS; **49** © Lindsay Hebberd/CORBIS; **50—51** Jupiter Images; **54** © Ulf Andersen/Getty Images; **55** National Archives NARA; **56—57** Courtesy of Library of Congress; **61** Jupiter Unlimited; **63** © Eddie Adams/Sygma/CORBIS; **64** (top) © Lake County Museum/CORBIS; **64—65** (bottom) Jupiter Unlimited; **67** © William Gottlieb/CORBIS; **71** © John Springer Collection/CORBIS; **72** Jupiter Unlimited; **74** (top) Courtesy of Library of Congress; (bottom) PhotoDisc; **78** (top) Courtesy of Cynthia Rylant; (bottom) Courtesy of Gary Soto; **79** iStockphoto; **80** © Geoffrey Clements/CORBIS; **81, 82** PhotoDisc; **84** (top) © Todd Gipstein/CORBIS; (bottom) PhotoDisc; **86** Courtesy of Jerry Bauer; **87** © Morton Beebe/CORBIS; **89** Jupiter Unlimited; **91** Image Source; **92** © Bettmann/CORBIS; **96** (bottom) © William J. Weber; **96, 97** Royalty-Free/CORBIS; **98** Jupiter Unlimited; **101** © Images.com/CORBIS; **102** © Alice Attie/Jupiter Images; **104** Jupiter Unlimited; **106** iStockphoto; **107** Jupiter Unlimited; **108—109** Jupiter Unlimited; **111** Jupiter Unlimited; **112** Jupiter Unlimited; **114—115** Jupiter Unlimited; **116** iStockphoto; **118, 119** Jupiter Unlimited; **120** iStockphoto; **122, 125, 127** Jupiter Unlimited; **129** Jacket Cover from *The Outside Shot* by Walter Dean Myers. Used by permission of Random House Children's Books, a division of Random House, Inc.; Jacket Cover from *Dandelion Wine* by Ray Bradbury. Copyright © 1957 by Ray Bradbury. Reprinted by permission; Book cover from *Missing May* by Cynthia Rylant. Reprinted by permission of Orchard Books, an imprint of Scholastic

Inc.; Cover from *A Tree Grows in Brooklyn* by Betty Smith. Copyright © 1947 by Betty Smith. Reprinted by permission; Jacket Cover from *Tunes for Bears to Dance to* by Robert Cormier. Copyright © 1992 by Robert Cormier. Used by permission of Dell Publishing, a division of Random House, Inc.; Jacket Cover from *Siddhartha* by Herman Hesse. Used by permission of Bantam Books, a division of Random House, Inc.; **130** (left) Shutterstock; (right) Getty Images; **131** Jupiter Unlimited; **136** Eileen Ryan Photography.

Unit 2

142 (top) © Tom Till/Alamy; (bottom left) Courtesy of Library of Congress; (bottom middle) Courtesy of Eugenia Collier; (bottom right) Courtesy of AP Images; **143** (top) *Ogalalla Sioux 'Indian Scout' Sioux* (oil on canvas), Sharp, Joseph Henry (1859–1953)/© Butler Institute of American Art, Youngstown, OH, USA, Museum Purchase 1913/The Bridgeman Art Library; (bottom left) Courtesy of Gary Soto; (bottom middle) Courtesy of Library of Congress; (bottom right) Courtesy of Helga Hoel; **144** (top) © Robert Millman/CORBIS; (bottom) © Karl Weatherly/CORBIS; **145** Courtesy of Library of Congress; **146** Image Source; **147** Jupiter Unlimited; **149** © Francis G. Mayer/CORBIS; **151** Jupiter Royalty Free; **153** © Blue Lantern Studio/CORBIS; **154** Courtesy of Gary Soto; **155** © David Turnley/CORBIS; **157** © Jupiter Images; **159, 160** © Jupiter Images; **164** Jupiter Unlimited; **168** Courtesy of Eugenia Collier; **169** Smithsonian American Art Museum, Washington, DC/Art Resource, NY; **170–171** Jupiter Images; **173** Smithsonian American Art Museum, Washington, DC/Art Resource, NY; **174, 177** iStockphoto; **180** © Heyday Books; **181** © Blaine Harrington III/Alamy; **182** © Jupiter Images; **183** © John Kershaw/Alamy; **185, 186** iStockphoto; **188** Courtesy of Library of Congress; **189** (top) iStockphoto; (bottom) RHI Films; **192** Jupiter Images; **200** AP Images; **201, 202, 203, 205** Jupiter Unlimited; **206** © Kevin Fleming/CORBIS; **208** PhotoDisc; **209** © SuperStock, Inc./SuperStock; **211** (top) Courtesy of Helga Hoel; (bottom) Courtesy of Library of Congress; **212** *Ogalalla Sioux 'Indian Scout' Sioux* (oil on canvas), Sharp, Joseph Henry (1859–1953)/© Butler Institute of American Art, Youngstown, OH, USA, Museum Purchase 1913/The Bridgeman Art Library; **213** iStockphoto; **217** © Brooklyn Museum/CORBIS; **218** iStockphoto; **220** *An old man and his dog seated by a road side,* Landseer, Sir Edwin (1802–1873)/Private Collection, Photo © Christie's Images/The Bridgeman Art Library; **222** Getty Images; **223** © Copyright Irinaland ueber dem Balkan—*Irinaland over the Balkans.* Mixed technique on aluminum foil (1966). Private Collection, Vienna, Austria; **225** Jupiter Unlimited; **229** Getty Images; **232** PhotoDisc; **238** Jupiter Unlimited; **240** AP Images; **244** (top) *An Autumn Day at the Farm,* 1919 (oil on canvas), Waite, Edward Wilkins (1864–1924)/Private Collection/The Bridgeman Art Library; (bottom) AP Images; **249** *Companions,* Charles, James (1851–1906)/© Gallery Oldham, UK/The Bridgeman Art Library; **250** *On a Sussex Farm,* Charles, James (1851–1906)/© Warrington Museum and Art Gallery, Cheshire, UK/The Bridgeman Art Library; **254** © Tom Till/Alamy; **256–257, 259, 262** (left) Jupiter Unlimited; **261** Jacket Cover from *The Face on the Milk Carton* by Caroline B. Cooney. Used by permission of Bantam Books, a division of Random House, Inc.; Book cover from *Nothing But the Truth* by Avi. Jacket Art © 1991 by Peter Catalanotto. Reprinted by permission of Orchard Books, an imprint of Scholastic Inc.; Cover from *Dragon's Gate* by Lawrence Yep. Copyright © 1993 by Lawrence Yep. Used with permission of HarperCollins Publishers; Cover from *Under the Baseball Moon* by John H. Ritter. Copyright © 2006 by John H. Ritter. Reprinted by permission; Cover from *So Yesterday* by Scott Westerfield. Copyright © 2005 by Scott Westerfield. Reprinted by permission; *The Watcher* by James Howe. Reprinted by permission of Betsy Imershien; **262** (right) Courtesy of Gary Soto; **263** Jupiter Unlimited; **266** AP Images; **270** Eileen Ryan Photography.

Unit 3

276 (top) Getty Images; (bottom left) © Mitchell Gerber/CORBIS; (bottom middle) © Paul Bishop, Jr.; (bottom right) Courtesy of Lucha Corpi; **277** (top) *Little Girl with her Doll* (oil on canvas), Puy, Jean (1876–1960)/Musee Antoine Lecuyer, Saint-Quentin, France, © DACS/The Bridgeman Art Library; (bottom left) Getty Images; (bottom middle) Courtesy of Ruth T. Wong; (bottom right) © Hans Gedda/Sygma/CORBIS; **278** Getty Images; **279** Jupiter Unlimited; **281** (top) Shutterstock; (bottom) © Mitchell Gerber/CORBIS; **282** © Hyacinth Manning /SuperStock; **284, 286** Jupiter Unlimited; **290** Paul Bishop, Jr.; **291** Bancroft Library; **293** AP Images; **296** PhotoDisc;

299 Media Bakery; **301** Media Bakery; **302** Courtesy of New Georgia Encyclopedia; **303** Jupiter Images; **304** iStockphoto; **306** Jupiter Images; **310** Jupiter Unlimited; **312** Courtesy of Paul Rogat Loeb; **313** © Wally McNamee/CORBIS; **322** © Bettmann/CORBIS; **325** Courtesy of Lucha Corpi; **326** *Little Girl with her Doll* (oil on canvas), Puy, Jean (1876–1960)/Musee Antoine Lecuyer, Saint-Quentin, France, © DACS/The Bridgeman Art Library; **329** *The Princess consulting the bird Bulbulhezar,* illustration for 'The Two Jealous Sisters,' from *The Arabian Nights,* 1939 (colour engraving), Broders, Roger (1883–1953)/Private Collection, © DACS/Roger Perrin/The Bridgeman Art Library; **330** © Lili K./zefa/CORBIS; **335** Courtesy of Ruth T. Wong; **336** © Nik Wheeler/CORBIS; **338** Shutterstock; **342** © Bettmann/CORBIS; **344** Courtesy of Library of Congress; **347** (top) AP Images; (bottom) © Hans Gedda/Sygma/CORBIS; **348–349** The Jacob and Gwendolyn Lawrence Foundation/Art Resource, NY; **350–351** © Bettmann/CORBIS; **351** (background) iStockphoto; **354** © Contemporary African Art Collection Limited/CORBIS; **355** Courtesy of Library of Congress; **356** Courtesy of Library of Congress; **357** Courtesy of Library of Congress; **360** Getty Images; **361** © Nathan Benn/CORBIS; **364** SuperStock; **367** Jupiter Images; **369** iStockphoto; **370** © JP Laffont/Sygma/CORBIS; **372** (top) SuperStock; (bottom) Getty Images; **374** Getty Images; **376** (top) © Jeffry W. Myers/CORBIS; (bottom) Getty Images; **377** Getty Images; **379** Cover from *The Voice that Challenged a Nation: Marian Anderson and the Struggle for Equal Rights* by Russell Freedman. Copyright © 2004 by Russell Freedman. Reprinted by permission of Clarion Books, an imprint of Houghton Mifflin Company. All rights reserved; Cover from *Escape! The Story of the Great Houdini* by Sid Fleischman. Copyright © 2006 by Sid Fleischman. Used by permission of HarperCollins Publishers; Cover from *Something Out of Nothing: Marie Curie and Radium* by Carla Killough McClafferty. Copyright © 2006 by Carla Killough McClafferty. Reprinted by permission; "Secrets of a Civil War Submarine" by Sally M. Walker. Text copyright © 2005 by Sally M. Walker. Reprinted with the permission of Carolrhoda Books, a division of Lerner Publishing Group, Inc. All rights reserved. No part of this excerpt may be used or reproduced in any manner whatsoever without the prior written permission of Lerner Publishing Group, Inc.; Jacket cover design by Nancy Goldberg from *Something Out of Nothing: Marie Curie and Radium* by Carla Killough McClafferty. Jacket design copyright © 1998 by Nancy Goldenberg. Used by permission of Farrar, Straus and Giroux, LLC; Cover from *Close to Shore: The Terrifying Shark Attacks of 1916* by Michael Capuzzo and illustrated by Lars Hokanson. Used by permission of Crown Publishers, an imprint of Random House Children's Books, a division of Random House, Inc.; Cover from *The Poet Slave of Cuba: A Biography of Juan Francisco Manzano* by Margarita Engle. Copyright © 2006 by Margarita Engle. Reprinted by permission; **380** Getty Images; **381, 384** Jupiter Unlimited; **386** Eileen Ryan Photography.

Unit 4

392 (top) *The Persistence of Memory,* 1931 (oil on canvas), Dali, Salvador (1904–1989)/Museum of Modern Art, New York, USA, © DACS/The Bridgeman Art Library; (bottom left) Courtesy of Mansfield Library; **393** (top) Jupiter Images; (bottom left) Courtesy of Elio Schaechter; (bottom middle) Courtesy of Mansfield Library; (bottom right) Courtesy of Kjetil Kjernsmo; **394** Paul Collins Art; **397** © Reuters/CORBIS; **399** © Jerome Minet/Kipa/CORBIS; **400** Jupiter Images; **404** PhotoDisc; **407–408** (background) Jupiter Images; **409** © DK Limited/CORBIS; **410** Jupiter Images; **411** *The Persistence of Memory,* 1931 (oil on canvas), Dali, Salvador (1904–1989)/Museum of Modern Art, New York, USA, © DACS/The Bridgeman Art Library; **412, 414** Ken Garland Photography; (bottom middle) © Wildlife Conservation Society; (bottom right) 2004 Phaeton Group, C. Evan Gelista; **415, 419, 420** Jupiter Images; **423** (top) Courtesy of Elio Schaechter; (bottom) Courtesy of Mansfield Library; **424** *Fly Agaric* (oil on canvas), Martin du Mesnil, Dorothee/Private Collection/The Bridgeman Art Library; **426** *Seeking the New Home* (oil on canvas), Wyeth, Newell Convers (1882–1945)/Private Collection, Photo © Christie's Images/The Bridgeman Art Library; **430** Shutterstock; **433** Courtesy of Kjetil Kjernsmo; **434** Jupiter Images; **437** Jupiter Unlimited; **438** David LaRochelle; **440** 2004 Phaeton Group, C. Evan Gelista; **441** Courtesy of Photofest; **444, 445** The Picture Desk; **448** (top) SuperStock, *Growling Jaguar,* 2000. John Bunker; (bottom) © Wildlife Conservation Society; **452–453** Jupiter Images; **456–457** Victoria & Albert Museum, London/Art Resource, NY; **458** Courtesy of Ken Garland Photography; **459** Cover from *Write Your Own Fantasy Story* by Tish

Farrell. Copyright © Tick Tock Entertainment Ltd. 2006. Reprinted by permission; From *Peanut Butter, Milk, and other Deadly Threats: What you should know about Food Allergies* by Sherry Mabry Gordon. Published by Enslow Publishers, Inc., Berkely Heights, N.J. All rights reserved; Cover from *e.guides Rock and Mineral* by John Farndon. Copyright © 2005 Dorling Kindersley Ltd. Reprinted by permission; Book cover from *Understanding the Holy Land: Answering questions about the Israeli-Palestinian Conflict* by Mitch Frank. Reprinted by permission of Penguin Group (USA) Inc.; Cover from *September 11, 2001: Attack on New York City* by Wilborn Hampton. Copyright © 2003 by Wilborn Hampton. Reprinted by permission; Cover from *Harlem Stomp! A Cultural History of the Harlem Renaissance* by Laban Carrick Hill. Copyright © 2003 by Laban Carrick Hill. Reprinted by permission; **460** (left) Jupiter Unlimited; (right) Courtesy of Stuart Dybek; **461** Jupiter Unlimited; **466** Eileen Ryan Photography.

Unit 5

472 (top) *Road to Taos at the Rio Grande* (oil on canvas), Henderson, William Penhallow (1877–1943)/Fred Jones Jr. Museum of Art, University of Oklahoma, USA, Richard H. and Adeline J. Fleischaker Collection, 1996/The Bridgeman Art Library; (bottom left and middle) Courtesy of Library of Congress; (bottom right) Getty Images; **473** (top) SuperStock; (bottom left and middle) © Bettmann/CORBIS; (bottom right) Writer Pictures; **475** Jupiter Images; **476** fol.94v *Beehives* (vellum), Italian School, (14th century)/Osterreichische Nationalbibliothek, Vienna, Austria, Alinari/The Bridgeman Art Library; **478** Library of Congress; **479** *Lake Scene by Moonlight*, 1879 (board), Gilbert, Arthur (1819–1995)/Private Collection, © The Maas Gallery, London, UK/The Bridgeman Art Library; **481** Courtesy of Library of Congress; **482** *The Falling Star*, 1909 (oil on canvas), Hay, James Hamilton (1874–1916)/© Walker Art Gallery, National Museums Liverpool/The Bridgeman Art Library; **484** Image Source; **485** Jupiter Unlimited; **486** *Olympia*, 1863 (oil on canvas) (detail of 64183), Manet, Edouard (1832–1883)/Musee d'Orsay, Paris, France, Giraudon/The Bridgeman Art Library; **487** *Snowdon by Moonlight*, 1792, Wright of Derby, Joseph (1734–1797)/© University of Liverpool Art Gallery & Collections, UK/The Bridgeman Art Library; **488** Courtesy of Library of Congress; **490** Getty

Images; **493** Getty Images; **494** *Goldfish*, Seligman, Lincoln (Contemporary Artist)/Private Collection/The Bridgeman Art Library; **498** Getty Images; **499** *The Unveiling of the Statue of Liberty, Enlightening the World*, 1886 (oil on canvas), Moran, Edward (1829–1901)/© Museum of the City of New York, USA/The Bridgeman Art Library; **500** (all) Jupiter Images; **501** Courtesy of Library of Congress; **503** Courtesy of Library of Congress; **506** *Road to Taos at the Rio Grande* (oil on canvas), Henderson, William Penhallow (1877–1943)/Fred Jones Jr. Museum of Art, University of Oklahoma, USA, Richard H. and Adeline J. Fleischaker Collection, 1996/The Bridgeman Art Library; **507** Jupiter Images; **509** Courtesy of Leslie Marmon Silko; **510** SuperStock; **512** © Bettmann/CORBIS; **513** *Robin*, from *The Farnley Book of Birds*, c. 1816 (pencil and w/c on paper), Turner, Joseph Mallord William (1775–1851)/© Leeds Museums and Galleries (City Art Gallery) U.K./The Bridgeman Art Library; **514** *The Day of Rest*, c. 1926, Robinson, Frederick Cayley (1862–1927)/© Bury Art Gallery and Museum, Lancashire, UK/The Bridgeman Art Library; **516** (top) © Bettmann/CORBIS; (bottom) Writer Pictures; **517** Superstock; **518** Jupiter Unlimited; **519** *Camels Watering in front of the Gates of Pekin—Visiting the Extreme Orient*/Paul Bremen Collection, USA/The Bridgeman Art Library; **520** Jupiter Images; **523** (top) *Woman on the Telephone*, 1948 (acrylic paper), Avery, Milton Clark (1893–1965)/Private Collection, © DACS/The Bridgeman Art Library; (bottom) © Bettmann/CORBIS; **524** PhotoDisc; **525** (foreground) *Fawn*, from *Drawings of Animals, Insects and Reptiles from Malacca*, c. 1805–1818 (w/c and gouache on paper), Chinese School, (19th century)/© Royal Asiatic Society, London, UK/The Bridgeman Art Library; (background) Jupiter Unlimited; (bottom) © Albertin, Walter/LOC/Writer Pictures; **526** PhotoDisc; **527** *This Same Sky: A Collection of Poems from Around the World* by Naomi Shihab Nye. Reprinted by permission of the author; Cover from *Poems from Homeroom: A Writer's Place to Start* by Kathi Appelt. Copyright © 2002 by Kathi Appelt. Reprinted by permission; Cover from *Here in Harlem: Poems in Many Voices* by Walter Dean Myers. Copyright © 2004 by Walter Dean Myers. Reprinted by permission; Reprinted with the permission of Simon & Schuster Books for Young Readers, an imprint of Simon & Schuster Children's Publishing Division from *My America: A Poetry Atlas of the United States* selected by Lee Bennett Hopkins, illustrated

by Stephen Alcorn. Jacket illustrations copyright ©
2000 Stephen Alcorn; Book cover from *The Complete
Collected Poems of Maya Angelou* by Maya Angelou,
copyright © 1994. Used by permission of Random
House, Inc.; Book cover from *It's a Woman's World: A
Century of Women's Voices in Poetry* by Neil Philip.
Reprinted by permission of Penguin Group (USA) Inc.;
528 AP Photos; **534** Eileen Ryan Photography.

Unit 6

540 (top) *Living Room Lounge*, 2000 (oil on canvas),
Bootman, Colin (Contemporary Artist)/Private
Collection/The Bridgeman Art Library; (bottom left)
Courtesy of Leslie Marmon Silko; (bottom middle)
Portrait of Joseph Bruchac, © Martin Benjamin 2007;
(bottom right) © Oscar White/CORBIS; **541** (top) Tom
Jenz/Jupiter Images; (bottom left) Courtesy Judith
Ortiz Cofer; (bottom middle and right) © Bettmann/
CORBIS; **542** © Judith Collins/Alamy; **543** © Oscar
White/CORBIS; **544–545** Tom Jenz/ Jupiter Images;
548 Schomburg Center; **549** © Stuart Abraham/
Alamy; **551** © Bettmann/CORBIS; **552** Jupiter
Unlimited; **553** iStockphoto; **554** Jupiter Unlimited;
557, 558, 560 © Bettmann/CORBIS; **561** Elin
Pendleton; **562–563** PhotoDisc; **567** SuperStock;
568 Jupiter Unlimited; **571** (bottom) Courtesy of
Library of Congress; **571–577** (background) Jupiter
Unlimited; **572** © Stock Montage, Inc./Alamy; **576**
Porringer, 1760 (silver), Revere, Paul (1735–1818)/
Private Collection, Photo © Boltin Picture Library/The
Bridgeman Art Library; **578** SuperStock; **579** Jupiter
Unlimited; **583** SuperStock; **585** Jupiter Unlimited;
587 (top) PhotoDisc; (bottom) Courtesy of Judith
Ortiz Cofer; **588** PhotoDisc; **590** (top) Portrait of
Joseph Bruchac, © Martin Benjamin 2007; (bottom)
Courtesy of Leslie Marmon Silko; **591** (foreground)
© LOOK Die Bildagentur der Fotografen GmbH/
Alamy; (background) Jupiter Images; **592, 594** (top)
Jupiter Images; **594** (bottom) © Writer Pictures; **596**
Jupiter Images; **598** *Living Room Lounge*, 2000 (oil
on canvas), Bootman, Colin (Contemporary Artist)/
Private Collection/The Bridgeman Art Library; **599**
© Bettmann/CORBIS; **601** Cover from *The Space
Between Our Footsteps: Poems and Painitngs from
the Middle East* by Naomi Shihab Nye. Copyright ©
1998 by Naomi Shihab Nye. Reprinted by permission;
Cover from *The Rime of the Ancient Mariner* by Samuel
Taylor Coleridge. Copyright © Cassel & Co, 2001.
Reprinted by permission; Cover from *Heart to Heart:*

*New Poems Inspired by Twentieth-Century American
Art* by Jan Greenberg. Copyright © Harry N. Abrams,
Inc. Reprinted by permission; Book cover from *Step
Lightly: Poems for the Journey*, copyright © 1998 by
Nancy Willard, reprinted by permission of Harcourt,
Inc.; Cover from *William Butler Yeats: Poetry for Young
People* edited by Jonathan Allison. Copyright ©
2002 by Jonathan Allison. Reprinted by permission;
Cover from *Imaginary Animals: Poetry and Art for
Young People* edited by Charles Sullivan. Copyright
© 1996 Charles Sullivan. Reprinted by permission;
602 AP Images; **603** Media Bakery; **608** Eileen Ryan
Photography.

Unit 7

614 (top) Media Bakery; (bottom left and middle)
© Bettmann/CORBIS; **615** (top) © Hulton-Deutsch
Collection/CORBIS; (bottom left and middle) Getty
Images; (bottom right) © Hulton-Deutsch Collection/
CORBIS; **616** Jupiter Unlimited; **617** Courtesy
of Library of Congress; **619** © Hulton-Deutsch
Collection/CORBIS; **620** © H. Armstrong Roberts/
CORBIS; **629** © Bettmann/CORBIS; **634** PhotoDisc;
636 Mary Evans Picture Library; **637** Shutterstock;
640 © Bettmann/CORBIS; **641** Courtesy of
Photofest; **644** The Picture Desk; **648** Courtesy of
Photofest; **655** The Picture Desk; **663** Courtesy of
Photofest; **667** 20th Century-Fox/Photofest; **676**
The Picture Desk; **678, 680** Getty Images; **682** ©
Reuters/CORBIS; **685** The Picture Desk; **690, 693,
700** Courtesy of Photofest; **708** Media Bakery; **709,
710** Courtesy of Library of Congress; **714** (top)
Jupiter Unlimited; (bottom) Getty Images; **719** Jupiter
Images; **725** Jupiter Unlimited; **729** Book cover *The
Glass Menagerie* by Tennessee Williams. Used courtesy
of New Directions Publishing Corp.; From *The Working
Life—An Actor on the Elizabethan Stage* 1st Edition
by Currie, Stephen (author). 2002. Reprinted with
permission of Gale, a division of Thomson Learning:
www.thomsonrights.com.; Fax 1-800-730-2215;
Cover from *Children of a Lesser God* by Mark Medoff.
Copyright © 1980 Westmark Productions. Reprinted
by permission; Cover from *Shakespeare: His Work and
His World* by Michael Rosen. Copyright © 2001 by
Michael Rosen. Reprinted by permission; Cover from
Backstage at a Play by Kimberly M. Miller. Copyright
© 2003 by Rosen Book Works, Inc. Reprinted by
permission; Cover from *Break a Leg! The Kids' Guide
to Acting and Stagecraft* by Lise Friedman. Copyright

© 2002 Lise Friedman. Reprinted by permission; **730** (right) Courtesy of Library of Congress; (left) Jupiter Unlimited; **731** Jupiter Unlimited; **736** Eileen Ryan Photography.

Unit 8

742 (top) Jupiter Unlimited; (bottom left) Portrait of Joseph Bruchac, © Martin Benjamin 2007; (bottom middle and right) Courtesy of Library of Congress; **743** (top) *Eva and Greenie,* 1904 (oil on canvas), Hudson, Grace Carpenter (1836–1937)/ Private Collection, Photo © Christie's Images/The Bridgeman Art Library; (bottom left) Courtesy of Judith Ortiz Cofer; (bottom middle) Courtesy of Najib Joe Hakim; (bottom right) © CORBIS; **744** © Catherine Karnow/CORBIS; **745** Woodfin Camp; **748–749** Jupiter Images; **752, 754, 757** Courtesy of Library of Congress; **761** (foreground) Courtesy of Library of Congress; (background) PhotoDisc; **764** Jupiter Unlimited; **766** Courtesy of Library of Congress; **770** Jupiter Unlimited; **773** © BASSOULS SOPHIE/CORBIS SYGMA; **774** SuperStock; **776** Shutterstock; **778** (top) Portrait of Joseph Bruchac, © Martin Benjamin 2007; **779** *Chief 'Crazy Horse'* (1838–1877) (oil on canvas), Lindneux, Robert Ottokar (1871–1970)/ Private Collection, Peter Newark American Pictures/ The Bridgeman Art Library; **781, 782** Jupiter Images; **786** Courtesy of Ron Rovtar Photography **787** *Dance,* 1996 (mixed media on canvas), Deceus, Francks (Contemporary Artist)/Private Collection/ The Bridgeman Art Library; **789** Jupiter Images; **791** *Eva and Greenie,* 1904 (oil on canvas), Hudson, Grace Carpenter (1836–1937)/Private Collection, Photo © Christie's Images/The Bridgeman Art Library; **793** Richard G. Walser papers, P-4168, photograph of Walser; **794** *The Capture of the Pirate Blackbeard,* 1718, Ferris, Jean Leon Jerome (1863–1930)/ Private Collection/The Bridgeman Art Library; **798** © CORBIS; **799** The Granger Collection, New York; **800** © Bettmann/CORBIS; **800–801** Jupiter Unlimited;

802 © Christie's Images/SuperStock; **804** Najib Joe Hakim; **805** Dan Dutton; **806** Jupiter Images; **808** SuperStock; **810** Shutterstock; **812** Jupiter Unlimited; **814** Courtesy of Library of Congress; **815** (top) Jupiter Unlimited; (bottom) © Lowell Georgia/ CORBIS; **818** Jupiter Unlimited; **823** SuperStock; **825, 830,** Jupiter Unlimited; **842** Shutterstock; **836** (top) © Michael Nicholson/CORBIS; (bottom) Courtesy of Library of Congress; **841** *In the Forest with a Barrel* from *Rip Van Winkle* written by Washington Irving (1783–1859), 1905, Rackham, Arthur (1867–1939)/ Private Collection, © The Fine Art Society, London, UK/The Bridgeman Art Library; **844** © Bettmann/ CORBIS; **847** *New Year's Cakes* from *Rip van Winkle* by Washington Irving (1783–1859), 1905, Rackham, Arthur (1867–1939)/Private Collection/ The Bridgeman Art Library; **850** (top) iStockphoto; (bottom) Courtesy of Judith Ortiz Cofer; **852** Jupiter Images; **855** Cover from *White Wolf Woman: Native American Transformation Myths* by Teresa Pijoan. Copyright © 1992 by Teresa Pijoan. Reprinted by permission; Cover from *Solomon and the Ant: And Other Jewish Folktales* retold by Sheldon Oberman, jacket art by Lloyd Bloom. (Boyds Mills Press, 2006.) Reprinted with the permission of Boyds Mills Press, Inc.; Book cover from *Golden Tales* by Lulu Delacre. Copyright © 1995 by Lulu Delacre. Reprinted by permission of Scholastic Inc.; Cover from *Spider Spins a Story: Fourteen Legends from Native America* edited by Jill Max. Copyright © 1997 by Jill Max. Reprinted by permission; Book cover from *The Legend of the Wandering King* by Laura Gallego Garcia. Jacket painting © 2005 by Tim O'Brien. Reprinted by permission of Arthur A. Levine Books, an imprint of Scholastic Inc.; Cover from *The Legend of the White Buffalo Woman* by Paul Goble. Reprinted by permission of National Geographic Society; **856** Courtesy of Ron Rovtar Photography; **864** Eileen Ryan Photography.

870 (top left) © William A. Bake/CORBIS; (top right) © Reuters/CORBIS; (bottom left) Jupiter Unlimited; (bottom right) PhotoDisc

Vocabulary

Grammar & Style

Writing

Research & Documentation

Applied English

Speaking & Listening

Index of Titles & Authors

For Your Reading List